BASEBALL PROSPECTUS

2016

The Essential Guide to the 2016 Season

Edited by Patrick Dubuque, Sam Miller, and Jason Wojciechowski

R.J. Anderson, Nick Ashbourne, Paul Boye, J.P. Breen, Ben Carsley, Ken Funck, Brendan Gawlowski, Mike Gianella, Craig Goldstein, Bryan Grosnick, Wilson Karaman, David Lee, Kate Morrison, Chris Mosch, Jeffrey Paternostro, Tommy Rancel, Daniel Rathman, Dan Rozenson, Mauricio Rubio Jr., Bret Sayre, Matt Sussman, David Temple, Doug Thorburn, Matt Trueblood, Bradley Woodrum, Will Woods, Geoff Young

James Walsh and Dave Pease, Consultants

TURNER PUBLISHING COMPANY

Turner Publishing Company
424 Church Street • Suite 2240 • Nashville, Tennessee 37219
445 Park Avenue • 9th Floor • New York, New York 10022
www.turnerpublishing.com

Library of Congress Cataloging-in-Publication Data:
ISBN 9781681621180 (pbk); 9781681621111 (hbk);
9781681622668 (ebk)

Project Credits
Cover Design: Maddie Cothren
Interior design and production: Bryan Davidson
Layout: Misty Horten & Colleen Cunningham

Manufactured in the United States of America
10 9 8 7 6 5 4 3 2 1

TABLE OF CONTENTS

Foreword

by David Forst, General Manager of the Oakland Athletics

There was a time, not all that long ago, when Baseball Prospectus wasn't a website that had traffic in the hundreds of thousands of fans; rather, it was a hidden little corner of the internet for hardcore sabermetrics. And it certainly wasn't the book you're holding in your hands (or reading on a tablet) that lands on the *New York Times* bestseller list every year; it was something more akin to a yearly pamphlet that, by one of its own writer's admission, was "pretty terrible."

When I started working for the A's in January 2000, followers of BP were in something of a limited club. BP was a place where smart, interesting people wrote smart, interesting things about the game, but the Baseball Prospectus "brand" wasn't something you casually found on ESPN.com or stumbled across on Twitter because someone retweeted it. You had to be someone who thought about the game in a certain objective and insightful way, and you had to actively seek out that type of content. Baseball Prospectus was an attempt to see the game differently. It was trying to quantify and explain what had been happening on the field for decades, beyond the accounts and daily reporting of beat writers and columnists. It hoped to give voice to those fans who, for years, advocated for a smarter way of accounting for the results of every outcome on the field but never had a forum in which to do it.

That wasn't an easy thing to accomplish. Baseball has been around for 150 years and has been viewed through mostly the same lens for all that time. There were, of course, exceptions inside the game (Earl Weaver comes to mind) and outside the game (Bill James's writing deserves credit for paving the way for just about everything in this book)—individuals whose intelligence and passion allowed them to break through with a different perspective. But they were outliers. BP's success made this outside-the-box vision of the game accessible on an infinitely larger scale, using the reach of the internet to help create a generation of fans and hopeful GMs-in-training who were hungry for such information and to find others who viewed the game on this level.

So, how did BP separate itself and become the model for numerous other sites and blogs that were and still are trying to replicate its success? Like any great company, it relied on great people. Just look at the people who've been under the BP banner at one time or another and the work they've gone on to do since. People like Gary Huckabay, Joe Sheehan (SI) and Christina Kahrl (ESPN) founded this book, and almost 20 years later are still writing some of the best stuff out there on baseball. They gave way to the likes of Will Carroll (SI), Keith Law (ESPN), Jonah Keri (ESPN) and Nate Silver (FiveThirtyEight), all of whom continue to influence baseball and its decision makers with their writing today. (And, in Nate's case, seem to have had powerful insights into things far greater than the outcome of a baseball game.) In many cases, former Baseball Prospectus authors have gone on to become those decision makers and work for clubs, most notably Law (Blue Jays), Kevin Goldstein (Astros), Keith Woolner (Indians) and James Click (Rays). I have, out of necessity, left many names out; there are countless others who have taken that path.

The job that I was lucky enough to land in 2000 would look about as different today as this book does from those early BP pamphlets. While the game itself has changed in very visible ways in those 16 years on the field—infields shifting, relievers throwing ever harder, strikeout rates steadily increasing, homers going up and then down and then back up again last summer—it has become even more different off the field. Those of us tasked with making the decisions on 25- and 40-man rosters, on player development systems and on drafting and signing amateur players have access to so much more information than we did when I first walked in the door. We have the ability and freedom to dissect that information and implement it in ways that would never have been understood or accepted by a different generation of fans. Today, there's no end in sight to the intelligent, thoughtful and diverse voices out there looking to discuss, debate and deconstruct every nuance of our game. That avid discourse is a big part of what makes this job so much fun and so interesting on a day-to-day and year-to-year basis. The year-round passion of baseball fans is fueled in the winter months by the writing within these pages, but luckily for us all, it's just about time for another offseason to come to a close as we inch closer to Opening Day. I, for one, can't wait for the 2016 season to start. ■

Baseball Prospectus 2016
Statistical Introduction

Why don't you get your nose out of those numbers and watch a game?

It's a false dilemma, of course. We would wager that Baseball Prospectus readers watch more games than the typical fan. They also probably pay better attention when they watch. The numbers do not replace observation; they supplement it. Having the numbers allows you to learn things not readily seen by mere watching and to keep up on many more players than any one person otherwise could.

This book doesn't ask you to choose between the two. Instead, we combine numerical analysis with the observations of a lot of very bright people. They won't always agree. Just as the eyes don't always see what the numbers do, the reverse can be true. In order to get the most out of this book, however, it helps to understand the numbers we're presenting and why.

Offense

The core of our offense measurements is True Average, which attempts to quantify everything a player does at the plate—hitting for power, taking walks, striking out and even "productive" outs—and scale it to batting average. A player with a TAv of .260 is average, .300 exceptional, .200 rather awful.

True Average also accounts for the context a player performs in. That means we adjust it based on the mix of parks a player plays in. Also, rather than use a blanket park adjustment for every player on a team, a player who plays a disproportionate number of his games at home will see that reflected in his numbers. We also adjust based on league quality: The average player in the AL is better than the average player in the NL, and True Average accounts for this.

Because hitting isn't the entirety of scoring runs, we also look at a player's Baserunning Runs. BRR accounts for the value of a player's ability to steal bases, of course, but also accounts for his ability to go first to third on a single, or advance on a flyball.

Defense

Defense is a much thornier issue. The general move in the sabermetric community has been toward stats based on zone data, where human stringers record the type of batted ball (grounder, liner, flyball) and its presumed landing location. That data is used to compile expected outs for comparing a fielder's actual performance.

The trouble with zone data is twofold. First, unlike the data we use in the calculation of the statistics you see in this book, zone data wasn't made publicly available; it was recorded by commercial providers who kept the raw data private, only disclosing it to a select few who paid for it. Second, as we've seen the field of zone-based defensive analysis open up—more data and more metrics based upon that data coming to light—we see that the conclusions of zone-based defensive metrics don't hold up to outside scrutiny. Different data providers can come to very different conclusions about the same events. Even two metrics based on the same data set can come to radically different conclusions based on their starting assumptions, assumptions that haven't been tested, using methods that can't be duplicated or verified by outside analysts.

The quality of the fielder can bias the data: Zone-based fielding metrics will tend to attribute more expected outs to good fielders than bad fielders, irrespective of the distribution of batted balls. Scorers who work in parks with high press boxes will tend to score more line drives than scorers who work in parks with low press boxes.

Our Field Runs Above Average (FRAA) incorporates play-by-play data, allowing us to study the issue of defense at a granular level without resorting to the sorts of subjective data used in some other fielding metrics. We count how many plays a player made, as well as expected plays for the average player at that position based on a pitcher's estimated groundball tendencies and the handedness of the batter. There are also adjustments for park and base-out situations.

In addition, catchers have different defensive responsibilities than other defensive players, in particular framing pitches to make umpires more likely to call them strikes and blocking errant pitches. We incorporate PITCHf/x data, where available, and adjust for the pitcher, umpire, batter (including handedness) and home-field advantage using a mixed-model approach to determine how many strikes a catcher is adding to or subtracting from his pitchers' ledgers, and then convert those extra or lost strikes to runs using simple linear weights. We use a similar approach to determine how much better or worse than average a catcher is at letting errant pitches past him (regardless of whether the official scorer labels it a passed ball or a wild pitch)—PITCHf/x is a particularly powerful tool in this regard because we can tell which pitches end up in the dirt (and at what angle and speed) even though basic play-by-play data simply records the pitch as a ball or a swinging strike because the catcher successfully blocked it.

These metrics, as well as the catcher's abilities to prevent steals, are incorporated into catchers' FRAA along with their ball-in-play fielding (e.g. popups and bunts near home plate).

Pitching

Of course, how we measure fielding influences how we measure pitching.

Most sabermetric analysis of pitching has been inspired by Voros McCracken, who stated, "There is little if any difference among major-league pitchers in their ability to prevent hits on balls hit in the field of play." When first published, this statement was extremely controversial, but later research has, by and large, validated it. McCracken (and others) went forth from that finding to create a variety of defense-independent pitching measures. One that you'll see in the book is FIP, Fielding Independent Pitching, which accounts for walks, strikeouts, hit-by-pitches and homers accumulated by a pitcher and puts them into one number on an ERA scale. Another is cFIP, which takes those FIP inputs, makes a variety of adjustments (including the batter, catcher, umpire, stadium, home-field advantage and handedness) and puts the whole thing on a "100 minus" scale in which the lower the number the better. The standard deviation of cFIP is forced to 15, so you know that a 56 cFIP, like Clayton Kershaw posted in 2015, is nearly three standard deviations from the mean.

The trouble is that many efforts to separate pitching from fielding have ended up separating pitching from pitching—looking at only a handful of variables in isolation from the situation in which they occurred. What we've done instead is take a pitcher's actual results, event by event, and adjust each event based on the environment in which it occurred, including park factor, batter, catcher, umpire, base-out situation, run differential, inning, defense, home-field advantage, whether the pitcher is a starter or reliever and game-time temperature. DRA also considers the pitcher's effect on basestealing (both in terms of likelihood of stealing and likelihood of success) and the pitcher's effect on passed balls and wild pitches. Out of all this comes Deserved Run Average (DRA), our core pitching metric, which is making its first appearance in this Annual this year. It is the rate stat on which pitcher Wins Above Replacement Player is determined.

One key point to note is that DRA is set on the same scale as runs allowed per nine innings, not ERA. Looking only at earned runs tends to overrate three kinds of pitchers:

1. Pitchers who play in parks where scorers hand out more errors. Looking at error rates between parks tells us scorers differ significantly in how likely they are to score any given play as an error (as opposed to an infield hit);
2. Groundball pitchers, because a substantial proportion of errors occurs on groundballs; and
3. Pitchers who aren't very good. Good pitchers tend to allow fewer unearned runs than bad pitchers, because good pitchers have more ways to get out of jams than bad pitchers. They're more likely to get a strikeout to end the inning, and less likely to give up a home run.

Projections

Many of you aren't turning to this book just for a look at what a player has done, but a look at what a player is going to do: the PECOTA projections.

PECOTA, initially developed by Nate Silver (who has moved on to greater fame as a political analyst), consists of three parts:

1. Major-league equivalencies, to allow us to use minor-league stats to project how a player will perform in the majors;
2. Baseline forecasts, which use weighted averages and regression to the mean to produce an estimate of a player's true talent level; and
3. A career-path adjustment, which incorporates information on how comparable players' stats changed over time.

Now that we've gone over the core stats, let's go over what's in the book.

Team Prospectus

The bulk of this book comprises team chapters, with one for each of the 30 major-league franchises. On the first page of each chapter, you will be greeted by a box laying out some key statistics for each team. You can see Atlanta's box on the right

At the top, 2015 W-L is exactly as it sounds, the unadjusted tally of wins and losses. Pythag presents an adjusted 2015 win percentage by taking the runs scored per game (RS/G) and allowed (RA/G) by the team last season and running them through a version of Bill James' Pythagorean formula refined and developed by David Smyth and Brandon Heipp, called "Pythagenpat."

A team's runs scored is accompanied by True Average (TAv) and Baserunning Runs (BRR), both of which were described above, to give a picture of how a team scores its runs. In terms of run-prevention ability, we present a team's TAv allowed (TAv-P), FIP and Defensive Efficiency

BRAVES PROSPECTUS

2015 W-L: 67-95, 4TH IN NL EAST

Pythag	.374	30th	DER	.695	26th
RS/G	3.54	30th	B-Age	28.8	24th
RA/G	4.69	27th	P-Age	25.7	1st
TAv	.254	23rd	Salary	$97.1M	22nd
BRR	2.93	14th	M$/MW	$4.5M	8th
TAv-P	.284	29th	DL Days	1169	20th
FIP	4.37	27th	$ on DL	14%	12th

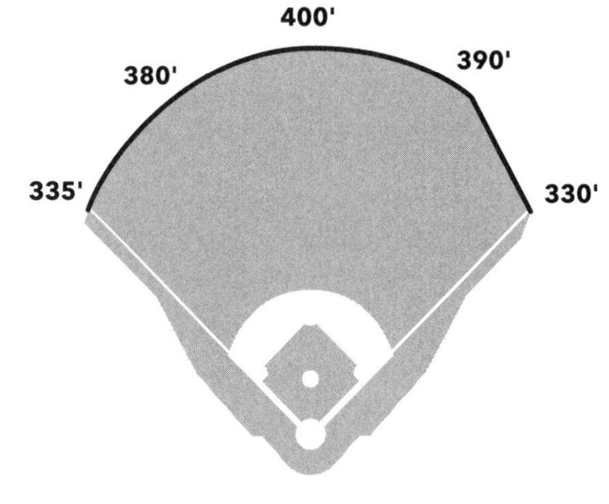

Outfield wall profile: **8'**

Three-Year Park Factors

Runs	Runs/RH	Runs/LH	HR/RH	HR/LH
93	99	101	99	95

Top Hitter WARP	2.9	Andrelton Simmons
Top Pitcher WARP	2.1	Shelby Miller
Top Prospect		Dansby Swanson

Rating (DER), which is simply its rate of balls in play turned into outs.

Then we have several measures not directly related to on-field performance. B-Age and P-Age tell us the average age of a team's batters and pitchers, respectively. Salary tells us how much the team cost to put on the field, and Doug Pappas' Marginal Dollars per Marginal Win (M$/MW) tells us how much a team paid above the bare minimum it had to pay and how much production above replacement it received for that money.

Finally, we count up the number of disabled-list days a team had, as well as the amount of salary paid to players while they were on the DL, expressed as a percentage of the total payroll.

Next to each of these stats, you see the team's MLB rank in that category, where 1st signifies a good outcome (e.g. highest TAv, lowest Tav-P) and 30th a bad outcome (highest $ on DL, lowest DER), except for salary, where we make no value judgments—1st is highest.

After the team information comes a variety of data about the home ballpark: a diagram of the park's dimensions showing distances to the outfield wall; a graphic that shows the height of the wall from the left-field pole to the right-field pole, reading left to right; and a table showing the three-year park factors presented in their usual 100-scale fashion, with 100 being average, 110 meaning that the park inflates the stat by 10 percent and 90 meaning the stat deflates the stat by 10 percent.

On the second page of each chapter, you will see three graphs. The first graph, titled "2015 Hit List Ranking," shows the Hit List Rank for this team on every day of the 2015 season and is intended to give you an idea of the shape of the season. Hit List Rank is a measure of overall team performance that drives the Prospectus Hit List power ranking at baseballprospectus.com. It is based on team run differential and includes adjustments for park, league and quality of opposition. You can see more about Hit List Ranking at http://bbp.cx/a/4383.

The second graph is entitled "Committed Payroll" and is intended to give you an idea of how this team's player budgets match up with the competition historically and going forward. The payroll figures are current as of January 1, 2016; with several big-ticket free agents still unsigned as of this writing, keep in mind the final 2016 figure will be significantly different for many teams. You can always find current data at Baseball Prospectus' Cot's Baseball Contracts page. MLB and division averages are also plotted to allow for quick comparison.

The third graph is entitled "Farm System Ranking" and shows the Baseball Prospectus prospect team's ranking of this team's farm system for the last several years.

Following the graphs is the "Personnel" section. Here you'll find some of the important people in the organization, and any former Baseball Prospectus staff who are currently part of the team's front office or scouting staff

Position Players

After a bylined opening essay about each team, the chapters move to the player comments, which are also bylined, though the vagaries of player movement and the group-project nature of the book means that the names you see at the head of each chapter are more a rough guide than a precise accounting of the division of labor.

Jason Heyward RF

Born: 8/9/89 Age: 26 Bats: L Throws: L Height: 6'5" Weight: 245

YEAR	TEAM	LVL	AGE	PA	R	2B	3B	HR	RBI	BB	K	SB	CS	AVG/OBP/SLG	TAv	BABIP	BRR	FRAA	WARP
2013	ATL	MLB	23	440	67	22	1	14	38	48	73	2	4	.254/.349/.427	.280	.281	1.2	RF(86): 6.7, CF(20): -0.0	2.7
2013	GWN	AAA	23	26	1	1	0	0	6	4	7	1	0	.300/.423/.350	.308	.429	0.0	RF(3): 0.1	0.2
2014	ATL	MLB	24	649	74	26	3	11	58	67	98	20	4	.271/.351/.384	.288	.308	1.0	RF(149): 27.6	6.2
2015	SLN	MLB	25	610	79	33	4	13	60	56	90	23	3	.293/.359/.439	.294	.329	6.1	RF(144): 15.9, CF(10): 2.1	5.9
2016	*CHN*	*MLB*	*26*	*643*	*90*	*30*	*3*	*21*	*72*	*65*	*114*	*18*	*4*	*.263/.343/.436*	*.279*	*.295*	*2.5*	*CF -6*	*3.2*
2017	*CHN*	*MLB*	*27*	*593*	*78*	*27*	*2*	*19*	*74*	*61*	*103*	*16*	*4*	*.264/.346/.436*	*.284*	*.293*	*2.7*	*CF -6*	*3.0*

Breakout: 4% Improve: 57% Collapse: 1% Attrition: 4% MLB: 98% *Comparables: Nick Markakis, Gary Sheffield, Rusty Staub*

Each player is listed with the major-league team by whom he was employed as of mid-December 2015, meaning that players who changed teams via free agency, trade or otherwise later in the offseason will be listed under their previous employer.

As an example, take a look at this winter's major free-agent hitter, Jason Heyward. His stat block is at the top of the page.

The player-specific sections begin with biographical information before moving onto the column headers and actual data. The column headers begin with standard information like year, team, level (majors or level of the minors), and the raw, untranslated tallies found on the back of a baseball card: PA (plate appearances), R (runs), 2B (doubles), 3B (triples), HR (home runs), RBI (runs batted in), BB (walks), K (strikeouts), SB (stolen bases) and CS (caught stealing).

Following those are untranslated "slash" statistics: batting average (AVG), on-base percentage (OBP) and slugging percentage (SLG). The slash line is followed by True Average (TAv), which, as described above, rolls all those things and more into one easy-to-digest number.

BABIP stands for Batting Average on Balls in Play, and is what it sounds like: How often did a ball put in play by the hitter fall for a hit? An especially low or high BABIP may mean a hitter was especially lucky or unlucky. However, hitters who hit the ball hard tend to have especially high BABIPs from season to season; so do speedy hitters who are able to beat out more grounders for base hits.

Next is Baserunning Runs (BRR) which, as mentioned earlier, covers all sorts of baserunning accomplishments, not just stolen bases. Then comes Fielding Runs Above Average (FRAA); for historical stats, we have the number of games played at each position in parenthesis. For multi-position players, we are only able to display the two positions the fielder played most frequently that season.

The last column is Wins Above Replacement Player. WARP is our total-value stat that, for a hitter, combines a player's batting runs above average (derived from True Average), BRR, FRAA, an adjustment for positions played and a credit for plate appearances based upon the difference between the "replacement level" (derived by looking at the quality of players added to a team's roster after the start of the season) and the league average.

The final line below the comment is PECOTA data, which is discussed further below.

Catchers

New this year is a separate box for catchers showing some of the defensive metrics that apply particularly to them. As an example, let's check out Russell Martin.

Russell Martin

YEAR	TEAM	P. COUNT	FRM RUNS	BLK RUNS	THRW RUNS	TOT RUNS
2013	PIT	16495	10.6	0.4	1.7	12.7
2014	PIT	14470	15.1	-0.1	2.4	17.5
2015	TOR	15667	11.6	-0.5	2.5	13.6
2016	*TOR*	*18439*	*15.7*	*-0.3*	*2.8*	*18.2*
2017	*TOR*	*16071*	*12.8*	*-0.3*	*2.3*	*14.9*

The YEAR and TEAM columns are what you'd expect. P. COUNT is the number of pitches the catcher "received," though really it's the number of pitches thrown by pitchers when the catcher was in the battery; that is, it includes swinging strikes, fouls and balls in play. FRM RUNS is the total runs the catcher added by getting the umpire to call strikes where the average catcher did not (or vice versa). The calculation of this statistic is described above. BLK RUNS, also described above, expresses in runs above or below average the catcher's ability to prevent wild pitches and passed balls. Finally, THRW RUNS sums the catcher's ability to dissuade runners from stealing and to catch them when they do run. This statistic is calculated similarly to the Framing and Blocking stats, and takes into account various factors, including the pitcher (who may have a quick or slow delivery, or a good or bad pickoff move) and the baserunner (who may be Billy Hamilton or Billy Butler). The final column, TOT RUNS, is the sum of the previous three.

Pitchers

Now let's look at how pitchers are presented, using the biggest free-agent splash of the offseason, Zack Greinke. His stat block is at the top of the facing page.

The first line and the YEAR, TEAM, LVL and AGE columns are the same as in the hitters example above. The next set of columns—W (wins), L (losses), SV (saves), G (games pitched), GS (games started), IP (innings pitched), H (hits), HR (home runs), BB9 (walks per nine innings), K9 (strikeouts per nine innings)—are the actual, unadjusted stats compiled by the pitcher during each season.

Next is GB%, which is the percentage of all batted balls that were hit on the ground, including both outs and hits. The average GB% for a major-league pitcher in 2015 was about 45 percent; a pitcher anywhere north of 50 percent can be considered a good groundball pitcher. As

Zack Greinke RHP

Born: 10/21/83 Age: 32 Bats: R Throws: R Height: 6'2" Weight: 195

YEAR	TEAM	LVL	AGE	W	L	SV	G	GS	IP	H	HR	BB/9	K/9	GB%	BABIP	WHIP	ERA	FIP	DRA	WARP	CFIP	MPH
2013	LAN	MLB	29	15	4	0	28	28	177^2	152	13	2.3	7.5	48%	.276	1.11	2.63	3.20	3.27	3.5	95	94.8
2014	LAN	MLB	30	17	8	0	32	32	202^1	190	19	1.9	9.2	50%	.311	1.15	2.71	2.94	3.47	3.3	82	94.6
2015	LAN	MLB	31	19	3	0	32	32	222^2	148	14	1.6	8.1	49%	.229	0.84	1.66	2.79	2.17	7.6	85	94.7
2016	*ARI*	*MLB*	*32*	*14*	*10*	*0*	*32*	*32*	214^1	*188*	*21*	*2.2*	*8.4*	*49%*	*.304*	*1.12*	*3.24*	*3.27*	*3.87*	*3.6*	*86*	
2017	*ARI*	*MLB*	*33*	*11*	*10*	*0*	*29*	*29*	*179*	*159*	*17*	*2.3*	*7.9*	*49%*	*.303*	*1.14*	*3.34*	*3.66*	*3.99*	*2.9*	*89*	

Breakout: 13% Improve: 32% Collapse: 34% Attrition: 7% MLB: 88% *Comparables: Kelvim Escobar, Jason Schmidt, Chris Carpenter*

mentioned above, this is based on observation by human stringers and can be skewed based upon a number of factors. We've included the number as a guide, but please approach it skeptically.

BABIP is the same statistic as for batters, but often tells you more in the case of pitchers, because most major-league pitchers have little control over their batting average on balls in play. A high BABIP is often due to a poor defense or bad luck rather than a pitcher's own abilities, and may be a good indicator of a potential rebound. A typical league-average BABIP is around .290–.300.

WHIP and ERA are common to most fans, with the former measuring the number of walks and hits allowed on a per-inning basis while the latter prorates earned runs allowed on a nine-innings basis. Neither is translated or adjusted in any way.

FIP was discussed above: It puts onto an ERA scale a measurement of how the pitcher performed on the events that do not involve the fielders behind him.

Deserved Run Average (DRA) was also described above. It is the basis of pitcher WARP and measures how many runs (not earned runs) the pitcher "deserved" to allow per nine innings. For the sake of comparison, the average runs allowed per nine in MLB in 2015 was 4.28. One important point about minor leaguers is that because we do not have all the data we would need to fully calculate minor-league DRA, what is listed under "DRA" for minor leaguers is really a runs-allowed-per-nine figure calculated based on cFIP's components.

Because, as has been true of BP's pitching metrics in the past, neither DRA nor the conversion from DRA to WARP contains a "leverage" multiplier, WARP for relief pitchers (especially closers) may seem lower than you might see elsewhere and may conflict with how we feel about relief aces coming in and "saving" the game. This is by design: Saves give extra credit to the closer for what his teammates did to put him in a save spot to begin with; WARP is incapable of feeling excitement over a successful save, and judges them dispassionately. Furthermore, DRA controls for players who have the benefit of pitching in short durations and at maximum ability.

cFIP, described above, adjusts FIP for a variety of factors and scales it on the familiar 100 scale; because these are pitchers preventing runs, below 100 is good, and above 100 is bad.

MPH, which is also new for 2015, is the pitcher's 95th percentile velocity for that season—the goal is to give you a sense of the pitcher's peak fastball velocity, not his average. This comes from PITCHf/x data, and thus is not publicly available for minor leaguers.

PECOTA

Both pitchers and hitters have PECOTA projections for next season, as well as a set of biographical details that describe the performance of that player's comparable players according to PECOTA. For the first time, this book contains two years of PECOTA projections for every player.

The 2016 and 2017 lines are the PECOTA projection for the player at the date we went to press in late December. The player is projected into the league and park context as indicated by his team abbreviation. All PECOTAs represent a player's projected major-league performance. The numbers beneath the player's stats—Breakout, Improve, Collapse, Attrition—are a part of PECOTA. These estimate the likelihood of changes in performance relative to a player's previously established level of production, based upon the performance of the comparable players:

Breakout Rate is the percent chance that a player's production will improve by at least 20 percent relative to the weighted average of his performance over his most recent seasons.

Improve Rate is the percent chance that a player's production will improve at all relative to his baseline performance. A player who is expected to perform just the same as he has in the recent past will have an Improve Rate of 50 percent.

Collapse Rate is the percent chance that a position player's runs produced per plate appearance will decline by at least 25 percent relative to his baseline performance.

Attrition Rate operates on playing time rather than performance. Specifically, it measures the likelihood that a player's playing time will decrease by at least 50 percent relative to his established level.

Breakout Rate and Collapse Rate can sometimes be counterintuitive for players who have already experienced a radical change in performance level. It's also worth noting that the projected decline in a player's rate performances might not be indicative of an expected decline in underlying ability or skill, but rather something of an anticipated correction following a breakout season.

MLB% is the percentage of similar players who played in the major leagues in their relevant season.

The final pieces of information are the player's three highest-scoring comparable players as determined by

PECOTA. Occasionally, a player's top comparables will not be representative of the larger sample that PECOTA uses. All comparables represent a snapshot of how the listed player was performing at the same age as the current player, so if a 23-year-old hitter is compared to Sammy Sosa, he's actually being compared to a 23-year-old Sammy Sosa, not the decrepit Orioles version of Sosa, nor to Sosa's career as a whole.

A few points about pitcher projections. First, we aren't yet projecting peak velocity, so that column will be blank in the PECOTA lines. Second, projecting DRA is trickier than evaluating past performance, because it is unclear how deserving each pitcher will be of his anticipated outcomes. However, we know that cFIP estimates future run-scoring very well, and that cFIP and DRA are based on a similar structure and model. Thus, the projected DRA figures you see are based on the past cFIPs generated by the pitcher and comparable players over time, along with the other factors described above.

Lineouts

The stats box in the Lineouts section contains all the same information, but only has the 2015 stats for each player.

Managers

Each team chapter ends with a manager's comment and data breaking down his tactical tendencies. Though it's often difficult to isolate a manager's contribution to a team, comparing specific data modeled after well-documented plays and styles to the league average helps determine what a manager likes to do, even if we are still unable to translate that information into actual wins and losses.

Following the year, team and the actual record, Pythag +/- lets us know by how many games the team under- or over-performed its Pythagenpat record. That isn't necessarily a reflection on the manager, but it does tell us how well a team performed compared to a somewhat less noisy assessment of the underlying talent.

Pitching staff usage follows, first with AVG PC reporting the average pitch count of his starting pitchers; 100+P and 120+P track the number of games in which the starters exceeded those thresholds. QS is the number of quality starts—a start of at least six innings and with no more than three runs allowed—that a manager received from his starting pitchers. BQS is Blown Quality Starts, a Baseball Prospectus stat that measures games in which the starter delivered a quality start through six innings before losing it in the seventh inning or later. A Blown Quality Start is not necessarily an indictment of a manager's abilities or tactics—a number of factors, ranging from excellent offensive support to extremely poor bullpen support, can lead a manager to leave his starter in a game after he's thrown six quality innings. Conversely, the decision by a manager to "bank" quality starts by restricting his starters to only six innings can have downsides as well, as it increases the bullpen's workload and gives it more opportunities to blow games in which the starter was cruising.

The next stats in the manager table tally how many pitching changes a manager made over the course of the season (REL) and how many times the reliever called upon didn't allow any runners, his own or inherited, to score (REL w Zero R). Bequeathed runners also count against "REL w Zero R," meaning that relievers who exit with runners on who subsequently score prevent a manager from "padding" his tally here. Concluding the pitching section, IBB is simply the number of intentional walks the manager ordered during the given season, which can be a mark of managerial strategy so long as outlying intentional-walk recipients like Miguel Cabrera are accounted for.

Managers do more than manage pitchers, however; their usage of the bench can lead to added or lost performance. PH is the number of pinch-hitters used, and PH Avg and PH HR report the offensive statistics of pinch-hitters called upon.

We then turn to the so-called small-ball tactics, starting with the running game. The manager's aggressiveness on the bases is broken down by successful steals of second and third base (SB2, SB3) and times caught (CS2, CS3). We also provide the number of sacrifices a team attempted (SAC Att) and their success rate (SAC %). Be sure to keep in mind the differences between leagues, as National League sacrifice attempts, like pinch-hitter usage, are greatly inflated by the fact that pitchers bat. To correct for this, we list the number of times a manager got a successful sacrifice from a position player (POS SAC), which allows for comparisons between the two leagues. Squeeze counts the number of successful squeeze plays the team executed over the season.

Finally, we have a couple of statistics that attempt to measure the manager's hit-and-run tactics. Swing is the number of times a hitter swung at a pitch while the runners were in motion, while In Play reflects how many times hitters swung and made contact while those runners were off to the races. Granted, swings on steal attempts do not always translate to hit-and-run attempts, but managers who greatly deviate from the average can be assumed to be staunch proponents or opponents of the strategy.

PECOTA Leaderboards

As a result of the way it weights previous seasons, PECOTA can tend to appear bullish on players coming off a bad year and bearish on players coming off a great year. And because we list the 50th percentile projections—the middle of the range the system thinks this player is capable of producing—it rarely predicts any player will hit 40 home runs or strike out 250 batters. At the end of this book, though, we've ranked the top players according to their projections. It's often as helpful to know who the system thinks will be the top second baseman as what his actual stats are likely to be. ■

ARIZONA DIAMONDBACKS

Essay by Zachary Levine

Player comments by Matt Sussman, Craig Goldstein, and BP authors

The phrase "mystery team" entered our vocabulary courtesy of then-*Sports Illustrated* writer and Arby's enthusiast Jon Heyman in 2010, putting its date of birth sometime after "walk-off" but before "churro dog." The original context was the Cliff Lee pursuit, the hot story of the winter meetings, with reporters using sources from agents to executives to flight-tracking systems to monitor the race between the Yankees and the Rangers for the services of the top free-agent pitcher in baseball. In the final stretches of the race, there emerged a mystery team, thought to be a ploy by an agent to drive up Lee's price, but proven to be legitimate when the Phillies swooped in and signed their former ace back.

In a way, the Diamondbacks of this offseason were the perfect mystery team in their pursuit and eventual signing of Zack Greinke. Not only was this supposed to be another two-team race, but had the Diamondbacks been the focus of any chatter, it could have easily been explained away by their trying to raise the price for the Giants and Dodgers.

But in another way, there's something ultimately flawed about the mystery team concept. The largely unspoken part of the phenomenon is that while no. 1 and 2 teams may be at the top of the list of probabilities, there are 28 other organizations that could at least theoretically sign the player; when you add up the small probabilities for those 28, there's a very substantial chance that a supposedly mystery team will sign *any* free agent. Perhaps in years past, the 28 probabilities were negligible next to the odds of the Yankees or Red Sox getting the player, but in this era of relative balance in spending, the mystery team has ceased to be all that interesting.

The Diamondbacks, with the Greinke signing and the trade of no. 1 overall pick Dansby Swanson (among others) to Atlanta for Shelby Miller, are more representative of another recent phenomenon, the birth of which came almost exactly one year later, also at the winter meetings. The key moment was Jose Reyes putting on a Miami Marlins jersey days after Heath Bell signed and days before Mark Buehrle gave their rotation sudden credibility.

It's the team that appears out of nowhere—not in terms of likelihood of signing players but in terms of national relevance—to make a huge winter splash, win the offseason, become a trendy pick, become a trendier pick-

DIAMONDBACKS PROSPECTUS

2015 W-L: 79-83, 3RD IN NL WEST

Pythag	.505	15th	DER	.706	11th
RS/G	4.44	8th	B-Age	26.4	2nd
RA/G	4.40	19th	P-Age	26.7	3rd
TAv	.266	7th	Salary	$88.2M	25th
BRR	14.69	3rd	M$/MW	$2.5M	22nd
TAv-P	.267	21st	DL Days	1071	17th
FIP	4.24	24th	$ on DL	15%	14th

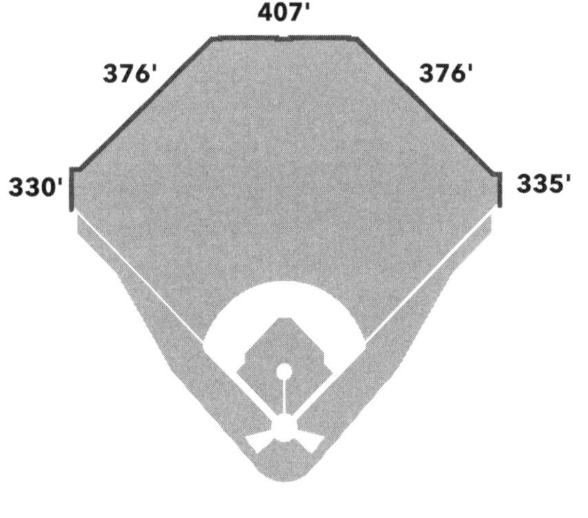

Outfield wall profile: **7'6"** to **25'**

Three-Year Park Factors

Runs	Runs/RH	Runs/LH	HR/RH	HR/LH
101	108	110	104	103

Top Hitter WARP	9.2	Paul Goldschmidt
Top Pitcher WARP	2.0	Brad Ziegler
Top Prospect		Braden Shipley

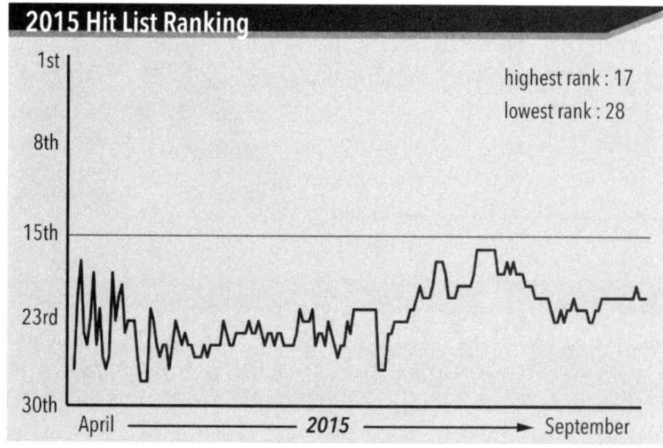

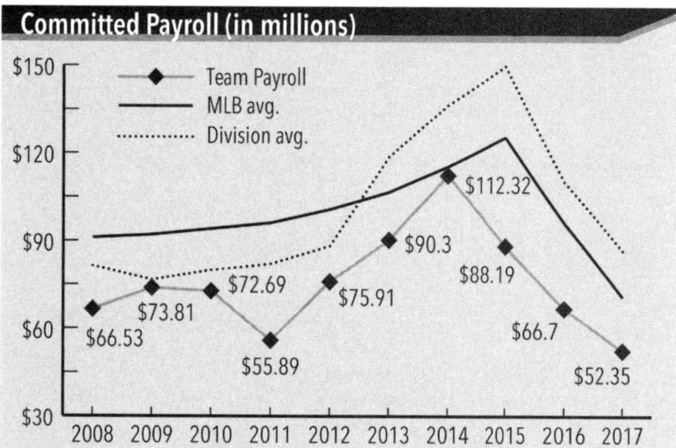

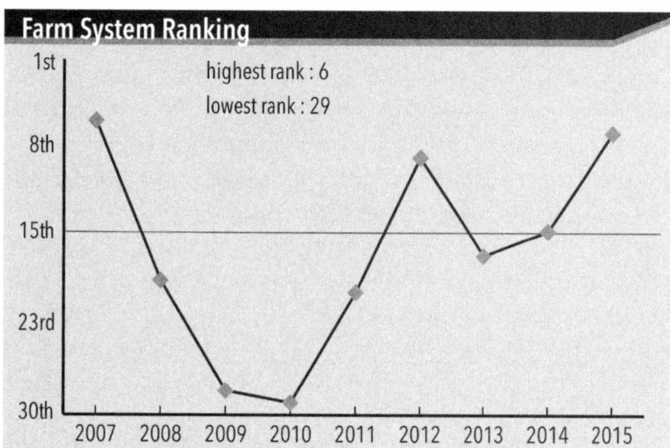

Personnel

President: Derrick Hall

General Manager: Dave Stewart

Manager: Chip Hale

against and enter the season as a massive story. Being Baseball Prospectus, we're probably supposed to give it a name from baseball history, so how about we call it the "Surprise Team Acquiring New Talent Outta Nowhere"?

The 2012 Marlins were the STANTON (named after former Yankees reliever Mike, of course) that we all saw coming, the master-planned STANTON. They were moving into a new stadium and loading up on names to put in promotional items, all while having the most important attribute of any true STANTON: They were a bad team.

Since the Marlins, there have been three other previously low-spenders who became instant buyers, whether by trade or free-agent signing, despite a poor prior-year record. The 2013 Blue Jays grabbed headlines with their acquisitions of R.A. Dickey and the 2012 Marlins, and last year, the illustriously bad Padres and White Sox had huge offseasons and were popular picks in their respective playoff races.

And now we have the Diamondbacks, coming off a year better than any of the STANTONs of yesteryear. They won 79 games, while none of the other four topped 75, and finished 2015 with a positive run differential, an MVP runner-up in Paul Goldschmidt and a young core that makes their offseason spending feel closer to final pieces than overhauls.

What should we expect from the latest of these big-mover sub-.500 teams? For one, attendance should go up. The other four averaged a 21 percent increase at the box office in the year after their big spends, though the 13 percent from the three teams not opening new stadiums might be a fairer estimate for where the Diamondbacks could be headed from their average 2015 attendance of 25,680, which ranked 23rd in baseball.

But if you believe in the n=4 (which, granted, you shouldn't do), Arizona isn't headed for much on the field. None of those four surprise offseason winners went up or down by more than three games. (See Table 1.) All that anticipation led to nothing: None of the teams was in contention in July, and none came all that close to a winning season, much less the playoffs.

Table 1: Selected teams following offseasons of increased spending

Year/Team	RECORD			AVERAGE ATTENDANCE		
	Before	After	Change	Before	After	Change
2012 Marlins	72-90	69-93	-3	18,772	27,401	+46%
2013 Blue Jays	73-89	74-88	+1	25,922	31,316	+21%
2015 Padres	77-85	74-88	-3	27,103	30,367	+12%
2015 White Sox	73-89	76-86	+3	20,381	21,677	+6%

Fine. How about the fact that the Diamondbacks are historically young and on the upward slope of their aging curves? They were just the seventh team since 1950 to have their primary starter at every position and all five of their primary starting pitchers be 28 or younger. Like the records of the big spenders, this is a less encouraging tidbit than it sounds at first. (See Table 2.) Ever since the late-1960s Athletics, whose players like Reggie Jackson, Blue Moon Odom and Catfish Hunter would become centerpieces of the early-1970s powerhouses, young teams are bad teams that take a long time to be competitive.

Table 2: Teams with primary starter at all eight positions and top five starters 28 and under

Team	Record	Years to .500	Years to 90+ wins
1967 Athletics	62-99	1	4
1968 Athletics	82-80	-	3
1982 Twins	60-102	2	6
1989 Mariners	73-89	2	8
1996 Tigers	53-109	10	10
1999 Expos	68-94	3	13
2015 Diamondbacks	79-83		

The encouraging part, if you're looking at it through Sedona red-colored glasses, is that there is a potential mixup of cause and effect in that chart. It's not that teams are noncompetitive because they relied on young players. In a lot of cases, it was just the opposite: They had a lot of young players because they were making no effort to be competitive.

For the Diamondbacks, who are, by contrast, making an *accelerated* effort to be competitive, this fun fact might be a very good thing. One talent they've had as an organization is turning late picks and non-elite prospects into outstanding major leaguers, Goldschmidt and David Peralta being among the best examples recently. Even first-rounder A.J. Pollock has considerably outplayed his projections, breaking out as a five-plus-win player. With a team that trailed only the Rockies in the National League in runs scored, adding pitching was clearly the way to go, and the Diamondbacks should therefore be better positioned to win than both the previous surprise teams and the previous hyper-young teams.

Given the differences between the Diamondbacks and previous STANTONs, and with the "S" in STANTON standing for "Surprise," it's fair to ask: Was Arizona's splurge legitimately a surprise?

In the sense that the Diamondbacks have never spent like this before, absolutely. They'd never paid anything close to the highest per-year salary in baseball, and, more strikingly, they came into this offseason as one of eight teams never to come to terms on a nine-figure deal. (See Table 3.)

Table 3: Most and fewest $100 million total value contracts signed by team, entering 2015-16 offseason

Team	$100M Contracts
Yankees	9
Red Sox	4
Tigers	4
Dodgers	4
...	...
Diamondbacks, Orioles, White Sox, Indians, Royals, Athletics, Pirates, Padres	0

Therefore, it's easy to think of the Diamondbacks as the picture of baseball's middle class, both in ways immeasurable—you'd never put them in a sentence with the Yankees and Red Sox, but they've historically never appeared with the Pirates and Royals either—and in their demographics:

- They play in the 13th-largest market in baseball, which puts them 17th in market size if you're willing to give full credit in the shared markets.
- Since their World Series postscript year of 2002, they haven't finished in the top five in attendance, but in their whole lifespan, they've never been a bottom-five team either.
- Of the 30 current home stadiums, theirs ranks as the 15th oldest.

In other words, yo ballclub so middle class, it might as well have two and a half children and a Costco membership.

But for a middle-class team, they've played every role imaginable. The idea of a long-term plan does not seem to be the Diamondbacks Way, to the extent you're allowed to have a Way if your franchise debuted more recently than Fastball's "The Way." If Arizona has established any pattern, it is rapidly changing approaches to roster-building.

One day, they're constructing the game's best farm system: Heading into their NL West title year of 2007, the Diamondbacks had four prospects listed in BP's Top 50—Chris Young, Stephen Drew, Carlos Quentin, Justin Upton—and honorable mentions in Carlos Gonzalez and Conor Jackson. Less than a decade later, they've already charged through mini-phases of mid-tier free-agent binging, spending cool-offs, win-now trades and prospect-dumping to end up where they are now: playing in the deep end of the pool with an eye toward doing the same in late October. The ownership hasn't changed, but even within the Ken Kendrick reign, it's as if they've gone through every ownership archetype in the past 10 seasons alone, and it's not clear anything is going to settle down anytime soon: Far be it from any of us to miss low on Tony La Russa's longevity, but a 69-year-old is not typically someone you'd hire for a nice long-term plan.

Arguably, though, those last two phases, prospect-dumping and big-splash acquiring, fit together, or at least coincide. See, for instance, Yasmany Tomas, a $68.5 million free-agent investment that came between the trades of Trevor Bauer and the straight sale of Touki Toussaint's contract. In other words, the Diamondbacks were foregoing dinner every night to save up for a Ferrari, but when they finally saved enough, they decided that topping out at 225 mph was for pikers, cashed in with a monster new television deal and headed to the Gulfstream dealership instead.

The Greinke signing was a surprising spend in the sense that you didn't hear Arizona's name leading up to it. They were the mystery team and fit that role well, especially as a division rival of the only two non-mystery teams. The Miller acquisition turned a move into a movement, a sure sign that their aim is 2016. Out of nowhere, though? No. These are moves launched out of a young roster, an impatient and frequently adjusting owner and the "everyone can play" economic structure of the MLBAM era.

The Diamondbacks' offseason campaign of "Evolution" couldn't fit this franchise any worse. They don't evolve; they change course dramatically, surge and collapse to last place and start all over again with the moves and results of next year having little to do with the last.

In that sense, the surprise offseason of the Diamondbacks was no surprise at all. ■

—Zachary Levine lives in Las Vegas and is a contributor to Baseball Prospectus.

HITTERS

Nick Ahmed SS

Born: 3/15/90 Age: 26 Bats: R Throws: R Height: 6'2" Weight: 195

YEAR	TEAM	LVL	AGE	PA	R	2B	3B	HR	RBI	BB	K	SB	CS	AVG/OBP/SLG	TAv	BABIP	BRR	FRAA	WARP
2013	MOB	AA	23	538	58	21	5	4	46	33	72	26	7	.236/.288/.324	.231	.266	1.3	SS(133): 21.7, 2B(2): -0.6	3.0
2014	RNO	AAA	24	452	57	26	4	4	47	37	55	14	6	.312/.373/.425	.272	.352	0.3	SS(91): 14.6, 2B(14): -0.8	3.9
2014	ARI	MLB	24	75	9	2	0	1	4	3	10	0	1	.200/.233/.271	.200	.220	1.0	SS(18): -1.7, 2B(2): -0.3	-0.3
2015	ARI	MLB	25	459	49	17	6	9	34	29	81	4	5	.226/.275/.359	.236	.257	4.6	SS(129): 5.2	1.8
2016	*ARI*	*MLB*	*26*	*495*	*53*	*22*	*4*	*7*	*41*	*28*	*86*	*9*	*5*	*.242/.287/.359*	*.226*	*.277*	*3.7*	*SS 8*	*2.0*
2017	*ARI*	*MLB*	*27*	*511*	*52*	*21*	*4*	*9*	*49*	*30*	*94*	*9*	*5*	*.235/.282/.355*	*.231*	*.270*	*4.2*	*SS 8*	*2.2*

Breakout: 6% Improve: 40% Collapse: 10% Attrition: 26% MLB: 73% *Comparables: Ramiro Pena, Brendan Ryan, Pete Kozma*

Being the one to replace Jeter is a daunting task. Being the one to replace the one who replaced Jeter? Less so. The Didi Gregorius trade paved a sandy path for Ahmed to become the full-time shortstop. He has the range of a Roomba, but he hits like one, too. A seedling of power (nine home runs was ninth among NL shortstops) and a better-than-average strikeout rate mean the average should improve, though he's not going to hit any higher than seventh on a good team. But if another shortstop comes along who can hit, the Snakes will probably let that one replace the one who replaced the one who replaced Jeter.

Jason Bourgeois LF

Born: 1/4/82 Age: 34 Bats: R Throws: R Height: 5'9" Weight: 200

YEAR	TEAM	LVL	AGE	PA	R	2B	3B	HR	RBI	BB	K	SB	CS	AVG/OBP/SLG	TAv	BABIP	BRR	FRAA	WARP
2013	DUR	AAA	31	391	52	15	3	2	61	31	38	22	6	.290/.343/.368	.251	.315	3.8	LF(40): 4.9, CF(39): 2.1	1.7
2013	TBA	MLB	31	18	2	0	0	1	2	2	4	0	0	.188/.278/.375	.335	.182	0.5	LF(6): -0.2, RF(1): -0.0	0.2
2014	CIN	MLB	32	34	5	0	1	0	1	1	6	0	0	.242/.265/.303	.221	.296	0.2	LF(8): -0.4, CF(2): -0.0	-0.1
2014	LOU	AAA	32	600	76	29	3	4	43	40	51	24	9	.278/.328/.363	.232	.299	5.1	CF(112): -3.4, LF(18): -2.7	-0.2
2015	LOU	AAA	33	60	8	2	1	0	7	3	5	1	1	.309/.356/.382	.261	.340	0.1	CF(8): -0.5, LF(5): -0.4	0.1
2015	CIN	MLB	33	212	28	5	2	3	14	14	33	3	1	.240/.294/.332	.243	.275	0.3	CF(35): -2.3, LF(18): 0.6	0.0
2016	*ARI*	*MLB*	*34*	*250*	*27*	*10*	*2*	*2*	*18*	*14*	*35*	*7*	*3*	*.254/.296/.341*	*.225*	*.285*	*0.2*	*CF -2, LF 0*	*-0.3*
2017	*ARI*	*MLB*	*35*	*277*	*26*	*10*	*2*	*2*	*22*	*15*	*40*	*6*	*3*	*.246/.289/.323*	*.225*	*.280*	*0.4*	*CF -2, LF 0*	*-0.3*

Breakout: 1% Improve: 16% Collapse: 8% Attrition: 15% MLB: 44% *Comparables: Kerry Robinson, Jesus Feliciano, Calvin Murray*

As Lincoln once didn't say, "It is better to be thought a punchless out-maker than to get enough playing time and remove all doubt." When Bourgeois filled in for the injured Billy Hamilton last summer he displayed a similar inability to steal first base, along with a dissimilar inability to steal any other base or run down flyballs. Bourgeois has parlayed his good wheels into center field reserve stints for six teams over the last eight seasons, but now that he's 34 and seems to have lost a step he's looking more and more like a donut tire.

Socrates Brito RF

Born: 9/6/92 Age: 23 Bats: L Throws: L Height: 6'1" Weight: 200

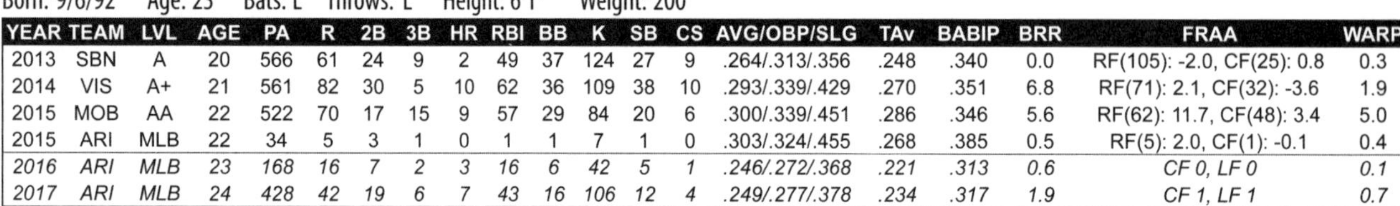

YEAR	TEAM	LVL	AGE	PA	R	2B	3B	HR	RBI	BB	K	SB	CS	AVG/OBP/SLG	TAv	BABIP	BRR	FRAA	WARP
2013	SBN	A	20	566	61	24	9	2	49	37	124	27	9	.264/.313/.356	.248	.340	0.0	RF(105): -2.0, CF(25): 0.8	0.3
2014	VIS	A+	21	561	82	30	5	10	62	36	109	38	10	.293/.339/.429	.270	.351	6.8	RF(71): 2.1, CF(32): -3.6	1.9
2015	MOB	AA	22	522	70	17	15	9	57	29	84	20	6	.300/.339/.451	.286	.346	5.6	RF(62): 11.7, CF(48): 3.4	5.0
2015	ARI	MLB	22	34	5	3	1	0	1	1	7	1	0	.303/.324/.455	.268	.385	0.5	RF(5): 2.0, CF(1): -0.1	0.4
2016	*ARI*	*MLB*	*23*	*168*	*16*	*7*	*2*	*3*	*16*	*6*	*42*	*5*	*1*	*.246/.272/.368*	*.221*	*.313*	*0.6*	*CF 0, LF 0*	*0.1*
2017	*ARI*	*MLB*	*24*	*428*	*42*	*19*	*6*	*7*	*43*	*16*	*106*	*12*	*4*	*.249/.277/.378*	*.234*	*.317*	*1.9*	*CF 1, LF 1*	*0.7*

Breakout: 0% Improve: 0% Collapse: 2% Attrition: 4% MLB: 4% *Comparables: Kyle Waldrop, Scott Cousins, Mikie Mahtook*

Let's say you have a friend who is knowledgeable about baseball, and prospects in particular. It's not merely that he knows who the good ones are, but he knows why they are good. You, well, you know some—enough to know that you don't know enough. You and your friend are talking, and Brito's name comes up. You say, "I like him. He's got a good name." Your friend is aghast. He begins to lecture you sternly:

"Brito? That's the guy you like? Sure he's not bad, but he barely walks! He doesn't strike out a ton either, but you're still stuck with a guy who is going to *have* to hit in the .280s or above to be of much use offensively, because he's not going to provide power. There just isn't much lower-half involvement in his swing. The glove is nice, and he's got a nice arm, but he's most likely a corner guy, which means he's going to have to be in the vein of Jason Heyward on defense to be a first-division player. I'd like him more in center. There's a lot of risk in Brito because if his hit tool isn't plus, he becomes more of a fourth outfielder. If he does hit, though, there's a lot to like."

First things first: Your friend is kind of a tool. But he makes some good points. Still, what you know most about prospects is that no one knows anything. Now, your friend, he fancies he knows something, although he knows nothing; whereas you, as you do not know anything, do not fancy that you do. In this trifling particular, then, you appear to be wiser than he, because you do not fancy you know what you do not know.

As you walk away from the conversation, you say to yourself, "Although I do not suppose that either of us knows anything really beautiful and good, I am better off than he is."

Welington Castillo C

Born: 4/24/87 Age: 29 Bats: R Throws: R Height: 5'10" Weight: 210

YEAR	TEAM	LVL	AGE	PA	R	2B	3B	HR	RBI	BB	K	SB	CS	AVG/OBP/SLG	TAv	BABIP	BRR	FRAA	WARP
2013	CHN	MLB	26	428	41	23	0	8	32	34	97	2	0	.274/.349/.397	.266	.347	-1.0	C(111): -19.7	0.0
2014	CHN	MLB	27	417	28	19	0	13	46	26	102	0	0	.237/.296/.389	.261	.288	-1.9	C(106): -15.0	0.1
2015	SEA	MLB	28	28	3	0	0	0	2	1	5	0	0	.160/.179/.160	.134	.182	0.0	C(5): -1.0	-0.4
2015	CHN	MLB	28	47	5	2	0	2	5	3	12	0	0	.163/.234/.349	.233	.172	0.0	C(9): 0.3	0.1
2015	ARI	MLB	28	303	34	13	1	17	50	21	75	0	0	.255/.317/.496	.284	.286	-0.9	C(74): -10.8	0.9
2016	*ARI*	*MLB*	*29*	*535*	*60*	*24*	*1*	*19*	*69*	*41*	*132*	*1*	*0*	*.250/.319/.422*	*.261*	*.304*	*-1.4*	*C -23*	*-0.2*
2017	*ARI*	*MLB*	*30*	*452*	*56*	*20*	*1*	*16*	*56*	*34*	*115*	*0*	*0*	*.247/.314/.414*	*.263*	*.302*	*-1.4*	*C -20*	*-0.2*

Breakout: 4% Improve: 36% Collapse: 6% Attrition: 14% MLB: 92% *Comparables: Ryan Doumit, Nick Hundley, Ben Broussard*

YEAR	TEAM	P. COUNT	FRM RUNS	BLK RUNS	THRW RUNS	TOT RUNS
2013	CHN	15558	-21.5	1.2	0.4	-20.0
2014	CHN	15118	-15.5	0.7	-0.7	-15.6
2015	CHN	1119	0.4	0.0	0.0	0.4
2015	SEA	860	-0.8	0.0	0.0	-0.9
2015	ARI	10394	-10.8	0.0	-0.2	-11.0
2016	*ARI*	*19412*	*-23.3*	*0.6*	*-0.3*	*-23.0*
2017	*ARI*	*16386*	*-20.7*	*0.5*	*-0.3*	*-20.6*

The man they call Beef had never actually tried steak coated with pâté and duxelles wrapped in puff pastry until last year, when Fox Sports Arizona arranged the meal for a TV segment. Which means he might have never tasted the delicacy at all had Jon Lester not brought his own personal catcher to the Cubs, making Castillo an expendable third man, causing his bosses to ice floe him first toward catcher-starved Seattle and finally to the desert, where coyote wellington is just too gamy. Get him enough playing time and he'll pop 20-plus baseballs over the fence—he was just one shy in 2015, conclusive proof that he didn't get enough playing time—but given the low OBP it's best to match him with a left-handed catcher, preferably one who enjoys chicken divan.

Isan Diaz MI

Born: 5/27/96 Age: 20 Bats: L Throws: R Height: 5'10" Weight: 185

YEAR	TEAM	LVL	AGE	PA	R	2B	3B	HR	RBI	BB	K	SB	CS	AVG/OBP/SLG	TAv	BABIP	BRR	FRAA	WARP
2016	*ARI*	*MLB*	*20*	*250*	*27*	*9*	*1*	*6*	*23*	*15*	*79*	*2*	*1*	*.205/.255/.337*	*.206*	*.277*	*-0.2*	*SS -1, 2B -0*	*-0.3*
2017	*ARI*	*MLB*	*21*	*344*	*36*	*14*	*2*	*9*	*36*	*22*	*106*	*3*	*2*	*.215/.269/.356*	*.225*	*.287*	*-0.2*	*SS -1, 2B 0*	*0.2*

Breakout: 0% Improve: 1% Collapse: 0% Attrition: 3% MLB: 3% *Comparables: Eugenio Suarez, Brad Harman, Yamaico Navarro*

It's long been assumed that Diaz, a 2014 second-rounder, will drift across the bag and spend his career at the keystone. The Diamondbacks think differently, at least for now, as he spent 93 percent of his innings at shortstop. Either way, defense isn't the selling point here, as Diaz excels at the plate with a sweet swing in the style of Carlos Gonzalez. Last year his contact and power skills erupted in the Pioneer League, which he led in OPS. His package of tools indicates a jack of all trades, master of none: He should be average to slightly above across the board, but is unlikely to find the equilibrium that makes him more than a starter on a bad team.

Brandon Drury 3B

Born: 8/21/92 Age: 23 Bats: R Throws: R Height: 6'1" Weight: 215

YEAR	TEAM	LVL	AGE	PA	R	2B	3B	HR	RBI	BB	K	SB	CS	AVG/OBP/SLG	TAv	BABIP	BRR	FRAA	WARP
2013	SBN	A	20	583	78	51	4	15	85	47	92	1	1	.302/.362/.500	.308	.340	-3.8	3B(108): 5.5	4.9
2014	VIS	A+	21	478	73	35	1	19	81	41	76	4	3	.300/.366/.519	.299	.326	-2.7	3B(84): 1.3, 3B(4): 1.3	3.3
2014	MOB	AA	21	116	12	7	0	4	14	7	19	0	0	.295/.345/.476	.302	.321	0.8	3B(28): -1.5, 2B(2): 0.3	0.9
2015	RNO	AAA	22	276	43	26	0	2	25	21	35	0	2	.331/.384/.458	.278	.375	-1.0	3B(28): -3.1, 2B(27): -1.6	0.9
2015	MOB	AA	22	291	22	14	1	3	36	11	41	4	5	.278/.306/.370	.252	.312	-0.7	2B(35): 2.2, 3B(32): 1.9	1.0
2015	ARI	MLB	22	59	3	3	0	2	8	2	8	0	0	.214/.254/.375	.205	.217	-1.5	3B(11): -0.6, 2B(6): -0.1	-0.4
2016	*ARI*	*MLB*	*23*	*32*	*3*	*2*	*0*	*1*	*4*	*2*	*7*	*0*	*0*	*.257/.294/.407*	*.241*	*.303*	*-0.1*	*3B -0*	*0.0*
2017	*ARI*	*MLB*	*24*	*325*	*36*	*20*	*1*	*8*	*36*	*17*	*67*	*1*	*1*	*.259/.302/.408*	*.253*	*.307*	*-0.8*	*3B -1*	*0.4*

Breakout: 5% Improve: 21% Collapse: 1% Attrition: 11% MLB: 31% *Comparables: Tommy La Stella, Stefen Romero, German Duran*

With Martin Prado several years gone, Randall Delgado mired in the 'pen and Nick Ahmed proving to be the no-hit shortstop he was billed as, it's likely that Drury becomes the most valuable piece from the disappointing Justin Upton package. Drury's whole is more than the sum of his parts, as he doesn't truly excel at anything, nor is he truly poor at anything (though he's slow). His power outburst of yesteryear proved to be a Cal League mirage—though it's worth noting he does have above-average raw. While his power generally plays down, Chase Field is a bigger booster than T. Boone Pickens, so we could see a 20-homer season somewhere down the line. He's a better defender at the hot corner than the keystone, but the latter provides a more direct path to playing time at present.

Paul Goldschmidt 1B

Born: 9/10/87 Age: 28 Bats: R Throws: R Height: 6'3" Weight: 225

YEAR	TEAM	LVL	AGE	PA	R	2B	3B	HR	RBI	BB	K	SB	CS	AVG/OBP/SLG	TAv	BABIP	BRR	FRAA	WARP
2013	ARI	MLB	25	710	103	36	3	36	125	99	145	15	7	.302/.401/.551	.325	.343	-0.3	1B(159): 18.0	7.5
2014	ARI	MLB	26	479	75	39	1	19	69	64	110	9	3	.300/.396/.542	.332	.368	3.9	1B(109): 3.1	4.8
2015	ARI	MLB	27	695	103	38	2	33	110	118	151	21	5	.321/.435/.570	.348	.382	2.4	1B(157): 17.0	9.2
2016	*ARI*	*MLB*	*28*	*645*	*95*	*37*	*2*	*30*	*99*	*89*	*146*	*15*	*5*	*.290/.388/.531*	*.316*	*.342*	*1.7*	*1B 10*	*6.2*
2017	*ARI*	*MLB*	*29*	*585*	*89*	*34*	*2*	*26*	*89*	*80*	*132*	*13*	*4*	*.290/.387/.523*	*.320*	*.343*	*1.8*	*1B 9*	*5.7*

Breakout: 1% Improve: 47% Collapse: 2% Attrition: 1% MLB: 99% *Comparables: Joey Votto, Miguel Cabrera, Prince Fielder*

If we're going to blame anyone for glossing over the accomplishments of Goldschmidt, perhaps it's our fault for getting too used to big, burly first basemen in the 90s. Mark McGwire became the spokesslugger for ludicrous home run totals, and did it so (sideeyes) well that it diluted the brilliance of Jeff Bagwell, Todd Helton, Fred McGriff and Carlos Delgado. We're not sure that even Albert Pujols, who produced stupendous year after stupendouser year, *really* gets credit for what he did—he had more WARP by age 28 than Derek Jeter did in his career, for goodness sakes.

That era's gone, but still we write more about the Zobrists and the Gordons and the Molinas than we do about Goldschmidt, who last year produced, by WARP, the eighth-best season by a first baseman since 1950, behind Norm Cash and six Pujols seasons. The culture of the game is getting younger, Vinier and stratospherically more athletic (all good things!). None of those descriptors leaps to mind when discussing Goldschmidt, though in addition to hitting for power and average, he plays great defense and can even run. He contains all desired qualities in a baseball star, except he can't play the middle of the field. (Bryce Harper having a legendary year didn't help either.)

What's it going to take to get him noticed? A 50-homer season? An indelible postseason moment? Converting him to right field, which he could probably do and do well? Perhaps all of the above. But the most clinical and correct way for him to force the issue, of course, is to just produce stupendous year after stupendouser year.

Tuffy Gosewisch C

Born: 8/17/83 Age: 32 Bats: R Throws: R Height: 5'11" Weight: 200

YEAR	TEAM	LVL	AGE	PA	R	2B	3B	HR	RBI	BB	K	SB	CS	AVG/OBP/SLG	TAv	BABIP	BRR	FRAA	WARP
2013	RNO	AAA	29	272	30	20	1	7	33	17	40	1	1	.284/.327/.456	.264	.309	-0.8	C(68): 10.9	2.4
2013	ARI	MLB	29	47	1	2	0	0	3	0	8	0	0	.178/.174/.222	.146	.211	-0.1	C(13): 0.7	-0.3
2014	ARI	MLB	30	132	6	8	0	1	7	3	24	0	0	.225/.242/.310	.211	.269	0.5	C(35): -1.0	-0.1
2015	ARI	MLB	31	138	9	6	0	1	13	8	23	2	1	.211/.261/.281	.240	.248	1.4	C(37): -1.3	0.4
2016	*ARI*	*MLB*	*32*	*65*	*6*	*3*	*0*	*1*	*6*	*3*	*12*	*0*	*0*	*.239/.274/.353*	*.225*	*.279*	*0.2*	*C 0*	*0.1*
2017	*ARI*	*MLB*	*33*	*145*	*13*	*7*	*0*	*2*	*13*	*6*	*28*	*1*	*0*	*.220/.257/.323*	*.217*	*.259*	*0.4*	*C 0*	*0.0*

Breakout: 3% Improve: 15% Collapse: 12% Attrition: 26% MLB: 68% *Comparables: Wil Nieves, Koyie Hill, Omir Santos*

It's not often that something like Tuffy Gosewisch is Plan A, but Arizona followed the fantasy strategy of punting catcher and made Gosewisch the starting backstop. His throwing arm is his one loud tool, which is probably enough for him to compete for a backup spot, but he hits like Triple-A depth. After a torn ACL ended his season in late May, the Diamondbacks were forced into action and acquired Welington Castillo and Jarrod Saltalamacchia. From June 1st on, Arizona catchers hit .253/.317/.500. We don't all know what our purpose in life is, but surely some of us were put here to fall off a cliff so that the county finally puts a "no climbing" sign up there.

YEAR	TEAM	P. COUNT	FRM RUNS	BLK RUNS	THRW RUNS	TOT RUNS
2013	ARI	1789	1.0	0.1	0.0	1.1
2013	RNO	9169	8.3	1.5	2.6	12.4
2014	ARI	4630	-1.7	0.1	0.4	-1.2
2015	ARI	5113	-1.2	0.0	0.0	-1.2
2016	*ARI*	*2411*	*-0.3*	*0.1*	*0.3*	*0.1*
2017	*ARI*	*5374*	*-0.9*	*0.3*	*0.6*	*0.0*

Phil Gosselin 2B

Born: 10/3/88 Age: 27 Bats: R Throws: R Height: 6'1" Weight: 200

YEAR	TEAM	LVL	AGE	PA	R	2B	3B	HR	RBI	BB	K	SB	CS	AVG/OBP/SLG	TAv	BABIP	BRR	FRAA	WARP
2013	ATL	MLB	24	7	2	0	0	0	0	1	2	0	0	.333/.429/.333	.258	.500	0.2	2B(3): -0.0	0.0
2013	MIS	AA	24	241	27	10	1	1	23	12	31	5	1	.243/.291/.312	.244	.275	0.4	2B(35): 4.4, LF(16): -2.5	0.4
2013	GWN	AAA	24	228	17	4	1	2	15	12	38	1	0	.266/.308/.324	.234	.315	1.3	2B(46): 5.3, LF(4): 0.1	0.6
2014	ATL	MLB	25	136	17	4	0	1	3	5	27	2	2	.266/.304/.320	.268	.330	1.5	2B(26): -0.8, 3B(9): 1.3	0.7
2014	GWN	AAA	25	407	58	29	5	5	31	19	62	6	1	.344/.379/.487	.293	.401	2.1	3B(41): 1.9, 2B(25): -1.0	2.7
2015	VIS	A+	26	23	3	0	0	0	2	1	5	0	0	.318/.348/.318	.227	.412	0.2	2B(2): -0.1, 3B(1): 0.0	0.0
2015	ARI	MLB	26	76	17	5	1	3	13	7	11	0	1	.303/.382/.545	.327	.321	1.0	2B(13): -0.4, LF(3): -0.1	0.8
2015	RNO	AAA	26	22	4	4	0	0	5	1	2	0	0	.333/.364/.524	.288	.368	0.1	2B(3): 0.4, 3B(1): -0.3	0.1
2015	ATL	MLB	26	42	2	4	0	0	2	2	5	2	0	.325/.357/.425	.282	.371	0.0	3B(5): 0.3, 2B(3): -0.2	0.2
2016	*ARI*	*MLB*	*27*	*220*	*24*	*12*	*2*	*3*	*20*	*10*	*42*	*2*	*1*	*.276/.313/.400*	*.250*	*.323*	*1.3*	*2B 2, LF -0*	*0.9*
2017	*ARI*	*MLB*	*28*	*327*	*34*	*17*	*2*	*5*	*33*	*14*	*65*	*3*	*1*	*.267/.304/.392*	*.253*	*.315*	*1.9*	*2B 3, LF 0*	*1.3*

Breakout: 4% Improve: 23% Collapse: 13% Attrition: 27% MLB: 63% *Comparables: Eugenio Velez, Danny Richar, Tony Abreu*

Perhaps the most esoteric trade in recent memory involved Gosselin, who was sent from Atlanta in exchange for Touki Toussaint and Bronson Arroyo—a high-risk first rounder and a dead-weight contract for a broken-thumbed 26th man. Why Gosselin? Presumably, because it would have felt weird to give away two players for *literally* nothing, rather than figuratively nothing. His bat-to-ball skills might be better than originally thought, but he will continue to feel like that free U2 album on your playlist.

Gabriel Guerrero RF

Born: 12/11/93 Age: 22 Bats: R Throws: R Height: 6'3" Weight: 190

YEAR	TEAM	LVL	AGE	PA	R	2B	3B	HR	RBI	BB	K	SB	CS	AVG/OBP/SLG	TAv	BABIP	BRR	FRAA	WARP
2013	CLN	A	19	499	60	23	3	4	50	21	113	12	3	.271/.303/.358	.251	.344	1.8	RF(121): 10.5	1.7
2014	HDS	A+	20	580	97	28	2	18	96	34	131	18	6	.307/.347/.467	.267	.373	3.6	RF(94): -1.9, CF(9): -2.6	0.9
2015	MOB	AA	21	297	29	15	5	5	32	11	60	8	2	.226/.256/.367	.242	.268	2.5	RF(58): 0.9, CF(19): 3.6	0.8
2015	WTN	AA	21	191	22	10	0	2	15	12	48	3	0	.215/.262/.305	.206	.279	1.5	CF(28): 3.6, RF(22): 3.5	0.3
2016	*ARI*	*MLB*	*22*	*250*	*21*	*11*	*2*	*4*	*24*	*7*	*72*	*3*	*1*	*.221/.243/.333*	*.201*	*.292*	*0.2*	*RF 1, CF -0*	*-0.7*
2017	*ARI*	*MLB*	*23*	*394*	*38*	*19*	*3*	*8*	*39*	*12*	*108*	*5*	*1*	*.233/.257/.359*	*.223*	*.303*	*0.4*	*RF 2, CF 0*	*-0.3*

Breakout: 5% Improve: 5% Collapse: 0% Attrition: 4% MLB: 5% *Comparables: Socrates Brito, Brennan Boesch, Alex Hassan*

Long on tools but short on patience, Guerrero struggled in his first taste of the upper minors, where a steady diet of breaking balls (and a hack-tastic approach) left him hungry. A slow starter in 2013 and a fast starter in 2014, Guerrero was a non-starter last year. He didn't clear a .250 batting average nor .275 OBP in any month, and his struggles made it easier for Seattle to part with him in the Mark Trumbo trade. Guerrero's inability to adjust in-season is a bit concerning, but it's too soon to give up on a 22-year-old with his raw ability and makeup—he's said to love the game. The 2016 season is a make-or-break one; we'll find out just how much the game loves Guerrero back.

Aaron Hill 2B

Born: 3/21/82 Age: 34 Bats: R Throws: R Height: 5'11" Weight: 200

YEAR	TEAM	LVL	AGE	PA	R	2B	3B	HR	RBI	BB	K	SB	CS	AVG/OBP/SLG	TAv	BABIP	BRR	FRAA	WARP
2013	ARI	MLB	31	362	45	21	1	11	41	29	48	1	4	.291/.356/.462	.288	.312	-0.1	2B(84): -2.3	1.8
2013	RNO	AAA	31	26	8	1	1	0	6	1	3	0	0	.375/.385/.500	.281	.409	0.1	2B(6): 0.5	0.2
2014	ARI	MLB	32	541	52	26	3	10	60	28	92	4	3	.244/.287/.367	.234	.276	-2.6	2B(116): 4.2, 3B(7): -0.1	0.2
2015	ARI	MLB	33	353	32	18	0	6	39	31	54	7	2	.230/.295/.345	.241	.253	2.1	2B(47): 2.4, 3B(38): -1.1	0.7
2016	*ARI*	*MLB*	*34*	*367*	*44*	*19*	*2*	*8*	*36*	*25*	*56*	*5*	*2*	*.259/.314/.403*	*.248*	*.285*	*0.0*	*2B 2, 3B -1*	*1.0*
2017	*ARI*	*MLB*	*35*	*300*	*33*	*16*	*1*	*6*	*31*	*21*	*48*	*3*	*2*	*.251/.307/.384*	*.249*	*.282*	*0.0*	*2B 1, 3B -1*	*0.7*

Breakout: 0% Improve: 33% Collapse: 11% Attrition: 13% MLB: 92% *Comparables: Bill Madlock, Denny Walling, Chone Figgins*

For several years, Hill racked up counting stats to match those of the league's best second basemen. He played good defense, and his power was impressive (though regrettably inconsistent). Of late, though, he's declined so sharply that he barely fits as a big-league backup infielder. The final remnant of Kevin Towers' spendencies, he was the biggest earner on last year's D'backs payroll. Second and third on that list were salary dumps, and the most likely reason Hill didn't join them on the train out of town was the $12 million that he's owed this year, too.

Jake Lamb 3B

Born: 10/9/90 Age: 25 Bats: L Throws: R Height: 6'3" Weight: 205

YEAR	TEAM	LVL	AGE	PA	R	2B	3B	HR	RBI	BB	K	SB	CS	AVG/OBP/SLG	TAv	BABIP	BRR	FRAA	WARP
2013	VIS	A+	22	283	44	20	0	13	47	48	70	0	0	.303/.424/.558	.331	.380	-0.1	3B(55): -2.5	2.8
2014	MOB	AA	23	439	60	35	5	14	79	50	99	0	0	.318/.399/.551	.334	.389	-1.1	3B(97): -3.0	4.6
2014	ARI	MLB	23	133	15	4	1	4	11	6	37	1	1	.230/.263/.373	.226	.291	0.4	3B(34): -0.4	0.0
2014	RNO	AAA	23	21	3	4	0	1	5	3	4	2	0	.500/.571/.889	.471	.615	0.1	3B(5): -0.5, 1B(1): -0.1	0.5
2015	ARI	MLB	24	390	38	15	5	6	34	36	97	3	2	.263/.331/.386	.263	.344	-1.7	3B(95): 9.8, 1B(8): 0.4	2.3
2016	*ARI*	*MLB*	*25*	*610*	*66*	*31*	*5*	*17*	*74*	*57*	*162*	*4*	*2*	*.259/.329/.426*	*.264*	*.334*	*-0.6*	*3B 8, 1B 0*	*2.7*
2017	*ARI*	*MLB*	*26*	*536*	*63*	*26*	*4*	*14*	*61*	*48*	*140*	*3*	*2*	*.252/.320/.410*	*.263*	*.322*	*-0.6*	*3B 7, 1B 0*	*2.2*

Breakout: 4% Improve: 41% Collapse: 9% Attrition: 22% MLB: 91% *Comparables: Pedro Alvarez, Cody Asche, Ian Stewart*

Lamb basically won Arizona's third base job last year over Yasmany Tomas, and we say "basically" because he didn't actually start Opening Day, due to his tragic flaw: The Diamondbacks were facing a lefty, and he simply can't hit like a starting third baseman against those guys (.200/.275/.267). The overall production is enough to stick in the bigs, thanks to his defensive chops—particularly his excellent range. Sometimes players grow out of platoon splits, and Chip Hale protected him enough that we don't have a conclusive sample yet.

Peter O'Brien C

Born: 7/15/90 Age: 25 Bats: R Throws: R Height: 6'4" Weight: 235

YEAR	TEAM	LVL	AGE	PA	R	2B	3B	HR	RBI	BB	K	SB	CS	AVG/OBP/SLG	TAv	BABIP	BRR	FRAA	WARP
2013	TAM	A+	22	280	31	17	3	11	55	19	76	0	1	.265/.314/.486	.280	.326	0.1	3B(38): -4.8, C(12): -0.1	1.0
2013	CSC	A	22	226	47	22	1	11	41	22	58	0	0	.325/.394/.619	.396	.397	0.9	C(53): -0.4	4.5
2014	TRN	AA	23	294	47	14	1	23	51	16	77	0	0	.245/.296/.555	.291	.253	-0.9	1B(27): -1.1, C(19): -3.3	0.9
2014	TAM	A+	23	119	19	9	1	10	19	4	29	0	0	.321/.353/.688	.349	.351	-0.1	C(24): -0.2, RF(6): 2.2	1.9
2015	RNO	AAA	24	534	77	35	9	26	107	31	124	1	3	.284/.332/.551	.292	.328	-0.1	LF(57): -7.7, RF(47): 0.0	2.2
2015	ARI	MLB	24	12	1	1	0	1	3	2	5	0	0	.400/.500/.800	.433	.750	-0.3	LF(3): -0.2	0.2
2016	*ARI*	*MLB*	*25*	*73*	*9*	*4*	*1*	*4*	*11*	*4*	*23*	*0*	*0*	*.243/.286/.486*	*.264*	*.299*	*-0.1*	*RF 0*	*0.3*
2017	*ARI*	*MLB*	*26*	*296*	*39*	*15*	*2*	*15*	*45*	*16*	*93*	*0*	*0*	*.239/.286/.478*	*.268*	*.298*	*-0.5*	*RF 0*	*1.0*

Breakout: 2% Improve: 18% Collapse: 9% Attrition: 23% MLB: 53% *Comparables: Carlos Peguero, Matt Clark, Bryce Brentz*

In July of 1961, psychologist Stanley Milgram conducted experiments on obedience to authority. He set out to discover how much pain a person would inflict on another if a man in a uniform ordered it. The answer, it turned out, was a lot—most subjects were willing to send 450 volts of electricity into a helpless and innocent stranger. And so we get to understand the poor, cowed soul who carried out the task of keeping the stiff-handed, yips-stricken O'Brien behind the plate in spring

YEAR	TEAM	P. COUNT	FRM RUNS	BLK RUNS	THRW RUNS	TOT RUNS
2014	TRN	2618	-2.1	-0.4	-1.0	-3.5
2014	MOB	235	0.6	-0.2	0.1	0.5
2015	RNO	1630	0.3	0.0	0.1	0.4

training. Thankfully, the Diamondbacks ended the experiment late in camp, after which O'Brien flourished, swatting 70 extra-base hits at Triple-A Reno and earning a cup of coffee as an outfielder. The length in his swing will always result in strikeouts by the bushel, but when he makes contact, he usually puts a charge into the ball. O'Brien profiles best at first base, but he's expected to break in as a corner outfielder. That's likely to be a short-lived experiment, too, but this one will be more like a 10-volt charge at worst.

Chris Owings 2B

Born: 8/12/91 Age: 24 Bats: R Throws: R Height: 5'10" Weight: 190

YEAR	TEAM	LVL	AGE	PA	R	2B	3B	HR	RBI	BB	K	SB	CS	AVG/OBP/SLG	TAv	BABIP	BRR	FRAA	WARP
2013	RNO	AAA	21	575	104	31	8	12	81	22	99	20	7	.330/.359/.482	.272	.386	6.3	SS(111): 5.9, 2B(11): -1.0	4.2
2013	ARI	MLB	21	61	5	5	0	0	5	6	10	2	0	.291/.361/.382	.254	.356	-0.9	SS(13): -0.9, 2B(3): 0.2	0.0
2014	ARI	MLB	22	332	34	15	6	6	26	16	67	8	1	.261/.300/.406	.250	.314	-0.8	SS(61): -3.7, 2B(18): -1.3	0.3
2014	RNO	AAA	22	40	6	1	0	0	1	0	9	3	0	.250/.250/.275	.178	.323	0.8	2B(8): -0.1, SS(1): -0.0	-0.2
2015	ARI	MLB	23	552	59	27	5	4	43	26	144	16	4	.227/.264/.322	.213	.305	1.9	2B(115): -5.0, SS(35): -4.9	-1.9
2016	*ARI*	*MLB*	*24*	*509*	*58*	*25*	*5*	*8*	*44*	*22*	*114*	*14*	*4*	*.257/.290/.382*	*.233*	*.315*	*-0.2*	*2B -4, SS -1*	*0.1*
2017	*ARI*	*MLB*	*25*	*513*	*53*	*25*	*4*	*9*	*52*	*24*	*116*	*14*	*4*	*.258/.294/.383*	*.243*	*.318*	*0.2*	*2B -4, SS -1*	*0.6*

Breakout: 7% Improve: 46% Collapse: 4% Attrition: 15% MLB: 89% *Comparables: Omar Infante, Robinson Cano, Josh Barfield*

Owings wasn't just disappointing in 2015; he was historically abysmal. He reached base exactly as many times (144) as he struck out, becoming only the 21st player ever to qualify for the batting title without reaching more than he whiffed. Most of Owings' predecessors were thoroughly vexed power hitters (Mark Reynolds, Adam Dunn, Rob Deer) who nonetheless tatered a bunch. To find somebody with Owings' mass of suck *and* lack of slug, go all the way back to Bill Cunningham in 1911. Owings had curiously low splits against lefties, so if it's all BABIP luck, then perhaps he'll bounce back better than Cunningham, who would go on to play eight more games in his career and eventually die.

David Peralta LF

Born: 8/14/87 Age: 28 Bats: L Throws: L Height: 6'1" Weight: 215

YEAR	TEAM	LVL	AGE	PA	R	2B	3B	HR	RBI	BB	K	SB	CS	AVG/OBP/SLG	TAv	BABIP	BRR	FRAA	WARP
2013	VIS	A+	25	219	29	15	0	8	42	9	28	1	0	.346/.370/.534	.300	.368	0.5	LF(36): 1.9, RF(8): -1.1	1.6
2014	ARI	MLB	26	348	40	12	9	8	36	16	60	6	3	.286/.320/.450	.272	.328	0.1	RF(40): 3.2, LF(36): -4.5	0.8
2014	MOB	AA	26	223	33	17	1	6	46	18	21	2	0	.297/.359/.480	.311	.307	1.8	LF(43): 1.8, CF(4): -0.6	2.0
2015	ARI	MLB	27	517	61	26	10	17	78	44	107	9	4	.312/.371/.522	.320	.368	-1.2	LF(124): 4.4, RF(9): -0.3	4.7
2016	*ARI*	*MLB*	*28*	*593*	*68*	*30*	*8*	*17*	*76*	*38*	*111*	*8*	*4*	*.285/.333/.466*	*.275*	*.327*	*-0.5*	*LF 3, CF -1*	*2.9*
2017	*ARI*	*MLB*	*29*	*527*	*64*	*25*	*7*	*15*	*65*	*34*	*99*	*7*	*3*	*.277/.326/.452*	*.276*	*.318*	*-0.3*	*LF 2, CF -1*	*2.5*

Breakout: 0% Improve: 49% Collapse: 8% Attrition: 21% MLB: 92% *Comparables: Ben Francisco, Juan Rivera, David Murphy*

Pop quiz: Who led all left fielders in TAv? Pencils down. You already saw the name, so you're welcome on the gimme. The ex-pitcher-cum-indie-league-outfielder keeps surpassing expectations—so far he's the Rick Ankiel we wanted all along—but at some point Peralta has to be approaching his ceiling for both power and defense. If you're looking for a bold prediction, how about this: He led the NL with 10 triples. He probably won't do that again.

A.J. Pollock CF

Born: 12/5/87 Age: 28 Bats: R Throws: R Height: 6'1" Weight: 195

YEAR	TEAM	LVL	AGE	PA	R	2B	3B	HR	RBI	BB	K	SB	CS	AVG/OBP/SLG	TAv	BABIP	BRR	FRAA	WARP
2013	ARI	MLB	25	482	64	28	5	8	38	33	82	12	3	.269/.322/.409	.259	.314	2.8	CF(110): -3.3, LF(7): -0.2	1.3
2014	RNO	AAA	26	52	4	1	1	0	9	2	4	0	0	.163/.192/.224	.146	.174	1.1	CF(13): 1.6	-0.2
2014	ARI	MLB	26	287	41	19	6	7	24	19	46	14	3	.302/.353/.498	.308	.344	1.9	CF(68): -2.4, LF(2): -0.2	2.2
2015	ARI	MLB	27	673	111	39	6	20	76	53	89	39	7	.315/.367/.498	.306	.338	7.9	CF(151): -7.8	5.4
2016	*ARI*	*MLB*	*28*	*639*	*86*	*35*	*6*	*14*	*63*	*46*	*100*	*28*	*6*	*.281/.333/.435*	*.267*	*.314*	*4.0*	*CF -3*	*2.8*
2017	*ARI*	*MLB*	*29*	*552*	*65*	*29*	*6*	*12*	*63*	*41*	*85*	*23*	*6*	*.276/.330/.430*	*.272*	*.308*	*4.0*	*CF -3*	*2.7*

Breakout: 2% Improve: 50% Collapse: 2% Attrition: 9% MLB: 94% *Comparables: Shane Victorino, Jacoby Ellsbury, Jon Jay*

If you coded a baseball video game but didn't have the rights to use real major-league player names, A.J. Pollock would be a tremendous Jon Dowd-style knockoff name for Mike Trout. Fortuitously for Arizona, the existent Pollock's real skill set, on a smaller scale, feels comparable to the game's best player: premium center-field defense, speed and extra-base power. His only leg up on Trout's overall game is a noticeably smaller strikeout rate. He is, of course, four years Trout's senior, so 2015 was probably peak Pollock. But with three more years of team control, the Diamondbacks control an underpaid, dynamic outfielder, while most other teams go fish.

Yasmany Tomas RF

Born: 11/14/90 Age: 25 Bats: R Throws: R Height: 6'2" Weight: 255

YEAR	TEAM	LVL	AGE	PA	R	2B	3B	HR	RBI	BB	K	SB	CS	AVG/OBP/SLG	TAv	BABIP	BRR	FRAA	WARP
2015	RNO	AAA	24	23	2	1	0	1	3	2	5	0	0	.190/.261/.381	.171	.200	-0.5	RF(5): -1.4	-0.4
2015	ARI	MLB	24	426	40	19	3	9	48	17	110	5	2	.273/.305/.401	.246	.354	-0.1	RF(57): -1.9, 3B(31): -2.5	-0.2
2016	*ARI*	*MLB*	*25*	*614*	*66*	*29*	*4*	*16*	*68*	*31*	*154*	*7*	*3*	*.259/.299/.408*	*.245*	*.325*	*-0.2*	*RF -1*	*0.4*
2017	*ARI*	*MLB*	*26*	*493*	*56*	*23*	*3*	*13*	*57*	*27*	*122*	*5*	*2*	*.256/.299/.407*	*.253*	*.318*	*-0.1*	*RF 0*	*0.6*

Breakout: 6% Improve: 69% Collapse: 1% Attrition: 2% MLB: 100% *Comparables: Jeff Francoeur, Ellis Valentine, Dave Winfield*

A thought experiment:

Imagine Tomas as a college draft pick fast-tracked into the majors. Imagine, after maybe two years and a week the minors, he got called up in April to make his major-league debut, and in his rookie year produced those numbers above. Not so much a bust, right? Blame his Cuban predecessors for setting the bar for immediate success in the States so very high. Yes, he was inked for $68 million over six years, and if this doesn't work out in a couple years he'll be a tough boulder to budge. But the thick corner outfielder (the Diamondbacks liked him in right field most of all) had, in all, a very fine first half before fizzling as the calendar ripened. His potential still lies in his home run total.

He isn't Puig, Cespedes or Abreu. But he's not Henry Urrutia either. He's Yasmany Tomas, whatever that is.

Jamie Westbrook 2B

Born: 6/18/95 Age: 21 Bats: R Throws: R Height: 5'9" Weight: 170

YEAR	TEAM	LVL	AGE	PA	R	2B	3B	HR	RBI	BB	K	SB	CS	AVG/OBP/SLG	TAv	BABIP	BRR	FRAA	WARP
2014	SBN	A	19	565	69	27	4	8	49	38	98	6	3	.259/.314/.375	.268	.303	0.2	2B(119): 0.4, 1B(1): -0.1	2.0
2015	VIS	A+	20	527	75	33	4	17	72	24	69	14	4	.319/.357/.510	.331	.337	0.8	2B(93): -2.3	5.1
2016	*ARI*	*MLB*	*21*	*250*	*23*	*12*	*2*	*6*	*27*	*10*	*53*	*1*	*1*	*.244/.279/.381*	*.230*	*.289*	*-0.1*	*2B 0*	*0.2*
2017	*ARI*	*MLB*	*22*	*486*	*52*	*24*	*4*	*11*	*53*	*21*	*97*	*3*	*1*	*.253/.290/.394*	*.248*	*.295*	*-0.3*	*2B 0, LF 0*	*1.1*

Breakout: 6% Improve: 19% Collapse: 0% Attrition: 8% MLB: 21% *Comparables: Kolten Wong, Jose Altuve, Johnny Giavotella*

An undersized keystoner with a knack for hard contact, Westbrook wins the award for most obvious Dustin Pedroia comp. His ability to put the barrel on the ball played exceedingly well in the California League, though a look at his production from 2014, in a more neutral setting, gives us a better idea of his long-term output. He receives high grades for his makeup, as he shows intensity on the field and never relents at the plate, battling for every pitch—just like Pedroia, would you look at that. Realistically, the comp is nuttily optimistic, as Pedroia comps tend to be. One scout summed him up: "Not an all-star or first-division regular, but I want him as part of that 25."

Marcus Wilson CF

Born: 8/15/96 Age: 19 Bats: R Throws: R Height: 6'3" Weight: 175

YEAR	TEAM	LVL	AGE	PA	R	2B	3B	HR	RBI	BB	K	SB	CS	AVG/OBP/SLG	TAv	BABIP	BRR	FRAA	WARP
2016	*ARI*	*MLB*	*19*	*250*	*19*	*9*	*1*	*3*	*18*	*17*	*84*	*1*	*0*	*.183/.240/.262*	*.180*	*.269*	*-0.3*	*CF -1, LF -0*	*-1.6*
2017	*ARI*	*MLB*	*20*	*320*	*28*	*11*	*2*	*4*	*25*	*22*	*105*	*1*	*1*	*.187/.246/.275*	*.194*	*.270*	*-0.4*	*CF -2, LF 0*	*-1.6*

Breakout: 0% Improve: 0% Collapse: 0% Attrition: 0% MLB: 0% *Comparables: Che-Hsuan Lin, Derrick Robinson, Austin Jackson*

Wilson was a young pick—only 17—when the Diamondbacks plucked him in the second round in 2014 and bought him out of his Arizona State commitment for $1 million. He hasn't cracked short-season ball yet, and if there are positive signs in his approach and excuses baked into his age, there are also serious concerns about his lack of power. To be fair, his home run total (one) might have doubled if not for an opponent's insane leap/glove/juggle/secure catch against one of his opposite-field drives, but Wilson is nonetheless still looking to crack triple digits with his ISO. He has plus speed that he pairs with a plus arm, and he puts both to use in center field. He remains a candidate to explode in any given season, as adding bulk will help the lack of power; so should his willingness to elongate his swing to compensate for that lack of power.

PITCHERS

Chase Anderson RHP

Born: 11/30/87 Age: 28 Bats: R Throws: R Height: 6'1" Weight: 194

YEAR	TEAM	LVL	AGE	W	L	SV	G	GS	IP	H	HR	BB/9	K/9	GB%	BABIP	WHIP	ERA	FIP	DRA	WARP	CFIP	MPH
2013	RNO	AAA	25	4	7	0	26	13	88	107	11	3.4	8.2	38%	.350	1.59	5.73	4.54	4.83	0.7	94	
2014	MOB	AA	26	4	2	0	6	6	39	22	1	1.4	8.8	48%	.212	0.72	0.69	2.19				
2014	ARI	MLB	26	9	7	0	21	21	114^{1}	117	16	3.1	8.3	42%	.313	1.37	4.01	4.19	4.49	0.4	104	93.6
2015	ARI	MLB	27	6	6	0	27	27	152^{2}	158	18	2.4	6.5	44%	.302	1.30	4.30	4.16	4.23	1.4	110	94.3
2016	*ARI*	*MLB*	*28*	*3*	*3*	*0*	*8*	*8*	45^{2}	*45*	*6*	*2.7*	*7.1*	*43%*	*.311*	*1.29*	*4.00*	*4.22*	*4.71*	*0.3*	*110*	
2017	*ARI*	*MLB*	*29*	*4*	*5*	*0*	*14*	*14*	83^{2}	*82*	*11*	*2.7*	*7.3*	*43%*	*.309*	*1.28*	*4.08*	*4.48*	*4.81*	*0.4*	*113*	

Breakout: 20% Improve: 49% Collapse: 16% Attrition: 23% MLB: 87% *Comparables: Chris Young, David Phelps, Jake Arrieta*

Unfortunately for him, "Chase Anderson" doubled as an easy accomplishment last year, as he departed a full third of his starts prior to the sixth inning. Anderson's changeup has more tumble than a first-grade gymnastics class, but that only gives him one swing-and-miss offering to pair with a pedestrian fastball. He already uses two different changeups depending on the situation, and unless he can pull another one out of his wallet, a fifth starter is likely all he is. It's tough to succeed in a hitter's park without premium stuff, something the Diamondbacks won't seem to acknowledge.

Silvino Bracho RHP

Born: 7/17/92 Age: 23 Bats: R Throws: R Height: 5'10" Weight: 190

YEAR	TEAM	LVL	AGE	W	L	SV	G	GS	IP	H	HR	BB/9	K/9	GB%	BABIP	WHIP	ERA	FIP	DRA	WARP	CFIP	MPH
2014	SBN	A	21	3	2	26	45	0	43^{1}	25	3	1.7	14.5	40%	.275	0.76	2.08	1.85	2.98	0.9	46	
2015	ARI	MLB	22	0	0	1	13	0	12^{1}	9	2	2.9	12.4	21%	.269	1.05	1.46	3.73	3.22	0.2	84	94.9
2015	MOB	AA	22	2	1	16	37	0	44^{2}	34	3	1.8	11.9	25%	.295	0.96	1.81	2.21	0.39	2.3	54	
2016	*ARI*	*MLB*	*23*	*2*	*1*	*0*	*45*	*0*	47^{2}	*39*	*5*	*2.8*	*10.9*	*23%*	*.315*	*1.12*	*3.04*	*3.04*	*3.66*	*0.8*	*77*	
2017	*ARI*	*MLB*	*24*	*3*	*1*	*1*	*51*	*0*	55^{1}	*44*	*7*	*2.6*	*11.2*	*23%*	*.309*	*1.08*	*3.03*	*3.32*	*3.65*	*0.8*	*76*	

Breakout: 20% Improve: 28% Collapse: 15% Attrition: 20% MLB: 49% *Comparables: Addison Reed, Yimi Garcia, R.J. Alvarez*

Bracho's delivery looks like his body is moving at one-and-a-half speed. So has his career—it took just three seasons to advance from the Dominican Summer League to the majors, striking out at least a batter per inning each step of the way. His big-league inaugural was the first time his WHIP has ever topped 1.00, and then just barely. He's a shorty whose fastball sits at 93 up in the zone, and the effect—like he's throwing uphill—is of a ball that almost jumps over bats. The slider doesn't yet get the whiff rate you'd like from a good bullpen secondary. Think Ernesto Frieri with control.

Archie Bradley RHP

Born: 8/10/92 Age: 23 Bats: R Throws: R Height: 6'4" Weight: 230

YEAR	TEAM	LVL	AGE	W	L	SV	G	GS	IP	H	HR	BB/9	K/9	GB%	BABIP	WHIP	ERA	FIP	DRA	WARP	CFIP	MPH
2013	VIS	A+	20	2	0	0	5	5	28^{2}	22	1	3.1	13.5	44%	.362	1.12	1.26	2.48	4.37	0.5	68	
2013	MOB	AA	20	12	5	0	21	21	123^{1}	93	5	4.3	8.7	47%	.276	1.23	1.97	3.04	3.97	1.0	97	
2014	MOB	AA	21	2	3	0	12	12	54^{2}	45	2	5.9	7.6	44%	.285	1.48	4.12	4.23				
2014	RNO	AAA	21	1	4	0	5	5	24^{1}	26	0	4.4	8.5	46%	.373	1.56	5.18	3.78	5.13	0.0	96	
2015	RNO	AAA	22	1	0	0	4	4	21^{1}	26	3	2.1	8.4	40%	.359	1.45	2.95	4.26	4.27	0.3	92	
2015	ARI	MLB	22	2	3	0	8	8	35^{2}	36	3	5.6	5.8	60%	.297	1.63	5.80	4.98	5.18	-0.1	122	94.4
2016	*ARI*	*MLB*	*23*	*3*	*3*	*0*	*8*	*8*	42^{1}	*40*	*5*	*3.9*	*7.5*	*51%*	*.309*	*1.38*	*4.23*	*4.34*	*4.96*	*0.2*	*117*	
2017	*ARI*	*MLB*	*24*	*5*	*6*	*0*	*18*	*18*	104^{2}	*96*	*12*	*4.1*	*8.1*	*51%*	*.308*	*1.38*	*4.19*	*4.61*	*4.91*	*0.4*	*115*	

Breakout: 15% Improve: 30% Collapse: 17% Attrition: 30% MLB: 50% *Comparables: Mauricio Robles, Aaron Poreda, Dan Cortes*

Nothing can haze a rookie like dumb luck. Arizona's former top pitching prospect rolled into the season as Arizona's no. 5 starter, posting three quality starts before a line drive to his jaw sidelined him. Before Carlos Gonzalez took that fateful swing, Bradley's ERA was 1.35 and the first result in a Google Images search was of a handsome young country boy. But after returning he never got going again; his ERA is the abomination you see above and his first Google result is now a swoll-jawed hospital selfie. Eventually tendinitis and a slow rehab stumped him, and the Diamondbacks shut him down, healthy, in September.

Enrique Burgos RHP

Born: 11/23/90 Age: 25 Bats: R Throws: R Height: 6'3" Weight: 250

YEAR	TEAM	LVL	AGE	W	L	SV	G	GS	IP	H	HR	BB/9	K/9	GB%	BABIP	WHIP	ERA	FIP	DRA	WARP	CFIP	MPH
2013	SBN	A	22	2	2	17	49	0	46^{1}	29	1	9.5	9.7	58%	.243	1.68	3.88	4.70	5.58	-0.4	128	
2014	VIS	A+	23	3	3	29	55	0	54^{2}	37	5	4.3	13.7	47%	.275	1.15	2.47	3.43	4.28	0.7	72	
2015	ARI	MLB	24	2	2	2	30	0	27	27	2	5.0	13.0	36%	.385	1.56	4.67	2.90	4.18	0.2	84	98.3
2015	RNO	AAA	24	0	1	5	15	0	15	19	3	7.2	13.8	42%	.421	2.07	6.00	5.93	4.60	0.1	92	
2016	*ARI*	*MLB*	*25*	*2*	*1*	*0*	*36*	*0*	38^{1}	*33*	*4*	*4.2*	*10.3*	*39%*	*.319*	*1.33*	*3.69*	*3.59*	*4.36*	*0.3*	*99*	
2017	*ARI*	*MLB*	*26*	*2*	*1*	*2*	*45*	*0*	46^{2}	*38*	*5*	*4.4*	*11.1*	*39%*	*.315*	*1.29*	*3.61*	*3.97*	*4.27*	*0.3*	*96*	

Breakout: 16% Improve: 29% Collapse: 19% Attrition: 34% MLB: 51% *Comparables: Jose Ceda, Michael Kohn, Brad Boxberger*

After seven-plus years of Burgos sometimes throwing strikes in the Diamondbacks system, the team could no longer neglect the spiking strikeout rate and called him up. He struck out half the batters he faced in a seven-game stretch of May, and back-to-back saves put him in the closer's conversation. Shoulder tendinitis and continued control issues took him out of it. His fastball tops out at 99 mph and he balances it with a nice hard slider, which is the five-dollar shake of reliever repertoires. If he can devise a plan to handle lefties (who got on base at a .431 rate against him), Arizona might have a special Panamanian reliever, not that anyone can think of another one.

Andrew Chafin LHP

Born: 6/17/90 Age: 26 Bats: R Throws: L Height: 6'2" Weight: 225

YEAR	TEAM	LVL	AGE	W	L	SV	G	GS	IP	H	HR	BB/9	K/9	GB%	BABIP	WHIP	ERA	FIP	DRA	WARP	CFIP	MPH
2013	VIS	A+	23	3	1	0	6	6	31	32	1	4.1	9.3	47%	.341	1.48	4.65	3.48	5.29	0.3	98	
2013	MOB	AA	23	10	7	0	21	21	126^{1}	118	5	2.9	6.2	53%	.292	1.26	2.85	3.09	4.09	0.8	101	
2014	MOB	AA	24	4	1	0	9	9	55	49	4	3.1	6.7	46%	.280	1.24	1.96	3.73				
2014	ARI	MLB	24	0	1	0	3	3	14	13	0	5.1	6.4	56%	.317	1.50	3.86	3.60	4.15	0.1	108	92.9
2014	RNO	AAA	24	5	6	0	17	16	92^{2}	111	11	3.8	7.1	52%	.339	1.62	5.34	4.99	5.23	0.5	100	
2015	ARI	MLB	25	5	1	2	66	0	75	56	3	3.6	7.0	60%	.248	1.15	2.76	3.38	2.72	1.8	104	95.6
2016	*ARI*	*MLB*	*26*	*2*	*1*	*0*	*36*	*0*	38^{1}	*37*	*4*	*3.1*	*6.7*	*56%*	*.303*	*1.30*	*4.02*	*3.98*	*4.73*	*0.1*	*109*	
2017	*ARI*	*MLB*	*27*	*3*	*3*	*0*	*18*	*9*	64^{1}	*60*	*7*	*3.1*	*7.2*	*56%*	*.301*	*1.28*	*4.05*	*4.45*	*4.77*	*0.3*	*110*	

Breakout: 13% Improve: 30% Collapse: 15% Attrition: 22% MLB: 60% *Comparables: Esmerling Vasquez, Josh Collmenter, Michael Bowden*

Save for the closer, the phone rang in Arizona for no hurler more frequently than for Chafin, and that's going to happen when you're a left-hander who can get anyone out. The Kent Stater with a history of starting went multiple innings in relief, holding righties to a skinny .233 TAv and lefties to an emaciated .205. The walk rate looks alarming, but a fifth of those were intentional. He could start if needed, but might flourish better in a fireman role, which would work out perfectly—fewer numbers to dial.

Taylor Clarke RHP

Born: 5/13/93 Age: 23 Bats: R Throws: R Height: 6'4" Weight: 195

YEAR	TEAM	LVL	AGE	W	L	SV	G	GS	IP	H	HR	BB/9	K/9	GB%	BABIP	WHIP	ERA	FIP	DRA	WARP	CFIP	MPH
2015	YAK	A-	22	0	0	3	13	0	21	8	0	1.7	11.6	51%	.186	0.57	0.00	1.75	2.41	0.6	72	
2016	*ARI*	*MLB*	*23*	*2*	*1*	*1*	*34*	*0*	36^{2}	*32*	*5*	*3.7*	*8.7*	*41%*	*.292*	*1.29*	*4.12*	*4.21*	*4.86*	*0.0*	*113*	
2017	*ARI*	*MLB*	*24*	*2*	*1*	*1*	*33*	*0*	*54*	*45*	*7*	*4.2*	*8.8*	*41%*	*.281*	*1.30*	*4.31*	*4.74*	*5.09*	*-0.1*	*118*	

Breakout: 0% Improve: 0% Collapse: 0% Attrition: 0% MLB: 0% *Comparables: Jaye Chapman, Wesley Wright, Eddie Kunz*

Clarke will not be stopped. Tommy John surgery in 2013 couldn't do it. His school announcing the shuttering of its baseball program couldn't. After transferring to College of Charleston, Clarke put together his best year yet, including an 18-strikeout complete game against Radford in March. While most find command the last thing to return following TJ, it's already a strength for Clarke. He boasts an impressive fastball that has ticked up to the 90-94 range, and supplements it with both a slider and a changeup that he's shown some feel for. Clarke's three-pitch mix gives him the tools to start, but he was relief-only in his pro debut, which could give you an idea of what the organization intends to do with its third-round pick.

Josh Collmenter RHP

Born: 2/7/86 Age: 30 Bats: R Throws: R Height: 6'4" Weight: 235

YEAR	TEAM	LVL	AGE	W	L	SV	G	GS	IP	H	HR	BB/9	K/9	GB%	BABIP	WHIP	ERA	FIP	DRA	WARP	CFIP	MPH
2013	ARI	MLB	27	5	5	0	49	0	92	79	8	3.2	8.3	36%	.277	1.22	3.13	3.44	3.46	1.3	91	90.1
2014	ARI	MLB	28	11	9	1	33	28	179^{1}	163	18	2.0	5.8	41%	.267	1.13	3.46	3.84	3.79	2.2	113	88.8
2015	ARI	MLB	29	4	6	1	44	12	121	129	18	1.8	4.7	36%	.282	1.26	3.79	4.67	4.57	0.4	120	87.7
2016	*ARI*	*MLB*	*30*	*3*	*1*	*0*	*50*	*0*	52^{2}	*51*	*7*	*2.3*	*6.0*	*38%*	*.292*	*1.24*	*4.16*	*4.29*	*4.89*	*0.0*	*115*	
2017	*ARI*	*MLB*	*31*	*4*	*4*	*0*	*29*	*10*	92^{2}	*90*	*12*	*2.5*	*5.9*	*38%*	*.290*	*1.25*	*4.30*	*4.73*	*5.06*	*0.1*	*120*	

Breakout: 6% Improve: 43% Collapse: 19% Attrition: 6% MLB: 95% *Comparables: Billy O'Dell, Pat Jarvis, Gary Peters*

If you need to demote a starter to the bullpen and your choices are Collmenter or a non-Collmenter, go with the former. He's taken the demotion many times, and always earns his way back. His ERA in 110 career relief appearances sits at 2.32, and in 75 career starts at 4.03, meaning he's both much better in short bursts and credibly qualified in longer ones. Whether that makes him your starter (as he was for the Diamondbacks on Opening Day 2015), your swingman or your set-up guy depends on your team's needs, rather than some universally correct application of an arm like this. He has a pet rodent named Slider, despite not throwing one, which means he has the most untouchable slider in the game.

Patrick Corbin LHP

Born: 7/19/89 Age: 26 Bats: L Throws: L Height: 6'3" Weight: 210

YEAR	TEAM	LVL	AGE	W	L	SV	G	GS	IP	H	HR	BB/9	K/9	GB%	BABIP	WHIP	ERA	FIP	DRA	WARP	CFIP	MPH
2013	ARI	MLB	23	14	8	0	32	32	208^{1}	189	19	2.3	7.7	48%	.283	1.17	3.41	3.40	3.75	2.9	92	94.8
2015	MOB	AA	25	1	0	0	3	3	16^{1}	13	1	2.8	6.1	41%	.290	1.10	2.76	3.85	3.89	-0.1	96	
2015	ARI	MLB	25	6	5	0	16	16	85	91	9	1.8	8.3	48%	.327	1.27	3.60	3.37	4.45	0.6	94	95.0
2016	*ARI*	*MLB*	*26*	*11*	*9*	*0*	*28*	*28*	*168*	*159*	*18*	*2.2*	*8.1*	*48%*	*.313*	*1.19*	*3.49*	*3.47*	*4.14*	*2.3*	*94*	
2017	*ARI*	*MLB*	*27*	*11*	*10*	*0*	*29*	*29*	182^{2}	*169*	*21*	*2.0*	*8.4*	*48%*	*.310*	*1.15*	*3.44*	*3.77*	*4.08*	*2.5*	*92*	

Breakout: 29% Improve: 65% Collapse: 11% Attrition: 7% MLB: 93% *Comparables: Jordan Zimmermann, Ricky Nolasco, Chris Tillman*

After a one-and-a-half-year excused absence, the Tommy John patient rejoined Arizona's rotation in July and, facing a 90-pitch limit per outing, looked super similar to the pre-scarred Corbin. Heck, the strikeouts were actually up, the walks were actually down, and the groundballs were actually—well, down, on the ground, like groundballs will be, but they were up in frequency of occurrence. So add an inning to each of his 16 starts, extrapolate it to a full season and he's back to his 200-inning workload. He'd be good enough to start Opening Day for a third of the league's teams, if no longer the Diamondbacks.

Rubby De La Rosa RHP

Born: 3/4/89 Age: 27 Bats: R Throws: R Height: 6'1" Weight: 225

YEAR	TEAM	LVL	AGE	W	L	SV	G	GS	IP	H	HR	BB/9	K/9	GB%	BABIP	WHIP	ERA	FIP	DRA	WARP	CFIP	MPH
2013	PAW	AAA	24	3	3	0	24	20	80^{1}	65	9	5.4	8.5	44%	.265	1.41	4.26	4.82	4.89	0.1	115	
2013	BOS	MLB	24	0	2	0	11	0	11^{1}	15	2	1.6	4.8	48%	.325	1.50	5.56	5.63	8.03	-0.5	113	98.8
2014	PAW	AAA	25	2	4	0	12	12	60	50	1	3.8	8.6	55%	.299	1.25	3.45	2.97	4.28	0.6	91	
2014	BOS	MLB	25	4	8	0	19	18	101^{2}	116	12	3.1	6.6	47%	.327	1.49	4.43	4.33	5.32	-0.7	106	98.1
2015	ARI	MLB	26	14	9	0	32	32	188^{2}	193	32	3.0	7.2	51%	.287	1.36	4.67	4.84	4.74	0.7	113	97.9
2016	*ARI*	*MLB*	*27*	*9*	*10*	*0*	*28*	*28*	159^{2}	*155*	*22*	*2.9*	*7.3*	*50%*	*.305*	*1.30*	*4.22*	*4.29*	*4.96*	*0.6*	*118*	
2017	*ARI*	*MLB*	*28*	*7*	*9*	*0*	*25*	*25*	146^{2}	*143*	*20*	*2.8*	*7.4*	*50%*	*.306*	*1.29*	*4.18*	*4.60*	*4.91*	*0.6*	*117*	

Breakout: 21% Improve: 57% Collapse: 14% Attrition: 15% MLB: 88% *Comparables: Chris Tillman, Ross Ohlendorf, Cliff Lee*

It's not so much who won the Wade Miley trade, but rather who survived it. De La Rosa battled through the season healthy and happy—not much more you can ask for, existentially speaking—but, goodness, could he have been kinder to left-handed hitting? Despite his vaunted changeup, lefties were not fooled and raked a .315/.382/.567 mark against him. If that subset of baseballers are going to wine and dine on all his pitches, his occasional moments of brilliance just won't matter, and he'll eventually be deconstructed into a righty specialist. Time is ticking, existentially speaking.

Randall Delgado RHP

Born: 2/9/90 Age: 26 Bats: R Throws: R Height: 6'4" Weight: 220

YEAR	TEAM	LVL	AGE	W	L	SV	G	GS	IP	H	HR	BB/9	K/9	GB%	BABIP	WHIP	ERA	FIP	DRA	WARP	CFIP	MPH
2013	RNO	AAA	23	2	5	0	13	13	64	69	9	4.9	8.0	54%	.327	1.62	5.91	5.44	5.34	-0.2	108	
2013	ARI	MLB	23	5	7	0	20	19	116^{1}	116	24	1.8	6.1	43%	.266	1.19	4.26	4.96	4.79	0.2	112	94.8
2014	ARI	MLB	24	4	4	0	47	4	77^{2}	71	6	4.1	10.0	37%	.311	1.36	4.87	3.36	3.66	0.8	95	95.9
2015	ARI	MLB	25	8	4	1	64	1	72	63	7	4.1	9.1	44%	.290	1.33	3.25	3.81	3.69	0.9	99	96.0
2016	*ARI*	*MLB*	*26*	*2*	*1*	*0*	*45*	*0*	47^{2}	*43*	*6*	*3.2*	*8.4*	*43%*	*.306*	*1.26*	*3.82*	*3.92*	*4.51*	*0.3*	*104*	
2017	*ARI*	*MLB*	*27*	*5*	*5*	*0*	*36*	*12*	102^{1}	*91*	*12*	*3.1*	*8.6*	*43%*	*.303*	*1.23*	*3.77*	*4.14*	*4.45*	*0.8*	*102*	

Breakout: 33% Improve: 64% Collapse: 11% Attrition: 7% MLB: 93% *Comparables: Chris Tillman, Jeff Francis, Danny Duffy*

Sometimes it takes a few years of shifting roles and backpacking through the Andes before you truly find yourself and realize what you should be. Delgado, initially groomed to be a starter with a good curveball, is now a late-inning reliever who abandoned his curveball at the last rest stop. Getting primarily seventh-inning assignments, he threw changeups to lefties and a new pesky slider to right-handers and didn't show much platoon flaw. The arsenal overhaul helped generate more Ks and put him in the mix to be a setup man or long reliever. He might not have found himself quite yet, but man is he close.

Zachary Godley RHP

Born: 4/21/90 Age: 26 Bats: R Throws: R Height: 6'3" Weight: 245

YEAR	TEAM	LVL	AGE	W	L	SV	G	GS	IP	H	HR	BB/9	K/9	GB%	BABIP	WHIP	ERA	FIP	DRA	WARP	CFIP	MPH
2013	BOI	A-	23	2	0	0	13	0	25^2	20	0	1.8	9.5	63%	.299	0.97	1.75	1.80	3.57	0.3	77	
2014	KNC	A	24	1	1	7	11	0	15	9	0	4.2	15.0	52%	.310	1.07	1.80	1.55	3.63	0.2	71	
2014	DAY	A+	24	3	2	8	29	0	40^1	40	3	3.8	11.6	56%	.349	1.41	3.57	3.19	3.76	0.4	82	
2015	VIS	A+	25	8	3	0	14	12	75^1	64	3	2.3	9.3	56%	.300	1.10	2.27	3.10	3.95	1.4	89	
2015	ARI	MLB	25	5	1	0	9	6	36^2	29	4	4.2	8.3	47%	.272	1.25	3.19	4.36	4.26	0.3	105	93.8
2015	MOB	AA	25	2	1	0	7	5	24^1	21	2	3.7	4.4	61%	.260	1.27	4.07	4.99	5.68	-0.2	116	
2016	*ARI*	*MLB*	*26*	*2*	*2*	*0*	*5*	*5*	*25*	*24*	*3*	*3.4*	*7.6*	*49%*	*.311*	*1.34*	*4.19*	*4.24*	*4.90*	*0.1*	*115*	
2017	*ARI*	*MLB*	*27*	*2*	*2*	*0*	*18*	*4*	*46^2*	*45*	*6*	*3.6*	*7.8*	*49%*	*.307*	*1.35*	*4.38*	*4.81*	*5.12*	*0.0*	*121*	

Breakout: 18% Improve: 30% Collapse: 12% Attrition: 21% MLB: 50% *Comparables: Michael Stutes, Randor Bierd, John Maine*

A 10th-round pick by the Cubs in 2013, Godley came to Arizona in the Miguel Montero trade without much hype—he was a 24-year-old stuck in High-A relief work. Within three months of his assignment to Visalia, where he was stretched out to become a starter, Godley was in the Diamondbacks' rotation and using low-90s sinkers and cutters to toy with grown men. In September, the club that let him go pasted him for his worst outing of the year, and with a guy like Godley—drafted as a college senior, short history of success, long history of being undesired—there will be a tendency to treat each bad outing as the chime of midnight. But he's got no platoon splits, a starter's body and one of the league's hardest cutters.

Zack Greinke RHP

Born: 10/21/83 Age: 32 Bats: R Throws: R Height: 6'2" Weight: 195

YEAR	TEAM	LVL	AGE	W	L	SV	G	GS	IP	H	HR	BB/9	K/9	GB%	BABIP	WHIP	ERA	FIP	DRA	WARP	CFIP	MPH
2013	LAN	MLB	29	15	4	0	28	28	177^2	152	13	2.3	7.5	48%	.276	1.11	2.63	3.20	3.27	3.5	95	94.8
2014	LAN	MLB	30	17	8	0	32	32	202^1	190	19	1.9	9.2	50%	.311	1.15	2.71	2.94	3.47	3.3	82	94.6
2015	LAN	MLB	31	19	3	0	32	32	222^2	148	14	1.6	8.1	49%	.229	0.84	1.66	2.79	2.17	7.6	85	94.7
2016	*ARI*	*MLB*	*32*	*14*	*10*	*0*	*32*	*32*	*214^1*	*188*	*21*	*2.2*	*8.4*	*49%*	*.304*	*1.12*	*3.24*	*3.27*	*3.87*	*3.6*	*86*	
2017	*ARI*	*MLB*	*33*	*11*	*10*	*0*	*29*	*29*	*179*	*159*	*17*	*2.3*	*7.9*	*49%*	*.303*	*1.14*	*3.34*	*3.66*	*3.99*	*2.9*	*89*	

Breakout: 13% Improve: 32% Collapse: 34% Attrition: 7% MLB: 88% *Comparables: Kelvim Escobar, Jason Schmidt, Chris Carpenter*

Greinke has long received praise for being one of the game's smartest pitchers, and he sure picked a wise time to have his best season ever. Pitching in his opt-out year, Greinke posted personal-best marks in DRA, hit rate, and walk rate while throwing the second-most innings and earning the second-lowest homer rate of his career. He has become among the game's most impressive command artists despite still boasting stuff good enough to let him get away with missed locations. He didn't miss his spots very often in 2015, throwing his changeup more and his fastball less en route to what would likely be a Cy Young Award in a world he didn't have to share with both Clayton Kershaw *and* Jake Arrieta. Greinke did benefit from some good luck, to be sure, and his .229 BABIP and 87 percent strand rate are likely unsustainable. Still, if the Diamondbacks have to settle for the pitcher who averaged 3.8 WARP per season in 2012–14 instead of the 7.6-WARP monster of 2015, they'll live.

Keith Hessler LHP

Born: 3/15/89 Age: 27 Bats: L Throws: L Height: 6'4" Weight: 215

YEAR	TEAM	LVL	AGE	W	L	SV	G	GS	IP	H	HR	BB/9	K/9	GB%	BABIP	WHIP	ERA	FIP	DRA	WARP	CFIP	MPH
2013	VIS	A+	24	8	7	0	26	26	137	161	24	4.2	8.3	44%	.343	1.64	5.85	5.83	5.87	0.5	116	
2014	VIS	A+	25	4	2	1	44	0	59^1	79	3	2.7	11.8	57%	.408	1.63	4.40	2.93	4.34	0.6	73	
2015	ARI	MLB	26	0	1	0	18	0	12^1	16	4	2.9	8.8	37%	.324	1.62	8.03	6.41	7.23	-0.4	102	95.0
2015	MOB	AA	26	3	1	1	24	0	25^1	17	1	1.8	11.4	66%	.281	0.87	0.71	1.88	0.96	1.1	60	
2015	VIS	A+	26	1	0	0	10	0	14^2	11	0	1.2	12.3	55%	.333	0.89	0.00	1.46	2.78	0.4	73	
2015	RNO	AAA	26	1	1	0	17	0	19	14	3	3.8	6.2	46%	.216	1.16	5.68	5.55	5.35	0.0	108	
2016	*ARI*	*MLB*	*27*	*1*	*0*	*0*	*18*	*0*	*19*	*19*	*3*	*3.2*	*8.0*	*45%*	*.325*	*1.37*	*4.19*	*4.57*	*4.90*	*0.0*	*114*	
2017	*ARI*	*MLB*	*28*	*2*	*1*	*1*	*17*	*3*	*35^2*	*35*	*5*	*3.3*	*8.3*	*45%*	*.319*	*1.34*	*4.20*	*4.61*	*4.91*	*0.1*	*115*	

Breakout: 10% Improve: 12% Collapse: 8% Attrition: 15% MLB: 24% *Comparables: Evan Reed, Humberto Sanchez, Jose Veras*

Hessler, a 28th-round pick in 2010 from Coastal Carolina, began the year in High-A and finished it in Arizona, with his ERA progression—0.00, 0.71, 5.68, 8.03—resembling some sort of staggering-drunk Fibonacci sequence. While he showed no real platoon malady in the minors, his splits in the majors were extreme enough to have their own energy drink: .622 OPS vs. lefties, 1.288 vs. righties. The FIP splits are more even across the board, which equates to something closer to the truth: He's just okay against everyone.

Daniel Hudson RHP

Born: 3/9/87 Age: 29 Bats: R Throws: R Height: 6'3" Weight: 235

YEAR	TEAM	LVL	AGE	W	L	SV	G	GS	IP	H	HR	BB/9	K/9	GB%	BABIP	WHIP	ERA	FIP	DRA	WARP	CFIP	MPH
2014	ARI	MLB	27	0	1	0	3	0	2^2	4	0	0.0	6.8	46%	.364	1.50	13.50	1.60	5.21	0.0	102	96.8
2015	ARI	MLB	28	4	3	4	64	1	67^2	64	7	3.3	9.4	43%	.305	1.32	3.86	3.52	3.99	0.6	91	98.6
2016	*ARI*	*MLB*	*29*	*3*	*1*	*0*	*50*	*0*	*52^2*	*48*	*6*	*2.9*	*8.7*	*43%*	*.313*	*1.23*	*3.49*	*3.61*	*4.15*	*0.5*	*94*	
2017	*ARI*	*MLB*	*30*	*4*	*3*	*1*	*54*	*7*	*90^1*	*84*	*10*	*2.9*	*8.5*	*43%*	*.316*	*1.25*	*3.54*	*3.89*	*4.21*	*0.7*	*96*	

Breakout: 18% Improve: 43% Collapse: 19% Attrition: 4% MLB: 98% *Comparables: Erik Hanson, Don Drysdale, Len Barker*

Simply getting back to the major leagues after consecutive Tommy John-branded operations was a mountain climb for Hudson. Last year was the lumbering peak above that—a full year in the bullpen—and the righthander scaled that too. The ex-starter settled in as the setup man, gripping and ripping his fastball at a career-best 97 mph (touching triple digits), and while his future (given his injury history) is probably in the bullpen, he did make a three-inning scoreless spot start. If you see a surgeon on the street, shake his hand and congratulate him on his handiwork. Statistically, you have a good chance of it being one of Hudson's doctors.

Dominic Leone RHP

Born: 10/26/91 Age: 24 Bats: R Throws: R Height: 5'11" Weight: 210

YEAR	TEAM	LVL	AGE	W	L	SV	G	GS	IP	H	HR	BB/9	K/9	GB%	BABIP	WHIP	ERA	FIP	DRA	WARP	CFIP	MPH
2013	WTN	AA	21	1	2	4	16	0	18	12	2	2.5	8.5	49%	.213	0.94	2.50	3.30	3.74	0.1	90	
2013	HDS	A+	21	0	1	12	29	0	39^{2}	31	2	2.0	8.4	57%	.274	1.01	2.50	3.32	4.68	0.5	79	
2014	SEA	MLB	22	8	2	0	57	0	66^{1}	52	4	3.4	9.5	57%	.282	1.16	2.17	3.10	3.34	0.9	91	97.2
2015	SEA	MLB	23	0	4	0	10	0	11^{1}	11	1	7.1	5.6	50%	.270	1.76	6.35	5.40	5.86	-0.2	119	96.3
2015	MOB	AA	23	1	2	0	19	0	27^{2}	22	1	3.9	9.1	44%	.292	1.23	3.90	3.16	3.42	0.3	90	
2015	ARI	MLB	23	0	1	0	3	0	3^{2}	8	1	0.0	4.9	35%	.438	2.18	14.73	6.43	10.98	-0.3	117	95.1
2016	*ARI*	*MLB*	*24*	*1*	*0*	*0*	*14*	*0*	14^{1}	*13*	*2*	*3.4*	*8.2*	*51%*	*.307*	*1.29*	*3.87*	*4.09*	*4.57*	*0.1*	*103*	
2017	*ARI*	*MLB*	*25*	*1*	*0*	*1*	*25*	*0*	32^{1}	*28*	*4*	*3.4*	*8.4*	*51%*	*.299*	*1.26*	*3.94*	*4.32*	*4.65*	*0.1*	*105*	

Breakout: 24% Improve: 38% Collapse: 14% Attrition: 27% MLB: 67% *Comparables: Josh Spence, Cody Allen, Daniel Schlereth*

Put it this way: The only time Leone was accused of hitting his spot was in July, when he was ejected for plunking Christian Yelich. Otherwise, his control deserted him, his fastball lost velo, his slider lost bite, and his promising career as a middle-inning stalwart took detours to Triple- and then Double-A. In between those assignments, the Mariners gave him the change-of-scenery golden ticket by sending him to Arizona in a "flotsam for jetsam" blockbuster. Whether he turns out to have been the flotsam (floating wreckage) or jetsam (goods thrown overboard) will depend on whether he can locate the strike zone again. Here's hoping for jetsam.

Adam Loewen LHP

Born: 4/9/84 Age: 32 Bats: L Throws: L Height: 6'6" Weight: 235

YEAR	TEAM	LVL	AGE	W	L	SV	G	GS	IP	H	HR	BB/9	K/9	GB%	BABIP	WHIP	ERA	FIP	DRA	WARP	CFIP	MPH
2014	CLR	A+	30	1	0	0	2	2	10^{1}	7	0	6.1	7.8	52%	.259	1.35	2.61	3.68	4.60	0.0	108	
2014	REA	AA	30	4	5	0	17	17	103^{1}	84	7	4.6	6.5	52%	.255	1.33	3.31	4.50	4.82	0.4	110	
2015	PHI	MLB	31	1	0	0	20	0	19^{1}	20	3	7.9	10.2	37%	.354	1.91	6.98	6.01	5.60	-0.2	107	94.0
2015	LEH	AAA	31	1	3	10	33	0	46	29	1	6.3	11.7	48%	.277	1.33	2.15	3.05	3.53	0.5	93	
2015	REA	AA	31	1	0	0	7	0	12^{1}	10	1	3.6	9.5	31%	.290	1.22	1.46	3.67	3.51	0.1	91	
2016	*ARI*	*MLB*	*32*	*4*	*3*	*0*	*37*	*8*	*76*	*68*	*8*	*4.3*	*8.5*	*42%*	*.307*	*1.37*	*4.04*	*4.05*	*4.73*	*0.4*	*110*	
2017	*ARI*	*MLB*	*33*	*4*	*3*	*0*	*31*	*7*	73^{2}	*67*	*9*	*4.4*	*8.6*	*42%*	*.309*	*1.40*	*4.22*	*4.64*	*4.94*	*0.2*	*115*	

Breakout: 9% Improve: 10% Collapse: 9% Attrition: 20% MLB: 24% *Comparables: Sean Henn, Marty McLeary, Bill Murphy*

A story that should be considered nothing short of remarkable no matter the end result, Loewen completed his second reinvention in 2015, returning to his roots as a pitcher. Serious thoughts that he would step back onto a major-league mound started surfacing late in 2014, when Loewen was with Double-A Reading. The numbers weren't gorgeous, but he had rediscovered his breaking ball and was touching the mid-90s with his fastball. Add in an injury to Mario Hollands in the spring and, just like that, another comeback was within reach. Loewen flashed impressive stuff at times, but more often looked like pitching was still new to him, allowing a hit and a walk per inning. He did strike out about a quarter of the batters he faced, so even after all that, an effective reliever may yet be dormant within him.

Yoan Lopez RHP

Born: 1/2/93 Age: 23 Bats: R Throws: R Height: 6'3" Weight: 185

YEAR	TEAM	LVL	AGE	W	L	SV	G	GS	IP	H	HR	BB/9	K/9	GB%	BABIP	WHIP	ERA	FIP	DRA	WARP	CFIP	MPH
2015	MOB	AA	22	1	6	0	10	9	48	46	4	4.5	6.0	40%	.290	1.46	4.69	4.55	5.44	-0.4	113	
2016	*ARI*	*MLB*	*23*	*2*	*2*	*0*	*7*	*7*	35^{2}	*37*	*4*	*4.2*	*6.2*	*37%*	*.314*	*1.50*	*4.57*	*4.61*	*5.30*	*0.0*	*126*	
2017	*ARI*	*MLB*	*24*	*7*	*10*	*0*	*28*	*28*	169^{2}	*175*	*21*	*4.2*	*6.5*	*37%*	*.313*	*1.50*	*4.64*	*5.11*	*5.38*	*-0.2*	*129*	

Breakout: 0% Improve: 0% Collapse: 0% Attrition: 0% MLB: 0% *Comparables: Andrew Carpenter, Mayckol Guaipe, Sam LeCure*

The decision to sign Lopez to an $8.25 mil contract was an interesting one on several levels. The Diamondbacks hadn't spent more than $1.06 million (Jose Herrera) on any non-exempt international free agents in recent memory, and here they were setting the record (briefly) for bonuses awarded to any IFA under 23. Not only was it a continuation of spending on Cuban talent—following Yasmany Tomas' signing, which was exempt from international free agent spending restrictions—but it also effectively prevented the D'backs from participating in the next two IFA periods (2015-16, 2016-17), which are expected to be thick with Cuban talent.

Was it worth it? It's difficult to say at this point. Lopez's Double-A performance didn't live up to the "first-round talent" grades that some evaluators put on him in the offseason, with an inflated ERA and a strikeout rate hovering just over 15 percent. The quality of his stuff *did* receive plaudits, as he would sit in the 92-94 mph range with some run on his fastball. His best secondary is a slider that he likes to frontdoor to right-handed batters for called strikes, or drop out of the zone for swings and misses. In Cuban footage, he could be seen dropping his arm and throwing his breaking ball from close to a side-armed angle, but he has made progress in replicating the arm slot of his fastball since arriving Stateside. The changeup is nascent and its development will be crucial to his ability to remain in the rotation. There are some who believe he's destined to end up in the bullpen.

Complicating matters as the year went on was the organization's apparent thriftiness in the draft—they were $1.7 million under their draft allotment, which just doesn't happen—and in dealing away fellow pitching prospect Touki Toussaint just to rid themselves of the remainder of Bronson Arroyo's contract. In essence, they traded Toussaint to save roughly the same money they committed to Lopez, and pretty much nobody thinks Lopez is better than Toussaint. Thus the question going forward isn't merely "Can Lopez justify Dave Stewart's decision to sign him?" but rather "Can Lopez justify *everything* Stewart gave up?"

Evan Marshall RHP

Born: 4/18/90 Age: 26 Bats: R Throws: R Height: 6'2" Weight: 225

YEAR	TEAM	LVL	AGE	W	L	SV	G	GS	IP	H	HR	BB/9	K/9	GB%	BABIP	WHIP	ERA	FIP	DRA	WARP	CFIP	MPH
2013	RNO	AAA	23	3	6	3	54	0	58	75	2	4.7	9.2	60%	.412	1.81	4.34	3.79	4.69	0.4	89	
2014	RNO	AAA	24	0	1	1	14	0	16^{2}	10	0	2.7	10.3	61%	.303	0.90	0.54	2.32	4.67	0.0	81	
2014	ARI	MLB	24	4	4	0	57	0	49^{1}	50	3	3.1	9.9	61%	.351	1.36	2.74	2.86	3.95	0.3	89	95.9
2015	ARI	MLB	25	0	2	0	13	0	13^{1}	20	3	3.4	4.7	51%	.370	1.88	6.07	6.16	8.47	-0.6	117	96.3
2015	RNO	AAA	25	3	2	0	31	0	32^{1}	47	1	3.6	7.0	66%	.380	1.86	6.40	3.94	5.24	0.0	99	
2016	*ARI*	*MLB*	*26*	*1*	*0*	*0*	*18*	*0*	*19*	*20*	*2*	*3.3*	*7.8*	*60%*	*.331*	*1.39*	*3.94*	*3.88*	*4.66*	*0.1*	*104*	
2017	*ARI*	*MLB*	*27*	*1*	*1*	*0*	*27*	*0*	*28*	*28*	*3*	*3.2*	*8.1*	*60%*	*.330*	*1.37*	*3.97*	*4.36*	*4.69*	*0.1*	*105*	

Breakout: 16% Improve: 23% Collapse: 20% Attrition: 20% MLB: 50% *Comparables: Ramon Troncoso, Sam Demel, Scott Maine*

The Diamondbacks' Opening Day setup guy added giddyup to his fastball but lost sink, and that made all the difference: pitches got left up, Marshall got sent down. All that's of secondary concern now, after a line drive fractured his skull while he was pitching for Reno in August. Marshall walked off the field steadily, seemingly fine, but later that night doctors found bleeding in his brain and performed an emergency, life-saving surgery. He'll wear the funny hat this year, hopefully another step toward a future in which all pitchers are at least partially protected by padded headwear. "I was minutes away from not making it," Marshall told the AP. "And if the worst thing that happens from all this is I have to wear a funny-looking hat to continue my career, I'll take it."

Shelby Miller RHP

Born: 9/20/90 Age: 25 Bats: R Throws: R Height: 6'2" Weight: 205

YEAR	TEAM	LVL	AGE	W	L	SV	G	GS	IP	H	HR	BB/9	K/9	GB%	BABIP	WHIP	ERA	FIP	DRA	WARP	CFIP	MPH
2013	SLN	MLB	22	15	9	0	31	31	173^{1}	152	20	3.0	8.8	40%	.280	1.21	3.06	3.64	4.07	1.7	98	96.6
2014	SLN	MLB	23	10	9	0	32	31	183	160	22	3.6	6.2	42%	.256	1.27	3.74	4.51	3.99	1.8	118	96.0
2015	ATL	MLB	24	6	17	0	33	33	205^{1}	183	13	3.2	7.5	49%	.285	1.25	3.02	3.47	3.14	4.6	97	96.7
2016	*ARI*	*MLB*	*25*	*12*	*11*	*0*	*32*	*32*	*192*	*178*	*21*	*2.9*	*7.7*	*46%*	*.302*	*1.25*	*3.80*	*3.80*	*4.49*	*1.8*	*103*	
2017	*ARI*	*MLB*	*26*	*9*	*9*	*0*	*27*	*27*	*165^{2}*	*153*	*19*	*2.8*	*7.8*	*46%*	*.301*	*1.23*	*3.80*	*4.16*	*4.49*	*1.5*	*104*	

Breakout: 25% Improve: 63% Collapse: 20% Attrition: 12% MLB: 96% *Comparables: David Price, Jarrod Parker, Jose Quintana*

What a trade *that* was. We won't take an Official Position in this book on who ripped off whom in the Diamondbacks-Braves blockbuster that brought Miller to the Copper State, but say this about Dave Stewart: His approach to team-building so far is as in-your-face as his famously intense mound presence.

Weird as it looks for a rebuilding team to trade away a cheap 25-year-old starter, the Braves should probably be applauded for, one year earlier, flipping a one-year outfielder for a heralded pitcher coming off a (relative) sophomore slump; they came out smelling like roses after Miller turned in one of the best 2015 seasons in the league by DRA's lights. He brought his strikeouts back within reason and amped his grounder rate by the seeming paradox of diversifying his arsenal at the same time that he reduced his curve deployment to below 10 percent: Miller went from being a fastball-dominant pitcher to a fastball**s**-dominant one, throwing a sinker and a cutter about a fifth of the time apiece, turning pitches that had previously been mere seasoning into full-fledged ingredients. Miller's win-loss record, and his 24-start winless streak, were an unfortunate sideshow in 2015; if he holds his actual pitching steady, or continues to make the kinds of improvements that you hope someone his age will make, this year could see the W and L columns flipped.

Robbie Ray LHP

Born: 10/1/91 Age: 24 Bats: L Throws: L Height: 6'2" Weight: 195

YEAR	TEAM	LVL	AGE	W	L	SV	G	GS	IP	H	HR	BB/9	K/9	GB%	BABIP	WHIP	ERA	FIP	DRA	WARP	CFIP	MPH
2013	HAR	AA	21	5	2	0	11	11	58	56	4	3.3	9.3	45%	.317	1.33	3.72	3.55	4.51	0.5	96	
2013	POT	A+	21	6	3	0	16	16	84	60	9	4.4	10.7	45%	.273	1.20	3.11	3.97	4.25	1.0	85	
2014	TOL	AAA	22	7	6	0	20	19	100^{1}	106	6	3.9	6.7	36%	.326	1.50	4.22	4.05	4.82	0.3	110	
2014	DET	MLB	22	1	4	0	9	6	28^{2}	43	5	3.5	6.0	40%	.376	1.88	8.16	5.25	7.72	-1.0	114	95.5
2015	RNO	AAA	23	2	3	0	9	9	41^{2}	44	1	5.8	12.3	44%	.422	1.70	3.67	3.12	3.41	1.0	82	
2015	ARI	MLB	23	5	12	0	23	23	127^{2}	121	9	3.5	8.4	45%	.311	1.33	3.52	3.55	4.10	1.4	98	96.4
2016	*ARI*	*MLB*	*24*	*7*	*7*	*0*	*21*	*21*	*119^{2}*	*116*	*12*	*3.3*	*8.3*	*43%*	*.325*	*1.33*	*3.71*	*3.72*	*4.39*	*1.3*	*100*	
2017	*ARI*	*MLB*	*25*	*7*	*7*	*0*	*22*	*22*	*127^{2}*	*119*	*14*	*3.2*	*8.7*	*43%*	*.320*	*1.29*	*3.71*	*4.08*	*4.39*	*1.2*	*101*	

Breakout: 25% Improve: 50% Collapse: 16% Attrition: 25% MLB: 85% *Comparables: Vance Worley, Rubby De La Rosa, Andrew Cashner*

Detroit might have won the Doug Fister trade after all; problem is, they flipped the spoils to Arizona before realizing it. The former trade bait with the suspect curveball turned it into a sort of slurvy-curvy amalgam that was an effective swing-and-miss offering, dispelling the belief that his destiny was the bullpen. He also added two points of zip on his fastball, bringing it to 94, and both of these pleasant surprises arguably made Ray the desert's most consistent—dare we say, best?—starter. Young enough to not remember the O.J. trial, Ray has time to learn to pitch deeper into games (he seldom finished seven and only once went past) and, with no discernible platoon splits, emerge as a borderline ace. For now, he's a solid no. 3.

Braden Shipley RHP

Born: 2/22/92 Age: 24 Bats: R Throws: R Height: 6'2" Weight: 185

YEAR	TEAM	LVL	AGE	W	L	SV	G	GS	IP	H	HR	BB/9	K/9	GB%	BABIP	WHIP	ERA	FIP	DRA	WARP	CFIP	MPH
2013	SBN	A	21	0	1	0	4	4	20^2	14	2	3.5	7.0	46%	.218	1.06	2.61	4.35	4.68	0.1	104	
2013	YAK	A-	21	0	2	0	8	8	19	30	1	2.8	11.4	44%	.475	1.89	7.58	2.58	3.70	0.3	84	
2014	MOB	AA	22	1	2	0	4	4	20	14	3	4.5	8.1	56%	.216	1.20	3.60	4.84				
2014	VIS	A+	22	2	4	0	10	10	60^1	57	7	3.1	10.1	48%	.331	1.29	4.03	4.39	4.82	0.5	89	
2014	SBN	A	22	4	2	0	8	8	45^2	46	1	2.2	8.1	47%	.336	1.25	3.74	2.83	4.08	0.6	87	
2015	MOB	AA	23	9	11	0	28	27	156^2	147	7	3.2	6.8	46%	.294	1.30	3.50	3.55	3.93	1.7	96	
2016	*ARI*	*MLB*	*24*	*8*	*8*	*0*	*25*	*25*	*126^2*	*127*	*14*	*3.4*	*6.8*	*42%*	*.314*	*1.37*	*4.14*	*4.19*	*4.84*	*0.7*	*114*	
2017	*ARI*	*MLB*	*25*	*6*	*8*	*0*	*21*	*21*	*123^1*	*124*	*15*	*3.6*	*7.0*	*42%*	*.313*	*1.41*	*4.39*	*4.82*	*5.13*	*0.2*	*121*	

Breakout: 0% Improve: 0% Collapse: 0% Attrition: 0% MLB: 0% *Comparables: Roenis Elias, Jose Ramirez, J.R. Graham*

Shipley has been on the express track as a prospect since he was drafted, and with good reason. A late comer to the mound—he started pitching his sophomore year—he adapted quickly, showing his old shortstop athleticism and three potentially plus pitches. You could call Shipley's curveball "Teddy Pendergrass" because he didn't use it much in college but later learned how it helps to undress batters. He can drop it in the zone for strikes or out of the zone for whiffs, though his command of the spike grip waxes and wanes. His changeup is his best secondary, occasionally flashing plus-plus. He didn't miss as many bats in 2015, and the quality of his stuff was known to fluctuate (more than normal) start-to-start, perhaps a side effect of his relatively recent conversion.

Matt Stites RHP

Born: 5/28/90 Age: 26 Bats: L Throws: R Height: 5'11" Weight: 195

YEAR	TEAM	LVL	AGE	W	L	SV	G	GS	IP	H	HR	BB/9	K/9	GB%	BABIP	WHIP	ERA	FIP	DRA	WARP	CFIP	MPH
2013	SAN	AA	23	2	2	14	46	0	52	37	6	1.4	8.8	47%	.228	0.87	2.08	3.11	3.71	0.6	81	
2014	MOB	AA	24	0	1	3	12	0	12	10	0	2.2	6.0	54%	.286	1.08	3.75	2.60				
2014	ARI	MLB	24	0	0	0	37	0	33	33	6	4.4	7.1	45%	.273	1.48	5.73	5.44	5.59	-0.4	116	98.7
2014	RNO	AAA	24	0	0	12	17	0	16	13	1	3.4	8.4	49%	.286	1.19	2.25	3.76	4.98	0.1	92	
2015	RNO	AAA	25	1	1	3	23	0	25^2	31	2	4.9	4.9	56%	.326	1.75	3.86	5.16	6.64	-0.4	117	
2015	ARI	MLB	25	0	0	0	11	0	8^2	14	1	5.2	6.2	46%	.406	2.19	12.46	5.01	7.63	-0.3	113	97.1
2016	*ARI*	*MLB*	*26*	*1*	*0*	*0*	*14*	*0*	*14^1*	*14*	*2*	*3.2*	*6.8*	*48%*	*.301*	*1.33*	*4.31*	*4.37*	*5.04*	*0.0*	*119*	
2017	*ARI*	*MLB*	*27*	*2*	*1*	*0*	*31*	*0*	*32^1*	*30*	*4*	*3.2*	*7.3*	*48%*	*.296*	*1.29*	*4.29*	*4.71*	*5.02*	*-0.1*	*119*	

Breakout: 16% Improve: 29% Collapse: 13% Attrition: 22% MLB: 44% *Comparables: Josh Spence, Preston Claiborne, Warner Madrigal*

Stites began the season on the disabled list with elbow inflammation, which in Bad News Power Rankings is second only to waking up terrified of polyester pants. It cost him April and May and, one might speculate, the mph missing from his fastball when he did come back. He was wild as buckshot and couldn't fool a soul, which leaves us three possibilities: (1) he just can't hit his spots at the top level, confirming *those* fears; (2) the elbow never got right, confirming *that* fear; (3) polyesterphobia, confirming *that* joke. He'll have to prove himself in the dog-eat-dog world of spring training reliever battles.

Alex Young LHP

Born: 9/9/93 Age: 22 Bats: L Throws: L Height: 6'2" Weight: 205

In the months before last June's draft, Young transitioned from reliever to starter at TCU. The move was a success on multiple fronts, not only adding depth to the Horned Frogs' rotation, but also uncovering a third pitch for Young. That, as much as anything, is what propelled him to his second-round selection. He doesn't have premium velocity from the left side, generally sitting in the low 90s, but shows impressive command and manipulation of the normally troublesome knuckle-curve. As a starter he was forced to develop a changeup, and it turned quickly into an above-average offering with depth and late fade. The lack of velocity probably limits his upside, but with two mature secondaries he stands to be a quick mover and a realistic back-end starter.

Brad Ziegler RHP

Born: 10/10/79 Age: 36 Bats: R Throws: R Height: 6'4" Weight: 220

YEAR	TEAM	LVL	AGE	W	L	SV	G	GS	IP	H	HR	BB/9	K/9	GB%	BABIP	WHIP	ERA	FIP	DRA	WARP	CFIP	MPH
2013	ARI	MLB	33	8	1	13	78	0	73	61	3	2.7	5.4	71%	.258	1.14	2.22	3.38	3.04	1.4	106	88.3
2014	ARI	MLB	34	5	3	1	68	0	67	60	5	3.2	7.3	65%	.284	1.25	3.49	3.67	3.48	0.8	104	86.9
2015	ARI	MLB	35	0	3	30	66	0	68	48	3	2.2	4.8	74%	.220	0.96	1.85	3.47	2.27	2.0	111	86.4
2016	*ARI*	*MLB*	*36*	*3*	*1*	*32*	*54*	*0*	*57^1*	*52*	*6*	*2.8*	*6.2*	*71%*	*.288*	*1.22*	*3.99*	*4.05*	*4.70*	*0.1*	*107*	
2017	*ARI*	*MLB*	*37*	*3*	*1*	*8*	*54*	*0*	*51^1*	*48*	*5*	*2.6*	*5.9*	*71%*	*.290*	*1.22*	*3.97*	*4.35*	*4.68*	*0.1*	*106*	

Breakout: 22% Improve: 41% Collapse: 30% Attrition: 6% MLB: 85% *Comparables: Roberto Hernandez, Scott Downs, Kent Tekulve*

The last closer to notch 30 saves and strike out fewer than five per nine innings was the Todd Jones Experience in 2007. The comparison stops there for Ziegler, the sidewinder done right, who had knocked on the door for seemingly eons to be the ninth-inning guy (but always conspicuously from the bottom hinge). Addison Reed's meltdown was his gain. Ziggy keeps everything on the ground, and opponents hit .111 off his changeup—a pitch most sidearmers simply don't throw, but that Ziegler has incorporated a little more every year. The excruciatingly low, career-best BABIP means more of those bleeders probably turn to singles this year, but the aging Ziegler still has the oddball arsenal to saw off batters in the late innings.

Lineouts

Hitters

NAME	POS	TEAM	LVL	AGE	PA	R	2B	3B	HR	RBI	BB	K	SB	CS	AVG/OBP/SLG	TAv	BABIP	BRR	FRAA	WARP
Sergio Alcantara	SS	KNC	A	18	79	5	1	0	0	5	4	17	1	0	.113/.169/.127	.177	.145	-0.1	SS(20): 1.2	-0.3
	SS	YAK	A-	18	287	34	12	2	1	23	24	46	6	0	.253/.314/.327	.263	.302	2.4	SS(52): 4.8, 2B(20): 1.9	2.1
Colin Bray	CF	KNC	A	22	560	78	25	8	3	52	47	109	27	9	.308/.370/.410	.286	.385	7.1	CF(125): 4.3, RF(1): 1.8	4.8
Oscar Hernandez	C	ARI	MLB	21	36	4	1	0	0	1	3	15	0	0	.161/.257/.194	.180	.313	0.2	C(13): -1.7	-0.3
	C	RNO	AAA	21	27	2	3	0	0	1	1	5	0	0	.240/.269/.360	.208	.300	-0.3	C(8): 0.0	-0.1
Chris Herrmann	C	MIN	MLB	27	113	13	5	1	2	10	7	37	0	0	.146/.214/.272	.186	.203	1.0	C(38): -4.9, 1B(2): 0.0	-0.8
	C	ROC	AAA	27	88	9	3	0	1	6	11	13	3	0	.260/.364/.342	.266	.295	-0.4	C(17): 1.8, LF(1): -0.0	0.5
Gerald Laird	C	ARI	MLB	35	2	0	0	0	0	0	0	0	0	0	.000/.000/.000	.007	.000	0.0	C(1): -0.0	0.0
Domingo Leyba	2B	VIS	A+	19	562	60	21	5	2	43	26	90	10	6	.237/.277/.309	.239	.278	4.2	SS(123): 0.5	1.6
Cody Ransom	3B	RNO	AAA	39	181	14	8	1	6	30	10	44	1	0	.210/.249/.377	.226	.240	0.1	SS(39): 1.3, 3B(3): 0.2	0.2
Jack Reinheimer	SS	MOB	AA	22	328	39	14	2	4	26	37	54	9	5	.265/.355/.371	.283	.311	-0.2	SS(72): 0.4, 2B(5): 0.3	2.2
	SS	WTN	AA	22	219	25	10	1	1	16	14	39	12	1	.277/.323/.351	.261	.337	2.5	SS(44): 0.7, 2B(4): 0.0	1.3
Victor Reyes	LF	KNC	A	20	458	57	17	5	2	59	22	58	13	4	.311/.343/.389	.269	.352	4.4	LF(60): 6.3, RF(52): 4.1	3.2

Sergio Alcantara has all the ingredients for a good-field, no-hit shortstop: He's a good fielder, and he gets no hits. ❖ A broken foot in 2014 slowed **Colin Bray** by a year and allowed his (older, actually) brother Tyler to catch up to him in the Midwest League. Colin has enough speed to be a rangy fourth outfielder, and to beat his sidearming brother to The Show. ❖ Rule 5 selectee **Oscar Hernandez** spent half the season with a broken hand, half the season playing over his head, and the whole season telling people he is Felix Hernandez's messy roommate. ❖ **Chris Herrmann** is versatile, in that he bats left-handed (terribly), and can play catcher (poorly) or either outfield spot (badly). ❖ **Gerald Laird** missed most of the year with a bad back, then worked hard to get back. Once his back healed, the 'backs, who were way back in the standings, didn't want him back, even as a backup. ❖ Part of the Didi Gregorius get, **Domingo Leyba** struggled in what is normally a hitter's haven, and might ultimately be nothing more than a Sunday player. ❖ A third-round pick in 2014, **Matt Railey** has across-the-board tools but has been slowed by amphetamines, completely missing the point. ❖ Around the time you're reading this, **Cody Ransom**, who returned stateside after a year in Japan, is becoming the world's first documented 40-year-old Cody. ❖ Whether he sticks at shortstop, light-hitting utility speedy guy **Jack Reinheimer** is like the exact inverse of the man he was acquired for. It's like the Diamondbacks traded Mark Trumbo for Trumbo's butt groove. ❖ Long and lean, **Victor Reyes** took 1,220 professional plate appearances to hit his first home run. Naturally, he hit his second 14 PAs later, in his final at-bat of the season, and no doubt spent the offseason sketching trendlines on napkins.

Pitchers

NAME	TEAM	LVL	AGE	W	L	SV	G	GS	IP	H	HR	BB/9	K/9	GB%	BABIP	WHIP	ERA	FIP	FRA	WARP	CFIP	MPH
Anthony Banda	VIS	A+	21	8	8	0	28	27	151^2	150	8	2.3	9.0	48%	.336	1.25	3.32	3.31	3.72	3.4	86	
Jake Barrett	RNO	AAA	23	1	3	11	22	0	23	27	1	4.7	8.2	49%	.371	1.70	5.09	3.90	5.03	0.0	100	
	MOB	AA	23	3	0	4	25	0	30	34	2	3.3	9.0	47%	.364	1.50	4.20	3.27	3.27	0.5	88	
Daniel Gibson	VIS	A+	23	2	1	1	27	0	28	16	1	2.2	12.2	44%	.268	0.82	1.61	2.28	2.47	0.9	69	
	MOB	AA	23	1	0	2	26	0	24	18	0	5.2	7.5	44%	.273	1.33	1.50	3.39	4.79	-0.1	106	
Brad Keller	KNC	A	19	8	9	0	26	25	142	128	3	2.3	6.9	58%	.293	1.16	2.60	3.13	3.69	2.1	94	
Cody Reed	YAK	A-	19	5	4	0	15	14	63^1	51	5	3.0	10.2	39%	.287	1.14	3.27	3.40	3.24	1.6	84	
Matt Reynolds	ARI	MLB	30	0	0	0	18	0	13^2	14	6	4.6	11.9	44%	.267	1.54	4.61	7.99	6.67	-0.3	96	90.2
	RNO	AAA	30	3	6	0	45	0	50	54	5	3.2	7.7	42%	.331	1.44	5.58	4.50	4.80	0.2	98	
Jimmie Sherfy	MOB	AA	23	1	6	2	44	0	49^2	50	3	5.1	9.1	50%	.336	1.57	6.52	3.95	4.59	0.0	102	
Tim Stauffer	NYN	MLB	33	0	0	0	5	0	5^2	8	2	3.2	12.7	50%	.429	1.76	7.94	6.51	7.71	-0.2	97	91.6
	LVG	AAA	33	4	1	0	8	8	54^1	46	4	1.7	5.8	59%	.253	1.03	2.48	3.99	4.39	0.7	95	
	MIN	MLB	33	1	0	0	13	0	15	24	4	4.2	3.6	53%	.357	2.07	6.60	7.17	11.67	-1.2	119	91.1
Allen Webster	RNO	AAA	25	4	6	0	15	15	77	117	8	3.0	7.2	50%	.405	1.86	8.18	4.47	5.18	0.3	100	
	ARI	MLB	25	1	1	0	9	5	31	32	10	5.8	4.9	48%	.237	1.68	5.81	8.39	7.34	-0.9	134	94.5

Texas native and crafty lefty in training **Anthony Banda** has the size, athleticism and values you'd look for in a fine young man from the Lone Star State. What we're saying is he's Easy Company for his teammates to keep, but you'd expect nothing less from a Banda brother. ❖ Already chained to a middle-relief profile, **Jake Barrett** endured a difficult season, including a demotion from Triple-A to Double-A (with, as it turned out, no return ticket). He was done in by inconsistent command of a fastball that's flat as day-old soda. ❖ Daniel Gibson the NBA player retired, changed his name to Boobie and is now a rapper featuring a song called "Funk." **Daniel Gibson** the 2013 seventh-round pick also features funk, which he used to hold lefties to a .151/.237/.186 line last year. ❖ **Brad Keller** has an inconsistent changeup, an unfortunately consistent (it's always bad) slider, and an enviable set of glutes. He still doesn't miss bats but will eat innings. ❖ Former second-rounder **Cody Reed** is a big, left-handed starting pitcher with a chance for an above-average fastball and slider. Reminds some of Cody Reed. ❖ **Matt Reynolds** returned from Tommy John surgery throwing 88 mph (a tick slower than pre-surgery) and allowing a home run every two innings. With a killer curve he throws almost 40 percent of the time, he can survive the velo drop, but not the other thing. ❖ The second-best part of having the first-overall pick is the big-slot spillover for later-round picks like **Wesley Rodriguez**. The 12th-rounder/$350,000 sign consistently hits 97 and shows a power curve, or at least did, before his June Tommy John surgery. ❖ **Jimmie Sherfy** and his wipeout slider held batters to .220/.280/.294 with bases empty and .325/.471/.475 with men on, i.e. it wasn't great but he'll never have another season this bad, either. ❖ **Tim Stauffer** joined the Mets from independent ball in 2015, but his existence was mostly theoretical. ❖ None of **Allen Webster**'s numbers cast him in a positive light. There weren't many good words to say about his performance either, and hieroglyphics speak very little about baseball in general.

Manager

Chip Hale

After the Diamondbacks' 12-17 start to the 2009 season, their brass decided it was time to shake things up. In baseball terms, that meant it was time to fire manager Bob Melvin. Rather than promote one of Melvin's coaches to fill the void, the front office opted for a member of its own: A.J. Hinch, whose official title had been director of player development. Hinch would last until the following July, when the Diamondbacks underwent a front-office makeover and decided it was time to shake things up.

The Diamondbacks have since undergone another front-office makeover. Led by Dave Stewart and Tony La Russa, this group decided at the conclusion of the 2014 season that it was their time to shake things up, so they fired Kirk Gibson and began a managerial search. Who did they settle on? Hale, a member of Melvin's staff in Oakland. That isn't the funny part. This is: Hale was on Melvin's Arizona staff too, and had previously managed in the system for six seasons. Hale was, in other words, seemingly more qualified to run the Diamondbacks at the time than Hinch was, but didn't get the job because he didn't have the right supporters. Ain't business something?

Anyway, justice eventually prevailed, Hale got the job and we all lived happily ever after. No, but really, Hale made the most his first year in the desert, guiding much of the same team that had notched the majors' worst record the previous season to a near-.500 mark and a third-place finish. Nitpicking managers is sort of our thing, though, so what does a deeper dive say about Hale? It says Hale likes to call for intentional walks (he tied Mike Scioscia for the most in the majors) and position-player sacrifices. Many will find it tough to accept the former (though it's more tolerable in the National League, where walking the eighth-place hitter to get to the pitcher is at times the right call), but the latter is easy to explain away by focusing on the who, not the what. The four D'backs who finished with five-plus bunts were Chris Owings, Nick Ahmed, Cliff Pennington and Ender Inciarte—or three no-hit infielders and an outfielder who is wont to bunt for hits. Nothing upsetting there.

Depending on your perspective, what is upsetting is that Hale seemed to pay homage to La Russa by making obsessive pitching changes. Oliver Perez pitched to one batter in 18 of his 48 appearances (including, at one point, five consecutive one-batter appearances), and Arizona's relievers as a whole ranked fifth in the majors in one-and-done appearances. Hale, for his part, looks like he could stick around for a few years.

ATLANTA BRAVES

Essay by Mark Bradley

Player comments by David Lee and BP authors

John Coppolella never played much baseball. He was the football manager at Notre Dame. He graduated with a degree in business and had a six-figure job with Intel waiting. He accepted a paid internship with the Yankees instead. His parents were not pleased.

In 2006, Braves general manager John Schuerholz hired Coppolella to be the team's director of baseball operations. Coppolella is among that generation of baseball lovers drawn to process above pine tar. The guy known as "Coppy" was working under his idol.

Eight years later, Schuerholz—then the Braves' president—essentially charged Coppolella with the task of razing and restoring a franchise that had fallen into what Schuerholz regarded as rack and ruin under Frank Wren, who'd succeeded him as GM in October 2007. Not that this collapse was entirely evident to the outside eye: From Opening Day 2010 through Sept. 17, 2014, Wren's Braves won more games than any other National League team.

But this was how deeply the Braves soured on Wren. On Sept. 22, 2013, his team clinched the National League East, marking Atlanta's first division title since the record run of 14 in succession ended in 2005. On Sept. 22, 2014, he was fired. Schuerholz opened the press conference by saying, "We have terminated Frank Wren." Terminated? Was this *Apocalypse Now*?

The Braves did not thank Wren for his diligent service. They did not wish the best for him and his family. Later that day, Schuerholz fired Jeff Wren, Frank's brother and a Braves scout, via voicemail. (On assignment, Jeff Wren was in the shower at his hotel.) Seven weeks later, they traded Kyle Wren, a minor-league outfielder and Frank's son, to Milwaukee.

(Footnote: The Braves wanted to fire Frank Wren on Sunday, Sept. 21, but were informed that Kyle was scheduled to receive an award in pregame ceremonies. It was decided that firing his dad on such a day would be, you know, cold-blooded. So the Braves waited until Monday to be cold-blooded.)

Into the breach stepped John Hart, lured from his Orlando home and MLB Network studios to be president of baseball operations. The corporate stance was that Hart, who'd done great work in Cleveland in the '90s, would serve as the new public face and as Coppolella's mentor;

BRAVES PROSPECTUS

2015 W-L: 67-95, 4th in NL East

Pythag	.374	30th	DER	.695	26th
RS/G	3.54	30th	B-Age	28.8	24th
RA/G	4.69	27th	P-Age	25.7	1st
TAv	.254	23rd	Salary	$97.1M	22nd
BRR	2.93	14th	M$/MW	$4.5M	8th
TAv-P	.284	29th	DL Days	1169	20th
FIP	4.37	27th	$ on DL	14%	12th

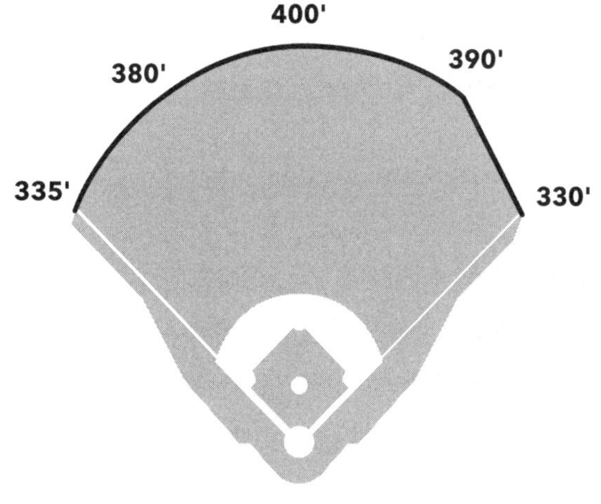

Outfield wall profile: **8'**

Three-Year Park Factors

Runs	Runs/RH	Runs/LH	HR/RH	HR/LH
93	99	101	99	95

Top Hitter WARP	2.9	Andrelton Simmons
Top Pitcher WARP	4.6	Shelby Miller
Top Prospect	Dansby Swanson	

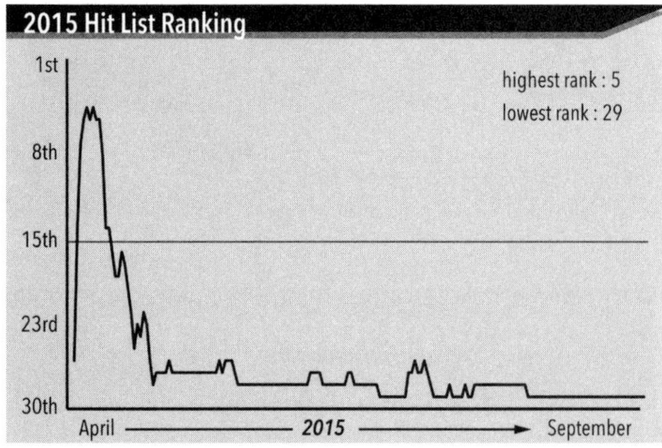

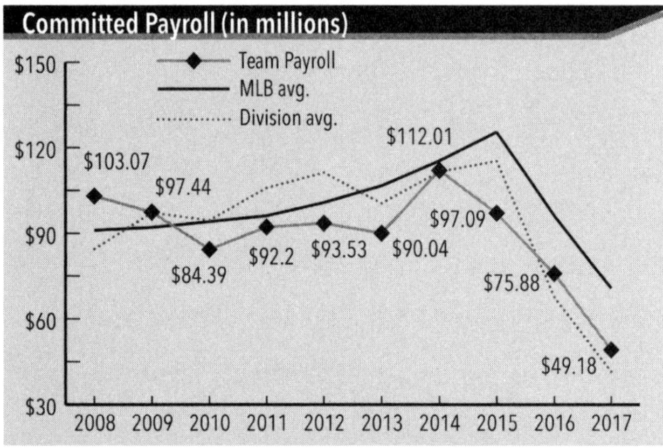

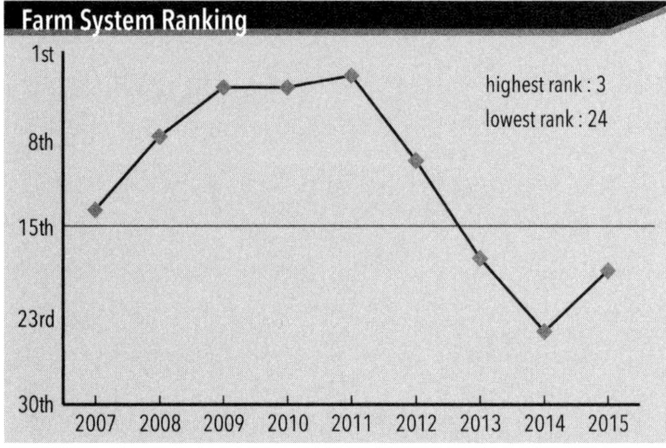

Personnel

President: John Schuerholz
President, Baseball Operations: John Hart
General Manager: John Coppolella
Manager: Fredi Gonzalez

Baseball Prospectus Alumni
Kiley McDaniel
Noah Woodward

in-house, it was generally held that Coppy—officially the assistant GM—would soon be Top Cat.

Sure enough, Coppolella was named GM on Oct. 1, 2015—even as many in the organization admitted he'd been doing GM things for the past year. Three days after his promotion, the Braves closed the season at 67-95, their worst record in a quarter-century. In two years they'd gone from 96 wins to 95 losses, but the higher-ups were happier with the guy who'd presided over the 95 losses than with his predecessor, whose sin was in not winning to specification. As Schuerholz said of Wren's dismissal: "We want to get back to doing things the Braves' Way."

That meant with homegrown talent and a bountiful farm system. That meant without the money-for-nothing contracts Wren handed Dan Uggla and Melvin (nee B.J.) Upton. Above all, that meant with young pitching.

Coppolella is 37. He's an advocate of analytics—he reads "Baseball Prospectus" daily—but people-savvy enough that Wren put him in charge of professional scouting. Not to dredge up the old divide, but he speaks the language on both sides of the *Moneyball* fence.

Even so, he hadn't been granted full access to Wren's inner circle. He'd formulate trade scenarios—two or three a day, according to someone who worked with him—but was never asked to vote yea or nay on any major deal. Post-Wren, Coppolella became the guy calling and texting other clubs: "Would you be willing to do this? Or this? Or even that?" Sometimes the solicitations would come at 2 a.m., sometimes at 6 a.m. Every week for a year, Coppolella asked the general manager of another National League team what it would take to work a deal for a particular All-Star. (That trade hasn't yet been made, FYI.)

Now Coppolella had the big red button. The new Braves' first big move was trading Jason Heyward, once projected as the face of the franchise, to St. Louis for Shelby Miller and Tyrell Jenkins. It made sense—Heyward was set become a free agent in November 2015 and surely wouldn't re-up with a mid-market team in rebuild mode, while Miller and Jenkins were the sort of pitchers on whom the rebuild would hang—but it had the effect of a punch in the nose. By trading Heyward, the Braves told us they weren't concerned about winning in 2015 or 2016.

The Braves, see, aren't just a team in administrative transition. After the 2016 season, the movement will become literal. They're leaving Turner Field, which came into being in 1997 after Atlanta's Olympic Stadium was cut in half, for SunTrust Park in suburban Cobb County. We could spend a week discussing the move, but here's the condensed version: The Braves got mad at the city of Atlanta, which labored long to help the NFL Falcons build a new downtown stadium but did little to placate the baseball team, and they found another government entity willing—nay, eager—to grant their every wish.

For public consumption, the Braves have never said, "The heck with downtown; we're waiting until we get to

Cobb County to win again." But knowing they're moving surely made the teardown easier. The Braves as inherited by Coppolella and Hart weren't good enough to win big and had too many bad contracts to be nimble in their reconstruction. Half-measures weren't an option.

After trading Heyward, the Braves sent Evan Gattis, a liability with any sort of glove, to Houston; Justin Upton, who was also ticketed for free agency, to San Diego; and, on the eve of Opening Day and also to San Diego, the peerless closer Craig Kimbrel and the pricy dud Melvin Upton. By then, the Atlanta audience was aghast: Would the last real player left inside I-285 turn out the lights? But by the time of the Kimbrel trade there should have been no shock to anything the Braves did. They were executing their stated plan. They were slashing payroll and restocking the farm and loading up on young pitching.

The only snag in Year 1 of what Hart called "the reset" was that the Braves played better longer than anyone expected. On July 7th, they were 3 ½ games behind the first-place Nationals, a half-game behind the Mets. The Braves blew a four-run lead in Milwaukee on July 8th to slip below .500 and were swept in a four-game series by Colorado, making them 42-47 at the All-Star break. Jason Grilli, pressed into closer service after Kimbrel was traded, tore his Achilles in Denver. Freddie Freeman, the best Braves hitter by three miles, was on the disabled list.

Privately, the Braves insisted they would make no in-season trade in the attempt to win 81 games, as opposed to 76. Still, Hart felt he owed his hovering-around-.500 team a little something, so the front office kept buying relievers on the cheap—with a bit better bullpen over the first half, the Braves might have been in first place—while surely yearning for the clarity a losing streak would bring. Those five losses before the break gave Hart/Coppolella their license to deal. As a sop, the Braves handed manager Fredi Gonzalez and his coaches a year's contract extension over the break, as if to say, "We're not going to hold you responsible for what's about to happen."

On July 24th, the Braves traded journeymen Kelly Johnson and Juan Uribe to the Mets for a couple of middling pitching prospects. On July 30th, Coppolella and Hart stumped the band: They sent their latest closer (Jim Johnson), their longtime LOOGY (Luis Avilan), their as-rated-by-some no. 1 prospect Jose Peraza and a 24-year-old left-handed starting pitcher with an ERA of 3.10 (Alex Wood) to the Dodgers for Hector Olivera, a 30-year-old who hadn't taken a major-league at-bat. Three big-leaguers and a top prospect for a Cuban defector who'd been fighting injuries since signing with Los Angeles. Worst trade in baseball history, or just of the new millennium?

There was, believe it or not, thought involved. Johnson and Avilan were expendable. The Braves themselves didn't regard Peraza, a middle infielder who doesn't hit for power and doesn't walk, their top prospect; they preferred Ozzie Albies, further down the chain. They fretted that Wood's delivery—invariably described, even by Wood himself, as "funky"—would lead to a physical breakdown. And they'd surveyed the bats apt to be available in free agency and concluded that Olivera, on whom they'd bid $40 million in the spring, would be a cheaper option. (The Dodgers bought him for $62.5 million and were on the hook for his $28 million signing bonus; the Braves wound up getting him for around $32 million over five-plus years.)

By then, the New Braves had made enough clever moves—prying the teenage pitcher Touki Toussaint from Arizona for utility man Phil Gosselin and the absorption of Bronson Arroyo's salary (subsequently off-loaded in the Olivera deal) was a master stroke—to earn the benefit of some doubt. Indeed, the machinations of Braves executives were more entertaining than anything their bare-bones team was doing. Coppolella was conjuring exotic trades left and right, and he was persuasive enough that Hart would eventually say, "Know what? That just might work."

Most of the time, anyway. It's believed Hart vetoed at least one other deadline deal, leading us to wonder: Who was left to trade?

Er, Andrelton Simmons? On Nov. 12th, the Braves made the first major move of the offseason by sending the once-in-a-generation shortstop to the Angels for Erick Aybar, but mostly for more pitching. Lefty Sean Newcomb and righty Chris Ellis were ranked no. 1 and no. 2 in the Angels' chain. The Braves believe the massive Newcomb is now the no. 1 pitching prospect in their suddenly bountiful—in arms if not yet bats—system.

In his youth, Coppolella wanted to be John Schuerholz. Having been entrusted with Schuerholz's franchise, he became Hercules unchained. (Though the slender Coppolella in no way resembles Hercules and, given that he's bald, doesn't favor Samson, either.) The Braves, who'd risen to eminence on the arms of Tom Glavine and Steve Avery and John Smoltz, said they wanted young pitching. Coppolella was delivering it on a heaping pallet.

By season's end, Matt Wisler and Mike Foltynewicz and Manny Banuelos—all acquired post-Wren—had taken turns in the rotation. Miller posted maybe the best 6-17 season ever. (He finished with an ERA of 3.02 but, owing to his team's inability to score, went four calendar months between victories.) After the Simmons trade, the Braves had visions of moving into SunTrust Park with Miller heading a rotation that would also include Julio Teheran, Wisler, Newcomb and Lucas Sims—none of whom would be older than 26 on Opening Day 2017. And that was with Toussaint, the 2015 Round 1 draftee Kolby Allard and Max Fried, acquired in the Justin Upton trade, presumably coming fast.

Hitting is another matter. Under Wren, the Braves were a clout-or-out offense. In 2013, they led the National League in home runs and strikeouts. (They also won those 96 games.) In 2014, they stopped hitting homers but kept whiffing apace. This dire combo left Schuerholz wanting a more contact-oriented lineup. Mission accomplished, sort of. The 2015 Braves had the second-fewest strikeouts among big-league teams, second only to the Royals. In the here and now, this recalibration availed the Braves naught: They finished last in runs. Indeed, they scored the same number (573) as in 2014, when they finished next-to-last.

The absence of offense was one of the reasons—not the biggest, but a reason all the same—they were moved to part with Simmons: He's the best in the business at saving runs, but he's not much at creating them. In 2015, he ranked 13th-worst in the majors among qualifying hitters in OPS; in 2014, he was the sixth worst.

The Braves are gorging on young arms not because they want to adopt a 12-man rotation but because they plan to use the excess to buy the bats they lack. As of Christmas Eve, their projected everyday eight included only three proven big-league hitters—Freeman, Nick Markakis and Aybar—and it was unknown if they planned to keep the latter or flip him for still more pitching. As for Olivera: Acquired as a third baseman, the Braves now project him as a left fielder. Wherever he plays, he'd better hit.

After the Simmons trade, the consensus among Braves fans was that the organization had lost its collective mind. Social media was awash with various forms of, "I'm never spending another dime on this team!" That the Braves cared so little for what was being said/written was, in an odd way, refreshing. Coppolella isn't doing what he's doing to be loved; he's doing it because he absolutely believes this is the only way it can be done.

For inspiration, he looks to recent events. The Royals traded Zack Greinke a year after a Cy Young season and landed Lorenzo Cain and Alcides Escobar, MVPs of the 2014 and 2015 ALCS, respectively. They traded Wil Myers, the no. 3 prospect in baseball, to Tampa Bay for James Shields, who would help lift Kansas City to the 2014 World Series, and Wade Davis, who would record the Series-clinching out in 2015. The Mets traded R.A. Dickey to Toronto a month after he'd won a Cy Young; that trade yielded Noah Syndergaard and Travis d'Arnaud, the starting battery in Game Three of the 2015 Series.

And then, as if on cue, Coppolella consummated a deal that, at least for daring, rivaled any of the above. On Dec. 8, he traded Miller—the young pitcher whose arrival in exchange for Heyward touched off this frenzy, the only Brave to make the 2015 All-Star team—to Arizona for Ender Inciarte, an outfielder whose WAR value for 2015 was 5.3 (way better than any Brave); for Aaron Blair, rated the best pitcher in the D-backs' system, and for shortstop Dansby Swanson, the first player taken in the June draft.

A lot of fans—and even some folks who write about baseball for a living—hated the Olivera and Simmons trades. Almost everyone loved this one. From the Braves' perspective, this made such sweeping sense that it was possible to feel sorry for the Diamondbacks. They'd given away Swanson, whom they'd made the no. 1 of no. 1's not six months earlier, for a pitcher yet to receive a Cy Young vote.

The Braves' second Miller trade in 13 months went a ways toward calming Coppolella's constituency. This time his daring was underpinned by an obvious design. Maybe there was really method to his manic deal-making.

Minutes after the Simmons trade was announced, this correspondent sent Coppolella a message: "You are fearless, sir."

Within seconds came his response: "We are going to win by being bold."

Maybe they will. Or maybe they'll win nothing and Coppolella will be gone in three years, a dreamer who failed so spectacularly as to become a cautionary tale. (The ancient Greeks had Icarus; 21st Century baseball fans could have Coppy.) In 2016, the Braves will again be one of the worst teams in the majors, but that's a considered choice. If the price of eventual greatness is being worse than mediocre now, that's a bill Coppolella will be glad to pay.

He has spent half his life dreaming of such an assignment. All those trade scenarios he'd offer to Wren on a daily basis? Coppolella now holds the power to make them happen—and he has, on almost a daily basis. He might be new to the job, but he is not afraid. ■

—Mark Bradley has been a sports columnist at the Atlanta Journal-Constitution *since 1984.*

Hitters

Ronald Acuna CF

Born: 12/18/97 Age: 18 Bats: R Throws: R Height: 6'0" Weight: 180

Isranel Wilson RF

Born: 3/6/98 Age: 18 Bats: L Throws: R Height: 6'3" Weight: 185

Juan Yepez 1B

Born: 2/19/98 Age: 18 Bats: R Throws: R Height: 6'1" Weight: 200

If the Braves get back strong in the international market, this could be the trio that signaled the return. Yepez was Atlanta's top signing in 2014 at $1 million. He's advanced physically, and he experienced short-season success at 17. He took steps to shore up his conditioning before signing, and scouts praise his quick, loose swing with power potential. He's a corner guy who might be best suited for first base.

Acuna, a six-figure sign in 2014, has garnered perhaps the most buzz of the three, and it's tough to find an evaluator who doesn't come away impressed. He has the potential for a solid power-speed combination while playing a rangy center field. Wilson, another six-figure sign in 2014, is different from the other two based on more projection and a lengthier frame. He stayed back at the complex because of a lack of polish in his approach, but double-digit home runs at the age of a high school junior are difficult to ignore. He's likely destined for a corner-outfield spot, and has a chance for impact power.

Braves executives have noted that their lower-level affiliates are going to be fun to watch in 2016, and these three are a big reason why.

Ozhaino Albies SS

Born: 1/7/97 Age: 19 Bats: B Throws: R Height: 5'9" Weight: 150

YEAR	TEAM	LVL	AGE	PA	R	2B	3B	HR	RBI	BB	K	SB	CS	AVG/OBP/SLG	TAv	BABIP	BRR	FRAA	WARP
2015	ROM	A	18	439	64	21	8	0	37	36	56	29	8	.310/.368/.404	.304	.358	4.7	SS(93): 6.0	5.1
2016	*ATL*	*MLB*	*19*	*250*	*27*	*10*	*2*	*3*	*18*	*14*	*59*	*7*	*3*	*.230/.275/.323*	*.221*	*.292*	*0.4*	*SS 3*	*0.5*
2017	*ATL*	*MLB*	*20*	*408*	*41*	*17*	*3*	*6*	*38*	*23*	*88*	*12*	*4*	*.245/.289/.354*	*.243*	*.299*	*1.3*	*SS 4*	*1.4*

Breakout: 0% Improve: 2% Collapse: 0% Attrition: 2% MLB: 3% *Comparables: Francisco Lindor, Elvis Andrus, Addison Russell*

There were whispers entering 2015 that Albies could become a top Braves prospect; well, here we are. He has such a loose, easy feel for both baseball and life that you can't help but love the kid. He has an advanced ability to barrel baseballs based on loose hands that find pitches in all quadrants of the zone, and he takes what pitchers give him by shooting contact to all fields. He does this from both sides of the plate, although it comes a little more naturally as a lefty. He occasionally lacks extension through the ball, which limits hard contact, and his power is well below average, but his plus-plus speed could manufacture "power," adding extra bases on balls in the gaps. Albies also has the skills to play shortstop at a high level: His arm is strong enough for the left side, but the key is again his hands, which eat grounders alive. The bow on the physical package is that his bright personality is a positive influence in the clubhouse and his great work ethic should allow him to continue adjusting and improving as he climbs the ladder.

Erick Aybar SS

Born: 1/14/84 Age: 32 Bats: B Throws: R Height: 5'10" Weight: 180

YEAR	TEAM	LVL	AGE	PA	R	2B	3B	HR	RBI	BB	K	SB	CS	AVG/OBP/SLG	TAv	BABIP	BRR	FRAA	WARP
2013	ANA	MLB	29	589	68	33	5	6	54	23	59	12	7	.271/.301/.382	.250	.292	4.0	SS(138): -10.8	1.1
2014	ANA	MLB	30	641	77	30	4	7	68	36	62	16	9	.278/.321/.379	.270	.297	5.5	SS(155): -14.6	2.3
2015	ANA	MLB	31	638	74	30	1	3	44	25	73	15	6	.270/.301/.338	.237	.300	3.2	SS(154): -13.2	0.1
2016	*ATL*	*MLB*	*32*	*618*	*62*	*32*	*4*	*6*	*54*	*31*	*73*	*15*	*7*	*.268/.310/.372*	*.248*	*.293*	*3.6*	*SS -13*	*1.2*
2017	*ATL*	*MLB*	*33*	*516*	*51*	*27*	*3*	*4*	*45*	*27*	*64*	*11*	*5*	*.262/.304/.358*	*.250*	*.288*	*3.5*	*SS -11*	*0.5*

Breakout: 0% Improve: 39% Collapse: 8% Attrition: 7% MLB: 96% *Comparables: Alexei Ramirez, Ryan Theriot, Rafael Furcal*

Aybar's defensive reputation has outpaced the metrics for years now: His FRAA has finished in the red in four straight seasons. The defenders of his glove are receding as he ages, just like his utility to a contending club is receding with his offense. Aybar's secondary skills completely vanished in 2015, resulting in the third-worst walk rate and the third-lowest home run frequency in the American League. He has the bat-to-ball talents to provide a .270 average on the regular (he's only finished below that mark in a full season once), but putting 37 percent of the pitches you see in play, as Aybar did to rank second in the league last year, carries little value with such weak results on contact.

Michael Bourn CF

Born: 12/27/82 Age: 33 Bats: L Throws: R Height: 5'10" Weight: 180

YEAR	TEAM	LVL	AGE	PA	R	2B	3B	HR	RBI	BB	K	SB	CS	AVG/OBP/SLG	TAv	BABIP	BRR	FRAA	WARP
2013	CLE	MLB	30	575	75	21	6	6	50	40	132	23	12	.263/.316/.360	.251	.338	5.4	CF(128): -4.9	1.3
2014	AKR	AA	31	25	0	0	0	0	0	2	10	1	0	.087/.160/.087	.120	.154	-1.0	CF(6): -0.0	-0.4
2014	COH	AAA	31	20	1	1	0	0	2	0	3	0	0	.150/.150/.200	.118	.176	-0.6	CF(3): 0.3	-0.3
2014	CLE	MLB	31	487	57	17	10	3	28	35	114	10	6	.257/.314/.360	.246	.337	1.8	CF(105): -6.6	0.3
2015	CLE	MLB	32	326	29	12	1	0	19	29	76	13	5	.246/.313/.294	.224	.332	2.1	CF(88): 0.6, LF(1): -0.0	0.1
2015	ATL	MLB	32	156	10	3	1	0	11	17	31	4	2	.221/.303/.257	.229	.280	-0.3	LF(28): 2.8, CF(18): 1.7	0.4
2016	*ATL*	*MLB*	*33*	*382*	*43*	*14*	*4*	*2*	*26*	*32*	*87*	*13*	*6*	*.248/.313/.330*	*.236*	*.320*	*1.8*	*CF -3*	*0.3*
2017	*ATL*	*MLB*	*34*	*419*	*40*	*15*	*4*	*2*	*32*	*33*	*100*	*13*	*6*	*.238/.300/.316*	*.234*	*.310*	*2.5*	*CF -3*	*-0.2*

Breakout: 1% Improve: 32% Collapse: 6% Attrition: 13% MLB: 95% *Comparables: Chuck Hinton, Kenny Lofton, Reed Johnson*

Bourn went from major Cleveland free-agent signing to salary-dump candidate faster than he used to go home to first on a drag bunt. The wheels, both metaphorically and literally, are off. Cleveland traded him with Nick Swisher to Atlanta for Chris Johnson in a swap of bad contracts that opened payroll for the Indians now while doing the same for the Braves in the future. He came off the bench in Atlanta and looked every bit the declining bat with diminished speed. His role for the last year of his contract is probably fourth outfielder (and maybe waiver bait toward the end of the season), and if he manages the 550 plate appearances needed to vest his 2017 option, someone should be sued for malpractice, malfeasance and malicious infliction of distress on Atlanta's fans.

Daniel Castro INF

Born: 11/14/92 Age: 23 Bats: R Throws: R Height: 5'11" Weight: 175

YEAR	TEAM	LVL	AGE	PA	R	2B	3B	HR	RBI	BB	K	SB	CS	AVG/OBP/SLG	TAv	BABIP	BRR	FRAA	WARP
2013	LYN	A+	20	96	10	1	1	0	7	7	6	3	1	.284/.337/.318	.240	.305	-0.5	2B(17): -1.3, SS(6): -0.4	-0.1
2014	LYN	A+	21	279	33	16	3	1	34	10	20	7	4	.292/.320/.389	.253	.312	2.0	SS(70): 5.6	1.8
2014	MIS	AA	21	180	23	9	1	4	20	5	18	2	1	.277/.300/.410	.268	.289	-0.1	SS(44): 5.1, 2B(3): 0.1	1.5
2015	MIS	AA	22	98	17	5	0	0	10	4	8	4	2	.389/.411/.444	.322	.422	2.6	SS(21): -4.2, 2B(1): 0.1	0.9
2015	GWN	AAA	22	345	19	9	0	0	36	22	32	1	1	.268/.314/.297	.231	.293	0.0	SS(88): 7.6, 2B(1): 0.1	1.1
2015	ATL	MLB	22	100	14	2	1	2	5	3	15	0	0	.240/.263/.344	.232	.266	1.2	2B(12): 1.3, SS(10): -0.0	0.3
2016	*ATL*	*MLB*	*23*	*58*	*5*	*2*	*0*	*1*	*5*	*2*	*9*	*0*	*0*	*.256/.287/.357*	*.232*	*.283*	*-0.1*	*2B -0*	*0.0*
2017	*ATL*	*MLB*	*24*	*348*	*35*	*13*	*2*	*5*	*33*	*15*	*51*	*2*	*1*	*.251/.287/.354*	*.237*	*.276*	*-0.4*	*2B -1*	*-0.1*

Breakout: 14% Improve: 42% Collapse: 9% Attrition: 24% MLB: 66% *Comparables: Alcides Escobar, Erick Aybar, Jose Iglesias*

If MLB ever implements a bat boy–lookalike contest among its players, Atlanta has a surefire candidate in Castro. The baby-faced utilityman from Mexico made his major-league debut with the Braves in 2015 along with the rest of civilization and showed some contact skills on occasion. "And he hit two homers in 100 PAs! That's double digits over a full season!" you're probably shouting because you looked at the stat box above. Well, sure, fine, but first of all, please use your inside voice, and second of all, pair that with the zero homers in 443 PAs in Double- and Triple-A last year and you come out with a less impressive total. He knows his way around a glove and can play multiple positions, including shortstop, but that's pretty much what you get.

Pedro Ciriaco INF

Born: 9/27/85 Age: 30 Bats: R Throws: R Height: 6'0" Weight: 180

YEAR	TEAM	LVL	AGE	PA	R	2B	3B	HR	RBI	BB	K	SB	CS	AVG/OBP/SLG	TAv	BABIP	BRR	FRAA	WARP
2013	SDN	MLB	27	68	5	1	1	1	4	3	10	6	0	.238/.284/.333	.221	.269	-0.4	SS(18): -0.4, 2B(2): 0.2	-0.1
2013	BOS	MLB	27	58	4	2	1	1	4	6	12	2	1	.216/.293/.353	.258	.256	-0.8	3B(10): -1.0, SS(8): -2.2	-0.2
2013	OMA	AAA	27	171	19	8	1	1	15	6	22	4	1	.281/.310/.363	.250	.319	2.7	SS(30): -2.8, 3B(7): 2.4	0.6
2013	KCA	MLB	27	11	0	1	0	0	0	0	1	1	0	.182/.182/.273	.229	.200	0.5	SS(3): 0.1	0.1
2014	OMA	AAA	28	215	27	17	3	2	24	6	35	6	0	.302/.322/.444	.263	.353	2.8	SS(28): -0.5, 2B(21): 0.7	1.4
2014	KCA	MLB	28	49	7	2	0	0	2	0	9	4	0	.213/.229/.255	.168	.263	1.3	2B(13): 0.7, 3B(3): -0.4	-0.2
2015	GWN	AAA	29	80	8	1	0	1	7	1	15	1	0	.234/.253/.286	.196	.279	0.2	3B(13): 1.8, SS(5): -0.1	-0.1
2015	ATL	MLB	29	151	14	8	1	1	15	2	38	4	2	.261/.275/.352	.239	.340	1.2	3B(24): -0.2, SS(9): -0.1	0.3
2016	*ATL*	*MLB*	*30*	*250*	*24*	*11*	*2*	*2*	*19*	*7*	*51*	*9*	*2*	*.246/.270/.333*	*.220*	*.297*	*0.5*	*3B 1, SS -2*	*-0.2*
2017	*ATL*	*MLB*	*31*	*296*	*26*	*12*	*2*	*2*	*24*	*8*	*61*	*9*	*2*	*.238/.262/.319*	*.217*	*.288*	*0.8*	*3B 2, SS -2*	*-0.6*

Breakout: 1% Improve: 17% Collapse: 8% Attrition: 16% MLB: 41% *Comparables: Bo Hart, Napoleon Calzado, Matt Kata*

Ciriaco played the most games of his career in 2015, which says more about Atlanta's season than Ciriaco's. The last time he got significant playing time was for the lowly 2012 Red Sox. He was on the move in 2013 and played most of 2014 in the minors because he worked for better teams. It's a fact of life. Ciriaco didn't do much with his opportunity and, while he wasn't signed at press time, he will likely continue to move around as depth.

Braxton Davidson RF

Born: 6/18/96 Age: 20 Bats: L Throws: L Height: 6'2" Weight: 210

YEAR	TEAM	LVL	AGE	PA	R	2B	3B	HR	RBI	BB	K	SB	CS	AVG/OBP/SLG	TAv	BABIP	BRR	FRAA	WARP
2015	ROM	A	19	494	51	23	0	10	45	84	135	1	6	.242/.381/.374	.283	.337	-1.6	RF(109): 3.7	2.3
2016	*ATL*	*MLB*	*20*	*250*	*23*	*8*	*0*	*5*	*24*	*31*	*88*	*0*	*0*	*.187/.294/.300*	*.222*	*.281*	*-0.5*	*RF 1*	*-0.3*
2017	*ATL*	*MLB*	*21*	*377*	*44*	*14*	*1*	*8*	*36*	*50*	*125*	*0*	*0*	*.199/.312/.325*	*.245*	*.292*	*-1.0*	*RF 2*	*0.0*

Breakout: 2% Improve: 2% Collapse: 0% Attrition: 2% MLB: 2% *Comparables: Caleb Gindl, Chris Parmelee, Daniel Fields*

Davidson has a young face and boyish charm, playfully jabbing at teammate Ozhaino Albies and stealing players' caps, but don't mistake that for immaturity. Davidson carries himself like a pro far beyond his years and possesses so much confidence that it becomes contagious. He has an advanced approach and should hit for average, but he needs to be more aggressive on hittable pitches early in the count. The power should develop into 20-plus home runs per year. Davidson is a bat-first player without the range to handle right field, but hiding him in left isn't out of the question if it means a position other than first base. He laid out for a diving catch in a mud puddle down the line last season and played the rest of the game in a Pigpennish state, an amusing moment that highlights both life in the minor leagues and Davidson's desire to excel.

Tyler Flowers C

Born: 1/24/86 Age: 30 Bats: R Throws: R Height: 6'4" Weight: 245

YEAR	TEAM	LVL	AGE	PA	R	2B	3B	HR	RBI	BB	K	SB	CS	AVG/OBP/SLG	TAv	BABIP	BRR	FRAA	WARP
2013	CHA	MLB	27	275	24	11	0	10	24	14	94	0	1	.195/.247/.355	.212	.261	-1.0	C(84): 3.9	0.2
2014	CHA	MLB	28	442	42	16	1	15	50	25	159	0	1	.241/.297/.396	.250	.355	-0.5	C(124): 5.1	2.1
2015	CHA	MLB	29	361	21	12	0	9	39	21	104	0	1	.239/.295/.356	.239	.320	-1.8	C(110): 13.6, 1B(2): 0.0	2.1
2016	*ATL*	*MLB*	*30*	*124*	*13*	*4*	*0*	*4*	*14*	*9*	*41*	*0*	*0*	*.219/.290/.370*	*.241*	*.303*	*-0.2*	*C 3*	*0.6*
2017	*ATL*	*MLB*	*31*	*216*	*25*	*8*	*0*	*7*	*24*	*17*	*73*	*0*	*0*	*.212/.286/.360*	*.244*	*.294*	*-0.5*	*C 4*	*0.8*

Breakout: 2% Improve: 47% Collapse: 8% Attrition: 14% MLB: 97% *Comparables: Jarrod Saltalamacchia, Stan Lopata, David Ross*

YEAR	TEAM	P. COUNT	FRM RUNS	BLK RUNS	THRW RUNS	TOT RUNS
2013	CHA	11465	3.8	-0.5	0.0	3.3
2014	CHA	17840	7.0	-1.6	1.7	7.1
2015	CHA	14504	16.3	-0.8	-1.0	14.4
2016	*ATL*	*4980*	*3.1*	*-0.3*	*0.0*	*2.8*
2017	*ATL*	*8693*	*4.9*	*-0.5*	*0.0*	*4.3*

For a guy whose most important defensive responsibility is shaping the strike zone, Flowers seems strangely powerless to control it as a hitter. He has a little thump but strikes out way too much to make substantial use of it, and he's come in on the wrong side of a .300 OBP four years running. All that said, he's an excellent framer and only a slightly below-average thrower, so the minimal value he provides at the plate is gravy, anyway.

Freddie Freeman 1B

Born: 9/12/89 Age: 26 Bats: L Throws: R Height: 6'5" Weight: 225

YEAR	TEAM	LVL	AGE	PA	R	2B	3B	HR	RBI	BB	K	SB	CS	AVG/OBP/SLG	TAv	BABIP	BRR	FRAA	WARP
2013	ATL	MLB	23	629	89	27	2	23	109	66	121	1	0	.319/.396/.501	.324	.371	-2.6	1B(147): 3.8	5.0
2014	ATL	MLB	24	708	93	43	4	18	78	90	145	3	4	.288/.386/.461	.315	.351	-1.4	1B(162): -4.4	4.1
2015	ATL	MLB	25	481	62	27	0	18	66	56	98	3	1	.276/.370/.471	.316	.321	1.4	1B(117): -9.7	2.4
2016	*ATL*	*MLB*	*26*	*604*	*74*	*32*	*1*	*21*	*81*	*66*	*123*	*3*	*1*	*.280/.365/.463*	*.297*	*.327*	*-0.7*	*1B -2*	*3.1*
2017	*ATL*	*MLB*	*27*	*540*	*75*	*29*	*1*	*18*	*70*	*64*	*109*	*2*	*1*	*.278/.369/.460*	*.309*	*.325*	*-0.7*	*1B -2*	*2.5*

Breakout: 5% Improve: 54% Collapse: 0% Attrition: 5% MLB: 99% *Comparables: Ike Davis, Miguel Cabrera, Mark Teixeira*

Freeman's season of frustration was a microcosm of Atlanta's year as a whole. His two major injuries affected his right wrist and right oblique; both lingered, and both hampered. The wrist injury was said to be a bone bruise that he felt from June through the end of the year, and the oblique strain came just nine days after he returned from the disabled list for the initial wrist injury. Considering what he dealt with, it's impressive Freeman produced like he did—like they say, he could fall out of (a hospital) bed and hit .276. His ideal scenario is a clean bill of health and a return to 20-plus homers as Atlanta's lineup anchor, face of the franchise and all-around good hugger.

Adonis Garcia 3B

Born: 4/12/85 Age: 31 Bats: R Throws: R Height: 5'9" Weight: 190

YEAR	TEAM	LVL	AGE	PA	R	2B	3B	HR	RBI	BB	K	SB	CS	AVG/OBP/SLG	TAv	BABIP	BRR	FRAA	WARP
2013	SWB	AAA	28	216	17	9	1	3	10	11	21	4	4	.256/.312/.357	.242	.274	-0.7	CF(26): -0.5, RF(14): 0.1	0.0
2014	SWB	AAA	29	368	58	20	3	9	45	17	51	11	3	.319/.353/.474	.282	.348	4.3	CF(25): 1.7, RF(24): 0.7	2.4
2015	GWN	AAA	30	350	43	17	1	3	47	15	41	5	1	.284/.314/.369	.247	.314	3.4	3B(66): 2.2, LF(9): 1.0	1.2
2015	ATL	MLB	30	198	20	12	0	10	26	5	35	0	0	.277/.293/.497	.287	.291	0.1	3B(42): -3.0, LF(10): 0.4	0.9
2016	*ATL*	*MLB*	*31*	*572*	*57*	*28*	*2*	*14*	*65*	*22*	*100*	*6*	*2*	*.261/.293/.399*	*.250*	*.294*	*-0.3*	*3B 0*	*1.0*
2017	*ATL*	*MLB*	*32*	*520*	*56*	*26*	*2*	*12*	*57*	*20*	*92*	*4*	*2*	*.258/.290/.392*	*.254*	*.292*	*-0.5*	*3B 0*	*0.4*

Breakout: 0% Improve: 9% Collapse: 8% Attrition: 15% MLB: 25% *Comparables: Terry Tiffee, Andy Marte, Hector Luna*

This Adonis is the God of the Opposite-Field Home Run: His first six dingers in the major leagues were to center or right field. The Braves had picked up the Cuban as a minor-league free agent after the Yankees released him less than a week before the season opener. It proved to be another shrewd move for Atlanta's scouting department, as Garcia proceeded to show plus power at Triple-A and carried it to double-digit home runs in his first major-league season. He's the definition of a true pinch-hitter, seeing opposite-hand pitchers well and staying aggressive on fastballs early, so, despite his late debut, he could carve out a multi-year career on National League benches as the guy who makes you think twice before calling on your LOOGY.

Ender Inciarte CF

Born: 10/29/90 Age: 25 Bats: L Throws: L Height: 5'10" Weight: 185

YEAR	TEAM	LVL	AGE	PA	R	2B	3B	HR	RBI	BB	K	SB	CS	AVG/OBP/SLG	TAv	BABIP	BRR	FRAA	WARP
2013	MOB	AA	22	516	68	17	3	5	25	27	47	43	8	.281/.327/.362	.269	.303	8.4	CF(94): 11.2, RF(22): -0.2	4.1
2014	RNO	AAA	23	120	22	4	2	2	12	10	21	7	2	.312/.367/.440	.276	.368	2.2	CF(25): -2.1	0.6
2014	ARI	MLB	23	447	54	18	2	4	27	25	53	19	3	.278/.318/.359	.252	.310	2.3	CF(76): 9.3, LF(37): 6.9	2.9
2015	MOB	AA	24	23	3	1	1	1	1	3	2	0	0	.300/.391/.600	.369	.294	0.0	CF(4): 0.5, RF(1): 0.1	0.4
2015	ARI	MLB	24	561	73	27	5	6	45	26	58	21	10	.303/.338/.408	.277	.329	6.5	RF(77): 2.7, LF(47): 7.9	4.1
2016	*ATL*	*MLB*	*25*	*275*	*33*	*12*	*1*	*4*	*22*	*14*	*35*	*11*	*3*	*.274/.315/.372*	*.252*	*.300*	*1.7*	*CF 5*	*1.5*
2017	*ATL*	*MLB*	*26*	*429*	*45*	*18*	*2*	*5*	*40*	*22*	*53*	*17*	*6*	*.271/.312/.365*	*.255*	*.296*	*3.4*	*CF 8*	*2.0*

Breakout: 0% Improve: 53% Collapse: 3% Attrition: 17% MLB: 96% *Comparables: Ben Revere, Ryan Sweeney, Jacoby Ellsbury*

If you need to reach him, don't bother calling; he'll contact you. Inciarte had the league's sixth-best contact rate (89 percent), resulting in the eighth-lowest strikeout rate (10 percent) and the ninth-best batting average. His defense and baserunning polish his profile to a high shine. That Atlanta was able to get two top prospects *and* Inciarte for Shelby Miller, who finished just 0.5 WARP ahead of Inciarte last year, is why the resounding reaction from both inside and outside the game was that the Braves pulled off a coup. The only reason Inciarte isn't your typical middle-of-the-road leadoff hitter is because most teams don't begin with an Ender.

Nick Markakis RF

Born: 11/17/83 Age: 32 Bats: L Throws: L Height: 6'1" Weight: 190

YEAR	TEAM	LVL	AGE	PA	R	2B	3B	HR	RBI	BB	K	SB	CS	AVG/OBP/SLG	TAv	BABIP	BRR	FRAA	WARP
2013	BAL	MLB	29	700	89	24	0	10	59	55	76	1	2	.271/.329/.356	.255	.291	1.9	RF(155): 0.7	1.2
2014	BAL	MLB	30	710	81	27	1	14	50	62	84	4	2	.276/.342/.386	.272	.299	-1.8	RF(147): 7.1, 1B(2): -0.2	2.7
2015	ATL	MLB	31	686	73	38	1	3	53	70	83	2	1	.296/.370/.376	.283	.338	-1.8	RF(153): -8.0	1.9
2016	*ATL*	*MLB*	*32*	*624*	*70*	*28*	*1*	*8*	*54*	*56*	*79*	*2*	*1*	*.272/.341/.371*	*.262*	*.302*	*-0.4*	*RF 1*	*1.6*
2017	*ATL*	*MLB*	*33*	*545*	*61*	*26*	*1*	*7*	*52*	*47*	*70*	*1*	*0*	*.271/.336/.372*	*.269*	*.300*	*-0.4*	*RF 0*	*1.1*

Breakout: 0% Improve: 31% Collapse: 2% Attrition: 13% MLB: 100% *Comparables: Tony Gwynn, David DeJesus, Floyd Robinson*

The Braves' rebuilding process has been a straightforward affair, but the one move that drew some confusion, to be charitable, was the Markakis signing, which totaled $44 million over four years starting in his age-31 season. The Braves like Markakis for his quiet confidence and leadership, and they see him as someone the younger players can look to as an example of how to carry themselves on and off the field. Markakis' on-field value remains up for discussion. His offseason neck surgery cut short his preparation time, and that was the reason given for his lack of power. There are two problems with that line of reasoning. First, his 2015 ISO of .080 isn't *that* far from his 2013-14 ISO of .097, and as far as we know he hasn't been having neck surgery every year. Second, his 2015 swing was extremely short and level, geared for contact, not power. On the other hand, he posted his best OBP since 2010 and $11 million per year doesn't buy so very much anymore. It's not like Atlanta could have plowed that money into the draft, after all.

Hector Olivera 3B

Born: 4/5/85 Age: 31 Bats: R Throws: R Height: 6'2" Weight: 220

YEAR	TEAM	LVL	AGE	PA	R	2B	3B	HR	RBI	BB	K	SB	CS	AVG/OBP/SLG	TAv	BABIP	BRR	FRAA	WARP
2015	OKL	AAA	30	31	5	1	1	1	1	0	3	0	0	.387/.387/.581	.337	.407	0.0	3B(5): -0.3, 2B(2): -0.3	0.3
2015	TUL	AA	30	25	3	0	0	1	6	3	5	0	0	.318/.400/.455	.293	.375	0.4	3B(4): 0.2, 2B(2): -0.2	0.2
2015	GWN	AAA	30	42	5	3	0	0	3	2	4	0	0	.231/.286/.308	.211	.257	0.1	3B(9): 0.1	-0.1
2015	ATL	MLB	30	87	4	4	1	2	11	5	12	0	0	.253/.310/.405	.261	.273	-1.0	3B(21): -3.7	-0.2
2016	*ATL*	*MLB*	*31*	*453*	*46*	*20*	*3*	*11*	*48*	*28*	*80*	*1*	*0*	*.251/.305/.389*	*.253*	*.284*	*-0.4*		*1.0*
2017	*ATL*	*MLB*	*32*	*358*	*39*	*15*	*2*	*8*	*37*	*22*	*65*	*0*	*0*	*.242/.297/.370*	*.253*	*.278*	*-0.6*	-	*0.3*

Breakout: 2% Improve: 24% Collapse: 10% Attrition: 22% MLB: 59% *Comparables: Hector Luna, Sean Burroughs, Chris Denorfia*

The Braves wanted Olivera. They tried during the free-agent process but came up short to the Dodgers' Bag of Holding full of money. When the opportunity came around again at the trade deadline, they used a resource in which they were a bit richer: Young talent, including Jose Peraza and Alex Wood, Olivera soon made his major-league debut, playing 24 games down the stretch and at least flashing the skills that drew teams to him in the first place. His swing has some length and he tends to bar out by hitting around the ball, but his inside-out approach should produce consistent contact to all fields with over-the-fence pop to the pull side. His third-base defense was hit or miss, but he also lacked reps at that point. The Braves have a lot riding on Olivera, and they expect him to be a middle-of-the-order hitter. At least he looks the part: He could easily win Most Ripped Player if that were a thing.

Eury Perez CF

Born: 5/30/90 Age: 26 Bats: R Throws: R Height: 6'0" Weight: 190

YEAR	TEAM	LVL	AGE	PA	R	2B	3B	HR	RBI	BB	K	SB	CS	AVG/OBP/SLG	TAv	BABIP	BRR	FRAA	WARP
2013	SYR	AAA	23	433	55	18	5	7	28	13	64	23	8	.300/.336/.422	.263	.343	2.2	CF(68): -8.1, LF(15): 1.4	0.9
2013	WAS	MLB	23	8	1	0	0	0	0	0	3	1	0	.125/.125/.125	.082	.200	0.1	CF(4): -0.1, LF(3): -0.1	-0.1
2014	POT	A+	24	33	6	1	0	1	4	3	4	6	1	.321/.387/.464	.317	.348	0.4	CF(9): 1.4	0.5
2014	SYR	AAA	24	238	30	13	2	1	11	13	35	20	3	.311/.372/.406	.271	.367	3.3	RF(29): -2.6, CF(18): -1.2	0.8
2014	NYA	MLB	24	10	2	0	0	0	0	0	3	1	0	.200/.200/.200	.144	.286	0.2	CF(2): 0.0, RF(2): -0.2	-0.1
2015	GWN	AAA	25	271	35	8	2	2	21	22	39	28	8	.297/.370/.373	.278	.347	2.6	CF(25): -0.9, RF(23): -0.9	1.4
2015	ATL	MLB	25	133	10	4	0	0	5	7	23	3	1	.269/.331/.303	.229	.333	1.4	LF(29): 1.0, RF(6): 1.1	0.1
2016	*ATL*	*MLB*	*26*	*250*	*31*	*10*	*1*	*3*	*19*	*10*	*47*	*14*	*4*	*.268/.311/.358*	*.242*	*.315*	*1.3*	*LF 1, RF -1*	*0.3*
2017	*ATL*	*MLB*	*27*	*328*	*34*	*12*	*2*	*4*	*29*	*14*	*61*	*18*	*5*	*.260/.305/.351*	*.245*	*.304*	*2.4*	*LF 1, RF -1*	*0.2*

Breakout: 2% Improve: 15% Collapse: 12% Attrition: 20% MLB: 39% *Comparables: Jeff Kobernus, Roger Bernadina, Chris Duffy*

Perez was claimed off waivers by the Braves and did exactly what the world thought he'd do, which is produce at a fourth-outfielder level. He received quite a bit of playing time because the Braves had little else to throw out in left field early in the season, and the result was a few slapped singles before he eventually broke his hand on a Triple-A hit by a pitch. A team typically wants its fourth outfielder to play steady defense and run a little, but Perez remains a raw outfielder with little arm strength, and he didn't run in the majors, despite possessing the speed to do so. He's one of those "can I keep the shirt?" players who might wind up passing through 10 organizations before he's done.

Jace Peterson 2B

Born: 5/9/90 Age: 26 Bats: L Throws: R Height: 6'0" Weight: 200

YEAR	TEAM	LVL	AGE	PA	R	2B	3B	HR	RBI	BB	K	SB	CS	AVG/OBP/SLG	TAv	BABIP	BRR	FRAA	WARP
2013	LEL	A+	23	496	78	17	13	7	66	54	58	42	10	.303/.382/.454	.314	.332	4.7	SS(106): -6.3	4.8
2014	SAN	AA	24	83	10	3	0	1	7	9	9	4	3	.311/.386/.392	.291	.344	1.3	SS(17): -0.8, 3B(1): 0.0	0.7
2014	ELP	AAA	24	299	44	21	6	2	39	42	50	12	6	.306/.406/.464	.356	.374	0.1	SS(28): -0.5, 2B(25): 1.8	0.9
2014	SDN	MLB	24	58	3	0	0	0	0	2	18	2	0	.113/.161/.113	.107	.171	0.3	2B(14): 1.1, 3B(10): 0.4	-0.5
2015	ATL	MLB	25	597	55	23	5	6	52	56	120	12	10	.239/.314/.335	.251	.296	2.3	2B(144): -3.4	1.0
2016	*ATL*	*MLB*	*26*	*583*	*68*	*23*	*5*	*6*	*44*	*57*	*114*	*16*	*9*	*.238/.316/.340*	*.239*	*.285*	*1.4*	*2B 2, SS -0*	*1.5*
2017	*ATL*	*MLB*	*27*	*560*	*59*	*21*	*5*	*7*	*49*	*55*	*113*	*15*	*9*	*.231/.310/.334*	*.242*	*.277*	*2.2*	*2B 2, SS 0*	*1.0*

Breakout: 4% Improve: 49% Collapse: 14% Attrition: 33% MLB: 82% *Comparables: Kevin Frandsen, Russ Adams, Chris Getz*

Major-league teams know what they have with Peterson at this point. He has no carrying tool but does enough to be a big leaguer based on some contact ability and a grinder mentality that might tie to his days as a defensive back in college. He started strong in his rookie season for the Braves before wearing down late and getting beat by advanced pitching that became familiar with him. Peterson set a nice table for a while, and even got creative with the dishes by hitting some home runs, but his overall skill set is more suited to a utility role. He plays a good second base, can play multiple positions in a pinch and is an outstanding teammate.

A.J. Pierzynski C

Born: 12/30/76 Age: 39 Bats: L Throws: R Height: 6'3" Weight: 235

YEAR	TEAM	LVL	AGE	PA	R	2B	3B	HR	RBI	BB	K	SB	CS	AVG/OBP/SLG	TAv	BABIP	BRR	FRAA	WARP
2013	TEX	MLB	36	529	48	24	1	17	70	11	76	1	1	.272/.297/.425	.262	.288	-2.8	C(119): -9.4	1.0
2014	SLN	MLB	37	88	6	2	0	1	6	5	14	0	1	.244/.295/.305	.224	.284	-1.0	C(23): -5.9	-0.7
2014	BOS	MLB	37	274	19	10	1	4	31	9	40	0	0	.254/.286/.348	.233	.282	-2.0	C(64): -3.5	-0.2
2015	ATL	MLB	38	436	38	24	1	9	49	19	37	0	2	.300/.339/.430	.281	.310	-2.4	C(107): -12.1	1.4
2016	*ATL*	*MLB*	*39*	*520*	*47*	*23*	*2*	*11*	*56*	*19*	*71*	*1*	*1*	*.256/.290/.378*	*.240*	*.276*	*-2.3*	*C -16*	*-0.7*
2017	*ATL*	*MLB*	*40*	*392*	*40*	*16*	*1*	*8*	*39*	*14*	*58*	*0*	*0*	*.240/.275/.353*	*.233*	*.262*	*-1.8*	*C -13*	*-1.3*

Breakout: 2% Improve: 18% Collapse: 11% Attrition: 22% MLB: 70% *Comparables: Yogi Berra, Mike Redmond, Smoky Burgess*

The Braves signed Pierzynski to groom Christian Bethancourt behind the plate and help guide a young pitching staff. Instead, he took Bethancourt's spot when the young catcher struggled, became like an extra coach on a young Braves team and, oh yeah, had his most productive season at the plate since 2003 (by TAv). The best symbol of how the season went for both Pierzynski and the Braves? How about 205 plate appearances in the cleanup spot after just 152 PAs in that spot in his entire career prior to 2015. Maybe taking a dip in the Fountain of Youth kept him cool during the hot Atlanta summer.

YEAR	TEAM	P. COUNT	FRM RUNS	BLK RUNS	THRW RUNS	TOT RUNS
2013	TEX	16052	-8.5	-0.5	0.7	-8.3
2014	BOS	8804	-1.6	-0.1	-1.0	-2.7
2014	SLN	2922	-4.5	-0.2	-0.9	-5.6
2015	ATL	14752	-9.7	0.1	-1.0	-10.6
2016	*ATL*	*18252*	*-12.5*	*-0.3*	*-1.4*	*-14.1*
2017	*ATL*	*13757*	*-10.3*	*-0.2*	*-1.2*	*-11.7*

Rio Ruiz 3B

Born: 5/22/94 Age: 22 Bats: L Throws: R Height: 6'2" Weight: 215

YEAR	TEAM	LVL	AGE	PA	R	2B	3B	HR	RBI	BB	K	SB	CS	AVG/OBP/SLG	TAv	BABIP	BRR	FRAA	WARP
2013	QUD	A	19	472	46	33	1	12	63	50	92	12	3	.260/.335/.430	.275	.303	-3.6	3B(111): -6.7	1.3
2014	LNC	A+	20	602	76	37	2	11	77	82	91	4	4	.293/.387/.436	.293	.335	-3.7	3B(105): -6.1, 3B(11): -6.1	2.4
2015	MIS	AA	21	489	48	21	1	5	46	63	94	2	2	.233/.333/.324	.259	.288	-2.8	3B(119): 6.7	1.9
2016	*ATL*	*MLB*	*22*	*250*	*22*	*11*	*0*	*4*	*24*	*25*	*59*	*0*	*0*	*.220/.298/.330*	*.231*	*.276*	*-0.5*	*3B -2*	*-0.3*
2017	*ATL*	*MLB*	*23*	*428*	*47*	*20*	*1*	*8*	*41*	*44*	*99*	*0*	*0*	*.221/.302/.340*	*.243*	*.275*	*-1.1*	*3B -4*	*-0.5*

Breakout: 2% Improve: 9% Collapse: 1% Attrition: 10% MLB: 12% *Comparables: Taylor Green, Garin Cecchini, Jake Smolinski*

Ruiz's lack of power sent Braves fans into a tizzy, justified considering he's a corner infielder, but unjustified considering it was his first year in the system and his Double-A debut. That said, he will need to make adjustments to reach the role of an average regular at third base. *That* said, he's young enough to provide hope that he can make them. His swing can get long and loopy at times because of a deep hand load, and his lower half can leak and get rotational, causing him to pull off the ball, sap his plate coverage and lose power to all fields. The Double-A monster lives to eat up shortcomings, and it fed off Ruiz for much of the season. For his part, he showed the ability to adjust in-season and produced more as the season progressed. He has a solid approach and feel at the plate, and there's enough in the glove to stay at third. While 2016 won't be precisely a make-or-break season, struggling in his first taste of the high minors has put Ruiz at something of a crossroads.

Mallex Smith CF

Born: 5/6/93 Age: 23 Bats: L Throws: R Height: 5'9" Weight: 170

YEAR	TEAM	LVL	AGE	PA	R	2B	3B	HR	RBI	BB	K	SB	CS	AVG/OBP/SLG	TAv	BABIP	BRR	FRAA	WARP
2013	FTW	A	20	507	81	17	2	4	29	59	84	64	16	.262/.367/.340	.275	.318	8.6	CF(61): 0.2, LF(6): 1.4	3.1
2014	FTW	A	21	303	56	13	6	0	15	38	55	48	16	.295/.393/.394	.286	.373	3.9	CF(63): -0.5	2.2
2014	LEL	A+	21	261	43	16	1	5	16	31	48	40	10	.327/.414/.475	.330	.400	2.1	CF(33): -4.0, RF(4): -0.8	1.8
2015	MIS	AA	22	241	35	5	2	2	22	27	41	23	6	.340/.418/.413	.335	.412	4.1	CF(54): -0.5	3.1
2015	GWN	AAA	22	307	49	12	6	0	13	24	44	34	7	.281/.339/.367	.268	.332	4.4	CF(68): 1.0	1.8
2016	*ATL*	*MLB*	*23*	*72*	*10*	*3*	*0*	*1*	*5*	*6*	*16*	*6*	*2*	*.247/.319/.343*	*.245*	*.311*	*0.6*	*CF 0*	*0.2*
2017	*ATL*	*MLB*	*24*	*409*	*43*	*14*	*3*	*4*	*35*	*34*	*89*	*33*	*9*	*.244/.313/.334*	*.246*	*.301*	*4.7*	*CF 1*	*0.9*

Breakout: 2% Improve: 18% Collapse: 3% Attrition: 11% MLB: 33% *Comparables: Ezequiel Carrera, Billy Hamilton, Billy Burns*

Teams generally like the players they acquire (seeing as how they acquired them and all), but there seems to be a special kind of joy in the Braves organization for Smith. For one, he's mature beyond his years. Second, he has that don't-blink-or-you'll-miss-me speed that produced eye-popping stolen-base totals in 2014 and continued against more advanced catchers in 2015. The question is how much Smith will hit and whether it's enough to lead off every day. He's put up a fine batting average at every stop, and his swing is short and quick to the zone, but he needs to avoid the empty average that comes with slap hitting if he's to be a weapon, rather than an adequacy, on offense. On the other side of the ball, he's taking steps to shore up the raw parts of his game in center field and should be fine long term.

Dansby Swanson SS

Born: 2/11/94 Age: 22 Bats: R Throws: R Height: 6'0" Weight: 190

On his first day on the field, the best Swanson since Ron took one to the face from fellow high-priced acquisition Yoan Lopez. He reportedly got up and said, "That's a pretty good first day, huh?" Love this kid.

While he may lack the impact tools of previous 1:1 selections Carlos Correa and Gerrit Cole, Swanson should contribute ably on both sides of the ball. He has a short stroke that enables him to generate plenty of hard contact, auguring an above-average hit tool down the line. He'll never be mistaken for a power hitter, but his swing should get him into the double digits for homers, and his plus speed will help him both on the bases and in the field. He won't be a premium defender at shortstop, but should last at the position, and he has college experience at the keystone should he need to move over.

Swanson's greatest strength may be his makeup. He propelled both his college and short-season squads to championship series last season, routinely stayed 20 minutes or more after games to sign autographs and has gone on record saying he'd like to make world the better place. Lest he bite off more than he can chew, he should start with the Braves franchise.

Nick Swisher 1B

Born: 11/25/80 Age: 35 Bats: B Throws: L Height: 6'0" Weight: 195

YEAR	TEAM	LVL	AGE	PA	R	2B	3B	HR	RBI	BB	K	SB	CS	AVG/OBP/SLG	TAv	BABIP	BRR	FRAA	WARP
2013	CLE	MLB	32	634	74	27	2	22	63	77	138	1	0	.246/.341/.423	.283	.288	-1.6	1B(112): 9.4, RF(27): 1.8	3.3
2014	CLE	MLB	33	401	33	20	0	8	42	36	111	0	0	.208/.278/.331	.235	.273	-1.7	1B(52): -1.8, RF(4): -0.7	-1.1
2015	LKC	A	34	20	5	2	0	0	1	5	2	0	0	.429/.600/.571	.419	.500	0.5	RF(3): -0.4	0.4
2015	COH	AAA	34	37	6	2	0	1	5	5	8	0	0	.375/.459/.531	.313	.478	0.2	RF(6): -1.3	0.2
2015	CLE	MLB	34	111	6	4	0	2	8	8	24	0	0	.198/.261/.297	.205	.237	-1.0	RF(1): -0.2	-0.6
2015	ATL	MLB	34	149	8	5	0	4	17	27	30	0	0	.195/.349/.339	.268	.221	-0.2	LF(25): 0.5, 1B(12): -1.5	0.2
2016	*ATL*	*MLB*	*35*	*496*	*60*	*22*	*1*	*13*	*50*	*61*	*116*	*1*	*0*	*.234/.331/.382*	*.261*	*.286*	*-1.4*	*LF 2, 1B 0*	*1.3*
2017	*ATL*	*MLB*	*36*	*363*	*44*	*15*	*0*	*9*	*38*	*44*	*87*	*0*	*0*	*.224/.321/.366*	*.261*	*.275*	*-1.2*	*LF 2, 1B 0*	*0.4*

Breakout: 1% Improve: 25% Collapse: 8% Attrition: 17% MLB: 92% *Comparables: Lyle Overbay, Mark Teixeira, Rafael Palmeiro*

Swisher joined Michael Bourn as Cleveland teammates who became Atlanta teammates in a contract swap. Like Bourn, Swisher didn't change his fortunes with his new team, but he had a heck of a fun time trying. He greeted his new clubhouse companions with the same joy and eternal optimism that he takes everywhere he goes. He even took part in the Tomahawk Chop after his first hit as a Brave, and he did the Chop with each arm after hitting a home run from each side of the plate in one day at Wrigley Field. Swisher has been the definition of an every-day player throughout his career, but he's now playing the part of a declining corner man hindered by knee surgeries. As with Bourn, don't expect his 2017 option (based on 550 PAs) to vest.

PITCHERS

David Aardsma RHP

Born: 12/27/81 Age: 34 Bats: R Throws: R Height: 6'3" Weight: 220

YEAR	TEAM	LVL	AGE	W	L	SV	G	GS	IP	H	HR	BB/9	K/9	GB%	BABIP	WHIP	ERA	FIP	DRA	WARP	CFIP	MPH
2013	NWO	AAA	31	1	0	0	10	0	14	9	2	5.1	7.7	32%	.194	1.21	2.57	5.43	4.56	0.1	101	
2013	NYN	MLB	31	2	2	0	43	0	39^{2}	39	7	4.3	8.2	34%	.286	1.46	4.31	5.24	5.05	-0.2	106	93.8
2014	MEM	AAA	32	4	0	11	33	0	35	20	1	4.4	9.3	34%	.216	1.06	1.29	3.73	5.08	0.1	93	
2015	OKL	AAA	33	0	1	15	20	0	18^{2}	12	0	3.4	11.1	27%	.267	1.02	2.41	2.26	3.36	0.4	82	
2015	ATL	MLB	33	1	1	0	33	0	30^{2}	25	6	4.1	10.3	30%	.264	1.27	4.70	4.89	4.44	0.1	94	94.0
2016	*ATL*	*MLB*	*34*	*2*	*1*	*1*	*39*	*0*	*41^{2}*	*35*	*5*	*3.7*	*8.7*	*33%*	*.290*	*1.24*	*4.00*	*4.05*	*4.72*	*0.1*	*105*	
2017	*ATL*	*MLB*	*35*	*3*	*1*	*2*	*61*	*0*	*61*	*53*	*8*	*3.6*	*8.6*	*33%*	*.291*	*1.26*	*4.14*	*4.54*	*4.88*	*0.0*	*110*	

Breakout: 21% Improve: 31% Collapse: 16% Attrition: 14% MLB: 60% *Comparables: Juan Rincon, Tim Byrdak, Aquilino Lopez*

Aardsma's return to the majors didn't go well, and ended with a September release, but he'll always come first in mom's heart. Also on alphabetical lists. But mainly mom's heart. He opted out of his minor-league deal with the Dodgers early in the year and signed with the Braves, who gave him more than enough chances. The fastball velocity was around 92 but seriously lacked life, which doesn't mix well with poor command. Calling him "AAArdsma" might be unnecessarily rude, but it does reflect his present talent level.

Kolby Allard LHP

Born: 8/13/97 Age: 18 Bats: L Throws: L Height: 6'1" Weight: 180

If there's a single example of Atlanta's renewed mindset of targeting and developing high school pitching, the mindset on which the Braves built much of their previous success, it could end up being Allard. The California lefty was seen as perhaps the top high school arm in the 2015 draft class before a stress reaction in his back cut short his senior year. He fell to the Braves at no. 14 overall, signed for just above slot and was moved along slowly in his first pro season, with the expectation that the reins would be loosened soon. Allard works in the low to mid-90s with life from a smooth delivery, paired with a biting curveball that projects as plus. He needs to further develop his changeup, but his solid command profile and effortless motion provide a foundation for optimism.

Manny Banuelos LHP

Born: 3/13/91 Age: 25 Bats: R Throws: L Height: 5'10" Weight: 205

YEAR	TEAM	LVL	AGE	W	L	SV	G	GS	IP	H	HR	BB/9	K/9	GB%	BABIP	WHIP	ERA	FIP	DRA	WARP	CFIP	MPH
2014	TAM	A+	23	0	0	0	5	5	12^2	10	0	1.4	9.9	36%	.303	0.95	2.84	1.89	3.93	0.2	86	
2014	TRN	AA	23	1	3	0	17	16	49	40	8	3.5	8.1	42%	.242	1.20	4.59	5.03	4.64	0.3	104	
2014	SWB	AAA	23	1	0	0	4	4	15	14	2	6.0	7.8	39%	.273	1.60	3.60	5.56	4.97	0.0	113	
2015	GWN	AAA	24	6	2	0	16	16	84^2	64	2	4.3	7.3	42%	.266	1.23	2.23	3.46	4.70	-0.1	108	
2015	ATL	MLB	24	1	4	0	7	6	26^1	30	4	4.1	6.5	41%	.313	1.59	5.13	5.40	5.73	-0.2	115	91.4
2016	*ATL*	*MLB*	*25*	*7*	*9*	*0*	*24*	*24*	*127^1*	*117*	*13*	*3.6*	*7.4*	*40%*	*.300*	*1.32*	*4.15*	*4.08*	*4.88*	*0.6*	*115*	
2017	*ATL*	*MLB*	*26*	*5*	*7*	*0*	*23*	*23*	*135^1*	*128*	*18*	*4.0*	*7.7*	*40%*	*.305*	*1.39*	*4.41*	*4.87*	*5.19*	*0.1*	*123*	

Breakout: 24% Improve: 34% Collapse: 13% Attrition: 37% MLB: 60% *Comparables: Andy Oliver, Anthony Ranaudo, Chris Dwyer*

Banuelos' story is one of patience and hoping like crazy that he can stay healthy enough to be effective. The little lefty has transformed from hard-throwing Yankees prospect to buy-low acquisition to Braves rotation hopeful in the span of five years. Atlanta let Banuelos go back to his old arsenal of fastballs, curveballs and changeups (after the Yankees had him drop the curve in favor of a cutter-slider hybrid), and early 2015 was the first time he expressed confidence in his elbow since 2012 Tommy John surgery. The fastball sat in the low 90s with better command, and he threw his secondaries with more conviction until his elbow barked again in late July. He returned, perhaps prematurely, in late August, and was soon shut down with a bone chip that ended his season. When healthy, Banuelos has the stuff to be a back-end starter, but he's yet to prove he'll ever satisfy that condition.

Aaron Blair RHP

Born: 5/26/92 Age: 24 Bats: R Throws: R Height: 6'5" Weight: 230

YEAR	TEAM	LVL	AGE	W	L	SV	G	GS	IP	H	HR	BB/9	K/9	GB%	BABIP	WHIP	ERA	FIP	DRA	WARP	CFIP	MPH
2013	YAK	A-	21	1	1	0	8	8	31	25	2	3.8	8.1	42%	.280	1.23	2.90	3.80	4.23	0.3	98	
2013	SBN	A	21	0	2	0	3	3	17^2	19	0	2.0	6.6	45%	.328	1.30	3.57	2.72	4.47	0.2	96	
2014	SBN	A	22	1	2	0	6	6	35^2	25	2	3.5	11.1	42%	.258	1.09	4.04	3.01	4.01	0.5	84	
2014	VIS	A+	22	4	2	0	13	13	72^1	70	6	2.6	10.1	41%	.338	1.26	4.35	3.86	4.82	0.0	86	
2014	MOB	AA	22	4	1	0	8	8	46^1	30	4	3.1	8.9	44%	.228	0.99	1.94	3.49				
2015	MOB	AA	23	6	3	0	13	13	83^1	70	8	2.5	6.9	55%	.265	1.12	2.70	3.95	3.56	1.4	92	
2015	RNO	AAA	23	7	2	0	13	12	77	67	5	3.2	6.5	48%	.273	1.22	3.16	4.08	4.47	0.9	95	
2016	*ATL*	*MLB*	*24*	*7*	*9*	*0*	*23*	*23*	*132^1*	*117*	*15*	*3.2*	*7.4*	*45%*	*.289*	*1.24*	*4.10*	*4.04*	*4.82*	*0.7*	*114*	
2017	*ATL*	*MLB*	*25*	*6*	*7*	*0*	*19*	*19*	*113^2*	*108*	*16*	*3.4*	*7.7*	*45%*	*.304*	*1.33*	*4.30*	*4.73*	*5.06*	*0.3*	*120*	

Breakout: 10% Improve: 18% Collapse: 19% Attrition: 32% MLB: 51% *Comparables: Brian Johnson, Eric Hurley, James Houser*

The prospect world is funny sometimes. Someone like Blair, who was drafted with the 36th-overall pick, has performed as expected thus far, which is to say: extremely well. You don't get drafted at that spot without talent, especially if you're not signing at a discount. (Blair got $1.435 million.) He can hum a fastball in as high as 96 mph, and will generally sit 91-94 with movement. He's flashed plus with both of his secondaries (curve, change), is consistently average or better with both and will mix in a slider as well. His command suffers at the behest of the heavy movement on his heater and he'll walk around league-average totals, but he doesn't lack for control. So where is the hype? He lacks the reputation of former organization-mate Archie Bradley (though he's got a good résumé) and the panache of Braden Shipley (though he'll work with three plus pitches at times), but could be a better prospect than either of them. There might not be as much ceiling with Blair as there is with the other players, but don't take that to mean there isn't any at all. Blair could be a mid-rotation starter, and he could be that as soon as mid-2016. That might not excite you right now, but Mike Leake just got $80 million, and not from a dumb team. This Coppolella knows what he's doing.

Danny Burawa RHP

Born: 12/30/88 Age: 27 Bats: R Throws: R Height: 6'2" Weight: 210

YEAR	TEAM	LVL	AGE	W	L	SV	G	GS	IP	H	HR	BB/9	K/9	GB%	BABIP	WHIP	ERA	FIP	DRA	WARP	CFIP	MPH
2013	TRN	AA	24	6	3	4	46	0	66	47	1	5.7	9.0	54%	.271	1.35	2.59	3.43	4.84	0.0	108	
2014	TRN	AA	25	0	0	1	11	0	17	13	0	2.1	9.5	57%	.295	1.00	1.59	2.30	4.10	0.1	86	
2014	SWB	AAA	25	3	1	3	31	0	42^1	47	3	5.5	11.7	60%	.386	1.72	5.95	3.52	4.28	0.3	89	
2015	TRN	AA	26	0	0	0	3	3	11	5	1	7.4	10.6	48%	.167	1.27	3.27	4.81	4.89	0.0	108	
2015	SWB	AAA	26	1	3	1	32	1	49^1	37	2	3.8	7.1	56%	.254	1.18	2.55	3.56	2.89	0.9	100	
2015	NYA	MLB	26	0	0	0	1	0	0^2	3	1	13.5	13.5	50%	.667	6.00	54.00	24.10	32.99	-0.2	104	97.8
2015	ATL	MLB	26	0	0	0	12	0	12^1	8	1	2.9	7.3	55%	.219	0.97	3.65	3.81	0.98	0.5	103	96.8
2016	*ATL*	*MLB*	*27*	*3*	*1*	*0*	*63*	*0*	*67*	*58*	*7*	*3.8*	*8.0*	*55%*	*.296*	*1.29*	*3.97*	*4.04*	*4.66*	*0.3*	*108*	
2017	*ATL*	*MLB*	*28*	*2*	*1*	*0*	*33*	*0*	*46^2*	*42*	*5*	*3.7*	*8.5*	*55%*	*.306*	*1.30*	*3.90*	*4.28*	*4.58*	*0.2*	*106*	

Breakout: 5% Improve: 11% Collapse: 17% Attrition: 23% MLB: 33% *Comparables: Roy Corcoran, Erik Hamren, Pedro Viola*

Quiz questions: (1) Where did this guy come from? (2) And why isn't he throwing late innings for a major-league team yet?

Suggested answers: (1) The Yankees designated Burawa for assignment in early August and the Braves scooped him up nine days later. He struggled throwing strikes in New York's system, but when Atlanta's scouting department spies an arm they like, there's probably something there. In his 12 appearances out of the Braves' bullpen down the stretch, he threw in the mid-90s with sink and arm-side run, and paired the fastball with a biting slider that generated a considerable number of swinging strikes. (2) Occasional bouts of wildness have held him back, though he didn't allow a walk in his final six appearances last year. If that's a signal that some teaching got through to him, the Braves might have found themselves an electric bullpen contributor for essentially free.

Mauricio Cabrera RHP

Born: 9/22/93 Age: 22 Bats: R Throws: R Height: 6'3" Weight: 230

YEAR	TEAM	LVL	AGE	W	L	SV	G	GS	IP	H	HR	BB/9	K/9	GB%	BABIP	WHIP	ERA	FIP	DRA	WARP	CFIP	MPH
2013	ROM	A	19	3	8	0	24	24	131^1	118	3	4.9	7.3	51%	.298	1.44	4.18	3.91	4.88	0.3	112	
2014	LYN	A+	20	1	1	0	19	3	29	24	1	5.9	8.7	65%	.295	1.48	5.59	4.41	5.08	0.0	114	
2015	CAR	A+	21	2	2	1	23	0	31	30	1	4.9	8.1	61%	.309	1.52	5.52	3.51	4.77	-0.2	106	
2015	MIS	AA	21	0	1	0	13	0	17^1	12	1	9.3	13.0	46%	.289	1.73	5.71	4.46	5.09	-0.1	106	
2016	*ATL*	*MLB*	*22*	*2*	*3*	*0*	*17*	*6*	*42^1*	*40*	*4*	*5.0*	*7.1*	*47%*	*.306*	*1.49*	*4.55*	*4.55*	*5.29*	*-0.1*	*126*	
2017	*ATL*	*MLB*	*23*	*6*	*7*	*1*	*46*	*18*	*143^2*	*138*	*16*	*5.3*	*7.5*	*47%*	*.313*	*1.55*	*4.66*	*5.15*	*5.42*	*-0.4*	*129*	

Breakout: 0% Improve: 0% Collapse: 0% Attrition: 0% MLB: 0% *Comparables: Rafael Dolis, Deunte Heath, Ryan Pressly*

You've read this comment before. Cabrera is a flamethrower who needs to harness his control to have a chance. The fastball is a sight to behold, sitting in the upper 90s and touching triple digits, and Cabrera shows feel for turning over a changeup that could play in the majors. He also has a curveball that flashes a power break. Add all this up and you see late-innings relief potential, but his below-average control, forget about command, lowers the probability of reaching that ceiling. He's much rawer than you'd think given that he's already 22, and the same issues show up on his scouting reports year after year. Cabrera still has time and immense arm strength on his side, but ... well, you've read this comment before.

Jhoulys Chacin RHP

Born: 1/7/88 Age: 28 Bats: R Throws: R Height: 6'3" Weight: 215

YEAR	TEAM	LVL	AGE	W	L	SV	G	GS	IP	H	HR	BB/9	K/9	GB%	BABIP	WHIP	ERA	FIP	DRA	WARP	CFIP	MPH
2013	COL	MLB	25	14	10	0	31	31	197^1	188	11	2.8	5.7	48%	.288	1.26	3.47	3.44	3.51	3.3	104	93.0
2014	CSP	AAA	26	1	1	0	2	2	10^2	9	0	4.2	6.8	52%	.273	1.31	2.53	3.89	5.39	0.1	103	
2014	COL	MLB	26	1	7	0	11	11	63^1	63	8	4.0	6.0	44%	.285	1.44	5.40	4.79	4.17	0.5	113	91.4
2015	COH	AAA	27	1	3	0	7	7	42	39	3	3.2	5.4	45%	.271	1.29	3.21	3.97	4.60	0.0	106	
2015	ARI	MLB	27	2	1	0	5	4	26^2	24	4	3.4	7.1	51%	.263	1.27	3.38	4.66	4.50	0.2	108	90.9
2015	RNO	AAA	27	6	3	0	13	13	86^2	79	3	3.1	6.5	51%	.292	1.26	3.22	3.81	4.62	0.9	97	
2016	*ATL*	*MLB*	*28*	*1*	*2*	*0*	*5*	*5*	*25*	*21*	*2*	*3.0*	*6.9*	*48%*	*.279*	*1.19*	*3.94*	*3.64*	*4.63*	*0.2*	*109*	
2017	*ATL*	*MLB*	*29*	*11*	*12*	*0*	*32*	*32*	*204^1*	*189*	*25*	*2.9*	*6.8*	*48%*	*.291*	*1.25*	*4.13*	*4.53*	*4.85*	*1.0*	*115*	

Breakout: 18% Improve: 51% Collapse: 20% Attrition: 7% MLB: 92% *Comparables: Clay Buchholz, Dustin McGowan, Whitey Ford*

Second on the Rockies' career ERA list, Chacin was cut from the team last year as mechanical and velocity concerns piled up. (And when the Rockies are ready to cut ties, then *oh man.*) On came the minor-league deals: first with the Indians, where he opted out after a month in Columbus, then to Arizona and the promise of sixth-man shuttle service. Success showed up in small doses, and he added a cutter that got strong whiff and groundball action and turned him into a true six-pitch pitcher. He also recovered one of the 2 mph that his sinker lost in 2014. Spring trainings are going to be competitive for him for the foreseeable future, though.

Brandon Cunniff RHP

Born: 10/7/88 Age: 27 Bats: R Throws: R Height: 6'0" Weight: 185

YEAR	TEAM	LVL	AGE	W	L	SV	G	GS	IP	H	HR	BB/9	K/9	GB%	BABIP	WHIP	ERA	FIP	DRA	WARP	CFIP	MPH
2013	LYN	A+	24	1	0	0	20	0	31^2	20	2	6.0	11.1	43%	.257	1.29	1.99	3.79	4.53	0.2	95	
2014	LYN	A+	25	1	0	3	9	0	15^2	5	0	4.0	12.1	50%	.167	0.77	0.00	2.18	3.94	0.2	79	
2014	MIS	AA	25	3	0	0	33	0	52^2	39	2	3.4	8.5	48%	.262	1.12	2.05	2.98				
2015	ATL	MLB	26	2	2	0	39	0	35	27	4	5.7	9.5	47%	.261	1.40	4.63	4.42	3.74	0.4	101	96.0
2016	*ATL*	*MLB*	*27*	*1*	*0*	*0*	*20*	*0*	*21^1*	*18*	*2*	*4.1*	*8.5*	*46%*	*.295*	*1.30*	*4.06*	*3.93*	*4.79*	*0.0*	*109*	
2017	*ATL*	*MLB*	*28*	*1*	*0*	*1*	*25*	*0*	*33*	*28*	*4*	*4.1*	*8.8*	*46%*	*.299*	*1.32*	*4.03*	*4.43*	*4.76*	*0.0*	*108*	

Breakout: 19% Improve: 26% Collapse: 19% Attrition: 25% MLB: 56% *Comparables: Evan Meek, Royce Ring, Josh Edgin*

The Braves unearthed Cunniff in the independent Frontier League in 2013 after he threw heat for the Southern Illinois Miners. In fact, he pitched parts of three seasons in the league after quickly bowing out of the Marlins' system. However, because they're the Braves and he's a pitcher, Cunniff debuted in the majors last year. The organization liked what it saw from the strong right-hander, including a low-to-mid-90s fastball with some sink and a slider that flashed sharp break. Producing strikeouts hasn't been a problem; the issue is that when he struggles to find the zone, he can't adjust, resulting in a 15 percent walk rate in the majors. Cunniff also missed a couple of months with a groin injury. You keep someone like this around and keep trying to coach him up to fix the control issues, especially in a lost season or two, but you'll wind up cutting bait nine times out of 10, and that's fine, too.

Ross Detwiler LHP

Born: 3/6/86 Age: 30 Bats: R Throws: L Height: 6'3" Weight: 215

YEAR	TEAM	LVL	AGE	W	L	SV	G	GS	IP	H	HR	BB/9	K/9	GB%	BABIP	WHIP	ERA	FIP	DRA	WARP	CFIP	MPH
2013	WAS	MLB	27	2	7	0	13	13	71^1	92	5	1.8	4.9	48%	.344	1.49	4.04	3.64	5.57	-0.6	113	95.1
2014	WAS	MLB	28	2	3	1	47	0	63	68	5	3.0	5.6	47%	.309	1.41	4.00	4.13	4.96	-0.4	116	95.6
2015	ATL	MLB	29	1	0	0	24	0	15^1	20	1	9.4	7.6	71%	.404	2.35	7.63	6.03	6.23	-0.2	139	95.2
2015	TEX	MLB	29	0	5	0	17	7	43	62	9	4.2	5.9	38%	.358	1.91	7.12	6.13	8.52	-1.9	122	94.8
2016	*ATL*	*MLB*	*30*	*3*	*3*	*0*	*25*	*8*	*63*	*63*	*7*	*3.2*	*6.3*	*48%*	*.306*	*1.36*	*4.37*	*4.33*	*5.17*	*0.0*	*121*	
2017	*ATL*	*MLB*	*31*	*7*	*7*	*1*	*51*	*17*	*139^2*	*149*	*18*	*3.1*	*6.2*	*48%*	*.317*	*1.41*	*4.46*	*4.94*	*5.28*	*-0.2*	*124*	

Breakout: 15% Improve: 40% Collapse: 17% Attrition: 13% MLB: 82% *Comparables: Sergio Mitre, Charlie Morton, Mike Caldwell*

On the Atlanta bullpen carousel, Detwiler was the busted horse no one wanted to ride. The Braves picked him up midseason after the Rangers released him, and the fact that Texas cut its losses on his $3.4 million contract in July says plenty. The Braves signed him for the minimum and got less than the minimum in return. He suddenly lost the ability to find the zone and the results when he did throw strikes (check that BABIP) raised the question of whether he'd be better off missing wide with everything. He was bounced between LOOGY and long relief until a strained hamstring mercifully sent his season to the glue factory in mid-September.

All that said, he's still just 30, throws pretty hard and was the sixth overall pick once upon a time. He might spend another decade getting written up in this book.

Chris Ellis RHP

Born: 9/22/92 Age: 23 Bats: R Throws: R Height: 6'5" Weight: 205

YEAR	TEAM	LVL	AGE	W	L	SV	G	GS	IP	H	HR	BB/9	K/9	GB%	BABIP	WHIP	ERA	FIP	DRA	WARP	CFIP	MPH
2015	INL	A+	22	4	5	0	11	11	62^2	53	6	2.9	10.1	36%	.290	1.16	3.88	3.79	3.81	1.3	87	
2015	ARK	AA	22	7	4	0	15	15	78	77	9	5.0	7.2	36%	.296	1.54	3.92	4.98	6.17	-0.9	119	
2016	*ATL*	*MLB*	*23*	*5*	*8*	*0*	*20*	*20*	*103*	*98*	*15*	*4.1*	*7.5*	*33%*	*.301*	*1.41*	*4.79*	*4.75*	*5.59*	*-0.4*	*135*	
2017	*ATL*	*MLB*	*24*	*6*	*9*	*0*	*24*	*24*	*141^2*	*144*	*24*	*4.1*	*7.7*	*33%*	*.314*	*1.48*	*4.94*	*5.45*	*5.76*	*-0.7*	*139*	

Breakout: 0% Improve: 0% Collapse: 0% Attrition: 0% MLB: 0% *Comparables: Ricky Nolasco, Tyler Wagner, Justin Marks*

Ellis has a major-league fastball and a usable change, but his breaking ball hasn't come around and he has a tendency to battle his command. His frame and heater will give him a shot, but overall he doesn't figure to grow into anything more than a back-end starter; even if his curve takes a step forward, he has major work to do cleaning up those command issues. It would be fun to tell you, at this point, something weird and interesting and distinguishing about Ellis because so far he's exactly the same as nine out of 10 pitching prospects in this book, but he's the guy who retweeted the Pirates Water Cooler account, so...

Mike Foltynewicz RHP

Born: 10/7/91 Age: 24 Bats: R Throws: R Height: 6'4" Weight: 220

YEAR	TEAM	LVL	AGE	W	L	SV	G	GS	IP	H	HR	BB/9	K/9	GB%	BABIP	WHIP	ERA	FIP	DRA	WARP	CFIP	MPH
2013	LNC	A+	21	1	0	0	7	5	26	31	4	4.8	10.0	46%	.360	1.73	3.81	5.16	5.41	0.2	100	
2013	CCH	AA	21	5	3	3	23	16	103^1	75	8	4.5	8.3	55%	.254	1.23	2.87	3.88	4.54	0.5	107	
2014	OKL	AAA	22	7	7	0	21	18	102^2	98	10	4.6	8.9	49%	.322	1.46	5.08	4.79	5.38	0.4	103	
2014	HOU	MLB	22	0	1	0	16	0	18^2	23	3	3.4	6.8	29%	.333	1.61	5.30	4.87	6.85	-0.5	110	100.0
2015	GWN	AAA	23	1	6	0	10	10	56^2	52	7	4.1	10.0	42%	.308	1.38	3.49	3.92	3.67	0.7	94	
2015	ATL	MLB	23	4	6	0	18	15	86^2	112	17	3.0	8.0	36%	.349	1.63	5.71	5.08	6.72	-1.8	111	99.0
2016	*ATL*	*MLB*	*24*	*7*	*8*	*0*	*24*	*24*	*120*	*111*	*14*	*3.3*	*8.1*	*39%*	*.308*	*1.29*	*4.08*	*3.98*	*4.80*	*0.7*	*113*	
2017	*ATL*	*MLB*	*25*	*6*	*7*	*0*	*27*	*20*	*128^1*	*121*	*17*	*3.2*	*8.4*	*39%*	*.311*	*1.30*	*4.05*	*4.45*	*4.76*	*0.7*	*112*	

Breakout: 26% Improve: 38% Collapse: 14% Attrition: 26% MLB: 66% *Comparables: Ricky Nolasco, Tyson Ross, Nathan Adcock*

Foltynewicz changed organizations, tweaked his delivery multiple times, backed some off the fastball velocity and dabbled with a new pitch: The Braves, who acquired him from Houston for Evan Gattis, tinkered with the big right-hander's delivery to slow his actions and help him remain in sync; he sat closer to the mid-90s with a slight increase in movement on his fastball; and he started throwing a downward-breaking slider to complement his slower curveball. Despite all these changes over the course of one season, the needle didn't move on his potential role down the road: His command never improved, and he struggled getting through major-league lineups multiple times. His season ended in scary fashion, as he went to the emergency room in September for what turned out to be blood clots in his arm; doctors removed one of his ribs to help alleviate the problem. Alex Cobb had the same procedure and is now one of the better pitchers in the league when he's healthy, but there's probably not a causal link there.

Enderson Franco RHP

Born: 12/29/92 Age: 23 Bats: R Throws: R Height: 6'2" Weight: 170

YEAR	TEAM	LVL	AGE	W	L	SV	G	GS	IP	H	HR	BB/9	K/9	GB%	BABIP	WHIP	ERA	FIP	DRA	WARP	CFIP	MPH
2014	HUD	A-	21	7	3	0	13	13	68^2	74	4	1.0	6.6	51%	.318	1.19	3.28	3.14	4.18	0.6	96	
2015	BGR	A	22	5	6	0	13	13	71^2	82	4	1.0	5.9	54%	.321	1.26	3.89	3.19	3.15	1.6	88	
2015	GRB	A	22	1	6	0	12	12	54^1	74	6	4.1	6.1	44%	.360	1.82	7.29	5.05	5.99	-0.5	113	
2016	*ATL*	*MLB*	*23*	*5*	*8*	*0*	*21*	*21*	*105*	*117*	*13*	*3.3*	*5.3*	*41%*	*.321*	*1.49*	*4.70*	*4.72*	*5.49*	*-0.3*	*131*	
2017	*ATL*	*MLB*	*24*	*6*	*8*	*0*	*21*	*21*	*121*	*140*	*15*	*3.6*	*5.5*	*41%*	*.329*	*1.55*	*4.69*	*5.21*	*5.48*	*-0.2*	*130*	

Breakout: 0% Improve: 0% Collapse: 0% Attrition: 0% MLB: 0% *Comparables: Brett Sinkbeil, Cole DeVries, Alan Johnson*

Three teams saw fit to purchase Franco's services since December 2014, as the Rays snagged him in the minor-league Rule 5 draft before turning around and selling him to the Marlins for an international bonus slot in July. Finally, the Braves picked him up in *this* winter's minor-league Rule 5. Franco can command a low-90s fastball and has feel for a changeup, though the production has never quite been there and his control backed up noticeably after changing organizations for a second time. This might suggest the Marlins did him no favors, and the Braves may be able to fix him, but it might also suggest that all this shuttling around from organization to organization is going to stunt his growth. There's a modest baseline of talent here, but he'll be 23 this year and "gain consistency in A-ball" is not the most aggressive of goals.

Max Fried LHP

Born: 1/18/94 Age: 22 Bats: L Throws: L Height: 6'4" Weight: 185

YEAR	TEAM	LVL	AGE	W	L	SV	G	GS	IP	H	HR	BB/9	K/9	GB%	BABIP	WHIP	ERA	FIP	DRA	WARP	CFIP	MPH
2013	FTW	A	19	6	7	0	23	23	118^{2}	107	7	4.2	7.6	59%	.304	1.37	3.49	4.04	4.91	0.5	110	
2016	*ATL*	*MLB*	*22*	*2*	*3*	*0*	*9*	*9*	*35^{1}*	*36*	*4*	*4.6*	*6.0*	*50%*	*.307*	*1.53*	*5.03*	*4.91*	*5.86*	*-0.2*	*140*	
2017	*ATL*	*MLB*	*23*	*6*	*10*	*0*	*28*	*28*	*172^{2}*	*186*	*24*	*4.4*	*6.2*	*50%*	*.321*	*1.57*	*4.99*	*5.52*	*5.81*	*-0.7*	*139*	

Breakout: 0% Improve: 0% Collapse: 0% Attrition: 0% MLB: 0% *Comparables: Chad Bettis, Shane Greene, Mario Hollands*

The Braves acquired Fried while he was rehabbing from Tommy John surgery, so occasional reminders throughout the year that he was in the system would have been helpful to remember just how deep Atlanta's minor-league pitching runs. Fried's talent when healthy is undeniable. He has feel for three pitches that could all reach plus, projects for a solid command profile and has tons of projection in his frame. The consensus since he was drafted seventh overall in 2012 is that Fried is a sure-fire top-five left-handed pitching prospect, and he was in the running for the top spot before his elbow barked in 2014. There's always risk coming off of arm surgery, but age and aptitude are on his side.

Jason Grilli RHP

Born: 11/11/76 Age: 39 Bats: R Throws: R Height: 6'4" Weight: 230

YEAR	TEAM	LVL	AGE	W	L	SV	G	GS	IP	H	HR	BB/9	K/9	GB%	BABIP	WHIP	ERA	FIP	DRA	WARP	CFIP	MPH
2013	PIT	MLB	36	0	2	33	54	0	50	40	4	2.3	13.3	36%	.327	1.06	2.70	1.94	3.13	0.9	56	95.8
2014	PIT	MLB	37	0	2	11	22	0	20^{1}	22	4	4.9	9.3	28%	.321	1.62	4.87	5.36	6.87	-0.6	103	95.7
2014	ANA	MLB	37	1	3	1	40	0	33^{2}	29	0	2.7	9.6	42%	.312	1.16	3.48	2.18	2.09	1.0	84	95.4
2015	ATL	MLB	38	3	4	24	36	0	33^{2}	28	2	2.7	12.0	27%	.313	1.13	2.94	2.15	3.61	0.4	71	96.0
2016	*ATL*	*MLB*	*39*	*3*	*1*	*34*	*55*	*0*	*58^{2}*	*47*	*6*	*3.1*	*10.5*	*32%*	*.308*	*1.15*	*3.29*	*3.14*	*3.93*	*0.7*	*84*	
2017	*ATL*	*MLB*	*40*	*3*	*1*	*19*	*64*	*0*	*58^{2}*	*50*	*7*	*3.1*	*10.1*	*32%*	*.309*	*1.20*	*3.49*	*3.81*	*4.17*	*0.5*	*90*	

Breakout: 13% Improve: 32% Collapse: 28% Attrition: 15% MLB: 75% *Comparables: Octavio Dotel, Joel Peralta, Rudy Seanez*

The supposedly simple act of covering first base ended Grilli's season and kept him in Atlanta longer than anticipated when he ruptured his left Achilles on his way to the bag in July. Before the injury, his stuff was sharp, he was throwing strikes and he was among the league leaders in saves. Which meant that, given the Braves' place in the standings, he was extremely likely to be dealt to a contender. Instead, he's forced to work his way back at 39 and prove, once again, that he can pitch in the late innings. He's done it before, most recently after missing all of 2010 because of a torn quadriceps, but his first hurdle will be pitchers' fielding practice in spring training.

Edwin Jackson RHP

Born: 9/9/83 Age: 32 Bats: R Throws: R Height: 6'3" Weight: 210

YEAR	TEAM	LVL	AGE	W	L	SV	G	GS	IP	H	HR	BB/9	K/9	GB%	BABIP	WHIP	ERA	FIP	DRA	WARP	CFIP	MPH
2013	CHN	MLB	29	8	18	0	31	31	175^{1}	197	16	3.0	6.9	53%	.322	1.46	4.98	3.76	4.77	0.3	103	95.8
2014	CHN	MLB	30	6	15	0	28	27	140^{2}	168	18	4.0	7.9	41%	.352	1.64	6.33	4.42	5.90	-1.9	116	95.9
2015	CHN	MLB	31	2	1	0	23	0	31	30	0	3.5	6.7	46%	.306	1.35	3.19	2.94	3.64	0.4	107	97.2
2015	ATL	MLB	31	2	2	1	24	0	24^{2}	14	4	3.3	6.2	35%	.156	0.93	2.92	4.99	2.65	0.6	116	96.7
2016	*ATL*	*MLB*	*32*	*3*	*1*	*0*	*57*	*0*	*60*	*60*	*7*	*3.3*	*7.2*	*44%*	*.317*	*1.37*	*4.15*	*4.16*	*4.91*	*0.0*	*113*	
2017	*ATL*	*MLB*	*33*	*9*	*10*	*0*	*40*	*25*	*172^{1}*	*183*	*21*	*3.2*	*7.0*	*44%*	*.325*	*1.41*	*4.17*	*4.59*	*4.93*	*0.6*	*114*	

Breakout: 19% Improve: 51% Collapse: 14% Attrition: 9% MLB: 89% *Comparables: Ervin Santana, Jerry Koosman, Frank Tanana*

Entering spring training last year, the Cubs' front office committed to Jackson in the bullpen. The decision paid off: For 31 innings, he pitched like a high-quality middle reliever. However, when the time came for Chicago to call up Rafael Soriano, Jackson was designated for assignment. After signing with the Braves, Jackson's home run rate, and thus his FIP, skyrocketed, but his ERA held steady. He's essentially a four-seam/slider pitcher now, throwing one of those two pitches 93 percent of the time against righties. He reduced that number to 68 percent against lefties, throwing more sinkers, curves, and changeups to keep lefties from teeing off, which worked, as Jackson actually had a reverse split. (Small sample alarm, of course.) Jackson's not *good*, exactly, but if his name were Bryan Morris or Trevor Gott, to pick a couple of relievers with similar ERAs and FIPs, we'd be perfectly pleased with a reasonably steady 60 innings for the league minimum salary. On the other hand, if his name were Bryan Morris, the Cubs might have trouble figuring out where to send the final $11 million they owe him.

Tyrell Jenkins RHP

Born: 7/20/92 Age: 23 Bats: R Throws: R Height: 6'4" Weight: 180

YEAR	TEAM	LVL	AGE	W	L	SV	G	GS	IP	H	HR	BB/9	K/9	GB%	BABIP	WHIP	ERA	FIP	DRA	WARP	CFIP	MPH
2013	PEO	A	20	4	4	0	10	10	49^{1}	51	4	4.4	6.2	58%	.303	1.52	4.74	4.53	5.04	0.1	113	
2013	PMB	A+	20	0	0	0	3	3	10	13	0	0.9	5.4	58%	.361	1.40	4.50	2.34	4.17	0.1	96	
2014	PMB	A+	21	6	5	0	13	13	74	74	6	2.8	5.0	50%	.286	1.31	3.28	4.31	4.71	0.2	111	
2015	MIS	AA	22	5	5	0	16	16	93	84	3	4.0	5.7	53%	.278	1.34	3.00	3.84	5.71	-0.9	116	
2015	GWN	AAA	22	3	4	0	9	9	45^{1}	43	4	4.0	5.8	55%	.277	1.39	3.57	4.48	5.83	-0.7	120	
2016	*ATL*	*MLB*	*23*	*1*	*1*	*0*	*3*	*3*	*16*	*16*	*2*	*3.9*	*5.4*	*51%*	*.304*	*1.45*	*4.65*	*4.91*	*5.41*	*0.0*	*130*	
2017	*ATL*	*MLB*	*24*	*3*	*4*	*0*	*10*	*10*	*56*	*61*	*7*	*4.1*	*5.5*	*51%*	*.318*	*1.55*	*4.85*	*5.36*	*5.64*	*-0.2*	*135*	

Breakout: 0% Improve: 0% Collapse: 0% Attrition: 0% MLB: 0% *Comparables: Zach Jackson, Daniel Corcino, Ryan Pressly*

Perhaps the biggest takeaway from Jenkins' first season in the Braves' system is that he stayed mostly healthy. (He blew away his previous season-high in innings by 56.) Despite middling component stats, he's now approaching the major-league door. Maybe knocking on it. Maybe ringing the bell. Maybe just standing there and shouting! However he plans to alert the inhabitants of the major-league house, Jenkins has the potential for two standout pitches: a running fastball that gets into the mid-90s and a power curve. His changeup, which lacked major-league quality in the past, is still a tick below average, but it flashed enough to give him a third pitch he can occasionally offer. He still needs to cut down the walks and further develop his command to be a no. 4 starter, but he's a premium athlete with effortless velocity, and that plays.

Jim Johnson RHP

Born: 6/27/83 Age: 33 Bats: R Throws: R Height: 6'6" Weight: 240

YEAR	TEAM	LVL	AGE	W	L	SV	G	GS	IP	H	HR	BB/9	K/9	GB%	BABIP	WHIP	ERA	FIP	DRA	WARP	CFIP	MPH
2013	BAL	MLB	30	3	8	50	74	0	70^{1}	72	5	2.3	7.2	59%	.327	1.28	2.94	3.47	4.22	0.3	98	96.1
2014	OAK	MLB	31	4	2	2	38	0	40^{1}	60	5	5.1	6.2	60%	.390	2.06	7.14	5.32	7.02	-1.3	121	96.2
2014	DET	MLB	31	1	0	0	16	0	13	9	0	8.3	9.7	68%	.265	1.62	6.92	4.47	4.23	0.0	118	95.4
2015	LAN	MLB	32	0	3	1	23	0	18^{2}	32	3	2.9	8.2	65%	.446	2.04	10.12	5.04	7.06	-0.5	109	96.9
2015	ATL	MLB	32	2	3	9	49	0	48	45	2	2.6	6.2	64%	.295	1.23	2.25	3.27	3.30	0.8	103	96.5
2016	*ATL*	*MLB*	*33*	*3*	*1*	*0*	*50*	*0*	53^{1}	*50*	*5*	*3.1*	*7.1*	*62%*	*.306*	*1.29*	*3.98*	*3.92*	*4.73*	*0.1*	*107*	
2017	*ATL*	*MLB*	*34*	*2*	*1*	*3*	*50*	*0*	47^{2}	*49*	*5*	*3.2*	*6.9*	*62%*	*.319*	*1.37*	*4.15*	*4.57*	*4.93*	*0.0*	*112*	

Breakout: 24% Improve: 40% Collapse: 28% Attrition: 7% MLB: 91% *Comparables: Bob Wickman, Brad Ziegler, Sparky Lyle*

Investing in relievers is like buying a two-pack of Starburst. Math dictates you have a 75 percent shot at hitting on one red or pink or *at least* finding a replacement-level orange, but goddamn if you don't come up double yellows time and again. Johnson was cherry with the Braves, posting a 2.25 ERA in 49 innings and resuming his former closer role, but after the Dodgers acquired him as part of the Alex Wood deal, he turned out to be a total lemon, surrendering 21 runs in 18 innings and failing to make the postseason roster. This is why teams that can afford it take the 12-piece-stick approach to bullpen-building: When you grab a dozen arms at once, odds are at least a few won't leave a sour taste in your mouth.

Ian Krol LHP

Born: 5/9/91 Age: 25 Bats: L Throws: L Height: 6'1" Weight: 210

YEAR	TEAM	LVL	AGE	W	L	SV	G	GS	IP	H	HR	BB/9	K/9	GB%	BABIP	WHIP	ERA	FIP	DRA	WARP	CFIP	MPH
2013	HAR	AA	22	0	0	1	21	0	26	14	1	2.4	10.0	48%	.210	0.81	0.69	2.63	4.12	0.2	85	
2013	WAS	MLB	22	2	1	0	32	0	27^{1}	28	5	2.6	7.2	40%	.280	1.32	3.95	4.67	5.13	-0.2	106	95.9
2014	DET	MLB	23	0	0	1	45	0	32^{2}	42	6	3.6	7.7	42%	.343	1.68	4.96	5.21	6.43	-0.8	102	94.9
2015	TOL	AAA	24	1	1	1	28	0	31^{1}	21	0	3.7	9.8	56%	.259	1.09	2.30	2.23	2.98	0.5	86	
2015	DET	MLB	24	2	3	0	33	0	28	31	4	5.5	8.4	46%	.338	1.71	5.79	5.14	5.12	-0.1	109	96.5
2016	*ATL*	*MLB*	*25*	*3*	*1*	*0*	*50*	*0*	53^{1}	*48*	*6*	*3.3*	*8.2*	*46%*	*.305*	*1.27*	*3.89*	*3.94*	*4.60*	*0.2*	*104*	
2017	*ATL*	*MLB*	*26*	*3*	*2*	*1*	*49*	*3*	*62*	*62*	*9*	*3.1*	*8.4*	*46%*	*.323*	*1.33*	*4.07*	*4.47*	*4.81*	*0.1*	*110*	

Breakout: 33% Improve: 49% Collapse: 19% Attrition: 27% MLB: 71% *Comparables: Chris Britton, Chris Ray, Mike Zagurski*

You've probably seen this type of pitcher before: At times, Krol looks like the best left-handed reliever not named Aroldis Chapman. You get to wondering why he's not a setup man. A couple days later, *thud*, multiple runs come trotting home with Krol on the mound. The impact of the shelling leaves you bewildered. This phenomenon is known as a Krolover Accident. It's perfectly normal for the promising lefty with mid-90s heat and mid-level secondary slop. But for this particular hurler, the Krolovers don't outweigh the days he's Invincible Ian. Fun fact, depending on your team of preference: All four home runs he gave up last year were to the Yankees.

Sugar Ray Marimon RHP

Born: 9/30/88 Age: 27 Bats: R Throws: R Height: 6'1" Weight: 195

YEAR	TEAM	LVL	AGE	W	L	SV	G	GS	IP	H	HR	BB/9	K/9	GB%	BABIP	WHIP	ERA	FIP	DRA	WARP	CFIP	MPH
2013	NWA	AA	24	6	14	0	27	26	148^{1}	159	26	2.7	7.2	40%	.296	1.38	4.31	4.72	4.74	0.4	111	
2014	NWA	AA	25	0	1	0	4	4	21	18	0	3.0	3.9	58%	.269	1.19	2.14	3.26				
2014	OMA	AAA	25	5	4	0	15	15	83^{1}	88	10	2.8	7.2	40%	.318	1.37	3.56	4.77	5.30	0.5	103	
2015	GWN	AAA	26	5	4	0	17	14	81^{2}	75	4	2.9	5.3	42%	.276	1.24	3.31	3.68	4.44	0.2	106	
2015	ATL	MLB	26	0	1	0	16	0	25^{2}	30	3	4.9	4.9	40%	.314	1.71	7.36	5.23	6.46	-0.5	123	93.7
2016	*ATL*	*MLB*	*27*	*5*	*6*	*0*	*25*	*15*	93^{2}	*90*	*11*	*3.0*	*6.1*	*41%*	*.294*	*1.30*	*4.36*	*4.32*	*5.12*	*0.1*	*122*	
2017	*ATL*	*MLB*	*28*	*6*	*7*	*0*	*26*	*19*	126^{2}	*129*	*18*	*3.0*	*6.2*	*41%*	*.301*	*1.35*	*4.58*	*5.05*	*5.38*	*-0.2*	*129*	

Breakout: 3% Improve: 5% Collapse: 9% Attrition: 11% MLB: 18% *Comparables: Chris Seddon, Shane Komine, Jay Jackson*

What's in a name? That which we call Sugar by any other name would pitch as sweet; so Ray Marimon would, were he not Ray Marimon call'd, retain that dear perfection which—

Sorry, what? Marimon's stuff is actually kind of mediocre? Awwww, nuts. You can understand the initial confusion: Soak in his Triple-A numbers and you get a rush, but then the seven-plus ERA and 1:1 strikeout-to-walk ratio in his MLB cup of coffee leave a bitter taste. Marimon is best suited to be minor-league depth due to an unsavory lack of command, and any team that has him under contract should be filling its bullpen with meatier options. Taking the route many players of his caliber do, he signed with a team in Korea this winter.

Matt Marksberry LHP

Born: 8/25/90 Age: 25 Bats: L Throws: L Height: 6'1" Weight: 200

YEAR	TEAM	LVL	AGE	W	L	SV	G	GS	IP	H	HR	BB/9	K/9	GB%	BABIP	WHIP	ERA	FIP	DRA	WARP	CFIP	MPH
2014	ROM	A	23	5	10	0	22	22	111^2	100	10	4.1	7.9	49%	.286	1.35	3.55	4.45	4.91	0.6	106	
2015	CAR	A+	24	3	1	2	22	0	35^2	22	2	3.3	8.8	52%	.220	0.98	2.78	3.28	3.54	0.4	94	
2015	GWN	AAA	24	0	0	1	11	0	10^1	10	0	0.9	7.0	62%	.312	1.06	2.61	1.90	3.38	0.1	91	
2015	ATL	MLB	24	0	3	0	31	0	23^1	22	2	6.2	8.1	39%	.294	1.63	5.01	4.66	4.89	-0.1	109	94.9
2016	*ATL*	*MLB*	*25*	*2*	*1*	*0*	*30*	*0*	*32*	*30*	*4*	*4.0*	*7.1*	*42%*	*.299*	*1.38*	*4.42*	*4.51*	*5.19*	*-0.1*	*122*	
2017	*ATL*	*MLB*	*26*	*3*	*3*	*1*	*27*	*6*	*62^1*	*59*	*8*	*4.2*	*7.4*	*42%*	*.304*	*1.42*	*4.53*	*5.00*	*5.32*	*-0.1*	*124*	

Breakout: 19% Improve: 20% Collapse: 5% Attrition: 23% MLB: 35% *Comparables: Nick Maronde, Jorge De La Rosa, Felipe Paulino*

Matt Marksberry is a lefty with above-average fastball velocity, feel for two pitches and minor-league success, so the Braves fast-tracked him as a reliever in 2015 and threw him into the bullpen fire. There were few good things to say about Mark Mattsberry's debut assignment over 31 appearances. His fastball averaged 93 and touched 96, but it was straight and lacked downhill plane despite his high release. The result was it getting rocked when in the zone. Mort Morksberry gets his curveball into the low 80s and flashes downward break, but it lacks bite and mostly rolls, which limits his swing-and-miss impact. The framework is there to stick in the major leagues as a specialist, but Mirk Mirtsberry needs to improve in at least one or two areas to reach that potential.

Andrew McKirahan LHP

Born: 2/8/90 Age: 26 Bats: R Throws: L Height: 6'2" Weight: 195

YEAR	TEAM	LVL	AGE	W	L	SV	G	GS	IP	H	HR	BB/9	K/9	GB%	BABIP	WHIP	ERA	FIP	DRA	WARP	CFIP	MPH
2013	KNC	A	23	2	0	0	14	0	19^2	14	0	3.2	10.1	62%	.292	1.07	2.75	2.63	4.10	0.2	84	
2014	DAY	A+	24	2	1	8	23	0	36^1	29	1	2.0	8.2	53%	.269	1.02	0.99	2.76	4.06	0.2	91	
2014	TEN	AA	24	0	3	2	21	0	28^2	28	3	1.9	7.5	48%	.298	1.19	3.45	3.50				
2015	ATL	MLB	25	1	0	0	27	0	27^1	40	2	3.3	7.2	53%	.409	1.83	5.93	3.82	5.18	-0.2	107	95.4
2016	*ATL*	*MLB*	*26*	*2*	*1*	*0*	*30*	*0*	*32*	*31*	*3*	*2.9*	*7.0*	*51%*	*.311*	*1.30*	*3.99*	*3.73*	*4.72*	*0.1*	*109*	
2017	*ATL*	*MLB*	*27*	*1*	*1*	*1*	*30*	*0*	*38*	*39*	*5*	*2.8*	*7.3*	*51%*	*.320*	*1.33*	*4.04*	*4.45*	*4.78*	*0.0*	*111*	

Breakout: 13% Improve: 15% Collapse: 16% Attrition: 21% MLB: 39% *Comparables: Sam Demel, Lucas Luetge, Tanner Scheppers*

McKirahan had a whirlwind season, but his hair remained top notch, a Samardzjian mass of dark tresses peeking around from behind like a nervous toddler on Bring Your Child To Work Day. He was selected by the Marlins from the Cubs in the Rule 5 draft in December 2014, but was placed on waivers in spring training. The Braves won the claim battle among several interested teams and inserted him into the bullpen. After only three appearances, he was suspended 80 games for testing positive for the growth hormone Ipamorelin. (The test dated back to his time with the Marlins, for whatever that's worth.) On the bright side for the Braves, this ate three months off the Rule 5 clock. McKirahan struggled when he returned, but the team, having no real urgency to do anything so quotidian as win baseball games, let him ride it out. Now 26, he'll have to prove capable of holding a role to avoid an unceremonious removal from the roster, but an above-average fastball, decent slider and gorgeous locks are on his side.

Mike Minor LHP

Born: 12/26/87 Age: 28 Bats: R Throws: L Height: 6'4" Weight: 220

YEAR	TEAM	LVL	AGE	W	L	SV	G	GS	IP	H	HR	BB/9	K/9	GB%	BABIP	WHIP	ERA	FIP	DRA	WARP	CFIP	MPH
2013	ATL	MLB	25	13	9	0	32	32	204^2	177	22	2.0	8.0	37%	.272	1.09	3.21	3.34	4.01	2.2	93	92.9
2014	ATL	MLB	26	6	12	0	25	25	145^1	165	21	2.7	7.4	43%	.323	1.44	4.77	4.36	5.22	-0.8	113	92.9
2016	*ATL*	*MLB*	*28*	*2*	*2*	*0*	*6*	*6*	*38^1*	*34*	*5*	*2.5*	*7.4*	*40%*	*.291*	*1.18*	*3.96*	*4.06*	*4.67*	*0.3*	*109*	
2017	*ATL*	*MLB*	*29*	*10*	*10*	*0*	*28*	*28*	*170^2*	*163*	*22*	*2.1*	*7.1*	*40%*	*.301*	*1.19*	*3.84*	*4.22*	*4.53*	*1.5*	*105*	

Breakout: 12% Improve: 44% Collapse: 16% Attrition: 5% MLB: 76% *Comparables: Jeff Francis, Cliff Lee, Jeremy Hellickson*

Minor's career has fallen down a hole. After a promising start as a first-round pick who developed as every team hopes their first-round picks will, he struggled repeating his mechanics and saw his stuff flatten in 2014. He also dealt with left-shoulder inflammation in spring training and soreness late in the year. The nightmares engendered by those issues came to life when his shoulder caved in, requiring surgery to repair a torn labrum in May. As you can see in the stats box above, it cost him the season. How much more it will cost him is, as with all shoulder injuries, unknown. Someone toss him a rope.

Peter Moylan RHP

Born: 12/2/78 Age: 37 Bats: R Throws: R Height: 6'2" Weight: 225

YEAR	TEAM	LVL	AGE	W	L	SV	G	GS	IP	H	HR	BB/9	K/9	GB%	BABIP	WHIP	ERA	FIP	DRA	WARP	CFIP	MPH
2013	ABQ	AAA	34	4	1	4	38	0	46	38	1	3.9	8.8	52%	.294	1.26	2.74	3.33	4.42	0.4	81	
2013	LAN	MLB	34	1	0	0	14	0	15^1	23	3	4.1	3.5	28%	.370	1.96	6.46	6.15	9.11	-0.8	124	92.7
2015	GWN	AAA	36	2	0	6	27	0	28^2	22	1	2.8	7.5	57%	.269	1.08	3.14	3.19	3.57	0.3	94	
2015	ATL	MLB	36	1	0	0	22	0	10^1	12	1	0.0	7.0	69%	.314	1.16	3.48	2.87	4.34	0.0	103	92.6
2016	*ATL*	*MLB*	*37*	*2*	*1*	*1*	*35*	*0*	*37^1*	*35*	*4*	*3.1*	*7.4*	*55%*	*.306*	*1.28*	*3.92*	*4.03*	*4.63*	*0.1*	*106*	
2017	*ATL*	*MLB*	*38*	*3*	*1*	*1*	*53*	*0*	*52^1*	*52*	*6*	*3.0*	*7.2*	*55%*	*.317*	*1.34*	*4.04*	*4.44*	*4.77*	*0.1*	*110*	

Breakout: 14% Improve: 29% Collapse: 14% Attrition: 9% MLB: 48% *Comparables: Vic Darensbourg, Bryan Corey, Yasuhiko Yabuta*

Moylan was hired by the Braves to help coach the Rookie-level Danville affiliate in 2015. Instead, he ended up appearing in 22 games in the majors. That's the result of a good news–bad news scenario. The good news is that Moylan bounced back from a second Tommy John surgery enough to be effective again and earn major-league time. The bad news is that the Braves were desperate enough to give him high-leverage opportunities in September. Moylan threw well, though. He didn't walk anyone in 10-plus innings and induced groundballs by getting the movement back on his sinker. Moylan's career was kaput not long ago, right up until the moment it wasn't. Trying to predict what happens from here is folly.

Sean Newcomb LHP

Born: 6/12/93 Age: 23 Bats: L Throws: L Height: 6'5" Weight: 245

YEAR	TEAM	LVL	AGE	W	L	SV	G	GS	IP	H	HR	BB/9	K/9	GB%	BABIP	WHIP	ERA	FIP	DRA	WARP	CFIP	MPH
2014	BUR	A	21	0	1	0	4	4	11^2	13	1	3.9	11.6	28%	.387	1.54	6.94	3.31	4.19	0.1	90	
2015	BUR	A	22	1	0	0	7	7	34^1	25	1	5.0	11.8	66%	.308	1.28	1.83	2.90	3.32	0.7	90	
2015	INL	A+	22	6	1	0	13	13	65^2	50	2	4.5	11.5	49%	.300	1.26	2.47	3.17	3.81	1.4	87	
2015	ARK	AA	22	2	2	0	7	7	36	22	2	6.0	9.8	47%	.235	1.28	2.75	3.94	5.16	0.0	109	
2016	*ATL*	*MLB*	*23*	*5*	*7*	*0*	*22*	*22*	100^2	*87*	*12*	*4.6*	*9.1*	*49%*	*.303*	*1.37*	*4.30*	*4.20*	*5.01*	*0.3*	*119*	
2017	*ATL*	*MLB*	*24*	*7*	*9*	*0*	*28*	*28*	170^2	*151*	*23*	*4.6*	*9.4*	*49%*	*.309*	*1.40*	*4.27*	*4.69*	*4.97*	*0.5*	*117*	

Breakout: 10% Improve: 18% Collapse: 8% Attrition: 21% MLB: 31% *Comparables: Jake Arrieta, Wilmer Font, Max Scherzer*

Half of the prospect return in the Andrelton Simmons trade, Newcomb's fastball is the big weapon in his three-pitch arsenal. His slider and changeup can develop into solid offerings, and there's hope that his command can get to average, which would allow the whole profile to play up. His frame certainly looks like it can carry a starter's load, which is another way of saying "he's really friggin' big." Newcomb was the Angels' best prospect before the trade, and he's the Braves' best prospect now. That's how it works when you're a lefty starter who can touch the high 90s.

Williams Perez RHP

Born: 5/21/91 Age: 25 Bats: R Throws: R Height: 6'1" Weight: 230

YEAR	TEAM	LVL	AGE	W	L	SV	G	GS	IP	H	HR	BB/9	K/9	GB%	BABIP	WHIP	ERA	FIP	DRA	WARP	CFIP	MPH
2013	ROM	A	22	5	4	0	14	13	70	73	5	2.3	7.6	57%	.329	1.30	4.24	3.62	4.19	0.7	91	
2013	LYN	A+	22	6	2	0	9	9	55	50	4	2.9	7.7	53%	.287	1.24	2.62	3.68	4.48	0.5	93	
2014	MIS	AA	23	7	6	0	26	25	133	119	4	2.6	6.4	59%	.283	1.19	2.91	3.29				
2015	GWN	AAA	24	3	1	0	8	8	38^2	32	1	2.3	8.4	52%	.292	1.09	1.16	2.48	2.73	0.9	83	
2015	ATL	MLB	24	7	6	1	23	20	116^2	130	13	3.9	5.6	51%	.318	1.55	4.78	4.90	5.10	-0.1	125	93.4
2016	*ATL*	*MLB*	*25*	*3*	*3*	*0*	*33*	*8*	*69*	*69*	*7*	*3.2*	*6.2*	*51%*	*.308*	*1.35*	*4.35*	*4.21*	*5.12*	*0.1*	*121*	
2017	*ATL*	*MLB*	*26*	*4*	*5*	*0*	*14*	*14*	82^1	*84*	*10*	*3.2*	*6.6*	*51%*	*.314*	*1.37*	*4.38*	*4.84*	*5.16*	*0.1*	*123*	

Breakout: 12% Improve: 35% Collapse: 24% Attrition: 35% MLB: 72% *Comparables: Hayden Penn, Junichi Tazawa, Justin Germano*

If Perez's sinker sank any more, it'd submerge like a submarine in the South Seas. If it had any more downward movement, it'd head underground and become God Emperor of Dune. What we're trying to tell you is that Perez gets a lot of movement on his fastball, which is why he threw it 72 percent of the time. He earned a shot in the thin Braves rotation, but his 20 starts were an up-and-down affair depending on whether he could command his fastball that day. Perez is, as you surely guessed, effective when locating the pitch down in the zone and on the corners, but the question is whether that will happen often enough for him to remain a starter. Best guess is that his future lies in middle relief, but he's still young, so dream what dreams you will.

Jose Ramirez RHP

Born: 1/21/90 Age: 26 Bats: R Throws: R Height: 6'3" Weight: 190

YEAR	TEAM	LVL	AGE	W	L	SV	G	GS	IP	H	HR	BB/9	K/9	GB%	BABIP	WHIP	ERA	FIP	DRA	WARP	CFIP	MPH
2013	TRN	AA	23	1	3	1	9	8	42^1	28	7	3.2	10.6	44%	.233	1.02	2.76	4.39	4.06	0.6	83	
2013	SWB	AAA	23	1	3	0	8	8	31^1	29	3	6.0	8.0	46%	.321	1.60	4.88	5.06	5.07	0.0	121	
2014	SWB	AAA	24	3	0	1	9	0	12^1	13	0	7.3	11.7	48%	.394	1.86	1.46	3.44	4.38	0.1	92	
2014	NYA	MLB	24	0	2	0	8	0	10	11	2	6.3	9.0	23%	.321	1.80	5.40	6.46	6.21	-0.2	108	97.5
2015	SWB	AAA	25	3	0	10	32	0	49^2	40	1	4.2	10.1	46%	.305	1.27	2.90	2.67	2.73	1.0	83	
2015	NYA	MLB	25	0	0	0	3	0	3	6	0	12.0	6.0	46%	.462	3.33	15.00	6.77	16.09	-0.4	113	98.2
2015	SEA	MLB	25	1	0	0	5	0	4^2	9	0	11.6	5.8	43%	.429	3.21	11.57	6.96	11.07	-0.4	128	98.5
2015	TAC	AAA	25	1	1	0	9	0	13	16	5	4.8	6.9	32%	.282	1.77	9.00	8.68	6.49	-0.2	115	
2016	*ATL*	*MLB*	*26*	*1*	*1*	*0*	*25*	*0*	26^2	*24*	*3*	*3.7*	*8.6*	*40%*	*.309*	*1.30*	*3.85*	*3.98*	*4.54*	*0.2*	*104*	
2017	*ATL*	*MLB*	*27*	*2*	*2*	*0*	*20*	*6*	55^2	*51*	*6*	*3.4*	*9.3*	*40%*	*.322*	*1.30*	*3.71*	*4.08*	*4.38*	*0.4*	*99*	

Breakout: 22% Improve: 27% Collapse: 15% Attrition: 29% MLB: 46% *Comparables: Jon Huber, Tom Mastny, Cory Rasmus*

Armed with a 100 mph fastball and only a cursory idea of where it was going, Ramirez produced more baserunners than outs in his cup of coffee last season. Unlike most big-armed hurlers with control problems, Ramirez works with three pitches and actually has a decent track record of throwing strikes. His tumbling changeup in particular fooled a couple of decent hitters last September. While neither the change nor his slider projects as the kind of weapon that portends a future in the very back of the bullpen, both can be effective offerings when he locates effectively. Still, for a rookie who will be 26 on Opening Day, there's an uncomfortably large gap between that rosy projection and his current strike-throwing abilities.

Paco Rodriguez LHP

Born: 4/16/91 Age: 25 Bats: L Throws: L Height: 6'3" Weight: 220

YEAR	TEAM	LVL	AGE	W	L	SV	G	GS	IP	H	HR	BB/9	K/9	GB%	BABIP	WHIP	ERA	FIP	DRA	WARP	CFIP	MPH
2013	LAN	MLB	22	3	4	2	76	0	54^{1}	30	5	3.1	10.4	50%	.210	0.90	2.32	3.06	2.18	1.6	82	91.4
2014	ABQ	AAA	23	2	3	1	32	0	28^{2}	25	4	5.3	11.0	51%	.300	1.47	4.40	4.85	4.88	0.2	87	
2014	LAN	MLB	23	1	0	0	19	0	14	12	1	2.6	9.0	51%	.324	1.14	3.86	2.89	4.12	0.1	94	90.8
2015	LAN	MLB	24	0	0	0	18	0	10^{1}	10	0	2.6	7.0	48%	.323	1.26	2.61	2.48	3.61	0.1	105	89.7
2016	*ATL*	*MLB*	*25*	*2*	*1*	*1*	*36*	*0*	*38^{1}*	*31*	*4*	*3.2*	*9.1*	*51%*	*.290*	*1.16*	*3.66*	*3.54*	*4.33*	*0.2*	*96*	
2017	*ATL*	*MLB*	*26*	*4*	*2*	*1*	*84*	*0*	*63^{1}*	*53*	*7*	*3.1*	*9.1*	*51%*	*.296*	*1.18*	*3.60*	*3.94*	*4.26*	*0.5*	*94*	

Breakout: 28% Improve: 55% Collapse: 25% Attrition: 21% MLB: 89% *Comparables: Addison Reed, Tim Collins, Cody Allen*

Rodriguez was, like Chris Withrow, a low-key addition for the Braves as an injured reliever they hope will throw high-leverage innings in the future. They'll have to wait a while to find out if he can help, though, as he had Tommy John surgery at the end of the 2015 season. The lefty is known for a big stab in his arm motion, but left-handed hitters probably feel something like a stab in their hearts when stepping in against him. (Please see your doctor immediately if you're feeling this any time you're not batting against Rodriguez.) He's also proven capable against righties, which could make him a legitimate full-inning option, or at least a situational lefty you're not afraid to leave in for a three-batter stretch. Regardless of the upside, the first task is to regain health. [Insert periodic reminder that Tommy John surgery doesn't have a 100 percent recovery rate.]

Shae Simmons RHP

Born: 9/3/90 Age: 25 Bats: R Throws: R Height: 5'11" Weight: 175

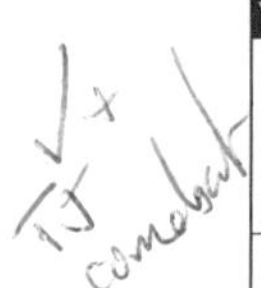

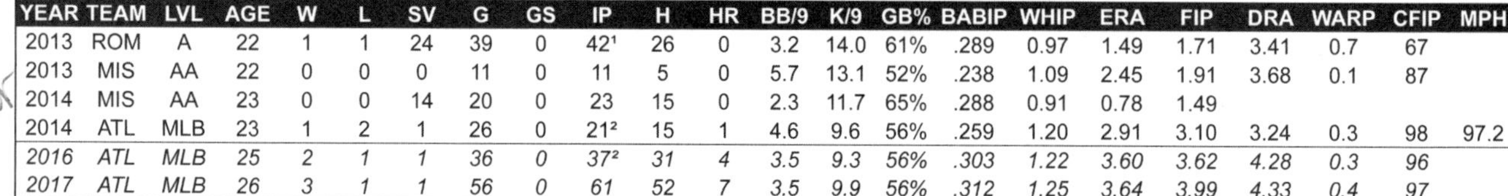

YEAR	TEAM	LVL	AGE	W	L	SV	G	GS	IP	H	HR	BB/9	K/9	GB%	BABIP	WHIP	ERA	FIP	DRA	WARP	CFIP	MPH
2013	ROM	A	22	1	1	24	39	0	42^{1}	26	0	3.2	14.0	61%	.289	0.97	1.49	1.71	3.41	0.7	67	
2013	MIS	AA	22	0	0	0	11	0	11	5	0	5.7	13.1	52%	.238	1.09	2.45	1.91	3.68	0.1	87	
2014	MIS	AA	23	0	0	14	20	0	23	15	0	2.3	11.7	65%	.288	0.91	0.78	1.49				
2014	ATL	MLB	23	1	2	1	26	0	21^{2}	15	1	4.6	9.6	56%	.259	1.20	2.91	3.10	3.24	0.3	98	97.2
2016	*ATL*	*MLB*	*25*	*2*	*1*	*1*	*36*	*0*	*37^{2}*	*31*	*4*	*3.5*	*9.3*	*56%*	*.303*	*1.22*	*3.60*	*3.62*	*4.28*	*0.3*	*96*	
2017	*ATL*	*MLB*	*26*	*3*	*1*	*1*	*56*	*0*	*61*	*52*	*7*	*3.5*	*9.9*	*56%*	*.312*	*1.25*	*3.64*	*3.99*	*4.33*	*0.4*	*97*	

Breakout: 16% Improve: 26% Collapse: 23% Attrition: 43% MLB: 54% *Comparables: Michael Kohn, Rich Thompson, Brad Boxberger*

Simmons was on his way to being a potential Craig Kimbrel replacement until he went down with Tommy John surgery just before spring training last season. He shares Kimbrel's stature, but he sits around 95 mph with his fastball, not 98, and his breaking pitch is a slider, not a curve. So, really, they're pretty different. That fastball comes with serious arm-side movement, though, and the slider bites hard. The Braves built a stockpile of injured relievers (Paco Rodriguez, Chris Withrow, Jason Grilli), but the one who was already in the organization could have the brightest future.

Lucas Sims RHP

Born: 5/10/94 Age: 22 Bats: R Throws: R Height: 6'2" Weight: 225

YEAR	TEAM	LVL	AGE	W	L	SV	G	GS	IP	H	HR	BB/9	K/9	GB%	BABIP	WHIP	ERA	FIP	DRA	WARP	CFIP	MPH
2013	ROM	A	19	12	4	0	28	18	116^{2}	83	3	3.5	10.3	44%	.284	1.11	2.62	3.09	4.03	1.3	86	
2014	LYN	A+	20	8	11	0	28	28	156^{2}	146	12	3.3	6.1	42%	.277	1.30	4.19	4.56	5.05	0.2	114	
2015	CAR	A+	21	3	4	0	9	9	40	39	2	5.2	8.3	47%	.325	1.55	5.18	4.00	5.16	-0.3	110	
2015	MIS	AA	21	4	2	0	9	9	47^{2}	29	1	5.5	10.6	48%	.257	1.22	3.21	3.30	3.98	0.5	97	
2016	*ATL*	*MLB*	*22*	*1*	*1*	*0*	*3*	*3*	*16*	*14*	*2*	*4.2*	*7.3*	*40%*	*.296*	*1.36*	*4.30*	*4.54*	*5.00*	*0.1*	*119*	
2017	*ATL*	*MLB*	*23*	*3*	*5*	*0*	*13*	*13*	*74^{2}*	*71*	*9*	*4.9*	*7.6*	*40%*	*.310*	*1.50*	*4.75*	*5.23*	*5.52*	*-0.2*	*132*	

Breakout: 4% Improve: 9% Collapse: 10% Attrition: 14% MLB: 27% *Comparables: Chaz Roe, Robbie Ray, Sean Gallagher*

Sims struggled in April in a return taste of the Carolina League, but was starting to make strides when a team bus crash put him on the disabled list for much of May and June with an undisclosed injury, a crash that also affected several teammates. He didn't let that unfortunate incident halt the momentum in his development, and he received rave reviews within the organization during two rehab outings at the spring complex in late June. He was eventually promoted to Double-A, where he put together a solid nine-start stretch to end the season. Sims has two pitches with plus potential, a mid-90s fastball with run and a hard curveball, and he's slowly making strides with his changeup and command. His mid-rotation potential remains.

Mike Soroka RHP

Born: 8/4/97 Age: 18 Bats: R Throws: R Height: 6'4" Weight: 195

YEAR	TEAM	LVL	AGE	W	L	SV	G	GS	IP	H	HR	BB/9	K/9	GB%	BABIP	WHIP	ERA	FIP	DRA	WARP	CFIP	MPH
2016	*ATL*	*MLB*	*18*	*2*	*3*	*0*	*9*	*9*	*36^{1}*	*37*	*5*	*3.3*	*6.8*	*30%*	*.313*	*1.38*	*4.47*	*4.53*	*5.20*	*0.0*	*125*	
2017	*ATL*	*MLB*	*19*	*6*	*8*	*0*	*26*	*26*	*152^{1}*	*165*	*21*	*3.0*	*6.6*	*30%*	*.323*	*1.41*	*4.45*	*4.92*	*5.18*	*0.1*	*124*	

Breakout: 0% Improve: 0% Collapse: 0% Attrition: 0% MLB: 0% *Comparables: Roberto Osuna, Jordan Lyles, Deolis Guerra*

Soroka flew under the radar entering the 2015 draft. For one, he was a Canadian high school pitcher. In addition, he was a Canadian high school pitcher. He became the first Canadian high school pitcher taken in the first round since 2007 when the Braves popped him 28th overall. The former Canadian high school pitcher's fastball sits in the low 90s with arm-side movement, and his tight slider with true two-plane break is a potential weapon made even more dangerous for right-handed batters by Soroka's crossfire motion and three-quarters arm slot. Add his projectable frame and some feel for a changeup, and Soroka is a potential mid-rotation candidate down the road; not bad for a Canadian high school pitcher.

Julio Teheran RHP

Born: 1/27/91 Age: 25 Bats: R Throws: R Height: 6'2" Weight: 200

YEAR	TEAM	LVL	AGE	W	L	SV	G	GS	IP	H	HR	BB/9	K/9	GB%	BABIP	WHIP	ERA	FIP	DRA	WARP	CFIP	MPH
2013	ATL	MLB	22	14	8	0	30	30	185^{2}	173	22	2.2	8.2	39%	.288	1.17	3.20	3.67	4.15	1.7	98	94.7
2014	ATL	MLB	23	14	13	0	33	33	221	188	22	2.1	7.6	37%	.267	1.08	2.89	3.46	3.35	3.9	99	93.8
2015	ATL	MLB	24	11	8	0	33	33	200^{2}	189	27	3.3	7.7	42%	.288	1.31	4.04	4.43	4.21	2.0	108	94.3
2016	*ATL*	*MLB*	*25*	*11*	*12*	*0*	*33*	*33*	*208*	*183*	*24*	*2.6*	*7.7*	*40%*	*.291*	*1.17*	*3.86*	*3.83*	*4.56*	*1.8*	*106*	
2017	*ATL*	*MLB*	*26*	*10*	*10*	*0*	*28*	*28*	*168^{1}*	*159*	*22*	*2.5*	*7.7*	*40%*	*.301*	*1.22*	*3.95*	*4.34*	*4.67*	*1.2*	*109*	

Breakout: 25% Improve: 60% Collapse: 20% Attrition: 9% MLB: 95% *Comparables: Jair Jurrjens, Mike Minor, Micah Owings*

There was more virtual ink spilled trying to figure out Teheran's season than over any other Braves pitcher in 2015. Atlanta's former top prospect signed a six-year extension in February 2014 and responded by establishing himself as a borderline no. 1 starter with a sub-three ERA that year. Fade out happily on 2014, fade back in on mid-June 2015 and you see a 5.07 ERA. Teheran's lopsided home-road splits were analyzed to death, but all that did was muddy the fact that he couldn't command his fastball or get bite on his slider. Smash cut to August and he's throwing from the first-base side of the rubber instead of the middle, spotting his four-seam fastball while throwing it with more conviction and getting sharper break on his slider. He even improved the feel for his change-up, which helped slow the bashing from both left-handed hitters and switch-hitting bloggers. Closing montage: seven total runs allowed in his final six starts. Stick a Post-it next to Teheran's season line to remind you that development isn't always linear and leave the worrying whether he sleeps as soundly with fluffy hotel pillows to those unfortunate souls who don't buy this book..

Touki Toussaint RHP

Born: 6/20/96 Age: 20 Bats: R Throws: R Height: 6'3" Weight: 185

YEAR	TEAM	LVL	AGE	W	L	SV	G	GS	IP	H	HR	BB/9	K/9	GB%	BABIP	WHIP	ERA	FIP	DRA	WARP	CFIP	MPH
2015	ROM	A	19	3	5	0	10	10	48^{2}	40	6	6.1	7.0	41%	.252	1.50	5.73	5.74	7.09	-1.1	127	
2015	KNC	A	19	2	2	0	7	7	39	31	4	3.5	6.7	38%	.243	1.18	3.69	4.55	5.14	-0.1	109	
2016	*ATL*	*MLB*	*20*	*3*	*5*	*0*	*15*	*15*	*61^{2}*	*62*	*8*	*5.1*	*6.0*	*34%*	*.298*	*1.56*	*5.34*	*5.25*	*6.23*	*-0.7*	*150*	
2017	*ATL*	*MLB*	*21*	*6*	*10*	*0*	*27*	*27*	*165^{2}*	*172*	*26*	*5.1*	*6.2*	*34%*	*.304*	*1.60*	*5.43*	*6.01*	*6.33*	*-1.5*	*153*	

Breakout: 0% Improve: 0% Collapse: 0% Attrition: 0% MLB: 0% *Comparables: Tyler Matzek, Jeurys Familia, Drew Hutchison*

Rarely is a baseball decision so far off the grid that the industry collectively scratches its head, but Arizona did its best to get there by essentially selling Toussaint to Atlanta for the $10 million represented by the Braves' willingness to take on Bronson Arroyo's contract. Toussaint remains crudo-raw, but when he pulls the talent together at moments here and there, it's enough to make a grown scout blush. He's an elite athlete with arm strength to die for. The fastball ranges widely around the zone and on the gun, but ticks up to 96 mph, and Toussaint has shown the ability to sit 93-95 for a couple of innings. The curve induces expletives in the stands and the batter's box: It's one of the best in the minors when it works, and has double-plus potential. Add feel for a plus-potential changeup and you get a no. 2 ceiling. He won't leave his teens until midway through this year, though the vagaries of cutoff dates mean that we call this his age-20 season. Accordingly, Toussaint has a long way to go to reach his ceiling; the path starts with improving his command and tightening up his mechanics.

Arodys Vizcaino RHP

Born: 11/13/90 Age: 25 Bats: R Throws: R Height: 6'0" Weight: 190

YEAR	TEAM	LVL	AGE	W	L	SV	G	GS	IP	H	HR	BB/9	K/9	GB%	BABIP	WHIP	ERA	FIP	DRA	WARP	CFIP	MPH
2014	TEN	AA	23	1	1	1	14	0	13^{2}	7	1	2.0	10.5	52%	.200	0.73	2.63	2.67				
2014	IOW	AAA	23	0	0	0	17	0	18^{1}	25	1	5.4	7.9	47%	.393	1.96	5.40	4.79	5.61	0.0	109	
2014	CHN	MLB	23	0	0	0	5	0	5	5	1	5.4	7.2	40%	.286	1.60	5.40	5.90	5.50	-0.1	107	98.0
2015	ATL	MLB	24	3	1	9	36	0	33^{2}	27	1	3.5	9.9	37%	.295	1.19	1.60	2.51	3.35	0.5	85	100.2
2016	*ATL*	*MLB*	*25*	*3*	*1*	*3*	*50*	*0*	*53^{1}*	*46*	*5*	*3.1*	*8.8*	*38%*	*.301*	*1.20*	*3.56*	*3.49*	*4.22*	*0.5*	*94*	
2017	*ATL*	*MLB*	*26*	*3*	*1*	*5*	*53*	*0*	*53^{1}*	*48*	*6*	*3.3*	*8.8*	*38%*	*.312*	*1.27*	*3.71*	*4.06*	*4.40*	*0.3*	*98*	

Breakout: 33% Improve: 60% Collapse: 16% Attrition: 23% MLB: 85% *Comparables: Jose Arredondo, Jordan Walden, Josh Spence*

Vizcaino was one of the bright spots of Atlanta's season, which may seem odd considering he lost 80 games after getting popped for Stanozolol, that most hilarious of steroids. Well, hilarious right up until the moment it shows up on the report of your pee test. The Braves' patience (in a sense, anyway; they were the ones who traded him away in 2012 before reacquiring him last offseason) finally paid off when Vizcaino established himself as a late-innings reliever down the stretch. He maintained upper-90s velocity, kept it in the zone and struck out 27 percent of batters faced while getting closing experience. He's been around forever, but check the age column above: There's still reason to hope for further refinements in his game. Vizcaino's injury report still follows him like a puppy who misses its mom, but with a cleaner delivery that cuts down on wasted momentum and tightens his release point, he's finally on track to take that puppy to the no-kill shelter and leave it there for someone else to adopt. That's a metaphor for "stay healthy."

Ryan Weber RHP

Born: 8/12/90 Age: 25 Bats: R Throws: R Height: 6'0" Weight: 180

YEAR	TEAM	LVL	AGE	W	L	SV	G	GS	IP	H	HR	BB/9	K/9	GB%	BABIP	WHIP	ERA	FIP	DRA	WARP	CFIP	MPH
2013	LYN	A+	22	6	5	0	22	15	93^{2}	90	6	1.4	7.8	62%	.303	1.12	3.84	3.29	4.01	1.3	77	
2014	MIS	AA	23	5	6	0	32	13	101^{1}	129	7	1.4	5.5	58%	.349	1.43	4.53	3.36				
2015	MIS	AA	24	0	2	1	11	3	26^{1}	23	1	0.3	8.2	43%	.293	0.91	2.73	2.09	2.44	0.7	79	
2015	GWN	AAA	24	6	3	3	27	6	73^{1}	60	7	1.1	4.3	61%	.233	0.94	2.21	3.93	4.35	0.1	105	
2015	ATL	MLB	24	0	3	0	5	5	28^{1}	25	3	1.9	6.0	66%	.278	1.09	4.76	4.04	3.95	0.4	110	91.5
2016	*ATL*	*MLB*	*25*	*2*	*1*	*0*	*18*	*3*	*32*	*32*	*3*	*2.3*	*5.8*	*59%*	*.306*	*1.27*	*4.08*	*3.79*	*4.83*	*0.1*	*113*	
2017	*ATL*	*MLB*	*26*	*2*	*2*	*0*	*16*	*6*	*57*	*62*	*7*	*2.4*	*5.5*	*59%*	*.314*	*1.35*	*4.34*	*4.78*	*5.14*	*0.0*	*121*	

Breakout: 9% Improve: 13% Collapse: 19% Attrition: 26% MLB: 33% *Comparables: Jose Alvarez, Graham Taylor, Sean Gilmartin*

The undersized Weber has had a gorilla-sized chip on his shoulder since reaching the upper levels in 2014. He slowly progressed through the system and was bouncing between starting and relieving until a call to the majors in September 2015 made the long wait worth it. Weber is listed at six feet, but that's on one of those weird perfect-posture days when he slept fantastically the night before and has a spring in his step. Even on those days, though, he doesn't get much spring in his fastball, sitting around 90 mph. That doesn't sell tickets, but he gets impressive sink and run on the pitch, and he spots it well enough to get by.

Daniel Winkler RHP

Born: 2/2/90 Age: 26 Bats: R Throws: R Height: 6'3" Weight: 200

YEAR	TEAM	LVL	AGE	W	L	SV	G	GS	IP	H	HR	BB/9	K/9	GB%	BABIP	WHIP	ERA	FIP	DRA	WARP	CFIP	MPH
2013	MOD	A+	23	12	5	0	22	22	130^{1}	84	15	2.6	10.5	42%	.232	0.93	2.97	3.99	4.58	2.2	75	
2013	TUL	AA	23	1	2	0	5	5	26^{2}	23	3	3.4	7.8	42%	.282	1.24	3.04	4.03	4.37	0.2	102	
2014	TUL	AA	24	5	2	0	12	12	70	33	5	2.2	9.1	38%	.172	0.71	1.41	3.01				
2015	ATL	MLB	25	0	0	0	2	0	1^{2}	2	2	5.4	10.8	40%	.000	1.80	10.80	18.16	14.33	-0.2	103	92.7
2016	*ATL*	*MLB*	*26*	*3*	*2*	*0*	*43*	*3*	57^{2}	*47*	*7*	*2.9*	*8.7*	*36%*	*.286*	*1.14*	*3.81*	*3.77*	*4.49*	*0.1*	*104*	
2017	*ATL*	*MLB*	*27*	*7*	*8*	*0*	*21*	*21*	121^{2}	*106*	*18*	*2.8*	*8.7*	*36%*	*.293*	*1.18*	*4.07*	*4.46*	*4.80*	*0.7*	*113*	

Breakout: 8% Improve: 19% Collapse: 14% Attrition: 27% MLB: 41% *Comparables: Asher Wojciechowski, Ryan Verdugo, Jeff Niemann*

The Braves plucked Winkler from the Rockies in the Rule 5 draft before 2015 in spite of (or perhaps because of) his Tommy John surgery in June 2014, then stashed him on the disabled list until he finished his rehab in September. You probably know that a Rule 5 pick has to stay on the 25-man roster or the disabled list for the full year; what you might not know is that the full year doesn't count unless the player spends at least 90 days on the active roster. Because Winkler was not activated until a few weeks before the season ended, the remainder of his 90-day sentence carries over into 2016. In a helpful turn of events, Winkler could have what it takes to stick in a major-league bullpen right now based on deception and command; he's suited for middle relief, if probably not much more. Here's hoping it's 90 happy days for Winkler and the Braves.

Matt Wisler RHP

Born: 9/12/92 Age: 23 Bats: R Throws: R Height: 6'3" Weight: 195

YEAR	TEAM	LVL	AGE	W	L	SV	G	GS	IP	H	HR	BB/9	K/9	GB%	BABIP	WHIP	ERA	FIP	DRA	WARP	CFIP	MPH
2013	LEL	A+	20	2	1	0	6	6	31	22	1	1.7	8.1	43%	.253	0.90	2.03	3.06	4.89	0.4	87	
2013	SAN	AA	20	8	5	0	20	20	105	85	7	2.3	8.8	39%	.281	1.07	3.00	2.79	3.80	1.5	84	
2014	SAN	AA	21	1	0	0	6	6	30	26	2	1.8	10.5	47%	.312	1.07	2.10	2.25				
2014	ELP	AAA	21	9	5	0	22	22	116^{2}	131	19	2.8	7.8	44%	.317	1.43	5.01	5.14	4.51	1.2	88	
2015	GWN	AAA	22	3	4	0	12	12	65	68	5	1.8	6.8	40%	.307	1.25	4.29	3.30	3.26	1.1	89	
2016	*ATL*	*MLB*	*23*	*10*	*12*	*0*	*32*	*32*	182^{1}	*174*	*22*	*2.6*	*6.8*	*37%*	*.299*	*1.25*	*4.10*	*4.07*	*4.85*	*0.9*	*114*	
2017	*ATL*	*MLB*	*24*	*6*	*8*	*0*	*26*	*21*	150^{1}	*155*	*22*	*2.7*	*7.0*	*37%*	*.314*	*1.33*	*4.29*	*4.74*	*5.08*	*0.2*	*120*	

Breakout: XX% Improve: XX% Collapse: XX% Attrition: XX% MLB: XX% *Comparables: XXXXXX, XXXXX, XXXXX*

As with Hector Olivera, the Braves are nothing if not persistent. They wanted Wisler badly, but swung and missed when they dealt Justin Upton to San Diego. When the Padres called back in April, the Braves took another hack and this time connected in the Craig Kimbrel trade. Wisler has the prototypical no. 3 starter's arsenal: a plus-potential fastball, plus-potential slider, developing changeup that could be above average and a fringy curveball. His greatest present attribute is plus control, which is a good bit ahead of his command, and that's why he'll occasionally get rocked as he matures. He had his share of growing pains over 19 starts in his major-league debut, but he finished strong and looked increasingly comfortable. There's no sexy, ace upside here, but Wisler is mid-rotation worthy and should be for a long time. If you're skeptical about the value of that kind of pitcher, check out the last three years of free-agent dollars for starters.

Lineouts

Hitters

NAME	POS	TEAM	LVL	AGE	PA	R	2B	3B	HR	RBI	BB	K	SB	CS	AVG/OBP/SLG	TAv	BABIP	BRR	FRAA	WARP
Gordon Beckham	2B	CHA	MLB	28	237	24	8	0	6	20	19	43	0	1	.209/.275/.332	.225	.229	1.8	3B(76): -2.3, 2B(11): 0.4	-0.1
Jordy Lara	1B	WTN	AA	24	494	48	27	6	7	56	37	85	0	0	.242/.308/.377	.254	.281	-3.9	3B(76): -13.2, 1B(22): 1.1	-0.8
Ryan Lavarnway	C	BAL	MLB	27	32	1	1	0	0	0	4	7	0	0	.107/.219/.143	.142	.143	0.1	C(9): -1.5	-0.4
	C	GWN	AAA	27	49	5	2	0	2	8	8	7	0	0	.268/.388/.463	.336	.281	-0.6	1B(5): 1.0, C(5): -0.1	0.6
	C	ATL	MLB	27	74	5	5	0	2	6	8	21	0	0	.227/.311/.394	.239	.302	0.7	C(21): -2.8, 1B(1): -0.0	0.0
Dustin Peterson	LF	CAR	A+	20	498	58	15	2	8	62	44	91	6	3	.251/.317/.348	.253	.295	2.0	LF(114): -10.5	-0.2
Joey Terdoslavich	PH	GWN	AAA	26	179	23	11	1	4	24	29	33	1	1	.281/.391/.452	.316	.327	1.3	1B(21): 0.7, LF(8): -0.6	1.4
	PH	ATL	MLB	26	59	5	4	1	1	4	3	14	0	0	.214/.254/.375	.227	.268	0.2	1B(12): -0.3, LF(2): -0.1	-0.1

Gordon Beckham's bat started going backward years ago and, as 28-year-olds will, he faded defensively in 2015, leaving something more like a punchline and less like a big leaguer. ❖ **Derian Cruz**, Atlanta's 2015 international splash at $2 million, is a switch-hitting infielder who projects as a plus-plus runner with contact skills, which is why he got the aforementioned $2 million. ❖ **Lucas Herbert**, the Braves' 2015 second-round pick and Kolby Allard's batterymate in high school, has leadership skills and a strong defensive profile at catcher while offering some power. ❖ As a first baseman with a strong arm and no other above-average tools, **Jordy Lara** is good enough to play baseball for the next few seasons and not good enough to spend many of them in the majors. ❖ **Ryan Lavarnway** is now merely minor-league depth, an experienced catcher to wait in Triple-A for emergencies, but his occasional home run power is still pretty. ❖ The Braves saw the writing on the wall about **Dustin Peterson**'s third-base defense and moved him to left field, where he'll need to max out his bat's above-average raw power to be a regular in the majors. ❖ **Austin Riley** was a two-way player in high school, but he settled in at third base after the Braves drafted him 41st overall last year; he offers big raw power and, as you might guess, arm strength. ❖ **Joey Terdoslavich**'s opportunities in the majors have been scant, and he was hampered in 2015 by a two-month wrist injury, but he hasn't done much to seize the day when called, either. He's one year and three days older than Freddie Freeman. ❖ **Dian Toscano** signed a four-year contract out of Cuba, but became a ghost when paperwork issues prevented the projected fourth outfielder from playing all year.

Pitchers

NAME	TEAM	LVL	AGE	W	L	SV	G	GS	IP	H	HR	BB/9	K/9	GB%	BABIP	WHIP	ERA	FIP	FRA	WARP	CFIP	MPH
Zachary Bird	RCU	A+	20	5	7	0	19	17	89	74	6	4.9	9.6	40%	.293	1.37	4.75	4.24	5.63	0.1	108	
	MIS	AA	20	1	1	0	3	3	12^{2}	8	0	8.5	5.7	29%	.229	1.58	4.26	4.88	6.50	-0.2	124	
David Carpenter	NYA	MLB	29	0	1	0	22	0	18^{2}	20	3	3.4	5.3	46%	.283	1.45	4.82	5.30	6.73	-0.4	117	97.2
	WAS	MLB	29	0	0	0	8	0	6	5	1	3.0	6.0	26%	.222	1.17	1.50	5.00	0.81	0.3	114	97.0
John Gant	SLU	A+	22	2	0	0	6	6	40^{1}	27	4	2.2	10.7	50%	.232	0.92	1.79	2.89	1.94	1.3	76	
	BIN	AA	22	4	5	0	11	11	59^{1}	67	2	3.9	6.5	47%	.337	1.57	4.70	3.62	5.11	-0.2	111	
	MIS	AA	22	4	0	0	7	7	40^{2}	28	1	3.1	9.5	43%	.273	1.03	1.99	2.54	2.65	1.1	81	
David Holmberg	LOU	AAA	23	7	7	0	21	19	120^{1}	142	14	3.1	5.3	45%	.322	1.52	4.34	4.59	5.73	-1.6	119	
	CIN	MLB	23	1	4	0	6	6	28^{1}	36	10	5.1	4.8	44%	.280	1.84	7.62	8.60	7.82	-0.9	136	90.0
Jason Hursh	MIS	AA	23	3	6	2	24	15	82^{1}	111	3	3.5	6.6	54%	.380	1.74	5.14	3.49	5.29	-0.4	109	
	GWN	AAA	23	1	0	0	10	0	15	16	2	3.0	3.0	53%	.275	1.40	5.40	5.42	5.55	-0.2	117	
Casey Kelly	SAN	AA	25	1	8	1	27	14	82	94	7	3.7	6.6	51%	.323	1.56	4.94	4.26	5.58	-0.5	111	
	ELP	AAA	25	1	2	0	4	3	15^{2}	20	0	2.9	8.0	47%	.408	1.60	6.32	3.15	3.97	0.3	88	
	SDN	MLB	25	0	2	0	3	2	11^{1}	19	1	2.4	5.6	47%	.409	1.94	7.94	4.13	7.65	-0.4	113	93.2
Ryan Kelly	MIS	AA	27	1	1	10	17	0	18^{2}	13	0	2.9	8.7	47%	.255	1.02	0.48	2.34	3.63	0.2	93	
	GWN	AAA	27	3	1	13	24	0	28^{1}	12	0	2.2	9.5	42%	.188	0.67	0.95	1.89	1.97	0.8	71	
	ATL	MLB	27	0	0	0	17	0	16^{2}	21	5	3.2	5.4	47%	.302	1.62	7.02	6.94	6.88	-0.4	115	94.9
Michael Kohn	GWN	AAA	29	0	1	0	7	0	10	9	0	4.5	9.9	44%	.360	1.40	4.50	2.46	3.51	0.1	93	
	ATL	MLB	29	0	0	0	6	0	4^{2}	0	0	11.6	7.7	22%	.000	1.29	0.00	5.30	0.76	0.2	108	96.6
Ethan Martin	REA	AA	26	3	1	0	21	5	51^{2}	46	3	2.6	5.4	49%	.267	1.18	3.14	3.87	4.77	-0.1	108	
Bud Norris	SDN	MLB	30	1	2	0	20	0	16^{2}	16	1	3.2	11.3	61%	.349	1.32	5.40	2.68	1.85	0.6	77	97.8
	BAL	MLB	30	2	9	0	18	11	66^{1}	84	14	3.4	6.8	44%	.329	1.64	7.06	5.61	7.58	-2.1	113	96.3
Max Povse	ROM	A	21	4	2	0	12	12	59^{2}	50	2	2.4	7.5	45%	.279	1.11	2.56	3.20	3.18	1.4	85	
	CAR	A+	21	1	3	0	5	5	18^{1}	24	0	3.4	4.9	52%	.364	1.69	9.33	3.80	4.60	0.0	104	
Ricardo Sanchez	ROM	A	18	1	6	0	10	10	39^{2}	37	3	4.8	7.0	47%	.286	1.46	5.45	4.95	6.06	-0.4	115	
Andrew Thurman	CAR	A+	23	5	4	0	11	11	57^{1}	57	2	1.7	6.8	43%	.306	1.19	3.77	2.99	3.15	1.1	90	
	MIS	AA	23	1	4	0	5	5	24^{1}	29	0	5.9	5.2	39%	.341	1.85	5.18	4.12	6.58	-0.5	121	

Zachary Bird is an athlete with the potential for two above-average offerings, but he hasn't solidified a future as a starter because he walks too many and lacks a reliable third pitch. ❖ The Nationals acquired hard-throwing **David Carpenter** in June to fix their bullpen, only to see shoulder inflammation shut him down. Now Atlanta will try to fix *him*. ❖ **Brady Feigl** is a hard-throwing lefty reliever who missed his sophomore year in college with a labrum tear and his sophomore year in the minors with Tommy John surgery. ❖ **John Gant** shows enough in a four-pitch mix to project as a back-end starter or reliever, but his inconsistent delivery and thin frame may prevent him from getting there. ❖ Super-sized lefty **David Holmberg** looks like an innings eater, but too frequently his low-velocity fastball, changeup and curve look like a Super Deluxe Combo Meal with Pibb Xtra and ranch on the side. ❖ **Jason Hursh**'s lack of impact stuff beyond a hard sinking fastball limits his projection, and his move to the bullpen midway through the Double-A season put the nail in the coffin of any rotation dreams. ❖ **Casey Kelly** spent most of 2015 building up arm strength and toughening character. He got hit hard in the minors before enjoying more public degradation in the majors in September. ❖ **Ryan Kelly** is a former 26th-round pick who has pitched in four organizations and made his major-league debut last year at 27; if you're waiting for the part of this where he's not actually a journeyman, well, the fairy godmother must have gotten stuck in traffic. ❖ When he was 10, **Michael Kohn** predicted he'd pitch for the Braves. That's cute. He can't throw strikes and a strained shoulder cost him much of 2015. That's not cute. ❖ His days as a prospect now far behind him, his fastball hardly even a facsimile of what it once was, 2015 passed without a major-league appearance for **Ethan Martin**. ❖ After flopping in Baltimore as a starter, **Bud Norris** went to San Diego, where he flopped as a reliever and shared some controversial thoughts with *USA Today* on how baseball players of certain ethnicities should behave; he's a regular Bud of all trades. ❖ The 6-foot-8 **Max Povse**, who goes by @TallWall22 on Twitter, generated buzz for his size and lively stuff, but his first full season was hampered by disabled list stints for undisclosed injuries. ❖ The best version of **Ricardo Sanchez** has mid-rotation potential based on two plus-potential pitches and a developing third, but if you've ever had a teenager in your house, you know how often the best version of Sanchez shows up. Exercise patience: We all get over being young. ❖ **Andrew Thurman** throws more strikes than a union in the '40s and offers a deep arsenal with no standout pitch, making him a polished prospect who should reach the majors and be entirely forgettable once he's there. ❖ **Chris Withrow** spent all of 2015 recovering from Tommy John surgery; the Braves grabbed him in the Juan Uribe trade with the hope of future impact innings of the type he provided the Dodgers in 2013.

MANAGER

Fredi Gonzalez

YEAR	TEAM	W	L	Pythag +/-	Avg PC	100+ P	120+ P	QS	BQS	REL	REL w Zero R	IBB	PH	PH Avg	PH HR	SB2	CS2	SB3	CS3	SAC Att	SAC%	POS SAC	Squeeze	Swing	In Play
2013	ATL	96	66	-3	95.3	48	1	102	5	466	422	35	213	.247	6	60	28	4	2	99	58.6	21	3	241	76
2014	ATL	79	83	1	98.1	78	3	110	6	472	393	36	205	.180	2	90	29	5	3	89	59.6	19	3	273	78
2015	ATL	67	95	8	93.3	49	0	79	5	532	421	45	252	.200	5	62	31	7	2	87	77.0	18	1	243	73

After a surprisingly competitive first half that saw the Braves go 42-47, Gonzalez and his coaching staff received extensions through the 2016 season that included a club option for 2017. The Braves celebrated Gonzalez's fortune by going 25-48 in the second half and igniting tanking allegations.

If the Braves intended to lose games, nobody told Gonzalez. He continued to field lineups as good as could have been expected given the roster and his at-times odd predilections—remember, he used to hit Melvin Upton Jr. leadoff when he *wanted* to win. Likewise, he did the best he could with the majors' worst bullpen—a leaky mess that housed myriad waiver claims—and a rotation that featured Williams Perez and Ryan Weber, among others. In short, the Braves' problem was talent, not effort.

What the second half proved was not that the Braves had pulled the plug, but that Gonzalez's predicament is hands down one of the oddest in the game. Typically, teams fire their manager before moving from competitive mode to a full rebuild—in part because a disappointing season tends to trigger the switch. The Braves had that disappointing season—see 2014—and even changed front office personnel, yet nonetheless kept Gonzalez around. That's rare, and many would argue pointless, since there's little chance he survives the entire rebuild process.

BALTIMORE ORIOLES

Essay by Jonathan Bernhardt

Player comments by Doug Thorburn, Mauricio Rubio and BP authors

What do you do when you've only got one trick? Because that's the Dan Duquette Baltimore Orioles. It's a very good trick, but more and more it seems like it won't be enough. That trick: Cautiously chasing the deal.

In fairness to the unit Duquette has put together, it's not a trick without merit. Nelson Cruz's one-year, $8 million deal late in the 2013–14 offseason gave the Orioles an MVP-caliber player on the cheap, and in 2012 the Orioles signed Taiwanese lefty Wei-Yin Chen to a three-year contract with a club option for 2015. They ended up paying Chen about $16 million for four years of 110 ERA+ pitching, an absolute steal considering the current market, and an unalloyed victory for Baltimore's international-scouting group.

But then there was the Ubaldo Jimenez signing. Four years and $50 million sounds like a good deal for a 30-year-old starter who threw 182 innings with a 3.77 DRA, if you don't know that said starter is Ubaldo Jimenez, a pitcher with less consistent success than next month's weather forecast. The Jimenez signing was also chasing the deal: Like Cruz's, it came in late February 2014, and also like Cruz, Jimenez's value had been sapped by the qualifying offer. If the Orioles could keep him at least a league-average starter over the life of his contract, he was probably more useful to them than the first-round pick it cost to sign him.

Instead, Jimenez pitched below replacement level in 125 innings in his first year in Baltimore, and the thought that he might maintain the serviceable 4.11 ERA he managed last season is undercut by his obscene splits: He allowed an .805 OPS to hitters in the second half (think Hunter Pence or Matt Holliday), leading to a 5.63 ERA. That's what happens when you only buy things that are on sale: Sometimes you get more value than you paid for, and sometimes you get less.

+++

That spending philosophy wouldn't be an issue for Baltimore except that this Orioles regime appears fundamentally unable to develop its own ballplayers internally. The few success stories of the developmental system—players drafted, developed and promoted to the bigs by the Orioles—over the last five years are Manny Machado, Matt Wieters, Zach Britton and Jim Johnson.

ORIOLES PROSPECTUS

2015 W-L: 81-81, 3rd in AL East

Pythag	.513	13th	DER	.702	17th
RS/G	4.40	9th	B-Age	27.9	6th
RA/G	4.28	15th	P-Age	28.2	13th
TAv	.253	24th	Salary	$119M	14th
BRR	-6.58	24th	M$/MW	$3.3M	18th
TAv-P	.258	13th	DL Days	566	2nd
FIP	4.09	19th	$ on DL	8%	4th

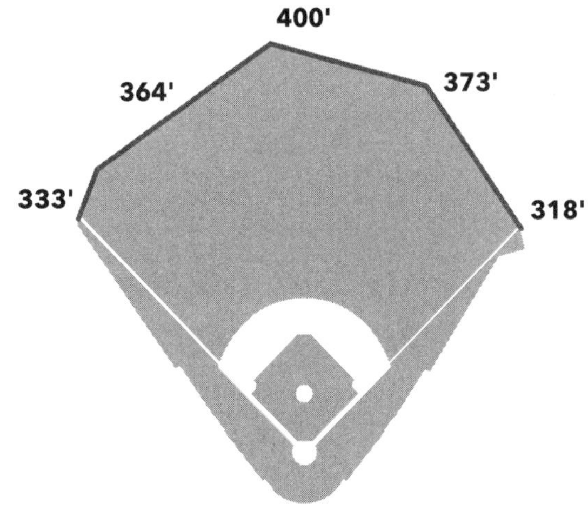

Outfield wall profile: **7'** to **21'**

Three-Year Park Factors

Runs	Runs/RH	Runs/LH	HR/RH	HR/LH
108	123	117	130	124

Top Hitter WARP	7.3	Manny Machado
Top Pitcher WARP	2.0	Zach Britton
Top Prospect	Hunter Harvey	

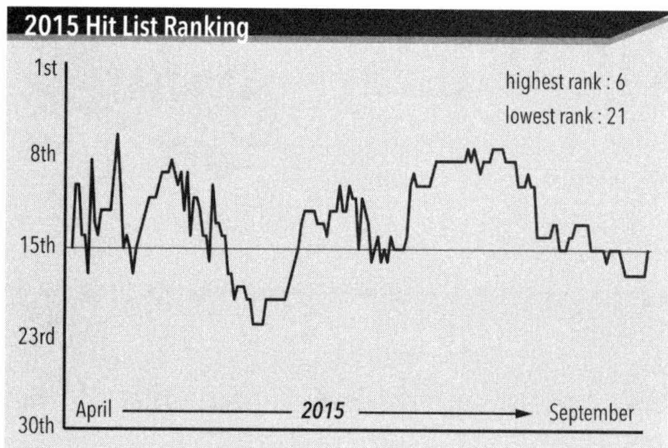

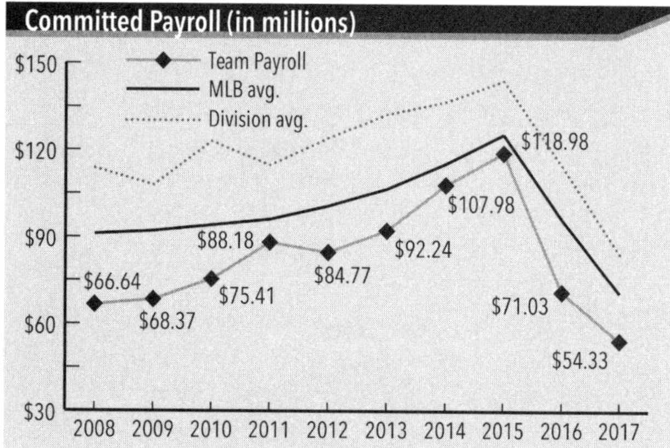

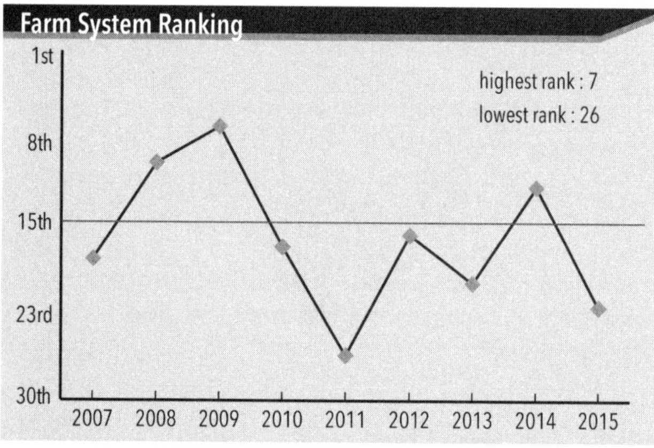

Personnel

General Manager: Dan Duquette

Manager: Buck Showalter

We're not counting Jake Arrieta, the man who just won the 2015 Cy Young Award with the Cubs, for the obvious reason that he only became a good pitcher when he changed organizations and was allowed to throw the pitches he wanted to throw, the way he wanted to throw them.

Duquette's team, which started its work in the 2011-12 offseason, can take partial credit, at most, for those four successes. Machado was the no. 3 pick in his draft and debuted in 2012; Wieters was a no. 5 pick and made the All-Star team in 2011; Britton came up in 2011 and failed as a starter in both the majors and Triple-A for three years before the organization finally made him an ace reliever in 2014; and Johnson had 256 innings with a 145 ERA+ out of the bullpen in the four years leading up to Duquette's hiring—making him a closer was not exactly a stroke of genius. That's two obvious studs on whom Duquette's regime put the finishing touches, one desperation move to the bullpen and one long-established relief pitcher.

Contrast those with the current regime's first-round picks: Kevin Gausman (2012), Hunter Harvey (2013), Josh Hart (2013) and D.J. Stewart (2015). Gausman, a polished pitcher out of LSU, was only supposed to need work on something bendy to complement a devastating fastball-changeup combination. Instead he's bounced all over the minors, moved constantly between starting and relief and struggled to command the two pitches he already had when he was drafted. Harvey had a promising start to 2014 in the minors and has been hurt ever since. Hart played at High-A as a 20-year-old center fielder last year, but the sub-.600 OPS he puts up every season means he's not earning his promotions with performance. It's too early to say anything about Stewart, but if you wanted to be uncharitable you'd point out that the Florida State outfielder didn't hit in his 62-game introduction to pro ball.

But first-rounders aren't everything; what about the rest of those drafts? Here's where the real problem is: Those four guys basically are Baltimore's drafts. Baseball Prospectus' prospect team rates just three players drafted under Duquette as likely average-or-better major leaguers: Harvey (assuming health), catcher Chance Sisco and first baseman Trey Mancini. And despite taking eight college players in their first 10 picks, first baseman Christian Walker is the only Orioles 2012 draftee aside from Gausman to see the majors—he got thimbles of coffee the last two seasons.

It's only been four drafts, though. Has the front office done a better job developing the previous regime's prospects?

The 2008 draft saw seven players make the big leagues, including a guy who should be the poster child for the success of the system: catcher Caleb Joseph, drafted in the seventh round. Joseph arrived on the scene in 2014 after Matt Wieters went down with an arm injury that eventually required Tommy John surgery; he was... serviceable. Sure, Joseph has never caught over 100 games in an MLB season, will be 30 next year and has a career TAv of .237, but he's either a good defensive catcher or, if you like pitch-framing data, a great one, so it's okay if the bat doesn't play so well.

But here's the thing: The Orioles' development people hated Joseph's defense. In 2013, when the starting catcher was an uninspiring and arguably overworked Wieters (.262 TAv and 85 more innings caught than the next-highest total) and the backup was a galling mishmash of Taylor Teagarden, Steve Clevenger and Chris Snyder, Joseph was in Double-A with an .840 OPS in 135 games at age 27, a performance practically begging for at least a promotion to Triple-A, if not an immediate slot in the Orioles' catcher/first base/designated hitter carousel. When fans asked, though, the word from the beat writers was: The Orioles don't think Joseph's fundamentals are good enough to catch in the majors. His frame is too big. He's not an option. Maybe those anonymous quotes spurred Joseph to improve his game, or maybe he improved in spite of them. But maybe his defensive game was never a problem to begin with.

Besides Joseph, Duquette's team inherited the 2008 first-rounder, Brian Matusz, after he put up the worst ERA for a starting pitcher (min. 10 starts) in recorded history. They made him into a moderately successful LOOGY. The other five major leaguers from that draft are Xavier Avery, L.J. Hoes, Kyle Hudson, Chris Herrmann and Jason Gurka. They were without impact.

The 2009 draft gave Baltimore Mychal Givens. He flunked out as a shortstop, and the regime deserves credit for managing his 2013 conversion to pitching because, what do you know, he was pretty good last year! Thirty innings of high-strikeout, low-walk baseball and a likely spot in the middle innings for 2016—not bad for the individual. The flip side? He's his draft year's sole big-league representative.

The next draft was better because it has Machado, but it also has nobody else; 21st-rounder Scott Copeland was released just over two years after signing but managed 15 bad innings for the Blue Jays last year. Neat!

Finally, ex-GM Andy MacPhail's last draft, in 2011, has produced four major leaguers so far: Dylan Bundy, Mike Wright, Tyler Wilson and Zach Davies. Bundy remains a good prospect, but he signed a major-league contract out of the draft. Thus the Orioles find themselves without minor-league options on a pitcher whose high-minors experience totals 38 solid innings in Double-A because of Tommy John surgery and calcification in his shoulder. Davies put up the second-best ERA of any starting pitcher on the Orioles last season, except he did it for the Brewers after being traded for Gerardo Parra and his .218 TAv. Wilson and Wright appeared for Baltimore in very limited action as spot starters and occasional long men. If you sum their K/9 rates, you get something a bit above the league average.

The amateur draft is a major gamble, and very, very few picks ever pan out. That's why a lot of teams supplement it with international signings. Baltimore hasn't. After being banned from South Korea for the Seong-min Kim debacle, the most inspiring international free agent the Orioles have signed is Cuban outfielder Dariel Alvarez, whose only standout tool is power. He's been unimpressive in his brief time in the majors. Jomar Reyes is also worth noting as a top-five prospect in the Orioles' system, but he's a 19-year-old third baseman who won't stay at that corner for long.

If the Orioles are going to continue emphasizing veteran continuity on the major-league roster and taking an extremely cautious wait-and-see approach to free agency, if their biggest concern over the first two months of the 2015-16 winter is the re-signing of reliever Darren O'Day, if their most aggressive move is acquiring a poor man's Chris Davis in Mark Trumbo, then the organization has to effectively turn its draft picks into contributors. Over the last eight draft classes, there has been an institutional failure to make that happen.

There is no longer any margin for error in Baltimore; the AL East is awake. The Red Sox have remembered they're a premiere franchise, hiring Dave Dombrowski to run baseball operations and, accordingly, spending the blood and treasure to acquire Craig Kimbrel and David Price. The Rays continue to draft, sign and develop young pitching with infuriating consistency. Despite the tumult in their front office, the Blue Jays should still have the best offense in baseball. Even this new, underwhelming version of the Yankees manages to win 85 games and fight for a Wild Card, and in any event they have $60 million coming off their payroll after 2016.

And the Orioles? They'll hope that Chris Tillman bounces back into at least an acceptable MLB starter, and that Gausman takes the step forward that Arrieta never did in Baltimore. They'll hope they can maximize Trumbo's value as a slugger in Camden Yards, that J.J. Hardy stays healthy and that Jonathan Schoop's injury-shortened 2015 was a breakout, not a flash in the pan. They'll hope Givens is as good as his 30-inning stint last year, and that none of the other young pitchers are as bad as theirs. They will hope for Chaz Roe to be a contributor.

It is tempting to posit that the Orioles are still addicted to the spirit of 2012—constantly chasing 99th percentile outcomes, assuming the legacy of Lew Ford, Nate McLouth and Robert Andino means that all their fringe guys will play well when it matters—but it's more likely the case that Baltimore's front office just doesn't ever, ever want to be on the wrong side of paying a man too much money to play professional baseball. In some places, in some times, if Bundy and Harvey hadn't gotten hurt, that might have been enough.

But the modern AL East is neither that time nor that

place, and both of those pitchers play for a team that hasn't successfully groomed a starter since Erik Bedard. If you can't develop, you have to spend. The doom hanging over the heads of the Orioles is this: They will get what they pay for. ■

—Jonathan Bernhardt (@jonbernhardt) is a freelance baseball writer whose work has appeared at Sports on Earth, The Guardian, VICE Sports and, of course, Baseball Prospectus.

Hitters

Chris Davis 1B

Born: 3/17/86 Age: 30 Bats: L Throws: R Height: 6'3" Weight: 230

YEAR	TEAM	LVL	AGE	PA	R	2B	3B	HR	RBI	BB	K	SB	CS	AVG/OBP/SLG	TAv	BABIP	BRR	FRAA	WARP
2013	BAL	MLB	27	673	103	42	1	53	138	72	199	4	1	.286/.370/.634	.358	.336	1.9	1B(155): -7.6	7.0
2014	BAL	MLB	28	525	65	16	0	26	72	60	173	2	1	.196/.300/.404	.272	.242	-3.1	1B(115): -3.1, 3B(21): 0.6	0.7
2015	BAL	MLB	29	670	100	31	0	47	117	84	208	2	3	.262/.361/.562	.316	.319	-0.9	1B(111): -4.9, RF(30): -2.4	3.9
2016	*BAL*	*MLB*	*30*	*600*	*86*	*26*	*1*	*38*	*103*	*57*	*186*	*3*	*2*	*.257/.335/.523*	*.295*	*.316*	*-0.7*	*1B -6, RF -3*	*2.2*
2017	*BAL*	*MLB*	*31*	*545*	*81*	*25*	*0*	*32*	*89*	*51*	*165*	*2*	*1*	*.252/.329/.503*	*.283*	*.309*	*-0.7*	*1B -5, RF -3*	*1.8*

Breakout: 0% Improve: 63% Collapse: 2% Attrition: 6% MLB: 98% *Comparables: Ryan Howard, Adam Dunn, Harmon Killebrew*

The disparity between his 2013 and '14 seasons was so wide that the lazy analysis of "he'll hit somewhere between" was nigh unavoidable. Davis acquiesced for much of the year, and on July 28th his .240/.323/.480 slash was just six points askew of PECOTA's 50th percentile projection. And then he caught fire: 15 home runs in the span of 23 games, 35 runs driven in, a slugging percentage raised by 100 points. He continued to mash for the rest of the season, and when the dust had settled Davis led the American League with a .300 ISO and topped the majors in homers for the second time in three years. It was less a fantastic walk year than a fantastic walk half, but Davis' raw power is unquestioned and his Adderall drama is in the rearview. Now he can focus on the game and collect his considerable paycheck.

Ryan Flaherty UT

Born: 7/27/86 Age: 29 Bats: L Throws: R Height: 6'3" Weight: 220

YEAR	TEAM	LVL	AGE	PA	R	2B	3B	HR	RBI	BB	K	SB	CS	AVG/OBP/SLG	TAv	BABIP	BRR	FRAA	WARP
2013	BAL	MLB	26	271	28	11	0	10	27	19	62	2	0	.224/.293/.390	.247	.259	0.6	2B(65): -1.1, SS(9): -1.4	0.1
2013	NOR	AAA	26	35	4	1	0	2	5	1	8	0	0	.265/.286/.471	.287	.292	0.5	2B(8): -1.3	0.1
2014	BAL	MLB	27	312	33	15	1	7	32	22	68	1	0	.221/.288/.356	.242	.266	0.8	3B(43): 1.7, 2B(30): 1.5	0.6
2015	BAL	MLB	28	301	34	8	3	9	31	26	81	0	0	.202/.281/.356	.220	.251	0.7	2B(56): -1.9, SS(15): -0.8	-0.6
2016	*BAL*	*MLB*	*29*	*211*	*23*	*8*	*1*	*7*	*25*	*15*	*51*	*1*	*0*	*.228/.291/.390*	*.236*	*.269*	*0.3*	*2B -1, SS -1*	*0.0*
2017	*BAL*	*MLB*	*30*	*243*	*29*	*9*	*1*	*8*	*28*	*18*	*60*	*0*	*0*	*.223/.289/.382*	*.234*	*.264*	*0.2*	*2B -1, SS -2*	*0.0*

Breakout: 1% Improve: 45% Collapse: 9% Attrition: 15% MLB: 100% *Comparables: Felipe Lopez, Ryne Sandberg, Brandon Phillips*

Flaherty's 2015 performance was a dead ringer for the previous season, and it would take some serious wishcasting to expect anything higher than a .300 OBP at this point. He was helpless against breaking pitches, finishing 2-for-49 with 30 strikeouts in at-bats that concluded with a breaker—which explains his dedicated approach to attacking early fastballs. Flaherty has been bleeding out power since his mid-20s while the empty swings have become more frequent, and his only real value is the utility to play any of the non-battery positions on the diamond.

J.J. Hardy SS

Born: 8/19/82 Age: 33 Bats: R Throws: R Height: 6'1" Weight: 200

YEAR	TEAM	LVL	AGE	PA	R	2B	3B	HR	RBI	BB	K	SB	CS	AVG/OBP/SLG	TAv	BABIP	BRR	FRAA	WARP
2013	BAL	MLB	30	644	66	27	0	25	76	38	73	2	1	.263/.306/.433	.268	.263	-3.8	SS(159): -12.1	1.5
2014	BAL	MLB	31	569	56	28	0	9	52	29	104	0	0	.268/.309/.372	.256	.317	-0.9	SS(141): 1.9	2.2
2015	BAL	MLB	32	437	45	14	0	8	37	20	88	0	0	.219/.253/.311	.209	.257	-2.1	SS(114): -2.0	-0.9
2016	*BAL*	*MLB*	*33*	*563*	*56*	*24*	*1*	*17*	*68*	*29*	*93*	*1*	*0*	*.251/.291/.398*	*.240*	*.272*	*-1.9*	*SS -6*	*0.7*
2017	*BAL*	*MLB*	*34*	*466*	*51*	*18*	*1*	*13*	*51*	*22*	*82*	*0*	*0*	*.238/.275/.373*	*.229*	*.262*	*-1.8*	*SS -5*	*0.2*

Breakout: 0% Improve: 37% Collapse: 6% Attrition: 7% MLB: 94% *Comparables: Alex Gonzalez, Edgar Renteria, Jason Bartlett*

A left-shoulder injury landed Hardy on the disabled list coming out of spring training and likely compromised him at the plate upon his return. It was a recurrence of the labrum tear that he endured back in 2004, and he told MASN's Roch Kubatko in October that "it's weak, it's not as strong as I'd like it to be, so I'm protecting it. And when I say protecting it, it's just like I'm not letting go with my top hand if I get fooled by a pitch, where before I can let it go. It's hard to hit and not get extended."

But he remained committed to avoiding offseason surgery, citing his experiences with a similar surgery 12 years ago ("it was miserable"). With more than $28 million remaining on his contract through 2017 (including a 2018 buyout), Hardy will need to be tremendous defensively to justify not just the contract but the roster spot. But last year's Fielding Bible voters dropped him to his lowest finish (eighth) since 2011, and FRAA isn't optimistic.

Jonah Heim C

Born: 6/27/95 Age: 21 Bats: B Throws: R Height: 6'3" Weight: 190

YEAR	TEAM	LVL	AGE	PA	R	2B	3B	HR	RBI	BB	K	SB	CS	AVG/OBP/SLG	TAv	BABIP	BRR	FRAA	WARP
2014	ABE	A-	19	73	2	2	0	1	2	2	15	0	0	.143/.164/.214	.138	.164	0.2	C(18): -0.1	-0.6
2015	DEL	A	20	157	13	8	1	1	16	6	26	0	0	.248/.280/.336	.229	.293	-1.0	C(35): -0.7	-0.1
2016	*BAL*	*MLB*	*21*	*250*	*20*	*10*	*1*	*5*	*22*	*8*	*64*	*0*	*0*	*.206/.235/.311*	*.189*	*.258*	*-0.3*	*C -0*	*-0.9*
2017	*BAL*	*MLB*	*22*	*229*	*22*	*9*	*1*	*5*	*22*	*9*	*57*	*0*	*0*	*.212/.247/.325*	*.202*	*.261*	*-0.4*	*C 0*	*-0.4*

Breakout: 1% Improve: 3% Collapse: 1% Attrition: 3% MLB: 3% *Comparables: Elias Diaz, Miguel Gonzalez, Pedro Severino*

Hard work and an up-the-middle home will do a lot for a prospect's stock, but when the bat doesn't profile as an impact tool, they're *asked* to do a lot. Heim shows aptitude for catching, with strong lateral movement, a feel for framing and coordinated footwork. His arm strength is a plus, but his accuracy can get loose at times. His offensive game lags behind his defensive promise, which isn't surprising for a kid raised in an upstate New York hamlet called Snyder, which gets "measurable precipitation" 166 days a year. Sure, Heim gained countless hours working on his squat by a fireplace, but it's hard to replace reps against good velocity.

Adam Jones CF

Born: 8/1/85 Age: 30 Bats: R Throws: R Height: 6'2" Weight: 215

YEAR	TEAM	LVL	AGE	PA	R	2B	3B	HR	RBI	BB	K	SB	CS	AVG/OBP/SLG	TAv	BABIP	BRR	FRAA	WARP
2013	BAL	MLB	27	689	100	35	1	33	108	25	136	14	3	.285/.318/.493	.294	.314	2.2	CF(156): -16.3	3.0
2014	BAL	MLB	28	682	88	30	2	29	96	19	133	7	1	.281/.311/.469	.291	.311	2.1	CF(155): -1.5	4.3
2015	BAL	MLB	29	581	74	25	3	27	82	24	102	3	1	.269/.308/.474	.259	.286	1.4	CF(134): 7.6	2.7
2016	*BAL*	*MLB*	*30*	*671*	*84*	*31*	*2*	*30*	*98*	*27*	*127*	*8*	*2*	*.279/.317/.481*	*.276*	*.304*	*1.4*	*CF -7*	*2.9*
2017	*BAL*	*MLB*	*31*	*577*	*77*	*28*	*2*	*26*	*84*	*23*	*112*	*6*	*2*	*.278/.315/.481*	*.274*	*.304*	*1.1*	*CF -6*	*2.8*

Breakout: 2% Improve: 45% Collapse: 3% Attrition: 11% MLB: 100% *Comparables: Hunter Pence, Corey Hart, Alex Rios*

If you throw it, Jones will swing. He swung at the highest frequency of strikes in baseball (87 percent) as well as the highest rate of overall pitches (61 percent), an ongoing trend of challenging the defense that ups the ante on his ridiculously consistent production over the past six seasons. He did break a couple of strings in 2015, as it was the first time since 2009 that Jones failed to play at least 149 games and the first time he didn't hit above .280, but otherwise Mr. Consistency was good for his usual .780 OPS and avoided the disabled list again. It wasn't a single injury but various dings and dents—including knocks to his ankle, shoulder and head—that kept him out of the lineup more times in 2015 than the previous four seasons combined.

Caleb Joseph C

Born: 6/18/86 Age: 30 Bats: R Throws: R Height: 6'3" Weight: 180

YEAR	TEAM	LVL	AGE	PA	R	2B	3B	HR	RBI	BB	K	SB	CS	AVG/OBP/SLG	TAv	BABIP	BRR	FRAA	WARP
2013	BOW	AA	27	570	74	31	2	22	97	39	92	4	2	.299/.346/.494	.302	.321	0.8	C(64): 14.5, LF(16): -1.5	5.8
2014	NOR	AAA	28	95	8	7	0	2	11	3	22	0	0	.261/.284/.402	.254	.324	0.6	C(21): 3.6	0.8
2014	BAL	MLB	28	275	22	9	0	9	28	17	69	0	1	.207/.264/.354	.231	.246	-1.4	C(78): 16.1, 1B(4): -0.0	2.0
2015	BAL	MLB	29	355	38	16	1	11	49	27	72	0	0	.234/.299/.394	.242	.269	-1.5	C(94): 10.9, 1B(1): 0.1	2.0
2016	*BAL*	*MLB*	*30*	*97*	*10*	*4*	*0*	*3*	*12*	*5*	*21*	*0*	*0*	*.244/.290/.410*	*.242*	*.279*	*-0.3*	*C 3*	*0.6*
2017	*BAL*	*MLB*	*31*	*291*	*33*	*12*	*1*	*9*	*34*	*17*	*66*	*0*	*0*	*.234/.281/.387*	*.233*	*.271*	*-0.9*	*C 9*	*1.5*

Breakout: 3% Improve: 20% Collapse: 9% Attrition: 22% MLB: 62% *Comparables: Robby Hammock, Javier Valentin, Michael McKenry*

YEAR	TEAM	P. COUNT	FRM RUNS	BLK RUNS	THRW RUNS	TOT RUNS
2013	BOW	8712	15.8	-1.8	-0.2	13.9
2014	BAL	10859	13.1	-0.2	1.3	14.2
2014	NOR	3082	3.1	0.0	0.6	3.7
2015	BAL	13197	10.0	0.1	0.5	10.5
2016	*BAL*	*3733*	*3.1*	*-0.2*	*0.1*	*3.0*
2017	*BAL*	*11212*	*8.7*	*-0.7*	*0.2*	*8.2*

Plenty of players enjoy a hot week at some point during the season, but Joseph has added a twist to the conventional path, having caught fire during the *same* week for two years in a row. He hit five homers in five consecutive games played from August 2nd to 9th of 2014, and last year posted multi-hit games in all four of his starts from August 1st to 8th, with three jacks and three doubles. It's probably a fluke, but DFS gamers might target Caleb Joseph in the first week of August 2016... just in case.

Manny Machado 3B

Born: 7/6/92 Age: 23 Bats: R Throws: R Height: 6'3" Weight: 185

YEAR	TEAM	LVL	AGE	PA	R	2B	3B	HR	RBI	BB	K	SB	CS	AVG/OBP/SLG	TAv	BABIP	BRR	FRAA	WARP
2013	BAL	MLB	20	710	88	51	3	14	71	29	113	6	7	.283/.314/.432	.268	.322	0.7	3B(156): 27.3	6.0
2014	BAL	MLB	21	354	38	14	0	12	32	20	68	2	0	.278/.324/.431	.274	.317	-1.2	3B(82): 7.7	2.4
2015	BAL	MLB	22	713	102	30	1	35	86	70	111	20	8	.286/.359/.502	.292	.297	3.4	3B(156): 21.3, SS(7): -0.8	7.3
2016	*BAL*	*MLB*	*23*	*630*	*87*	*33*	*3*	*23*	*77*	*42*	*104*	*11*	*5*	*.283/.334/.469*	*.277*	*.307*	*1.0*	*3B 20*	*5.3*
2017	*BAL*	*MLB*	*24*	*581*	*78*	*30*	*2*	*23*	*81*	*42*	*94*	*11*	*5*	*.285/.340/.479*	*.281*	*.306*	*1.3*	*3B 19*	*5.6*

Breakout: 4% Improve: 54% Collapse: 0% Attrition: 3% MLB: 97% *Comparables: Ryan Zimmerman, Gordon Beckham, Brett Lawrie*

The legend is growing. Machado didn't just come back from knee surgery (his second in two years), he came back as the bionic man. He possessed the same elite defense that he had before the injury. He added speed to his game, as the player with 10 combined steals through his first three seasons (and with surgical scars on both knees) swiped 20 bags. And he started turning all those doubles into home runs, resulting in the first 30-homer, 20-steal season in Baltimore since Luke Perry was cool.

Just 23, Machado could probably move over to short and still be one of the top defenders in the league; meanwhile, he has the offensive clout to justify a position much further down the defensive spectrum. He took advantage of his home environs and its friendliness to right-handed pop, knocking 21 of his home runs at Camden Yards, and the burgeoning power profile likely means that 2015 was both the beginning and the end of his time as a leadoff hitter. One would imagine that a player coming back from major surgery could use a breather here or there, but Machado played every game and led the majors in plate appearances, making enemies in multiple cities along the way. Maybe that's the ultimate endorsement: He must be doing something right for Jon Papelbon to hate his guts.

Trey Mancini 1B

Born: 3/18/92 Age: 24 Bats: R Throws: R Height: 6'4" Weight: 215

YEAR	TEAM	LVL	AGE	PA	R	2B	3B	HR	RBI	BB	K	SB	CS	AVG/OBP/SLG	TAv	BABIP	BRR	FRAA	WARP
2013	ABE	A-	21	285	43	18	2	3	35	20	43	3	1	.328/.382/.449	.327	.379	0.1	1B(61): 9.6	3.4
2014	DEL	A	22	291	30	13	3	3	42	14	52	1	1	.317/.357/.422	.292	.378	-1.1	1B(66): 1.8	1.4
2014	FRD	A+	22	295	37	19	0	7	41	14	43	0	1	.251/.295/.396	.243	.273	-0.4	1B(69): -6.7	-1.0
2015	FRD	A+	23	217	28	14	3	8	32	9	35	4	2	.314/.341/.527	.299	.345	-0.1	1B(51): 2.9	1.5
2015	BOW	AA	23	354	60	29	3	13	57	22	58	2	1	.359/.395/.586	.340	.400	0.2	1B(75): -0.8	3.4
2016	*BAL*	*MLB*	*24*	*250*	*26*	*13*	*1*	*8*	*32*	*10*	*56*	*0*	*0*	*.264/.296/.431*	*.251*	*.312*	*-0.4*	*1B 0*	*0.1*
2017	*BAL*	*MLB*	*25*	*378*	*44*	*19*	*1*	*12*	*47*	*15*	*87*	*0*	*0*	*.262/.295/.429*	*.250*	*.311*	*-0.8*	*1B 0*	*0.3*

Breakout: 0% Improve: 11% Collapse: 15% Attrition: 24% MLB: 30% *Comparables: Wes Bankston, Mark Trumbo, Neftali Soto*

As Sam Fuld is to Wikipedia, Mancini is to the college team website bio: At Notre Dame, his stretched for 2,700 words, including 1,100 on his freshman campaign alone. ("Went 0-for-4 (.000) with the bases loaded.") He's coming off a breakout year, with a simplified swing that knocked Double-A pitching around and put Mancini on the third row of the big-league club's depth chart. The bat gives him more upside than Christian Walker, but his skill set can be summed up in four words: Hits, and that's it.

Ryan Mountcastle SS

Born: 2/18/97 Age: 19 Bats: R Throws: R Height: 6'3" Weight: 195

YEAR	TEAM	LVL	AGE	PA	R	2B	3B	HR	RBI	BB	K	SB	CS	AVG/OBP/SLG	TAv	BABIP	BRR	FRAA	WARP
2015	ABE	A-	18	34	2	0	0	1	5	0	10	0	1	.212/.206/.303	.193	.261	-0.5	SS(6): -1.0	-0.3
2016	*BAL*	*MLB*	*19*	*250*	*23*	*8*	*1*	*6*	*23*	*8*	*79*	*3*	*2*	*.199/.225/.314*	*.186*	*.265*	*-0.2*	*SS -1, 3B 0*	*-0.9*
2017	*BAL*	*MLB*	*20*	*331*	*31*	*12*	*1*	*8*	*33*	*9*	*104*	*5*	*3*	*.207/.231/.331*	*.198*	*.274*	*0.0*	*SS -1, 3B 0*	*-0.6*

Breakout: 0% Improve: 0% Collapse: 0% Attrition: 0% MLB: 0% *Comparables: Hernan Perez, Arismendy Alcantara, Carlos Rivero*

Mountcastle can make the easy plays and has an accurate enough arm. *Whoa, fellas, slow down the hype train!* Indeed. He's got middling foot speed and his physical projection suggests a goldfish's lifespan at the position. His swing gets long and it's going to need some work. He can find the barrel, so there's some potential here, but not the kind you'd want with the same overall pick (no. 36) that landed Johnny Bench and Randy Johnson.

Cedric Mullins CF

Born: 10/1/94 Age: 21 Bats: B Throws: L Height: 5'8" Weight: 175

YEAR	TEAM	LVL	AGE	PA	R	2B	3B	HR	RBI	BB	K	SB	CS	AVG/OBP/SLG	TAv	BABIP	BRR	FRAA	WARP
2015	ABE	A-	20	309	34	15	5	2	32	22	33	17	4	.264/.333/.375	.293	.293	0.9	CF(66): -9.5	1.2
2016	*BAL*	*MLB*	*21*	*250*	*25*	*10*	*1*	*5*	*23*	*12*	*57*	*5*	*2*	*.221/.265/.340*	*.211*	*.265*	*0.2*	*CF -3*	*-0.7*
2017	*BAL*	*MLB*	*22*	*320*	*33*	*12*	*2*	*7*	*32*	*17*	*69*	*7*	*3*	*.229/.277/.353*	*.222*	*.272*	*0.6*	*CF -4*	*0.0*

Breakout: 3% Improve: 4% Collapse: 0% Attrition: 3% MLB: 4% *Comparables: Abraham Almonte, Ben Revere, Cedric Hunter*

He's on the short end, but Mullins has some pretty elite company in the 5-8 club. Now, he doesn't have the profile to outproduce 'Ye or Eminem, and he couldn't reach Robin Williams with a ladder. Given his feel for the barrel, plus speed and defense in center field, there's a chance that Mullins can work his way into Mark Ruffalo territory, a solid performer with limitations but a fair bit of charm. That is to say, he's no Muammar Gaddafi.

Jimmy Paredes 3B

Born: 11/25/88 Age: 27 Bats: B Throws: R Height: 6'3" Weight: 200

YEAR	TEAM	LVL	AGE	PA	R	2B	3B	HR	RBI	BB	K	SB	CS	AVG/OBP/SLG	TAv	BABIP	BRR	FRAA	WARP
2013	OKL	AAA	24	358	50	21	6	8	37	28	67	16	7	.287/.345/.462	.284	.340	6.2	RF(35): -2.9, SS(20): 2.2	2.6
2013	HOU	MLB	24	135	8	4	0	1	10	6	44	4	4	.192/.231/.248	.189	.280	-0.3	RF(39): -5.0, 2B(3): 0.2	-1.3
2014	KCA	MLB	25	10	3	0	0	0	0	0	3	2	0	.200/.200/.200	.162	.286	0.1	3B(3): -0.3, 2B(2): -0.0	-0.1
2014	OMA	AAA	25	280	37	18	4	5	36	11	78	17	1	.305/.332/.457	.275	.414	1.3	3B(28): 3.0, SS(14): -1.5	1.6
2014	BAL	MLB	25	55	9	4	0	2	8	2	13	2	0	.302/.327/.491	.297	.368	0.2	3B(13): -0.1, 2B(1): -0.0	0.4
2014	NOR	AAA	25	140	11	7	1	3	23	6	31	4	0	.258/.286/.394	.228	.310	0.7	3B(27): -3.6, 2B(5): -0.2	-0.4
2015	BAL	MLB	26	384	46	17	2	10	42	19	111	4	4	.275/.310/.416	.253	.369	-1.0	3B(8): -0.3, 2B(6): -0.3	0.0
2016	*BAL*	*MLB*	*27*	*614*	*65*	*28*	*4*	*14*	*66*	*25*	*159*	*17*	*6*	*.257/.287/.395*	*.238*	*.325*	*0.2*	*2B -0, 3B -0*	*-0.2*
2017	*BAL*	*MLB*	*28*	*544*	*58*	*26*	*4*	*12*	*59*	*23*	*143*	*15*	*6*	*.257/.289/.396*	*.239*	*.330*	*0.6*	*2B 0, 3B 0*	*0.8*

Breakout: 4% Improve: 18% Collapse: 10% Attrition: 20% MLB: 45% *Comparables: Lance Niekro, Jeff Baker, Joe Mahoney*

The strike zone belongs to the pitcher when Paredes digs in the batter's box. He struck out nearly six times for every walk last season, with a 29 percent strikeout rate that would have ranked second in the American League (behind Chris Davis) if Paredes had merited enough plate appearances to qualify. He managed hits in 26 of his first 29 games and on May 23rd was hitting .352/.383/.590 in 128 plate appearances, but he wilted to .237/.273/.328 with a strikeout for every three plate appearances after that. There's some emerging pop here—10 home runs effectively tripled his career total—but his defense isn't good enough to support a superutility rep.

Gerardo Parra RF

Born: 5/6/87 Age: 29 Bats: L Throws: L Height: 5'11" Weight: 210

YEAR	TEAM	LVL	AGE	PA	R	2B	3B	HR	RBI	BB	K	SB	CS	AVG/OBP/SLG	TAv	BABIP	BRR	FRAA	WARP
2013	ARI	MLB	26	663	79	43	4	10	48	48	100	10	10	.268/.323/.403	.257	.305	0.8	RF(123): 23.1, CF(33): 2.7	4.1
2014	MIL	MLB	27	134	13	4	1	3	10	8	28	4	2	.268/.318/.390	.249	.326	0.1	LF(27): 0.1, CF(9): -0.1	0.5
2014	ARI	MLB	27	440	51	18	3	6	30	24	72	5	5	.259/.305/.362	.248	.300	1.1	RF(102): 0.8, CF(3): 0.8	0.5
2015	MIL	MLB	28	351	53	24	5	9	31	20	57	9	3	.328/.369/.517	.309	.372	-1.8	LF(46): -2.2, CF(31): 0.1	2.3
2015	BAL	MLB	28	238	30	12	0	5	20	8	35	5	1	.237/.268/.357	.218	.259	-0.1	RF(47): -0.4, CF(10): 1.1	-0.4
2016	*BAL*	*MLB*	*29*	*600*	*75*	*29*	*4*	*13*	*59*	*39*	*100*	*13*	*7*	*.272/.324/.412*	*.254*	*.306*	*0.0*	*RF 2, LF 1*	*1.8*
2017	*BAL*	*MLB*	*30*	*547*	*63*	*27*	*3*	*12*	*59*	*36*	*91*	*10*	*6*	*.269/.322/.406*	*.251*	*.304*	*0.5*	*RF 2, LF 1*	*1.8*

Breakout: 2% Improve: 43% Collapse: 4% Attrition: 6% MLB: 98% *Comparables: Melky Cabrera, Rusty Greer, Gene Woodling*

In 2013, Defensive Runs Saved assigned Parra a +41 in right field, which (if you believe it) is the best season by a right fielder in history. The next year he was -1; last year, -10. Partly that's a story about defensive metrics, but Gold Glove voters, UZR, our own FRAA and the Fielding Bible have all pretty much agreed about the trajectory (if not quite the scale). More than that, it's the story of Parra, who has a lot of tools that show up in fantastic bursts but never seem to show up all at once. In 2015, with Parra taking a more aggressive approach on pitches in the zone, it was his power's turn to shine, until roughly exactly the day Milwaukee pitched him to Baltimore. That made it the second year in a row he got flipped for long-term value on July 31st, and the second year in a row he struggled with his new club. His value going forward largely depends on whether we ignore the more recent negative readings of his defense as noisy outputs from inexact metrics.

Steve Pearce OF

Born: 4/13/83 Age: 33 Bats: R Throws: R Height: 5'11" Weight: 200

YEAR	TEAM	LVL	AGE	PA	R	2B	3B	HR	RBI	BB	K	SB	CS	AVG/OBP/SLG	TAv	BABIP	BRR	FRAA	WARP
2013	BAL	MLB	30	138	14	7	0	4	13	15	25	1	0	.261/.362/.420	.301	.300	-0.7	LF(15): -0.6, RF(3): 0.0	0.6
2014	BAL	MLB	31	383	51	26	0	21	49	40	76	5	0	.293/.373/.556	.346	.322	-2.1	1B(51): 7.5, LF(35): 4.1	5.0
2015	BAL	MLB	32	325	42	13	1	15	40	23	69	1	1	.218/.289/.422	.244	.232	2.0	LF(41): -0.5, 1B(28): 1.0	0.3
2016	*BAL*	*MLB*	*33*	*319*	*39*	*15*	*1*	*13*	*44*	*29*	*66*	*2*	*1*	*.254/.331/.452*	*.274*	*.284*	*-0.5*	*LF 2, 1B 2*	*1.7*
2017	*BAL*	*MLB*	*34*	*257*	*33*	*12*	*0*	*9*	*32*	*22*	*55*	*1*	*1*	*.245/.321/.419*	*.259*	*.281*	*-0.4*	*LF 1, 1B 2*	*1.1*

Breakout: 0% Improve: 25% Collapse: 6% Attrition: 9% MLB: 90% *Comparables: Ryan Ludwick, Milton Bradley, Sid Gordon*

At least it's never boring. A year after overshooting his 90th percentile projection, Pearce undershot his 10th percentile. He played the outfield, some first base and even a handful of games at the keystone (for the first time in his professional career), as he tried to convince Buck Showalter to justify writing "Pearce" on the lineup card long enough for him to figure this thing out. The destruction of southpaws was the predominant aspect of his 2014 breakout, but he summoned Mendoza for a .623 OPS against them in 2015. The stat line gives the impression that Pearce reverted to old tactics, but there was at least one subtle improvement in his game: He figured out the curveball. He hit six bombs off the bender last season, after failing to leave the yard against *any* of the 500-plus curves he had seen in his career.

Nolan Reimold LF

Born: 10/12/83 Age: 32 Bats: R Throws: R Height: 6'4" Weight: 205

YEAR	TEAM	LVL	AGE	PA	R	2B	3B	HR	RBI	BB	K	SB	CS	AVG/OBP/SLG	TAv	BABIP	BRR	FRAA	WARP
2013	BOW	AA	29	51	3	0	1	1	5	4	13	0	0	.196/.255/.304	.201	.242	0.0	LF(7): -0.7	-0.3
2013	BAL	MLB	29	140	17	3	0	5	12	10	41	0	1	.195/.250/.336	.226	.238	1.3	LF(11): 1.5	0.0
2014	BOW	AA	30	69	10	3	0	2	9	12	13	1	1	.315/.420/.481	.348	.357	-0.9	LF(8): 0.4	0.7
2014	ARI	MLB	30	18	2	1	0	1	4	0	10	0	0	.294/.278/.529	.280	.571	0.0	LF(4): -0.1	0.1
2014	TOR	MLB	30	60	3	4	0	2	9	6	22	1	0	.212/.283/.404	.265	.300	0.4	RF(10): 1.0	0.3
2015	BAL	MLB	31	195	24	5	1	6	20	23	47	0	0	.247/.344/.394	.260	.308	-0.2	LF(37): -1.8, RF(13): 0.7	0.2
2015	NOR	AAA	31	226	25	13	0	2	15	26	42	5	1	.274/.363/.371	.270	.338	1.2	LF(37): 1.3, RF(6): -0.7	0.9
2016	*BAL*	*MLB*	*32*	*304*	*34*	*12*	*1*	*10*	*38*	*27*	*77*	*2*	*1*	*.239/.312/.405*	*.254*	*.290*	*0.8*	*RF 2, LF 0*	*0.8*
2017	*BAL*	*MLB*	*33*	*269*	*32*	*10*	*1*	*9*	*31*	*24*	*69*	*1*	*0*	*.232/.304/.388*	*.246*	*.285*	*0.6*	*RF 2, LF 0*	*0.8*

Breakout: 1% Improve: 21% Collapse: 4% Attrition: 16% MLB: 71% *Comparables: Fred Lewis, Josh Phelps, Casey Blake*

Reimold found his way back home after a year spent abroad, splitting time between Baltimore and Norfolk, AKA the two places on earth where everyone knows his name. His platoon splits have been essentially neutral for most of his career, but he favored lefties by 100 points of OPS in 2015 and Buck Showalter rewarded him with time in the leadoff spot against southpaws down the stretch.

Jomar Reyes 3B

Born: 2/20/97 Age: 19 Bats: R Throws: R Height: 6'3" Weight: 220

YEAR	TEAM	LVL	AGE	PA	R	2B	3B	HR	RBI	BB	K	SB	CS	AVG/OBP/SLG	TAv	BABIP	BRR	FRAA	WARP
2015	DEL	A	18	335	36	27	4	5	44	18	73	1	0	.278/.334/.440	.309	.351	-3.4	3B(74): -6.5	1.8
2016	*BAL*	*MLB*	*19*	*250*	*22*	*11*	*1*	*6*	*27*	*9*	*72*	*0*	*0*	*.224/.261/.358*	*.219*	*.292*	*-0.3*	*3B -3*	*-0.8*
2017	*BAL*	*MLB*	*20*	*387*	*42*	*20*	*1*	*11*	*44*	*15*	*107*	*0*	*0*	*.232/.272/.386*	*.233*	*.296*	*-0.7*	*3B -4*	*-0.4*

Breakout: 0% Improve: 1% Collapse: 0% Attrition: 0% MLB: 1% *Comparables: Matt Dominguez, Cheslor Cuthbert, Miguel Sano*

Reyes has three flaws when it comes to baseball: He runs like a toddler on codeine, he fields like his glove is a Gucci flip flop and he takes batting practice to Lloyd's "You." And we can forgive it all, for Reyes possesses potential plus power, a hit tool that can get to average and a Kromuskit of an arm. He impressed after an aggressive assignment to Delmarva and his bat profiles to be a weapon at the major-league level, even at his eventual home at first.

Jonathan Schoop 2B

Born: 10/16/91 Age: 24 Bats: R Throws: R Height: 6'1" Weight: 225

YEAR	TEAM	LVL	AGE	PA	R	2B	3B	HR	RBI	BB	K	SB	CS	AVG/OBP/SLG	TAv	BABIP	BRR	FRAA	WARP
2013	NOR	AAA	21	289	30	11	0	9	34	13	55	1	2	.256/.301/.396	.247	.290	0.1	2B(48): -1.1, SS(20): 2.6	0.7
2013	BAL	MLB	21	15	5	0	0	1	1	1	2	0	0	.286/.333/.500	.257	.273	0.0	2B(4): -0.0	0.0
2014	BAL	MLB	22	481	48	18	0	16	45	13	122	2	0	.209/.244/.354	.220	.249	0.3	2B(123): 1.8, 3B(17): -1.5	-0.6
2015	BOW	AA	23	26	3	2	0	3	6	1	6	0	0	.240/.269/.680	.308	.188	-0.8	2B(7): 0.3	0.2
2015	BAL	MLB	23	321	34	17	0	15	39	9	79	2	0	.279/.306/.482	.271	.329	-2.9	2B(84): -0.0	1.0
2016	*BAL*	*MLB*	*24*	*516*	*60*	*23*	*1*	*22*	*69*	*18*	*123*	*2*	*1*	*.250/.285/.436*	*.251*	*.287*	*-1.4*	*2B 0*	*1.4*
2017	*BAL*	*MLB*	*25*	*455*	*56*	*19*	*0*	*20*	*61*	*18*	*108*	*2*	*1*	*.245/.285/.430*	*.249*	*.280*	*-1.4*	*2B 0*	*1.4*

Breakout: 4% Improve: 45% Collapse: 2% Attrition: 4% MLB: 99% *Comparables: Jorge Cantu, Howie Kendrick, Robinson Cano*

The Orioles have a knack for rostering right-handed batters with reverse platoon splits, and Schoop toes the company line. He has slugged 161 points higher against right-handed pitchers in his career, though that relative success has come at the expense of a walk rate that is cut from thin to anemic. Schoop hit 15 of his doubles and 13 of his homers against righties in roughly two-thirds of his 2015 plate appearances, joining the likes of Adam Jones and Manny Machado among Baltimore's reverse-splitted batsmen.

Chance Sisco C

Born: 2/24/95 Age: 21 Bats: L Throws: R Height: 6'2" Weight: 193

YEAR	TEAM	LVL	AGE	PA	R	2B	3B	HR	RBI	BB	K	SB	CS	AVG/OBP/SLG	TAv	BABIP	BRR	FRAA	WARP
2014	DEL	A	19	478	56	27	2	5	63	42	79	1	2	.340/.406/.448	.312	.406	-1.2	C(74): -2.0	4.0
2015	FRD	A+	20	300	30	12	3	4	26	33	41	8	1	.308/.387/.422	.299	.350	-0.7	C(57): -0.0	2.3
2015	BOW	AA	20	84	9	4	0	2	8	9	14	0	1	.257/.337/.392	.268	.293	-1.9	C(17): -0.1	0.2
2016	*BAL*	*MLB*	*21*	*250*	*24*	*11*	*1*	*5*	*27*	*19*	*57*	*1*	*0*	*.253/.313/.377*	*.241*	*.311*	*-0.4*	*C -8*	*-0.3*
2017	*BAL*	*MLB*	*22*	*331*	*39*	*15*	*1*	*8*	*36*	*26*	*74*	*1*	*0*	*.260/.322/.394*	*.250*	*.317*	*-0.6*	*C -10*	*0.1*

Breakout: 2% Improve: 10% Collapse: 0% Attrition: 8% MLB: 14% *Comparables: Travis d'Arnaud, Austin Hedges, Christian Vazquez*

YEAR	TEAM	P. COUNT	FRM RUNS	BLK RUNS	THRW RUNS	TOT RUNS
2015	BOW	2140	0.0	-0.1	0.1	0.0
2016	*BAL*	*8669*	*-5.5*	*-0.7*	*-1.3*	*-7.5*
2017	*BAL*	*11480*	*-7.6*	*-0.8*	*-1.7*	*-10.1*

Athleticism is an asset for catchers: It gives them the mobility to block pitches, helps with footwork and is just generally a net positive when donning the tools of ignorance. It's also not *quite* the same as having catching skills. Sisco has athleticism, but like a rapper with great rhymes and zero flow, he has very little feel for the position. That's okay, because, unlike catching skills, athleticism travels around the diamond, and Sisco's solid-average hit tool will allow him to play second, third or a corner-outfield spot in a pinch.

D.J. Stewart LF

Born: 11/30/93 Age: 22 Bats: L Throws: R Height: 6'0" Weight: 230

YEAR	TEAM	LVL	AGE	PA	R	2B	3B	HR	RBI	BB	K	SB	CS	AVG/OBP/SLG	TAv	BABIP	BRR	FRAA	WARP
2015	ABE	A-	21	268	25	8	2	6	24	23	52	4	1	.218/.288/.345	.247	.250	-0.3	LF(52): -0.3	0.1
2016	*BAL*	*MLB*	*22*	*250*	*23*	*8*	*1*	*7*	*25*	*14*	*70*	*0*	*0*	*.206/.253/.335*	*.205*	*.258*	*-0.3*	*LF 1*	*-0.7*
2017	*BAL*	*MLB*	*23*	*326*	*36*	*12*	*1*	*11*	*37*	*19*	*92*	*0*	*0*	*.212/.264/.365*	*.221*	*.264*	*-0.5*	*LF 1*	*-0.3*

Breakout: 1% Improve: 1% Collapse: 0% Attrition: 1% MLB: 1% *Comparables: Corey Dickerson, Daniel Dorn, Kyle Waldrop*

Coming into any situation with high expectations can be tough, and trying to live up to a high draft selection is a daunting way to start any career. But when it comes to Stewart, the 25th-overall pick last June, his debut would have been disappointing even for a 20th-round senior sign. His profile coming out of college was that of a polished hitter with a solid approach at the plate. But his swing was exposed quickly against professional pitching—against, frankly, the lowest-quality professional pitching. He's probably not .633-OPS-in-the-Penn-League bad, and there is a potential major leaguer in here. But his swing, poor athleticism, position and lack of carrying tool all point toward a best-case future as a role player.

Mark Trumbo 1B

Born: 1/16/86 Age: 30 Bats: R Throws: R Height: 6'4" Weight: 225

YEAR	TEAM	LVL	AGE	PA	R	2B	3B	HR	RBI	BB	K	SB	CS	AVG/OBP/SLG	TAv	BABIP	BRR	FRAA	WARP
2013	ANA	MLB	27	678	85	30	2	34	100	54	184	5	2	.234/.294/.453	.274	.273	-3.5	1B(123): 5.3, RF(19): -0.3	2.0
2014	ARI	MLB	28	362	37	15	1	14	61	28	89	2	3	.235/.293/.415	.254	.274	-2.2	1B(43): -4.6, LF(41): -0.2	-0.4
2015	SEA	MLB	29	361	39	13	0	13	41	26	93	0	0	.263/.316/.419	.274	.328	1.9	RF(34): -3.0, 1B(22): 0.1	0.9
2015	ARI	MLB	29	184	23	10	3	9	23	10	39	0	0	.259/.299/.506	.282	.286	-1.5	RF(42): -2.1, 1B(1): 0.0	0.4
2016	*BAL*	*MLB*	*30*	*576*	*71*	*24*	*2*	*30*	*88*	*38*	*141*	*2*	*2*	*.254/.305/.473*	*.270*	*.289*	*-1.7*	*1B -0*	*1.3*
2017	*BAL*	*MLB*	*31*	*498*	*65*	*21*	*1*	*24*	*72*	*33*	*126*	*2*	*1*	*.245/.297/.453*	*.260*	*.283*	*-1.5*	*1B 0*	*0.9*

Breakout: 2% Improve: 42% Collapse: 2% Attrition: 12% MLB: 100% *Comparables: Corey Hart, Dave Parker, Juan Gonzalez*

Trumbo found his way to a new destination once again in 2015. After another organizational sea change, the Diamondbacks had too many outfielders and Trumbo was the odd man out. The Mariners took him on, and Trumbo repeated his usual pattern of being inconsistent on a day-to-day basis yet putting up fairly consistent numbers across the board. With the exception of his injury-marred 2014, Trumbo has put up a TAv between .274 and .287 since his major-league debut in 2011. The problem with Trumbo has never been with his performance but with how teams utilize him. He's stretched as a corner outfielder, which is putting it politely, but was blocked at first in Arizona by a guy named Paul Goldschmidt.

New Mariners GM Jerry Dipoto stayed true to his principles, trading an inherited Trumbo for a second time. Baltimore is somewhat more likely to use him at first base and DH, which is good for him.

Christian Walker 1B

Born: 3/28/91 Age: 25 Bats: R Throws: R Height: 6'0" Weight: 220

YEAR	TEAM	LVL	AGE	PA	R	2B	3B	HR	RBI	BB	K	SB	CS	AVG/OBP/SLG	TAv	BABIP	BRR	FRAA	WARP
2013	BOW	AA	22	69	7	5	0	0	1	6	10	0	0	.242/.319/.323	.266	.288	-1.6	1B(14): -0.8	-0.1
2013	FRD	A+	22	239	25	17	0	8	35	17	41	2	0	.288/.343/.479	.283	.318	-1.0	1B(52): -2.5	0.5
2013	DEL	A	22	131	19	5	0	3	20	11	16	0	3	.353/.420/.474	.345	.388	-1.9	1B(29): 4.8	1.6
2014	BAL	MLB	23	19	1	1	0	1	1	1	9	0	0	.167/.211/.389	.227	.250	0.0	1B(6): 0.0	0.0
2014	NOR	AAA	23	188	15	10	0	6	19	18	49	0	0	.259/.335/.428	.271	.327	-2.8	1B(44): -2.0, 3B(1): -0.0	0.0
2014	BOW	AA	23	411	58	15	2	20	77	38	83	2	1	.301/.367/.516	.314	.337	0.9	1B(91): 1.4	3.1
2015	NOR	AAA	24	592	68	33	1	18	74	49	136	1	3	.257/.324/.423	.262	.311	1.4	1B(130): -2.7	0.6
2015	BAL	MLB	24	12	0	0	0	0	0	3	4	0	0	.111/.333/.111	.208	.200	0.0	1B(2): -0.0	-0.1
2016	*BAL*	*MLB*	*25*	*134*	*15*	*6*	*0*	*5*	*18*	*9*	*35*	*0*	*0*	*.248/.305/.427*	*.255*	*.302*	*-0.3*	*1B -0*	*0.1*
2017	*BAL*	*MLB*	*26*	*353*	*44*	*17*	*1*	*13*	*45*	*25*	*94*	*0*	*0*	*.245/.302/.425*	*.253*	*.301*	*-0.9*	*1B 0*	*0.8*

Breakout: 5% Improve: 16% Collapse: 8% Attrition: 22% MLB: 35% *Comparables: Tommy Medica, Andy Wilkins, Mark Hamilton*

Another year, another cup of coffee so brief that his rookie status remains intact. Walker's in a bit of an odd situation: He's closer to the majors than fellow corner prospect Trey Mancini, so he will get first crack at Baltimore's 1B/DH at-bats, even though Mancini (and, a few levels behind him, Jomar Reyes) is a better prospect. It's as though there's one Cabbage Patch Doll left and Walker is at the front of the line, but he might not have brought enough money to pay for it. He has firmed up his body and improved his swing dramatically, but there remain concerns about his ultimate power output. With Mancini just one promotion behind him, this is a big year.

Matt Wieters C

Born: 5/21/86 Age: 30 Bats: B Throws: R Height: 6'5" Weight: 230

YEAR	TEAM	LVL	AGE	PA	R	2B	3B	HR	RBI	BB	K	SB	CS	AVG/OBP/SLG	TAv	BABIP	BRR	FRAA	WARP
2013	BAL	MLB	27	579	59	29	0	22	79	43	104	2	0	.235/.287/.417	.262	.247	0.7	C(140): -5.7	2.2
2014	BAL	MLB	28	112	13	5	0	5	18	6	19	0	1	.308/.339/.500	.314	.329	-0.2	C(22): -2.3	0.8
2015	BAL	MLB	29	282	24	14	1	8	25	21	67	0	0	.267/.319/.422	.257	.328	-1.3	C(55): -1.4, 1B(3): -0.1	0.7
2016	*BAL*	*MLB*	*30*	*553*	*63*	*26*	*1*	*21*	*74*	*46*	*102*	*1*	*1*	*.257/.318/.438*	*.262*	*.280*	*-0.3*	*C -10*	*1.5*
2017	*BAL*	*MLB*	*31*	*386*	*48*	*17*	*0*	*14*	*49*	*31*	*73*	*0*	*0*	*.249/.310/.423*	*.254*	*.273*	*-0.4*	*C -7*	*0.9*

Breakout: 3% Improve: 46% Collapse: 5% Attrition: 6% MLB: 96% *Comparables: Miguel Montero, Gary Carter, Yogi Berra*

YEAR	TEAM	P. COUNT	FRM RUNS	BLK RUNS	THRW RUNS	TOT RUNS
2013	BAL	19760	-8.1	0.8	0.4	-6.9
2014	BAL	3357	-2.0	0.0	0.0	-2.0
2015	BAL	8132	-3.6	0.1	0.0	-3.5
2016	*BAL*	*20023*	*-10.6*	*0.6*	*-0.6*	*-10.7*
2017	*BAL*	*13967*	*-8.3*	*0.3*	*-0.5*	*-8.5*

Wieters made a successful return less than 12 months after Tommy John surgery on his throwing elbow, nailing baserunners at a league-average rate (31 percent) and posting the same hitting stats that have become standard issue for the former wunderkind. The switch-hitter overcame his platoon issues, at least for a season, posting nearly identical batting and slugging averages on each side—good news, as the heavy half was always his weakness. There's a laundry list of complicating factors when trying to peg Wieters' future performance, from the skewed aging patterns of catcher offense to the question marks surrounding the longevity of tall backstops. Let's start small: Consider that Wieters had LASIK surgery and then whiffed at a career-high pace in his first season with laser-enhanced corneas.

Mike Yastrzemski RF

Born: 8/23/90 Age: 25 Bats: L Throws: L Height: 5'11" Weight: 180

YEAR	TEAM	LVL	AGE	PA	R	2B	3B	HR	RBI	BB	K	SB	CS	AVG/OBP/SLG	TAv	BABIP	BRR	FRAA	WARP
2013	ABE	A-	22	235	28	13	4	3	25	24	44	8	8	.273/.362/.420	.309	.333	-2.2	CF(34): 6.7, RF(14): 0.0	2.6
2014	BOW	AA	23	201	23	13	4	3	12	14	34	1	2	.250/.310/.413	.256	.293	-0.5	CF(38): 2.8, LF(4): -0.8	0.7
2014	FRD	A+	23	107	21	7	2	1	19	8	16	5	0	.312/.364/.462	.304	.350	0.5	LF(14): -0.8, RF(9): -0.4	0.6
2014	DEL	A	23	288	52	14	10	10	44	19	64	12	4	.306/.365/.554	.319	.371	4.3	RF(54): 6.5, CF(6): 4.1	3.9
2015	BOW	AA	24	536	63	30	6	6	59	43	100	8	7	.246/.316/.372	.266	.294	0.5	LF(53): -3.7, RF(40): -1.7	0.7
2016	*BAL*	*MLB*	*25*	*250*	*28*	*11*	*2*	*6*	*24*	*15*	*62*	*2*	*2*	*.232/.287/.379*	*.233*	*.287*	*-0.1*	*LF -2, RF 0*	*-0.2*
2017	*BAL*	*MLB*	*26*	*340*	*36*	*15*	*4*	*8*	*36*	*21*	*84*	*3*	*2*	*.228/.284/.376*	*.233*	*.283*	*0.0*	*LF -3, RF 0*	*-0.1*

Breakout: 3% Improve: 9% Collapse: 2% Attrition: 9% MLB: 18% *Comparables: Chris Pettit, Bryan Petersen, Tyler Collins*

To paraphrase Hawk Harrelson, in all my years writing up these comments I have never seen a player go home to first in 4.2 seconds as well as Yaz does. Rico Petrocelli was a close second. I tell you what Stone Pony, you know who was the best I ever saw at playing all three outfield positions as a 40 OFP prospect? Yaz. You know I played with his grandaddy on those Red Sox teams when I invented batting gloves and I can tell you first hand that Mike Yastrzemski is the best I ever saw at being a solid bench option for a competitive team. (Three minutes of silence.) Yaz.

PITCHERS

Brad Brach RHP

Born: 4/12/86 Age: 30 Bats: R Throws: R Height: 6'6" Weight: 215

YEAR	TEAM	LVL	AGE	W	L	SV	G	GS	IP	H	HR	BB/9	K/9	GB%	BABIP	WHIP	ERA	FIP	DRA	WARP	CFIP	MPH
2013	TUC	AAA	27	4	3	3	33	0	44^{1}	43	5	2.8	8.9	40%	.306	1.29	2.84	4.13	4.54	0.4	85	
2013	SDN	MLB	27	1	0	0	33	0	31	36	3	5.5	9.0	40%	.375	1.77	3.19	4.12	5.72	-0.4	104	94.5
2014	BAL	MLB	28	7	1	0	46	0	62^{1}	48	6	3.6	7.8	41%	.250	1.17	3.18	3.93	3.14	1.0	101	96.0
2014	NOR	AAA	28	3	1	1	17	0	23^{1}	26	1	2.3	16.6	31%	.490	1.37	3.47	1.00	2.90	0.5	39	
2015	BAL	MLB	29	5	3	1	62	0	79^{1}	57	7	4.3	10.1	46%	.263	1.20	2.72	3.44	3.11	1.5	83	96.5
2016	*BAL*	*MLB*	*30*	*3*	*1*	*0*	*55*	*0*	*57^{2}*	*52*	*7*	*3.9*	*9.5*	*43%*	*.293*	*1.33*	*4.13*	*4.11*	*4.20*	*0.5*	*91*	
2017	*BAL*	*MLB*	*31*	*2*	*1*	*0*	*38*	*0*	*44^{2}*	*40*	*6*	*4.3*	*9.4*	*43%*	*.291*	*1.38*	*4.52*	*4.24*	*4.60*	*0.1*	*101*	

Breakout: 24% Improve: 50% Collapse: 20% Attrition: 16% MLB: 86% *Comparables: Will Ohman, Derrick Turnbow, Jason Motte*

Brach's pitch speed has been on an uphill climb over the past few years, with each season representing a new plateau and the compound interest adding up to 2.3 clicks since 2012. His ERA and FIP have both dropped in each of those years, too, and the combinations of sentences one and two hint at something better than regression-minded PECOTA has forecast. The right-hander has quick leg movements and a heavy drop-and-drive pattern to his delivery, hunching over during his stride before popping up with an upright release point, borrowing from deliveries both new and old in an evolved interpretation of high-speed funk.

Parker Bridwell RHP

Born: 8/2/91 Age: 24 Bats: R Throws: R Height: 6'4" Weight: 190

YEAR	TEAM	LVL	AGE	W	L	SV	G	GS	IP	H	HR	BB/9	K/9	GB%	BABIP	WHIP	ERA	FIP	DRA	WARP	CFIP	MPH
2013	DEL	A	21	8	9	0	26	26	142^{2}	141	9	3.7	9.1	42%	.322	1.40	4.73	3.71	4.45	1.0	99	
2014	FRD	A+	22	7	10	0	26	26	141^{2}	123	11	4.4	9.0	41%	.299	1.36	4.45	4.20	4.67	0.9	103	
2015	BOW	AA	23	4	5	0	18	18	97	96	7	3.5	8.6	40%	.320	1.38	3.99	3.53	4.02	0.9	97	
2016	*BAL*	*MLB*	*24*	*5*	*6*	*0*	*16*	*16*	*87^{1}*	*94*	*12*	*4.1*	*7.2*	*36%*	*.305*	*1.52*	*4.91*	*4.87*	*4.92*	*0.2*	*115*	
2017	*BAL*	*MLB*	*25*	*6*	*7*	*0*	*21*	*21*	*122*	*128*	*16*	*4.5*	*8.0*	*36%*	*.311*	*1.55*	*4.97*	*4.67*	*4.98*	*0.2*	*116*	

Breakout: 0% Improve: 0% Collapse: 0% Attrition: 0% MLB: 0% *Comparables: Steve Johnson, Chris Carpenter, Jimmy Nelson*

The mercurial pitching prospect was moving right along at Double-A Bowie, racking up the strikeouts, serving the base in a bad way and further confounding prospect evaluators with regard to what his eventual role will be. He's been a great big tease over his professional career, flashing signs of competence with a curve that wants to be plus and a slider that looks like it can be solid-average. He'd mix in the occasional 7 IP, 0 BB, 8 K game but give up four runs in the process. Bridwell's flirtations with competence became more intriguing as the season progressed and then he landed on the DL and didn't pitch an inning after July 26th. We still don't have the answers when it comes to Bridwell, furthering the idea that you just can't trust a dude who has a name that sounds like a high-end furniture store.

Zach Britton LHP

Born: 12/22/87 Age: 28 Bats: L Throws: L Height: 6'3" Weight: 195

YEAR	TEAM	LVL	AGE	W	L	SV	G	GS	IP	H	HR	BB/9	K/9	GB%	BABIP	WHIP	ERA	FIP	DRA	WARP	CFIP	MPH
2013	NOR	AAA	25	6	5	0	19	19	103^{1}	112	5	4.0	6.5	63%	.324	1.53	4.27	3.86	4.56	0.5	106	
2013	BAL	MLB	25	2	3	0	8	7	40	52	4	3.8	4.1	59%	.338	1.73	4.95	4.83	4.73	0.1	127	94.3
2014	BAL	MLB	26	3	2	37	71	0	76^{1}	46	4	2.7	7.3	76%	.215	0.90	1.65	3.16	2.03	2.3	93	97.8
2015	BAL	MLB	27	4	1	36	64	0	65^{2}	51	3	1.9	10.8	81%	.308	0.99	1.92	1.98	2.19	2.0	64	98.7
2016	*BAL*	*MLB*	*28*	*3*	*1*	*35*	*59*	*0*	*63*	*58*	*7*	*2.7*	*8.7*	*76%*	*.295*	*1.22*	*3.73*	*3.75*	*3.79*	*0.8*	*82*	
2017	*BAL*	*MLB*	*29*	*5*	*4*	*15*	*41*	*10*	*92^{1}*	*85*	*9*	*2.8*	*8.8*	*76%*	*.301*	*1.23*	*3.70*	*3.45*	*3.76*	*1.3*	*82*	

Breakout: 31% Improve: 64% Collapse: 19% Attrition: 11% MLB: 93% *Comparables: Bobby Parnell, Brandon Webb, Jonny Venters*

Britton entered the 2015 season as an unconventional closer, given his left-handedness and history of low strikeout rates, but he has continued to build on the three-tick velocity bump he got transitioning to relief. By the final months of 2015 he was approaching 98 with a sinking fastball that he throws 90 percent of the time, and that helped him marry a newly elite FIP with an already-elite ERA. Nobody questions his handedness anymore.

Dylan Bundy RHP

Born: 11/15/92 Age: 23 Bats: B Throws: R Height: 6'1" Weight: 200

YEAR	TEAM	LVL	AGE	W	L	SV	G	GS	IP	H	HR	BB/9	K/9	GB%	BABIP	WHIP	ERA	FIP	DRA	WARP	CFIP	MPH
2014	ABE	A-	21	0	1	0	3	3	15	10	0	1.8	13.2	55%	.323	0.87	0.60	1.11	3.56	0.2	69	
2014	FRD	A+	21	1	2	0	6	6	26^{1}	28	0	4.4	5.1	47%	.318	1.56	4.78	3.97	5.08	0.0	114	
2015	BOW	AA	22	0	3	0	8	8	22	21	0	2.0	10.2	42%	.356	1.18	3.68	1.81	2.61	0.6	79	
2016	*BAL*	*MLB*	*23*	*4*	*4*	*0*	*13*	*13*	*69*	*70*	*9*	*3.3*	*7.1*	*41%*	*.295*	*1.39*	*4.60*	*4.56*	*4.63*	*0.4*	*107*	
2017	*BAL*	*MLB*	*24*	*5*	*6*	*0*	*18*	*18*	*107*	*110*	*14*	*3.3*	*7.1*	*41%*	*.298*	*1.40*	*4.72*	*4.42*	*4.75*	*0.3*	*111*	

Breakout: 0% Improve: 0% Collapse: 0% Attrition: 0% MLB: 0% *Comparables: Andrew Heaney, Dellin Betances, Max Scherzer*

To look back at the Orioles' history with pitching prospects is to take a long, sad and draining journey through the paths of despair, broken promises and clipped wings. Bundy was an extremely highly regarded prospect coming out of the 2011 draft, though some teams were spooked by his brutal high school workload. In his professional debut the next spring, he didn't allow an earned run until his 34th professional inning, and debuted in the majors at age 19 that same season. He hasn't been back since. No major leaguer in the past 35 years has played his final MLB game at 19 or younger.

It's been injuries of course—first Tommy John, then shoulder woes that shut him down last summer—and the biggest shame of it all remains that Bundy impresses when he's healthy. Our scouting report had him throwing an easy 95 with excellent plane and two plus secondary offerings with a workable cutter. That's top-of-the-rotation upside and it's what makes Bundy's current situation so difficult. The Orioles will have to make a decision regarding Bundy now. He's out of minor-league options, so he will have to be placed on the 25-man (or disabled list) as a giant unknown. This could be the year we finally see what Bundy's got. Perhaps just as likely, it could be another year we don't see him at all.

Wei-Yin Chen LHP

Born: 7/21/85 Age: 30 Bats: L Throws: L Height: 6'0" Weight: 195

YEAR	TEAM	LVL	AGE	W	L	SV	G	GS	IP	H	HR	BB/9	K/9	GB%	BABIP	WHIP	ERA	FIP	DRA	WARP	CFIP	MPH
2013	BAL	MLB	27	7	7	0	23	23	137	142	17	2.6	6.8	36%	.305	1.32	4.07	4.07	4.31	1.0	102	94.2
2013	BOW	AA	27	1	0	0	2	2	12	9	0	1.5	6.0	50%	.265	0.92	3.00	2.49	4.38	0.1	95	
2014	BAL	MLB	28	16	6	0	31	31	185^{2}	193	23	1.7	6.6	42%	.296	1.23	3.54	3.92	4.26	1.2	98	94.4
2015	BAL	MLB	29	11	8	0	31	31	191^{1}	192	28	1.9	7.2	43%	.290	1.22	3.34	4.13	4.20	1.9	97	94.3
2016	*BAL*	*MLB*	*30*	*11*	*11*	*0*	*31*	*31*	*185*	*187*	*27*	*2.1*	*7.1*	*42%*	*.289*	*1.24*	*4.27*	*4.33*	*4.31*	*1.8*	*99*	
2017	*BAL*	*MLB*	*31*	*8*	*8*	*0*	*22*	*22*	*127*	*131*	*17*	*2.3*	*7.0*	*42%*	*.295*	*1.29*	*4.54*	*4.24*	*4.58*	*0.8*	*106*	

Breakout: 16% Improve: 49% Collapse: 20% Attrition: 4% MLB: 93% *Comparables: Howie Pollet, Javier Vazquez, Gil Meche*

Chen fit the mold of a 2015 Orioles starting pitcher, giving up homers by the bushel and yet cracking his FIP by a healthy margin. His ERA was good for seventh in the AL among qualified starters, all the while his home run count climbing to within one of the league's lead. The key to Chen's game is in minimizing the walks, because batters *are* going to leave the yard against him—his 10.4 percent rate of extra-base hits was the highest in the circuit. He has the mechanical underpinnings to keep hitting spots well into his 30s.

Jason Garcia RHP

Born: 11/21/92 Age: 23 Bats: R Throws: R Height: 6'0" Weight: 185

YEAR	TEAM	LVL	AGE	W	L	SV	G	GS	IP	H	HR	BB/9	K/9	GB%	BABIP	WHIP	ERA	FIP	DRA	WARP	CFIP	MPH
2013	GRN	A	20	2	2	1	9	1	36^{1}	33	3	4.0	8.9	44%	.300	1.35	4.21	4.14	4.44	0.1	99	
2014	GRN	A	21	2	1	3	9	3	35^{2}	31	0	4.3	9.3	54%	.326	1.35	3.79	3.11	4.54	0.3	94	
2014	LOW	A-	21	1	1	0	5	4	20^{2}	19	0	3.0	9.6	50%	.328	1.26	3.48	2.76	4.07	0.2	92	
2015	BAL	MLB	22	1	0	0	21	0	29^{2}	25	3	5.2	6.7	44%	.250	1.42	4.25	4.86	4.52	0.1	110	95.7
2015	BOW	AA	22	1	2	0	9	0	15	12	2	5.4	8.4	57%	.250	1.40	4.20	5.14	4.56	0.0	104	
2016	*BAL*	*MLB*	*23*	*1*	*0*	*0*	*20*	*0*	*21*	*22*	*3*	*3.9*	*7.2*	*44%*	*.301*	*1.48*	*4.79*	*4.91*	*4.82*	*0.0*	*112*	
2017	*BAL*	*MLB*	*24*	*2*	*2*	*0*	*13*	*4*	*46^{1}*	*48*	*6*	*4.3*	*7.8*	*44%*	*.308*	*1.52*	*5.01*	*4.71*	*5.04*	*-0.1*	*118*	

Breakout: 8% Improve: 14% Collapse: 7% Attrition: 20% MLB: 26% *Comparables: Cam Bedrosian, Gregory Infante, Anthony Lerew*

As FanGraphs' Kiley McDaniel told it, the Orioles by sorta-random chance had video of a bunch of Garcia's post-TJ outings in instructs. In six innings of footage he struck out 15, so Baltimore nabbed him in the Rule 5 draft—most teams wouldn't have had nearly the same exposure to this new and improved Garcia. His velocity has spiked since the surgery, and if the slider and command ever come around he'll be a weapon out of the pen.

Kevin Gausman RHP

Born: 5/13/90 Age: 26 Bats: R Throws: R Height: 6'0" Weight: 210

YEAR	TEAM	LVL	AGE	W	L	SV	G	GS	IP	H	HR	BB/9	K/9	GB%	BABIP	WHIP	ERA	FIP	DRA	WARP	CFIP	MPH
2013	BOW	AA	22	2	4	0	8	8	46^{1}	44	3	1.0	9.5	54%	.313	1.06	3.11	2.57	3.65	0.9	69	
2013	BAL	MLB	22	3	5	0	20	5	47^{2}	51	8	2.5	9.3	45%	.328	1.34	5.66	4.02	3.85	0.5	86	99.3
2013	NOR	AAA	22	1	2	0	8	7	35^{2}	36	1	2.3	8.3	48%	.354	1.26	4.04	2.56	3.79	0.5	80	
2014	NOR	AAA	23	1	3	0	11	11	43^{1}	41	5	3.7	9.1	47%	.298	1.36	3.32	4.07	4.28	0.4	90	
2014	BAL	MLB	23	7	7	0	20	20	113^{1}	111	7	3.0	7.0	44%	.304	1.31	3.57	3.44	4.19	0.8	100	98.2
2015	BAL	MLB	24	4	7	0	25	17	112^{1}	109	17	2.3	8.3	46%	.288	1.23	4.25	4.07	4.31	0.9	90	98.7
2015	NOR	AAA	24	0	1	0	3	3	14	10	2	3.9	9.0	51%	.242	1.14	1.29	4.30	3.90	0.1	98	
2016	*BAL*	*MLB*	*25*	*11*	*11*	*0*	*31*	*31*	*186*	*183*	*25*	*2.7*	*8.1*	*46%*	*.296*	*1.28*	*4.11*	*4.18*	*4.16*	*2.1*	*94*	
2017	*BAL*	*MLB*	*26*	*9*	*9*	*0*	*30*	*30*	*186^{1}*	*181*	*22*	*2.5*	*8.4*	*46%*	*.301*	*1.25*	*4.01*	*3.75*	*4.06*	*1.9*	*91*	

Breakout: 23% Improve: 65% Collapse: 17% Attrition: 10% MLB: 99% *Comparables: Matt Garza, Andy Sonnanstine, John Danks*

Gausman has displayed incredible resilience through his pitching career, showing the ability and the willingness to alter his mechanics as well as his approach from high school to college and then the pros, where he has bounced between roles in the rotation and the bullpen. And from where, incidentally, he has been demoted seven times since his much-hyped 2013 debut. He has the repertoire to succeed in a starting role, the frame to theoretically withstand the rigors of the job and enough dollars invested in him to justify some patience. But some patience has been necessary, both with his performance—he's got a 4.27 ERA and just 7.5 strikeouts per nine in 42 career starts—and with the Orioles, who can't seem to make up their minds. If he doesn't turn into something good fast (he's already 25), we'll spend a long time debating whether the Orioles' front office foresaw his struggles or caused them.

Mychal Givens RHP

Born: 5/13/90 Age: 26 Bats: R Throws: R Height: 6'0" Weight: 210

YEAR	TEAM	LVL	AGE	W	L	SV	G	GS	IP	H	HR	BB/9	K/9	GB%	BABIP	WHIP	ERA	FIP	DRA	WARP	CFIP	MPH
2013	DEL	A	23	2	3	3	28	0	42^{2}	34	1	4.0	7.6	53%	.275	1.24	4.22	3.65	4.65	0.0	105	
2014	BOW	AA	24	0	0	0	18	0	25^{1}	19	0	8.2	9.9	66%	.292	1.66	3.91	4.58	5.05	-0.1	114	
2014	FRD	A+	24	1	2	3	18	0	33^{1}	21	2	4.3	7.3	62%	.202	1.11	3.24	4.30	4.83	0.0	108	
2015	BOW	AA	25	4	2	15	35	0	57^{1}	38	1	2.5	12.4	42%	.289	0.94	1.73	1.73	1.20	2.3	58	
2015	BAL	MLB	25	2	0	0	22	0	30	20	1	1.8	11.4	42%	.268	0.87	1.80	1.70	1.84	1.0	71	97.1
2016	*BAL*	*MLB*	*26*	*3*	*1*	*0*	*50*	*0*	52^{1}	*46*	*6*	*3.3*	*9.5*	*43%*	*.288*	*1.24*	*3.86*	*3.83*	*3.94*	*0.8*	*87*	
2017	*BAL*	*MLB*	*27*	*2*	*1*	*0*	*30*	*0*	*46*	*40*	*5*	*3.6*	*9.9*	*43%*	*.294*	*1.28*	*4.02*	*3.77*	*4.10*	*0.3*	*91*	

Breakout: 24% Improve: 37% Collapse: 21% Attrition: 26% MLB: 65% *Comparables: Vic Black, Cory Burns, Michael Schwimer*

Givens was a shortstop who hit .286/.402/.452 in his professional debut, but the bat deserted him and he converted to the mound three years ago. His raw stuff alone flashes the potential for him to be a useful bullpen arm in the majors. He can hit 96 with some serious run and his slider features plus movement with tightness in the break. He continues the Orioles tradition of pitching prospects with designer names having poor command, casting his overall future into questionable territory.

Miguel Gonzalez RHP

Born: 11/21/92 Age: 23 Bats: R Throws: R Height: 6'0" Weight: 185

YEAR	TEAM	LVL	AGE	W	L	SV	G	GS	IP	H	HR	BB/9	K/9	GB%	BABIP	WHIP	ERA	FIP	DRA	WARP	CFIP	MPH
2013	BAL	MLB	29	11	8	0	30	28	171^{1}	157	24	2.8	6.3	41%	.260	1.23	3.78	4.48	3.73	2.4	108	93.7
2014	BAL	MLB	30	10	9	0	27	26	159	155	25	2.9	6.3	39%	.273	1.30	3.23	4.92	4.91	-0.2	116	93.3
2015	BAL	MLB	31	9	12	0	26	26	144^{2}	151	24	3.2	6.8	42%	.295	1.40	4.91	4.98	4.80	0.4	112	93.8
2016	*BAL*	*MLB*	*32*	*9*	*10*	*0*	*28*	*28*	159^{2}	*157*	*24*	*3.0*	*6.6*	*41%*	*.277*	*1.32*	*4.86*	*4.86*	*4.89*	*0.4*	*116*	
2017	*BAL*	*MLB*	*33*	*8*	*10*	*0*	*26*	*26*	154^{2}	*158*	*23*	*3.1*	*6.5*	*41%*	*.286*	*1.37*	*5.09*	*4.79*	*5.12*	*0.0*	*122*	

Breakout: 24% Improve: 37% Collapse: 21% Attrition: 26% MLB: 65% *Comparables: Vic Black, Cory Burns, Michael Schwimer*

After three years defying the laws of FIPsics, Gonzalez's ERA finally caught up to the expectations laid forth by his peripheral stats. Yardballs have been his greatest weakness throughout his big-league tenure, and on that front he reached new lows (or, more literally, highs—the bad one) in 2015. Besides the quantity was the context: His home run rate traditionally drops by almost half when runners are on, a disparity that he couldn't maintain last year. Part of what keeps his head above water is his static pattern of pitch sequencing, maintaining his frequency of pitch types regardless of count, situation or batter handedness, rather than falling into a predictable pattern such as early fastballs and late secondaries. As for the predictable pattern of allowing a home run every 25th batter, however...

Hunter Harvey RHP

Born: 12/9/94 Age: 21 Bats: R Throws: R Height: 6'3" Weight: 175

YEAR	TEAM	LVL	AGE	W	L	SV	G	GS	IP	H	HR	BB/9	K/9	GB%	BABIP	WHIP	ERA	FIP	DRA	WARP	CFIP	MPH
2013	ABE	A-	18	0	1	0	3	3	12	11	0	3.0	11.2	68%	.355	1.25	2.25	1.60	3.68	0.1	88	
2014	DEL	A	19	7	5	0	17	17	87^{2}	66	5	3.4	10.9	46%	.290	1.13	3.18	3.42	4.12	1.3	79	
2016	*BAL*	*MLB*	*21*	*2*	*2*	*0*	*7*	*7*	33^{2}	*33*	*5*	*4.0*	*8.7*	*38%*	*.300*	*1.42*	*4.89*	*4.99*	*4.94*	*0.1*	*115*	
2017	*BAL*	*MLB*	*22*	*7*	*10*	*0*	*29*	*29*	178^{1}	*167*	*25*	*4.3*	*9.1*	*38%*	*.295*	*1.41*	*5.09*	*4.80*	*5.14*	*0.0*	*121*	

Breakout: 0% Improve: 0% Collapse: 0% Attrition: 0% MLB: 0% *Comparables: Keyvius Sampson, Luis Severino, Danny Duffy*

Some things sound great in theory and just don't work out in practice: Future and Drake making a mixtape, marrying your high school sweetheart and, apparently, the Baltimore Orioles developing well-regarded pitching prospects. Harvey has a high octane arsenal but he missed an important developmental year with right-elbow discomfort—not surgery, mind you, just discomfort, which kept him from throwing a single competitive pitch during his age-20 season. The Orioles finally shut him down for the year when the pain returned in instructs, and Harvey had a second visit with Dr. Andrews. It's just rest and rehab for now, after which the Orioles will see whether Harvey's two double-plus pitches, a fastball and a curve, are still in there. If they are, he's got top-of-the-rotation potential, though he's still with the Orioles, so...

Ubaldo Jimenez RHP

Born: 1/22/84 Age: 32 Bats: R Throws: R Height: 6'5" Weight: 210

YEAR	TEAM	LVL	AGE	W	L	SV	G	GS	IP	H	HR	BB/9	K/9	GB%	BABIP	WHIP	ERA	FIP	DRA	WARP	CFIP	MPH
2013	CLE	MLB	29	13	9	0	32	32	182^{2}	163	16	3.9	9.6	45%	.304	1.33	3.30	3.45	3.77	2.5	89	95.3
2014	BAL	MLB	30	6	9	0	25	22	125^{1}	113	14	5.5	8.3	43%	.289	1.52	4.81	4.70	4.91	-0.2	112	93.7
2015	BAL	MLB	31	12	10	0	32	32	184	182	20	3.3	8.2	50%	.309	1.36	4.11	3.98	4.20	1.8	96	93.7
2016	*BAL*	*MLB*	*32*	*11*	*11*	*0*	*32*	*32*	182^{1}	*175*	*23*	*3.8*	*8.7*	*48%*	*.298*	*1.38*	*4.29*	*4.32*	*4.34*	*1.7*	*99*	
2017	*BAL*	*MLB*	*33*	*9*	*9*	*0*	*28*	*28*	*168*	*162*	*19*	*3.6*	*8.7*	*48%*	*.301*	*1.37*	*4.30*	*4.04*	*4.35*	*1.4*	*100*	

Breakout: 18% Improve: 55% Collapse: 17% Attrition: 7% MLB: 89% *Comparables: Mark Langston, Sam Jones, Ted Lilly*

Jimenez has one of the least consistent deliveries in the majors, suffering from volatile timing as well as positioning. His saloon-door stride has been known to swing into wildly different landing spots, turning the mound into a minefield on days that he pitches. When everything is going right, such as during the first half of 2015, Jimenez is able to maximize stability and keep the top half closed until he has both feet in contact with the ground; when he's off, there's no telling where his stride will be directed and his front shoulder opens up earlier than a Vegas strip club. He tied with Jered Weaver for the most stolen bases surrendered among AL pitchers, as opposing baserunners were a tidy 22-for-25 in taking advantage of the unpredictable motion and the unpredictable location of Ubaldo's pitches.

Lazaro Leyva RHP

Born: 8/8/94 Age: 21 Bats: R Throws: R Height: 6'2" Weight: 190

YEAR	TEAM	LVL	AGE	W	L	SV	G	GS	IP	H	HR	BB/9	K/9	GB%	BABIP	WHIP	ERA	FIP	DRA	WARP	CFIP	MPH
2015	ABE	A-	20	0	3	1	15	7	40^1	31	0	3.6	8.0	50%	.270	1.17	2.90	3.07	4.77	0.0	105	
2016	*BAL*	*MLB*	*21*	*2*	*2*	*1*	*19*	*4*	*32^1*	*38*	*5*	*4.6*	*5.3*	*37%*	*.304*	*1.68*	*5.64*	*5.75*	*5.60*	*-0.3*	*134*	
2017	*BAL*	*MLB*	*22*	*3*	*3*	*1*	*31*	*9*	*103^2*	*120*	*13*	*4.3*	*5.5*	*37%*	*.308*	*1.64*	*5.49*	*5.18*	*5.45*	*-0.5*	*130*	

Breakout: 0% Improve: 0% Collapse: 0% Attrition: 0% MLB: 0% *Comparables: Kyle McPherson, Waldis Joaquin, Jon Meloan*

At 20 years old and fresh out of Cuba, Leyva was an abstraction coming into the year, the type of urban myth with potentially exaggerated powers that tends to be produced by communists. But Leyva's myth came honestly, as he touches elite-level velocity and pairs it with a curveball that has 11-5 shape and the type of snap and depth that leaves swings longing. He's no starter, as the effort and overall aesthetic of his delivery preclude any type of role that requires more than four outs. But he can be a solid-average closer, which is a tremendous find for $725,000.

Brian Matusz LHP

Born: 2/11/87 Age: 29 Bats: L Throws: L Height: 6'5" Weight: 190

YEAR	TEAM	LVL	AGE	W	L	SV	G	GS	IP	H	HR	BB/9	K/9	GB%	BABIP	WHIP	ERA	FIP	DRA	WARP	CFIP	MPH
2013	BAL	MLB	26	2	1	0	65	0	51	43	3	2.8	8.8	40%	.292	1.16	3.53	2.94	2.46	1.3	92	93.9
2014	BAL	MLB	27	2	3	0	63	0	51^2	51	7	3.0	9.2	36%	.301	1.32	3.48	4.03	4.63	-0.1	90	93.4
2015	BAL	MLB	28	1	4	0	58	0	49	38	5	3.7	10.3	36%	.270	1.18	2.94	3.55	3.48	0.7	85	93.2
2016	*BAL*	*MLB*	*29*	*3*	*1*	*0*	*55*	*0*	*57^2*	*55*	*7*	*3.0*	*9.1*	*37%*	*.300*	*1.28*	*3.97*	*3.90*	*4.03*	*0.4*	*88*	
2017	*BAL*	*MLB*	*30*	*4*	*3*	*1*	*57*	*5*	*73*	*68*	*9*	*3.0*	*9.0*	*37%*	*.295*	*1.26*	*4.05*	*3.78*	*4.11*	*0.7*	*90*	

Breakout: 43% Improve: 64% Collapse: 10% Attrition: 10% MLB: 89% *Comparables: Chris Capuano, Jeff Samardzija, Felipe Paulino*

The more Matusz relieves, the more he *looks* like a reliever. His delivery has devolved to resemble those of his short-burst brethren, as he sells out stability for power and uses a hurried motion that lacks balance during the most critical phases. He brings the fastball at a modest 90-93 mph, but by invoking a tall release point—manipulating his arm slot with extra spine tilt—he nevertheless gets big whiffs with the pitch. What he won't get are 6-3 putouts; two consecutive seasons of a 36 percent groundball rate further blur the theoretical connection between downhill plane and grounders.

T.J. McFarland LHP

Born: 2/11/87 Age: 29 Bats: L Throws: L Height: 6'5" Weight: 190

YEAR	TEAM	LVL	AGE	W	L	SV	G	GS	IP	H	HR	BB/9	K/9	GB%	BABIP	WHIP	ERA	FIP	DRA	WARP	CFIP	MPH
2013	BAL	MLB	24	4	1	0	38	1	74^2	83	7	3.4	7.0	60%	.319	1.49	4.22	3.87	4.20	0.4	104	91.4
2014	BAL	MLB	25	4	2	0	37	1	58^2	70	2	2.0	5.2	65%	.337	1.41	2.76	3.31	4.63	-0.1	109	93.3
2014	NOR	AAA	25	0	1	0	5	5	24	21	0	3.0	9.4	71%	.309	1.21	3.75	2.77	4.28	0.2	90	
2015	NOR	AAA	26	2	3	1	16	9	52^2	42	0	2.4	5.3	66%	.255	1.06	2.91	2.78	3.85	0.5	97	
2015	BAL	MLB	26	2	2	0	30	0	40^1	52	4	4.0	5.8	65%	.343	1.74	4.91	4.44	5.13	-0.2	113	94.2
2016	*BAL*	*MLB*	*27*	*2*	*1*	*0*	*50*	*0*	*52^1*	*57*	*7*	*2.8*	*6.0*	*64%*	*.303*	*1.41*	*4.58*	*4.67*	*4.60*	*0.1*	*105*	
2017	*BAL*	*MLB*	*28*	*4*	*3*	*0*	*32*	*8*	*88^2*	*96*	*10*	*3.0*	*6.4*	*64%*	*.308*	*1.42*	*4.61*	*4.31*	*4.63*	*0.3*	*106*	

Breakout: 30% Improve: 53% Collapse: 18% Attrition: 29% MLB: 83% *Comparables: Roberto Hernandez, Brian Duensing, Adam Warren*

McFarland has one of the best groundball rates in baseball and one of the worst BABIPs in baseball over the past three years, which might lead one to blame the grounders. In fact, he does quite well when he gets his kind of contact. Rather, he has the league's fourth-worst BABIP on flies (min. 100 balls in play), and the fifth-worst on line drives (ditto), since 2013. His high-contact approach danced between the rain drops in 2014, but he was unable to harness the same magic last season. With low-90s velocity and a non-threatening changeup/breaking ball combination, the low-slot lefty's path to success is to keep the ball down in the zone and under opponent bats *even more than he does now*, which is an awfully big ask.

Darren O'Day RHP

Born: 10/22/82 Age: 33 Bats: R Throws: R Height: 6'4" Weight: 220

YEAR	TEAM	LVL	AGE	W	L	SV	G	GS	IP	H	HR	BB/9	K/9	GB%	BABIP	WHIP	ERA	FIP	DRA	WARP	CFIP	MPH
2013	BAL	MLB	30	5	3	2	68	0	62	47	7	2.2	8.6	40%	.250	1.00	2.18	3.61	2.78	1.4	88	88.3
2014	BAL	MLB	31	5	2	4	68	0	68^2	42	6	2.5	9.6	47%	.218	0.89	1.70	3.35	2.61	1.6	80	89.6
2015	BAL	MLB	32	6	2	6	68	0	65^1	47	5	1.9	11.3	36%	.278	0.93	1.52	2.46	2.82	1.5	67	89.1
2016	*BAL*	*MLB*	*33*	*3*	*1*	*2*	*59*	*0*	*63*	*51*	*8*	*2.5*	*9.8*	*40%*	*.271*	*1.08*	*3.53*	*3.65*	*3.63*	*0.9*	*76*	
2017	*BAL*	*MLB*	*34*	*3*	*1*	*3*	*64*	*0*	*61^2*	*52*	*7*	*2.4*	*9.2*	*40%*	*.276*	*1.11*	*3.75*	*3.51*	*3.86*	*0.6*	*83*	

Breakout: 19% Improve: 47% Collapse: 28% Attrition: 8% MLB: 97% *Comparables: Rafael Soriano, Damaso Marte, George Sherrill*

O'Day uses the hunched-over stride of a submarine pitcher and finishes with a below-sidearm slot to generate one of the lowest release points in the major leagues, just three and a half feet off the ground when the ball leaves his hand. He relies on movement more than velocity to keep baseballs away from the sweet spot of opponent lumber, including a frisbee-style slider that he throws 44 percent of the time. But it was his high-80s four-seamer that was virtually unhittable in 2015. In 90 at-bats that concluded with a four-seamer, O'Day registered 40 strikeouts and held opponents to a .156 slugging percentage. That boosted his strikeout rate to new heights, boosted O'Day to All-Star status and boosted his bank account by $31 million.

Chaz Roe RHP

Born: 10/9/86 Age: 29 Bats: R Throws: R Height: 6'5" Weight: 190

YEAR	TEAM	LVL	AGE	W	L	SV	G	GS	IP	H	HR	BB/9	K/9	GB%	BABIP	WHIP	ERA	FIP	DRA	WARP	CFIP	MPH
2013	RNO	AAA	26	0	0	7	22	0	22	15	0	1.6	8.2	55%	.250	0.86	1.23	2.71	4.42	0.2	82	
2013	ARI	MLB	26	1	0	0	21	0	22^{1}	18	3	5.2	9.7	59%	.273	1.39	4.03	4.36	4.14	0.1	97	93.6
2014	NWO	AAA	27	3	3	14	47	0	64	53	5	3.0	10.1	60%	.304	1.16	3.66	3.73	4.92	0.4	88	
2014	NYA	MLB	27	0	0	0	3	0	2	3	0	13.5	18.0	17%	.500	3.00	9.00	3.66	11.97	-0.2	102	94.1
2015	BAL	MLB	28	4	2	0	36	0	41^{1}	44	4	3.7	8.3	55%	.342	1.48	4.14	3.83	4.83	-0.1	99	94.9
2015	NOR	AAA	28	3	1	2	17	0	24^{2}	17	0	3.3	8.0	67%	.258	1.05	2.19	2.83	3.26	0.3	89	
2016	*BAL*	*MLB*	*29*	*2*	*1*	*0*	*40*	*0*	*42*	*42*	*5*	*3.3*	*8.0*	*57%*	*.301*	*1.37*	*4.35*	*4.24*	*4.40*	*0.2*	*99*	
2017	*BAL*	*MLB*	*30*	*2*	*1*	*0*	*34*	*0*	40^{2}	*41*	*5*	*3.5*	*8.3*	*57%*	*.305*	*1.39*	*4.53*	*4.25*	*4.58*	*0.1*	*104*	

Breakout: 13% Improve: 20% Collapse: 23% Attrition: 28% MLB: 46% *Comparables: Evan Reed, Chris Leroux, Donnie Veal*

Roe has a delivery that breaks into distinct phases, starting with a robotic line to the plate in which he keeps his shoulders on a straight rail toward the target, followed by a rotational phase in which the forward momentum gives way to an upper half that spins like a top. It's a motion with simple roots but a potentially complicated usage pattern, further confused by egregious spine tilt that directs his kinetic energy to the first-base side of the mound. What all that means, for the uninitiated: His motion's working against his efforts to hit targets. A two-pitch pitcher, Roe leans on 92-96 mph velocity and a sporadically sharp breaking ball to keep the bats quiet, or at least try.

Chris Tillman RHP

Born: 4/15/88 Age: 28 Bats: R Throws: R Height: 6'5" Weight: 200

YEAR	TEAM	LVL	AGE	W	L	SV	G	GS	IP	H	HR	BB/9	K/9	GB%	BABIP	WHIP	ERA	FIP	DRA	WARP	CFIP	MPH
2013	BAL	MLB	25	16	7	0	33	33	206^{1}	184	33	3.0	7.8	40%	.269	1.22	3.71	4.45	3.61	3.2	98	94.6
2014	BAL	MLB	26	13	6	0	34	34	207^{1}	189	21	2.9	6.5	42%	.267	1.23	3.34	4.04	3.67	2.8	106	94.0
2015	BAL	MLB	27	11	11	0	31	31	173	176	20	3.3	6.2	46%	.294	1.39	4.99	4.42	4.21	1.7	110	94.4
2016	*BAL*	*MLB*	*28*	*11*	*11*	*0*	*31*	*31*	*186*	*181*	*25*	*3.0*	*7.0*	*44%*	*.280*	*1.31*	*4.50*	*4.54*	*4.53*	*1.3*	*106*	
2017	*BAL*	*MLB*	*29*	*10*	*10*	*0*	*28*	*28*	171^{1}	*171*	*22*	*3.1*	*7.1*	*44%*	*.288*	*1.34*	*4.66*	*4.37*	*4.69*	*0.8*	*110*	

Breakout: 19% Improve: 59% Collapse: 21% Attrition: 5% MLB: 90% *Comparables: Andrew Cashner, Homer Bailey, Joe Blanton*

Tillman has had one of baseball's tallest release points for the past few years, reaching almost seven feet of vertical distance, but in 2015 the arm slot dropped to a release four inches lower. Whether or not this was tied to the collapse of his ERA is the subject of debate, but the numbers indicate that all of his pitches were compromised despite velocity in line with his previously established pitch speeds. He walked too many, struck out too few and when the ball was put in play it was hit hard, resulting in the second-highest ERA and the third-worst strikeout-to-walk ratio among qualifying AL starters last season. The big question is whether the answer could be as simple as the problem.

Mike Wright RHP

Born: 1/3/90 Age: 26 Bats: R Throws: R Height: 6'6" Weight: 215

YEAR	TEAM	LVL	AGE	W	L	SV	G	GS	IP	H	HR	BB/9	K/9	GB%	BABIP	WHIP	ERA	FIP	DRA	WARP	CFIP	MPH
2013	BOW	AA	23	11	3	0	26	26	143^{2}	152	9	2.4	8.5	44%	.332	1.33	3.26	3.27	3.97	2.1	79	
2014	NOR	AAA	24	5	11	0	26	26	142^{2}	159	10	2.6	6.5	39%	.322	1.40	4.61	3.79	4.45	1.1	96	
2015	NOR	AAA	25	9	1	0	15	14	81	59	4	2.8	7.0	45%	.250	1.04	2.22	3.28	3.49	1.2	93	
2015	BAL	MLB	25	3	5	0	12	9	44^{2}	52	9	3.6	5.2	39%	.295	1.57	6.04	6.10	6.34	-0.7	120	97.6
2016	*BAL*	*MLB*	*26*	*5*	*6*	*0*	*18*	*18*	*90*	*98*	*12*	*2.9*	*6.3*	*40%*	*.301*	*1.41*	*4.68*	*4.67*	*4.71*	*0.4*	*108*	
2017	*BAL*	*MLB*	*27*	*5*	*6*	*0*	*17*	*17*	*101*	*113*	*15*	*3.0*	*6.4*	*40%*	*.305*	*1.45*	*5.09*	*4.77*	*5.12*	*0.0*	*120*	

Breakout: 14% Improve: 30% Collapse: 18% Attrition: 34% MLB: 60% *Comparables: Pat Misch, Robert Ray, Kyle Gibson*

Wright had an excellent introduction to the highest level last summer, spinning consecutive starts of seven-inning, shutout baseball to start his career. But because nobody retires after two starts, he stuck around for brutal reality, allowing 17 runs in just 15 innings over the next four starts, and just like that his career ERA had gone from Sidd Finch's to Brian Bohanon's. The Orioles quickly pulled the plug on the Wright experiment until rosters expanded in September, at which point he opened the floodgates a little wider and his ERA was drowned in a sea of home runs. The good news is there's nowhere to go now but up. Except maybe down.

Lineouts

Hitters

NAME	POS	TEAM	LVL	AGE	PA	R	2B	3B	HR	RBI	BB	K	SB	CS	AVG/OBP/SLG	TAv	BABIP	BRR	FRAA	WARP
Dariel Alvarez	OF	BAL	MLB	26	31	3	1	0	1	1	2	8	0	0	.241/.290/.379	.251	.300	0.6	RF(12): 1.9, CF(1): -0.0	0.3
	OF	NOR	AAA	26	541	61	24	2	16	72	16	63	7	3	.275/.305/.424	.265	.285	2.8	RF(95): 10.5, CF(47): -2.0	2.7
Drew Dosch	3B	BOW	AA	23	251	17	7	3	1	21	15	45	2	1	.238/.286/.307	.217	.290	-2.0	3B(68): -1.7	-0.8
	3B	FRD	A+	23	233	30	8	3	2	34	23	37	4	2	.275/.348/.372	.288	.324	-1.1	3B(52): -0.5, SS(1): 0.0	1.3
Josh Hart	OF	FRD	A+	20	445	43	15	3	1	28	11	81	30	15	.255/.282/.311	.227	.310	2.9	CF(82): -3.0, LF(21): -1.6	-0.4
L.J. Hoes	LF	FRE	AAA	25	429	69	24	3	3	53	52	62	26	8	.295/.383/.400	.278	.344	0.4	RF(48): -4.4, LF(26): 3.3	1.8
	LF	HOU	MLB	25	16	1	0	0	0	1	1	3	0	0	.267/.313/.267	.222	.333	0.2	RF(5): -0.3, LF(3): -0.2	-0.1
Paul Janish	INF	BAL	MLB	32	36	4	3	0	0	3	0	3	0	0	.286/.278/.371	.257	.303	0.3	SS(13): -0.1, 2B(1): -0.3	0.1
	INF	NOR	AAA	32	344	29	7	2	0	21	31	41	2	1	.235/.313/.272	.231	.270	0.6	SS(95): 7.3	1.2
Rey Navarro	2B	BAL	MLB	25	30	5	2	0	1	3	0	3	0	0	.276/.276/.448	.249	.280	-0.5	2B(9): -0.6	-0.1
	2B	NOR	AAA	25	394	49	20	1	6	23	27	48	4	4	.261/.310/.372	.256	.285	-0.1	2B(49): -0.7, SS(40): 7.3	1.8
Francisco Pena	C	KCA	MLB	25	7	0	0	0	0	0	0	3	0	0	.143/.143/.143	.158	.250	0.0	C(8): -0.2	-0.1
	C	OMA	AAA	25	374	42	20	1	13	48	23	56	4	1	.251/.305/.430	.252	.265	2.8	C(89): 7.4	2.3
Joey Rickard	OF	DUR	AAA	24	104	16	6	2	0	11	10	20	1	0	.360/.437/.472	.334	.457	-1.3	LF(13): -0.2, RF(11): -0.6	0.8
	OF	MNT	AA	24	282	38	19	6	2	32	39	42	19	4	.322/.420/.479	.327	.379	1.5	LF(24): -1.7, RF(19): 2.8	2.8
	OF	PCH	A+	24	94	8	3	0	0	12	20	13	3	2	.268/.436/.310	.308	.322	-0.5	LF(11): -1.8, RF(6): 1.2	0.7
Henry Urrutia	OF	BAL	MLB	28	36	3	1	0	1	6	2	3	0	0	.265/.306/.382	.227	.267	-0.1	LF(8): 1.1	0.1
	OF	NOR	AAA	28	505	58	22	1	10	53	40	81	1	3	.291/.345/.409	.273	.332	0.7	LF(38): -0.3, RF(27): -0.3	1.5
Delmon Young	DH	BAL	MLB	29	180	20	6	0	2	16	4	29	0	0	.270/.289/.339	.220	.313	1.0	RF(40): -1.1, LF(2): 0.4	-0.4

A profound phobia of walks has effectively capped the value of **Dariel Alvarez** since he came stateside; the bat-to-ball skills will need to translate and the in-game power will need to grow if he's to avoid drowning in the player pool. ❖ The troll who lives under Double-A claimed another victim, as **Drew Dosch** was exposed as a player who can't recognize spin, lacks natural gifts and probably tops out at org soldier. ❖ **Josh Hart** shows plus defense and finds the barrel well enough to predict an average hit tool, but the bat has about as much power as the Green Party. ❖ **L.J. Hoes** became a victim of the Great Houston Outfield Logjam and Bake-Off of 2015, appearing in only eight games in the majors. He got sent back to Baltimore and everybody's a winner. ❖ Professional defensive replacement **Paul Janish** hasn't gone yard in the majors since Obama's first term, and there's not a three to be found in his career slash line. ❖ Maine native **Ryan McKenna** features some feel for hitting, a solid defensive profile in center and a lot more winter coats than your typical prep hitting prospect. ❖ **Rey Navarro** put the ball in play in 26 of his 30 big-league plate appearances last season, one of which was a longball that went nearly as high as it went deep, giving the coaching staff ample opportunity to see how hard he runs on both groundouts and home run trots. ❖ **Francisco Pena** can be poison to would-be base thieves and his bat sometimes has things to say, but his latent inability to beat out Drew Butera for a backup-catcher job doesn't bode well for his future. ❖ **Joey** "Bags" **Rickard** is a speedster with on-base chops and the glove to cover all three outfield positions. The ninth-rounder also has triples power and a blank page for a scouting report, so temper optimism. ❖ **Henry Urrutia** hits baseballs for breakfast, but then he boots baseballs for lunch and chases slowly after baseballs for dinner. ❖ **Delmon Young** will emerge with some contender this fall, ready to steal 15 more seconds of fame. He's due.

Pitchers

NAME	TEAM	LVL	AGE	W	L	SV	G	GS	IP	H	HR	BB/9	K/9	GB%	BABIP	WHIP	ERA	FIP	FRA	WARP	CFIP	MPH
Jeff Beliveau	TBA	MLB	28	0	0	0	5	0	2^{2}	6	1	3.4	6.8	25%	.455	2.62	13.50	7.60	14.86	-0.3	106	89.7
Tim Berry	BOW	AA	24	2	7	0	23	15	82^{1}	107	8	3.7	6.2	46%	.351	1.71	7.32	4.53	5.42	-0.6	115	
Garrett Cleavinger	ABE	A-	21	6	1	1	19	0	25	14	2	6.5	11.5	44%	.231	1.28	2.16	4.39	5.46	-0.2	112	
Oliver Drake	BAL	MLB	28	0	0	0	13	0	15^{2}	16	1	5.2	9.8	50%	.333	1.60	2.87	3.49	4.18	0.1	101	93.0
	NOR	AAA	28	1	2	23	42	0	44	23	1	3.3	13.5	47%	.256	0.89	0.82	1.54	0.49	2.1	52	
Brian Gonzalez	DEL	A	19	4	9	0	23	23	105^{2}	98	8	5.0	6.9	45%	.288	1.49	5.71	4.84	7.10	-2.4	127	
Joe Gunkel	PME	AA	23	2	1	0	4	3	18^{1}	26	1	3.9	10.8	40%	.481	1.85	3.93	2.89	2.78	0.4	78	
	SLM	A+	23	1	1	2	8	2	22	16	2	1.6	9.0	47%	.250	0.91	2.05	2.98	2.47	0.6	81	
	BOW	AA	23	8	4	0	17	17	104^{1}	85	7	1.3	6.0	40%	.250	0.96	2.59	3.39	3.15	2.1	88	
David Hess	BOW	AA	21	1	1	0	2	2	10	10	0	3.6	10.8	30%	.370	1.40	4.50	2.07	3.72	0.1	93	
	FRD	A+	21	9	4	0	26	25	133^{1}	112	8	3.6	7.4	35%	.268	1.24	3.58	3.64	3.91	1.3	98	
Steve Johnson	BAL	MLB	27	0	0	0	6	0	5^{1}	8	2	8.4	5.1	43%	.316	2.44	10.12	9.67	11.99	-0.5	114	90.8
	NOR	AAA	27	4	1	1	32	3	54^{2}	43	2	2.6	11.0	34%	.323	1.08	2.30	2.11	1.17	2.2	62	
Jon Keller	BOW	AA	22	0	0	0	7	0	12^{2}	6	0	5.7	5.7	46%	.182	1.11	3.55	4.14	5.54	-0.2	120	
	FRD	A+	22	3	4	4	30	0	63^{2}	65	1	3.8	7.1	63%	.317	1.45	3.82	3.49	4.35	0.0	102	
Branden Kline	BOW	AA	23	3	3	0	8	8	39^{1}	35	4	4.3	6.2	47%	.261	1.37	3.66	4.90	5.95	-0.5	122	
Christopher Lee	FRD	A+	22	3	6	0	14	14	76^{1}	76	1	3.4	5.7	57%	.306	1.38	3.07	3.42	4.29	0.4	102	
	QUD	A	22	3	2	0	7	6	30^{2}	36	1	2.9	7.0	68%	.333	1.50	4.11	3.43	4.80	0.0	104	
	BOW	AA	22	4	2	0	7	7	38	32	0	4.7	6.2	62%	.283	1.37	3.08	3.56	5.86	-0.5	122	
Edgar Olmos	TAC	AAA	25	1	1	1	20	2	33	32	0	3.5	9.3	40%	.344	1.36	3.55	3.27	3.72	0.6	85	
	SEA	MLB	25	1	0	0	6	2	14	16	1	5.1	2.6	50%	.283	1.71	4.50	5.39	6.23	-0.2	124	95.4
C.J. Riefenhauser	DUR	AAA	25	4	2	1	29	0	34^{2}	25	1	1.8	8.8	48%	.255	0.92	2.86	2.44	2.40	0.9	78	
	TBA	MLB	25	1	0	0	17	0	14^{2}	15	3	4.3	4.3	42%	.267	1.50	5.52	6.24	6.00	-0.2	121	91.5
Tanner Scott	ABE	A-	20	4	0	0	9	1	21^{1}	16	0	5.1	13.1	64%	.340	1.31	3.38	2.72	4.13	0.2	98	
	DEL	A	20	0	3	2	9	2	21	19	0	4.3	12.4	57%	.373	1.38	4.29	2.15	3.28	0.4	86	
Andrew Triggs	BOW	AA	26	0	2	17	43	0	61	42	0	1.6	10.3	61%	.286	0.87	1.03	1.86	1.54	2.2	61	
Christian Turnipseed	ABE	A-	23	0	0	4	10	0	18	9	0	1.5	8.5	52%	.205	0.67	0.00	2.13	3.27	0.3	87	

NAME	TEAM	LVL	AGE	W	L	SV	G	GS	IP	H	HR	BB/9	K/9	GB%	BABIP	WHIP	ERA	FIP	FRA	WARP	CFIP	MPH
Tyler Wilson	NOR	AAA	25	5	5	0	17	17	94[1]	94	8	1.7	6.0	50%	.295	1.19	3.24	3.62	3.57	1.3	93	
	BAL	MLB	25	2	2	0	9	5	36	39	1	2.8	3.2	54%	.309	1.39	3.50	3.74	4.90	0.0	121	92.4
Vance Worley	IND	AAA	27	3	1	0	5	5	34	30	4	1.3	5.6	53%	.255	1.03	2.38	4.07	4.01	0.3	100	
	PIT	MLB	27	4	6	0	23	8	71[2]	81	6	2.6	6.2	48%	.323	1.42	4.02	3.85	5.56	-0.6	113	92.0

Soft-tossing lefty **Jeff Beliveau** underwent surgery to repair a torn rotator cuff. It will be a rough journey, Jeff. Don't stop beli... never mind. ❖ **Tim Berry** is left-handed and throws in the low-to-mid-90s with a solid change, earning him the "Crafty Lefty" achievement. He's starting to creep into Roger Murtaugh territory, though. ❖ **Garrett Cleavinger** sits in the mid-90s with a power curve and has the makings of a solid relief arm, but he'll always be misremembered by casual Orioles fans as the guy Baltimore traded Jake Arrieta for [sic]. ❖ **Oliver Drake** has one of the goofier deliveries in the game. He starts bent over the front side before he strides completely open, and then veers his head hard to the glove side until it's nearly perpendicular to the ground, with his throwing arm coming through the hitter's visual window at 12 o'clock. ❖ Seventh-rounder **Gray Fenter** is much more than that, having signed for a million bucks. He hits 96 occasionally, sits more comfortable around 90-94, has fringe command and tweets pictures of babies in penguin outfits. ❖ Meh-stuff southpaw **Brian Gonzalez** struggled badly in his full-season debut, but he was the youngest pitcher on his team. That means the third-rounder's got a lot of time still to grow or, because he has such limited projection, a lot of time still to disappoint. ❖ Necessity is the mother of gimmickry: **Joe Gunkel** is quick to home, works deceptively and hides his fastball. That'll have to do, because he doesn't have a standout pitch and his slider is a non-factor against lefties. ❖ **David Hess**' repertoire suffers from what plagues most internet trade proposals: Just because you added a lot of stuff doesn't mean it actually adds up. ❖ Despite a rebound performance at Triple-A, **Steve Johnson**'s grasp on a big-league future is slipping as the game becomes increasingly intolerant of subpar velocity. ❖ As recently as 1933, a 6-foot-5 pitcher would have been the tallest player in all of baseball. Now, it's just, oh, whatever. Same with big fastball/average slider reliever profiles, and same with **Jon Keller**. ❖ **Branden Kline**'s got a wide velocity band, ranging from 89 to 95 with mixed results. The fastball finds barrels when the movement dulls, and his slider features fringe command with middling bite. ❖ **Christopher Lee** *looks* like an Astros farmhand, tall and long and athletic and blessed with a fastball that touches 95. He looks *less* like an Astros farmhand now that he wears an O's jersey at spring training. ❖ Control has always been **Edgar Olmos**' problem; last year his control improved while his strikeouts plummeted, so at least his struggles have some variety. As a left-handed pitcher, he will keep getting chances. ❖ **C.J. Riefenhauser** bounced between Durham and St. Petersburg around a stint on the disabled list with shoulder inflammation. Coincidently, it is the first time a synonym for heat or fire has been mentioned in regards to him throwing a baseball. ❖ **Tanner Scott** has a pretty solid reliever starter kit, but the command sucks and his inconsistent release point makes him risky. Obviously should be named Scott Tanner; if he makes it, will replace Clayton Richard as MLB's most backward name. ❖ **Andrew Triggs** is a reliever who doesn't really have the sort of profile that plays up in relief, with a little sink and a little deception and not much stuff at all. ❖ **Christian Turnipseed**, y'all. ❖ **Tyler Wilson** has a major-league-quality fastball and enough command for a middle-relief career, which sounds ehhh but relative to where he was three years ago it's yeaaaah. ❖ **Vance Worley** split the season between the majors and the minors, the rotation and the bullpen and relevancy and irrelevancy. The way his career has played out, it's anyone's guess which sides he winds up on in 2016.

Manager

Buck Showalter

YEAR	TEAM	W	L	Pythag +/-	Avg PC	100+ P	120+ P	QS	BQS	REL	REL w Zero R	IBB	PH	PH Avg	PH HR	SB2	CS2	SB3	CS3	SAC Att	SAC%	POS SAC	Squeeze	Swing	In Play
2013	BAL	85	77	0	95.9	75	0	78	5	473	380	32	65	.143	0	70	26	9	2	39	69.2	23	0	236	68
2014	BAL	96	66	1	97.8	78	1	78	7	479	405	25	74	.308	2	37	16	6	3	56	62.5	32	1	205	60
2015	BAL	81	81	-2	93.7	63	0	72	4	453	369	27	79	.208	1	34	22	9	2	33	60.6	18	0	191	58

When Showalter was a young coach with the Yankees, he learned a saying from Billy Martin: "Preparation always shows itself in the spontaneity of the moment." That anecdote comes courtesy of Bill Pennington's book on Martin, subtitled *Baseball's Flawed Genius*. Based on his managing style, it's fair to say Showalter took Martin's proverb to heart.

Showalter took something besides the apothegm from his mentor: the tag of a flawed baseball genius. *Men's Journal* once asked if he was too smart for the sport, and rumors have persisted that he's tough to work with because he wants more power than the typical manager—during his time with the Diamondbacks he altered the in-construction stadium's blueprints to his liking. (Yes, really.) Regardless of the merit of the flawed part, detective is a more apt term for Showalter than genius. He's willing to search every nook and cranny for a clue that might help his team scratch out a potentially important run at some indeterminable future date. Showalter is untied to the status quo and has no use for the brand of misoneism endorsed by most baseball lifers. Rather, he'll do just about anything to gain an advantage; hence piping in crowd noise during spring training drills; hence trying the absurd (Steve Pearce at second base, anyone?); and hence his obsessive attention to detail.

Showalter's monomaniacal tendencies are most apparent in his bullpen management, since he takes a hands-off approach with the offense. The O's bullpen finished last season with the 11th-most innings, yet pitched the fewest games on zero days' rest. Credit those ranks to Showalter's decision to trade appearance totals for appearance length, as Baltimore ranked second in the majors in multi-inning relief stints. The bargain included Zach Britton, who tied for the most saves of five-plus outs, and who had the eighth-most multi-inning appearances among the 21 closers with more than 30 saves.

But Martin's saying lends itself to Showalter's involvement in subjects of greater importance than baseball. Showalter was raised in the segregated south by a father who the writer Pat Jordan once compared to Atticus Finch. As a result, Showalter grew up more open-minded and curious about racial inequalities and issues than the average person born and raised during that time. You figure Showalter's childhood served as the preparation that showed itself in the spontaneity of the moment during the Baltimore riots. Well positioned to offer a nuanced take, Showalter delivered by saying, in part, "I've never been black, okay? So I don't know, I can't put myself there. I've never faced the challenges that they face, so I understand the emotion ... I want us to learn from some stuff that's gone on on both sides of it." Flawed whatever, we could all learn from Showalter.

BOSTON RED SOX

Essay by Brian MacPherson

Player comments by Ben Carsley and BP authors

Rebuilding is not possible in Boston, or so say both conventional wisdom and the newest executive in residence at Columbia University. Even a slight hint at a preference for the future over the present meets with scorn and ridicule. What ex-GM Theo Epstein once tried to describe as a "bridge period"—a comment that preceded an 89-win season, it should be noted; a win total that would have earned the Red Sox the second wild card had only the second wild card then been in existence—are, within Fenway's walls, anathema on par with Yankees caps.

And yet here the Red Sox stand, looking back at their third last-place finish in four seasons, albeit with a World Series title sprinkled into the mix like a cherry on top of a trash can. For a franchise driven by the idea that last place is unacceptable and rebuilding is impossible, the depths to which they have fallen are remarkable. In spite of trying to win every year—or, perhaps, because of trying to win every year—the Red Sox have won even one postseason game only once in the last seven years.

And so, rather than traveling to Fort Myers, Fla., as he did for more than 15 years, New England native Ben Cherington will spend the spring teaching Ivy League master's degree students just a stone's throw from Yankee Stadium. It falls to accomplished team architect Dave Dombrowski to blend strategies forged in Montreal, Miami and Detroit to build the sustainable winner in Boston that Cherington could not.

Were the notoriously methodical Cherington at the helm of a team like Kansas City, he too might have had the patience to wait for a wave of young players to blossom. Instead, because of the pressures that come with Boston—be they real, perceived or a mix of the two—Cherington jettisoned his stated long-term plan in favor of short-term solutions. It cost him his job.

"We're in a unique baseball market with fans and support that's different than a lot of places," Cherington said in July, a little more than a month before the hiring of Dombrowski prompted his exit. "We respect that. We have an obligation to give the fans our best shot every year. That's the way the business model is set up, and the baseball model is a reflection of that."

Upstart teams like the Astros, Cubs and Royals have demonstrated the rewards a team can reap if patient enough to see the rebuilding process through. There's

RED SOX PROSPECTUS

2015 W-L: 78-84, 5th in AL East

Pythag	.497	17th	DER	.695	26th
RS/G	4.62	4th	B-Age	28.3	14th
RA/G	4.65	25th	P-Age	28	10th
TAv	.258	20th	Salary	$180.4M	3rd
BRR	3.13	12th	M$/MW	$5.7M	5th
TAv-P	.260	15th	DL Days	1200	21st
FIP	4.14	22nd	$ on DL	15%	14th

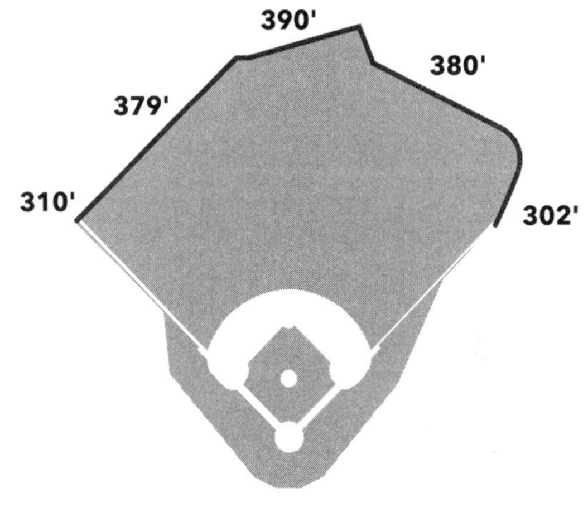

Outfield wall profile: **3'** to **37'**

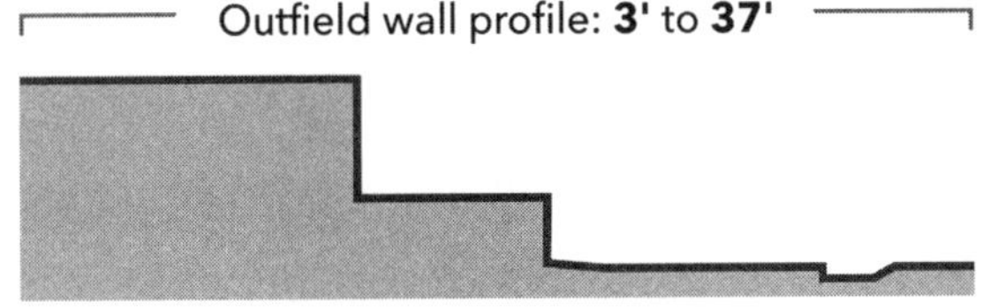

Three-Year Park Factors

Runs	Runs/RH	Runs/LH	HR/RH	HR/LH
110	120	124	114	107

Top Hitter WARP	5.5	Mookie Betts
Top Pitcher WARP	2.5	Wade Miley
Top Prospect	Yoan Moncada	

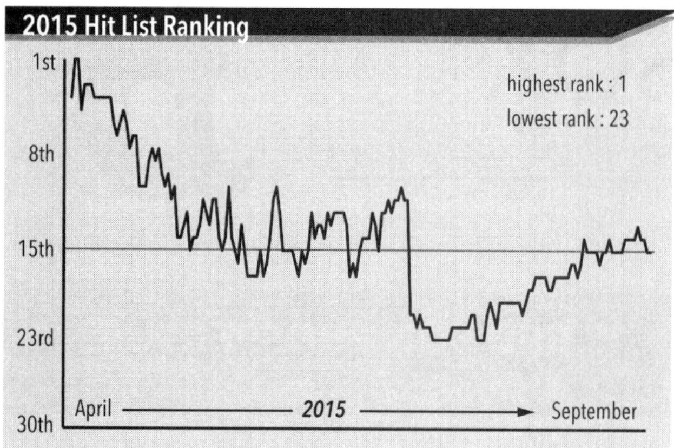

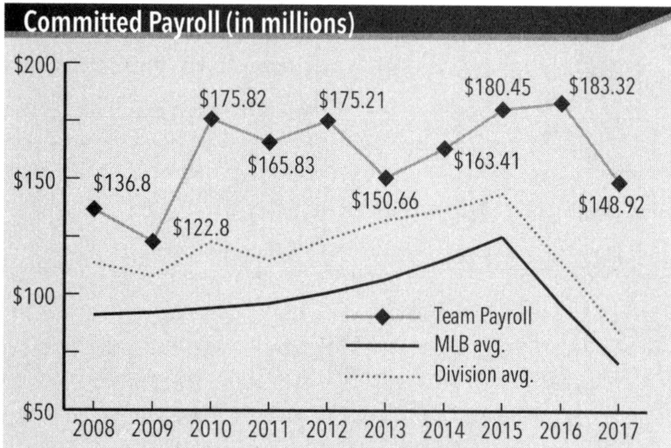

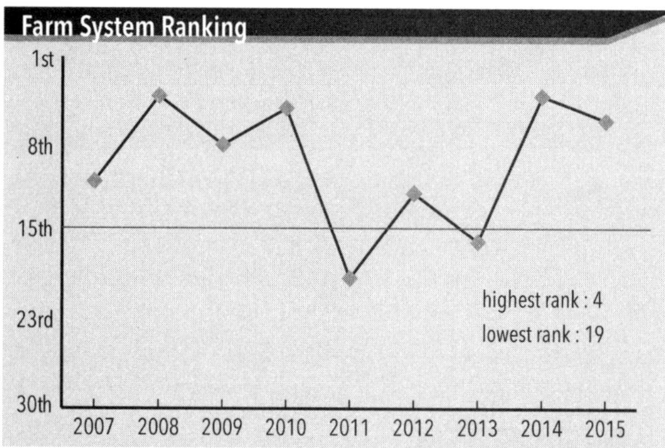

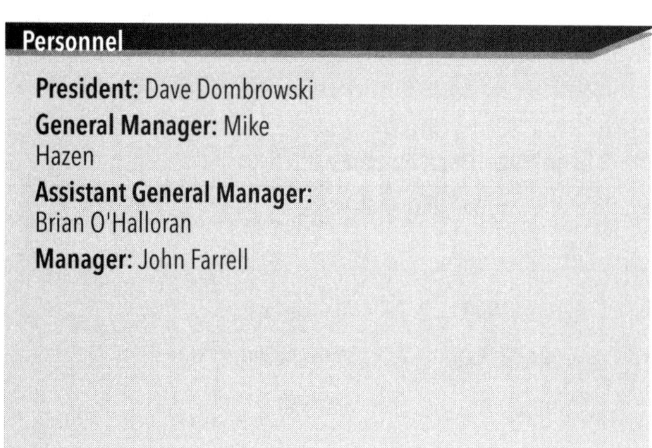
Personnel

President: Dave Dombrowski

General Manager: Mike Hazen

Assistant General Manager: Brian O'Halloran

Manager: John Farrell

more than one way to exercise patience: The Astros and Cubs—Epstein's Cubs, it should be noted—took a more direct and strategic approach, trading away veterans for prospects and enjoying the numerous top-10 draft picks that came with the mountains of losses. It perhaps is telling that Epstein made a more staunch commitment to the long-term plan with the sad-sack Cubs than he did when he was signing Carl Crawford and trading Anthony Rizzo for Adrian Gonzalez in Boston.

The Royals took a more indirect path, their tradition of losing allowing them to ride out the early struggles of the young players who became the core of back-to-back American League pennant winners. They couldn't afford to pay for big-ticket stars to replace underachieving youngsters. They had no choice but to wait and hope—and to get more than a little bit fortunate with a development arc or two.

Just as a periodic forest fire can have a long-term benefit to an ecosystem, a periodic embrace of the second division can have positive long-term effects for a franchise. Trading veterans for prospects can inject young talent otherwise unobtainable beyond the amateur draft. That's how Houston acquired Jake Marisnick (in a trade for Jarred Cosart). That's how Chicago acquired Addison Russell (in a trade for Jeff Samardzija). That's how Kansas City acquired Lorenzo Cain (in a trade for Zack Greinke). That's how the New York Mets acquired Travis D'Arnaud and Noah Syndergaard (in a trade for R.A. Dickey). These deals don't always work out—Dombrowski has made a career out of trading prospects who fail to blossom with their new teams—but, then, no kind of trade *always* works out.

The downfall of the Cherington regime began more than a year before his departure from the team. The failure of youngsters Xander Bogaerts, Jackie Bradley Jr. and Will Middlebrooks to produce during the 2014 season—challenges not dissimilar to those faced by the likes of Alex Gordon, Eric Hosmer and Mike Moustakas early in their respective careers—dropped the Red Sox into last place by late July. A repeat of their magical run to the World Series the previous October was not going to happen. The Cherington regime was in no peril, but even the most fervent of the win-now crowd in Boston acknowledged that it was time to sell.

Cherington had two obvious and valuable trade chips at his disposal in Andrew Miller, who had resurrected his career as a dominant reliever with the Red Sox, and ace starter Jon Lester. He had an under-the-radar trade chip in John Lackey, whose Tommy John surgery after the 2011 season had triggered a clause in his contract giving his team an option on his services at the big-league minimum in 2015. Lackey would help a team in 2014, but that clause seemingly made him at least as valuable a trade commodity as Lester.

If the Red Sox ever were going to make a landscape-altering veteran-for-prospects trade—something they hadn't done since trading away Heathcliff Slocumb for Derek Lowe and Jason Varitek in 1997—this would be their opportunity. Such a trade also would fly in the face of their implicit edict to compete every year, however.

Cherington traded Miller to Baltimore for pitching prospect Eduardo Rodriguez, a move that looked terrific at the time and only looked better as time passed. Boston pitching instructors revamped the way Rodriguez threw his changeup, allowing him to throw it as hard as he could rather than aiming for maximum separation from his fastball. The velocity of the pitch increased, but so too did the ferociousness of the sink, and it became a weapon for him. He posted a 3.85 ERA in 21 starts after his call-up in late May last season.

But in trading Lackey and Lester, Cherington targeted established major-league players rather than prospects. He tried to do again what he'd done so well two years earlier, a flash-turnaround of a last-place team into a World Series contender—without, perhaps, considering how unlikely such an accomplishment was in the first place. He didn't do what almost every other team would have done in the same position. He traded Lester and Jonny Gomes to Oakland for Yoenis Cespedes, a slugger nobody outside the game had known was even available. He traded Lackey to St. Louis for Allen Craig and Joe Kelly, two contributors to the St. Louis team his Red Sox had defeated in the 2013 World Series.

"There were attractive prospect packages that were available to us for both guys," he said the day of the trades. "We just felt like what made the most sense for us was to try to focus on impact major-league talent that's ready. Although there were some prospects that were available to us that were very attractive, we wanted to add to the major-league team and really give ourselves a head-start on building again and becoming as good as we can as quickly as possible."

The devil takes a hand, or so says an old Turkish proverb, in what is done in haste.

Rather than trading Lester for the next Varitek or Cain (or, at least, trying), the Red Sox traded Lester for a slugger who became superfluous (at least on the depth chart) in Boston as soon as Cuban defector Rusney Castillo signed his long-term contract three weeks later. Rather than trading Lackey for the next Syndergaard or Russell—or even another Rodriguez—the Red Sox traded Lackey for a middling big-league starter and a negative-value contract. Craig went almost immediately from a buy-low sleeper to an albatross, unclaimed on waivers and outrighted off the 40-man roster less than a year after the trade. Kelly yet has promise, especially after a strong close to his season, but he was sent to Triple-A Pawtucket in late June thanks to a 5.67 ERA and a refusal to throw pitches other than 99 mph fastballs. Lackey posted a sub-3.00 ERA in 33 starts for the Cardinals, and he pitched 7 1/3 shutout innings in the opening game of the NLDS. It was a near-total squandering of a valuable asset.

Part of the reason Cherington targeted Cespedes and Craig was the devastating lack of production the team had gotten from its youngest hitters—Bogaerts, Bradley and Middlebrooks. Bogaerts showed flashes of stardom in April and May before losing his way for three months, and Bradley and Middlebrooks would have ranked second-to-last and last in the American League in OPS+, respectively, had they been permitted enough plate appearances to qualify.

Perhaps Cherington could have been patient with his young players the way Kansas City was with its young players—with Cain, with Gordon, with Hosmer, with Moustakas. Perhaps he should have been that patient. Because he operated in what he saw as a unique baseball market, however, Cherington decided he couldn't afford such patience. He invested more than $70 million in Castillo that August, an apparent reflection of a lack of confidence in Bradley's hit tool. He invested more than $90 million in Pablo Sandoval in November, a move that necessitated a trade of Middlebrooks. He then spent close to $90 million on Hanley Ramirez, with the hope that the longtime shortstop could play an adequate left field for a year or two before taking over for David Ortiz as the team's designated hitter.

Those three signings represented classic big-market strategy, the type of strategy not often seen from small-market teams or sabermetric darlings. It bore greater resemblance to the spending sprees made by the Angels and the Marlins in 2011, or the Blue Jays in 2012. For Boston, those three signings represented the team's first foray into the high end of the free-agent market since an ill-advised $142 million investment in Crawford in 2010. That move had required a trade of miraculous proportions to escape. At least two of the three signings—if one feels generous, one might say the jury is still out on Castillo—have worked out about as well as the Crawford signing did.

Rather than controlling a roster of underachieving but cheap young players, Cherington found himself by midseason coping with a roster top-heavy with underachieving and expensive veterans—the type of inflexibility he'd pledged to avoid after he traded Crawford and Gonzalez to Los Angeles in 2012.

At the same time, in a nod to long-term sustainability, Cherington eschewed the high-end pitching market. He didn't go aggressively after Max Scherzer or James Shields. He didn't trade Mookie Betts or Blake Swihart for Cole Hamels. He declined to bid the $150 million or more it would have taken to bring back Lester, though the $135 million he did bid made all the more curious the team's reluctance to engage seriously with Lester the previous spring.

Instead, Cherington tried to acquire an ace-in-waiting

rather than an ace-in-name. Many felt Kelly had such potential thanks to an upper-90s fastball and three average or better secondary pitches. Given a second bite at trading a valuable veteran, he spun the now-redundant Cespedes not into prospects but into Rick Porcello. The pitcher was at the age when one could hope for a breakout rather than regression. But neither he nor Kelly performed anywhere close to expectations.

As the Red Sox sank into last place for a second straight season, Henry made the decision that the Cherington strategy had run its course. There's no room for patience in Boston, and Henry had run out of patience with his GM. The soft-spoken former commodities trader jumped on the opportunity to hire a potential Hall of Fame executive in Dombrowski, who had been let go by the Detroit Tigers. Cherington exited stage left.

Unlike Epstein or Cherington, Dombrowski comes to the Red Sox without deep New England roots. How he perceives and approaches the pressure to win immediately and consistently remains to be seen. He repeatedly made clear he believes a Red Sox team that prominently features Bogaerts, Rodriguez, Mookie Betts, and catching tandem Blake Swihart and Christian Vazquez has little need for a total tear-down. He went further than that in late November, when he signed his name on a contract that promised $217 million to David Price. Forget aces in waiting, Boston was saying. Just give us the ace.

"We're in a position that we should be in a spot to compete," Dombrowski said a week after the season ended. "There are cycles that are attached to that. You have a hard time collecting young talent at times when you're a big-market club because a lot of times you're trading that talent, or you're impatient with them. It's hard to get them over the hump because of the added pressures of being in a big market. (But) we have some of those players, which is a tremendous plus for us."

Rebuilding might not be possible in Boston. As the Dombrowski era dawns, the Red Sox will try to figure out whether, at the very least, some patience is. ■

— Brian MacPherson is a Red Sox beat writer for the Providence Journal

Hitters

Andrew Benintendi OF

Born: 7/6/94 Age: 21 Bats: L Throws: L Height: 5'10" Weight: 170

YEAR	TEAM	LVL	AGE	PA	R	2B	3B	HR	RBI	BB	K	SB	CS	AVG/OBP/SLG	TAv	BABIP	BRR	FRAA	WARP
2015	LOW	A-	20	153	19	2	4	7	15	25	15	7	1	.290/.408/.540	.317	.279	1.6	CF(31): 8.4	2.4
2015	GRN	A	20	86	17	5	0	4	16	10	9	3	2	.351/.430/.581	.374	.355	1.0	CF(18): -2.5	1.2
2016	*BOS*	*MLB*	*21*	*250*	*30*	*10*	*1*	*9*	*30*	*21*	*56*	*3*	*2*	*.244/.310/.412*	*.250*	*.283*	*-0.2*	*CF 1*	*0.7*
2017	*BOS*	*MLB*	*22*	*373*	*48*	*14*	*2*	*14*	*48*	*34*	*83*	*5*	*3*	*.253/.324/.432*	*.260*	*.294*	*-0.1*	*CF 2*	*1.6*

Breakout: 8% Improve: 19% Collapse: 2% Attrition: 8% MLB: 32% *Comparables: Joc Pederson, Christian Yelich, Byron Buxton*

You have to think former Red Sox GM Ben Cherington was thrilled when Benintendi, the SEC Player of the Year, was there for the taking with the seventh pick in the 2015 draft; in fact, one could say the board fell *exactly* as Benintendi did. A five-tool outfielder who dominated as a sophomore at Arkansas, Benintendi raked in small samples at both Lowell and Greenville, showcasing an advanced approach and more pop than his frame would suggest. While he's got the speed and instincts to make it work in center, his above-average arm makes him perhaps best suited to Fenway's spacious right field, where he can spend his entire career being compared (favorably) to Trot Nixon or (unfavorably) to J.D. Drew, depending on how he emotes post-strikeouts.

Mookie Betts CF

Born: 10/7/92 Age: 23 Bats: R Throws: R Height: 5'9" Weight: 180

YEAR	TEAM	LVL	AGE	PA	R	2B	3B	HR	RBI	BB	K	SB	CS	AVG/OBP/SLG	TAv	BABIP	BRR	FRAA	WARP
2013	SLM	A+	20	211	30	12	3	7	39	23	17	20	2	.341/.414/.551	.331	.346	3.0	2B(50): 9.4	3.5
2013	GRN	A	20	340	63	24	1	8	26	58	40	18	2	.296/.418/.477	.329	.322	4.7	2B(76): -6.3	3.4
2014	PME	AA	21	253	56	18	3	6	34	35	20	22	3	.355/.443/.551	.346	.366	6.2	2B(40): 1.7, CF(12): -0.7	3.9
2014	PAW	AAA	21	211	31	12	2	5	31	26	30	11	4	.335/.417/.503	.314	.380	2.4	CF(33): -0.5, 2B(6): -0.5	2.0
2014	BOS	MLB	21	213	34	12	1	5	18	21	31	7	3	.291/.368/.444	.300	.327	3.2	CF(28): 0.2, 2B(14): -0.8	1.8
2015	BOS	MLB	22	654	92	42	8	18	77	46	82	21	6	.291/.341/.479	.291	.310	2.3	CF(133): 11.9, RF(11): -0.9	5.5
2016	*BOS*	*MLB*	*23*	*651*	*94*	*38*	*5*	*18*	*73*	*59*	*89*	*25*	*7*	*.299/.364/.477*	*.291*	*.324*	*3.3*	*RF 3, CF 1*	*4.6*
2017	*BOS*	*MLB*	*24*	*591*	*77*	*35*	*4*	*17*	*75*	*56*	*83*	*23*	*6*	*.295/.363/.474*	*.287*	*.319*	*3.9*	*RF 3, CF 1*	*4.6*

Breakout: 2% Improve: 48% Collapse: 2% Attrition: 12% MLB: 87% *Comparables: Grady Sizemore, Andrew McCutchen, Logan Morrison*

Baseball isn't supposed to be this easy. Betts has gone from a breakout prospect in Greenville to a first-division starter in two years, and he appears to be on the cusp of something altogether more. The then-22-year-old almost joined the 20/20 club in his first full campaign, showing off more power than most thought he possessed. He displayed the skills needed to be a plus-plus defender in center, despite very little outfield experience. He also got better in the second half, demonstrating that he knows how to adjust, and he did all this with the quiet confidence and selective aggressiveness that define many of the game's best players. Rather than go a few months without dominating a sphere-hurling sport, Betts spent his offseason participating in the PBA's World Series of Bowling, proving that he's always hunting quality strikes. Whether you prefer Betts or Xander Bogaerts is a question of taste, but there's no doubt that this is what a franchise cornerstone looks like in today's game.

Xander Bogaerts SS

Born: 10/1/92 Age: 23 Bats: R Throws: R Height: 6'1" Weight: 210

YEAR	TEAM	LVL	AGE	PA	R	2B	3B	HR	RBI	BB	K	SB	CS	AVG/OBP/SLG	TAv	BABIP	BRR	FRAA	WARP
2013	BOS	MLB	20	50	7	2	0	1	5	5	13	1	0	.250/.320/.364	.300	.323	1.1	3B(9): -1.4, SS(8): 1.6	0.5
2013	PME	AA	20	259	40	12	6	6	35	35	51	5	1	.311/.407/.502	.324	.378	1.9	SS(47): -5.4	2.4
2013	PAW	AAA	20	256	32	11	0	9	32	28	44	2	2	.284/.369/.453	.285	.320	1.5	SS(49): -5.6, 3B(10): -1.0	1.2
2014	BOS	MLB	21	594	60	28	1	12	46	39	138	2	3	.240/.297/.362	.247	.296	3.0	SS(99): -8.2, 3B(44): -1.9	0.7
2015	BOS	MLB	22	654	84	35	3	7	81	32	101	10	2	.320/.355/.421	.266	.372	4.8	SS(156): -1.4	3.5
2016	*BOS*	*MLB*	*23*	*620*	*66*	*31*	*3*	*13*	*71*	*42*	*120*	*6*	*2*	*.284/.337/.420*	*.265*	*.336*	*3.4*	*SS -8*	*3.0*
2017	*BOS*	*MLB*	*24*	*568*	*71*	*28*	*2*	*15*	*67*	*43*	*109*	*6*	*2*	*.286/.345/.435*	*.271*	*.336*	*3.1*	*SS -7*	*3.6*

Breakout: 9% Improve: 59% Collapse: 1% Attrition: 6% MLB: 98% *Comparables: Troy Tulowitzki, Starlin Castro, Hanley Ramirez*

This is not the Xander Bogaerts we were promised. As a prospect, Bogaerts was labeled as a third baseman masquerading as a shortstop, but one whose plus power would yield immediate results. In 2015, the Sox were gifted a competent defensive shortstop with an impressive hit tool, but one whose power failed to shine. Homers are at a premium in the game today, and you can argue that the Bogaerts who existed in the minds of so many scouts would be the superior version. But legitimate shortstops who can bat in the top third of the order are something altogether more rare, and that's very much who Bogaerts is already at the age of 23.

His transformation is remarkable for several reasons, first among them his glove work. In 2014, he was a defensive trainwreck, showing poor range and an inability to make accurate throws in high-pressure situations. It turns out renowned infielder coach Brian Butterfield is renowned for a reason, and Bogaerts is now a legitimate shortstop through and through, capable of making every routine play and the occasional spectacular one. But he didn't just show up a new fielder in 2015; he also totally changed his approach to hitting. Known for power and patience in the minors, he cut down his walks and strikeouts by swinging earlier in the count, pushing the ball the other way a ton and riding a .372 BABIP to the majors' fifth-best average. The Aruban even ran a bit, going 10-for-12 in steal attempts and posting positive baserunning numbers.

The hope, of course, is that it all comes together. That Bogaerts remains a staunch defender, above-average runner and good hitter while allowing his natural plus power to surface. The fear is that he's lost his pop and is too reliant on weak contact, making him a solid player but not altogether special. Odds dictate he'll end up somewhere between those two outcomes, but when you see the ease with which he can generate loft and how he makes adjustments, it's tough to bet against him blossoming into a star. Whether you prefer Bogaerts or Mookie Betts is a question of taste, but there's no doubt that either iteration of Bogaerts is what a franchise cornerstone looks like in today's game.

Jackie Bradley CF

Born: 4/19/90 Age: 26 Bats: L Throws: R Height: 5'10" Weight: 200

YEAR	TEAM	LVL	AGE	PA	R	2B	3B	HR	RBI	BB	K	SB	CS	AVG/OBP/SLG	TAv	BABIP	BRR	FRAA	WARP
2013	PAW	AAA	23	374	57	26	3	10	35	41	75	7	7	.275/.374/.469	.302	.331	0.1	CF(58): 2.7, RF(7): 0.5	3.3
2013	BOS	MLB	23	107	18	5	0	3	10	10	31	2	0	.189/.280/.337	.236	.246	-2.2	CF(19): -0.7, LF(14): -0.2	-0.3
2014	PAW	AAA	24	69	6	1	0	1	5	3	18	0	1	.212/.246/.273	.185	.277	0.3	CF(14): 1.6	-0.2
2014	BOS	MLB	24	423	45	19	2	1	30	31	121	8	0	.198/.265/.266	.198	.284	0.4	CF(113): 21.0, RF(12): -0.8	0.8
2015	BOS	MLB	25	255	43	17	4	10	43	27	69	3	0	.249/.335/.498	.280	.310	2.0	RF(32): 3.6, CF(27): -1.7	2.1
2015	PAW	AAA	25	318	38	18	1	9	29	30	44	4	4	.305/.382/.472	.322	.336	-0.2	CF(67): -3.0, RF(2): 0.1	2.7
2016	*BOS*	*MLB*	*26*	*511*	*63*	*28*	*3*	*13*	*52*	*43*	*126*	*7*	*3*	*.247/.320/.405*	*.253*	*.310*	*-1.0*	*CF 6*	*2.0*
2017	*BOS*	*MLB*	*27*	*491*	*59*	*27*	*3*	*13*	*56*	*43*	*118*	*6*	*3*	*.249/.324/.413*	*.256*	*.310*	*-0.8*	*CF 6*	*2.4*

Breakout: 7% Improve: 59% Collapse: 8% Attrition: 14% MLB: 91% *Comparables: Jose Bautista, Curtis Granderson, Kirk Nieuwenhuis*

That may be Bradley's 2015 triple-slash line, but it's rarely the type of hitter he truly represents. Sometimes, like in August when he hit .354/.429/.734, Bradley looks like an offensive force few predicted he could become even as a high-profile prospect. More often, like in September when he hit .216/.308/.431, he still appears to be utterly incompetent. Bradley has nearly 800 career PA, but it's hard to figure out exactly who he is. He remains a generational defensive talent and he showed surprising pop last year... but he's just soooo bad sometimes. Is he Mike Cameron without speed? Fred Lynn with a crappy average? Or maybe just Juan Lagares with a better draft pedigree? We don't know yet, but if Bradley takes as big a leap forward in 2016 as he did in 2015, he's a uniquely valuable asset. And hey, if there's anything JBJ excels at, it's his irreproachable first step.

Rusney Castillo RF

Born: 7/9/87 Age: 28 Bats: R Throws: R Height: 5'9" Weight: 195

YEAR	TEAM	LVL	AGE	PA	R	2B	3B	HR	RBI	BB	K	SB	CS	AVG/OBP/SLG	TAv	BABIP	BRR	FRAA	WARP
2014	BOS	MLB	26	40	6	1	0	2	6	3	6	3	0	.333/.400/.528	.319	.357	0.7	CF(10): 1.3	0.6
2015	BOS	MLB	27	289	35	10	2	5	29	13	54	4	5	.253/.288/.359	.213	.298	1.3	RF(48): 4.3, LF(24): 4.6	0.3
2015	PAW	AAA	27	172	17	7	0	3	17	14	28	10	2	.282/.337/.385	.292	.323	0.0	CF(17): 1.6, RF(16): -1.6	1.0
2016	*BOS*	*MLB*	*28*	*570*	*67*	*26*	*3*	*14*	*60*	*34*	*109*	*15*	*7*	*.267/.314/.406*	*.249*	*.310*	*1.8*	*LF 2, RF 1*	*1.6*
2017	*BOS*	*MLB*	*29*	*486*	*57*	*23*	*2*	*13*	*56*	*29*	*93*	*12*	*6*	*.266/.313/.411*	*.251*	*.307*	*2.1*	*LF 2, RF 1*	*1.9*

Breakout: 3% Improve: 48% Collapse: 8% Attrition: 16% MLB: 88% *Comparables: Charlie Blackmon, Chris Duffy, Felix Pie*

Castillo has more raw power and a better arm than Mookie Betts and more speed and better bat-to-ball ability than Jackie Bradley Jr. He's quickly becoming the poster boy for the argument that tools aren't everything. Coming out of Cuba, Castillo was lauded for his glove, arm and speed, and we were told the hit tool and power would be good enough to play. He's come as advertised in the outfield and in terms of pop, but breaking pitches befuddle him, he's a horrendous baserunner and he makes mental mistakes that Dewey Crowe would find amateurish. You can cite a lack of MLB experience, but Castillo will turn 29 this season, and there's no explaining away his .202 TAv against right-handed pitching. Maybe the unique circumstances make it unfair to grade Castillo against standard aging curves and we all know development isn't linear, but as of now it looks like the Red Sox spent $72.5 million on a short-side platoon player.

Michael Chavis 3B

Born: 8/11/95 Age: 20 Bats: R Throws: R Height: 5'10" Weight: 190

YEAR	TEAM	LVL	AGE	PA	R	2B	3B	HR	RBI	BB	K	SB	CS	AVG/OBP/SLG	TAv	BABIP	BRR	FRAA	WARP
2015	GRN	A	19	471	56	29	1	16	58	29	144	8	5	.223/.277/.405	.244	.293	-1.2	3B(68): 3.7, SS(1): -0.1	0.6
2016	*BOS*	*MLB*	*20*	*250*	*23*	*10*	*0*	*8*	*28*	*11*	*92*	*2*	*1*	*.198/.236/.344*	*.201*	*.281*	*-0.4*	*3B 2, SS -0*	*-0.8*
2017	*BOS*	*MLB*	*21*	*368*	*40*	*17*	*1*	*13*	*43*	*18*	*130*	*3*	*1*	*.208/.251/.371*	*.218*	*.288*	*-0.6*	*3B 3, SS 0*	*-0.2*

Breakout: 1% Improve: 2% Collapse: 0% Attrition: 2% MLB: 2% *Comparables: Matt Davidson, Marcell Ozuna, Nick Castellanos*

When Chavis was drafted in the first round in 2014, we were told he possessed a relatively mature hit tool and developing power. In his first taste of full-season ball, the Georgia native flipped the script on those reports, mashing 16 homers and 29 doubles but hitting for a poor average and striking out at a Tim Beckham-esque pace. A Tim Beckham-esque K% is the same as a Kris Bryant K%, to be fair, but players who whiff like that bust more often than they turn into handsome franchise cornerstones. That being said, Chavis *is* handsome, so if he learns to walk more than once a week that's half the battle right there.

Allen Craig RF

Born: 7/18/84 Age: 31 Bats: R Throws: R Height: 6'2" Weight: 215

YEAR	TEAM	LVL	AGE	PA	R	2B	3B	HR	RBI	BB	K	SB	CS	AVG/OBP/SLG	TAv	BABIP	BRR	FRAA	WARP
2013	SLN	MLB	28	563	71	29	2	13	97	40	100	2	0	.315/.373/.457	.297	.368	-2.5	1B(95): 0.4, LF(25): -0.8	2.3
2014	SLN	MLB	29	398	34	17	1	7	44	26	77	1	1	.237/.291/.346	.233	.281	-3.6	RF(70): -5.0, 1B(24): 1.4	-1.3
2014	BOS	MLB	29	107	7	3	0	1	2	9	36	1	0	.128/.234/.191	.177	.193	-0.2	1B(17): 1.1, RF(12): -1.3	-0.8
2015	PAW	AAA	30	399	29	14	0	4	30	49	70	0	0	.274/.368/.350	.277	.331	-3.0	1B(46): -3.4, RF(21): -2.0	0.3
2015	BOS	MLB	30	88	6	1	0	1	3	7	26	0	0	.152/.239/.203	.181	.212	-0.2	RF(9): -0.0, LF(7): -0.1	-0.6
2016	*BOS*	*MLB*	*31*	*250*	*27*	*13*	*0*	*7*	*31*	*19*	*52*	*1*	*0*	*.272/.334/.426*	*.265*	*.322*	*-1.1*	*1B 1, RF -1*	*0.5*
2017	*BOS*	*MLB*	*32*	*226*	*27*	*12*	*0*	*6*	*26*	*18*	*48*	*0*	*0*	*.261/.324/.412*	*.257*	*.310*	*-1.1*	*1B 1, RF -1*	*0.4*

Breakout: 2% Improve: 31% Collapse: 8% Attrition: 10% MLB: 85% *Comparables: Jesus Guzman, Mike Lamb, Adam Lind*

Everything came up Allen Craig in 2015... except for Allen Craig himself. Buried beneath a glut of first-base/corner-outfield types when the season began, Craig saw the likes of Mike Napoli, Shane Victorino, Hanley Ramirez, Rusney Castillo and Daniel Nava all get hurt, traded, demoted or some combination thereof. Craig also saw the Red Sox stink, increasing the likelihood they'd be willing to play him to see what he had left in the tank. What Craig didn't see was any semblance of his old power, and while he reached base at a good clip in Pawtucket, he lacks the thunder you need from a corner bat. Unless he finds the Fountain of Youth and its accompanying gold stein, Craig's best days are behind him.

Rafael Devers 3B

Born: 10/24/96 Age: 19 Bats: L Throws: R Height: 6'0" Weight: 195

YEAR	TEAM	LVL	AGE	PA	R	2B	3B	HR	RBI	BB	K	SB	CS	AVG/OBP/SLG	TAv	BABIP	BRR	FRAA	WARP
2015	GRN	A	18	508	71	38	1	11	70	24	84	3	2	.288/.329/.443	.282	.326	1.6	3B(72): -9.1	1.7
2016	*BOS*	*MLB*	*19*	*250*	*22*	*13*	*0*	*6*	*28*	*8*	*63*	*0*	*0*	*.235/.265/.374*	*.219*	*.290*	*-0.5*	*3B -3*	*-0.8*
2017	*BOS*	*MLB*	*20*	*429*	*46*	*25*	*1*	*12*	*49*	*14*	*103*	*0*	*0*	*.242/.273/.395*	*.231*	*.293*	*-1.1*	*3B -5*	*-0.5*

Breakout: 0% Improve: 1% Collapse: 0% Attrition: 0% MLB: 1% *Comparables: Matt Dominguez, Cheslor Cuthbert, Jefry Marte*

Articles about Devers lend themselves to the same hyperbolic headlines as particularly brutal Jon Stewart takedowns: *Watch Rafael Devers Absolutely Destroy This Baseball. This Fastball Was Eviscerated By Rafael Devers. Rafael Devers Is Molecularly Deconstructing Low-A Pitching.* Given the sweet-swinging lefty bat's power, age and results, it's easy to understand why; anytime a teenager dominates at the plate the way Devers has before his 19th birthday, there's going to be excitement. But despite his youth, pop and bat-to-barrel skills, Devers isn't perfect. His walk rate fell below 5 percent last year, he's not terribly athletic and so far he looks more like a first baseman than a third baseman. Power comes at a premium today, and if his hit *and* pop both grade out as plus, not a lot else will matter. Still, he'll need to at least refine his approach if he wants to put on a daily show in the big leagues.

Ryan Hanigan C

Born: 8/16/80 Age: 35 Bats: R Throws: R Height: 6'0" Weight: 215

YEAR	TEAM	LVL	AGE	PA	R	2B	3B	HR	RBI	BB	K	SB	CS	AVG/OBP/SLG	TAv	BABIP	BRR	FRAA	WARP
2013	CIN	MLB	32	260	17	8	0	2	21	29	27	0	1	.198/.306/.261	.219	.216	-1.1	C(72): 5.2	0.5
2014	PCH	A+	33	24	4	0	0	1	2	2	3	0	0	.250/.375/.400	.294	.250	-0.1	C(3): -0.0	0.1
2014	TBA	MLB	33	263	18	9	0	5	34	31	39	1	0	.218/.318/.324	.251	.240	-1.6	C(79): 5.9	1.4
2015	BOS	MLB	34	201	28	8	0	2	16	20	39	0	0	.247/.337/.328	.242	.306	-1.9	C(53): 0.7	0.4
2016	*BOS*	*MLB*	*35*	*90*	*9*	*4*	*0*	*1*	*8*	*10*	*12*	*0*	*0*	*.252/.342/.340*	*.245*	*.283*	*-0.4*	*C 1*	*0.3*
2017	*BOS*	*MLB*	*36*	*94*	*10*	*3*	*0*	*1*	*8*	*10*	*13*	*0*	*0*	*.245/.335/.324*	*.239*	*.276*	*-0.4*	*C 1*	*0.3*

Breakout: 2% Improve: 26% Collapse: 7% Attrition: 17% MLB: 86% *Comparables: Jason Kendall, Brian Schneider, Paul Lo Duca*

YEAR	TEAM	P. COUNT	FRM RUNS	BLK RUNS	THRW RUNS	TOT RUNS
2013	CIN	9151	4.4	-0.3	0.4	4.6
2014	TBA	10071	6.3	0.3	0.1	6.6
2015	BOS	7692	1.3	0.0	0.3	1.5
2016	*BOS*	*3378*	*1.1*	*0.0*	*0.1*	*1.1*
2017	*BOS*	*3514*	*0.9*	*0.0*	*0.1*	*0.9*

It's truly amazing that everyone keeps walking Hanigan, because he can't really do anything with balls thrown over the plate; the veteran backstop has just 34 extra-base hits over the past three seasons. Yet he still somehow managed a 10 percent walk rate last year, proof that it can just be hard to throw three strikes in baseball. Hanigan is still a relevant roster piece thanks to his defense, respect as a game-caller and OBP that's tolerable for a no. 9 hitter. That being said, it may be best if Blake Swihart and/or Christian Vazquez conspire to make him obsolete before opposing pitchers finish the job.

Marco Hernandez SS

Born: 9/6/92 Age: 23 Bats: L Throws: R Height: 6'0" Weight: 170

YEAR	TEAM	LVL	AGE	PA	R	2B	3B	HR	RBI	BB	K	SB	CS	AVG/OBP/SLG	TAv	BABIP	BRR	FRAA	WARP
2013	KNC	A	20	443	45	17	3	4	34	16	72	21	7	.254/.287/.338	.234	.297	-0.6	SS(100): 8.6	1.3
2014	DAY	A+	21	486	61	13	7	3	55	30	90	22	8	.270/.315/.351	.246	.328	0.0	SS(122): 4.3	1.8
2015	PAW	AAA	22	190	27	9	2	4	22	8	39	1	0	.271/.300/.409	.268	.324	-1.2	SS(22): -4.4, 2B(15): -0.6	0.2
2015	PME	AA	22	294	30	21	4	5	31	9	49	4	2	.326/.349/.482	.289	.382	-1.9	SS(67): -3.0	1.6
2016	*BOS*	*MLB*	*23*	*250*	*23*	*11*	*2*	*4*	*24*	*7*	*61*	*3*	*1*	*.250/.272/.369*	*.219*	*.311*	*0.1*	*SS -0, 2B -0*	*0.1*
2017	*BOS*	*MLB*	*24*	*359*	*35*	*17*	*3*	*6*	*36*	*12*	*85*	*4*	*2*	*.246/.274/.372*	*.225*	*.304*	*0.3*	*SS -1, 2B 0*	*0.5*

Breakout: 17% Improve: 30% Collapse: 10% Attrition: 23% MLB: 46% *Comparables: Danny Santana, Jeff Bianchi, Hector Gomez*

Single-A was cruel to Hernandez. The then-Cub struggled in a small sample there in 2012 and again for a full season in 2013, largely erasing himself from the prospect scene. Since then, however, he's hit at every stop, including a 46-game demonstration at Pawtucket to end last season. There's not much power in his profile, but there is some speed and some bat-to-ball ability. It's enough that as someone who can legitimately hold down the shortstop position he should make for a viable utility infielder. You read that right: The Red Sox system is so deep they even have Deven Marrero insurance. Given that Hernandez was acquired for the low, low price of one Felix Doubront, it's pretty clear in retrospect that Boston won the Theo Epstein trade.

Brock Holt UT

Born: 6/11/88 Age: 28 Bats: L Throws: R Height: 5'10" Weight: 180

YEAR	TEAM	LVL	AGE	PA	R	2B	3B	HR	RBI	BB	K	SB	CS	AVG/OBP/SLG	TAv	BABIP	BRR	FRAA	WARP
2013	BOS	MLB	25	72	9	2	0	0	11	7	4	1	0	.203/.275/.237	.230	.207	0.7	3B(20): -0.5, 2B(5): 0.0	0.0
2013	PAW	AAA	25	329	35	6	0	3	24	30	54	8	3	.258/.327/.309	.244	.303	-0.1	2B(44): -5.5, SS(32): -2.5	-0.2
2014	PAW	AAA	26	121	21	8	2	1	7	8	12	7	1	.315/.380/.454	.302	.344	0.5	SS(19): -0.2, 3B(4): -0.1	1.2
2014	BOS	MLB	26	492	68	23	5	4	29	33	98	12	2	.281/.331/.381	.261	.349	3.8	3B(39): -1.5, RF(35): -0.4	1.5
2015	BOS	MLB	27	509	56	27	6	2	45	46	97	8	1	.280/.349/.379	.256	.350	3.8	2B(58): 0.8, 3B(33): -1.3	1.6
2016	*BOS*	*MLB*	*28*	*356*	*41*	*17*	*3*	*3*	*30*	*27*	*63*	*7*	*2*	*.282/.338/.386*	*.251*	*.334*	*1.9*	*2B -0, SS -0*	*1.2*
2017	*BOS*	*MLB*	*29*	*500*	*54*	*25*	*4*	*5*	*46*	*38*	*90*	*9*	*2*	*.280/.337/.383*	*.250*	*.334*	*2.7*	*2B 0, SS 0*	*1.9*

Breakout: 5% Improve: 37% Collapse: 7% Attrition: 17% MLB: 82% *Comparables: Chris Burke, Jemile Weeks, Brandon Phillips*

The Red Sox were tough to watch during the first half of 2015. Their young players weren't thriving, their new additions were floundering and their pitching sent most of New England into a state of denial. Who could Boston look to in this time of need? None other than Brock Holt and Brock Holt's hair, who together hit .292/.379/.412 en route to an All-Star Game appearance. For the second straight year, Brock Holt, All-Star continued to serve as baseball's most versatile player, appearing at every defensive spot save pitcher and catcher at least once. Unfortunately, as the Red Sox got better in the second half, Brock Holt, All-Star got much worse, continuing a more ominous trend. Chances are we've seen Brock Holt, All-Star's peak, but so long as he continues to serve as Boston's Swiss Army knife he's a uniquely valuable and incredibly fun asset.

Deven Marrero SS

Born: 8/25/90 Age: 25 Bats: R Throws: R Height: 6'1" Weight: 195

YEAR	TEAM	LVL	AGE	PA	R	2B	3B	HR	RBI	BB	K	SB	CS	AVG/OBP/SLG	TAv	BABIP	BRR	FRAA	WARP
2013	SLM	A+	22	376	50	20	0	2	21	42	60	21	2	.256/.341/.334	.238	.307	-0.5	SS(85): 6.1	1.3
2013	PME	AA	22	85	7	0	0	0	5	10	16	6	0	.236/.321/.236	.229	.293	1.9	SS(19): 4.7	0.8
2014	PAW	AAA	23	202	23	11	0	1	20	12	37	4	1	.210/.260/.285	.189	.255	0.7	SS(50): -0.8	-0.8
2014	PME	AA	23	307	42	19	2	5	39	34	57	12	7	.291/.371/.433	.290	.349	-1.3	SS(66): -2.5	1.9
2015	BOS	MLB	24	56	8	0	0	1	3	3	19	2	1	.226/.268/.283	.202	.333	0.8	3B(13): 0.3, SS(6): 0.3	0.0
2015	PAW	AAA	24	419	49	13	1	6	29	33	87	12	5	.256/.316/.344	.259	.315	2.7	SS(90): 6.4, 2B(8): -1.2	2.5
2016	*BOS*	*MLB*	*25*	*32*	*4*	*1*	*0*	*1*	*3*	*2*	*8*	*1*	*0*	*.241/.300/.347*	*.227*	*.304*	*0.0*	*SS 0*	*0.1*
2017	*BOS*	*MLB*	*26*	*290*	*31*	*13*	*1*	*5*	*28*	*22*	*70*	*7*	*3*	*.242/.300/.354*	*.231*	*.306*	*0.3*	*SS 2*	*0.9*

Breakout: 1% Improve: 17% Collapse: 9% Attrition: 21% MLB: 44% *Comparables: Chris Nelson, Tyler Saladino, Argenis Diaz*

The Red Sox went back to the well one too many times when they popped Marrero in the first round in 2012; not every middle infielder from ASU turns into a franchise cornerstone, it seems. Marrero hit well enough in Portland in 2014 for some to think he could be a second-division starter, but really, the book's been out on him for a while now. He's a utility infielder through and through, talented with the glove but bereft of offensive upside and not fleet-of-foot enough to be an impact pinch-runner. While such a player has some value, it's still a disappointing outcome for someone with Marrero's draft pedigree.

Yoan Moncada 2B

Born: 5/27/95 Age: 21 Bats: B Throws: R Height: 6'2" Weight: 205

YEAR	TEAM	LVL	AGE	PA	R	2B	3B	HR	RBI	BB	K	SB	CS	AVG/OBP/SLG	TAv	BABIP	BRR	FRAA	WARP
2015	GRN	A	20	363	61	19	3	8	38	42	83	49	3	.278/.380/.438	.312	.353	7.6	2B(71): -5.5	3.2
2016	*BOS*	*MLB*	*21*	*250*	*32*	*10*	*1*	*6*	*23*	*21*	*75*	*17*	*3*	*.220/.296/.351*	*.229*	*.297*	*2.3*	*2B -3*	*0.1*
2017	*BOS*	*MLB*	*22*	*300*	*34*	*13*	*1*	*8*	*32*	*25*	*89*	*21*	*4*	*.225/.300/.368*	*.236*	*.301*	*3.5*	*2B -3*	*1.0*

Breakout: 2% Improve: 5% Collapse: 0% Attrition: 5% MLB: 9% *Comparables: Brett Lawrie, Jonathan Schoop, Dilson Herrera*

Moncada spent his first professional season reaffirming truths that many baseball fans hold to be self-evident: You don't draft or sign young talent based on need, you can't take small sample sizes seriously and MLB's international signing restrictions are for suckers. The concern among Red Sox Nation members was palpable when Moncada hit just .229/.311/.321 in his first 30 games, because it's shocking, really, that a 20-year-old in a new country in full-season ball who hadn't played professionally in nearly two years might show a little rust. Oddly enough, from July 1st on, Moncada hit .305/.414/.503, and he finished the year in Greenville an absurd 49-for-52 in stolen base attempts. We won't know for the better part of a decade whether Moncada will justify the $63 million the Red Sox spent on him, but he's off to one hell of a start. If nothing else, it doesn't seem like anyone's too worried about Pablo Sandoval blocking him now.

David Ortiz DH

Born: 11/18/75 Age: 40 Bats: L Throws: L Height: 6'3" Weight: 230

YEAR	TEAM	LVL	AGE	PA	R	2B	3B	HR	RBI	BB	K	SB	CS	AVG/OBP/SLG	TAv	BABIP	BRR	FRAA	WARP
2013	BOS	MLB	37	600	84	38	2	30	103	76	88	4	0	.309/.395/.564	.332	.321	-2.2	1B(6): -0.4	4.9
2014	BOS	MLB	38	602	59	27	0	35	104	75	95	0	0	.263/.355/.517	.307	.256	-7.7	1B(5): 0.0	2.7
2015	BOS	MLB	39	614	73	37	0	37	108	77	95	0	1	.273/.360/.553	.304	.264	-6.6	1B(9): -0.0	2.8
2016	*BOS*	*MLB*	*40*	*608*	*83*	*32*	*1*	*31*	*96*	*72*	*97*	*1*	*1*	*.278/.363/.514*	*.298*	*.287*	*-4.8*	-	*3.0*
2017	*BOS*	*MLB*	*41*	*465*	*66*	*23*	*0*	*20*	*67*	*53*	*79*	*0*	*0*	*.265/.349/.474*	*.278*	*.281*	*-3.9*	-	*1.7*

Breakout: 0% Improve: 16% Collapse: 8% Attrition: 13% MLB: 77% *Comparables: Frank Thomas, Chipper Jones, Hank Aaron*

Throw out anything you think you know about aging curves or the rules of baseball in general; they don't apply to Ortiz. Since the last Annual publication, Ortiz added another 37 homers to his total, joined the 500 home run club, logged his most innings in the field since 2006 (still just 60, but hey) and turned 40 years old. Just about everything that could've gone right for Ortiz in 2015 did. He stayed on the field, continued to post an absurdly good K/BB% for a power hitter, recorded his most plate appearances since 2009 and padded what should be a Hall of Fame resume. If you want to nitpick, Ortiz's stats against southpaws took a turn for the worse, but his 1.008 OPS against right-handers is enough to justify his role and salary. Big Papi chose to hang up the cleats after 2016, but it looks as though we'll be spared a Jeterian limp to the finish line. Enjoy this ride while it lasts, because there's never going to be anyone quite like Ortiz ever again.

Dustin Pedroia 2B

Born: 8/17/83 Age: 32 Bats: R Throws: R Height: 5'9" Weight: 175

YEAR	TEAM	LVL	AGE	PA	R	2B	3B	HR	RBI	BB	K	SB	CS	AVG/OBP/SLG	TAv	BABIP	BRR	FRAA	WARP
2013	BOS	MLB	29	724	91	42	2	9	84	73	75	17	5	.301/.372/.415	.289	.326	-1.4	2B(160): 4.6	4.5
2014	BOS	MLB	30	609	72	33	0	7	53	51	75	6	6	.278/.337/.376	.268	.307	2.9	2B(135): 10.0	3.6
2015	BOS	MLB	31	425	46	19	1	12	42	38	51	2	2	.291/.356/.441	.271	.308	-0.4	2B(92): 2.6	1.9
2016	*BOS*	*MLB*	*32*	*599*	*67*	*32*	*2*	*12*	*67*	*55*	*71*	*9*	*4*	*.291/.357/.425*	*.273*	*.313*	*0.1*	*2B 5*	*3.9*
2017	*BOS*	*MLB*	*33*	*480*	*57*	*24*	*1*	*9*	*50*	*42*	*60*	*6*	*3*	*.283/.346/.403*	*.263*	*.309*	*0.3*	*2B 4*	*3.0*

Breakout: 1% Improve: 36% Collapse: 2% Attrition: 9% MLB: 98% *Comparables: Ian Kinsler, Placido Polanco, Jose Vidro*

Pedroia was on pace to have one of his better offensive seasons in recent history until a hamstring injury forced him to the DL in late June. The Muddy Chicken pushed himself to return in mid-July, but he clearly pushed too hard, re-aggravating the injury after six games and subsequently missing the next six weeks. When healthy, Pedroia showed surprising power, and he could have challenged for 20 bombs for the first time since 2011 if he had received 600-plus PA. Unfortunately, Pedroia also took a small step back in the field, proved that his base-stealing days are over and missed at least 20 games for the third time in the past five seasons. We knew all about second basemen and aging curves when he signed his eight-year extension in 2014. Pedroia still has the hit tool, glove and low AAV to make that deal look good, but we may need to start referencing his contract as "merely good" rather than "a massive steal" for the Red Sox. That's still a hell of a thing, and he is poised to remain an impact contributor even if, thanks to Mookie Betts and Xander Bogaerts, he's no longer Boston's best overall player.

Hanley Ramirez 1B

Born: 12/23/83 Age: 32 Bats: R Throws: R Height: 6'2" Weight: 225

YEAR	TEAM	LVL	AGE	PA	R	2B	3B	HR	RBI	BB	K	SB	CS	AVG/OBP/SLG	TAv	BABIP	BRR	FRAA	WARP
2013	LAN	MLB	29	336	62	25	2	20	57	27	52	10	2	.345/.402/.638	.360	.363	-1.6	SS(76): 1.2	4.8
2014	LAN	MLB	30	512	64	35	0	13	71	56	84	14	5	.283/.369/.448	.305	.323	0.9	SS(115): -16.2	2.8
2015	BOS	MLB	31	430	59	12	1	19	53	21	71	6	3	.249/.291/.426	.252	.257	0.0	LF(92): -15.9, 3B(1): -0.0	-1.2
2016	*BOS*	*MLB*	*32*	*562*	*72*	*29*	*2*	*20*	*74*	*48*	*100*	*13*	*5*	*.274/.341/.460*	*.279*	*.304*	*-0.6*	*1B 0*	*2.0*
2017	*BOS*	*MLB*	*33*	*491*	*64*	*25*	*1*	*17*	*64*	*40*	*88*	*10*	*4*	*.273/.337/.451*	*.272*	*.303*	*-0.2*	-	*2.0*

Breakout: 0% Improve: 35% Collapse: 2% Attrition: 9% MLB: 95% *Comparables: Carlos Quentin, Carlos Lee, Hideki Matsui*

Welp, that didn't go so well. You can understand the thought process Ben Cherington and Co. had when signing Ramirez to a four-year, $88 million deal. The Sox needed a proven hitter to complement all of their youngsters, and they wanted insurance for their oft-injured and/or unproven outfielders. Sure, Ramirez lacked outfield experience, but he was a shortstop in 2014, for cryin' out loud. A lousy shortstop, granted, but the Sox moved him as far down the defensive spectrum as you can go before you hit "DH" or "bench" or "Wily Mo Pena." It was a sound plan and it failed spectacularly, as Christopher Darden had better luck with gloves. Whether Ramirez didn't care or lacked aptitude or both, his -11 FRAA doesn't do justice the butchery he committed in left field. He was a walking (he rarely moved faster than a jog) Red Wedding. Oh, and Ramirez didn't even hit all that well! And he got hurt again. And now he's moving to first base, where the ball will come his way even more often. What could possibly go wrong?

Josh Rutledge SS

Born: 4/21/89 Age: 27 Bats: R Throws: R Height: 6'1" Weight: 190

YEAR	TEAM	LVL	AGE	PA	R	2B	3B	HR	RBI	BB	K	SB	CS	AVG/OBP/SLG	TAv	BABIP	BRR	FRAA	WARP
2013	CSP	AAA	24	162	24	17	1	4	24	12	21	1	2	.371/.444/.587	.336	.415	-0.4	SS(22): -1.5, 2B(16): 0.5	1.8
2013	COL	MLB	24	314	45	6	1	7	19	22	62	12	0	.235/.294/.337	.229	.276	4.2	2B(58): 2.5, SS(14): 0.3	0.7
2014	COL	MLB	25	342	44	16	7	4	33	20	83	2	3	.269/.323/.405	.242	.353	2.2	SS(69): -5.1, 2B(17): -0.9	0.2
2014	CSP	AAA	25	64	7	3	0	1	5	7	12	3	3	.333/.413/.444	.307	.405	1.2	SS(13): -1.3, 2B(2): -0.1	0.6
2015	BOS	MLB	26	85	11	1	0	1	10	5	26	0	0	.284/.333/.338	.246	.400	-0.8	2B(30): -0.9, 3B(5): -0.6	-0.1
2015	SLC	AAA	26	337	45	19	3	5	32	19	67	2	1	.274/.323/.403	.249	.332	1.1	SS(38): -2.4, 2B(14): 1.1	0.6
2016	*BOS*	*MLB*	*27*	*250*	*29*	*13*	*2*	*5*	*24*	*13*	*58*	*3*	*1*	*.258/.306/.399*	*.244*	*.317*	*1.1*	*SS -2, 2B 0*	*0.5*
2017	*BOS*	*MLB*	*28*	*193*	*21*	*10*	*1*	*4*	*20*	*11*	*46*	*2*	*1*	*.250/.299/.387*	*.239*	*.310*	*0.9*	*SS -1, 2B 0*	*0.4*

Breakout: 2% Improve: 34% Collapse: 10% Attrition: 18% MLB: 89% *Comparables: Jason Donald, Zack Cozart, Brendan Harris*

Rutledge is the baseball version of a spare tire; it's intrinsically a bummer when you have to use him as it means something has gone awry, but you can roll him out there without damaging the foundation of your team. After falling flat with the Angels, Rutledge had a good year filling in for Dustin Pedroia and Pablo Sandoval in Boston, hitting well thanks to a .400 BABIP. A 39-game sample isn't enough for him to gain traction over Brock Holt, of course, but it's not hard to envision Rutledge bouncing around the league as a retread utility infielder for years to come.

Pablo Sandoval 3B

Born: 8/11/86 Age: 29 Bats: L Throws: R Height: 5'11" Weight: 255

YEAR	TEAM	LVL	AGE	PA	R	2B	3B	HR	RBI	BB	K	SB	CS	AVG/OBP/SLG	TAv	BABIP	BRR	FRAA	WARP
2013	SFN	MLB	26	584	52	27	2	14	79	47	79	0	0	.278/.341/.417	.275	.301	-4.8	3B(137): -17.5	0.4
2014	SFN	MLB	27	638	68	26	3	16	73	39	85	0	0	.279/.324/.415	.283	.300	-4.7	3B(151): -0.1	3.0
2015	BOS	MLB	28	505	43	25	1	10	47	25	73	0	0	.245/.292/.366	.229	.270	-5.5	3B(123): -7.6	-1.4
2016	*BOS*	*MLB*	*29*	*584*	*65*	*30*	*2*	*19*	*77*	*40*	*81*	*0*	*0*	*.284/.336/.454*	*.272*	*.302*	*-4.3*	*3B -8*	*1.1*
2017	*BOS*	*MLB*	*30*	*501*	*63*	*27*	*1*	*16*	*63*	*35*	*72*	*0*	*0*	*.280/.333/.445*	*.267*	*.300*	*-4.0*	*3B -7*	*1.1*

Breakout: 2% Improve: 38% Collapse: 3% Attrition: 8% MLB: 98% *Comparables: Aramis Ramirez, George Brett, Bill Madlock*

There was something strange about the Red Sox signing Sandoval from the moment the ink dried, a general incredulity that this was the guy the organization would pony up for in the post–Nick Punto Trade era. Sandoval's on-base percentage and slugging had declined steadily over the three years prior to his five-year pact, and his struggles against left-handed pitching were becoming more prominent. All those negative trends continued last year, and Sandoval's once-strong defense also regressed in a hurry, rendering him one of the worst every-day players in the league. The artist formerly known as Kung Fu Panda will only be entering his age-29 season, and if he skipped a few snacks this offseason, it's easy to envision him rebounding into an asset. Still, his 2015 was a horrendous first impression in a city that will love you for pissing in the Green Monster if you hit like Manny, but will crucify you for bathroom Instagraming if you're batting .245.

Travis Shaw 1B

Born: 4/16/90 Age: 26 Bats: L Throws: R Height: 6'4" Weight: 225

YEAR	TEAM	LVL	AGE	PA	R	2B	3B	HR	RBI	BB	K	SB	CS	AVG/OBP/SLG	TAv	BABIP	BRR	FRAA	WARP
2013	PME	AA	23	529	57	21	4	16	50	78	117	7	3	.221/.342/.394	.270	.262	-2.4	1B(111): -3.7, 3B(4): -0.0	0.5
2014	PME	AA	24	208	35	8	1	11	37	29	23	5	3	.305/.406/.548	.319	.301	-1.8	1B(35): -3.3, 3B(6): -0.4	1.0
2014	PAW	AAA	24	346	43	21	1	10	41	28	76	2	0	.262/.321/.431	.260	.312	-2.1	1B(75): 4.6, 3B(6): -0.4	0.6
2015	PAW	AAA	25	322	29	12	2	5	30	26	54	0	1	.249/.318/.356	.252	.289	-1.3	3B(43): 4.5, 1B(31): -2.9	0.6
2015	BOS	MLB	25	248	31	10	0	13	36	18	57	0	1	.270/.327/.487	.278	.304	-1.0	1B(55): -0.3, 3B(8): 0.4	0.7
2016	*BOS*	*MLB*	*26*	*239*	*27*	*10*	*1*	*8*	*31*	*22*	*54*	*1*	*1*	*.248/.321/.423*	*.257*	*.292*	*-0.3*	*1B -1, 3B 0*	*0.3*
2017	*BOS*	*MLB*	*27*	*454*	*57*	*19*	*2*	*15*	*55*	*45*	*102*	*1*	*1*	*.245/.324/.411*	*.254*	*.291*	*-0.7*	*1B -2, 3B 1*	*0.7*

Breakout: 3% Improve: 26% Collapse: 8% Attrition: 20% MLB: 51% *Comparables: Ryan Garko, Jeff Clement, Juan Miranda*

"Innocent until proven guilty" is not a tenet that applies to young, successful major leaguers without a prospect pedigree. Instead, we tend to assume this subset of the big-league population is due for regression. Most of the time we're right, but we're wrong often enough to keep things interesting. Seen as a one-trick prospect who could do little but hit right-handed pitching for power, Shaw was pressed into major-league duty last year and thrived, producing a higher slugging percentage than Albert Pujols or Adrian Gonzalez. There are lots of red flags here, from Shaw's out-of-nowhere reverse platoon splits to his lofty flyball rate to his penchant for the swing-and-miss. But Shaw showed that his power is real, that he's a capable defender at first and that he can even play a little hot corner if need be. Is he more likely to be the next Chad Tracy than the next, say, Paul Goldschmidt? Sure. But any outcome there within would make him a huge developmental success.

Blake Swihart C

Born: 4/3/92 Age: 24 Bats: B Throws: R Height: 6'1" Weight: 205

YEAR	TEAM	LVL	AGE	PA	R	2B	3B	HR	RBI	BB	K	SB	CS	AVG/OBP/SLG	TAv	BABIP	BRR	FRAA	WARP
2013	SLM	A+	21	422	45	29	7	2	42	41	63	7	8	.298/.366/.428	.271	.350	-6.9	C(101): 6.0	2.4
2014	PME	AA	22	380	47	23	3	12	55	29	65	7	1	.300/.353/.487	.303	.337	2.2	C(81): 19.5	5.7
2014	PAW	AAA	22	71	6	3	1	1	9	2	15	1	0	.261/.282/.377	.212	.321	0.1	C(16): 0.8	0.0
2015	PAW	AAA	23	80	7	3	0	0	11	6	14	1	1	.311/.363/.351	.272	.383	-1.4	C(16): 1.6	0.4
2015	BOS	MLB	23	309	47	17	1	5	31	18	77	4	2	.274/.319/.392	.241	.359	2.4	C(83): -6.1	0.4
2016	*BOS*	*MLB*	*24*	*449*	*45*	*24*	*3*	*9*	*48*	*28*	*102*	*5*	*2*	*.267/.313/.399*	*.247*	*.331*	*1.8*	*C -1*	*1.5*
2017	*BOS*	*MLB*	*25*	*503*	*56*	*27*	*3*	*11*	*55*	*31*	*119*	*5*	*2*	*.266/.312/.404*	*.249*	*.332*	*2.1*	*C -2*	*2.1*

Breakout: 10% Improve: 34% Collapse: 11% Attrition: 23% MLB: 69% *Comparables: Guillermo Quiroz, J.R. Murphy, Hank Conger*

YEAR	TEAM	P. COUNT	FRM RUNS	BLK RUNS	THRW RUNS	TOT RUNS
2014	PAW	2329	0.7	0.0	-0.1	0.7
2014	PME	10418	15.8	0.3	2.1	18.2
2015	BOS	11445	-5.9	-0.6	0.3	-6.2
2015	PAW	2261	0.4	-0.1	0.0	0.4
2016	*BOS*	*16678*	*-3.1*	*-0.3*	*0.8*	*-2.6*
2017	*BOS*	*18701*	*-4.6*	*-0.3*	*0.8*	*-4.1*

In any given season there are rarely more than a dozen-or-so catchers who are legitimate offensive and defensive assets. Swihart isn't there quite yet, but, as a 23-year-old rookie pressed into full-time duty much sooner than the Red Sox would have preferred, he showed that he has the stuff to someday join those hallowed ranks. Prospect development isn't linear, and that's doubly true for catchers, yet Swihart has made steady, measured progress at every stop since being drafted in the first round in 2011. The switch-hitter initially looked overmatched at the plate, but he adjusted to bat .310/.364/.457 in 141 PA from August on, throwing in three stolen bases for good measure. He's no Christian Vazquez defensively, but Swihart is athletic and quick for a backstop, with the arm to improve upon his 28 percent caught-stealing percentage and the receiving skills to improve upon mediocre pitch-framing metrics. Xander Bogaerts and Mookie Betts may be Boston's two most important young players, but Swihart belongs in the conversation.

Sam Travis 1B

Born: 8/21/90 Age: 25 Bats: R Throws: R Height: 5'9" Weight: 200

YEAR	TEAM	LVL	AGE	PA	R	2B	3B	HR	RBI	BB	K	SB	CS	AVG/OBP/SLG	TAv	BABIP	BRR	FRAA	WARP
2014	LOW	A-	20	174	28	5	1	4	30	4	18	5	1	.333/.364/.448	.291	.357	-0.7	1B(33): -1.7	0.5
2014	GRN	A	20	115	12	11	1	3	14	7	14	0	1	.290/.330/.495	.276	.308	-1.3	1B(23): 0.3	0.2
2015	SLM	A+	21	278	35	15	4	5	40	26	43	10	6	.313/.378/.467	.306	.356	2.0	1B(46): 2.4	2.2
2015	PME	AA	21	281	35	17	2	4	38	33	34	9	6	.300/.384/.436	.297	.332	2.7	1B(63): 8.5	2.6
2016	*BOS*	*MLB*	*22*	*250*	*27*	*13*	*1*	*6*	*28*	*18*	*52*	*4*	*3*	*.263/.320/.410*	*.253*	*.312*	*-0.3*	*1B 2*	*0.4*
2017	*BOS*	*MLB*	*23*	*350*	*41*	*18*	*2*	*8*	*39*	*27*	*72*	*6*	*4*	*.259/.319/.408*	*.253*	*.307*	*-0.1*	*1B 3*	*0.9*

Breakout: 10% Improve: 26% Collapse: 4% Attrition: 21% MLB: 45% *Comparables: Logan Morrison, Chris Marrero, Nick Evans*

As a first baseman without big power or an explosive hit tool, Travis' profile is fairly boring. No one gets worked up over the next, oh, let's say, James Loney. So why, other than his status as a second-round draft pick, are we paying him any mind? Because he keeps hitting. Maybe you could write off his success in Lowell, Greenville and Salem as a college bat taking advantage of inferior competition, but you're entering big boy territory once you hit Portland and the Indiana product raked there, too. Travis is now a .310/.371/.457 hitter in 761 professional PA, and while scouting the stat line is a fool's errand, so is ignoring success. There's not a ton of projection left here but if even a few of his doubles start leaving the yard he becomes a much more intriguing proposition. Perhaps he and Travis Shaw can form some sort of homegrown all-Travis platoon some day.

Christian Vazquez C

Born: 8/21/90 Age: 25 Bats: R Throws: R Height: 5'9" Weight: 200

YEAR	TEAM	LVL	AGE	PA	R	2B	3B	HR	RBI	BB	K	SB	CS	AVG/OBP/SLG	TAv	BABIP	BRR	FRAA	WARP
2013	PME	AA	22	399	48	19	1	5	48	47	44	7	5	.289/.376/.395	.285	.316	1.2	C(93): 20.3	5.2
2014	PAW	AAA	23	270	35	17	0	3	20	21	52	0	1	.279/.336/.385	.252	.340	0.8	C(52): 7.6	1.7
2014	BOS	MLB	23	201	15	9	0	1	20	19	33	0	0	.240/.308/.309	.239	.283	-1.8	C(54): 14.8	1.9
2016	*BOS*	*MLB*	*25*	*96*	*9*	*5*	*0*	*1*	*9*	*8*	*16*	*0*	*0*	*.264/.327/.369*	*.244*	*.306*	*-0.4*	*C 4*	*0.6*
2017	*BOS*	*MLB*	*26*	*186*	*20*	*10*	*0*	*3*	*18*	*15*	*32*	*1*	*0*	*.263/.326/.373*	*.245*	*.306*	*-0.7*	*C 7*	*1.3*

Breakout: 7% Improve: 19% Collapse: 4% Attrition: 36% MLB: 60% *Comparables: Curtis Thigpen, Jonathan Lucroy, Lou Marson*

YEAR	TEAM	P. COUNT	FRM RUNS	BLK RUNS	THRW RUNS	TOT RUNS
2013	PME	13217	17.3	-0.5	2.5	19.4
2014	BOS	7331	13.7	-0.2	1.2	14.7
2014	PAW	7253	8.4	0.0	0.9	9.2
2016	*BOS*	*3523*	*3.6*	*-0.2*	*0.4*	*3.8*
2017	*BOS*	*6843*	*6.5*	*-0.4*	*0.8*	*6.9*

The Red Sox feature no shortage of exciting young players, but fans who'd suffered through Victor Martinez, Jarrod Saltalamacchia and A.J. Pierzynski were especially excited to watch Vazquez's defensive prowess last season. They were robbed of that chance on March 13th, when Vazquez threw out True Yankee Tyler Wade in a Grapefruit League matchup and his elbow popped. The good news is he will have had just about a full year to recover from Tommy John surgery, and he's expected to be ready for spring training. The bad news is his arm was his best weapon, and while his bat isn't so lifeless as to preclude the possibility of him starting for a first-division team, defense—specifically his ability to mow down runners—is his calling card. Vazquez showed great promise as a pitch-framer and game-caller in his rookie campaign, so even if his arm doesn't come all the way back, he's in for a long career. Any lingering TJ effects would be a damn shame, though, because he had the Molina Starter Kit in his toolbag before he went under the knife.

Chris Young LF

Born: 9/5/83 Age: 32 Bats: R Throws: R Height: 6'2" Weight: 200

YEAR	TEAM	LVL	AGE	PA	R	2B	3B	HR	RBI	BB	K	SB	CS	AVG/OBP/SLG	TAv	BABIP	BRR	FRAA	WARP
2013	OAK	MLB	29	375	46	18	3	12	40	36	93	10	3	.200/.280/.379	.247	.237	1.0	CF(54): 0.6, RF(26): 2.5	0.9
2014	NYN	MLB	30	287	31	12	0	8	28	25	54	7	3	.205/.283/.346	.252	.226	1.1	LF(55): 3.3, CF(27): -1.8	0.7
2014	NYA	MLB	30	79	9	8	0	3	10	7	16	1	0	.282/.354/.521	.311	.327	0.6	LF(18): 1.4, RF(1): 0.0	0.8
2015	NYA	MLB	31	356	53	20	1	14	42	30	73	3	1	.252/.320/.453	.272	.283	-2.0	RF(76): -3.0, LF(55): -2.2	0.4
2016	*BOS*	*MLB*	*32*	*200*	*23*	*11*	*1*	*6*	*25*	*20*	*44*	*4*	*1*	*.239/.318/.418*	*.258*	*.279*	*0.0*	*LF 1, RF 1*	*0.8*
2017	*BOS*	*MLB*	*33*	*233*	*28*	*13*	*0*	*7*	*27*	*21*	*51*	*4*	*1*	*.234/.308/.404*	*.250*	*.274*	*0.1*	*LF 2, RF 1*	*0.9*

Breakout: 0% Improve: 27% Collapse: 2% Attrition: 10% MLB: 91% *Comparables: Andy Pafko, Seth Smith, Billy Williams*

Young is one of those guys that embodies the creeping insidiousness of time's unstoppable advance and fills you with existential dread. One day, he's a toolsy 30-30 threat promising championships and you have your whole life in front of you. Next thing you know, he's just another lefty-mashing role player, and you're walking home drunk thinking about whether you're willing to lower your standards to the level where you'll eat something under the heat lamps at the 7-Eleven. For what it's worth, the Yankees deployed the aging, depressingly mundane version of Young very well in 2015, and the results were solid. For almost all of us, growing old is all about learning to accept a limited role.

PITCHERS

Trey Ball LHP

Born: 6/27/94 Age: 22 Bats: L Throws: L Height: 6'6" Weight: 185

YEAR	TEAM	LVL	AGE	W	L	SV	G	GS	IP	H	HR	BB/9	K/9	GB%	BABIP	WHIP	ERA	FIP	DRA	WARP	CFIP	MPH
2014	GRN	A	20	5	10	0	22	22	100	111	9	3.5	6.1	38%	.309	1.50	4.68	4.66	5.14	0.2	113	
2015	SLM	A+	21	9	13	0	25	25	129^1	129	16	4.2	5.4	40%	.277	1.46	4.73	5.13	7.55	-4.8	135	
2016	*BOS*	*MLB*	*22*	*5*	*8*	*0*	*21*	*21*	*97^2*	*126*	*18*	*4.9*	*4.0*	*33%*	*.307*	*1.83*	*6.51*	*6.49*	*6.63*	*-1.8*	*159*	
2017	*BOS*	*MLB*	*23*	*3*	*6*	*0*	*13*	*13*	*77*	*95*	*15*	*5.0*	*4.7*	*33%*	*.301*	*1.80*	*6.71*	*6.49*	*6.83*	*-1.2*	*164*	

Breakout: 0% Improve: 0% Collapse: 0% Attrition: 0% MLB: 0% *Comparables: Ariel Pena, Sugar Ray Marimon, David Buchanan*

Ball's 2015 comment focused on his late-season surge and ultimate upside as reasons for optimism despite a poor 2014 showing. It's hardly unusual for a prep pitcher to struggle in his first taste of full-season action, and that was doubly true for Ball, who was relatively new to pitching full-time as a two-way draft prospect. After a totally uninspiring 2015 season in High-A, it's harder to make excuses for him. He is imposing, left-handed and shows some promise with his secondaries; those traits alone will afford him plenty of chances. That said, he's already used up his first one, and it would behoove him to get his last name rolling if he wants to remain a legitimate prospect. His first-round pedigree will only take him so far.

Matt Barnes RHP

Born: 6/17/90 Age: 26 Bats: R Throws: R Height: 6'4" Weight: 210

YEAR	TEAM	LVL	AGE	W	L	SV	G	GS	IP	H	HR	BB/9	K/9	GB%	BABIP	WHIP	ERA	FIP	DRA	WARP	CFIP	MPH
2013	PME	AA	23	5	10	0	24	24	108	112	11	3.8	11.2	46%	.356	1.46	4.33	3.54	4.10	1.4	84	
2014	BOS	MLB	24	0	0	0	5	0	9	11	1	2.0	8.0	34%	.357	1.44	4.00	3.49	5.40	-0.1	99	96.5
2014	PAW	AAA	24	8	9	0	23	22	127^2	119	8	3.2	7.3	44%	.294	1.29	3.95	3.71	4.45	0.9	98	
2015	BOS	MLB	25	3	4	0	32	2	43	56	9	3.1	8.2	42%	.351	1.65	5.44	5.20	5.90	-0.6	104	97.7
2015	PAW	AAA	25	1	1	0	17	5	37^2	36	3	5.3	9.8	42%	.320	1.54	4.06	3.85	4.32	0.1	101	
2016	*BOS*	*MLB*	*26*	*1*	*0*	*0*	*23*	*0*	*24*	*26*	*3*	*3.5*	*8.0*	*42%*	*.318*	*1.48*	*4.46*	*4.37*	*4.64*	*0.0*	*107*	
2017	*BOS*	*MLB*	*27*	*2*	*3*	*0*	*13*	*7*	*51^1*	*53*	*7*	*3.7*	*8.0*	*42%*	*.307*	*1.45*	*4.61*	*4.47*	*4.80*	*0.1*	*112*	

Breakout: 17% Improve: 30% Collapse: 30% Attrition: 37% MLB: 70% *Comparables: Brad Peacock, P.J. Walters, Christian Friedrich*

It's getting harder and harder to be optimistic about Barnes' future as an impact major leaguer. He throws hard and has pitched well in the upper minors in the past, but the UConn product is inconsistent, hasn't mastered a third pitch and frequently loses his command. It's long been assumed that Barnes could be a dominant late-inning weapon as a reliever, but the right-hander was shellacked to the tune of a .304/.362/.511 line in 32 innings out of the 'pen in the majors. Barnes is just 25, has an ideal build and throws hard, so he's far from out of chances. But if he hadn't been a first-round pick there wouldn't be much differentiating him from the myriad dime-a-dozen flamethrowers who can't hit their spots and wash out in Triple-A.

Craig Breslow LHP

Born: 8/8/80 Age: 35 Bats: L Throws: L Height: 6'1" Weight: 185

YEAR	TEAM	LVL	AGE	W	L	SV	G	GS	IP	H	HR	BB/9	K/9	GB%	BABIP	WHIP	ERA	FIP	DRA	WARP	CFIP	MPH
2013	BOS	MLB	32	5	2	0	61	0	59^2	49	3	2.7	5.0	45%	.254	1.12	1.81	3.63	3.15	1.0	115	92.6
2014	BOS	MLB	33	2	4	1	60	0	54^1	73	8	4.6	6.1	38%	.351	1.86	5.96	5.37	6.55	-1.4	124	91.1
2015	BOS	MLB	34	0	4	1	45	2	65	69	12	3.2	6.4	38%	.289	1.42	4.15	5.24	4.94	-0.1	111	92.5
2016	*BOS*	*MLB*	*35*	*2*	*1*	*1*	*51*	*0*	*53^2*	*61*	*8*	*3.3*	*6.4*	*39%*	*.306*	*1.50*	*4.92*	*4.99*	*5.09*	*-0.2*	*119*	
2017	*BOS*	*MLB*	*36*	*2*	*1*	*1*	*36*	*0*	*36^2*	*40*	*5*	*3.3*	*6.5*	*39%*	*.302*	*1.47*	*4.89*	*4.74*	*5.06*	*-0.1*	*118*	

Breakout: 19% Improve: 38% Collapse: 30% Attrition: 12% MLB: 82% *Comparables: Larry Andersen, Joe Grzenda, Jim Gott*

Breslow came up huge for the Red Sox in the 2013 postseason. Since then, he's posted a 4.98 ERA in 119 innings, *costing* the Sox 1.5 WARP. That's worse than what Eric Gagne, Rudy Seanez, Andrew Bailey and Edward Mujica did in Boston *combined*. Breslow doesn't strike anyone out, gives up a ton of homers and has allowed well over a hit per inning over the last two seasons. He's equally inept against lefties as against righties, and at 35 there's little reason to think he'll rebound. Can Breslow soak up innings for a bad team? Sure. In fact, that's kind of what defines a bad team. But he doesn't belong in a contending bullpen anymore, and he might not belong in the league. We're contractually obligated to mention that he went to Yale.

Clay Buchholz RHP

Born: 8/14/84 Age: 31 Bats: L Throws: R Height: 6'3" Weight: 190

YEAR	TEAM	LVL	AGE	W	L	SV	G	GS	IP	H	HR	BB/9	K/9	GB%	BABIP	WHIP	ERA	FIP	DRA	WARP	CFIP	MPH
2013	BOS	MLB	28	12	1	0	16	16	108^1	75	4	3.0	8.0	49%	.254	1.02	1.74	2.81	2.63	3.0	88	94.7
2014	PAW	AAA	29	0	1	0	2	2	10^2	6	2	1.7	8.4	42%	.167	0.75	2.53	4.76	4.30	0.1	94	
2014	BOS	MLB	29	8	11	0	28	28	170^1	182	17	2.9	7.0	48%	.315	1.39	5.34	4.03	4.44	0.7	103	93.9
2015	BOS	MLB	30	7	7	0	18	18	113^1	114	6	1.8	8.5	49%	.329	1.21	3.26	2.65	3.37	2.2	82	94.3
2016	*BOS*	*MLB*	*31*	*10*	*8*	*0*	*26*	*26*	*156*	*149*	*16*	*2.5*	*7.9*	*48%*	*.296*	*1.23*	*3.77*	*3.78*	*3.97*	*2.1*	*89*	
2017	*BOS*	*MLB*	*32*	*10*	*9*	*0*	*27*	*27*	*165*	*156*	*18*	*2.5*	*7.7*	*48%*	*.291*	*1.22*	*3.89*	*3.77*	*4.10*	*2.1*	*92*	

Breakout: 11% Improve: 46% Collapse: 22% Attrition: 8% MLB: 94% *Comparables: Warren Spahn, Bob Gibson, Kevin Millwood*

After nine seasons and 1,028 innings in the majors, here's Buchholz: He's one of the game's most frustrating, talented and inconsistent pitchers, dazzling in a half-season's worth of work before hitting the DL with an elbow injury never to return. When he is on the mound and it's all clicking he looks like a legit no. 1 starter, but he's averaged just 20 starts/126 innings a year since 2008, and his career FIP illustrates that he often has trouble tapping into his talent. There's too much upside here to decline his $13 million option for 2016, but that doesn't mean anyone should feel great about picking it up. Elevators have fewer ups and downs.

Roenis Elias LHP

Born: 8/1/88 Age: 27 Bats: L Throws: L Height: 6'1" Weight: 190

YEAR	TEAM	LVL	AGE	W	L	SV	G	GS	IP	H	HR	BB/9	K/9	GB%	BABIP	WHIP	ERA	FIP	DRA	WARP	CFIP	MPH
2013	WTN	AA	24	6	11	0	22	22	130	112	9	3.5	8.4	44%	.286	1.25	3.18	3.20	3.73	1.5	89	
2014	SEA	MLB	25	10	12	0	29	29	163^2	151	16	3.5	7.9	48%	.294	1.31	3.85	4.06	5.04	-0.5	106	94.3
2015	TAC	AAA	26	4	2	0	12	12	61^1	80	9	2.6	6.9	43%	.350	1.60	7.34	5.05	5.14	0.3	101	
2015	SEA	MLB	26	5	8	0	22	20	115^1	106	15	3.4	7.6	45%	.280	1.30	4.14	4.49	4.40	0.9	108	94.5
2016	*BOS*	*MLB*	*27*	*3*	*2*	*0*	*29*	*6*	*56*	*58*	*7*	*3.3*	*7.3*	*45%*	*.302*	*1.40*	*4.54*	*4.49*	*4.71*	*0.2*	*110*	
2017	*BOS*	*MLB*	*28*	*4*	*4*	*0*	*12*	*12*	*72*	*73*	*9*	*3.2*	*7.6*	*45%*	*.301*	*1.38*	*4.52*	*4.37*	*4.69*	*0.4*	*109*	

Breakout: 22% Improve: 52% Collapse: 22% Attrition: 21% MLB: 93% *Comparables: John Maine, Jake Arrieta, Carlos Carrasco*

Elias is one of those fungible starting pitchers who gets dubbed Quad-A by fans who don't own him in any of their nine fantasy leagues. Among a herd of fragile Seattle starters in 2015, it was his round-trip light rail pass that was his most valuable feature. His fastball is adequate but it's the curve, magical on random days, that will decide whether his career is of the four- or the 10-year varieties. It's likely he'll find himself back in Triple-A in April, practicing that breaking ball and waiting for the first elbow to strain. Just don't call Elias Quad-A. He's much better than mere organizational filler.

Anderson Espinoza RHP

Born: 3/9/98 Age: 18 Bats: R Throws: R Height: 6'0" Weight: 160

YEAR	TEAM	LVL	AGE	W	L	SV	G	GS	IP	H	HR	BB/9	K/9	GB%	BABIP	WHIP	ERA	FIP	DRA	WARP	CFIP	MPH
2016	*BOS*	*MLB*	*18*	*2*	*3*	*0*	*9*	*9*	36^1	*42*	*5*	*3.9*	*6.5*	*48%*	*.313*	*1.57*	*5.15*	*5.08*	*5.25*	*-0.1*	*126*	
2017	*BOS*	*MLB*	*19*	*5*	*8*	*0*	*24*	*24*	142^2	*164*	*21*	*3.6*	*6.3*	*48%*	*.311*	*1.55*	*5.22*	*5.05*	*5.32*	*-0.2*	*128*	

Breakout: 0% Improve: 0% Collapse: 0% Attrition: 0% MLB: 0% *Comparables: Roberto Osuna, Deolis Guerra, Jordan Lyles*

Espinoza is *not* Pedro Martinez. They have different names, of course, but it bears mentioning because you are almost certainly going to see Espinoza compared to the all-time Red Sox great as he progresses through his prospect career. The teenager was so dominant in Rookie ball that the Sox bumped him up to Greenville at the very end of the season, where he was briefly the youngest player in the Sally League by more than a year. (Rafael Devers was next youngest.) In fact, Espinoza was the first 17-year-old in the Sally League in nearly a decade. On the mound, the Venezuelan can reach triple digits, boasts two potential plus off-speed weapons in his curve and his change and has a repeatable delivery that helped him walk just 14 batters all year. The Red Sox can't put him in an "I'm the Ace" shirt just yet, but that's apparel he may be able to wear sans irony in a few years.

Brian Johnson LHP

Born: 12/7/90 Age: 25 Bats: L Throws: L Height: 6'4" Weight: 235

YEAR	TEAM	LVL	AGE	W	L	SV	G	GS	IP	H	HR	BB/9	K/9	GB%	BABIP	WHIP	ERA	FIP	DRA	WARP	CFIP	MPH
2013	SLM	A+	22	1	0	0	2	2	11	9	0	4.1	6.5	59%	.281	1.27	1.64	3.26	4.69	0.1	101	
2013	GRN	A	22	1	6	0	15	15	69	50	4	3.7	9.0	47%	.251	1.13	2.87	3.63	4.27	0.6	94	
2014	PME	AA	23	10	2	0	20	20	118	78	6	2.4	7.6	48%	.229	0.93	1.75	3.15	3.93	1.6	80	
2014	SLM	A+	23	3	1	0	5	5	25^2	23	0	2.5	11.6	41%	.333	1.17	3.86	1.76	3.75	0.4	74	
2015	PAW	AAA	24	9	6	0	18	18	96	74	6	3.0	8.4	47%	.264	1.10	2.53	3.22	3.16	1.8	88	
2015	BOS	MLB	24	0	1	0	1	1	4^1	3	0	8.3	6.2	33%	.250	1.62	8.31	4.49	1.72	0.2	109	91.7
2016	*BOS*	*MLB*	*25*	*3*	*2*	*0*	*8*	*8*	42^1	*40*	*5*	*3.2*	*7.9*	*43%*	*.286*	*1.29*	*4.12*	*4.23*	*4.30*	*0.4*	*98*	
2017	*BOS*	*MLB*	*26*	*6*	*6*	*0*	*19*	*19*	109^1	*99*	*13*	*3.3*	*8.2*	*43%*	*.280*	*1.27*	*4.23*	*4.10*	*4.42*	*0.8*	*101*	

Breakout: 21% Improve: 31% Collapse: 16% Attrition: 35% MLB: 61% *Comparables: Scott Barnes, Matt Maloney, Alex Meyer*

For several years now, there's been some disparity in how national scouts and writers described Johnson and what those who watched him on a routine basis had to say. Bereft of a true out pitch or premium velocity, his primary virtues are that he's big and left-handed, portending a starter who can soak up innings. Those qualities alone aren't enough to yield a 2.32 ERA in 330 minor-league innings, however, and to study Johnson is to understand that he is a pitcher with truly remarkable feel for and command of four average pitches. That's not a wonderful profile for Fenway Park, and Johnson experienced elbow issues toward the end of last year that added another red flag to his resume. Still, he is straight out of central casting for "crafty lefty," and it's easy to envision him sticking around the back end of a major-league rotation for the better part of the next decade.

Joe Kelly RHP

Born: 6/9/88 Age: 28 Bats: R Throws: R Height: 6'1" Weight: 190

YEAR	TEAM	LVL	AGE	W	L	SV	G	GS	IP	H	HR	BB/9	K/9	GB%	BABIP	WHIP	ERA	FIP	DRA	WARP	CFIP	MPH
2013	SLN	MLB	25	10	5	0	37	15	124	124	10	3.2	5.7	52%	.289	1.35	2.69	3.98	4.57	0.4	118	97.8
2014	SLN	MLB	26	2	2	0	7	7	35	41	3	2.6	6.4	55%	.330	1.46	4.37	3.90	5.38	-0.3	108	97.8
2014	MEM	AAA	26	0	0	0	3	3	10^{1}	8	1	5.2	3.5	56%	.226	1.35	2.61	5.93	5.74	0.0	121	
2014	BOS	MLB	26	4	2	0	10	10	61^{1}	47	5	4.7	6.0	57%	.237	1.29	4.11	4.64	3.47	1.0	124	98.3
2015	BOS	MLB	27	10	6	0	25	25	134^{1}	145	15	3.3	7.4	46%	.319	1.44	4.82	4.15	4.30	1.2	104	98.6
2015	PAW	AAA	27	1	1	0	4	4	19	14	1	2.8	8.5	58%	.265	1.05	2.84	3.05	3.40	0.3	91	
2016	*BOS*	*MLB*	*28*	*8*	*8*	*0*	*24*	*24*	127^{1}	*135*	*15*	*3.4*	*7.0*	*50%*	*.308*	*1.44*	*4.46*	*4.47*	*4.65*	*0.7*	*108*	
2017	*BOS*	*MLB*	*29*	*6*	*7*	*0*	*20*	*20*	*117*	*120*	*14*	*3.4*	*7.1*	*50%*	*.299*	*1.40*	*4.52*	*4.38*	*4.71*	*0.5*	*110*	

Breakout: 15% Improve: 50% Collapse: 21% Attrition: 14% MLB: 90% *Comparables: Sergio Mitre, Zach Miner, Tyson Ross*

"Joe Kelly has great stuff" is a joke, you see. Not because it isn't true, but because to praise the quality of Kelly's offerings without citing his other attributes misses the big picture in the same manner as asking how Mrs. Lincoln enjoyed the play. Pitch movement and velocity are mighty trees, but command, control and sequencing make up much of the starting-pitcher forest, and only minding the former can make you miss the latter entirely. After predicting he'd win the Cy Young in spring training, Kelly pitched poorly enough to be demoted to Pawtucket in June. Most thought he'd move to the bullpen, but he was recalled as a starter in July, pitched horribly three times... and then inexplicably embarked on the best eight-game run of his career. Kelly went 7–0 with a 2.35 ERA from August 7th to September 15th before sitting out the rest of the season with shoulder soreness. That's why this is funny. Joe Kelly really does have great stuff. You just never know if he'll be able to use it.

Craig Kimbrel RHP

Born: 5/28/88 Age: 28 Bats: R Throws: R Height: 5'11" Weight: 220

YEAR	TEAM	LVL	AGE	W	L	SV	G	GS	IP	H	HR	BB/9	K/9	GB%	BABIP	WHIP	ERA	FIP	DRA	WARP	CFIP	MPH
2013	ATL	MLB	25	4	3	50	68	0	67	39	4	2.7	13.2	47%	.263	0.88	1.21	1.90	2.63	1.6	55	99.3
2014	ATL	MLB	26	0	3	47	63	0	61^{2}	30	2	3.8	13.9	43%	.237	0.91	1.61	1.81	1.54	2.2	67	99.6
2015	SDN	MLB	27	4	2	39	61	0	59^{1}	40	6	3.3	13.2	46%	.276	1.04	2.58	2.71	3.05	1.2	65	99.5
2016	*BOS*	*MLB*	*28*	*3*	*1*	*41*	*55*	*0*	57^{2}	*45*	*7*	*3.2*	*12.3*	*46%*	*.290*	*1.13*	*3.29*	*3.22*	*3.52*	*0.9*	*74*	
2017	*BOS*	*MLB*	*29*	*3*	*1*	*45*	*60*	*0*	59^{1}	*47*	*8*	*3.5*	*11.6*	*46%*	*.280*	*1.18*	*3.76*	*3.64*	*4.02*	*0.5*	*88*	

Breakout: 25% Improve: 44% Collapse: 39% Attrition: 12% MLB: 95% *Comparables: Francisco Rodriguez, Jonathan Broxton, Troy Percival*

On the one hand, Kimbrel's worst season to date was still better than most relievers' best. On the other, he pitched 60 innings for a team that lost 88 games and is owed $24 million over the next two years. Factor in that the Padres' acquisition cost included Melvin Upton's salary (less Cameron Maybin's and Carlos Quentin's) and you're looking at a $23 million per year closer for a team that hasn't sniffed .500 since 2010. It was hardly a surprise, then, that the Padres delivered him to a relevant Red Sox club in the offseason. Kimbrel returned to his old tricks after the All-Star break, holding opponents to a ridiculous .120/.198/.228 line. Despite his "down year," he remains an elite closer, a howitzer among ninth-inning weapons.

Michael Kopech RHP

Born: 4/30/96 Age: 20 Bats: R Throws: R Height: 6'3" Weight: 205

YEAR	TEAM	LVL	AGE	W	L	SV	G	GS	IP	H	HR	BB/9	K/9	GB%	BABIP	WHIP	ERA	FIP	DRA	WARP	CFIP	MPH
2015	GRN	A	19	4	5	0	16	15	65	53	2	3.7	9.7	47%	.313	1.23	2.63	3.35	3.90	0.9	93	
2016	*BOS*	*MLB*	*20*	*3*	*3*	*0*	*12*	*12*	*42*	*44*	*5*	*4.6*	*7.7*	*40%*	*.313*	*1.57*	*4.91*	*4.86*	*5.03*	*0.0*	*119*	
2017	*BOS*	*MLB*	*21*	*6*	*8*	*0*	*28*	*28*	171^{1}	*170*	*22*	*4.3*	*7.7*	*40%*	*.297*	*1.47*	*4.88*	*4.72*	*5.00*	*0.1*	*119*	

Breakout: 0% Improve: 0% Collapse: 0% Attrition: 0% MLB: 0% *Comparables: Justin Nicolino, Trevor Cahill, Zach Braddock*

Approximately 86 percent of all pitching prospects are big right-handers from Texas. Kopech rose above the masses by pitching very well, earning rave reviews for an upper-90s fastball and power breaking ball while dominating as a 19-year-old in Low-A. Kopech was so impressive, in fact, that when BP staffers redrafted the 2014 class in mid-June, Kopech went sixth overall, a stark improvement from where the Red Sox cast him at 33 as compensation for losing Jacoby Ellsbury. The other shoe dropping here is that Kopech was suspended for 50 games for testing positive for Oxilofrine in July. He pled ignorance but accepted exile all the same. Still, the arrow is pointing up.

Tommy Layne LHP

Born: 11/2/84 Age: 31 Bats: L Throws: L Height: 6'2" Weight: 190

YEAR	TEAM	LVL	AGE	W	L	SV	G	GS	IP	H	HR	BB/9	K/9	GB%	BABIP	WHIP	ERA	FIP	DRA	WARP	CFIP	MPH
2013	TUC	AAA	28	2	4	0	49	0	46	49	1	5.3	8.0	52%	.338	1.65	4.50	4.09	5.33	0.0	108	
2013	SDN	MLB	28	0	2	0	14	0	8^2	10	1	5.2	6.2	54%	.360	1.73	2.08	5.56	8.09	-0.4	113	91.0
2014	PAW	AAA	29	5	1	11	37	0	48	29	1	3.8	9.9	61%	.243	1.02	1.50	2.73	4.10	0.4	84	
2014	BOS	MLB	29	2	1	0	30	0	19	14	0	3.8	6.6	51%	.264	1.16	0.95	3.11	3.12	0.3	105	91.9
2015	BOS	MLB	30	2	1	1	64	0	47^2	41	3	5.1	8.5	56%	.292	1.43	3.97	3.86	3.56	0.7	102	92.8
2016	*BOS*	*MLB*	*31*	*2*	*1*	*0*	*41*	*0*	43^1	*43*	*5*	*4.0*	*7.9*	*56%*	*.302*	*1.43*	*4.37*	*4.44*	*4.55*	*0.1*	*104*	
2017	*BOS*	*MLB*	*32*	*3*	*1*	*1*	*52*	*2*	*53*	*54*	*7*	*4.0*	*7.8*	*56%*	*.304*	*1.47*	*4.64*	*4.50*	*4.83*	*0.0*	*111*	

Breakout: 9% Improve: 14% Collapse: 9% Attrition: 17% MLB: 34% *Comparables: Ross Wolf, Justin Lehr, Randy Choate*

You can't predict baseball, and you really can't predict bullpens. Layne has logged 66 innings for the Red Sox since they picked him off the scrap heap in San Diego, and the should-be LOOGY has exceeded all reasonable expectations. He held left-handed batters to a .144/.248/.170 line in 26 innings last season, and while righties feasted on him, it's clear he can be effective when deployed properly. Layne needs to limit his walks if he wants to stick in an MLB bullpen long term, but so far so good for the man who nearly walked away from the game three years ago.

Patrick Light RHP

Born: 3/29/91 Age: 25 Bats: R Throws: R Height: 6'5" Weight: 195

YEAR	TEAM	LVL	AGE	W	L	SV	G	GS	IP	H	HR	BB/9	K/9	GB%	BABIP	WHIP	ERA	FIP	DRA	WARP	CFIP	MPH
2013	GRN	A	22	1	4	0	10	9	28^1	44	4	4.4	8.9	47%	.417	2.05	8.89	4.93	4.67	0.1	103	
2014	GRN	A	23	2	0	0	3	3	17^1	15	1	2.1	9.9	60%	.304	1.10	4.15	2.84	4.25	0.2	83	
2014	SLM	A+	23	6	6	0	22	22	115	135	10	2.6	4.5	45%	.311	1.46	4.93	4.67	5.05	0.1	114	
2015	PAW	AAA	24	2	4	2	26	0	33	31	2	7.1	9.5	53%	.322	1.73	5.18	4.28	5.79	-0.6	117	
2015	PME	AA	24	1	1	3	21	0	29^2	18	3	3.3	9.7	63%	.208	0.98	2.43	3.54	3.26	0.4	88	
2016	*BOS*	*MLB*	*25*	*1*	*0*	*0*	*18*	*0*	19^1	*22*	*2*	*4.1*	*6.3*	*50%*	*.313*	*1.59*	*4.96*	*4.69*	*5.09*	*-0.1*	*120*	
2017	*BOS*	*MLB*	*26*	*2*	*2*	*0*	*14*	*6*	*46*	*52*	*6*	*4.4*	*6.5*	*50%*	*.312*	*1.62*	*5.21*	*5.05*	*5.35*	*-0.1*	*127*	

Breakout: 0% Improve: 0% Collapse: 0% Attrition: 0% MLB: 0% *Comparables: Daniel Moskos, Geno Espineli, Daniel Davidson*

Since he was drafted 37th overall in 2012, Light's been labeled by many as a future reliever. After struggling mightily as a starter in the low minors, he lived up to his reputation: The Red Sox finally moved him to the 'pen last season, and Light, well, shined. He struck out more than a batter per inning between Portland and Pawtucket, using a mid-to-high-90s fastball and a devastating splitter to great effect. His 17 percent walk rate in Triple-A is concerning, but his MiLB track record suggests that's largely a fluke. The Red Sox lack much impact reliever talent in the high minors, and it's easy to see Light logging substantial major-league innings in the near future. If reading this made you miss Daniel Bard, you're not alone.

Jorge Marban RHP

Born: 12/5/88 Age: 27 Bats: R Throws: R Height: 6'1" Weight: 215

YEAR	TEAM	LVL	AGE	W	L	SV	G	GS	IP	H	HR	BB/9	K/9	GB%	BABIP	WHIP	ERA	FIP	DRA	WARP	CFIP	MPH
2015	PME	AA	26	2	1	5	24	0	33	25	0	6.0	7.1	36%	.258	1.42	1.36	3.78	5.90	-0.6	121	
2015	SLM	A+	26	2	1	1	8	0	16	14	1	3.9	7.3	33%	.271	1.31	1.69	3.94	4.27	0.0	101	
2015	PAW	AAA	26	3	0	0	6	0	13	6	0	2.8	9.0	24%	.207	0.77	0.69	2.31	2.93	0.2	85	
2016	*BOS*	*MLB*	*27*	*2*	*1*	*2*	*39*	*0*	40^2	*44*	*5*	*4.5*	*6.9*	*28%*	*.305*	*1.58*	*4.97*	*5.01*	*5.10*	*-0.2*	*120*	
2017	*BOS*	*MLB*	*28*	*1*	*0*	*1*	*26*	*0*	41^2	*43*	*6*	*4.6*	*7.1*	*28%*	*.297*	*1.55*	*5.11*	*4.95*	*5.24*	*-0.2*	*123*	

Breakout: 3% Improve: 3% Collapse: 3% Attrition: 3% MLB: 7% *Comparables: Jumbo Diaz, Josh Kinney, Santiago Ramirez*

Jorge Marban flunked out of the Rangers' system and was floundering in stateside independent ball before a last-ditch effort in the Australian Baseball League, where he pitched for part-time Red Sox scout Steve Fish. Marban struck out 44 batters in 32 innings and got his walks down under control, and Fish hooked him to a contract with the Sox. Despite some lingering command issues, Marban pitched well in Salem, Portland and Pawtucket last season, and there's a nonzero chance he stars in the sequel to Boston's first indy-league success story, The Legend of Daniel Nava. Marban is still a long shot, but purely from a mileage standpoint that term seems awfully relative.

Justin Masterson RHP

Born: 3/22/85 Age: 31 Bats: R Throws: R Height: 6'6" Weight: 260

YEAR	TEAM	LVL	AGE	W	L	SV	G	GS	IP	H	HR	BB/9	K/9	GB%	BABIP	WHIP	ERA	FIP	DRA	WARP	CFIP	MPH
2013	CLE	MLB	28	14	10	0	32	29	193	156	13	3.5	9.1	60%	.285	1.20	3.45	3.38	3.15	4.1	89	95.8
2014	COH	AAA	29	0	1	0	2	2	11^2	9	0	6.2	7.7	47%	.281	1.46	5.40	3.70	4.62	0.1	103	
2014	CLE	MLB	29	4	6	0	19	19	98	106	6	5.1	8.5	61%	.350	1.65	5.51	4.11	5.40	-0.7	110	93.0
2014	SLN	MLB	29	3	3	0	9	6	30^2	35	6	3.8	6.8	59%	.309	1.57	7.04	5.81	6.89	-0.8	142	93.0
2015	PAW	AAA	30	0	2	0	3	3	13^2	8	0	4.6	7.9	65%	.235	1.10	3.29	3.16	4.24	0.1	103	
2015	BOS	MLB	30	4	2	0	18	9	59^1	68	7	4.1	7.4	52%	.339	1.60	5.61	4.86	6.17	-0.9	116	91.0
2016	*BOS*	*MLB*	*31*	*5*	*4*	*0*	*14*	*14*	*78*	*80*	*9*	*3.9*	*8.0*	*57%*	*.312*	*1.46*	*4.46*	*4.48*	*4.64*	*0.4*	*108*	
2017	*BOS*	*MLB*	*32*	*9*	*10*	*0*	*28*	*28*	174^1	*181*	*20*	*3.9*	*7.8*	*57%*	*.312*	*1.47*	*4.55*	*4.40*	*4.73*	*0.8*	*109*	

Breakout: 13% Improve: 44% Collapse: 20% Attrition: 15% MLB: 94% *Comparables: Carlos Zambrano, Doug Davis, Jim Beattie*

Game of Thrones fans will be familiar with Beric "The Lightning Lord" Dondarrion, a good and just knight who's used to introduce resurrection into the series. Unfortunately, Beric's tale turns sour when we learn that each time he's brought back, he loses more and more of his old self. So it goes with Masterson, whose own comeback tale with the Red Sox met a gory end in August after he struggled all season long. Masterson's drastically reduced velocity has rendered his once-potent fastball/slider combo lifeless, and his ability to log 200-plus innings is a fading relic as well. The former Red Sox farmhand has always had trouble with lefties, but in 2015 southpaws hit like Babe Ruth against him, batting .307/.409/.508 with 17 XBH. Masterson will be just 31 this season and perhaps deserves one more shot as a ROOGY or a long man, but as Arya Stark will remind you, all pitching careers must die.

Alexi Ogando RHP

Born: 10/5/83 Age: 32 Bats: R Throws: R Height: 6'4" Weight: 195

YEAR	TEAM	LVL	AGE	W	L	SV	G	GS	IP	H	HR	BB/9	K/9	GB%	BABIP	WHIP	ERA	FIP	DRA	WARP	CFIP	MPH
2013	TEX	MLB	29	7	4	0	23	18	104^{1}	87	11	3.5	6.2	43%	.254	1.23	3.11	4.39	3.61	1.6	114	96.8
2013	ROU	AAA	29	0	1	0	3	3	13	12	4	2.8	2.8	38%	.186	1.23	6.23	7.88	5.47	0.0	117	
2014	TEX	MLB	30	2	3	1	27	0	25	33	1	5.4	7.9	37%	.386	1.92	6.84	3.84	5.10	-0.2	107	96.6
2015	BOS	MLB	31	3	1	0	64	0	65^{1}	59	12	3.9	7.3	44%	.260	1.33	3.99	5.29	4.57	0.1	111	96.8
2016	*BOS*	*MLB*	*32*	*3*	*2*	*0*	*31*	*4*	*50*	*49*	*7*	*3.5*	*6.9*	*42%*	*.282*	*1.36*	*4.72*	*4.80*	*4.90*	*0.0*	*116*	
2017	*BOS*	*MLB*	*33*	*5*	*4*	*1*	*65*	*8*	104^{2}	*106*	*16*	*3.7*	*6.4*	*42%*	*.282*	*1.42*	*5.18*	*5.03*	*5.38*	*-0.6*	*128*	

Breakout: 12% Improve: 40% Collapse: 33% Attrition: 12% MLB: 92% *Comparables: Andy Messersmith, Andy McGaffigan, Matt Clement*

The good news is Ogando regained some velocity last season. That's it. That's all the good news. The former Ranger gave up 12 homers in 64 games and allowed nearly a hit per inning while posting a DRA north of 4.50 and a FIP north of 5.00 with Boston. Ogando is now two seasons removed from being mildly useful and four seasons removed from being good, which means he should probably be removed from the big leagues altogether. Instead, he'll end up closing for the A's or the Marlins or something.

Henry Owens LHP

Born: 7/21/92 Age: 23 Bats: L Throws: L Height: 6'6" Weight: 220

YEAR	TEAM	LVL	AGE	W	L	SV	G	GS	IP	H	HR	BB/9	K/9	GB%	BABIP	WHIP	ERA	FIP	DRA	WARP	CFIP	MPH
2013	PME	AA	20	3	1	0	6	6	30^{1}	18	3	4.5	13.6	29%	.254	1.09	1.78	3.26	3.95	0.4	79	
2013	SLM	A+	20	8	5	0	20	20	104^{2}	66	6	4.6	10.6	45%	.249	1.14	2.92	3.46	4.15	1.4	82	
2014	PAW	AAA	21	3	1	0	6	6	38	32	4	2.8	10.4	44%	.301	1.16	4.03	3.59	4.02	0.5	81	
2014	PME	AA	21	14	4	0	20	20	121	89	6	3.5	9.4	48%	.267	1.12	2.60	3.16	3.92	1.7	79	
2015	PAW	AAA	22	3	8	0	21	21	122^{1}	84	7	4.1	7.6	41%	.233	1.14	3.16	3.66	4.65	0.0	107	
2015	BOS	MLB	22	4	4	0	11	11	63	62	7	3.4	7.1	37%	.293	1.37	4.57	4.25	3.78	0.9	105	92.5
2016	*BOS*	*MLB*	*23*	*3*	*3*	*0*	*8*	*8*	45^{2}	*43*	*5*	*3.7*	*8.0*	*39%*	*.289*	*1.36*	*4.31*	*4.29*	*4.49*	*0.3*	*104*	
2017	*BOS*	*MLB*	*24*	*4*	*4*	*0*	*13*	*13*	77^{2}	*69*	*9*	*3.9*	*8.6*	*39%*	*.283*	*1.33*	*4.22*	*4.09*	*4.40*	*0.6*	*101*	

Breakout: 18% Improve: 36% Collapse: 19% Attrition: 30% MLB: 67% *Comparables: Ian Kennedy, Keyvius Sampson, Jake Odorizzi*

For years now we've all wondered if Owens was destined to be a rotation anchor or more of a complementary back-end piece. We've got another year or two of wondering ahead, as Owens did just enough to keep the no. 3 starter dream alive while performing more along the lines of a no. 4/5. Owens' Triple-A numbers don't jump off the page, but he was dominant over his final 10 starts in Pawtucket, holding batters to a .188/.248/.293 line. Once he reached the majors, the lanky lefty was maddeningly inconsistent in his 11 starts, hitting game scores of over 70 three times but also twice bottoming out at 15. Despite being left-handed, tall and deceptive as all hell, Owens allowed same-side hitters to mash to the tune of .293/.396/.463 against him in the bigs (in 48 PA, to be fair), suggesting he needs to come up with a weapon that prevents southpaws from sitting on his change. He's already proven capable of unleashing some of the best f-bombs on the mound this side of John Lackey, so let's hope he pans out.

Rick Porcello RHP

Born: 12/27/88 Age: 27 Bats: R Throws: R Height: 6'5" Weight: 200

YEAR	TEAM	LVL	AGE	W	L	SV	G	GS	IP	H	HR	BB/9	K/9	GB%	BABIP	WHIP	ERA	FIP	DRA	WARP	CFIP	MPH
2013	DET	MLB	24	13	8	0	32	29	177	185	18	2.1	7.2	56%	.315	1.28	4.32	3.56	3.76	2.4	93	94.3
2014	DET	MLB	25	15	13	0	32	31	204^{2}	211	18	1.8	5.7	51%	.298	1.23	3.43	3.70	3.93	2.1	99	93.2
2015	BOS	MLB	26	9	15	0	28	28	172	196	25	2.0	7.8	47%	.332	1.36	4.92	4.10	4.69	0.7	97	94.2
2016	*BOS*	*MLB*	*27*	*11*	*8*	*0*	*26*	*26*	163^{2}	*177*	*20*	*2.1*	*7.4*	*50%*	*.317*	*1.32*	*4.00*	*4.02*	*4.19*	*1.8*	*95*	
2017	*BOS*	*MLB*	*28*	*10*	*9*	*0*	*27*	*27*	166^{1}	*177*	*21*	*2.1*	*7.2*	*50%*	*.311*	*1.30*	*4.10*	*3.97*	*4.29*	*1.6*	*98*	

Breakout: 23% Improve: 56% Collapse: 24% Attrition: 9% MLB: 98% *Comparables: Bob Rush, Charles Nagy, Dwight Gooden*

Ben Cherington had a natural obsession,
for acquiring some groundball SPs.
He gave Rick money for a workload to handle,
but Porcello brought no stability.
One day he started throwing high in the zone,
and it's true he bumped up his strikeout pace.
But hitters teed off and he didn't know why,
took a DL stint for him to save some face.
(Y'all can't cut me.)
Don't go chasing strikeout calls,
just stick to the sinkers and the groundouts you're used to.
I know that the results got better when you pitched in the fall,
but it's hard to look at your stats.

David Price LHP

Born: 8/26/85 Age: 30 Bats: L Throws: L Height: 6'6" Weight: 210

YEAR	TEAM	LVL	AGE	W	L	SV	G	GS	IP	H	HR	BB/9	K/9	GB%	BABIP	WHIP	ERA	FIP	DRA	WARP	CFIP	MPH
2013	TBA	MLB	27	10	8	0	27	27	186^{2}	178	16	1.3	7.3	47%	.298	1.10	3.33	3.05	3.89	2.3	86	96.1
2014	DET	MLB	28	4	4	0	11	11	77^{2}	74	5	1.7	9.5	45%	.317	1.15	3.59	2.46	2.79	1.9	61	96.3
2014	TBA	MLB	28	11	8	0	23	23	170^{2}	156	20	1.2	10.0	42%	.301	1.05	3.11	2.96	3.56	2.6	76	95.9
2015	DET	MLB	29	9	4	0	21	21	146	133	13	1.8	8.5	41%	.293	1.11	2.53	3.03	2.87	3.8	75	96.5
2015	TOR	MLB	29	9	1	0	11	11	74^{1}	57	4	2.2	10.5	44%	.283	1.01	2.30	2.19	2.73	2.0	60	97.2
2016	*BOS*	*MLB*	*30*	*15*	*9*	*0*	*33*	*33*	*221*	*208*	*24*	*1.7*	*9.2*	*43%*	*.305*	*1.13*	*3.24*	*3.26*	*3.45*	*4.4*	*72*	
2017	*BOS*	*MLB*	*31*	*13*	*9*	*0*	*29*	*29*	*179^{1}*	*165*	*19*	*1.7*	*8.9*	*43%*	*.296*	*1.11*	*3.32*	*3.21*	*3.53*	*3.8*	*75*	

Breakout: 17% Improve: 52% Collapse: 19% Attrition: 12% MLB: 98% *Comparables: Jose Rijo, Adam Wainwright, Erik Bedard*

Just like Mark McGwire's 62nd home run, the moon landing and Janet Jackson's wardrobe malfunction, we all remember where we were when we saw David Price storm out of the bullpen in Game Four of the ALDS. In fact, it's still as befuddling today as it was on October 12th, even knowing the Blue Jays went on to win the series. Before he was relegated to mop-up duty that day, Price finished second in the AL Cy Young voting after coming over from Detroit at the trade deadline. A true workhorse, Price has faced more batters over the last six years than Clayton Kershaw, Cole Hamels and Justin Verlander; nobody has faced more than him since the start of 2014. He also found himself immune, at least during the regular season, to two major tenets of the modern pitching age: the velocity aging curve (Price saw his highest mark since 2012) and the third-time-through-the-order penalty (his .533 OPS against third-time opponents was lower than his first or second). The playoffs continued to be his bugaboo, but there's no reason to believe this won't resolve itself over the life of his massive new contract.

Eduardo Rodriguez LHP

Born: 4/7/93 Age: 23 Bats: L Throws: L Height: 6'2" Weight: 210

YEAR	TEAM	LVL	AGE	W	L	SV	G	GS	IP	H	HR	BB/9	K/9	GB%	BABIP	WHIP	ERA	FIP	DRA	WARP	CFIP	MPH
2013	BOW	AA	20	4	3	0	11	11	59^{2}	53	5	3.6	8.9	42%	.296	1.29	4.22	3.74	4.32	0.6	91	
2013	FRD	A+	20	6	4	0	14	14	85^{1}	78	4	2.6	7.0	48%	.292	1.21	2.85	3.36	4.27	1.0	86	
2014	PME	AA	21	3	1	0	6	6	37^{1}	30	1	1.9	9.4	47%	.299	1.02	0.96	2.42	3.21	0.8	66	
2014	BOW	AA	21	3	7	0	16	16	82^{2}	90	5	3.2	7.5	46%	.328	1.44	4.79	3.52	4.25	0.8	88	
2015	BOS	MLB	22	10	6	0	21	21	121^{2}	120	13	2.7	7.2	45%	.290	1.29	3.85	3.89	3.44	2.3	99	96.8
2015	PAW	AAA	22	4	3	0	8	8	48^{1}	46	2	1.3	8.2	50%	.321	1.10	2.98	2.31	2.09	1.5	74	
2016	*BOS*	*MLB*	*23*	*10*	*8*	*0*	*26*	*26*	*148^{1}*	*152*	*17*	*2.7*	*7.5*	*45%*	*.304*	*1.33*	*4.07*	*4.08*	*4.26*	*1.5*	*97*	
2017	*BOS*	*MLB*	*24*	*8*	*8*	*0*	*25*	*25*	*144^{2}*	*145*	*17*	*2.8*	*7.7*	*45%*	*.303*	*1.32*	*4.15*	*4.02*	*4.34*	*1.3*	*99*	

Breakout: 26% Improve: 47% Collapse: 19% Attrition: 22% MLB: 77% *Comparables: Patrick Corbin, Drew Pomeranz, Alex Sanabia*

The Red Sox and Orioles have both had trouble developing quality MLB starting pitchers over the past half-decade, but Rodriguez looks poised to break that trend after a very promising rookie campaign. The Venezuelan southpaw relied heavily on a potent mid-90s fastball and an inconsistent slider/changeup mix to finish slightly better than league average, per cFIP. At his best, such as his May 28th debut against Texas, Rodriguez is a strikeout machine who gets ahead, pounds the zone and limits walks. At his worst, such as his five-out mid-July implosion against the Angels, Rodriguez loses his command, leaves the ball up, tips his pitches and surrenders a ton of hard contact. Still, for a 22-year-old with no experience above Triple-A heading into 2015, E-Rod's (don't blame us: He picked that nickname) debut was nothing short of a success, portending a best-case future as a no. 2 starter. Holding up over 200-plus innings will be Rodriguez's next big test, as the 170 he logged last season were a career high.

Robbie Ross LHP

Born: 6/24/89 Age: 27 Bats: L Throws: L Height: 5'11" Weight: 215

YEAR	TEAM	LVL	AGE	W	L	SV	G	GS	IP	H	HR	BB/9	K/9	GB%	BABIP	WHIP	ERA	FIP	DRA	WARP	CFIP	MPH
2013	TEX	MLB	24	4	2	0	65	0	62^{1}	63	4	2.7	8.4	45%	.326	1.32	3.03	3.20	3.97	0.5	94	95.1
2014	ROU	AAA	25	5	4	0	12	9	60^{1}	66	7	2.4	6.4	58%	.319	1.36	4.33	4.73	5.31	0.3	101	
2014	TEX	MLB	25	3	6	0	27	12	78^{1}	103	9	3.4	5.9	54%	.352	1.70	6.20	4.77	6.25	-1.5	118	92.9
2015	BOS	MLB	26	0	2	6	54	0	60^{2}	59	7	3.0	7.9	51%	.295	1.30	3.86	3.99	4.07	0.5	100	95.1
2016	*BOS*	*MLB*	*27*	*2*	*1*	*0*	*50*	*0*	*53*	*56*	*6*	*3.0*	*7.1*	*53%*	*.308*	*1.40*	*4.42*	*4.32*	*4.60*	*0.1*	*106*	
2017	*BOS*	*MLB*	*28*	*4*	*2*	*1*	*48*	*4*	*73^{1}*	*75*	*9*	*2.9*	*7.5*	*53%*	*.303*	*1.35*	*4.29*	*4.15*	*4.46*	*0.3*	*102*	

Breakout: 20% Improve: 48% Collapse: 26% Attrition: 15% MLB: 87% *Comparables: Ryan Rowland-Smith, Wade Davis, Andrew Cashner*

Your options are pretty limited once your parents name you Robbie Ross Jr., really. You can be an NFL punt return specialist, a NASCAR driver, a middle reliever or a Confederate Civil War reenactor. Thankfully our protagonist chose the career with the most security, and he had an adequate first season as a member of the Red Sox. While his overall line wasn't pretty, Ross did hold lefties to a .214/.284/.360 line, and though his ERA ticked up in the second half nearly all of his peripherals were better. He's a southpaw, throws fairly hard and is young, so he'll have plenty of chances to make it as a LOOGY before resorting to running left, turning left or pretending to fight the left.

Carson Smith RHP

Born: 10/19/89 Age: 26 Bats: R Throws: R Height: 6'6" Weight: 215

YEAR	TEAM	LVL	AGE	W	L	SV	G	GS	IP	H	HR	BB/9	K/9	GB%	BABIP	WHIP	ERA	FIP	DRA	WARP	CFIP	MPH
2013	WTN	AA	23	1	3	15	44	0	50	33	1	3.1	12.8	72%	.294	1.00	1.80	1.65	2.87	0.9	60	
2014	TAC	AAA	24	1	3	10	39	0	43	44	1	2.7	9.4	70%	.352	1.33	2.93	2.89	4.73	0.3	80	
2014	SEA	MLB	24	1	0	0	9	0	8^1	2	0	3.2	10.8	81%	.125	0.60	0.00	1.84	-1.50	0.6	90	96.2
2015	SEA	MLB	25	2	5	13	70	0	70	49	2	2.8	11.8	66%	.292	1.01	2.31	2.09	2.67	1.7	67	95.9
2016	*BOS*	*MLB*	*26*	*3*	*1*	*0*	*50*	*0*	*53*	*46*	*5*	*3.0*	*10.7*	*67%*	*.309*	*1.21*	*3.25*	*3.28*	*3.47*	*1.0*	*70*	
2017	*BOS*	*MLB*	*27*	*3*	*1*	*5*	*50*	*0*	*55^2*	*46*	*5*	*3.1*	*10.9*	*67%*	*.302*	*1.18*	*3.16*	*3.06*	*3.37*	*0.9*	*67*	

Breakout: 36% Improve: 53% Collapse: 24% Attrition: 18% MLB: 91% *Comparables: Luke Gregerson, Kevin Quackenbush, Jose Arredondo*

How bullpens change: A year ago, the Mariners seemed so stocked at reliever that Smith earned only a lineout in this book, his talent almost an extravagance. Then, 2015. After Fernando Rodney threw himself out of a job and with every other member of the staff scuffling, manager Lloyd McClendon turned to to Smith on June 6th. For a while, he ran with the job, but a dip in velocity combined with some command issues pushed him back into a lower profile role. When he's on, he dominates with a 91-93 mph fastball that can play up to 95 and a hard slider that is difficult to make contact against. His velocity and results rallied in September, and he enters this season as the best seventh-inning pitcher in baseball.

Junichi Tazawa RHP

Born: 6/6/86 Age: 30 Bats: R Throws: R Height: 5'11" Weight: 200

YEAR	TEAM	LVL	AGE	W	L	SV	G	GS	IP	H	HR	BB/9	K/9	GB%	BABIP	WHIP	ERA	FIP	DRA	WARP	CFIP	MPH
2013	BOS	MLB	27	5	4	0	71	0	68^1	70	9	1.6	9.5	35%	.321	1.20	3.16	3.25	4.24	0.3	77	96.4
2014	BOS	MLB	28	4	3	0	71	0	63	58	5	2.4	9.1	38%	.303	1.19	2.86	2.97	3.17	1.0	82	96.2
2015	BOS	MLB	29	2	7	3	61	0	58^2	65	5	2.0	8.6	42%	.349	1.33	4.14	3.02	4.11	0.4	88	95.9
2016	*BOS*	*MLB*	*30*	*3*	*1*	*0*	*50*	*0*	*53*	*54*	*6*	*2.4*	*8.8*	*40%*	*.313*	*1.28*	*3.69*	*3.66*	*3.90*	*0.6*	*86*	
2017	*BOS*	*MLB*	*31*	*3*	*1*	*2*	*52*	*0*	*53^2*	*51*	*6*	*2.3*	*8.8*	*40%*	*.298*	*1.20*	*3.69*	*3.58*	*3.90*	*0.5*	*86*	

Breakout: 28% Improve: 60% Collapse: 20% Attrition: 11% MLB: 92% *Comparables: Scott Stewart, Jerry Blevins, Jason Motte*

Joe Torre : Scott Proctor :: John Farrell : Junichi Tazawa. After logging 138 innings (including the postseason) between 2013 and 2014, Tazawa took the mound 46 more times before August last year. By July his workload had caught up to him, as the righty posted a 7.08 ERA in 20 innings in the second half. He has been the picture of health since recovering from Tommy John surgery in 2010, but after dealing with hip, groin and shoulder soreness at various points last season, and with the Red Sox having no real incentive to crack the whip, he was shut down in early September. He's still just 29 and showed a negligible loss in velocity, so general reliever fluctuation aside, he should be back to his old self for his contract year.

Koji Uehara RHP

Born: 4/3/75 Age: 41 Bats: R Throws: R Height: 6'2" Weight: 195

YEAR	TEAM	LVL	AGE	W	L	SV	G	GS	IP	H	HR	BB/9	K/9	GB%	BABIP	WHIP	ERA	FIP	DRA	WARP	CFIP	MPH
2013	BOS	MLB	38	4	1	21	73	0	74^1	33	5	1.1	12.2	42%	.188	0.57	1.09	1.64	1.73	2.6	41	91.2
2014	BOS	MLB	39	6	5	26	64	0	64^1	51	10	1.1	11.2	35%	.273	0.92	2.52	3.11	2.86	1.3	63	90.3
2015	BOS	MLB	40	2	4	25	43	0	40^1	28	3	2.0	10.5	29%	.248	0.92	2.23	2.41	2.38	1.1	74	89.1
2016	*BOS*	*MLB*	*41*	*2*	*1*	*0*	*41*	*0*	*43^1*	*34*	*5*	*2.1*	*10.5*	*33%*	*.271*	*1.02*	*3.23*	*3.19*	*3.46*	*0.8*	*71*	
2017	*BOS*	*MLB*	*42*	*4*	*2*	*15*	*40*	*5*	*66*	*53*	*9*	*2.1*	*9.8*	*33%*	*.263*	*1.04*	*3.61*	*3.51*	*3.87*	*0.8*	*83*	

Breakout: 21% Improve: 40% Collapse: 26% Attrition: 14% MLB: 75% *Comparables: Takashi Saito, Trevor Hoffman, Russ Springer*

Given the way Uehara tired at the end of 2014 and the finite number of bullets one assumes he has in his right arm, the Red Sox had to at least be considering shutting down their closer altogether in the season's final months. Ian Kinsler made that decision for the Boston brass in early August, when he ended Uehara's dominant 2015 via a line drive that broke Koji's wrist. While he was still very much a high-five catalyst last year, his strikeout rate, walk rate, velocity and flyball percentage were all trending in the wrong direction, and there's an excellent chance that 2016 is his last season. There's also an excellent chance that his last season is excellent, as his splitter and incredible command continue to prove that velocity is not the end-all be-all, even for bullpenners.

Steven Wright RHP

Born: 8/30/84 Age: 31 Bats: R Throws: R Height: 6'1" Weight: 215

YEAR	TEAM	LVL	AGE	W	L	SV	G	GS	IP	H	HR	BB/9	K/9	GB%	BABIP	WHIP	ERA	FIP	DRA	WARP	CFIP	MPH
2013	BOS	MLB	28	2	0	0	4	1	13^1	12	0	6.1	6.8	38%	.308	1.58	5.40	3.83	4.91	0.0	110	88.7
2013	PAW	AAA	28	8	7	0	24	24	135^1	130	10	4.3	6.6	53%	.294	1.44	3.46	4.23	4.76	0.3	111	
2014	BOS	MLB	29	0	1	0	6	1	21	21	2	1.7	9.4	57%	.328	1.19	2.57	2.87	3.34	0.3	88	87.2
2014	PAW	AAA	29	5	5	0	15	15	95	86	9	2.1	6.4	48%	.269	1.14	3.41	3.88	4.47	0.7	99	
2015	PAW	AAA	30	2	5	0	8	8	52	55	2	2.6	7.3	51%	.331	1.35	3.81	3.02	3.51	0.7	92	
2015	BOS	MLB	30	5	4	0	16	9	72^2	67	12	3.3	6.4	45%	.252	1.29	4.09	4.98	4.11	0.7	110	88.2
2016	*BOS*	*MLB*	*31*	*3*	*2*	*0*	*41*	*5*	*65*	*67*	*8*	*3.3*	*6.7*	*47%*	*.296*	*1.40*	*4.57*	*4.53*	*4.75*	*0.1*	*112*	
2017	*BOS*	*MLB*	*32*	*4*	*5*	*0*	*13*	*13*	*74^1*	*77*	*10*	*3.3*	*6.7*	*47%*	*.294*	*1.41*	*4.83*	*4.68*	*5.02*	*0.1*	*119*	

Breakout: 6% Improve: 8% Collapse: 5% Attrition: 14% MLB: 24% *Comparables: Jason Stanford, Matt Palmer, Justin Lehr*

Predicting pitcher performance is a precarious endeavor to begin with. Add a knuckleball into the equation—a pitch that Wright throws nearly 90% of the time—and you're basically left with guesswork. That's why it's difficult to say that Wright exceeded expectations last season—none existed to begin with—and yet his 70-plus innings of quality baseball-throwing are notable nonetheless. Wright probably would've kept logging innings, too, but he was shelved in early August after being struck just below the head by an errant fly ball while running sprints. As Wright's comedic counterpart would tell you, that just goes to prove that working out is a pain in the neck.

Lineouts

Hitters

NAME	POS	TEAM	LVL	AGE	PA	R	2B	3B	HR	RBI	BB	K	SB	CS	AVG/OBP/SLG	TAv	BABIP	BRR	FRAA	WARP
Luis Alexander Basabe	OF	LOW	A-	18	256	36	8	3	7	23	32	67	15	4	.243/.340/.401	.273	.315	4.1	CF(28): 4.9, RF(25): 5.8	2.9
Sean Coyle	2B	PAW	AAA	23	148	21	3	0	5	16	20	44	4	1	.159/.274/.302	.235	.195	2.4	2B(28): 0.5, 3B(10): -0.7	0.2
Mauricio Dubon	SS	GRN	A	20	262	43	12	3	4	29	18	34	18	4	.301/.354/.428	.294	.337	6.3	2B(38): 8.9, SS(18): 1.0	3.5
	SS	SLM	A+	20	269	27	9	0	1	18	23	38	12	3	.274/.343/.325	.240	.320	2.1	SS(52): -2.2, 2B(5): 0.1	0.5
Ryan LaMarre	CF	CIN	MLB	26	26	2	0	0	0	0	0	9	0	0	.080/.080/.080	.069	.125	0.4	CF(13): 1.3, LF(2): -0.1	-0.3
	CF	LOU	AAA	26	329	33	17	1	8	18	18	88	11	4	.257/.307/.400	.251	.333	-0.5	CF(80): 10.2, RF(1): -0.0	1.7
Sandy Leon	C	BOS	MLB	26	128	8	2	0	0	3	7	28	0	1	.184/.238/.202	.170	.244	-0.5	C(37): -3.6, 3B(1): -0.0	-1.1
	C	PAW	AAA	26	111	8	4	0	1	13	10	23	0	1	.263/.342/.333	.259	.333	0.6	C(21): 0.3	0.5
Nick Longhi	OF	GRN	A	19	488	52	27	3	7	62	34	88	2	0	.281/.338/.403	.282	.334	-8.7	1B(71): 2.1, RF(50): -5.9	0.5
Austin Rei	C	LOW	A-	21	130	14	5	1	2	12	11	39	1	0	.179/.285/.295	.230	.250	0.4	C(31): 1.3	0.3
Wendell Rijo	2B	SLM	A+	19	455	47	27	2	6	47	34	94	15	7	.260/.324/.381	.265	.321	-2.0	2B(97): 6.3, SS(4): -0.2	1.9

Not to be confused with his brother, **Luis** *Alexander* **Basabe**, **Luis** *Alejandro* **Basabe** is a somewhat fast, switch-hitting middle infielder with a good eye and enough youth to forgive the rest. ❖ Not to be confused with his brother, Luis *Alejandro* Basabe, **Luis** *Alexander* **Basabe** is a fast, switch-hitting center fielder with some power and enough youth to forgive the rest. ❖ **Sean Coyle** can run a bit, has more pop than you'd think and has some defensive versatility, but injuries and a lackluster hit tool derailed his season. This isn't a reprint of his 2015 Annual comment, but it may as well be. ❖ If you like utility infielders but hate instant gratification, **Mauricio Dubon** is your guy. Yes, he stole 30 bases between Greenville and Salem, but his ultimate profile suggests he'll largely serve as insurance for Marco Hernandez, who serves as insurance for Deven Marrero, who serves as insurance for Brock Holt, who serves as insurance for everything. ❖ **Ryan LaMarre** has shed the dreaded "tweener" label and earned fifth outfielder consideration by playing a surprisingly adept center field; even more surprising is the fact he's been written up in this book every year since 2011, and yet we've never included a *Blazing Saddles* quote. ❖ Literally Spanish for "a beached sea lion," **Sandy Leon** is a 70-grade defender and a 20-grade everything else. Fifty percent of the time he threw out would-be base-stealers every time. ❖ **Nick Longhi** is a Springfield, MA, native and former 30th-round pick who put together a nice season in Greenville after an injury-shortened 2014. He's a corner outfielder/first baseman so the bat will have to play, but it has to this point. ❖ The Red Sox popped arguably the best defensive catcher in the 2015 draft when they grabbed **Austin Rei** in the third round. His bat has a long way to go, but his glove will buy him plenty of time. ❖ **Wendell Rijo** has been a popular sleeper among Red Sox followers for a few seasons now, and while the second baseman has done enough to keep the dream alive he's yet to truly flourish. Good thing he's only 20.

Pitchers

NAME	TEAM	LVL	AGE	W	L	SV	G	GS	IP	H	HR	BB/9	K/9	GB%	BABIP	WHIP	ERA	FIP	FRA	WARP	CFIP	MPH
Ty Buttrey	GRN	A	22	1	0	0	4	4	22	17	2	1.2	9.0	57%	.259	0.91	2.45	3.21	3.05	0.5	83	
Ryan Cook	OAK	MLB	28	0	2	0	4	0	4^1	7	0	6.2	6.2	59%	.412	2.31	10.38	3.80	13.39	-0.4	108	95.6
	NAS	AAA	28	4	1	8	30	0	33^1	32	3	3.8	7.0	53%	.299	1.38	4.05	4.74	5.48	-0.1	106	
	BOS	MLB	28	0	0	0	5	0	4^1	13	4	8.3	6.2	50%	.450	3.92	27.00	16.49	17.65	-0.7	129	96.2
Edwin Escobar	PAW	AAA	23	3	3	0	19	6	49^2	52	8	4.5	4.3	38%	.272	1.55	5.07	5.92	7.45	-1.8	138	
Heath Hembree	BOS	MLB	26	2	0	0	22	0	25^1	25	5	3.2	5.3	30%	.260	1.34	3.55	5.55	4.75	0.0	113	97.7
	PAW	AAA	26	0	5	8	29	0	31^2	23	1	2.8	9.1	36%	.265	1.04	2.27	2.68	2.83	0.6	84	
Williams Jerez	GRN	A	23	3	1	3	14	0	39^1	43	3	2.3	9.8	49%	.367	1.35	2.06	3.13	3.07	0.8	84	
	PME	AA	23	1	2	1	22	0	37	34	2	4.1	7.5	49%	.294	1.38	3.65	3.67	4.50	0.0	104	
	SLM	A+	23	1	0	0	5	0	12^1	11	0	2.9	8.8	57%	.314	1.22	0.73	2.52	3.56	0.1	94	
Roman Mendez	BOS	MLB	24	0	0	0	3	0	2	3	1	4.5	4.5	57%	.333	2.00	4.50	10.10	11.85	-0.2	137	95.9
	TEX	MLB	24	0	1	0	12	0	11^2	11	1	5.4	6.9	12%	.323	1.54	5.40	4.73	7.07	-0.3	102	95.8
	ROU	AAA	24	3	2	5	30	0	35^2	31	5	2.3	8.3	36%	.268	1.12	2.78	4.41	3.96	0.5	89	
Sean O'Sullivan	PHI	MLB	27	1	6	0	13	13	71	94	16	2.5	4.4	44%	.312	1.61	6.08	6.20	6.23	-1.0	129	92.5
	LEH	AAA	27	5	2	0	9	9	56^1	48	3	3.0	6.6	39%	.266	1.19	3.20	3.46	4.02	0.5	99	
Noe Ramirez	PAW	AAA	25	4	1	3	30	1	42^2	33	1	3.8	8.0	44%	.271	1.20	2.32	3.02	3.76	0.3	96	
	BOS	MLB	25	0	1	0	17	0	13	13	3	4.8	9.0	38%	.278	1.54	4.15	6.18	6.14	-0.2	105	91.9
Teddy Stankiewicz	SLM	A+	21	5	11	0	25	25	141^1	149	11	2.0	4.9	45%	.302	1.28	4.01	4.02	4.95	-0.5	109	
Anthony Varvaro	BOS	MLB	30	0	1	0	9	0	11	14	0	4.9	6.5	49%	.378	1.82	4.09	3.29	5.32	-0.1	109	94.2
Luis Ysla	SJO	A+	23	3	6	0	33	9	79^2	109	9	4.6	10.7	40%	.433	1.88	6.21	4.52	5.46	0.1	104	

Fellow 2014 international signee Anderson Espinoza stole all the headlines last season, but don't forget about right-hander **Christopher Acosta**, who has substantial upside despite being younger than the first Harry Potter book. ❖ **Ty Buttrey**'s decent performance in High-A and revamped delivery are reasons enough to view him as a legit starter prospect, but it's the projectability due to his massive size that scouts are really excited about. In other words, they love big Buttreys and they cannot lie. Somewhere, Brett Lawrie is nodding. ❖ It takes a lot to make a bullpen, but even one Cook was too many for the Red Sox, as **Ryan Cook** allowed 18 runs in eight-plus innings after being picked off the scrap heap. Where's Smarf when you need him? ❖ Sometimes you trade for lefty pitching prospects, and they become Eduardo Rodriguez. More often than not they turn into **Edwin Escobar**, who was both hurt and bad last season. ❖ **Heath Hembree**'s heavenly high heat had heralds harboring hope he'd hang around; however, his horrific homer habit has hamstrung him horribly. ❖ Turns out **Williams Jerez** is better at throwing fastballs than he is at hitting them, and the former outfielder has impressed since converting to the mound in 2014. He has the two last names of a man who could make it as a LOOGY. ❖ **Roman Mendez** long hovered around the periphery of Rangers pitching prospects, but a freak arm injury in 2013 slowed his development. Despite some success with the major-league club in 2014, he struggled enough in 2015 to be demoted and eventually designated for assignment, leading to a reunion with the Red Sox. ❖ Among those blessed enough to have faced 1,300 or more major-league hitters in the modern era, only four pitchers have a higher career FIP than **Sean O'Sullivan**'s 5.73. ❖

Noe Ramirez had a terrific season in Triple-A before promptly surrendering three homers in his first 13 MLB innings. He'll enjoy a long career as someone's ninth or 10th best reliever, though hopefully they'll be too polite to tell him. ❖ **Teddy Stankiewicz** hasn't done anything particularly impressive since being drafted 45th overall in 2013, but he hasn't disappointed, either. He's got the frame and feel for his craft to start, but he needs to miss more bats. ❖ The Red Sox forgot to call "no takezies backzies" when dealing **Anthony Varvaro** to the Cubs in May. Chicago promptly returned the reliever to Boston upon realizing he required right flexor tendon surgery, which knocked him out for the remainder of the year. ❖ Early arm woes led to mid-June Tommy John surgery for **Brandon Workman**, whose similarity scores lend a whole new meaning to underwhelming Workman's comp cases. ❖ "Keep calm and acquire potential bullpen arms from the Giants" appears to be Boston's motto when they're out of the race. So it was last year with **Luis Ysla**, a talented 23-year-old lefty whom the Sox grabbed in exchange for Alejandro De Aza.

Manager

John Farrell

YEAR	TEAM	W	L	Pythag +/-	Avg PC	100+ P	120+ P	QS	BQS	REL	REL w Zero R	IBB	PH	PH Avg	PH HR	SB2	CS2	SB3	CS3	SAC Att	SAC%	POS SAC	Squeeze	Swing	In Play
2013	BOS	97	65	-5	100.0	88	5	95	6	450	355	10	81	.235	6	104	17	17	2	38	63.2	21	0	336	104
2014	BOS	71	91	0	97.7	73	1	87	6	493	410	19	91	.231	2	43	21	19	3	34	58.8	19	1	301	79
2015	BOS	51	64	0	93.7	48	0	53	2	328	251	12	51	.244	0	40	12	9	1	29	79.3	21	0	222	98

Farrell's name appears above, but it was bench coach Torey Lovullo who finished the season as the Red Sox manager. Beginning in mid-August, Farrell took a leave of absence to receive treatment for stage one lymphoma, which had been discovered during a surgery to repair a hernia.

Thankfully, Farrell, who had signed a contract extension in February, announced on the season's final day that he would return to his post come spring. The Red Sox coupled that announcement with another: They had signed Lovullo to a two-year contract extension. Nothing odd there, except that part of the new deal stipulated Lovullo would waive his right to interview for any job openings—a shocking development for someone who had tried time and again to land a managerial gig of his own. Speculation about Dave Dombrowski's motives focused on him being uncomfortable with Farrell's health, or wanting to groom Lovullo as the Red Sox' future manager. There's probably validity to both theories, but we'd like to think friendship and loyalty played a role, too—and not just because Fenway Park houses a statue honoring the four players immortalized in David Halberstam's The Teammates.

Lovullo and Farrell don't have a relationship on that level—not yet—but their history dates back more than two decades, to their shared playing days with the Angels. When Farrell became the manager in Toronto, he tabbed Lovullo to join him; and when Farrell returned to Boston, he made sure Lovullo returned as well. It would be an odd, antiquated move if Lovullo indeed sacrificed his career aspirations to remain in Boston alongside his ailing friend. We can't help but hope that was the case.

CHICAGO CUBS

Essay by Mark Armour and Daniel R. Levitt

Player comments by Bradley Woodrum and BP authors

"The only thing I know for sure," said Cubs president Theo Epstein before the 2015 NLCS, "is that whatever team wins the World Series, their particular style of play will be completely en vogue and trumpeted from the rooftops by the media all offseason—and in front offices—as the way to win."

1. The Plan

Epstein's honesty and candor have always been refreshing. When he became GM of the Red Sox at age 28 in late 2002, he did not hide his plans. He would use his team's revenue advantages to build a "$100 million player development machine," to provide young talent to the big-league club, depth to deal with injuries or poor performance, and trade assets to fill developmental holes. The process all started, Epstein felt, with the amateur draft and young international free agents. Ably assisted by farm director Ben Cherington, Epstein ran Boston's machine for nine years.

The Red Sox' 2004 title happened so quickly that it owed little to an increased emphasis on development but much to Epstein's acquisitions of David Ortiz, Curt Schilling, Keith Foulke, and several others. But Boston-era Epstein took advantage of the existing draft rules, letting many of his free agents walk away while stockpiling draft picks. (The compensation for losing a free agent in this period was much higher than today—as much as a first rounder plus a sandwich pick between the first two rounds.)

After drafting Jonathan Papelbon in 2003 and Dustin Pedroia in 2004, the Red Sox lost Pedro Martinez, Derek Lowe and Orlando Cabrera to free agency later that year but ended up with five of the first 50 picks in the 2005 draft. The resultant bounty included Jacoby Ellsbury, Clay Buchholz, and Jed Lowrie. The Red Sox did not always draft this well, but they often had extra draft picks to hedge their bets. In Epstein's nine years in charge, the Red Sox had 23 picks before the start of the second round. The 2007 champions included several players from their system.

Things unraveled in Boston, Epstein later claimed, because he gave in to pressure from ownership to forego waiting for the next crop from the system in lieu of signing or acquiring high-priced veterans. The culmination of this shift came after the 2010 season with the signing of Carl Crawford and the trade for Adrian Gonzalez. The pair cost a $300 million commitment over seven years, several

CUBS PROSPECTUS

2015 W-L: 97-65, 3rd in NL Central

Pythag	.557	5th	DER	.713	7th
RS/G	4.25	15th	B-Age	26.6	3rd
RA/G	3.75	4th	P-Age	29.4	26th
TAv	.265	8th	Salary	$120.3M	13th
BRR	-4.53	19th	M$/MW	$2.2M	24th
TAv-P	.244	3rd	DL Days	1200	21st
FIP	3.33	1st	$ on DL	8%	4th

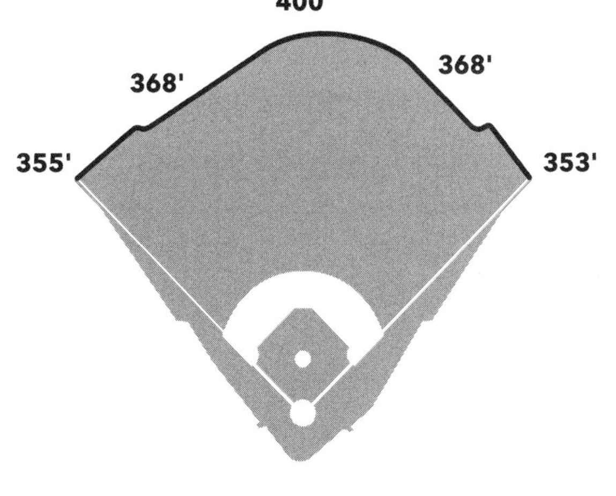

Outfield wall profile: **11'6"** to **15'**

Three-Year Park Factors

Runs	Runs/RH	Runs/LH	HR/RH	HR/LH
98	106	102	120	110

Top Hitter WARP	5.9	Kris Bryant
Top Pitcher WARP	7.3	Jake Arrieta
Top Prospect		Gleyber Torres

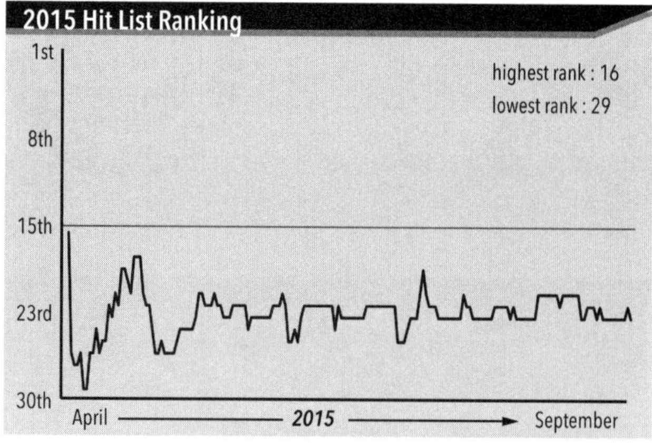

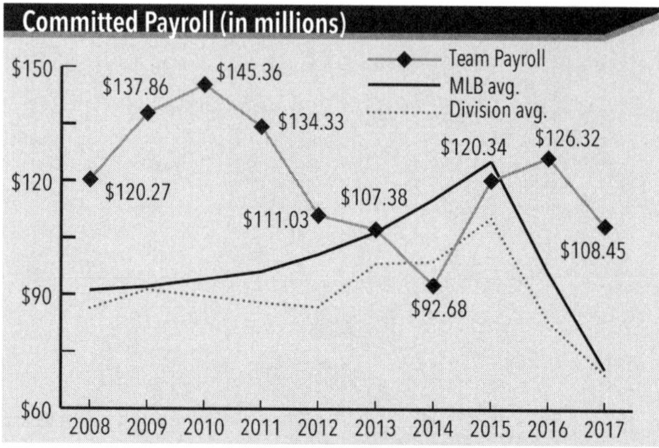

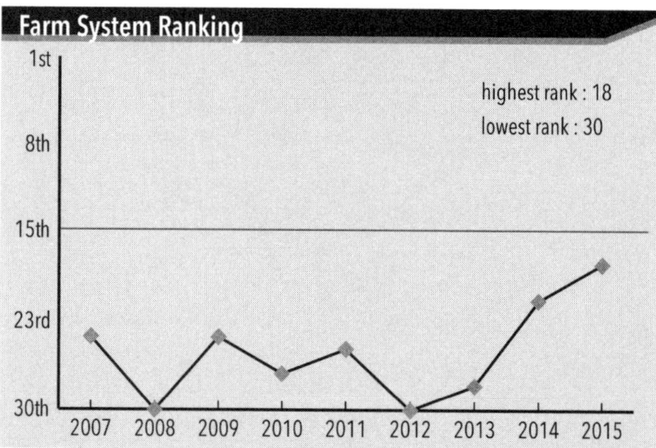

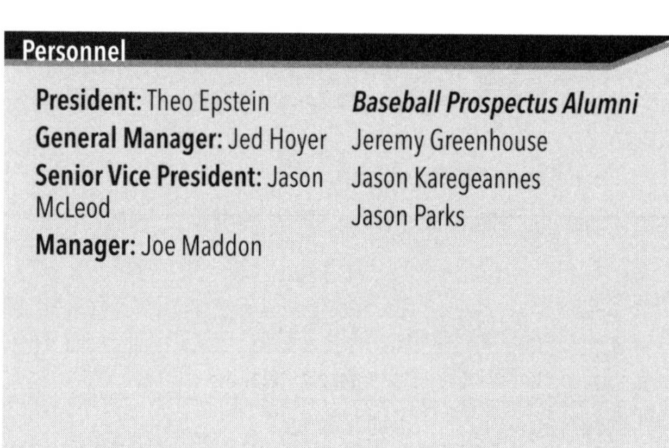
Personnel

President: Theo Epstein
General Manager: Jed Hoyer
Senior Vice President: Jason McLeod
Manager: Joe Maddon

Baseball Prospectus Alumni
Jeremy Greenhouse
Jason Karegeannes
Jason Parks

prospects (including Anthony Rizzo), and the 24th pick in the 2011 draft. "I fucked up," Epstein admitted a couple years later. By that time he was in Chicago, with a new title (President of Baseball Ops) and a total commitment from ownership to build and trust his machine.

The 2012 Collective Bargaining Agreement changed the free agent rules considerably. Teams now receive compensation only if they are willing to make a "qualified" offer, and the compensation is just a single sandwich pick. There is no compensation if the player was acquired during the recently concluded season—the Red Sox' selection of Ellsbury in 2005 was compensation for losing Cabrera, a July 2004 acquisition. Moreover, overpaying for later picks became much more difficult because of proscribed draft "pools." With all of these changes, a team is basically left with "drafting well," which is easier said than done. There are also new restrictions on how much teams can spend on international signings.

Instead of differentiating themselves by spending more to build a homegrown core, the Cubs under Epstein have done it by focusing on a specific category of young players: position players. "The reason we focus on position players in the draft," he said, "and the bigger trades that we made, it's not just because we anticipated the decline in offense, it's also because position players are more predictable." As measured by WAR produced by hitters under 25, the 2015 Cubs (with Anthony Rizzo, Kris Bryant, Addison Russell, Kyle Schwarber, and Starlin Castro), boasted the ninth-best collection of young hitting talent since the advent of free agency. With the cost-control these players provide, the Cubs were free to supplement with top free agents Jason Heyward, Ben Zobrist and John Lackey this winter, and to trade Castro from depth. The plan came together.

2. The Promise

An interesting question relevant to the Cubs is how a team assembled this way is likely to perform in the years ahead. The problem in creating such a study is that teams that win 97 games, as the Cubs did, are not likely to improve, as they fight the inexorable pull toward .500. By separating all team-seasons since 1976 into winning percentage blocks (cohorts) of .025 (e.g. .475 to .500), we created cohorts between .400 and .600, and looked at where each group of teams was three years later:

.400-.425: .487
.425-.450: .491
.450-.475: .486
.475-.500: .498
.500-.525: .496
.525-.550: .514
.550-.575: .510
.575-.600: .516

All teams feel the tug toward .500, but a team that wins 40 percent of its games this year is, on average, likely to win 48.7 percent of its games three years from now. A team that wins 59 percent of its games, like the Cubs did, usually finds itself just a few games over .500.

In evaluating the effectiveness over time of any strategy—such as stockpiling young position players—the key is not so much the absolute record several years later, but whether it helps a team remain, or advance, further than its starting point would suggest.

A more realistic goal for the Cubs is to outpace their cohort expectation and remain close to their 2015 level, at least for the next few years. How likely is that? Table 1 shows us how teams with comparable young hitting talent have done.

Table 1 - Most WAR from Position Players 25 and Under Since 1976

Team	Year	WAR <=25	Year 0	Year 1	Year 2	Year 3	Cohort Year 3
Montreal	1978	23.2	.469	.594	.556	.556	.486
Kansas City	1999	20.6	.398	.475	.401	.383	.473
Montreal	1979	19.8	.594	.556	.556	.531	.516
Atlanta	2013	19.2	.593	.488	.374		.516
Kansas City	1977	18.9	.630	.568	.525	.599	.540
Minnesota	1984	18.7	.500	.475	.438	.525	.496
Toronto	1985	18.7	.615	.531	.593	.537	.541
Montreal	1992	18.5	.537	.580	.649	.458	.514
CUBS	2015	18.3	.586				.516
Cleveland	1992	18.3	.469	.469	.584	.694	.486
St. Louis	2001	18.0	.574	.599	.525	.648	.510
Detroit	1978	17.7	.531	.528	.519	.550	.514
Cincinnati	1988	17.7	.540	.463	.562	.457	.514
Tampa Bay	2010	17.6	.593	.562	.556	.564	.516

Note: Players with negative WAR are summed as if 0.

The average winning percentage of the 14 teams in Table 1 is .545. This makes sense—if a team can get 17.5 or more WAR from three to five arbitrarily categorized players, modest production from the rest of the team should produce a competitive ballclub. Of the 12 teams, every one except the 1999 Royals can be said to have outperformed its "cohort" expectation. The Atlanta Braves will this year likely join them as underperformers. The only other two teams to finish below .500 three years later were the 1992 Expos and the 1988 Reds, but both had considerable success in Year 2. The Expos had the best record in baseball in the strike-shortened 1994 season, before slashing payroll, while the 1990 Reds won the World Series. Obviously these were both successes, even though each then faded in Year 3.

The 1977 Royals "declined," but did so with two division titles and the 1980 pennant. The 1978 Expos would come within a ninth-inning Rick Monday home run of the 1981 pennant. The 1978 Tigers could only hang around .500 with their young, but they competed for a division title in Year 3. The 1984 Twins would lead to the 1987 World Series winners. The 1985 Blue Jays would average 90 wins over the next three seasons, and make the ALCS in the fourth.

The 1992 Indians' core produced one of the AL's best teams of the decade, as John Hart not only accumulated young position players but pioneered the practice of signing them to long contracts, gaining cost certainty and payroll stability. Three years later the team won the AL pennant with the best record in baseball, losing a close six-game World Series to the Braves. The 2001 Cardinals went to the NLCS in two of the next three seasons and reached the World Series in 2004. The 2010 Rays would twice reach the playoffs in the next three seasons.

There is no guarantee that any players will develop as hoped or projected. But history suggests that if a team can come up with a core of young quality position players, it will outperform teams of similar quality over subsequent seasons. Epstein has created a team that should be able to push back against the inevitable pull toward .500.

3. The Cubs

That all said, Chicago Cubs fans can be forgiven for their caution. Over the past 40 years, Wrigley Field has seen other young teams leap forward, only to slink back to mediocrity just as their rooters were getting comfortable.

After more than a decade of irrelevance, the 1984 Cubs (96-66) improved by 25 games to post their best record in 39 years. Ryne Sandberg (24) was the league's best player, and the lineup also contained Leon Durham (26), Jody Davis (27), and Bob Dernier (27). Rick Sutcliffe, Dennis Eckersley, Scott Sanderson, and Steve Trout, none yet 30, were the top starters and Lee Smith (26) was their closer. They were the league's best team, and seemed primed for a run of contention. Some guys got hurt, some guys regressed, and the team dropped back below .500 for a few years.

In 1989 the team won 93 games and was back on top. Sandberg (29) was still a star, and the Cubs had added Mark Grace (25), Shawon Dunston (26), Greg Maddux (23), Mitch Williams (24), and rookies Dwight Smith and Jerome Walton. They again had the league's best record and a promising core that was sure to keep them near the top. Instead, a few regressions (permanent in the case of the two rookies) and they were back to 77 wins and would not contend for another decade.

The 2003 Cubs (88-74) won an NLDS before losing the famous seven-game NLCS to the Marlins. The unquestioned stars of this team were starting pitchers Mark Prior (22), Kerry Wood (26), and Carlos Zambrano (22). Though Wood and Prior got hurt and never regained their stardom, the club actually won 89 games the next year, the first time the Cubs had finished over .500 two years in a row in 32 years. But two years of contention was all they got.

The 2015 Cubs won 97 games, the third highest total in baseball. With all their young positional talent, the past tells us that the future is promising. But, as any Cubs would tell you, one can never be sure. ■

—Mark Armour and Daniel R. Levitt are the authors of In Pursuit of Pennants—Baseball Operations from Deadball to Moneyball. *They have written many other books and articles together and separately over the past 15 years.*

HITTERS

Arismendy Alcantara CF

Born: 10/29/91 Age: 24 Bats: B Throws: R Height: 5'10" Weight: 170

YEAR	TEAM	LVL	AGE	PA	R	2B	3B	HR	RBI	BB	K	SB	CS	AVG/OBP/SLG	TAv	BABIP	BRR	FRAA	WARP
2013	TEN	AA	21	571	69	36	4	15	69	62	125	31	6	.271/.352/.451	.287	.332	5.2	SS(66): 1.4, 2B(64): -0.5	4.2
2014	CHN	MLB	22	300	31	11	2	10	29	17	93	8	5	.205/.254/.367	.227	.266	0.7	CF(48): -4.2, 2B(25): 1.3	-0.4
2014	IOW	AAA	22	366	62	25	11	10	41	25	83	21	3	.307/.353/.537	.303	.380	3.8	2B(70): -4.5, CF(11): -1.0	2.7
2015	IOW	AAA	23	499	72	20	10	12	36	35	125	16	6	.231/.285/.399	.249	.291	4.3	2B(74): 6.9, CF(16): -0.7	1.8
2015	CHN	MLB	23	32	5	0	0	0	1	5	11	1	0	.077/.226/.077	.161	.133	0.4	2B(8): 0.1, 3B(2): 0.4	-0.1
2016	*CHN*	*MLB*	*24*	*95*	*12*	*4*	*1*	*3*	*10*	*6*	*26*	*3*	*1*	*.229/.282/.397*	*.238*	*.288*	*0.3*	*CF -1, RF -0*	*0.0*
2017	*CHN*	*MLB*	*25*	*312*	*35*	*14*	*3*	*9*	*36*	*21*	*87*	*10*	*3*	*.227/.283/.396*	*.246*	*.287*	*1.3*	*CF -2, RF -1*	*0.1*

Breakout: 3% Improve: 30% Collapse: 10% Attrition: 27% MLB: 60% *Comparables: Derek Dietrich, Sean Rodriguez, Delwyn Young*

After rocketing through the Cubs' minor-league system and earning 300 plate appearances as a 22-year-old utility player, Alcantara looked like a key feature of the team's rapidly improving outlook. Then he finished 2014 cold and started 2015 icy, collecting only two hits through his first 32 PA, and tumbled down to Triple-A, where he warmed up before again finishing cold, missing the cut for a September call-up. It's enough to send you scrambling for a flu shot. Dire as all this looks, the book isn't closed on Alcantara: He has raw power, great athleticism and positional flexibility. In the right situation, he should at least have Emilio Bonifacio–type utility (though shaped a little differently: Alcantara has nearly reached Bonifacio's career homers total in about one-eighth the playing time), but in his present situation, which is to say with a load of talented position players ahead of him, Alcantara will need to recapture his earlier form to have any hope of substantial playing time.

Albert Almora CF

Born: 12/1/92 Age: 23 Bats: R Throws: R Height: 6'0" Weight: 190

YEAR	TEAM	LVL	AGE	PA	R	2B	3B	HR	RBI	BB	K	SB	CS	AVG/OBP/SLG	TAv	BABIP	BRR	FRAA	WARP
2013	KNC	A	19	272	39	17	4	3	23	17	30	4	4	.329/.376/.466	.286	.362	-0.7	CF(59): 12.6	2.9
2014	DAY	A+	20	385	55	20	2	7	50	12	46	6	3	.283/.306/.406	.254	.305	0.9	CF(87): 5.9	1.7
2014	TEN	AA	20	144	20	7	2	2	10	2	23	0	1	.234/.250/.355	.212	.267	-0.1	CF(32): -1.8	-0.5
2015	TEN	AA	21	452	69	26	4	6	46	32	47	8	4	.272/.327/.400	.271	.291	1.2	CF(69): 3.4, LF(18): -0.4	2.3
2016	*CHN*	*MLB*	*22*	*250*	*26*	*12*	*1*	*5*	*23*	*8*	*46*	*2*	*1*	*.242/.270/.371*	*.228*	*.275*	*-0.2*	*CF 2, LF 0*	*0.3*
2017	*CHN*	*MLB*	*23*	*379*	*38*	*18*	*2*	*8*	*38*	*15*	*69*	*2*	*1*	*.242/.277/.366*	*.237*	*.276*	*-0.5*	*CF 4, LF 1*	*0.5*

Breakout: 3% Improve: 9% Collapse: 3% Attrition: 10% MLB: 17% *Comparables: Matt Szczur, Mason Williams, Gerardo Parra*

The no. 6 overall selection in the 2012 draft should reach Triple-A this year at 22 despite zero professional seasons with double-digit homers. He earned his way there with doubles pop and superior defensive chops. While his prospect star has degraded a touch, Almora could still make the leap into the majors as soon as this season, though likely not as an every-day starter. He maintains a solid contact rate and good speed (despite little activity in his SB column), but he will need to make continued adjustments at the plate. For fantasy owners looking to build a roster of outfield prospects, know that Almora's real-life value is likely to far outstrip his roto performance.

Javier Baez 2B

Born: 12/1/92 Age: 23 Bats: R Throws: R Height: 6'0" Weight: 190

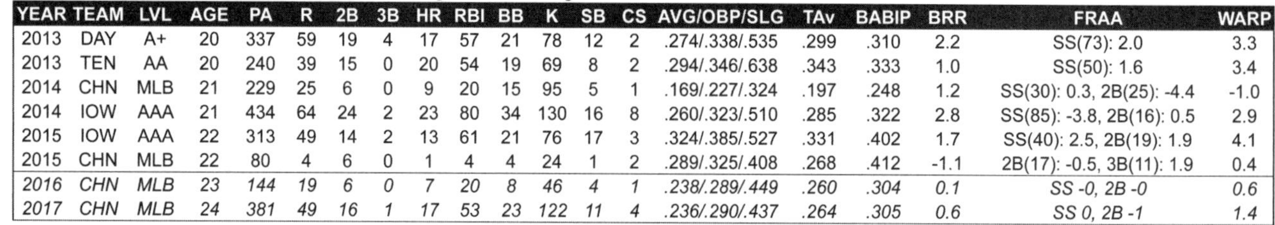

YEAR	TEAM	LVL	AGE	PA	R	2B	3B	HR	RBI	BB	K	SB	CS	AVG/OBP/SLG	TAv	BABIP	BRR	FRAA	WARP
2013	DAY	A+	20	337	59	19	4	17	57	21	78	12	2	.274/.338/.535	.299	.310	2.2	SS(73): 2.0	3.3
2013	TEN	AA	20	240	39	15	0	20	54	19	69	8	2	.294/.346/.638	.343	.333	1.0	SS(50): 1.6	3.4
2014	CHN	MLB	21	229	25	6	0	9	20	15	95	5	1	.169/.227/.324	.197	.248	1.2	SS(30): 0.3, 2B(25): -4.4	-1.0
2014	IOW	AAA	21	434	64	24	2	23	80	34	130	16	8	.260/.323/.510	.285	.322	2.8	SS(85): -3.8, 2B(16): 0.5	2.9
2015	IOW	AAA	22	313	49	14	2	13	61	21	76	17	3	.324/.385/.527	.331	.402	1.7	SS(40): 2.5, 2B(19): 1.9	4.1
2015	CHN	MLB	22	80	4	6	0	1	4	4	24	1	2	.289/.325/.408	.268	.412	-1.1	2B(17): -0.5, 3B(11): 1.9	0.4
2016	*CHN*	*MLB*	*23*	*144*	*19*	*6*	*0*	*7*	*20*	*8*	*46*	*4*	*1*	*.238/.289/.449*	*.260*	*.304*	*0.1*	*SS -0, 2B -0*	*0.6*
2017	*CHN*	*MLB*	*24*	*381*	*49*	*16*	*1*	*17*	*53*	*23*	*122*	*11*	*4*	*.236/.290/.437*	*.264*	*.305*	*0.6*	*SS 0, 2B -1*	*1.4*

Breakout: 1% Improve: 31% Collapse: 4% Attrition: 15% MLB: 63% *Comparables: Chris Davis, Mark Reynolds, Oswaldo Arcia*

Because so much has gone well for Cubs prospects of late, it is easy to forget that perhaps the most powerful hitter in the system has yet to find his footing in the majors. Scouts have emptied a metric ton of ballpoint pens describing his power stroke from his time at Arlington Country Day through the minors, but in his brief major-league experience, it's his strikeouts that have marked him most. He did chop a fifth of them off his rate in his second tour of the PCL, but a fractured finger erased most of his June and July and may have kept Starlin Castro from being traded at the deadline. Now, with little left to learn in the minors and a much more successful (if still strikeout-prone) September 2015 call-up behind him, Baez appears back on track to be *someone's* infielder of the present and future. At press time, with Ben Zobrist in the fold, trade rumors swirled around Baez, but he was still a Cub, albeit one without a clear path to consistent playing time. While his OBP may never crack .310 for any sustained period, he has legitimate 40–home run power and he could be the league's best-hitting second baseman before his 25th birthday. In December 2018.

Kris Bryant 3B

Born: 1/4/92 Age: 24 Bats: R Throws: R Height: 6'5" Weight: 215

YEAR	TEAM	LVL	AGE	PA	R	2B	3B	HR	RBI	BB	K	SB	CS	AVG/OBP/SLG	TAv	BABIP	BRR	FRAA	WARP
2013	BOI	A-	21	77	13	8	1	4	16	8	17	0	0	.354/.416/.692	.372	.404	-0.2	3B(16): -0.2	1.1
2013	DAY	A+	21	62	9	5	1	5	14	3	17	1	0	.333/.387/.719	.362	.400	-0.6	3B(13): 1.7	1.0
2014	TEN	AA	22	297	61	20	0	22	58	43	77	8	2	.355/.458/.702	.397	.440	0.1	3B(62): 3.7	5.8
2014	IOW	AAA	22	297	57	14	1	21	52	43	85	7	2	.295/.418/.619	.363	.367	-2.2	3B(67): 3.5	4.6
2015	IOW	AAA	23	33	7	1	0	3	10	2	9	2	0	.321/.364/.679	.411	.333	0.5	3B(7): -1.0	0.6
2015	CHN	MLB	23	650	87	31	5	26	99	77	199	13	4	.275/.369/.488	.317	.378	2.3	3B(144): -2.6, LF(8): -0.3	5.9
2016	*CHN*	*MLB*	*24*	*612*	*89*	*27*	*3*	*32*	*96*	*69*	*188*	*11*	*3*	*.266/.359/.510*	*.307*	*.346*	*1.4*	*3B 1*	*5.2*
2017	*CHN*	*MLB*	*25*	*593*	*92*	*27*	*2*	*33*	*96*	*69*	*178*	*11*	*3*	*.269/.365/.521*	*.322*	*.344*	*1.6*	*3B 1*	*5.3*

Breakout: 6% Improve: 49% Collapse: 12% Attrition: 14% MLB: 88% *Comparables: Ryan Braun, Giancarlo Stanton, Eddie Mathews*

Nothing says "exciting start to the baseball season" like a protracted, angry dialogue between agents and executives in the press, but that's how Bryant's 2015 began. After a spring training in which he led the majors with nine homers (in only 40 at-bats) and hit a slash that would make a Game Genie blush (.425/.477/1.175), Bryant went to the minors, not the cleanup spot for a Cubs team expected to contend. The front office made the expected noises about Bryant needing to work on his defense, then called him up on the very day that would guarantee that 2015 would not count as a full season of service time for free-agency purposes. Over the winter, news broke that the MLBPA had filed grievances over alleged service-time shenanigans regarding Bryant and the Phillies' Maikel Franco. Whether a system can be created that does not result in these weird, obvious manipulations remains to be seen.

On the field, Bryant was stellar. He whiffed a lot, but did it in the way you're supposed to: as a trade-off for hard contact and walks. In the end, the top-20 TAv matters more than how Bryant got there unless there's reason to believe the strikeouts foretell a coming cliff. PECOTA sees no cause for concern: The system doesn't hand out five-WARP projections to just any 24-year-old. Oh, and his defense was fine.

Jeimer Candelario 3B

Born: 11/24/93 Age: 22 Bats: B Throws: R Height: 6'1" Weight: 210

YEAR	TEAM	LVL	AGE	PA	R	2B	3B	HR	RBI	BB	K	SB	CS	AVG/OBP/SLG	TAv	BABIP	BRR	FRAA	WARP
2013	KNC	A	19	572	71	35	1	11	57	68	88	1	0	.256/.346/.396	.257	.290	-0.6	3B(121): -3.2	1.2
2014	KNC	A	20	263	32	19	3	6	37	18	45	0	1	.250/.300/.426	.264	.284	-0.6	3B(62): 5.7	1.5
2014	DAY	A+	20	244	24	10	2	5	26	23	44	0	3	.193/.275/.326	.224	.218	-2.1	3B(57): 8.1	0.4
2015	TEN	AA	21	182	21	10	1	5	25	22	21	0	0	.291/.379/.462	.306	.308	0.2	3B(44): -3.6	1.1
2015	MYR	A+	21	343	42	25	3	5	39	20	62	0	1	.270/.318/.415	.270	.320	-0.5	3B(77): -8.6	0.5
2016	*CHN*	*MLB*	*22*	*250*	*22*	*12*	*1*	*6*	*27*	*17*	*57*	*0*	*0*	*.218/.273/.357*	*.225*	*.261*	*-0.5*	*3B -1*	*-0.4*
2017	*CHN*	*MLB*	*23*	*423*	*46*	*21*	*1*	*11*	*45*	*32*	*95*	*0*	*0*	*.220/.282/.366*	*.238*	*.260*	*-1.0*	*3B -3*	*-0.5*

Breakout: 4% Improve: 11% Collapse: 1% Attrition: 12% MLB: 14% *Comparables: Jake Smolinski, Neil Walker, Stephen Piscotty*

Candelario hasn't converted his doubles power into the over-the-fence stuff (despite an average raw power tool) and he hasn't convinced observers that he can handle third base in the majors. He doesn't necessarily need to do *both* to have a career, but he probably needs to do one of them. Word is that he's worked hard on his defense at third, so that's a good sign, as is the fact that he's just 22, so the switch-hitting prospect could still grow into the pop he'd need to play first base or DH. That's the optimistic side. This is real life, though, so a Quad-A career is probably the most likely outcome.

Chris Coghlan LF

Born: 6/18/85 Age: 31 Bats: L Throws: R Height: 6'0" Weight: 195

YEAR	TEAM	LVL	AGE	PA	R	2B	3B	HR	RBI	BB	K	SB	CS	AVG/OBP/SLG	TAv	BABIP	BRR	FRAA	WARP
2013	MIA	MLB	28	214	10	10	3	1	10	17	43	2	0	.256/.318/.354	.263	.322	-0.1	LF(18): 1.3, CF(17): 1.2	0.8
2013	JUP	A+	28	28	1	0	1	0	2	1	6	0	0	.185/.214/.259	.165	.238	0.4	3B(6): -0.9	-0.3
2014	IOW	AAA	29	88	9	5	0	0	6	13	18	6	1	.243/.379/.314	.267	.321	0.5	RF(16): -0.7, 1B(5): -0.0	0.2
2014	CHN	MLB	29	432	50	28	5	9	41	39	81	7	4	.283/.352/.452	.292	.337	2.4	LF(101): 4.5, RF(4): 0.2	3.2
2015	CHN	MLB	30	503	64	25	6	16	41	58	94	11	2	.250/.341/.443	.279	.284	1.4	LF(99): 2.2, RF(21): 0.3	2.5
2016	*CHN*	*MLB*	*31*	*333*	*36*	*16*	*2*	*7*	*36*	*32*	*60*	*6*	*2*	*.243/.320/.390*	*.252*	*.277*	*0.8*	*LF 2, RF 1*	*1.2*
2017	*CHN*	*MLB*	*32*	*375*	*42*	*17*	*2*	*8*	*38*	*36*	*73*	*6*	*2*	*.225/.305/.363*	*.246*	*.262*	*0.9*	*LF 3, RF 1*	*0.8*

Breakout: 1% Improve: 38% Collapse: 5% Attrition: 15% MLB: 79% *Comparables: Nate McLouth, Esteban German, Alejandro De Aza*

Despite winning the Rookie of the Year Award in 2009, knee and back injuries hampered Coghlan's career with the Marlins. He failed to crack the 100-games mark from 2010 to 2013 before finally regaining some health in 2014 with the Cubs. Last year was more of the same, albeit with a slight drop-off in hitting, though the result still left Coghlan a slightly above-average player overall. He hits for good power, gets on base and plays a solid left field. Fortunately for him, he seems to be pulling it all together just in time for his post-2016 free agency; unfortunately for him, he seems to be pulling it all together just in time for his decline phase.

Willson Contreras C

Born: 5/13/92 Age: 24 Bats: R Throws: R Height: 6'1" Weight: 175

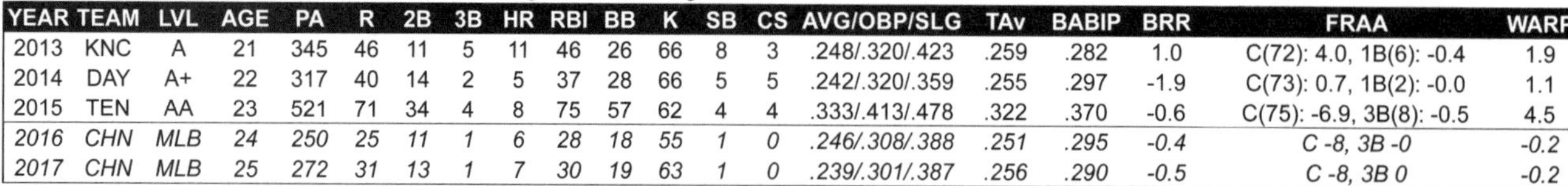

YEAR	TEAM	LVL	AGE	PA	R	2B	3B	HR	RBI	BB	K	SB	CS	AVG/OBP/SLG	TAv	BABIP	BRR	FRAA	WARP
2013	KNC	A	21	345	46	11	5	11	46	26	66	8	3	.248/.320/.423	.259	.282	1.0	C(72): 4.0, 1B(6): -0.4	1.9
2014	DAY	A+	22	317	40	14	2	5	37	28	66	5	5	.242/.320/.359	.255	.297	-1.9	C(73): 0.7, 1B(2): -0.0	1.1
2015	TEN	AA	23	521	71	34	4	8	75	57	62	4	4	.333/.413/.478	.322	.370	-0.6	C(75): -6.9, 3B(8): -0.5	4.5
2016	*CHN*	*MLB*	*24*	*250*	*25*	*11*	*1*	*6*	*28*	*18*	*55*	*1*	*0*	*.246/.308/.388*	*.251*	*.295*	*-0.4*	*C -8, 3B -0*	*-0.2*
2017	*CHN*	*MLB*	*25*	*272*	*31*	*13*	*1*	*7*	*30*	*19*	*63*	*1*	*0*	*.239/.301/.387*	*.256*	*.290*	*-0.5*	*C -8, 3B 0*	*-0.2*

Breakout: 4% Improve: 10% Collapse: 16% Attrition: 17% MLB: 40% *Comparables: J.R. Towles, Andrew Susac, Jonathan Lucroy*

YEAR	TEAM	P. COUNT	FRM RUNS	BLK RUNS	THRW RUNS	TOT RUNS
2015	TEN	10381	-6.2	1.2	-0.7	-5.7
2016	*CHN*	*7465*	*-8.4*	*0.6*	*-0.4*	*-8.2*
2017	*CHN*	*8136*	*-7.9*	*0.5*	*-0.3*	*-7.7*

Contreras showed perhaps the biggest improvement among any Cubs prospect in the 2015 season. The catcher halved his strikeout rate and bopped an extra-base hit in nearly 10 percent of his plate appearances. He has the chops and athleticism to stick behind the plate and may be the long-term answer for the Cubs at the position, particularly because his age and timetable match up well with the current catching situation: If he spends this year at Triple-A, he could replace David Ross as Miguel Montero's backup in 2017, then assume the starting job in 2018, when he'll be 26. Then again, you know what they say about the best-laid plans.

Dexter Fowler CF

Born: 3/22/86 Age: 30 Bats: B Throws: R Height: 6'5" Weight: 195

YEAR	TEAM	LVL	AGE	PA	R	2B	3B	HR	RBI	BB	K	SB	CS	AVG/OBP/SLG	TAv	BABIP	BRR	FRAA	WARP
2013	COL	MLB	27	492	71	18	3	12	42	65	105	19	9	.263/.369/.407	.265	.323	3.9	CF(110): -10.4	1.1
2014	HOU	MLB	28	505	61	21	4	8	35	66	108	11	4	.276/.375/.399	.292	.351	-0.9	CF(111): -15.3	1.4
2015	CHN	MLB	29	690	102	29	8	17	46	84	154	20	7	.250/.346/.411	.281	.308	-1.0	CF(152): 1.0	3.7
2016	*CHN*	*MLB*	*30*	*600*	*78*	*24*	*6*	*12*	*56*	*74*	*142*	*16*	*6*	*.249/.348/.393*	*.267*	*.314*	*0.4*	*CF -8*	*1.7*
2017	*CHN*	*MLB*	*31*	*585*	*71*	*24*	*6*	*12*	*61*	*72*	*139*	*14*	*6*	*.247/.345/.392*	*.274*	*.313*	*0.9*	*CF -8*	*1.7*

Breakout: 3% Improve: 49% Collapse: 4% Attrition: 6% MLB: 100% *Comparables: Nate McLouth, Chris Young, Chet Lemon*

Fowler started his age-29 season cold, slashing an uncharacteristic .232/.308/.369 through the first half of the year. Having already read his season totals in the stat box above, you can now deduce that he turned on the jets in the second half, and indeed: .272/.389/.463 from July 17th through October 4th. Two post-Coors years later, any fears that a career in Colorado inflated his moderate hitting ability are securely dead. Nothing about Fowler's recent history suggests his production will nosedive in his 30s, but, as for so many first-time free agents, his best years (2014 and 2015, specifically) are likely behind him.

Ian Happ OF

Born: 8/12/94 Age: 21 Bats: B Throws: R Height: 6'0" Weight: 205

YEAR	TEAM	LVL	AGE	PA	R	2B	3B	HR	RBI	BB	K	SB	CS	AVG/OBP/SLG	TAv	BABIP	BRR	FRAA	WARP
2013	COL	MLB	27	492	71	18	3	12	42	65	105	19	9	.263/.369/.407	.265	.323	3.9	CF(110): -10.4	1.1
2014	HOU	MLB	28	505	61	21	4	8	35	66	108	11	4	.276/.375/.399	.292	.351	-0.9	CF(111): -15.3	1.4
2015	CHN	MLB	29	690	102	29	8	17	46	84	154	20	7	.250/.346/.411	.281	.308	-1.0	CF(152): 1.0	3.7
2016	*CHN*	*MLB*	*21*	*250*	*25*	*9*	*1*	*7*	*27*	*20*	*73*	*1*	*0*	*.208/.275/.354*	*.225*	*.268*	*-0.2*	*CF -1, LF 1*	*-0.2*
2017	*CHN*	*MLB*	*22*	*297*	*34*	*12*	*2*	*9*	*33*	*25*	*87*	*1*	*1*	*.211/.282/.367*	*.238*	*.270*	*-0.3*	*CF -1, LF 1*	*0.0*

Breakout: 0% Improve: 0% Collapse: 0% Attrition: 2% MLB: 3% *Comparables: Andrew Lambo, Chris Davis, Ramon Flores*

Happ was the no. 9 overall pick last year out of the the University of Cincinnati (Sandy Koufax's alma mater) on the basis of a reputation for polish rather than tools. Polish alone doesn't make you a single-digit pick, though, and polish alone won't give you an ISO over .200 in your pro debut. As a switch-hitter with an advanced approach and a focus by the Cubs on getting him time at all three outfield spots, Happ could move quickly. It's worth noting that moving quickly in Chicago may just be the fast track to getting stuck in Triple-A behind other good players, like drag racing from stoplight to stoplight in downtown traffic.

Jason Heyward RF

Born: 8/9/89 Age: 26 Bats: L Throws: L Height: 6'5" Weight: 245

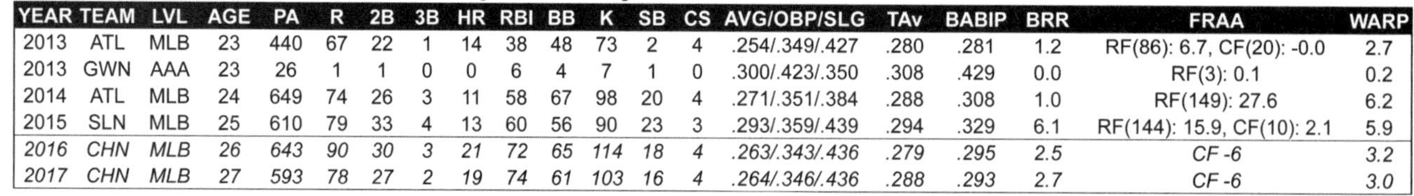

YEAR	TEAM	LVL	AGE	PA	R	2B	3B	HR	RBI	BB	K	SB	CS	AVG/OBP/SLG	TAv	BABIP	BRR	FRAA	WARP
2013	ATL	MLB	23	440	67	22	1	14	38	48	73	2	4	.254/.349/.427	.280	.281	1.2	RF(86): 6.7, CF(20): -0.0	2.7
2013	GWN	AAA	23	26	1	1	0	0	6	4	7	1	0	.300/.423/.350	.308	.429	0.0	RF(3): 0.1	0.2
2014	ATL	MLB	24	649	74	26	3	11	58	67	98	20	4	.271/.351/.384	.288	.308	1.0	RF(149): 27.6	6.2
2015	SLN	MLB	25	610	79	33	4	13	60	56	90	23	3	.293/.359/.439	.294	.329	6.1	RF(144): 15.9, CF(10): 2.1	5.9
2016	*CHN*	*MLB*	*26*	*643*	*90*	*30*	*3*	*21*	*72*	*65*	*114*	*18*	*4*	*.263/.343/.436*	*.279*	*.295*	*2.5*	*CF -6*	*3.2*
2017	*CHN*	*MLB*	*27*	*593*	*78*	*27*	*2*	*19*	*74*	*61*	*103*	*16*	*4*	*.264/.346/.436*	*.288*	*.293*	*2.7*	*CF -6*	*3.0*

Breakout: 4% Improve: 57% Collapse: 1% Attrition: 4% MLB: 98% *Comparables: Nick Markakis, Gary Sheffield, Rusty Staub*

Is there any good young player besides Bryce Harper who is as polarizing as Heyward? Unlike Harper, whose 'tude rubs people wrong, Heyward's biggest defect seems to be that he isn't Mike Trout. What he is, though, is remarkable enough: a freaky-deaky 6-foot-5 athooolete who plays D better than The Edge. While Heyward's glove is hosannaed by fans and foes alike, his offensive game causes folks to pick sides, mostly because his big frame is supposed to result in big power numbers. Alas, Heyward doesn't see it that way, so rather than swing for the fences early and often, he prioritizes contact and employs a patient, disciplined approach. That combo makes him a productive hitter (which, along with his defense and baserunning, makes him one of the better players in all of baseball, and a perennial MVP snub), but not the mean, lean, home run swatting machine that would earn him universal approval. Basically, this is a classic case of great being the enemy of perfect. Oh well. He's now nine-figures rich, and with moolah like that, who needs harmony among the railbirds?

Austin Jackson CF

Born: 8/23/94 Age: 21 Bats: L Throws: L Height: 6'1" Weight: 205

YEAR	TEAM	LVL	AGE	PA	R	2B	3B	HR	RBI	BB	K	SB	CS	AVG/OBP/SLG	TAv	BABIP	BRR	FRAA	WARP
2013	DET	MLB	26	614	99	30	7	12	49	52	129	8	4	.272/.337/.417	.277	.333	4.4	CF(129): -8.5	2.6
2014	DET	MLB	27	420	52	25	5	4	33	35	85	9	4	.273/.332/.398	.265	.334	2.4	CF(100): -5.9	1.1
2014	SEA	MLB	27	236	19	5	1	0	14	12	59	11	2	.229/.267/.260	.195	.309	0.4	CF(54): 0.1	-0.8
2015	SEA	MLB	28	448	46	18	3	8	38	24	107	15	9	.272/.312/.387	.255	.348	-2.6	CF(107): 4.8	1.4
2015	CHN	MLB	28	79	10	7	0	1	10	5	19	2	1	.236/.304/.375	.247	.308	0.2	RF(22): 1.2, CF(8): -0.6	0.1
2015	TAC	AAA	28	42	4	1	0	0	1	4	12	1	0	.263/.333/.289	.230	.385	0.4	CF(4): -1.1	-0.1
2016	*CHN*	*MLB*	*29*	*605*	*74*	*26*	*6*	*11*	*54*	*51*	*144*	*16*	*7*	*.257/.324/.388*	*.254*	*.324*	*0.9*	*CF -3, RF 1*	*1.6*
2017	*CHN*	*MLB*	*30*	*551*	*62*	*24*	*5*	*11*	*57*	*47*	*137*	*13*	*7*	*.255/.322/.389*	*.262*	*.325*	*1.4*	*CF -2, RF 1*	*1.5*

Breakout: 3% Improve: 38% Collapse: 2% Attrition: 10% MLB: 100% *Comparables: Chet Lemon, Amos Otis, Franklin Gutierrez*

Only a few years ago, there was talk that Jackson might be the rare player to sustain a BABIP above .350. As that talk muted, so did the expectations for his career. Entering his age-29 season, Jackson has now shuttled through three different teams over the last two years, and he's rapidly reaching the stage where we *expect* multiple uniforms per season. He has a steady reputation as a strong defender who can also pop a few homers and stretch singles into doubles at a steady clip, but as his star potential has faded to the point of being snuffed out, so goes his playing time. The steady depreciation of his speed and offensive expectations increase the odds of his settling into a fourth outfielder or platoon role sooner rather than later.

Billy McKinney CF

Born: 8/23/94 Age: 21 Bats: L Throws: L Height: 6'1" Weight: 205

YEAR	TEAM	LVL	AGE	PA	R	2B	3B	HR	RBI	BB	K	SB	CS	AVG/OBP/SLG	TAv	BABIP	BRR	FRAA	WARP
2013	VER	A-	18	37	5	2	1	1	6	3	4	1	1	.353/.405/.559	.371	.379	-0.5	CF(9): 0.5	0.6
2014	DAY	A+	19	210	30	12	4	1	36	25	42	1	0	.301/.390/.432	.306	.377	2.4	RF(29): 0.2, CF(4): -0.3	1.7
2014	STO	A+	19	333	42	12	2	10	33	36	58	5	3	.241/.330/.400	.249	.267	0.1	CF(65): -7.9, RF(7): 0.1	-0.2
2015	TEN	AA	20	308	29	26	1	3	39	27	47	0	0	.285/.346/.420	.286	.329	0.0	RF(60): -2.0, LF(12): 0.6	1.3
2015	MYR	A+	20	125	19	5	2	4	25	17	13	0	2	.340/.432/.544	.332	.348	0.0	RF(13): -0.0, LF(4): 1.9	1.4
2016	*CHN*	*MLB*	*21*	*250*	*26*	*11*	*1*	*5*	*23*	*19*	*55*	*0*	*0*	*.234/.298/.362*	*.235*	*.283*	*-0.3*	*RF -0, LF 0*	*-0.1*
2017	*CHN*	*MLB*	*22*	*424*	*49*	*21*	*3*	*11*	*47*	*36*	*94*	*0*	*0*	*.243/.312/.396*	*.258*	*.290*	*-0.8*	*RF 0, LF 1*	*0.6*

Breakout: 2% Improve: 10% Collapse: 1% Attrition: 6% MLB: 14% *Comparables: Jorge Soler, Jose Tabata, Wil Myers*

McKinney finally broke into Double-A after a season and a half in High-A, and his showing in Tennessee was solid. The former Oakland farmhand has done well to revive expectations that he could contribute to the Cubs as an all-around outfielder, one of those OBP-and-doubles-power types that, especially without basestealing, isn't the sexiest player on the roster but *is* a valuable member of the team. A midseason promotion in 2016 is probably the most aggressive possibility, and with Jason Heyward now anchoring one outfield spot, there shouldn't be any real rush on McKinney.

Miguel Montero C

Born: 7/9/83 Age: 32 Bats: L Throws: R Height: 5'11" Weight: 210

YEAR	TEAM	LVL	AGE	PA	R	2B	3B	HR	RBI	BB	K	SB	CS	AVG/OBP/SLG	TAv	BABIP	BRR	FRAA	WARP
2013	ARI	MLB	29	475	44	14	0	11	42	51	110	0	0	.230/.318/.344	.240	.282	-2.0	C(112): 2.0	1.2
2014	ARI	MLB	30	560	40	23	0	13	72	56	97	0	4	.243/.329/.370	.260	.275	-4.6	C(131): 11.7	3.3
2015	CHN	MLB	31	403	36	11	0	15	53	49	103	1	1	.248/.345/.409	.279	.306	-1.1	C(109): 13.4	3.9
2016	*CHN*	*MLB*	*32*	*482*	*53*	*19*	*0*	*14*	*57*	*51*	*105*	*1*	*1*	*.246/.334/.391*	*.262*	*.293*	*-1.8*	*C 11*	*3.3*
2017	*CHN*	*MLB*	*33*	*446*	*54*	*17*	*0*	*12*	*48*	*45*	*102*	*0*	*0*	*.239/.324/.372*	*.258*	*.289*	*-1.7*	*C 9*	*2.4*

Breakout: 2% Improve: 20% Collapse: 8% Attrition: 11% MLB: 95% *Comparables: Russell Martin, Ted Simmons, Gary Carter*

YEAR	TEAM	P. COUNT	FRM RUNS	BLK RUNS	THRW RUNS	TOT RUNS
2013	ARI	16048	2.4	-0.6	-0.2	1.7
2014	ARI	18483	11.4	-0.2	0.0	11.3
2015	CHN	13007	16.0	0.2	-2.0	14.1
2016	*CHN*	*16534*	*12.5*	*-0.2*	*-1.5*	*10.8*
2017	*CHN*	*15314*	*10.7*	*-0.2*	*-1.5*	*9.0*

When the Cubs traded for Montero last winter, the practical expectation was solid defense and good-for-a-catcher offense. What they got were the best defensive rates of his career and flat-out-good offense, albeit at a reduced quantity due to an injured thumb that cost Montero most of July. His current contract pays out $14 million in both his age-32 and age-33 seasons. When the Diamondbacks originally crafted this deal with their franchise backstop, the thought, as with most long-term deals, was probably that these final years would be the bitter medicine necessary to secure his services on the cheap while he was young. Now, though, 2016–17 looks more like the cherry on the sundae. Unless you don't like the cherry, in which case it's the whipped cream. The point is it's sweet and good.

Anthony Rizzo 1B

Born: 8/8/89 Age: 26 Bats: L Throws: L Height: 6'3" Weight: 240

YEAR	TEAM	LVL	AGE	PA	R	2B	3B	HR	RBI	BB	K	SB	CS	AVG/OBP/SLG	TAv	BABIP	BRR	FRAA	WARP
2013	CHN	MLB	23	690	71	40	2	23	80	76	127	6	5	.233/.323/.419	.264	.258	-1.8	1B(159): 13.9	2.3
2014	CHN	MLB	24	616	89	28	1	32	78	73	116	5	4	.286/.386/.527	.335	.311	2.1	1B(140): -0.9	5.5
2015	CHN	MLB	25	701	94	38	3	31	101	78	105	17	6	.278/.387/.512	.328	.289	-5.1	1B(160): 1.5	5.3
2016	*CHN*	*MLB*	*26*	*662*	*91*	*33*	*2*	*32*	*100*	*68*	*126*	*9*	*5*	*.266/.355/.495*	*.300*	*.287*	*-1.4*	*1B 3*	*4.0*
2017	*CHN*	*MLB*	*27*	*590*	*87*	*29*	*1*	*28*	*88*	*66*	*111*	*8*	*4*	*.266/.361/.493*	*.310*	*.287*	*-1.0*	*1B 2*	*3.6*

Breakout: 5% Improve: 55% Collapse: 0% Attrition: 5% MLB: 99% *Comparables: Paul Goldschmidt, Joey Votto, Prince Fielder*

The Cubs front office, back when it was the Padres front office, and back when it was the Red Sox front office, had high hopes for Rizzo. When they moved, Rizzo moved with them. Now, four years into the Cubs-Rizzo marriage, all of Chicagoland can see why the suits believed in him for so long. With two consecutive five-WARP seasons under his belt at a position with high offensive standards and little opportunity to distinguish oneself on defense, Rizzo has established himself as not just the first baseman of the future, but the lineup anchor of the next era. A key facet of his game is the .340 career OBP against lefties, which means Joe Maddon can print out 162 lineup cards with Rizzo's name prefilled and spend his mental energy worrying about the other 24 guys on the roster. Low-cost team options will keep him in Chicago through 2021, when he'll be all of 31.

David Ross C

Born: 3/19/77 Age: 39 Bats: R Throws: R Height: 6'2" Weight: 230

YEAR	TEAM	LVL	AGE	PA	R	2B	3B	HR	RBI	BB	K	SB	CS	AVG/OBP/SLG	TAv	BABIP	BRR	FRAA	WARP
2013	BOS	MLB	36	116	11	5	0	4	10	11	42	1	0	.216/.298/.382	.240	.321	0.0	C(36): 5.7	0.9
2014	BOS	MLB	37	171	16	7	0	7	15	16	58	0	1	.184/.260/.368	.230	.239	-0.8	C(50): 3.9	0.6
2015	CHN	MLB	38	182	6	9	0	1	9	20	61	1	0	.176/.267/.252	.203	.276	0.0	C(59): 4.3, P(2): -0.0	0.2
2016	*CHN*	*MLB*	*39*	*100*	*10*	*4*	*0*	*3*	*10*	*9*	*33*	*0*	*0*	*.202/.275/.343*	*.220*	*.276*	*-0.1*	*C 2*	*0.3*
2017	*CHN*	*MLB*	*40*	*29*	*3*	*1*	*0*	*1*	*3*	*2*	*10*	*0*	*0*	*.192/.264/.324*	*.216*	*.267*	*0.0*	*C 1*	*0.1*

Breakout: 1% Improve: 14% Collapse: 5% Attrition: 18% MLB: 69% *Comparables: Jason Varitek, Todd Pratt, Kirk Gibson*

YEAR	TEAM	P. COUNT	FRM RUNS	BLK RUNS	THRW RUNS	TOT RUNS
2013	BOS	4691	5.5	0.1	0.5	6.1
2014	BOS	6832	5.8	-0.1	-0.4	5.3
2015	CHN	6326	4.3	-0.1	-0.1	4.2
2015	CHN	6326	4.3	-0.1	-0.1	4.2
2016	*CHN*	*3853*	*2.8*	*0.0*	*0.0*	*2.7*
2017	*CHN*	*1108*	*0.7*	*0.0*	*0.0*	*0.7*

Little was asked of Ross in 2015, and little did he provide. A strong pitch-framer and an otherwise capable defender, Ross had no more than backup-duty aspirations for his 2015 season, so his .544 OPS wasn't so much a failure as a minor bummer, especially for those of us who remember his .579 SLG in 2006 with the Reds. Ross has said that 2016 is the end of the line for him on the field, and it's been a neat run, but given the high regard in which his baseball smarts are held, expect to hear his name as a coach and manager for years to come. Tidbit to watch for in his final year: Ross has never attempted more than one stolen base in a season, and he needs one success to square his career record at four steals and four times caught.

Addison Russell SS

Born: 1/23/94 Age: 22 Bats: R Throws: R Height: 6'0" Weight: 200

YEAR	TEAM	LVL	AGE	PA	R	2B	3B	HR	RBI	BB	K	SB	CS	AVG/OBP/SLG	TAv	BABIP	BRR	FRAA	WARP
2013	STO	A+	19	504	85	29	10	17	60	61	116	21	3	.275/.377/.508	.321	.338	1.0	SS(105): -3.6	5.3
2014	TEN	AA	20	205	32	11	0	12	36	9	35	2	2	.294/.332/.536	.304	.306	0.2	SS(47): 5.7	2.5
2014	MID	AA	20	57	7	3	1	1	8	8	8	3	2	.333/.439/.500	.304	.385	-0.3	SS(11): -0.9	0.4
2015	IOW	AAA	21	46	7	4	0	1	9	1	7	1	0	.318/.326/.477	.300	.351	-0.8	SS(6): -1.0, 2B(5): 0.3	0.2
2015	CHN	MLB	21	523	60	29	1	13	54	42	149	4	3	.242/.307/.389	.252	.324	-1.7	2B(86): 6.9, SS(61): -2.5	1.6
2016	*CHN*	*MLB*	*22*	*547*	*68*	*26*	*2*	*17*	*59*	*41*	*145*	*6*	*3*	*.242/.304/.406*	*.253*	*.304*	*-1.0*	*SS -3*	*1.9*
2017	*CHN*	*MLB*	*23*	*588*	*69*	*28*	*2*	*17*	*68*	*44*	*151*	*7*	*3*	*.243/.306/.400*	*.259*	*.304*	*-1.0*	*SS -3*	*2.0*

Breakout: 4% Improve: 39% Collapse: 0% Attrition: 12% MLB: 69% *Comparables: Xander Bogaerts, Melvin Upton, Freddie Freeman*

A consensus top-five prospect heading into the 2015 season, Russell may have been something of a disappointment for fans hoping for a record-busting rookie season. Even though his offensive performance did not measure up to the hype, the middle infielder still had an impressive campaign. His defense at short and second was somewhere between capable and great, and his offense—while not on par with his near-.900 OPS throughout the minors—was still above average for a shortstop and well above average for a 21-year-old.

Having displaced starting shortstop Starlin Castro so definitively that Castro was traded to the Yankees this offseason, Russell has no obstacles preventing him from becoming one of the league's regular six-holers. While he may take a few years to fully adjust to major-league pitching, there is nothing in his pedigree, minor-league numbers or demeanor to suggest he is a high-volatility asset. Injuries and surprises do happen, but Russell feels like the first can't-miss shortstop in Chicago since, well, Starlin Castro.

Brendan Ryan SS

Born: 3/26/82 Age: 34 Bats: R Throws: R Height: 6'2" Weight: 195

YEAR	TEAM	LVL	AGE	PA	R	2B	3B	HR	RBI	BB	K	SB	CS	AVG/OBP/SLG	TAv	BABIP	BRR	FRAA	WARP
2013	NYA	MLB	31	62	7	2	0	1	1	2	13	0	0	.220/.258/.305	.209	.267	0.7	SS(17): 2.1	0.2
2013	SEA	MLB	31	287	23	10	0	3	21	21	60	4	2	.192/.254/.265	.201	.237	-2.1	SS(84): 8.5	0.1
2014	NYA	MLB	32	124	5	4	0	0	8	4	30	0	2	.167/.211/.202	.164	.221	-0.5	SS(25): -1.5, 2B(19): 1.7	-0.8
2015	TRN	AA	33	29	1	1	0	0	1	3	6	0	0	.240/.345/.280	.240	.316	0.0	SS(3): 0.5, 3B(2): 0.2	0.1
2015	NYA	MLB	33	103	10	6	2	0	8	5	29	0	0	.229/.275/.333	.218	.328	0.0	2B(26): -0.8, 3B(14): 0.2	-0.2
2016	*CHN*	*MLB*	*34*	*78*	*7*	*3*	*0*	*1*	*6*	*6*	*16*	*1*	*1*	*.217/.285/.307*	*.215*	*.265*	*-0.2*	*SS 1, 3B 0*	*0.0*
2017	*CHN*	*MLB*	*35*	*36*	*3*	*1*	*0*	*0*	*3*	*3*	*8*	*0*	*0*	*.206/.278/.287*	*.213*	*.255*	*-0.1*	*SS 0, 3B 0*	*0.0*

Breakout: 3% Improve: 27% Collapse: 11% Attrition: 23% MLB: 86% *Comparables: Bobby Avila, Tom Herr, Delino DeShields*

For years people thought they knew Ryan to be a charming, one-dimensional, glove-first utility infielder. Those "people" were incomprehensibly wrong. Although he did appear in 47 games as his humble everyday persona, Ryan showed a whole new side, making his major-league debut as a pitcher in August. He dialed it up to 84 mph and baffled a powerful Astros lineup over two scoreless innings with a bold changeup-heavy strategy, pulling the string 68 percent of the time. After years of hitting like a pitcher, deciding to pitch like one was a brilliant move. Or so it seemed until the Cubs released him two days before Christmas.

Kyle Schwarber C

Born: 3/5/93 Age: 23 Bats: L Throws: R Height: 6'0" Weight: 235

YEAR	TEAM	LVL	AGE	PA	R	2B	3B	HR	RBI	BB	K	SB	CS	AVG/OBP/SLG	TAv	BABIP	BRR	FRAA	WARP
2014	BOI	A-	21	24	7	1	1	4	10	2	2	0	1	.600/.625/1.350	.612	.533	0.0		0.0
2014	KNC	A	21	96	17	8	0	4	15	11	17	1	1	.361/.448/.602	.297	.419	-0.1	LF(2): 0.0, C(1): -0.0	0.1
2014	DAY	A+	21	191	31	9	1	10	28	26	38	4	0	.302/.393/.560	.324	.328	-0.7	LF(26): 1.9, C(9): -0.1	2.0
2015	CHN	MLB	22	273	52	6	1	16	43	36	77	3	3	.246/.355/.487	.307	.293	3.4	LF(41): -3.1, C(21): -1.4	2.0
2015	TEN	AA	22	243	39	10	1	13	39	42	49	1	0	.320/.438/.579	.371	.365	0.3	C(37): 1.9	4.0
2015	IOW	AAA	22	67	7	7	1	3	10	7	23	0	0	.333/.403/.633	.387	.500	0.1	C(15): 0.0	1.2
2016	*CHN*	*MLB*	*23*	*605*	*83*	*22*	*2*	*32*	*94*	*73*	*167*	*4*	*2*	*.253/.349/.487*	*.293*	*.305*	*4.2*	*LF -4, C -1*	*4.0*
2017	*CHN*	*MLB*	*24*	*534*	*80*	*20*	*2*	*27*	*81*	*66*	*145*	*4*	*2*	*.253/.352/.482*	*.301*	*.307*	*3.7*	*LF -4, C -1*	*3.5*

Breakout: 2% Improve: 42% Collapse: 2% Attrition: 13% MLB: 86% *Comparables: Anthony Rizzo, Evan Longoria, Chris Carter*

YEAR	TEAM	P. COUNT	FRM RUNS	BLK RUNS	THRW RUNS	TOT RUNS
2015	CHN	2400	-0.9	0.0	-0.1	-1.1
2015	IOW	1863	0.7	-0.2	-0.1	0.5
2015	TEN	4884	2.9	-0.3	-1.2	1.4
2016	*CHN*	*4065*	*-0.1*	*-0.6*	*-0.5*	*-1.2*
2017	*CHN*	*3588*	*-0.1*	*-0.1*	*-0.1*	*-0.2*

When the Cubs needed a designated hitter for a stretch of games in the middle of June, the choice was both obvious and unusual. Unusual because the typical Double-A catcher cannot contribute immediately to an MLB lineup. Obvious because Schwarber was no typical Double-A catcher. In only 58 games in the Southern League, Schwarber clapped 13 homers. His first professional season, 2014, lasted only 72 games, but he still managed to knock 18 dongs and 18 doubles. Following his week as the Cubs' DH, he went to Triple-A, where he hit another three homers in just 17 games. Behind the plate, a Molina he is not, but Schwarber's bat should continue to force its way into Joe Maddon's lineup even with Miguel Montero as the team's no. 1 catcher. Lucky for Maddon, then, that the Cubs' front office has provided him with a roster chock full of positional flexibility.

Jorge Soler RF

Born: 2/25/92 Age: 24 Bats: R Throws: R Height: 6'4" Weight: 215

YEAR	TEAM	LVL	AGE	PA	R	2B	3B	HR	RBI	BB	K	SB	CS	AVG/OBP/SLG	TAv	BABIP	BRR	FRAA	WARP
2013	DAY	A+	21	237	38	13	1	8	35	21	38	5	1	.281/.343/.467	.283	.304	1.8	RF(55): -2.5	1.0
2014	CHN	MLB	22	97	11	8	1	5	20	6	24	1	0	.292/.330/.573	.324	.339	-0.2	RF(24): -0.7	0.7
2014	TEN	AA	22	79	13	9	1	6	22	12	15	0	0	.415/.494/.862	.450	.457	-0.3	RF(16): -2.8	1.4
2014	IOW	AAA	22	127	22	11	1	8	29	17	26	0	1	.282/.378/.618	.324	.303	-0.1	RF(27): -1.2	1.0
2015	CHN	MLB	23	404	39	18	1	10	47	32	121	3	1	.262/.324/.399	.263	.361	-0.2	RF(95): -8.7	-0.1
2016	*CHN*	*MLB*	*24*	*579*	*67*	*29*	*2*	*22*	*78*	*47*	*152*	*3*	*1*	*.255/.318/.444*	*.269*	*.314*	*-0.4*	*RF -9*	*0.9*
2017	*CHN*	*MLB*	*25*	*499*	*65*	*25*	*2*	*20*	*67*	*42*	*130*	*3*	*1*	*.251/.317/.446*	*.277*	*.307*	*-0.5*	*RF -8*	*0.7*

Breakout: 3% Improve: 40% Collapse: 8% Attrition: 16% MLB: 94% *Comparables: Oswaldo Arcia, Wil Myers, Travis Snider*

Injuries have slowed the ascent of the Cubs' Cuban right fielder, but he is only entering his age-24 season and none of his injuries (oblique, ankle, hamstring) appear to be recurring or long-term concerns. That said, it is hard to frame Soler's first full season in the majors as anything but a disappointment. Among rookies with at least 300 PA, Soler's 30 percent strikeout rate ranked sixth, but his .137 ISO ranked just 18th. In other words: lots of whiffs, and not enough power to make up for it. But the story for Soler is a developing one. His scouting reports and minor-league performance suggest he will take a step forward in 2016. Keep expectations muted and you're more likely to be happy with the outcome.

Gleyber Torres SS

Born: 12/13/96 Age: 19 Bats: R Throws: R Height: 6'1" Weight: 175

YEAR	TEAM	LVL	AGE	PA	R	2B	3B	HR	RBI	BB	K	SB	CS	AVG/OBP/SLG	TAv	BABIP	BRR	FRAA	WARP
2014	BOI	A-	17	32	4	2	3	1	4	4	7	2	0	.393/.469/.786	.373	.500	0.6	SS(7): 0.4	0.6
2015	SBN	A	18	514	53	24	5	3	62	43	108	22	13	.293/.353/.386	.266	.373	-2.0	SS(119): -9.5	1.3
2015	MYR	A+	18	24	1	0	0	0	2	1	7	0	1	.174/.208/.174	.151	.250	-0.3	SS(7): 0.2	-0.2
2016	*CHN*	*MLB*	*19*	*250*	*26*	*10*	*1*	*4*	*20*	*14*	*73*	*4*	*3*	*.216/.264/.322*	*.210*	*.292*	*-0.3*	*SS -4*	*-0.5*
2017	*CHN*	*MLB*	*20*	*428*	*44*	*18*	*3*	*8*	*42*	*25*	*117*	*8*	*6*	*.236/.283/.360*	*.236*	*.308*	*0.0*	*SS -6*	*0.0*

Breakout: 0% Improve: 1% Collapse: 0% Attrition: 0% MLB: 1% *Comparables: Addison Russell, Corey Seager, Jonathan Schoop*

Profiled as an above-average defender heading into the season, Torres continued to build on the hopes that he can hit as well. If he gets there, it'll be on the strength of an above-average hit tool rather than power, which will likely be of the more gap-to-gap variety. When you're scouting his stat line, remember the following key considerations: age relative to level, position and the fact that you really shouldn't be scouting his stat line. Torres is still several years from the majors and, like every Cubs position-player prospect, he's blocked. Still, there's plenty of time during which the middle-infield logjam could resolve itself through injury, ineffectiveness, trade or wanderlust.

Christian Villanueva 3B

Born: 6/19/91 Age: 25 Bats: R Throws: R Height: 5'11" Weight: 210

YEAR	TEAM	LVL	AGE	PA	R	2B	3B	HR	RBI	BB	K	SB	CS	AVG/OBP/SLG	TAv	BABIP	BRR	FRAA	WARP
2013	TEN	AA	22	542	60	41	2	19	72	34	117	5	7	.261/.317/.469	.275	.303	1.8	3B(124): -4.8	2.3
2014	TEN	AA	23	259	31	20	0	4	32	19	42	0	1	.248/.310/.385	.249	.284	-1.0	3B(61): 1.0, 2B(3): 0.3	0.6
2014	IOW	AAA	23	248	22	18	0	6	26	21	64	2	1	.211/.283/.372	.231	.266	-0.1	3B(63): 7.2	0.7
2015	TEN	AA	24	28	5	0	0	2	7	4	5	0	0	.208/.321/.458	.324	.176	0.4	3B(6): -0.4	0.3
2015	IOW	AAA	24	508	56	23	2	18	88	35	80	2	3	.259/.313/.437	.274	.273	-2.2	3B(85): 3.7, 1B(35): 1.3	2.3
2016	*CHN*	*MLB*	*25*	*250*	*25*	*13*	*0*	*8*	*31*	*13*	*59*	*1*	*1*	*.227/.276/.396*	*.236*	*.264*	*-0.5*	*3B 2, 1B 0*	*0.1*
2017	*CHN*	*MLB*	*26*	*369*	*42*	*19*	*1*	*12*	*44*	*21*	*89*	*1*	*1*	*.229/.279/.397*	*.245*	*.270*	*-0.9*	*3B 3, 1B 0*	*0.3*

Breakout: 4% Improve: 10% Collapse: 9% Attrition: 22% MLB: 28% *Comparables: Carlos Rivero, Matthew Duffy, Adam Duvall*

Not long ago, Villanueva looked like a solid prospect, briefly blipping onto *Baseball America*'s list as Mr. 100. He arrived in the Cubs' organization along with Kyle Hendricks in the Ryan Dempster trade, and while he wasn't the blue chip of that deal, he had a strong minor-league history and age on his side. Now stagnation has his age creeping to... well, not on his side, his minor-league numbers have been weak two seasons running and—biggest of all—Kris Bryant is firmly entrenched at third base in the majors. Villanueva carries a reputation as a strong defender and has shown decent pop, so on another team you might see a path toward a starting job, if not exactly a slew of All-Star bids. The name "Luis Valbuena" springs to mind.

Dan Vogelbach 1B

Born: 12/17/92 Age: 23 Bats: L Throws: R Height: 6'0" Weight: 250

YEAR	TEAM	LVL	AGE	PA	R	2B	3B	HR	RBI	BB	K	SB	CS	AVG/OBP/SLG	TAv	BABIP	BRR	FRAA	WARP
2013	DAY	A+	20	66	13	2	0	2	5	16	13	1	0	.280/.455/.440	.322	.343	0.7	1B(7): -0.2	0.6
2013	KNC	A	20	502	55	21	0	17	71	57	76	4	4	.284/.364/.450	.288	.305	-5.6	1B(85): -0.6	1.4
2014	DAY	A+	21	560	71	28	1	16	76	66	91	4	4	.268/.357/.429	.280	.296	-3.1	1B(103): -9.9	0.6
2015	TEN	AA	22	313	41	16	1	7	39	57	61	1	1	.272/.403/.425	.310	.330	-3.0	1B(75): 1.4	1.9
2016	*CHN*	*MLB*	*23*	*250*	*27*	*10*	*0*	*8*	*30*	*27*	*59*	*0*	*0*	*.231/.317/.386*	*.252*	*.275*	*-0.5*	*1B -2*	*-0.1*
2017	*CHN*	*MLB*	*24*	*383*	*48*	*16*	*0*	*13*	*46*	*40*	*92*	*0*	*0*	*.236/.317/.400*	*.262*	*.282*	*-1.0*	*1B -3*	*-0.1*

Breakout: 10% Improve: 14% Collapse: 7% Attrition: 19% MLB: 33% *Comparables: Justin Smoak, Yonder Alonso, Mike Carp*

While his home run totals have never quite matched his pre-draft hype, Vogelbach has done nothing but smush minor-league pitching, especially right-handers, against whom he's hit .298/.393/.498. His defense, baserunning and contact skills all range from hopeless to not great; he hustles, but it's a slow hustle. Still, his total hitting ability should be more than enough to propel him to the majors. The bigger issue for Vogelbach is with whom he will debut. As an NL team that employs Anthony Rizzo, the Cubs will be hard-pressed to find playing time for a bat-only player. If Vogelbach remains stuck in the Cubs' system, he may not even reach the big leagues until 2017 or later. We can dream of him being the heir apparent to David Ortiz, but he'll need to find his way to a DH team to reach that destiny.

Ben Zobrist 2B

Born: 5/26/81 Age: 35 Bats: B Throws: R Height: 6'3" Weight: 210

YEAR	TEAM	LVL	AGE	PA	R	2B	3B	HR	RBI	BB	K	SB	CS	AVG/OBP/SLG	TAv	BABIP	BRR	FRAA	WARP
2013	TBA	MLB	32	698	77	36	3	12	71	72	91	11	3	.275/.354/.402	.283	.303	-0.9	2B(125): -3.0, RF(39): 1.2	3.5
2014	TBA	MLB	33	654	83	34	3	10	52	75	84	10	5	.272/.354/.395	.288	.301	2.4	2B(79): 4.6, LF(38): 2.6	4.7
2015	OAK	MLB	34	271	39	20	2	6	33	33	26	1	1	.268/.354/.447	.298	.277	-0.2	2B(34): -0.1, LF(27): -0.9	1.6
2015	KCA	MLB	34	264	37	16	1	7	23	29	30	2	3	.284/.364/.453	.293	.299	1.2	2B(35): -2.3, LF(18): -1.4	1.3
2016	*CHN*	*MLB*	*35*	*655*	*84*	*36*	*4*	*15*	*67*	*75*	*99*	*8*	*5*	*.266/.352/.422*	*.277*	*.294*	*0.4*	*2B 0*	*3.9*
2017	*CHN*	*MLB*	*36*	*528*	*61*	*28*	*3*	*10*	*54*	*58*	*84*	*5*	*3*	*.249/.333/.388*	*.268*	*.282*	*0.4*	*2B 0*	*2.2*

Breakout: 1% Improve: 28% Collapse: 6% Attrition: 13% MLB: 91% *Comparables: Chase Utley, Carlos Guillen, Brian Roberts*

One of the league's most versatile players, Zobrist missed a month last summer with a balky knee but still managed to post his usual outstanding offensive numbers while bouncing between second base and the corner outfield. As he's moved into his mid-thirties Zobrist is no longer a threat to launch 20 bombs or steal double-digit bases, but his ability to make contact, draw walks and line doubles into the gap allows him to produce anywhere in the lineup. His glove caught a case of the vapors last summer, which may be the first sign of age-related decline, but Zobrist remains the archetype of a "professional hitter" in the sabermetric era.

PITCHERS

Jake Arrieta RHP

Born: 3/6/86 Age: 30 Bats: R Throws: R Height: 6'4" Weight: 225

YEAR	TEAM	LVL	AGE	W	L	SV	G	GS	IP	H	HR	BB/9	K/9	GB%	BABIP	WHIP	ERA	FIP	DRA	WARP	CFIP	MPH
2013	BAL	MLB	27	1	2	0	5	5	23^2	25	2	6.5	8.7	33%	.343	1.77	7.23	4.64	5.61	-0.2	102	96.3
2013	IOW	AAA	27	2	2	0	7	7	30^1	32	2	4.7	11.6	51%	.390	1.58	3.56	3.64	4.82	0.3	93	
2013	CHN	MLB	27	4	2	0	9	9	51^2	34	7	4.2	6.4	46%	.190	1.12	3.66	4.92	2.80	1.3	122	96.5
2013	NOR	AAA	27	5	3	0	9	8	49	45	4	2.6	7.0	52%	.285	1.20	4.41	3.63	4.34	0.4	101	
2014	CHN	MLB	28	10	5	0	25	25	156^2	114	5	2.4	9.6	51%	.272	0.99	2.53	2.23	2.42	4.6	77	95.9
2014	TEN	AA	28	1	1	0	4	4	14^1	8	0	3.1	6.9	62%	.200	0.91	1.26	2.70				
2015	CHN	MLB	29	22	6	0	33	33	229	150	10	1.9	9.3	58%	.246	0.86	1.77	2.38	2.31	7.4	74	97.0
2016	*CHN*	*MLB*	*30*	*14*	*9*	*0*	*32*	*32*	*214^1*	*163*	*19*	*2.4*	*9.2*	*55%*	*.281*	*1.03*	*3.05*	*3.06*	*3.56*	*4.4*	*75*	
2017	*CHN*	*MLB*	*31*	*11*	*9*	*0*	*30*	*30*	*188*	*151*	*17*	*2.4*	*9.1*	*55%*	*.293*	*1.06*	*3.13*	*3.32*	*3.65*	*3.5*	*78*	

Breakout: 18% Improve: 49% Collapse: 23% Attrition: 15% MLB: 94% *Comparables: A.J. Burnett, Kevin Appier, Warren Spahn*

You know the basics of the story: Orioles prospect with two top-100 rankings under his belt spends three and a half years trying to get it together in the majors before Baltimore pulls the plug and sends him to Chicago for the steadier Scott Feldman; it's in the Cubs organization where the talent finally comes together, as Arrieta posts a 3.56 ERA in Iowa and a 3.66 ERA in Chicago in 2013. After a shoulder injury caused him to miss April 2014, Arrieta's been nothing but stellar: In 385 innings over the last two seasons, he's got a 2.08 ERA and 4.5 strikeouts to every walk while inducing grounders on well over half his balls in play. The culmination was his Cy Young Award victory over Zack Greinke and Clayton Kershaw, though any of the three would have been an excellent choice for the honor.

Arrieta relies nearly three-quarters of the time on his sinker or his slider/cutter. The latter weapon was not a new invention in Chicago, not something he stumbled on during a vision quest in the Himalayas, but rather a pitch that simply began clicking. He uses the same grip and same arm slot, but generates effectively two pitches, throwing a low-90s cutter against righties and a high-80s slider with more depth to sink under lefties' bats. Arrieta was so far beyond excellent in 2015 that, while it's almost certain to stand as his best year, he has a lot of room to regress while still pitching like an All-Star.

Rex Brothers LHP

Born: 12/18/87 Age: 28 Bats: L Throws: L Height: 6'0" Weight: 210

YEAR	TEAM	LVL	AGE	W	L	SV	G	GS	IP	H	HR	BB/9	K/9	GB%	BABIP	WHIP	ERA	FIP	DRA	WARP	CFIP	MPH
2013	COL	MLB	25	2	1	19	72	0	67^1	51	5	4.8	10.2	50%	.280	1.29	1.74	3.33	3.20	1.1	84	96.2
2014	COL	MLB	26	4	6	0	74	0	56^1	65	7	6.2	8.8	41%	.343	1.85	5.59	4.95	5.22	-0.5	112	95.8
2015	COL	MLB	27	1	0	0	17	0	10^1	9	0	7.0	4.4	58%	.273	1.65	1.74	4.52	3.33	0.2	119	95.5
2015	ABQ	AAA	27	5	2	3	45	0	42^1	27	1	9.4	13.0	50%	.292	1.68	4.46	4.28	5.83	-0.3	108	
2016	*CHN*	*MLB*	*28*	*2*	*1*	*1*	*49*	*0*	*51^1*	*43*	*6*	*5.0*	*9.7*	*47%*	*.305*	*1.40*	*4.23*	*4.23*	*4.88*	*0.0*	*112*	
2017	*CHN*	*MLB*	*29*	*2*	*1*	*1*	*49*	*0*	*43*	*38*	*5*	*4.9*	*9.8*	*47%*	*.322*	*1.43*	*4.18*	*4.52*	*4.82*	*0.0*	*111*	

Breakout: 23% Improve: 44% Collapse: 28% Attrition: 12% MLB: 91% *Comparables: Brian Bruney, Frank Francisco, John Rocker*

There was a time when Brothers was seen as the closer of the future in Colorado, but the problem with pitchers who are effectively wild is that adverbs are the first thing an editor cuts. Brothers spent the majority of last season walking a batter per inning at Triple-A and his brief stints in the majors were no better; he walked more men than he struck out in 10 innings, continuing a yearly trend in the wrong direction for his strikeout and walk rates. You don't have to be a control artist to thrive in a bullpen role, but Brothers' paint is no longer even hitting the canvas.

Trevor Cahill RHP

Born: 3/1/88 Age: 28 Bats: R Throws: R Height: 6'4" Weight: 240

YEAR	TEAM	LVL	AGE	W	L	SV	G	GS	IP	H	HR	BB/9	K/9	GB%	BABIP	WHIP	ERA	FIP	DRA	WARP	CFIP	MPH
2013	RNO	AAA	25	0	2	0	3	3	16^2	16	3	4.9	7.0	60%	.289	1.50	5.94	5.97	5.18	0.1	107	
2013	ARI	MLB	25	8	10	0	26	25	146^2	143	13	4.0	6.3	58%	.289	1.42	3.99	4.23	4.43	0.8	118	92.5
2014	ARI	MLB	26	3	12	1	32	17	110^2	123	9	4.5	8.5	50%	.350	1.61	5.61	3.86	5.19	-0.6	110	93.0
2014	RNO	AAA	26	2	2	0	6	6	28^1	21	4	6.4	8.6	63%	.254	1.45	3.49	5.75	5.57	0.1	112	
2015	ATL	MLB	27	0	3	0	15	3	26^1	36	2	3.8	4.8	64%	.354	1.78	7.52	4.45	6.83	-0.6	123	94.1
2015	CHN	MLB	27	1	0	0	11	0	17	8	2	2.6	11.6	63%	.182	0.76	2.12	3.16	2.03	0.6	81	95.2
2015	OKL	AAA	27	1	3	0	6	6	28^2	32	3	4.4	5.3	51%	.299	1.60	6.28	5.24	6.12	-0.2	124	
2016	*CHN*	*MLB*	*28*	*2*	*1*	*0*	*43*	*0*	*46*	*43*	*5*	*3.6*	*7.4*	*56%*	*.302*	*1.33*	*4.17*	*4.11*	*4.82*	*0.1*	*113*	
2017	*CHN*	*MLB*	*29*	*4*	*5*	*0*	*18*	*12*	*81^1*	*78*	*10*	*3.6*	*7.2*	*56%*	*.305*	*1.35*	*4.31*	*4.65*	*4.98*	*0.2*	*118*	

Breakout: 20% Improve: 55% Collapse: 19% Attrition: 10% MLB: 94% *Comparables: Chuck Finley, Jason Jennings, Pat Hentgen*

The only thing that's clearly true about Cahill at this point is that he's not a starting pitcher. The question we're left with is whether he's even a big-league reliever. His Chicago work was very good, but that BABIP isn't staying that low, and his career 3.53 ERA out of the bullpen is fine but hardly something to jump for joy about: NL relievers as a whole put up a 3.66 ERA in 2015. The movement on Cahill's sinker has long been preposterous, but it doesn't matter if he's not inducing swings: Cahill was in the bottom 15 percent of the league in swing rate on his sinker last season. He did do a better job getting called strikes on the pitch, and that showed up in his walk rates, but not enough better to squarely put to rest the uncertainty around Cahill's future.

Carl Edwards Jr RHP

Born: 8/16/88 Age: 27 Bats: R Throws: R Height: 6'3" Weight: 210

YEAR	TEAM	LVL	AGE	W	L	SV	G	GS	IP	H	HR	BB/9	K/9	GB%	BABIP	WHIP	ERA	FIP	DRA	WARP	CFIP	MPH
2013	HIC	A	21	8	2	0	18	18	93^1	62	0	3.3	11.8	54%	.268	1.03	1.83	2.06	3.41	1.5	67	
2013	DAY	A+	21	0	0	0	6	6	23	14	1	2.7	12.9	43%	.260	0.91	1.96	1.85	3.33	0.4	67	
2014	TEN	AA	22	1	2	0	10	10	48	30	1	3.9	8.6	47%	.234	1.06	2.44	2.92				
2015	IOW	AAA	23	3	1	2	23	0	31^2	15	0	6.8	11.1	44%	.221	1.23	2.84	3.50	4.33	0.3	94	
2015	TEN	AA	23	2	2	4	13	0	23^2	11	1	6.5	13.7	67%	.222	1.18	2.66	2.96	2.59	0.6	81	
2015	CHN	MLB	23	0	0	0	5	0	4^2	3	0	5.8	7.7	58%	.250	1.29	3.86	3.38	6.24	-0.1	105	96.0
2016	*CHN*	*MLB*	*24*	*1*	*1*	*0*	*24*	*0*	*25*	*19*	*3*	*4.0*	*9.5*	*48%*	*.283*	*1.20*	*3.65*	*3.88*	*4.22*	*0.3*	*96*	
2017	*CHN*	*MLB*	*25*	*4*	*4*	*0*	*24*	*12*	*87^2*	*69*	*10*	*4.2*	*9.9*	*48%*	*.298*	*1.26*	*3.82*	*4.11*	*4.42*	*0.7*	*101*	

Breakout: 12% Improve: 25% Collapse: 25% Attrition: 36% MLB: 63% *Comparables: Scott Barnes, Matt Magill, Brian Johnson*

Edwards has gone from unknown 48th-round pick to highly touted starting prospect to—perhaps most surprisingly—reliever. Despite expectations among the scouting community that Edwards could crack the Cubs' 2016 rotation, the wiry righty started 2015 in relief, and then never left. It's hard to argue with the results: 55 innings of sub-three ERA in Double-A and Triple-A. It's easy to argue with the process: Check out those 2015 walk rates. Edwards averaged an inning and a half in his appearances, syncing with the front office's claims that he would pitch shorter bursts, but remain somewhat extended. According to Jed Hoyer last April, they "in no way, shape or form have given up on him as a starter." That's dandy, but since so few pitchers make the move back to the rotation following a full-season shift to the bullpen, it is easier now to imagine Edwards as a shutdown reliever forevermore. Assuming he can reel those walks in, anyway. If he can't, delete "shutdown."

Justin Grimm RHP

Born: 8/16/88 Age: 27 Bats: R Throws: R Height: 6'3" Weight: 210

YEAR	TEAM	LVL	AGE	W	L	SV	G	GS	IP	H	HR	BB/9	K/9	GB%	BABIP	WHIP	ERA	FIP	DRA	WARP	CFIP	MPH
2013	CHN	MLB	24	0	2	0	10	0	9	4	0	3.0	8.0	38%	.167	0.78	2.00	2.58	-0.42	0.6	100	95.8
2013	TEX	MLB	24	7	7	0	17	17	89	116	15	3.1	6.9	45%	.347	1.65	6.37	4.82	6.41	-1.6	108	94.5
2013	IOW	AAA	24	2	3	0	8	8	42^1	46	1	3.6	8.7	51%	.354	1.49	4.68	3.14	4.61	0.5	89	
2014	CHN	MLB	25	5	2	0	73	0	69	59	4	3.5	9.1	51%	.294	1.25	3.78	3.18	3.17	1.1	96	96.8
2015	CHN	MLB	26	3	5	3	62	0	49^2	31	4	4.7	12.1	46%	.255	1.15	1.99	3.14	3.53	0.7	86	97.8
2016	*CHN*	*MLB*	*27*	*2*	*1*	*0*	*43*	*0*	*46*	*40*	*5*	*3.3*	*9.0*	*47%*	*.306*	*1.23*	*3.64*	*3.69*	*4.22*	*0.4*	*95*	
2017	*CHN*	*MLB*	*28*	*5*	*4*	*1*	*41*	*10*	*86^2*	*76*	*9*	*3.1*	*9.4*	*47%*	*.313*	*1.21*	*3.50*	*3.75*	*4.06*	*1.0*	*91*	

Breakout: 25% Improve: 54% Collapse: 21% Attrition: 15% MLB: 92% *Comparables: John Maine, Blaine Boyer, David Hernandez*

Forearm inflammation kept Grimm under 50 innings on the year, but the fastball-curveball reliever dominated when healthy. Initially acquired from the Rangers to help shore up a thin rotation, Grimm appears to have settled into a long-term position in the bullpen, where he has pitched exclusively since the end of 2013. If his forearm issues subside, and if he can cut the walks back to his old rate while maintaining his gain in strikeouts, Grimm could be poised for a move up the leverage ladder in 2016. If he works his way into a closer role, he'll need a nickname; may we suggest "King Thrushbeard"?.

Jason Hammel RHP

Born: 9/2/82 Age: 33 Bats: R Throws: R Height: 6'6" Weight: 225

YEAR	TEAM	LVL	AGE	W	L	SV	G	GS	IP	H	HR	BB/9	K/9	GB%	BABIP	WHIP	ERA	FIP	DRA	WARP	CFIP	MPH
2013	BAL	MLB	30	7	8	1	26	23	139^1	155	22	3.1	6.2	42%	.304	1.46	4.97	4.96	4.91	0.0	114	95.1
2014	CHN	MLB	31	8	5	0	17	17	108^2	88	10	1.9	8.6	41%	.272	1.02	2.98	3.16	3.13	2.2	89	94.7
2014	OAK	MLB	31	2	6	0	13	12	67^2	66	13	2.8	7.2	38%	.272	1.29	4.26	5.13	5.18	-0.3	116	94.9
2015	CHN	MLB	32	10	7	0	31	31	170^2	158	23	2.1	9.1	41%	.288	1.16	3.74	3.71	4.61	0.9	91	94.4
2016	*CHN*	*MLB*	*33*	*11*	*9*	*0*	*29*	*29*	*174*	*151*	*22*	*2.3*	*8.1*	*41%*	*.289*	*1.12*	*3.74*	*3.78*	*4.33*	*2.0*	*99*	
2017	*CHN*	*MLB*	*34*	*10*	*10*	*0*	*30*	*30*	*188^2*	*171*	*24*	*2.2*	*7.9*	*41%*	*.297*	*1.14*	*3.83*	*4.09*	*4.43*	*1.7*	*102*	

Breakout: 22% Improve: 50% Collapse: 23% Attrition: 16% MLB: 93% *Comparables: John Lackey, Randy Wolf, Luis Tiant*

Entering his age-33 season, Hammel is healthy and as average-ish as ever. It might be worth watching if there are long-term results from the apparent increase in velocity on his no. 2 pitch, the slider. Brooks Baseball data shows the speed steadily increased each month, but did not appear to have appreciable impact on his results. If the change was deliberate, Hammel may have retooled his approach, which could pay dividends in 2016. If it wasn't deliberate, losing control over your second-most-important pitch is never really a harbinger of success.

Dan Haren RHP

Born: 9/17/80 Age: 35 Bats: R Throws: R Height: 6'5" Weight: 215

YEAR	TEAM	LVL	AGE	W	L	SV	G	GS	IP	H	HR	BB/9	K/9	GB%	BABIP	WHIP	ERA	FIP	DRA	WARP	CFIP	MPH
2013	WAS	MLB	32	10	14	1	31	30	169^2	179	28	1.6	8.0	39%	.302	1.24	4.67	4.06	4.60	0.6	99	91.0
2014	LAN	MLB	33	13	11	0	32	32	186	183	27	1.7	7.0	43%	.277	1.18	4.02	4.06	4.13	1.5	103	89.6
2015	CHN	MLB	34	4	2	0	11	11	58^1	58	10	2.0	6.8	30%	.273	1.22	4.01	4.60	4.73	0.2	114	88.4
2015	MIA	MLB	34	7	7	0	21	21	129	116	21	1.7	6.1	34%	.248	1.09	3.42	4.66	4.44	0.9	114	87.9
2016	*CHN*	*MLB*	*35*	*10*	*9*	*0*	*27*	*27*	*156^2*	*149*	*23*	*2.0*	*6.9*	*36%*	*.287*	*1.17*	*4.20*	*4.20*	*4.88*	*0.7*	*115*	
2017	*CHN*	*MLB*	*36*	*7*	*8*	*0*	*22*	*22*	*132*	*130*	*20*	*2.1*	*6.8*	*36%*	*.297*	*1.21*	*4.27*	*4.61*	*4.96*	*0.5*	*117*	

Breakout: 12% Improve: 39% Collapse: 14% Attrition: 10% MLB: 90% *Comparables: Billy Pierce, Ron Guidry, Bartolo Colon*

Haren did not initially want to play in 2015, preferring to retire and stay with his family on the west coast, but the Marlins convinced him to lace up the cleats one more time, then traded him to the Cubs once they finished their annual realization of mediocrity. Haren ate innings for five different teams over the last four years, and his results were... They were. They existed. You can't deny that. As his strikeout rate eroded, he relied more heavily on his history of inducing soft contact in the air. It made him a perfectly acceptable pitcher: 3.3 WARP in four years sums him up as well as any single number can sum up any single person. While he's still just 35, his velocity did a swan dive the last two years, resulting in an 87 mph fastball last season; according to Brooks Baseball, the only 2015 righties who threw at least 200 four-seamers or sinkers and averaged a lower velocity than Haren were Jered Weaver, Doug Fister and Brad Ziegler, the latter of whom throws underhand.

But Haren deserves better treatment in this, his final send-off. He was above-average for the A's from 2005 to 2007, instantly replacing the production of Mark Mulder in what turned out to be a massively lopsided trade for Oakland. Upon his next trade, this time to Arizona, he took another step forward, producing three excellent seasons in his next four years split between the Diamondbacks and Angels: He ranked seventh, ninth, 51st and 11th in WARP over those years. Age came for him then, but he's still retiring on his own terms, coming off a 32-start season, not sent packing by injury (he spent a total of 32 days on the disabled list in his career) or sub-replacement pitching into a fretful forced free agency..

Kyle Hendricks RHP

Born: 12/7/89 Age: 26 Bats: R Throws: R Height: 6'3" Weight: 190

YEAR	TEAM	LVL	AGE	W	L	SV	G	GS	IP	H	HR	BB/9	K/9	GB%	BABIP	WHIP	ERA	FIP	DRA	WARP	CFIP	MPH
2013	IOW	AAA	23	3	1	0	6	6	40	35	2	1.8	6.1	62%	.273	1.08	2.47	3.54	4.84	0.4	97	
2013	TEN	AA	23	10	3	0	21	21	126^1	107	3	1.9	7.2	59%	.279	1.05	1.85	2.36	3.46	1.8	80	
2014	CHN	MLB	24	7	2	0	13	13	80^1	72	4	1.7	5.3	51%	.271	1.08	2.46	3.29	2.89	1.9	107	90.6
2014	IOW	AAA	24	10	5	0	17	17	102^2	98	5	2.0	8.5	56%	.322	1.18	3.59	3.17	4.60	1.3	74	
2015	CHN	MLB	25	8	7	0	32	32	180	166	17	2.2	8.4	54%	.296	1.16	3.95	3.38	3.87	2.5	93	90.7
2016	*CHN*	*MLB*	*26*	*10*	*8*	*0*	*28*	*28*	*159^2*	*141*	*17*	*2.3*	*7.6*	*54%*	*.294*	*1.14*	*3.58*	*3.62*	*4.14*	*2.2*	*93*	
2017	*CHN*	*MLB*	*27*	*10*	*9*	*0*	*27*	*27*	*160^2*	*144*	*17*	*2.3*	*8.2*	*54%*	*.304*	*1.15*	*3.56*	*3.81*	*4.12*	*2.2*	*93*	

Breakout: 25% Improve: 53% Collapse: 17% Attrition: 13% MLB: 86% *Comparables: Wade Miley, Alex Cobb, Josh Collmenter*

In his first full season in the majors, Hendricks was kept on a tight leash, but put up a league-average ERA and slightly better components. An area of concern, however, is the contact rates he has maintained through the last two seasons. He tends to allow contact on about 80 percent of swings, which puts his whiffs-per-pitch rate eighth-lowest among qualified NL pitchers. For a pitcher who maintains an above-average strikeout rate, missing so few bats is a bit of paradox. His top two pitches, an 89 mph sinker and an 80 mph changeup, generate a lot of groundballs, so it is not out of the question for Hendricks to continue to pitch well, but without generating more whiffs, it is hard to imagine he will continue to do so through a strikeout-heavy approach..

Pierce Johnson RHP

Born: 5/10/91 Age: 25 Bats: R Throws: R Height: 6'3" Weight: 200

YEAR	TEAM	LVL	AGE	W	L	SV	G	GS	IP	H	HR	BB/9	K/9	GB%	BABIP	WHIP	ERA	FIP	DRA	WARP	CFIP	MPH
2013	DAY	A+	22	6	1	0	10	8	48^2	41	1	3.9	9.2	43%	.333	1.27	2.22	2.99	3.91	0.5	87	
2013	KNC	A	22	5	5	0	13	13	69^2	68	4	2.8	9.6	52%	.335	1.29	3.10	3.12	3.99	1.0	80	
2014	TEN	AA	23	5	4	0	18	17	91^2	60	8	5.3	8.9	44%	.242	1.24	2.55	4.27				
2014	KNC	A	23	0	1	0	2	2	11	4	1	2.5	6.5	63%	.115	0.64	2.45	4.30	4.36	0.1	97	
2015	TEN	AA	24	6	2	0	16	16	95	76	4	3.0	6.8	42%	.266	1.14	2.08	3.47	3.73	1.3	94	
2016	*CHN*	*MLB*	*25*	*5*	*5*	*0*	*16*	*16*	*80*	*72*	*9*	*3.7*	*7.3*	*40%*	*.293*	*1.31*	*4.19*	*4.26*	*4.81*	*0.5*	*113*	
2017	*CHN*	*MLB*	*26*	*8*	*10*	*0*	*27*	*27*	*164^1*	*152*	*20*	*4.0*	*7.6*	*40%*	*.303*	*1.37*	*4.43*	*4.77*	*5.09*	*0.3*	*121*	

Breakout: 19% Improve: 28% Collapse: 13% Attrition: 31% MLB: 49% *Comparables: Andrew Bailey, Brian Bannister, Chris Dwyer*

The no. 43 pick in the 2012 draft, Johnson perhaps spent more time in the low minors than the Cubs originally envisioned. He will be 25 this year, yet will be getting his first taste of Triple-A hitting. Johnson struggles with his command and has sustained a variety of leg injuries. However, he has three solid pitches, including a possibly elite curveball, he has stymied hitters at every level he's visited and he has the ability to shore up the back end of the Cubs' rotation as soon as this year. Given all the negatives, Johnson is still very much a net positive in the Cubs' system.

John Lackey RHP

Born: 10/23/78 Age: 37 Bats: R Throws: R Height: 6'6" Weight: 235

YEAR	TEAM	LVL	AGE	W	L	SV	G	GS	IP	H	HR	BB/9	K/9	GB%	BABIP	WHIP	ERA	FIP	DRA	WARP	CFIP	MPH
2013	BOS	MLB	34	10	13	0	29	29	189^1	179	26	1.9	7.7	48%	.281	1.16	3.52	3.89	3.86	2.4	92	94.5
2014	SLN	MLB	35	3	3	0	10	10	60^2	69	9	2.2	7.1	43%	.319	1.38	4.30	4.24	4.63	0.1	105	93.6
2014	BOS	MLB	35	11	7	0	21	21	137^1	137	15	2.1	7.6	49%	.298	1.23	3.60	3.59	3.89	1.5	93	94.8
2015	SLN	MLB	36	13	10	0	33	33	218	211	21	2.2	7.2	48%	.295	1.21	2.77	3.59	4.16	2.2	100	94.4
2016	*CHN*	*MLB*	*37*	*12*	*9*	*0*	*29*	*29*	*194^1*	*179*	*24*	*2.2*	*7.6*	*47%*	*.298*	*1.17*	*3.74*	*3.80*	*4.33*	*2.2*	*99*	
2017	*CHN*	*MLB*	*38*	*10*	*10*	*0*	*27*	*27*	*160^2*	*153*	*19*	*2.2*	*7.5*	*47%*	*.308*	*1.20*	*3.77*	*4.04*	*4.37*	*1.9*	*100*	

Breakout: 10% Improve: 33% Collapse: 19% Attrition: 13% MLB: 82% *Comparables: Jerry Koosman, John Burkett, Sal Maglie*

"If he's able to survive the workload, he'll be a good major-league pitcher." Similar sentiments are dispersed throughout this book, but that sentence is from the 2002 edition, which hit stores about seven months before its subject, Lackey, stomped onto the national stage. He was 23 years old when he appeared in three World Series games (including two starts) in seven days. Some 2,400-plus innings, 14 seasons and one Tommy John surgery later, Lackey ranks fourth in frames completed since his rookie year. The pitchers who rank first, third, fifth, seventh and 10th all threw their final pitches last season. Lackey? He was busy posting the best ERA of his career and starting Games One and Four of the NLDS for the team with the best record in baseball. Safe to say he was able to survive the workload..

Jon Lester LHP

Born: 5/10/91 Age: 25 Bats: R Throws: R Height: 6'3" Weight: 200

YEAR	TEAM	LVL	AGE	W	L	SV	G	GS	IP	H	HR	BB/9	K/9	GB%	BABIP	WHIP	ERA	FIP	DRA	WARP	CFIP	MPH
2013	BOS	MLB	29	15	8	0	33	33	213^{1}	209	19	2.8	7.5	46%	.300	1.29	3.75	3.61	4.06	2.2	94	95.3
2014	OAK	MLB	30	6	4	0	11	11	76^{2}	66	7	1.9	8.3	43%	.281	1.07	2.35	3.16	3.38	1.3	80	93.7
2014	BOS	MLB	30	10	7	0	21	21	143	128	9	2.0	9.4	46%	.308	1.12	2.52	2.65	3.38	2.5	74	94.4
2015	CHN	MLB	31	11	12	0	32	32	205	183	16	2.1	9.1	50%	.304	1.12	3.34	2.95	3.89	2.8	82	94.3
2016	*CHN*	*MLB*	*32*	*15*	*10*	*0*	*32*	*32*	*224*	*189*	*23*	*2.1*	*8.9*	*48%*	*.299*	*1.08*	*3.18*	*3.20*	*3.70*	*4.2*	*81*	
2017	*CHN*	*MLB*	*33*	*12*	*10*	*0*	*30*	*30*	*190*	*170*	*19*	*2.1*	*8.6*	*48%*	*.311*	*1.13*	*3.29*	*3.51*	*3.83*	*3.4*	*84*	

Breakout: 17% Improve: 47% Collapse: 23% Attrition: 8% MLB: 94% *Comparables: Vic Raschi, A.J. Burnett, Adam Wainwright*

The Cubs' big 2015 free-agent splash, Lester began the season cold, with a 6.23 ERA in his first month of action. Poor performance combined with pitching the day before Jake Arrieta every trip through the rotation caused Lester's grip on the "ace" title to evaporate quicker than a snow bank in July. The result was an end-of-season DRA that ranked just 30th among MLB's 78 ERA-title qualifiers; without getting too deeply into the semantics, it's fair to say he pitched like a no. 2 starter overall. If that's a disappointment, remember that from 2011 to 2013, he looked like a no. 2 *at best*. The Cubs signed him for six years, sure, but his annual salary, in the context of where the free-agent market now takes contracts, doesn't require him to be an ace for the team to walk away happy. His history of health (just one DL trip in the eight years since his recovery from cancer) and last year's component stats (which best resemble his 2009 season, when he *was* an ace) lend plenty of hope that he'll be a positive force in every year of that deal.

Jean Machi RHP

Born: 2/1/82 Age: 34 Bats: R Throws: R Height: 6'0" Weight: 255

YEAR	TEAM	LVL	AGE	W	L	SV	G	GS	IP	H	HR	BB/9	K/9	GB%	BABIP	WHIP	ERA	FIP	DRA	WARP	CFIP	MPH
2013	FRE	AAA	31	3	1	2	16	0	18^{1}	13	0	1.5	9.3	47%	.289	0.87	0.98	2.15	4.40	0.2	82	
2013	SFN	MLB	31	3	1	0	51	0	53	46	2	2.0	8.7	54%	.301	1.09	2.38	2.27	2.51	1.3	82	95.4
2014	SFN	MLB	32	7	1	2	71	0	66^{1}	45	5	2.4	6.9	55%	.230	0.95	2.58	3.40	2.85	1.3	100	94.7
2015	SFN	MLB	33	1	0	0	33	0	35	38	3	3.6	5.7	52%	.294	1.49	5.14	4.30	5.59	-0.4	118	95.0
2015	BOS	MLB	33	1	0	4	26	0	23	21	5	3.1	7.8	49%	.246	1.26	5.09	5.23	4.88	0.0	108	95.1
2016	*CHN*	*MLB*	*34*	*3*	*1*	*1*	*55*	*0*	58^{2}	*52*	*7*	*2.9*	*7.2*	*52%*	*.286*	*1.21*	*4.04*	*4.06*	*4.70*	*0.1*	*108*	
2017	*CHN*	*MLB*	*35*	*2*	*1*	*1*	*38*	*0*	38^{1}	*35*	*4*	*2.9*	*7.2*	*52%*	*.298*	*1.24*	*4.01*	*4.31*	*4.66*	*0.1*	*107*	

Breakout: 16% Improve: 29% Collapse: 27% Attrition: 7% MLB: 75% *Comparables: Dale Thayer, Trever Miller, Pat Neshek*

Machi is an easy pitcher to root for, what with his eight-year minor-league career, Sandoval-esque physique, infamous bullpen flatulence and funky forkball. Unfortunately, Machi is also an easy pitcher to hit against, as evidenced by the 33 earned runs in 59 innings between San Francisco and Boston last year. After spending the first chapter of his MLB career in the pitcher-friendly NL West, Machi struggled with the Red Sox, handing out home runs like propaganda leaflets. That he only managed a minor-league deal with the Cubs despite ending the year as Boston's de facto closer says all you need to know about the state of the sorry Sox bullpen.

Spencer Patton RHP

Born: 2/20/88 Age: 28 Bats: R Throws: R Height: 6'1" Weight: 200

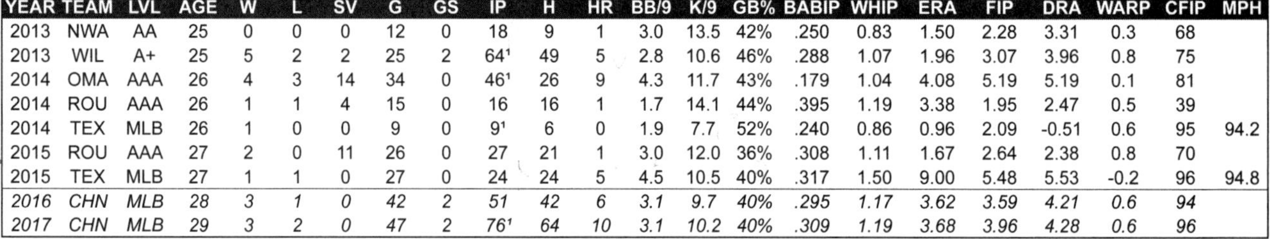

YEAR	TEAM	LVL	AGE	W	L	SV	G	GS	IP	H	HR	BB/9	K/9	GB%	BABIP	WHIP	ERA	FIP	DRA	WARP	CFIP	MPH
2013	NWA	AA	25	0	0	0	12	0	18	9	1	3.0	13.5	42%	.250	0.83	1.50	2.28	3.31	0.3	68	
2013	WIL	A+	25	5	2	2	25	2	64^{1}	49	5	2.8	10.6	46%	.288	1.07	1.96	3.07	3.96	0.8	75	
2014	OMA	AAA	26	4	3	14	34	0	46^{1}	26	9	4.3	11.7	43%	.179	1.04	4.08	5.19	5.19	0.1	81	
2014	ROU	AAA	26	1	1	4	15	0	16	16	1	1.7	14.1	44%	.395	1.19	3.38	1.95	2.47	0.5	39	
2014	TEX	MLB	26	1	0	0	9	0	9^{1}	6	0	1.9	7.7	52%	.240	0.86	0.96	2.09	-0.51	0.6	95	94.2
2015	ROU	AAA	27	2	0	11	26	0	27	21	1	3.0	12.0	36%	.308	1.11	1.67	2.64	2.38	0.8	70	
2015	TEX	MLB	27	1	1	0	27	0	24	24	5	4.5	10.5	40%	.317	1.50	9.00	5.48	5.53	-0.2	96	94.8
2016	*CHN*	*MLB*	*28*	*3*	*1*	*0*	*42*	*2*	*51*	*42*	*6*	*3.1*	*9.7*	*40%*	*.295*	*1.17*	*3.62*	*3.59*	*4.21*	*0.6*	*94*	
2017	*CHN*	*MLB*	*29*	*3*	*2*	*0*	*47*	*2*	76^{1}	*64*	*10*	*3.1*	*10.2*	*40%*	*.309*	*1.19*	*3.68*	*3.96*	*4.28*	*0.6*	*96*	

Breakout: 12% Improve: 20% Collapse: 27% Attrition: 29% MLB: 56% *Comparables: Kirby Yates, Ian Thomas, C.C. Lee*

A middle reliever with a 9.00 ERA in 24 major-league innings hardly seems worthy of a profile, but Patton's disastrous-looking line is the result of 11 earned runs sprinkled across two horrific outings when he was asked to take one (or in this case, two) for the team. The Rangers' recent track record of success with seemingly fungible relievers at a minimum would have made Patton worth keeping an eye on in 2016; that the Cubs bothered to acquired him this winter adds some additional intrigue. If that isn't enough to cheer you up, indulge a little and scout the minor-league stats.

Neil Ramirez RHP

Born: 5/25/89 Age: 27 Bats: R Throws: R Height: 6'4" Weight: 190

YEAR	TEAM	LVL	AGE	W	L	SV	G	GS	IP	H	HR	BB/9	K/9	GB%	BABIP	WHIP	ERA	FIP	DRA	WARP	CFIP	MPH
2013	FRI	AA	24	9	3	0	21	21	103	77	8	3.7	11.1	44%	.295	1.16	3.84	2.97	3.64	1.6	79	
2014	CHN	MLB	25	3	3	3	50	0	43^{2}	29	2	3.5	10.9	30%	.262	1.05	1.44	2.58	2.28	1.2	83	97.2
2015	CHN	MLB	26	1	0	0	19	0	14	12	1	3.9	9.6	38%	.289	1.29	3.21	3.23	4.09	0.1	94	95.7
2016	*CHN*	*MLB*	*27*	*2*	*1*	*0*	*36*	*0*	37^{2}	*31*	*4*	*3.2*	*9.5*	*43%*	*.295*	*1.17*	*3.49*	*3.49*	*4.06*	*0.4*	*91*	
2017	*CHN*	*MLB*	*28*	*4*	*3*	*0*	*28*	*9*	69^{1}	*58*	*8*	*3.3*	*9.6*	*43%*	*.300*	*1.21*	*3.72*	*4.00*	*4.33*	*0.6*	*98*	

Breakout: 17% Improve: 39% Collapse: 16% Attrition: 22% MLB: 64% *Comparables: Dylan Axelrod, Dustin Nippert, Steven Shell*

To make money playing baseball, you have to (a) play baseball well and (b) play baseball. Ramirez has done the former, but failed in the latter, missing most of the season with shoulder inflammation and abdominal soreness. The ab issue was apparently incurred via a July sneeze; probably nobody was around to bless him. His right shoulder also caused him to hit the minor-league DL in 2012 and 2013, and triceps soreness cost him 15 days in 2014. If he can stay on the mound, which is a big "if," and assuming his velocity recovers to pre-2015 rates, arguably an even bigger "if," he has setup-man talent, despite a flyball rate that will cause terror in the late innings on days the wind is blowing out at Wrigley.

Fernando Rodney RHP

Born: 3/18/77 Age: 39 Bats: R Throws: R Height: 5'11" Weight: 220

YEAR	TEAM	LVL	AGE	W	L	SV	G	GS	IP	H	HR	BB/9	K/9	GB%	BABIP	WHIP	ERA	FIP	DRA	WARP	CFIP	MPH
2013	TBA	MLB	36	5	4	37	68	0	66^{2}	53	3	4.9	11.1	50%	.298	1.34	3.38	2.87	4.30	0.2	83	99.8
2014	SEA	MLB	37	1	6	48	69	0	66^{1}	61	3	3.8	10.3	51%	.330	1.34	2.85	2.86	4.28	0.2	88	98.0
2015	CHN	MLB	38	2	0	0	14	0	12	8	1	3.0	11.2	57%	.259	1.00	0.75	3.50	3.37	0.2	89	97.0
2015	SEA	MLB	38	5	5	16	54	0	50^{2}	51	8	4.4	7.6	51%	.295	1.50	5.68	5.24	6.12	-0.9	111	98.0
2016	*CHN*	*MLB*	*39*	*8*	*8*	*0*	*117*	*60*	*60*	*51*	*7*	*3.5*	*9.0*	*51%*	*.296*	*1.25*	*3.89*	*3.86*	*4.52*	*0.3*	*102*	
2017	*CHN*	*MLB*	*40*	*2*	*1*	*14*	*35*	*0*	*33^{2}*	*32*	*4*	*3.4*	*8.6*	*51%*	*.313*	*1.32*	*4.13*	*4.44*	*4.80*	*0.0*	*109*	

Breakout: 12% Improve: 46% Collapse: 17% Attrition: 13% MLB: 78% *Comparables: Randy Choate, Jeff Nelson, Al Worthington*

A late-season stint with the Cubs may have saved Rodney's offseason. The fireballer was struggling through his second season with the Mariners when Chicago acquired him in August. Through his final 12 innings, he twirled a 30 percent strikeout rate to just 8 percent walks, and he shined in a public way during the Cubs' impressive playoff push. Are 12 innings enough to undo 50 innings of putridity in Seattle? No, especially not for a pitcher on the verge of 40. On the other hand, outside of a little bit less drop on his sinker and changeup, Rodney's velocity, movement and usage of his pitches hardly moved from 2014 to 2015, so it's entirely possible that the massive fall-off in his strikeout rate is more "he's a reliever!" blip than "he's old!" sign of doom.

Hector Rondon RHP

Born: 2/26/88 Age: 28 Bats: R Throws: R Height: 6'3" Weight: 180

YEAR	TEAM	LVL	AGE	W	L	SV	G	GS	IP	H	HR	BB/9	K/9	GB%	BABIP	WHIP	ERA	FIP	DRA	WARP	CFIP	MPH
2013	CHN	MLB	25	2	1	0	45	0	54^{2}	52	6	4.1	7.2	46%	.280	1.41	4.77	4.37	4.22	0.2	105	98.0
2014	CHN	MLB	26	4	4	29	64	0	63^{1}	52	2	2.1	9.0	50%	.286	1.06	2.42	2.23	2.37	1.6	86	98.7
2015	CHN	MLB	27	6	4	30	72	0	70	55	4	1.9	8.9	53%	.268	1.00	1.67	2.70	3.18	1.3	85	99.0
2016	*CHN*	*MLB*	*28*	*2*	*1*	*38*	*47*	*0*	*50*	*42*	*5*	*2.5*	*8.6*	*51%*	*.290*	*1.12*	*3.44*	*3.38*	*4.00*	*0.6*	*87*	
2017	*CHN*	*MLB*	*29*	*3*	*1*	*19*	*53*	*0*	*55^{2}*	*49*	*6*	*2.5*	*8.4*	*51%*	*.299*	*1.16*	*3.58*	*3.82*	*4.16*	*0.5*	*92*	

Breakout: 21% Improve: 51% Collapse: 26% Attrition: 11% MLB: 95% *Comparables: Jesse Orosco, Doug Corbett, Tug McGraw*

The most successful Rule 5 pick in recent Cubs history (the only competition being Josh Hamilton, who, oops, they traded to Cincinnati), Rondon has elevated from fringe Indians prospect to shutdown closer. His 2015 innovation was to lean more heavily on his high-90s hard sinker, which in retrospect is kind of obvious: My dude, you've got a 97 mph sinker—throw it! The result of listening to our sage advice was an ERA in the Chapman-Greinke-Arrieta-Giles zone. FIP suggests his improvement wasn't necessarily in his sphere of influence, but still grades him as excellent: He was sandwiched between Gerrit Cole, Chris Sale, Craig Kimbrel and Jacob deGrom on the FIP leaderboards. He's 28 and hasn't hit the DL in the major leagues, but we won't hold it against you if you're still not buying; There Is No Such Thing As A Consistent Relief Pitcher, after all.

Pedro Strop RHP

Born: 6/13/85 Age: 31 Bats: R Throws: R Height: 6'1" Weight: 220

YEAR	TEAM	LVL	AGE	W	L	SV	G	GS	IP	H	HR	BB/9	K/9	GB%	BABIP	WHIP	ERA	FIP	DRA	WARP	CFIP	MPH
2013	BAL	MLB	28	0	3	0	29	0	22^{1}	23	4	6.0	9.7	52%	.292	1.70	7.25	5.54	7.50	-0.8	99	97.7
2013	CHN	MLB	28	2	2	1	37	0	35	22	1	2.8	10.8	54%	.247	0.94	2.83	2.28	0.95	1.5	76	98.2
2014	CHN	MLB	29	2	4	2	65	0	61	40	2	3.7	10.5	56%	.268	1.07	2.21	2.63	2.35	1.6	83	97.3
2015	CHN	MLB	30	2	6	3	76	0	68	39	5	3.8	10.7	53%	.225	1.00	2.91	3.19	2.67	1.6	81	97.5
2016	*CHN*	*MLB*	*31*	*2*	*1*	*3*	*43*	*0*	*46*	*34*	*5*	*3.3*	*10.3*	*53%*	*.286*	*1.11*	*3.34*	*3.43*	*3.90*	*0.5*	*82*	
2017	*CHN*	*MLB*	*32*	*3*	*1*	*1*	*55*	*0*	*50*	*38*	*5*	*3.3*	*10.4*	*53%*	*.298*	*1.13*	*3.25*	*3.48*	*3.80*	*0.6*	*79*	

Breakout: 20% Improve: 38% Collapse: 31% Attrition: 13% MLB: 90% *Comparables: Francisco Cordero, Jim Kern, Scot Shields*

Part of the Scott Feldman–Jake Arrieta trade in 2013, Strop has been exceptional in his time with the Cubs, posting a 2.63 ERA since moving to the north side, but with Hector Rondon locking down the closer role, Strop is not in line to receive many closing opportunities. Strop increased his slider usage each of the last three years, but in 2015 crossed the Rubicon, tossing the pitch just shy of 50 percent of the time, making it his most-used pitch for the first time since 2011. The pitch's characteristics (velocity, movement) haven't changed much in recent years, and there's no reason to mess with it: Among relievers who threw at least 200 sliders last year, only Will Smith induced more whiffs per swing on his slider than Strop (and in 2014, Strop was way out in front, 3 percentage points ahead of Smith), and just four got more grounders per ball in play. It's a weapon, in other words, and as long as he can keep throwing it effectively, he can keep locking down the eighth inning for the Cubs.

Duane Underwood RHP

Born: 7/20/94 Age: 21 Bats: R Throws: R Height: 6'2" Weight: 215

YEAR	TEAM	LVL	AGE	W	L	SV	G	GS	IP	H	HR	BB/9	K/9	GB%	BABIP	WHIP	ERA	FIP	DRA	WARP	CFIP	MPH
2013	BOI	A-	18	3	4	0	14	11	54^{1}	62	4	4.5	6.0	58%	.310	1.64	4.97	4.77	5.04	-0.1	118	
2014	KNC	A	19	6	4	0	22	21	100^{2}	85	10	3.2	7.5	50%	.273	1.20	2.50	4.42	4.57	0.6	103	
2015	MYR	A+	20	6	3	0	14	14	73^{1}	52	6	2.9	5.9	55%	.223	1.04	2.58	4.15	4.88	-0.2	109	
2016	*CHN*	*MLB*	*21*	*4*	*5*	*0*	*15*	*15*	*67^{2}*	*68*	*9*	*3.8*	*5.6*	*45%*	*.294*	*1.43*	*4.95*	*4.95*	*5.66*	*-0.3*	*137*	
2017	*CHN*	*MLB*	*22*	*7*	*10*	*0*	*29*	*29*	*176^{1}*	*180*	*26*	*3.9*	*6.0*	*45%*	*.301*	*1.46*	*5.05*	*5.49*	*5.78*	*-0.7*	*141*	

Breakout: 0% Improve: 0% Collapse: 0% Attrition: 0% MLB: 0% *Comparables: Aaron Sanchez, Carlos Carrasco, Joe Ross*

Elbow inflammation kept Underwood to just 16 starts last year, but the limited playing time did not curb expectations for one of the Cubs' top arms. He features three strong pitches—fastball, curve and change—and has limited competition on his way up a Cubs system that features few high-level pitching prospects. The points of concern: Underwood has not maintained very high strikeout rates and he has struggled to stay healthy. How quickly he addresses those issues will determine how quickly you see him in Chicago. Or, not to be pessimistic except TINSTAAPP and all, *whether* you see him in Chicago.

Tsuyoshi Wada LHP

Born: 2/21/81 Age: 35 Bats: L Throws: L Height: 5'11" Weight: 180

YEAR	TEAM	LVL	AGE	W	L	SV	G	GS	IP	H	HR	BB/9	K/9	GB%	BABIP	WHIP	ERA	FIP	DRA	WARP	CFIP	MPH
2013	NOR	AAA	32	5	6	0	19	19	102^2	112	9	3.1	7.0	39%	.328	1.43	4.03	3.93	4.37	0.7	100	
2014	IOW	AAA	33	10	6	0	19	18	113^2	104	13	2.2	9.5	42%	.302	1.16	2.77	3.87	4.74	1.3	80	
2014	CHN	MLB	33	4	4	0	13	13	69^1	67	7	2.5	7.4	39%	.296	1.24	3.25	3.72	4.44	0.3	100	91.4
2015	IOW	AAA	34	4	5	0	16	16	86^2	93	4	2.7	6.4	44%	.318	1.37	3.95	3.67	4.62	0.9	96	
2015	CHN	MLB	34	1	1	0	8	7	32^1	30	5	3.1	8.6	50%	.284	1.27	3.62	4.37	5.52	-0.2	99	90.6
2016	*CHN*	*MLB*	*35*	*7*	*6*	*0*	*18*	*18*	115^1	*112*	*14*	*2.6*	*7.1*	*42%*	*.305*	*1.26*	*4.03*	*4.04*	*4.65*	*0.9*	*108*	
2017	*CHN*	*MLB*	*36*	*5*	*5*	*0*	*14*	*14*	84^2	*86*	*11*	*2.6*	*7.1*	*42%*	*.314*	*1.31*	*4.22*	*4.54*	*4.87*	*0.4*	*114*	

Breakout: 10% Improve: 24% Collapse: 12% Attrition: 10% MLB: 52% *Comparables: Travis Smith, Seth Etherton, Nelson Figueroa*

After an impressive 13-start rookie season in 2014, Wada returned to the Cubs on a one-year, $4 million deal. He looked like the top candidate to take the fifth spot in the rotation out of spring training, but injuries pushed his season debut back to May 20th. He only made seven starts before succumbing to shoulder inflammation in his throwing arm. After another month on the DL, Wada spent the next two months starting games in Triple-A before returning to the majors as a September call-up. Wada signed quickly in the offseason, opting to return to Japan rather than battle once again for a roster spot in the majors. He could conceivably make a return to North America after proving his health in Japan, but he's 35 and few make the trip twice.

Adam Warren RHP

Born: 8/25/87 Age: 28 Bats: R Throws: R Height: 6'1" Weight: 225

YEAR	TEAM	LVL	AGE	W	L	SV	G	GS	IP	H	HR	BB/9	K/9	GB%	BABIP	WHIP	ERA	FIP	DRA	WARP	CFIP	MPH
2013	NYA	MLB	25	3	2	1	34	2	77	80	10	3.5	7.5	47%	.311	1.43	3.39	4.35	4.81	-0.2	105	95.2
2014	NYA	MLB	26	3	6	3	69	0	78^2	63	4	2.7	8.7	48%	.272	1.11	2.97	2.92	2.94	1.5	92	96.4
2015	NYA	MLB	27	7	7	1	43	17	131^1	114	10	2.7	7.1	46%	.278	1.16	3.29	3.56	3.40	2.4	99	95.4
2016	*CHN*	*MLB*	*28*	*4*	*2*	*0*	*45*	*5*	66^2	*59*	*7*	*2.8*	*7.8*	*46%*	*.296*	*1.19*	*3.61*	*3.70*	*4.18*	*0.9*	*94*	
2017	*CHN*	*MLB*	*29*	*4*	*3*	*1*	*34*	*9*	88^2	*78*	*8*	*2.6*	*8.1*	*46%*	*.303*	*1.17*	*3.52*	*3.76*	*4.07*	*1.1*	*91*	

Breakout: 27% Improve: 53% Collapse: 15% Attrition: 16% MLB: 87% *Comparables: Josh Collmenter, Troy Patton, Jeff Samardzija*

The best adjectives to describe Warren are ones that don't exactly shoot for the stars. Cheap. Useful. Versatile. Dependable. Consistent. Most people hope their superiors have more glowing things to say about them, but in professional baseball those descriptors can put you on the road to millions of dollars and a long career. Warren was better than most realize in a starting role in 2015, and deserves another shot to stick in the rotation, which he may not get with the pitchers in front of him in Chicago. As a reliever he was yet another arm that allowed Joe Girardi to shorten games. He doesn't throw especially hard, but he's no Mark Buehrle, and he's got four legitimate pitches. You could do worse, and there are teams this year that certainly will.

Travis Wood LHP

Born: 2/6/87 Age: 29 Bats: R Throws: L Height: 5'11" Weight: 175

YEAR	TEAM	LVL	AGE	W	L	SV	G	GS	IP	H	HR	BB/9	K/9	GB%	BABIP	WHIP	ERA	FIP	DRA	WARP	CFIP	MPH
2013	CHN	MLB	26	9	12	0	32	32	200	163	18	3.0	6.5	35%	.248	1.14	3.11	3.86	3.20	4.1	105	91.5
2014	CHN	MLB	27	8	13	0	31	31	173^2	190	20	3.9	7.6	37%	.320	1.53	5.03	4.35	5.05	-0.6	112	91.1
2015	CHN	MLB	28	5	4	4	54	9	100^2	86	11	3.5	10.5	37%	.300	1.24	3.84	3.43	3.91	1.1	85	93.3
2016	*CHN*	*MLB*	*29*	*2*	*1*	*0*	*40*	*0*	41^2	*36*	*5*	*3.1*	*8.3*	*36%*	*.293*	*1.21*	*3.82*	*3.93*	*4.42*	*0.0*	*101*	
2017	*CHN*	*MLB*	*30*	*6*	*6*	*0*	*18*	*18*	*104*	*95*	*12*	*3.0*	*8.3*	*36%*	*.306*	*1.24*	*3.85*	*4.13*	*4.45*	*1.0*	*102*	

Breakout: 31% Improve: 51% Collapse: 17% Attrition: 9% MLB: 95% *Comparables: Tom Gorzelanny, Kevin Correia, Edwin Jackson*

Wood's career-best strikeout rate entering 2015 was his rookie season 20.5% K-rate. An extra-full rotation pushed Wood into relief, and the move to the bullpen pushed him to a 28.2% K-rate. In his work as a reliever, Wood managed a 30.2% K-rate. Given his success from the bullpen and the continued strength of the Cubs rotation — to say nothing of his recent struggles as a starter — Wood may have moved to relief for good.

That may not be the worst news for fantasy owners because Wood had become a negative asset as a starter. With a career 4.11 ERA entering the 2015 season, Wood essentially had only one good, full year in the rotation, 2013, and that required a career-low BABIP and an unusual suppression of his natural home run rate. In the bullpen, Wood could suppress his home run rate in a more sustainable way, and he can also limit the damage righties inflict on him. The move may not help fantasy owners looking for traditional counting results from Wood — wins or Ks — but the move should be a positive one for his rate numbers and his career.

Lineouts

Hitters

NAME	POS	TEAM	LVL	AGE	PA	R	2B	3B	HR	RBI	BB	K	SB	CS	AVG/OBP/SLG	TAv	BABIP	BRR	FRAA	WARP
Chris Denorfia	RF	CHN	MLB	34	231	18	11	1	3	18	15	56	0	1	.269/.319/.373	.249	.351	0.7	LF(43): 4.1, RF(28): -0.1	0.7
Donnie Dewees	OF	EUG	A-	21	303	42	14	1	5	30	14	54	19	7	.266/.306/.376	.270	.311	2.5	CF(42): 1.7, LF(16): 1.7	1.8
Jonathan Herrera	SS	CHN	MLB	30	132	14	5	1	2	14	2	23	3	0	.230/.242/.333	.206	.267	0.7	2B(29): -2.3, 3B(16): -1.2	-0.7
Eloy Jimenez	OF	EUG	A-	18	250	36	10	0	7	33	15	43	3	2	.284/.328/.418	.300	.321	-0.2	LF(46): -4.8, RF(8): 3.1	1.4
Tommy La Stella	2B	CHN	MLB	26	75	4	6	0	1	11	5	7	2	0	.269/.324/.403	.269	.283	-0.4	2B(14): 0.5, 3B(12): -0.7	0.2
	2B	IOW	AAA	26	38	3	2	1	1	6	4	3	0	0	.333/.395/.545	.312	.333	-0.7	2B(5): 0.1	0.2
	2B	TEN	AA	26	41	9	3	0	0	3	3	1	0	0	.250/.325/.333	.261	.257	-0.7	2B(5): 0.4, 3B(4): 0.9	0.2
Mike O'Neill	OF	MEM	AAA	27	85	4	1	0	0	5	12	4	1	0	.257/.373/.271	.261	.273	-0.6	LF(21): -1.9	-0.1
	OF	SFD	AA	27	239	26	7	0	0	19	37	19	3	5	.301/.409/.337	.289	.330	-3.0	LF(32): -0.3, CF(1): -0.2	0.8
Juan Perez	LF	SAC	AAA	28	344	41	24	3	7	37	17	62	17	2	.265/.306/.424	.251	.310	2.8	RF(33): 1.8, LF(32): -2.1	0.6
	LF	SFN	MLB	28	40	5	3	0	0	2	1	6	1	0	.282/.300/.359	.229	.333	0.8	LF(8): -0.5, CF(5): -0.2	0.0
	LF	SJO	A+	28	28	2	2	0	0	3	1	4	0	0	.192/.214/.269	.163	.217	-0.3	CF(3): 0.0, RF(1): 0.2	-0.2
Matt Szczur	OF	CHN	MLB	25	80	5	5	0	1	8	6	15	2	0	.222/.278/.333	.229	.263	0.5	LF(26): -1.0, CF(6): -0.9	-0.2
	OF	IOW	AAA	25	305	40	12	2	8	31	22	51	20	5	.292/.355/.442	.306	.330	-0.3	CF(50): 0.2, LF(10): -0.5	2.2
Chesny Young	2B	MYR	A+	22	452	65	18	3	1	30	45	44	12	5	.321/.394/.388	.301	.358	2.6	3B(23): 0.7, 2B(21): -1.4	3.2
	2B	SBN	A	22	122	23	5	1	0	14	12	7	9	3	.315/.385/.380	.275	.333	2.7	2B(26): 0.8, SS(4): -0.8	0.8
Mark Zagunis	OF	MYR	A+	22	512	78	24	5	8	54	80	86	12	10	.271/.406/.412	.317	.323	1.4	RF(80): -10.4, LF(13): 1.5	3.1

Chris Denorfia is now 35 and seems to be holding his corner-outfield defense steady, but his lefty-mashing days might be over. One of those skills is a lot easier to replace than the other. ❖ A 2015 second-rounder out of North Florida, **Donnie Dewees**' bat could and should develop into a serious asset in center field, but his initial taste of pro ball was uninspiring. ❖ **Jonathan Herrera** is a glove-first, bat-last infielder whose talents include playing anywhere in the infield, not hitting for power, not taking walks and not hitting very well. ❖ **Eloy Jimenez** is a 19-year-old outfielder with serious power upside and no chance of ever winning a Gold Glove. Comps to Jorge Soler are an excellent illustration of why lots of people hate comps. ❖ **Tommy La Stella** does little but avoid strikeouts, which is enough for some to see a second-division second baseman, while others see Will Rhymes. ❖ **Mike O'Neill** isn't considered a real prospect, but he walks so much that Johnny Appleseed is all, "Get a bike, bruh." ❖ **Juan Perez** was rushed to the majors in mid-August by the Giants, pressed into emergency duty at second base two weeks later and shelved with a torn oblique before the season was out. ❖ Dominican outfielder **Yonathan Sierra Estiwal** got $2.5 million from the Cubs, one of the 10 or so biggest bonuses in the J2 class, on the basis of good hit and power tools. He should, most likely, end up somewhere between low-minors washout and Hall of Famer. ❖ **Matt Sczcur** revived hopes of a fourth-outfielder future with a good season in Triple-A, but remember: "Men in general are quick to believe that which they wish to be true." ❖ **Chesny Young** is a 2014 14th-rounder who walked more than he struck out in High-A while hitting .321 and playing the four corners and second base; you've heard of this profile before, so you can guess how little power he has. ❖ **Mark Zagunis** is an underpowered ex-catcher with sterling OBPs in the low minors. Every once in a while a guy like that manages to maintain his walk rate when he moves up to leagues where pitchers actually know how to pitch.

Pitchers

NAME	TEAM	LVL	AGE	W	L	SV	G	GS	IP	H	HR	BB/9	K/9	GB%	BABIP	WHIP	ERA	FIP	FRA	WARP	CFIP	MPH
Tommy Hunter	CHN	MLB	28	2	0	1	19	0	15^2	20	4	1.7	8.6	41%	.340	1.47	5.74	5.14	6.01	-0.2	98	99.0
	BAL	MLB	28	2	2	0	39	0	44^2	41	3	2.2	6.4	48%	.286	1.16	3.63	3.35	3.34	0.7	100	98.7
Eric Jokisch	IOW	AAA	25	5	4	0	14	14	70	81	6	3.0	5.0	51%	.311	1.49	4.37	4.63	5.95	-0.3	111	
Jack Leathersich	NYN	MLB	24	0	1	0	17	0	11^2	12	0	5.4	10.8	47%	.400	1.63	2.31	2.82	5.83	-0.2	99	94.2
	LVG	AAA	24	0	0	0	13	0	13^1	10	3	4.7	14.9	33%	.292	1.27	5.40	5.02	3.20	0.3	80	
Yoervis Medina	IOW	AAA	26	0	2	1	28	0	34^1	40	3	5.5	9.2	50%	.370	1.78	6.29	4.71	5.00	0.1	102	
	CHN	MLB	26	0	0	0	5	0	9	12	1	4.0	7.0	44%	.355	1.78	7.00	4.38	4.79	0.0	115	95.1
	SEA	MLB	26	1	0	1	12	0	12	11	1	5.2	6.8	34%	.270	1.50	3.00	4.44	7.26	-0.4	117	94.6
Yoanner Negrin	YUC	AAA	31	4	1	0	15	5	36	33	0	4.0	4.5	0%	.273	1.36	2.00	4.02				
	IOW	AAA	31	1	0	0	13	2	30^1	24	4	2.4	8.9	51%	.267	1.05	2.97	4.62	3.79	0.5	87	
Carlos Pimentel	IOW	AAA	25	12	6	0	27	26	143^1	121	12	4.3	7.4	38%	.268	1.32	2.95	4.51	5.72	-0.2	110	
Clayton Richard	IND	AAA	31	4	2	0	9	9	56	53	3	2.1	4.0	57%	.260	1.18	2.09	3.87	4.93	-0.2	110	
	CHN	MLB	31	4	2	0	23	3	42^1	47	3	1.5	4.7	60%	.297	1.28	3.83	3.61	4.89	0.0	116	94.2
Zac Rosscup	CHN	MLB	27	2	1	0	33	0	26^2	26	5	4.4	9.8	38%	.296	1.46	4.39	4.89	6.22	-0.5	99	95.5
	IOW	AAA	27	0	0	0	11	0	11^1	8	1	3.2	15.9	30%	.318	1.06	4.76	2.54	2.35	0.4	69	
Carson Sands	EUG	A-	20	3	4	0	14	14	57^1	62	0	3.3	6.4	53%	.332	1.45	3.92	3.58	5.89	-0.3	112	
Rafael Soriano	CHN	MLB	35	2	0	0	6	0	5^2	8	2	1.6	6.4	30%	.333	1.59	6.35	6.87	9.02	-0.3	106	93.3
Justin Steele	EUG	A-	19	3	1	0	10	10	40^2	38	0	3.3	8.4	60%	.311	1.30	2.66	2.84	4.36	0.5	97	
Jen-Ho Tseng	MYR	A+	20	7	7	0	22	22	119	115	5	2.3	6.6	40%	.301	1.22	3.55	3.29	3.74	1.4	96	

Dylan Cease needs either a comma or better command of his high-90s heat. ❖ **Bryan Hudson** is a tall, lanky left-hander who went to the Cubs in the third round last June; he could climb quickly if he can add bulk to his frame and develop a third pitch. ❖ **Tommy Hunter** is the poster child for reliever conversions, what with his 4 mph velocity bump, which he's maintained for the last three years, and his 139-point OPS difference; not everyone with the body to withstand a starter's workload stays a starter. ❖ **Eric Jokisch** made a start for the Cubs in 2014 but spent all of 2015 in Triple-A (and injured), the difference being less about his performance than about what his usage signals about the success of the major-league squad; expect more of the same in 2016. ❖ **Jack Leathersich** made his major-league debut before undergoing Tommy John surgery in late July. When healthy, he's a high-effort strikeout machine with a sharp curveball that could go anywhere. ❖ The main beef from the Welington Castillo trade, **Yoervis Medina** throws a scintillating fastball and a mid-80s curveball that generates a hefty load of whiffs, but his walk rates suggest he has been fortunate to keep his runs-allowed figures as low as he has. ❖ Since 2012, **Yoanner Negrin** has oscillated between the Cubs' high minors and the Mexican League after starting his career in Cuba; all along, he's been a swingman with solid strikeout numbers and no real calling card. Time is running short. ❖ **Carlos Pimentel** deserves mention for sustaining a 2.95 ERA as a starter in the PCL, where the average is 4.37. The pitchers with at least 20 starts sandwiched around him on the leaderboards were Clayton Blackburn and Barry Zito. ❖ **Clayton Richard** is an ex-prospect who's now 32 but made something of his first extended look in the bullpen last year, turning in a bat-seeking, groundball-heavy performance that won't impress ERA estimators but might make him a little middle-relief cash before age takes away his fastball. ❖ **Zac Rosscup** throws with his left hand. ❖ **Carson Sands** is a lefty with a strong curve and changeup who possesses all the tools necessary to hold a place on the upper end of the Cubs' rotation someday in the distant, distant, distant future. ❖ **Rafael Soriano** signed with the Cubs midseason, went down with shoulder inflammation 11 days later and eventually got cut. You know all about the old Soriano, but this isn't the old Soriano. ❖ **Justin Steele** was an overslot 2014 fifth-rounder; he can hump it up to 95 mph from the left side but is working on a changeup. He is, in other words, a pitching prospect. ❖ **Jen-Ho Tseng** has a solid fastball, solid curve, solid changeup and solid command. This translates to a future as a gelatinous no. 4 starter.

Manager

Joe Maddon

YEAR	TEAM	W	L	Pythag +/-	Avg PC	100+ P	120+ P	QS	BQS	REL	REL w Zero R	IBB	PH	PH Avg	PH HR	SB2	CS2	SB3	CS3	SAC Att	SAC%	POS SAC	Squeeze	Swing	In Play
2013	TBA	92	71	4	94.9	65	2	80	2	485	399	38	169	.235	1	61	34	12	3	39	61.5	24	0	292	93
2014	TBA	77	85	-2	97.1	77	0	84	1	494	418	27	130	.218	1	52	24	11	2	73	58.9	42	3	313	106
2015	CHN	97	65	6	91.1	53	2	81	3	551	459	38	287	.201	5	82	32	13	3	53	60.4	15	2	330	105

You've probably heard the Hermetic saying, "As above, so below." Maddon put his own spin on that in 2015: "As below, so above." He brought most of his signature tricks with him to Chicago from St. Petersburg—be it exotic animals, telling an overworked reliever to enjoy a "beach day" or canceling batting practice throughout the season. The biggest differences were 1) a larger audience and 2) the fact that Maddon was bringing home more papaya than Princess Poo-Poo-ly.

Okay, that's not true. The biggest difference was that Maddon had no designated hitter in the National League, meaning he could double-switch to his heart's content (not that the DH ever stopped him before). He also had to contend with where to bat the pitcher. Maddon settled on the eighth slot, placing his pitcher in the customary ninth spot just 12 times all year, many of those occurring in September.

Maddon has always had small-ball tendencies—he got them honest from Gene Mauch's teachings in Anaheim. He didn't go bunt-crazy in his first season in the National League, but he did lead the majors in hit-and-run attempts. Maddon stayed true to himself in other ways by embracing all the young Cubs—although, it's not as if he had a say in the matter—and by deploying Kris Bryant at five positions, including center field. Whether Maddon's influence helped the rookies make a quick transition to the majors is unclear; however, the same seemed to be true in Tampa Bay and might be worth pondering.

If Maddon's first year in Chicago had a gray area or blemish, it had to be his handling of Jake Arrieta. The Cubs rode their ace something fierce down the stretch, at one point allowing him to throw more than 110 pitches in five consecutive outings. Maddon resorted to the same talking points he used to apply to David Price and James Shields—how a high pitch count isn't the same physiologically for every pitcher, how the stress of pitches matters more than the raw count and so on. All sensible, if unverifiable. Still, that kind of management will give you pause in 2015—especially when the pitcher in question tops his previous single-season high for big-league innings by more than 70.

Otherwise, Maddon was everything the Cubs wanted and expected. He was creative with how he handled lineups and positioning, he was calming and empowering to the young core and he was kooky enough to take the spotlight and pressure off the kids when it proved necessary. The season didn't end in a World Series visit or victory, but the future indeed seems bright in Chicago.

CHICAGO WHITE SOX

Essay by R.J. Anderson

Player comments by Matthew Trueblood and BP authors

On July 22, 2002, the White Sox replaced pitching coach Nardi Contreras with pitching coordinator Don Cooper.

Cooper has since become an organizational fixture, as recognizable and identifiable with White Sox baseball as Southpaw or the scoreboard pinwheels. He's salvaged numerous careers by teaching his charges the cutter, and prolonged countless others with his league-renowned strength and conditioning program; he's taken part in a championship parade; and he's even outlasted two managers and a general manager. His official team bio runs more than 1,500 words—and that's *excluding* 2015 and the parts about his personal life and playing career. In the most basic terms, Cooper has been the White Sox pitching coach for a long time, and has all the accomplishments to prove it.

Yet Cooper isn't the focus here. Rather, his appointment to pitching coach and subsequent term serves as a reference point for an event that happened five days later. On July 27, the White Sox traded second baseman Ray Durham to the Athletics for Jon Adkins. A homegrown talent and multiple-time All-Star, Durham is symbolic in his own right. But whereas Cooper represents organizational success, Durham stands for organizational failure—an old reminder that the White Sox have tried and tried again for 13-plus years to find a second baseman as good and reliable as the one they once traded away.

This is the part where youngsters in the audience might require a refresher course on (or an introduction to) Durham's career. In the plainest terms, he was a short, switch-hitting second baseman who was picked in the fifth round of the 1990 draft. The White Sox pushed him aggressively throughout his minor-league days, yet he managed to hold his own against older competition. Durham broke out in 1994 by hitting .296/.363/.495 in Triple-A—a performance that led *Baseball America* to name him the 28th-best prospect in the game. The White Sox were also impressed, and Durham never returned to the minors again, save for a rehab stint a decade later.

Though Durham struggled during his rookie season and was never considered a skilled fielder, he would become a reliable offensive quantity. He posted his first above-average season in his second try, and would subsequently top the .260 True Average mark in 10 of his

WHITE SOX PROSPECTUS

2015 W-L: 76-86, 4th in AL Central

Pythag	.446	23rd	DER	.689	28th
RS/G	3.84	28th	B-Age	28.2	12th
RA/G	4.33	18th	P-Age	27.5	7th
TAv	.247	30th	Salary	$118.6M	15th
BRR	-4.74	21st	M$/MW	$3.8M	13th
TAv-P	.261	16th	DL Days	750	9th
FIP	3.79	9th	$ on DL	3%	1st

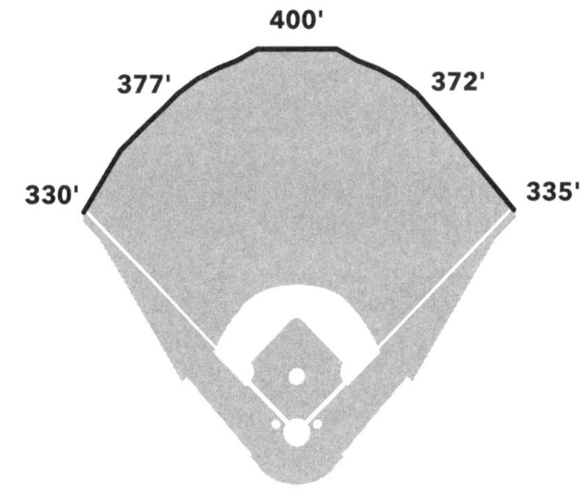

Outfield wall profile: **8'**

Three-Year Park Factors

Runs	Runs/RH	Runs/LH	HR/RH	HR/LH
102	115	105	111	108

Top Hitter WARP	4.6	Adam Eaton
Top Pitcher WARP	4.0	Chris Sale
Top Prospect		Tim Anderson

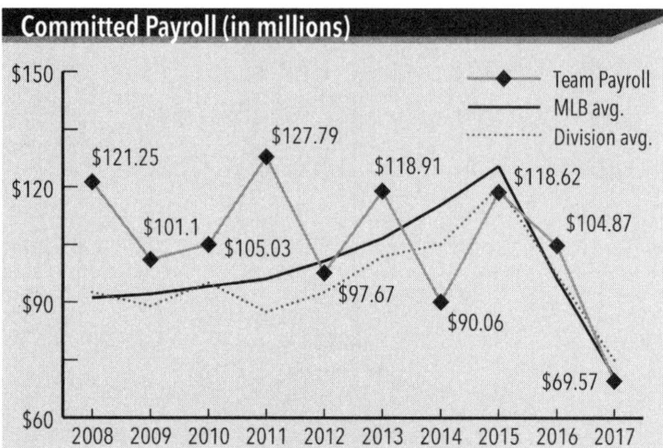

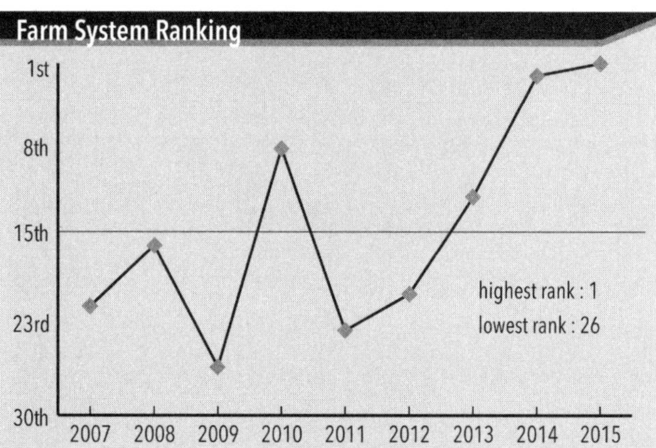

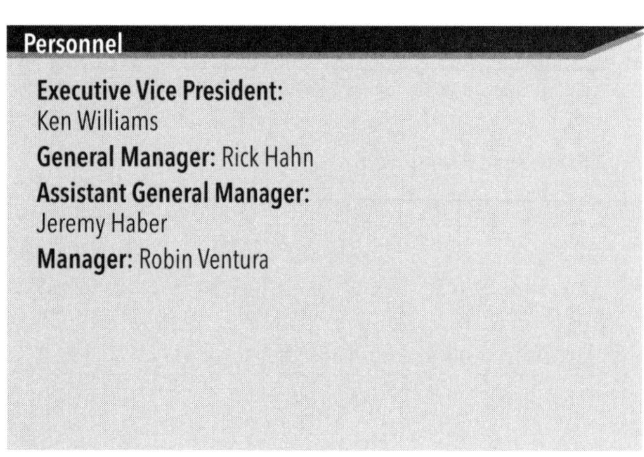
Personnel

Executive Vice President:
Ken Williams

General Manager: Rick Hahn

Assistant General Manager:
Jeremy Haber

Manager: Robin Ventura

next 12 full seasons. Bill James wrote in *The New Historical Abstract* that he considered Durham one of the top-100 second basemen of all time through the 2000 season—an impressive accomplishment, considering Durham accumulated nearly 60 percent of his career 36 Wins Above Replacement Player *after* that season. In short, Durham could hit and was one of the best second basemen of his era because of it. Replacing a player like that is never easy, but it isn't the impossible task you would think it is based on the White Sox' attempts.

To better understand the degree of the White Sox' keystone problems following the Durham trade, you have to look at the big picture. Since 2003, the White Sox rank 29th in WARP accumulated by their second basemen. The Royals, the only team to finish below the White Sox, enjoyed a reprieve from their longstanding positional despair when they acquired Ben Zobrist at the deadline. The White Sox are still waiting for their Zobrist, as evidenced by their 2015: Chicago's second second basemen combined to serve as the fifth-least productive position in the majors.

The White Sox' struggles to find a reliable second baseman haven't stemmed from a lack of effort. Between Ken Williams and Rick Hahn, the White Sox have obsessively plugged away at finding a fit. In the 13 full seasons since Durham's departure, the White Sox have had 16 distinct second basemen record more than 200 plate appearances during a season; additionally, seven different players have received the lion's share of playing time. The law of averages suggests *one* of those players should have turned into a decent stopgap; reality informs us otherwise.

How did things get this bad—and is there hope for the future? Let's start by recapping the past, season-by-season, all the while comparing the White Sox' WARP totals to Durham's median total during his years spent in Chicago (3.2).

In 2003... the White Sox opened the season with D'Angelo Jimenez, a 25-year-old they'd acquired the previous July, as their everyday starter. Jimenez showed potential with the bat (he finished his White Sox career as a roughly league-average hitter), but was dumped in a July trade after Williams landed Roberto Alomar from the Mets. Jimenez would outhit Alomar the rest of the season. Total: 1.4 WARP, 44 percent of Durham.

In 2004... Williams pinned his hopes on another pair of trade acquisitions: Willie Harris (added in January 2002) and Juan Uribe (December 2003). Uribe proved to be the better of the two, but his services were also required at shortstop, meaning Harris got more time at the keystone. Williams again acquired Alomar down the stretch, who, this go around, was outhit by Wilson Valdez and Kelly Dransfeldt. Total: 1.5 WARP, 47 percent of Durham.

In 2005... Williams signed Tadahito Iguchi from the Fukuoka Diei Hawks, with whom Iguchi had hit better than

.330 in consecutive seasons. His bat translated enough to make him an asset in spite of a shaky glove. By this point, Uribe had slid over to shortstop permanently, while Harris was used as a sub to keep Iguchi fresh. The White Sox won the World Series and all seemed well. Total: 1.5 WARP, 47 percent of Durham.

In 2006... Iguchi had another solid if unspectacular season. Total: 0.8 WARP, 25 percent of Durham.

In 2007... Iguchi's bat slipped and the White Sox could no longer tolerate his defense. Williams dumped him on Philadelphia and inserted Danny Richar, who they had acquired in a prospect-for-prospect trade with the Diamondbacks. Richar's line-drive swing was supposed to make up for his lacking plate discipline. It didn't, and he was shipped out the following July as part of the Ken Griffey Jr. deal. Total: -0.3 WARP.

In 2008... Uribe moved to second base out of deference to Orlando Cabrera. Later, when Uribe had to move to third base to cover for Joe Crede's injury, Williams again turned to an international free-agent. This time it was Alexei Ramirez, a Cuban shortstop who everyone reading this is familiar with. Total: 0.9 WARP, 28 percent of Durham.

In 2009... with Ramirez at shortstop and Uribe on another team, the White Sox turned to a variety of untested options. They opened the season leaning on Chris Getz (25) and Brent Lillibridge (25), before later inserting Jayson Nix (26). None of them hit, but the defense was pretty good. Total: 1.9 WARP, 59 percent of Durham.

In 2010... the White Sox once more moved a young player to fill a need. This time it was Gordon Beckham, the eighth-overall pick in the 2008 draft. Beckham had played shortstop in college and third base the previous season. Unfortunately, he left his bat on the left side of the infield. Total: -0.1 WARP.

In 2011... Beckham couldn't hit. Total: 0.6 WARP, 19 percent of Durham.

In 2012... Beckham still couldn't hit. Total: 0.1 WARP, 3 percent of Durham.

In 2013... bad bat or not, Beckham continued to serve as Chicago's Plan A. An injury caused him to miss time, however, during which Jeff Keppinger and Tyler Greene filled in. This may surprise you, but none of them were the solution. Total: 0.6 WARP, 19 percent of Durham.

In 2014... the White Sox tired of Beckham. Hahn, now the GM, traded him to the Angels in August and inserted Carlos Sanchez, who hit worse than Beckham did. Total: 0.5 WARP, 16 percent of Durham.

In 2015... Beckham was back. Seriously. But not as a second baseman. Instead Hahn tried out 24-yer-old top prospect Micah Johnson. By mid-May, the White Sox decided to demote Johnson and reinsert Sanchez. Sanchez hit about as poorly as Johnson did. Total: -1.6 WARP.

TABLE: WARP Accumulated by Drafted Position Players, 2003-15

Team	WARP	Team	WARP
Braves	202	Indians	22
Cardinals	196	White Sox	26
Brewers	166	Cubs	32
Rockies	162	Padres	53
Phillies	161	Mariners	53
Median		**98**	

The natural inclination when a team fails this often is to look for a pattern—some trend that highlights an illogical obsession with a certain skill set, or a steady miscalculation. There is a pattern in the White Sox' misses, but it's not the one you would expect. More often than not the White Sox have employed youngsters at second base. Young players carry a lot of obvious benefits—they're cheaper, often better at defense and funner to dream on—but the negative is that you can hold onto hope that they're going to work out for longer than you might with an older player.

As a result, the White Sox have wasted a lot of time over the past decade-plus by just giving their kids ample opportunity to succeed—not just at second base, either. The White Sox have become one of the league's worst teams at drafting and developing hitters. Beckham, that massive bust who couldn't hold down the second-base job? He's accrued the most positional-player WAR of anyone drafted by the White Sox since 2002, according to *The Catbird Seat*'s Ethan Spalding.

Entering the offseason, then, the question for Hahn and the White Sox was whether they would stick to their usual homegrown route by giving Sanchez and Johnson another chance, or if they would divert and sign a veteran—one like Howard Kendrick or Daniel Murphy. They chose to stay the course.

While rolling with the younger player is always an agreeable strategy in this era, there's good reason for caution with both of the involved players. Evaluators consider Sanchez both the more polished and less intriguing of the two prospects. He's a quality defender who doesn't have the bat speed, approach or strength to be a good hitter. Most second basemen with his profile are minor leaguers. Johnson, on the other hand, is a premium athlete with near-elite speed and enough offensive skill to be a solid hitter. Yet on the defensive side of things, Johnson has bad hands, making him a better fit for the outfield.

Neither player is a sure thing—or even a sure thing so far as second-base prospects go. If the White Sox could meld those two together—pairing Johnson's bat and wheels with Sanchez's defense—then they'd have a solid, complete talent who could make Durham proud. They can't—not legally, anyway—meaning they're almost certain to favor Johnson for the long haul. Maybe that'll work out fine, with Johnson becoming the fix for the White Sox' decade-plus-long problems.

You can't help but wonder, though, if the White Sox will regret not splurging for a veteran. For the fans' sake, here's hoping they learn from their mistakes someday soon—preferably before Cooper retires and/or the Durham trades turn 20 years old. ■

—R.J. Anderson lives in Florida and joined Prospectus in 2011. In the past, Anderson's work has appeared on ESPN and Wired.com, as well as in Newsweek.

Hitters

Jose Abreu 1B

Born: 1/29/87 Age: 29 Bats: R Throws: R Height: 6'3" Weight: 255

YEAR	TEAM	LVL	AGE	PA	R	2B	3B	HR	RBI	BB	K	SB	CS	AVG/OBP/SLG	TAv	BABIP	BRR	FRAA	WARP
2014	CHA	MLB	27	622	80	35	2	36	107	51	131	3	1	.317/.383/.581	.343	.356	-1.0	1B(109): -2.0	5.7
2015	CHA	MLB	28	668	88	34	3	30	101	39	140	0	0	.290/.347/.502	.291	.333	-2.9	1B(115): 6.2	3.2
2016	*CHA*	*MLB*	*29*	*638*	*84*	*32*	*3*	*31*	*99*	*45*	*136*	*1*	*1*	*.289/.352/.514*	*.305*	*.329*	*-1.6*	*1B 2*	*4.1*
2017	*CHA*	*MLB*	*30*	*566*	*81*	*28*	*2*	*26*	*85*	*41*	*117*	*0*	*0*	*.286/.350/.502*	*.299*	*.325*	*-1.7*	*1B 1*	*3.3*

Breakout: 4% Improve: 61% Collapse: 1% Attrition: 4% MLB: 99% *Comparables: Miguel Cabrera, Mark Teixeira, Adrian Gonzalez*

The puzzling question isn't so much what happened to Abreu's control of the strike zone (he walked a third less often in 2015 than in his stellar rookie showing), but how he ever had that control. A free swinger, Abreu walked 51 times in 2014, mostly because pitchers were afraid of his fairly awesome power. Once they started testing him more, though, they found that he was human—if only just. Abreu tried a more patient tack (he nearly halved his first-pitch swing rate) even as AL pitchers decided to go after him more aggressively. He's a good hitter, but 1,300 PA into his career, the seesaw of adjustments between Abreu and his opponents is still tilting pretty steeply. The exact shape and extent of his greatness next season is hard to forecast.

Micker Adolfo OF

Born: 9/11/96 Age: 19 Bats: R Throws: R Height: 6'3" Weight: 200

YEAR	TEAM	LVL	AGE	PA	R	2B	3B	HR	RBI	BB	K	SB	CS	AVG/OBP/SLG	TAv	BABIP	BRR	FRAA	WARP
2016	*CHA*	*MLB*	*19*	*250*	*18*	*8*	*1*	*3*	*20*	*12*	*84*	*2*	*1*	*.180/.224/.264*	*.178*	*.259*	*-0.2*	*RF -0, CF -0*	*-1.6*
2017	*CHA*	*MLB*	*20*	*316*	*29*	*11*	*1*	*6*	*27*	*16*	*104*	*3*	*1*	*.193/.239/.295*	*.195*	*.271*	*-0.2*	*RF 0, CF 0*	*-1.5*

Breakout: 0% Improve: 0% Collapse: 0% Attrition: 0% MLB: 0% *Comparables: Zoilo Almonte, Gregory Polanco, Marcell Ozuna*

Nothing has gone right so far in the career of the White Sox's big Latin American signee of 2013. Adolfo is a hulking guy with a swing that will allow him to access every bit of his potential power—but only if and when he can consistently make contact. He's physically mature, but that adjective doesn't carry over to mental or emotional descriptions of him yet. That's okay; he turned 19 in September, which is to say he would have been in high school last June if he'd been born in Des Moines. They don't make movies about high schoolers behaving responsibly and rationally, do they? Your *Can'ts Hardly Wait* and your *Feetloose* and your *Rebels Without a Cause* and so on—not a well-developed frontal lobe among them.

And yet, the pressure's on, and this winter will be a crucible for him, as he'll need to show discipline and resiliency to recover from a badly broken leg suffered in August. He needs to make measurable progress in 2016 in order to get back on track.

Tim Anderson SS

Born: 6/23/93 Age: 23 Bats: R Throws: R Height: 6'1" Weight: 185

YEAR	TEAM	LVL	AGE	PA	R	2B	3B	HR	RBI	BB	K	SB	CS	AVG/OBP/SLG	TAv	BABIP	BRR	FRAA	WARP
2013	KAN	A	20	301	45	10	5	1	21	23	78	24	4	.277/.348/.363	.272	.384	6.3	SS(63): 2.7	2.6
2014	BIR	AA	21	45	7	3	0	1	7	0	9	0	1	.364/.364/.500	.322	.441	-0.1	SS(10): 0.3	0.5
2014	WNS	A+	21	300	48	18	7	6	31	7	68	10	3	.297/.323/.472	.267	.369	3.6	SS(66): -1.1	1.8
2015	BIR	AA	22	550	79	21	12	5	46	24	114	49	13	.312/.350/.429	.289	.391	10.9	SS(110): 0.6	5.1
2016	*CHA*	*MLB*	*23*	*250*	*31*	*10*	*3*	*4*	*21*	*7*	*70*	*12*	*4*	*.251/.279/.371*	*.229*	*.333*	*1.5*	*SS 0*	*0.6*
2017	*CHA*	*MLB*	*24*	*351*	*35*	*13*	*4*	*7*	*36*	*11*	*96*	*17*	*5*	*.248/.279/.374*	*.232*	*.323*	*3.0*	*SS 0*	*1.0*

Breakout: 13% Improve: 23% Collapse: 5% Attrition: 15% MLB: 36% *Comparables: Junior Lake, Grant Green, Brandon Crawford*

In his first two (truncated) seasons of pro ball, Anderson proved he had some feel for the barrel of the bat and the power to make that a problem for opposing pitchers, not to mention speed that would play all the way up to its raw 70 grade. That left only the questions of whether his approach would mature enough to make those raw offensive tools work, and where he would land defensively. In 2015, he began to provide an encouraging answer to the first question, as his lack of "plate discipline" began to look more like Adam Jones' controlled aggression and less like Jake Marisnick's garbage barge disaster. The second will dog him until he makes the majors. He's a great athlete; he's not a shortstop.

Alex Avila C

Born: 1/29/87 Age: 29 Bats: L Throws: R Height: 5'11" Weight: 210

YEAR	TEAM	LVL	AGE	PA	R	2B	3B	HR	RBI	BB	K	SB	CS	AVG/OBP/SLG	TAv	BABIP	BRR	FRAA	WARP
2013	TOL	AAA	26	51	5	3	0	1	5	7	12	0	0	.250/.353/.386	.260	.323	0.4	C(6): -0.2	0.2
2013	DET	MLB	26	379	39	14	1	11	47	44	112	0	0	.227/.317/.376	.253	.305	-2.8	C(98): 5.3	1.7
2014	DET	MLB	27	457	44	22	0	11	47	61	151	0	3	.218/.327/.359	.250	.322	-5.5	C(122): -1.5, 1B(1): -0.0	0.8
2015	TOL	AAA	28	22	2	0	0	1	5	0	8	0	0	.300/.273/.450	.253	.385	0.0	C(4): -0.1	0.0
2015	DET	MLB	28	219	21	5	0	4	13	40	66	0	1	.191/.339/.287	.235	.278	-3.3	C(44): -9.3, 1B(23): -0.1	-1.1
2016	*CHA*	*MLB*	*29*	*409*	*46*	*17*	*1*	*10*	*43*	*56*	*119*	*1*	*1*	*.230/.338/.376*	*.258*	*.312*	*-3.2*	*C -6*	*0.8*
2017	*CHA*	*MLB*	*30*	*299*	*37*	*12*	*1*	*7*	*30*	*43*	*87*	*0*	*0*	*.223/.338/.360*	*.253*	*.306*	*-2.4*	*C -5*	*0.3*

Breakout: 4% Improve: 40% Collapse: 5% Attrition: 7% MLB: 99% *Comparables: Gene Tenace, Chris Iannetta, Dick Dietz*

YEAR	TEAM	P. COUNT	FRM RUNS	BLK RUNS	THRW RUNS	TOT RUNS
2013	DET	13523	6.7	-0.9	-0.8	5.0
2014	DET	16914	-3.4	1.2	1.4	-0.7
2015	DET	5969	-8.4	0.0	0.0	-8.3
2016	*CHA*	*15039*	*-4.9*	*0.0*	*0.2*	*-4.7*
2017	*CHA*	*11008*	*-4.3*	*0.0*	*0.1*	*-4.2*

Here's the good news: After six-plus seasons of foul-tip welts and concussion symptoms, Avila played the season symptom-free. Part of that is the bad news: A knee injury, which sent him to the disabled list, Wally Pipped the former All-Star into reserve status behind the younger, sprier James McCann. Even his father Al assuming the Detroit general manager's office in a pizza-sauced front-office coup couldn't grease the wheels on the lineup card. Offense-wise, Avila churned out his most dismal season, save for his trademark wealth of walks. His catching arm remains strong enough to thwart a third of all baserunners, and he played a skosh at first to diversify his portfolio, but the dead-pull hitter has been devoured by defensive shifts and needs to adjust if he wants to keep a significant portion of his new timeshare with Dioner Navarro.

Melky Cabrera LF

Born: 8/11/84 Age: 31 Bats: B Throws: L Height: 5'10" Weight: 210

YEAR	TEAM	LVL	AGE	PA	R	2B	3B	HR	RBI	BB	K	SB	CS	AVG/OBP/SLG	TAv	BABIP	BRR	FRAA	WARP
2013	TOR	MLB	28	372	39	15	2	3	30	23	47	2	2	.279/.322/.360	.252	.313	-0.2	LF(77): -5.4	-0.2
2014	TOR	MLB	29	621	81	35	3	16	73	43	67	6	2	.301/.351/.458	.293	.316	-1.8	LF(133): 2.7, RF(4): -0.2	3.5
2015	CHA	MLB	30	683	70	36	2	12	77	40	88	3	0	.273/.314/.394	.253	.297	-2.6	LF(150): -7.7	-0.2
2016	*CHA*	*MLB*	*31*	*617*	*73*	*31*	*4*	*13*	*62*	*38*	*84*	*5*	*2*	*.290/.333/.425*	*.271*	*.317*	*-1.4*	*LF -5*	*1.9*
2017	*CHA*	*MLB*	*32*	*569*	*64*	*27*	*3*	*10*	*60*	*35*	*79*	*3*	*1*	*.285/.328/.408*	*.265*	*.313*	*-1.4*	*LF -4*	*1.3*

Breakout: 0% Improve: 39% Collapse: 1% Attrition: 4% MLB: 94% *Comparables: Juan Rivera, Carl Crawford, David Murphy*

The fragility of a BABIP-driven profile was on display at two positions at U.S. Cellular Field in 2015, but there's no question Cabrera's was the headline act. For the second time in three years, his shaky defense in left field and failure to produce the power required of a shaky defensive left fielder made Cabrera an overpaid replacement-level player. In 2015, his strikeouts ticked up, his BABIP dipped lower than it had been in half a decade, he walked as rarely as ever and—well, we've pretty much named all the parts of baseball. (He's a bad baserunner, too. Okay, now we've named 'em all.) It's a high-variance game he plays, and he could bounce back in 2016. At 32 and in need of some shelter from even a corner outfielder's defensive responsibilities, though, he's no longer a good bet.

Matt Davidson 3B

Born: 3/26/91 Age: 25 Bats: R Throws: R Height: 6'3" Weight: 230

YEAR	TEAM	LVL	AGE	PA	R	2B	3B	HR	RBI	BB	K	SB	CS	AVG/OBP/SLG	TAv	BABIP	BRR	FRAA	WARP
2013	RNO	AAA	22	500	55	32	3	17	74	46	134	1	0	.280/.350/.481	.264	.359	-2.6	3B(108): -0.9	1.5
2013	ARI	MLB	22	87	8	6	0	3	12	10	24	0	1	.237/.333/.434	.258	.306	-0.8	3B(20): -3.3	-0.2
2014	CHR	AAA	23	539	59	18	0	20	55	49	164	0	0	.199/.283/.362	.222	.253	-5.2	3B(111): -4.6, SS(2): 0.0	-1.6
2015	CHR	AAA	24	602	63	22	0	23	74	62	191	1	0	.203/.293/.375	.236	.264	-3.6	3B(130): 15.5, SS(2): -0.1	1.5
2016	*CHA*	*MLB*	*25*	*62*	*6*	*2*	*0*	*2*	*7*	*5*	*21*	*0*	*0*	*.203/.277/.363*	*.231*	*.275*	*-0.1*	*3B 0*	*-0.1*
2017	*CHA*	*MLB*	*26*	*300*	*34*	*11*	*1*	*10*	*34*	*25*	*98*	*0*	*0*	*.202/.277/.358*	*.230*	*.271*	*-0.7*	*3B 0*	*-0.2*

Breakout: 5% Improve: 9% Collapse: 11% Attrition: 20% MLB: 25% *Comparables: Mike Costanzo, Matthew Brown, Jamie Romak*

Davidson is the exact opposite of a "change-of-scenery" guy: He was developing just fine, then got plucked up, whisked off, and has been suffering through an extremely painful series of probes ever since. The power is still there (well, some of it is), and Davidson still takes his walks. He even acquits himself at third base, which we all used to think was his only remaining challenge. He's fanning at an untenable clip, though, and that's in Triple-A.

Adam Eaton CF

Born: 12/6/88 Age: 27 Bats: L Throws: L Height: 5'8" Weight: 185

YEAR	TEAM	LVL	AGE	PA	R	2B	3B	HR	RBI	BB	K	SB	CS	AVG/OBP/SLG	TAv	BABIP	BRR	FRAA	WARP
2013	ARI	MLB	24	277	40	10	4	3	22	17	44	5	2	.252/.314/.360	.239	.294	2.1	LF(35): -0.8, CF(30): -5.3	-0.2
2013	VIS	A+	24	64	12	3	0	1	6	10	6	8	1	.321/.438/.434	.298	.348	1.8	CF(4): -0.5	0.5
2013	RNO	AAA	24	40	5	2	0	1	5	3	8	0	0	.143/.225/.286	.180	.148	-0.7	CF(2): -0.2	-0.4
2014	CHA	MLB	25	538	76	26	10	1	35	43	83	15	9	.300/.362/.401	.283	.359	0.6	CF(121): 0.0	3.0
2015	CHA	MLB	26	689	98	28	9	14	56	58	131	18	8	.287/.361/.431	.282	.345	5.9	CF(145): 2.1	4.6
2016	*CHA*	*MLB*	*27*	*633*	*80*	*29*	*7*	*8*	*55*	*52*	*111*	*18*	*8*	*.282/.354/.403*	*.272*	*.333*	*2.9*	*CF -1*	*3.3*
2017	*CHA*	*MLB*	*28*	*571*	*66*	*26*	*6*	*8*	*57*	*48*	*100*	*15*	*7*	*.279/.351/.399*	*.270*	*.329*	*3.3*	*CF -1*	*2.8*

Breakout: 9% Improve: 38% Collapse: 6% Attrition: 15% MLB: 97% *Comparables: Jacoby Ellsbury, Desmond Jennings, Matt Murton*

The White Sox raised eyebrows by signing Eaton to a spring extension in 2015. He was precisely the kind of player whose skill set the arbitration process fails to properly reward. With six homers in nearly 1,000 big-league plate appearances, he appeared to have a low ceiling because of his sheer lack of power.

Then the season began, and in this one regard, at least, the Sox were made to look brilliant. The 5-foot-8 Eaton rebuilt his swing to allow him to pull the ball more, and specifically, to pull it in the air. The changes worked, and Eaton yanked several pitches into seats in the AL's right-field corners, in addition to putting a few more in the gaps. The new swing cost him some contact, but he also started drawing more walks, a consequence as well of pitchers respecting him enough to nibble. Pair all of that with solid defense in center field, and Eaton ended 2015 looking like a steal at any price for the next six years.

Todd Frazier 3B

Born: 2/12/86 Age: 30 Bats: R Throws: R Height: 6'3" Weight: 220

YEAR	TEAM	LVL	AGE	PA	R	2B	3B	HR	RBI	BB	K	SB	CS	AVG/OBP/SLG	TAv	BABIP	BRR	FRAA	WARP
2013	CIN	MLB	27	600	63	29	3	19	73	50	125	6	5	.234/.314/.407	.260	.269	1.7	3B(147): -1.8, LF(2): -0.2	1.9
2014	CIN	MLB	28	660	88	22	1	29	80	52	139	20	8	.273/.336/.459	.297	.309	3.2	3B(124): -3.3, 1B(43): 0.6	4.4
2015	CIN	MLB	29	678	82	43	1	35	89	44	137	13	8	.255/.309/.498	.293	.271	-1.1	3B(155): 2.4	4.7
2016	*CHA*	*MLB*	*30*	*590*	*74*	*27*	*3*	*23*	*78*	*45*	*130*	*12*	*6*	*.251/.316/.444*	*.272*	*.287*	*0.8*	*3B -2*	*2.4*
2017	*CHA*	*MLB*	*31*	*535*	*66*	*25*	*2*	*19*	*67*	*39*	*118*	*10*	*6*	*.246/.309/.419*	*.263*	*.285*	*1.2*	*3B -2*	*1.6*

Breakout: 1% Improve: 43% Collapse: 3% Attrition: 13% MLB: 95% *Comparables: David Freese, Ty Wigginton, Adrian Beltre*

Everyone loves seeing a hometown hero make good, so we could go on and on about Frazier's electric Home Run Derby win at Great American Ballpark last July. That would be much more fun than discussing Frazier's forgettable .220/.274/.390 second half, but alas, that happened too. We also could engage in some Small Sample Theater to tease out through his peripherals why Frazier went from Babe to Bum so quickly, but the fact is Frazier's true talent level lies between those two extremes. He's a solid defensive third baseman nearing the end of his prime with tremendous power and sketchy on-base skills, likely to produce for the White Sox at a level well beyond his reasonable salary until he hits free agency in 2018. At that point he'll have earned enough to finance a *real* Small Sample Theater, where patrons can eat tapas, drink beer flights and watch one-act plays featuring protagonists that quickly jump to unsupported conclusions. Food for thought, Todd.

Avisail Garcia RF

Born: 6/12/91 Age: 25 Bats: R Throws: R Height: 6'4" Weight: 240

YEAR	TEAM	LVL	AGE	PA	R	2B	3B	HR	RBI	BB	K	SB	CS	AVG/OBP/SLG	TAv	BABIP	BRR	FRAA	WARP
2013	DET	MLB	22	88	12	3	1	2	10	4	21	0	1	.241/.273/.373	.246	.295	0.3	CF(23): -2.0, RF(5): -0.4	-0.2
2013	TOL	AAA	22	156	23	7	1	5	23	8	32	4	2	.374/.410/.537	.342	.455	0.6	CF(25): -0.9, RF(6): -1.1	1.7
2013	CHR	AAA	22	32	6	0	1	1	9	4	4	0	0	.370/.469/.556	.387	.409	-0.4	CF(7): -1.1	0.4
2013	LAK	A+	22	28	9	0	2	1	4	4	1	2	0	.417/.500/.708	.393	.409	0.7	CF(2): -0.4, RF(2): -0.2	0.5
2013	CHA	MLB	22	168	19	4	2	5	21	5	38	3	2	.304/.327/.447	.272	.370	-1.1	RF(36): -2.6, CF(8): -1.2	0.0
2014	CHA	MLB	23	190	19	8	0	7	29	14	44	4	1	.244/.305/.413	.257	.285	-1.8	RF(46): -1.0	0.0
2014	CHR	AAA	23	53	9	3	0	1	3	1	16	0	0	.340/.377/.460	.280	.485	0.8	RF(7): 0.2	0.3
2015	CHA	MLB	24	601	66	17	2	13	59	36	141	7	7	.257/.309/.365	.245	.320	-0.3	RF(130): 3.6	0.4
2016	*CHA*	*MLB*	*25*	*574*	*62*	*20*	*4*	*15*	*66*	*29*	*134*	*8*	*5*	*.268/.312/.405*	*.259*	*.329*	*-1.3*	*RF -5*	*0.5*
2017	*CHA*	*MLB*	*26*	*533*	*63*	*18*	*3*	*15*	*61*	*28*	*120*	*7*	*5*	*.265/.310/.405*	*.258*	*.319*	*-0.8*	*RF -5*	*0.4*

Breakout: 1% Improve: 56% Collapse: 3% Attrition: 14% MLB: 97% *Comparables: Travis Buck, Alex Rios, Dayan Viciedo*

Bereft of plate discipline, Garcia hasn't come anywhere close to tapping his power potential—and doesn't appear to be on the verge of changing that. There are players with much worse contact problems, but few with greater difficulty consistently making *good* contact. Garcia is a 25-year-old with the offensive profile of a decent middle infielder, but the defensive value (and the frame) of a rolltop desk. He's toolsy and projectable, but those words become backhanded compliments at roughly his age. He could figure things out and grow into a superstar, but the Jeff Francoeur and Delmon Young rookie cards gathering dust inside *your* rolltop desk are good reminders that it's unlikely to happen.

Courtney Hawkins LF

Born: 11/12/93 Age: 22 Bats: R Throws: R Height: 6'3" Weight: 230

YEAR	TEAM	LVL	AGE	PA	R	2B	3B	HR	RBI	BB	K	SB	CS	AVG/OBP/SLG	TAv	BABIP	BRR	FRAA	WARP
2013	WNS	A+	19	425	48	16	3	19	62	29	160	10	5	.178/.249/.384	.216	.236	1.7	CF(100): -3.4	-0.9
2014	WNS	A+	20	515	65	25	4	19	84	53	143	11	3	.249/.331/.450	.275	.316	2.0	LF(108): -3.5, CF(6): -0.7	1.8
2015	BIR	AA	21	330	39	19	2	9	41	20	100	1	4	.243/.300/.410	.260	.332	-1.6	LF(62): -0.9	0.4
2016	*CHA*	*MLB*	*22*	*250*	*24*	*9*	*1*	*9*	*29*	*14*	*93*	*1*	*1*	*.196/.248/.356*	*.216*	*.277*	*-0.3*	*LF -0*	*-0.5*
2017	*CHA*	*MLB*	*23*	*274*	*29*	*11*	*1*	*9*	*30*	*16*	*102*	*2*	*1*	*.196/.251/.352*	*.218*	*.281*	*-0.3*	*LF -1, RF 0*	*-0.6*

Breakout: 2% Improve: 6% Collapse: 2% Attrition: 8% MLB: 11% *Comparables: Jamie Romak, Jeremy Moore, Trayce Thompson*

The more one-dimensional a profile is, the better a player must be in that one dimension to make it work. That's just simple physics—Newton's third law of prospects. Hawkins has seen any chances of being a defensive asset disappear as he's added weight to his already-hulking frame. He struck out 30 percent of the time in Double-A this season and doesn't walk. His hit tool is dull, and he can't run the bases. Given all those things, his 30 extra-base hits (and in particular, his nine home runs) in half a season of playing time just aren't enough to fill a package. From this point in his development, you can see Hawkins' big-league dream: It's the short side of a left-field platoon.

Adam LaRoche 1B

Born: 11/6/79 Age: 36 Bats: L Throws: L Height: 6'3" Weight: 205

YEAR	TEAM	LVL	AGE	PA	R	2B	3B	HR	RBI	BB	K	SB	CS	AVG/OBP/SLG	TAv	BABIP	BRR	FRAA	WARP
2013	WAS	MLB	33	590	70	19	3	20	62	72	131	4	1	.237/.332/.403	.265	.277	-0.6	1B(149): -0.7	0.8
2014	WAS	MLB	34	586	73	19	0	26	92	82	108	3	0	.259/.362/.455	.304	.277	-2.6	1B(136): 6.4	3.7
2015	CHA	MLB	35	484	41	21	0	12	44	49	133	0	0	.207/.293/.340	.233	.269	-4.7	1B(48): 0.9, P(1): -0.0	-1.2
2016	*CHA*	*MLB*	*36*	*570*	*65*	*21*	*1*	*20*	*72*	*66*	*134*	*2*	*0*	*.229/.320/.399*	*.259*	*.269*	*-2.4*	*1B 1*	*0.7*
2017	*CHA*	*MLB*	*37*	*471*	*59*	*16*	*1*	*16*	*55*	*54*	*114*	*0*	*0*	*.218/.309/.380*	*.250*	*.258*	*-2.3*	*1B 1*	*0.5*

Breakout: 0% Improve: 24% Collapse: 13% Attrition: 14% MLB: 84% *Comparables: Cliff Floyd, Ryan Klesko, Rafael Palmeiro*

In about 100 fewer plate appearances than he'd taken with Washington in 2014, LaRoche managed 25 *more* strikeouts for the 2015 White Sox. He didn't totally lose his grasp on the strike zone and start chasing an inordinate number of bad ones. He didn't see a radically different mix of pitches or pitchers. He didn't try to rebuild his approach. At 35, LaRoche simply Lost It. He swung roughly as often as ever, but missed much more. By the end of the season, pitchers were thoroughly unafraid to challenge him, and they won ever more of those challenges as the year wound down. If he can't find a new way of doing things that accounts for his age, LaRoche's career as an acceptable big-league hitter is over.

Brett Lawrie 2B

Born: 1/18/90 Age: 26 Bats: R Throws: R Height: 6'0" Weight: 210

YEAR	TEAM	LVL	AGE	PA	R	2B	3B	HR	RBI	BB	K	SB	CS	AVG/OBP/SLG	TAv	BABIP	BRR	FRAA	WARP
2013	TOR	MLB	23	442	41	18	3	11	46	30	68	9	5	.254/.315/.397	.263	.280	0.3	3B(103): 1.6, 2B(6): -0.4	1.7
2014	TOR	MLB	24	282	27	9	0	12	38	16	49	0	0	.247/.301/.421	.264	.260	-0.2	3B(63): 1.1, 2B(32): 1.7	1.3
2015	OAK	MLB	25	602	64	29	3	16	60	28	144	5	2	.260/.299/.407	.266	.320	-2.9	3B(109): 3.5, 2B(42): -3.4	1.9
2016	*CHA*	*MLB*	*26*	*517*	*58*	*23*	*4*	*16*	*63*	*33*	*100*	*6*	*3*	*.266/.321/.428*	*.268*	*.304*	*-1.0*	*2B -1*	*2.3*
2017	*CHA*	*MLB*	*27*	*512*	*65*	*22*	*3*	*17*	*65*	*35*	*98*	*6*	*3*	*.268/.325/.441*	*.273*	*.301*	*-0.9*	*2B -1*	*2.4*

Breakout: 2% Improve: 53% Collapse: 4% Attrition: 12% MLB: 100% *Comparables: Edwin Encarnacion, Minnie Minoso, Bill Madlock*

Lawrie plays baseball like a man who just drank an entire pot of coffee and can't decide whether to do everything all at once or just run to the bathroom. His reflexes are incredible, which should make him an ideal fit for third base. Problem is, he reacts so quickly that he forgets to slow down before throwing to first, which often results in hilarity. Second base seems less natural, which forces him to be more deliberate and actually execute plays rather than rely on superior athleticism. At the plate, Lawrie makes hard contact but also has days like April 7th, when he went 0-for-4 with four strikeouts on a total of 12 pitches. He is dynamic, energetic and entertaining, though the disconnect between his abundant physical tools and his pedestrian production also makes him profoundly frustrating.

Jacob May CF

Born: 1/23/92 Age: 24 Bats: B Throws: R Height: 5'10" Weight: 180

YEAR	TEAM	LVL	AGE	PA	R	2B	3B	HR	RBI	BB	K	SB	CS	AVG/OBP/SLG	TAv	BABIP	BRR	FRAA	WARP
2013	KAN	A	21	230	36	6	3	8	28	16	43	19	5	.286/.346/.461	.309	.325	1.6	CF(50): -4.6	1.6
2014	WNS	A+	22	472	66	31	10	2	27	42	71	37	8	.258/.326/.395	.255	.305	5.3	CF(92): -8.7, LF(2): -0.3	0.8
2015	BIR	AA	23	432	47	15	1	2	32	29	73	37	17	.275/.329/.334	.252	.332	-1.3	CF(98): -13.2	-0.6
2016	*CHA*	*MLB*	*24*	*250*	*32*	*10*	*2*	*4*	*18*	*14*	*57*	*14*	*6*	*.232/.278/.337*	*.218*	*.283*	*1.1*	*CF -5*	*-0.7*
2017	*CHA*	*MLB*	*25*	*324*	*33*	*13*	*2*	*6*	*31*	*19*	*74*	*19*	*7*	*.235/.283/.350*	*.224*	*.286*	*2.4*	*CF -7*	*-0.6*

Breakout: 8% Improve: 16% Collapse: 3% Attrition: 15% MLB: 21% *Comparables: Abraham Almonte, Logan Schafer, Ryan Strausborger*

May has a lot of chances to help a big-league team on some level, but a narrowing path to becoming a regular contributor. He can run, but he's not a true burner, and he doesn't maximize the value of his legs with instincts and efficiency. He can put the bat on the ball a bit, but he's neither patient nor powerful. He looks better in left field than in center, but there's no way the bat works in left. He'll be 24 this year, and has had some success at Double-A, but it'll take at least one more developmental jump to turn him into more than a fourth outfielder.

Trey Michalczewski 3B

Born: 2/27/95 Age: 21 Bats: B Throws: R Height: 6'3" Weight: 210

YEAR	TEAM	LVL	AGE	PA	R	2B	3B	HR	RBI	BB	K	SB	CS	AVG/OBP/SLG	TAv	BABIP	BRR	FRAA	WARP
2014	KAN	A	19	495	57	25	7	10	70	45	140	6	3	.273/.348/.433	.278	.375	0.9	3B(114): -7.7	1.9
2014	WNS	A+	19	84	5	2	0	0	5	9	21	1	0	.194/.293/.222	.222	.275	-0.7	3B(17): -0.9	-0.3
2015	WNS	A+	20	532	59	35	4	7	75	50	114	4	3	.259/.335/.395	.256	.326	0.9	3B(127): 3.8	2.0
2016	*CHA*	*MLB*	*21*	*250*	*21*	*10*	*1*	*4*	*24*	*18*	*80*	*0*	*0*	*.208/.270/.321*	*.213*	*.293*	*-0.3*	*3B -1, 1B 0*	*-0.7*
2017	*CHA*	*MLB*	*22*	*392*	*41*	*19*	*2*	*9*	*39*	*28*	*124*	*0*	*0*	*.209/.275/.349*	*.225*	*.289*	*-0.7*	*3B -2, 1B 0*	*-0.7*

Breakout: 0% Improve: 0% Collapse: 0% Attrition: 1% MLB: 1% *Comparables: Alex Liddi, Will Middlebrooks, Kaleb Cowart*

Thirty-five of the 46 extra-base hits Michalczewski notched in the Carolina League last year were doubles, but it's a faith too important to lose that doubles turn into homers down the road. Just 20 years old for most of 2015, Michalczewski is already big, strong and surprisingly good at maintaining his swing from each side of the plate. His approach isn't a total loss; it just needs the polish so many players lack at this stage of development. He's inconsistent at third base, but the goal will be to keep him there, because the stakes of his offensive development go way up if he's trying to fit the profile of an average-minus defensive left fielder.

Dioner Navarro C

Born: 2/9/84 Age: 32 Bats: B Throws: R Height: 5'9" Weight: 205

YEAR	TEAM	LVL	AGE	PA	R	2B	3B	HR	RBI	BB	K	SB	CS	AVG/OBP/SLG	TAv	BABIP	BRR	FRAA	WARP
2013	CHN	MLB	29	266	31	7	0	13	34	23	36	0	1	.300/.365/.492	.301	.307	-5.3	C(55): 0.3	1.7
2014	TOR	MLB	30	520	40	22	0	12	69	32	76	3	0	.274/.317/.395	.260	.301	-1.3	C(112): -20.5	-0.4
2015	TOR	MLB	31	192	17	7	0	5	20	17	29	0	0	.246/.307/.374	.255	.262	-1.2	C(39): -3.2	0.2
2016	*CHA*	*MLB*	*32*	*134*	*14*	*5*	*0*	*4*	*16*	*10*	*21*	*0*	*0*	*.263/.318/.399*	*.255*	*.287*	*-0.8*	*C -5*	*-0.1*
2017	*CHA*	*MLB*	*33*	*151*	*17*	*5*	*0*	*4*	*16*	*11*	*26*	*0*	*0*	*.253/.307/.375*	*.244*	*.280*	*-1.0*	*C -5*	*-0.3*

Breakout: 1% Improve: 17% Collapse: 13% Attrition: 20% MLB: 87% *Comparables: Johnny Estrada, John Baker, Carlos Ruiz*

YEAR	TEAM	P. COUNT	FRM RUNS	BLK RUNS	THRW RUNS	TOT RUNS
2013	CHN	7704	0.1	-0.1	0.1	0.1
2014	TOR	14932	-19.4	0.4	0.2	-18.8
2015	TOR	4992	-3.5	0.0	0.3	-3.3
2016	*CHA*	*4744*	*-4.6*	*0.0*	*0.1*	*-4.5*
2017	*CHA*	*5339*	*-5.4*	*0.0*	*0.0*	*-5.3*

They say the devil's greatest trick was convincing Marco Estrada he was better off with Navarro behind the plate than Russell Martin in 2015. The former top-50 prospect caught 19 of Estrada's 34 appearances and coaxed him to a 2.63 ERA, a vast improvement over the 4.11 ERA he had with "that other catcher." Many theories surfaced. Maybe Navarro made Estrada feel more comfortable. Maybe he's a great framer. (He's not.) Maybe it was the pitch-calling. Maybe it was his .182 BABIP with Navarro catching. (If *that's* a catching skill, then pay him all the money.) At the plate, Navarro continued to hit southpaws well with a .894 OPS, just not as well as Martin and his .937 OPS. "It's all about Martin. Martin, Martin, Martin," he might say if he hadn't just made $5 million to play once every three days. He's out from under Martin now, though, and into a likely and entirely appropriate platoon with Alex Avila in Chicago.

Mike Olt 3B

Born: 8/27/88 Age: 27 Bats: R Throws: R Height: 6'2" Weight: 210

YEAR	TEAM	LVL	AGE	PA	R	2B	3B	HR	RBI	BB	K	SB	CS	AVG/OBP/SLG	TAv	BABIP	BRR	FRAA	WARP
2013	ROU	AAA	24	268	37	15	0	11	32	35	89	0	0	.213/.317/.422	.268	.288	0.6	3B(63): 3.2	1.5
2013	IOW	AAA	24	152	11	3	1	3	8	20	37	0	0	.168/.276/.275	.213	.207	-0.9	3B(38): 3.7	0.0
2014	IOW	AAA	25	115	16	9	0	7	24	8	33	1	0	.302/.348/.585	.324	.373	-0.7	1B(26): 0.0, 3B(2): 0.0	0.9
2014	CHN	MLB	25	258	23	8	0	12	33	25	100	0	1	.160/.248/.356	.234	.203	-0.3	3B(52): -2.6, 1B(12): -0.2	-0.3
2015	CHA	MLB	26	86	6	0	0	3	4	7	29	0	1	.203/.267/.316	.205	.277	-0.4	3B(20): -2.0, 1B(5): -0.2	-0.5
2015	IOW	AAA	26	235	30	14	0	9	25	20	71	0	1	.265/.333/.460	.297	.356	-0.1	3B(33): 1.9, 1B(20): -3.7	1.3
2015	CHN	MLB	26	16	1	0	0	1	1	0	6	0	0	.133/.188/.333	.163	.125	0.0	3B(6): 0.0	-0.1
2016	*CHA*	*MLB*	*27*	*160*	*18*	*6*	*0*	*7*	*21*	*16*	*53*	*0*	*0*	*.214/.296/.407*	*.253*	*.282*	*0.0*	*3B 0, 1B -0*	*0.2*
2017	*CHA*	*MLB*	*28*	*284*	*36*	*11*	*0*	*12*	*36*	*28*	*93*	*0*	*0*	*.210/.291/.394*	*.247*	*.276*	*-0.1*	*3B 0, 1B 0*	*0.3*

Breakout: 3% Improve: 19% Collapse: 8% Attrition: 22% MLB: 50% *Comparables: Josh Fields, Zach Lutz, Jason Dubois*

Olt still has some of the tools that made him a plus defensive third baseman. He still has a modicum of the power that made him an elite prospect as late as the end of the 2012 season. Unfortunately, he also has, or has had: a broken clavicle (2011), plantar fasciitis (2012), a concussion from a pitch that hit him in the head (later 2012), vision problems that appear to have started with that concussion (2013), a hamstring strain (2014), and a broken right wrist (2015). Quietly, he has simply missed too much development time, had to do too much rehab and recovery and conditioning work to keep improving as a hitter. Further, the injuries listed above aren't the heal-up-and-put-it-behind-you kind. It's a shame, but there's not even a dream left here. Too much swing-and-miss, too little time.

Jake Peter 2B

Born: 4/5/93 Age: 23 Bats: L Throws: R Height: 6'1" Weight: 185

YEAR	TEAM	LVL	AGE	PA	R	2B	3B	HR	RBI	BB	K	SB	CS	AVG/OBP/SLG	TAv	BABIP	BRR	FRAA	WARP
2014	WNS	A+	21	94	8	4	1	0	5	4	13	1	0	.236/.277/.303	.201	.276	1.6	2B(23): 3.8	0.2
2015	WNS	A+	22	562	76	25	5	3	57	53	89	23	3	.260/.330/.348	.253	.307	2.4	2B(107): 4.6, SS(13): 2.3	2.2
2016	*CHA*	*MLB*	*23*	*250*	*22*	*10*	*1*	*4*	*23*	*17*	*59*	*4*	*1*	*.222/.277/.323*	*.218*	*.278*	*0.3*	*2B 4, SS 0*	*0.3*
2017	*CHA*	*MLB*	*24*	*332*	*33*	*13*	*2*	*5*	*30*	*22*	*75*	*5*	*1*	*.224/.280/.330*	*.222*	*.276*	*0.5*	*2B 5, SS 0*	*0.5*

Breakout: 2% Improve: 4% Collapse: 0% Attrition: 2% MLB: 5% *Comparables: Phil Gosselin, Justin Turner, Chris Coghlan*

He's a little light on power, but Peter does everything else well enough to be a regular second baseman if his development stays on track. Left-handed hitters at the right-leaning infield positions always have a little extra value, and ones with plate discipline can be especially useful. Peter is versatile (he played 13 games at shortstop in 2015, though he's no more than a fill-in option at that spot in the bigs; he does have the arm for an outfield corner if he lands in a utility role) and his game is well rounded. There's no vaulted ceiling here, but you don't have to hunch over or duck under light fixtures, either.

Alexei Ramirez SS

Born: 9/22/81 Age: 34 Bats: R Throws: R Height: 6'2" Weight: 180

YEAR	TEAM	LVL	AGE	PA	R	2B	3B	HR	RBI	BB	K	SB	CS	AVG/OBP/SLG	TAv	BABIP	BRR	FRAA	WARP
2013	CHA	MLB	31	674	68	39	2	6	48	26	68	30	9	.284/.313/.380	.254	.309	1.6	SS(158): -1.6	2.4
2014	CHA	MLB	32	657	82	35	2	15	74	24	81	21	4	.273/.305/.408	.253	.292	-0.1	SS(158): 9.8	3.3
2015	CHA	MLB	33	622	54	33	0	10	62	31	68	17	7	.249/.285/.357	.236	.264	-4.4	SS(152): 4.3, P(1): -0.0	1.0
2016	*CHA*	*MLB*	*34*	*591*	*67*	*29*	*2*	*8*	*47*	*26*	*76*	*19*	*6*	*.259/.294/.360*	*.236*	*.285*	*-1.2*	*SS 2*	*1.5*
2017	*CHA*	*MLB*	*35*	*516*	*49*	*24*	*2*	*6*	*45*	*21*	*69*	*14*	*5*	*.249/.282/.340*	*.227*	*.276*	*-0.8*	*SS 2*	*0.7*

Breakout: 0% Improve: 27% Collapse: 9% Attrition: 12% MLB: 91% *Comparables: Willie Bloomquist, Julio Lugo, Orlando Cabrera*

At his peak, Ramirez was a metronome. His low-walk, low-strikeout, .290ish-BABIP, low-power (but not no-power) profile produced quiet value for seven solid seasons. In 2015, his value cratered when, while the rest of those skills remained, the bottom fell out from under his BABIP. The knee-jerk response is to chalk that up to luck, but jerk not your knee, dear reader, because it's not as simple as "he hit into some rot." It's that his groundball BABIP was the lowest of his career; his flyball BABIP was the lowest of his career; and his line drive BABIP was the lowest of his career. Hence, the lowest BABIP of his career. BABIP is the first skill to fade for most hitters; Ramirez made it almost to his mid-30s before his fell off a cliff. Don't expect it to come back.

Tyler Saladino 3B

Born: 7/20/89 Age: 26 Bats: R Throws: R Height: 6'0" Weight: 200

YEAR	TEAM	LVL	AGE	PA	R	2B	3B	HR	RBI	BB	K	SB	CS	AVG/OBP/SLG	TAv	BABIP	BRR	FRAA	WARP
2013	BIR	AA	23	493	49	17	2	5	55	51	86	28	8	.229/.316/.314	.237	.271	0.7	SS(75): 0.6, 2B(43): 2.4	1.0
2014	CHR	AAA	24	325	41	16	4	9	43	27	50	7	1	.310/.367/.483	.275	.346	1.3	SS(50): 3.4, 1B(10): 0.3	2.2
2015	CHA	MLB	25	254	33	6	4	4	20	12	51	8	2	.225/.267/.335	.210	.269	1.1	3B(60): 5.3, SS(11): -0.7	0.1
2015	CHR	AAA	25	231	28	7	2	4	29	22	33	25	2	.255/.332/.372	.255	.277	1.7	SS(34): 2.3, 3B(2): -0.3	1.0
2016	*CHA*	*MLB*	*26*	*516*	*63*	*18*	*4*	*9*	*43*	*37*	*106*	*22*	*4*	*.239/.298/.356*	*.236*	*.283*	*1.8*	*SS -0*	*1.4*
2017	*CHA*	*MLB*	*27*	*544*	*59*	*20*	*4*	*10*	*54*	*43*	*116*	*23*	*5*	*.239/.305/.363*	*.242*	*.287*	*2.5*	*SS 0*	*1.8*

Breakout: 5% Improve: 24% Collapse: 6% Attrition: 20% MLB: 39% *Comparables: Danny Worth, Michael Morse, Travis Metcalf*

For a tragically telling fortnight, Saladino was trumpeted as like an important thing. Sixty-two plate appearances of a .286/.317/.464 line shouldn't set fans to drooling, but such was the desperation felt by the faltering South Siders' fan base. In truth (and in all the games after that quasi-promising debut), Saladino is just a player out of time to grow into much more than a utilityman. He can run a bit and he'll be a defensive asset on the left side of the infield. He just can't hit enough to play regularly for a good team.

Carlos Sanchez 2B

Born: 6/29/92 Age: 24 Bats: B Throws: R Height: 5'11" Weight: 195

YEAR	TEAM	LVL	AGE	PA	R	2B	3B	HR	RBI	BB	K	SB	CS	AVG/OBP/SLG	TAv	BABIP	BRR	FRAA	WARP
2013	CHR	AAA	21	479	50	20	2	0	28	29	76	16	7	.241/.293/.296	.220	.290	-1.9	2B(61): -4.3, SS(52): -1.6	-1.2
2014	CHR	AAA	22	494	60	19	6	7	57	36	84	16	4	.293/.349/.412	.249	.344	1.8	2B(64): -0.2, SS(44): 0.1	1.2
2014	CHA	MLB	22	104	6	5	0	0	5	3	25	1	1	.250/.269/.300	.221	.329	-1.5	2B(27): -3.4, SS(1): -0.1	-0.7
2015	CHR	AAA	23	137	17	10	0	2	17	4	28	5	2	.344/.368/.466	.279	.426	0.6	2B(26): -0.7, SS(3): 1.3	0.8
2015	CHA	MLB	23	420	40	23	1	5	31	19	81	2	2	.224/.268/.326	.218	.270	1.5	2B(117): -2.3	-0.8
2016	*CHA*	*MLB*	*24*	*178*	*19*	*8*	*1*	*2*	*14*	*9*	*35*	*3*	*1*	*.248/.292/.347*	*.230*	*.297*	*0.1*	*2B -1, SS 0*	*0.1*
2017	*CHA*	*MLB*	*25*	*424*	*42*	*18*	*2*	*5*	*37*	*22*	*86*	*7*	*3*	*.249/.294/.342*	*.230*	*.300*	*0.4*	*2B -3, SS 1*	*0.2*

Breakout: 6% Improve: 29% Collapse: 6% Attrition: 16% MLB: 55% *Comparables: Ruben Gotay, Alexi Amarista, Kolten Wong*

For better and for worse, the White Sox are an unstoppable manufacturer (and, bizarrely, also a pretty aggressive purchaser) of Sanchez-type players. There's not much power or plate discipline here, but there's a modicum of speed, average contact ability and a knack for finding gaps now and then. Sanchez's glove is a bit worse than one hopes such players' gloves will be; he's solely a second baseman, and then not a very good one. In the big picture, it's a big-league profile. It's not an especially helpful one.

Hector Sanchez C

Born: 11/17/89 Age: 26 Bats: B Throws: R Height: 6'0" Weight: 235

YEAR	TEAM	LVL	AGE	PA	R	2B	3B	HR	RBI	BB	K	SB	CS	AVG/OBP/SLG	TAv	BABIP	BRR	FRAA	WARP
2013	SFN	MLB	23	140	8	4	0	3	19	7	29	0	0	.248/.300/.349	.241	.296	-0.9	C(33): 2.0	0.4
2013	FRE	AAA	23	99	10	4	0	3	11	12	15	0	0	.271/.364/.424	.275	.294	-0.3	C(18): -0.8	0.4
2014	FRE	AAA	24	20	1	0	0	1	3	1	3	0	0	.158/.200/.316	.187	.133	-0.1	C(5): -0.0	-0.1
2014	SFN	MLB	24	177	8	8	0	3	28	8	55	0	1	.196/.237/.301	.208	.266	-0.2	C(45): 1.6, 1B(1): -0.3	-0.1
2015	SAC	AAA	25	152	18	6	0	4	14	9	25	0	0	.273/.318/.403	.256	.304	-2.1	C(30): -3.9	-0.1
2015	SFN	MLB	25	59	5	4	0	1	5	2	14	0	0	.179/.207/.304	.183	.220	-0.8	C(16): -1.5	-0.5
2016	*CHA*	*MLB*	*26*	*250*	*22*	*11*	*0*	*6*	*27*	*13*	*58*	*0*	*0*	*.235/.279/.363*	*.228*	*.284*	*-0.6*	*C -3*	*-0.1*
2017	*CHA*	*MLB*	*27*	*159*	*17*	*7*	*0*	*4*	*16*	*9*	*38*	*0*	*0*	*.227/.274/.356*	*.225*	*.276*	*-0.4*	*C -2*	*-0.2*

Breakout: 8% Improve: 27% Collapse: 17% Attrition: 25% MLB: 64% *Comparables: Jeff Mathis, Tony Cruz, Ronny Paulino*

Backup catchers are a fungible lot, and fair or not, durability and defense often determine their fates. Sanchez can endear himself to a manager as a switch-hitter with raw pop, but concussions derailed him in 2014 and a leg injury snatched his shot to fill in when Andrew Susac hit the shelf last year. The Maracay native also fails the second criterion with subpar blocking and framing, along with inconsistent footwork that impedes his strong arm. He's still young, but in the time it took you to read this three backups just like him sent the White Sox resumes.

YEAR	TEAM	P. COUNT	FRM RUNS	BLK RUNS	THRW RUNS	TOT RUNS
2013	FRE	2502	-0.3	-0.2	0.0	-0.5
2013	SFN	3590	2.4	-0.2	-0.1	2.1
2014	SFN	5051	2.5	-0.3	-0.5	1.7
2015	SAC	4506	-3.3	-0.2	-0.5	-4.0
2015	SFN	1578	-1.3	0.0	-0.1	-1.3
2016	*CHA*	*8553*	*-2.0*	*-0.4*	*-0.4*	*-2.8*
2017	*CHA*	*5431*	*-1.5*	*-0.3*	*-0.3*	*-2.1*

PITCHERS

Spencer Adams RHP

Born: 4/13/96 Age: 20 Bats: R Throws: R Height: 6'3" Weight: 171

YEAR	TEAM	LVL	AGE	W	L	SV	G	GS	IP	H	HR	BB/9	K/9	GB%	BABIP	WHIP	ERA	FIP	DRA	WARP	CFIP	MPH
2015	WNS	A+	19	3	0	0	5	5	29^{1}	31	1	2.1	7.1	49%	.323	1.30	2.15	2.95	3.34	0.5	92	
2015	KAN	A	19	9	5	0	19	19	100	111	7	1.0	6.6	52%	.311	1.22	3.24	3.29	3.15	2.4	85	
2016	*CHA*	*MLB*	*20*	*5*	*6*	*0*	*17*	*17*	*87*	*102*	*13*	*2.6*	*5.4*	*44%*	*.304*	*1.46*	*5.07*	*5.13*	*5.40*	*-0.3*	*128*	
2017	*CHA*	*MLB*	*21*	*7*	*10*	*0*	*26*	*26*	*152*	*181*	*24*	*2.4*	*5.1*	*44%*	*.304*	*1.46*	*5.11*	*5.10*	*5.44*	*-0.5*	*130*	

Breakout: 0% Improve: 0% Collapse: 0% Attrition: 0% MLB: 0% *Comparables: Hector Rondon, Henderson Alvarez, Kyle Ryan*

Having used their first pick of the 2014 draft on the highly polished, quick-to-the-majors arm of Carlos Rodon, the White Sox spent their next one on Adams, a projectable high schooler who is more polished and could be quicker to the majors than any of us foresaw. There are four pitches here, highlighted by a fastball-slider pairing that seems to set "late-inning difference maker" as a floor. Adams saw High-A ball for a significant stretch as a 19-year-old, and hung. The command is surprisingly advanced, and the reports on his makeup (especially competitive swagger) are strong. Finding this blend of risk and reward in the second round is how scouting directors end up (relatively) famous.

Matt Albers RHP

Born: 1/20/83 Age: 33 Bats: L Throws: R Height: 6'1" Weight: 225

YEAR	TEAM	LVL	AGE	W	L	SV	G	GS	IP	H	HR	BB/9	K/9	GB%	BABIP	WHIP	ERA	FIP	DRA	WARP	CFIP	MPH
2013	CLE	MLB	30	3	1	0	56	0	63	57	2	3.3	5.0	66%	.274	1.27	3.14	3.52	3.62	0.7	115	95.9
2014	HOU	MLB	31	0	0	0	8	0	10	10	0	2.7	7.2	53%	.333	1.30	0.90	2.76	3.54	0.1	99	96.2
2015	CHA	MLB	32	2	0	0	30	0	37^{1}	31	3	2.2	6.8	59%	.259	1.07	1.21	3.45	3.18	0.7	101	93.0
2016	*CHA*	*MLB*	*33*	*2*	*1*	*0*	*33*	*0*	35^{1}	*34*	*4*	*3.0*	*6.8*	*60%*	*.279*	*1.29*	*4.28*	*4.29*	*4.60*	*0.1*	*105*	
2017	*CHA*	*MLB*	*34*	*2*	*1*	*0*	*42*	*0*	*46*	*47*	*6*	*3.1*	*6.6*	*60%*	*.290*	*1.37*	*4.49*	*4.48*	*4.83*	*-0.1*	*110*	

Breakout: 29% Improve: 43% Collapse: 25% Attrition: 8% MLB: 89% *Comparables: Matt Lindstrom, Brad Ziegler, Bob Wickman*

Only Wade Davis has a lower ERA over the past two years than Albers, who has done it not by dominating so much as by building an impassable moat between third base and home. His strand rate last year, at 95 percent, was the league's best, and explains how he could climb so high on the ERA leaderboard despite the next *21* names all having lower FIPs than his. That said, his FIPs are also much improved since he added a changeup to the mix two years ago, and that first career save could come anytime.

Chris Beck RHP

Born: 9/4/90 Age: 25 Bats: R Throws: R Height: 6'3" Weight: 225

YEAR	TEAM	LVL	AGE	W	L	SV	G	GS	IP	H	HR	BB/9	K/9	GB%	BABIP	WHIP	ERA	FIP	DRA	WARP	CFIP	MPH
2013	BIR	AA	22	2	2	0	5	5	28	26	0	1.0	7.1	45%	.313	1.04	2.89	1.88	3.58	0.4	84	
2013	WNS	A+	22	11	8	0	21	21	118^{2}	117	11	3.2	4.3	59%	.275	1.34	3.11	4.76	5.21	0.2	118	
2014	CHR	AAA	23	1	3	0	7	7	33^{1}	36	1	3.5	7.6	49%	.324	1.47	4.05	3.42	4.41	0.3	94	
2014	BIR	AA	23	5	8	0	20	20	116^{2}	116	7	2.4	4.4	49%	.278	1.26	3.39	3.92				
2015	CHR	AAA	24	3	2	0	10	10	54^{1}	50	3	2.3	6.6	46%	.281	1.18	3.15	3.29	3.72	0.6	95	
2015	CHA	MLB	24	0	1	0	1	1	6	10	0	6.0	4.5	50%	.417	2.33	6.00	4.10	7.78	-0.2	113	94.5
2016	*CHA*	*MLB*	*25*	*4*	*4*	*0*	*28*	*10*	76^{1}	*81*	*8*	*3.1*	*5.3*	*46%*	*.290*	*1.41*	*4.62*	*4.56*	*4.92*	*0.1*	*116*	
2017	*CHA*	*MLB*	*26*	*5*	*7*	*0*	*18*	*18*	104^{2}	*116*	*13*	*3.2*	*5.4*	*46%*	*.297*	*1.46*	*4.81*	*4.79*	*5.12*	*0.0*	*121*	

Breakout: 20% Improve: 24% Collapse: 7% Attrition: 25% MLB: 37% *Comparables: Chaz Roe, Doug Mathis, D.J. Mitchell*

Elbow inflammation cut Beck's season short in mid-June. Before that happened, he'd built up some developmental momentum with a string of strong starts in the International League. He routinely touches the mid-90s with his fastball and has the body and delivery to do so as a starter. He even keeps that pitch down and induces groundballs. What he doesn't do is get pitches past good hitters, largely because neither his curveball nor his changeup has blossomed into anything like an out pitch. He's young, so there's time, but it's hard to improve feel for spin or an off-speed pitch while working through a balky elbow.

Tyler Danish RHP

Born: 9/12/94 Age: 21 Bats: R Throws: R Height: 6'0" Weight: 205

YEAR	TEAM	LVL	AGE	W	L	SV	G	GS	IP	H	HR	BB/9	K/9	GB%	BABIP	WHIP	ERA	FIP	DRA	WARP	CFIP	MPH
2014	WNS	A+	19	5	3	0	18	18	91^{2}	87	7	2.3	7.7	62%	.301	1.20	2.65	3.69	4.28	1.0	91	
2014	KAN	A	19	3	0	0	7	7	38	28	0	2.4	5.9	66%	.252	1.00	0.71	3.06	4.59	0.3	96	
2015	BIR	AA	20	8	12	0	26	26	142	175	13	3.8	5.7	56%	.347	1.65	4.50	4.60	5.72	-1.4	114	
2016	*CHA*	*MLB*	*21*	*6*	*8*	*0*	*23*	*23*	118^{2}	*136*	*15*	*3.7*	*5.4*	*55%*	*.307*	*1.56*	*5.05*	*5.05*	*5.30*	*-0.3*	*127*	
2017	*CHA*	*MLB*	*22*	*5*	*7*	*0*	*17*	*17*	100^{1}	*120*	*15*	*3.8*	*5.0*	*55%*	*.309*	*1.61*	*5.38*	*5.36*	*5.65*	*-0.6*	*137*	

Breakout: 0% Improve: 0% Collapse: 0% Attrition: 0% MLB: 0% *Comparables: Steve Garrison, Henderson Alvarez, Collin Balester*

Danish's cheese was a little too appetizing for Southern League hitters in 2015. He didn't miss enough bats with his sinker-slider blend, and troublingly, that problem only grew more pronounced as the season progressed. Danish has youth and a decent changeup on which to lean, but he's short, throws from a fairly low arm slot (with some unorthodox mechanics) and profiles as a guy who'll have platoon issues against good hitters—though, in fairness, he hasn't to this point. The White Sox pride themselves on working past such issues when they can, but Danish's future might well be in the bullpen. His is the sort of repertoire that most consistently plays up in relief.

John Danks LHP

Born: 4/15/85 Age: 31 Bats: L Throws: L Height: 6'1" Weight: 210

YEAR	TEAM	LVL	AGE	W	L	SV	G	GS	IP	H	HR	BB/9	K/9	GB%	BABIP	WHIP	ERA	FIP	DRA	WARP	CFIP	MPH
2013	CHR	AAA	28	1	0	0	3	3	15^{2}	13	1	6.9	8.0	49%	.286	1.60	3.45	4.93	5.01	0.0	118	
2013	CHA	MLB	28	4	14	0	22	22	138^{1}	151	28	1.8	5.8	42%	.283	1.29	4.75	5.09	4.63	0.5	114	92.0
2014	CHA	MLB	29	11	11	0	32	32	193^{2}	205	25	3.4	6.0	44%	.291	1.44	4.74	4.79	4.54	0.6	117	91.3
2015	CHA	MLB	30	7	15	0	30	30	177^{2}	195	24	2.8	6.3	40%	.305	1.41	4.71	4.46	4.79	0.5	110	92.2
2016	*CHA*	*MLB*	*31*	*10*	*11*	*0*	*29*	*29*	*174*	*182*	*23*	*2.8*	*6.5*	*41%*	*.292*	*1.35*	*4.54*	*4.54*	*4.85*	*0.6*	*114*	
2017	*CHA*	*MLB*	*32*	*9*	*10*	*0*	*26*	*26*	*156^{2}*	*174*	*24*	*2.7*	*6.3*	*41%*	*.301*	*1.42*	*4.74*	*4.73*	*5.06*	*0.1*	*120*	

Breakout: 19% Improve: 52% Collapse: 10% Attrition: 10% MLB: 92% *Comparables: Jason Vargas, Hal Newhouser, Pascual Perez*

Danks has settled comfortably (though White Sox fans would use a different adverb) into the space between average and replacement level, churning out three seasons of almost precisely half-win performance. The inspiration for the Danks Theory no longer has a reverse split. In fact, he's now so vulnerable to right-handed batters that he arguably requires exodus to bullpen work, where he can find his footing on the leeward side of platoon hostility. This isn't what one hopes for when one signs a starter to a five-year, $65 million extension, but in a sense, the fact that Danks is still racking up innings and not killing the team is a win.

No it's not.

But maybe a little.

Zach Duke LHP

Born: 4/19/83 Age: 33 Bats: L Throws: L Height: 6'2" Weight: 210

YEAR	TEAM	LVL	AGE	W	L	SV	G	GS	IP	H	HR	BB/9	K/9	GB%	BABIP	WHIP	ERA	FIP	DRA	WARP	CFIP	MPH
2013	LOU	AAA	30	2	0	2	26	0	27^{2}	19	2	1.6	11.1	52%	.274	0.87	1.30	2.34	3.37	0.4	65	
2013	CIN	MLB	30	0	1	0	14	0	10^{2}	8	1	1.7	5.9	41%	.226	0.94	0.84	3.49	-0.34	0.6	113	92.5
2013	WAS	MLB	30	1	1	0	12	1	20^{2}	31	2	3.5	4.8	54%	.367	1.89	8.71	4.52	9.47	-1.2	117	90.9
2014	MIL	MLB	31	5	1	0	74	0	58^{2}	49	3	2.6	11.4	60%	.322	1.12	2.45	2.11	3.01	1.1	72	92.2
2015	CHA	MLB	32	3	6	1	71	0	60^{2}	47	9	4.7	9.8	59%	.264	1.30	3.41	4.59	4.50	0.1	97	92.0
2016	*CHA*	*MLB*	*33*	*3*	*1*	*0*	*50*	*0*	*53*	*48*	*6*	*3.3*	*9.0*	*58%*	*.298*	*1.28*	*3.82*	*3.90*	*4.12*	*0.4*	*92*	
2017	*CHA*	*MLB*	*34*	*5*	*3*	*1*	*51*	*6*	*78^{1}*	*72*	*9*	*3.2*	*9.1*	*58%*	*.300*	*1.28*	*3.88*	*3.87*	*4.19*	*0.7*	*93*	

Breakout: 26% Improve: 44% Collapse: 11% Attrition: 11% MLB: 65% *Comparables: Scott Downs, D.J. Carrasco, Jean Machi*

Of the 252 pitchers who threw at least 1,000 pitches in 2015, only one threw a lower percentage of theirs through the zone than did Duke. Unfortunately for the nobleman, 219 pitchers got higher out-of-zone chase rates. Even as batters continued to struggle with Duke's new arm slot and more intense stuff, they found themselves walking in an eighth of their plate appearances against him. Late in the season, Duke scrapped his slider, and he's now quite close to being a true, traditional two-pitch reliever: sinker and curve. His success from here on out will depend on his ability to use the zone more without getting hit harder.

Jace Fry LHP

Born: 7/9/93 Age: 22 Bats: L Throws: L Height: 6'1" Weight: 190

YEAR	TEAM	LVL	AGE	W	L	SV	G	GS	IP	H	HR	BB/9	K/9	GB%	BABIP	WHIP	ERA	FIP	DRA	WARP	CFIP	MPH
2015	WNS	A+	21	1	8	0	10	10	52	60	1	2.9	6.8	54%	.339	1.48	3.63	2.98	3.84	0.5	97	
2016	*CHA*	*MLB*	*22*	*2*	*2*	*0*	*11*	*6*	*36*	*41*	*4*	*3.7*	*5.3*	*50%*	*.305*	*1.55*	*4.73*	*4.85*	*4.99*	*0.0*	*117*	
2017	*CHA*	*MLB*	*23*	*7*	*8*	*1*	*39*	*22*	*151^{1}*	*178*	*17*	*3.6*	*4.8*	*50%*	*.307*	*1.57*	*4.87*	*4.85*	*5.14*	*-0.1*	*122*	

Breakout: 0% Improve: 0% Collapse: 0% Attrition: 0% MLB: 0% *Comparables: Ricky Romero, Colin Rea, Cody Anderson*

Tommy John surgery shot a hole through the middle of Fry's college career, but he pitched well enough as a junior at Oregon State to be a draft prospect of some renown in 2014. The White Sox pounced on him in the third round, betting that being a short left-hander without any standout offering or plus velocity would be no impediment to a kid with a dream. He was 10 starts into nicely rewarding that investment, this summer, looking like he could be in Double-A by July, when Tommy John came back for him. It'll be late 2016 before he takes the mound again, and he'll now be fighting to make a relief career work.

Carson Fulmer RHP

Born: 12/13/93 Age: 22 Bats: R Throws: R Height: 6'1" Weight: 190

YEAR	TEAM	LVL	AGE	W	L	SV	G	GS	IP	H	HR	BB/9	K/9	GB%	BABIP	WHIP	ERA	FIP	DRA	WARP	CFIP	MPH
2015	WNS	A+	21	0	0	0	8	8	22	16	2	3.7	10.2	43%	.269	1.14	2.05	3.66	3.62	0.3	95	
2016	*CHA*	*MLB*	*22*	*2*	*3*	*0*	*9*	*9*	*33^{2}*	*34*	*4*	*4.4*	*7.6*	*38%*	*.301*	*1.50*	*4.66*	*4.73*	*4.92*	*0.1*	*116*	
2017	*CHA*	*MLB*	*23*	*4*	*7*	*0*	*26*	*26*	*156^{2}*	*164*	*20*	*4.2*	*7.5*	*38%*	*.306*	*1.51*	*4.71*	*4.69*	*4.97*	*0.2*	*117*	

Breakout: 0% Improve: 0% Collapse: 0% Attrition: 0% MLB: 0% *Comparables: Josh Lindblom, Adam Wilk, Ricky Romero*

Fulmer pitches fast, and that's a comment on more than his fastball velocity. Watching video of him can send one scrambling to fix the playback speed ("Surely I've got this on 1.5x," one might say, to one's wife, who doesn't care, but she's around, and this is what marriage is, talking to yourself, calling it a conversation), but for the most part, he hits his timing markers and isn't truly rushing anything. Once the ball leaves his hand, it sizzles at up to 97 mph, or snaps downward on a sharp, deep plane. It's worth rewinding and watching it again, maybe in slow motion.

Fulmer had the best season of any college starter and was probably the best pitcher in the class. The seven teams above the White Sox lacked the appetite for risk to take him, thanks to that hyper-speed delivery, his short stature and a few questions about his third pitch (a changeup). Given the organization with which he landed, though, it'd be no surprise if Fulmer at least reached the majors as a starter, and given his scouting report and track record, it'd be no surprise if he succeeds in that role.

Jordan Guerrero LHP

Born: 5/31/94 Age: 22 Bats: L Throws: L Height: 6'3" Weight: 190

YEAR	TEAM	LVL	AGE	W	L	SV	G	GS	IP	H	HR	BB/9	K/9	GB%	BABIP	WHIP	ERA	FIP	DRA	WARP	CFIP	MPH
2014	KAN	A	20	6	2	0	27	9	78	81	5	3.1	9.2	48%	.344	1.38	3.46	3.52	4.49	0.6	92	
2015	KAN	A	21	6	1	0	9	9	55^1	42	1	1.6	9.8	44%	.293	0.94	2.28	2.20	1.77	2.2	67	
2015	WNS	A+	21	7	3	0	16	16	93^2	82	6	2.0	8.5	45%	.298	1.10	3.56	3.04	2.42	2.6	81	
2016	CHA	MLB	22	6	6	1	34	16	108	112	13	3.2	7.4	39%	.304	1.39	4.38	4.37	4.70	0.5	109	
2017	CHA	MLB	23	6	6	0	28	17	121	130	16	3.2	6.9	39%	.305	1.43	4.59	4.57	4.92	0.2	115	

Breakout: 0% Improve: 0% Collapse: 0% Attrition: 0% MLB: 0% *Comparables: Sean Nolin, Simon Castro, Vincent Velasquez*

The White Sox lean toward bringing young players along quickly, but Guerrero came to them after an uneven senior year that included whispers of arm trouble, so they kept the southpaw on a slow simmer until 2015. Once they let the leash out, though, the Sox got to see an unqualified breakout. He doesn't throw hard enough to profile as a top-of-the-rotation arm, but his command and feel for a good changeup allowed him to mow down hitters at both levels of Class A in 2015. He's the rising star in a system fraught with promising but slow-developing arms.

Myles Jaye RHP

Born: 12/28/91 Age: 24 Bats: B Throws: R Height: 6'3" Weight: 170

YEAR	TEAM	LVL	AGE	W	L	SV	G	GS	IP	H	HR	BB/9	K/9	GB%	BABIP	WHIP	ERA	FIP	DRA	WARP	CFIP	MPH
2013	WNS	A+	21	9	6	0	20	20	118^1	122	8	3.3	6.8	51%	.312	1.40	4.11	4.02	4.80	0.7	103	
2013	KAN	A	21	4	1	0	7	7	41	36	2	3.7	8.1	55%	.301	1.29	2.20	3.70	4.41	0.3	99	
2014	WNS	A+	22	3	0	0	4	4	29	22	2	1.6	4.7	53%	.215	0.93	1.55	3.90	4.53	0.2	99	
2014	BIR	AA	22	4	12	0	24	24	132	146	10	3.6	5.0	46%	.311	1.51	5.32	4.47				
2015	BIR	AA	23	12	9	0	26	26	147^2	135	8	2.9	6.3	48%	.284	1.23	3.29	3.70	3.99	1.6	97	
2016	CHA	MLB	24	7	8	0	22	22	122^2	134	14	3.5	5.7	45%	.299	1.48	4.78	4.79	5.06	0.1	120	
2017	CHA	MLB	25	6	7	0	19	19	110^2	126	15	3.5	5.4	45%	.305	1.53	4.98	4.97	5.27	-0.2	126	

Breakout: 0% Improve: 0% Collapse: 0% Attrition: 0% MLB: 0% *Comparables: Alan Johnson, D.J. Mitchell, Williams Perez*

How many guys with some actual prospect sheen on them make 50 starts in Double-A? That's what the White Sox have had Jaye do over the past two seasons. Ask White Sox people, though, and they'll tell you the repeated level assignment was less about Jaye's struggles in 2014 than about the challenge they gave him by putting him in Birmingham so soon. Jaye was primarily a shortstop in high school and took a long time to find his footing as a pitcher in the pros, but the Sox like the raw package and love the concrete steps he took toward his ceiling as a back-end starter in 2015.

Dan Jennings LHP

Born: 4/17/87 Age: 29 Bats: L Throws: L Height: 6'3" Weight: 210

YEAR	TEAM	LVL	AGE	W	L	SV	G	GS	IP	H	HR	BB/9	K/9	GB%	BABIP	WHIP	ERA	FIP	DRA	WARP	CFIP	MPH
2013	MIA	MLB	26	2	4	0	47	0	40^2	39	1	3.5	8.4	49%	.328	1.35	3.76	2.65	3.60	0.5	96	94.3
2013	NWO	AAA	26	4	2	1	18	0	25	19	1	4.0	9.0	68%	.265	1.20	1.80	3.41	4.78	0.1	93	
2014	MIA	MLB	27	0	2	0	47	0	40^1	45	3	3.8	8.5	50%	.339	1.54	1.34	3.45	4.61	-0.1	103	94.5
2015	CHA	MLB	28	2	3	0	53	0	56^1	55	3	3.8	7.3	65%	.304	1.40	3.99	3.44	3.64	0.7	100	95.0
2016	CHA	MLB	29	3	1	0	50	0	53	53	6	3.4	7.7	59%	.302	1.38	4.20	4.26	4.51	0.2	101	
2017	CHA	MLB	30	2	1	1	48	0	49^2	51	6	3.4	7.6	59%	.306	1.42	4.27	4.25	4.58	0.1	103	

Breakout: 31% Improve: 52% Collapse: 24% Attrition: 25% MLB: 81% *Comparables: Evan Meek, Ramon Troncoso, Chad Qualls*

The story of Jennings' first season with Don Cooper as his pitching coach reads like that of a hundred other pitchers' first encounters with a dozen other famous pitching coaches: learned a sinker, induced a ton of groundballs, made only marginal improvements. Jennings still doesn't miss bats the way elite (or even above-average) relievers do, but at least he has some newfound tactical utility. If there's a tough lefty coming up in the seventh inning and you need a double play, Jennings is your man. In the other 140 games per year, his value is harder to articulate.

Erik Johnson RHP

Born: 12/30/89 Age: 26 Bats: R Throws: R Height: 6'3" Weight: 230

YEAR	TEAM	LVL	AGE	W	L	SV	G	GS	IP	H	HR	BB/9	K/9	GB%	BABIP	WHIP	ERA	FIP	DRA	WARP	CFIP	MPH
2013	BIR	AA	23	8	2	0	14	14	84^2	57	6	2.2	7.9	50%	.228	0.92	2.23	2.90	3.47	1.3	80	
2013	CHA	MLB	23	3	2	0	5	5	27^2	32	5	3.6	5.9	48%	.290	1.55	3.25	5.42	4.77	0.0	112	94.9
2013	CHR	AAA	23	4	1	0	10	10	57^1	43	1	3.0	8.9	48%	.295	1.08	1.57	2.59	3.88	0.4	83	
2014	CHR	AAA	24	5	7	0	20	20	105^2	136	11	4.6	5.4	45%	.346	1.80	6.73	5.19	5.26	-0.2	123	
2014	CHA	MLB	24	1	1	0	5	5	23^2	27	1	5.7	6.8	40%	.356	1.77	6.46	4.34	6.03	-0.4	112	92.4
2015	CHA	MLB	25	3	1	0	6	6	35	32	8	4.4	7.7	26%	.253	1.40	3.34	5.90	4.99	0.0	110	94.1
2015	CHR	AAA	25	11	8	0	23	22	132^2	108	5	2.8	9.2	42%	.293	1.12	2.37	2.57	1.71	4.9	69	
2016	CHA	MLB	26	8	8	0	24	24	136^2	131	15	3.3	7.7	38%	.293	1.33	4.10	4.17	4.41	1.2	101	
2017	CHA	MLB	27	8	8	0	24	24	140^1	136	17	3.5	7.9	38%	.295	1.36	4.25	4.24	4.57	0.9	105	

Breakout: 17% Improve: 36% Collapse: 23% Attrition: 27% MLB: 82% *Comparables: Jimmy Nelson, Adam Warren, David Phelps*

After a disastrous 2014 that left Johnson seemingly in danger of totally falling out of the picture, 2015 was... better. That's damning with faint praise, but better faint praise than none at all. (Right?) Johnson's ability to touch the mid-90s, at least as a starter, is gone.

His slider was once a high-80s bat misser that would start on the same plane as the heat and then just disappear; that pitch is gone, too. Johnson still throws a slider, but it now sits in the low-to-mid-80s, and he uses it more as a changer of speeds and eye levels than as an inducer of whiffs. The change has been good for his command profile, but it might not be enough to put him back on the map.

Nate Jones RHP

Born: 1/28/86 Age: 30 Bats: R Throws: R Height: 6'5" Weight: 220

YEAR	TEAM	LVL	AGE	W	L	SV	G	GS	IP	H	HR	BB/9	K/9	GB%	BABIP	WHIP	ERA	FIP	DRA	WARP	CFIP	MPH
2013	CHA	MLB	27	4	5	0	70	0	78	69	5	3.0	10.3	52%	.330	1.22	4.15	2.66	3.42	1.1	74	100.4
2014	CHA	MLB	28	0	0	0	2	0	0	2	0			0%	1.000				14.04		116	98.3
2015	CHA	MLB	29	2	2	0	19	0	19	12	5	2.8	12.8	49%	.206	0.95	3.32	4.63	3.52	0.3	77	100.0
2016	*CHA*	*MLB*	*30*	*3*	*1*	*0*	*55*	*0*	*57^2*	*51*	*6*	*3.0*	*10.1*	*50%*	*.302*	*1.21*	*3.47*	*3.43*	*3.77*	*0.8*	*81*	
2017	*CHA*	*MLB*	*31*	*3*	*1*	*2*	*53*	*0*	*57*	*51*	*7*	*3.1*	*9.7*	*50%*	*.298*	*1.24*	*3.69*	*3.68*	*4.01*	*0.5*	*87*	

Breakout: 22% Improve: 53% Collapse: 20% Attrition: 13% MLB: 88% *Comparables: Jason Frasor, Will Ohman, Brian Fuentes*

Jones' 2014 was the kind of injury nightmare from which hardly any pitcher can be expected to make it back. He had back surgery in May and Tommy John surgery in late July. The fact that he even returned to a big-league mound in August 2015, then, is a fairly major victory. The fact that he was still sitting 98 with his fastball and near 90 with his slider borders on miraculous. The fact that he struck out 27 and walked six in 19 appearances is downright ridiculous. This says as much about 2015 on the South Side as about Jones, but he was one of the best stories of the Sox's season.

Tommy Kahnle RHP

Born: 8/7/89 Age: 26 Bats: R Throws: R Height: 6'1" Weight: 235

YEAR	TEAM	LVL	AGE	W	L	SV	G	GS	IP	H	HR	BB/9	K/9	GB%	BABIP	WHIP	ERA	FIP	DRA	WARP	CFIP	MPH
2013	TRN	AA	23	1	3	15	46	0	60	38	4	6.8	11.1	45%	.254	1.38	2.85	3.97	4.87	0.0	109	
2014	COL	MLB	24	2	1	0	54	0	68^2	51	7	4.1	8.3	48%	.240	1.19	4.19	3.99	2.51	1.7	95	97.5
2015	ABQ	AAA	25	1	3	6	21	0	27	19	3	4.0	9.3	38%	.235	1.15	4.67	4.41	4.40	0.2	94	
2015	COL	MLB	25	0	1	2	36	0	33^1	31	3	7.6	10.5	59%	.329	1.77	4.86	4.51	4.42	0.1	99	99.1
2016	*CHA*	*MLB*	*26*	*2*	*1*	*0*	*36*	*0*	*38^2*	*33*	*4*	*4.5*	*9.2*	*50%*	*.278*	*1.35*	*4.28*	*4.12*	*4.57*	*0.1*	*105*	
2017	*CHA*	*MLB*	*27*	*2*	*1*	*1*	*31*	*0*	*40^2*	*34*	*4*	*4.9*	*9.6*	*50%*	*.278*	*1.37*	*4.21*	*4.19*	*4.49*	*0.1*	*103*	

Breakout: 22% Improve: 38% Collapse: 26% Attrition: 25% MLB: 71% *Comparables: Henry Rodriguez, Gary Majewski, Daniel Schlereth*

A year ago, Kahnle was a clear Rule 5 success, thriving in multi-inning stints to be, by Deserved Run Average, a top-30 reliever. Hitting cherries on a Rule 5er means the club is essentially playing with house money, but that didn't make Kahnle's step backward in 2015 any easier for the Rockies to stomach. He lost control of his four-seamer and all but junked his slider, forcing him to lean on a changeup and pitch backward—throwing, in one two-week stretch of August, 65 percent cambios. Batters walked against him at a Harper-ian rate, more than offsetting gains to his K and GB rates. Indeed, no pitcher with at least 30 innings had a worse walk rate than Kahnle, who was optioned back to Triple-A by the end of August and traded to Chicago in the winter.

Robin Leyer RHP

Born: 3/13/93 Age: 23 Bats: R Throws: R Height: 6'2" Weight: 175

YEAR	TEAM	LVL	AGE	W	L	SV	G	GS	IP	H	HR	BB/9	K/9	GB%	BABIP	WHIP	ERA	FIP	DRA	WARP	CFIP	MPH
2014	KAN	A	21	5	9	0	25	25	134^2	144	9	2.9	5.7	44%	.317	1.39	3.81	4.25	4.94	0.7	108	
2015	WNS	A+	22	3	6	0	16	16	83^2	79	7	2.8	6.9	42%	.275	1.25	4.30	3.81	4.07	0.6	99	
2015	BIR	AA	22	3	1	0	12	6	38^1	42	3	4.0	7.0	34%	.328	1.54	4.93	4.16	4.69	0.1	103	
2016	*CHA*	*MLB*	*23*	*6*	*8*	*0*	*21*	*21*	*103*	*118*	*13*	*3.9*	*5.5*	*35%*	*.305*	*1.57*	*5.12*	*5.06*	*5.38*	*-0.3*	*128*	
2017	*CHA*	*MLB*	*24*	*5*	*6*	*0*	*17*	*17*	*103*	*123*	*14*	*4.1*	*5.6*	*35%*	*.315*	*1.65*	*5.24*	*5.22*	*5.51*	*-0.4*	*131*	

Breakout: 0% Improve: 0% Collapse: 0% Attrition: 0% MLB: 0% *Comparables: Brett Sinkbeil, Ryan Cook, Chris Heston*

Scouts are split (more than split, really; utterly non-committal) on the question of whether there's a useful breaking ball in Leyer's arm, which is peculiar, because after two full, healthy seasons it's not like anyone is hurting for looks at the guy, and its not like a guy with his fastball is ever under the radar. If there is a breaking pitch coming, it hasn't shown up yet, and Leyer isn't missing many bats without one. Maybe the answer is to let the life in the arm work for him, without challenging him to develop a brand-new feel for spin, and just add a cutter. If that happens, and if the pitch takes, Leyer is a closer in the making.

Thaddius Lowry RHP

Born: 10/4/94 Age: 21 Bats: R Throws: R Height: 6'4" Weight: 215

YEAR	TEAM	LVL	AGE	W	L	SV	G	GS	IP	H	HR	BB/9	K/9	GB%	BABIP	WHIP	ERA	FIP	DRA	WARP	CFIP	MPH
2014	KAN	A	19	4	6	0	17	17	87	103	5	3.0	4.4	46%	.328	1.52	4.76	4.52	5.21	0.2	118	
2015	KAN	A	20	12	8	0	26	26	150^2	158	8	2.4	5.6	47%	.306	1.31	4.48	3.88	4.53	1.1	100	
2016	*CHA*	*MLB*	*21*	*6*	*8*	*0*	*21*	*21*	*112^2*	*136*	*16*	*3.6*	*4.3*	*39%*	*.305*	*1.61*	*5.44*	*5.46*	*5.71*	*-0.8*	*137*	
2017	*CHA*	*MLB*	*22*	*5*	*7*	*0*	*19*	*19*	*109*	*137*	*17*	*3.6*	*4.3*	*39%*	*.311*	*1.65*	*5.54*	*5.53*	*5.82*	*-0.8*	*140*	

Breakout: 0% Improve: 0% Collapse: 0% Attrition: 0% MLB: 0% *Comparables: Ryan Webb, Osiris Matos, Andrew Faulkner*

Through his age-20 season, Lowry already has the better part of two years in full-season ball under his belt. After starting to show better consistency in 2015, he's ready for an assignment to the Carolina League. Hitters there will see a very big human with a sinker that can touch 95, a slider that mimics the fastball's action well through release, and a changeup that will remind them this is still a high school catcher with a lot of tightening up left to do. There doesn't appear to be front-line upside, but with his arm strength and workhorse size Lowry feels like a potential mid-rotation starter.

Jake Petricka RHP

Born: 6/5/88 Age: 28 Bats: R Throws: R Height: 6'5" Weight: 205

YEAR	TEAM	LVL	AGE	W	L	SV	G	GS	IP	H	HR	BB/9	K/9	GB%	BABIP	WHIP	ERA	FIP	DRA	WARP	CFIP	MPH
2013	CHA	MLB	25	1	1	0	16	0	19^1	20	0	4.7	4.7	64%	.312	1.55	3.26	3.75	3.50	0.3	115	96.4
2013	CHR	AAA	25	2	0	1	10	0	15^1	9	0	4.1	10.0	60%	.237	1.04	1.17	2.36	4.09	0.1	91	
2013	BIR	AA	25	3	0	0	21	1	39^1	36	1	4.1	9.4	57%	.350	1.37	2.06	2.61	3.73	0.3	89	
2014	CHA	MLB	26	1	6	14	67	0	73	67	3	4.1	6.8	65%	.299	1.37	2.96	3.63	3.40	1.0	106	97.2
2015	CHA	MLB	27	4	3	2	62	0	52	56	2	3.1	5.7	66%	.325	1.42	3.63	3.43	3.96	0.5	110	97.2
2016	*CHA*	*MLB*	*28*	*3*	*1*	*0*	*50*	*0*	*53*	*55*	*6*	*3.5*	*6.9*	*65%*	*.307*	*1.43*	*4.30*	*4.47*	*4.61*	*0.1*	*105*	
2017	*CHA*	*MLB*	*29*	*3*	*2*	*3*	*42*	*5*	70^2	*73*	*7*	*3.4*	*7.0*	*65%*	*.306*	*1.41*	*4.23*	*4.21*	*4.53*	*0.3*	*103*	

Breakout: 28% Improve: 46% Collapse: 14% Attrition: 26% MLB: 72% *Comparables: Chad Qualls, Bryan Morris, Jared Hughes*

Petricka is Seth Maness without the good press: a sinker-mad right-handed middle reliever with a big platoon split and a bigger groundball rate. They even share the quirk of a surname that looks easy to pronounce but isn't (that's Pet-RICH-ka). Of course, there are two perfectly good reasons why Maness is more famous. One: He's gotten big outs in the playoffs, while Petricka's never been there. Two: Maness has good, or at least average, control. Petricka is all over the place. Unless Item Two changes, Petricka will remain a much more limited asset than Maness, and a much, much more anonymous one.

Zach Putnam RHP

Born: 7/3/87 Age: 28 Bats: R Throws: R Height: 6'2" Weight: 225

YEAR	TEAM	LVL	AGE	W	L	SV	G	GS	IP	H	HR	BB/9	K/9	GB%	BABIP	WHIP	ERA	FIP	DRA	WARP	CFIP	MPH
2013	CHN	MLB	25	0	0	0	5	0	3^1	9	1	0.0	10.8	53%	.571	2.70	18.90	4.52	11.55	-0.3	100	92.4
2013	IOW	AAA	25	1	1	4	17	0	19^1	20	0	2.8	10.2	73%	.364	1.34	3.26	2.22	4.43	0.2	81	
2014	CHA	MLB	26	5	3	6	49	0	54^2	39	2	3.3	7.6	56%	.257	1.08	1.98	3.10	2.16	1.6	95	91.9
2015	CHA	MLB	27	3	3	0	49	0	48^2	42	7	4.4	11.8	47%	.310	1.36	4.07	4.07	4.44	0.2	84	92.4
2016	*CHA*	*MLB*	*28*	*2*	*1*	*0*	*46*	*0*	48^1	*43*	*5*	*3.5*	*9.8*	*50%*	*.297*	*1.28*	*3.76*	*3.74*	*4.06*	*0.5*	*88*	
2017	*CHA*	*MLB*	*29*	*3*	*1*	*2*	*48*	*0*	53^2	*45*	*6*	*3.4*	*10.1*	*50%*	*.288*	*1.23*	*3.57*	*3.56*	*3.86*	*0.6*	*83*	

Breakout: 31% Improve: 46% Collapse: 20% Attrition: 18% MLB: 78% *Comparables: Mark Melancon, Evan Meek, Derrick Turnbow*

Putnam doesn't throw overwhelmingly hard, but since arriving on the South Side in early 2014 he's gone to extremely heavy splitter usage, and batters haven't solved that pitch yet. In 2015, he threw the splitter over 63 percent of the time, and nearly a quarter of those offerings (not just the ones batters swung at) resulted in swings and misses. There's nothing else he does especially well, but if he can even maintain this skill he's a good middle reliever.

Jose Quintana LHP

Born: 1/24/89 Age: 27 Bats: R Throws: L Height: 6'1" Weight: 220

YEAR	TEAM	LVL	AGE	W	L	SV	G	GS	IP	H	HR	BB/9	K/9	GB%	BABIP	WHIP	ERA	FIP	DRA	WARP	CFIP	MPH
2013	CHA	MLB	24	9	7	0	33	33	200	188	23	2.5	7.4	44%	.283	1.22	3.51	3.85	3.78	2.7	93	93.9
2014	CHA	MLB	25	9	11	0	32	32	200^1	197	10	2.3	8.0	47%	.318	1.24	3.32	2.84	3.37	3.5	84	93.9
2015	CHA	MLB	26	9	10	0	32	32	206^1	218	16	1.9	7.7	48%	.327	1.27	3.36	3.15	4.21	2.0	89	94.1
2016	*CHA*	*MLB*	*27*	*12*	*10*	*0*	*31*	*31*	195^1	*189*	*19*	*2.1*	*7.9*	*47%*	*.299*	*1.20*	*3.52*	*3.54*	*3.83*	*3.0*	*83*	
2017	*CHA*	*MLB*	*28*	*11*	*9*	*0*	*29*	*29*	180^2	*176*	*19*	*1.7*	*8.0*	*47%*	*.302*	*1.17*	*3.36*	*3.36*	*3.66*	*3.1*	*79*	

Breakout: 21% Improve: 45% Collapse: 26% Attrition: 12% MLB: 93% *Comparables: Adam Wainwright, Joe Blanton, Johnny Cueto*

Entering 2015, Quintana didn't have a lot of hurdles left to clear in his quest to establish himself as a no. 2 starter. He needed mostly to be more consistent from one start to the next, and to get ahead of opposing hitters a bit more often. He went out and did both, posting just one Game Score south of 32 (and none south of 34 after April), turning in 25 Quality Starts, and throwing a strike on the first pitch against 68.9 percent of batters he faced. He threw his curveball at a career-high rate, and batters showed no sign of warming to it with the increased exposure. Quintana might be the best recovering minor-league free agent in baseball history.

David Robertson RHP

Born: 4/9/85 Age: 31 Bats: R Throws: R Height: 5'11" Weight: 195

YEAR	TEAM	LVL	AGE	W	L	SV	G	GS	IP	H	HR	BB/9	K/9	GB%	BABIP	WHIP	ERA	FIP	DRA	WARP	CFIP	MPH
2013	NYA	MLB	28	5	1	3	70	0	66^1	51	5	2.4	10.4	52%	.287	1.04	2.04	2.64	2.63	1.6	70	94.6
2014	NYA	MLB	29	4	5	39	63	0	64^1	45	7	3.2	13.4	47%	.288	1.06	3.08	2.71	2.64	1.5	64	94.4
2015	CHA	MLB	30	6	5	34	60	0	63^1	46	7	1.8	12.2	38%	.275	0.93	3.41	2.49	2.77	1.5	63	94.7
2016	*CHA*	*MLB*	*31*	*3*	*1*	*37*	*59*	*0*	62^2	*50*	*7*	*2.7*	*11.5*	*42%*	*.293*	*1.10*	*3.12*	*3.15*	*3.44*	*1.1*	*69*	
2017	*CHA*	*MLB*	*32*	*3*	*1*	*40*	*63*	*0*	62^1	*53*	*8*	*2.8*	*11.0*	*42%*	*.299*	*1.16*	*3.32*	*3.31*	*3.66*	*0.8*	*75*	

Breakout: 24% Improve: 38% Collapse: 29% Attrition: 11% MLB: 92% *Comparables: Ryne Duren, Jose Valverde, Michael Gonzalez*

Robertson posted a career-low walk rate and racked up the strikeouts yet again in 2015. Free of Yankee Stadium, he allowed himself to use the upper half of the zone a bit more often, and his flyball rate rose. He's still a cutter-curveball guy, which is a unique and aesthetically delightful blend. One red flag: Robertson's velocity dropped in the second half, and his numbers went the wrong direction in consequence. Robertson's a reliever over 30, so despite his good track record benefit of the doubt is in short supply here. He'll need to show that he's his usual, healthy self in spring training.

Carlos Rodon LHP

Born: 12/10/92 Age: 23 Bats: L Throws: L Height: 6'3" Weight: 235

YEAR	TEAM	LVL	AGE	W	L	SV	G	GS	IP	H	HR	BB/9	K/9	GB%	BABIP	WHIP	ERA	FIP	DRA	WARP	CFIP	MPH
2014	CHR	AAA	21	0	0	0	3	3	12	9	0	6.0	13.5	42%	.346	1.42	3.00	2.61	4.01	0.2	80	
2015	CHR	AAA	22	1	0	0	2	2	10	8	0	3.6	11.7	42%	.333	1.20	3.60	2.36	2.81	0.2	84	
2015	CHA	MLB	22	9	6	0	26	23	139^{1}	130	11	4.6	9.0	49%	.315	1.44	3.75	3.84	4.49	0.9	101	97.1
2016	*CHA*	*MLB*	*23*	*9*	*9*	*0*	*28*	*28*	*148^{1}*	*137*	*15*	*3.9*	*8.9*	*49%*	*.301*	*1.36*	*4.02*	*4.04*	*4.31*	*1.4*	*99*	
2017	*CHA*	*MLB*	*24*	*9*	*9*	*0*	*27*	*27*	*164^{2}*	*154*	*19*	*3.8*	*8.7*	*49%*	*.298*	*1.36*	*4.11*	*4.09*	*4.41*	*1.2*	*102*	

Breakout: 27% Improve: 64% Collapse: 22% Attrition: 7% MLB: 97% *Comparables: Scott Kazmir, Curt Simmons, Rich Harden*

Rodon didn't demonstrate the command he will need to dominate in the majors during his rookie campaign, but there's no denying the progress he did show. The left-hander developed his four-seamer and sinker into distinct, equally useful, significant offerings, and he began to trust his changeup enough to keep right-handed hitters honest. That took him from a pitcher with only two surefire big-league pitches to one with four, and given the closer-caliber sexiness of his original heater and slider, that's a scary proposition. Most of the role-related risk in Rodon's profile is now gone, and all that's left is to continue the refinements he made in his first full year under Don Cooper's tutelage. (No, "Don Cooper's tutelage" is not officially required text in anything written about the White Sox.)

Chris Sale LHP

Born: 3/30/89 Age: 27 Bats: L Throws: L Height: 6'6" Weight: 180

YEAR	TEAM	LVL	AGE	W	L	SV	G	GS	IP	H	HR	BB/9	K/9	GB%	BABIP	WHIP	ERA	FIP	DRA	WARP	CFIP	MPH
2013	CHA	MLB	24	11	14	0	30	30	214^{1}	184	23	1.9	9.5	47%	.289	1.07	3.07	3.20	3.12	4.6	71	97.1
2014	CHA	MLB	25	12	4	0	26	26	174	129	13	2.0	10.8	43%	.280	0.97	2.17	2.60	2.58	4.7	63	97.5
2015	CHA	MLB	26	13	11	0	31	31	208^{2}	185	23	1.8	11.8	43%	.323	1.09	3.41	2.70	3.43	4.0	64	98.4
2016	*CHA*	*MLB*	*27*	*13*	*9*	*0*	*30*	*30*	*201*	*163*	*21*	*1.9*	*11.0*	*44%*	*.292*	*1.02*	*2.89*	*2.94*	*3.20*	*4.6*	*63*	
2017	*CHA*	*MLB*	*28*	*13*	*10*	*0*	*31*	*31*	*195*	*160*	*22*	*1.9*	*10.6*	*44%*	*.289*	*1.03*	*3.03*	*3.02*	*3.35*	*4.4*	*68*	

Breakout: 25% Improve: 56% Collapse: 19% Attrition: 5% MLB: 98% *Comparables: Sam McDowell, CC Sabathia, Felix Hernandez*

If it weren't for Max Scherzer (who got to face pitchers), Sale would have set a record in 2015. He allowed a 75.9-percent contact rate on pitches in the strike zone, a number bested (among starters) only by Scherzer since the dawn of the PITCHf/x Era. That's the kind of pitcher Sale has become: capable of pounding the zone without fear, and still missing bats at a stunning rate. He did give up a bit more power and hard contact than is his custom, but so many batters made no contact at all that it didn't really matter. Oh, and despite the terrifying delivery and the sky-high pitch counts, he made a career-high 31 starts, without incident.

Jacob Turner RHP

Born: 5/21/91 Age: 25 Bats: R Throws: R Height: 6'5" Weight: 215

YEAR	TEAM	LVL	AGE	W	L	SV	G	GS	IP	H	HR	BB/9	K/9	GB%	BABIP	WHIP	ERA	FIP	DRA	WARP	CFIP	MPH
2013	NWO	AAA	22	3	4	0	10	10	56^{1}	59	7	2.2	5.6	54%	.284	1.30	4.47	4.85	5.16	0.3	106	
2013	MIA	MLB	22	3	8	0	20	20	118	116	11	4.1	5.9	48%	.285	1.44	3.74	4.40	4.70	0.3	123	94.6
2014	MIA	MLB	23	4	7	0	20	12	78^{1}	106	8	2.6	6.2	52%	.368	1.65	5.97	3.97	5.82	-1.0	115	95.6
2014	JUP	A+	23	1	1	0	2	2	11	7	1	0.8	8.2	69%	.214	0.73	2.45	3.03	3.88	0.1	84	
2014	CHN	MLB	23	2	4	0	8	6	34^{2}	42	4	2.6	4.4	49%	.322	1.50	6.49	4.49	4.71	0.0	124	95.0
2016	*CHA*	*MLB*	*25*	*2*	*1*	*0*	*29*	*2*	*39*	*42*	*5*	*3.2*	*5.9*	*51%*	*.294*	*1.43*	*4.74*	*4.78*	*5.06*	*0.0*	*118*	
2017	*CHA*	*MLB*	*26*	*5*	*6*	*0*	*15*	*15*	*91^{1}*	*97*	*12*	*3.1*	*6.1*	*51%*	*.295*	*1.41*	*4.64*	*4.62*	*4.95*	*0.2*	*116*	

Breakout: 25% Improve: 50% Collapse: 20% Attrition: 22% MLB: 89% *Comparables: Zach Duke, Casey Janssen, Tommy Hunter*

A strained right flexor in his elbow sabotaged Turner's bounceback hopes for the 2015 season. He made all of two starts in the minor leagues before hitting the DL for the rest of the year. Having thus failed to crack the Cubs roster, he'll try again this year 10 miles to the south. Unfortunately for him, Turner finds himself once again trying to break into one of the stronger rotations in the league. If he's healthy, there's reason to believe in his talent: He was the no. 9 overall pick and a top-25 prospect three years running; he has shown the ability to avoid the free pass and get grounders; and he isn't velocityless. What he hasn't done, even in this whiffy era, is miss bats. All the other stuff falls away if he's going to post strikeout rates that would've been pedestrian in the '90s.

Lineouts

Hitters

NAME	POS	TEAM	LVL	AGE	PA	R	2B	3B	HR	RBI	BB	K	SB	CS	AVG/OBP/SLG	TAv	BABIP	BRR	FRAA	WARP
Keon Barnum	1B	WNS	A+	22	428	40	24	0	9	67	35	112	0	1	.257/.322/.390	.256	.335	-3.3	1B(96): -8.6	-1.0
Rob Brantly	C	BIR	AA	25	121	13	6	1	4	22	3	14	0	1	.325/.347/.496	.290	.343	-1.5	C(29): -3.8	0.4
	C	CHA	MLB	25	36	3	1	0	1	6	2	8	0	0	.121/.167/.242	.154	.120	0.0	C(14): -2.4	-0.5
	C	CHR	AAA	25	94	11	3	0	4	16	5	17	0	0	.291/.319/.465	.268	.309	-1.3	C(14): -0.6	0.2
Nick Delmonico	3B	BIR	AA	22	253	26	24	0	3	26	25	52	2	1	.238/.313/.386	.261	.292	1.1	3B(59): 6.7	1.7
	3B	KAN	A	22	22	4	1	1	1	8	1	4	0	0	.400/.409/.700	.458	.438	-0.5	3B(4): 0.4	0.5
Adam Engel	OF	WNS	A+	23	608	90	23	9	7	43	62	132	65	11	.251/.335/.369	.259	.321	10.3	CF(136): -0.3	2.9
Leury Garcia	3B	CHA	MLB	24	15	0	0	0	0	1	1	7	1	0	.214/.267/.214	.171	.429	0.7	CF(4): -0.5, SS(3): -0.1	-0.1
	3B	CHR	AAA	24	385	57	19	3	3	31	20	66	30	12	.298/.340/.395	.260	.357	3.0	SS(43): 0.3, CF(22): 5.7	2.3
J.B. Shuck	LF	CHA	MLB	28	165	15	8	2	0	15	16	16	7	5	.266/.340/.350	.263	.295	1.3	RF(27): -0.3, CF(11): 0.6	0.6
Kevan Smith	C	CHR	AAA	27	361	41	13	2	6	36	29	66	0	1	.260/.330/.370	.246	.309	-1.5	C(93): -7.9	0.1

Jhoandro Alfaro looks like his brother Jorge, only in some squashed video format that makes everything shorter, wider and worse. ❖ **Keon Barnum** is a really big guy with a really big guy's defensive profile but a regular-sized guy's power production. ❖ Catchers develop late, and there's promise in his past, but the failures at the plate are piling up for **Rob Brantly**. ❖ **Nick Delmonico** ran into a developmental brick wall almost the moment he was traded in mid-2013, and spraypainting a tunnel on that wall hasn't worked. ❖ **Adam Engel** is an absolute burner with an idea of the strike zone, but needs to pass the Double-A test at the plate before things get real. ❖ **Leury Garcia** still has a chance to be a helpful big-league utility man, but if that's going to happen, his bat must improve before his speed goes. And speed goes fast. ❖ **J.B. Shuck** is half of a good corner outfielder, and half of a pretty good buddy cop show. ❖ **Kevan Smith** is a former college QB, current minor-league depth piece and future coach or instructor. Somewhere between the present and the near-certain future lies the hazy possibility that he's a backup backstop in the majors.

Pitchers

NAME	TEAM	LVL	AGE	W	L	SV	G	GS	IP	H	HR	BB/9	K/9	GB%	BABIP	WHIP	ERA	FIP	FRA	WARP	CFIP	MPH
Scott Carroll	CHR	AAA	30	7	4	0	16	16	83	85	8	3.1	4.9	56%	.278	1.37	3.47	4.45	5.36	-0.7	115	
	CHA	MLB	30	1	1	0	18	0	36^{2}	40	2	3.2	6.6	60%	.325	1.45	3.44	3.65	4.81	0.0	107	92.2
Matt Cooper	WNS	A+	23	1	0	1	8	0	12^{2}	11	0	2.1	8.5	40%	.297	1.11	1.42	2.07	3.15	0.2	90	
	KAN	A	23	3	0	11	30	0	39^{2}	20	2	2.0	14.5	45%	.247	0.73	1.59	1.59	0.02	2.2	45	
Zack Erwin	KAN	A	21	0	2	0	7	3	19	15	0	1.9	7.1	51%	.263	1.00	1.89	2.69	4.00	0.2	94	
Nolan Sanburn	BIR	AA	23	0	2	2	22	1	30	26	1	6.9	9.0	64%	.287	1.63	6.60	4.14	5.58	-0.4	111	
Daniel Webb	CHR	AAA	25	2	1	2	18	0	28^{1}	25	3	4.8	7.6	60%	.272	1.41	3.81	4.64	5.12	-0.3	111	
	CHA	MLB	25	1	0	0	27	0	30	41	3	6.6	6.6	50%	.373	2.10	6.30	5.24	6.22	-0.5	124	97.2
Michael Ynoa	WNS	A+	23	0	2	6	28	0	38	37	2	3.8	9.5	44%	.337	1.39	2.61	3.65	3.70	0.3	95	

Scott Carroll was Kyle Orton's backup quarterback at Purdue, which still has a chance to be the first line of his obituary. ❖ **Matt Cooper** appears to launch the ball out of his own right ear, which positively melted the young players in the low minors but won't scare more advanced hitters. ❖ **Jesse Crain**'s stuff is so good that he merits a passing mention here despite two full seasons (and counting) lost to shoulder problems. ❖ It's early, but **Zack Erwin**'s long levers and strong start in pro ball suggest that the White Sox found something with their fourth-round pick. ❖ **Nolan Sanburn**'s excellent velocity won't help him if he doesn't rediscover his command. ❖ **Daniel Webb** has the whiff rate and the groundball profile to be a useful reliever, and the walk rate to be a *really* good leadoff hitter. ❖ **Michael Ynoa** is still big, oft-injured and lacking nuance, but he's pitched well in relief the past two years and is inching toward the majors. This is his seventh book comment; Corey Kluber has six.

Manager

Robin Ventura

YEAR	TEAM	W	L	Pythag +/-	Avg PC	100+ P	120+ P	QS	BQS	REL	REL w Zero R	IBB	PH	PH Avg	PH HR	SB2	CS2	SB3	CS3	SAC Att	SAC%	POS SAC	Squeeze	Swing	In Play
2013	CHA	63	99	-3	100.5	96	4	90	3	470	389	24	67	.125	1	102	41	2	1	27	70.4	15	0	315	102
2014	CHA	73	89	3	100.0	91	4	89	5	453	332	42	72	.290	1	81	33	4	2	28	67.9	18	0	276	80
2015	CHA	76	86	5	102.2	105	2	98	5	414	329	34	109	.198	2	68	39	0	3	42	71.4	27	1	296	101

In most cases where an expensive, veteran-laden team fails to meet expectations, the manager takes the fall; in Chicago, it was the bench coach. Rick Hahn elected to keep Ventura around, choosing instead to dismiss Mark Parent. Hahn cited Ventura's communication skills, growth potential and outside-the-game management as pros, but admitted that Ventura's in-game work hasn't met expectations—a surprisingly frank assessment in the era of executive prattle.

Hahn didn't specify what about Ventura's tactical choices were unsatisfactory to him, possibly because there were too many to pick through. The White Sox were a poor baserunning club (they made the most outs on the basepaths), a poor fielding club (they had the third-lowest defensive efficiency), a poor hitting club (they had the lowest team True Average) and so on. Placing all the team's ills and ails on Ventura would be unfair, but he probably deserves the blame for *some* of it.

Something else Ventura deserves blame for is his reckless approach to pitcher workloads. Remember, the White Sox' playoff odds dipped below 5 percent in mid-June and never rebounded; this was a team that knew it was playing for the future before the Futures Game took place. So it's concerning that Ventura was the only manager who allowed his starters to turn over lineups more than twice in more than 30 percent of their games. What's more is the White Sox led the majors in starts exceeding 120 pitches, with seven—no other team topped four—and had *four* pitchers finish in the top 13 in the American League in average pitch count: Chris Sale (second), Jose Quintana (fifth), Jeff Samardzija (sixth) and Carlos Rodon (13th). Makes you wonder how many more pitches Ventura would have demanded if the White Sox were in the race.

Maybe you can excuse three-fourths of the quartet because they were veterans with track records and certain expectations. But Rodon? He was 22 years old and less than a year into his career when Ventura had him work past the century mark in four consecutive starts (he completed 22 innings in those games). Rodon was the youngest qualified pitcher in the majors to average more than 100 pitches, with 24-year-old Gerrit Cole (in his *third* big-league season) finishing second. There's a time and a place to teach a starter how to work deep into games; that time and place for Rodon was not in 2015.

This isn't meant to resemble the PAP-bleating of yesteryear, either. There's much we don't know about pitcher workloads and stress-management levels—much that Don Cooper and the White Sox' ace medical staff *do* know. Rodon could have a long, injury-free career. But from the outside, Ventura's decision to ride Rodon so hard appears to be the latest in a line of questionable decision-making. Perhaps Hahn is correct and Ventura can improve upon his flaws. As of right now, though, it seems more likely that the White Sox will be conducting managerial interviews come October.

CINCINNATI REDS

Essay by Russell Carleton

Player comments by Ken Funck and BP authors

Let's preview the 2016 Reds season: It's going to be rough.

Those are the only five words you really need to know.

Now, moving on to the only question worth asking about the 2016 Reds: Should they trade Joey Votto? It's a weird thing to ask when Votto has been a Redleg all of his baseball life and the team recently signed him to a major long-term extension with a no-trade clause that could keep him in Cincinnati through the entirety of his 30s. In fact, Votto is signed for the next eight years—with a team option for the 2024 season, just to be safe—and in each of those years, he will take home a check for north of $20 million for his efforts. It's good work if you can get it.

On top of that, Votto is in the gravitational field of the "best player in baseball" discussion. Since and including his 2010 MVP season, he has finished in the top 10 in WARP among NL hitters in five out of six seasons, the exception being his injury-riddled 2014, and even then he was still a top-25 hitter in the league per True Average. Votto will be 32 on Opening Day 2016, generally considered past the peak age for hitters, but if he's going to decline, it's going to be from quite a height. If Votto has a few reasonably good seasons—not MVP level, just pretty good—he starts to enter the conversation for the Hall of Fame. In some sense, he becomes this generation's Todd Helton. Why would the Reds *want* to trade someone like that?

Of course, to everything there is a season and a time to every trade rumor under heaven. The Reds traded Johnny Cueto last year, and everyone understood why. Cueto was in the final year of his contract and the Reds were obviously in bad shape heading into the trade deadline. They dealt him to the Royals and all he got was a lousy World Series ring. It doesn't take a rocket scientist to figure out which veterans have expiring contracts and who would make a good trade candidate this season. Expect to see a few more trades and for the Reds to stockpile a few more prospects in return.

The Reds have already shown that they are going for a youth movement, essentially ending last season with an all-rookie starting rotation of Anthony DeSclafani, Raisel Iglesias, Keyvius Sampson, John Lamb, Brandon Finnegan and Michael Lorenzen. Billy Hamilton and Eugenio Suarez have become regulars. It makes sense that they might

REDS PROSPECTUS

2015 W-L: 64-98, 5TH IN NL CENTRAL

Pythag	.425	27th	DER	.703	15th
RS/G	3.95	26th	B-Age	29.5	27th
RA/G	4.65	25th	P-Age	27.1	4th
TAv	.262	14th	Salary	$115.4M	16th
BRR	1.95	16th	M$/MW	$6.6M	2nd
TAv-P	.277	27th	DL Days	946	14th
FIP	4.26	25th	$ on DL	19%	20th

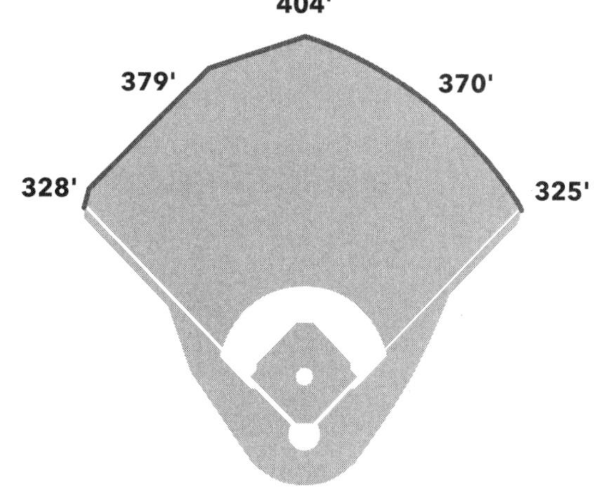

Outfield wall profile: **8'** to **12'**

Three-Year Park Factors

Runs	Runs/RH	Runs/LH	HR/RH	HR/LH
96	104	108	113	114

Top Hitter WARP	7.6	Joey Votto
Top Pitcher WARP	3.8	Johnny Cueto
Top Prospect	Robert Stephenson	

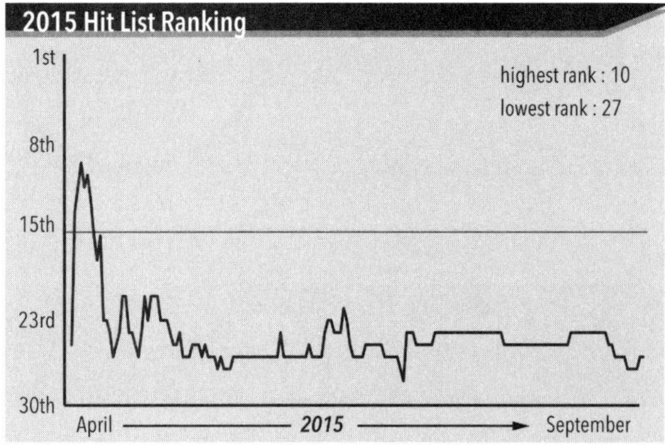

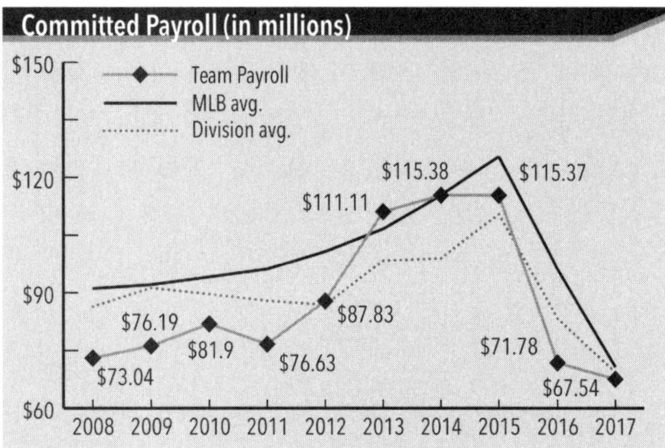

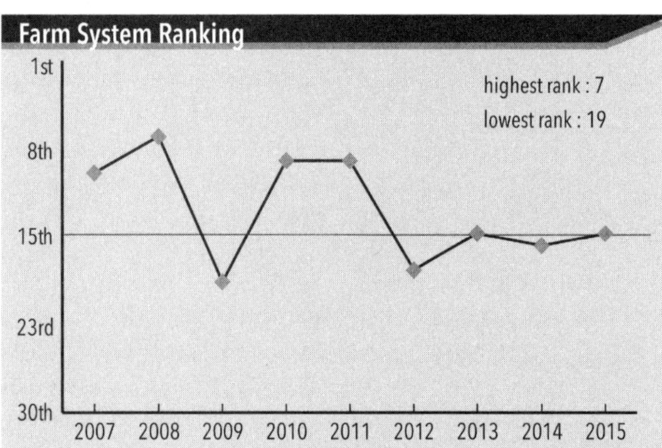

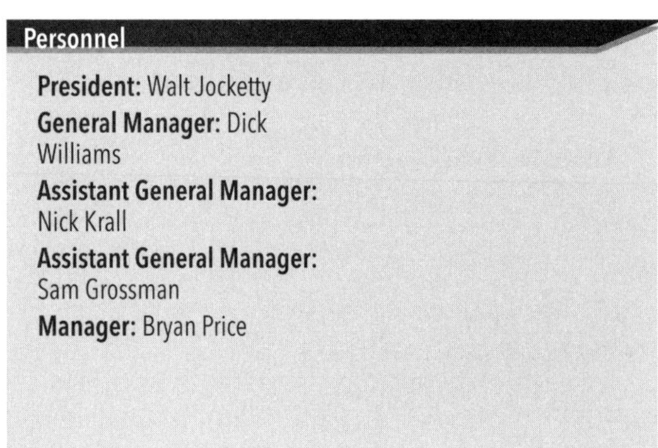
Personnel

President: Walt Jocketty
General Manager: Dick Williams
Assistant General Manager: Nick Krall
Assistant General Manager: Sam Grossman
Manager: Bryan Price

want to lay low for a bit given that they happen to be in the same division as the teams with the three best records in baseball last year. Best that they not put too many resources into the next couple of years. Prospects for contending aren't so good, so they might as well play the prospects. And Joey Votto.

There comes a point when a team might look at a guy like Votto and say, "Hey, we can lose 90 games with or without him!" He's 32, and it's going to take a few years for the Reds to build themselves up again; by then Votto will not only be on the wrong side of 30, but on the wrong side of 35. Surely someone out there would give the Reds something of value for Votto, and better to get it now and save the money, right?

Warning! Gory Mathematical Details Ahead!

Before we trade Votto the player, let's also assess Votto the contract and Votto the scarce resource. One nice thing about acquiring a player who is at the very end of his deal is that it's a low-risk move. If you sign a player to a one-year deal (or trade for a player with one year left on his contact), you don't have to worry about his performance suddenly drying up, leaving you stuck paying him for the next few years. Most big free-agent contracts are signed in the knowledge that the team will regret those last few years, but at the front of the contract, they'll reap the rewards of a player in his prime.

Of course, in this case, we've got a different situation. Any team trading for Votto would get his contract along with him, and for better or worse, Votto would be on the books for the next eight years. Even for a team that runs a $200 million payroll, his salary would represent an eighth of the budget. So what are the chances that a player like Votto—a star now—will still be shining in a few years?

I looked at all position players in baseball from 1999 onward who had ranked in the top five at their position, according to Baseball Prospectus' WARP, for the previous three years, and who were between 27 and 32 years old in the first of those three years. These are guys like Votto who have proven themselves to be exceptional performers. There were 66 of them in the data set, and in the first year after their three-year run of dominance, more than two-thirds were still in the top five at their position. By year three, though, that was down to less than half (36 percent), and by year five, it was fewer than 10 percent who had maintained their high level of play.

Now, all was not lost. I categorized players as All-Stars (top five in the league at their position), first-division regulars (nos. 6 through 15 at their positions), second-division regulars (16 through 30) or fringe/bench guys (31 and up). Table 1 breaks down what the 66 players I looked at were doing at each point.

	Year 1	Year 3	Year 5
All-Star	68%	36%	9%
First-Division Regular	20%	32%	30%
Second-Division Regular	11%	15%	24%
Fringe/Bench	2%	3%	3%
Out of Baseball/Injured	0%	14%	33%

If these guys are any sort of comp for Votto, his chances of remaining an All-Star player, even into 2018, are a little better than a third, and his chances of being better than average are about 70 percent. Even by 2020, he's got a 40 percent chance of being better than the average starter. In other words, a player like Votto isn't a good bet to remain at an All-Star level, but he *is* a good bet to remain a pretty good player. Long-term mega-contracts are often criticized as bad investments on the part of teams. If you view the point of the contract as securing All-Star performance forever and ever, then it's pretty clearly not a good gamble.

But let's look at it the other way around. Suppose the Reds had simply let Votto walk away. Someone would have to hit in the second spot in the lineup and play first base, if only because it's hard to record a 5-3 putout without the "3." It's tempting to think that if the Reds were to pick one of the 30 best first basemen in any given year, they'd have a 50/50 shot at getting one who was better than average. However, there's a big flaw in that logic: The Reds don't get to randomly pick from the 30 best first basemen in the league. Generally, when teams have one of the good ones, they try to lock him up and he isn't available to everyone else. The rest of the league is left sifting through the remainders. The Reds have to either hope that a good first baseman shows up in their farm system or go out on the free-agent market—and pay free-agent prices—for a replacement.

In that sense, Votto doesn't have a *bad* contract; he has a contract that does something boring that isn't always discussed. It's likely that Votto will remain a good player and keep the Reds from having to dredge the bottom of the barrel for a first baseman or pay something close to Votto's salary for a free-agent replacement, and he comes with the potential upside of remaining a superstar. Not to mention all that "Face of the Team" stuff. That insurance comes with a hefty price tag, but given the going rate for talent in the game right now, it's not out of line.

And that brings us to Votto the scarce resource. In baseball, offense is down. To give some context, Votto finished 2015 with a .459 on-base percentage just a smidge behind Bryce Harper on the leaderboard. In 10th place on the 2015 OBP list was Prince Fielder, with a .378 mark. In 2005, Votto would have been among 11 hitters with at least a .400 OBP. There just aren't as many good hitters around now. The Reds are locking in what appears to be a rare commodity, a guy who can hit one clear to Clermont County *and* get on base at one of the best rates in baseball. So if you're tempted to say that Votto should be traded because he has a "bad contract," think twice.

They Won't Be Bad Forever

You might suggest trading Votto because he's a beautiful swan on what will be some hard-to-watch Reds teams. If it were the last year of his contract, that would make sense, but because he's signed for most of a decade, we need to remember that while the next few years will be tough, nothing in baseball lasts forever.

How long will the Reds have to wait? Less time than you might think. I took all teams from 1988 to 2015 and looked at how well their winning percentage in one year correlated with the next year. A correlation of zero means that one year tells you absolutely nothing about the next. A correlation of one means that knowing a team's winning percentage in one year perfectly predicts the next year. In this case, the answer was .46. How well does this year's winning percentage predict two years from now? The correlation is .34. By year three, it's down to .19. In other words, by the third year, the league kind of re-shuffles itself. It doesn't mean that the good teams become bad in three years and the bad become good. It just means that no one has any clue what's going to happen in three years.

For the Reds, that's a reasonable time frame. Cincinnati's farm system is a bit lacking in "WOW!" prospects, but they do have a small mass of guys who project to be solid-but-not-spectacular players. Third and fourth starters, hitters who can hold down a regular lineup place and not embarrass themselves, that type. In a few years, some of those pieces will be in place and the Reds will have a good foundation for a contending team. It might help if they have a good veteran first baseman around, one who might still be an elite-level hitter, or somewhere in the neighborhood. A guy like Votto, say.

The Reds will probably be awful this year, but if history is any guide, there is hope for the future. Many of the players who were worth trading in the last year or so (and who might still be traded) were homegrown products. In fact, over the last few years, the Reds have brought Homer Bailey, Jay Bruce, Johnny Cueto, Paul Janish, Mike Leake, Todd Frazier, Billy Hamilton, Zack Cozart and Devin Mesoraco through their system, along with that first baseman they have. Aroldis Chapman was a slightly different case in that he came from Cuba with four years in the top league there, but he was still seasoned in the Reds' high minors before making his big-league debut. On top of that, Cincinnati has developed Travis Wood, Drew Stubbs, Yonder Alonso, Chris Heisey and Brad Boxberger, all of whom have made reasonable contributions to other teams. The Reds seem to have a knack for developing the types of pieces you need to fill out a roster.

So, should the Reds be looking to trade their first baseman? Aside from the usual "We'll listen on anyone" line, it doesn't make sense for them to be actively pursuing the idea. They'd need to find someone who would otherwise be willing to sign one player for eight years and $20-25 million per year, who needs a first baseman and who would be willing to part with the sort of prospects who would be a better bet to be good in three years than Votto will likely still be. And Votto would have to waive his no-trade clause. That's a lot to ask. For now, Reds fans, just enjoy the fact that you get to watch one of the best hitters in the game play for your team.

(And no, they're not going to trade Homer Bailey's contract.) ■

—Russell Carleton is an author of Baseball Prospectus who grew up in Ohio... even if it was Cleveland

HITTERS

Tucker Barnhart C

Born: 1/7/91 Age: 25 Bats: B Throws: R Height: 5'11" Weight: 190

YEAR	TEAM	LVL	AGE	PA	R	2B	3B	HR	RBI	BB	K	SB	CS	AVG/OBP/SLG	TAv	BABIP	BRR	FRAA	WARP
2013	PEN	AA	22	395	31	19	1	3	44	45	57	1	0	.260/.348/.348	.262	.300	-2.3	C(96): -11.8	0.4
2014	LOU	AAA	23	292	18	9	3	1	29	28	34	0	1	.246/.319/.316	.230	.277	-3.0	C(75): -7.2	-0.6
2014	CIN	MLB	23	60	3	0	0	1	1	4	10	0	0	.185/.241/.241	.206	.209	-0.4	C(20): -1.3	-0.2
2015	CIN	MLB	24	274	23	9	0	3	18	25	45	0	1	.252/.324/.326	.245	.294	2.4	C(73): 3.3, RF(1): 0.2	1.5
2016	*CIN*	*MLB*	*25*	*61*	*6*	*2*	*0*	*1*	*6*	*5*	*11*	*0*	*0*	*.240/.307/.341*	*.232*	*.277*	*0.2*	*C -2*	*-0.1*
2017	*CIN*	*MLB*	*26*	*272*	*29*	*11*	*1*	*4*	*25*	*23*	*48*	*0*	*0*	*.242/.310/.344*	*.242*	*.279*	*0.9*	*C -8*	*-0.2*

Breakout: 5% Improve: 17% Collapse: 7% Attrition: 28% MLB: 49% *Comparables: Curtis Thigpen, Rob Brantly, Lou Marson*

YEAR	TEAM	P. COUNT	FRM RUNS	BLK RUNS	THRW RUNS	TOT RUNS
2013	PEN	12799	-16.9	0.7	1.8	-14.3
2014	CIN	2291	-2.0	0.0	0.4	-1.6
2014	LOU	10597	-7.4	0.5	0.9	-6.0
2015	CIN	10131	2.0	0.1	0.6	2.6
2015	LOU	676	-0.1	-0.2	0.0	-0.4
2016	*CIN*	*2297*	*-1.9*	*0.0*	*0.1*	*-1.8*
2017	*CIN*	*10253*	*-9.2*	*0.2*	*0.4*	*-8.5*

A league-wide emphasis on catcher defense, familiarity with the Reds' late-summer rookie rotation and Devin Mesoraco's hip conspired last summer to give Barnhart a long enough run behind the plate to imprint the phrase "big leaguer" next to his image in the minds of baseball staff. A punchless switch-hitter with a strong arm and estimable receiving skills, he'll never produce enough offense to be a good team's primary backstop but should enjoy a long, wandering career as a backup for hire. In a dozen years he'll be some future ace's "personal catcher," and in 20 he'll be a St. Louis bench coach and manager-in-waiting.

Alex Blandino SS

Born: 11/6/92 Age: 23 Bats: R Throws: R Height: 6'0" Weight: 190

YEAR	TEAM	LVL	AGE	PA	R	2B	3B	HR	RBI	BB	K	SB	CS	AVG/OBP/SLG	TAv	BABIP	BRR	FRAA	WARP
2014	DYT	A	21	152	20	10	1	4	16	13	42	1	2	.261/.329/.440	.291	.341	0.3	SS(34): 5.1	1.7
2015	DAY	A+	22	342	46	18	2	7	35	31	56	7	10	.294/.370/.438	.317	.338	0.5	SS(68): -0.2, 2B(6): 0.1	3.5
2015	PEN	AA	22	138	15	7	0	3	18	18	21	2	2	.235/.350/.374	.283	.261	0.3	SS(24): 1.9, 2B(6): -0.4	1.1
2016	*CIN*	*MLB*	*23*	*250*	*30*	*11*	*1*	*7*	*26*	*20*	*61*	*2*	*2*	*.237/.307/.389*	*.249*	*.289*	*-0.7*	*SS 2, 2B -0*	*1.0*
2017	*CIN*	*MLB*	*24*	*329*	*39*	*15*	*1*	*9*	*38*	*26*	*81*	*3*	*3*	*.244/.314/.399*	*.264*	*.301*	*-0.8*	*SS 3, 2B -1*	*1.6*

Breakout: 4% Improve: 24% Collapse: 2% Attrition: 15% MLB: 39% *Comparables: Brad Miller, Marcus Semien, Josh Rodriguez*

Blandino displayed an advanced approach, solid hit tool and power potential during his successful full-season debut—all the makings of a bat-first shortstop, assuming he really is a shortstop. Most scouts doubted that the former Stanford third baseman could make that transition, but Blandino has used good instincts and solid fundamentals to compensate for his subpar range, and so far he's looked the part. Should the position prove too hard, he'll hit well enough to play second. If everything comes together, he could grow up to be Jeff Blauser.

Brennan Boesch RF

Born: 4/12/85 Age: 31 Bats: L Throws: L Height: 6'4" Weight: 225

YEAR	TEAM	LVL	AGE	PA	R	2B	3B	HR	RBI	BB	K	SB	CS	AVG/OBP/SLG	TAv	BABIP	BRR	FRAA	WARP
2013	SWB	AAA	28	37	6	2	0	0	2	7	8	0	0	.200/.351/.267	.283	.273	0.6	RF(7): -0.2	0.2
2013	NYA	MLB	28	53	6	2	1	3	8	2	9	0	0	.275/.302/.529	.273	.282	-1.2	RF(15): 1.1	0.2
2014	SLC	AAA	29	407	68	25	7	25	85	29	86	10	4	.332/.381/.636	.327	.374	1.8	RF(56): -11.2, CF(20): -2.8	2.6
2014	ANA	MLB	29	79	6	2	0	2	7	2	19	3	0	.187/.203/.293	.203	.214	0.2	RF(9): -0.1, LF(3): 0.1	-0.3
2015	LOU	AAA	30	208	17	9	0	4	30	19	41	0	2	.326/.386/.439	.294	.399	-1.5	RF(24): -3.6, LF(8): 2.8	0.8
2015	CIN	MLB	30	94	4	2	0	1	5	4	30	1	0	.146/.191/.202	.148	.207	0.2	CF(8): -1.6, RF(8): -0.6	-1.0
2016	*CIN*	*MLB*	*31*	*250*	*27*	*11*	*1*	*8*	*31*	*16*	*58*	*3*	*1*	*.247/.300/.409*	*.252*	*.294*	*-0.8*	*RF -3, LF -1*	*-0.1*
2017	*CIN*	*MLB*	*32*	*184*	*21*	*8*	*1*	*6*	*22*	*11*	*44*	*2*	*1*	*.242/.292/.401*	*.254*	*.292*	*-0.5*	*RF -2, LF -1*	*-0.1*

Breakout: 1% Improve: 38% Collapse: 11% Attrition: 14% MLB: 82% *Comparables: Garrett Jones, Emil Brown, John Mayberry*

Remember those magical days of 2011, when Will married Kate, Adele arrived, Charlie Sheen imploded and Boesch tore into major-league pitching like a warlock with tiger blood? Since that one heady season in Detroit, the lanky outfielder has posted a .225/.266/.353 line with four different teams and last year managed the lowest WARP on a 64-win Reds squad. Teams continue to dream on the power in his bat but his free-swinging ways make unleashing it an accident, not a planned result. But he'll always have 2011, so expect to find Boesch on lists of spring non-roster invitees for years to come.

Jay Bruce RF

Born: 4/3/87 Age: 29 Bats: L Throws: L Height: 6'3" Weight: 225

YEAR	TEAM	LVL	AGE	PA	R	2B	3B	HR	RBI	BB	K	SB	CS	AVG/OBP/SLG	TAv	BABIP	BRR	FRAA	WARP
2013	CIN	MLB	26	697	89	43	1	30	109	63	185	7	3	.262/.329/.478	.290	.322	1.9	RF(160): 18.5	5.6
2014	CIN	MLB	27	545	71	21	1	18	66	44	149	12	3	.217/.281/.373	.244	.269	4.2	RF(131): 1.4, 1B(3): -0.1	0.7
2015	CIN	MLB	28	649	72	35	4	26	87	58	145	9	5	.226/.294/.434	.261	.251	-2.7	RF(150): 3.0	1.3
2016	*CIN*	*MLB*	*29*	*600*	*75*	*29*	*2*	*26*	*82*	*56*	*151*	*10*	*4*	*.239/.313/.445*	*.265*	*.281*	*0.7*	*RF 6*	*2.5*
2017	*CIN*	*MLB*	*30*	*531*	*70*	*26*	*1*	*23*	*72*	*52*	*137*	*7*	*3*	*.234/.310/.440*	*.270*	*.277*	*0.8*	*RF 5*	*2.0*

Breakout: 3% Improve: 51% Collapse: 1% Attrition: 2% MLB: 98% *Comparables: Larry Walker, David Justice, Vic Wertz*

Bruce was slashing .257/.341/.486 at last year's trade deadline, when word came down that the Reds nearly traded him to the pennant-chasing Mets. Perhaps his .178/.219/.357 line after that was brought on by a late-summer emotional malaise playing behind Michael Lorenzen in half-empty stadiums rather than Noah Syndergaard in a sold-out Citi Field; more likely, it was just another bad patch for one of the league's most notoriously streaky players. Bruce regained some of his power stroke last year and improved his contact rate, but posted another damagingly low on-base percentage fueled by a minuscule batting average on balls in play. If there's a silver lining it's that his BABIP wasn't worse when hitting into the frequent defensive shifts he faces, which means some of that might just be bad luck. It wouldn't be shocking to see Bruce turn back the clock, hit a few more where they ain't and put up All-Star numbers. Nor would it be shocking to see him hit like a replacement-level outfielder. Most likely, being Jay Bruce, he'll do both.

Ramon Cabrera C

Born: 11/5/89 Age: 26 Bats: B Throws: R Height: 5'8" Weight: 195

YEAR	TEAM	LVL	AGE	PA	R	2B	3B	HR	RBI	BB	K	SB	CS	AVG/OBP/SLG	TAv	BABIP	BRR	FRAA	WARP
2013	TOL	AAA	23	165	13	9	1	1	15	14	21	0	1	.242/.311/.336	.248	.276	-1.5	C(19): -1.2	0.0
2013	ERI	AA	23	362	44	22	2	0	54	44	34	4	0	.304/.392/.388	.294	.338	-4.3	C(31): -2.4	1.5
2014	ALT	AA	24	49	5	5	0	1	5	3	6	0	1	.239/.286/.413	.266	.256	-1.8	C(11): -6.6	-0.6
2014	ERI	AA	24	431	42	17	0	5	47	33	37	1	0	.277/.329/.358	.247	.292	-1.1	C(73): -17.8	-1.1
2015	CIN	MLB	25	30	4	1	0	1	3	0	5	0	0	.367/.367/.500	.362	.417	-1.0	C(8): -1.3	0.2
2015	LOU	AAA	25	351	29	14	0	2	35	27	44	1	1	.290/.343/.353	.259	.328	-2.3	C(84): -16.0	-0.3
2016	*CIN*	*MLB*	*26*	*66*	*6*	*3*	*0*	*1*	*7*	*5*	*10*	*0*	*0*	*.256/.311/.359*	*.242*	*.289*	*-0.1*	*C -4*	*-0.3*
2017	*CIN*	*MLB*	*27*	*232*	*25*	*10*	*0*	*4*	*22*	*17*	*38*	*0*	*0*	*.247/.303/.349*	*.244*	*.282*	*-0.6*	*C -14*	*-1.1*

Breakout: 2% Improve: 14% Collapse: 7% Attrition: 14% MLB: 29% *Comparables: Jordan Pacheco, Manny Pina, Steve Clevenger*

YEAR	TEAM	P. COUNT	FRM RUNS	BLK RUNS	THRW RUNS	TOT RUNS
2013	ERI	4281	-1.9	-0.1	0.0	-2.1
2013	TOL	2958	-0.2	0.3	-0.5	-0.5
2014	ERI	10284	-15.5	1.1	-2.5	-17.0
2014	ALT	1491	-7.1	-0.1	0.8	-6.4
2015	CIN	836	-1.3	0.0	0.1	-1.2
2015	LOU	12245	-13.7	0.3	-1.2	-14.6
2016	*CIN*	*2401*	*-3.5*	*0.1*	*-0.3*	*-3.7*
2017	*CIN*	*8450*	*-12.8*	*0.3*	*-1.0*	*-13.5*

Cabrera was named the MVP of the Louisville Bats and earned his first September call-up last year, but the switch-hitting catcher shouldn't grow too accustomed to big-league meal money. A contact hitter with limp-noodle power, Cabrera has some on-base ability but doesn't hit enough to be a starter in The Show or flash the standout catch-and-throw skills that teams often value in a backup. With 58 more big-league plate appearances he'll finally earn some bragging rights by passing his father Alex, who toiled for the Diamondbacks back in 2000 and has outhit his son in the Venezuelan Winter League each of the past four years. And you thought *you* dreaded family dinners.

Jake Cave CF

Born: 12/4/92 Age: 23 Bats: L Throws: L Height: 6'0" Weight: 200

YEAR	TEAM	LVL	AGE	PA	R	2B	3B	HR	RBI	BB	K	SB	CS	AVG/OBP/SLG	TAv	BABIP	BRR	FRAA	WARP
2013	CSC	A	20	520	69	37	6	2	31	40	110	18	9	.282/.347/.401	.280	.362	-1.3	CF(111): 1.5, RF(2): 0.6	2.9
2014	TAM	A+	21	416	50	18	4	3	24	28	80	10	3	.304/.354/.395	.269	.377	0.5	CF(89): -2.4	1.5
2014	TRN	AA	21	197	24	10	5	4	18	18	44	2	3	.273/.344/.455	.279	.344	1.9	CF(20): -2.2, LF(8): -1.7	0.6
2015	TRN	AA	22	563	68	22	5	2	37	43	98	17	3	.269/.330/.345	.261	.327	0.5	CF(101): -3.2, LF(16): 1.7	1.6
2015	SWB	AAA	22	29	4	3	1	0	2	3	8	0	0	.458/.517/.667	.408	.647	0.1	CF(4): 0.2, LF(2): -0.1	0.6
2016	*CIN*	*MLB*	*23*	*230*	*24*	*10*	*2*	*3*	*19*	*14*	*59*	*3*	*1*	*.243/.293/.354*	*.230*	*.314*	*0.1*	*CF -0, LF 1*	*0.1*
2017	*CIN*	*MLB*	*24*	*445*	*46*	*20*	*3*	*6*	*42*	*29*	*113*	*6*	*2*	*.247/.300/.359*	*.241*	*.319*	*0.3*	*CF -1, LF 1*	*0.3*

Breakout: 2% Improve: 8% Collapse: 1% Attrition: 3% MLB: 13% *Comparables: Xavier Paul, Darrell Ceciliani, Bryan Petersen*

August 27, 2016:
A ballplayer wanders into the familiar Scranton locker room. It is dark. He cannot see his teammates. Daylight spills through the open doorway, casting each man's shadow against his locker.

"I'm back. And you won't believe what I have seen," the ballplayer calls out, excitedly. "The major leagues! The way the cameras sparkle in the second decks. The jets. The way men eat meals. Not burgers, but meals," he says, a catch in his throat, "with nutritional value." The men do not turn, but continue to put on their socks and shoes, tape up their ankles.

"Come with me! Leave this place and come with me to the major leagues. I know it is bright there, and the pitchers fierce. But it is the real world, not this shadow life, this lie." He grabs the shoulder of Slade Heathcott, but his former friend only looks away. No one speaks, no one moves. The shadows are all that are real to them.

Zack Cozart SS

Born: 8/12/85 Age: 30 Bats: R Throws: R Height: 6'0" Weight: 195

YEAR	TEAM	LVL	AGE	PA	R	2B	3B	HR	RBI	BB	K	SB	CS	AVG/OBP/SLG	TAv	BABIP	BRR	FRAA	WARP
2013	CIN	MLB	27	618	74	30	3	12	63	26	102	0	0	.254/.284/.381	.242	.285	6.9	SS(150): -1.5	2.0
2014	CIN	MLB	28	543	48	18	5	4	38	25	79	7	0	.221/.268/.300	.212	.255	2.0	SS(147): 9.1	0.8
2015	CIN	MLB	29	214	28	10	1	9	28	14	29	3	3	.258/.310/.459	.288	.258	0.8	SS(52): 0.9	1.7
2016	*CIN*	*MLB*	*30*	*534*	*58*	*25*	*3*	*11*	*50*	*28*	*89*	*5*	*2*	*.247/.290/.378*	*.237*	*.275*	*3.0*	*SS -0*	*1.7*
2017	*CIN*	*MLB*	*31*	*385*	*39*	*17*	*1*	*8*	*38*	*19*	*70*	*3*	*1*	*.235/.275/.353*	*.232*	*.266*	*2.1*	*SS 0*	*0.7*

Breakout: 2% Improve: 42% Collapse: 5% Attrition: 13% MLB: 92% *Comparables: Cliff Pennington, Brendan Ryan, Jack Wilson*

A brutal injury suffered at the first-base bag ended Cozart's season in June, teaching us all that we have a biceps tendon in our knee (who knew?) and ending what had been easily his most productive big-league season. Cozart was drawing more walks and launching more bombs than at any point in his career, posting a .201 ISO that came in five points higher than those of Andrew McCutchen and Miguel Cabrera. He didn't have a snowball's chance of remaining in such lofty company over a full season but even incremental improvement at the dish, paired with his often-stellar shortstop defense, would make a healthy Cozart a valuable commodity. We'll find out this summer how much of his range and newfound offensive competence have survived the knife.

Ivan De Jesus SS

Born: 5/1/87 Age: 29 Bats: R Throws: R Height: 5'11" Weight: 200

YEAR	TEAM	LVL	AGE	PA	R	2B	3B	HR	RBI	BB	K	SB	CS	AVG/OBP/SLG	TAv	BABIP	BRR	FRAA	WARP
2013	IND	AAA	26	345	36	27	3	3	32	29	65	5	2	.319/.380/.457	.299	.390	0.7	2B(67): 1.3, 3B(11): 0.9	2.7
2014	NOR	AAA	27	469	54	19	5	5	56	50	84	2	1	.282/.358/.389	.257	.340	-2.9	SS(98): -8.5, 2B(8): -0.1	0.6
2015	LOU	AAA	28	209	22	9	3	0	16	22	43	2	1	.303/.378/.384	.279	.392	1.7	3B(31): 1.6, 1B(22): 0.2	1.3
2015	CIN	MLB	28	222	15	10	2	4	28	19	55	0	2	.244/.311/.373	.259	.315	-0.4	2B(20): 1.5, LF(18): 0.7	0.8
2016	*CIN*	*MLB*	*29*	*177*	*17*	*8*	*1*	*2*	*16*	*14*	*41*	*1*	*1*	*.250/.313/.355*	*.240*	*.317*	*0.1*	*3B 0, SS -1*	*0.2*
2017	*CIN*	*MLB*	*30*	*341*	*37*	*15*	*2*	*5*	*32*	*28*	*80*	*1*	*1*	*.250/.314/.359*	*.248*	*.317*	*0.1*	*3B 1, SS -2*	*0.4*

Breakout: 1% Improve: 7% Collapse: 5% Attrition: 16% MLB: 21% *Comparables: Kory Casto, Brian Barden, Josh Rodriguez*

De Jesus the Younger is past the point where he'll ever get a chance to be an every-day infielder like his pops (let alone get traded for a Hall of Famer), but his defensive versatility and ability to not quite be an automatic out showed Reds fans what a true utility guy looks like. He's steady in the field, provides professional at-bats, works cheap and gives managers a fun name to say when reporting a double-switch, a category in which De Jesus could lead the league. Most importantly he gets paid handsomely to do what he loves, so weep not for Ivan De Jesus.

Adam Duvall 3B

Born: 9/4/88 Age: 27 Bats: R Throws: R Height: 6'1" Weight: 205

YEAR	TEAM	LVL	AGE	PA	R	2B	3B	HR	RBI	BB	K	SB	CS	AVG/OBP/SLG	TAv	BABIP	BRR	FRAA	WARP
2013	RIC	AA	24	430	61	23	4	17	58	35	72	2	1	.252/.320/.465	.288	.268	0.2	3B(90): 6.0, 1B(7): -0.2	3.3
2014	FRE	AAA	25	394	67	21	3	27	90	30	82	2	0	.298/.360/.599	.326	.320	1.7	3B(52): 2.1, 1B(41): 2.0	4.4
2014	SFN	MLB	25	77	8	2	0	3	5	3	20	0	0	.192/.234/.342	.222	.220	0.4	1B(21): -1.0, 3B(1): -0.0	-0.3
2015	LOU	AAA	26	104	11	4	0	4	7	6	23	1	0	.189/.260/.358	.212	.206	-1.1	LF(16): 0.2, 1B(8): 2.2	-0.2
2015	CIN	MLB	26	72	6	2	0	5	9	6	26	0	0	.219/.306/.484	.286	.273	0.4	LF(15): -0.7, 1B(4): -0.0	0.3
2016	*CIN*	*MLB*	*27*	*504*	*62*	*22*	*2*	*27*	*78*	*30*	*126*	*1*	*0*	*.238/.291/.467*	*.264*	*.264*	*-0.6*	*LF -2, 1B 0*	*1.5*
2017	*CIN*	*MLB*	*28*	*502*	*68*	*21*	*2*	*28*	*77*	*31*	*126*	*1*	*0*	*.236/.291/.469*	*.273*	*.260*	*-0.9*	*LF -2, 1B 0*	*1.6*

Breakout: 2% Improve: 13% Collapse: 9% Attrition: 19% MLB: 38% *Comparables: Jake Fox, Mat Gamel, Mauro Gomez*

Duvall is a one-dimensional player who came to Cincinnati last summer as part of the Mike Leake trade, but since that one dimension is right-handed power, he has a chance. The baseball world has finally agreed they can no longer stomach watching him at third base, so the latest plan is for Duvall to live out his dreams in left field; unfortunately, those dreams are often the ones where you're chasing after something but never quite catch it. He doesn't make enough contact or draw enough walks to post a serviceable on-base percentage, but when he catches up to an ill-placed fastball he can put a serious hurt on it. Duvall is a poor man's Mark Trumbo, making him a reasonable enough outfield placeholder for a rebuilding team but not a long-term solution.

Billy Hamilton CF

Born: 9/9/90 Age: 25 Bats: B Throws: R Height: 6'0" Weight: 160

YEAR	TEAM	LVL	AGE	PA	R	2B	3B	HR	RBI	BB	K	SB	CS	AVG/OBP/SLG	TAv	BABIP	BRR	FRAA	WARP
2013	CIN	MLB	22	22	9	2	0	0	1	2	4	13	1	.368/.429/.474	.358	.467	1.1	CF(7): 0.3	0.5
2013	LOU	AAA	22	547	75	18	4	6	41	38	102	75	15	.256/.308/.343	.232	.310	10.7	CF(118): 18.3, SS(1): 0.0	3.0
2014	CIN	MLB	23	611	72	25	8	6	48	34	117	56	23	.250/.292/.355	.243	.304	5.4	CF(144): 16.3	3.2
2015	CIN	MLB	24	454	56	8	3	4	28	28	75	57	8	.226/.274/.289	.215	.264	10.9	CF(110): 1.5	0.6
2016	*CIN*	*MLB*	*25*	*611*	*90*	*22*	*5*	*9*	*41*	*37*	*115*	*67*	*16*	*.246/.293/.349*	*.228*	*.287*	*7.1*	*CF 12*	*2.2*
2017	*CIN*	*MLB*	*26*	*548*	*55*	*18*	*4*	*8*	*50*	*34*	*103*	*59*	*15*	*.241/.289/.344*	*.232*	*.280*	*8.8*	*CF 11*	*2.0*

Breakout: 2% Improve: 60% Collapse: 2% Attrition: 13% MLB: 98% *Comparables: Willy Taveras, Julio Borbon, Jordan Schafer*

The amazing thing about Hamilton isn't that he led the majors in our Baserunning Runs metric last season; it's that he did so while never getting on base in the month he missed with a bum shoulder, and rarely getting on base in any other month. Maury Wills posted the highest BRR total in our database back in 1962, but he reached base more than twice as many times as Hamilton; on a per-chance basis, Hamilton was better on the basepaths last year than anyone we've ever measured. Add in center-field defense that earned him Gold Glove consideration and you have a position player who provides value despite wielding one of the weakest sticks in the game. If Hamilton ever stops lofting lazy pop flies and starts slapping the ball on the ground, he might get on base enough to break baseball.

Devin Mesoraco C

Born: 6/19/88 Age: 28 Bats: R Throws: R Height: 6'1" Weight: 220

YEAR	TEAM	LVL	AGE	PA	R	2B	3B	HR	RBI	BB	K	SB	CS	AVG/OBP/SLG	TAv	BABIP	BRR	FRAA	WARP
2013	CIN	MLB	25	352	31	13	0	9	42	24	61	0	2	.238/.287/.362	.233	.264	-1.2	C(97): -9.9	-0.6
2014	CIN	MLB	26	440	54	25	0	25	80	41	103	1	3	.273/.359/.534	.333	.309	-6.2	C(109): -6.1	4.0
2015	CIN	MLB	27	51	2	1	1	0	2	5	9	1	0	.178/.275/.244	.203	.222	0.3	C(6): -0.5	-0.2
2016	*CIN*	*MLB*	*28*	*544*	*64*	*27*	*1*	*20*	*68*	*48*	*108*	*3*	*2*	*.248/.321/.427*	*.265*	*.278*	*-3.0*	*C -13*	*1.0*
2017	*CIN*	*MLB*	*29*	*304*	*38*	*13*	*0*	*10*	*37*	*27*	*61*	*1*	*1*	*.237/.311/.404*	*.262*	*.266*	*-1.7*	*C -8*	*0.2*

Breakout: 0% Improve: 47% Collapse: 6% Attrition: 17% MLB: 95% *Comparables: Victor Martinez, Ryan Garko, Ronny Paulino*

YEAR	TEAM	P. COUNT	FRM RUNS	BLK RUNS	THRW RUNS	TOT RUNS
2013	CIN	12439	-11.0	0.4	-0.1	-10.7
2014	CIN	14953	-5.9	0.5	-0.8	-6.3
2014	PEN	212	-0.1	0.0	0.1	0.0
2015	CIN	777	-0.3	0.0	0.0	-0.3
2016	*CIN*	*19556*	*-13.7*	*0.6*	*-1.0*	*-14.1*
2017	*CIN*	*10924*	*-8.3*	*0.3*	*-0.6*	*-8.6*

The Reds drew significant flak over their curious handling of Mesoraco's hip impingement last summer, but in retrospect... yeah, they probably deserved some flak. An inability to squat without hip pain pushed the slugging catcher into a limited PH/DH role for a month, as the club hoped in vain that partial rest would heal him. Then Mesoraco was sent to Louisville to learn how to play left field because, you know, outfielders don't have to squat, but obviously that didn't do his hip any good. The inevitable result was surgery in June, and Mesoraco should be on schedule to don his shin guards again this spring. Even before the injury his work behind the dish was merely adequate, so left field might be his destiny. If his 2014 breakout wasn't a fluke—and that's a big if—his bat will play anywhere; otherwise he'll need to catch to provide value. Both Mesoraco and the Reds have a lot of questions to answer this summer.

Kris Negron SS

Born: 2/1/86 Age: 30 Bats: R Throws: R Height: 6'0" Weight: 190

YEAR	TEAM	LVL	AGE	PA	R	2B	3B	HR	RBI	BB	K	SB	CS	AVG/OBP/SLG	TAv	BABIP	BRR	FRAA	WARP
2013	LOU	AAA	27	379	31	14	1	5	30	26	93	11	3	.225/.295/.317	.223	.292	1.3	SS(73): -6.6, 3B(12): 1.2	-0.2
2014	LOU	AAA	28	240	33	15	3	3	25	14	54	9	2	.269/.328/.406	.248	.346	2.5	SS(47): 0.9, CF(14): -1.4	0.9
2014	CIN	MLB	28	158	19	10	1	6	17	12	40	5	0	.271/.331/.479	.289	.337	2.6	3B(25): 1.0, 2B(17): 0.5	1.4
2015	LOU	AAA	29	230	13	5	1	4	15	15	47	3	1	.216/.280/.309	.211	.258	-2.1	SS(46): -5.3, CF(8): 0.1	-1.1
2015	CIN	MLB	29	107	5	2	0	0	2	9	23	2	0	.140/.238/.161	.155	.186	0.7	SS(10): 0.9, LF(10): -0.2	-0.7
2016	*CIN*	*MLB*	*30*	*250*	*26*	*9*	*1*	*5*	*23*	*15*	*67*	*5*	*1*	*.214/.274/.334*	*.218*	*.272*	*1.3*	*SS -1, CF -0*	*0.0*
2017	*CIN*	*MLB*	*31*	*306*	*31*	*12*	*1*	*6*	*29*	*19*	*83*	*6*	*1*	*.214/.273/.334*	*.223*	*.272*	*1.6*	*SS -1, CF 0*	*0.0*

Breakout: 0% Improve: 10% Collapse: 4% Attrition: 7% MLB: 20% *Comparables: Tommy Manzella, Brian Barden, Omar Quintanilla*

We were right, of course, but that doesn't mean we're happy about it. When Negron managed to randomly display some fleeting ability with the bat during a two-month stint with the Reds back in 2014, we called it exactly that: random and fleeting. Sometimes players like Negron with long and sordid minor-league track records turn into solid major leaguers. Sometimes storm clouds deliver frogs instead of rain. Sometimes the conspiracy theory turns out to be true. Sometimes we let our affinity for effort and attitude and a redemptive narrative cloud our judgment, and we hope someone like Negron will carve out a big-league career, because he'll appreciate it, and so will we. Almost always, we're disappointed.

Jose Peraza SS

Born: 4/30/94 Age: 22 Bats: R Throws: R Height: 6'0" Weight: 180

YEAR	TEAM	LVL	AGE	PA	R	2B	3B	HR	RBI	BB	K	SB	CS	AVG/OBP/SLG	TAv	BABIP	BRR	FRAA	WARP
2013	ROM	A	19	504	72	18	8	1	47	34	64	64	15	.288/.341/.371	.275	.328	7.0	SS(104): 19.5	5.6
2014	MIS	AA	20	195	35	7	3	1	17	7	15	25	8	.335/.363/.422	.291	.361	5.2	2B(41): -3.7	1.3
2014	LYN	A+	20	304	44	13	8	1	27	10	32	35	7	.342/.365/.454	.308	.376	5.0	2B(58): -6.1, SS(7): 0.6	2.4
2015	OKL	AAA	21	94	11	3	1	1	5	2	10	7	0	.289/.304/.378	.264	.316	1.6	2B(14): 0.2, SS(4): -0.5	0.4
2015	LAN	MLB	21	25	3	1	1	0	1	2	2	3	0	.182/.250/.318	.224	.200	0.7	2B(6): 0.6, CF(1): -0.0	0.1
2015	GWN	AAA	21	427	52	10	7	3	37	15	35	26	7	.294/.318/.379	.254	.311	0.9	2B(81): -1.2, CF(13): -2.5	0.6
2016	*CIN*	*MLB*	*22*	*200*	*26*	*7*	*2*	*3*	*16*	*6*	*31*	*13*	*3*	*.268/.292/.382*	*.234*	*.297*	*1.7*	*2B -1, SS 1*	*0.4*
2017	*CIN*	*MLB*	*23*	*434*	*45*	*14*	*5*	*8*	*44*	*15*	*69*	*29*	*7*	*.267/.294/.384*	*.243*	*.296*	*5.0*	*2B -1, SS 2*	*1.1*

Breakout: 4% Improve: 24% Collapse: 9% Attrition: 22% MLB: 44% *Comparables: Ryan Brett, Carlos Sanchez, Howie Kendrick*

Peraza's comment in this book last year referred to the Braves moving the plus defensive shortstop to second base in order to accommodate defensive wizard Andrelton Simmons. Now Peraza is a Red and Simmons is an Angel and Atlanta has... Erick Aybar? Yikes. Peraza has been remarkably consistent during his career, hitting for a high average, refusing to walk, stealing bases and playing great defense at every stop. He more than held his own in Triple-A as a 21-year-old last season, eventually getting a cup of coffee in LA after being sent west in the Alex Wood/Hector Olivera trade. He came partway back east in this winter's Todd Frazier deal, and his path to a job in the majors is clearer in an organization that he doesn't share with Corey Seager and whatever baubles $300 million buys. Sure, Peraza's one of those twice-traded prospects now, but when it's the frenetic Braves and Dodgers sending him packing, you apply a discount factor. He's more like a 1.4-times-traded prospect.

Brandon Phillips 2B

Born: 6/28/81 Age: 35 Bats: R Throws: R Height: 6'0" Weight: 210

YEAR	TEAM	LVL	AGE	PA	R	2B	3B	HR	RBI	BB	K	SB	CS	AVG/OBP/SLG	TAv	BABIP	BRR	FRAA	WARP
2013	CIN	MLB	32	666	80	24	2	18	103	39	98	5	3	.261/.310/.396	.257	.281	-1.1	2B(151): 6.4	2.2
2014	CIN	MLB	33	499	44	25	0	8	51	23	74	2	3	.266/.306/.372	.253	.298	-2.2	2B(121): -7.4	-0.1
2015	CIN	MLB	34	623	69	19	2	12	70	27	68	23	3	.294/.328/.395	.270	.315	2.3	2B(141): 0.2, SS(1): -0.0	2.7
2016	*CIN*	*MLB*	*35*	*596*	*63*	*26*	*1*	*13*	*64*	*31*	*84*	*11*	*3*	*.269/.312/.390*	*.251*	*.292*	*-0.2*	*2B -0*	*1.8*
2017	*CIN*	*MLB*	*36*	*486*	*52*	*19*	*1*	*9*	*48*	*24*	*73*	*8*	*3*	*.261/.304/.368*	*.249*	*.289*	*-0.2*	*2B 0*	*1.0*

Breakout: 0% Improve: 31% Collapse: 6% Attrition: 12% MLB: 82% *Comparables: Mark Ellis, Orlando Hudson, Ronnie Belliard*

It's always an honor to be placed on a list whose only other entry is Willie Mays, and last year Phillips joined the Say Hey Kid as the only players in MLB history to nab 20 steals during their age-34 season or later after two consecutive years swiping five or fewer bags. (Note that Mays did it at age 40 while posting a league-leading .425 on-base percentage, because Willie Mays.) His resurgent wheels helped Phillips log his best season since 2011, earning Gold Glove consideration and once again ranking among the best second-sackers in baseball. His power and defensive range are both starting to wane and he's never been one to draw walks, but he can still line balls into the gap, take the extra base and flash his infectious grin after yet another unlikely defensive gem. Here's hoping joy can inoculate him against the cruel second-base aging curve for years to come.

Yorman Rodriguez CF

Born: 8/12/85 Age: 30 Bats: R Throws: R Height: 6'0" Weight: 195

YEAR	TEAM	LVL	AGE	PA	R	2B	3B	HR	RBI	BB	K	SB	CS	AVG/OBP/SLG	TAv	BABIP	BRR	FRAA	WARP
2013	PEN	AA	20	289	30	15	2	4	31	25	76	4	0	.267/.329/.385	.261	.359	-0.3	RF(66): 2.5	0.8
2013	BAK	A+	20	278	41	20	4	9	35	22	77	6	3	.251/.319/.470	.265	.327	0.9	CF(55): -12.3, RF(1): -0.2	-0.2
2014	PEN	AA	21	502	69	20	5	9	40	47	117	12	5	.262/.331/.389	.265	.333	2.7	CF(88): -1.8, RF(20): 0.2	2.0
2014	CIN	MLB	21	29	3	0	0	0	2	1	12	0	1	.222/.276/.222	.193	.400	0.5	RF(4): 0.7, CF(2): -0.1	0.0
2015	LOU	AAA	22	326	42	13	3	10	41	17	80	4	1	.269/.308/.429	.255	.335	0.1	RF(55): -4.1, CF(30): -4.9	-0.4
2016	*CIN*	*MLB*	*23*	*150*	*15*	*6*	*1*	*4*	*16*	*9*	*45*	*1*	*1*	*.233/.280/.370*	*.231*	*.311*	*0.0*	*LF -0*	*0.0*
2017	*CIN*	*MLB*	*24*	*333*	*37*	*14*	*2*	*9*	*36*	*22*	*98*	*3*	*1*	*.239/.290/.381*	*.245*	*.318*	*-0.1*	*LF -1*	*0.2*

Breakout: 1% Improve: 6% Collapse: 1% Attrition: 3% MLB: 11% *Comparables: Josh Kroeger, Roger Kieschnick, Nate Schierholtz*

Rodriguez lost the second half of his inaugural Triple-A season to a calf strain, but when he was healthy he continued to tantalize with his drool-worthy tools and frustrate with his mundane production. He has the ideal right-field starter kit, with lean strength, speed and one of the strongest and most accurate arms in the minor leagues. Yet as easy as everything looks for him in the field, he can be a mess at the plate, struggling to make contact and unable to convert his prodigious power potential into game-day thump. His 2014 cup of coffee already gave him more big-league plate appearances than any Yorman in history, edging out reliever Yorman Bazardo. If he can ever learn to consistently find his pitch and tattoo it, he'll be able to put some more distance between himself and all the Yormen to come.

Skip Schumaker LF

Born: 2/3/80 Age: 36 Bats: L Throws: R Height: 5'10" Weight: 190

YEAR	TEAM	LVL	AGE	PA	R	2B	3B	HR	RBI	BB	K	SB	CS	AVG/OBP/SLG	TAv	BABIP	BRR	FRAA	WARP
2013	LAN	MLB	33	356	31	16	0	2	30	28	54	2	2	.263/.332/.332	.242	.312	-1.6	2B(44): -5.7, LF(35): -2.2	-0.9
2014	CIN	MLB	34	271	22	12	0	2	22	18	50	2	1	.235/.287/.308	.233	.284	0.8	LF(33): -2.8, 2B(19): -0.4	-0.4
2015	CIN	MLB	35	268	23	20	0	1	21	23	51	2	2	.242/.306/.336	.236	.301	-2.1	LF(40): -0.5, 2B(12): 0.4	-0.3
2016	*CIN*	*MLB*	*36*	*254*	*23*	*13*	*1*	*2*	*21*	*20*	*45*	*2*	*1*	*.248/.309/.333*	*.232*	*.296*	*-0.6*	*LF -1, 2B -1*	*-0.3*
2017	*CIN*	*MLB*	*37*	*202*	*20*	*11*	*0*	*1*	*16*	*16*	*36*	*1*	*1*	*.243/.309/.323*	*.237*	*.294*	*-0.5*	*LF -1, 2B -1*	*-0.3*

Breakout: 0% Improve: 39% Collapse: 9% Attrition: 20% MLB: 75% *Comparables: Tim Raines, Jay Payton, Harvey Kuenn*

We've learned a lot from Schumaker over his long, varied and occasionally inexplicable career, especially the reminder that a baseball clubhouse is a workplace, and positional versatility, selflessness, dirty uniforms and likability can keep you employed at a higher rate of pay than your raw production might otherwise predict. Last year's lesson involved the difference between counting and rate stats, illuminated by his league-leading 19 pinch-hits, which sounds wonderful until you learn he had half-again as many chances as the next guy on the list (Alex Guerrero) and actually posted a woeful .592 OPS in the pinch. The Reds paid a cool half-million to buy out the end of Schumaker's three-year deal (his 2014 seminar was entitled *Your Agent, Your Friend*), but we wouldn't be surprised to find him haunting the end of another National League bench this year.

Eugenio Suarez SS

Born: 7/18/91 Age: 24 Bats: R Throws: R Height: 5'11" Weight: 180

YEAR	TEAM	LVL	AGE	PA	R	2B	3B	HR	RBI	BB	K	SB	CS	AVG/OBP/SLG	TAv	BABIP	BRR	FRAA	WARP
2013	LAK	A+	21	122	17	6	2	1	12	14	25	2	3	.311/.410/.437	.305	.397	-0.3	SS(24): 3.3, 2B(1): 0.2	1.4
2013	ERI	AA	21	496	53	24	4	9	45	46	98	9	11	.253/.332/.387	.268	.307	-0.3	SS(111): 6.5	3.2
2014	ERI	AA	22	170	26	14	1	6	29	15	38	7	2	.284/.347/.503	.293	.342	-0.5	SS(42): -0.7	1.2
2014	DET	MLB	22	277	33	9	1	4	23	22	67	3	2	.242/.316/.336	.247	.316	1.1	SS(81): 0.5, 3B(2): -0.1	0.9
2014	TOL	AAA	22	52	6	4	0	2	7	6	9	2	0	.302/.404/.535	.300	.333	0.6	SS(12): -0.8	0.5
2015	LOU	AAA	23	238	30	9	2	8	25	26	40	3	4	.256/.348/.438	.285	.282	0.5	SS(55): -3.0	1.3
2015	CIN	MLB	23	398	42	19	2	13	48	17	94	4	1	.280/.315/.446	.283	.341	0.3	SS(96): -2.6, 3B(1): -0.0	2.4
2016	*CIN*	*MLB*	*24*	*558*	*69*	*25*	*2*	*16*	*58*	*40*	*133*	*7*	*4*	*.249/.311/.403*	*.253*	*.302*	*0.3*	*3B -4*	*0.8*
2017	*CIN*	*MLB*	*25*	*574*	*69*	*27*	*2*	*17*	*68*	*42*	*136*	*7*	*4*	*.252/.314/.412*	*.265*	*.304*	*0.5*	*3B -4*	*1.1*

Breakout: 7% Improve: 43% Collapse: 10% Attrition: 20% MLB: 93% *Comparables: Stephen Drew, Jhonny Peralta, Brad Miller*

It was *déjà vu* all over again for Suarez, who once again was tapped to fill in for an injured big-league shortstop (first Jose Iglesias, now Zack Cozart) and held his own. The young Venezuelan has been best known for his iffy defense, solid hit tool and inconsistent results, but last year he broke out his boom stick and launched 21 bombs between Louisville and Cincinnati. Suarez is allergic to ball four and his glove is a better fit for second base, but if his power is for realsies he can be an asset in the middle infield. With lots of moving parts on Cincinnati's rebuilding roster, Suarez is perfectly positioned to slot in wherever he's asked, work on his defense and prove the thunder in his bat is here to stay.

Joey Votto 1B

Born: 9/10/83 Age: 32 Bats: L Throws: R Height: 6'2" Weight: 220

YEAR	TEAM	LVL	AGE	PA	R	2B	3B	HR	RBI	BB	K	SB	CS	AVG/OBP/SLG	TAv	BABIP	BRR	FRAA	WARP
2013	CIN	MLB	29	726	101	30	3	24	73	135	138	6	3	.305/.435/.491	.329	.360	0.5	1B(161): 6.3	6.7
2014	CIN	MLB	30	272	32	16	0	6	23	47	49	1	1	.255/.390/.409	.303	.299	-0.7	1B(61): 2.6	1.7
2015	CIN	MLB	31	695	95	33	2	29	80	143	135	11	3	.314/.459/.541	.360	.371	-5.7	1B(156): 1.4	7.6
2016	*CIN*	*MLB*	*32*	*646*	*90*	*34*	*1*	*22*	*88*	*116*	*125*	*7*	*3*	*.291/.421/.486*	*.321*	*.343*	*-2.0*	*1B 3*	*5.4*
2017	*CIN*	*MLB*	*33*	*535*	*79*	*26*	*1*	*16*	*67*	*94*	*108*	*4*	*2*	*.276/.407/.453*	*.316*	*.330*	*-1.7*	*1B 3*	*3.6*

Breakout: 1% Improve: 28% Collapse: 2% Attrition: 5% MLB: 97% *Comparables: Lance Berkman, Todd Helton, Albert Pujols*

As the Six-Fingered Man once told Prince Humperdinck, "If you haven't got your health, you haven't got anything." Now that Votto has his legs underneath him, he's once again torturing big-league pitchers, getting on base at a historic pace, launching bombs, leading the league in walks, sorting through pitches like a pile of unripe avocados and generally doing whatever the hell he wants at the plate. Last year he offered at fewer pitches than at any point in his career, and when he did put the ball in play he got out of his recent pull habit and used the whole field without sacrificing his plus power. Votto currently ranks 14th on the all-time OBP list, first among active players and trailing only Barry Bonds among those who debuted after 1950. If there's a pool somewhere to pick the next player to post a five-win season in his 40s, Votto would be a fine choice.

Kyle Waldrop LF

Born: 11/26/91 Age: 24 Bats: L Throws: L Height: 6'2" Weight: 215

YEAR	TEAM	LVL	AGE	PA	R	2B	3B	HR	RBI	BB	K	SB	CS	AVG/OBP/SLG	TAv	BABIP	BRR	FRAA	WARP
2013	BAK	A+	21	540	66	32	4	21	54	32	121	20	8	.258/.304/.462	.268	.299	0.2	LF(113): -6.9, RF(4): -0.5	0.9
2014	BAK	A+	22	289	54	20	1	6	32	22	56	11	2	.359/.409/.516	.312	.432	0.7	RF(44): -0.8, LF(8): -0.2	2.0
2014	PEN	AA	22	252	27	17	3	8	35	17	44	3	4	.315/.359/.517	.305	.357	-0.5	RF(30): 0.6, LF(29): 1.2	1.9
2015	CIN	MLB	23	1	0	0	0	0	0	0	1	0	0	.000/.000/.000	-.009	--	0.0		0.0
2015	PEN	AA	23	259	21	13	3	6	31	12	61	2	2	.277/.313/.430	.284	.343	0.8	RF(47): 4.3, 1B(15): -0.3	1.7
2015	LOU	AAA	23	213	8	6	0	1	13	7	54	0	1	.185/.211/.229	.169	.245	-2.0	LF(20): -0.7, 1B(20): -0.0	-2.2
2016	*CIN*	*MLB*	*24*	*250*	*23*	*11*	*1*	*6*	*27*	*10*	*67*	*2*	*1*	*.234/.265/.371*	*.223*	*.295*	*-0.3*	*RF -1, 1B -0*	*-0.6*
2017	*CIN*	*MLB*	*25*	*292*	*31*	*13*	*1*	*8*	*32*	*13*	*80*	*2*	*1*	*.231/.267/.375*	*.233*	*.292*	*-0.4*	*RF -1, 1B 0*	*-0.6*

Breakout: 8% Improve: 9% Collapse: 0% Attrition: 5% MLB: 11% *Comparables: Tyler Colvin, Roger Kieschnick, Josh Kroeger*

A bat-first prospect limited to left field or first base, Waldrop struggled through a tough year at the plate and is running out of time to figure things out. Blessed with prodigious raw power, Waldrop continually struggles to command the strike zone and make contact, as evidenced by his 6:1 strikeout-to-walk ratio in the high minors last year. Since batting practice homers don't show up in the boxscore, Waldrop is looking more and more like organizational fodder, a prospect zombie existing only to consume the hopes of younger pitchers.

Jesse Winker LF

Born: 8/17/93 Age: 22 Bats: L Throws: L Height: 6'3" Weight: 210

YEAR	TEAM	LVL	AGE	PA	R	2B	3B	HR	RBI	BB	K	SB	CS	AVG/OBP/SLG	TAv	BABIP	BRR	FRAA	WARP
2013	DYT	A	19	486	73	18	5	16	76	63	75	6	1	.281/.379/.463	.290	.308	-1.6	LF(100): -2.9, RF(1): -0.3	2.1
2014	BAK	A+	20	249	42	15	0	13	49	40	46	5	1	.317/.426/.580	.319	.349	-2.2	LF(46): -2.2, LF(2): -2.2	1.5
2014	PEN	AA	20	92	15	5	0	2	8	14	22	0	0	.208/.326/.351	.256	.259	0.4	LF(20): 1.8	0.4
2015	PEN	AA	21	526	69	24	2	13	55	74	83	8	4	.282/.390/.433	.308	.320	-2.0	LF(83): -4.7, RF(39): -2.7	2.8
2016	*CIN*	*MLB*	*22*	*99*	*11*	*4*	*0*	*3*	*12*	*11*	*22*	*0*	*0*	*.240/.326/.404*	*.260*	*.281*	*-0.1*	*LF -1*	*0.2*
2017	*CIN*	*MLB*	*23*	*332*	*42*	*14*	*1*	*10*	*39*	*37*	*75*	*1*	*1*	*.238/.326/.398*	*.267*	*.285*	*-0.5*	*LF -3*	*0.6*

Breakout: 6% Improve: 25% Collapse: 3% Attrition: 16% MLB: 45% *Comparables: Thomas Neal, Jaff Decker, Colby Rasmus*

The after-effects of his 2014 wrist injury may have contributed to a punchless first half, but once July rolled around Winker torched Double-A pitching to the tune of .306/.417/.505 the rest of the way. An advanced hitter who waits for his pitch, makes contact and sprays line shots to all fields, Winker has the on-base skills to bat near the top of a big-league lineup. Defensively he's a prototypical left fielder, and if you can find any fainter praise to damn him with, please let us know. If Winker can develop a little more power he could become a star; if not, he's a sure bet to reach his floor as a gloveless Nick Markakis.

PITCHERS

Burke Badenhop RHP

Born: 2/8/83 Age: 33 Bats: R Throws: R Height: 6'5" Weight: 210

YEAR	TEAM	LVL	AGE	W	L	SV	G	GS	IP	H	HR	BB/9	K/9	GB%	BABIP	WHIP	ERA	FIP	DRA	WARP	CFIP	MPH
2013	MIL	MLB	30	2	3	1	63	0	62^1	62	6	1.7	6.1	56%	.289	1.19	3.47	3.50	4.10	0.4	98	91.5
2014	BOS	MLB	31	0	3	1	70	0	70^2	70	1	2.4	5.1	62%	.304	1.26	2.29	3.10	3.27	1.1	108	92.0
2015	CIN	MLB	32	2	4	0	68	0	66^1	71	4	2.7	4.9	48%	.298	1.37	3.93	3.76	3.65	0.8	115	91.0
2016	*CIN*	*MLB*	*33*	*3*	*1*	*0*	*57*	*0*	*60*	*61*	*7*	*2.7*	*5.7*	*53%*	*.301*	*1.31*	*4.22*	*4.29*	*4.80*	*0.1*	*108*	
2017	*CIN*	*MLB*	*34*	*2*	*1*	*0*	*33*	*0*	*32^1*	*35*	*4*	*2.7*	*5.4*	*53%*	*.313*	*1.38*	*4.41*	*4.67*	*5.02*	*-0.1*	*113*	

Breakout: 26% Improve: 43% Collapse: 21% Attrition: 6% MLB: 90% *Comparables: Joe Beimel, Matt Lindstrom, Tim Burke*

Groundballs sound like a wobbly base on which to construct something substantial, but Badenhop has used them to build a solid career. Last year, however, his vaunted sinker wasn't delivering the ground-pounding goodness to which we've grown accustomed; fewer than half of them put into play resulted in a groundball, compared to nearly two-thirds in 2014 and for his career. With a high-wage middle-innings groundball specialist about as critical to a rebuilding team as a vestigial tail, Cincinnati understandably bought out his contract, but Badenhop is a solid bet to continue inducing valuable seventh-inning double plays this summer.

Homer Bailey RHP

Born: 5/3/86 Age: 30 Bats: R Throws: R Height: 6'4" Weight: 225

YEAR	TEAM	LVL	AGE	W	L	SV	G	GS	IP	H	HR	BB/9	K/9	GB%	BABIP	WHIP	ERA	FIP	DRA	WARP	CFIP	MPH
2013	CIN	MLB	27	11	12	0	32	32	209	181	20	2.3	8.6	48%	.284	1.12	3.49	3.28	3.74	2.9	91	97.2
2014	CIN	MLB	28	9	5	0	23	23	145^2	134	16	2.8	7.7	52%	.286	1.23	3.71	3.90	4.07	1.3	104	96.8
2015	CIN	MLB	29	0	1	0	2	2	11^1	16	3	3.2	2.4	59%	.317	1.76	5.56	7.13	7.91	-0.4	120	94.5
2016	*CIN*	*MLB*	*30*	*2*	*2*	*0*	*6*	*6*	*38*	*34*	*4*	*2.7*	*7.7*	*51%*	*.297*	*1.20*	*3.84*	*3.67*	*4.37*	*0.4*	*100*	
2017	*CIN*	*MLB*	*31*	*12*	*12*	*0*	*32*	*32*	*202^2*	*195*	*24*	*2.7*	*7.5*	*51%*	*.310*	*1.26*	*4.03*	*4.26*	*4.59*	*1.6*	*106*	

Breakout: 14% Improve: 43% Collapse: 24% Attrition: 8% MLB: 95% *Comparables: Shaun Marcum, Jeff Francis, Freddy Garcia*

In some other dimension of our multiverse, Bailey is healthy and last year posted his fourth straight solid season in the Reds' rotation. That isn't as good as the competing dimension where he makes good on his stuff and pedigree and spends a decade as a *bona fide* ace, let alone the ideal one where his birth name is Hom-El, he can fly and John Candy just retired after a 20-year run as the king of late-night television. Unfortunately, Reds fans reading this comment live in the one where the perennially frustrating Bailey has made only 25 starts over the last two years, won't return to the mound until midseason and is set to earn an average of $20 million annually through 2019. Before being bitten by the injury bug, Bailey had seen a velocity spike and was getting more mileage out of his two-seamer and splitter. If he can be that guy again, he'll earn his salary as a solid mid-rotation starter.

Aroldis Chapman LHP

Born: 2/28/88 Age: 28 Bats: L Throws: L Height: 6'4" Weight: 215

YEAR	TEAM	LVL	AGE	W	L	SV	G	GS	IP	H	HR	BB/9	K/9	GB%	BABIP	WHIP	ERA	FIP	DRA	WARP	CFIP	MPH
2013	CIN	MLB	25	4	5	38	68	0	63^2	37	7	4.1	15.8	34%	.280	1.04	2.54	2.44	3.10	1.1	52	102.4
2014	CIN	MLB	26	0	3	36	54	0	54	21	1	4.0	17.7	44%	.290	0.83	2.00	0.86	1.35	2.1	36	103.2
2015	CIN	MLB	27	4	4	33	65	0	66^1	43	3	4.5	15.7	38%	.331	1.15	1.63	1.97	2.47	1.8	56	103.0
2016	*CIN*	*MLB*	*28*	*4*	*2*	*38*	*65*	*0*	*68^1*	*43*	*7*	*3.4*	*14.2*	*38%*	*.304*	*1.00*	*2.56*	*2.48*	*3.01*	*2.0*	*58*	
2017	*CIN*	*MLB*	*29*	*4*	*3*	*14*	*35*	*8*	*77^2*	*52*	*9*	*3.6*	*13.6*	*38%*	*.307*	*1.07*	*2.93*	*3.07*	*3.44*	*1.4*	*71*	

Breakout: 27% Improve: 43% Collapse: 39% Attrition: 12% MLB: 94% *Comparables: Francisco Rodriguez, David Robertson, Armando Benitez*

There's something about Chapman for everyone to love. Adrenaline junkies appreciate the visceral thrill of his triple-digit heat. Capitalists dig on his escape from Cuba to earn what the market will bear. Trivia masters enjoy knowing Chapman is a citizen of the Pyreneean nation of Andorra. Stats nerds flip over the fact he threw the 62 fastest pitches in baseball last year, causing the MLB.com Statcast Leaderboard to implement a button entitled "Enable the Chapman Filter." Most importantly, big-league managers love that Chapman shortens virtually every game in which he appears by a full inning. Guys like Craig Kimbrel and Kanley Jansen may be equally productive, but nothing causes more disquiet to opposing hitters than the sight and sound of Chapman warming up. In a sense it might be a good thing he was never converted into an ace starter, since everyone who buys a ticket to see his team play knows they have a chance to experience the Aroldis Show.

Tony Cingrani LHP

Born: 7/5/89 Age: 26 Bats: L Throws: L Height: 6'4" Weight: 210

YEAR	TEAM	LVL	AGE	W	L	SV	G	GS	IP	H	HR	BB/9	K/9	GB%	BABIP	WHIP	ERA	FIP	DRA	WARP	CFIP	MPH
2013	CIN	MLB	23	7	4	0	23	18	104^2	72	14	3.7	10.3	36%	.241	1.10	2.92	3.76	3.60	1.6	89	95.1
2013	LOU	AAA	23	3	0	0	6	6	31^1	14	1	3.2	14.1	50%	.236	0.80	1.15	1.64	3.14	0.7	56	
2014	CIN	MLB	24	2	8	0	13	11	63^1	62	12	5.0	8.7	37%	.292	1.53	4.55	5.34	6.13	-1.1	110	94.4
2015	CIN	MLB	25	0	3	0	35	1	33^1	31	3	6.8	10.5	41%	.329	1.68	5.67	4.51	5.49	-0.3	102	94.7
2015	LOU	AAA	25	0	1	0	9	6	24^2	20	2	4.0	11.7	45%	.310	1.26	1.82	3.20	2.67	0.6	82	
2016	*CIN*	*MLB*	*26*	*3*	*1*	*0*	*59*	*0*	*62^2*	*51*	*8*	*3.6*	*9.3*	*40%*	*.287*	*1.21*	*3.92*	*3.92*	*4.47*	*0.4*	*102*	
2017	*CIN*	*MLB*	*27*	*6*	*6*	*0*	*31*	*17*	*117*	*96*	*15*	*3.5*	*9.2*	*40%*	*.289*	*1.21*	*3.98*	*4.22*	*4.54*	*0.9*	*104*	

Breakout: 34% Improve: 61% Collapse: 18% Attrition: 11% MLB: 95% *Comparables: Matt Moore, Hong-Chih Kuo, Marc Rzepczynski*

Cingrani posted some cringe-inducing numbers last season, but we're willing to grade his first full season in the bullpen as an "Incomplete." His lack of reliable secondary offerings have long meant his days in the rotation were numbered, and as expected his low-90s fastball played up in relief and led to increased strikeout and swinging strike rates. However, he struggled with both command and control, and between the walks and the line drives and two stints on the DL he never found his groove. Cingrani has the goods to get big outs in the 'pen, and if he's healthy this summer he's well positioned to start proving it.

Carlos Contreras RHP

Born: 1/8/91 Age: 25 Bats: R Throws: R Height: 5'11" Weight: 215

YEAR	TEAM	LVL	AGE	W	L	SV	G	GS	IP	H	HR	BB/9	K/9	GB%	BABIP	WHIP	ERA	FIP	DRA	WARP	CFIP	MPH
2013	PEN	AA	22	3	2	0	8	8	42^1	36	2	4.5	5.5	48%	.262	1.35	2.76	4.07	4.62	0.0	117	
2013	BAK	A+	22	5	7	0	18	18	90	70	9	4.1	9.6	43%	.269	1.23	3.80	4.44	5.10	1.1	93	
2014	PEN	AA	23	2	1	0	9	3	20	15	0	4.9	12.1	40%	.300	1.30	2.70	2.29				
2014	CIN	MLB	23	0	1	0	17	0	19^1	19	2	7.9	8.8	36%	.304	1.86	6.52	5.12	5.52	-0.2	117	96.3
2015	CIN	MLB	24	0	0	0	22	0	28	22	3	6.4	6.1	41%	.232	1.50	4.82	5.45	4.74	0.0	125	94.9
2015	LOU	AAA	24	2	2	3	31	0	39^2	32	3	6.8	12.5	37%	.322	1.56	2.95	3.64	3.33	0.5	90	
2016	*CIN*	*MLB*	*25*	*3*	*1*	*0*	*65*	*0*	68^1	*59*	*8*	*4.4*	*8.2*	*38%*	*.290*	*1.35*	*4.31*	*4.25*	*4.89*	*0.0*	*113*	
2017	*CIN*	*MLB*	*26*	*4*	*3*	*0*	*46*	*7*	92^2	*81*	*11*	*4.5*	*8.8*	*38%*	*.301*	*1.37*	*4.27*	*4.54*	*4.85*	*0.2*	*112*	

Breakout: 14% Improve: 31% Collapse: 17% Attrition: 27% MLB: 50% *Comparables: Emiliano Fruto, Jeremy Jeffress, Josh Rupe*

Over the last two seasons, Contreras has managed to not only fulfill his dreams of pitching in the major leagues but post the highest score in a critical statistical category. Unfortunately, that category is walk percentage, where Contreras' 16.9 percent edged out the appropriately named Grant Balfour. When a pitcher walks seven batters per nine innings over his short big-league career, it's fair to ask whether that pitcher should ever be allowed to work nine *more* big-league innings. Contreras doesn't miss enough bats to survive his addiction to ball four, and shouldn't be tabbed for more than mop-up duty in a major-league 'pen.

Anthony DeSclafani RHP

Born: 4/18/90 Age: 26 Bats: R Throws: R Height: 6'1" Weight: 190

YEAR	TEAM	LVL	AGE	W	L	SV	G	GS	IP	H	HR	BB/9	K/9	GB%	BABIP	WHIP	ERA	FIP	DRA	WARP	CFIP	MPH
2013	JAX	AA	23	5	4	0	13	13	75	74	7	1.7	7.4	49%	.309	1.17	3.36	3.19	3.80	0.8	91	
2013	JUP	A+	23	4	2	0	12	12	54	48	3	1.5	8.8	54%	.304	1.06	1.67	2.56	3.55	0.9	74	
2014	MIA	MLB	24	2	2	0	13	5	33	40	4	1.4	7.1	42%	.330	1.36	6.27	3.74	5.02	-0.1	102	95.5
2014	NWO	AAA	24	3	3	0	12	11	59^1	48	2	3.2	8.9	44%	.284	1.16	3.49	3.41	5.03	0.5	93	
2014	JAX	AA	24	3	4	0	8	8	43	45	4	2.1	8.0	46%	.333	1.28	4.19	3.33				
2015	CIN	MLB	25	9	13	0	31	31	184^2	194	17	2.7	7.4	47%	.318	1.35	4.05	3.70	3.95	2.4	100	95.3
2016	*CIN*	*MLB*	*26*	*10*	*10*	*0*	*29*	*29*	*174*	*173*	*19*	*2.5*	*7.1*	*46%*	*.316*	*1.27*	*3.85*	*3.82*	*4.39*	*1.8*	*100*	
2017	*CIN*	*MLB*	*27*	*8*	*9*	*0*	*27*	*27*	158^2	*162*	*18*	*2.4*	*7.4*	*46%*	*.327*	*1.29*	*3.85*	*4.07*	*4.39*	*1.5*	*100*	

Breakout: 32% Improve: 58% Collapse: 20% Attrition: 14% MLB: 93% *Comparables: Scott Baker, Zach McAllister, Wade Miley*

Kids these days, they grow up so fast. On July 29th, DeSclafani was a rookie pitcher taking his 25th turn in a big-league rotation. Yet he was also by far the veteran of the starting staff, as the other seven pitchers who would work in the Reds' rotation from that point on had started only 30 games between them. DeSclafani held his own and showed promise as a mid-rotation anchor, making believers of those who thought his stuff and frame wouldn't bear up to a starter's workload. He depends on a plus slider and decent curveball to help keep hitters off his mundane low-90s heater, but his dodgy changeup left him vulnerable to lefties. If DeSclafani can find something to help tame the oppo-handed, he should find work munching innings for years to come.

Jumbo Diaz RHP

Born: 4/18/90 Age: 26 Bats: R Throws: R Height: 6'1" Weight: 190

YEAR	TEAM	LVL	AGE	W	L	SV	G	GS	IP	H	HR	BB/9	K/9	GB%	BABIP	WHIP	ERA	FIP	DRA	WARP	CFIP	MPH
2013	LOU	AAA	29	3	4	13	44	0	54^1	35	5	3.5	9.9	51%	.231	1.03	1.66	3.41	3.84	0.5	82	
2014	LOU	AAA	30	2	2	18	30	0	33^1	25	1	2.7	8.4	48%	.267	1.05	1.35	2.97	4.09	0.3	84	
2014	CIN	MLB	30	0	1	0	36	0	34^2	29	3	3.6	9.6	41%	.295	1.24	3.38	3.30	3.28	0.5	87	99.6
2015	LOU	AAA	31	0	1	8	13	0	16	11	0	2.2	6.8	42%	.229	0.94	1.12	2.59	3.69	0.1	95	
2015	CIN	MLB	31	2	1	1	61	0	60^1	58	9	2.7	10.4	47%	.316	1.26	4.18	3.82	4.35	0.3	85	100.0
2016	*CIN*	*MLB*	*32*	*3*	*1*	*0*	*59*	*0*	62^2	*53*	*7*	*2.9*	*9.0*	*45%*	*.295*	*1.18*	*3.69*	*3.53*	*4.23*	*0.6*	*92*	
2017	*CIN*	*MLB*	*33*	*3*	*1*	*1*	*53*	*0*	*57*	*50*	*7*	*2.8*	*9.2*	*45%*	*.301*	*1.19*	*3.75*	*3.97*	*4.30*	*0.4*	*94*	

Breakout: 15% Improve: 28% Collapse: 13% Attrition: 22% MLB: 51% *Comparables: Jean Machi, Wil Ledezma, Clay Rapada*

To be a reliever is to be plagued by the curse of small samples. Take Diaz, who by many measures pitched better in the first half of last season than he did later on, allowing fewer walks and fewer hard-hit balls, while generating more groundball outs and posting an excellent whiff rate. But he was undone by the gopher ball, as fully 25 percent of the flyballs he allowed landed in the bleachers, and in early June he was sent to Louisville for fine-tuning. When Diaz returned in mid-July he had lost his setup gig, but after yielding a more normal number of home runs per flyball (a notoriously fickle metric) the rest of the way, he was considered "cured." Through it all the big righty continued to unleash his overpowering upper-90s heat and darting slider, making him a valuable and inexpensive late-innings weapon no matter what some random 20-inning sample might say.

Brandon Finnegan LHP

Born: 4/14/93 Age: 23 Bats: L Throws: L Height: 5'11" Weight: 185

YEAR	TEAM	LVL	AGE	W	L	SV	G	GS	IP	H	HR	BB/9	K/9	GB%	BABIP	WHIP	ERA	FIP	DRA	WARP	CFIP	MPH
2014	NWA	AA	21	0	3	0	8	0	12	15	2	1.5	9.8	52%	.342	1.42	2.25	3.87				
2014	WIL	A+	21	0	1	0	5	5	15	5	1	1.2	7.8	50%	.121	0.47	0.60	3.05	4.13	0.2	85	
2014	KCA	MLB	21	0	1	0	7	0	7	6	0	1.3	12.9	59%	.353	1.00	1.29	0.73	0.74	0.3	83	95.3
2015	NWA	AA	22	0	1	1	5	3	13	10	1	8.3	9.0	42%	.257	1.69	2.77	5.07	6.67	-0.2	122	
2015	LOU	AAA	22	0	3	0	8	8	30^1	31	3	5.0	8.9	45%	.318	1.58	6.23	4.34	4.57	0.0	104	
2015	CIN	MLB	22	2	2	0	6	4	23^2	21	5	3.0	9.1	52%	.262	1.23	4.18	4.89	5.00	0.0	98	94.6
2015	OMA	AAA	22	0	2	0	6	4	14	17	1	4.5	12.2	46%	.421	1.71	7.07	3.31	3.74	0.3	85	
2015	KCA	MLB	22	3	0	0	14	0	24^1	16	3	4.8	7.8	59%	.213	1.19	2.96	4.71	3.55	0.4	105	96.0
2016	*CIN*	*MLB*	*23*	*7*	*8*	*0*	*24*	*24*	*120*	*105*	*15*	*3.5*	*8.4*	*51%*	*.295*	*1.26*	*4.10*	*4.03*	*4.68*	*0.9*	*109*	
2017	*CIN*	*MLB*	*24*	*4*	*4*	*1*	*45*	*13*	126^2	*113*	*16*	*3.4*	*8.2*	*51%*	*.296*	*1.26*	*4.19*	*4.44*	*4.78*	*0.4*	*112*	

Breakout: 14% Improve: 42% Collapse: 19% Attrition: 24% MLB: 68% *Comparables: Matt Garza, Scott Olsen, Johnny Cueto*

Finnegan's game log last season bore a worrisome resemblance to an American Eagle flight attendant's log, which may not be the best thing for a pitcher in his first full professional season. The Royals kept him bouncing between minor-league stops and the big club, and between the rotation and the bullpen, never letting him find his rhythm or follow a normal development path. His new employers in Cincinnati seem committed to using him as a starter, and with a fastball that can reach the mid-90s, an excellent slider and a solid changeup, he has the goods to succeed. Focusing on repeating his delivery, rather than his role or which uniform he'll be wearing tomorrow, will help him reduce the walks that currently plague him and allow him to mature into a solid third starter.

Amir Garrett LHP

Born: 5/3/92 Age: 24 Bats: L Throws: L Height: 6'5" Weight: 210

YEAR	TEAM	LVL	AGE	W	L	SV	G	GS	IP	H	HR	BB/9	K/9	GB%	BABIP	WHIP	ERA	FIP	DRA	WARP	CFIP	MPH
2013	DYT	A	21	1	3	0	8	8	34	40	4	4.2	4.0	40%	.305	1.65	6.88	5.57	5.44	-0.1	125	
2014	DYT	A	22	7	8	0	27	27	133^1	115	11	3.4	8.6	50%	.282	1.25	3.64	3.87	4.61	0.9	104	
2015	DAY	A+	23	9	7	0	26	26	140^1	117	4	3.5	8.5	45%	.298	1.23	2.44	2.90	3.55	1.6	97	
2016	*CIN*	*MLB*	*24*	*1*	*0*	*0*	*27*	*0*	28^1	*28*	*3*	*4.1*	*6.7*	*41%*	*.305*	*1.43*	*4.56*	*4.42*	*5.16*	*0.0*	*122*	
2017	*CIN*	*MLB*	*25*	*3*	*4*	*0*	*11*	*11*	66^2	*66*	*8*	*4.4*	*6.8*	*41%*	*.309*	*1.47*	*4.80*	*5.10*	*5.43*	*-0.1*	*129*	

Breakout: 0% Improve: 0% Collapse: 0% Attrition: 0% MLB: 0% *Comparables: Cody Anderson, Chris Carpenter, Angel Guzman*

A former St. John's hoopster, Garrett continues to flash impressive upside as he completes his transition from athlete to pitcher. The towering lefty can reach back for high-90s heat that could make him a bullpen weapon on its own, but his slider and changeup are both improving and give him a chance to stay in the rotation. He'll need to shore up his command as he starts to face more advanced hitters in the high minors, but if it all comes together Garrett has mid-rotation potential.

J.J. Hoover RHP

Born: 8/13/87 Age: 28 Bats: R Throws: R Height: 6'3" Weight: 245

YEAR	TEAM	LVL	AGE	W	L	SV	G	GS	IP	H	HR	BB/9	K/9	GB%	BABIP	WHIP	ERA	FIP	DRA	WARP	CFIP	MPH
2013	CIN	MLB	25	5	5	3	69	0	66	47	6	3.5	9.1	33%	.244	1.11	2.86	3.44	3.27	1.1	92	95.3
2014	CIN	MLB	26	1	10	0	54	0	62^2	56	13	4.5	10.8	29%	.277	1.39	4.88	4.94	5.19	-0.5	96	95.3
2015	CIN	MLB	27	8	2	1	67	0	64^1	44	7	4.3	7.3	44%	.215	1.17	2.94	4.50	3.58	0.9	109	95.8
2016	*CIN*	*MLB*	*28*	*3*	*1*	*2*	*54*	*0*	*57*	*46*	*7*	*3.6*	*8.3*	*38%*	*.270*	*1.20*	*4.12*	*4.09*	*4.69*	*0.1*	*108*	
2017	*CIN*	*MLB*	*29*	*3*	*1*	*1*	*55*	*0*	58^1	*47*	*7*	*3.5*	*8.3*	*38%*	*.274*	*1.20*	*4.10*	*4.35*	*4.67*	*0.1*	*108*	

Breakout: 23% Improve: 52% Collapse: 18% Attrition: 10% MLB: 84% *Comparables: Jose Arredondo, Neal Cotts, Wesley Wright*

Hoover has a long tradition of existence in the Reds' bullpen, both to its members and the community at large, but a rough 2014 season had him on double-secret probation last spring. He responded with the most productive stretch of his career, posting a 30-appearance scoreless streak, holding batters to a .172/.271/.292 line through the end of August and earning the role of eighth-inning palate cleanser before opponents are force-fed Aroldis Chapman. His success was due both to keeping the ball low in the zone (to counter his chronic gopheritis) and an unsustainably low .215 BABIP that overcame a precipitous drop in his strikeout rate. As the season wore on the flyballs became more and more frequent until a four-tater September reminded us of the fine line Hoover often walks. He'll either need to increase his strikeout rate or remember how to keep the ball in the park in order to remain a solid late-inning option.

Raisel Iglesias RHP

Born: 1/4/90 Age: 26 Bats: R Throws: R Height: 6'2" Weight: 185

YEAR	TEAM	LVL	AGE	W	L	SV	G	GS	IP	H	HR	BB/9	K/9	GB%	BABIP	WHIP	ERA	FIP	DRA	WARP	CFIP	MPH
2015	CIN	MLB	25	3	7	0	18	16	95^1	81	11	2.6	9.8	48%	.286	1.14	4.15	3.58	3.77	1.4	87	95.4
2015	LOU	AAA	25	1	3	0	6	6	29	26	4	2.5	6.5	53%	.250	1.17	3.41	4.33	4.34	0.1	103	
2016	*CIN*	*MLB*	*26*	*10*	*9*	*0*	*28*	*28*	159^2	*135*	*19*	*2.6*	*8.8*	*48%*	*.295*	*1.13*	*3.61*	*3.63*	*4.12*	*2.2*	*94*	
2017	*CIN*	*MLB*	*27*	*9*	*9*	*0*	*28*	*28*	169^1	*148*	*20*	*2.5*	*8.8*	*48%*	*.303*	*1.15*	*3.64*	*3.84*	*4.15*	*2.0*	*95*	

Breakout: 21% Improve: 52% Collapse: 16% Attrition: 10% MLB: 98% *Comparables: Mike Minor, Max Scherzer, Josh Beckett*

The Reds signed Iglesias to a seven-year, $27 million contract back in 2014, and the young Cuban is already making good. Iglesias is primarily a sinker-slider pitcher who works in a four-seamer and a changeup, but he consistently varies his release point to give each offering different movement and keep hitters off-balance. Primarily a reliever in Cuba, Iglesias has worked hard to build up his stamina and was at his best down the stretch, when he became the first Reds starter in over a century to post double-digit strikeouts in three consecutive starts. He'll need to gain more consistency with his changeup to tame lefty batters, but Iglesias looks primed to settle in as a solid mid-rotation option who can occasionally dominate.

John Lamb LHP

Born: 7/10/90 Age: 25 Bats: L Throws: L Height: 6'4" Weight: 205

YEAR	TEAM	LVL	AGE	W	L	SV	G	GS	IP	H	HR	BB/9	K/9	GB%	BABIP	WHIP	ERA	FIP	DRA	WARP	CFIP	MPH
2013	WIL	A+	22	4	12	0	19	19	92^{2}	109	13	1.8	7.4	38%	.334	1.38	5.63	4.28	4.38	1.0	89	
2013	OMA	AAA	22	1	2	0	3	3	16	15	1	3.9	5.6	42%	.269	1.38	6.75	4.82	5.30	0.1	109	
2014	OMA	AAA	23	8	10	0	27	26	138^{1}	137	19	4.4	8.5	41%	.303	1.48	3.97	5.26	5.62	0.3	113	
2015	LOU	AAA	24	1	1	0	3	3	17	14	0	3.7	11.1	23%	.326	1.24	2.65	2.10	2.70	0.4	82	
2015	OMA	AAA	24	9	1	0	17	17	94^{1}	80	7	2.8	9.2	36%	.297	1.16	2.67	3.58	3.06	2.6	78	
2015	CIN	MLB	24	1	5	0	10	10	49^{2}	58	8	3.4	10.5	40%	.376	1.55	5.80	4.19	5.85	-0.5	93	93.7
2016	*CIN*	*MLB*	*25*	*8*	*8*	*0*	*26*	*26*	*137^{2}*	*126*	*17*	*3.0*	*8.5*	*37%*	*.305*	*1.25*	*3.93*	*3.91*	*4.48*	*1.3*	*103*	
2017	*CIN*	*MLB*	*26*	*7*	*7*	*0*	*23*	*23*	*132^{2}*	*124*	*18*	*3.1*	*8.8*	*37%*	*.314*	*1.28*	*4.06*	*4.31*	*4.63*	*0.9*	*107*	

Breakout: 24% Improve: 35% Collapse: 29% Attrition: 32% MLB: 71% *Comparables: Andre Rienzo, Brandon Workman, Jose Cisnero*

A former top prospect whose arrival was delayed by Tommy John surgery, Lamb has been better than advertised since coming to Cincinnati in the Johnny Cueto trade. The mid-90s velocity of his youth is no longer there, but Lamb has compensated with a cutter that can be a true swing-and-miss offering and a plus changeup that proofs him against righty bats. His flyball tendencies are a bad fit for Cincinnati and will lead to some disasterpiece outings, as they did in 2015, but if the illustrated man can continue to strike out a batter per inning he has a chance to settle in at the back of the rotation.

Sam LeCure RHP

Born: 5/4/84 Age: 32 Bats: R Throws: R Height: 6'0" Weight: 210

YEAR	TEAM	LVL	AGE	W	L	SV	G	GS	IP	H	HR	BB/9	K/9	GB%	BABIP	WHIP	ERA	FIP	DRA	WARP	CFIP	MPH
2013	CIN	MLB	29	2	1	1	63	0	61	50	4	3.5	9.7	44%	.295	1.21	2.66	2.94	4.04	0.4	92	91.9
2014	CIN	MLB	30	1	4	0	62	0	56^{2}	62	6	3.8	7.6	45%	.329	1.52	3.81	4.21	5.17	-0.5	110	90.3
2015	CIN	MLB	31	0	2	0	19	0	20	16	2	3.2	6.8	59%	.237	1.15	3.15	4.01	4.24	0.1	109	89.8
2015	LOU	AAA	31	5	4	1	41	0	60	63	7	3.6	6.6	42%	.304	1.45	5.25	4.51	4.95	-0.4	110	
2016	*CIN*	*MLB*	*32*	*3*	*1*	*0*	*65*	*0*	*69*	*64*	*9*	*3.3*	*7.3*	*46%*	*.294*	*1.29*	*4.24*	*4.29*	*4.82*	*0.1*	*112*	
2017	*CIN*	*MLB*	*33*	*1*	*0*	*0*	*26*	*0*	*29*	*27*	*3*	*3.4*	*7.2*	*46%*	*.296*	*1.30*	*4.31*	*4.57*	*4.90*	*0.0*	*115*	

Breakout: 25% Improve: 49% Collapse: 22% Attrition: 17% MLB: 86% *Comparables: Todd Coffey, Aaron Fultz, Santiago Casilla*

"The stuff returned to my norm, which is unremarkable, but still good enough." That was LeCure the day he returned to Cincinnati after spending most of the summer in Louisville, displaying the self-awareness that has helped make him a bullpen fixture for the better part of six seasons. LeCure uses a million tricks to keep hitters from sitting on his combustible upper-80s fastball; last year he started replacing more of his knuckle-curves with an improved splitter and turned into a true worm-killer down the stretch. That bodes well for his future, so we should expect to see even more sluggers trudging back to the dugout sporting the classic "how'd that guy get me out?" expression in the middle innings this summer.

Michael Lorenzen RHP

Born: 5/4/84 Age: 32 Bats: R Throws: R Height: 6'0" Weight: 210

YEAR	TEAM	LVL	AGE	W	L	SV	G	GS	IP	H	HR	BB/9	K/9	GB%	BABIP	WHIP	ERA	FIP	DRA	WARP	CFIP	MPH
2014	PEN	AA	22	4	6	0	24	24	120^{2}	112	9	3.3	6.3	53%	.285	1.29	3.13	4.01				
2015	CIN	MLB	23	4	9	0	27	21	113^{1}	131	18	4.5	6.6	42%	.322	1.66	5.40	5.43	6.42	-1.9	125	97.1
2015	LOU	AAA	23	4	2	0	6	6	43	34	3	1.7	4.0	49%	.231	0.98	1.88	3.74	4.38	0.2	105	
2016	*CIN*	*MLB*	*24*	*8*	*11*	*0*	*29*	*29*	*153^{2}*	*157*	*21*	*3.5*	*6.0*	*44%*	*.304*	*1.41*	*4.74*	*4.76*	*5.37*	*-0.2*	*127*	
2017	*CIN*	*MLB*	*25*	*7*	*9*	*0*	*24*	*24*	*143^{2}*	*148*	*19*	*3.5*	*6.7*	*44%*	*.315*	*1.42*	*4.68*	*4.98*	*5.30*	*0.0*	*124*	

Breakout: 14% Improve: 31% Collapse: 7% Attrition: 17% MLB: 44% *Comparables: Nick Martinez, Jimmy Gobble, Ryan Feierabend*

Big-league hitters have no problem turning around mid-90s fastballs over the plate if they don't have something else to worry about, as Lorenzen found out in his rookie season. The young right-hander struggled with his command and was hit hard, causing him to nibble, walk too many men and post a FIP that was barely on the good side of Jeremy Guthrie. His slider and changeup remain works in progress, in the Crazy Horse Memorial sense, but if you squint you can still see the outlines of a future fourth starter. Youth and velocity will continue to convince the Reds to give him chances, but Lorenzen will need to figure out new ways to make batters uncomfortable if he wants to avoid becoming just another middle reliever with a big fastball and inconsistent results.

Ryan Mattheus RHP

Born: 11/10/83 Age: 32 Bats: R Throws: R Height: 6'3" Weight: 220

YEAR	TEAM	LVL	AGE	W	L	SV	G	GS	IP	H	HR	BB/9	K/9	GB%	BABIP	WHIP	ERA	FIP	DRA	WARP	CFIP	MPH
2013	WAS	MLB	29	0	2	0	37	0	35^{1}	52	1	3.8	5.6	57%	.398	1.90	6.37	3.42	6.34	-0.7	117	95.2
2014	SYR	AAA	30	1	3	2	34	0	40^{1}	47	5	2.7	7.1	57%	.321	1.46	5.80	4.28	4.49	0.1	97	
2014	WAS	MLB	30	0	0	0	7	0	8^{2}	7	0	4.2	4.2	50%	.269	1.27	1.04	3.91	3.94	0.1	115	95.2
2015	ANA	MLB	31	0	0	0	1	0	1	0	0	9.0	18.0	100%	.000	1.00	0.00	2.10	1.28	0.0	95	95.2
2015	CIN	MLB	31	2	4	0	57	0	55	67	3	2.8	5.7	56%	.333	1.53	4.09	3.63	4.64	0.0	112	95.4
2015	SLC	AAA	31	0	2	1	11	0	12^{2}	10	2	1.4	8.5	57%	.229	0.95	2.84	4.23	3.66	0.2	86	
2016	*CIN*	*MLB*	*32*	*3*	*1*	*0*	*57*	*0*	*60^{1}*	*58*	*7*	*3.1*	*6.3*	*55%*	*.296*	*1.30*	*4.26*	*4.30*	*4.84*	*0.0*	*111*	
2017	*CIN*	*MLB*	*33*	*2*	*1*	*0*	*39*	*0*	*40^{2}*	*40*	*4*	*3.0*	*6.2*	*55%*	*.304*	*1.33*	*4.29*	*4.54*	*4.87*	*0.0*	*112*	

Breakout: 28% Improve: 44% Collapse: 26% Attrition: 27% MLB: 81% *Comparables: Joe Beimel, Saul Rivera, Rafael Perez*

Mattheus doesn't strike anybody out or walk anybody. He doesn't allow a lot of flyballs or home runs. He doesn't throw particularly hard or have great secondary stuff or throw a screwball or a knuckler or an eephus. He doesn't start or finish games, and he rarely ever wins or loses them. What he does do is throw hundreds of low-leverage pitches out of the roughly 24,000 a bad team needs to throw each year, saving the arms of better or more aspirational pitchers, sometimes inducing a useful double-play grounder while allowing fans to take a bathroom break without worrying they'll miss something special. Many pitchers could do this, but Mattheus *does* do this, and in a perfectly acceptable way. It's good work if you can get it.

Jon Moscot RHP

Born: 8/15/91 Age: 24 Bats: R Throws: R Height: 6'4" Weight: 210

YEAR	TEAM	LVL	AGE	W	L	SV	G	GS	IP	H	HR	BB/9	K/9	GB%	BABIP	WHIP	ERA	FIP	DRA	WARP	CFIP	MPH
2013	PEN	AA	21	2	1	0	6	6	31	34	3	3.5	8.1	32%	.337	1.48	3.19	3.82	4.19	0.2	103	
2013	BAK	A+	21	2	14	0	22	22	115^{2}	109	17	2.8	8.7	47%	.287	1.25	4.59	4.83	4.92	1.6	86	
2014	PEN	AA	22	7	10	0	25	25	149^{1}	145	11	2.6	6.7	38%	.291	1.26	3.13	3.68				
2014	LOU	AAA	22	1	1	0	3	3	17^{1}	15	5	3.6	4.7	22%	.189	1.27	5.71	7.28	5.10	0.0	121	
2015	CIN	MLB	23	1	1	0	3	3	11^{2}	11	2	3.9	4.6	44%	.243	1.37	4.63	5.65	4.77	0.0	117	94.1
2015	LOU	AAA	23	7	1	0	9	9	54^{1}	50	5	3.1	5.6	40%	.269	1.27	3.15	4.15	5.18	-0.3	114	
2016	*CIN*	*MLB*	*24*	*3*	*3*	*0*	*24*	*8*	*57*	*55*	*7*	*3.0*	*6.2*	*37%*	*.293*	*1.30*	*4.42*	*4.37*	*5.00*	*0.1*	*118*	
2017	*CIN*	*MLB*	*25*	*4*	*5*	*0*	*14*	*14*	*84^{2}*	*86*	*11*	*3.1*	*6.5*	*37%*	*.308*	*1.36*	*4.61*	*4.88*	*5.21*	*0.1*	*123*	

Breakout: 9% Improve: 19% Collapse: 18% Attrition: 36% MLB: 51% *Comparables: Kevin Mulvey, Anthony Ranaudo, Stolmy Pimentel*

Moscot earned his first big-league call-up last June and was making his third start when he separated his non-throwing shoulder diving to tag Anthony Gose in a rundown at second base. The injury couldn't have come at a worse time for the former fourth-rounder, as it kept him from strutting his stuff in Cincinnati's late-season rookie showcase. Moscot isn't overpowering but does a decent job of commanding his 50-grade four-pitch mix and profiles as a possible fifth starter or swingman, a role he should be healthy enough to audition for this spring.

Manny Parra LHP

Born: 10/30/82 Age: 33 Bats: L Throws: L Height: 6'3" Weight: 215

YEAR	TEAM	LVL	AGE	W	L	SV	G	GS	IP	H	HR	BB/9	K/9	GB%	BABIP	WHIP	ERA	FIP	DRA	WARP	CFIP	MPH
2013	CIN	MLB	30	2	3	0	57	0	46	40	5	2.9	11.0	46%	.315	1.20	3.33	3.04	3.57	0.6	88	95.9
2014	CIN	MLB	31	0	3	1	53	0	36^{2}	39	4	4.4	8.3	54%	.327	1.55	4.66	4.22	5.14	-0.3	107	95.8
2015	CIN	MLB	32	1	2	0	40	0	32^{1}	32	2	1.7	6.4	48%	.303	1.18	3.90	3.10	3.46	0.5	104	94.9
2016	*CIN*	*MLB*	*33*	*2*	*1*	*0*	*35*	*0*	*37*	*36*	*5*	*2.9*	*7.8*	*49%*	*.311*	*1.28*	*4.02*	*4.12*	*4.58*	*0.1*	*105*	
2017	*CIN*	*MLB*	*34*	*3*	*1*	*0*	*54*	*0*	*44*	*45*	*6*	*3.0*	*7.2*	*49%*	*.319*	*1.37*	*4.47*	*4.73*	*5.09*	*-0.1*	*118*	

Breakout: 30% Improve: 48% Collapse: 22% Attrition: 8% MLB: 89% *Comparables: Aaron Fultz, Tippy Martinez, Nick Masset*

Between stints on the disabled list with neck, elbow and shoulder woes, Parra managed to put together another useful season in the Reds' bullpen. He threw more fastballs and fewer splitters than in years past, winding up with both the lowest walk and strikeout rates of his career and improving his results against right-handed batters. Having completed his conversion from mercurial starter to reliable reliever, Parra now seems determined to become a pitch-to-contact guy; if that doesn't work, maybe his next move will be to focus on becoming a LOOGY. With Parra, you never know.

Cody Reed LHP

Born: 4/15/93 Age: 23 Bats: L Throws: L Height: 6'5" Weight: 220

YEAR	TEAM	LVL	AGE	W	L	SV	G	GS	IP	H	HR	BB/9	K/9	GB%	BABIP	WHIP	ERA	FIP	DRA	WARP	CFIP	MPH
2014	LEX	A	21	3	9	0	19	19	84	105	5	3.9	6.2	59%	.351	1.68	5.46	4.37	5.23	0.2	115	
2015	PEN	AA	22	6	2	0	8	8	49^{2}	39	1	2.9	10.9	50%	.311	1.11	2.17	2.24	1.82	1.9	72	
2015	WIL	A+	22	5	5	1	13	10	67^{1}	62	3	2.4	8.7	46%	.309	1.19	2.14	2.75	2.88	1.5	87	
2015	NWA	AA	22	2	2	0	5	5	28^{2}	26	3	2.5	6.0	45%	.258	1.19	3.45	4.27	4.82	0.1	105	
2016	*CIN*	*MLB*	*23*	*7*	*8*	*0*	*24*	*24*	*116^{2}*	*116*	*14*	*3.3*	*7.0*	*46%*	*.310*	*1.37*	*4.34*	*4.27*	*4.92*	*0.5*	*115*	
2017	*CIN*	*MLB*	*24*	*7*	*8*	*0*	*24*	*24*	*141*	*143*	*17*	*3.3*	*7.3*	*46%*	*.320*	*1.38*	*4.33*	*4.59*	*4.91*	*0.5*	*115*	

Breakout: 0% Improve: 0% Collapse: 0% Attrition: 0% MLB: 0% *Comparables: Lance Lynn, Chris Reed, Yoervis Medina*

One-third of Cincinnati's Johnny Cueto haul, Reed is a massive left-handed starter with moving mid-90s heat and a slider that can flash plus. Many prospects struggle in their first taste of the high minors, but Reed got better as the season went on and looked like a major steal by season's end. Cleaner mechanics helped him to repeat his delivery and cut a huge chunk out of his walk rate, while an improving changeup gives right-handed batters something to think about. Not many southpaws can match Reed's size and stuff, and if he continues to avoid ball four he'll grow into a mid-rotation stalwart.

Keyvius Sampson RHP

Born: 1/6/91 Age: 25 Bats: R Throws: R Height: 6'2" Weight: 225

YEAR	TEAM	LVL	AGE	W	L	SV	G	GS	IP	H	HR	BB/9	K/9	GB%	BABIP	WHIP	ERA	FIP	DRA	WARP	CFIP	MPH
2013	TUC	AAA	22	2	3	0	9	9	38	44	5	6.9	5.9	38%	.320	1.92	7.11	6.33	6.02	-0.1	128	
2013	SAN	AA	22	10	4	0	19	18	103^1	74	9	2.9	9.6	44%	.254	1.04	2.26	3.10	3.86	1.4	86	
2014	ELP	AAA	23	2	5	0	38	14	91^2	91	19	6.7	9.2	40%	.297	1.73	6.68	6.67	4.49	0.9	105	
2015	CIN	MLB	24	2	6	0	13	12	52^1	67	7	4.5	7.2	42%	.341	1.78	6.54	4.79	6.36	-0.8	117	94.8
2015	LOU	AAA	24	2	4	0	8	7	39	40	1	5.1	7.6	49%	.325	1.59	5.08	3.64	5.44	-0.4	114	
2015	PEN	AA	24	1	2	0	8	8	43^2	35	2	4.9	8.5	45%	.277	1.35	1.85	3.81	4.66	0.1	103	
2016	*CIN*	*MLB*	*25*	*4*	*4*	*0*	*26*	*10*	*67*	*62*	*8*	*3.8*	*7.2*	*42%*	*.292*	*1.35*	*4.43*	*4.32*	*5.01*	*0.1*	*118*	
2017	*CIN*	*MLB*	*26*	*3*	*4*	*0*	*16*	*10*	*72^1*	*69*	*9*	*3.9*	*7.5*	*42%*	*.302*	*1.39*	*4.55*	*4.83*	*5.15*	*0.0*	*121*	

Breakout: 20% Improve: 38% Collapse: 16% Attrition: 34% MLB: 61% *Comparables: Fabio Castro, Michael Kirkman, Michael Blazek*

Sampson joined the Reds' Rookie Rotation Review at the end of July and spent the rest of the year showing the same combination of promise and frustration that has defined his career. The former Padres farmhand can dial up mid-90s heat but struggles to command it, and his off-speed offerings remain more garnish than complementary side dish. Sampson doesn't seem likely to ever develop the consistency he'll need to thrive in a big-league rotation, but he could carve out a role in the seventh inning, especially ones when the fans started leaving in the fifth.

Josh Smith RHP

Born: 8/7/87 Age: 28 Bats: R Throws: R Height: 6'2" Weight: 220

YEAR	TEAM	LVL	AGE	W	L	SV	G	GS	IP	H	HR	BB/9	K/9	GB%	BABIP	WHIP	ERA	FIP	DRA	WARP	CFIP	MPH
2013	PEN	AA	25	11	9	0	28	28	160	148	16	2.8	7.8	40%	.286	1.24	3.26	3.54	3.99	1.4	97	
2014	LOU	AAA	26	10	7	0	28	24	159	174	8	3.7	7.0	32%	.322	1.51	4.70	3.84	4.58	1.0	100	
2015	CIN	MLB	27	0	4	0	9	7	32^2	42	5	5.8	8.3	39%	.370	1.93	6.89	5.70	7.34	-0.9	115	93.1
2015	LOU	AAA	27	3	5	0	15	12	86^1	84	2	2.5	7.2	42%	.311	1.25	3.75	2.90	3.19	1.6	88	
2015	PEN	AA	27	5	4	0	9	9	56	51	5	1.4	8.5	42%	.293	1.07	3.05	3.16	2.30	1.8	77	
2016	*CIN*	*MLB*	*28*	*9*	*9*	*0*	*27*	*27*	*152*	*149*	*18*	*3.1*	*7.2*	*37%*	*.306*	*1.32*	*4.13*	*4.13*	*4.69*	*1.1*	*108*	
2017	*CIN*	*MLB*	*29*	*4*	*5*	*0*	*13*	*13*	*75^1*	*77*	*10*	*3.1*	*7.4*	*37%*	*.317*	*1.36*	*4.36*	*4.62*	*4.95*	*0.3*	*115*	

Breakout: 7% Improve: 19% Collapse: 5% Attrition: 16% MLB: 28% *Comparables: Robert Ray, Phil Irwin, Philip Humber*

Major League Baseball is in the entertainment business, and with so few things to differentiate the scores of mediocre players who could qualify for a swingman role it's surprising that more players like Smith don't change their names to something more memorable or ingratiating, like Freedom Smith or Masterpiece Smith or Pedro Martinez Jr. As it is, Smith's commonplace repertoire matches his commonplace name, with a low-90s fastball and average breaking stuff that can baffle the farm kids but gets crushed by the best hitters in the world. On the plus side, Smith can tell his grandkids about the time he struck out Kris Bryant twice on six pitches.

Robert Stephenson RHP

Born: 2/24/93 Age: 23 Bats: R Throws: R Height: 6'2" Weight: 200

YEAR	TEAM	LVL	AGE	W	L	SV	G	GS	IP	H	HR	BB/9	K/9	GB%	BABIP	WHIP	ERA	FIP	DRA	WARP	CFIP	MPH
2013	BAK	A+	20	2	2	0	4	4	20^2	19	3	0.9	9.6	39%	.286	1.02	3.05	3.82	4.67	0.3	79	
2013	DYT	A	20	5	3	0	14	14	77	56	5	2.3	11.2	51%	.279	0.99	2.57	2.59	3.57	1.5	65	
2013	PEN	AA	20	0	2	0	4	4	16^2	17	2	7.0	9.7	34%	.357	1.80	4.86	4.65	4.35	0.1	107	
2014	PEN	AA	21	7	10	0	27	26	136^2	114	18	4.9	9.2	38%	.264	1.38	4.74	4.58				
2015	LOU	AAA	22	4	4	0	11	11	55^2	51	2	4.4	8.2	41%	.306	1.40	4.04	3.35	4.37	0.2	103	
2015	PEN	AA	22	4	7	0	14	14	78^1	53	8	4.9	10.2	39%	.249	1.23	3.68	4.16	3.81	1.0	95	
2016	*CIN*	*MLB*	*23*	*2*	*3*	*0*	*8*	*8*	*40*	*34*	*5*	*4.1*	*8.5*	*37%*	*.292*	*1.31*	*4.18*	*4.26*	*4.73*	*0.3*	*111*	
2017	*CIN*	*MLB*	*24*	*4*	*5*	*0*	*13*	*13*	*78^1*	*68*	*9*	*4.4*	*9.2*	*37%*	*.306*	*1.36*	*4.22*	*4.48*	*4.78*	*0.4*	*112*	

Breakout: 12% Improve: 19% Collapse: 10% Attrition: 18% MLB: 34% *Comparables: Neil Ramirez, Mauricio Robles, Zack Wheeler*

Few minor leaguers have as much raw stuff as Stephenson, who can dial his fastball into the mid-90s and work in a devastating curveball and a much improved changeup, but his Jekyll and Hyde command continues to undermine him. When he repeats his delivery, hits his spots and works ahead in the count Stephenson looks for all the world like a future ace. When he doesn't, advanced hitters wait him out and tattoo his mistakes or gladly accept ball four. The Reds are wisely letting him work out the kinks in the high minors before exposing him to the Bryce Harpers of the world, but if his production starts to match his projection he'll arrive with a bang this summer.

Pedro Villarreal RHP

Born: 12/9/87 Age: 28 Bats: R Throws: R Height: 6'1" Weight: 235

YEAR	TEAM	LVL	AGE	W	L	SV	G	GS	IP	H	HR	BB/9	K/9	GB%	BABIP	WHIP	ERA	FIP	DRA	WARP	CFIP	MPH
2013	CIN	MLB	25	0	1	0	2	1	5^2	13	4	4.8	6.4	28%	.429	2.82	12.71	12.37	14.82	-0.7	119	94.0
2013	LOU	AAA	25	4	9	2	33	18	109^2	115	17	2.3	6.9	47%	.296	1.30	4.43	4.59	4.60	0.5	107	
2014	LOU	AAA	26	6	2	2	42	2	56^1	57	5	2.1	8.0	40%	.313	1.24	3.20	3.59	4.09	0.5	83	
2014	CIN	MLB	26	0	2	0	12	0	14^2	11	1	4.3	7.4	36%	.244	1.23	4.30	3.99	3.55	0.2	107	94.9
2015	LOU	AAA	27	1	0	1	19	0	26	26	0	1.4	7.3	54%	.317	1.15	3.81	2.00	2.81	0.5	84	
2015	CIN	MLB	27	1	3	0	29	0	50	57	6	2.2	5.2	43%	.311	1.38	3.42	4.46	4.65	0.0	117	94.5
2016	*CIN*	*MLB*	*28*	*4*	*3*	*0*	*32*	*7*	*65^1*	*65*	*8*	*2.5*	*6.5*	*43%*	*.302*	*1.28*	*4.19*	*4.11*	*4.77*	*0.3*	*110*	
2017	*CIN*	*MLB*	*29*	*5*	*5*	*0*	*41*	*11*	*106^2*	*112*	*15*	*2.6*	*6.4*	*43%*	*.309*	*1.34*	*4.57*	*4.85*	*5.20*	*-0.1*	*122*	

Breakout: 6% Improve: 15% Collapse: 1% Attrition: 12% MLB: 24% *Comparables: Steven Shell, Tyler Cloyd, Esmailin Caridad*

For the first time in his career, Villarreal spent more time in Cincinnati than in Louisville, due more to the Reds' pitching fire sale than Villarreal setting the world on fire. He works multiple innings, throws strikes, avoids walks, keeps his fielders involved and cleans up his own messes without requiring his team to burn *another* bullpen arm—essentially everything he can do to keep his manager from wondering if there's someone else around who won't make a bad day even worse. As long as he does that, and as long as the team doesn't require anything more, Villarreal should be able to survive a few more years at the back of a big-league bullpen.

LINEOUTS

Hitters

NAME	POS	TEAM	LVL	AGE	PA	R	2B	3B	HR	RBI	BB	K	SB	CS	AVG/OBP/SLG	TAv	BABIP	BRR	FRAA	WARP
Aristides Aquino	RF	DYT	A	21	249	25	9	3	5	27	11	53	6	1	.234/.281/.364	.236	.280	2.0	RF(60): 1.1	0.1
Juan Duran	RF	PEN	AA	23	238	29	16	3	6	43	12	88	2	1	.256/.290/.438	.278	.382	-0.5	RF(53): 5.2	1.4
Phil Ervin	OF	DAY	A+	22	475	68	18	0	12	63	53	83	30	7	.242/.338/.375	.277	.271	4.2	LF(83): 10.3, CF(26): 1.3	3.8
	OF	PEN	AA	22	66	7	3	0	2	8	13	15	4	3	.235/.409/.412	.296	.294	-1.5	LF(12): -0.2, CF(5): 1.1	0.4
Gavin LaValley	3B	DYT	A	20	530	52	29	1	4	53	50	114	4	1	.267/.343/.358	.262	.341	-2.4	3B(113): -6.2, 1B(9): -0.2	0.9
Scott Schebler	OF	LAN	MLB	24	40	6	0	0	3	4	3	13	2	1	.250/.325/.500	.325	.300	0.4	LF(7): -0.2, RF(6): -0.0	0.4
	OF	OKL	AAA	24	485	57	16	9	13	50	40	93	15	2	.241/.322/.410	.276	.278	2.3	RF(48): -5.3, CF(38): 2.1	1.8
Blake Trahan	SS	DAY	A+	21	36	1	0	0	0	0	0	5	0	0	.114/.139/.114	.097	.133	0.2	SS(11): 0.1	-0.5

Now the story of the lanky outfielder who has the tools to be a prototypical big-league right fielder, and the one season he had no choice but to sit two months with a broken wrist and ponder his need to develop a better plate approach altogether; it's **Aristides Aquino**'s development. ❖ Man/mountain **Juan Duran** also missed half of last season with a wrist injury, depriving disappointed Southern League pitchers of the opportunity to pad their strikeout totals. He'll likely never make enough contact to be a Cincinnati mainstay, but his enviable longball thump should keep him wanderin' the outfields of the high minors for years to come. ❖ **Phil Ervin** bounced back from a rough 2014 full-season debut to show an improved approach and great wheels; defensively stretched in center field, he'll need to further develop his power stroke to survive in an outfield corner. ❖ During his first spin through the Midwest League **Gavin LaValley** flashed a surprisingly solid glove at the hot corner, made contact and controlled the strike zone. The power bat most expected to be his calling card, however, was nowhere to be seen; with most scouts still expecting him to float down the defensive spectrum, he'll need that paddle. ❖ If you've ever watched Kole Calhoun and thought, "God, I wish this player were 25 percent worse at everything," you'd love **Scott Schebler**, who found Oklahoma City and Los Angeles much more daunting than Chattanooga. ❖ First-round pick **Tyler Stephenson** impressed in his Rookie league debut, flashing solid receiving skills and enough agility behind the plate to lower some of the warning flags about his wantonly excessive height. At the plate he showed a good eye, and if he learns to unleash his power potential he could grow into a first-division catcher. ❖ Louisiana-Lafayette star **Blake Trahan** showed expected polish in his debut, answering questions about his glove (might stick at short), bat (grinder with solid OBP skills, no power) and the best place for cajun in Billings (Café Zydeco for sit down, Cajun Phatty's for cart food or catering).

Pitchers

NAME	TEAM	LVL	AGE	W	L	SV	G	GS	IP	H	HR	BB/9	K/9	GB%	BABIP	WHIP	ERA	FIP	FRA	WARP	CFIP	MPH
Nathan Adcock	LOU	AAA	27	0	2	11	22	0	24^{1}	23	0	2.6	7.4	72%	.303	1.23	2.96	2.75	3.84	0.2	96	
	CIN	MLB	27	1	2	0	13	0	18	15	3	6.0	6.5	51%	.222	1.50	6.00	6.05	4.78	0.0	118	96.4
Mark Armstrong	DYT	A	20	3	3	0	13	12	64^{2}	71	1	1.9	6.1	51%	.332	1.31	3.20	3.03	4.11	0.6	98	
Collin Balester	CIN	MLB	29	1	1	0	15	0	15^{2}	17	3	7.5	7.5	30%	.298	1.91	7.47	6.67	6.79	-0.4	119	94.7
	LOU	AAA	29	0	0	7	21	0	22	16	1	1.2	5.3	40%	.227	0.86	2.05	2.98	3.13	0.3	93	
	ALT	AA	29	1	0	4	13	0	20^{1}	14	1	2.7	6.2	53%	.228	0.98	1.77	3.56	4.08	0.1	99	
	IND	AAA	29	0	0	0	8	0	14^{2}	12	1	3.1	4.9	44%	.224	1.16	3.07	3.98	3.91	0.1	116	
Alejandro Chacin	DAY	A+	22	2	0	10	29	0	36^{2}	23	3	2.7	13.7	48%	.263	0.93	2.45	2.32	1.14	1.4	66	
	DYT	A	22	1	0	1	10	0	14^{2}	16	0	2.5	9.8	58%	.390	1.36	5.52	2.24	3.30	0.2	90	
Dayan Diaz	PME	AA	26	0	0	2	9	0	15^{2}	7	0	1.1	9.8	32%	.189	0.57	1.15	1.48	2.40	0.4	74	
	PAW	AAA	26	2	1	4	28	0	57	47	3	4.4	7.7	41%	.267	1.32	1.89	3.70	4.51	-0.1	104	
Nick Howard	DAY	A+	22	3	2	2	24	5	38	34	0	11.8	7.3	45%	.327	2.21	6.63	5.80	11.00	-3.4	175	
Stephen Johnson	RIC	AA	24	3	0	0	44	0	58	45	2	4.5	10.6	48%	.297	1.28	3.41	3.13	3.78	0.5	94	
Tyler Mahle	DYT	A	20	13	8	0	27	26	152	145	7	1.5	8.0	53%	.313	1.12	2.43	2.93	2.69	4.1	83	
Jason Marquis	CIN	MLB	36	3	4	0	9	9	47^{1}	64	10	2.7	7.0	49%	.351	1.65	6.46	5.30	7.16	-1.2	111	90.0
Keury Mella	DAY	A+	21	3	1	0	4	4	21^{1}	11	2	6.3	9.7	41%	.184	1.22	2.95	4.62	4.70	-0.1	111	
	SJO	A+	21	5	3	0	16	16	81^{2}	66	5	2.9	9.1	44%	.272	1.13	3.31	3.79	4.48	1.1	95	
J.C. Ramirez	ARI	MLB	26	1	1	0	12	0	15^{1}	15	1	2.3	6.5	62%	.298	1.24	4.11	3.36	2.42	0.4	103	97.7
	RNO	AAA	26	0	1	1	23	0	25	22	0	3.6	6.5	55%	.282	1.28	2.88	3.36	3.42	0.5	86	
	SEA	MLB	26	0	1	0	8	0	8^{1}	10	2	7.6	5.4	17%	.286	2.04	7.56	7.90	6.81	-0.2	129	99.1
	TAC	AAA	26	1	1	0	14	0	18	17	2	3.5	9.0	40%	.312	1.33	2.50	4.38	4.22	0.2	106	
Salvatore Romano	DAY	A+	21	6	5	0	19	18	104	103	2	2.9	6.8	59%	.318	1.31	3.46	2.91	3.97	0.6	102	
	PEN	AA	21	0	4	0	7	7	23	35	4	4.7	3.5	47%	.348	2.04	10.96	6.35	7.30	-0.7	126	
Nick Travieso	DAY	A+	21	6	6	0	19	19	93^{1}	82	4	2.9	7.3	44%	.282	1.20	2.70	3.32	4.46	-0.1	108	
Blake Wood	IND	AAA	29	2	5	29	57	0	58^{2}	52	2	3.8	10.7	50%	.327	1.31	3.53	2.54	2.61	1.3	81	

Nate Adcock was toiling away in middle relief when his elbow went sproing last July, resulting in Tommy John surgery; his previous return from thoracic outlet surgery featured two extra ticks on his fastball, so perhaps he'll be hitting the high-90s when we see him again in 2017. ❖ Scouts describe **Mark Armstrong** as a big man in that weirdly positive scouting way, and while his name is a bit of an oversell at present, he's shown good command in his nascent career. ❖ It was nice to see **Collin Balester** work his way back from Tommy John surgery and appear in his first big-league games since 2012, unless you were a Reds fan watching him walk as many men as he struck out and post a wide-body ERA that points toward a career starting its final descent. ❖ Daytona closer **Alejandro Chacin** doesn't have great size or velocity, but he's dominated the low minors with his deceptive three-quarters delivery and his groundball tendencies, which could someday make him the last reliever on a big-league roster. ❖ Former Tigers first-rounder **Jonathon Crawford** missed most of the season with shoulder woes, making it even more likely his lack of a usable third pitch will precipitate a move to the bullpen. ❖ **Dayan Diaz** has done a good job of limiting homers over the past two years and now sits on the precipice of the majors, making this a potentially less bittersweet ditty about jacks and Dayan. ❖ **Nick Howard**'s season was an unmitigated disaster, as the former college closer survived only five turns in the rotation before moving back to the 'pen, walked more batters than he whiffed and was shelved for the entire second half with shoulder soreness. His uniform this spring will sport more question marks than the Riddler's. ❖ Rocket-armed reliever **Stephen Johnson** can unleash triple-digit fastballs and power breakers, meaning they're off the leash and running wild. If he can domesticate them even a little, he can work high-leverage innings in the Cincinnati bullpen. ❖ Despite not being old enough to buy a Warped Wing Creepshow Smoked Porter, **Tyler Mahle** commanded his low-90s fastball and developing secondary stuff during an impressive Dayton debut; his ceiling is limited, but he has a chance. ❖ **Jason Marquis** hasn't posted a positive WARP since 2009, yet broke camp with the rebuilding Reds and made nine starts last year because lefty hurlers always get... wait a minute, he only *bats* lefty? Then we have no words. ❖ After missing most of the 2013 and 2014 seasons with shoulder woes, **Sean Marshall** avoided that fate by missing *all* of 2015. If he seems healthy some team may try to catch lightning in a bottle, which from a probability standpoint is one of the most accurate metaphors around. ❖ Former San Francisco farmhand **Keury Mella** uses a crossfire delivery to fling his heavy mid-90s fastball and power curve, generating copious awkward swings and groundball outs; if he can develop a workable changeup to help keep lefties at bay, he could grow into a mid-rotation horse. ❖ The Reds moved college closer/first baseman **Tanner Rainey** to the rotation, where he used his mid-90s heat to strike out nearly a man per inning in his Rookie league debut. If this starting thing doesn't pan out, he could still move fast as a reliever. ❖ **J.C. Ramirez** has always had a live arm, but in the five years since the Mariners traded him to the Phillies in the Cliff Lee deal, he remains one of the guys traded in the Cliff Lee deal. ❖ **Sal Romano** was torched in his first taste of Double-A, but improved mechanics, decent command and a worm-killing mid-90s heater give him the tools he needs to succeed; if he continues to do the right things he could fit into the back end of the Cincinnati rotation, at which point we'll finally be able to say Sal's famous. ❖ Prep fireballer **Antonio Santillan** is bigger than Texas, although he's from Texas so the physics of that are a little difficult, and he can throw his four-seamer clean through this book, assuming it was held tightly and we soaked it in a bathtub for six hours first. Clearly we're bad at legend-making around here, but if Santillan can harness his high-90s heat and pair it with his hammer curve, he could be, like, really good. ❖ Former top pick **Nick Travieso** has paid his dues—including two months lost last summer to a line drive off his forearm—and is ready for Double-A to teach him whether his workmanlike three-pitch mix can baffle more advanced hitters. ❖ Drafted in the same round as former Nationals farmhand Stephen King, we think **Blake Wood's** career would make good fodder for the *other* Stephen King. Working title: *The Reliever Who Loved Triple-A.*

MANAGER

Bryan Price

YEAR	TEAM	W	L	Pythag +/-	Avg PC	100+ P	120+ P	QS	BQS	REL	REL w Zero R	IBB	PH	PH Avg	PH HR	SB2	CS2	SB3	CS3	SAC Att	SAC%	POS SAC	Squeeze	Swing	In Play
2014	CIN	76	86	-3	97.3	74	1	103	2	428	337	33	219	.246	6	103	42	19	7	103	73.8	38	1	309	77

Pitching coaches are often overlooked as serious managerial candidates. For years prior to his promotion, Price seemed like the exception. His name surfaced each winter, with details about his stellar communication skills and his promising future as a skipper. Heck, even *Slate* got in on the act, publishing a 2009 article in which Price demonstrated his interpersonal savvy by helping author Eric Liu work through a mental hurdle on the mound. Price seemed like the real deal—so real that the Reds didn't interview other candidates before appointing him manager following Dusty Baker's dismissal.

So how then do you explain Price's April and May? During the first two months of the season, he dropped 77 f-bombs in an ignorant rant concerning the media's job—i.e. reporting things like injuries, whether they helped the team or not. Weeks later, he was ejected from a game before it started. The rest of Price's season went without fireworks, but again, how do you explain the erosion of his communication skills? Had the pressures of managing a losing club pushed him over the line? Was he feeling the heat? Or did he awaken from a fugue in June with no recollection of his previous outbursts?

Whatever the case, Price was not dismissed after the season despite finishing with the majors' second-worst record. Walt Jocketty cited the Reds' injuries and trades over the past two years as reasons why Price shouldn't be held accountable for the club's poor marks. Both are fair points. In 2015, the Reds received just 23 games from prospective catcher Devin Mesoraco, 53 games from shortstop Zack Cozart and 114 games from Billy Hamilton. Additionally, Jocketty stripped the rotation, trading Johnny Cueto, Mike Leake, Alfredo Simon and Mat Latos. The Reds, as a result, started a rookie pitcher in each game after July 28th. Price, in theory, should be a positive influence on those youngsters.

Still, that's not to suggest Price's on-the-field management is all aces. No manager requested more pitchouts—a strategy that may hinder those pitchers' ability to counter the running game on their own—and the rest of his tactical decisions were a mixed bag at best. Batting Joey Votto second is a smart, progressive move; batting Jason Bourgeois leadoff is neither. The conservative usage of Aroldis Chapman has always been a sore spot in Cincinnati, and Price stuck with the status quo. Maybe he would've been more aggressive had the team been competitive? Who knows; that's the difficulty of evaluating managers—especially those leading transitioning or rebuilding squads. With Price and Jocketty's contracts each ending after the 2016 season, both will enter spring as lame ducks. Barring a dramatic turnaround, they'll enter the fall as sitting ducks.

CLEVELAND INDIANS

Essay by Pete Beatty

Player comments by Bryan Grosnick and BP authors

In 2015, the Indians had a chance to prove Mark Shapiro's genius once and for all. A young, frisky club eyed a playoff run that could validate the long-time team boss in his thrifty, sober style: develop draft picks, swap veterans for prospects, and patch the whole thing together with chicken wire and modest free-agent signings. Shapiro-ism: It isn't pretty, but *it can work* (with a lot of luck)!

Dreaming on a title run wasn't just astigmatic optimism: Plenty of non-Clevelanders saw the 2015 Indians as a sneaky playoff contender. *Sports Illustrated* went so far as to predict the club as World Series winners in March. This potential proved out, in some sense: At season's end, third-order winning percentage said Cleveland should have won 93 games and paced the AL Central.

Unfortunately, they don't play games in the third order.

In between hot-stove tasseography and postseason forensics, first-order reality did a number on the Tribe. The team stepped in a bucket in April (7 wins to 14 losses) and spent the rest of the season extricating their foot. Atrocious first acts have become a trend for Terry Francona's Cleveland teams. Since taking over in 2013, Francona has lead the club to a .532 winning percentage overall, nothing to sneeze at. But if you take away a grody 29–44 mark before May 1, his teams have played to a .556 mark—a four-win difference for a team that lives on the fringes of playoff qualification.

As narrative, "starting bad → getting better" satisfies. Manny Acta's Indians teams habitually posted a strong first fifty games and just as often faded down the stretch. Watching the Francona-managed clubs find themselves in early summer generates warm fuzzies. But both as narrative and as a baseball strategy, playing well for the entire season works better.

With the Tribe set to return a similar 25-man in 2016, we can reasonably expect that they'll play to the same underlying talent as 2015. The final result will be down to dice-rolls like sequencing and BABIP. If we want to know what 2016 is going to look like, we should start by asking how Cleveland wound up 81–80 in 2015.

Starting pitching didn't stop the Tribe from winning consistently. In Corey Kluber, Carlos Carrasco and Danny Salazar, the Indians had (and have) three frontline starters who strike out nearly 10 batters per 9 innings. Even the isotopic Trevor Bauer, still just 25, threatened early in the

INDIANS PROSPECTUS

2015 W-L: 81-80, 3rd in AL Central

Pythag	.517	12th	DER	.712	8th
RS/G	4.13	18th	B-Age	27.9	6th
RA/G	3.95	9th	P-Age	27.3	6th
TAv	.256	22nd	Salary	$88M	26th
BRR	-8.47	25th	M$/MW	$2.3M	23rd
TAv-P	.240	1st	DL Days	899	11th
FIP	3.59	7th	$ on DL	21%	24th

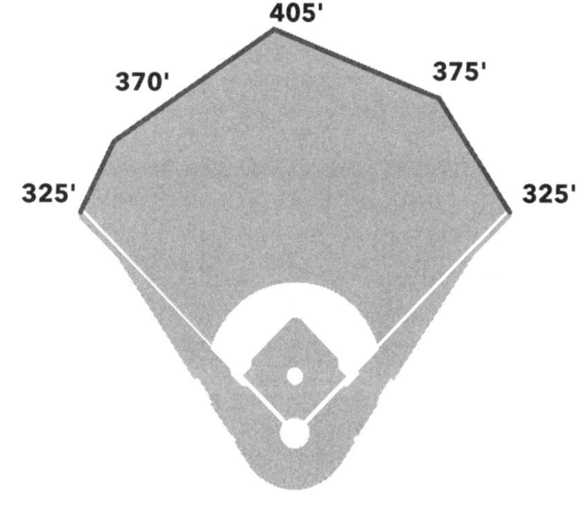

Outfield wall profile: **9'** to **19'**

Three-Year Park Factors

Runs	Runs/RH	Runs/LH	HR/RH	HR/LH
106	114	116	106	103

Top Hitter WARP	3.3	Francisco Lindor
Top Pitcher WARP	4.5	Corey Kluber
Top Prospect		Bradley Zimmer

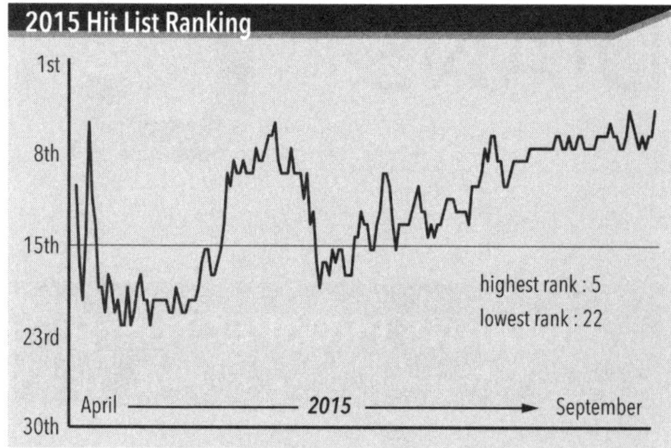

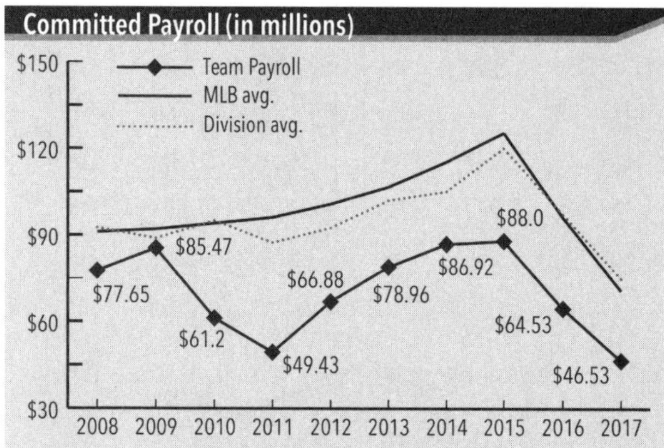

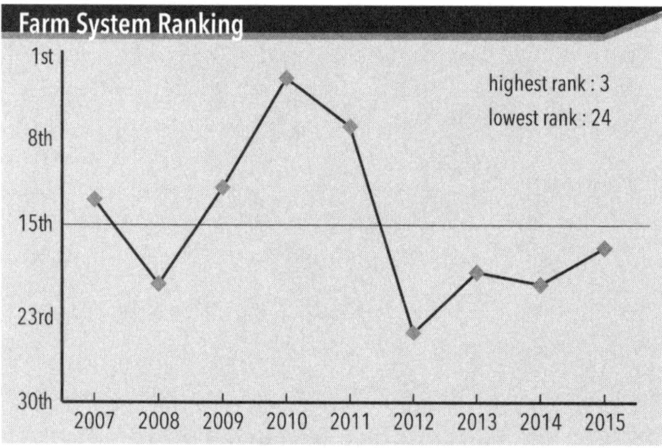

Personnel

President: Chris Antonetti
General Manager: Mike Chernoff
Assistant General Manager: Derek Falvey
Manager: Terry Francona

Baseball Prospectus Alumni
Max Marchi
Steffan Segui
Keith Woolner

season to stabilize as a reliable above-average starter.

The bullpen wasn't the problem, either. Cleveland relievers posted 4.9 WARP, good for sixth overall in MLB. Closer Cody Allen dominated after a bumpy start, striking out more than a third of the batters he faced. The usual bullpen volatility manifested, but for every Scott Atchison (2014: 72 stellar innings; 2015: released before July 1) there was a Jeff Manship (1.5 WARP in under 40 innings!?).

In the spirit of the police procedural, let's narrow down our remaining suspects. The pitching staff has solid alibis. So the murderer was either the offense's run-creation, at home plate, with the bat –or– the defense's run-prevention, in the field, with the glove.

After the awfulness of April, it sure looked like the defense was the culprit. Cleveland's fielding stunk for the second half of 2014, and very little was done to shore a shaky unit up. The southpaw side of the infield (then Lonnie Chisenhall at third base and Jose Ramirez at short) was hamfisted. The right side wasn't much better (soppressata-fisted?). Post-2014 breakout, Michael Brantley's bat more than excuses his mediocre left-field defense, but with Michael Bourn no longer a plus glove in center and Brandon Moss's limited range in right, the outfield was as well-ventilated as the infield. In May, *Sports Illustrated* could ask with a straight face whether the Indians' defense was on track to be the worst in modern MLB history, two months after predicting they could win the whole fracking thing.

But as we know from decades of *Law and Order*, it's never the first suspect. A funny thing happened on the way to the defensive hall of shame. The left side of the infield was recast midseason, with superprospect Francisco Lindor and glove-first Giovanny Urshela taking over from Ramirez and Chisenhall. Bourn and Moss were traded, replaced by driftwood in the form of Abraham Almonte and … Lonnie Chisenhall.

Lindor and Urshela were always expected to provide premium defense. But Chisenhall was a revelation (or possibly a small-sample-size fever dream) in right field. After volunteering for a crash-course outfield conversion during a mid-season Triple-A demotion, Lonnie Baseball saved 5.6 runs in 50 games—a rate that puts him right there with Jason Heyward for the best right fielder in MLB over a full season.

So, we're down to one suspect. By process of elimination: Offense murked the 2015 Indians. Tribe hitters plated 669 runs, which would be respectable in the National League. In the American League, it was good for 11th place. The five AL playoff qualifiers averaged more than 770 runs. (Even with Toronto's curve-smashing taken out of the figuring, it's 747, plenty more than Cleveland managed).

Part of the problem was just bum luck. The Indians were toward the rear of the middle of the pack in slugging percentage and home runs, but they took plenty of walks.

Q: How good was Francisco Lindor?
Hell of good. His 3.3 WARP may have been aided by a breezy .348 BABIP, and his .169 ISO outpaced anything he showed in the minors, but it's possible Lindor needed the big stage to break all the way out. Also, he won't turn 23 until after the 2016 season.

Q: How good will Francisco Lindor be?
His glovework is already plus-plus, just shy of the Andrelton Simmons god-tier. Lindor may not always hit as well as his freshman classmate Carlos Correa, but he'll hit enough to be the best Indians shortstop since prime Omar Vizquel, if not better.

Q: So are we saying Francisco or Frankie?
A: Frankie has more snap, more vinegar, but I think we should stick with Francisco until we have a chance to ask him in person. Although Francona says Frankie, whatever that counts for.

Unfortunately, the tolerable number of hits the team compiled were poorly sequenced. A .305 BABIP with no runners sank to .292 with men on, and .278 with runners in scoring position. (For comparison, league average BABIP was .294 bases empty, .306 with men on, .298 with RISP.)

That's a lot to fit on the gravestone for the 2015 Indians. While the engravers are busy, we can dream on the 2016 Indians. There are plenty of reasons the team should contend in 2016 and beyond. The aforementioned trio of Kluber, Carrasco, and Salazar. Plenty of serviceable arms to fill out the rest of the rotation, and a solid 'pen. The electrifying Lindor. Jason Kipnis, who had 51 hits *in May*. Brantley. A bounceback year from Carlos Santana, whose very real value is obscured by ugly batting averages and clumsy defense, and a healthy Yan Gomes behind the plate.

Math majors will notice that Lindor + Kipnis + Brantley + Santana + Gomes = 5. Sports science majors will know that the number of offensive players in a baseball lineup traditionally ≥ 9. Giovanny Urshela's glove plays, but it remains to be seen whether his bat does. That leaves two outfielders and a platoon-y first base/DH type to be determined.

With just six spots settled, there was a lot of task for the Cleveland front office between the writing of this essay and Opening Day. They had to figure it out without the help of Mark Shapiro.

For the first time since 1991, Shapiro isn't part of the Indians organization, having joined the Blue Jays as team president in late August. Shapiro had been with Cleveland since the Municipal Stadium era. Shapiro took over the GM role in November 2001, a few weeks after Jamie Moyer outdueled Chuck Finley to end the Tribe's attempt to upset the 116-win Mariners in the ALDS. (Bartolo Colon was Cleveland's best pitcher in that series.)

That defeat was the end of the John Hart Indians, a shadow dynasty that regularly made deep playoff runs but came two outs and one Jose Mesa short of ending Cleveland's long championship drought. New boss Shapiro inherited an unenviable task—his first task was dismantling the best Indians team in a half-century. He was never going to be popular with fans.

And he never was. Shapiro did occasionally stellar work as GM and subsequently team president, collecting multiple executive of the year awards. He put the team in a position to come within one win of the World Series, just six years removed from empty cupboards. Even when the promising Travis Hafner-Grady Sizemore core fizzled post 2007, Shapiro ably rebuilt on the fly.

But the fanbase never warmed up to the cold #process-mongering of those quick rebuilds. There is a litany of "I never forgave Shapiro for…" moments among Tribe fans. Some early-bird grouses loathed Shapiro for dealing away Robbie Alomar, whose expiration date was rapidly approaching, in 2002. Trading reigning Cy Young winners CC Sabathia and Cliff Lee in successive seasons incinerated all of the good vibes generated by the 2007 playoff run. Sending Victor Martinez to Boston in 2009 was piling on.

Decisive trades like this have helped the Indians retool rapidly over the past 15 years, but they also earned Shapiro & Co. a reputation as penny-pinchers who frequently flipped dollars for three quarters. This logic requires ignoring the times when those quarters grew up to be dollars, as with one-time PTBNL Brantley and late bloomer Carrasco. But the skinflint accusation is a hard one to beat. Under Shapiro and the ownership of the Dolan family, the Indians threw around free agent dollars like family-heirloom manhole covers.

And the few times the team did spend, whoo boy did it backfire. In the aftermath of a juicy TV deal between the 2012 and 2013 seasons, the Tribe went on a spree in a fairly soft free-agent class. The result was the disastrous double-dip of Nick Swisher and Michael Bourn. Both deals amounted to buying at the top of the market. In August of last season, Cleveland sold at the bottom, shipping the two overpaid and gimpy veterans and a dump truck full of cash to Atlanta for Chris Johnson and his terrible contract.

New general manager Mike Chernoff and newly inaugurated club president Chris Antonetti (kicked upstairs from the GM seat) face the same problem that Shapiro did during his tenure in Cleveland—the franchise

Who are we blaming for 67 years of not winning the World Series?

- Mark Shapiro: 39%
- Supernatural forces: 27%
- Random variability of universe: 14%
- Other teams being better: 10%
- Flo from Progressive: 9%
- Bad karma from the continued use of Chief Wahoo: 1%

will only build through trades, draft, and international development. There will be no premium a la carte improvements through free agency.

This makes for a roster-construction Kobayashi Maru: You have a good pitching staff, with multiple above-average arms under team control for several years (Kluber, Carrasco, Salazar, Allen). You have half of a decent set of position players. Without the brute-force option of bringing in talent via free agency, your choices are lose-lose: You can roll with jobbers at power positions, or you can deal from strength to patch the holes (for instance, swapping a controllable plus arm for a bat). Is it possible to actually make your team meaningfully better, or just re-shuffle the talent?

The Shapiro-era Indians faced this same scenario more than once. When the team was good enough to contend, Shapiro opted for minor repairs instead of splashy trades or signings, relying on a mix of Señor Spielbergo-esque discount free agents and youngsters to plug the gaps. The new regime has continued this rich tradition of kludges, adding affordable veteran pieces Mike Napoli and Rajai Davis to the 2016 club.

In the wrong light, the Shapiro school of roster construction could read like cheapness. A lot of Tribe fans chose to see the team's cautious moves that way. But if we set aside the sour aftertaste of bad luck and unmet expectations, the Shapiro era was a qualified success, and the outgoing boss left the franchise in far better shape than he found it.

The current Indians core may be the posthumous pudding that proves Shapiro's genius. Through development, canny trading, and scratch-and-dent free agent signings, the team has a realistic shot at the postseason for the next few seasons. Even with some missing pieces, the 2016 version has a puncher's odds at a title run, given their strong starting pitching and the compressed zaniness of playoff performance.

The 2015 World Series featured two payrolls not that far north of Cleveland's, and 98-win Pittsburgh had nearly the same cap figure as the Indians. The playing field isn't completely even for acutely thrifty franchises, but neither is the game entirely rigged. During his years in Cleveland, Mark Shapiro wrote a book on how a small-market club can compete without spending beyond its means. Even though that book's author has departed for the big bucks and socialized healthcare of Toronto, the Indians have one last shot to write a happy ending to his story. ■

— Pete Beatty is (probably) the most dedicated Cleveland Indians fan in Tuscaloosa, Alabama, where he is studying for an MFA in creative writing.

WHY AREN'T WE GOING TO INDIANS GAMES?

From June 1995 to April 2001, the Indians sold out 455 consecutive regular-season games. The sellout streak ran on the excitement of a team full of stars. Fans couldn't get enough of the first consistently competitive Indians squad in three decades.

Skip ahead 15 years from the end of the streak: Cleveland has been mired in the bottom third of MLB in home attendance since 2003, and the the last four years have been particularly ugly. Only Tampa Bay and Miami have filled fewer seats than the Tribe since 2012. Tampa has the excuse of a ballpark that half the fanbase can't get to easily; Miami has the excuse of being the Marlins.

A decline in attendance is inevitable when a perennial contending club finally breaks down. But Indians attendance hasn't declined so much as cratered. What exactly happened here?

The answer isn't that complicated: The strong attendance of the 1990s was an outlier. Lousy attendance is historically normal for the Indians. For their Westeros-winter-sized bad stretch from 1959 to 1994, the team drew poorly in a rapidly shrinking city. Those six magical years of a butt in every seat required a long list of coincidences: A very good team, a shiny new stadium, a booming economy, and the three-year disappearance of the NFL's Browns. Apart from the Shawn Kemp-era Cavs, the '90s Tribe didn't face much competition for the entertainment dollars of sports-loving Clevelanders.

The past decade-plus has been a different, crappier story: The Browns are back (and psychedelically bad), the economy stinks, and the Indians are inconsistent. What else is new?

HITTERS

Abraham Almonte CF

Born: 6/27/89 Age: 27 Bats: B Throws: R Height: 5'9" Weight: 210

YEAR	TEAM	LVL	AGE	PA	R	2B	3B	HR	RBI	BB	K	SB	CS	AVG/OBP/SLG	TAv	BABIP	BRR	FRAA	WARP
2013	SEA	MLB	24	82	10	4	0	2	9	6	21	1	0	.264/.313/.403	.262	.333	1.5	CF(15): -2.0, RF(7): -0.4	0.1
2013	WTN	AA	24	120	18	6	1	4	18	18	28	6	1	.255/.367/.451	.281	.314	-2.4	CF(11): -0.4, RF(8): 0.5	0.3
2013	TAC	AAA	24	396	63	17	5	11	50	49	66	20	7	.314/.403/.491	.325	.363	1.6	CF(83): 4.0, LF(5): 0.4	4.7
2014	SDN	MLB	25	107	9	5	0	2	7	6	20	1	2	.265/.305/.378	.257	.312	-1.7	LF(16): -0.4, CF(15): 7.4	0.9
2014	TAC	AAA	25	312	42	10	3	6	31	28	66	7	4	.267/.333/.390	.261	.330	-0.2	CF(69): 1.7	1.2
2014	SEA	MLB	25	113	10	5	1	1	8	6	40	3	1	.198/.248/.292	.218	.308	1.1	CF(26): 0.3	0.0
2015	CLE	MLB	26	196	30	9	5	5	20	16	33	6	0	.264/.321/.455	.264	.296	1.2	CF(50): 3.7	1.2
2015	SDN	MLB	26	62	6	3	0	0	4	5	19	1	1	.204/.271/.259	.215	.314	-1.8	LF(6): -1.0, CF(6): -0.5	-0.5
2015	ELP	AAA	26	282	43	18	2	4	35	33	46	11	4	.275/.361/.414	.285	.325	1.3	CF(59): -10.4, LF(3): -0.5	0.6
2016	*CLE*	*MLB*	*27*	*491*	*61*	*22*	*4*	*10*	*46*	*44*	*111*	*13*	*5*	*.253/.321/.393*	*.252*	*.308*	*-0.2*	*CF -4*	*0.9*
2017	*CLE*	*MLB*	*28*	*516*	*58*	*23*	*4*	*10*	*54*	*46*	*119*	*13*	*5*	*.249/.316/.386*	*.248*	*.306*	*0.2*	*CF -4*	*0.9*

Breakout: 3% Improve: 34% Collapse: 8% Attrition: 19% MLB: 77% *Comparables: Lorenzo Cain, Ryan Kalish, Charlie Blackmon*

Almonte is no team's first choice as an everyday center fielder, but in Cleveland all he had to do to win over the fanbase was not be Michael Bourn, a task billions of unexceptional people succeed at daily. Once installed as a regular after the trade deadline, Almonte actually thrived, with solid range in center and a power spike that boosted his slugging percentage 76 points from 2014. Nominally a switch-hitter, Almonte scalded right-handed pitching—all but one of his 22 extra-base hits came against righties—and flailed to a microscopic .017 ISO against lefties. PECOTA expects his bat to regress to something between his San Diego and Cleveland iterations, so he profiles as a good secondary option, not a consistent starter, still not Michael Bourn, and still never gonna be Bradley Zimmer.

Bobby Bradley 1B

Born: 5/29/96 Age: 20 Bats: L Throws: R Height: 6'1" Weight: 225

YEAR	TEAM	LVL	AGE	PA	R	2B	3B	HR	RBI	BB	K	SB	CS	AVG/OBP/SLG	TAv	BABIP	BRR	FRAA	WARP
2015	LKC	A	19	465	62	15	4	27	92	56	148	3	0	.269/.361/.529	.314	.352	-2.1	1B(101): 4.8	3.5
2016	*CLE*	*MLB*	*20*	*250*	*28*	*8*	*1*	*11*	*35*	*21*	*91*	*0*	*0*	*.214/.284/.412*	*.243*	*.293*	*-0.2*	*1B 2*	*0.1*
2017	*CLE*	*MLB*	*21*	*381*	*50*	*14*	*2*	*18*	*53*	*37*	*134*	*0*	*0*	*.223/.301/.430*	*.254*	*.303*	*-0.6*	*1B 2*	*0.7*

Breakout: 5% Improve: 16% Collapse: 0% Attrition: 5% MLB: 18% *Comparables: Giancarlo Stanton, Miguel Sano, Mike Carp*

Bradley finally made the leap from high-power curiosity to legitimate prospect, as he thrived against Midwest League pitching despite not turning 19 until after Memorial Day. Not only did he put up the finest hitting numbers of any Midwest regular, he led the entire Cleveland organization in home runs. Now let your eye wander up to those PECOTA comes up above his stats. Mhm.

The road between Lake City and Cleveland is surprisingly long and treacherous—he'll have to improve on his nearly league-leading strikeout rate, and he's a designated hitter trying to pass as a first baseman. (With 24 errors in 2015, he's inconspicuous like a dog driving.) It's more likely he eventually reminds Indians fans of Russell Branyan than of Jim Thome, but at least his recent performance put Bradley on the map.

Michael Brantley LF

Born: 5/15/87 Age: 29 Bats: L Throws: L Height: 6'2" Weight: 200

YEAR	TEAM	LVL	AGE	PA	R	2B	3B	HR	RBI	BB	K	SB	CS	AVG/OBP/SLG	TAv	BABIP	BRR	FRAA	WARP
2013	CLE	MLB	26	611	66	26	3	10	73	40	67	17	4	.284/.332/.396	.271	.304	2.4	LF(151): 4.1, CF(1): -0.1	2.7
2014	CLE	MLB	27	676	94	45	2	20	97	52	56	23	1	.327/.385/.506	.320	.333	5.1	LF(107): -2.4, CF(46): -0.1	6.1
2015	CLE	MLB	28	596	68	45	0	15	84	60	51	15	1	.310/.379/.480	.294	.318	-3.2	LF(101): 3.4, CF(28): -3.9	3.0
2016	*CLE*	*MLB*	*29*	*472*	*55*	*29*	*2*	*9*	*54*	*39*	*51*	*13*	*2*	*.297/.356/.442*	*.278*	*.316*	*0.5*	*LF 2, CF -1*	*2.4*
2017	*CLE*	*MLB*	*30*	*536*	*64*	*32*	*2*	*10*	*59*	*43*	*61*	*12*	*2*	*.288/.346/.427*	*.269*	*.308*	*0.5*	*LF 2, CF -1*	*2.5*

Breakout: 0% Improve: 37% Collapse: 3% Attrition: 3% MLB: 99% *Comparables: Conor Jackson, Martin Prado, Nick Markakis*

No, he didn't repeat as an MVP finalist, but Brantley's 2015 campaign was as well rounded as safety scissors. He stole bases without getting caught—he has the game's second-best success rate since 2013, min. 30 steals—and played a confident left field while the rest of the Indians looked like they were fielding a greased-up pig. He is a unique and dangerous hitter, with elite bat-to-ball skills (his 93 percent contact rate was the best in baseball last year), controlled aggression on early-count fastballs, and an overall approach that produced his first double-digit walk rate. Only three guys walked more than they struck out last year, and they comprise a strange trio: Joey Votto, Nori Aoki and Brantley, who has some of the best of both of those guys in his game. Naturally; he has some of everything in his game.

He'll start 2016 with a new challenge: offseason shoulder surgery, which puts the start of his season in doubt.

Joey Butler DH

Born: 3/12/86 Age: 30 Bats: R Throws: R Height: 6'2" Weight: 220

YEAR	TEAM	LVL	AGE	PA	R	2B	3B	HR	RBI	BB	K	SB	CS	AVG/OBP/SLG	TAv	BABIP	BRR	FRAA	WARP
2013	ROU	AAA	27	505	71	26	0	12	51	69	119	1	2	.291/.395/.437	.306	.376	-3.9	RF(53): -3.3, LF(47): 0.4	2.8
2013	TEX	MLB	27	15	3	2	0	0	1	3	6	0	0	.333/.467/.500	.348	.667	0.3	LF(3): -0.1, RF(2): -0.0	0.2
2014	SLN	MLB	28	6	0	0	0	0	0	1	3	0	0	.000/.167/.000	.106	.000	-0.1	RF(1): -0.2	-0.1
2014	MEM	AAA	28	106	16	4	0	4	20	19	16	0	0	.360/.481/.547	.368	.409	1.0	LF(14): -1.3	1.5
2015	TBA	MLB	29	276	30	12	0	8	30	16	82	5	2	.276/.326/.416	.253	.377	-1.1	LF(30): 0.9, RF(6): 0.1	0.2
2015	DUR	AAA	29	137	21	9	1	6	24	14	31	0	0	.333/.416/.575	.348	.410	1.4	RF(17): -1.4, LF(6): -0.5	1.5
2016	*CLE*	*MLB*	*30*	*250*	*28*	*12*	*0*	*7*	*30*	*25*	*67*	*2*	*1*	*.264/.345/.416*	*.272*	*.348*	*-0.4*	*LF -1, RF 0*	*0.8*
2017	*CLE*	*MLB*	*31*	*367*	*45*	*17*	*0*	*9*	*41*	*37*	*100*	*2*	*1*	*.257/.339/.398*	*.264*	*.343*	*-0.7*	*LF -2, RF 0*	*1.1*

Breakout: 2% Improve: 11% Collapse: 10% Attrition: 20% MLB: 42% *Comparables: Ryan Shealy, Jason Botts, Kila Ka'aihue*

There was a moment in late June when Rays manager Kevin Cash said he was considering (with apparent sincerity) commissioning t-shirts that had Butler's face on the front and a koan on the back: Joey Can Hit. Butler had a .325/.368/.497 line at the time. But if those shirts were ever made, they likely ended up in the same shipping containers as the Super Bowl XLIX Champion Seattle Seahawks merch. That very night, Butler went 0-for-4, then went into a tailspin befitting his quad-A profile and org-soldier resume. He hit .191/.255/.277 in 102 PA the rest of the way, including his two-homer game in the season's finale. Cleveland will give him a shot, if not quite yet a shirt.

Lonnie Chisenhall 3B

Born: 10/4/88 Age: 27 Bats: L Throws: R Height: 6'2" Weight: 190

YEAR	TEAM	LVL	AGE	PA	R	2B	3B	HR	RBI	BB	K	SB	CS	AVG/OBP/SLG	TAv	BABIP	BRR	FRAA	WARP
2013	CLE	MLB	24	308	30	17	0	11	36	16	56	1	0	.225/.270/.398	.251	.243	0.6	3B(88): -0.9	0.7
2013	COH	AAA	24	125	21	8	2	6	26	12	24	2	0	.390/.456/.676	.388	.443	-1.3	3B(27): 1.0	2.2
2014	CLE	MLB	25	533	62	29	1	13	59	39	99	3	1	.280/.343/.427	.278	.328	-1.8	3B(114): -9.3, 1B(11): -0.7	1.3
2015	COH	AAA	26	171	18	13	0	3	21	11	35	1	0	.280/.329/.420	.256	.342	-2.0	3B(32): -1.6, RF(4): 1.2	0.2
2015	CLE	MLB	26	362	38	19	1	7	44	23	69	4	1	.246/.294/.372	.238	.288	1.6	RF(51): 5.6, 3B(50): 2.5	1.1
2016	*CLE*	*MLB*	*27*	*567*	*62*	*32*	*2*	*15*	*65*	*36*	*112*	*4*	*1*	*.263/.316/.423*	*.257*	*.304*	*0.1*	*RF 16*	*3.0*
2017	*CLE*	*MLB*	*28*	*496*	*58*	*28*	*2*	*14*	*59*	*32*	*98*	*3*	*1*	*.261/.314/.423*	*.257*	*.302*	*-0.1*	*RF 14*	*2.7*

Breakout: 5% Improve: 43% Collapse: 6% Attrition: 13% MLB: 95% *Comparables: Danny Valencia, Jorge Cantu, Josh Harrison*

Upon returning from a demotion to Triple-A mid-season, Chisenhall looked like an entirely different ballplayer. His move from third base to right field transformed him from an indifferent defender to, so far, an excellent one. Playing deep in right allows him to show off good range coming in on flyballs and a powerful arm, flipping his defense from liability to asset on the team's balance sheet. Meanwhile, a productive August (.403/.474/.552) salvaged the offensive side of his season, and there is reason to think 2016 could see a bit of positive regression. Chiz hurt his own offense in 2015 by popping a lot of balls up; 21 percent of his flies (of which there were many) didn't leave the infield, which was the fourth-highest rate among hitters with 200+ PA. The league-average popup rate was only 9.5 percent, and this was a dramatic shift from his rate during previous seasons. Expect fewer automatic outs, and fewer demotions to Triple-A mid-season, going forward.

Rajai Davis LF

Born: 10/19/80 Age: 35 Bats: R Throws: R Height: 5'9" Weight: 195

YEAR	TEAM	LVL	AGE	PA	R	2B	3B	HR	RBI	BB	K	SB	CS	AVG/OBP/SLG	TAv	BABIP	BRR	FRAA	WARP
2013	TOR	MLB	32	360	49	16	2	6	24	21	67	45	6	.260/.312/.375	.251	.308	6.7	LF(57): 4.2, RF(35): -2.0	1.6
2014	DET	MLB	33	494	64	27	2	8	51	22	75	36	11	.282/.320/.401	.263	.320	4.8	LF(99): 0.8, CF(48): -1.5	1.9
2015	DET	MLB	34	370	55	16	11	8	30	22	76	18	8	.258/.306/.440	.263	.308	0.9	CF(46): -1.0, LF(39): -2.0	0.8
2016	*CLE*	*MLB*	*35*	*284*	*38*	*14*	*3*	*4*	*21*	*15*	*57*	*21*	*6*	*.254/.299/.368*	*.235*	*.307*	*1.7*	*LF 2*	*0.5*
2017	*CLE*	*MLB*	*36*	*310*	*30*	*15*	*3*	*3*	*28*	*16*	*63*	*21*	*7*	*.250/.295/.359*	*.233*	*.305*	*2.4*	*LF 2*	*0.6*

Breakout: 0% Improve: 23% Collapse: 10% Attrition: 23% MLB: 86% *Comparables: Felipe Alou, Darin Erstad, Marlon Byrd*

You know that feeling where you wake up on a school day and realize you forgot to study? Davis looked at the calendar last year and said, "Oh, it's September of my contract year." It's the only explanation for why half of his eight homers came that month, as did a .973 OPS, which led him to career highs in slugging and triples. Now 35, Davis can still burn through the bags, but it's his advanced hitting for extra bases that makes him a valuable bench presence. The bigger the ballpark, the better he can split the gap and reach third, but then he has to defend that same space; given the routes he's been observed taking, he may want to study up on some of the finer points of defense rather than cram the night before.

Yandy Diaz 3B

Born: 8/8/91 Age: 24 Bats: R Throws: R Height: 6'2" Weight: 185

YEAR	TEAM	LVL	AGE	PA	R	2B	3B	HR	RBI	BB	K	SB	CS	AVG/OBP/SLG	TAv	BABIP	BRR	FRAA	WARP
2014	CAR	A+	22	338	42	7	5	2	37	49	35	3	3	.286/.396/.367	.293	.320	0.6	3B(74): -2.3	2.2
2015	AKR	AA	23	564	61	13	5	7	55	78	65	8	7	.315/.412/.408	.306	.350	-2.3	3B(122): -9.6	3.3
2016	*CLE*	*MLB*	*24*	*250*	*27*	*9*	*2*	*5*	*27*	*30*	*45*	*1*	*1*	*.265/.355/.386*	*.266*	*.311*	*-0.2*	*3B -4*	*0.4*
2017	*CLE*	*MLB*	*25*	*322*	*40*	*11*	*2*	*7*	*34*	*39*	*59*	*1*	*1*	*.266/.357/.394*	*.268*	*.312*	*-0.3*	*3B -5*	*0.7*

Breakout: 3% Improve: 16% Collapse: 14% Attrition: 24% MLB: 50% *Comparables: Greg Garcia, James Darnell, Alex Hassan*

Whooooooo's ready to scout the stat line? This Cuban import has little prospect pedigree, but has shown remarkable control of the plate during his two years in the Cleveland organization. Last season, he had the second-highest walk rate in the Eastern League (13.8 percent), which outpaced his strikeout rate (11.1 percent) and gives the impression of a guy who could reach base even at the highest level. He'll need that OBP, as his plate coverage comes from a short swing that robs him of game power.

He has another calling card that the stat line doesn't show: He's one of the best defensive third basemen in the minor leagues. Diaz didn't wow in a cup of coffee with Columbus at the end of the season, but this Eastern League All-Star has enough going for him that a solid showing at the start of 2016 could tip him ahead of Giovanny Urshela.

Clint Frazier CF

Born: 9/6/94 Age: 21 Bats: R Throws: R Height: 6'1" Weight: 190

YEAR	TEAM	LVL	AGE	PA	R	2B	3B	HR	RBI	BB	K	SB	CS	AVG/OBP/SLG	TAv	BABIP	BRR	FRAA	WARP
2014	LKC	A	19	542	70	18	6	13	50	56	161	12	6	.266/.349/.411	.277	.372	0.8	CF(111): -18.9, RF(1): 0.0	0.8
2015	LYN	A+	20	588	88	36	3	16	72	68	125	15	7	.285/.377/.465	.297	.348	-2.3	CF(93): -5.1, RF(35): 0.4	3.2
2016	*CLE*	*MLB*	*21*	*250*	*29*	*10*	*1*	*6*	*24*	*21*	*80*	*2*	*1*	*.224/.294/.366*	*.234*	*.311*	*-0.3*	*CF -3, RF 0*	*-0.2*
2017	*CLE*	*MLB*	*22*	*444*	*51*	*19*	*2*	*11*	*48*	*39*	*139*	*4*	*2*	*.233/.307/.380*	*.243*	*.322*	*-0.3*	*CF -5, RF 0*	*0.2*

Breakout: 7% Improve: 10% Collapse: 1% Attrition: 5% MLB: 18% *Comparables: Brett Jackson, Christian Yelich, Michael Choice*

From his mop of crimson hair to his 80-grade bat speed, Frazier certainly stands out, even among other talented prospects. While 2015 began with Red Thunder earning the wrong kind of attention—he struggled and broke a couple bats over his knee in anger—he claims that watching fellow elite prospect Bradley Zimmer succeed gave him a newfound appreciation for reaching base and staying focused. The stats matched his updated approach, and by the time his muse had been promoted out of Lynchburg, Frazier had drastically cut his strikeout rate from the past two seasons (from 30 percent to 21 percent in 2015) and re-established himself as a premier prospect. He stood out during the Arizona Fall League as well, earning a starting spot in the Fall Stars game, and looks poised to draw more eyes in 2016.

Yan Gomes C

Born: 7/19/87 Age: 28 Bats: R Throws: R Height: 6'2" Weight: 215

YEAR	TEAM	LVL	AGE	PA	R	2B	3B	HR	RBI	BB	K	SB	CS	AVG/OBP/SLG	TAv	BABIP	BRR	FRAA	WARP
2013	CLE	MLB	25	322	45	18	2	11	38	18	67	2	0	.294/.345/.481	.296	.342	0.1	C(85): 18.0, 1B(1): -0.0	4.6
2013	COH	AAA	25	24	2	4	0	0	3	4	4	0	0	.300/.417/.500	.309	.375	-0.4	C(6): 0.3	0.2
2014	CLE	MLB	26	518	61	25	3	21	74	24	120	0	0	.278/.313/.472	.281	.326	-0.1	C(126): 13.4	4.8
2015	CLE	MLB	27	389	38	22	0	12	45	13	104	0	0	.231/.267/.391	.237	.285	-0.7	C(91): -3.1	0.4
2016	*CLE*	*MLB*	*28*	*510*	*57*	*28*	*2*	*18*	*64*	*27*	*125*	*1*	*0*	*.263/.309/.442*	*.262*	*.318*	*-0.3*	*C 9*	*3.4*
2017	*CLE*	*MLB*	*29*	*513*	*63*	*28*	*2*	*18*	*66*	*28*	*129*	*0*	*0*	*.261/.309/.439*	*.260*	*.320*	*-0.6*	*C 8*	*3.3*

Breakout: 1% Improve: 40% Collapse: 8% Attrition: 9% MLB: 96% *Comparables: Nick Hundley, J.P. Arencibia, Ryan Doumit*

YEAR	TEAM	P. COUNT	FRM RUNS	BLK RUNS	THRW RUNS	TOT RUNS
2013	CLE	11402	14.7	0.3	0.5	15.6
2013	COH	785	0.4	0.0	0.0	0.4
2014	CLE	17511	9.9	1.3	2.4	13.6
2015	CLE	12205	-2.7	-0.1	-0.2	-3.0
2016	*CLE*	*18135*	*7.0*	*0.4*	*0.8*	*8.2*
2017	*CLE*	*18236*	*5.9*	*0.4*	*0.7*	*7.0*

Coming into 2015, Gomes was every team's dream: an above-average catcher on both sides of the ball, with a contract that paid him just $22 million over the next six seasons. But seven games into his season, Gomes wrecked his MCL on a play at the plate; his body returned to the team at the end of May, but the bat didn't recover until... July, when he returned to league-average production for his position? Or maybe September, when his slugging finally returned to 2014 levels? Eventually he got there, at least. Though his whiff percentage didn't change much in the aggregate, he was swinging and missing on fastballs 14 percent of the time, which is a large tick up from his 2014 Silver Slugger season. Breaking pitches tend to put his bat to rest, so he'll need to go back to feasting on hard stuff in order to reclaim his position as one of the best catchers (and bargains) in the league.

Erik Gonzalez SS

Born: 8/31/91 Age: 24 Bats: R Throws: R Height: 6'3" Weight: 195

YEAR	TEAM	LVL	AGE	PA	R	2B	3B	HR	RBI	BB	K	SB	CS	AVG/OBP/SLG	TAv	BABIP	BRR	FRAA	WARP
2013	LKC	A	21	383	59	23	7	9	49	24	71	10	4	.259/.307/.439	.261	.301	2.4	3B(65): 10.6, SS(16): -1.7	2.7
2013	CAR	A+	21	163	16	9	5	0	27	5	38	1	2	.242/.259/.366	.207	.311	-0.5	SS(39): 2.9	0.0
2014	AKR	AA	22	136	21	6	3	1	16	7	23	6	1	.357/.390/.473	.292	.429	2.9	SS(30): -3.9	0.9
2014	CAR	A+	22	336	44	14	7	3	46	23	65	15	6	.289/.336/.409	.265	.355	1.3	SS(74): -3.2	1.5
2015	COH	AAA	23	261	32	6	3	3	23	15	47	8	2	.223/.277/.311	.220	.266	2.7	SS(62): 8.9	1.1
2015	AKR	AA	23	327	38	18	4	6	46	11	56	10	5	.280/.304/.421	.263	.321	0.5	SS(71): 4.1	2.0
2016	*CLE*	*MLB*	*24*	*250*	*23*	*11*	*3*	*5*	*25*	*10*	*62*	*5*	*2*	*.240/.270/.366*	*.223*	*.301*	*0.4*	*SS 2, 2B 0*	*0.5*
2017	*CLE*	*MLB*	*25*	*368*	*36*	*16*	*4*	*7*	*37*	*15*	*91*	*7*	*3*	*.243/.276/.369*	*.228*	*.305*	*0.9*	*SS 2, 2B 0*	*1.0*

Breakout: 1% Improve: 9% Collapse: 3% Attrition: 15% MLB: 25% *Comparables: Grant Green, Hector Gomez, Jordany Valdespin*

Every team needs a defensive-minded middle infield backup like Gonzalez, except perhaps the team that currently has him. After starting his professional career as a jack-of-all-trades on defense, he has built himself into a plus defensive shortstop and developed an average hit tool, earning raves for his makeup. After hitting well at Akron, he struggled at the plate after being called up to replace Francisco Lindor at Columbus, but got back on track thanks to a great 11-game run during the International League playoffs (.326/.340/.609), the first time he had shown such power. On any other team he could be pegged as a future regular at best, and a utility option at worst, but in Cleveland he's just another middle infielder in the shadow of Lindor.

Chris Johnson 3B

Born: 10/1/84 Age: 31 Bats: R Throws: R Height: 6'3" Weight: 225

YEAR	TEAM	LVL	AGE	PA	R	2B	3B	HR	RBI	BB	K	SB	CS	AVG/OBP/SLG	TAv	BABIP	BRR	FRAA	WARP
2013	ATL	MLB	28	547	54	34	0	12	68	29	116	0	0	.321/.358/.457	.283	.394	2.3	3B(125): -4.2, 1B(12): 0.4	2.9
2014	ATL	MLB	29	611	43	27	0	10	58	23	159	6	0	.263/.292/.361	.239	.345	-0.3	3B(150): -22.6, 1B(1): -0.0	-1.9
2015	ATL	MLB	30	162	12	7	0	2	11	7	49	2	1	.235/.272/.320	.228	.330	-0.8	3B(23): -1.0, 1B(20): 0.9	-0.3
2015	CLE	MLB	30	93	6	4	0	1	7	3	25	0	0	.289/.312/.367	.232	.391	0.1	1B(10): -0.3, 3B(4): -0.0	-0.2
2016	*CLE*	*MLB*	*31*	*312*	*30*	*17*	*1*	*7*	*34*	*15*	*78*	*2*	*0*	*.269/.308/.399*	*.246*	*.342*	*0.2*	*3B -3, 1B 0*	*-0.1*
2017	*CLE*	*MLB*	*32*	*316*	*35*	*16*	*1*	*7*	*34*	*17*	*82*	*1*	*0*	*.260/.304/.391*	*.244*	*.334*	*0.0*	*3B -4, 1B 0*	*-0.1*

Breakout: 1% Improve: 47% Collapse: 11% Attrition: 12% MLB: 97% *Comparables: Jeff Baker, Wes Helms, Eric Karros*

Acquired from the Braves in a July contract swap (the Braves got awful Michael Bourn contract and awful Nick Swisher contract; the winner in the trade was all 28 other teams), Johnson was at his one-tool best in his first two starts for the Tribe. He leveraged his contact ability into five singles and two just-inside-the-line doubles in eight plate appearances, then swiftly reverted to the hitter we've come to know. C.J. demonstrated a wispy contact percentage (69.6 percent in 2015) that would be appropriate for a power hitter, but distressing for a third baseman with a .131 career ISO. He avoids walks and is persistently negative in both baserunning (-4 career BRR) and defense (-57.4 career FRAA), so his only useful role is as a low-upside pinch-hitting option against lefties. Missing time with an ugly infected spider bite in September didn't grant him the powers of Spider-Man, something he'd need in order to stick in a team's starting lineup.

Jason Kipnis 2B

Born: 4/3/87 Age: 29 Bats: L Throws: R Height: 5'11" Weight: 195

YEAR	TEAM	LVL	AGE	PA	R	2B	3B	HR	RBI	BB	K	SB	CS	AVG/OBP/SLG	TAv	BABIP	BRR	FRAA	WARP
2013	CLE	MLB	26	658	86	36	4	17	84	76	143	30	7	.284/.366/.452	.309	.345	-0.8	2B(147): -1.8	4.9
2014	CLE	MLB	27	555	61	25	1	6	41	50	100	22	3	.240/.310/.330	.238	.288	4.6	2B(123): 11.8	2.0
2015	CLE	MLB	28	641	86	43	7	9	52	57	107	12	8	.303/.372/.451	.290	.356	0.9	2B(124): -5.6	3.2
2016	*CLE*	*MLB*	*29*	*642*	*74*	*32*	*5*	*13*	*69*	*63*	*122*	*20*	*6*	*.268/.343/.412*	*.266*	*.316*	*0.8*	*2B 0*	*3.2*
2017	*CLE*	*MLB*	*30*	*565*	*66*	*30*	*4*	*11*	*60*	*55*	*109*	*16*	*6*	*.265/.340/.405*	*.262*	*.314*	*1.2*	*2B 0*	*2.8*

Breakout: 1% Improve: 40% Collapse: 2% Attrition: 6% MLB: 99% *Comparables: Neil Walker, Ian Kinsler, Marcus Giles*

In May 2015, Bryce Harper put up an OPS of 1.379, Max Scherzer threw 43 innings with a 1.67 ERA, and both were arguably less valuable than Jason Kipnis. He had 22 extra-base hits, played his usual fair defense up the middle, put up an OPS of 1.217, and produced nearly three wins, like some kind of peak Rogers Hornsby resuscitated for a 31-day tour.

On the other side, there was the August shoulder injury he rushed back from. The Indians called it inflammation, but Kipnis commented "there's more to it" on his way back. He did not look like himself after taking a few weeks to recover. He stopped putting balls in the air, and his diminishing speed did him no favors on balls in play. For a player who had always earned extra bases not from home runs but from gap doubles and sterling stolen base success rates, it was a sad montage.

Both versions of Dirtbag are the real thing. Despite the now-frequent minor injuries and a shifting skill set, he remains one of the top pivots in the sport. He'll never be Hornsby for a full year, but even faced with a few bad months, he led all AL second basemen in WARP last year.

Francisco Lindor SS

Born: 11/14/93 Age: 22 Bats: B Throws: R Height: 5'11" Weight: 190

YEAR	TEAM	LVL	AGE	PA	R	2B	3B	HR	RBI	BB	K	SB	CS	AVG/OBP/SLG	TAv	BABIP	BRR	FRAA	WARP
2013	CAR	A+	19	373	51	19	6	1	27	35	39	20	5	.306/.373/.410	.274	.341	-2.3	SS(82): 5.6	2.5
2013	AKR	AA	19	91	14	3	1	1	7	14	7	5	2	.289/.407/.395	.305	.309	-0.8	SS(21): -2.3	0.5
2014	AKR	AA	20	387	51	12	4	6	48	40	61	25	9	.278/.352/.389	.273	.320	0.1	SS(88): 7.3	3.0
2014	COH	AAA	20	180	24	4	0	5	14	9	36	3	7	.273/.307/.388	.230	.317	0.7	SS(38): 2.5	0.5
2015	CLE	MLB	21	438	50	22	4	12	51	27	69	12	2	.313/.353/.482	.286	.348	-0.6	SS(98): 3.4	3.3
2015	COH	AAA	21	262	26	11	5	2	22	25	38	9	7	.284/.350/.402	.270	.328	0.4	SS(56): -1.2	1.3
2016	*CLE*	*MLB*	*22*	*634*	*80*	*27*	*6*	*12*	*59*	*46*	*116*	*19*	*8*	*.273/.327/.406*	*.255*	*.313*	*-2.2*	*SS 2*	*2.8*
2017	*CLE*	*MLB*	*23*	*625*	*71*	*27*	*5*	*12*	*67*	*45*	*109*	*19*	*8*	*.275/.327/.406*	*.256*	*.313*	*-1.3*	*SS 2*	*3.0*

Breakout: 8% Improve: 54% Collapse: 9% Attrition: 20% MLB: 74% *Comparables: Troy Tulowitzki, Asdrubal Cabrera, Melvin Upton*

The runner-up for the 2015 AL Rookie of the Year made a pretty good case that he, not Carlos Correa, was not only the league's top rookie, but also the most valuable shortstop in baseball. Of course, Correa made a pretty good case, too. The world is generous to us, and this is going to be really, really fun.

The case for Lindor relies a bit on defensive value, which we all know is less nourishing in single servings than offensive value. But Lindor's exceptional ratings (DRS had him worth 10 runs; UZR, 15) are just confirmation of what scouts and prospect mavens have been promising: Ultraathleticism, supergrace, megarange, etc. Lindor stands out most on a particular type of play, the one that off the bat looks neither routine nor *necessarily* a hit, the tweener groundball. On plays judged by the video-scouting company Inside Edge to be either Unlikely plays (10-40 percent of shortstops would convert it) or Even plays (40-60 percent), Lindor was the best in baseball last year. Of the Unlikely variety, he succeeded *67* percent of the time. This is a small bucket of plays and this was only a glimpse, to be sure, but glimpses have powered carnal fantasies for millenia.

Of course, that's what we had expected from Lindor. The headline, really, was that he can really hit. Despite bringing his groundball tendencies with him to The Show, he took 14 balls out of the park in 2015, a new professional career high. His power might regress some—51 percent is a lot of grounders for an aspiring slugger—but his advanced approach and bat-to-ball skills look strong enough to make those Elvis Andrus comps look stingy: At 22, he's already the better hitter. And probably the better shortstop. And maybe, just maybe, the best shortstop.

Francisco Mejia C

Born: 10/27/95 Age: 20 Bats: B Throws: R Height: 5'10" Weight: 175

YEAR	TEAM	LVL	AGE	PA	R	2B	3B	HR	RBI	BB	K	SB	CS	AVG/OBP/SLG	TAv	BABIP	BRR	FRAA	WARP
2014	MHV	A-	18	274	32	17	4	2	36	18	47	2	4	.282/.339/.407	.277	.337	0.0	C(52): 0.5	1.6
2015	LKC	A	19	446	45	13	0	9	53	38	78	4	1	.243/.324/.345	.259	.281	-1.8	C(94): 1.8	1.8
2016	*CLE*	*MLB*	*20*	*250*	*21*	*10*	*1*	*5*	*25*	*13*	*63*	*0*	*0*	*.219/.269/.338*	*.213*	*.274*	*-0.4*	*C 0*	*-0.1*
2017	*CLE*	*MLB*	*21*	*356*	*37*	*16*	*1*	*8*	*36*	*18*	*89*	*0*	*0*	*.225/.273/.355*	*.223*	*.277*	*-0.8*	*C 1*	*0.2*

Breakout: 0% Improve: 0% Collapse: 0% Attrition: 0% MLB: 0% *Comparables: J.R. Murphy, Travis d'Arnaud, Wilson Ramos*

YEAR	TEAM	P. COUNT	FRM RUNS	BLK RUNS	THRW RUNS	TOT RUNS
2016	*CLE*	*8790*	*0.0*	*0.0*	*0.0*	*0.0*
2017	*CLE*	*12514*	*0.0*	*0.0*	*0.0*	*0.0*

Just surviving as the Lake County Captains' starting catcher at the age of 19 with no obvious signs the he was overmatched counts as an achievement. But Mejia was the no. 84 prospect on BP's pre-2015 Top 101 list, and his special combination of switch-hitting raw, plus-plus arm strength and veteran makeup means that expectations are already very high. While his overall offensive performance wasn't stellar, he improved as the year went on, with a dismal April start (.155/.222/.276) dragging down his seasonal line. Catchers can take a long time to matriculate, but if Mejia figures out how to attack high-quality breaking pitches and can learn to handle a pitching staff he'll have a combination of skills that few backstops in the game could match.

Mike Napoli 1B

Born: 10/31/81 Age: 34 Bats: R Throws: R Height: 6'1" Weight: 225

YEAR	TEAM	LVL	AGE	PA	R	2B	3B	HR	RBI	BB	K	SB	CS	AVG/OBP/SLG	TAv	BABIP	BRR	FRAA	WARP
2013	BOS	MLB	31	578	79	38	2	23	92	73	187	1	1	.259/.360/.482	.294	.367	-0.3	1B(131): 0.7	2.7
2014	BOS	MLB	32	500	49	20	0	17	55	78	133	3	2	.248/.370/.419	.295	.321	-1.8	1B(110): -0.1	2.1
2015	TEX	MLB	33	91	9	2	0	5	10	12	19	0	2	.295/.396/.513	.318	.333	-0.3	1B(15): 0.6, LF(11): -1.2	0.6
2015	BOS	MLB	33	378	37	18	1	13	40	45	99	3	1	.207/.307/.386	.247	.252	-0.1	1B(96): 5.2	0.4
2016	*CLE*	*MLB*	*34*	*593*	*76*	*26*	*1*	*26*	*83*	*77*	*167*	*3*	*2*	*.245/.349/.452*	*.284*	*.311*	*-0.7*	*1B 2*	*2.6*
2017	*CLE*	*MLB*	*35*	*476*	*63*	*20*	*1*	*18*	*60*	*57*	*135*	*1*	*1*	*.235/.334/.417*	*.267*	*.304*	*-0.6*	*1B 2*	*1.4*

Breakout: 1% Improve: 25% Collapse: 8% Attrition: 11% MLB: 95% *Comparables: Carlos Pena, Ryan Howard, Carlos Delgado*

Napoli started 2015 looking like all of the health-related maladies of the past few years were finally catching up with him in a big way. He slashed his way to a paltry .193/.294/.353 line in the first half of the season, with fastballs streaking past him before he could get the bat out over the plate. Napoli recovered in the second half, posting his more typically dominant power numbers down the stretch and pulling balls at a much more customary rate. A trade to Texas at the deadline pushed Napoli into a part-time role in August and September, which may have helped Nap get a second wind and recover.

At 34, it's by no means clear he's done as a full-time starter, but given his avascular necrosis—the degenerative hip condition that was diagnosed back in 2013—prospective teams hedged their bets, and the Indians got him on a one-year deal. A crumbling OPS against righties (.816, .739, and .603 from 2013-2015) is equally discouraging. Moving out from behind the plate prolonged Nap's career, but as with any degenerative condition (including old age), there is no cure.

Tyler Naquin CF

Born: 4/24/91 Age: 25 Bats: L Throws: R Height: 6'2" Weight: 190

YEAR	TEAM	LVL	AGE	PA	R	2B	3B	HR	RBI	BB	K	SB	CS	AVG/OBP/SLG	TAv	BABIP	BRR	FRAA	WARP
2013	CAR	A+	22	498	69	27	6	9	42	41	112	14	7	.277/.345/.424	.264	.351	0.9	CF(102): 11.0	3.0
2013	AKR	AA	22	85	9	3	0	1	6	5	22	1	3	.225/.271/.300	.237	.298	-1.0	CF(18): -1.7	-0.2
2014	AKR	AA	23	341	54	12	5	4	30	29	71	14	3	.313/.371/.424	.290	.389	-0.1	CF(73): 4.0, RF(1): 0.1	2.6
2015	COH	AAA	24	218	34	13	0	6	17	25	49	6	2	.263/.353/.430	.268	.323	0.8	CF(47): 2.1	1.1
2015	AKR	AA	24	160	16	12	1	1	10	15	24	7	1	.348/.419/.468	.336	.410	-1.4	CF(33): 1.6	1.9
2016	*CLE*	*MLB*	*25*	*250*	*29*	*12*	*1*	*5*	*22*	*18*	*67*	*5*	*2*	*.248/.307/.374*	*.240*	*.326*	*0.2*	*CF 1, RF 0*	*0.5*
2017	*CLE*	*MLB*	*26*	*248*	*27*	*11*	*1*	*5*	*25*	*18*	*69*	*5*	*2*	*.244/.304/.368*	*.238*	*.325*	*0.4*	*CF 1, RF 0*	*0.5*

Breakout: 12% Improve: 27% Collapse: 3% Attrition: 31% MLB: 48% *Comparables: Xavier Paul, Mikie Mahtook, Lane Adams*

Naquin has one standout tool—a 70-grade arm—which would be enough if he were a pitching prospect. Instead, the former Aggie will need to rely on other skills to separate himself from the Trevor Crowes and Travis Bucks of past Cleveland outfields. While he has barreled minor-league pitching and lifted his walk rate to a solid 11 percent last year, his level swing plane robs him of in-game power and underscores his lack of other standout tools. If he can break free of the "jack-of-all-trades, master-of-none" stigma and perform when he gets a shot in the bigs, his rifle arm will be more exclamation point than consolatory at-least-he's-got-a...

Mike Papi LF

Born: 9/19/92 Age: 23 Bats: L Throws: R Height: 6'2" Weight: 190

YEAR	TEAM	LVL	AGE	PA	R	2B	3B	HR	RBI	BB	K	SB	CS	AVG/OBP/SLG	TAv	BABIP	BRR	FRAA	WARP
2014	LKC	A	21	166	21	4	0	3	15	26	32	2	0	.178/.305/.274	.232	.204	0.7	RF(33): -1.4, 1B(2): -0.1	-0.3
2015	LYN	A+	22	506	53	34	2	4	45	81	118	6	7	.236/.362/.356	.272	.316	-3.6	LF(74): -3.8, RF(44): -0.8	0.8
2016	*CLE*	*MLB*	*23*	*250*	*23*	*11*	*0*	*4*	*23*	*31*	*71*	*1*	*1*	*.201/.303/.311*	*.224*	*.276*	*-0.5*	*LF -3, RF -1*	*-0.7*
2017	*CLE*	*MLB*	*24*	*344*	*38*	*16*	*1*	*6*	*31*	*42*	*98*	*1*	*1*	*.208/.307/.328*	*.230*	*.283*	*-0.7*	*LF -4, RF -1*	*-0.7*

Breakout: 0% Improve: 0% Collapse: 1% Attrition: 1% MLB: 1% *Comparables: Alex Hassan, Eric Thames, Matt Young*

Papi is the off-brand Michael Conforto and the Hydrox to Kyle Schwarber's Oreo. He's the same type of college "bat-first" player as the aforementioned no-position 2014 draftees/2015 breakouts: He has a quest to have a bat in his hand. Without that, it's like Kryptonite and Superman. Unfortunately, while Lynchburg is no friend to power hitters (it ranks in the top quartile of MiLB ballparks that suppress homers), a good 2015 showing for the bat-only Papi would have included more than four dingers. There's still hope, as he's incredibly patient and his swing is short to the ball and covers a lot of plate. But unless he can take another step forward, Little Papi's career will be marked by unflattering comparisons to his draft-class peers.

Roberto Perez C

Born: 12/23/88 Age: 27 Bats: R Throws: R Height: 5'11" Weight: 225

YEAR	TEAM	LVL	AGE	PA	R	2B	3B	HR	RBI	BB	K	SB	CS	AVG/OBP/SLG	TAv	BABIP	BRR	FRAA	WARP
2013	COH	AAA	24	222	16	12	0	0	24	22	59	0	1	.176/.269/.241	.184	.250	-0.9	C(66): 17.8	0.9
2013	AKR	AA	24	128	10	6	0	2	10	32	25	1	1	.247/.453/.376	.317	.318	-1.0	C(32): 0.2	1.3
2014	COH	AAA	25	209	29	11	1	8	43	29	51	1	0	.305/.405/.517	.296	.388	-1.2	C(53): 15.0	3.2
2014	CLE	MLB	25	95	10	5	0	1	4	5	26	0	0	.271/.311/.365	.244	.379	-1.5	C(29): 2.2	0.4
2015	CLE	MLB	26	226	30	9	1	7	21	33	64	0	0	.228/.348/.402	.257	.304	-0.8	C(69): 5.0	1.4
2016	*CLE*	*MLB*	*27*	*124*	*13*	*6*	*0*	*3*	*13*	*15*	*34*	*0*	*0*	*.230/.330/.367*	*.246*	*.300*	*-0.4*	*C 4*	*0.8*
2017	*CLE*	*MLB*	*28*	*209*	*25*	*9*	*1*	*5*	*21*	*26*	*58*	*0*	*0*	*.227/.328/.363*	*.244*	*.297*	*-0.8*	*C 6*	*1.3*

Breakout: 8% Improve: 30% Collapse: 15% Attrition: 32% MLB: 69% *Comparables: Rob Bowen, Hank Conger, George Kottaras*

YEAR	TEAM	P. COUNT	FRM RUNS	BLK RUNS	THRW RUNS	TOT RUNS
2013	COH	8525	17.4	0.9	0.6	18.9
2014	CLE	3667	1.9	0.2	0.5	2.6
2014	COH	7159	12.8	0.5	1.1	14.4
2015	CLE	8759	4.7	0.0	0.8	5.6
2016	*CLE*	*4716*	*3.8*	*0.1*	*0.3*	*4.3*
2017	*CLE*	*7952*	*6.0*	*0.2*	*0.5*	*6.7*

Perez seems to be cobbled together from the best pieces of Cleveland's last two receivers. First, he mimicked Carlos Santana's approach at the plate. He swung at fewer pitches outside of the zone (15.7 percent) than any other hitter in baseball with 200 plate appearances—fewer even than celebrated connoisseur Joey Votto—which allowed him to maintain a solid OBP. Then, he coupled that with his carrying trait: a defensive profile that may even surpass Yan Gomes. His strong arm cut down 42 percent of would-be basestealers (second in the AL among catchers with as many attempts), and his solid framing saved about three runs in 2015—four runs better than what Gomes provided. Sure, Perez's 2015 may be an example of everything going right for this never-was prospect, but there's also a chance this Frankencatcher could be baseball's best backup backstop this season.

Ryan Raburn RF

Born: 4/17/81 Age: 35 Bats: R Throws: R Height: 6'0" Weight: 185

YEAR	TEAM	LVL	AGE	PA	R	2B	3B	HR	RBI	BB	K	SB	CS	AVG/OBP/SLG	TAv	BABIP	BRR	FRAA	WARP
2013	CLE	MLB	32	277	40	18	0	16	55	29	67	0	0	.272/.357/.543	.327	.311	0.7	RF(54): 2.5, LF(13): -0.6	2.7
2014	CLE	MLB	33	212	18	7	0	4	22	13	51	0	0	.200/.250/.297	.198	.245	-0.4	RF(25): -0.3, LF(20): 0.1	-1.1
2015	CLE	MLB	34	201	22	16	1	8	29	23	44	0	0	.301/.393/.543	.320	.361	0.2	LF(18): 0.7, RF(17): -0.7	1.6
2016	*CLE*	*MLB*	*35*	*200*	*21*	*10*	*1*	*6*	*23*	*15*	*52*	*0*	*0*	*.235/.299/.396*	*.244*	*.292*	*0.1*	*RF -1, LF -0*	*0.0*
2017	*CLE*	*MLB*	*36*	*146*	*16*	*7*	*0*	*4*	*16*	*11*	*38*	*0*	*0*	*.224/.291/.374*	*.234*	*.280*	*0.0*	*RF -1, LF 0*	*-0.1*

Breakout: 0% Improve: 23% Collapse: 11% Attrition: 17% MLB: 90% *Comparables: Olmedo Saenz, Phil Nevin, Carl Everett*

If your favorite team is facing a left-handed pitcher, who would you rather have at the dish: Raburn or Bryce Harper? Before you answer, consider this: Raburn's slash line against lefties was .325/.415/.589 in 176 PA, compared to Harper's .318/.434/.552 in 189. Over the past three seasons, his unadjusted OPS against lefties tops Buster Posey, Justin Upton, Adam Jones... and Harper. Now, unlike Harper, Raburn has historically been awful against right-handed pitchers; Cleveland offset this by restricting him to just 25 trips against his stronger foe in 2015. As he comes into his age-35 season, it's safe to expect his performance to regress closer to his career norms, and he's nearly played himself out of any defensive role.

Okay, now what's your answer? Yeah, Harper. Obviously. Probably.

Jose Ramirez SS

Born: 9/17/92 Age: 23 Bats: B Throws: R Height: 5'9" Weight: 180

YEAR	TEAM	LVL	AGE	PA	R	2B	3B	HR	RBI	BB	K	SB	CS	AVG/OBP/SLG	TAv	BABIP	BRR	FRAA	WARP
2013	CLE	MLB	20	14	5	0	1	0	0	2	2	0	1	.333/.429/.500	.338	.400	0.5	2B(5): 0.4, SS(2): -0.0	0.3
2013	AKR	AA	20	533	78	16	6	3	38	39	41	38	16	.272/.325/.349	.261	.290	3.0	2B(53): 0.6, SS(50): 3.9	3.0
2014	CLE	MLB	21	266	27	10	2	2	17	13	35	10	1	.262/.300/.346	.233	.297	2.1	SS(56): 1.8, 2B(11): -0.5	0.7
2014	COH	AAA	21	277	37	15	2	5	29	25	30	19	11	.302/.360/.441	.268	.321	-1.8	2B(35): 6.0, SS(21): 1.3	1.7
2015	CLE	MLB	22	355	50	14	3	6	27	32	39	10	4	.219/.291/.340	.238	.232	1.0	SS(46): -4.2, 2B(33): 2.5	0.5
2015	COH	AAA	22	195	29	13	2	1	12	17	9	15	4	.293/.354/.408	.268	.303	1.6	2B(28): 2.1, SS(10): -0.5	1.0
2016	*CLE*	*MLB*	*23*	*368*	*46*	*16*	*3*	*5*	*30*	*25*	*45*	*16*	*6*	*.260/.312/.375*	*.239*	*.278*	*0.8*	*3B 3, 2B 2*	*1.1*
2017	*CLE*	*MLB*	*24*	*526*	*57*	*22*	*4*	*8*	*52*	*35*	*62*	*23*	*9*	*.264/.313/.382*	*.243*	*.280*	*2.3*	*3B 4, 2B 3*	*2.0*

Breakout: 4% Improve: 33% Collapse: 3% Attrition: 19% MLB: 56% *Comparables: J.J. Hardy, Ruben Tejada, Dustin Pedroia*

Ramirez checks all the boxes for an instant fan favorite: His height makes him easily identifiable on the field, he fills in with good-enough defense all over the infield, and he plays so frenetically he's even earned a killer nickname: the Angry Hamster. The barrier between *fan favorite* and plain old *favorite* is his potential, which he's yet to tap. With plus speed, he should be stealing more bases and improving on 2015's 71 percent success rate. He's shown good effort in working counts (3.99 pitches seen per PA, above league average), and there are glimpses of a legitimate hit tool (90 percent contact rate), but neither has translated to hits yet. Ramirez has had worse-than-average production on both flyballs (.549 OPS) and grounders (.472 OPS) in the majors, an unfortunate combination. If he doesn't have enough power to convert flies into extra-base hits, or can't sneak enough singles on those grounders, then he risks running the utility-infielder wheel for the next several seasons. That would make hamster very angry indeed.

Jerry Sands DH

Born: 9/28/87 Age: 28 Bats: R Throws: R Height: 6'4" Weight: 225

YEAR	TEAM	LVL	AGE	PA	R	2B	3B	HR	RBI	BB	K	SB	CS	AVG/OBP/SLG	TAv	BABIP	BRR	FRAA	WARP
2013	IND	AAA	25	397	37	17	2	7	34	50	105	0	1	.207/.311/.329	.229	.276	0.0	RF(73): 13.7, LF(15): 0.6	0.9
2014	TBA	MLB	26	22	1	0	0	1	4	0	6	0	0	.190/.227/.333	.187	.214	-0.1		-0.1
2014	DUR	AAA	26	219	32	12	0	9	36	26	53	1	0	.268/.352/.474	.272	.321	-0.4	RF(31): 4.4, 1B(12): 0.3	1.2
2015	COH	AAA	27	276	41	12	1	14	46	45	40	1	2	.287/.409/.538	.327	.289	-0.1	RF(24): -0.4, 1B(14): -0.0	2.3
2015	CLE	MLB	27	133	11	5	1	4	19	9	36	0	0	.236/.286/.390	.238	.298	-0.6	RF(32): -1.6, 1B(11): 1.4	-0.2
2016	*CLE*	*MLB*	*28*	*250*	*28*	*11*	*1*	*9*	*33*	*25*	*64*	*0*	*0*	*.237/.316/.423*	*.260*	*.285*	*-0.4*	*RF 1, 1B 0*	*0.6*
2017	*CLE*	*MLB*	*29*	*333*	*42*	*15*	*1*	*13*	*43*	*33*	*85*	*0*	*0*	*.235/.312/.421*	*.257*	*.282*	*-0.8*	*RF 1, 1B 1*	*0.9*

Breakout: 4% Improve: 14% Collapse: 14% Attrition: 24% MLB: 45% *Comparables: Michael Taylor, Joe Mather, Ryan Ludwick*

A crowded Cleveland outfield pushed Sands to the minors despite a ripping hot start to 2015, and he drubbed Triple-A pitching during a long run in Columbus. Which is what he does. Which has always, sort of, been the problem. It'd be so much easier for everybody if he'd just stop doing *that*.

After being called back up to the bigs in the Indians' new post-Bourn-and-Swisher world, Sands couldn't leverage any of the power and patience that made him so dangerous in the minors. He was overmatched by hard stuff, as 25 percent of his swings on fastballs were whiffs. And he demonstrated why scouts have historically placed a low grade on his hit tool, swinging most egregiously at pitches up and in—pitcher's pitches as much as any other. Combine that with the troubles everybody has on low and away, and he's only a mistake hitter at this point in his career. That's a great way to end up on another minor-league contract, where, son of a gun, he'll probably drub Triple-A pitching again.

Carlos Santana 1B

Born: 4/8/86 Age: 30 Bats: B Throws: R Height: 5'11" Weight: 210

YEAR	TEAM	LVL	AGE	PA	R	2B	3B	HR	RBI	BB	K	SB	CS	AVG/OBP/SLG	TAv	BABIP	BRR	FRAA	WARP
2013	CLE	MLB	27	642	75	39	1	20	74	93	110	3	1	.268/.377/.455	.312	.301	-2.6	C(84): -14.1, 1B(29): 0.5	3.6
2014	CLE	MLB	28	660	68	25	0	27	85	113	124	5	2	.231/.365/.427	.292	.249	-1.8	1B(94): 5.0, 3B(26): -0.9	3.1
2015	CLE	MLB	29	666	72	29	2	19	85	108	122	11	3	.231/.357/.395	.265	.261	-2.3	1B(132): -3.4	0.4
2016	*CLE*	*MLB*	*30*	*678*	*85*	*33*	*2*	*22*	*86*	*105*	*128*	*7*	*3*	*.246/.364/.429*	*.283*	*.278*	*-2.3*	*1B -0*	*2.5*
2017	*CLE*	*MLB*	*31*	*576*	*78*	*28*	*2*	*18*	*69*	*91*	*112*	*5*	*2*	*.236/.358/.413*	*.274*	*.269*	*-2.0*	*1B 0*	*2.5*

Breakout: 2% Improve: 50% Collapse: 5% Attrition: 5% MLB: 98% *Comparables: Nick Johnson, Edwin Encarnacion, Todd Helton*

Now firmly entrenched as Cleveland's first baseman, it's no longer good enough to be a good hitter *for a catcher*. At the end of the year, Santana claimed that a nagging back injury—perhaps from shouldering a greater offensive burden?—was to blame for a dip in power and the worst offensive performance of his career. Fortunately, Santana remains a world-class plate discipline savant, with league-wide top-five marks in pitches seen per plate appearance (4.30) and walk rate (16.2 percent); he hacked at fewer pitches outside the strike zone (19.2 percent) than anyone in the game. If he can get that slugging percentage back above .420, as PECOTA foresees, he's a top-20 hitter in the AL. The question is whether you'd rather have a guy with a good excuse, or without a nagging back injury.

Giovanny Urshela 3B

Born: 10/11/91 Age: 24 Bats: R Throws: R Height: 6'0" Weight: 215

YEAR	TEAM	LVL	AGE	PA	R	2B	3B	HR	RBI	BB	K	SB	CS	AVG/OBP/SLG	TAv	BABIP	BRR	FRAA	WARP
2013	AKR	AA	21	466	42	23	2	8	43	14	48	1	1	.270/.292/.384	.240	.286	-2.7	3B(107): 2.0, SS(3): -0.1	0.4
2014	AKR	AA	22	98	15	9	0	5	19	6	16	1	1	.300/.347/.567	.303	.314	2.2	3B(23): 0.6	1.1
2014	COH	AAA	22	430	63	27	6	13	65	30	51	0	2	.276/.331/.473	.265	.289	-0.6	3B(98): 0.1, SS(1): -0.1	1.6
2015	COH	AAA	23	84	12	5	1	3	9	3	12	0	0	.272/.298/.469	.244	.288	0.6	3B(17): 3.2	0.5
2015	CLE	MLB	23	288	25	8	1	6	21	18	58	0	1	.225/.279/.330	.217	.266	-1.4	3B(80): 7.6	0.3
2016	*CLE*	*MLB*	*24*	*489*	*46*	*24*	*3*	*13*	*57*	*22*	*83*	*1*	*1*	*.253/.289/.401*	*.242*	*.280*	*-0.9*	*3B 4*	*0.8*
2017	*CLE*	*MLB*	*25*	*520*	*57*	*26*	*3*	*14*	*59*	*24*	*92*	*1*	*1*	*.249/.288/.398*	*.242*	*.279*	*-1.1*	*3B 4*	*0.9*

Breakout: 4% Improve: 24% Collapse: 7% Attrition: 14% MLB: 51% *Comparables: Willy Aybar, Daniel Murphy, Josh Vitters*

It only took a complete mid-season makeover of Cleveland's awful defense to get Urshela his shot. The young Colombian showed smooth motions and plus range from the jump; for Indians fans who spent a year and a half watching Carlos Santana and Lonnie Chisenhall at third base, this was like going from pool to hot tub. Unfortunately, he didn't hit, and with Yandy Diaz breathing down his neck (metaphorically, we hope), he'll need to turn his bat-to-ball skills and power potential into actual production if he's to keep a regular job. If he can't, he's more likely the next Matt Dominguez than the next Pedro Feliz, though neither comparison is particularly inspiring.

Bradley Zimmer OF

Born: 11/27/92 Age: 23 Bats: L Throws: R Height: 6'4" Weight: 185

YEAR	TEAM	LVL	AGE	PA	R	2B	3B	HR	RBI	BB	K	SB	CS	AVG/OBP/SLG	TAv	BABIP	BRR	FRAA	WARP
2014	MHV	A-	21	197	32	11	2	4	30	19	30	11	4	.304/.401/.464	.327	.348	2.4	CF(42): 1.4	2.4
2015	LYN	A+	22	335	60	17	3	10	39	37	77	32	5	.308/.403/.493	.322	.388	3.1	CF(41): 7.9, RF(22): 0.3	4.3
2015	AKR	AA	22	214	24	9	1	6	24	18	54	12	2	.219/.313/.374	.257	.273	-0.2	CF(42): 0.7	0.6
2016	*CLE*	*MLB*	*23*	*250*	*32*	*10*	*1*	*8*	*29*	*20*	*73*	*12*	*3*	*.231/.311/.396*	*.250*	*.303*	*1.3*	*CF 4, RF 0*	*1.2*
2017	*CLE*	*MLB*	*24*	*383*	*46*	*16*	*2*	*12*	*44*	*30*	*113*	*18*	*4*	*.230/.307/.391*	*.247*	*.305*	*2.7*	*CF 6, RF 1*	*1.8*

Breakout: 1% Improve: 15% Collapse: 5% Attrition: 13% MLB: 41% *Comparables: Brett Jackson, Chris Young, Michael Choice*

The Danny Glover to Clint Frazier's Mel Gibson, Zimmer is older, wiser, and arguably better than his flashier counterpart. His stay at Lynchburg was phenomenal (.322 True Average, great defense, high cheekbones), and cemented him among the game's top 25 prospects thanks to a lethal combination of skills and tools: plus power, speed, range and approach. A hairline fracture in his foot slowed him late and prevented him from showing his stuff during the Arizona Fall League, but Zimmer remains on track to patrol Progressive Field by the start of 2017. His ceiling is Grady Sizemore. His floor... well, that's Grady Sizemore, too.

PITCHERS

Brady Aiken LHP

Born: 8/16/96 Age: 19 Bats: L Throws: L Height: 6'4" Weight: 210

Say you're building a pitching prospect in *MLB: The Show*. You get a pool of points and can assign them to any number of skills and talents. You load up on fastball velocity, curveball movement, and an overall broad repertoire. You add points for intelligence and command, and even assign whatever's left to give your avatar a lean, tall pitcher's frame, with room to grow. And, heck, why not make him a lefty? There's just one last rating to fill in: "Elbow ligament." And, whoops, you're out of points.

In what felt almost like self-fulfilling prophecy, the atypically sized UCL that scuttled negotiations between the Astros and Aiken tore during the pitcher's first appearance at the IMG Academy. He was, by that point, already something of a huge star: He broke the news of his injury on Derek Jeter's website and had his Tommy John surgery performed by the Yankees' surgeon, David Altchek. But he was also a spectacularly unpredictable commodity, slipping from first overall in 2014 to 17th overall a year later. It was a gutsy move by the Indians, who will now undoubtedly act very conservatively bringing him along. If he comes back fully healthy—and roughly 80 percent of TJ patients do—he ought to once against have those plus ratings across the board, but now with a more typical ulnar collateral ligament holding it all together. That's a) a big "if" but b) a hell of a prospect.

Cody Allen RHP

Born: 11/20/88 Age: 27 Bats: R Throws: R Height: 6'1" Weight: 210

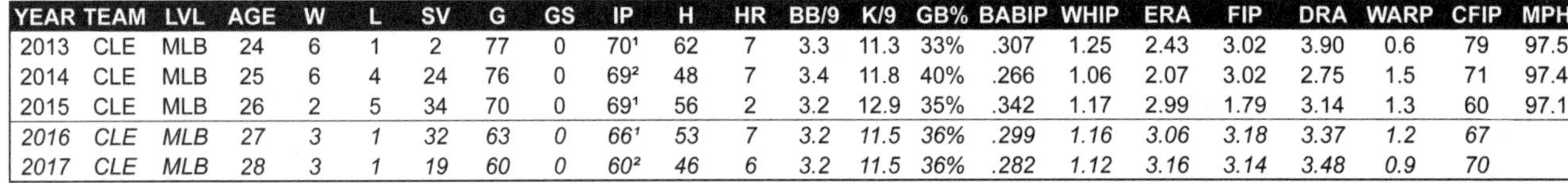

YEAR	TEAM	LVL	AGE	W	L	SV	G	GS	IP	H	HR	BB/9	K/9	GB%	BABIP	WHIP	ERA	FIP	DRA	WARP	CFIP	MPH
2013	CLE	MLB	24	6	1	2	77	0	70^{1}	62	7	3.3	11.3	33%	.307	1.25	2.43	3.02	3.90	0.6	79	97.5
2014	CLE	MLB	25	6	4	24	76	0	69^{2}	48	7	3.4	11.8	40%	.266	1.06	2.07	3.02	2.75	1.5	71	97.4
2015	CLE	MLB	26	2	5	34	70	0	69^{1}	56	2	3.2	12.9	35%	.342	1.17	2.99	1.79	3.14	1.3	60	97.1
2016	*CLE*	*MLB*	*27*	*3*	*1*	*32*	*63*	*0*	*66^{1}*	*53*	*7*	*3.2*	*11.5*	*36%*	*.299*	*1.16*	*3.06*	*3.18*	*3.37*	*1.2*	*67*	
2017	*CLE*	*MLB*	*28*	*3*	*1*	*19*	*60*	*0*	*60^{2}*	*46*	*6*	*3.2*	*11.5*	*36%*	*.282*	*1.12*	*3.16*	*3.14*	*3.48*	*0.9*	*70*	

Breakout: 36% Improve: 56% Collapse: 26% Attrition: 17% MLB: 98% *Comparables: Hong-Chih Kuo, Jordan Walden, David Robertson*

Allen had a sneaky-great season as Cleveland's closer last season, using an ugly April (1.043 OPS against) to lull hitters into a false sense of security for the rest of the year. His out-pitch, a ridiculous spiked curveball, is a sleeper in the Best Pitch In Baseball conversation. It's the second-hardest curve in the game (behind Craig Kimbrel) and, last year, got the highest whiff/swing results, at 64 percent. It's also his primary groundball inducer, and batters managed an isolated power of .020 when they did put it in play. Oh, and it's platoon proof.

Allen has a bit of a reputation as a "cardiac closer," which is really just further proof that no fan trusts his closer unless it's Mo. All has proven as reliable as any late-inning option in the American League, and the only white knuckles fans should worry about the ones sticking out from one of baseball's finest pitches.

Cody Anderson RHP

Born: 9/14/90 Age: 25 Bats: R Throws: R Height: 6'4" Weight: 235

YEAR	TEAM	LVL	AGE	W	L	SV	G	GS	IP	H	HR	BB/9	K/9	GB%	BABIP	WHIP	ERA	FIP	DRA	WARP	CFIP	MPH
2013	AKR	AA	22	0	0	0	3	3	12^{2}	16	2	6.4	7.1	24%	.359	1.97	5.68	5.93	5.17	0.0	115	
2013	CAR	A+	22	9	4	0	23	23	123^{1}	105	6	2.3	8.2	40%	.296	1.10	2.34	3.04	4.09	1.8	80	
2014	AKR	AA	23	4	11	0	25	25	125^{2}	141	17	3.2	5.8	46%	.312	1.48	5.44	4.99	5.05	0.1	120	
2015	CLE	MLB	24	7	3	0	15	15	91^{1}	77	9	2.4	4.3	47%	.237	1.11	3.05	4.24	3.59	1.6	119	94.8
2015	COH	AAA	24	1	1	0	3	3	19^{1}	17	0	2.3	8.4	41%	.315	1.14	2.33	2.23	2.94	0.4	85	
2015	AKR	AA	24	3	2	0	10	10	52	44	2	1.6	6.2	46%	.273	1.02	1.73	2.96	3.55	0.8	92	
2016	*CLE*	*MLB*	*25*	*10*	*11*	*0*	*29*	*29*	*174*	*184*	*22*	*3.0*	*5.7*	*45%*	*.292*	*1.39*	*4.64*	*4.71*	*4.94*	*0.4*	*117*	
2017	*CLE*	*MLB*	*26*	*7*	*8*	*0*	*24*	*24*	*138^{2}*	*144*	*18*	*3.1*	*6.0*	*45%*	*.289*	*1.38*	*4.66*	*4.64*	*4.96*	*0.2*	*118*	

Breakout: 19% Improve: 35% Collapse: 15% Attrition: 31% MLB: 62% *Comparables: Philip Humber, Justin Germano, Anthony Bass*

On June 17th, Shaun Marcum had an absolute disaster of a start (two-plus innings, six earned runs) and inadvertently jump-started Cody Anderson's big-league career. Forced into duty as Cleveland's new no. 5, Anderson promptly navigated lineups the way the Millenium Falcon dodged asteroids, never more than one step away from disaster but never closer, either. Big Country has the stuff of a swingman, with a pedestrian fastball and good-but-not-elite control, so it would be a mistake to expect him to replicate the runaway success of his 2015 season—especially the 1.38 ERA in September that won him the AL Pitcher of the Month honors. (Despite a 3.85 FIP, harumph.) Predictive metrics like cFIP see the big righty as a fringy starter going forward, but he'll always have 2015.

Shawn Armstrong RHP

Born: 9/11/90 Age: 25 Bats: R Throws: R Height: 6'2" Weight: 225

YEAR	TEAM	LVL	AGE	W	L	SV	G	GS	IP	H	HR	BB/9	K/9	GB%	BABIP	WHIP	ERA	FIP	DRA	WARP	CFIP	MPH
2013	AKR	AA	22	2	3	0	30	0	33	32	2	5.7	11.7	36%	.353	1.61	4.09	3.60	4.58	0.1	98	
2014	AKR	AA	23	6	2	15	44	0	51	39	3	3.4	12.0	41%	.310	1.14	2.12	2.63	3.57	0.7	66	
2015	COH	AAA	24	1	2	16	46	0	49^{2}	37	0	4.7	14.5	43%	.363	1.27	2.36	1.63	0.42	2.4	54	
2015	CLE	MLB	24	0	0	0	8	0	8	5	1	2.2	12.4	35%	.250	0.88	2.25	2.73	2.87	0.2	87	96.5
2016	*CLE*	*MLB*	*25*	*2*	*1*	*0*	*34*	*0*	35^{2}	*30*	*3*	*3.9*	*11.2*	*40%*	*.308*	*1.27*	*3.30*	*3.16*	*3.61*	*0.6*	*75*	
2017	*CLE*	*MLB*	*26*	*2*	*1*	*0*	*33*	*0*	39^{2}	*33*	*4*	*4.0*	*11.4*	*40%*	*.302*	*1.27*	*3.39*	*3.39*	*3.71*	*0.5*	*78*	

Breakout: 24% Improve: 33% Collapse: 16% Attrition: 37% MLB: 55% *Comparables: Kevin Quackenbush, Donnie Joseph, Steven Ames*

His name puts too fine a point on it, but *man* can Armstrong throw. Like many relief-only prospects, he lives and dies on two pitches: a humming fastball and a wipeout slider with strong tilt. In Columbus, hitters couldn't touch him—he struck out 38 percent of hitters faced and was selected to the International League All-Star Game. After being called up to The Show, he looked like an All-Star at the highest level, averaging 94.5 mph on his four-seamer and touching 97. If he keeps the control gains he demonstrated in 2015, he'll settle in at the back of the Tribe's bullpen.

Trevor Bauer RHP

Born: 1/17/91 Age: 25 Bats: R Throws: R Height: 6'1" Weight: 200

YEAR	TEAM	LVL	AGE	W	L	SV	G	GS	IP	H	HR	BB/9	K/9	GB%	BABIP	WHIP	ERA	FIP	DRA	WARP	CFIP	MPH
2013	CLE	MLB	22	1	2	0	4	4	17	15	3	8.5	5.8	36%	.240	1.82	5.29	7.08	6.68	-0.4	129	95.1
2013	COH	AAA	22	6	7	0	22	22	121^{1}	119	14	5.4	7.9	43%	.307	1.58	4.15	5.08	5.24	-0.3	125	
2014	COH	AAA	23	4	1	0	7	7	46	36	5	2.7	8.6	40%	.263	1.09	2.15	3.84	4.20	0.5	88	
2014	CLE	MLB	23	5	8	0	26	26	153	151	16	3.5	8.4	37%	.312	1.38	4.18	4.04	4.34	0.8	102	96.5
2015	CLE	MLB	24	11	12	0	31	30	176	152	23	4.0	8.7	41%	.276	1.31	4.55	4.30	4.17	1.8	102	95.6
2016	*CLE*	*MLB*	*25*	*9*	*10*	*0*	*29*	*29*	153^{2}	*145*	*19*	*3.9*	*8.7*	*40%*	*.294*	*1.37*	*4.27*	*4.31*	*4.57*	*1.0*	*106*	
2017	*CLE*	*MLB*	*26*	*9*	*9*	*0*	*26*	*26*	150^{2}	*136*	*19*	*3.7*	*9.0*	*40%*	*.287*	*1.31*	*4.11*	*4.09*	*4.40*	*1.3*	*102*	

Breakout: 34% Improve: 64% Collapse: 19% Attrition: 15% MLB: 91% *Comparables: Gio Gonzalez, Josh Johnson, Chad Gaudin*

Subscribing to the theory of "effective velocity," Bauer usually tries to craft his pitches for maximum separation in velocity; by throwing up and in his hard stuff looks faster, and his soft stuff looks slower. It's new branding, but pitchers have been playing that game for years. But in Bauer's case, this approach and his wide variety of pitches lead to some pretty fascinating outcomes: Even in his best start, on April 9th, Bauer walked five, struck out 11, and threw 111 pitches in just six no-hit innings. His tinkering approach has appeared to lead to inconsistency, and Terry Francona briefly pulled him from the Cleveland rotation during a late-season playoff charge. Is he overthinking his approach to pitching? Maybe, but smart guys like Zack Greinke and Greg Maddux could adjust without walking four batters per nine. Perhaps the next shift in approach he should consider is this: Get the ball over the damn plate more often.

Carlos Carrasco RHP

Born: 3/21/87 Age: 29 Bats: R Throws: R Height: 6'4" Weight: 210

YEAR	TEAM	LVL	AGE	W	L	SV	G	GS	IP	H	HR	BB/9	K/9	GB%	BABIP	WHIP	ERA	FIP	DRA	WARP	CFIP	MPH
2013	CLE	MLB	26	1	4	0	15	7	46^{2}	64	4	3.5	5.8	50%	.364	1.76	6.75	4.13	5.81	-0.6	116	98.0
2013	COH	AAA	26	3	1	1	16	14	71^{2}	59	6	2.6	9.9	45%	.285	1.12	3.14	3.22	3.77	1.0	80	
2014	CLE	MLB	27	8	7	1	40	14	134	103	7	1.9	9.4	54%	.274	0.99	2.55	2.47	2.60	3.4	78	98.4
2015	CLE	MLB	28	14	12	0	30	30	183^{2}	154	18	2.1	10.6	53%	.304	1.07	3.63	2.81	3.40	3.5	66	97.5
2016	*CLE*	*MLB*	*29*	*11*	*8*	*0*	*29*	*29*	165^{1}	*143*	*17*	*2.4*	*10.1*	*52%*	*.299*	*1.14*	*3.14*	*3.23*	*3.44*	*3.3*	*71*	
2017	*CLE*	*MLB*	*30*	*10*	*7*	*0*	*38*	*24*	*170*	*145*	*17*	*2.3*	*10.2*	*52%*	*.297*	*1.11*	*3.03*	*3.02*	*3.32*	*3.3*	*68*	

Breakout: 19% Improve: 46% Collapse: 15% Attrition: 1% MLB: 98% *Comparables: John Lackey, Sean Marshall, Adam Wainwright*

He's the ace-level starter you've heard the least about over the past two years. He's the master of an unbelievable slider with serious break and startling velocity—one of the best pitches in baseball. He's the guy with the best Corey Kluber impression in baseball, and who is darned close to overtaking the original. Last season it was Cookie, not Kluber, who set the Cleveland franchise record for strikeout rate in a season for a starter (30 percent), who led the team in cFIP (66). He's signed to an unbelievably team-friendly contract, an extension signed on the basis of 14 good starts in 2014. It was aggressive and gutsy for the Indians to commit to a pitcher who, one year earlier, had seemed a fair bet to fade out of the league entirely. Today? He still doesn't get the recognition his skills deserve, but after another season like the last one he'll finally burst free of Kluber's shadow and start casting a long one of his own.

Joba Chamberlain RHP

Born: 9/23/85 Age: 30 Bats: R Throws: R Height: 6'2" Weight: 250

YEAR	TEAM	LVL	AGE	W	L	SV	G	GS	IP	H	HR	BB/9	K/9	GB%	BABIP	WHIP	ERA	FIP	DRA	WARP	CFIP	MPH
2013	NYA	MLB	27	2	1	1	45	0	42	47	8	5.6	8.1	43%	.315	1.74	4.93	5.67	5.55	-0.5	115	97.6
2014	DET	MLB	28	2	5	2	69	0	63	57	3	3.4	8.4	55%	.310	1.29	3.57	3.19	3.20	1.0	90	96.1
2015	DET	MLB	29	0	2	0	30	0	22	32	5	2.0	6.1	45%	.360	1.68	4.09	5.51	8.35	-1.0	107	96.6
2015	KCA	MLB	29	0	0	0	6	0	5^{2}	6	1	6.4	12.7	47%	.357	1.76	7.94	4.69	1.50	0.2	92	97.8
2016	*CLE*	*MLB*	*30*	*2*	*1*	*1*	*38*	*0*	*40*	*42*	*5*	*3.5*	*8.2*	*50%*	*.315*	*1.43*	*4.27*	*4.29*	*4.59*	*0.1*	*104*	
2017	*CLE*	*MLB*	*31*	*3*	*1*	*1*	*59*	*0*	52^{2}	*56*	*7*	*3.5*	*8.0*	*50%*	*.318*	*1.46*	*4.33*	*4.31*	*4.65*	*0.0*	*105*	

Breakout: 22% Improve: 58% Collapse: 14% Attrition: 3% MLB: 90% *Comparables: Juan Gutierrez, Mike Stanton, Logan Ondrusek*

Let's take the optimistic view, since a player as seemingly hexed as Chamberlain deserves a little optimism. His 2014 rebound in the Tigers 'pen actually happened—it was a real thing that occurred not too long ago—and Chamberlain has avoided significant injury for two consecutive seasons. There are no longer any questions about his role. He can still pump his fastball into the mid-90s, and his breaking stuff can be crisp. While last year was a certifiable disaster from a results standpoint, earning his release from both the Tigers and Blue Jays before struggling in Kansas City, his BABIP and percentage of home runs per fly ball were extremely high and have the potential for regression. Almost anything can happen over a 50-inning span, so Chamberlain has as much chance of thriving in middle relief this year as any other hard-throwing veteran.

Michael Clevinger RHP

Born: 12/21/90 Age: 25 Bats: R Throws: R Height: 6'4" Weight: 220

YEAR	TEAM	LVL	AGE	W	L	SV	G	GS	IP	H	HR	BB/9	K/9	GB%	BABIP	WHIP	ERA	FIP	DRA	WARP	CFIP	MPH
2014	INL	A+	23	1	3	0	13	13	55^{1}	58	8	4.4	9.4	0%	.331	1.54	5.37	5.20				
2014	BUR	A	23	3	0	0	5	5	24	16	2	1.9	10.1	48%	.241	0.88	1.88	2.94	3.87	0.4	79	
2014	CAR	A+	23	0	1	0	5	4	20^{2}	20	1	4.8	6.5	41%	.328	1.50	4.79	4.73	5.07	0.0	115	
2015	AKR	AA	24	9	8	0	27	26	158	127	8	2.3	8.3	37%	.272	1.06	2.73	3.02	2.95	3.6	83	
2016	*CLE*	*MLB*	*25*	*7*	*7*	*0*	*22*	*22*	*111^{1}*	*112*	*13*	*3.0*	*7.7*	*30%*	*.297*	*1.33*	*4.18*	*4.18*	*4.49*	*0.8*	*103*	
2017	*CLE*	*MLB*	*26*	*6*	*7*	*0*	*21*	*21*	*122^{2}*	*125*	*18*	*3.0*	*7.8*	*30%*	*.296*	*1.35*	*4.45*	*4.43*	*4.78*	*0.4*	*111*	

Breakout: 10% Improve: 17% Collapse: 12% Attrition: 22% MLB: 32% *Comparables: Red Patterson, Roenis Elias, Neil Ramirez*

Every year, prospect hounds and fantasy mavens pick up this very Annual to look for their white whale: sleeper picks that will, come late September, make the general populace shiver with envy at their scouting acumen. Of course, now that nearly every Low-A ballclub has scout types writing up reports on them, it's become nearly impossible to find the truly unknowns. It's like looking for a clean-shaven dude in Brooklyn. But be happy, deep-divers: Clevinger could be your guy.

A former top-10 prospect with the Angels, his development stalled during every hurler's requisite first Tommy John surgery. But 2015 was a revelation—he posted 158 strong innings at Akron and tallied nearly a strikeout per inning. His strengths: a four-pitch arsenal and legit mid-90s heat, not the sort of pyrite mid-90s heat that faux scouts hype because they saw 94 on a nearby gun once. The red flags: delivery (awkward) and durability (untested). Nevertheless, the return for Vinnie Pestano looks like a steal so far. This is the latest in a stretch of savvy trades for starting pitching talent made by Chris Antonetti and staff. Maybe next time you should just ask the Cleveland front office for starting pitcher sleeper picks.

Kyle Crockett LHP

Born: 12/15/91 Age: 24 Bats: L Throws: L Height: 6'2" Weight: 175

YEAR	TEAM	LVL	AGE	W	L	SV	G	GS	IP	H	HR	BB/9	K/9	GB%	BABIP	WHIP	ERA	FIP	DRA	WARP	CFIP	MPH
2013	AKR	AA	21	1	0	0	9	0	10^{1}	7	0	1.7	7.8	67%	.259	0.87	0.00	2.16	4.27	0.1	91	
2014	AKR	AA	22	0	0	6	15	0	15^{2}	8	0	1.7	9.8	60%	.211	0.70	0.57	1.95	3.86	0.2	77	
2014	CLE	MLB	22	4	1	0	43	0	30	26	2	2.4	8.4	57%	.296	1.13	1.80	3.26	3.06	0.5	97	92.1
2015	COH	AAA	23	3	1	0	29	0	28^{2}	42	3	3.5	8.5	50%	.406	1.85	5.97	3.89	4.01	0.1	97	
2015	CLE	MLB	23	0	0	0	31	0	17^{2}	17	1	3.6	7.6	55%	.320	1.36	4.08	3.50	4.72	0.0	103	92.5
2016	*CLE*	*MLB*	*24*	*2*	*1*	*0*	*43*	*0*	*46*	*47*	*5*	*3.1*	*7.7*	*53%*	*.305*	*1.37*	*4.18*	*4.13*	*4.49*	*0.1*	*102*	
2017	*CLE*	*MLB*	*25*	*3*	*1*	*1*	*54*	*0*	*46^{2}*	*47*	*6*	*3.3*	*7.9*	*53%*	*.301*	*1.38*	*4.35*	*4.33*	*4.67*	*0.0*	*107*	

Breakout: 23% Improve: 35% Collapse: 13% Attrition: 28% MLB: 62% *Comparables: Bill Bray, Mike Morin, Daniel Schlereth*

Crockett was the Indians' designated Columbus-to-Cleveland shuttle lefty, optioned thrice to the minors during the 2015 season (April, June and July). In between his travels up and down I-71, Crockett delivered a fastball-slider combo from a low three-quarters arm slot on the left side. While he's not an extreme specialist like other funk-armed southpaws (hey there, Randy Choate!), he still hasn't found a knack for retiring righties, who posted an .803 OPS against him over the past two seasons. Even though he was a college closer, Crockett's likely long-term role is shuffling up and down the Ohio corridor, trying to induce groundball outs in middle-leverage situations and waiting to run out of minor-league options.

Tom Gorzelanny LHP

Born: 7/12/82 Age: 33 Bats: R Throws: L Height: 6'2" Weight: 210

YEAR	TEAM	LVL	AGE	W	L	SV	G	GS	IP	H	HR	BB/9	K/9	GB%	BABIP	WHIP	ERA	FIP	DRA	WARP	CFIP	MPH
2013	MIL	MLB	30	3	6	0	43	10	85^{1}	77	11	3.3	8.8	45%	.288	1.27	3.90	3.91	4.04	0.7	93	93.5
2014	MIL	MLB	31	0	0	0	23	0	21	22	1	3.4	9.9	47%	.344	1.43	0.86	2.96	4.21	0.1	99	92.4
2015	DET	MLB	32	2	2	0	48	0	39^{1}	45	4	5.3	8.2	42%	.353	1.73	5.95	4.50	5.81	-0.5	106	93.5
2016	*CLE*	*MLB*	*33*	*2*	*1*	*0*	*32*	*2*	*41^{1}*	*40*	*5*	*3.6*	*8.1*	*43%*	*.297*	*1.38*	*4.32*	*4.40*	*4.62*	*0.1*	*106*	
2017	*CLE*	*MLB*	*34*	*4*	*2*	*0*	*58*	*3*	*80^{1}*	*79*	*10*	*3.7*	*7.7*	*43%*	*.294*	*1.40*	*4.49*	*4.47*	*4.80*	*0.0*	*111*	

Breakout: 25% Improve: 50% Collapse: 20% Attrition: 13% MLB: 83% *Comparables: Alfredo Simon, Randy Myers, Aaron Heilman*

Several bargain-bin relievers have had regrettable seasons with the Tigers over the years, and Gorzelanny is no exception. The veteran lefty was designated for assignment in June with a 1.96 WHIP, but accepted a Triple-A assignment and began throwing from a different (lower) arm angle, because the alternative was beer-league softball. While his walk rate ballooned, so did his strikeout rate, and a second chance with Detroit confirmed both trends. If he can harness the new delivery, his new-look secondary pitches might miss enough maple to win an Opening Day job with Cleveland—his fifth stop in the tour of baseball's central-division cities.

Ben Heller RHP

Born: 8/5/91 Age: 24 Bats: R Throws: R Height: 6'3" Weight: 205

YEAR	TEAM	LVL	AGE	W	L	SV	G	GS	IP	H	HR	BB/9	K/9	GB%	BABIP	WHIP	ERA	FIP	DRA	WARP	CFIP	MPH
2013	MHV	A-	21	1	3	2	21	1	37^1	37	0	3.4	9.4	52%	.343	1.37	3.13	2.29	3.78	0.2	92	
2014	CAR	A+	22	1	0	1	17	0	16	8	1	7.3	9.6	49%	.194	1.31	2.25	5.21	5.13	-0.1	116	
2014	LKC	A	22	4	1	4	28	0	37	19	3	3.9	15.6	46%	.254	0.95	2.43	2.54	3.32	0.6	60	
2015	LYN	A+	23	0	2	12	36	0	34^1	30	0	3.4	11.3	37%	.333	1.25	4.46	2.06	2.39	0.8	82	
2016	*CLE*	*MLB*	*24*	*2*	*1*	*1*	*34*	*0*	*35^2*	*35*	*4*	*4.3*	*9.0*	*38%*	*.309*	*1.45*	*4.20*	*4.33*	*4.51*	*0.1*	*103*	
2017	*CLE*	*MLB*	*25*	*2*	*1*	*2*	*35*	*0*	*43*	*41*	*5*	*4.2*	*9.5*	*38%*	*.313*	*1.43*	*4.06*	*4.05*	*4.36*	*0.2*	*99*	

Breakout: 0% Improve: 0% Collapse: 0% Attrition: 0% MLB: 0% *Comparables: Mickey Storey, Rob Wooten, Robbie Weinhardt*

Until this year, Heller was barely a blip on anyone's radar, a 20th-round relief-pitching pick out of the obscure Olivet Nazarene University back in 2013. While he's still not exactly lighting the prospecting world on fire, his minor-league production should raise an eyebrow or two. His sharp strikeout numbers in High-A Lynchburg earned him a promotion to Double-A, where Heller promptly hit the gas and punched out 15 hitters in six innings. Though he's unlikely to ever be the most famous baseball-playing Ben to come out of Olivet (the last guy to be drafted from the school prior to Heller was Ben Zobrist), he now has an outside chance to reach the bigs in an impact relief role.

Juan Hillman LHP

Born: 5/15/97 Age: 19 Bats: L Throws: L Height: 6'2" Weight: 183

YEAR	TEAM	LVL	AGE	W	L	SV	G	GS	IP	H	HR	BB/9	K/9	GB%	BABIP	WHIP	ERA	FIP	DRA	WARP	CFIP	MPH
2016	*CLE*	*MLB*	*19*	*1*	*2*	*0*	*14*	*5*	*30^2*	*40*	*5*	*5.8*	*3.8*	*19%*	*.313*	*1.95*	*6.66*	*6.66*	*7.16*	*-0.8*	*165*	
2017	*CLE*	*MLB*	*20*	*2*	*5*	*0*	*23*	*14*	*113^2*	*141*	*19*	*5.2*	*4.1*	*19%*	*.305*	*1.82*	*6.33*	*6.30*	*6.81*	*-1.5*	*159*	

Breakout: 0% Improve: 0% Collapse: 0% Attrition: 0% MLB: 0% *Comparables: Alberto Cabrera, Josh Stinson, Dan Cortes*

The Indians were thrilled that Hillman fell all the way to 59th overall in the 2015 draft—a host of talent evaluators, including BP's Christopher Crawford, had him ranked 20 or more picks higher on their boards. While Hillman doesn't have top-end velocity, he has far more going for him than the average prep arm. He comes to the table with two good off-speed pitches, a change with deception and fade and a solid curveball. In addition, he's already mastered locating his low-90s fastball down in the zone. He even has a pretty impressive mentor and godfather in Tom "Flash" Gordon, who became Hillman's legal guardian when the pitcher turned 14. Gordon also coached him and guided him through the competitive showcase circuit. It's a strange twist on the old notion of "bloodlines," as Hillman shares none of Gordon's ancestry but spent years learning from a major-league veteran, not to mention an active major leaguer (Dee) and a first-round draft pick (Nick). "Without Mr. Gordon and the support of his family," Hillman told MLB.com's Jordan Bastian, "I don't know where I'd be today." Or where he'll be in five years. Despite the risks inherent in prep arms, we bet it'll be Cleveland.

T.J. House LHP

Born: 9/29/89 Age: 26 Bats: R Throws: L Height: 6'1" Weight: 205

YEAR	TEAM	LVL	AGE	W	L	SV	G	GS	IP	H	HR	BB/9	K/9	GB%	BABIP	WHIP	ERA	FIP	DRA	WARP	CFIP	MPH
2013	COH	AAA	23	7	10	0	24	24	141^2	163	11	3.4	7.0	56%	.338	1.53	4.32	3.89	4.45	0.9	102	
2013	AKR	AA	23	2	1	0	4	4	22^1	20	1	1.2	10.9	57%	.333	1.03	3.22	1.89	3.67	0.4	69	
2014	COH	AAA	24	1	4	0	10	10	57	56	3	2.5	6.6	60%	.312	1.26	3.79	3.52	4.41	0.5	96	
2014	CLE	MLB	24	5	3	0	19	18	102	113	10	1.9	7.1	62%	.332	1.32	3.35	3.72	4.91	-0.2	101	93.6
2015	CLE	MLB	25	0	4	0	4	4	13	21	1	8.3	4.8	60%	.392	2.54	13.15	6.26	9.23	-0.7	122	92.0
2015	COH	AAA	25	0	2	0	4	4	21	21	3	5.6	5.6	56%	.286	1.62	3.86	5.78	6.13	-0.4	123	
2016	*CLE*	*MLB*	*26*	*2*	*2*	*0*	*5*	*5*	*28^2*	*31*	*3*	*2.9*	*6.6*	*59%*	*.310*	*1.41*	*4.34*	*4.18*	*4.64*	*0.2*	*108*	
2017	*CLE*	*MLB*	*27*	*5*	*5*	*0*	*16*	*16*	*92^1*	*98*	*11*	*2.9*	*6.6*	*59%*	*.303*	*1.38*	*4.32*	*4.31*	*4.62*	*0.5*	*108*	

Breakout: 24% Improve: 44% Collapse: 22% Attrition: 31% MLB: 79% *Comparables: Zach Jackson, Adam Warren, Luis Mendoza*

To call Tiger Junior's 2015 a disappointment undersells the damage and overlooks the danger. He had the worst ERA in baseball (min. 10 innings) and allowed as many runs in four starts as Zack Greinke allowed in his first 19. He was demoted, then disabled by shoulder inflammation, and to top it off he had to file a grievance against the Indians to get service credit for time in the big-league infirmary. Without the velocity spike that led to his ascendance in 2014, he's unlikely to duplicate his balmy peak, which means this all hinges on the success of a shoulder rehab that the Indians admit has taken much longer than expected. Nice knowing ya, kid.

Rob Kaminsky LHP

Born: 9/2/94 Age: 21 Bats: R Throws: L Height: 5'11" Weight: 190

YEAR	TEAM	LVL	AGE	W	L	SV	G	GS	IP	H	HR	BB/9	K/9	GB%	BABIP	WHIP	ERA	FIP	DRA	WARP	CFIP	MPH
2014	PEO	A	19	8	2	0	18	18	100^2	71	2	2.8	7.1	53%	.239	1.01	1.88	3.28	4.52	0.8	102	
2015	PMB	A+	20	6	5	0	17	17	94^2	82	0	2.7	7.5	63%	.291	1.16	2.09	2.51	3.37	1.3	94	
2016	*CLE*	*MLB*	*21*	*5*	*6*	*0*	*16*	*16*	*84*	*91*	*9*	*3.6*	*5.5*	*52%*	*.300*	*1.49*	*4.66*	*4.72*	*4.96*	*0.2*	*117*	
2017	*CLE*	*MLB*	*22*	*8*	*10*	*0*	*27*	*27*	*163^2*	*173*	*20*	*3.7*	*5.8*	*52%*	*.292*	*1.47*	*4.77*	*4.76*	*5.08*	*0.1*	*120*	

Breakout: 0% Improve: 0% Collapse: 0% Attrition: 0% MLB: 0% *Comparables: Ian Krol, Mike Montgomery, Jordan Walden*

The magician holds up something plain, something ordinary, a hat or a deck of cards or an undersized, 5-foot-11 pitching prospect without upper-end velocity. Then he makes that that ordinary thing do something extraordinary. Kaminsky's turn is a trap-door curveball, a true deceiver with stellar break, one of the best breaking pitches in the minors. Performance at High-A Palm Beach drew solid reviews, and the youngster showed a preternatural ability to induce weak contact and get hitters to put the ball on the ground. Now, make no mistake: Kaminsky could bust. He could max out at Triple-A. The fastball is straight and he's already dealing with a season cut short by back stiffness. But the Cleveland front office pulled off a pretty slick sleight-of-hand trick here, transforming Joey Wendle into a legitimate left-handed pitching prospect at the low, low cost of feeding Brandon Moss for a half-season. If a team could repeat that trick every night it would get a lot of applause.

Corey Kluber RHP

Born: 4/10/86 Age: 30 Bats: R Throws: R Height: 6'4" Weight: 215

YEAR	TEAM	LVL	AGE	W	L	SV	G	GS	IP	H	HR	BB/9	K/9	GB%	BABIP	WHIP	ERA	FIP	DRA	WARP	CFIP	MPH
2013	CLE	MLB	27	11	5	0	26	24	147^{1}	153	15	2.0	8.3	48%	.329	1.26	3.85	3.33	4.10	1.4	87	95.8
2013	COH	AAA	27	1	1	0	2	2	12^{1}	14	2	2.2	8.8	51%	.343	1.38	6.57	4.10	4.19	0.1	94	
2014	CLE	MLB	28	18	9	0	34	34	235^{2}	207	14	1.9	10.3	50%	.316	1.09	2.44	2.37	2.89	5.5	66	95.7
2015	CLE	MLB	29	9	16	0	32	32	222	189	22	1.8	9.9	44%	.297	1.05	3.49	2.94	3.32	4.5	72	95.2
2016	*CLE*	*MLB*	*30*	*9*	*7*	*0*	*24*	*24*	*144*	*131*	*15*	*2.2*	*10.0*	*46%*	*.310*	*1.15*	*3.10*	*3.19*	*3.41*	*2.9*	*71*	
2017	*CLE*	*MLB*	*31*	*10*	*7*	*0*	*24*	*24*	*142*	*126*	*15*	*2.1*	*9.8*	*46%*	*.300*	*1.12*	*3.15*	*3.15*	*3.46*	*3.0*	*72*	

Breakout: 19% Improve: 54% Collapse: 13% Attrition: 6% MLB: 96% *Comparables: Marco Estrada, Anibal Sanchez, Erik Bedard*

For the past two seasons, Kluber has pitched the way June Carter described Johnny Cash's music: "Sharp like a razor, steady like a train." The razor is his ability to take over a game, which gave baseball one of 2015's signature moments: his chase for a 21-strikeout game on May 13, 2015. He was pulled before he could hope to complete the feat—18 strikeouts in eight innings, tantalizingly close—and then struck out the side in the first inning of his next outing. To undersell it: Dude was sharp. Like a razor.

And then there's the steadiness. He throws tons of innings by keeping his mechanics tight and limiting bad pitches, producing a stellar walk rate and requiring just 3.7 pitches per plate appearance. He shows all the telltale signs of a contact-inducing control artist, while *also* competing for the league's strikeout crown. The total package produced the AL's best FIP over the past two seasons and the second-most regular-season innings in baseball. Not bad for a boy named Klu.

Jeff Manship RHP

Born: 1/16/85 Age: 31 Bats: R Throws: R Height: 6'2" Weight: 205

YEAR	TEAM	LVL	AGE	W	L	SV	G	GS	IP	H	HR	BB/9	K/9	GB%	BABIP	WHIP	ERA	FIP	DRA	WARP	CFIP	MPH
2013	CSP	AAA	28	6	8	0	24	17	104	114	8	2.8	6.1	53%	.314	1.40	4.85	4.16	4.84	0.9	95	
2013	COL	MLB	28	0	5	0	11	4	30^{2}	37	6	3.5	5.3	46%	.301	1.60	7.04	5.56	5.78	-0.4	120	91.7
2014	LEH	AAA	29	0	1	0	8	5	25^{1}	29	1	6.4	7.5	54%	.354	1.86	4.62	4.34	5.07	0.0	116	
2014	PHI	MLB	29	1	2	0	20	0	23	24	1	5.5	6.3	45%	.311	1.65	6.65	4.10	5.07	-0.2	115	94.2
2015	COH	AAA	30	0	2	2	23	0	31^{2}	25	3	2.6	8.8	57%	.262	1.07	1.99	3.28	2.68	0.7	82	
2015	CLE	MLB	30	1	0	0	32	0	39^{1}	20	1	2.3	7.6	52%	.192	0.76	0.92	2.60	1.53	1.5	91	94.5
2016	*CLE*	*MLB*	*31*	*2*	*1*	*0*	*48*	*0*	*51*	*51*	*6*	*3.3*	*7.2*	*51%*	*.296*	*1.35*	*4.20*	*4.34*	*4.50*	*0.2*	*102*	
2017	*CLE*	*MLB*	*32*	*3*	*3*	*0*	*32*	*7*	*77^{2}*	*80*	*9*	*3.3*	*7.2*	*51%*	*.302*	*1.40*	*4.31*	*4.30*	*4.62*	*0.3*	*105*	

Breakout: 12% Improve: 17% Collapse: 10% Attrition: 17% MLB: 38% *Comparables: Jeff Fulchino, Everett Teaford, Jason Grilli*

Success is always just one adjustment away, or so pitching coaches and chiropractors would have us believe. In baseball, small changes are often sound and fury, signifying no permanent changes to an overall career arc, but Manship's shift to the third-base side of the pitching rubber came with unprecedented success. Those few feet not only dramatically changed his horizontal release point (and his control), they dropped his ERA nearly six runs between 2014 and 2015. Manship's resume still reads "failed starter," but now it also comes with a fun fact—he's one of just 14 relief pitchers since 1988 to throw 30 or more innings and keep an ERA under 1.00—and a season-long stint as an effective setup man. Sometimes a tiny shift can make all the difference.

Zach McAllister RHP

Born: 12/8/87 Age: 28 Bats: R Throws: R Height: 6'6" Weight: 240

YEAR	TEAM	LVL	AGE	W	L	SV	G	GS	IP	H	HR	BB/9	K/9	GB%	BABIP	WHIP	ERA	FIP	DRA	WARP	CFIP	MPH
2013	CLE	MLB	25	9	9	0	24	24	134^{1}	134	13	3.3	6.8	39%	.295	1.36	3.75	4.06	4.55	0.6	109	94.7
2014	COH	AAA	26	7	1	0	11	11	69	57	3	1.8	7.7	44%	.276	1.03	2.09	2.86	3.98	0.9	79	
2014	CLE	MLB	26	4	7	0	22	15	86	96	7	2.9	7.7	43%	.332	1.44	5.23	3.47	4.89	-0.2	99	97.1
2015	CLE	MLB	27	4	4	1	61	1	69	70	7	3.0	11.0	46%	.346	1.35	3.00	3.12	4.26	0.4	80	97.9
2016	*CLE*	*MLB*	*28*	*3*	*1*	*0*	*53*	*0*	*56^{1}*	*56*	*6*	*2.9*	*8.3*	*43%*	*.306*	*1.31*	*3.83*	*3.84*	*4.13*	*0.5*	*93*	
2017	*CLE*	*MLB*	*29*	*6*	*5*	*0*	*27*	*15*	*101^{2}*	*103*	*12*	*2.8*	*8.5*	*43%*	*.312*	*1.32*	*3.83*	*3.81*	*4.13*	*1.1*	*92*	

Breakout: 22% Improve: 64% Collapse: 10% Attrition: 6% MLB: 91% *Comparables: Carlos Carrasco, John Maine, Jeff Niemann*

After years of trying to establish himself as a full-time starter for the Tribe, Cleveland bumped McAllister from the rotation after just one start in 2015. Fortunately, the conversion to relief worked out for both parties, as a starter-to-reliever velocity bump transformed him from a no. 5 starter to solid setup option. Not only did he add almost three ticks to both his fastball and curve, he scrapped his dismal slider for a cutter that zoomed in on hitters nearly 11 percent faster than his old offering. The velocity gains bought him more whiffs and many more strikeouts (up to 28 percent from 20 percent). Now entrenched in the 'pen, McAllister might not be Wade Davis, but he is another guy who could provide far more value in 70 innings per season than he ever did in 140.

Triston McKenzie RHP

Born: 8/2/97 Age: 18 Bats: R Throws: R Height: 6'5" Weight: 165

The 42nd pick in the 2015 draft, McKenzie was bought out of his commitment to Vanderbilt thanks to an $800,000 raise over the recommended slot amount. Why would the Tribe break the bank for another hard-throwing prep pitcher when their system is already loaded with high-risk, high-reward arms? One recalls the old adage about how to develop a good pitcher: Start with three good prospects. McKenzie qualifies. His performance during his final year of high school was predictably dominant (157 strikeouts in 91 innings in a baseball-rich region), and he is tall and lean with a wicked fastball—essentially the prototype for a front-of-the-rotation starter. Best of all, he is already armed with three solid offerings (fastball, curve and change). He made his pro debut two days after turning 18, and the Arizona League didn't have a chance: 17 strikeouts, four hits, 12 innings. Sure, he's risky, but it's a numbers game, and every number in this comment says McKenzie could be a dude.

Ryan Merritt LHP

Born: 2/21/92 Age: 24 Bats: L Throws: L Height: 6'0" Weight: 170

YEAR	TEAM	LVL	AGE	W	L	SV	G	GS	IP	H	HR	BB/9	K/9	GB%	BABIP	WHIP	ERA	FIP	DRA	WARP	CFIP	MPH
2013	LKC	A	21	6	9	0	24	23	126^{1}	142	10	1.3	6.5	50%	.331	1.27	3.42	3.47	4.37	1.3	93	
2014	CAR	A+	22	13	3	0	25	25	160^{1}	128	12	1.4	7.1	47%	.251	0.95	2.58	3.47	4.04	2.2	83	
2015	AKR	AA	23	10	7	0	22	22	141	145	8	1.0	5.7	44%	.304	1.14	3.51	3.25	3.25	2.7	87	
2015	COH	AAA	23	2	0	0	5	5	30	38	1	1.8	4.8	49%	.343	1.47	4.20	3.22	4.27	0.2	101	
2016	*CLE*	*MLB*	*24*	*8*	*9*	*0*	*24*	*24*	*137^{2}*	*157*	*17*	*2.1*	*5.2*	*43%*	*.303*	*1.37*	*4.50*	*4.51*	*4.83*	*0.5*	*112*	
2017	*CLE*	*MLB*	*25*	*6*	*6*	*0*	*17*	*17*	*102*	*119*	*14*	*2.2*	*5.2*	*43%*	*.307*	*1.42*	*4.65*	*4.64*	*4.99*	*0.2*	*116*	

Breakout: 18% Improve: 25% Collapse: 3% Attrition: 26% MLB: 36% *Comparables: Seth Maness, Tim Cooney, Mike Wright*

Welcome to the crafty left-hander club, where every eligible young thing has limited stuff and sea-level upside. It can be pretty tough to succeed with such a skinny strikeout rate, but Merritt has found a way to post solid minor-league numbers with the tools he has at his disposal. The southpaw possesses three solid offerings, and his command is exceptional, especially with his fastball. If he ever finds a way to turn his slurvy breaking pitch into an out-getter, he could certainly turn his success in the low minors into a semi-regular job as a back-end starter. The ceiling is low here—the best case scenario is a late-career Mark Buehrle with a nice uniform number. The worst-case scenario? He pulls a Keyser Soze and like that ... he's gone.

Danny Salazar RHP

Born: 1/11/90 Age: 26 Bats: L Throws: R Height: 6'0" Weight: 195

YEAR	TEAM	LVL	AGE	W	L	SV	G	GS	IP	H	HR	BB/9	K/9	GB%	BABIP	WHIP	ERA	FIP	DRA	WARP	CFIP	MPH
2013	CLE	MLB	23	2	3	0	10	10	52	44	7	2.6	11.2	37%	.298	1.13	3.12	3.19	2.54	1.5	73	99.5
2013	COH	AAA	23	4	2	1	14	13	59^{1}	44	4	2.1	11.8	42%	.303	0.98	2.73	2.26	3.24	1.2	61	
2013	AKR	AA	23	2	3	0	7	7	33^{2}	27	1	2.7	13.6	33%	.366	1.10	2.67	1.57	3.42	0.7	60	
2014	CLE	MLB	24	6	8	0	20	20	110	117	13	2.9	9.8	36%	.343	1.38	4.25	3.55	4.44	0.5	87	97.8
2014	COH	AAA	24	4	6	0	11	11	60^{2}	58	7	4.2	11.3	38%	.323	1.42	3.71	3.79	4.02	0.8	80	
2015	CLE	MLB	25	14	10	0	30	30	185	156	23	2.6	9.5	45%	.278	1.13	3.45	3.59	3.66	3.0	83	97.9
2016	*CLE*	*MLB*	*26*	*10*	*9*	*0*	*28*	*28*	*159^{2}*	*145*	*19*	*2.9*	*9.9*	*42%*	*.303*	*1.23*	*3.59*	*3.65*	*3.90*	*2.3*	*86*	
2017	*CLE*	*MLB*	*27*	*8*	*8*	*0*	*26*	*26*	*153^{2}*	*139*	*19*	*2.8*	*9.9*	*42%*	*.299*	*1.21*	*3.63*	*3.62*	*3.94*	*1.9*	*87*	

Breakout: 30% Improve: 59% Collapse: 13% Attrition: 5% MLB: 95% *Comparables: Jonathan Sanchez, Jordan Zimmermann, Hong-Chih Kuo*

In 2014, Salazar was an impressive upstart looking to break out, but he also was among the bottom 10 starting pitchers in groundball rate. In 2015, he kept the rest of his repertoire the same, but threw his sinker more often and more effectively. The pitch generated grounders on 64 percent of balls in play, up from 41 percent a year earlier. We're conditioned to look at HR rates as the proxy for flyball damage, but it was doubles that were killing Salazar before the tweak: He allowed one every four innings in '14, but one in every seven frames last year. Armed with wipeout breaking stuff, high velocity, and now a sinker that he can lean on early in counts, The Dzar could well be poised to anchor the front of a rotation for half a decade, especially if he proves he can keep making adjustments on the fly.

Bryan Shaw RHP

Born: 11/8/87 Age: 28 Bats: B Throws: R Height: 6'1" Weight: 210

YEAR	TEAM	LVL	AGE	W	L	SV	G	GS	IP	H	HR	BB/9	K/9	GB%	BABIP	WHIP	ERA	FIP	DRA	WARP	CFIP	MPH
2013	CLE	MLB	25	7	3	1	70	0	75	60	4	3.4	8.8	46%	.271	1.17	3.24	3.10	3.05	1.4	93	95.9
2014	CLE	MLB	26	5	5	2	80	0	76^{1}	61	6	2.6	7.5	50%	.251	1.09	2.59	3.45	2.92	1.5	98	95.5
2015	CLE	MLB	27	3	3	2	74	0	64	59	8	2.7	7.6	47%	.279	1.22	2.95	3.98	4.25	0.4	99	94.3
2016	*CLE*	*MLB*	*28*	*3*	*1*	*5*	*58*	*0*	*61^{1}*	*57*	*7*	*3.0*	*7.9*	*48%*	*.285*	*1.26*	*4.01*	*4.04*	*4.32*	*0.3*	*97*	
2017	*CLE*	*MLB*	*29*	*3*	*1*	*2*	*61*	*0*	*57^{2}*	*52*	*7*	*2.9*	*7.7*	*48%*	*.274*	*1.23*	*4.21*	*4.20*	*4.54*	*0.1*	*105*	

Breakout: 33% Improve: 57% Collapse: 20% Attrition: 19% MLB: 94% *Comparables: Eric O'Flaherty, Joe Smith, Jesse Crain*

There's an old adage that half of success is just showing up, and Shaw has that half down pat. Since joining the Indians in 2013, no reliever has more appearances than Cleveland's right-handed setup man. The other half of his moderate success comes from his pitch mix: He lives and dies by a low-90s cutter that he throws two-thirds of the time, but he also features a slider that moves a remarkable nine inches side-to-side. If you want to see one of those dancing high-spin sliders, just flip on your television anytime between April and September; as with syndicated *Simpsons* reruns, odds are he'll be on.

Justus Sheffield LHP

Born: 5/13/96 Age: 20 Bats: L Throws: L Height: 5'10" Weight: 196

YEAR	TEAM	LVL	AGE	W	L	SV	G	GS	IP	H	HR	BB/9	K/9	GB%	BABIP	WHIP	ERA	FIP	DRA	WARP	CFIP	MPH
2015	LKC	A	19	9	4	0	26	26	127^{2}	135	8	2.7	9.7	48%	.344	1.36	3.31	2.99	2.77	3.3	84	
2016	*CLE*	*MLB*	*20*	*5*	*6*	*0*	*19*	*19*	*88^{2}*	*98*	*12*	*3.4*	*7.4*	*41%*	*.317*	*1.48*	*4.50*	*4.59*	*4.79*	*0.3*	*112*	
2017	*CLE*	*MLB*	*21*	*7*	*9*	*0*	*26*	*26*	*155*	*170*	*21*	*3.2*	*7.1*	*41%*	*.310*	*1.45*	*4.53*	*4.51*	*4.82*	*0.4*	*113*	

Breakout: 0% Improve: 0% Collapse: 0% Attrition: 0% MLB: 0% *Comparables: Jarrod Parker, Tyler Robertson, Justin Nicolino*

Every team wants a pitcher with professional bloodlines and a mid-90s fastball coming from the left side. Every team worries about a young starter who's only 5-foot-10 and already has legal issues on his record. So where does that leave Sheffield? Last year was certainly a step in the right direction, as the former prep arm showed flashes that he could stick in the middle of a rotation. His first full season was peppered with outings in which his command was an issue, but he settled in during the final two months of the season and notched a 0.96 ERA in his last five starts of the year. A 3.63 strikeout-to-walk rate shows he has the raw talent to eclipse his cousin Tony's minor-league career. (Oh, you thought when we mentioned bloodlines we meant Gary? That's a belief so widely held it deserves a Snopes rebuttal. Justus tells people "at least once a day" that he and the nine-time All-Star aren't related.)

Giovanni Soto LHP

Born: 5/18/91 Age: 25 Bats: L Throws: L Height: 6'2" Weight: 190

YEAR	TEAM	LVL	AGE	W	L	SV	G	GS	IP	H	HR	BB/9	K/9	GB%	BABIP	WHIP	ERA	FIP	DRA	WARP	CFIP	MPH
2014	AKR	AA	23	0	2	1	37	0	53	45	2	2.0	8.3	59%	.291	1.08	3.23	2.73	3.82	0.6	75	
2015	COH	AAA	24	2	1	2	46	1	53^2	35	1	4.9	8.6	58%	.248	1.19	2.68	3.18	4.05	0.2	100	
2015	CLE	MLB	24	0	0	0	6	0	3^1	3	0	0.0	0.0	69%	.231	0.90	0.00	3.10	0.54	0.2	111	92.2
2016	*CLE*	*MLB*	*25*	*1*	*0*	*0*	*19*	*0*	*20^1*	*19*	*2*	*3.9*	*8.0*	*57%*	*.295*	*1.37*	*4.09*	*4.22*	*4.36*	*0.1*	*100*	
2017	*CLE*	*MLB*	*26*	*3*	*2*	*0*	*26*	*5*	*53^1*	*49*	*6*	*3.9*	*8.4*	*57%*	*.292*	*1.35*	*4.14*	*4.11*	*4.41*	*0.3*	*101*	

Breakout: 15% Improve: 24% Collapse: 11% Attrition: 29% MLB: 46% *Comparables: Zach Phillips, C.J. Riefenhauser, Jose Capellan*

Five years ago, BP's Kevin Goldstein claimed that with his command and secondary pitches, baseball's second "Gio Soto" could eventually become a strong starting pitcher—if his sub-90 velocity ever ticked up. He never did figure out that trick—few do—but his secondary pitches (a slider and a classic molasses-slow curve) keep same-handed hitters off balance, and he should still become a strong *relief* pitcher. During his age-24 season, Soto was lights-out to start the year at Triple-A Columbus as a LOOGY (with a 2.15 ERA in the first half), and his six-appearance September call-up was a run-free success. Lefty specialists tend to stay in the game even longer than backup catchers, so this Soto should outlast the other.

Josh Tomlin RHP

Born: 10/19/84 Age: 31 Bats: R Throws: R Height: 6'1" Weight: 190

YEAR	TEAM	LVL	AGE	W	L	SV	G	GS	IP	H	HR	BB/9	K/9	GB%	BABIP	WHIP	ERA	FIP	DRA	WARP	CFIP	MPH
2013	CLE	MLB	28	0	0	0	1	0	2	2	0	0.0	0.0	38%	.250	1.00	0.00	3.08	5.40	0.0	108	93.0
2013	COH	AAA	28	2	0	0	3	3	15	12	0	0.0	6.6	28%	.279	0.80	2.40	2.14	3.98	0.2	88	
2014	CLE	MLB	29	6	9	0	25	16	104	120	18	1.2	8.1	39%	.320	1.29	4.76	4.03	5.16	-0.5	91	91.3
2014	COH	AAA	29	2	1	0	6	6	40	26	5	2.2	7.4	37%	.210	0.90	2.25	4.08	4.28	0.4	93	
2015	COH	AAA	30	1	2	0	4	4	21^1	25	3	0.4	7.2	43%	.328	1.22	4.22	3.53	2.64	0.5	81	
2015	CLE	MLB	30	7	2	0	10	10	65^2	47	13	1.1	7.8	39%	.199	0.84	3.02	4.40	3.51	1.2	89	91.2
2016	*CLE*	*MLB*	*31*	*7*	*6*	*0*	*18*	*18*	*108*	*101*	*14*	*2.1*	*7.9*	*38%*	*.282*	*1.16*	*3.89*	*3.96*	*4.20*	*1.2*	*95*	
2017	*CLE*	*MLB*	*32*	*7*	*7*	*0*	*21*	*21*	*123^1*	*117*	*17*	*2.1*	*7.8*	*38%*	*.285*	*1.18*	*3.95*	*3.93*	*4.26*	*1.2*	*97*	

Breakout: 19% Improve: 52% Collapse: 21% Attrition: 13% MLB: 92% *Comparables: Brandon McCarthy, Jeff Karstens, Dennis Eckersley*

For the third time in his career, Tomlin allowed more home runs (13) than walks (eight). If he can just let four more balls escape Cleveland's gravitational tug, he'll be (at least temporarily) the only pitcher ever to feature such a fun fact over an entire career. Which is to say, Tomlin is unique even in the weird world of baseball. Early season shoulder surgery delayed the start to his year, but when he came back in August he had no trouble returning to his patented brand of pinpoint control and monstrous parabolas. A run of success at the end of the season was due to incredible luck: He had the most favorable BABIP (.199) and strand rate (90.2 percent) of any starter in baseball. With Tomlin's history of allowing medium-to-hard contact about 80 percent of the time—and most of it in the air—you should expect that luck to run out just in time for him to hit free agency at the end of this season.

Ryan Webb RHP

Born: 2/5/86 Age: 30 Bats: R Throws: R Height: 6'6" Weight: 245

YEAR	TEAM	LVL	AGE	W	L	SV	G	GS	IP	H	HR	BB/9	K/9	GB%	BABIP	WHIP	ERA	FIP	DRA	WARP	CFIP	MPH
2013	MIA	MLB	27	2	6	0	66	0	80^1	70	5	3.0	6.0	59%	.266	1.21	2.91	3.57	4.14	0.4	107	95.0
2014	NOR	AAA	28	0	2	0	11	0	11^1	13	1	1.6	7.9	50%	.324	1.32	4.76	3.27	4.33	0.1	92	
2014	BAL	MLB	28	3	3	0	51	0	49^1	50	2	2.2	6.8	52%	.310	1.26	3.83	2.98	2.91	1.0	97	94.5
2015	CLE	MLB	29	1	0	0	40	0	50^2	46	4	2.1	5.5	60%	.271	1.14	3.20	3.74	3.80	0.5	108	94.5
2016	*CLE*	*MLB*	*30*	*2*	*1*	*0*	*45*	*0*	*47^2*	*49*	*5*	*3.0*	*6.6*	*58%*	*.298*	*1.37*	*4.30*	*4.27*	*4.62*	*0.1*	*103*	
2017	*CLE*	*MLB*	*31*	*2*	*1*	*0*	*41*	*0*	*45^1*	*49*	*5*	*3.2*	*6.3*	*58%*	*.306*	*1.44*	*4.40*	*4.39*	*4.73*	*0.0*	*105*	

Breakout: 34% Improve: 58% Collapse: 19% Attrition: 10% MLB: 90% *Comparables: Brandon League, Burke Badenhop, Kent Tekulve*

Webb is more than just the world leader in finishing games without a save, more than just the unofficial mascot of BP's Effectively Wild podcast. He also taught us all something interesting about how teams value compensation picks. The Dodgers briefly acquired Webb and his $2.75 million salary in exchange for a competitive balance draft pick (and a couple of non-prospects). Then they released him, effectively purchasing that draft pick for the cost of his contract. If the Dodgers were *really* smart, perhaps they would have kept the tall righty as well as the pick—his ability to induce groundballs was on full display last season, and he out-WARPed all of L.A.'s relievers save Kenley Jansen and Yimi Garcia. Webb will move on to a new 'pen in 2016, but scores of baseball nerds will follow him wherever he goes.

Lineouts

Hitters

NAME	POS	TEAM	LVL	AGE	PA	R	2B	3B	HR	RBI	BB	K	SB	CS	AVG/OBP/SLG	TAv	BABIP	BRR	FRAA	WARP
Jesus Aguilar	1B	CLE	MLB	25	20	0	1	0	0	2	0	7	0	0	.316/.350/.368	.256	.500	-0.3	1B(4): -0.1	0.0
	1B	COH	AAA	25	570	57	29	1	19	93	47	115	0	0	.267/.332/.439	.254	.305	-3.4	1B(98): -3.7	-0.5
Michael Choice	LF	COH	AAA	25	62	5	5	0	1	7	5	22	1	0	.204/.306/.352	.235	.323	-0.5	RF(8): 1.0, LF(2): 0.3	0.0
	LF	ROU	AAA	25	447	53	25	1	12	60	32	115	2	0	.244/.309/.399	.261	.310	0.6	LF(62): -11.3, RF(16): -1.6	-0.4
Michael Choice	LF	TEX	MLB	25	1	0	0	0	0	0	0	1	0	0	.000/.000/.000	.011	--	0.0	RF(1): -0.0	0.0
Collin Cowgill	RF	ANA	MLB	29	74	10	2	1	1	2	4	19	2	1	.188/.233/.290	.195	.245	1.5	LF(41): 0.8, RF(4): 0.7	0.0
	RF	SLC	AAA	29	47	5	3	0	1	4	2	5	0	0	.364/.404/.500	.304	.395	-0.2	LF(5): 1.0, RF(2): 0.1	0.4
Michael Martinez	PH	CLE	MLB	32	32	7	2	0	0	2	1	12	0	1	.267/.290/.333	.255	.444	-0.4	LF(9): 0.3, CF(2): 0.0	0.0
	PH	COH	AAA	32	401	53	24	5	5	42	32	60	11	3	.289/.344/.424	.269	.332	2.3	2B(66): -5.0, CF(19): -0.6	1.7
Mark Mathias	2B	MHV	A-	20	294	38	19	3	2	32	35	36	5	4	.282/.382/.408	.309	.316	0.2	2B(61): 6.5	3.0
Dorssys Paulino	SS	LKC	A	20	348	38	12	2	6	39	22	61	11	5	.256/.319/.364	.263	.298	-0.6	LF(80): -6.8, SS(1): 0.0	0.1
	SS	LYN	A+	20	177	27	10	6	4	30	17	30	5	2	.305/.371/.526	.301	.350	-0.9	LF(36): -1.7	0.9
James Ramsey	CF	COH	AAA	25	503	46	21	2	12	42	53	128	3	4	.243/.327/.382	.256	.315	-2.9	LF(52): 0.5, CF(41): -2.2	0.4
Anthony Recker	C	LVG	AAA	31	108	17	3	1	8	21	12	26	0	0	.245/.343/.553	.286	.250	-0.3	C(21): 0.7, 1B(2): -0.1	0.7
	C	NYN	MLB	31	92	6	1	0	2	5	11	35	1	0	.125/.239/.213	.180	.186	-0.1	C(28): -4.5, 1B(1): -0.0	-0.9
Shane Robinson	OF	MIN	MLB	30	197	28	7	3	0	16	12	29	6	1	.250/.299/.322	.230	.296	-0.3	LF(55): 0.5, CF(15): 0.2	0.0
Zach Walters	PH	CLE	MLB	25	30	0	0	0	0	3	0	15	0	0	.133/.133/.133	.113	.267	0.3	LF(3): -0.3, SS(2): 0.0	-0.4
	PH	COH	AAA	25	379	39	21	3	10	48	30	79	3	0	.249/.310/.416	.248	.292	-0.5	LF(37): 5.2, 3B(24): -2.5	0.5
Tony Wolters	2B	AKR	AA	23	271	23	7	2	2	17	21	63	3	2	.209/.290/.280	.219	.273	1.8	C(56): 9.1, SS(3): 0.2	1.1

Hmmmm, how to remember generic dude **Jesus Aguilar**? Thing of your typical Quad-A first baseman, remove any pedigree or top-tier power, and calibrate your expectations based on how many universities rejected you. ❖ In his only major-league plate appearance last season, **Michael Choice** struck out; considering his Triple-A experience, that qualifies as the *highlight* of his season. He's gone from "the next Matt Holliday" to "the next Fernando Martinez" in the time it takes to say "dammmn, sick burn." ❖ **Collin Cowgill** sports the Rickey Henderson disadvantage of being a left-handed thrower and right-handed hitter, and he's a corner outfielder whose key asset is his glove, which is a luxury best afforded by expanded rosters. ❖ **Michael Martinez** is the rusty Swiss Army Knife you've had since Cub Scouts: He does everything and nothing, and the tweezers are missing. ❖ A third-round draftee last June, **Mark Mathias** has raked so far in short-season ball, but outgoing college juniors are supposed to do that at the *very* least. If he keeps it up in full-season ball, perhaps he'll earn the 100-word comment in next year's Annual. ❖ You spend three years in the Midwest League, as **Dorssys Paulino** did, and you'd better be a coach, because you're sure as heck not a prospect anymore. He finally hit a bit in the second half, but he also left shortstop for good. ❖ **James Ramsey** is rapidly aging out of the prospect pool, and his bat took a downturn despite decent power and patience at Columbus. Of course, we now know Cleveland got out of the Justin Masterson business at just the right time, so anything from Ramsey is gravy. ❖ It was a great run, but **Anthony Recker** is rounding into the "keep your bags packed in case someone gets hurt" phase of his career. On the other hand, as a catcher, he could survive in that phase for a decade if he wants. ❖ **Shane Robinson** is a very fine fifth outfielder, which only sounds like a backhanded compliment because you've never been handed a fifth outfielder's paycheck. ❖ **Luke Wakamatsu**, son of Royals bench coach Don Wakamatsu, surprised everyone by taking a $290,000 bonus and passing on Rice University after Cleveland popped him in round 20. He's a switch hitter with good offensive projection and the ability to stick at short, but we're still waiting to see whether or not we'll hate his nickname: Luke Sky-Waka. ❖ **Zach Walters** is versatile! He could be the next Ben Zobrist! if he just learns to make more contact! hit for more power, walk more often, run faster! play better defense, and! find a way out of Triple-A! ❖ Poor **Tony Wolters** moved to catcher, injured his right knee twice and stopped hitting entirely. The most likely scenario in which he reaches his potential involves a flux capacitor.

Pitchers

NAME	TEAM	LVL	AGE	W	L	SV	G	GS	IP	H	HR	BB/9	K/9	GB%	BABIP	WHIP	ERA	FIP	FRA	WARP	CFIP	MPH
Austin Adams	COH	AAA	28	2	2	4	13	0	12	13	1	5.2	12.8	48%	.400	1.67	4.50	3.16	2.77	0.2	83	
	CLE	MLB	28	2	0	1	28	0	33^{1}	37	2	3.5	6.2	48%	.315	1.50	3.78	3.67	4.76	0.0	112	99.4
Mitch Brown	LYN	A+	21	9	12	0	27	26	141^{2}	147	15	4.9	6.9	52%	.315	1.58	5.15	4.89	7.41	-4.9	132	
Gavin Floyd	CLE	MLB	32	0	0	0	7	0	13^{1}	11	0	2.7	4.7	46%	.256	1.12	2.70	3.18	2.46	0.4	109	95.1
Luis Lugo	LYN	A+	21	8	10	0	25	25	125^{2}	129	11	3.7	8.5	39%	.325	1.44	4.15	3.81	4.66	0.0	105	
Shaun Marcum	CLE	MLB	33	3	2	0	7	6	35	32	9	2.8	7.7	33%	.253	1.23	5.40	5.76	5.24	-0.1	102	87.5
	COH	AAA	33	7	4	0	16	14	88^{1}	85	7	2.1	6.8	34%	.295	1.20	3.26	3.38	2.94	1.9	85	
Carlos Marmol	COH	AAA	32	3	1	13	28	0	31	19	1	7.8	13.9	36%	.295	1.48	2.03	3.09	3.29	0.4	89	
Nick Maronde	COH	AAA	25	0	8	0	28	11	85	102	9	3.5	8.4	39%	.360	1.59	4.76	3.84	4.02	0.6	98	
Shawn Morimando	AKR	AA	22	10	12	0	28	28	158^{2}	139	9	3.7	7.3	39%	.288	1.29	3.18	3.64	4.47	0.7	104	
Toru Murata	COH	AAA	30	15	4	0	27	26	164^{1}	148	16	2.5	5.5	44%	.265	1.17	2.90	4.11	4.58	0.2	107	
	CLE	MLB	30	0	1	0	1	1	3^{1}	4	2	2.7	5.4	38%	.182	1.50	8.10	10.60	12.08	-0.3	110	89.6
Dan Otero	NAS	AAA	30	2	0	0	15	2	27^{2}	23	1	1.3	6.2	60%	.262	0.98	1.95	3.13	3.91	0.4	89	
	OAK	MLB	30	2	4	0	41	0	46^{2}	64	7	1.2	5.4	50%	.354	1.50	6.75	4.37	5.89	-0.7	108	92.1
Felipe Paulino	IOW	AAA	31	5	9	0	20	20	104	108	9	4.5	7.2	50%	.321	1.54	4.93	4.89	6.66	-1.2	119	
Ryan Perez	MHV	A-	21	0	1	0	22	0	25	30	4	7.9	7.9	40%	.347	2.08	6.48	6.59	7.63	-0.9	129	
Adam Plutko	AKR	AA	23	9	5	0	19	19	116^{1}	96	9	1.8	7.0	31%	.256	1.02	2.86	3.37	3.21	2.3	87	
	LYN	A+	23	4	2	0	8	8	49^{2}	30	3	0.9	8.5	36%	.214	0.70	1.27	2.51	1.81	1.8	73	
Enosil Tejeda	AKR	AA	26	1	1	2	31	0	35^{1}	24	0	3.8	7.4	38%	.250	1.10	1.27	3.07	4.52	0.0	105	
Joe Thatcher	HOU	MLB	33	1	3	0	43	0	22^{2}	23	1	4.8	10.3	47%	.361	1.54	3.18	2.97	4.66	0.0	96	86.9
Kirby Yates	TBA	MLB	28	1	0	0	20	0	20^{1}	23	10	3.1	9.3	30%	.245	1.48	7.97	8.61	7.98	-0.8	103	94.7
	DUR	AAA	28	1	2	6	23	0	25^{1}	27	5	4.3	12.1	39%	.344	1.54	5.33	4.70	3.53	0.3	92	

Possessed of a fastball that clears 100 mph, you'd imagine **Austin Adams** would be a dominant relief arm. Unfortunately for the Indians, imagination doesn't get whiffs, and Adams is a boring replacement-level middle reliever. ❖ Ohio is famous for its roller-coasters, so it fits that Cleveland prospect **Mitch Brown** had an up-and-down season that ended with a (metaphorical) lost flipflop and a (who knows, perhaps literal?) bunch of puke. Whether he gets back in line at Lake City or moves on to Akron, he'll need to improve command and consistency at some point. ❖ **Gavin Floyd** fractured his olecranon—a bony protrusion of the ulna—for the second straight season during spring training; a shaky September comeback ensued. It's been three years since he was healthy, and danged if his career isn't starting to look like a parabola reaching its touchdown. ❖ **Luis Lugo** is huge (6-foot-5) and has plus velocity, so if the starting pitcher thing doesn't work out he can either be a reliever or, as a fallback, a Marvel Comics superhero secret identity. (Peter Parker, Bruce Banner, Matt Murdock ... they're almost always alliterative.) ❖ The most compelling example of the Good-Or-Injured fallacy, **Shaun Marcum** demonstrates how the "injured" usually destroys the "good" while we're not looking. It's been three years since he was either. ❖ **Carlos Marmol** led all International League regulars in walks per nine innings. The last time a Columbus clipper was this far off the mark, the *Santa María* made landfall on Guanahani instead of India. ❖ One of the first members of the 2011 draft class to reach The Show, **Nick Maronde** is attempting to convert back to starting after a few disastrously wild stints in Anaheim's bullpen. It hasn't worked yet, so for now he's marooned in the high-minors friend zone ❖ **Shawn Morimando** has average command of an average fastball/slider combo, and yet his performance in Double-A was actually above average. In a Cleveland system stacked with arms, he'd need to lower his walk rate to really stand out. ❖ **Toru Murata** pitched in such exotic locales as Japan, Panama, Venezuela and Akron before getting called up to make his big-league debut as the 26th man in a doubleheader... at the age of 30. He got hit hard and was DFA'ed immediately, but goddammit now the world knows he lived. ❖ After two years as a key bullpen cog for the A's, **Dan Otero** turned into a punching bag, the unfortunate sinkerballer whose ball doesn't sink until it's on the other side of the outfield fence. ❖ **Felipe Paulino**'s scintillating fastball landed him briefly on the Cubs' 40-man roster last year; his dull everything else ensured no major-league appearances. ❖ Twelfth-rounder **Ryan Perez** is Diet Pat Venditte: all the fizz of an ambidextrous switch-pitcher, none of the effectiveness! ❖ **Adam Plu o** pitched in the same rotation as Gerrit Cole and Trevor Bauer in college, and he's still not conceding rank: He absolutely dominated High-A, then pitched well in Double-A. But the BABIP, and he doesn't carry top-end stuff, and... yeah, we'd still rather have Cole. ❖ **Enosil Tejeda** is allergic to allowing home runs—he's allowed just seven in 296 minor-league innings, and zero in 2015—and has strikeout stuff, so he might emerge in the Cleveland 'pen next year. ❖ **Joe Thatcher** has both the name and the looks of a guy who would do a really good job fixing your brakes, but, like, for a very fair price. Instead, he's a relief pitcher who has a strong strikeout rate, has lived in too many apartments, and will most likely pitch until he's 40 given what hand he throws with. ❖ **Kirby Yates** was voted most likely to be Brandon Gomes by the 2017 edition of this book.

MANAGER

Terry Francona

YEAR	TEAM	W	L	Pythag +/-	Avg PC	100+ P	120+ P	QS	BQS	REL	REL w Zero R	IBB	PH	PH Avg	PH HR	SB2	CS2	SB3	CS3	SAC Att	SAC%	POS SAC	Squeeze	Swing	In Play
2013	CLE	92	70	1	94.9	68	0	73	5	540	454	26	58	.255	3	96	33	21	3	41	75.6	30	0	332	85
2014	CLE	85	77	2	94.6	61	0	78	5	573	507	51	103	.233	0	96	23	8	4	63	81.0	49	0	290	92
2015	CLE	81	80	-3	94.5	77	2	91	4	476	391	27	106	.240	4	79	26	7	1	65	72.3	45	0	274	58

Figuring out why a manager does certain things is always more art than science. Take Francona, who seems to straddle the line between traditional and progressive. In some cases, Francona's tendencies jive with what you'd expect from someone who worked under a sabermetrically inclined front office in Boston and now works under another in Cleveland. He finished third in the majors in pinch-hitters used, and wisely deployed lefty specialists like Kyle Crockett and Marc Rzepczynski against more than 60 percent of same-handed batters; additionally, he deployed closer Cody Allen for a majors-leading seven saves of at least four outs. Each of those is a testament to his willingness to maximize the effectiveness of his players and improve his club's chances of winning.

In other cases, though, Francona's predilections stray from analytical convention. The most glaring example of this in 2015 was how the Indians ranked second in position-player sacrifice attempts. Asking Michael Bourn, Jose Ramirez and Mike Aviles—none enjoying good offensive seasons—to lay one down here and there makes sense. But having Francisco Lindor sacrifice an American League-leading 13 times over 99 games? That's sketchy at best and silly at worst. So who or what gives?

Evidently not Francona, not when it comes to the bunt sign. Rather, Lindor was often the one behind the decision to square around. "I like the idea that he's thinking about trying to play the game right," Francona told MLB.com's Jordan Bastian. "There's actually times where I think it's better served to let him swing. But again, as we get to know each other, those things will be a lot easier. There's going to be times where a guy doesn't have a good feel for that pitcher and he's like, 'You know what? I can lay a bunt down here.'"

You might prefer that Francona have talked to Lindor about curbing the bunting during the season. But viewed in a different light, you have to appreciate how he provides his players, even the rookies, freedom to play the game as they see fit. What's more, you have to like how Francona handled the question: acknowledging his objection in a positive, respectful way. Those are small things, and things that players value more than fans, yet things that explain why Francona is known as a player's manager. Besides, there's probably an added benefit to Francona's behavior. By allowing Lindor (and others) breathing room, Francona's words likely carry more weight when he does provide them. Perhaps that stuff isn't worth the irritation it causes us outsiders, but there's probably a method to the madness.

COLORADO ROCKIES

Essay by Tom Ley

Player comments by Chris Mosch and BP authors

Any discussion of the Rockies will inevitably lead to talking about The Trade, so let's dive right in.

On July 28th, Colorado traded Troy Tulowitzki to the Blue Jays for Jose Reyes, Jeff Hoffman, Miguel Castro and Jesus Tinoco. There's a near-limitless number of angles from which to view the decision to jettison an all-world shortstop who is still relatively young and on a bargain long-term contract in order to scoop up a few pitching prospects—"Tulo's injury-prone and on the wrong side of 30!" shouts the savvy guy; "It's the stupidest thing the Rockies have ever done!" shouts the angry guy—but the only viewpoint that really matters is GM Jeff Bridich's. It's not hard to make out the logic that drove the trade, which essentially boils down to, "Dear God, we could really *really* use some pitching!"

If there was ever a pitching staff bad enough to justify trading a future Hall of Famer, it's the staff the Rockies put out in 2015. The team's squadron of human pitching machines put together a league-worst team ERA of 5.04 while striking out just seven batters per nine innings. Those numbers aren't great in any context, but they are particularly ghastly in an era when strikeout rates are higher than they've ever been and the league-average ERA has settled around 3.85. It seemed like every team in the league employed two or three brutes who throw 98 and have two wicked breaking pitches; the Rockies had Kyle Kendrick.

If you buy into the idea that no ace free-agent pitcher in his right mind would willingly choose to pitch at altitude, then the only way to solve a problem like this is to stock the farm system with as many potential impact arms as possible. Enter: Tinoco, Castro and Hoffman. Exit: Tulowitzki.

Given how quickly teams like the Astros, Mets and Cubs managed to ride back into relevancy on the shoulders of their young talent, it's easy to find ways to feel optimistic about the direction of the Rockies. Trading Tulowitzki may end being a massive mistake, but the deal at least set the organization on a clear path; gone are the days of being a bad team that annually deluded itself into thinking it could compete. The Rockies have a very clear goal: to develop the farm as quickly as possible and become the next Astros. But that kind of optimism discounts the Rockies' gloomy history of trying and failing to secure

ROCKIES PROSPECTUS

2015 W-L: 68-94, 5th in NL West

Pythag	.435	26th	DER	.682	30th
RS/G	4.55	5th	B-Age	27.9	6th
RA/G	5.21	30th	P-Age	28.4	16th
TAv	.253	24th	Salary	$97.1M	23rd
BRR	10.71	5th	M$/MW	$4.3M	11th
TAv-P	.277	27th	DL Days	1388	26th
FIP	4.59	30th	$ on DL	13%	11th

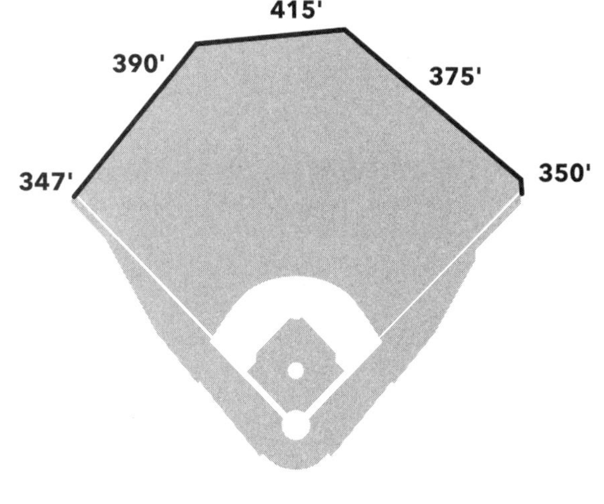

Outfield wall profile: **8'** to **14'**

Three-Year Park Factors

Runs	Runs/RH	Runs/LH	HR/RH	HR/LH
112	123	118	117	110

Top Hitter WARP	7.4	Nolan Arenado
Top Pitcher WARP	1.9	Jorge De La Rosa
Top Prospect	Brendan Rodgers	

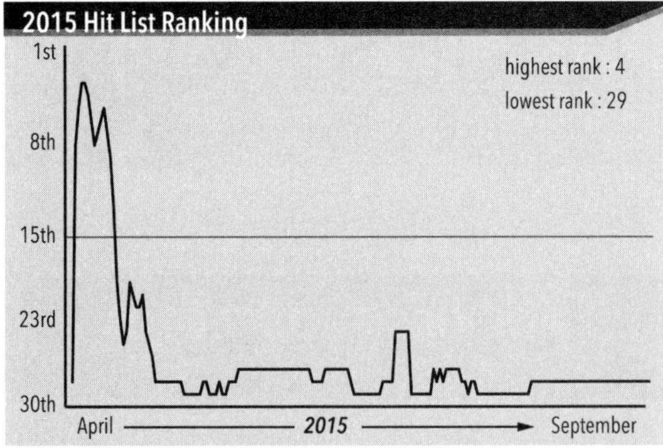

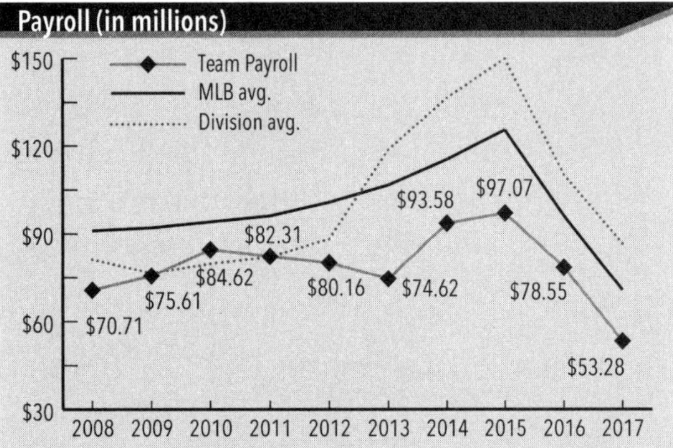

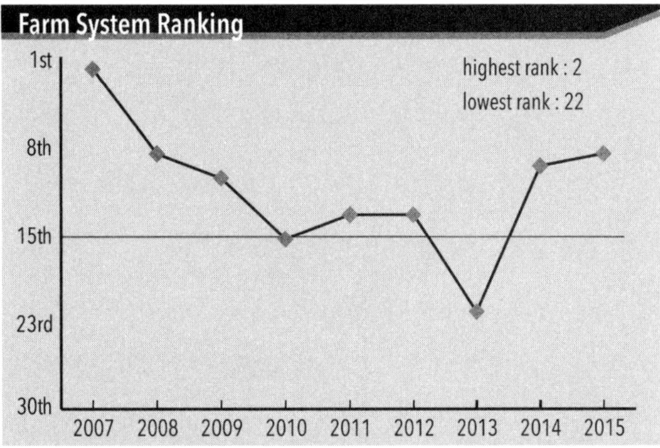

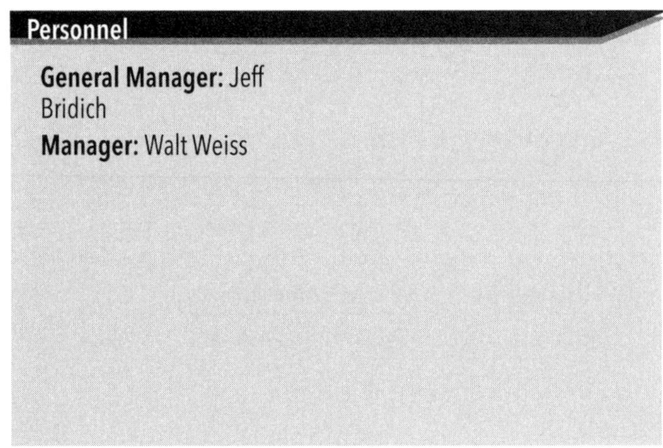
Personnel

General Manager: Jeff Bridich

Manager: Walt Weiss

good pitching. In the context of that history, the Tulowitzki trade isn't just a big gamble; it's a sign that the franchise is running out of ideas.

The Rockies don't have the same relationship with pitching prospects that most teams do, and that's because they've never really successfully developed one. Colorado has used its first-round pick on a pitcher 17 times, and Jamey Wright has the highest career WARP of that group, at 14.2. (Just 4.1 wins of that total came in his initial stint with the Rockies.) Call it the Curse of David Nied, the would-be ace the Rockies snatched from the Braves with the first pick of the 1992 expansion draft, and the guy *The New York Times* once casually dubbed "sort of the Shaquille O'Neal of Major League Baseball." Nied posted a career 5.06 ERA and was out of the league by 1996. Just about every heralded pitching prospect to land in Colorado since then, from Jeff Francis to Greg Reynolds to Tyler Matzek, has followed Nied's legacy.

It's not just prospect development where things have gone wrong, either. Who can forget the time the team threw $172 million at Mike Hampton and Denny Neagle in 2001, only to see them amass a combined four WARP in Rockies uniforms? They've tried raiding other teams' prospect cabinets as well, most recently when Ubaldo Jimenez was flipped for Alex White and Drew Pomeranz. White was released by the Braves last summer and hasn't been seen in the majors since 2012; Pomeranz was traded by the A's this winter for Yonder Alonso, a first baseman who can't even slug .400. The best season either of the two had for the Rockies was Pomeranz's 4.93 ERA in 96 innings on 2012. In short: It didn't work.

All of that failure is what led to Tulowitzki putting on a Blue Jays uniform. If drafting pitchers hasn't worked, and buying pitchers hasn't worked, and flipping the closest thing they've ever had to an ace for young arms hasn't worked, then maybe trading the Hall-of-Fame shortstop in his prime will be the thing that finally brings in some top-flight pitching talent.

What you make of this largely depends on how you feel about player development in general. All prospects are, to some extent, lottery tickets, so it's possible the Rockies have just had a much worse run of luck than most teams. Any organization unfortunate enough to be developing pitching prospects in pre-humidor Coors Field deserves at least a small break. Still, a track record this poor suggests there are systemic flaws in the way the Rockies go about cultivating pitchers, both young and old. The most recent development strategy has seen the Rockies preaching a Groundballs Over Everything philosophy, which didn't result in much but a few not-terrible campaigns from Aaron Cook and Jhoulys Chacin, as well as Greg Reynolds getting drafted ahead of Tim Lincecum (Christ), Max Scherzer (kill me) and Clayton Kershaw (I'm dead) in 2006.

Hoffman, Tinoco and Castro may very well have the talent to save the Rockies' pitching staff, but that talent doesn't exist in a vacuum. They will have to outrun whatever it is in the Rockies' system that doomed all those who came before them. History, recent and ancient, suggests they are being chased by more than just bad luck.

As for that recent history, look no further than the 2015 campaigns of Eddie Butler and Jon Gray, the latest pair of promising young starters to have made it to the big-league rotation. Butler, the 15th-overall pick in the 2012 draft, has only seen his walk rate increase as he's progressed through the Rockies' system. He was given multiple chances to grab a permanent spot in the big-league rotation in 2015 and proceeded to walk almost five batters per nine innings, finishing with a 5.90 ERA. Butler was one of the organization's most prized prospects coming into the season, and out of nowhere became Worse Aaron Cook. Gray made nine starts in the majors, in which he struck out about eight batters per nine innings and posted a 3.65 FIP while on a severe pitch-count restriction. All fine, except for the ERA nearly two runs higher and the fact that he consistently threw 100 mph in college, but had his velocity reduced to the 93–96 mph range after the team messed with his mechanics. These are real problems, and just the latest indicators that there is something broken about the way the team rears its young pitchers.

There's an even bigger cloud hanging over the organization in the shape of All-Star third baseman Nolan Arenado's future ambitions. Arenado is one of the best young players in the league, a masher with 89 extra-base hits last year (42 of them on the road) and defense that inspires Homeric odes. This is exactly the kind of guy a rebuilding team like the Rockies needs to lock up with a long-term deal—exactly like the one they gave Troy Tulowitzki, even; maybe they should have kept that guy!—but that's going to be a tall task if the team doesn't see some meaningful player development in the next season or two. Arenado is entering his first year of arbitration eligibility, and if the team stays bad, it's easy to imagine him going year-to-year in arbitration and then bolting as soon as he hits the open market.

This, aside from never having any good arms, is what's so frustrating about the Rockies' continued failure to develop talented pitchers. Teams that can draft and develop their own talent don't find themselves in situations like this. They don't have to turn their world-class shortstop and franchise cornerstone into a Hail Mary trade chip, and they don't have to worry about their hotshot third baseman being next out the door, because why would he want to play on a team whose best shot at getting better is to trade the cornerstone? When a team fails so completely at developing talent—the most important thing there is in a small- or mid-size market—the failure trickles down.

The good news is that the Rockies have never been in a better position to remove the rot from the roots. The farm system is as stocked with young talent as it's ever been, and it could get even richer if the team manages to pull off a few more key trades. If Hoffman and Gray and the rest of the youngsters can become solid major-league players, and if the Rockies can finally become a franchise with a functioning talent pipeline, then maybe the Tulowitzki trade will have been worth it after all. If all that falls apart, though, and Arenado leaves, then the franchise will end up in as dark a place as it's ever been. ■

—Tom Ley is a writer at Deadspin.

HITTERS

Nolan Arenado 3B

Born: 4/16/91 Age: 25 Bats: R Throws: R Height: 6'2" Weight: 205

YEAR	TEAM	LVL	AGE	PA	R	2B	3B	HR	RBI	BB	K	SB	CS	AVG/OBP/SLG	TAv	BABIP	BRR	FRAA	WARP
2013	COL	MLB	22	514	49	29	4	10	52	23	72	2	0	.267/.301/.405	.236	.296	1.1	3B(130): 17.8	2.4
2013	CSP	AAA	22	75	14	11	0	3	21	5	9	0	2	.364/.392/.667	.337	.368	-1.6	3B(17): 4.6	1.2
2014	CSP	AAA	23	20	2	2	0	0	3	0	3	0	0	.350/.350/.450	.246	.412	0.1	3B(4): -0.0	0.0
2014	COL	MLB	23	467	58	34	2	18	61	25	58	2	1	.287/.328/.500	.273	.294	1.3	3B(111): 18.5	4.3
2015	COL	MLB	24	665	97	43	4	42	130	34	110	2	5	.287/.323/.575	.299	.284	1.5	3B(156): 22.2	7.4
2016	*COL*	*MLB*	*25*	*594*	*72*	*38*	*3*	*26*	*90*	*30*	*89*	*3*	*2*	*.288/.324/.513*	*.271*	*.298*	*1.1*	*3B 17*	*4.4*
2017	*COL*	*MLB*	*26*	*527*	*71*	*32*	*3*	*24*	*80*	*31*	*80*	*2*	*2*	*.287/.329/.512*	*.280*	*.296*	*1.0*	*3B 15*	*5.0*

Breakout: 1% Improve: 61% Collapse: 2% Attrition: 3% MLB: 99% *Comparables: Jim Ray Hart, Ryan Zimmerman, Robinson Cano*

Arenado's progression from promising youngster to full-fledged superstar was the culmination of the astonishing transformation he's undergone since his days as a Rockies farmhand. The consensus was that he was a bat-first prospect who might even have to abandon the hot corner (e.g. "...projects as no more than acceptable at third base." —KG, 1/18/11). A thick lower half and slow feet accompanied good hands and a strong arm. Emphasis from the coaching staff on his lateral movement and admirable work by Arenado on his diet turned him into a premier defender upon reaching Colorado, all the while his bat having more or less stalled. But last year the power spiked from good to elite, with accusations of his offense being a product of Coors Field put to rest; he launched more homers and posted a better True Average on the road.

Combine the bat with his impersonation of a human vacuum at third base and you get a top-10 player by WARP. Defensive metrics are in awe of him, and so is Brooks Robinson. The man who handled the hot corner better than anyone in history told *The Denver Post* last June, "No one plays any better than he does." Quite the compliment, especially considering that Arenado's closest competition for the superlative plays for Robinson's long-time employer.

Brandon Barnes LF

Born: 5/15/86 Age: 30 Bats: R Throws: R Height: 6'2" Weight: 210

YEAR	TEAM	LVL	AGE	PA	R	2B	3B	HR	RBI	BB	K	SB	CS	AVG/OBP/SLG	TAv	BABIP	BRR	FRAA	WARP
2013	HOU	MLB	27	445	46	17	1	8	41	21	127	11	11	.240/.289/.346	.242	.327	0.5	CF(116): 14.1, RF(13): 0.3	2.1
2014	COL	MLB	28	313	37	17	4	8	27	15	100	5	4	.257/.293/.425	.235	.364	0.2	RF(55): 0.6, LF(18): -2.1	-0.4
2015	COL	MLB	29	281	30	13	2	2	17	21	67	4	2	.251/.314/.341	.229	.332	1.7	LF(75): 1.3, RF(21): -1.1	0.0
2015	ABQ	AAA	29	143	19	6	0	5	12	10	34	7	3	.205/.266/.364	.210	.237	0.6	LF(1): -0.1, RF(1): -0.1	-0.3
2016	*COL*	*MLB*	*30*	*260*	*29*	*13*	*1*	*6*	*26*	*15*	*70*	*6*	*3*	*.253/.301/.391*	*.232*	*.328*	*0.6*	*CF 2, RF -0*	*0.3*
2017	*COL*	*MLB*	*31*	*305*	*34*	*15*	*2*	*7*	*34*	*19*	*84*	*6*	*4*	*.250/.303/.395*	*.242*	*.324*	*1.1*	*CF 2, RF 0*	*0.9*

Breakout: 1% Improve: 42% Collapse: 4% Attrition: 16% MLB: 91% *Comparables: Eric Byrnes, Fred Lewis, Chris Heisey*

Incredible athleticism, an affinity for highlight-reel catches and around 25 different tattoos distinguish Barnes from your run-of-the-mill fourth outfielder. So did an astronomical strikeout rate, a flaw he vowed to cut down in the spring, a vow that showed how much effort it actually takes to rearrange deck chairs.

First, Barnes completely overhauled his swing—adding a leg kick akin to Matt Holliday's—but was squeezed off the big-league roster when camp ended. He returned in May with the leg kick gone, but a rethunk approach that showed commitment to his pledge: He cut his swing rate significantly and his plate discipline trended in the right direction. His contract rate didn't budge, but gains in strike-zone control cut the strikeout rate from 32 percent to 24 percent. And yet, power and weaker contact accompanied the shift in approach, effectively just rearranging where the holes in his game lay. Weaknesses turn out to be difficult to scrub away, like so many tattoos.

Charlie Blackmon CF

Born: 7/1/86 Age: 29 Bats: L Throws: L Height: 6'3" Weight: 210

YEAR	TEAM	LVL	AGE	PA	R	2B	3B	HR	RBI	BB	K	SB	CS	AVG/OBP/SLG	TAv	BABIP	BRR	FRAA	WARP
2013	COL	MLB	26	258	35	17	2	6	22	7	49	7	0	.309/.336/.467	.273	.366	3.0	RF(34): -0.1, CF(25): -2.2	0.9
2013	CSP	AAA	26	299	56	15	6	3	40	35	41	7	5	.288/.376/.428	.266	.329	2.0	CF(65): -3.7	1.0
2014	COL	MLB	27	648	82	27	3	19	72	31	96	28	10	.288/.335/.440	.260	.315	0.0	RF(73): -4.6, CF(69): -0.9	1.0
2015	COL	MLB	28	682	93	31	9	17	58	46	112	43	13	.287/.347/.450	.272	.325	3.4	LF(14): -1.1, RF(7): -0.0	2.7
2016	*COL*	*MLB*	*29*	*636*	*88*	*31*	*6*	*16*	*64*	*39*	*107*	*29*	*9*	*.279/.332/.434*	*.252*	*.313*	*1.4*	*CF -6*	*1.2*
2017	*COL*	*MLB*	*30*	*576*	*68*	*26*	*5*	*14*	*65*	*38*	*101*	*25*	*9*	*.267/.326/.417*	*.255*	*.302*	*2.1*	*CF -6*	*1.8*

Breakout: 0% Improve: 37% Collapse: 15% Attrition: 18% MLB: 90% *Comparables: Roger Bernadina, Chone Figgins, Rajai Davis*

Blackmon, like Barnes, also revamped his entire philosophy last spring, vowing that he would see more pitches to give both himself and his teammates increased looks at the opposing pitcher's arsenal. After swinging at the first pitch slightly more often than the league average rate in 2014, he became the most passive hitter in baseball in 2015. Pitchers noticed, responding with more first-pitch fastballs as the season wore on. What could be classified as an approach that was too passive at times morphed into one better described as aggressively selective in other counts. He continued to jump on pitches in his happy zone—down and in—while increasingly laying off strikes if they didn't fit his liking. More walks and strikeouts were predictable byproducts of working deeper counts, along with a slight uptick in power. His embrace of the leadoff spot further manifested itself on the basepaths; only Dee Gordon and Billy Hamilton swiped more bags than Blackmon, who pledged in March to leverage his newfound familiarity with NL pitchers to "open up the playbook a little." If Barnes is your reminder that most spring training storylines are empty calories, Blackmon is a reminder that some stick.

David Dahl CF

Born: 4/1/94 Age: 22 Bats: L Throws: R Height: 6'2" Weight: 195

YEAR	TEAM	LVL	AGE	PA	R	2B	3B	HR	RBI	BB	K	SB	CS	AVG/OBP/SLG	TAv	BABIP	BRR	FRAA	WARP
2013	ASH	A	19	42	9	4	1	0	7	2	8	2	0	.275/.310/.425	.259	.344	-0.1	CF(8): -1.4	0.0
2014	MOD	A+	20	125	14	8	2	4	14	5	27	3	0	.267/.296/.467	.269	.315	1.7	CF(25): 3.3, CF(4): 3.3	1.0
2014	ASH	A	20	422	69	33	6	10	41	23	65	18	5	.309/.347/.500	.279	.348	3.3	CF(70): 11.8, LF(7): 0.5	3.8
2015	NBR	AA	21	302	46	16	3	6	24	11	72	22	7	.278/.304/.417	.262	.352	4.8	RF(3): -0.4	1.0
2015	BOI	A-	21	24	1	1	0	0	1	0	9	0	0	.125/.125/.167	.113	.200	0.2		-0.2
2016	*COL*	*MLB*	*22*	*250*	*31*	*13*	*2*	*6*	*23*	*8*	*65*	*10*	*3*	*.251/.275/.398*	*.220*	*.316*	*1.0*	*CF 0, RF -0*	*0.0*
2017	*COL*	*MLB*	*23*	*369*	*39*	*18*	*4*	*9*	*41*	*14*	*94*	*15*	*5*	*.253/.283/.402*	*.234*	*.317*	*2.2*	*CF 1, RF 0*	*0.8*

Breakout: 1% Improve: 5% Collapse: 1% Attrition: 5% MLB: 14% *Comparables: Tyler Colvin, Felix Pie, Yorman Rodriguez*

A scary on-field collision with Double-A teammate Juan Ciriaco sent Dahl to the hospital with a lacerated spleen in May, and his season appeared to be over. Instead, he made the decision to have the spleen removed, which raises all sorts of questions a non-doctor such as yourself might have: What? How? They can do that? To which we answer: Yes, via a splenectomy, leaving Dahl a bit more prone to dangerous bacterial infections (strep, meningitis) but otherwise fully human. The most important question, of course, was how long it would take to recover, and the answer—seven weeks—brought him back around the All-Star break. He hit .292/.318/.481 at Double-A after the surgery, compared to .269/.296/.379 before, raising the possibility that spleen removal should be either mandatory or illegal.

"Physically gifted" only begins to describe Dahl, who has a five-tool skill set headlined by a line-drive swing with an all-fields approach. That raises his ceiling; his elite up-the-middle defense lifts his floor. It's unfair to ding him for a freak spleen accident, but at some point the laundry list of injuries and lost development time has to raise moderate concern, and after just 29 games back he was felled by patella tendinitis, a much more pedestrian injury. Dahl's stock holds steady, but a healthy 2016 would go a long way to demonstrating that he's not made of paper.

Daniel Descalso SS

Born: 10/19/86 Age: 29 Bats: L Throws: R Height: 5'10" Weight: 190

YEAR	TEAM	LVL	AGE	PA	R	2B	3B	HR	RBI	BB	K	SB	CS	AVG/OBP/SLG	TAv	BABIP	BRR	FRAA	WARP
2013	SLN	MLB	26	358	43	25	1	5	43	22	56	6	3	.238/.290/.366	.243	.271	3.9	SS(55): 1.2, 2B(39): 1.1	1.5
2014	SLN	MLB	27	184	20	11	0	0	10	20	33	1	3	.242/.333/.311	.244	.305	-0.6	2B(21): 2.7, SS(19): -2.1	0.1
2015	COL	MLB	28	209	22	3	2	5	22	20	45	1	2	.205/.283/.324	.225	.244	-0.6	SS(33): 0.8, 2B(14): -1.3	-0.2
2016	*COL*	*MLB*	*29*	*258*	*27*	*12*	*2*	*4*	*25*	*22*	*47*	*3*	*2*	*.255/.323/.384*	*.236*	*.297*	*0.6*	*3B -0, SS 0*	*0.5*
2017	*COL*	*MLB*	*30*	*163*	*18*	*8*	*1*	*3*	*17*	*14*	*30*	*2*	*1*	*.259/.329/.391*	*.249*	*.303*	*0.5*	*3B 0, SS 0*	*0.6*

Breakout: 5% Improve: 46% Collapse: 3% Attrition: 9% MLB: 98% *Comparables: Alan Trammell, Edgar Renteria, Barry Larkin*

The pronunciation of the Rockies utility man's last name is the Spanish translation for "barefoot." Rest assured, Descalso sports Nike cleats like many of his Rockies teammates, but "bare" *is* a fairly accurate description of his offensive production during the first year with his new club. His slash line during his tenure as the Cardinals' Swiss Army knife was never anything to write home about, but it was usually enough to justify half a season's worth of playing time given his defensive versatility. With the Rockies, his park-adjusted numbers were among the worst in the league. He started chasing pitches out of the zone at a career-high rate, couldn't catch up to fastballs at the letters and developed a knack for weak contact. A rebuilding franchise with intriguing infield prospects in the upper minors has better ways to allocate 200 PAs.

Corey Dickerson LF

Born: 5/22/89 Age: 27 Bats: L Throws: R Height: 6'1" Weight: 205

YEAR	TEAM	LVL	AGE	PA	R	2B	3B	HR	RBI	BB	K	SB	CS	AVG/OBP/SLG	TAv	BABIP	BRR	FRAA	WARP
2013	CSP	AAA	24	345	61	21	14	11	50	26	49	6	10	.371/.414/.632	.332	.409	-1.1	LF(63): -1.1, RF(5): -1.0	3.2
2013	COL	MLB	24	213	32	13	5	5	17	16	41	2	2	.263/.316/.459	.269	.307	0.3	LF(36): 0.2, CF(15): -0.6	0.6
2014	COL	MLB	25	478	74	27	6	24	76	37	101	8	7	.312/.364/.567	.303	.356	-2.4	LF(99): -7.0, CF(9): -1.3	1.9
2015	ABQ	AAA	26	29	3	1	0	1	3	1	4	0	0	.286/.310/.429	.247	.304	-0.8	LF(5): -0.8	-0.1
2015	COL	MLB	26	234	30	18	2	10	31	10	56	0	1	.304/.333/.536	.288	.367	-0.5	LF(53): -1.8	1.0
2016	*COL*	*MLB*	*27*	*582*	*74*	*33*	*9*	*23*	*86*	*39*	*120*	*7*	*6*	*.299/.345/.524*	*.285*	*.345*	*-1.5*	*LF -1, RF -0*	*3.0*
2017	*COL*	*MLB*	*28*	*403*	*52*	*23*	*6*	*15*	*57*	*27*	*84*	*4*	*4*	*.289/.335/.502*	*.281*	*.335*	*-0.7*	*LF -1, RF 0*	*2.4*

Breakout: 4% Improve: 52% Collapse: 4% Attrition: 8% MLB: 99% *Comparables: Mark Trumbo, Carlos Gonzalez, Khris Davis*

So 2014 wasn't a fluke: Dickerson once again showed the same blend of power and all-fields ability, both on the ground and in the air. But neither was 2015 a proper follow-up, as his inability to stay on the field made this feel like a lost season. He developed plantar fasciitis in his right foot in April, played through it for a month, then needed two separate month-long DL stints to finally heal up. He returned for a week at the end of July, just long enough to fracture two ribs laying out for a line drive, and just like that he was shelved another month. He's never been attractive to injury bugs before, so we'd chalk it up as an anomalous season. Expect more righty mashing at the plate and cringe-worthy routes in the outfield in 2016.

Carlos Gonzalez RF

Born: 10/17/85 Age: 30 Bats: L Throws: L Height: 6'1" Weight: 220

YEAR	TEAM	LVL	AGE	PA	R	2B	3B	HR	RBI	BB	K	SB	CS	AVG/OBP/SLG	TAv	BABIP	BRR	FRAA	WARP
2013	COL	MLB	27	436	72	23	6	26	70	41	118	21	3	.302/.367/.591	.313	.368	1.9	LF(106): 4.0	4.1
2014	COL	MLB	28	281	35	15	1	11	38	19	70	3	0	.238/.292/.431	.233	.283	1.2	LF(48): -5.5, RF(17): 0.1	-0.6
2015	COL	MLB	29	608	87	25	2	40	97	46	133	2	0	.271/.325/.540	.284	.284	-0.1	RF(150): -4.2	2.2
2016	*COL*	*MLB*	*30*	*536*	*74*	*26*	*3*	*27*	*84*	*44*	*123*	*9*	*2*	*.278/.339/.514*	*.279*	*.318*	*0.7*	*RF -3*	*2.1*
2017	*COL*	*MLB*	*31*	*495*	*68*	*24*	*3*	*23*	*73*	*40*	*117*	*7*	*1*	*.269/.329/.489*	*.274*	*.313*	*0.5*	*RF -3*	*2.2*

Breakout: 1% Improve: 42% Collapse: 0% Attrition: 10% MLB: 100% *Comparables: Matt Kemp, Corey Hart, Roger Maris*

Over the years, we've grown accustomed to both CarGo the superstar and CarGo the frequent visitor of the disabled list. The first few months of last season offered us a glimpse at his photo negative: healthy and unproductive. Part of his miserable first half could be attributed to one of the worst two-strike approaches in baseball (lowest OPS split with two strikes relative to other counts; min. 400 PAs). Adjustments were made to avoid situations where he was prone to chasing breaking balls out of the zone; as the season wore on he became more aggressive early in at-bats. This resulted in fewer two-strike counts,

Career two-strike rate: 46 percent
April–June 2015: 49 percent
July–October 2015: 43 percent

which helped fuel a three-month tear over which he launched 30 of his 40 dingers. Gonzalez's early struggles and the lack of his usual elevated BABIP deflated his overall line, but his second half reinforced that, despite his fragility and loss of speed and bad road splits and ultra-aggressiveness, he remains one of the most feared sluggers in the game.

Pedro Gonzalez SS

Born: 10/27/97 Age: 18 Bats: R Throws: R Height: 6'3" Weight: 160

Manny Machado and Alex Rios are the most common physical comparisons for this seven-figure international signee, whose frame and exceptional body control promise— well, promise nothing except that scouts will love him for at least a couple years. He's unlikely to stick at short, but projects to hit enough for a reasonable third base profile. Long levers add some swing-and-miss to his game—as seen in an otherwise promising debut in the Dominican Summer League—but if he adds strength as expected there will be plenty of swing-and-trot, too.

Nick Hundley C

Born: 9/8/83 Age: 32 Bats: R Throws: R Height: 6'1" Weight: 205

YEAR	TEAM	LVL	AGE	PA	R	2B	3B	HR	RBI	BB	K	SB	CS	AVG/OBP/SLG	TAv	BABIP	BRR	FRAA	WARP
2013	SDN	MLB	29	408	35	19	0	13	44	26	98	1	0	.233/.290/.389	.251	.279	-1.9	C(112): -13.9	-0.3
2014	SDN	MLB	30	59	1	3	0	1	3	0	13	0	0	.271/.271/.373	.238	.333	-0.6	C(14): 2.2	0.3
2014	BAL	MLB	30	174	17	4	0	5	19	10	50	1	0	.233/.273/.352	.245	.299	-0.4	C(49): 0.7	0.6
2015	COL	MLB	31	389	45	21	5	10	43	21	76	5	6	.301/.339/.467	.268	.356	0.5	C(102): -13.3	0.8
2016	*COL*	*MLB*	*32*	*507*	*56*	*24*	*4*	*14*	*58*	*30*	*118*	*4*	*3*	*.258/.307/.416*	*.240*	*.314*	*-1.1*	*C -15*	*-0.5*
2017	*COL*	*MLB*	*33*	*411*	*46*	*18*	*3*	*10*	*45*	*26*	*99*	*3*	*2*	*.250/.301/.392*	*.241*	*.311*	*-0.8*	*C -12*	*-0.1*

Breakout: 7% Improve: 36% Collapse: 8% Attrition: 13% MLB: 95% *Comparables: Brandon Inge, Ivan Rodriguez, Javy Lopez*

YEAR	TEAM	P. COUNT	FRM RUNS	BLK RUNS	THRW RUNS	TOT RUNS
2013	SDN	15467	-14.8	0.5	-0.7	-15.0
2014	SDN	1462	1.8	0.1	0.0	1.9
2014	BAL	6605	-0.2	0.4	-1.1	-1.0
2015	COL	14669	-16.2	0.2	0.9	-15.1
2016	*COL*	*19262*	*-16.0*	*0.4*	*-0.1*	*-15.8*
2017	*COL*	*15616*	*-13.8*	*0.3*	*-0.2*	*-13.7*

One of the most sensible pairings of last offseason put Hundley in Denver for a two-year commitment. The veteran catcher wanted to avoid toiling away as a backup and the Rockies wanted anyone who could plausibly catch a thrown baseball better than Wilin Rosario (who couldn't). The first year of the marriage went better than anyone could have expected. Hundley quit chasing fastballs off the plate and connected with more pitches inside the zone, leading to a career-best strikeout rate and his best offensive season since his monster second half in 2011. We wouldn't bet on him being the team's fourth-best hitter again, and going forward the Rockies will be more concerned with how he handles their young—and frequently erratic—pitching staff. After all, he's already been well worth the $6.25 million investment.

DJ LeMahieu 2B

Born: 7/13/88 Age: 27 Bats: R Throws: R Height: 6'4" Weight: 215

YEAR	TEAM	LVL	AGE	PA	R	2B	3B	HR	RBI	BB	K	SB	CS	AVG/OBP/SLG	TAv	BABIP	BRR	FRAA	WARP
2013	CSP	AAA	24	158	34	8	5	1	22	10	19	8	2	.364/.405/.510	.292	.405	3.4	SS(30): 6.3, 2B(2): -0.2	2.2
2013	COL	MLB	24	434	39	21	3	2	28	19	67	18	7	.280/.311/.361	.228	.328	0.7	2B(90): 3.6, 3B(14): -0.9	0.2
2014	COL	MLB	25	538	59	15	5	5	42	33	97	10	10	.267/.315/.348	.226	.322	3.7	2B(144): 2.7, 3B(7): -0.8	0.2
2015	COL	MLB	26	620	85	21	5	6	61	50	107	23	3	.301/.358/.388	.253	.362	4.9	2B(149): -0.9	1.7
2016	*COL*	*MLB*	*27*	*567*	*61*	*24*	*5*	*7*	*51*	*33*	*95*	*17*	*6*	*.285/.327/.387*	*.237*	*.332*	*2.7*	*2B 2*	*1.4*
2017	*COL*	*MLB*	*28*	*529*	*56*	*21*	*5*	*6*	*50*	*32*	*90*	*14*	*6*	*.277/.320/.377*	*.241*	*.322*	*3.0*	*2B 2*	*2.0*

Breakout: 7% Improve: 43% Collapse: 6% Attrition: 19% MLB: 95% *Comparables: Darwin Barney, Donovan Solano, Brandon Phillips*

LeMahieu spent the offseason working out with teammate Charlie Blackmon, adopting a regimen the outfielder christened "Body by Blackmon." In a pair of stunning upsets, no Best Shape Of My Life quotes were uttered by the second baseman during spring training and he came away from Chuck Nazty's program devoid of any discernable improvements to his facial hair. However, he did take cues from the outfielder's revamped hitting philosophy and employed a more selective approach at the plate; his walk rate climbed for a second straight season.

That being said, it's hard to view LeMahieu's "breakout" at the plate through any lens uncolored by skepticism. Nearly all of his offensive gains came through an inflated BABIP that was unaccompanied by significant changes in his batted ball profile: No uptick in power; no extra contact; no higher percentage of hard-hit balls. More concerning was that the defensive metrics previously enamored with his slick glove work at the keystone saw him as merely average compared to his peers. We know not to treat a year's worth of defensive data as sacrosanct, but given his age, it's not crazy to think his peak defensive years could be in the rear-view mirror.

Ryan McMahon 3B

Born: 12/14/94 Age: 21 Bats: L Throws: R Height: 6'2" Weight: 185

YEAR	TEAM	LVL	AGE	PA	R	2B	3B	HR	RBI	BB	K	SB	CS	AVG/OBP/SLG	TAv	BABIP	BRR	FRAA	WARP
2014	ASH	A	19	552	93	46	3	18	102	54	143	8	5	.282/.358/.502	.284	.360	-0.3	3B(118): 7.9	4.0
2015	MOD	A+	20	556	85	43	6	18	75	49	153	6	13	.300/.372/.520	.358	.401	1.5	3B(129): 26.1	10.7
2016	*COL*	*MLB*	*21*	*250*	*27*	*14*	*1*	*8*	*31*	*18*	*78*	*1*	*2*	*.245/.305/.421*	*.241*	*.333*	*-0.6*	*3B 6*	*0.8*
2017	*COL*	*MLB*	*22*	*427*	*51*	*25*	*2*	*13*	*52*	*33*	*129*	*2*	*3*	*.249/.312/.425*	*.253*	*.335*	*-1.0*	*3B 10*	*2.3*

Breakout: 3% Improve: 10% Collapse: 5% Attrition: 9% MLB: 21% *Comparables: Ian Stewart, Corey Seager, Travis Snider*

For the second year, McMahon took opposing pitchers' lunch money despite being one of the youngest players at his level. That he's done nothing but mash since entering professional ball is even more remarkable given that he split time between the diamond and the gridiron during high school. An inflated strikeout rate is one of the few blemishes in his well-rounded game; some scouts believe his approach actually took a step backward down the stretch, when he appeared to fall into the trap of swinging for dingers in the dinger-happy California League. His strikeout rate went up and his OBP dropped from .405 through May to .353 the rest of the way. In his defense, he hit a bunch more dingers!

Justin Morneau 1B

Born: 5/15/81 Age: 35 Bats: L Throws: R Height: 6'4" Weight: 220

YEAR	TEAM	LVL	AGE	PA	R	2B	3B	HR	RBI	BB	K	SB	CS	AVG/OBP/SLG	TAv	BABIP	BRR	FRAA	WARP
2013	PIT	MLB	32	92	6	4	0	0	3	13	12	0	0	.260/.370/.312	.246	.303	-0.4	1B(25): -0.7	-0.2
2013	MIN	MLB	32	543	56	32	0	17	74	37	98	0	0	.259/.315/.426	.274	.288	-0.6	1B(112): -5.7	0.6
2014	COL	MLB	33	550	62	32	3	17	82	34	60	0	3	.319/.364/.496	.297	.330	-0.7	1B(131): 3.6	3.0
2015	COL	MLB	34	182	19	10	3	3	15	13	25	0	0	.310/.363/.458	.279	.350	0.2	1B(44): -1.7	0.4
2016	*COL*	*MLB*	*35*	*250*	*27*	*14*	*1*	*7*	*31*	*18*	*40*	*0*	*0*	*.280/.334/.440*	*.255*	*.309*	*-0.1*	*1B -1*	*0.1*
2017	*COL*	*MLB*	*36*	*237*	*29*	*12*	*1*	*7*	*28*	*17*	*39*	*0*	*0*	*.272/.328/.430*	*.259*	*.301*	*-0.2*	*1B -1*	*0.4*

Breakout: 1% Improve: 29% Collapse: 9% Attrition: 23% MLB: 89% *Comparables: Ty Wigginton, Mike Sweeney, Michael Young*

Sometimes it's impossible for a player to get past his worst days. For Morneau, the concussion that cut his MVP-pace 2010 season short was a chronic issue the following year and nearly forced him into retirement. Even after winning the NL batting crowd in 2014—the highest point of his redemption story—he admitted the injury still haunted him. "It's something that will always be with me," he told ESPN.com last spring, comparing it to the dread a pitcher might sense when he feels a twinge in his elbow after Tommy John surgery. That's what made the concussion Morneau suffered in May all the more disheartening. Lingering symptoms accompanied a cervical neck strain and kept him on the shelf until September. Fortunately, he returned to action free of any further complications, but the Rockies understandably declined to pick up his 2016 option.

Tom Murphy C

Born: 4/3/91 Age: 25 Bats: R Throws: R Height: 6'1" Weight: 220

YEAR	TEAM	LVL	AGE	PA	R	2B	3B	HR	RBI	BB	K	SB	CS	AVG/OBP/SLG	TAv	BABIP	BRR	FRAA	WARP
2013	ASH	A	22	341	55	26	2	19	74	37	87	4	5	.288/.385/.590	.324	.346	-3.2	C(69): -0.8	3.5
2013	TUL	AA	22	74	9	5	0	3	9	4	16	0	0	.290/.338/.493	.294	.340	-1.9	C(14): -0.2	0.4
2014	TUL	AA	23	109	16	4	0	5	15	14	27	0	0	.213/.321/.415	.261	.242	-0.6	C(23): -0.1	0.2
2015	ABQ	AAA	24	136	19	9	2	7	19	5	43	0	1	.271/.301/.535	.257	.350	0.5	C(27): 0.4	0.4
2015	NBR	AA	24	294	36	17	1	13	44	23	80	5	2	.249/.320/.468	.273	.306	0.1	C(58): -1.1	1.7
2015	COL	MLB	24	39	5	1	0	3	9	4	10	0	0	.257/.333/.543	.281	.273	0.5	C(11): -2.9	0.0
2016	*COL*	*MLB*	*25*	*32*	*4*	*2*	*0*	*2*	*5*	*2*	*10*	*0*	*0*	*.242/.303/.461*	*.252*	*.305*	*0.0*	*C -1*	*0.0*
2017	*COL*	*MLB*	*26*	*250*	*33*	*12*	*1*	*11*	*36*	*16*	*78*	*1*	*1*	*.242/.301/.457*	*.256*	*.311*	*-0.4*	*C -8*	*0.4*

Breakout: 4% Improve: 19% Collapse: 5% Attrition: 17% MLB: 47% *Comparables: Taylor Teagarden, Dusty Ryan, Max Ramirez*

YEAR	TEAM	P. COUNT	FRM RUNS	BLK RUNS	THRW RUNS	TOT RUNS
2014	TUL	2740	1.9	-0.1	0.2	2.0
2015	ABQ	4087	-0.6	-0.3	-0.2	-1.1
2015	COL	1584	-2.1	0.0	-0.1	-2.1
2015	NBR	7358	1.3	-0.3	0.3	1.4
2016	*COL*	*1191*	*-0.7*	*-0.1*	*-0.1*	*-0.9*
2017	*COL*	*9316*	*-6.4*	*-1.1*	*-0.5*	*-8.0*

Shoulder injuries cost Murphy most of the 2014 season, but a strong showing in the upper minors and with Team USA at the Pan-American Games eventually earned him a cup of coffee with the big-league club. The backstop is built like a Clydesdale, showing above-average power at every stop and enough defensive grace to ease previous concerns about his sticking at the position long-term. Now the concern is the 29 percent strikeout rate that surfaced in the high minors, a result of the length in his swing and fringy bat speed that makes him susceptible to hard stuff on the hands. With Nick Hundley entering the final year of his contract, Murphy is being groomed to be the catcher of the future and could even wrestle away playing time from the veteran at some point this season. But he's not quite there yet.

Tyler Nevin 2B

Born: 5/29/97 Age: 19 Bats: R Throws: R Height: 6'4" Weight: 200

YEAR	TEAM	LVL	AGE	PA	R	2B	3B	HR	RBI	BB	K	SB	CS	AVG/OBP/SLG	TAv	BABIP	BRR	FRAA	WARP
2016	*COL*	*MLB*	*19*	*250*	*20*	*9*	*1*	*3*	*20*	*16*	*75*	*1*	*1*	*.200/.255/.294*	*.183*	*.275*	*-0.5*	*3B -1*	*-1.5*
2017	*COL*	*MLB*	*20*	*381*	*38*	*15*	*1*	*7*	*35*	*27*	*109*	*1*	*1*	*.215/.274/.329*	*.212*	*.287*	*-0.8*	*3B -2*	*-0.8*

Breakout: 0% Improve: 0% Collapse: 0% Attrition: 0% MLB: 0% *Comparables: Maikel Franco, Matt Davidson, Nolan Arenado*

Want to know how much times have changed? As the 38th overall pick last year, Nevin signed for $2 million. Adjusting for inflation, his dad, Phil, signed for a little more than half that much as the first overall pick in 1992.

Nevin the younger has an advanced approach at the plate but a stiffer swing than one would expect from a compensation-round pick taken primarily for his bat. As is the case with many 18-year-olds, there is plenty of room to add strength to the build, but as is the case with many 18-year-olds, there is a risk that that same added bulk would force a move down the defensive spectrum.

Dom Nunez C

Born: 1/17/95 Age: 21 Bats: L Throws: R Height: 6'0" Weight: 175

YEAR	TEAM	LVL	AGE	PA	R	2B	3B	HR	RBI	BB	K	SB	CS	AVG/OBP/SLG	TAv	BABIP	BRR	FRAA	WARP
2015	ASH	A	20	441	61	23	0	13	53	53	55	7	7	.282/.373/.448	.281	.298	-0.8	C(99): 0.4	2.0
2016	*COL*	*MLB*	*21*	*250*	*25*	*11*	*1*	*7*	*29*	*20*	*54*	*1*	*1*	*.233/.295/.380*	*.221*	*.269*	*-0.5*	*C -0*	*0.0*
2017	*COL*	*MLB*	*22*	*277*	*33*	*12*	*1*	*9*	*33*	*22*	*58*	*1*	*1*	*.240/.303/.403*	*.240*	*.273*	*-0.6*	*C 0*	*0.8*

Breakout: 0% Improve: 2% Collapse: 0% Attrition: 2% MLB: 2% *Comparables: Travis d'Arnaud, Tucker Barnhart, J.R. Murphy*

YEAR	TEAM	P. COUNT	FRM RUNS	BLK RUNS	THRW RUNS	TOT RUNS
2016	*COL*	*9034*	*0.0*	*0.0*	*0.0*	*0.0*
2017	*COL*	*9998*	*0.0*	*0.0*	*0.0*	*0.0*

Timing can be everything in a developing hitter's swing. Nunez found that out the hard way when he stumbled out of the gate in his first full-season assignment. Early on, he swapped his leg kick for a toe tap and cut down the length in his swing by getting his hands in a better position for fire, but trouble syncing the two changes led to a .531 OPS in the first half. Once the timing issues were sorted out, his bat took off. He smacked all 13 of his home runs in the second half, walked 37 times against just 24 strikeouts and posted a 1.050 OPS. Nunez isn't the second coming of Mike Piazza, but the bat could play average at the big-league level with some occasional pull-side pop. Pair that with rapidly improving defense behind the plate and off the charts makeup and you've got a player with a chance to be a second-division backstop.

Kevin Padlo 3B

Born: 7/15/96 Age: 19 Bats: R Throws: R Height: 6'2" Weight: 200

YEAR	TEAM	LVL	AGE	PA	R	2B	3B	HR	RBI	BB	K	SB	CS	AVG/OBP/SLG	TAv	BABIP	BRR	FRAA	WARP
2015	BOI	A-	18	308	44	22	2	9	46	45	62	33	5	.294/.404/.502	.325	.353	1.3	3B(59): 0.1	3.2
2015	ASH	A	18	99	11	5	0	2	7	14	26	2	1	.145/.273/.277	.209	.179	0.2	3B(25): 3.6	0.2
2016	*COL*	*MLB*	*19*	*250*	*28*	*10*	*1*	*7*	*26*	*22*	*73*	*8*	*3*	*.216/.290/.360*	*.218*	*.284*	*0.5*	*3B 3*	*0.0*
2017	*COL*	*MLB*	*20*	*395*	*46*	*18*	*2*	*12*	*45*	*34*	*110*	*12*	*4*	*.227/.297/.386*	*.236*	*.291*	*1.3*	*3B 5*	*1.1*

Breakout: 0% Improve: 2% Collapse: 0% Attrition: 1% MLB: 3% *Comparables: Cheslor Cuthbert, Matt Dominguez, Miguel Sano*

Most high school prospects never deal with failure. The 2014 fifth-round pick was given an aggressive Sally League assignment, against players more than three years his elder, and got flat-out smoked for the first time in his life. The Rockies quickly decided to hit the reset button and try again at short-season ball. Padlo proceeded to rake in the pitching-friendly Northwest League, showing the type of resilience that earns him universally high praise for his makeup. The former San Diego commit has a long swing but a sound approach at the plate and enough power to profile just fine at the hot corner, where his athleticism and improving footwork give him a real chance to stick. A system stacked with promising position players makes it difficult for Padlo to stand out, but he's an intriguing blue chipper who could shoot up prospect lists in the coming years.

Kyle Parker LF

Born: 9/30/89 Age: 26 Bats: R Throws: R Height: 6'0" Weight: 205

YEAR	TEAM	LVL	AGE	PA	R	2B	3B	HR	RBI	BB	K	SB	CS	AVG/OBP/SLG	TAv	BABIP	BRR	FRAA	WARP
2013	TUL	AA	23	528	70	23	3	23	74	40	99	6	6	.288/.345/.492	.300	.318	-2.0	LF(77): -6.2, RF(20): -2.3	1.9
2014	COL	MLB	24	26	1	1	0	0	1	0	14	0	0	.192/.192/.231	.154	.417	-0.1	RF(4): 0.1, 1B(2): -0.1	-0.3
2014	CSP	AAA	24	542	73	30	3	15	72	33	102	4	3	.289/.336/.450	.262	.335	-3.3	RF(74): -11.1, 1B(40): 0.8	-0.4
2015	COL	MLB	25	112	10	3	1	3	11	6	37	1	0	.179/.223/.311	.172	.242	1.1	LF(28): -2.7, RF(4): -0.2	-1.0
2015	ABQ	AAA	25	388	53	19	4	9	58	24	102	6	4	.280/.326/.431	.236	.365	0.5	1B(48): 3.0, LF(39): -6.3	-0.7
2016	*COL*	*MLB*	*26*	*188*	*19*	*8*	*1*	*6*	*23*	*10*	*49*	*1*	*1*	*.253/.294/.409*	*.233*	*.316*	*-0.2*	*LF -3*	*-0.2*
2017	*COL*	*MLB*	*27*	*343*	*40*	*15*	*2*	*11*	*41*	*19*	*89*	*2*	*1*	*.254/.299/.415*	*.244*	*.318*	*-0.3*	*LF -5*	*0.2*

Breakout: 2% Improve: 6% Collapse: 6% Attrition: 13% MLB: 23% *Comparables: Zoilo Almonte, Donald Lutz, Cole Garner*

At 26, Parker, the late-blooming former college quarterback, finally got an extended look at big-league pitching. It went as well an extended look straight into the sun. Among hitters with at least 100 plate appearances, Parker ranked fifth worst in True Average and only Joey Gallo made less contact on pitches in the strike zone. His game always had moderate swing-and-miss, which was excused because of his plus raw power. But, as some scouts predicted, the holes in his swing were exacerbated against premium velocity and quality breaking balls. Yes, it's a small sample. It's also a very discouraging first impression for a player who is ancient by prospect standards and whose carrying tool was supposed to be his bat.

Jordan Patterson RF

Born: 2/12/92 Age: 24 Bats: L Throws: L Height: 6'4" Weight: 215

YEAR	TEAM	LVL	AGE	PA	R	2B	3B	HR	RBI	BB	K	SB	CS	AVG/OBP/SLG	TAv	BABIP	BRR	FRAA	WARP
2014	ASH	A	22	532	69	27	0	14	66	46	118	25	8	.278/.359/.430	.269	.338	-1.5	RF(102): -1.1, 1B(11): 2.3	1.4
2015	NBR	AA	23	202	26	19	0	7	32	11	42	9	4	.286/.342/.503	.293	.336	0.7	RF(22): 2.8, 1B(21): 0.8	1.4
2015	MOD	A+	23	339	62	26	12	10	43	19	88	9	6	.304/.378/.568	.358	.400	6.8	RF(52): -3.4, LF(9): -0.2	4.7
2016	*COL*	*MLB*	*24*	*250*	*29*	*12*	*2*	*7*	*29*	*13*	*70*	*6*	*3*	*.246/.305/.416*	*.239*	*.316*	*0.1*	*RF 0, 1B 1*	*0.2*
2017	*COL*	*MLB*	*25*	*332*	*39*	*17*	*2*	*10*	*40*	*17*	*92*	*8*	*4*	*.250/.308/.417*	*.249*	*.322*	*0.5*	*RF 0, 1B 2*	*0.9*

Breakout: 3% Improve: 7% Collapse: 2% Attrition: 9% MLB: 15% *Comparables: Steven Souza, Casper Wells, Zoilo Almonte*

Colorado's system is thick with outfield prospects in its lower levels, so Patterson was squeezed off prospect depth charts before breaking through with a .297/.364/.543 line across two levels last year. The 2013 fourth-rounder stays balanced with the help of a wide base, and he displays solid barrel control with plus raw power. Pitch recognition issues and an overly aggressive approach in the zone have undercut a solid-average hit tool, though he did cut his strikeout rate considerably after the promotion to Double-A New Britain. The corner profile will limit Patterson's ultimate ceiling, but Colorado has been turning prospects like him into fantasy studs for two decades.

Ben Paulsen 1B

Born: 10/27/87 Age: 28 Bats: L Throws: R Height: 6'4" Weight: 210

YEAR	TEAM	LVL	AGE	PA	R	2B	3B	HR	RBI	BB	K	SB	CS	AVG/OBP/SLG	TAv	BABIP	BRR	FRAA	WARP
2013	CSP	AAA	25	502	64	32	10	18	79	37	128	2	2	.292/.345/.523	.291	.366	0.8	1B(116): 5.3	2.9
2014	CSP	AAA	26	497	76	32	6	20	76	58	119	4	5	.294/.378/.533	.298	.362	-1.5	1B(93): 9.6, RF(4): -0.3	3.4
2014	COL	MLB	26	66	8	4	0	4	10	2	19	0	0	.317/.348/.571	.294	.400	-1.5	1B(15): 0.7, RF(3): -0.0	0.2
2015	ABQ	AAA	27	141	19	8	2	3	15	15	34	1	0	.256/.340/.424	.239	.330	-2.7	1B(18): 2.0, RF(5): -0.7	-0.2
2015	COL	MLB	27	354	42	19	4	11	49	23	92	1	2	.277/.326/.462	.269	.351	1.0	1B(90): -0.1, LF(19): -1.2	0.8
2016	*COL*	*MLB*	*28*	*489*	*54*	*25*	*5*	*17*	*65*	*36*	*136*	*2*	*2*	*.260/.316/.455*	*.255*	*.332*	*-0.1*	*1B 6, RF 0*	*1.2*
2017	*COL*	*MLB*	*29*	*531*	*65*	*28*	*5*	*17*	*68*	*40*	*148*	*2*	*1*	*.257/.315/.445*	*.259*	*.332*	*-0.2*	*1B 6, RF 0*	*2.0*

Breakout: 7% Improve: 21% Collapse: 11% Attrition: 29% MLB: 52% *Comparables: Jake Fox, Victor Diaz, Tyler Moore*

Sporting a thick, grizzly beard that could fell a tree by its mere approach, Paulsen hit enough to lock down the strong side of a platoon at first base once Justin Morneau went down with a concussion in May. A shaving mishap in August forced him to get rid of the full beard, to which manager Walt Weiss quipped, "There's some wildlife that lost some habitat when that thing came off." A clean-shaven Paulsen hit just .264/.301/.425 the rest of the way, compared to his .282/.335/.475 bearded line. A pair of university economists once found that handsome quarterbacks in the NFL outperformed their normal-faced peers; maybe appearance is destiny, one could claim. Paulsen's season makes the case that PECOTA should quit ignoring the Samson effect.

Jose Reyes SS

Born: 6/11/83 Age: 33 Bats: B Throws: R Height: 6'0" Weight: 195

YEAR	TEAM	LVL	AGE	PA	R	2B	3B	HR	RBI	BB	K	SB	CS	AVG/OBP/SLG	TAv	BABIP	BRR	FRAA	WARP
2013	TOR	MLB	30	419	58	20	0	10	37	34	47	15	6	.296/.353/.427	.283	.315	2.2	SS(92): 2.7	3.3
2014	TOR	MLB	31	655	94	33	4	9	51	38	73	30	2	.287/.328/.398	.274	.312	6.4	SS(142): -12.7	3.0
2015	COL	MLB	32	208	21	8	2	3	19	9	24	8	4	.259/.291/.368	.224	.281	0.4	SS(46): 0.6	0.2
2015	TOR	MLB	32	311	36	17	0	4	34	17	38	16	2	.285/.322/.385	.252	.315	2.6	SS(69): -2.8	1.0
2016	*COL*	*MLB*	*33*	*623*	*84*	*32*	*8*	*11*	*60*	*41*	*61*	*29*	*6*	*.308/.353/.448*	*.264*	*.324*	*3.5*	*SS -5*	*3.1*
2017	*COL*	*MLB*	*34*	*530*	*59*	*26*	*6*	*7*	*55*	*34*	*55*	*22*	*6*	*.299/.342/.421*	*.261*	*.319*	*3.3*	*SS -5*	*3.1*

Breakout: 1% Improve: 26% Collapse: 4% Attrition: 9% MLB: 94% *Comparables: Jimmy Rollins, Rafael Furcal, Placido Polanco*

Just how far Reyes has fallen from Most Exciting Player In Baseball was made clear at the trade deadline, when his inclusion in the Troy Tulowitzki blockbuster deal was merely a way for the Blue Jays to offset the burden of Tulo's rather large contract. Reyes is a few years removed from losing his first step and now entering the phase of his career where the second and third steps follow. His baserunning acumen should keep his value on the bases afloat for the time being. The same cannot be said for his defense, however, as he continues to be a liability at the six-hole. To make matters worse, his power is all but gone (last among qualified hitters in average flyball distance) and his overall production at the plate sank below league average for the first time since 2005. The deterioration over the years has been gradual, but Reyes is approaching the decline stage where things can get ugly quick.

Mark Reynolds 1B

Born: 8/3/83 Age: 32 Bats: R Throws: R Height: 6'2" Weight: 220

YEAR	TEAM	LVL	AGE	PA	R	2B	3B	HR	RBI	BB	K	SB	CS	AVG/OBP/SLG	TAv	BABIP	BRR	FRAA	WARP
2013	CLE	MLB	29	384	40	8	0	15	48	43	123	3	0	.215/.307/.373	.255	.285	0.0	1B(41): 0.6, 3B(40): -3.5	0.2
2014	MIL	MLB	30	433	47	9	0	22	45	47	122	5	1	.196/.287/.394	.256	.218	1.0	1B(91): 1.7, 3B(42): 1.7	1.1
2015	SLN	MLB	31	432	35	21	2	13	48	44	121	2	3	.230/.315/.398	.253	.300	-4.5	1B(100): 1.6, 3B(22): -0.8	-0.1
2016	*COL*	*MLB*	*32*	*276*	*35*	*11*	*1*	*12*	*37*	*31*	*82*	*2*	*1*	*.231/.322/.436*	*.256*	*.291*	*-0.7*	*1B 1*	*0.4*
2017	*COL*	*MLB*	*33*	*381*	*51*	*14*	*1*	*16*	*50*	*42*	*114*	*2*	*1*	*.225/.315/.419*	*.254*	*.286*	*-1.0*	*1B 2*	*0.8*

Breakout: 0% Improve: 23% Collapse: 5% Attrition: 8% MLB: 92% *Comparables: Richie Sexson, Gil Hodges, Jim Gentile*

By reaching double-digit home runs last season, Reynolds joined a select group of players who had homered at least 10 times in each year since 2007—a group comprising future Hall of Famers, former All-Stars and um... Reynolds. In retrospect, it's hard to believe a third baseman who homered 30-plus times in three consecutive seasons never made an appearance in the Midsummer Classic, but that's the danger of looking at history backward. What's with all this talk about Reynolds' past anyway—he's only 32, so what about his future? Alas, players with Reynolds' skill set tend to age worse than our pop-culture references. To wit, even in 2015—a successful season by his standards—he set new career-worst marks in homers per at-bat and per flyball. He still walks and runs into enough pitches to stick around and extend his streak in 2016. After that? Hey, most people would *love* to retire before their mid-30s.

Brendan Rodgers SS

Born: 8/9/96 Age: 19 Bats: R Throws: R Height: 6'0" Weight: 180

Widely considered the most talented player in the draft, Rodgers "fell" to third overall as the Diamondbacks and Astros opted for college talents with higher floors. In his pro debut, he banged out four hits, including a home run, and when the post-game spread didn't show up he fed the entire team with just a few fish and—well, that's the legend, anyway. Rodgers has a compact swing that generates easy bat speed, giving him a potential plus hit tool and pop that projects to be above average. Combine that with actions smooth enough to stick up the middle and an arm that makes all the throws from deep in the hole and you have the makings of a superstar. He wore a red bowtie to his prom.

Wilin Rosario C

Born: 2/23/89 Age: 27 Bats: R Throws: R Height: 5'11" Weight: 220

YEAR	TEAM	LVL	AGE	PA	R	2B	3B	HR	RBI	BB	K	SB	CS	AVG/OBP/SLG	TAv	BABIP	BRR	FRAA	WARP
2013	COL	MLB	24	466	63	22	1	21	79	15	109	4	1	.292/.315/.486	.268	.344	3.1	C(106): -19.4, 1B(4): 0.1	0.6
2014	COL	MLB	25	410	46	25	0	13	54	23	70	1	0	.267/.305/.435	.237	.293	-1.8	C(96): -10.2, 1B(4): -0.1	-0.5
2015	ABQ	AAA	26	155	18	12	1	7	23	5	31	1	1	.297/.329/.534	.263	.336	-1.0	1B(34): -3.0	-0.2
2015	COL	MLB	26	242	22	14	1	6	29	8	56	2	1	.268/.295/.416	.229	.329	-1.4	1B(52): -2.5, C(2): 0.1	-0.8
2016	*COL*	*MLB*	*27*	*41*	*5*	*2*	*0*	*2*	*6*	*2*	*9*	*0*	*0*	*.267/.299/.469*	*.251*	*.306*	*0.0*		*0.1*
2017	*COL*	*MLB*	*28*	*178*	*22*	*9*	*1*	*8*	*25*	*8*	*43*	*1*	*0*	*.262/.296/.456*	*.254*	*.306*	*-0.1*	*-*	*0.7*

Breakout: 3% Improve: 52% Collapse: 6% Attrition: 7% MLB: 95% *Comparables: Mike Jacobs, Wilson Betemit, Chris Shelton*

YEAR	TEAM	P. COUNT	FRM RUNS	BLK RUNS	THRW RUNS	TOT RUNS
2013	COL	14872	-16.6	-1.0	-0.1	-17.7
2014	COL	13807	-5.4	-1.5	-0.8	-7.7
2015	COL	252	0.1	0.0	0.0	0.1

The Rosario catching experience was put to rest after three seasons of awkward framing attempts and imperiled umpires. There were 197 passed balls and wild pitches on his watch from 2012–14—45 more than the next worst catcher during that span. Unfortunately for the Rockies, first basemen have to catch thrown baseball, too, and sloppy footwork and poor decisions made him a liability at the cold corner. Teams commonly attempted to exploit him with bunts guided in his general direction. Declining power at the dish loosened his grip on the starting job further and he eventually settled into the weak side of a platoon. At this point, he would fit better on a team with an available DH spot and a Triple-A schedule.

Trevor Story SS

Born: 11/15/92 Age: 23 Bats: R Throws: R Height: 6'1" Weight: 180

YEAR	TEAM	LVL	AGE	PA	R	2B	3B	HR	RBI	BB	K	SB	CS	AVG/OBP/SLG	TAv	BABIP	BRR	FRAA	WARP
2013	MOD	A+	20	554	71	34	5	12	65	45	183	23	1	.233/.305/.394	.270	.343	1.8	SS(125): -0.9, 3B(4): -0.1	3.0
2014	TUL	AA	21	237	29	8	1	9	20	28	82	3	1	.200/.302/.380	.255	.281	0.8	SS(43): -8.9, 3B(6): 0.7	0.0
2014	MOD	A+	21	218	38	17	7	5	28	31	59	20	4	.332/.436/.582	.341	.467	2.8	SS(39): -0.1, 3B(8): -0.9	3.0
2015	NBR	AA	22	300	46	20	6	10	40	35	73	15	2	.281/.373/.523	.330	.350	3.4	SS(50): 3.2, 2B(12): -0.1	4.3
2015	ABQ	AAA	22	275	37	20	4	10	40	16	68	7	1	.277/.324/.504	.272	.341	3.0	SS(35): 1.9, 3B(14): -0.1	1.9
2016	*COL*	*MLB*	*23*	*250*	*29*	*13*	*2*	*8*	*30*	*20*	*81*	*6*	*1*	*.238/.304/.419*	*.242*	*.330*	*0.9*	*SS -2, 2B -0*	*0.6*
2017	*COL*	*MLB*	*24*	*420*	*50*	*21*	*4*	*13*	*50*	*34*	*137*	*11*	*2*	*.235/.303/.415*	*.248*	*.327*	*1.7*	*SS -3, 2B 0*	*1.6*

Breakout: 2% Improve: 20% Collapse: 2% Attrition: 9% MLB: 39% *Comparables: Mark Reynolds, Brandon Hicks, Alex Liddi*

Story took two tries at both High- and Double-A before conquering each level, with strikeout rates north of 33 percent in each initial go. But he took to Triple-A immediately, cutting back on the Ks and adding strength to affirm his legit-prospect status. Pitch recognition issues will be a constant, but in between some awkward flails at wayward breaking balls he'll inflict serious damage. The wet-feet struggles he went through in earlier promotions undoubtedly await him in Denver—where he should get a look at some point in 2016—but his power and speed combo should be enough to clear the low offensive bar set by his middle-infield peers.

Raimel Tapia CF

Born: 2/4/94 Age: 22 Bats: L Throws: L Height: 6'2" Weight: 160

YEAR	TEAM	LVL	AGE	PA	R	2B	3B	HR	RBI	BB	K	SB	CS	AVG/OBP/SLG	TAv	BABIP	BRR	FRAA	WARP
2014	ASH	A	20	539	93	32	1	9	72	35	90	33	16	.326/.382/.453	.288	.383	3.1	LF(43): -4.7, CF(42): -2.4	2.0
2015	MOD	A+	21	593	74	34	9	12	71	24	105	26	10	.305/.333/.467	.317	.350	-0.7	LF(46): 0.4	5.6
2016	*COL*	*MLB*	*22*	*250*	*27*	*12*	*2*	*5*	*27*	*9*	*55*	*7*	*4*	*.268/.298/.403*	*.229*	*.322*	*0.1*	*CF 1, LF -0*	*0.1*
2017	*COL*	*MLB*	*23*	*450*	*49*	*22*	*3*	*9*	*48*	*19*	*97*	*14*	*7*	*.273/.308/.404*	*.243*	*.327*	*0.9*	*CF 2, LF 0*	*1.3*

Breakout: 3% Improve: 11% Collapse: 3% Attrition: 14% MLB: 24% *Comparables: Felix Pie, Matt Szczur, Xavier Avery*

Tapia is one of the more polarizing names you'll see on this year's Top 100s, due in part to unorthodox swing mechanics that get even weirder when he drops down into an exaggerated two-strike crouch. His contact skills rival any prospect's, but they don't *always* benefit him: He tries to hit everything and will expand the zone even with the count in his favor, limiting the utility of his hit tool. That being said, it's easier (if still difficult) for a hitter to learn to be more selective than it is for a hitter to learn how to barrel top-level stuff the way Tapia does. His ETA is at least a year off, but all the ingredients are there for a first-division regular.

Forrest Wall 2B

Born: 11/20/95 Age: 20 Bats: L Throws: R Height: 6'0" Weight: 176

YEAR	TEAM	LVL	AGE	PA	R	2B	3B	HR	RBI	BB	K	SB	CS	AVG/OBP/SLG	TAv	BABIP	BRR	FRAA	WARP
2015	ASH	A	19	416	57	16	10	7	46	41	72	23	9	.280/.355/.438	.284	.329	1.4	2B(92): 1.3	2.5
2016	*COL*	*MLB*	*20*	*250*	*31*	*9*	*3*	*5*	*23*	*17*	*61*	*7*	*3*	*.238/.294/.377*	*.221*	*.295*	*0.4*	*2B -0*	*-0.1*
2017	*COL*	*MLB*	*21*	*378*	*44*	*15*	*5*	*10*	*43*	*29*	*90*	*11*	*6*	*.252/.313/.410*	*.247*	*.307*	*1.2*	*2B -1*	*1.3*

Breakout: 5% Improve: 10% Collapse: 0% Attrition: 7% MLB: 10% *Comparables: Luis Valbuena, Delino DeShields, Brett Lawrie*

If statheads have TINSTAAPP, scouts have TINSTAA2BP, which posits that anybody playing second base at 18 probably lacks the tools to be a premium defender or hitter. That undoubtedly played a role in Wall falling to 35th overall, but he's the exception that proves the rule: He has excellent bat-to-ball skills, makes loud contact, is a plus-plus runner and sticks to the keystone not because he lacks the athleticism for the six hole (he doesn't) but because high school labrum surgery sapped his arm strength. Put his tools at any other position and he'd get mid-first round consideration, but of course the league needs 30 starting second basemen, too. With every extra-base hit that Wall rips into the opposite-field gap, it becomes clear that many of the teams that passed over him focused too much on his one deficiency at the expense of an otherwise enticing overall package. If only there was an expression for that.

PITCHERS

Yency Almonte RHP

Born: 6/4/94 Age: 22 Bats: B Throws: R Height: 6'3" Weight: 205

YEAR	TEAM	LVL	AGE	W	L	SV	G	GS	IP	H	HR	BB/9	K/9	GB%	BABIP	WHIP	ERA	FIP	DRA	WARP	CFIP	MPH
2014	BUR	A	20	2	5	0	9	9	42	40	5	3.0	6.9	46%	.280	1.29	4.93	4.65	4.59	0.3	104	
2015	WNS	A+	21	3	3	0	7	6	44^{2}	28	1	2.4	7.9	52%	.231	0.90	2.42	2.67	2.64	1.1	83	
2015	KAN	A	21	8	4	0	17	16	92^{2}	92	8	2.5	6.9	45%	.295	1.27	3.88	4.17	4.55	0.7	100	
2016	*COL*	*MLB*	*22*	*6*	*7*	*0*	*20*	*20*	*101^{2}*	*115*	*15*	*3.3*	*5.9*	*40%*	*.324*	*1.51*	*4.80*	*4.82*	*5.34*	*-0.1*	*128*	
2017	*COL*	*MLB*	*23*	*7*	*9*	*0*	*24*	*24*	*143^{2}*	*149*	*21*	*3.6*	*6.4*	*40%*	*.306*	*1.43*	*5.00*	*5.24*	*5.56*	*-0.4*	*134*	

Breakout: 0% Improve: 0% Collapse: 0% Attrition: 0% MLB: 0% *Comparables: James Houser, Adam Ottavino, Joe Ross*

Consistency eludes Almonte, as it eludes so many of us, but especially and particularly young pitching prospects. When things go well, he can reach the mid-90s and his slider becomes a terrific out pitch. Almonte is big and sturdy, and he thrived at a tender age in both halves of Class A baseball in 2015. The next step will be developing a third pitch that really makes the first two pop.

Tyler Anderson LHP

Born: 12/30/89 Age: 26 Bats: L Throws: L Height: 6'4" Weight: 210

YEAR	TEAM	LVL	AGE	W	L	SV	G	GS	IP	H	HR	BB/9	K/9	GB%	BABIP	WHIP	ERA	FIP	DRA	WARP	CFIP	MPH
2013	MOD	A+	23	3	2	0	13	13	74^{2}	62	10	2.9	7.6	47%	.250	1.15	3.25	4.87	5.45	0.6	106	
2013	TRI	A-	23	1	1	0	3	3	15	9	0	1.8	7.8	66%	.205	0.80	0.60	2.18	3.88	0.2	87	
2014	TUL	AA	24	7	4	0	23	23	118^{1}	91	3	3.0	8.1	52%	.274	1.11	1.98	2.77				
2016	*COL*	*MLB*	*26*	*2*	*2*	*0*	*7*	*7*	*36^{2}*	*37*	*4*	*3.1*	*6.7*	*47%*	*.312*	*1.35*	*4.09*	*4.13*	*4.60*	*0.3*	*106*	
2017	*COL*	*MLB*	*27*	*10*	*11*	*0*	*31*	*31*	*198^{2}*	*190*	*24*	*3.2*	*7.0*	*47%*	*.302*	*1.31*	*4.39*	*4.59*	*4.94*	*0.7*	*115*	

Breakout: 6% Improve: 13% Collapse: 4% Attrition: 18% MLB: 23% *Comparables: Graham Taylor, Chris Dwyer, Mitch Talbot*

When the Rockies selected Anderson with the 20th overall pick in 2011, they thought they were getting a polished talent who would move quickly. The University of Oregon product lacked dominating stuff but had a deceptive motion and refined command that made him likely to achieve his back-of-the-rotation profile. Instead, a wide variety of injuries have stalled his progress. The latest blow was a stress fracture in his pitching elbow, which cost him the entire 2015 season. He admitted to the *Las Vegas Review-Journal* that the injury first affected him at High-A Modesto in 2013 and that he pitched through the pain in 2014 (and still managed a 1.98 ERA at Double-A!) before being shut down during the Texas League playoffs. Now 26, Anderson will compete for a spot in the big-league rotation this spring. If he makes it, he'll be the 22nd first-rounder from his class to reach The Show.

Christian Bergman RHP

Born: 5/4/88 Age: 28 Bats: R Throws: R Height: 6'1" Weight: 180

YEAR	TEAM	LVL	AGE	W	L	SV	G	GS	IP	H	HR	BB/9	K/9	GB%	BABIP	WHIP	ERA	FIP	DRA	WARP	CFIP	MPH
2013	TUL	AA	25	8	7	0	27	27	171	162	25	1.2	5.8	50%	.265	1.08	3.37	4.15	4.29	1.4	100	
2014	CSP	AAA	26	5	5	0	15	15	92^{1}	96	11	1.8	5.8	43%	.287	1.23	4.19	4.60	5.32	0.5	102	
2014	COL	MLB	26	3	5	0	10	10	54^{2}	75	9	1.6	5.1	33%	.333	1.55	5.93	4.71	5.71	-0.6	109	91.6
2015	COL	MLB	27	3	1	0	30	4	68^{1}	82	8	2.0	4.9	41%	.327	1.42	4.74	4.26	4.54	0.2	112	92.3
2016	*COL*	*MLB*	*28*	*3*	*2*	*0*	*50*	*3*	*64^{2}*	*71*	*9*	*2.2*	*5.6*	*39%*	*.316*	*1.34*	*4.31*	*4.45*	*4.81*	*0.1*	*114*	
2017	*COL*	*MLB*	*29*	*5*	*5*	*0*	*14*	*14*	*82*	*87*	*12*	*2.2*	*5.9*	*39%*	*.309*	*1.30*	*4.58*	*4.77*	*5.11*	*0.2*	*122*	

Breakout: 7% Improve: 20% Collapse: 7% Attrition: 20% MLB: 38% *Comparables: Andrew Albers, Cha Seung Baek, John Ely*

The handful of uninspiring starts Bergman made in late 2014 convinced the Rockies that his zone-pounding, contact-heavy approach was best off in a long-relief role. Of his 26 relief appearances last season, 19 were of the multiple-inning variety. Several of those were spent cleaning up messes left behind by a group of starting pitchers that threw the fewest innings in baseball. Fellow mop-up man Yohan Flande got the chance to crack the rotation down the stretch before Bergman did, which is about all that needs to be said about his place on the depth chart.

Rafael Betancourt RHP

Born: 4/29/75 Age: 41 Bats: R Throws: R Height: 6'2" Weight: 215

YEAR	TEAM	LVL	AGE	W	L	SV	G	GS	IP	H	HR	BB/9	K/9	GB%	BABIP	WHIP	ERA	FIP	DRA	WARP	CFIP	MPH
2013	COL	MLB	38	2	5	16	32	0	28^{2}	26	2	3.5	8.5	39%	.289	1.29	4.08	3.19	3.16	0.5	91	92.1
2015	COL	MLB	40	2	4	1	45	0	39^{1}	43	4	2.7	9.2	24%	.328	1.40	6.18	3.37	3.98	0.3	86	93.0
2016	*COL*	*MLB*	*41*	*2*	*1*	*1*	*35*	*0*	*37*	*36*	*5*	*2.8*	*8.2*	*27%*	*.315*	*1.28*	*3.87*	*3.93*	*4.36*	*0.2*	*97*	
2017	*COL*	*MLB*	*42*	*3*	*1*	*1*	*59*	*0*	*54^{1}*	*51*	*7*	*2.9*	*7.9*	*27%*	*.301*	*1.26*	*4.19*	*4.36*	*4.72*	*0.1*	*106*	

Breakout: 15% Improve: 33% Collapse: 37% Attrition: 28% MLB: 76% *Comparables: Tom Gordon, Russ Springer, Trevor Hoffman*

"Nobody would have blamed Betancourt if he had called it a career when he learned at the end of 2013 that he'd completely torn his ulnar collateral ligament. He was 38 and had earned $23 million over the course of a career that started in the 1990s as a failed shortstop prospect with the Red Sox, took a detour through Japan, and included a previous elbow surgery, all before his first pitch in the majors for the Indians at the age of 28.

But instead of hanging up his cleats, he underwent Tommy John surgery, hoping to regain the impeccable command that had led to a vastly underrated tenure with Cleveland and allowed him to be one of the few relievers to so successfully navigate the thin air of Coors Field. Upon his return, he discovered a new penchant for grooving 90 mph fastballs, which eventually led to his release in August. The peripherals still reflect a pitcher worthy of a roster spot, but after you turn 40 teams don't want to wait for your luck to bounce back."

Chad Bettis RHP

Born: 4/26/89 Age: 27 Bats: R Throws: R Height: 6'1" Weight: 200

YEAR	TEAM	LVL	AGE	W	L	SV	G	GS	IP	H	HR	BB/9	K/9	GB%	BABIP	WHIP	ERA	FIP	DRA	WARP	CFIP	MPH
2013	COL	MLB	24	1	3	0	16	8	44^{2}	55	6	4.0	6.0	49%	.327	1.68	5.64	4.90	5.00	-0.1	115	96.8
2013	TUL	AA	24	3	4	0	12	12	63	60	9	1.9	9.7	50%	.307	1.16	3.71	3.52	3.71	1.0	81	
2014	COL	MLB	25	0	2	0	21	0	24^{2}	42	4	3.6	4.7	53%	.384	2.11	9.12	5.49	7.42	-0.9	116	96.4
2014	CSP	AAA	25	3	4	3	20	5	55^{1}	45	1	3.4	8.9	60%	.303	1.19	3.09	3.25	4.97	0.4	90	
2015	ABQ	AAA	26	3	2	0	7	7	39	41	5	2.3	7.6	47%	.319	1.31	3.46	4.42	4.41	0.5	94	
2015	COL	MLB	26	8	6	0	20	20	115	120	11	3.3	7.7	53%	.313	1.41	4.23	3.87	3.77	1.7	98	95.7
2016	*COL*	*MLB*	*27*	*9*	*8*	*0*	*26*	*26*	*137^{2}*	*141*	*17*	*2.9*	*7.4*	*52%*	*.322*	*1.35*	*4.02*	*4.09*	*4.51*	*1.3*	*104*	
2017	*COL*	*MLB*	*28*	*6*	*6*	*0*	*34*	*18*	*129*	*124*	*15*	*2.9*	*7.7*	*52%*	*.312*	*1.28*	*4.10*	*4.28*	*4.60*	*0.8*	*107*	

Breakout: 25% Improve: 55% Collapse: 22% Attrition: 21% MLB: 93% *Comparables: John Maine, Garrett Mock, Carlos Carrasco*

It was another ugly year for pitching at Coors Field, but a breakout season by Bettis was one of the few positives to take away from the big-league rotation. The former second-round pick had been written off after a string of shoulder injuries and dreadful stints in Denver but got another crack at the rotation in May. He took a perfect game into the seventh inning against the Phillies in his fourth start, then served as the co-ace of the staff with Jorge De La Rosa the rest of the season. Bettis did a better job consistently burying his slider low and away to right-handers, giving him two secondary pitches (the changeup is the other) that drew whiffs 20 percent of the time and produced two grounders for every three balls put in play. Salvaging a league-average starter out of what was thought to be a failed prospect is a development the Rockies will gladly take.

Eddie Butler RHP

Born: 3/13/91 Age: 25 Bats: R Throws: R Height: 6'2" Weight: 180

YEAR	TEAM	LVL	AGE	W	L	SV	G	GS	IP	H	HR	BB/9	K/9	GB%	BABIP	WHIP	ERA	FIP	DRA	WARP	CFIP	MPH
2013	ASH	A	22	5	1	0	9	9	54^1	25	2	4.1	8.4	76%	.172	0.92	1.66	3.63	4.47	0.3	100	
2013	TUL	AA	22	1	0	0	6	6	27^2	13	0	2.0	8.1	58%	.188	0.69	0.65	2.01	3.77	0.4	84	
2013	MOD	A+	22	3	4	0	13	13	67^2	58	7	2.8	8.9	49%	.280	1.17	2.39	4.16	5.01	0.9	90	
2014	TUL	AA	23	6	9	0	18	18	108	104	10	2.7	5.2	47%	.274	1.26	3.58	4.10				
2014	COL	MLB	23	1	1	0	3	3	16	23	2	3.9	1.7	56%	.328	1.88	6.75	5.67	6.29	-0.3	127	96.7
2015	ABQ	AAA	24	2	6	0	11	11	63^1	71	6	3.6	5.3	54%	.314	1.52	5.40	4.99	6.09	-0.4	113	
2016	*COL*	*MLB*	*25*	*2*	*3*	*0*	*8*	*8*	*40*	*44*	*6*	*3.4*	*5.4*	*51%*	*.314*	*1.47*	*4.80*	*4.99*	*5.35*	*0.0*	*128*	
2017	*COL*	*MLB*	*26*	*4*	*5*	*0*	*14*	*14*	80^2	*79*	*10*	*3.5*	*6.0*	*51%*	*.296*	*1.37*	*4.81*	*5.04*	*5.36*	*-0.1*	*128*	

Breakout: 16% Improve: 28% Collapse: 13% Attrition: 32% MLB: 54% *Comparables: Justin Germano, Jeff Samardzija, Sergio Mitre*

We can't say for sure that the shoulder complications that set Butler back in 2014 directly robbed him of his stuff (he continued to complain about shoulder fatigue last spring), but his disastrous rookie season suggests something wasn't right. The fastball still sat in the mid-90s but with diminished life. The slider lost bite. The changeup—his money pitch as a prospect—fooled nobody in the majors. Among changeups thrown at least 200 times, Butler's had the seventh-lowest whiff rate and the highest line-drive rate, resulting in an absurd .404 True Average against the pitch. He struck out only two more batters than he walked and finished the season with a DRA that ranked third-to-last among pitchers who threw at least 70 innings. Youth and a strong groundball profile are points in his favor but none of that will matter if he can't miss more bats.

Miguel Castro RHP

Born: 12/24/94 Age: 21 Bats: R Throws: R Height: 6'5" Weight: 190

YEAR	TEAM	LVL	AGE	W	L	SV	G	GS	IP	H	HR	BB/9	K/9	GB%	BABIP	WHIP	ERA	FIP	DRA	WARP	CFIP	MPH
2014	VAN	A-	19	6	2	0	10	10	50^1	36	2	3.6	9.5	49%	.272	1.11	2.15	3.48	4.45	0.7	88	
2014	LNS	A	19	1	1	0	4	4	21^2	10	2	2.9	8.3	55%	.151	0.78	3.74	3.95	4.21	0.2	91	
2015	TOR	MLB	20	0	2	4	13	0	12^1	15	2	4.4	8.8	41%	.351	1.70	4.38	4.73	7.90	-0.5	93	99.5
2015	BUF	AAA	20	1	3	0	13	5	19^2	26	4	5.5	9.6	42%	.367	1.93	4.58	5.80	5.24	-0.2	109	
2015	COL	MLB	20	0	1	0	5	0	5^1	6	2	6.8	10.1	25%	.286	1.88	10.12	8.04	8.12	-0.2	108	99.0
2015	ABQ	AAA	20	2	0	0	11	0	13^2	6	0	4.6	6.6	57%	.162	0.95	1.32	3.89	4.48	0.1	96	
2016	*COL*	*MLB*	*21*	*2*	*1*	*0*	*31*	*0*	*33*	*33*	*4*	*3.6*	*7.6*	*42%*	*.314*	*1.39*	*4.27*	*4.19*	*4.80*	*0.0*	*110*	
2017	*COL*	*MLB*	*22*	*3*	*3*	*3*	*27*	*8*	71^1	*66*	*9*	*3.8*	*7.8*	*42%*	*.300*	*1.35*	*4.52*	*4.73*	*5.08*	*0.0*	*118*	

Breakout: 6% Improve: 10% Collapse: 3% Attrition: 8% MLB: 16% *Comparables: Tommy Hanson, Jake Odorizzi, Severino Gonzalez*

When a team takes a 20-year-old with an electric fastball and no experience above High-A and thrusts him into a major-league bullpen, the best-case scenario is Roberto Osuna's 2015 season: enough fastball command to avoid blowups, some gradual development of an elite secondary offering, and a breakout season as Toronto's closer. More common, however, is how his Opening Day teammate Castro's season unfolded: flashes of bat-missing stuff that rarely found the strike zone. The Blue Jays quickly realized Castro wasn't big-league ready, sent him back to the minors in May and then flipped him to Colorado in the Troy Tulowitzki deal. The promise of a potential above-average cambio and a developing slider provides hope for a live-armed starter; the backup plan is that he'll develop enough control to become what Osuna was immediately. Plan C is to hope Jeff Hoffman becomes an ace and Castro can be remembered as the trade's throw-in.

Jorge De La Rosa LHP

Born: 4/5/81 Age: 35 Bats: L Throws: L Height: 6'1" Weight: 215

YEAR	TEAM	LVL	AGE	W	L	SV	G	GS	IP	H	HR	BB/9	K/9	GB%	BABIP	WHIP	ERA	FIP	DRA	WARP	CFIP	MPH
2013	COL	MLB	32	16	6	0	30	30	167^2	170	11	3.3	6.0	50%	.303	1.38	3.49	3.74	3.81	2.2	106	93.6
2014	COL	MLB	33	14	11	0	32	32	184^1	161	21	3.3	6.8	53%	.264	1.24	4.10	4.31	3.44	3.1	104	94.7
2015	COL	MLB	34	9	7	0	26	26	149	137	17	3.9	8.1	54%	.289	1.36	4.17	4.22	4.00	1.8	101	94.6
2016	*COL*	*MLB*	*35*	*11*	*9*	*0*	*30*	*30*	*171*	*164*	*21*	*3.2*	*7.4*	*53%*	*.310*	*1.31*	*4.10*	*4.15*	*4.60*	*1.4*	*107*	
2017	*COL*	*MLB*	*36*	*9*	*10*	*0*	*28*	*28*	*170*	*154*	*20*	*3.1*	*7.5*	*53%*	*.298*	*1.25*	*4.17*	*4.35*	*4.68*	*1.1*	*109*	

Breakout: 15% Improve: 43% Collapse: 25% Attrition: 13% MLB: 91% *Comparables: Chuck Finley, Mark Langston, Jim Bibby*

When de la Rosa returned from Tommy John surgery at the end of the 2012 season, not many expected a career revival. Command was never his strength to begin with, and he had a checkered injury history even before going under knife. That made the zip he lost on his fastball upon returning all the more concerning. Instead of leaning on his fastball as a crutch, he recognized that he needed to give hitters more varied looks in order to survive. So he goes to a high-80s cutter just as often as his four-seamer and sprinkles in a handful of sinkers every start. He terrorizes hitters with a nasty splitter one out of every three pitches, and uses it both as an out pitch and to generate weak grounders in hitter's counts. If your kids ever ask you that awkward question "where do crafty lefties come from," here's your answer.

Jairo Diaz RHP

Born: 5/27/91 Age: 25 Bats: R Throws: R Height: 6'0" Weight: 200

YEAR	TEAM	LVL	AGE	W	L	SV	G	GS	IP	H	HR	BB/9	K/9	GB%	BABIP	WHIP	ERA	FIP	DRA	WARP	CFIP	MPH
2013	SBR	AFA	22	0	2	0	13	0	22^1	38	3	5.6	8.5	53%	.438	2.33	8.87	5.52				
2013	BUR	A	22	0	3	8	32	0	34	27	3	2.9	7.4	54%	.253	1.12	3.97	4.16	4.54	0.1	98	
2014	INL	A+	23	2	3	4	29	0	32	31	2	2.8	10.4	0%	.322	1.28	4.78	3.27				
2014	ANA	MLB	23	0	0	0	5	0	5^2	4	0	4.8	12.7	46%	.308	1.24	3.18	1.92	2.76	0.1	94	99.9
2014	ARK	AA	23	2	1	11	27	0	32^2	30	2	2.8	13.2	53%	.384	1.22	2.20	1.99				
2015	ABQ	AAA	24	3	5	8	47	0	55	51	6	6.1	8.2	58%	.292	1.60	4.58	5.44	6.73	-0.9	118	
2015	COL	MLB	24	0	1	0	21	0	19	16	2	2.8	8.5	56%	.269	1.16	2.37	3.58	2.50	0.5	93	100.1
2016	*COL*	*MLB*	*25*	*3*	*1*	*0*	*52*	*0*	55^1	*58*	*7*	*3.9*	*8.0*	*52%*	*.337*	*1.48*	*4.28*	*4.32*	*4.79*	*0.1*	*111*	
2017	*COL*	*MLB*	*26*	*3*	*2*	*0*	*36*	*5*	63^2	*59*	*8*	*3.8*	*8.6*	*52%*	*.316*	*1.36*	*4.33*	*4.54*	*4.85*	*0.1*	*113*	

Breakout: 11% Improve: 11% Collapse: 4% Attrition: 17% MLB: 20% *Comparables: Alberto Cabrera, Merkin Valdez, Randy Wells*

With tree trunks for legs, ridiculous arm strength and a high-effort delivery, Diaz checks all the boxes you'd expect from a catcher-turned-reliever. The looming question mark when the Rockies acquired him for Josh Rutledge was his ability to throw strikes, a flaw that resurfaced during his stint at Triple-A. Upon his callup at the end of August, tweaks were made to compact his delivery, which allowed him to hide the ball longer. He also added a two-seam fastball, which he was able to grip and rip with the same velocity as his four-seamer. The walks went down noticeably and the Venezuelan fanned nearly a batter per inning while generating grounders on over half his balls in play. If the control can be harnessed—and make no mistake, that's a tree-trunks-sized if—there's a potential impact bullpen arm here.

Yohan Flande LHP

Born: 1/27/86 Age: 30 Bats: L Throws: L Height: 6'2" Weight: 180

YEAR	TEAM	LVL	AGE	W	L	SV	G	GS	IP	H	HR	BB/9	K/9	GB%	BABIP	WHIP	ERA	FIP	DRA	WARP	CFIP	MPH
2013	GWN	AAA	27	9	7	1	31	19	131^1	142	9	3.2	6.3	53%	.314	1.43	4.18	3.84	4.41	0.8	100	
2014	COL	MLB	28	0	6	0	16	10	59	55	5	2.4	5.2	60%	.272	1.20	5.19	3.97	3.05	1.2	108	92.9
2014	CSP	AAA	28	3	11	0	18	16	88^1	112	9	3.4	6.8	55%	.361	1.64	5.60	4.70	5.56	0.2	109	
2015	NBR	AA	29	5	0	0	6	6	39^2	27	1	0.9	6.8	65%	.234	0.78	1.36	2.39	2.73	1.0	80	
2015	COL	MLB	29	3	3	0	19	10	68^1	73	14	3.3	5.7	61%	.277	1.43	4.74	5.71	4.80	0.1	117	93.0
2015	ABQ	AAA	29	3	3	0	6	6	31^2	55	8	2.0	3.1	44%	.370	1.96	7.11	6.95	7.12	-0.6	120	
2016	*COL*	*MLB*	*30*	*7*	*7*	*0*	*32*	*20*	118^2	*134*	*17*	*2.7*	*5.8*	*56%*	*.326*	*1.43*	*4.54*	*4.61*	*5.07*	*0.2*	*119*	
2017	*COL*	*MLB*	*31*	*4*	*5*	*0*	*18*	*13*	*86*	*93*	*13*	*2.7*	*6.0*	*56%*	*.315*	*1.38*	*4.84*	*5.06*	*5.40*	*-0.1*	*128*	

Breakout: 0% Improve: 10% Collapse: 3% Attrition: 11% MLB: 19% *Comparables: Jason Stanford, Billy Buckner, Eric Stults*

Flande doesn't miss bats, but he has more or less limited contact to two outcomes: A groundball, or the longest home run you ever saw. Specifically, one out of every four flyballs went for a home run, double the rate against him the previous season, and more than double the league's average. (All but three topped 400 feet, and Michael Taylor landed one 479 feet away.) Dare we say that batters maul Flande's fastb—no, we daren't. We'll dare instead to say it's unlikely he outgrows his current status as a long reliever who can fill the back of a rotation in a pinch.

Kyle Freeland LHP

Born: 5/14/93 Age: 23 Bats: L Throws: L Height: 6'3" Weight: 170

YEAR	TEAM	LVL	AGE	W	L	SV	G	GS	IP	H	HR	BB/9	K/9	GB%	BABIP	WHIP	ERA	FIP	DRA	WARP	CFIP	MPH
2014	ASH	A	21	2	0	0	5	5	21^2	14	1	1.7	7.5	52%	.220	0.83	0.83	3.08	4.47	0.2	92	
2015	MOD	A+	22	3	2	0	7	7	39^2	48	5	1.8	4.3	49%	.314	1.41	4.76	5.06	6.22	-0.2	115	
2016	*COL*	*MLB*	*23*	*2*	*3*	*0*	*8*	*8*	35^1	*44*	*7*	*3.1*	*4.6*	*45%*	*.326*	*1.58*	*5.56*	*5.70*	*6.15*	*-0.4*	*150*	
2017	*COL*	*MLB*	*24*	*6*	*11*	*0*	*28*	*28*	174^1	*200*	*33*	*3.2*	*4.9*	*45%*	*.307*	*1.51*	*5.85*	*6.14*	*6.47*	*-1.8*	*158*	

Breakout: 0% Improve: 0% Collapse: 0% Attrition: 0% MLB: 0% *Comparables: Brooks Raley, Mike Hinckley, Ryan Tepera*

Concerns over Freeland's mechanics and the elbow surgery on his resume scared some teams off the polished University of Evansville product before the 2014 draft. The Rockies bit at no. 8 overall, and got bit right back: He dealt with shoulder fatigue this spring, then surgery to remove bone chips from his elbow, and didn't make his first start of the season until August. The results once he returned were vague, but between his tremendous command and three-pitch mix he's back on track for a mid-rotation ceiling. That's if he stays healthy, of course. Between his polish and the very real chance he breaks again, the Rockies will be wise to put him on the express.

Jonathan Gray RHP

Born: 11/5/91 Age: 24 Bats: R Throws: R Height: 6'4" Weight: 235

YEAR	TEAM	LVL	AGE	W	L	SV	G	GS	IP	H	HR	BB/9	K/9	GB%	BABIP	WHIP	ERA	FIP	DRA	WARP	CFIP	MPH
2013	MOD	A+	21	4	0	0	5	5	24	10	0	2.2	13.5	50%	.227	0.67	0.75	1.52	4.12	0.5	57	
2014	TUL	AA	22	10	5	0	24	24	124^1	107	10	3.0	8.2	40%	.285	1.19	3.91	3.43				
2015	ABQ	AAA	23	6	6	0	21	20	114^1	129	9	3.2	8.7	44%	.350	1.49	4.33	3.88	3.83	2.1	87	
2015	COL	MLB	23	0	2	0	9	9	40^2	52	4	3.1	8.9	46%	.384	1.62	5.53	3.65	4.74	0.1	93	97.4
2016	*COL*	*MLB*	*24*	*8*	*7*	*0*	*24*	*24*	*127^1*	*132*	*16*	*3.0*	*7.9*	*43%*	*.332*	*1.37*	*3.93*	*4.02*	*4.42*	*1.3*	*100*	
2017	*COL*	*MLB*	*25*	*7*	*7*	*0*	*22*	*22*	*129^2*	*120*	*15*	*2.9*	*8.7*	*43%*	*.316*	*1.25*	*3.85*	*4.02*	*4.33*	*1.3*	*98*	

Breakout: 19% Improve: 41% Collapse: 15% Attrition: 26% MLB: 76% *Comparables: Andrew Heaney, Carlos Carrasco, Danny Salazar*

When you're christened a potential top-of-the-rotation monster, the type who throws triple-digit heat and a wipeout slider and has the good body and the fancy pedigree, the guy with 7s across his scouting report, like a slot machine spitting nickels, anything less than complete domination is inevitably met with disappointment. Such has been the case for Gray, who, two years after being selected third overall in the 2013 draft, has seen his raw stuff back up and struggled with bouts of inconsistency. Seeing arguably the most hyped pitching prospect in Rockies history now tabbed as a likely mid-rotation arm is frustrating, so it's to the organization's credit that they remained patient with him in 2015. Instead of giving in to the temptation of asking him to save a dreadful major-league staff, they let him ripen at Triple-A before finally giving him the call in the nobody's-still-watching days of August and September. There were some scuffles, and a .390 BABIP, but Gray's excellent strikeout-to-walk ratio and gaudy whiff rate on his slider provide reason for optimism. Previous expectations should be adjusted, but there's still a live arm and a ton of potential within.

David Hale RHP

Born: 9/27/87 Age: 28 Bats: R Throws: R Height: 6'2 Weight: 210

YEAR	TEAM	LVL	AGE	W	L	SV	G	GS	IP	H	HR	BB/9	K/9	GB%	BABIP	WHIP	ERA	FIP	DRA	WARP	CFIP	MPH
2013	ATL	MLB	25	1	0	0	2	2	11	11	0	0.8	11.5	61%	.355	1.09	0.82	0.75	4.07	0.1	89	94.4
2013	GWN	AAA	25	6	9	0	22	20	114^2	123	8	2.8	6.0	54%	.313	1.39	3.22	3.89	4.41	0.7	100	
2014	ATL	MLB	26	4	5	0	45	6	87^1	89	5	4.0	4.5	57%	.288	1.47	3.30	4.28	4.77	-0.2	131	93.8
2015	COL	MLB	27	5	5	0	17	12	78^1	95	14	2.3	7.0	49%	.325	1.47	6.09	4.77	4.96	0.0	103	93.1
2015	ABQ	AAA	27	0	3	0	11	11	50	68	4	3.8	6.7	55%	.383	1.78	6.66	4.54	5.29	0.1	102	
2016	*COL*	*MLB*	*28*	*3*	*2*	*0*	*27*	*6*	*56^1*	*63*	*8*	*2.9*	*6.1*	*52%*	*.329*	*1.44*	*4.41*	*4.60*	*4.93*	*0.1*	*114*	
2017	*COL*	*MLB*	*29*	*4*	*4*	*0*	*18*	*11*	*75*	*78*	*9*	*2.9*	*6.6*	*52%*	*.315*	*1.36*	*4.46*	*4.66*	*4.99*	*0.2*	*115*	

Breakout: 27% Improve: 38% Collapse: 19% Attrition: 29% MLB: 67% *Comparables: Jeremy Hefner, Tim Stauffer, Craig Stammen*

All the pieces are in place for Hale to be a decent pitcher. He has good fastball command and respectable velocity, plus a changeup and slider that each draw whiffs and groundballs. Yet you look up at the end of the year and his ERA starts with a "6." Weird. Hale's prevailing issue was a dinger problem (not to be confused with the team's mascot situation) that wasn't just a product of Coors Field. Six of the 14 homers he served up were on the road, where he threw only one-third of his innings. The rest of his peripherals trended in the right direction, with a passable strikeout rate accompanying a minimal number of free passes. There's nothing too sexy about the way he goes about his business, but with the right breaks he could be a useful arm.

Jeff Hoffman RHP

Born: 1/8/93 Age: 23 Bats: R Throws: R Height: 6'5" Weight: 225

YEAR	TEAM	LVL	AGE	W	L	SV	G	GS	IP	H	HR	BB/9	K/9	GB%	BABIP	WHIP	ERA	FIP	DRA	WARP	CFIP	MPH
2015	NHP	AA	22	0	0	0	2	2	11^2	9	0	1.5	6.2	43%	.257	0.94	1.54	2.41	2.47	0.3	72	
2015	DUN	A+	22	3	3	0	11	11	56	59	4	2.4	6.1	53%	.329	1.32	3.21	3.70	4.19	0.1	105	
2015	NBR	AA	22	2	2	0	7	7	36^1	27	3	2.5	7.2	58%	.242	1.02	3.22	3.74	3.44	0.6	100	
2016	*COL*	*MLB*	*23*	*5*	*4*	*0*	*14*	*14*	*71*	*77*	*9*	*3.0*	*5.8*	*50%*	*.322*	*1.42*	*4.36*	*4.49*	*4.87*	*0.3*	*114*	
2017	*COL*	*MLB*	*24*	*9*	*11*	*0*	*31*	*31*	*193^1*	*198*	*24*	*3.0*	*6.1*	*50%*	*.309*	*1.36*	*4.57*	*4.77*	*5.10*	*0.3*	*120*	

Breakout: 0% Improve: 0% Collapse: 0% Attrition: 0% MLB: 0% *Comparables: Garrett Olson, Michael Stutes, Jered Weaver*

As noted in Kyle Freeland's comment, the Rockies took a risky college pitcher with a troubling injury history eighth overall in the 2014 draft. The Blue Jays, meanwhile, took a risky college pitcher with a troubling injury history ninth in that same draft, and as the stars would have it the Rockies now have that guy, too. Before the trade that sent Hoffman to Colorado, to be forever known by many as "the trade that cost us Troy Tulowitzki grrrrrr," the Blue Jays tweaked his delivery. He's more upright than he was in college, which helps him get downhill plane. That costs his fastball some explosiveness, but it's a more repeatable motion and puts less stress on his elbow. Command of his mid- to high-90s smoke is still the glaring concern, one that dates back to his days at East Carolina. However, this is still a starting pitcher who, at his best, has two pitches that flash double plus: the aforementioned heater and a curveball he can locate both in and out of the zone. There are still wrinkles to iron out but Hoffman has legitimate no. 2 starter upside.

Kyle Kendrick RHP

Born: 8/26/84 Age: 31 Bats: R Throws: R Height: 6'3" Weight: 210

YEAR	TEAM	LVL	AGE	W	L	SV	G	GS	IP	H	HR	BB/9	K/9	GB%	BABIP	WHIP	ERA	FIP	DRA	WARP	CFIP	MPH
2013	PHI	MLB	28	10	13	0	30	30	182	207	18	2.3	5.4	52%	.306	1.40	4.70	3.99	4.15	1.7	113	92.2
2014	PHI	MLB	29	10	13	0	32	32	199	214	25	2.6	5.5	47%	.290	1.36	4.61	4.54	4.68	0.3	124	92.3
2015	COL	MLB	30	7	13	0	27	27	142^{1}	172	33	2.8	5.1	41%	.300	1.52	6.32	6.15	5.61	-1.0	129	91.2
2016	*COL*	*MLB*	*31*	*8*	*8*	*0*	*22*	*22*	*129^{2}*	*148*	*20*	*2.6*	*5.2*	*45%*	*.316*	*1.43*	*4.84*	*4.88*	*5.39*	*-0.2*	*129*	
2017	*COL*	*MLB*	*32*	*7*	*10*	*0*	*22*	*22*	*132^{2}*	*145*	*22*	*2.9*	*5.2*	*45%*	*.305*	*1.42*	*5.29*	*5.54*	*5.89*	*-1.0*	*141*	

Breakout: 17% Improve: 54% Collapse: 13% Attrition: 8% MLB: 93% *Comparables: Paul Minner, Mark Clark, Saul Rogovin*

Good heavens, what a signing. Colorado's been trying to isolate the attributes of a successful Coors Field pitcher for going on 20 years now, and it got them to Kyle Kendrick? A contact-oriented pitcher who can't even boast a good walk or groundball rate? Perhaps the Rockies liked that he got by without the heavy use of a curveball, a pitch *Baseball Prospectus* author Dan Rozenson found suffers disproportionately negative effects at their home park. No matter the reason for the experiment, it failed miserably—unless you were part of BP's Hacking Mass fantasy game, where sucking is the key and where Kendrick was the preseason's most popular pick. (Good move; he was the format's MVP.)

He lost a tick off his fastball and his splitter didn't have its same bottoming-out action in Denver's thin air, leading to a career-low groundball rate and the most contact yielded since 2011. What followed were two home runs allowed every nine innings (bad, but not park-adjusted) and one of the 10 highest DRAs among starting pitchers with at least 100 innings pitched (bad *and* park-adjusted). Luckily for the Rockies, they only signed up for a one-year pact, meaning daily fantasy players will have to find a new pitcher to stack their lineups against.

Boone Logan LHP

Born: 8/13/84 Age: 31 Bats: R Throws: L Height: 6'5" Weight: 215

YEAR	TEAM	LVL	AGE	W	L	SV	G	GS	IP	H	HR	BB/9	K/9	GB%	BABIP	WHIP	ERA	FIP	DRA	WARP	CFIP	MPH
2013	NYA	MLB	28	5	2	0	61	0	39	33	7	3.0	11.5	51%	.292	1.18	3.23	3.84	3.15	0.7	80	96.4
2014	COL	MLB	29	2	3	0	35	0	25	31	6	4.0	11.5	54%	.379	1.68	6.84	5.10	6.53	-0.6	86	95.0
2015	COL	MLB	30	0	3	0	60	0	35^{1}	40	3	4.3	11.2	45%	.374	1.61	4.33	3.64	4.24	0.2	89	95.5
2016	*COL*	*MLB*	*31*	*3*	*1*	*2*	*57*	*0*	*60^{2}*	*59*	*8*	*3.4*	*9.6*	*48%*	*.334*	*1.35*	*3.88*	*3.85*	*4.38*	*0.3*	*96*	
2017	*COL*	*MLB*	*32*	*4*	*2*	*3*	*88*	*0*	*58*	*52*	*7*	*3.4*	*9.7*	*48%*	*.317*	*1.28*	*3.96*	*4.13*	*4.47*	*0.3*	*98*	

Breakout: 26% Improve: 44% Collapse: 29% Attrition: 16% MLB: 94% *Comparables: Sergio Santos, Matt Mantei, Kyle Farnsworth*

Figuring out how to reliably construct a bullpen remains one of baseball's great mysteries. Logan's tenure in Colorado is a blunt reminder that simply throwing money at relievers isn't always a quick fix. His slider is still a terror on lefties, who saw the pitch a whopping 58 percent of the time and whiffed on more than half their hacks at it. After working as the team's primary setup man early in the season, he was relegated to situational stuff down the stretch. With the Rockies in rebuilding mode and 2016 likely Logan's final year with the club, there's a good chance they keep him in a similar role and give more intriguing power arms like Justin Miller and Jairo Diaz shots to stick at the back of the pen. It's not a bad use of Logan, considering his strengths. It's just not what you'd have hoped from a guy brought in on a three-year deal.

Tyler Matzek LHP

Born: 10/19/90 Age: 25 Bats: L Throws: L Height: 6'3" Weight: 230

YEAR	TEAM	LVL	AGE	W	L	SV	G	GS	IP	H	HR	BB/9	K/9	GB%	BABIP	WHIP	ERA	FIP	DRA	WARP	CFIP	MPH
2013	TUL	AA	22	8	9	0	26	26	142^{1}	147	13	4.8	6.0	42%	.306	1.57	3.79	4.62	5.14	-0.3	122	
2014	CSP	AAA	23	5	4	0	12	12	66^{2}	70	8	4.2	8.2	51%	.302	1.51	4.05	4.82	5.24	0.4	99	
2014	COL	MLB	23	6	11	0	20	19	117^{2}	120	9	3.4	7.0	52%	.312	1.39	4.05	3.75	3.89	1.3	104	95.4
2015	ABQ	AAA	24	0	1	1	10	1	11^{1}	5	1	13.5	11.9	54%	.174	1.94	8.74	6.86	7.48	-0.3	122	
2015	COL	MLB	24	2	1	0	5	5	22	21	2	7.8	6.1	43%	.302	1.82	4.09	5.98	5.67	-0.2	123	95.0
2016	*COL*	*MLB*	*25*	*2*	*2*	*0*	*6*	*6*	*34^{1}*	*36*	*4*	*3.7*	*7.1*	*49%*	*.324*	*1.45*	*4.35*	*4.29*	*4.85*	*0.2*	*114*	
2017	*COL*	*MLB*	*26*	*4*	*4*	*0*	*12*	*12*	*69^{1}*	*66*	*9*	*3.7*	*8.0*	*49%*	*.311*	*1.36*	*4.37*	*4.57*	*4.87*	*0.3*	*115*	

Breakout: 22% Improve: 39% Collapse: 17% Attrition: 33% MLB: 72% *Comparables: Allen Webster, Erik Johnson, Anthony Ranaudo*

Matzek was like a Bill Bryson book: He walked all the way to Alburquerque (issuing a free pass per inning in his first five starts at Colorado), then walked all the way to extended spring training (after giving away seven in his first outing with the Isotopes), and then (after a disastrous rehab stint with Boise) he walked all the way to Southern California, where the Rockies gave him part of the summer off from baseball activities. To "get a blow," as they say (and as they said).

It was just a year earlier that Matzek, the 11th overall pick in the 2009 draft, seemed to have clicked, with a promising rookie campaign and a third consecutive season improving his walk rate. But he has always struggled with mechanical inconsistency and, in turn, the threat of extreme wildness—as a prospect he once walked 36 batters in a 22-inning stretch comprising seven starts. Matzek said in 2015 that he had been dealing with "mental triggers" that caused him to "lock up" on the mound. In California, he worked with a sports psychologist who helped him with the anxiety he was experiencing on the field. He returned to Albuquerque a month and a half later to make nine relief appearances down the stretch. The walks were still there, but he was open about being in a better place mentally and ready to move on.

The Rockies stress that they still view his long-term future as a starter, and it's not difficult to see why. The four months that he spent as roughly a league-average starter in 2014 offer a glimpse into what he can be when everything stays in line. But what Matzek dealt with this past season is the starkest reminder that baseball players are human beings first and foremost. That's the joy of this game, and at times also the cuss of it.

Justin Miller RHP

Born: 6/13/87 Age: 29 Bats: R Throws: R Height: 6'3" Weight: 215

YEAR	TEAM	LVL	AGE	W	L	SV	G	GS	IP	H	HR	BB/9	K/9	GB%	BABIP	WHIP	ERA	FIP	DRA	WARP	CFIP	MPH
2013	ROU	AAA	26	0	1	1	11	0	11	14	4	7.4	9.8	32%	.303	2.09	9.82	8.57	5.64	0.0	113	
2013	FRI	AA	26	1	0	2	16	0	16	16	1	3.9	11.8	37%	.357	1.44	6.19	3.31	4.01	0.1	89	
2014	TOL	AAA	27	2	1	5	38	0	44^{2}	30	2	2.4	7.9	42%	.241	0.94	1.81	3.27	4.22	0.3	89	
2014	DET	MLB	27	1	0	0	8	0	12^{1}	14	2	1.5	3.6	41%	.273	1.30	5.11	4.94	5.61	-0.2	114	94.4
2015	ABQ	AAA	28	0	2	7	25	0	27^{1}	20	2	2.6	10.9	44%	.261	1.02	2.30	3.23	2.96	0.7	77	
2015	NBR	AA	28	1	1	0	6	0	10^{2}	7	0	3.4	8.4	50%	.233	1.03	0.84	3.08	3.90	0.1	96	
2015	COL	MLB	28	3	3	1	34	0	33^{1}	21	2	3.0	10.3	38%	.244	0.96	4.05	2.65	1.74	1.2	79	96.4
2016	*COL*	*MLB*	*29*	*2*	*1*	*0*	*47*	*0*	49^{2}	*46*	*6*	*2.9*	*8.5*	*39%*	*.307*	*1.24*	*3.73*	*3.81*	*4.20*	*0.5*	*94*	
2017	*COL*	*MLB*	*30*	*2*	*1*	*1*	*42*	*0*	*47*	*42*	*6*	*3.0*	*8.9*	*39%*	*.303*	*1.22*	*3.92*	*4.08*	*4.41*	*0.3*	*100*	

Breakout: 14% Improve: 23% Collapse: 28% Attrition: 27% MLB: 53% *Comparables: Blake Parker, Mickey Storey, Marcus McBeth*

Miller signed a minor-league deal with the Rox and, after dominating at New Britain and Albuquerque, forced his way onto the big-league roster in June. By September he was getting high-leverage innings for the Rockies (a loose definition of "high leverage") and at one point he struck out eight consecutive batters, breaking a franchise record previously co-owned by bullpen legends Manny Corpas, Rex Brothers and Luis Vizcaino. The average velocity on Miller's slider spiked to 87 mph, nearly four ticks faster than what it was during his awful 2014 stint with the Tigers. With the pitch emerging as a legitimate weapon to complement his mid-90s fastball, he should get the chance to carve out a permanent spot at the back of Colorado's bullpen.

Jason Motte RHP

Born: 6/22/82 Age: 34 Bats: R Throws: R Height: 6'0" Weight: 205

Motte came back from Tommy John surgery in 2014 minus about 3 mph across the board. Last year, he chopped his cutter usage by two-thirds and got almost a mile back on his four-seam fastball. Whether that explains his semi-adequate results is one question; whether the increased velocity was the last gasp of a mid-30s reliever is probably the more important one. At just $5 million per annum, the Rockies haven't committed much money to Motte, but a two-year deal certainly seems aggressive for a flyball middle reliever who missed September and the postseason with a shoulder injury.

Mike Nikorak RHP

Born: 9/16/96 Age: 19 Bats: R Throws: R Height: 6'5" Weight: 205

Nikorak was considered one of the top prep arms in his draft class, but control issues and inconsistent fastball velocity during his senior year sunk his stock. He fell from a top-10 talent to the 27th-overall pick, which was only the start of his Very Bad Summer. He walked nearly two batters *per inning*, including walking more than 35 percent of the righties he faced. There's a lot of raw talent there, starting with a big fastball and a hook with swing-and-miss potential, but there is also a WHIP that looks like a pretty good ERA.

Adam Ottavino RHP

Born: 11/22/85 Age: 30 Bats: B Throws: R Height: 6'5" Weight: 220

YEAR	TEAM	LVL	AGE	W	L	SV	G	GS	IP	H	HR	BB/9	K/9	GB%	BABIP	WHIP	ERA	FIP	DRA	WARP	CFIP	MPH
2013	COL	MLB	27	1	3	0	51	0	78^{1}	73	5	3.6	9.0	48%	.311	1.33	2.64	3.12	3.03	1.5	84	94.4
2014	COL	MLB	28	1	4	1	75	0	65	67	6	2.2	9.7	47%	.347	1.28	3.60	3.07	3.15	1.1	77	98.2
2015	COL	MLB	29	1	0	3	10	0	10^{1}	3	0	1.7	11.3	63%	.158	0.48	0.00	1.52	0.17	0.6	79	98.1
2016	*COL*	*MLB*	*30*	*2*	*1*	*0*	*38*	*0*	*40*	*37*	*4*	*2.9*	*9.4*	*50%*	*.329*	*1.24*	*3.42*	*3.29*	*3.88*	*0.6*	*83*	
2017	*COL*	*MLB*	*31*	*2*	*1*	*1*	*35*	*0*	*44*	*38*	*5*	*3.1*	*9.8*	*50%*	*.314*	*1.20*	*3.55*	*3.69*	*4.03*	*0.4*	*86*	

Breakout: 28% Improve: 59% Collapse: 17% Attrition: 18% MLB: 88% *Comparables: Kevin Gregg, Scot Shields, Sam LeCure*

Ottavino endeared himself to statheads everywhere when he went on MLB Now with Brian Kenny last offseason and revealed that he had elevated his fastball more in the second half of 2014 after reading a FanGraphs post that detailed Sean Doolittle's success with the tactic. Namedropping Brooks Baseball and PITCHf/x in subsequent interviews solidified him in a tier just behind Zack Greinke, Brandon McCarthy and Trevor Bauer among the Internet's favorite sabermetrically-inclined pitchers. Unfortunately, Ottavino's elbow blew out after a dominant April, forcing him to undergo Tommy John surgery—and becoming, in a sense, just another statistic.

Chris Rusin LHP

Born: 10/22/86 Age: 29 Bats: L Throws: L Height: 6'2" Weight: 195

YEAR	TEAM	LVL	AGE	W	L	SV	G	GS	IP	H	HR	BB/9	K/9	GB%	BABIP	WHIP	ERA	FIP	DRA	WARP	CFIP	MPH
2013	IOW	AAA	26	8	7	0	19	18	121	113	8	2.0	5.1	50%	.272	1.16	3.35	4.03	5.06	0.8	104	
2013	CHN	MLB	26	2	6	0	13	13	66^{1}	66	8	3.3	4.9	50%	.275	1.36	3.93	4.72	4.02	0.7	119	89.9
2014	IOW	AAA	27	8	13	0	23	23	146^{1}	163	15	2.3	6.0	55%	.320	1.37	4.31	4.63	5.43	0.6	106	
2014	CHN	MLB	27	0	0	0	4	0	12^{2}	16	1	3.6	5.7	49%	.341	1.66	7.11	4.05	5.19	-0.1	107	90.5
2015	ABQ	AAA	28	3	2	0	7	6	34^{1}	47	6	2.9	4.7	54%	.325	1.69	6.29	5.78	6.17	-0.2	111	
2015	COL	MLB	28	6	10	0	24	22	131^{2}	170	19	2.8	5.9	53%	.339	1.60	5.33	4.73	5.62	-1.0	112	91.9
2016	*COL*	*MLB*	*29*	*4*	*3*	*0*	*57*	*5*	80^{1}	*91*	*11*	*2.5*	*5.5*	*53%*	*.323*	*1.41*	*4.50*	*4.53*	*5.02*	*0.1*	*118*	
2017	*COL*	*MLB*	*30*	*4*	*5*	*0*	*13*	*13*	76^{2}	*84*	*11*	*2.6*	*5.8*	*53%*	*.314*	*1.38*	*4.77*	*4.99*	*5.32*	*0.0*	*126*	

Breakout: 12% Improve: 24% Collapse: 14% Attrition: 20% MLB: 44% *Comparables: David Pauley, Clayton Mortensen, Pat Misch*

One thing DRA's process tells us is that Rusin lived in a cold-crueler world than any pitcher in baseball—his ledger had the most "runs" rebated for tough pitching conditions beyond his control. This was largely a product of making half his starts at Coors Field, but he also threw to a clumsy receiver and was tasked with retiring a challenging collection of hitters. Even controlling for all those factors couldn't change the fact that he was *also* one of the worst starting pitchers in baseball. Given his left-handedness, there's always hope he could be put to good use in the bullpen. Then again, same-sided hitters posted a .303 TAv against him, so even that's not a clear course of action. DRA helps those who help themselves.

Antonio Senzatela RHP

Born: 1/21/95 Age: 21 Bats: R Throws: R Height: 6'1" Weight: 180

YEAR	TEAM	LVL	AGE	W	L	SV	G	GS	IP	H	HR	BB/9	K/9	GB%	BABIP	WHIP	ERA	FIP	DRA	WARP	CFIP	MPH
2013	TRI	A-	18	2	4	0	8	8	42[1]	48	1	2.8	4.3	59%	.309	1.44	3.83	3.81	4.61	0.2	108	
2014	ASH	A	19	15	2	0	26	26	144[2]	134	11	2.2	5.5	47%	.267	1.18	3.11	4.19	4.79	0.9	103	
2015	MOD	A+	20	9	9	0	26	26	154	131	10	1.9	8.4	47%	.282	1.06	2.51	3.56	4.17	2.6	91	
2016	*COL*	*MLB*	*21*	*8*	*8*	*0*	*23*	*23*	*128*	*141*	*21*	*3.0*	*5.7*	*41%*	*.313*	*1.44*	*4.93*	*5.03*	*5.45*	*-0.3*	*132*	
2017	*COL*	*MLB*	*22*	*7*	*9*	*0*	*23*	*23*	*137[1]*	*137*	*22*	*3.1*	*6.5*	*41%*	*.297*	*1.34*	*4.98*	*5.21*	*5.50*	*-0.3*	*134*	

Breakout: 0% Improve: 0% Collapse: 0% Attrition: 0% MLB: 0% *Comparables: Jonathan Pettibone, Carlos Carrasco, Sean O'Sullivan*

You wouldn't expect a ton of velocity out of Senzatela's normal-human frame and low-effort delivery, but the Venezuelan regularly pumps low- to mid-90s fastballs with late life and can reach 98 for show. The absence of a secondary offering that can even flash average is troubling, but that just puts a brighter shine on his heater, as he still struck out nearly a batter per inning while dominating the Cal League. Presently constructed, you're looking at a pitcher who would fit best in a bullpen, but time and physics are on his side.

Lineouts

Hitters

NAME	POS	TEAM	LVL	AGE	PA	R	2B	3B	HR	RBI	BB	K	SB	CS	AVG/OBP/SLG	TAv	BABIP	BRR	FRAA	WARP
Cristhian Adames	SS	ABQ	AAA	23	511	62	20	3	11	51	36	56	11	7	.311/.362/.438	.271	.334	2.8	SS(79): -8.0, 2B(20): -2.0	2.0
	SS	COL	MLB	23	58	4	1	1	0	3	3	11	0	1	.245/.298/.302	.215	.310	-1.4	SS(13): 0.4, 2B(2): -0.0	-0.2
Jeremy Barfield	OF	ABQ	AAA	26	132	10	7	1	3	15	10	25	0	0	.267/.318/.417	.249	.309	-1.3	RF(29): -3.1, LF(5): -0.8	-0.4
	OF	NBR	AA	26	92	9	4	0	2	8	8	18	0	0	.195/.272/.317	.232	.222	0.7	RF(24): -0.2	-0.1
	OF	QUI	AAA	26	47	3	1	0	1	8	9	11	0	0	.105/.277/.211	.188	.115	0.0		0.0
Rosell Herrera	OF	MOD	A+	22	512	55	20	6	4	36	37	97	9	8	.260/.314/.354	.268	.319	-1.4	CF(62): -14.2, RF(22): -0.2	-0.2
Michael McKenry	C	COL	MLB	30	152	20	7	3	4	17	22	41	2	2	.205/.329/.402	.253	.265	-1.3	C(32): -1.3	0.3
Roberto Ramos	1B	ASH	A	20	190	33	14	0	10	40	18	39	4	0	.341/.413/.610	.345	.390	0.2	1B(41): -1.9	1.8
Rafael Ynoa	2B	ABQ	AAA	27	243	29	12	4	1	11	16	36	5	1	.286/.333/.388	.245	.337	0.5	2B(26): -0.4, 3B(24): -0.1	0.3
	2B	COL	MLB	27	131	14	8	1	0	9	3	28	1	0	.260/.277/.339	.210	.333	0.9	LF(19): -1.2, 3B(10): -0.4	-0.3

Cristhian Adames is out of minor-league options. He'll get the chance to be a glove-only super-utility type if he breaks camp, or a have-glove-will-travel type if he doesn't. ❖ **Jeremy Barfield** endured two separate independent league stints and a cameo in Mexico before signing with the Rockies and finishing the season with Albuquerque. Time is running out on the outfielder-turned-pitcher-turned-back-outfielder's dreams of ever reaching the majors, same as yours. ❖ **Rosell Herrera** showed little progress at the plate during his repeat of High-A and was extremely raw navigating the outfield for the first time. His 2013 Sally League MVP season feels like it was eons ago. ❖ The BABIP magic **Michael McKenry** experienced in 2014 faded away, a lateral meniscus tear in his right knee required surgery in late August, and that K in his last name continued to not be an H. It all made Colorado's decision to clear him from their 40-man roster easier. ❖ **Daniel Montano** doesn't have any particular tool that grabs your attention but his projectable frame and fluid swing were enough to earn the J2 signee a $2 million signing bonus. ❖ A hulking frame allows **Roberto Ramos** to generate the type of plus raw power he exhibited while mashing at Asheville. It also exacerbates his dreadful footwork, which he'll need to work hard to improve in order to stay on the field. ❖ **Rafael Ynoa**'s versatility and scrappiness earned him a spot on Walt Weiss' bench for four months. During that time he drew one fewer walk than his teammate and starting pitcher Chad Bettis, in four times the plate appearances.

Pitchers

NAME	TEAM	LVL	AGE	W	L	SV	G	GS	IP	H	HR	BB/9	K/9	GB%	BABIP	WHIP	ERA	FIP	FRA	WARP	CFIP	MPH
Ryan Castellani	ASH	A	19	2	7	0	27	27	113[1]	134	5	2.3	7.5	49%	.348	1.44	4.45	3.27	3.58	2.1	89	
Simon Castro	ABQ	AAA	27	5	5	0	36	0	57	53	6	3.2	11.7	40%	.326	1.28	3.79	3.58	2.66	1.6	73	
	COL	MLB	27	2	0	0	11	0	10[1]	11	0	4.4	7.8	56%	.344	1.55	6.10	3.16	3.73	0.1	105	94.2
Carlos Estevez	MOD	A+	22	5	0	5	14	0	19[2]	12	0	2.3	11.4	55%	.286	0.86	1.37	2.00	2.85	0.5	74	
	NBR	AA	22	0	3	13	34	0	36	39	2	2.2	10.8	42%	.363	1.33	4.50	2.44	2.20	1.0	74	
Christian Friedrich	COL	MLB	27	0	4	0	68	0	58[1]	75	5	3.9	6.9	49%	.361	1.71	5.25	4.07	4.19	0.4	106	93.7
Gonzalez Germen	CHN	MLB	27	0	0	0	6	0	6	8	0	7.5	12.0	56%	.500	2.17	7.50	3.00	13.88	-0.7	94	95.8
	COL	MLB	27	0	0	1	29	1	32[2]	33	4	5.8	6.9	48%	.299	1.65	3.86	5.15	3.44	0.5	112	96.3
	IOW	AAA	27	5	1	4	24	0	33[1]	29	3	4.6	7.3	46%	.268	1.38	3.78	4.77	3.14	0.8	112	
Jordan Lyles	COL	MLB	24	2	5	0	10	10	49	54	2	3.5	5.5	51%	.329	1.49	5.14	3.81	4.15	0.5	112	95.2
Sam Moll	MOD	A+	23	0	1	2	25	0	53[2]	40	7	2.0	9.6	56%	.250	0.97	3.02	4.13	3.62	1.0	85	
	NBR	AA	23	0	0	0	13	0	14[2]	7	0	2.5	10.4	42%	.212	0.75	1.23	1.77	2.83	0.3	81	
Scott Oberg	COL	MLB	25	3	4	1	64	0	58[1]	58	10	4.8	6.8	56%	.286	1.53	5.09	5.78	4.70	0.0	118	97.7
Chad Qualls	HOU	MLB	36	3	5	4	60	0	49[1]	46	6	1.6	8.4	61%	.288	1.11	4.38	3.49	3.95	0.4	93	94.2
Jesus Tinoco	LNS	A	20	2	6	0	15	15	81[1]	88	1	2.4	7.5	44%	.335	1.35	3.54	2.77	3.40	1.5	91	
	ASH	A	20	5	0	0	7	7	40	36	2	1.8	8.3	43%	.309	1.10	1.80	3.03	3.04	1.0	83	

Ryan Castellani was kept on a strict workload during his first full-season assignment but held his own against competition three years older than him. He shows surprisingly good feel for a curve and change to complement his low-90s sinker. ❖ For four Annuals in a row (2010–2013) we pleaded with pitching prospect **Simon Castro** to beg, borrow or steal a changeup, or be doomed to middle relief. He didn't, and he is. ❖ Recovering from his second Tommy John surgery, **Tyler Chatwood** made two rehab starts with Asheville in September (including Game Three of the Sally League championship series) and is on schedule to be ready for the start of the season. ❖ **Carlos Estevez** has a mid-90s fastball, a decent breaking ball and shares the birth name of Charlie Sheen. His stuff isn't as electric as Rick Vaughn's but comes without the wildness; for a second straight season, he walked fewer than Two and a Half Men per nine. ❖ **Christian Friedrich**'s slider lacked the same hellacious bite it had during his promising LOOGY stint at the end of 2014. Colorado's abysmal bullpen depth pushed him into a crossover role, further exposing his hefty platoon split. ❖ Enough teams employed **Gonzalez Germen** last year to merit consideration for an HBO sequel, "Germen Takes The Field." Instead, he settled for a low-leverage role in "A Very Bad Rockies Bullpen." ❖ One of five prep talents the Rockies selected in the first three rounds, **Peter Lambert** is not like most high school arms, as his appeal is his polish and three pitches with average to above-average potential. ❖ **Jordan Lyles** was two months into his typical season (ton of grounders, lackluster strikeout rate, bland breaking ball) when he suffered a season-ending torn ligament in his left big toe. ❖ **Sam Moll** is left-handed, has two above-average pitches and is bound for the bullpen. He's smaller than your typical back-end reliever but the last thing anyone wants to see is another *Southpaw* that sticks so strictly to its genre. ❖ **Scott Oberg** didn't miss bats, couldn't throw strikes and watched one out of every five fly balls leave the park. Among the other 29 teams' bullpen-innings leaders, only Philadelphia's Justin De Fratus managed a worse DRA. ❖ From the bullpeeeeeeeen, it's **Chad Qualls**! He had a penchant for ground balls! All others cleared the walls! Decent secondary numbeeeeeeers! Bad strand rate, God, God dang! ❖ It's easy to dream on **Jesus Tinoco**'s mid-90s fastball fitting perfectly in Denver's thin air with its heavy sinking action. He's also as close to Coors as an imperial stout and his lackluster secondary pitches cap his upside at back-end starter.

Manager

Walt Weiss

YEAR	TEAM	W	L	Pythag +/-	Avg PC	100+ P	120+ P	QS	BQS	REL	REL w Zero R	IBB	PH	PH Avg	PH HR	SB2	CS2	SB3	CS3	SAC Att	SAC%	POS SAC	Squeeze	Swing	In Play
2013	COL	74	88	-1	90.2	22	0	65	0	502	366	52	257	.282	6	97	28	15	4	100	65.0	34	2	301	91
2014	COL	66	96	-9	91.9	32	0	70	4	547	404	32	265	.259	5	70	40	15	6	92	64.1	33	2	313	79
2015	COL	68	94	-2	86.7	32	0	54	3	584	451	42	262	.250	4	81	37	16	5	66	66.7	26	3	295	88

The Rockies are not regarded as a "smart" organization by the cognoscenti, even though they employ objectively "smart" staffers. The times might be changing, however. New general manager Jeff Bridich (an Ivy League graduate) seemed to empower those employees more than his predecessors did. How can we tell? Look no further than Weiss' transformation, from generic and uninspiring in 2014, to co-opting many of the league's hottest strategical trends in 2015.

Weiss' tweaks were most apparent in how he constructed his lineups and positioned his defenders. The Rockies joined a growing number of National League teams who bat their pitcher eighth—a strategy that seemed to fit the Rockies better than anyone else, since their starters were more likely to be done before their second plate appearance anyway. Yet Weiss didn't stick to it, and after batting the pitcher eighth five times in April, he did so just twice thereafter. To his credit, he *did* show a greater commitment to improved defensive positioning. The Rockies topped their 2014 seasonal total in shifts during April, according to the *Denver Post*, and ended up shifting more than any other NL team.

You might suspect that the Rockies in return played better defense and turned more balls in play into outs than before. Nope; Colorado's defensive efficiency *declined* from its 2014 mark, and finished as the worst in the majors. It brings to mind Greg Maddux's old quote about how locating his pitches is what made him look smart, not his intelligence or approach. The same thinking applies to teams and managers: You can try seemingly smart things—in this instance, positioning your fielders where the opposition tends to hit the ball—but nobody will call you smart *unless* it leads to better results.

The Rockies' shifts might not have benefited the team in 2015, but they did benefit Weiss, who found himself retained through the winter. You wonder if Bridich has come to view filling the manager position the same way he views filling his rotation: No qualified, established talent is going to go to a place that routinely makes them look stupid, so the Rockies will have to develop their own if they want to keep pace with everyone else. If so, Weiss might be around to stay.

DETROIT TIGERS

Essay by Rob Arthur

Player comments by Matt Sussman, Craig Goldstein, and BP authors

The Detroit Tigers were once a great team. From 2011-2014, the Tigers posted four straight division-winning seasons, ascending once to the World Series. In that time, the Tigers boasted two Most Valuable Players and 18 All-Star selections, finishing first in their division each year. It's largely the chaos of MLB's short-series playoff system that prevented them from earning a championship.

The Tigers are a great team no more. After a 74-win campaign in 2015, Detroit is saddled with an aging, underperforming core. Nor is help on the way: between an exhausted farm system and a $170 million payroll, the Tigers cannot count on serious reinforcements by way of prospects or from free agency. The future is not bright.

Although their current window is closing, the Tigers have a crucial ingredient that may enable them to avoid the downside of the competitive cycle: money. The Tigers were once a great team, and may soon be again.

The Competitive Cycle

Embedded in the notion of a championship window is the idea that strong performance over a series of years necessarily entails a cost to the future. What goes up, must come down: the best teams in year one become ground under the wheel of competitive balance into the worst teams in year three (or five, or seven, and so on). A team like the Tigers, who enjoyed a period of strong contention, will have to pay their dues in the basement in order to return.

We've seen successful applications of this theory in several recent rebuilds. The Cubs and Astros were surprise playoff contenders this year, after going through extended spells of putrid performance that enabled them to build prospects and develop undervalued players. Conversely, we've witnessed teams like the Phillies try to delay the inevitable closing of the championship window, only to end prolonging the misery of the rebuild.

The competitive cycle exists because teams often have to balance choices which prioritize current versus future value. Teams on the edge of contention have a strong incentive to make decisions that expedite wins now over wins in the future. There are many ways to do so.

Former Tigers GM Dave Dombrowski was famous for trading away prospects to acquire veterans. Since prospects are cheap but mostly contribute in subsequent

TIGERS PROSPECTUS

2015 W-L: 74-87, 5th in AL Central

Pythag	.425	27th	DER	.702	17th
RS/G	4.25	15th	B-Age	28.4	17th
RA/G	4.96	28th	P-Age	28.8	22nd
TAv	.262	14th	Salary	$172.8M	5th
BRR	-21.86	29th	M$/MW	$6.2M	3rd
TAv-P	.272	26th	DL Days	645	4th
FIP	4.43	28th	$ on DL	20%	21st

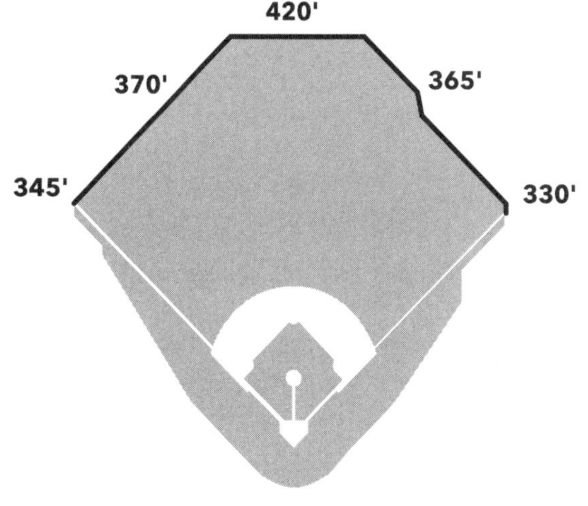

Outfield wall profile: **6'10"** to **14'**

Three-Year Park Factors

Runs	Runs/RH	Runs/LH	HR/RH	HR/LH
103	115	111	105	103

Top Hitter WARP	4.8	Miguel Cabrera
Top Pitcher WARP	3.8	Justin Verlander
Top Prospect	Michael Fulmer	

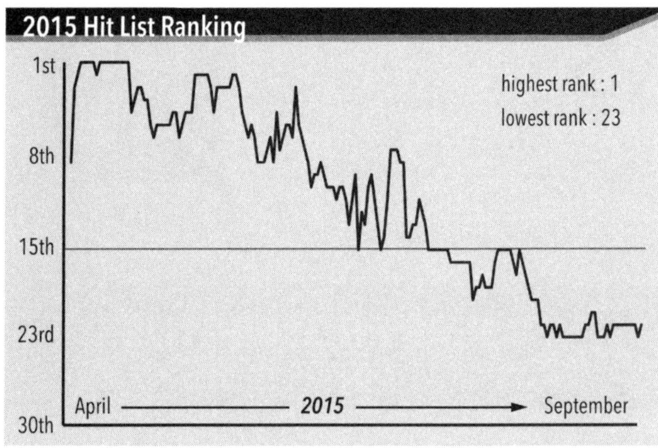

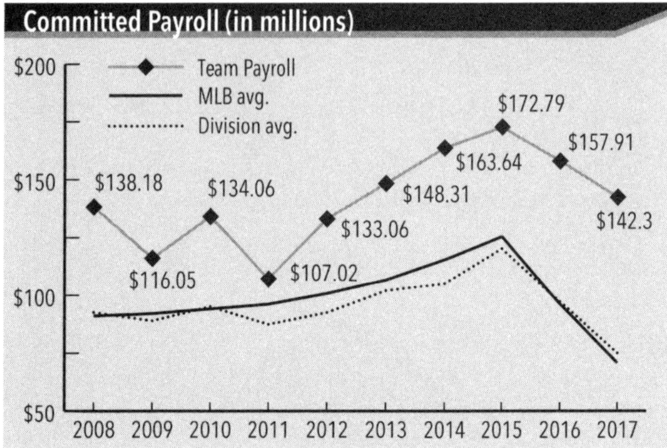

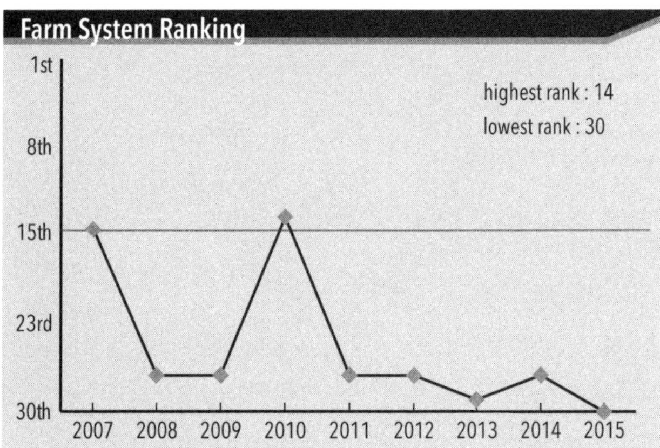

Personnel

General Manager: Al Avila

Assistant General Manager: David Chadd

Assistant General Manager: John Westhoff

Manager: Brad Ausmus

Baseball Prospectus Alumni

Andrew Koo

years—whereas veterans are expensive contributors available now—this tactic was an obvious exchange of future for present value. Dombrowski's penchant for prospect swaps had devastating effects on the farm system. At the beginning of the 2015 season, the Tigers' farm ranked last in all of baseball, according to both Baseball America and Baseball Prospectus. Trade deadline deals boosted that system and got an early start on the rebuilding, but even with the added prospects, this farm is not especially good.

Another mechanism leading to the Tigers downfall was their fondness for expensive extensions. Like most big contracts, these served to lock up talent at affordable rates in the short term while paying too much on the back end of the deal. Two contracts stand out in that regard, for their magnitude in both dollars and time: the Justin Verlander and Miguel Cabrera extensions. Each player is a former MVP, and while both had solid seasons in 2015, neither is likely to have their best days ahead. And yet, both are owed at least $28 million a year into the 2020s, at which point we can't expect them to be much more than marginal players.

On top of the bad contracts and the inferior farm, the Tigers dealt with front office turnover, losing top-notch general manager and noted trade wizard Dave Dombrowski. While Dombrowski was largely responsible for getting Detroit into the mess in which they now find themselves, he also built the competitive core of Detroit's roster and was well on his way to revitalizing the farm when he left. Many of the most toxic free agent extensions and contracts were reportedly foisted upon him by ownership, a challenge the next regime will struggle to negotiate as deftly as Dombrowski did. Al Avila, Dombrowski's replacement, could be just as good, but he's unlikely to be substantially better, and so this replacement must be counted as a net negative.

Foretelling The Tigers' Future

There's no question that Detroit is currently in a bad way. Less clear is their fate going forward: are they destined to suffer the downside of the competitive cycle, and if so, how long will it take for them to return to relevance?

I looked for comparable teams to the 2015 edition of the Detroit Tigers, going back to 1988. In order to find teams with a closed championship window, I limited my search to only losing seasons in which the team possessed a farm system ranked in the bottom third of the league by Baseball America.

On average, such teams do not fare well in the following term (Graph 1). The median winning percentage over the next five years is .471, for a 74-win pace over a full year. Such a season makes for some hard watching, often with nary a hope of contention. It takes 12 full years for the median winning percentage to rise over .500, which is an awful long time to wait from a fan's perspective.

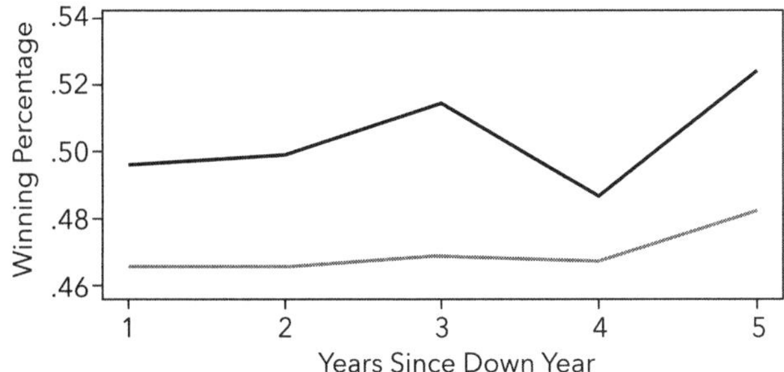

Some of this delay is undoubtedly due to front office turnover, as teams gamble on unproven GMs only to discard them when they make mistakes. This turnover effectively restarts the rebuild over again. Unfortunately, that's a risk the Tigers are taking in Avila, and since GM skill is so hard to measure, we will not know whether the new front office is any good for several years.

So at first glance, it appears that the Tigers are in bad shape going into the future. But they have money working in their favor. Over the last decade, the Tigers have had the 6th-highest normalized payroll in the league, behind only the Yankees, Red Sox, Dodgers, Phillies, and Angels. Detroit has consistently spent more than even some teams we tend to consider big market forces, like the Cubs and Mets.

The relative wealth of the Tigers grants them a measure of contention that other rebuilding teams do not have. Let's add an additional criterion to the list I mentioned above: that a team has to have a payroll 0.5 standard deviations above the average. This constraint gives us a list of 19 team-seasons, including most recently the 2013-2014 Philadelphia Phillies.

Intuitively, you might imagine that a team with an inadequate farm system and a losing record which still managed to spend a bit more than average would be in even worse shape. But that's not the case: in the very next year, and in dramatic contrast to the poorer teams in Graph 1, these wealthy teams tended to rebound to almost 81 wins. In three of the next four years, the median performance of the wealthy teams breaks .500.

Granted, teams which spend more tend to win more games generally. But that isn't enough to account for the way rich teams bounce back so rapidly from bad seasons. By Year Five following a 2015-Tigers-like season, the wealthy teams are only two wins shy of their overall average performance—basically, they are back to normal.

So although rich teams go through competitive cycles like all franchises, they aren't nearly as severe. Whereas for all teams those cycles tend to lead to multiple years of sub-.500 futility, rich teams tend to rise towards mediocrity immediately. Their competitive cycles not only start from a higher point, they are also more rapid.

In addition to the obvious ability to afford marquee free agents like Jordan Zimmerman, there are several reasons rich teams do not suffer oscillations on the same scale. Wealthy outfits can leverage their larger payrolls to build prospect depth faster. One way to do this is by taking on the anchor contracts of other teams in exchange for younger depth. Another is through savvy high-risk, high-reward signings, a tactic the Chicago Cubs employed several times to acquire some notable breakout players (e.g. Jake Arrieta and Pedro Strop for Scott Feldman and Steve Clevenger).

It's worth noting that Dombrowski didn't employ these strategies in his tenure as GM, opting instead for brilliant trades and pricy free agents. But the Tigers are clearly entering a new era, both in terms of management and championship aspirations. Avila is not guaranteed to be anything like Dombrowski in this novel situation, and has the flexibility to employ a different set of tactics.

More speculatively, rich teams may be better able to attract the best and brightest GM candidates. Often—as we saw with the Dodgers (Andrew Friedman) and Red Sox (Dombrowski's new home)—wealthy owners are able to poach the most successful GMs from down-market franchises. That the moneyed teams get their pick of front offices may enable them to more quickly find reliable and competent management, which is ultimately what propels teams out of the bottom of a competitive cycle. This last hypothesis probably doesn't apply to the Tigers, who opted to promote their GM from within rather than appropriate a successful front office from without.

Will the Tigers Keep Spending?

Detroit's current payroll makes them able to bear a set of millstone contracts and still compete with the most affluent teams in the league for free agents, but Tigers owner Mike Ilitch wasn't always so willing to spend. Since he bought the team in 1992, the Tigers have tended to run a much tighter ship, putting them 15th in MLB in spending over that longer timespan.

That's more along the lines of the Seattle Mariners than the Chicago Cubs. It's also more in line with Detroit's market size, which ranks between 12th and 15th in the league, depending on whose numbers you consult. If the team's fortunes fall, and the gate receipts begin to dry up, Ilitch could decide to withdraw some of the Tigers' spending power, which would have a disastrous effect on their ability to retool. Alternatively, if Ilitch passes away, a new ownership may be less willing to spend.

Predicting the actions of the kind of eccentric billionaire who owns a sports team is difficult enough without complications, but in this case, there are several additional factors which play a role. Ilitch's health may be failing, and he put a strong premium on seeing this team's core come to championship fruition. How those opposing motivations resolve themselves may determine Detroit's 2016-2020 budgets, and consequentially how long they remain in the cellar.

Whatever becomes of the Tigers—and we have little knowledge of what will—the current core of the roster will be celebrated for years to come. Although not a dynasty in any strict sense of the word, Dombrowski's Tigers were a formidable team, year in and year out. There's a special joy in seeing a roster with a well-constructed core excel for several years in a row, and that is almost certainly over for now. But provided Ilitch continues to spend, we may yet see the Tigers in contention while Cabrera and Verlander are still playing. ■

Thanks to Ben Lindbergh and Rob McQuown for assembling the underlying data used in this article.

—Rob Arthur is a Chicago-based contributor to FiveThirtyEight whose work has appeared in ESPN The Magazine *and* Slate.

Hitters

Mike Aviles 3B

Born: 3/13/81 Age: 35 Bats: R Throws: R Height: 5'10" Weight: 205

YEAR	TEAM	LVL	AGE	PA	R	2B	3B	HR	RBI	BB	K	SB	CS	AVG/OBP/SLG	TAv	BABIP	BRR	FRAA	WARP
2013	CLE	MLB	32	394	54	15	0	9	46	15	41	8	5	.252/.282/.368	.241	.257	1.4	3B(56): -2.0, SS(46): -0.3	0.5
2014	CLE	MLB	33	374	38	16	1	5	39	13	49	14	5	.247/.273/.343	.230	.271	2.0	3B(36): -0.6, 2B(33): 2.8	0.1
2015	CLE	MLB	34	317	37	10	0	5	17	20	38	3	1	.231/.282/.317	.208	.250	-0.7	LF(34): 0.4, 3B(28): 0.9	-0.4
2016	*DET*	*MLB*	*35*	*106*	*11*	*4*	*0*	*2*	*10*	*5*	*14*	*2*	*1*	*.244/.277/.356*	*.223*	*.260*	*0.2*	*SS 0, 3B -0*	*0.0*
2017	*DET*	*MLB*	*36*	*170*	*16*	*7*	*1*	*3*	*16*	*7*	*24*	*3*	*2*	*.237/.269/.340*	*.216*	*.256*	*0.4*	*SS 0, 3B 0*	*-0.2*

Breakout: 0% Improve: 30% Collapse: 11% Attrition: 23% MLB: 76% *Comparables: Jack Wilson, Jerry Hairston, John McDonald*

By True Average, Aviles was the fifth-worst hitter in baseball with 300 or more plate appearances last season. The only remedy to this kind of inefficacy? *Stop giving Mike Aviles so many plate appearances*. He hasn't posted a decent on-base percentage since 2010, and his calling card ability to fill in at many positions isn't as rare as it once was. (Fourteen other ballplayers made multiple appearances at five or more positions in 2015.) Is Aviles good for a clubhouse? Sure: The way the Indians rallied around Mike and his leukemia-diagnosed daughter last season was wonderful to watch. Is he still capable of helping a team on the field? Probably not.

Miguel Cabrera 1B

Born: 4/18/83 Age: 33 Bats: R Throws: R Height: 6'4" Weight: 240

YEAR	TEAM	LVL	AGE	PA	R	2B	3B	HR	RBI	BB	K	SB	CS	AVG/OBP/SLG	TAv	BABIP	BRR	FRAA	WARP
2013	DET	MLB	30	652	103	26	1	44	137	90	94	3	0	.348/.442/.636	.372	.356	-3.0	3B(145): -13.2	7.9
2014	DET	MLB	31	685	101	52	1	25	109	60	117	1	1	.313/.371/.524	.308	.346	3.0	1B(126): 8.3, 3B(10): 0.3	5.5
2015	DET	MLB	32	511	64	28	1	18	76	77	82	1	1	.338/.440/.534	.333	.384	-3.0	1B(107): 6.9	4.8
2016	*DET*	*MLB*	*33*	*622*	*87*	*35*	*2*	*28*	*97*	*76*	*99*	*2*	*1*	*.317/.402/.542*	*.326*	*.342*	*-0.9*	*1B 6*	*5.9*
2017	*DET*	*MLB*	*34*	*518*	*77*	*28*	*1*	*21*	*76*	*58*	*88*	*0*	*0*	*.302/.383/.510*	*.309*	*.332*	*-1.0*	*1B 5*	*4.0*

Breakout: 2% Improve: 19% Collapse: 7% Attrition: 10% MLB: 98% *Comparables: Albert Pujols, David Ortiz, Lance Berkman*

You are going to be defined by your greatest accomplishment, and whenever your current accomplishment is inferior to your greatest, people aren't going to care very much. This is the unwavering cruelty of public opinion: We're never happy, and the former MVP and Triple Crown–doffing Cabrera must have gone off the grid with a down year. He was displaced to the disabled list for the first time in his 13-year career, missing almost two months with a calf strain. The decline in his power motored the aging husk of a last-place team. We're all just a bunch of Regina Georges, because despite the bad news, Cabrera still won the MLB batting title and led the AL in on-base percentage. He now has an identical OPS+ to Joe DiMaggio (in an identical number of seasons) and with one more good year he is going to reach 2,500 hits, 500 doubles and 1,000 walks to go along with the 400 homers he's already amassed.

But there's little disagreement about his status among the great hitters in history, and his career numbers will compile in due time. The challenges lie in the eight more guaranteed years on his ginormous contract. Like a TV drama in its second decade, the groundwork has already been laid for Miguel Cabrera, Hall of Famer, but past greatness doesn't provide present production. The cast of characters around him has shifted, and the central plot is no longer Cabrera versus pitchers (he won that war), but Cabrera versus his own mortality. It's almost impossible to expect his strong but round frame to play in mint condition moving forward, and Cabreraheads are always going to prefer the early years, so let's treat the rest of his career as a spinoff and find out if this rare baseball talent reaches the final season of his deal before bowing out of the sport as a broken-down heap of confusing plots and escalating tragedy.

Nick Castellanos 3B

Born: 3/4/92 Age: 24 Bats: R Throws: R Height: 6'4" Weight: 210

YEAR	TEAM	LVL	AGE	PA	R	2B	3B	HR	RBI	BB	K	SB	CS	AVG/OBP/SLG	TAv	BABIP	BRR	FRAA	WARP
2013	TOL	AAA	21	595	81	37	1	18	76	54	100	4	1	.276/.343/.450	.282	.307	-0.6	LF(130): 3.1	3.0
2013	DET	MLB	21	18	1	0	0	0	0	0	1	0	0	.278/.278/.278	.206	.294	-0.1	LF(9): -1.0	-0.2
2014	DET	MLB	22	579	50	31	4	11	66	36	140	2	2	.259/.306/.394	.254	.326	-3.0	3B(145): -1.9	1.0
2015	DET	MLB	23	595	42	33	6	15	73	39	152	0	3	.255/.303/.419	.251	.322	-2.4	3B(145): 2.1	1.3
2016	*DET*	*MLB*	*24*	*583*	*58*	*31*	*4*	*15*	*68*	*40*	*132*	*2*	*2*	*.259/.310/.414*	*.255*	*.314*	*-1.8*	*3B -2*	*0.9*
2017	*DET*	*MLB*	*25*	*565*	*66*	*29*	*3*	*15*	*65*	*41*	*127*	*2*	*2*	*.257/.311/.413*	*.257*	*.309*	*-1.8*	*3B -2*	*0.9*

Breakout: 5% Improve: 53% Collapse: 4% Attrition: 6% MLB: 98% *Comparables: Alex Gordon, Mike Moustakas, Edwin Encarnacion*

The defensive metrics agree that Castellanos improved from 2014; only FRAA thinks he was above average in 2015, but only FRAA didn't find him a literal butcher playing the position with ham hocks and knives instead of a glove in the first place. The eye test says FRAA has rose-colored glasses: The former top-40 prospect noticeably improved his range from "statue" to "someone pushing a statue on a dolly." Gold Gloves are not in this man's future, but every made play will help excuse him for not hitting .300 yet. Speaking of his bat (the whole reason he was ranked as a prospect in the first place), he's not showing great progress swinging the stick, but when he does make contact he's an all-fields hitter, and more power looks to be on its way. This season being his final pre-arbitration year would be a good time to hold onto his defensive gains while making the next leap with the bat; the so-called "platform season" is very important.

Harold Castro 2B

Born: 11/30/93 Age: 22 Bats: L Throws: R Height: 6'0" Weight: 165

YEAR	TEAM	LVL	AGE	PA	R	2B	3B	HR	RBI	BB	K	SB	CS	AVG/OBP/SLG	TAv	BABIP	BRR	FRAA	WARP
2013	WMI	A	19	153	17	7	1	1	11	2	40	5	1	.231/.240/.313	.202	.308	-0.2	2B(40): 5.3	0.0
2013	LAK	A+	19	80	8	2	1	0	11	5	22	3	2	.274/.316/.329	.267	.385	-0.4	2B(21): -2.2	0.0
2014	WMI	A	20	83	8	5	0	0	3	5	7	3	2	.250/.304/.319	.224	.273	0.3	2B(11): 0.8	0.0
2014	LAK	A+	20	232	17	5	0	0	10	9	40	8	8	.299/.335/.322	.251	.366	-1.9	2B(48): -0.9, 3B(7): -0.1	0.1
2015	ERI	AA	21	363	41	12	2	1	26	14	63	17	9	.256/.283/.313	.226	.306	-1.7	2B(59): -3.0, SS(22): 1.9	-0.4
2016	*DET*	*MLB*	*22*	*250*	*25*	*9*	*1*	*2*	*17*	*8*	*61*	*7*	*4*	*.229/.255/.308*	*.198*	*.288*	*0.0*	*2B -0, 3B -0*	*-0.7*
2017	*DET*	*MLB*	*23*	*366*	*33*	*14*	*2*	*4*	*30*	*13*	*83*	*11*	*6*	*.238/.267/.324*	*.210*	*.294*	*0.7*	*2B -1, 3B 0*	*-0.6*

Breakout: 1% Improve: 10% Collapse: 0% Attrition: 8% MLB: 10% *Comparables: Hernan Perez, Charlie Culberson, Nick Noonan*

Last year's comment for Castro ended with "this is a prospect." That holds true today, but only in a technical sense: His rookie eligibility is intact. In an evaluative sense, he's much more of an organizational player. True, he reached Double-A at 21, but he hasn't reached league-average production on offense in any stop since Rookie ball in 2012. Castro's below-average arm limits him to the right side of the infield, and anyone dreaming of a transition to the outfield should note that he's more agile than he is fast. His bottom-of-the-scale power makes his upside that of an empty-average wizard; while there is a place for those guys in the majors, his low-energy style makes his odds of reaching his ceiling seem poor.

Tyler Collins OF

Born: 6/6/90 Age: 26 Bats: L Throws: L Height: 5'11" Weight: 215

YEAR	TEAM	LVL	AGE	PA	R	2B	3B	HR	RBI	BB	K	SB	CS	AVG/OBP/SLG	TAv	BABIP	BRR	FRAA	WARP
2013	ERI	AA	23	530	67	29	0	21	79	51	122	4	5	.240/.323/.438	.282	.277	0.9	LF(88): -4.5, RF(18): -1.5	1.7
2014	DET	MLB	24	25	3	0	0	1	4	1	4	0	0	.250/.280/.375	.229	.263	-0.4	LF(5): -0.1, RF(5): -0.3	-0.1
2014	TOL	AAA	24	526	63	17	2	18	62	49	116	12	4	.263/.335/.423	.259	.310	-1.8	LF(92): -0.8, RF(22): 2.5	1.0
2015	TOL	AAA	25	218	21	10	0	2	20	22	40	9	2	.247/.330/.332	.243	.298	1.1	LF(17): 0.9, RF(17): 1.4	0.2
2015	DET	MLB	25	207	18	11	3	4	25	13	43	2	1	.266/.316/.417	.255	.324	0.0	LF(37): 1.9, RF(7): -1.2	0.4
2016	*DET*	*MLB*	*26*	*295*	*32*	*12*	*1*	*9*	*35*	*22*	*70*	*4*	*2*	*.240/.301/.396*	*.246*	*.288*	*-0.2*	*LF 0, RF 0*	*0.5*
2017	*DET*	*MLB*	*27*	*402*	*47*	*16*	*2*	*12*	*46*	*31*	*98*	*5*	*2*	*.235/.298/.389*	*.244*	*.285*	*-0.2*	*LF 0, RF 0*	*0.5*

Breakout: 9% Improve: 22% Collapse: 9% Attrition: 26% MLB: 54% *Comparables: Brandon Jones, Alfredo Marte, Xavier Paul*

The door hasn't slammed on Collins' face as a starter, but he does have "fourth outfielder" scrawled across his forehead. Last year he spelled an injured Victor Martinez as DH against right-handers, then was called back up to replace Yoenis Cespedes on the roster. The native Texan gives maximum effort every time he steps on the dirt (making him a manager's dream), but sometimes that's too much, resulting in overaggressive gambits at the plate, in the field and on the basepaths. Assuming he can regulate his head of steam and defend like a defensive replacement should, Collins should be a dependable bench guy whose name any manager would enjoy calling out.

Michael Gerber RF

Born: 7/8/92 Age: 23 Bats: L Throws: R Height: 6'2" Weight: 175

YEAR	TEAM	LVL	AGE	PA	R	2B	3B	HR	RBI	BB	K	SB	CS	AVG/OBP/SLG	TAv	BABIP	BRR	FRAA	WARP
2014	ONE	A-	21	243	40	16	4	7	37	17	48	8	4	.286/.354/.493	.309	.335	1.5	RF(52): 0.1, CF(1): -0.0	1.9
2014	WMI	A	21	35	4	3	0	0	5	4	3	1	0	.387/.457/.484	.298	.429	0.2	RF(6): 1.1, LF(2): -0.5	0.3
2015	WMI	A	22	583	74	31	10	13	76	49	97	16	4	.292/.355/.468	.301	.330	-0.2	RF(80): -1.1, LF(3): -0.7	3.4
2016	*DET*	*MLB*	*23*	*250*	*24*	*11*	*2*	*6*	*28*	*14*	*61*	*2*	*1*	*.233/.282/.381*	*.232*	*.284*	*0.0*	*RF 2, CF -0*	*0.1*
2017	*DET*	*MLB*	*24*	*379*	*42*	*17*	*4*	*10*	*42*	*25*	*90*	*3*	*1*	*.240/.296/.397*	*.244*	*.292*	*0.1*	*RF 4, CF 0*	*0.7*

Breakout: 2% Improve: 5% Collapse: 2% Attrition: 4% MLB: 10% *Comparables: Andrew Lambo, J.D. Martinez, Matt Joyce*

Drafted in in the 15th round in 2014, Gerber didn't experience many growing pains transitioning to the minors. His stats have been there the whole time, but the Tigers had to spoon-feed him some adjustments. Gerber shortened his swing upon turning pro, and while there's still length to it, baby steps do constitute progress. Despite the shorter hack there's still juice in his bat, as he can mash to the pull side. Gerber is stretched in center and might not have the stick for a corner outfield spot, but he's good enough to provide insurance at all three positions, *i.e.* he profiles as a fourth outfielder. We just hope he's not the butt of infantile jokes in the locker room.

Anthony Gose CF

Born: 8/10/90 Age: 25 Bats: L Throws: L Height: 6'1" Weight: 190

YEAR	TEAM	LVL	AGE	PA	R	2B	3B	HR	RBI	BB	K	SB	CS	AVG/OBP/SLG	TAv	BABIP	BRR	FRAA	WARP
2013	TOR	MLB	22	153	15	6	5	2	12	5	37	4	3	.259/.283/.408	.233	.333	0.0	CF(34): -1.8, LF(15): 0.2	-0.2
2013	BUF	AAA	22	448	64	17	6	3	27	38	121	22	13	.239/.316/.336	.233	.336	4.0	CF(85): -1.0, RF(14): 1.8	0.6
2014	TOR	MLB	23	274	31	8	1	2	13	25	74	15	5	.226/.311/.293	.227	.317	4.3	CF(65): -1.5, RF(14): 0.3	0.2
2014	BUF	AAA	23	224	29	5	2	4	25	17	65	21	8	.244/.305/.346	.222	.338	1.4	CF(31): 2.2, RF(18): -0.1	0.0
2015	DET	MLB	24	535	73	24	8	5	26	45	145	23	11	.254/.321/.367	.248	.352	2.6	CF(137): 1.7	1.5
2016	*DET*	*MLB*	*25*	*639*	*78*	*23*	*9*	*6*	*45*	*50*	*173*	*31*	*13*	*.240/.306/.343*	*.233*	*.326*	*2.9*	*CF -0*	*0.7*
2017	*DET*	*MLB*	*26*	*537*	*54*	*20*	*7*	*6*	*47*	*43*	*144*	*26*	*11*	*.238/.305/.344*	*.235*	*.322*	*3.8*	*CF 0*	*0.8*

Breakout: 5% Improve: 57% Collapse: 6% Attrition: 20% MLB: 85% *Comparables: Felix Pie, Michael Saunders, Jordan Schafer*

Numbers don't lie, except sometimes defensive metrics. They label Gose as a poor, or at best average, defender, but watch a week of him roving around center and you might expect the spreadsheet's nose to start growing. The only new-age metric that commended him was Statcast's route efficiency. What gives? Consider that Gose's predecessor, Austin Jackson, had a reputation beyond the numbers, and that once he played in Seattle for a while those numbers shot up. Same with Curtis Granderson before that. Perhaps Comerica Park, which has the deepest center field this side of Tal's Hill, is hindering the advanced defensive matrix beyond what park adjustments are capable of catching? The numbers are lying; Gose is a superior defender. His batting line is absolutely telling the truth, however, and perhaps too brutally.

Derek Hill CF

Born: 12/30/95 Age: 20 Bats: R Throws: R Height: 6'2" Weight: 195

YEAR	TEAM	LVL	AGE	PA	R	2B	3B	HR	RBI	BB	K	SB	CS	AVG/OBP/SLG	TAv	BABIP	BRR	FRAA	WARP
2014	ONE	A-	18	78	8	1	1	0	3	2	26	2	1	.203/.244/.243	.178	.313	0.0		0.0
2015	WMI	A	19	235	33	6	5	0	16	20	44	25	7	.238/.305/.314	.258	.298	1.2	CF(51): 2.8	1.1
2016	*DET*	*MLB*	*20*	*250*	*30*	*9*	*2*	*3*	*17*	*15*	*65*	*14*	*5*	*.217/.264/.313*	*.210*	*.282*	*1.2*	*CF -1*	*-0.4*
2017	*DET*	*MLB*	*21*	*311*	*30*	*11*	*3*	*4*	*26*	*21*	*79*	*18*	*7*	*.224/.279/.321*	*.219*	*.290*	*2.4*	*CF -1*	*-0.1*

Breakout: 0% Improve: 0% Collapse: 2% Attrition: 2% MLB: 2% *Comparables: Anthony Gose, Andrew McCutchen, Mason Williams*

It should come as no surprise that Hill, the son of Dodgers area scout Orsino Hill, is viewed as a natural, instinctive player; it is the family business after all. Despite the inborn talent and professional upbringing, Hill hasn't exactly been a monster to this point as a pro. It's reasonable to expect the Tigers to continue to take it slow with one of the few prospects in the system with legitimate upside. A gifted defender with plus-plus speed, Hill covers large swaths of ground in center and regularly earns rave reviews there. He is less polished at the plate, but projects to have an average hit tool. He has strong hands, but he gets them high pre-swing and lacks leverage, opting for a line-drive stroke rather than muscling up. The bag, in other words, is mixed, but you can count on no hands the number of 20-year-olds, in baseball or out, for whom that's not true.

Jose Iglesias SS

Born: 1/5/90 Age: 26 Bats: R Throws: R Height: 5'11" Weight: 185

YEAR	TEAM	LVL	AGE	PA	R	2B	3B	HR	RBI	BB	K	SB	CS	AVG/OBP/SLG	TAv	BABIP	BRR	FRAA	WARP
2013	BOS	MLB	23	234	27	10	2	1	19	11	30	3	1	.330/.376/.409	.285	.376	0.1	3B(34): -0.7, SS(29): 1.0	1.5
2013	PAW	AAA	23	133	17	2	0	4	15	9	18	5	3	.202/.262/.319	.203	.204	1.2	SS(32): 1.4, 3B(1): -0.1	0.0
2013	DET	MLB	23	148	12	6	0	2	10	4	30	2	1	.259/.306/.348	.236	.320	-0.4	SS(42): 2.2, 3B(3): 0.5	0.5
2015	DET	MLB	25	454	44	17	3	2	23	25	44	11	8	.300/.347/.370	.252	.330	-4.3	SS(119): -6.6	0.4
2016	*DET*	*MLB*	*26*	*527*	*52*	*19*	*3*	*4*	*43*	*28*	*72*	*11*	*6*	*.268/.315/.347*	*.239*	*.300*	*-2.4*	*SS -2*	*0.9*
2017	*DET*	*MLB*	*27*	*527*	*54*	*19*	*3*	*5*	*46*	*27*	*74*	*11*	*6*	*.268/.313/.354*	*.241*	*.300*	*-1.9*	*SS -2*	*1.1*

Breakout: 4% Improve: 45% Collapse: 13% Attrition: 21% MLB: 90% *Comparables: Emmanuel Burriss, Dee Gordon, Eduardo Nunez*

Good things come to shortstops who wait, and Iglesias waited a year with shin injuries to get back and reel off those flashy plays. While the metrics weren't impressed, Iglesias' reputation has superseded the numbers. He may lack the range of Andrelton Simmons or Brandon Crawford, but his arm is no joke; anyone who has seen him make a strong throw with merely a flick of his wrist can verify that. His shins are great, too, and that he was able to last the whole year (until a finger injury shut his September down) is proof he'll be fine in the long run. He was also an All-Star last year, driven by the facet of his game always thought to be a question mark: his hitting. A .314 first-half average turned him into a reliable no. 9 hitter, though the only people who rely more on singles than Iglesias does are exotic dancers.

Jacoby Jones SS

Born: 5/10/92 Age: 24 Bats: R Throws: R Height: 6'2" Weight: 205

YEAR	TEAM	LVL	AGE	PA	R	2B	3B	HR	RBI	BB	K	SB	CS	AVG/OBP/SLG	TAv	BABIP	BRR	FRAA	WARP
2013	JAM	A-	21	67	14	2	2	1	10	3	14	3	2	.311/.358/.459	.329	.383	1.9	CF(10): -0.8, SS(5): -0.3	0.8
2014	WVA	A	22	501	72	21	3	23	70	33	132	17	9	.288/.347/.503	.291	.352	5.7	SS(99): 4.1	4.6
2015	BRD	A+	23	423	48	18	3	10	58	31	113	14	4	.253/.313/.396	.261	.330	-1.8	SS(84): 11.0	2.7
2015	ERI	AA	23	160	26	7	2	6	20	17	52	10	3	.250/.331/.463	.282	.337	1.5	SS(37): 3.6	1.6
2016	*DET*	*MLB*	*24*	*250*	*31*	*9*	*2*	*8*	*26*	*15*	*83*	*6*	*2*	*.222/.274/.383*	*.230*	*.299*	*0.4*	*SS 3, 3B 0*	*0.8*
2017	*DET*	*MLB*	*25*	*347*	*38*	*13*	*2*	*11*	*39*	*20*	*115*	*8*	*3*	*.220/.271/.375*	*.228*	*.299*	*0.9*	*SS 4, 3B 0*	*1.0*

Breakout: 2% Improve: 13% Collapse: 11% Attrition: 17% MLB: 27% *Comparables: Zach Walters, Brandon Hicks, Brandon Wood*

Acquired for Joakim Soria, Jones has more tools than Tinder. He's a big-time athlete, complete with above-average speed and raw power (though consistency eludes him). He's able to differentiate between which pitches are DTF (down to fly) and which are just teases, and he certainly enjoys rounding the bases when he makes a connection, but he swings through too many pitches in the zone to post a high average. Predictably, pictures of him playing the middle infield are carefully chosen to hide the stiffness and clumsiness that might keep him from playing shortstop full time down the line. That said, if you're looking for a guy with a power stroke who can fill multiple positions, feel free to swipe right.

Ian Kinsler 2B

Born: 6/22/82 Age: 34 Bats: R Throws: R Height: 6'0" Weight: 200

YEAR	TEAM	LVL	AGE	PA	R	2B	3B	HR	RBI	BB	K	SB	CS	AVG/OBP/SLG	TAv	BABIP	BRR	FRAA	WARP
2013	TEX	MLB	31	614	85	31	2	13	72	51	59	15	11	.277/.344/.413	.291	.288	3.5	2B(124): 13.5	5.4
2014	DET	MLB	32	726	100	40	4	17	92	29	79	15	4	.275/.307/.420	.256	.288	3.0	2B(160): 3.1	2.4
2015	DET	MLB	33	675	94	35	7	11	73	43	80	10	6	.296/.342/.428	.269	.323	2.1	2B(153): -0.2	2.7
2016	*DET*	*MLB*	*34*	*637*	*78*	*32*	*4*	*13*	*61*	*49*	*76*	*13*	*6*	*.264/.326/.405*	*.261*	*.281*	*2.3*	*2B 6*	*3.6*
2017	*DET*	*MLB*	*35*	*547*	*61*	*26*	*4*	*10*	*56*	*42*	*67*	*9*	*5*	*.256/.317/.385*	*.252*	*.275*	*2.3*	*2B 5*	*2.5*

Breakout: 1% Improve: 30% Collapse: 11% Attrition: 13% MLB: 90% *Comparables: Mark Loretta, Placido Polanco, Ben Zobrist*

Kinsler's not so old when you consider he's still too young to run for president, but that he was still a first-division second baseman in his 11th season is important because he looked to be burning out a few years ago. Also burning is his plate approach: His entire offensive value, at this point, is tied to batting average, with walks and homers being treated more like bugs than features. The wily veteran is still adding value on the basepaths, though he should be cutting back the steal attempts to just a handful a year. His defense is the subject of statistical controversy, but subjectively, he seemed to pick it with the best of 'em. Of all his abilities, the glove should be the last to wilt. He can probably squeeze out one more above-average year on all fronts before becoming another recognizable name stuck in the bottom of the order who looks good diving for lots of balls and even catching a few.

Jefry Marte 3B

Born: 6/21/91 Age: 25 Bats: R Throws: R Height: 6'1" Weight: 220

YEAR	TEAM	LVL	AGE	PA	R	2B	3B	HR	RBI	BB	K	SB	CS	AVG/OBP/SLG	TAv	BABIP	BRR	FRAA	WARP
2013	MID	AA	22	278	33	17	1	2	28	25	49	8	1	.278/.349/.380	.273	.333	-1.4	3B(47): -6.9, 1B(2): -0.2	0.2
2014	MID	AA	23	460	50	17	0	10	53	45	69	9	3	.259/.333/.375	.268	.286	-1.4	3B(91): 6.5, 1B(3): 0.3	2.3
2015	DET	MLB	24	90	9	4	0	4	11	8	22	0	0	.213/.284/.413	.250	.241	0.2	1B(22): 0.7, 3B(7): 0.6	0.2
2015	TOL	AAA	24	399	49	25	3	15	65	31	64	8	5	.275/.341/.487	.284	.294	-0.4	3B(91): 0.5, 1B(4): -0.1	2.2
2016	*DET*	*MLB*	*25*	*67*	*7*	*3*	*0*	*2*	*8*	*5*	*14*	*1*	*0*	*.246/.307/.398*	*.251*	*.285*	*0.0*	*1B -0*	*0.0*
2017	*DET*	*MLB*	*26*	*307*	*36*	*14*	*1*	*9*	*36*	*22*	*64*	*4*	*2*	*.249/.308/.407*	*.254*	*.289*	*-0.1*	*1B 0*	*0.4*

Breakout: 8% Improve: 15% Collapse: 15% Attrition: 40% MLB: 52% *Comparables: Yamaico Navarro, Jesus Guzman, Matt Carpenter*

Even if he accomplishes little else, Marte will be the answer to the trivia question, "Who was Miguel Cabrera's first DL replacement?" After eight seasons, three organizations and one stint in our Top 100 prospects (seven years ago!), the natural third baseman finally showed enough extra-base clout to be asked to learn major-league first base on the fly. He was passable, albeit with unconventional and exorbitant effort, and at times displayed the footwork of a centipede with vertigo. His primary value to a roster is whacking baseballs thrown by lefties (1.115 OPS in 2015, both levels combined). Now 25, the raw corner-infield project has the career arc of a full-time pinch-hitter, or would have if those still existed.

J.D. Martinez LF

Born: 8/21/87 Age: 28 Bats: R Throws: R Height: 6'3" Weight: 220

YEAR	TEAM	LVL	AGE	PA	R	2B	3B	HR	RBI	BB	K	SB	CS	AVG/OBP/SLG	TAv	BABIP	BRR	FRAA	WARP
2013	CCH	AA	25	20	1	2	0	1	5	0	1	0	0	.300/.300/.550	.287	.278	0.0	LF(2): -0.4, RF(2): -0.3	0.0
2013	HOU	MLB	25	310	24	17	0	7	36	10	82	2	0	.250/.272/.378	.244	.319	-2.3	LF(50): -6.5, RF(25): -2.6	-1.2
2014	TOL	AAA	26	71	16	3	1	10	22	3	17	2	0	.308/.366/.846	.349	.263	-0.5	LF(12): -0.2	0.8
2014	DET	MLB	26	480	57	30	3	23	76	30	126	6	3	.315/.358/.553	.319	.389	0.6	LF(83): -2.1, RF(34): -1.4	3.6
2015	DET	MLB	27	657	93	33	2	38	102	53	178	3	2	.282/.344/.535	.304	.339	-3.9	RF(148): -7.6	2.9
2016	*DET*	*MLB*	*28*	*599*	*71*	*30*	*3*	*23*	*83*	*42*	*144*	*4*	*2*	*.271/.324/.465*	*.276*	*.324*	*-2.0*	*RF -11*	*1.0*
2017	*DET*	*MLB*	*29*	*563*	*73*	*27*	*2*	*21*	*75*	*42*	*135*	*3*	*2*	*.267/.324/.454*	*.274*	*.320*	*-1.9*	*RF -11*	*0.9*

Breakout: 0% Improve: 49% Collapse: 6% Attrition: 9% MLB: 98% *Comparables: Jeremy Hermida, Rocco Baldelli, Brad Hawpe*

Just when we thought 2014 was a breakout/overachievement year, Martinez broke out again in '15; who knows how many more boxes he's trapped inside. The All-Star set the Tigers mark for most home runs in a season by a right fielder, and that was Al Kaline's position. Nine of Martinez's homers were in the eighth inning or later, and 17 of them were to the right of dead center. He is now an elite two-tool player, the second being the throwing arm, one of the most accurate on the corners. He swings far too much to get the OBP beyond .350 and possesses unremarkable speed and defensive range. He cannot carry a lineup, but he can be the Roger Maris. It has now been two years since Martinez was released by the Astros to make room for Robbie Grossman.

Victor Martinez 1B

Born: 12/23/78 Age: 37 Bats: B Throws: R Height: 6'2" Weight: 210

YEAR	TEAM	LVL	AGE	PA	R	2B	3B	HR	RBI	BB	K	SB	CS	AVG/OBP/SLG	TAv	BABIP	BRR	FRAA	WARP
2013	DET	MLB	34	668	68	36	0	14	83	54	62	0	2	.301/.355/.430	.280	.313	-6.2	1B(11): 0.8, C(3): 0.2	1.6
2014	DET	MLB	35	641	87	33	0	32	103	70	42	3	2	.335/.409/.565	.335	.316	-5.9	1B(35): -2.8, C(2): -0.2	4.7
2015	DET	MLB	36	485	39	20	0	11	64	31	52	0	0	.245/.301/.366	.232	.253	-3.5	1B(10): 0.5	-1.2
2016	*DET*	*MLB*	*37*	*608*	*65*	*31*	*2*	*14*	*72*	*49*	*61*	*1*	*1*	*.288/.348/.428*	*.273*	*.299*	*-4.3*		*1.4*
2017	*DET*	*MLB*	*38*	*404*	*46*	*19*	*1*	*8*	*42*	*30*	*44*	*0*	*0*	*.266/.322/.389*	*.253*	*.281*	*-3.0*	-	*0.0*

Breakout: 0% Improve: 19% Collapse: 8% Attrition: 5% MLB: 73% *Comparables: Carlos Lee, Todd Helton, John Olerud*

A year after runnering-up for MVP, Martinez began spring training on the wrong foot, specifically the left one, the accompanying knee of which underwent its second surgery in four years. His bat and body could never recover, and he eventually went on the DL for general healing purposes. That respite had short-term success (.923 OPS over his next 25 games) but his legs eventually wore out in September. The lone bright spot is his high average batting right-handed, although it was mostly singles. (A second bright spot is the $51 million left on his contract. But maybe that's just from his perspective.) Few predicted repeat success from a 30-homer season, but hopes of a David Ortiz–style late-career charge are fading: Ortiz never had a season this bad, and his worst in a Red Sox uniform still featured a .263 TAv. At least V-Mart now knows to start subsequent seasons off on the *right* foot.

Cameron Maybin CF

Born: 4/4/87 Age: 29 Bats: R Throws: R Height: 6'3" Weight: 215

2013	SDN	MLB	26	57	7	1	0	1	5	4	9	4	1	.157/.232/.235	.158	.171	0.8	CF(14): -1.0	-0.4
2013	TUC	AAA	26	56	7	1	0	4	5	10	9	1	1	.261/.393/.543	.338	.242	-0.1	CF(13): -0.4	0.6
2014	ELP	AAA	27	61	8	2	1	1	6	6	10	1	0	.264/.328/.396	.241	.295	-0.7	CF(15): -0.8	-0.1
2014	SDN	MLB	27	272	24	13	4	1	15	19	56	4	3	.235/.290/.331	.233	.297	1.1	CF(86): -4.7	-0.3
2015	ATL	MLB	28	555	65	18	2	10	59	45	102	23	6	.267/.327/.370	.264	.316	3.5	CF(139): 0.8	2.5
2016	*DET*	*MLB*	*29*	*482*	*55*	*19*	*4*	*9*	*46*	*38*	*92*	*16*	*5*	*.255/.315/.378*	*.250*	*.301*	*2.1*		*1.2*
2017	*DET*	*MLB*	*30*	*500*	*55*	*19*	*5*	*9*	*50*	*40*	*101*	*16*	*6*	*.250/.313/.373*	*.248*	*.300*	*2.6*	*LF 0, CF -1*	*1.1*

Breakout: 0% Improve: 48% Collapse: 5% Attrition: 9% MLB: 98% *Comparables: Aaron Rowand, Franklin Gutierrez, Ryan Sweeney*

Poll the Braves on the player who benefited the most from hitting coach Kevin Seitzer's first year with the team and a popular answer is Maybin. The former highly touted prospect and no. 10 overall pick has largely disappointed, putting together just one season (2011) that's come close to fulfilling his lofty scouting reports. He got halfway back in 2015, posting a .774 OPS in the first half, which is basically what MLB first basemen hit in 2015. Unfortunately, his .600 second-half OPS was *well* below what MLB catchers hit. Half splits don't tend to provide much predictive value, so focus instead on Maybin's .264 overall TAv, his success in keeping his swing short and sweet and his first-ever double-digit home run season. The Tigers, who drafted him before sending him away in the Miguel Cabrera trade, will hope he can consolidate, or even build on, his gains even without Seitzer.

James McCann C

Born: 6/13/90 Age: 26 Bats: R Throws: R Height: 6'2" Weight: 210

YEAR	TEAM	LVL	AGE	PA	R	2B	3B	HR	RBI	BB	K	SB	CS	AVG/OBP/SLG	TAv	BABIP	BRR	FRAA	WARP
2013	ERI	AA	23	486	50	30	1	8	54	30	85	3	3	.277/.328/.404	.266	.321	-0.5	C(100): 5.0	2.8
2014	TOL	AAA	24	460	49	34	0	7	54	25	90	9	2	.295/.343/.427	.262	.355	0.7	C(98): 0.6, 3B(1): 0.0	2.3
2014	DET	MLB	24	12	2	1	0	0	0	0	2	1	0	.250/.250/.333	.211	.300	0.1	C(6): -0.3	0.0
2015	DET	MLB	25	425	32	18	5	7	41	16	90	0	1	.264/.297/.387	.230	.325	-4.7	C(112): -17.6	-1.8
2016	*DET*	*MLB*	*26*	*532*	*48*	*28*	*3*	*9*	*55*	*23*	*113*	*3*	*1*	*.258/.296/.380*	*.238*	*.312*	*-3.2*	*C -15*	*-0.9*
2017	*DET*	*MLB*	*27*	*503*	*52*	*25*	*3*	*9*	*50*	*23*	*112*	*2*	*1*	*.251/.291/.375*	*.235*	*.307*	*-3.2*	*C -15*	*-1.1*

Breakout: 5% Improve: 23% Collapse: 18% Attrition: 30% MLB: 66% *Comparables: Tony Cruz, Ronny Paulino, Jeff Mathis*

YEAR	TEAM	P. COUNT	FRM RUNS	BLK RUNS	THRW RUNS	TOT RUNS
2013	ERI	12722	4.9	0.5	0.0	5.5
2014	DET	356	-0.2	0.0	0.0	-0.3
2014	TOL	13647	-4.6	0.3	5.5	1.2
2015	DET	15395	-16.6	0.3	0.8	-15.6
2016	*DET*	*19538*	*-15.9*	*0.3*	*1.7*	*-13.9*
2017	*DET*	*18485*	*-16.2*	*0.3*	*1.5*	*-14.3*

Being good is 70 percent opportunity and 30 percent... well, actually being good. McCann was thrust into the starting role when Alex Avila rusted up for a few weeks, and the athletic backstop did enough impressive things (knocking his fair share of extra-base hits; demonstrating the coveted leadership intangible through a season in which Tigers pitching was far too tangible) to seize the starting job in Detroit, but nowhere near enough impressive things to actually be *good*. The defensive stat you see above is almost entirely framing: On a per-pitch basis, the only worse catchers with a similar amount of playing time in 2015 were Welington Castillo, Carlos Ruiz and Nick Hundley. Even if you're skeptical of these newfangled framing metrics, back them completely out of his WARP and you're still left with a replacement-level player; even for a catcher, that OBP (and consequently that TAv) won't get McCann much more than a participation ribbon. If he hits like he did in Triple-A, we've got a different story; same if he picks up a few catching tips from Brad Ausmus—the data we have on Ausmus, which is limited, suggests that he was a pretty good framer at the tail end of his career. Exercise hope, and exercise skepticism. Both are healthy.

Steven Moya RF

Born: 8/9/91 Age: 24 Bats: L Throws: R Height: 6'7" Weight: 260

YEAR	TEAM	LVL	AGE	PA	R	2B	3B	HR	RBI	BB	K	SB	CS	AVG/OBP/SLG	TAv	BABIP	BRR	FRAA	WARP
2013	LAK	A+	21	388	52	19	5	12	55	18	106	6	0	.255/.296/.433	.254	.327	1.3	RF(78): -5.3	0.0
2014	ERI	AA	22	549	81	33	3	35	105	23	161	16	4	.276/.306/.555	.295	.327	1.4	RF(131): 2.0	3.5
2014	DET	MLB	22	8	2	0	0	0	0	0	2	0	0	.375/.375/.375	.284	.500	0.0	RF(5): -0.2	0.0
2015	TOL	AAA	23	535	53	30	0	20	74	27	162	5	4	.240/.283/.420	.241	.312	-0.5	RF(97): -11.7, LF(13): -0.1	-1.4
2015	LAK	A+	23	42	3	3	0	3	8	1	13	0	0	.275/.286/.575	.291	.320	0.1	RF(9): 0.1	0.2
2015	DET	MLB	23	25	1	0	1	0	0	3	10	0	0	.182/.280/.273	.199	.333	-0.3	RF(5): 0.3, LF(2): 1.7	0.1
2016	*DET*	*MLB*	*24*	*129*	*14*	*6*	*1*	*6*	*17*	*5*	*44*	*1*	*1*	*.229/.260/.425*	*.238*	*.301*	*0.0*	*RF -0*	*-0.1*
2017	*DET*	*MLB*	*25*	*363*	*43*	*17*	*2*	*16*	*49*	*14*	*121*	*4*	*2*	*.231/.266/.430*	*.243*	*.303*	*0.0*	*RF -1*	*0.0*

Breakout: 3% Improve: 10% Collapse: 6% Attrition: 17% MLB: 25% *Comparables: Bryce Brentz, Carlos Peguero, Greg Halman*

Moya's stock took a hard tumble toward the X axis when he couldn't build on his 2014 Eastern League MVP success, or correct any of his obvious flaws. He still strikes out like it's his job, he refuses to take ball four for an answer and the power isn't real enough to justify those two things. Is any of this correctable? For a young man who has trouble protecting the strike zone, being 6-foot-7 is a hindrance; it would take time to learn the McGwire Crouch. Power is this sport's panacea, and there are still enough Moya believers to think he can add depth to an outfield; for the rest he can only add height.

Jarrod Saltalamacchia C

Born: 5/2/85 Age: 31 Bats: B Throws: R Height: 6'4" Weight: 235

YEAR	TEAM	LVL	AGE	PA	R	2B	3B	HR	RBI	BB	K	SB	CS	AVG/OBP/SLG	TAv	BABIP	BRR	FRAA	WARP
2013	BOS	MLB	28	470	68	40	0	14	65	43	139	4	1	.273/.338/.466	.288	.372	0.8	C(119): -4.8	3.1
2014	MIA	MLB	29	435	43	20	0	11	44	55	143	0	1	.220/.320/.362	.258	.317	0.1	C(107): -37.7	-2.3
2015	ARI	MLB	30	194	23	14	0	8	23	19	57	0	0	.251/.332/.474	.280	.327	-0.6	C(38): -7.9, 1B(4): -0.1	0.3
2015	RNO	AAA	30	36	2	0	0	2	7	2	13	0	0	.188/.222/.375	.228	.211	-0.1	C(5): -0.0	0.0
2015	MIA	MLB	30	33	3	1	0	1	1	4	12	0	0	.069/.182/.207	.140	.063	-0.2	C(9): -0.5	-0.3
2016	*DET*	*MLB*	*31*	*104*	*11*	*5*	*0*	*4*	*13*	*10*	*32*	*0*	*0*	*.229/.303/.412*	*.252*	*.303*	*0.0*	*C -6*	*-0.2*
2017	*DET*	*MLB*	*32*	*192*	*23*	*9*	*1*	*7*	*23*	*18*	*60*	*0*	*0*	*.222/.299/.400*	*.247*	*.297*	*-0.1*	*C -10*	*-0.6*

Breakout: 3% Improve: 37% Collapse: 8% Attrition: 12% MLB: 97% *Comparables: Kelly Shoppach, Johnny Bench, Stan Lopata*

The fraternity of thirtysomething catchers is one of noble wanderers who espouse the virtues of intangibles and cool-looking helmets. The sodium-packed backstop has now entered that secret society, thanks to an otherwise forgettable tenure with the Marlins. Following an April in which his hit total equaled his error count, Miami parted ways a day after Salty's paternity leave ended. (He had reportedly declined a DL stint to "work on his swing.") Arizona picked him up because, whoa, did you say you can catch? He'll bring low averages, bad defense and a poor arm to Detroit, but otherwise he's a fine veteran backup.

YEAR	TEAM	P. COUNT	FRM RUNS	BLK RUNS	THRW RUNS	TOT RUNS
2013	BOS	16457	-5.1	0.4	0.0	-4.7
2014	MIA	14700	-34.0	-0.5	-2.4	-36.9
2015	MIA	1187	-0.7	0.0	0.0	-0.7
2015	RNO	659	0.1	0.0	0.0	0.1
2015	ARI	5288	-7.4	0.1	-0.3	-7.6
2016	*DET*	*3698*	*-5.2*	*0.0*	*-0.2*	*-5.4*
2017	*DET*	*6814*	*-9.9*	*0.0*	*-0.5*	*-10.4*

A.J. Simcox SS

Born: 6/22/94 Age: 22 Bats: R Throws: R Height: 6'3" Weight: 185

YEAR	TEAM	LVL	AGE	PA	R	2B	3B	HR	RBI	BB	K	SB	CS	AVG/OBP/SLG	TAv	BABIP	BRR	FRAA	WARP
2015	ONE	A-	21	108	14	5	1	0	12	5	14	5	2	.270/.306/.340	.255	.307	2.0	SS(25): 4.8	1.1
2015	WMI	A	21	91	11	3	0	1	8	5	11	4	2	.400/.440/.471	.323	.452	1.0	SS(20): -0.3	1.1
2016	*DET*	*MLB*	*22*	*250*	*23*	*10*	*1*	*4*	*22*	*10*	*58*	*3*	*2*	*.233/.267/.337*	*.214*	*.288*	*-0.1*	*SS 1*	*0.1*
2017	*DET*	*MLB*	*23*	*299*	*30*	*12*	*2*	*5*	*28*	*13*	*66*	*4*	*2*	*.243/.280/.354*	*.226*	*.297*	*0.0*	*SS 1*	*0.4*

Breakout: 4% Improve: 10% Collapse: 3% Attrition: 9% MLB: 15% *Comparables: Trevor Plouffe, Danny Worth, Hanley Ramirez*

It's not often that 14th-round picks receive mention in the Annual the year they're drafted, but your standard late-round draftee doesn't get a $600,000 signing bonus. Much of that money was earmarked for Nick Shumpert, who ended up declining to sign. Detroit then redirected funds to buy Simcox out of his return to Tennessee, where his father is a coach. Scouts like his chances of sticking at shortstop thanks to smooth actions and an above-average arm. They hate his chances of hitting for power, as there's little loft in his swing. Overall, it's a bit of a toss-up, as some see the hit tool playing above average, while others see it limiting Simcox to second-division starter.

Christin Stewart LF

Born: 12/10/93 Age: 22 Bats: L Throws: R Height: 6'0" Weight: 205

YEAR	TEAM	LVL	AGE	PA	R	2B	3B	HR	RBI	BB	K	SB	CS	AVG/OBP/SLG	TAv	BABIP	BRR	FRAA	WARP
2015	WMI	A	21	216	29	9	4	7	31	18	45	3	2	.286/.375/.492	.316	.338	-0.5	LF(39): -5.8	1.1
2015	ONE	A-	21	59	7	2	2	2	11	5	18	0	0	.245/.322/.490	.315	.313	-0.6	LF(13): -0.2	0.4
2016	*DET*	*MLB*	*22*	*250*	*25*	*9*	*2*	*7*	*27*	*15*	*72*	*0*	*0*	*.217/.279/.369*	*.229*	*.278*	*-0.1*	*LF -3*	*-0.4*
2017	*DET*	*MLB*	*23*	*251*	*28*	*9*	*2*	*7*	*27*	*15*	*73*	*0*	*0*	*.214/.278/.366*	*.230*	*.277*	*-0.2*	*LF -3*	*-0.1*

Breakout: 2% Improve: 7% Collapse: 0% Attrition: 7% MLB: 11% *Comparables: Andrew Lambo, Thomas Neal, Jamie Romak*

One of two first-round picks by Detroit, Stewart's selection likely had long-time draft followers wondering "what just happened?" as he wasn't a hard-throwing right-handed pitcher. A 2015 preseason All-American, "ultra-aggressive" is one way to describe Stewart's approach at the plate. Fans of the walk shouldn't head to the panic room just yet though, as Stewart showed the ability to discern balls from strikes in the lower minors. Defense is a bit of an adventureland, as he's currently limited to left field thanks to a below-average arm. He's on the road to establishing himself as one of Detroit's better prospects, and some might consider him a gift from the twilight of the Dombrowski era.

PITCHERS

Al Alburquerque RHP

Born: 6/10/86 Age: 30 Bats: R Throws: R Height: 6'0" Weight: 195

YEAR	TEAM	LVL	AGE	W	L	SV	G	GS	IP	H	HR	BB/9	K/9	GB%	BABIP	WHIP	ERA	FIP	DRA	WARP	CFIP	MPH
2013	TOL	AAA	27	0	1	1	10	0	14^{1}	9	2	8.2	17.0	17%	.318	1.53	3.14	3.97	4.13	0.1	91	
2013	DET	MLB	27	4	3	0	53	0	49	39	5	6.2	12.9	40%	.312	1.49	4.59	3.75	3.65	0.6	82	97.4
2014	DET	MLB	28	3	1	1	72	0	57^{1}	46	7	3.3	9.9	46%	.275	1.17	2.51	3.81	2.99	1.1	84	96.3
2015	DET	MLB	29	4	1	0	67	0	62	63	4	4.8	8.4	50%	.337	1.55	4.21	3.72	4.03	0.5	101	96.1
2016	*DET*	*MLB*	*30*	*2*	*1*	*0*	*50*	*0*	52^{2}	*49*	*6*	*4.2*	*9.3*	*47%*	*.302*	*1.40*	*4.24*	*4.15*	*4.51*	*0.1*	*100*	
2017	*DET*	*MLB*	*31*	*2*	*1*	*0*	*34*	*0*	31^{2}	*31*	*4*	*4.5*	*9.4*	*47%*	*.306*	*1.46*	*4.48*	*4.40*	*4.76*	*0.0*	*106*	

Breakout: 25% Improve: 46% Collapse: 29% Attrition: 13% MLB: 90% *Comparables: Brian Wilson, Hong-Chih Kuo, Sergio Santos*

Alburquerque proves that even a young pitcher whose upside is limited by a lack of breadth of pitches or a lack of fastball can still carve out a perfectly reasonable career in relief. The Sultan of Slider now has nearly three full seasons under his belt despite a one-note arsenal, banking on that pitch nearly 60 percent of the time historically, though it's worth noting that the usage dipped to a career-low 56 percent last year. The slider's swing-and-miss rate is also in steady decline, and his sinker isn't sinky enough to get him out of trouble; one or the other of those things is going to have to change if he wants to keep carving that career. His arbitration years might also price him out of a job, as cheaper seventh-inning options can be found without too much exertion.

Matt Boyd LHP

Born: 2/2/91 Age: 25 Bats: L Throws: L Height: 6'3" Weight: 215

YEAR	TEAM	LVL	AGE	W	L	SV	G	GS	IP	H	HR	BB/9	K/9	GB%	BABIP	WHIP	ERA	FIP	DRA	WARP	CFIP	MPH
2013	DUN	A+	22	0	2	0	3	2	10	7	2	2.7	9.9	39%	.238	1.00	5.40	4.54	3.98	0.1	90	
2013	LNS	A	22	0	1	0	5	3	14	7	0	0.6	7.7	37%	.184	0.57	0.64	1.84	4.14	0.2	85	
2014	NHP	AA	23	1	4	0	10	10	42^{2}	55	5	2.7	9.3	31%	.379	1.59	6.96	3.94	4.07	0.5	84	
2014	DUN	A+	23	5	3	0	16	16	90^{2}	65	4	2.0	10.2	42%	.270	0.94	1.39	2.49	3.52	1.6	72	
2015	BUF	AAA	24	3	1	0	6	6	39	32	5	1.4	8.5	41%	.260	0.97	2.77	3.46	2.89	0.9	83	
2015	TOR	MLB	24	0	2	0	2	2	6^{2}	15	5	1.4	9.4	43%	.435	2.40	14.85	11.20	15.82	-0.9	106	94.8
2015	NHP	AA	24	6	1	0	12	12	73^{2}	39	3	2.2	8.6	24%	.199	0.77	1.10	2.67	2.34	2.2	74	
2015	DET	MLB	24	1	4	0	11	10	50^{2}	56	12	3.4	6.4	32%	.297	1.48	6.57	5.95	5.44	-0.3	113	94.6
2016	*DET*	*MLB*	*25*	*2*	*3*	*0*	*8*	*8*	42^{1}	*41*	*6*	*2.8*	*7.5*	*33%*	*.290*	*1.29*	*4.39*	*4.42*	*4.66*	*0.2*	*109*	
2017	*DET*	*MLB*	*26*	*4*	*4*	*0*	*13*	*13*	*77*	*74*	*11*	*2.8*	*8.3*	*33%*	*.290*	*1.27*	*4.31*	*4.24*	*4.57*	*0.4*	*106*	

Breakout: 15% Improve: 31% Collapse: 35% Attrition: 31% MLB: 73% *Comparables: Chad Bettis, Hector Noesi, Ramon Ramirez*

You know that dream where you have a 7.53 ERA in your first major-league season, then notice you were in your underwear? Boyd lived half that nightmare, which undercut an otherwise stellar minor-league campaign. His 5.6 hits-per-nine mark doubled when donning a major-league uniform and the homer rate more than quadrupled. Still, the not-ready-for-prime-time player was the penultimate prospect Detroit received in the David Price deal, and even at 25 he has upside. Be it nerves or tight-binding britches, Boyd needs to move the fastball away from the nucleus of the strike zone if he wants back in the rotation.

Beau Burrows RHP

Born: 9/18/96 Age: 19 Bats: R Throws: R Height: 6'2" Weight: 200

YEAR	TEAM	LVL	AGE	W	L	SV	G	GS	IP	H	HR	BB/9	K/9	GB%	BABIP	WHIP	ERA	FIP	DRA	WARP	CFIP	MPH
2016	*DET*	*MLB*	*19*	*2*	*3*	*0*	*11*	*8*	*33*	*36*	*4*	*4.6*	*6.9*	*18%*	*.309*	*1.59*	*5.09*	*4.94*	*5.30*	*-0.1*	*126*	
2017	*DET*	*MLB*	*20*	*5*	*6*	*0*	*30*	*24*	162^{1}	*173*	*21*	*4.0*	*7.2*	*18%*	*.307*	*1.51*	*4.74*	*4.70*	*4.94*	*0.2*	*118*	

Breakout: 0% Improve: 0% Collapse: 0% Attrition: 0% MLB: 0% *Comparables: Julio Teheran, Will Smith, Eduardo Rodriguez*

The Tigers love drafting right-handed pitchers with velocity in the first round (e.g. Sleeth, Verlander, Porcello, Perry, Turner, Ruffin, Crawford) and Burrows is the latest addition. There's a case to be made that he never should have lasted to the 22nd-overall pick, but perhaps teams are just scared of alliteration. What they should be frightened of is looking silly. Burrows peppers the strike zone with a three-pitch mix, starting with that dynamic fastball, and working in a swing-and-miss power curve and a nascent changeup. He can get downhill plane on his fastball, but it takes a conscious effort to do so, as he's likely a couple inches shy of his listed 6-foot-2. Despite the lack of vertical aptitude, Burrows is physically mature and has a durable frame that looks capable of logging substantial innings. Progress will come from improving the consistency and command of his secondary offerings. If he can do so, the Tigers found a mid-rotation workhorse late in the first round.

Neftali Feliz RHP

Born: 5/2/88 Age: 28 Bats: R Throws: R Height: 6'3" Weight: 225

YEAR	TEAM	LVL	AGE	W	L	SV	G	GS	IP	H	HR	BB/9	K/9	GB%	BABIP	WHIP	ERA	FIP	DRA	WARP	CFIP	MPH
2013	TEX	MLB	25	0	0	0	6	0	4^{2}	5	0	3.9	7.7	29%	.357	1.50	0.00	3.29	5.62	-0.1	104	96.8
2014	ROU	AAA	26	1	1	7	24	0	28^{2}	19	6	2.5	9.7	30%	.203	0.94	3.14	5.20	5.02	0.1	94	
2014	TEX	MLB	26	2	1	13	30	0	31^{2}	20	5	3.1	6.0	29%	.176	0.98	1.99	4.93	2.47	0.8	108	97.2
2015	DET	MLB	27	2	2	4	30	0	28^{1}	33	3	2.9	7.3	40%	.353	1.48	7.62	3.92	4.62	0.0	96	98.6
2015	TEX	MLB	27	1	2	6	18	0	19^{2}	24	2	4.1	7.3	36%	.344	1.68	4.58	4.17	5.27	-0.1	100	97.1
2015	ROU	AAA	27	0	1	0	10	0	11	15	1	3.3	9.0	23%	.368	1.73	7.36	4.14	4.70	0.1	94	
2016	*DET*	*MLB*	*28*	*6*	*7*	*0*	*97*	*50*	*50*	*47*	*6*	*3.0*	*7.1*	*34%*	*.278*	*1.26*	*4.25*	*4.28*	*4.54*	*0.1*	*103*	
2017	*DET*	*MLB*	*29*	*4*	*2*	*12*	*58*	*4*	79^{2}	*76*	*11*	*3.0*	*7.3*	*34%*	*.282*	*1.29*	*4.43*	*4.37*	*4.73*	*0.1*	*109*	

Breakout: 16% Improve: 45% Collapse: 31% Attrition: 12% MLB: 94% *Comparables: Manny Delcarmen, Joe Smith, Jeremy Accardo*

When someone with a legendary fastball can't throw said fastball anymore, you just want to reach out and hug the guy. That's Feliz: Concerns about his velocity cost him his closer's role in Texas and eventually his roster spot. The Tigers picked him up because that's what the Tigers do with cheap free-agent relievers. The fastball played up to 98 on occasion, but Feliz had difficulty reaching into his bag of tricks and always finding the *really* fast fastball. Sometimes he came up with a rabbit or a whoopee cushion, though more often it was just a lesser fastball. He needs to donate the rabbits and the slow fastballs to a shelter or he'll keep bounding around teams, looking for that hug.

Michael Fulmer RHP

Born: 3/15/93 Age: 23 Bats: R Throws: R Height: 6'3" Weight: 200

YEAR	TEAM	LVL	AGE	W	L	SV	G	GS	IP	H	HR	BB/9	K/9	GB%	BABIP	WHIP	ERA	FIP	DRA	WARP	CFIP	MPH
2013	SLU	A+	20	2	2	0	7	7	34	24	1	4.8	7.7	38%	.245	1.24	3.44	3.86	4.48	0.2	106	
2014	SLU	A+	21	6	10	0	19	19	95^{1}	112	7	2.9	8.1	50%	.347	1.50	3.97	3.77	4.13	0.9	93	
2015	BIN	AA	22	6	2	0	15	15	86	73	3	2.4	8.7	52%	.293	1.12	1.88	2.63	2.55	2.4	73	
2015	ERI	AA	22	4	1	0	6	6	31^{2}	27	4	2.0	9.4	48%	.287	1.07	2.84	3.49	3.15	0.6	91	
2016	*DET*	*MLB*	*23*	*2*	*1*	*0*	*18*	*3*	30^{2}	*31*	*3*	*3.0*	*7.3*	*48%*	*.302*	*1.36*	*4.17*	*3.96*	*4.43*	*0.1*	*101*	
2017	*DET*	*MLB*	*24*	*3*	*4*	*0*	*11*	*11*	64^{2}	*66*	*8*	*3.0*	*7.6*	*48%*	*.302*	*1.36*	*4.26*	*4.21*	*4.53*	*0.4*	*104*	

Breakout: 18% Improve: 23% Collapse: 12% Attrition: 26% MLB: 42% *Comparables: Matt Magill, Wily Peralta, Alex Cobb*

A midseason trade is often a boon for a prospect's standing; Fulmer proved no exception, arriving as the top piece in the trade that sent Yoenis Cespedes to New York. Plucked from the pitching-rich Mets and sent to the prospect-destitute Tigers, Fulmer went from relative obscurity to the upper reaches of his new organization's rankings. He employs a fastball that sits in the mid-90s (drink!) and pairs it with a slider nearing the 90s; his look matches his stuff, thanks to his flowing hair and goatee. His changeup lags behind his top two offerings (drink!), but has average potential. While the quality of stuff may hint at more, the consistency of his command and secondaries (drink!) will determine whether he becomes more than a mid-rotation starter.

Shane Greene RHP

Born: 11/17/88 Age: 27 Bats: R Throws: R Height: 6'4" Weight: 210

YEAR	TEAM	LVL	AGE	W	L	SV	G	GS	IP	H	HR	BB/9	K/9	GB%	BABIP	WHIP	ERA	FIP	DRA	WARP	CFIP	MPH
2013	TRN	AA	24	8	4	0	14	13	79^{1}	92	6	2.3	7.7	51%	.347	1.41	3.18	3.61	4.50	0.7	96	
2013	TAM	A+	24	4	6	0	13	13	75	83	4	1.2	8.3	49%	.348	1.24	3.60	2.61	3.51	1.2	74	
2014	SWB	AAA	25	5	2	0	15	13	66^{1}	79	3	3.5	7.7	52%	.360	1.58	4.61	3.40	4.37	0.6	95	
2014	NYA	MLB	25	5	4	0	15	14	78^{2}	81	8	3.3	9.3	51%	.330	1.40	3.78	3.76	4.51	0.3	96	95.3
2015	DET	MLB	26	4	8	0	18	16	83^{2}	103	13	2.9	5.4	46%	.325	1.55	6.88	5.11	6.33	-1.3	118	94.2
2015	TOL	AAA	26	1	1	0	7	7	35	37	2	2.8	5.4	44%	.304	1.37	3.86	3.90	4.67	0.0	106	
2016	*DET*	*MLB*	*27*	*3*	*3*	*0*	*26*	*6*	*55*	*63*	*7*	*3.1*	*6.5*	*47%*	*.321*	*1.49*	*4.54*	*4.64*	*4.81*	*0.1*	*111*	
2017	*DET*	*MLB*	*28*	*4*	*5*	*0*	*15*	*15*	87^{2}	*99*	*12*	*3.1*	*7.1*	*47%*	*.317*	*1.46*	*4.62*	*4.56*	*4.89*	*0.2*	*114*	

Breakout: 29% Improve: 44% Collapse: 9% Attrition: 19% MLB: 64% *Comparables: Christian Friedrich, Billy Buckner, Jason Berken*

The season is long and unforgiving, evidenced by how Greene led the American League in ERA (0.39) after three starts, then by season's end owned the worst mark (min. 50 IP). Following that Cy Youngish opening act, Greene failed to complete five innings in nine of his final 13 starts. He was shuttled to the minors twice but never could reproduce his April ace arsenal. Greene always displayed inconsistent minor-league numbers that never translated cleanly to major-league success, and 2015 was the all-time puzzler. That is, until a medical explanation was diagnosed. A pseudoaneurysm was causing numbness in his throwing hand, requiring a surgical fix and no more baseball for the year. Simply getting back into the rotation, any rotation, would be a success for the quick-working five-pitchman, given that he, y'know, just had arterial surgery.

Blaine Hardy LHP

Born: 3/14/87 Age: 29 Bats: L Throws: L Height: 6'2" Weight: 230

YEAR	TEAM	LVL	AGE	W	L	SV	G	GS	IP	H	HR	BB/9	K/9	GB%	BABIP	WHIP	ERA	FIP	DRA	WARP	CFIP	MPH
2013	ERI	AA	26	2	2	1	16	0	27^{2}	16	1	3.9	8.5	34%	.217	1.01	1.63	3.21	4.36	0.2	93	
2013	TOL	AAA	26	6	1	0	14	9	64	46	7	2.7	7.5	29%	.227	1.02	1.69	3.95	4.34	0.5	100	
2014	DET	MLB	27	2	1	0	38	0	39	34	1	4.6	7.2	54%	.289	1.38	2.54	3.52	2.41	1.0	105	91.3
2014	TOL	AAA	27	3	2	0	20	6	47	35	2	2.5	10.1	50%	.284	1.02	2.68	2.55	3.77	0.6	71	
2015	DET	MLB	28	5	3	0	70	0	61^{1}	61	2	3.2	8.1	42%	.319	1.35	3.08	2.86	3.30	1.0	94	91.0
2016	*DET*	*MLB*	*29*	*3*	*1*	*0*	*54*	*0*	*57*	*54*	*6*	*3.3*	*7.5*	*44%*	*.288*	*1.31*	*4.05*	*4.14*	*4.32*	*0.4*	*97*	
2017	*DET*	*MLB*	*30*	*3*	*2*	*1*	*37*	*3*	*60*	*60*	*7*	*3.4*	*7.9*	*44%*	*.300*	*1.38*	*4.22*	*4.17*	*4.50*	*0.2*	*101*	

Breakout: 21% Improve: 29% Collapse: 22% Attrition: 20% MLB: 55% *Comparables: Anthony Varvaro, Blake Parker, Cory Wade*

There are three pitchers since 2014 who have thrown 100 innings while allowing three or fewer home runs. Ken Giles and Wade Davis are both closers. You're looking at Stingy Homer Pitcher No. 3, who looks like he should belong on the back of *Highlights* magazine with those two superiors. The unassuming lefty lacks the pedigree, firepower or other peripherals to lock down the ninth inning, so he can hang his hat on being the left-hander best at limiting home runs. As a flyball pitcher traipsing about Detroit, this all about park factors, right? That's where the curveball comes in: When Hardy's hook—a true 12-to-6 offering—is hit into play, 80 percent of the time it's a groundball, the highest rate in the majors (min. 100 curves). If his curve stays down, he'll stick around town.

Joe Jimenez RHP

Born: 1/17/95 Age: 21 Bats: R Throws: R Height: 6'3" Weight: 220

YEAR	TEAM	LVL	AGE	W	L	SV	G	GS	IP	H	HR	BB/9	K/9	GB%	BABIP	WHIP	ERA	FIP	DRA	WARP	CFIP	MPH
2014	ONE	A-	19	3	2	4	23	0	26^{2}	22	1	2.0	13.8	44%	.350	1.05	2.70	1.75	3.21	0.4	58	
2015	WMI	A	20	5	1	17	40	0	43	23	2	2.3	12.8	34%	.239	0.79	1.47	1.93	0.80	2.0	60	
2016	*DET*	*MLB*	*21*	*2*	*1*	*1*	*33*	*0*	*35*	*32*	*4*	*3.6*	*9.5*	*28%*	*.303*	*1.32*	*3.92*	*3.98*	*4.29*	*0.2*	*94*	
2017	*DET*	*MLB*	*22*	*2*	*1*	*1*	*34*	*0*	*42^{2}*	*43*	*5*	*3.9*	*10.0*	*28%*	*.326*	*1.44*	*4.02*	*3.96*	*4.40*	*0.2*	*96*	

Breakout: 0% Improve: 0% Collapse: 0% Attrition: 0% MLB: 0% *Comparables: Tim Collins, Joe Ortiz, Eduardo Sanchez*

The duality of man tells us that just because a man is one thing, it does not preclude him from being another, quite different, possibly opposite thing. It is through this lens that we come to understand Jimenez. He went undrafted out of Puerto Rico in 2013, but signed for $100,000. Prior to the draft he had gone from pitching in the upper 80s to touching 94 mph. In 2014 his fastball sat 94-97 and ventured into the triple digits on occasion, all while showing above-average life. He complements his fastball with a slow slider that will show plus and a rarely used changeup. Add those qualities up and you get a hard-throwing relief prospect who has a chance to anchor a bullpen, something as seemingly common as the air we breathe.

Mark Lowe RHP

Born: 6/7/83 Age: 33 Bats: L Throws: R Height: 6'3" Weight: 210

YEAR	TEAM	LVL	AGE	W	L	SV	G	GS	IP	H	HR	BB/9	K/9	GB%	BABIP	WHIP	ERA	FIP	DRA	WARP	CFIP	MPH
2013	ANA	MLB	30	1	0	0	11	0	11^{2}	11	1	8.5	5.4	42%	.270	1.89	9.26	5.82	7.57	-0.4	122	95.4
2013	SYR	AAA	30	3	1	1	24	0	28^{2}	31	3	3.1	11.6	33%	.373	1.43	3.14	3.03	3.84	0.3	82	
2014	COH	AAA	31	4	3	17	41	0	41^{2}	46	4	3.7	10.2	48%	.368	1.51	5.62	3.65	4.06	0.4	82	
2014	CLE	MLB	31	0	1	0	7	0	7	10	2	7.7	7.7	30%	.320	2.29	3.86	7.73	10.59	-0.5	107	94.6
2015	SEA	MLB	32	0	1	0	34	0	36	31	1	2.8	11.8	38%	.357	1.17	1.00	1.85	2.75	0.8	72	97.8
2015	TOR	MLB	32	1	2	1	23	0	19	15	3	0.5	6.6	47%	.231	0.84	3.79	3.84	2.90	0.4	81	98.8
2016	*DET*	*MLB*	*33*	*3*	*1*	*0*	*54*	*0*	*57*	*54*	*6*	*3.1*	*8.9*	*41%*	*.303*	*1.28*	*3.71*	*3.77*	*3.98*	*0.6*	*85*	
2017	*DET*	*MLB*	*34*	*3*	*1*	*1*	*50*	*0*	*53^{2}*	*51*	*7*	*3.2*	*9.3*	*41%*	*.305*	*1.31*	*3.96*	*3.90*	*4.25*	*0.3*	*92*	

Breakout: 30% Improve: 44% Collapse: 17% Attrition: 12% MLB: 80% *Comparables: Alberto Castillo, Randy Flores, Aaron Fultz*

After throwing only 18 innings between 2013 and 2014 due to a combination of injury and ineffectiveness, Lowe took full advantage of Safeco Field for four months before ending the season as a key cog in the Blue Jays' bullpen. Right-handed hitters have historically loathed facing Lowe, who serves up sliders like a White Castle line cook, but their collective .523 OPS against him was over 100 points lower than his career mark. More importantly, he struck out David Freese twice this past summer, which was undoubtedly good for Lowe's confidence, but in reality was more like having your first girlfriend finally see you out with someone new... four years after she broke up with you.

Daniel Norris LHP

Born: 4/25/93 Age: 23 Bats: L Throws: L Height: 6'2" Weight: 195

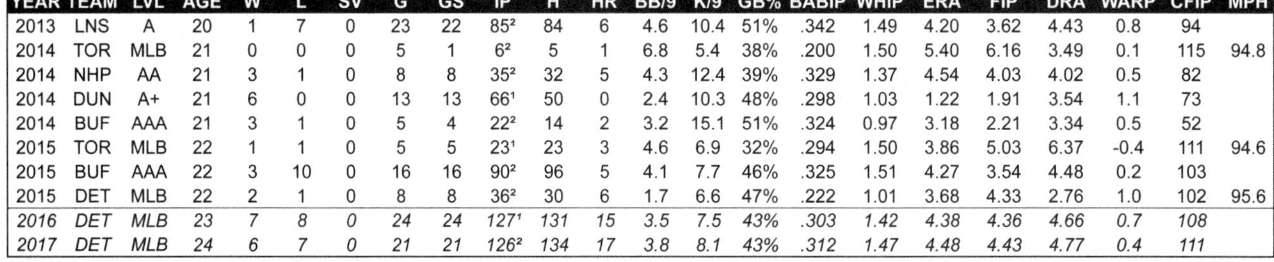

YEAR	TEAM	LVL	AGE	W	L	SV	G	GS	IP	H	HR	BB/9	K/9	GB%	BABIP	WHIP	ERA	FIP	DRA	WARP	CFIP	MPH
2013	LNS	A	20	1	7	0	23	22	85^{2}	84	6	4.6	10.4	51%	.342	1.49	4.20	3.62	4.43	0.8	94	
2014	TOR	MLB	21	0	0	0	5	1	6^{2}	5	1	6.8	5.4	38%	.200	1.50	5.40	6.16	3.49	0.1	115	94.8
2014	NHP	AA	21	3	1	0	8	8	35^{2}	32	5	4.3	12.4	39%	.329	1.37	4.54	4.03	4.02	0.5	82	
2014	DUN	A+	21	6	0	0	13	13	66^{1}	50	0	2.4	10.3	48%	.298	1.03	1.22	1.91	3.54	1.1	73	
2014	BUF	AAA	21	3	1	0	5	4	22^{2}	14	2	3.2	15.1	51%	.324	0.97	3.18	2.21	3.34	0.5	52	
2015	TOR	MLB	22	1	1	0	5	5	23^{1}	23	3	4.6	6.9	32%	.294	1.50	3.86	5.03	6.37	-0.4	111	94.6
2015	BUF	AAA	22	3	10	0	16	16	90^{2}	96	5	4.1	7.7	46%	.325	1.51	4.27	3.54	4.48	0.2	103	
2015	DET	MLB	22	2	1	0	8	8	36^{2}	30	6	1.7	6.6	47%	.222	1.01	3.68	4.33	2.76	1.0	102	95.6
2016	*DET*	*MLB*	*23*	*7*	*8*	*0*	*24*	*24*	*127^{1}*	*131*	*15*	*3.5*	*7.5*	*43%*	*.303*	*1.42*	*4.38*	*4.36*	*4.66*	*0.7*	*108*	
2017	*DET*	*MLB*	*24*	*6*	*7*	*0*	*21*	*21*	*126^{2}*	*134*	*17*	*3.8*	*8.1*	*43%*	*.312*	*1.47*	*4.48*	*4.43*	*4.77*	*0.4*	*111*	

Breakout: 8% Improve: 25% Collapse: 15% Attrition: 26% MLB: 47% *Comparables: Nick Maronde, Danny Duffy, Andy Oliver*

You thought your year was full of tumult? Norris began spring training with an ESPN feature story about him living in a van in the offseason. He made the Blue Jays' rotation, then after a month was kicked to Triple-A. He was told by doctors he had thyroid cancer. He fought command issues in Buffalo while striking out 15 per nine. He became the centerpiece of the David Price trade and immediately joined Detroit in the rotation. He hit a 419-foot home run in Wrigley Field and suffered an oblique injury in the same game. A month later, he threw five perfect innings. A couple outings after that, it took 54 pitches to get out of the first. At season's end he told the world about his cancer and beat it. As a pitcher with mid-rotation potential, all Norris probably wants is fewer peaks and valleys.

Mike Pelfrey RHP

Born: 1/14/84 Age: 32 Bats: R Throws: R Height: 6'7" Weight: 240

YEAR	TEAM	LVL	AGE	W	L	SV	G	GS	IP	H	HR	BB/9	K/9	GB%	BABIP	WHIP	ERA	FIP	DRA	WARP	CFIP	MPH
2013	MIN	MLB	29	5	13	0	29	29	152^{2}	184	13	3.1	6.0	45%	.337	1.55	5.19	4.02	4.49	0.8	109	95.2
2014	ROC	AAA	30	1	0	0	2	2	10	9	0	2.7	2.7	41%	.250	1.20	0.90	3.96	4.75	0.0	111	
2014	MIN	MLB	30	0	3	0	5	5	23^{2}	29	5	6.8	3.8	45%	.286	1.99	7.99	7.60	6.91	-0.6	132	93.5
2015	MIN	MLB	31	6	11	0	30	30	164^{2}	198	11	2.5	4.7	53%	.334	1.48	4.26	3.97	4.56	0.9	114	96.0
2016	*DET*	*MLB*	*32*	*7*	*8*	*0*	*24*	*24*	*120*	*134*	*11*	*3.0*	*5.6*	*51%*	*.310*	*1.44*	*4.38*	*4.31*	*4.65*	*0.7*	*108*	
2017	*DET*	*MLB*	*33*	*8*	*8*	*0*	*24*	*24*	*142^{2}*	*166*	*16*	*3.0*	*5.7*	*51%*	*.317*	*1.49*	*4.47*	*4.42*	*4.75*	*0.6*	*110*	

Breakout: 7% Improve: 43% Collapse: 20% Attrition: 7% MLB: 92% *Comparables: Jim Clancy, Scott Feldman, Charlie Leibrandt*

Pelfrey balked at the Twins' attempt to demote him to the bullpen toward the end of spring training, but thanks to Ervin Santana's suspension, he never actually had to make that move. Given just a quick look at Pelfrey's pitch usage, though, you might be forgiven for assuming he *did* move into short relief in 2015. He shelved his four-seam fastball and his curve, going with a full-force power approach. His sinker usage skyrocketed past 70 percent, and his slider and splitter played off the pitch much better as part of a limited arsenal. He actually added velocity, too, sitting on the high side of 94 mph with that sinker. He still gives up too much hard contact and misses too few bats, but he's reestablished himself as a viable starter. Not a *good* starter. But viable.

Francisco Rodriguez RHP

Born: 1/7/82 Age: 34 Bats: R Throws: R Height: 6'0" Weight: 195

YEAR	TEAM	LVL	AGE	W	L	SV	G	GS	IP	H	HR	BB/9	K/9	GB%	BABIP	WHIP	ERA	FIP	DRA	WARP	CFIP	MPH
2013	BAL	MLB	31	2	1	0	23	0	22	25	5	2.0	11.5	48%	.351	1.36	4.50	4.30	5.41	-0.2	73	93.8
2013	MIL	MLB	31	1	1	10	25	0	24^2	17	2	3.3	9.5	34%	.250	1.05	1.09	3.06	2.19	0.7	83	93.2
2014	MIL	MLB	32	5	5	44	69	0	68	49	14	2.4	9.7	46%	.216	0.99	3.04	4.47	3.58	0.8	88	93.0
2015	MIL	MLB	33	1	3	38	60	0	57	38	6	1.7	9.8	48%	.235	0.86	2.21	2.93	2.24	1.7	77	91.5
2016	*DET*	*MLB*	*34*	*3*	*1*	*39*	*54*	*0*	*57*	*49*	*7*	*2.6*	*9.3*	*46%*	*.282*	*1.16*	*3.73*	*3.77*	*4.00*	*0.5*	*88*	
2017	*DET*	*MLB*	*35*	*3*	*1*	*38*	*60*	*0*	*57^2*	*51*	*8*	*2.8*	*9.1*	*46%*	*.279*	*1.19*	*3.95*	*3.90*	*4.24*	*0.3*	*94*	

Breakout: 19% Improve: 38% Collapse: 33% Attrition: 10% MLB: 91% *Comparables: Kazuhiro Sasaki, Jim Brewer, John Hiller*

In baseball, as in life, success is sustained through constant adaptation. K-Rod was supposed to be finished. He no longer worked in the mid-90s, had seen his swinging-strike rate drop and had become increasingly home run prone. Instead Rodriguez posted his best ERA since 2010 by completely abandoning his power profile. He dramatically decreased the frequency of his fastballs and threw his changeup 43 percent of the time in 2015. What's crazy about that is the right-hander didn't even develop a changeup until approximately a half-dozen years ago, an afterthought that has suddenly become his lifeline, the only reason he still has a big-league job. He transitioned to this approach, though not as extreme, several years ago, but his inability to consistently get ahead of hitters limited his effectiveness. Hence the home run issues. In 2015, Rodriguez had a 63 percent strike rate on the first pitch, a career high and almost six percentage points higher than his career norm. Essentially, he's a changeup specialist with above-average command at this point. Seven years ago, when he saved 62 games for Los Angeles, that would have seemed incomprehensible. Baseball is about adaptation.

Bruce Rondon RHP

Born: 12/9/90 Age: 25 Bats: R Throws: R Height: 6'3" Weight: 275

YEAR	TEAM	LVL	AGE	W	L	SV	G	GS	IP	H	HR	BB/9	K/9	GB%	BABIP	WHIP	ERA	FIP	DRA	WARP	CFIP	MPH
2013	DET	MLB	22	1	2	1	30	0	28^2	28	2	3.5	9.4	47%	.329	1.36	3.45	3.04	3.96	0.2	90	102.6
2013	TOL	AAA	22	1	1	14	30	0	29^2	14	1	3.9	12.1	51%	.210	0.91	1.52	2.46	3.72	0.3	78	
2015	TOL	AAA	24	2	2	1	13	0	12^2	16	1	4.3	9.9	44%	.375	1.74	7.11	3.39	3.93	0.1	96	
2015	DET	MLB	24	1	0	5	35	0	31	31	3	5.5	10.5	44%	.329	1.61	5.81	4.07	4.65	0.0	95	101.1
2016	*DET*	*MLB*	*25*	*2*	*1*	*0*	*49*	*0*	*51^2*	*47*	*6*	*3.7*	*8.9*	*45%*	*.294*	*1.32*	*3.99*	*4.11*	*4.24*	*0.3*	*95*	
2017	*DET*	*MLB*	*26*	*3*	*1*	*5*	*50*	*0*	*49^1*	*47*	*7*	*4.1*	*9.2*	*45%*	*.302*	*1.42*	*4.42*	*4.36*	*4.70*	*0.0*	*106*	

Breakout: 29% Improve: 48% Collapse: 21% Attrition: 34% MLB: 76% *Comparables: Daniel Schlereth, Jose Mijares, Josh Spence*

The phrase "something to prove" gets thrown around more often in baseball than, well, baseballs. But if we had to pick someone to embody the phrase, let it be Rondon. It's no secret to anyone that the latest Tigers Closer Of The Future No Really We Mean It This Time is blessed with a triple-digit fastball and some dipping secondary offerings, but following Tommy John rehab he needed more Triple-A work to hone his command. Once handed the closing duties, he struggled. The biggest infraction was averaging 93 mph on his heater in a mid-September outing: The team sent him home for the year. While that effort level put him in the doghouse, he should have no problem getting back in the team's good graces and the closer's job because he, you know, throws 100.

Kyle Ryan LHP

Born: 9/25/91 Age: 24 Bats: L Throws: L Height: 6'5" Weight: 210

YEAR	TEAM	LVL	AGE	W	L	SV	G	GS	IP	H	HR	BB/9	K/9	GB%	BABIP	WHIP	ERA	FIP	DRA	WARP	CFIP	MPH
2013	LAK	A+	21	12	7	0	24	24	142	132	12	2.3	5.7	49%	.275	1.19	3.17	4.02	4.41	0.8	105	
2014	DET	MLB	22	2	0	0	6	1	10^1	10	0	1.7	3.5	77%	.286	1.16	2.61	2.97	2.31	0.3	111	92.8
2014	TOL	AAA	22	3	0	0	5	5	33	21	0	1.4	5.5	52%	.221	0.79	1.64	2.60	4.28	0.3	93	
2014	ERI	AA	22	7	10	0	21	21	126^2	140	15	2.3	5.5	49%	.309	1.36	4.55	4.44	4.71	0.6	107	
2015	DET	MLB	23	2	4	0	16	6	56^1	60	9	3.2	4.8	49%	.288	1.42	4.47	5.23	4.44	0.3	119	90.8
2015	TOL	AAA	23	4	9	0	17	17	103	117	3	2.9	5.5	61%	.335	1.46	4.19	3.30	4.23	0.6	101	
2016	*DET*	*MLB*	*24*	*3*	*2*	*0*	*29*	*5*	*50^2*	*56*	*6*	*3.0*	*5.2*	*53%*	*.301*	*1.44*	*4.72*	*4.76*	*4.99*	*0.0*	*118*	
2017	*DET*	*MLB*	*25*	*4*	*5*	*0*	*12*	*12*	*70^1*	*80*	*10*	*3.0*	*5.6*	*53%*	*.307*	*1.47*	*4.85*	*4.81*	*5.13*	*0.0*	*122*	

Breakout: 13% Improve: 28% Collapse: 12% Attrition: 25% MLB: 51% *Comparables: Zeke Spruill, Anthony Swarzak, Anthony Ortega*

In a thicker system, Ryan is still a prospect with fringy rotation potential, but he was a Tigers pitching prospect who wasn't traded, so he was thrown straight into the fire to find out about his fringiness the hard way. None of his pitches are particularly swing-and-miss, but the lanky lefty hasn't shown extreme platoon splits, as his changeup (thrown exclusively to righties) kept those numbers consistent enough. He's therefore not automatically being built up as a career LOOGY, but there are only so many pitchers out there with Mark Buehrle–like peripherals not named Mark Buehrle. Fortunately, the world *does* need more Tony Sipps.

Anibal Sanchez RHP

Born: 2/27/84 Age: 32 Bats: R Throws: R Height: 6'0" Weight: 205

YEAR	TEAM	LVL	AGE	W	L	SV	G	GS	IP	H	HR	BB/9	K/9	GB%	BABIP	WHIP	ERA	FIP	DRA	WARP	CFIP	MPH
2013	DET	MLB	29	14	8	0	29	29	182	156	9	2.7	10.0	48%	.307	1.15	2.57	2.42	2.76	4.7	71	96.4
2014	DET	MLB	30	8	5	0	22	21	126	108	4	2.1	7.3	48%	.277	1.10	3.43	2.74	3.11	2.6	83	94.8
2015	DET	MLB	31	10	10	0	25	25	157	152	29	2.8	7.9	41%	.278	1.28	4.99	4.70	4.34	1.3	101	94.5
2016	*DET*	*MLB*	*32*	*9*	*9*	*0*	*28*	*28*	*159^{2}*	*153*	*19*	*2.8*	*8.3*	*44%*	*.295*	*1.27*	*3.96*	*3.95*	*4.22*	*1.7*	*96*	
2017	*DET*	*MLB*	*33*	*10*	*10*	*0*	*27*	*27*	*166*	*166*	*23*	*2.9*	*8.4*	*44%*	*.302*	*1.32*	*4.16*	*4.10*	*4.43*	*1.4*	*101*	

Breakout: 10% Improve: 40% Collapse: 28% Attrition: 7% MLB: 91% *Comparables: Josh Beckett, Erik Bedard, Ted Lilly*

Sure, flyball pitchers are going to have seasons like this, but extremely low on the list of pitchers likely to allow 29 dingers was Sanchez, who gave up fewer than half that total in the last two seasons combined. He became the first pitcher to allow 15 home runs in Comerica Park since 2006. Then an inflamed rotator cuff ended his campaign in mid-August as benevolently as possible. If that sore shoulder lingered all season (and reports indicate it did), it might help explain the gopher problem. Velocity, secondary pitches: All the obvious indicators resembled the 2013 ERA/FIP league leader. With two expensive years left on the contract, the team can only hope an offseason of rest (and a break from turning one's neck all the time) is all that's needed to bring his numbers back down to earth.

Alfredo Simon RHP

Born: 5/8/81 Age: 35 Bats: R Throws: R Height: 6'6" Weight: 265

YEAR	TEAM	LVL	AGE	W	L	SV	G	GS	IP	H	HR	BB/9	K/9	GB%	BABIP	WHIP	ERA	FIP	DRA	WARP	CFIP	MPH
2013	CIN	MLB	32	6	4	1	63	0	87^{2}	68	8	2.7	6.5	47%	.236	1.07	2.87	3.93	3.74	0.9	110	96.7
2014	CIN	MLB	33	15	10	0	32	32	196^{1}	181	22	2.6	5.8	50%	.265	1.21	3.44	4.30	3.77	2.5	114	96.2
2015	DET	MLB	34	13	12	0	31	31	187	201	24	3.3	5.6	46%	.294	1.44	5.05	4.74	4.53	1.1	117	95.2
2016	*DET*	*MLB*	*35*	*10*	*12*	*0*	*30*	*30*	*180*	*190*	*22*	*3.2*	*5.8*	*47%*	*.290*	*1.41*	*4.75*	*4.74*	*5.02*	*0.2*	*118*	
2017	*DET*	*MLB*	*36*	*3*	*3*	*0*	*17*	*7*	*56^{1}*	*62*	*8*	*3.2*	*6.1*	*47%*	*.300*	*1.46*	*4.84*	*4.78*	*5.11*	*-0.1*	*119*	

Breakout: 13% Improve: 39% Collapse: 18% Attrition: 13% MLB: 83% *Comparables: Cory Lidle, Elmer Dessens, Ryan Franklin*

In a walk year, Simon picked the absolute worst time for his luck pendulum to swing back into underperforming his FIP. All Big Pasta could accomplish last year was devouring enough innings to lead the 2015 Tigers, but any cardiologist will tell you not to fill up on carbohydrates. He stayed uninjured, though after the season he admitted to pitching all year with a bad knee. For someone with such a large frame, his strategy is surprisingly pitch-to-contact-and-pray. He works slowly on the mound, goes deep in counts and throws an occasional eephus because :shrug:. He is store-bought back-end starting pitching that is durable, yet verges on bullpen depth, and if he projects to lead your team in innings, consider a nice leafy salad instead.

Spencer Turnbull RHP

Born: 9/18/92 Age: 23 Bats: R Throws: R Height: 6'3" Weight: 215

YEAR	TEAM	LVL	AGE	W	L	SV	G	GS	IP	H	HR	BB/9	K/9	GB%	BABIP	WHIP	ERA	FIP	DRA	WARP	CFIP	MPH
2014	ONE	A-	21	0	2	0	11	11	28^{1}	31	1	4.4	6.0	68%	.347	1.59	4.45	4.15	4.40	-0.7	104	
2015	WMI	A	22	11	3	0	22	22	116^{2}	106	0	4.0	8.2	53%	.314	1.35	3.01	3.10	4.41	0.8	101	
2016	*DET*	*MLB*	*23*	*4*	*6*	*0*	*17*	*17*	*80*	*86*	*8*	*5.0*	*6.1*	*45%*	*.306*	*1.64*	*4.93*	*4.99*	*5.14*	*0.0*	*121*	
2017	*DET*	*MLB*	*24*	*7*	*9*	*0*	*26*	*26*	*154^{2}*	*160*	*16*	*5.0*	*6.7*	*45%*	*.301*	*1.60*	*4.83*	*4.79*	*5.04*	*0.1*	*119*	

Breakout: 0% Improve: 0% Collapse: 0% Attrition: 0% MLB: 0% *Comparables: Bryan Mitchell, Renyel Pinto, Steve Johnson*

One of a bevy of Tigers prospects whose future lies on the fault line between back-end starter and high-octane reliever, Turnbull touches triple digits with his four-seamer. He gets big life when he works below the century mark, and can reach the mid-90s with his two-seam as well. He'll mix in a slider that features hard bite when it's on, but lacks consistency. His changeup lags behind the slider and might never be more than a fringe-average offering. If he can cut down on the free passes and refine his command, he just might turn the prospect hounds bullish.

Jose Valdez RHP

Born: 3/1/90 Age: 26 Bats: R Throws: R Height: 6'1" Weight: 200

YEAR	TEAM	LVL	AGE	W	L	SV	G	GS	IP	H	HR	BB/9	K/9	GB%	BABIP	WHIP	ERA	FIP	DRA	WARP	CFIP	MPH
2013	WMI	A	23	1	1	16	27	0	26^{1}	16	0	6.8	12.0	36%	.291	1.37	2.73	2.96	4.46	0.1	95	
2013	LAK	A+	23	1	1	17	23	0	23	16	1	5.5	12.5	42%	.306	1.30	2.74	2.98	3.80	0.2	84	
2014	ERI	AA	24	2	3	18	47	0	57	56	6	4.1	10.4	43%	.340	1.44	4.11	3.83	4.27	0.3	91	
2015	TOL	AAA	25	4	5	5	43	0	57	49	3	6.0	6.8	49%	.282	1.53	3.32	4.33	5.96	-1.1	122	
2015	DET	MLB	25	0	1	0	7	0	9	10	2	4.0	4.0	36%	.276	1.56	4.00	6.44	5.73	-0.1	116	98.4
2016	*DET*	*MLB*	*26*	*1*	*0*	*0*	*24*	*0*	*25^{2}*	*27*	*3*	*4.6*	*6.9*	*43%*	*.301*	*1.54*	*4.83*	*4.84*	*5.07*	*-0.1*	*119*	
2017	*DET*	*MLB*	*27*	*1*	*0*	*1*	*24*	*0*	*28*	*29*	*4*	*5.1*	*7.7*	*43%*	*.303*	*1.60*	*5.10*	*5.04*	*5.35*	*-0.2*	*125*	

Breakout: 8% Improve: 9% Collapse: 3% Attrition: 10% MLB: 15% *Comparables: Arquimedes Caminero, Brandon Cunniff, Taylor Thompson*

Valdez became the first pitcher in four years to retire none of the four batters he faced in his major-league debut. Whether it was jitters or him accidentally blurting out each pitch and location before throwing it, a month following that dubious debut (just the 31st of its type in history), he settled down and threw some effective no-leverage innings. With an upper-90s fastball, a plus slider and an experimental changeup, there's middle relief potential here, but he might want to start back in Triple-A and see where he misplaced that high strikeout rate. Hint: It's not behind the Barcalounger.

Drew VerHagen RHP

Born: 10/22/90 Age: 25 Bats: R Throws: R Height: 6'6" Weight: 230

YEAR	TEAM	LVL	AGE	W	L	SV	G	GS	IP	H	HR	BB/9	K/9	GB%	BABIP	WHIP	ERA	FIP	DRA	WARP	CFIP	MPH
2013	ERI	AA	22	2	5	0	12	12	60	53	3	2.5	6.0	60%	.272	1.17	3.00	3.69	4.47	0.5	96	
2013	LAK	A+	22	5	3	0	12	11	67^1	49	1	3.6	4.7	58%	.231	1.13	2.81	3.82	4.58	0.2	111	
2014	DET	MLB	23	0	1	0	1	1	5	5	0	5.4	7.2	46%	.385	1.60	5.40	3.36	5.23	0.0	100	92.9
2014	TOL	AAA	23	6	7	0	19	19	110^1	117	5	2.0	5.1	56%	.308	1.29	3.67	3.70	4.57	0.7	102	
2015	DET	MLB	24	2	0	0	20	0	26^1	18	1	4.8	4.4	76%	.221	1.22	2.05	4.32	2.61	0.7	117	96.6
2015	TOL	AAA	24	1	3	1	15	0	27^2	26	0	3.6	6.8	60%	.310	1.34	3.58	2.94	4.18	0.1	101	
2016	*DET*	*MLB*	*25*	*1*	*0*	*0*	*24*	*0*	25^2	*27*	*3*	*3.1*	*5.2*	*61%*	*.286*	*1.37*	*4.56*	*4.76*	*4.83*	*0.0*	*113*	
2017	*DET*	*MLB*	*26*	*3*	*3*	*0*	*17*	*8*	*65*	*68*	*8*	*3.3*	*5.7*	*61%*	*.289*	*1.41*	*4.82*	*4.77*	*5.11*	*-0.1*	*120*	

Breakout: 19% Improve: 27% Collapse: 13% Attrition: 28% MLB: 48% *Comparables: James Houser, Fabio Castro, Mike Montgomery*

When a team uses 22 different pitchers out of the bullpen in a year, someone, *anyone* has to come out of nowhere and make his case for being a dependable middle reliever. The one with the inside track for the Tigers just happens to be tallest. VerHagen, probably 10th on the team's starting-pitcher depth chart, was converted to the 'pen to maximize his velocity and likelihood of a big-league check. His fastball became faster, heavier and ultimately a Drowning Pool song: Everything hit the floor. His FIP (and K:BB ratio) may tell us VerHagen is simply Zach Britton who can't throw a strike, but as long as nobody can launch his fastball into low orbit, he fits the mold of a sixth-inning fireman.

Justin Verlander RHP

Born: 2/20/83 Age: 33 Bats: R Throws: R Height: 6'5" Weight: 225

YEAR	TEAM	LVL	AGE	W	L	SV	G	GS	IP	H	HR	BB/9	K/9	GB%	BABIP	WHIP	ERA	FIP	DRA	WARP	CFIP	MPH
2013	DET	MLB	30	13	12	0	34	34	218^1	212	19	3.1	8.9	40%	.316	1.31	3.46	3.30	3.71	3.2	85	97.9
2014	DET	MLB	31	15	12	0	32	32	206	223	18	2.8	6.9	41%	.317	1.40	4.54	3.77	4.12	1.7	99	96.1
2015	DET	MLB	32	5	8	0	20	20	133^1	113	13	2.2	7.6	37%	.267	1.09	3.38	3.46	2.62	3.8	86	96.5
2016	*DET*	*MLB*	*33*	*12*	*11*	*0*	*31*	*31*	207^2	*191*	*22*	*2.7*	*7.9*	*39%*	*.284*	*1.22*	*3.86*	*3.86*	*4.12*	*2.5*	*94*	
2017	*DET*	*MLB*	*34*	*12*	*11*	*0*	*29*	*29*	183^1	*177*	*23*	*2.7*	*7.9*	*39%*	*.290*	*1.26*	*4.08*	*4.01*	*4.35*	*1.8*	*100*	

Breakout: 14% Improve: 38% Collapse: 26% Attrition: 20% MLB: 96% *Comparables: Jason Schmidt, Ryan Dempster, David Cone*

Gone are the days of Verlander throwing upper-90s fastballs in the seventh inning and basically being unfair to the entire sport; we can blame age, injury or whatever social crisis is out there. But after five straight years of average velocity decline, his fastball remained steady at 93-94, maxing out at 99. Once he knew his physical limitations, he learned to pitch with them: Verlander landed with the fourth-best DRA in 2015 (min. 100 IP; behind Greinke, Kershaw and Arrieta). That may overstate how "back" he is, because a triceps injury landed him on the DL, and lack of recovery time was an explanation given for his poor 2014. If he can marry the quantity of 2014 with the quality of a regressed version of 2015, he can easily be a staff's no. 2.

Alex Wilson RHP

Born: 11/3/86 Age: 29 Bats: R Throws: R Height: 6'0" Weight: 215

YEAR	TEAM	LVL	AGE	W	L	SV	G	GS	IP	H	HR	BB/9	K/9	GB%	BABIP	WHIP	ERA	FIP	DRA	WARP	CFIP	MPH
2013	PAW	AAA	26	3	1	0	14	0	17	17	2	2.6	8.5	42%	.312	1.29	3.71	3.73	4.11	0.1	91	
2013	BOS	MLB	26	1	1	0	26	0	27^2	34	0	4.6	7.2	31%	.378	1.73	4.88	3.11	6.25	-0.6	106	94.8
2014	BOS	MLB	27	1	0	0	18	0	28^1	20	3	1.6	6.0	45%	.213	0.88	1.91	3.94	3.06	0.5	102	94.7
2014	PAW	AAA	27	6	1	5	35	0	41^1	38	2	5.0	8.7	38%	.316	1.48	4.35	3.87	4.54	0.1	100	
2015	DET	MLB	28	3	3	2	59	1	70	61	5	1.4	4.9	53%	.258	1.03	2.19	3.50	2.67	1.7	105	94.5
2016	*DET*	*MLB*	*29*	*2*	*1*	*0*	*49*	*0*	51^2	*54*	*5*	*2.7*	*6.3*	*48%*	*.298*	*1.35*	*4.26*	*4.15*	*4.55*	*0.2*	*104*	
2017	*DET*	*MLB*	*30*	*2*	*1*	*1*	*40*	*0*	51^1	*54*	*7*	*2.7*	*7.0*	*48%*	*.302*	*1.37*	*4.38*	*4.34*	*4.68*	*0.0*	*107*	

Breakout: 19% Improve: 28% Collapse: 21% Attrition: 19% MLB: 51% *Comparables: Tim Dillard, Mike Ekstrom, Frank Herrmann*

The spider in the corner is weaving into her web "SOME THROW-IN." Rick Porcello for Yoenis Cespedes felt like a fair swap, but this Chris Pratt dead ringer was added to sweeten the transaction. Wilson's atrocious spring made him an Opening Day Mud Hen, but come June 1st, he had already thrown 26 innings in the majors, a portent that his emergency strike-throwing services would be needed early and often. Like the lone competent employee in an office, he kept receiving more duties, from a spot start to save situations to refilling the coffee machine. If the low strikeout rate is any indication, versatility and a lack of walks (a red flag from yesteryear that has disappeared of late) will remain his towering strengths.

Justin Wilson LHP

Born: 8/18/87 Age: 28 Bats: L Throws: L Height: 6'2" Weight: 205

YEAR	TEAM	LVL	AGE	W	L	SV	G	GS	IP	H	HR	BB/9	K/9	GB%	BABIP	WHIP	ERA	FIP	DRA	WARP	CFIP	MPH
2013	PIT	MLB	25	6	1	0	58	0	73^2	50	4	3.4	7.2	55%	.229	1.06	2.08	3.39	3.19	1.2	102	98.7
2014	PIT	MLB	26	3	4	0	70	0	60	49	4	4.5	9.1	52%	.285	1.32	4.20	3.59	3.47	0.7	92	97.9
2015	NYA	MLB	27	5	0	0	74	0	61	49	3	3.0	9.7	46%	.301	1.13	3.10	2.66	2.83	1.4	82	97.6
2016	*DET*	*MLB*	*28*	*3*	*1*	*0*	*49*	*0*	51^2	*43*	*5*	*3.3*	*8.9*	*49%*	*.278*	*1.20*	*3.70*	*3.74*	*3.96*	*0.5*	*87*	
2017	*DET*	*MLB*	*29*	*4*	*3*	*0*	*55*	*5*	*78*	*64*	*9*	*3.2*	*9.7*	*49%*	*.274*	*1.17*	*3.75*	*3.69*	*4.01*	*0.8*	*89*	

Breakout: 23% Improve: 42% Collapse: 27% Attrition: 28% MLB: 82% *Comparables: Ryan Cook, Andrew Bailey, Jonny Venters*

Wilson was a victim of circumstance, that circumstance being the existence of Dellin Betances and Andrew Miller. In New York he was doomed to be overshadowed so long as his numbers didn't jump off the page and perform a traditional Irish jig. Nonetheless, he put in a dominant season's work lengthening the bullpen and ensuring that the Yankees basically played in six-inning games, which are much easier on commuters and casual fans. He still won't be the closer in Detroit on Opening Day, but it's a lot easier to imagine him winding up in the role with the competition being Francisco Rodriguez and Mark Lowe than it was with Betances and Miller.

Randy Wolf LHP

Born: 8/22/76 Age: 39 Bats: L Throws: L Height: 6'0" Weight: 205

YEAR	TEAM	LVL	AGE	W	L	SV	G	GS	IP	H	HR	BB/9	K/9	GB%	BABIP	WHIP	ERA	FIP	DRA	WARP	CFIP	MPH
2014	SLC	AAA	37	1	1	0	7	7	37^{2}	45	5	2.9	7.4	46%	.342	1.51	4.78	4.81	5.21	0.3	102	
2014	NOR	AAA	37	0	0	0	6	1	15	18	1	3.0	7.2	36%	.347	1.53	4.20	3.62	4.64	0.0	102	
2014	MIA	MLB	37	1	3	1	6	4	25^{2}	33	4	2.1	6.7	41%	.345	1.52	5.26	4.35	7.00	-0.7	107	90.2
2014	RNO	AAA	37	5	1	0	6	6	34	40	1	4.8	9.3	46%	.398	1.71	4.50	3.61	4.14	0.6	81	
2015	DET	MLB	38	0	5	0	8	7	34^{2}	46	5	3.9	7.3	46%	.366	1.76	6.23	4.75	6.69	-0.7	107	90.7
2015	BUF	AAA	38	9	2	0	23	23	139^{2}	139	4	2.6	6.8	46%	.324	1.28	2.58	2.96	3.14	2.7	88	
2016	*DET*	*MLB*	*39*	*8*	*9*	*0*	*24*	*24*	*137*	*147*	*14*	*3.0*	*6.7*	*43%*	*.310*	*1.41*	*4.24*	*4.20*	*4.51*	*1.0*	*104*	
2017	*DET*	*MLB*	*40*	*4*	*5*	*0*	*13*	*13*	*76^{1}*	*85*	*9*	*3.0*	*6.6*	*43%*	*.314*	*1.45*	*4.46*	*4.41*	*4.74*	*0.3*	*110*	

Breakout: 11% Improve: 26% Collapse: 11% Attrition: 2% MLB: 52% *Comparables: Brett Tomko, Kevin Millwood, Kevin Appier*

This is why Dory from *Finding Nemo* would make a good life-skills coach for aging hurlers: "Just keep pitching, just keep pitching..." Wolf signed with Toronto last year and accepted an assignment in Buffalo's rotation, dutifully throwing strikes for four months and keeping a tidy ERA in the hopes of a big-league spot start. But Toronto burst into a contender while Detroit simply burst. A simple cash trade put Wolf into the Tigers' rotation for the final six weeks. Perhaps his most impressive feat was throwing 50 pitches in an inning and only allowing two runs in a game the team eventually won. Just keep pitching, Randy. Just keep pitching.

Jordan Zimmermann RHP

Born: 5/23/86 Age: 30 Bats: R Throws: R Height: 6'2" Weight: 225

YEAR	TEAM	LVL	AGE	W	L	SV	G	GS	IP	H	HR	BB/9	K/9	GB%	BABIP	WHIP	ERA	FIP	DRA	WARP	CFIP	MPH
2013	WAS	MLB	27	19	9	0	32	32	213^{1}	192	19	1.7	6.8	49%	.271	1.09	3.25	3.33	3.83	2.8	98	96.2
2014	WAS	MLB	28	14	5	0	32	32	199^{2}	185	13	1.3	8.2	42%	.302	1.07	2.66	2.65	3.42	3.3	84	95.9
2015	WAS	MLB	29	13	10	0	33	33	201^{2}	204	24	1.7	7.3	44%	.302	1.20	3.66	3.78	4.12	2.2	100	95.2
2016	*DET*	*MLB*	*30*	*11*	*11*	*0*	*31*	*31*	*186*	*183*	*21*	*2.0*	*7.0*	*44%*	*.290*	*1.20*	*3.90*	*3.91*	*4.17*	*2.1*	*95*	
2017	*DET*	*MLB*	*31*	*11*	*10*	*0*	*28*	*28*	*172*	*171*	*22*	*2.0*	*7.2*	*44%*	*.290*	*1.22*	*4.03*	*3.99*	*4.31*	*1.7*	*100*	

Breakout: 8% Improve: 45% Collapse: 23% Attrition: 8% MLB: 95% *Comparables: Brad Penny, Freddy Garcia, Jered Weaver*

From 2012 to 2014, Zimmermann struck out 7.3 batters per nine and walked 1.7. He twice made the All-Star team, twice received Cy Young votes and produced a 2.90 ERA. Last year's walk season might look like a step back at just the wrong time, but Zimmermann struck out 7.3 batters per nine and walked 1.7. BABIP a little up, strand rate a little down, HR/FB rate a little up. The Big Three Of Bad Luck.

You could say it's especially bad luck that Zimmermann's bad luck came with such bad timing, but if he'd been born 25 years earlier, the rise in his ERA and the relatively low win total would have hurt his market value. Today, GMs are smart enough to know consistency (and strong peripherals) when they see it. Since the beginning of that 2012 season only four pitchers have started more games than Zimmermann. Only one of the four, Max Scherzer, has a better ERA over those years, and he by just a single hundredth of a run. Zimmermann might be the best pitcher in baseball whom nobody calls an ace. At least now he's got the nine-figure contract to prove he is one.

Kevin Ziomek LHP

Born: 3/21/92 Age: 24 Bats: R Throws: L Height: 6'3" Weight: 200

YEAR	TEAM	LVL	AGE	W	L	SV	G	GS	IP	H	HR	BB/9	K/9	GB%	BABIP	WHIP	ERA	FIP	DRA	WARP	CFIP	MPH
2014	WMI	A	22	10	6	0	23	23	123	89	5	3.9	11.1	47%	.286	1.15	2.27	2.98	4.05	1.6	86	
2015	LAK	A+	23	9	11	0	27	27	154^{2}	142	3	2.0	8.3	54%	.312	1.14	3.43	2.38	2.22	4.4	80	
2016	*DET*	*MLB*	*24*	*7*	*8*	*0*	*23*	*23*	*121*	*124*	*12*	*3.5*	*7.2*	*45%*	*.304*	*1.41*	*4.22*	*4.24*	*4.52*	*0.9*	*102*	
2017	*DET*	*MLB*	*25*	*6*	*7*	*0*	*20*	*20*	*115^{1}*	*117*	*13*	*3.8*	*7.7*	*45%*	*.304*	*1.44*	*4.35*	*4.30*	*4.66*	*0.6*	*107*	

Breakout: 0% Improve: 0% Collapse: 0% Attrition: 0% MLB: 0% *Comparables: Steven Matz, Bud Norris, George Kontos*

There is a plot summary of the film *Memento* on IMDB authored by Scion013, in which the last line states, "One story line moves forward in time while the other tells the story backwards revealing more each time." This doubles as an explanation of Ziomek's career thus far. In one sense, there's been nothing but progress for the 58th-overall pick. He spent the entirety of last season in High-A Lakeland, a bit curiously given his age and success there. Production and stuff tell different stories, though: While one advanced, the other regressed. His fastball backed up to the high 80s, occasionally scraping 90 mph; his breaking balls lacked bite and consistency; and his change was depthless when he deigned to throw it at all. While Ziomek can attack the zone at will, his command within it is loose. There's a fifth starter in there somewhere, and he should ink the route there soon, lest upper-minors hitters tattoo him in an altogether different manner.

Lineouts

Hitters

NAME	POS	TEAM	LVL	AGE	PA	R	2B	3B	HR	RBI	BB	K	SB	CS	AVG/OBP/SLG	TAv	BABIP	BRR	FRAA	WARP
Wynton Bernard	CF	ERI	AA	24	587	78	29	8	4	36	38	73	43	16	.301/.352/.408	.281	.344	2.6	CF(83): -3.4, LF(47): -0.0	2.9
Grayson Greiner	C	LAK	A+	22	343	24	12	0	3	21	27	90	0	0	.183/.254/.250	.199	.247	-0.1	C(88): -2.2	-0.9
Mike Hessman	1B	TOL	AAA	37	475	48	25	4	16	57	57	103	3	0	.237/.341/.437	.283	.276	-3.3	1B(47): 1.1, 3B(18): -1.0	1.5
Bryan Holaday	C	DET	MLB	27	65	3	5	0	2	13	1	13	0	0	.281/.292/.453	.259	.327	-0.2	C(18): -3.4, 2B(1): -0.0	-0.1
	C	TOL	AAA	27	179	18	8	0	2	17	10	35	1	1	.224/.282/.311	.217	.270	0.4	C(48): -9.6, P(1): -0.0	-1.0
Dixon Machado	SS	DET	MLB	23	78	6	3	0	0	5	7	14	1	0	.235/.307/.279	.208	.296	-0.7	SS(24): -0.8	-0.3
	SS	TOL	AAA	23	567	61	22	1	4	48	36	85	15	3	.261/.313/.332	.229	.305	2.0	SS(125): -5.6, 3B(2): -0.1	0.1
Andrew Romine	SS	DET	MLB	29	203	25	5	0	2	15	11	46	10	5	.255/.307/.315	.227	.328	-1.0	3B(59): 1.1, SS(27): 1.5	0.1
Kade Scivicque	C	ONE	A-	22	36	5	3	0	0	1	3	3	0	0	.406/.472/.500	.343	.448	-0.5	C(8): -0.2	0.4
	C	WMI	A	22	180	21	4	0	5	17	9	26	2	1	.242/.306/.358	.241	.261	-0.7	C(35): 0.8	0.4
Zach Shepherd	3B	WMI	A	19	443	48	17	2	5	51	47	117	4	3	.245/.327/.339	.262	.332	0.5	3B(105): -5.7	0.9
Josh Wilson	2B	DET	MLB	34	41	4	3	0	0	5	0	15	0	0	.316/.350/.395	.259	.522	-0.4	2B(11): -0.2, 3B(10): -0.3	0.0
	2B	TOL	AAA	34	293	30	14	1	3	30	22	70	10	2	.252/.316/.347	.237	.328	-3.5	2B(34): 2.8, 3B(24): 1.2	0.2

Wynton Bernard's plus-plus speed couldn't help him avoid being labeled a "nasty little fella" by Steve Harvey when he was on the Family Feud, but it *was* good enough to net him a spot on the 40-man roster. ❖ You know when you're walking down the stairs, something you've done 10 million times in your life, and you miss the step you've landed on 9,999,999 other times, and you land awkwardly, fall down and then lay there not knowing what just happened or what to do next? That was **Grayson Greiner**'s 2015. ❖ As his body limped to the finish line of a peripatetic baseball career, Triple-A virtuoso **Mike Hessman** broke a 79-year-old record with his 433rd career minor-league home run. Tune into *Baseball Prospectus 2095* to see who hits no. 434. ❖ **Bryan Holaday** is good enough as a backup catcher to both hide in the shadows of the dugout and maintain a steady sports paycheck, which means once he retires he can coach varsity at The Milford School. ❖ "Failed" shortstop prospect **Dixon Machado** forced his way back onto the 40-man and finished out the season as the Tigers' big-league shortstop. He's still not a threat to hit, but his delicious defense will keep him a useful backup. ❖ **Andrew Romine** has a magnificent head of hair, Roger Dorn levels of luxury, and this best separates him from your garden-variety utility infielder. ❖ If you judged by name alone, you might think that **Kade Scivicque** was a character in a soap opera, and his performance in Low-A wouldn't tell you differently. Fortunately he's young and restless, so these forthcoming days of our lives could allow the 2015 fourth-rounder to see the guiding light. ❖ A solidly built Australian, **Zach Shepherd** pairs his power to all fields with a solid approach, but notches too many strikeouts and is more likely to man left field than the hot corner. ❖ Allspice infielder **Josh Wilson** made the Tigers his ninth big-league team and fourth for whom he pitched. The best small sample of his career will make him randomly appear on a big-league roster near you.

Pitchers

NAME	TEAM	LVL	AGE	W	L	SV	G	GS	IP	H	HR	BB/9	K/9	GB%	BABIP	WHIP	ERA	FIP	FRA	WARP	CFIP	MPH
Tyler Alexander	ONE	A-	20	0	2	0	12	12	37	17	3	1.2	8.0	67%	.151	0.59	0.97	3.27	2.63	1.1	80	
Sandy Baez	ONE	A-	21	3	4	0	14	14	65^{1}	73	4	3.0	7.2	41%	.343	1.45	4.13	3.96	4.55	0.4	102	
Endrys Briceno	LAK	A+	23	2	3	0	8	6	33	39	2	3.8	4.4	52%	.327	1.61	4.09	4.89	6.14	-0.8	126	
Edgar De La Rosa	ERI	AA	24	0	1	1	13	0	16^{2}	21	1	9.7	6.5	29%	.370	2.34	7.56	6.03	7.57	-0.6	134	
Buck Farmer	DET	MLB	24	0	4	0	14	5	40^{1}	53	10	3.8	5.4	48%	.326	1.74	7.36	6.63	6.79	-0.9	120	95.2
	TOL	AAA	24	7	3	0	16	16	86^{2}	85	6	2.6	7.9	44%	.306	1.27	4.15	3.27	3.20	1.6	89	
Jeff Ferrell	DET	MLB	24	0	0	0	9	0	11^{1}	12	3	3.2	4.8	40%	.243	1.41	6.35	6.55	5.28	-0.1	112	95.3
	TOL	AAA	24	0	1	4	11	0	11^{1}	8	3	4.0	7.9	36%	.179	1.15	4.76	6.16	3.80	0.1	98	
	ERI	AA	24	0	0	12	17	1	27	21	4	1.3	11.7	32%	.279	0.93	1.67	3.16	1.31	1.1	59	
Austin Kubitza	ERI	AA	23	9	13	0	27	27	133^{2}	191	6	3.2	6.5	62%	.388	1.79	5.79	3.65	5.12	-0.5	109	
Jairo Labourt	LAK	A+	21	1	5	0	7	7	35^{2}	45	3	3.8	8.6	44%	.375	1.68	6.31	3.70	3.86	0.3	106	
	DUN	A+	21	2	7	0	18	18	80^{1}	83	6	4.9	7.8	43%	.314	1.58	4.59	4.15	4.23	0.2	116	
Confesor Lara	LAK	A+	24	1	0	3	9	0	16^{1}	10	1	1.7	11.0	40%	.243	0.80	1.10	2.06	2.44	0.4	79	
	ERI	AA	24	1	2	0	26	0	42^{1}	51	3	2.3	4.9	40%	.322	1.46	4.68	4.02	4.84	-0.2	107	
Joe Nathan	DET	MLB	40	0	0	1	1	0	0^{1}	0	0	0.0	27.0	0%	.000	0.00	0.00	-2.90	3.86	0.0	98	92.5
Angel Nesbitt	TOL	AAA	24	1	5	0	27	0	40^{1}	54	3	4.7	6.7	41%	.375	1.86	6.25	4.20	5.59	-0.6	115	
	DET	MLB	24	1	1	0	24	0	21^{2}	22	2	3.3	5.8	53%	.286	1.38	5.40	4.67	4.23	0.1	110	96.5
Drew Smith	ONE	A-	21	2	0	2	11	0	27^{2}	15	0	1.3	10.7	39%	.234	0.69	0.33	1.67	1.71	1.0	69	
Josh Zeid	TOL	AAA	28	4	3	2	42	4	70^{2}	68	4	5.0	7.5	42%	.309	1.51	4.46	4.01	5.16	-0.6	112	

A southpaw who would engender "Rembrandt" descriptions from a GMC commercial, **Tyler Alexander** has pitchability for days, helping his pedestrian fastball play up; his secondaries flash above-average. ❖ **Sandy Baez** is destined for the bullpen, but he could still be an impact arm if his potentially plus slider can become filthy enough to make "Sandy Baez" a euphemism. ❖ **Endrys Briceno** underwent Tommy John surgery in early 2014, but was healthy enough by July to return to the Land o' Lakes, where his smooth-as-butter delivery allowed him to knife through the opposition with mid-90s fastballs. ❖ **Edgar De La Rosa** missed most of 2015 with a torn lat. He touches 100 mph when healthy, though his secondary offerings are so down-market that teenagers ask him, "WHAT ARE THOOOOOSE?" ❖ **Buck Farmer** became the second Tigers relief pitcher in the designated-hitter era to record a base hit, which may explain his pitching numbers. ❖ **Jeff Ferrell** may not have big-league staying power, but he made this book thanks to an overnight conversion from ineffective Double-A starter to sizzling Double-A closer, resulting in his rapid promotion. ❖ **Austin Kubitza** has the frame of a starter, the pitch selection of a reliever and the stuff of an org arm. He's also insufferable when his teammates try to play spades. ❖ Acquired as part of the David Price trade, southpaw **Jairo Labourt** can run his fastball up to 97 mph. His slider will flash above-average at times, but both his changeup and command play 56k to his fastball's broadband. ❖ **Confesor Lara**'s name could play anywhere from *Metal Gear Solid* to *Mad Max: Fury Road*, but his stuff plays best in the middle innings.

❖ **Joe Nathan** experienced twice the elbow injuries (2) as batters faced (1) in 2015, with a torn UCL among the maladies. If he calls it a career, the man who ranks eighth in saves will hang it up anticlimactically, though that one batter was a strikeout and a save, so it's as "going out on top" as an elder closer can get. ❖ We were wrong last year. It turns out **Angel Nesbitt** *couldn't* help a team in the bullpen. ❖ Perhaps **Drew Smith** is an Otis Redding fan, as he came down with a tender arm after being selected in the third round. When healthy, he throws 95 to 98 mph and has a chance at a plus breaking ball. ❖ **Josh Zeid** was the only Tigers pitcher on the 40-man never to reach the big leagues, either because of chronic control issues or because he was alphabetically at the end. He was also outrighted in September.

Manager

Brad Ausmus

YEAR	TEAM	W	L	Pythag +/-	Avg PC	100+ P	120+ P	QS	BQS	REL	REL w Zero R	IBB	PH	PH Avg	PH HR	SB2	CS2	SB3	CS3	SAC Att	SAC%	POS SAC	Squeeze	Swing	In Play
2014	DET	90	72	3	101.0	103	3	90	9	473	367	34	71	.164	1	90	34	16	7	40	60.0	20	1	296	83
2015	DET	74	87	6	94.1	77	2	72	10	505	396	32	74	.121	1	66	44	17	5	43	53.5	23	1	293	86

We noted last year that Ausmus' Tigers led the majors in blown quality starts. We couldn't figure out why, though we offered three theories: 1) Ausmus hadn't adjusted to the pace of the game from the bench; 2) Ausmus figured his bullpen would blow the game anyway; and/or 3) Ausmus was too darn stubborn to change pitchers. Whatever explanation or combination of explanations applied in 2014 probably worked for 2015 as well, because the Tigers again led the majors in blown quality starts. You would have thought that such stagnation, plus the Tigers' change at general manager—Al Avila took over for Dave Dombrowski late in the season—would have equaled curtains for Ausmus. Nope. There were rumors before the season ended that Ausmus would be dismissed and Ron Gardenhire would be pursued, but those proved false—or, perhaps, premature. Hence Ausmus gets a shot at the hat trick.

One of the leading explanations behind Ausmus' retention is that he's good with the young players. That's probably true on a personal level. For instance, George Sipple of the Detroit Free Press reported in May that Ausmus flipped catcher James McCann a ball during BP, and on the ball was a note letting McCann know he'd be starting that night. Cute, right?

Less cute is what Ausmus did to Daniel Norris. The gem of the David Price payout, Norris was allowed to throw 54 pitches in the first inning of a late September start. We know as well as anyone that raw pitch count isn't the end-all, be-all for evaluating stress, but look, anytime a pitcher is topping 45, 50 pitches in the first, it's time to get him out of there. Ausmus didn't even remove Norris after the frame, either. Instead he let a 22-year-old—one who will literally help determine his and his organization's fate—return to the mound for only God knows what reason. The worst part? Ausmus removed Norris 17 pitches later, so he couldn't even claim "saving the bullpen" as a justification. Smart.

Ausmus has one guaranteed year remaining on his contract before the Tigers have to make a call on his 2017 option. Presumably, Avila will use 2016 as an evaluation year—for the team and its manager—meaning Ausmus will have to seek a new employer if he has another season like his last.

HOUSTON ASTROS

Essay by Evan Drellich

Player comments by David Temple and BP authors

The Astros were six outs from eliminating the Royals in Game 4 of the American League Division Series, an afternoon when Carlos Correa homered twice and also failed to glove a grounder up the middle. The series took a turn for the worse, but Correa won American League Rookie of the Year and the franchise won credibility—both deservedly so. By at least a year, the Astros and their phenom shortstop arrived ahead of schedule.

Expectations will soar now, because the misery of 2012-14 was sold to the public as the path to sustainability. Annual relevance is more and more elusive, as the *Providence Journal*'s Tim Britton detailed in these pages last year. But Astros general manager Jeff Luhnow's old Cardinals saddled the unicorn of annual success in part because of his blueprint, so he has his own standard to meet.

The Astros' rebuilding "Process"—a term sold on t-shirts at Minute Maid Park—has unfolded unlike any other strategy before it, even in comparison to the Cubs' simultaneous effort. Since Luhnow and owner Jim Crane took over the Astros, their Process has posed new questions of business ethics, and the merit of baseball's rules has been tested to a degree not seen in years.

Fifteen years ago, the Yankees pushed the envelope of baseball capitalism. They couldn't win a pennant or sign a free agent without a new round of "Now is it too much? How about now? Now?"

"Reward your fans," George Steinbrenner told the *New York Times* for a story that ran in January 2003. "You don't need to put it in your pocket like 90 percent of the rest of the owners may do. I feel we're very heavily loaded with revenue sharing. We're not going to go against it. We're trying to figure out ways to go around it and still contribute. We're not trying to avoid, we're not breaking any rules, but we're just trying to make sure we put the money back into our team."

The Astros too found an envelope to push; it just had a lot less cash in it. Without the resources of the Yankees and Dodgers, Luhnow turned to the unique advantage presented by outgoing general manager Ed Wade: the draft. Nothing is more central to the Astros' identity, and there is no better context to frame their operation than the drafts of 2012-14, when they selected first overall each time.

ASTROS PROSPECTUS

2015 W-L: 86-76, 2ND IN AL WEST

Pythag	.575	3rd	DER	.715	4th
RS/G	4.50	6th	B-Age	26.3	1st
RA/G	3.81	6th	P-Age	28.8	22nd
TAv	.267	6th	Salary	$72.5M	29th
BRR	5.13	8th	M$/MW	$1.6M	29th
TAv-P	.243	2nd	DL Days	599	3rd
FIP	3.63	8th	$ on DL	14%	12th

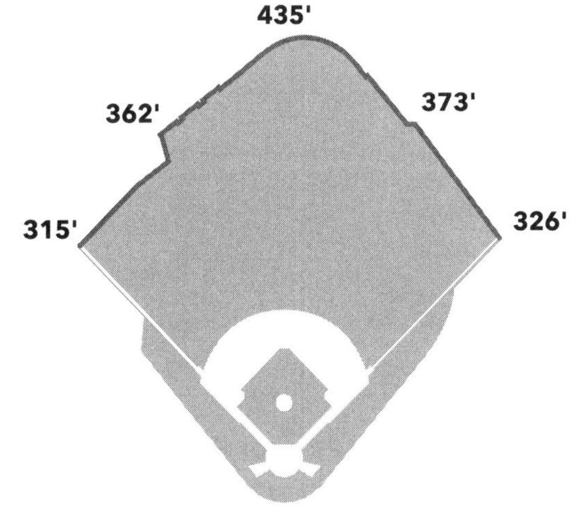

Outfield wall profile: **5'** to **25'**

Three-Year Park Factors

Runs	Runs/RH	Runs/LH	HR/RH	HR/LH
103	118	107	120	121

Top Hitter WARP	3.6	George Springer
Top Pitcher WARP	6.2	Dallas Keuchel
Top Prospect		Alex Bregman

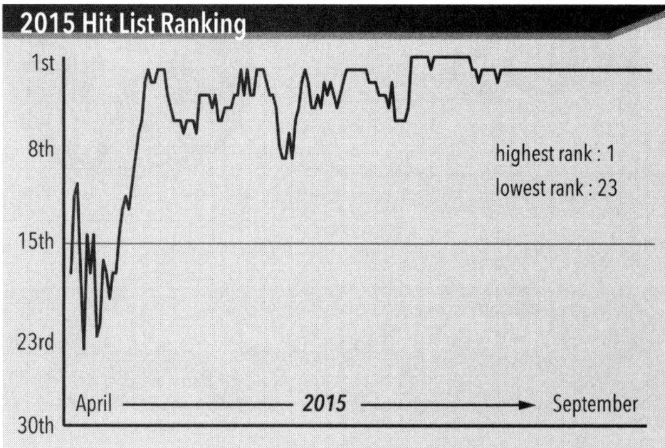

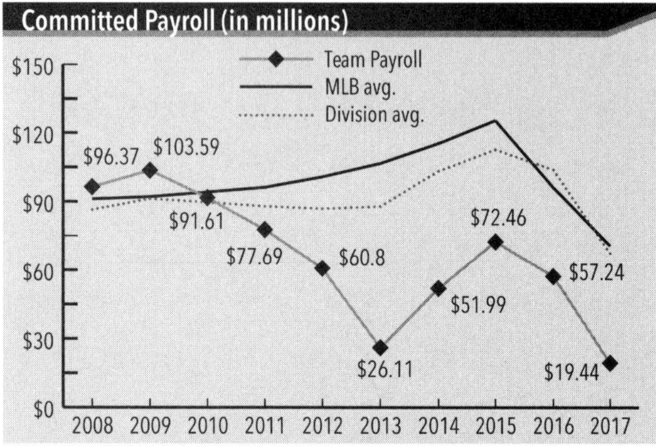

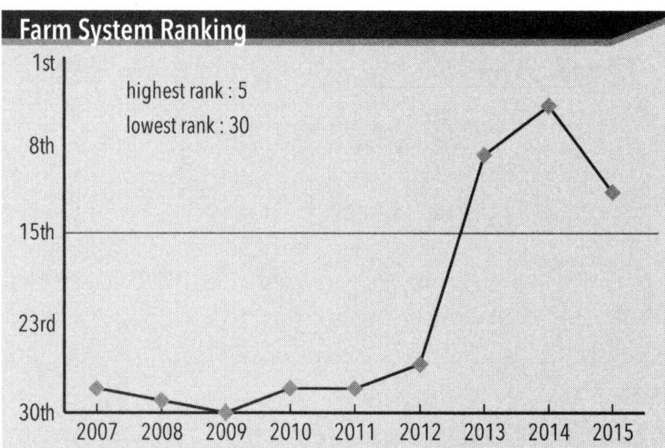

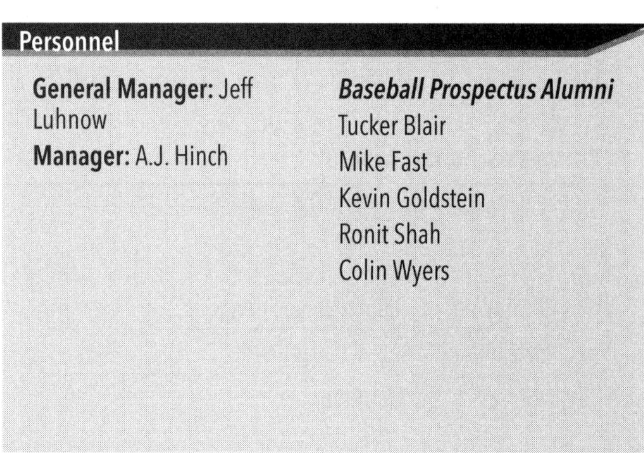

Personnel
General Manager: Jeff Luhnow
Manager: A.J. Hinch
Baseball Prospectus Alumni
Tucker Blair
Mike Fast
Kevin Goldstein
Ronit Shah
Colin Wyers

The Astros haven't been shown to have broken a rule. Yet how they have maneuvered and molded draft plans to the collective bargaining agreement is fodder for sports management courses. How should major league teams—big businesses acting as public trusts—morally operate? And even in situations absent any moral question, where do baseball's rules prove the most opportunistic or weakest? Where does shrewdness cross over into impropriety?

2012

Athlete worship is ugly. People are people, some are just muscular and inconceivably well paid and we don't know what they're like at home.

And with no further hedging, please join in gushing over Carlos Correa. There will be no greater development in 2016 than his continued success, and drafting him was a stroke of genius. How the Astros landed Correa four years ago, when they took him first overall and masterfully navigated the first amateur draft of the current CBA—well, it's lurid.

The Astros found themselves in a perfect storm of their own approach and good fortune. They used the lack of industry consensus over the No. 1 pick to convince the player they thought was the best to sign at a price, $4.8 million, suggesting they too had their doubts. The Astros had a tangible gain from saving money on that pick because of a new signing-bonus pool system, a gain that did not exist in the previous CBA—and a gain they were prepared for.

Mark Appel got $6.35 million from the Astros as the top pick a year after Correa. A year before Correa's draft, Gerrit Cole received $8 million from the Pirates. Including Cole, there were five players in 2011 who received higher bonuses than Houston's star shortstop.

Correa is the outlier. Starting with Correa's draft class, baseball's rules attached a dollar value to every pick in the top-10 rounds. Teams have a limited bonus pool to work from, but money saved on one pick can be applied elsewhere. Correa's pick was allotted $7.2 million, so his $4.8 million bonus banked the Astros $3.4 million. Voila: the Astros took a "tough sign" in Lance McCullers at No. 41 overall, and had the room to give him a bonus of $2.5 million.

The Astros' negotiating skills alone didn't make this happen. Hyper-competitive, Correa greatly wanted to be the first overall pick, which comes with prestige (as well as financial opportunities on the side). The belief is that if Correa did not agree to sign at a discounted rate, he may have slid as far as No. 6 or 7. The Astros saw him as the best player available, but kept everyone guessing, including the media, in part because their brain trust was undecided until very near to draft day.

Correa's upbringing in Puerto Rico actually helped erase the Astros' trail. There are certain dates when all teams watch Puerto Rican amateurs. Because every club is on hand, it's not easy for scouts to notice their rivals—to get a sense of which team is watching which players. Had Correa grown up in the continental U.S., the Astros' presence at his games would have been much more obvious. So the Astros kept their cards close to the vest, Correa reasonably didn't have much leverage to demand a higher bonus, and the Astros not only got their man, they got him on the cheap.

From the very beginning of this CBA, the Astros showed the new system was porous. The players' union probably didn't intend for top amateurs to be commonly selected with the intent of saving money. That's happened over and over in this current draft system, not just with the first overall pick. College seniors will sign for barely any money in the top-10 rounds, often far ahead of where they would likely be drafted based on talent alone, because they'll take a low bonus.

Everyone knows the strategy now. Everyone uses it. The Astros were the first to execute it.

2013

If the 2012 draft is the Astros' great success story, 2013 is the great failure. Tanking to earn a top draft pick, it turns out, does not bring automatic success. You can put your fans through four years of misery only to end up with Mark Appel. Or, more accurately, you can put your fans through four years of misery only to deal Appel, among others, to the Phillies for not another starting pitcher, not an every-day position player, but a reliever. The careers of Appel and Kris Bryant, the second overall pick in 2013, remain young and the tables could turn. But to this point, the Astros got it wrong. Bryant won National League Rookie of the Year for the Cubs. Appel hasn't won a spot on a 40-man roster.

Part of the impetus for any team to pick first overall three consecutive times is playing the odds. Someone might not work out. Appel was a dud, Correa blossomed. That's not what fans are sold on, though. The billboard never said, "We just want to get one of these guys right."

The failure of Appel flies in the face of the promise of the Astros' rebuild, the message that was hammered home to fans over and over: the team would be bad, but losing would get big draft picks who would make the team better. That's a tiny, shrouded slice of the picture. Most of the credit for the Astros' 2015 revival—contrary to the narrative—was not the draft-and-rebuild (with Correa and McCullers very notable exceptions).

Luhnow's roster assembly at the big league level and the development of players already in place made the Astros contenders again. Luhnow made strong moves with very limited resources in free agency (Luke Gregerson and Colby Rasmus). He swung creative trades (Luis Valbuena) and some great waiver claims (Collin McHugh and Will Harris). He also held on to many of the right players signed by the previous administration, from Dallas Keuchel to Jose Altuve to George Springer.

So why the misdirection around the value of picking so high in the draft?

When a team is tanking, it has a low payroll. Owners save gobs of money—and yes, there's an outside shot at a generational talent. But that approach is no more automatic a means to winning than the Yankees' old addiction to spend-spend-spend. The Astros have pocketed money in the exact way that Steinbrenner refused to.

If they're to keep winning, the drafts will have to pay off beyond high picks. They won't even have top picks to make anymore. So drafting and developing better than the competition is important. But while tanking isn't a golden ticket for success, it can be great for business—and what's great for business isn't necessarily what's best for players and fans.

2014

Can hardball go too far in negotiations?

Brady Aiken had Tommy John surgery less than a year after the Astros demonstrated concern over the ligament in question. He's with the Indians now, a first-round pick for them in 2015 after he went unsigned by the Astros as the first overall pick in 2014.

The litany of issues the Aiken-Astros soap opera surfaced could be a riot act for some corners of the CBA. From the availability of medical information before the draft to who determines the health of a drafted player—the team doctor has that power solely right now—Aiken and the Astros found themselves in a situation that highlighted an array of potential shortcomings in baseball's governance.

But what made the Aiken drama so contentious were the events after a $6.5 million signing bonus was agreed upon and the Astros didn't like what they saw in Aiken's physical. Aiken's agent, Casey Close, torched the Astros to FOXSports.com a month before the August draft signing deadline in 2014. The allegation was the Astros were using Aiken's elbow condition to manipulate the draft, leveraging a medical condition beyond what was fair, what was right—and doing so for the club's betterment. A reduced offer to Aiken would not only save them money, it potentially could have helped them land an additional pitcher in the draft.

As the drama unfolded, Luhnow was asked if he was following the rules. "Of course we are," he said.

Executives and baseball people exist in a small, insular world. The common opinion is that there is a baseline of respect that must be maintained. "Baseball has its nuances," Luhnow told the *Houston Chronicle* in 2013 on the subject of negotiation philosophy, before the Aiken drama. "You've got 30 teams negotiating with one another. You've got agents. The one thing that kind of levels the playing field in baseball is the fact that whether it's an agent or another team, you're going to be at the table again. So (if) you feel like you win this one, and you took advantage of the party, it's going to hurt you. You're going to be back at the table with some other deal that you really need." The Astros have dealt with Close's agency, Excel, many times since the Aiken mess.

So much remains unknown about the Aiken drama. The only significant supporting evidence for either party—verbal accusations aside—is that Aiken went for surgery. The concern surrounding Aiken's elbow was not limited to the need for Tommy John surgery, however—it was also how well he would recover from it. (Aiken could go on to have a brilliant career and the Astros could still have had their diagnosis spot on, because perhaps Aiken's hypothetical brilliant career will come against great hypothetical odds.)

It is possible that Close and union head Tony Clark, who also criticized the Astros verbally, were using their own form of manipulative negotiation—pressure via the press. The Astros stayed silent.

The ugliest part of the drama is that the beginning of another player's career hung in the balance. Pitcher Jacob Nix, a fifth-round pick of the Astros that year, passed his physical and went unsigned—collateral damage when Aiken didn't take his own deal. If the Astros had signed Nix without signing Aiken, the team would have blown way past its bonus pool and lost future draft picks. The total money slotted for the first overall pick disappeared when Aiken didn't sign, and the Astros needed the savings on Aiken's deal to finalize Nix's deal.

Nix received a six-figure sum to settle a grievance filed on his behalf.

Agents of Change?

What makes the Astros so compelling is not so much how they've performed as the kinds of questions they make us ask. They're questions that are ultimately answerable only by the reader.

It's true that somewhere along the way, the Astros probably went too far. The tanking effort hit a bottom that no organization has reached before, and the empty 2013 season was a direct slap in the face of competitiveness. As Mark Appel's situation shows us, the merits of tanking are debatable, and the benefits that do come from it aren't always spread evenly among the team, its players and fans.

Somewhere along the way, too, the Astros probably caught a bad rap for just doing things that benefited them and not others. When it comes to Correa's draft, all the Astros did was plan well and start to expose areas where the union may have miscalculated. Universally, the 2012 draft is rightly regarded as a stroke of genius.

Can genius become unfair? Is that what happened with Aiken?

Rules are what define sports, what separate them from Calvinball and art. Fans of opposing teams may have different feelings about a game, but they are bound by the same objective results. Without them, clear victory and champions can't exist. But where the Astros have operated and at times succeeded is the grey realm inside the framework of those rules—one where few precedents exist.

This leads to a broader discussion of moral weight. When rules are created, are the Astros still bound to a code of ethics greater than those stipulated by the league's constitution? Or is it now upon the rule-makers, the parties hashing out the next CBA in 2016, to create rules that foster ethics they desire?

We cannot say. What we can say, with assurance, is that the Astros, alone, did not make the rules. They may singularly make us re-think some. ■

—Evan Drellich is in his third season covering the Astros for the Houston Chronicle. He grew up in New York City and graduated from Binghamton University, alma mater of Tony Kornheiser and Flo from Progressive.

Hitters

Jose Altuve 2B

Born: 5/6/90 Age: 26 Bats: R Throws: R Height: 5'6" Weight: 165

YEAR	TEAM	LVL	AGE	PA	R	2B	3B	HR	RBI	BB	K	SB	CS	AVG/OBP/SLG	TAv	BABIP	BRR	FRAA	WARP
2013	HOU	MLB	23	672	64	31	2	5	52	32	85	35	13	.283/.316/.363	.243	.316	0.9	2B(145): -6.6	-0.1
2014	HOU	MLB	24	707	85	47	3	7	59	36	53	56	9	.341/.377/.453	.302	.360	5.9	2B(156): -7.5	4.8
2015	HOU	MLB	25	689	86	40	4	15	66	33	67	38	13	.313/.353/.459	.285	.329	-2.0	2B(153): -3.1	3.2
2016	*HOU*	*MLB*	*26*	*677*	*92*	*38*	*4*	*11*	*61*	*34*	*75*	*39*	*11*	*.305/.341/.432*	*.272*	*.326*	*0.6*	*2B -6*	*3.0*
2017	*HOU*	*MLB*	*27*	*583*	*69*	*32*	*3*	*12*	*67*	*29*	*64*	*33*	*10*	*.303/.339/.444*	*.275*	*.319*	*1.8*	*2B -5*	*3.0*

Breakout: 1% Improve: 52% Collapse: 7% Attrition: 16% MLB: 97% *Comparables: Aaron Hill, Martin Prado, Jose Lopez*

One might not predict a player coming off a batting title to change a lot about his batting approach, but that's exactly what Altuve did. The three-time All-Star pulled the ball more and took to the skies, converting some singles into long outs and some doubles into homers. He hit more home runs (15) in 2015 than he did in 2014 and 2013 combined; his ISO jumped 30 points; and his stolen-base totals (and success rate) took a drastic drop. He also hit his way into a new Gold Glove, to add to the changes in his game. This is not to say that Altuve has suddenly transformed into Chase Utley (that would seemingly upset the families of both players), but his new approach is worth noting.

Andrew Aplin CF

Born: 3/21/91 Age: 25 Bats: L Throws: L Height: 6'0" Weight: 205

YEAR	TEAM	LVL	AGE	PA	R	2B	3B	HR	RBI	BB	K	SB	CS	AVG/OBP/SLG	TAv	BABIP	BRR	FRAA	WARP
2013	LNC	A+	22	598	102	32	7	9	107	83	63	24	6	.278/.376/.424	.281	.297	4.4	CF(125): 9.8	4.7
2014	CCH	AA	23	434	49	11	1	6	50	65	56	21	8	.267/.379/.354	.280	.298	0.4	RF(55): 8.8, CF(42): -4.5	2.5
2014	OKL	AAA	23	116	14	3	1	0	15	15	15	5	3	.260/.348/.313	.249	.294	-0.3	CF(23): 5.5, RF(6): 0.2	0.7
2015	FRE	AAA	24	285	37	7	2	2	28	45	41	20	7	.275/.392/.348	.287	.326	1.5	CF(67): -7.4, RF(5): 0.0	1.2
2015	CCH	AA	24	134	27	3	4	0	12	24	13	12	3	.343/.458/.448	.313	.383	2.3	CF(21): -1.4, RF(10): -0.5	1.2
2016	*HOU*	*MLB*	*25*	*250*	*27*	*9*	*2*	*3*	*21*	*31*	*44*	*10*	*3*	*.236/.331/.331*	*.243*	*.277*	*0.6*	*CF 0, RF 0*	*0.5*
2017	*HOU*	*MLB*	*26*	*325*	*37*	*11*	*2*	*4*	*29*	*41*	*57*	*13*	*5*	*.234/.331/.335*	*.244*	*.273*	*1.3*	*CF 0, RF 0*	*0.7*

Breakout: 3% Improve: 14% Collapse: 5% Attrition: 20% MLB: 26% *Comparables: Che-Hsuan Lin, Cedric Hunter, Jake Smolinski*

Aplin has played some form of professional baseball for three years at this point, and has used that time to prove that he has better-than-average plate discipline, good range in the outfield, speed on the basepaths and not very much power. He's basically Jake Marisnick with a better command of the strike zone. And since Marisnick spent most of 2015 with the Houston club, it would be reasonable to expect that a slightly better version of him would be welcome in the Astros' lineup. Houston seems to agree, since they added Aplin to the 40-man roster to keep him away from the Rule 5 draft. He'll be 25 in 2016, and might have an outside shot of breaking camp on the big-league club. If not, he would be in the front of the line for a midseason injury replacement.

Alex Bregman SS

Born: 3/30/94 Age: 22 Bats: R Throws: R Height: 6'0" Weight: 180

YEAR	TEAM	LVL	AGE	PA	R	2B	3B	HR	RBI	BB	K	SB	CS	AVG/OBP/SLG	TAv	BABIP	BRR	FRAA	WARP
2015	QUD	A	21	133	18	5	0	1	13	17	13	5	2	.259/.368/.330	.263	.283	2.4	SS(26): 3.2	1.2
2015	LNC	A+	21	178	19	8	4	3	21	12	17	8	4	.319/.364/.475	.289	.336	-2.0	SS(37): -1.9	0.9
2016	*HOU*	*MLB*	*22*	*250*	*26*	*10*	*2*	*5*	*23*	*16*	*48*	*5*	*2*	*.236/.291/.355*	*.231*	*.276*	*0.0*	*SS 0*	*0.5*
2017	*HOU*	*MLB*	*23*	*348*	*38*	*14*	*2*	*7*	*35*	*23*	*65*	*7*	*4*	*.248/.303/.370*	*.242*	*.288*	*0.3*	*SS 0*	*1.1*

Breakout: 2% Improve: 18% Collapse: 9% Attrition: 14% MLB: 28% *Comparables: Joe Panik, Tyler Pastornicky, Jose Pirela*

If 66 games of low-level professional baseball are a good indication (they aren't), then Bregman should turn out to be a fine baseball player (he still may). He was certainly highly valued coming out of LSU, and forced the Astros to select him second overall lest they miss out on his talent. The Astros' brass seems to think he can stick at short, though there appears to be someone ensconced in that position already. He could move to second but—wouldn't you know it?—there appears to be a mainstay in that position, as well. There isn't necessarily a clear future for him quite yet, but there really isn't a clear future for any of us, so we probably shouldn't worry about it unless we enjoy mild depression and panic attacks. Maybe you do. If so, worry about Alex Bregman all you'd like.

Daz Cameron OF

Born: 1/15/97 Age: 19 Bats: R Throws: R Height: 6'2" Weight: 185

YEAR	TEAM	LVL	AGE	PA	R	2B	3B	HR	RBI	BB	K	SB	CS	AVG/OBP/SLG	TAv	BABIP	BRR	FRAA	WARP
2016	*HOU*	*MLB*	*19*	*250*	*25*	*8*	*1*	*4*	*18*	*15*	*85*	*10*	*5*	*.181/.234/.269*	*.183*	*.262*	*0.4*	*CF 2, LF 0*	*-0.9*
2017	*HOU*	*MLB*	*20*	*317*	*29*	*9*	*2*	*5*	*26*	*20*	*105*	*13*	*7*	*.185/.241/.279*	*.191*	*.264*	*1.4*	*CF 3, LF 0*	*-1.1*

Breakout: 0% Improve: 0% Collapse: 0% Attrition: 0% MLB: 0% *Comparables: Che-Hsuan Lin, Dalton Pompey, Abraham Almonte*

Cameron was a bit of a wildcard coming into the 2015 draft, as inconsistency at the plate and a high asking price turned some teams off. The Astros had the willingness and, more importantly, the bonus pool money to bring him into the fold, and so they nabbed him with the 37th pick. The son of former major-league outfielder Mike Cameron, Daz brings what many think is a complete, if not totally explosive, tool set. He has shown a good deal of speed in his limited time as a pro, and acquits himself well in center field. He gets high marks for his bat speed, but doesn't project to necessarily bring a lot of power to the plate. He's still a teenager, so he'll have lots of time to prove himself. He'll also have lots of time to incur the enormous weight of the task that we call living, but at least he'll have his $4 million signing bonus to pad his fall.

Chris Carter 1B

Born: 12/18/86 Age: 29 Bats: R Throws: R Height: 6'4" Weight: 250

YEAR	TEAM	LVL	AGE	PA	R	2B	3B	HR	RBI	BB	K	SB	CS	AVG/OBP/SLG	TAv	BABIP	BRR	FRAA	WARP
2013	HOU	MLB	26	585	64	24	2	29	82	70	212	2	0	.223/.320/.451	.281	.311	-2.0	1B(61): -5.1, LF(49): -6.4	0.6
2014	HOU	MLB	27	572	68	21	1	37	88	56	182	5	2	.227/.308/.491	.293	.267	0.3	1B(14): -0.5, LF(6): 0.1	2.6
2015	HOU	MLB	28	460	50	17	0	24	64	57	151	1	2	.199/.307/.427	.266	.244	-2.7	1B(115): -0.7	0.4
2016	*HOU*	*MLB*	*29*	*454*	*58*	*18*	*1*	*23*	*68*	*51*	*149*	*2*	*1*	*.222/.313/.452*	*.270*	*.283*	*-1.1*	*1B -2*	*0.8*
2017	*HOU*	*MLB*	*30*	*477*	*67*	*18*	*1*	*25*	*70*	*56*	*157*	*2*	*1*	*.220/.314/.449*	*.268*	*.280*	*-1.2*	*1B -2*	*0.8*

Breakout: 6% Improve: 58% Collapse: 2% Attrition: 3% MLB: 90% *Comparables: Chris Davis, Mark Reynolds, Travis Hafner*

If we learned anything from the 1996 Micheal Keaton movie *Multiplicity*, it's that making copies of copies leads to results of lesser quality than the original. This is the situation with Carter. Baseball's attempts to keep copying the three-true-outcome demigods of yesteryear have yielded them a barn of a man with tremendous power and atrocious contact skills. Since 2012, he hasn't had a season in which he struck out in less than 30 percent of his plate appearances. He did take his share of walks in 2015, but could not put up the same impressive power numbers from 2014 that made him a valuable asset. The things that kept him on the field in the past—his power potential, his winning smile, the fact that he was employed by the Astros—aren't good enough any more. Carter has gone from iffy prospect to a poor-hitting, poor-defending right-handed first baseman pushing 30. How many beakers must explode in a ball of glass and fire before an experiment can be deemed a failure?

Jason Castro C

Born: 6/18/87 Age: 29 Bats: L Throws: R Height: 6'3" Weight: 215

YEAR	TEAM	LVL	AGE	PA	R	2B	3B	HR	RBI	BB	K	SB	CS	AVG/OBP/SLG	TAv	BABIP	BRR	FRAA	WARP
2013	HOU	MLB	26	491	63	35	1	18	56	50	130	2	1	.276/.350/.485	.305	.351	2.1	C(98): -3.9	4.0
2014	HOU	MLB	27	512	43	21	2	14	56	34	151	1	0	.222/.286/.366	.245	.294	-2.3	C(114): 9.5	2.2
2015	HOU	MLB	28	375	38	19	0	11	31	33	115	0	0	.211/.283/.365	.231	.280	-1.2	C(103): 11.5	1.7
2016	*HOU*	*MLB*	*29*	*429*	*45*	*22*	*2*	*13*	*52*	*38*	*118*	*1*	*0*	*.238/.309/.405*	*.254*	*.305*	*-0.3*	*C 7*	*2.4*
2017	*HOU*	*MLB*	*30*	*418*	*50*	*20*	*1*	*12*	*48*	*40*	*115*	*0*	*0*	*.230/.308/.391*	*.249*	*.296*	*-0.5*	*C 6*	*2.0*

Breakout: 2% Improve: 36% Collapse: 6% Attrition: 8% MLB: 97% *Comparables: Carlton Fisk, Johnny Bench, Gary Carter*

YEAR	TEAM	P. COUNT	FRM RUNS	BLK RUNS	THRW RUNS	TOT RUNS
2013	HOU	13994	-1.0	-0.6	-0.5	-2.1
2014	HOU	16021	11.6	0.8	-1.0	11.5
2015	HOU	14019	10.9	-0.1	1.1	11.9
2016	*HOU*	*15255*	*7.7*	*-0.1*	*0.2*	*7.8*
2017	*HOU*	*14847*	*6.5*	*-0.1*	*0.1*	*6.5*

It's a bit of a shame that Castro's career year occurred during a time (2013) when his team was busy pouring gasoline onto fire at Santa's workshop. Having been long known to be an asset defensively, the promise he showed at the plate in 2013 would have been a welcome sight for the Astros in 2015. Alas, it seems as if his disappointing 2014 season wasn't just a fluke as he carried a lot of that disappointment over to 2015. In fact, between 2014 and 2015, he was the AL's worst starting catcher with the bat not named Caleb Joseph or Mike Zunino. He was, coincidentally, both the AL's best and the AL's worst catcher named Jason Castro during that same timeframe. He still provides enough value defensively that, unless Max Stassi suddenly learns how to hit, he'll most likely be the Astros' backstop for the near future.

Carlos Correa SS

Born: 9/22/94 Age: 21 Bats: R Throws: R Height: 6'4" Weight: 210

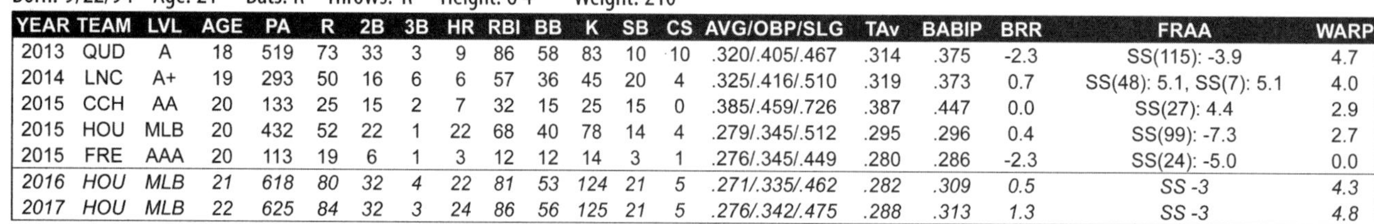

YEAR	TEAM	LVL	AGE	PA	R	2B	3B	HR	RBI	BB	K	SB	CS	AVG/OBP/SLG	TAv	BABIP	BRR	FRAA	WARP
2013	QUD	A	18	519	73	33	3	9	86	58	83	10	10	.320/.405/.467	.314	.375	-2.3	SS(115): -3.9	4.7
2014	LNC	A+	19	293	50	16	6	6	57	36	45	20	4	.325/.416/.510	.319	.373	0.7	SS(48): 5.1, SS(7): 5.1	4.0
2015	CCH	AA	20	133	25	15	2	7	32	15	25	15	0	.385/.459/.726	.387	.447	0.0	SS(27): 4.4	2.9
2015	HOU	MLB	20	432	52	22	1	22	68	40	78	14	4	.279/.345/.512	.295	.296	0.4	SS(99): -7.3	2.7
2015	FRE	AAA	20	113	19	6	1	3	12	12	14	3	1	.276/.345/.449	.280	.286	-2.3	SS(24): -5.0	0.0
2016	*HOU*	*MLB*	*21*	*618*	*80*	*32*	*4*	*22*	*81*	*53*	*124*	*21*	*5*	*.271/.335/.462*	*.282*	*.309*	*0.5*	*SS -3*	*4.3*
2017	*HOU*	*MLB*	*22*	*625*	*84*	*32*	*3*	*24*	*86*	*56*	*125*	*21*	*5*	*.276/.342/.475*	*.288*	*.313*	*1.3*	*SS -3*	*4.8*

Breakout: 8% Improve: 36% Collapse: 6% Attrition: 13% MLB: 59% *Comparables: Jason Heyward, Xander Bogaerts, Mike Trout*

Correa is a Saturday morning, a cup of coffee and the second chapter of your new favorite book. He's the 20 dollars you forgot you put in your winter coat. He's the sound of someone you love pulling into your driveway. Correa is a hand-knit afghan and a wanted kiss on the neck and extra-thick socks on a cold day. He's the smell of a puppy's head. He's a bump up to first class when you could really use a drink. He's that eye twitch finally going away. Correa is your favorite sweatshirt and your childhood swing set and a handful of jelly beans. He's that episode of *Survivor* where your least-favorite contestant gets voted off. He's a four-day weekend and a short line at the DMV and a pot of mac and cheese that you don't have to share. To see Correa swing a bat is to witness both a tornado and a calm winter evening. To see him field is an exercise in eye widening. His arm is a series of bungee cords wrapped around a Dead Sea Scroll. His legs are two-for-one Mad Dog margaritas. A video of him barehanding a grounder is on display right now at the Louvre. Correa built the pyramids and he wrote the first two seasons of *Deadwood* and he invented the plastic thing that keeps your shoelaces from fraying. He talked George Lucas into selling the *Star Wars* franchise. Correa is a fist pump. He's your best friend.

J.D. Davis 3B

Born: 4/27/93 Age: 23 Bats: R Throws: R Height: 6'3" Weight: 215

YEAR	TEAM	LVL	AGE	PA	R	2B	3B	HR	RBI	BB	K	SB	CS	AVG/OBP/SLG	TAv	BABIP	BRR	FRAA	WARP
2014	QUD	A	21	171	20	9	0	8	32	13	41	4	0	.303/.363/.516	.312	.364	0.5	3B(41): -1.9	1.4
2014	TCV	A-	21	131	18	7	1	5	20	15	25	1	0	.279/.382/.495	.320	.317	-0.3	3B(27): 3.9, RF(1): 0.0	1.6
2015	LNC	A+	22	552	93	28	3	26	101	54	157	5	2	.289/.370/.520	.294	.374	-1.3	3B(117): -1.6	3.5
2016	*HOU*	*MLB*	*23*	*250*	*27*	*10*	*1*	*10*	*32*	*17*	*82*	*0*	*0*	*.223/.285/.398*	*.243*	*.296*	*-0.4*	*3B -1*	*0.1*
2017	*HOU*	*MLB*	*24*	*410*	*49*	*16*	*1*	*15*	*50*	*29*	*135*	*0*	*0*	*.218/.282/.387*	*.239*	*.294*	*-0.8*	*3B -2*	*0.0*

Breakout: 1% Improve: 16% Collapse: 2% Attrition: 10% MLB: 47% *Comparables: Alex Gordon, Alex Liddi, Josh Bell*

Davis was a two-way player at Cal State Fullerton, but the Astros liked his bat enough to convert him to a full-time hitter. Though scouts predict he'll have to move to first at some point, he and his big arm have clung to third so far. He hit well at High-A Lancaster, featuring raw power and contact struggles, which probably makes him the perfect candidate for a Houston uniform. He'll have to wait a bit, however, as he'll be starting only his age-23 season in 2016. A move to Double-A should be in the plans to see if his bat can still work at a higher level. Also, seeing as the Astros have about 400 candidates that can only play first base or DH, they'll want to make sure Davis gets as many chances to stick at third as possible.

Matthew Duffy 3B

Born: 2/6/89 Age: 27 Bats: R Throws: R Height: 6'3" Weight: 215

YEAR	TEAM	LVL	AGE	PA	R	2B	3B	HR	RBI	BB	K	SB	CS	AVG/OBP/SLG	TAv	BABIP	BRR	FRAA	WARP
2013	LNC	A+	24	424	74	20	4	19	84	30	80	0	2	.323/.397/.553	.318	.366	-1.0	3B(95): 14.8, 1B(5): 0.1	5.5
2013	CCH	AA	24	95	11	4	0	5	10	3	22	1	1	.247/.295/.461	.277	.274	-0.3	3B(7): -0.1, 1B(4): 0.1	0.3
2014	CCH	AA	25	216	23	11	1	6	35	7	36	2	1	.302/.340/.455	.281	.342	-0.2	3B(35): 3.3, 1B(16): 1.1	1.5
2014	OKL	AAA	25	352	47	11	3	12	49	21	70	0	3	.279/.333/.448	.270	.319	-1.3	1B(55): 0.2, 3B(35): -0.8	0.9
2015	HOU	MLB	26	9	0	1	0	0	3	1	2	0	0	.375/.444/.500	.333	.500	0.0	1B(2): -0.0, 3B(2): -0.4	0.1
2015	FRE	AAA	26	557	94	29	2	20	104	48	90	4	1	.294/.366/.484	.291	.320	2.4	3B(75): 5.4, 1B(33): 0.3	4.0
2016	*HOU*	*MLB*	*27*	*162*	*17*	*7*	*1*	*6*	*21*	*9*	*38*	*0*	*0*	*.249/.302/.418*	*.256*	*.293*	*-0.2*	*1B 0, 3B 1*	*0.3*
2017	*HOU*	*MLB*	*28*	*322*	*39*	*13*	*1*	*11*	*40*	*18*	*75*	*0*	*0*	*.246/.302/.416*	*.255*	*.290*	*-0.6*	*1B 0, 3B 1*	*0.8*

Breakout: 1% Improve: 16% Collapse: 8% Attrition: 8% MLB: 24% *Comparables: James D'Antona, Jesus Guzman, Jason Rogers*

The Astros' Matt Duffy will most likely be referred to as The Astros' Matt Duffy for some time, thanks to the rise to prominence of the Giants' third sacker. TAMD isn't necessarily a slouch in his own right, though Houston really needs him to stick at third instead of the outfield given their lack of depth at the former and seemingly never-ending supply of it at the latter. He had a cup of coffee with Houston in 2015, though since he only logged eight games it was more like one of those tiny espresso cups. Though he lacks the love of the scouts, his walk and strikeout rates in the minors have been steadily improving since Double-A, and he looks to be yet another option for Houston to mull over come spring training.

Nolan Fontana SS

Born: 6/6/91 Age: 25 Bats: L Throws: R Height: 5'11" Weight: 205

YEAR	TEAM	LVL	AGE	PA	R	2B	3B	HR	RBI	BB	K	SB	CS	AVG/OBP/SLG	TAv	BABIP	BRR	FRAA	WARP
2013	LNC	A+	22	499	88	18	6	8	60	102	100	16	5	.259/.415/.399	.283	.327	3.9	SS(95): -9.4	2.8
2014	CCH	AA	23	305	33	21	1	1	26	61	76	5	8	.262/.418/.376	.304	.383	-2.7	2B(41): -0.2, SS(25): 1.3	2.3
2015	FRE	AAA	24	456	56	21	6	3	40	74	99	6	11	.241/.369/.357	.277	.317	0.1	SS(57): -6.3, 2B(31): -0.9	1.9
2016	*HOU*	*MLB*	*25*	*60*	*7*	*2*	*0*	*1*	*4*	*9*	*16*	*1*	*1*	*.210/.339/.314*	*.241*	*.288*	*-0.2*	*SS -0, 2B 0*	*0.1*
2017	*HOU*	*MLB*	*26*	*259*	*29*	*10*	*2*	*3*	*21*	*41*	*70*	*3*	*3*	*.213/.341/.318*	*.242*	*.291*	*-0.6*	*SS -2, 2B 0*	*0.4*

Breakout: 1% Improve: 9% Collapse: 3% Attrition: 12% MLB: 22% *Comparables: Daniel Muno, Andy Parrino, Greg Garcia*

Fontana's plate discipline might be his saving grace. Reports say he plays an almost-kind-of-decent infield—good positioning and footwork make up for an average arm and range—and has a swing that's made for contact. As previously noted, the shortstop position will be occupied in Houston for a little while, but Fontana could find himself in a utility role before too long. If he can prove that he can still draw walks in the majors, it will be hard to keep him down much longer; there's not much left for him to show. An infielder with on-base skills is like seeing *Die Hard* while flipping through channels: You didn't necessarily go searching for it, but are certainly glad you found it.

Evan Gattis DH

Born: 8/18/86 Age: 29 Bats: R Throws: R Height: 6'4" Weight: 260

YEAR	TEAM	LVL	AGE	PA	R	2B	3B	HR	RBI	BB	K	SB	CS	AVG/OBP/SLG	TAv	BABIP	BRR	FRAA	WARP
2013	GWN	AAA	26	22	1	4	0	1	1	0	4	0	0	.333/.364/.667	.344	.375	-0.6	LF(1): 0.6, C(1): -0.0	0.3
2013	ATL	MLB	26	382	44	21	0	21	65	21	81	0	0	.243/.291/.480	.271	.255	0.6	LF(48): 2.5, C(42): 7.0	2.7
2014	ATL	MLB	27	401	41	17	1	22	52	22	97	0	0	.263/.317/.493	.298	.298	-5.1	C(93): 0.3	2.8
2015	HOU	MLB	28	604	66	20	11	27	88	30	119	0	1	.246/.285/.463	.262	.264	0.0	LF(11): -1.7	0.6
2016	*HOU*	*MLB*	*29*	*593*	*70*	*26*	*5*	*29*	*90*	*32*	*129*	*1*	*0*	*.252/.299/.477*	*.272*	*.276*	*-1.4*		*1.6*
2017	*HOU*	*MLB*	*30*	*531*	*68*	*23*	*4*	*24*	*76*	*31*	*115*	*0*	*0*	*.248/.299/.459*	*.266*	*.274*	*-1.5*	-	*1.1*

Breakout: 6% Improve: 58% Collapse: 2% Attrition: 7% MLB: 96% *Comparables: Orlando Cepeda, Glenn Davis, Adam LaRoche*

YEAR	TEAM	P. COUNT	FRM RUNS	BLK RUNS	THRW RUNS	TOT RUNS
2013	ATL	5254	6.1	0.0	0.1	6.2
2014	ATL	12794	3.5	-1.0	-1.6	0.9

Gattis swings a bat like he believes that if he doesn't hit a home run, the bank will take his pa's farm away. That approach seemed to work for him in 2014 with Atlanta, but he turned back into a grizzly pumpkin when he made the move to Houston. He did achieve one of the most fun fun facts of the year by becoming the first player in 60 years to triple 11 times without stealing a base. Otherwise, he hit a few more dingers and even managed to cut down on his strikeout rate a bit, but a depressed BABIP and an inability to get on base severely cut into his value. The fact that he hung up the catcher's gear for a full-time DH role also depressed his worth. He'll have time to redeem himself, but somebody should tell him that a single or a walk still might still save his family's land.

Carlos Gomez CF

Born: 8/18/86 Age: 29 Bats: R Throws: R Height: 6'4" Weight: 260

YEAR	TEAM	LVL	AGE	PA	R	2B	3B	HR	RBI	BB	K	SB	CS	AVG/OBP/SLG	TAv	BABIP	BRR	FRAA	WARP
2013	MIL	MLB	27	590	80	27	10	24	73	37	146	40	7	.284/.338/.506	.293	.344	2.1	CF(145): 21.2	6.4
2014	MIL	MLB	28	644	95	34	4	23	73	47	141	34	12	.284/.356/.477	.300	.339	1.7	CF(145): 3.6	5.2
2015	MIL	MLB	29	314	42	20	1	8	43	23	70	7	6	.262/.328/.423	.273	.322	0.0	CF(72): -0.2, 2B(1): -0.0	1.4
2015	HOU	MLB	29	163	19	9	0	4	13	8	31	10	3	.242/.288/.383	.241	.278	2.0	CF(39): 4.4	0.9
2016	*HOU*	*MLB*	*30*	*604*	*89*	*29*	*5*	*21*	*67*	*38*	*145*	*29*	*10*	*.256/.314/.443*	*.266*	*.305*	*1.1*	*CF 9*	*3.6*
2017	*HOU*	*MLB*	*31*	*536*	*66*	*26*	*4*	*19*	*69*	*33*	*131*	*24*	*9*	*.255/.311/.442*	*.263*	*.305*	*1.9*	*CF 8*	*3.2*

Breakout: 2% Improve: 46% Collapse: 3% Attrition: 9% MLB: 100% *Comparables: Carlos Beltran, Curtis Granderson, Aaron Rowand*

Gomez's injury-riddled 2015 was a disappointment for both Milwaukee and Houston fans. Specifically, his injury down the stretch was a big hindrance to Houston's productivity at the end of the regular season and into the playoffs, as he struggled with an intercostal injury—damage to the muscles that lie between the ribs. If you haven't noticed, Gomez swings the bat hard all the time, every time. An injury to the body's trunk could be seen as a barrier to his batting approach. He still provided defensive value where he could, and there's really no reason to think he'll cease doing so in 2016. He should also be good for at least a dozen GIF-able moments, too, which provides another, if not different, kind of value.

Marwin Gonzalez SS

Born: 3/14/89 Age: 27 Bats: B Throws: R Height: 6'1" Weight: 205

YEAR	TEAM	LVL	AGE	PA	R	2B	3B	HR	RBI	BB	K	SB	CS	AVG/OBP/SLG	TAv	BABIP	BRR	FRAA	WARP
2013	OKL	AAA	24	183	16	10	1	1	15	8	23	4	1	.262/.293/.349	.234	.295	-0.5	SS(29): -4.1, 2B(13): 2.3	-0.1
2013	HOU	MLB	24	222	22	8	0	4	14	9	37	6	2	.221/.252/.319	.222	.250	1.1	SS(53): -1.0, 2B(10): 0.9	0.1
2014	HOU	MLB	25	310	33	15	1	6	23	17	58	2	4	.277/.327/.400	.261	.330	-0.6	SS(71): 1.0, 2B(11): 1.5	1.4
2015	HOU	MLB	26	370	44	18	1	12	34	16	74	4	5	.279/.317/.442	.261	.326	0.7	1B(43): 2.0, SS(32): -1.3	1.4
2016	*HOU*	*MLB*	*27*	*264*	*28*	*13*	*1*	*6*	*28*	*13*	*47*	*3*	*3*	*.258/.300/.395*	*.245*	*.291*	*0.3*	*3B -2, SS -1*	*0.3*
2017	*HOU*	*MLB*	*28*	*315*	*35*	*16*	*1*	*8*	*35*	*16*	*59*	*4*	*3*	*.253/.297/.398*	*.245*	*.285*	*0.6*	*3B -2, SS -1*	*0.4*

Breakout: 2% Improve: 49% Collapse: 5% Attrition: 9% MLB: 99% *Comparables: Brandon Crawford, Yuniesky Betancourt, Stephen Drew*

Gonzalez might still be best known as that dude who broke up Yu Darvish's no-hitter with two outs in the ninth back in 2013, but he's quietly turned himself into a pretty useful player. He played short after Jed Lowrie went down and before Carlos Correa came up, then moved to third for a spell while also relieving Jose Altuve at second every now and then. And while playing him at either first or in left field would seem like the moves of a manager either in an extra-innings affair or high on PCP, he actually started 32 games at one of those two positions. For a team stricken with injury and occasional ineffectiveness, Gonzalez served the superutility role nicely.

Though still sporting a laughable K/BB ratio, he had the most power-heavy season of his career. He belted a dozen dingers while adding almost 50 points of slug. He's not a late-blooming Albert Pujols or anything, but he's taken to his utility role well and could serve in that function for some time.

Teoscar Hernandez CF

Born: 10/15/92 Age: 23 Bats: R Throws: R Height: 6'2" Weight: 180

YEAR	TEAM	LVL	AGE	PA	R	2B	3B	HR	RBI	BB	K	SB	CS	AVG/OBP/SLG	TAv	BABIP	BRR	FRAA	WARP
2013	QUD	A	20	565	97	25	9	13	55	41	135	24	11	.271/.328/.435	.280	.344	6.4	CF(108): -8.5, RF(15): 2.2	3.0
2014	CCH	AA	21	98	12	4	1	4	10	2	36	2	3	.284/.299/.474	.291	.418	-1.0	CF(21): 0.4, RF(2): 0.1	0.6
2014	LNC	A+	21	455	72	33	8	17	75	49	117	31	6	.294/.376/.550	.327	.374	3.2	CF(82): 4.7, CF(10): 4.7	5.9
2015	CCH	AA	22	514	92	12	2	17	48	33	126	33	7	.219/.275/.362	.237	.261	7.4	CF(79): -1.1, RF(39): 3.8	1.2
2016	*HOU*	*MLB*	*23*	*250*	*32*	*10*	*2*	*8*	*25*	*12*	*78*	*9*	*3*	*.221/.261/.378*	*.227*	*.288*	*1.1*	*CF -1, RF 1*	*0.1*
2017	*HOU*	*MLB*	*24*	*345*	*38*	*13*	*3*	*11*	*41*	*17*	*106*	*13*	*4*	*.228/.268/.392*	*.234*	*.294*	*2.2*	*CF -1, RF 1*	*0.4*

Breakout: 2% Improve: 9% Collapse: 3% Attrition: 11% MLB: 26% *Comparables: Slade Heathcott, Franklin Gutierrez, Kirk Nieuwenhuis*

Hernandez had a pretty good minor-league season in 2014, and then had essentially the opposite of that in 2015. He maintained his home run power but lost more than 100 points off his BABIP, while his strike-zone judgment failed to improve. Meanwhile, his routes and his arm conspired to move him from center to right. Scouts still talk about all his other tools, and his power-speed combination entices, but he'll simply have to fill some of those holes in his swing before he'll be able to stick out in a crowded outfield-prospect pool.

Jon Kemmer RF

Born: 11/17/90 Age: 25 Bats: L Throws: L Height: 6'2" Weight: 220

YEAR	TEAM	LVL	AGE	PA	R	2B	3B	HR	RBI	BB	K	SB	CS	AVG/OBP/SLG	TAv	BABIP	BRR	FRAA	WARP
2013	TCV	A-	22	225	29	7	1	4	16	17	41	1	2	.221/.304/.327	.251	.258	0.1	LF(55): 1.4, RF(14): 0.7	0.5
2014	QUD	A	23	204	29	15	1	4	17	20	39	3	1	.289/.369/.450	.306	.350	1.8	1B(22): 0.6, LF(20): -0.1	1.7
2014	LNC	A+	23	159	32	10	1	12	33	4	33	0	1	.294/.314/.608	.299	.303	3.0	RF(19): -0.1, 1B(2): -0.1	1.1
2015	CCH	AA	24	425	67	28	4	18	65	45	89	9	1	.327/.414/.574	.338	.387	0.8	RF(48): 2.8, LF(21): -0.8	4.6
2016	*HOU*	*MLB*	*25*	*250*	*28*	*12*	*1*	*10*	*33*	*16*	*66*	*1*	*0*	*.246/.307/.437*	*.264*	*.301*	*-0.1*	*RF -1, LF 0*	*0.6*
2017	*HOU*	*MLB*	*26*	*303*	*38*	*14*	*2*	*12*	*39*	*22*	*83*	*1*	*0*	*.241/.308/.432*	*.262*	*.300*	*-0.3*	*RF -1, LF 0*	*0.8*

Breakout: 6% Improve: 24% Collapse: 6% Attrition: 29% MLB: 49% *Comparables: Steven Souza, Nolan Reimold, Bryce Brentz*

Kemmer needs to hire a brand manager or something. The 21st-rounder logged a .988 OPS in 2015 and still managed to fly under the radar. True, he did spend the entire season at Double-A, but he also didn't appear on many (if any) organizational lists coming into the season. Not to say he should have—he had merely an okay time in 2014 in A-ball, and he's old for pretty much all levels. But he greatly expanded his on-base abilities by significantly improving his walk rate and getting hit by a lot of pitches. His bat will be what keeps him interesting, as he doesn't provide much in the way of defensive value. He'll be given his age-25 season to prove himself—i.e., duplicate his 2015 season entirely—to finally get someone's attention.

Tony Kemp 2B

Born: 10/31/91 Age: 24 Bats: L Throws: R Height: 5'6" Weight: 165

YEAR	TEAM	LVL	AGE	PA	R	2B	3B	HR	RBI	BB	K	SB	CS	AVG/OBP/SLG	TAv	BABIP	BRR	FRAA	WARP
2013	QUD	A	21	120	21	1	1	1	9	19	18	4	2	.255/.387/.316	.269	.304	0.9	2B(17): 2.4, CF(3): -0.5	0.7
2013	TCV	A-	21	204	25	7	2	1	13	21	29	17	9	.282/.355/.362	.278	.325	-1.1	2B(47): 0.7, LF(3): -0.4	0.9
2014	LNC	A+	22	356	79	19	4	4	37	45	35	28	7	.336/.433/.468	.318	.367	7.0	2B(54): -1.6, 2B(7): -1.6	3.4
2014	CCH	AA	22	275	42	11	4	4	21	28	32	13	6	.292/.381/.425	.293	.322	5.7	2B(56): -2.3, LF(3): -0.1	2.1
2015	FRE	AAA	23	311	42	9	3	3	29	21	37	20	6	.273/.334/.362	.254	.305	1.8	2B(51): 0.2, CF(20): -0.7	0.8
2015	CCH	AA	23	230	36	10	1	0	19	35	28	15	8	.358/.457/.420	.303	.416	2.0	2B(39): -3.6, CF(7): -1.6	1.3
2016	*HOU*	*MLB*	*24*	*250*	*31*	*10*	*2*	*3*	*20*	*22*	*45*	*11*	*4*	*.255/.330/.360*	*.245*	*.297*	*0.5*	*2B -2, CF -1*	*0.4*
2017	*HOU*	*MLB*	*25*	*380*	*43*	*14*	*3*	*5*	*36*	*35*	*67*	*16*	*6*	*.255/.334/.364*	*.249*	*.294*	*1.7*	*2B -3, CF -1*	*0.8*

Breakout: 10% Improve: 14% Collapse: 5% Attrition: 17% MLB: 27% *Comparables: Eric Sogard, Cole Figueroa, Chris Coghlan*

Kemp's past successes got him pushed to Triple-A when he was only 23, and for the first time in his pro career he did not excel. His small stature won't bring him many dingers, but he's built a good swing that produces solid contact and helps him play into his speed. Before 2015, Kemp walked about as many times as he struck out, and his plate discipline is what will eventually land him a job on a big-league club. His main position is second, but he can play some outfield. He most likely just needs to grow (no pun intended) into his current level, but could very well be considered trade bait or the first infield call-up for Houston in 2016. He's cute as a button.

Jake Marisnick CF

Born: 3/30/91 Age: 25 Bats: R Throws: R Height: 6'4" Weight: 220

YEAR	TEAM	LVL	AGE	PA	R	2B	3B	HR	RBI	BB	K	SB	CS	AVG/OBP/SLG	TAv	BABIP	BRR	FRAA	WARP
2013	MIA	MLB	22	118	6	2	1	1	5	6	27	3	1	.183/.231/.248	.193	.232	0.4	CF(32): 5.2	0.1
2013	JAX	AA	22	298	43	13	3	12	46	17	68	11	6	.294/.358/.502	.311	.351	1.9	CF(54): 4.6, LF(11): -0.2	3.2
2014	NWO	AAA	23	377	50	16	4	10	40	17	64	24	6	.277/.326/.434	.276	.314	1.7	CF(81): -2.1, RF(4): 2.9	2.2
2014	MIA	MLB	23	51	3	0	0	0	0	3	19	5	0	.167/.216/.167	.151	.276	0.1	CF(13): 3.3	0.0
2014	HOU	MLB	23	186	18	8	0	3	19	5	48	6	3	.272/.299/.370	.246	.352	1.1	RF(31): 3.3, CF(17): 1.7	0.9
2015	HOU	MLB	24	372	46	15	4	9	36	18	105	24	9	.236/.281/.383	.243	.310	3.1	CF(99): 5.6, LF(16): 2.3	1.7
2016	*HOU*	*MLB*	*25*	*186*	*25*	*8*	*1*	*5*	*17*	*8*	*48*	*9*	*3*	*.242/.285/.385*	*.236*	*.298*	*0.7*	*LF 4, RF 2*	*0.8*
2017	*HOU*	*MLB*	*26*	*313*	*34*	*13*	*2*	*8*	*35*	*14*	*80*	*15*	*5*	*.240/.284/.391*	*.238*	*.294*	*1.9*	*LF 7, RF 3*	*1.4*

Breakout: 4% Improve: 54% Collapse: 8% Attrition: 19% MLB: 90% *Comparables: Felix Pie, Michael Saunders, Brian Anderson*

In terms of fringy Astros outfielders, Marisnick is a rich man's Robbie Grossman. In fairness to both parties, a labradoodle dressed as a member of the 1919 White Sox would still be considered a rich man's Robbie Grossman, but the point is that Houston seemingly found their ideal not-terrible fourth outfielder in Marisnick. For example, he can kiiiiind of hit. He's young enough that there's a chance he might even get better at kiiiiind-of-hitting. He's fast and can cover a lot of ground in any outfield spot. If you've got a case of Robbie Grossman, Jake Marisnick is just what the doctor ordered. It's not all sterling silver, however: He didn't get on base a whole lot, due to the fact that he was concentrating on swinging at every pitch that came his way. He still has the speed to snag some bags and beat out some weak grounders, but will have to learn to take a pitch every now and again if he wants to avoid being a poor man's somebody else soon.

Colby Rasmus CF

Born: 8/11/86 Age: 29 Bats: L Throws: L Height: 6'2" Weight: 195

YEAR	TEAM	LVL	AGE	PA	R	2B	3B	HR	RBI	BB	K	SB	CS	AVG/OBP/SLG	TAv	BABIP	BRR	FRAA	WARP
2013	TOR	MLB	26	458	57	26	1	22	66	37	135	0	1	.276/.338/.501	.297	.356	1.0	CF(114): 5.2	3.9
2014	TOR	MLB	27	376	45	21	1	18	40	29	124	4	0	.225/.287/.448	.270	.294	-0.5	CF(87): 1.7	1.6
2014	BUF	AAA	27	24	0	0	0	0	2	1	9	0	0	.130/.167/.130	.126	.214	0.0	CF(4): 0.3	-0.3
2015	HOU	MLB	28	485	67	23	2	25	61	47	154	2	1	.238/.314/.475	.283	.305	1.9	LF(72): -3.5, RF(43): 7.3	3.0
2016	*HOU*	*MLB*	*29*	*582*	*69*	*25*	*4*	*24*	*75*	*49*	*166*	*3*	*1*	*.233/.300/.431*	*.257*	*.290*	*0.8*	*LF -4, RF 2*	*1.6*
2017	*HOU*	*MLB*	*30*	*464*	*58*	*20*	*3*	*19*	*61*	*41*	*135*	*2*	*1*	*.228/.299/.425*	*.254*	*.285*	*0.5*	*LF -3, RF 1*	*1.1*

Breakout: 3% Improve: 49% Collapse: 1% Attrition: 1% MLB: 96% *Comparables: Vic Wertz, Larry Walker, Craig Wilson*

In 2015, Rasmus packed up his drum of canola oil, headed down to Houston and plugged himself nicely into the Astros' swing-happy, dinger-mashing lineup. He hit the most home runs of his career, had a nice bounceback from his 2014 season, and even managed some postseason heroics. Not bad for a guy whose personal style leads one to believe he makes his living buying Zima for high school kids. Because he's been around for so long, it's easy to forget that Rasmus is only entering his age-29 year. He's had his ups and downs, some of which have been chalked up to differences with management, or to his all-or-nothing approach. But he's always had the tools, and has appeared lately to be a happy camper.

A.J. Reed 1B

Born: 5/10/93 Age: 23 Bats: L Throws: L Height: 6'4" Weight: 240

YEAR	TEAM	LVL	AGE	PA	R	2B	3B	HR	RBI	BB	K	SB	CS	AVG/OBP/SLG	TAv	BABIP	BRR	FRAA	WARP
2014	TCV	A-	21	150	22	11	0	5	30	22	22	2	0	.306/.420/.516	.349	.337	-1.8	1B(31): -1.2	1.3
2014	QUD	A	21	135	21	9	1	7	24	8	32	0	0	.272/.326/.528	.298	.314	-2.3	1B(18): -1.0	0.4
2015	CCH	AA	22	237	38	14	1	11	46	27	49	0	0	.332/.405/.571	.334	.383	-4.5	1B(32): -1.6	1.5
2015	LNC	A+	22	385	75	16	4	23	81	59	73	0	0	.346/.449/.638	.360	.385	1.2	1B(64): 3.4	5.1
2016	*HOU*	*MLB*	*23*	*102*	*13*	*4*	*0*	*5*	*15*	*10*	*26*	*0*	*0*	*.256/.331/.471*	*.283*	*.306*	*-0.1*	*1B -0*	*0.4*
2017	*HOU*	*MLB*	*24*	*360*	*49*	*16*	*2*	*16*	*51*	*35*	*93*	*0*	*0*	*.257/.332/.464*	*.279*	*.311*	*-0.6*	*1B -1*	*1.2*

Breakout: 2% Improve: 25% Collapse: 3% Attrition: 22% MLB: 66% *Comparables: Chris Carter, Jerry Sands, Brandon Belt*

As Houston fans watched some version of Chris Carter or Jon Singleton or Luis Valbuena probably strike out in 2015, their groans of frustration were stifled by a very loud whisper coming from both nowhere and everywhere at the same time: "Rest easy, child. A.J. Reed is coming… ." Reed's minor-league numbers from 2015 could be categorized as "stupid good" by anyone who likes baseball and using the word "stupid" as a both an adjective and a positive modifier. He has done pretty much everything in his power (pun 84 percent intended) to convince Houston brass to let him have a shot at fixing the cosmic suck the team suffered at first base in 2015. He may not be the savior Houston is looking for, but considering that Marwin Gonzalez logged the second-most plate appearances at first base for the Astros last year, the coming of Reed should at least bring some relief for the organization.

George Springer RF

Born: 9/19/89 Age: 26 Bats: R Throws: R Height: 6'3" Weight: 215

YEAR	TEAM	LVL	AGE	PA	R	2B	3B	HR	RBI	BB	K	SB	CS	AVG/OBP/SLG	TAv	BABIP	BRR	FRAA	WARP
2013	OKL	AAA	23	267	50	7	4	18	53	41	65	22	3	.311/.425/.626	.373	.362	1.6	CF(47): -2.2, RF(11): -0.3	4.0
2013	CCH	AA	23	323	56	20	0	19	55	42	96	23	5	.297/.399/.579	.350	.390	4.9	CF(70): -6.0, LF(3): 0.4	4.1
2014	HOU	MLB	24	345	45	8	1	20	51	39	114	5	2	.231/.336/.468	.304	.294	0.5	RF(71): 2.0, CF(8): 0.3	2.6
2014	OKL	AAA	24	61	17	4	1	3	9	9	15	4	0	.353/.459/.647	.372	.455	1.4	RF(7): 0.1, CF(6): -0.5	1.0
2015	HOU	MLB	25	451	59	19	2	16	41	50	109	16	4	.276/.367/.459	.299	.342	2.3	RF(93): 5.6, CF(10): 0.6	3.6
2015	CCH	AA	25	20	4	1	0	0	0	2	6	1	0	.278/.350/.333	.232	.417	0.2	RF(3): -0.2	0.0
2016	*HOU*	*MLB*	*26*	*568*	*83*	*22*	*3*	*28*	*84*	*66*	*166*	*19*	*5*	*.258/.354/.485*	*.300*	*.328*	*1.8*	*RF 0, CF 0*	*4.0*
2017	*HOU*	*MLB*	*27*	*531*	*80*	*20*	*2*	*27*	*82*	*64*	*155*	*18*	*4*	*.259/.359/.494*	*.301*	*.327*	*2.1*	*RF 0, CF 0*	*3.9*

Breakout: 6% Improve: 54% Collapse: 8% Attrition: 11% MLB: 99% *Comparables: Paul Goldschmidt, Steven Souza, Kyle Blanks*

Though hampered a bit by injury in 2015, Springer took the roux of his 2014 season and used it to mix up a pretty good gumbo. His strikeout numbers were still high, though much improved from his previous year's spit-take-level rate. He suffered a broken wrist in the middle of the season, which not only knocked him out for a while, but impacted his power numbers when he returned. The homers were fewer, but he still managed to sprinkle in some tape-measure shots here and there, along with a helping of doubles. He also saw his average and on-base percentage rise while continuing to play an excellent right field. He's an incredibly fun player to watch, whether you're a Houston fan or not.

Kyle Tucker OF

Born: 1/17/97 Age: 19 Bats: L Throws: R Height: 6'4" Weight: 190

YEAR	TEAM	LVL	AGE	PA	R	2B	3B	HR	RBI	BB	K	SB	CS	AVG/OBP/SLG	TAv	BABIP	BRR	FRAA	WARP
2016	*HOU*	*MLB*	*19*	*250*	*24*	*9*	*1*	*5*	*21*	*9*	*71*	*7*	*2*	*.195/.226/.302*	*.188*	*.252*	*0.5*	*RF 1, CF 0*	*-1.2*
2017	*HOU*	*MLB*	*20*	*337*	*32*	*13*	*2*	*8*	*34*	*13*	*95*	*9*	*3*	*.210/.242/.338*	*.207*	*.266*	*1.2*	*RF 1, CF 0*	*-1.0*

Breakout: 0% Improve: 0% Collapse: 0% Attrition: 0% MLB: 0% *Comparables: Oswaldo Arcia, Ramon Flores, Caleb Gindl*

Tucker was the fifth-overall pick in the 2015 draft, and is considered a better talent than his brother and current Astros outfielder, Preston. The Gatorade Florida Player of the Year shows power to all fields and demonstrates a swing that sends beat writers to the thesaurus. And unlike the elder Tucker, his defensive profile ranks in the comfortable "potential for center but with the arm to be good in right" range. A downside: Kyle and Preston's parents have almost certainly become insufferable braggarts who people now avoid at the grocery store. Their yearly Christmas card is not even opened by more than 50 percent of its recipients. Thanks for ruining Christmas, Kyle.

Preston Tucker LF

Born: 7/6/90 Age: 25 Bats: L Throws: L Height: 6'0" Weight: 215

YEAR	TEAM	LVL	AGE	PA	R	2B	3B	HR	RBI	BB	K	SB	CS	AVG/OBP/SLG	TAv	BABIP	BRR	FRAA	WARP
2013	OKL	AAA	23	267	50	7	4	18	53	41	65	22	3	.311/.425/.626	.373	.362	1.6	CF(47): -2.2, RF(11): -0.3	4.0
2013	CCH	AA	23	323	56	20	0	19	55	42	96	23	5	.297/.399/.579	.350	.390	4.9	CF(70): -6.0, LF(3): 0.4	4.1
2014	HOU	MLB	24	345	45	8	1	20	51	39	114	5	2	.231/.336/.468	.304	.294	0.5	RF(71): 2.0, CF(8): 0.3	2.6
2014	OKL	AAA	24	61	17	4	1	3	9	9	15	4	0	.353/.459/.647	.372	.455	1.4	RF(7): 0.1, CF(6): -0.5	1.0
2015	HOU	MLB	25	451	59	19	2	16	41	50	109	16	4	.276/.367/.459	.299	.342	2.3	RF(93): 5.6, CF(10): 0.6	3.6
2015	CCH	AA	25	20	4	1	0	0	0	2	6	1	0	.278/.350/.333	.232	.417	0.2	RF(3): -0.2	0.0
2016	*HOU*	*MLB*	*25*	*187*	*21*	*9*	*0*	*8*	*26*	*13*	*42*	*0*	*0*	*.248/.305/.438*	*.262*	*.283*	*-0.1*	*LF -0, RF 0*	*0.5*
2017	*HOU*	*MLB*	*26*	*401*	*51*	*19*	*0*	*16*	*53*	*29*	*91*	*1*	*1*	*.250/.307/.437*	*.262*	*.288*	*-0.4*	*LF -1, RF 0*	*1.1*

Breakout: 9% Improve: 38% Collapse: 12% Attrition: 30% MLB: 83% *Comparables: Eric Thames, Corey Dickerson, Matt LaPorta*

In 2015, Tucker proved, against all odds, that it is scientifically possible to have a dad bod as a 24-year-old. He was not able to prove, however, that he has the ability to hit left-handed pitching or play very good defense. Tucker is a bopper by trade, although one who doesn't strike out as much as the colors on his uniform suggest. Summoned to fill the Springer-sized void in the outfield, he's also had experience playing first base, and is probably better suited there. His limited upside suggests a life of wandering the waiver wire, but as a member of one of the less jeans-oriented franchises, he'll get a chance.

Luis Valbuena 3B

Born: 11/30/85 Age: 30 Bats: L Throws: R Height: 5'10" Weight: 200

YEAR	TEAM	LVL	AGE	PA	R	2B	3B	HR	RBI	BB	K	SB	CS	AVG/OBP/SLG	TAv	BABIP	BRR	FRAA	WARP
2013	CHN	MLB	27	391	34	15	1	12	37	53	63	1	4	.218/.331/.378	.260	.233	-0.2	3B(94): -0.3, 2B(6): -0.1	1.2
2014	CHN	MLB	28	547	68	33	4	16	51	65	113	1	2	.249/.341/.435	.292	.294	-0.2	3B(124): -11.1, 2B(21): -1.3	2.2
2015	HOU	MLB	29	493	62	18	0	25	56	50	106	1	0	.224/.310/.438	.267	.235	1.9	3B(99): -6.2, 1B(31): 1.9	1.5
2016	*HOU*	*MLB*	*30*	*543*	*60*	*25*	*2*	*18*	*68*	*58*	*115*	*1*	*2*	*.237/.322/.410*	*.262*	*.273*	*0.7*	*3B -6, 1B 0*	*1.0*
2017	*HOU*	*MLB*	*31*	*504*	*62*	*23*	*1*	*16*	*59*	*55*	*110*	*1*	*1*	*.230/.315/.395*	*.255*	*.267*	*0.6*	*3B -6, 1B 0*	*0.5*

Breakout: 0% Improve: 32% Collapse: 7% Attrition: 12% MLB: 83% *Comparables: Morgan Ensberg, Justin Turner, Brendan Harris*

Valbuena came to the Astros in 2015 to do two things: hit home runs and chew bubble gum. And he was all out of bubble gum. Then, he ran out of home runs, too. In the first half of 2015, Valbuena didn't spend a lot of time on base, because he was either making outs (which he did a lot) or hitting home runs. Despite being on pace for a 40-homer season through the first half, his copius flaws rendered him basically a replacement-level player, if not worse. After the break he actually started *hitting* better, improving his batting average, on-base percentage and slugging percentage. He did all of this while playing bad-but-not-terrible third base. One can assume he also ate and slept, as well. Despite concluding as one of his more ragged seasons, Valbuena is slated for a full-time job at third this season. PECOTA is bearish, but after a couple years of Matt Dominguez, even 25 good plate appearances a year feels like a reprieve.

Danry Vasquez LF

Born: 1/8/94 Age: 22 Bats: L Throws: R Height: 6'3" Weight: 190

YEAR	TEAM	LVL	AGE	PA	R	2B	3B	HR	RBI	BB	K	SB	CS	AVG/OBP/SLG	TAv	BABIP	BRR	FRAA	WARP
2013	WMI	A	19	423	47	16	5	6	40	31	56	9	8	.283/.334/.400	.279	.313	-0.7	LF(96): -2.4	1.5
2013	QUD	A	19	128	12	2	1	3	20	6	15	2	0	.288/.323/.398	.285	.304	-1.1	LF(32): 0.5	0.6
2014	LNC	A+	20	475	67	30	2	5	47	40	68	1	2	.291/.353/.407	.272	.335	-1.7	RF(53): -8.8, LF(25): 1.5	-0.3
2015	LNC	A+	21	182	21	13	2	3	21	13	24	6	4	.315/.365/.470	.297	.355	1.2	LF(38): 3.3	1.6
2015	CCH	AA	21	296	30	13	1	0	19	16	42	3	7	.245/.294/.300	.214	.289	-2.5	LF(54): 1.2, RF(3): -0.1	-1.1
2016	*HOU*	*MLB*	*22*	*250*	*20*	*11*	*1*	*3*	*23*	*11*	*51*	*2*	*2*	*.231/.267/.332*	*.214*	*.275*	*-0.6*	*LF 2, RF -0*	*-0.3*
2017	*HOU*	*MLB*	*23*	*313*	*30*	*14*	*2*	*4*	*28*	*15*	*63*	*2*	*2*	*.233/.273/.341*	*.221*	*.277*	*-0.6*	*LF 3, RF 0*	*-0.2*

Breakout: 1% Improve: 3% Collapse: 1% Attrition: 5% MLB: 6% *Comparables: Alex Romero, Adron Chambers, Cedric Hunter*

Some prospects are young for their level; Vasquez has always been thin for his. The lanky left fielder has failed to add to his frame, or his résumé, over the past couple of years, especially after getting obliterated by opposing pitchers at Double-A. It's not a good sign for a player who sorely needs his bat to carry him: His defense in the corners is indifferent at best, his baserunning is lackluster and his eye average. Vasquez is young enough to turn it around, and has shown the ability to pick up the spare when repeating levels. Given his flaws, the ceiling here is old friend Frank Catalonotto. Given his performance, that ceiling is nearly out of view.

Tyler White 3B

Born: 10/29/90 Age: 25 Bats: R Throws: R Height: 5'11" Weight: 225

YEAR	TEAM	LVL	AGE	PA	R	2B	3B	HR	RBI	BB	K	SB	CS	AVG/OBP/SLG	TAv	BABIP	BRR	FRAA	WARP
2013	TCV	A-	22	127	19	2	0	3	25	13	9	1	0	.286/.362/.384	.312	.287	0.3	3B(26): -1.2, 1B(8): -0.1	1.0
2014	QUD	A	23	290	41	20	1	7	41	35	40	0	1	.305/.414/.485	.335	.337	-3.6	3B(62): -3.6, 1B(2): 0.4	2.6
2014	LNC	A+	23	186	28	13	1	8	23	28	27	0	0	.267/.403/.527	.313	.276	-2.5	1B(31): -0.2, 1B(4): -0.2	0.9
2015	FRE	AAA	24	259	37	19	1	7	59	42	38	0	1	.362/.467/.559	.354	.412	-3.0	1B(25): -1.5, 3B(3): -0.1	2.4
2015	CCH	AA	24	236	33	6	0	7	40	42	35	1	0	.284/.415/.426	.297	.313	0.2	3B(44): -2.6, 1B(3): -0.2	1.3
2016	*HOU*	*MLB*	*25*	*250*	*28*	*12*	*1*	*7*	*31*	*30*	*51*	*0*	*0*	*.255/.352/.420*	*.276*	*.298*	*-0.4*	*3B -1, 1B -1*	*0.7*
2017	*HOU*	*MLB*	*26*	*283*	*36*	*14*	*1*	*8*	*33*	*31*	*58*	*0*	*0*	*.254/.344/.413*	*.269*	*.300*	*-0.7*	*3B -1, 1B -1*	*0.7*

Breakout: 3% Improve: 19% Collapse: 12% Attrition: 32% MLB: 60% *Comparables: James Darnell, Kila Ka'aihue, Zelous Wheeler*

Players picked in the 33rd round with Billy Jo Robidoux–like facial hair and physique and no natural defensive position aren't supposed to even make the Annual, yet here we are. White was drafted as someone for live arms to strike out in Rookie leagues, but he never stopped hitting, capping his rise through the system with an otherworldly two months at Triple-A Fresno. His batting eye is as sharp as they come, but his power is gap at best and he offers nothing outside the 24 square feet of the batter's box. Even if the bat were real, he's at the back of a fairly long line, and doesn't need to be added to the 40-man until next winter.

PITCHERS

Scott Feldman RHP

Born: 2/7/83 Age: 33 Bats: L Throws: R Height: 6'7" Weight: 220

YEAR	TEAM	LVL	AGE	W	L	SV	G	GS	IP	H	HR	BB/9	K/9	GB%	BABIP	WHIP	ERA	FIP	DRA	WARP	CFIP	MPH
2013	CHN	MLB	30	7	6	0	15	15	91	79	10	2.5	6.6	53%	.255	1.14	3.46	3.90	3.20	1.9	104	92.4
2013	BAL	MLB	30	5	6	0	15	15	90^2	80	9	3.1	6.5	51%	.262	1.22	4.27	4.16	3.88	1.1	105	92.0
2014	HOU	MLB	31	8	12	0	29	29	180^1	185	16	2.5	5.3	49%	.291	1.30	3.74	4.14	3.99	1.8	111	90.9
2015	HOU	MLB	32	5	5	0	18	18	108^1	115	13	2.2	5.1	51%	.291	1.31	3.90	4.29	4.72	0.4	115	92.6
2016	*HOU*	*MLB*	*33*	*10*	*10*	*0*	*29*	*29*	*174*	*178*	*22*	*2.6*	*6.1*	*50%*	*.286*	*1.31*	*4.51*	*4.53*	*4.73*	*0.8*	*110*	
2017	*HOU*	*MLB*	*34*	*9*	*11*	*0*	*29*	*29*	*175*	*193*	*23*	*2.9*	*5.8*	*50%*	*.300*	*1.42*	*4.77*	*4.65*	*5.00*	*0.2*	*117*	

Breakout: 16% Improve: 46% Collapse: 16% Attrition: 9% MLB: 92% *Comparables: Orel Hershiser, Bob Rush, Karl Drews*

Feldman was signed in 2013 to shut up the people who realized that the Astros' payroll could barely cover the price of a scalped Taylor Swift concert ticket. Until he got hurt, he was perfectly serviceable in 2015, which was exactly what the Astros needed him to be (serviceable, that is, not hurt). He's in the final year of his contract, and probably even nearer to the end of his usefulness to the pitching-rich Astros; soon he'll strap on the bindle and find another bad team to perform for, giving the fans six innings per game to think there's still a chance of winning.

Riley Ferrell RHP

Born: 10/18/93 Age: 22 Bats: R Throws: R Height: 6'2" Weight: 200

YEAR	TEAM	LVL	AGE	W	L	SV	G	GS	IP	H	HR	BB/9	K/9	GB%	BABIP	WHIP	ERA	FIP	DRA	WARP	CFIP	MPH
2015	QUD	A	21	0	0	1	12	0	16^2	10	0	7.0	9.2	58%	.244	1.38	1.08	3.70	5.37	-0.2	111	
2016	*HOU*	*MLB*	*22*	*1*	*0*	*1*	*31*	*0*	32^1	*33*	*4*	*6.0*	*7.1*	*50%*	*.299*	*1.70*	*5.38*	*5.34*	*5.55*	*-0.3*	*132*	
2017	*HOU*	*MLB*	*23*	*1*	*0*	*1*	*27*	*0*	*38*	*39*	*4*	*5.7*	*7.0*	*50%*	*.301*	*1.67*	*5.15*	*5.05*	*5.31*	*-0.2*	*126*	

Breakout: 0% Improve: 0% Collapse: 0% Attrition: 0% MLB: 0% *Comparables: Colton Murray, Brian Ellington, Brandon Cunniff*

Ferrell hails from the same TCU relief corps that produced Brandon Finnegan, and was about as dominant as a college reliever could be. He gave up far too many walks, but also managed to strike out 15 batters per nine, which, according to our spreadsheets, is a very good number. The third-rounder's fastball sits in the mid-90s and he can hump it up to around 98, with the customary lagging secondaries. His strikeout numbers will be enough to keep him around for a while, but his career path will hinge on whether he can start controlling his pitches better.

Josh Fields RHP

Born: 8/19/85 Age: 30 Bats: R Throws: R Height: 6'0" Weight: 195

YEAR	TEAM	LVL	AGE	W	L	SV	G	GS	IP	H	HR	BB/9	K/9	GB%	BABIP	WHIP	ERA	FIP	DRA	WARP	CFIP	MPH
2013	HOU	MLB	27	1	3	5	41	0	38	31	8	4.3	9.5	38%	.245	1.29	4.97	5.13	4.44	0.1	94	96.7
2014	HOU	MLB	28	4	6	4	54	0	54^2	50	2	2.8	11.5	33%	.343	1.23	4.45	2.12	2.61	1.3	70	96.9
2015	HOU	MLB	29	4	1	0	54	0	50^2	39	2	3.4	11.9	37%	.308	1.14	3.55	2.16	2.69	1.2	71	97.1
2016	*HOU*	*MLB*	*30*	*2*	*1*	*0*	*44*	*0*	*47*	*39*	*5*	*3.1*	*10.3*	*37%*	*.287*	*1.18*	*3.49*	*3.47*	*3.74*	*0.6*	*78*	
2017	*HOU*	*MLB*	*31*	*2*	*1*	*2*	*45*	*0*	47^2	*41*	*5*	*3.5*	*10.0*	*37%*	*.286*	*1.24*	*3.74*	*3.66*	*4.01*	*0.4*	*84*	

Breakout: 29% Improve: 53% Collapse: 17% Attrition: 12% MLB: 90% *Comparables: John Axford, Derrick Turnbow, Jason Motte*

September was rough on all the Astros, but until that point Fields was finally seeing results approach his excellent peripherals over the past two years. The former Rule 5 pick can light up the radar gun pretty well, and his mechanics have improved over time from horror show to acceptable, leaving the Astros with one of the better setup men in baseball. It's the kind of under-the-radar move that illustrates the importance of not only finding talent, but cultivating it: The 2014-15 Astros were the recipients of the Josh Fields that the Seattle Mariners expected in 2010, when they drafted him as a college reliever and fast-tracked him to the majors. Not all happy accidents are accidental.

Mike Fiers RHP

Born: 6/15/85 Age: 31 Bats: R Throws: R Height: 6'2" Weight: 200

YEAR	TEAM	LVL	AGE	W	L	SV	G	GS	IP	H	HR	BB/9	K/9	GB%	BABIP	WHIP	ERA	FIP	DRA	WARP	CFIP	MPH
2013	MIL	MLB	28	1	4	0	11	3	22^1	28	8	2.4	6.0	37%	.270	1.52	7.25	7.14	8.40	-1.0	114	90.9
2013	NAS	AAA	28	1	2	0	5	5	28^2	24	3	3.8	9.4	47%	.284	1.26	2.20	4.09	4.78	0.3	93	
2014	NAS	AAA	29	8	5	0	17	17	102^1	80	8	1.5	11.3	46%	.289	0.95	2.55	2.90	4.23	1.8	58	
2014	MIL	MLB	29	6	5	0	14	10	71^2	46	7	2.1	9.5	36%	.224	0.88	2.13	2.96	2.33	2.1	80	92.0
2015	HOU	MLB	30	2	1	0	10	9	62^1	45	10	3.0	8.5	39%	.217	1.06	3.32	4.36	3.42	1.2	100	92.2
2015	MIL	MLB	30	5	9	0	21	21	118	117	14	3.3	9.2	41%	.316	1.36	3.89	3.87	4.19	1.2	89	91.8
2016	*HOU*	*MLB*	*31*	*10*	*9*	*0*	*29*	*29*	165^1	*144*	*21*	*2.8*	*8.9*	*40%*	*.276*	*1.19*	*3.96*	*3.97*	*4.21*	*1.8*	*95*	
2017	*HOU*	*MLB*	*32*	*9*	*9*	*0*	*27*	*27*	*159*	*147*	*21*	*2.9*	*8.3*	*40%*	*.281*	*1.25*	*4.20*	*4.12*	*4.47*	*1.2*	*102*	

Breakout: 14% Improve: 37% Collapse: 22% Attrition: 13% MLB: 86% *Comparables: Colby Lewis, Adam Bernero, Kevin Appier*

When Carlos Gomez was traded from Milwaukee to Houston at the 2015 trade deadline, a common topic for discussion was whether the Astros gave up too much. But they didn't trade four prospects for Gomez. They traded four prospects for Gomez and Fiers. The king of the slow high fastball has settled into a role as a Very Useful Engine, taking the mound every fifth day and producing mid-rotation results, and once in a while a no-hitter. If there's a flaw in his game, it's everything: That 90 mph fastball shouldn't work, his control isn't *that* great for a junkballer and his home run rate will always be unsettling, especially in his new cozy confines. And yet Fiers gets it done, and does it cheap. He's under team control until he's old enough to run for President. By then he'll probably figure out how to throw a pitch that splits the ball in half, and he'll still be striking out a batter an inning.

Ken Giles RHP

Born: 9/20/90 Age: 25 Bats: R Throws: R Height: 6'2" Weight: 205

YEAR	TEAM	LVL	AGE	W	L	SV	G	GS	IP	H	HR	BB/9	K/9	GB%	BABIP	WHIP	ERA	FIP	DRA	WARP	CFIP	MPH
2013	CLR	A+	22	2	2	6	24	0	25²	23	4	6.7	11.9	32%	.306	1.64	6.31	4.96	4.42	0.0	103	
2014	LEH	AAA	23	2	0	5	11	0	13²	10	0	5.3	5.9	31%	.256	1.32	2.63	4.02	4.79	0.0	111	
2014	REA	AA	23	0	0	7	13	0	15	8	0	3.0	17.4	44%	.348	0.87	1.20	0.49	3.16	0.3	49	
2014	PHI	MLB	23	3	1	1	44	0	45²	25	1	2.2	12.6	46%	.267	0.79	1.18	1.31	1.38	1.7	58	100.3
2015	PHI	MLB	24	6	3	15	69	0	70	59	2	3.2	11.2	47%	.311	1.20	1.80	2.16	2.41	1.9	74	99.8
2016	*HOU*	*MLB*	*25*	*3*	*1*	*37*	*54*	*0*	*57¹*	*48*	*6*	*3.0*	*10.7*	*46%*	*.294*	*1.17*	*3.28*	*3.33*	*3.52*	*1.1*	*73*	
2017	*HOU*	*MLB*	*26*	*3*	*1*	*4*	*50*	*0*	*59¹*	*50*	*6*	*3.0*	*10.8*	*46%*	*.300*	*1.17*	*3.11*	*3.04*	*3.34*	*1.0*	*68*	

Breakout: 34% Improve: 57% Collapse: 19% Attrition: 19% MLB: 87% *Comparables: Joey Devine, David Robertson, Trevor Rosenthal*

Giles followed up his breakout 2014 with a reputation-cementing 2015: He's hard-throwing and hard to hit. An early-season velocity dip was the biggest concern that faced him all year, and as the temperature warmed and 95 turned back into 98 and 99, so too did fears of potential arm trouble subside. The Phillies didn't *need* to trade Giles—he's not a free agent until after the 2020 season, and surely they'd like to be competitive enough to need a top-notch closer sometime in the next five years—but they apparently felt that the Velasquez-Appel-Eshelman-Arauz-Oberholtzer package was too good to turn down. On the flip side, the Astros have built a system deep enough that they could make the deal to strengthen an already-strong bullpen without entirely mortgaging their future. We can't call it a win-win because there are too many ways for the trade to go wrong for both sides, but you can at least see the logic all around. For his part, Giles will surely appreciate the additional opportunities for saves that will burnish his arbitration cases come 2017 and beyond.

Luke Gregerson RHP

Born: 5/14/84 Age: 32 Bats: L Throws: R Height: 6'3" Weight: 200

YEAR	TEAM	LVL	AGE	W	L	SV	G	GS	IP	H	HR	BB/9	K/9	GB%	BABIP	WHIP	ERA	FIP	DRA	WARP	CFIP	MPH
2013	SDN	MLB	29	6	8	4	73	0	66¹	49	3	2.4	8.7	47%	.257	1.01	2.71	2.67	2.68	1.5	83	90.3
2014	OAK	MLB	30	5	5	3	72	0	72¹	58	6	1.9	7.3	54%	.256	1.01	2.12	3.27	2.85	1.5	91	90.3
2015	HOU	MLB	31	7	3	31	64	0	61	48	5	1.5	8.7	62%	.264	0.95	3.10	2.83	3.06	1.2	84	91.4
2016	*HOU*	*MLB*	*32*	*3*	*1*	*5*	*59*	*0*	*62²*	*55*	*7*	*2.4*	*8.4*	*57%*	*.279*	*1.15*	*3.73*	*3.72*	*3.97*	*0.6*	*86*	
2017	*HOU*	*MLB*	*33*	*3*	*1*	*12*	*61*	*0*	*57²*	*56*	*7*	*2.7*	*7.5*	*57%*	*.289*	*1.27*	*4.17*	*4.07*	*4.44*	*0.2*	*99*	

Breakout: 20% Improve: 42% Collapse: 31% Attrition: 8% MLB: 98% *Comparables: LaTroy Hawkins, Jeff Montgomery, Mike Marshall*

Gregerson is the poster child for the "closers are made not born" argument. After signing a three-year deal with Houston after the 2014 season, the long-time setup man was given his first full-time closer role at the age of 31. He responded by posting the best K/BB rate of his career while managing to navigate most late-inning situations very well. His home run problems from 2014 haven't gone away quite yet, but the sinker sunk better than ever, helping set a career-high groundball rate. His fastball rarely goes much above 90 mph, but good command and an ability to induce weak contact with late movement help make up for that. Barring injury or a wacky trade, he should be part of Houston's high-leverage relief corps for a while.

Will Harris LHP

Born: 1/24/84 Age: 32 Bats: L Throws: L Height: 6'0" Weight: 185

YEAR	TEAM	LVL	AGE	W	L	SV	G	GS	IP	H	HR	BB/9	K/9	GB%	BABIP	WHIP	ERA	FIP	DRA	WARP	CFIP	MPH
2016	*HOU*	*MLB*	*31*	*3*	*1*	*0*	*54*	*0*	*57¹*	*51*	*7*	*3.1*	*9.0*	*48%*	*.284*	*1.24*	*3.99*	*3.99*	*4.23*	*0.4*	*95*	
2017	*HOU*	*MLB*	*32*	*3*	*1*	*1*	*52*	*0*	*53*	*49*	*7*	*3.5*	*8.7*	*48%*	*.287*	*1.31*	*4.33*	*4.24*	*4.59*	*0.1*	*104*	

Breakout: 23% Improve: 36% Collapse: 27% Attrition: 19% MLB: 80% *Comparables: Brian Tallet, Jim Henderson, Jared Burton*

When Harris joined Houston in 2015, he was a 30-year-old reliever claimed off waivers three times. With the Astros, he blossomed into a reliever with a safe job and a slight home run problem. He may continue to succeed or fail from this point forward because Relievers Are Just Like Us (subject to the human condition and unpredictable as a species)!

Scott Kazmir LHP

Born: 8/28/84 Age: 31 Bats: R Throws: R Height: 6'4" Weight: 225

YEAR	TEAM	LVL	AGE	W	L	SV	G	GS	IP	H	HR	BB/9	K/9	GB%	BABIP	WHIP	ERA	FIP	DRA	WARP	CFIP	MPH
2013	CLE	MLB	29	10	9	0	29	29	158	162	19	2.7	9.2	42%	.324	1.32	4.04	3.54	4.44	0.9	89	95.7
2014	OAK	MLB	30	15	9	0	32	32	190¹	171	16	2.4	7.8	44%	.285	1.16	3.55	3.38	3.55	2.9	91	94.3
2015	HOU	MLB	31	2	6	0	13	13	73¹	78	13	2.9	6.6	40%	.288	1.39	4.17	5.16	5.02	0.0	115	94.4
2015	OAK	MLB	31	5	5	0	18	18	109²	84	7	2.9	8.3	48%	.262	1.09	2.38	3.13	3.11	2.5	90	94.7
2016	*HOU*	*MLB*	*32*	*10*	*9*	*0*	*28*	*28*	*168*	*160*	*21*	*2.7*	*8.3*	*44%*	*.294*	*1.25*	*4.03*	*4.01*	*4.28*	*1.7*	*98*	
2017	*HOU*	*MLB*	*33*	*9*	*9*	*0*	*28*	*28*	*167²*	*166*	*21*	*2.7*	*7.8*	*44%*	*.297*	*1.29*	*4.14*	*4.06*	*4.40*	*1.4*	*101*	

Breakout: 15% Improve: 52% Collapse: 26% Attrition: 14% MLB: 94% *Comparables: Vic Raschi, Wandy Rodriguez, Gavin Floyd*

For a pitcher who spent two years out of baseball, Kazmir has been remarkably consistent upon his return. His pitches have maintained near-constant velocity and he's employed them with near-constant command, while perhaps most surprisingly taking the hill almost every fifth day. His last contract was one of the riskiest two-year deals in recent memory; his next will be both longer and safer. Kazmir caught gopheritis in the stale summer Houston air, nearly tripling his home run rate after a July trade, but there was little mechanically different on which to blame it. Once he resumes his third-starter status, few outside Houston will remember his poor end to 2015. And if the Astros continue their ascent, even their own fans will have forgotten the Kazmir Era by next October.

Dallas Keuchel LHP

Born: 1/1/88 Age: 28 Bats: L Throws: L Height: 6'3" Weight: 210

YEAR	TEAM	LVL	AGE	W	L	SV	G	GS	IP	H	HR	BB/9	K/9	GB%	BABIP	WHIP	ERA	FIP	DRA	WARP	CFIP	MPH
2013	HOU	MLB	25	6	10	0	31	22	153^{2}	184	20	3.0	7.2	58%	.340	1.54	5.15	4.28	4.85	0.0	101	91.7
2014	HOU	MLB	26	12	9	0	29	29	200	187	11	2.2	6.6	65%	.296	1.17	2.92	3.24	3.33	3.6	95	92.0
2015	HOU	MLB	27	20	8	0	33	33	232	185	17	2.0	8.4	62%	.269	1.02	2.48	2.88	2.78	6.2	81	91.8
2016	*HOU*	*MLB*	*28*	*12*	*10*	*0*	*32*	*32*	*192*	*173*	*19*	*2.2*	*7.9*	*63%*	*.287*	*1.14*	*3.56*	*3.58*	*3.78*	*3.1*	*83*	
2017	*HOU*	*MLB*	*29*	*11*	*9*	*0*	*29*	*29*	*177*	*167*	*17*	*2.1*	*7.6*	*63%*	*.295*	*1.17*	*3.60*	*3.50*	*3.82*	*2.8*	*84*	

Breakout: 23% Improve: 61% Collapse: 18% Attrition: 6% MLB: 94% *Comparables: Brandon Webb, Brandon McCarthy, Roy Halladay*

There's an argument to be made that Dallas Keuchel wouldn't be a Gold Glove-caliber defender if he weren't a Cy Young-caliber pitcher. The pitcher can really only make a play if the ball is hit directly at him or very near him—there's no reaction time allowed to make many diving stops or the like. So for him to show off his defensive prowess, he needs to get chances. To get chances, he needs to get hitters to hit the ball at him. In order to maximize his chances of making a play, it would help if those balls were softly hit. This is all a roundabout way to talk about what makes him such a good pitcher. It's not that he simply induces groundballs. He induces *soft* groundballs. He does this by avoiding the heart of the plate like Wesley Snipes avoids roundhouses and taxes. This is why he gets the most soft tappers to the mound, and why he gets the most chances to turn those into outs. If you cross your eyes, you can almost see that Keuchel won two pitching awards in 2015.

Francis Martes RHP

Born: 11/24/95 Age: 20 Bats: R Throws: R Height: 6'1" Weight: 225

YEAR	TEAM	LVL	AGE	W	L	SV	G	GS	IP	H	HR	BB/9	K/9	GB%	BABIP	WHIP	ERA	FIP	DRA	WARP	CFIP	MPH
2015	QUD	A	19	3	2	2	10	8	52	33	1	2.2	7.8	48%	.229	0.88	1.04	2.78	3.21	1.1	88	
2015	CCH	AA	19	1	0	0	3	3	14^{2}	19	2	4.3	9.8	30%	.386	1.77	4.91	4.32	4.56	0.1	99	
2015	LNC	A+	19	4	1	0	6	5	35	31	1	2.1	9.5	55%	.309	1.11	2.31	2.81	3.20	1.0	79	
2016	*HOU*	*MLB*	*20*	*4*	*4*	*0*	*20*	*11*	*67^{2}*	*68*	*9*	*3.4*	*7.4*	*42%*	*.294*	*1.39*	*4.63*	*4.51*	*4.82*	*0.2*	*114*	
2017	*HOU*	*MLB*	*21*	*7*	*8*	*0*	*29*	*23*	*156^{2}*	*166*	*23*	*3.4*	*6.9*	*42%*	*.299*	*1.44*	*4.86*	*4.75*	*5.06*	*0.0*	*120*	

Breakout: 0% Improve: 0% Collapse: 0% Attrition: 0% MLB: 0% *Comparables: Manny Banuelos, Jacob Turner, Sean Gallagher*

Martes might win the award for Most Improved Astro of 2015. After getting thrown into the Jarred Cosart deal, he was seen as a stuff-first prospect who needed a lot of refinement. Mechanical changes boosted velocity on his fastball, and he can now bring it in the mid-to-high 90s with late life. He's also working on a change resembling average, which will nicely complement his already-devastating curveball. He'll only be 20 in 2016, so his arrival is probably still more than a year away as he develops the stamina to match his stuff. If Houston makes another playoff run, however, they have a potential weapon for the late innings if they need it.

Lance McCullers RHP

Born: 10/2/93 Age: 22 Bats: L Throws: R Height: 6'2" Weight: 205

YEAR	TEAM	LVL	AGE	W	L	SV	G	GS	IP	H	HR	BB/9	K/9	GB%	BABIP	WHIP	ERA	FIP	DRA	WARP	CFIP	MPH
2013	QUD	A	19	6	5	0	25	19	104^{2}	92	3	4.2	10.1	57%	.327	1.35	3.18	3.05	4.24	1.2	88	
2014	LNC	A+	20	3	6	4	25	18	97	95	18	5.2	10.7	48%	.311	1.56	5.47	5.73	5.77	-0.6	109	
2015	CCH	AA	21	3	1	1	7	5	32	16	1	3.9	13.5	42%	.234	0.94	0.56	2.20	2.26	1.1	73	
2015	HOU	MLB	21	6	7	0	22	22	125^{2}	106	10	3.1	9.2	48%	.288	1.19	3.22	3.23	3.62	2.1	87	97.4
2016	*HOU*	*MLB*	*22*	*9*	*8*	*0*	*28*	*28*	*140*	*123*	*16*	*3.5*	*9.4*	*48%*	*.292*	*1.28*	*3.89*	*3.93*	*4.12*	*1.7*	*92*	
2017	*HOU*	*MLB*	*23*	*7*	*7*	*0*	*29*	*23*	*155*	*141*	*18*	*3.6*	*9.6*	*48%*	*.299*	*1.30*	*3.89*	*3.80*	*4.12*	*1.4*	*92*	

Breakout: 24% Improve: 36% Collapse: 16% Attrition: 17% MLB: 66% *Comparables: Matt Cain, Michael Wacha, Joel Zumaya*

If any one player was the embodiment of the 2015 Astros' season, it was McCullers. Everyone saw promise and potential, but also youth—he and they both seemed at least a year away. It was fitting, then, that when the Astros went HAM McCullers played a big part. The 21-year-old did not break camp with the big-league club, and was seen as a spot starter when he got called up in May. He then proceeded to triple-dog dare the front office to send him back down. The former first-rounder relied on an impressive fastball, nasty curve and the occasional changeup to strike out more than a batter per inning. His one blemish was a good deal of walks, which led to high pitch counts and disappointing early exits—hey, we said he was just like the 2015 Astros, didn't we?

Collin McHugh RHP

Born: 6/19/87 Age: 29 Bats: R Throws: R Height: 6'2" Weight: 190

YEAR	TEAM	LVL	AGE	W	L	SV	G	GS	IP	H	HR	BB/9	K/9	GB%	BABIP	WHIP	ERA	FIP	DRA	WARP	CFIP	MPH
2013	TUL	AA	26	1	1	0	2	2	13	9	1	0.0	8.3	48%	.250	0.69	1.38	2.21	3.75	0.2	83	
2013	CSP	AAA	26	2	2	0	9	9	46^{2}	52	2	2.7	9.1	46%	.355	1.41	4.63	3.21	4.01	0.9	74	
2013	COL	MLB	26	0	3	0	4	4	19	33	4	0.9	3.8	40%	.377	1.84	9.95	5.23	6.63	-0.4	125	92.6
2013	LVG	AAA	26	3	2	0	9	9	53^{1}	57	3	2.2	6.9	47%	.329	1.31	2.87	3.72	4.49	0.7	83	
2013	NYN	MLB	26	0	1	0	3	1	7	12	2	3.9	3.9	50%	.385	2.14	10.29	7.16	11.24	-0.5	114	92.7
2014	OKL	AAA	27	0	0	0	5	3	19	15	0	2.8	6.2	33%	.263	1.11	3.79	3.28	5.28	0.1	102	
2014	HOU	MLB	27	11	9	0	25	25	154^{2}	117	13	2.4	9.1	45%	.259	1.02	2.73	3.13	2.75	3.9	79	93.8
2015	HOU	MLB	28	19	7	0	32	32	203^{2}	207	19	2.3	7.6	47%	.310	1.28	3.89	3.55	3.98	2.5	97	92.7
2016	*HOU*	*MLB*	*29*	*12*	*10*	*0*	*31*	*31*	*186*	*178*	*21*	*2.5*	*7.9*	*46%*	*.292*	*1.24*	*3.87*	*3.90*	*4.10*	*2.3*	*92*	
2017	*HOU*	*MLB*	*30*	*10*	*9*	*0*	*27*	*27*	*164^{2}*	*163*	*19*	*2.7*	*8.0*	*46%*	*.299*	*1.29*	*3.99*	*3.90*	*4.23*	*1.7*	*94*	

Breakout: 22% Improve: 52% Collapse: 18% Attrition: 10% MLB: 93% *Comparables: Marco Estrada, Phil Coke, Aaron Heilman*

Had a few things not happened, the discussion around McHugh would have revolved around the questions of whether he was a has-been or a never-was. Given his draft position (554th overall), the latter probably would have fit more. But after being claimed off of waivers by the Astros, he's gone from eighth starter to eighth in the AL Cy Young vote in just two years. According to the stories, Houston saw potential in the spin rate of his curveball, and thought that he could utilize that weapon more. About a quarter of his pitches thrown in 2014 and 2015 were yakkers, and they saw more movement and generated more swinging strikes than nearly anyone around. Though he didn't replicate the high-strikeout/low-BABIP craziness of 2014, he provided plenty of quality innings for a young playoff team, and is under team control well into his 30s.

Joe Musgrove RHP

Born: 12/4/92 Age: 23 Bats: R Throws: R Height: 6'5" Weight: 255

YEAR	TEAM	LVL	AGE	W	L	SV	G	GS	IP	H	HR	BB/9	K/9	GB%	BABIP	WHIP	ERA	FIP	DRA	WARP	CFIP	MPH
2014	TCV	A-	21	7	1	0	15	13	77	64	4	1.2	7.8	53%	.275	0.96	2.81	2.84	3.80	1.0	80	
2015	QUD	A	22	4	1	0	5	3	25^2	22	0	0.4	8.1	51%	.293	0.90	0.70	1.84	2.39	0.8	79	
2015	CCH	AA	22	4	0	1	8	7	45	35	7	1.2	6.6	45%	.219	0.91	2.20	4.25	2.95	1.1	82	
2015	LNC	A+	22	4	0	0	6	4	30	28	2	0.3	12.9	52%	.366	0.97	2.40	2.08	1.90	1.2	57	
2016	*HOU*	*MLB*	*23*	*1*	*0*	*0*	*20*	*0*	*21*	*22*	*3*	*2.5*	*7.0*	*43%*	*.293*	*1.31*	*4.65*	*4.57*	*4.92*	*-0.1*	*115*	
2017	*HOU*	*MLB*	*24*	*4*	*4*	*0*	*18*	*10*	*83*	*87*	*13*	*2.4*	*7.0*	*43%*	*.294*	*1.32*	*4.65*	*4.56*	*4.92*	*0.1*	*115*	

Breakout: 7% Improve: 10% Collapse: 8% Attrition: 14% MLB: 23% *Comparables: Josh Lindblom, Kyle Hendricks, Dan Straily*

Like Frances Martes, Musgrove made some huge strides in 2015. Drafted by the Blue Jays in 2011, shoulder woes robbed him of time and toil, and at the nadir he'd seen 10 miles shaved off his fastball. The former supplemental pick restored that velocity to the low-to-mid-90s, and combines a good downward plane with ridiculous, fourth-wall-shattering command to put up excellent numbers in the minors. Despite his extended convalescence he is still plenty young, and his progress is encouraging.

Pat Neshek RHP

Born: 9/4/80 Age: 35 Bats: B Throws: R Height: 6'3" Weight: 210

YEAR	TEAM	LVL	AGE	W	L	SV	G	GS	IP	H	HR	BB/9	K/9	GB%	BABIP	WHIP	ERA	FIP	DRA	WARP	CFIP	MPH
2013	OAK	MLB	32	2	1	0	45	0	40^1	40	6	3.3	6.5	35%	.268	1.36	3.35	4.69	4.64	0.0	110	92.2
2014	SLN	MLB	33	7	2	6	71	0	67^1	44	4	1.2	9.1	37%	.233	0.79	1.87	2.35	1.53	2.4	74	93.5
2015	HOU	MLB	34	3	6	1	66	0	54^2	49	8	2.0	8.4	34%	.273	1.12	3.62	3.91	4.20	0.3	92	93.1
2016	*HOU*	*MLB*	*35*	*3*	*1*	*0*	*59*	*0*	*62*^{2}	*55*	*8*	*2.4*	*8.5*	*34%*	*.276*	*1.15*	*3.88*	*3.93*	*4.11*	*0.5*	*91*	
2017	*HOU*	*MLB*	*36*	*3*	*1*	*2*	*59*	*0*	*55*	*51*	*7*	*2.5*	*8.3*	*34%*	*.285*	*1.21*	*3.98*	*3.88*	*4.22*	*0.3*	*94*	

Breakout: 24% Improve: 44% Collapse: 24% Attrition: 15% MLB: 83% *Comparables: Tyler Walker, Neal Cotts, Joe Borowski*

Coming off a career year with the Cardinals in 2014, Neshek signed with the Astros to pitch the eighth and fell somewhere between superb and very good from March through August. September exploded his season like a scrap of cesium in a bowl of water. He struck out four of the 42 batters he faced, and put nearly half of them on base. As his team limped to the finish line and the bullpen lay in tatters, he continued to lob fastballs directly at the heart of the plate. Baseball is better with Neshek and his super-goofy delivery in it, so here's hoping he can fight his way back to something like his former self, if only to give him more time to add to his prodigious autograph collection.

Tony Sipp LHP

Born: 7/12/83 Age: 32 Bats: L Throws: L Height: 6'0" Weight: 190

YEAR	TEAM	LVL	AGE	W	L	SV	G	GS	IP	H	HR	BB/9	K/9	GB%	BABIP	WHIP	ERA	FIP	DRA	WARP	CFIP	MPH
2013	RNO	AAA	29	1	0	1	9	0	10	3	0	4.5	10.8	44%	.130	0.80	0.00	2.67	4.67	0.1	91	
2013	ARI	MLB	29	3	2	0	56	0	37^2	35	6	5.3	10.0	28%	.284	1.51	4.78	4.85	4.77	-0.1	103	92.5
2014	ELP	AAA	30	1	1	0	11	0	14^2	14	1	1.2	12.9	38%	.361	1.09	4.30	2.34	4.52	0.1	96	
2014	HOU	MLB	30	4	3	4	56	0	50^2	28	5	3.0	11.2	35%	.205	0.89	3.38	2.96	1.81	1.7	71	94.9
2015	HOU	MLB	31	3	4	0	60	0	54^1	41	5	2.5	10.3	41%	.271	1.03	1.99	2.90	3.10	1.0	80	93.2
2016	*HOU*	*MLB*	*32*	*3*	*1*	*0*	*54*	*0*	*57*^{1}	*46*	*7*	*3.1*	*10.0*	*38%*	*.269*	*1.14*	*3.73*	*3.75*	*3.97*	*0.5*	*87*	
2017	*HOU*	*MLB*	*33*	*3*	*1*	*2*	*60*	*0*	*52*	*45*	*7*	*3.2*	*9.3*	*38%*	*.277*	*1.22*	*4.02*	*3.94*	*4.28*	*0.3*	*95*	

Breakout: 25% Improve: 43% Collapse: 24% Attrition: 4% MLB: 87% *Comparables: Frank Francisco, Skip Lockwood, Francisco Rodriguez*

Sipp saw his best season in 2015 as a 32-year-old, chastising lefties and righties alike. In not falling apart during September, he was one of the most valuable pieces of the Houston bullpen—enough so that he netted himself a three-year deal. To watch Sipp work is to watch an even mixture of pitching, breakdancing and performance art. His delivery is jerky, rushed, compact and always features a little hot step afterward. It's hard to say whether he's just readjusting his feet in preparation to field the ball, or if he's simply ecstatic that he lives in a time when middle relievers can earn $18 million. It's a delight to see, regardless.

Lineouts

Hitters

NAME	POS	TEAM	LVL	AGE	PA	R	2B	3B	HR	RBI	BB	K	SB	CS	AVG/OBP/SLG	TAv	BABIP	BRR	FRAA	WARP
Derek Fisher	LF	LNC	A+	21	398	74	10	7	16	63	47	95	23	5	.262/.354/.471	.295	.314	4.3	LF(43): -1.5, CF(35): -1.6	2.7
	LF	QUD	A	21	171	32	11	1	6	24	19	37	8	2	.305/.386/.510	.326	.370	-0.5	CF(30): -2.8, LF(3): -0.8	1.3
Colin Moran	3B	CCH	AA	22	417	47	25	2	9	67	43	79	1	0	.306/.381/.459	.293	.365	-0.6	3B(78): 0.4	2.7
Jon Singleton	1B	FRE	AAA	23	448	72	25	2	22	83	64	99	2	1	.254/.359/.505	.301	.282	-1.5	1B(84): 3.2	2.6
	1B	HOU	MLB	23	58	6	2	0	1	6	10	17	1	0	.191/.328/.298	.245	.267	0.3	1B(14): -1.0	-0.1
Max Stassi	C	FRE	AAA	24	328	37	8	2	13	43	26	93	1	1	.211/.279/.384	.237	.257	2.2	C(83): 11.5	2.1
	C	HOU	MLB	24	17	4	0	0	1	2	1	5	0	0	.400/.438/.600	.340	.556	0.5	C(10): -0.7	0.2

International signee and charming teenager **Gilberto Celestino** did his best work when the camera was on him, excelling in major tournaments. His defense in center is universally praised; his swing, occasionally contested. ❖ **Derek Fisher** was a supplemental first-round pick in the 2014 draft, and he has hit at every level at which he's played. He's a free swinger with the range and arm to be relegated to left field, though he did manage to swipe bases (at an 82 percent success rate) with the agility of a point guard. ❖ **Colin Moran** is a skinny third baseman who can make good contact, but is fairly unremarkable in all the other tools. He could become a solid infielder, a middling utility guy, or Secretary of the Interior. These are but three options, as Colin Moran contains multitudes. ❖ **Miguelangel Sierra** was a 16-year-old July 2nd international signing who garnered high marks for his ability to play shortstop. He tore up the Dominican Summer League, slugging .476, but did cool down substantially (albeit in limited games) once he reached the Gulf Coast League. ❖ It has been said that **Jon Singleton** flosses with telephone poles, can body slam a coach bus full of broken jackhammers, and even once beat the Ayatollah at a game of pachinko. It has never been said that Singleton possesses the pitch-recognition skills to stick in the major leagues. ❖ **Max Stassi** has never really proven he can hit above the Double-A level, save for some strong showings in *very* short stints in the majors. Unless his bat picks up (he's still 25, which is 21 in catcher years), he seems destined for a career as a backup catcher, which is still a cooler job than yours.

Pitchers

NAME	TEAM	LVL	AGE	W	L	SV	G	GS	IP	H	HR	BB/9	K/9	GB%	BABIP	WHIP	ERA	FIP	FRA	WARP	CFIP	MPH
Kevin Chapman	FRE	AAA	27	3	2	8	49	0	53	60	3	4.4	10.4	44%	.373	1.62	4.75	3.62	4.14	0.6	90	
	HOU	MLB	27	0	0	0	3	0	5^{1}	4	1	5.1	13.5	18%	.300	1.31	3.38	4.23	4.83	0.0	94	94.3
Luis Cruz	FRE	AAA	24	7	5	0	28	19	116	119	18	4.0	7.2	38%	.296	1.47	4.27	5.51	6.36	-1.1	116	
Dean Deetz	TCV	A-	21	4	2	0	7	5	28^{1}	22	1	3.2	6.7	60%	.244	1.13	2.86	4.08	4.71	0.1	104	
	QUD	A	21	5	1	0	7	6	35^{1}	17	0	3.3	7.4	65%	.175	0.85	0.76	2.86	4.15	0.3	99	
Chris Devenski	CCH	AA	24	7	4	2	24	17	119^{2}	117	12	2.5	7.8	34%	.300	1.25	3.01	3.74	3.26	2.5	85	
Michael Feliz	LNC	A+	22	1	1	0	8	5	32^{2}	30	2	3.3	9.1	48%	.298	1.29	4.41	3.84	4.59	0.4	96	
	HOU	MLB	22	0	0	0	5	0	8	9	2	4.5	7.9	38%	.292	1.62	7.88	6.48	5.98	-0.1	106	96.7
	CCH	AA	22	6	3	1	15	12	78^{2}	52	5	2.3	8.0	43%	.228	0.92	2.17	3.11	3.18	1.8	85	
Reymin Guduan	QUD	A	23	3	0	0	6	0	12	6	0	2.2	11.2	58%	.231	0.75	0.75	1.90	2.84	0.3	84	
	CCH	AA	23	1	3	0	16	0	16^{1}	20	3	10.5	10.5	49%	.354	2.39	11.57	6.85	8.37	-0.7	132	
	LNC	A+	23	0	3	4	13	0	17^{1}	12	0	5.7	13.0	54%	.293	1.33	3.12	2.80	3.69	0.3	85	
Will Harris	HOU	MLB	30	5	5	2	68	0	71	42	8	2.8	8.6	52%	.192	0.90	1.90	3.63	2.36	2.0	92	94.2
David Paulino	QUD	A	21	3	2	0	5	5	28^{2}	21	0	2.2	10.0	47%	.292	0.98	1.57	2.00	2.19	1.0	77	
	LNC	A+	21	1	1	1	6	5	29^{1}	24	1	3.1	9.2	40%	.295	1.16	4.91	3.40	3.89	0.6	88	
Brad Peacock	HOU	MLB	27	0	1	0	1	1	5	5	0	3.6	5.4	31%	.312	1.40	5.40	3.70	6.33	-0.1	108	92.3
Brady Rodgers	FRE	AAA	24	9	7	0	21	21	115^{2}	136	13	1.9	6.9	49%	.327	1.39	4.51	4.20	4.23	1.7	91	
Asher Wojciechowski	HOU	MLB	26	0	1	0	5	3	16^{1}	23	2	3.9	8.8	21%	.389	1.84	7.16	4.02	8.35	-0.7	103	93.5
	FRE	AAA	26	8	4	0	20	20	115^{1}	129	13	3.2	6.8	38%	.319	1.47	4.92	4.78	5.65	-0.1	107	

Kevin Chapman failed to be a person of much interest in 2015, spending most of the season in Triple-A. He's sinister enough to be useful, if he can stop walking the world. ❖ After spring training in 2015, the Astros sent **Luis Cruz** back to Triple-A to work on his curve. Based on the results, next time they'll ask him to do his cross-training in TV/VCR repair. ❖ **Dean Deetz** is a hard-throwing right-hander who underwent Tommy John surgery in high school, but is showing promise with his fastball and newfound slider. The takeaway? Deetz: New Ucl Throwing Sliders. ❖ Hailed by his friends as "Devo," his teammates as "The Dragon," and his foes as "the pitcher," **Chris Devenski** capped a successful 2015 season by getting called up to Triple-A and winning the league's championship game in his only start. That might be his zenith, but there are worse. ❖ **Michael Feliz** spent a good deal of time as a forgotten reliever on the big-league squad in 2015, but his size, velocity and track record in the minors make him a prime candidate for starting someday. Feliz's fastball sits in the mid-90s, and he's had success limiting walks while pitching in the minors. ❖ **Reymin Guduan** is a hard-throwing lefty with control problems. He needs to figure it out, if only to draw attention away from his name being an anagram for "damn urine guy.". ❖ **David Paulino**, the PTBNL in the Jose Veras trade with the Tigers, bounced back from Tommy John surgery to pitch at three different levels in 2015. He had limited time in each, but posted good strikeout and walk rates the whole season. ❖ **Brad Peacock** was looking to improve upon his replacement-level 2014 season, but an intercostal strain suffered in his first start, along with various rehab setbacks, erased his 2015 season. A flyball pitcher with a penchant for walks, there are many question marks attached to his future. ❖ **Brady Rodgers** grew up outside Houston and rooted for the 'stros in the team's 2005 World Series run. He'll need to pitch well to win his name back in the search engines from NFL preview articles. ❖ **Asher Wojciechowski** is essentially Oberholtzer-lite, a flyball pitcher who gives up too much contact. He made it, though, meaning two of this book's three editors can now get an MLB jersey with their name on the back without having to pay extra money like a dork.

Manager

A.J. Hinch

YEAR	TEAM	W	L	Pythag +/-	Avg PC	100+ P	120+ P	QS	BQS	REL	REL w Zero R	IBB	PH	PH Avg	PH HR	SB2	CS2	SB3	CS3	SAC Att	SAC%	POS SAC	Squeeze	Swing	In Play
2015	HOU	86	76	-8	98.0	74	4	94	4	482	412	17	114	.224	5	99	41	21	5	40	70.0	25	2	300	83

In calling Hinch and the Astros a logical match in last year's book, we questioned whether Houston's front office could make it work. After all, Jeff Luhnow had gone through two managers already, dismissing lame duck Brad Mills after a season, and handpicked Bo Porter after most of two. The Luhnow-era Astros were unreliable in other regards, too. Houston had become the organization most prone to seemingly preventable PR- and communication-related failings. Asking Hinch, whose stint with the D'Backs hadn't gone perfectly, to heal all that ailed the Astros seemed overzealous at best and borderline dangerous at worst.

But while the 2015 Astros retained some of their amateur-hour feel off the field—their surprising postseason run was followed by a Jon Heyman report that front-office morale was at an all-time low due to poor pay and a slashed pension plan—Hinch did fix Houston's on-the-field problems. In the most simple terms, he accomplished this by embracing youth. Whereas many managers like to break rookies in by batting them near the bottom of the order for a few weeks (if not longer), Hinch slotted Carlos Correa into the no. 2 spot after four big-league games. The week before Correa arrived, Hinch had taken to using Preston Tucker, another rookie, as his no. 3 hitter. Perhaps those decisions were unavoidable and would have been made by anyone else in the same situation. But Hinch also adopted a slew of offensive strategies that you would expect from a young and athletic roster: tons of stolen-base attempts (including double steals), tons of hit-and-runs and so on.

Since Hinch is another former catcher with slight managerial experience, you might wonder where he falls on the Cash-Ausmus hook scale. The answer in 2015 was to the Ausmus side. The Astros had the second-most starts of 120 or more pitches, and featured the highest individual pitch count of the season: the 134-pitch, no-hit effort spun by Mike Fiers. Hinch opted to ride his starters—particularly Dallas Keuchel, who was gifted the long leash in the postseason as well—in spite of having the best bullpen in the majors, according to DRA. Therein is the beat-or-the-chorus question: Did Hinch get more out of his bullpen because he minimized their activity, or did he get less out of his roster than he could have by not following the increasing trend of limiting starters' times through the order? Ponder that while the Astros calculate how to avoid another late-season (and postseason) collapse.

KANSAS CITY ROYALS

Essay by Sam Mellinger

Player comments by Ken Funck and BP authors

The face of the last great Royals moment is wrinkled now. George Brett is 62 years old, and he stands on the field with a cup of beer in his hand surrounded by a celebration that for most of the last two decades seemed entirely impossible.

All around him, the Royals smile and high-five and drink champagne and, perhaps most of all, hug each other and ask, "Can you believe it?" They are World Series champions, somehow, a result that for most of the last 30 years seemed far less plausible than the Cubs championship predicted for this season in Back to the Future.

Brett had watched this from the beginning. Like all Royals fans, even those who are not among the greatest 30 or so baseball players of all-time, there were years he did not brag about the team. It's hard to love something that doesn't love itself, but he kept hoping, kept watching, and even spent every spring training instructing and many summers scouting and even one summer as the team's hitting coach.

He has tried to help Mike Moustakas through slumps, and Eric Hosmer understand how pitchers want to attack him, and told Alex Gordon he would've loved to trade talent. Brett is as connected and invested in the Royals as any all-time great is in his former team, so after the Royals won the World Series—and that still sounds a little strange, right?—it only felt natural to ask Brett how this team would fare against his 1985 team that beat the Cardinals for the franchise's first championship.

"They'd beat us," he said. "I really believe they're a better team. They're a better team than we were. They have more depth throughout the lineup. They have better speed. Defensively, I think they're better. We could probably beat them in some positions, but they're a better ballclub."

If you know a Royals fan who occasionally goes silent in conversation, drifting off and staring into space, there is at least a 50-50 chance he or she is daydreaming about the eighth inning against Houston, or Eric Hosmer's dash home in New York, or the fact that 800,000 people—nearly twice the population of Kansas City—showed up for a parade in which Brett, for so long the symbol of a glorious past that could never be matched, doubled down and

ROYALS PROSPECTUS

2015 W-L: 95-67, 1st in AL Central

Pythag	.556	6th	DER	.714	6th
RS/G	4.47	7th	B-Age	29.1	26th
RA/G	3.96	10th	P-Age	30	28th
TAv	.263	13th	Salary	$112.9M	17th
BRR	4.43	9th	M$/MW	$2.1M	25th
TAv-P	.255	10th	DL Days	710	6th
FIP	4.01	14th	$ on DL	16%	17th

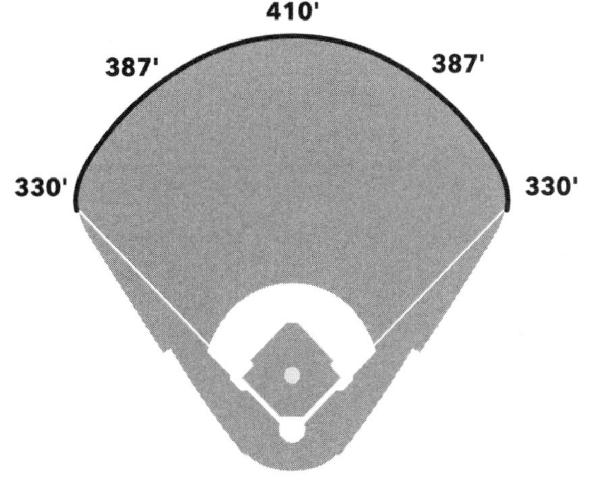

Outfield wall profile: **8'**

Three-Year Park Factors

Runs	Runs/RH	Runs/LH	HR/RH	HR/LH
101	110	119	96	115

Top Hitter WARP	6.7	Lorenzo Cain
Top Pitcher WARP	2.5	Wade Davis
Top Prospect	Raul Mondesi	

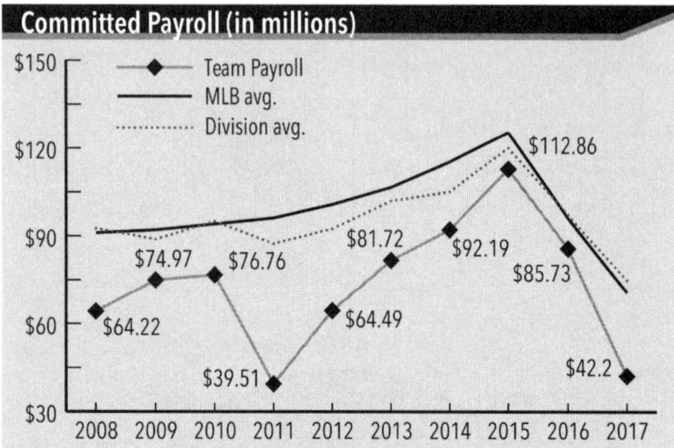

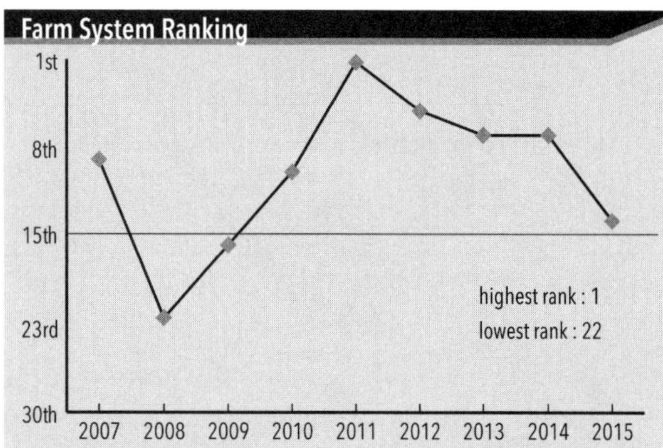

Personnel

General Manager: Dayton Moore

Assistant General Manager: J.J. Picollo

Assistant General Manager: Rene Francisco

Assistant General Manager: Scott Sharp

Manager: Ned Yost

Baseball Prospectus Alumni

Mike Groopman

Daniel Mack

called the 2015 Royals the best team in franchise history.

Pfew.

These words are being typed in November, just a few days after the Royals paraded through downtown with visual evidence of the commissioner's trophy, and you are unlikely to read this before February, when pitchers and catchers report, but the feeling then will largely be the same as the feeling now—how in the actual hell did we find ourselves in a world in which the Royals not only won the World Series, but won it convincingly, because they are now some sort of playoff machine?

The Royals are not the first small-money team to succeed in the modern big-money era of baseball, of course. You may have heard there was a book and Brad Pitt movie done about the A's. The Rays toppled the fortunes of the Yankees and Red Sox in the American League East, earning many of their players enormous raises, and landing Andrew Friedman a job with the filthy rich Dodgers.

But the A's never made the World Series. Since 2000, their postseason record is 19-27 in games, and 2-9 in rounds (including Wild Card game loss to the Royals). The Rays made one World Series, and lost in five games. Their postseason record (again, including Wild Card games) is 13-14 in games, and 3-4 in rounds. In the last two years, the Royals' postseason record is 22-9 in games, and 6-1 in rounds.

The Royals play in baseball's third-smallest market, and had the 17th biggest payroll in 2015. Since the strike, World Series winners have had, on average, the seventh biggest payroll. The only team to do it on less money, relative to their peers, was the 1997 Marlins—and they went 80-82 the year before their title, and lost 108 games the year after.

Over the last three seasons, only three teams have won more games than the Royals. None have won more playoff games than the Royals, who entered the offseason among the betting favorites for the 2016 World Series championship. But just with the success of the last two years, the Royals have succeeded in building a winner within a budget in a way that is unprecedented in modern baseball.

So, it's an entirely appropriate question: how in the actual hell did this happen?

The answer is as simple or as complicated as you want it to be, so let's start with the simple: the Royals have aced virtually every important personnel decision for years, building a team that knows exactly what it is, with players who believe completely in the cause and each other, pushed forward with loads of talent.

The juice is in the details, though, and you would not be reading a book like this without interest in the details. Here, then, are six details crucial to the Royals' long journey from punchline to champions:

1. David Glass' patience. This is listed first on purpose, because without it, nothing else matters. Glass was one of baseball's most empty owners from his purchase of the team in 2000 to the firing of general manager Allard Baird in 2006. Internally, there has been some revisionist history that Baird and his predecessor Herk Robinson did not ask for enough resources or support from ownership, but the organization lacked funding for basic tools, all the way down to cell phones for scouts.

But just as criticizing Glass for his bumbling first six years in charge is fair, so too is giving him credit for the last nine years. He identified and hired a top general manager candidate, and then—with few exceptions—supported and funded his work.

There are many owners in many markets who would've fired Moore in 2010. That was Moore's fourth full season in charge. The Royals lost 95 games, Moore fired his hand-picked manager, and most of the big league moves—from free agent contracts to Gil Meche and Jose Guillen, to trades for Mike Jacobs and Yuniesky Betancourt—had flopped. And there are many owners in many markets who would've fired Moore in 2012. That was Moore's sixth full season in charge. The Royals lost 90 games, turning an "Our Time" marketing slogan into a cruel joke, and golden prospect Eric Hosmer had suffered through a miserable second season in the big leagues.

Over and over, Moore and his assistants acknowledge that they got more time than could've been expected. If it didn't work out, Glass would be criticized for inactivity. When it does work out, he should be praised for patience.

2. Royals' previous ineptitude. This is a bit counterintuitive, but true nonetheless. The Royals had been so bad for so long that Glass had no choice but to give Moore virtual autonomy over baseball operations. There would be a budget, of course, but Moore had the freedom to build without any cultural inertia.

The organization's infrastructure was so outdated that the improvements were clean, and in many ways complete. It's easier to build a nice house from an empty lot, rather than purchasing a crumbling tear-down inhabited by a hoarder.

Moore beefed up the scouting and support staff without having to fire anyone, because the staff was so small. He could build an international scouting department in exactly the way he wanted, because there was nothing pre-existing to work around. The Royals had nothing to lose, in other words.

3. A Moneyball approach, sort of. That description will cause some members of the Royals' baseball operations department to cringe or curse or perhaps both. But it's true, even if there are still some who believe the point of the book was that you need to take walks and not bunt.

The Royals—whether they intended it this way or not, and you get different answers on that from different people at different times—found their own form of Moneyball, just with different market inefficiencies. They valued athleticism, defense, power arms in the bullpen, and a strong clubhouse culture in a time when all of those things were being passed over by most clubs in favor of analytics, power hitters, and workhorse starting pitchers.

They zigged while other teams zagged, in other words. The result is the game's best defense, a roster loaded with athletes, a freakishly good back end of the bullpen, and a bunch of professional athletes who genuinely care for each other. It's easy to draw a connection between that profile and a team that wins so many games late.

4. The James Shields trade. In the beginning, at least in Kansas City, it was the Wil Myers trade. And now, at least in Kansas City, it is more appropriately called the Wade Davis trade. But whatever the name, it marked a very clear turn for a franchise that for decades had been building for a vague future just out of reach.

The tangible parts are obvious. Shields provided more than 450 innings of 3.18 ERA pitching across two seasons, and Davis has developed into one of the game's best relief pitchers. But there are important intangible benefits here, too.

The Royals needed to know what winning looked like and felt like, and more than anyone else, Shields brought that. Many players have cited that trade as the moment they fully believed the Royals were absolutely serious about winning. None of that should be overlooked.

5. The Zack Greinke trade. This one never got as much attention as the Shields trade, but at least in terms of the baseball product, was probably more important.

Cain is one of the game's best centerfielders, a particularly effective weapon in one of baseball's biggest outfields. He has also developed into a very good hitter, and an elite athlete with a knack for the moment.

Alcides Escobar is a very good shortstop who plays with an infectious joy and an unrelenting drive. Nobody even attempts to explain why the team is so much better with him batting leadoff, but it speaks to his importance and the peculiar way this team has found its place.

Royals management actually wanted to trade Greinke to Washington for a package that included Jordan Zimmerman, Drew Storen, and Danny Espinosa. But Greinke would not sign an extension that would've finalized the deal. As it turned out, the Royals would've done fine with that trade. But not as well as the trade that filled significant organizational holes with an All-Star shortstop and centerfielder.

But, hey. Everybody needs a little luck along the way.

6. International scouting. This one's probably the most boring, but crucial all the same. Moore hired Rene

Francisco to build an international scouting department essentially from the ground up. For years and years, the Royals had ignored the international market, cutting themselves off from one of the sport's great talent pools.

The most important thing Francisco had was money. The Royals went from what was effectively a non-existent presence in Latin America to one of baseball's top spenders. But he also brought experience, credibility, and connections. He knew where to look for the best players, which was critical for a franchise that had been a non-factor there.

On his first official scouting trip for the Royals, Francisco signed Kelvin Herrera in the Dominican Republic and Salvador Perez in Venezuela. In the years since, the Royals have hit on Yordano Ventura, Raul A. Mondesi, Miguel Almonte and others. A glaring weakness is turned to an undeniable strength.

This list could go on and on. The Royals have operated with a general humility, even while often growing agitated at what they perceived to be negative treatment in the local media. They have done a good job of signing their best young players to long-term deals, and of cultivating an environment where coaches are cherished and supported and allowed to work.

They spent big on the draft, taking advantage of loopholes (like drafting Wil Myers in the third round and signing him with first-round money) until baseball closed them. They also had their fair share of good fortune, like moving Alex Gordon to left field out of desperation and watching him turn into one of the game's great all-around players. There is no list that could be comprehensive and fit in the pages of this section.

The best part for Royals fans is that this is a discussion that can be had over ribs and beer all throughout the winter, their team finally the subject of praise rather than ridicule. Like any team, they have work to do in the offseason, but a core that is largely in place for at least another season.

So, who knows? Maybe we'll be asking George Brett if the 2016 Royals are even better than 2015. ■

—Sam Mellinger is a sports columnist at the Kansas City Star, *where he's worked since 2000.*

Hitters

Lane Adams OF

Born: 11/13/89 Age: 26 Bats: R Throws: R Height: 6'4" Weight: 190

YEAR	TEAM	LVL	AGE	PA	R	2B	3B	HR	RBI	BB	K	SB	CS	AVG/OBP/SLG	TAv	BABIP	BRR	FRAA	WARP
2013	WIL	A+	23	370	56	23	2	7	39	43	66	23	6	.276/.362/.424	.294	.325	2.6	CF(85): 1.8	3.0
2013	NWA	AA	23	177	30	7	1	5	26	18	45	15	0	.244/.333/.397	.272	.311	2.9	RF(18): -2.4, LF(15): -0.6	0.6
2014	KCA	MLB	24	3	1	0	0	0	0	0	2	0	0	.000/.000/.000	.010	.000	0.1	LF(2): 0.0, CF(2): 0.0	-0.1
2014	NWA	AA	24	465	65	25	3	11	36	45	86	38	9	.269/.352/.427	.287	.314	3.2	CF(104): 3.9	3.6
2015	OMA	AAA	25	132	14	5	0	4	13	13	21	2	1	.226/.305/.374	.249	.239	1.6	CF(21): 1.5, RF(11): -0.5	0.5
2015	NWA	AA	25	414	58	21	3	12	49	36	98	29	6	.298/.360/.466	.291	.372	2.0	CF(40): -0.1, LF(34): 0.1	2.5
2016	*KCA*	*MLB*	*26*	*88*	*10*	*4*	*0*	*2*	*9*	*7*	*21*	*4*	*1*	*.241/.305/.384*	*.248*	*.298*	*0.5*	*LF 1, RF -0*	*0.3*
2017	*KCA*	*MLB*	*27*	*313*	*36*	*15*	*1*	*8*	*34*	*24*	*75*	*15*	*3*	*.241/.307/.386*	*.251*	*.298*	*2.1*	*LF 3, RF 0*	*1.0*

Breakout: 5% Improve: 26% Collapse: 14% Attrition: 29% MLB: 48% *Comparables: Thomas Pham, Scott Cousins, Ben Francisco*

With 69 stolen bases in the high minors over the last two seasons, Adams has the type of speed that gets labeled "game-breaking" outside the Royals organization and "mundane" within it. Rangy and athletic, Adams is a solid center fielder with some juice in his bat, but can struggle to make consistent contact. If you squint you can almost see the outlines of a 20/20 center fielder, but the realistic outcome here is a Choctaw version of Paulo Orlando, which is still pretty cool.

Jorge Bonifacio RF

Born: 6/4/93 Age: 23 Bats: R Throws: R Height: 6'1" Weight: 195

YEAR	TEAM	LVL	AGE	PA	R	2B	3B	HR	RBI	BB	K	SB	CS	AVG/OBP/SLG	TAv	BABIP	BRR	FRAA	WARP
2013	WIL	A+	20	234	32	11	3	2	29	23	40	0	2	.296/.368/.408	.289	.353	-1.7	RF(50): 2.1	1.2
2013	NWA	AA	20	105	15	7	0	2	19	11	23	2	1	.301/.371/.441	.302	.377	0.8	RF(23): 0.0	0.8
2014	NWA	AA	21	566	49	20	4	4	51	50	127	8	3	.230/.302/.309	.232	.295	3.3	RF(125): -12.5, LF(2): -0.1	-1.7
2015	NWA	AA	22	536	60	30	2	17	64	42	126	3	2	.240/.305/.416	.256	.287	0.1	RF(97): -5.9, LF(18): -1.3	0.0
2016	*KCA*	*MLB*	*23*	*250*	*22*	*11*	*2*	*4*	*25*	*16*	*63*	*1*	*0*	*.226/.280/.347*	*.226*	*.288*	*-0.2*	*RF -3, LF -1*	*-0.7*
2017	*KCA*	*MLB*	*24*	*362*	*38*	*18*	*3*	*8*	*37*	*24*	*92*	*1*	*1*	*.234/.290/.374*	*.240*	*.297*	*-0.4*	*RF -5, LF -1*	*-0.7*

Breakout: 2% Improve: 3% Collapse: 3% Attrition: 3% MLB: 7% *Comparables: Scott Van Slyke, Andrew Lambo, Bronson Sardinha*

Bonifacio found a little more success during his second spin through the Texas League, as the young Dominican began turning some measure of his power potential into game-day thump. He lacks his brother Emilio's quickness, but his cannon arm and burgeoning power make him an ideal fit for right field. However, advanced pitchers still take advantage of his over-aggressive approach and fool him with spin, so there's plenty of doubt whether he'll ever get on base enough to be more than a minor-league lifer.

Drew Butera C

Born: 8/9/83 Age: 32 Bats: R Throws: R Height: 6'1" Weight: 200

YEAR	TEAM	LVL	AGE	PA	R	2B	3B	HR	RBI	BB	K	SB	CS	AVG/OBP/SLG	TAv	BABIP	BRR	FRAA	WARP
2013	ROC	AAA	29	94	8	2	0	2	10	2	15	0	0	.218/.247/.310	.209	.236	0.2	C(22): 1.1	0.0
2013	ABQ	AAA	29	57	3	3	1	0	3	4	14	0	0	.135/.196/.231	.151	.184	0.4	C(16): -0.3	-0.4
2013	MIN	MLB	29	3	0	0	0	0	0	0	1	0	0	.000/.000/.000	-.016	.000	0.0	C(2): -0.3	-0.1
2013	LAN	MLB	29	7	0	0	0	0	0	0	4	0	0	.143/.143/.143	.052	.333	-0.3	1B(2): -0.1, C(2): 0.1	-0.2
2014	LAN	MLB	30	192	16	6	1	3	14	17	41	0	0	.188/.267/.288	.214	.227	-0.2	C(57): 5.6, P(2): -0.0	0.5
2015	KCA	MLB	31	99	6	3	0	1	5	6	24	0	0	.198/.266/.267	.202	.262	-1.0	C(42): -2.2, 1B(5): 0.0	-0.5
2015	ANA	MLB	31	21	3	0	0	0	0	0	2	0	1	.190/.190/.190	.180	.211	-0.2	C(7): -0.9, 1B(3): -0.0	-0.2
2016	*KCA*	*MLB*	*32*	*31*	*2*	*1*	*0*	*0*	*2*	*2*	*6*	*0*	*0*	*.201/.256/.289*	*.198*	*.241*	*-0.1*	*C -0*	*-0.1*
2017	*KCA*	*MLB*	*33*	*84*	*7*	*3*	*0*	*1*	*6*	*6*	*18*	*0*	*0*	*.193/.256/.277*	*.195*	*.235*	*-0.2*	*C 0*	*-0.3*

Breakout: 4% Improve: 30% Collapse: 10% Attrition: 23% MLB: 94% *Comparables: Brent Mayne, Charlie Lau, Joe Ginsberg*

YEAR	TEAM	P. COUNT	FRM RUNS	BLK RUNS	THRW RUNS	TOT RUNS
2013	MIN	137	-0.3	0.0	0.0	-0.3
2013	ROC	2782	1.5	0.2	0.0	1.7
2013	ABQ	2380	-1.5	0.2	1.0	-0.3
2013	LAN	93	0.1	0.0	0.0	0.1
2014	LAN	7366	4.9	-0.2	0.1	4.9
2014	LAN	7366	4.9	-0.2	0.1	4.9
2015	ANA	933	-0.8	0.0	0.0	-0.8
2015	KCA	3765	-3.1	0.1	0.2	-2.8
2016	*KCA*	*1204*	*-0.2*	*0.0*	*0.1*	*-0.1*
2017	*KCA*	*3259*	*-0.7*	*0.0*	*0.1*	*-0.6*

When Butera coaxed his unprecedented walk to load the bases last October, it was the first time the punchless receiver had ever drawn a free pass after facing 10 or more pitches. That he did so again, only two plate appearances (and eight days) later, to keep the line moving in Kansas City's amazing ALCS Game Four comeback: That was just another slab of Royals Magic. The proud owner of a career .188 TAv, Butera is perhaps the worst hitter ever to become a postseason offensive hero, but his solid catch-and-throw skills and enviable wavy locks will keep him caddying for better receivers for years to come.

Lorenzo Cain CF

Born: 4/13/86 Age: 30 Bats: R Throws: R Height: 6'2" Weight: 205

YEAR	TEAM	LVL	AGE	PA	R	2B	3B	HR	RBI	BB	K	SB	CS	AVG/OBP/SLG	TAv	BABIP	BRR	FRAA	WARP
2013	KCA	MLB	27	442	54	21	3	4	46	33	90	14	6	.251/.310/.348	.245	.309	-1.3	CF(92): 9.0, RF(32): 0.8	1.5
2014	KCA	MLB	28	502	55	29	4	5	53	24	108	28	5	.301/.339/.412	.269	.380	3.2	CF(93): 2.5, RF(77): 4.1	2.9
2015	KCA	MLB	29	604	101	34	6	16	72	37	98	28	6	.307/.361/.477	.301	.347	4.0	CF(136): 17.3, RF(5): -0.3	6.7
2016	*KCA*	*MLB*	*30*	*605*	*69*	*31*	*5*	*11*	*62*	*36*	*123*	*26*	*6*	*.272/.323/.404*	*.261*	*.327*	*1.7*	*CF 14*	*3.9*
2017	*KCA*	*MLB*	*31*	*548*	*60*	*28*	*4*	*10*	*57*	*31*	*114*	*21*	*6*	*.266/.316/.399*	*.257*	*.322*	*2.1*	*CF 12*	*3.2*

Breakout: 2% Improve: 45% Collapse: 6% Attrition: 16% MLB: 97% *Comparables: Marlon Byrd, Aaron Rowand, Rajai Davis*

Cain was able to build on his breakout 2014 postseason with an electrifying campaign that placed him among the best in baseball at the plate, on the basepaths and in center field. He's the modern-day master of the Mad Dash Home, with instant acceleration and long strides that make him a joy to watch whether he's stealing bases, scoring from first on a single or laying out to rob someone of a double in the gap. At the plate he made more frequent hard contact, leading to fewer strikeouts and a 65-point jump in his slugging percentage, and the ball made more frequent hard contact with him, leading to a HBP-fueled bump in his on-base percentage. None of this seems like a fluke, and with two years left before hitting free agency Cain currently ranks among the most valuable commodities in baseball.

Orlando Calixte SS

Born: 2/3/92 Age: 24 Bats: R Throws: R Height: 5'11" Weight: 160

YEAR	TEAM	LVL	AGE	PA	R	2B	3B	HR	RBI	BB	K	SB	CS	AVG/OBP/SLG	TAv	BABIP	BRR	FRAA	WARP
2013	NWA	AA	21	536	59	25	4	8	36	42	131	14	11	.250/.312/.368	.243	.325	1.0	SS(101): -6.7, 3B(11): -0.2	0.5
2014	NWA	AA	22	412	43	15	1	11	37	27	92	9	5	.241/.288/.374	.249	.286	-0.9	SS(92): -3.1, 3B(1): 0.0	0.8
2015	OMA	AAA	23	394	38	11	2	8	27	27	84	22	3	.229/.287/.339	.230	.279	0.7	SS(55): -5.4, 3B(21): -0.1	-0.3
2015	KCA	MLB	23	3	1	0	0	0	0	0	0	0	0	.000/.000/.000	.001	.000	0.5	SS(1): 0.0	0.0
2016	*KCA*	*MLB*	*24*	*250*	*28*	*10*	*1*	*5*	*20*	*14*	*64*	*7*	*2*	*.221/.267/.335*	*.216*	*.277*	*0.5*	*SS -2, 2B 0*	*-0.3*
2017	*KCA*	*MLB*	*25*	*294*	*29*	*12*	*1*	*5*	*27*	*17*	*74*	*8*	*3*	*.222/.270/.335*	*.218*	*.278*	*0.8*	*SS -2, 2B 0*	*-0.4*

Breakout: 2% Improve: 5% Collapse: 1% Attrition: 16% MLB: 17% *Comparables: Zack Cozart, Diory Hernandez, Lance Zawadzki*

A solid defender with good range and the ability to swipe a bag, Calixte has decent pop for a middle infielder and can look like a future big-league shortstop. Then you'll see him repeatedly hack away at off-speed junk outside the zone and doubt he can ever survive long-term exposure to big-league pitching when Triple-A journeymen can torture him so. The hardest things for young hitters to learn are patience and pitch recognition, so Calixte is likely at best a utility infielder in waiting.

Dusty Coleman UT

Born: 4/20/87 Age: 29 Bats: R Throws: R Height: 6'2" Weight: 205

YEAR	TEAM	LVL	AGE	PA	R	2B	3B	HR	RBI	BB	K	SB	CS	AVG/OBP/SLG	TAv	BABIP	BRR	FRAA	WARP
2013	MID	AA	26	554	65	34	10	3	61	57	155	17	10	.260/.344/.390	.265	.375	4.8	SS(66): 8.6, 2B(52): -3.7	3.4
2013	SAC	AAA	26	22	4	1	0	0	1	0	5	1	0	.143/.182/.190	.183	.188	0.4	3B(4): -0.7, 2B(2): 0.0	-0.2
2014	MID	AA	27	554	79	27	2	18	81	47	202	16	5	.223/.300/.397	.254	.332	0.9	SS(125): 7.2, 2B(9): 0.2	2.9
2015	KCA	MLB	28	5	0	0	0	0	0	0	3	0	0	.000/.000/.000	-.008	.000	-1.2	3B(2): 0.1	-0.2
2015	OMA	AAA	28	276	31	11	2	7	27	14	69	8	2	.275/.323/.418	.272	.354	0.7	SS(36): 0.5, 2B(27): 1.7	1.8
2015	NWA	AA	28	114	12	9	0	2	18	14	23	4	4	.341/.460/.505	.354	.433	0.0	SS(24): 3.7, 2B(2): -0.3	2.0
2016	*KCA*	*MLB*	*29*	*250*	*25*	*11*	*2*	*5*	*22*	*17*	*85*	*5*	*2*	*.214/.280/.338*	*.223*	*.313*	*0.2*	*SS 3, 2B 0*	*0.5*
2017	*KCA*	*MLB*	*30*	*264*	*27*	*12*	*2*	*5*	*25*	*18*	*90*	*5*	*2*	*.212/.278/.336*	*.223*	*.310*	*0.2*	*SS 3, 2B 0*	*0.4*

Breakout: 0% Improve: 2% Collapse: 2% Attrition: 7% MLB: 7% *Comparables: Brent Dlugach, John Nelson, Matt Macri*

Coleman made his major-league debut last year in unforgettable fashion, entering the July 3rd game against the Twins as a pinch-runner. He moved to third base and looked ready to score the winning run on a Mike Moustakas sacrifice fly before inexplicably channeling his inner Jack Cust, stopping halfway down the line and getting tagged out. His team survived his epic TOOTBLAN and went on to win anyway, because Royals, and Coleman went back to the minors. Like most journeyman minor-league infielders, he's not likely to see the majors again; unlike most, he's likely to someday get a standing ovation at a Royals old-timer's game.

Christian Colon UT

Born: 5/14/89 Age: 27 Bats: R Throws: R Height: 5'10" Weight: 190

YEAR	TEAM	LVL	AGE	PA	R	2B	3B	HR	RBI	BB	K	SB	CS	AVG/OBP/SLG	TAv	BABIP	BRR	FRAA	WARP
2013	OMA	AAA	24	577	72	12	3	12	58	41	57	15	4	.273/.335/.379	.256	.288	2.1	2B(75): 2.5, SS(54): -3.0	1.9
2014	OMA	AAA	25	388	55	18	0	8	47	30	29	15	4	.311/.366/.433	.278	.317	0.6	SS(35): 2.0, 2B(35): 0.6	2.4
2014	KCA	MLB	25	49	8	5	1	0	6	3	4	2	0	.333/.375/.489	.316	.366	0.8	2B(11): 0.4, 3B(5): 0.2	0.6
2015	OMA	AAA	26	217	19	9	0	1	17	21	18	8	2	.281/.353/.344	.248	.305	-1.2	SS(26): 3.3, 2B(16): 0.2	0.6
2015	KCA	MLB	26	119	8	5	0	0	6	11	17	3	2	.290/.356/.336	.249	.344	-1.3	SS(21): 0.4, 2B(14): -0.3	0.3
2016	*KCA*	*MLB*	*27*	*183*	*21*	*8*	*1*	*2*	*15*	*12*	*22*	*5*	*1*	*.262/.315/.357*	*.242*	*.283*	*0.2*	*2B 0, SS -0*	*0.4*
2017	*KCA*	*MLB*	*28*	*359*	*38*	*14*	*1*	*5*	*33*	*26*	*44*	*8*	*3*	*.259/.316/.354*	*.240*	*.281*	*0.5*	*2B 1, SS 0*	*0.7*

Breakout: 2% Improve: 21% Collapse: 9% Attrition: 20% MLB: 47% *Comparables: Matt Tolbert, Jeff Keppinger, Andy Cannizaro*

If you need someone to make a play in the 12th inning of a postseason game, Colon has proven to be the perfect tool for the job. He only has two career postseason at-bats, but has used them to drive home and then score the tying and winning runs of the 2014 Wild Card playoff game and drive in the go-ahead run in last year's Series-clinching victory, both times in the 12th frame. He's also a steady infield glove, provides professional at-bats and gets on base, making him an ideal fit for a utility gig. Colon could also function as a stop-gap starter at second base, but wouldn't be an asset if he had to play every day. After all, most games don't go into extras.

Tony Cruz C

Born: 8/18/86 Age: 29 Bats: R Throws: R Height: 5'11" Weight: 215

YEAR	TEAM	LVL	AGE	PA	R	2B	3B	HR	RBI	BB	K	SB	CS	AVG/OBP/SLG	TAv	BABIP	BRR	FRAA	WARP
2013	SLN	MLB	26	129	13	6	1	1	13	4	25	0	0	.203/.240/.293	.178	.247	0.7	C(44): 1.2, 3B(3): -0.0	-0.3
2014	SLN	MLB	27	150	11	5	0	1	17	13	28	0	3	.200/.270/.259	.190	.245	-0.2	C(47): -8.9, 1B(2): 0.0	-1.4
2015	SLN	MLB	28	151	6	7	1	2	11	6	32	0	0	.204/.235/.310	.179	.248	0.2	C(51): -0.5, 3B(3): 0.1	-0.7
2016	*KCA*	*MLB*	*29*	*63*	*5*	*3*	*0*	*1*	*5*	*3*	*12*	*0*	*0*	*.227/.271/.331*	*.216*	*.270*	*0.1*	*C -1*	*-0.2*
2017	*KCA*	*MLB*	*30*	*161*	*15*	*8*	*1*	*2*	*14*	*10*	*32*	*0*	*1*	*.222/.272/.323*	*.214*	*.267*	*0.3*	*C -4*	*-0.5*

Breakout: 0% Improve: 30% Collapse: 14% Attrition: 18% MLB: 90% *Comparables: Drew Butera, Jordan Pacheco, Jeff Mathis*

YEAR	TEAM	P. COUNT	FRM RUNS	BLK RUNS	THRW RUNS	TOT RUNS
2013	SLN	4457	1.4	0.2	-0.1	1.5
2014	SLN	5298	-7.4	-0.1	-0.2	-7.7
2015	SLN	4705	-0.6	0.0	-0.3	-0.8
2016	*KCA*	*2402*	*-1.1*	*0.0*	*-0.1*	*-1.2*
2017	*KCA*	*6134*	*-3.2*	*0.1*	*-0.4*	*-3.6*

When you think about it, Cruz would make for the worst roommate ever. At best, he works for a few hours once a week; otherwise, he spends his time sitting around, snacking and waiting for his friends to go play catch, as if he were yanked straight from an Apatow film. Cruz the ballplayer isn't much better; he can't hit, and his defense isn't so good that he's guaranteed a job for as long as he can cop a squat. Yet, like that annoying roomie, he's managed to stick around well beyond his welcome. The Cardinals tried for years to replace him without much success, so they did the next-best thing: use him as little as possible. To wit, last season marked the fourth time Cruz had appeared in more than 50 games while recording fewer than 200 trips to the plate; that's one shy of Henry Blanco's career mark, and five short of David Ross' modern record. Those guys played into their late 30s (and beyond, in Blanco's case); Cruz is 29, so he could have another 10 years to shatter those marks—though, knowing the type, he'll probably leave the record-breaking for someone else to do. At least the Cardinals were kind enough to put him in the best possible situation to succeed.

Cheslor Cuthbert 3B

Born: 11/16/92 Age: 23 Bats: R Throws: R Height: 6'1" Weight: 190

YEAR	TEAM	LVL	AGE	PA	R	2B	3B	HR	RBI	BB	K	SB	CS	AVG/OBP/SLG	TAv	BABIP	BRR	FRAA	WARP
2013	NWA	AA	20	264	25	16	0	6	28	20	51	5	2	.215/.279/.359	.218	.246	-2.9	3B(59): 3.1	-0.3
2013	WIL	A+	20	254	32	21	2	2	31	27	37	1	2	.280/.354/.418	.283	.324	-2.2	3B(57): -2.3	1.0
2014	NWA	AA	21	395	35	19	1	10	48	36	67	9	3	.276/.342/.420	.275	.313	-2.1	3B(60): -1.8, 1B(28): 1.6	1.3
2014	OMA	AAA	21	100	12	5	0	2	16	9	12	1	1	.264/.330/.385	.232	.286	0.3	3B(15): -0.8, 1B(9): -0.9	-0.2
2015	OMA	AAA	22	438	55	22	1	11	51	37	60	5	2	.277/.339/.421	.276	.302	-1.8	3B(75): 4.7, 1B(25): 0.5	2.2
2015	KCA	MLB	22	50	6	2	1	1	8	4	9	0	0	.217/.280/.370	.236	.250	-0.2	3B(17): 1.1, 2B(1): -0.0	0.1
2016	*KCA*	*MLB*	*23*	*129*	*12*	*7*	*1*	*3*	*14*	*9*	*24*	*1*	*0*	*.242/.295/.372*	*.241*	*.280*	*-0.1*	*1B 0, 2B -0*	*0.1*
2017	*KCA*	*MLB*	*24*	*394*	*43*	*20*	*1*	*9*	*41*	*27*	*75*	*3*	*1*	*.243/.296/.376*	*.243*	*.281*	*-0.4*	*1B 1, 2B -1*	*0.1*

Breakout: 5% Improve: 30% Collapse: 3% Attrition: 17% MLB: 42% *Comparables: Matt Dominguez, Willy Aybar, Taylor Green*

There are still far more questions than answers when it comes to Cuthbert, who made his big-league debut last summer and earned another September look-see. The organization continues to pencil him in at third base, and he's improved defensively to the point where some scouts feel he may be adequate there. Otherwise he'll need to slide across the diamond to first, where his position will be writing checks that his bat can't cash. He's provided consistent production in the high minors, which is a polite way to say he gets on base a little, hits the occasional home run and generally hasn't shown the offensive potential you'd hope for from a future corner man. Cuthbert is still young, but the expiration date on that excuse is fast approaching.

Hunter Dozier 3B

Born: 8/22/91 Age: 24 Bats: R Throws: R Height: 6'4" Weight: 220

YEAR	TEAM	LVL	AGE	PA	R	2B	3B	HR	RBI	BB	K	SB	CS	AVG/OBP/SLG	TAv	BABIP	BRR	FRAA	WARP
2013	LEX	A	21	59	6	6	0	0	9	3	5	0	0	.327/.373/.436	.322	.360	-0.5	3B(13): 1.1	0.6
2014	WIL	A+	22	267	36	18	0	4	39	35	56	7	3	.295/.397/.429	.324	.371	2.2	3B(62): -7.8	2.2
2014	NWA	AA	22	267	33	12	0	4	21	31	70	3	2	.209/.303/.312	.222	.280	0.9	3B(61): -6.2	-0.8
2015	NWA	AA	23	523	65	27	1	12	53	45	151	6	2	.213/.281/.349	.241	.283	-0.7	3B(115): -4.1	0.0
2016	*KCA*	*MLB*	*24*	*250*	*22*	*12*	*1*	*5*	*24*	*19*	*72*	*1*	*1*	*.212/.277/.331*	*.223*	*.285*	*-0.3*	*3B -3*	*-0.7*
2017	*KCA*	*MLB*	*25*	*351*	*36*	*17*	*1*	*7*	*34*	*28*	*104*	*2*	*1*	*.211/.278/.337*	*.226*	*.287*	*-0.5*	*3B -5*	*-0.9*

Breakout: 0% Improve: 5% Collapse: 3% Attrition: 9% MLB: 12% *Comparables: Richie Shaffer, Matthew Duffy, Travis Metcalf*

Dozier was unable to solve the mysteries of the Texas League last summer, as the former top pick spent a full season failing to assemble consistent at-bats or make consistent hard contact against more advanced pitchers. It was an especially troubling season for a college product like Dozier, who is short on tools and projection but should show more polish, especially in his approach at the plate. He did start launching a few bombs and has plus power potential for a third baseman, but his defense at the hot corner is still a work in progress. This already feels like a make-or-break season for Dozier's career, and if he keeps posting middle-infield batting lines with a corner-man's glove he'll soon become organizational fodder.

Jarrod Dyson CF

Born: 8/15/84 Age: 31 Bats: L Throws: R Height: 5'10" Weight: 160

YEAR	TEAM	LVL	AGE	PA	R	2B	3B	HR	RBI	BB	K	SB	CS	AVG/OBP/SLG	TAv	BABIP	BRR	FRAA	WARP
2013	KCA	MLB	28	239	30	9	4	2	17	21	45	34	6	.258/.326/.366	.246	.317	3.2	CF(73): 1.7	0.9
2013	OMA	AAA	28	58	8	2	0	0	1	3	12	5	0	.154/.228/.192	.185	.200	0.6	CF(14): 1.6	-0.1
2014	KCA	MLB	29	290	33	4	4	1	24	22	52	36	7	.269/.324/.327	.242	.330	4.7	CF(106): 4.2, LF(3): 0.1	1.3
2015	KCA	MLB	30	225	31	8	6	2	18	14	37	26	3	.250/.311/.380	.249	.296	4.7	CF(37): 4.0, LF(27): 5.9	1.9
2016	*KCA*	*MLB*	*31*	*485*	*61*	*15*	*7*	*2*	*31*	*37*	*88*	*54*	*9*	*.246/.309/.326*	*.231*	*.294*	*5.4*	*LF 7, CF 1*	*1.5*
2017	*KCA*	*MLB*	*32*	*349*	*33*	*11*	*4*	*1*	*26*	*27*	*64*	*37*	*7*	*.237/.301/.312*	*.224*	*.284*	*4.8*	*LF 5, CF 1*	*0.8*

Breakout: 1% Improve: 27% Collapse: 12% Attrition: 24% MLB: 83% *Comparables: Craig Gentry, Tony Gwynn, Alfredo Amezaga*

It's appropriate that when the Royals needed to manufacture a run to clinch their first title in a generation, the primary raw material was Dyson, who pinch-ran, stole second, went to third on a groundout and scored the go-ahead run. That's what Dyson and Kansas City do. Ned Yost has often been chided for his decision-making (see: leadoff hitter Alcides Escobar), but how many speedy, punch-less fourth-outfielder types litter major-league rosters without providing the impact Yost gets from Dyson? The Royals have wisely minimized his exposure at the plate and maximized his impact on the basepaths and in the field, which sure sounds like smart management to us. Kansas City fans had best hope Dyson doesn't have to spend the season as a platoon corner outfielder, since every game he starts is a game he's not able to enter in a key situation after a better hitter works his way on base.

Alcides Escobar SS

Born: 12/16/86 Age: 29 Bats: R Throws: R Height: 6'1" Weight: 185

YEAR	TEAM	LVL	AGE	PA	R	2B	3B	HR	RBI	BB	K	SB	CS	AVG/OBP/SLG	TAv	BABIP	BRR	FRAA	WARP
2013	KCA	MLB	26	642	57	20	4	4	52	19	84	22	0	.234/.259/.300	.205	.264	2.2	SS(158): 1.1	-0.7
2014	KCA	MLB	27	620	74	34	5	3	50	23	83	31	6	.285/.317/.377	.255	.326	5.3	SS(162): -3.3	2.5
2015	KCA	MLB	28	662	76	20	5	3	47	26	75	17	5	.257/.293/.320	.224	.286	5.3	SS(148): 7.2	1.7
2016	*KCA*	*MLB*	*29*	*672*	*66*	*28*	*6*	*4*	*52*	*27*	*92*	*24*	*5*	*.259/.295/.346*	*.230*	*.290*	*3.2*	*SS 0*	*1.6*
2017	*KCA*	*MLB*	*30*	*548*	*52*	*24*	*4*	*3*	*45*	*25*	*78*	*18*	*4*	*.254/.295/.337*	*.227*	*.286*	*2.9*	*SS 0*	*1.0*

Breakout: 2% Improve: 44% Collapse: 4% Attrition: 11% MLB: 99% *Comparables: Jack Wilson, Tony Fernandez, Yuniesky Betancourt*

Last year Escobar was a worthy Gold Glove–winner at shortstop, a world champion and a millstone around the neck of the Royals' offense. An unrepentant hacker, Escobar rarely strikes out but has little power and considers walks to be a badge of cowardice. When his bleeders sneak through the infield or his flares find the outfield grass he can post a high enough BABIP to avoid utter offensive ruination; when they don't, he's among the worst hitters in baseball. Yet Ned Yost saw fit to lead Escobar off 131 times last season, not only depriving the actual hitters in the Kansas City lineup more chances to drive in runs but ensuring he would come to the plate more than he had in any season of his career. There are those who will follow the "if it ain't broke, don't fix it" maxim and see no reason to drop Escobar to the bottom of the order where he belongs. To them we say: The fact you once made a putt with your sand wedge doesn't prove you should throw away your old Billy Baroo.

Reymond Fuentes OF

Born: 2/12/91 Age: 25 Bats: L Throws: L Height: 6'0" Weight: 160

YEAR	TEAM	LVL	AGE	PA	R	2B	3B	HR	RBI	BB	K	SB	CS	AVG/OBP/SLG	TAv	BABIP	BRR	FRAA	WARP
2013	SDN	MLB	22	36	4	0	0	0	1	3	16	3	0	.152/.222/.152	.145	.294	0.8	CF(15): -0.3, LF(2): 0.1	-0.3
2013	SAN	AA	22	403	56	21	2	6	35	41	71	29	10	.316/.396/.441	.324	.381	1.2	RF(41): -8.5, LF(26): 3.1	3.0
2013	TUC	AAA	22	67	17	4	0	0	8	10	10	6	1	.418/.515/.491	.357	.511	1.4	CF(14): 0.6	1.1
2014	ELP	AAA	23	178	29	9	3	1	16	17	27	13	2	.261/.337/.376	.288	.310	1.4	LF(27): 1.1, CF(17): -1.1	0.2
2014	SAN	AA	23	194	25	6	2	4	17	16	37	12	1	.324/.386/.453	.315	.392	0.9	CF(39): 1.0, LF(2): -0.0	2.0
2015	OMA	AAA	24	445	70	10	4	9	46	30	72	29	6	.308/.360/.422	.281	.356	2.7	CF(53): 4.4, LF(47): 2.4	3.3
2016	*KCA*	*MLB*	*25*	*157*	*20*	*6*	*1*	*2*	*13*	*12*	*33*	*8*	*2*	*.268/.328/.382*	*.252*	*.322*	*0.9*	*LF 2, RF -1*	*0.6*
2017	*KCA*	*MLB*	*26*	*388*	*43*	*15*	*3*	*6*	*38*	*30*	*85*	*19*	*4*	*.262/.325/.380*	*.252*	*.317*	*2.9*	*LF 6, RF -2*	*1.3*

Breakout: 11% Improve: 39% Collapse: 9% Attrition: 40% MLB: 65% *Comparables: Ben Francisco, Abraham Almonte, Adron Chambers*

Kansas City collects speedy outfielders with the frenzied abandon of squirrels collecting acorns, so it was no surprise to see the Royals trade for Fuentes back in 2014. A former top pick in Boston, Fuentes is a true center fielder who can make contact, draw a few walks, lash gappers and run like the wind. He doesn't have significant power, but his on-base skills could play at the top of the order. Compared to the other fourth outfielder types in Kansas City's employ, he's younger than Lane Adams, older than Bubba Starling, slower than Terrance Gore, less fluent in Portuguese than Paulo Orlando and less fluent in cool than Jarrod Dyson.

Jonny Gomes OF

Born: 11/22/80 Age: 35 Bats: R Throws: R Height: 6'1" Weight: 230

YEAR	TEAM	LVL	AGE	PA	R	2B	3B	HR	RBI	BB	K	SB	CS	AVG/OBP/SLG	TAv	BABIP	BRR	FRAA	WARP
2013	BOS	MLB	32	366	49	17	0	13	52	43	89	1	0	.247/.344/.426	.283	.298	2.5	LF(98): -0.4, RF(4): -0.4	1.9
2014	OAK	MLB	33	75	6	1	0	0	5	9	18	0	0	.234/.320/.250	.235	.313	0.2	LF(19): -0.2	0.0
2014	BOS	MLB	33	246	22	7	0	6	32	26	70	0	0	.234/.329/.354	.265	.312	-0.3	LF(65): -3.3, RF(11): 1.2	0.4
2015	ATL	MLB	34	228	27	7	0	7	22	28	67	1	1	.221/.325/.364	.261	.293	0.7	LF(59): -6.1, RF(2): -0.0	0.0
2015	KCA	MLB	34	34	2	2	0	0	4	3	14	0	0	.167/.235/.233	.202	.294	-0.1	RF(6): -0.3	-0.2
2016	*KCA*	*MLB*	*35*	*257*	*28*	*9*	*1*	*8*	*30*	*29*	*73*	*1*	*0*	*.225/.325/.379*	*.257*	*.292*	*0.6*	*LF -5, RF 0*	*0.2*
2017	*KCA*	*MLB*	*36*	*182*	*22*	*6*	*0*	*5*	*19*	*21*	*53*	*0*	*0*	*.215/.315/.352*	*.246*	*.285*	*0.4*	*LF -4, RF 0*	*-0.2*

Breakout: 2% Improve: 22% Collapse: 13% Attrition: 19% MLB: 90% *Comparables: Jason Bay, Andruw Jones, Jimmy Wynn*

Over his 13-year career Gomes has evolved from full-time outfielder to lefty masher to gritty veteran presence to professional teammate. His personal highlight reel for last season consists primarily of words, not deeds: Christian Colon after his Series-winning pinch-hit immediately praising Gomes for teaching him how to prepare; Josh Donaldson describing how Gomes exhorted him to be more aggressive at the plate, eventually leading to his MVP season; and Gomes himself stealing the show with his impassioned speech at the Royals' championship rally. Between the lines he's a shadow of his former self, a statue in the field, hopeless against same-side pitching and lacking punch against lefties. Yet he'll still likely find a home on a contender's bench, because his lessons about grit and hustle and toughness and professionalism seemingly go down better when his number could theoretically be penciled into the lineup.

Alex Gordon LF

Born: 2/10/84 Age: 32 Bats: L Throws: R Height: 6'1" Weight: 220

YEAR	TEAM	LVL	AGE	PA	R	2B	3B	HR	RBI	BB	K	SB	CS	AVG/OBP/SLG	TAv	BABIP	BRR	FRAA	WARP
2013	KCA	MLB	29	700	90	27	6	20	81	52	141	11	3	.265/.327/.422	.277	.310	4.2	LF(155): 12.9	4.6
2014	KCA	MLB	30	643	87	34	1	19	74	65	126	12	3	.266/.351/.432	.287	.310	4.2	LF(156): 15.7	5.4
2015	OMA	AAA	31	37	6	2	0	1	5	8	6	0	0	.429/.568/.607	.428	.524	-1.1	LF(4): 1.0	0.7
2015	KCA	MLB	31	422	40	18	0	13	48	49	92	2	5	.271/.377/.432	.299	.327	-1.7	LF(101): 4.0	2.9
2016	*KCA*	*MLB*	*32*	*600*	*68*	*32*	*3*	*15*	*71*	*57*	*126*	*7*	*4*	*.268/.346/.427*	*.276*	*.322*	*1.7*	*LF 8*	*3.9*
2017	*KCA*	*MLB*	*33*	*510*	*62*	*26*	*3*	*12*	*57*	*48*	*110*	*5*	*3*	*.263/.340/.413*	*.271*	*.320*	*1.6*	*LF 7*	*2.9*

Breakout: 0% Improve: 31% Collapse: 3% Attrition: 8% MLB: 95% *Comparables: Josh Willingham, Shin-Soo Choo, David Justice*

If Gordon hadn't missed nearly two months with a groin strain last summer, he likely would have joined Miguel Cabrera and Andrew McCutchen as the only players to post at least four WARP in each of the past five seasons. The best player on the best Royals team in a generation, Gordon's biggest strength is his lack of weaknesses. He's a savvy baserunner who plays stellar defense in left field, gets on base, hits home runs and punishes same-side pitching. Gordon isn't immune to Father Time, however, and as he closes out his peak he's already started to leak a little range and much of his basestealing burst, and will likely start to lose more time to strains and stresses. Even a diminished Gordon will be a very good player, and should be a solid contributor (though not a superstar) for the foreseeable future.

Terrance Gore OF

Born: 6/8/91 Age: 25 Bats: R Throws: R Height: 5'7" Weight: 165

YEAR	TEAM	LVL	AGE	PA	R	2B	3B	HR	RBI	BB	K	SB	CS	AVG/OBP/SLG	TAv	BABIP	BRR	FRAA	WARP
2013	LEX	A	22	541	76	6	3	0	24	62	120	68	8	.215/.334/.242	.244	.293	12.3	LF(119): 10.1, CF(10): -0.7	2.6
2014	KCA	MLB	23	2	5	0	0	0	0	0	0	5	0	.000/.500/.000	.296	.000	1.0	LF(2): -0.0	0.1
2014	WIL	A+	23	287	34	8	1	0	15	20	66	36	4	.218/.284/.258	.242	.293	4.3	LF(81): 17.7, CF(8): -1.4	2.2
2014	OMA	AAA	23	26	8	0	0	0	0	2	4	11	3	.250/.348/.250	.231	.313	1.9	LF(7): -0.7	0.1
2015	NWA	AA	24	259	42	4	1	0	16	26	50	39	2	.284/.367/.311	.256	.366	4.1	LF(51): 0.3, CF(21): -2.9	0.7
2015	KCA	MLB	24	4	1	0	0	0	0	0	1	3	0	.000/.250/.000	.147	.000	0.9	LF(4): -0.4	0.0
2016	*KCA*	*MLB*	*25*	*250*	*31*	*7*	*1*	*1*	*12*	*18*	*62*	*24*	*3*	*.215/.286/.268*	*.207*	*.282*	*3.7*	*LF 6, CF -1*	*0.3*
2017	*KCA*	*MLB*	*26*	*251*	*24*	*6*	*1*	*1*	*17*	*19*	*62*	*24*	*3*	*.218/.292/.270*	*.209*	*.286*	*4.5*	*LF 6, CF -1*	*0.4*

Breakout: 4% Improve: 13% Collapse: 3% Attrition: 13% MLB: 19% *Comparables: Derrick Robinson, Kyle Hudson, Jerry Owens*

Blessed with basestealing prowess and raw speed that can bend the fabric of space-time, Gore made a few strides at the plate last season hoping to become more than just a perennial playoff pinch-runner. He increased his walk rate and posted a credible on-base percentage in the Texas League, lending a little credence to the thought that he might be able to carry his weight all season on a big-league bench. However, Gore's swing generates less power than a 10-year-old D cell and a weak arm limits him to left field, meaning he's still about 20 points of OBP below where he can realistically be considered for a fourth-outfielder job.

Eric Hosmer 1B

Born: 10/24/89 Age: 26 Bats: L Throws: L Height: 6'4" Weight: 225

YEAR	TEAM	LVL	AGE	PA	R	2B	3B	HR	RBI	BB	K	SB	CS	AVG/OBP/SLG	TAv	BABIP	BRR	FRAA	WARP
2013	KCA	MLB	23	680	86	34	3	17	79	51	100	11	4	.302/.353/.448	.291	.335	-0.4	1B(158): 8.0, RF(1): -0.1	3.7
2014	KCA	MLB	24	547	54	35	1	9	58	35	93	4	2	.270/.318/.398	.262	.312	-1.9	1B(130): 8.1	1.4
2015	KCA	MLB	25	667	98	33	5	18	93	61	108	7	3	.297/.363/.459	.289	.336	2.7	1B(154): 3.7, RF(1): 0.0	3.4
2016	*KCA*	*MLB*	*26*	*634*	*71*	*32*	*3*	*16*	*75*	*51*	*101*	*8*	*3*	*.279/.338/.430*	*.273*	*.311*	*0.2*	*1B 5*	*2.5*
2017	*KCA*	*MLB*	*27*	*581*	*71*	*28*	*2*	*14*	*66*	*51*	*92*	*7*	*3*	*.271/.337/.416*	*.270*	*.303*	*0.2*	*1B 5*	*1.9*

Breakout: 4% Improve: 52% Collapse: 0% Attrition: 6% MLB: 100% *Comparables: Wally Joyner, Ron Blomberg, Brian Giles*

Hosmer's Polaroid moment occurred during Kansas City's championship-clinching Game Five victory, when he lined an RBI double to left that spoiled Matt Harvey's shutout bid in the ninth before playing chicken with David Wright's eyes and Lucas Duda's arm to dash home with the game-tying run. That sequence perfectly illustrates Hosmer's value, as the young first baseman supplements his mundane power by playing Gold Glove defense, running the bases well, showing tremendous baseball instincts and never shying away from the big moment. His contact-oriented groundball approach can render him subject to the merciless gods of BABIP, and as he enters his prime it would be nice to see him ditch his tradition of following up solid seasons with stinkers. Still two years shy of free agency, Hosmer's well-rounded game is a perfect fit in Kansas City.

Omar Infante 2B

Born: 12/26/81 Age: 34 Bats: R Throws: R Height: 5'11" Weight: 195

YEAR	TEAM	LVL	AGE	PA	R	2B	3B	HR	RBI	BB	K	SB	CS	AVG/OBP/SLG	TAv	BABIP	BRR	FRAA	WARP
2013	DET	MLB	31	476	54	24	3	10	51	20	44	5	2	.318/.345/.450	.285	.333	-0.2	2B(118): 5.3	3.1
2013	TOL	AAA	31	21	1	0	0	0	1	2	2	0	0	.211/.286/.211	.160	.235	0.3	2B(4): -0.7	-0.2
2014	KCA	MLB	32	575	50	21	3	6	66	33	68	9	3	.252/.295/.337	.234	.275	2.9	2B(134): -13.6	-1.2
2015	KCA	MLB	33	455	39	23	7	2	44	9	69	2	2	.220/.234/.318	.202	.255	-0.8	2B(124): -6.5	-2.3
2016	*KCA*	*MLB*	*34*	*558*	*57*	*25*	*5*	*6*	*45*	*23*	*67*	*7*	*3*	*.259/.290/.364*	*.235*	*.280*	*0.5*	*2B -7*	*0.1*
2017	*KCA*	*MLB*	*35*	*448*	*41*	*19*	*4*	*4*	*38*	*19*	*59*	*4*	*2*	*.245/.277/.337*	*.222*	*.270*	*0.4*	*2B -5*	*-0.7*

Breakout: 0% Improve: 28% Collapse: 14% Attrition: 16% MLB: 88% *Comparables: Jack Wilson, Mike Aviles, Freddy Sanchez*

It can't all be sunshine and lollipops. Since the Y2K scare, only five players have posted a TAv worse than Infante's score last season: Angel Berroa (Royals), Neifi Perez (Royals), Cesar Izturis (twice!), Yadi Molina (seriously, not Jose?) and Darwin Barney (Gold Glove). Even worse, those players "earned" a little under $10 million combined for those six seasons, while Infante pocketed a cool $7.5 million all on his own last year, and will have been paid $17.75 million more after his 2018 option is bought out. His two seasons in Kansas City have been plagued by injuries, most notably bone spurs in his elbow that called for offseason surgery. In theory, a healthy Infante can provide solid defense at the keystone and a little pop at the bottom of the lineup; in practice, we'll believe it when we see it.

Raul Mondesi SS

Born: 7/27/95 Age: 20 Bats: B Throws: R Height: 6'1" Weight: 185

YEAR	TEAM	LVL	AGE	PA	R	2B	3B	HR	RBI	BB	K	SB	CS	AVG/OBP/SLG	TAv	BABIP	BRR	FRAA	WARP
2013	LEX	A	17	536	61	13	7	7	47	34	118	24	10	.261/.311/.361	.257	.331	1.1	SS(108): -0.0	2.0
2014	WIL	A+	18	472	54	14	12	8	33	24	122	17	4	.211/.256/.354	.232	.274	1.4	SS(106): 2.2	0.9
2015	NWA	AA	19	338	36	11	5	6	33	17	88	19	6	.243/.279/.372	.239	.316	0.8	SS(63): -2.0, 2B(18): -3.3	0.0
2016	*KCA*	*MLB*	*20*	*250*	*27*	*8*	*3*	*4*	*19*	*8*	*70*	*8*	*3*	*.215/.241/.328*	*.200*	*.277*	*1.2*	*SS -0, 2B -1*	*-0.4*
2017	*KCA*	*MLB*	*21*	*437*	*41*	*15*	*6*	*8*	*43*	*16*	*116*	*15*	*5*	*.227/.256/.354*	*.214*	*.283*	*2.7*	*SS 0, 2B -2*	*0.1*

Breakout: 0% Improve: 1% Collapse: 0% Attrition: 4% MLB: 5% *Comparables: Adam Jones, Tim Beckham, Chris Owings*

When Mondesi became the first player in history to make his MLB debut in the World Series last fall, it was only the latest in a series of aggressive assignments for the young shortstop. He spent the entire summer playing Double-A ball, half of it while still a teenager, despite looking overmatched at the plate the season before in High-A. Scouts salivate over his speed, build and defensive chops, and see him growing into a power-hitting middle infielder with multiple All-Star appearances, though he's yet to find even a modicum of success at the plate. To do that he'll need to learn how to make contact and control the strike zone, which is easier said than done when you're habitually facing pitchers with a half-decade of baseball experience on you.

Kendrys Morales DH

Born: 6/20/83 Age: 33 Bats: B Throws: R Height: 6'1" Weight: 225

YEAR	TEAM	LVL	AGE	PA	R	2B	3B	HR	RBI	BB	K	SB	CS	AVG/OBP/SLG	TAv	BABIP	BRR	FRAA	WARP
2013	SEA	MLB	30	657	64	34	0	23	80	49	114	0	0	.277/.336/.449	.290	.309	-4.5	1B(31): -2.1	2.0
2014	SEA	MLB	31	239	16	9	0	7	24	21	41	0	0	.207/.285/.347	.251	.222	-1.2	1B(14): -1.1	-0.2
2014	MIN	MLB	31	162	12	11	0	1	18	6	27	0	0	.234/.259/.325	.223	.273	-0.3	1B(13): -1.0	-0.6
2015	KCA	MLB	32	639	81	41	2	22	106	58	103	0	0	.290/.362/.485	.294	.319	-5.5	1B(9): -0.4	2.3
2016	*KCA*	*MLB*	*33*	*580*	*62*	*31*	*2*	*18*	*73*	*43*	*105*	*0*	*0*	*.265/.325/.431*	*.272*	*.298*	*-3.3*		*1.4*
2017	*KCA*	*MLB*	*34*	*511*	*61*	*26*	*2*	*14*	*59*	*36*	*94*	*0*	*0*	*.262/.319/.416*	*.266*	*.299*	*-3.2*	-	*0.7*

Breakout: 2% Improve: 28% Collapse: 4% Attrition: 9% MLB: 97% *Comparables: Justin Morneau, Mike Sweeney, Adrian Gonzalez*

We can't tell you with any certainty that the deal Morales signed before last season was the largest ever handed out to an aging, bat-only player who had just been out-slugged by Billy Hamilton, let alone Billy Butler. Researching that would cause us to ingest so many horrible player-seasons we'd probably feel like Michael Clarke Duncan in *The Green Mile*, and who needs that? Suffice it to say his two-year, $17 million deal caused some justifiable hand-wringing, but Kansas City was rewarded with a Silver Slugger season from their new DH. Morales has always hit when healthy, both physically and emotionally, and with the embarrassment of his 2014 contract fail firmly in the rearview mirror, and the luxury of an actual spring training, he was free to concentrate on putting a hurt on pitchers from both sides of the plate. If he can do it again this year, and there are plenty of reasons to think he should, the Royals may well be willing to exercise their side of an $11 million mutual option for 2017—an offer you would think Morales would now be inclined to accept.

Mike Moustakas 3B

Born: 9/11/88 Age: 27 Bats: L Throws: R Height: 6'0" Weight: 215

YEAR	TEAM	LVL	AGE	PA	R	2B	3B	HR	RBI	BB	K	SB	CS	AVG/OBP/SLG	TAv	BABIP	BRR	FRAA	WARP
2013	KCA	MLB	24	514	42	26	0	12	42	32	83	2	4	.233/.287/.364	.234	.257	-3.0	3B(134): 5.1	0.5
2014	KCA	MLB	25	500	45	21	1	15	54	35	74	1	0	.212/.271/.361	.233	.220	1.7	3B(138): 7.1	1.2
2014	OMA	AAA	25	34	3	3	0	1	5	3	6	0	0	.355/.412/.548	.328	.417	0.1	3B(7): 1.6	0.5
2015	KCA	MLB	26	614	73	34	1	22	82	43	76	1	2	.284/.348/.470	.291	.294	-1.3	3B(146): 7.5	4.6
2016	*KCA*	*MLB*	*27*	*609*	*62*	*32*	*2*	*17*	*72*	*41*	*99*	*2*	*2*	*.247/.305/.404*	*.254*	*.269*	*-0.6*	*3B 5*	*1.8*
2017	*KCA*	*MLB*	*28*	*535*	*61*	*28*	*1*	*15*	*61*	*35*	*88*	*1*	*1*	*.241/.298/.396*	*.249*	*.263*	*-0.6*	*3B 4*	*1.1*

Breakout: 5% Improve: 48% Collapse: 3% Attrition: 11% MLB: 99% *Comparables: Chad Tracy, Puddin Head Jones, George Brett*

"I fully believe in Moustakas' rebirth this year as an all-fields hitter." So wrote Baseball Prospectus co-founder Rany Jazayerli while shopping the longtime Royals (and Wichita Whiffers) third basemen in his Strat-O-Matic baseball league, and if you can't believe Rany on the Royals, who can you believe? His newfound ability to drive the ball the opposite way helped Moustakas beat the shift and post career highs in virtually every offensive category, and he remains one of the league's better defensive third sackers. He grew more pull-happy as the season wore on and remains a flyball hitter with middling raw power, so there's always the chance he regresses at the plate when some of those souvenirs start dying at the right-field warning track. Just now entering his peak with two years to go before free agency, even with a little regression he'll put the dark malaise of his early career behind him.

Paulo Orlando OF

Born: 11/1/85 Age: 30 Bats: R Throws: R Height: 6'2" Weight: 210

YEAR	TEAM	LVL	AGE	PA	R	2B	3B	HR	RBI	BB	K	SB	CS	AVG/OBP/SLG	TAv	BABIP	BRR	FRAA	WARP
2013	OMA	AAA	27	326	41	9	3	5	46	22	56	8	3	.276/.326/.379	.268	.323	1.0	CF(70): 8.7, RF(21): 2.7	2.5
2014	OMA	AAA	28	554	61	21	9	6	63	39	86	34	9	.301/.355/.415	.277	.351	3.6	CF(80): 12.4, RF(42): 4.7	4.5
2015	KCA	MLB	29	251	31	14	6	7	27	5	53	3	3	.249/.269/.444	.254	.291	0.1	RF(45): -1.7, LF(37): 2.1	0.5
2015	OMA	AAA	29	182	20	11	0	3	17	8	32	9	0	.276/.309/.394	.256	.321	2.1	CF(18): -1.1, RF(11): 0.4	0.8
2016	*KCA*	*MLB*	*30*	*552*	*53*	*23*	*6*	*7*	*50*	*24*	*110*	*17*	*6*	*.249/.286/.357*	*.230*	*.298*	*0.9*	*RF 8*	*0.5*
2017	*KCA*	*MLB*	*31*	*525*	*50*	*22*	*6*	*6*	*46*	*23*	*107*	*16*	*5*	*.246/.283/.348*	*.227*	*.297*	*1.4*	*RF 7*	*0.2*

Breakout: 0% Improve: 7% Collapse: 9% Attrition: 16% MLB: 24% *Comparables: Jason Ellison, Buck Coats, Dewayne Wise*

Perhaps the first sign that the Royals had a magical season in store was Orlando's April arrival, when the veteran minor leaguer completed his 29-year, 5,000-mile trek from Sao Paolo to Kansas City by tripling in his first official at-bat. There were cheers and smiles and fist pumps and joy and the spectacle of yet another Royals outfielder morphing into a blur rounding second. There was Salvy Perez laughing as he capriciously pretended to throw Orlando's precious souvenir into the stands. There was Orlando himself channeling Kansas City's poet laureate, proclaiming, "That what speed do," before enduring his first big-league Gatorade shower. And, not coincidentally, there was a win over a division rival.

Orlando is a perfectly serviceable fourth outfielder with great wheels, a plus glove, some thump in his bat and a penchant for making too many outs. He's like Jordan Danks, which is to say he's essentially fungible and easily forgettable. But he isn't really like Jordan Danks, because he had That Moment during That Season, and because baseball is tribal and Orlando is now forever a member of that tribe.

Salvador Perez C

Born: 5/10/90 Age: 26 Bats: R Throws: R Height: 6'3" Weight: 240

YEAR	TEAM	LVL	AGE	PA	R	2B	3B	HR	RBI	BB	K	SB	CS	AVG/OBP/SLG	TAv	BABIP	BRR	FRAA	WARP
2013	KCA	MLB	23	526	48	25	3	13	79	21	63	0	0	.292/.323/.433	.277	.311	-2.3	C(137): -2.4, 1B(1): -0.1	2.8
2014	KCA	MLB	24	606	57	28	2	17	70	22	85	1	0	.260/.289/.403	.251	.278	-3.6	C(146): -14.2	0.2
2015	KCA	MLB	25	553	52	25	0	21	70	13	82	1	0	.260/.280/.426	.251	.270	-2.5	C(139): -8.4, 1B(1): -0.0	0.8
2016	*KCA*	*MLB*	*26*	*606*	*62*	*31*	*3*	*17*	*75*	*23*	*79*	*1*	*0*	*.275/.306/.429*	*.264*	*.291*	*-2.6*	*C -10*	*1.5*
2017	*KCA*	*MLB*	*27*	*564*	*66*	*28*	*2*	*17*	*68*	*23*	*76*	*0*	*0*	*.271/.304/.426*	*.262*	*.287*	*-2.7*	*C -10*	*1.1*

Breakout: 8% Improve: 50% Collapse: 3% Attrition: 9% MLB: 98% *Comparables: Wilson Ramos, Ted Simmons, Kurt Suzuki*

YEAR	TEAM	P. COUNT	FRM RUNS	BLK RUNS	THRW RUNS	TOT RUNS
2013	KCA	17991	-1.7	0.1	0.6	-1.0
2014	KCA	20329	-13.5	0.5	1.7	-11.3
2015	KCA	19339	-8.2	0.4	1.4	-6.4
2016	*KCA*	*20063*	*-10.3*	*0.5*	*1.5*	*-8.4*
2017	*KCA*	*18660*	*-10.1*	*0.4*	*1.2*	*-8.5*

Take a look at the numbers above, and you'll see remarkable consistency across the board between Perez's 2014 and 2015 campaigns. That consistency can be extended to include another All-Star Game appearance, another Gold Glove and another season as one of the most hacktastic players in the game. Last year's World Series MVP was among the league leaders in swinging at pitches out of the zone, and posted the lowest walk rate in a league that also features Alcides Escobar. Of course, he also launched 21 bombs while adding to his reputation for toughness, durability and leadership behind the dish. Perez is poised to enter his prime as the premier backstop in the Junior Circuit; if he can just learn to lay off those sliders low and away, the sky will be the limit.

Alex Rios RF

Born: 2/18/81 Age: 35 Bats: R Throws: R Height: 6'5" Weight: 210

YEAR	TEAM	LVL	AGE	PA	R	2B	3B	HR	RBI	BB	K	SB	CS	AVG/OBP/SLG	TAv	BABIP	BRR	FRAA	WARP
2013	TEX	MLB	32	197	26	11	2	6	26	9	30	16	1	.280/.315/.457	.276	.305	2.1	RF(47): 1.3, CF(1): -0.1	1.1
2013	CHA	MLB	32	465	57	22	2	12	55	32	78	26	6	.277/.328/.421	.267	.314	3.0	RF(108): 5.8	2.2
2014	TEX	MLB	33	521	54	30	8	4	54	23	93	17	9	.280/.311/.398	.254	.335	-2.5	RF(114): 1.2	0.4
2015	KCA	MLB	34	411	40	22	2	4	32	15	67	9	0	.255/.287/.353	.231	.294	0.9	RF(105): 1.0	-0.3
2016	*KCA*	*MLB*	*35*	*411*	*43*	*22*	*4*	*7*	*41*	*18*	*66*	*14*	*4*	*.260/.294/.388*	*.243*	*.295*	*0.4*	*RF 4*	*0.7*
2017	*KCA*	*MLB*	*36*	*311*	*31*	*16*	*3*	*5*	*30*	*14*	*51*	*10*	*3*	*.253/.288/.373*	*.236*	*.288*	*0.4*	*RF 3*	*0.2*

Breakout: 0% Improve: 25% Collapse: 12% Attrition: 25% MLB: 85% *Comparables: Carl Furillo, Reed Johnson, Brian Jordan*

The Royals ponied up $11 million for Rios to add some power to their outfield mix, since he's rangy and athletic and actually anchors himself when he swings, instead of doing that Nori Aoki thing where he's already running to first while slapping the ball to the left side of the infield. Yet after homering on Opening Day, Rios went 43 games before going yard again and posted a .224/.255/.256 line during that span while missing seven weeks with a hand injury. Overall, Rios managed a lower slugging percentage than Aoki had the previous year with none of the commensurate on-base percentage. Rios used to post solid numbers in alternating years, but now the delay seems to be following a Fibonacci sequence that describes the plummeting spiral of his career.

Bubba Starling CF

Born: 8/3/92 Age: 23 Bats: R Throws: R Height: 6'4" Weight: 210

YEAR	TEAM	LVL	AGE	PA	R	2B	3B	HR	RBI	BB	K	SB	CS	AVG/OBP/SLG	TAv	BABIP	BRR	FRAA	WARP
2013	LEX	A	20	498	51	21	4	13	63	53	128	22	3	.241/.329/.398	.287	.309	1.0	CF(117): 0.2	3.1
2014	WIL	A+	21	549	67	23	4	9	54	49	150	17	2	.218/.304/.338	.260	.293	4.9	CF(130): 1.8	2.4
2015	NWA	AA	22	367	51	19	4	10	32	30	91	4	5	.254/.318/.426	.272	.319	0.9	CF(75): -3.4, RF(9): -0.4	1.2
2015	WIL	A+	22	51	6	4	0	2	12	7	17	2	1	.386/.471/.614	.388	.600	-0.1	CF(11): -0.1	0.8
2016	*KCA*	*MLB*	*23*	*250*	*24*	*10*	*2*	*6*	*26*	*17*	*75*	*3*	*1*	*.217/.276/.352*	*.227*	*.290*	*0.0*	*CF -1, RF 1*	*-0.1*
2017	*KCA*	*MLB*	*24*	*370*	*40*	*15*	*3*	*9*	*39*	*25*	*111*	*4*	*2*	*.224/.283/.368*	*.235*	*.299*	*0.1*	*CF -2, RF 1*	*0.0*

Breakout: 1% Improve: 6% Collapse: 3% Attrition: 6% MLB: 20% *Comparables: Franklin Gutierrez, Jordan Danks, Bryan Petersen*

Starling made enough progress last summer for the Royals to stash him away on their 40-man roster, but he still has a long way to go. The former top pick oozes athleticism, plays a plus center field and is making more consistent contact but has yet to turn his power potential into production between the lines. The Royals will give him another chance to conquer Double-A, and if the light comes on he could grow into a fourth outfielder—not that Kansas City has any shortage of those.

PITCHERS

Miguel Almonte RHP

Born: 4/4/93 Age: 23 Bats: R Throws: R Height: 6'2" Weight: 180

YEAR	TEAM	LVL	AGE	W	L	SV	G	GS	IP	H	HR	BB/9	K/9	GB%	BABIP	WHIP	ERA	FIP	DRA	WARP	CFIP	MPH
2013	LEX	A	20	6	9	0	25	25	130^{2}	115	6	2.5	9.1	47%	.297	1.16	3.10	3.04	3.99	1.5	85	
2014	WIL	A+	21	6	8	0	23	22	110^{1}	107	9	2.6	8.2	48%	.316	1.26	4.49	3.92	4.38	1.0	94	
2015	OMA	AAA	22	2	2	0	11	6	36^{2}	33	3	3.7	10.1	43%	.323	1.31	5.40	3.90	3.83	0.7	87	
2015	NWA	AA	22	4	4	0	17	17	67	65	4	3.6	7.4	43%	.307	1.37	4.03	4.00	4.77	0.3	103	
2015	KCA	MLB	22	0	2	0	9	0	8^{2}	7	4	7.3	10.4	52%	.158	1.62	6.23	9.57	6.66	-0.2	106	98.9
2016	*KCA*	*MLB*	*23*	*3*	*3*	*0*	*34*	*8*	*67^{1}*	*68*	*8*	*3.3*	*7.0*	*42%*	*.296*	*1.39*	*4.44*	*4.53*	*4.87*	*0.1*	*114*	
2017	*KCA*	*MLB*	*24*	*4*	*6*	*0*	*16*	*16*	*92*	*97*	*14*	*3.8*	*7.3*	*42%*	*.301*	*1.48*	*4.79*	*4.91*	*5.25*	*-0.1*	*125*	

Breakout: 9% Improve: 10% Collapse: 6% Attrition: 10% MLB: 20% *Comparables: Michael Blazek, Cody Anderson, Jay Jackson*

Almonte spent his first big-league stint working out of the Kansas City 'pen, and scouts continue to wonder if that's the place he'll eventually call home. His mid-90s fastball and plus changeup can dominate, but fleeting command and a continually sketchy breaking ball cause him to be far more hittable than his stuff should otherwise allow. His script for success involves getting ahead of hitters with well-placed heat and punching them out with his change, but far too often advanced hitters make Almonte pay when he leaves his fastball over the plate early in the count. He's still young, and if he starts hitting his spots he has mid-rotation potential.

Wade Davis RHP

Born: 9/7/85 Age: 30 Bats: R Throws: R Height: 6'5" Weight: 220

YEAR	TEAM	LVL	AGE	W	L	SV	G	GS	IP	H	HR	BB/9	K/9	GB%	BABIP	WHIP	ERA	FIP	DRA	WARP	CFIP	MPH
2013	KCA	MLB	27	8	11	0	31	24	135^{1}	169	15	3.9	7.6	42%	.361	1.68	5.32	4.21	5.71	-1.4	105	95.6
2014	KCA	MLB	28	9	2	3	71	0	72	38	0	2.9	13.6	49%	.264	0.85	1.00	1.22	1.34	2.8	50	98.5
2015	KCA	MLB	29	8	1	17	69	0	67^{1}	33	3	2.7	10.4	39%	.200	0.79	0.94	2.26	1.64	2.5	67	98.4
2016	*KCA*	*MLB*	*30*	*4*	*2*	*43*	*67*	*0*	*70^{2}*	*59*	*6*	*3.0*	*10.0*	*43%*	*.291*	*1.16*	*3.15*	*3.25*	*3.57*	*1.2*	*76*	
2017	*KCA*	*MLB*	*31*	*4*	*3*	*3*	*56*	*5*	*86^{1}*	*72*	*8*	*3.0*	*10.3*	*43%*	*.293*	*1.17*	*3.11*	*3.22*	*3.52*	*1.3*	*74*	

Breakout: 30% Improve: 63% Collapse: 16% Attrition: 11% MLB: 97% *Comparables: Kelvim Escobar, Joe Nathan, Norm Charlton*

Davis allowed the lowest TAv of any pitcher in baseball last year (.172, essentially turning every hitter into Michael Wacha at the plate), so let's spend a moment basking in the glory of his arsenal. His fastball sits in the mid-90s and can edge near triple digits when needed, commanded high in the zone where batters can't get on top of it. His cutter arrives at a snarling 93 mph with heavy sink and a chip on its shoulder. His knuckle-curve bends low to kiss the earth, generating awkward swings and groundball outs with equal frequency. Liquid bliss, taking shape as a dominant closer under club control for two more value-priced seasons.

Danny Duffy LHP

Born: 12/21/88 Age: 27 Bats: L Throws: L Height: 6'3" Weight: 205

YEAR	TEAM	LVL	AGE	W	L	SV	G	GS	IP	H	HR	BB/9	K/9	GB%	BABIP	WHIP	ERA	FIP	DRA	WARP	CFIP	MPH
2013	NWA	AA	24	0	2	0	4	4	16	16	3	2.8	15.8	38%	.448	1.31	3.94	3.49	3.18	0.3	66	
2013	KCA	MLB	24	2	0	0	5	5	24^{1}	19	0	5.2	8.1	31%	.284	1.36	1.85	3.12	2.24	0.8	102	96.9
2013	OMA	AAA	24	3	0	0	12	10	53	50	4	4.2	10.0	38%	.329	1.42	4.08	3.85	4.83	0.5	94	
2014	KCA	MLB	25	9	12	0	31	25	149^{1}	113	12	3.2	6.8	38%	.239	1.11	2.53	3.86	3.28	2.7	105	96.7
2015	KCA	MLB	26	7	8	1	30	24	136^{2}	137	15	3.5	6.7	41%	.298	1.39	4.08	4.40	4.82	0.3	108	97.0
2016	*KCA*	*MLB*	*27*	*9*	*11*	*0*	*29*	*29*	*165^{1}*	*159*	*18*	*3.2*	*7.2*	*39%*	*.287*	*1.32*	*4.17*	*4.28*	*4.61*	*1.0*	*107*	
2017	*KCA*	*MLB*	*28*	*8*	*9*	*0*	*26*	*26*	*155^{2}*	*154*	*18*	*3.2*	*7.7*	*39%*	*.298*	*1.35*	*4.05*	*4.17*	*4.48*	*1.0*	*104*	

Breakout: 18% Improve: 45% Collapse: 25% Attrition: 14% MLB: 91% *Comparables: Chad Gaudin, Daniel Cabrera, Dustin McGowan*

You should have known better than to tell your brother-in-law you weren't surprised by Duffy's struggles last year because he had outpitched his peripherals in 2014. Of course he was going to shoot you that propeller-head look and spray you with the hose, something you could have avoided by instead saying he gives up a lot of flyballs that were due to start turning into more home runs, or that he walks too many and strikes out too few to be an ace. So at this year's family picnic remember to tell him that Duffy will be just fine at the end of the rotation, and he'll be more valuable there than in long relief. Just don't say "third pitch" or "leverage" or "BABIP" or "home runs per flyball," or you'll get the hose again.

Dillon Gee RHP

Born: 4/28/86 Age: 30 Bats: R Throws: R Height: 6'1" Weight: 205

YEAR	TEAM	LVL	AGE	W	L	SV	G	GS	IP	H	HR	BB/9	K/9	GB%	BABIP	WHIP	ERA	FIP	DRA	WARP	CFIP	MPH
2013	NYN	MLB	27	12	11	0	32	32	199	208	24	2.1	6.4	45%	.296	1.28	3.62	3.98	4.24	1.6	108	92.0
2014	NYN	MLB	28	7	8	0	22	22	137^{1}	128	18	2.8	6.2	45%	.268	1.25	4.00	4.49	4.39	0.7	118	91.7
2015	SLU	A+	29	0	0	0	2	2	10^{1}	9	0	0.0	10.5	59%	.333	0.87	0.87	0.84	2.03	0.3	75	
2015	NYN	MLB	29	0	3	0	8	7	39^{2}	55	5	2.5	5.7	53%	.355	1.66	5.90	4.45	7.18	-1.0	117	92.2
2015	LVG	AAA	29	8	3	0	14	14	88^{1}	105	7	1.8	6.4	45%	.338	1.39	4.58	3.88	4.41	1.1	94	
2016	*KCA*	*MLB*	*30*	*3*	*2*	*0*	*48*	*2*	*59*	*63*	*7*	*2.5*	*5.7*	*47%*	*.293*	*1.36*	*4.43*	*4.50*	*4.88*	*0.0*	*116*	
2017	*KCA*	*MLB*	*31*	*5*	*6*	*0*	*15*	*15*	*87^{2}*	*98*	*12*	*2.7*	*6.0*	*47%*	*.302*	*1.42*	*4.49*	*4.63*	*4.95*	*0.2*	*117*	

Breakout: 15% Improve: 44% Collapse: 16% Attrition: 8% MLB: 83% *Comparables: Jeff Karstens, Sergio Mitre, Vicente Padilla*

This is a long slog to ignominy. First sent to the bullpen by the Mets during spring training, Gee was granted a reprieve when Zack Wheeler succumbed to a torn UCL. He made five starts before missing a month with a groin injury; with so many young pitchers on the come-up, he came back on a short leash, got bombed and took his walking papers. That would be brutal enough, but no team would rescue this perfectly serviceable starter. Gee cleared waivers and accepted his Triple-A assignment, pitching out the season thousands of miles away while the kids took the city by storm. It's sad because this was a fait accompli: There was simply too much young talent coming too quickly for Gee to keep up. Not least because he never relied on velocity, Gee has some good years in him yet. Here's hoping they aren't spent in Omaha.

Foster Griffin LHP

Born: 7/27/95 Age: 20 Bats: R Throws: L Height: 6'3" Weight: 200

YEAR	TEAM	LVL	AGE	W	L	SV	G	GS	IP	H	HR	BB/9	K/9	GB%	BABIP	WHIP	ERA	FIP	DRA	WARP	CFIP	MPH
2015	LEX	A	19	4	6	0	22	22	102^{2}	123	8	3.1	6.2	55%	.337	1.54	5.44	4.22	5.21	0.0	107	
2016	*KCA*	*MLB*	*20*	*3*	*6*	*0*	*17*	*17*	70^{1}	*87*	*10*	*3.7*	*4.0*	*48%*	*.306*	*1.65*	*5.49*	*5.57*	*5.92*	*-0.7*	*142*	
2017	*KCA*	*MLB*	*21*	*6*	*9*	*0*	*27*	*27*	*160*	*203*	*26*	*3.7*	*4.3*	*48%*	*.312*	*1.68*	*5.48*	*5.61*	*5.91*	*-1.0*	*142*	

Breakout: 0% Improve: 0% Collapse: 0% Attrition: 0% MLB: 0% *Comparables: Kyle Waldrop, Dan Cortes, Jon Niese*

Griffin got knocked around in his full-season debut, but he flashed the potential that made him a first-round pick in 2014 and made incremental progress throughout the year. He lacked command of his low-90s fastball and his secondary offerings were raw but he did generate plenty of groundballs. Watching a prep draftee struggle in his first full season is about as surprising and enlightening as watching Kevin Millar eat a McRib sandwich, so let's agree to talk about Griffin again next year after the Royals' development staff has a chance to spend a little more quality time with him.

Jeremy Guthrie RHP

Born: 4/8/79 Age: 37 Bats: R Throws: R Height: 6'1" Weight: 205

YEAR	TEAM	LVL	AGE	W	L	SV	G	GS	IP	H	HR	BB/9	K/9	GB%	BABIP	WHIP	ERA	FIP	DRA	WARP	CFIP	MPH
2013	KCA	MLB	34	15	12	0	33	33	211^{2}	236	30	2.5	4.7	45%	.296	1.39	4.04	4.82	4.49	1.1	123	95.7
2014	KCA	MLB	35	13	11	0	32	32	202^{2}	215	23	2.2	5.5	45%	.294	1.30	4.13	4.34	4.38	1.0	117	94.8
2015	KCA	MLB	36	8	8	0	30	24	148^{1}	186	29	2.7	5.1	37%	.315	1.55	5.95	5.59	6.28	-2.3	126	94.7
2016	*KCA*	*MLB*	*37*	*7*	*10*	*0*	*23*	*23*	139^{1}	*152*	*19*	*2.5*	*5.3*	*41%*	*.291*	*1.37*	*4.75*	*4.83*	*5.19*	*-0.1*	*124*	
2017	*KCA*	*MLB*	*38*	*6*	*7*	*0*	*17*	*17*	100^{1}	*114*	*15*	*2.6*	*5.6*	*41%*	*.299*	*1.43*	*4.79*	*4.91*	*5.23*	*-0.1*	*125*	

Breakout: 12% Improve: 41% Collapse: 15% Attrition: 14% MLB: 76% *Comparables: Woody Williams, John Tudor, Randy Wolf*

Guthrie's career has been a high-wire act for several years now and last season he finally lost his balance, as the veteran innings-eater pitched his way out of the Royals' rotation while putting up a Lovecraftian stat-line. The league posted a .312 TAv when facing him, fueled by his league-high line-drive rate, a groundball blackout and a home run spike. Guthrie has managed to pull his career back from the brink before, but as he enters his late 30s it's fair to question whether a team will ever again stomach watching him pitch every fifth day.

Kelvin Herrera RHP

Born: 12/31/89 Age: 26 Bats: R Throws: R Height: 5'10" Weight: 200

YEAR	TEAM	LVL	AGE	W	L	SV	G	GS	IP	H	HR	BB/9	K/9	GB%	BABIP	WHIP	ERA	FIP	DRA	WARP	CFIP	MPH
2013	KCA	MLB	23	5	7	2	59	0	58^{1}	48	9	3.2	11.4	49%	.281	1.18	3.86	3.73	4.32	0.2	80	101.0
2013	OMA	AAA	23	0	1	2	10	3	16	6	1	3.4	12.4	47%	.161	0.75	1.12	3.13	4.34	0.2	79	
2014	KCA	MLB	24	4	3	0	70	0	70	54	0	3.3	7.6	52%	.274	1.14	1.41	2.72	2.38	1.8	100	101.0
2015	KCA	MLB	25	4	3	0	72	0	69^{2}	52	5	3.4	8.3	46%	.249	1.12	2.71	3.41	2.93	1.5	93	101.0
2016	*KCA*	*MLB*	*26*	*3*	*1*	*0*	*57*	*0*	*60*	*52*	*6*	*3.3*	*8.4*	*48%*	*.275*	*1.23*	*3.79*	*3.87*	*4.23*	*0.4*	*94*	
2017	*KCA*	*MLB*	*27*	*3*	*1*	*1*	*57*	*0*	58^{2}	*55*	*7*	*3.6*	*8.6*	*48%*	*.289*	*1.34*	*4.06*	*4.18*	*4.53*	*0.1*	*102*	

Breakout: 34% Improve: 56% Collapse: 21% Attrition: 8% MLB: 94% *Comparables: Drew Storen, Gregg Olson, Neftali Feliz*

Already a dominant force in the late innings, Herrera stepped up his game last September when Greg Holland's injury forced everyone in the Kansas City 'pen to move one peg up the pecking order. His triple-digit heater and devastating changeup were already racking up plenty of strikeouts and even more weak groundballs, but the slider he unveiled late in the season rendered him virtually unhittable. Herrera struck out over 40 percent of the batters he faced in the playoffs and posted a 61 percent groundball rate, holding batters to a .200/.241/.240 line. With another offseason to refine his arsenal and another potential weapon to make hitters' knees knock, there's every reason to believe Herrera could be even more of a beast this year.

Luke Hochevar RHP

Born: 9/15/83 Age: 32 Bats: R Throws: R Height: 6'5" Weight: 225

YEAR	TEAM	LVL	AGE	W	L	SV	G	GS	IP	H	HR	BB/9	K/9	GB%	BABIP	WHIP	ERA	FIP	DRA	WARP	CFIP	MPH
2013	KCA	MLB	29	5	2	2	58	0	70^{1}	41	8	2.2	10.5	36%	.214	0.82	1.92	2.99	2.48	1.8	67	97.9
2015	KCA	MLB	31	1	1	1	49	0	50^{2}	49	7	2.8	8.7	38%	.298	1.28	3.73	3.97	4.70	0.0	95	96.6
2015	OMA	AAA	31	0	1	0	9	4	10^{1}	16	2	7.0	8.7	47%	.438	2.32	7.84	6.50	6.05	-0.1	107	
2016	*KCA*	*MLB*	*32*	*3*	*1*	*0*	*51*	*0*	54^{1}	*48*	*6*	*2.9*	*8.5*	*38%*	*.285*	*1.21*	*3.72*	*3.87*	*4.13*	*0.5*	*93*	
2017	*KCA*	*MLB*	*33*	*4*	*3*	*1*	*40*	*9*	*87*	*79*	*11*	*2.8*	*8.7*	*38%*	*.287*	*1.22*	*3.78*	*3.88*	*4.20*	*0.7*	*95*	

Breakout: 19% Improve: 55% Collapse: 19% Attrition: 6% MLB: 91% *Comparables: Steve Carlton, Bert Blyleven, Mark Langston*

"There can be no life without change, and to be afraid of what is different or unfamiliar is to be afraid of life." From top overall draft pick to rotation washout to bullpen phoenix to Tommy John survivor, Hochevar seems to have taken Teddy Roosevelt's words to heart as he reinvents himself for the next phase of his checkered career. The jump in his fastball and the bite on his cutter survived the knife, and when Hochevar's command returned in late June he proved to be a quality bullpen arm. To cherry-pick a random turning point, batters torched him at a .349/.370/.605 rate through the middle of June, but posted a .222/.292/.379 line the rest of the way. Hochevar's three-pitch mix looks pedestrian next to the jaw-dropping arsenals of his fellow bullpen mates, but it appears more than capable of holding its own in the seventh inning.

Greg Holland RHP

Born: 11/20/85 Age: 30 Bats: R Throws: R Height: 5'10" Weight: 205

YEAR	TEAM	LVL	AGE	W	L	SV	G	GS	IP	H	HR	BB/9	K/9	GB%	BABIP	WHIP	ERA	FIP	DRA	WARP	CFIP	MPH
2013	KCA	MLB	27	2	1	47	68	0	67	40	3	2.4	13.8	40%	.282	0.87	1.21	1.39	2.37	1.8	39	99.4
2014	KCA	MLB	28	1	3	46	65	0	62^1	37	3	2.9	13.0	49%	.268	0.91	1.44	1.86	1.76	2.1	58	98.4
2015	KCA	MLB	29	3	2	32	48	0	44^2	39	2	5.2	9.9	51%	.319	1.46	3.83	3.24	4.31	0.2	93	96.7
2016	*KCA*	*MLB*	*30*	*2*	*1*	*29*	*40*	*0*	*42^1*	*34*	*4*	*3.5*	*11.0*	*49%*	*.288*	*1.19*	*3.30*	*3.26*	*3.72*	*0.5*	*78*	
2017	*KCA*	*MLB*	*31*	*3*	*1*	*46*	*63*	*0*	*61^1*	*50*	*8*	*3.5*	*11.1*	*49%*	*.292*	*1.21*	*3.42*	*3.52*	*3.86*	*0.6*	*82*	

Breakout: 27% Improve: 45% Collapse: 32% Attrition: 8% MLB: 94% *Comparables: Michael Gonzalez, David Robertson, Francisco Rodriguez*

Holland just never seemed right all season, as the Kansas City closer soldiered through bouts of sketchy control and shockingly reduced velocity to post 32 saves before it was discovered that he had been pitching with a partially torn ligament in his elbow; he'll miss the entire 2016 campaign after undergoing Tommy John surgery last October. While baseball is replete with cases of TJ survivors returning stronger than ever, there are no guarantees, especially for a pitcher as slider-reliant as Holland. Whether his otherworldly slide piece helped to speed the fray in his elbow, and whether he'll still be able to throw it with such wild abandon upon his return are open questions. What's certain is that the timing couldn't be worse for Holland, as he'll spend what would have been his walk year building up his strength in anonymous training facilities instead of sending muttering batsmen back to the bench in the heat of another pennant race.

Kris Medlen RHP

Born: 10/7/85 Age: 30 Bats: B Throws: R Height: 5'10" Weight: 190

YEAR	TEAM	LVL	AGE	W	L	SV	G	GS	IP	H	HR	BB/9	K/9	GB%	BABIP	WHIP	ERA	FIP	DRA	WARP	CFIP	MPH
2013	ATL	MLB	27	15	12	0	32	31	197	194	18	2.1	7.2	47%	.299	1.22	3.11	3.45	4.35	1.3	104	91.9
2015	KCA	MLB	29	6	2	0	15	8	58^1	56	6	2.8	6.2	51%	.282	1.27	4.01	4.10	4.53	0.3	109	93.5
2015	OMA	AAA	29	1	0	0	3	3	15^1	16	6	0.6	5.3	51%	.222	1.11	4.11	8.10	5.64	0.0	110	
2015	NWA	AA	29	0	1	0	3	3	15	13	2	2.4	6.6	67%	.250	1.13	3.00	4.76	4.06	0.2	95	
2016	*KCA*	*MLB*	*30*	*8*	*10*	*0*	*28*	*28*	*148^1*	*146*	*17*	*2.5*	*6.3*	*50%*	*.284*	*1.27*	*4.16*	*4.30*	*4.60*	*0.9*	*108*	
2017	*KCA*	*MLB*	*31*	*8*	*9*	*0*	*39*	*22*	*157*	*162*	*23*	*2.7*	*6.9*	*50%*	*.294*	*1.34*	*4.37*	*4.50*	*4.83*	*0.4*	*115*	

Breakout: 9% Improve: 43% Collapse: 21% Attrition: 8% MLB: 93% *Comparables: Billy O'Dell, Ben McDonald, Jack McDowell*

Medlen falls into the "productive or hurt" camp of big-league hurlers, ping-ponging between effective campaigns in the rotation or the 'pen and trips to the surgical ward. The Royals signed him during his second Tommy John rehab and the diminutive righty thrived in relief, struggled as a starter and showed enough to make him a candidate for the 2016 rotation. Medlen has never been overpowering but he knows how to pitch, painting the black with his low-90s heater and keeping hitters off-balance with a slow-motion curve and a plus changeup. He's only managed to spend one full season in the rotation, so his durability will always be in question, but he's a solid upside play if his employers can manage his innings wisely.

Franklin Morales LHP

Born: 1/24/86 Age: 30 Bats: L Throws: L Height: 6'1" Weight: 210

YEAR	TEAM	LVL	AGE	W	L	SV	G	GS	IP	H	HR	BB/9	K/9	GB%	BABIP	WHIP	ERA	FIP	DRA	WARP	CFIP	MPH
2013	BOS	MLB	27	2	2	0	20	1	25^1	24	2	5.3	7.5	40%	.310	1.54	4.62	4.58	5.02	-0.1	109	96.1
2013	PAW	AAA	27	0	1	0	5	2	11^1	5	3	2.4	9.5	35%	.087	0.71	4.76	5.32	4.09	0.1	92	
2014	COL	MLB	28	6	9	0	38	22	142^1	166	24	4.1	6.3	45%	.315	1.62	5.37	5.39	5.10	-0.6	117	93.9
2015	KCA	MLB	29	4	2	0	67	0	62^1	58	4	2.0	5.9	51%	.277	1.16	3.18	3.49	3.84	0.6	106	95.0
2016	*KCA*	*MLB*	*30*	*3*	*1*	*0*	*57*	*0*	*60*	*60*	*8*	*3.3*	*6.5*	*47%*	*.284*	*1.37*	*4.56*	*4.79*	*5.00*	*-0.1*	*118*	
2017	*KCA*	*MLB*	*31*	*6*	*5*	*0*	*63*	*12*	*125*	*127*	*18*	*3.4*	*6.7*	*47%*	*.286*	*1.40*	*4.70*	*4.82*	*5.15*	*-0.3*	*122*	

Breakout: 20% Improve: 53% Collapse: 22% Attrition: 7% MLB: 97% *Comparables: Todd Wellemeyer, Chad Gaudin, Steve Bedrosian*

Once again pitching at a more reasonable distance from the Earth's core, Morales used his second parole from Rockies prison to reinvent himself in Kansas City. Between the thick air and the Gold Glove fielders behind him, the veteran lefty felt comfortable cutting down on both his walks and strikeouts, inducing more groundballs and reaping the reward of a low BABIP to become a reliable cog in middle relief. Royals fans may long argue whether his indecisive dance after fielding a comebacker in Game Three of the World Series was more reminiscent of a panicky squirrel in traffic or Bluto scouting for witnesses in front of the Faber College administration building.

Joakim Soria RHP

Born: 5/18/84 Age: 32 Bats: R Throws: R Height: 6'3" Weight: 200

YEAR	TEAM	LVL	AGE	W	L	SV	G	GS	IP	H	HR	BB/9	K/9	GB%	BABIP	WHIP	ERA	FIP	DRA	WARP	CFIP	MPH
2013	TEX	MLB	29	1	0	0	26	0	23^2	18	2	5.3	10.6	53%	.286	1.35	3.80	3.71	3.18	0.4	92	93.6
2014	DET	MLB	30	1	1	1	13	0	11	13	2	1.6	4.9	52%	.289	1.36	4.91	5.25	4.81	0.0	102	92.8
2014	TEX	MLB	30	1	3	17	35	0	33^1	25	0	1.1	11.3	42%	.291	0.87	2.70	1.09	1.85	1.1	60	92.6
2015	PIT	MLB	31	0	0	1	29	0	26^2	23	0	2.7	9.4	41%	.329	1.16	2.03	1.96	2.71	0.6	86	94.7
2015	DET	MLB	31	3	1	23	43	0	41	32	8	2.4	7.9	46%	.222	1.05	2.85	4.84	3.46	0.6	95	95.2
2016	*KCA*	*MLB*	*32*	*3*	*1*	*2*	*62*	*0*	*65^1*	*59*	*7*	*2.7*	*8.4*	*44%*	*.286*	*1.21*	*3.72*	*3.78*	*4.18*	*0.4*	*93*	
2017	*KCA*	*MLB*	*33*	*3*	*1*	*16*	*63*	*0*	*58^1*	*56*	*8*	*2.8*	*8.1*	*44%*	*.289*	*1.27*	*4.03*	*4.16*	*4.53*	*0.1*	*103*	

Breakout: 23% Improve: 49% Collapse: 25% Attrition: 4% MLB: 94% *Comparables: Francisco Rodriguez, Paul Shuey, Jason Frasor*

You always hear about how it's difficult to build a bullpen, and Soria's past two seasons are a good example of why that is. He started the 2014 season in Texas, where he lasted 33 innings without allowing a home run. The Rangers were out of the race at the deadline, so they sent Soria to Detroit. He spent the next year there, accumulating 52 innings and allowing 10 home runs. The Tigers were out of the race at the subsequent deadline, so they sent Soria to Pittsburgh. From then until the season ended, he didn't allow a home run. If you're Brad Ausmus, fighting for another year in the dugout, how do you explain this? Soria didn't change who he was as a pitcher; maybe he tweaked this or that, but for his cold and hot spells to line up perfectly with his team changes? It doesn't make sense. None of this makes sense.

Jason Vargas LHP

Born: 2/2/83 Age: 33 Bats: L Throws: L Height: 6'0" Weight: 215

YEAR	TEAM	LVL	AGE	W	L	SV	G	GS	IP	H	HR	BB/9	K/9	GB%	BABIP	WHIP	ERA	FIP	DRA	WARP	CFIP	MPH
2013	ANA	MLB	30	9	8	0	24	24	150	162	17	2.8	6.5	42%	.310	1.39	4.02	4.12	4.46	0.8	106	90.1
2014	KCA	MLB	31	11	10	0	30	30	187	197	19	2.0	6.2	41%	.299	1.27	3.71	3.87	4.11	1.6	103	89.7
2015	KCA	MLB	32	5	2	0	9	9	43	46	5	2.5	5.7	41%	.297	1.35	3.98	4.27	5.36	-0.2	109	90.3
2016	*KCA*	*MLB*	*33*	*4*	*4*	*0*	*10*	*10*	*64^1*	*64*	*7*	*2.3*	*6.2*	*41%*	*.285*	*1.26*	*4.08*	*4.14*	*4.52*	*0.5*	*105*	
2017	*KCA*	*MLB*	*34*	*11*	*11*	*0*	*30*	*30*	*192^1*	*200*	*25*	*2.4*	*6.3*	*41%*	*.291*	*1.31*	*4.23*	*4.36*	*4.69*	*1.0*	*110*	

Breakout: 21% Improve: 46% Collapse: 22% Attrition: 14% MLB: 90% *Comparables: Jarrod Washburn, Ron Reed, John Burkett*

You're probably as tired of reading about Tommy John surgery as we are writing about it, so let's just say Vargas came down with a complaint he called Night Hoss, underwent cupping and blistering last August to help balance his humors and should return to the mound in 2017. At that point Vargas will have one year left to fill out the back of the Royals' rotation and use his low-velocity lefty stylings to make good on his four-year, $32 million deal.

Yordano Ventura RHP

Born: 6/3/91 Age: 25 Bats: R Throws: R Height: 6'0" Weight: 180

YEAR	TEAM	LVL	AGE	W	L	SV	G	GS	IP	H	HR	BB/9	K/9	GB%	BABIP	WHIP	ERA	FIP	DRA	WARP	CFIP	MPH
2013	KCA	MLB	22	0	1	0	3	3	15^1	13	3	3.5	6.5	51%	.227	1.24	3.52	5.36	4.69	0.0	109	100.3
2013	OMA	AAA	22	5	4	0	15	14	77	80	4	3.9	9.5	42%	.357	1.47	3.74	3.54	4.54	0.9	85	
2013	NWA	AA	22	3	2	0	11	11	57^2	39	3	3.1	11.5	43%	.279	1.02	2.34	2.41	3.49	1.0	75	
2014	KCA	MLB	23	14	10	0	31	30	183	168	14	3.4	7.8	48%	.288	1.30	3.20	3.63	4.03	1.7	103	100.3
2015	KCA	MLB	24	13	8	0	28	28	163^1	154	14	3.2	8.6	53%	.307	1.30	4.08	3.54	4.07	1.9	91	99.8
2016	*KCA*	*MLB*	*25*	*11*	*11*	*0*	*31*	*31*	*186*	*174*	*19*	*3.2*	*8.3*	*51%*	*.295*	*1.29*	*3.76*	*3.92*	*4.20*	*2.0*	*95*	
2017	*KCA*	*MLB*	*26*	*9*	*9*	*0*	*28*	*28*	*166^2*	*158*	*19*	*3.1*	*8.9*	*51%*	*.301*	*1.29*	*3.68*	*3.80*	*4.11*	*1.8*	*93*	

Breakout: 30% Improve: 62% Collapse: 21% Attrition: 16% MLB: 94% *Comparables: Tommy Hanson, Josh Johnson, Daniel Hudson*

The surface narrative for Ventura's 2015 season seems like a step back from his rookie campaign, featuring early-season run prevention woes, a month-long head-clearing sojourn in Triple-A, and a solid (if unspectacular) return. Dig a little deeper, though, and it's easy to see that Ventura actually took a few major steps forward, cutting into his walk rate, amping up his strikeouts, getting more groundouts and building a more sustainable arsenal. Ventura can still lob lightning bolts, but he did lose a full tick off his otherworldly fastball. He made up for this through liberal application of an improved curveball that can generate nearly pornographic whiff and groundball rates, and sets him up with another weapon to unleash against both righties and lefties. Ventura has yet to fully translate his overpowering stuff into dominant production, but he's poised to get there. Patience, my friends.

Edinson Volquez RHP

Born: 7/3/83 Age: 32 Bats: R Throws: R Height: 6'0" Weight: 220

YEAR	TEAM	LVL	AGE	W	L	SV	G	GS	IP	H	HR	BB/9	K/9	GB%	BABIP	WHIP	ERA	FIP	DRA	WARP	CFIP	MPH
2013	LAN	MLB	29	0	2	0	6	5	28	25	5	2.6	8.4	48%	.253	1.18	4.18	4.34	2.78	0.7	111	95.4
2013	SDN	MLB	29	9	10	0	27	27	142^1	168	14	4.4	7.3	49%	.337	1.67	6.01	4.19	5.46	-1.0	113	95.1
2014	PIT	MLB	30	13	7	0	32	31	192^2	166	17	3.3	6.5	53%	.263	1.23	3.04	4.12	4.07	1.7	112	96.0
2015	KCA	MLB	31	13	9	0	34	33	200^1	190	16	3.2	7.0	47%	.290	1.31	3.55	3.79	4.15	2.1	104	96.3
2016	*KCA*	*MLB*	*32*	*10*	*12*	*0*	*30*	*30*	*180*	*178*	*20*	*3.4*	*6.9*	*49%*	*.290*	*1.37*	*4.29*	*4.42*	*4.74*	*0.8*	*110*	
2017	*KCA*	*MLB*	*33*	*8*	*9*	*0*	*25*	*25*	*145*	*144*	*18*	*3.4*	*7.1*	*49%*	*.290*	*1.37*	*4.26*	*4.38*	*4.71*	*0.7*	*109*	

Breakout: 13% Improve: 51% Collapse: 19% Attrition: 13% MLB: 88% *Comparables: Chuck Finley, Vicente Padilla, Doug Davis*

The fabric of baseball is woven through with personal stories of triumph and loss, and few will forget the sight of Volquez gutting through six innings of Kansas City's Series-clinching Game Five just days after the death of his father. That moment was the capstone of what had been his best season since the Bush administration, as the veteran starter proved his 2014 Pittsburgh revival wasn't a fluke. Long known for his sky-high walk and strikeout rates, Volquez is now committed to avoiding free passes, inducing weak contact and letting his defense do the work. It's not sexy, but it works well enough to make Volquez a solid mid-rotation option at a bargain price.

Chris Young RHP

Born: 5/25/79 Age: 37 Bats: R Throws: R Height: 6'10" Weight: 255

YEAR	TEAM	LVL	AGE	W	L	SV	G	GS	IP	H	HR	BB/9	K/9	GB%	BABIP	WHIP	ERA	FIP	DRA	WARP	CFIP	MPH
2013	SYR	AAA	34	1	2	0	7	7	32	50	9	3.9	4.5	30%	.342	2.00	7.88	7.17	5.64	-0.2	132	
2014	SEA	MLB	35	12	9	0	30	29	165	143	26	3.3	5.9	25%	.238	1.23	3.65	5.04	4.76	0.1	121	88.0
2015	KCA	MLB	36	11	6	0	34	18	123^{1}	91	16	3.1	6.1	28%	.209	1.09	3.06	4.49	3.54	2.1	109	88.9
2016	*KCA*	*MLB*	*37*	*7*	*10*	*0*	*26*	*26*	*130*	*121*	*17*	*3.3*	*6.2*	*27%*	*.262*	*1.30*	*4.60*	*4.75*	*5.04*	*0.1*	*120*	
2017	*KCA*	*MLB*	*38*	*7*	*8*	*0*	*21*	*21*	*126^{2}*	*124*	*19*	*3.4*	*6.5*	*27%*	*.271*	*1.35*	*4.70*	*4.82*	*5.15*	*0.0*	*122*	

Breakout: 8% Improve: 30% Collapse: 20% Attrition: 21% MLB: 73% *Comparables: Bruce Chen, Freddy Garcia, Randy Wolf*

In retrospect, it all makes perfect sense. Young has long been one of the most extreme flyball pitchers in baseball; Royals outfielders cover more ground than Proust; bring them together, and *hey presto!* you've got yourself a cheap, effective starter. Young remains one of the most incongruous and fascinating players in the game: a giant of a man with a fantastic pitchface and a soft-tossing repertoire, one who annually posts the lowest BABIPs in recent history. Put him in an environment where the fences are distant and the fielders are gazelles, and he can be a solid fourth starter. Like the bumblebee, we don't fully understand his secret, and we're happier not knowing.

Kyle Zimmer RHP

Born: 9/13/91 Age: 24 Bats: R Throws: R Height: 6'3" Weight: 215

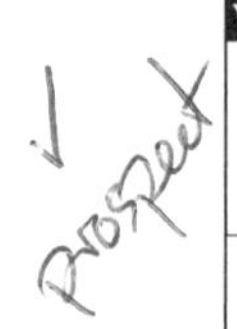

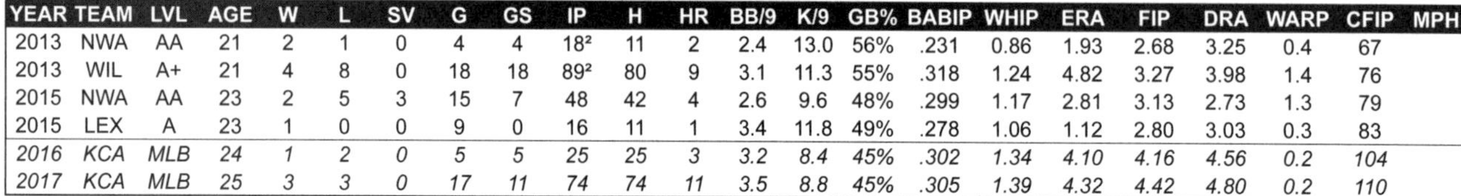

YEAR	TEAM	LVL	AGE	W	L	SV	G	GS	IP	H	HR	BB/9	K/9	GB%	BABIP	WHIP	ERA	FIP	DRA	WARP	CFIP	MPH
2013	NWA	AA	21	2	1	0	4	4	18^{2}	11	2	2.4	13.0	56%	.231	0.86	1.93	2.68	3.25	0.4	67	
2013	WIL	A+	21	4	8	0	18	18	89^{2}	80	9	3.1	11.3	55%	.318	1.24	4.82	3.27	3.98	1.4	76	
2015	NWA	AA	23	2	5	3	15	7	48	42	4	2.6	9.6	48%	.299	1.17	2.81	3.13	2.73	1.3	79	
2015	LEX	A	23	1	0	0	9	0	16	11	1	3.4	11.8	49%	.278	1.06	1.12	2.80	3.03	0.3	83	
2016	*KCA*	*MLB*	*24*	*1*	*2*	*0*	*5*	*5*	*25*	*25*	*3*	*3.2*	*8.4*	*45%*	*.302*	*1.34*	*4.10*	*4.16*	*4.56*	*0.2*	*104*	
2017	*KCA*	*MLB*	*25*	*3*	*3*	*0*	*17*	*11*	*74*	*74*	*11*	*3.5*	*8.8*	*45%*	*.305*	*1.39*	*4.32*	*4.42*	*4.80*	*0.2*	*110*	

Breakout: 16% Improve: 22% Collapse: 13% Attrition: 29% MLB: 46% *Comparables: Alex Meyer, Sean Nolin, J.J. Hoover*

Armed with a worm-killing fastball that can reach the upper 90s and a sharp-breaking power curve, Zimmer has the stuff to front a big-league rotation but has yet to display the health or durability to take the ball every fifth day. The Royals handled him with care last summer after offseason surgery to clean up his shoulder, merely the latest setback in an injury history that's longer and more unsettling than an Apple EULA. When Zimmer did take the mound he drank the tears of overmatched Double-A hitters, and most scouts think his stuff is ready to play at the highest level if he can stay healthy and build up his stamina. If not, he could still join Kansas City's stable of bullpen leviathans.

LINEOUTS

Hitters

NAME	POS	TEAM	LVL	AGE	PA	R	2B	3B	HR	RBI	BB	K	SB	CS	AVG/OBP/SLG	TAv	BABIP	BRR	FRAA	WARP
Cody Decker	1B	ELP	AAA	28	421	52	23	1	21	75	42	107	1	0	.252/.335/.488	.275	.297	-0.6	1B(56): 0.7, 3B(30): -2.8	1.2
	1B	SDN	MLB	28	12	0	0	0	0	1	0	5	0	0	.000/.000/.000	.011	.000	0.0	1B(3): -0.5	-0.3
Brett Eibner	CF	OMA	AAA	26	431	65	23	1	19	81	38	79	10	0	.303/.364/.514	.312	.338	3.0	CF(53): -6.3, RF(34): -4.8	2.8
Alfredo Escalera-Maldonado	OF	LEX	A	20	285	40	13	3	8	33	10	58	12	2	.313/.356/.477	.303	.372	3.4	LF(36): 2.5, CF(22): -3.2	2.8
	OF	WIL	A+	20	222	18	7	2	2	14	17	61	7	3	.206/.285/.291	.230	.287	1.6	LF(38): 0.6, CF(12): 1.2	0.1
Balbino Fuenmayor	1B	NWA	AA	25	308	50	22	1	15	51	12	46	1	0	.354/.386/.591	.340	.381	-2.2	1B(65): -1.1	2.7
	1B	OMA	AAA	25	70	12	6	1	2	15	0	13	0	0	.377/.371/.580	.348	.436	-0.7	1B(14): -1.6	0.5
Elier Hernandez	OF	LEX	A	20	314	37	19	2	5	42	14	73	6	5	.290/.331/.421	.283	.369	-2.3	RF(70): -10.7, CF(5): -0.4	0.0
	OF	WIL	A+	20	196	15	7	2	1	12	10	47	4	2	.232/.281/.311	.233	.299	-1.2	RF(45): 7.3	0.4
Jose Martinez	OF	OMA	AAA	26	396	57	25	3	10	60	48	55	8	2	.384/.461/.563	.351	.434	-3.6	RF(28): -1.1, LF(27): 0.8	4.1
Ryan O'Hearn	1B	LEX	A	21	356	44	11	0	19	56	36	87	7	2	.277/.351/.494	.295	.321	-1.5	1B(64): 2.5, RF(3): 0.3	1.9
	1B	WIL	A+	21	181	14	10	0	8	21	19	54	0	0	.236/.315/.447	.286	.300	-0.4	1B(42): 0.3	0.7
Chase Vallot	C	LEX	A	18	333	46	13	3	13	40	41	105	1	0	.219/.331/.427	.274	.291	-2.8	C(44): -1.4	1.1

As a reward for hitting at least 15 homers in each of his seven professional seasons, **Cody Decker** finally got called up to San Diego, where for a few weeks he savored the feel of a bona fide big-league bench. ❖ **Brett Eibner** has always flashed plus power, a strong arm and solid defensive chops but last summer he finally stopped chasing sliders out of the zone and reduced his disastrous whiff rate, earning fourth-outfielder consideration. ❖ Speedy outfielder **Alfredo Escalera-Maldonado** displayed good baseball instincts, plus makeup and surprising pop in his second spin through Low-A. If he reaches the bigs he'll have the longest name in MLB history, along with (1) what is likely the longest Wikipedia entry for a relatively anonymous minor leaguer, covering such topics as his parents' first meeting at Long Island College Hospital, his philanthropic efforts, that one time he met Ramon Orta, Puerto Rico's Secretary-Designate of Sports and Recreation, and the fact his younger sister Gabriela is one of his closest advisors; and (2) what is now almost certainly the longest Lineout in Baseball Prospectus history. We're pulling for him. ❖ Indy-league find **Balbino Fuenmayor** was tearing up the high minors before tearing up his knee in August; his aggressive approach may yet become a millstone, but if he can continue to pair his newfound hit tool with his ever-present power, his comeback story might have a happy ending. ❖ Italian bonus baby **Marten Gasparini** bounced back from a series of leg problems to display some, ahem, sick wheels in the Pioneer League, swiping 26 bags and logging 10 triples; if he can stay at shortstop he has a chance to be something special. ❖ **Elier Hernandez** made some strides last summer towards turning his estimable physical tools into production before hitting a wall in High-A; like the ghost pepper, a little bit of plate discipline can go a long, long way. ❖ Former White Sox and Braves farmhand

Jose Martinez got everyone's attention by winning the PCL batting title; he lacks the power you'd expect from someone his size, but he controls the strike zone and could yet spend some time on a big-league bench. ❖ **Ryan O'Hearn** followed up his Pioneer League MVP season with a power-packed full-season debut, launching 27 bombs and settling in at first base; if he continues to dent baseballs in the high minors, he might have a career. ❖ **Chase Vallot** chases a lot, striking out in fully one-third of his professional plate appearances; his work behind the dish is still raw, but the possibility of light-tower power from the catcher position will earn him many more chances.

Pitchers

NAME	TEAM	LVL	AGE	W	L	SV	G	GS	IP	H	HR	BB/9	K/9	GB%	BABIP	WHIP	ERA	FIP	FRA	WARP	CFIP	MPH
Scott Alexander	KCA	MLB	25	0	0	0	4	0	6	5	0	4.5	4.5	72%	.278	1.33	4.50	4.10	3.43	0.1	109	95.0
	OMA	AAA	25	2	3	14	41	0	63^{1}	48	5	2.4	7.1	64%	.243	1.03	2.56	3.90	3.93	0.9	89	
Christian Binford	OMA	AAA	22	1	4	0	6	6	27^{2}	31	4	4.9	2.9	41%	.276	1.66	5.86	6.45	7.54	-0.6	127	
	NWA	AA	22	4	7	0	16	16	91^{1}	118	6	2.3	5.9	40%	.358	1.54	5.03	3.66	4.44	0.8	99	
Scott Blewett	LEX	A	19	3	5	0	18	18	81^{1}	88	6	2.7	6.6	48%	.317	1.38	5.20	3.96	4.37	0.8	98	
Louis Coleman	KCA	MLB	29	1	0	0	4	0	3	1	0	6.0	3.0	38%	.125	1.00	0.00	4.44	2.64	0.1	109	91.6
	OMA	AAA	29	8	2	9	38	0	64	48	4	3.2	8.9	34%	.267	1.11	1.69	3.57	3.17	1.4	80	
Alec Mills	WIL	A+	23	7	7	0	21	21	113^{1}	122	3	1.1	8.8	52%	.350	1.20	3.02	2.09	1.03	5.2	67	
Sam Selman	NWA	AA	24	3	5	3	41	0	56^{1}	56	3	6.7	11.0	53%	.361	1.74	5.27	4.10	5.63	-0.5	110	
Eric Skoglund	WIL	A+	22	6	3	0	15	15	84^{1}	83	2	1.2	7.0	50%	.314	1.11	3.52	2.53	2.43	2.4	82	
Glenn Sparkman	NWA	AA	23	2	2	0	4	4	20	17	1	4.1	9.4	41%	.302	1.30	3.60	3.35	4.04	0.3	95	

Triple-A closer **Scott Alexander** uses his low-90s sinker to generate double-play bouncers and doesn't hurt himself with walks and home runs. He'll get a look-see for a middle relief role this spring, but he has a lot of bodies to climb over. ❖ **Christian Binford**'s best tool—pinpoint fastball command—deserted him last year, as the towering righty walked more men than he whiffed in Omaha and continued to struggle after a demotion to Double-A. He's young enough to adjust, but his low-velocity repertoire will always walk a razor line. ❖ Not to damn him with too much context, but **Scott Blewett** put together a surprisingly solid season for a cold-climate teenager making his full-season debut before melting in the August heat; with a solid frame, a fastball that can touch the mid-90s and a bat-missing bender he could grow into a prototypical rotation workhorse. ❖ Veteran slider-slinger **Louis Coleman** was the best option in the Omaha 'pen last summer; unfortunately for him, the best option for the Kansas City 'pen was to leave him there. ❖ Scale model lefty **Tim Collins** blew out his UCL last spring and underwent Tommy John surgery; you'll know he's returned this summer when you first hear someone mutter "how can someone that size throw that hard?" ❖ Disappointment descended on **Brian Flynn** when he missed the year with a torn lat muscle after nearly breaking camp with the big club; the Royals will still need to sort out whether his sinker-slider mix works best at the back of the rotation or in middle relief. ❖ Armed with a low-90s fastball and an excellent changeup, **Alec Mills** put up solid numbers at High-A Wilmington and would rather chew glass than hand out a free pass; he'll get his first crack at passing the Double-A exam this summer. ❖ First-rounder **Ashe Russell** wows with his mid-90s fastball and darting slider, but his cross-body delivery gives some scouts the willies; an Indiana prep school product, the Royals will build him up slowly. ❖ Disney Pixar is producing an animated feature called *Stop And Go* featuring anthropomorphic traffic signals that set aside their differences to help guide a young man home; **Sam Selman** spent last summer auditioning for the part of "Walk." ❖ Lefty **Eric Skoglund** used solid command of a low-90s fastball and a plus changeup to mow down the kids in High-A, but missed the second half of the year with an elbow injury; if he can get healthy and pull the same tricks in Double-A, he could become a mid-rotation option. ❖ Elbow woes that culminated in Tommy John surgery will keep control specialist **Glenn Sparkman** off the mound until at least midseason, so in the meantime he wants you to picture him striding across a football field wearing a houndstooth overcoat and a diamond earring to the strains of the Simple Minds classic *Don't You (Forget About Me)*. ❖ Second-round pick **Josh Staumont** channeled Nuke LaLoosh during his Rookie league debut, unleashing easy triple-digit thunderbolts and a hammer curve while filling the scorecard with strikeouts, walks, wild pitches, hit batsmen and bruised mascots. The Royals think they can improve his control without forcing him to breathe through his eyelids, and if they're right they'll have another bullpen leviathan on their hands. ❖ The Royals finally achieved their dream of cornering the Indianapolis prep arm market when they drafted **Nolan Watson** a dozen picks after Ashe Russell. This here Hoosier has more pitches in his arsenal, less jump in his fastball, a lower ceiling and a higher floor than that there other Hoosier.

MANAGER

Ned Yost

YEAR	TEAM	W	L	Pythag +/-	Avg PC	100+ P	120+ P	QS	BQS	REL	REL w Zero R	IBB	PH	PH Avg	PH HR	SB2	CS2	SB3	CS3	SAC Att	SAC%	POS SAC	Squeeze	Swing	In Play
2013	KCA	86	76	-1	98.6	79	2	95	5	427	374	21	74	.210	1	133	30	19	2	56	66.1	36	1	369	99
2014	KCA	89	73	5	98.6	90	2	95	4	451	399	14	43	.250	2	124	29	29	7	55	60.0	30	1	344	112
2015	KCA	95	67	4	92.8	52	0	71	3	493	418	10	36	.188	0	76	30	27	2	48	70.8	32	0	257	86

To those who spend every postseason first- and second-guessing managerial decisions, Yost's World Series victory might have sparked an existential crisis, or served as a belief-altering occasion. After all, just how could this happen given our perception of Yost and his managing abilities? Obviously, Yost's recent success doesn't make him a brilliant skipper—at least not tactically. What the postseason did do a good job of was highlighting all his tendencies, be it good or bad. He continued to deploy his bullpen aggressively, as he had throughout the regular season—a smart call, given the Royals' rotation had been ravaged by injury and shaky performance. Yost also stayed true to his starting nine; so true, in fact, that Yost used as many or fewer pinch-hitters for positional players than the likes of Ryne Sandberg and Bud Black—neither of whom managed the entire season. Whether that's a good thing or not depends on your beliefs when it comes to playing the matchups and resting your regulars.

Rest assured, Yost retained some of his easier-to-critique tics, too. In spite of having options like Alex Gordon and Ben Zobrist available to bat leadoff, Yost chose to roll with Alcides Escobar—an inexplicable decision by most reasoning, yet one that somehow paid off, since Escobar went on an unexpected tear during the postseason. Yost has always liked to bunt, and 2015 was no exception: the Royals finished eighth in the majors in position-player sacrifices—though, as the Lorenzo Cain's efforts in the postseason taught us, not all of those were called from the dugout.

If there's a lesson from Yost's portion of the World Series victory, it's a reminder that managers aren't as important as we make them out to be. They're fun to nitpick and criticize when things go bad, but they're not the difference-markers; not really—those are the players. The managers? They have to be supportive of the players, they have to put them in positions where they can succeed and they have to otherwise stay out of the way. Yost isn't perfect and he might not even be good, but he's seemingly competent at two, and maybe all three of those things. In 2015, that was enough to win a ring.

LOS ANGELES ANGELS

Essay by David Roth

Player comments by Doug Thorburn, Mauricio Rubio, and BP authors

There is no one thing that a baseball team is supposed to be. There are the basics—it's important to have enough players on the roster, just in a practical sense, and most teams at least like to have a scrappy shortish utility player and a quippy veteran reliever. If a given team wants to mix in a few centimillionaires with strain-prone obliques or a half-dozen platoon goofs or guys named Cuauhtemoc or Kale or Kole or Yerwin, that's on them. We mostly trust the market and gravity to work it all out, and it mostly works itself out.

Or, anyway, it works out well enough that those of us who peg our emotional well-being to baseball teams are able to get from them what we need. Each team means a different thing to the people who care about it, and can mean an infinite number of things—they grow or shrink to fill the space we make for them. This does not give us any say in how good or bad our team will be, not at all or even a little bit, which is the foremost and fundamental frustration of the whole thing. Our manifest devotion will never, ever change the direction of the thing to which we're devoted, because it doesn't work like that and because the people with the power to change it are not listening.

There is a bleak existential parallel there—just absolutely right there, it's not even subtext—but this is an essay about the Los Angeles Angels of Anaheim, and so there's no reason to overcomplicate it. If we get from our teams what we need, the teams themselves can be whatever the people running them want them to be. We can see these teams as an expression of the desires and ambitions and biases and limitations and myriad hamstrung weirdnesses of the powerful people who run them.

So: Take the Angels. Here is a team with a rich and ambitious owner whose wealth is bolstered by an exceptionally lucrative television deal. They play their home games in a beautiful part of the country, give or take some extremely toxic traffic and the seething, strange local politics. They have the exclusive rights to the single most valuable player in baseball. They literally have a guy named Kole on the roster, and he's even pretty good.

This is, in short, a team that fans could quite reasonably dream some extremely wild dreams about. The Angels could be anything at all, up to and including World Series

ANGELS PROSPECTUS

2015 W-L: 85-77, 3rd in AL West

Pythag	.490	19th	DER	.715	4th
RS/G	4.08	20th	B-Age	28.7	21st
RA/G	4.17	13th	P-Age	28.3	15th
TAv	.257	21st	Salary	$141.7M	9th
BRR	2.28	15th	M$/MW	$3.5M	16th
TAv-P	.262	18th	DL Days	672	5th
FIP	4.03	16th	$ on DL	15%	14th

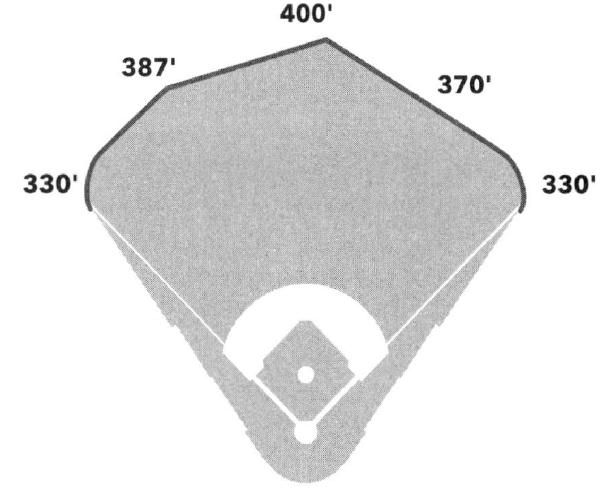

Three-Year Park Factors

Runs	Runs/RH	Runs/LH	HR/RH	HR/LH
98	110	105	115	107

Top Hitter WARP	10	Mike Trout
Top Pitcher WARP	3.3	Garrett Richards
Top Prospect		Joe Gatto

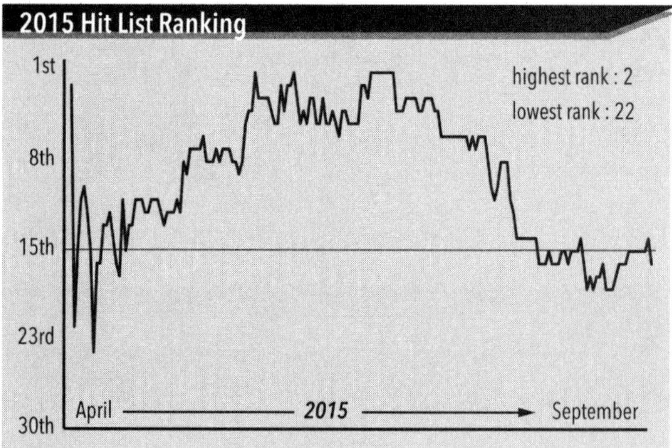

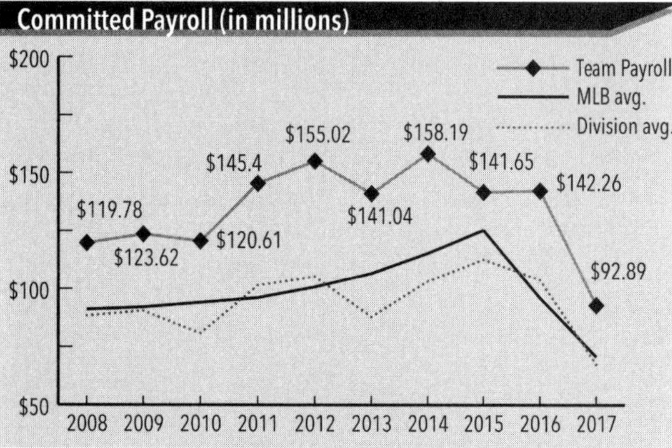

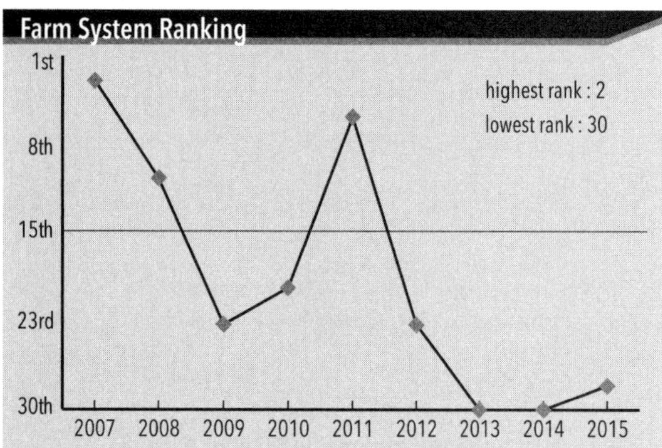

Personnel

President: John Carpino
General Manager: Billy Eppler
Assistant General Manager: Steve Martone
Assistant General Manager: Jonathan Strangio
Manager: Mike Scioscia

Baseball Prospectus Alumni
Chris Mosch

champions. They could be anything they want to be, and somehow the people in charge of picking an identity settled on "internet comment section." It is not any more satisfying than it sounds.

You, of course, are smart enough to stop when you get to the end of something that you have been reading online. You value your time on earth and understand how precious and brief it is, and know not to spend any of those hours walking the superheated miles of irradiated ungrammatical ragebarf that unspool in the comments under every item that presently exists on the internet. I, on the other hand, am a total idiot, just a real dope who does not value his time in any meaningful way. So I can tell you a little bit about what you'll find in those comment sections.

First things first: They're bad. The Comments are not a conversation, and despite being argumentative in the extreme they're not even an argument. They are a cacophony of furious and fuming assertion, a thousand monologues screamed at the same time in something like the same pitch, all day and all night, forever and ever, amen. It is, finally and most fundamentally, a pose-off. The Comments are a space in which to righteously make every single thing happening in the world about the manifest righteousness and rightness of your own crabbed and crabby self. The Comments are an echo chamber in which to lay out your own armchair biases—luxuriously inflexible and unfailingly certain, one way or the other—and make the world conform to and reflect them. It is a sad and angry place, simultaneously intimate to the point of claustrophobia and as bloodlessly abstract as drone warfare. To reiterate: pretty bad.

This sort of aggrieved and casually reasoned grouchiness cannot and will not live long outside the comments, but then it's not meant to. It's meant to be pure, and to stay where it is—the idea is to be *right*, not strictly correct. This is the point of it: The Comments are performative, a place to play at being as draconian and uncompromising and dictatorial as your smallest and shittiest and most merciless dreams will let you be, and as the world mostly will not. If you want your favorite team to cut loose a disappointing player for some reason or other, or to play in a certain style that you deem to be right, or to mandate that relievers throw sliders every third pitch no matter what, that is absolutely the sort of thing you are welcome to lay out, at length, in The Comments.

That is what The Comments are for, if they have a purpose—they are a safe space for people to share their passionately held idiocies and gripes and fixes. No one is listening, and no one should, but the comments are not there to be read. Think of them as the ghost vault in *Ghostbusters*—all those restless, rageful shades are trapped, removed from the world through which we all walk, and then dumped into a tank where they can slime each other forever, safely sequestered from everyone else. This is a fine way to store the ghosts power-eating hot dogs in the city's hotel ballrooms and haunting Sigourney Weaver's refrigerator. It is not any sort of way for a baseball team to operate.

The Angels are a baseball team with the corporate culture and philosophy and general ambient vibe of The Comments. As a team, they're pretty good—good enough to be in the playoff mix until the last day of the 2015 season, in large part because they're lucky enough to employ Mike Trout. As a broader enterprise, though, they are in much worse shape. The team is not the problem here. The problem is how joyless, paranoid, proudly backward, overdetermined and under-reasoned the organization is. The Angels are talented enough to win a decent number of baseball games; they are a solid offseason and a bit of luck away from winning a lot more than that. They're also enough of a self-thwarting mess to make those strengths not matter; it's tough to imagine a team this surly, secretive and strange as champions. That's a problem that doesn't get solved in an offseason.

+++

The baseball stuff is the baseball stuff, and the baseball stuff has been secondary to the not-quite-baseball stuff for about as long as Arte Moreno has owned the team. Moreno has spent the last three seasons not quite negotiating a schism between his team's front office and dugout. Last year, manager Mike Scioscia won this exceptionally passive-aggressive double-bank power struggle when GM Jerry Dipoto resigned on July 1st; Dipoto is now the GM in Seattle, and his former chief deputy, fellow big leaguer Scott Servais, is that team's manager.

Dipoto made some mistakes, although the most costly of those—the since-bought-out contract of Josh Hamilton and the slow-burning whiff of a deal given to Albert Pujols—have a strong Overcompensating Owner Decides To Make A Splash vibe to them. (Moreno's vindictive and weirdly personal response to Hamilton's relapse before 2015, a disastrously public campaign to get the contract nullified, did much to reveal the type of person in the owner's suite.) The team's farm system is a wreck, too—after new GM Billy Eppler flipped top prospect Sean Newcomb in a deal with Atlanta for Andrelton Simmons, Baseball Prospectus ranked it as the worst in the majors. This is not ideal, but it would be worse for an organization that couldn't afford mistakes. The Angels absolutely can, and have long seemed—going back to the Signing Gary Matthews Jr./Trading For Vernon Wells days—to make these sorts of mistakes as a conspicuous-consumption ritual.

Anyway, the Angels are more than the sum of their bad contracts. Mike Trout is so much better than any other player in baseball that it is both unfair and objectively ridiculous, and he won't turn 25 until after the All-Star break. Dipoto left the team with a wealth of young, inexpensive starting pitching, and the rotation will be better in 2016 when Tyler Skaggs rejoins the mix after Tommy John surgery cost him all of 2015. The team did well to get Simmons, the best defensive shortstop in a generation, and Kole Calhoun won a Gold Glove of his own in 2015. Eppler's other offseason moves suggest an emphasis on defense and positional flexibility, which is at least contemporary.

This is all good, but for a team that entered the offseason one big contract away from paying the luxury tax, there are also a striking number of holes. Johnny Giavotella played second base all year long, on purpose, at roughly a Johnny Giavotellan level. The list of Angels left fielders in 2015—Matt Joyce, David DeJesus, Shane Victorino, David Murphy—looks uncomfortably like the waiver moves of a desperate fantasy owner. As I write this, those problems have not been solved; what has been solved, at least in name, is third base, where Yunel Escobar will play despite every publicly available metric rating his defense somewhere between "horrific" and "actually it's just horrific." There is a great deal of very expensive dead weight on the roster, too; that will largely clear up after 2016, but the 2016 season hasn't happened yet, and it is presently slated to happen with Jered Weaver and C.J. Wilson each making $20 million. On the other hand, there is also Mike Trout, who was admittedly mentioned earlier but is worth mentioning again because he is so hilariously good at baseball, which is the sport the Angels play.

Again, though, this is just the baseball stuff. Baseball-wise, the Angels missed the playoffs in 2015 on the last day of the season, and won the division a year earlier. Baseball-wise, they have their issues but in no way appear to be a team in crisis. And yet the Angels are more or less a team in crisis, not for any prosaic baseball-related reason but because they are just so fraught and weird and *angry*. By dint of Moreno's decisions and abdications—Dipoto and Scioscia had been at odds since 2012, and never quite figured out a way to work together—the Angels have become a conflicted and proudly prehistoric failed state. But this is not quite right—failed states are failed states, and the Angels chose to be this way.

+++

Here is where we return to The Comments. The long-running dispute between Dipoto and Scioscia was not the stereotypical nerds vs. jocks binary so beloved of The Comments. Dipoto and Servais and pro scouting director Hal Morris were all long-tenured MLB players, like Scioscia, and the information they passed along—basic analytical stuff like scouting reports and suggestions regarding defensive shifts—was repeatedly kept from anyone who might have used it by Scioscia's staff. At some point, Moreno had to make a choice between the employees providing this information and the employees refusing even to look at it. He went with the latter, which was if nothing else the most Comments choice available—in the rhetorical vacuum of The Comments, a stand on principle, no matter how infected or discredited the principle, trumps all. It will always feel right.

And so the Angels continue to rely on what is invariably described as "feel." This sounds like a synonym for the old managerial intuition but is actually something else—an unscientific and arbitrary and extremely rigid alternate-universe vision of Playing The Right Way, which Scioscia will not see compromised by things like scouting reports or outside information. Starting pitchers were not allowed to throw up in the zone, full stop; right-handed relievers were required to throw sliders, whether or not that was a pitch they threw with much effectiveness; the defense mostly did not shift and pitchers did not use scouting data to attack opposing hitters' weaknesses; lineups were constructed by mysticism and gut.

All of which is to say that Scioscia and since-deposed pitching coach Mike Butcher effectively embargoed not just the printouts and suggestions of Dipoto's front office, but the last couple decades of baseball modernity. They did this not because their approach worked—the Angels have made the postseason just once since 2009, despite payrolls that rank among the league's elite—but because they believed it was right, and because their instincts and intuition and experience and *values* told them that poor Cam Bedrosian should throw his bummy slider 25 percent of the time. The Angels looked at the data and decided to do what they thought was right—to take Hamilton's relapse personally and slime him in public, to stick to the old Jurassic Macho when times got tough. They stood on principle, even where the principle was shot through and moldy and honestly more of a strident cliché than anything that could be called a principle. They did this because it was the right thing to do. Upvote if you agree.

The secret sadness of The Comments as a way of being is how false-bottomed and fake it all is. What appears to be a stand on principle or some damn-the-torpedoes assertion of bravery is, finally, a retreat: In response to the unpredictability and inconvenience and stubborn slippery elusiveness of the present, The Comments seek refuge in false certitude, authoritarian mysticism, glass-jawed denial and all misbegotten species of future-fighting grievance.

It is not principled, although it poses as such. It is mostly an elevation of reactions and hunches and received wisdom and under-examined biases over anything and everything that might challenge them. It is intellectually coherent, but only insofar as it exists in denial of anything that might challenge that coherence. The people positing and posturing and sternly saying "no" in The Comments are there because it is the easiest, safest, most isolated place to be. It is difficult to imagine them negotiating daily life with much success, or much joy.

Which is fine, as far as it goes. Life is hard, and that is part of why we need this game, and these teams. Baseball is a thing that gets us out of this world—it is an escape into hope and languor and happy abstraction, and there's beer. To see a baseball team turned into a grim and grouchy reification of The Comments at every level, to see it turned upside down and inside out by its refusal to join the game as it is played because it is easier to be right in a vacuum than compromise in the world—well, it's a waste, mostly. There is no one thing that a baseball team is supposed to be, but it's sure supposed to be a lot more fun than this. ■

—David Roth is a contributing editor at Vice Sports and a co-founder of The Classical.

HITTERS

Roberto Baldoquin MI

Born: 5/14/94 Age: 22 Bats: R Throws: R Height: 5'11" Weight: 185

YEAR	TEAM	LVL	AGE	PA	R	2B	3B	HR	RBI	BB	K	SB	CS	AVG/OBP/SLG	TAv	BABIP	BRR	FRAA	WARP
2015	INL	A+	21	309	23	12	1	1	27	9	70	4	5	.235/.266/.294	.229	.303	0.4	SS(75): -17.9	-1.7
2016	*ANA*	*MLB*	*22*	*250*	*20*	*9*	*1*	*3*	*20*	*7*	*67*	*2*	*1*	*.210/.238/.295*	*.196*	*.272*	*-0.4*	*SS -8*	*-1.4*
2017	*ANA*	*MLB*	*23*	*297*	*27*	*11*	*1*	*4*	*25*	*10*	*76*	*2*	*2*	*.215/.250/.304*	*.204*	*.275*	*-0.4*	*SS -10*	*-0.5*

Breakout: 1% Improve: 1% Collapse: 0% Attrition: 2% MLB: 2% *Comparables: Argenis Diaz, German Duran, Zack Cozart*

When Common was just a rapper, he was solid, doing just enough to make you ponder the issues without extending outside his box. Then someone put him on *Girlfriends* and the man hasn't been the same since. Baldoquin as a second baseman is a fine option—he'll do well enough in the field and you don't have to think too hard about anything—but Baldoquin at short will end up like Common in *Smokin' Aces*; no one's cuing that up for a second viewing. He is aggressive at the plate as well, which will undermine his natural power and hit tools.

Quintin Berry LF

Born: 11/21/84 Age: 31 Bats: L Throws: L Height: 6'1" Weight: 190

YEAR	TEAM	LVL	AGE	PA	R	2B	3B	HR	RBI	BB	K	SB	CS	AVG/OBP/SLG	TAv	BABIP	BRR	FRAA	WARP
2013	BOS	MLB	28	9	5	0	0	1	4	1	2	3	0	.625/.667/1.000	.566	.800	0.5	RF(4): -0.2, LF(4): -0.1	0.3
2013	TOL	AAA	28	199	16	8	0	1	15	23	45	15	2	.168/.278/.234	.209	.221	-0.8	CF(47): -0.3	-0.6
2013	OMA	AAA	28	172	18	2	1	2	16	26	34	13	2	.222/.343/.292	.250	.275	2.0	LF(40): -3.4, RF(3): 0.3	0.1
2014	BAL	MLB	29	2	3	0	0	0	0	0	1	1	0	.000/.000/.000	-.008	.000	0.6	LF(3): -0.0, RF(1): -0.0	0.0
2014	NOR	AAA	29	432	53	19	1	3	35	57	84	25	6	.285/.382/.367	.264	.359	-1.7	LF(76): 12.2, CF(23): 1.2	2.6
2015	PAW	AAA	30	426	44	7	1	4	36	51	89	35	6	.228/.329/.287	.246	.288	2.2	RF(42): -4.1, CF(33): 1.1	0.7
2015	CHN	MLB	30	1	1	0	0	0	0	0	1	2	1	.000/.000/.000	-.006	--	-0.4	CF(2): -0.1, LF(2): -0.1	-0.1
2016	*ANA*	*MLB*	*31*	*250*	*31*	*8*	*1*	*3*	*17*	*25*	*64*	*15*	*3*	*.224/.310/.306*	*.231*	*.294*	*1.7*	*RF -1, CF 1*	*0.4*
2017	*ANA*	*MLB*	*32*	*235*	*24*	*7*	*1*	*2*	*19*	*23*	*61*	*13*	*3*	*.220/.307/.299*	*.228*	*.291*	*1.8*	*RF -1, CF 1*	*0.1*

Breakout: 2% Improve: 10% Collapse: 11% Attrition: 20% MLB: 27% *Comparables: Jason Repko, Ron Calloway, Mike Edwards*

The last time Berry appeared in the majors when it wasn't September was back in 2012 with the Tigers, but he's managed 31 games played and six stolen bases over the last three seasons, plus three postseason steals and a ring with the Red Sox in 2013. Check out his Triple-A slugging percentages above if you've got a hankering for more Berry. There's little reason to think he can't keep latching on as a designated runner with a new random contender every August 31st until the calendar turns to the 2020s. The one hiccup last year was his September 20th caught stealing, his first in the major leagues, and of course it was the Cardinals who got him. That Yadier Mol—what's that? It was Tony Cruz? Oh.

Kole Calhoun RF

Born: 10/14/87 Age: 28 Bats: L Throws: L Height: 5'10" Weight: 200

YEAR	TEAM	LVL	AGE	PA	R	2B	3B	HR	RBI	BB	K	SB	CS	AVG/OBP/SLG	TAv	BABIP	BRR	FRAA	WARP
2013	SLC	AAA	25	274	48	15	6	12	49	32	32	10	2	.354/.431/.617	.332	.371	-0.4	CF(31): -4.2, RF(17): -1.9	2.2
2013	ANA	MLB	25	222	29	7	2	8	32	21	41	2	2	.282/.347/.462	.294	.311	1.5	RF(54): 6.5, 1B(6): 0.3	2.1
2014	SLC	AAA	26	22	7	2	1	1	5	0	3	0	1	.500/.500/.818	.391	.556	-0.3	RF(4): -0.4	0.3
2014	ANA	MLB	26	537	90	31	3	17	58	38	104	5	3	.272/.325/.450	.293	.313	3.9	RF(123): -1.2, 1B(2): -0.0	3.1
2015	ANA	MLB	27	686	78	23	2	26	83	45	164	4	1	.256/.308/.422	.267	.304	-2.3	RF(157): 13.9, 1B(1): 0.0	3.0
2016	*ANA*	*MLB*	*28*	*640*	*83*	*28*	*4*	*22*	*75*	*49*	*138*	*6*	*3*	*.262/.322/.439*	*.273*	*.304*	*1.3*	*RF 6*	*3.3*
2017	*ANA*	*MLB*	*29*	*592*	*74*	*25*	*3*	*20*	*74*	*48*	*129*	*5*	*2*	*.259/.323/.428*	*.271*	*.304*	*1.1*	*RF 6*	*2.5*

Breakout: 0% Improve: 50% Collapse: 6% Attrition: 15% MLB: 96% *Comparables: Josh Reddick, Jeremy Hermida, Matt Joyce*

Calhoun was a fixture in the Angels' pasture last season, where he logged more innings than any other outfielder in the game, an effort that included Gold Glove–worthy range and 11 outfield kills. He turned up the intensity on the risk-reward dial at the plate, selling out for home runs in return for a lot more empty swings, an approach that got out of hand in his final month, with 45 strikeouts and just five walks over his last 120 plate appearances. The rake-and-rake philosophy did yield the hoped-for higher output of dingers, and he hit 19 of his 26 bombs over the final three months of the season, but he's not an ideal fit at the top of the batting order, where he played much of the year: 124 of his 157 starts came in the first or second slot. On the other hand, we're talking about a three-win player in a lineup that featured David Freese's .323 mark as its second-best OBP, so maybe we shouldn't quibble too much about who hits where.

Kaleb Cowart 3B

Born: 6/2/92 Age: 24 Bats: B Throws: R Height: 6'3" Weight: 225

YEAR	TEAM	LVL	AGE	PA	R	2B	3B	HR	RBI	BB	K	SB	CS	AVG/OBP/SLG	TAv	BABIP	BRR	FRAA	WARP
2013	ARK	AA	21	546	48	20	1	6	42	38	124	14	5	.221/.279/.301	.216	.280	3.1	3B(131): -9.5	-1.5
2014	ARK	AA	22	487	48	18	4	6	54	43	99	26	7	.223/.295/.324	.234	.272	1.7	3B(120): -2.3	0.1
2015	INL	A+	23	221	32	14	4	2	23	22	43	10	2	.242/.326/.387	.273	.298	1.7	3B(42): 6.4, SS(4): -0.1	1.8
2015	ANA	MLB	23	52	8	2	0	1	4	5	19	1	1	.174/.255/.283	.195	.269	0.0	3B(33): 1.1	-0.1
2015	SLC	AAA	23	253	35	13	3	6	45	29	64	2	1	.323/.395/.491	.294	.422	0.3	3B(49): -1.5, LF(5): 0.5	1.7
2016	*ANA*	*MLB*	*24*	*100*	*9*	*4*	*0*	*2*	*9*	*7*	*27*	*2*	*1*	*.215/.273/.321*	*.219*	*.280*	*0.1*	*LF -1, 2B 0*	*-0.1*
2017	*ANA*	*MLB*	*25*	*381*	*38*	*15*	*2*	*6*	*35*	*27*	*100*	*8*	*3*	*.219/.277/.328*	*.223*	*.284*	*0.7*	*LF -2*	*-0.3*

Breakout: 0% Improve: 3% Collapse: 2% Attrition: 6% MLB: 8% *Comparables: Matt Carpenter, Matthew Duffy, Matt Mangini*

Cowart has been around for a long time, and took an unusual step backward to the Cal League after two miserable seasons with the bat at Double-A. After the Kyle Kubitza acquisition in January, Cowart was rumored to be moving to the mound, but then he went and hit at both High- and Triple-A (check out the TAv column for his two minor-league stints to get a sense of how things look with park and league issues stripped out), though his brief major-league stint didn't turn out quite as well. After all this, he still won't turn 24 until the middle of this season, but unless Kubitza makes a smooth transition to second base, the Angels will have to make a decision soon on which glove-first, meh-bat third-base option to keep around.

C.J. Cron DH

Born: 1/5/90 Age: 26 Bats: R Throws: R Height: 6'4" Weight: 235

YEAR	TEAM	LVL	AGE	PA	R	2B	3B	HR	RBI	BB	K	SB	CS	AVG/OBP/SLG	TAv	BABIP	BRR	FRAA	WARP
2013	ARK	AA	23	565	56	36	1	14	83	23	83	8	4	.274/.319/.428	.278	.298	-1.5	1B(124): -0.4	1.5
2014	SLC	AAA	24	213	30	14	1	7	33	18	40	2	1	.316/.385/.511	.299	.368	1.7	1B(42): -0.4	1.3
2014	ANA	MLB	24	253	28	12	1	11	37	10	61	0	0	.256/.289/.450	.265	.300	-1.6	1B(36): -0.9	0.1
2015	SLC	AAA	25	98	15	10	2	6	23	4	14	0	0	.323/.347/.667	.313	.324	-1.4	1B(16): -1.4	0.4
2015	ANA	MLB	25	404	37	17	1	16	51	17	82	3	1	.262/.300/.439	.262	.293	1.4	1B(58): -0.4	0.6
2016	*ANA*	*MLB*	*26*	*589*	*64*	*30*	*2*	*21*	*76*	*25*	*123*	*3*	*1*	*.258/.297/.432*	*.260*	*.293*	*-0.2*	*1B -2*	*0.7*
2017	*ANA*	*MLB*	*27*	*528*	*64*	*26*	*1*	*19*	*68*	*24*	*111*	*3*	*1*	*.254/.296/.429*	*.260*	*.288*	*-0.3*	*1B -2*	*0.5*

Breakout: 2% Improve: 49% Collapse: 1% Attrition: 11% MLB: 77% *Comparables: Mitch Moreland, Kendrys Morales, Brett Wallace*

Cron's sophomore season was similar to the first: light on patience and heavy on power. The pop disappeared with a southpaw on the mound, though. The split may have been a single-year blip, but Cron's low walk rate has been part of his profile since the minor leagues, a weak spot in his game that effectively caps his utility as a one-dimensional slugger. To his credit, Cron demonstrated no discretion or preference for pitch type, hitting multiple homers on fastballs, changeups, curves, sliders and cutters last season.

David DeJesus OF

Born: 12/20/79 Age: 36 Bats: L Throws: L Height: 5'11" Weight: 190

YEAR	TEAM	LVL	AGE	PA	R	2B	3B	HR	RBI	BB	K	SB	CS	AVG/OBP/SLG	TAv	BABIP	BRR	FRAA	WARP
2013	CHN	MLB	33	318	39	19	3	6	27	29	55	3	0	.250/.330/.401	.268	.291	3.0	CF(73): 3.1, LF(3): 1.2	2.0
2013	WAS	MLB	33	4	0	0	0	0	0	0	1	0	0	.000/.000/.000	.079	.000	0.0	RF(2): -0.1, CF(1): -0.0	-0.1
2014	TBA	MLB	34	273	24	15	2	6	19	30	43	0	3	.248/.344/.403	.278	.280	0.0	LF(13): 0.8, CF(3): -0.4	0.9
2014	PCH	A+	34	28	1	0	0	0	2	4	4	1	1	.227/.357/.227	.247	.263	0.4	LF(3): -0.4	0.0
2015	TBA	MLB	35	257	24	8	2	5	26	19	39	3	2	.259/.323/.375	.251	.289	0.9	LF(52): 2.1, RF(2): -0.0	0.6
2015	ANA	MLB	35	60	3	1	0	0	4	2	13	0	0	.125/.183/.143	.148	.163	-0.3	LF(11): -1.9, CF(2): -0.1	-0.8
2016	*ANA*	*MLB*	*36*	*292*	*33*	*13*	*2*	*5*	*26*	*25*	*53*	*3*	*2*	*.240/.316/.362*	*.251*	*.278*	*0.5*	*LF -1, RF -0*	*0.5*
2017	*ANA*	*MLB*	*37*	*255*	*28*	*11*	*2*	*4*	*24*	*22*	*48*	*2*	*2*	*.229/.307/.347*	*.244*	*.269*	*0.6*	*LF -1, RF 0*	*0.1*

Breakout: 0% Improve: 28% Collapse: 9% Attrition: 17% MLB: 78% *Comparables: Brian Downing, Moises Alou, Minnie Minoso*

DeJesus apparently grew up on a sandlot where left field was out of bounds: Only two of his 75 homers during the PITCHf/x era have left the yard to the opposite field. (Okay, fine, maybe it's just that he doesn't have the pop to hit the ball out the opposite way.) He continued to play his usual brand of pull-heavy baseball last season, but the evolving world of defensive shifts provided a tougher gauntlet for DeJesus to run. He offered at pitches outside the strike zone at his highest rate since we've had that metric available to us, a bad sign regardless of whether the liberal approach was due to angst or a slip in pitch recognition. He was traded to Anaheim at the deadline, and the Halos finished one game behind the second Wild Card spot. WARP doesn't really work this way, but DeJesus cost the team nearly a full win in his 60 plate appearances. We're only saying!

Yunel Escobar SS

Born: 11/2/82 Age: 33 Bats: R Throws: R Height: 6'2" Weight: 215

YEAR	TEAM	LVL	AGE	PA	R	2B	3B	HR	RBI	BB	K	SB	CS	AVG/OBP/SLG	TAv	BABIP	BRR	FRAA	WARP
2013	TBA	MLB	30	578	61	27	1	9	56	57	73	4	4	.256/.332/.366	.264	.281	1.0	SS(153): -0.0	2.8
2014	TBA	MLB	31	529	33	18	0	7	39	43	60	1	1	.258/.324/.340	.257	.282	1.5	SS(136): -13.9, LF(1): -0.0	0.7
2015	WAS	MLB	32	591	75	25	1	9	56	45	70	2	2	.314/.375/.415	.284	.347	-0.8	3B(134): -21.3	1.0
2016	*ANA*	*MLB*	*33*	*629*	*63*	*24*	*1*	*9*	*58*	*49*	*83*	*3*	*2*	*.264/.326/.358*	*.254*	*.290*	*0.8*	*3B -21*	*-0.9*
2017	*ANA*	*MLB*	*34*	*529*	*57*	*19*	*1*	*7*	*47*	*43*	*73*	*1*	*1*	*.250/.317/.336*	*.246*	*.278*	*0.6*	*3B -18*	*0.5*

Breakout: 2% Improve: 27% Collapse: 5% Attrition: 10% MLB: 94% *Comparables: Bill Madlock, Carney Lansford, Harvey Kuenn*

It was a year of surprises for Escobar, who was brought to Washington to play second base with the potential to move back to his native shortstop once Ian Desmond took off in free agency. Instead, Escobar filled in for Anthony Rendon at third and, somewhat surprisingly, was a terrible third baseman, though he stayed there (and Rendon moved) upon the incumbent's return. Further surprising, he had his best offensive output in years, notwithstanding his league-leading 24 double plays grounded into. His contract—which carries a team option after this year—isn't exactly a burden, but Danny Espinosa and Trea Turner are far cheaper options, which is why the Nationals flipped him to the Angels for Trevor Gott.

Taylor Featherston UT

Born: 10/8/1989 Age: 26 Bats: R Throws: R Height: 6'11" Weight: 185

YEAR	TEAM	LVL	AGE	PA	R	2B	3B	HR	RBI	BB	K	SB	CS	AVG/OBP/SLG	TAv	BABIP	BRR	FRAA	WARP
2013	MOD	A+	23	516	87	31	10	13	81	30	110	17	4	.292/.342/.484	.307	.352	4.7	2B(109): 6.7, SS(5): 0.3	5.3
2014	TUL	AA	24	550	69	33	4	16	57	38	114	14	6	.260/.322/.439	.279	.305	-2.1	2B(72): 10.3, SS(39): -0.8	3.6
2015	SLC	AAA	25	32	4	1	1	0	1	2	8	0	0	.172/.219/.276	.166	.227	0.2	SS(4): 0.4, 2B(3): 0.8	-0.1
2015	ANA	MLB	25	169	23	5	1	2	9	7	46	4	2	.162/.212/.247	.177	.215	1.0	3B(39): 0.9, 2B(33): -1.1	-0.8
2016	*ANA*	*MLB*	*26*	*63*	*6*	*3*	*0*	*1*	*6*	*3*	*16*	*1*	*0*	*.225/.269/.360*	*.228*	*.280*	*0.0*	*2B 1*	*0.1*
2017	*ANA*	*MLB*	*27*	*283*	*28*	*12*	*2*	*6*	*28*	*13*	*75*	*5*	*2*	*.219/.264/.351*	*.222*	*.276*	*0.4*	*2B 3*	*0.3*

Breakout: 4% Improve: 27% Collapse: 8% Attrition: 25% MLB: 47% *Comparables: Pedro Florimon, J.J. Furmaniak, Lance Zawadzki*

The bat wasn't ready, but the Halos were in need of a backup middle infielder, and Featherston was, like the mountain, there after being selected in the Rule 5 draft from Colorado (technically by the Cubs, who traded him to the Angels). Featherston broke camp with the big club and filled in as a late-inning replacement on defense. With Johnny Giavotella out of action and Grant Green sidelined down the stretch, Featherston played like a man over his head for three weeks of starting duty; he predictably struggled to barrel up big-league fastballs and was generally left vulnerable to the authoritative presence of MLB pitchers. Another year of seasoning might be nice, but he's 26 at this point and last year was essentially a waste. Maybe Rule 5 isn't such a hot idea after all.

David Freese 3B

Born: 4/28/83 Age: 33 Bats: R Throws: R Height: 6'2" Weight: 225

YEAR	TEAM	LVL	AGE	PA	R	2B	3B	HR	RBI	BB	K	SB	CS	AVG/OBP/SLG	TAv	BABIP	BRR	FRAA	WARP
2013	SLN	MLB	30	521	53	26	1	9	60	47	106	1	2	.262/.340/.381	.252	.320	-1.6	3B(132): -14.1	-0.4
2014	ANA	MLB	31	511	53	25	1	10	55	38	124	1	3	.260/.321/.383	.269	.330	-0.4	3B(122): -8.5	1.1
2015	ANA	MLB	32	470	53	27	0	14	56	31	107	1	1	.257/.323/.420	.268	.310	0.3	3B(113): 0.3	1.9
2015	SLC	AAA	32	25	2	0	0	1	6	3	4	0	0	.286/.400/.429	.285	.313	-0.3	3B(3): -0.2	0.1
2016	*ANA*	*MLB*	*33*	*455*	*48*	*20*	*1*	*12*	*53*	*37*	*107*	*1*	*1*	*.256/.326/.397*	*.265*	*.316*	*-0.2*	*3B -7*	*0.7*
2017	*ANA*	*MLB*	*34*	*449*	*53*	*20*	*0*	*11*	*48*	*34*	*106*	*1*	*1*	*.254/.320/.384*	*.259*	*.315*	*-0.2*	*3B -7*	*0.2*

Breakout: 0% Improve: 28% Collapse: 3% Attrition: 3% MLB: 90% *Comparables: Al Rosen, Bobby Bonilla, Carlos Guillen*

After two straight seasons of slugging like a middle infielder, Freese was able to rebound in 2015 with his best power output since his twenties, setting him up nicely to inhale the pungent air of free agency for the first time. At a minimum, he has contributed league-average offense at the plate even in his down years, and though the late-blossoming infielder appears to have passed his short peak, even the decline phase should include a couple more productive seasons.

Julio Garcia SS

Born: 7/31/97 Age: 18 Bats: R Throws: R Height: 6'0" Weight: 175

Having a plus glove-arm combination is enough to land a player high on an Angels prospect list, but Garcia would be at least an intriguing player to keep an eye on in any system. A potentially average hit tool and no power at all don't add up to a future All-Star, but pair that possible bat with praise-worthy defense and you've got a better shot at being a major leaguer than most teenagers with a .509 OPS in Rookie ball.

Johnny Giavotella 2B

Born: 7/10/87 Age: 28 Bats: R Throws: R Height: 5'8" Weight: 185

YEAR	TEAM	LVL	AGE	PA	R	2B	3B	HR	RBI	BB	K	SB	CS	AVG/OBP/SLG	TAv	BABIP	BRR	FRAA	WARP
2013	OMA	AAA	25	426	48	24	0	7	46	51	59	8	4	.286/.369/.408	.286	.320	0.2	2B(46): -2.4, 3B(29): 3.4	2.4
2013	KCA	MLB	25	48	4	3	0	0	4	5	4	0	0	.220/.333/.293	.253	.243	-0.6	2B(13): -0.5	0.0
2014	KCA	MLB	26	41	8	1	0	1	5	1	5	0	1	.216/.268/.324	.259	.219	0.8	2B(12): 0.5	0.2
2014	OMA	AAA	26	493	66	33	2	7	61	47	36	20	4	.308/.373/.440	.293	.321	0.5	2B(65): -4.9, 3B(29): 0.4	2.8
2015	ANA	MLB	27	502	51	25	5	4	49	32	59	2	1	.272/.318/.375	.257	.301	1.0	2B(128): -3.3, SS(1): -0.0	1.0
2016	*ANA*	*MLB*	*28*	*454*	*43*	*22*	*2*	*6*	*44*	*33*	*66*	*6*	*2*	*.260/.316/.367*	*.250*	*.292*	*0.9*	*2B -4*	*1.0*
2017	*ANA*	*MLB*	*29*	*516*	*53*	*23*	*2*	*6*	*47*	*34*	*77*	*6*	*2*	*.254/.307/.355*	*.244*	*.287*	*1.0*	*2B -4*	*0.5*

Breakout: 2% Improve: 17% Collapse: 7% Attrition: 18% MLB: 72% *Comparables: Eric Sogard, Matt Tolbert, Justin Turner*

Giavotella woke up one morning in late August suffering from double vision with no apparent cause, a malady that was eventually diagnosed as fourth-cranial-nerve palsy. It knocked him from the Angels' lineup for a month down the stretch. He was a beast upon his return, launching an extra-base hit in each of his first six games back in action, helping to ease concerns about the long-term impact of the issue. For the season, his lack of power was on par with that of Erick Aybar, and the holes in Giavotella's defense were exposed during his first taste of extended playing time. For all that, you could do worse at second base. Here's lookin' at you, Stephen Drew.

Jahmai Jones OF

Born: 8/4/97 Age: 18 Bats: R Throws: R Height: 5'11" Weight: 210

Bloodlines and natural athleticism are the main draws for Jones, who offers an unrefined but exciting collection of tools. He is a plus runner who can develop into a solid hitter, albeit one without much power projection. The arm might be a bit light for center, but Jones' glove has the potential to mitigate that problem. (That bloodlines list, by the way: Dad was drafted by the Pittsburgh Steelers in 1991; one brother was drafted by the Detroit Lions in 2014; another brother may be drafted by an NFL team this year; an uncle on the other side played 15 years in the NFL; and a cousin signed with the Minnesota Vikings as an undrafted free agent in 2015.)

Matt Joyce LF

Born: 8/3/84 Age: 31 Bats: L Throws: R Height: 6'2" Weight: 200

YEAR	TEAM	LVL	AGE	PA	R	2B	3B	HR	RBI	BB	K	SB	CS	AVG/OBP/SLG	TAv	BABIP	BRR	FRAA	WARP
2013	TBA	MLB	28	481	61	22	0	18	47	59	87	7	3	.235/.328/.419	.285	.251	-1.2	LF(58): 0.6, RF(58): -5.5	1.5
2014	TBA	MLB	29	493	51	23	2	9	52	62	111	2	5	.254/.349/.383	.278	.316	-0.3	LF(81): 2.1, RF(15): -1.3	1.9
2015	SLC	AAA	30	43	3	1	0	2	6	5	9	0	0	.333/.419/.528	.328	.385	0.1	LF(7): -0.6	0.3
2015	ANA	MLB	30	284	17	12	1	5	21	30	67	0	3	.174/.272/.291	.217	.215	0.5	LF(64): -0.4, RF(2): -0.1	-0.7
2016	*ANA*	*MLB*	*31*	*315*	*35*	*14*	*1*	*9*	*37*	*34*	*69*	*2*	*2*	*.240/.328/.400*	*.264*	*.283*	*-0.2*	*LF 1, RF -0*	*1.2*
2017	*ANA*	*MLB*	*32*	*269*	*33*	*12*	*1*	*8*	*30*	*30*	*60*	*1*	*2*	*.234/.324/.389*	*.260*	*.277*	*0.0*	*LF 1, RF 0*	*0.8*

Breakout: 0% Improve: 35% Collapse: 4% Attrition: 6% MLB: 91% *Comparables: Chris Young, Billy Williams, Brian Giles*

Joyce kept walking and swatting home runs at essentially the same pace that he maintained in 2014, but his batting average cratered and brought his OPS components down with it, contributing to the league-worst offense that the Angels got out of their left fielders in 2015. The Halos followed the usage manual that the Rays had deployed, sparing Joyce versus left-handed pitching (just 24 of his plate appearances last season occurred with the platoon disadvantage), but his vulnerability against secondary pitches was still exploited: He hit just .124 with a .044 ISO and zero homers in the 113 at-bats that ended on non-fastballs.

Kyle Kubitza 3B

Born: 7/15/90 Age: 25 Bats: L Throws: R Height: 6'3" Weight: 210

YEAR	TEAM	LVL	AGE	PA	R	2B	3B	HR	RBI	BB	K	SB	CS	AVG/OBP/SLG	TAv	BABIP	BRR	FRAA	WARP
2013	LYN	A+	22	527	75	28	6	12	57	80	132	8	16	.260/.380/.434	.283	.344	-2.9	3B(125): 0.8	2.8
2014	MIS	AA	23	529	76	31	11	8	55	77	133	21	6	.295/.405/.470	.330	.401	3.7	3B(120): -5.9, LF(1): -0.0	5.5
2015	SLC	AAA	24	526	63	43	5	7	50	60	125	7	1	.271/.357/.433	.270	.355	-1.2	3B(73): -4.0, LF(18): -0.4	1.4
2015	ANA	MLB	24	39	6	0	0	0	1	3	15	0	0	.194/.256/.194	.166	.333	0.0	3B(13): -1.1, 2B(2): -0.0	-0.4
2016	*ANA*	*MLB*	*25*	*241*	*24*	*11*	*2*	*4*	*24*	*27*	*74*	*3*	*1*	*.224/.315/.357*	*.247*	*.317*	*0.0*	*3B -1, LF -1*	*0.1*
2017	*ANA*	*MLB*	*26*	*407*	*46*	*18*	*3*	*8*	*40*	*45*	*126*	*5*	*2*	*.223/.314/.356*	*.247*	*.318*	*0.1*	*3B -1, LF -1*	*0.1*

Breakout: 10% Improve: 13% Collapse: 12% Attrition: 29% MLB: 34% *Comparables: Zach Lutz, Matthew Brown, Jeff Baker*

Kubitza is another player in a hodgepodge of Angels prospects with broad but middling skill sets. He has every-day upside, as he does have a smooth stroke and a plus arm, but even at his ceiling, he's just not going to be terribly exciting. A small sample of major-league experience exposed a long swing that leads to strikeouts; it's the primary concern about the big lefty's profile.

David Murphy RF

Born: 10/18/81 Age: 34 Bats: L Throws: L Height: 6'3" Weight: 210

YEAR	TEAM	LVL	AGE	PA	R	2B	3B	HR	RBI	BB	K	SB	CS	AVG/OBP/SLG	TAv	BABIP	BRR	FRAA	WARP
2013	TEX	MLB	31	476	51	26	1	13	45	37	59	1	4	.220/.282/.374	.234	.227	-0.9	LF(128): -1.7, P(1): -0.0	-0.5
2014	CLE	MLB	32	462	40	25	1	8	58	36	61	2	3	.262/.319/.385	.266	.285	-4.4	RF(120): -2.6, LF(2): -0.2	0.3
2015	CLE	MLB	33	229	22	12	1	5	27	16	29	0	1	.296/.344/.437	.276	.318	-0.2	LF(21): -2.0, RF(17): -0.8	0.5
2015	ANA	MLB	33	162	16	6	0	5	23	4	20	0	1	.265/.281/.400	.243	.275	-1.2	LF(32): -1.7	-0.3
2016	*ANA*	*MLB*	*34*	*379*	*39*	*17*	*1*	*8*	*39*	*28*	*56*	*2*	*2*	*.255/.312/.384*	*.254*	*.279*	*-1.4*	*LF -2, RF -0*	*0.4*
2017	*ANA*	*MLB*	*35*	*281*	*31*	*12*	*1*	*6*	*28*	*20*	*45*	*1*	*1*	*.247/.302/.367*	*.247*	*.276*	*-1.0*	*LF -1, RF 0*	*-0.1*

Breakout: 1% Improve: 31% Collapse: 4% Attrition: 14% MLB: 83% *Comparables: Juan Rivera, Johnny Damon, Jose Vidro*

Murphy was the American League's top pinch-hitter in 2015, bar none. He had the most pinch-hits (11), -homers (three), and -RBIs (nine) in the circuit. None of this means you should expect him, at 34, to match his 2012 peak with the Rangers, when he posted an .859 OPS that remains his career high (ignoring his 112-PA 2007) by over 50 points. However, all of those accolades *can* be found under the "special skills" heading of his resume. References available upon request.

Cliff Pennington SS

Born: 6/15/84 Age: 32 Bats: B Throws: R Height: 5'10" Weight: 195

YEAR	TEAM	LVL	AGE	PA	R	2B	3B	HR	RBI	BB	K	SB	CS	AVG/OBP/SLG	TAv	BABIP	BRR	FRAA	WARP
2013	ARI	MLB	29	299	25	13	1	1	18	26	54	2	0	.242/.310/.309	.233	.298	3.0	SS(51): 2.5, 2B(29): 0.6	0.9
2014	ARI	MLB	30	201	21	5	3	2	10	20	36	6	1	.254/.340/.350	.272	.309	0.2	SS(23): 0.2, 2B(18): 0.4	1.1
2015	TOR	MLB	31	92	9	3	0	2	11	11	20	0	0	.160/.270/.280	.218	.182	0.5	2B(22): 1.6, 3B(6): -0.0	0.1
2015	ARI	MLB	31	157	15	3	0	1	10	16	29	3	0	.237/.314/.281	.216	.290	-0.6	SS(24): 2.9, 3B(12): -0.1	0.1
2016	*ANA*	*MLB*	*32*	*148*	*15*	*5*	*1*	*2*	*13*	*12*	*30*	*3*	*1*	*.236/.303/.328*	*.234*	*.282*	*0.4*	*SS 1, 2B 1*	*0.5*
2017	*ANA*	*MLB*	*33*	*111*	*11*	*4*	*0*	*1*	*9*	*10*	*23*	*2*	*0*	*.234/.305/.325*	*.235*	*.286*	*0.3*	*SS 1, 2B 1*	*0.3*

Breakout: 2% Improve: 41% Collapse: 11% Attrition: 11% MLB: 92% *Comparables: Nick Punto, Brendan Ryan, Julio Lugo*

Whether it's more surprising that Pennington now has a career 0.00 postseason ERA or that he signed a two-year contract this offseason comes down to personal preference and the experiences you've accumulated in your life. Perhaps the former would be less surprising if you knew he topped out at 91 mph in his one ALCS appearance, or perhaps the latter would be more surprising if you glanced up at his 2015 TAv. Either way, the Angels get a reasonable defensive replacement who, by the end of this contract, should only be seeing at-bats from the dugout. Or the bullpen!

Carlos Perez C

Born: 10/27/90 Age: 25 Bats: R Throws: R Height: 6'0" Weight: 210

YEAR	TEAM	LVL	AGE	PA	R	2B	3B	HR	RBI	BB	K	SB	CS	AVG/OBP/SLG	TAv	BABIP	BRR	FRAA	WARP
2013	OKL	AAA	22	296	29	14	0	2	32	25	39	1	1	.269/.328/.345	.254	.304	-1.0	C(71): 8.6	1.9
2013	CCH	AA	22	60	6	4	0	1	5	4	11	0	0	.283/.356/.415	.259	.341	0.0	C(12): -0.2	0.2
2014	OKL	AAA	23	340	33	16	2	6	34	29	54	3	0	.259/.323/.385	.254	.295	-0.5	C(74): 7.5, 1B(5): -0.2	1.9
2015	SLC	AAA	24	79	11	8	0	2	12	7	7	1	0	.361/.418/.556	.329	.381	0.4	C(16): 1.7	1.1
2015	ANA	MLB	24	283	20	13	0	4	21	19	49	2	0	.250/.299/.346	.249	.292	-2.2	C(80): 2.1, 1B(2): -0.6	0.9
2016	*ANA*	*MLB*	*25*	*533*	*51*	*25*	*1*	*9*	*50*	*36*	*97*	*2*	*1*	*.246/.299/.353*	*.241*	*.284*	*-2.2*	*C 3*	*1.4*
2017	*ANA*	*MLB*	*26*	*499*	*52*	*24*	*1*	*8*	*47*	*34*	*92*	*2*	*0*	*.244/.297/.353*	*.240*	*.283*	*-2.2*	*C 2*	*0.9*

Breakout: 6% Improve: 21% Collapse: 7% Attrition: 35% MLB: 64% *Comparables: Curtis Thigpen, Jonathan Lucroy, Austin Romine*

YEAR	TEAM	P. COUNT	FRM RUNS	BLK RUNS	THRW RUNS	TOT RUNS
2013	OKL	10240	6.3	-2.6	4.8	8.6
2014	OKL	9874	8.4	0.0	-0.6	7.8
2015	ANA	10676	-0.6	-0.1	0.6	0.0
2015	SLC	2392	2.1	0.0	0.0	2.2
2016	*ANA*	*20058*	*1.7*	*-1.1*	*1.2*	*1.8*
2017	*ANA*	*18791*	*0.5*	*-1.0*	*1.1*	*0.5*

Perez hit about as well as could be expected from a 24-year-old who had slashed .275/.336/.388 in 180 games at the Triple-A level, and he even managed a walk-off homer in his debut, but more importantly he held his own behind the dish in his first handling of a big-league pitching staff. Perez threw out 25 of 66 attempted basestealers (38 percent), the fifth-most collars in the American League, and he earned slightly above-average marks in the framing metrics during his rookie year. Offense is the least concern at this stage of development, and backstops are often late to develop at the plate, but Perez has a career as a backup catcher even if the bat never comes around.

Albert Pujols 1B

Born: 1/16/80 Age: 36 Bats: R Throws: R Height: 6'3" Weight: 230

YEAR	TEAM	LVL	AGE	PA	R	2B	3B	HR	RBI	BB	K	SB	CS	AVG/OBP/SLG	TAv	BABIP	BRR	FRAA	WARP
2013	ANA	MLB	33	443	49	19	0	17	64	40	55	1	1	.258/.330/.437	.285	.258	1.7	1B(34): 3.3	2.2
2014	ANA	MLB	34	695	89	37	1	28	105	48	71	5	1	.272/.324/.466	.295	.265	-2.1	1B(116): -1.6, 3B(1): 0.0	2.8
2015	ANA	MLB	35	661	85	22	0	40	95	50	72	5	3	.244/.307/.480	.279	.217	-1.0	1B(95): 6.2, 3B(1): -0.0	2.6
2016	*ANA*	*MLB*	*36*	*495*	*62*	*23*	*0*	*23*	*72*	*38*	*60*	*4*	*1*	*.262/.323/.470*	*.283*	*.256*	*-0.3*	*1B 0*	*2.1*
2017	*ANA*	*MLB*	*37*	*467*	*61*	*21*	*0*	*20*	*64*	*30*	*57*	*2*	*1*	*.255/.307/.448*	*.271*	*.250*	*-0.4*	*1B 0*	*1.5*

Breakout: 1% Improve: 21% Collapse: 9% Attrition: 5% MLB: 86% *Comparables: Vladimir Guerrero, Victor Martinez, Hideki Matsui*

Pujols possesses some of the key ingredients for a low BABIP, from his pedestrian foot speed to his glaring flyball tendencies, but that fails to explain a .217 mark that qualified as the lowest BABIP in baseball by 18 points. The only way past the defense was to hit it over the wall, which he did with the greatest frequency we've seen since his Cardinals days. The fact that Pujols crushes high fastballs is on page one of the scouting handbook, and he'll pull the trigger regardless of count, a combination that led to 28 percent of the pitches against him missing low and away. His devolution to such a simplified approach is a disappointing development from a player who, in his prime, epitomized the value of pitch recognition and reaction time.

Andrelton Simmons SS

Born: 9/4/89 Age: 26 Bats: R Throws: R Height: 6'2" Weight: 195

YEAR	TEAM	LVL	AGE	PA	R	2B	3B	HR	RBI	BB	K	SB	CS	AVG/OBP/SLG	TAv	BABIP	BRR	FRAA	WARP
2013	ATL	MLB	23	658	76	27	6	17	59	40	55	6	5	.248/.296/.396	.257	.247	-1.0	SS(156): 27.3	5.4
2014	ATL	MLB	24	576	44	18	4	7	46	32	60	4	5	.244/.286/.331	.230	.263	3.6	SS(146): 10.3	2.2
2015	ATL	MLB	25	583	60	23	2	4	44	39	48	5	3	.265/.321/.338	.248	.285	0.7	SS(147): 10.5	2.9
2016	*ANA*	*MLB*	*26*	*568*	*58*	*23*	*3*	*12*	*57*	*34*	*54*	*5*	*3*	*.258/.307/.381*	*.252*	*.266*	*1.1*	*SS 12*	*3.8*
2017	*ANA*	*MLB*	*27*	*546*	*61*	*22*	*3*	*12*	*58*	*34*	*55*	*5*	*3*	*.259/.307/.387*	*.255*	*.267*	*1.2*	*SS 12*	*3.5*

Breakout: 2% Improve: 46% Collapse: 6% Attrition: 14% MLB: 98% *Comparables: Elvis Andrus, Yunel Escobar, Melky Cabrera*

The world knows what Simmons can do with the glove. If life exists on other planets, they probably know what Simmons can do with the glove, too. (Come to think of it, are we *sure* he's from here?) He's consistently rated as the best defensive shortstop in baseball, and 2015 was no exception. On the other side, he had a different type of season at the plate for the third consecutive year, this time for the better. That may sound odd, considering his power went to nothing, but new Braves hitting coach Kevin Seitzer's focus on cutting down swings and making more contact greatly impacted Simmons. He toned down his ferocious cuts, stayed more balanced, worked the other way with a higher line-drive rate and put the ball in play more often. If he can maintain consistently solid contact and avoid popups, he'll hit enough to be above average overall; if he can do that while adding a little bit of strength, he'll be an All Star–caliber player, by WARP even if not by the fan vote. Whether Dave Hansen and Paul Sorrento, the Angels' hitting coaches, reverse or reinforce those changes, and whether they do so for the better or the worse, remains to be seen.

Geovany Soto C

Born: 1/20/83 Age: 33 Bats: R Throws: R Height: 6'1" Weight: 235

YEAR	TEAM	LVL	AGE	PA	R	2B	3B	HR	RBI	BB	K	SB	CS	AVG/OBP/SLG	TAv	BABIP	BRR	FRAA	WARP
2013	TEX	MLB	30	184	20	9	0	9	22	20	60	1	2	.245/.328/.466	.289	.330	-3.3	C(53): 1.9, 3B(1): -0.0	1.3
2014	TEX	MLB	31	38	5	2	0	1	3	0	11	0	0	.237/.237/.368	.212	.308	-0.6	C(10): -0.3	-0.1
2014	FRI	AA	31	22	4	2	0	0	1	3	6	0	0	.368/.455/.474	.343	.538	-0.8	C(4): 0.1	0.2
2014	ROU	AAA	31	33	2	2	0	1	2	1	10	0	0	.188/.212/.344	.175	.238	0.0	C(7): 0.5	-0.2
2014	OAK	MLB	31	49	3	4	0	0	8	6	8	0	0	.262/.354/.357	.249	.324	-0.2	C(14): -1.3	0.0
2015	CHA	MLB	32	210	20	8	0	9	21	21	63	0	1	.219/.301/.406	.255	.278	-0.4	C(73): -2.4	0.5
2016	*ANA*	*MLB*	*33*	*59*	*6*	*2*	*0*	*2*	*7*	*5*	*16*	*0*	*0*	*.216/.289/.373*	*.244*	*.269*	*-0.3*	*C -0*	*0.1*
2017	*ANA*	*MLB*	*34*	*86*	*10*	*3*	*0*	*3*	*10*	*7*	*24*	*0*	*0*	*.214/.286/.362*	*.241*	*.266*	*-0.4*	*C 0*	*0.1*

Breakout: 5% Improve: 28% Collapse: 7% Attrition: 18% MLB: 90% *Comparables: John Buck, Ramon Castro, David Ross*

There are those who will never forgive Soto for not growing into a star. What he is, though, is a very valuable role player, not quite a regular but an overqualified backup. He's an average framer, he draws some walks and he can blast a mistake pitch with the best of them (though well-executed pitches give him fits). He's not a liability in the running game, either. Which is weird, because here's the thing: Soto can just barely throw the ball back to the pitcher. After receiving a pitch, he drops to his knees (one at a time), then catapults the ball to the mound as he half-falls forward onto home plate. He then brushes the dirt away from the dish in a lame covering maneuver, but... something is going on there. It probably doesn't count as the yips, because it has no detrimental effect to his team, but it's fascinating. Fascinating!

YEAR	TEAM	P. COUNT	FRM RUNS	BLK RUNS	THRW RUNS	TOT RUNS
2013	TEX	7078	0.8	0.1	0.1	1.0
2014	ROU	713	0.5	0.0	0.1	0.6
2014	TEX	1524	-0.2	-0.1	0.0	-0.3
2014	OAK	1700	-1.8	0.0	0.5	-1.3
2015	CHA	7902	-0.8	-0.1	-0.3	-1.2
2016	*ANA*	*2264*	*-0.3*	*0.0*	*0.0*	*-0.3*
2017	*ANA*	*3297*	*-0.6*	*0.0*	*0.0*	*-0.7*

Mike Trout CF

Born: 8/7/91 Age: 24 Bats: R Throws: R Height: 6'2" Weight: 235

YEAR	TEAM	LVL	AGE	PA	R	2B	3B	HR	RBI	BB	K	SB	CS	AVG/OBP/SLG	TAv	BABIP	BRR	FRAA	WARP
2013	ANA	MLB	21	716	109	39	9	27	97	110	136	33	7	.323/.432/.557	.367	.376	1.7	CF(111): -3.2, LF(47): 1.5	10.0
2014	ANA	MLB	22	705	115	39	9	36	111	83	184	16	2	.287/.377/.561	.352	.349	4.7	CF(149): -1.7	9.2
2015	ANA	MLB	23	682	104	32	6	41	90	92	158	11	7	.299/.402/.590	.353	.344	1.6	CF(156): 9.8	10.0
2016	*ANA*	*MLB*	*24*	*650*	*107*	*31*	*7*	*30*	*93*	*79*	*147*	*19*	*5*	*.299/.390/.546*	*.331*	*.350*	*1.9*	*CF 3*	*7.9*
2017	*ANA*	*MLB*	*25*	*584*	*91*	*27*	*6*	*28*	*94*	*75*	*126*	*17*	*5*	*.299/.395/.551*	*.336*	*.343*	*2.3*	*CF 3*	*6.9*

Breakout: 4% Improve: 58% Collapse: 5% Attrition: 8% MLB: 95% *Comparables: Giancarlo Stanton, Yasiel Puig, Frank Thomas*

This Angelfish is an ostentatious example of the breed, showing off its brilliance with theatrics in the field and at the plate. Trout's game continues to morph as he ages, with 2015 representing a new platform of power that led to career highs in slugging percentage and ISO. He epitomized the take-and-rake approach, seeing an AL-high 4.4 pitches per plate appearance and swinging at just 38 percent of the pitches he saw. Bringing the tool kit full circle, FRAA rated Trout's defense in 2015 as the best of his career, built on the second-most outfield putouts in the game (with a tip of the cap to the flyball-heavy staff in Anaheim).

Trout has been a perennial MVP candidate since his first full season, with a level of instant domination that hadn't been seen since... well, Albert Pujols, actually, so Trout has an ideal mentor hitting behind him in the lineup every day. His enthusiasm and intensity are infectious; his learning curve is off the chart; and he can't be defeated with conventional weapons. Pitchers are just going to have to get creative, and judging by Trout's utter domination of the likes of Yu Darvish and Felix Hernandez, whose unique repertoires have terrorized the rest of the league, creative ain't going to be enough.

Shane Victorino RF

Born: 11/30/80 Age: 35 Bats: R Throws: R Height: 5'9" Weight: 190

YEAR	TEAM	LVL	AGE	PA	R	2B	3B	HR	RBI	BB	K	SB	CS	AVG/OBP/SLG	TAv	BABIP	BRR	FRAA	WARP
2013	BOS	MLB	32	532	82	26	2	15	61	25	75	21	3	.294/.351/.451	.292	.321	-0.6	RF(110): 24.8, CF(15): 1.0	5.5
2014	PAW	AAA	33	29	3	1	0	0	0	0	6	0	0	.138/.138/.172	.113	.174	0.3	RF(9): -1.9	-0.6
2014	BOS	MLB	33	133	14	6	1	2	12	6	21	2	0	.268/.303/.382	.251	.304	-0.7	RF(30): -1.0	-0.1
2015	BOS	MLB	34	106	10	2	0	1	4	9	14	5	0	.245/.324/.298	.240	.278	1.4	RF(32): 2.8	0.4
2015	ANA	MLB	34	98	9	2	2	0	3	7	18	2	0	.214/.292/.286	.215	.265	-0.6	LF(29): 1.1, CF(3): -0.1	-0.2
2016	*ANA*	*MLB*	*35*	*250*	*32*	*10*	*2*	*5*	*23*	*17*	*35*	*9*	*1*	*.255/.317/.392*	*.257*	*.275*	*-0.2*	*RF 5, LF 0*	*1.2*
2017	*ANA*	*MLB*	*36*	*99*	*11*	*4*	*1*	*2*	*10*	*7*	*15*	*3*	*1*	*.246/.308/.371*	*.248*	*.269*	*-0.1*	*RF 2, LF 0*	*0.3*

Breakout: 1% Improve: 28% Collapse: 7% Attrition: 14% MLB: 77% *Comparables: Tony Gwynn, Randy Winn, Gabe Kapler*

If 2014 was a stumble, then 2015 was a crash and burn for Victorino. He's now had two and a half seasons of practice hitting exclusively from the right side, but the extra reps against same-side pitchers didn't help: He produced a paltry .211/.269/.225 line in 80 plate appearances against them last year. He battled injuries and suffered a power outage in Boston, and a subsequent relocation to Anaheim did little to heal his offensive woes, as he was merely next in line in a bucket brigade full of empty pails. The former triple threat has endured a precipitous decline in which his skills have rapidly deteriorated. He hasn't been caught stealing in two years, which is superficially neat until you remember he hasn't been on base enough to be caught.

Taylor Ward C

Born: 12/14/93 Age: 22 Bats: R Throws: R Height: 6'1" Weight: 190

YEAR	TEAM	LVL	AGE	PA	R	2B	3B	HR	RBI	BB	K	SB	CS	AVG/OBP/SLG	TAv	BABIP	BRR	FRAA	WARP
2016	*ANA*	*MLB*	*22*	*250*	*22*	*9*	*1*	*4*	*22*	*20*	*60*	*0*	*0*	*.219/.285/.317*	*.223*	*.275*	*-0.4*	*C -0*	*0.1*
2017	*ANA*	*MLB*	*23*	*270*	*29*	*9*	*1*	*5*	*25*	*23*	*63*	*0*	*0*	*.223/.295/.329*	*.232*	*.276*	*-0.6*	*C 0*	*0.2*

Breakout: 8% Improve: 10% Collapse: 4% Attrition: 13% MLB: 15% *Comparables: Bryan Anderson, Carlos Perez, Carlos Santana*

YEAR	TEAM	P. COUNT	FRM RUNS	BLK RUNS	THRW RUNS	TOT RUNS
2016	*ANA*	*8825*	*0.0*	*0.0*	*0.0*	*0.0*

Sure, the 2015 draft was bereft of the high-octane talent previous drafts have yielded, but we're not talking about the level of hopelessness and shortage of skill signified by 50 Cent, world's no. 1 rapper, or Marcelo Rios, world's no. 1 tennis player. Ward is symbolic of the type of talent that was available in the second through fifth rounds last year. He has catch-and-throw skills and enough bat to start if it all comes together, but let's be honest: It probably won't.

PITCHERS

Victor Alcantara RHP

Born: 4/3/93 Age: 23 Bats: R Throws: R Height: 6'2" Weight: 190

YEAR	TEAM	LVL	AGE	W	L	SV	G	GS	IP	H	HR	BB/9	K/9	GB%	BABIP	WHIP	ERA	FIP	DRA	WARP	CFIP	MPH
2014	BUR	A	21	7	6	1	27	20	125^{1}	98	6	4.3	8.4	58%	.277	1.26	3.81	3.77	4.53	0.8	102	
2015	INL	A+	22	7	12	0	27	27	136	152	10	3.8	8.3	52%	.345	1.54	5.62	4.37	5.65	0.1	108	
2016	*ANA*	*MLB*	*23*	*6*	*9*	*0*	*23*	*23*	*114*	*123*	*18*	*4.4*	*6.8*	*48%*	*.299*	*1.57*	*5.38*	*5.40*	*5.69*	*-0.8*	*137*	
2017	*ANA*	*MLB*	*24*	*4*	*6*	*0*	*14*	*14*	*84^{2}*	*93*	*14*	*5.0*	*7.2*	*48%*	*.307*	*1.65*	*5.51*	*5.54*	*5.83*	*-0.6*	*140*	

Breakout: 0% Improve: 0% Collapse: 0% Attrition: 0% MLB: 0% *Comparables: Luke Jackson, Fernando Nieve, Edgar Olmos*

Twista is known as the fastest rapper alive (he's not actually, but he did hold the Guiness World Record for a while, so close enough); he has to write twice as many bars as a normal rapper because his flow is so overwhelming that a normal-sized portion of lyrics would leave him with song lengths more befitting the latest Puig Destroyer record. He's also never caught on in the mainstream because speed isn't everything. That's a lesson Alcantara is still trying to learn. The still-young-but-not-that-young Alcantara can put up triple digits and make all the scouts go "oh oh oh oh oh..." with his fastball, but he still lacks command and secondary offerings. It's probably too much to ask Alcantara to fill a starting role but hey, Twista was pretty good dropping in on "Slow Jamz," so a relief role is not the end of the world.

Jose Alvarez LHP

Born: 5/6/89 Age: 27 Bats: L Throws: L Height: 5'11" Weight: 180

YEAR	TEAM	LVL	AGE	W	L	SV	G	GS	IP	H	HR	BB/9	K/9	GB%	BABIP	WHIP	ERA	FIP	DRA	WARP	CFIP	MPH
2013	TOL	AAA	24	8	6	1	21	20	128^{2}	114	11	1.7	8.0	47%	.283	1.08	2.80	3.18	3.87	1.7	83	
2013	DET	MLB	24	1	5	0	14	6	38^{2}	42	7	3.7	7.2	42%	.302	1.50	5.82	5.22	4.78	0.0	108	92.1
2014	ANA	MLB	25	0	0	0	2	0	0^{2}	1	0	0.0	13.5	0%	.500	1.50	0.00	0.16	4.79	0.0	100	91.0
2014	SLC	AAA	25	0	2	0	6	6	30^{2}	35	8	4.4	5.0	55%	.276	1.63	6.75	7.84	6.24	-0.1	132	
2016	*ANA*	*MLB*	*27*	*2*	*1*	*0*	*47*	*0*	*50*	*48*	*6*	*2.6*	*7.2*	*49%*	*.287*	*1.25*	*4.10*	*4.22*	*4.42*	*0.2*	*101*	
2017	*ANA*	*MLB*	*28*	*4*	*4*	*0*	*26*	*11*	*81^{2}*	*82*	*10*	*3.0*	*7.3*	*49%*	*.295*	*1.34*	*4.29*	*4.29*	*4.62*	*0.4*	*106*	

Breakout: 19% Improve: 39% Collapse: 22% Attrition: 33% MLB: 74% *Comparables: Burke Badenhop, Joe Saunders, Phil Coke*

Successful pitchers who lack ideal size are more likely to exhibit strong pitching mechanics in order to overcome biological disadvantages. Alvarez exemplifies this tenet with an efficient delivery that helps the southpaw get the most out of his modest frame and low-90s velocity. With strong momentum that carves an efficient path to the plate and near-perfect posture, Alvarez releases the ball at greater depth than pitchers who tower over him in the locker room. The tactic allows him to disguise the arrows in his four-pitch quiver by shrinking the window opposing batters have in which to identify the incoming pitch.

Cam Bedrosian RHP

Born: 10/2/91 Age: 24 Bats: R Throws: R Height: 6'0" Weight: 230

YEAR	TEAM	LVL	AGE	W	L	SV	G	GS	IP	H	HR	BB/9	K/9	GB%	BABIP	WHIP	ERA	FIP	DRA	WARP	CFIP	MPH
2013	BUR	A	21	1	5	7	37	2	54^{1}	55	4	3.6	11.4	57%	.362	1.42	5.30	3.25	4.05	0.6	82	
2014	ARK	AA	22	1	0	15	30	0	32^{1}	10	1	2.8	15.9	57%	.196	0.62	1.11	0.92				
2014	ANA	MLB	22	0	1	0	17	0	19^{1}	23	2	5.6	9.3	43%	.356	1.81	6.52	4.30	6.43	-0.5	105	97.2
2015	ANA	MLB	23	1	0	0	34	0	33^{1}	40	3	5.1	9.2	45%	.378	1.77	5.40	4.12	5.76	-0.4	104	97.0
2015	SLC	AAA	23	1	1	3	24	0	35^{2}	32	0	3.5	10.6	54%	.348	1.29	2.78	2.51	2.78	1.0	75	
2016	*ANA*	*MLB*	*24*	*2*	*1*	*0*	*47*	*0*	*50*	*48*	*6*	*3.6*	*9.1*	*47%*	*.304*	*1.35*	*4.00*	*4.12*	*4.33*	*0.3*	*97*	
2017	*ANA*	*MLB*	*25*	*2*	*1*	*0*	*33*	*3*	*53^{2}*	*51*	*7*	*3.9*	*9.7*	*47%*	*.306*	*1.38*	*4.16*	*4.17*	*4.50*	*0.2*	*102*	

Breakout: 29% Improve: 41% Collapse: 9% Attrition: 26% MLB: 64% *Comparables: Stephen Pryor, Chris Ray, Hong-Chih Kuo*

Bedrosian was carved from the Garrett Richards mold of hard-throwing, over-the-top right-handers with 12-6 breaking balls, though by the time he reaches his release point it becomes clear that Cam did his undergrad work at the Steve Bedrosian School of Pitching. Batters picked up the breaking ball early in its flight path last season, teeing off on the pitch like they knew it was coming. This minimized the effectiveness of his 95 mph fastball. The lines between the concepts of command and control are often blurry, but it's a clear sign that command is in trouble when an over-the-top thrower walks five batters per nine.

Joe Gatto RHP

Born: 6/14/95 Age: 21 Bats: R Throws: R Height: 6'3" Weight: 204

YEAR	TEAM	LVL	AGE	W	L	SV	G	GS	IP	H	HR	BB/9	K/9	GB%	BABIP	WHIP	ERA	FIP	DRA	WARP	CFIP	MPH
2016	*ANA*	*MLB*	*21*	*1*	*3*	*0*	*11*	*7*	*34*	*44*	*6*	*5.6*	*3.5*	*41%*	*.307*	*1.91*	*6.69*	*6.80*	*7.27*	*-0.9*	*167*	
2017	*ANA*	*MLB*	*22*	*3*	*8*	*0*	*25*	*19*	*126^{2}*	*169*	*21*	*5.7*	*3.5*	*41%*	*.317*	*1.97*	*6.60*	*6.63*	*7.17*	*-2.1*	*165*	

Breakout: 0% Improve: 0% Collapse: 0% Attrition: 0% MLB: 0% *Comparables: Jairo Diaz, Esmil Rogers, Jared Hughes*

The current most famous Joe Gatto is a member of the comedy troupe The Tenderloins, a group so noteworthy that its Wikipedia page currently states, "Q is on Tell em steve dave podcast with bryan J from comic book men." (Sic, as they say, throughout.) This Joe Gatto was a three-sport athlete popped in the second round in 2014 who spent his age-20 season putting up bad numbers in Rookie ball. His curve is well ahead of his change, but his frame and projectability leave some room for hope that he can someday supplant the former star of "Impractical Jokers" at the top of the Google rankings.

Andrew Heaney LHP

Born: 6/5/91 Age: 25 Bats: L Throws: L Height: 6'2" Weight: 185

YEAR	TEAM	LVL	AGE	W	L	SV	G	GS	IP	H	HR	BB/9	K/9	GB%	BABIP	WHIP	ERA	FIP	DRA	WARP	CFIP	MPH
2013	JAX	AA	22	4	1	0	6	6	33^2	31	2	2.4	6.1	41%	.279	1.19	2.94	3.12	4.07	0.2	100	
2013	JUP	A+	22	5	2	0	13	12	61^2	45	2	2.5	9.6	49%	.257	1.01	0.88	2.64	3.72	0.8	81	
2014	NWO	AAA	23	5	4	0	15	15	83^2	75	9	2.5	9.8	45%	.296	1.17	3.87	3.89	4.71	1.0	79	
2014	JAX	AA	23	4	2	0	9	8	53^2	45	2	2.2	8.7	47%	.285	1.08	2.35	2.46				
2014	MIA	MLB	23	0	3	0	7	5	29^1	32	6	2.1	6.1	48%	.289	1.33	5.83	5.42	6.24	-0.5	111	93.8
2015	SLC	AAA	24	6	2	0	14	14	78^1	95	2	2.9	8.5	48%	.372	1.53	4.71	3.11	3.22	2.0	80	
2015	ANA	MLB	24	6	4	0	18	18	105^2	99	9	2.4	6.6	41%	.284	1.20	3.49	3.70	3.75	1.6	105	94.1
2016	*ANA*	*MLB*	*25*	*8*	*9*	*0*	*26*	*26*	137^2	*136*	*16*	*2.6*	*7.2*	*43%*	*.290*	*1.27*	*4.06*	*4.14*	*4.39*	*1.2*	*101*	
2017	*ANA*	*MLB*	*26*	*8*	*8*	*0*	*23*	*23*	*138*	*137*	*17*	*2.6*	*7.5*	*43%*	*.292*	*1.27*	*4.02*	*4.03*	*4.35*	*1.2*	*100*	

Breakout: 19% Improve: 45% Collapse: 22% Attrition: 18% MLB: 84% *Comparables: Travis Wood, Jake Odorizzi, Dan Straily*

Heaney has been precisely as advertised, an advanced arm who can slip right into the no. 3 spot in a major-league rotation. The ceiling might be limited, as his current strengths of mechanical stability and pitch command are reaching maximum effectiveness, while his power attributes are less likely to improve, but his high floor substantiates the optimism surrounding his future. The southpaw has a repertoire that will be theoretically difficult on right-handed bats, with an arsenal that includes a low-90s sinker and a changeup, but Heaney throws just about everything with natural cut, and fellow lefties were the ones who were effectively silenced last season, slashing just .228/.261/.307.

Jake Jewell RHP

Born: 5/16/93 Age: 23 Bats: R Throws: R Height: 6'3" Weight: 200

YEAR	TEAM	LVL	AGE	W	L	SV	G	GS	IP	H	HR	BB/9	K/9	GB%	BABIP	WHIP	ERA	FIP	DRA	WARP	CFIP	MPH
2015	BUR	A	22	6	8	2	31	15	111^1	110	8	2.5	8.9	53%	.325	1.27	4.77	3.51	3.51	1.7	92	
2016	*ANA*	*MLB*	*23*	*4*	*4*	*1*	*34*	*12*	*76*	*81*	*11*	*3.3*	*7.0*	*45%*	*.302*	*1.44*	*4.78*	*4.87*	*5.08*	*-0.1*	*120*	
2017	*ANA*	*MLB*	*24*	*4*	*5*	*1*	*30*	*15*	*125*	*135*	*18*	*3.5*	*7.0*	*45%*	*.305*	*1.47*	*4.76*	*4.78*	*5.06*	*-0.1*	*120*	

Breakout: 0% Improve: 0% Collapse: 0% Attrition: 0% MLB: 0% *Comparables: Dallas Braden, Hiram Burgos, Stephen Fife*

Jewell's frame and arsenal indicate a starter's future and, after a half-season in the bullpen in Burlington, the Angels indicated a starter's present, putting him in the rotation on June 18th and leaving him there the rest of the year, even as he posted a 4.99 ERA as a starter in a 4.2-runs-per-game league. Jewell was a project arm in the 2014 draft, with a big fastball and two breaking pitches that came and went. At 23 and having not exactly mastered Low-A, Jewell has a long way to go, but if he can avoid foolish games like the two-inning, seven-run disasterpiece on July 5th against Cedar Rapids, he may someday be an Angel standing by for a rotation spot.

Mat Latos RHP

Born: 12/9/87 Age: 28 Bats: R Throws: R Height: 6'6" Weight: 245

YEAR	TEAM	LVL	AGE	W	L	SV	G	GS	IP	H	HR	BB/9	K/9	GB%	BABIP	WHIP	ERA	FIP	DRA	WARP	CFIP	MPH
2013	CIN	MLB	25	14	7	0	32	32	210^2	197	14	2.5	8.0	47%	.299	1.21	3.16	3.08	3.74	3.0	90	96.0
2014	CIN	MLB	26	5	5	0	16	16	102^1	92	9	2.3	6.5	41%	.269	1.15	3.25	3.62	3.61	1.5	106	94.1
2014	LOU	AAA	26	2	0	0	4	4	19^1	17	1	3.3	6.1	43%	.281	1.24	2.33	3.77	4.60	0.1	104	
2015	LAN	MLB	27	0	3	0	6	5	24^1	31	3	2.2	6.7	52%	.354	1.52	6.66	4.02	5.27	-0.1	108	95.3
2015	MIA	MLB	27	4	7	0	16	16	88^1	85	8	2.5	8.0	45%	.297	1.25	4.48	3.43	3.90	1.2	98	94.8
2015	ANA	MLB	27	0	0	0	2	0	3^2	4	2	2.5	7.4	42%	.200	1.36	4.91	9.38	11.21	-0.3	137	96.2
2016	*ANA*	*MLB*	*28*	*10*	*10*	*0*	*30*	*30*	*165*	*159*	*19*	*2.6*	*7.3*	*45%*	*.286*	*1.25*	*4.04*	*4.09*	*4.39*	*1.4*	*99*	
2017	*ANA*	*MLB*	*29*	*11*	*11*	*0*	*30*	*30*	*187*	*196*	*23*	*2.8*	*6.7*	*45%*	*.298*	*1.36*	*4.28*	*4.30*	*4.65*	*1.0*	*106*	

Breakout: 18% Improve: 59% Collapse: 20% Attrition: 3% MLB: 93% *Comparables: John Danks, Jon Matlack, Bartolo Colon*

Alanis Morissette thinks it's ironic that Mat Latos finished 2015 with the Angels because he's developed a reputation as being... let's go with difficult to deal with. More like Brat Latos, if you will. It's tempting to roll with that narrative as an explanation for why he's already found himself a part of five different organizations, but, as always, performance is the true key. The big righty posted just north of two WARP in 2014 and 2015 combined, has become increasingly homer-prone despite leaving the Great American Ball Park and has dealt with myriad injuries. He's young enough and talented enough that he'll likely earn sixth and seventh and eighth chances, but he comes with more red flags than a Swiss slalom course. At least he's good at naming cats.

Mike Morin RHP

Born: 5/3/91 Age: 25 Bats: R Throws: R Height: 6'4" Weight: 220

YEAR	TEAM	LVL	AGE	W	L	SV	G	GS	IP	H	HR	BB/9	K/9	GB%	BABIP	WHIP	ERA	FIP	DRA	WARP	CFIP	MPH
2013	SBR	AFA	22	3	1	13	30	0	39	30	2	1.2	9.9	42%	.297	0.90	1.85	2.69				
2013	ARK	AA	22	0	2	10	26	0	31	26	2	1.5	9.6	51%	.296	1.00	2.03	2.44	3.58	0.4	77	
2014	ANA	MLB	23	4	4	0	60	0	59	51	3	2.9	8.2	48%	.287	1.19	2.90	3.11	3.40	0.8	94	94.7
2015	ANA	MLB	24	4	2	1	47	0	35^1	36	3	2.3	10.4	41%	.344	1.27	6.37	2.82	4.17	0.2	86	95.0
2015	SLC	AAA	24	4	2	1	14	0	17^1	25	3	3.1	9.9	39%	.415	1.79	6.23	5.04	4.54	0.1	93	
2016	*ANA*	*MLB*	*25*	*2*	*1*	*0*	*43*	*0*	*45*	*43*	*5*	*2.8*	*8.5*	*43%*	*.299*	*1.26*	*3.86*	*3.84*	*4.20*	*0.3*	*92*	
2017	*ANA*	*MLB*	*26*	*2*	*1*	*0*	*43*	*0*	46^1	*47*	*6*	*2.9*	*8.6*	*43%*	*.310*	*1.33*	*3.90*	*3.91*	*4.24*	*0.3*	*92*	

Breakout: 32% Improve: 52% Collapse: 16% Attrition: 27% MLB: 79% *Comparables: Kyle McClellan, Jerry Blevins, Bill Bray*

Morin has long thrown straight over the top, and last season he elevated his release point by about four inches, a factor that likely contributed to the elevation of his pitches as well: Morin doubled his frequency of pitches that finished in the upper third of the strike zone. His command was not nearly as strong as his 6 percent walk rate might indicate (see also: the high BABIP despite a good defense behind him), but the emphasis on verticality in his fastball helped Morin's changeup, as he buried it underneath the strike zone, making it his go-to pitch for strikeouts.

Cesar Ramos LHP

Born: 6/22/84 Age: 32 Bats: L Throws: L Height: 6'2" Weight: 200

YEAR	TEAM	LVL	AGE	W	L	SV	G	GS	IP	H	HR	BB/9	K/9	GB%	BABIP	WHIP	ERA	FIP	DRA	WARP	CFIP	MPH
2013	TBA	MLB	29	2	2	1	48	0	67^1	66	6	2.9	7.1	42%	.293	1.31	4.14	3.73	4.01	0.5	101	93.8
2014	TBA	MLB	30	2	6	0	43	7	82^2	73	8	4.2	7.2	46%	.265	1.35	3.70	4.27	4.00	0.6	109	92.4
2015	ANA	MLB	31	2	1	0	65	0	52^1	55	2	2.6	7.4	49%	.335	1.34	2.75	2.99	3.92	0.5	99	92.2
2016	*ANA*	*MLB*	*32*	*3*	*1*	*0*	*52*	*0*	*55*	*52*	*6*	*3.2*	*7.2*	*47%*	*.281*	*1.31*	*4.29*	*4.26*	*4.63*	*0.1*	*104*	
2017	*ANA*	*MLB*	*33*	*2*	*1*	*0*	*40*	*2*	*60*	*64*	*8*	*3.4*	*6.9*	*47%*	*.301*	*1.43*	*4.48*	*4.48*	*4.83*	*0.0*	*109*	

Breakout: 25% Improve: 42% Collapse: 32% Attrition: 19% MLB: 92% *Comparables: Geoff Geary, Brad Ziegler, Ramon Ramirez*

The curveball emerged as Ramos' most potent pitch last season, accounting for 28 of his strikeouts (versus just eight curves put into play all season). The southpaw kept the pitch hidden from view until he got two strikes on a batter, resulting in a usage rate of just 12 percent. The slow breaker comes in at 71 mph and never stood out of his repertoire prior to last season. The deadly curve was necessary because every other blade in his bag was dull.

Garrett Richards RHP

Born: 5/27/88 Age: 28 Bats: R Throws: R Height: 6'3" Weight: 210

YEAR	TEAM	LVL	AGE	W	L	SV	G	GS	IP	H	HR	BB/9	K/9	GB%	BABIP	WHIP	ERA	FIP	DRA	WARP	CFIP	MPH
2013	ANA	MLB	25	7	8	1	47	17	145	151	12	2.7	6.3	60%	.302	1.34	4.16	3.69	4.11	1.2	99	97.2
2014	ANA	MLB	26	13	4	0	26	26	168^2	124	5	2.7	8.8	52%	.264	1.04	2.61	2.63	2.53	4.7	86	98.8
2015	ANA	MLB	27	15	12	0	32	32	207^1	181	20	3.3	7.6	56%	.274	1.24	3.65	3.83	3.69	3.3	101	97.8
2016	*ANA*	*MLB*	*28*	*12*	*11*	*0*	*31*	*31*	195^1	*178*	*20*	*3.0*	*7.8*	*56%*	*.282*	*1.24*	*3.90*	*3.94*	*4.22*	*2.1*	*96*	
2017	*ANA*	*MLB*	*29*	*11*	*10*	*0*	*29*	*29*	*180*	*178*	*21*	*3.0*	*7.5*	*56%*	*.294*	*1.32*	*4.08*	*4.09*	*4.42*	*1.5*	*102*	

Breakout: 23% Improve: 58% Collapse: 22% Attrition: 8% MLB: 95% *Comparables: Brandon Webb, Justin Masterson, Johnny Cueto*

After defying traditional trends in 2014 by simultaneously adding velocity while transitioning to longer outings, Richards gave a bit of the bump back in 2015, though his average speed of 96 mph was still higher than it was during his years in relief. The big question surrounding his 2015 performance wasn't velocity, but how his surgically repaired knee would hold up to the rigors of pitching, and he responded by setting a career high in innings pitched. Richards had weak balance in his delivery prior to the injury and the knee woes didn't do his stability any favors. All of his ratios took a step backward, and he led the majors in wild pitches for the second consecutive season, but the scope of Richards' lack of command continued to be obscured by a decent walk rate, as his electric stuff can invoke swings regardless of whether he hits his target.

Fernando Salas RHP

Born: 5/30/85 Age: 31 Bats: R Throws: R Height: 6'2" Weight: 200

YEAR	TEAM	LVL	AGE	W	L	SV	G	GS	IP	H	HR	BB/9	K/9	GB%	BABIP	WHIP	ERA	FIP	DRA	WARP	CFIP	MPH
2013	MEM	AAA	28	1	2	12	22	0	23^2	15	1	1.9	8.0	36%	.222	0.85	1.90	3.10	4.60	0.2	89	
2013	SLN	MLB	28	0	3	0	27	0	28	27	3	1.9	7.1	34%	.279	1.18	4.50	3.59	4.67	0.0	102	92.7
2014	ANA	MLB	29	5	0	0	57	0	58^2	50	5	2.1	9.4	32%	.285	1.09	3.38	2.96	3.29	0.9	86	93.9
2015	ANA	MLB	30	5	2	0	72	0	63^2	61	8	1.7	10.5	38%	.308	1.15	4.24	3.12	4.40	0.2	77	93.6
2016	*ANA*	*MLB*	*31*	*3*	*1*	*0*	*52*	*0*	*55*	*48*	*7*	*2.4*	*9.0*	*36%*	*.279*	*1.14*	*3.66*	*3.82*	*4.00*	*0.5*	*85*	
2017	*ANA*	*MLB*	*32*	*3*	*1*	*0*	*56*	*0*	53^2	*49*	*7*	*2.5*	*9.1*	*36%*	*.290*	*1.20*	*3.71*	*3.72*	*4.05*	*0.4*	*87*	

Breakout: 28% Improve: 53% Collapse: 22% Attrition: 14% MLB: 94% *Comparables: Jerry Blevins, Dan Wheeler, Al Holland*

Something went wrong with Salas' sabermetric chemistry set last season, as he set personal bests in walk and strikeout rates, only to post another ERA in the mid-4.00s. The career high in homers certainly didn't help his case, but Salas' traditional numbers only seem to suffer as his advanced stats continue to improve. He's no Dave Borkowski (career ERA 1.03 higher than his FIP) or Jim Walkup (1.13), to say nothing of Hal Elliot (1.69), in part because in Salas' first two seasons, his ERA beat his FIP by not-insubstantial amounts. Still, a couple more years like he's gone and Salas could start challenging the career marks of Boof Bonser or Jesse Winters.

Hector Santiago LHP

Born: 12/16/87 Age: 28 Bats: R Throws: L Height: 6'0" Weight: 215

YEAR	TEAM	LVL	AGE	W	L	SV	G	GS	IP	H	HR	BB/9	K/9	GB%	BABIP	WHIP	ERA	FIP	DRA	WARP	CFIP	MPH
2013	CHA	MLB	25	4	9	0	34	23	149	137	17	4.3	8.3	39%	.289	1.40	3.56	4.47	4.28	1.1	107	95.5
2014	ANA	MLB	26	6	9	0	30	24	127^1	120	15	3.7	7.6	32%	.288	1.36	3.75	4.31	4.76	0.0	111	94.6
2014	SLC	AAA	26	1	1	0	3	3	14	23	0	4.5	5.8	48%	.426	2.14	6.43	4.13	5.76	0.0	111	
2015	ANA	MLB	27	9	9	0	33	32	180^2	156	29	3.5	8.1	31%	.252	1.26	3.59	4.74	4.67	0.7	107	93.8
2016	*ANA*	*MLB*	*28*	*8*	*9*	*0*	*26*	*26*	148^1	*136*	*21*	*3.3*	*8.1*	*32%*	*.276*	*1.28*	*4.46*	*4.54*	*4.80*	*0.6*	*112*	
2017	*ANA*	*MLB*	*29*	*7*	*7*	*0*	*32*	*19*	*132*	*123*	*18*	*3.4*	*8.3*	*32%*	*.283*	*1.31*	*4.36*	*4.38*	*4.69*	*0.5*	*109*	

Breakout: 16% Improve: 53% Collapse: 20% Attrition: 9% MLB: 89% *Comparables: Wade Davis, Juan Cruz, Byung-Hyun Kim*

Santiago conjured a convincing mirage of run prevention for the first few months of the season, coaxing his first-ever All-Star appearance in the process, but the sheep emerged from wolf's clothing in the second half. Comparing the two sides of the break, Santiago pitched 37 additional innings in the first half, but he gave up 20 more runs, 11 more extra-base hits and three more walks in the shorter second half. When all was said and done, his walk and homer rates were second-highest in the American League, while a .252 BABIP helped the southpaw's ERA best his FIP by more than half a run for the fourth consecutive season.

Matt Shoemaker RHP

Born: 9/27/86 Age: 29 Bats: R Throws: R Height: 6'2" Weight: 225

YEAR	TEAM	LVL	AGE	W	L	SV	G	GS	IP	H	HR	BB/9	K/9	GB%	BABIP	WHIP	ERA	FIP	DRA	WARP	CFIP	MPH
2013	SLC	AAA	26	11	13	0	29	29	184^1	212	27	1.4	7.8	44%	.332	1.31	4.64	4.34	4.54	2.2	85	
2013	ANA	MLB	26	0	0	0	1	1	5	2	0	3.6	9.0	42%	.167	0.80	0.00	2.28	2.94	0.1	100	94.5
2014	SLC	AAA	27	1	0	0	5	5	25^2	34	2	3.2	9.1	47%	.421	1.68	6.31	3.97	4.96	0.2	86	
2014	ANA	MLB	27	16	4	0	27	20	136	122	14	1.6	8.2	43%	.286	1.07	3.04	3.29	3.89	1.4	89	93.7
2015	ANA	MLB	28	7	10	0	25	24	135^1	135	24	2.3	7.7	42%	.285	1.26	4.46	4.56	4.79	0.4	102	93.5
2016	*ANA*	*MLB*	*29*	*4*	*4*	*0*	*11*	*11*	*62^2*	*61*	*9*	*2.2*	*7.8*	*42%*	*.288*	*1.22*	*4.10*	*4.20*	*4.43*	*0.5*	*102*	
2017	*ANA*	*MLB*	*30*	*5*	*5*	*0*	*13*	*13*	*77^1*	*81*	*13*	*2.4*	*7.7*	*42%*	*.298*	*1.31*	*4.41*	*4.43*	*4.77*	*0.3*	*111*	

Breakout: 15% Improve: 39% Collapse: 15% Attrition: 17% MLB: 68% *Comparables: Yusmeiro Petit, Guillermo Moscoso, Scott Richmond*

It didn't take long for the cobbler to fashion another shoe, and the sound when it dropped was deafening. Following his eye-popping opening salvo of 2014, Shoemaker experienced the regression that everyone saw coming: All of his rate stats cratered and he began offering up home runs like hot-tub coupons at a housing expo. The splitter was Shoemaker's most effective pitch in his rookie season, finishing off more than half of his strikeouts and inducing grounders even when batters did make contact, but it fell apart last season. He coughed up nine dongers on the pitch and hitters enjoyed an ISO of .231 against it, turning his most potent (or maybe only) weapon into kryptonite.

Tyler Skaggs LHP

Born: 7/13/91 Age: 24 Bats: L Throws: L Height: 6'4" Weight: 215

YEAR	TEAM	LVL	AGE	W	L	SV	G	GS	IP	H	HR	BB/9	K/9	GB%	BABIP	WHIP	ERA	FIP	DRA	WARP	CFIP	MPH
2013	RNO	AAA	21	6	10	0	19	17	104	114	5	3.4	9.3	45%	.353	1.47	4.59	3.44	4.52	1.2	84	
2013	ARI	MLB	21	2	3	0	7	7	38^2	38	7	3.5	8.4	45%	.282	1.37	5.12	4.83	4.24	0.3	101	91.9
2014	ANA	MLB	22	5	5	0	18	18	113	107	9	2.4	6.8	51%	.293	1.21	4.30	3.58	3.91	1.2	102	94.6
2016	*ANA*	*MLB*	*24*	*3*	*3*	*0*	*10*	*10*	*53*	*52*	*6*	*2.7*	*7.5*	*48%*	*.289*	*1.27*	*4.12*	*4.07*	*4.45*	*0.4*	*102*	
2017	*ANA*	*MLB*	*25*	*7*	*7*	*0*	*21*	*21*	*121^1*	*123*	*14*	*2.7*	*7.8*	*48%*	*.305*	*1.32*	*3.92*	*3.93*	*4.23*	*1.2*	*96*	

Breakout: 15% Improve: 44% Collapse: 18% Attrition: 22% MLB: 83% *Comparables: Dallas Braden, Jaime Garcia, Justin Masterson*

Once the proud owner of the one of the game's ugliest deliveries, including what might have been the shallowest release point in the game, Skaggs made substantial progress honing his mechanics while dealing with the differing demands of the coaching staffs of the Diamondbacks and Angels. He was enjoying a career-best season at the highest level when his UCL blew a gasket in August 2014. The late-summer timing means that he will have 20 months of rehabilitation between pitches in the major leagues.

Joe Smith RHP

Born: 3/22/84 Age: 32 Bats: R Throws: R Height: 6'2" Weight: 205

YEAR	TEAM	LVL	AGE	W	L	SV	G	GS	IP	H	HR	BB/9	K/9	GB%	BABIP	WHIP	ERA	FIP	DRA	WARP	CFIP	MPH
2013	CLE	MLB	29	6	2	3	70	0	63	54	5	3.3	7.7	52%	.282	1.22	2.29	3.63	3.41	0.9	99	92.1
2014	ANA	MLB	30	7	2	15	76	0	74^2	45	4	1.8	8.2	61%	.214	0.80	1.81	2.88	2.12	2.2	85	91.2
2015	ANA	MLB	31	5	5	5	70	0	65^1	64	4	2.6	7.9	54%	.317	1.27	3.58	3.12	4.39	0.2	95	90.8
2016	*ANA*	*MLB*	*32*	*3*	*1*	*3*	*61*	*0*	*65*	*57*	*7*	*2.6*	*7.8*	*56%*	*.273*	*1.16*	*3.86*	*3.90*	*4.19*	*0.4*	*93*	
2017	*ANA*	*MLB*	*33*	*3*	*1*	*5*	*67*	*0*	*62^1*	*59*	*7*	*2.8*	*7.1*	*56%*	*.282*	*1.26*	*4.14*	*4.14*	*4.49*	*0.2*	*101*	

Breakout: 16% Improve: 43% Collapse: 26% Attrition: 9% MLB: 94% *Comparables: Chad Bradford, Jim Mecir, Hoyt Wilhelm*

You're forgiven if Smith slipped under your radar when perusing the stat sheet, but if you've ever seen him pitch then an image of the sidewinding right-hander is likely etched into memory. Despite the five-cent name and seven-cent stuff, Smith has quietly performed the same diligent duty for the last five seasons, keeping hitters off balance with his style rather than his substance. He keeps the homers down and the walks in line, and he's good for an automatic 70 appearances per year, bringing uncommon stability to a volatile role. This adds up to the rare reliever worthy of a multi-year commitment even when you've got no intention of using him as a closer.

Nate Smith LHP

Born: 8/28/91 Age: 24 Bats: L Throws: L Height: 6'3" Weight: 205

YEAR	TEAM	LVL	AGE	W	L	SV	G	GS	IP	H	HR	BB/9	K/9	GB%	BABIP	WHIP	ERA	FIP	DRA	WARP	CFIP	MPH
2014	INL	A+	22	6	3	0	10	10	55^2	41	3	2.3	8.2	0%	.250	0.99	3.07	3.36				
2014	ARK	AA	22	5	3	0	11	11	62^1	48	3	4.3	9.7	34%	.290	1.25	2.89	3.04				
2015	SLC	AAA	23	2	4	0	7	7	36	48	7	3.8	5.8	42%	.320	1.75	7.75	6.10	6.57	-0.4	114	
2015	ARK	AA	23	8	4	0	17	17	101^2	82	10	2.5	7.2	44%	.247	1.08	2.48	3.90	3.88	1.5	93	
2016	*ANA*	*MLB*	*24*	*6*	*8*	*0*	*21*	*21*	*105*	*106*	*16*	*3.2*	*6.7*	*36%*	*.283*	*1.36*	*4.81*	*4.91*	*5.16*	*-0.1*	*123*	
2017	*ANA*	*MLB*	*25*	*5*	*7*	*0*	*20*	*20*	*116*	*129*	*19*	*3.7*	*6.9*	*36%*	*.304*	*1.52*	*5.10*	*5.12*	*5.47*	*-0.4*	*130*	

Breakout: 9% Improve: 20% Collapse: 13% Attrition: 36% MLB: 44% *Comparables: Anthony Ranaudo, Eric Jokisch, David Rollins*

Around BP's newsroom, Smith is known as "Anonynate" for his generic profile: low-90s fastball, above-average change, middling bendy stuff, only avoids "crafty lefty" on his scouting reports because clichés have fallen out of favor. Some wags insisted on calling him "John" to really hammer the point home until those wags started getting fired. The Angels may tolerate generic prospect profiles, but BP doesn't.

Huston Street RHP

Born: 8/2/83 Age: 32 Bats: R Throws: R Height: 6'0" Weight: 195

YEAR	TEAM	LVL	AGE	W	L	SV	G	GS	IP	H	HR	BB/9	K/9	GB%	BABIP	WHIP	ERA	FIP	DRA	WARP	CFIP	MPH
2013	SDN	MLB	29	2	5	33	58	0	56^2	44	12	2.2	7.3	32%	.213	1.02	2.70	4.89	3.99	0.4	99	92.1
2014	ANA	MLB	30	1	2	17	28	0	26^1	24	1	2.4	7.9	33%	.299	1.18	1.71	2.70	2.40	0.7	84	92.1
2014	SDN	MLB	30	1	0	24	33	0	33	18	3	1.9	9.3	42%	.195	0.76	1.09	2.86	2.39	0.8	85	91.7
2015	ANA	MLB	31	3	3	40	62	0	62^1	52	7	2.9	8.2	36%	.263	1.16	3.18	3.70	3.68	0.8	97	91.6
2016	*ANA*	*MLB*	*32*	*3*	*1*	*33*	*57*	*0*	*60*	*52*	*8*	*2.6*	*7.8*	*36%*	*.267*	*1.16*	*4.06*	*4.19*	*4.41*	*0.2*	*100*	
2017	*ANA*	*MLB*	*33*	*3*	*1*	*39*	*58*	*0*	*56^2*	*52*	*8*	*2.8*	*7.4*	*36%*	*.272*	*1.24*	*4.39*	*4.41*	*4.77*	*0.0*	*111*	

Breakout: 25% Improve: 40% Collapse: 36% Attrition: 3% MLB: 94% *Comparables: Scott Linebrink, Cliff Politte, Rick Aguilera*

Street was born a closer. He climbed to no. 20 on the all-time saves list last season, sitting at 315 by season's end, as his electric slide continued to mesmerize opposing batters. He has retained velocity reasonably well as he ages, though missing behind the bat was never Street's game in the first place. Right-handed batters received heavy doses of the slider, a pitch that was nearly automatic with two strikes (95 percent frequency) yet still coaxed a whiff on 35 percent of swings.

Nick Tropeano RHP

Born: 8/27/90 Age: 25 Bats: R Throws: R Height: 6'4" Weight: 200

YEAR	TEAM	LVL	AGE	W	L	SV	G	GS	IP	H	HR	BB/9	K/9	GB%	BABIP	WHIP	ERA	FIP	DRA	WARP	CFIP	MPH
2013	CCH	AA	22	7	10	5	28	20	133^2	140	15	2.6	8.8	45%	.333	1.34	4.11	3.51	3.96	1.5	89	
2014	HOU	MLB	23	1	3	0	4	4	21^2	19	0	3.7	5.4	43%	.279	1.29	4.57	3.34	3.07	0.5	111	92.7
2014	OKL	AAA	23	9	5	0	23	20	124^2	90	11	2.4	8.7	40%	.248	0.99	3.03	3.81	4.73	1.4	79	
2015	ANA	MLB	24	3	2	0	8	7	37^2	40	2	2.4	9.1	42%	.342	1.33	3.82	2.57	4.45	0.3	91	93.4
2015	SLC	AAA	24	3	6	0	16	16	88	97	9	3.7	9.8	42%	.353	1.51	4.81	4.08	3.89	1.6	87	
2016	*ANA*	*MLB*	*25*	*2*	*1*	*0*	*22*	*3*	*37*	*35*	*4*	*2.9*	*8.4*	*40%*	*.292*	*1.25*	*3.96*	*3.86*	*4.29*	*0.2*	*98*	
2017	*ANA*	*MLB*	*26*	*4*	*4*	*0*	*11*	*11*	*64^1*	*61*	*9*	*3.1*	*8.8*	*40%*	*.296*	*1.29*	*4.04*	*4.06*	*4.38*	*0.5*	*100*	

Breakout: 21% Improve: 41% Collapse: 21% Attrition: 32% MLB: 74% *Comparables: Scott Barnes, A.J. Griffin, J.J. Hoover*

With such a powerful delivery, one might expect Tropeano to channel the Ricky Vaughn cliché and unleash 100 mph bullets with no idea where the ball is going, but the right-hander's velocity stays parked in the low 90s and he flirts with solid command. He also mirrors the high elbows of Chris Sale and struggles with balance during his stride. There's a lot of flail in Tropeano's delivery, but his lack of limb control after release point is a poor indicator given that he stays reasonably on line to the target. Tropeano will travel as far as his secondary pitches will carry him, but the changeup and the slider both need refinement before he can prevent opposing batters from sitting on heat.

Jered Weaver RHP

Born: 10/4/82 Age: 33 Bats: R Throws: R Height: 6'7" Weight: 210

YEAR	TEAM	LVL	AGE	W	L	SV	G	GS	IP	H	HR	BB/9	K/9	GB%	BABIP	WHIP	ERA	FIP	DRA	WARP	CFIP	MPH
2013	ANA	MLB	30	11	8	0	24	24	154^1	139	17	2.2	6.8	32%	.268	1.14	3.27	3.85	3.48	2.7	98	90.0
2014	ANA	MLB	31	18	9	0	34	34	213^1	193	27	2.7	7.1	35%	.267	1.21	3.59	4.22	3.92	2.3	108	89.7
2015	ANA	MLB	32	7	12	0	26	26	159	163	24	1.9	5.1	37%	.273	1.23	4.64	4.78	4.81	0.4	119	87.2
2016	*ANA*	*MLB*	*33*	*10*	*11*	*0*	*29*	*29*	*174*	*163*	*24*	*2.2*	*6.1*	*36%*	*.261*	*1.19*	*4.53*	*4.56*	*4.86*	*0.5*	*116*	
2017	*ANA*	*MLB*	*34*	*10*	*11*	*0*	*28*	*28*	*174^2*	*178*	*26*	*2.5*	*5.8*	*36%*	*.277*	*1.30*	*4.74*	*4.75*	*5.08*	*0.1*	*122*	

Breakout: 15% Improve: 41% Collapse: 22% Attrition: 12% MLB: 96% *Comparables: Gaylord Perry, Orel Hershiser, Jack Morris*

Weaver is tumbling deeper into the rabbit hole of Jamie Moyer velocity, including an average fastball of just 84 mph last season, but he's following the path about 10 years premature. He can only get by for so long with deceptive angles and the masking abilities of Pride Rock, even though his tightly closed stride and exaggerated spine tilt coax a release point that is unique among his cohort of big-league hurlers. He strides far toward the third-base side and opposing baserunners attempted to take advantage with 32 steal attempts last season (tied for most in the American League), though a league-leading 10 of those would-be thieves were stopped in their tracks.

C.J. Wilson LHP

Born: 11/18/80 Age: 35 Bats: L Throws: L Height: 6'1" Weight: 210

YEAR	TEAM	LVL	AGE	W	L	SV	G	GS	IP	H	HR	BB/9	K/9	GB%	BABIP	WHIP	ERA	FIP	DRA	WARP	CFIP	MPH
2013	ANA	MLB	32	17	7	0	33	33	212^1	200	15	3.6	8.0	46%	.300	1.34	3.39	3.54	3.92	2.5	99	93.5
2014	ANA	MLB	33	13	10	0	31	31	175^2	169	17	4.4	7.7	49%	.306	1.45	4.51	4.34	4.78	0.0	113	93.1
2015	ANA	MLB	34	8	8	0	21	21	132	118	13	3.1	7.5	45%	.281	1.24	3.89	3.99	4.09	1.5	105	92.6
2016	*ANA*	*MLB*	*35*	*9*	*9*	*0*	*26*	*26*	*156*	*149*	*18*	*3.3*	*7.6*	*46%*	*.288*	*1.32*	*4.31*	*4.33*	*4.65*	*0.9*	*108*	
2017	*ANA*	*MLB*	*36*	*9*	*10*	*0*	*27*	*27*	*162^1*	*168*	*20*	*3.3*	*7.2*	*46%*	*.303*	*1.41*	*4.39*	*4.41*	*4.74*	*0.7*	*110*	

Breakout: 16% Improve: 45% Collapse: 29% Attrition: 9% MLB: 93% *Comparables: Al Leiter, Jose Contreras, Chuck Finley*

Bone spurs in Wilson's left elbow aggravated him over the summer and he shut it down in late July. He had pitched well despite the discomfort, including an 8 percent walk rate that was the second-best mark of his career, but his familiarity and experience with elbow ailments—including two separate surgical procedures to remove bone spurs in addition to a 2003 Tommy John surgery—reinforced Wilson's decision to stop pitching before more damage was done and his 2016 season was put in jeopardy. Two consecutive seasons of second-half disappointments have led to concerns about his fortitude. The questions are silly, but may have factored into Wilson's hope that getting himself fully right for 2016 can avoid a third year of the same. From a public-relations perspective, cracking the $20 million mark in salary this year will probably bring extra scrutiny, but regardless of the dollars in play, questioning any player's attempts to preserve his own body isn't a good look.

Lineouts

Hitters

NAME	POS	TEAM	LVL	AGE	PA	R	2B	3B	HR	RBI	BB	K	SB	CS	AVG/OBP/SLG	TAv	BABIP	BRR	FRAA	WARP
Todd Cunningham	OF	ATL	MLB	26	93	13	4	0	0	4	5	17	2	1	.221/.280/.267	.214	.275	-0.1	LF(22): -0.2, RF(4): -0.3	0.0
	OF	GWN	AAA	26	375	42	13	3	2	31	23	34	9	4	.261/.325/.337	.257	.283	-0.1	RF(53): -0.9, CF(36): 4.8	1.1
Natanael Delgado	OF	BUR	A	19	438	32	19	5	6	46	19	104	2	2	.241/.276/.355	.232	.304	-1.1	RF(90): -11.4, LF(1): 0.2	-1.9
Craig Gentry	CF	NAS	AAA	31	450	64	13	0	5	25	36	76	25	7	.256/.319/.327	.263	.301	3.5	CF(101): -2.5	1.6
	CF	OAK	MLB	31	56	6	0	2	0	3	4	15	1	1	.120/.196/.200	.184	.167	0.4	LF(13): -0.6, CF(8): 0.5	-0.2
Conor Gillaspie	3B	ANA	MLB	27	68	4	4	1	1	9	4	13	0	0	.203/.250/.344	.218	.240	-0.8	3B(17): -2.5, 2B(1): -0.0	-0.4
	3B	CHA	MLB	27	185	10	11	1	3	15	9	34	0	1	.237/.276/.364	.227	.275	-0.7	3B(52): 0.6, 1B(2): 0.3	0.0
Daniel Nava	RF	BOS	MLB	32	78	6	2	0	0	7	8	17	0	0	.152/.260/.182	.194	.200	1.6	RF(15): 0.5, LF(7): -0.1	-0.2
	RF	PAW	AAA	32	42	4	1	0	1	8	4	11	2	0	.250/.357/.361	.271	.333	0.0	RF(6): -0.1, 1B(3): 0.1	0.1
	RF	TBA	MLB	32	88	7	2	0	1	3	12	19	1	0	.233/.364/.301	.269	.302	-0.7	RF(19): 0.5, 1B(7): 0.0	0.2
Efren Navarro	1B	ANA	MLB	29	88	9	4	0	0	5	5	16	0	2	.253/.295/.301	.205	.313	0.9	1B(29): 0.5, LF(15): 1.0	-0.1
	1B	SLC	AAA	29	316	53	24	1	2	29	27	55	0	1	.329/.380/.442	.274	.392	0.0	1B(60): -0.1, LF(5): 0.2	0.8
Alex Yarbrough	2B	SLC	AAA	23	545	56	29	3	3	48	26	136	1	1	.236/.274/.324	.207	.313	1.5	2B(115): -18.5, 3B(4): -0.4	-3.4

Todd Cunningham had a brief cup of coffee with the Braves in 2013 and a venti latte in 2015; he has hung around thanks to his contact skills and speed, but overall there's not much here. ❖ **Natanael Delgado** was pushed to right field as a teenager, which places a lot of pressure on his bat, but he does show a functional approach at the plate that will help him tap into his plus raw power. ❖ Despite facing inferior pitching, **Craig Gentry** fared no better at Triple-A Nashville last season than he had for Oakland a year earlier, before changes in demographic and consumption patterns forced him back to the farm. ❖ Acquired by the Angels to fill in for the injured David Freese, **Conor Gillaspie** did nothing during his three-week cameo to suggest that the change of scenery had worked any miracles for his bat, and his full-season performance fell dangerously close to his 10th-percentile PECOTA projection. ❖ In the Baseball Prospectus comment management system, it lists the following: **Daniel Nava** (0 words). Indeed. ❖ **Efren Navarro** has been sheltered from southpaws in 85 percent of his plate appearances, but such a usage pattern may be unnecessary, as he has shown himself equally inept against pitchers from both sides. ❖ There's a broad base of average tools in **Johan Sala**'s shed, and he projects to have a long-term life in center field despite bulking up, but at just 18 and having not yet debuted stateside, he's a long way from playing on your living room TV. ❖ **Brendon Sanger** has a solid approach and a wide set of tools, but none of them stand out, so he's a fourth outfielder. There are worse fates (digging ditches), but there are also better ones (billionaire trust-fund baby). ❖ Once a steady performer, **Alex Yarbrough** slipped after a disappointing (read: genuinely awful) PCL campaign in 2015. He's looking at second-division upside.

Pitchers

NAME	TEAM	LVL	AGE	W	L	SV	G	GS	IP	H	HR	BB/9	K/9	GB%	BABIP	WHIP	ERA	FIP	FRA	WARP	CFIP	MPH
A.J. Achter	ROC	AAA	26	4	2	14	43	0	48	28	5	2.4	8.8	44%	.192	0.85	2.62	3.43	2.69	1.0	82	
	MIN	MLB	26	0	1	0	11	0	13^{1}	12	4	4.1	9.4	24%	.235	1.35	6.75	6.25	5.62	-0.1	99	92.3
Deolis Guerra	IND	AAA	26	2	1	4	25	0	36^{2}	21	1	2.0	9.1	38%	.220	0.79	1.23	2.15	2.02	1.1	72	
	PIT	MLB	26	2	0	0	10	0	16^{2}	26	5	1.6	9.2	40%	.438	1.74	6.48	5.74	9.13	-0.9	98	93.3
Greg Mahle	ARK	AA	22	3	3	16	31	0	35^{1}	34	1	2.8	9.2	55%	.333	1.27	3.06	2.56	3.26	0.6	85	
	INL	A+	22	0	1	9	21	0	22^{2}	26	1	1.2	12.3	46%	.446	1.28	3.57	2.28	2.36	0.7	69	
Kyle McGowin	ARK	AA	23	9	9	0	27	27	154	148	16	2.9	7.3	45%	.295	1.29	4.38	4.14	4.59	1.0	102	
Vinnie Pestano	SLC	AAA	30	1	3	10	35	0	34^{1}	18	1	2.1	11.0	35%	.224	0.76	2.10	2.58	1.91	1.2	63	
	ANA	MLB	30	1	0	0	19	0	11^{2}	15	3	6.2	10.0	24%	.343	1.97	5.40	6.53	8.42	-0.5	102	91.8
Cory Rasmus	SLC	AAA	27	0	1	1	10	3	15^{1}	9	0	1.2	14.7	44%	.281	0.72	2.35	0.73	1.29	0.7	55	
	ANA	MLB	27	0	0	0	16	1	20^{2}	15	3	4.8	11.8	39%	.261	1.26	5.23	4.12	3.91	0.2	88	94.5
Jeremy Rhoades	BUR	A	22	5	5	0	16	15	87	75	4	2.0	8.1	59%	.290	1.08	2.69	3.03	2.99	2.0	86	
	INL	A+	22	4	5	0	10	10	50^{2}	65	14	3.2	10.1	50%	.359	1.64	8.35	6.54	5.64	0.1	109	
Austin Robichaux	BUR	A	22	9	8	0	28	28	142	136	12	3.2	5.8	57%	.284	1.31	3.74	4.40	5.92	-1.6	117	

A.J. Achter is a Quadruple-A relief arm, but every team needs two or three or seven of those. ❖ Seven years and four Triple-A stints later, **Deolis Guerra** made his major-league debut, then threw more regular-season innings than Johan Santana had in the previous three seasons combined. Makes you wonder who *really* won that trade. ❖ Emily Thorne/Amanda Clarke made it her mission to wipe out the Grayson family, but thankfully spared **Grayson Long**, who touches 93 with mediocre command and a good changeup. ❖ **Greg Mahle** has average stuff and a decepti—hey, do you think it's "mail" or "maul" or "mah-lay" or what? Boy, really gets you wondering. ❖ Where's **Kyle McGowin**? He pitched all year at Double-A Arkansas, throws 95 with sink, has an above-average slider and might develop a changeup, which means he's McTryin' to be a major-league starter, but he'll be McNeedin' to stay healthy if he really plans on McMakin' it. ❖ **Vinnie Pestano**'s recent bouts of success have occurred against inferior competition; he was serving up cookies like a Keebler Elf with 89 mph fastballs over the heart of the plate during his brief time in the big leagues last year. ❖ **Cory Rasmus** missed the first few months of the season after recovering from abdominal surgery, but he was absolutely dominant for Salt Lake upon his return, striking out 25 of the 59 batters he faced to earn his ticket back to Anaheim. ❖ **Jeremy Rhoades** is tall, doesn't have the changeup or command necessary to start, has been 12 years in the making, can make the majors as a reliever with a solid fastball-slider combination and will surely last 54 years in that role until a massive earthquake ends his career. ❖ Tall and projectable (*i.e.* kind of terrifyingly skinny), **Austin Robichaux** has a solid feel for pitching and features an average fastball-breaker pair.

Manager

Mike Scioscia

YEAR	TEAM	W	L	Pythag +/-	Avg PC	100+ P	120+ P	QS	BQS	REL	REL w Zero R	IBB	PH	PH Avg	PH HR	SB2	CS2	SB3	CS3	SAC Att	SAC%	POS SAC	Squeeze	Swing	In Play
2013	ANA	78	84	-3	97.5	77	6	87	5	496	400	36	83	.214	3	71	32	10	1	54	68.5	35	0	349	110
2014	ANA	98	64	1	94.1	71	3	80	5	543	467	41	103	.233	1	72	37	9	2	42	61.9	24	1	315	88
2015	ANA	85	77	6	95.0	55	2	88	5	518	429	45	102	.217	2	45	31	6	2	50	74.0	36	3	297	91

The highlight of Scioscia's 2015 doubled as the organization's nadir. A tug of war between Scioscia and general manager Jerry Dipoto ended midway through the season with the latter's resignation. Philosophical and personality clashes are bound to happen, that's life, but the tipping point was reportedly Scioscia's unwillingness to provide his coaches and players with additional scouting info.

"Additional scouting info" isn't a subject that should cause rifts between the front office and field staff. But just as marriages don't end over one argument about the bills, Scioscia and Dipoto's relationship didn't reach irreconcilability over some data packets. In fact, Ken Rosenthal reported that communication between the two was "strained" and that they were nearing a "breaking point" as far back as September 2012—or less than a year into Dipoto's tenure.

It wasn't a coincidence that the real breaking point arrived in 2015. Scioscia was approaching the end of the seventh year of his decade-long contract, significant because it allowed him to opt out at season's end. Owner Arte Moreno was probably concerned that if he pushed back against Scioscia, or ruled in Dipoto's favor, Scioscia would bolt to his hometown Phillies or the rival Dodgers—you figure Scioscia would have loved Andrew Friedman if he found Dipoto's information peddling too aggressive.

What Scioscia is then, is the game's final manager king. He's outlasted three GMs in the era of the executive, and has done so without owning a chunk of the team. His staying power is more remarkable considering he lacks a surefire Hall of Fame résumé. Scioscia won the 2002 World Series, of course, but has advanced past the divisional round just twice since—the most recent time coming in 2009. He's never delivered fewer than 75 wins a season, yet he's one for his last six at securing 90-plus wins. Scioscia's longevity is amazing and unusual—he remains the one skipper hired since the strike to record more than 15 years on the bench—but we have to ask: Would he still be the Angels manager if it weren't for that ill-advised contract? Probably not.

LOS ANGELES DODGERS

Essay by Eric Nusbaum

Player comments by Ben Carsley and BP authors

Every so often over the past two seasons, the LED ribbon wrapping around the Loge level façade at Dodger Stadium has displayed an odd, turf-colored advertisement. The ad lingers for a while, then flashes away to some other sponsor, or the score, or an entreaty to get loud. It might even go by unnoticed, lost amid the eating, the drinking, amid the planes and helicopters drifting overhead and the ballgame happening below.

Modernity crept up gradually on Chavez Ravine. The sightlines are still pristine, and the baseball itself has plenty of room to breathe in the spacious park. But the future is always rounding third base, sometimes in the form of very shiny stuff like LED billboards or very weird stuff like in-stadium hosts on the video screens.

As much as the team loves to embrace its history, there isn't much quaint about the Dodgers in 2016. The Guggenheim ownership group has been transparent in turning the franchise into a far-reaching and ruthless entertainment brand. Time, money, and the baseball operations department led by Andrew Friedman have been unsentimental in their remaking of a franchise that has hung its hat on what you could call nostalgia for a better future. The Dodgers have always been on the cutting edge of history—Jackie Robinson, the great move West, Nomomania, even the sleek, chromatic design of the stadium itself—and always been happy to exploit that fact.

Departed last offseason were Hanley Ramirez, Matt Kemp, and many millions of TV viewers who don't have Time Warner. Departed this offseason were Zack Greinke and Don Mattingly. Departing soon will be many of the living ghosts who have given Dodger Stadium its character over six decades: Tommy Lasorda, Don Newcomb, and the soon-to-retire Vin Scully among them.

The subject of ghosts calls to mind the bright green advertisements that have appearing in Dodger Stadium lately. They say:

PLAN AHEAD. FOREST LAWN. 800-2-FOREST.

Forest Lawn is Southern California's largest and most influential chain of memorial parks (not cemeteries). It is the company more responsible than any other for what

DODGERS PROSPECTUS

2015 W-L: 92-70, 1st in NL West

Pythag	.551	7th	DER	.704	14th
RS/G	4.12	19th	B-Age	29.6	28th
RA/G	3.67	2nd	P-Age	28	10th
TAv	.274	2nd	Salary	$282.2M	1st
BRR	-5.26	22nd	M$/MW	$6.2M	4th
TAv-P	.248	4th	DL Days	1383	25th
FIP	3.43	3rd	$ on DL	16%	17th

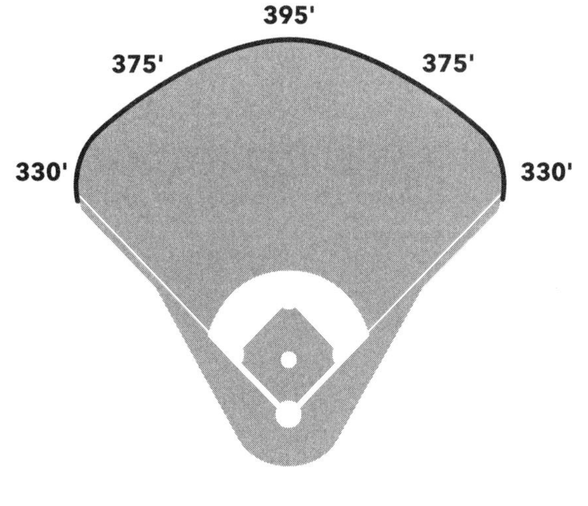

Outfield wall profile: **4'** to **8'**

Three-Year Park Factors

Runs	Runs/RH	Runs/LH	HR/RH	HR/LH
94	102	101	106	115

Top Hitter WARP	4.9	Yasmani Grandal
Top Pitcher WARP	8.0	Clayton Kershaw
Top Prospect	Corey Seager	

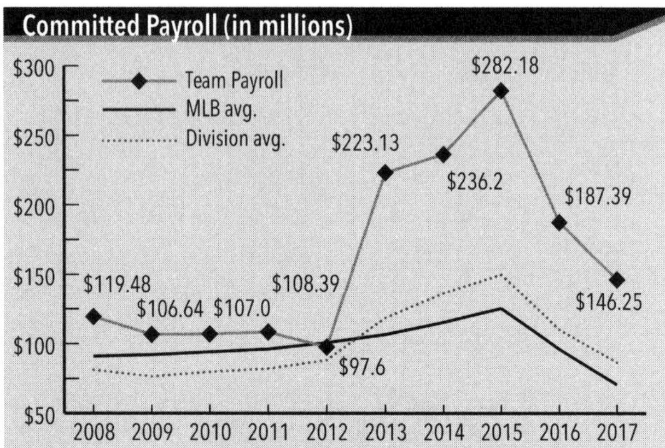

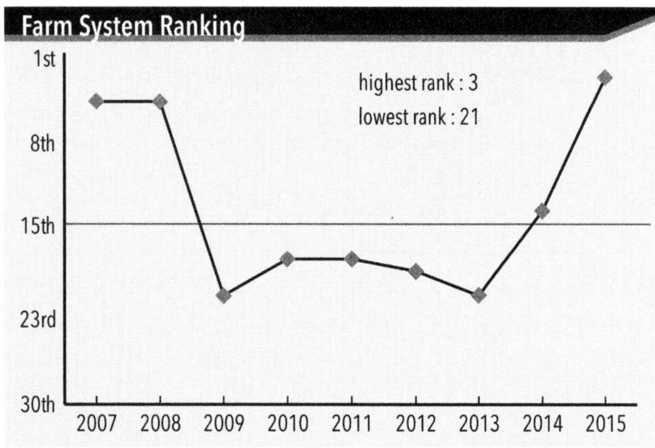

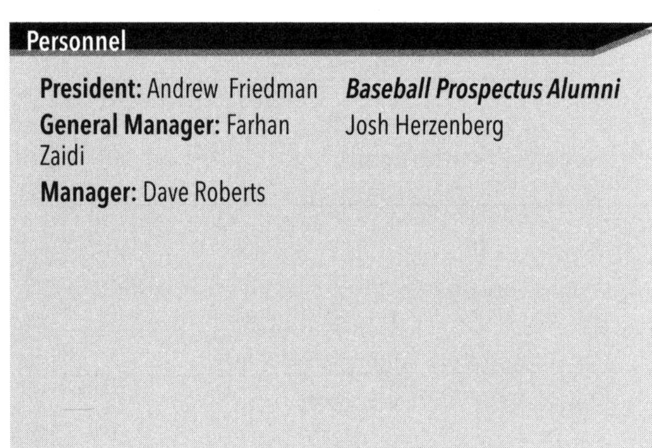
Personnel

President: Andrew Friedman

General Manager: Farhan Zaidi

Manager: Dave Roberts

Baseball Prospectus Alumni

Josh Herzenberg

death looks like in America today, and for that we have a man named Hubert Eaton to thank. Eaton, an Englishman, took over Forest Lawn Cemetery in 1917, and implemented something called the Builder's Creed, which said, among other things:

> *I Shall Endeavor To Build Forest Lawn As Different, As Unlike Other Cemeteries As Sunshine Is To Darkness, As Eternal Life Is Unlike Death. I Shall Try To Build At Forest Lawn A Great Park, Devoid Of Misshapen Monuments And Other Customary Signs Of Earthly Death, But Filled With Towering Trees, Sweeping Lawns, Splashing Fountains, Singing Birds, Beautiful Statuary, Cheerful Flowers, Noble Memorial Architecture With Interiors Full Of Light And Color, And Redolent Of The World's Best History And Romances.*

Eaton saw Forest Lawn, then just a small cemetery in Glendale, as a canvas onto which he could paint his soft-edged vision of death. He invented those flat bronze markers you see in modern cemeteries, and was the first person to put the funeral chapel inside the cemetery park for one-stop shopping.

In this way, Eaton was not unlike another ambitious Angeleno transplant: Walter O'Malley, whose vision of baseball was as sweeping and pastoral as Eaton's vision of death, and who had his own blank canvas in the form of a brand new stadium. O'Malley was obsessive about the design of Dodger Stadium. No view-obstructing columns. Thousands of parking spots. Open concourses. Immaculate and careful landscaping. At the time of its opening, Dodger Stadium was unlike any other ballpark in America.

Despite the best efforts of Frank McCourt and Rupert Murdoch to squash any traces, O'Malley's fastidiousness about presentation and branding and the fan experience still lingers in the Dodgers DNA. Which leads one to wonder what the hell the team was doing running ads for a cemetery in the middle of a playoff race. It seemed off-brand, and more than a little unusual.

Just the opposite, said Michael Young, the Dodgers Senior Vice President of Corporate Partnerships. The ads, which grew out of a Spanish-language radio partnership (complete with Fernando Valenzuela endorsement!), were actually targeted at Dodger Stadium's massive Latino fan base.

"For many non-Latinos, the idea of promoting a cemetery seems out of place in a place where you're having fun and celebrating," said Young. "But within the Latino community, cemeteries/memorial parks are a place where they to go to celebrate and be with their loved ones for hours or an entire day. Understanding that part of their culture, we thought it just made a lot of sense."

At the end of the McCourt years, when the stadium was a desolate, it would have been easy to make a joke about how Dodger fans didn't have to go all the way to Forest Lawn to experience a graveyard. But now, the Guggenheim

Dodgers are actually trying to create something not unlike the graveyard that advertises in their stadium. They want to create a Dodgers franchise that transcends the year to year title quest. The Guggenheim version of "Noble Memorial Architecture With Interiors Full Of Light And Color" is a brand that outlives individual seasons or players.

This begins with Dodger Stadium itself, which has undergone major renovations, and where the fan experience is engineered with very specific goals in mind. Young says when it comes to in-game advertising, the idea is to make money without sacrificing the atmosphere that makes Dodger Stadium a special place to watch a ballgame. That means accenting the natural symmetry of the architecture, and creating branded fan experiences that play up Dodger history, like the retired numbers plaza on the top deck (sponsored by Bank of America).

"Even though we've created more places to advertise, it really hasn't impacted the feel of the building," Young said. "Your eye isn't going to all these different signs, your eye is going to where your eye has always gone when you walk into Dodger Stadium." He means the field of play, and LED ribbon notwithstanding, that remains mostly true.

The obligation extends from the business side to the baseball side. Andrew Friedman, Farhan Zaidi, and their many sub-lieutenants are tasked with creating a more sustainable winning baseball team without sacrificing the intangibles of Dodgerdom. Fundamentally, that means doing good baseball things that also feel like "Dodger" baseball things: investing heavily in international talent, developing a deep farm system, and having really good pitchers. They have done all three of those—although inheriting Clayton Kershaw didn't hurt.

The Friedman front office is also forced to contend with a relatively recent Dodger tradition: lavish, ineffectual spending. Ever since Kevin Brown landed in L.A. in 1998 with baseball's first $100 million contract in his pocket (landed, by the way, in a chartered jet that was actually provided as a clause in the deal), the Dodgers have spent big and spent foolishly.

The Guggenheim group and Stan Kasten didn't help matters by going out and acquiring the contracts of Josh Beckett, Carl Crawford, and Adrian Gonzalez immediately after taking control of the franchise. In doing so, they acquired some useful players (on and off the field, as Gonzalez is the team's fist big Mexican star since Fernando Valenzuela), but they also shifted the team into an awkward purgatorial space that it is still struggling to get out of. As Kasten repeatedly said, the idea was that the Dodgers could use their considerable financial resources to both rebuild and go for broke simultaneously.

This has led to gaudy spending on Cuban imports, and an unprecedented willingness to pay money to players to not wear the Dodger uniform. (The Mike Morse era will be remembered fondly in LA). But it has also put Friedman and company in an awkward place. The Dodgers were willing to spend $19.5 million in 2015 for Brian Wilson and Dan Haren to not pitch in Los Angeles, but they aren't willing to cough up an extra $20 or 30 million to match Arizona's offer to Zack Greinke?

There is an obvious difference, of course: Greinke is a long-term financial commitment, and the new regime seems more interested in creating a deep, sustainable roster than the kind of problematic top-heavy team that it inherited. In this sense, they are building something more akin to the Dodgers of the '60s and '70s than any of the recent teams that have crumbled in the postseason: talented rosters that back up their stars with a seemingly endless supply of homegrown talent.

The idea is to live in the past and future at the same time. In new manager Dave Roberts, the Dodgers have hired a man who perfectly embodies this ambition. Roberts is a progressive-minded baseball man who will carry out the vision of his bosses upstairs. But he is also a former fan favorite as a Dodger. And the club's first minority manager, he is an instant reminder of all the best parts of Dodger lore.

Roberts will be equipped with a roster that further exemplifies the Friedman/Zaidi model: while we are still in the process of discovering what exactly that model is, the front office has shown itself to value depth, flexibility, and short term contracts like the one given to Hisahi Iwakuma. The Dodgers may not look so threatening on paper without Greinke in the fold and with a sudden reticence to spend their way into first place, but they are bursting at the seams with useful position players. Rotation help is on the way in the form of super prospect Julio Urias and his late blooming sidekick Jose De Leon.

What this approach represents is something that the Dodgers have been immune to for many years: progress. Nothing exemplified this better than Dodger Stadium itself. For decades, there was organ music and DiamondVision and the 76 station in in the parking lot behind center field was a full service operation. But longtime organist Nancy Bea Hefley retired after 2015, and the instant replays are in high definition now, and the 76 station hasn't been anything more than decorative since Frank McCourt ripped out the gas tanks.

Win or lose, the Dodgers, like Forest Lawn, are still selling the pastoral fantasy. It's just that now, part of that sales pitch involves reminding us that their stadium is the second most Instragrammed place on earth. The past we idealize and the future we always wanted remain in perfect harmony. The fan experience second to none. The advertisements tastefully rendered. The ball club winning no matter who is on it. Noble Memorial Architecture. O'Malley and Hubert Eaton would both be proud. ■

—Eric Nusbaum is the West Coast Editor for VICE Sports. His writing has appeared in Sports Illustrated, ESPN the Magazine, *and* Pitchers & Poets.

Hitters

Austin Barnes C

Born: 12/28/89 Age: 26 Bats: R Throws: R Height: 5'10" Weight: 185

YEAR	TEAM	LVL	AGE	PA	R	2B	3B	HR	RBI	BB	K	SB	CS	AVG/OBP/SLG	TAv	BABIP	BRR	FRAA	WARP
2013	JUP	A+	23	417	42	15	1	4	38	52	59	5	2	.260/.367/.343	.272	.298	-0.1	C(64): -0.4	2.0
2013	JAX	AA	23	74	10	2	2	1	7	12	10	0	0	.339/.446/.484	.346	.392	0.0	C(11): -0.5, 2B(4): 0.1	0.9
2014	JUP	A+	24	200	24	11	2	1	14	19	25	3	3	.317/.385/.417	.285	.364	-3.3	C(44): -0.7	1.1
2014	JAX	AA	24	348	56	20	2	12	43	50	36	8	0	.296/.406/.507	.332	.299	0.7	2B(30): 0.1, C(29): 2.0	4.2
2015	LAN	MLB	25	37	4	2	0	0	1	6	6	1	0	.207/.361/.276	.257	.261	-0.2	C(11): 0.5, 3B(1): -0.0	0.2
2015	OKL	AAA	25	335	40	17	2	9	42	35	36	12	2	.315/.389/.479	.333	.331	-1.5	C(78): 15.9	5.6
2016	*LAN*	*MLB*	*26*	*250*	*32*	*11*	*1*	*6*	*26*	*25*	*45*	*3*	*1*	*.258/.339/.406*	*.271*	*.292*	*0.1*	*C 7, 2B -0*	*2.2*
2017	*LAN*	*MLB*	*27*	*340*	*42*	*16*	*1*	*9*	*39*	*33*	*62*	*4*	*1*	*.260/.340/.411*	*.282*	*.297*	*0.0*	*C 9, 2B 0*	*2.9*

Breakout: 1% Improve: 18% Collapse: 15% Attrition: 23% MLB: 44% *Comparables: John Jaso, Gaby Sanchez, Matt Carpenter*

YEAR	TEAM	P. COUNT	FRM RUNS	BLK RUNS	THRW RUNS	TOT RUNS
2014	JAX	3562	3.2	0.0	-0.3	2.9
2015	LAN	1229	0.5	0.0	-0.1	0.5
2015	OKL	10507	17.0	0.2	0.3	17.4
2016	*LAN*	*9267*	*8.1*	*0.1*	*-0.6*	*7.5*
2017	*LAN*	*12600*	*10.0*	*0.1*	*-0.9*	*9.2*

Barnes continued his run as one of baseball's most interesting, most overlooked prospects in 2015. He focused on logging innings behind the plate in Triple-A, and after playing in the infield 45 times in 2014, Barnes did so just twice last year. It's certainly true that he lacks an impact profile, but a backup catcher/second baseman/third baseman who can routinely make solid contact? That's a valuable asset in an era when teams need 17-man bullpens to roster all their specialists, like the arm reserved for lefties under six feet tall and that guy with a particular talent for inducing groundballs *right* to the bag at third base. Given the way Barnes handled Oklahoma City last season, it shouldn't be a surprise to see him spend considerable time with the Dodgers this year, though his prospects for seeing routine playing time are more dubious.

Cody Bellinger 1B

Born: 7/13/95 Age: 20 Bats: L Throws: L Height: 6'4" Weight: 180

YEAR	TEAM	LVL	AGE	PA	R	2B	3B	HR	RBI	BB	K	SB	CS	AVG/OBP/SLG	TAv	BABIP	BRR	FRAA	WARP
2015	RCU	A+	19	544	97	33	4	30	103	52	150	10	2	.264/.336/.538	.315	.314	2.5	1B(91): 9.2, CF(26): 0.0	5.3
2016	*LAN*	*MLB*	*20*	*250*	*28*	*10*	*1*	*11*	*33*	*18*	*81*	*1*	*0*	*.214/.276/.409*	*.245*	*.273*	*-0.1*	*1B 4, CF 0*	*0.5*
2017	*LAN*	*MLB*	*21*	*400*	*50*	*17*	*1*	*17*	*53*	*34*	*124*	*3*	*1*	*.221/.290/.419*	*.262*	*.280*	*-0.4*	*1B 6, CF 1*	*1.0*

Breakout: 6% Improve: 13% Collapse: 0% Attrition: 7% MLB: 15% *Comparables: Mike Carp, Miguel Sano, Giancarlo Stanton*

Bellinger smashed 67 extra-base hits—including 30 homers—at Rancho Cucamonga last season. Any time someone hits that many bombs in this day and age we have to pay attention, but Bellinger mashed in the Cal League, which does to power output what gym class does to high school GPAs. Scouts seem convinced that some of Bellinger's pop is real, and spending 26 games in center field instead of at first base is a promising sign for his future. At the same time, striking out in over a quarter of your PAs is never ideal, and neither are reports about how Bellinger looks against breaking balls. He's the son of former big leaguer Clay Bellinger, and dad's best single-season homer output was just 16, so at least Cody has some bragging rights.

Carl Crawford LF

Born: 8/5/81 Age: 34 Bats: L Throws: L Height: 6'2" Weight: 230

YEAR	TEAM	LVL	AGE	PA	R	2B	3B	HR	RBI	BB	K	SB	CS	AVG/OBP/SLG	TAv	BABIP	BRR	FRAA	WARP
2013	LAN	MLB	31	469	62	30	3	6	31	28	66	15	4	.283/.329/.407	.273	.321	1.9	LF(107): 5.2	2.4
2014	LAN	MLB	32	370	56	14	3	8	46	16	55	23	6	.300/.339/.429	.297	.335	3.9	LF(94): -1.0	2.6
2015	OKL	AAA	33	32	8	2	1	1	6	1	3	0	0	.367/.375/.600	.342	.370	0.4	LF(6): -0.4	0.3
2015	LAN	MLB	33	193	19	9	2	4	16	10	41	10	2	.265/.304/.403	.251	.324	0.6	LF(51): -8.8	-0.6
2017	LAN	MLB	35	213	22	10	2	4	21	10	41	8	2	.256/.295/.379	.251	.302	1.0	LF 0	0.3

Breakout: 0% Improve: 27% Collapse: 14% Attrition: 19% MLB: 92% *Comparables: Al Oliver, Eric Byrnes, Rondell White*

The Dodgers paid Crawford just north of $21 million to actively hurt their team last season, as he finally dipped into negative-WARP territory. We're so used to Crawford being a massive disappointment that it's easy to lose sight of just how disastrous his contract is, but the shell of what was once among the game's most exciting players has received nearly $96 million to produce 5.8 WARP since 2011. Last season, Crawford's strikeout rate reached an all-time high, his defensive metrics registered at an all-time low and he hit the DL for the fifth straight year. He's got two years and $49.5 million left on his deal, but if he keeps decaying faster than Hydrogen-7 he might not get much playing time even against right-handers.

A.J. Ellis C

Born: 4/9/81 Age: 35 Bats: R Throws: R Height: 6'2" Weight: 230

YEAR	TEAM	LVL	AGE	PA	R	2B	3B	HR	RBI	BB	K	SB	CS	AVG/OBP/SLG	TAv	BABIP	BRR	FRAA	WARP
2013	LAN	MLB	32	448	43	17	1	10	52	45	78	0	2	.238/.318/.364	.265	.269	-0.6	C(113): -4.5	1.7
2014	LAN	MLB	33	347	21	9	0	3	25	53	57	0	0	.191/.323/.254	.227	.225	-4.1	C(92): -14.8	-1.7
2015	LAN	MLB	34	217	24	9	0	7	21	32	38	0	0	.238/.355/.403	.293	.265	-2.7	C(62): -2.2	1.2
2016	*LAN*	*MLB*	*35*	*163*	*17*	*6*	*0*	*3*	*16*	*20*	*31*	*0*	*0*	*.234/.338/.358*	*.258*	*.272*	*-0.8*	*C -4*	*0.1*
2017	*LAN*	*MLB*	*36*	*120*	*14*	*4*	*0*	*2*	*12*	*14*	*23*	*0*	*0*	*.225/.325/.343*	*.256*	*.262*	*-0.7*	*C -3*	*-0.1*

Breakout: 2% Improve: 29% Collapse: 6% Attrition: 17% MLB: 82% *Comparables: Carlos Ruiz, Brian Schneider, Trot Nixon*

YEAR	TEAM	P. COUNT	FRM RUNS	BLK RUNS	THRW RUNS	TOT RUNS
2013	LAN	15539	-2.9	-0.8	1.2	-2.5
2014	LAN	12138	-12.3	-0.3	-1.3	-13.8
2015	LAN	7583	-5.9	0.0	0.7	-5.1
2016	*LAN*	*5754*	*-4.2*	*-0.2*	*0.2*	*-4.3*
2017	*LAN*	*4219*	*-3.3*	*-0.1*	*0.1*	*-3.4*

It may seem strange to look at Ellis' numbers from 2015 and think "what a rebound," but that's where we are with the veteran backstop. After a dismal 2014 in which Ellis was among the majors' worst catchers to receive regular playing time, he posted the third-best WARP of his career last season. Ellis reached base at an impressive clip, rediscovered his modest power and upgraded his framing numbers from "oh god look away" to "well, okay." He'll turn 35 in April and has a modest skill set to begin with so there's little margin for error, but when you carry enough clout to write the foreword to Clayton Kershaw's book, perhaps your margins are a little wider than they first appear.

Andre Ethier CF

Born: 4/10/82 Age: 34 Bats: L Throws: L Height: 6'2" Weight: 210

YEAR	TEAM	LVL	AGE	PA	R	2B	3B	HR	RBI	BB	K	SB	CS	AVG/OBP/SLG	TAv	BABIP	BRR	FRAA	WARP
2013	LAN	MLB	31	553	54	33	2	12	52	61	95	4	3	.272/.360/.423	.284	.315	-2.0	CF(74): -5.9, RF(54): 1.6	2.1
2014	LAN	MLB	32	380	29	17	6	4	42	31	74	2	2	.249/.322/.370	.263	.307	-4.3	CF(68): -3.0, LF(16): -2.1	0.1
2015	LAN	MLB	33	445	54	20	7	14	53	43	75	2	3	.294/.366/.486	.314	.330	-2.7	RF(80): -2.3, LF(51): -0.2	2.8
2016	*LAN*	*MLB*	*34*	*523*	*57*	*26*	*3*	*13*	*62*	*46*	*103*	*3*	*2*	*.267/.338/.421*	*.275*	*.315*	*-2.7*	*LF -7, RF 0*	*1.2*
2017	*LAN*	*MLB*	*35*	*414*	*49*	*20*	*2*	*9*	*45*	*35*	*83*	*2*	*1*	*.263/.331/.402*	*.275*	*.314*	*-2.0*	*LF -6, RF 0*	*0.4*

Breakout: 0% Improve: 38% Collapse: 6% Attrition: 10% MLB: 96% *Comparables: Michael Cuddyer, Magglio Ordonez, Larry Walker*

It feels like the Dodgers have wanted to rid themselves of Ethier since the day he signed his ill-advised five-year, $85 million extension. They were glad to still have Ethier around last year, though, as the 33-year-old earned more WARP than any other Dodgers outfielder and had his best campaign since 2012. We're all aware that Ethier is an acutely flawed player who shouldn't ever be allowed to face a left-handed pitcher or position himself in center field, but the man hit .306/.383/.517 against righties and didn't embarrass himself with the glove in a corner in 2015. If this is more than just a dead-cat bounce, the Dodgers could use his stabilizing force in a lineup awash with inconsistent assets. Between the southpaw struggles that plague Ethier, Joc Pederson and the sentient remains of Carl Crawford, the Dodgers really, *really* need a right-handed platoon outfielder.

Also: Ethier is still *hella* handsome.

Adrian Gonzalez 1B

Born: 5/8/82 Age: 34 Bats: L Throws: L Height: 6'2" Weight: 220

YEAR	TEAM	LVL	AGE	PA	R	2B	3B	HR	RBI	BB	K	SB	CS	AVG/OBP/SLG	TAv	BABIP	BRR	FRAA	WARP
2013	LAN	MLB	31	641	69	32	0	22	100	47	98	1	0	.293/.342/.461	.293	.315	-3.8	1B(151): -3.1	2.1
2014	LAN	MLB	32	660	83	41	0	27	116	56	112	1	1	.276/.335/.482	.301	.294	-5.3	1B(157): 10.9	4.1
2015	LAN	MLB	33	643	76	33	0	28	90	62	107	0	1	.275/.350/.480	.302	.294	-2.1	1B(149): 10.9	4.5
2016	*LAN*	*MLB*	*34*	*659*	*76*	*35*	*1*	*24*	*89*	*52*	*117*	*1*	*1*	*.281/.339/.463*	*.283*	*.311*	*-3.2*	*1B 6*	*3.0*
2017	*LAN*	*MLB*	*35*	*552*	*71*	*28*	*1*	*19*	*71*	*46*	*99*	*0*	*0*	*.275/.336/.448*	*.288*	*.306*	*-2.9*	*1B 5*	*2.0*

Breakout: 0% Improve: 32% Collapse: 3% Attrition: 9% MLB: 94% *Comparables: Paul Konerko, Mark Teixeira, Ted Kluszewski*

It's already been more than three years since the Dodgers gave away prospects who have amounted to nothing and absorbed a staggering amount of money in the name of acquiring Gonzalez. Time flies when you consistently make the playoffs. Since returning to the west, Gonzalez has played in 508 games, hit .283/.342/.472, mashed 116 doubles and 80 homers and continued to provide a good glove. He essentially repeated his 2014 campaign in 2015, finishing as Los Angeles' most valuable position player. His days as one of the game's preeminent sluggers are over, to be sure, but Gonzalez did finish in the top-50 in TAv among qualified batters and made his first All-Star Game since 2011. He is still owed $66.5 million for the final three years of his deal, and when you add in the costs of Carl Crawford and Josh Beckett, the Dodgers certainly paid a premium for his performance. But perform he has.

Yasmani Grandal C

Born: 11/8/88 Age: 27 Bats: B Throws: R Height: 6'1" Weight: 225

YEAR	TEAM	LVL	AGE	PA	R	2B	3B	HR	RBI	BB	K	SB	CS	AVG/OBP/SLG	TAv	BABIP	BRR	FRAA	WARP
2013	TUC	AAA	24	38	3	3	0	0	2	2	8	0	0	.306/.342/.389	.262	.393	-1.5	C(5): 0.4	0.0
2013	SDN	MLB	24	108	13	8	0	1	9	18	18	0	0	.216/.352/.341	.260	.257	0.9	C(26): 6.2, 1B(1): -0.0	1.3
2014	SDN	MLB	25	443	47	19	1	15	49	58	115	3	0	.225/.327/.401	.286	.277	-3.1	C(76): 11.5, 1B(37): -1.2	3.5
2015	LAN	MLB	26	426	43	12	0	16	47	65	92	0	1	.234/.353/.403	.276	.268	-4.0	C(107): 25.2, 1B(6): -0.1	4.9
2016	*LAN*	*MLB*	*27*	*510*	*61*	*22*	*1*	*18*	*65*	*68*	*112*	*1*	*1*	*.245/.350/.421*	*.278*	*.289*	*-2.5*	*C 32*	*6.6*
2017	*LAN*	*MLB*	*28*	*463*	*63*	*19*	*0*	*16*	*57*	*64*	*103*	*1*	*0*	*.240/.346/.415*	*.285*	*.282*	*-2.5*	*C 28*	*5.5*

Breakout: 3% Improve: 48% Collapse: 7% Attrition: 8% MLB: 99% *Comparables: Carlos Santana, Chris Iannetta, Alex Avila*

YEAR	TEAM	P. COUNT	FRM RUNS	BLK RUNS	THRW RUNS	TOT RUNS
2013	SDN	3656	6.0	0.1	-0.4	5.7
2013	TUC	586	0.3	0.0	0.0	0.3
2014	SDN	9898	14.5	-0.3	-2.3	11.9
2015	LAN	13767	25.5	-0.2	-0.4	25.0
2016	*LAN*	*17914*	*32.6*	*-0.3*	*-1.6*	*30.7*
2017	*LAN*	*16266*	*28.5*	*-0.2*	*-1.5*	*26.8*

It feels like Grandal has been around—and mostly disappointing—forever, but the backstop only turned 27 in November. That's why his 2015 season, which was the best of his career by WARP, is so exciting: There's a chance Grandal's best days still lie ahead. With his ACL injury and PED suspension firmly in the rear-view mirror, Grandal logged nearly 900 innings behind the plate, by far the most of his career. He posted good framing numbers, average defensive metrics, set a new personal best for homers and finished with the fifth-best OBP of any catcher with at least 200 PA. Grandal performs better against lefties and will never be confused with a Molina defensively, but he's relatively young, has an advanced skill set on offense, at least for a backstop, and is under team control for three more years, at which point Matt Kemp will still be owed $22 million.

Alex Guerrero OF

Born: 11/20/86 Age: 29 Bats: R Throws: R Height: 6'0" Weight: 215

YEAR	TEAM	LVL	AGE	PA	R	2B	3B	HR	RBI	BB	K	SB	CS	AVG/OBP/SLG	TAv	BABIP	BRR	FRAA	WARP
2014	ABQ	AAA	27	258	38	14	5	15	49	10	44	4	0	.329/.364/.613	.313	.351	1.5	2B(51): -4.9, LF(9): 0.8	1.9
2014	RCU	A+	27	21	3	4	1	0	2	2	2	0	0	.368/.429/.684	.356	.412	-0.1	3B(2): -0.0, 2B(2): -0.2	0.3
2014	LAN	MLB	27	13	0	0	0	0	0	0	6	0	0	.077/.077/.077	.059	.143	0.2	LF(3): -0.3	-0.3
2015	LAN	MLB	28	230	25	9	1	11	36	7	57	1	0	.233/.261/.434	.253	.261	-1.3	LF(29): -1.3, 3B(22): -0.8	0.1
2016	*LAN*	*MLB*	*29*	*159*	*18*	*7*	*1*	*7*	*22*	*6*	*38*	*1*	*0*	*.246/.279/.443*	*.257*	*.284*	*-0.3*	*3B -1*	*0.3*
2017	*LAN*	*MLB*	*30*	*199*	*24*	*8*	*1*	*8*	*26*	*7*	*49*	*1*	*0*	*.237/.270/.423*	*.256*	*.275*	*-0.5*	*3B -1*	*0.1*

Breakout: 4% Improve: 22% Collapse: 7% Attrition: 15% MLB: 66% *Comparables: Laynce Nix, Xavier Paul, Casper Wells*

For the first time in his stateside career, Guerrero finished a season with as much of his ears intact as when that season began. Unfortunately, that was the Cuban's most notable achievement in 2015, as the $28 million man floundered at the plate after a hot April and made more appearances in the outfield than the infield, which was very much not the plan when he was signed. Guerrero probably needs to be demoted or traded to see playing time moving forward, but his contract makes it difficult for the Dodgers to do either. A sunk cost is a sunk cost, so perhaps Guerrero will just be released, but at 29 there's still time for him to become a worthwhile bench option.

Enrique Hernandez OF

Born: 8/24/91 Age: 24 Bats: R Throws: R Height: 5'11" Weight: 200

YEAR	TEAM	LVL	AGE	PA	R	2B	3B	HR	RBI	BB	K	SB	CS	AVG/OBP/SLG	TAv	BABIP	BRR	FRAA	WARP
2013	CCH	AA	21	483	53	18	2	13	46	34	70	5	3	.236/.297/.375	.240	.253	-0.5	2B(104): -4.7, SS(5): 0.3	-0.2
2014	MIA	MLB	22	45	3	2	1	2	6	4	10	0	0	.175/.267/.425	.267	.179	0.0	CF(7): 0.9, 3B(3): 0.0	0.4
2014	OKL	AAA	22	289	41	17	2	8	31	18	25	6	5	.337/.380/.508	.295	.346	1.7	2B(26): -0.4, 3B(14): 0.7	2.4
2014	HOU	MLB	22	89	10	4	2	1	8	8	11	0	0	.284/.348/.420	.283	.319	0.3	CF(11): 0.3, LF(8): 1.0	0.6
2014	NWO	AAA	22	84	8	5	0	2	6	10	13	0	1	.250/.345/.403	.286	.276	-0.5	2B(11): 0.1, SS(8): -0.3	0.5
2014	CCH	AA	22	43	9	3	0	1	5	3	3	0	0	.325/.372/.475	.298	.333	0.1	2B(10): 0.7	0.4
2015	OKL	AAA	23	64	6	2	0	1	9	4	14	1	0	.169/.219/.254	.188	.200	0.6	SS(8): -0.3, CF(4): -0.2	-0.3
2015	LAN	MLB	23	218	24	12	2	7	22	11	46	0	2	.307/.346/.490	.315	.364	0.1	2B(20): 1.1, CF(19): -1.4	2.0
2016	*LAN*	*MLB*	*24*	*390*	*41*	*18*	*2*	*11*	*44*	*22*	*70*	*2*	*2*	*.253/.299/.405*	*.251*	*.283*	*0.3*	*2B -1, CF 0*	*1.1*
2017	*LAN*	*MLB*	*25*	*486*	*56*	*23*	*2*	*13*	*56*	*27*	*87*	*3*	*2*	*.255/.301/.406*	*.260*	*.286*	*0.5*	*2B -2, CF 0*	*1.2*

Breakout: 3% Improve: 37% Collapse: 11% Attrition: 20% MLB: 81% *Comparables: Didi Gregorius, Brad Miller, Aaron Hill*

It feels like Hernandez saw a highlight reel featuring Brock Holt and Brock Holt's hair and thought, "You know what, that looks pretty fun." For the second year in the row, the super-utilityman played every position save first base, catcher and pitcher, and this time around Hernandez contributed with the bat, too. Despite walking less and striking out more, he improved in nearly every offensive category, riding a .364 BABIP to a .315 TAv. Can we reasonably expect Kiké to hit like that again? Probably not, but Hernandez's versatility and knack for hitting left-handed pitching make him an asset, even if he's miscast in the every-day-center-fielder role he assumed once Joc Pederson's struggles became too much to bear.

Micah Johnson 2B

Born: 12/18/90 Age: 25 Bats: L Throws: R Height: 6'0" Weight: 210

YEAR	TEAM	LVL	AGE	PA	R	2B	3B	HR	RBI	BB	K	SB	CS	AVG/OBP/SLG	TAv	BABIP	BRR	FRAA	WARP
2013	WNS	A+	22	228	28	7	4	1	15	10	27	22	7	.275/.309/.360	.234	.310	-1.0	2B(47): 5.2	0.4
2013	KAN	A	22	351	76	17	11	6	42	40	67	61	19	.342/.422/.530	.357	.422	5.5	2B(72): 7.5	6.0
2013	BIR	AA	22	22	2	0	0	0	1	0	4	1	0	.238/.227/.238	.175	.278	0.3	2B(5): 0.2	-0.1
2014	CHR	AAA	23	302	30	10	5	2	28	16	42	12	6	.275/.314/.370	.240	.315	1.5	2B(58): -7.0	-0.4
2014	BIR	AA	23	170	18	9	1	3	16	21	27	10	7	.329/.414/.466	.312	.385	1.1	2B(30): -1.0	1.4
2015	CHA	MLB	24	114	10	4	0	0	4	9	30	3	2	.230/.306/.270	.222	.329	-1.2	2B(33): -2.0	-0.5
2015	CHR	AAA	24	353	54	17	3	8	36	32	63	28	7	.315/.375/.466	.299	.369	2.3	2B(75): 7.0	3.3
2016	*LAN*	*MLB*	*25*	*250*	*32*	*10*	*2*	*4*	*21*	*15*	*55*	*12*	*5*	*.261/.308/.381*	*.247*	*.315*	*0.8*	*2B 2*	*1.0*
2017	*LAN*	*MLB*	*26*	*401*	*43*	*15*	*4*	*7*	*40*	*25*	*88*	*19*	*8*	*.260/.307/.378*	*.253*	*.314*	*2.2*	*2B 3*	*1.5*

Breakout: 2% Improve: 20% Collapse: 15% Attrition: 35% MLB: 60% *Comparables: Eric Young, Jose Pirela, Kevin Russo*

If he can stick around long enough and find the right role, Johnson will figure out how to hit big-league pitchers. He can run and he can sting the ball, though his over-the-fence power is limited. He controls the strike zone well enough. He's a craftsman at the plate: dedicated, intelligent, willing to adjust. He's a poor defender at second base, though, so poor that the White Sox cut his first audition for the job short and stuck the stickless Carlos Sanchez there for much of 2015. Johnson's future as anything more than a bench bat (an endangered species, that) rides on whether he can find a home in center field.

Howie Kendrick 2B

Born: 7/12/83 Age: 32 Bats: R Throws: R Height: 5'11" Weight: 220

YEAR	TEAM	LVL	AGE	PA	R	2B	3B	HR	RBI	BB	K	SB	CS	AVG/OBP/SLG	TAv	BABIP	BRR	FRAA	WARP
2013	ANA	MLB	29	513	55	21	4	13	54	23	89	6	3	.297/.335/.439	.290	.340	-6.6	2B(118): -2.0, LF(1): -0.0	2.0
2014	ANA	MLB	30	674	85	33	5	7	75	48	110	14	5	.293/.347/.397	.278	.347	-2.2	2B(154): 0.8	2.9
2015	LAN	MLB	31	495	64	22	2	9	54	27	82	6	2	.295/.336/.409	.272	.342	3.1	2B(113): -1.2	2.2
2016	*LAN*	*MLB*	*32*	*600*	*63*	*30*	*4*	*12*	*67*	*32*	*115*	*9*	*3*	*.281/.324/.415*	*.266*	*.331*	*-1.9*	*2B 0*	*2.6*
2017	*LAN*	*MLB*	*33*	*505*	*56*	*25*	*3*	*9*	*52*	*26*	*99*	*6*	*3*	*.277/.319/.397*	*.267*	*.331*	*-1.5*	*2B 0*	*1.6*

Breakout: 2% Improve: 46% Collapse: 4% Attrition: 10% MLB: 96% *Comparables: Ryne Sandberg, Brandon Phillips, Aaron Hill*

The juxtaposition between the expectations laid upon Kendrick as a prospect and the solid but unspectacular success he's enjoyed has been discussed for the better part of his 10-year career. Even now, after the second baseman reached free agency for the first time, we're often reminded that Howie Kendrick: Future Batting Title Champ never came to be. (This is the seventh time the term "batting title" has appeared in a Kendrick comment in this annual.) Yet what Kendrick lacks in upside he compensates for in stability. He has produced between 2.0 and 3.5 WARP in each of the last five years, shows no signs of regression and has the type of contact-oriented profile that ages well. The 32-year-old is still a capable defender at the keystone, has just enough power to keep pitchers honest and figures to be a set-it-and-forget-it option for the next three to five years.

Joc Pederson OF

Born: 4/21/92 Age: 24 Bats: L Throws: L Height: 6'1" Weight: 215

YEAR	TEAM	LVL	AGE	PA	R	2B	3B	HR	RBI	BB	K	SB	CS	AVG/OBP/SLG	TAv	BABIP	BRR	FRAA	WARP
2013	CHT	AA	21	519	81	24	3	22	58	70	114	31	8	.278/.381/.497	.313	.327	3.9	CF(106): 1.2, LF(6): 1.0	5.3
2014	LAN	MLB	22	38	1	0	0	0	0	9	11	0	0	.143/.351/.143	.210	.235	-0.4	CF(7): 0.8, RF(5): -0.2	-0.1
2014	ABQ	AAA	22	553	106	17	4	33	78	100	149	30	13	.303/.435/.582	.329	.385	3.7	CF(99): -2.6, LF(12): 1.9	6.4
2015	LAN	MLB	23	585	67	19	1	26	54	92	170	4	7	.210/.346/.417	.287	.262	0.3	CF(147): -21.4	1.2
2016	*LAN*	*MLB*	*24*	*631*	*97*	*21*	*2*	*29*	*80*	*88*	*182*	*14*	*8*	*.235/.349/.447*	*.285*	*.294*	*0.3*	*CF -11*	*2.8*
2017	*LAN*	*MLB*	*25*	*602*	*86*	*21*	*2*	*27*	*83*	*84*	*176*	*13*	*7*	*.231/.345/.438*	*.290*	*.291*	*1.0*	*CF -10*	*2.2*

Breakout: 4% Improve: 46% Collapse: 12% Attrition: 16% MLB: 85% *Comparables: Brandon Belt, Pedro Alvarez, Oswaldo Arcia*

If you enjoyed *Strange Case of Dr. Jekyll and Mr. Hyde*, you'll love the sequel, *Joc Pederson's 2015 Season*. Pederson hit .230/.364/.487 with 20 homers in the first half, earning a spot on the All-Star team and finishing second in the Home Run Derby. But in the second half Pederson was astonishingly bad, posting a .178/.317/.300 line and suffering a .232 BABIP despite doing little to change his approach. He lost regular playing time to Enrique Hernandez, barely played at all against southpaws and received just eight plate appearances in the postseason. At the very least, Pederson appears a safe bet to be a Colby Rasmus–type player, but with even more power and much better hair. If you're an optimist, you still see a potential star who usually passes the eye test in center (metrics disagree) and is dominant enough against right-handers to make his deficiencies well worth bearing. He'll be 24 this year, so it's reasonable to hope Dr. Jocyll's ugly transformation is only temporary.

Yasiel Puig RF

Born: 12/7/90 Age: 25 Bats: R Throws: R Height: 6'2" Weight: 255

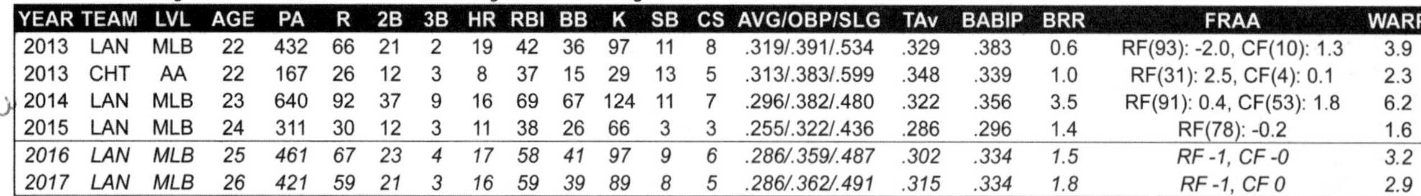

YEAR	TEAM	LVL	AGE	PA	R	2B	3B	HR	RBI	BB	K	SB	CS	AVG/OBP/SLG	TAv	BABIP	BRR	FRAA	WARP
2013	LAN	MLB	22	432	66	21	2	19	42	36	97	11	8	.319/.391/.534	.329	.383	0.6	RF(93): -2.0, CF(10): 1.3	3.9
2013	CHT	AA	22	167	26	12	3	8	37	15	29	13	5	.313/.383/.599	.348	.339	1.0	RF(31): 2.5, CF(4): 0.1	2.3
2014	LAN	MLB	23	640	92	37	9	16	69	67	124	11	7	.296/.382/.480	.322	.356	3.5	RF(91): 0.4, CF(53): 1.8	6.2
2015	LAN	MLB	24	311	30	12	3	11	38	26	66	3	3	.255/.322/.436	.286	.296	1.4	RF(78): -0.2	1.6
2016	*LAN*	*MLB*	*25*	*461*	*67*	*23*	*4*	*17*	*58*	*41*	*97*	*9*	*6*	*.286/.359/.487*	*.302*	*.334*	*1.5*	*RF -1, CF -0*	*3.2*
2017	*LAN*	*MLB*	*26*	*421*	*59*	*21*	*3*	*16*	*59*	*39*	*89*	*8*	*5*	*.286/.362/.491*	*.315*	*.334*	*1.8*	*RF -1, CF 0*	*2.9*

Breakout: 3% Improve: 64% Collapse: 1% Attrition: 4% MLB: 100% *Comparables: Justin Upton, Hanley Ramirez, Ryan Braun*

You might have thought you'd seen and heard it all with Puig. He can TOOTBLAN one moment and unleash one of the most athletic plays you'll see on a baseball diamond the next. He'll flail helplessly at balls in the dirt during one at-bat, then launch a homer to the moon. He'll seem an affable, childlike wonder on the field, then get pulled over for doing 110, presumably because he was late for something. Yes, Puig has mystified ever since arriving from Cuba, but we saw something altogether new in 2015: We saw him fail.

All the progress Puig made in terms of walking more and striking out less evaporated last season. He hit the ball on a line and in the air more than he did in 2014, but while his homer-per-fly rate spiked, everything else regressed. He had to deal with a mortal .296 BABIP after posting marks of .383 and .356 his first two years, but that alone doesn't account for his astounding drop in TAv and slugging. That Puig was still able to earn 1.5 WARP in a poor half-season speaks to his upside, but didn't much help a Dodgers team that was probably hoping for three or four times that impact.

Puig's hamstrings are to blame for his two extended absences last year, and we've already heard about how he's going to try to drop weight to mold his body in the vision of a strong safety rather than a middle linebacker. Any changes that keep him on the field are welcome both for Dodgers fans and baseball nerds worldwide, as he's one of the league's most entertaining players and one of two or three Dodgers under contract who can actually hit left-handed pitching.

For some reason, shouting "YAS PUIG!" when he does good things is less widespread than you'd think in this *Broad City*–dominated world we live in. Be the change that you wish to see in the baseball stadium.

Jimmy Rollins SS

Born: 11/27/78 Age: 37 Bats: B Throws: R Height: 5'7" Weight: 175

YEAR	TEAM	LVL	AGE	PA	R	2B	3B	HR	RBI	BB	K	SB	CS	AVG/OBP/SLG	TAv	BABIP	BRR	FRAA	WARP
2013	PHI	MLB	34	666	65	36	2	6	39	59	93	22	6	.252/.318/.348	.241	.288	1.9	SS(153): -3.8	1.2
2014	PHI	MLB	35	609	78	22	4	17	55	64	100	28	6	.243/.323/.394	.274	.269	-0.8	SS(131): 8.2	4.2
2015	LAN	MLB	36	563	71	24	3	13	41	44	86	12	8	.224/.285/.358	.237	.246	4.0	SS(134): -8.6	0.5
2016	*LAN*	*MLB*	*37*	*538*	*67*	*23*	*2*	*12*	*49*	*44*	*80*	*18*	*6*	*.238/.300/.369*	*.243*	*.259*	*1.0*	*SS -2*	*1.6*
2017	*LAN*	*MLB*	*38*	*491*	*51*	*20*	*2*	*9*	*47*	*37*	*75*	*14*	*5*	*.227/.285/.341*	*.236*	*.251*	*1.2*	*SS -2*	*0.6*

Breakout: 0% Improve: 27% Collapse: 15% Attrition: 17% MLB: 79% *Comparables: Barry Larkin, Jamey Carroll, Marco Scutaro*

Los Angeles was counting on Rollins to be a role player, not a key cog, meaning that some regression from his last performance in Philly would have been fine. Unfortunately, he "regressed" the way your car "regresses" when you drive it into a pole, or like your cookies "regress" when you leave them in the oven for six hours. Career lows in average, OBP and stolen bases dropped his TAv to an embarrassing level, and he lost more than a step in the field, too. Given how good Rollins was in 2014 you can't blame him if he wants to give it one more shot, perhaps serving as a mentor in a reserve role. Then again, it's always painful to watch one of the greats limp to the finish line, and if Rollins decides to hang 'em up that would be just as easy to justify. If this was his last ride, let's remember him as the heart and soul of many a talented Phillies team, and purge the grizzled veteran who lost his job to Corey Seager from our minds.

Corey Seager SS

Born: 4/27/94 Age: 22 Bats: L Throws: R Height: 6'4" Weight: 215

YEAR	TEAM	LVL	AGE	PA	R	2B	3B	HR	RBI	BB	K	SB	CS	AVG/OBP/SLG	TAv	BABIP	BRR	FRAA	WARP
2013	RCU	A+	19	114	10	2	1	4	15	12	31	1	0	.160/.246/.320	.221	.179	0.2	SS(25): -5.7, 3B(1): -0.0	-0.6
2013	GRL	A	19	312	45	18	3	12	57	34	58	9	4	.309/.389/.529	.330	.353	-0.5	SS(74): -5.1	3.2
2014	CHT	AA	20	161	28	16	3	2	27	10	39	1	1	.345/.381/.534	.305	.450	1.4	SS(35): -1.0	1.5
2014	RCU	A+	20	365	61	34	2	18	70	30	76	5	1	.352/.411/.633	.355	.411	2.4	SS(64): 10.2, SS(7): 10.2	7.3
2015	OKL	AAA	21	464	64	30	2	13	61	32	65	3	0	.278/.332/.451	.285	.298	2.2	SS(90): 8.3, 3B(15): 1.0	4.3
2015	LAN	MLB	21	113	17	8	1	4	17	14	19	2	0	.337/.425/.561	.356	.387	0.4	SS(21): 1.6, 3B(6): 0.7	1.9
2015	TUL	AA	21	86	17	7	1	5	15	5	11	1	1	.375/.407/.675	.393	.385	0.5	SS(15): 0.1, 3B(4): -0.2	1.6
2016	*LAN*	*MLB*	*22*	*565*	*63*	*31*	*3*	*21*	*76*	*34*	*128*	*2*	*1*	*.263/.311/.452*	*.271*	*.309*	*-0.5*	*SS 1*	*3.5*
2017	*LAN*	*MLB*	*23*	*572*	*70*	*31*	*3*	*21*	*75*	*35*	*131*	*2*	*1*	*.256/.306/.443*	*.275*	*.301*	*-0.8*	*SS 1*	*3.0*

Breakout: 4% Improve: 39% Collapse: 4% Attrition: 19% MLB: 73% *Comparables: Brett Lawrie, Evan Longoria, Andy Marte*

Seager was a card-carrying member of the Too Big To Stay At Shortstop Club, hanging out with Xander Bogaerts and Carlos Correa as visions of a move to third base danced in scouts' heads. Maybe that shift will come someday, but for now Seager looks just fine at short, and that upgrades him from "great" to "elite" on the prospect scale. He dominated in Tulsa and hit well in Oklahoma City before Jimmy Rollins' ineptitude forced Seager to the bigs at the tender age of 21. He responded by producing nearly two WARP in just 27 games, which means that at this pace he'd only need two seasons to out-WARP older brother Kyle, who, remember, is one of the better third basemen in the league. That goal may be a bit lofty, but Corey is poised to be a key contributor for the boys in blue in 2016, and will likely open the season as the prohibitive Rookie of the Year favorite.

Trayce Thompson CF

Born: 3/15/91 Age: 25 Bats: R Throws: R Height: 6'3" Weight: 210

YEAR	TEAM	LVL	AGE	PA	R	2B	3B	HR	RBI	BB	K	SB	CS	AVG/OBP/SLG	TAv	BABIP	BRR	FRAA	WARP
2013	BIR	AA	22	590	78	23	5	15	73	60	139	25	8	.229/.321/.383	.274	.280	3.8	CF(67): -8.9, RF(62): 2.6	2.1
2014	BIR	AA	23	595	86	34	6	16	59	65	151	20	5	.237/.324/.419	.269	.301	4.0	CF(81): 4.1, LF(48): 0.7	3.2
2015	CHA	MLB	24	135	17	8	3	5	16	13	26	1	0	.295/.363/.533	.308	.341	1.5	RF(18): 0.2, LF(12): 0.8	1.1
2015	CHR	AAA	24	417	53	23	4	13	39	23	79	11	5	.260/.304/.441	.258	.295	1.5	CF(94): 1.6, RF(5): 2.4	1.7
2016	*LAN*	*MLB*	*25*	*305*	*33*	*14*	*2*	*9*	*35*	*21*	*85*	*6*	*2*	*.225/.283/.391*	*.243*	*.284*	*0.4*	*CF -0, RF 1*	*0.6*
2017	*LAN*	*MLB*	*26*	*454*	*51*	*21*	*3*	*13*	*52*	*32*	*128*	*9*	*3*	*.225/.286/.390*	*.251*	*.287*	*0.9*	*CF 0, RF 1*	*0.8*

Breakout: 9% Improve: 25% Collapse: 11% Attrition: 41% MLB: 61% *Comparables: Curtis Granderson, Joe Benson, Blake Tekotte*

Early in his development, Thompson was passive (not patient; passive) at the plate, leading to fewer hard-hit balls and less contact than a player with his tool kit should have managed. He found a more aggressive approach that sort of worked in 2015, though there are holes in his swing as yet unexplored by the few big leaguers who saw him. With iffy strike-zone command, average power and good speed he doesn't use very well, Thompson figures to be an uneven regular outfielder or competent backup, not unlike fellow Alliteration All-Stars Brandon Barnes and Collin Cowgill.

Justin Turner 3B

Born: 11/23/84 Age: 31 Bats: R Throws: R Height: 5'11" Weight: 205

YEAR	TEAM	LVL	AGE	PA	R	2B	3B	HR	RBI	BB	K	SB	CS	AVG/OBP/SLG	TAv	BABIP	BRR	FRAA	WARP
2013	NYN	MLB	28	214	12	13	1	2	16	11	34	0	1	.280/.319/.385	.262	.327	0.3	3B(23): -0.9, SS(18): -1.4	0.4
2014	LAN	MLB	29	322	46	21	1	7	43	28	58	6	1	.340/.404/.493	.340	.404	1.0	3B(59): 3.1, SS(15): -0.2	4.0
2015	LAN	MLB	30	439	55	26	1	16	60	36	71	5	2	.294/.370/.491	.321	.321	1.2	3B(100): -0.9, 1B(10): -0.1	4.2
2016	*LAN*	*MLB*	*31*	*617*	*67*	*36*	*2*	*13*	*70*	*44*	*98*	*7*	*3*	*.279/.341/.422*	*.276*	*.314*	*1.1*	*3B -0, SS -0*	*3.0*
2017	*LAN*	*MLB*	*32*	*502*	*57*	*28*	*1*	*9*	*52*	*33*	*85*	*4*	*2*	*.269/.330/.397*	*.273*	*.309*	*0.8*	*3B 0, SS 0*	*1.6*

Breakout: 0% Improve: 37% Collapse: 5% Attrition: 5% MLB: 96% *Comparables: Martin Prado, Sal Bando, Bill Madlock*

The age of #lolMets may be behind us, but Turner has produced 8.4 WARP for the Dodgers since New York decided to non-tender him after 2013. Baseball's Tormund Giantsbane was outstanding once again in 2015, hitting new career highs in homers, ISO, plate appearances and facial hair. He primarily manned the hot corner, but also filled in at first and second and even made a brief cameo at short. Despite his atypical career, Turner has done enough over the past three years to prove that his bat is real, and he can be used either as a solid starter or one of the best utilitymen in the game. The only real concern here is his knee. No, not because of the infected ingrown hair that cost Turner a midseason DL stint, but the microfracture surgery he required after the season ended. He survived Hardhome, though, so this shouldn't sideline him for long.

Chase Utley 2B

Born: 12/17/78 Age: 37 Bats: L Throws: R Height: 6'1" Weight: 190

YEAR	TEAM	LVL	AGE	PA	R	2B	3B	HR	RBI	BB	K	SB	CS	AVG/OBP/SLG	TAv	BABIP	BRR	FRAA	WARP
2013	PHI	MLB	34	531	73	25	6	18	69	45	79	8	3	.284/.348/.475	.292	.305	1.6	2B(125): 0.2	3.4
2014	PHI	MLB	35	664	74	36	6	11	78	53	85	10	1	.270/.339/.407	.287	.295	2.8	2B(147): 4.7, 1B(1): -0.0	4.5
2015	PHI	MLB	36	282	23	12	1	5	30	22	35	3	0	.217/.284/.333	.240	.227	-1.1	2B(62): -2.0, 1B(4): -0.1	-0.2
2015	LAN	MLB	36	141	14	9	1	3	9	10	29	1	0	.202/.291/.363	.241	.237	-0.4	2B(26): 1.8, 3B(3): -0.1	0.2
2016	*LAN*	*MLB*	*37*	*584*	*62*	*27*	*4*	*14*	*65*	*45*	*85*	*8*	*1*	*.246/.317/.393*	*.255*	*.267*	*0.8*	*2B 4*	*2.6*
2017	*LAN*	*MLB*	*38*	*410*	*45*	*19*	*2*	*9*	*42*	*30*	*62*	*4*	*1*	*.236/.304/.373*	*.252*	*.258*	*0.4*	*2B 3*	*1.2*

Breakout: 0% Improve: 23% Collapse: 18% Attrition: 9% MLB: 76% *Comparables: Jerry Hairston, Marco Scutaro, Mark Loretta*

When Utley agreed to a trade that let him join his old double-play partner in Los Angeles, it was easy to imagine the duo winning another ring, hanging up the cleats and waiting patiently for the results of their Hall of Fame ballots in 2020. Instead, Rollins lost his job and Utley lost quite a few fans thanks to a slide that a middle infielder should know better than to make. With all due respect to a player who's had a wonderful career, Utley looked entirely washed up in 2015. He's got a little power left, but he struck out at his highest rate since 2009, wasn't great in the field and shouldn't be let within 100 feet of a left-handed pitcher. The question, looking at his drop-off from 2014 to 2015, is whether the cliff was real and the fall deadly or if there's some bounceback left in the old coot. It's probably worth the Dodgers' $7 million to find out given the upside, and as far as Plan Bs and platoon partners go, Enrique Hernandez is pretty sturdy. Certainly a lot sturdier than Ruben Tejada's fibula.

Scott Van Slyke LF

Born: 7/24/86 Age: 29 Bats: R Throws: R Height: 6'4" Weight: 220

YEAR	TEAM	LVL	AGE	PA	R	2B	3B	HR	RBI	BB	K	SB	CS	AVG/OBP/SLG	TAv	BABIP	BRR	FRAA	WARP
2013	ABQ	AAA	26	263	55	17	2	12	48	50	61	8	2	.348/.479/.627	.338	.437	1.0	1B(51): 3.1, LF(8): 0.5	3.1
2013	LAN	MLB	26	152	13	8	0	7	19	20	37	1	1	.240/.342/.465	.285	.276	-1.0	LF(30): 0.2, RF(13): 0.2	0.6
2014	LAN	MLB	27	246	32	13	1	11	29	28	71	4	2	.297/.386/.524	.332	.394	-0.1	LF(32): 1.2, CF(21): -1.0	2.5
2015	LAN	MLB	28	253	19	14	0	6	30	23	62	3	1	.239/.317/.383	.271	.299	0.0	LF(55): 5.9, RF(22): -1.3	1.2
2016	*LAN*	*MLB*	*29*	*354*	*44*	*18*	*0*	*13*	*47*	*38*	*89*	*5*	*2*	*.253/.339/.446*	*.282*	*.309*	*-0.4*	*LF 2, 1B 0*	*2.0*
2017	*LAN*	*MLB*	*30*	*335*	*44*	*17*	*0*	*12*	*42*	*35*	*88*	*4*	*2*	*.243/.330/.422*	*.281*	*.303*	*-0.3*	*LF 2, 1B 0*	*1.3*

Breakout: 3% Improve: 33% Collapse: 5% Attrition: 10% MLB: 80% *Comparables: Ryan Raburn, Josh Willingham, Ryan Church*

Some thought Van Slyke might be on the verge of a breakout after his strong 2014, but the Abraham Lincoln impersonator just broke instead. Though he hit well enough against right-handers in 2014 to suggest he needn't be used strictly as a platoon player, the Dodgers really pushed their luck in 2015, giving him 139 plate appearances against same-side pitching. The result: a

.225/.261/.375 line versus righties that weighed down his overall numbers, though it's worth noting that Van Slyke's .258/.386/.396 line against southpaws was hardly elite in its own right. He dealt with back and wrist issues at various points, so perhaps health is to blame for Van Slyke's dramatic drop in ISO, but the Dodgers may very well decide they need a more consistent right-handed complement to Andre Ethier, Joc Pederson and Carl Crawford moving forward.

Alex Verdugo OF

Born: 5/15/96 Age: 20 Bats: L Throws: L Height: 6'0" Weight: 205

YEAR	TEAM	LVL	AGE	PA	R	2B	3B	HR	RBI	BB	K	SB	CS	AVG/OBP/SLG	TAv	BABIP	BRR	FRAA	WARP
2015	RCU	A+	19	96	20	9	2	4	19	4	12	1	0	.385/.406/.659	.372	.408	0.4	CF(23): 2.2	1.8
2015	GRL	A	19	444	50	23	2	5	42	17	53	13	5	.295/.325/.394	.258	.326	-0.7	CF(89): 16.6, RF(11): 1.4	3.1
2016	*LAN*	*MLB*	*20*	*250*	*23*	*12*	*1*	*6*	*28*	*5*	*51*	*2*	*1*	*.245/.261/.381*	*.227*	*.283*	*-0.2*	*CF 3, RF -0*	*0.3*
2017	*LAN*	*MLB*	*21*	*388*	*41*	*20*	*2*	*10*	*44*	*9*	*75*	*3*	*1*	*.251/.271/.398*	*.243*	*.285*	*-0.3*	*CF 4, RF 0*	*0.6*

Breakout: 2% Improve: 5% Collapse: 0% Attrition: 5% MLB: 8% *Comparables: Fernando Martinez, Eddie Rosario, Oswaldo Arcia*

Verdugo hit just .213/.254/.274 in April and May as the 2014 second-rounder acclimated to his first full season of professional ball. Look up at his final batting line at Great Lakes for an idea of how he hit from June on. Then consider his brief performance as a 19-year-old in High-A. Then remember that he was a raw, two-way player coming out of high school. Not too shabby, eh? There's a lot to like with Verdugo, who's moving fast and devoid of any glaring flaws as a prospect. He should spend most of the season in the Cal League, where hitter-friendly environments stand to make Verdugo an expensive but effective minor-league DFS play.

PITCHERS

Brett Anderson LHP

Born: 2/1/88 Age: 28 Bats: L Throws: L Height: 6'3" Weight: 240

YEAR	TEAM	LVL	AGE	W	L	SV	G	GS	IP	H	HR	BB/9	K/9	GB%	BABIP	WHIP	ERA	FIP	DRA	WARP	CFIP	MPH
2013	OAK	MLB	25	1	4	3	16	5	44^{2}	51	5	4.2	9.3	62%	.359	1.61	6.04	3.88	5.19	-0.2	99	95.0
2014	COL	MLB	26	1	3	0	8	8	43^{1}	44	1	2.7	6.0	63%	.314	1.32	2.91	2.96	3.31	0.8	99	92.9
2015	LAN	MLB	27	10	9	0	31	31	180^{1}	194	18	2.3	5.8	67%	.310	1.33	3.69	3.97	4.39	1.4	114	93.5
2016	*LAN*	*MLB*	*28*	*8*	*7*	*0*	*24*	*24*	*127^{1}*	*128*	*15*	*2.3*	*6.4*	*67%*	*.310*	*1.26*	*4.03*	*4.01*	*4.72*	*0.9*	*110*	
2017	*LAN*	*MLB*	*29*	*7*	*8*	*0*	*24*	*24*	*138^{2}*	*145*	*16*	*2.5*	*6.4*	*67%*	*.320*	*1.32*	*4.02*	*4.39*	*4.71*	*0.9*	*110*	

Breakout: 24% Improve: 51% Collapse: 16% Attrition: 9% MLB: 89% *Comparables: Jaime Garcia, Charles Nagy, Paul Maholm*

Listen, you already know where this comment is going, but it's got to be said. Brett Anderson threw 180 innings in 2015. That's the most he's thrown in one season in his career. It's only the second time he's crossed the 150-innings mark; the first time was in 2009. Anderson's 180 innings were just 25 fewer than he threw from 2011 to 2014 combined. He avoided the disabled list. He finally did it. Yet as happy as you have to be for Anderson, it's hard not to feel a little let down by his very average performance, to combat the sense that for five years we held our collective breath for Jon Niese with a better Twitter account. There's more upside here to be sure—Anderson is still just 28 and appeared more potent with the Rockies in 2014—but he's going to need a team that loves to gamble that he'll be both healthy and impactful moving forward. Give Anderson props for being self-aware on that last point: He accepted the Dodgers' qualifying offer despite reportedly having a multi-year deal on the table.

Chris Anderson RHP

Born: 7/29/92 Age: 23 Bats: R Throws: R Height: 6'3" Weight: 235

YEAR	TEAM	LVL	AGE	W	L	SV	G	GS	IP	H	HR	BB/9	K/9	GB%	BABIP	WHIP	ERA	FIP	DRA	WARP	CFIP	MPH
2013	GRL	A	20	3	0	0	12	12	46	32	0	4.7	9.8	40%	.288	1.22	1.96	2.79	4.38	0.5	93	
2014	RCU	A+	21	7	7	0	27	25	134^{1}	147	11	4.2	9.8	45%	.370	1.56	4.62	4.26	5.53	-0.8	103	
2015	TUL	AA	22	9	7	0	23	23	126^{2}	123	12	4.2	7.0	46%	.297	1.44	4.05	4.57	5.66	-0.7	113	
2016	*LAN*	*MLB*	*23*	*7*	*8*	*0*	*23*	*23*	*114^{2}*	*120*	*17*	*3.8*	*6.9*	*43%*	*.320*	*1.47*	*4.91*	*4.87*	*5.69*	*-0.6*	*136*	
2017	*LAN*	*MLB*	*24*	*4*	*7*	*0*	*17*	*17*	*100^{2}*	*108*	*15*	*4.8*	*7.4*	*43%*	*.333*	*1.60*	*5.13*	*5.64*	*5.94*	*-0.7*	*141*	

Breakout: 0% Improve: 0% Collapse: 0% Attrition: 0% MLB: 0% *Comparables: Daniel Corcino, Fernando Nieve, Tyler Wagner*

When the Dodgers popped Anderson with the 18th-overall pick in 2013, the hope was that he'd be a fast-moving mid-rotation starter who would provide depth in relatively short order. Anderson has moved somewhat quickly, so he held up that end of the bargain, but he's been bad, which makes this comment a classic case of burying the lede. Anderson had big-time control issues in High-A in 2014, but at least he was missing bats. The big righty stopped doing that in Tulsa last year, but the walks didn't concomitantly disappear, so he's living off his first-round pedigree at this point. He may be a viable reliever if his velocity ticks up and his command improves in shorter stints. That is not how you want your comment to end after just three professional seasons.

Bronson Arroyo RHP

Born: 2/24/77 Age: 39 Bats: R Throws: R Height: 6'3" Weight: 185

YEAR	TEAM	LVL	AGE	W	L	SV	G	GS	IP	H	HR	BB/9	K/9	GB%	BABIP	WHIP	ERA	FIP	DRA	WARP	CFIP	MPH
2013	CIN	MLB	36	14	12	0	32	32	202	199	32	1.5	5.5	47%	.267	1.15	3.79	4.46	4.40	1.2	116	90.1
2014	ARI	MLB	37	7	4	0	14	14	86	92	10	2.0	4.9	55%	.295	1.29	4.08	4.29	4.59	0.2	119	88.5
2016	*LAN*	*MLB*	*39*	*2*	*2*	*0*	*6*	*6*	*38^{1}*	*37*	*5*	*1.8*	*5.7*	*49%*	*.291*	*1.17*	*4.15*	*4.11*	*4.84*	*0.2*	*115*	
2017	*LAN*	*MLB*	*40*	*11*	*12*	*0*	*32*	*32*	*202^{1}*	*208*	*26*	*2.0*	*5.4*	*49%*	*.300*	*1.25*	*4.28*	*4.66*	*4.99*	*0.7*	*119*	

Breakout: 6% Improve: 20% Collapse: 16% Attrition: 2% MLB: 52% *Comparables: Paul Byrd, Harry Brecheen, Preacher Roe*

Over the last two seasons, Arroyo has thrown 86 innings, been traded three times, hit the DL for the first time in his career and earned $23.5 million, including his 2016 buyout. If you want to get granular, that's $273,255 per inning, $500,000 per strikeout, $3.4

million per win and $1.9 million per abandoned cornrow. The Guy Fieri of back-end starters (in both quality and looks) is about to enter his age-39 season, but when we last saw him on the mound he was still limiting walks, giving up gopher balls and doing just enough to skate by. Unless he retires, some team will likely let Arroyo eat up innings on the cheap once more, though the unfortunate realities of dead-tree media mean that we went to press without knowing his fate.

Luis Avilan LHP

Born: 7/19/89 Age: 26 Bats: L Throws: L Height: 6'2" Weight: 220

YEAR	TEAM	LVL	AGE	W	L	SV	G	GS	IP	H	HR	BB/9	K/9	GB%	BABIP	WHIP	ERA	FIP	DRA	WARP	CFIP	MPH
2013	ATL	MLB	23	5	0	0	75	0	65	40	1	3.0	5.3	58%	.204	0.95	1.52	3.25	2.62	1.6	116	95.6
2014	ATL	MLB	24	4	1	0	62	0	43^{1}	47	2	4.4	5.2	58%	.317	1.57	4.57	4.21	5.00	-0.3	123	95.7
2014	GWN	AAA	24	0	1	0	9	0	11^{2}	13	0	8.5	4.6	50%	.342	2.06	5.40	5.16	5.36	-0.1	126	
2015	LAN	MLB	25	0	1	0	23	0	15^{2}	13	2	2.9	10.3	55%	.275	1.15	5.17	3.67	3.26	0.3	93	95.5
2015	ATL	MLB	25	2	4	0	50	0	37^{2}	35	4	2.4	7.4	49%	.284	1.19	3.58	3.69	4.32	0.2	99	95.8
2016	*LAN*	*MLB*	*26*	*3*	*1*	*0*	*51*	*0*	*54*	*48*	*6*	*2.7*	*7.1*	*54%*	*.286*	*1.19*	*4.00*	*3.89*	*4.70*	*0.1*	*107*	
2017	*LAN*	*MLB*	*27*	*4*	*2*	*1*	*67*	*2*	*68^{2}*	*62*	*8*	*2.9*	*7.1*	*54%*	*.289*	*1.22*	*4.02*	*4.38*	*4.72*	*0.2*	*107*	

Breakout: 24% Improve: 47% Collapse: 21% Attrition: 21% MLB: 78% *Comparables: Jeremy Accardo, Jesse Crain, Alberto Arias*

If you're wondering why bullpens are so hard to construct and maintain, consider Avilan. At various points in his four-year career, he's looked like a dominant late-inning asset, a fringy LOOGY, a strikeout artist and a groundball specialist. From 2012 to 2014, he gave up just four homers; last season he gave up six. The most anonymous player who headed to LA as part of the Alex Wood deal, Avilan gave up nine runs in just 15 innings with the Dodgers but was better than his ERA suggests when used as a strict one-and-done matchups guy. That role makes his spot on the roster inherently tenuous, but hey, at least he out-pitched fellow trade piece Jim Johnson.

Pedro Baez RHP

Born: 3/11/88 Age: 28 Bats: R Throws: R Height: 6'0" Weight: 230

YEAR	TEAM	LVL	AGE	W	L	SV	G	GS	IP	H	HR	BB/9	K/9	GB%	BABIP	WHIP	ERA	FIP	DRA	WARP	CFIP	MPH
2013	RCU	A+	25	2	2	2	32	0	34^{2}	41	3	3.9	8.3	39%	.349	1.62	3.63	4.69	5.45	0.2	103	
2013	CHT	AA	25	1	1	0	16	0	23^{1}	26	3	3.1	8.9	44%	.338	1.46	4.24	3.64	4.05	0.1	98	
2014	CHT	AA	26	2	1	6	17	0	19^{1}	15	0	4.2	8.4	35%	.278	1.24	2.79	2.88				
2014	LAN	MLB	26	0	0	0	20	0	24	16	3	1.9	6.8	38%	.197	0.88	2.62	3.85	2.57	0.6	105	98.4
2014	ABQ	AAA	26	0	0	6	23	0	22^{2}	27	4	1.6	7.9	46%	.343	1.37	4.76	5.02	5.14	0.1	96	
2015	LAN	MLB	27	4	2	0	52	0	51	47	4	1.9	10.6	41%	.326	1.14	3.35	2.53	4.00	0.4	80	99.8
2016	*LAN*	*MLB*	*28*	*2*	*1*	*0*	*46*	*0*	*49*	*43*	*5*	*2.5*	*8.8*	*41%*	*.305*	*1.16*	*3.54*	*3.39*	*4.17*	*0.5*	*93*	
2017	*LAN*	*MLB*	*29*	*2*	*1*	*0*	*46*	*0*	*50^{1}*	*44*	*6*	*2.9*	*8.7*	*41%*	*.301*	*1.20*	*3.68*	*4.00*	*4.33*	*0.3*	*98*	

Breakout: 24% Improve: 49% Collapse: 16% Attrition: 16% MLB: 73% *Comparables: David Carpenter, Rich Thompson, Matt Reynolds*

Death, taxes and Baez getting pounded after relieving Clayton Kershaw in the playoffs. Before Baez decided to make David Wright a postseason hero, he was quite good for the Dodgers, striking out nearly 30 percent of opposing batters and lowering his homer rate from 2014, but the former position player seemed to wear down as the season dragged on, allowing nine earned runs in his final 14 regular-season innings and ceding his setup role to Chris Hatcher. When Baez is on, his fastball is devastating and his slider keeps hitters honest, but when Baez is off, the only thing devastated is the Dodgers' fanbase; see, in this regard, the seven (including postseason) appearances in which he allowed two or more earned runs. That's not an atypical profile for a reliever, but it's one the Dodgers are likely tired of seeing in October.

Mike Bolsinger RHP

Born: 1/29/88 Age: 28 Bats: R Throws: R Height: 6'1" Weight: 215

YEAR	TEAM	LVL	AGE	W	L	SV	G	GS	IP	H	HR	BB/9	K/9	GB%	BABIP	WHIP	ERA	FIP	DRA	WARP	CFIP	MPH
2013	MOB	AA	25	4	0	0	9	6	43	35	0	3.1	6.5	57%	.271	1.16	2.51	2.59	4.10	0.3	101	
2013	RNO	AAA	25	7	7	0	17	17	101	116	12	3.5	8.6	53%	.348	1.53	4.72	4.47	4.86	0.9	96	
2014	ARI	MLB	26	1	6	0	10	9	52^{1}	66	7	2.9	8.3	54%	.355	1.59	5.50	3.98	6.63	-1.2	107	90.5
2014	RNO	AAA	26	8	3	0	17	16	91^{2}	92	6	3.1	8.6	56%	.331	1.35	3.93	3.78	4.68	1.1	78	
2015	OKL	AAA	27	3	3	0	10	8	46^{2}	30	2	3.5	11.8	47%	.272	1.03	2.31	2.89	2.62	1.5	73	
2015	LAN	MLB	27	6	6	0	21	21	109^{1}	104	11	3.7	8.1	56%	.299	1.36	3.62	3.94	4.26	1.0	105	89.7
2016	*LAN*	*MLB*	*28*	*9*	*8*	*0*	*26*	*26*	*137^{2}*	*127*	*16*	*3.0*	*8.3*	*54%*	*.311*	*1.25*	*3.82*	*3.81*	*4.49*	*1.3*	*103*	
2017	*LAN*	*MLB*	*29*	*7*	*7*	*0*	*22*	*22*	*126^{2}*	*113*	*15*	*3.5*	*8.5*	*54%*	*.307*	*1.29*	*3.92*	*4.29*	*4.61*	*0.9*	*106*	

Breakout: 23% Improve: 44% Collapse: 13% Attrition: 20% MLB: 71% *Comparables: Dan Meyer, Sam LeCure, Tom Wilhelmsen*

One imagines that the last 15 or so months, depending on when you read this, have been an emotional roller coaster for Bolsinger. First he was traded from the Diamondbacks to the Dodgers; that qualifies as a positive. Next, he saw the Dodgers add arms like Brandon McCarthy and Brett Anderson, utterly burying him on the depth chart. Improbably, injuries forced Bolsinger to make 16 starts, and the right-hander surprised everyone, posting a 2.83 ERA across 89 innings. That didn't stop the Dodgers from acquiring Alex Wood and Mat Latos at the trade deadline, bumping Bolsinger to Triple-A until September, when he got five more MLB starts and was terrible. Is life more unfair because Bolsinger wasn't rewarded for his impressive midseason efforts, or is life more unfair because Bolsinger, who was completely unremarkable in Triple-A, lucked into being traded to one of the best teams in the league in the first place? Philosophers will debate this quandary for decades, but we know two things for sure: Life is unfair and Bolsinger is a decent fifth or sixth starting option.

Brooks Brown RHP

Born: 6/20/85 Age: 31 Bats: L Throws: R Height: 6'3" Weight: 205

YEAR	TEAM	LVL	AGE	W	L	SV	G	GS	IP	H	HR	BB/9	K/9	GB%	BABIP	WHIP	ERA	FIP	DRA	WARP	CFIP	MPH
2013	IND	AAA	28	6	5	0	37	8	91	95	11	2.4	6.8	52%	.316	1.31	4.75	4.12	4.34	0.3	99	
2014	CSP	AAA	29	1	1	7	37	0	47^{1}	50	4	3.2	8.7	52%	.336	1.42	4.18	4.25	5.11	0.2	92	
2014	COL	MLB	29	0	1	0	28	0	26	20	3	1.7	7.3	60%	.230	0.96	2.77	3.68	1.69	0.9	90	96.2
2015	ABQ	AAA	30	0	0	0	16	0	15	20	1	3.0	10.2	30%	.422	1.67	6.00	3.20	3.76	0.2	86	
2015	COL	MLB	30	1	3	0	36	0	33	32	2	4.4	5.5	53%	.278	1.45	4.91	4.28	3.18	0.6	117	95.9
2016	*LAN*	*MLB*	*31*	*3*	*2*	*0*	*33*	*4*	*49^{1}*	*47*	*6*	*2.7*	*7.4*	*50%*	*.307*	*1.26*	*3.96*	*4.03*	*4.63*	*0.3*	*107*	
2017	*LAN*	*MLB*	*32*	*4*	*3*	*1*	*56*	*7*	*101^{1}*	*102*	*13*	*3.0*	*7.3*	*50%*	*.316*	*1.35*	*4.20*	*4.58*	*4.91*	*0.1*	*114*	

Breakout: 7% Improve: 10% Collapse: 3% Attrition: 9% MLB: 20% *Comparables: Jarrett Grube, Michael O'Connor, Dusty Hughes*

At 29 in 2014, Brown was a rookie going on washed up, and the turn came quickly: The Rockies dropped him from high leverage to the back of the bullpen by June last year, as it had become clear he wasn't the same pitcher at 30. The separation between his fastball and changeup closed, and the latter lost its tumble, limiting the effectiveness of his best secondary pitch. He missed fewer bats, killed fewer worms, started handing out free passes like BOGO coupons and was on waivers by October. The Dodgers claimed him, but there's no particular reason to think he won't be waived a couple more times before this book hits your hands.

Jharel Cotton RHP

Born: 1/19/92 Age: 24 Bats: R Throws: R Height: 5'11" Weight: 195

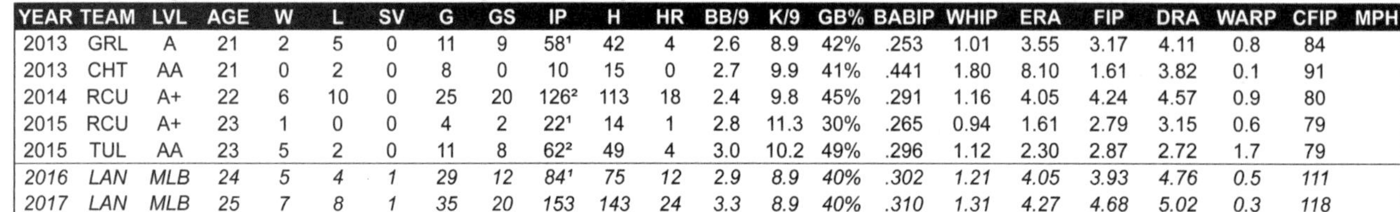

YEAR	TEAM	LVL	AGE	W	L	SV	G	GS	IP	H	HR	BB/9	K/9	GB%	BABIP	WHIP	ERA	FIP	DRA	WARP	CFIP	MPH
2013	GRL	A	21	2	5	0	11	9	58^{1}	42	4	2.6	8.9	42%	.253	1.01	3.55	3.17	4.11	0.8	84	
2013	CHT	AA	21	0	2	0	8	0	10	15	0	2.7	9.9	41%	.441	1.80	8.10	1.61	3.82	0.1	91	
2014	RCU	A+	22	6	10	0	25	20	126^{2}	113	18	2.4	9.8	45%	.291	1.16	4.05	4.24	4.57	0.9	80	
2015	RCU	A+	23	1	0	0	4	2	22^{1}	14	1	2.8	11.3	30%	.265	0.94	1.61	2.79	3.15	0.6	79	
2015	TUL	AA	23	5	2	0	11	8	62^{2}	49	4	3.0	10.2	49%	.296	1.12	2.30	2.87	2.72	1.7	79	
2016	*LAN*	*MLB*	*24*	*5*	*4*	*1*	*29*	*12*	*84^{1}*	*75*	*12*	*2.9*	*8.9*	*40%*	*.302*	*1.21*	*4.05*	*3.93*	*4.76*	*0.5*	*111*	
2017	*LAN*	*MLB*	*25*	*7*	*8*	*1*	*35*	*20*	*153*	*143*	*24*	*3.3*	*8.9*	*40%*	*.310*	*1.31*	*4.27*	*4.68*	*5.02*	*0.3*	*118*	

Breakout: 16% Improve: 22% Collapse: 11% Attrition: 22% MLB: 47% *Comparables: Scott Lewis, James McDonald, David Hernandez*

It was easy to pick Cotton as a breakout candidate headed into last year. His fastball had already earned him some acclaim, but the Cotton ball that took the biggest step forward was his changeup; it's like Cotton eyed Joe Blanton's off-speed pitch and thought, "I need to do better." Cotton bowled through the competition in Rancho Cucamonga and Tulsa with his new weapon and low-90s heater, eventually landing in Oklahoma City, where he figures to start in 2016. There's a chance that what we saw last season wasn't the 100 percent real Cotton, and it's possible that the lack of a plus breaking ball will plant Cotton in the bullpen long term. Still, Cotton can declare himself a legit starting prospect if he excels in the rotation in Triple-A, and the Dodgers have done a terrific job cultivating Cotton to this point.

Jose De Leon RHP

Born: 8/7/92 Age: 23 Bats: R Throws: R Height: 6'2" Weight: 185

YEAR	TEAM	LVL	AGE	W	L	SV	G	GS	IP	H	HR	BB/9	K/9	GB%	BABIP	WHIP	ERA	FIP	DRA	WARP	CFIP	MPH
2014	GRL	A	21	2	0	0	4	4	22^{2}	14	1	0.8	16.7	31%	.317	0.71	1.19	0.62	2.93	0.6	44	
2015	TUL	AA	22	2	6	0	16	16	76^{2}	61	11	3.4	12.3	36%	.294	1.17	3.64	3.64	2.11	2.7	71	
2015	RCU	A+	22	4	1	0	7	7	37^{2}	26	1	1.9	13.9	45%	.325	0.90	1.67	2.00	1.02	1.9	52	
2016	*LAN*	*MLB*	*23*	*6*	*5*	*0*	*18*	*18*	*86^{2}*	*71*	*12*	*3.0*	*11.0*	*37%*	*.312*	*1.14*	*3.50*	*3.47*	*4.17*	*1.1*	*92*	
2017	*LAN*	*MLB*	*24*	*9*	*9*	*0*	*30*	*30*	*184^{2}*	*158*	*26*	*3.4*	*10.8*	*37%*	*.319*	*1.23*	*3.63*	*3.97*	*4.33*	*1.6*	*97*	

Breakout: 10% Improve: 22% Collapse: 13% Attrition: 20% MLB: 41% *Comparables: James Paxton, Burch Smith, Adam Morgan*

It doesn't really seem fair that the Dodgers, what with their unseemly wealth, genius front office and productive farm system, should also get to unearth gems in the 24th round of the draft. Yet here we are with De Leon, who has gone from "interesting arm" to "top-flight prospect" in just two seasons. After a breakout 2014, De Leon was even more impressive last season, decimating High-A hitters before missing bats but also allowing more contact in Double-A. De Leon routinely sits in the mid-90s with his fastball, can devastate with his slider and shows more than enough promise with his change to portend success in the rotation. He was surprisingly homer-prone in Tulsa and his command and control both need to take a step forward, but he's got all the ingredients you look for in a stud starting prospect. De Leon has lived in Julio Urias' shadow to this point but could sniff the majors in 2016 all the same.

Pablo Fernandez RHP

Born: 8/5/89 Age: 26 Bats: R Throws: R Height: 6'1" Weight: 185

YEAR	TEAM	LVL	AGE	W	L	SV	G	GS	IP	H	HR	BB/9	K/9	GB%	BABIP	WHIP	ERA	FIP	DRA	WARP	CFIP	MPH
2015	RCU	A+	25	2	1	0	4	4	21^{1}	26	3	1.7	7.6	35%	.354	1.41	4.22	4.90	4.96	0.2	100	
2015	GRL	A	25	1	1	0	4	4	17^{2}	20	2	1.0	8.2	39%	.333	1.25	4.08	3.40	3.31	0.3	90	
2016	*LAN*	*MLB*	*26*	*2*	*3*	*0*	*8*	*8*	*36^{2}*	*38*	*6*	*2.9*	*6.9*	*30%*	*.312*	*1.35*	*4.66*	*4.79*	*5.38*	*0.0*	*130*	
2017	*LAN*	*MLB*	*27*	*7*	*10*	*0*	*30*	*30*	*183^{2}*	*196*	*29*	*3.2*	*6.8*	*30%*	*.319*	*1.42*	*4.76*	*5.23*	*5.50*	*-0.3*	*133*	

Breakout: 0% Improve: 6% Collapse: 1% Attrition: 2% MLB: 8% *Comparables: Sammy Solis, Chris Smith, Eddie Bonine*

Hector Olivera received just a bit more press, but the Dodgers also signed Fernandez out of Cuba last season, inking him to an $8 million minor-league deal in May. Fernandez wasn't a hot commodity on the market, and he's got an atypical profile as a former command/control artist who gained velocity in his mid-20s. Most of his Cuban National Series experience came in the 'pen—he has

40 career saves—but apparently the Proven Closer tag didn't mean much to the Dodgers, who seem intent on stretching him out. Fernandez threw just 43 innings across three levels before being shut down with elbow soreness, so what was undoubtedly a very eventful year in his life was pretty uneventful on the mound.

Carlos Frias RHP

Born: 11/13/89 Age: 26 Bats: R Throws: R Height: 6'4" Weight: 195

YEAR	TEAM	LVL	AGE	W	L	SV	G	GS	IP	H	HR	BB/9	K/9	GB%	BABIP	WHIP	ERA	FIP	DRA	WARP	CFIP	MPH
2013	RCU	A+	23	2	3	0	8	8	46	52	4	2.2	9.4	47%	.353	1.37	4.11	3.60	4.83	0.7	83	
2013	GRL	A	23	5	3	0	12	12	68^1	66	3	3.0	6.5	48%	.304	1.30	2.63	3.66	4.72	0.4	106	
2013	CHT	AA	23	1	1	0	8	2	16	15	2	3.9	4.5	55%	.265	1.38	3.94	5.23	4.48	0.0	113	
2014	CHT	AA	24	2	1	0	5	5	32	34	2	2.5	3.9	55%	.294	1.34	3.38	4.16				
2014	LAN	MLB	24	1	1	0	15	2	32^1	33	4	1.9	8.1	52%	.299	1.24	6.12	3.57	3.63	0.4	100	96.8
2014	ABQ	AAA	24	8	4	0	16	15	91^2	114	4	2.1	6.4	50%	.358	1.47	5.01	3.60	4.97	0.8	91	
2015	OKL	AAA	25	2	0	0	8	3	21^1	24	2	2.1	8.0	46%	.344	1.36	2.95	3.74	4.22	0.3	92	
2015	LAN	MLB	25	5	5	0	17	13	77^2	88	7	3.0	5.0	58%	.319	1.47	4.06	4.35	5.26	-0.2	123	97.7
2016	*LAN*	*MLB*	*26*	*2*	*2*	*0*	*15*	*6*	*39^2*	*42*	*5*	*2.7*	*6.1*	*53%*	*.315*	*1.34*	*4.28*	*4.30*	*5.00*	*0.1*	*117*	
2017	*LAN*	*MLB*	*27*	*4*	*4*	*0*	*16*	*11*	*73^1*	*79*	*9*	*2.9*	*6.2*	*53%*	*.322*	*1.41*	*4.34*	*4.74*	*5.07*	*0.1*	*119*	

Breakout: 24% Improve: 48% Collapse: 18% Attrition: 32% MLB: 81% *Comparables: Trevor Bell, Dustin Moseley, Joe Saunders*

Frias is your third-favorite pair of jeans or a turkey-and-cheese on white or a Domino's pizza; he lets you get by, but he's never what you want. It seems obvious that the 26-year-old Dominican belongs in the 'pen, yet the Dodgers wound up needing to start Frias 13 times and the results were as expected. Batters hit .303/.369/.404 against him as a starter; that's basically Jose Altuve's slash line. Despite not being terribly effective, Frias logged the fifth-most innings of any Dodger last season, and despite averaging nearly 95 mph on his fastball, he struck out just 13 percent of the batters he faced. Perhaps he can aspire to more as a full-time reliever, but the Dodgers will need to keep him out of the rotation to find out.

Yimi Garcia RHP

Born: 8/18/90 Age: 25 Bats: R Throws: R Height: 6'1" Weight: 210

YEAR	TEAM	LVL	AGE	W	L	SV	G	GS	IP	H	HR	BB/9	K/9	GB%	BABIP	WHIP	ERA	FIP	DRA	WARP	CFIP	MPH
2013	CHT	AA	22	4	6	19	49	0	60^1	35	9	2.1	12.7	31%	.217	0.81	2.54	2.83	2.93	1.1	60	
2014	LAN	MLB	23	0	0	0	8	0	10	6	2	0.9	8.1	42%	.167	0.70	1.80	4.20	1.84	0.3	98	94.4
2014	ABQ	AAA	23	4	2	5	47	0	61	58	5	2.7	10.2	30%	.327	1.25	3.10	3.63	4.48	0.6	68	
2015	LAN	MLB	24	3	5	1	59	1	56^2	44	8	1.6	10.8	30%	.263	0.95	3.34	3.23	3.10	1.1	78	96.4
2015	OKL	AAA	24	0	0	0	9	0	10^2	9	1	4.2	10.1	29%	.296	1.31	4.22	3.97	4.29	0.1	93	
2016	*LAN*	*MLB*	*25*	*2*	*1*	*0*	*32*	*0*	*34^1*	*28*	*4*	*2.2*	*9.9*	*30%*	*.295*	*1.06*	*3.29*	*3.21*	*3.90*	*0.5*	*85*	
2017	*LAN*	*MLB*	*26*	*2*	*1*	*1*	*38*	*0*	*42^2*	*34*	*5*	*2.5*	*10.1*	*30%*	*.295*	*1.08*	*3.23*	*3.52*	*3.83*	*0.5*	*83*	

Breakout: 25% Improve: 41% Collapse: 27% Attrition: 35% MLB: 77% *Comparables: Sammy Gervacio, Carson Smith, C.C. Lee*

Pretty much every organization has a Yimi Garcia, but nearly every organization's Yimi Garcia enjoys anonymity. A failed starting-pitcher prospect who toiled in the Dodgers' system for four years before getting a cup of coffee in 2014, Garcia put together a very solid campaign out of the bullpen last year. Despite not throwing particularly hard by today's standards, he struck out 30 percent of batters faced, and despite only throwing one breaking pitch (a slider), he was better against southpaws than righties. Garcia struggles with the long ball and lacks closer upside, but he soaked up the third-most innings of any Dodgers reliever last year while returning above-average results. That might make him sound like a roll of paper towels, but what better to help you clean up after starters?

Chris Hatcher RHP

Born: 1/12/85 Age: 31 Bats: B Throws: R Height: 6'1" Weight: 200

YEAR	TEAM	LVL	AGE	W	L	SV	G	GS	IP	H	HR	BB/9	K/9	GB%	BABIP	WHIP	ERA	FIP	DRA	WARP	CFIP	MPH
2013	NWO	AAA	28	4	3	33	60	0	67^1	69	8	3.7	8.7	46%	.314	1.44	3.61	4.48	4.80	0.4	93	
2013	MIA	MLB	28	0	1	0	7	0	8^2	13	1	4.2	7.3	39%	.375	1.96	12.46	4.29	9.20	-0.5	108	97.0
2014	NWO	AAA	29	1	2	5	15	0	22^1	16	2	2.4	10.1	48%	.259	0.99	2.01	3.43	4.85	0.1	85	
2014	MIA	MLB	29	0	3	0	52	0	56	55	4	1.9	9.6	49%	.327	1.20	3.38	2.53	2.93	1.1	82	97.1
2015	LAN	MLB	30	3	5	4	49	0	39	35	4	3.0	10.4	44%	.307	1.23	3.69	3.42	4.48	0.1	90	98.1
2016	*LAN*	*MLB*	*31*	*3*	*1*	*0*	*51*	*0*	*54*	*47*	*6*	*2.6*	*8.8*	*46%*	*.302*	*1.17*	*3.60*	*3.52*	*4.24*	*0.5*	*94*	
2017	*LAN*	*MLB*	*32*	*2*	*1*	*1*	*48*	*0*	*53^1*	*49*	*6*	*3.0*	*8.9*	*46%*	*.311*	*1.25*	*3.74*	*4.07*	*4.40*	*0.3*	*98*	

Breakout: 17% Improve: 25% Collapse: 15% Attrition: 16% MLB: 50% *Comparables: Aquilino Lopez, Brian Sanches, Jairo Asencio*

With Kenley Jansen on the DL, Hatcher, like Jansen a former catcher, got his first career save on Opening Day. For a long while, that looked like it would be the highlight of his season. As of June 17th, he had allowed 13 earned runs in 18 innings, with opposing hitters teeing off to a .293/.365/.400 line. Hatcher went on the DL with a left-oblique strain and compound fracture of his pride, and didn't resurface until two months later. What'd he do when he got back? Post a 1.31 ERA in 20 innings en route to assuming setup duties, of course. Hatcher is 31, and his command remains an issue, but he throws super hard and has a very good beard, so at least some of the ingredients for sustained bullpen success are there.

Grant Holmes RHP

Born: 3/22/96 Age: 20 Bats: L Throws: R Height: 6'1" Weight: 215

YEAR	TEAM	LVL	AGE	W	L	SV	G	GS	IP	H	HR	BB/9	K/9	GB%	BABIP	WHIP	ERA	FIP	DRA	WARP	CFIP	MPH
2015	GRL	A	19	6	4	0	24	24	103^{1}	86	6	4.7	10.2	44%	.307	1.35	3.14	3.48	4.07	1.1	98	
2016	*LAN*	*MLB*	*20*	*5*	*5*	*0*	*17*	*17*	74^{2}	*67*	*9*	*4.8*	*8.7*	*37%*	*.309*	*1.43*	*4.39*	*4.37*	*5.08*	*0.2*	*120*	
2017	*LAN*	*MLB*	*21*	*8*	*10*	*0*	*30*	*30*	*190*	*167*	*22*	*4.9*	*9.1*	*37%*	*.308*	*1.42*	*4.21*	*4.62*	*4.87*	*0.7*	*116*	

Breakout: 0% Improve: 0% Collapse: 0% Attrition: 0% MLB: 0% *Comparables: Trevor Cahill, Lance McCullers, Justin Nicolino*

It doesn't take great powers of observation to discover that Holmes was an absolute steal at no. 22 overall in the 2014 draft. The burly right-hander made quite the impression in 2015, dispatching hitters like a Midwest League of red-headed stepchildren while logging in excess of 100 innings. Holmes sits in the low-to-mid-90s with his fastball but can touch 98, and while his changeup needs to take a step forward, his curve already has scouts dreaming about a future as a no. 2/3 starter—it is a curious incident indeed when the hammer does nothing in the nighttime. He's not a sure lock to reach his upside, though: To improve his game he'll need to stop missing a foot outside—Holmes walked over 12 percent of batters faced last year. From the workhorse build to the repeatable delivery to the excellent hair, Holmes already looks the part. If the Dodgers had any sense, they'd bring back De Jon Watson to help him finish his development.

J.P. Howell LHP

Born: 4/25/83 Age: 33 Bats: L Throws: L Height: 6'0" Weight: 180

YEAR	TEAM	LVL	AGE	W	L	SV	G	GS	IP	H	HR	BB/9	K/9	GB%	BABIP	WHIP	ERA	FIP	DRA	WARP	CFIP	MPH
2013	LAN	MLB	30	4	1	0	67	0	62	42	2	3.3	7.8	59%	.241	1.05	2.03	2.86	2.54	1.5	98	89.7
2014	LAN	MLB	31	3	3	0	68	0	49	31	2	4.6	8.8	59%	.236	1.14	2.39	3.27	2.63	1.1	105	88.7
2015	LAN	MLB	32	6	1	1	65	0	44	47	3	2.9	8.0	60%	.333	1.39	1.43	3.37	4.31	0.2	103	89.2
2016	*LAN*	*MLB*	*33*	*3*	*1*	*2*	*56*	*0*	*59*	*50*	*7*	*3.0*	*8.0*	*60%*	*.290*	*1.19*	*3.91*	*3.94*	*4.59*	*0.2*	*105*	
2017	*LAN*	*MLB*	*34*	*3*	*1*	*1*	*67*	*0*	54^{1}	*49*	*6*	*3.4*	*7.7*	*60%*	*.299*	*1.29*	*4.11*	*4.48*	*4.82*	*0.0*	*111*	

Breakout: 26% Improve: 38% Collapse: 31% Attrition: 15% MLB: 92% *Comparables: Peter Moylan, Bruce Ruffin, Hoyt Wilhelm*

They don't make 'em much more consistent than Howell. For the third straight year, the seasoned southpaw served as a reliable option for the Dodgers, holding left-handed hitters to a .224/.295/.224 line in 95 plate appearances. Curiously, Howell was used in equal measure against righties, whose .318/.368/.455 performance tells us he's probably best off as a LOOGY moving forward. Howell limped to the finish line in 2014 and history threatened to repeat itself this past August, but he pulled it together late, pitching well in September and in his lone postseason appearance. Lefty relievers live forever and velocity has never been a part of Howell's game, so while he's about to turn 33 he and the Dodgers should continue Hollywood's most stable relationship this side of Brad and Angeli... aww dammit.

Kenley Jansen RHP

Born: 9/30/87 Age: 28 Bats: B Throws: R Height: 6'5" Weight: 265

YEAR	TEAM	LVL	AGE	W	L	SV	G	GS	IP	H	HR	BB/9	K/9	GB%	BABIP	WHIP	ERA	FIP	DRA	WARP	CFIP	MPH
2013	LAN	MLB	25	4	3	28	75	0	76^{2}	48	6	2.1	13.0	39%	.273	0.86	1.88	1.96	2.42	2.0	49	95.9
2014	LAN	MLB	26	2	3	44	68	0	65^{1}	55	5	2.6	13.9	36%	.350	1.13	2.76	1.88	3.08	1.1	60	97.4
2015	LAN	MLB	27	2	1	36	54	0	52^{1}	33	6	1.4	13.8	36%	.260	0.78	2.41	2.17	2.19	1.6	55	95.6
2016	*LAN*	*MLB*	*28*	*3*	*2*	*40*	*60*	*0*	63^{2}	*44*	*7*	*2.1*	*12.5*	*37%*	*.296*	*0.92*	*2.61*	*2.51*	*3.16*	*1.4*	*62*	
2017	*LAN*	*MLB*	*29*	*4*	*2*	*46*	*68*	*0*	67^{2}	*50*	*8*	*2.5*	*11.7*	*37%*	*.296*	*1.01*	*3.00*	*3.25*	*3.63*	*1.0*	*76*	

Breakout: 25% Improve: 44% Collapse: 40% Attrition: 11% MLB: 95% *Comparables: Armando Benitez, Francisco Rodriguez, Troy Percival*

Despite pitching in the Golden Age of Bullpens, Jansen has never received quite as much fanfare as, say, Aroldis Chapman, Craig Kimbrel or even Andrew Miller. That's a shame, because the burly right-hander is just as good as any of them. Jansen didn't throw a pitch until May 15th last year thanks to foot surgery, but he was as dominant as ever once he returned, striking out a stupefying 40 percent of the batters he faced. Only Chapman and Miller struck out a higher percentage among pitchers with at least 40 innings, but Jansen walked fewer than either of those two southpaws. He upped his slider usage a bit in 2015, yet still relied on his cutter nearly 90 percent of the time, and despite throwing that pitch more than a mile per hour slower than he did in 2014, it did not lose its effectiveness. Jansen is slated for free agency after this season, and while he may prove to be exorbitantly expensive to most, this is the Dodgers we're talking about. He should stay in Hollywood (or Echo Park, whatever) for a long time.

Clayton Kershaw LHP

Born: 3/19/88 Age: 28 Bats: L Throws: L Height: 6'4" Weight: 225

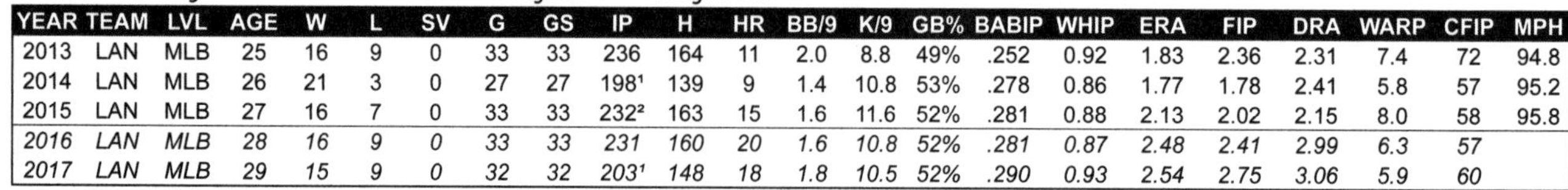

YEAR	TEAM	LVL	AGE	W	L	SV	G	GS	IP	H	HR	BB/9	K/9	GB%	BABIP	WHIP	ERA	FIP	DRA	WARP	CFIP	MPH
2013	LAN	MLB	25	16	9	0	33	33	236	164	11	2.0	8.8	49%	.252	0.92	1.83	2.36	2.31	7.4	72	94.8
2014	LAN	MLB	26	21	3	0	27	27	198^{1}	139	9	1.4	10.8	53%	.278	0.86	1.77	1.78	2.41	5.8	57	95.2
2015	LAN	MLB	27	16	7	0	33	33	232^{2}	163	15	1.6	11.6	52%	.281	0.88	2.13	2.02	2.15	8.0	58	95.8
2016	*LAN*	*MLB*	*28*	*16*	*9*	*0*	*33*	*33*	*231*	*160*	*20*	*1.6*	*10.8*	*52%*	*.281*	*0.87*	*2.48*	*2.41*	*2.99*	*6.3*	*57*	
2017	*LAN*	*MLB*	*29*	*15*	*9*	*0*	*32*	*32*	203^{1}	*148*	*18*	*1.8*	*10.5*	*52%*	*.290*	*0.93*	*2.54*	*2.75*	*3.06*	*5.9*	*60*	

Breakout: 22% Improve: 42% Collapse: 26% Attrition: 9% MLB: 99% *Comparables: Roger Clemens, Kevin Appier, Ron Guidry*

You know how everyone freaked out about how good Zack Greinke was last season? Kershaw was still better. People forget that, because Kershaw's dominance has become... mundane isn't right, but perhaps expected? Taken for granted, at least. He took his MVP- and Cy Young–winning 2014 campaign and basically hit Ctrl-C Ctrl-V, posting a 2.16 DRA while throwing more innings and striking out a higher percentage of those who dared oppose him. Kershaw was quite good in the postseason as well, which still feels worthy of note even though the narrative that he melts in October should've been put to bed in 2013. It's hard to imagine anything but injury slowing Kershaw down, and as the lanky lefty deals in his prime years we simply have the good fortune of watching one of the greatest pitching careers of all time. He's already more than a third of the way to Roger Clemens' career PWARP, yet Kershaw won't turn 30 until 2018.

Zach Lee RHP

Born: 9/13/91 Age: 24 Bats: R Throws: R Height: 6'4" Weight: 210

YEAR	TEAM	LVL	AGE	W	L	SV	G	GS	IP	H	HR	BB/9	K/9	GB%	BABIP	WHIP	ERA	FIP	DRA	WARP	CFIP	MPH
2013	CHT	AA	21	10	10	0	28	25	142^{2}	132	13	2.2	8.3	49%	.298	1.17	3.22	3.08	3.71	1.7	89	
2014	ABQ	AAA	22	7	13	0	28	27	150^{2}	177	18	3.2	5.8	52%	.323	1.53	5.38	5.16	5.42	0.6	110	
2015	OKL	AAA	23	11	6	0	19	19	113^{1}	107	5	1.5	6.4	50%	.298	1.11	2.70	3.35	3.75	2.3	87	
2015	LAN	MLB	23	0	1	0	1	1	4^{2}	11	1	1.9	5.8	55%	.526	2.57	13.50	5.30	13.86	-0.5	109	92.2
2016	*LAN*	*MLB*	*24*	*3*	*3*	*0*	*8*	*8*	45^{2}	*45*	*6*	*2.1*	*6.5*	*49%*	*.303*	*1.22*	*4.13*	*4.16*	*4.83*	*0.2*	*113*	
2017	*LAN*	*MLB*	*25*	*4*	*5*	*0*	*13*	*13*	75^{2}	*81*	*10*	*2.6*	*6.2*	*49%*	*.318*	*1.36*	*4.41*	*4.81*	*5.16*	*0.1*	*122*	

Breakout: 15% Improve: 24% Collapse: 11% Attrition: 29% MLB: 47% *Comparables: Jay Jackson, Kyle McPherson, Tim Cooney*

It's been over five years since the Dodgers drafted Lee in the first round and gave him $5.25 million to not throw footballs for a living. It's been about three years since we figured out he probably wasn't headed to the top of an MLB rotation, but that doesn't mean Lee is without value. The lack of a true out pitch is a glaring flaw, but Lee had a fine season at Oklahoma City, and while he missed time with tingly fingers (medical term), he's got the athleticism and build of a workhorse. You can do worse than to have a cost-controlled version of such a pitcher as your fifth or sixth starter, and Lee could finally put more MLB innings than trade rumors under his belt in 2016.

Adam Liberatore LHP

Born: 5/12/87 Age: 29 Bats: L Throws: L Height: 6'3" Weight: 240

YEAR	TEAM	LVL	AGE	W	L	SV	G	GS	IP	H	HR	BB/9	K/9	GB%	BABIP	WHIP	ERA	FIP	DRA	WARP	CFIP	MPH
2013	DUR	AAA	26	5	3	0	43	0	60^{1}	50	1	3.7	10.3	49%	.308	1.24	3.58	2.43	3.84	0.6	82	
2014	DUR	AAA	27	6	1	4	54	0	65	43	1	2.1	11.9	46%	.292	0.89	1.66	1.65	3.32	1.1	51	
2015	OKL	AAA	28	0	1	3	19	0	21^{2}	18	2	4.2	7.5	44%	.267	1.29	3.74	4.66	5.08	0.0	102	
2015	LAN	MLB	28	2	2	0	39	0	29^{2}	26	3	2.7	8.8	45%	.284	1.18	4.25	3.43	3.58	0.4	90	96.3
2016	*LAN*	*MLB*	*29*	*1*	*1*	*0*	*23*	*0*	24^{2}	*21*	*3*	*2.6*	*8.8*	*44%*	*.301*	*1.14*	*3.47*	*3.65*	*4.10*	*0.3*	*90*	
2017	*LAN*	*MLB*	*30*	*2*	*1*	*1*	*34*	*0*	41^{2}	*36*	*5*	*3.0*	*9.1*	*44%*	*.308*	*1.20*	*3.58*	*3.90*	*4.23*	*0.3*	*94*	

Breakout: 10% Improve: 14% Collapse: 17% Attrition: 22% MLB: 33% *Comparables: Marcus McBeth, Brad Salmon, Mickey Storey*

Not content to rely on J.P. Howell and Joel Peralta alone, Andrew Friedman also picked up Liberatore to round out a bullpen replete with former Rays, but the lefty never made it to the majors in Tampa. His debut with the Dodgers was fine, okay, nondescript, average, middle of the road, vanilla. Still, the large lefty will need to miss a few more bats if he wants to earn his name à la Simon Bolivar, Emperor Alexander II and Pedro I of Brazil. Now *those* were some Liberatores who knew how to provide relief.

Brandon McCarthy RHP

Born: 7/7/83 Age: 32 Bats: R Throws: R Height: 6'7" Weight: 225

YEAR	TEAM	LVL	AGE	W	L	SV	G	GS	IP	H	HR	BB/9	K/9	GB%	BABIP	WHIP	ERA	FIP	DRA	WARP	CFIP	MPH
2013	ARI	MLB	29	5	11	0	22	22	135	161	13	1.4	5.1	50%	.320	1.35	4.53	3.72	4.55	0.6	110	93.2
2013	RNO	AAA	29	0	0	0	2	2	10^{1}	15	2	2.6	3.5	55%	.325	1.74	6.97	6.47	5.42	0.0	110	
2014	NYA	MLB	30	7	5	0	14	14	90^{1}	91	10	1.3	8.2	51%	.307	1.15	2.89	3.25	3.30	1.7	82	95.1
2014	ARI	MLB	30	3	10	0	18	18	109^{2}	131	15	1.6	7.6	56%	.345	1.38	5.01	3.79	4.98	-0.3	98	95.2
2015	LAN	MLB	31	3	0	0	4	4	23	24	9	1.6	11.3	39%	.288	1.22	5.87	6.25	7.07	-0.6	90	96.0
2016	*LAN*	*MLB*	*32*	*3*	*2*	*0*	*8*	*8*	48^{1}	*48*	*6*	*1.6*	*7.5*	*51%*	*.314*	*1.16*	*3.64*	*3.62*	*4.29*	*0.6*	*97*	
2017	*LAN*	*MLB*	*33*	*12*	*11*	*0*	*32*	*32*	*207*	*210*	*25*	*1.8*	*7.3*	*51%*	*.321*	*1.22*	*3.67*	*3.99*	*4.32*	*2.2*	*98*	

Breakout: 12% Improve: 46% Collapse: 27% Attrition: 10% MLB: 90% *Comparables: David Wells, Larry Jansen, Esteban Loaiza*

The Dodgers know that pitchers break, which is why they bought so many pitchers who'd been broken last offseason. They hit on Brett Anderson but not so with McCarthy, who has all the luck of Charlie Brown: Punter or Roy Sullivan: Lightning Rod (look it up). McCarthy had missed time thanks to his fingers, shoulder, forearm and head in his 11-year career, but had yet to suffer a torn UCL. He checked that off the list just four starts into his four-year, $48 million contract, undergoing Tommy John surgery that figures to keep him out until late 2016 at the earliest. We'll all benefit from his rehab tweets, but once again we're left wondering what McCarthy's career might have looked like if he could just stay on the mound.

Frankie Montas RHP

Born: 3/21/93 Age: 23 Bats: R Throws: R Height: 6'2" Weight: 185

YEAR	TEAM	LVL	AGE	W	L	SV	G	GS	IP	H	HR	BB/9	K/9	GB%	BABIP	WHIP	ERA	FIP	DRA	WARP	CFIP	MPH
2013	GRN	A	20	2	9	0	19	18	85^{1}	94	10	3.4	10.1	39%	.349	1.48	5.70	3.98	4.23	0.8	92	
2013	KAN	A	20	3	2	0	5	5	25^{2}	20	1	6.3	10.9	47%	.302	1.48	4.56	3.68	3.97	0.3	86	
2014	WNS	A+	21	4	0	0	10	10	62	45	2	2.0	8.1	54%	.256	0.95	1.60	2.90	3.99	0.9	81	
2015	CHA	MLB	22	0	2	0	7	2	15	14	1	5.4	12.0	38%	.361	1.53	4.80	3.10	3.75	0.2	92	99.8
2015	BIR	AA	22	5	5	0	23	23	112	89	3	3.9	8.7	43%	.282	1.22	2.97	3.03	3.10	2.5	86	
2016	*LAN*	*MLB*	*23*	*2*	*1*	*0*	*26*	*3*	39^{2}	*35*	*4*	*3.3*	*8.5*	*39%*	*.304*	*1.25*	*3.79*	*3.62*	*4.44*	*0.2*	*102*	
2017	*LAN*	*MLB*	*24*	*5*	*5*	*0*	*17*	*17*	99^{2}	*93*	*12*	*3.6*	*8.6*	*39%*	*.316*	*1.33*	*3.90*	*4.26*	*4.57*	*0.7*	*106*	

Breakout: 10% Improve: 20% Collapse: 13% Attrition: 25% MLB: 39% *Comparables: Nick Maronde, Jordan Zimmermann, Drew Smyly*

The absolute low-end projection for a healthy Montas is lights-out relief arm. In short bursts, he can spend as much time on the high side of 100 as on the low side, with a slider that sits 89–90 and misses (enough) bats. His command is a little loose, but his sheer stuff overwhelms that issue. He's got a good, starter-ready body, too, though keeping it from ballooning is a matter of some concern. The question is whether, since he has little left to prove in the minors, the Dodgers are willing to slow him down and force the development of a third pitch. If he can find one that works, damn the torpedoes (and the questions about his delivery): He's a starter. If not, he'll be able to shorten games for however long he remains healthy.

Joel Peralta RHP

Born: 3/23/76 Age: 40 Bats: R Throws: R Height: 5'10" Weight: 210

YEAR	TEAM	LVL	AGE	W	L	SV	G	GS	IP	H	HR	BB/9	K/9	GB%	BABIP	WHIP	ERA	FIP	DRA	WARP	CFIP	MPH
2013	TBA	MLB	37	3	8	1	80	0	71^1	47	7	4.3	9.3	27%	.227	1.14	3.41	3.71	3.33	1.1	94	92.7
2014	TBA	MLB	38	3	4	1	69	0	63^1	60	9	2.1	10.5	35%	.307	1.18	4.41	3.43	4.26	0.2	79	92.2
2015	LAN	MLB	39	3	1	3	33	0	29	28	6	2.5	7.4	34%	.265	1.24	4.34	5.02	4.43	0.1	104	92.2
2016	*LAN*	*MLB*	*40*	*2*	*1*	*1*	*37*	*0*	*38^2*	*32*	*5*	*2.6*	*8.7*	*32%*	*.282*	*1.11*	*3.75*	*3.74*	*4.42*	*0.2*	*101*	
2017	*LAN*	*MLB*	*41*	*3*	*1*	*2*	*68*	*0*	*60^2*	*52*	*8*	*2.9*	*8.4*	*32%*	*.289*	*1.18*	*3.87*	*4.22*	*4.56*	*0.2*	*104*	

Breakout: 15% Improve: 25% Collapse: 12% Attrition: 7% MLB: 61% *Comparables: Mike Remlinger, Octavio Dotel, Rudy Seanez*

Providing so-so innings in bulk out of the bullpen is supposed to be Peralta's thing. But, in a reminder that time waits for no middle reliever, Peralta was out-Peralta'd by several of his Dodgers teammates in 2015. The veteran right-hander missed most of May and June with a neck injury, came back to surrender 12 earned runs in 14 innings, then missed most of August with a neck injury again. Peralta is about to turn 40 and we're about three seasons removed from him being truly good, which explains why the Dodgers declined his modest $2.5 million option for 2016. Odds are someone will give him a shot unless he retires (they hadn't yet when we sent this book to the printer), but the former staple of many a Joe Maddon bullpen is nearing the end. He's put together a nice career for someone who didn't reach the majors until 29.

Hyun-jin Ryu LHP

Born: 3/25/87 Age: 29 Bats: R Throws: L Height: 6'2" Weight: 255

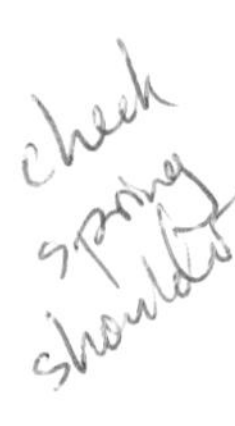

YEAR	TEAM	LVL	AGE	W	L	SV	G	GS	IP	H	HR	BB/9	K/9	GB%	BABIP	WHIP	ERA	FIP	DRA	WARP	CFIP	MPH
2013	LAN	MLB	26	14	8	0	30	30	192	182	15	2.3	7.2	52%	.296	1.20	3.00	3.21	3.70	2.8	93	93.7
2014	LAN	MLB	27	14	7	0	26	26	152	152	8	1.7	8.2	50%	.319	1.19	3.38	2.59	3.87	1.7	87	94.3
2016	*LAN*	*MLB*	*29*	*11*	*8*	*0*	*28*	*28*	*168*	*151*	*17*	*1.8*	*8.1*	*52%*	*.306*	*1.10*	*3.29*	*3.25*	*3.89*	*2.8*	*86*	
2017	*LAN*	*MLB*	*30*	*11*	*9*	*0*	*29*	*29*	*176^2*	*168*	*17*	*2.0*	*8.0*	*52%*	*.318*	*1.17*	*3.28*	*3.56*	*3.88*	*2.9*	*85*	

Breakout: 6% Improve: 40% Collapse: 21% Attrition: 5% MLB: 98% *Comparables: Jon Matlack, Mark Buehrle, Curt Schilling*

The hope for Ryu was that he'd combine his 2013 innings total with his 2014 production, leading to a true breakout year. Instead, the left-shoulder soreness that plagued him in 2014 reared its ugly head again, and Ryu underwent season-ending labrum-repair surgery on May 21st without throwing a regular-season pitch. Shoulder injuries are infinitely more terrifying than their elbow counterparts, but Ryu is supposed to be ready for spring training. He's only going into his age-29 season, which is a point in his favor, but counting on him for bulk innings may not be wise. Counting on him to be bulky is a safe bet, though.

Ross Stripling RHP

Born: 11/23/89 Age: 26 Bats: R Throws: R Height: 6'3" Weight: 190

YEAR	TEAM	LVL	AGE	W	L	SV	G	GS	IP	H	HR	BB/9	K/9	GB%	BABIP	WHIP	ERA	FIP	DRA	WARP	CFIP	MPH
2013	CHT	AA	23	6	4	1	21	16	94	91	4	1.8	7.9	54%	.310	1.17	2.78	2.31	3.50	1.3	81	
2013	RCU	A+	23	2	0	0	6	6	33^2	24	1	2.9	9.1	57%	.261	1.04	2.94	3.12	4.96	0.5	89	
2015	TUL	AA	25	3	6	0	13	13	67^1	61	7	2.5	7.4	55%	.281	1.19	3.88	3.86	3.83	1.1	93	
2016	*LAN*	*MLB*	*26*	*1*	*1*	*0*	*3*	*3*	*15*	*15*	*2*	*2.5*	*7.0*	*52%*	*.304*	*1.26*	*4.21*	*3.97*	*4.93*	*0.1*	*116*	
2017	*LAN*	*MLB*	*27*	*2*	*3*	*0*	*10*	*10*	*56^2*	*58*	*9*	*2.9*	*7.0*	*52%*	*.311*	*1.35*	*4.49*	*4.91*	*5.26*	*0.0*	*125*	

Breakout: 8% Improve: 14% Collapse: 7% Attrition: 22% MLB: 29% *Comparables: Tony Watson, Hector Ambriz, Mike Bolsinger*

Stripling missed all of 2014 and half of 2015 thanks to Tommy John surgery and its laborious recovery process. He allowed 12 runs in his first four Double-A starts after resurfacing in June, but allowed just 17 runs in nine starts thereafter. Upside was never the draw with Stripling, but given how many of his fellow Dodgers starting prospects have washed out or moved to the bullpen, his 2013 emergence as a potential back-end arm is more meaningful than you might think. This season should give us a better indication of whether the right-hander will be worth the wait or if this has just been one big Stripling-tease.

Chin-hui Tsao RHP

Born: 6/2/81 Age: 35 Bats: R Throws: R Height: 6'1" Weight: 210

YEAR	TEAM	LVL	AGE	W	L	SV	G	GS	IP	H	HR	BB/9	K/9	GB%	BABIP	WHIP	ERA	FIP	DRA	WARP	CFIP	MPH
2015	OKL	AAA	34	2	1	7	30	0	39	31	3	2.5	9.7	28%	.283	1.08	2.77	3.29	2.93	1.0	77	
2015	LAN	MLB	34	1	1	0	5	0	7	15	3	3.9	9.0	33%	.500	2.57	10.29	8.02	13.73	-0.8	107	95.9
2016	*LAN*	*MLB*	*35*	*2*	*1*	*2*	*36*	*0*	*38*	*34*	*5*	*2.7*	*8.7*	*28%*	*.306*	*1.20*	*3.82*	*3.75*	*4.49*	*0.2*	*102*	
2017	*LAN*	*MLB*	*36*	*2*	*1*	*2*	*42*	*0*	*55*	*51*	*7*	*2.9*	*8.7*	*28%*	*.312*	*1.24*	*3.83*	*4.17*	*4.50*	*0.2*	*102*	

Breakout: 15% Improve: 30% Collapse: 16% Attrition: 10% MLB: 53% *Comparables: Buddy Carlyle, Tim Hamulack, Julio Manon*

Tsao's Wikipedia page alleges that, in no particular order, he accepted "wine and sex" from the mafia in exchange for throwing games in the Taiwan Series; once spoiled a Steve Trachsel no-hitter; embezzled $1.6 million as part of a beef-noodle-soup restaurant scandal; recorded the fastest-ever pitch by a Taiwanese pitcher (100 mph); made two Olympic teams; was banned from the Australian Baseball League; and went eight years between MLB appearances. Can you believe Steve Trachsel almost threw a no-hitter?

Julio Urias LHP

Born: 8/12/96 Age: 19 Bats: L Throws: L Height: 6'2" Weight: 205

YEAR	TEAM	LVL	AGE	W	L	SV	G	GS	IP	H	HR	BB/9	K/9	GB%	BABIP	WHIP	ERA	FIP	DRA	WARP	CFIP	MPH
2013	GRL	A	16	2	0	0	18	18	54^{1}	44	5	2.7	11.1	54%	.320	1.10	2.48	3.01	3.91	0.9	76	
2014	RCU	A+	17	2	2	0	25	20	87^{2}	60	4	3.8	11.2	46%	.314	1.11	2.36	3.35	4.90	-0.1	89	
2015	TUL	AA	18	3	4	0	13	13	68^{1}	53	4	2.0	9.7	47%	.282	1.00	2.77	2.60	2.00	2.5	69	
2016	*LAN*	*MLB*	*19*	*5*	*5*	*0*	*18*	*18*	*68*	*62*	*9*	*2.8*	*9.1*	*44%*	*.313*	*1.23*	*3.92*	*3.78*	*4.61*	*0.5*	*107*	
2017	*LAN*	*MLB*	*20*	*7*	*9*	*0*	*31*	*31*	*196^{2}*	*182*	*26*	*2.7*	*8.9*	*44%*	*.313*	*1.23*	*3.79*	*4.14*	*4.46*	*1.2*	*104*	

Breakout: 0% Improve: 0% Collapse: 0% Attrition: 0% MLB: 0% *Comparables: Madison Bumgarner, Taijuan Walker, Jordan Lyles*

Torii Hunter was drafted before Urias was born. There, we've now fulfilled our "Urias is young" reference quota, but it's time to stop thinking of him primarily in terms of his age. In a way, all of the "it's amazing what Urias is doing at X level as a Y-year-old" comments undersell how good he's been, especially last season. Urias took some planned time off after midseason cosmetic eye surgery but was flat-out dominant when on the mound, striking out 28 percent of all batters he faced in Tulsa. With three plus pitches, universal respect for his feel for pitching and a tiny bit of projection left in his 19-year-old body, Urias is as close to perfect as a pitching prospect can get; all that's really left for him is to build his innings count. A 2016 debut is a distinct possibility, as is immediate success as at least a mid-rotation arm.

Alex Wood LHP

Born: 1/12/91 Age: 25 Bats: R Throws: L Height: 6'4" Weight: 215

YEAR	TEAM	LVL	AGE	W	L	SV	G	GS	IP	H	HR	BB/9	K/9	GB%	BABIP	WHIP	ERA	FIP	DRA	WARP	CFIP	MPH
2013	ATL	MLB	22	3	3	0	31	11	77^{2}	76	3	3.1	8.9	50%	.333	1.33	3.13	2.62	4.18	0.6	94	94.6
2013	MIS	AA	22	4	2	0	10	10	57	41	1	2.4	9.0	56%	.261	0.98	1.26	1.98	3.23	1.0	71	
2014	ATL	MLB	23	11	11	0	35	24	171^{2}	151	16	2.4	8.9	48%	.295	1.14	2.78	3.22	3.95	1.7	93	92.5
2015	ATL	MLB	24	7	6	0	20	20	119^{1}	132	8	2.7	6.8	49%	.332	1.41	3.54	3.48	4.11	1.3	102	91.9
2015	LAN	MLB	24	5	6	0	12	12	70^{1}	66	7	2.9	6.3	57%	.280	1.27	4.35	4.13	3.49	1.3	111	91.0
2016	*LAN*	*MLB*	*25*	*11*	*9*	*0*	*28*	*28*	*168*	*159*	*18*	*2.2*	*7.5*	*51%*	*.307*	*1.19*	*3.72*	*3.62*	*4.39*	*1.8*	*100*	
2017	*LAN*	*MLB*	*26*	*9*	*9*	*0*	*28*	*28*	*168^{2}*	*168*	*19*	*2.5*	*7.3*	*51%*	*.318*	*1.27*	*3.75*	*4.08*	*4.43*	*1.6*	*101*	

Breakout: 16% Improve: 54% Collapse: 21% Attrition: 6% MLB: 99% *Comparables: Matt Garza, Jose Quintana, Chad Billingsley*

Alex Wood the Brave may have had DirecTV, but Alex Wood the Dodger had cable. The southpaw owned a 3.48 ERA and near-matching FIP before heading west, but coughed up a 4.35 ERA and 4.15 FIP with Los Angeles. Wood generated more groundballs and enjoyed a lower BABIP in LA, but he also struck out fewer batters while walking more, and surrendered seven homers in 70 innings after allowing just eight in 119 in Atlanta. Wood's overall Dodgers performance is a bit skewed by two horrible starts in which he allowed 14 earned runs, but he was inconsistent enough that the overall theme holds true. If he stays on the mound, Wood is a perfectly acceptable mid-rotation starter who's under team control for the next four years, but it would be nice if he got back to his bat-missing halcyon days of 2014.

LINEOUTS

Hitters

NAME	POS	TEAM	LVL	AGE	PA	R	2B	3B	HR	RBI	BB	K	SB	CS	AVG/OBP/SLG	TAv	BABIP	BRR	FRAA	WARP
Willie Calhoun	2B	GRL	A	20	66	9	3	0	1	8	5	7	0	0	.393/.439/.492	.346	.434	0.0	2B(12): -1.6	0.6
	2B	RCU	A+	20	82	11	7	0	3	14	7	13	0	0	.329/.390/.548	.321	.362	0.9	2B(20): -1.3	0.7
Charlie Culberson	INF	ABQ	AAA	26	20	3	1	0	1	2	0	6	0	0	.200/.200/.400	.198	.231	0.2	SS(5): -0.0	0.0
Daniel Fields	OF	DET	MLB	24	3	1	1	0	0	0	0	2	0	0	.333/.333/.667	.327	1.000	0.2	LF(1): -0.3	0.0
	OF	TOL	AAA	24	526	59	25	8	7	41	66	146	17	7	.228/.335/.367	.244	.320	1.7	CF(92): -3.3, LF(24): 4.2	0.9
Kyle Garlick	OF	GRL	A	23	162	24	12	2	4	24	10	35	2	2	.327/.385/.517	.310	.407	-1.3	RF(27): 1.2, LF(7): 1.1	1.3
	OF	RCU	A+	23	61	16	4	0	5	14	4	20	0	0	.389/.426/.741	.395	.516	1.1	RF(7): -0.9, LF(4): 0.2	1.0
Johan Mieses	OF	GRL	A	19	181	16	10	1	5	20	11	31	7	4	.277/.320/.440	.292	.308	-0.8	CF(24): 0.0, RF(18): 0.9	1.1
	OF	RCU	A+	19	214	35	18	1	6	19	13	57	3	1	.245/.299/.439	.258	.316	0.6	CF(25): 3.3, LF(15): -0.5	1.1
Jacob Scavuzzo	OF	GRL	A	21	226	30	14	3	5	20	7	44	4	1	.263/.292/.427	.267	.305	1.0	LF(52): -6.4	0.1
	OF	RCU	A+	21	255	47	18	1	13	49	21	54	3	4	.308/.376/.568	.346	.352	0.5	LF(42): -5.7, CF(4): -0.3	2.3
Jose Tabata	PH	IND	AAA	26	165	19	6	1	0	5	16	16	2	2	.291/.364/.345	.252	.326	1.3	RF(34): -1.5	0.1
	PH	OKL	AAA	26	99	6	4	0	2	8	8	13	1	0	.225/.286/.337	.254	.240	-0.4	LF(12): 0.4, RF(10): -1.2	0.0
	PH	PIT	MLB	26	41	2	0	0	0	4	2	7	0	1	.289/.341/.289	.233	.355	0.0	RF(5): -0.2, LF(3): -0.1	-0.1
Ronald Torreyes	2B	FRE	AAA	22	72	7	1	0	0	5	1	9	0	1	.200/.211/.214	.157	.230	-0.7	2B(13): -1.2, SS(5): -0.5	-0.8
	2B	LAN	MLB	22	8	1	1	0	0	1	1	1	0	0	.333/.429/.500	.328	.400	0.0	2B(4): 0.2, 3B(3): -0.0	0.1
	2B	NHP	AA	22	54	4	2	0	0	9	4	2	2	0	.140/.204/.180	.134	.146	-0.1	2B(14): -0.7, SS(1): -0.0	-0.7
	2B	OKL	AAA	22	53	10	2	1	0	3	2	4	0	0	.306/.340/.388	.282	.326	-0.1	2B(7): -0.7, SS(5): 1.4	0.4
	2B	TUL	AA	22	274	39	13	2	4	19	20	23	3	3	.293/.348/.410	.289	.308	1.6	SS(48): 0.3, 3B(7): -0.8	2.0

2015 fourth-round pick **Willie Calhoun** is a power-hitting second-base prospect who's probably not a second baseman but really can hit for power. He reached High-A just 241 plate appearances into his career. ❖ A pair of back surgeries limited **Charlie Culberson** to just five games with Albuquerque last year. His claim to fame would be that he leads San Francisco's 2007 draft class in career home runs, except that distinction belongs to Madison Bumgarner. ❖ **Brendon Davis**, a 2015 fifth-rounder, is a rail-thin shortstop who projects as a power-packed third baseman if he eats a few snacks. A wrist injury and his current size conspired to limit his pop in his professional debut. ❖ **Daniel Fields** triples as a complete sentence, a complete self-description and the name of a center fielder who led the International League in walks, then bounced from Detroit to Milwaukee to Los Angeles on waivers. ❖ Baseball has long been a superstitious sport, but the Dodgers took things to the next level when they drafted outfielder **Kyle Garlick** in the hopes of improving their luck with bats. ❖ **Mitch Hansen** was a 2015 second-rounder who didn't do much MMMBopping in Rookie ball, so he'll need to produce some offense This Time Around if he wants to be taken seriously as a prospect. ❖ Considered one of the crown jewels of the 2015 J2 crop, **Starling Heredia** is a big, toolsy 16-year-old Dominican outfielder. He'll look to follow more in the footsteps of Starling Marte than Bubba Starling. ❖ **Johan Mieses** was pretty impressive as a 19-year-old at Great Lakes and mostly held his own as a 20-year-old in Rancho Cucamonga, which is more of a compliment and less of a Taco Bell order than it sounds like, respectively. ❖ Since being drafted in the second round in 2013, **Jordan Paroubeck** has played in just 69 games (not so nice) and has been traded twice, but he's toolsy, crushed the Pioneer League and has reportedly trained with Barry Bonds, so he's more intriguing than your standard "dealt for a bonus slot" prospect. ❖ **Jacob Scavuzzo** is a toolsy outfield prospect who parlayed a strong, Cal League–aided season into an AFL invite. He's unlikely to make it up in 2016, which will, sadly, rob us of Vin Scully saying his name. ❖ **Jose Tabata** is a career .275/.336/.377 hitter who's produced just 1.5 WARP in 407 contests since 2010, which tells you all you need to know about the rest of his game. Not every "team-friendly" extension works out. ❖ **Ronald Torreyes** has been traded more times than a holofoil Pokemon card, but finally reached the majors with his fifth organization, the Dodgers, last year. He's got a tough profile as a right-handed utility option who is limited at shortstop, but he's hit well at every stop.

Pitchers

NAME	TEAM	LVL	AGE	W	L	SV	G	GS	IP	H	HR	BB/9	K/9	GB%	BABIP	WHIP	ERA	FIP	FRA	WARP	CFIP	MPH
Scott Baker	LAN	MLB	33	0	1	0	2	2	11	11	4	2.5	6.5	41%	.233	1.27	5.73	7.25	7.21	-0.3	110	91.6
	OKL	AAA	33	7	3	0	13	13	77	64	6	0.8	6.0	44%	.251	0.92	3.39	3.64	3.75	1.6	87	
Brandon Beachy	OKL	AAA	28	1	1	0	10	9	47	40	4	4.0	6.9	48%	.269	1.30	3.64	4.64	5.64	0.0	109	
	LAN	MLB	28	0	1	0	2	2	8	10	1	6.8	5.6	29%	.333	2.00	7.88	5.79	7.33	-0.2	110	92.0
Tommy Bergjans	GRL	A	22	1	3	0	9	9	40	43	2	2.5	8.3	48%	.350	1.35	3.60	3.02	3.14	0.9	88	
Chase DeJong	LNS	A	21	7	4	0	14	14	86^{1}	75	9	1.9	8.0	42%	.270	1.08	3.13	3.70	3.32	1.7	90	
	RCU	A+	21	4	3	0	11	10	50	44	6	2.7	9.4	37%	.277	1.18	3.96	4.22	4.15	0.9	91	
Caleb Dirks	TUL	AA	22	0	0	0	14	0	13^{1}	7	0	4.1	11.5	29%	.226	0.98	1.35	2.32	3.73	0.2	91	
	ROM	A	22	1	2	1	6	0	10	12	0	1.8	9.9	55%	.387	1.40	1.80	2.18	3.45	0.2	88	
	CAR	A+	22	0	0	2	11	0	16^{2}	8	0	6.5	9.7	62%	.205	1.20	0.00	3.25	4.28	0.0	102	
	RCU	A+	22	2	0	3	9	0	10	8	1	1.8	16.2	40%	.368	1.00	0.90	2.08	2.11	0.4	66	
Tyler Olson	TAC	AAA	25	3	5	1	25	6	54^{1}	61	7	2.8	8.8	46%	.329	1.44	4.47	4.37	3.98	0.8	88	
	SEA	MLB	25	1	1	0	11	0	13^{1}	18	2	6.8	5.4	48%	.364	2.10	5.40	6.33	8.22	-0.6	114	91.0
Josh Ravin	LAN	MLB	27	2	1	0	9	0	9^{1}	13	3	3.9	11.6	43%	.370	1.82	6.75	6.38	6.96	-0.3	99	99.4
	OKL	AAA	27	3	1	3	22	0	28	23	2	5.1	12.2	45%	.313	1.39	3.86	3.64	3.83	0.4	86	
Jacob Rhame	TUL	AA	22	3	3	2	39	0	50	34	5	3.4	10.3	32%	.244	1.06	3.06	3.52	3.02	1.0	83	
Joe Wieland	OKL	AAA	25	10	5	0	22	21	113^{2}	135	7	2.0	7.3	44%	.355	1.41	4.59	3.52	3.82	2.2	87	
	LAN	MLB	25	0	1	0	2	2	8^{2}	10	2	5.2	4.2	39%	.276	1.73	8.31	6.97	6.69	-0.2	116	93.4

The Dodgers made yet another international splash when they signed Cuban right-hander **Yadier Alvarez** to a $16 million deal last July. He's 19, throws in the upper 90s and has already received three MVP votes from confused St. Louis sportswriters. ❖ Former decent starter **Scott Baker** tossed 11 frames for the Dodgers in 2015, simultaneously finishing one and two innings short of a Baker's dozen. ❖ The Dodgers paid **Brandon Beachy** $2.75 million to allow seven runs in eight innings, proving that they treat real money like you treat FAAB dollars. ❖ **Tommy Bergjans**, the Dodgers' 2015 eighth-round pick, was plucked from Haverford College, also the alma mater of Josh Byrnes, the third head of the Dodgers' many-GMs front office. Bergjans reached Great Lakes in his first professional season, which puts yet another Tommy Haverford fairly close to Pawnee. ❖ **Lisalverto Bonilla** had surprising success in a starting role toward the end of 2014, but Tommy John surgery in April derailed any momentum the medium-sized righty might have built up. ❖ The Dodgers popped Vanderbilt product **Walker Buehler** 24th overall in the 2015 draft only to learn the right-hander would need Tommy John surgery immediately thereafter. Buehler should get between 365 and 547 Days Off. ❖ **Chase DeJong** was acquired from the Blue Jays for what amounts to money, which the Dodgers can print more easily than back-end starter prospects. ❖ Acquired from the Braves for an international-bonus-pool slot, **Caleb Dirks** stuck 'em with the pointy end across three levels, posting 11.5 K/9 as a reliever. ❖ When it comes to unbreakable records, **Tyler Olson** and his 0.52 intentional walks per inning pitched belongs in the rarefied air beside Cy Young and Joe DiMaggio. ❖ **Josh Ravin** can miss bats with the best of them, but his control and homer-prone ways are a huge problem. He struck out 12 in nine innings for the Dodgers but also walked four and gave up three bombs, and since that's so Ravin there's no real future we can see. ❖ **Jacob Rhame** throws hard and misses bats, and while he gave up a few too many homers and walks, he was quite good in Tulsa last season. Relievers with this profile almost never fail to live up to expectations, so he's a lock to be closing for the Dodgers by 2017. ❖ The good news is **Joe Wieland** threw over 100 innings for the first time since 2011; the bad news is quantity isn't everything.

Manager

Dave Roberts

Here's a surprise.

When the Dodgers announced that Don Mattingly wouldn't return as skipper, the natural response was to pencil Gabe Kapler into the spot. After all, Kapler had previous managerial experience, and had worked alongside Andrew Friedman in some capacity or another for most of his post-playing career. Sure enough, Kapler was named a candidate, and was later identified as a finalist for the job. Yet in the end, the Dodgers went with a different ex-outfielder who had ties to one of their executives: Roberts.

Roberts had previously served in various roles for the Padres, where he inevitably ran into Josh Byrnes from time to time. Most recently, Roberts had been San Diego's bench coach for the past two seasons. He'd even interviewed for their managerial opening when Bud Black was fired. Alas, the Padres passed on him not once, but twice: first in naming an interim skipper, and again after the season, when he didn't receive another courtesy interview. You could say, then, that Roberts entered the process with the Dodgers as an underdog. Nevertheless, he made a big enough impression on the Dodgers' brass to become the franchise's first minority skipper.

The question now is whether Roberts can continue to turn heads. Those in the know praise him foremost for his people skills—a good thing, given the bold personalities that often inhabit the Dodgers clubhouse. Not as much is said or known about Roberts' strategical bents, but he figures to be tolerable in that regard, considering he served as Bud Black's right-hand man and has access to the Dodgers front office. In other words, this has the chance to be a successful long-term relationship.

MIAMI MARLINS

Essay by Matt Trueblood

Player comments by Wilson Karaman and BP authors

Giancarlo Stanton took some convincing, but the Marlins sold him on the notion that they were serious about contending. That's why he signed a six-year, $107 million contract extension, giving up three years that would have been part of his first free-agent deal. (Ignore the hype and the feigned secondary commitment. Stanton is going to opt out after 2020.) Stanton signed that deal, though, and at that point, the Marlins owed him nothing more than they owe everyone in their organization: an honest effort to improve the team as much as possible, for as long as possible. Any other organization might have heaved a sigh of relief at having six seasons, instead of three, to capitalize on a remarkable talent like Stanton, and continued building a team and system that could sustainably support its generational talent throughout those years. Instead, Jeffrey Loria ruined everything.

The Miami McCourt, Pt. 1: The Shortsighted Offseason

The Marlins traded the long term for the short term in multiple transactions, swapping out Nathan Eovaldi, Andrew Heaney, Kiké Hernandez, Chris Hatcher, Anthony DeSclafani and Austin Barnes for Dee Gordon, Dan Haren, Martin Prado, Mat Latos and David Phelps. (They also gave up a fairly high draft pick and two prospects to land starting pitcher Jarred Cosart at the 2014 trade deadline.) Staying firmly on brand, they got the Dodgers to pay the full salaries of Gordon and Haren, even though Gordon was arbitration-eligible and hadn't yet had his salary set, and even if Haren retired rather than accept his assignment to Miami. They also got $3 million per year for each of the two years left on Prado's contract, and they took Latos to arbitration rather than bridge the $1 million gap between his asking price and their offer. (They won.)

Those deals didn't make the organization stronger, but there's no denying that they made the big-league roster better in the short term. Prado and Gordon, especially, improved on what they had in-house at their respective positions, and addressed the team's biggest offensive deficiency of 2014: contact rate. The pitching additions amounted, perhaps, to a lateral move, but if they gave away team control and upside, they likely got some reliability in return. Their position was tenuous and they

MARLINS PROSPECTUS

2015 W-L: 71-91, 3rd in NL East

Pythag	.454	21st	DER	.706	11th
RS/G	3.78	29th	B-Age	27.8	5th
RA/G	4.19	14th	P-Age	27.2	5th
TAv	.261	17th	Salary	$69M	30th
BRR	13.61	4th	M$/MW	$2.5M	21st
TAv-P	.270	25th	DL Days	1133	19th
FIP	4.01	14th	$ on DL	24%	26th

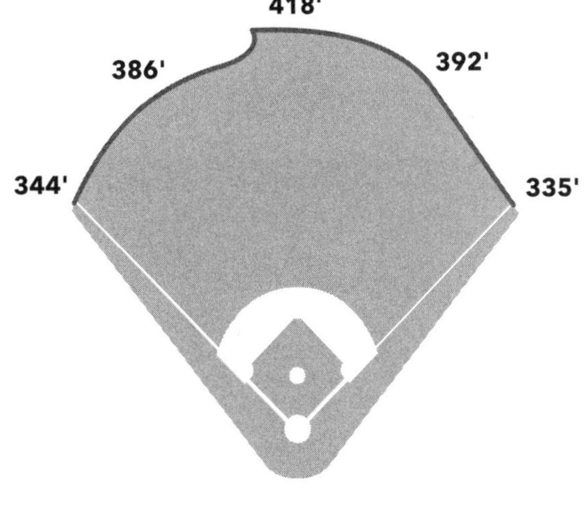

Outfield wall profile: **10'** to **16'**

Three-Year Park Factors

Runs	Runs/RH	Runs/LH	HR/RH	HR/LH
92	95	103	95	96

Top Hitter WARP	4.6	Giancarlo Stanton
Top Pitcher WARP	1.4	A.J. Ramos
Top Prospect	Tyler Kolek	

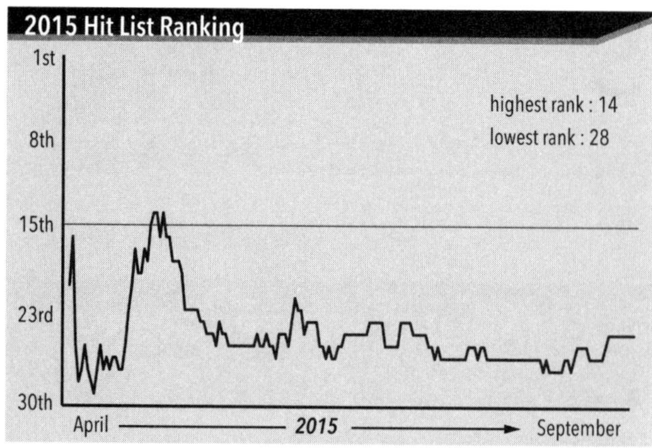

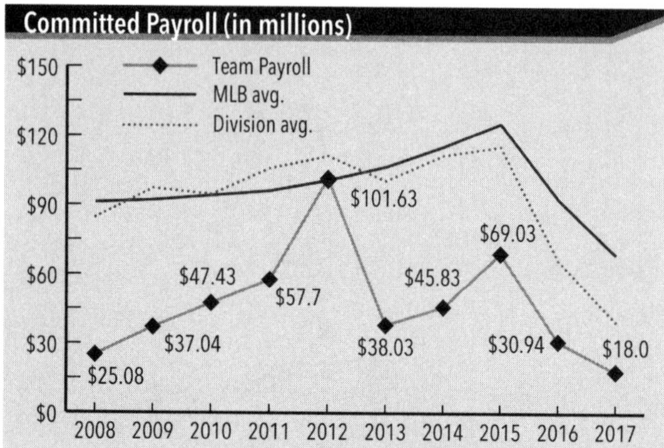

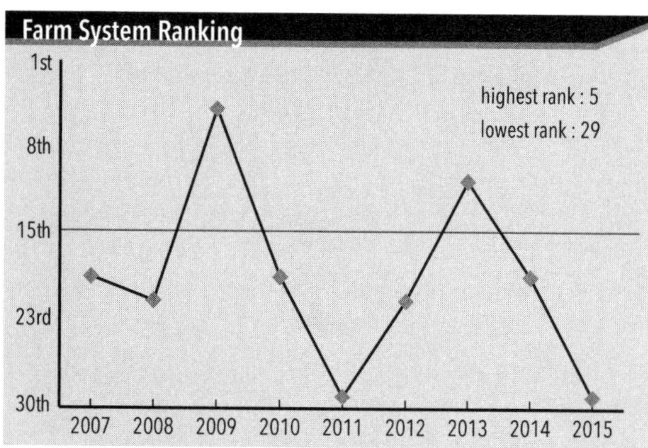

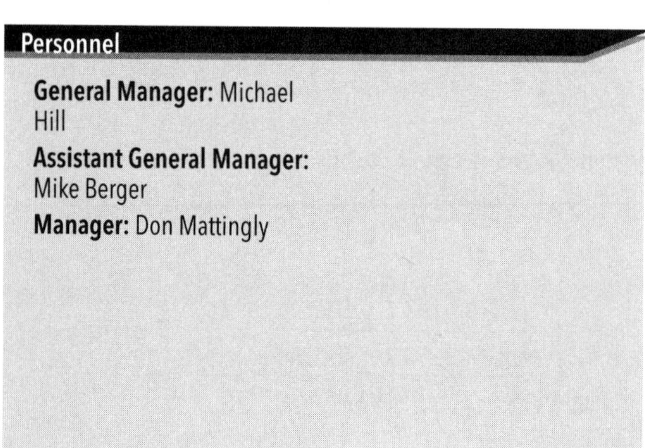
Personnel

General Manager: Michael Hill

Assistant General Manager: Mike Berger

Manager: Don Mattingly

paid a long-term price to get there, but yes, the 2015 Marlins were in position to compete.

The Miami McCourt, Pt. 2: The Bizarre Manager

If Loria's winter seemed myopic, though, his spring put it to shame. Rumors about the job security of manager Mike Redmond cropped up as the team stumbled to a 3-11 start, and though they briefly pulled out of that spiral, the next three-game losing streak was enough to earn Redmond his walking papers. Suddenly, the Fighting Stantons were destabilized, with a clear message from ownership that they weren't doing enough but no clear directives for fixing the problem.

There was no reason to fire the manager of an even modestly talented 16-22 team. On the day of Redmond's last game at the helm in Miami, the Blue Jays were 17-22. The Rangers were 16-22. The Pirates were 18-20. Loria was so fixated on winning in 2015, though, that he pulled the trigger, and installed GM Dan Jennings as manager. (Read that twice, even though you already knew it. Revel in the absurdity of it. Embrace the lunacy.)

Here's something you should know about the Marlins: They employed Andy Barkett for five years, including 2015. Barkett is a former big leaguer (though only very briefly, for the 2001 Pirates) and a Miami native, and from 2007 through 2014, he managed full-season minor-league teams in the Tigers' and Marlins' systems. He's 41, and as of the start of the 2015 season, he was the team's roving minor-league hitting coordinator. He briefly managed a Dominican Winter League team, too. There might have been a more qualified managerial candidate than Barkett available, or a more natural role from which to promote a valued member of the organization, but it's hard to imagine one.

If Loria hired good executives or trusted the ones he had, surely the Marlins would have installed Barkett, or someone similarly ready, and maybe their season would have gotten back on track. (Or maybe not, but even those who strongly believe managers have little effect would acknowledge that the odds would be better with a more conventional candidate.) If they felt Redmond wasn't doing the job and wanted an in-house replacement, Barkett was as clear a choice as could possibly have presented itself. Instead, Loria installed GM Dan Jennings as manager. Reports have indicated that Loria tried for years to convince Jennings to manage the team, and finally won the argument in May. If true, that makes the decision even more inscrutable: It wasn't an emergency backup, a contingency plan. To some extent, this midstream tectonic change in organizational structure, this season-derailing distraction and disruption, was all part of Loria's master plan.

In October, by the way, Barkett turned down the Marlins' contract offer for 2016; he signed on with the Pirates in December.

The Miami McCourt, Pt. 3: The Declining Catcher

There is no season in which firing one's manager and demoting the GM to that position despite the GM's lack of experience or demonstrated proficiency in that role wouldn't be the most bizarre decision. Loria, Jennings and President of Baseball Operations Michael Hill made other peculiar calls, though. There was, for instance, the decision to cut bait and release Jarrod Saltalamacchia on May 5th, with the majority of the $21 million they had committed to him prior to 2014 still owed. Saltalamacchia is a catcher in name only these days, and turned in -2.6 WARP during his Marlins tenure, but cutting a player nine games and 33 plate appearances into the season is an extraordinary choice. Two days after being released, Saltalamacchia signed with the Diamondbacks, and turned in a .280 True Average for Arizona. Equalizing playing time, Jeff Mathis, the Marlins' primary backup catcher, was worth all of one run more than Saltalamacchia, including framing.

The Miami McCourt, Pt. 4: The Promising Outfielder

Then there was Marcell Ozuna, who became the annual Marlin to be jerked around, abused or blackballed by ownership for reasons beyond understanding. Ozuna struggled throughout the first half, batting .249/.301/.337 and cracking only four home runs. That's an unfortunate line for a young hitter on whom the team had counted heavily as they built their aspiring contender, but it's far short of a catastrophe. Ozuna's first-half OPS was better than those of Ian Desmond, Starlin Castro, Angel Pagan and Juan Lagares, among others who got similar playing time. Defensively, Ozuna continued to acquit himself well in center field, not impressing but not hurting the team. There was cause for concern, and perhaps cause for a brief benching, but because these are the Marlins, Ozuna was demoted to Triple-A New Orleans.

No, strike that. Because this is Loria, Ozuna was demoted. We learned after the season that Jennings, Loria's dragooned skipper, stood in defiance of the owner's mandate that Ozuna be benched. He continued playing Ozuna, so Loria ordered the demotion to wrest away the discretionary choice. Ozuna would stay with New Orleans through August 14th, batting .317/.379/.558 in 132 plate appearances. According to Scott Boras, who represents Ozuna, players groused about the absence of his client throughout the Marlins' miserable July, and Jennings openly told them that he wanted Ozuna on the club and in the lineup, but was overruled.

It shouldn't surprise you to hear this next part. The Marlins recalled Ozuna in mid-August (six days after Ozuna's Super Two cutoff date, saving the Marlins a year of arbitration salary and suppressing his awards for 2017-19), and he hit just fine (a .789 OPS, right in line with the second half of, to take one example, Kyle Seager). It didn't matter, though. The Marlins were 46-69 by the first game of his return; the problems with the team ran far deeper than Ozuna.

The Miami McCourt, Pt. 5: The Capitulation Trades

That the team traded away Haren, Latos, Michael Morse, erstwhile closer Steve Cishek and even Sam Dyson (a reliever making the league-minimum salary, though in line for Super Two status after 2017) is not surprising, nor laudable, nor especially despicable. It was a rational reaction to the very logical conclusion drawn by management at the All-Star break: This team was going nowhere. There are two things we should note about that sequence, however, that bespeak the problems that remain unsolved.

First, every move saved the Marlins money. Eating the bad salary attached to Latos and Morse could have allowed the team to get some real talent in return, but instead, the two were packaged in a three-team deal that also sent the Marlins' 2016 competitive-balance pick to the Braves, and while they did get three minor leaguers back, there's a strong case to be made that the Marlins' greatest benefit in that trade was saving the remaining money owed to Latos and Morse. That also means they more or less sold their competitive-balance pick for the third year out of four. All of which would be fine, except that Loria's next demonstration of a willingness to roll savings in one spot into increased spending in another will be his first.

Second, seeing those players traded away was a stinging reminder that they were the Marlins' idea of a renewed commitment to winning, and winning now. Haren was a near-retiree. Latos was coming off a season riddled with arm injuries and bad clubhouse juju. Morse was a role player, a one-dimensional lefty-masher, not a full-time starter on any credible contender. Sure, Miami also acquired Gordon and Prado, and those moves worked out fairly well, but the fact remains: This executive team is either completely hamstrung by the tightness of Loria's budgets or fundamentally incapable of identifying and assembling the crucial elements of a winning team.

✦✦✦

That's the cruelest twist on the Marlins' narrative. For all of Loria's egomania and meddling, for all the thievery from and mistreatment of a community and market they haven't bothered to really understand, for all the feigned effort to contend that still left them spending less on payroll in 2015 than any other team, the Marlins' story still isn't a simple tale of corruption. There's a healthy dose of honest-to-God towering incompetence here, spoiling even the sincere efforts Loria and his lackeys make to win. They have no idea what makes a good manager. They have no idea how to value assets in trades or free agency. They have no idea how to create sustainable growth, coherent processes or a well-rounded big-league team. When stirred to action for some cause other than cost-cutting, they tend to lurch in the direction of solving whatever problem presents itself most obviously. After being the second-most strikeout-prone team in MLB in 2014, they paid dearly to get their hands on Prado and Gordon, and they did improve their contact rate—but not their run production. They don't understand the vagaries of sample size, which is why they perennially mishandle their own players—not only Ozuna and Saltalamacchia, but guys like Logan Morrison and Chris Coghlan. Maybe the baseball-operations team gets these things, but if so, they've been unable to override Loria's capricious will.

The 2015 Marlins won 71 games, with half-seasons of Stanton and Jose Fernandez, and with a midseason sell-off. They could be competitive if both players are healthy and at full strength in 2016. Unfortunately, with Stanton owed $9 million and Fernandez hitting arbitration for the first time, there's no guarantee that either player is even a Marlin on Opening Day. (Remember the maltreatment of Ozuna, a Boras client who spurned the Marlins' advances on extension talks prior to the 2015 season? Fernandez is in the same boat.) Ditto for Gordon, who should make $6 million or so via arbitration. (Book-production realities mean that this essay was written amid swirling rumors but no consummated action on these fronts.) If you trust the Marlins to keep those players just because they look like a potentially excellent core, ignoring or working around a collective price tag pushing $20 million, Loria has a fresco of the Brooklyn Bridge he would love to sell you. Da Vinci painted it! And even if the team does keep all three of their would-be leaders and stars, who can guarantee that Miami will spend enough (and wisely enough) to supplement them and add 20 wins to the ledger? There's not a clear path to that kind of progress in this organization.

The Marlins always seem to come up with good players. Their minor-league system operates smoothly, perhaps because it exists below the threshold of Loria's attention and interest. They're a good amateur-scouting organization with a consistent high-risk, high-reward approach, which is how they come up with so many superstars. At the end of the day, though, winning takes either a wide-open checkbook or very sharp talent evaluation and deployment. The Marlins are the cheapest and the dumbest team in baseball, which is why not even Giancarlo Stanton and Jose Fernandez can save them. ■

—Matt Trueblood is an author of Baseball Prospectus, armed for the task of surveying the Marlins' systemic failure primarily by the formative years he wasted on the Andy MacPhail-era Cubs.

Hitters

Jeff Baker 1B

Born: 6/21/81 Age: 35 Bats: R Throws: R Height: 6'2" Weight: 220

YEAR	TEAM	LVL	AGE	PA	R	2B	3B	HR	RBI	BB	K	SB	CS	AVG/OBP/SLG	TAv	BABIP	BRR	FRAA	WARP
2013	TEX	MLB	32	175	21	8	0	11	21	18	48	1	0	.279/.360/.545	.318	.333	-1.8	1B(21): -1.5, LF(21): -0.6	0.9
2014	MIA	MLB	33	225	27	10	4	3	28	13	51	1	0	.264/.307/.394	.266	.331	-2.0	1B(43): -3.2, 2B(21): 1.1	0.1
2015	MIA	MLB	34	80	11	3	0	3	8	8	25	0	0	.208/.288/.375	.273	.273	0.1	1B(17): -1.3, LF(1): -0.0	0.1
2016	*MIA*	*MLB*	*35*	*250*	*24*	*11*	*2*	*6*	*28*	*16*	*63*	*1*	*0*	*.242/.293/.381*	*.250*	*.304*	*-1.3*	*1B -5, 2B 0*	*-0.4*
2017	*MIA*	*MLB*	*36*	*36*	*4*	*1*	*0*	*1*	*4*	*2*	*9*	*0*	*0*	*.228/.283/.355*	*.244*	*.288*	*-0.2*	*1B -1, 2B 0*	*-0.1*

Breakout: 1% Improve: 25% Collapse: 12% Attrition: 18% MLB: 93% *Comparables: Olmedo Saenz, Gil Hodges, Phil Nevin*

There comes a time in every man's life when the battle bests him. Baker still managed to run into a couple against southpaws—his career's hallmark utility—but the bat looked lethargic and his contact rates plummeted before an oblique injury shelved him in early July. What happened next will be left for labor historians to debate: Baker was released from the team for "conveying an anti-front office message." For his troubles he learned something he didn't know then but he certainly knows now: Nobody f#%&s with The Loria.

Justin Bour 1B

Born: 5/28/88 Age: 28 Bats: L Throws: R Height: 6'4" Weight: 250

YEAR	TEAM	LVL	AGE	PA	R	2B	3B	HR	RBI	BB	K	SB	CS	AVG/OBP/SLG	TAv	BABIP	BRR	FRAA	WARP
2013	TEN	AA	25	361	48	17	0	18	64	36	63	0	2	.237/.313/.461	.274	.236	-1.3	1B(74): -1.7	0.6
2014	NWO	AAA	26	430	59	27	0	18	72	39	57	3	1	.306/.372/.517	.320	.319	-1.6	1B(91): 5.0	3.7
2014	MIA	MLB	26	83	10	3	0	1	11	9	19	0	0	.284/.361/.365	.278	.370	-0.6	1B(15): 1.0	0.3
2015	MIA	MLB	27	446	42	20	0	23	73	34	101	0	0	.262/.321/.479	.289	.294	-4.1	1B(111): -6.3	0.7
2015	NWO	AAA	27	62	8	1	0	1	5	11	6	1	0	.275/.403/.353	.284	.295	0.2	1B(13): -0.0	0.2
2016	*MIA*	*MLB*	*28*	*562*	*64*	*25*	*1*	*23*	*77*	*45*	*114*	*1*	*0*	*.253/.314/.439*	*.269*	*.282*	*-3.1*	*1B -0*	*1.1*
2017	*MIA*	*MLB*	*29*	*542*	*69*	*25*	*1*	*20*	*69*	*46*	*113*	*0*	*0*	*.250/.315/.425*	*.275*	*.285*	*-3.3*	*1B 0*	*0.5*

Breakout: 8% Improve: 29% Collapse: 9% Attrition: 23% MLB: 68% *Comparables: Ryan Shealy, Nate Freiman, Matt LaPorta*

The Marlins saw the opportunity to snag some defense-be-damned production on the cheap a couple winters ago and plucked Bour in the Triple-A Rule 5 draft. "Lumber" is both his preferred weapon and the best verb to describe his fieldwork—depending on your preferred metric, his performance at the cold corner was somewhere between "bad" and "that batting dummy Charlie Sheen beheads in *Major League* could've done better." But his exit velocity cracked the top 20, and while he proved over-aggressive against breaking pitches he managed to pummel a decent number of the ones he made contact with. Sometimes hitters just kind of end up having a solid season without much advance notice that they're ripe to have a solid season. What you saw last year is pretty much what the Marlins should get for another couple seasons, before his arbitration clock starts ticking.

Derek Dietrich 2B

Born: 7/18/89 Age: 26 Bats: L Throws: R Height: 6'0" Weight: 210

YEAR	TEAM	LVL	AGE	PA	R	2B	3B	HR	RBI	BB	K	SB	CS	AVG/OBP/SLG	TAv	BABIP	BRR	FRAA	WARP
2013	JAX	AA	23	257	35	13	3	11	38	29	60	3	0	.271/.381/.509	.316	.327	0.2	2B(50): -2.9, 3B(8): -0.7	1.9
2013	MIA	MLB	23	233	32	10	2	9	23	11	56	1	0	.214/.275/.405	.260	.247	0.7	2B(57): -3.6	0.3
2014	NWO	AAA	24	92	15	3	0	7	16	4	18	1	0	.317/.391/.610	.360	.333	0.0	2B(21): -0.4	1.3
2014	MIA	MLB	24	183	31	6	2	5	17	13	38	1	0	.228/.326/.386	.277	.270	2.9	2B(44): 1.4, 3B(1): -0.3	1.3
2015	NWO	AAA	25	224	25	13	2	7	27	15	45	0	2	.260/.357/.458	.306	.303	-0.7	2B(35): -5.2, 1B(8): -0.8	1.2
2015	MIA	MLB	25	289	38	14	3	10	24	23	65	0	2	.256/.346/.456	.301	.303	0.8	LF(46): -3.9, 3B(26): 0.5	1.7
2016	*MIA*	*MLB*	*26*	*273*	*31*	*12*	*2*	*10*	*36*	*18*	*64*	*1*	*1*	*.242/.322/.438*	*.273*	*.284*	*1.3*	*3B -1, SS 0*	*1.2*
2017	*MIA*	*MLB*	*27*	*270*	*34*	*11*	*2*	*9*	*34*	*18*	*62*	*1*	*1*	*.238/.318/.421*	*.276*	*.280*	*1.2*	*3B -1, SS 0*	*0.8*

Breakout: 4% Improve: 48% Collapse: 8% Attrition: 10% MLB: 97% *Comparables: Sean Rodriguez, Jedd Gyorko, Chase Headley*

For a long time, Dietrich was just a bat-first keystoner with a questionable hitting approach and severe glove-clunk. He remains aggressive but earns his keep with ample power and tons of OBP-padding HBPs. In a way he kind of improved defensively, insofar as Miami management abandoned virtually all hope of developing him into their second baseman of the future and instead used him to plug holes in left field and third base, where his contributions with the leather didn't rate nearly as poorly. Miami made him available at the trade deadline but ultimately kept him around; as an in-his-prime, cost-controlled offensive asset with some newfound defensive versatility, Dietrich figures this year to play a regular role in some capacity for the, ahem, budget-conscious Marlins.

Cole Gillespie RF

Born: 6/20/84 Age: 32 Bats: R Throws: R Height: 6'2" Weight: 205

YEAR	TEAM	LVL	AGE	PA	R	2B	3B	HR	RBI	BB	K	SB	CS	AVG/OBP/SLG	TAv	BABIP	BRR	FRAA	WARP
2013	FRE	AAA	29	269	35	11	2	9	31	32	52	7	0	.277/.361/.455	.286	.318	-0.6	LF(46): 0.6, 2B(12): -0.7	1.3
2013	CHN	MLB	29	59	6	2	0	0	4	6	13	0	0	.240/.328/.280	.233	.316	0.0	RF(13): 1.7, LF(3): -0.5	0.1
2013	SFN	MLB	29	10	0	0	0	0	0	1	0	0	0	.000/.100/.000	.038	.000	0.0	LF(3): -0.1	-0.2
2014	SEA	MLB	30	78	9	2	0	1	5	6	13	2	2	.254/.312/.324	.228	.298	0.6	LF(16): -0.0, RF(9): -0.4	-0.1
2014	TOR	MLB	30	3	0	0	0	0	0	0	0	0	0	.000/.000/.000	-.012	.000	0.0	RF(1): -0.4	-0.1
2014	BUF	AAA	30	104	15	4	1	2	16	14	14	3	0	.354/.423/.500	.338	.370	-1.0	RF(11): 0.8, LF(9): 0.5	1.1
2014	TAC	AAA	30	68	14	5	1	5	14	9	9	2	0	.362/.456/.741	.432	.364	1.2	LF(9): -0.3, RF(6): -0.7	1.5
2015	MIA	MLB	31	157	17	10	2	2	16	10	27	4	1	.290/.333/.428	.269	.342	2.4	CF(31): -1.2, RF(17): -1.3	0.5
2015	NWO	AAA	31	281	30	15	1	0	23	27	31	7	2	.291/.356/.360	.283	.324	1.4	RF(49): -3.2, CF(5): -0.8	0.9
2016	*MIA*	*MLB*	*32*	*197*	*20*	*7*	*2*	*3*	*19*	*19*	*38*	*4*	*1*	*.248/.322/.363*	*.253*	*.296*	*1.2*	*CF -0, LF 0*	*0.7*
2017	*MIA*	*MLB*	*33*	*296*	*32*	*11*	*3*	*4*	*27*	*28*	*58*	*5*	*2*	*.242/.317/.349*	*.254*	*.291*	*1.8*	*CF -1, LF 0*	*0.6*

Breakout: 1% Improve: 8% Collapse: 3% Attrition: 18% MLB: 26% *Comparables: Raul Gonzalez, Jeff Salazar, Justin Christian*

Tell 'em about that grind, kid. Gillespie has wandered the minor leagues like Kwai Chang Caine for over a decade now, and chances are that at some point he's appeared at a baseball field near you. Every so often during that time, however, his head has bobbed above water with a big-league cap on its brow, and in 2015 he set (ever-so-modest) career highs in games and PAs. He did just enough to flip his career WARP balance back into the black, with passable defense in all three outfield spots and a smattering of decent at-bats. What the future holds for Gillespie is anybody's guess, but wherever he goes, there he'll be. (Probably not for long.)

Dee Gordon 2B

Born: 4/22/88 Age: 28 Bats: L Throws: R Height: 5'11" Weight: 170

YEAR	TEAM	LVL	AGE	PA	R	2B	3B	HR	RBI	BB	K	SB	CS	AVG/OBP/SLG	TAv	BABIP	BRR	FRAA	WARP
2013	ABQ	AAA	25	433	65	17	9	0	33	51	70	49	11	.297/.385/.390	.277	.364	7.2	SS(73): 10.9, 2B(20): -0.7	4.3
2013	LAN	MLB	25	106	9	1	1	1	6	10	21	10	2	.234/.314/.298	.234	.292	1.4	SS(27): 1.1, 2B(3): 0.3	0.5
2014	LAN	MLB	26	650	92	24	12	2	34	31	107	64	19	.289/.326/.378	.268	.346	4.0	2B(144): -2.8	2.4
2015	MIA	MLB	27	653	88	24	8	4	46	25	91	58	20	.333/.359/.418	.292	.383	4.1	2B(145): -0.6	4.3
2016	*MIA*	*MLB*	*28*	*641*	*85*	*22*	*8*	*3*	*41*	*36*	*102*	*56*	*17*	*.280/.322/.360*	*.249*	*.328*	*2.7*	*2B -0*	*2.1*
2017	*MIA*	*MLB*	*29*	*574*	*57*	*20*	*7*	*3*	*48*	*32*	*91*	*48*	*16*	*.278/.319/.357*	*.252*	*.323*	*4.3*	*2B 0*	*1.5*

Breakout: 2% Improve: 42% Collapse: 2% Attrition: 12% MLB: 90% *Comparables: Chris Getz, Brendan Ryan, Emilio Bonifacio*

Take that, haters.

In the aftermath of That Night in the winter meetings, when we surveyed the de facto three-way deal that sent Andrew Heaney to Anaheim, Howie Kendrick to Los Angeles, Gordon to Miami and some other stuff to some other places, only one thing was near universally agreed upon: The Marlins got tooken. But Gordon responded with across-the-board improvements to set the WARP pace for all MLB keystoners, all while playing on the Dodgers' dime. There was surely some happy fortune involved in Gordon's batting title, as he gained nearly 40 points of BABIP despite a consistent batted ball distribution. Still, when you're one of the faster burners in the league (he is), and you hit groundballs at one of the highest rates in the league (he does), you're never without potential to luck into a few more knocks every now and again.

Furthering the batting average cause, he also continued an enviable trend of lopping whiffs off his ledger, though he accomplished the feat simply by swinging a lot more and making contact at a standard rate. It was an impressive exercise in creativity to prop up his on-base profile in spite of an ongoing aversion to free passes. Add in continuing defensive improvements and an above-board FRAA, and you had one of the more valuable senior circuit assets in 2015. There are enough warning signs about sustainability in the profile that the smart money banks on some modest regression in 2016, but the "smart" money is still smarting from That Night.

Adeiny Hechavarria SS

Born: 4/15/89 Age: 27 Bats: R Throws: R Height: 6'2" Weight: 215

YEAR	TEAM	LVL	AGE	PA	R	2B	3B	HR	RBI	BB	K	SB	CS	AVG/OBP/SLG	TAv	BABIP	BRR	FRAA	WARP
2013	MIA	MLB	24	578	30	14	8	3	42	30	96	11	10	.227/.267/.298	.204	.270	-5.5	SS(148): -6.3	-2.3
2014	MIA	MLB	25	574	53	20	10	1	34	26	86	7	5	.276/.308/.356	.243	.323	3.6	SS(146): 9.2	2.8
2015	MIA	MLB	26	499	54	17	6	5	48	23	78	7	2	.281/.315/.374	.249	.325	3.2	SS(130): 6.2	2.5
2016	*MIA*	*MLB*	*27*	*566*	*52*	*20*	*6*	*6*	*48*	*29*	*99*	*8*	*4*	*.256/.295/.350*	*.235*	*.300*	*0.7*	*SS 1*	*1.5*
2017	*MIA*	*MLB*	*28*	*516*	*50*	*18*	*5*	*6*	*45*	*28*	*93*	*6*	*4*	*.248/.289/.344*	*.237*	*.293*	*0.8*	*SS 1*	*0.9*

Breakout: 4% Improve: 47% Collapse: 8% Attrition: 12% MLB: 99% *Comparables: Alcides Escobar, Ronny Cedeno, Erick Aybar*

For a couple years there Hechavarria looked like one of those rip-off arcade games from the 80s: The Marlins kept pumping in quarters even though there was no next level to get to. Things changed dramatically in 2015, as the young Cuban broke out defensively to produce one of the better statistical seasons of any big-league shortstop. His efficiency improved across the board, especially on the plays he was supposed to make—those routine ones having long vexed observers who saw his arm, his range, his highlights. Perhaps that's a credit to better positioning and anticipation. Maybe somebody fixed a software glitch. Whatever it was, Hechavarria emerged as the key cog in a spectacularly upgraded Miami defense, a development which overshadowed notable gains in his offensive output as well. He turned down a contract extension before the season began, and given his employer's tendencies he might have priced himself out of a second offer.

Jeff Mathis C

Born: 3/31/83 Age: 33 Bats: R Throws: R Height: 6'0" Weight: 205

YEAR	TEAM	LVL	AGE	PA	R	2B	3B	HR	RBI	BB	K	SB	CS	AVG/OBP/SLG	TAv	BABIP	BRR	FRAA	WARP
2013	MIA	MLB	30	256	14	7	1	5	29	21	76	0	0	.181/.251/.284	.204	.243	1.0	C(73): 6.4	0.5
2014	MIA	MLB	31	195	12	7	0	2	12	15	64	0	0	.200/.263/.274	.204	.303	0.8	C(62): 3.0	0.2
2015	JAX	AA	32	20	2	1	0	0	2	2	6	0	0	.294/.350/.353	.305	.417	-0.1	C(2): 0.0	0.2
2015	MIA	MLB	32	103	9	4	1	2	12	7	24	0	0	.161/.214/.290	.202	.186	-0.2	C(30): 4.3	0.3
2016	*MIA*	*MLB*	*33*	*121*	*10*	*5*	*0*	*2*	*11*	*8*	*36*	*0*	*0*	*.195/.248/.305*	*.202*	*.257*	*0.2*	*C 2*	*0.0*
2017	*MIA*	*MLB*	*34*	*167*	*16*	*6*	*1*	*3*	*15*	*11*	*50*	*0*	*0*	*.193/.247/.301*	*.204*	*.253*	*0.2*	*C 2*	*-0.2*

Breakout: 0% Improve: 39% Collapse: 12% Attrition: 25% MLB: 89% *Comparables: Hank Foiles, Damian Miller, Eddie Taubensee*

YEAR	TEAM	P. COUNT	FRM RUNS	BLK RUNS	THRW RUNS	TOT RUNS
2013	MIA	9391	7.1	-0.1	0.4	7.4
2014	MIA	7570	1.2	0.1	1.0	2.4
2015	MIA	4146	3.5	0.1	0.1	3.6
2016	*MIA*	*3529*	*1.7*	*0.0*	*0.2*	*1.9*
2017	*MIA*	*4883*	*1.7*	*0.0*	*0.2*	*1.8*

When he was on the field, Mathis continued to do what he's annually paid seven figures to do: steal a bunch of extra strikes and prevent errant pitches from touring the tender pastures of foul territory. He also continued to do what he's annually ripped to shreds by team-specific bloggers for, posting the worst on-base percentage of his career—no easy task for the man with the lowest TAv (min. 2,000 PA) in the 21st century. A fluky broken finger in April cost him 53 days, but he's generally still healthy for his age and position. He and Adam Jones are tied with 14 career intentional walks.

Casey McGehee 3B

Born: 10/12/82 Age: 33 Bats: R Throws: R Height: 6'1" Weight: 220

YEAR	TEAM	LVL	AGE	PA	R	2B	3B	HR	RBI	BB	K	SB	CS	AVG/OBP/SLG	TAv	BABIP	BRR	FRAA	WARP
2014	MIA	MLB	31	691	56	29	1	4	76	67	102	4	2	.287/.355/.357	.264	.335	-6.0	3B(158): -17.1	0.0
2015	MIA	MLB	32	120	7	7	0	0	9	10	22	1	0	.182/.250/.245	.187	.227	0.8	1B(20): -1.0, 3B(10): -0.7	-0.7
2015	SFN	MLB	32	138	7	5	0	2	11	11	28	0	1	.213/.275/.299	.178	.258	-0.7	3B(32): -0.7, 1B(1): -0.0	-0.9
2015	SAC	AAA	32	46	7	3	0	2	7	3	5	0	0	.357/.391/.571	.318	.361	0.1	3B(10): -0.8	0.4
2016	*MIA*	*MLB*	*33*	*336*	*30*	*14*	*1*	*5*	*31*	*28*	*60*	*2*	*1*	*.236/.298/.332*	*.235*	*.276*	*-1.6*	*3B -7, 1B -1*	*-1.1*
2017	*MIA*	*MLB*	*34*	*281*	*29*	*11*	*0*	*3*	*23*	*25*	*51*	*1*	*0*	*.225/.294/.311*	*.233*	*.266*	*-1.4*	*3B -6, 1B 0*	*-1.3*

Breakout: 5% Improve: 39% Collapse: 4% Attrition: 11% MLB: 92% *Comparables: Harvey Kuenn, George Kell, John Valentin*

In six years, when we all finally realize that the Marlins were just playing a diabolical long game this whole time, we very well may look back on McGehee's tenure with the club as the symbol of the era. A year after turning in one of the more surprisingly competent seasons anyone'd seen come out of nowhere in quite some time, the veteran third-sacker fetched additional value for the franchise in an off-season trade to San Francisco that netted a couple prospects. Upon arriving in the Bay Area he promptly reverted to pre-Japan form, got himself released, latched back on with Miami, and went on to help the team secure a protected draft slot by posting a negative WARP. "Not bad, McGehee," they'll say with a note of nostalgia on their breath. "Not bad at all." Which will be ironic, of course, because he was really, really bad last year.

Tommy Medica 1B

Born: 4/9/88 Age: 28 Bats: R Throws: R Height: 6'1" Weight: 209

YEAR	TEAM	LVL	AGE	PA	R	2B	3B	HR	RBI	BB	K	SB	CS	AVG/OBP/SLG	TAv	BABIP	BRR	FRAA	WARP
2013	SAN	AA	25	320	48	20	3	18	57	28	67	4	2	.296/.372/.582	.334	.327	-1.4	1B(51): 3.2, LF(1): -0.3	3.1
2013	SDN	MLB	25	79	9	2	0	3	10	10	23	0	0	.290/.380/.449	.312	.395	0.2	1B(19): -1.0	0.4
2014	SDN	MLB	26	259	31	11	2	9	27	14	75	6	1	.233/.286/.408	.280	.299	1.1	1B(46): -0.4, LF(22): -0.8	0.9
2014	ELP	AAA	26	101	8	6	2	3	18	9	24	0	0	.213/.307/.427	.396	.258	1.1	1B(15): -0.8, LF(10): 0.8	0.3
2015	ELP	AAA	27	363	47	16	2	5	39	23	70	5	2	.259/.314/.364	.239	.312	1.9	1B(59): -1.3, LF(28): -0.2	-0.3
2016	*MIA*	*MLB*	*28*	*172*	*18*	*7*	*1*	*5*	*21*	*12*	*45*	*2*	*1*	*.236/.298/.399*	*.254*	*.293*	*0.2*	*1B -0*	*0.3*
2017	*MIA*	*MLB*	*29*	*299*	*35*	*13*	*2*	*9*	*34*	*22*	*79*	*3*	*1*	*.235/.299/.390*	*.261*	*.297*	*0.4*	*1B 0*	*0.3*

Breakout: 10% Improve: 24% Collapse: 12% Attrition: 30% MLB: 55% *Comparables: Jake Fox, Ryan Shealy, Brett Wallace*

For the second straight year, Medica put up Ruthian numbers in spring training and hit like a journeyman bench bat once the games counted. The Marlins scooped him up out of the Padres' recycling bin in September because, well, why not? With no real defensive value to speak of, he'll face increasingly long odds to log substantial playing time for a big-league club in 2016.

Josh Naylor 1B

Born: 6/22/97 Age: 19 Bats: L Throws: L Height: 6'0" Weight: 225

YEAR	TEAM	LVL	AGE	PA	R	2B	3B	HR	RBI	BB	K	SB	CS	AVG/OBP/SLG	TAv	BABIP	BRR	FRAA	WARP
2016	*MIA*	*MLB*	*19*	*250*	*19*	*9*	*1*	*4*	*21*	*9*	*71*	*1*	*0*	*.196/.228/.287*	*.188*	*.257*	*-0.3*	*1B -2*	*-1.7*
2017	*MIA*	*MLB*	*20*	*339*	*31*	*13*	*1*	*6*	*31*	*13*	*89*	*1*	*0*	*.210/.243/.316*	*.207*	*.267*	*-0.6*	*1B -2*	*-1.7*

Breakout: 0% Improve: 0% Collapse: 0% Attrition: 0% MLB: 0% *Comparables: Cedric Hunter, Oswaldo Arcia, Brandon Drury*

"Naylor is *listed* at 225 pounds." Get used to those words, and to the side-eye inflection of "listed," because as long as Naylor is playing professional baseball there will be concern about his body and skepticism about what that listed weight purports. High schoolers with Prince Fielder body comps typically aren't popped 12th overall, but Naylor has an atypical offensive ceiling. (Also, he signed for an under-slot $2.2 million.) Canadian germination infused his wrists and shoulders with lumberjack strength, which produces spectacular power binges in batting practice. Limited amateur exposure left him behind the learning curve and overaggressive against even the most pedestrian of bendy pitches, however. He performed well in Rookie ball despite the raw approach, but he'll face a more daunting test in his full-season assignment this year. He'll never contribute much in the field or on the bases, so the pressure on his bat will be enormous.

Marcell Ozuna CF

Born: 11/12/90 Age: 25 Bats: R Throws: R Height: 6'1" Weight: 225

YEAR	TEAM	LVL	AGE	PA	R	2B	3B	HR	RBI	BB	K	SB	CS	AVG/OBP/SLG	TAv	BABIP	BRR	FRAA	WARP
2013	JAX	AA	22	47	6	3	1	5	15	3	9	1	0	.333/.383/.810	.414	.310	0.4	RF(10): -0.6	0.9
2013	MIA	MLB	22	291	31	17	4	3	32	13	57	5	1	.265/.303/.389	.258	.326	1.4	RF(36): 7.1, CF(33): 0.6	1.6
2014	MIA	MLB	23	612	72	26	5	23	85	41	164	3	1	.269/.317/.455	.285	.337	-1.0	CF(140): -6.1, LF(11): 4.3	3.1
2015	MIA	MLB	24	494	47	27	0	10	44	30	110	2	3	.259/.308/.383	.255	.320	3.8	CF(111): -11.2, RF(15): 0.7	0.5
2015	NWO	AAA	24	132	21	12	1	5	11	11	23	1	0	.317/.379/.558	.362	.359	0.7	CF(29): -1.6	1.7
2016	*MIA*	*MLB*	*25*	*585*	*63*	*30*	*3*	*18*	*73*	*36*	*137*	*4*	*2*	*.263/.311/.431*	*.267*	*.316*	*1.4*	*CF -13*	*1.3*
2017	*MIA*	*MLB*	*26*	*541*	*67*	*28*	*3*	*18*	*69*	*36*	*125*	*3*	*2*	*.265/.316/.441*	*.282*	*.317*	*1.3*	*CF -12*	*1.2*

Breakout: 2% Improve: 67% Collapse: 2% Attrition: 2% MLB: 100% *Comparables: Matt Kemp, Cesar Cedeno, Chris Young*

After bouncing back from a nasty thumb injury with a 23-homer outburst and one of the larger spikes in batted ball distance in 2014, all offensive systems sure looked like a go for Ozuna heading into the season. But there were whispers in spring of less-than-stellar conditioning, and once the games started he was passive in April, aggressive in May and just plain terrible in June. That led to one of the more surprising demotions of the season—one which just so happened to last long enough to add an extra year of arbitration eligibility to his tab. Sure, his approach had taken a couple steps in the wrong direction: He chased a bit more often, and the quality of his contact fell a bit. Still, the excellent bat speed held, he hit more line drives and his overall exit velocity cracked the top 20 leaguewide. Despite the lost season there's still an awful lot of thump in his bat, and a 25-year-old under suspiciously team-friendly control adds up to an intriguing asset—whether in Miami or elsewhere in 2016.

Martin Prado 3B

Born: 10/27/83 Age: 32 Bats: R Throws: R Height: 6'1" Weight: 190

YEAR	TEAM	LVL	AGE	PA	R	2B	3B	HR	RBI	BB	K	SB	CS	AVG/OBP/SLG	TAv	BABIP	BRR	FRAA	WARP
2013	ARI	MLB	29	664	70	36	2	14	82	47	53	3	5	.282/.333/.417	.264	.288	-5.6	3B(113): 3.3, 2B(32): -3.9	1.3
2014	NYA	MLB	30	137	18	9	0	7	16	3	23	1	0	.316/.336/.541	.327	.340	0.3	2B(17): 1.7, 3B(11): 1.3	1.5
2014	ARI	MLB	30	436	44	17	4	5	42	23	57	2	1	.270/.317/.370	.246	.301	0.7	3B(99): -6.7, 2B(4): -1.0	0.0
2015	MIA	MLB	31	551	52	22	2	9	63	37	68	1	0	.288/.338/.394	.283	.313	0.2	3B(124): 0.1, 2B(11): -0.2	3.1
2016	*MIA*	*MLB*	*32*	*587*	*65*	*27*	*3*	*10*	*54*	*38*	*66*	*3*	*2*	*.271/.320/.387*	*.260*	*.290*	*-1.0*	*3B -2, 2B -0*	*1.4*
2017	*MIA*	*MLB*	*33*	*521*	*55*	*24*	*2*	*8*	*50*	*33*	*60*	*2*	*1*	*.259/.307/.366*	*.257*	*.278*	*-1.0*	*3B -2, 2B 0*	*0.3*

Breakout: 1% Improve: 39% Collapse: 7% Attrition: 11% MLB: 98% *Comparables: Maicer Izturis, Bill Madlock, Edgardo Alfonzo*

The guy who plays every position stuck to mostly just one in 2015. The stability agreed with him, as he posted his best WARP since 2012, maintaining his borderline-elite contact rates while tightening up against bad balls. His hot corner defense was good enough that it wasn't bad. A handful of bumps and bangs over the course of the summer—including a disabling blow to his shoulder—served to remind that nothing lasts forever, not even in the hot Miami swamp. But while Prado will at some point cease to be a useful big league player, it doesn't appear we're there just yet.

J.T. Realmuto C

Born: 3/18/91 Age: 25 Bats: R Throws: R Height: 6'1" Weight: 205

YEAR	TEAM	LVL	AGE	PA	R	2B	3B	HR	RBI	BB	K	SB	CS	AVG/OBP/SLG	TAv	BABIP	BRR	FRAA	WARP
2013	JAX	AA	22	416	41	21	3	5	39	36	68	9	1	.239/.310/.353	.253	.275	-1.6	C(99): 16.4	3.2
2014	JAX	AA	23	423	66	25	6	8	62	41	59	18	5	.299/.369/.461	.302	.333	5.6	C(88): 17.6	6.3
2014	MIA	MLB	23	30	4	1	1	0	9	1	8	0	0	.241/.267/.345	.227	.333	0.0	C(9): -0.6	0.0
2015	MIA	MLB	24	467	49	21	7	10	47	19	70	8	4	.259/.290/.406	.260	.285	0.5	C(118): -16.1	0.5
2016	*MIA*	*MLB*	*25*	*472*	*47*	*22*	*5*	*9*	*49*	*27*	*84*	*9*	*3*	*.251/.296/.385*	*.247*	*.288*	*0.6*	*C -7*	*0.8*
2017	*MIA*	*MLB*	*26*	*515*	*55*	*25*	*5*	*10*	*54*	*31*	*94*	*10*	*3*	*.251/.299/.390*	*.256*	*.289*	*0.9*	*C -9*	*0.6*

Breakout: 2% Improve: 34% Collapse: 13% Attrition: 33% MLB: 93% *Comparables: Chris Snyder, Curtis Thigpen, Jonathan Lucroy*

YEAR	TEAM	P. COUNT	FRM RUNS	BLK RUNS	THRW RUNS	TOT RUNS
2013	JAX	11832	16.4	0.3	-0.6	16.1
2014	JAX	11404	17.3	-0.3	0.6	17.7
2014	MIA	996	-0.4	0.0	0.0	-0.4
2015	MIA	16187	-15.6	-0.5	0.1	-15.9
2015	NWO	416	-0.1	-0.2	0.0	-0.3
2016	*MIA*	*16805*	*-5.3*	*-0.5*	*-0.2*	*-6.0*
2017	*MIA*	*18342*	*-7.0*	*-0.5*	*-0.3*	*-7.8*

Young catchers rarely evolve into starters at the major-league level without some growing pains along the way, but if his rookie campaign was the pains then we're *very* excited to see the growing. He struggled initially when the team handed over the keys to the castle in May, but after producing just a .213/.243/.346 slash line through the end of that month he rebounded to close his debut campaign with a top-20 TAv among backstops. Advanced metrics see a below-average receiver and one of the worst framers in the game, but he drew praise for his game-calling and development as the season progressed. Now that he's firmly entrenched behind the dish, the only danger for the Marlins is that Realmuto's blend of pop, leadership and athleticism will someday make him expensive.

Miguel Rojas SS

Born: 2/24/89 Age: 27 Bats: R Throws: R Height: 6'0" Weight: 150

YEAR	TEAM	LVL	AGE	PA	R	2B	3B	HR	RBI	BB	K	SB	CS	AVG/OBP/SLG	TAv	BABIP	BRR	FRAA	WARP
2013	CHT	AA	24	478	45	12	2	5	32	40	49	10	4	.233/.303/.307	.227	.253	3.1	SS(129): 20.9, 2B(3): -0.0	2.9
2014	LAN	MLB	25	162	16	3	0	1	9	10	28	0	0	.181/.242/.221	.174	.217	0.5	SS(66): 3.3, 3B(19): -0.0	-0.4
2014	ABQ	AAA	25	173	27	9	0	4	13	10	21	7	3	.302/.353/.434	.273	.326	1.2	SS(23): -0.6, 3B(16): 0.5	1.1
2015	MIA	MLB	26	157	13	7	1	1	17	11	16	0	1	.282/.329/.366	.273	.307	1.9	SS(32): -1.9, 2B(9): -0.6	0.8
2015	NWO	AAA	26	275	32	15	4	3	23	13	26	2	5	.301/.343/.430	.286	.324	-0.4	SS(63): 7.5, 3B(1): 0.2	2.6
2016	*MIA*	*MLB*	*27*	*105*	*10*	*4*	*1*	*1*	*9*	*6*	*15*	*1*	*1*	*.242/.290/.336*	*.228*	*.266*	*0.3*	*SS 1, 2B 1*	*0.4*
2017	*MIA*	*MLB*	*28*	*285*	*29*	*10*	*1*	*4*	*25*	*17*	*42*	*2*	*2*	*.237/.288/.332*	*.231*	*.262*	*1.0*	*SS 4, 2B 2*	*0.9*

Breakout: 7% Improve: 17% Collapse: 7% Attrition: 25% MLB: 54% *Comparables: Brandon Fahey, Alberto Gonzalez, Ray Olmedo*

Sometimes in life, being really good at just one thing can be enough. One of the premier glove men around town, Rojas slotted in as an adequate utility infielder after a midseason recall. His bat will never strike more than mild awareness into any pitcher's heart, though his offense was pleasantly tolerable in a limited sample of at-bats last season. The leather and rock-bottom price will keep him gainfully employed for the foreseeable future, though his limitations with the stick are such that he's likely to rack up all the frequent flyer points he needs along the way to publish a travelogue of Triple-A ballparks.

Avery Romero 2B

Born: 5/11/93 Age: 23 Bats: R Throws: R Height: 5'11" Weight: 195

YEAR	TEAM	LVL	AGE	PA	R	2B	3B	HR	RBI	BB	K	SB	CS	AVG/OBP/SLG	TAv	BABIP	BRR	FRAA	WARP
2013	BAT	A-	20	235	27	18	0	2	30	15	34	3	4	.297/.357/.411	.289	.339	-1.2	2B(53): 6.6	2.0
2013	GRB	A	20	40	5	1	0	1	5	4	5	0	0	.147/.237/.265	.204	.143	-0.1	2B(9): -0.7	-0.2
2014	GRB	A	21	399	51	23	1	5	46	25	47	6	4	.320/.366/.429	.287	.354	-0.2	2B(77): -3.7	1.8
2014	JUP	A+	21	108	12	8	0	0	10	7	13	4	1	.320/.370/.400	.284	.368	0.9	2B(16): 0.4, 3B(6): -0.3	0.7
2015	JUP	A+	22	505	47	14	1	3	42	38	71	3	4	.259/.315/.314	.257	.297	0.4	2B(109): -9.7	0.1
2016	*MIA*	*MLB*	*23*	*250*	*20*	*11*	*1*	*3*	*23*	*13*	*51*	*0*	*0*	*.238/.279/.332*	*.224*	*.285*	*-0.4*	*2B -2*	*-0.3*
2017	*MIA*	*MLB*	*24*	*360*	*36*	*16*	*1*	*5*	*33*	*20*	*71*	*1*	*0*	*.241/.287/.341*	*.236*	*.287*	*-0.8*	*2B -3*	*-0.4*

Breakout: 5% Improve: 11% Collapse: 1% Attrition: 4% MLB: 13% *Comparables: Justin Turner, Phil Gosselin, Austin Barnes*

Another season, another winter write-up emphasizing projection over production. After a solid two-level campaign in 2014, Romero's feet got stuck in the swampy mud of the age-appropriate Florida State League last summer. He still flashes the quick bat and sneaky strength that carried prior predictions of an above-average hitter, but that anticipated power still hasn't materialized in games and the unrefined approach is looking less and less like a youthful indiscretion. Reports of stagnation at the keystone cloud what was already a borderline defensive profile. There's still a broad underlying skill set to suggest the former third-rounder could eventually earn regular big-league playing time, but there'll be pressure to show improvements on at least one side of the ball in Double-A this year.

Xavier Scruggs 1B

Born: 9/23/87 Age: 28 Bats: R Throws: R Height: 6'1" Weight: 220

YEAR	TEAM	LVL	AGE	PA	R	2B	3B	HR	RBI	BB	K	SB	CS	AVG/OBP/SLG	TAv	BABIP	BRR	FRAA	WARP
2013	SFD	AA	25	546	67	18	1	29	81	82	177	11	7	.248/.376/.487	.302	.335	-1.1	1B(129): 3.4, LF(1): -0.0	3.3
2014	SLN	MLB	26	18	0	1	0	0	2	2	7	0	0	.200/.333/.267	.219	.375	-0.7	1B(5): -0.2	-0.1
2014	MEM	AAA	26	538	82	29	3	21	87	53	114	3	5	.286/.370/.494	.303	.336	0.3	1B(133): 2.5, RF(1): -0.4	3.5
2015	SLN	MLB	27	43	5	2	0	0	7	0	10	1	0	.262/.279/.310	.213	.344	-0.2	1B(11): 1.1	-0.1
2015	MEM	AAA	27	449	54	22	1	14	57	54	103	4	3	.238/.341/.410	.289	.285	0.9	1B(57): 2.0, LF(38): -2.1	2.1
2016	*MIA*	*MLB*	*28*	*250*	*28*	*10*	*1*	*8*	*30*	*25*	*72*	*2*	*1*	*.229/.318/.397*	*.262*	*.297*	*-0.4*	*1B 0, LF -2*	*0.4*
2017	*MIA*	*MLB*	*29*	*324*	*40*	*13*	*1*	*10*	*37*	*33*	*94*	*2*	*1*	*.220/.311/.381*	*.263*	*.289*	*-0.6*	*1B 0, LF -2*	*0.0*

Breakout: 3% Improve: 11% Collapse: 11% Attrition: 20% MLB: 31% *Comparables: Matt Clark, Josh Whitesell, Jeff Bailey*

Although Scruggs has shown power and on-base skills against left-handed pitchers throughout his minor-league career, the Cardinals continued to overlook him for bench jobs. In 2015, that meant bypassing Scruggs in favor of Mark Reynolds, who offered more defensive flexibility. For a younger player, the snub would be no big deal; an ant in the dirt, so to speak. Alas, Scruggs celebrated his 28th birthday in September, which means he's beginning to perceive Triple-A as less of a resting place and more of a purgatory. How can you tell? He added 46 outfield appearances to his tally during the season, pushing his career total to ... carry the one ... uh, 47. The takeaway from last season is clear: Scruggs' bat isn't enough by itself to secure him a spot in the majors—though the chances are better in Miami than they were in St. Louis.

Donovan Solano 2B

Born: 12/17/87 Age: 28 Bats: R Throws: R Height: 5'9" Weight: 205

YEAR	TEAM	LVL	AGE	PA	R	2B	3B	HR	RBI	BB	K	SB	CS	AVG/OBP/SLG	TAv	BABIP	BRR	FRAA	WARP
2013	MIA	MLB	25	395	33	13	1	3	34	23	57	3	1	.249/.305/.316	.230	.287	-1.8	2B(93): 8.3, 3B(2): -0.0	0.5
2013	NWO	AAA	25	73	8	3	1	2	9	4	11	0	0	.379/.411/.545	.366	.418	0.0	2B(9): 1.0, 3B(4): 0.0	1.2
2014	NWO	AAA	26	22	2	1	0	0	3	0	5	0	0	.095/.091/.143	.064	.118	0.1	3B(3): 1.1, 2B(1): 0.1	-0.3
2014	MIA	MLB	26	340	26	11	1	3	28	19	61	1	2	.252/.300/.323	.239	.304	-1.3	2B(73): 1.1, SS(4): -0.9	0.1
2015	NWO	AAA	27	147	10	3	0	0	6	4	24	0	1	.271/.288/.293	.214	.322	-0.8	SS(16): -0.6, 2B(9): -0.2	-0.5
2015	MIA	MLB	27	94	6	3	1	0	7	1	18	0	0	.189/.215/.244	.186	.236	-0.7	3B(10): 0.2, SS(10): -0.0	-0.5
2016	*MIA*	*MLB*	*28*	*250*	*25*	*9*	*1*	*3*	*20*	*13*	*45*	*1*	*1*	*.252/.298/.340*	*.234*	*.295*	*-0.8*	*SS -1, 2B 1*	*0.3*
2017	*MIA*	*MLB*	*29*	*147*	*15*	*5*	*1*	*2*	*13*	*8*	*27*	*1*	*0*	*.250/.299/.342*	*.241*	*.293*	*-0.5*	*SS 0, 2B 1*	*0.1*

Breakout: 4% Improve: 35% Collapse: 9% Attrition: 14% MLB: 91% *Comparables: Daniel Descalso, Everth Cabrera, Alex Cintron*

For two years running the Marlins just couldn't seem to quit Solano, granting him curiously outsized allotments of playing time despite just a borderline-useful glove and terrible offensive performance. Then he made the club again out of spring training because of course he did—these are the Marlins after all—and here we were poised to go again. It took almost three months—with Solano tallying just nine hits—before the roster finally crunched him, setting off a prolific series of options and recalls that single-handedly kept one MLB paper-pusher from making it home in time for dinner all summer. The dying embers A1:D1331 a love remembered may yet compel the Marlins to commit even *more* playing time in 2016, but younger, cheaper and very likely better options dot the farm landscape. Or else maybe they'll just give his older brother Jhonatan another shot.

Isael Soto RF

Born: 11/2/96 Age: 19 Bats: L Throws: L Height: 6'0" Weight: 190

YEAR	TEAM	LVL	AGE	PA	R	2B	3B	HR	RBI	BB	K	SB	CS	AVG/OBP/SLG	TAv	BABIP	BRR	FRAA	WARP
2015	BAT	A-	18	22	1	0	0	0	0	1	10	0	0	.095/.136/.095	.088	.182	-0.7	RF(4): -0.2	-0.5
2015	GRB	A	18	67	2	1	0	0	1	3	27	0	0	.125/.164/.141	.110	.216	-0.8	RF(12): 0.7, CF(3): -0.5	-1.0
2016	*MIA*	*MLB*	*19*	*250*	*17*	*8*	*1*	*3*	*20*	*12*	*91*	*1*	*0*	*.177/.217/.260*	*.176*	*.265*	*-0.3*	*RF 1, CF -0*	*-1.5*
2017	*MIA*	*MLB*	*20*	*314*	*28*	*11*	*1*	*5*	*27*	*14*	*114*	*1*	*0*	*.188/.229/.291*	*.193*	*.279*	*-0.4*	*RF 2, CF 0*	*-1.6*

Breakout: 0% Improve: 0% Collapse: 0% Attrition: 0% MLB: 0% *Comparables: Marcell Ozuna, Michael Saunders, Zoilo Almonte*

The Marlins are nothing if not aggressive with their promising minor leaguers, and assigning Soto to full-season ball at age 18 kept with company policy. He was greeted rudely, and after a moribund April that included just one lonely extra-base hit, he went down with a knee injury that sidelined him until the end of August. Scouts see a well-rounded player without a standout skill or much physical projection. He'll remain a lumpy ball of clay heading into 2016, but one capable of resembling an every-day right fielder in due time.

Giancarlo Stanton RF

Born: 11/8/89 Age: 26 Bats: R Throws: R Height: 6'6" Weight: 240

YEAR	TEAM	LVL	AGE	PA	R	2B	3B	HR	RBI	BB	K	SB	CS	AVG/OBP/SLG	TAv	BABIP	BRR	FRAA	WARP
2013	MIA	MLB	23	504	62	26	0	24	62	74	140	1	0	.249/.365/.480	.316	.313	0.2	RF(116): -0.5	3.8
2014	MIA	MLB	24	638	89	31	1	37	105	94	170	13	1	.288/.395/.555	.342	.353	2.3	RF(143): 13.6	8.3
2015	MIA	MLB	25	318	47	12	1	27	67	34	95	4	2	.265/.346/.606	.353	.294	0.5	RF(71): 7.7	4.6
2016	*MIA*	*MLB*	*26*	*611*	*93*	*28*	*2*	*38*	*106*	*74*	*169*	*8*	*2*	*.266/.360/.545*	*.317*	*.314*	*0.8*	*RF 6*	*6.0*
2017	*MIA*	*MLB*	*27*	*507*	*82*	*23*	*1*	*32*	*89*	*63*	*139*	*6*	*2*	*.266/.362/.546*	*.333*	*.312*	*0.6*	*RF 5*	*4.7*

Breakout: 4% Improve: 63% Collapse: 3% Attrition: 5% MLB: 98% *Comparables: Mickey Mantle, Adam Dunn, Darryl Strawberry*

There are power hitters, and there is Stanton. We always knew his tree trunk made a special kind of thump, and thanks to the dawn of public exit velocity data now we know just how special his lumber really is. He hit the ball harder and farther than anyone else in baseball in 2015, duh, but with the average speed of a ball off his bat clocking in *more than three full mph faster than any other hitter*. To put that in perspective, the gap between him and second place equaled that between numbers two and *47*. Sometimes, stats tell you who is best. Sometimes, they help you appreciate the extremely best.

Unfortunately, in what has become a real bummer of a semi-annual tradition, we also lost the opportunity to witness him perform his feats of strength for a significant chunk of the season. Felled for the entire second half—this time by a dreaded hamate fracture and sketchy recovery on the back end—he'll enter a season for the first time with questions swirling about his expected power output. He'll also return to uncertainty about just what kind of hitter he'll be as he climbs into his physical prime. Perhaps concluding that nuanced approaches are best left for the normals, he featured when healthy all the hallmarks of a man selling out for the long ball: a huge spike in his pull and fly-ball rates, a big jump for in-zone whiffs, and fewer strolls to first base. A greedy man's profile, that. But hey, you can't make an omelet without cracking a few balls out of the stadium along the way, right? Stanton's return to good health and productivity would be a welcome sight for fans of all stripes, none more so than the fishy kind.

Ichiro Suzuki RF

Born: 10/22/73 Age: 42 Bats: L Throws: R Height: 5'11" Weight: 170

YEAR	TEAM	LVL	AGE	PA	R	2B	3B	HR	RBI	BB	K	SB	CS	AVG/OBP/SLG	TAv	BABIP	BRR	FRAA	WARP
2013	NYA	MLB	39	555	57	15	3	7	35	26	63	20	4	.262/.297/.342	.240	.285	4.1	RF(128): -4.2, CF(13): -0.8	-0.2
2014	NYA	MLB	40	385	42	13	2	1	22	21	68	15	3	.284/.324/.340	.252	.346	2.6	RF(119): -4.0, LF(9): -0.3	0.2
2015	MIA	MLB	41	438	45	5	6	1	21	31	51	11	5	.229/.282/.279	.218	.257	3.5	RF(73): 8.5, LF(30): -0.1	0.2
2016	*MIA*	*MLB*	*42*	*234*	*21*	*7*	*2*	*0*	*15*	*11*	*29*	*7*	*2*	*.248/.284/.296*	*.214*	*.281*	*1.2*	*RF 0, LF 1*	*-0.2*
2017	*MIA*	*MLB*	*43*	*220*	*18*	*6*	*1*	*0*	*14*	*10*	*30*	*6*	*2*	*.228/.263/.270*	*.205*	*.262*	*1.3*	*RF 0, LF 1*	*-0.7*

Breakout: 0% Improve: 12% Collapse: 16% Attrition: 22% MLB: 55% *Comparables: Paul Molitor, Enos Slaughter, Tony Gwynn*

At times it's tough to see an all-timer like Ichiro in this way. One of the most dynamic players of this or any generation, reduced to Desi Relaford levels of offensive futility. It's awkward. And not in an ultimately-redemptive teen comedy kind of way. In a cold, starkly mortal way.

Yet even in the throes of unmitigated failure there were little nuggets of greatness in Ichiro's swan dive. He reversed his recent trends on a dime and posted the lowest swing-and-miss rate of his entire 15-year career. At 41! And he pitched! After years—*years*—of begging, pleading with managers to let him take the ball, he was finally deemed expendable enough as an organizational asset to climb onto the bump in a big league game. Even made a big league hitter look silly with a half-decent slider when he did. At times it's an outright *blessing* to see Ichiro getting to do the things his greatness, paradoxically, wouldn't let him do when he was too valuable to mess around with. Think about these things when you think of Ichiro's 2015 campaign—and, for that matter, while you watch him lurch uncomfortably along toward a couple well-deserved milestones in 2016.

Tomas Telis C

Born: 6/18/91 Age: 25 Bats: B Throws: R Height: 5'8" Weight: 215

YEAR	TEAM	LVL	AGE	PA	R	2B	3B	HR	RBI	BB	K	SB	CS	AVG/OBP/SLG	TAv	BABIP	BRR	FRAA	WARP
2013	FRI	AA	22	369	32	19	0	4	43	10	46	8	2	.264/.290/.353	.229	.291	-2.1	C(82): -15.8	-1.6
2014	TEX	MLB	23	71	7	2	0	0	8	1	10	0	0	.250/.271/.279	.234	.293	-0.1	C(17): -7.9	-0.8
2014	ROU	AAA	23	147	18	7	2	3	17	6	12	1	1	.345/.377/.489	.296	.363	0.2	C(19): -1.3, 1B(9): 0.5	0.9
2014	FRI	AA	23	295	31	16	2	2	33	17	29	7	1	.303/.339/.401	.274	.325	-2.7	C(46): 0.9, 1B(1): 0.1	1.3
2015	NWO	AAA	24	55	3	0	0	0	4	5	6	2	0	.333/.389/.333	.285	.372	0.5	C(12): -7.4	-0.3
2015	TEX	MLB	24	12	1	0	0	0	2	0	1	0	0	.182/.250/.182	.194	.200	-0.3	C(4): -1.3	-0.2
2015	MIA	MLB	24	29	1	0	0	0	0	1	3	0	0	.148/.207/.148	.171	.167	-0.7	C(7): -1.9	-0.4
2015	ROU	AAA	24	300	43	15	1	5	25	14	31	1	2	.291/.327/.404	.251	.313	-1.3	C(50): -1.1, 1B(3): 0.1	0.5
2016	*MIA*	*MLB*	*25*	*62*	*5*	*3*	*0*	*1*	*6*	*2*	*9*	*0*	*0*	*.258/.285/.346*	*.232*	*.289*	*-0.1*	*C -4*	*-0.4*
2017	*MIA*	*MLB*	*26*	*263*	*25*	*12*	*1*	*3*	*23*	*9*	*39*	*2*	*1*	*.253/.280/.346*	*.237*	*.284*	*-0.3*	*C -17*	*-1.7*

Breakout: 9% Improve: 17% Collapse: 12% Attrition: 26% MLB: 40% *Comparables: Robinzon Diaz, Jhonatan Solano, Juan Centeno*

For a second straight season Telis wiggled his way onto a big-league roster in September, this time after landing with the Marlins in a deadline deal. (For Sam Dyson.) And he earned it, man. After years of questionable leather work he willed his way to respectability behind the dish, highlighted by dramatic improvements in his footwork and release that culminated in an impressive 43 percent capture rate of would-be base-stealers. He's always been able to hit a little bit, and the newfound defensive viability gives him the full collector's set of late-blooming backup skills heading into 2016.

YEAR	TEAM	P. COUNT	FRM RUNS	BLK RUNS	THRW RUNS	TOT RUNS
2013	FRI	11279	-14.6	-0.6	0.2	-15.0
2014	FRI	6004	0.9	0.1	-0.6	0.4
2014	ROU	2202	-0.8	0.0	-0.2	-1.0
2014	TEX	2268	-7.2	-0.1	-0.4	-7.6
2015	ROU	7286	-5.1	0.3	1.8	-3.0
2015	TEX	402	-1.2	0.0	0.0	-1.2
2015	MIA	557	-1.8	0.0	0.0	-1.8
2015	NWO	1789	-6.7	0.0	-0.3	-7.0
2016	*MIA*	*2238*	*-4.0*	*-0.1*	*0.0*	*-4.0*
2017	*MIA*	*9479*	*-17.4*	*-0.3*	*-0.1*	*-17.8*

Christian Yelich LF

Born: 12/5/91 Age: 24 Bats: L Throws: R Height: 6'2" Weight: 195

YEAR	TEAM	LVL	AGE	PA	R	2B	3B	HR	RBI	BB	K	SB	CS	AVG/OBP/SLG	TAv	BABIP	BRR	FRAA	WARP
2013	MIA	MLB	21	273	34	12	1	4	16	31	66	10	0	.288/.370/.396	.295	.380	3.3	LF(59): -3.5, CF(5): -0.5	1.5
2013	JUP	A+	21	30	3	0	0	2	4	4	8	0	0	.231/.333/.462	.271	.250	0.2	CF(6): -1.0	0.0
2013	JAX	AA	21	222	33	13	6	7	29	26	52	5	5	.280/.365/.518	.322	.346	-1.0	CF(27): -2.0, LF(22): 0.4	1.8
2014	MIA	MLB	22	660	94	30	6	9	54	70	137	21	7	.284/.362/.402	.286	.356	2.6	LF(138): -5.2, CF(12): -1.7	2.8
2015	MIA	MLB	23	525	63	30	2	7	44	47	101	16	5	.300/.366/.416	.288	.370	1.4	LF(103): 5.0, CF(36): -3.3	3.2
2016	*MIA*	*MLB*	*24*	*625*	*82*	*31*	*4*	*13*	*60*	*62*	*135*	*18*	*6*	*.277/.350/.414*	*.279*	*.342*	*1.9*	*LF 2*	*3.6*
2017	*MIA*	*MLB*	*25*	*571*	*71*	*28*	*3*	*12*	*63*	*58*	*123*	*16*	*5*	*.280/.354/.418*	*.291*	*.345*	*2.4*	*LF 2*	*3.1*

Breakout: 1% Improve: 62% Collapse: 0% Attrition: 0% MLB: 100% *Comparables: Travis Buck, Mike Greenwell, Jeremy Hermida*

Yelich's full-season debut in 2014 was so exquisite that his 3.2 WARP last year—an improvement!—somehow feels unfulfilled. How's *that* for the burden of expectations? He did struggle through most of May—mightily, at times—and two DL stints before the All-Star break didn't help matters. But after settling in healthy he found his way on base at a near-.400 clip in the second half while continuing to hone an instinctual defensive game on the grass. There's a good deal of horsepower under the hood of his swing, but his bat's trajectory continues to limit his projection for over-the-fence power: He hit groundballs at a more prolific clip than any other batter in the majors last season, and his oppo approach rivals Derek Jeter's. He hit 'em hard, at least, and the batted ball profile has produced well above-average BABIP numbers for him in consecutive years. He'll play out 2016 at the tender age of 24, his status as one of the most promising young outfielders in the game intact.

Pitchers

Kyle Barraclough RHP

Born: 5/23/90 Age: 26 Bats: R Throws: R Height: 6'3" Weight: 225

YEAR	TEAM	LVL	AGE	W	L	SV	G	GS	IP	H	HR	BB/9	K/9	GB%	BABIP	WHIP	ERA	FIP	DRA	WARP	CFIP	MPH
2014	PMB	A+	24	1	1	1	16	0	18^2	28	0	5.3	8.7	57%	.459	2.09	5.30	3.39	4.59	0.0	105	
2014	PEO	A	24	1	1	10	32	0	40	21	0	5.2	13.5	51%	.259	1.10	1.12	2.21	3.96	0.4	82	
2015	PMB	A+	25	1	0	4	11	0	15	9	0	5.4	13.8	32%	.290	1.20	0.60	1.90	2.79	0.3	87	
2015	MIA	MLB	25	2	1	0	25	0	24^1	12	1	6.7	11.1	34%	.224	1.23	2.59	3.45	3.08	0.5	93	
2015	SFD	AA	25	2	0	8	23	0	24^2	19	0	7.3	10.2	49%	.302	1.58	3.28	3.70	6.28	-0.4	119	
2016	*MIA*	*MLB*	*26*	*2*	*1*	*0*	*46*	*0*	48^1	*42*	*5*	*4.6*	*9.1*	*38%*	*.307*	*1.37*	*4.02*	*4.03*	*4.74*	*0.1*	*108*	
2017	*MIA*	*MLB*	*27*	*2*	*1*	*1*	*40*	*0*	47^1	*41*	*5*	*4.7*	*9.6*	*38%*	*.314*	*1.39*	*3.95*	*4.36*	*4.66*	*0.1*	*106*	

Breakout: 17% Improve: 23% Collapse: 10% Attrition: 18% MLB: 36% *Comparables: Royce Ring, Pedro Strop, Santiago Casilla*

The return in the July trade that cast off former closer Steve Cishek, Barraclough joined the tail of the Marlins' "all stuff, no finesse" reliever parade. His fastball will sit comfortably in the mid-90s, but while his slider shows an above-average tilt it frequently fails to snap off properly. His bugaboo control was on full display across his first 24 big-league innings, as he issued an uncomfortable 18 free passes. He's a tough hurler to square up, so if he can stumble into even modest improvement with his pitch location there is high-leverage potential here. He'll turn 26 at the front end of the 2016 season, however, making him a borderline stubborn old coot by baseball's "live-arm" standards, and limiting the likelihood of significant skill improvement.

Carter Capps RHP

Born: 8/7/90 Age: 25 Bats: R Throws: R Height: 6'5" Weight: 220

YEAR	TEAM	LVL	AGE	W	L	SV	G	GS	IP	H	HR	BB/9	K/9	GB%	BABIP	WHIP	ERA	FIP	DRA	WARP	CFIP	MPH
2014	PMB	A+	23	1	1	1	16	0	18^2	28	0	5.3	8.7	57%	.459	2.09	5.30	3.39	4.59	0.0	105	
2014	PEO	A	23	1	1	10	32	0	40	21	0	5.2	13.5	51%	.259	1.10	1.12	2.21	3.96	0.4	82	
2015	PMB	A+	24	1	0	4	11	0	15	9	0	5.4	13.8	32%	.290	1.20	0.60	1.90	2.79	0.3	87	
2015	MIA	MLB	24	2	1	0	25	0	24^1	12	1	6.7	11.1	34%	.224	1.23	2.59	3.45	3.08	0.5	93	
2015	SFD	AA	24	2	0	8	23	0	24^2	19	0	7.3	10.2	49%	.302	1.58	3.28	3.70	6.28	-0.4	119	
2016	*MIA*	*MLB*	*25*	*3*	*1*	*0*	*51*	*0*	53^2	*44*	*6*	*2.8*	*10.8*	*44%*	*.319*	*1.13*	*3.12*	*3.17*	*3.72*	*1.0*	*79*	
2017	*MIA*	*MLB*	*26*	*2*	*1*	*1*	*46*	*0*	56^1	*46*	*6*	*2.9*	*11.4*	*44%*	*.326*	*1.14*	*2.97*	*3.24*	*3.54*	*0.9*	*74*	

Breakout: 28% Improve: 51% Collapse: 20% Attrition: 18% MLB: 86% *Comparables: Cody Allen, Rex Brothers, Hong-Chih Kuo*

If he were healthy, it's entirely possible that Capps would have struck you out while you were reading this sentence. His statistical wonders of 2015 are subject to requisite sample size warnings, but he arm-stabbed and crow-hopped his way to world-leading strikeout and cFIP rates before his elbow broke (again) after just 31 innings. The delivery shenanigans—you've surely seen them, but in case not: He leaps—were not without controversy, as they shaved an extra two feet off the distance Capps' pitches traveled to the plate. His raw arsenal featured plenty of giddy-up and wiggle in its own right, but the advantageous release point helped him pair the hardest perceived velocity of any big league fastball with a dive-bombing deuce that missed three out of every four swinging bats. If his ligaments remain unsprained and his muscles unstrained, the potential for a truly special full season of relief resides within.

Adam Conley LHP

Born: 5/24/90 Age: 26 Bats: L Throws: L Height: 6'3" Weight: 185

YEAR	TEAM	LVL	AGE	W	L	SV	G	GS	IP	H	HR	BB/9	K/9	GB%	BABIP	WHIP	ERA	FIP	DRA	WARP	CFIP	MPH
2013	JAX	AA	23	11	7	0	26	25	138^2	125	7	2.4	8.4	48%	.295	1.17	3.25	2.66	3.63	1.7	86	
2014	NWO	AAA	24	3	5	0	12	11	60	65	3	3.9	7.2	53%	.333	1.52	6.00	4.20	5.60	0.1	111	
2015	NWO	AAA	25	9	3	0	19	18	107	85	4	3.4	6.8	48%	.265	1.17	2.52	3.83	4.57	1.1	97	
2015	MIA	MLB	25	4	1	0	15	11	67	65	7	2.8	7.9	41%	.304	1.28	3.76	3.83	4.95	0.0	99	95.2
2016	*MIA*	*MLB*	*26*	*7*	*8*	*0*	*24*	*24*	*120*	*113*	*12*	*2.9*	*7.1*	*44%*	*.305*	*1.26*	*3.93*	*3.81*	*4.65*	*0.9*	*108*	
2017	*MIA*	*MLB*	*27*	*6*	*7*	*0*	*21*	*21*	*124*	*121*	*15*	*2.9*	*7.2*	*44%*	*.311*	*1.30*	*4.09*	*4.51*	*4.84*	*0.6*	*114*	

Breakout: 17% Improve: 29% Collapse: 29% Attrition: 39% MLB: 75% *Comparables: Adam Warren, Kyle Gibson, Brad Peacock*

Conley's trajectory as hulking mid-90s left-hander went black in 2014, and now we have Conley's new trajectory as hulking low-90s left-hander. As is often the case, it was a classic story of Man vs. Ligament; Conley's couldn't handle the dare of throwing that hard that often, but he rebounded non-surgically last year to force his way into the Marlins' second-half rotation. Even missing three ticks, the fastball still missed plenty of bats, and the rest of his arsenal played up because of it. Between a solid strikeout rate and weak flyball contact, Conley's results were solid enough to keep the 25-year-old squarely in the mix for starts this spring.

Erik Cordier RHP

Born: 2/25/86 Age: 30 Bats: R Throws: R Height: 6'4" Weight: 215

YEAR	TEAM	LVL	AGE	W	L	SV	G	GS	IP	H	HR	BB/9	K/9	GB%	BABIP	WHIP	ERA	FIP	DRA	WARP	CFIP	MPH
2013	IND	AAA	27	4	2	4	44	0	53	51	3	4.8	11.0	48%	.351	1.49	4.58	3.19	4.04	0.3	89	
2014	SFN	MLB	28	0	0	0	7	0	6	5	0	3.0	13.5	43%	.357	1.17	1.50	2.60	4.32	0.0	93	101.6
2014	FRE	AAA	28	4	3	3	47	0	52^2	40	4	5.3	11.6	40%	.295	1.35	3.59	4.04	4.85	0.3	85	
2015	MIA	MLB	29	0	0	0	8	0	12^1	13	1	4.4	5.1	45%	.293	1.54	5.84	4.78	5.57	-0.1	115	99.8
2015	SAC	AAA	29	2	1	9	31	0	34^2	20	0	6.5	11.2	42%	.244	1.30	1.04	3.28	4.30	0.3	96	
2016	*MIA*	*MLB*	*30*	*3*	*1*	*0*	*45*	*1*	*51^1*	*44*	*5*	*3.8*	*8.9*	*42%*	*.307*	*1.28*	*3.78*	*3.72*	*4.46*	*0.3*	*102*	
2017	*MIA*	*MLB*	*31*	*2*	*1*	*0*	*47*	*1*	*59^1*	*52*	*7*	*4.0*	*9.4*	*42%*	*.315*	*1.33*	*3.91*	*4.29*	*4.61*	*0.2*	*106*	

Breakout: 8% Improve: 14% Collapse: 4% Attrition: 6% MLB: 21% *Comparables: Atahualpa Severino, Dustin Richardson, Brad Salmon*

Triple-digit heat is a kind of social privilege: Guys who have it tend to get a *lot* of chances. Case in point Cordier, whose debut in 2014 came a full decade and three team-switches after he was drafted. He returned to The Show last year, now playing for his fifth org, and logged the third-hottest average heater when he did. And...well, thus concludes the highlight reel. He struggled to miss bats in his dozen prime time innings, controlled his pitches poorly and got knocked about rather rudely by big-league hitters. He'll get another chance, although in 2016 it will be for the Orix Buffaloes of the Nippon Professional Baseball League. Check your privilege, kid.

Jarred Cosart RHP

Born: 5/25/90 Age: 26 Bats: R Throws: R Height: 6'3" Weight: 195

YEAR	TEAM	LVL	AGE	W	L	SV	G	GS	IP	H	HR	BB/9	K/9	GB%	BABIP	WHIP	ERA	FIP	DRA	WARP	CFIP	MPH
2013	OKL	AAA	23	7	4	0	18	17	93	74	5	4.8	9.0	60%	.276	1.33	3.29	3.98	4.86	0.8	95	
2013	HOU	MLB	23	1	1	0	10	10	60	46	3	5.2	4.9	55%	.246	1.35	1.95	4.38	2.65	1.6	122	97.1
2014	HOU	MLB	24	9	7	0	20	20	116^1	119	7	3.9	5.8	58%	.302	1.46	4.41	4.05	3.89	1.3	116	96.4
2014	MIA	MLB	24	4	4	0	10	10	64	54	2	3.1	5.6	52%	.267	1.19	2.39	3.29	2.92	1.5	116	96.0
2015	NWO	AAA	25	0	1	0	4	4	16^1	21	2	4.4	6.1	53%	.339	1.78	6.06	5.31	6.37	-0.1	113	
2015	MIA	MLB	25	2	5	0	14	13	69^2	63	10	4.3	6.1	55%	.259	1.38	4.52	5.14	5.40	-0.3	123	96.7
2016	*MIA*	*MLB*	*26*	*9*	*11*	*0*	*29*	*29*	*165^1*	*148*	*16*	*3.5*	*6.4*	*56%*	*.288*	*1.29*	*4.16*	*4.12*	*4.92*	*0.7*	*116*	
2017	*MIA*	*MLB*	*27*	*9*	*10*	*0*	*28*	*28*	*172^2*	*159*	*18*	*3.7*	*6.9*	*56%*	*.298*	*1.33*	*4.11*	*4.53*	*4.86*	*0.8*	*115*	

Breakout: 29% Improve: 48% Collapse: 16% Attrition: 18% MLB: 81% *Comparables: Dana Eveland, Robbie Ross, Chris Archer*

The only pitcher in baseball last year to miss time with vertigo *and* get dinged for illegal gambling... and those might have been the high points. Cosart allowed the league's second-hardest average exit velocity, to go with his traditionally atavistic peripherals. Despite a fastball that sits 95, he has never had even an average strikeout rate as a pro, and while he burns his share of worms his spotty command has had predictable consequences for his consistency. Cosart has had a handful of peripheral-defying stretches of competent production as a big leaguer, but he's perilously close to that one 6.83-ERA season that causes everybody to give up on him (until he reemerges two years later as a relief ace).

Mike Dunn LHP

Born: 5/23/85 Age: 31 Bats: L Throws: L Height: 6'0" Weight: 210

YEAR	TEAM	LVL	AGE	W	L	SV	G	GS	IP	H	HR	BB/9	K/9	GB%	BABIP	WHIP	ERA	FIP	DRA	WARP	CFIP	MPH
2013	MIA	MLB	28	3	4	2	75	0	67^2	53	5	3.7	9.6	42%	.271	1.20	2.66	3.09	3.00	1.3	87	96.5
2014	MIA	MLB	29	10	6	1	75	0	57	47	4	3.5	10.6	37%	.291	1.21	3.16	3.03	3.40	0.8	88	97.0
2015	MIA	MLB	30	2	5	0	72	0	54	46	6	4.8	10.8	40%	.301	1.39	4.50	3.92	4.54	0.1	89	96.7
2016	*MIA*	*MLB*	*31*	*3*	*1*	*3*	*66*	*0*	*69^2*	*57*	*7*	*3.5*	*9.8*	*39%*	*.302*	*1.21*	*3.60*	*3.41*	*4.28*	*0.5*	*94*	
2017	*MIA*	*MLB*	*32*	*4*	*2*	*1*	*79*	*0*	*64^1*	*54*	*8*	*3.6*	*9.9*	*39%*	*.305*	*1.24*	*3.69*	*4.05*	*4.39*	*0.4*	*97*	

Breakout: 27% Improve: 44% Collapse: 35% Attrition: 19% MLB: 95% *Comparables: Chad Fox, Matt Mantei, Kyle Farnsworth*

Some trailblazers get their faces printed on currency, or an elementary school named in their honor. Others get two-year deals. The Marlins hadn't negotiated with an eligible player after the arbitration deadline in over a decade, so Dunn's deal last winter was a noteworthy moment for franchise historians. Unfortunately, it was one of few he produced in 2015. The southpaw was once again deployed to take on all comers despite some historical vulnerability to right-handed power. He managed to maintain a strong whiff rate with his mid-90s fastball, but hitters tuned up the pitch pretty well when they did lay wood on it, driving his worst DRA in three years. He'll head into his walk year with a year's salary guaranteed and a wide open road ahead.

Jose Fernandez RHP

Born: 7/31/92 Age: 23 Bats: R Throws: R Height: 6'2" Weight: 215

YEAR	TEAM	LVL	AGE	W	L	SV	G	GS	IP	H	HR	BB/9	K/9	GB%	BABIP	WHIP	ERA	FIP	DRA	WARP	CFIP	MPH
2013	MIA	MLB	20	12	6	0	28	28	172^{2}	111	10	3.0	9.7	47%	.240	0.98	2.19	2.70	2.38	5.3	76	98.2
2014	MIA	MLB	21	4	2	0	8	8	51^{2}	36	4	2.3	12.2	50%	.271	0.95	2.44	2.15	2.60	1.4	68	98.6
2015	MIA	MLB	22	6	1	0	11	11	64^{2}	61	4	1.9	11.0	44%	.343	1.16	2.92	2.26	3.49	1.2	74	99.2
2015	JUP	A+	22	1	1	0	4	4	19^{2}	18	1	1.8	11.4	38%	.370	1.12	3.20	1.89	1.77	0.7	72	
2016	*MIA*	*MLB*	*23*	*11*	*9*	*0*	*28*	*28*	*187*	*144*	*17*	*2.4*	*10.0*	*46%*	*.294*	*1.04*	*3.03*	*2.92*	*3.63*	*3.7*	*77*	
2017	*MIA*	*MLB*	*24*	*11*	*10*	*0*	*31*	*31*	*197*	*154*	*21*	*2.4*	*10.0*	*46%*	*.295*	*1.05*	*3.10*	*3.38*	*3.71*	*3.3*	*79*	

Breakout: 25% Improve: 52% Collapse: 14% Attrition: 4% MLB: 96% *Comparables: Stephen Strasburg, Scott Kazmir, Michael Wacha*

In a year with precious few causes for exclamation in Miami, Fernandez's return to health and (for the most part) form was something to scream about. His control was as good as ever! The four-seam velocity was back! The curveball known as "The Defector" didn't *quite* defect as inscrutably on two planes as it did in the past, but it was close enough for one to declare that "The Defector" defected once more! Sure, there was some rust. His fastball got a little too adventurous in the middle of the zone, he didn't miss quite as many bats, and his BABIP was inflated by an abnormal amount of line-drive contact. But this is a feel-good story, damn it, and it isn't every day that a pitcher just hops out of his hospital bad and posts a top-20 cFIP. It's a testament to the absurdity of the talent level here, and while the Marlins will likely be careful with Fernandez's 2016 workload, his reconstructed right arm dramatically upgrades everything about being a Marlins fan, at least for the next few seasons of club control.

Kendry Flores RHP

Born: 11/24/91 Age: 24 Bats: R Throws: R Height: 6'2" Weight: 175

YEAR	TEAM	LVL	AGE	W	L	SV	G	GS	IP	H	HR	BB/9	K/9	GB%	BABIP	WHIP	ERA	FIP	DRA	WARP	CFIP	MPH
2013	AUG	A	21	10	6	0	22	22	141^{2}	113	11	1.1	8.7	39%	.267	0.92	2.73	3.00	3.72	2.2	76	
2014	SJO	A+	22	4	6	0	20	20	105^{2}	101	14	2.7	9.5	40%	.306	1.26	4.09	4.39	5.03	0.5	91	
2015	MIA	MLB	23	1	2	0	7	1	12^{2}	16	0	2.8	6.4	37%	.372	1.58	4.97	2.93	5.27	-0.1	106	93.4
2015	NWO	AAA	23	3	2	0	10	10	58^{2}	49	3	2.1	6.4	46%	.264	1.07	2.61	3.60	4.45	0.7	96	
2015	JAX	AA	23	3	3	0	9	9	56^{2}	33	3	2.4	6.7	46%	.201	0.85	2.06	3.41	3.67	0.8	94	
2016	*MIA*	*MLB*	*24*	*1*	*1*	*0*	*3*	*3*	*15*	*14*	*2*	*2.7*	*6.8*	*40%*	*.291*	*1.22*	*4.11*	*4.51*	*4.83*	*0.1*	*114*	
2017	*MIA*	*MLB*	*25*	*3*	*3*	*0*	*9*	*9*	*53^{1}*	*53*	*8*	*3.0*	*6.9*	*40%*	*.307*	*1.34*	*4.40*	*4.85*	*5.17*	*0.1*	*122*	

Breakout: 14% Improve: 21% Collapse: 17% Attrition: 27% MLB: 52% *Comparables: Kyle Hendricks, Tim Cooney, Troy Patton*

In another system Flores' precarious back-of-the-rotation upside probably wouldn't warrant as much attention, but this is the Marlins so he's kind of a big deal. He'll work off a low-90s fastball, with ample attention also devoted to a curve, change and newly-acquired cutter to supplement. None projects as a standout offering—the changeup probably comes closest—but he'll generally command the ball well and mix speed and location enough to stay ahead of hitters. He gave up a bunch of hard contact in his first live look at big-league hitters, but whatever, it was a brief look. More concerning, he's now the owner of a dubious streak of prematurely ending seasons—he hit the shelf with shoulder woes for a second consecutive August. The opportunity should be there for Flores in 2016, and if the body is willing the mind may just be able to coax him into the shape of a useful big leaguer.

Jarlin Garcia LHP

Born: 1/18/93 Age: 23 Bats: L Throws: L Height: 6'2" Weight: 170

YEAR	TEAM	LVL	AGE	W	L	SV	G	GS	IP	H	HR	BB/9	K/9	GB%	BABIP	WHIP	ERA	FIP	DRA	WARP	CFIP	MPH
2013	BAT	A-	20	2	3	0	15	15	69^{2}	58	7	2.3	9.6	48%	.279	1.09	3.10	3.14	3.65	0.8	86	
2014	GRB	A	21	10	5	0	25	25	133^{2}	152	13	1.4	7.5	49%	.332	1.29	4.38	3.77	4.38	1.5	88	
2015	JAX	AA	22	1	3	0	7	7	36^{2}	38	4	4.2	8.6	41%	.324	1.50	4.91	4.20	4.68	0.1	103	
2015	JUP	A+	22	3	5	0	18	18	97	96	4	2.1	6.4	41%	.303	1.23	3.06	3.05	3.57	1.0	97	
2016	*MIA*	*MLB*	*23*	*6*	*8*	*0*	*23*	*23*	*117^{1}*	*123*	*12*	*3.0*	*5.8*	*39%*	*.315*	*1.38*	*4.22*	*4.15*	*4.98*	*0.4*	*117*	
2017	*MIA*	*MLB*	*24*	*7*	*8*	*0*	*23*	*23*	*137^{1}*	*151*	*18*	*3.0*	*5.9*	*39%*	*.321*	*1.43*	*4.42*	*4.90*	*5.22*	*0.1*	*124*	

Breakout: 0% Improve: 0% Collapse: 0% Attrition: 0% MLB: 0% *Comparables: Williams Perez, Josh Tomlin, Jensen Lewis*

Garcia's fastball and slider project as plus offerings, but his changeup lags and his slider doesn't bite quite enough to lock up right-handers. Between the potential platoon issues, his Ric Ocasek frame and an arduous delivery, chances are he ends up in a bullpen, spitting sunflower seeds and telling yarns about the year he pitched pretty well in High-A before Double-A hitters bombed all over his limited arsenal.

Brad Hand LHP

Born: 3/20/90 Age: 26 Bats: L Throws: L Height: 6'3" Weight: 215

YEAR	TEAM	LVL	AGE	W	L	SV	G	GS	IP	H	HR	BB/9	K/9	GB%	BABIP	WHIP	ERA	FIP	DRA	WARP	CFIP	MPH
2013	NWO	AAA	23	3	5	0	15	15	81^{2}	69	7	5.0	8.9	50%	.287	1.40	3.42	4.43	5.08	0.5	105	
2013	MIA	MLB	23	1	1	0	7	2	20^{2}	13	2	3.5	6.5	42%	.193	1.02	3.05	3.99	2.60	0.5	109	95.6
2014	MIA	MLB	24	3	8	1	32	16	111	112	10	3.2	5.4	53%	.287	1.36	4.38	4.17	4.40	0.4	121	95.3
2014	NWO	AAA	24	2	0	0	4	4	22	18	3	3.7	9.0	54%	.268	1.23	3.27	4.70	5.27	0.1	101	
2014	JUP	A+	24	0	0	0	2	2	12	4	0	1.5	10.5	84%	.160	0.50	0.75	1.56	3.68	0.2	76	
2015	MIA	MLB	25	4	7	0	38	12	93^{1}	107	9	3.1	6.5	48%	.330	1.49	5.30	4.10	5.80	-1.0	113	95.1
2016	*MIA*	*MLB*	*26*	*4*	*3*	*0*	*56*	*5*	*80^{1}*	*72*	*8*	*2.9*	*6.5*	*50%*	*.286*	*1.23*	*4.12*	*3.94*	*4.86*	*0.2*	*114*	
2017	*MIA*	*MLB*	*27*	*6*	*6*	*0*	*27*	*17*	*113^{2}*	*110*	*14*	*2.9*	*6.8*	*50%*	*.301*	*1.29*	*4.16*	*4.59*	*4.91*	*0.4*	*116*	

Breakout: 24% Improve: 48% Collapse: 21% Attrition: 26% MLB: 89% *Comparables: Franklin Morales, Travis Wood, Casey Coleman*

A sturdy southpaw from Minnesota, Hand settled in as a not-good swingman for Miami. He tamed some of the the control demons that had tormented his younger days, but he also posted one of the worst DRA figures in baseball and essentially turned every right-handed hitter he faced—and swingmen face a lot of them—into Andrew McCutchen. A more specialized role might be just the cure for what's ailed him, though Miami has shown little past inclination to explore that path and his lack of minor-league options places him at something of a crossroads with the team that drafted him.

Jose Jose LHP

Born: 7/21/90 Age: 25 Bats: L Throws: L Height: 6'2" Weight: 175

YEAR	TEAM	LVL	AGE	W	L	SV	G	GS	IP	H	HR	BB/9	K/9	GB%	BABIP	WHIP	ERA	FIP	DRA	WARP	CFIP	MPH
2013	SBN	A	22	0	1	5	16	0	15^{1}	19	2	4.1	8.8	35%	.386	1.70	5.28	5.03	4.63	0.1	100	
2014	SBN	A	23	1	1	0	38	0	45^{1}	28	2	3.4	10.1	29%	.241	0.99	2.58	3.00	4.00	0.4	84	
2015	VIS	A+	24	0	1	0	9	0	10^{1}	10	0	1.7	12.2	42%	.385	1.16	1.74	1.65	3.32	0.2	81	
2016	*MIA*	*MLB*	*25*	*2*	*1*	*2*	*35*	*0*	*37^{1}*	*34*	*4*	*3.5*	*8.3*	*31%*	*.309*	*1.30*	*3.99*	*3.90*	*4.71*	*0.1*	*108*	
2017	*MIA*	*MLB*	*26*	*2*	*1*	*2*	*41*	*0*	*49^{2}*	*44*	*6*	*3.7*	*8.8*	*31%*	*.308*	*1.30*	*4.02*	*4.42*	*4.74*	*0.1*	*109*	

Breakout: 0% Improve: 0% Collapse: 0% Attrition: 0% MLB: 0% *Comparables: Josh Edgin, B.J. Rosenberg, Colton Murray*

An outfield bust in his much younger days, the man with a name so nice you have to say it twice now makes his minor-league living by filling up the zone with a three-pitch mix from the left side. What Jose Jose lacks in standout velocity he makes up for with precision, and a solid fading change gives rise to the possibility that he might just be able to get right-handers out every now and again. Southpaws with double-digit strikeout-to-walk ratios don't grow on trees, and especially when you factor in the marketing potential (can't you just *feel* the stadium chants?) there's a strong case to be made for a club to give this guy a shot.

Tom Koehler RHP

Born: 6/29/86 Age: 30 Bats: R Throws: R Height: 6'3" Weight: 235

YEAR	TEAM	LVL	AGE	W	L	SV	G	GS	IP	H	HR	BB/9	K/9	GB%	BABIP	WHIP	ERA	FIP	DRA	WARP	CFIP	MPH
2013	NWO	AAA	27	0	2	0	4	4	23	16	2	4.7	7.0	48%	.230	1.22	2.74	4.70	5.20	0.1	109	
2013	MIA	MLB	27	5	10	0	29	23	143	140	14	3.4	5.8	49%	.289	1.36	4.41	4.24	4.59	0.5	120	95.6
2014	MIA	MLB	28	10	10	0	32	32	191^{1}	177	16	3.3	7.2	46%	.290	1.30	3.81	3.81	3.81	2.3	110	95.6
2015	MIA	MLB	29	11	14	0	32	31	187^{1}	180	22	3.7	6.6	49%	.283	1.37	4.08	4.56	4.69	0.7	117	94.6
2016	*MIA*	*MLB*	*30*	*9*	*11*	*0*	*31*	*31*	*164^{1}*	*151*	*18*	*3.3*	*6.7*	*48%*	*.293*	*1.28*	*4.23*	*4.18*	*4.98*	*0.6*	*118*	
2017	*MIA*	*MLB*	*31*	*7*	*9*	*0*	*23*	*23*	*136^{2}*	*136*	*18*	*3.4*	*6.8*	*48%*	*.307*	*1.37*	*4.43*	*4.88*	*5.22*	*0.1*	*124*	

Breakout: 3% Improve: 24% Collapse: 24% Attrition: 23% MLB: 58% *Comparables: Chris Narveson, Tim Stauffer, Ryan Drese*

Like one of those movies where an everyman stumbles into the presidency of the United States, so it was that injuries, awfulness and trades conspired to make Tom Koehler—nice guy, loving husband and father, works out there in his garage most nights just trying to make sure his 1985 Volvo will be able to start up for at least one more cold winter morning—the Marlins' nominal ace. It went...not great. He walked more, struck out fewer, allowed more home runs, his cFIP sank to the lowest rungs of qualified starters. Highlights of his season? He recorded the hardest-hit out of the year (a 117-mph Hanley Ramirez liner) and he ran his streak of big-league innings without surrendering a balk to 535. Every team needs an everyman to clock in, clock out, and keep the complaining to a minimum, so in that sense Koehler's a hero. He's just miscast as an ace, as we pretty much all are.

Tyler Kolek RHP

Born: 12/15/95 Age: 20 Bats: R Throws: R Height: 6'5" Weight: 260

YEAR	TEAM	LVL	AGE	W	L	SV	G	GS	IP	H	HR	BB/9	K/9	GB%	BABIP	WHIP	ERA	FIP	DRA	WARP	CFIP	MPH
2015	GRB	A	19	4	10	0	25	25	108^{2}	108	7	5.1	6.7	51%	.298	1.56	4.56	4.87	6.54	-1.8	119	
2016	*MIA*	*MLB*	*20*	*4*	*7*	*0*	*20*	*20*	*81^{1}*	*84*	*8*	*5.3*	*5.5*	*44%*	*.308*	*1.61*	*5.17*	*5.04*	*6.06*	*-0.8*	*144*	
2017	*MIA*	*MLB*	*21*	*5*	*9*	*0*	*26*	*26*	*153*	*162*	*19*	*5.3*	*5.8*	*44%*	*.313*	*1.65*	*5.19*	*5.78*	*6.08*	*-1.0*	*145*	

Breakout: 0% Improve: 0% Collapse: 0% Attrition: 0% MLB: 0% *Comparables: Scott Elbert, Brandon Maurer, Enny Romero*

Kolek went second overall in 2014 on the strength of a triple-digit fastball and dreamy Texan frame, but only the Texan frame showed up for his full-season debut. His sitting velocity was down 4-6 mph, depending on which day you caught him, and his underdeveloped secondaries didn't miss bats. There's always been effort in his delivery and unease about his command, so his clumsy inaugural has led to the first whispers among evaluators of a bullpen future. That transition certainly won't happen soon—he's young, his assignment to A-Ball was aggressive, and there's a *lot* invested in his upside—but 2016 will be a pivotal one for his development. As it is, though, a dozen or so 2014 first-rounders have surpassed him as a prospect.

Raudel Lazo LHP

Born: 4/12/89 Age: 27 Bats: L Throws: L Height: 5'9" Weight: 165

YEAR	TEAM	LVL	AGE	W	L	SV	G	GS	IP	H	HR	BB/9	K/9	GB%	BABIP	WHIP	ERA	FIP	DRA	WARP	CFIP	MPH
2015	MIA	MLB	26	0	0	0	7	0	5^{2}	5	1	3.2	7.9	29%	.250	1.24	3.18	4.75	5.76	-0.1	104	92.3
2015	JAX	AA	26	3	2	0	18	0	29^{1}	29	2	2.1	9.8	39%	.351	1.23	2.15	2.83	3.03	0.5	86	
2015	JUP	A+	26	1	1	1	8	0	12	7	0	1.5	9.0	43%	.233	0.75	1.50	1.67	2.53	0.2	82	
2016	*MIA*	*MLB*	*27*	*2*	*1*	*0*	*30*	*0*	*32^{1}*	*30*	*3*	*3.0*	*7.4*	*34%*	*.308*	*1.27*	*3.87*	*3.75*	*4.58*	*0.2*	*105*	
2017	*MIA*	*MLB*	*28*	*1*	*1*	*0*	*28*	*0*	*39*	*37*	*4*	*3.2*	*7.7*	*34%*	*.308*	*1.30*	*3.95*	*4.36*	*4.68*	*0.1*	*108*	

Breakout: 11% Improve: 12% Collapse: 11% Attrition: 14% MLB: 25% *Comparables: Jorge Vasquez, Sandy Rosario, Chris Leroux*

When you've got good bloodlines in the game anything is possible, and as the nephew of an all-time Serie Nacional great Lazo has those. But the southpaw can also lay claim to his own awesome resume of perseverance after surviving a 2011 defection and battling back from consecutive Tommy John surgeries to finally force a big-league debut last summer. When he's been able to take the hill the 26-year-old has produced outstanding results against minor-league lefties on the strength of a lively 90 mph fastball and biting slider. There's also a changeup that has solid tumble, providing hope for more than a situational lot in life—assuming his third elbow ligament will allow it.

Brett Lilek LHP

Born: 8/10/93 Age: 22 Bats: L Throws: L Height: 6'4" Weight: 220

YEAR	TEAM	LVL	AGE	W	L	SV	G	GS	IP	H	HR	BB/9	K/9	GB%	BABIP	WHIP	ERA	FIP	DRA	WARP	CFIP	MPH
2015	BAT	A-	21	1	2	0	11	10	35	30	1	1.8	11.1	44%	.333	1.06	3.34	2.20	1.52	1.4	69	
2016	*MIA*	*MLB*	*22*	*2*	*3*	*0*	*9*	*9*	*37^2*	*34*	*4*	*2.9*	*8.4*	*34%*	*.312*	*1.23*	*3.62*	*3.60*	*4.30*	*0.4*	*97*	
2017	*MIA*	*MLB*	*23*	*7*	*8*	*0*	*31*	*31*	*197^1*	*188*	*24*	*3.0*	*8.4*	*34%*	*.317*	*1.28*	*3.85*	*4.24*	*4.57*	*1.0*	*105*	

Breakout: 0% Improve: 0% Collapse: 0% Attrition: 0% MLB: 0% *Comparables: Michael Feliz, Sean Gilmartin, Adam Wilk*

Miami popped Lilek in the second round after his uneven spring at Arizona State caused his draft stock to slump, and when healthy he'll sit in the low 90s, snap a solid curveball and deceive with a tumbling changeup. His command will take a stroll from time to time and he doesn't have enough stuff to repeatedly beat hitters in the zone, so taming the ball consistently will have to be his meal ticket. As a polished college arm, he threw as well as he should have against NYPL hitters before shoulder inflammation cut his debut short. He'll move as fast as his command and health will allow, and is as good a bet to be in this book 10 years from now as we are to still be producing it.

Scott McGough RHP

Born: 10/31/89 Age: 26 Bats: R Throws: R Height: 6'0" Weight: 170

YEAR	TEAM	LVL	AGE	W	L	SV	G	GS	IP	H	HR	BB/9	K/9	GB%	BABIP	WHIP	ERA	FIP	DRA	WARP	CFIP	MPH
2013	JAX	AA	23	4	3	1	36	0	61^2	48	4	2.6	8.2	54%	.254	1.07	2.63	2.82	3.66	0.5	87	
2015	MIA	MLB	25	0	0	0	6	0	6^2	12	0	5.4	5.4	63%	.444	2.40	9.45	3.76	9.27	-0.4	113	95.5
2015	NWO	AAA	25	0	1	1	13	0	17	9	1	4.8	6.4	40%	.174	1.06	2.12	4.54	5.29	0.0	106	
2015	JAX	AA	25	0	0	0	10	0	13^1	14	1	4.1	2.7	54%	.277	1.50	2.70	5.03	6.22	-0.3	121	
2016	*MIA*	*MLB*	*26*	*1*	*0*	*0*	*20*	*0*	*21^2*	*21*	*2*	*3.5*	*6.4*	*49%*	*.302*	*1.35*	*4.29*	*4.10*	*5.05*	*0.0*	*117*	
2017	*MIA*	*MLB*	*27*	*1*	*0*	*0*	*22*	*0*	*31^1*	*31*	*4*	*3.6*	*6.9*	*49%*	*.304*	*1.39*	*4.45*	*4.92*	*5.24*	*-0.1*	*122*	

Breakout: 4% Improve: 6% Collapse: 1% Attrition: 7% MLB: 9% *Comparables: Erik Hamren, Josh Fields, Jay Buente*

When little kids the world over act out their backyard big-league debuts, they rarely go quite as poorly as McGough's did: He faced seven batters and left with an ERA of 40.50. Still, the man made a big-league debut, and if kids aren't play-acting falling into a plush hotel bed or receiving a $100.50 per diem, that's their own fault. Making It was an especially impressive achievement for McGough, who had undergone Tommy John surgery in 2014 and reached the Miami rubber after just 32 innings of rehab. The velocity on his normally mid-90's fastball flagged in his September audition, suggesting some potential fatigue on the back end of that recovery, but if it rebounds after a winter of rest he has the kind of solid stuff and marginal control to round out the soft underbelly of the bullpen.

Bryan Morris RHP

Born: 3/28/87 Age: 29 Bats: L Throws: R Height: 6'3" Weight: 225

YEAR	TEAM	LVL	AGE	W	L	SV	G	GS	IP	H	HR	BB/9	K/9	GB%	BABIP	WHIP	ERA	FIP	DRA	WARP	CFIP	MPH
2013	PIT	MLB	26	5	7	0	55	0	65	57	8	3.9	5.1	58%	.251	1.31	3.46	4.87	4.64	0.0	122	96.2
2014	MIA	MLB	27	4	1	0	39	0	40^2	33	2	2.7	8.0	57%	.265	1.11	0.66	3.00	2.10	1.2	99	98.0
2014	PIT	MLB	27	4	0	0	21	0	23^2	25	4	4.6	5.3	68%	.296	1.56	3.80	5.89	6.17	-0.5	117	97.8
2015	MIA	MLB	28	5	4	0	67	0	63	67	3	3.7	6.7	63%	.323	1.48	3.14	3.67	5.00	-0.2	113	97.5
2016	*MIA*	*MLB*	*29*	*3*	*1*	*0*	*61*	*0*	*64^2*	*60*	*7*	*3.2*	*6.7*	*62%*	*.295*	*1.28*	*4.14*	*4.12*	*4.90*	*0.0*	*113*	
2017	*MIA*	*MLB*	*30*	*2*	*1*	*1*	*46*	*0*	*54^1*	*53*	*7*	*3.2*	*6.8*	*62%*	*.303*	*1.33*	*4.20*	*4.63*	*4.97*	*-0.1*	*115*	

Breakout: 32% Improve: 47% Collapse: 25% Attrition: 25% MLB: 77% *Comparables: Ramon Troncoso, Javy Guerra, Javier Lopez*

There are expectations for first-rounders that don't get put on fifth- or 10th- or 39th-round guys, but the journey toward reaching that level is often as jagged and piecemeal as any other aspiring professional's career path. In Morris' case it took six years to make the bigs, and along the way were a Tommy John rehab, disappointing results and, ultimately, a decision to reroute his path toward the bullpen. The whole thing has worked out reasonably well, as he's now three full years and nigh-on 200 innings into a big-league career that has produced a better ERA+ since 2013 than Glen Perkins, Drew Storen, Steve Cishek, and so on. He keeps a decent sinker/slider combination down in the zone, gets grounders at a strong clip and neutralizes right-handed hitters enough that he can reliably inherit runners in the middle innings. It's not the glitziest or most glamorous endpoint for the 26th-overall draft slot, but what's important is that he got there.

Chris Narveson LHP

Born: 12/20/81 Age: 34 Bats: L Throws: L Height: 6'3" Weight: 205

YEAR	TEAM	LVL	AGE	W	L	SV	G	GS	IP	H	HR	BB/9	K/9	GB%	BABIP	WHIP	ERA	FIP	DRA	WARP	CFIP	MPH
2013	NAS	AAA	31	4	7	0	15	15	77	85	9	2.8	6.9	41%	.310	1.42	5.14	4.57	5.27	0.3	108	
2013	MIL	MLB	31	0	0	0	2	0	2	1	0	4.5	0.0	57%	.143	1.00	0.00	4.52	4.94	0.0	109	87.6
2015	NWO	AAA	33	0	3	0	10	4	26	38	4	3.5	10.0	38%	.425	1.85	5.19	4.52	4.90	0.1	97	
2015	JUP	A+	33	2	0	0	2	2	11^1	11	0	1.6	7.9	28%	.344	1.15	3.18	2.19	3.09	0.2	90	
2015	MIA	MLB	33	3	1	0	15	2	30^1	24	7	2.7	9.5	41%	.233	1.09	4.45	4.94	4.59	0.1	96	90.9
2016	*MIA*	*MLB*	*34*	*3*	*3*	*0*	*17*	*8*	*48^2*	*45*	*6*	*2.8*	*7.5*	*38%*	*.302*	*1.24*	*3.98*	*4.05*	*4.70*	*0.3*	*110*	
2017	*MIA*	*MLB*	*35*	*7*	*8*	*0*	*44*	*22*	*164^2*	*165*	*23*	*2.8*	*7.4*	*38%*	*.312*	*1.31*	*4.20*	*4.63*	*4.96*	*0.4*	*118*	

Breakout: 11% Improve: 30% Collapse: 13% Attrition: 10% MLB: 62% *Comparables: Claudio Vargas, Eric Stults, Tim Redding*

Come to think of it, there sure were a lot of stories of perseverance on last year's awful Marlins team—not, most likely, a coincidence, and not, necessarily, a winning strategy. Absent for most of the previous three seasons, Narveson has now suffered through a Tommy John surgery, two major shoulder procedures, another on his hip, a relatively unsuccessful turn in Japan and a bunch of annoying hot dog/sandwich debates without losing his career (or sanity). He finally got back on the mound in the Western hemisphere with the best velocity he'd shown since 2009 and a markedly deeper curveball that suddenly generated whiffs at a borderline-elite rate in his two months with Miami. (The home runs, though. Whoa, the home runs.) Say what you will about the Marlins' way of doing things, but it does create opportunities for guys willing to play for relative scraps, and those guys are often the ones you root for.

Justin Nicolino LHP

Born: 11/22/91 Age: 24 Bats: L Throws: L Height: 6'3" Weight: 190

YEAR	TEAM	LVL	AGE	W	L	SV	G	GS	IP	H	HR	BB/9	K/9	GB%	BABIP	WHIP	ERA	FIP	DRA	WARP	CFIP	MPH
2013	JUP	A+	21	5	2	0	18	18	96^{2}	89	4	1.7	6.0	50%	.286	1.11	2.23	3.08	4.04	0.9	92	
2013	JAX	AA	21	3	2	0	9	9	45^{1}	63	2	2.4	6.2	42%	.386	1.65	4.96	3.04	4.17	0.3	101	
2014	JAX	AA	22	14	4	0	28	28	170^{1}	162	10	1.1	4.3	49%	.267	1.07	2.85	3.44				
2015	NWO	AAA	23	7	7	0	20	20	115	134	11	2.3	4.9	52%	.324	1.42	3.52	4.61	5.74	-0.3	110	
2015	MIA	MLB	23	5	4	0	12	12	74	72	8	2.4	2.8	46%	.259	1.24	4.01	4.88	5.12	-0.1	132	91.8
2016	*MIA*	*MLB*	*24*	*8*	*10*	*0*	*26*	*26*	148^{1}	*156*	*16*	*2.2*	*4.3*	*48%*	*.300*	*1.30*	*4.42*	*4.31*	*5.23*	*0.1*	*125*	
2017	*MIA*	*MLB*	*25*	*7*	*9*	*0*	*23*	*23*	134^{2}	*154*	*19*	*2.3*	*4.5*	*48%*	*.315*	*1.40*	*4.61*	*5.11*	*5.45*	*-0.3*	*130*	

Breakout: 14% Improve: 25% Collapse: 14% Attrition: 28% MLB: 52% *Comparables: Anthony Swarzak, Jeanmar Gomez, Alex Sanabia*

As a prospect Nicolino was frequently heralded for his lofty floor, but the southpaw's advanced metrics tested the foundation in his first 12 starts for Miami. He posted the worst strikeout rate (by a lot) of any hurler to log at least his 74 innings, and that exercise in bat-missing futility fueled the worst cFIP in baseball. His back-of-the-baseball-card numbers looked mercifully more pleasant, thanks in large part to a BABIP 37 points south of league-average. There was something to that low rate, as he managed to leverage his decent changeup and passable sinker into a reasonably benign contact profile. Big-league hitters tend to run out of patience for hurlers who ask *that* much of the defense behind them, however, and Nicolino will walk a fine line into his battle for a rotation spot in spring training.

Nefi Ogando RHP

Born: 6/3/89 Age: 27 Bats: R Throws: R Height: 6'2" Weight: 220

YEAR	TEAM	LVL	AGE	W	L	SV	G	GS	IP	H	HR	BB/9	K/9	GB%	BABIP	WHIP	ERA	FIP	DRA	WARP	CFIP	MPH
2013	SLM	A+	24	2	3	3	33	0	55	49	5	4.4	7.2	50%	.272	1.38	4.09	4.51	4.87	0.1	107	
2014	REA	AA	25	5	1	7	48	0	56	64	6	4.5	9.2	51%	.352	1.64	6.27	4.53	4.64	0.1	102	
2015	REA	AA	26	2	3	2	24	0	34^{2}	25	2	4.9	8.6	44%	.258	1.27	2.86	3.85	4.49	0.0	104	
2015	PHI	MLB	26	0	0	0	4	0	4	7	0	4.5	4.5	47%	.412	2.25	9.00	3.66	7.78	-0.1	111	97.6
2015	LEH	AAA	26	2	2	1	21	0	28^{1}	27	1	3.8	7.0	46%	.295	1.38	2.86	3.76	4.38	0.0	102	
2016	*MIA*	*MLB*	*27*	*3*	*1*	*1*	*56*	*0*	59^{2}	*57*	*6*	*3.6*	*7.1*	*44%*	*.307*	*1.36*	*4.18*	*4.08*	*4.91*	*0.0*	*114*	
2017	*MIA*	*MLB*	*28*	*1*	*0*	*0*	*25*	*0*	*37*	*36*	*5*	*4.0*	*7.4*	*44%*	*.313*	*1.43*	*4.39*	*4.85*	*5.16*	*-0.1*	*121*	

Breakout: 2% Improve: 3% Collapse: 5% Attrition: 7% MLB: 8% *Comparables: Ryan Kelly, Rommie Lewis, Bo Schultz*

Called up to The Show but barely called upon, Ogando fits the description of a middle reliever who could either hang around in the majors with a low profile for a few years or get shuttled back and forth until his options run out. Ogando is a bit atypical in that he was already 21 when he was signed in 2010 out of the Dominican Republic, and while his minor-league performance won't put stars in anyone's eyes, his stuff looks to be just average enough to the point that the idea of him winning a spot in the 'pen out of spring training doesn't seem so far-fetched. At his best, he'll sit 93 to 94 mph with his fastball and generate a good chunk of groundballs, but his command remains suspect, as does his ability to sustain even an average whiff rate.

David Phelps RHP

Born: 10/9/86 Age: 29 Bats: R Throws: R Height: 6'2" Weight: 200

YEAR	TEAM	LVL	AGE	W	L	SV	G	GS	IP	H	HR	BB/9	K/9	GB%	BABIP	WHIP	ERA	FIP	DRA	WARP	CFIP	MPH
2013	NYA	MLB	26	6	5	0	22	12	86^{2}	88	8	3.6	8.2	44%	.323	1.42	4.98	3.84	4.59	0.2	99	92.5
2014	NYA	MLB	27	5	5	1	32	17	113	115	13	3.7	7.3	44%	.301	1.42	4.38	4.43	4.63	0.2	110	92.7
2015	MIA	MLB	28	4	8	0	23	19	112	119	11	2.7	6.2	43%	.303	1.36	4.50	4.05	4.80	0.3	112	93.0
2016	*MIA*	*MLB*	*29*	*3*	*3*	*0*	*10*	*10*	*50*	*47*	*5*	*2.9*	*7.0*	*43%*	*.301*	*1.26*	*4.00*	*3.86*	*4.74*	*0.3*	*111*	
2017	*MIA*	*MLB*	*30*	*4*	*4*	*0*	*19*	*10*	*74*	*74*	*9*	*3.0*	*7.0*	*43%*	*.310*	*1.33*	*4.10*	*4.53*	*4.86*	*0.3*	*114*	

Breakout: 30% Improve: 51% Collapse: 23% Attrition: 17% MLB: 97% *Comparables: Jake Arrieta, John Maine, Brian Bannister*

The swingman's swingman continued his sneak-assault on his role, reaching a career-high 19 starts to continue an interesting trend:

- 2012: 57 percent of his innings as a starter
- 2013: 76 percent
- 2014: 86 percent
- 2015: 96 percent

While you might speculate that we're watching the Peter Principle played out in bullet-time, the curious thing is that Phelps had pretty much already found the level of his own incompetence in the bullpen, where over the past three years he has allowed 5.91 runs per nine. He's been a little better when he starts—4.78 RA, with better control and slightly fewer homers—but is, in fact, not the master of this niche role that we might generously have called him at some point. Rather, he's just not great.

A.J. Ramos RHP

Born: 9/20/86 Age: 29 Bats: R Throws: R Height: 5'10" Weight: 205

YEAR	TEAM	LVL	AGE	W	L	SV	G	GS	IP	H	HR	BB/9	K/9	GB%	BABIP	WHIP	ERA	FIP	DRA	WARP	CFIP	MPH
2013	MIA	MLB	26	3	4	0	68	0	80	58	4	4.8	9.7	40%	.266	1.26	3.15	3.21	3.16	1.4	91	96.4
2014	MIA	MLB	27	7	0	0	68	0	64	36	1	6.0	10.3	45%	.233	1.23	2.11	3.18	2.18	1.8	97	94.4
2015	MIA	MLB	28	2	4	32	71	0	70^{1}	45	6	3.3	11.1	44%	.252	1.01	2.30	3.03	3.02	1.4	77	95.8
2016	*MIA*	*MLB*	*29*	*3*	*1*	*25*	*66*	*0*	69^{2}	*50*	*7*	*3.7*	*10.2*	*44%*	*.280*	*1.13*	*3.45*	*3.37*	*4.09*	*0.8*	*90*	
2017	*MIA*	*MLB*	*30*	*3*	*1*	*9*	*59*	*0*	*63*	*47*	*7*	*3.5*	*10.5*	*44%*	*.284*	*1.13*	*3.47*	*3.78*	*4.11*	*0.6*	*90*	

Breakout: 31% Improve: 50% Collapse: 24% Attrition: 15% MLB: 96% *Comparables: Al Alburquerque, Michael Gonzalez, Steve Cishek*

Mercy me, we seem to have stumbled upon an actual success story on the 2015 Marlins! Ramos traded in his book of homer-suppressing spells for significantly better control of his three-pitch arsenal, and it made for a much more viscerally appealing (if similarly productive) experience after his promotion from setup man to closer. Ongoing improvement with his changeup played a big role, helping him keep left-handed hitters off base at a better-than-70 percent clip for the first time. He'll be due a hefty raise this winter, but even with the bump all signs point to him providing bullpen stability at a reasonable price again in 2016.

Chris Reed LHP

Born: 5/20/90 Age: 26 Bats: L Throws: L Height: 6'3" Weight: 225

YEAR	TEAM	LVL	AGE	W	L	SV	G	GS	IP	H	HR	BB/9	K/9	GB%	BABIP	WHIP	ERA	FIP	DRA	WARP	CFIP	MPH
2013	CHT	AA	23	4	11	0	29	25	137^{2}	128	9	4.1	6.9	62%	.295	1.39	3.86	3.73	4.34	0.5	111	
2014	CHT	AA	24	4	8	0	23	23	137	114	10	3.6	7.6	54%	.267	1.23	3.22	3.80				
2014	ABQ	AAA	24	0	3	0	5	5	21^{1}	37	5	4.6	7.6	49%	.416	2.25	10.97	6.89	5.90	0.0	113	
2015	OKL	AAA	25	0	0	0	8	0	11	11	0	3.3	4.1	41%	.324	1.36	3.27	3.78	3.03	0.3	89	
2015	TUL	AA	25	2	2	1	16	0	23^{2}	22	2	6.8	6.1	44%	.274	1.69	7.23	5.33	7.16	-0.6	128	
2015	NWO	AAA	25	1	0	0	14	0	20^{2}	18	3	5.7	10.0	31%	.288	1.50	3.92	5.29	3.99	0.3	117	
2015	MIA	MLB	25	0	0	0	2	0	4	6	0	2.2	2.2	50%	.375	1.75	4.50	3.41	5.90	-0.1	112	93.3
2016	*MIA*	*MLB*	*26*	*4*	*4*	*0*	*23*	*11*	69^{2}	*67*	*8*	*3.6*	*6.4*	*44%*	*.302*	*1.36*	*4.39*	*4.43*	*5.17*	*0.0*	*122*	
2017	*MIA*	*MLB*	*27*	*6*	*8*	*0*	*37*	*21*	149^{2}	*152*	*21*	*3.9*	*6.8*	*44%*	*.313*	*1.45*	*4.69*	*5.19*	*5.52*	*-0.5*	*131*	

Breakout: 8% Improve: 15% Collapse: 3% Attrition: 16% MLB: 25% *Comparables: Doug Mathis, Kevin Mulvey, Mitch Talbot*

The Dodgers finally ran out of patience with their former first-rounder's soggy control and shipped Reed to the Marlins in a sparsely noted swap of struggling southpaws in July. Rare strikeouts rained down in triumphant celebration at Triple-A after the scenery change, but he otherwise remained ineffectively wild on the farm. He snuck in a big-league debut along the way, becoming the first Chris Reed in history to do so, but he'll need to find significantly greater consistency around the zone if he's to further add to the legacy.

Andre Rienzo RHP

Born: 7/5/88 Age: 27 Bats: R Throws: R Height: 6'3" Weight: 190

YEAR	TEAM	LVL	AGE	W	L	SV	G	GS	IP	H	HR	BB/9	K/9	GB%	BABIP	WHIP	ERA	FIP	DRA	WARP	CFIP	MPH
2013	CHA	MLB	24	2	3	0	10	10	56	55	11	4.5	6.1	50%	.257	1.48	4.82	5.88	4.24	0.4	120	93.7
2013	CHR	AAA	24	8	6	0	20	20	113	105	7	3.7	9.0	53%	.308	1.34	4.06	3.34	4.06	1.2	90	
2014	CHR	AAA	25	1	4	0	10	9	46^{2}	44	4	4.6	8.3	47%	.290	1.46	4.05	4.24	4.67	0.2	104	
2014	CHA	MLB	25	4	5	0	18	11	64^{2}	82	12	4.6	7.1	47%	.332	1.78	6.82	5.76	6.77	-1.6	116	93.8
2015	NWO	AAA	26	2	6	0	15	14	77^{2}	66	5	3.7	6.5	46%	.271	1.26	3.01	4.35	5.65	-0.1	110	
2015	MIA	MLB	26	0	1	0	14	0	19^{2}	17	2	5.9	6.9	48%	.259	1.53	5.95	5.09	4.94	-0.1	114	92.3
2016	*MIA*	*MLB*	*27*	*3*	*1*	*0*	*56*	*0*	*59*	*55*	*7*	*3.5*	*7.1*	*47%*	*.297*	*1.32*	*4.29*	*4.26*	*5.05*	*0.0*	*119*	
2017	*MIA*	*MLB*	*28*	*5*	*5*	*0*	*15*	*15*	*88*	*83*	*11*	*3.6*	*7.7*	*47%*	*.301*	*1.35*	*4.30*	*4.75*	*5.06*	*0.2*	*120*	

Breakout: 17% Improve: 33% Collapse: 25% Attrition: 34% MLB: 65% *Comparables: Josh Outman, David Purcey, Mitchell Boggs*

Rienzo holds distinction as the first (and to date only) Brazilian to toe a big-league rubber, and for being the guy Dan Jennings traded Dan Jennings for. He had earned his swingman's wings with a respectable enough effort in mixed-use duty for the White Sox, but despite decent work in a starting gig at Triple-A he was strictly bullpen-bound for the Fish. Despite continuing to generate ample whiffs and grounders with his curve he remained cutter- and sinker-dominant, betting his lot on two pitches he commands poorly. After a wild pitch in August, he covered home plate and got plowed like snow by a sliding Yoenis Cespedes, which might finally be the motivation he needs to *quit throwing so many wild pitches*. He throws a ton.

So, to recap: Brazilian, Dan Jennings thing, wild pitches.

Jose Urena RHP

Born: 9/12/91 Age: 24 Bats: R Throws: R Height: 6'3" Weight: 175

YEAR	TEAM	LVL	AGE	W	L	SV	G	GS	IP	H	HR	BB/9	K/9	GB%	BABIP	WHIP	ERA	FIP	DRA	WARP	CFIP	MPH
2013	JUP	A+	21	10	7	0	27	26	149^{2}	148	8	1.7	6.4	50%	.299	1.18	3.73	3.21	4.02	1.5	91	
2014	JAX	AA	22	13	8	0	26	25	162	155	14	1.6	6.7	48%	.290	1.14	3.33	3.39				
2015	NWO	AAA	23	6	1	0	11	11	67^{2}	65	4	2.5	5.5	54%	.292	1.24	2.66	4.13	5.18	0.3	104	
2015	MIA	MLB	23	1	5	0	20	9	61^{2}	73	5	3.6	4.1	49%	.319	1.59	5.25	4.67	5.60	-0.5	129	97.1
2016	*MIA*	*MLB*	*24*	*3*	*2*	*0*	*26*	*6*	51^{2}	*52*	*5*	*2.6*	*5.4*	*49%*	*.301*	*1.30*	*4.25*	*4.09*	*5.02*	*0.1*	*119*	
2017	*MIA*	*MLB*	*25*	*5*	*6*	*0*	*16*	*16*	*97*	*102*	*13*	*2.9*	*5.6*	*49%*	*.309*	*1.37*	*4.46*	*4.93*	*5.27*	*0.0*	*125*	

Breakout: 13% Improve: 24% Collapse: 14% Attrition: 23% MLB: 47% *Comparables: Elih Villanueva, Dillon Gee, Daryl Thompson*

Urena's stellar control didn't translate from the minors in his first go on the big stage, but a lack of whiffs did and the combination made for an uncomfortable introduction. He can hang out in the mid-90s and fade a changeup some, but big-league hitters had no trouble squaring up either pitch last summer, slugging a combined .552 against his two best weapons. His slider took an intriguing step forward, but while interesting pieces abound the puzzle has some gaps. He figures to be in the mix for innings somewhere in 2016, though a general consensus among evaluators continues to point toward a future in the bullpen.

LINEOUTS

Hitters

NAME	POS	TEAM	LVL	AGE	PA	R	2B	3B	HR	RBI	BB	K	SB	CS	AVG/OBP/SLG	TAv	BABIP	BRR	FRAA	WARP
Brian Anderson	2B	JUP	A+	22	530	50	22	2	8	62	40	109	2	2	.235/.304/.340	.269	.287	-0.9	3B(121): 4.3	2.5
Austin Dean	LF	JUP	A+	21	578	67	32	2	5	52	39	76	18	10	.268/.318/.366	.285	.299	2.9	LF(67): -0.5, RF(66): -2.7	2.7
Stone Garrett	CF	BAT	A-	19	247	36	18	6	11	46	19	60	8	5	.297/.352/.581	.339	.355	-1.0	CF(58): -2.0	2.6
Justin Maxwell	RF	SFN	MLB	31	274	26	8	2	7	26	20	76	2	1	.209/.275/.341	.233	.269	1.0	RF(58): 4.9, LF(19): 0.1	0.4
Adrian Nieto	C	BIR	AA	25	315	27	9	2	5	27	52	77	0	0	.207/.344/.316	.263	.274	0.4	C(77): 1.2	1.7
Yefri Perez	CF	JUP	A+	24	563	74	10	1	1	22	31	95	71	21	.240/.286/.269	.230	.290	10.3	CF(133): 13.8	2.5
Joshua Riddle	SS	JAX	AA	23	189	26	6	1	5	20	8	24	0	0	.289/.323/.422	.293	.306	0.3	SS(42): -4.6	1.0
	SS	JUP	A+	23	198	30	6	1	0	9	11	29	7	3	.270/.311/.314	.274	.321	2.7	SS(42): 4.6	1.9
Anfernee Seymour	SS	BAT	A-	20	266	39	10	4	0	14	20	52	29	6	.273/.338/.349	.254	.348	3.4	SS(61): -3.8	0.9
Justin Twine	2B	GRB	A	19	473	44	20	3	7	39	6	108	8	4	.206/.235/.310	.210	.253	1.0	SS(116): -18.8	-2.5
K.J. Woods	1B	GRB	A	19	439	53	28	1	18	58	45	133	1	3	.277/.364/.496	.306	.376	-3.2	1B(64): 0.3	2.4

Brian Anderson held his own in the offense-starved Florida State League, but between a limited defensive profile and modest potential with the stick he projects as a borderline big leaguer. ❖ An unheralded international signing in 2014, 17-year-old **Samuel Castro**'s stateside debut showcased a decent stroke from both sides of the plate and the arm and hands to play shortstop. ❖ **Austin Dean** can control the bat and hit a little bit, but as a stocky kid without game power he projects as a fourth outfielder without centerfield speed, and with the wrong-handed swing for a platooner. ❖ **Stone Garrett**'s power, speed and top-shelf makeup proved too Texan a combination for the NYPL to handle, and questions about his hit tool and defense will have to instead seek their answers in full-season ball. ❖ If you look up "irony" in a baseball dictionary instead of Merriam-Webster's, you'll find **Justin Maxwell**, who survived cut day in April but not roster expansion in September. ❖ **Adrian Nieto** weathered the storm of being thrown into the majors in 2014, but requires major defensive progress to get back. ❖ **Yefri Perez** can't hit—he put up the third-worst OPS in the Florida State League last year despite an advanced age for the level—but he could outrun the cops and has solid baserunning acumen, a combination that would make him an interesting postseason roster piece in another team's chapter. ❖ **J.T. Riddle** has the defensive chops of a starting shortstop, but even after solving Double-A his bat has more question marks than a Jim Carrey-sized unitard. ❖ A local high school product, shortstop **Anfernee Seymour** was popped in the seventh round in 2014 because he's fast. He swiped the second-most bags in the New York-Penn League also because he's fast. He's fast. ❖ **Justin Twine** posted the second-worst qualifying OPS in A-Ball, amid reports of bad weight gain. He's a 20-year-old shortstop, in the sense that he's only allowed to play shortstop because he's 20. ❖ Third-rounder **Isaiah White** will chase baseballs and steal bases, but professional pitchers laid bare his extremely raw offensive skill set. This is a long way from playable, but he's a long way from it needing to be. ❖ **K.J. Woods** can drop hot butter on your breakfast toast when he gets ahold of one, but a long swing and severe contact issues threaten to leave you choking on your proverbial butterless bread product.

Pitchers

NAME	TEAM	LVL	AGE	W	L	SV	G	GS	IP	H	HR	BB/9	K/9	GB%	BABIP	WHIP	ERA	FIP	FRA	WARP	CFIP	MPH
Austin Brice	JAX	AA	23	6	9	0	25	25	125^{1}	114	11	5.0	9.1	34%	.307	1.46	4.67	4.36	5.29	-0.6	110	
Jeff Brigham	JUP	A+	23	2	2	0	6	5	33^{2}	34	0	2.4	5.9	52%	.324	1.28	1.87	2.75	3.73	0.3	99	
	RCU	A+	23	4	5	0	17	14	68	78	8	4.8	8.5	57%	.340	1.68	5.96	5.28	6.31	-0.4	113	
Brian Ellington	JAX	AA	24	4	1	0	25	0	43	28	0	2.7	9.8	37%	.259	0.95	2.51	2.09	2.26	1.2	76	
	MIA	MLB	24	2	1	0	23	0	25	17	1	4.7	6.5	39%	.225	1.20	2.88	4.04	3.76	0.3	111	99.5
Kevin Guzman	GRL	A	20	5	7	0	17	15	83	94	5	3.1	6.7	41%	.341	1.48	3.90	3.81	4.74	0.2	104	
Justin Jacome	BAT	A-	21	0	1	0	12	11	32^{2}	37	1	1.9	8.0	43%	.367	1.35	2.48	2.87	3.29	0.7	89	
Michael Mader	GRB	A	21	6	12	0	27	27	140^{2}	141	8	3.6	5.5	51%	.294	1.41	4.73	4.41	5.94	-1.2	115	
Dustin McGowan	PHI	MLB	33	1	2	0	14	1	23^{1}	29	7	7.7	8.1	42%	.314	2.10	6.94	7.83	7.69	-0.8	119	97.3
	LEH	AAA	33	2	2	15	31	1	39^{2}	41	2	5.4	6.4	45%	.300	1.64	4.08	4.29	6.12	-0.9	121	
Nick Wittgren	NWO	AAA	24	1	6	19	51	0	62^{1}	58	6	1.2	9.2	35%	.302	1.06	3.03	3.23	2.55	1.8	72	

Acquired in a deadline deal from the Dodgers, **Victor Araujo** commands a solid fastball-slider tandem that took well to the thick Florida air. He might sneak into the bullpen mix in 2016. ❖ The Marlins continued to develop **Austin Brice** as a starter at Double-A in 2015, but, surprise surprise, poor command and lack of progress on a third pitch will force his move to the bullpen sooner than later. That's okay for a guy capable of hitting 98 and flashing a plus curveball. ❖ Acquired in a deadline deal from the Dodgers, **Jeff Brigham** can touch 99 with wandering command and little feel for the rest of his arsenal. ❖ **Aaron Crow**'s precipitous fall from first-round grace smacked the pavement elbow first in 2015, as he succumbed to Tommy John surgery without throwing a single pitch for his new organization. ❖ **Brian Ellington** is an arm-strength reliever who can pop triple digits with a moving heater but lacks the command or secondary support to pitch at the back of a bullpen. ❖ Acquired in a deadline deal from the Dodgers, **Kevin Guzman** is tall, skinny, throws strikes and was curiously and immediately demoted by the Marlins to the Gulf Coast League. ❖ **Justin Jacome** parlayed a nice summer on the Cape and a solid junior season at UCSB into a fifth-round slot bonus. The polished lefty commands a solid, unspectacular arsenal with some deception from the left side, and should move quickly through the low minors. ❖ Former third-rounder **Michael Mader** can hit 95 with a complementary deuce, but he walked a bunch of guys in his full-season debut while also not striking very many out, and that is the opposite of what pitchers generally try to do. ❖ To watch **Dustin McGowan** pitch is to be absolutely convinced that he has the stuff to be a major-league reliever. To watch him pitch is to also be absolutely unconvinced he'll rein any of it in enough to be effective in any role. ❖ Last year's Triple-A closer **Nick Wittgren** tops out in the low-90s but succeeds with deception and strong command of a three-pitch mix. He'll be neither a closer nor in Triple-A this year, a net profit.

Manager

Don Mattingly

YEAR	TEAM	W	L	Pythag +/-	Avg PC	100+ P	120+ P	QS	BQS	REL	REL w Zero R	IBB	PH	PH Avg	PH HR	SB2	CS2	SB3	CS3	SAC Att	SAC%	POS SAC	Squeeze	Swing	In Play
2013	LAN	92	70	2	95.1	69	2	93	2	504	424	44	208	.209	4	74	22	4	5	113	62.8	32	0	283	93
2014	LAN	94	68	1	95.1	70	1	100	1	496	395	35	235	.231	1	123	46	14	3	82	57.3	15	1	340	104
2015	LAN	92	70	2	91.3	47	2	95	3	515	408	32	269	.215	8	51	26	8	8	69	71.0	15	1	250	76

Mattingly can't seem to escape eccentric owners. He played under George Steinbrenner, managed for Frank McCourt and now he's the latest skipper tasked with keeping Jeffrey Loria satisfied. Good luck.

You can understand why a low-pressure environment like Miami would appeal to Mattingly. He's spent his entire managerial career in Los Angeles, where his every decision was second-guessed and where he never seemed to escape the hot seat. Moving to a less-frenzied market where he can work with younger (and presumably less-entitled) players sounds wonderful by comparison. There's just one problem:Tthe one person with outsized expectations for the Marlins is the team's owner, making Mattingly's locale change the equivalent of hopping out of the frying pan and into the dragon's mouth.

Loria has never liked a manager for more than a few months at a time. Fredi Gonzalez is the only skipper hired under Loria to last three consecutive seasons on the job. Otherwise, the Fish have changed managers at an obsessive rate: Mattingly will be their eighth different Opening Day manager in the past 15 years. Mattingly's four-year deal doesn't ensure his job is secure, either—if anything, it puts more pressure on him to produce immediate results. Remember that Loria canned Ozzie Guillen and Mike Redmond within 13 months of signing them to multi-year deals. The best news for Mattingly, then, is that he's likely to receive checks from the Marlins long after he's been fired.

That reads like a joke, but it's not. Mattingly has his pluses as a manager: He's a calming influence, someone who excels at the person-to-person interactions that make up a lot of the gig. But his biggest negative is that he falters when he's asked to make in-game strategic choices. As a result, Mattingly is unlikely to turn the Marlins into contenders on the strength of his wits and foresight. No big deal, right? Except that makes him an easy target for external and (more likely) internal criticism. Loria might claim to be a huge Donnie Baseball fan today, but Mattingly will be just another scapegoat tomorrow.

MILWAUKEE BREWERS

Essay by Ryan Romano

Player comments by J.P. Breen and BP authors

"It has to be, like, wayyy a ball for us to not swing," said Carlos Gomez, swiping his hand about a foot off the edge of an imaginary plate. "If it's close to the zone and we can drive the ball, we're going to swing. Everybody here has the green light."
–The New York Times, *on the Brewers*

Innovation in baseball is a complicated thing. There are only three ways to get ahead: Luck, which can't be replicated; doing the same thing as everybody else better, which calls to mind that old wisdom that if it were easy everybody would do it; or finding a new way. The disadvantage to the last is that others will undoubtedly notice and copy, which leads to an interesting result: Other facets of the game, the ones that aren't in style, become underappreciated and thus undervalued. And the cycle continues. If one falls far enough behind the curve, one might eventually find oneself ahead of it.

It's a cliché by now to say that *Moneyball* wasn't about any particular tactic—it wasn't about drafting college arms or giving up defense, but about making decisions based on empirical measures. But it's probably fair to say it was also at least sort of about OBP. At least, that's one of the lessons the rest of the league took. In the October issue of the *Journal of Sports Economics*, three economists demonstrated convincingly that the league really was blind to the value of OBP before Michael Lewis' book came out. After the A's "secret" was revealed, the rest of the league quickly "fixed" a market that had been undercompensating players who reached base.

That has made it frustrating for the Milwaukee fan who has watched the Brewers resist this fairly simple revelation. Over the past five years, no NL team has walked less often than the Brewers, and not by accident. It has been their defining characteristic. The *Milwaukee Journal-Sentinel* referred to the club's "swing-first, ask-questions-later approach" as "a source of contention," while the *Times* quoted former manager Ron Roenicke thusly: "If your personnel works out better by being aggressive on the first thing they see, then you go with it."

They went with it. Roenicke is gone now, and so is the general manager who acquired all those personnel who (theoretically) worked out better by being aggressive on

BREWERS PROSPECTUS

2015 W-L: 68-94, 4th in NL Central

Pythag	.446	23rd	DER	.696	25th
RS/G	4.04	22nd	B-Age	28.2	12th
RA/G	4.55	24th	P-Age	28.4	16th
TAv	.251	27th	Salary	$104.2M	20th
BRR	-2.11	18th	M$/MW	$4.7M	7th
TAv-P	0.269	23rd	DL Days	477	1st
FIP	4.20	23rd	$ on DL	4%	2nd

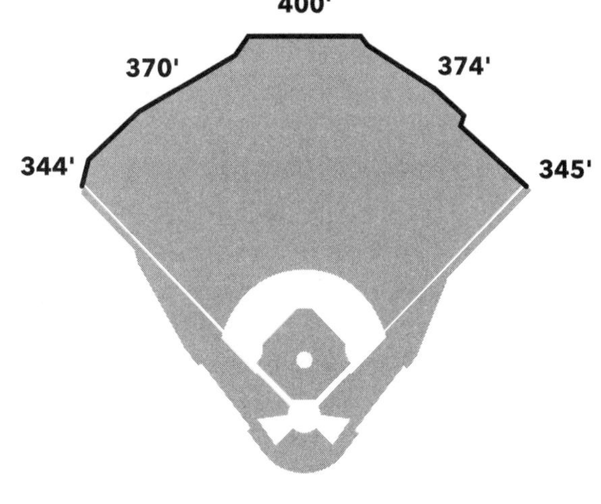

Outfield wall profile: **8'**

Three-Year Park Factors

Runs	Runs/RH	Runs/LH	HR/RH	HR/LH
101	103	113	113	121

Top Hitter WARP	2.4	Ryan Braun
Top Pitcher WARP	2.4	Jimmy Nelson
Top Prospect		Orlando Arcia

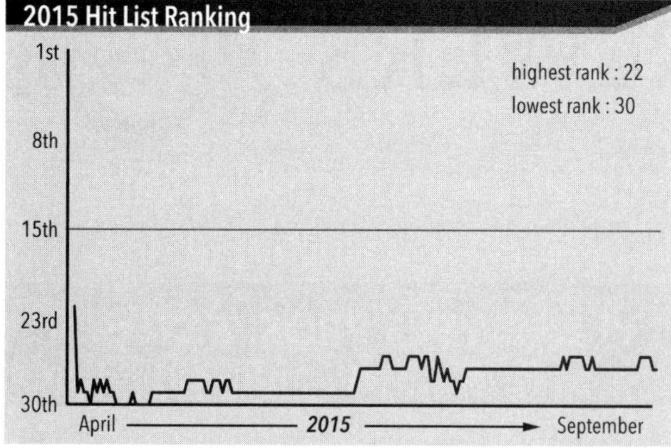

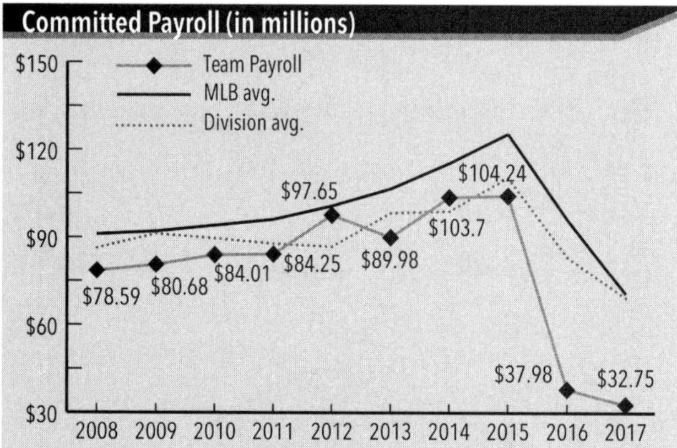

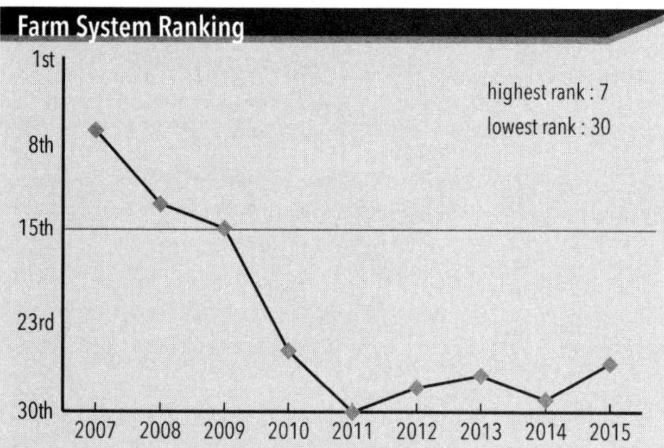

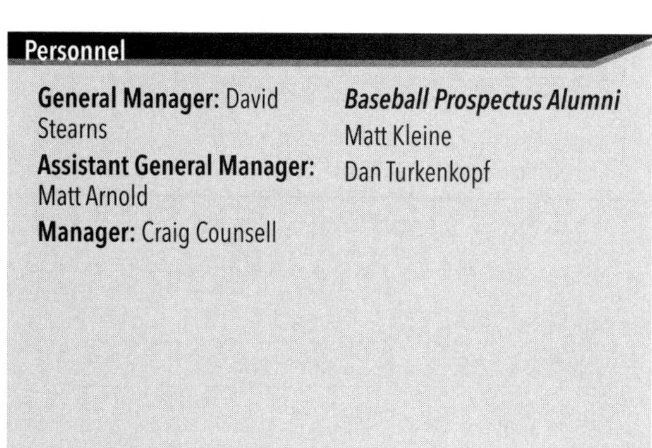
Personnel

General Manager: David Stearns
Assistant General Manager: Matt Arnold
Manager: Craig Counsell

Baseball Prospectus Alumni
Matt Kleine
Dan Turkenkopf

the first thing they saw. As new GM David Stearns takes over for Doug Melvin in the Milwaukee front office—bringing with him analytical bona fides—it's worth asking how much the Brewers' pre-*Moneyball* philosophy really hurt them, if it indeed did at all.

✦✦✦

Walks have always, undeniably been undervalued. For the first century-plus of baseball, statistical analysis focused on the "Triple Crown" metrics: batting average, home runs, and runs batted in, all of which to some degree discouraged the practice of fighting for ball four. Not all baserunners were created equal, and while walks might have been a byproduct of good hitting—fear might lead to a free pass—they weren't the goal. The players who eschewed this reasoning went mostly under the radar.

Take, for example, two seemingly similar players from the days of yore: Washington Senators third baseman Eddie Yost, and Philadelphia Phillies center fielder Richie Ashburn. Both played primarily in the 1950s, each retiring in 1962. They compiled a similar number of plate appearances (9,175 for Yost, 9,736 for Ashburn), and produced similarly in those chances.

- Yost: .394 OBP, .371 SLG, .362 wOBA
- Ashburn: .396 OBP, .382 SLG, .362 wOBA

Why did one man become a star and the other vanish? Yost's offense depended on an astonishing 17.6 percent walk rate, which won him the moniker "The Walking Man." Ashburn also drew plenty of walks, but he used a .308 batting average to produce a similar career OBP. Yost made one All-Star team and never finished higher than 20th in MVP voting; Ashburn made five and finished in the top 20 six times. The prejudice against walks made one a star and the other relatively anonymous.

Similar disparities existed throughout history, and Orioles manager Earl Weaver famously took advantage of the industry's blindspot. Outs, he posited, were incredibly valuable, the most valuable (and finite) resource a team had. He thus prioritized the hitters who made the fewest outs, which is to say, the hitters who reached base the most often. Sometimes, like with Eddie Murray or Al Bumbry, that meant hitters who had a high batting average. More often, however, it entailed a high walk rate. Weaver looked at men such as Don Buford and Bobby Grich, recognized their potential, and plugged them into the lineup, where they posted spectacular on-base percentages and excelled overall. Under Weaver, the Orioles always reached base at a heavy clip despite inconsistent averages.

And, yet, Weaver's revelation took nearly three more decades to catch on, and it took a bestselling book to do so. The '00s saw many teams hoard players who earned walks, in many instances finding the same success that Oakland did. It was common knowledge that, to consistently win games, a club most likely needs to walk.

✦✦✦

This narrative looks nice. A somewhat-minute aspect of the game rises in popularity, slowly but surely, until people finally acknowledge its worth. For Scott Hatteberg and Jeremy Brown's legacy, it'd be nice if the story ended there, but then what we would all make of the Kansas City Royals?

Over the past three years, the Royals have won the fourth-most regular season games in the majors, at 270. They also rank dead last in walk rate over that span. The absence of bases on balls in Kansas City is anything but a new development: Rany Jazayerli, a baseball writer and Royals fan, once quipped that "the people of Kansas City have no concept of what it means to have a lineup that grinds out at-bats—you might as well ask them if they want to go to the beach after the ballgame."

Putting as many men on base as possible, in whatever manner available, obviously helps an offense. However, it's important to not overstate the impact. Since 1900, on-base percentage accounts for about one-fifth of the variability of a club's record. Which isn't to say that walks make no difference, but that other areas of performance count, as well. Baserunning Runs (BsR) accounts for about 18.8 percent of team winning percentage since 1900, while defense (as measured primarily by Total Zone runs) has been responsible for about 24 percent. These all fluctuate from season to season, but the effects have been fairly consistent throughout a century-plus of baseball.

So let's return to our emblematic player comparison. Did Yost receive too little credit—and Ashburn, too much—for his offensive performance? Certainly; the biases of the day are no longer any secret. But Yost was also *awful* in other, non-hitting aspects of the game: He cost his teams eight runs with his baserunning (according to BsR), and 113 runs with his glove (according to TZ). Ashburn, on the other hand, was worth 16 runs on the bases and 59 runs in the field over the course of his career. By Baseball Prospectus' measure of total value, this all made Yost a very good ballplayer (45 career WARP) and Richie Ashburn a Hall of Famer (69 WARP). This is probably a pretty obvious point, but it's meant to be: There are tons of ways to be good at baseball. Getting hung up on just one of them is the best way to be bad at baseball analysis.

It's the same with Weaver's Orioles: Walks were only one of the ways he innovated, and walks were only one of the ways his team outclassed the rest of the league. He treasured outs in every way, building good defenses to collect more of them and drilling good baserunning to preserve his own.

And Beane's A's, famous in the *Moneyball* years for punting defense and speed, somewhat less famously embraced those skills by the mid-00s. (They still draw tons of walks.)

Which brings us back to the Brewers, the subject of this overly circuitous essay. Currently, they resemble the champion Royals in two key ways: They don't spend very much, with the 18th-highest player expenditure since 2013; and they don't walk very often. Kansas City has demonstrated that this doesn't necessarily beget failure. They catch the baseball and they take extra bases without giving away outs. And here, at last, is where we get to the reason that the beleaguered Brewers fan is so beleaguered: It isn't that the Brewers have been bad at drawing walks, but that they've been bad at everything.

- Baserunning: 12th in the NL in 2015
- Defensive Efficiency: 12th in the NL in 2015
- ERA: 11th in the NL in 2015
- Isolated Power: Ninth in the NL in 2015
- Batting Average: Seventh in the NL in 2015
- And, yes, Walks: 12th in the NL in 2015

There's the cruel twist for the Brewers fan. Milwaukee hung on to its principles long enough to see those principles come back into vogue. It's not just the Royals, with their first-pitch swinging and Esky Magic. The near-dynastic Giants have drawn, over the past five years, only 95 more walks than Milwaukee, the 12th most in the NL. The Rays, as documented elsewhere in this book, reversed their longtime strategy of working counts and exhausting pitchers, and now swing early and often. Even the Astros—the SABR-orthodox Astros, from whom the Brewers plucked David Stearns—offered at more first pitches this year than any team in baseball. When Stearns' Astros went looking for an impact player at the trade deadline, they chose Carlos "If it's close to the zone we're going to swing" Gomez. Hack is back, baby. The Brewers are at the cool kid's table once again.

And that's why GM Doug Melvin deserved so much blame for the Brewers' struggles, and why he was fired: Not the walks—obsess as many fans did over that narrow sliver of the team's performance—but the whole package. In 10 years, when you ask a tuned-in Brewers fan what went wrong during the late Melvin era, he or she will undoubtedly mention the Brewers' approach. But lack of innovation in baseball is a complicated thing. ■

—Ryan Romano is a baseball writer for BP Milwaukee, Beyond the Box Score, and Camden Depot, and a journalism student at the University of Maryland.

HITTERS

Orlando Arcia SS

Born: 8/4/94 Age: 21 Bats: R Throws: R Height: 6'0" Weight: 165

YEAR	TEAM	LVL	AGE	PA	R	2B	3B	HR	RBI	BB	K	SB	CS	AVG/OBP/SLG	TAv	BABIP	BRR	FRAA	WARP
2013	WIS	A	18	486	67	14	5	4	39	35	40	20	9	.251/.314/.333	.241	.268	1.8	SS(120): 10.9	2.4
2014	BRV	A+	19	546	65	29	5	4	50	42	65	31	11	.289/.346/.392	.263	.326	4.3	SS(90): 7.3, 2B(36): -0.0	3.5
2015	BLX	AA	20	552	74	37	7	8	69	30	73	25	8	.307/.347/.453	.294	.343	1.3	SS(123): 15.7, 2B(3): 0.2	6.2
2016	*MIL*	*MLB*	*21*	*69*	*8*	*3*	*0*	*1*	*6*	*3*	*12*	*2*	*1*	*.254/.286/.381*	*.232*	*.292*	*0.1*	*2B 1*	*0.1*
2017	*MIL*	*MLB*	*22*	*387*	*42*	*20*	*3*	*8*	*42*	*18*	*66*	*12*	*4*	*.267/.303/.406*	*.255*	*.303*	*1.3*	*2B 3*	*1.7*

Breakout: 8% Improve: 19% Collapse: 1% Attrition: 13% MLB: 22% *Comparables: Carlos Sanchez, Jorge Polanco, Joe Panik*

Intangibles matter. Arcia's performance at the plate belies his years, but it's his mannerisms that stand out. He was the eighth-youngest player in Double-A but kept a healthy amount of swagger, aware that he belongs at the highest level of competition. He has good rapport with his teammates and reportedly keeps the clubhouse loose with a big personality. Pair that positive makeup with a potentially above-average bat at a premium position, and you've got an elite prospect. The Brewers haven't produced a young talent like this since Braun and Fielder.

Ryan Braun RF

Born: 11/17/83 Age: 32 Bats: R Throws: R Height: 6'2" Weight: 205

YEAR	TEAM	LVL	AGE	PA	R	2B	3B	HR	RBI	BB	K	SB	CS	AVG/OBP/SLG	TAv	BABIP	BRR	FRAA	WARP
2013	MIL	MLB	29	253	30	14	2	9	38	27	56	4	5	.298/.372/.498	.300	.360	1.8	LF(59): 4.7	2.3
2014	MIL	MLB	30	580	68	30	6	19	81	41	113	11	5	.266/.324/.453	.278	.304	-3.1	RF(134): 2.9, CF(1): -0.0	2.1
2015	MIL	MLB	31	568	87	27	3	25	84	54	115	24	4	.285/.356/.498	.298	.322	3.5	RF(130): -11.5	2.4
2016	*MIL*	*MLB*	*32*	*574*	*81*	*29*	*3*	*26*	*85*	*49*	*110*	*18*	*5*	*.288/.354/.509*	*.298*	*.320*	*0.9*	*RF -4*	*3.4*
2017	*MIL*	*MLB*	*33*	*516*	*72*	*26*	*3*	*22*	*75*	*44*	*102*	*15*	*5*	*.283/.349/.496*	*.301*	*.317*	*1.2*	*RF -4*	*3.0*

Breakout: 0% Improve: 26% Collapse: 2% Attrition: 6% MLB: 99% *Comparables: Hank Aaron, Frank Robinson, Matt Holliday*

The stigma of performance-enhancing drugs will dog Braun for years, even after his playing days have ended, but his return to form on offense should dampen the criticism a bit. Still, that doesn't mean that he'll enter 2016 without question marks. Instead of concerns about his post-PED performance, the uncertainy will stem from his health. Beyond the nerve issues in his hand that require regular treatment, he played through a back injury that necessitated a surgical procedure after the season. It's not ideal timing, given that his five-year, $105 million contract extension is just now kicking in. The deal puzzled many when it was announced five years ago, and given his recent issues, it surely evokes a severe case of heartburn for ownership and the new front office. Braun remains a talented hitter who can anchor a lineup. Unfortunately, this just feels like it's gonna mirror the latter half of Carlos Beltran's career: flashes of immense talent interrupted by sporadic, frustrating stints on the disabled list.

Keon Broxton OF

Born: 5/7/90 Age: 26 Bats: R Throws: R Height: 6'3" Weight: 195

YEAR	TEAM	LVL	AGE	PA	R	2B	3B	HR	RBI	BB	K	SB	CS	AVG/OBP/SLG	TAv	BABIP	BRR	FRAA	WARP
2013	MOB	AA	23	372	40	13	3	8	41	30	116	5	1	.231/.296/.359	.239	.325	1.8	CF(48): 0.7, RF(35): -0.2	0.2
2014	ALT	AA	24	471	67	22	9	15	52	59	122	25	6	.275/.369/.484	.299	.357	4.4	CF(80): 1.3, LF(43): 4.0	4.4
2015	IND	AAA	25	367	51	15	8	7	42	47	105	28	9	.256/.352/.423	.275	.356	0.1	LF(46): 3.6, CF(31): -2.9	1.8
2015	ALT	AA	25	204	35	12	4	3	26	19	51	11	6	.302/.365/.464	.292	.395	3.5	CF(43): 4.5, RF(1): -0.3	2.2
2015	PIT	MLB	25	2	3	0	0	0	0	0	1	1	1	.000/.000/.000	.001	.000	0.1	RF(1): -0.0, CF(1): -0.0	0.0
2016	*MIL*	*MLB*	*26*	*145*	*18*	*6*	*2*	*4*	*16*	*13*	*47*	*6*	*2*	*.230/.303/.395*	*.243*	*.319*	*0.6*	*CF 1, RF -0*	*0.3*
2017	*MIL*	*MLB*	*27*	*279*	*33*	*11*	*3*	*8*	*33*	*25*	*90*	*11*	*4*	*.232/.305/.402*	*.252*	*.323*	*1.5*	*CF 1, RF -1*	*0.7*

Breakout: 14% Improve: 25% Collapse: 12% Attrition: 34% MLB: 48% *Comparables: Melky Mesa, Justin Maxwell, Ben Johnson*

Acquired from Pittsburgh for Jason Rogers, the athletic Broxton demonstrates speed, power, and defense at all three outfield positions. He's also helpless against any pitch with movement; during his cold streaks, that includes the movement forward toward the plate. Broxton's strikeout rate was the highest on the team, and one of the most severe in the International League. As a reserve outfielder and pinch hitter, he'll provide the unconstrained possibilities of the human spirit, as well as the profound limitations of the human flesh.

Garin Cecchini 3B

Born: 4/20/91 Age: 25 Bats: L Throws: R Height: 6'3" Weight: 220

YEAR	TEAM	LVL	AGE	PA	R	2B	3B	HR	RBI	BB	K	SB	CS	AVG/OBP/SLG	TAv	BABIP	BRR	FRAA	WARP
2013	SLM	A+	22	262	44	19	4	5	33	43	34	15	7	.350/.469/.547	.349	.400	2.2	3B(59): -7.6	2.9
2013	PME	AA	22	295	36	14	3	2	28	51	52	8	2	.296/.420/.404	.312	.367	0.6	3B(44): 6.3	3.2
2014	BOS	MLB	23	36	6	3	0	1	4	3	11	0	0	.258/.361/.452	.311	.368	-0.5	3B(9): 0.6	0.3
2014	PAW	AAA	23	458	52	21	1	7	57	44	99	11	1	.263/.341/.371	.256	.331	2.0	3B(84): -5.2, LF(26): -1.0	0.7
2015	BOS	MLB	24	4	0	0	0	0	0	0	3	0	0	.000/.000/.000	.042	.000	0.0	1B(1): 0.9	0.0
2015	PAW	AAA	24	469	34	14	0	7	28	40	100	9	0	.213/.286/.296	.216	.262	0.2	LF(65): -4.1, 1B(23): -2.8	-2.0
2016	*MIL*	*MLB*	*25*	*227*	*24*	*10*	*1*	*5*	*24*	*22*	*53*	*3*	*1*	*.246/.325/.374*	*.249*	*.306*	*0.2*	*1B -1, 3B -1*	*0.1*
2017	*MIL*	*MLB*	*26*	*407*	*46*	*18*	*2*	*8*	*41*	*38*	*96*	*6*	*1*	*.244/.321/.369*	*.254*	*.308*	*0.3*	*3B -2*	*0.4*

Breakout: 8% Improve: 20% Collapse: 13% Attrition: 31% MLB: 42% *Comparables: Shane Peterson, Cole Gillespie, Jaff Decker*

It was never supposed to be the bat. Scouts have long had questions about Cecchini's defensive home, power and the pronunciation of his last name, but the bat was safe. His career OBP was north of .400 heading into 2014, and his penchant for getting on base made it easy to overlook his lack of pop and strange profile. Unfortunately, he left his on-base ability in Portland; the former top prospect has hit just .238/.314/.333 in more than 900 PA in Pawtucket, and was especially bad last season. Cecchini has added some versatility to his defensive game, but deck chairs, Titanic, etc. He wouldn't be the first 25-year-old to turn it around in Triple-A, nor would he be the first to stall out at that level. We may never know what undid him as a prospect, but at least we'll be able to eliminate "scenery" as one of the variables as the 2016 season progresses.

Trent Clark OF

Born: 11/1/96 Age: 19 Bats: L Throws: L Height: 6'0" Weight: 205

YEAR	TEAM	LVL	AGE	PA	R	2B	3B	HR	RBI	BB	K	SB	CS	AVG/OBP/SLG	TAv	BABIP	BRR	FRAA	WARP
2016	*MIL*	*MLB*	*19*	*250*	*26*	*8*	*1*	*4*	*20*	*20*	*73*	*8*	*3*	*.197/.266/.300*	*.202*	*.265*	*0.3*	*CF -2, LF 0*	*-0.8*
2017	*MIL*	*MLB*	*20*	*351*	*36*	*12*	*2*	*7*	*33*	*29*	*98*	*11*	*5*	*.208/.277/.325*	*.221*	*.273*	*1.2*	*-*	*-0.2*

Breakout: 0% Improve: 0% Collapse: 0% Attrition: 0% MLB: 0% *Comparables: Aaron Hicks, Andrew McCutchen, Dalton Pompey*

After drafting Clark 15th overall, scouting director Ray Montgomery called him a "prodigal hitter." The comment referred to more than his impressive hit tool. He utilizes an awkward grip, somewhat like a golfer's grip, but his control of the barrel and his ability to square up the baseball makes scouts quickly forget about the mechanical optics. Clark is more than a free-swinger, however, and his ability to command the zone makes him one of the system's safest hitting prospects. If he proves able to handle center field, he's an elite prospect. If he ultimately needs to move to a corner spot, his power will have to develop more to be able to carry the position. One scout suggested that Clark has a little bit of Michael Brantley in him. Coincidentally, the organization has lacked a prospect with true plus-hit potential since Brantley went to Cleveland as the PTBNL in the CC Sabathia deal.

Khris Davis LF

Born: 12/21/87 Age: 28 Bats: R Throws: R Height: 5'10" Weight: 195

YEAR	TEAM	LVL	AGE	PA	R	2B	3B	HR	RBI	BB	K	SB	CS	AVG/OBP/SLG	TAv	BABIP	BRR	FRAA	WARP
2013	MIL	MLB	25	153	27	10	0	11	27	11	34	3	0	.279/.353/.596	.322	.293	1.2	LF(34): -2.3	1.2
2013	NAS	AAA	25	281	35	12	1	13	37	31	59	6	4	.255/.349/.473	.295	.283	-1.3	LF(55): 2.1, RF(10): 0.4	1.8
2014	MIL	MLB	26	549	70	37	2	22	69	32	122	4	1	.244/.299/.457	.281	.275	-0.6	LF(134): 3.3	2.7
2015	MIL	MLB	27	440	54	16	2	27	66	44	122	6	2	.247/.323/.505	.286	.285	-1.3	LF(108): -5.2	1.5
2015	WIS	A	27	24	1	0	0	0	2	3	2	0	1	.100/.208/.100	.152	.105	0.0	LF(3): -0.0	-0.2
2016	*MIL*	*MLB*	*28*	*563*	*74*	*28*	*2*	*29*	*85*	*45*	*135*	*7*	*2*	*.249/.316/.480*	*.276*	*.280*	*-0.7*	*LF 3*	*3.0*
2017	*MIL*	*MLB*	*29*	*518*	*70*	*24*	*1*	*25*	*75*	*41*	*122*	*5*	*2*	*.243/.310/.461*	*.276*	*.273*	*-0.6*	*LF 3*	*2.5*

Breakout: 1% Improve: 50% Collapse: 7% Attrition: 8% MLB: 98% *Comparables: Chris Duncan, Alex Gordon, Carlos Gonzalez*

For Davis, the 2015 campaign went from a lost season to one that shattered conceptions. He meandered through the first two months of the year, only to injure his knee and land on the disabled list. Milwaukee firmly transitioned to rebuilding mode in his absence, and conversation hovered around whether the Brewers needed a platoon left fielder with questionable defensive skills. Upon returning from injury, Davis submitted his opinion on the subject. He launched 21 homers in the second half—good for seventh in the majors—and did almost all his damage against right-handed pitching. Those monstrous two months flipped the script entirely. Rather than being known as a fringe player without a defensive home, he has now flashed an ability to rank among the top 25 or so power hitters in the game.

David Denson 1B

Born: 1/17/95 Age: 21 Bats: L Throws: R Height: 6'3" Weight: 254

YEAR	TEAM	LVL	AGE	PA	R	2B	3B	HR	RBI	BB	K	SB	CS	AVG/OBP/SLG	TAv	BABIP	BRR	FRAA	WARP
2014	WIS	A	19	269	37	10	1	4	29	43	80	3	3	.243/.364/.350	.272	.359	0.6	1B(66): -1.0	0.6
2015	WIS	A	20	151	18	7	1	3	16	17	49	1	1	.226/.311/.361	.247	.329	1.2	1B(28): -1.0, LF(5): -0.5	-0.1
2016	*MIL*	*MLB*	*21*	*250*	*22*	*8*	*1*	*5*	*24*	*25*	*88*	*0*	*0*	*.190/.272/.305*	*.208*	*.279*	*-0.4*	*1B -1, LF -0*	*-1.0*
2017	*MIL*	*MLB*	*22*	*368*	*40*	*14*	*1*	*9*	*36*	*38*	*126*	*0*	*0*	*.200/.285/.329*	*.227*	*.291*	*-0.9*	*1B -1*	*-0.8*

Breakout: 0% Improve: 0% Collapse: 0% Attrition: 0% MLB: 0% *Comparables: Max Stassi, Thomas Neal, Russ Canzler*

On August 15th, Denson made history by being the first active organized-baseball player to come out as gay. He's obviously not the first gay baseball player and almost certainly not the only active one, either. However, it was still a positive moment for the sport, and one the Brewers handled with empathy and grace—exactly as any team should. This will hopefully embolden other players to take the same steps, if desired.

Denson chronicled his depression, anxiety and self-doubt, all of which impacted the 20-year-old's performance on the diamond. He only hit .224/.337/.435 after the announcement, though, which knots up the attractive narrative that we'd all like to weave. One assumes that the real litmus test will be 2016, his third season with Low-A Wisconsin. He possesses the power/patience potential that teams covet at first base, yet still strikes out almost 30 percent of the time. He's also terrible against lefties, hitting just .165/.275/.241 against them. Denson represents a momentous victory for baseball, and his courageous announcement was surely a huge personal weight off his shoulders. Here's hoping his on-field production makes the story perfect in 2016.

Josh Fellhauer OF

Born: 3/24/88 Age: 28 Bats: L Throws: L Height: 5'11" Weight: 175

YEAR	TEAM	LVL	AGE	PA	R	2B	3B	HR	RBI	BB	K	SB	CS	AVG/OBP/SLG	TAv	BABIP	BRR	FRAA	WARP
2013	PEN	AA	25	26	2	3	0	0	2	1	6	0	0	.250/.308/.375	.236	.333	0.5	LF(6): -0.6, CF(1): -0.1	0.0
2013	LOU	AAA	25	289	33	10	0	4	26	35	58	3	2	.268/.359/.358	.265	.330	-0.5	RF(43): 3.3, LF(21): -1.5	0.8
2014	LOU	AAA	26	29	4	3	0	0	4	2	7	0	0	.222/.276/.333	.205	.300	-0.2	LF(5): -1.1, RF(2): 0.0	-0.3
2014	HUN	AA	26	147	12	9	2	0	9	16	32	1	1	.289/.366/.391	.283	.381	-2.4	CF(22): 3.7, LF(14): 3.2	1.1
2014	PEN	AA	26	126	12	3	2	0	10	18	28	1	1	.243/.352/.308	.256	.329	-0.6	CF(21): 2.5, LF(6): -0.6	0.4
2015	BLX	AA	27	236	20	8	0	2	25	28	43	8	2	.240/.342/.310	.266	.293	0.7	RF(29): 2.0, LF(27): 2.0	1.1
2016	*MIL*	*MLB*	*28*	*250*	*27*	*10*	*1*	*4*	*20*	*23*	*62*	*2*	*1*	*.232/.309/.336*	*.229*	*.301*	*-0.2*	*RF -1, LF -2*	*-0.5*
2017	*MIL*	*MLB*	*29*	*222*	*24*	*9*	*1*	*3*	*20*	*21*	*55*	*2*	*1*	*.232/.309/.335*	*.236*	*.300*	*-0.2*	*RF -1, LF -2*	*-0.4*

Breakout: 1% Improve: 2% Collapse: 7% Attrition: 9% MLB: 10% *Comparables: Reid Gorecki, Luke Allen, Colin Curtis*

Few 27-year-olds who hit like Fellhauer did in Double-A make sporting headlines without being arrested. Last year was an exception. Fellhauer had been through a turbulent year, losing his mother to cancer. An *ESPN The Magazine* article that chronicled the Biloxi Shuckers' mammoth 54-game road trip to begin the 2015 season showed how Fellhauer went from feeling broken and lost to finding a family in his fellow Shucker teammates. Minor-league journeymen are key cogs in the baseball machine, something that isn't truly appreciated outside the clubhouse. Fellhauer led the Biloxi Shuckers to a Southern League division title, no matter what his slash line said. He shaped the team through his passion and his pain, and his teammates rallied around him. These types of stories deserve to be heard, too, as guys like him epitomize the soul of baseball.

Jake Gatewood SS

Born: 9/25/95 Age: 20 Bats: R Throws: R Height: 6'5" Weight: 190

YEAR	TEAM	LVL	AGE	PA	R	2B	3B	HR	RBI	BB	K	SB	CS	AVG/OBP/SLG	TAv	BABIP	BRR	FRAA	WARP
2015	WIS	A	19	193	16	5	1	4	16	14	65	5	0	.209/.275/.316	.226	.306	-0.8	SS(52): -4.0	-0.4
2016	*MIL*	*MLB*	*20*	*250*	*24*	*8*	*1*	*6*	*21*	*12*	*93*	*1*	*0*	*.187/.230/.304*	*.188*	*.275*	*-0.2*	*SS -2*	*-1.0*
2017	*MIL*	*MLB*	*21*	*327*	*32*	*11*	*1*	*8*	*31*	*16*	*116*	*1*	*0*	*.195/.239/.316*	*.203*	*.280*	*-0.4*	*SS -3*	*-0.9*

Breakout: 0% Improve: 0% Collapse: 0% Attrition: 1% MLB: 1% *Comparables: Jonathan Villar, Reid Brignac, Yamaico Navarro*

The majority opinion on Gatewood has been that he'll never develop the hit tool necessary to succeed at the higher levels. He was duly exposed when the organization bequeathed upon him a controversial promotion to Low-A Wisconsin. After he hovered near the Mendoza Line for the first couple months, the Brewers recanted and sent him to Rookie ball, where he came alive. He hit .274/.331/.476 with 23 doubles in just 54 games. Moreover, his strikeout rate dropped below 30 percent. Believing Gatewood had turned a corner in his professional journey, the club promoted him back to Low-A and watched him relapse. In two painful weeks, he hit .170/.250/.362 with 16 strikeouts in 52 plate appearances. It's overly rash to consider his struggles in A-ball to be career-defining, as very few 19-year-olds dominate the level, but it does suggest that we should pump the brakes on the bandwagon. Ultimately, his season is a baseball Rorschach test. If you didn't believe in him prior to 2015, you'll look at the skill set and see a butterfly. If not, you'll look at the results and see a skull.

Scooter Gennett 2B

Born: 5/1/90 Age: 26 Bats: L Throws: R Height: 5'10" Weight: 185

YEAR	TEAM	LVL	AGE	PA	R	2B	3B	HR	RBI	BB	K	SB	CS	AVG/OBP/SLG	TAv	BABIP	BRR	FRAA	WARP
2013	NAS	AAA	23	350	44	10	5	3	22	21	59	10	5	.280/.327/.371	.264	.333	-1.4	2B(77): 10.1	2.0
2013	MIL	MLB	23	230	29	11	2	6	21	10	42	2	1	.324/.356/.479	.308	.380	2.2	2B(59): -1.9	1.8
2014	MIL	MLB	24	474	55	31	3	9	54	22	67	6	3	.289/.320/.434	.269	.321	-1.1	2B(119): -11.1, RF(1): -0.0	0.4
2015	MIL	MLB	25	391	42	18	4	6	29	12	68	1	3	.264/.294/.381	.233	.309	1.1	2B(108): -2.9	-0.2
2015	CSP	AAA	25	79	12	7	1	2	11	4	10	0	1	.307/.342/.507	.275	.333	-0.7	2B(17): -0.2	0.3
2016	*MIL*	*MLB*	*26*	*496*	*50*	*26*	*4*	*11*	*57*	*22*	*82*	*5*	*3*	*.279/.313/.422*	*.252*	*.313*	*0.7*	*2B -6*	*1.0*
2017	*MIL*	*MLB*	*27*	*460*	*51*	*23*	*3*	*11*	*52*	*20*	*77*	*4*	*3*	*.274/.309/.417*	*.258*	*.307*	*0.8*	*2B -5*	*1.1*

Breakout: 6% Improve: 53% Collapse: 6% Attrition: 20% MLB: 96% *Comparables: Josh Barfield, Ronny Cedeno, Howie Kendrick*

They say second basemen are born of deficiency. Not enough range for shortstop. Not enough arm for third base. Not enough bat to carry a corner profile. In this sense, Gennett is really a second baseman. Not only is he incapable of playing shortstop, but he's questionable defensively even at second base. This puts significant pressure on his bat to carry him, which isn't possible because the 26-year-old is an instant out against lefties (career .297 OPS). As such, his value wholly depends on his offensive production on those days he gets to face right-handed pitchers. Even in those situations, he was a below-average hitter last season. Unsurprisingly, that leaves Gennett as being below replacement level, nothing but a shaky platoon option on a non-contending club.

Monte Harrison RF

Born: 8/10/95 Age: 20 Bats: R Throws: R Height: 6'3" Weight: 220

YEAR	TEAM	LVL	AGE	PA	R	2B	3B	HR	RBI	BB	K	SB	CS	AVG/OBP/SLG	TAv	BABIP	BRR	FRAA	WARP
2015	WIS	A	19	184	18	6	2	2	11	14	77	6	4	.148/.246/.247	.184	.265	1.0	CF(42): -5.7, RF(4): 0.0	-1.5
2016	*MIL*	*MLB*	*20*	*250*	*26*	*7*	*1*	*5*	*18*	*14*	*100*	*5*	*3*	*.169/.231/.270*	*.179*	*.268*	*0.0*	*CF -1, RF 0*	*-1.4*
2017	*MIL*	*MLB*	*21*	*347*	*34*	*11*	*2*	*7*	*31*	*21*	*137*	*8*	*5*	*.184/.250/.299*	*.202*	*.291*	*0.5*	*CF -1, RF 0*	*-1.1*

Breakout: 0% Improve: 0% Collapse: 0% Attrition: 0% MLB: 0% *Comparables: Michael Saunders, Keon Broxton, Trayce Thompson*

Raw, athletic prospects often arrest our attention in Rookie ball, and Harrison, a former football star, is no exception. It's hard not to daydream about what he could be, especially after he posted a .402 OBP and stole 32 bases in just 224 plate appearances. The Brewers pushed him, promoting him to full-season ball at just 19 years old, and it backfired. He struck out twice every five times up, hit so rarely it became kind of novel and quickly found himself back in Helena. To his credit, the young man turned it around in the Pioneer League, showing some sneaky power before ending his season with a gruesome broken ankle. Of course, it's about the long view with Harrison. He's beyond raw, still learning how to play baseball instead of just out-athleting the competition. The swing is a work in progress, and he must utilize his lower half better while also developing some pitch recognition. The tools exist for a power-speed guy who can handle center field, and the makeup is positive. Those profiles are rare. We're just realistically two presidential elections away from seeing it realized in any meaningful way.

Gilbert Lara SS

Born: 10/30/97 Age: 18 Bats: R Throws: R Height: 6'2" Weight: 190

YEAR	TEAM	LVL	AGE	PA	R	2B	3B	HR	RBI	BB	K	SB	CS	AVG/OBP/SLG	TAv	BABIP	BRR	FRAA	WARP
2015	BRR	Rk	17	214	29	4	5	1	25	9	41	3	3	.248/.285/.332	.244	.304	2.6	SS(50): 8.3	1.6
2015	HEL	Rk	17	49	2	3	0	0	5	5	12	0	0	.205/.286/.273	.189	.281	-0.3	SS(12): 1.9	0.0
2016	*MIL*	*MLB*	*18*	*250*	*18*	*8*	*1*	*4*	*21*	*9*	*77*	*0*	*0*	*.192/.224/.285*	*.178*	*.261*	*-0.3*	*SS 3*	*-0.7*
2017	*MIL*	*MLB*	*19*	*320*	*27*	*10*	*1*	*4*	*26*	*10*	*94*	*0*	*0*	*.195/.222/.280*	*.184*	*.260*	*-0.5*	*-*	*-1.2*

Breakout: 0% Improve: 0% Collapse: 0% Attrition: 0% MLB: 0% *Comparables: Jose Peraza, Eduardo Escobar, Wilfredo Tovar*

Lara isn't just one of the most exciting prospects in baseball; he also represents a re-commitment to the international market in Milwaukee. The Brewers went from not having a Latin American training complex in 2011 to suddenly spending $3.2 million on Lara in 2014. It's not an isolated incident, either, as Milwaukee has made sincere bids on Jose Abreu, Yoan Moncada, and Byung-Ho Park in the past two years. With Lara, at least, the strategy seems to be paying off. He started off hitting over .400 with three triples in his first 12 professional games, and although he tired and struggled mightily down the stretch, he flashed loud tools as a 17-year-old playing professionally in the United States. The raw power is huge, the hitting aptitude is present, and there isn't as much swing-and-miss as one would expect. It's now a question of growth, consistency, and recognizing spin. He's ages away and the finished product is abstract, but if you're searching for a potential perennial All-Star in the Brewers' system, Lara is near the top of the list.

Jonathan Lucroy C

Born: 6/13/86 Age: 30 Bats: R Throws: R Height: 6'0" Weight: 195

YEAR	TEAM	LVL	AGE	PA	R	2B	3B	HR	RBI	BB	K	SB	CS	AVG/OBP/SLG	TAv	BABIP	BRR	FRAA	WARP
2013	MIL	MLB	27	580	59	25	6	18	82	46	69	9	1	.280/.340/.455	.274	.290	-7.6	C(126): 29.0, 1B(14): 0.1	5.7
2014	MIL	MLB	28	655	73	53	2	13	69	66	71	4	4	.301/.373/.465	.305	.324	2.1	C(136): 16.7, 1B(19): 0.2	7.9
2015	MIL	MLB	29	415	51	20	3	7	43	36	64	1	0	.264/.326/.391	.254	.297	-2.4	C(86): 1.0, 1B(7): 0.1	1.4
2016	*MIL*	*MLB*	*30*	*587*	*65*	*31*	*3*	*15*	*71*	*48*	*84*	*4*	*2*	*.279/.339/.436*	*.270*	*.303*	*-2.5*	*C 14, 1B -1*	*4.1*
2017	*MIL*	*MLB*	*31*	*514*	*62*	*26*	*2*	*13*	*59*	*39*	*77*	*3*	*1*	*.272/.330/.420*	*.271*	*.298*	*-2.3*	*C 10, 1B 0*	*3.2*

Breakout: 1% Improve: 41% Collapse: 6% Attrition: 6% MLB: 97% *Comparables: Victor Martinez, Ted Simmons, Yadier Molina*

YEAR	TEAM	P. COUNT	FRM RUNS	BLK RUNS	THRW RUNS	TOT RUNS
2013	MIL	17427	31.6	1.3	-0.9	31.9
2014	MIL	18951	16.4	1.7	-1.3	16.8
2015	MIL	12038	1.2	0.1	-0.1	1.2
2016	*MIL*	*14956*	*14.5*	*0.9*	*-0.5*	*14.9*
2017	*MIL*	*13091*	*9.0*	*0.5*	*-0.4*	*9.2*

Last season proved to be a disappointing performance from Lucroy, previously one of the NL's best players. It was George Clooney's *Tomorrowland*, or *Battlefield Earth* showing up on Forrest Whitaker's resume. Lucroy hit under .280 for the first time since 2011, saw his ISO drop almost 40 points and his framing numbers dramatically declined. Myriad injuries—a hamstring, a broken toe and a concussion—surely affected his performance; however, he also began hinting at his discontent in Milwaukee. He revealed that the Brewers resisted his overtures for a long-term contract extension (on top of his current one) and gave multiple radio interviews in which he indicated that he'd be happier playing baseball elsewhere if the club couldn't compete in the immediate future. Which, realistically, it probably can't, with or without him.

Will Middlebrooks 3B

Born: 9/9/88 Age: 27 Bats: R Throws: R Height: 6'3" Weight: 220

YEAR	TEAM	LVL	AGE	PA	R	2B	3B	HR	RBI	BB	K	SB	CS	AVG/OBP/SLG	TAv	BABIP	BRR	FRAA	WARP
2013	BOS	MLB	24	374	41	18	0	17	49	20	98	3	1	.227/.271/.425	.240	.263	1.5	3B(92): 1.9, 2B(2): 0.0	0.8
2013	PAW	AAA	24	196	25	5	0	10	35	16	38	1	0	.268/.327/.464	.272	.288	-0.2	3B(40): 3.6	1.2
2014	BOS	MLB	25	234	14	10	0	2	19	15	70	1	1	.191/.256/.265	.188	.273	-0.2	3B(62): -1.5, 1B(1): -0.0	-1.2
2014	PAW	AAA	25	112	13	1	1	4	8	6	30	0	0	.231/.277/.375	.218	.282	0.8	3B(17): 0.4	-0.1
2015	SDN	MLB	26	270	23	7	2	9	29	11	60	2	1	.212/.241/.361	.221	.237	0.1	3B(69): -2.8, SS(8): 0.9	-0.4
2015	ELP	AAA	26	164	13	5	1	4	19	8	35	1	2	.255/.287/.379	.227	.299	-1.0	3B(33): -2.9, 1B(4): 0.4	-0.4
2016	*MIL*	*MLB*	*27*	*458*	*52*	*17*	*1*	*19*	*62*	*25*	*113*	*3*	*2*	*.240/.284/.424*	*.243*	*.277*	*0.4*	*3B -2*	*0.3*
2017	*MIL*	*MLB*	*28*	*391*	*48*	*15*	*1*	*16*	*51*	*22*	*96*	*2*	*1*	*.237/.283/.416*	*.249*	*.276*	*0.3*	*3B -2*	*0.3*

Breakout: 6% Improve: 41% Collapse: 7% Attrition: 11% MLB: 90% *Comparables: Chris Johnson, Chase Headley, Jorge Cantu*

In spring training, Middlebrooks' former teammate Cody Ross told Padres.com that the young third baseman acquired from Boston in December 2014 had "good strike zone awareness." This is like Steven Seagal declaring that an actor has "good emotional range." Despite Ross' vote of confidence, the former phenom followed his track record, swinging at everything and hitting little. A trip to the more forgiving PCL produced similarly dismal results. Middlebrooks, who played a handful of games at shortstop for the desperate

Padres before his demotion, would need to reach base 42 straight times to raise his career OBP to .300. Failing that, he can hope for a sequel to *Into the Sun*, which coincidentally is where his career is headed.

Demi Orimoloye OF

Born: 1/6/97 Age: 19 Bats: R Throws: R Height: 6'4" Weight: 225

YEAR	TEAM	LVL	AGE	PA	R	2B	3B	HR	RBI	BB	K	SB	CS	AVG/OBP/SLG	TAv	BABIP	BRR	FRAA	WARP
2016	*MIL*	*MLB*	*19*	*250*	*29*	*8*	*1*	*7*	*22*	*9*	*82*	*11*	*5*	*.193/.227/.319*	*.189*	*.260*	*0.9*	*RF -1, LF -0*	*-1.3*
2017	*MIL*	*MLB*	*20*	*321*	*34*	*12*	*1*	*10*	*36*	*13*	*106*	*16*	*7*	*.216/.251/.368*	*.222*	*.290*	*2.1*	*-*	*-0.4*

Breakout: 0% Improve: 0% Collapse: 0% Attrition: 0% MLB: 0% *Comparables: Jay Bruce, Chris Parmelee, Marcell Ozuna*

The Brewers selected the Canadian prepster in the fourth round and managed to sign him under slot at $450,000. He had flashed five-tool potential and was on his way to a first-round grade before a disappointing spring hurt his stock, but after he signed he was one of the brightest stars in the Arizona League. He's a prototypical, big-bodied right fielder with the ability to hit for power and average. His pitch recognition and knowledge of the strike zone must improve, as with most teenagers, but the tools are shiny. Orimoloye could also be the first African-born individual to play in the majors, something that would bring increased attention to the growth of the game in Africa. His play might also draw notice to the fact that it's dangerous to place such heavy emphasis on spring performance for prep players in the northern climates.

Brett Phillips CF

Born: 5/30/94 Age: 22 Bats: L Throws: R Height: 6'0" Weight: 180

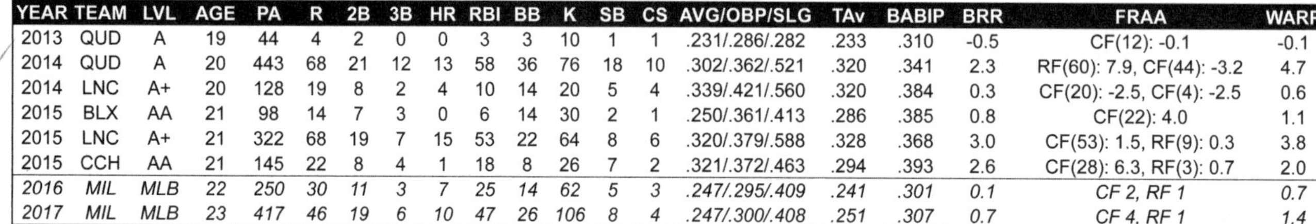

YEAR	TEAM	LVL	AGE	PA	R	2B	3B	HR	RBI	BB	K	SB	CS	AVG/OBP/SLG	TAv	BABIP	BRR	FRAA	WARP
2013	QUD	A	19	44	4	2	0	0	3	3	10	1	1	.231/.286/.282	.233	.310	-0.5	CF(12): -0.1	-0.1
2014	QUD	A	20	443	68	21	12	13	58	36	76	18	10	.302/.362/.521	.320	.341	2.3	RF(60): 7.9, CF(44): -3.2	4.7
2014	LNC	A+	20	128	19	8	2	4	10	14	20	5	4	.339/.421/.560	.320	.384	0.3	CF(20): -2.5, CF(4): -2.5	0.6
2015	BLX	AA	21	98	14	7	3	0	6	14	30	2	1	.250/.361/.413	.286	.385	0.8	CF(22): 4.0	1.1
2015	LNC	A+	21	322	68	19	7	15	53	22	64	8	6	.320/.379/.588	.328	.368	3.0	CF(53): 1.5, RF(9): 0.3	3.8
2015	CCH	AA	21	145	22	8	4	1	18	8	26	7	2	.321/.372/.463	.294	.393	2.6	CF(28): 6.3, RF(3): 0.7	2.0
2016	*MIL*	*MLB*	*22*	*250*	*30*	*11*	*3*	*7*	*25*	*14*	*62*	*5*	*3*	*.247/.295/.409*	*.241*	*.301*	*0.1*	*CF 2, RF 1*	*0.7*
2017	*MIL*	*MLB*	*23*	*417*	*46*	*19*	*6*	*10*	*47*	*26*	*106*	*8*	*4*	*.247/.300/.408*	*.251*	*.307*	*0.7*	*CF 4, RF 1*	*1.4*

Breakout: 5% Improve: 23% Collapse: 1% Attrition: 19% MLB: 46% *Comparables: Austin Jackson, Jordan Schafer, Kirk Nieuwenhuis*

Phillips burst onto the prospect scene on the strength of back-to-back power showcases in the Cal League. Once he graduated to Double-A and then headed to Milwaukee in the Carlos Gomez/Mike Fiers deal, the extra-base hits began to dry up. Fortunately, his value doesn't lie in his ability to hit 20-plus homers. His profile is attractive because he's a legitimate center-field prospect with solid plate discipline and great speed. He's well rounded and still managed to post a .361 on-base percentage when he "struggled" in Double-A Biloxi. Phillips added muscle to his frame and some scouts believe he has become a true five-tool prospect—or maybe a four-tool guy, depending on one's views about his future power production. Either way, he was the best prospect traded at the 2015 deadline and could be patrolling a big-league outfield by the end of this year.

Victor Roache LF

Born: 9/17/91 Age: 24 Bats: R Throws: R Height: 6'1" Weight: 225

YEAR	TEAM	LVL	AGE	PA	R	2B	3B	HR	RBI	BB	K	SB	CS	AVG/OBP/SLG	TAv	BABIP	BRR	FRAA	WARP
2013	WIS	A	21	519	62	14	4	22	74	46	137	6	2	.248/.322/.440	.274	.302	-1.0	LF(86): 0.3	1.7
2014	BRV	A+	22	481	46	17	2	18	54	37	138	11	4	.226/.298/.400	.247	.287	-0.7	LF(106): -6.6, RF(1): -0.0	-0.4
2015	BRV	A+	23	264	23	11	2	10	36	21	94	3	3	.259/.326/.448	.303	.382	-1.0	LF(52): 3.8	2.1
2015	BLX	AA	23	249	23	11	3	8	35	23	64	2	1	.247/.321/.430	.266	.309	1.1	LF(57): -1.3	0.7
2016	*MIL*	*MLB*	*24*	*250*	*26*	*8*	*1*	*10*	*32*	*15*	*87*	*1*	*0*	*.211/.265/.385*	*.226*	*.285*	*-0.2*	*LF -0*	*-0.2*
2017	*MIL*	*MLB*	*25*	*307*	*37*	*11*	*1*	*13*	*39*	*20*	*105*	*1*	*1*	*.215/.272/.395*	*.240*	*.289*	*-0.4*	*LF 0*	*0.1*

Breakout: 3% Improve: 6% Collapse: 2% Attrition: 7% MLB: 16% *Comparables: Carlos Peguero, Scott Schebler, Donald Lutz*

Known since his days at Georgia Southern University for his gargantuan raw power, Roache's home run column has done nothing to dispel the notion. Singles, though—maybe mix in a few? Roache will never be a high-contact player and is limited to a corner-outfield position. The best-case scenario is the Chris Carter type—a guy who hits between .200 and .230 with 20-plus homers. He'll have to sustain the improvements he showed in 2015 to reach that ceiling, though, as he currently projects as a injury replacement for a franchise down on its luck.

Domingo Santana LF

Born: 8/5/92 Age: 23 Bats: R Throws: R Height: 6'5" Weight: 225

YEAR	TEAM	LVL	AGE	PA	R	2B	3B	HR	RBI	BB	K	SB	CS	AVG/OBP/SLG	TAv	BABIP	BRR	FRAA	WARP
2013	CCH	AA	20	476	72	23	2	25	64	46	139	12	5	.252/.345/.498	.296	.316	0.2	RF(100): 0.2, CF(8): 1.7	3.0
2014	HOU	MLB	21	18	1	0	0	0	0	1	14	0	0	.000/.056/.000	.066	.000	0.1	LF(3): -0.8, RF(2): -0.1	-0.4
2014	OKL	AAA	21	513	63	27	2	16	81	64	149	6	4	.296/.384/.474	.304	.408	0.7	RF(59): -0.3, LF(49): -0.0	3.6
2015	FRE	AAA	22	326	62	18	3	16	59	48	91	1	4	.320/.426/.582	.348	.429	0.6	RF(59): -6.8, LF(1): 0.1	2.9
2015	MIL	MLB	22	145	14	5	0	6	18	18	46	2	0	.231/.345/.421	.299	.310	0.6	CF(23): -2.9, RF(16): -1.4	0.5
2015	CSP	AAA	22	85	13	5	1	2	18	6	17	1	1	.380/.424/.544	.318	.467	-0.1	LF(14): -1.5, RF(4): -0.4	0.5
2015	HOU	MLB	22	42	6	2	0	2	8	2	17	2	1	.256/.310/.462	.256	.400	0.3	RF(9): -0.2, LF(3): -0.8	0.0
2016	*MIL*	*MLB*	*23*	*518*	*64*	*22*	*2*	*21*	*71*	*52*	*168*	*5*	*3*	*.248/.332/.443*	*.274*	*.339*	*0.4*	*CF -8*	*1.8*
2017	*MIL*	*MLB*	*24*	*528*	*70*	*22*	*2*	*20*	*68*	*54*	*168*	*5*	*3*	*.246/.331/.431*	*.277*	*.337*	*0.6*	*CF -8*	*1.9*

Breakout: 1% Improve: 34% Collapse: 4% Attrition: 15% MLB: 71% *Comparables: Wil Myers, Chris Carter, Jorge Soler*

Few things scream *rebuild* like a 6-foot-5 mountain of muscle being thrust into center field on a daily basis. Santana had played only 12 professional games there before the Brewers tried it for 23 meaningless late-summer games. The club isn't delusional enough to believe the 23-year-old is a long-term solution in center; however, he did need regular playing time against big-league pitching and had no other avenue available. They didn't learn much: Santana didn't hit for average, showed off light-tower raw power and struck out over 30 percent of the time. That sounds like another Brewers legend, come to think of it. Maybe the Brew Crew acquired Stormin' Gorman Thomas of the 21st century. Santana needs to step up his facial-hair game for that to be possible, but the raw follicle tools are available. It's just about consistency and creativity at this point.

Jean Segura SS

Born: 3/17/90 Age: 26 Bats: R Throws: R Height: 5'10" Weight: 205

YEAR	TEAM	LVL	AGE	PA	R	2B	3B	HR	RBI	BB	K	SB	CS	AVG/OBP/SLG	TAv	BABIP	BRR	FRAA	WARP
2013	MIL	MLB	23	623	74	20	10	12	49	25	84	44	13	.294/.329/.423	.265	.326	2.6	SS(144): 22.0	5.6
2014	MIL	MLB	24	557	61	14	6	5	31	28	70	20	9	.246/.289/.326	.233	.275	4.8	SS(144): 22.2	3.8
2015	MIL	MLB	25	584	57	16	5	6	50	13	93	25	6	.257/.281/.336	.217	.298	5.3	SS(140): 12.5	1.8
2013	ROC	AAA	22	155	25	6	0	10	30	22	37	2	1	.313/.426/.594	.338	.366	-0.7	RF(17): -0.7, LF(2): 0.1	1.4
2016	*MIL*	*MLB*	*26*	*537*	*68*	*18*	*6*	*9*	*46*	*23*	*78*	*25*	*8*	*.270/.306/.384*	*.241*	*.298*	*2.9*	*SS 17*	*3.7*
2017	*MIL*	*MLB*	*27*	*540*	*58*	*18*	*6*	*10*	*56*	*23*	*77*	*25*	*8*	*.270/.306/.391*	*.252*	*.296*	*3.9*	*SS 17*	*4.3*

Breakout: 4% Improve: 50% Collapse: 5% Attrition: 11% MLB: 97% *Comparables: Erick Aybar, Alcides Escobar, Yuniesky Betancourt*

Few harbor any real expectations for Segura anymore. The promise he showed early in 2013 has long passed, as he's hitting .252/.285/.331 with 11 homers and a .226 TAv over the past two seasons. While both his skills with the glove and his ability to steal 25 bases per year give him value, the overall putrid state of the shortstop position is what should keep the 26-year-old in a starting lineup for the foreseeable future. He falls into poor habits, drifting into the baseball and becoming too rotational with his swing, and he isn't able to consistently implement the adjustments that helped him hit .286/.344/.482 in the first month of last season. As such, Segura serves as a prime example of how baseball is more about consistency than it is raw skills.

PITCHERS

Zach Davies RHP

Born: 2/7/93 Age: 23 Bats: R Throws: R Height: 6'0" Weight: 160

YEAR	TEAM	LVL	AGE	W	L	SV	G	GS	IP	H	HR	BB/9	K/9	GB%	BABIP	WHIP	ERA	FIP	DRA	WARP	CFIP	MPH
2013	FRD	A+	20	7	9	0	26	26	148^{2}	145	10	2.3	8.0	52%	.310	1.23	3.69	3.28	4.09	2.1	80	
2014	BOW	AA	21	10	7	0	21	20	110	106	8	2.6	8.9	54%	.314	1.25	3.35	3.30	3.97	1.5	81	
2015	MIL	MLB	22	3	2	0	6	6	34	26	2	4.0	6.4	58%	.245	1.21	3.71	3.84	3.33	0.7	114	90.9
2015	CSP	AAA	22	1	2	0	5	5	27	38	2	4.0	7.0	57%	.391	1.85	5.00	4.45	5.59	0.0	105	
2015	NOR	AAA	22	5	6	0	19	18	101^{1}	91	4	2.9	7.2	54%	.290	1.22	2.84	3.08	3.41	1.6	91	
2016	*MIL*	*MLB*	*23*	*8*	*8*	*0*	*26*	*26*	*130*	*127*	*15*	*2.9*	*7.0*	*54%*	*.306*	*1.30*	*4.07*	*4.06*	*4.55*	*1.1*	*105*	
2017	*MIL*	*MLB*	*24*	*7*	*8*	*0*	*22*	*22*	*130*	*126*	*15*	*3.2*	*7.4*	*54%*	*.310*	*1.33*	*4.24*	*4.41*	*4.74*	*0.8*	*110*	

Breakout: 16% Improve: 25% Collapse: 16% Attrition: 25% MLB: 48% *Comparables: Matt Magill, Michael Bowden, Troy Patton*

First things first: Spelling matters. Zachary Davis is a serial killer from Tennessee. Zachary Davies is a professional baseball player who made his major-league debut in 2015. The Milwaukee Brewers sent Gerardo Parra to Baltimore to acquire the young right-hander, largely at the bequest of the club's analytics department. The fact that he strikes out nearly a batter per inning, maintains a respectable walk rate and is a former 26th-round pick makes him a sabermetric dream. He relies on location and an above-average changeup. His high-80s fastball actually makes him quite similar to former Brewers starter Marco Estrada. As a bonus, though, Davies lets us know what the average IT guy would look like if he played professional baseball, and that *feels* important.

Miguel Diaz RHP

Born: 11/28/94 Age: 21 Bats: R Throws: R Height: 6'1" Weight: 175

YEAR	TEAM	LVL	AGE	W	L	SV	G	GS	IP	H	HR	BB/9	K/9	GB%	BABIP	WHIP	ERA	FIP	DRA	WARP	CFIP	MPH
2016	*MIL*	*MLB*	*21*	*1*	*2*	*1*	*22*	*3*	33^{1}	*39*	*5*	*5.5*	*5.1*	*32%*	*.320*	*1.77*	*5.99*	*5.83*	*6.86*	*-0.9*	*158*	
2017	*MIL*	*MLB*	*22*	*2*	*2*	*1*	*29*	*6*	86^{2}	*99*	*13*	*4.6*	*5.6*	*32%*	*.324*	*1.65*	*5.53*	*5.86*	*6.33*	*-1.0*	*147*	

Breakout: 0% Improve: 0% Collapse: 0% Attrition: 0% MLB: 0% *Comparables: Michael Blazek, Abel De Los Santos, Brian Broderick*

Diaz turned heads as a 19-year-old in 2014, showing easy velocity and a curveball that flashed above-average potential. Slowed by injuries this past year, though, his stock stagnated a bit. He returned with a bit more weight on his shoulders and more effort in his delivery. The bullpen beckons him like the Reaper in an Ingmar Bergman film, as it does with all control-challenged teenagers. But the right-hander might have a plot twist or two left in him, dominating somewhat younger competition in the Arizona League after returning from the disabled list.

Tim Dillard RHP

Born: 7/19/83 Age: 32 Bats: R Throws: R Height: 6'4" Weight: 220

YEAR	TEAM	LVL	AGE	W	L	SV	G	GS	IP	H	HR	BB/9	K/9	GB%	BABIP	WHIP	ERA	FIP	DRA	WARP	CFIP	MPH
2013	NAS	AAA	29	4	2	0	38	0	47	43	2	4.8	5.6	62%	.265	1.45	4.40	4.74	5.63	-0.2	118	
2014	HUN	AA	30	5	3	1	43	0	60^{1}	44	3	2.4	7.9	54%	.247	0.99	3.13	3.32				
2015	CSP	AAA	31	3	2	0	27	6	54	62	3	3.5	7.3	49%	.345	1.54	5.50	4.14	4.47	0.5	94	
2016	*MIL*	*MLB*	*32*	*2*	*1*	*2*	*44*	*1*	*50^{1}*	*50*	*6*	*3.2*	*6.7*	*50%*	*.307*	*1.36*	*4.48*	*4.33*	*5.00*	*0.0*	*116*	
2017	*MIL*	*MLB*	*33*	*2*	*1*	*1*	*37*	*1*	*51^{1}*	*52*	*7*	*3.2*	*7.1*	*50%*	*.311*	*1.36*	*4.57*	*4.77*	*5.10*	*-0.1*	*119*	

Breakout: 16% Improve: 21% Collapse: 12% Attrition: 26% MLB: 37% *Comparables: Randy Choate, Francisley Bueno, Royce Ring*

Dillard returned to the organization as a grizzled tricenarian to serve as mentor and pseudo-player-coach in Triple-A Colorado Springs. He appeared in the majors for the Brewers in four separate seasons—the last coming in 2012—and struggled to a 5.50 ERA for the Sky Sox, making him an unlikely candidate for the *BP Annual*. However, his impact became readily apparent as the season progressed, as the right-hander kept the clubhouse (of a team 19 games under .500) relaxed and connected. Multiple times per week, Dillard directed short "Dubsmash" movies on Twitter starring Sky Sox teammates, who clearly enjoyed participating and planned future acts on Twitter. The highlights included masterpieces like remakes of *Jurassic Park*, *Mighty Morphin Power Rangers*, and *The Waterboy*. He even surreptitiously filmed a brief Korn music video behind a trio of teammates on a clubhouse couch. Minor-league baseball ain't Hollywood, but Dillard made an early claim to Oscar consideration in 2015.

Marcos Diplan RHP

Born: 9/18/96 Age: 19 Bats: R Throws: R Height: 6'0" Weight: 160

YEAR	TEAM	LVL	AGE	W	L	SV	G	GS	IP	H	HR	BB/9	K/9	GB%	BABIP	WHIP	ERA	FIP	DRA	WARP	CFIP	MPH
2016	*MIL*	*MLB*	*19*	*2*	*2*	*0*	*12*	*6*	*33^{2}*	*38*	*5*	*5.4*	*5.4*	*30%*	*.316*	*1.72*	*5.83*	*5.74*	*6.67*	*-0.7*	*155*	
2017	*MIL*	*MLB*	*20*	*4*	*7*	*0*	*24*	*17*	*123*	*143*	*19*	*5.1*	*5.3*	*30%*	*.325*	*1.73*	*5.87*	*6.22*	*6.72*	*-1.7*	*156*	

Breakout: 0% Improve: 0% Collapse: 0% Attrition: 0% MLB: 0% *Comparables: Michael Feliz, Andrew Faulkner, Kelvin Herrera*

An overlooked part of the Yovani Gallardo trade, Diplan can throw in the mid-90s with his fastball and shows feel for both his curveball and his changeup. If he were a couple inches taller or carried 10 to 15 additional pounds of good weight, the right-hander would garner much more attention from scouts and prospect fanatics. Having a slight build generally means velocity is created with much more force, and Diplan fits the mold. His prospect stock will wholly depend on his ability to hold velocity in the middle innings and how he copes with the stresses of full-season ball. His results with Rookie-level Helena were impressive—he struck out more than a batter per inning and posted a 3.75 ERA as an 18-year-old—but accomplishments won't be enough. He'll have to outlive all the potential failures that have been prescribed to him. It's hard to be young sometimes.

Matt Garza RHP

Born: 11/26/83 Age: 32 Bats: R Throws: R Height: 6'4" Weight: 215

YEAR	TEAM	LVL	AGE	W	L	SV	G	GS	IP	H	HR	BB/9	K/9	GB%	BABIP	WHIP	ERA	FIP	DRA	WARP	CFIP	MPH
2013	TEX	MLB	29	4	5	0	13	13	84^{1}	89	12	2.3	7.9	41%	.308	1.32	4.38	3.99	4.89	0.0	94	96.1
2013	CHN	MLB	29	6	1	0	11	11	71	61	8	2.5	7.9	43%	.266	1.14	3.17	3.75	3.00	1.6	92	95.4
2014	MIL	MLB	30	8	8	0	27	27	163^{1}	143	12	2.8	6.9	46%	.268	1.18	3.64	3.51	3.82	1.9	107	95.2
2015	MIL	MLB	31	6	14	0	26	25	148^{2}	176	23	3.5	6.3	47%	.319	1.57	5.63	4.96	5.33	-0.5	119	95.1
2016	*MIL*	*MLB*	*32*	*8*	*8*	*0*	*22*	*22*	*131^{1}*	*129*	*18*	*2.8*	*6.6*	*46%*	*.299*	*1.30*	*4.36*	*4.39*	*4.87*	*0.6*	*114*	
2017	*MIL*	*MLB*	*33*	*8*	*9*	*0*	*24*	*24*	*140^{2}*	*141*	*18*	*2.8*	*6.5*	*46%*	*.304*	*1.31*	*4.47*	*4.66*	*4.99*	*0.5*	*118*	

Breakout: 11% Improve: 52% Collapse: 28% Attrition: 18% MLB: 95% *Comparables: Gavin Floyd, John Tudor, Doug Davis*

Garza responded to a league-worst ERA (among qualified starters) by lashing out at the unkind world—and, more specifically, in the direction of his employers—in what might have been his best pitch of the year. He refused to work out of the bullpen and castigated the front office for shutting him down out of mercy with a month remaining. Perhaps Garza failed to appreciate who was receiving the mercy. The righthander saw his strikeout rate drop for the fourth-consecutive year and his home run issues returned. His velocity remained constant—sitting just above 93 mph—but his movement and ability to induce whiffs have waned. Like myriad thirty-somethings before him, Garza must learn how to compete and find success with diminished stuff and a body that can't physically do what it could in his prime. The problem is that he has always had a penchant for missing in the zone, for throwing rather than pitching. A winter of reflection is in order.

Josh Hader LHP

Born: 4/7/94 Age: 22 Bats: L Throws: L Height: 6'3" Weight: 160

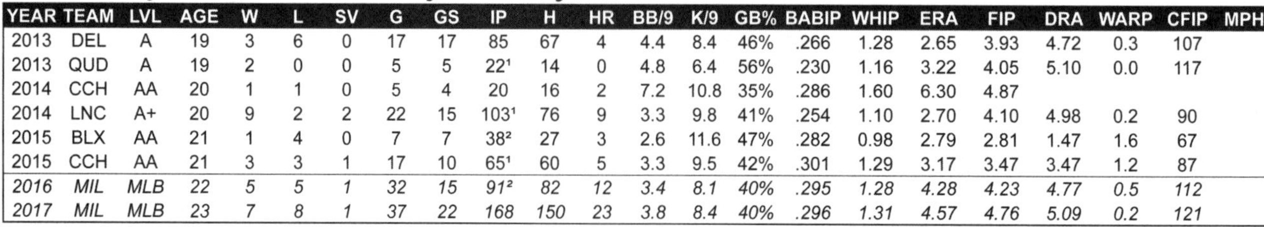

YEAR	TEAM	LVL	AGE	W	L	SV	G	GS	IP	H	HR	BB/9	K/9	GB%	BABIP	WHIP	ERA	FIP	DRA	WARP	CFIP	MPH
2013	DEL	A	19	3	6	0	17	17	85	67	4	4.4	8.4	46%	.266	1.28	2.65	3.93	4.72	0.3	107	
2013	QUD	A	19	2	0	0	5	5	22^{1}	14	0	4.8	6.4	56%	.230	1.16	3.22	4.05	5.10	0.0	117	
2014	CCH	AA	20	1	1	0	5	4	20	16	2	7.2	10.8	35%	.286	1.60	6.30	4.87				
2014	LNC	A+	20	9	2	2	22	15	103^{1}	76	9	3.3	9.8	41%	.254	1.10	2.70	4.10	4.98	0.2	90	
2015	BLX	AA	21	1	4	0	7	7	38^{2}	27	3	2.6	11.6	47%	.282	0.98	2.79	2.81	1.47	1.6	67	
2015	CCH	AA	21	3	3	1	17	10	65^{1}	60	5	3.3	9.5	42%	.301	1.29	3.17	3.47	3.47	1.2	87	
2016	*MIL*	*MLB*	*22*	*5*	*5*	*1*	*32*	*15*	*91^{2}*	*82*	*12*	*3.4*	*8.1*	*40%*	*.295*	*1.28*	*4.28*	*4.23*	*4.77*	*0.5*	*112*	
2017	*MIL*	*MLB*	*23*	*7*	*8*	*1*	*37*	*22*	*168*	*150*	*23*	*3.8*	*8.4*	*40%*	*.296*	*1.31*	*4.57*	*4.76*	*5.09*	*0.2*	*121*	

Breakout: 6% Improve: 19% Collapse: 17% Attrition: 26% MLB: 53% *Comparables: Eric Hurley, Jhoulys Chacin, Mike Montgomery*

For the second time in three seasons, Hader found himself swapping caps. Baltimore traded the left-hander to Houston in the infamous Bud Norris acquisition, who then passed him along to Milwaukee in the Carlos Gomez deal. The 6-foot-3 southpaw has a lofty ceiling—shown by his numbers in Double-A Biloxi, especially that eye-popping 32.9 percent strikeout rate—but reaching it will depend on his physical stamina. Hader features a low, unorthodox delivery and doesn't have a sturdy build. He can hit 96-98 mph early in starts, but the gun cools off notably in the middle innings. The Brewers will continue to develop him as a starter, based on his three usable pitches, including a changeup that should keep righties honest. However, letting him go max-effort for an inning or two could result in a nasty reliever. Considering he wasn't the headline piece in the Gomez trade, though, the Brewers could afford to take a physical flier like Hader, hoping he defies the odds and taps some inner source of endurance.

Adrian Houser RHP

Born: 2/2/93 Age: 23 Bats: R Throws: R Height: 6'4" Weight: 230

2013	TCV	A-	20	0	4	0	14	9	50	57	1	1.8	7.0	54%	.348	1.34	3.42	2.70	3.88	0.4	96	
2014	QUD	A	21	5	6	0	25	17	108^{2}	99	5	3.1	7.7	54%	.301	1.25	4.14	3.70	4.48	0.7	100	
2015	LNC	A+	22	2	2	0	12	8	49^{2}	48	3	3.6	10.0	56%	.338	1.37	4.35	4.04	4.09	0.9	90	
2015	BLX	AA	22	4	1	0	7	7	37	33	4	1.5	7.8	58%	.266	1.05	2.92	3.55	2.90	0.9	84	
2015	MIL	MLB	22	0	0	0	2	0	2	1	0	9.0	0.0	83%	.167	1.50	0.00	6.16	3.98	0.0	111	97.1
2015	CCH	AA	22	1	2	0	7	5	33^{1}	39	6	4.1	6.2	51%	.308	1.62	6.21	5.70	6.15	-0.4	117	
2016	*MIL*	*MLB*	*23*	*6*	*7*	*0*	*36*	*18*	106^{2}	*110*	*15*	*3.4*	*6.6*	*50%*	*.311*	*1.41*	*4.67*	*4.67*	*5.17*	*0.0*	*123*	
2017	*MIL*	*MLB*	*24*	*6*	*7*	*0*	*28*	*20*	139^{1}	*143*	*20*	*3.4*	*6.8*	*50%*	*.313*	*1.40*	*4.79*	*5.01*	*5.30*	*-0.1*	*127*	

Breakout: 0% Improve: 0% Collapse: 0% Attrition: 0% MLB: 0% *Comparables: Giovanni Soto, Jered Weaver, Zach Phillips*

At 6-foot-4 with a fastball that hits 98 mph and an above-average curveball, Houser already projects as a useful big-league reliever. His ultimate ceiling depends on the development of his changeup and his command. The changeup flashes average and has a similar release point to his fastball. He worked heavily on *el cambio* during his stint with the Surprise Saguaros in the Arizona Fall League, which indicates that he's aware of the need to develop that pitch. The Brewers believed in the right-hander's recent progression, and nabbed him in the Gomes/Fiers trade. They continued to groom him as a starter, and Houser rewarded the organization with a 2.92 ERA in seven starts. He's more stuff over utility at this point, but he's only 22 and showed signs of getting it in 2015. If you're prone to dreaming on pull tabs and big arms with command issues, Houser might be your breakout candidate of choice in 2016

Jeremy Jeffress RHP

Born: 9/21/87 Age: 28 Bats: R Throws: R Height: 6'0" Weight: 215

YEAR	TEAM	LVL	AGE	W	L	SV	G	GS	IP	H	HR	BB/9	K/9	GB%	BABIP	WHIP	ERA	FIP	DRA	WARP	CFIP	MPH
2013	BUF	AAA	25	1	0	7	25	0	27^{1}	22	0	4.3	9.2	56%	.324	1.28	1.65	2.58	4.15	0.2	93	
2013	TOR	MLB	25	1	0	0	10	0	10^{1}	8	1	4.4	10.5	69%	.280	1.26	0.87	3.46	3.83	0.1	92	99.6
2014	MIL	MLB	26	1	1	0	29	0	28^{2}	27	1	2.2	7.8	65%	.321	1.19	1.88	2.54	1.48	1.1	94	98.8
2014	TOR	MLB	26	0	0	0	3	0	3^{1}	8	0	8.1	10.8	33%	.667	3.30	10.80	5.26	27.32	-0.9	105	97.8
2014	NAS	AAA	26	4	1	5	30	0	41^{2}	33	0	3.9	9.7	64%	.317	1.22	1.51	2.84	4.80	0.3	82	
2015	MIL	MLB	27	5	0	0	72	0	68	64	5	2.9	8.9	60%	.314	1.26	2.65	3.25	3.77	0.8	91	97.7
2016	*MIL*	*MLB*	*28*	*3*	*1*	*5*	*55*	*0*	58^{1}	*53*	*7*	*2.9*	*8.5*	*60%*	*.312*	*1.23*	*3.73*	*3.79*	*4.19*	*0.6*	*92*	
2017	*MIL*	*MLB*	*29*	*2*	*1*	*1*	*47*	*0*	54^{1}	*47*	*5*	*2.9*	*9.2*	*60%*	*.311*	*1.18*	*3.53*	*3.67*	*3.97*	*0.6*	*86*	

Breakout: 32% Improve: 47% Collapse: 17% Attrition: 19% MLB: 77% *Comparables: Mark Melancon, Pedro Strop, Javy Guerra*

From 2010 to 2014, Jeffress bounced around way more than you'd expect of a first-rounder with a heavy upper-90s fastball. He just couldn't consistently find the strike zone. Since re-joining the Brewers in 2014, the Virginia native has peppered the zone and transformed himself into a mainstay in the bullpen. Since the prodigal son returned, however, he's keeping the ball near the plate while still evading some swings. He's yet another example of why guys with premium arm strength always find jobs, even when they keep losing them.

Cesar Jimenez LHP

Born: 11/12/84 Age: 31 Bats: L Throws: L Height: 6'0" Weight: 215

YEAR	TEAM	LVL	AGE	W	L	SV	G	GS	IP	H	HR	BB/9	K/9	GB%	BABIP	WHIP	ERA	FIP	DRA	WARP	CFIP	MPH
2013	PHI	MLB	28	1	1	0	19	0	17	14	1	5.3	5.8	41%	.245	1.41	3.71	4.43	3.61	0.2	119	91.6
2013	LEH	AAA	28	4	2	3	36	3	66^{1}	61	3	3.5	8.7	42%	.314	1.31	3.12	3.04	4.01	0.6	88	
2014	PHI	MLB	29	0	0	0	16	0	16	14	1	3.9	4.5	42%	.265	1.31	1.69	4.23	4.01	0.1	117	91.0
2014	LEH	AAA	29	3	2	3	38	2	49^{2}	34	0	2.7	8.3	44%	.256	0.99	1.45	2.41	3.99	0.5	80	
2015	PHI	MLB	30	0	0	0	3	0	3^{1}	1	0	0.0	10.8	67%	.167	0.30	0.00	0.76	-1.45	0.2	91	92.2
2015	LEH	AAA	30	3	5	4	41	1	57^{1}	61	4	2.8	6.3	44%	.315	1.38	3.61	3.61	4.05	0.2	99	
2015	MIL	MLB	30	0	0	0	16	0	19^{2}	16	2	3.7	9.6	52%	.280	1.22	3.66	3.57	2.77	0.5	89	91.6
2016	*MIL*	*MLB*	*31*	*3*	*1*	*0*	*64*	*0*	67^{2}	*65*	*8*	*3.0*	*7.4*	*44%*	*.307*	*1.30*	*4.07*	*3.99*	*4.56*	*0.4*	*104*	
2017	*MIL*	*MLB*	*32*	*2*	*1*	*0*	*34*	*0*	44^{2}	*44*	*6*	*3.0*	*8.0*	*44%*	*.320*	*1.31*	*4.13*	*4.29*	*4.63*	*0.1*	*105*	

Breakout: 7% Improve: 13% Collapse: 9% Attrition: 13% MLB: 29% *Comparables: Jim Miller, Dale Thayer, Ross Wolf*

Sure, acquiring a 30-year-old reliever off waivers isn't about to boost the attendance numbers, but at least Jimenez is the rare journeyman lefty who can handle full-inning duty. His fastball-changeup combination held righties to a .208/.276/.358 line and punched out 29 percent of them. It's not a case of reverse platoon splits, either, as illustrated by lefties only managing a .200 slugging percentage in 2015. Not overpowering, the Venezuelan native relies on a dynamic changeup that draws whiffs at a rate higher than James Shields'.

Taylor Jungmann RHP

Born: 12/18/89 Age: 26 Bats: R Throws: R Height: 6'6" Weight: 220

YEAR	TEAM	LVL	AGE	W	L	SV	G	GS	IP	H	HR	BB/9	K/9	GB%	BABIP	WHIP	ERA	FIP	DRA	WARP	CFIP	MPH
2013	HUN	AA	23	10	10	0	26	26	139^1	117	11	4.7	5.3	58%	.253	1.36	4.33	4.55	4.78	-0.2	124	
2014	NAS	AAA	24	8	6	0	19	18	101^2	88	7	4.1	8.9	57%	.301	1.32	3.98	4.32	5.29	0.6	100	
2014	HUN	AA	24	4	4	0	9	9	52	52	4	2.6	8.0	60%	.316	1.29	2.77	3.46				
2015	CSP	AAA	25	2	3	0	11	9	59^1	61	2	4.4	8.2	60%	.349	1.52	6.37	3.89	4.64	0.6	96	
2015	MIL	MLB	25	9	8	0	21	21	119^1	106	11	3.5	8.1	48%	.290	1.28	3.77	3.95	3.84	1.7	105	94.5
2016	*MIL*	*MLB*	*26*	*10*	*11*	*0*	*31*	*31*	*176^2*	*163*	*20*	*3.4*	*7.4*	*51%*	*.301*	*1.30*	*4.19*	*4.16*	*4.67*	*1.3*	*109*	
2017	*MIL*	*MLB*	*27*	*8*	*9*	*0*	*26*	*26*	*156*	*144*	*18*	*3.5*	*7.7*	*51%*	*.306*	*1.32*	*4.32*	*4.50*	*4.82*	*0.8*	*113*	

Breakout: 19% Improve: 36% Collapse: 13% Attrition: 28% MLB: 69% *Comparables: Jimmy Nelson, Clay Hensley, Michael Kirkman*

Jungmann was fool's gold for the weary. Brewers fans, wandering the wastelands of a lost season, saw a forgotten former first-round pick get promoted and surprisingly glide his way through his first couple months. He won games, showing unexpected gains in his command and secondary offerings. Still, guys rarely average a double-digit walk rate in the minors and miraculously cut it to 6.6 percent, as he did in June. Then, his character reasserted itself and he began to fall behind batters. His walk rate climbed to 9.5 percent in July, then 10 percent in August and 11.4 percent in September and October. Jungmann offered glimpses of hope; however, his true self is probably closer to what we saw in Double-A and Triple-A than what he did in June and July. His 105 cFIP reflects that back-end projection.

Nathan Kirby LHP

Born: 11/23/93 Age: 22 Bats: L Throws: L Height: 6'2" Weight: 200

YEAR	TEAM	LVL	AGE	W	L	SV	G	GS	IP	H	HR	BB/9	K/9	GB%	BABIP	WHIP	ERA	FIP	DRA	WARP	CFIP	MPH
2015	WIS	A	21	0	1	0	5	2	12^2	15	0	5.0	5.0	62%	.357	1.74	5.68	4.19	5.66	-0.1	113	
2016	*MIL*	*MLB*	*22*	*2*	*2*	*1*	*19*	*4*	*34^2*	*39*	*5*	*4.3*	*4.9*	*54%*	*.313*	*1.60*	*5.23*	*5.46*	*5.80*	*-0.3*	*138*	
2017	*MIL*	*MLB*	*23*	*3*	*3*	*1*	*35*	*10*	*107*	*120*	*13*	*4.4*	*5.2*	*54%*	*.319*	*1.61*	*5.24*	*5.52*	*5.81*	*-0.6*	*138*	

Breakout: 0% Improve: 0% Collapse: 0% Attrition: 0% MLB: 0% *Comparables: Carlos Frias, Jon Link, Nick Greenwood*

After opening the season as a top-10 talent, Kirby fell to the Brewers with the 40th-overall pick. Despite a lost season stemming from a strained lat and its aftershocks, it appeared scouting director Ray Montgomery and his staff had capitalized on a massive value-buy. A pre-signing medical unveiled an unexpected issue that slashed his bonus over $300,000, and he underwent Tommy John surgery after just five professional appearances. Heavily investing in an injured player has become somewhat commonplace in recent drafts, with guys like Jeff Hoffman and Michael Matuella signing for at least $2 million, but this type of creativity and commitment has historically been absent from the Brewers organization until the past couple years. A better balance of risk and reward is a significant reason why Milwaukee's farm system has vastly improved.

Kyle Lohse RHP

Born: 10/4/78 Age: 37 Bats: R Throws: R Height: 6'2" Weight: 215

YEAR	TEAM	LVL	AGE	W	L	SV	G	GS	IP	H	HR	BB/9	K/9	GB%	BABIP	WHIP	ERA	FIP	DRA	WARP	CFIP	MPH
2013	MIL	MLB	34	11	10	0	32	32	198^2	196	26	1.6	5.7	44%	.276	1.17	3.35	4.05	4.02	2.1	105	91.9
2014	MIL	MLB	35	13	9	0	31	31	198^1	183	22	2.0	6.4	42%	.268	1.15	3.54	3.92	4.06	1.8	110	91.7
2015	MIL	MLB	36	5	13	2	37	22	152^1	180	29	2.5	6.4	41%	.314	1.46	5.85	5.14	5.60	-1.1	116	91.5
2016	*MIL*	*MLB*	*37*	*8*	*8*	*0*	*23*	*23*	*139^2*	*137*	*20*	*2.2*	*6.1*	*41%*	*.290*	*1.23*	*4.36*	*4.38*	*4.85*	*0.7*	*116*	
2017	*MIL*	*MLB*	*38*	*9*	*9*	*0*	*25*	*25*	*146^2*	*146*	*19*	*2.3*	*6.2*	*41%*	*.298*	*1.25*	*4.40*	*4.57*	*4.89*	*0.7*	*116*	

Breakout: 8% Improve: 33% Collapse: 19% Attrition: 15% MLB: 82% *Comparables: Dennis Martinez, Bronson Arroyo, Doyle Alexander*

Lohse had the worst home run rate (1.7 HR/9) of any starter in baseball who threw at least 150 innings, higher than his reported golf handicap of 1.3. Some have pointed toward his 3.81 ERA as a reliever—and his 2.25 ERA in the final month of the campaign—as evidence that he may be an under-the-radar candidate for a bullpen role. Of course, he also compiled a 1.45 WHIP as a reliever, and they do tend to frown on home runs in the late innings. On the positive side, his velocity held solid and his swinging-strike rate actually increased to 9 percent, so it is important to recognize the potential for a bounce-back season. It also might not be a bad idea for Lohse to spend a bit more time on the golf course, shaving the last couple strokes off his game. You know, just in case.

Jorge Lopez RHP

Born: 2/10/93 Age: 23 Bats: R Throws: R Height: 6'3" Weight: 190

YEAR	TEAM	LVL	AGE	W	L	SV	G	GS	IP	H	HR	BB/9	K/9	GB%	BABIP	WHIP	ERA	FIP	DRA	WARP	CFIP	MPH
2013	WIS	A	20	7	8	2	25	22	117	120	13	3.7	7.1	48%	.305	1.44	5.23	4.67	4.92	0.5	110	
2014	BRV	A+	21	10	10	0	25	25	137^2	144	12	3.0	7.8	50%	.328	1.38	4.58	3.88	4.23	1.2	96	
2015	BLX	AA	22	12	5	0	24	24	143^1	105	9	3.3	8.6	54%	.259	1.10	2.26	3.36	3.02	3.3	86	
2015	MIL	MLB	22	1	1	0	2	2	10	14	0	4.5	9.0	57%	.467	1.90	5.40	2.96	7.58	-0.3	106	96.0
2016	*MIL*	*MLB*	*23*	*7*	*8*	*0*	*23*	*23*	*124^2*	*120*	*15*	*3.4*	*7.5*	*50%*	*.310*	*1.34*	*4.22*	*4.19*	*4.70*	*0.9*	*110*	
2017	*MIL*	*MLB*	*24*	*6*	*7*	*0*	*20*	*20*	*115^2*	*112*	*15*	*3.8*	*7.9*	*50%*	*.315*	*1.39*	*4.50*	*4.69*	*5.01*	*0.3*	*118*	

Breakout: 12% Improve: 14% Collapse: 7% Attrition: 12% MLB: 26% *Comparables: Michael Blazek, Jay Jackson, Jarrod Parker*

Drafted out of Puerto Rico in the second round of the 2011 draft, Lopez instantly became a darling of scouts. He oozed projectability and poise. After four professional seasons, though, the velocity jump never materialized, and he couldn't miss bats. To be fair,

Lopez dealt with far more than any 22-year-old should have to handle. His infant son battled a mysterious autoimmune disease and desperately needed an intestinal transplant. It left him frequently traveling to Puerto Rico to help, but without much money (given minor-league wages), he had little hope for his son's survival. Fortunately, his teammates in Brevard County organized a charity golf tournament to raise money. A year later, his son finally got a diagnosis and might not need a transplant after all. On the field, the right-hander catapulted up the Brewers' system, as his expected velocity jump finally came and he began throwing more strikes. It resulted in a call-up in September. On and off the field, Lopez couldn't have asked for a better year, and the outlooks for both Lopezes are bright.

Kodi Medeiros LHP

Born: 5/25/96 Age: 20 Bats: L Throws: L Height: 6'2" Weight: 180

YEAR	TEAM	LVL	AGE	W	L	SV	G	GS	IP	H	HR	BB/9	K/9	GB%	BABIP	WHIP	ERA	FIP	DRA	WARP	CFIP	MPH
2015	WIS	A	19	4	5	1	25	16	93^1	79	0	3.9	9.1	65%	.307	1.27	4.44	2.96	3.54	1.5	92	
2016	*MIL*	*MLB*	*20*	*4*	*4*	*1*	*29*	*12*	67^2	*67*	*7*	*3.8*	*6.9*	*57%*	*.312*	*1.41*	*4.28*	*4.31*	*4.74*	*0.4*	*111*	
2017	*MIL*	*MLB*	*21*	*6*	*6*	*1*	*39*	*19*	155^2	*146*	*15*	*3.7*	*7.2*	*57%*	*.307*	*1.35*	*4.24*	*4.44*	*4.70*	*0.6*	*111*	

Breakout: 0% Improve: 0% Collapse: 0% Attrition: 0% MLB: 0% *Comparables: Zach Davies, Aaron Sanchez, Trevor Cahill*

Medeiros is one of the more polarizing prospects in the minors. The Brewers shocked the industry when they grabbed him with the 12th-overall pick of the 2014 draft, and then challenged him with an aggressive promotion to the Midwest League as a 19-year-old. He adroitly handled it, striking out more than a batter per inning and not allowing a *single home run* in 93 innings. The southpaw features an unorthodox low delivery and has extreme life on all of his pitches, especially his wicked slider that routinely locks the knees of left-handed hitters. His accuracy resembles buckshot, and his delivery and stature suggest that it's unlikely he'll be able to hold up over 200 innings year after year. They said this about Chris Sale; they also said it about dozens of pitchers you've never heard of, because they were right. Medeiros has ample time to prove skeptics wrong and demonstrate that his slight frame can handle a strenuous workload. Still, given his electric fastball-slider combination, his realistic floor is a very good substitute in the big leagues, something increasingly valuable in this, the Era of the the Relief Pitcher.

Jimmy Nelson RHP

Born: 6/5/89 Age: 27 Bats: R Throws: R Height: 6'6" Weight: 245

YEAR	TEAM	LVL	AGE	W	L	SV	G	GS	IP	H	HR	BB/9	K/9	GB%	BABIP	WHIP	ERA	FIP	DRA	WARP	CFIP	MPH
2013	HUN	AA	24	5	4	0	12	12	69	63	5	2.0	9.4	52%	.320	1.13	2.74	2.81	3.39	0.7	78	
2013	MIL	MLB	24	0	0	0	4	1	10	2	0	4.5	7.2	42%	.083	0.70	0.90	2.92	1.33	0.4	102	96.1
2013	NAS	AAA	24	5	6	0	15	15	83^1	74	2	5.4	9.8	63%	.327	1.49	3.67	3.64	4.89	0.7	96	
2014	NAS	AAA	25	10	2	0	17	16	111	70	3	2.6	9.2	62%	.241	0.92	1.46	2.97	4.57	1.5	72	
2014	MIL	MLB	25	2	9	0	14	12	69^1	82	6	2.5	7.4	50%	.344	1.46	4.93	3.75	6.14	-1.2	108	96.0
2015	MIL	MLB	26	11	13	0	30	30	177^1	163	18	3.3	7.5	52%	.285	1.29	4.11	4.13	3.89	2.4	108	96.0
2016	*MIL*	*MLB*	*27*	*11*	*10*	*0*	*30*	*30*	*180*	*167*	*21*	*3.0*	*7.5*	*53%*	*.301*	*1.26*	*4.05*	*4.04*	*4.53*	*1.6*	*104*	
2017	*MIL*	*MLB*	*28*	*9*	*9*	*0*	*27*	*27*	158^1	*142*	*18*	*3.2*	*7.9*	*53%*	*.299*	*1.25*	*4.09*	*4.26*	*4.58*	*1.3*	*106*	

Breakout: 25% Improve: 56% Collapse: 23% Attrition: 28% MLB: 92% *Comparables: David Phelps, Tyson Ross, Josh Outman*

Pockets of people in the industry adore Nelson, and in 2015 it became apparent why. The right-hander flashed hints of brilliance, especially given his new knuckle-curve that gave him a true third pitch that he could throw for strikes. His swinging-strike rate eclipsed the double-digit mark and he continued to induce a copious number of groundballs—everything a team targets in a young hurler. Still, the old bugaboos remained. His walk rate continues to suffer, but the more significant problem lies in the fact that lefties hit .298/.381/.495 against him. He occasionally found success with fastballs away and hard sliders on the hands to them, but it left a narrow margin for error. Ideally, Nelson would get a bit more vertical movement on his knuckle-curve over the winter, which would help him change eye levels better. A relentless worker, he's poised for a true breakout.

Wily Peralta RHP

Born: 5/8/89 Age: 27 Bats: R Throws: R Height: 6'1" Weight: 245

YEAR	TEAM	LVL	AGE	W	L	SV	G	GS	IP	H	HR	BB/9	K/9	GB%	BABIP	WHIP	ERA	FIP	DRA	WARP	CFIP	MPH
2013	MIL	MLB	24	11	15	0	32	32	183^1	187	19	3.6	6.3	52%	.293	1.42	4.37	4.27	4.54	0.8	112	97.6
2014	MIL	MLB	25	17	11	0	32	32	198^2	198	23	2.8	7.0	56%	.295	1.30	3.53	4.08	4.20	1.4	110	98.5
2015	MIL	MLB	26	5	10	0	20	20	108^2	130	14	3.1	5.0	53%	.320	1.54	4.72	4.86	5.85	-1.1	125	97.1
2016	*MIL*	*MLB*	*27*	*10*	*11*	*0*	*31*	*31*	176^2	*183*	*23*	*2.9*	*6.2*	*54%*	*.312*	*1.35*	*4.39*	*4.40*	*4.90*	*0.8*	*116*	
2017	*MIL*	*MLB*	*28*	*9*	*10*	*0*	*28*	*28*	*172*	*176*	*20*	*2.8*	*6.8*	*54%*	*.320*	*1.33*	*4.22*	*4.40*	*4.71*	*1.1*	*111*	

Breakout: 23% Improve: 53% Collapse: 18% Attrition: 16% MLB: 88% *Comparables: Ivan Nova, Clayton Richard, Manny Parra*

It's easy to pin down Peralta's gameplan on the mound, thanks to a mid-90s sinker and a groundball rate around 51 percent: He thrives on weak contact and limiting walks. The problem is that the right-hander owns a career 8.2 percent walk rate and has given up more than a home run per nine innings the past two seasons. In other words, like John Mayer, he has the tools to be brilliant, but the end product always ends up being underwhelming and a little annoying. His slider was less effective, only missing bats 11 percent of the time—a career low by four percentage points. No wonder his strikeout rate dropped to 12.6 percent, the fourth-worst in baseballl (min 100 IP). He'd likely benefit from a year or two at the Ray Searage Academy in Pittsburgh, throwing fastballs in on the hands of mannequins in one of their secret laboratories.

Cody Ponce RHP

Born: 4/25/94 Age: 22 Bats: R Throws: R Height: 6'6" Weight: 240

YEAR	TEAM	LVL	AGE	W	L	SV	G	GS	IP	H	HR	BB/9	K/9	GB%	BABIP	WHIP	ERA	FIP	DRA	WARP	CFIP	MPH
2015	WIS	A	21	2	1	3	12	7	46	43	1	1.8	7.0	52%	.300	1.13	2.15	2.77	3.34	0.8	90	
2016	*MIL*	*MLB*	*22*	*2*	*2*	*0*	*16*	*6*	*36^{1}*	*39*	*4*	*2.9*	*5.7*	*45%*	*.311*	*1.38*	*4.43*	*4.28*	*4.90*	*0.1*	*116*	
2017	*MIL*	*MLB*	*23*	*5*	*6*	*1*	*32*	*17*	*145^{2}*	*157*	*17*	*3.0*	*5.7*	*45%*	*.317*	*1.41*	*4.59*	*4.79*	*5.08*	*0.1*	*120*	

Breakout: 0% Improve: 0% Collapse: 0% Attrition: 0% MLB: 0% *Comparables: Justin De Fratus, Andrew Faulkner, Colin Rea*

Rumors circulated prior to the 2015 amateur draft that Ponce could go to the Brewers at no. 15 overall. In fact, the Brewers did select the burly right-hander, just a round later. Some scouts wondered what his inconsistent performance against DII talent said about the quality of his stuff, which appeared great on paper. Those who saw Ponce on the right day, however, came away with inklings that he could be something special—a non-Brewers scout opined that the 6-foot-6 righty was the best value-pick of the whole draft. Ponce can hit 98 mph with his fastball and features a potentially devastating slider/cutter that flashes plus. Though the changeup is a work in progress, he already has the building blocks of a mid-rotation starter. The body will need maintaining and he has mechanics that put unneeded stress on his elbow, but the profile is eye-catching. He could jump up prospect lists in 2016 once he explores the pitcher-friendly Florida State League, as it's tailor-made for a power-armed strike-thrower like him.

Will Smith LHP

Born: 7/10/89 Age: 26 Bats: R Throws: L Height: 6'5" Weight: 260

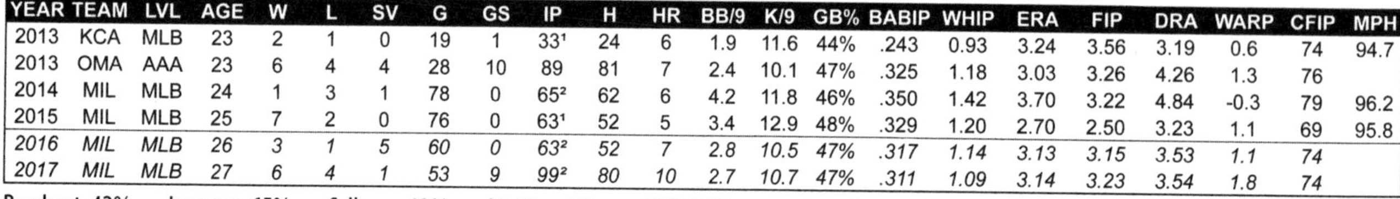

YEAR	TEAM	LVL	AGE	W	L	SV	G	GS	IP	H	HR	BB/9	K/9	GB%	BABIP	WHIP	ERA	FIP	DRA	WARP	CFIP	MPH
2013	KCA	MLB	23	2	1	0	19	1	33^{1}	24	6	1.9	11.6	44%	.243	0.93	3.24	3.56	3.19	0.6	74	94.7
2013	OMA	AAA	23	6	4	4	28	10	89	81	7	2.4	10.1	47%	.325	1.18	3.03	3.26	4.26	1.3	76	
2014	MIL	MLB	24	1	3	1	78	0	65^{2}	62	6	4.2	11.8	46%	.350	1.42	3.70	3.22	4.84	-0.3	79	96.2
2015	MIL	MLB	25	7	2	0	76	0	63^{1}	52	5	3.4	12.9	48%	.329	1.20	2.70	2.50	3.23	1.1	69	95.8
2016	*MIL*	*MLB*	*26*	*3*	*1*	*5*	*60*	*0*	*63^{2}*	*52*	*7*	*2.8*	*10.5*	*47%*	*.317*	*1.14*	*3.13*	*3.15*	*3.53*	*1.1*	*74*	
2017	*MIL*	*MLB*	*27*	*6*	*4*	*1*	*53*	*9*	*99^{2}*	*80*	*10*	*2.7*	*10.7*	*47%*	*.311*	*1.09*	*3.14*	*3.23*	*3.54*	*1.8*	*74*	

Breakout: 42% Improve: 65% Collapse: 13% Attrition: 9% MLB: 93% *Comparables: Aaron Crow, Marc Rzepczynski, Kris Medlen*

The golden lancehead viper, located off the coast of Brazil, is one of the deadliest snakes in the whole world. Its bite has a seven-percent death rate—though that has nothing on the potency of Smith's slider, which has cut down more than 30 percent of individuals who have been unfortunate enough to encounter it. That makes it more lethal than those thrown by Aroldis Chapman, Tyson Ross, and Francisco Liriano. It's illegal to buy or sell lancehead vipers in the United States, and rumor has it that states like Illinois, Missouri, Pennsylvania, and Ohio are exploring what legal avenues are available as a means to deal with Smith's slider. Until then, it seems that NL Central clubs should keep a supply of anti-venom at the ready.

Tyler Thornburg RHP

Born: 9/29/88 Age: 27 Bats: R Throws: R Height: 5'11" Weight: 190

YEAR	TEAM	LVL	AGE	W	L	SV	G	GS	IP	H	HR	BB/9	K/9	GB%	BABIP	WHIP	ERA	FIP	DRA	WARP	CFIP	MPH
2013	NAS	AAA	24	0	9	0	15	15	74^{2}	90	11	3.5	10.5	36%	.380	1.59	5.79	4.48	4.80	0.7	92	
2013	MIL	MLB	24	3	1	0	18	7	66^{2}	53	1	3.5	6.5	38%	.271	1.18	2.03	3.08	2.82	1.6	101	94.6
2014	MIL	MLB	25	3	1	0	27	0	29^{2}	24	1	6.4	8.5	37%	.284	1.52	4.25	3.78	4.35	0.0	112	96.3
2015	MIL	MLB	26	0	2	0	24	0	34^{1}	31	7	3.1	8.9	35%	.253	1.25	3.67	5.14	4.71	0.0	103	95.2
2015	CSP	AAA	26	2	7	0	17	17	88^{2}	106	16	3.7	5.8	42%	.315	1.60	5.28	5.91	6.64	-1.0	118	
2016	*MIL*	*MLB*	*27*	*3*	*1*	*0*	*55*	*0*	*58^{1}*	*56*	*8*	*3.2*	*7.3*	*38%*	*.298*	*1.31*	*4.39*	*4.36*	*4.88*	*0.0*	*115*	
2017	*MIL*	*MLB*	*28*	*4*	*4*	*0*	*22*	*10*	*75^{1}*	*73*	*10*	*3.2*	*7.8*	*38%*	*.308*	*1.32*	*4.43*	*4.63*	*4.93*	*0.2*	*116*	

Breakout: 13% Improve: 40% Collapse: 22% Attrition: 33% MLB: 76% *Comparables: J.A. Happ, Josh Lindblom, Rick VandenHurk*

People bristle at the stereotypes of short pitchers. It's uncomfortable to project talented pitchers, who've often experienced nothing but success, to be future relievers based solely on the fact that they stand at or less than six feet tall. Everywhere else, six is plenty of feet! People point to Tim Lincecum as a counter-example, but even he was breaking down before age 30. And that's the anomaly. Scenarios like Thornburg's are far more common: big stuff, flashes of dominance, and then injuries. The right-hander lost two ticks off his fastball and is no longer considered for a starting role, just two years after posting a 2.03 ERA in a third of a season. It's just too difficult for a small frame to cope with the demands of professional baseball, year after year, especially as a starter. Thus, when your favorite pitching prospect is getting "unfairly" downgraded for his short stature, it's important to remember that we've seen this genre of movie before. It rarely ends well.

Wei-Chung Wang LHP

Born: 4/25/92 Age: 24 Bats: L Throws: L Height: 6'2" Weight: 185

YEAR	TEAM	LVL	AGE	W	L	SV	G	GS	IP	H	HR	BB/9	K/9	GB%	BABIP	WHIP	ERA	FIP	DRA	WARP	CFIP	MPH
2014	WIS	A	22	0	2	0	3	3	13^{2}	13	0	2.6	6.6	50%	.310	1.24	3.29	2.90	4.54	0.1	102	
2014	MIL	MLB	22	0	0	0	14	0	17^{1}	30	6	4.2	6.8	40%	.375	2.19	10.90	7.66	10.61	-1.3	117	94.3
2015	BRV	A+	23	10	6	0	25	25	139^{2}	146	9	2.5	5.9	44%	.303	1.32	3.54	3.58	4.27	0.3	106	
2016	*MIL*	*MLB*	*24*	*6*	*8*	*0*	*22*	*22*	*110*	*120*	*14*	*3.1*	*5.4*	*44%*	*.312*	*1.44*	*4.65*	*4.64*	*5.16*	*0.2*	*122*	
2017	*MIL*	*MLB*	*25*	*5*	*7*	*0*	*18*	*18*	*107*	*112*	*13*	*3.3*	*5.4*	*44%*	*.305*	*1.41*	*4.80*	*5.02*	*5.33*	*-0.1*	*127*	

Breakout: 0% Improve: 0% Collapse: 0% Attrition: 0% MLB: 0% *Comparables: Joe Martinez, Bobby LaFromboise, Marco Estrada*

In 2014, the Brewers saw an opportunity to nab a prospect from the hated Pirates, and got creative. They selected Rookie-ball hurler Wang in the Rule 5 draft. The plan: Stash him in the back of the bullpen for a year, then continue his development in the minors the year after. It got messy. With a mere 47 innings in the Gulf Cost League, Wang was unsurprisingly overmatched in the big leagues. He lasted 14 games before heading to the DL with a nasty case of inferiority. Once the ordeal was over, however, Wang reminded everybody in 2015 why he was worth the trouble, compiling a 1.97 ERA at High-A from June on. His low-90s fastball, changeup and curveball are all potentially league-average offerings, and he projects as a back-end starter with a chance to reward the Brewers for their cunning and patience.

Devin Williams RHP

Born: 9/21/94 Age: 21 Bats: R Throws: R Height: 6'3" Weight: 165

YEAR	TEAM	LVL	AGE	W	L	SV	G	GS	IP	H	HR	BB/9	K/9	GB%	BABIP	WHIP	ERA	FIP	DRA	WARP	CFIP	MPH
2015	WIS	A	20	3	9	0	22	13	89	75	3	3.6	9.0	40%	.295	1.25	3.44	3.28	3.56	1.4	93	
2016	*MIL*	*MLB*	*21*	*4*	*3*	*1*	*31*	*9*	*64*	*62*	*7*	*4.1*	*7.5*	*35%*	*.311*	*1.42*	*4.36*	*4.31*	*4.83*	*0.3*	*113*	
2017	*MIL*	*MLB*	*22*	*5*	*5*	*1*	*33*	*16*	*142*[2]	*129*	*15*	*4.0*	*7.8*	*35%*	*.303*	*1.35*	*4.28*	*4.47*	*4.74*	*0.5*	*111*	

Breakout: 0% Improve: 0% Collapse: 0% Attrition: 0% MLB: 0% *Comparables: Ethan Martin, Scott Barnes, Zach Braddock*

Williams is a sleeper for next year's top 100 lists. His fastball currently bumps 93-94 mph with projection to grow. He has the ideal athletic frame to add positive weight, which should help him avoid overtaxing his body in future years. The changeup flashes average potential, which gives him the tools to develop into a mid-rotation starter. His mechanics smoothed out over the summer, giving him better and more consistent shape on his breaking ball and improving his ability to dot in and around the strike zone. He's ready to throw 100-plus innings for the first time as a professional.

Lineouts

Hitters

NAME	POS	TEAM	LVL	AGE	PA	R	2B	3B	HR	RBI	BB	K	SB	CS	AVG/OBP/SLG	TAv	BABIP	BRR	FRAA	WARP
Nevin Ashley	C	CSP	AAA	30	381	52	14	4	8	61	32	72	0	2	.306/.374/.442	.287	.364	-1.5	C(85): -4.0, 1B(3): 0.0	2.2
	C	MIL	MLB	30	21	2	1	0	0	1	0	8	0	0	.100/.143/.150	.154	.167	-0.2	C(8): -0.0	-0.2
Javier Betancourt	2B	LAK	A+	20	531	45	17	5	3	48	29	44	4	1	.263/.304/.336	.242	.281	-2.8	2B(116): 8.6	1.0
Matt Clark	1B	CSP	AAA	28	548	70	34	1	20	77	58	106	1	0	.291/.367/.492	.287	.331	-2.4	1B(106): 7.3, LF(22): 0.3	2.7
Clint Coulter	C	BRV	A+	21	569	63	30	3	13	59	46	92	6	6	.246/.329/.397	.285	.275	-0.5	RF(117): 5.0, CF(3): 0.2	3.1
Jake Elmore	SS	DUR	AAA	28	240	20	4	0	0	12	38	30	4	4	.247/.377/.268	.256	.292	-2.1	3B(38): 1.0, 1B(13): -0.3	0.5
	SS	TBA	MLB	28	158	10	5	0	2	16	12	25	1	1	.206/.263/.284	.204	.231	0.4	1B(25): -0.5, 3B(9): -0.7	-0.8
Ramon Flores	OF	NYA	MLB	23	33	3	1	0	0	0	0	4	0	0	.219/.219/.250	.192	.250	0.5	LF(11): 2.5, RF(1): -0.0	0.2
	OF	SWB	AAA	23	321	43	11	2	7	34	39	43	3	2	.286/.377/.417	.302	.314	-0.8	LF(45): -2.0, RF(15): -0.3	1.7
	OF	TAC	AAA	23	63	11	6	0	2	7	11	6	0	0	.423/.524/.654	.373	.455	1.2	CF(12): -0.9, LF(2): -0.2	1.0
Elian Herrera	RF	CSP	AAA	30	233	33	15	2	3	27	20	29	4	1	.357/.413/.490	.312	.404	-1.2	2B(23): 0.0, LF(13): 1.2	2.2
	RF	MIL	MLB	30	277	29	18	0	7	33	18	72	3	1	.242/.290/.395	.242	.307	-0.1	3B(47): 2.7, 2B(36): 4.3	1.1
Martin Maldonado	C	MIL	MLB	28	256	19	7	0	4	22	23	65	0	1	.210/.282/.293	.208	.272	-0.5	C(74): 4.3, 1B(1): -0.0	0.2
Hernan Perez	2B	DET	MLB	24	34	1	0	0	0	0	1	11	1	0	.061/.088/.061	.039	.091	-0.3	3B(8): -0.0, 2B(5): -0.1	-0.7
	2B	MIL	MLB	24	238	13	15	2	1	21	4	48	4	1	.270/.281/.365	.227	.335	-1.3	3B(72): 0.6, 2B(14): -1.0	-0.3
Shane Peterson	OF	CSP	AAA	27	194	26	10	2	7	27	17	41	0	1	.320/.387/.523	.297	.387	1.2	RF(26): 0.1, LF(14): -0.1	1.2
	OF	MIL	MLB	27	226	22	7	3	2	16	20	55	0	1	.259/.324/.353	.247	.345	-2.3	LF(33): 2.0, CF(20): 1.1	0.2
Alex Presley	OF	HOU	MLB	29	13	1	0	0	0	1	1	5	0	0	.250/.308/.250	.210	.429	0.0	LF(4): -0.3, RF(1): -0.4	-0.1
	OF	FRE	AAA	29	367	48	14	1	3	49	27	41	15	4	.292/.345/.367	.253	.324	2.0	CF(41): 4.4, RF(28): -1.3	1.0
Michael Reed	OF	BLX	AA	22	377	43	20	5	5	49	53	80	25	7	.278/.379/.422	.309	.347	-3.0	RF(76): 4.0, CF(8): 0.1	2.9
	OF	CSP	AAA	22	148	19	13	2	0	21	20	31	1	0	.246/.351/.381	.245	.323	1.4	RF(30): -3.5, CF(5): -1.4	-0.3
	OF	MIL	MLB	22	6	2	1	0	0	0	0	3	0	0	.333/.333/.500	.304	.667	-1.0	RF(3): -0.1	-0.1
Yadiel Rivera	SS	BLX	AA	23	208	23	9	3	1	16	17	30	8	7	.277/.345/.375	.265	.327	-1.9	2B(38): 1.9, 3B(10): -1.3	0.5
	SS	CSP	AAA	23	306	32	8	4	1	28	10	53	4	3	.238/.266/.303	.199	.286	1.3	SS(71): -0.6, 2B(8): -1.3	-0.7
	SS	MIL	MLB	23	15	0	0	0	0	0	0	4	0	0	.071/.071/.071	.073	.100	-0.3	2B(4): -0.2, SS(2): 0.4	-0.3
Tyrone Taylor	CF	BLX	AA	21	504	48	20	3	3	43	31	55	10	6	.260/.312/.337	.243	.288	1.1	CF(84): 2.3, RF(29): -1.9	0.5
Jonathan Villar	SS	FRE	AAA	24	313	59	13	5	5	32	27	77	35	9	.271/.342/.407	.276	.359	6.7	SS(59): -4.5, 3B(6): -0.5	1.9
	SS	HOU	MLB	24	128	18	7	1	2	11	10	29	7	2	.284/.339/.414	.270	.360	-0.4	SS(22): 1.3, 3B(12): 1.1	0.8
Colin Walsh	2B	MID	AA	25	619	97	39	2	13	49	124	131	17	7	.302/.447/.470	.304	.390	2.0	2B(117): -7.9, LF(10): -0.5	4.0
Kyle Wren	OF	BLX	AA	24	258	26	6	0	0	13	24	29	20	9	.300/.370/.326	.286	.342	-0.9	LF(34): 1.7, CF(25): 1.2	1.6
	OF	CSP	AAA	24	314	33	11	3	1	26	19	45	16	4	.251/.298/.320	.225	.293	-0.3	CF(54): 1.3, LF(19): -2.8	-0.4

Nevin Ashley doubled in his major-league debut on September 9th. After 870 minor-league games over 10 years, the 31-year-old couldn't have cared less about the Brewers' overall record; standing at second, he basked in the warmth of realized dreams. (He was stranded on second and the Brewers lost the game.) ❖ If **Javier Betancourt** were any more fringe, he'd be Dr. Walter Bishop. On the upside he's got great instincts and Edgardo Alfonzo for an uncle. ❖ **Matt Clark** hit nearly .300 with 20 homers in Triple-A and was on the 40-man roster, but didn't see Miller Park in September. It's poor timing for the Quad-A slugger, who is exactly the player the Brewers needed in the dark Yuniesky Times of 2013. ❖ **Clint Coulter** took the prospecting world by storm with a scorching-hot April; afterward, the storm receded as the converted catcher only hit .232/.310/.351 with seven homers. ❖ Utilityman **Jake Elmore** played six positions for the Rays, including 25 games at first base and one on the mound. The Brewers are his sixth organization since the start of 2014. ❖ Provided that **Ramon Flores** recovers from a ghastly ankle injury, he'll provide organizational depth as a corner outfielder. Flores can hit a little bit and he'll take his walks, which makes him perfect for saber-friendly fringe prospect lists and the 2002 Oakland A's. ❖ **Elian Herrera** became the third player to ever hit a grand slam off Burke Badenhop, the other two being Ryan Theriot and Brooks Conrad. And that's the worst Sporcle quiz in the history of mankind. You're welcome. ❖ **Martin Maldonado** may be the team barber, but he also cuts down runners with startling precision. His 38 percent caught-stealing rate was 10 percent better than the league's average and near Molina-level. ❖ **Yerison Pena** hit .327/.424/.551 with 20 extra-base hits in 43 games for the DSL Brewers. Sadly, it was at age 23. He was the DSL's equivalent of that 16-year-old middle schooler who was held back a few years and won the eighth-grade football MVP award. ❖ **Hernan Perez** represents the second Hernan to play in the majors. Hernan Iribarren is currently winning with a career WARP of -0.1. ❖ **Shane Peterson** is the human embodiment of the 90-loss season. He's a physically unimpressive white guy who plays the game the "right way," though, so internet commenters quickly fell in love with the 27-year-old and his finite, finite potential. ❖ **Alex Presley** saw very limited time on the big-league club, partly due to the plethora of outfielders in Houston and partly due to the fact that he's Alex Presley. ❖ **Michael Reed** had a 13.9 percent walk rate in 2015, which makes the sabermetrically inclined fan squirm with delight. It's the other 86.1 percent that may limit him from being anything more than a fourth outfielder, even with his notable gap-power improvement. ❖ **Yadiel Rivera** barely bested a .300 slugging percentage in the thin air of Colorado Springs. He's like a Puerto Rican MacGyver with the glove, though, beautiful and toolsy. ❖ **Tyrone Taylor** entered the 2015 season as one of the Brewers' prized prospects, but a disappointing year combined with a massive influx of minor-league talent has left the 21-year-old looking more like a Toyota Camry in a parking lot crammed with BMWs and Lexuses. ❖ **Jonathan Villar** went to the Astros in the Roy Oswalt trade, and all these years later it's still the most interesting thing about him. ❖ **Colin Walsh** has never posted a full-season OBP lower than .356, but he's 26 and spent 2015 in Double-A. PECOTA comps him to Kevin Melillo, which is downright eerie. ❖ **Kyle Wren** was traded to Milwaukee after the Braves relieved his father, Frank Wren, of his general manager duties. As the old adage goes, when you break up with someone, you break up with all their friends. Don't let anyone tell you that baseball doesn't reflect society.

Pitchers

NAME	TEAM	LVL	AGE	W	L	SV	G	GS	IP	H	HR	BB/9	K/9	GB%	BABIP	WHIP	ERA	FIP	FRA	WARP	CFIP	MPH
Yhonathan Barrios	ALT	AA	23	0	1	10	20	0	24^{2}	17	1	3.3	4.4	47%	.211	1.05	1.46	3.92	5.15	-0.2	114	
	BLX	AA	23	3	2	6	16	0	20	22	1	2.2	7.2	48%	.344	1.35	3.15	3.25	3.62	0.2	92	
	IND	AAA	23	1	2	1	13	0	15^{2}	19	0	4.6	5.2	36%	.345	1.72	4.60	3.54	5.32	-0.2	112	
	MIL	MLB	23	0	0	0	5	0	6^{2}	3	0	0.0	9.4	60%	.200	0.45	0.00	1.06	-1.06	0.5	93	98.9
Michael Blazek	MIL	MLB	26	5	3	0	45	0	55^{2}	40	3	2.9	7.6	49%	.242	1.04	2.43	3.20	2.46	1.5	97	95.8
Jed Bradley	CSP	AAA	25	2	4	0	20	1	26	45	1	3.5	5.2	52%	.431	2.12	9.00	4.10	6.01	-0.2	108	
	BLX	AA	25	1	1	0	23	0	32^{2}	29	1	2.8	8.5	55%	.311	1.19	3.31	3.09	3.24	0.5	88	
Tyler Cravy	MIL	MLB	25	0	8	0	14	7	42^{2}	47	5	4.6	7.4	42%	.326	1.62	5.70	4.73	6.20	-0.6	113	93.7
	CSP	AAA	25	7	7	0	17	17	95^{1}	92	6	2.9	7.1	41%	.303	1.29	3.97	3.95	4.43	1.2	94	
David Goforth	MIL	MLB	26	1	0	0	20	0	24^{2}	32	4	2.9	8.8	52%	.373	1.62	4.01	4.30	5.82	-0.3	100	96.4
	CSP	AAA	26	0	4	4	38	0	47	36	2	5.2	6.5	58%	.252	1.34	2.68	4.43	5.64	-0.2	109	
Junior Guerra	CHA	MLB	30	0	0	0	3	0	4	7	1	2.2	6.8	57%	.462	2.00	6.75	5.60	9.30	-0.2	105	96.6
	CHR	AAA	30	2	4	7	26	8	63^{2}	44	5	4.1	11.2	44%	.260	1.15	3.39	3.11	2.46	1.7	79	
	BIR	AA	30	2	3	0	5	3	19^{2}	15	2	1.8	11.9	48%	.325	0.97	2.29	2.90	1.44	0.8	66	
Nick Hagadone	CLE	MLB	29	0	1	0	36	0	27^{1}	30	3	4.0	9.2	38%	.333	1.54	4.28	3.80	4.88	-0.1	101	96.6
Corey Knebel	MIL	MLB	23	0	0	0	48	0	50^{1}	44	8	3.0	10.4	50%	.290	1.21	3.22	4.06	4.11	0.4	87	97.5
	CSP	AAA	23	1	2	6	16	0	15^{1}	14	1	4.1	12.9	42%	.371	1.37	4.70	2.95	2.66	0.4	73	
Ariel Pena	MIL	MLB	26	2	1	0	6	5	27^{1}	24	2	4.6	8.9	40%	.293	1.39	4.28	3.89	4.74	0.1	102	94.1
	CSP	AAA	26	2	2	0	43	7	82^{2}	77	7	3.5	9.0	39%	.312	1.32	4.14	3.96	3.70	1.5	86	
Tyler Wagner	BLX	AA	24	11	5	0	25	25	152^{1}	130	7	2.7	7.1	64%	.283	1.15	2.25	3.27	3.45	2.7	91	
	MIL	MLB	24	0	2	0	3	3	13^{2}	22	1	4.6	3.3	53%	.389	2.12	7.24	4.92	8.86	-0.6	127	92.0

Acquired from Pittsburgh in the Aramis Ramirez deal, **Yhonathan Barrios** is a 5-foot-10, converted infielder who can touch triple-digits with the fastball. That's all he can throw, but it has some sink and he isn't missing with it, so it could very well be enough. ❖ **Michael Blazek** is, if not a diamond in the rough, a cool geode. He showed three legit pitches and an ability to avoid basehits, despite not seeing many high-leverage innings. His 2.46 DRA was 15th best in baseball (min. 40 IP). ❖ **Jed Bradley**'s career has mirrored Nic Cage's performance in *The Weatherman*. The viewer's emotions shift from anger to pity, culminating in a brisk departure from the theatre in the middle of the film, hand shielding one's eyes from the pain. ❖ **Tyler Cravy** is a pleasant reminder that the majors are in some part a meritocracy. He went without a victory in 2015, in both the statistical and the moral sense. ❖ **David Goforth** dialed down his velocity for the sake of command, in an attempt to be a pitcher rather than a thrower. His walk rate (13.6% in Triple-A) indicates that it was, in fact, a false dichotomy all along. ❖ **Junior Guerra** pitched in 12 different leagues, in five time zones, over nine years, before finally reaching the big leagues in 2015. One can only imagine how he felt after giving up singles to the first three batters. ❖ Southpaw **Nick Hagadone** was halfway through a disappointing 2015 when he fractured the medial epicondyle in his left elbow. We joke about the eternal life one receives after committing one's soul to LOOGYdom, but truth is that mid-90s from the left side just doesn't go as far as it used to. ❖ **Corey Knebel** is a potential back-end reliever who stands 6-foot-4 with a mid-to-high-90s fastball and a no-shit curveball. With only that information provided, you already know he's a Texan. [baseball] As a two-pitch, flyball reliever with command problems and career platoon splits, **Ariel Pena**'s name on a lineup card (A. Pena) is quite fitting. ❖ A sinker-slider pitcher with plus-makeup isn't the sexiest profile, but guys like **Tyler Wagner** often make up the back-end of starting rotations on contending clubs. A combined 2.05 ERA over his last 303 innings will earn him chances. ❖ **Taylor Williams** soared up prospect charts in 2014, but missed all of 2015 with elbow issues and finally had Tommy John surgery in August—which means he likely won't return until 2017 as a 26-year-old hurler who has never pitched above High-A. Not great, Bob.

Manager

Craig Counsell

YEAR	TEAM	W	L	Pythag +/-	Avg PC	100+ P	120+ P	QS	BQS	REL	REL w Zero R	IBB	PH	PH Avg	PH HR	SB2	CS2	SB3	CS3	SAC Att	SAC%	POS SAC	Squeeze	Swing	In Play
2015	MIL	61	76	-3	92.4	40	0	53	6	424	338	30	244	.259	5	67	20	9	3	59	72.9	16	1	197	63

When Counsell took over in May following Ron Roenicke's dismissal, his managerial experience comprised one interview (with the Rays the previous winter) and zero on-the-bench training. What Counsell had done was work in the Brewers' front office, where he became familiar with analytics.

Figuring out whether Counsell put his education to good use is difficult. The Brewers weren't a good club when he came into power, and got worse at the deadline by trading Carlos Gomez and Gerardo Parra. Still, this much is clear: Counsell liked to pinch-hit for his position players. If you prorate Counsell's numbers to a full season, he would've ranked third in the National League, behind Don Mattingly and Joe Maddon—each of whom had playoff races to worry about. The Brewers weren't jockeying for postseason position, yet Counsell did his best to keep Scooter Gennett, Shane Peterson and Adam Lind away from left-handed pitchers—a sign that he appreciates platoon splits.

Counsell also dropped hints that he values an out more than his predecessor did. Undoubtedly the biggest difference between Counsell and Roenicke was his willingness to have a position player drop down a bunt. Counsell notched 44 position player sacrifices in 137 games; Roenicke, meanwhile, somehow tallied 18 in 25 games—or 41 percent as many in less than a fifth as many games.

Of course, that's just two examples. For the most part, it remains to be seen whether Counsell has what it takes to manage for the long haul. Nonetheless, it looks like he'll receive at least another season to make his case. New general manager David Stearns kept Counsell on board and—to make a comparison to Stearn's old employer in Houston—there's a chance the Brewers already have their A.J. Hinch in place.

MINNESOTA TWINS

Essay by Ken Funck

Player comments by Matthew Trueblood and BP authors

Despite failing to make the postseason for the fifth straight season, there were plenty of positive signs on display in Minnesota last summer. The Twins enjoyed their first winning season since claiming a division title in 2010 and remained in contention late into September, surfing the positive vibes of an energetic new manager and the first flowering of a farm system that has been carefully cultivated to deliver the franchise from its recent irrelevance. It should feel like *déjà vu* all over again for Terry Ryan, whose first stint as general manager featured six straight losing seasons before an influx of home-grown talent helped Minnesota finally post a winning record in 2001. The Twins used that season, and those players, as a springboard to win six division titles over the next 10 seasons; now that Ryan has returned to the corner office after a four-year hiatus and the farm system is once again ranked among baseball's best there's hope in the Twin Cities that history can repeat itself.

But will it? Can perhaps the most aggressively old-school franchise in the league once again become a perennial winner in today's analytics-driven environment? Last spring, we ran a series of articles on our website called "Every Team's Moneyball" that attempted to describe the unique strategy each franchise employs to gain an advantage. Here's the money quote from our piece on Minnesota: "The Twins have no Moneyball. They're committed to building the next great Twins team the same way they built the last one. ... Ryan says that the Twins are invested in many of the new approaches other clubs have adopted ... [b]ut it's clear that, in the Twins' eyes, those things are merely gravy; player acquisition and development are still the meat. ... Can the Twins pull themselves back into contention by doing the one thing every other team tries to do, only better?"

To help answer that question, we happily have a number of case studies against which we can compare the current Twins. Last season saw the playoff arrival of rebuilding teams in Chicago and Houston that not only created farm systems as well regarded as Minnesota's, but also famously embrace analytics. As a counterpoint, the reigning world champion Royals are considered to be at the opposite end of the sabermetric spectrum, following an approach that in the popular imagination should have

TWINS PROSPECTUS

2015 W-L: 83-79, 2nd in AL Central

Pythag	.497	17th	DER	.700	20th
RS/G	4.30	11th	B-Age	28.3	14th
RA/G	4.32	17th	P-Age	28.9	24th
TAv	.248	29th	Salary	$108.3M	19th
BRR	-4.70	20th	M$/MW	$2.8M	19th
TAv-P	.259	14th	DL Days	730	7th
FIP	4.07	18th	$ on DL	12%	10th

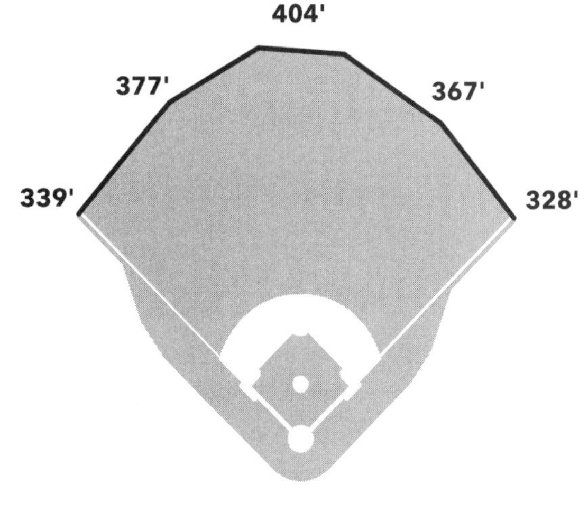

Outfield wall profile: **8'** to **23'**

Three-Year Park Factors

Runs	Runs/RH	Runs/LH	HR/RH	HR/LH
106	118	115	119	104

Top Hitter WARP	2.4	Eddie Rosario
Top Pitcher WARP	2.8	Kyle Gibson
Top Prospect		Byron Buxton

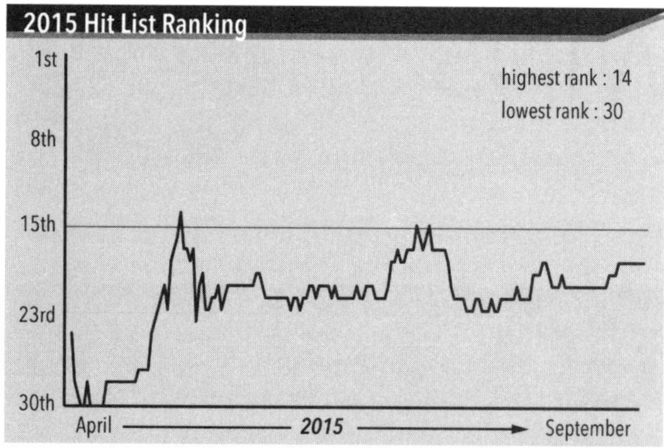

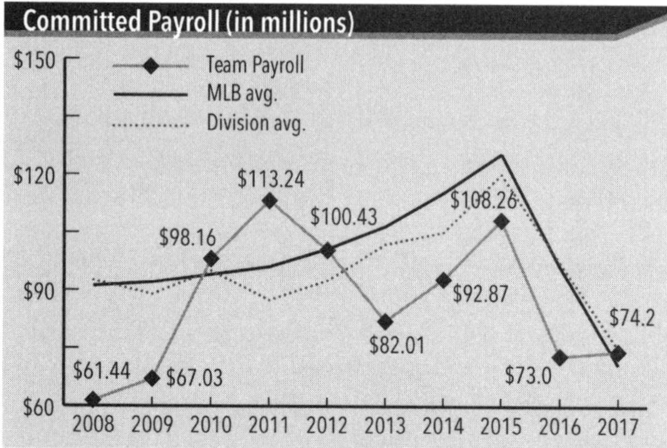

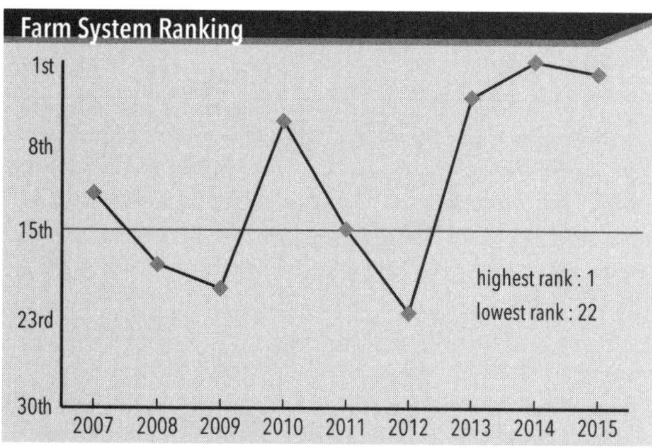

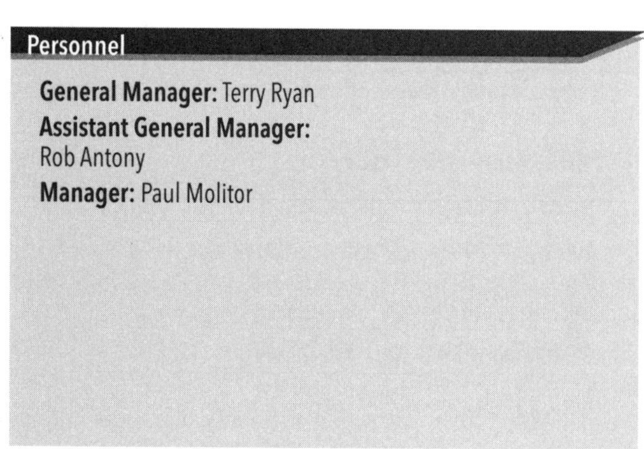
Personnel

General Manager: Terry Ryan

Assistant General Manager: Rob Antony

Manager: Paul Molitor

gone out of style with whalebone corsets and hairnets. (Of course, the Royals have an analytics department, as every team does, but the perception remains what it is, in part because of how the team has branded itself under the leadership of Dayton Moore and Ned Yost.) Last year's playoffs also featured the current platonic ideal of a baseball organization, the Cardinals. Each of these teams is further down the road of turning exceptional minor-league talent into playoff success than the Twins are.

To give some idea of how the Twins, Cubs, Astros, Royals and Cardinals were constructed, Table 1 shows the WARP total for each team broken down by the method used to add each player to the organization. "Farm" includes both draftees and amateur-free-agent signings; "FA" includes free agents, Rule 5 picks, waiver claims and players acquired through cash-only trades; "Trade" is further broken down by whether the primary players given up were originally acquired through either the Farm or FA route, sometimes by tracking back through a chain of transactions. Some of this is a little arbitrary, most is alarmingly inexact and none requires the type of Gory Mathematical Details that Russell Carleton admirably produces. We're talking in broad strokes here. Let's sit back, enjoy an adult beverage, eyeball the numbers and see what jumps out.

Team	WARP					Percentage				
	Farm	FA	Trade	Trade Farm	Trade FA	Farm	FA	Trade	Trade Farm	Trade FA
Twins	11.2	2.7	5.9	4.6	1.3	57%	14%	30%	23%	7%
Cubs	9.2	11.6	24.6	11.9	12.7	20%	26%	54%	26%	28%
Astros	17.6	11.9	8.6	6.8	1.8	46%	31%	23%	18%	5%
Royals	18.0	3.5	11.2	11.9	-0.7	55%	11%	34%	36%	-2%
Cardinals	23.2	5.8	11.8	12.0	-0.2	57%	14%	29%	29%	0%

Going To Rehab: Chicago Cubs

If the Twins have a developmental *doppelganger* in this comparison, it's the Cubs. Minnesota and Chicago were the top two farm systems in both our 2014 and 2015 organizational rankings, they both employ some of the most highly regarded prospects in the game and neither were expected to compete for a playoff spot last season. Yet the Cubs managed to win 14 more games than the Twins, and the difference doesn't lie in a quicker emergence of their high-octane talent, despite the October highlight reels produced by Kyle Schwarber and Jorge Soler. The Twins got more production from their home-grown talent, including veterans Trevor Plouffe and Brian Dozier and newcomers Miguel Sano and Eddie Rosario, than the Cubs received from their in-house options. However, Chicago received significantly more from their free-agent signees, and not just because of their deep pockets. Sure, quirky mega-millionaire Jon Lester gave them a boost, but so did clearance-rack items Chris Coghlan and Jason Hammel.

The major difference, however, lies in the efforts Chicago made to enhance its roster while the organizational dough had yet to rise. By far the biggest slice of Chicago's deep-dish WARP pie is the value received from players acquired through trades, especially free-agent acquisitions who were flipped for younger, cost-controlled talent. During their fallow years Theo Epstein and company made a cottage industry of signing undervalued veteran pitchers, assigning pitching coach Chris Bosio to polish them up and then trading them for prospects or down-on-their-luck veterans with upside. The most famous of these moves involved coaxing 15 good starts from Scott Feldman before spinning him into Cy Young–winner Jake Arrieta and bullpen cog Pedro Strop; signing players like Hammel and Paul Maholm and claiming Luis Valbuena off waivers also helped bring Dexter Fowler, Tommy La Stella and (in part) Addison Russell into the fold. Not every move paid off, but they cost essentially nothing, and if the world is willing to hand you a basketful of free scratch-offs you might as well reach in and grab a few.

In comparison, Minnesota's free agents were brought in to help the Twins compete in the short term, but often challenged beat writers to find new synonyms for "forgettable." Ricky Nolasco has been a disaster, Ervin Santana has been either mediocre or suspended, Mike Pelfrey was either mediocre or hurt and Kevin Correia was Kevin Correia (hey look, another synonym for "forgettable!"). Only Phil Hughes and catcher Kurt Suzuki produced out of the gate, and instead of cashing them in and heading for the buffet the Twins doubled down and signed them to instantly regrettable extensions. This puts even more pressure on the farm system to produce.

Adding The Right Spice: Houston Astros

Houston has also received high marks in our organizational rankings, and since they visited Chernobyl upon their roster several years ago and devoted themselves to a complete rebuild, their home-grown talent is at least a year ahead of Minnesota's. The most productive players on the Astros are young veterans like George Springer, Dallas Keuchel, Jose Altuve and Jason Castro, while otherworldly tyro Carlos Correa and starter Lance McCullers arrived last summer. Given this head start, it's not surprising that Houston is getting more value from its home-grown talent than Minnesota, and the Twins can take heart in the thought that Sano, Byron Buxton, Max Kepler and Jose Berrios are just starting to arrive.

However, the timely lesson here for the Twins is how to react once you are approaching contention. When it became clear they were ready to make a run, the Astros didn't stand pat and slot in all the young talent they've obsessively hoarded; instead, they made smart, responsible moves to fill out the roster around them. Colby Rasmus and Luke Gregerson were signed as relatively big-ticket free agents. Trades of players whose provenance had their roots in the Houston system brought back complementary pieces Jake Marisnick, Valbuena, Evan Gattis and Hank Conger, and provided the fodder for trade-deadline acquisitions Carlos Gomez and Mike Fiers. The contending-team moves took an aggressive step forward this winter with the acquisition of fireballing closer Ken Giles for a large package of youngsters.

Rarely do all the pieces needed for a playoff team arrive fully assembled from the farm system, and over the next two years Ryan will need to make judicious free-agent signings and trade redundant minor-league parts if he wants to transform Minnesota's pulsating mass of potentiality into a consistent big-league winner. The signing of Byung-ho Park is a good start, as the Korean slugger typifies the bold moves Minnesota will need to make to add spice to the roster.

Missouri Loves Company: Kansas City Royals and St. Louis Cardinals

Minnesota's Midwestern neighbors embody the ideals to which the Twins clearly aspire, as both franchises have found success while building primarily from within. The Royals were so committed to their process that it became a proper noun, first mockingly as the Royals suffered through six losing seasons, then with grudging respect as Dayton Moore brought Kansas City fans their first championship in a generation. Further down the Big Muddy, the Cardinals have their own proper noun for the ever-evolving player-development process that has made them baseball's most consistent winners: The Cardinal Way.

When you add together the wins they've earned from home-grown players, both currently on the roster or indirectly through trades, the Royals and especially the Cardinals are the modern-day masters of self-sufficiency. Yet even these teams, the ones tending the most fertile soil in baseball, can't survive completely off the grid; they still need to be successful buyers and traders in order to collect all the goods needed to thrive. While the Royals were waiting patiently for Eric Hosmer and Mike Moustakas to turn into championship cogs, they traded first veterans (Zack Greinke for Lorenzo Cain and Alcides Escobar), then prospects (Jake Odorizzi and Wil Myers for Wade Davis and James Shields) to fill out the roster. The list of Cardinals players acquired through trades includes Jason Heyward, Adam Wainwright, John Lackey, Randal Grichuk and Matt Holliday (before he re-signed as a free agent). In comparison, Minnesota's list of trade acquisitions reads like a list of toothpaste flavors: useful, uninspiring and a pale imitation of something better. There's a good chance Trevor May, Eduardo Escobar, Tommy Milone, Eduardo Nunez, Kevin Jepsen and Alex Meyer will collect as many All-Star appearances as you will, and none of the Twins' free agents produced significantly more than one win last year.

✦✦✦

It may be that Buxton and Sano are on the verge of becoming this generation's Mays and McCovey, and perhaps prospects like Berrios, Kepler and Nick Gordon will all grow into stars. Even so, that on its own won't be enough for the Twins to win a title. (Mays himself, after all, collected just one ring, five years before McCovey arrived on the scene.) To do that Minnesota will need to improve on its recent record of free-agent and trade-market failures. This isn't news to Ryan, who once traded local produce for David Ortiz, Eric Milton, Joe Mays, Kyle Lohse and Shannon Stewart to complement the primarily home-grown roster of his early-aughties division champs, but it is an imperative. The problem is that there's no obvious prescription: What makes one signing a Feldman (who turns into an Arrieta) and another move a Pelfrey? There are identifiable mistakes (not trading Hughes), but then there are the moves in which the Twins did "the one thing every other team tries to do" but *didn't* do it better (Ben Revere for May; Denard Span for Meyer). The Twins are right to consider player development the most important thing, but it can't ever be the only thing, and even if they do everything, they've still got to do it at a higher level than their competition in order to win. ■

—Ken Funck is an author of Baseball Prospectus and has contributed to the Annual since 2010.

Hitters

Oswaldo Arcia RF

Born: 5/9/91 Age: 25 Bats: L Throws: R Height: 6'0" Weight: 225

YEAR	TEAM	LVL	AGE	PA	R	2B	3B	HR	RBI	BB	K	SB	CS	AVG/OBP/SLG	TAv	BABIP	BRR	FRAA	WARP
2013	ROC	AAA	22	155	25	6	0	10	30	22	37	2	1	.313/.426/.594	.338	.366	-0.7	RF(17): -0.7, LF(2): 0.1	1.4
2013	MIN	MLB	22	378	34	17	2	14	43	23	117	1	2	.251/.304/.430	.267	.336	-1.6	LF(56): 4.1, RF(29): -2.4	1.0
2014	ROC	AAA	23	85	16	7	0	5	18	5	17	1	0	.312/.365/.597	.288	.339	0.6	RF(16): 0.4	0.5
2014	MIN	MLB	23	410	46	16	3	20	57	31	127	1	2	.231/.300/.452	.271	.292	-0.6	RF(100): -3.0	0.8
2015	ROC	AAA	24	311	31	13	0	12	41	18	82	0	1	.199/.257/.372	.235	.228	-1.0	RF(55): -5.1, LF(5): -0.2	-1.0
2015	MIN	MLB	24	65	6	0	0	2	8	4	15	0	0	.276/.338/.379	.245	.333	-1.4	LF(15): 0.9, RF(4): -0.0	0.0
2016	*MIN*	*MLB*	*25*	*232*	*27*	*10*	*1*	*10*	*33*	*16*	*67*	*1*	*1*	*.241/.304/.443*	*.261*	*.300*	*-0.6*	*LF 2, RF -0*	*0.8*
2017	*MIN*	*MLB*	*26*	*296*	*39*	*12*	*1*	*13*	*41*	*21*	*84*	*1*	*1*	*.238/.302/.440*	*.259*	*.291*	*-0.8*	*LF 3, RF 0*	*0.9*

Breakout: 1% Improve: 50% Collapse: 4% Attrition: 8% MLB: 90% *Comparables: Wily Mo Pena, Jay Bruce, Chris Davis*

Arcia has big-time power, and though his approach has been uneven, he has flashed patience and the ability to sting the ball to the opposite field. He swings and misses a lot, though. He's also a very poor defensive outfielder, even in left field. The Twins dislike both of those things, which is why Arcia's playing time was endangered and sometimes encroached upon even when he was healthy and productive. In 2015, he suffered a hip injury in April and scuffled throughout his rehab assignment, so his playing time went extinct. During one blazing fortnight around the Fourth of July, Arcia nearly pushed his way back into the picture. When that failed, many felt he got frustrated and lost his alignment. The rest of the season was a disaster, and while there's time yet, Arcia's development seems entirely off the rails. If ever there was a change-of-scenery candidate, Arcia might be that.

Travis Blankenhorn 3B

Born: 8/3/96 Age: 19 Bats: L Throws: R Height: 6'2" Weight: 208

YEAR	TEAM	LVL	AGE	PA	R	2B	3B	HR	RBI	BB	K	SB	CS	AVG/OBP/SLG	TAv	BABIP	BRR	FRAA	WARP
2016	*MIN*	*MLB*	*19*	*250*	*19*	*8*	*1*	*4*	*21*	*11*	*77*	*0*	*0*	*.191/.232/.283*	*.183*	*.260*	*-0.3*	*3B -2, LF 0*	*-1.6*
2017	*MIN*	*MLB*	*20*	*363*	*34*	*13*	*1*	*7*	*33*	*17*	*106*	*1*	*0*	*.204/.246/.313*	*.201*	*.269*	*-0.6*	*3B -3, LF 0*	*0.6*

Breakout: 0% Improve: 0% Collapse: 0% Attrition: 0% MLB: 0% *Comparables: Matt Davidson, Maikel Franco, Steven Souza*

The Matterhorn is one of the deadliest peaks in the world, claiming the lives of more than 500 climbers in the last 150 years. The Blankenhorn is a teenager. Which of the two is more terrifying remains a toss-up. The Twins surmounted their fear and spent their third-round pick in June on Blankenhorn, a high school shortstop whose frame and skill set will keep him firmly on the corners of the diamond in pro ball. That he won't play in the middle is one of the few bad things one can say about him, though. He bats left-handed, showing good raw power and the hit tool he'll need in order to actualize it. He still moves like a recently converted shortstop and has an above-average arm for a third baseman. A good spring could put him in full-season ball right away in 2016.

Byron Buxton CF

Born: 12/18/93 Age: 22 Bats: R Throws: R Height: 6'2" Weight: 190

YEAR	TEAM	LVL	AGE	PA	R	2B	3B	HR	RBI	BB	K	SB	CS	AVG/OBP/SLG	TAv	BABIP	BRR	FRAA	WARP
2013	FTM	A+	19	253	41	4	8	4	22	32	49	23	8	.326/.415/.472	.320	.404	5.0	CF(55): 9.1	3.9
2013	CDR	A	19	321	68	15	10	8	55	44	56	32	11	.341/.431/.559	.349	.402	4.6	CF(66): 2.8	4.9
2014	FTM	A+	20	134	19	4	2	4	16	10	33	6	2	.240/.313/.405	.254	.298	1.5	CF(28): 6.0, RF(2): -0.4	1.0
2015	ROC	AAA	21	59	11	3	1	1	8	4	12	2	1	.400/.441/.545	.378	.500	0.9	CF(11): 1.1	1.1
2015	MIN	MLB	21	138	16	7	1	2	6	6	44	2	2	.209/.250/.326	.214	.301	1.3	CF(44): 6.4	0.6
2015	CHT	AA	21	268	44	7	12	6	37	26	51	20	2	.283/.351/.489	.305	.332	2.4	CF(58): 14.2	4.0
2016	*MIN*	*MLB*	*22*	*624*	*82*	*22*	*10*	*15*	*60*	*47*	*162*	*25*	*8*	*.255/.313/.407*	*.255*	*.327*	*3.1*	*CF 26*	*5.1*
2017	*MIN*	*MLB*	*23*	*591*	*68*	*20*	*9*	*13*	*65*	*45*	*151*	*25*	*8*	*.258/.318/.403*	*.255*	*.330*	*4.0*	*CF 24*	*5.0*

Breakout: 6% Improve: 42% Collapse: 1% Attrition: 18% MLB: 69% *Comparables: Cameron Maybin, Anthony Gose, Adam Jones*

Snakebitten and stuck in an organization that has institutionally forgotten how to develop position players, Buxton has encountered a lot of adversity over the last two seasons. In 2015, that included some utterly inscrutable promotions and demotions, a significant hand injury and a rough introduction to big-league pitching. (Very rough. "Please don't compare it to 2011 Trout" rough.

Really, really bad.) Through all that, though, shone a player with absolutely electric skills. Buxton will probably be the best defensive center fielder in the American League this year, and the American League is where Kevins Pillar and Kiermaier play. Buxton's speed and power are also evident, even if his control of the strike zone seems to be lagging behind. He's still a better bet to win an MVP Award than the vast majority of 22-year-olds.

Brian Dozier 2B

Born: 5/15/87 Age: 29 Bats: R Throws: R Height: 5'11" Weight: 200

YEAR	TEAM	LVL	AGE	PA	R	2B	3B	HR	RBI	BB	K	SB	CS	AVG/OBP/SLG	TAv	BABIP	BRR	FRAA	WARP
2013	MIN	MLB	26	623	72	33	4	18	66	51	120	14	7	.244/.312/.414	.263	.278	3.9	2B(146): 13.4	3.8
2014	MIN	MLB	27	707	112	33	1	23	71	89	129	21	7	.242/.345/.416	.279	.269	4.3	2B(156): 5.5	4.4
2015	MIN	MLB	28	704	101	39	4	28	77	61	148	12	4	.236/.307/.444	.260	.261	4.8	2B(157): -8.6	1.6
2016	*MIN*	*MLB*	*29*	*635*	*83*	*31*	*3*	*19*	*67*	*57*	*124*	*14*	*5*	*.240/.313/.406*	*.256*	*.270*	*3.4*	*2B 0*	*2.7*
2017	*MIN*	*MLB*	*30*	*594*	*71*	*29*	*2*	*18*	*69*	*53*	*117*	*12*	*5*	*.236/.310/.401*	*.253*	*.267*	*3.5*	*2B 0*	*2.5*

Breakout: 1% Improve: 41% Collapse: 2% Attrition: 6% MLB: 99% *Comparables: Marcus Giles, Mark Ellis, Neil Walker*

For some reason, on the heels of a breakout 2014 that carried into the early part of 2015, Dozier began aggressively trying to fix what wasn't broken. He doubled the rate at which he swung at the first pitch. He sat dead red on every pitch, to the detriment of his ability to adjust to anything else. As the season wore on, his power dried up, he whiffed more and more within the strike zone, his defense got worse and his baserunning got worse. A borderline star second baseman withered into a replacement-level player.

Obviously, that kind of total collapse begets questions about unmentioned injuries, and Dozier did have an MRI on his hip just after the end of the season. No serious injury was reported, but it would be a surprise if he wasn't playing hurt in the second half. Is Dozier to be trusted going forward? It's terribly hard to say. Injury or no, he's been a weird player much longer than he's been a violently disappointing one. For the second straight season, Dozier did worse each time he saw a starter within a game, and did by far his best work against relievers. That's unorthodox to the point of incredibility, and underscores that Dozier has always built his value on manhandling heaters. That's a skill that requires good health to be viable, so whatever ailed Dozier late in the season, it had better be gone come spring training.

Eduardo Escobar SS

Born: 1/5/89 Age: 27 Bats: B Throws: R Height: 5'10" Weight: 185

YEAR	TEAM	LVL	AGE	PA	R	2B	3B	HR	RBI	BB	K	SB	CS	AVG/OBP/SLG	TAv	BABIP	BRR	FRAA	WARP
2013	MIN	MLB	24	179	23	5	2	3	10	11	34	0	2	.236/.282/.345	.241	.279	-2.0	SS(38): -0.2, 3B(23): -2.9	-0.3
2013	ROC	AAA	24	188	22	16	2	4	27	17	37	6	2	.307/.380/.500	.290	.373	0.1	SS(29): 1.6, 2B(6): 1.0	1.7
2014	MIN	MLB	25	465	52	35	2	6	37	24	93	1	1	.275/.315/.406	.252	.336	0.7	SS(98): -8.7, 3B(25): -1.4	0.5
2015	MIN	MLB	26	446	48	31	4	12	58	28	86	2	3	.262/.309/.445	.266	.301	-1.4	SS(71): -5.9, LF(35): 4.1	1.5
2016	*MIN*	*MLB*	*27*	*479*	*45*	*26*	*4*	*7*	*46*	*27*	*94*	*3*	*2*	*.256/.300/.382*	*.238*	*.302*	*-0.8*	*SS -9*	*0.2*
2017	*MIN*	*MLB*	*28*	*470*	*47*	*24*	*4*	*7*	*45*	*28*	*96*	*2*	*2*	*.245/.290/.369*	*.231*	*.292*	*-0.7*	*SS -9*	*1.1*

Breakout: 6% Improve: 38% Collapse: 12% Attrition: 22% MLB: 93% *Comparables: Ronny Cedeno, Luis Gonzalez, Brandon Phillips*

Escobar is a fringy defensive shortstop, but for any kind of shortstop, he's a really good hitter. Last season, he made the marginal improvement in plate discipline he needed to really tap into his natural power and roughly average hit tool, and he should have been Paul Molitor's starting shortstop almost right away. Instead, Molitor stuck Escobar in left field in over half his games through the end of June. That was like using an iPhone as a compass: technically possible, but wasteful, frustrating and disorienting. To Molitor's credit, he figured that out by the trade deadline. From July 28th through the end of the year, Escobar was the Twins' starting shortstop, and he batted .278/.338/.505 over that span. Given his age, there's no reason he can't have a successful full season as a regular shortstop in 2016.

Nick Gordon SS

Born: 10/24/95 Age: 20 Bats: L Throws: R Height: 6'0" Weight: 160

YEAR	TEAM	LVL	AGE	PA	R	2B	3B	HR	RBI	BB	K	SB	CS	AVG/OBP/SLG	TAv	BABIP	BRR	FRAA	WARP
2015	CDR	A	19	535	79	23	7	1	58	39	88	25	8	.277/.336/.360	.258	.333	2.9	SS(118): 8.4	3.3
2016	*MIN*	*MLB*	*20*	*250*	*25*	*10*	*2*	*3*	*19*	*13*	*61*	*5*	*2*	*.228/.271/.323*	*.214*	*.292*	*0.1*	*SS 3*	*0.4*
2017	*MIN*	*MLB*	*21*	*385*	*37*	*17*	*3*	*5*	*34*	*19*	*90*	*7*	*3*	*.236/.279/.337*	*.223*	*.298*	*0.5*	*SS 5*	*2.4*

Breakout: 2% Improve: 6% Collapse: 0% Attrition: 2% MLB: 7% *Comparables: Lonnie Chisenhall, Eugenio Suarez, Brad Harman*

Whatever trace doubts remained about Gordon's long-term position, he firmly dispelled them in 2015. He's a shortstop, and a good one. He also has a solid-average hit tool, can drive the ball into the gaps and runs quite well. He's rail-thin like his brother Dee, but only because he's so young. He's going to grow into a slightly stronger frame, and his swing and approach give him a chance to develop over-the-fence pull power. He didn't have a strong second half, but Gordon remains the best shortstop prospect in the Twins' system and maintains a first-division ceiling.

Travis Harrison OF

Born: 10/17/92 Age: 23 Bats: R Throws: R Height: 6'1" Weight: 215

YEAR	TEAM	LVL	AGE	PA	R	2B	3B	HR	RBI	BB	K	SB	CS	AVG/OBP/SLG	TAv	BABIP	BRR	FRAA	WARP
2013	CDR	A	20	537	66	28	0	15	59	68	125	2	4	.253/.366/.416	.282	.316	1.2	3B(112): -9.6, LF(1): -0.0	2.1
2014	FTM	A+	21	537	80	33	1	3	59	64	86	7	5	.269/.361/.365	.281	.318	0.0	LF(98): -7.3, 3B(15): -2.0	1.5
2015	CHT	AA	22	479	64	23	4	5	54	65	102	3	9	.240/.363/.356	.276	.307	0.4	RF(97): -16.5, 1B(1): 0.0	0.0
2016	*MIN*	*MLB*	*23*	*250*	*23*	*11*	*1*	*4*	*24*	*24*	*64*	*1*	*1*	*.221/.309/.338*	*.235*	*.289*	*-0.6*	*RF -7, LF -0*	*-0.9*
2017	*MIN*	*MLB*	*24*	*368*	*41*	*17*	*1*	*7*	*35*	*36*	*96*	*1*	*1*	*.226/.313/.350*	*.241*	*.297*	*-0.9*	*RF -10, LF 0*	*-0.4*

Breakout: 2% Improve: 6% Collapse: 3% Attrition: 5% MLB: 12% *Comparables: Ramon Flores, Rene Tosoni, Jarrett Parker*

Harrison was a first-round pick for the Twins back in 2011, but after failing to cut it at third base, he's become a fringy corner-outfield prospect. He owns a .366 career OBP, but he's never been wildly young for his level, and the power and athleticism one hopes to get from a corner guy are absent from Harrison's profile. He still has the arm of a third baseman, but his range is poor and he's shown mostly gap power at the plate. Maintaining the strike-zone control that has propped him up as he's risen to the high minors will be critical (and very difficult) going forward. When OBP > SLG for a major leaguer, it's a curiosity; when OBP > SLG for a minor leaguer, it's a red flag.

Torii Hunter RF

Born: 7/18/75 Age: 40 Bats: R Throws: R Height: 6'2" Weight: 220

YEAR	TEAM	LVL	AGE	PA	R	2B	3B	HR	RBI	BB	K	SB	CS	AVG/OBP/SLG	TAv	BABIP	BRR	FRAA	WARP
2013	DET	MLB	37	652	90	37	5	17	84	26	113	3	2	.304/.334/.465	.292	.344	0.8	RF(143): -13.2	2.0
2014	DET	MLB	38	586	71	33	2	17	83	23	89	4	3	.286/.319/.446	.266	.311	0.4	RF(128): -8.2	0.5
2015	MIN	MLB	39	567	67	22	0	22	81	35	105	2	5	.240/.293/.409	.246	.258	1.3	RF(123): 1.7	0.5
2016	*MIN*	*MLB*	*40*	*537*	*64*	*24*	*2*	*14*	*56*	*30*	*104*	*4*	*3*	*.265/.311/.407*	*.252*	*.305*	*0.7*	*RF -8*	*0.0*
2017	*MIN*	*MLB*	*41*	*428*	*48*	*18*	*1*	*10*	*46*	*22*	*87*	*2*	*2*	*.257/.301/.385*	*.241*	*.302*	*0.6*	*RF -6*	*0.2*

Breakout: 1% Improve: 22% Collapse: 9% Attrition: 15% MLB: 70% *Comparables: Dave Winfield, Moises Alou, Dwight Evans*

Hunter spent 2015 with the organization that drafted him in the first round in 1993 and was his home when he rose to prominence with spectacular center-field defense and consistent output at the plate: From 2002 to 2007, his OBP strayed from the .330s just once and his slugging stayed within a 75-point band. That we're dredging up this ancient history can only mean one thing: Hunter called it a career in late October. It was a pretty successful and enjoyable valedictory campaign: Hunter recovered somewhat from the (apparent) loss of plate discipline and fielding skills that had marked his previous two seasons. He hit 22 home runs, posting his highest ISO since 2010. He took almost an assistant role alongside rookie skipper Paul Molitor. His age showed in slowness (in both his legs and swing), leading to his first BABIP south of .297 since 2003. That pinned down his total WARP, but in addition to whatever value he had off the field, he made a small on-field contribution to a surprising season for the Twins. Give Hunter credit for a career spent defying the aging curve, mentoring players who still swear by his counsel and smiling almost constantly.

Max Kepler CF

Born: 2/10/93 Age: 23 Bats: L Throws: L Height: 6'4" Weight: 205

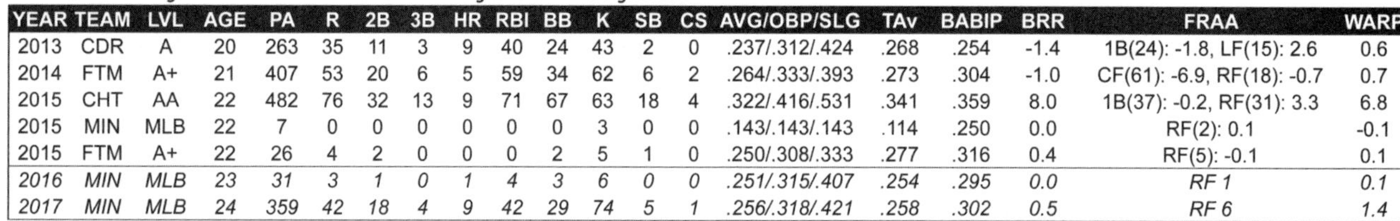

YEAR	TEAM	LVL	AGE	PA	R	2B	3B	HR	RBI	BB	K	SB	CS	AVG/OBP/SLG	TAv	BABIP	BRR	FRAA	WARP
2013	CDR	A	20	263	35	11	3	9	40	24	43	2	0	.237/.312/.424	.268	.254	-1.4	1B(24): -1.8, LF(15): 2.6	0.6
2014	FTM	A+	21	407	53	20	6	5	59	34	62	6	2	.264/.333/.393	.273	.304	-1.0	CF(61): -6.9, RF(18): -0.7	0.7
2015	CHT	AA	22	482	76	32	13	9	71	67	63	18	4	.322/.416/.531	.341	.359	8.0	1B(37): -0.2, RF(31): 3.3	6.8
2015	MIN	MLB	22	7	0	0	0	0	0	0	3	0	0	.143/.143/.143	.114	.250	0.0	RF(2): 0.1	-0.1
2015	FTM	A+	22	26	4	2	0	0	0	2	5	1	0	.250/.308/.333	.277	.316	0.4	RF(5): -0.1	0.1
2016	*MIN*	*MLB*	*23*	*31*	*3*	*1*	*0*	*1*	*4*	*3*	*6*	*0*	*0*	*.251/.315/.407*	*.254*	*.295*	*0.0*	*RF 1*	*0.1*
2017	*MIN*	*MLB*	*24*	*359*	*42*	*18*	*4*	*9*	*42*	*29*	*74*	*5*	*1*	*.256/.318/.421*	*.258*	*.302*	*0.5*	*RF 6*	*1.4*

Breakout: 11% Improve: 15% Collapse: 10% Attrition: 25% MLB: 36% *Comparables: Yonder Alonso, Mike Carp, Andy Wilkins*

We're still waiting for the homers to show up, but Kepler is a standout in all other aspects, and at this point, there's no reason he can't graduate into the majors for good sometime during the first half of 2016. He's patient, doesn't compromise his well-built swing to chase dingers, runs the bases well and should be at least an average corner outfielder. One never knows what to expect from a player plucked out of a culture in which baseball plays only a small part, but Kepler's approach, demeanor and instincts have wowed the skeptics mostly into silence. If he can find the right adjustments as he acquaints himself with big-league pitching, he should be able to tap into the pop suggested by his large frame, and if that happens, he's headed for stardom.

Joe Mauer 1B

Born: 4/19/83 Age: 33 Bats: L Throws: R Height: 6'5" Weight: 225

YEAR	TEAM	LVL	AGE	PA	R	2B	3B	HR	RBI	BB	K	SB	CS	AVG/OBP/SLG	TAv	BABIP	BRR	FRAA	WARP
2013	MIN	MLB	30	508	62	35	0	11	47	61	89	0	1	.324/.404/.476	.315	.383	-0.5	C(75): -2.3, 1B(8): -0.3	4.3
2014	MIN	MLB	31	518	60	27	2	4	55	60	96	3	0	.277/.361/.371	.261	.342	4.2	1B(100): 2.8	1.4
2015	MIN	MLB	32	666	69	34	2	10	66	67	112	2	1	.265/.338/.380	.258	.309	-2.6	1B(137): -1.6	0.1
2016	*MIN*	*MLB*	*33*	*610*	*63*	*31*	*2*	*8*	*62*	*68*	*102*	*3*	*1*	*.282/.362/.393*	*.271*	*.333*	*0.3*	*1B -0*	*1.7*
2017	*MIN*	*MLB*	*34*	*520*	*60*	*26*	*1*	*6*	*48*	*55*	*88*	*1*	*0*	*.277/.353/.377*	*.262*	*.329*	*0.1*	*1B 0*	*0.8*

Breakout: 2% Improve: 26% Collapse: 2% Attrition: 10% MLB: 96% *Comparables: John Olerud, Kent Hrbek, Lyle Overbay*

Walter White grew a beard in the final season of *Breaking Bad*, not only to disguise his visage but to send the audience a clear signal: Things are different now. They can't go back to the way they were, and this Heisenberg is not to be confused with the force of nature we saw in previous seasons. So it is with Mauer. His story isn't over; this might even be the most interesting part. It's just not the most *exciting* part. There's nothing special left in his tank, and from now on, Mauer's story will be about what makes us all human, instead of what makes some of us seem to be more. Age stole his positional value, then his power and now it has taken his on-base skills. He's an excellent illustration of the reason we don't anoint Hall of Famers until they're well into their 30s.

J.R. Murphy C

Born: 5/13/91 Age: 25 Bats: R Throws: R Height: 5'11" Weight: 205

YEAR	TEAM	LVL	AGE	PA	R	2B	3B	HR	RBI	BB	K	SB	CS	AVG/OBP/SLG	TAv	BABIP	BRR	FRAA	WARP
2013	NYA	MLB	22	27	3	1	0	0	1	1	9	0	0	.154/.185/.192	.146	.235	0.0	C(15): 1.1	-0.1
2013	TRN	AA	22	211	34	10	0	6	25	24	32	1	0	.268/.352/.421	.307	.293	1.4	C(49): -0.2	2.2
2013	SWB	AAA	22	257	26	19	0	6	21	23	41	0	1	.270/.342/.430	.264	.304	0.6	C(56): 10.2	2.4
2014	SWB	AAA	23	196	17	9	0	6	28	13	42	0	0	.246/.292/.397	.238	.284	1.0	C(46): 9.8	1.5
2014	NYA	MLB	23	85	7	4	0	1	9	4	22	0	0	.284/.318/.370	.267	.379	-1.1	C(30): 1.0	0.4
2015	NYA	MLB	24	172	21	9	1	3	14	12	43	0	0	.277/.327/.406	.258	.357	0.2	C(65): -1.8	0.6
2016	*MIN*	*MLB*	*25*	*471*	*46*	*24*	*1*	*11*	*54*	*32*	*99*	*0*	*0*	*.257/.308/.396*	*.249*	*.304*	*-0.6*	*C 3*	*1.9*
2017	*MIN*	*MLB*	*26*	*420*	*48*	*22*	*1*	*11*	*47*	*29*	*92*	*0*	*0*	*.254/.308/.399*	*.249*	*.303*	*-0.7*	*C 2*	*1.9*

Breakout: 5% Improve: 31% Collapse: 11% Attrition: 29% MLB: 84% *Comparables: Ryan Doumit, Chris Snyder, J.R. Towles*

YEAR	TEAM	P. COUNT	FRM RUNS	BLK RUNS	THRW RUNS	TOT RUNS
2013	NYA	1079	1.1	0.0	0.0	1.1
2013	SWB	8000	7.9	0.9	1.2	10.0
2014	NYA	3213	1.7	-0.1	-0.2	1.4
2014	SWB	6727	11.7	-0.2	-0.7	10.7
2015	NYA	6891	-0.8	-0.1	-0.2	-1.1
2016	*MIN*	*18417*	*4.5*	*-0.1*	*0.1*	*4.5*
2017	*MIN*	*16431*	*3.1*	*0.0*	*0.0*	*3.0*

Murphy is a competent backup who's young enough to have some promise and is coming off a solid season with the bat. That's all well and good, but under the "Personal" section of his Wikipedia page literally the only thing written is, "Murphy grew up as a fan of the Boston Red Sox." As a result, he was a fraud in pinstripes who spent his nights staring at his ceiling fan wondering if there was anything he could do to repel the waves of self-loathing he felt every time he donned a Yankees uniform. Probably. Luckily for Murphy, he was shipped to the Twins in exchange for Aaron Hicks, where his love of Boston will be a misdemeanor rather than a felony.

Eduardo Nunez SS

Born: 6/15/87 Age: 29 Bats: R Throws: R Height: 6'0" Weight: 195

YEAR	TEAM	LVL	AGE	PA	R	2B	3B	HR	RBI	BB	K	SB	CS	AVG/OBP/SLG	TAv	BABIP	BRR	FRAA	WARP
2013	NYA	MLB	26	336	38	17	4	3	28	20	51	10	3	.260/.307/.372	.255	.298	-0.2	SS(75): -10.7, 3B(14): -0.9	-0.1
2014	ROC	AAA	27	41	7	1	0	1	6	1	8	1	0	.282/.293/.385	.225	.323	-0.2	3B(4): -0.3, SS(4): -0.0	-0.1
2014	MIN	MLB	27	213	26	7	4	4	24	5	31	9	3	.250/.271/.382	.226	.278	0.9	3B(20): -0.1, SS(20): -1.4	0.3
2015	MIN	MLB	28	204	23	14	1	4	20	12	29	8	4	.282/.327/.431	.262	.314	0.8	SS(27): 2.3, 3B(16): -1.1	0.9
2016	*MIN*	*MLB*	*29*	*251*	*28*	*12*	*2*	*3*	*22*	*13*	*36*	*11*	*4*	*.262/.304/.377*	*.238*	*.291*	*0.3*	*2B -1, 1B 0*	*-0.1*
2017	*MIN*	*MLB*	*30*	*151*	*15*	*7*	*1*	*2*	*14*	*8*	*23*	*6*	*2*	*.255/.297/.367*	*.234*	*.287*	*0.4*	*2B -1, SS 0*	*0.2*

Breakout: 3% Improve: 48% Collapse: 10% Attrition: 22% MLB: 97% *Comparables: Brendan Ryan, Zack Cozart, Angel Berroa*

Often maligned for his lack of strengths, Nunez has done a laudable job of shoring up his weaknesses. He's unimpressive but passable at either position on the left side of an infield. He did a much better job of working at-bats with a purpose in 2015, expanding his strike zone less often and making harder contact once he got his pitch. He can't keep his helmet on when he runs the bases and he makes some downright strange mistakes in the field, but he's a tenable bench player, the kind that allows teams to carry talented, fragile players, or bet a little more aggressively on young and unproven guys.

Daniel Palka OF

Born: 10/28/91 Age: 24 Bats: L Throws: L Height: 6'2" Weight: 220

YEAR	TEAM	LVL	AGE	PA	R	2B	3B	HR	RBI	BB	K	SB	CS	AVG/OBP/SLG	TAv	BABIP	BRR	FRAA	WARP
2013	YAK	A-	21	55	10	1	2	2	10	7	16	1	0	.340/.418/.574	.385	.467	0.8	1B(10): 1.4	1.0
2014	SBN	A	22	521	63	23	5	22	82	56	129	9	3	.248/.332/.466	.288	.294	-1.4	1B(93): 8.9, RF(11): 4.9	3.5
2015	VIS	A+	23	576	95	36	3	29	90	56	164	24	7	.280/.352/.532	.329	.353	1.1	RF(69): 3.5, 1B(37): -0.6	5.4
2016	*MIN*	*MLB*	*24*	*250*	*29*	*10*	*1*	*10*	*32*	*20*	*77*	*4*	*1*	*.224/.287/.409*	*.243*	*.286*	*0.1*	*RF 1, 1B 1*	*0.2*
2017	*MIN*	*MLB*	*25*	*368*	*46*	*16*	*1*	*15*	*48*	*29*	*111*	*6*	*2*	*.225/.289/.417*	*.247*	*.285*	*0.2*	*RF 1, 1B 1*	*0.8*

Breakout: 2% Improve: 9% Collapse: 2% Attrition: 9% MLB: 21% *Comparables: Casper Wells, Bryce Brentz, Nolan Reimold*

Prior to 2015, Palka had played 12 games as a professional in the outfield. One of several natural first basemen that Arizona has pushed to the outfield, he started 88 games on the grass, including one in center field. The D'backs appeared content to trade defense for offense and Palka packs plenty of the latter, though he was aided by the Cal League's charms. The downside? He whiffed in close to 29 percent of his plate appearances despite being a little old for the level. Then again, once upon a time another Diamondbacks first-base prospect struck out way too much and was dismissed as a product of his environment, and now he's the reason Palka was deemed expendable: The Snakes traded him to Minnesota in November.

Byung-ho Park 1B

Born: 7/10/86 Age: 29 Bats: R Throws: R Height: 6'1" Weight: 194

YEAR	TEAM	LVL	AGE	PA	R	2B	3B	HR	RBI	BB	K	SB	CS	AVG/OBP/SLG	TAv	BABIP	BRR	FRAA	WARP
2013	NEX	KBO	26	556	91	17	0	37	117	92	96	10	2	.318/.437/.602	-	.000	-	-	-
2014	NEX	KBO	27	571	126	16	2	52	124	96	142	8	3	.303/.433/.686	-	.000	-	-	-
2015	NEX	KBO	28	622	129	35	1	53	146	78	161	10	3	.343/.436/.714	-	.000	-	-	-
2016	*MIN*	*MLB*	*29*	*517*	*63*	*25*	*4*	*17*	*64*	*37*	*126*	*5*	*2*	*.254/.323/.448*	*.275*	*.329*	*-0.3*	*1B -3*	*2.0*
2017	*MIN*	*MLB*	*30*	*485*	*60*	*23*	*3*	*16*	*61*	*36*	*121*	*4*	*2*	*.251/.320/.441*	*.270*	*.326*	*0.1*	*1B -3*	*1.1*

Breakout: 3% Improve: 46% Collapse: 4% Attrition: 9% MLB: 90% *Comparables: Glenn Davis, Mike Napoli, Ted Kluszewski*

Great organizations are flexible and opportunistic. For years, the Twins' greatest weaknesses have been their institutional, obdurate inflexibility and conservatism. Park provides evidence, though, that the old dogs who have run the team for 30-plus years can still learn new tricks. The Pirates profited from the league's wariness of Korean players and their track records last winter, and in November, the Twins gobbled up Park for less than $25 million over four years, including the posting fee. His strikeout rates and lack of defensive value raise red flags, but if the power Park used to launch 105 home runs in his last two seasons in the KBO traverses the Pacific, Terry Ryan is going to look like a very savvy gambler.

Trevor Plouffe 3B

Born: 6/15/86 Age: 30 Bats: R Throws: R Height: 6'2" Weight: 215

YEAR	TEAM	LVL	AGE	PA	R	2B	3B	HR	RBI	BB	K	SB	CS	AVG/OBP/SLG	TAv	BABIP	BRR	FRAA	WARP
2013	MIN	MLB	27	522	44	22	1	14	52	34	112	2	1	.254/.309/.392	.261	.301	-0.4	3B(120): -14.3, 1B(2): -0.0	0.1
2014	MIN	MLB	28	582	69	40	2	14	80	53	109	2	1	.258/.328/.423	.272	.299	-0.6	3B(127): 0.0	2.5
2015	MIN	MLB	29	632	74	35	4	22	86	50	124	2	1	.244/.307/.435	.261	.274	-5.4	3B(140): 5.1, 1B(17): 0.7	2.1
2016	*MIN*	*MLB*	*30*	*582*	*63*	*29*	*2*	*19*	*74*	*46*	*119*	*2*	*1*	*.248/.312/.424*	*.262*	*.283*	*-1.9*	*3B -4*	*1.1*
2017	*MIN*	*MLB*	*31*	*527*	*63*	*27*	*2*	*16*	*63*	*41*	*108*	*1*	*1*	*.244/.306/.410*	*.254*	*.280*	*-1.8*	*3B -4*	*0.7*

Breakout: 2% Improve: 36% Collapse: 5% Attrition: 16% MLB: 89% *Comparables: Ty Wigginton, Hank Blalock, Kevin Kouzmanoff*

Life is so cruel. No matter how hard one works and how diligently one earns every ounce of progress, time still comes and takes away the best of us all. Plouffe won't turn 30 until June, but his late bloom didn't save him from the creeping corrosion of age. Over the course of his first three years at third base, he made himself into a well-above-average fielder, but he regressed there in 2015. (FRAA disagrees, but you've long since learned to exercise skepticism about single-season fielding stats, right?) In 2014, he finally found balance in driving the ball, controlling the strike zone and hitting to all fields, but in 2015, he put the ball on the ground more often than he had in years, and his offense dropped back to its pre-2014 levels. (Literally: Check the identical 2013 and 2015 TAvs.) Plouffe is in danger of looking like a flash in the pan, but what he should be is a reminder that we all get old much too young.

Jorge Polanco SS

Born: 7/5/93 Age: 22 Bats: B Throws: R Height: 5'11" Weight: 200

YEAR	TEAM	LVL	AGE	PA	R	2B	3B	HR	RBI	BB	K	SB	CS	AVG/OBP/SLG	TAv	BABIP	BRR	FRAA	WARP
2013	CDR	A	19	523	76	32	10	5	78	42	59	4	4	.308/.362/.452	.297	.336	-0.4	2B(57): -2.0, SS(49): -6.6	2.9
2014	NBR	AA	20	157	13	6	0	1	16	9	28	7	3	.281/.323/.342	.244	.342	0.8	SS(33): 1.0, 2B(4): -0.1	0.6
2014	MIN	MLB	20	8	2	1	1	0	3	2	2	0	0	.333/.500/.833	.452	.500	0.1	SS(4): 0.2	0.2
2014	FTM	A+	20	432	61	17	6	6	45	46	60	10	8	.291/.364/.415	.282	.327	1.0	SS(86): 0.1, 2B(6): -1.3	2.8
2015	MIN	MLB	21	12	1	0	0	0	1	2	1	1	0	.300/.417/.300	.270	.333	0.3	SS(4): -0.5	0.0
2015	CHT	AA	21	431	55	17	3	6	47	35	63	18	10	.289/.346/.393	.261	.330	1.5	SS(83): 2.5, 2B(8): -0.5	2.2
2015	ROC	AAA	21	94	7	6	0	0	6	4	10	1	0	.284/.309/.352	.232	.313	0.2	SS(19): -0.5	0.0
2016	*MIN*	*MLB*	*22*	*59*	*7*	*3*	*0*	*1*	*5*	*3*	*11*	*1*	*1*	*.256/.298/.367*	*.234*	*.302*	*0.0*	*SS 0*	*0.1*
2017	*MIN*	*MLB*	*23*	*419*	*45*	*18*	*3*	*7*	*42*	*27*	*76*	*9*	*4*	*.268/.315/.386*	*.248*	*.314*	*0.4*	*SS 1*	*2.0*

Breakout: 5% Improve: 25% Collapse: 9% Attrition: 23% MLB: 39% *Comparables: Jose Pirela, Tyler Pastornicky, Jean Segura*

The Twins make weird personnel decisions under pressure sometimes, and Polanco's uneven development over the last two years is at least somewhat attributable to the thoroughly bizarre way the team has pinballed him around the organization over that span. Four big-league stints in two years, for a total of two weeks. A one-day call-up from High-A to Double-A in May 2014. Promoted to Triple-A in early July 2015, then sent back to Double-A after one of the aforementioned cups of big-league coffee at the end of the month. He's not really a shortstop and he has no power, but Polanco probably profiles as a solid second-division second baseman based on his contact skills and athletic ability if he ever gets left alone long enough to get comfortable again.

Eddie Rosario OF

Born: 9/28/91 Age: 24 Bats: L Throws: R Height: 6'1" Weight: 180

YEAR	TEAM	LVL	AGE	PA	R	2B	3B	HR	RBI	BB	K	SB	CS	AVG/OBP/SLG	TAv	BABIP	BRR	FRAA	WARP
2013	FTM	A+	21	231	40	13	5	6	35	17	29	3	6	.329/.377/.527	.317	.350	-2.5	2B(50): 9.9	2.9
2013	NBR	AA	21	313	40	19	3	4	38	21	67	7	4	.284/.330/.412	.269	.355	-1.0	2B(65): -4.2	0.6
2014	FTM	A+	22	34	5	0	0	0	4	4	5	1	1	.300/.382/.300	.265	.360	-1.1	CF(7): -0.7, 2B(2): 0.1	0.0
2014	NBR	AA	22	336	40	20	3	8	36	17	68	8	4	.237/.277/.396	.237	.277	-1.9	CF(43): 2.8, LF(18): 3.3	0.5
2015	ROC	AAA	23	100	11	2	1	3	12	5	17	1	1	.242/.280/.379	.249	.267	-0.5	CF(11): -0.8, RF(10): -0.5	-0.1
2015	MIN	MLB	23	474	60	18	15	13	50	15	118	11	6	.267/.289/.459	.252	.332	4.1	LF(86): 12.4, RF(34): -0.3	2.4
2016	*MIN*	*MLB*	*24*	*569*	*59*	*25*	*8*	*14*	*64*	*24*	*133*	*11*	*6*	*.252/.283/.408*	*.238*	*.306*	*2.7*	*RF -11*	*-1.0*
2017	*MIN*	*MLB*	*25*	*591*	*64*	*26*	*9*	*16*	*69*	*28*	*137*	*12*	*7*	*.253/.288/.416*	*.244*	*.306*	*3.3*	*RF -12*	*0.2*

Breakout: 6% Improve: 22% Collapse: 10% Attrition: 15% MLB: 50% *Comparables: Michael Saunders, Kelly Johnson, Fernando Martinez*

Rosario is exactly why statistical analysis is vital in baseball. As a 23-year-old rookie, he led the league in both outfield assists and triples, the two most exciting plays in baseball. He also hit some home runs that would make Vladimir Guerrero raise an appreciative eyebrow. He's electrifying, and there's absolutely no way, without numbers, that you'd realize he only walked as many times as he tripled, leading to a .289 OBP. For now, at least, that puts an unfortunately low ceiling on an otherwise thrilling player.

Miguel Sano 3B

Born: 5/11/93 Age: 23 Bats: R Throws: R Height: 6'4" Weight: 260

YEAR	TEAM	LVL	AGE	PA	R	2B	3B	HR	RBI	BB	K	SB	CS	AVG/OBP/SLG	TAv	BABIP	BRR	FRAA	WARP
2013	NBR	AA	20	276	35	15	3	19	55	36	81	2	1	.236/.344/.571	.312	.265	-0.9	3B(64): 0.5	2.4
2013	FTM	A+	20	243	51	15	2	16	48	29	61	9	2	.330/.424/.655	.366	.397	2.8	3B(56): -2.9	3.7
2015	MIN	MLB	22	335	46	17	1	18	52	53	119	1	1	.269/.385/.530	.314	.396	-4.0	3B(9): -0.4, 1B(2): 0.0	1.9
2015	CHT	AA	22	286	55	18	1	15	48	38	68	5	1	.274/.374/.544	.332	.315	1.0	3B(62): -1.1	3.2
2016	*MIN*	*MLB*	*23*	*594*	*82*	*26*	*2*	*33*	*95*	*71*	*189*	*3*	*1*	*.247/.342/.500*	*.291*	*.316*	*-3.4*		*3.4*
2017	*MIN*	*MLB*	*24*	*527*	*79*	*23*	*2*	*28*	*81*	*67*	*167*	*3*	*1*	*.245/.346/.489*	*.287*	*.318*	*-3.2*	*3B 0*	*1.0*

Breakout: 1% Improve: 38% Collapse: 3% Attrition: 13% MLB: 82% *Comparables: Giancarlo Stanton, Chris Davis, Eddie Mathews*

Let's just enjoy this. Let's savor the unmitigated mashfest that was Sano's rookie season, the thrilling way he throttled baseballs as the improbable Twins came within a weekend of reaching the playoffs. Sano was magnificent, launching home runs of majestic distance and trajectory, drawing walks, getting big hits seemingly at every opportunity. Yes, he fanned over 35 percent of the time. No, he didn't answer any of the questions about his long-term position, as the Twins mostly played him at DH and he was unimpressive when he did man the hot corner. Yes, he was hobbled by a hamstring injury that made him Jim Thome–slow for the last month of the season. But there will be rainouts and off days and gray winter months in which to ponder those things. Here, in the spring, let us remember the Summer of Sano.

Danny Santana SS

Born: 11/7/90 Age: 25 Bats: B Throws: R Height: 5'11" Weight: 185

YEAR	TEAM	LVL	AGE	PA	R	2B	3B	HR	RBI	BB	K	SB	CS	AVG/OBP/SLG	TAv	BABIP	BRR	FRAA	WARP
2013	NBR	AA	22	588	66	22	10	2	45	24	94	30	13	.297/.333/.386	.268	.353	1.5	SS(125): -1.3, 2B(3): 0.0	3.0
2014	ROC	AAA	23	105	15	7	2	0	7	6	28	4	1	.268/.311/.381	.239	.377	-0.7	SS(20): -2.5	-0.2
2014	MIN	MLB	23	430	70	27	7	7	40	19	98	20	4	.319/.353/.472	.291	.405	2.0	CF(69): 0.2, SS(34): -7.0	2.3
2015	MIN	MLB	24	277	30	10	5	0	21	6	68	8	4	.215/.241/.291	.194	.290	1.4	SS(66): -0.6, CF(5): -0.0	-0.7
2015	ROC	AAA	24	162	24	10	4	3	15	7	25	6	3	.322/.348/.500	.310	.365	-0.5	SS(30): 2.6, CF(2): -0.1	1.7
2016	*MIN*	*MLB*	*25*	*112*	*13*	*5*	*2*	*1*	*9*	*4*	*25*	*4*	*1*	*.269/.299/.386*	*.238*	*.332*	*0.2*	*CF 0, SS -0*	*0.2*
2017	*MIN*	*MLB*	*26*	*300*	*30*	*14*	*4*	*4*	*30*	*10*	*65*	*11*	*4*	*.269/.299/.394*	*.241*	*.330*	*1.1*	*CF 1, SS -1*	*1.2*

Breakout: 4% Improve: 52% Collapse: 10% Attrition: 29% MLB: 94% *Comparables: Ian Desmond, Ronny Cedeno, Scooter Gennett*

One of the ways in which Bill James first devised the defensive spectrum we know was by examining the relative offensive performance at various positions by guys who changed positions during their careers. It's a nebulous notion, but there's something to the idea that increased defensive responsibility or an attempt to play a tougher defensive spot can cut into the time a player has to dedicate to his offensive game. Santana might (or might not) be a worthwhile case study. A long-time minor-league shortstop with a balsa bat, Santana found success on both sides of the ledger when Minnesota thrust him into the starting center-field job in 2014. In 2015, with Aaron Hicks finding his way and Byron Buxton healthy, Santana moved back to shortstop and completely stopped doing positive things at the plate. Oh, and it turns out he's a pretty bad shortstop now.

Kurt Suzuki C

Born: 10/4/83 Age: 32 Bats: R Throws: R Height: 5'11" Weight: 205

YEAR	TEAM	LVL	AGE	PA	R	2B	3B	HR	RBI	BB	K	SB	CS	AVG/OBP/SLG	TAv	BABIP	BRR	FRAA	WARP
2013	WAS	MLB	29	281	19	11	1	3	25	20	32	2	0	.222/.283/.310	.227	.240	1.0	C(78): -10.0	-0.6
2013	OAK	MLB	29	35	6	2	0	2	7	2	3	0	0	.303/.343/.545	.343	.286	-1.1	C(15): 1.2	0.5
2014	MIN	MLB	30	503	37	34	0	3	61	34	46	0	1	.288/.345/.383	.265	.310	-4.7	C(119): -18.3	0.0
2015	MIN	MLB	31	479	36	17	0	5	50	29	59	0	0	.240/.296/.314	.216	.265	-1.8	C(130): -12.8	-1.5
2016	*MIN*	*MLB*	*32*	*140*	*13*	*7*	*0*	*2*	*13*	*9*	*18*	*0*	*0*	*.250/.304/.356*	*.235*	*.271*	*-0.6*	*C -5*	*-0.3*
2017	*MIN*	*MLB*	*33*	*254*	*26*	*11*	*0*	*3*	*23*	*16*	*34*	*0*	*0*	*.244/.299/.340*	*.228*	*.267*	*-1.2*	*C -9*	*0.0*

Breakout: 2% Improve: 35% Collapse: 9% Attrition: 18% MLB: 98% *Comparables: Paul Lo Duca, Brian Schneider, Earl Battey*

YEAR	TEAM	P. COUNT	FRM RUNS	BLK RUNS	THRW RUNS	TOT RUNS
2013	WAS	10767	-9.3	0.8	-1.6	-10.1
2013	OAK	1567	0.8	-0.2	0.3	0.9
2014	MIN	16027	-19.5	0.4	0.0	-19.0
2015	MIN	17433	-8.9	0.4	-3.8	-12.4
2016	*MIN*	*5065*	*-4.3*	*0.1*	*-0.7*	*-4.8*
2017	*MIN*	*9206*	*-8.3*	*0.2*	*-1.3*	*-9.3*

Suzuki was a pleasant surprise for the 2014 Twins, posting his best offensive season since his rookie campaign in 2007. Minnesota professed its faith in Suzuki by signing him to a two-year extension in the middle of that season, whereupon, entirely predictably, he had his *worst* offensive season on record. Suzuki claims not to buy into pitch-framing stats, and who can blame a guy who our system dinged more than 20 runs in 2014? He's alternated bad framing years with *really* bad framing years since 2011, so PECOTA's bet about where he ends up defensively this season looks like a fair bet; if it's right, he's not even worth a backup slot.

Kennys Vargas DH

Born: 8/1/90 Age: 25 Bats: B Throws: R Height: 6'5" Weight: 290

YEAR	TEAM	LVL	AGE	PA	R	2B	3B	HR	RBI	BB	K	SB	CS	AVG/OBP/SLG	TAv	BABIP	BRR	FRAA	WARP
2013	FTM	A+	22	520	68	33	1	19	93	50	105	0	0	.267/.344/.468	.284	.304	-0.9	1B(81): -3.5	1.5
2014	MIN	MLB	23	234	26	10	1	9	38	12	63	0	0	.274/.316/.456	.275	.340	0.1	1B(13): -0.3	0.6
2014	NBR	AA	23	405	50	17	0	17	63	43	68	0	2	.281/.360/.472	.297	.303	-1.0	1B(81): 6.3	2.6
2015	CHT	AA	24	151	20	3	2	7	24	26	32	0	0	.287/.417/.516	.339	.333	-0.7	1B(27): 2.3	1.7
2015	ROC	AAA	24	151	20	6	0	6	22	26	39	0	0	.279/.411/.475	.326	.359	-1.0	1B(26): 1.0	1.2
2015	MIN	MLB	24	184	18	4	0	5	17	9	54	0	0	.240/.277/.349	.212	.319	-1.1	1B(18): 0.2	-0.8
2016	*MIN*	*MLB*	*25*	*105*	*12*	*4*	*0*	*4*	*14*	*9*	*27*	*0*	*0*	*.249/.316/.424*	*.261*	*.303*	*-0.1*	*1B 0*	*0.2*
2017	*MIN*	*MLB*	*26*	*312*	*39*	*13*	*1*	*11*	*39*	*25*	*81*	*0*	*0*	*.242/.306/.411*	*.253*	*.297*	*-0.5*	*1B 1*	*0.4*

Breakout: 5% Improve: 33% Collapse: 8% Attrition: 23% MLB: 68% *Comparables: Brett Wallace, Brandon Moss, Nick Evans*

Vargas is a huge Latino first baseman/designated hitter, so naturally, he's drawn David Ortiz comps. He's drawn David Ortiz comps, so naturally, the Twins are irrationally pessimistic about him. The Twins are irrationally pessimistic about him, so naturally, they sent him to Double-A Chattanooga at the first sign of trouble in 2015. Vargas only used his time in the minors to prove conclusively that they pose no challenge for him; this year, he will have to either earn a spot in the majors somewhere or slide slowly into Kila Ka'aihue territory. Ka'aihue was born in Hawaii, so in a sense "Kila Ka'aihue territory" could be quite nice, but that's not the sense we mean. No, what we mean is, in reverse order, going back to 2012: New Orleans, Syracuse, Hiroshima, Reno, Sacramento. That sense.

Adam Walker OF

Born: 10/18/91 Age: 24 Bats: R Throws: R Height: 6'4" Weight: 225

YEAR	TEAM	LVL	AGE	PA	R	2B	3B	HR	RBI	BB	K	SB	CS	AVG/OBP/SLG	TAv	BABIP	BRR	FRAA	WARP
2013	CDR	A	21	553	83	31	7	27	109	31	115	10	0	.278/.319/.526	.287	.304	0.2	RF(122): -9.1	1.7
2014	FTM	A+	22	555	78	19	1	25	94	44	156	9	5	.246/.307/.436	.267	.303	0.6	RF(110): 0.9	1.6
2015	CHT	AA	23	560	75	31	3	31	106	51	195	13	4	.239/.309/.498	.283	.317	0.5	LF(110): -22.0, RF(6): -0.6	0.2
2016	*MIN*	*MLB*	*24*	*250*	*29*	*10*	*1*	*12*	*35*	*13*	*86*	*3*	*1*	*.218/.259/.422*	*.235*	*.282*	*0.0*	*LF -8, RF -0*	*-0.8*
2017	*MIN*	*MLB*	*25*	*337*	*42*	*14*	*1*	*17*	*48*	*19*	*115*	*4*	*1*	*.223/.269/.434*	*.243*	*.288*	*0.0*	*LF -10, RF 0*	*-0.3*

Breakout: 4% Improve: 12% Collapse: 5% Attrition: 14% MLB: 26% *Comparables: Carlos Peguero, Greg Halman, Xavier Scruggs*

A butterfly can't spread its wings from inside its cocoon, so eventually, a prospect whose trail through the minors was blazed with an unsustainable approach has to start making difficult adjustments. That sums up Walker's 2015. In the first half, he slugged .612 with 23 home runs, but fanned 37 percent of the time and walked less than a fifth as often. He adjusted, whiffing less and walking more in the second half, but his ability to drive the ball disappeared. He kills fastballs, but struggles to recognize other stuff, and his attempts to wait longer and pick up spin seem to be coming at the cost of that attacking mentality. His future rides on being able to find a balance.

PITCHERS

Fernando Abad LHP

Born: 12/17/85 Age: 30 Bats: L Throws: L Height: 6'1" Weight: 220

YEAR	TEAM	LVL	AGE	W	L	SV	G	GS	IP	H	HR	BB/9	K/9	GB%	BABIP	WHIP	ERA	FIP	DRA	WARP	CFIP	MPH
2013	SYR	AAA	27	1	0	0	17	0	17	17	0	1.1	6.4	53%	.309	1.12	1.06	2.15	4.13	0.1	92	
2013	WAS	MLB	27	0	3	0	39	0	37^{2}	42	3	2.4	7.6	41%	.325	1.38	3.35	3.23	3.74	0.4	100	96.6
2014	OAK	MLB	28	2	4	0	69	0	57^{1}	34	4	2.4	8.0	42%	.211	0.85	1.57	3.28	2.20	1.6	91	95.4
2015	OAK	MLB	29	2	2	0	62	0	47^{2}	45	11	3.6	8.5	41%	.264	1.34	4.15	5.48	4.95	-0.1	104	94.5
2016	*MIN*	*MLB*	*30*	*3*	*1*	*0*	*50*	*0*	*53*	*54*	*7*	*3.0*	*7.7*	*41%*	*.298*	*1.34*	*4.34*	*4.30*	*4.54*	*0.1*	*103*	
2017	*MIN*	*MLB*	*31*	*3*	*2*	*1*	*58*	*2*	57^{2}	*58*	*8*	*3.0*	*8.1*	*41%*	*.297*	*1.33*	*4.34*	*4.22*	*4.54*	*0.2*	*103*	

Breakout: 14% Improve: 50% Collapse: 16% Attrition: 11% MLB: 82% *Comparables: Santiago Casilla, Jerry Blevins, Scott Stewart*

Abad was a-terrible in April and May (5.93 ERA, .993 OPS), brilliant in June and July (1.15, .424) and terrible again from August onward (5.40, .956). Back pain caused him to miss a few days in early July, but that was during his hottest stretch, and although Abad's fastball velocity slipped for the second straight season, it didn't vary from month to month. Whatever the cause of his inconsistency, it earned him low-leverage duty and two extended stretches of being available but unused. Meanwhile, lefties beat him like one of those drums in the Oakland bleachers. Opposing managers noticed and didn't bother to pinch-hit. The implications for a LOOGY are troubling, to put it mildly.

Jose Berrios RHP

Born: 5/27/94 Age: 22 Bats: R Throws: R Height: 6'0" Weight: 185

YEAR	TEAM	LVL	AGE	W	L	SV	G	GS	IP	H	HR	BB/9	K/9	GB%	BABIP	WHIP	ERA	FIP	DRA	WARP	CFIP	MPH
2013	CDR	A	19	7	7	0	19	19	103^{2}	105	6	3.5	8.7	45%	.330	1.40	3.99	3.58	4.25	1.2	88	
2014	NBR	AA	20	3	4	0	8	8	40^{2}	33	2	2.7	6.2	45%	.261	1.11	3.54	3.65	4.54	0.3	102	
2014	FTM	A+	20	9	3	0	16	16	96^{1}	78	4	2.1	10.2	38%	.297	1.05	1.96	2.51	3.40	1.8	69	
2015	CHT	AA	21	8	3	0	15	15	90^{2}	77	6	2.4	9.1	49%	.296	1.11	3.08	3.09	2.07	3.1	74	
2015	ROC	AAA	21	6	2	0	12	12	75^{2}	59	6	1.7	9.9	40%	.277	0.96	2.62	2.79	1.69	2.8	69	
2016	*MIN*	*MLB*	*22*	*8*	*8*	*0*	*23*	*23*	129^{2}	*123*	*14*	*2.8*	*8.3*	*39%*	*.297*	*1.26*	*3.87*	*3.87*	*4.09*	*1.6*	*91*	
2017	*MIN*	*MLB*	*23*	*8*	*8*	*0*	*24*	*24*	144^{1}	*135*	*18*	*3.0*	*8.7*	*39%*	*.295*	*1.27*	*4.05*	*3.95*	*4.28*	*1.4*	*97*	

Breakout: 13% Improve: 23% Collapse: 17% Attrition: 19% MLB: 56% *Comparables: Tommy Hanson, Michael Bowden, Henry Owens*

Despite something less than prototypical height, Berrios has all the physicality one could want in a budding starter. He's a workout warrior with power in his lower half, and he has pitchability and a major competitive motor. These things help overcome any concerns about his youth or the minor shoulder pangs that took a bite out of his 2014 season. Of course, so do three pitches that need no more projection to earn 60 grades. (His changeup is killer, with unbelievable arm speed, and it only got better in 2015.) Add his impressive command to that mix and the drool starts flowing. Berrios dominated both levels of the high minors in 2015, and barring a setback or an injury in camp, he's headed for the big things in the majors in 2016.

Blaine Boyer RHP

Born: 7/11/81 Age: 34 Bats: R Throws: R Height: 6'3" Weight: 225

YEAR	TEAM	LVL	AGE	W	L	SV	G	GS	IP	H	HR	BB/9	K/9	GB%	BABIP	WHIP	ERA	FIP	DRA	WARP	CFIP	MPH
2013	OMA	AAA	31	0	1	1	13	0	15	15	3	1.8	10.8	54%	.300	1.20	3.00	4.37	4.54	0.1	85	
2014	SDN	MLB	32	0	1	0	32	0	40^{1}	34	2	1.8	6.5	45%	.264	1.04	3.57	2.90	3.25	0.6	103	95.7
2014	ELP	AAA	32	1	2	7	25	0	29	26	2	1.9	8.7	55%	.316	1.10	3.10	3.39	4.45	0.2	101	
2015	MIN	MLB	33	3	6	1	68	0	65	62	5	2.6	4.6	49%	.270	1.25	2.49	3.97	3.61	0.9	113	95.5
2016	*MIN*	*MLB*	*34*	*3*	*1*	*0*	*57*	*0*	*60*	*65*	*7*	*2.8*	*5.7*	*48%*	*.297*	*1.40*	*4.49*	*4.54*	*4.71*	*0.0*	*108*	
2017	*MIN*	*MLB*	*35*	*1*	*1*	*0*	*28*	*0*	*30^{1}*	*34*	*4*	*2.9*	*6.0*	*48%*	*.301*	*1.43*	*4.70*	*4.59*	*4.93*	*-0.1*	*114*	

Breakout: 11% Improve: 18% Collapse: 22% Attrition: 9% MLB: 54% *Comparables: D.J. Carrasco, Geoff Geary, Clay Condrey*

If describing your strikeout rate requires rendering Larry Gura's surname into an adjective ("Guranian," "Guralicious," "Gurarrific"), you might be a Twins reliever. It's not terribly surprising that Boyer saw his strikeout rate fall off the table in 2015. That just happens sometimes, especially to middling middle relievers. What's surprising (and oh so revealing) is that the Twins allowed Boyer to pitch high-leverage innings for roughly four months. DRA liked Boyer for his ability to keep the ball on the ground and in the park, but his average control and inability to miss bats should push him into mop-up work, if not off MLB rosters altogether.

Nick Burdi RHP

Born: 1/19/93 Age: 23 Bats: R Throws: R Height: 6'5" Weight: 215

YEAR	TEAM	LVL	AGE	W	L	SV	G	GS	IP	H	HR	BB/9	K/9	GB%	BABIP	WHIP	ERA	FIP	DRA	WARP	CFIP	MPH
2014	CDR	A	21	0	0	4	13	0	13	8	0	5.5	18.0	55%	.400	1.23	4.15	1.33	3.52	0.2	68	
2015	FTM	A+	22	2	2	2	13	0	20	12	1	1.4	13.1	44%	.275	0.75	2.25	1.37	0.98	0.8	60	
2015	CHT	AA	22	3	4	2	30	0	43^{2}	40	3	6.6	11.1	49%	.322	1.65	4.53	3.99	4.37	0.1	99	
2016	*MIN*	*MLB*	*23*	*2*	*1*	*2*	*45*	*0*	*47^{2}*	*45*	*5*	*4.6*	*9.0*	*45%*	*.306*	*1.46*	*4.25*	*4.23*	*4.41*	*0.3*	*101*	
2017	*MIN*	*MLB*	*24*	*2*	*1*	*2*	*39*	*0*	*52*	*47*	*5*	*4.7*	*10.0*	*45%*	*.305*	*1.42*	*4.00*	*3.88*	*4.15*	*0.3*	*94*	

Breakout: 0% Improve: 0% Collapse: 0% Attrition: 0% MLB: 0% *Comparables: Donnie Joseph, Cory Burns, Carson Smith*

Burdi was a college closer, succeeding with blazing velocity and a wicked, diving slider. He looked like a future big-league relief ace, and the Twins were so eager for the future that they started Burdi in Double-A in 2015. That only served as a reminder, though, that the future is promised to no one. Burdi had an ERA near six before being demoted to the Florida State League, and even after dominating there, he walked 10 of 58 batters in a second stint. He showed better in the Arizona Fall League, but until he delivers consistent evidence of command against advanced hitters, he's as much suspect as prospect.

Neal Cotts LHP

Born: 3/25/80 Age: 36 Bats: L Throws: L Height: 6'2" Weight: 200

YEAR	TEAM	LVL	AGE	W	L	SV	G	GS	IP	H	HR	BB/9	K/9	GB%	BABIP	WHIP	ERA	FIP	DRA	WARP	CFIP	MPH
2013	ROU	AAA	33	3	1	2	15	0	23	13	1	2.0	16.4	54%	.353	0.78	0.78	1.13	3.45	0.5	44	
2013	TEX	MLB	33	8	3	1	58	0	57	36	2	2.8	10.3	46%	.246	0.95	1.11	2.20	1.98	1.8	77	94.3
2014	TEX	MLB	34	2	9	2	73	0	66^{2}	66	6	3.1	8.5	36%	.314	1.34	4.32	3.61	3.85	0.5	91	93.1
2015	MIL	MLB	35	1	0	0	51	0	49^{2}	44	9	3.1	8.9	46%	.269	1.23	3.26	4.75	4.08	0.4	98	92.1
2015	MIN	MLB	35	0	0	0	17	0	13^{2}	14	3	3.3	5.9	24%	.262	1.39	3.95	5.96	4.99	0.0	124	92.3
2016	*MIN*	*MLB*	*36*	*3*	*1*	*1*	*51*	*0*	*53^{2}*	*53*	*7*	*3.0*	*8.2*	*40%*	*.296*	*1.31*	*4.26*	*4.23*	*4.49*	*0.2*	*102*	
2017	*MIN*	*MLB*	*37*	*2*	*1*	*0*	*33*	*0*	*33*	*33*	*5*	*3.3*	*8.1*	*40%*	*.298*	*1.38*	*4.59*	*4.48*	*4.84*	*0.0*	*111*	

Breakout: 21% Improve: 40% Collapse: 27% Attrition: 8% MLB: 76% *Comparables: Hector Carrasco, Joel Peralta, Yoshinori Tateyama*

At this point in our ever-evolving understanding of baseball (generally) and pitching (specifically), it's uncommon that a relief pitcher will have a four-seam fastball, a cutter *and* a slider. Short-relief hurlers tend to develop either a cutter that stands in for a more traditional fastball, or a good old-fashioned heater-slider mix. Cotts is among those who genuinely employ all three pitches, throwing them in different situations and different velocity bands, leaving no doubt of their distinction from one another. In 2015, he also developed a sinker to play off his four-seamer against right-handed batters. This is how one weathers four years between big-league stints and makes an honest second shot at a career: unique approach and eager adaptation.

Tyler Duffey RHP

Born: 12/27/90 Age: 25 Bats: R Throws: R Height: 6'3" Weight: 220

YEAR	TEAM	LVL	AGE	W	L	SV	G	GS	IP	H	HR	BB/9	K/9	GB%	BABIP	WHIP	ERA	FIP	DRA	WARP	CFIP	MPH
2013	FTM	A+	22	4	5	0	15	9	62^{2}	67	3	2.4	6.3	42%	.315	1.34	4.45	3.46	4.16	0.5	96	
2013	CDR	A	22	3	2	0	9	9	58^{1}	49	5	0.9	7.3	53%	.259	0.94	2.78	3.20	3.90	0.9	76	
2014	ROC	AAA	23	2	0	0	3	3	16	16	3	3.4	9.0	28%	.302	1.38	3.94	5.11	4.45	0.1	97	
2014	NBR	AA	23	8	3	0	18	18	111^{1}	104	14	1.5	6.8	47%	.274	1.10	3.80	4.13	4.47	0.9	99	
2014	FTM	A+	23	3	0	0	4	4	22^{1}	22	0	2.0	5.2	36%	.286	1.21	2.82	2.90	4.29	0.2	98	
2015	MIN	MLB	24	5	1	0	10	10	58	56	4	3.1	8.2	51%	.315	1.31	3.10	3.21	3.95	0.7	93	93.3
2015	ROC	AAA	24	5	6	0	14	14	85^{1}	73	1	1.9	7.2	47%	.276	1.07	2.53	2.38	2.60	2.2	81	
2015	CHT	AA	24	2	2	0	8	8	52^{2}	46	0	2.1	9.2	54%	.322	1.10	2.56	1.99	1.73	2.0	70	
2016	*MIN*	*MLB*	*25*	*6*	*7*	*0*	*21*	*21*	*105*	*104*	*11*	*2.7*	*6.9*	*47%*	*.293*	*1.29*	*4.08*	*4.06*	*4.29*	*1.0*	*98*	
2017	*MIN*	*MLB*	*26*	*6*	*6*	*0*	*17*	*17*	*102*	*100*	*13*	*2.9*	*7.4*	*47%*	*.290*	*1.31*	*4.34*	*4.23*	*4.56*	*0.7*	*106*	

Breakout: 20% Improve: 35% Collapse: 21% Attrition: 27% MLB: 68% *Comparables: J.J. Hoover, Brandon Workman, Simon Castro*

Duffey is the first success story to come out of the Twins' experiment with drafting college relievers and turning them into starters. With only low-90s velocity and a slightly above-average curveball, he flew below the prospect radar, but he made steady progress and stayed healthy. In 2015, though, he really found something, and rode it all the way to a successful second-half showing for the Twins. He'll need to develop more than the simple blend of four-seamer, sinker and curve he used on his first circuit of the league, but he's proved himself an MLB-caliber arm. You'll forgive us *Justified* fans shouting "Win, Duffey!" when he puts up a W in the major leagues.

Casey Fien RHP

Born: 10/21/83 Age: 32 Bats: R Throws: R Height: 6'2" Weight: 210

YEAR	TEAM	LVL	AGE	W	L	SV	G	GS	IP	H	HR	BB/9	K/9	GB%	BABIP	WHIP	ERA	FIP	DRA	WARP	CFIP	MPH
2013	MIN	MLB	29	5	2	0	73	0	62	51	9	1.7	10.6	40%	.280	1.02	3.92	3.19	2.65	1.5	67	93.6
2014	MIN	MLB	30	5	6	1	73	0	63^{1}	64	7	1.4	7.2	35%	.297	1.17	3.98	3.46	3.26	1.0	89	95.2
2015	MIN	MLB	31	4	6	0	62	0	63^{1}	61	6	1.1	5.8	38%	.272	1.09	3.55	3.42	2.82	1.4	99	94.8
2016	*MIN*	*MLB*	*32*	*3*	*1*	*0*	*55*	*0*	*58^{1}*	*56*	*7*	*2.3*	*7.3*	*37%*	*.284*	*1.21*	*3.98*	*4.06*	*4.20*	*0.4*	*93*	
2017	*MIN*	*MLB*	*33*	*3*	*1*	*1*	*56*	*0*	*55*	*53*	*7*	*2.3*	*7.5*	*37%*	*.282*	*1.22*	*4.15*	*4.04*	*4.38*	*0.2*	*99*	

Breakout: 24% Improve: 44% Collapse: 30% Attrition: 7% MLB: 89% *Comparables: Bobby Seay, Bob Howry, Justin Speier*

Fien doesn't have a whiff-inducing widowmaker of a pitch, and he doesn't have an especially complicated arsenal. He throws a four-seam fastball and a cutter, and he relies on their good velocity and his excellent control to get outs. (Since 2013, there have been 307 pitchers with at least 150 innings pitched. Only 10 have a lower walk rate than Fien's 3.9 percent.) In the first half of 2015, Fien's velocity was down: He was averaging 92.6 miles per hour on his four-seamer, and 88.1 on his cutter, down from 94.1 and 88.8 mph, respectively, in 2014. That might seem a small difference, but given Fien's style and his flyball proclivity, it wasn't. When Fien rediscovered his velocity down the stretch, the fearless strike-throwing machine retook a well-earned setup role and thrived.

Kyle Gibson RHP

Born: 10/23/87 Age: 28 Bats: R Throws: R Height: 6'6" Weight: 215

YEAR	TEAM	LVL	AGE	W	L	SV	G	GS	IP	H	HR	BB/9	K/9	GB%	BABIP	WHIP	ERA	FIP	DRA	WARP	CFIP	MPH
2013	MIN	MLB	25	2	4	0	10	10	51	69	7	3.5	5.1	51%	.350	1.75	6.53	5.19	6.40	-0.9	125	94.6
2013	ROC	AAA	25	7	5	0	17	17	101^{2}	85	5	2.9	7.7	57%	.279	1.16	2.92	3.11	3.92	1.3	85	
2014	MIN	MLB	26	13	12	0	31	31	179^{1}	178	12	2.9	5.4	57%	.287	1.31	4.47	3.82	3.44	3.0	109	94.1
2015	MIN	MLB	27	11	11	0	32	32	194^{2}	186	18	3.0	6.7	56%	.287	1.29	3.84	3.93	3.83	2.8	100	94.5
2016	*MIN*	*MLB*	*28*	*9*	*10*	*0*	*29*	*29*	*165^{1}*	*166*	*17*	*2.9*	*6.7*	*56%*	*.295*	*1.33*	*4.19*	*4.17*	*4.40*	*1.4*	*101*	
2017	*MIN*	*MLB*	*29*	*8*	*9*	*0*	*26*	*26*	*152*	*156*	*18*	*2.9*	*7.0*	*56%*	*.300*	*1.35*	*4.29*	*4.19*	*4.51*	*1.0*	*104*	

Breakout: 17% Improve: 58% Collapse: 16% Attrition: 8% MLB: 92% *Comparables: Brandon McCarthy, Sergio Mitre, Randy Wells*

Among pitchers who threw at least 1,500 pitches in 2015, only Francisco Liriano threw a lower percentage of his through the strike zone than did Gibson. For both pitchers, this says something about their skill set (they're not blessed with razor-sharp control) and something about their approach (they work the edges of the zone, trying to induce weak contact, working down, working in, hoping to pull hitters out of their preferred approaches). Gibson isn't Liriano, whose superior stuff earns him significantly more whiffs, but he did start using his changeup considerably more against righties in 2015. With three true weapons now in his arsenal, Gibson is emerging as a grounder-heavy mid-rotation starter, and a pretty good one.

Stephen Gonsalves LHP

Born: 7/8/94 Age: 21 Bats: L Throws: L Height: 6'5" Weight: 190

YEAR	TEAM	LVL	AGE	W	L	SV	G	GS	IP	H	HR	BB/9	K/9	GB%	BABIP	WHIP	ERA	FIP	DRA	WARP	CFIP	MPH
2014	CDR	A	19	2	3	0	8	8	36^{2}	31	1	2.7	10.8	36%	.326	1.15	3.19	2.50	3.91	0.5	81	
2015	FTM	A+	20	7	2	0	15	15	79^{1}	66	2	4.3	6.2	39%	.270	1.31	2.61	3.58	5.07	-0.7	115	
2015	CDR	A	20	6	1	0	9	9	55	29	2	2.5	12.6	41%	.243	0.80	1.15	2.11	1.07	2.6	64	
2016	*MIN*	*MLB*	*21*	*5*	*6*	*0*	*18*	*18*	*92^{1}*	*94*	*10*	*4.1*	*7.2*	*36%*	*.300*	*1.47*	*4.51*	*4.51*	*4.67*	*0.5*	*109*	
2017	*MIN*	*MLB*	*22*	*8*	*9*	*0*	*26*	*26*	*154^{1}*	*154*	*19*	*4.3*	*7.9*	*36%*	*.299*	*1.48*	*4.61*	*4.49*	*4.77*	*0.6*	*112*	

Breakout: 0% Improve: 0% Collapse: 0% Attrition: 0% MLB: 0% *Comparables: Matt Magill, Homer Bailey, Trevor May*

Midseason promotions are important, especially for pitching prospects. Developmental momentum is real, and progression doesn't always line up with the progress of the earth around the sun. When Gonsalves proved his long levers and advanced changeup were too much for Midwest League hitters, the Twins made the right call by promoting him to their High-A affiliate. Alas, even correct decisions are often fraught with risk, and pitching prospects are always, always fraught with risk. Gonsalves hit a serious speed bump in Fort Myers. His stuff didn't back up, and he didn't lose his command; he just found himself a weapon short. Until he finds consistency with a breaking ball, it will stay that way. The good news is that by the end of the season, a sharp curveball was starting to take shape, and he had a few very strong outings.

J.R. Graham RHP

Born: 1/14/90 Age: 26 Bats: R Throws: R Height: 6'0" Weight: 210

YEAR	TEAM	LVL	AGE	W	L	SV	G	GS	IP	H	HR	BB/9	K/9	GB%	BABIP	WHIP	ERA	FIP	DRA	WARP	CFIP	MPH
2013	MIS	AA	23	1	3	0	8	8	35^2	39	0	2.5	7.1	68%	.348	1.37	4.04	2.18	3.79	0.4	91	
2014	MIS	AA	24	1	5	0	27	19	71^1	79	2	3.3	6.3	53%	.328	1.47	5.55	3.50				
2015	MIN	MLB	25	1	1	0	39	1	63^2	73	10	3.0	7.5	51%	.323	1.48	4.95	4.66	5.12	-0.3	104	97.6
2016	*MIN*	*MLB*	*26*	*2*	*3*	*0*	*8*	*8*	*40*	*43*	*5*	*3.1*	*6.8*	*51%*	*.308*	*1.43*	*4.53*	*4.57*	*4.73*	*0.2*	*110*	
2017	*MIN*	*MLB*	*27*	*3*	*4*	*0*	*22*	*11*	*79^1*	*84*	*10*	*3.3*	*7.5*	*51%*	*.309*	*1.42*	*4.48*	*4.37*	*4.68*	*0.3*	*109*	

Breakout: 20% Improve: 37% Collapse: 22% Attrition: 31% MLB: 68% *Comparables: Bobby Parnell, Jeff Manship, Billy Traber*

The Twins looked at Graham, a former top prospect in the Braves' system whose pedigree took a huge hit due to shoulder trouble in 2013, and saw a fastball that still reaches the very high 90s, a sinker that helps him induce grounders and a hard slider, and decided he was worth a Rule 5 pick. They slotted him into a long-relief role he would fill all season, one in which he averaged 27 pitches per appearance and appeared almost exclusively in low-leverage situations. That role barely exists in modern baseball, and nothing Graham did made reviving it just for him seem viable. In fact, he lost three weeks to shoulder fatigue late in the season. At this point, the prudent thing would be to let go of any hopes that he can start and move him into a more traditional, short-burst relief gig.

Phil Hughes RHP

Born: 6/24/86 Age: 30 Bats: R Throws: R Height: 6'5" Weight: 250

YEAR	TEAM	LVL	AGE	W	L	SV	G	GS	IP	H	HR	BB/9	K/9	GB%	BABIP	WHIP	ERA	FIP	DRA	WARP	CFIP	MPH
2013	NYA	MLB	27	4	14	0	30	29	145^2	170	24	2.6	7.5	32%	.324	1.46	5.19	4.52	5.06	-0.3	101	94.7
2014	MIN	MLB	28	16	10	0	32	32	209^2	221	16	0.7	8.0	38%	.324	1.13	3.52	2.68	3.12	4.3	70	94.6
2015	MIN	MLB	29	11	9	0	27	25	155^1	184	29	0.9	5.4	37%	.304	1.29	4.40	4.67	4.95	0.1	107	93.1
2016	*MIN*	*MLB*	*30*	*9*	*9*	*0*	*26*	*26*	*148^1*	*160*	*20*	*1.5*	*6.8*	*36%*	*.303*	*1.24*	*4.06*	*4.06*	*4.27*	*1.5*	*97*	
2017	*MIN*	*MLB*	*31*	*8*	*8*	*0*	*24*	*24*	*142^1*	*155*	*21*	*1.7*	*7.0*	*36%*	*.305*	*1.28*	*4.22*	*4.10*	*4.44*	*1.2*	*102*	

Breakout: 16% Improve: 50% Collapse: 12% Attrition: 4% MLB: 90% *Comparables: John Candelaria, Howie Pollet, Warren Hacker*

Hughes' helplessness against his own impulse to tinker was well documented in New York. After their newest free-agent pitching investment broke the all-time record for strikeout-to-walk ratio in 2014, the Twins felt so sure that insecurity was behind Hughes that they doubled down on their initial three-year commitment to him, extending him through 2019. Thereupon, Hughes showed up at spring training with a renewed commitment to his changeup and his sinker, a notion about changing his cutter usage and an intentionally lower arm slot. What followed—the return of his gopheritis, slumping velocity, a back injury that might have been there all along but didn't sideline him until mid-summer; in short, a nightmarish season that throws his future back into doubt—was tragically predictable. Some people will never be convinced of their own sufficiency.

Tyler Jay LHP

Born: 4/19/94 Age: 22 Bats: L Throws: L Height: 6'1" Weight: 180

YEAR	TEAM	LVL	AGE	W	L	SV	G	GS	IP	H	HR	BB/9	K/9	GB%	BABIP	WHIP	ERA	FIP	DRA	WARP	CFIP	MPH
2015	FTM	A+	21	0	1	1	19	0	18^1	18	0	3.9	10.8	41%	.353	1.42	3.93	2.07	2.85	0.3	88	
2016	*MIN*	*MLB*	*22*	*2*	*1*	*1*	*32*	*0*	*34*	*35*	*3*	*3.8*	*7.1*	*37%*	*.308*	*1.46*	*4.18*	*4.21*	*4.40*	*0.1*	*100*	
2017	*MIN*	*MLB*	*23*	*3*	*1*	*2*	*52*	*0*	*50^1*	*50*	*5*	*3.7*	*7.8*	*37%*	*.306*	*1.41*	*4.09*	*3.99*	*4.31*	*0.3*	*96*	

Breakout: 0% Improve: 0% Collapse: 0% Attrition: 0% MLB: 0% *Comparables: Scott McGough, Lester Oliveros, R.J. Alvarez*

Three years after the Twins made college relievers who could convert to the rotation as pros the theme running through many of their early draft picks, Minnesota tried the same thing with the eighth-overall pick in June. Jay made cameo appearances as a starter at the University of Illinois, but primarily relieved. His command gave Twins scouts cause to believe he can turn a lineup card over without racking up an ugly pitch count, and the organization liked his ability to throw his budding changeup without any alteration to his short, simple arm stroke. Nonetheless, he relieved throughout his stint in the Florida State League, so he'll head to spring training without significant starting experience. As such, he's likely to be a slower climber than most college arms taken this high in the draft.

Kevin Jepsen RHP

Born: 7/26/84 Age: 31 Bats: R Throws: R Height: 6'3" Weight: 235

YEAR	TEAM	LVL	AGE	W	L	SV	G	GS	IP	H	HR	BB/9	K/9	GB%	BABIP	WHIP	ERA	FIP	DRA	WARP	CFIP	MPH
2013	ANA	MLB	28	1	3	0	45	0	36	41	3	3.5	9.0	42%	.345	1.53	4.50	3.41	4.31	0.1	92	98.1
2014	ANA	MLB	29	0	2	2	74	0	65	45	4	3.2	10.4	50%	.263	1.05	2.63	2.81	2.47	1.6	83	98.2
2015	TBA	MLB	30	2	5	5	46	0	41^2	34	4	4.3	7.3	50%	.254	1.30	2.81	4.16	4.52	0.1	109	97.4
2015	MIN	MLB	30	1	1	10	29	0	28	18	1	2.2	8.0	42%	.224	0.89	1.61	2.53	0.47	1.4	84	97.0
2016	*MIN*	*MLB*	*31*	*3*	*1*	*2*	*55*	*0*	*58^1*	*55*	*6*	*3.4*	*8.0*	*47%*	*.291*	*1.31*	*4.12*	*4.03*	*4.35*	*0.3*	*96*	
2017	*MIN*	*MLB*	*32*	*3*	*1*	*3*	*60*	*0*	*54*	*50*	*6*	*3.6*	*8.2*	*47%*	*.293*	*1.33*	*4.15*	*4.03*	*4.38*	*0.2*	*96*	

Breakout: 24% Improve: 46% Collapse: 28% Attrition: 16% MLB: 90% *Comparables: Craig Breslow, Ronald Belisario, Jason Isringhausen*

Jepsen's simplified way of doing things has paid off two years in a row. With mid-90s heat and a very sharp curveball, he's found the ability to keep the ball down, earning plenty of strikeouts and a healthy share of groundballs. The changeup he tries to use to keep left-handed hitters honest is a poor pitch, but Jepsen so dominates righties that he's an asset even on the change's worst days. Because of his large platoon split, though, don't bet on him sticking in the closer role he took on at the end of 2015.

Trevor May RHP

Born: 9/23/89 Age: 26 Bats: R Throws: R Height: 6'5" Weight: 240

YEAR	TEAM	LVL	AGE	W	L	SV	G	GS	IP	H	HR	BB/9	K/9	GB%	BABIP	WHIP	ERA	FIP	DRA	WARP	CFIP	MPH
2013	NBR	AA	23	9	9	0	27	27	151^2	149	14	4.0	9.4	40%	.328	1.42	4.51	3.91	4.48	1.3	96	
2014	MIN	MLB	24	3	6	0	10	9	45^2	59	7	4.3	8.7	39%	.377	1.77	7.88	4.80	6.05	-0.7	101	94.7
2014	ROC	AAA	24	8	6	0	18	18	98^1	75	4	3.6	8.6	38%	.270	1.16	2.84	3.16	4.14	1.1	86	
2015	MIN	MLB	25	8	9	0	48	16	114^2	127	11	2.0	8.6	41%	.340	1.33	4.00	3.22	4.41	0.7	82	96.8
2016	*MIN*	*MLB*	*26*	*3*	*1*	*1*	*55*	*0*	*58^1*	*58*	*7*	*2.9*	*8.5*	*40%*	*.308*	*1.32*	*3.88*	*4.00*	*4.09*	*0.0*	*91*	
2017	*MIN*	*MLB*	*27*	*5*	*5*	*0*	*15*	*15*	*88^2*	*85*	*10*	*3.0*	*9.0*	*40%*	*.306*	*1.30*	*3.86*	*3.75*	*4.07*	*1.0*	*91*	

Breakout: 26% Improve: 41% Collapse: 30% Attrition: 25% MLB: 88% *Comparables: Juan Nicasio, Hector Rondon, Brandon Workman*

The Twins decided that Trevor May never solve the puzzle of consistency in the starting rotation, so they shifted him to the bullpen for the second half. The experiment panned out pretty well. Trevor May have a fastball that hung around 93 mph as a starter, but Trevor May sit 96 and often reach higher in short bursts. The extra speed accentuated the pitch's strong swing-and-miss rates, and Trevor May throw a curve and change that play up slightly with the switch, too. Trevor May still work up in the zone with his heat and give up a lot of hard contact, but Trevor May encourage belief going forward with the whiff frequency he achieved over the final two months.

Alex Meyer RHP

Born: 1/3/90 Age: 26 Bats: R Throws: R Height: 6'9" Weight: 225

YEAR	TEAM	LVL	AGE	W	L	SV	G	GS	IP	H	HR	BB/9	K/9	GB%	BABIP	WHIP	ERA	FIP	DRA	WARP	CFIP	MPH
2013	NBR	AA	23	4	3	0	13	13	70	60	3	3.7	10.8	61%	.317	1.27	3.21	2.85	3.90	1.1	77	
2014	ROC	AAA	24	7	7	0	27	27	130^1	116	10	4.4	10.6	49%	.321	1.38	3.52	3.66	4.28	1.3	90	
2015	ROC	AAA	25	4	5	0	38	8	92	101	4	4.7	9.8	47%	.372	1.62	4.79	3.28	3.89	0.7	96	
2015	MIN	MLB	25	0	0	0	2	0	2^2	4	2	10.1	10.1	22%	.286	2.62	16.88	13.98	15.51	-0.3	107	98.6
2016	*MIN*	*MLB*	*26*	*2*	*1*	*0*	*35*	*0*	*37^1*	*37*	*4*	*4.0*	*8.7*	*46%*	*.312*	*1.43*	*4.11*	*4.23*	*4.31*	*0.3*	*98*	
2017	*MIN*	*MLB*	*27*	*4*	*4*	*0*	*17*	*11*	*74^2*	*71*	*9*	*4.1*	*9.5*	*46%*	*.309*	*1.42*	*4.26*	*4.15*	*4.47*	*0.4*	*102*	

Breakout: 20% Improve: 24% Collapse: 22% Attrition: 41% MLB: 60% *Comparables: Nate Karns, Corey Kluber, Dustin Richardson*

There's something to be said for being proactive in player development. If Meyer's 2014 (in which he struck out 27 percent of the batters he faced, all as a starter, all in Triple-A) didn't impress the Twins enough to give him a look in the majors, either at the end of that season or heading into 2015, they probably should have moved him into relief right away. They didn't, and they ended up having to make that move after Meyer posted an ERA on the wrong side of seven in eight starts. They promoted him to the parent club in June, gave up on him after two appearances there and sent him back to Rochester to finish stalling out.

Tommy Milone LHP

Born: 2/16/87 Age: 29 Bats: L Throws: L Height: 6'0" Weight: 220

YEAR	TEAM	LVL	AGE	W	L	SV	G	GS	IP	H	HR	BB/9	K/9	GB%	BABIP	WHIP	ERA	FIP	DRA	WARP	CFIP	MPH
2013	OAK	MLB	26	12	9	0	28	26	156^1	160	25	2.2	7.3	36%	.284	1.27	4.14	4.33	4.63	0.5	102	89.4
2013	SAC	AAA	26	0	0	0	2	2	10^1	16	0	0.9	13.1	52%	.516	1.65	1.74	0.96	4.26	0.2	75	
2014	MIN	MLB	27	0	1	0	6	5	21^2	37	4	4.6	5.8	46%	.393	2.22	7.06	5.93	8.01	-0.9	131	88.7
2014	OAK	MLB	27	6	3	0	16	16	96^1	91	12	2.4	5.7	39%	.262	1.21	3.55	4.45	4.24	0.6	108	88.6
2014	SAC	AAA	27	1	1	0	4	4	21	28	5	3.9	7.3	46%	.343	1.76	6.43	6.46	5.56	0.1	121	
2015	MIN	MLB	28	9	5	1	24	23	128^2	128	17	2.5	6.4	44%	.279	1.27	3.92	4.27	4.01	1.6	104	90.0
2015	ROC	AAA	28	4	0	0	5	5	38^2	25	2	0.7	10.9	47%	.261	0.72	0.70	1.63	0.51	2.0	50	
2016	*MIN*	*MLB*	*29*	*7*	*8*	*0*	*23*	*23*	*122*	*128*	*16*	*2.5*	*6.9*	*42%*	*.298*	*1.33*	*4.35*	*4.34*	*4.56*	*0.8*	*105*	
2017	*MIN*	*MLB*	*30*	*7*	*7*	*0*	*21*	*21*	*124*	*129*	*17*	*2.5*	*7.2*	*42%*	*.296*	*1.32*	*4.39*	*4.27*	*4.60*	*0.8*	*107*	

Breakout: 33% Improve: 52% Collapse: 17% Attrition: 12% MLB: 94% *Comparables: Jason Vargas, Boof Bonser, Tom Gorzelanny*

Milone survived a month-long demotion to Triple-A and an elbow strain that cost him much of August to turn in a decent season in 2015. He's still trying to prove that, despite a fastball that sits in the high 80s and a lack of any exceptional skill that mitigates that limitation, he can be a solid back-end starter in the majors. He has a decent shot at it, because his curveball and changeup are both bona fide big-league offerings and he doesn't have glaring weaknesses. Those hopes took a hit, though, when Milone lost touch with his cutter. He threw it zero times in his final start before hitting the DL, and very sparingly after returning. Without that pitch, he's a weapon short. John McClane would just strangle a bad guy and take his cutter, but Milone is more of an Al Powell.

Ricky Nolasco RHP

Born: 12/13/82 Age: 33 Bats: R Throws: R Height: 6'2" Weight: 235

YEAR	TEAM	LVL	AGE	W	L	SV	G	GS	IP	H	HR	BB/9	K/9	GB%	BABIP	WHIP	ERA	FIP	DRA	WARP	CFIP	MPH
2013	MIA	MLB	30	5	8	0	18	18	112^1	112	11	2.0	7.2	43%	.299	1.22	3.85	3.47	4.19	1.0	93	92.9
2013	LAN	MLB	30	8	3	0	16	15	87	83	6	2.2	7.8	46%	.298	1.20	3.52	3.12	3.70	1.3	93	93.5
2014	MIN	MLB	31	6	12	0	27	27	159	203	22	2.2	6.5	44%	.351	1.52	5.38	4.32	5.02	-0.4	100	92.8
2015	MIN	MLB	32	5	2	0	9	8	37^1	50	3	3.4	8.4	42%	.392	1.71	6.75	3.48	6.52	-0.7	93	93.5
2016	*MIN*	*MLB*	*33*	*8*	*9*	*0*	*24*	*24*	*144*	*157*	*17*	*2.5*	*7.2*	*44%*	*.316*	*1.37*	*4.15*	*4.14*	*4.36*	*1.3*	*98*	
2017	*MIN*	*MLB*	*34*	*9*	*9*	*0*	*27*	*27*	*164^2*	*180*	*21*	*2.6*	*7.3*	*44%*	*.317*	*1.38*	*4.23*	*4.11*	*4.44*	*1.3*	*101*	

Breakout: 21% Improve: 45% Collapse: 19% Attrition: 11% MLB: 86% *Comparables: Brett Myers, John Smiley, Rodrigo Lopez*

The huge mistake teams make when pricing and paying starting pitchers in the free-agent market is underestimating risk. Guys like Nolasco—and there's an entire class of Nolascos out there who have signed multi-year contracts in the last five years—appeal to teams because they feel safe, but that feeling is a dangerous delusion. Over the first half of what was the richest free-agent deal in

Twins history when he signed it, Nolasco has been haunted by both nagging injuries and poor performance even when he's been on the mound. His once-dominant splitter is now closer to dormant. His stuff has softened. Mid-rotation starters are always closer to implosion than you think, and Nolasco has become a cautionary tale.

Glen Perkins LHP

Born: 3/2/83 Age: 33 Bats: L Throws: L Height: 6'0" Weight: 215

YEAR	TEAM	LVL	AGE	W	L	SV	G	GS	IP	H	HR	BB/9	K/9	GB%	BABIP	WHIP	ERA	FIP	DRA	WARP	CFIP	MPH
2013	MIN	MLB	30	2	0	36	61	0	62^{2}	43	5	2.2	11.1	37%	.271	0.93	2.30	2.52	2.42	1.6	63	97.5
2014	MIN	MLB	31	4	3	34	63	0	61^{2}	62	7	1.6	9.6	36%	.316	1.18	3.65	3.13	3.49	0.8	74	95.6
2015	MIN	MLB	32	3	5	32	60	0	57	58	9	1.6	8.5	34%	.297	1.19	3.32	3.79	3.56	0.8	84	96.1
2016	*MIN*	*MLB*	*33*	*3*	*1*	*37*	*55*	*0*	*58^{1}*	*54*	*7*	*2.3*	*9.0*	*35%*	*.297*	*1.19*	*3.71*	*3.69*	*3.93*	*0.6*	*85*	
2017	*MIN*	*MLB*	*34*	*3*	*1*	*29*	*57*	*0*	*56*	*53*	*7*	*2.4*	*8.7*	*35%*	*.293*	*1.20*	*3.89*	*3.77*	*4.12*	*0.4*	*90*	

Breakout: 21% Improve: 47% Collapse: 26% Attrition: 11% MLB: 96% *Comparables: Skip Lockwood, Troy Percival, Kiko Calero*

Perkins' full-season stats paint the picture of an effective but unexceptional reliever, perhaps a dependable seventh-inning guy. Hardly anything could be farther from the truth. A healthy, dominant Perkins was a huge reason for the Twins' first-half success. He fanned a quarter of opposing batters, walked next to nobody and allowed a .463 OPS. Then, stricken with neck problems and back spasms for the entire second half, Perkins was a huge reason for the team's sub-.500 finish and failure to reach the playoffs. He was too slow to admit he was compromised, and the Twins were much, *much* too slow to take serious relief responsibilities away from him. Perkins had -1.8 Win Probability Added after the All-Star break, reflecting both how dreadful he was and how much Paul Molitor foolishly continued to trust him.

Ryan Pressly RHP

Born: 12/15/88 Age: 27 Bats: R Throws: R Height: 6'3" Weight: 210

YEAR	TEAM	LVL	AGE	W	L	SV	G	GS	IP	H	HR	BB/9	K/9	GB%	BABIP	WHIP	ERA	FIP	DRA	WARP	CFIP	MPH
2013	MIN	MLB	24	3	3	0	49	0	76^{2}	71	5	3.2	5.8	45%	.282	1.28	3.87	3.70	3.47	1.0	111	95.9
2014	ROC	AAA	25	1	4	6	35	0	60^{1}	55	1	3.1	9.4	44%	.318	1.26	2.98	2.58	4.01	0.5	80	
2014	MIN	MLB	25	2	0	0	25	0	28^{1}	30	3	2.5	4.4	50%	.281	1.34	2.86	4.50	3.97	0.2	112	95.5
2015	MIN	MLB	26	3	2	0	27	0	27^{2}	27	0	3.9	7.2	49%	.318	1.41	2.93	2.82	3.43	0.4	101	97.0
2015	ROC	AAA	26	0	2	0	7	0	10	6	1	5.4	13.5	35%	.263	1.20	4.50	3.26	2.99	0.2	86	
2016	*MIN*	*MLB*	*27*	*2*	*1*	*0*	*45*	*0*	*47^{2}*	*48*	*5*	*3.2*	*7.1*	*46%*	*.294*	*1.35*	*4.21*	*4.21*	*4.42*	*0.3*	*100*	
2017	*MIN*	*MLB*	*28*	*2*	*1*	*0*	*33*	*2*	*58^{1}*	*58*	*7*	*3.2*	*7.8*	*46%*	*.297*	*1.35*	*4.20*	*4.10*	*4.41*	*0.3*	*100*	

Breakout: 22% Improve: 45% Collapse: 16% Attrition: 29% MLB: 73% *Comparables: Jim Johnson, Michael Bowden, Adam Warren*

Pressly can reach the mid-90s with his fastball, and he has three solid pitches he can throw to right-handed batters (heater, slider, curve), adding a sinker into the mix against lefties. Despite less-than-eye-popping strikeout numbers, he consistently prevents runs well, avoiding walks and keeping the ball on the ground. DRA loves him. (You're waiting for the "but." Here comes the "but.") *But* there's no way he could throw 180 innings in a season. If Pressly could handle it from a durability perspective, one could almost imagine him stretching out as a starter, but he's had two straight seasons halved by injuries (in 2015, a lat strain was the culprit), so he seems doomed to remain an anonymous middle reliever.

Ervin Santana RHP

Born: 12/12/82 Age: 33 Bats: R Throws: R Height: 6'2" Weight: 175

YEAR	TEAM	LVL	AGE	W	L	SV	G	GS	IP	H	HR	BB/9	K/9	GB%	BABIP	WHIP	ERA	FIP	DRA	WARP	CFIP	MPH
2013	KCA	MLB	30	9	10	0	32	32	211	190	26	2.2	6.9	47%	.267	1.14	3.24	3.96	3.83	2.7	97	95.5
2014	ATL	MLB	31	14	10	0	31	31	196	193	16	2.9	8.2	45%	.319	1.31	3.95	3.36	4.24	1.3	101	95.8
2015	MIN	MLB	32	7	5	0	17	17	108	104	12	3.0	6.8	43%	.285	1.30	4.00	4.14	3.79	1.6	103	95.8
2015	ROC	AAA	32	3	0	0	3	3	20^{2}	17	2	1.7	4.8	41%	.242	1.02	1.74	4.08	4.31	0.1	104	
2016	*MIN*	*MLB*	*33*	*9*	*10*	*0*	*26*	*26*	*163^{2}*	*157*	*19*	*2.7*	*6.9*	*44%*	*.280*	*1.26*	*4.26*	*4.23*	*4.46*	*1.3*	*103*	
2017	*MIN*	*MLB*	*34*	*11*	*10*	*0*	*29*	*29*	*176^{1}*	*169*	*23*	*2.6*	*7.0*	*44%*	*.280*	*1.25*	*4.34*	*4.22*	*4.54*	*1.2*	*105*	

Breakout: 18% Improve: 45% Collapse: 24% Attrition: 16% MLB: 89% *Comparables: John Lackey, Randy Wolf, Bartolo Colon*

When Santana was suspended for 80 games after a positive PED test on the eve of the 2015 season, the most fun was had by the jokesters who pointed out that the suspension also rendered him ineligible for postseason play. By the time Santana returned, the jokes had turned to half-hearted outrage: The Twins actually stood on the edge of the playoffs, and their $55 million man wouldn't be able to pitch if they got there. After a six-start stretch in which Santana's opponents had an OPS of 1.056, anger turned to apathy (or at least apathetic anger). Then, as if in defiance of fans' dismissiveness, Santana finished with seven straight starts of at least seven innings and two or fewer runs allowed. Only Clayton Kershaw matched that streak in 2015. In other words, Santana remains maddeningly inconsistent, and the Twins remain on the hook for $40.5 million over the next three years as Santana pitches into his mid-30s. For normal humans, that's an age of settling down and mellowing out. Pitchers aren't normal humans.

Kohl Stewart RHP

Born: 10/7/94 Age: 21 Bats: R Throws: R Height: 6'3" Weight: 195

YEAR	TEAM	LVL	AGE	W	L	SV	G	GS	IP	H	HR	BB/9	K/9	GB%	BABIP	WHIP	ERA	FIP	DRA	WARP	CFIP	MPH
2014	CDR	A	19	3	5	0	19	19	87	75	4	2.5	6.4	57%	.270	1.14	2.59	3.73	4.51	0.7	101	
2015	FTM	A+	20	7	8	0	22	22	129^{1}	134	2	3.1	4.9	59%	.308	1.38	3.20	3.45	5.13	-1.2	116	
2016	*MIN*	*MLB*	*21*	*5*	*7*	*0*	*19*	*19*	*98^{2}*	*117*	*11*	*3.7*	*3.7*	*52%*	*.303*	*1.60*	*5.19*	*5.23*	*5.33*	*-0.2*	*128*	
2017	*MIN*	*MLB*	*22*	*6*	*8*	*0*	*21*	*21*	*126*	*145*	*15*	*3.9*	*4.3*	*52%*	*.297*	*1.58*	*5.31*	*5.18*	*5.45*	*-0.4*	*131*	

Breakout: 0% Improve: 0% Collapse: 0% Attrition: 0% MLB: 0% *Comparables: Joe Ross, Andrew Faulkner, Collin Balester*

There's a chance (no, really) that Stewart has four plus pitches in his arsenal. He's the perfect size for a right-handed starter. He competes on the mound, he gets groundballs and he's smart. His command is where most 21-year-olds' command is, which is to say underdeveloped, but he's not a lost cause. That's what makes the whole prospecting business so difficult. Stewart simply hasn't missed bats at an acceptable level anywhere he's been. In 2015, he fanned three or fewer batters in 13 of his 22 starts. (His season high in strikeouts was seven.) Absent performance to match the scouting reports, Stewart's star might dim badly in 2016.

Lewis Thorpe LHP

Born: 11/23/95 Age: 20 Bats: R Throws: L Height: 6'1" Weight: 160

YEAR	TEAM	LVL	AGE	W	L	SV	G	GS	IP	H	HR	BB/9	K/9	GB%	BABIP	WHIP	ERA	FIP	DRA	WARP	CFIP	MPH
2014	CDR	A	18	3	2	0	16	16	71^2	62	7	4.5	10.0	44%	.297	1.37	3.52	4.24	4.42	0.6	98	
2016	*MIN*	*MLB*	*20*	*2*	*3*	*0*	*8*	*8*	*34*	*35*	*5*	*4.2*	*7.8*	*35%*	*.306*	*1.50*	*4.72*	*4.80*	*4.83*	*0.1*	*115*	
2017	*MIN*	*MLB*	*21*	*7*	*9*	*0*	*28*	*28*	*172^2*	*170*	*24*	*4.1*	*8.5*	*35%*	*.299*	*1.44*	*4.58*	*4.45*	*4.69*	*0.6*	*112*	

Breakout: 0% Improve: 0% Collapse: 0% Attrition: 0% MLB: 0% *Comparables: Justin Nicolino, Trevor Cahill, Lance McCullers*

Thorpe chose rehab for a sprained UCL in his elbow late in 2014, but he tore the ligament outright in spring training 2015, so the Twins' Australian southpaw underwent Tommy John surgery. Once he heals up, he'll try to show the good fastball with which he has already demonstrated advanced command, and the feel for a changeup a lefty needs to make it as a starter. He also has a pair of breaking balls, though he might have to choose just one soon so as to get it really up to par. He doesn't throw from down under, and his curveball spins the same way American pitchers' do, but Thorpe has a chance to be the best Australian pitcher to date. He just needs time, health and 15 good pounds.

Michael Tonkin RHP

Born: 11/19/89 Age: 26 Bats: R Throws: R Height: 6'7" Weight: 220

YEAR	TEAM	LVL	AGE	W	L	SV	G	GS	IP	H	HR	BB/9	K/9	GB%	BABIP	WHIP	ERA	FIP	DRA	WARP	CFIP	MPH
2013	NBR	AA	23	1	2	7	22	0	24^1	21	0	3.0	11.1	60%	.313	1.19	2.22	2.21	3.98	0.3	80	
2013	MIN	MLB	23	0	0	0	9	0	11^1	9	0	2.4	7.9	44%	.265	1.06	0.79	2.10	2.74	0.3	94	96.8
2013	ROC	AAA	23	1	2	14	30	0	32^2	33	3	2.2	9.9	49%	.330	1.26	4.41	3.02	3.69	0.4	77	
2014	ROC	AAA	24	3	4	10	39	0	45	41	2	2.4	9.2	48%	.305	1.18	2.80	2.82	3.87	0.5	75	
2014	MIN	MLB	24	0	0	0	25	0	19	23	2	2.8	7.6	50%	.350	1.53	4.74	4.11	5.74	-0.3	102	96.2
2015	MIN	MLB	25	0	0	0	26	0	23^1	21	4	3.5	7.3	57%	.258	1.29	3.47	4.99	3.87	0.2	104	96.7
2015	ROC	AAA	25	2	1	14	33	0	41	25	2	1.1	10.1	54%	.240	0.73	1.10	1.99	1.16	1.6	60	
2016	*MIN*	*MLB*	*26*	*3*	*1*	*0*	*50*	*0*	*53*	*52*	*6*	*2.8*	*8.2*	*52%*	*.302*	*1.30*	*3.94*	*3.92*	*4.16*	*0.5*	*92*	
2017	*MIN*	*MLB*	*27*	*2*	*1*	*0*	*45*	*0*	*52^1*	*51*	*6*	*2.9*	*9.1*	*52%*	*.305*	*1.29*	*3.91*	*3.81*	*4.13*	*0.4*	*91*	

Breakout: 28% Improve: 38% Collapse: 25% Attrition: 23% MLB: 68% *Comparables: Jonathan Albaladejo, Kam Mickolio, Cory Burns*

Because of the timing of Tonkin's development, he briefly became a symbol of the Twins' move away from pitching to contact and toward an appreciation of velocity in line with the rest of the league. Perhaps it's fitting, then, that the team has treated Tonkin with mistrust, demoting him every time he's struggled in the majors. He has nothing whatsoever left to prove in the minors, which is good, because he's finally out of options. Tonkin is finally due for a fair shake this year.

LINEOUTS

Hitters

NAME	POS	TEAM	LVL	AGE	PA	R	2B	3B	HR	RBI	BB	K	SB	CS	AVG/OBP/SLG	TAv	BABIP	BRR	FRAA	WARP
Juan Centeno	C	CSP	AAA	25	187	11	6	3	0	24	5	19	2	2	.295/.312/.364	.227	.323	0.9	C(45): -9.4	-0.7
	C	MIL	MLB	25	23	0	1	0	0	0	2	7	0	0	.048/.130/.095	.107	.071	0.3	C(7): -1.1	-0.4
John Hicks	C	SEA	MLB	25	34	1	1	0	0	1	1	18	1	1	.063/.091/.094	.063	.143	0.0	C(14): -0.7, 3B(1): -0.0	-0.6
	C	TAC	AAA	25	320	39	15	1	6	35	17	71	9	2	.245/.282/.362	.235	.298	3.0	C(67): -0.1, 1B(11): 0.2	0.7
Levi Michael	2B	CHT	AA	24	264	43	12	5	5	31	31	53	18	3	.267/.369/.434	.302	.327	1.5	2B(52): 1.5	2.2
Stuart Turner	C	CHT	AA	23	379	40	13	1	4	37	45	69	5	2	.223/.322/.306	.251	.268	-1.4	C(96): -12.6	-0.2
Engelb Vielma	SS	FTM	A+	21	501	49	9	2	1	29	35	71	35	12	.270/.321/.306	.255	.315	1.5	SS(120): 15.7	3.8

Trey Cabbage is very green right now, but with plus potential in his offensive profile and a good shot to stick at third base, he has a chance to end up the head of the Twins' 2015 draft class. ❖ The true Catcher in the Rye, **Juan Centeno**, continued to wander through the wet fields, heading west-northwest for his next warm cup of coffee. ❖ Fare thee well, **Lewin Diaz**, as you travel the green, green rocky road that is the minors with your frame, fluidity and power potential. ❖ **John Hicks** profiles as a perennial back-up catcher, but the Twins used a December waiver claim on him to maintain their legally mandated Hicks Quota. ❖ The Twins spent big money on 16-year-old Dominican shortstop **Wander Javier**, so you've got about seven years to build your list of puns in preparation. Don't forget soundalikes: "A Fish Called Wander" is fair game if he's traded to the Marlins. ❖ If backup second basemen still fit onto big-league rosters, **Levi Michael** would look downright promising. They don't, so he's fringy. ❖ **Stuart Turner**'s best tool on offense is his patience, but that's something, and his strong defensive profile behind the plate is the real hook, anyway. ❖ **Engelb Vielma** will have the bat knocked out of his hands in the majors, but he's a sensational defensive shortstop and he can run. We're still pretty sure his name is the result of an unfortunately timed interruption.

Pitchers

NAME	TEAM	LVL	AGE	W	L	SV	G	GS	IP	H	HR	BB/9	K/9	GB%	BABIP	WHIP	ERA	FIP	FRA	WARP	CFIP	MPH
Mat Batts	FTM	A+	23	8	4	0	17	17	100^2	96	3	1.5	7.6	44%	.303	1.12	2.77	2.52	2.15	3.0	79	
	CDR	A	23	3	2	0	7	7	40^2	31	0	2.4	9.7	47%	.295	1.03	2.21	2.19	2.61	1.1	82	
Michael Cederoth	CDR	A	22	1	4	0	11	6	35^1	33	2	4.6	9.4	56%	.298	1.44	4.08	3.74	4.58	0.1	102	
J.T. Chargois	CHT	AA	24	1	1	11	32	0	33	26	1	5.5	9.3	56%	.298	1.39	2.73	3.64	4.20	0.1	99	
	FTM	A+	24	1	0	4	16	0	15	12	0	3.0	11.4	48%	.286	1.13	2.40	1.63	2.39	0.3	83	
Logan Darnell	ROC	AAA	26	5	1	0	35	7	77^2	77	3	2.9	7.6	49%	.319	1.31	2.78	2.96	3.64	0.9	94	
Brian Duensing	MIN	MLB	32	4	1	1	55	0	48^2	46	5	3.9	4.4	53%	.265	1.38	4.25	4.99	4.31	0.2	122	93.9
Ryan O'Rourke	ROC	AAA	27	0	0	0	20	0	13^2	13	1	4.6	14.5	22%	.387	1.46	5.93	2.43	2.65	0.3	82	
	MIN	MLB	27	0	0	0	28	0	22	16	3	6.1	9.8	43%	.236	1.41	6.14	4.74	3.15	0.4	98	92.8
Taylor Rogers	ROC	AAA	24	11	12	0	28	27	174	190	9	2.3	6.5	53%	.330	1.34	3.98	3.21	3.67	2.2	94	
Jason Wheeler	ROC	AAA	24	1	7	0	15	15	78	104	11	2.8	4.6	41%	.338	1.64	6.58	5.08	6.09	-1.4	122	
	CHT	AA	24	4	3	0	10	10	59^2	58	7	2.4	7.5	41%	.295	1.24	3.92	4.11	3.53	1.0	91	

Mat Batts is a terrible name for a pitcher, mostly because that's not how you spell Matt. ❖ With a Kyle Farnsworth–like body, a Kyle Farnsworth–like fastball and a Kyle-Farnsworth–like slider, **Michael Cederoth** has as good a chance as anyone to be the next Matt Anderson. ❖ Finally healthy after two full seasons lost and one Tommy John surgery, **J.T. Chargois** resumed his march toward a middle-relief role that will feel disappointing given his raw velocity (sits mid-90s) and his birthplace (Sulphur, Louisiana). ❖ **Logan Darnell** has one option year left to develop as a starter in the minors, but if he's smart, he'll focus on his nickname options: Logan the LOOGY and LOOGY Logan are fine, but LOOGan Darnell should be his choice. ❖ "LOOGY" is used as a neutral descriptor these days, but back when it was mostly derisive, it would have applied nicely to **Brian Duensing**. ❖ **Mason Melotakis** is talented, but any reliever who has Tommy John surgery before he reaches the majors carries a lot of questions. One example of such questions is, "Will he reach the majors?" We're not sure. ❖ Lefties are helpless against **Ryan O'Rourke**'s slider, but he has neither a second weapon nor sufficient control to be more than a LOOGY. ❖ Soft-tossing lefty starter **Taylor Rogers** is valuable as long as he can be kept in the minors as a seventh or eighth starter. ❖ **Jason Wheeler** is huge, but his stuff isn't, and after a promising 2014, his 2015 follow-up was a harsh reminder of what advanced hitters do with lefties who can't break a wet tissue.

Manager

Paul Molitor

YEAR	TEAM	W	L	Pythag +/-	Avg PC	100+ P	120+ P	QS	BQS	REL	REL w Zero R	IBB	PH	PH Avg	PH HR	SB2	CS2	SB3	CS3	SAC Att	SAC%	POS SAC	Squeeze	Swing	In Play
2015	MIN	83	79	2	91.2	55	0	76	6	520	420	34	72	.129	1	59	34	11	3	57	52.6	30	3	279	100

The Twins don't change managers often—they've had just two since 1986, after all. So when Terry Ryan dismissed Ron Gardenhire in favor of Molitor, you knew there had to be legitimate reasons.

For the cynical, those reasons were marinated in nostalgia. Molitor is Mr. Minnesota. He grew up there, attended the University of Minnesota, played for the Twins and has filled every role imaginable with the club since. Factor in the Twins' subsequent reunion with Torii Hunter, and the organization appeared more concerned with reliving the past than building a future. (Molitor's spring declaration banning cellphones and tablets 30 minutes before game time probably didn't help with that perception.) But one surprisingly competitive season later, the Twins seemed to have better reasons for hiring Molitor than a wistful desire to return to the old days. Throughout the year, he earned a reputation as a stickler for details—someone who studies tape alongside his players, and who examines the field as intently as he did when he played. Yet unlike others of that ilk who have earned the control-freak label, Molitor's humility and consistency were both pluses. He served as the ultimate rarity: a Hall of Fame-level player who can crack jokes when things go wrong and who would rather take blame than credit.

Molitor's modest approach extended to his preparation. He stayed true to his previous analytical interest, often explaining his decisions within the context of the numbers—for instance, arguing that he batted Joe Mauer second instead of leadoff because, while he recognized the importance of getting on base, he wanted Mauer to come to the plate with a runner on more often. It might be a surprise, then, to learn that the Twins attempted more sacrifices than all but two other teams. How could that be?

Rest assured, Molitor wasn't just throwing away outs. Most of the bunting was done by Danny Santana and Kurt Suzuki—neither good hitters—and seemed to be left up to the hitters. Additionally, Molitor made a point a lot of analytical types have made before: There's value in bunting for a hit. "They always have the option of using a bunt if they don't feel comfortable trying to hit to the right side," Molitor told Phil Miller of the *Minneapolis Star Tribune*. "They also learned that neither of those bunts were particularly good, but they got the job done. And I hope it makes them realize that they made close plays out of not-really-good bunts. If you can get the ball into a good spot, everybody should think about it now and then."

That same open mind and resourcefulness has Molitor looking like a solid hire.

NEW YORK METS

Essay by Mike Pesca

Player comments by Will Woods and BP authors

The Queens, NY enclave of Jamaica Estates features spacious yards, Tudor-style homes and the serenity offered by a neighborhood so leafy that there are entire blocks you can traverse without spotting a high-rise, elevated train or street numbered in the triple digits. Donald Trump is from Jamaica Estates. The place is classy.

To begin the 2015 season the Mets, another notable Queens denizen, found themselves metaphorically in a neighborhood much like Jamaica Estates—or, more accurately, on the edge of Jamaica Estates. They professed a 11432 zip code, but they were actually dwelling in neighboring Jamaica, the Queens neighborhood with one of the highest foreclosure rates in the city. It was all sylvan lawns and rolling hills, but in truth the Mets were struggling against a less-than-stable undercurrent.

For years the Mets had been living above their means. In 2008 they had the second-highest Opening Day payroll in baseball, behind only the Yankees. But in December 2008 it was revealed that the Wilpon family, owner of the Mets, had been taken for about half a billion dollars in Bernard Madoff's Ponzi scheme. At the time, public pronouncements from Fred Wilpon and his co-owner and brother-in-law Saul Katz were of the "Move along, nothing to be seen here" ilk. (They were backed up by the commissioner's office.) "The individual partners lost some money at Madoff. It doesn't affect the Mets," said Jeff Wilpon, Fred's son and the team's chief operating officer, at the time. "It doesn't affect the Citi Field project. It doesn't affect SNY or any of our other operating businesses."

But even a casual accounting of the Mets' accounting would have found the Madoff money accounting for a large percentage of their fortune. However, there's no accounting for hubris, or desperation, or, if you want to be generous, salesmanship born of necessity. Just a few months after the Madoff scheme was revealed, the Mets would be opening their new park, built at a cost of around $900 million, of which the Mets paid around $400 million.

Within a week of Madoff's arrest, *The New York Times* covered the Mets' 2008 Christmas party. In the sixth paragraph of a nine-paragraph story, the *Times* tossed off this sentence: "Wilpon and Major League Baseball officials have insisted that Wilpon's losses are bearable and will have no effect on the operation of the Mets, who have one

METS PROSPECTUS

2015 W-L: 90-72, 1st in NL East

Pythag	.549	8th	DER	.712	8th
RS/G	4.22	17th	B-Age	28.7	21st
RA/G	3.78	5th	P-Age	28.5	19th
TAv	.271	4th	Salary	$101.3M	21st
BRR	3.97	10th	M$/MW	$2.1M	26th
TAv-P	.257	12th	DL Days	1799	30th
FIP	3.56	6th	$ on DL	27%	28th

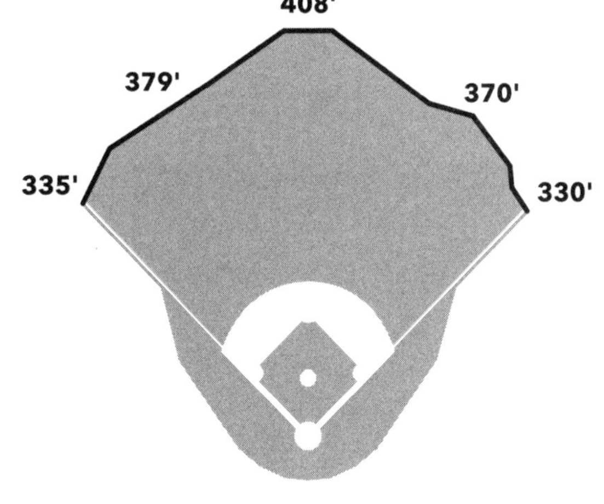

Outfield wall profile: **8'**

Three-Year Park Factors

Runs	Runs/RH	Runs/LH	HR/RH	HR/LH
90	92	104	101	125

Top Hitter WARP	5.5	Curtis Granderson
Top Pitcher WARP	4.4	Jacob deGrom
Top Prospect		Steven Matz

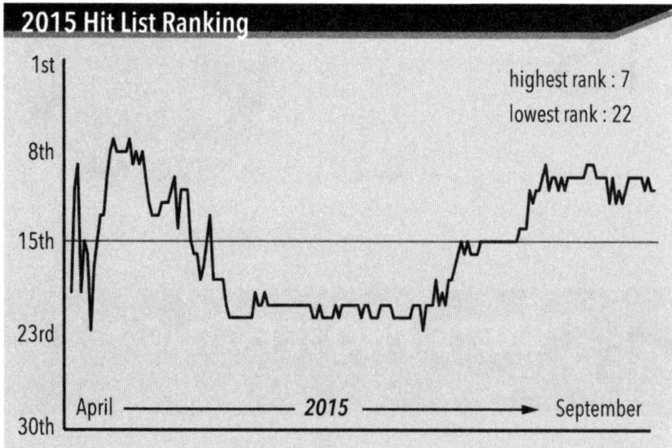

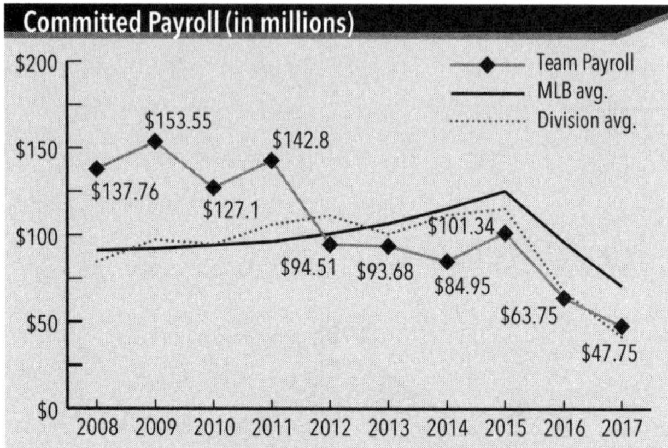

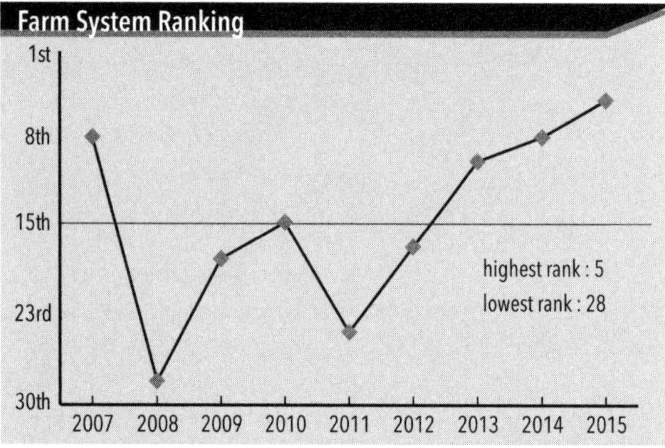

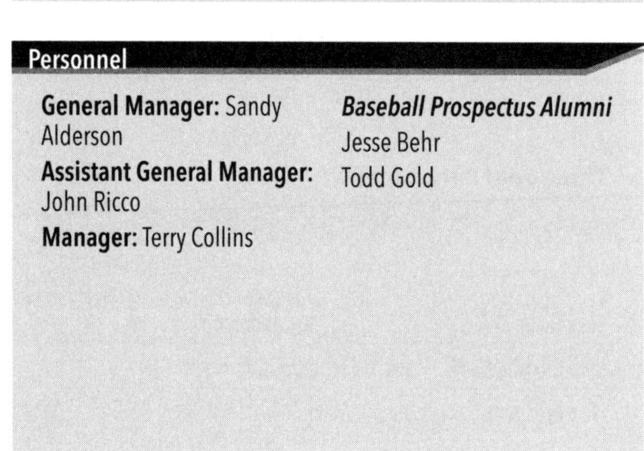

of the sport's highest payrolls."

Personnel
General Manager: Sandy Alderson
Assistant General Manager: John Ricco
Manager: Terry Collins
Baseball Prospectus Alumni
Jesse Behr
Todd Gold

The story ended with the hope that the newly acquired Francisco Rodriguez would forestall a third September collapse in a row. The Mets did indeed avoid a September collapse; they finished K-Rod's first season 22 games under .500. In 2010, as the novelty of Citi Field wore off and attendance declined by almost 20 percent, the Mets saw their payroll slip to fifth in baseball. This was a huge-market team whose naming rights went for $20 million per annum and whose regional sports network, two-thirds owned by the Wilpons themselves, is worth an estimated billion dollars. Over the next five years the Mets payroll ranked seventh, 14th, 23rd, 22nd, and 21st in baseball.

The Mets had never had a winning team at Citi Field, had drawn 13th out of the 15 teams in the National League two years in a row, and were still digging out of the Madoff-induced penury. This is how the Mets headed into 2015, evincing an ill-warranted Jamaica Estates confidence with bills and payments only they could fathom.

On the baseball side, they assured fans—and, it would seem, themselves, judging by their paucity of offseason moves—that they were on solid footing, that they'd built on a sturdy foundation and prime real estate. Their young arms would see them through. Matt Harvey had, before missing a year due to injury, already established himself as a premier pitcher. Jacob deGrom was the 2014 Rookie of the Year. And when another young hurler, Zack Wheeler, was lost to Tommy John surgery, eyes easily drifted to flame-throwing prospects Steven Matz and Noah Syndergaard.

Mets management assured fans that the latter two would be given time to blossom in the minors, owing to a dedicated timetable for their development, and not the prospect of pushing back their free agencies. "For their own good." It was hard to know which strain of Mets mendacity to attend to: The Mets were undeniably cheap, and most plausibly greedy. On the other hand, keeping fine young prospects in the minors to extend team control is actually a prudent financial move, and the Mets had not, as of late, shown the capacity for such acumen.

But it was no matter early, as the Mets ripped off 10 straight April wins, a streak carried along by great pitching and a schedule stuffed with Phillies, Marlins and Braves. As the saying goes, you have to play the teams before you, and with a 13-3 record the Mets were feeling less Jamaica Estates and more Douglaston—an even wealthier neighborhood, right across the Nassau County border. John McEnroe is from Douglaston. Douglaston is ritzy, and expensive, but the Mets had a nest egg. Heck, at 13-3, they could go .500 the rest of the way and still have a shot at a playoff slot!

In fact the Mets went 23-34 over the next two months and found themselves a game below .500. The seeds of the collapse were sewn during that early win streak. David Wright went down to injury, and while it's true that he was coming off a season in which his slugging percentage looked like a typical David Wright OBP, his loss was nevertheless profound. That's because his replacement was Eric Campbell, nicknamed "Soup," who proceeded to compile a .295 slug over the next two months, an outcome that was in the lowest 10 percent of even Campbell's own PECOTA projections. Meanwhile, Anthony Recker and Kevin Plawecki were filling in just as sluglessly for injured catcher Travis d'Arnaud. The nicknames "Broth" and "Remouillage" were available.

By late June, it was clear that the move to Douglaston was ill-advised, and perhaps the Mets ought seek shelter in Ridgewood, or possibly Astoria—good rental markets, but nowhere near the exclusivity of top addresses. The team's plan of eking out low-scoring victories behind amazing arms was not working, even though the arms *were* amazing. Syndergaard was called up in mid-May, and his strikeout rate rose in each of his first three months as he led the majors in average fastball velocity. DeGrom was again dominant, and Harvey injury-free. Matz debuted with two fill-in starts at the end of June and won both. Yet the Mets were 4 1/2 games back of the Nationals, and only 1 1/2 ahead of the Braves.

Around this time, WFAN's Mike Francesa declared, "If you are a Met fan who has been happy with this season, you are no longer happy. The needs are everything except starting pitching. No bullpen. No bench. No offense. No defense."

This assessment was perfectly accurate, and hardly even high dudgeon for the legendary New York sportscaster. The Francesa Scale of Fury is modeled after Moh's Scale of Hardness. where the softest mineral, talc, is assigned a value of 1 and the hardest, diamond, is rated a 7. This evisceration of the Mets' sorry state rated a 2, one above grouse and not even within sight of roar, bellow or thunder (5, 6, 7 on the scale). An inert offense is a thing of pity, not rage, even to a maestro of hypertension.

Soon thereafter *The New York Post* ran an article under the headline "The reason the Mets aren't planning to fire Terry Collins." A careful reading of the article does not yield *one* reason per se, but the following players are listed in order: Dilson Herrera, Darrell Ceciliani, Plawecki and Campbell. From Nuts to Soup, the Mets lineup was such a desperate goulash as to stretch the memories of the Elias Sports Bureau, which noted that on July 23rd the Mets' nos. 4 and 5 hitters, John Mayberry and Soup Campbell, brought batting averages of .170 and .179 into the game. The Bureau told us it was the second time in the live-ball era an actual major-league team started 4/5 hitters with averages that low—and the 1975 A's had done it only to staff a post-clinch hangover lineup. Oakland's comparably inept tandem drove in both of the club's runs that day; Mayberry and Soup, on the other hand, were pureed by Clayton Kershaw, who threw a three-hitter.

Through July, the Mets were last in runs scored, at 3.5 per game. Their offensive anemia laid bare a few truths. The first is that fine pitching alone cannot be relied on to win games. The Mets were actually doing well in low-scoring games. When they scored exactly two runs, they had the eighth-best winning percentage in baseball. When they scored exactly three, they were fourth best. Their pitching was such that they actually went 14-5 when scoring four runs—a .736 winning percentage when scoring a quarter-run *below* league average. But they also lost an MLB-high four 1-0 games. Over the first 100 games of the season, the Mets demonstrated just how far good pitching can go, and the extent to which it can go no further.

They were also leading baseball in the ignominious "games missed" statistic, with 23 players spending more than 1,800 games inactive. This demonstrates the true use of payroll, and what it means to be a team of means. Cash to spend, it is assumed, is useful in paying for big free agents, or to at least ensure that no roster spot goes to a horrifically inferior player. While it is nice to ink the splashy veteran, the real value of money is making up for mistakes in all the other areas.

Teams with actual financial ballast are able to absorb a misstep of the Josh Hamilton variety. They are not undone when a Carl Crawford underperforms, or, more accurately, performs poorly in a fairly predictable manner. But for a team like the Mets, paying off a Douglaston mortgage with only a Ridgewood income, a lone mistake becomes insurmountable. For example, the offseason signing of Michael Cuddyer at $21 million was not unreasonable. It became disastrous when Cuddyer quit slugging but had to keep playing. And when the Mets suffered injuries, and the replacement players failed to deliver, or were subject to a valid debate over whether they could be eaten with a fork like a meal, it was a debacle. Even more frustrating for Mets fans was management's habit of constantly downplaying debilitating injuries. *The Wall Street Journal* assembled a half-dozen examples of how the Mets initially described player injuries as bumps and scrapes, when they turned out to be tears and sprains. "We don't expect it's going to be a major issue" became Wheeler's Tommy John surgery four days later. "It's not real serious" was 22 missed games for Daniel Murphy. And so on.

All this conspired to slot Mayberry and Soup into Elias Fun Fact history. It made for a popless offense, the worst in baseball. Citi Field crowds, which had topped 40,000 in April and early May, were in the low 20Ks by June and July. Dazzling pitchers saw their starts wasted. The Mets were like restaurant owners with a team of brilliant young chefs turning out four-star dishes, only to have a bumbling wait staff trip and spill Consommé in customers' laps.

But then, a few days before the trade deadline, there was a rumbling. At least a whimpering: Wilmer Flores, emotional on the field after hearing rumors he'd been traded. While this was sad for the 23-year-old Venezuelan, who'd signed at 16, and who said he believed he'd be a "Met for life," it did represent hope. The Mets seemed to be going all-in, trading not just the lachrymose middle infielder but Wheeler, too. The returnee would be Carlos Gomez, a superb defensive outfielder with speed and power. The deal was done, Twitter was ablaze, Flores was apuddle.

And then, the deal was not done. Scotched over health and finances, if not compassion for weeping Wilmer. But at the last minute, the Mets decided to play major-league baseball. They acquired Yoenis Cespedes. From that point forward nothing was the same.

✦✦✦

Cespedes was hitless in his first game as a Met, then went 1-for-4 with a run scored in his second, then whacked three doubles in his third. The Mets fought back to first place, a spot they'd never relinquish. In the 50 games Cespedes started between his acquisition and the Mets' clinching victory, he hit .294/.338/.624 with 17 homers. He wore a garish neon yellow arm brace, which became a thing. He embraced a "rally parakeet," which became a thing. He commissioned his own walk-up song titled "The Power," which became a thing. The Mets offense became a thing. By this point Soup was consigned to pinch-hitter status, and here was Cespedes to stir the pot. The team averaged six runs per game in August. With the return of Wright and d'Arnaud, they averaged 6.5 in 20 pre-clinch September games. They had gone from fakin' Jamaica Estates to getting in over their heads in Douglaston to actually owning one of those new buildings that just went up overlooking Midtown Manhattan in Hunter's Point. Or maybe one of those rarified neighborhoods people in the other parts of Queens haven't even heard of. Little Neck. A $3 million five-bed, five-bath in Little Neck.

In the playoffs the Mets surged, and to a casual observer who had not witnessed the crazy gumbo of lies and tears it all seemed logical, maybe even inevitable. The Mets were built on aces, so why would it surprise anyone that such a team would run October? Their rotation, now including Matz, had a combined salary of around $2 million, or what their NLDS opponent Clayton Kershaw is paid for approximately 15 innings. But the fireballers did, in fact, ball fire. The Mets won the pennant and were, in one way of looking at it, were eight outs away from winning the World Series—an admittedly odd thing to say about a team that lost in five games, thanks to a bunch of late leads blown.

Financially, times seemed better, as well, with the Wilpons having sold several 4 percent shares of the team at $20 million each a few years ago. (Among the perks of ownership, as laid out in a leaked prospectus, are business cards listing you as "Owner" and guaranteed access to Mr. Met.) The Wilpon family has also reportedly re-financed its loans at lower rates. Still, it's unclear whether they will look at this season and learn a lesson. Why not be parsimonious to a fault until the very last moment, if you can get a *Deus Cesp Machina* out of your one authentically gutsy acquisition? Why not rely on your young aces, all under suppressed-salary control for years to come, and hope to scrounge up a couple of runs like tiny chunks of lobster in an otherwise highly strained bisque? Oh, and let's not forget the benefits of playing in the NL East, where the rest of the division was a combined 80 games under .500.

When the season ended, the Mets and four other teams were listed by Las Vegas as 10/1 shots to win the 2016 World Series. The Dodgers led all teams at 8/1. With offense still a big question mark, and their division rivals poised to do better simply by reverting to the mean, there's a lot riding on those young arms. That's especially true if the owners' fists remain closed. ■

—*xxxxxxx*urnal.

Hitters

Wuilmer Becerra OF

Born: 10/1/94 Age: 21 Bats: R Throws: R Height: 6'4" Weight: 190

YEAR	TEAM	LVL	AGE	PA	R	2B	3B	HR	RBI	BB	K	SB	CS	AVG/OBP/SLG	TAv	BABIP	BRR	FRAA	WARP
2015	SAV	A	20	487	67	27	3	9	63	33	96	16	8	.290/.342/.423	.294	.351	-0.2	RF(100): -5.1	2.1
2016	*NYN*	*MLB*	*21*	*250*	*23*	*10*	*1*	*6*	*25*	*12*	*73*	*3*	*2*	*.210/.252/.328*	*.216*	*.276*	*-0.3*	*RF -1*	*-0.7*
2017	*NYN*	*MLB*	*22*	*303*	*32*	*12*	*1*	*8*	*32*	*16*	*89*	*4*	*2*	*.216/.263/.349*	*.232*	*.283*	*-0.2*	*RF -1, LF 0*	*0.5*

Breakout: 3% Improve: 5% Collapse: 0% Attrition: 7% MLB: 11% *Comparables: Rymer Liriano, Yorman Rodriguez, Carlos Gonzalez*

It's somewhat contradictory for a 17-year-old, seven-figure signee to be called a "throw-in" in a trade, yet that's the go-to narrative with Becerra, who took a fastball to the face just games after signing with Toronto and found himself in the R.A. Dickey trade when he came to. Since then he has justified his signing bonus, if not the lack of hype: His strikeout rate, thought to be a weakness, has declined in each of three seasons with the Mets. His real offensive shortcoming may be his honesty; he struggles with off-speed stuff, and seems to want to react to a pitch rather than make a plan and jump on it. But he's strong, with good hands and a great arm. Besides, how many 21-year-olds do you know who can plan ahead?

Asdrubal Cabrera SS

Born: 11/13/85 Age: 30 Bats: B Throws: R Height: 6'0" Weight: 205

YEAR	TEAM	LVL	AGE	PA	R	2B	3B	HR	RBI	BB	K	SB	CS	AVG/OBP/SLG	TAv	BABIP	BRR	FRAA	WARP
2013	CLE	MLB	27	562	66	35	2	14	64	35	114	9	3	.242/.299/.402	.262	.283	-2.8	SS(129): -5.0	1.5
2014	CLE	MLB	28	416	54	22	2	9	40	27	79	7	2	.246/.305/.386	.252	.286	-0.7	SS(92): -2.0	1.1
2014	WAS	MLB	28	200	20	9	2	5	21	22	29	3	0	.229/.312/.389	.274	.245	0.7	2B(48): -2.8, SS(1): 0.0	0.6
2015	TBA	MLB	29	551	66	28	5	15	58	36	107	6	3	.265/.315/.430	.261	.306	-0.4	SS(136): -8.2	1.4
2016	*NYN*	*MLB*	*30*	*530*	*65*	*27*	*2*	*15*	*55*	*38*	*101*	*7*	*3*	*.244/.305/.401*	*.259*	*.277*	*-1.0*	*SS -5*	*1.9*
2017	*NYN*	*MLB*	*31*	*503*	*57*	*26*	*2*	*13*	*55*	*36*	*101*	*6*	*2*	*.233/.294/.384*	*.257*	*.267*	*-0.9*	*SS -5*	*1.7*

Breakout: 2% Improve: 49% Collapse: 2% Attrition: 6% MLB: 95% *Comparables: Stephen Drew, Carlos Guillen, Jhonny Peralta*

The reported demise of Cabrera As Shortstop was either exaggerated or just premature. Signed by the Rays to essentially replace Ben Zobrist in the lineup, Cabrera held his own at the six spot for Tampa Bay, re-establishing himself as a viable option up the middle. He beat out younger, more athletic players in a spring competition with solid, maybe even boring, play at the position. Everyone loves flash, but it is important to have someone who can make most plays; Cabrera can still do that. Although he was a subpar hitter during the first half, he rebounded: In the season's twilight, he was not just a good hitter for his position, but one of the best hitters overall. The sum of both halves resulted in the slightest of above-average seasons, which is apt. He should continue on a similar path as he joins a new team for the third time since July 2014 and enters a new decade on the planet.

Gavin Cecchini SS

Born: 12/22/93 Age: 22 Bats: R Throws: R Height: 6'2" Weight: 200

YEAR	TEAM	LVL	AGE	PA	R	2B	3B	HR	RBI	BB	K	SB	CS	AVG/OBP/SLG	TAv	BABIP	BRR	FRAA	WARP
2013	BRO	A-	19	212	18	8	0	0	14	14	30	2	3	.273/.319/.314	.277	.319	0.1	SS(50): 5.6	1.9
2014	SLU	A+	20	271	36	10	1	5	31	32	40	3	3	.236/.325/.352	.246	.259	0.3	SS(59): -5.1	0.2
2014	SAV	A	20	259	42	17	4	3	25	25	41	7	1	.259/.333/.408	.276	.299	3.5	SS(53): 3.4	2.2
2015	BIN	AA	21	485	64	26	4	7	51	42	55	3	4	.317/.377/.442	.300	.348	-2.3	SS(109): 2.3	4.2
2016	*NYN*	*MLB*	*22*	*250*	*26*	*11*	*1*	*5*	*23*	*18*	*52*	*0*	*0*	*.235/.291/.361*	*.243*	*.277*	*-0.4*	*SS 1*	*0.9*
2017	*NYN*	*MLB*	*23*	*452*	*50*	*20*	*2*	*10*	*47*	*33*	*92*	*1*	*1*	*.243/.299/.373*	*.257*	*.286*	*-0.9*	*SS 2*	*2.2*

Breakout: 5% Improve: 29% Collapse: 10% Attrition: 23% MLB: 40% *Comparables: Marcus Semien, Eugenio Suarez, Reid Brignac*

It's pronounced "cheh-KEE-nee," and you might actually need to know that now. The major takeaway from Cecchini's breakout hitting campaign is that he was able to make more contact without sacrificing power. He opened his stance last year to provide a timing mechanism, and while the numbers may be a bit inflated, they made him a top prospect once again. Now, where would he stand on defense? Cecchini still has yet to play anywhere but shortstop, but scouts are divided on his potential to stay there, and a move probably makes him a bench player. He could possibly grade out average, if you're used to watching Wilmer Flores and Ruben Tejada. Oh, you are? Fantastic! (Of note: His combination of chinstrap and high-and-tight makes for some of the worst overall hair in the system.)

Yoenis Cespedes LF

Born: 10/18/85 Age: 30 Bats: R Throws: R Height: 5'10" Weight: 210

YEAR	TEAM	LVL	AGE	PA	R	2B	3B	HR	RBI	BB	K	SB	CS	AVG/OBP/SLG	TAv	BABIP	BRR	FRAA	WARP
2013	OAK	MLB	27	574	74	21	4	26	80	37	137	7	7	.240/.294/.442	.279	.274	-0.1	LF(94): 3.3, CF(18): -1.7	2.4
2014	OAK	MLB	28	432	62	26	3	17	67	28	80	3	2	.256/.303/.464	.290	.278	1.7	LF(82): 7.0, CF(9): -0.4	3.1
2014	BOS	MLB	28	213	27	10	3	5	33	7	48	4	0	.269/.296/.423	.269	.325	-0.1	LF(43): 4.3	1.1
2015	DET	MLB	29	427	62	28	2	18	61	19	87	3	4	.293/.323/.506	.293	.331	0.6	LF(99): 12.7	3.8
2015	NYN	MLB	29	249	39	14	4	17	44	14	54	4	1	.287/.337/.604	.334	.306	0.6	CF(40): -2.3, LF(35): 1.1	2.6
2016	*NYN*	*MLB*	*30*	*610*	*75*	*29*	*4*	*27*	*87*	*37*	*135*	*8*	*4*	*.258/.308/.468*	*.283*	*.292*	*0.9*	*LF 6, CF -2*	*4.0*
2017	*NYN*	*MLB*	*31*	*574*	*74*	*28*	*4*	*25*	*81*	*35*	*130*	*7*	*4*	*.255/.305/.462*	*.290*	*.290*	*1.0*	*LF 6, CF -2*	*2.1*

Breakout: 0% Improve: 41% Collapse: 0% Attrition: 10% MLB: 100% *Comparables: Josh Hamilton, Matt Holliday, Jason Bay*

Cespedes joined the Mets at the trade deadline and, fireworks aside, posted an on-base percentage all of 14 points higher than with the Tigers. It is likely that for 29 teams Cespedes will be money well unspent. He is now 30, and having relied on his natural athleticism more than perhaps any other position player, that number may be especially meaningful. He seems to get slower afoot, or perhaps just less interested, with each passing year. While his arm will always play, he needs his speed to overcome his merely average outfield instincts. On offense, the "swing hard in case you hit it" philosophy does not have many mid-30s case studies. This isn't to say the fall is coming this season. It isn't. But he didn't sign a one-year deal, either. (We hope. He was still a free agent when we went to press.)

Michael Conforto LF

Born: 3/1/93 Age: 23 Bats: L Throws: R Height: 6'1" Weight: 215

YEAR	TEAM	LVL	AGE	PA	R	2B	3B	HR	RBI	BB	K	SB	CS	AVG/OBP/SLG	TAv	BABIP	BRR	FRAA	WARP
2014	BRO	A-	21	186	30	10	0	3	19	16	29	3	0	.331/.403/.448	.315	.383	1.9	LF(41): 0.8	1.8
2015	BIN	AA	22	197	21	12	3	5	26	23	35	1	0	.312/.396/.503	.312	.368	-2.4	LF(45): -0.1	1.3
2015	SLU	A+	22	206	25	12	0	7	28	17	26	0	1	.283/.350/.462	.292	.294	-1.7	LF(41): 7.1	1.7
2015	NYN	MLB	22	194	30	14	0	9	26	17	39	0	1	.270/.335/.506	.315	.297	0.6	LF(50): 2.8	1.9
2016	*NYN*	*MLB*	*23*	*587*	*66*	*29*	*2*	*22*	*78*	*48*	*129*	*1*	*1*	*.250/.316/.438*	*.273*	*.287*	*-1.1*	*LF 8*	*3.4*
2017	*NYN*	*MLB*	*24*	*527*	*67*	*26*	*2*	*20*	*68*	*42*	*117*	*1*	*1*	*.247/.313/.431*	*.280*	*.285*	*-1.2*	*LF 7*	*2.0*

Breakout: 2% Improve: 34% Collapse: 5% Attrition: 12% MLB: 68% *Comparables: Adam Lind, Oswaldo Arcia, Jorge Soler*

The first rookie to hit two home runs in a World Series game in 19 years. The third player of all time to play in the Little League World Series, the College World Series and the adults-only World Series. Most importantly, not a bad outfielder! The book on Conforto was that his defense could be problematic, but with six outfield assists, he was a plus on both sides of the ball. With the bat, like a more powerful Rico Brogna, he's a line-drive spray hitter who defies a single plan of attack; he forces the pitcher to play to his own strengths through a lack of obvious weaknesses. That's not something you can typically say about a rookie, and while he's unlikely to keep up last year's pace over a full season—he had only 15 plate appearances against lefties over 56 games—he's such a natural that the adaptation shouldn't take long. He's also Italian, which you wouldn't think would be a big deal, but this is the city that's still coming to terms with Steven Matz not being Jewish.

Michael Cuddyer RF

Born: 3/27/79 Age: 37 Bats: R Throws: R Height: 6'2" Weight: 220

YEAR	TEAM	LVL	AGE	PA	R	2B	3B	HR	RBI	BB	K	SB	CS	AVG/OBP/SLG	TAv	BABIP	BRR	FRAA	WARP
2013	COL	MLB	34	540	74	31	3	20	84	46	100	10	3	.331/.389/.530	.304	.382	1.0	RF(118): -15.0, 1B(15): 0.3	1.9
2014	COL	MLB	35	205	32	15	1	10	31	14	30	3	0	.332/.376/.579	.315	.351	0.6	RF(35): -0.1, 1B(14): 0.0	1.6
2015	NYN	MLB	36	408	44	18	1	10	41	24	88	2	0	.259/.309/.391	.272	.312	0.3	LF(69): -3.0, 1B(18): 1.0	1.1
2016	*NYN*	*MLB*	*37*	*346*	*39*	*17*	*1*	*11*	*43*	*25*	*72*	*4*	*1*	*.258/.314/.423*	*.276*	*.298*	*0.3*	*LF -5, 1B 0*	*1.0*
2017	*NYN*	*MLB*	*38*	*263*	*30*	*13*	*0*	*8*	*30*	*18*	*56*	*2*	*1*	*.246/.300/.396*	*.270*	*.288*	*0.2*	*LF -4, 1B 0*	*0.2*

Breakout: 0% Improve: 27% Collapse: 8% Attrition: 14% MLB: 84% *Comparables: Raul Ibanez, Torii Hunter, Hank Aaron*

Cuddyer turned down $15 million for one year in Colorado in favor of $21 million for two years in New York. The stinker of a season he turned in, bad and ugly in equal measure, would have made that decision look savvy, except that he decided to retire this winter. Exactly how much of his foregone (backloaded) 2016 salary was made up in a buyout is unknown as of this writing, but it seems very likely that he would have taken home more dough on the one-year deal, though for the opposite reason than you'd have guessed a year ago. Maybe it was worth those millions to get to his first World Series, though.

You can understand Cuddyer hanging 'em up now, even when he's shown himself still capable of hitting like a second-division first baseman overall: Take a look at his injury history when you have a chance, and compare its length to Bugsy Siegel's rap sheet, to get a sense of the toll his job for the last 17 years has taken on his body. At least he'll always have his September 20, 2009 AL Player of the Week Award.

Travis d'Arnaud C

Born: 2/10/89 Age: 27 Bats: R Throws: R Height: 6'2" Weight: 210

YEAR	TEAM	LVL	AGE	PA	R	2B	3B	HR	RBI	BB	K	SB	CS	AVG/OBP/SLG	TAv	BABIP	BRR	FRAA	WARP
2013	LVG	AAA	24	78	19	8	0	2	12	21	12	0	0	.304/.487/.554	.355	.349	-1.2	C(18): 4.6	1.5
2013	BIN	AA	24	30	2	2	1	1	3	3	9	0	0	.222/.300/.481	.266	.294	-0.8	C(7): 0.1	0.1
2013	NYN	MLB	24	112	4	3	0	1	5	12	21	0	0	.202/.286/.263	.205	.244	-0.5	C(30): 3.8	0.2
2014	LVG	AAA	25	59	13	8	0	6	16	3	5	0	0	.436/.475/.909	.412	.409	-0.5	C(10): 1.4	1.3
2014	NYN	MLB	25	421	48	22	3	13	41	32	64	1	0	.242/.302/.416	.268	.259	-0.3	C(105): 6.0	2.9
2015	NYN	MLB	26	268	31	14	1	12	41	23	49	0	0	.268/.340/.485	.312	.289	-0.1	C(64): 12.0	4.0
2015	BIN	AA	26	20	3	1	0	0	1	0	2	0	0	.300/.300/.350	.220	.333	-0.3	C(4): -0.0	0.0
2016	*NYN*	*MLB*	*27*	*522*	*59*	*27*	*2*	*19*	*69*	*47*	*90*	*1*	*0*	*.249/.321/.435*	*.276*	*.270*	*-0.5*	*C 15*	*4.9*
2017	*NYN*	*MLB*	*28*	*414*	*53*	*20*	*1*	*15*	*53*	*37*	*73*	*0*	*0*	*.245/.316/.429*	*.282*	*.264*	*-0.6*	*C 12*	*2.9*

Breakout: 3% Improve: 42% Collapse: 7% Attrition: 11% MLB: 100% *Comparables: Victor Martinez, Miguel Montero, Buster Posey*

YEAR	TEAM	P. COUNT	FRM RUNS	BLK RUNS	THRW RUNS	TOT RUNS
2013	LVG	2454	3.7	-0.2	0.2	3.7
2013	NYN	4198	4.3	-0.1	-0.1	4.1
2014	LVG	1338	1.6	0.0	-0.2	1.5
2014	NYN	14765	9.1	-1.7	-1.8	5.6
2015	NYN	9002	12.6	0.1	0.0	12.7
2016	*NYN*	*18601*	*17.9*	*-0.6*	*-1.2*	*16.0*
2017	*NYN*	*14738*	*13.2*	*-0.5*	*-1.1*	*11.6*

We are in an era when d'Arnaud's hitting represents exceptional value from a catcher. In just 68 games, he added over two and a half wins on offense alone. Finally, we can say the bat is real. The question is whether his defense is as good as our system thinks. He rated third in baseball in stolen-strike percentage, but it's possible that the quality of the staff he was catching skewed that figure in a way our adjustments aren't catching—Kevin Plawecki, no Jose Molina himself, finished fourth. Subjectively, d'Arnaud is closer to average than excellent. The real concern is over his throws, which have been on a steady downward trajectory, literally and figuratively, since his 2013 debut. Do not be fooled by the 33 percent caught-stealing percentage; by season's end, something was very, very wrong.

Alejandro De Aza OF

Born: 4/11/84 Age: 32 Bats: L Throws: L Height: 6'0" Weight: 195

YEAR	TEAM	LVL	AGE	PA	R	2B	3B	HR	RBI	BB	K	SB	CS	AVG/OBP/SLG	TAv	BABIP	BRR	FRAA	WARP
2013	CHA	MLB	29	675	84	27	4	17	62	50	147	20	8	.264/.323/.405	.266	.318	1.8	CF(107): 4.3, LF(79): -1.0	2.9
2014	CHA	MLB	30	439	45	19	5	5	31	33	100	15	7	.243/.309/.354	.245	.311	-2.0	LF(112): -0.1, CF(14): 3.3	0.4
2014	BAL	MLB	30	89	11	5	3	3	10	6	19	2	3	.293/.341/.537	.312	.350	-1.3	LF(20): 2.0, CF(2): -0.1	0.7
2015	SFN	MLB	31	75	12	4	1	0	3	12	14	2	2	.262/.387/.361	.285	.333	-0.5	LF(17): 0.7	0.4
2015	BOS	MLB	31	178	23	9	5	4	25	12	36	3	1	.292/.347/.484	.298	.352	0.9	LF(33): -0.8, RF(24): -1.6	0.9
2015	BAL	MLB	31	112	16	4	1	3	7	7	34	2	2	.214/.277/.359	.229	.288	-1.0	LF(19): 1.7, RF(13): -0.0	-0.1
2016	*NYN*	*MLB*	*32*	*510*	*62*	*24*	*5*	*9*	*45*	*38*	*112*	*14*	*8*	*.252/.313/.383*	*.257*	*.308*	*-1.0*	*CF 8, RF -1*	*2.2*
2017	*NYN*	*MLB*	*33*	*380*	*40*	*17*	*3*	*6*	*36*	*27*	*84*	*9*	*5*	*.241/.300/.363*	*.253*	*.295*	*-0.2*	*CF 6, RF -1*	*1.6*

Breakout: 0% Improve: 29% Collapse: 3% Attrition: 16% MLB: 83% *Comparables: Ben Francisco, Emil Brown, Fred Lewis*

Baltimore to Boston to San Francisco is a route you'd expect a second-tier presidential candidate from Maryland to fly, so if De Aza had known his itinerary, he and Martin O'Malley could've shared a plane. Both have had their tepid heydays—O'Malley as mayor

and governor and *Wire* character, De Aza as a fantasy sleeper who once nearly went 20/20—but these days De Aza could spend days in your team's clubhouse without being noticed, like O'Malley on a nationally televised debate stage. They'll both do a lot of traveling and make an occasional headline, but neither will do great things in 2016.

Lucas Duda 1B

Born: 2/3/86 Age: 30 Bats: L Throws: R Height: 6'4" Weight: 255

YEAR	TEAM	LVL	AGE	PA	R	2B	3B	HR	RBI	BB	K	SB	CS	AVG/OBP/SLG	TAv	BABIP	BRR	FRAA	WARP
2013	LVG	AAA	27	78	13	3	0	0	8	14	15	1	0	.306/.423/.355	.272	.388	-0.9	1B(12): 0.4, LF(3): 0.8	0.2
2013	SLU	A+	27	30	4	2	0	1	5	2	7	0	0	.250/.300/.429	.235	.300	-0.7	LF(5): -0.7	-0.2
2013	NYN	MLB	27	384	42	16	0	15	33	55	102	0	3	.223/.352/.415	.286	.276	0.6	LF(58): -5.3, 1B(34): -0.9	1.1
2014	NYN	MLB	28	596	74	27	0	30	92	69	135	3	2	.253/.349/.481	.311	.283	-2.4	1B(146): -6.9, LF(1): -0.2	2.7
2015	NYN	MLB	29	554	67	33	0	27	73	66	138	0	2	.244/.352/.486	.320	.285	1.0	1B(129): -7.9	3.3
2016	*NYN*	*MLB*	*30*	*605*	*74*	*27*	*1*	*25*	*83*	*69*	*145*	*2*	*2*	*.239/.336/.436*	*.281*	*.279*	*0.2*	*1B -7*	*1.6*
2017	*NYN*	*MLB*	*31*	*531*	*72*	*22*	*0*	*21*	*69*	*63*	*129*	*1*	*1*	*.232/.335/.424*	*.288*	*.272*	*0.1*	*1B -6*	*0.0*

Breakout: 2% Improve: 49% Collapse: 4% Attrition: 8% MLB: 99% *Comparables: David Ortiz, Derrek Lee, Kevin Youkilis*

Duda's red-hot April featured one opposite-field double after another, spawning a barrage of wistful "He's completely changed his approach!" stories. But in the end... no. Hitters of the Duda/Adam Dunn/Jim Thome fraternity never completely change. What makes Duda interesting—insofar as baseball's least-interesting man is capable of being interesting—is how such a steady, patient approach can yield such a maddeningly inconsistent end product. Duda hardly ever expands the zone, whiffing at just 55 pitches out of the strike zone in 135 games, and his spray charts are also far more even than you would expect. This is not the kind of hitter you'd expect to be the streakiest on his team. Defensively, he gets a bad rap. He's big and slow, but he's got great hands and, yes, a good arm.

Wilmer Flores SS

Born: 10/1/94 Age: 21 Bats: R Throws: R Height: 6'4" Weight: 190

YEAR	TEAM	LVL	AGE	PA	R	2B	3B	HR	RBI	BB	K	SB	CS	AVG/OBP/SLG	TAv	BABIP	BRR	FRAA	WARP
2013	NYN	MLB	21	101	8	5	0	1	13	5	23	0	0	.211/.248/.295	.200	.264	-0.3	3B(26): 1.2, 2B(2): -0.1	-0.2
2013	LVG	AAA	21	463	69	36	4	15	86	25	63	1	3	.321/.357/.531	.300	.342	-1.2	2B(79): -4.7, 1B(11): 0.4	2.7
2014	NYN	MLB	22	274	28	13	1	6	29	12	31	1	0	.251/.286/.378	.249	.265	-0.2	SS(51): 2.4, 2B(19): -1.4	0.8
2014	LVG	AAA	22	241	43	11	2	13	57	16	39	0	2	.323/.367/.568	.311	.339	-0.3	SS(32): 6.2, 2B(12): 0.3	2.9
2015	NYN	MLB	23	510	55	22	0	16	59	19	63	0	1	.263/.295/.408	.262	.273	-0.1	SS(103): -1.2, 2B(37): 2.4	2.2
2016	*NYN*	*MLB*	*24*	*244*	*25*	*12*	*1*	*8*	*31*	*10*	*38*	*0*	*0*	*.258/.292/.420*	*.261*	*.275*	*-0.1*	*2B -1, 3B 1*	*0.9*
2017	*NYN*	*MLB*	*25*	*417*	*49*	*21*	*1*	*14*	*51*	*18*	*64*	*1*	*1*	*.256/.291/.418*	*.267*	*.272*	*-0.4*	*2B -2, 3B 2*	*1.2*

Breakout: 3% Improve: 52% Collapse: 3% Attrition: 10% MLB: 99% *Comparables: Jean Segura, Asdrubal Cabrera, Robinson Cano*

What a year. Flores began the season an unfortunate guinea pig in Sandy Alderson's pitcher-hoarding, defense-Frankensteining experiment, then became the first person to cry on the field during a game since Evelyn Gardner, and eventually found himself on a late-night talk show. In the middle of all that, Flores somehow found time to make real strides. He nearly halved the whiff rates on the breaking pitches that dogged him in 2014, and while he'll never be a good shortstop, he showed outstanding work ethic to mostly avoid embarrassment. Looking forward, what would help Flores most would be a defined role. He yo-yoed between Triple-A and the majors in 2014, then yo-yoed around the infield in 2015. There is a reason closers pitch the ninth, the setup man the eighth, and so on. A cynic would say it's because the less these guys need to think, the better. We'll just say it's because it puts the players at ease. In Flores' case, being at ease is worth a lot, and it means he may have a higher ceiling than the raw numbers indicate. Unfortunately for him, the acquisitions of Neil Walker and Asdrubal Cabrera leave no room for him to settle into a position just yet.

Curtis Granderson RF

Born: 3/16/81 Age: 35 Bats: L Throws: R Height: 6'1" Weight: 200

YEAR	TEAM	LVL	AGE	PA	R	2B	3B	HR	RBI	BB	K	SB	CS	AVG/OBP/SLG	TAv	BABIP	BRR	FRAA	WARP
2013	SWB	AAA	32	21	2	0	0	1	3	1	4	0	0	.400/.429/.550	.339	.467	0.4	LF(2): -0.0, RF(2): -0.4	0.2
2013	NYA	MLB	32	245	31	13	2	7	15	27	69	8	2	.229/.317/.407	.264	.302	0.6	CF(25): 0.0, RF(14): 0.6	0.7
2014	NYN	MLB	33	654	73	27	2	20	66	79	141	8	2	.227/.326/.388	.275	.265	-0.9	RF(142): -5.0, CF(15): -0.4	1.8
2015	NYN	MLB	34	682	98	33	2	26	70	91	151	11	6	.259/.364/.457	.314	.305	1.3	RF(149): 1.3, CF(2): 0.7	5.5
2016	*NYN*	*MLB*	*35*	*649*	*91*	*24*	*4*	*27*	*79*	*75*	*165*	*10*	*4*	*.229/.324/.430*	*.274*	*.270*	*0.1*	*RF 2*	*2.7*
2017	*NYN*	*MLB*	*36*	*551*	*71*	*19*	*3*	*22*	*70*	*63*	*143*	*7*	*3*	*.218/.313/.406*	*.273*	*.257*	*0.1*	*RF 1*	*1.3*

Breakout: 2% Improve: 31% Collapse: 8% Attrition: 7% MLB: 94% *Comparables: Jayson Werth, J.D. Drew, Hank Aaron*

Granderson recently donated $5 million to build a baseball stadium for the University of Illinois at Chicago—the largest one-time gift ever from a pro athlete to his alma mater—and based on his previous two seasons, it wasn't clear how much longer he'd be good enough to crack *that* lineup. Yet Granderson improved in every aspect of the game, which makes us think he was simply, finally, healthy again. Offensive adjustments come and go without fanfare, but one does not magically improve one's outfield range at the age of 34. At the plate, he showed an ability to turn on the inside fastball while staying honest on off-speed pitches; previously, he had only been able to concentrate on one or the other. Of course, it's no more than he deserves as the consensus Nicest Guy in Baseball. Yes, we said he was done a year ago. File it under "Yeah, But Still."

Dilson Herrera 2B

Born: 3/3/94 Age: 22 Bats: R Throws: R Height: 5'10" Weight: 150

YEAR	TEAM	LVL	AGE	PA	R	2B	3B	HR	RBI	BB	K	SB	CS	AVG/OBP/SLG	TAv	BABIP	BRR	FRAA	WARP
2013	SAV	A	19	24	6	0	0	0	4	3	6	3	0	.316/.417/.316	.350	.429	0.2	2B(6): -0.1	0.3
2013	WVA	A	19	479	69	27	3	11	56	37	110	11	6	.265/.330/.421	.294	.328	-0.1	2B(103): 4.9	3.6
2014	NYN	MLB	20	66	6	0	1	3	11	7	17	0	0	.220/.303/.407	.254	.256	-0.9	2B(17): -0.1	0.0
2014	BIN	AA	20	278	50	17	3	10	48	29	52	9	4	.340/.406/.560	.330	.389	0.9	2B(55): -1.4, SS(8): -1.1	2.8
2014	SLU	A+	20	309	48	16	2	3	23	18	44	14	3	.307/.355/.410	.272	.353	0.3	2B(43): -3.5, SS(19): 1.5	1.2
2015	NYN	MLB	21	103	7	3	1	3	6	11	23	2	0	.211/.311/.367	.259	.250	0.2	2B(29): 2.1	0.5
2015	LVG	AAA	21	364	68	23	2	11	50	28	59	13	9	.327/.382/.511	.293	.369	2.7	2B(78): 2.1	2.7
2016	*NYN*	*MLB*	*22*	*31*	*4*	*1*	*0*	*1*	*3*	*2*	*8*	*1*	*0*	*.244/.301/.395*	*.256*	*.297*	*0.0*	*2B 0*	*0.1*
2017	*NYN*	*MLB*	*23*	*383*	*44*	*16*	*2*	*11*	*44*	*26*	*93*	*7*	*4*	*.244/.301/.395*	*.263*	*.297*	*0.2*	*2B 1*	*1.5*

Breakout: 7% Improve: 37% Collapse: 2% Attrition: 19% MLB: 63% *Comparables: Brett Lawrie, Arismendy Alcantara, Jonathan Schoop*

As recently as May of last year, Daniel Murphy was trade bait and Herrera was the Mets' second baseman of the present and future. But he didn't stake a claim to the job, and was forced to watch as Murphy's October aristeia helped send his career into flux. It's not so much that Murphy's possible return would have stifled Herrera's playing time—although of course it would have—as the fact that the Mets are, almost out of nowhere, in a kind of win-now situation. People expect things of them! And so, having expectations, and with Murphy having rejected their qualifying offer, the team does things like sign Asdrubal Cabrera and trade for Neil Walker, pushing Wilmer Flores and Ruben Tejada into backup roles and Herrera into purgatory. The good news is that, whenever the time comes and for whatever team it comes with, Herrera has all the tools to succeed.

Kelly Johnson 3B

Born: 2/22/82 Age: 34 Bats: L Throws: R Height: 6'1" Weight: 195

YEAR	TEAM	LVL	AGE	PA	R	2B	3B	HR	RBI	BB	K	SB	CS	AVG/OBP/SLG	TAv	BABIP	BRR	FRAA	WARP
2013	TBA	MLB	31	407	41	12	2	16	52	35	99	7	4	.235/.305/.410	.268	.276	1.5	LF(53): 1.6, 2B(22): 1.8	1.9
2014	BOS	MLB	32	25	1	1	0	0	1	0	10	0	0	.160/.160/.200	.120	.267	0.2	1B(5): -0.1, 3B(2): 0.3	-0.3
2014	BAL	MLB	32	45	7	4	0	1	4	6	11	0	1	.231/.333/.410	.304	.296	-0.9	3B(17): -1.3, 2B(3): -0.1	0.1
2014	NYA	MLB	32	227	21	9	2	6	22	23	50	2	1	.219/.304/.373	.256	.260	-4.8	3B(41): -0.0, 1B(27): 2.8	0.2
2015	ATL	MLB	33	197	20	5	0	9	34	13	43	1	1	.275/.321/.451	.286	.313	-2.8	LF(27): 1.3, 1B(20): 1.9	0.8
2015	NYN	MLB	33	138	18	6	0	5	13	10	38	1	0	.250/.304/.414	.271	.318	0.6	2B(27): 0.9, 1B(5): 0.3	0.7
2016	*NYN*	*MLB*	*34*	*309*	*34*	*11*	*1*	*9*	*33*	*27*	*83*	*3*	*2*	*.217/.290/.367*	*.244*	*.270*	*-1.3*	*LF -0, 1B 2*	*0.4*
2017	*NYN*	*MLB*	*35*	*237*	*26*	*8*	*1*	*6*	*24*	*21*	*66*	*2*	*1*	*.202/.274/.330*	*.233*	*.258*	*-1.0*	*LF 0, 1B 2*	*0.6*

Breakout: 0% Improve: 27% Collapse: 14% Attrition: 28% MLB: 90% *Comparables: Jerry Lynch, Charlie Maxwell, Ben Oglivie*

Not many players have joined the eventual league champions midseason, immediately assumed the third slot in the lineup, then found themselves out of the lineup come playoff time. A decade after his debut in Atlanta, which at the time had Mets fans strapping themselves in for a 15-year, Chipper Jones-esque adversarial relationship, Johnson found his way to Queens. It's difficult to peg him as a bona fide bench player because Johnson no longer does any one thing at an above-average level. He still has some pop, sure, but his groundball rates rose yet again in 2015, this time to critical levels. Worse still, he's only "defensively versatile" in the sense that he owns a lot of different gloves. Or maybe that he's just really defensive about how versatile he is.

Juan Lagares CF

Born: 3/17/89 Age: 27 Bats: R Throws: R Height: 6'1" Weight: 215

YEAR	TEAM	LVL	AGE	PA	R	2B	3B	HR	RBI	BB	K	SB	CS	AVG/OBP/SLG	TAv	BABIP	BRR	FRAA	WARP
2013	LVG	AAA	24	82	13	3	2	3	9	4	14	2	3	.346/.378/.551	.320	.393	0.4	CF(17): 2.7	1.1
2013	NYN	MLB	24	421	35	21	5	4	34	20	96	6	3	.242/.281/.352	.232	.310	0.3	CF(108): 20.4, RF(14): 1.1	2.4
2014	NYN	MLB	25	452	46	24	3	4	47	20	87	13	4	.281/.321/.382	.275	.341	1.0	CF(112): 10.9	3.4
2015	NYN	MLB	26	465	47	16	5	6	41	16	87	7	3	.259/.289/.358	.245	.308	1.4	CF(137): -0.7, RF(2): -0.3	0.7
2016	*NYN*	*MLB*	*27*	*206*	*23*	*9*	*2*	*3*	*18*	*9*	*42*	*4*	*2*	*.255/.293/.371*	*.247*	*.305*	*0.2*	*CF 3*	*0.8*
2017	*NYN*	*MLB*	*28*	*365*	*37*	*17*	*3*	*6*	*35*	*16*	*74*	*6*	*3*	*.251/.290/.366*	*.251*	*.299*	*0.6*	*CF 4*	*1.7*

Breakout: 6% Improve: 49% Collapse: 2% Attrition: 3% MLB: 100% *Comparables: Carlos Gomez, Ellis Burks, Mickey Brantley*

Lagares' season was a study in the value of arm strength to an outfielder. He was shut down in September 2014 with an elbow "sprain." (For the remainder of the book, you understand that quotations are assumed wherever Mets injuries are concerned.) We hope you're sitting down, because the problem resurfaced in June 2015! Now that the room has stopped spinning, you'll be further perturbed to learn that Lagares did not have an elbow procedure this winter, as was seemingly the plan. Either way, he'd better have this problem settled: Look above at the drop in FRAA his weakened state produced; the eye test says that was only a slight exaggeration. He also regressed at the plate, making no progress in his quest to start turning on the ball. You couldn't blame him for pressing a bit, though; he knows the arm, perhaps more even than his glove, is his calling card.

Desmond Lindsay OF

Born: 1/15/97 Age: 19 Bats: R Throws: R Height: 6'0" Weight: 200

YEAR	TEAM	LVL	AGE	PA	R	2B	3B	HR	RBI	BB	K	SB	CS	AVG/OBP/SLG	TAv	BABIP	BRR	FRAA	WARP
2015	BRO	A-	18	53	3	3	0	0	7	7	19	0	1	.200/.308/.267	.240	.346	-1.0	CF(14): -3.6	-0.4
2016	*NYN*	*MLB*	*19*	*250*	*20*	*8*	*1*	*4*	*20*	*15*	*86*	*1*	*1*	*.176/.230/.267*	*.189*	*.255*	*-0.4*	*CF -3*	*-1.4*
2017	*NYN*	*MLB*	*20*	*305*	*28*	*10*	*1*	*5*	*26*	*20*	*103*	*2*	*1*	*.186/.244/.286*	*.202*	*.267*	*-0.4*	*CF -3*	*0.6*

Breakout: 0% Improve: 0% Collapse: 0% Attrition: 0% MLB: 0% *Comparables: Dalton Pompey, Byron Buxton, Joe Benson*

A second-round draftee out of Sarasota's wonderfully named Out-of-Door Academy—a "Cum Laude Society School," hoho!—Lindsay is an athlete first and foremost, but the athleticism is already starting to transfer: His bat speed is freakish, and the compact power in his six-foot, 200-pound frame, which wouldn't look out of place at strong safety, gives four tools plus potential. (Not the arm, we're afraid. It's just not the most natural throwing motion.) Lindsay doesn't have the sweetest swing—the plane is especially odd—but now isn't the time to nitpick: He outclassed Rookie ball, and besides, if you had hands like that, you'd swing straight up, too. Given the Mets' recent history with Dominic Smith, Lindsay is a decent bet to start 2016 in the Sally League.

Daniel Murphy 2B

Born: 4/1/85 Age: 31 Bats: L Throws: R Height: 6'1" Weight: 215

YEAR	TEAM	LVL	AGE	PA	R	2B	3B	HR	RBI	BB	K	SB	CS	AVG/OBP/SLG	TAv	BABIP	BRR	FRAA	WARP
2013	NYN	MLB	28	697	92	38	4	13	78	32	95	23	3	.286/.319/.415	.265	.315	7.6	2B(150): -8.0, 1B(7): 0.3	2.2
2014	NYN	MLB	29	642	79	37	2	9	57	39	86	13	5	.289/.332/.403	.277	.322	-1.3	2B(126): -4.1, 3B(16): -0.9	2.2
2015	NYN	MLB	30	538	56	38	2	14	73	31	38	2	2	.281/.322/.449	.283	.278	-0.9	2B(69): -2.1, 3B(42): -2.1	2.1
2016	*NYN*	*MLB*	*31*	*529*	*61*	*31*	*2*	*10*	*50*	*29*	*67*	*9*	*3*	*.275/.315/.406*	*.264*	*.298*	*1.0*	*2B -4, 3B -2*	*1.6*
2017	*NYN*	*MLB*	*32*	*514*	*54*	*28*	*1*	*8*	*51*	*27*	*67*	*7*	*3*	*.268/.306/.382*	*.260*	*.293*	*1.0*	*2B -4, 3B -2*	*1.1*

Breakout: 0% Improve: 34% Collapse: 3% Attrition: 5% MLB: 95% *Comparables: Aaron Hill, Brandon Phillips, Jose Vidro*

Hey, we're romantics, too. We love to get caught up in the hoopla and take one crazy stretch completely out of context. That's what makes baseball fun. Which is why so many made such a big deal out of Murphy's... .198/.258/.346 line in April. Well, get it out of your mind now, reader; it put the whole season completely out of whack! There are plenty of better reasons to devalue Murphy: He's 31 this year, and he's already the league's worst defensive second baseman. But a team that believes in his bat might remember that he's played his entire career out of position to accommodate David Wright. A long-awaited return to third base could extend his career. Just don't go flying off the handle based on one month, okay? Come on, guys, sample size. We've been over this!

Kirk Nieuwenhuis OF

Born: 8/7/87 Age: 28 Bats: L Throws: R Height: 6'3" Weight: 225

YEAR	TEAM	LVL	AGE	PA	R	2B	3B	HR	RBI	BB	K	SB	CS	AVG/OBP/SLG	TAv	BABIP	BRR	FRAA	WARP
2013	NYN	MLB	25	108	10	3	1	3	14	12	32	2	0	.189/.278/.337	.233	.246	-0.8	CF(25): -1.0, LF(9): -0.5	-0.1
2013	LVG	AAA	25	330	60	15	2	14	37	40	78	6	2	.248/.345/.465	.264	.293	4.2	CF(42): 2.8, RF(29): 1.8	1.9
2014	NYN	MLB	26	130	16	14	1	3	16	16	39	4	0	.259/.346/.482	.306	.361	0.6	LF(17): 0.6, CF(14): 0.2	1.0
2014	LVG	AAA	26	229	34	13	3	11	32	15	56	3	3	.265/.319/.512	.274	.310	-0.3	LF(31): 8.5, CF(25): -0.8	1.7
2015	ANA	MLB	27	24	4	2	0	0	1	2	9	0	1	.136/.208/.227	.194	.231	0.1	LF(9): 0.6, CF(3): -0.2	-0.1
2015	NYN	MLB	27	117	17	9	0	4	13	8	40	2	1	.208/.282/.406	.268	.290	-0.1	LF(25): 0.1, CF(13): 1.8	0.6
2015	LVG	AAA	27	119	21	6	3	8	29	10	21	2	0	.324/.381/.667	.340	.333	1.0	CF(20): -3.0, RF(3): 0.6	1.2
2016	*NYN*	*MLB*	*28*	*107*	*14*	*5*	*0*	*4*	*12*	*9*	*32*	*2*	*1*	*.218/.290/.394*	*.250*	*.280*	*-0.2*	*CF -0, RF 1*	*0.3*
2017	*NYN*	*MLB*	*29*	*245*	*28*	*11*	*1*	*7*	*28*	*20*	*73*	*3*	*2*	*.215/.285/.375*	*.249*	*.281*	*-0.3*	*CF -1, RF 2*	*0.7*

Breakout: 3% Improve: 44% Collapse: 13% Attrition: 23% MLB: 85% *Comparables: Ryan Church, Tyler Colvin, Laynce Nix*

Baseball's greatest fraternity adds another member: With Ernie Young in 1996 and Darrin Fletcher in 2000, Nieuwenhuis becomes the third player in the BP era to hit three home runs in a major-league game and merit only a Lineout in the following year's Annual. Two other players had three-homer games and received no comment at all: Hee-Seop Choi (2005) spent a year in the minors before returning to Korea, and Kevin Elster (2000) retired. And now this has become a full comment for Kirk Nieuwenhuis. Foiled again.

Brandon Nimmo CF

Born: 3/27/93 Age: 23 Bats: L Throws: R Height: 6'3" Weight: 205

YEAR	TEAM	LVL	AGE	PA	R	2B	3B	HR	RBI	BB	K	SB	CS	AVG/OBP/SLG	TAv	BABIP	BRR	FRAA	WARP
2013	SAV	A	20	480	62	16	6	2	40	71	131	10	7	.273/.397/.359	.301	.402	2.0	CF(106): -0.9	3.8
2014	SLU	A+	21	279	59	9	5	4	25	50	51	9	3	.322/.448/.458	.318	.401	1.5	CF(56): -4.3	2.4
2014	BIN	AA	21	279	38	12	4	6	26	36	54	5	1	.238/.339/.396	.258	.283	0.1	CF(44): -0.1, LF(21): -3.5	0.4
2015	SLU	A+	22	20	3	1	0	0	2	4	3	0	0	.125/.300/.188	.211	.154	-0.4	CF(2): -0.5	-0.2
2015	LVG	AAA	22	112	19	3	1	3	8	18	20	5	4	.264/.393/.418	.283	.304	0.9	RF(17): 3.9, CF(13): -0.4	1.0
2015	BIN	AA	22	302	26	12	3	2	16	26	55	0	2	.279/.354/.368	.266	.343	-3.9	CF(57): -2.5, RF(10): 0.9	0.4
2016	*NYN*	*MLB*	*23*	*34*	*4*	*1*	*0*	*1*	*3*	*4*	*9*	*0*	*0*	*.219/.314/.332*	*.244*	*.293*	*0.0*	*LF -1*	*0.0*
2017	*NYN*	*MLB*	*24*	*352*	*39*	*12*	*2*	*6*	*32*	*41*	*95*	*3*	*2*	*.218/.317/.328*	*.252*	*.293*	*-0.3*	*LF -7*	*0.1*

Breakout: 2% Improve: 16% Collapse: 2% Attrition: 8% MLB: 45% *Comparables: Aaron Hicks, Robbie Grossman, Jackie Bradley*

Under other circumstances, an ACL sprain that kept Nimmo out a month might explain his lack of power. In reality, it's time to adjust our expectations: He's just not that kind of hitter. Like Christian Yelich or Nick Markakis, Nimmo has the body of a power hitter but not the mentality: He wants to hit the ball where it's pitched rather than try to yank it, and he seems hesitant to get more aggressive when ahead in the count. Helping the narrative, however, is his approach, which remains remarkably mature for his age and, given his lack of experience, could develop into something elite. He ought to be just about ready in a year, which means this should be the last Annual in which we note that Nimmo did not play high school baseball because—get this!—his native Wyoming does not offer the sport.

Haha, just kidding, he's going to have a 20-year career and go to the Hall of Fame and we're going to mention the Wyoming thing every single season.

Kevin Plawecki C

Born: 2/26/91 Age: 25 Bats: R Throws: R Height: 6'2" Weight: 225

YEAR	TEAM	LVL	AGE	PA	R	2B	3B	HR	RBI	BB	K	SB	CS	AVG/OBP/SLG	TAv	BABIP	BRR	FRAA	WARP
2013	SAV	A	22	282	35	24	1	6	43	23	32	1	0	.314/.390/.494	.355	.336	-3.7	C(46): 0.5	3.6
2013	SLU	A+	22	239	25	14	0	2	37	19	21	0	0	.294/.391/.392	.295	.319	-1.9	C(42): -1.1, 1B(17): 0.8	1.6
2014	LVG	AAA	23	170	25	6	0	5	21	14	21	0	0	.283/.345/.421	.266	.299	-0.3	C(40): 7.1, 1B(1): -0.0	1.6
2014	BIN	AA	23	249	33	18	0	6	43	16	27	0	0	.326/.378/.487	.304	.344	0.8	C(54): 6.4	3.1
2015	NYN	MLB	24	258	18	9	0	3	21	17	60	0	0	.219/.280/.296	.241	.277	-1.6	C(70): 11.9	1.8
2015	LVG	AAA	24	90	7	5	1	1	9	3	12	0	0	.224/.267/.341	.198	.250	-1.7	C(20): 0.3, 1B(1): -0.1	-0.4
2016	*NYN*	*MLB*	*25*	*175*	*16*	*8*	*0*	*4*	*18*	*10*	*33*	*0*	*0*	*.238/.296/.358*	*.247*	*.276*	*-0.4*	*C 2, 1B 0*	*0.7*
2017	*NYN*	*MLB*	*26*	*288*	*31*	*13*	*0*	*6*	*29*	*16*	*56*	*0*	*0*	*.234/.291/.357*	*.251*	*.273*	*-0.9*	*C 3, 1B 0*	*1.2*

Breakout: 6% Improve: 20% Collapse: 7% Attrition: 37% MLB: 66% *Comparables: Curtis Thigpen, Jonathan Lucroy, J.R. Towles*

YEAR	TEAM	P. COUNT	FRM RUNS	BLK RUNS	THRW RUNS	TOT RUNS
2014	BIN	7326	5.3	0.5	0.1	5.9
2014	LVG	5051	7.4	0.2	-1.0	6.6
2015	LVG	2811	0.5	0.1	0.0	0.6
2015	NYN	9093	12.3	0.1	-0.4	12.0
2016	*NYN*	*3569*	*2.7*	*0.1*	*-0.4*	*2.4*
2017	*NYN*	*5878*	*2.3*	*0.1*	*-0.4*	*2.0*

Plawecki needs playing time badly, but he's trapped behind one of the game's better offensive catchers. When Travis d'Arnaud added to his lengthy injury history in late April, Plawecki got a shot at the starting job. He didn't take his chance, though, and now seems destined for backup typecasting based on one bad season. Plawecki swung and missed at 42 percent of breaking pitches he saw in his debut season, but he isn't a free swinger, and he doesn't expand the zone. He just needs to acclimate. He's also a good example of how a soccer-style loan system might help some players gain much-needed playing time when injuries open up spots on other teams, but that's a topic for another book.

Matthew Reynolds INF

Born: 12/3/90 Age: 25 Bats: R Throws: R Height: 6'1" Weight: 205

YEAR	TEAM	LVL	AGE	PA	R	2B	3B	HR	RBI	BB	K	SB	CS	AVG/OBP/SLG	TAv	BABIP	BRR	FRAA	WARP
2013	SLU	A+	22	488	59	21	6	5	49	36	80	9	2	.226/.302/.337	.245	.263	2.1	SS(114): -3.0	1.2
2014	LVG	AAA	23	301	54	16	4	5	40	21	60	14	4	.333/.385/.479	.300	.404	4.6	SS(58): -0.1, 2B(8): 1.1	3.2
2014	BIN	AA	23	242	33	5	3	1	21	29	41	6	3	.355/.430/.422	.327	.433	1.7	SS(46): 0.2, 2B(13): -0.1	2.9
2015	LVG	AAA	24	490	70	32	5	6	65	32	92	13	4	.267/.319/.402	.247	.319	2.4	SS(92): 5.6, 2B(11): -0.9	1.8
2016	*NYN*	*MLB*	*25*	*250*	*27*	*10*	*2*	*3*	*20*	*16*	*61*	*5*	*2*	*.228/.284/.332*	*.233*	*.291*	*0.2*	*SS 0, 2B 0*	*0.5*
2017	*NYN*	*MLB*	*26*	*354*	*35*	*15*	*3*	*5*	*32*	*22*	*86*	*6*	*2*	*.231/.284/.339*	*.240*	*.293*	*0.5*	*SS 0, 2B 0*	*1.6*

Breakout: 1% Improve: 19% Collapse: 7% Attrition: 24% MLB: 43% *Comparables: Zack Cozart, Chris Nelson, Tyler Saladino*

It's unclear, given the middle-infielding woes that plagued the Mets at various points in 2015, exactly how Reynolds avoided a call-up during the regular season. Perhaps it's because his skill set is derivative of what the Mets already had; like Wilmer Flores (and even Ruben Tejada), Reynolds is one of those shortstops where you say, "Well, he makes all the plays over there," and hope no one asks any more questions. The other reason, of course, is that he didn't set the world on fire after a blistering 2014. He'll likely end up an invaluable bench option with his plate discipline, gap power, baserunning and defensive versatility. Fun note: Technically, Reynolds actually was called up, as Tejada's replacement during the NLDS. Had he appeared in a game, which he did not, he would have been the second player in the modern era to make his major-league debut in the postseason. Mark Kiger breathed a sigh of relief, but only for a minute: The Royals' Raul Mondesi wound up making his MLB debut in the World Series.

Amed Rosario SS

Born: 11/20/95 Age: 20 Bats: R Throws: R Height: 6'2" Weight: 170

YEAR	TEAM	LVL	AGE	PA	R	2B	3B	HR	RBI	BB	K	SB	CS	AVG/OBP/SLG	TAv	BABIP	BRR	FRAA	WARP
2014	SAV	A	18	31	2	0	1	1	4	1	11	0	0	.133/.161/.300	.157	.167	-0.1	SS(2): 0.1, 3B(1): -0.2	-0.3
2014	BRO	A-	18	290	39	11	5	1	23	17	47	7	3	.289/.337/.380	.274	.345	0.7	SS(64): 2.6	2.0
2015	SLU	A+	19	417	41	20	5	0	25	23	73	12	4	.257/.307/.335	.240	.316	0.9	SS(102): 14.2	2.5
2016	*NYN*	*MLB*	*20*	*250*	*23*	*10*	*2*	*4*	*19*	*9*	*69*	*3*	*1*	*.204/.238/.304*	*.203*	*.268*	*0.1*	*SS 3*	*0.1*
2017	*NYN*	*MLB*	*21*	*422*	*39*	*17*	*3*	*7*	*38*	*17*	*110*	*5*	*2*	*.212/.248/.323*	*.216*	*.269*	*0.3*	*SS 5*	*2.5*

Breakout: 0% Improve: 2% Collapse: 0% Attrition: 2% MLB: 3% *Comparables: Tim Beckham, Charlie Culberson, Yamaico Navarro*

Two years ago Rosario was a gangly teenager with a nice offensive profile, if only he could stay at shortstop. He's now 20, and the conversation has changed dramatically: The defense is carrying him, and his offensive ceiling is far lower. The assumption that Rosario would fill out with time was misguided; turns out he's just tall, with a narrow frame that allows him excellent range but limits his home run potential. Still, Rosario more than held his own as the youngest player in the High-A Florida State League, and showed reasonable gap power in doing so. He's unlikely to succeed in the high minors without better pitch recognition, but he does combine an aggressive approach with a nice feel for the strike zone. The most realistic ETA is still 2018, but depending on the Mets' shortstop situation, the tabloids will likely call for him sooner.

Dominic Smith 1B

Born: 6/15/95 Age: 21 Bats: L Throws: L Height: 6'0" Weight: 185

YEAR	TEAM	LVL	AGE	PA	R	2B	3B	HR	RBI	BB	K	SB	CS	AVG/OBP/SLG	TAv	BABIP	BRR	FRAA	WARP
2014	SAV	A	19	518	52	26	1	1	44	51	77	5	4	.271/.344/.338	.261	.321	-4.8	1B(110): -3.1	-0.2
2015	SLU	A+	20	497	58	33	0	6	79	35	75	2	1	.305/.354/.417	.279	.351	-6.5	1B(104): 9.4	1.8
2016	*NYN*	*MLB*	*21*	*250*	*20*	*12*	*0*	*4*	*24*	*15*	*60*	*0*	*0*	*.227/.273/.333*	*.226*	*.284*	*-0.5*	*1B 1*	*-0.4*
2017	*NYN*	*MLB*	*22*	*430*	*45*	*22*	*0*	*9*	*43*	*27*	*100*	*0*	*0*	*.237/.286/.361*	*.245*	*.293*	*-1.1*	*1B 2*	*0.7*

Breakout: 0% Improve: 2% Collapse: 0% Attrition: 2% MLB: 3% *Comparables: Max Kepler, Ryan Wheeler, Nick Evans*

You would think that being the Florida State League Player of the Year would be enough, but scouts remain divided on Smith's destiny. Perhaps it's because he seems bound and determined to spray everything to left center; he didn't pull a home run until July 11th. The concerns about his game power are valid, but they're also predicated on what Cito Gaston wanted John Olerud to be. To go as far as to make this a question of Smith's viability at first base is more than a bridge too far: It's putting the cart before the horse before letting the horse out of the barn to get to the bridge that leads to the runway. Smith rakes, and his defense is excellent to boot. For now, set your watches for 2017.

Ruben Tejada SS

Born: 10/27/89 Age: 26 Bats: R Throws: R Height: 5'11" Weight: 200

YEAR	TEAM	LVL	AGE	PA	R	2B	3B	HR	RBI	BB	K	SB	CS	AVG/OBP/SLG	TAv	BABIP	BRR	FRAA	WARP
2013	NYN	MLB	23	227	20	12	0	0	10	15	24	2	1	.202/.259/.260	.203	.228	1.8	SS(55): 3.0	0.1
2013	LVG	AAA	23	269	38	14	1	2	24	14	30	1	1	.288/.337/.379	.252	.316	2.7	SS(58): -0.4, 2B(1): -0.0	1.1
2014	NYN	MLB	24	419	30	11	0	5	34	50	73	1	2	.237/.342/.310	.260	.283	-2.5	SS(114): 13.1	2.9
2015	NYN	MLB	25	407	36	23	0	3	28	38	70	2	1	.261/.338/.350	.277	.315	0.6	SS(81): -2.7, 3B(19): -1.6	1.9
2016	*NYN*	*MLB*	*26*	*164*	*17*	*7*	*0*	*2*	*13*	*13*	*25*	*1*	*1*	*.248/.316/.337*	*.249*	*.284*	*0.0*	*SS 1*	*0.7*
2017	*NYN*	*MLB*	*27*	*292*	*31*	*13*	*0*	*4*	*26*	*24*	*47*	*1*	*1*	*.246/.315/.344*	*.259*	*.281*	*0.0*	*SS 2*	*1.5*

Breakout: 2% Improve: 42% Collapse: 9% Attrition: 17% MLB: 97% *Comparables: Elvis Andrus, Sean Burroughs, Erick Aybar*

Rarely has a man been so miscast as a martyr. Let us now remove ourselves from the romance and, frankly, the sheer narrative of Tejada's season-ending broken leg at the hands and feet of Chase Utley, and examine the irony of perhaps the least-loved Mets regular suddenly becoming the inspiration for his team and his city. There was an unspoken awkwardness even when it happened: Really, we have to mourn this guy? Because, you know, the guy behind him might actually be better. Is this all a little callous? Maybe. But if it's a happy ending you wanted, well, Jane Austen was a click away.

Juan Uribe 3B

Born: 3/22/79 Age: 37 Bats: R Throws: R Height: 6'0" Weight: 245

YEAR	TEAM	LVL	AGE	PA	R	2B	3B	HR	RBI	BB	K	SB	CS	AVG/OBP/SLG	TAv	BABIP	BRR	FRAA	WARP
2013	LAN	MLB	34	426	47	22	2	12	50	30	81	5	0	.278/.331/.438	.279	.322	1.9	3B(123): 13.3, 1B(4): 0.1	3.9
2014	LAN	MLB	35	404	36	23	0	9	54	15	77	0	1	.311/.337/.440	.281	.368	0.4	3B(102): 13.0	3.7
2015	ATL	MLB	36	167	17	6	0	7	17	15	37	1	0	.285/.353/.464	.298	.336	-0.2	3B(42): 4.4, 2B(1): 0.0	1.7
2015	NYN	MLB	36	143	17	9	0	6	20	14	34	0	0	.219/.301/.430	.277	.250	1.2	3B(26): -0.2, 2B(7): -0.1	0.8
2015	LAN	MLB	36	87	6	2	0	1	6	5	9	1	0	.247/.287/.309	.213	.264	-0.4	3B(24): 1.0	-0.1
2016	*NYN*	*MLB*	*37*	*375*	*38*	*17*	*1*	*9*	*39*	*23*	*79*	*2*	*0*	*.238/.289/.369*	*.244*	*.281*	*0.6*	*3B 7, 2B -0*	*1.3*
2017	*NYN*	*MLB*	*38*	*297*	*31*	*13*	*1*	*7*	*30*	*19*	*65*	*1*	*0*	*.228/.280/.351*	*.242*	*.272*	*0.3*	*3B 5, 2B 0*	*1.4*

Breakout: 0% Improve: 18% Collapse: 15% Attrition: 14% MLB: 67% *Comparables: Melvin Mora, Michael Young, Mark DeRosa*

All Juan Uribe wants to do is take fastballs out over the plate and send them right back where they came from. For some reason, pitchers remain willing to accommodate his blunt-force approach. Uribe was traded twice midseason in 2015, announcing his arrival in Queens with a wall-banging walk-off double against his former Dodgers teammates on July 26th. From there it was unremarkable, and he made just a cameo appearance in the playoffs due to injury. His hyper-aggression at the plate will make him a model pinch-hitter. Or maybe that's just what baseball thinks the ideal pinch-hitter is supposed to be.

Neil Walker 2B

Born: 9/10/85 Age: 30 Bats: B Throws: R Height: 6'3" Weight: 210

YEAR	TEAM	LVL	AGE	PA	R	2B	3B	HR	RBI	BB	K	SB	CS	AVG/OBP/SLG	TAv	BABIP	BRR	FRAA	WARP
2013	PIT	MLB	27	551	62	24	4	16	53	50	85	1	2	.251/.339/.418	.278	.274	0.8	2B(132): 2.8	2.9
2014	PIT	MLB	28	571	74	25	3	23	76	45	88	2	2	.271/.342/.467	.294	.288	0.4	2B(135): -2.6	3.3
2015	PIT	MLB	29	603	69	32	3	16	71	44	110	4	1	.269/.328/.427	.274	.306	1.8	2B(146): 4.7	3.3
2016	*NYN*	*MLB*	*30*	*595*	*65*	*28*	*2*	*18*	*72*	*49*	*113*	*3*	*2*	*.250/.319/.412*	*.268*	*.282*	*0.9*	*2B 1*	*3.1*
2017	*NYN*	*MLB*	*31*	*516*	*62*	*24*	*1*	*15*	*60*	*42*	*99*	*2*	*1*	*.246/.314/.402*	*.271*	*.279*	*0.7*	*2B 0*	*2.0*

Breakout: 0% Improve: 42% Collapse: 4% Attrition: 8% MLB: 96% *Comparables: Kelly Johnson, Marcus Giles, Aaron Hill*

It sounds like a backhanded compliment to call Walker one of the most boring players in the majors, but it's not meant to be. There's legitimate value in his consistent quality, in his always being healthy and productive, if always one monstrous May below All-Star levels. True to his nature, Walker had another year in which he took more than 500 trips to the plate and posted a TAv above .260, just as he had in each of his first four full big-league seasons. You can nitpick his defense or his numbers against left-handed pitchers, but that misses the point. No one is misreading Walker as a great player. He's merely a good, reliable one who got to live out everyone's childhood dream by helping his hometown team win games. Now he's on to the next phase, a year with the Mets, before yet another phase: free agency. Expect Walker to do what he always does, and for other teams to come knocking with multi-year offers afterward.

David Wright 3B

Born: 12/20/82 Age: 33 Bats: R Throws: R Height: 6'0" Weight: 205

YEAR	TEAM	LVL	AGE	PA	R	2B	3B	HR	RBI	BB	K	SB	CS	AVG/OBP/SLG	TAv	BABIP	BRR	FRAA	WARP
2013	NYN	MLB	30	492	63	23	6	18	58	55	79	17	3	.307/.390/.514	.326	.340	3.9	3B(111): 4.0	5.8
2014	NYN	MLB	31	586	54	30	1	8	63	42	113	8	5	.269/.324/.374	.258	.325	-2.2	3B(133): -3.2	1.2
2015	SLU	A+	32	33	5	0	0	0	1	5	6	0	0	.321/.424/.321	.330	.409	0.2	3B(7): -2.1	0.1
2015	NYN	MLB	32	174	24	7	0	5	17	22	36	2	1	.289/.379/.434	.315	.351	2.5	3B(38): -3.9	1.4
2016	*NYN*	*MLB*	*33*	*619*	*73*	*30*	*2*	*17*	*74*	*63*	*120*	*11*	*5*	*.267/.344/.423*	*.282*	*.310*	*1.1*	*3B -2*	*3.1*
2017	*NYN*	*MLB*	*34*	*421*	*52*	*21*	*1*	*11*	*48*	*41*	*82*	*6*	*3*	*.266/.340/.414*	*.288*	*.312*	*0.9*	*3B -1*	*1.0*

Breakout: 0% Improve: 30% Collapse: 3% Attrition: 4% MLB: 93% *Comparables: Carlos Guillen, Aramis Ramirez, George Brett*

The consensus seems to be that Wright's bout with spinal stenosis was just the latest chapter in his decline. The numbers don't quite bear that out; when he was on the field, Wright was actually quite good. Although he was visibly without his usual torque late in the season, his power numbers were relatively stable. So what do we make of his future, after a mostly lost season? Perhaps the same observation we made a year ago: Despite his struggles, Wright steadfastly refuses to change his approach to get around on more fastballs. Yes, he has struggled more with breaking pitches the last two seasons, but not out of overcompensation; it's as if he believes that, once finally healthy, he'll be his old self again. A year ago, this all smacked of maturity and confidence. As he ages, we must wonder if there isn't a bit of denial mixed in.

PITCHERS

Tyler Clippard RHP

Born: 2/14/85 Age: 31 Bats: R Throws: R Height: 6'3" Weight: 200

YEAR	TEAM	LVL	AGE	W	L	SV	G	GS	IP	H	HR	BB/9	K/9	GB%	BABIP	WHIP	ERA	FIP	DRA	WARP	CFIP	MPH
2013	WAS	MLB	28	6	3	0	72	0	71	37	9	3.0	9.3	29%	.170	0.86	2.41	3.80	2.59	1.7	88	94.3
2014	WAS	MLB	29	7	4	1	75	0	70^1	47	5	2.9	10.5	38%	.251	1.00	2.18	2.72	2.56	1.7	79	94.1
2015	OAK	MLB	30	1	3	17	37	0	38^2	25	3	4.9	8.8	22%	.214	1.19	2.79	3.93	3.16	0.7	102	93.6
2015	NYN	MLB	30	4	1	2	32	0	32^1	24	5	2.8	7.2	24%	.209	1.05	3.06	4.68	3.87	0.3	105	93.9
2016	*NYN*	*MLB*	*31*	*3*	*1*	*0*	*63*	*0*	*67*	*46*	*8*	*3.0*	*8.9*	*28%*	*.244*	*1.03*	*3.60*	*3.67*	*4.43*	*0.4*	*101*	
2017	*NYN*	*MLB*	*32*	*3*	*1*	*5*	*51*	*0*	50^2	*37*	*6*	*3.0*	*9.2*	*28%*	*.261*	*1.07*	*3.51*	*3.98*	*4.32*	*0.3*	*98*	

Breakout: 23% Improve: 42% Collapse: 28% Attrition: 11% MLB: 90% *Comparables: Francisco Rodriguez, Aaron Heilman, Brendan Donnelly*

Clippard's time with the Mets was illustrative of the blind spot many managers have about ad hoc player evaluation. At lower levels, after a leadoff walk or hanging changeup, you can get the bullpen going without causing a referendum on the player's status. On his bad days, Clippard showed early and with uncommon transparency that he didn't have it, yet Terry Collins would not offer a quick hook. This is not a matter of "bullpen management"; this is an inability to recognize, either through in-game performance or side sessions, that the man you acquired did not come as advertised. Clippard lost a full mile per hour off his fastball after joining the Mets in late July, likely due to a back injury that lingered through the playoffs, but he never missed significant time. It seems he simply reported that he was good to go, which was enough to maintain his hold on the eighth inning.

Bartolo Colon RHP

Born: 5/24/73 Age: 43 Bats: R Throws: R Height: 5'11" Weight: 285

YEAR	TEAM	LVL	AGE	W	L	SV	G	GS	IP	H	HR	BB/9	K/9	GB%	BABIP	WHIP	ERA	FIP	DRA	WARP	CFIP	MPH
2013	OAK	MLB	40	18	6	0	30	30	190^1	193	14	1.4	5.5	43%	.294	1.17	2.65	3.26	3.52	3.2	100	94.8
2014	NYN	MLB	41	15	13	0	31	31	202^1	218	22	1.3	6.7	41%	.307	1.23	4.09	3.54	4.29	1.2	100	93.1
2015	NYN	MLB	42	14	13	0	33	31	194^2	217	25	1.1	6.3	44%	.307	1.24	4.16	3.87	4.57	1.1	104	92.8
2016	*NYN*	*MLB*	*43*	*11*	*10*	*0*	*30*	*30*	*180*	*178*	*21*	*1.5*	*6.3*	*43%*	*.302*	*1.15*	*3.66*	*3.74*	*4.48*	*1.7*	*103*	
2017	*NYN*	*MLB*	*44*	*9*	*9*	*0*	*24*	*24*	141^2	*160*	*19*	*1.7*	*5.9*	*43%*	*.328*	*1.32*	*3.91*	*4.44*	*4.78*	*0.9*	*111*	

Breakout: 7% Improve: 9% Collapse: 16% Attrition: 27% MLB: 58% *Comparables: David Wells, Greg Maddux, Andy Pettitte*

Colon threw 83 percent fastballs, with an average of 89 mph, at the age of 42. He allowed 217 hits, the most in the league, yet pitched to a 3.87 FIP. He has been the same pitcher for the last five years, since his stem-cell treatment in 2010, yet no one has figured him out. That's because when you know what's coming, there's nothing to figure out. He made a natural transition to the bullpen during the playoffs, raising the question "If this is how the one-pitch wonder does in relief, would Mariano Rivera have made a league-average starter?" And Colon does all this with a physique that cannot possibly produce these results, and makes you wonder about stem-cell legislation. So what to make of Colon? Well, nothing. You ignore all this and make fun of him for being overweight and old and actually trying to hit when he's at bat. That's what a cultured fan would do.

Jacob deGrom RHP

Born: 6/19/88 Age: 28 Bats: L Throws: R Height: 6'4" Weight: 180

YEAR	TEAM	LVL	AGE	W	L	SV	G	GS	IP	H	HR	BB/9	K/9	GB%	BABIP	WHIP	ERA	FIP	DRA	WARP	CFIP	MPH
2013	BIN	AA	25	2	5	0	10	10	60	69	4	3.0	6.6	45%	.342	1.48	4.80	3.82	4.52	0.5	97	
2013	SLU	A+	25	1	0	0	2	2	12	12	1	1.5	9.8	47%	.333	1.17	3.00	2.91	3.92	0.1	88	
2013	LVG	AAA	25	4	2	0	14	14	75^2	87	6	2.9	7.5	47%	.342	1.47	4.52	3.93	4.65	0.9	88	
2014	NYN	MLB	26	9	6	0	22	22	140^1	117	7	2.8	9.2	47%	.297	1.14	2.69	2.64	3.34	2.5	86	96.4
2014	LVG	AAA	26	4	0	0	7	7	38^1	39	2	2.3	6.8	60%	.311	1.28	2.58	3.73	4.99	0.4	92	
2015	NYN	MLB	27	14	8	0	30	30	191	149	16	1.8	9.7	48%	.271	0.98	2.54	2.73	3.07	4.4	78	97.7
2016	*NYN*	*MLB*	*28*	*10*	*8*	*0*	*26*	*26*	*156*	*127*	*15*	*2.2*	*8.9*	*48%*	*.292*	*1.06*	*3.06*	*3.12*	*3.79*	*2.8*	*82*	
2017	*NYN*	*MLB*	*29*	*10*	*9*	*0*	*27*	*27*	159^1	*141*	*18*	*2.1*	*9.0*	*48%*	*.310*	*1.13*	*3.16*	*3.59*	*3.92*	*2.6*	*86*	

Breakout: 22% Improve: 56% Collapse: 14% Attrition: 12% MLB: 89% *Comparables: Josh Collmenter, Carlos Carrasco, Cory Luebke*

His curveball doesn't have much curve, his slider doesn't have much slide and his sinker hardly deserves the name, so at least we can explain why scouts weren't salivating over deGrom through the minors. His individual pitches don't seem to add up, and given his Tommy John surgery and overall inexperience on the mound, everything was going to have to go right. And that's deGrom's success in a nutshell, really, because in every start, on nearly every pitch, everything *does* go right. His elite ability to repeat his mechanics means he isn't making the mistakes that yield hittable pitches, and he won't walk anyone. That may not be the sexy answer, but it makes him a legitimate ace who is likely to stay healthy. Oh, there's also the velocity. That helps.

Jeurys Familia RHP

Born: 10/10/89 Age: 26 Bats: R Throws: R Height: 6'3" Weight: 240

YEAR	TEAM	LVL	AGE	W	L	SV	G	GS	IP	H	HR	BB/9	K/9	GB%	BABIP	WHIP	ERA	FIP	DRA	WARP	CFIP	MPH
2013	NYN	MLB	23	0	0	1	9	0	10^{2}	12	2	7.6	6.8	54%	.303	1.97	4.22	6.49	8.03	-0.4	117	98.0
2014	NYN	MLB	24	2	5	5	76	0	77^{1}	59	3	3.7	8.5	59%	.264	1.18	2.21	3.04	2.98	1.4	97	98.6
2015	NYN	MLB	25	2	2	43	76	0	78	59	6	2.2	9.9	61%	.272	1.00	1.85	2.76	3.02	1.6	83	100.1
2016	NYN	MLB	26	3	1	35	57	0	60^{1}	48	6	2.6	9.2	60%	.292	1.09	3.16	3.27	3.90	0.8	85	
2017	NYN	MLB	27	5	3	11	58	7	94^{2}	78	10	2.9	9.5	60%	.300	1.15	3.21	3.64	3.96	1.1	87	

Breakout: 35% Improve: 57% Collapse: 21% Attrition: 15% MLB: 91% *Comparables: Jose Arredondo, Aaron Crow, Drew Pomeranz*

Familia's pitching philosophy seems to be to throw whatever he wants, knowing no one can hit it, and thereby try to throw three strikes before ball four. He works almost exclusively front-to-back, establishing the sinker early in the count before mixing it up, with the only wrinkle being a penchant for quick pitching, which he learned from LaTroy Hawkins in 2013. In 2014, left-handed hitters reached base at a .377 clip; in 2015, that number went down to .291 largely because of his big revelation, a reliable splitter that gave lefties a different look that the slider wasn't providing. Familia posted three blown saves in the World Series, and you won't find a more misleading statistic in this book. The man did everything to deliver a championship but keep Jenrry Mejia clean.

Sean Gilmartin LHP

Born: 5/8/90 Age: 26 Bats: L Throws: L Height: 6'2" Weight: 205

YEAR	TEAM	LVL	AGE	W	L	SV	G	GS	IP	H	HR	BB/9	K/9	GB%	BABIP	WHIP	ERA	FIP	DRA	WARP	CFIP	MPH
2013	GWN	AAA	23	3	8	0	17	17	91	112	12	3.3	6.4	40%	.333	1.59	5.74	4.61	4.71	0.3	109	
2014	NBR	AA	24	7	3	0	12	12	72	76	2	2.0	9.2	43%	.357	1.28	3.12	2.45	3.64	1.3	69	
2014	ROC	AAA	24	2	4	0	14	14	73^{2}	69	7	3.4	7.2	39%	.291	1.32	4.28	4.17	4.63	0.4	104	
2015	NYN	MLB	25	3	2	0	50	1	57^{1}	50	2	2.8	8.5	46%	.302	1.19	2.67	2.78	3.80	0.6	94	91.2
2016	NYN	MLB	26	2	1	0	47	0	50^{1}	45	5	2.6	7.5	42%	.297	1.19	3.59	3.62	4.40	0.3	99	
2017	NYN	MLB	27	4	4	0	20	12	78	77	10	2.8	7.5	42%	.315	1.30	3.86	4.38	4.73	0.4	108	

Breakout: 15% Improve: 29% Collapse: 18% Attrition: 32% MLB: 68% *Comparables: Kyle Gibson, Adam Warren, David Phelps*

Some relievers are on the roster simply because they are left-handed. Then there's Gilmartin, who deserved a larger role but didn't get one, simply because he is left-handed. Injuries to Jerry Blevins and Jack Leathersich—the less said about Alex Torres, the better—left Gilmartin the lone lefty in the bullpen for most of the season. While game situations often called for him in LOOGY situations, his overall work suggests that the bullpen would have been better with no LOOGY at all. Gilmartin actually did better against righties in his debut season, although that goes against his entire minor-league career, and his sweeping slider indicates it could be an outlier. Still, his extremely slow changeup got enough groundballs that he deserved higher-leverage situations. The message, of course, is that we're creating a lefty glass ceiling by keeping so many lefties that don't deserve to be employed. Wait, what kind of book is this again?

Erik Goeddel RHP

Born: 12/20/88 Age: 27 Bats: R Throws: R Height: 6'3" Weight: 190

YEAR	TEAM	LVL	AGE	W	L	SV	G	GS	IP	H	HR	BB/9	K/9	GB%	BABIP	WHIP	ERA	FIP	DRA	WARP	CFIP	MPH
2013	BIN	AA	24	9	7	0	25	25	134	135	14	3.9	8.4	41%	.318	1.44	4.37	4.27	4.65	0.9	102	
2014	LVG	AAA	25	3	2	0	49	0	63^{2}	77	6	4.2	9.0	45%	.364	1.68	5.37	4.37	5.11	0.2	94	
2014	NYN	MLB	25	0	0	0	6	0	6^{2}	3	0	5.4	8.1	31%	.188	1.05	2.70	3.10	0.36	0.3	102	95.6
2015	NYN	MLB	26	1	1	0	35	0	33^{1}	24	1	2.4	9.2	44%	.267	0.99	2.43	2.50	3.10	0.6	92	95.7
2016	NYN	MLB	27	3	1	0	52	0	55^{1}	50	6	3.2	8.1	42%	.302	1.25	3.74	3.78	4.57	0.3	104	
2017	NYN	MLB	28	4	4	0	33	9	81^{2}	78	10	3.3	8.3	42%	.317	1.33	3.87	4.40	4.73	0.4	108	

Breakout: 14% Improve: 21% Collapse: 20% Attrition: 28% MLB: 50% *Comparables: Scott Barnes, Francisco Cruceta, Ramon A. Ramirez*

Finally, the Mets' doctors have an excuse. Goeddel has had so many arm injuries that, when the team was predictably vague in diagnosing his latest malady in mid-June, he admitted that there was so much scar tissue in his elbow that the doctors literally could not see what was wrong with it. Before then, though, Goeddel had seemed ticketed for high-leverage work, and was solid after returning in September as well. He makes for a different look as a reliever, featuring a splitter and sharp 12-to-6 curve that keep his splits relatively even. So why was he left off the NLCS and World Series rosters after one bad postseason outing, while certain others received chance after chance? You'd have to ask Terry Collins. Or, you know what, don't even bother.

Matt Harvey RHP

Born: 3/27/89 Age: 27 Bats: R Throws: R Height: 6'4" Weight: 215

YEAR	TEAM	LVL	AGE	W	L	SV	G	GS	IP	H	HR	BB/9	K/9	GB%	BABIP	WHIP	ERA	FIP	DRA	WARP	CFIP	MPH
2013	NYN	MLB	24	9	5	0	26	26	178^{1}	135	7	1.6	9.6	49%	.280	0.93	2.27	1.98	2.42	5.4	63	99.0
2015	NYN	MLB	26	13	8	0	29	29	189^{1}	156	18	1.8	8.9	49%	.273	1.02	2.71	3.08	3.48	3.5	86	98.8
2016	NYN	MLB	27	11	9	0	29	29	182^{2}	145	18	1.8	8.9	49%	.286	0.99	2.94	3.01	3.64	3.6	78	
2017	NYN	MLB	28	12	10	0	31	31	198^{1}	171	21	1.8	9.1	49%	.306	1.06	2.95	3.33	3.65	3.8	79	

Breakout: 19% Improve: 52% Collapse: 17% Attrition: 6% MLB: 89% *Comparables: Kris Medlen, J.P. Howell, Alex Cobb*

On October 23rd, David Wright, Jacob deGrom, Wilmer Flores and Harvey were guests on *Jimmy Kimmel Live* in front of a live crowd in Brooklyn. The former three could not stop grinning: The captain Wright did the bulk of the interview; Flores spoke of what it's like to cry in front of millions of people; and deGrom's hair had become a popular Halloween costume. Harvey trailed off after 10 words, all about Chase Utley. When the segment was over, Kimmel issued Harvey a quick apology, saying he'd run out of time. Harvey didn't seem offended, just uncomfortable, like he didn't want to be there. That's where he always fit with the 2015 Mets; for whatever reason, while everyone else was grinning, there was Harvey with a scowl, always with his own business to attend to. Nonsense story lines about innings limits and model girlfriends and missed workouts didn't make him look like a star; on this team, they made him look like an outcast. On the mound, he wasn't quite the same. The line-drive rates on his fastball and changeup soared in 2015, and he got lost in the crowd of so many other incredible young talents. Yet he adjusted and became a more complete pitcher with massively improved breaking stuff, and in the postseason we found out he has real guts. He is, in all likelihood, a good guy and a fine teammate. But now that the narrative ball is rolling, it will be tough to stop.

Steven Matz LHP

Born: 5/29/91 Age: 25 Bats: R Throws: L Height: 6'2" Weight: 200

YEAR	TEAM	LVL	AGE	W	L	SV	G	GS	IP	H	HR	BB/9	K/9	GB%	BABIP	WHIP	ERA	FIP	DRA	WARP	CFIP	MPH
2013	SAV	A	22	5	6	0	21	21	106^{1}	86	4	3.2	10.2	55%	.315	1.17	2.62	2.91	4.12	1.2	89	
2014	SLU	A+	23	4	4	0	12	12	69^{1}	66	0	2.7	8.0	59%	.328	1.25	2.21	2.73	4.07	0.7	91	
2014	BIN	AA	23	6	5	0	12	12	71^{1}	66	3	1.8	8.7	48%	.317	1.12	2.27	2.64	3.65	1.2	69	
2015	NYN	MLB	24	4	0	0	6	6	35^{2}	34	4	2.5	8.6	49%	.300	1.23	2.27	3.64	4.04	0.4	94	96.6
2015	LVG	AAA	24	7	4	0	15	14	90^{1}	69	6	3.1	9.4	57%	.278	1.11	2.19	3.44	2.98	2.6	77	
2015	BIN	AA	24	1	0	0	2	2	11^{1}	2	0	1.6	7.9	56%	.080	0.35	0.00	2.03	3.12	0.2	86	
2016	*NYN*	*MLB*	*25*	*9*	*8*	*0*	*26*	*26*	148^{1}	*123*	*16*	*2.8*	*8.5*	*52%*	*.290*	*1.14*	*3.49*	*3.59*	*4.28*	*1.8*	*98*	
2017	*NYN*	*MLB*	*26*	*8*	*8*	*0*	*25*	*25*	146^{1}	*130*	*18*	*2.9*	*8.9*	*52%*	*.308*	*1.22*	*3.60*	*4.09*	*4.42*	*1.4*	*101*	

Breakout: 22% Improve: 44% Collapse: 18% Attrition: 34% MLB: 71% *Comparables: Scott Barnes, Tyler Thornburg, Alex Meyer*

Matz started the year in Triple-A and ended it in the World Series; his six career regular-season starts were the third fewest of all time for a World Series starter, behind Joe Black (two) in 1952 and Marty Bystrom (five) in 1980. Matz got there by tying up what few loose ends he still had. His fastball generated far more movement in the big leagues than scouts had seen in years past. He gained substantial velocity differential on his changeup against his fastball—7 to 8 mph in years past versus 11 mph after his promotion—just in time to make it a serviceable show pitch to big-league righties. He experienced a Harvey-esque velocity explosion. Previously clocked in the low 90s, Matz's 94.6 mph average fastball velocity was behind only Chris Sale and David Price among left-handed starters. Best of all, the night before starting Game Four of the World Series, Matz slept at home on Long Island, in his own bed. Not a bad way to cap a year.

Jenrry Mejia RHP

Born: 10/11/89 Age: 26 Bats: R Throws: R Height: 6'0" Weight: 205

YEAR	TEAM	LVL	AGE	W	L	SV	G	GS	IP	H	HR	BB/9	K/9	GB%	BABIP	WHIP	ERA	FIP	DRA	WARP	CFIP	MPH
2013	BIN	AA	23	2	0	0	2	2	11	6	1	3.3	7.4	41%	.192	0.91	0.82	3.96	4.50	0.1	100	
2013	NYN	MLB	23	1	2	0	5	5	27^{1}	28	2	1.3	8.9	58%	.329	1.17	2.30	2.44	2.85	0.7	85	94.6
2014	NYN	MLB	24	6	6	28	63	7	93^{2}	98	9	3.9	9.4	52%	.336	1.48	3.65	3.70	4.75	-0.2	97	95.6
2015	NYN	MLB	25	1	0	0	7	0	7^{1}	4	0	2.5	8.6	50%	.222	0.82	0.00	2.07	0.50	0.4	95	95.8
2016	*NYN*	*MLB*	*26*	*2*	*1*	*0*	*33*	*0*	*35*	*30*	*4*	*2.9*	*8.5*	*53%*	*.297*	*1.18*	*3.51*	*3.67*	*4.30*	*0.3*	*96*	
2017	*NYN*	*MLB*	*27*	*8*	*6*	*16*	*67*	*17*	154^{2}	*141*	*17*	*3.0*	*8.6*	*53%*	*.314*	*1.25*	*3.54*	*4.01*	*4.34*	*1.3*	*96*	

Breakout: 35% Improve: 67% Collapse: 16% Attrition: 10% MLB: 95% *Comparables: Ryan Madson, Manny Parra, Ricky Romero*

Mejia's 162-game suspension for anabolic steroids—his second steroid suspension in two seasons—marked something of a first in our cultural conversation about PEDs. Rather than lamenting the integrity of the game, or debating the ethics of this drug versus that drug, everyone just called Mejia a selfish idiot. While it may not be an adequate defense either of his ethics or his idiocy, consider the long injury history and the bizarre way in which the Mets jerked him around from starter to reliever to starter to closer. At the very least, this was not a man secure about his health, his role or his future. Would that make stanozolol the right move? Well, maybe. But if he was insecure before, how's he feeling now?

Rafael Montero RHP

Born: 10/17/90 Age: 25 Bats: R Throws: R Height: 6'0" Weight: 185

YEAR	TEAM	LVL	AGE	W	L	SV	G	GS	IP	H	HR	BB/9	K/9	GB%	BABIP	WHIP	ERA	FIP	DRA	WARP	CFIP	MPH
2013	LVG	AAA	22	5	4	0	16	16	88^{2}	85	4	2.5	7.9	40%	.316	1.24	3.05	3.24	4.30	1.3	77	
2013	BIN	AA	22	7	3	0	11	11	66^{2}	51	2	1.4	9.7	40%	.277	0.92	2.43	2.00	3.41	1.4	59	
2014	LVG	AAA	23	6	4	0	16	16	80	69	4	3.8	9.0	44%	.297	1.29	3.60	3.66	4.91	0.8	87	
2014	NYN	MLB	23	1	3	0	10	8	44^{1}	44	8	4.7	8.5	36%	.298	1.51	4.06	5.11	6.52	-1.0	114	94.8
2015	NYN	MLB	24	0	1	0	5	1	10	9	0	4.5	11.7	50%	.321	1.40	4.50	2.06	4.79	0.0	90	95.0
2016	*NYN*	*MLB*	*25*	*2*	*2*	*0*	*6*	*6*	*30*	*25*	*3*	*2.9*	*8.1*	*44%*	*.281*	*1.15*	*3.66*	*3.64*	*4.47*	*0.3*	*102*	
2017	*NYN*	*MLB*	*26*	*5*	*6*	*0*	*16*	*16*	96^{2}	*86*	*13*	*3.1*	*8.5*	*44%*	*.297*	*1.23*	*3.80*	*4.31*	*4.64*	*0.7*	*107*	

Breakout: 21% Improve: 44% Collapse: 20% Attrition: 32% MLB: 73% *Comparables: Tyler Thornburg, Scott Lewis, Michael Bowden*

It was always going to be difficult for Montero, as the least sexy of a crop of young Mets starters that borders on baseball erotica. But 2015 was the double whammy: Not only was he (somewhat predictably) outshone by his fellow starlets; he also reprised the Mets' time-honored tradition of vague, season-long injury. Montero started the season in the bullpen, then made a spot start before succumbing to "shoulder inflammation." Some three months later, after a rehab stint yielded more "tightness," he was shut down. Assuming he returns this spring in good health, the Mets must learn from the Jenrry Mejia debacle in defining his role going forward. A fringy starter competing amid a gaggle of other top prospects while coming back from injury and being jerked around from starter to reliever—it all places unduly high expectations on the man for whom the Mets have the least expectation.

Bobby Parnell RHP

Born: 9/8/84 Age: 31 Bats: R Throws: R Height: 6'3" Weight: 205

YEAR	TEAM	LVL	AGE	W	L	SV	G	GS	IP	H	HR	BB/9	K/9	GB%	BABIP	WHIP	ERA	FIP	DRA	WARP	CFIP	MPH
2013	NYN	MLB	28	5	5	22	49	0	50	38	1	2.2	7.9	53%	.264	1.00	2.16	2.30	2.50	1.3	87	98.8
2014	NYN	MLB	29	0	0	0	1	0	1	2	0	9.0	9.0	25%	.500	3.00	9.00	4.10	11.33	-0.1	104	95.5
2015	NYN	MLB	30	2	4	1	30	0	24	30	0	6.4	4.9	55%	.366	1.96	6.38	4.20	7.42	-0.8	129	97.1
2016	*NYN*	*MLB*	*31*	*2*	*1*	*1*	*35*	*0*	*36^2*	*35*	*4*	*3.6*	*6.7*	*53%*	*.298*	*1.35*	*4.18*	*4.29*	*5.08*	*-0.1*	*118*	
2017	*NYN*	*MLB*	*32*	*2*	*1*	*2*	*48*	*0*	*44^2*	*46*	*5*	*3.5*	*6.2*	*53%*	*.311*	*1.42*	*4.24*	*4.83*	*5.15*	*-0.1*	*120*	

Breakout: 35% Improve: 52% Collapse: 17% Attrition: 16% MLB: 85% *Comparables: Rafael Perez, Brandon League, Dennys Reyes*

Before Tyler Clippard was a gleam in Terry Collins' eye, there was Parnell to take a bullpen role on name recognition over performance. His momentary success after returning in June from Tommy John surgery was a mirage, and the strikeout numbers (eight over his first 12 innings) hinted at what was to come. Parnell's season finally went off the rails in late July, just as Jenrry Mejia's season-long suspension opened the setup-man role for him. The silver lining is that he threw harder as the season went on, even as his lack of command condemned him. We're loathe to judge a pitcher on his velocity, but Parnell's sinker doesn't have enough movement to be reliable without it.

Addison Reed RHP

Born: 12/27/88 Age: 27 Bats: L Throws: R Height: 6'4" Weight: 230

YEAR	TEAM	LVL	AGE	W	L	SV	G	GS	IP	H	HR	BB/9	K/9	GB%	BABIP	WHIP	ERA	FIP	DRA	WARP	CFIP	MPH
2013	CHA	MLB	24	5	4	40	68	0	71^1	56	6	2.9	9.1	35%	.260	1.11	3.79	3.20	2.98	1.4	82	95.6
2014	ARI	MLB	25	1	7	32	62	0	59^1	57	11	2.3	10.5	28%	.295	1.21	4.25	4.00	4.41	0.1	86	95.0
2015	NYN	MLB	26	1	1	1	17	0	15^1	11	1	2.9	10.0	50%	.270	1.04	1.17	2.77	2.10	0.5	75	95.0
2015	RNO	AAA	26	1	1	5	11	0	10^1	8	1	4.4	9.6	48%	.250	1.26	1.74	4.18	4.29	0.1	92	
2015	ARI	MLB	26	2	2	3	38	0	40^2	47	2	3.1	7.5	41%	.344	1.50	4.20	3.16	4.86	-0.1	98	94.8
2016	*NYN*	*MLB*	*27*	*3*	*1*	*3*	*52*	*0*	*55^1*	*46*	*6*	*2.6*	*8.7*	*38%*	*.286*	*1.11*	*3.41*	*3.47*	*4.21*	*0.5*	*92*	
2017	*NYN*	*MLB*	*28*	*3*	*1*	*13*	*55*	*0*	*54*	*48*	*7*	*2.7*	*8.7*	*38%*	*.296*	*1.18*	*3.55*	*4.02*	*4.38*	*0.3*	*96*	

Breakout: 31% Improve: 52% Collapse: 25% Attrition: 13% MLB: 98% *Comparables: Hector Rondon, Jordan Walden, Manny Delcarmen*

While certain others struggled in high-leverage work earned on name value alone, Reed joined the Mets at the August trade deadline, immediately took over seventh-inning duty and was lights-out. For the second year in a row, Reed decided the changeup was surplus to requirements, and lefties haven't shown an ability to handle the slider (17 percent whiff rate versus 10 percent against righties in 2015). Strange, then, that Reed attacks hitters like a conventional righty rather than what he is; throwing 40 percent sliders to righties and just 24 percent to lefties may be playing by the book, but it doesn't maximize his potential. If any members of the Reed family are reading this: The Annual makes a great gift!

Hansel Robles RHP

Born: 8/13/90 Age: 25 Bats: R Throws: R Height: 5'11" Weight: 185

YEAR	TEAM	LVL	AGE	W	L	SV	G	GS	IP	H	HR	BB/9	K/9	GB%	BABIP	WHIP	ERA	FIP	DRA	WARP	CFIP	MPH
2013	SLU	A+	22	5	4	0	16	15	84^2	83	8	3.1	7.0	39%	.296	1.32	3.72	4.15	4.40	0.5	104	
2014	BIN	AA	23	7	6	0	30	18	110^2	107	10	3.5	8.6	38%	.312	1.36	4.31	3.97	4.46	0.8	97	
2015	NYN	MLB	24	4	3	0	57	0	54	37	8	3.0	10.2	34%	.227	1.02	3.67	3.94	3.70	0.6	89	98.7
2016	*NYN*	*MLB*	*25*	*2*	*1*	*0*	*43*	*0*	*45^1*	*37*	*5*	*3.0*	*8.6*	*34%*	*.286*	*1.16*	*3.66*	*3.70*	*4.46*	*0.3*	*103*	
2017	*NYN*	*MLB*	*26*	*4*	*3*	*0*	*26*	*9*	*74^2*	*65*	*9*	*3.0*	*9.0*	*34%*	*.303*	*1.21*	*3.62*	*4.11*	*4.41*	*0.6*	*101*	

Breakout: 15% Improve: 34% Collapse: 22% Attrition: 27% MLB: 62% *Comparables: Jonathan Papelbon, Hector Noesi, Chad Bettis*

The prize for most-improved reliever: You get the whole month of October off! From June 14th through the end of the season, Robles' line-drive rates on both the fastball and slider each fell by nearly a third. He was, all told, the Mets' most reliable reliever not named Jeurys Familia, and given the Mets' willingness to use rookie starters through the playoffs, it's perplexing that Robles threw only three innings in the postseason. This is a hot relief prospect who will take on a much larger role this season. Like Familia, he loves a good quick pitch. You would think noted quick pitchers wouldn't also throw 97 mph, but there you go.

Noah Syndergaard RHP

Born: 8/29/92 Age: 23 Bats: L Throws: R Height: 6'6" Weight: 240

YEAR	TEAM	LVL	AGE	W	L	SV	G	GS	IP	H	HR	BB/9	K/9	GB%	BABIP	WHIP	ERA	FIP	DRA	WARP	CFIP	MPH
2013	BIN	AA	20	6	1	0	11	11	54	46	8	2.0	11.5	43%	.304	1.07	3.00	3.36	3.60	1.0	65	
2013	SLU	A+	20	3	3	0	12	12	63^2	61	3	2.3	9.0	53%	.333	1.21	3.11	2.64	3.55	1.0	75	
2014	LVG	AAA	21	9	7	0	26	26	133	154	11	2.9	9.8	47%	.378	1.48	4.60	3.70	4.61	1.8	74	
2015	NYN	MLB	22	9	7	0	24	24	150	126	19	1.9	10.0	48%	.279	1.05	3.24	3.28	3.59	2.6	82	99.5
2015	LVG	AAA	22	3	0	0	5	5	29^2	20	2	2.4	10.3	52%	.261	0.94	1.82	2.99	2.85	0.9	76	
2016	*NYN*	*MLB*	*23*	*10*	*9*	*0*	*29*	*29*	*165^1*	*137*	*19*	*2.1*	*9.4*	*48%*	*.298*	*1.06*	*3.14*	*3.24*	*3.88*	*2.8*	*85*	
2017	*NYN*	*MLB*	*24*	*9*	*9*	*0*	*28*	*28*	*171*	*153*	*21*	*2.3*	*9.4*	*48%*	*.315*	*1.14*	*3.24*	*3.67*	*4.00*	*2.2*	*89*	

Breakout: 23% Improve: 55% Collapse: 13% Attrition: 15% MLB: 84% *Comparables: Brian Matusz, Francisco Liriano, Shelby Miller*

Just for fun, let's try to pick apart Syndergaard's debut season. His whiff rate on the fastball is surprisingly low, but then again, nobody hits it hard, either. His fastball command is more of a choice between "the high one" and "the low one," although he doesn't walk anyone and at 98 mph, who cares? Um, there exists an unflattering picture of him as a pudgy middle schooler. Okay, this is impossible. There is no model by which Syndergaard does not become a star.

Carlos Torres RHP

Born: 10/22/82 Age: 33 Bats: R Throws: R Height: 6'1" Weight: 180

YEAR	TEAM	LVL	AGE	W	L	SV	G	GS	IP	H	HR	BB/9	K/9	GB%	BABIP	WHIP	ERA	FIP	DRA	WARP	CFIP	MPH
2013	NYN	MLB	30	4	6	0	33	9	86^{1}	79	15	1.8	7.8	45%	.266	1.11	3.44	4.27	3.94	0.9	99	93.2
2013	LVG	AAA	30	6	3	0	12	12	71^{2}	71	7	2.4	8.4	52%	.308	1.26	3.89	3.85	4.39	1.0	80	
2014	NYN	MLB	31	8	6	2	73	1	97	89	11	3.5	8.9	49%	.302	1.31	3.06	3.83	4.12	0.5	100	94.3
2015	NYN	MLB	32	5	6	0	59	0	57^{2}	61	5	2.8	7.5	49%	.326	1.37	4.68	3.56	4.90	-0.1	102	94.8
2016	*NYN*	*MLB*	*33*	*2*	*1*	*0*	*47*	*0*	*50^{1}*	*44*	*6*	*2.6*	*7.8*	*48%*	*.292*	*1.17*	*3.72*	*3.85*	*4.55*	*0.3*	*104*	
2017	*NYN*	*MLB*	*34*	*4*	*3*	*0*	*40*	*6*	*80^{2}*	*77*	*11*	*2.7*	*7.7*	*48%*	*.307*	*1.26*	*3.88*	*4.39*	*4.74*	*0.3*	*108*	

Breakout: 30% Improve: 47% Collapse: 19% Attrition: 16% MLB: 76% *Comparables: Scott Downs, Gary Glover, Alberto Castillo*

Terry Collins seemed to forget about Torres as the Mets eased through September to the NL East crown. Perhaps you did too, but consider how conspicuous Torres was by his October absence. Likely Collins thought Bartolo Colon and Jon Niese would step in to fill the innings that would normally go to Torres, but that logic only further exposes his bizarre faith in Tyler Clippard to eat an inning by himself. With a more rational take on the rest of the bullpen, Torres becomes a more valuable piece. He's a rubber-armed righty with stable career splits, and he can go multiple innings if needed. Even the Mets' rotation needs that kind of guy.

Logan Verrett RHP

Born: 6/19/90 Age: 26 Bats: R Throws: R Height: 6'2" Weight: 190

YEAR	TEAM	LVL	AGE	W	L	SV	G	GS	IP	H	HR	BB/9	K/9	GB%	BABIP	WHIP	ERA	FIP	DRA	WARP	CFIP	MPH
2013	BIN	AA	23	12	6	0	24	24	146	136	21	1.9	8.1	45%	.288	1.14	4.25	4.08	4.16	1.8	86	
2014	LVG	AAA	24	11	5	0	28	28	162	188	17	1.9	6.6	47%	.328	1.37	4.33	4.35	5.03	1.4	94	
2015	TEX	MLB	25	0	1	0	4	0	9	11	1	4.0	3.0	57%	.294	1.67	6.00	5.22	6.78	-0.2	120	92.2
2015	LVG	AAA	25	5	3	0	18	11	64^{2}	69	6	2.6	7.4	42%	.325	1.36	4.59	4.09	4.48	0.7	95	
2015	NYN	MLB	25	1	1	1	14	4	38^{2}	23	5	2.6	8.4	42%	.191	0.88	3.03	3.99	2.31	1.2	96	93.4
2016	*NYN*	*MLB*	*26*	*4*	*3*	*0*	*32*	*8*	*65*	*57*	*8*	*2.3*	*7.0*	*44%*	*.280*	*1.13*	*3.82*	*3.95*	*4.67*	*0.3*	*108*	
2017	*NYN*	*MLB*	*27*	*6*	*7*	*0*	*17*	*17*	*103*	*101*	*15*	*2.4*	*7.0*	*44%*	*.301*	*1.25*	*4.08*	*4.64*	*4.99*	*0.3*	*117*	

Breakout: 12% Improve: 24% Collapse: 19% Attrition: 31% MLB: 58% *Comparables: Charles Brewer, Adam Wilk, Matt Maloney*

A first major-league start in Colorado for an extreme flyball pitcher of little acclaim is, to say the least, an unenviable circumstance. But Verrett forever endeared himself to Mets fans with a masterful showing on August 23rd, going eight innings for a win to put some space between New York and Washington in the NL East race. Whether he will get to reprise that performance is an open question; his is not the kind of arsenal that seems to be trending upward, and, as with Rafael Montero, the Mets don't have the innings to offer someone who needs to figure himself out at this level. But his exceptional command and sharp, slurvy breaking ball make you think that, somewhere, he will figure himself out.

Zack Wheeler RHP

Born: 5/30/90 Age: 26 Bats: L Throws: R Height: 6'4" Weight: 195

YEAR	TEAM	LVL	AGE	W	L	SV	G	GS	IP	H	HR	BB/9	K/9	GB%	BABIP	WHIP	ERA	FIP	DRA	WARP	CFIP	MPH
2013	LVG	AAA	23	4	2	0	13	13	68^{2}	61	9	3.5	9.6	42%	.289	1.28	3.93	4.41	4.64	0.8	88	
2013	NYN	MLB	23	7	5	0	17	17	100	90	10	4.1	7.6	45%	.279	1.36	3.42	4.14	4.11	1.0	109	97.3
2014	NYN	MLB	24	11	11	0	32	32	185^{1}	167	14	3.8	9.1	55%	.304	1.33	3.54	3.52	4.23	1.3	102	97.9
2016	*NYN*	*MLB*	*26*	*2*	*2*	*0*	*8*	*8*	*40*	*33*	*4*	*3.3*	*8.4*	*52%*	*.287*	*1.19*	*3.66*	*3.76*	*4.46*	*0.4*	*102*	
2017	*NYN*	*MLB*	*27*	*5*	*5*	*0*	*14*	*14*	*81^{1}*	*73*	*9*	*3.3*	*8.4*	*52%*	*.304*	*1.27*	*3.77*	*4.26*	*4.59*	*0.7*	*106*	

Breakout: 32% Improve: 62% Collapse: 20% Attrition: 12% MLB: 96% *Comparables: Chris Archer, Alex Cobb, Dustin McGowan*

While we watched Wilmer Flores break down in tears as news broke of his impending trade, hardly a thought was spared for Wheeler, who was to be traded along with Flores to Milwaukee for Carlos Gomez. Just as well: "Afterthought" is Wheeler's new stock-in-trade. The Mets' farm system turned out one of the great pitching classes of this generation, a class of which he was supposed to be a large part until a torn UCL shunted him aside. It's enough to make a man bitter, but when Wheeler again came up in trade rumors just days later, he called GM Sandy Alderson to plead his case. "[It] actually had quite an impact," Alderson said later. "Really expressed his desire to remain a Met, his excitement for being part of the organization and being part of what's happening here. Acknowledged it was a business but at the same time wanted to express his feelings to me."

Baseball is a business. This is the kind of thing scouts and sabermetricians say to each other when they've been arguing about the cut of a player's jib for five hours and for &*@#'s sake, can't we just agree on something? But the axiom implies that moments like Wheeler's call have no place in the discussion, no value to the organization. That isn't true; in a few minutes, Wheeler made himself more valuable to the Mets than he would be to another team, and increased the cost of trading him, as the remaining players might react negatively to the disposal of such a devoted teammate. Those things have real value, and we'll never have the information to determine that value, much less a metric to plug that missing information into.

Or at least, no metric through our traditional lenses. Maybe it's time to broaden our perspective; the Wheeler anecdote may not have helped the Mets on the field, but to say it didn't help the Mets at all assumes the team's only purpose is to win games. While you're cleaning the vomit out of your mouth, consider: Forbes puts out an annual list of most valuable brands, but it also publishes a list of most ethical companies, and best companies to work for. Why would companies (or teams) want to burn calories to make these lists? Because they have value beyond immediate profit; a story like Wheeler's, which endears the company to its other employees and makes it more attractive to outside talent, helps achieve that goal with no WAR added. Afterthought though he may have been at the time, spare a thought now for Wheeler, an employee who put his company to the test in a time of need, and provided at least a little counterweight to the drumbeat of stories illustrating how rough being a Mets employee is.

Gabriel Ynoa RHP

Born: 5/26/93 Age: 23 Bats: R Throws: R Height: 6'2" Weight: 160

YEAR	TEAM	LVL	AGE	W	L	SV	G	GS	IP	H	HR	BB/9	K/9	GB%	BABIP	WHIP	ERA	FIP	DRA	WARP	CFIP	MPH
2013	SAV	A	20	15	4	0	22	22	135^{2}	123	9	1.1	7.0	41%	.278	1.02	2.72	3.16	4.01	1.7	85	
2014	BIN	AA	21	3	2	0	11	11	66^{1}	74	9	1.6	5.7	40%	.304	1.30	4.21	4.53	4.65	0.4	105	
2014	SLU	A+	21	8	2	0	14	14	82	95	7	1.4	7.0	44%	.330	1.32	3.95	3.45	3.88	1.1	85	
2015	BIN	AA	22	9	9	0	25	24	152^{1}	157	14	1.8	4.8	47%	.283	1.23	3.90	4.12	4.67	0.3	106	
2016	*NYN*	*MLB*	*23*	*8*	*8*	*0*	*22*	*22*	134^{1}	*134*	*17*	*2.2*	*5.0*	*41%*	*.288*	*1.24*	*4.24*	*4.39*	*5.13*	*0.2*	*122*	
2017	*NYN*	*MLB*	*24*	*7*	*9*	*0*	*21*	*21*	125^{1}	*141*	*19*	*2.4*	*4.7*	*41%*	*.306*	*1.39*	*4.69*	*5.33*	*5.67*	*-0.6*	*136*	

Breakout: 8% Improve: 12% Collapse: 14% Attrition: 17% MLB: 29% *Comparables: Jose Urena, Zach Lee, Brad Bergesen*

Needs more seasoning. Ynoa projects to have a trio of at-least-average offerings in the majors, but right now the changeup is carrying too much of the load. In his first full season at Double-A, he didn't always seem comfortable attacking hitters with fastballs early in the count, and while his off-speed stuff induces a ton of weak contact, he has yet to show he can consistently work within his slim margin of error at higher levels. There is still middle-of-the-rotation potential here, given his impeccable control and low-effort delivery, but when he arrives, he needs to be completely ready. For now, remedial Double-A might not be a bad idea.

Lineouts

Hitters

NAME	POS	TEAM	LVL	AGE	PA	R	2B	3B	HR	RBI	BB	K	SB	CS	AVG/OBP/SLG	TAv	BABIP	BRR	FRAA	WARP
Jayce Boyd	UT	BIN	AA	24	175	18	16	0	1	16	13	16	2	1	.304/.360/.422	.277	.333	0.0	LF(26): -5.0, 1B(1): 0.0	0.1
	UT	LVG	AAA	24	151	12	11	0	0	12	12	23	0	2	.254/.313/.333	.237	.304	-0.8	LF(20): -3.2	-0.5
Eric Campbell	UT	LVG	AAA	28	142	28	9	1	5	18	25	20	7	2	.363/.493/.593	.372	.409	-0.1	3B(22): -0.9, LF(8): -0.2	1.9
	UT	NYN	MLB	28	206	28	8	0	3	19	26	37	5	3	.197/.312/.295	.227	.230	0.1	3B(48): -4.8, 1B(5): 0.0	-0.5
Darrell Ceciliani	CF	LVG	AAA	25	255	50	19	4	9	36	21	48	16	4	.345/.398/.581	.312	.400	3.4	CF(62): -0.3, LF(4): -0.0	2.5
	CF	NYN	MLB	25	75	5	2	0	1	3	4	25	5	1	.206/.270/.279	.243	.310	-1.0	LF(17): 2.5, CF(7): 0.3	0.3
Eudor Garcia	3B	SAV	A	21	429	57	23	4	9	59	22	95	5	2	.296/.340/.442	.306	.367	-0.1	3B(82): -10.0, 1B(1): -0.0	2.3
Luis Guillorme	SS	SAV	A	20	523	67	16	0	0	55	54	70	18	8	.318/.391/.354	.305	.374	0.4	SS(119): 8.1	5.6
Marc Krauss	1B	ANA	MLB	27	38	2	2	0	1	5	3	11	0	0	.143/.211/.286	.210	.174	-0.5	1B(4): -0.2, LF(1): -0.0	-0.2
	1B	DET	MLB	27	33	1	0	0	1	2	0	13	0	0	.152/.152/.242	.150	.211	-0.4	1B(12): 0.4	-0.3
	1B	SLC	AAA	27	195	23	8	3	4	29	35	38	0	1	.289/.415/.453	.295	.356	-1.6	1B(38): -2.5, LF(3): 0.5	0.6
	1B	TBA	MLB	27	10	0	1	0	0	1	0	7	0	0	.100/.100/.200	.102	.333	0.0	1B(4): -0.2	-0.2
	1B	TOL	AAA	27	103	14	4	2	0	9	18	26	2	2	.247/.379/.341	.260	.356	1.2	1B(23): 0.0	0.2
Champ Stuart	OF	SLU	A+	22	382	43	8	1	4	17	40	141	21	3	.176/.271/.242	.217	.287	4.2	CF(91): -14.0	-1.6
Jhoan Urena	3B	SLU	A+	20	222	15	5	3	0	18	11	40	2	0	.214/.257/.267	.187	.265	-1.0	3B(62): -0.3	-1.2

Jayce Boyd's bat is doing its damnedest to keep him on the prospect radar. His full-time switch to left field from first base mitigates his lack of power, but with the Mets' four-year outfielding apocalypse momentarily abated, his timing could have been better. ❖ **Eric Campbell** is probably considering a lawsuit for our essay at the front of this chapter, but truth is an absolute defense in libel cases. Soup will need to bring his Triple-A success to the big leagues if he's going to bring a case. ❖ Signed on his 16th birthday and with an impressive stint in the Appy League already under his belt, 18-year-old **Luis Carpio** is a slick-fielding infielder with a surprisingly mature approach at the plate. ❖ In June, Terry Collins said he was "shocked" no one had claimed **Darrell Ceciliani** in the Rule 5 draft. Eighteen days later, the Mets sent him down and never recalled him. Collins is probably less shocked now. ❖ **Eudor Garcia** is a natural hitter to all fields with no lack of power, and the hit tool is very, very real. Now, can he play third base? Oh... no, we were hoping you'd know. ❖ The best defensive shortstop in the Mets' system isn't Amed Rosario; it's **Luis Guillorme**, who will never, ever hit for power but may show enough plate discipline to put it all together. ❖ If Otto from *Airplane!* has a distant baseball cousin, it's **Marc Krauss**, emergency first baseman. His ability to draw walks in Triple-A hasn't translated to facing big-league pitching; after all, the major leagues is an entirely different kind of baseball... altogether! ❖ **Milton Ramos** did all he could with the bat, but we're holding back on the defensive superlatives that made him a prospect in the first place. Full-season ball will be a big test on both sides. ❖ **Champ Stuart** was born in the Bahamas and has 80 speed, so he'll continue to get a Lineout until he displays other, more baseball-relevant characteristics. He may yet, but the clock is ticking. ❖ **Jhoan Urena** made an unexpected jump from Low-A to High-A for 2015, and it showed in the hitting performance. He deserves a reprieve, but his defense may not play at any level. ❖ **Dash Winningham** led the Appalachian League in home runs and is more than just a masher, but with his glorious, major league–ready ginger flow and a name typically heard down at the hog races, it feels like we've buried the lede.

Pitchers

NAME	TEAM	LVL	AGE	W	L	SV	G	GS	IP	H	HR	BB/9	K/9	GB%	BABIP	WHIP	ERA	FIP	FRA	WARP	CFIP	MPH
Dario Alvarez	NYN	MLB	26	1	0	0	6	0	3^{2}	5	2	2.5	4.9	21%	.250	1.64	12.27	11.62	13.32	-0.4	111	94.0
	LVG	AAA	26	2	1	0	16	0	11	6	0	4.1	15.5	47%	.353	1.00	2.45	2.33	2.68	0.3	73	
	BIN	AA	26	1	1	0	32	0	31	21	2	4.6	12.5	46%	.271	1.19	3.19	3.17	2.77	0.7	81	
Jerry Blevins	NYN	MLB	31	1	0	0	7	0	5	0	0	0.0	7.2	55%	.000	0.00	0.00	1.56	-3.26	0.5	97	92.0
Robert Gsellman	SLU	A+	21	6	0	0	8	8	51	37	1	1.9	6.5	61%	.250	0.94	1.76	2.79	3.07	0.9	90	
	BIN	AA	21	7	7	0	16	16	92^{1}	89	4	2.5	4.8	54%	.277	1.25	3.51	3.65	4.89	-0.1	109	
Marcos Molina	SLU	A+	20	1	5	0	8	7	41^{1}	49	1	2.4	7.8	52%	.361	1.45	4.57	2.68	2.58	1.0	85	
Akeel Morris	SLU	A+	22	0	1	13	24	0	32	11	1	3.9	12.9	45%	.169	0.78	1.69	2.01	1.61	1.0	69	
	NYN	MLB	22	0	0	0	1	0	0^{2}	3	1	40.5	0.0	60%	.500	9.00	67.50	36.16	39.10	-0.3	113	95.0
	BIN	AA	22	0	1	0	23	0	29^{1}	17	1	4.6	10.7	43%	.242	1.09	2.45	2.86	3.39	0.4	89	
Eric O'Flaherty	NYN	MLB	30	0	0	0	16	0	8^{2}	18	1	5.2	6.2	47%	.459	2.65	13.50	5.70	8.38	-0.4	130	93.1
	OAK	MLB	30	1	2	0	25	0	21^{1}	29	1	5.5	6.3	68%	.354	1.97	5.91	4.14	7.01	-0.6	118	92.3
Josh Smoker	SLU	A+	26	1	0	6	14	0	21^{1}	12	1	2.5	11.0	50%	.216	0.84	1.69	2.18	1.93	0.6	75	
	BIN	AA	26	1	0	0	21	0	21	16	0	4.7	11.1	50%	.308	1.29	3.00	2.36	3.70	0.2	93	
Alex Torres	NYN	MLB	27	0	0	1	39	0	34^{1}	26	6	6.8	9.2	50%	.233	1.51	3.15	5.75	5.04	-0.1	115	94.5

Dario Alvarez didn't do enough to make the postseason roster, but he has the minor-league résumé for a possible LOOGY residency going forward. ❖ **Jerry Blevins** was spotless until a comebacker broke his pitching arm; he then slipped on a curb during rehab, broke the arm again and missed the remainder of the season. This was back when the Mets were more of a comedy act. ❖ **Nabil Crismatt** is a former Dominican Summer League standout from Colombia who made his stateside debut in 2014. He could pitch in full-season ball this year, and while he's not as young as most, he's a prospect until someone hits him, or until someone appropriates his name as a science-fiction expletive. ❖ **Robert Gsellman** doesn't throw hard enough to make headlines, but a gorgeous curveball and plus-plus, voluminous hair could keep him a starter all the way to The Show. He's already bullied his way to Double-A ahead of schedule. ❖ Did you hear the one about the Mets prospect who had Tommy John? Ask **Marcos Molina**. He tells it better than we do. ❖ **Akeel Morris** was called to the majors directly from High-A St. Lucie, for some reason, and was humbled by a Danny Valencia home run that may have traveled with him to Double-A Binghamton, where he continued to show eighth-inning relief potential. ❖ The Mets acquired **Eric O'Flaherty** in August to replace Alex Torres, and boy, did he ever. ❖ Former first-rounder **Josh Smoker** touched 99 from the left side at Double-A in his quest to resurrect his career after two arm surgeries and two years away from minor-league ball. Only health can hold him back. ❖ In any utopia, there must be pain, so the Mets continued to employ **Alex Torres**, whose walk rate reminded the rest of the pitching staff how wonderful they truly were. ❖ **Max Wotell** has one of the strangest deliveries you'll ever see, but isn't (quite) the injury risk that statement would indicate. The 2015 third-round pick figures to touch every part of the rubber in Brooklyn.

MANAGER

Terry Collins

YEAR	TEAM	W	L	Pythag +/-	Avg PC	100+ P	120+ P	QS	BQS	REL	REL w Zero R	IBB	PH	PH Avg	PH HR	SB2	CS2	SB3	CS3	SAC Att	SAC%	POS SAC	Squeeze	Swing	In Play
2013	NYN	74	88	1	95.7	69	2	94	3	534	417	38	262	.207	4	99	31	15	4	82	64.6	26	0	310	87
2014	NYN	79	83	-3	97.3	72	3	98	3	489	411	38	240	.181	3	90	27	10	7	86	68.6	18	3	274	64

Last year, we remarked on how Collins continued to feel like a bridge—around until the Mets completed their transition from rebuilding to competing, then removed for someone better. Naturally, Collins and the Mets responded by winning the pennant and coming within a few blown leads of capturing the title.

While Collins made his share of odd decisions—sticking by Matt Harvey deep into Game Five is going to haunt the Mets for a while—he made a number of encouraging calls, too. One of our chief complaints in the last book was how he didn't handle his young starters well—riding them too hard and showing no commitment to the organization's stated usage rules. That changed in 2015. The Mets were one of the 13 teams without a start of 120 or more pitches, and finished tied with the league-average amount of pitches per start. Perhaps Zack Wheeler's Tommy John surgery convinced Collins he had to change his ways, or maybe not. Who knows?

Collins did some solid work with his lineup and bullpen, too. No full-season manager asked his position players to sacrifice less than Collins did—a smart call, especially after the Mets reloaded at the deadline—and he showed an appreciable aggression in how he deployed closer Jeurys Familia, both during the regular season and the playoffs. But Collins shined the best when he was surrounded by reporters. Here were our three favorite quips of his from the season:

3) In response to Joe Maddon bringing in a magician: "I brought in a witch doctor to clean up the clubhouse. Get all the bad spirits out of there." (Credit: Mike Vorkunov)

2) In response to learning that Scott Boras represented Michael Conforto: "I wonder how many at-bats he is going to be allowed." (Credit: Mike Puma.)

1) In response to Wilmer Flores crying after learning he had been "traded": "Why would I have taken him out of the game? I've been in tears in the third inning and nobody has taken me out of the game!"(Credit: Every Mets beat writer.)

What can we say? Collins had a good year—so good that he received a two-year extension after the season to remain on board as the Mets skipper. Should Collins complete those two seasons, he would become the franchise's all-time leader in games managed. Some bridge, huh?

NEW YORK YANKEES

Essay by Kenny Ducey

Player comments by Nick Ashbourne and BP authors

After the Astros cleared the field following an American League Wild Card victory at Yankee Stadium, after thousands of energetic and passionate followers saw their posture reduced to a hopeless slouch, after Astros outfielder Carlos Gomez said he was feeling sexy yet again, Yankees General Manager Brian Cashman stood in the center of a hushed clubhouse. Writers surrounded him.

"I don't have any regrets," he said.

Alex Rodriguez had emerged from a season-long suspension to slug 33 home runs and post a TAv of .292, his highest since 2009. Mark Teixeira's wrist finally healed, and he, too, posted his highest TAv since 2009. In some act of sorcery, Carlos Beltran was able to OPS .862 after April in his 18th season in the major leagues; that would have been his highest full-season mark since 2011. Cashman was handed these three incredible gifts and his usual sky-high budget, yet only managed a Wild Card flame-out. So why didn't he have any regrets about how things turned out?

Because after literally decades of the same formula, the Yankees seem to be slowly transitioning into a younger, more defense-minded club. Gone are the days of sacrificing fielding, speed and contact for home runs, and gone are the days of sacrificing every last prospect to acquire veterans for short-term success. "At times we ran out four guys, five guys over 35 years old. I don't think that will happen next year," said manager Joe Girardi. "Who is going to be the next great Yankee people latch onto? I'm anxious to see some kids in the minor leagues come up and have some tremendous years." A Yankees manager declaring desire and excitement for prospects! How novel.

Defense

While the Yankees did not show well as a team-wide defense last season (see Table 1) things aren't as dire as they may seem, especially going forward. The team should field seven average-or-better defenders in 2016. Behind the plate, Brian McCann's framing numbers slipped last year, but he's still young enough that the slide from his top-notch defensive peak may not be irreversible, and he still blocks and throws well. Chase Headley and Didi Gregorius form a well-regarded defensive left side, and whether you think Starlin Castro is average or well below

YANKEES PROSPECTUS

2015 W-L: 87-75, 2nd in AL East

Pythag	.542	11th	DER	.699	22nd
RS/G	4.72	2nd	B-Age	31.5	30th
RA/G	4.31	16th	P-Age	27.5	7th
TAv	.265	8th	Salary	$217.8M	2nd
BRR	-8.67	26th	M$/MW	$5.3M	6th
TAv-P	.256	11th	DL Days	1214	23rd
FIP	3.94	11th	$ on DL	11%	9th

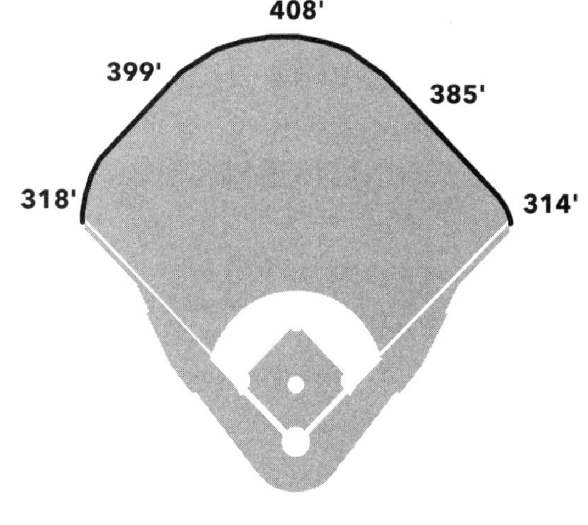

Outfield wall profile: **8'**

Three-Year Park Factors

Runs	Runs/RH	Runs/LH	HR/RH	HR/LH
106	113	121	119	132

Top Hitter WARP	3.0	Mark Teixeira
Top Pitcher WARP	3.1	Masahiro Tanakai
Top Prospect		Aaron Judge

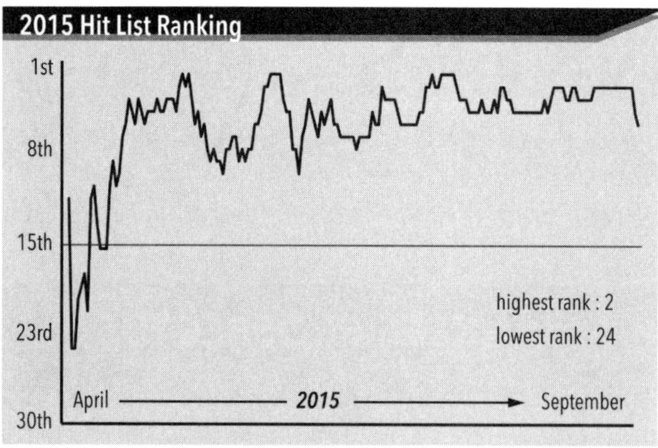

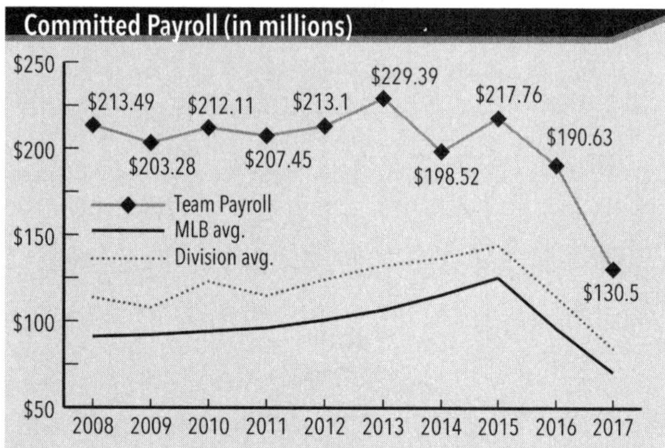

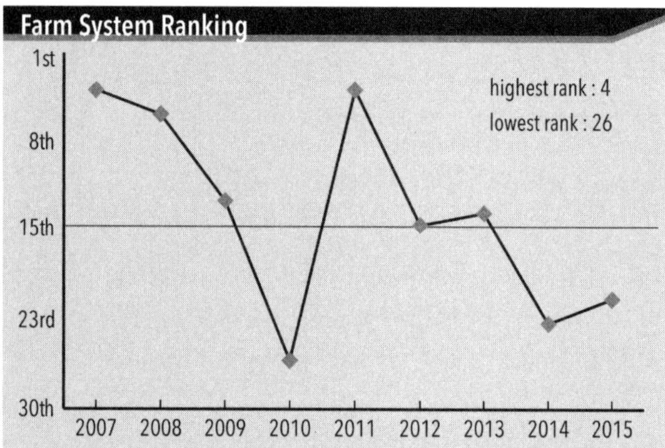

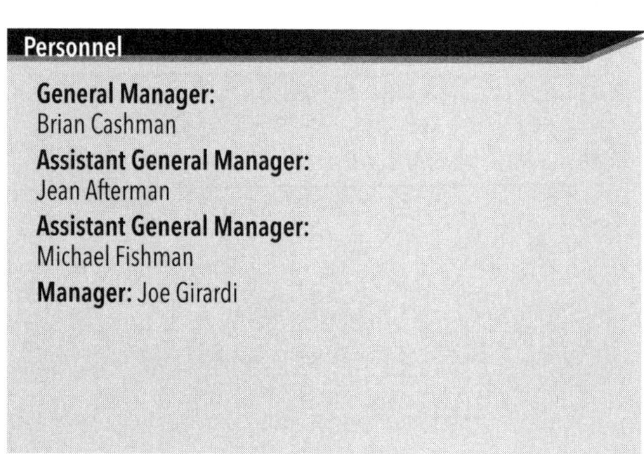
Personnel

General Manager:
Brian Cashman
Assistant General Manager:
Jean Afterman
Assistant General Manager:
Michael Fishman
Manager: Joe Girardi

at shortstop, his athleticism should play at second base. Teixeira has always been slick at first base, even if his movement resembles a jointless mannequin's. In left and center, the entire concept of Brett Gardner and Jacoby Ellsbury is that they run fast and defend.

TABLE 1

Year	Def. Eff.	Rank	Park-adjusted Def. Eff.	Rank
2012	.704	19th	0.01	15th
2013	.697	24th	-1.44	26th
2014	.702	18th	-0.21	17th
2015	.699	22nd	-0.47	21st

Unfortunately, the eighth regular defender for the Yankees is Beltran, who posted a bottom-10 season in all of baseball by FRAA last year, isn't any younger this season and still can't play his natural DH position. Beltran was never supposed to spend as much time in the outfield as he did, but that damn A-Rod, who always finds a way to hurt the team, hit too well in the DH role last year, played 151 games and solidified the spot for himself in 2016.

With 32-year-old Chris Young taking a two-year deal from the Red Sox this offseason, Cashman also got younger and better on defense at the fourth-outfielder spot, snagging Aaron Hicks from the Twins in exchange for John Ryan Murphy. Hicks' plus center-field defense will be useful if the Yankees find themselves with an injured Ellsbury again, and he'll be vastly overqualified to serve as Beltran's late-innings caddy.

Even Cashman's decisions about who *not* to play last season were made with defense in mind: Rob Refsnyder, who has hit .282/.370/.423 in one and a half seasons at Triple-A, received just 47 major-league plate appearances last year despite Stephen Drew's disastrous batting because the club felt Refsnyder's glove was not ready.

Things should only get better in 2017: Once Beltran's contract runs out at the end of the season, the Yankees will have the opportunity to replace him with Aaron Judge, who should be at least an average defender in right field despite the body of a defensive end.

Youth

The Yankees' average pitcher age in 2015 was 27.4, the lowest it's been since 1971, and despite everyone aging a year, as they will do, that number shouldn't change much this season, with 22-year-old Luis Severino taking a full-time spot. Of the projected Opening Day five, only CC Sabathia is over 30. The bullpen is even younger: The ridiculous three-headed beast of Aroldis Chapman, Andrew Miller and Dellin Betances top out at 31 and, as this essay is finalized in December, no aged vets are filling out the back end. Even long man/sixth starter Ivan Nova is just 29.

The position players are of a vintage more typically associated with the Yankees: They had the oldest average batter age in the bigs last season. That said, they also posted the lowest figure fielded by a Yankees team since 2011. If the projected nine stay healthy, that number will go up this year, notwithstanding the addition of Castro, but figures to drop precipitously come 2017, when Teixeira is replaced by Greg Bird and Beltran by Judge. Bird developed a cult following last year thanks to his towering home runs. He was called into action at just 22 due to Teixeira's injury, and clubbed 11 dingers to go with a sparkling .312 TAv. While it was immediately evident he could hit at the big-league level, he's almost certainly stuck in Triple-A this year, waiting for another injury.

Sincerity

In other times, you might wonder whether 2017 and 2018 (the first season after Rodriguez's deal expires) really would bring relief. Cashman can talk all he wants about gloves and table-setters, but with a Wild Card exit in 2015 and $60 million coming off the payroll after this year, is a youth movement really happening? Are the Yankees willing to be patient and let a young core develop?

As Ben Lindbergh laid out in last year's Annual, the Yankees have a long history of spending on aged talent to win championships, and it's possible their method will work again. Why would they deviate when they haven't had a losing season since 1992? Indeed, Cashman offered one of his top prospects, Jorge Mateo, for Craig Kimbrel at the deadline last year. Nobody would be shocked if Mateo, Bird, Severino or Judge headed out if the right player became available. Couple that with the fact that last year's 87 wins, driven by the elderly, was their best season since 2012, and the fact that the farm system is only decent, solid, okay; it's not bursting at the seams with talent in the manner of fellow big-market behemoths the Cubs. So, all told, perhaps skepticism is warranted.

As it stands right now, though, it's not just conceivable but likely that Beltran, Teixeira and Rodriguez will in fact leave, making room for more youthful vigor. Recent reassuring evidence is that Cashman let himself be outbid for Robinson Cano before 2014 despite no obvious candidate to replace him—he ought to be even less likely to panic and overpay for the aged when he has internal solutions available, as he does now.

Moreover, those in-house replacements are more likely to remain in the house between now and 2018 than at any prior point in Cashman's Yankees tenure. He's been hesitant to deal away his prospects in recent years in exchange for incremental veteran improvements; at the last trade deadline, he declined to send Adam Warren or Refsnyder packing in exchange for a few more wins. This doesn't mean he isn't making moves, or that he can be accused of hugging his own prospects, overvaluing the familiar to his detriment, because he *has* traded away youth. The difference is that he's been *acquiring* youth as well. When Cashman did eventually trade Warren, it was to get a young middle infielder in Castro who fits the team's future profile. He made similar acquisitions in the prior offseason: Trades for Nathan Eovaldi and Didi Gregorius fit into his on-the-fly rebuild, providing value in the present while still promising some upside in the future. Even the rejected Kimbrel offer would have netted the Yankees Kimbrel's age-28 through -30 seasons at reasonable salaries.

Aside from the Kimbrel attempt, Cashman held fast last July despite glaring holes, including at second base ("led" by Drew, the Yankees finished 28th in WARP at the position) and in the rotation (where Sabathia suffered through his third straight bad year, Nova failed to return to the heights of 2013 and Chris Capuano, of all people, made a start three days before the deadline). Nevertheless, the Yankees refused to pay the prices required to obtain top available talent like Ben Zobrist or David Price.

This winter's Aroldis Chapman trade runs somewhat counter to this narrative, but not much: The best player Cashman sent to Cincinnati is probably Eric Jagielo, who can hit but isn't much of a defender and may top out as a bench bat. Chapman's price was depressed by the domestic-violence accusation against him, so it's notable that Cashman waited until that price dropped to get into the bidding; ignoring quality of character to acquire talent on the cheap is a move more classically associated with the low-payroll, build-from-within Rays.

While the Yankees have over $100 million committed to the 32-year-old Ellsbury over the next five years, and McCann is also signed into his thirties, those deals don't necessarily defy the claims that the team wants to get younger and more athletic. McCann has been, as noted, a top defensive catcher, and he's only signed through his age-34 season, not into his late 30s like Beltran or Rodriguez. As to the center fielder, Cashman said, "The method to signing [Ellsbury] and [Gardner, also 32] were to be table-setters; to be those guys who can get on base and wreak havoc on the defense and steal some bases for us and provide great defense. It was supposed to start changing the evolution of the picture of this team being only home run oriented. We were trying to improve the defense, trying to improve some of the ways we could plate some runs." Youth, speed and defense is the ideal combination, in other words, but with Ellsbury the Yankees are hoping that he can continue to provide the latter two as he ages into his mid-30s. The execution may or may not work out, as all things in baseball are uncertain, but the theory of diversifying the offense and the roster, at least, is sound.

+++

Maybe the present contract doomsday that finally arrived as a result of the Yankees' spending in 2008 is enough for the team to stick with its professed re-thought tendencies. Maybe their fading offensive numbers in the final three months of the season (see Table 2) will convince them to consider their age just a bit. Maybe Bird's long home runs will entrance the front office, and they will fall out of love with players in their mid-thirties.

TABLE 2

Month	Team OPS+
March-April	110
May	99
June	124
July	126
August	93
September-October	91

Then again, maybe they're stuck in their ways. As the adage goes, denial is a river in the Bronx. ■

—Kenny Ducey (@KennyDucey) is a writer for Sports Illustrated *and Baseball Prospectus who is based in New York.*

HITTERS

Dustin Ackley LF

Born: 2/26/88 Age: 28 Bats: L Throws: R Height: 6'1" Weight: 205

YEAR	TEAM	LVL	AGE	PA	R	2B	3B	HR	RBI	BB	K	SB	CS	AVG/OBP/SLG	TAv	BABIP	BRR	FRAA	WARP
2013	TAC	AAA	25	126	21	8	0	2	14	19	14	0	0	.365/.472/.500	.339	.409	0.5	2B(12): -1.1, CF(9): -0.8	1.3
2013	SEA	MLB	25	427	40	18	2	4	31	37	72	2	3	.253/.319/.341	.251	.301	1.8	2B(53): 4.2, CF(50): -3.2	1.1
2014	SEA	MLB	26	542	64	27	4	14	65	32	90	8	4	.245/.293/.398	.262	.273	0.3	LF(133): 1.8	1.5
2015	SEA	MLB	27	207	22	8	1	6	19	14	38	2	2	.215/.270/.366	.240	.234	-0.2	LF(63): -4.4, CF(21): 0.0	-0.4
2015	NYA	MLB	27	57	6	3	2	4	11	4	7	0	0	.288/.333/.654	.358	.262	-1.4	2B(9): -0.8, 1B(4): 0.0	0.4
2016	*NYA*	*MLB*	*28*	*229*	*29*	*10*	*2*	*6*	*24*	*21*	*39*	*3*	*2*	*.258/.329/.412*	*.260*	*.288*	*0.1*	*LF 0, 1B 0*	*0.7*
2017	*NYA*	*MLB*	*29*	*264*	*31*	*12*	*2*	*7*	*30*	*23*	*45*	*3*	*2*	*.255/.323/.404*	*.255*	*.285*	*0.3*	*LF 0, 1B 1*	*0.7*

Breakout: 0% Improve: 45% Collapse: 4% Attrition: 11% MLB: 89% *Comparables: Andy Dirks, Conor Jackson, Kevin Mench*

Ackley is the kind of guy that people want to believe in. For certain stretches he looks like he knows what he's doing. He has the prospect pedigree, and he has demonstrated pretty much every baseball skill at least once. In his brief tenure with the Yankees he excelled, and although Yankee Stadium might have been something of a balm to what ailed him as a hitter, it's hard to expect a ton going forward. He has whispered many a promise to a fan lost in his smoky eyes, flicked just one extra second-half homer, but he never answers their calls next April. Ackley will let you down, but he's not important enough to break your heart. He's more like your deadbeat cousin who's never going to pay you your 20 bucks back.

Carlos Beltran DH

Born: 4/24/77 Age: 39 Bats: B Throws: R Height: 6'1" Weight: 210

YEAR	TEAM	LVL	AGE	PA	R	2B	3B	HR	RBI	BB	K	SB	CS	AVG/OBP/SLG	TAv	BABIP	BRR	FRAA	WARP
2013	SLN	MLB	36	600	79	30	3	24	84	38	90	2	1	.296/.339/.491	.289	.314	2.0	RF(137): -3.0	2.8
2014	NYA	MLB	37	449	46	23	0	15	49	37	80	3	1	.233/.301/.402	.260	.252	-2.8	RF(32): -0.5, 1B(1): -0.0	0.2
2015	NYA	MLB	38	531	57	34	1	19	67	45	85	0	0	.276/.337/.471	.280	.297	-0.4	RF(123): -15.3	0.4
2016	*NYA*	*MLB*	*39*	*558*	*66*	*27*	*2*	*22*	*76*	*48*	*100*	*3*	*1*	*.260/.325/.452*	*.269*	*.282*	*-0.4*	*RF -7*	*1.0*
2017	*NYA*	*MLB*	*40*	*379*	*46*	*17*	*1*	*12*	*46*	*31*	*68*	*1*	*1*	*.246/.308/.409*	*.250*	*.271*	*-0.4*	*RF -5*	*0.3*

Breakout: 0% Improve: 12% Collapse: 5% Attrition: 11% MLB: 72% *Comparables: Ken Griffey, Torii Hunter, Raul Ibanez*

If you are wringing out a towel, you always have the option of doing a good, thorough job, where you work at it until your hands hurt, or you can just give it a couple of twists and figure it's good enough. The St. Louis Cardinals probably knew there was a little value left in Beltran when they let him go at age 37, but their metaphorical linen closet was stocked. When the Yankees signed him they committed to the tough job of wringing out every drip of value left in his aging body. For a whole year it was a fruitless endeavor, but finally some usefulness oozed out of Beltran during a strong second half. It was a hopeful sign, even if he's a ghost of his former self in the outfield, in that his range is hampered by the curse that requires him to haunt the exact spot where he's positioned.

Greg Bird 1B

Born: 11/9/92 Age: 23 Bats: L Throws: R Height: 6'3" Weight: 220

YEAR	TEAM	LVL	AGE	PA	R	2B	3B	HR	RBI	BB	K	SB	CS	AVG/OBP/SLG	TAv	BABIP	BRR	FRAA	WARP
2013	CSC	A	20	573	84	36	3	20	84	107	132	1	1	.288/.428/.511	.347	.364	-0.5	1B(90): -6.3	5.4
2014	TRN	AA	21	116	16	8	0	7	11	18	27	0	0	.253/.379/.558	.329	.274	-1.0	1B(24): -1.2	0.8
2014	TAM	A+	21	325	36	22	1	7	32	45	70	1	0	.277/.375/.442	.297	.342	-1.2	1B(61): 1.1	1.7
2015	SWB	AAA	22	150	15	7	1	6	23	11	27	0	0	.301/.353/.500	.304	.333	-1.3	1B(29): 0.4	0.8
2015	NYA	MLB	22	178	26	9	0	11	31	19	53	0	0	.261/.343/.529	.312	.319	-1.4	1B(46): 1.0	1.1
2015	TRN	AA	22	212	29	16	0	6	29	24	30	1	1	.258/.358/.445	.302	.279	1.2	1B(41): 2.2	1.6
2016	*NYA*	*MLB*	*23*	*101*	*12*	*5*	*0*	*4*	*14*	*12*	*26*	*0*	*0*	*.246/.338/.454*	*.276*	*.298*	*-0.2*	*1B -0*	*0.3*
2017	*NYA*	*MLB*	*24*	*402*	*55*	*20*	*1*	*16*	*54*	*47*	*104*	*0*	*0*	*.248/.340/.449*	*.273*	*.304*	*-1.0*	*1B -1*	*0.4*

Breakout: 2% Improve: 25% Collapse: 5% Attrition: 20% MLB: 66% *Comparables: Brandon Belt, Jerry Sands, Anthony Rizzo*

If Helen of Troy had a face that launched a thousand ships, Bird had the name that launched a thousand hashtags. Sure, he's young and he can hit, but a large percentage of his meteoric rise to Yankees' folk hero status was the result of fans and headline writers getting enjoyment from the last name "Bird." One wonders whether he would have received the same reception if his name had been Greg Vole, Greg Shrew or Greg Common Suriname Toad. Probably not. Name aside, Bird showed a lot in the finishing stretch, and while it's hard to know exactly how the Yankees plan to fit him in with Teixeira and Rodriguez in place, they'd be wise to find a way.

Starlin Castro SS

Born: 3/24/90 Age: 26 Bats: R Throws: R Height: 6'0" Weight: 190

YEAR	TEAM	LVL	AGE	PA	R	2B	3B	HR	RBI	BB	K	SB	CS	AVG/OBP/SLG	TAv	BABIP	BRR	FRAA	WARP
2013	CHN	MLB	23	705	59	34	2	10	44	30	129	9	6	.245/.284/.347	.228	.290	0.1	SS(159): -5.4	0.0
2014	CHN	MLB	24	569	58	33	1	14	65	35	100	4	4	.292/.339/.438	.278	.337	-2.6	SS(133): 3.8	3.6
2015	CHN	MLB	25	578	52	23	2	11	69	21	91	5	5	.265/.296/.375	.243	.298	-2.2	SS(109): 2.8, 2B(38): 1.7	1.5
2016	*NYA*	*MLB*	*26*	*508*	*54*	*24*	*3*	*12*	*58*	*25*	*81*	*6*	*5*	*.277/.316/.418*	*.258*	*.309*	*-1.3*	*2B 9*	*2.8*
2017	*NYA*	*MLB*	*27*	*469*	*55*	*21*	*2*	*12*	*54*	*26*	*75*	*6*	*4*	*.274/.318/.416*	*.260*	*.305*	*-0.9*	*2B 8*	*2.5*

Breakout: 2% Improve: 52% Collapse: 1% Attrition: 10% MLB: 99% *Comparables: J.J. Hardy, Jose Reyes, Nomar Garciaparra*

"Don't give up yet. He's still young" was long the refrain for Cubs fans hoping Castro would turn a corner, unlock some hitherto-unseen power or plate discipline. Now they can stop worrying about his hitting because Castro is a Yankee, and we can stop fighting about his defense (FRAA, as you can see above, has liked him fine the last two years) because Castro is a second baseman. It's certainly a gamble for New York, as two of Castro's last three seasons have been disasters, but he's still just 26 and has a career .259 TAv, which is why PECOTA is taking the tack it is. There's talent here, enough talent that Castro has been a good player, not just okay but *good*, in four of his six major-league seasons, and his total salary commitment through 2019 is $38 million. Giving up a first-year arbitration-eligible no. 4/5 starter, in light of all that, looks like a worthwhile risk for the Yankees, even as the Cubs were essentially forced by their middle-infield logjam to make a trade.

Stephen Drew SS

Born: 3/16/83 Age: 33 Bats: L Throws: R Height: 6'0" Weight: 190

YEAR	TEAM	LVL	AGE	PA	R	2B	3B	HR	RBI	BB	K	SB	CS	AVG/OBP/SLG	TAv	BABIP	BRR	FRAA	WARP
2013	BOS	MLB	30	501	57	29	8	13	67	54	124	6	0	.253/.333/.443	.282	.320	-0.4	SS(124): -2.8	2.9
2013	PME	AA	30	23	1	2	0	1	4	2	4	0	0	.200/.261/.450	.297	.188	-0.3	SS(5): -0.3	0.1
2014	BOS	MLB	31	145	11	6	1	4	11	14	39	1	1	.176/.255/.328	.212	.216	-0.4	SS(39): 1.4	0.0
2014	NYA	MLB	31	155	7	8	0	3	15	13	36	0	0	.150/.219/.271	.195	.175	-1.7	2B(34): -1.0, SS(12): -0.3	-0.9
2015	NYA	MLB	32	428	43	16	1	17	44	37	71	0	2	.201/.271/.381	.236	.201	-2.7	2B(123): -2.9, SS(15): 0.7	-0.4
2016	*NYA*	*MLB*	*33*	*379*	*40*	*16*	*2*	*10*	*41*	*36*	*86*	*2*	*1*	*.221/.296/.375*	*.237*	*.260*	*-1.5*	*2B -2, SS -0*	*0.2*
2017	*NYA*	*MLB*	*34*	*358*	*40*	*14*	*2*	*10*	*39*	*34*	*83*	*1*	*1*	*.213/.287/.363*	*.231*	*.251*	*-1.4*	*2B -2, SS 0*	*0.9*

Breakout: 1% Improve: 37% Collapse: 8% Attrition: 11% MLB: 95% *Comparables: Lou Whitaker, Mark DeRosa, Mike Fontenot*

Drew managed a rare feat by hitting nearly 20 home runs and playing passable defense up the middle while not looking anything like a major league–caliber player. To achieve this he made a point of making incredibly weak contact on anything that wasn't pulled, and pulling nothing with any break. Yankee Stadium smiles on lefties who try to turn on fastballs, but as long as it remains legal for pitchers to make stuff bend, Drew would be wise to create some sort of backup plan. It's almost as if he thought the home runs he hit would act as flattering garment to hide the profoundly unappealing shape of his season. They did not.

Jacoby Ellsbury CF

Born: 9/11/83 Age: 32 Bats: L Throws: L Height: 6'1" Weight: 195

YEAR	TEAM	LVL	AGE	PA	R	2B	3B	HR	RBI	BB	K	SB	CS	AVG/OBP/SLG	TAv	BABIP	BRR	FRAA	WARP
2013	BOS	MLB	29	636	92	31	8	9	53	47	92	52	4	.298/.355/.426	.277	.341	5.3	CF(134): 5.6	4.3
2014	NYA	MLB	30	635	71	27	5	16	70	49	93	39	5	.271/.328/.419	.278	.296	-1.2	CF(141): 5.1	3.5
2015	NYA	MLB	31	501	66	15	2	7	33	35	86	21	9	.257/.318/.345	.249	.301	4.2	CF(110): -7.7	0.6
2016	*NYA*	*MLB*	*32*	*643*	*91*	*28*	*4*	*16*	*63*	*47*	*98*	*35*	*7*	*.277/.333/.420*	*.264*	*.306*	*1.2*	*CF 3*	*3.1*
2017	*NYA*	*MLB*	*33*	*517*	*62*	*21*	*2*	*13*	*58*	*36*	*82*	*26*	*6*	*.269/.323/.406*	*.256*	*.297*	*1.6*	*CF 3*	*2.1*

Breakout: 1% Improve: 47% Collapse: 2% Attrition: 9% MLB: 97% *Comparables: Angel Pagan, Coco Crisp, Vernon Wells*

It's always a scary moment when players in their 30s scuffle for the first time. It's similar to when you're a kid and you realize that your dad isn't an omnipotent and benevolent deity but just one of billions of guys who have figured out how to reproduce. Ellsbury played through some injuries and he's a good bet to bounce back to a degree, but the cat's out of the bag. No power, more strikeouts and less efficient baserunning are all in his near future. We all knew that Ellsbury was but a mortal man, but for the first time last season he forgot to pick us up from soccer practice.

Benjamin Gamel OF

Born: 5/17/92 Age: 24 Bats: L Throws: L Height: 5'11" Weight: 185

YEAR	TEAM	LVL	AGE	PA	R	2B	3B	HR	RBI	BB	K	SB	CS	AVG/OBP/SLG	TAv	BABIP	BRR	FRAA	WARP
2013	TRN	AA	21	72	5	4	0	1	5	4	18	1	0	.239/.282/.343	.238	.313	0.7	RF(6): -1.0, CF(5): 0.5	0.1
2013	TAM	A+	21	423	50	28	4	3	49	48	77	21	5	.272/.352/.396	.278	.330	1.5	LF(81): -4.1, CF(14): -1.2	1.5
2014	TRN	AA	22	586	58	31	3	2	51	36	88	13	5	.261/.308/.340	.238	.306	1.0	LF(99): -4.5, CF(16): -1.7	-0.7
2015	SWB	AAA	23	551	77	28	14	10	64	46	108	13	5	.300/.358/.472	.293	.364	1.8	CF(74): 1.0, LF(33): 3.5	4.4
2016	*NYA*	*MLB*	*24*	*250*	*29*	*12*	*2*	*5*	*23*	*17*	*57*	*4*	*1*	*.247/.298/.384*	*.237*	*.303*	*0.2*	*CF -0, LF 0*	*0.3*
2017	*NYA*	*MLB*	*25*	*372*	*40*	*19*	*3*	*8*	*39*	*23*	*88*	*6*	*2*	*.239/.289/.382*	*.234*	*.294*	*0.3*	*CF 0, LF 1*	*1.2*

Breakout: 14% Improve: 23% Collapse: 10% Attrition: 35% MLB: 46% *Comparables: Xavier Paul, Jason Pridie, Blake Tekotte*

The reigning International League Rookie of the Year, Gamel is a prototypical fourth outfielder with defensive versatility but no standout tools, unless you count "hitting 'em where they ain't" as a tool. He seemed headed for minor-league free agency, but all of a sudden he batted like a machine-gun turret at Triple-A, forcing himself into the brainstorming session of the Yankees' offseason plans. The former 10th-round pick was eligible for the Rule 5 draft, so the team added him to the 40-man this winter. It would be unfair to say guys like Gamel are a dime a dozen, because he could definitely be useful in the big leagues, but it's very difficult to imagine him succeeding in a full-time role.

Brett Gardner LF

Born: 8/24/83 Age: 32 Bats: L Throws: L Height: 5'10" Weight: 185

YEAR	TEAM	LVL	AGE	PA	R	2B	3B	HR	RBI	BB	K	SB	CS	AVG/OBP/SLG	TAv	BABIP	BRR	FRAA	WARP
2013	NYA	MLB	29	609	81	33	10	8	52	52	127	24	8	.273/.344/.416	.279	.342	3.4	CF(138): -9.2	2.5
2014	NYA	MLB	30	636	87	25	8	17	58	56	134	21	5	.256/.327/.422	.278	.305	4.5	LF(126): -0.6, CF(25): -0.6	3.1
2015	NYA	MLB	31	656	94	26	3	16	66	68	135	20	5	.259/.343/.399	.264	.312	4.7	LF(119): 0.6, CF(40): -2.2	2.3
2016	*NYA*	*MLB*	*32*	*631*	*81*	*25*	*6*	*12*	*58*	*60*	*127*	*21*	*6*	*.259/.336/.395*	*.255*	*.306*	*3.3*	*LF 0*	*2.0*
2017	*NYA*	*MLB*	*33*	*553*	*64*	*23*	*5*	*10*	*57*	*52*	*110*	*16*	*5*	*.252/.329/.384*	*.250*	*.296*	*3.3*	*LF 0*	*1.8*

Breakout: 2% Improve: 41% Collapse: 1% Attrition: 10% MLB: 95% *Comparables: Pete Rose, Minnie Minoso, Jose Cruz*

To say Gardner was Gardner-esque would be both a colossal cop-out and also by far the best way to describe his performance. A few home runs, a few steals, tough at-bats, solid defense... his routine is pretty much old hat by now. How you interpret that says a lot about you as a person. Perhaps you are bored by this predictability and watching him doesn't give you the kind of novel experiences you crave. Perhaps your life is a whirling vortex of frightening chaos and Gardner is the one constant you cling to as everything seems to fall apart around you. Either way works. The first one is probably a little bit healthier, as that vortex thing doesn't sound great, but really it's up to you.

Didi Gregorius SS

Born: 2/18/90 Age: 26 Bats: L Throws: R Height: 6'2" Weight: 205

YEAR	TEAM	LVL	AGE	PA	R	2B	3B	HR	RBI	BB	K	SB	CS	AVG/OBP/SLG	TAv	BABIP	BRR	FRAA	WARP
2013	RNO	AAA	23	33	7	2	0	2	2	2	1	1	0	.387/.424/.645	.332	.357	-0.6	SS(1): 0.2	0.3
2013	ARI	MLB	23	404	47	16	3	7	28	37	65	0	2	.252/.332/.373	.262	.290	-4.5	SS(100): -8.6	0.3
2014	ARI	MLB	24	299	35	9	5	6	27	22	52	3	0	.226/.290/.363	.245	.257	4.5	SS(67): 0.3, 2B(11): 1.2	1.4
2014	RNO	AAA	24	260	42	14	4	3	25	24	26	3	0	.310/.389/.447	.280	.338	1.0	2B(38): -2.8, SS(19): 1.8	1.4
2015	NYA	MLB	25	578	57	24	2	9	56	33	85	5	3	.265/.318/.370	.251	.297	1.0	SS(155): 1.2	2.1
2016	*NYA*	*MLB*	*26*	*553*	*63*	*22*	*4*	*12*	*53*	*37*	*89*	*4*	*2*	*.255/.314/.386*	*.248*	*.284*	*0.4*	*SS 0*	*2.1*
2017	*NYA*	*MLB*	*27*	*540*	*61*	*21*	*4*	*12*	*57*	*36*	*91*	*3*	*2*	*.253/.312/.386*	*.247*	*.284*	*0.4*	*SS 0*	*2.5*

Breakout: 3% Improve: 47% Collapse: 14% Attrition: 23% MLB: 97% *Comparables: Brandon Crawford, Daniel Descalso, Jemile Weeks*

Depending on what defensive metrics you use, or the color of your lenses, you could argue that Gregorius was the best every-day player on the Yankees last season. If you had predicted that coming into the year you would have been put in a straitjacket, frozen in carbonite and then shot directly into the sun. Excessive? Yes. Necessary? Definitely. No one wants to live in a world of hot takes. Gregorius succeeds in his role of first post-Jeter shortstop by being everything his predecessor wasn't offensively and defensively. He even has the decency to be left-handed as well. You couldn't ask for much more. Technically you could, but that's also punishable by freeze-drying.

Chase Headley 3B

Born: 5/9/84 Age: 32 Bats: B Throws: R Height: 6'2" Weight: 210

YEAR	TEAM	LVL	AGE	PA	R	2B	3B	HR	RBI	BB	K	SB	CS	AVG/OBP/SLG	TAv	BABIP	BRR	FRAA	WARP
2013	SDN	MLB	29	600	59	35	2	13	50	67	142	8	4	.250/.347/.400	.278	.319	-4.1	3B(140): -9.8	1.6
2014	SDN	MLB	30	307	27	12	1	7	32	22	73	4	1	.229/.296/.355	.243	.285	0.8	3B(76): -2.6	0.3
2014	NYA	MLB	30	224	28	8	0	6	17	29	49	3	2	.262/.371/.398	.286	.324	0.9	3B(51): 6.2, 1B(7): 1.3	2.2
2015	NYA	MLB	31	642	74	29	1	11	62	51	135	0	2	.259/.324/.369	.245	.317	-0.8	3B(155): 3.7, 1B(1): -0.0	1.4
2016	*NYA*	*MLB*	*32*	*568*	*65*	*26*	*1*	*16*	*67*	*58*	*128*	*5*	*3*	*.260/.342/.411*	*.267*	*.317*	*-0.9*	*3B 0*	*2.0*
2017	*NYA*	*MLB*	*33*	*533*	*66*	*25*	*1*	*14*	*59*	*54*	*122*	*4*	*2*	*.257/.340/.399*	*.261*	*.318*	*-0.8*	*3B 0*	*1.3*

Breakout: 2% Improve: 34% Collapse: 8% Attrition: 12% MLB: 97% *Comparables: Morgan Ensberg, David Freese, Scott Rolen*

To say Headley is stuck in a cosmic vortex of adequacy wouldn't be entirely fair to the third baseman, but it wouldn't be completely unfair either. While his production dipped a bit and he had some strange early-season fielding yips, he's still a fine starter, in all the admirable and pejorative uses of the word "fine." He's a good fielder, and his hitting is within spitting difference of average, but he's also too old to get better and relatively well compensated, so those characteristics don't get the blood pumping. With Headley at third you don't have to worry about the position, but he's unlikely to impact the fortunes of the Yankees in a profound way for good or ill in 2016.

Slade Heathcott OF

Born: 9/28/90 Age: 25 Bats: L Throws: L Height: 6'1" Weight: 190

YEAR	TEAM	LVL	AGE	PA	R	2B	3B	HR	RBI	BB	K	SB	CS	AVG/OBP/SLG	TAv	BABIP	BRR	FRAA	WARP
2013	TRN	AA	22	444	59	22	7	8	49	36	107	15	8	.261/.327/.411	.274	.336	1.7	CF(90): -2.2	2.0
2014	TRN	AA	23	37	4	2	0	0	1	3	13	0	1	.182/.250/.242	.207	.300	-0.7	RF(5): -0.3, CF(3): -0.3	-0.3
2015	SWB	AAA	24	271	25	7	3	2	27	18	61	6	5	.267/.315/.343	.242	.344	1.3	CF(36): 2.1, LF(15): -0.7	0.8
2015	NYA	MLB	24	30	6	2	0	2	8	2	5	0	1	.400/.429/.720	.386	.421	0.4	RF(9): -0.2, CF(8): 0.2	0.5
2016	*NYA*	*MLB*	*25*	*250*	*30*	*10*	*2*	*6*	*24*	*15*	*66*	*4*	*3*	*.240/.289/.380*	*.234*	*.305*	*-0.3*	*CF -1, LF -0*	*-0.1*
2017	*NYA*	*MLB*	*26*	*227*	*25*	*9*	*2*	*6*	*24*	*14*	*60*	*4*	*3*	*.241/.290/.376*	*.234*	*.307*	*-0.1*	*CF -1, LF 0*	*0.5*

Breakout: 9% Improve: 28% Collapse: 8% Attrition: 33% MLB: 51% *Comparables: Jason Pridie, Xavier Paul, Shane Victorino*

Heathcott battled everything from recurring injuries to alcohol-abuse issues to make the major leagues, and once there he hit the cover off the ball for a week before straining a quadriceps. What initially appeared to be a day-to-day injury turned into a month-long grade-two strain. It took Heathcott four months to heal. He's undoubtedly talented, with raw power and raw speed, but there's a reason it's still raw: Health is also a skill and he does not have it. While it's possible he finds his way and finds a role in the majors down the road, it's only a matter of time before these wounds start chipping away at his underlying skills. If they do, at least we'll have a week to remember him by; not everyone gets that.

Aaron Hicks CF

Born: 10/2/89 Age: 26 Bats: B Throws: R Height: 6'2" Weight: 210

YEAR	TEAM	LVL	AGE	PA	R	2B	3B	HR	RBI	BB	K	SB	CS	AVG/OBP/SLG	TAv	BABIP	BRR	FRAA	WARP
2013	ROC	AAA	23	82	7	4	2	0	5	10	21	1	0	.222/.317/.333	.242	.314	0.2	CF(19): -0.9	0.0
2013	MIN	MLB	23	313	37	11	3	8	27	24	84	9	3	.192/.259/.338	.237	.241	1.1	CF(81): 5.8	1.0
2014	MIN	MLB	24	225	22	8	0	1	18	36	56	4	3	.215/.341/.274	.245	.300	-0.8	CF(57): 6.8, LF(6): -0.5	0.9
2014	ROC	AAA	24	84	9	5	0	1	8	9	13	1	1	.278/.349/.389	.247	.317	-0.6	CF(16): -3.2, RF(4): -0.1	-0.2
2014	NBR	AA	24	178	30	11	1	4	21	28	27	2	3	.297/.404/.466	.311	.336	1.9	CF(27): 0.3, RF(9): 0.6	1.8
2015	MIN	MLB	25	390	48	11	3	11	33	34	66	13	3	.256/.323/.398	.253	.285	-0.9	CF(88): 6.5, RF(16): -0.6	1.5
2015	ROC	AAA	25	168	26	13	4	3	20	17	30	2	1	.342/.405/.544	.345	.407	1.4	CF(24): 4.3, RF(9): -0.3	2.5
2016	*NYA*	*MLB*	*26*	*278*	*36*	*11*	*2*	*7*	*27*	*29*	*62*	*6*	*2*	*.241/.323/.388*	*.253*	*.290*	*-0.3*	*RF -3, CF 2*	*0.4*
2017	*NYA*	*MLB*	*27*	*378*	*46*	*15*	*2*	*10*	*42*	*41*	*83*	*8*	*3*	*.238/.324/.388*	*.253*	*.284*	*-0.2*	*RF -4, CF 2*	*0.7*

Breakout: 6% Improve: 56% Collapse: 10% Attrition: 14% MLB: 97% *Comparables: David DeJesus, Dexter Fowler, Nate McLouth*

Good fourth outfielders have underrated value to contending teams, which is great news for Hicks. He was almost a SHINO (Switch Hitter In Name Only) from the time he first attained the high minors until the early part of 2015. He had a terrible swing from the left side, flat and long and slow all at the same time, but a brief experiment with becoming a full-time right-handed hitter only proved that Hicks needed the platoon advantage to maintain a decent approach. He rebuilt that swing over the winter prior to 2015, and the results were a bit better. Unfortunately, "a bit better" still leaves Hicks far short of an acceptable hitter against right-handed pitchers. He could be an asset with his glove and legs, but he's a short-side platoon bat. In his favor: He takes over for Chris Young, who was the same, only worse.

Eric Jagielo 3B

Born: 5/17/92 Age: 24 Bats: L Throws: R Height: 6'2" Weight: 215

YEAR	TEAM	LVL	AGE	PA	R	2B	3B	HR	RBI	BB	K	SB	CS	AVG/OBP/SLG	TAv	BABIP	BRR	FRAA	WARP
2013	STA	A-	21	218	19	14	1	6	27	26	54	0	0	.266/.376/.451	.315	.344	-1.9	3B(42): -0.5	1.6
2014	TAM	A+	22	359	43	14	0	16	54	38	93	0	0	.259/.354/.460	.282	.315	-1.1	3B(62): -9.8	0.8
2015	TRN	AA	23	248	36	16	2	9	35	18	58	0	0	.284/.347/.495	.316	.342	2.5	3B(39): -7.6, 1B(3): -0.1	1.6
2016	*NYA*	*MLB*	*24*	*250*	*28*	*10*	*1*	*10*	*33*	*18*	*76*	*0*	*0*	*.227/.297/.412*	*.249*	*.291*	*-0.4*	*3B -8, 1B 0*	*-0.5*
2017	*NYA*	*MLB*	*25*	*265*	*33*	*11*	*1*	*11*	*34*	*19*	*80*	*0*	*0*	*.223/.293/.406*	*.246*	*.283*	*-0.6*	*3B -8, 1B 0*	*-0.3*

Breakout: 2% Improve: 16% Collapse: 14% Attrition: 22% MLB: 41% *Comparables: Mat Gamel, Alex Liddi, Chase Headley*

Big left-handed power hitters are always going to look good in pinstripes, and Jagielo fits that description to a tee. Getting his first taste of the upper minors, he performed admirably until a knee injury ended his season in June. The 2013 first-rounder has moved quickly despite an uncommonly large lot of injuries, including a broken zygomatic arch (one of the most futuristic-sounding ailments in existence) in 2014. He can rake; staying on the field and proving he can field are the keys to his ascension.

Garrett Jones 1B

Born: 6/21/81 Age: 35 Bats: L Throws: L Height: 6'5" Weight: 235

YEAR	TEAM	LVL	AGE	PA	R	2B	3B	HR	RBI	BB	K	SB	CS	AVG/OBP/SLG	TAv	BABIP	BRR	FRAA	WARP
2013	PIT	MLB	32	440	41	26	2	15	51	31	101	2	0	.233/.289/.419	.260	.271	-3.7	1B(83): 0.7, RF(32): -3.0	-0.1
2014	MIA	MLB	33	547	59	33	2	15	53	46	116	0	1	.246/.309/.411	.267	.290	-2.1	1B(129): -4.9, RF(9): -1.4	0.1
2015	NYA	MLB	34	152	12	4	1	5	17	8	37	0	0	.215/.257/.361	.224	.255	-0.4	RF(24): -1.2, 1B(21): 1.2	-0.4
2016	*NYA*	*MLB*	*35*	*250*	*28*	*13*	*1*	*10*	*34*	*19*	*57*	*0*	*0*	*.241/.301/.432*	*.255*	*.276*	*-1.1*	*1B -0, RF -2*	*0.0*
2017	*NYA*	*MLB*	*36*	*217*	*26*	*11*	*1*	*8*	*27*	*17*	*50*	*0*	*0*	*.239/.299/.419*	*.251*	*.276*	*-1.0*	*1B 0, RF -2*	*0.0*

Breakout: 3% Improve: 32% Collapse: 9% Attrition: 16% MLB: 89% *Comparables: Dave Winfield, Cliff Floyd, Michael Cuddyer*

Put simply, the Yankees gambled on Jones last year and they lost. He had one job: He needed to hit right-handers hard to be valuable and he did not. It was not a disastrous outcome for the team, and if most people who gambled didn't lose, gambling wouldn't really exist. Once Ackley arrived at the trade deadline, the team found Jones expendable and released him, and he stayed released the rest of the season. The last time the left-handed slugger was useful was 2012 and it would be a surprise to see him help another team in the future. For a guy with the most stereotypical Welsh rugby player name imaginable he had a good run in the major leagues.

Aaron Judge RF

Born: 4/26/92 Age: 24 Bats: R Throws: R Height: 6'7" Weight: 275

YEAR	TEAM	LVL	AGE	PA	R	2B	3B	HR	RBI	BB	K	SB	CS	AVG/OBP/SLG	TAv	BABIP	BRR	FRAA	WARP
2014	CSC	A	22	278	36	15	2	9	45	39	59	1	0	.333/.428/.530	.341	.408	-2.8	RF(55): 2.1	2.9
2014	TAM	A+	22	285	44	9	2	8	33	50	72	0	0	.283/.411/.442	.302	.377	1.8	RF(61): 8.7	2.9
2015	TRN	AA	23	280	36	16	3	12	44	24	70	1	0	.284/.350/.516	.316	.345	2.6	RF(52): 10.5	3.6
2015	SWB	AAA	23	260	27	10	0	8	28	29	74	6	2	.224/.308/.373	.247	.289	-0.2	RF(50): 7.6, CF(8): -0.4	0.8
2016	*NYA*	*MLB*	*24*	*250*	*29*	*10*	*1*	*10*	*33*	*25*	*77*	*2*	*1*	*.233/.315/.415*	*.257*	*.307*	*-0.2*	*RF 5, CF -0*	*1.0*
2017	*NYA*	*MLB*	*25*	*397*	*52*	*16*	*1*	*16*	*52*	*41*	*121*	*2*	*1*	*.236/.318/.426*	*.260*	*.307*	*-0.4*	*RF 7, CF 0*	*1.5*

Breakout: 2% Improve: 14% Collapse: 9% Attrition: 14% MLB: 37% *Comparables: Nolan Reimold, Matt LaPorta, Casper Wells*

To say Judge is Dellin Betances with a big wooden stick would be a gross oversimplification, but it's not a bad way to conceptualize the Yankees' top prospect. The 24-year-old is massive, and his size has granted him power without robbing him of the athleticism to be a solid defensive outfielder. Considering the sheer volume of his strike zone it's also impressive how many walks he's been able to draw in the minor leagues. Judge didn't exactly light up Triple-A in his first exposure to the level, but that's nitpicking. He proved that he could excel in the high minors and there's very little reason to believe, based on his pedigree, that he can't be a big-league regular and a GIF mainstay as soon as this year.

Pete Kozma SS

Born: 4/11/88 Age: 28 Bats: R Throws: R Height: 6'0" Weight: 190

YEAR	TEAM	LVL	AGE	PA	R	2B	3B	HR	RBI	BB	K	SB	CS	AVG/OBP/SLG	TAv	BABIP	BRR	FRAA	WARP
2013	SLN	MLB	25	448	44	20	0	1	35	34	91	3	1	.217/.275/.273	.203	.274	3.2	SS(139): 19.0, LF(1): 0.0	1.6
2014	MEM	AAA	26	437	59	23	0	8	54	41	61	10	7	.248/.330/.372	.265	.275	1.6	SS(96): 5.1, 3B(11): 1.0	2.8
2014	SLN	MLB	26	26	4	3	0	0	0	3	4	0	0	.304/.385/.435	.297	.368	0.8	SS(8): 0.3, 2B(6): -0.3	0.3
2015	SLN	MLB	27	111	15	0	0	0	2	10	21	3	1	.152/.236/.152	.159	.192	2.7	SS(31): 1.2, 2B(17): 0.1	-0.4
2016	*NYA*	*MLB*	*28*	*154*	*14*	*6*	*0*	*2*	*13*	*12*	*31*	*2*	*1*	*.214/.277/.316*	*.211*	*.253*	*1.0*	*SS 3, 3B 1*	*0.3*
2017	*NYA*	*MLB*	*29*	*285*	*28*	*10*	*1*	*4*	*25*	*22*	*59*	*4*	*2*	*.214/.276/.315*	*.213*	*.255*	*2.0*	*SS 5, 3B 1*	*1.9*

Breakout: 6% Improve: 20% Collapse: 10% Attrition: 19% MLB: 44% *Comparables: Ramon Santiago, Anderson Hernandez, Brandon Fahey*

Sometimes the best summation of a player's season is his highlights page. Go to Baseball Savant, type in Kozma's name, and you'll find some impressive videos: a diving catch here, a stab and throw from deep in the hole there, and so on. All thrilling, all featuring Kozma in a cameo role as Frustrated Hitter. Small parts are often how stars begin their career—heck, Dave Chappelle was in *Con Air*—but Kozma is no star in the making. He instead serves as baseball's ultimate supporting cast member; around to help others achieve their glory without ever taking a moment to claim his own—not because he's unselfish, but because he can't; forget the season, that's the story of his entire career.

Jorge Mateo SS

Born: 6/23/95 Age: 21 Bats: R Throws: R Height: 6'0" Weight: 188

YEAR	TEAM	LVL	AGE	PA	R	2B	3B	HR	RBI	BB	K	SB	CS	AVG/OBP/SLG	TAv	BABIP	BRR	FRAA	WARP
2015	TAM	A+	20	91	15	5	3	0	7	7	18	11	2	.321/.374/.452	.313	.409	2.3	SS(20): 0.0	1.1
2015	CSC	A	20	409	51	18	8	2	33	36	80	71	15	.268/.338/.378	.277	.338	4.1	SS(78): -0.9	2.6
2016	*NYA*	*MLB*	*21*	*250*	*35*	*9*	*2*	*5*	*18*	*15*	*67*	*20*	*6*	*.222/.273/.340*	*.216*	*.288*	*2.3*	*SS 1*	*0.3*
2017	*NYA*	*MLB*	*22*	*341*	*36*	*13*	*3*	*7*	*34*	*22*	*88*	*28*	*8*	*.230/.283/.357*	*.226*	*.293*	*4.5*	*SS 1*	*2.1*

Breakout: 6% Improve: 8% Collapse: 0% Attrition: 3% MLB: 8% *Comparables: Tim Beckham, Yamaico Navarro, Asdrubal Cabrera*

On a team coming off two decades of Derek Jeter, being anointed the "shortstop of the future" is pretty daunting, but also quite the accomplishment. After missing most of 2014 with a broken finger, he bounced back to not only reach High-A but excel there. Some have graded Mateo's speed as a true 80 and it plays up on the basepaths and in the field, where his range is impressive. His ceiling is giving some kid 15 years from now very big shoes to fill.

Brian McCann C

Born: 2/20/84 Age: 32 Bats: L Throws: R Height: 6'3" Weight: 220

YEAR	TEAM	LVL	AGE	PA	R	2B	3B	HR	RBI	BB	K	SB	CS	AVG/OBP/SLG	TAv	BABIP	BRR	FRAA	WARP
2013	ATL	MLB	29	402	43	13	0	20	57	39	66	0	1	.256/.336/.461	.288	.261	-1.7	C(92): 9.8	3.9
2014	NYA	MLB	30	538	57	15	1	23	75	32	77	0	0	.232/.286/.406	.258	.231	-3.6	C(108): 15.7, 1B(16): -1.1	3.2
2015	NYA	MLB	31	535	68	15	1	26	94	52	97	0	0	.232/.320/.437	.270	.235	-4.5	C(126): -0.8, 1B(10): -0.1	2.4
2016	*NYA*	*MLB*	*32*	*599*	*73*	*19*	*1*	*28*	*86*	*53*	*100*	*1*	*0*	*.245/.318/.442*	*.264*	*.250*	*-3.2*	*C 8*	*3.5*
2017	*NYA*	*MLB*	*33*	*517*	*68*	*15*	*1*	*23*	*69*	*43*	*91*	*0*	*0*	*.234/.304/.417*	*.251*	*.242*	*-3.0*	*C 7*	*2.5*

Breakout: 1% Improve: 19% Collapse: 6% Attrition: 11% MLB: 97% *Comparables: Victor Martinez, Ramon Hernandez, Ted Simmons*

YEAR	TEAM	P. COUNT	FRM RUNS	BLK RUNS	THRW RUNS	TOT RUNS
2013	ATL	12622	10.3	0.5	-0.4	10.4
2014	NYA	14665	9.9	0.5	2.4	12.7
2015	NYA	17347	-3.9	0.6	0.6	-2.7
2016	*NYA*	*19455*	*4.3*	*0.7*	*1.2*	*6.2*
2017	*NYA*	*16802*	*2.6*	*0.5*	*0.9*	*4.0*

There's a widely held assumption that left-handed pull hitters and Yankee Stadium mix like olive oil and balsamic vinegar, thanks to the park's scandalously short porch and a perhaps Snopesable "air tunnel" effect. As a result, when McCann came to the Yankees it seemed like a forgone conclusion he would post career-high power numbers. He did, though 26 isn't the sexiest number and his overall production lagged behind his Atlanta days. After two years it seems clear McCann's home park won't elevate him to another offensive plane, and he may be doomed to be best known as a sheriff who dedicated his life to the unwritten law. Still a pretty great baseball player.

Rob Refsnyder 2B

Born: 3/26/91 Age: 25 Bats: R Throws: R Height: 6'1" Weight: 205

YEAR	TEAM	LVL	AGE	PA	R	2B	3B	HR	RBI	BB	K	SB	CS	AVG/OBP/SLG	TAv	BABIP	BRR	FRAA	WARP
2013	CSC	A	22	62	9	4	1	0	6	6	12	7	0	.370/.452/.481	.394	.476	0.1	2B(13): -1.5	0.9
2013	TAM	A+	22	511	66	28	2	6	51	78	70	16	6	.283/.408/.404	.303	.326	-1.6	2B(95): -8.3	2.7
2014	SWB	AAA	23	333	47	19	1	8	33	41	67	4	4	.300/.389/.456	.288	.364	-0.8	2B(64): -4.5, RF(9): -1.1	1.3
2014	TRN	AA	23	244	35	19	5	6	30	14	38	5	5	.342/.385/.548	.329	.391	-2.2	2B(58): 4.9	2.8
2015	SWB	AAA	24	525	66	28	2	9	56	56	73	12	2	.271/.359/.402	.284	.302	3.1	2B(107): 8.8	3.9
2015	NYA	MLB	24	47	3	3	0	2	5	3	7	2	0	.302/.348/.512	.268	.324	-0.8	2B(15): 0.5	0.1
2016	*NYA*	*MLB*	*25*	*89*	*10*	*5*	*0*	*2*	*11*	*9*	*18*	*1*	*1*	*.264/.344/.425*	*.272*	*.310*	*0.0*	*2B 0*	*0.5*
2017	*NYA*	*MLB*	*26*	*294*	*36*	*15*	*1*	*8*	*34*	*26*	*58*	*4*	*2*	*.263/.336/.421*	*.266*	*.307*	*-0.1*	*2B 1*	*1.1*

Breakout: 3% Improve: 17% Collapse: 15% Attrition: 35% MLB: 62% *Comparables: Cord Phelps, Tommy La Stella, Vince Belnome*

Refsnyder commands the strike zone very well, has a little power, a little speed and is learning to play a competent second base. He's got all the makings of a big-league contributor, and certainly looked the part in his brief cameo. He's probably not a star, but he's also probably not nothing. It's the second part of that sentence that had the faithful excited after the swamp of incompetency at the keystone since Robinson Cano skipped town. They were drawn to Refsnyder like a starving man to a hot dog. And then the Yankees went and got Starlin Castro, putting us all in the position of awkwardly putting the hot dog back.

Alex Rodriguez 3B

Born: 7/27/75 Age: 40 Bats: R Throws: R Height: 6'3" Weight: 225

YEAR	TEAM	LVL	AGE	PA	R	2B	3B	HR	RBI	BB	K	SB	CS	AVG/OBP/SLG	TAv	BABIP	BRR	FRAA	WARP
2013	NYA	MLB	37	181	21	7	0	7	19	23	43	4	2	.244/.348/.423	.273	.292	-1.0	3B(27): 0.7	0.7
2013	TAM	A+	37	20	2	1	0	0	3	1	5	0	0	.176/.300/.235	.193	.250	-0.6	3B(3): -0.0	-0.2
2015	NYA	MLB	39	620	83	22	1	33	86	84	145	4	0	.250/.356/.486	.292	.278	-2.1	3B(4): -0.1, 1B(2): -0.0	2.5
2016	*NYA*	*MLB*	*40*	*577*	*71*	*21*	*1*	*22*	*76*	*64*	*133*	*6*	*1*	*.245/.336/.422*	*.268*	*.287*	*-1.5*	*3B -0*	*1.3*
2017	*NYA*	*MLB*	*41*	*395*	*50*	*13*	*1*	*13*	*46*	*43*	*96*	*3*	*1*	*.229/.321/.384*	*.251*	*.275*	*-1.2*	*3B 0*	*0.9*

Breakout: 0% Improve: 17% Collapse: 9% Attrition: 14% MLB: 71% *Comparables: Jorge Posada, Matt Stairs, Edgar Martinez*

From a baseball perspective there is no way a sane person could describe Rodriguez's season as disappointing. Layoffs like his would destroy mortal men, but A-Rod returned to the lead with a vengeance and became the personification of "old man strength," even if he sputtered a bit down the stretch. However, from a fan's perspective there was a bit of a letdown as Rodriguez missed the chance to be the greatest villain in the North American sporting landscape. LeBron James dipped his toes in the waters of villainy with "The Decision" and the Tom Brady-Bill Belichick combo can always be counted on to be the baddies, but Rodriguez had transcendent potential. He had the chance to come back with his trademark detached arrogance with a heavy side of unapologetic bluster, but he did not. Sure, he attracted a few boos here and there, but he never leaned into them like a true heel. Instead he was kind of a model citizen, which was the biggest black mark on his season in terms of entertainment value. The worst thing he did all year was break a TV in the FOX studios with an errant throw of the football. What a wasted opportunity.

Austin Romine C

Born: 11/22/88 Age: 27 Bats: R Throws: R Height: 6'0" Weight: 215

YEAR	TEAM	LVL	AGE	PA	R	2B	3B	HR	RBI	BB	K	SB	CS	AVG/OBP/SLG	TAv	BABIP	BRR	FRAA	WARP
2013	NYA	MLB	24	148	15	9	0	1	10	8	37	1	0	.207/.255/.296	.189	.276	1.4	C(59): 3.0	0.1
2013	SWB	AAA	24	46	5	0	0	1	4	4	12	0	0	.333/.391/.405	.282	.448	-0.2	C(14): -0.1	0.3
2014	NYA	MLB	25	13	2	1	0	0	1	0	4	0	0	.231/.231/.308	.189	.333	-0.1	C(3): -0.2, 1B(1): -0.0	-0.1
2014	SWB	AAA	25	313	33	17	0	6	33	24	54	1	0	.242/.300/.365	.223	.279	-0.7	C(62): -2.4, 1B(13): -0.6	-0.4
2015	SWB	AAA	26	366	38	19	0	7	49	22	53	0	1	.260/.311/.379	.255	.289	1.3	C(75): 5.6, 1B(10): -0.7	1.9
2015	NYA	MLB	26	2	0	0	0	0	0	0	0	0	0	.000/.000/.000	.020	.000	0.0	1B(1): 0.2	0.0
2016	*NYA*	*MLB*	*27*	*97*	*10*	*4*	*0*	*2*	*10*	*6*	*20*	*0*	*0*	*.240/.290/.370*	*.231*	*.280*	*-0.2*	*C -0*	*0.1*
2017	*NYA*	*MLB*	*28*	*190*	*20*	*8*	*0*	*4*	*19*	*11*	*41*	*0*	*0*	*.227/.277/.353*	*.223*	*.266*	*-0.5*	*C -1*	*0.6*

Breakout: 6% Improve: 18% Collapse: 21% Attrition: 35% MLB: 46% *Comparables: Humberto Quintero, Koyie Hill, Wyatt Toregas*

YEAR	TEAM	P. COUNT	FRM RUNS	BLK RUNS	THRW RUNS	TOT RUNS
2013	NYA	6493	3.4	-0.3	-0.2	2.9
2013	SWB	1606	0.2	-0.1	0.0	0.2
2014	NYA	244	-0.2	0.0	0.0	-0.2
2014	SWB	8934	-0.3	-0.3	-1.7	-2.2
2015	SWB	10657	7.7	-0.1	-0.4	7.2
2016	*NYA*	*3883*	*0.2*	*-0.1*	*-0.2*	*-0.1*
2017	*NYA*	*7594*	*0.0*	*-0.2*	*-0.5*	*-0.7*

Romine has seen backup catchers come and go over the years, been leapfrogged by All-Stars and busts. Now, with J.R. Murphy gone to Minnesota, the 2010 All-Star Futures Game catcher finds himself competing for a roster spot again, but only until Gary Sanchez comes to take his locker. Then he'll be back in Triple-A, hitting just enough to avoid being booed and keeping the ball from rolling to the backstop with every pitch. It'll be enough to get him into the fourth row of team photographs for a few more years.

Gary Sanchez C

Born: 12/2/92 Age: 23 Bats: R Throws: R Height: 6'2" Weight: 230

YEAR	TEAM	LVL	AGE	PA	R	2B	3B	HR	RBI	BB	K	SB	CS	AVG/OBP/SLG	TAv	BABIP	BRR	FRAA	WARP
2013	TAM	A+	20	399	38	21	0	13	61	28	71	3	1	.254/.313/.420	.259	.280	-0.3	C(76): 0.8, 1B(1): -0.0	1.6
2013	TRN	AA	20	110	12	6	0	2	10	13	16	0	0	.250/.364/.380	.285	.280	-0.5	C(20): 0.1	0.7
2014	TRN	AA	21	477	48	19	0	13	65	43	91	1	1	.270/.338/.406	.283	.314	-2.6	C(93): 8.3	3.8
2015	NYA	MLB	22	2	0	0	0	0	0	0	1	0	0	.000/.000/.000	.033	.000	0.0		0.0
2015	TRN	AA	22	254	33	14	0	12	36	18	50	6	0	.262/.319/.476	.297	.285	-0.6	C(54): 1.4	2.2
2015	SWB	AAA	22	146	17	9	0	6	26	11	28	1	2	.295/.349/.500	.293	.330	-0.2	C(29): 2.7	1.3
2016	*NYA*	*MLB*	*23*	*33*	*4*	*1*	*0*	*1*	*4*	*2*	*8*	*0*	*0*	*.242/.298/.418*	*.253*	*.282*	*-0.1*	*C -0*	*0.1*
2017	*NYA*	*MLB*	*24*	*267*	*33*	*12*	*0*	*10*	*33*	*21*	*63*	*1*	*0*	*.235/.301/.405*	*.249*	*.275*	*-0.6*	*C -3*	*0.7*

Breakout: 8% Improve: 16% Collapse: 5% Attrition: 27% MLB: 45% *Comparables: Devin Mesoraco, Travis d'Arnaud, Yasmani Grandal*

YEAR	TEAM	P. COUNT	FRM RUNS	BLK RUNS	THRW RUNS	TOT RUNS
2014	TRN	13230	6.8	-1.4	1.9	7.3
2015	SWB	3954	3.0	0.0	0.0	3.0
2015	TRN	7918	0.5	0.3	0.7	1.5
2016	*NYA*	*1207*	*-0.4*	*0.0*	*0.0*	*-0.4*
2017	*NYA*	*9778*	*-3.6*	*-0.3*	*0.3*	*-3.5*

There's not a lot more Sanchez can do to prove he is capable of using a large piece of wood to propel baseballs a great distance. Unfortunately, as a catcher that's only one component of his job description. While he's not old for a prospect by any means, it does seem like he's been around for a long time. The debates about him are tired at this point and the consensus is simple: bat good; defense bad/apathetic/lazy. Can he turn the corner with the glove? If he doesn't, will the bat be enough to make an impact at first base or as a DH? It feels like we should have some answers by now, but we really don't. The excision of Murphy and Sanchez's performance in the AFL make the Magic 8 Ball optimistic.

Mark Teixeira 1B

Born: 4/11/80 Age: 36 Bats: B Throws: R Height: 6'3" Weight: 225

YEAR	TEAM	LVL	AGE	PA	R	2B	3B	HR	RBI	BB	K	SB	CS	AVG/OBP/SLG	TAv	BABIP	BRR	FRAA	WARP
2013	NYA	MLB	33	63	5	1	0	3	12	8	19	0	0	.151/.270/.340	.231	.156	0.1	1B(14): 0.5	-0.1
2014	NYA	MLB	34	508	56	14	0	22	62	58	109	1	1	.216/.313/.398	.265	.233	0.3	1B(117): -3.6	0.4
2015	NYA	MLB	35	462	57	22	0	31	79	59	85	2	0	.255/.357/.548	.313	.246	-3.8	1B(108): 3.3	3.0
2016	*NYA*	*MLB*	*36*	*543*	*70*	*21*	*1*	*27*	*81*	*60*	*103*	*2*	*1*	*.238/.330/.458*	*.275*	*.246*	*-1.4*	*1B 1*	*1.7*
2017	*NYA*	*MLB*	*37*	*422*	*57*	*15*	*1*	*19*	*58*	*43*	*80*	*0*	*0*	*.231/.316/.430*	*.261*	*.241*	*-1.3*	*1B 1*	*0.4*

Breakout: 1% Improve: 25% Collapse: 4% Attrition: 6% MLB: 87% *Comparables: Paul Konerko, Stan Musial, Travis Hafner*

When future baseball enthusiasts look back at the 2015 season, it's likely they'll forget that Teixeira was a legitimate MVP candidate for a time. In July, his last full month before going down with a leg fracture, he hit .333/.442/.724 and carried the Yankees to a 17-7 record. If he had been able to stay healthy, Teixeira's magnificent season might have been the magnum opus of a chronically under-appreciated star leading a group of resurgent veteran over-achievers to glory. Instead he was replaced by a more-than-competent Greg Bird and the Yankees ended up getting pulled into the violent riptide that was the Blue Jays' second-half run. Sometimes, life just isn't remotely fair.

Mason Williams CF

Born: 8/21/91 Age: 24 Bats: L Throws: R Height: 6'1" Weight: 185

YEAR	TEAM	LVL	AGE	PA	R	2B	3B	HR	RBI	BB	K	SB	CS	AVG/OBP/SLG	TAv	BABIP	BRR	FRAA	WARP
2013	TAM	A+	21	461	56	21	3	3	24	39	61	15	9	.261/.327/.350	.245	.299	3.3	CF(98): 9.7	2.0
2013	TRN	AA	21	76	7	3	1	1	4	1	18	0	0	.153/.164/.264	.146	.189	-0.5	CF(15): 0.2	-0.8
2014	TRN	AA	22	563	67	18	4	5	40	47	68	21	8	.223/.290/.304	.216	.248	2.9	CF(106): 4.5, RF(11): -0.7	-0.3
2015	NYA	MLB	23	22	3	3	0	1	3	1	3	0	0	.286/.318/.571	.300	.294	0.0	CF(8): -1.0	0.1
2015	TRN	AA	23	144	14	7	0	0	11	19	17	11	6	.317/.407/.375	.304	.365	-1.4	LF(14): 0.2, CF(13): -1.0	0.8
2015	SWB	AAA	23	91	12	7	1	0	11	8	6	2	1	.321/.382/.432	.299	.347	1.0	CF(20): 1.9	1.0
2016	*NYA*	*MLB*	*24*	*250*	*29*	*10*	*1*	*4*	*20*	*18*	*45*	*7*	*3*	*.229/.286/.341*	*.217*	*.260*	*0.1*	*CF 1, LF 1*	*-0.1*
2017	*NYA*	*MLB*	*25*	*366*	*39*	*15*	*2*	*7*	*36*	*27*	*67*	*10*	*4*	*.230/.290/.350*	*.225*	*.260*	*0.7*	*CF 2, LF 1*	*1.4*

Breakout: 3% Improve: 9% Collapse: 2% Attrition: 10% MLB: 15% *Comparables: Tony Gwynn, Rafael Ortega, Trevor Crowe*

Entering the year, Williams was out of prospect sizzle. He hadn't had a really productive year in the minor leagues since 2012 and hadn't figured out Double-A pitching at an age by which being able to hit Double-A pitching is fairly important. However, in his third stint at the level Williams really stepped on the classical gas, and then basically skipped Triple-A to reach the majors right on time. While this breakout seemed to come out of nowhere, the Yankees do deserve some credit for protecting him in the Rule 5 draft prior to the season, refusing to give up on their former top prospect. Unfortunately for Williams, he injured his shoulder diving back on a pickoff throw, ending what looked like a promising campaign after only eight games.

Pitchers

Dellin Betances RHP

Born: 3/23/88 Age: 28 Bats: R Throws: R Height: 6'8" Weight: 265

YEAR	TEAM	LVL	AGE	W	L	SV	G	GS	IP	H	HR	BB/9	K/9	GB%	BABIP	WHIP	ERA	FIP	DRA	WARP	CFIP	MPH
2013	SWB	AAA	25	6	4	5	38	6	84	52	2	4.5	11.6	45%	.269	1.12	2.68	2.69	3.88	0.9	84	
2013	NYA	MLB	25	0	0	0	6	0	5	9	1	3.6	18.0	36%	.615	2.20	10.80	2.88	8.92	-0.3	88	98.5
2014	NYA	MLB	26	5	0	1	70	0	90	46	4	2.4	13.5	49%	.241	0.78	1.40	1.67	1.22	3.6	48	99.5
2015	NYA	MLB	27	6	4	9	74	0	84	45	6	4.3	14.0	49%	.257	1.01	1.50	2.45	2.13	2.6	56	99.7
2016	*NYA*	*MLB*	*28*	*3*	*1*	*7*	*58*	*0*	*61^{1}*	*42*	*6*	*3.5*	*13.1*	*48%*	*.287*	*1.08*	*2.80*	*2.90*	*2.84*	*2.0*	*52*	
2017	*NYA*	*MLB*	*29*	*3*	*2*	*2*	*38*	*5*	*71^{1}*	*49*	*7*	*3.5*	*13.6*	*48%*	*.292*	*1.07*	*2.84*	*2.58*	*2.88*	*1.5*	*54*	

Breakout: 30% Improve: 49% Collapse: 28% Attrition: 20% MLB: 88% *Comparables: Andrew Bailey, Michael Gonzalez, Mike Fiers*

In the bizarre world of relievers, anyone can have a dominant season, so it was comforting for Yankees fans to see Betances remove any doubt about whether he got lucky in 2014 and confirm his status as a destroyer of worlds. His command lapsed at times, he struggled a bit down the stretch and he's A.J. Burnett-esque in his inability to control the running game, but what are small blemishes on the cheek of a giant? Betances is probably the scariest pitcher in the world right now, and when he's locating his pitches he's virtually unhittable. He's also the closest thing the baseball world has to the mythical 100-inning reliever. Watching him pitch is a pleasure and hitting against him must suck in the profoundest of ways.

Chris Capuano LHP

Born: 8/19/78 Age: 37 Bats: L Throws: L Height: 6'3" Weight: 220

YEAR	TEAM	LVL	AGE	W	L	SV	G	GS	IP	H	HR	BB/9	K/9	GB%	BABIP	WHIP	ERA	FIP	DRA	WARP	CFIP	MPH
2013	LAN	MLB	34	4	7	0	24	20	105^{2}	125	11	2.0	6.9	48%	.334	1.41	4.26	3.52	5.15	-0.3	100	91.4
2014	BOS	MLB	35	1	1	0	28	0	31^{2}	34	3	4.3	8.2	41%	.326	1.55	4.55	4.08	5.14	-0.2	101	92.7
2014	NYA	MLB	35	2	3	0	12	12	65^{2}	67	7	2.6	7.5	44%	.297	1.31	4.25	3.88	4.22	0.4	101	92.1
2014	CSP	AAA	35	1	0	0	3	3	14^{2}	12	2	1.8	8.6	51%	.256	1.02	3.07	4.18	5.10	0.1	95	
2015	NYA	MLB	36	0	4	0	22	4	40^{2}	52	6	4.9	8.4	46%	.362	1.82	7.97	5.00	6.51	-0.8	109	91.4
2015	SWB	AAA	36	2	1	0	6	6	28^{1}	20	0	2.2	7.9	51%	.267	0.95	1.27	2.13	2.64	0.7	81	
2016	*NYA*	*MLB*	*37*	*4*	*4*	*0*	*20*	*11*	*69^{2}*	*73*	*10*	*3.1*	*7.3*	*46%*	*.302*	*1.40*	*4.59*	*4.63*	*4.56*	*0.4*	*104*	
2017	*NYA*	*MLB*	*38*	*7*	*7*	*0*	*35*	*21*	*140^{1}*	*156*	*18*	*3.2*	*7.5*	*46%*	*.318*	*1.46*	*4.72*	*4.36*	*4.69*	*0.6*	*107*	

Breakout: 16% Improve: 38% Collapse: 11% Attrition: 11% MLB: 74% *Comparables: Brett Tomko, Harvey Haddix, Preacher Roe*

Capuano seems like he's been around forever, but in reality any human being has really only existed for a microscopic fraction of a blink of the universe's eye, so that characterization is unfair. In baseball terms... it's been a while. It may surprise you to note that Capuano was an All-Star in 2006 or that he appeared on an episode of *The Young and the Restless* in 2007. Nothing nearly that interesting happened in 2015. He was an old, ineffective bullpen lefty who made four starts. The longest went 5 1/3 innings. That about sums it up.

Ian Clarkin LHP

Born: 2/14/95 Age: 21 Bats: L Throws: L Height: 6'2" Weight: 190

YEAR	TEAM	LVL	AGE	W	L	SV	G	GS	IP	H	HR	BB/9	K/9	GB%	BABIP	WHIP	ERA	FIP	DRA	WARP	CFIP	MPH
2014	CSC	A	19	3	3	0	16	15	70	64	6	2.8	9.1	44%	.319	1.23	3.21	3.74	4.41	0.8	89	
2016	*NYA*	*MLB*	*21*	*2*	*3*	*0*	*8*	*8*	*33^{2}*	*37*	*5*	*3.7*	*6.4*	*36%*	*.303*	*1.51*	*5.26*	*5.17*	*5.20*	*0.0*	*123*	
2017	*NYA*	*MLB*	*22*	*6*	*9*	*0*	*28*	*28*	*169^{1}*	*182*	*24*	*4.1*	*6.5*	*36%*	*.300*	*1.53*	*5.48*	*5.09*	*5.42*	*-0.4*	*130*	

Breakout: 2% Improve: 3% Collapse: 2% Attrition: 5% MLB: 9% *Comparables: Jarred Cosart, Eric Hurley, Miguel Almonte*

Life is rough. One minute your elbow hurts a little, the next thing you know, it's October. Clarkin is the satisfied head nod of pitching prospects, a third or fourth starter-type with a workable low-90s fastball and plus curve and workable changeup. Things were progressing nicely for the former sandwich pick until inflammation forced him to spend the summer stretching and watching film. He returned in just enough time to shake off rust in the Arizona Fall League, which means he'll be back on course in 2016, still talented but no longer quite as young for his level.

Nathan Eovaldi RHP

Born: 2/13/90 Age: 26 Bats: R Throws: R Height: 6'2" Weight: 215

YEAR	TEAM	LVL	AGE	W	L	SV	G	GS	IP	H	HR	BB/9	K/9	GB%	BABIP	WHIP	ERA	FIP	DRA	WARP	CFIP	MPH
2013	MIA	MLB	23	4	6	0	18	18	106^{1}	100	7	3.4	6.6	46%	.287	1.32	3.39	3.57	3.83	1.4	108	99.2
2013	JAX	AA	23	1	0	0	3	3	11^{2}	13	0	3.1	6.9	50%	.342	1.46	5.40	2.40	4.06	0.1	99	
2014	MIA	MLB	24	6	14	0	33	33	199^{2}	223	14	1.9	6.4	46%	.323	1.33	4.37	3.34	4.20	1.5	105	98.9
2015	NYA	MLB	25	14	3	0	27	27	154^{1}	175	10	2.9	7.1	53%	.337	1.45	4.20	3.39	3.91	2.0	99	100.2
2016	*NYA*	*MLB*	*26*	*9*	*10*	*0*	*28*	*28*	*159^{2}*	*169*	*19*	*2.7*	*6.8*	*50%*	*.304*	*1.36*	*4.29*	*4.29*	*4.26*	*1.6*	*96*	
2017	*NYA*	*MLB*	*27*	*9*	*9*	*0*	*26*	*26*	*154^{1}*	*168*	*16*	*2.8*	*7.0*	*50%*	*.315*	*1.39*	*4.30*	*3.95*	*4.27*	*1.5*	*96*	

Breakout: 24% Improve: 62% Collapse: 14% Attrition: 10% MLB: 96% *Comparables: Matt Harrison, Edwin Jackson, Mike Pelfrey*

Eovaldi came to the Yankees as a guy with a reputation for throwing hard but giving up too many hits and failing to live up to his peripherals. He pretty much lived up, or down, to that reputation. The complaint here is that while he has top-notch heat, the secondary stuff just isn't there consistently. To his credit Eovaldi did develop a mightily intriguing splitter that did seem to help him down the stretch. He's old enough to no longer be considered a project, but unfortunately he still has all the characteristics of a project. The sterling 14-3 record might have helped him win friends with some over the course of the year, but frankly if you are reading this it's unlikely you are among them.

Drew Finley RHP

Born: 7/10/96 Age: 19 Bats: R Throws: R Height: 6'3" Weight: 200

YEAR	TEAM	LVL	AGE	W	L	SV	G	GS	IP	H	HR	BB/9	K/9	GB%	BABIP	WHIP	ERA	FIP	DRA	WARP	CFIP	MPH
2016	*NYA*	*MLB*	*19*	*1*	*3*	*0*	*9*	*9*	*31*	*37*	*6*	*5.9*	*5.3*	*20%*	*.304*	*1.86*	*6.71*	*6.72*	*6.78*	*-0.6*	*157*	
2017	*NYA*	*MLB*	*20*	*3*	*8*	*0*	*23*	*23*	*137^{2}*	*166*	*22*	*5.7*	*5.6*	*20%*	*.312*	*1.84*	*6.52*	*6.10*	*6.59*	*-1.5*	*153*	

On paper the Yankees' third-round pick checks most of the boxes for a pitching prospect. MLB bloodlines. Solid stuff. Pitchability. A Twitter profile that includes the words "Clear Eyes, Full Hearts, Can't Lose," indicating he's a fan of Friday Night Lights. But there are a lot of questions about Finley as a person that remain. Does he seem himself as more of a Matt Saracen or a Tim Riggins? How did he feel about the Landry/Tyra storyline in Season 2? Can he ultimately be at peace with Coach Taylor's decision to move to Philadelphia? Until these questions are answered it's going to be borderline impossible to evaluate him as a prospect.

James Kaprielian RHP

Born: 3/2/94 Age: 22 Bats: R Throws: R Height: 6'4" Weight: 200

James Kaprielian comes with heightened expectations even by Yankees prospect standards: At 16th overall, he was the highest draft pick made by the team since 1993. (Matt Drews, for perspective.) The tall right-hander started the year at UCLA and ended it with the Staten Island Yankees. In his brief taste of pro ball he didn't sink like a stone with cement blocks tied around it, and that's about all you can ask of your most recent draft picks, even the higher-rated ones. Kaprielian does not ooze raw upside, but he'll move relatively quickly through the system and is unlikely to bust completely.

Jacob Lindgren LHP

Born: 3/12/93 Age: 23 Bats: L Throws: L Height: 5'11" Weight: 205

YEAR	TEAM	LVL	AGE	W	L	SV	G	GS	IP	H	HR	BB/9	K/9	GB%	BABIP	WHIP	ERA	FIP	DRA	WARP	CFIP	MPH
2014	TRN	AA	21	1	1	0	8	0	11^{2}	6	0	6.9	13.9	73%	.273	1.29	3.86	2.58	4.08	0.1	85	
2015	NYA	MLB	22	0	0	0	7	0	7	5	3	5.1	10.3	41%	.143	1.29	5.14	8.10	7.22	-0.2	101	91.7
2015	SWB	AAA	22	1	1	3	15	0	22	16	0	4.1	11.9	70%	.302	1.18	1.23	1.88	2.19	0.6	76	
2016	*NYA*	*MLB*	*23*	*1*	*1*	*0*	*27*	*0*	*28^{1}*	*25*	*4*	*3.6*	*9.5*	*57%*	*.290*	*1.29*	*4.13*	*4.23*	*4.13*	*0.3*	*91*	
2017	*NYA*	*MLB*	*24*	*2*	*1*	*1*	*29*	*0*	*38^{1}*	*34*	*5*	*3.4*	*10.1*	*57%*	*.299*	*1.27*	*4.03*	*3.72*	*4.03*	*0.3*	*89*	

Breakout: 10% Improve: 13% Collapse: 9% Attrition: 15% MLB: 24% *Comparables: Jack Leathersich, Stephen Pryor, Chris Resop*

When the Yankees drafted Lindgren in the second round of the 2014 draft, he fulfilled one promise of the selection: He moved quickly, reaching the majors less than a year after the selection. He isn't especially big, doesn't throw extremely hard and is almost certainly a reliever long term, but a filthy one. Lindgren has a deceptive delivery and a nasty slider. It might have been a true breakout season had he not been a Yankees prospect, and thus legally obligated to have surgery. Fun fact: Lindgren's nickname is "The Strikeout Factory," which is lamer than people who use the word lame with regularity. Here's hoping his teammates just call him Jacob.

Chris Martin RHP

Born: 6/2/86 Age: 30 Bats: R Throws: R Height: 6'8" Weight: 215

YEAR	TEAM	LVL	AGE	W	L	SV	G	GS	IP	H	HR	BB/9	K/9	GB%	BABIP	WHIP	ERA	FIP	DRA	WARP	CFIP	MPH
2013	PAW	AAA	27	3	3	2	30	0	51	51	3	1.8	8.3	52%	.324	1.20	3.18	2.95	3.73	0.6	78	
2013	PME	AA	27	2	0	3	12	0	21	9	0	2.6	11.6	46%	.220	0.71	0.00	1.61	3.74	0.3	70	
2014	CSP	AAA	28	1	3	5	25	0	26^{2}	33	2	3.0	12.1	51%	.431	1.58	4.39	3.21	4.70	0.2	76	
2014	COL	MLB	28	0	0	0	16	0	15^{2}	22	2	2.3	8.0	61%	.408	1.66	6.89	3.74	5.98	-0.3	97	96.4
2015	NYA	MLB	29	0	2	1	24	0	20^{2}	28	2	2.6	7.8	55%	.361	1.65	5.66	3.64	5.49	-0.2	100	96.2
2015	SWB	AAA	29	0	1	2	20	0	28^{1}	26	1	3.2	7.9	52%	.294	1.27	3.18	3.02	3.66	0.2	94	
2016	*NYA*	*MLB*	*30*	*2*	*1*	*0*	*34*	*2*	*42^{2}*	*45*	*5*	*3.0*	*7.7*	*53%*	*.307*	*1.38*	*4.36*	*4.15*	*4.33*	*0.3*	*97*	
2017	*NYA*	*MLB*	*31*	*3*	*2*	*0*	*42*	*3*	*69*	*72*	*9*	*3.0*	*7.9*	*53%*	*.312*	*1.39*	*4.50*	*4.14*	*4.47*	*0.3*	*101*	

Breakout: 7% Improve: 12% Collapse: 16% Attrition: 16% MLB: 30% *Comparables: Neil Wagner, Jose Valdez, Greg Burke*

Martin is so little known that he doesn't appear on the first page of a Google search of his name. Some singer might have something to do with that (and a cricketer, and half a comedy-podcast duo), but it also shows that the tall right-hander fits firmly in the "just a guy" mold. He earned a role in the Yankees' bullpen early in the season, but faltered badly as the year went on and was ultimately demoted to Triple-A. That's a pretty mundane baseball tale, but Martin is adding some spice to his story by shipping off to Japan to play for the best-named team in the history of sports in 2016. If any Yankees fans remember Martin, they will be sure to wish him luck with the Nippon Ham Fighters.

Andrew Miller LHP

Born: 5/21/85 Age: 31 Bats: L Throws: L Height: 6'7" Weight: 210

YEAR	TEAM	LVL	AGE	W	L	SV	G	GS	IP	H	HR	BB/9	K/9	GB%	BABIP	WHIP	ERA	FIP	DRA	WARP	CFIP	MPH
2013	BOS	MLB	28	1	2	0	37	0	30^{2}	25	3	5.0	14.1	57%	.338	1.37	2.64	3.08	3.80	0.3	77	98.0
2014	BAL	MLB	29	2	0	1	23	0	20	8	1	1.8	15.3	36%	.219	0.60	1.35	1.16	1.29	0.8	25	96.9
2014	BOS	MLB	29	3	5	0	50	0	42^{1}	25	2	2.8	14.7	55%	.280	0.90	2.34	1.72	1.61	1.5	51	96.7
2015	NYA	MLB	30	3	2	36	60	0	61^{2}	33	5	2.9	14.6	50%	.241	0.86	2.04	2.13	2.23	1.8	50	97.6
2016	*NYA*	*MLB*	*31*	*3*	*1*	*35*	*54*	*0*	*56^{2}*	*38*	*6*	*2.8*	*13.3*	*50%*	*.281*	*0.99*	*2.71*	*2.76*	*2.74*	*1.3*	*49*	
2017	*NYA*	*MLB*	*32*	*4*	*2*	*11*	*69*	*0*	*61*	*43*	*6*	*3.0*	*13.0*	*50%*	*.289*	*1.04*	*2.88*	*2.61*	*2.91*	*1.3*	*53*	

Breakout: 17% Improve: 32% Collapse: 34% Attrition: 13% MLB: 89% *Comparables: Michael Wuertz, Jim Kern, Grant Balfour*

Dellin Betances is more imposing and more unusual, but Miller's slider would be worth its weight in gold if it weren't an abstract concept that couldn't be weighed. He backfoots the pitch as well as anybody in the game, throwing it with such frequency and such effectiveness that one wonders whether he could ditch his fastball completely and still post a sub-3 ERA. If his elbow can hold up to the strain of all those sliders, he'll be one of those rare relievers who easily justifies his four-year contract.

Ivan Nova RHP

Born: 1/12/87 Age: 29 Bats: R Throws: R Height: 6'4" Weight: 235

YEAR	TEAM	LVL	AGE	W	L	SV	G	GS	IP	H	HR	BB/9	K/9	GB%	BABIP	WHIP	ERA	FIP	DRA	WARP	CFIP	MPH
2013	SWB	AAA	26	2	0	0	3	3	17^{2}	15	1	2.0	8.7	56%	.298	1.08	2.04	2.70	4.04	0.2	89	
2013	NYA	MLB	26	9	6	0	23	20	139^{1}	135	9	2.8	7.5	54%	.313	1.28	3.10	3.50	3.38	2.5	96	96.1
2014	NYA	MLB	27	2	2	0	4	4	20^{2}	32	6	2.6	5.2	50%	.371	1.84	8.27	6.93	8.85	-1.0	120	94.9
2015	SWB	AAA	28	1	1	0	2	2	11	12	1	2.5	5.7	43%	.324	1.36	4.91	4.16	4.37	0.0	103	
2015	NYA	MLB	28	6	11	0	17	17	94	99	13	3.2	6.0	52%	.290	1.40	5.07	4.84	4.51	0.6	113	95.6
2016	*NYA*	*MLB*	*29*	*5*	*4*	*0*	*48*	*8*	*88*	*92*	*11*	*3.0*	*6.9*	*52%*	*.300*	*1.38*	*4.59*	*4.48*	*4.55*	*0.3*	*105*	
2017	*NYA*	*MLB*	*30*	*7*	*7*	*0*	*19*	*19*	*113^{2}*	*124*	*14*	*3.0*	*6.9*	*52%*	*.310*	*1.42*	*4.80*	*4.43*	*4.76*	*0.5*	*111*	

Breakout: 26% Improve: 49% Collapse: 19% Attrition: 11% MLB: 96% *Comparables: Vicente Padilla, Kyle Lohse, Ryan Dempster*

Nova returned from Tommy John surgery to provide some much-needed depth for the Yankees, but not much else. At this point he doesn't have the stuff to occupy any role more glamorous than "innings eater" and he's not durable enough take more than a couple of bites. Another year of recovery should help him with his command, but it might be time for him to transition to the dreaded swingman phase of his career. The ability to get groundballs is still there, but it's hard to identify any other aspect of pitching where he stands out.

Michael Pineda RHP

Born: 1/18/89 Age: 27 Bats: R Throws: R Height: 6'7" Weight: 260

YEAR	TEAM	LVL	AGE	W	L	SV	G	GS	IP	H	HR	BB/9	K/9	GB%	BABIP	WHIP	ERA	FIP	DRA	WARP	CFIP	MPH
2013	SWB	AAA	24	1	1	0	6	6	23^{1}	18	2	2.3	10.0	52%	.267	1.03	3.86	3.12	4.05	0.3	89	
2014	NYA	MLB	25	5	5	0	13	13	76^{1}	56	5	0.8	7.0	42%	.233	0.83	1.89	2.74	1.81	2.8	88	95.7
2015	NYA	MLB	26	12	10	0	27	27	160^{2}	176	21	1.2	8.7	50%	.332	1.23	4.37	3.31	3.95	2.1	80	95.7
2016	*NYA*	*MLB*	*27*	*12*	*10*	*0*	*31*	*31*	*186*	*175*	*23*	*1.7*	*8.3*	*49%*	*.287*	*1.13*	*3.72*	*3.69*	*3.71*	*3.1*	*81*	
2017	*NYA*	*MLB*	*28*	*10*	*9*	*0*	*30*	*30*	*191^{2}*	*184*	*22*	*1.5*	*8.0*	*49%*	*.292*	*1.12*	*3.75*	*3.42*	*3.74*	*2.7*	*82*	

Breakout: 22% Improve: 51% Collapse: 22% Attrition: 7% MLB: 95% *Comparables: Erik Hanson, Mat Latos, Tim Belcher*

The Yankees finally got a full(ish) season out of Pineda, but some bizarre splits blemished the final product. While the massive right-hander looked dominant at times and annexed the strike zone, he also allowed hitters to slash .302/.341/.575 with runners in scoring position. He also struggled as the season progressed, especially with the long ball. It was definitely a year to build on, and the 160 innings are the most important number on the stat line, but it has a bitter taste because of how strong Pineda initially looked. Ridiculously early awards speculation had him in the Cy Young conversation, but he ended up performing like a mid-rotation starter. His talent is hard to trust given what his body has been through, but on the plus side he's not Jesus Montero, nor will he be in the future.

Esmil Rogers RHP

Born: 8/14/85 Age: 30 Bats: R Throws: R Height: 6'3" Weight: 200

YEAR	TEAM	LVL	AGE	W	L	SV	G	GS	IP	H	HR	BB/9	K/9	GB%	BABIP	WHIP	ERA	FIP	DRA	WARP	CFIP	MPH
2013	TOR	MLB	27	5	9	0	44	20	137^2	152	21	2.9	6.3	48%	.304	1.42	4.77	4.75	4.83	0.0	110	96.5
2014	NYA	MLB	28	2	0	0	18	1	25	22	3	3.6	8.3	36%	.275	1.28	4.68	4.20	3.05	0.5	105	96.2
2014	TOR	MLB	28	0	0	0	16	0	20^2	28	5	3.0	9.1	46%	.371	1.69	6.97	5.43	7.81	-0.8	97	96.4
2014	BUF	AAA	28	2	2	0	12	7	48^2	42	2	3.3	7.6	47%	.294	1.23	3.14	3.44	4.39	0.4	95	
2015	SWB	AAA	29	1	1	0	7	7	34^2	37	0	3.1	7.3	51%	.349	1.41	3.38	2.67	3.75	0.4	95	
2015	NYA	MLB	29	1	1	0	18	0	33	41	5	3.8	8.5	43%	.356	1.67	6.27	4.65	5.79	-0.4	103	95.6
2016	*NYA*	*MLB*	*30*	*3*	*3*	*0*	*37*	*6*	*62^2*	*68*	*9*	*3.2*	*7.3*	*45%*	*.310*	*1.44*	*4.74*	*4.68*	*4.71*	*0.2*	*108*	
2017	*NYA*	*MLB*	*31*	*5*	*4*	*0*	*51*	*9*	*108*	*122*	*13*	*3.3*	*7.2*	*45%*	*.323*	*1.49*	*4.73*	*4.37*	*4.70*	*0.2*	*107*	

Breakout: 26% Improve: 50% Collapse: 14% Attrition: 7% MLB: 83% *Comparables: Gary Glover, Chad Gaudin, Boof Bonser*

At long last Rogers might have run out of chances. He's had seven seasons with four different franchises to prove he's capable of contributing in the big leagues, and finally in July the Yankees cut bait. ERA has its flaws, but it really is tough to stick around with a career 5.59 mark primarily as a reliever. While this could be an example of a guy who got more opportunities than he deserved because he threw hard, it's more fun to imagine a world in which Rogers is a skilled blackmailer and secret broker with safety deposit boxes in banks all over the world. Perhaps it took Brian Cashman's courage to let him go for the good of the Yankees, even though he knew that Rogers' wrath would destroy everything he held dear. There has yet to be definitive proof that any of that is false.

CC Sabathia LHP

Born: 7/21/80 Age: 35 Bats: L Throws: L Height: 6'7" Weight: 285

YEAR	TEAM	LVL	AGE	W	L	SV	G	GS	IP	H	HR	BB/9	K/9	GB%	BABIP	WHIP	ERA	FIP	DRA	WARP	CFIP	MPH
2013	NYA	MLB	32	14	13	0	32	32	211	224	28	2.8	7.5	47%	.308	1.37	4.78	4.12	4.29	1.6	100	94.2
2014	NYA	MLB	33	3	4	0	8	8	46	58	10	2.0	9.4	50%	.350	1.48	5.28	4.81	6.50	-1.0	94	91.6
2015	NYA	MLB	34	6	10	0	29	29	167^1	188	28	2.7	7.4	48%	.317	1.42	4.73	4.65	4.84	0.4	101	93.0
2016	*NYA*	*MLB*	*35*	*12*	*13*	*0*	*32*	*32*	*214^1*	*230*	*33*	*2.6*	*7.4*	*48%*	*.305*	*1.36*	*4.63*	*4.58*	*4.59*	*1.4*	*106*	
2017	*NYA*	*MLB*	*36*	*10*	*11*	*0*	*28*	*28*	*174^1*	*192*	*26*	*2.6*	*7.5*	*48%*	*.312*	*1.38*	*4.74*	*4.37*	*4.70*	*0.9*	*109*	

Breakout: 12% Improve: 34% Collapse: 21% Attrition: 14% MLB: 88% *Comparables: Vicente Padilla, Wandy Rodriguez, Steve Carlton*

It was a turbulent year for Sabathia, one that saw the perennial Cy Young candidate suffer through bone-on-bone arthritis in his right knee, an issue that would flare at random times as he planted his lead foot. Anchoring, in so many ways, a foundering Yankees rotation, Sabathia slapped on a brace and gritted out the injury, to his and the team's detriment. The former workhorse saw the eighth inning only twice in 29 starts, and only a late-season push got his ERA below five. Knee replacement is a near certainty. But few will remember this.

On October 5th, the day before the Yankees faced the Astros in the Wild Card game, Sabathia announced that he was leaving the team to enter rehabilitation for alcohol. "It hurts me deeply to do this now," he said in a statement, "but I owe it to myself and to my family to get myself right. I want to take control of my disease, and I want to be a better man, father and player." The Yankees lost the game, though Sabathia wouldn't have appeared regardless.

Our relationship with our players is necessarily one-sided, and the transactional nature of the business has imprinted itself on the fan. We cannot know Sabathia, and so he becomes defined by what he provides us, through his performance. To understand this, to face the New York media at the moment before the playoffs and to ask for help, for the sake of his family: This is a laudable thing. Sabathia plans to return to the club in 2016, though his health is not assured and rotation spot not reserved; given perspective, they're secondary concerns.

Sergio Santos RHP

Born: 7/4/83 Age: 32 Bats: R Throws: R Height: 6'4" Weight: 215

YEAR	TEAM	LVL	AGE	W	L	SV	G	GS	IP	H	HR	BB/9	K/9	GB%	BABIP	WHIP	ERA	FIP	DRA	WARP	CFIP	MPH
2013	TOR	MLB	29	1	1	1	29	0	25^2	11	1	1.4	9.8	50%	.175	0.58	1.75	1.87	1.27	1.0	72	97.1
2014	BUF	AAA	30	1	0	2	11	0	10^2	3	0	5.1	13.5	55%	.150	0.84	0.00	2.33	4.00	0.1	80	
2014	TOR	MLB	30	0	3	5	26	0	21	28	5	7.7	12.4	41%	.426	2.19	8.57	6.06	8.84	-1.1	98	96.4
2015	NYA	MLB	31	0	0	0	2	0	3	3	1	0.0	9.0	22%	.250	1.00	6.00	5.44	4.93	0.0	90	94.0
2015	LAN	MLB	31	0	0	0	12	0	13^1	13	2	4.7	10.1	46%	.297	1.50	4.72	4.44	5.51	-0.1	102	95.0
2016	*NYA*	*MLB*	*32*	*2*	*1*	*3*	*33*	*0*	*34^2*	*33*	*5*	*3.8*	*8.8*	*43%*	*.291*	*1.37*	*4.68*	*4.54*	*4.68*	*0.0*	*105*	
2017	*NYA*	*MLB*	*33*	*2*	*1*	*4*	*50*	*0*	*45^2*	*45*	*7*	*3.9*	*8.5*	*43%*	*.300*	*1.42*	*4.90*	*4.55*	*4.90*	*-0.1*	*111*	

Breakout: 20% Improve: 37% Collapse: 23% Attrition: 8% MLB: 76% *Comparables: John Axford, Matt Mantei, Scott Williamson*

Santos possesses a fastball in the mid-90s and the kind of slider Hercules would have developed if he hadn't been cleaning out stables all the time. As the Yankees found out in 2015, that's literally all he has. You'd think that would be enough to be a productive reliever, but durability actually goes a long way and command is a nifty thing to have, as well. The Bronx Bombers picked him up after he was dumped by the Dodgers as a no-risk flier, and after 10 days in pinstripes he was already on the shelf with a torn ACL. All in all it was a very "Sergio Santos" kind of season for Sergio Santos.

Luis Severino RHP

Born: 2/20/94 Age: 22 Bats: R Throws: R Height: 6'0" Weight: 195

YEAR	TEAM	LVL	AGE	W	L	SV	G	GS	IP	H	HR	BB/9	K/9	GB%	BABIP	WHIP	ERA	FIP	DRA	WARP	CFIP	MPH
2013	CSC	A	19	1	1	0	4	4	17^2	21	1	2.0	10.7	46%	.392	1.42	4.08	2.52	3.92	0.2	81	
2014	TRN	AA	20	2	2	0	6	6	25	20	1	2.2	10.4	48%	.297	1.04	2.52	2.27	3.90	0.4	78	
2014	TAM	A+	20	1	1	0	4	4	20^2	11	0	2.6	12.2	59%	.239	0.82	1.31	1.55	3.51	0.4	72	
2014	CSC	A	20	3	2	0	14	14	67^2	62	2	2.0	9.3	53%	.321	1.14	2.79	2.70	4.04	1.0	76	
2015	NYA	MLB	21	5	3	0	11	11	62^1	53	9	3.2	8.1	51%	.265	1.20	2.89	4.34	3.82	0.9	95	97.8
2015	SWB	AAA	21	7	0	0	11	11	61^1	40	0	2.5	7.3	42%	.237	0.93	1.91	2.51	3.01	1.3	86	
2015	TRN	AA	21	2	2	0	8	8	38	32	2	2.4	11.4	46%	.319	1.11	3.32	2.37	1.67	1.5	66	
2016	*NYA*	*MLB*	*22*	*10*	*10*	*0*	*31*	*31*	*164^1*	*154*	*21*	*3.0*	*8.3*	*47%*	*.287*	*1.27*	*4.25*	*4.18*	*4.24*	*1.7*	*96*	
2017	*NYA*	*MLB*	*23*	*8*	*9*	*0*	*28*	*28*	*167^2*	*156*	*21*	*2.9*	*8.7*	*47%*	*.292*	*1.26*	*4.26*	*3.92*	*4.25*	*1.4*	*97*	

Breakout: 13% Improve: 28% Collapse: 13% Attrition: 18% MLB: 58% *Comparables: Drew Hutchison, Arodys Vizcaino, Mat Latos*

Severino's first taste of big-league action was exactly what Yankees fans had been hoping for. The hard-throwing right-hander flashed impressive stuff and never seemed beaten. He allowed more than three runs in only one of his 11 starts and was an important cog in the rotation down the stretch. He's not without his warts, however. His secondary pitches aren't quite there yet, and as a fastball-slider guy he could open up some nasty platoon splits until his changeup catches up. That and concerns about his size might drive him to the bullpen still. Such nitpicking is missing the forest for the trees, and Severino's potential is undoubtedly exciting even if his early success was buoyed a bit by luck on balls in play and with runners in scoring position. Young power pitchers who can start aren't as common a commodity as Mets fans might think, and guys like Severino haven't come around often for the Yankees recently.

Chasen Shreve LHP

Born: 7/12/90 Age: 25 Bats: L Throws: L Height: 6'3" Weight: 185

YEAR	TEAM	LVL	AGE	W	L	SV	G	GS	IP	H	HR	BB/9	K/9	GB%	BABIP	WHIP	ERA	FIP	DRA	WARP	CFIP	MPH
2013	MIS	AA	22	3	1	0	36	0	42^2	43	1	4.6	5.9	47%	.298	1.52	4.43	3.45	4.25	0.0	105	
2013	LYN	A+	22	0	1	2	14	0	19^2	15	1	3.7	6.9	46%	.233	1.17	2.75	3.71	4.70	0.1	100	
2014	MIS	AA	23	3	2	7	36	0	54^1	42	2	1.5	12.6	46%	.336	0.94	2.48	1.42				
2014	ATL	MLB	23	0	0	0	15	0	12^1	10	0	2.2	10.9	50%	.312	1.05	0.73	1.40	2.75	0.3	90	93.8
2015	NYA	MLB	24	6	2	0	59	0	58^1	49	10	5.1	9.9	47%	.273	1.41	3.09	4.89	4.35	0.2	97	93.5
2016	*NYA*	*MLB*	*25*	*2*	*1*	*0*	*49*	*0*	*52*	*50*	*7*	*3.8*	*9.2*	*46%*	*.301*	*1.38*	*4.39*	*4.34*	*4.38*	*0.3*	*97*	
2017	*NYA*	*MLB*	*26*	*2*	*1*	*0*	*39*	*0*	*48*	*47*	*7*	*4.0*	*9.5*	*46%*	*.312*	*1.43*	*4.70*	*4.34*	*4.69*	*0.0*	*105*	

Breakout: 18% Improve: 25% Collapse: 20% Attrition: 37% MLB: 48% *Comparables: Sam Demel, Mike Zagurski, Robbie Weinhardt*

Part of the trade that sent Manny Banuelos to Atlanta, Shreve was a dependable reliever all season until he faced the mini-boss known as "September." In the final month of the year hitters smoked him for a .485/.600/.875 line in 41 plate appearances, which did a number on the back of his baseball card. His other five months of work, and his sinistral method of going about it, will offer him at least a couple of Septembers to avenge himself.

Masahiro Tanaka RHP

Born: 11/1/88 Age: 27 Bats: R Throws: R Height: 6'2" Weight: 210

YEAR	TEAM	LVL	AGE	W	L	SV	G	GS	IP	H	HR	BB/9	K/9	GB%	BABIP	WHIP	ERA	FIP	DRA	WARP	CFIP	MPH
2014	NYA	MLB	25	13	5	0	20	20	136^1	123	15	1.4	9.3	48%	.299	1.06	2.77	3.07	3.44	2.3	79	94.4
2015	NYA	MLB	26	12	7	0	24	24	154	126	25	1.6	8.1	48%	.243	0.99	3.51	3.96	3.33	3.1	86	94.6
2016	*NYA*	*MLB*	*27*	*12*	*11*	*0*	*32*	*32*	*201^2*	*182*	*28*	*1.8*	*8.4*	*48%*	*.280*	*1.11*	*3.86*	*3.87*	*3.86*	*3.0*	*86*	
2017	*NYA*	*MLB*	*28*	*13*	*10*	*0*	*30*	*30*	*187^2*	*175*	*24*	*1.7*	*8.4*	*48%*	*.290*	*1.12*	*3.90*	*3.57*	*3.90*	*3.1*	*87*	

Breakout: 26% Improve: 54% Collapse: 20% Attrition: 6% MLB: 99% *Comparables: Jim Bunning, John Montefusco, Ben Sheets*

Tanaka's 2015 was an excellent forgery of his original stateside performance. His innings, his record, his walk and strikeout and groundball rates all looked the same—but one flaw gave the whole thing away. When he got ahead in the count, batters were busy fighting off splitters for their lives. But when he got behind, Tanaka was forced to resort to the fastball, described by various scouts as "bad." Hitters squared up on it, exploding his home run rate. His ability to forge heroes out of opponents proved to be the Yankees' downfall in the Wild Card game, and it means that despite being a very good pitcher, he may not be the man to take the hill in a big game. Complaints aside, the Yankees deserve credit for having him available—their gambit with his elbow paid off, though he may never reach 200 innings.

Lineouts

Hitters

NAME	POS	TEAM	LVL	AGE	PA	R	2B	3B	HR	RBI	BB	K	SB	CS	AVG/OBP/SLG	TAv	BABIP	BRR	FRAA	WARP
Abiatal Avelino	SS	CSC	A	20	90	16	8	0	0	4	5	16	16	3	.301/.341/.398	.335	.373	3.0	SS(7): 0.6, 3B(7): 0.7	1.5
	SS	TAM	A+	20	446	64	12	2	4	23	32	63	38	15	.252/.309/.321	.245	.289	4.7	2B(58): 0.5, SS(41): 4.4	1.7
Kyle Holder	SS	STA	A-	21	250	23	7	1	0	12	17	34	6	2	.213/.273/.253	.206	.250	0.9	SS(56): -0.2	-0.4
Tyler Wade	SS	TAM	A+	20	418	51	11	5	2	28	39	65	31	15	.280/.349/.353	.274	.331	2.3	SS(72): 5.9, 2B(24): -0.9	3.0
	SS	TRN	AA	20	117	6	4	0	1	3	2	24	2	1	.204/.224/.265	.198	.250	0.3	SS(28): -1.3	-0.4

Abiatal Avelino bounced back from an injury-marred 2014 to show he can still excite with his tools, primarily his speed. He's a slap hitter, but at his age and stage there's nothing wrong with that. ❖ **Juan De Leon** was one of the highlights of the Yankees' international spending spree of 2014. He's also barely an adult, so this lineout is mostly just a reminder that as toolsy as they are, he and Dermis Garcia and Nelson Gomez are still years away. ❖ **Kyle Holder**, popped 30th overall, was the consensus best defensive shortstop in the draft. The only question about his glove going forward is whether he'll hit well enough to be allowed to wear one. ❖ **Hoy Yun Park** demonstrated patience at the plate, speed on the bases and a solid glove at short in his first professional action. ❖ **Luis Torrens** missed the 2015 season after tearing the labrum in his throwing shoulder. Fortunately, he had the good sense to be young for his level. ❖ He doesn't have Gregorius' range or Mateo's wheels, but the organization likes what it sees in **Tyler Wade**. He'll start 2016 at Double-A, but with little competition in front of him, he could reach the majors by the end of the year.

Pitchers

NAME	TEAM	LVL	AGE	W	L	SV	G	GS	IP	H	HR	BB/9	K/9	GB%	BABIP	WHIP	ERA	FIP	FRA	WARP	CFIP	MPH
Chance Adams	TAM	A+	20	1	0	0	5	0	14	12	0	1.3	10.3	38%	.324	1.00	1.29	1.74	2.57	0.3	84	
	CSC	A	20	1	1	0	5	0	11^2	7	0	3.1	12.3	64%	.250	0.94	3.09	1.77	3.76	0.1	92	
John Barbato	SWB	AAA	22	4	0	3	14	0	25	13	1	4.0	9.4	47%	.211	0.96	0.36	2.92	3.27	0.3	90	
	TRN	AA	22	2	2	0	26	0	42^1	42	4	3.0	9.4	41%	.330	1.32	4.04	3.62	2.85	0.8	82	
Luis Cessa	BIN	AA	23	7	4	0	13	13	77^1	77	2	2.0	7.1	50%	.315	1.22	2.56	2.69	3.24	1.5	87	
	LVG	AAA	23	0	3	0	5	5	24^1	40	3	1.5	8.9	56%	.425	1.81	8.51	3.85	4.16	0.4	89	
	TOL	AAA	23	1	3	0	7	7	37^2	46	2	3.6	8.1	49%	.376	1.62	5.97	3.40	4.01	0.3	100	
Cale Coshow	CSC	A	22	0	0	7	11	0	16	10	0	2.2	11.2	61%	.278	0.88	1.12	1.92	2.73	0.4	79	
	TRN	AA	22	2	3	0	6	6	33^1	29	1	3.5	5.7	48%	.262	1.26	3.51	3.84	5.14	-0.1	112	
	TAM	A+	22	7	2	1	16	9	64^2	46	2	1.5	7.8	53%	.254	0.88	2.23	2.48	2.72	1.4	85	
Caleb Cotham	TRN	AA	27	4	2	1	15	0	26	20	1	2.8	10.7	49%	.297	1.08	2.77	2.42	2.55	0.6	78	
	NYA	MLB	27	1	0	0	12	0	9^2	14	4	0.9	10.2	46%	.345	1.55	6.52	6.52	7.36	-0.3	94	94.8
	SWB	AAA	27	2	2	1	20	0	31	25	1	1.5	8.7	48%	.279	0.97	1.74	2.32	2.26	0.8	76	
William Davis	TRN	AA	22	2	1	0	6	5	33^1	38	1	2.2	6.5	47%	.343	1.38	4.32	3.21	4.09	0.3	98	
	TAM	A+	22	6	6	0	19	19	97^1	94	4	1.7	9.7	47%	.327	1.15	3.70	2.22	1.32	3.9	69	
Jeffrey Degano	STA	A-	22	0	0	0	4	2	10^2	10	0	4.2	11.8	30%	.370	1.41	2.53	2.86	3.75	0.1	94	
Nick Goody	NYA	MLB	23	0	0	0	7	0	5^2	6	0	4.8	4.8	47%	.316	1.59	4.76	4.16	6.11	-0.1	112	93.6
	SWB	AAA	23	1	1	4	14	0	20^2	14	0	3.0	10.9	30%	.280	1.02	1.31	1.75	2.29	0.5	77	
	TRN	AA	23	1	1	4	29	0	41^2	29	2	3.0	12.7	35%	.287	1.03	1.73	2.21	1.27	1.6	60	
Brady Lail	TRN	AA	21	6	4	0	20	19	106^1	91	2	2.2	5.3	44%	.262	1.10	2.45	3.06	4.14	0.9	100	
	SWB	AAA	21	3	2	0	7	7	37	46	4	4.1	3.2	46%	.318	1.70	4.62	5.32	6.91	-1.0	131	
Bryan Mitchell	NYA	MLB	24	0	2	1	20	2	29^2	37	4	4.9	8.8	50%	.359	1.79	6.37	4.72	5.91	-0.4	107	98.2
	SWB	AAA	24	5	5	0	15	15	75	63	1	4.4	7.3	54%	.286	1.33	3.12	3.18	4.44	0.2	104	
James Pazos	SWB	AAA	24	3	1	2	21	0	33	25	0	4.1	10.1	45%	.298	1.21	1.09	2.46	3.18	0.5	88	
	NYA	MLB	24	0	0	0	11	0	5	3	0	5.4	5.4	47%	.200	1.20	0.00	3.70	0.49	0.3	109	97.1
Branden Pinder	SWB	AAA	26	1	3	1	23	0	35^1	31	3	2.5	9.2	30%	.286	1.16	2.80	3.07	2.64	0.8	82	
	NYA	MLB	26	0	2	0	25	0	27^2	28	4	4.6	8.1	32%	.304	1.52	2.93	4.69	5.15	-0.1	105	97.4
Nick Rumbelow	SWB	AAA	23	2	3	8	37	0	52^2	47	4	2.2	9.7	47%	.295	1.14	4.27	2.72	2.11	1.5	75	
	NYA	MLB	23	1	1	0	17	0	15^2	16	2	2.9	8.6	46%	.304	1.34	4.02	3.81	4.93	0.0	97	96.3

Fifth-round reliever **Chance Adams** has the fastball and the slider to climb the minors quickly, but one can imagine he's aware what force the universe is operated by. ❖ **Johnny Barbato** is young, he throws hard and he posted a very shiny ERA at Triple-A last season. That's enough to put the return from the Shawn Kelley trade on the radar. ❖ **Luis Cessa** spent as much time in Detroit as the man he was traded for, Yoenis Cespedes, spent in New York. The impact was less. ❖ **Cale Coshow** will need to miss more bats in the upper minors if he wants to make an impact for the Yankees. But on the plus side, according to a 2014 interview he has a dog named Beefcake, which is objectively fantastic. ❖ A sinker-slider righty with a little bit of of juice, **Caleb Cotham** got a cup of coffee with the Yankees in 2015 and was knocked around pretty severely. ❖ **Rookie Davis** is a dual threat, in that he has a silly name and is an actual prospect of sorts. He can dial it up to 95 mph and posted stellar fielding-independent numbers as he moved up the ladder last year. ❖ Second-round 2015 draftee **Jeffrey Degano** sits comfortably in the low 90s with an interesting slider that misses bats. Considered a high-floor pick, he outperformed his projected low ceiling in year one and will aim for a spot in the middle of a rotation in a few years. ❖ Make no mistake, there is nothing extraordinary about **Icezack Flemming** except his given name. The 25th-round pick is worth cheering for anyway, simply because the image of all of Yankee Stadium on its feet chanting "Icezack!" "Icezack!" "Icezack!" is infinitely amusing. ❖ **Domingo German** was part of the Nathan Eovaldi-Martin Prado trade, but has yet to pitch in the Yankees organization after undergoing Tommy John surgery in April. He'll have a lot of makeup work to do when he gets back. ❖ A couple years removed from Tommy John surgery, **Nick Goody** ascended to the upper minors in 2015 and even got a taste of the big leagues in the wake of injuries. A two-pitch right-handed reliever with good strikeout numbers, he'll get another chance before too long. ❖ **Brady Lail** has a profile you could compare to David Phelps, if you were trying to explain why you don't think David Phelps will have a good year. ❖ **Bryan Mitchell** has youth and velocity going for him, but not only did he struggle in the majors in 2015, he also took an Eduardo Nunez line drive to the face. Tough year. ❖ LOOGY-in-training **James Pazos** was given a start in the second half of a doubleheader in 2014. He gave up a career-high four runs in a third of an inning, and never started again. The moral: Never fail at anything. ❖ **Branden Pinder** has a decent fastball and slider, but his best tool might be his knowledge of the commute between New York and Scranton. It's a skill he'll probably continue to hone in 2016. ❖ Undersized reliever **Nick Rumbelow** looked adequate in a Yankees uniform as a rookie in 2015, and adequacy is probably the fairest expectation for the right-hander going forward.

MANAGER

Joe Girardi

YEAR	TEAM	W	L	Pythag +/-	Avg PC	100+ P	120+ P	QS	BQS	REL	REL w Zero R	IBB	PH	PH Avg	PH HR	SB2	CS2	SB3	CS3	SAC Att	SAC%	POS SAC	Squeeze	Swing	In Play
2013	NYA	85	77	7	95.7	82	1	84	11	428	356	34	99	.242	1	96	27	18	4	53	67.9	35	0	302	94
2014	NYA	84	78	7	93.3	54	0	83	6	475	399	23	95	.244	2	97	23	13	3	45	64.4	27	0	311	85
2015	NYA	87	75	-1	92.5	42	0	72	9	497	400	16	111	.250	3	60	23	3	2	33	72.7	24	1	231	75

This will be Girardi's ninth season as Yankees manager, giving him the sixth-longest term in franchise history, and the second longest in the post-Stengel era. Joe Torre, the man Girardi trails, must be envious of his successor's job security. Whereas reports predicting Torre's imminent dismissal were never more than a losing streak away (in spite of his delivering four World Series titles, two other World Series appearances and 12 consecutive postseason berths), Girardi remains in good standing even though the Yankees haven't recorded a playoff win since 2012.

Times have changed in the Bronx, to the extent that Girardi deserves credit rather than blame for the Yankees' recent records. Although last season featured some failings on his part—he proved too loyal to Stephen Drew (second base) and Jacoby Ellsbury (leadoff)—his handling of the pitching staff might have made 2015 his finest managerial effort yet. The Yankees did not have a pitcher amass more than 180 innings, thereby forcing their bullpen to cover the third-most frames in the American League. Management supplied fresh arms throughout the year (culminating in a 13-man bullpen during September), but it was Girardi who made it all work.

The key to Girardi's deft bullpen handling is how he juggles opportunism with mindfulness: He's willing to use relievers in unconventional ways, but is careful to avoid overworking them. Consider Dellin Betances an example of the differences between Girardi and the standard manager. Any other skipper would have conferred Betances with the closer or eighth-inning-guy label and left him undisturbed until his designated outs rolled around. Not Girardi. Betances has appeared in the seventh, eighth and ninth, depending on the need, and has led baseball in multi-inning appearances two years in a row, including 2015, when he didn't pitch in more than two consecutive games all season.

This wasn't an instance of preferential treatment for the bullpen's hot young thing, either. Girardi abides by a self-imposed rule that forbids him from using any pitcher in three or more consecutive games; hence the Yankees leading the majors in multi-inning appearances while finishing 29th in appearances that came on zero days' rest. Girardi believes the method keeps his relievers fresher than they would be under normal usage, in part because it limits warm-up pitches made in vain. Of course, committing to the strategy requires a manager with foresight and discipline—how many skippers could resist using Betances in every close game?—and Girardi has shown he has enough of both. The Yankees just hope those well-rested arms can factor into a meaningful playoff run sometime soon.

OAKLAND ATHLETICS

Essay by Clair McNear

Player comments by Geoff Young, Craig Goldstein, and BP authors

Billy Beane is as close to a household name as there has ever been in a major-league front office, as close to a household name as any active player. He's the patron saint of sabermetrics, the Jesus to Bill James' John the Baptist. He gave the world *Moneyball*, the great baseball book, and Moneyball, the great baseball movement, and then was played by Brad Pitt—by *Brad Pitt*—in *Moneyball*, the great baseball movie. His name is synonymous with progress. He is the Man Who Changed Baseball Forever, a mastermind, a genius.

He's also, in some corners of Oakland, despised.

This is not unique to Beane. Every fan thinks his team's closer is unreliable, thinks his team never gets the runner in from third with one out, and thinks the front office is a bunch of crooks/idiots/cheapskates/hacks, depending on the particular blend of dissatisfaction. Beane is, in this respect, normal, but because Beane doesn't otherwise seem normal, this is surprising. *People think* that guy *is dumb*? You bet they do. Do they ever.

Maybe increasingly so. The 2015 season saw the franchise's worst record (68–94) since 1997, and the worst under Beane's watch. *Moneyball* the movie fades to black at the end: "Billy is still trying to win the last game of the season," it says. It's now been 18 years of waiting, for him; longer still for Oakland's fans. If he walked onto the O.co Coliseum's field now, some fans say, he would be booed. These are The Fans Who Hate Billy Beane.

The Angry Radio Fan

Brian Dixon is a lifelong A's fan and season ticket holder who co-hosts A's Fan Radio, a weekly internet radio show. Online, he goes by "Bauce Man"—pronounced "boss man"—a nickname he settled on after getting kicked off a couple Oakland fan pages for disagreeing, perhaps a little vocally, about the Oakland powers that be.

"It's Billy Beane, super-genius, who has a movie named after him, which I think made his head even bigger than it needed to be," Dixon says. "They're celebrating and hyping up this man. All these folks are making chicken salad out of chicken shit, saying he's so great. But he doesn't have the cojones, didn't have the stones, to take that extra step to make us a championship team for real."

ATHLETICS PROSPECTUS

2015 W-L: 68-94, 5TH IN AL WEST

Pythag	.477	20th	DER	.711	10th
RS/G	4.28	14th	B-Age	27.9	6th
RA/G	4.50	21st	P-Age	27.5	7th
TAv	.260	18th	Salary	$82.4M	27th
BRR	-22.28	30th	M$/MW	$3.6M	15th
TAv-P	.265	19th	DL Days	1330	24th
FIP	4.10	20th	$ on DL	17%	19th

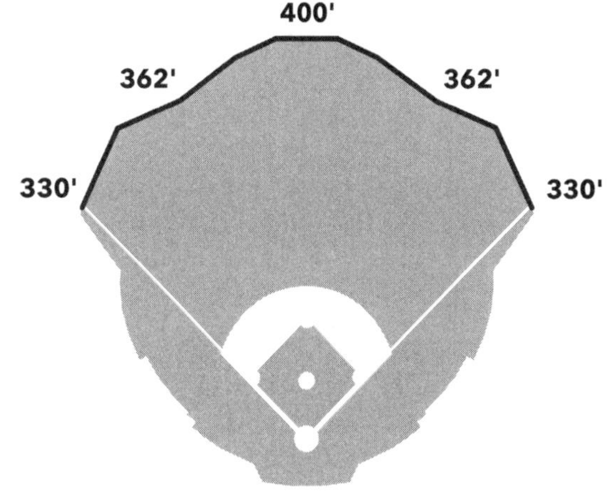

Outfield wall profile: **8'** to **15'**

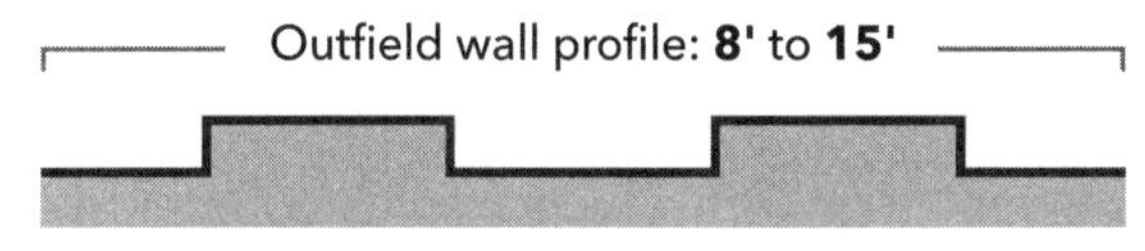

Three-Year Park Factors

Runs	Runs/RH	Runs/LH	HR/RH	HR/LH
98	111	107	102	100

Top Hitter WARP	1.9	Josh Reddick
Top Pitcher WARP	2.0	Sonny Gray
Top Prospect	Franklin Barreto	

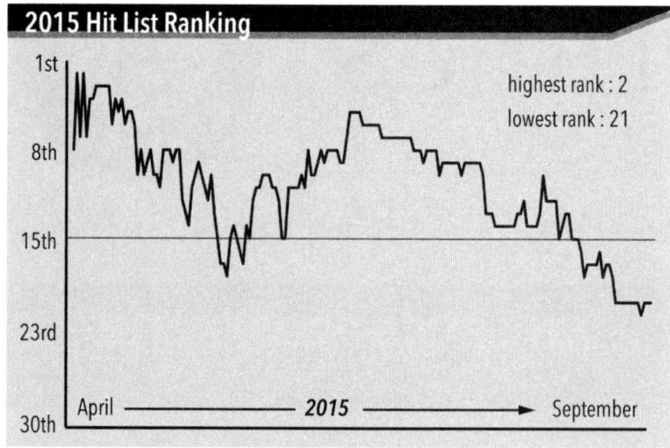

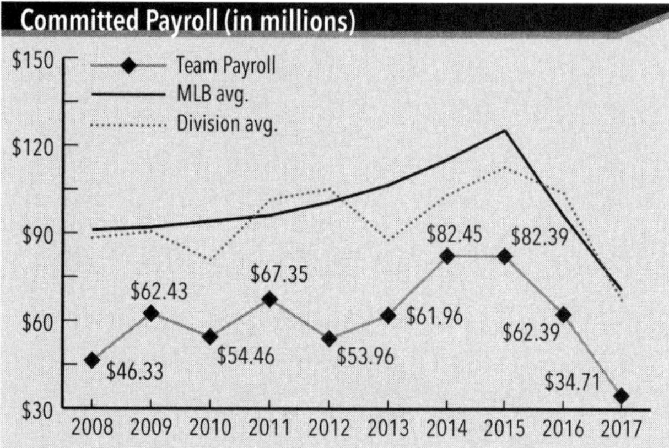

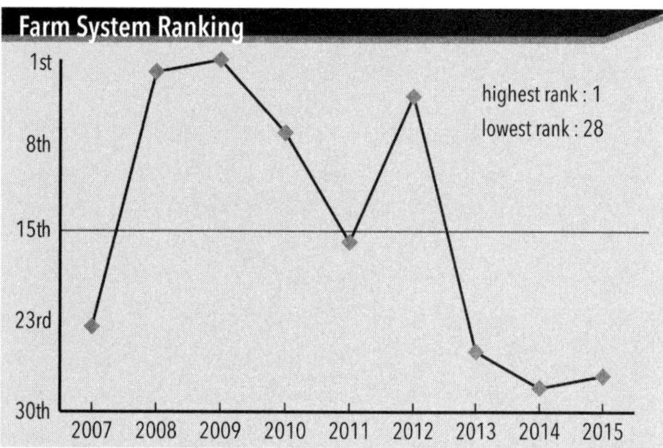

Personnel

Executive Vice President: Billy Beane

General Manager: David Forst

Manager: Bob Melvin

Baseball Prospectus Alumni
Al Skorupa

The Oakland A's are once again in the midst of total dismantling. It's a familiar cycle now: a few years of success—three, this time, beginning in 2012, with as many visits to the postseason. And then the trades begin. To fans like Dixon, each of these trade cycles comes just as the team is getting really good—and knocks everything down just before the team can get great.

"I'm somebody who cried my eyes out when Dennis Eckersley gave up that home run when I was six years old, playing the Dodgers in the '88 World Series," says Dixon. "But I've never felt worse in my life than July 31st."

That would be July 31st, 2014, the day Yoenis Cespedes was traded. Cespedes was in many ways a classic Billy Beane success: A potential star talent who, because there was a relatively short track record to go on, was available at mid-market prices. It was a gamble, but it paid off and he quickly became a star in Oakland. Then he was sent to the Red Sox for Jon Lester in a bid to shore up Oakland's playoff rotation. Many a *Baseball Prospectus* reader would consider this move the very definition of cojones, but when it didn't work, when the A's playoff bid ended four hours into the postseason, it set off the next rebuild. Josh Donaldson, fan favorite, the player who would go on to win the AL's MVP award and play in the ALCS in 2015, was shipped out. A team that seemed to be on the cusp was shaken up and reset on a course for low-cost okayness.

"Nobody fails like this and keeps doing it," says Dixon. "You know what the definition of insanity is? That's when you're doing the same thing over and over again, expecting different results. This guy is insane."

Dixon turns up at Oakland town hall meetings from time to time to exhort city and team officials to do what they need to keep the A's and Raiders in town. "It's like we are little pawns in a game of evil chess," he said from the podium in October. Here are the things he wants, in order: Stay in Oakland. Sell the team. Fire Billy Beane. Win.

"He's crazy if he thinks he can just get a bunch of cheap guys," says Dixon. "That that's ever going to bring forth a title. It's not going to happen. You're going to have to get some big-money guys that bring home the bacon.

"Not pork bacon," he says. "Beef bacon."

The Fan Who Just Wants Change

Kevin Holden moved to the Bay Area from the United Kingdom when he was 10 years old. It was 1988, and when the team made the World Series that year and won it all the following one, he thought, *Wow, I picked a good team!* Watching the A's provided some of his first lessons in American life, he says. He knows exactly how smart Beane was, and how much Beane built the franchise.

"He really got us on this path of spending wisely, and using this money to pluck guys off the scrap heap and put together amazing teams that did amazing things," he says. "I think if you look at what his legacy is, it's *Moneyball*."

But *Moneyball* is a period piece. Not one player from that team is still active, and not one team in baseball is run the same way now that it was then.

"I think a lot of the fans are a little bit tired of it now," says Holden. "Yeah, this is a great idea, but it doesn't get you far into the playoffs. Let somebody else try now."

There's little chance of that. As the 2015 season came to a close, the team announced that it would be Beane's last as GM—he would begin 2016 instead as Executive Vice President of Baseball Operations. The move is mostly symbolic; he continues to be active in day-to-day operations, and his successor, David Forst, was already heavily involved in all the responsibilities he now has.

"It feels a lot like what Vladimir Putin did in Russia, when he stepped down from being president and made his prime minister president for four years, and then he came back," says Kevin Holden. "You get the idea that Beane's still going to be pulling the strings. He's the one who's really calling the shots."

Which is great if you love Billy Beane.

The Unlikely Opposition

Danny Willis is a data journalist at the Bay Area News Group. He decided to study economics because of Bill James. During season after season sitting in the left field bleachers, he has looked and looked for signs of Billy Beane's greatness. He has studied his trades, the value of players over time, the WAR figures. And, he says, he just can't figure it out.

"Look at last season," he says. "Last season was a complete train wreck. He took a very, very good team, and he blew it up. He dismantled the team and last year they were just terrible. All his additions played terribly."

"And what happens?" asks Willis. "He gets a promotion. At that point it's like, no, he's never leaving. He's in there basically for life. He's like Connie Mack without the talent or the track record.

"I am not sure how he got the reputation he has other than the fact that he was played by Brad Pitt. The actual results of everything he has done haven't been good. He's done it cheap, but he also hasn't won anything, at least anything of note. And the times he has, it was essentially by accident."

The Conspiracy Theorists

In the darker corners of Oakland, they speak of conspiracy, of treason and sabotage just below the surface. There are many very sane, very reasonable reasons to dismiss the conspiracy. These are good reasons. But as with most conspiracies, these arguments rely on getting you to think just two little words: *But maybe*.

You are familiar, most probably, with baseball's collective bargaining agreement. The labor contract does many things for many people, among them laying out the rules of free agency, drug-testing, and in-game challenges. The CBA also tries to make amends for the variance in the 30 Major League baseball markets, offering a kind of reparations to teams in smaller markets. Under the most recent CBA, which took effect in 2012, the A's—with their perennially low attendance—get some $30 million a year.

The current CBA expires at the end of 2016. Team owners will spend the 2016 season renegotiating the terms of the agreement that will replace it. There is speculation that Oakland could lose its status as a shared revenue recipient, largely because of its location in the Bay Area—a team in a major metropolitan area, the thinking goes, even one that it shares, could hardly be considered to have a small market. If that happened, Oakland could lose its right to the $30 million a year that the team's owners say keeps the franchise afloat.

So, going into the 2016 negotiations, wouldn't the team have every reason to make things look as bleak as possible in Oakland? Wouldn't a team with low attendance, lower even than usual, strengthen the case that Oakland is a dismal market? And wouldn't a team with a losing record, its stars sold off a half-beat after they began to glimmer, with a crumbling stadium where the wind howls and concessions are few and toilets overflow—wouldn't all that keep fans away? Wouldn't you take a look at the way things are—the way things were in 2015—and think gosh, poor Oakland? Wouldn't Billy Beane, a minority owner of the team, look ahead to those 2016 negotiations and think about how much more difficult they would be if 2015 went well, if the fans of Oakland came alive, if they were made to?

And—of course, it's absurd. Billy Beane owns just a sliver of the team and scarcely stands to profit. Even if there were riches to be had, he's famously competitive, famously unable to handle losing, famously unable even to sit still while Oakland plays, watching from the TV in the team's gym. He obviously wants to see his strategy work, wants to see the A's get every last win they can, wants to cement his legacy. Of course, of course, of course, of course. Of these facts there can be no doubt.

But maybe?

After Donaldson was traded, Holden says, "I think a lot of fans are like, okay, here we go again. There was really no reason to blow this team up."

✦✦✦

Beane's November announcement that Oakland wasn't interested in trading young pitcher Sonny Gray, a lone bright spot in the team's grim 2015 season, was to these fans classic Billy Beane—how many clubs have to announce that they'll be hanging on to their ace, especially when that ace is due to make a league-minimum salary? But even the prospect of keeping Gray was little solace. The longer the A's hold on to him, they know, the more attached they're going to get, and they can be sure that eventually Gray is going to be traded.

Oakland fans watched the 2015 postseason from home. "I just want the smiled knocked off Billy Boy's face," wrote one on a fan page, cheering on Donaldson's Blue Jays and Cespedes' Mets all the way.

As for Dixon: he's never seen *Moneyball*, and he has no intention of doing so any time soon.

"I will watch *Moneyball 2* where the 2016 and 2017 A's win the title, and the story is about them," he said. "I'm not celebrating a movie about losing." ■

—Claire McNear is a staff writer at SB Nation who hails from Marin County, CA.

HITTERS

Yonder Alonso 1B

Born: 4/8/87 Age: 29 Bats: L Throws: R Height: 6'1" Weight: 220

YEAR	TEAM	LVL	AGE	PA	R	2B	3B	HR	RBI	BB	K	SB	CS	AVG/OBP/SLG	TAv	BABIP	BRR	FRAA	WARP
2013	SDN	MLB	26	375	34	11	0	6	45	32	47	6	0	.281/.341/.368	.262	.306	-3.0	1B(92): 4.2, 2B(1): -0.0	0.6
2014	SDN	MLB	27	288	27	19	1	7	27	17	36	6	1	.240/.285/.397	.253	.251	1.3	1B(77): 2.1, 3B(3): 0.0	0.5
2015	SDN	MLB	28	402	50	18	1	5	31	42	48	2	5	.282/.361/.381	.271	.313	-2.0	1B(102): 3.8, 3B(2): -0.0	1.1
2016	*OAK*	*MLB*	*29*	*510*	*53*	*26*	*1*	*10*	*54*	*46*	*72*	*5*	*3*	*.267/.333/.393*	*.263*	*.295*	*-1.6*	*1B 2*	*1.1*
2017	*OAK*	*MLB*	*30*	*451*	*52*	*22*	*1*	*9*	*47*	*40*	*68*	*4*	*2*	*.260/.326/.389*	*.259*	*.289*	*-1.4*	*1B 2*	*0.6*

Breakout: 3% Improve: 49% Collapse: 6% Attrition: 6% MLB: 96% *Comparables: James Loney, Casey Kotchman, John Jaso*

With an ISO similar to that of feared slugger Luis Rivas, Alonso lacks the offensive firepower of a prototypical first baseman. Add 30 points to his batting average and he becomes useful in a Hal Morris kind of way; otherwise his only awards are of the participation variety, when he's healthy enough to attend. It's a damning indictment of the Padres that they've spent the last four years starting him at a position that demands much more (don't mention Anthony Rizzo!) rather than developing or acquiring a legitimate starter; what that says about the A's, who sent some halfway decent pitching pieces to San Diego in order to acquire him, we'd rather not say. Alonso's season ended in early September, thanks to a stress reaction in his lower back resulting from an awkward slide into home that resembled nothing so much as a flop.

Franklin Barreto SS

Born: 2/27/96 Age: 20 Bats: R Throws: R Height: 5'9" Weight: 175

YEAR	TEAM	LVL	AGE	PA	R	2B	3B	HR	RBI	BB	K	SB	CS	AVG/OBP/SLG	TAv	BABIP	BRR	FRAA	WARP
2014	VAN	A-	18	328	65	23	4	6	61	26	64	29	5	.311/.384/.481	.314	.378	2.9	SS(68): -4.5	3.1
2015	STO	A+	19	364	50	22	3	13	47	15	67	8	3	.302/.333/.500	.318	.337	0.6	SS(86): -14.8	2.3
2016	*OAK*	*MLB*	*20*	*250*	*23*	*12*	*1*	*6*	*27*	*8*	*62*	*3*	*1*	*.235/.266/.371*	*.231*	*.290*	*0.1*	*SS -5*	*-0.1*
2017	*OAK*	*MLB*	*21*	*447*	*48*	*24*	*3*	*11*	*50*	*16*	*107*	*6*	*2*	*.249/.282/.401*	*.247*	*.303*	*0.3*	*SS -8*	*1.1*

Breakout: 4% Improve: 11% Collapse: 0% Attrition: 7% MLB: 14% *Comparables: Nick Franklin, Brad Harman, Corey Seager*

Deemed by many to be the key to the trade that sent Josh Donaldson to gather storms in Toronto, Barreto arrived in Oakland a polished prospect who had yet to be challenged. That changed in a hurry as management skipped him over Low-A and sent him directly to High-A Stockton. He stumbled early, posting a .448 OPS in April, but his bat warmed with the weather as he recorded a .933 mark the rest of the way. He's best on offense, where his barrel control compares favorably to Donkey Kong. He's made progress at shortstop, and his plus speed makes his range decent, but his hands might ultimately suit him better on the right side of the infield.

Billy Burns CF

Born: 8/30/89 Age: 26 Bats: B Throws: R Height: 5'9" Weight: 180

YEAR	TEAM	LVL	AGE	PA	R	2B	3B	HR	RBI	BB	K	SB	CS	AVG/OBP/SLG	TAv	BABIP	BRR	FRAA	WARP
2013	POT	A+	23	402	70	8	9	0	29	52	37	54	5	.312/.422/.391	.295	.349	0.1	LF(73): 3.6, CF(18): -1.6	2.7
2013	HAR	AA	23	138	26	4	0	0	8	20	17	20	2	.325/.434/.360	.305	.381	3.5	CF(17): 2.9, LF(13): 0.6	1.8
2014	SAC	AAA	24	121	17	2	0	0	5	9	19	3	1	.193/.254/.211	.174	.233	0.5	CF(28): 2.0	-0.5
2014	OAK	MLB	24	6	4	0	0	0	0	0	0	3	1	.167/.167/.167	.158	.167	-0.6	CF(1): -0.2	-0.1
2014	MID	AA	24	421	57	20	3	1	23	44	65	51	5	.250/.333/.330	.253	.298	4.9	CF(81): 7.0, LF(6): -1.8	2.1
2015	OAK	MLB	25	555	70	18	9	5	42	26	81	26	8	.294/.334/.392	.265	.339	2.4	CF(125): -12.9	0.9
2015	NAS	AAA	25	101	18	2	3	0	3	9	17	5	2	.308/.370/.396	.296	.378	0.5	CF(21): 0.3	0.8
2016	*OAK*	*MLB*	*26*	*641*	*78*	*22*	*7*	*4*	*43*	*46*	*105*	*38*	*8*	*.259/.318/.341*	*.243*	*.304*	*2.5*	*CF -2*	*1.2*
2017	*OAK*	*MLB*	*27*	*598*	*61*	*19*	*6*	*5*	*49*	*44*	*101*	*35*	*8*	*.251/.314/.335*	*.240*	*.295*	*3.5*	*CF -2*	*2.1*

Breakout: 5% Improve: 43% Collapse: 14% Attrition: 19% MLB: 71% *Comparables: Ezequiel Carrera, Brett Gardner, Julio Borbon*

A short, fast guy at the top of the order should be patient. He should work the count and wait for a good pitch to hit or take a walk so he can run wild on the bases. Burns never got the memo, averaging 3.5 pitches per plate appearance and hacking at first pitches like they were knotted vines blocking his path to buried treasure. Thing is, he destroyed first pitches, hitting .479 and slugging .718. Unorthodox though his strategy is, it's hard to argue with results. Burns was a hyper-efficient basestealer in the minors but hasn't used his speed to maximum advantage in the big leagues yet. He is a solid center fielder whose routes improved as the season progressed. His small size and large BABIP are concerns, but he has defied the odds by getting even this far. Don't bet against him.

Billy Butler DH

Born: 4/18/86 Age: 30 Bats: R Throws: R Height: 6'1" Weight: 240

YEAR	TEAM	LVL	AGE	PA	R	2B	3B	HR	RBI	BB	K	SB	CS	AVG/OBP/SLG	TAv	BABIP	BRR	FRAA	WARP
2013	KCA	MLB	27	668	62	27	0	15	82	79	102	0	0	.289/.374/.412	.283	.326	-6.3	1B(7): -0.0	1.6
2014	KCA	MLB	28	603	57	32	0	9	66	41	96	0	0	.271/.323/.379	.256	.310	-3.7	1B(37): 0.1	0.0
2015	OAK	MLB	29	601	63	28	1	15	65	52	101	0	0	.251/.323/.390	.255	.282	-9.1	1B(7): 0.2	-0.6
2016	*OAK*	*MLB*	*30*	*617*	*66*	*30*	*1*	*15*	*72*	*56*	*103*	*0*	*0*	*.270/.339/.412*	*.272*	*.304*	*-5.4*	*1B 0*	*1.3*
2017	*OAK*	*MLB*	*31*	*554*	*67*	*28*	*1*	*14*	*62*	*51*	*93*	*0*	*0*	*.266/.336/.409*	*.271*	*.301*	*-5.1*	*1B 0*	*0.9*

Breakout: 2% Improve: 46% Collapse: 7% Attrition: 7% MLB: 96% *Comparables: Kent Hrbek, Paul Konerko, Mike Sweeney*

Butler has hit a little better than Alexei Ramirez and a little worse than Starlin Castro over the last couple of years, the difference being that they provide defensive value up the middle and he seldom wields a glove at any position. Butler's home-to-first times can be measured on a tearaway calendar, and he routinely ranks among the game's top double-play victims. Only a strong September kept his overall numbers from declining for a third straight season. Butler once made a habit of getting into hitters' counts and then doing damage: In 2012 and 2013, 37 percent of his plate appearances ended in such counts and his OPS in them was a shade above 1.100. In 2014 and 2015, those numbers dipped to 30 percent and around .900. When your only asset is the ability to crush baseballs, losing that ability can have damaging consequences. Fortunately he's only owed an eight-figure salary through 2017.

Mark Canha 1B

Born: 2/15/89 Age: 27 Bats: R Throws: R Height: 6'1" Weight: 200

YEAR	TEAM	LVL	AGE	PA	R	2B	3B	HR	RBI	BB	K	SB	CS	AVG/OBP/SLG	TAv	BABIP	BRR	FRAA	WARP
2013	JAX	AA	24	504	63	32	2	13	58	54	102	6	1	.273/.371/.449	.313	.327	1.1	1B(110): -6.1, LF(12): 0.2	3.0
2014	NWO	AAA	25	537	83	28	3	20	82	57	112	3	1	.303/.384/.505	.322	.356	0.1	LF(61): 2.1, 1B(40): -1.7	4.6
2015	OAK	MLB	26	485	61	22	3	16	70	33	96	7	2	.254/.315/.426	.270	.289	0.8	1B(75): -1.9, LF(58): 5.4	1.7
2016	*OAK*	*MLB*	*27*	*201*	*22*	*10*	*1*	*6*	*24*	*16*	*44*	*2*	*1*	*.256/.325/.418*	*.272*	*.304*	*0.2*	*1B -1, RF -0*	*0.5*
2017	*OAK*	*MLB*	*28*	*332*	*39*	*16*	*2*	*9*	*37*	*26*	*73*	*2*	*1*	*.247/.318/.399*	*.264*	*.297*	*0.2*	*1B -1, RF -1*	*0.5*

Breakout: 5% Improve: 39% Collapse: 11% Attrition: 19% MLB: 70% *Comparables: Mike Carp, Nick Evans, Steve Pearce*

The A's grabbed Canha in the Rule 5 draft from Miami via Colorado, and the local kid (born in San Jose, college at Berkeley) ended up playing a larger role than anyone could have envisioned. His four-RBI debut and scorching first week made him *USA Today*'s Tuffy Rhodes Award winner, which appeared to be justified when his bat fell dormant for most of May through July. But in a plot twist, he started raking again in mid-August and never stopped. His defense was passable in left field and at first base, except for that one time Josh Reddick yelled at him for cutting a throw home. Lefties owned him, weirdly, although he showed in-season improvement. He'll never be mistaken for a star, but Canha is useful, maybe even as a starter.

Matt Chapman 3B

Born: 4/28/93 Age: 23 Bats: R Throws: R Height: 6'2" Weight: 205

YEAR	TEAM	LVL	AGE	PA	R	2B	3B	HR	RBI	BB	K	SB	CS	AVG/OBP/SLG	TAv	BABIP	BRR	FRAA	WARP
2014	BLT	A	21	202	22	8	3	5	20	7	46	2	1	.237/.282/.389	.221	.288	0.4	3B(21): 2.4	0.2
2015	STO	A+	22	352	60	21	3	23	57	39	79	4	1	.250/.341/.566	.335	.257	0.6	3B(77): 11.6	5.3
2016	*OAK*	*MLB*	*23*	*250*	*27*	*10*	*1*	*10*	*33*	*18*	*66*	*0*	*0*	*.219/.282/.409*	*.249*	*.259*	*-0.3*	*3B 5*	*1.0*
2017	*OAK*	*MLB*	*24*	*360*	*43*	*14*	*2*	*14*	*45*	*27*	*97*	*1*	*0*	*.215/.280/.400*	*.246*	*.257*	*-0.6*	*3B 8*	*1.7*

Breakout: 1% Improve: 17% Collapse: 3% Attrition: 11% MLB: 47% *Comparables: Alex Gordon, Josh Bell, Matt Davidson*

He's got that long swing, strong arm, good footwork,
And he's got that plus bat speed and he'll put in the work.
But when he makes weak contact, he grounds out every time,
And he gets thrown out by a mile, gets thrown out by a mile.

So it goes, he can't keep his quick bat in the zone,
Lacks a load. Lights are off, he's putting on a show.
They say, "I've seen that his raw power plays down in the games, in the games."
And well even if that's true,
he's got defensive value too,
and that should mean he'll be average in time.

Coco Crisp CF

Born: 11/1/79 Age: 36 Bats: B Throws: R Height: 5'10" Weight: 185

YEAR	TEAM	LVL	AGE	PA	R	2B	3B	HR	RBI	BB	K	SB	CS	AVG/OBP/SLG	TAv	BABIP	BRR	FRAA	WARP
2013	OAK	MLB	33	584	93	22	3	22	66	61	65	21	5	.261/.335/.444	.295	.258	4.1	CF(110): -0.9	4.1
2014	OAK	MLB	34	536	68	21	3	9	47	66	66	19	5	.246/.336/.363	.282	.266	0.4	CF(111): -19.2	0.7
2015	STO	A+	35	31	6	1	0	2	4	4	3	0	0	.222/.323/.481	.277	.182	0.6	LF(5): 0.2	0.2
2015	OAK	MLB	35	139	11	6	0	0	6	13	25	2	0	.175/.252/.222	.176	.218	1.5	LF(37): -2.8	-1.1
2016	*OAK*	*MLB*	*36*	*492*	*61*	*21*	*4*	*9*	*43*	*45*	*64*	*18*	*4*	*.248/.315/.377*	*.254*	*.266*	*2.0*	*LF -1*	*1.3*
2017	*OAK*	*MLB*	*37*	*313*	*34*	*13*	*2*	*5*	*30*	*28*	*42*	*10*	*3*	*.239/.306/.359*	*.246*	*.259*	*1.3*	*LF 0*	*0.9*

Breakout: 0% Improve: 25% Collapse: 8% Attrition: 15% MLB: 81% *Comparables: Frank Catalanotto, Johnny Damon, Tony Gwynn*

Crisp, who was a catalyst during the A's 2012-14 playoff runs, endured the worst season of his career. Never known for his durability, he reached new depths of fragility. He injured his right elbow in spring training, with subsequent surgery to remove a bone chip and spurs disabling him until early May. Two weeks after his season debut he was 2-for-45 and aggravated an old neck injury, causing him to miss the next 2½ months. He fared a little better on returning in August, although a .607 OPS is hardly cause for celebration. There is no way to put a positive spin on Crisp's lost 2015. Any possible future success depends entirely on his good health. At his age, and with his track record, that is a lot to ask.

Ike Davis 1B

Born: 3/22/87 Age: 29 Bats: L Throws: L Height: 6'4" Weight: 220

YEAR	TEAM	LVL	AGE	PA	R	2B	3B	HR	RBI	BB	K	SB	CS	AVG/OBP/SLG	TAv	BABIP	BRR	FRAA	WARP
2013	LVG	AAA	26	92	21	7	0	7	13	17	18	0	0	.293/.424/.667	.344	.300	-1.5	1B(19): 1.0	0.9
2013	NYN	MLB	26	377	37	14	0	9	33	57	101	4	0	.205/.326/.334	.249	.268	-0.6	1B(96): -3.8	-0.5
2014	PIT	MLB	27	397	39	18	0	10	46	57	74	0	4	.235/.343/.378	.263	.270	-1.7	1B(117): -1.6	0.2
2014	NYN	MLB	27	30	4	1	0	1	5	6	4	0	0	.208/.367/.375	.291	.211	0.1	1B(7): 0.9	0.2
2015	OAK	MLB	28	239	19	17	0	3	20	23	44	0	0	.229/.301/.350	.248	.272	-4.3	1B(65): 1.7, P(2): -0.0	-0.3
2015	NAS	AAA	28	21	2	1	0	0	5	0	5	0	0	.238/.238/.286	.170	.313	0.2	1B(4): 0.1	-0.2
2016	*OAK*	*MLB*	*29*	*265*	*30*	*12*	*0*	*9*	*33*	*32*	*58*	*1*	*1*	*.231/.324/.407*	*.266*	*.267*	*-1.2*	*1B -0*	*0.4*
2017	*OAK*	*MLB*	*30*	*271*	*35*	*12*	*0*	*9*	*33*	*33*	*59*	*1*	*0*	*.232/.326/.406*	*.267*	*.267*	*-1.3*	*1B 0*	*0.2*

Breakout: 6% Improve: 47% Collapse: 3% Attrition: 4% MLB: 97% *Comparables: Edwin Encarnacion, Todd Helton, Kent Hrbek*

Injuries have been part of the problem. Last year Davis missed 33 games in May and June with a strained left quadriceps, then saw his season end in August thanks to a torn left-hip labrum that required surgery. But even when healthy Davis has hit just .222/.328/.356 since his monster 2012. On the bright side, his pitching debut went well: He fired two scoreless innings, making him one of the A's most effective relievers and giving him bragging rights over his dad Ron on the ERA front.

Andrew Lambo PH

Born: 8/11/88 Age: 27 Bats: L Throws: L Height: 6'3" Weight: 215

YEAR	TEAM	LVL	AGE	PA	R	2B	3B	HR	RBI	BB	K	SB	CS	AVG/OBP/SLG	TAv	BABIP	BRR	FRAA	WARP
2013	PIT	MLB	24	33	4	2	0	1	2	3	11	0	1	.233/.303/.400	.253	.333	0.4	RF(6): -1.0, LF(2): 0.0	0.0
2013	IND	AAA	24	254	32	15	1	18	53	24	67	1	0	.272/.344/.589	.306	.303	0.7	RF(32): 0.3, LF(22): -0.3	1.8
2013	ALT	AA	24	247	35	9	4	14	46	20	60	6	1	.291/.351/.559	.319	.336	-0.3	LF(38): 2.8, 1B(18): -0.6	2.2
2014	PIT	MLB	25	39	3	4	0	0	1	0	8	0	0	.256/.256/.359	.207	.323	-0.1	RF(6): 0.2, 1B(1): -0.2	-0.1
2014	IND	AAA	25	262	44	19	2	11	42	22	47	3	2	.328/.389/.563	.305	.372	-0.8	1B(17): 0.4, LF(16): -1.3	1.5
2015	PIT	MLB	26	27	1	1	0	0	0	2	8	0	0	.040/.111/.080	.083	.059	0.0	RF(5): 0.3, LF(3): -0.1	-0.4
2016	*OAK*	*MLB*	*27*	*250*	*30*	*12*	*1*	*11*	*35*	*17*	*65*	*2*	*1*	*.249/.303/.457*	*.269*	*.295*	*-0.2*	*1B -0, RF -1*	*0.8*
2017	*OAK*	*MLB*	*28*	*194*	*24*	*10*	*1*	*8*	*27*	*13*	*50*	*1*	*1*	*.245/.298/.446*	*.266*	*.290*	*-0.2*	*1B 0, RF -1*	*0.3*

Breakout: 3% Improve: 14% Collapse: 12% Attrition: 25% MLB: 50% *Comparables: J.J. Davis, Justin Ruggiano, Alex Castellanos*

Lambo's Twitter bio (that's @Lambezzy35 for those interested) reads: "Take advantage of every oppurtunity [sic] that is presented to you." If only his body would heed the advice. Handed a bench job to begin the season, Lambo went down in May with a nagging case of plantar fasciitis and didn't return, thus ending his season after 27 plate appearances. The injury was the latest setback in a career known for them. While Lambo has shed his troubled reputation in recent years, he hasn't stayed healthy enough to claim a big-league job (he also missed significant time in 2012 and 2014). His above-average power and plate discipline augur a career as a platoon player, but, notably, just seven of his 67 batted balls in the majors have been classified as going the other way. A doubly helpful hint for you, Andrew: You can't spell "opportunity" without "oppo."

Jed Lowrie SS

Born: 4/17/84 Age: 32 Bats: B Throws: R Height: 6'0" Weight: 180

YEAR	TEAM	LVL	AGE	PA	R	2B	3B	HR	RBI	BB	K	SB	CS	AVG/OBP/SLG	TAv	BABIP	BRR	FRAA	WARP
2013	OAK	MLB	29	662	80	45	2	15	75	50	91	1	0	.290/.344/.446	.291	.319	-0.1	SS(119): -5.0, 2B(24): -3.1	3.7
2014	OAK	MLB	30	566	59	29	3	6	50	51	79	0	0	.249/.321/.355	.260	.281	-1.9	SS(130): -8.0	1.2
2015	HOU	MLB	31	263	35	14	0	9	30	28	43	1	0	.222/.312/.400	.263	.233	1.2	3B(47): -6.2, SS(17): 1.0	0.6
2016	*OAK*	*MLB*	*32*	*589*	*58*	*31*	*3*	*12*	*64*	*49*	*92*	*1*	*0*	*.253/.318/.388*	*.258*	*.281*	*-0.3*	*2B -19*	*0.2*
2017	*OAK*	*MLB*	*33*	*437*	*48*	*22*	*2*	*8*	*43*	*36*	*69*	*0*	*0*	*.244/.308/.367*	*.250*	*.274*	*-0.5*	*2B -14*	*0.0*

Breakout: 2% Improve: 37% Collapse: 6% Attrition: 10% MLB: 96% *Comparables: Brooks Robinson, Nomar Garciaparra, Bill Madlock*

Because this book will be printed in both paper and electronic form, there is an extremely good chance that some historian or anthropologist from the future will get their hands on it. I have a message for that person: If a means for time travel is a reality for you, please go back and tell us if Jed Lowrie was actually any good at baseball. I'm sure by now you've killed all your Baby Hitlers and whatnot, so please just do us in 2016 a solid and tell us what to think about Jed Lowrie. No doubt you've taken the methods put forward by the Astros, A's and others to enhance the science of baseball analysis and improved upon it. Please just tell us if we should appreciate Jed Lowrie or not. We honestly can't come to a consensus on it. We here in 2016 thank you in advance. Oh, also: Beyonce gets elected president, right?

Richie Martin SS

Born: 12/22/94 Age: 21 Bats: R Throws: R Height: 6'0" Weight: 192

YEAR	TEAM	LVL	AGE	PA	R	2B	3B	HR	RBI	BB	K	SB	CS	AVG/OBP/SLG	TAv	BABIP	BRR	FRAA	WARP
2015	VER	A-	20	226	31	6	4	2	16	25	47	7	7	.237/.353/.342	.280	.305	-0.3	SS(46): -0.5	1.3
2016	*OAK*	*MLB*	*21*	*250*	*22*	*8*	*1*	*3*	*20*	*16*	*73*	*3*	*2*	*.195/.256/.286*	*.203*	*.265*	*-0.4*	*SS -0*	*-0.4*
2017	*OAK*	*MLB*	*22*	*377*	*37*	*12*	*2*	*6*	*32*	*26*	*105*	*4*	*4*	*.199/.265/.298*	*.210*	*.264*	*-0.2*	*SS -1*	*1.6*

Breakout: 1% Improve: 2% Collapse: 0% Attrition: 1% MLB: 2% *Comparables: Tyler Saladino, Pete Kozma, Brad Harman*

Popped with the 20th-overall selection in the 2015 draft, Martin's profile won't make you get out of your seat and shake your bon-bon. La bomba isn't a major part of his game, as his bat isn't loaded and his swing lacks loft. You might say "I don't care" about the thunder in his bat and that would be fair; he is a shortstop after all. He does control the zone well, and his on-base abilities allow him to take advantage of his above-average speed. He's unlikely to be a plus defender, but it's alright, and his glove grades out as potentially average down the line. The whole shebang's a prospect who won't overwhelm but should provide value as long as he stays up the middle defensively.

Maxwell Muncy 1B

Born: 8/25/90 Age: 25 Bats: L Throws: R Height: 6'0" Weight: 205

YEAR	TEAM	LVL	AGE	PA	R	2B	3B	HR	RBI	BB	K	SB	CS	AVG/OBP/SLG	TAv	BABIP	BRR	FRAA	WARP
2013	STO	A+	22	428	67	13	1	21	76	64	68	1	1	.285/.400/.507	.330	.295	0.6	1B(85): -1.8	3.6
2013	MID	AA	22	197	22	12	2	4	24	24	34	0	1	.250/.340/.413	.257	.289	-1.0	1B(43): 2.2	0.3
2014	MID	AA	23	530	59	23	3	7	63	87	92	7	2	.264/.385/.379	.286	.316	-0.7	1B(86): 0.1, 3B(22): 2.2	2.4
2015	OAK	MLB	24	112	14	8	1	3	9	9	31	0	0	.206/.268/.392	.245	.261	-2.1	1B(23): 0.7, 3B(16): -0.6	-0.2
2015	NAS	AAA	24	243	24	14	1	4	35	26	58	0	1	.274/.350/.406	.293	.351	-0.8	3B(32): 3.1, 1B(26): 0.6	1.7
2016	*OAK*	*MLB*	*25*	*97*	*10*	*4*	*0*	*2*	*10*	*11*	*22*	*0*	*0*	*.230/.319/.362*	*.250*	*.281*	*-0.1*	*3B 1*	*0.3*
2017	*OAK*	*MLB*	*26*	*298*	*35*	*13*	*1*	*7*	*31*	*33*	*67*	*0*	*0*	*.233/.319/.371*	*.252*	*.285*	*-0.6*	*3B 4*	*1.1*

Breakout: 1% Improve: 10% Collapse: 17% Attrition: 30% MLB: 40% *Comparables: Matt Carpenter, Zelous Wheeler, Yamaico Navarro*

Muncy hasn't shown much pop since knocking 21 bombs in the California League in 2013, but the stocky left-handed hitter has an advanced approach at the plate, even if it didn't yield results in his MLB debut. He works counts and is strong enough to drive balls into the gaps. Primarily a first baseman in the minors, Muncy also played some third as a rookie and wasn't terrible. He worked out at second base with Ron Washington toward season's end and was scheduled to see game action there in the Mexican Pacific Winter League to increase his versatility and value. Those plans were interrupted by a rib injury that forced him out after seven games.

Yairo Munoz SS

Born: 1/23/95 Age: 21 Bats: R Throws: R Height: 6'1" Weight: 165

YEAR	TEAM	LVL	AGE	PA	R	2B	3B	HR	RBI	BB	K	SB	CS	AVG/OBP/SLG	TAv	BABIP	BRR	FRAA	WARP
2014	VER	A-	19	265	29	17	3	5	20	7	42	14	6	.298/.319/.448	.289	.338	0.9	SS(53): 6.6, 3B(8): 0.8	2.7
2015	BLT	A	20	400	48	14	3	9	48	22	62	10	2	.236/.278/.363	.247	.257	-0.2	SS(88): 0.9	1.1
2015	STO	A+	20	165	21	12	0	4	26	11	20	1	1	.320/.372/.480	.320	.346	0.3	SS(37): -3.8	1.4
2016	*OAK*	*MLB*	*21*	*250*	*22*	*10*	*1*	*5*	*24*	*9*	*54*	*2*	*1*	*.223/.254/.339*	*.219*	*.264*	*-0.2*	*SS -1*	*0.0*
2017	*OAK*	*MLB*	*22*	*402*	*40*	*17*	*2*	*9*	*41*	*16*	*84*	*2*	*1*	*.230/.264/.355*	*.227*	*.269*	*-0.4*	*SS -1*	*1.6*

Breakout: 8% Improve: 14% Collapse: 0% Attrition: 8% MLB: 14% *Comparables: Arismendy Alcantara, Jorge Polanco, Yamaico Navarro*

Benjamin Franklin famously said, "He that can have patience can have what he will." Munoz could test the A's in this regard, as he has all the tools to stick at shortstop, but questions remain about his focus after he committed 34 errors between Low- and High-A. He has a plus arm in the field and enough range for the position, but his sloppy footwork might cause him to shift to third as he advances. He'll show plus speed at times, though this is likely to play closer to average as he fills out his frame, so he won't be able to compensate for mistakes that way. But Franklin wasn't just thinking of Munoz's defense when he told us about patience; the prospect's approach at the plate needs work as well. He's got good feel for the barrel and above-average raw strength but hits off his front foot too often. Then again, Franklin also said, "Do not fear mistakes. You will know failure. Continue to reach out," so maybe Munoz is just doing his best in the face of conflicting coaching.

Jacob Nottingham C

Born: 4/3/95 Age: 21 Bats: R Throws: R Height: 6'3" Weight: 230

YEAR	TEAM	LVL	AGE	PA	R	2B	3B	HR	RBI	BB	K	SB	CS	AVG/OBP/SLG	TAv	BABIP	BRR	FRAA	WARP
2015	STO	A+	20	182	25	9	0	3	22	12	38	1	0	.299/.352/.409	.292	.365	0.4	C(34): -0.2, 1B(7): -0.1	1.3
2015	QUD	A	20	253	34	18	1	10	46	18	51	1	2	.326/.387/.543	.316	.385	-2.4	C(39): -0.9, 1B(10): -0.2	2.0
2015	LNC	A+	20	76	14	6	1	4	14	3	10	0	0	.324/.368/.606	.328	.333	-0.5	C(16): -0.2, 1B(1): 0.0	0.8
2016	*OAK*	*MLB*	*21*	*250*	*23*	*11*	*1*	*6*	*28*	*12*	*64*	*0*	*0*	*.235/.280/.374*	*.237*	*.293*	*-0.4*	*C -0, 1B -0*	*0.3*
2017	*OAK*	*MLB*	*22*	*307*	*35*	*15*	*1*	*9*	*35*	*17*	*76*	*0*	*0*	*.246/.295/.399*	*.253*	*.301*	*-0.7*	*C 0, 1B 0*	*1.0*

Breakout: 3% Improve: 8% Collapse: 1% Attrition: 7% MLB: 14% *Comparables: Gary Sanchez, Wilson Ramos, Chris Marrero*

YEAR	TEAM	P. COUNT	FRM RUNS	BLK RUNS	THRW RUNS	TOT RUNS
2016	*OAK*	*7576*	*0.0*	*0.0*	*0.0*	*0.0*
2017	*OAK*	*9306*	*0.0*	*0.0*	*0.0*	*0.0*

If history is going see the Astros having paid a king's ransom to acquire Scott Kazmir, it will rest on the broad shoulders of Nottingham. Known as an offense-minded catching prospect heading into the season, he took steps forward on both sides of the ball, though his advanced bat makes questions about his defense less relevant. Nottingham was lost in a forest of prospects in Houston, but is near the head of the class in Oakland. Some might see this as robbing the prospect-rich and giving to the prospect-poor. Nottingham doesn't look kindly upon stealing, though, nabbing 38 percent of his potential thieves across two levels and three teams last year. With the chance to have an average hit tool, plus power, and enough athleticism to stay behind the plate, Oakland might have found a long-term solution at catcher for a rental arm. That Sherwood be nice.

Renato Nunez 3B

Born: 4/4/94 Age: 22 Bats: R Throws: R Height: 6'1" Weight: 200

YEAR	TEAM	LVL	AGE	PA	R	2B	3B	HR	RBI	BB	K	SB	CS	AVG/OBP/SLG	TAv	BABIP	BRR	FRAA	WARP
2013	BLT	A	19	546	69	27	0	19	85	28	136	2	2	.258/.301/.423	.248	.315	-1.6	3B(114): 3.5	1.2
2014	STO	A+	20	563	75	28	3	29	96	34	113	2	0	.279/.336/.517	.280	.303	-1.6	3B(80): -0.4, 3B(3): -0.4	2.4
2015	MID	AA	21	416	62	23	0	18	61	28	66	1	0	.278/.332/.480	.277	.293	-0.9	3B(49): -0.7, 1B(16): -0.6	1.5
2016	*OAK*	*MLB*	*22*	*250*	*24*	*10*	*1*	*9*	*31*	*8*	*65*	*0*	*0*	*.224/.256/.385*	*.231*	*.267*	*-0.4*	*3B 0, 1B 1*	*-0.1*
2017	*OAK*	*MLB*	*23*	*367*	*40*	*15*	*1*	*13*	*43*	*13*	*98*	*0*	*0*	*.221/.255/.379*	*.230*	*.267*	*-0.8*	*3B 1, 1B 1*	*0.9*

Breakout: 4% Improve: 15% Collapse: 3% Attrition: 19% MLB: 29% *Comparables: Brandon Laird, Alex Liddi, Josh Bell*

Nunez has a quick bat that generates power to all fields when he isn't trying to pull everything. He cut down on his strikeouts last year and finished strong, hitting .352/.410/.620 over a final month interrupted by a hamstring strain, before continuing to rake in the Arizona Fall League. He might be more of a platoon type than an every-day player, and his sub-.900 fielding percentage in more than 300 games at third base suggests a position switch, though the A's haven't given up hope yet. Still, he saw action on the other side of the diamond last summer, and that's where many believe his future lies. The power excites, but Nunez must continue tightening his strike zone and improving his glovework if he's to have more than a bit role.

Matt Olson 1B

Born: 3/29/94 Age: 22 Bats: L Throws: R Height: 6'5" Weight: 230

YEAR	TEAM	LVL	AGE	PA	R	2B	3B	HR	RBI	BB	K	SB	CS	AVG/OBP/SLG	TAv	BABIP	BRR	FRAA	WARP
2013	BLT	A	19	558	69	32	0	23	93	72	148	4	3	.225/.326/.435	.266	.272	0.1	1B(127): 8.7	1.9
2014	STO	A+	20	634	111	31	1	37	97	117	137	2	0	.262/.404/.543	.326	.287	0.3	1B(102): -0.6, RF(6): 0.5	5.1
2015	MID	AA	21	585	82	37	0	17	75	105	139	5	1	.249/.388/.438	.285	.311	-0.4	1B(62): 12.2, RF(59): 15.2	5.3
2016	*OAK*	*MLB*	*22*	*250*	*28*	*10*	*0*	*9*	*31*	*33*	*72*	*0*	*0*	*.208/.315/.386*	*.256*	*.263*	*-0.5*	*1B 2, RF 3*	*0.8*
2017	*OAK*	*MLB*	*23*	*361*	*47*	*16*	*1*	*14*	*45*	*47*	*102*	*0*	*0*	*.211/.317/.399*	*.262*	*.263*	*-0.9*	*1B 2, RF 4*	*1.1*

Breakout: 1% Improve: 42% Collapse: 0% Attrition: 6% MLB: 58% *Comparables: Greg Bird, Jon Singleton, Anthony Rizzo*

Perhaps Olson thought Teddy Roosevelt said, "Walk often and carry a big stick," but either way it's working out well so far. The lanky lefty sports easy plus pull power but is widely known for his patience at the plate. Concerns about how his bat would play at the upper levels weren't really answered last year, as Olson slugged .500 or higher in three months and under .305 in the other two. His bat speed is just average, meaning he might have to cheat to catch premium velocity and access his power. A first baseman by trade, the A's have tried to take advantage of Olson's arm—he reached the low-90s on the mound—by playing him in right field, but despite the frame and a high-motor work ethic, Olson is not an impressive athlete and is better suited for the cold corner, where his lower-end power output will likely have him straddling the line between first- and second-division talent.

Josh Phegley C

Born: 2/12/88 Age: 28 Bats: R Throws: R Height: 5'10" Weight: 225

YEAR	TEAM	LVL	AGE	PA	R	2B	3B	HR	RBI	BB	K	SB	CS	AVG/OBP/SLG	TAv	BABIP	BRR	FRAA	WARP
2013	CHR	AAA	25	258	39	18	1	15	41	15	38	1	1	.316/.368/.597	.329	.317	-1.5	C(60): 8.6	3.9
2013	CHA	MLB	25	213	14	7	0	4	22	5	41	2	0	.206/.223/.299	.196	.236	-0.7	C(64): -0.5, 2B(1): -0.0	-0.6
2014	CHA	MLB	26	38	4	2	0	3	7	0	11	0	0	.216/.211/.514	.269	.208	-0.8	C(11): -2.6	-0.2
2014	CHR	AAA	26	467	69	30	4	23	75	31	72	0	1	.274/.331/.530	.268	.278	0.6	C(105): 4.7	3.2
2015	OAK	MLB	27	243	27	16	1	9	34	14	51	0	0	.249/.300/.449	.273	.283	-5.8	C(68): -6.6	0.1
2016	*OAK*	*MLB*	*28*	*193*	*20*	*10*	*1*	*7*	*26*	*9*	*37*	*0*	*0*	*.247/.289/.435*	*.259*	*.269*	*-1.9*	*C -2*	*0.4*
2017	*OAK*	*MLB*	*29*	*306*	*36*	*15*	*1*	*11*	*39*	*16*	*60*	*0*	*0*	*.244/.290/.423*	*.257*	*.269*	*-3.1*	*C -4*	*0.5*

Breakout: 7% Improve: 38% Collapse: 12% Attrition: 28% MLB: 82% *Comparables: Ryan Shealy, Welington Castillo, Xavier Paul*

Phegley was a pleasant surprise whose right-handed power and strong arm allowed the A's to rest Stephen Vogt as needed without sacrificing much on either side of the ball. Well, sort of: Phegley hit .383/.431/.830 from May 28th to June 26th, but a more stereotypically backup-catcherish .213/.266/.348 outside of those four weeks. He was at his best with men on base and in high-leverage situations, and his minor-league record suggests the power is legit. Phegley's season ended with a concussion incurred when Billy Butler accidentally whacked him during batting practice in September, which was arguably the most damage Butler did with his bat all year.

YEAR	TEAM	P. COUNT	FRM RUNS	BLK RUNS	THRW RUNS	TOT RUNS
2013	CHA	8625	-1.5	-0.3	0.2	-1.7
2013	CHR	8045	4.6	0.0	1.5	6.1
2014	CHA	1568	-2.5	0.0	0.0	-2.5
2014	CHR	15266	-1.7	-0.4	6.8	4.7
2015	OAK	8644	-6.2	0.0	0.5	-5.7
2016	*OAK*	*7378*	*-3.3*	*-0.1*	*0.9*	*-2.5*
2017	*OAK*	*11708*	*-6.0*	*-0.2*	*1.4*	*-4.8*

Chad Pinder MI

Born: 3/29/92 Age: 24 Bats: R Throws: R Height: 6'2" Weight: 190

YEAR	TEAM	LVL	AGE	PA	R	2B	3B	HR	RBI	BB	K	SB	CS	AVG/OBP/SLG	TAv	BABIP	BRR	FRAA	WARP
2013	VER	A-	21	161	14	4	0	3	8	12	41	1	0	.200/.286/.293	.262	.253	-0.9	SS(33): -4.1, 3B(2): 0.2	0.1
2014	STO	A+	22	436	61	32	5	13	55	22	99	12	9	.288/.336/.489	.286	.352	-1.0	2B(70): -4.4, SS(12): 1.5	1.7
2015	MID	AA	23	522	71	32	2	15	86	28	103	7	5	.317/.361/.486	.288	.374	-0.1	SS(111): -18.5	1.7
2016	*OAK*	*MLB*	*24*	*250*	*24*	*12*	*1*	*6*	*28*	*8*	*66*	*2*	*1*	*.242/.276/.380*	*.240*	*.306*	*-0.4*	*SS -5, 2B -0*	*0.0*
2017	*OAK*	*MLB*	*25*	*367*	*39*	*18*	*2*	*9*	*40*	*13*	*96*	*3*	*2*	*.244/.280/.386*	*.244*	*.308*	*-0.4*	*SS -8, 2B 0*	*0.7*

Breakout: 2% Improve: 16% Collapse: 7% Attrition: 19% MLB: 33% *Comparables: Zach Walters, Grant Green, Jordany Valdespin*

The Texas League's Player of the Year, Pinder is a great reason not to scout the stat line. While he's not looked down upon by scouts, he's thought of more as a utilityman than an every-day starter. It could be that his versatility is working against him in this regard, as Pinder played shortstop and third base in college before manning the keystone more often in 2014. His breakout season came back at shortstop, though, and his ability to play there will have a signficant impact on his role in the majors. With average hit and power tools, it's not hard to see Pinder outplaying expectations if he remains in the middle infield. That said, his aggressive approach can cause his power to play down, and it's not difficult to see this happening more frequently as he continues up the chain.

Josh Reddick RF

Born: 2/19/87 Age: 29 Bats: L Throws: R Height: 6'2" Weight: 180

YEAR	TEAM	LVL	AGE	PA	R	2B	3B	HR	RBI	BB	K	SB	CS	AVG/OBP/SLG	TAv	BABIP	BRR	FRAA	WARP
2013	OAK	MLB	26	441	54	19	2	12	56	46	86	9	2	.226/.307/.379	.263	.255	2.8	RF(113): 9.6	2.3
2014	OAK	MLB	27	396	53	16	7	12	54	28	63	1	1	.264/.316/.446	.294	.289	0.4	RF(107): 3.0, CF(1): -0.0	2.5
2014	STO	A+	27	22	6	2	0	3	8	1	6	0	0	.429/.455/.952	.502	.500	0.0	RF(3): -0.8	0.3
2015	OAK	MLB	28	582	67	25	4	20	77	49	65	10	2	.272/.333/.449	.287	.278	-0.1	RF(143): -6.7, CF(1): -0.0	1.9
2016	*OAK*	*MLB*	*29*	*609*	*71*	*27*	*5*	*21*	*78*	*52*	*107*	*8*	*2*	*.253/.317/.436*	*.273*	*.276*	*0.9*	*RF 1*	*2.5*
2017	*OAK*	*MLB*	*30*	*552*	*69*	*25*	*4*	*20*	*71*	*49*	*101*	*7*	*2*	*.250/.316/.435*	*.273*	*.274*	*0.8*	*RF 1*	*1.3*

Breakout: 5% Improve: 42% Collapse: 2% Attrition: 5% MLB: 97% *Comparables: Andre Ethier, Michael Cuddyer, Jason Kubel*

The shape of Reddick's offensive game has changed dramatically since his 32-homer outburst in 2012. While his over-the-fence power has declined, his ISO has remained respectable for a corner outfielder. At the same time, he makes better contact than he used to, whiffing a little less often each season. His strikeout rate in 2015 was half what it was three years earlier. The new Reddick might have fewer highs than the old one, but he also has fewer lows. In the field he still owns a strong arm, though few bother testing it anymore. Advanced defensive metrics weren't crazy about his work last year, but he still played a solid right field despite bouts of "happy feet" that cause him to clank a routine flyball once in a great while. Reddick is a borderline star with room for additional offensive growth, albeit in a different direction than was once expected.

Marcus Semien SS

Born: 9/17/90 Age: 25 Bats: R Throws: R Height: 6'1" Weight: 195

YEAR	TEAM	LVL	AGE	PA	R	2B	3B	HR	RBI	BB	K	SB	CS	AVG/OBP/SLG	TAv	BABIP	BRR	FRAA	WARP
2013	CHA	MLB	22	71	7	4	0	2	7	1	22	2	2	.261/.268/.406	.266	.348	-0.6	3B(17): -0.1, 2B(3): 0.1	0.3
2013	BIR	AA	22	484	90	21	5	15	49	84	66	20	5	.290/.420/.483	.329	.317	2.9	SS(47): 2.6, 2B(41): -1.8	5.9
2013	CHR	AAA	22	142	20	11	1	4	17	14	24	4	0	.264/.338/.464	.275	.293	-0.9	SS(25): -3.9, 3B(6): 1.6	0.5
2014	CHR	AAA	23	366	57	20	3	15	52	53	59	7	2	.267/.380/.502	.282	.282	2.8	SS(42): 0.9, 3B(17): 3.4	3.1
2014	CHA	MLB	23	255	30	10	2	6	28	21	70	3	0	.234/.300/.372	.248	.310	-1.3	3B(33): 2.3, 2B(26): 0.4	0.6
2015	OAK	MLB	24	601	65	23	7	15	45	42	132	11	5	.257/.310/.405	.253	.312	0.8	SS(152): -4.2	1.7
2016	*OAK*	*MLB*	*25*	*522*	*67*	*23*	*4*	*14*	*54*	*49*	*112*	*10*	*3*	*.250/.325/.409*	*.268*	*.298*	*-0.4*	*SS -3*	*2.7*
2017	*OAK*	*MLB*	*26*	*563*	*69*	*25*	*4*	*16*	*67*	*52*	*120*	*10*	*4*	*.251/.323/.417*	*.270*	*.296*	*-0.1*	*SS -3*	*2.2*

Breakout: 2% Improve: 54% Collapse: 5% Attrition: 10% MLB: 98% *Comparables: Brad Miller, Kyle Seager, Dustin Ackley*

The big question coming into 2015 was whether Semien could cut it as a starting big-league shortstop. His range and arm drew mixed reviews, with some evaluators suggesting a move to second base might be imminent. With the broad base of offensive skills he'd shown in the minors—plenty of walks and doubles, a few homers—the local product figured to be an asset with the bat on either side of the bag.

Semien's power translated well at the highest level, but his on-base skills didn't make the jump from Triple-A. Still, he played 152 games at shortstop and provided respectable offense from the position in his first full season. His glovework, as anticipated, was less respectable. As beat writer John Hickey observed, he committed more errors by the All-Star break (28) than the team's entire starting infield had at the same point in 2014.

Semien finished with an Oakland record 35 miscues, which sounds like—and is—a lot, but simple arithmetic shows that only 20 percent of his errors came in the second half. Heck, he made as many in a five-game stretch in May as he did from August onward. Breaking Semien's season into two-month chunks reveals the larger truth of his growth over time:

Month	G	E	Fldg%	OPS
Apr-May	53	18	.918	.770
Jun-Jul	48	11	.946	.527
Aug-Oct	51	6	.974	.830

What is OPS doing in a table about defense? Here's a theory, and it's only a theory: Semien struggled on defense early, but then began to improve, with attention on that aspect of his game causing him to take a short-term hit on offense. Then both sides of his game jelled at the same time, providing hope that a future at shortstop might yet be possible.

There are precedents: Jason Bartlett and David Eckstein enjoyed long careers at short despite the protests of those who believed they couldn't do it. Semien has enough athleticism to handle the position, and he drew praise throughout those early struggles for his maturity and his work ethic. One of the men praising Semien was Ron Washington, whom the A's hired toward the end of May to tutor the young infielder. The influence of Washington, who once helped Miguel Tejada refine his shortstop play, cannot be ignored. And while it's premature to declare Semien's shortcomings conquered, it's also premature to consider a shift further down the defensive spectrum.

Eric Sogard 2B

Born: 5/22/86 Age: 30 Bats: L Throws: R Height: 5'10" Weight: 190

YEAR	TEAM	LVL	AGE	PA	R	2B	3B	HR	RBI	BB	K	SB	CS	AVG/OBP/SLG	TAv	BABIP	BRR	FRAA	WARP
2013	OAK	MLB	27	410	45	24	3	2	35	27	51	10	5	.266/.322/.364	.266	.301	-1.5	2B(113): 0.0, SS(15): 0.2	1.3
2014	OAK	MLB	28	329	38	10	0	1	22	31	37	11	4	.223/.298/.268	.225	.251	0.3	2B(102): 8.2, SS(14): 0.2	0.7
2015	OAK	MLB	29	401	40	12	3	1	37	23	50	6	1	.247/.294/.304	.224	.283	2.2	2B(96): 5.7, SS(17): -0.0	0.5
2016	*OAK*	*MLB*	*30*	*148*	*14*	*6*	*1*	*1*	*12*	*11*	*19*	*3*	*1*	*.247/.306/.333*	*.238*	*.275*	*0.1*	*SS 0, 2B 1*	*0.5*
2017	*OAK*	*MLB*	*31*	*237*	*23*	*10*	*1*	*2*	*19*	*16*	*32*	*5*	*2*	*.242/.297/.327*	*.232*	*.271*	*0.3*	*SS 0, 2B 1*	*1.2*

Breakout: 0% Improve: 32% Collapse: 7% Attrition: 12% MLB: 88% *Comparables: Ryan Freel, Jonathan Herrera, Skip Schumaker*

When Sogard launched his only homer of the season, on September 23rd, the Oakland faithful went nuts. In addition to ending our national nightmare and having zero impact on a meaningless blowout loss at the end of a disappointing season, that momentous blast inched his slugging percentage toward .300, a mark he had not seen since late May. A capable second baseman with arm and range enough to make cameos at short, Sogard is an extreme contact hitter who seldom drives the ball with authority: Over the last three years, only Ben Revere and Ichiro Suzuki have a lower isolated power among the 233 players with at least 1,000 plate appearances. Sogard's glove, personality and cult following will sustain his career for a while, with perhaps fewer opportunities to inflict damage on his own team at the plate. He is well on his way to becoming the new Chuck Hiller, as everyone doubtless hoped.

Danny Valencia 3B

Born: 9/19/84 Age: 31 Bats: R Throws: R Height: 6'2" Weight: 220

YEAR	TEAM	LVL	AGE	PA	R	2B	3B	HR	RBI	BB	K	SB	CS	AVG/OBP/SLG	TAv	BABIP	BRR	FRAA	WARP
2013	BAL	MLB	28	170	20	14	1	8	23	8	33	0	2	.304/.335/.553	.307	.339	-0.4	3B(6): -0.4	1.0
2013	NOR	AAA	28	282	40	20	1	14	51	17	48	1	1	.286/.326/.531	.306	.300	1.6	3B(48): -2.4, 1B(6): -0.9	2.1
2014	TOR	MLB	29	165	12	11	1	2	19	7	35	1	1	.240/.273/.364	.225	.292	-1.3	3B(40): 1.1, 1B(20): -0.3	-0.2
2014	KCA	MLB	29	119	8	5	0	2	11	7	27	0	0	.282/.328/.382	.276	.354	-2.8	3B(26): 0.4, 2B(6): -0.6	0.2
2015	TOR	MLB	30	173	26	13	0	7	29	9	40	2	1	.296/.331/.506	.281	.353	-0.6	LF(32): -1.7, 3B(10): -1.0	0.4
2015	OAK	MLB	30	205	33	10	1	11	37	20	40	0	1	.284/.356/.530	.310	.308	0.5	3B(45): -2.0	1.6
2016	*OAK*	*MLB*	*31*	*563*	*56*	*29*	*2*	*16*	*67*	*32*	*111*	*3*	*3*	*.251/.293/.406*	*.255*	*.288*	*-2.0*	*3B -3*	*0.7*
2017	*OAK*	*MLB*	*32*	*470*	*53*	*25*	*1*	*13*	*55*	*25*	*95*	*2*	*2*	*.252/.294/.407*	*.256*	*.290*	*-1.6*	*3B -3*	*0.7*

Breakout: 0% Improve: 28% Collapse: 11% Attrition: 13% MLB: 83% *Comparables: Kevin Kouzmanoff, Ty Wigginton, Greg Dobbs*

The Blue Jays, suffering from an embarrassment of offensive riches, waived Valencia in August despite a slugging percentage north of .500. He did even better in Oakland, providing right-handed pop in the middle of a lineup that needed it. His defense at third base was less spectacular than Brett Lawrie's but also less erratic. Amusingly, we ended his comment last year by stating that Valencia couldn't replace Lawrie at the hot corner when both were in Toronto. Billy Beane disagreed and thus far looks the smarter for it. Valencia has teased at productivity in the past but never sustained it. With an average exit velocity on batted balls last year between those of Mike Trout and Nelson Cruz, his new level might not be an aberration.

Stephen Vogt C

Born: 11/1/84 Age: 31 Bats: L Throws: R Height: 6'0" Weight: 215

YEAR	TEAM	LVL	AGE	PA	R	2B	3B	HR	RBI	BB	K	SB	CS	AVG/OBP/SLG	TAv	BABIP	BRR	FRAA	WARP
2013	SAC	AAA	28	338	55	21	3	13	58	38	45	0	1	.324/.398/.547	.325	.344	-0.2	C(65): 15.8	5.4
2013	OAK	MLB	28	148	18	6	1	4	16	9	28	0	1	.252/.295/.400	.255	.286	-0.4	C(44): -4.7	0.0
2014	SAC	AAA	29	97	18	8	2	3	19	8	8	1	0	.364/.412/.602	.374	.372	1.3	C(19): 0.6, LF(1): -0.2	1.9
2014	OAK	MLB	29	287	26	10	2	9	35	16	39	1	0	.279/.321/.431	.287	.297	0.4	1B(47): -1.4, RF(17): -0.7	1.1
2015	OAK	MLB	30	511	58	21	3	18	71	56	97	0	2	.261/.341/.443	.286	.290	-7.0	C(99): -12.5, 1B(25): -1.1	1.1
2016	*OAK*	*MLB*	*31*	*582*	*62*	*25*	*4*	*17*	*71*	*49*	*101*	*1*	*1*	*.258/.321/.420*	*.266*	*.287*	*-2.9*	*C -8, 1B -1*	*1.4*
2017	*OAK*	*MLB*	*32*	*514*	*61*	*20*	*3*	*15*	*59*	*43*	*97*	*0*	*0*	*.245/.309/.398*	*.257*	*.276*	*-2.7*	*C -7, 1B -1*	*0.8*

Breakout: 5% Improve: 28% Collapse: 13% Attrition: 21% MLB: 86% *Comparables: Steve Pearce, Daniel Nava, Ryan Doumit*

YEAR	TEAM	P. COUNT	FRM RUNS	BLK RUNS	THRW RUNS	TOT RUNS
2013	OAK	5444	-3.7	-0.1	0.1	-3.7
2013	SAC	8905	13.2	-0.2	3.0	16.0
2014	OAK	1315	0.6	0.0	0.1	0.7
2014	SAC	2392	0.8	0.0	0.3	1.1
2015	OAK	13004	-10.2	-0.2	0.0	-10.4
2016	*OAK*	*17088*	*-6.6*	*-0.3*	*0.7*	*-6.1*
2017	*OAK*	*15093*	*-5.4*	*-0.3*	*0.5*	*-5.2*

Vogt proved that 2014 was no fluke, producing similar qualitative numbers in nearly twice the playing time en route to his first All-Star appearance. He carried the A's through May, hitting .322/.411/.611 over the first two months. The final four proved less kind, as the dinged-up backstop slipped to .230/.302/.358 the rest of the way, reminding us again that squatting behind home plate four days a week all summer is a tough way to make a living. Despite the slow fade in his first shot as a starting big-league catcher, Vogt remained a welcome presence in the lineup and in the clubhouse, with his Chris Farley impression bringing many laughs in a season that sorely needed them.

Mikey White SS

Born: 9/3/93 Age: 22 Bats: R Throws: R Height: 6'1" Weight: 200

YEAR	TEAM	LVL	AGE	PA	R	2B	3B	HR	RBI	BB	K	SB	CS	AVG/OBP/SLG	TAv	BABIP	BRR	FRAA	WARP
2015	BLT	A	21	145	16	5	0	1	12	10	30	0	1	.200/.283/.262	.212	.253	0.2	SS(35): -4.2	-0.6
2015	VER	A-	21	131	18	10	0	2	16	14	29	0	2	.315/.405/.459	.327	.402	0.7	SS(13): 0.2, 3B(11): 1.2	1.6
2016	*OAK*	*MLB*	*22*	*250*	*20*	*9*	*1*	*3*	*20*	*14*	*71*	*0*	*0*	*.197/.252/.286*	*.201*	*.265*	*-0.4*	*SS -2, 3B 0*	*-0.7*
2017	*OAK*	*MLB*	*23*	*327*	*31*	*13*	*1*	*5*	*28*	*19*	*89*	*0*	*0*	*.208/.265/.306*	*.213*	*.275*	*-0.7*	*SS -2, 3B 0*	*1.0*

Breakout: 0% Improve: 0% Collapse: 1% Attrition: 1% MLB: 1% *Comparables: Jed Lowrie, Taylor Featherston, Jason Donald*

The second SEC shortstop selected by the A's, White is less likely to stick at the position than first-rounder Richie Martin. Rather, Alabama's 2012 Mr. Baseball will probably make his sweet home at second base, where the grinder-style descriptions will fit a little more comfortably. White is the type to get the most out of his fringe-average tools thanks to an instinctive understanding of the game paired with a positive attitude and tremendous work ethic. Cliches aside, you don't get drafted in the second round on your makeup alone. While White may not be a walking tool shed, he's got more than enough to carve out a long career as a second-division second sacker.

Pitchers

Raul Alcantara RHP

Born: 12/4/92 Age: 23 Bats: R Throws: R Height: 6'3" Weight: 205

YEAR	TEAM	LVL	AGE	W	L	SV	G	GS	IP	H	HR	BB/9	K/9	GB%	BABIP	WHIP	ERA	FIP	DRA	WARP	CFIP	MPH
2013	BLT	A	20	7	1	0	13	13	77^1	84	3	0.8	6.8	47%	.324	1.18	2.44	2.77	4.05	1.1	82	
2013	STO	A+	20	5	5	0	14	14	79	73	8	1.9	7.5	41%	.280	1.14	3.76	4.21	5.09	1.0	93	
2014	MID	AA	21	2	0	0	3	3	19^2	17	0	2.3	4.6	54%	.288	1.12	2.29	3.17				
2015	STO	A+	22	0	2	0	15	15	48^2	54	3	1.5	5.4	46%	.319	1.27	3.88	4.00	5.72	0.0	110	
2016	*OAK*	*MLB*	*23*	*2*	*3*	*0*	*7*	*7*	35^1	*41*	*5*	*2.7*	*4.5*	*41%*	*.298*	*1.46*	*5.06*	*5.08*	*5.49*	*-0.2*	*133*	
2017	*OAK*	*MLB*	*24*	*7*	*10*	*0*	*26*	*26*	156^2	*198*	*29*	*3.0*	*4.6*	*41%*	*.312*	*1.60*	*5.51*	*5.68*	*5.98*	*-1.4*	*146*	

Breakout: 6% Improve: 8% Collapse: 3% Attrition: 11% MLB: 12% *Comparables: Jerad Eickhoff, Lance Broadway, Daniel Corcino*

Don't hold Alcantara's "demotion" against him too much. Yes, he reached Double-A in 2014 and spent all of last year in High-A, but he was also recovering from Tommy John surgery, so not overwhelming him might have been part of the plan. What you can hold against him is the utter lack of swing-and-miss stuff. Alcantara works with a plus fastball and can flash a plus changeup, but his slider is average at its best, and it isn't at its best often enough. He was viewed as a back-end starter even before he went under the knife; now he'll have to sharpen his stuff to reach even that modest ceiling.

Henderson Alvarez RHP

Born: 4/18/90 Age: 26 Bats: R Throws: R Height: 6'0" Weight: 205

2013	MIA	MLB	23	5	6	0	17	17	102^2	90	2	2.4	5.0	55%	.271	1.14	3.59	3.16	3.41	1.9	112	96.7
2013	JAX	AA	23	1	0	0	2	2	14^1	5	0	0.0	8.2	77%	.143	0.35	0.00	1.10	3.49	0.2	81	
2013	JUP	A+	23	1	0	0	2	2	10	9	1	0.9	1.8	53%	.242	1.00	2.70	4.44	4.52	0.0	111	
2014	MIA	MLB	24	12	7	0	30	30	187	198	14	1.6	5.3	56%	.304	1.24	2.65	3.55	3.93	2.0	110	96.4
2015	JUP	A+	25	0	1	0	3	3	11^1	11	0	1.6	6.4	57%	.297	1.15	1.59	2.28	3.51	0.1	96	
2015	MIA	MLB	25	0	4	0	4	4	22^1	28	1	2.8	3.6	60%	.318	1.57	6.45	3.88	5.55	-0.1	121	93.6
2016	*OAK*	*MLB*	*26*	*3*	*4*	*0*	*10*	*10*	*57*	*58*	*6*	*2.1*	*5.1*	*57%*	*.283*	*1.24*	*4.13*	*4.28*	*4.59*	*0.4*	*107*	
2017	*OAK*	*MLB*	*27*	*7*	*7*	*0*	*20*	*20*	*117*	*126*	*14*	*2.2*	*5.3*	*57%*	*.295*	*1.33*	*4.21*	*4.36*	*4.68*	*0.6*	*110*	

Breakout: 27% Improve: 57% Collapse: 15% Attrition: 8% MLB: 91% *Comparables: Mike Pelfrey, Mark Buehrle, Justin Thompson*

Like a post-apocalyptic hellscape or a Denny's corner booth on New Year's morning, Alvarez's season was disconsolate. He was 25, coming off an All-Star season, the Marlins' Opening Day starter in Jose Fernandez's absence, but his shoulder started barking during a pair of April starts, howled louder in a pair of May disasters and ultimately heeled at the icy hand of Dr. James Andrews in July. Unlike Tommy John surgery, there's no upside in a shoulder injury. The timetable that's been reported would have the A's sending him out on a rehab assignment in April.

John Axford RHP

Born: 4/1/83 Age: 33 Bats: R Throws: R Height: 6'5" Weight: 220

YEAR	TEAM	LVL	AGE	W	L	SV	G	GS	IP	H	HR	BB/9	K/9	GB%	BABIP	WHIP	ERA	FIP	DRA	WARP	CFIP	MPH
2013	SLN	MLB	30	1	0	0	13	0	10^1	11	0	2.6	9.6	55%	.379	1.35	1.74	2.05	5.67	-0.1	86	98.9
2013	MIL	MLB	30	6	7	0	62	0	54^2	62	10	3.8	8.9	46%	.331	1.55	4.45	4.74	5.47	-0.6	98	97.8
2014	PIT	MLB	31	0	1	0	13	0	11	9	0	4.9	9.8	54%	.321	1.36	4.09	2.83	4.40	0.0	109	97.4
2014	CLE	MLB	31	2	3	10	49	0	43^2	34	6	6.2	10.5	55%	.259	1.47	3.92	4.74	3.97	0.3	99	97.1
2015	COL	MLB	32	4	5	25	60	0	55^2	56	4	5.2	10.0	56%	.342	1.58	4.20	3.59	3.51	0.8	88	99.0
2016	*OAK*	*MLB*	*33*	*3*	*1*	*0*	*60*	*0*	*63*	*58*	*7*	*4.0*	*9.1*	*55%*	*.293*	*1.36*	*4.05*	*4.08*	*4.50*	*0.2*	*101*	
2017	*OAK*	*MLB*	*34*	*3*	*1*	*11*	*57*	*0*	51^2	*51*	*7*	*4.4*	*8.9*	*55%*	*.305*	*1.48*	*4.37*	*4.49*	*4.85*	*-0.1*	*110*	

Breakout: 21% Improve: 43% Collapse: 23% Attrition: 9% MLB: 89% *Comparables: Brian Wilson, Jose Valverde, Tippy Martinez*

The 2011 recipient of the Mustached American of the Year Award grew out a beard that he described to the *Denver Post* as having "a better cornucopia of colors" than beard rival Charlie Blackmon's. That was preseason, when things were fun. In an awful turn of events, Axford missed the first few weeks of the season to be with his 2-year-old son, who was in intensive care after being bitten by a rattlesnake during spring training. The father returned to the team just before Adam Ottavino underwent Tommy John surgery and subsequently took over ninth-inning duties. He adjusted well to Colorado's thin air, pitching lower in the zone and racking up grounders at a career-high rate. Walks remain the chief issue for Axford, and late innings with him can still be an adventure. That could eventually spell trouble for the coloring of his teammates' beards, though at least the A's won't have him pitching the ninth unless something goes badly awry.

Chris Bassitt RHP

Born: 2/22/89 Age: 27 Bats: R Throws: R Height: 6'5" Weight: 210

YEAR	TEAM	LVL	AGE	W	L	SV	G	GS	IP	H	HR	BB/9	K/9	GB%	BABIP	WHIP	ERA	FIP	DRA	WARP	CFIP	MPH
2013	BIR	AA	24	4	2	0	8	8	47^{2}	35	2	3.2	7.0	48%	.254	1.09	2.27	3.23	4.00	0.4	98	
2013	WNS	A+	24	7	2	0	18	18	101^{1}	90	9	3.7	9.0	50%	.283	1.30	3.46	3.90	4.51	1.0	93	
2014	BIR	AA	25	3	1	0	6	6	34^{2}	26	2	3.6	9.3	48%	.264	1.15	1.56	3.24				
2014	CHA	MLB	25	1	1	0	6	5	29^{2}	34	0	3.9	6.4	42%	.340	1.58	3.94	3.36	4.25	0.2	110	95.1
2015	OAK	MLB	26	1	8	0	18	13	86	78	5	3.1	6.7	46%	.289	1.26	3.56	3.73	4.04	1.0	107	96.3
2015	NAS	AAA	26	2	7	0	13	10	69	59	1	2.5	9.1	50%	.304	1.13	3.65	2.72	3.07	1.9	78	
2016	*OAK*	*MLB*	*27*	*6*	*6*	*0*	*19*	*19*	100^{2}	*94*	*10*	*3.1*	*7.3*	*46%*	*.283*	*1.28*	*3.98*	*4.10*	*4.43*	*0.8*	*101*	
2017	*OAK*	*MLB*	*28*	*5*	*5*	*0*	*24*	*15*	105^{1}	*100*	*12*	*3.4*	*7.9*	*46%*	*.287*	*1.32*	*4.05*	*4.19*	*4.51*	*0.6*	*104*	

Breakout: 18% Improve: 48% Collapse: 17% Attrition: 29% MLB: 75% *Comparables: David Phelps, Michael Kirkman, Dustin Nippert*

Bassitt was recalled in late April and made five relief appearances before returning to Triple-A two weeks later. Recalled again at the end of June, he pitched well as a starter before "shoulder soreness" kept him out for most of September. He did make three starts at season's end, but the rust showed, dragging down his overall numbers in an otherwise pleasantly surprising rookie campaign. Talk of a move to the bullpen has quieted for now, as Bassitt's velocity and funky delivery made for an effective combination deep into games, and fears that lefties would feast on his secondaries have been unwarranted thus far. He'll always have to prove doubters wrong, but that can be a powerful motivator.

Sean Doolittle LHP

Born: 9/26/86 Age: 29 Bats: L Throws: L Height: 6'3" Weight: 210

YEAR	TEAM	LVL	AGE	W	L	SV	G	GS	IP	H	HR	BB/9	K/9	GB%	BABIP	WHIP	ERA	FIP	DRA	WARP	CFIP	MPH
2013	OAK	MLB	26	5	5	2	70	0	69	53	4	1.7	7.8	35%	.262	0.96	3.13	2.74	2.69	1.6	85	97.2
2014	OAK	MLB	27	2	4	22	61	0	62^{2}	38	5	1.1	12.8	24%	.246	0.73	2.73	1.74	1.74	2.1	49	96.5
2015	OAK	MLB	28	1	0	4	12	0	13^{2}	12	1	3.3	9.9	35%	.306	1.24	3.95	2.96	3.42	0.2	93	95.0
2016	*OAK*	*MLB*	*29*	*3*	*1*	*35*	*50*	*0*	52^{2}	*44*	*6*	*2.1*	*9.7*	*28%*	*.281*	*1.07*	*3.15*	*3.39*	*3.59*	*0.8*	*76*	
2017	*OAK*	*MLB*	*30*	*3*	*1*	*14*	*54*	*0*	57^{2}	*49*	*7*	*2.3*	*9.8*	*28%*	*.282*	*1.11*	*3.26*	*3.38*	*3.72*	*0.7*	*80*	

Breakout: 23% Improve: 51% Collapse: 32% Attrition: 9% MLB: 100% *Comparables: Steve Cishek, Bobby Jenks, Frank Francisco*

True to his name, Doolittle did... well, not much in 2015. After receiving a platelet-rich plasma injection in January to treat what was reported to be a "slight rotator cuff tear" as part of a rest and rehab program designed to avoid surgery, he missed the A's first 48 games. He worked a scoreless inning in his season debut on May 27th, felt pain "in a slightly different area," and returned to the disabled list, where he remained until late August. By season's end his fastball was nearly back to normal, up a few ticks from his earlier abbreviated stint. Although Doolittle only worked consecutive days once, he went beyond a single inning three times in the final two weeks, providing further evidence of arm strength. Nothing is guaranteed, but the increased velocity and long outings are encouraging.

Ryan Dull RHP

Born: 10/2/89 Age: 26 Bats: R Throws: R Height: 5'10" Weight: 175

YEAR	TEAM	LVL	AGE	W	L	SV	G	GS	IP	H	HR	BB/9	K/9	GB%	BABIP	WHIP	ERA	FIP	DRA	WARP	CFIP	MPH
2013	STO	A+	23	1	3	6	15	0	22^{2}	13	0	1.2	12.3	31%	.255	0.71	1.59	1.57	4.28	0.4	64	
2013	BLT	A	23	1	1	12	20	0	25^{2}	16	1	1.1	12.3	47%	.263	0.74	2.10	1.47	3.49	0.4	59	
2013	MID	AA	23	0	1	1	10	0	11^{2}	15	2	2.3	9.3	38%	.351	1.54	4.63	4.00	4.05	0.1	90	
2014	MID	AA	24	5	5	6	40	0	56^{1}	52	6	2.4	9.7	40%	.299	1.19	2.88	3.30				
2015	OAK	MLB	25	1	2	1	13	0	17	12	4	3.2	8.5	39%	.200	1.06	4.24	5.34	3.72	0.2	95	92.9
2015	NAS	AAA	25	0	1	0	12	0	16	10	1	1.7	11.8	35%	.250	0.81	1.12	2.35	2.42	0.5	70	
2015	MID	AA	25	3	1	12	35	0	45	29	1	2.6	10.4	44%	.262	0.93	0.60	2.14	1.93	1.5	68	
2016	*OAK*	*MLB*	*26*	*2*	*1*	*0*	*35*	*0*	36^{2}	*33*	*4*	*2.9*	*8.7*	*37%*	*.284*	*1.23*	*3.87*	*3.76*	*4.34*	*0.3*	*96*	
2017	*OAK*	*MLB*	*27*	*1*	*1*	*1*	*29*	*0*	39^{1}	*36*	*6*	*3.4*	*9.3*	*37%*	*.290*	*1.30*	*4.03*	*4.16*	*4.52*	*0.1*	*100*	

Breakout: 18% Improve: 28% Collapse: 15% Attrition: 19% MLB: 50% *Comparables: Cory Burns, Michael Schwimer, A.J. Ramos*

Dull, a former 32nd-round pick whose late selection inspires him "to improve myself wherever I go," tore through two levels last year before a September recall. He dominated in his first eight outings with the A's before allowing four homers in his last five. The diminutive right-hander backs a low-90s heater with a slider and changeup. The keys to his success are fastball command down in the zone and a deceptive delivery that evolved at Midland under pitching coaches Don Schulze and John Wasdin. For Dull to thrive at the highest level, he'll need to solve lefties: Over the last two seasons they have an .850 OPS against him. Righties pose no such threat, as he has held them to a .431 OPS over that same period, with a scarcely believable 101:6 strikeout-to-walk ratio.

Kendall Graveman RHP

Born: 12/21/90 Age: 25 Bats: R Throws: R Height: 6'2" Weight: 185

YEAR	TEAM	LVL	AGE	W	L	SV	G	GS	IP	H	HR	BB/9	K/9	GB%	BABIP	WHIP	ERA	FIP	DRA	WARP	CFIP	MPH
2013	LNS	A	22	1	3	0	10	10	39^{2}	41	3	2.9	5.7	64%	.295	1.36	4.31	4.12	4.82	0.2	107	
2014	LNS	A	23	2	0	0	4	4	26^{1}	11	0	2.1	8.5	68%	.175	0.65	0.34	2.27	4.13	0.3	88	
2014	BUF	AAA	23	3	2	0	6	6	38^{1}	34	1	1.2	5.2	66%	.282	1.02	1.88	2.94	4.39	0.3	97	
2014	TOR	MLB	23	0	0	0	5	0	4^{2}	4	0	0.0	7.7	64%	.286	0.86	3.86	1.45	0.86	0.2	99	95.2
2014	DUN	A+	23	8	4	0	16	16	96^{2}	89	1	1.7	6.0	59%	.287	1.11	2.23	2.88	4.01	1.1	89	
2015	OAK	MLB	24	6	9	0	21	21	115^{2}	126	15	3.0	6.0	51%	.302	1.42	4.05	4.57	4.89	0.2	115	93.3
2015	NAS	AAA	24	2	1	0	4	4	24^{1}	20	1	3.3	5.2	64%	.241	1.19	1.85	4.09	6.09	-0.1	114	
2016	*OAK*	*MLB*	*25*	*2*	*2*	*0*	*6*	*6*	31^{2}	*32*	*4*	*2.9*	*5.7*	*54%*	*.286*	*1.34*	*4.42*	*4.66*	*4.88*	*0.1*	*116*	
2017	*OAK*	*MLB*	*26*	*4*	*5*	*0*	*13*	*13*	*75*	*78*	*10*	*2.8*	*6.2*	*54%*	*.293*	*1.36*	*4.34*	*4.48*	*4.79*	*0.3*	*113*	

Breakout: 14% Improve: 39% Collapse: 25% Attrition: 21% MLB: 83% *Comparables: Chris Tillman, Joe Blanton, Jeremy Sowers*

After making the A's rotation out of spring training, Graveman struggled, missing his spots, getting pounded and being shipped to Triple-A for a month. Nashville teammate Barry Zito helped him adjust his mental approach, and he returned to Oakland a different pitcher, notching a 1.78 ERA over his next nine starts. But success proved fleeting, as he dropped his final five decisions before ending the year on the disabled list with a strained oblique. As a sinker/cutter guy who pitches to contact, Graveman has little margin for error. He draws praise for the way he competes and the movement on his pitches, but unless he refines his command or develops a new pitch to shove past hitters, his ceiling is that of a back-end starter.

Sonny Gray RHP

Born: 11/7/89 Age: 26 Bats: R Throws: R Height: 5'11" Weight: 195

YEAR	TEAM	LVL	AGE	W	L	SV	G	GS	IP	H	HR	BB/9	K/9	GB%	BABIP	WHIP	ERA	FIP	DRA	WARP	CFIP	MPH
2013	OAK	MLB	23	5	3	0	12	10	64	51	4	2.8	9.4	52%	.276	1.11	2.67	2.73	2.71	1.7	86	95.6
2013	SAC	AAA	23	10	7	0	20	20	118^1	117	5	3.0	9.0	52%	.337	1.32	3.42	3.11	4.18	1.9	73	
2014	OAK	MLB	24	14	10	0	33	33	219	187	15	3.0	7.5	58%	.277	1.19	3.08	3.49	3.22	4.2	96	95.7
2015	OAK	MLB	25	14	7	0	31	31	208	166	17	2.6	7.3	53%	.255	1.08	2.73	3.42	2.76	5.6	92	95.6
2016	*OAK*	*MLB*	*26*	*11*	*11*	*0*	*31*	*31*	*186*	*164*	*17*	*2.7*	*7.8*	*55%*	*.280*	*1.18*	*3.58*	*3.68*	*4.02*	*2.4*	*90*	
2017	*OAK*	*MLB*	*27*	*11*	*10*	*0*	*29*	*29*	*177*	*163*	*19*	*2.7*	*8.3*	*55%*	*.291*	*1.22*	*3.59*	*3.71*	*4.03*	*2.3*	*91*	

Breakout: 24% Improve: 61% Collapse: 16% Attrition: 6% MLB: 92% *Comparables: Ubaldo Jimenez, Michael Pineda, Daniel Hudson*

When Gray lasted just three innings in a start against the White Sox on September 14th, it marked the only time all year he failed to go at least five, and just the third time in 74 career starts. The disaster outing was part of a rough final six weeks that saw his ERA climb from 2.06 to 2.73 and ended with a premature shutdown thanks to left-hip soreness. That's the bad news. The good news is everything else. A few tweaks elevated Gray's game from an already high level and cemented his ace status. Long known for an outstanding curve, Gray placed a greater emphasis on pounding fastballs down in the zone, explaining to Sahadev Sharma that his four-seamer's natural cutting action allows him to "get early contact and get deep in the game." The strategy worked. More impressively, the adjustments speak to a competitiveness that won't let him be satisfied until he's the best.

Jesse Hahn RHP

Born: 7/30/89 Age: 26 Bats: R Throws: R Height: 6'5" Weight: 190

YEAR	TEAM	LVL	AGE	W	L	SV	G	GS	IP	H	HR	BB/9	K/9	GB%	BABIP	WHIP	ERA	FIP	DRA	WARP	CFIP	MPH
2013	PCH	A+	23	2	1	0	19	19	67	55	1	2.4	8.5	63%	.284	1.09	2.15	2.49	3.54	1.1	74	
2014	SDN	MLB	24	7	4	0	14	12	73^1	57	4	3.9	8.6	52%	.270	1.21	3.07	3.38	3.78	0.9	102	93.9
2014	SAN	AA	24	2	1	0	13	10	42^1	34	1	3.2	8.1	66%	.282	1.16	1.91	2.77				
2015	OAK	MLB	25	6	6	0	16	16	96^2	88	5	2.3	6.0	53%	.273	1.17	3.35	3.48	4.08	1.1	108	94.8
2016	*OAK*	*MLB*	*26*	*10*	*10*	*0*	*28*	*28*	*168*	*161*	*16*	*2.9*	*6.8*	*53%*	*.284*	*1.29*	*4.01*	*4.09*	*4.47*	*1.3*	*103*	
2017	*OAK*	*MLB*	*27*	*8*	*9*	*0*	*28*	*28*	*174^2*	*173*	*20*	*3.0*	*7.4*	*53%*	*.294*	*1.33*	*4.03*	*4.17*	*4.49*	*1.0*	*104*	

Breakout: 35% Improve: 65% Collapse: 17% Attrition: 14% MLB: 94% *Comparables: Alex Cobb, Manny Parra, Dana Eveland*

Acquired from the Padres in December 2014, Hahn looked to build on his promising rookie campaign, but after a couple rough road outings in early May, his ERA stood at 4.73. He held opponents to a .220/.287/.303 line over his next 10 starts—including his first career shutout—and appeared to be finding himself before he was shut down with a forearm strain in early July. The injury was expected to keep him out two weeks, then a month, but ultimately cost him the rest of the season. Hahn had Tommy John surgery in 2010, so the caution is understandable. Still, in four professional seasons he has never thrown as many as 116 innings. The talent is real, as are the health concerns going forward.

Liam Hendriks RHP

Born: 2/10/89 Age: 27 Bats: R Throws: R Height: 6'1" Weight: 205

YEAR	TEAM	LVL	AGE	W	L	SV	G	GS	IP	H	HR	BB/9	K/9	GB%	BABIP	WHIP	ERA	FIP	DRA	WARP	CFIP	MPH
2013	ROC	AAA	24	4	8	0	16	16	98^1	115	9	1.4	5.7	45%	.324	1.32	4.67	3.68	4.23	0.9	95	
2013	MIN	MLB	24	1	3	0	10	8	47^1	67	10	2.7	6.5	38%	.350	1.71	6.85	5.46	5.65	-0.5	110	93.5
2014	TOR	MLB	25	1	0	0	3	3	13^1	12	3	2.7	5.4	35%	.225	1.20	6.07	6.23	4.63	0.0	112	93.2
2014	OMA	AAA	25	4	1	0	5	5	35	33	1	1.5	9.0	49%	.337	1.11	2.83	2.59	4.57	0.5	72	
2014	KCA	MLB	25	0	2	0	6	3	19^1	26	0	1.4	7.0	46%	.388	1.50	4.66	2.23	6.24	-0.4	107	94.2
2014	BUF	AAA	25	8	1	0	18	16	108^1	92	6	0.6	7.6	54%	.279	0.91	2.33	2.67	3.65	1.9	66	
2015	TOR	MLB	26	5	0	0	58	0	64^2	59	3	1.5	9.9	49%	.322	1.08	2.92	2.11	3.20	1.2	75	97.8
2016	*OAK*	*MLB*	*27*	*3*	*1*	*0*	*60*	*0*	*63*	*61*	*6*	*2.0*	*7.5*	*47%*	*.294*	*1.19*	*3.50*	*3.59*	*3.96*	*0.8*	*87*	
2017	*OAK*	*MLB*	*28*	*7*	*5*	*0*	*29*	*16*	*111^1*	*108*	*12*	*2.1*	*8.0*	*47%*	*.299*	*1.20*	*3.41*	*3.54*	*3.86*	*1.6*	*85*	

Breakout: 31% Improve: 58% Collapse: 13% Attrition: 15% MLB: 90% *Comparables: Scott Baker, Jacob deGrom, Cory Luebke*

Holy velocity jump, Batman! The right-handed Aussie had a well-established reputation as a command guy with fringy stuff heading into the 2015 season, which was destroyed when Hendriks was apparently bitten by a poisonous fastball last offseason. Reinvented as a power fastball/slider reliever (while still maintaining that command), he was dominant against same-side hitters, holding them to a .207/.242/.257 line on the season. Now able to hit 95 mph consistently, Hendriks should find himself third all time among Australia-born players in strikeouts by the end of 2016, likely passing Damian Moss, Peter Moylan and Ryan Rowland-Smith. So what caused Hendriks to punch his fastball up three ticks? The former half-back flank (that's a football position, not a steak) credits pilates, which is great news for studios in Triple-A cities across America. Watch out, Body Pure Pilates in Columbus, Ohio. Might want to add a few extra classes to the calendar in advance of the rush.

Rich Hill LHP

Born: 3/11/80 Age: 36 Bats: L Throws: L Height: 6'5" Weight: 220

YEAR	TEAM	LVL	AGE	W	L	SV	G	GS	IP	H	HR	BB/9	K/9	GB%	BABIP	WHIP	ERA	FIP	DRA	WARP	CFIP	MPH
2013	CLE	MLB	33	1	2	0	63	0	38^2	38	3	6.8	11.9	44%	.361	1.73	6.28	3.85	3.85	0.3	95	94.2
2014	NYA	MLB	34	0	0	0	14	0	5^1	6	0	5.1	15.2	42%	.500	1.69	1.69	2.03	5.69	-0.1	98	91.8
2014	PAW	AAA	34	3	3	2	25	0	39	29	0	3.9	10.4	50%	.299	1.18	3.23	2.51	4.17	0.3	79	
2014	ANA	MLB	34	0	0	0	2	0	0	1	0			0%	1.000				13.97	0.0	112	94.7
2015	SYR	AAA	35	2	2	0	25	0	21^2	12	1	8.7	13.3	54%	.262	1.52	2.91	4.40	3.69	0.2	108	
2015	BOS	MLB	35	2	1	0	4	4	29	14	2	1.6	11.2	51%	.197	0.66	1.55	2.24	1.46	1.2	71	92.7
2015	PAW	AAA	35	3	2	0	5	5	32^1	27	3	2.5	8.1	48%	.282	1.11	2.78	3.59	3.13	0.6	92	
2016	*OAK*	*MLB*	*36*	*7*	*8*	*0*	*24*	*24*	127^1	*110*	*13*	*3.8*	*9.6*	*48%*	*.290*	*1.29*	*3.77*	*3.85*	*4.21*	*1.4*	*92*	
2017	*OAK*	*MLB*	*37*	*6*	*4*	*2*	*93*	*6*	*107*	*96*	*13*	*3.9*	*9.7*	*48%*	*.296*	*1.33*	*3.87*	*3.99*	*4.32*	*0.6*	*95*	

Breakout: 16% Improve: 33% Collapse: 26% Attrition: 8% MLB: 69% *Comparables: Matt Miller, Randy Choate, Jose Valverde*

Tal's wasn't the only Hill to get a second life in 2015. On August 9th, Rich Hill made his second and final start with the Long Island Ducks of the independent Atlantic League. On September 13th, he was back in the majors, starting for the Red Sox. And on September 25th, the Milton, Massachusetts, native made his first career start at Fenway Park, where he proceeded to throw a 10-strikeout complete-game shutout. Hill was dominant in all four of his 2015 starts, and while it's tough to count on the injury prone 36-year-old for much of anything moving forward, odds are Hill has at least temporarily revived his fascinating MLB career. He's no LaTroy Hawkins in terms of longevity, but Hill has earned a comment in every BP Annual since 2006, which, given his career, is impressive in its own way. The Baseball Gods can be cruel sometimes, but this time they did us a solid.

Ryan Madson RHP

Born: 8/28/80 Age: 35 Bats: L Throws: R Height: 6'6" Weight: 210

YEAR	TEAM	LVL	AGE	W	L	SV	G	GS	IP	H	HR	BB/9	K/9	GB%	BABIP	WHIP	ERA	FIP	DRA	WARP	CFIP	MPH
2015	KCA	MLB	34	1	2	3	68	0	63^1	47	5	2.0	8.2	56%	.249	0.96	2.13	3.06	2.64	1.6	85	97.0
2016	*OAK*	*MLB*	*35*	*3*	*1*	*0*	*55*	*0*	*58*	*52*	*6*	*2.7*	*8.3*	*56%*	*.286*	*1.20*	*3.66*	*3.74*	*4.12*	*0.4*	*89*	
2017	*OAK*	*MLB*	*36*	*3*	*1*	*1*	*55*	*0*	51^1	*51*	*6*	*2.9*	*8.0*	*56%*	*.298*	*1.32*	*3.96*	*4.10*	*4.46*	*0.2*	*98*	

Breakout: 25% Improve: 46% Collapse: 27% Attrition: 13% MLB: 93% *Comparables: Akinori Otsuka, Heath Bell, Tom Gordon*

The former Philadelphia closer spent three years in the baseball wilderness struggling through intense pain, torturous workouts and emotional weariness before chancing upon an obscure electro-stimulus device that he credits with reviving his career. Last year he surprisingly made the Kansas City roster out of spring training and rewarded his new employers with just the latest in a long line of quietly dominant bullpen campaigns. Madson used his mid-90s heat, cutter and baffling changeup to hold batters to a minuscule .208 TAv last season, better than Craig Kimbrel, Jeurys Familia and teammate Kelvin Herrera, and there's no reason to think he can't continue on as a dominant setup man. The A's gave him a three-year deal to test that conclusion.

Sean Manaea LHP

Born: 2/1/92 Age: 24 Bats: L Throws: L Height: 6'5" Weight: 235

YEAR	TEAM	LVL	AGE	W	L	SV	G	GS	IP	H	HR	BB/9	K/9	GB%	BABIP	WHIP	ERA	FIP	DRA	WARP	CFIP	MPH
2014	WIL	A+	22	7	8	0	25	25	121^2	102	5	4.0	10.8	45%	.319	1.28	3.11	3.11	4.09	1.6	85	
2015	MID	AA	23	6	0	0	7	7	42^2	34	3	3.2	10.8	40%	.301	1.15	1.90	2.95	2.11	1.5	67	
2015	WIL	A+	23	1	0	0	4	4	19^2	22	0	1.8	10.1	44%	.407	1.32	3.66	1.78	2.40	0.6	82	
2016	*OAK*	*MLB*	*24*	*4*	*4*	*0*	*13*	*13*	65^2	*63*	*7*	*3.6*	*9.0*	*40%*	*.305*	*1.36*	*3.96*	*3.93*	*4.42*	*0.5*	*100*	
2017	*OAK*	*MLB*	*25*	*9*	*10*	*0*	*29*	*29*	183^2	*183*	*25*	*4.0*	*9.2*	*40%*	*.313*	*1.44*	*4.16*	*4.29*	*4.64*	*0.8*	*106*	

Breakout: 15% Improve: 22% Collapse: 11% Attrition: 25% MLB: 41% *Comparables: Alex Meyer, Andre Rienzo, Steven Matz*

Manipulation and deception are such core components of Manaea's game, you'd think he took lessons from Chin-hui Tsao. In addition to an ideal starter's frame, Manaea has a delivery that shows batters more joints than a Spike Lee marathon. He's all elbows, knees and ankles pre-pitch, and a big arcing finish with his trail leg after. These distractions help his already-quality stuff play up. Acquired for Ben Zobrist, Manaea attacks hitters with a 91-94 mph fastball that he will cut or sink depending on the situation. His slider is vampiric, mimicking the fastball before revealing its true nature with a sharp bite, and his changeup gives him a third above-average offering. Manaea's command flits between average and above, and if this is starting to sound a lot like a top-of-the-rotation pitcher, that's because he could be. Injuries (hip, foot, arm) have slowed his ascent dating back to college, but a healthy spring should have him knocking on the door to the majors.

Sean Nolin LHP

Born: 12/26/89 Age: 26 Bats: L Throws: L Height: 6'4" Weight: 230

YEAR	TEAM	LVL	AGE	W	L	SV	G	GS	IP	H	HR	BB/9	K/9	GB%	BABIP	WHIP	ERA	FIP	DRA	WARP	CFIP	MPH
2013	NHP	AA	23	8	3	0	17	17	92^2	89	6	2.4	10.0	36%	.333	1.23	3.01	2.82	3.71	1.6	71	
2013	TOR	MLB	23	0	1	0	1	1	1^1	7	1	6.8	0.0	30%	.667	6.00	40.50	15.08	20.07	-0.2	112	92.8
2013	BUF	AAA	23	1	1	0	3	3	17^2	13	1	5.1	6.6	39%	.267	1.30	1.53	4.34	4.68	0.1	112	
2014	BUF	AAA	24	4	6	0	17	17	87^1	74	6	3.6	7.6	42%	.270	1.25	3.50	3.86	4.46	0.7	97	
2014	TOR	MLB	24	0	0	0	1	0	1	1	1	0.0	0.0	25%	.000	1.00	9.00	16.16	9.69	-0.1	106	95.7
2015	OAK	MLB	25	1	2	0	6	6	29	35	4	3.7	4.7	43%	.301	1.62	5.28	5.10	4.94	0.0	121	91.2
2015	NAS	AAA	25	2	2	0	14	12	47^1	40	5	3.6	7.2	34%	.259	1.25	2.66	4.82	5.60	0.0	108	
2016	*OAK*	*MLB*	*26*	*10*	*12*	*0*	*31*	*31*	176^2	*178*	*20*	*3.2*	*6.5*	*40%*	*.287*	*1.36*	*4.39*	*4.44*	*4.84*	*0.6*	*113*	
2017	*OAK*	*MLB*	*27*	*8*	*10*	*0*	*29*	*29*	175^2	*187*	*26*	*3.4*	*6.9*	*40%*	*.297*	*1.44*	*4.64*	*4.79*	*5.12*	*0.0*	*121*	

Breakout: 13% Improve: 25% Collapse: 19% Attrition: 37% MLB: 62% *Comparables: Scott Barnes, Eric Surkamp, Charles Brewer*

If you liked Tommy Milone, you'll love Nolin, another southpaw who works in the high 80s and who relies on command in lieu of velocity. Nolin, part of the Josh Donaldson trade, missed most of spring training and all of April recovering from sports-hernia surgery. He then made 10 Triple-A appearances before being shut down for six weeks with shoulder tenderness, which made it difficult for him to find said command. Nolin's ability to hit spots other than the meaty part of bats has been sporadic in his brief big-league career. His stuff allows little margin for error, so he'll need to hone that ability if he's to stick at the back end of a rotation for any appreciable amount of time.

Jarrod Parker RHP

Born: 11/24/88 Age: 27 Bats: R Throws: R Height: 6'1" Weight: 195

YEAR	TEAM	LVL	AGE	W	L	SV	G	GS	IP	H	HR	BB/9	K/9	GB%	BABIP	WHIP	ERA	FIP	DRA	WARP	CFIP	MPH
2013	OAK	MLB	24	12	8	0	32	32	197	178	25	2.9	6.1	42%	.260	1.22	3.97	4.43	4.04	2.1	113	94.5
2015	NAS	AAA	26	1	0	0	2	2	10	14	2	1.8	6.3	54%	.343	1.60	6.30	5.40	5.52	0.0	105	
2016	*OAK*	*MLB*	*27*	*2*	*2*	*0*	*6*	*6*	*35^1*	*35*	*4*	*2.7*	*6.3*	*45%*	*.281*	*1.29*	*4.38*	*4.32*	*4.84*	*0.1*	*114*	
2017	*OAK*	*MLB*	*28*	*10*	*11*	*0*	*30*	*30*	*189^1*	*196*	*27*	*2.7*	*6.9*	*45%*	*.294*	*1.34*	*4.33*	*4.46*	*4.78*	*0.7*	*113*	

Breakout: 16% Improve: 36% Collapse: 26% Attrition: 14% MLB: 87% *Comparables: Jeremy Hellickson, Homer Bailey, Noah Lowry*

The good news is that Parker faced 84 batters last year, which is 84 more than he faced in 2014 while recovering from a second Tommy John surgery. The bad news is that during his fourth minor-league rehab start in early May, he sustained a gruesome medial epicondyle fracture (elbow) that ended his season and required him to go under the knife yet again. The latter procedure was downplayed as being merely to "clean up and repair" or "stabilize" the fracture, as opposed to a third TJ, but timetables have become pointless. Even before this last setback, the list of starting pitchers to make a successful return from a second TJ—it's an admittedly small sample—is basically Chris Capuano. Although Parker is entering what should be his physical prime, the human body has its limits.

Fernando Rodriguez RHP

Born: 6/18/84 Age: 32 Bats: R Throws: R Height: 6'3" Weight: 235

YEAR	TEAM	LVL	AGE	W	L	SV	G	GS	IP	H	HR	BB/9	K/9	GB%	BABIP	WHIP	ERA	FIP	DRA	WARP	CFIP	MPH
2014	OAK	MLB	30	1	0	0	7	0	9	4	0	2.0	4.0	33%	.148	0.67	1.00	2.94	-0.91	0.6	106	95.7
2014	SAC	AAA	30	3	0	0	38	0	45^2	40	2	3.2	10.4	39%	.328	1.23	1.97	3.20	4.59	0.4	74	
2015	NAS	AAA	31	0	0	0	10	1	16	8	2	3.4	10.1	44%	.162	0.88	2.81	4.10	3.79	0.3	88	
2015	OAK	MLB	31	4	2	0	56	0	58^2	43	4	3.7	10.0	41%	.264	1.14	3.84	3.05	2.71	1.4	87	95.8
2016	*OAK*	*MLB*	*32*	*3*	*1*	*0*	*50*	*0*	*52^2*	*46*	*5*	*3.6*	*9.1*	*40%*	*.284*	*1.27*	*3.78*	*3.77*	*4.22*	*0.4*	*92*	
2017	*OAK*	*MLB*	*33*	*2*	*1*	*0*	*45*	*0*	*49^1*	*46*	*6*	*4.0*	*9.1*	*40%*	*.299*	*1.37*	*3.92*	*4.05*	*4.38*	*0.2*	*96*	

Breakout: 23% Improve: 44% Collapse: 21% Attrition: 13% MLB: 81% *Comparables: Michael Wuertz, Joe Thatcher, Justin Miller*

Rodriguez, a journeyman who couldn't stick with an Astros team that lost 107 games in 2012, resurfaced with the A's in 2014 and last year became a key part of their beleaguered bullpen. His mid-90s fastball and low-80s curve hit their intended targets more often than in the past, though not enough to make him a serious option in high-leverage situations. He was deadly with nobody on base and had an extreme reverse platoon split, holding lefties to a .174/.268/.198 line. When Fernando Abad's back problems flared up in July, Rodriguez got the call against southpaws and responded. He's an asset in middle relief, where he can soak up innings and take pressure off the guys at the back end.

Barry Zito LHP

Born: 5/13/78 Age: 38 Bats: L Throws: L Height: 6'2" Weight: 205

YEAR	TEAM	LVL	AGE	W	L	SV	G	GS	IP	H	HR	BB/9	K/9	GB%	BABIP	WHIP	ERA	FIP	DRA	WARP	CFIP	MPH
2013	SFN	MLB	35	5	11	0	30	25	133^1	173	19	3.6	5.8	38%	.346	1.70	5.74	4.89	6.52	-2.6	126	85.4
2015	NAS	AAA	37	8	7	0	24	22	138	121	10	3.9	5.9	38%	.262	1.31	3.46	4.64	6.36	-1.2	117	
2015	OAK	MLB	37	0	0	0	3	2	7	12	4	7.7	2.6	41%	.320	2.57	10.29	12.53	14.51	-0.8	124	86.2
2016	*OAK*	*MLB*	*38*	*5*	*7*	*0*	*18*	*18*	*101*	*107*	*13*	*3.6*	*5.3*	*36%*	*.287*	*1.46*	*5.02*	*5.05*	*5.47*	*-0.4*	*131*	
2017	*OAK*	*MLB*	*39*	*6*	*8*	*0*	*20*	*20*	*119*	*133*	*18*	*3.7*	*5.3*	*36%*	*.297*	*1.54*	*5.17*	*5.31*	*5.63*	*-0.7*	*136*	

Breakout: 9% Improve: 27% Collapse: 11% Attrition: 17% MLB: 49% *Comparables: Ramon Ortiz, Jeff Suppan, Mike Hampton*

With no shortage of holes in the rotation all year, there were rumblings that the A's might summon prodigal son Zito from Triple-A, but it didn't happen until rosters expanded in September. With his team hopelessly out of contention, he started against former rotation-mate Tim Hudson. Though that start produced more good feelings than good baseball, there are benefits to feeling good. Having plied his pitching craft in Nashville over the summer, Zito—whose father conducted and arranged for Nat King Cole and whose mother sang backup for Cole—spent time there schmoozing with folks in the music business for his future career as a songwriter. Worse ballads have been written than this fond farewell to two Bay Area icons.

Lineouts

Hitters

NAME	POS	TEAM	LVL	AGE	PA	R	2B	3B	HR	RBI	BB	K	SB	CS	AVG/OBP/SLG	TAv	BABIP	BRR	FRAA	WARP
Carson Blair	C	MID	AA	25	208	24	15	4	6	29	33	62	1	0	.272/.389/.509	.296	.387	-3.3	C(38): -3.4, 1B(1): -0.0	0.8
	C	NAS	AAA	25	126	9	3	0	3	8	9	34	0	0	.221/.280/.327	.240	.282	-0.2	C(33): -7.6	-0.5
	C	OAK	MLB	25	35	3	0	0	1	3	4	18	0	0	.129/.229/.226	.163	.250	0.1	C(11): -4.5	-0.7
Skye Bolt	CF	VER	A-	21	206	26	10	2	4	19	24	44	2	1	.238/.325/.381	.271	.291	0.6	CF(31): 2.0, RF(13): -0.4	1.0
Sam Fuld	CF	OAK	MLB	33	325	34	16	3	2	22	30	55	9	3	.197/.276/.293	.224	.235	0.2	LF(57): 8.5, CF(43): 2.0	0.6
Tyler Ladendorf	UT	NAS	AAA	27	90	3	2	1	1	8	5	23	0	1	.265/.311/.349	.247	.350	0.5	SS(10): 0.6, LF(4): -0.4	0.2
	UT	OAK	MLB	27	18	3	0	1	0	2	1	2	0	0	.235/.278/.353	.240	.267	0.6	LF(3): -0.2, CF(2): -0.2	0.0
Sandber Pimentel	1B	BLT	A	20	471	50	17	0	13	41	50	104	1	2	.243/.335/.380	.258	.294	-3.4	1B(67): -4.0	-0.4
Rangel Ravelo	1B	MID	AA	23	98	13	6	1	2	17	9	17	0	1	.318/.378/.477	.279	.371	-0.5	1B(15): 0.4	0.3
	1B	NAS	AAA	23	112	10	5	1	1	18	7	22	0	0	.277/.324/.376	.268	.338	-0.4	1B(13): -0.9, LF(1): -0.0	0.1
Jake Smolinski	LF	NAS	AAA	26	97	16	9	0	5	17	8	9	2	1	.349/.402/.628	.426	.338	-0.2	LF(18): 0.5, RF(7): -1.0	1.9
	LF	OAK	MLB	26	118	12	6	2	5	20	8	19	0	1	.226/.288/.462	.295	.226	0.1	LF(27): -1.4, RF(10): 2.8	0.8
	LF	ROU	AAA	26	50	9	5	0	4	14	4	7	0	1	.422/.480/.800	.426	.441	0.3	RF(9): 0.1, LF(1): 0.9	1.1
	LF	TEX	MLB	26	74	12	1	0	1	6	11	20	1	0	.133/.270/.200	.204	.171	2.4	LF(25): 0.5, RF(6): 0.1	0.0
Joe Wendle	2B	NAS	AAA	25	618	80	42	8	10	57	22	114	12	2	.289/.323/.442	.292	.343	-2.0	2B(136): 1.8	3.8

Carson Blair was the final pick in the 35th round of the 2008 draft and last September became the first from that round to reach the big leagues, seeing limited action before a medial meniscus tear in his left knee ended his season less than three weeks later. ❖ They say lightning doesn't strike twice but **Skye Bolt** had six separate games with two strikeouts to his name. The outfielder also walks plenty, and shows four average or better tools. ❖ **Sam Fuld** has reached that point in his career where the only value he provides is on defense, which makes his 300-plus plate appearances last year both puzzling and unlikely to happen again. ❖ **Tyler Ladendorf** tripled in his first big-league at-bat, landed in Triple-A a few days later, and then spent most of the summer recovering from left-ankle surgery before returning to Oakland for a handful of games in September. ❖ After three seasons in the Dominican Summer League **Sandber Pimentel** beached stateside, but didn't show enough power in Low-A to profile at first base. ❖ Who was the last first-base prospect with below-average hit and in-game power tools who mattered? If you're drawing a blank, it's okay; you won't remember **Rangel Ravelo** either. ❖ After the A's selected **Jake Smolinski** off waivers in June from a Rangers team that had tired of watching him be less productive than an aulophobic flautist, he hit well enough in limited opportunities—especially against left-handers—to make the case for a more permanent role. ❖ While **Joe Wendle** has shown some semblance of pop throughout his minor-league career, it's more likely he's an empty-average Joe in the majors.

Pitchers

NAME	TEAM	LVL	AGE	W	L	SV	G	GS	IP	H	HR	BB/9	K/9	GB%	BABIP	WHIP	ERA	FIP	FRA	WARP	CFIP	MPH
R.J. Alvarez	NAS	AAA	24	3	3	5	31	0	35	36	2	4.4	10.5	42%	.358	1.51	4.11	3.54	3.92	0.5	88	
	OAK	MLB	24	0	0	0	21	0	20	27	7	5.8	10.4	25%	.351	2.00	9.90	7.30	8.49	-0.9	104	96.4
Aaron Brooks	NAS	AAA	25	1	0	0	2	2	12	9	1	0.0	8.2	42%	.250	0.75	2.25	2.85	2.36	0.4	64	
	OAK	MLB	25	3	4	0	11	9	51	67	9	2.5	6.2	46%	.341	1.59	6.71	5.08	6.12	-0.7	112	94.5
	OMA	AAA	25	6	5	0	18	17	106^{2}	118	9	1.8	7.8	48%	.337	1.30	3.71	3.59	2.81	3.2	76	
	KCA	MLB	25	0	0	0	2	0	4^{1}	6	0	0.0	6.2	27%	.400	1.38	6.23	1.72	8.41	-0.2	98	94.0
Daniel Coulombe	OAK	MLB	25	0	0	0	9	0	7^{2}	8	0	3.5	4.7	64%	.320	1.43	3.52	3.23	3.12	0.1	116	91.6
	OKL	AAA	25	3	1	1	38	0	41^{1}	35	1	5.2	8.9	50%	.309	1.43	3.27	3.82	4.89	0.1	99	
	LAN	MLB	25	0	0	0	5	0	8^{1}	9	0	6.5	7.6	48%	.333	1.80	7.56	3.64	6.26	-0.2	110	91.9
Dylan Covey	STO	A+	23	8	9	0	26	26	140^{1}	135	13	2.8	6.4	60%	.282	1.27	3.59	4.61	6.05	-0.4	113	
Felix Doubront	TOR	MLB	27	1	1	0	5	4	22^{2}	32	1	2.0	5.2	65%	.383	1.63	4.76	3.33	6.68	-0.5	106	93.4
	BUF	AAA	27	1	3	0	9	9	48	36	1	3.4	8.1	50%	.265	1.12	2.44	2.76	3.28	0.8	90	
	OAK	MLB	27	2	2	1	11	8	52^{2}	55	9	3.6	7.3	41%	.299	1.44	5.81	4.89	4.23	0.5	105	93.4
Aaron Kurcz	NAS	AAA	24	2	1	0	18	0	26	29	2	5.2	10.7	36%	.365	1.69	4.15	3.95	4.62	0.2	94	
	GWN	AAA	24	4	3	7	31	0	33	29	2	5.7	10.4	34%	.310	1.52	3.27	3.64	4.19	0.1	100	
Arnold Leon	NAS	AAA	26	2	5	1	20	6	58	52	7	2.9	8.5	42%	.281	1.22	2.95	4.36	4.56	0.5	96	
	OAK	MLB	26	0	2	0	19	0	26^{2}	30	3	3.0	6.4	47%	.321	1.46	4.39	4.15	4.37	0.1	104	94.2
Casey Meisner	STO	A+	20	3	1	0	7	7	32^{1}	27	1	1.9	6.7	28%	.265	1.05	2.78	3.35	4.96	0.3	101	
	SAV	A	20	7	2	0	12	12	76	59	6	2.2	7.8	46%	.256	1.03	2.13	3.64	3.75	1.3	91	
	SLU	A+	20	3	2	0	6	6	35	35	4	3.6	5.9	49%	.282	1.40	2.83	4.71	5.01	-0.3	114	
Daniel Mengden	QUD	A	22	4	1	0	8	6	38^{2}	30	1	1.9	8.4	49%	.274	0.98	1.16	2.65	2.84	0.9	85	
	LNC	A+	22	2	1	1	10	8	49^{2}	59	4	3.3	8.7	46%	.367	1.55	5.26	4.10	3.95	0.9	94	
	STO	A+	22	4	2	0	8	8	42^{1}	39	6	2.1	8.7	53%	.275	1.16	4.25	4.53	4.29	0.7	102	
Dillon Overton	MID	AA	23	5	2	0	13	13	64^{2}	65	4	2.1	6.5	34%	.305	1.24	3.06	3.34	3.75	1.1	92	
	STO	A+	23	2	4	0	14	12	61^{1}	62	7	1.8	8.7	34%	.331	1.21	3.82	4.07	3.98	1.1	89	
Marc Rzepczynski	SDN	MLB	29	0	1	0	27	0	14^{2}	17	2	2.5	10.4	66%	.385	1.43	7.36	3.84	4.16	0.1	92	94.3
	CLE	MLB	29	2	3	0	45	0	20^{1}	23	1	4.4	10.6	73%	.379	1.62	4.43	3.01	4.65	0.0	95	94.7
Bobby Wahl	MID	AA	23	2	0	4	24	0	32^{1}	36	2	3.9	10.0	50%	.374	1.55	4.18	3.17	3.42	0.5	87	
J.B. Wendelken	CHR	AAA	22	0	0	0	12	0	16	14	2	2.8	7.3	42%	.250	1.19	4.50	4.09	4.08	0.1	99	
	BIR	AA	22	6	2	5	27	0	43	36	4	2.3	11.7	28%	.305	1.09	2.72	2.67	1.03	1.8	62	

The lapses in command we mentioned last year became more than "occasional" for **R.J. Alvarez**, who alternated between catching way too much plate and none at all, undermining even his ability to neutralize righties. Lefties? Forget about lefties: .372/.415/.596 across two levels. ❖ **Aaron Brooks**, part of the return when Ben Zobrist was sent to Kansas City, lacks overpowering stuff and gets throttled when he misses his spots; he has allowed five runs or more in half of his 10 major-league starts. ❖ **Daniel Coulombe** is a take-charge lefty whose stuff lacks electricity; his fastball peaks in the high 80s even when he's fully amped. ❖ With four pitches that flash above average, **Dylan Covey** can look the part of a starter. His inconsistency in both quality and command, not to mention his inability to miss bats, says otherwise. ❖ **Felix Doubront** has been hittable (.180 ISO against) for four different teams in the last two years, which means that he's very popular, very left-handed, or both. ❖ You could judge **Aaron Kurcz** by the fact that three teams have traded for him in four years or by the fact that his returns have gone from Theo Epstein to Anthony Varvaro to international bonus money. ❖ In case of fire, break glass and call up **Arnold Leon**, who had brief stints with Oakland in each of the season's first five months before finally sticking when rosters expanded in September and the team was blazing out of control. ❖ The return for sending Tyler Clippard and his rec specs to the Mets, **Casey Meisner** has poor command but a great view in a crowd. ❖ **Daniel Mendgen** lacks ideal size and on most days lacks ideal stuff, which in some ways makes him an ideal Athletic. ❖ **Dillon Overton** continued his return from Tommy John surgery but he did so without the velocity he held previously, routinely sitting in the mid- to upper 80s. ❖ Journeyman **Marc Rzepczynski** was the Padres' lone trade-deadline acquisition and twice allowed three runs in a game while facing four batters, bookending a four-game stretch in which his ERA approached his word score; he came to Oakland with Yonder Alonso this winter. ❖ A flamed-out starter, **Bobby Wahl** hasn't lost any heat on his fastball, which sits 94-97 mph in relief. Add in his above-average slider and average change, and he could be a late-innings option. ❖ With a fastball that can reach the upper 90s in short bursts, **J.B. Wendelken** is on the verge of claiming a medium-leverage role in a big-league bullpen.

Manager

Bob Melvin

YEAR	TEAM	W	L	Pythag +/-	Avg PC	100+ P	120+ P	QS	BQS	REL	REL w Zero R	IBB	PH	PH Avg	PH HR	SB2	CS2	SB3	CS3	SAC Att	SAC%	POS SAC	Squeeze	Swing	In Play
2013	OAK	96	66	-1	94.8	56	0	92	2	447	370	23	130	.135	5	58	24	17	3	37	56.8	21	2	253	87
2014	OAK	88	74	-12	96.0	61	1	102	5	441	380	28	161	.201	3	67	16	16	4	41	46.3	15	2	253	83
2015	OAK	68	94	-9	92.4	61	0	83	3	487	368	19	152	.252	0	65	25	13	3	24	58.3	12	1	268	90

Melvin is almost unanimously regarded as one of the best managers in the game, so you had to feel for him as he suffered through a clunker of a season following the Athletics' latest reboot. Not only did the A's bottom out, posting the franchise's worst record since 1997 (the year before Billy Beane became general manager), but they did it in an inexplicable way. The difference between their third-order record—based on their underlying statistics—and their actual record was 12 wins, the second-largest gap in the majors. Just how does a team underperform to that degree? Many would start by investigating the manager; in this case, however, that seems fruitless.

Melvin remained true to his normal platoon-heavy ways. He micromanaged Max Muncy and Ike Davis so that more than 90 percent of their plate appearances came against righties, and he still found time to keep Sam Fuld and Eric Sogard over the 80 percent threshold. As a result, the A's finished second in the majors in pinch-hitters used, albeit to below-average results. You can blame that on a lack of talent, not a lack of effort. Ditto for the A's problematic bullpen, which finished 29th in the majors in DRA. If there's one area where Melvin might catch deserved heat, it's with his defense. The A's glovemen converted a higher rate of balls in play into outs than most realize (they finished top 10 in defensive efficiency), but nonetheless led the majors in errors. Things were so bad for a stretch that the A's sought out Ron Washington so that he could work his voodoo with nominal shortstop Marcus Semien, among others. You could theorize that the pre-Washington instruction just wasn't good enough, or you could chalk this up as the A's helping a talented old pal get back into the majors in a coaching capacity.

Whatever your verdict, the season wasn't all rotten for Melvin: He received a two-year extension in September that will keep him in Oakland through the 2018 season. He's earned that job security.

PHILADELPHIA PHILLIES

Essay by Holly M. Wendt

Player comments by Paul Boye and BP authors

To see a World in a Grain of Sand
And a Heaven in a Wild Flower
Hold Infinity in the palm of your hand
And Eternity in an hour
—William Blake, "Auguries of Innocence"

Since 2012, Phillies fans have done their share of auguring, looking for signs in the array of onions in their Whiz-Wits, conjuring portents in the flights of birds along the Schuylkill. But The Rotation could not save the fans; we were to wander again in the wilderness. Before the start of the most recent season, the predictions came easily: *doom*.

But William Blake's poem invites us to look closer, and we must not be afraid. And so, let us contemplate the world in a grain (or several) of sand; or rather, the Phillies and their future via a handful of games. As for heaven in a flower—well, there was plenty of time spent in the weeds. We'll find something.

7 June: The Gnat that sings his Summer's Song

On an unseasonably warm Sunday in early June, the Phillies set right-hander Sean O'Sullivan against Ryan Vogelsong and the Giants. Despite a 19-33 record through the first two months of the season, the Phillies had a chance at playing .500 baseball for that week. In this particular season, a one-week spate of not-awful was worth paying attention to, worth sitting through a stonefly hatch in the right-field seats.

The eventual 6-4 win felt surprisingly sweet, not only for its rarity and some late-inning excitement, but also because the Giants' early-season lineup had been destroying baseballs, and O'Sullivan—he of an end-of-season ERA north of six—managed to keep them in the ballpark. In relief, Ken Giles showed the excellent stuff that would see him in the closer's role by the end of July. The Phillies, in a way they didn't for most of the season, found a way to get timely, satisfying hits: homers from rookies Odubel Herrera and Maikel Franco, a double from Ryan Howard and important pinch-hit deliveries—not only Jeff Francouer's game-winning double, but also one from bench wizard Andres Blanco.

PHILLIES PROSPECTUS

2015 W-L: 63-99, 5th in NL East

Pythag	.382	29th	DER	.684	29th
RS/G	3.86	27th	B-Age	28	10th
RA/G	4.99	29th	P-Age	28.7	21st
TAv	.251	27th	Salary	$146.9M	7th
BRR	3.08	13th	M$/MW	$9.3M	1st
TAv-P	.286	30th	DL Days	1041	16th
FIP	4.43	28th	$ on DL	24%	26th

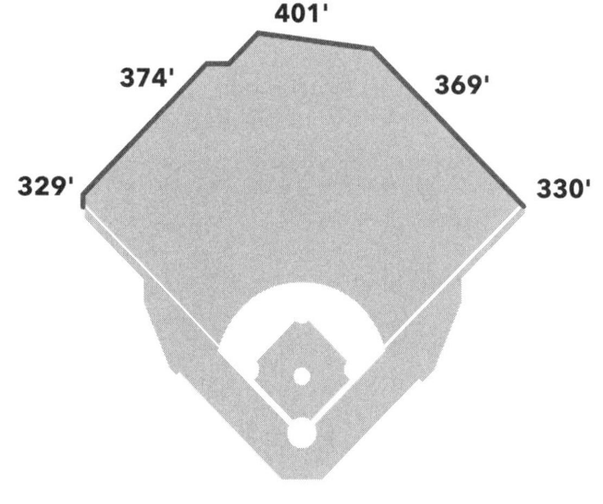

Outfield wall profile: **6'** to **19'**

Three-Year Park Factors

Runs	Runs/RH	Runs/LH	HR/RH	HR/LH
99	107	108	123	109

Top Hitter WARP	2.8	Odubel Herrera
Top Pitcher WARP	4.0	Cole Hamels
Top Prospect		J.P. Crawford

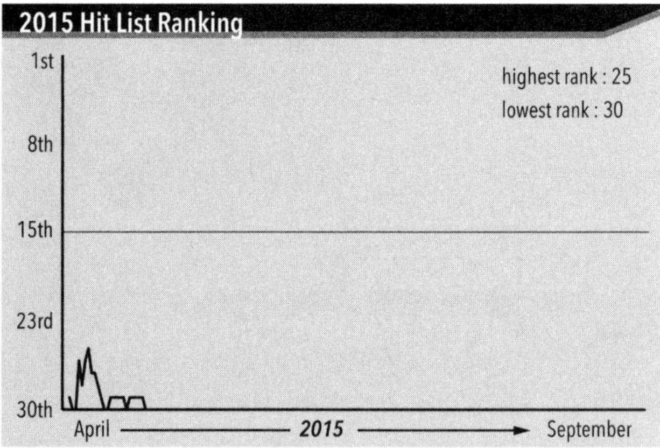

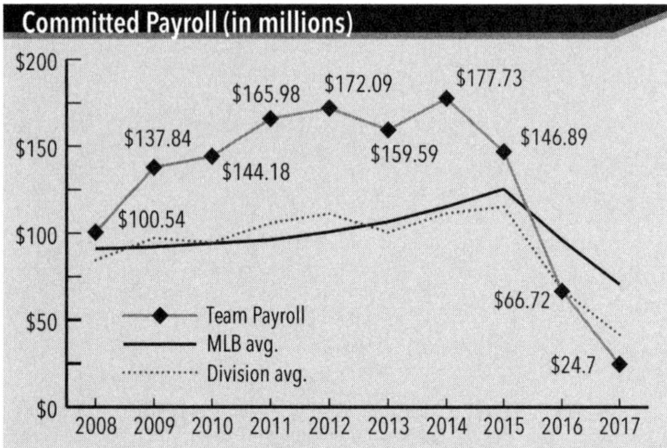

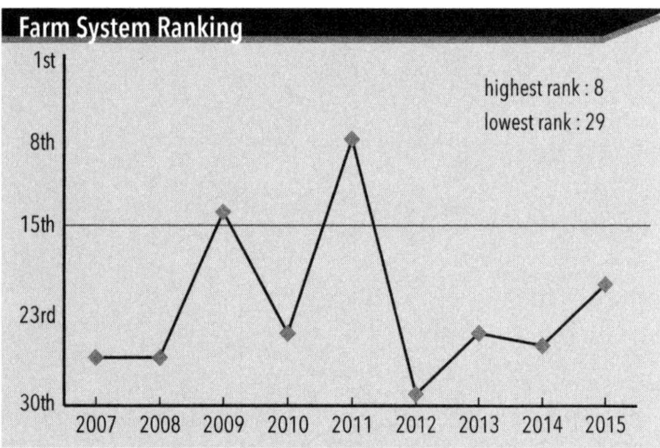

Personnel

President: Andy MacPhail

General Manager: Matt Klentak

Assistant General Manager: Benny Looper

Assistant General Manager: Scott Proefrock

Manager: Pete Mackanin

Baseball Prospectus Alumni

Lewie Pollis

Blanco played every non-battery position in the infield last year and slugged over .500. His 2015 numbers not only blew his career averages out of the water but were just plain great for a guy who started at least one game in every slot in the lineup.

Even more surprising, and more exciting for the long term, was the standout performance of Herrera. The Rule 5 pick from the Rangers was a revelation, hitting better than the average center fielder and posting the best slugging percentage of his professional career, down to and including his stint in Rookie ball. That afternoon's home run was one of eight on the year, and watching him crush a 1-1 Vogelsong offering into the Phillies' bullpen felt right for the day: a burst of tenacity that tied the game. There would be bright spots. There must be.

But on the Jumbotron, an image haunted the afternoon: Carlos Ruiz's lineup photo. No matter how I looked at it, he seemed like he was crying. The crinkling around his eyes wouldn't resolve into smile lines, and the white seam of his teeth seemed clenched, grit against something. Maybe it was a trick of the light; maybe my angle was bad; maybe a bad photo is a bad photo. Or maybe it was prescience.

Ruiz went go on to have his worst full season in the majors, and by the end, Cameron Rupp managed the bulk of the catching duties. Prospects Jorge Alfaro, who came to the Phillies from the Rangers in the Cole Hamels trade, and Andrew Knapp, who had a good half in Double-A, are in the pipeline; they or others like them are the future, as the youth always are. The question thus far unanswered by either portents or PECOTA is whether Ruiz, one of the last remnants of the team's run of excellence, has anything left in the present.

19 June: Some Squirrels to Misery are Born

Much as a squirrel had done in Game Four of the 2011 NLDS against the Cardinals, another squirrel stood as harbinger of a dire Phillies' fate. In 2011, the squirrel ran across the plate during the fifth inning of what would be a 5-3 Cardinals win, leaving Roy Halladay as the only hope in a must-win Game Five. We remember how that went: Halladay pitched eight innings of one-run baseball and Ryan Madson threw a scoreless ninth, but the Phillies, at home, could not conjure one paltry frigging run of support. On the final out of the game, Ryan Howard tore his Achilles tendon. As ill prophecy goes, 2011 was worse—there were expectations then.

In 2015, Phillippe Aumont, he of the brutal curve and frequent inability to find the strike zone, stood on the mound, re-invented as a starter—one of 14 different pitchers to fill that role for the Phillies. In the top of the second inning—when the Cardinals would hang four on the big righty—a squirrel that was trying to run along a wire above the Phillies' dugout fell. The little bad luck charm then made its way into the dugout, scattering players and giving viewers the momentary diversion of

Chase Utley's *squirrel!* face.

The rodent was caught and escorted out of the ballpark. No such escape for the team. Aumont gave up six runs in four innings, throwing more than 100 pitches, and though he precipitated this single-game tragedy, it was Justin DeFratus who was made to fall upon the sword in relief. Ryne Sandberg deployed him as a mop-up reliever last year, often using him to eat innings in lost causes—which, given the general state of the starting rotation, were many. As a result, DeFratus threw nearly 30 more innings in 2015 than he did in 2014, despite only a seven-game increase in appearances. His ERA more than doubled, as did the total number of home runs he allowed. His walks nearly tripled. DeFratus himself was (rightly) upset about the change in role, which Sandberg, apparently, never communicated to him.

DeFratus' individual plight is sad, but more relevantly, it stood as an encapsulation of Sandberg's tenure as manager, one that was rife with what Sandberg felt was naked disrespect for his authority by an entitled younger generation and with what his players felt was faulty decision-making and, worse, a failure to clearly convey those decisions. Perhaps the tight-rope squirrel presaged something else: Within a week of this game, Sandberg resigned. Pete Mackanin was named interim manager. After a rocky slide into the All-Star break, things looked a little better.

25 July: A Whole Patch of Wildflowers

In the heart of the Phillies' single real hot streak, a post-All-Star-break run of 11-2, Hamels faced Jake Arrieta and the Cubs. In 129 pitches, he reminded Phillies fans of the very best of times, delivering a 13-strikeout no-hitter against a Chicago team that would make it to the NLCS. The 5-0 win was backstopped by Ruiz and secured by Howard's third-inning three-run homer.

In that game, too, Franco doubled twice against Arrieta, continuing as a promising presence at the plate. Despite the Phillies' awful record in June, Franco was hottest then, helping him finish second on the team in home runs despite playing in only 80 games due to a hand fracture sustained on August 11th. Franco came back to play in the final three games of the season and collected three hits, including his final homer. After having spent a little part of 2014 and a big part of 2015 in the majors, Franco looks like he belongs. His third-base defense is maybe a cause for pause, but the Phillies tried him at first for two games, and he can have a long-term place there if his defense doesn't improve.

The week of July 19th as a whole was good. The Phillies went 5-1, and even the lone loss was its own kind of victory. On July 21st, pitching prospect Aaron Nola made his debut against the Rays, striking out six in as many innings, giving up just one run and five hits and notching his own first hit. The problem was that Nola's fifth-inning single was a quarter of the Phillies' total output. That the one run Nola gave up was a solo homer to Rays pitcher Nathan Karns was also less good, and indicative of a dinger issue over the rest of the season, but, generally, Nola's 13 starts bode well for the future.

It's to that future that the Phillies must look. No matter the time capsule Hamels opened on that windy Saturday in Chicago, by the time July ended, he was a Ranger. He and reliever Jake Diekman were traded for a passel of youngsters. Jonathan Papelbon went to the Nationals in return for another prospect. Ben Revere became a Blue Jay, bringing back two more. And on August 18th, in an 8-5 loss to Toronto, Utley played his last game as a Phillie.

4 October: The Winners Shout the Losers' Curse

The final game of the season dictated whether the Phillies would enter further ignominy: losses of two digits or three? The worst season since 1972 or the worst season since 1961? They faced the Marlins and Adam Conley, who'd beaten them in mid-September, but David Buchanan continued a productive final month to give the Phils a fighting chance.

In the bottom of the fourth inning, while the Phillies were losing 2-0 and between a Franco single and a Darin Ruf walk, a hawk fell from the sky—dead—and landed in foul territory. The game stood delayed for a moment until the grounds crew could remove the ex-raptor.

What sign this? How must it be read?

Against all odds, by the game's patterns of fortune, the dead hawk presaged luck for the Phillies. Franco went on to score their first run, doubled in by Blanco. Conley was lifted after the sixth, the game tied at two, and Marlins reliever Andre Rienzo coughed up four runs over five outless batters.

Admittedly, the game was a little peculiar, even beyond the bird. The Marlins' season went little better than the Phillies', and Miami only had individual markers for which to play: Dee Gordon's successful pursuit of the NL batting crown and Ichiro Suzuki's successful pursuit of awesomeness, as manifested in his one-run, two-hit performance as a reliever.

Maybe a lucky dead bird is the exact metaphor for the season. Except "lucky" is the wrong word—the hawk had nothing to do with Rienzo's inability to get an out. Mid-August call-up Aaron Altherr hit the ball hard and ran well in games not marked by strange avian circumstance. The Phillies scored one of their runs against a player who'd never pitched in an MLB game. But despite their record, despite a lot of signs that pegged the season as dead in the water before it even began (and *then* there was June), there was strange good fortune. Fortuitousness. How else to explain Herrera? How else to explain how well Nola and Jerad Eickhoff leapt into their roles as big-league starters? One half and one third of a season is not much upon which to judge, sure, but it's enough to get excited about, given the circumstances.

There are other signs of newness, too: Ruben Amaro Jr.'s contract was not renewed, and he's pursuing his own new path as first-base coach for the Red Sox. New President of Baseball Operations Andy MacPhail hired Matt Klentak, most recently an Angels assistant GM and formerly MacPhail's colleague in Baltimore, to replace Amaro. Klentak, at 35, is the youngest GM in Phillies history; he is younger than his big-ticket, low-productivity first baseman. But he already seems intent on meaningful change: In early November, Klentak reiterated the team's commitment to use "PHIL," a proprietary analytics and information system.

Mackanin no longer has "interim" attached to his title, and he'll be joined by new first-base and baserunning coach Mickey Morandini, who played second base for the Phillies through the '90s—really, the last notable Phillies second baseman before Utley took the position. Morandini also served as part of the coaching staff at the Phillies' Double-A affiliate, and it's surely no coincidence that he's with the big club as a significant number of former Reading Fightin Phils begin to dot the diamond in Philadelphia. One of those, shortstop J.P. Crawford, is certainly at the top of the list of players to watch for. Though Freddy Galvis has been holding down the position since Jimmy Rollins vacated it, Crawford is, barring anything catastrophic, the Phillies' future at short. Crawford is also their future, in short.

+++

All of this is hardly enough for a sandcastle, but 99 losses is not 100, and if the number of losses goes down instead of up in 2016, the castle will no longer be built upon the air. With luck, and time—an amount that no longer feels like an eternity—it could be a very fine castle indeed.

—Holly M. Wendt is Assistant Professor of English at Lebanon Valley College and an editor at The Classical.

HITTERS

Jorge Alfaro C

Born: 6/11/93 Age: 23 Bats: R Throws: R Height: 6'2" Weight: 225

YEAR	TEAM	LVL	AGE	PA	R	2B	3B	HR	RBI	BB	K	SB	CS	AVG/OBP/SLG	TAv	BABIP	BRR	FRAA	WARP
2013	HIC	A	20	420	63	22	1	16	53	28	111	16	3	.258/.338/.452	.280	.324	-0.4	C(82): 1.5, 1B(17): -0.8	2.6
2014	MYR	A+	21	437	63	22	5	13	73	23	100	6	5	.261/.318/.440	.268	.315	-1.7	C(75): 1.8, 1B(17): 0.0	2.1
2014	FRI	AA	21	99	12	4	0	4	14	6	23	0	0	.261/.343/.443	.271	.311	0.1	C(15): -0.9, 1B(1): -0.2	0.4
2015	FRI	AA	22	207	22	15	2	5	21	9	61	2	1	.253/.314/.432	.250	.347	0.6	C(35): -1.2, 1B(1): -0.0	0.5
2016	*PHI*	*MLB*	*23*	*33*	*3*	*1*	*0*	*1*	*4*	*1*	*10*	*0*	*0*	*.218/.267/.372*	*.226*	*.287*	*0.0*	*C -1*	*-0.1*
2017	*PHI*	*MLB*	*24*	*250*	*27*	*11*	*1*	*8*	*28*	*9*	*78*	*1*	*1*	*.214/.263/.370*	*.230*	*.283*	*-0.3*	*C -8*	*0.1*

Breakout: 4% Improve: 10% Collapse: 5% Attrition: 12% MLB: 17% *Comparables: Kyle Skipworth, Max Stassi, Tom Murphy*

YEAR	TEAM	P. COUNT	FRM RUNS	BLK RUNS	THRW RUNS	TOT RUNS
2014	FRI	2077	-0.4	-0.1	0.1	-0.4
2015	FRI	5306	-1.9	-0.3	0.4	-1.8
2016	*PHI*	*1207*	*-0.9*	*-0.1*	*-0.1*	*-1.2*
2017	*PHI*	*9130*	*-7.2*	*-1.1*	*-1.1*	*-9.3*

Ah, the allure of tools. The prize of the Cole Hamels trade return, Alfaro has a shed the size of a McMansion. Raw power? It's there. Otherworldly throwing arm? Got that. Questions about his eventual defensive position? Naturally. If Alfaro can shore up his defensive game, he stands a decent chance of becoming a star. Even if the best-laid plan fails, a future as a corner infielder isn't inconceivable, although dreams of him as a third baseman exist almost solely as a consequence of his arm. An early-season ankle injury cost Alfaro some development time, but he was able to return for a brief cameo in the Gulf Coast League, an encouraging sign heading into 2016.

Aaron Altherr OF

Born: 1/14/91 Age: 25 Bats: R Throws: R Height: 6'5" Weight: 215

YEAR	TEAM	LVL	AGE	PA	R	2B	3B	HR	RBI	BB	K	SB	CS	AVG/OBP/SLG	TAv	BABIP	BRR	FRAA	WARP
2013	CLR	A+	22	527	57	36	6	12	69	45	140	23	5	.275/.337/.455	.285	.360	0.5	CF(64): 4.8, LF(52): 2.7	3.6
2014	REA	AA	23	492	54	27	2	14	57	26	110	12	6	.236/.287/.399	.242	.279	-2.9	CF(100): 1.0, LF(12): 2.4	0.5
2014	PHI	MLB	23	5	0	0	0	0	0	0	2	0	0	.000/.000/.000	.005	.000	0.0	LF(1): 0.1	-0.1
2014	CLR	A+	23	33	6	1	2	0	2	5	8	1	0	.250/.364/.429	.278	.350	0.3	CF(6): 2.6, RF(1): -0.3	0.4
2015	REA	AA	24	260	29	19	3	6	29	28	40	8	3	.293/.371/.480	.302	.332	-0.4	RF(42): 4.0, CF(16): 1.3	2.3
2015	PHI	MLB	24	161	25	11	4	5	22	16	41	6	2	.241/.338/.489	.300	.301	0.0	LF(23): 0.5, RF(11): 0.6	1.4
2015	LEH	AAA	24	229	36	13	2	8	38	21	44	8	1	.294/.362/.495	.303	.338	1.7	CF(35): 2.7, RF(9): 0.2	2.2
2016	*PHI*	*MLB*	*25*	*542*	*60*	*28*	*4*	*16*	*63*	*36*	*148*	*12*	*4*	*.234/.291/.401*	*.245*	*.296*	*0.8*	*RF -0*	*0.5*
2017	*PHI*	*MLB*	*26*	*523*	*59*	*27*	*3*	*14*	*59*	*38*	*143*	*12*	*4*	*.231/.294/.394*	*.251*	*.295*	*1.1*	*RF 0*	*1.1*

Breakout: 5% Improve: 17% Collapse: 12% Attrition: 29% MLB: 46% *Comparables: Joey Terdoslavich, Josh Kroeger, Ben Johnson*

In 2014, Altherr was still very much a project, even at 23 in Double-A Reading. A wrist injury ate at his playing time early on, and his overall numbers were unimpressive at season's end, but his diligence and work ethic still earned him an espresso-size cup of coffee with the Phillies by the tail end of 2014. Then came a healthy 2015, and that diligent work began to manifest in drastically improved numbers. Altherr changed his approach to work deeper counts, quieted his hands in his stance and cleaned up his swing path, and a bump in walk rate and extra-base hits followed. Recalled to the big-league club when Maikel Franco hit the DL, Altherr's propensity for multi-baggers made itself visible from his first start onward. He'll still tend to swing a little long, given his size, and may be challenged to cover the inner part of the plate, but his mid- to outer-zone coverage is more than adequate. His athleticism makes him a fit for all three outfield positions, too, so 2016 figures to be the year he gets a good, long look in the majors.

J.P. Arencibia C

Born: 1/5/86 Age: 30 Bats: R Throws: R Height: 6'0" Weight: 205

YEAR	TEAM	LVL	AGE	PA	R	2B	3B	HR	RBI	BB	K	SB	CS	AVG/OBP/SLG	TAv	BABIP	BRR	FRAA	WARP
2013	TOR	MLB	27	497	45	18	0	21	55	18	148	0	2	.194/.227/.365	.217	.231	-1.9	C(131): 5.4	0.4
2014	ROU	AAA	28	203	31	8	0	14	41	10	53	1	0	.279/.320/.542	.294	.315	0.5	C(23): 3.3, 1B(20): 0.8	1.8
2014	TEX	MLB	28	222	20	9	0	10	35	10	62	0	0	.177/.239/.369	.228	.195	-1.8	C(22): 0.6, 1B(22): -2.0	-0.6
2015	TBA	MLB	29	73	9	3	0	6	17	1	22	0	0	.310/.315/.606	.318	.364	-0.7	C(23): -2.8	0.4
2015	DUR	AAA	29	405	52	17	0	22	65	15	125	0	0	.227/.259/.443	.252	.271	-1.9	1B(68): -3.6, C(10): -0.1	-0.4
2016	*PHI*	*MLB*	*30*	*250*	*27*	*9*	*0*	*12*	*35*	*11*	*75*	*0*	*0*	*.218/.259/.416*	*.238*	*.261*	*-0.8*	*1B -2, C 0*	*-0.2*
2017	*PHI*	*MLB*	*31*	*181*	*21*	*7*	*0*	*8*	*24*	*8*	*55*	*0*	*0*	*.209/.249/.392*	*.234*	*.252*	*-0.7*	*1B -1, C 0*	*0.2*

Breakout: 3% Improve: 37% Collapse: 9% Attrition: 18% MLB: 92% *Comparables: Mike Jacobs, Matthew Lecroy, Ben Broussard*

YEAR	TEAM	P. COUNT	FRM RUNS	BLK RUNS	THRW RUNS	TOT RUNS
2013	TOR	17407	6.5	-0.9	-0.2	5.4
2014	ROU	2783	2.6	-0.1	-0.1	2.4
2014	TEX	3167	1.2	-0.2	0.0	1.0
2014	TEX	3167	1.2	-0.2	0.0	1.0
2015	DUR	1180	-0.4	0.0	0.0	-0.5
2015	DUR	1180	-0.4	0.0	0.0	-0.5
2015	TBA	2589	-2.8	0.0	0.0	-2.7
2016	*PHI*	*2941*	*0.2*	*-0.1*	*-0.1*	*0.0*
2017	*PHI*	*2125*	*0.0*	*0.0*	*0.0*	*0.0*

Never known for taking his time at the plate, Arencibia's impatience may be tested when he hits free agency next offseason. Desperate for a warm body who owned a catcher's mitt late in the year, the Rays summoned the former first-round pick from Durham and enjoyed the most concentrated, potent solution of two true outcomes ever sold over the counter. Despite the small-sample heroics, he's the same JPA we all know and love: an offense-minded backup with oversize biceps and exploitable flaws. As long as he can put balls over fences, he should continue to receive compensation to sit on a bench and provide his team with a tiny glint of late-inning hope.

Cody Asche 3B

Born: 6/30/90 Age: 26 Bats: L Throws: R Height: 6'1" Weight: 200

YEAR	TEAM	LVL	AGE	PA	R	2B	3B	HR	RBI	BB	K	SB	CS	AVG/OBP/SLG	TAv	BABIP	BRR	FRAA	WARP
2013	PHI	MLB	23	179	18	8	1	5	22	15	43	1	0	.235/.302/.389	.250	.287	0.9	3B(44): 0.6	0.6
2013	LEH	AAA	23	446	52	24	4	15	68	35	95	11	3	.295/.352/.485	.285	.349	0.5	3B(103): 0.2	2.8
2014	PHI	MLB	24	434	43	25	0	10	46	33	102	0	1	.252/.309/.390	.260	.315	-0.3	3B(112): 0.4	1.4
2015	PHI	MLB	25	456	41	22	3	12	39	26	111	1	2	.245/.294/.395	.248	.304	-2.1	LF(63): -3.0, 3B(51): -2.4	-0.1
2015	LEH	AAA	25	67	7	3	0	1	3	6	9	0	0	.295/.358/.393	.270	.333	-1.0	LF(15): -1.2	0.0
2016	*PHI*	*MLB*	*26*	*534*	*57*	*26*	*2*	*17*	*66*	*36*	*124*	*3*	*2*	*.255/.309/.420*	*.256*	*.306*	*-0.5*	*LF -8*	*0.5*
2017	*PHI*	*MLB*	*27*	*536*	*68*	*27*	*2*	*19*	*69*	*39*	*127*	*3*	*2*	*.261/.319/.443*	*.274*	*.313*	*-0.6*	*LF -8*	*0.5*

Breakout: 11% Improve: 59% Collapse: 7% Attrition: 13% MLB: 96% *Comparables: J.D. Martinez, Matt Holliday, Lastings Milledge*

After two and a half seasons of roughly identical production, Asche is approaching predictability. Bumped off third base by the defensively superior and still-improving Maikel Franco, the Phillies tried Asche in left field in order to keep his bat in the lineup. That bat followed suit from 2014 and the abbreviated debut in 2013: a sub-.700 OPS, somewhere in the vicinity of a .250 TAv and a smattering of extra-base hits to complement unremarkable defense. In an organization that has other, younger corner players either graduating or rapidly accelerating toward The Show, Asche's future in Philadelphia is becoming tenuous and murky, no matter how predictable his production may be.

Andres Blanco INF

Born: 4/11/84 Age: 32 Bats: B Throws: R Height: 5'10" Weight: 195

YEAR	TEAM	LVL	AGE	PA	R	2B	3B	HR	RBI	BB	K	SB	CS	AVG/OBP/SLG	TAv	BABIP	BRR	FRAA	WARP
2014	PHI	MLB	30	53	4	5	0	1	3	2	6	0	0	.277/.306/.447	.267	.300	-0.6	3B(10): 0.5, SS(6): 0.2	0.3
2014	LEH	AAA	30	155	16	6	0	0	11	13	25	3	5	.241/.314/.285	.213	.292	1.2	SS(39): 1.6, 2B(5): -0.4	0.1
2015	PHI	MLB	31	261	32	22	3	7	25	21	44	1	1	.292/.360/.502	.303	.335	1.1	3B(36): -2.3, 2B(22): 0.8	2.0
2016	*PHI*	*MLB*	*32*	*310*	*32*	*17*	*1*	*6*	*32*	*21*	*56*	*3*	*2*	*.255/.314/.395*	*.250*	*.290*	*0.0*	*2B 1, SS 1*	*1.1*
2017	*PHI*	*MLB*	*33*	*290*	*30*	*16*	*1*	*5*	*28*	*19*	*52*	*2*	*2*	*.243/.299/.365*	*.246*	*.278*	*0.1*	*2B 1, SS 1*	*1.2*

Breakout: 3% Improve: 28% Collapse: 8% Attrition: 24% MLB: 80% *Comparables: Robb Quinlan, Esteban German, Greg Dobbs*

A stunningly effective find, Blanco quietly had one of the best seasons among part-time players in the entire league in 2015. Splitting time mostly between second and third base, the eight-year vet has emerged in Philadelphia after spending the full 2012 season in Triple-A and 2013 out of American pro ball entirely, casually putting up career-best offensive numbers in the meantime. His 261 plate appearances in 2015 were also a career high, his playing time aided by some conveniently untimely injuries, first to Maikel Franco, then to Cesar Hernandez. Blanco certainly made the most of the opportunity, and seems destined to find more time in the majors in 2016. He may just be depth in the end, but his resurgence has been nothing short of impressive nonetheless.

Peter Bourjos CF

Born: 3/31/87 Age: 29 Bats: R Throws: R Height: 6'1" Weight: 185

YEAR	TEAM	LVL	AGE	PA	R	2B	3B	HR	RBI	BB	K	SB	CS	AVG/OBP/SLG	TAv	BABIP	BRR	FRAA	WARP
2013	ANA	MLB	26	196	26	3	3	3	12	10	43	6	0	.274/.333/.377	.259	.346	1.9	CF(53): -2.2	0.6
2013	SLC	AAA	26	55	13	4	0	2	7	4	19	0	0	.208/.291/.417	.248	.286	0.9	CF(7): 0.7	0.2
2014	SLN	MLB	27	294	32	9	5	4	24	20	78	9	3	.231/.294/.348	.242	.311	3.5	CF(104): 1.3	0.9
2015	SLN	MLB	28	225	32	8	3	4	13	19	59	5	8	.200/.290/.333	.228	.263	0.7	CF(93): -2.4	-0.2
2016	*PHI*	*MLB*	*29*	*195*	*22*	*7*	*2*	*4*	*19*	*13*	*49*	*5*	*3*	*.240/.304/.382*	*.242*	*.300*	*0.9*	*CF 0*	*0.4*
2017	*PHI*	*MLB*	*30*	*226*	*25*	*8*	*3*	*5*	*24*	*15*	*59*	*5*	*4*	*.235/.298/.377*	*.246*	*.299*	*1.3*	*CF 0, LF 0*	*0.8*

Breakout: 1% Improve: 43% Collapse: 6% Attrition: 15% MLB: 98% *Comparables: Franklin Gutierrez, Aaron Rowand, Tony Gonzalez*

Remember when Bourjos, not Randal Grichuk, was the prize acquisition in the David Freese trade? That all changed in 2015. While Grichuk spent the season asserting himself as a major-league regular, Bourjos was busy doing his finest Jarrod Dyson impersonation, which, judging by that abysmal success rate on stolen-base attempts, isn't much better than your Christopher Walken impression. Having validated the widespread belief that he can't hit—not even half a dry lick—he started a career-low percentage of his appearances, instead entering games more often as a pinch-hitter, -runner and defensive sub. Bourjos probably isn't happy with the role change—he's a year away from free agency—but you can't blame the Cardinals for placing him in a position that minimized his weaknesses and maximized Grichuk's strengths, and little is likely to change even now that he's on the Phillies.

Domonic Brown LF

Born: 9/3/87 Age: 28 Bats: L Throws: L Height: 6'5" Weight: 225

YEAR	TEAM	LVL	AGE	PA	R	2B	3B	HR	RBI	BB	K	SB	CS	AVG/OBP/SLG	TAv	BABIP	BRR	FRAA	WARP
2013	PHI	MLB	25	540	65	21	4	27	83	39	97	8	3	.272/.324/.494	.292	.287	2.7	LF(132): -9.8, RF(2): -0.0	2.2
2014	PHI	MLB	26	512	47	22	1	10	63	34	91	7	1	.235/.285/.349	.245	.269	0.3	LF(127): -4.9	-0.2
2015	LEH	AAA	27	228	22	12	1	2	26	14	37	10	3	.257/.307/.352	.249	.301	1.6	RF(47): -3.0	0.0
2015	CLR	A+	27	20	2	1	0	1	3	2	7	0	0	.294/.400/.529	.355	.444	-0.2	RF(6): -0.5	0.2
2015	PHI	MLB	27	204	19	6	1	5	25	14	36	3	1	.228/.284/.349	.234	.257	-1.3	RF(50): 1.0	-0.2
2016	*PHI*	*MLB*	*28*	*290*	*33*	*13*	*1*	*9*	*35*	*23*	*53*	*5*	*2*	*.252/.312/.413*	*.258*	*.281*	*0.2*	*RF -2*	*0.4*
2017	*PHI*	*MLB*	*29*	*307*	*37*	*13*	*1*	*10*	*37*	*24*	*56*	*5*	*2*	*.248/.309/.411*	*.264*	*.274*	*0.2*	*RF -2*	*0.4*

Breakout: 1% Improve: 52% Collapse: 5% Attrition: 17% MLB: 92% *Comparables: Josh Reddick, Xavier Nady, Juan Rivera*

It's a cruel twist of fate, or maybe the most symbolically fitting thing in baseball history, that Brown's season came to an end after he crashed into a wall. Once more failing to replicate his two breakout months during the 2013 season, this particular chapter of the **What Could Have Been** saga saw Brown hindered by Achilles tendinitis in the spring, then shipped out to Lehigh Valley for two months to figure out, well, *something*, only to arrive back in the bigs in June and flop once more before concussion concerns from the literal crash ended his season. Even his most ardent defenders are now left dangling by their pinkie fingers, and Andy MacPhail's boot is on its way down: Brown was outrighted off the Phillies' 40-man roster before a new General Manager was even hired, and Brown will now turn his sights to rebuilding something from the ashes of the promise that once was.

J.P. Crawford SS

Born: 1/11/95 Age: 21 Bats: L Throws: R Height: 6'2" Weight: 180

YEAR	TEAM	LVL	AGE	PA	R	2B	3B	HR	RBI	BB	K	SB	CS	AVG/OBP/SLG	TAv	BABIP	BRR	FRAA	WARP
2013	LWD	A	18	60	10	1	0	0	2	7	10	2	1	.208/.300/.226	.220	.256	-0.3	SS(14): 0.8	0.1
2014	CLR	A+	19	271	32	7	0	8	29	28	37	10	7	.275/.352/.407	.284	.292	-2.9	SS(62): 0.2	1.6
2014	LWD	A	19	267	37	16	0	3	19	37	37	14	7	.295/.398/.405	.291	.342	1.2	SS(59): 0.8	2.3
2015	CLR	A+	20	95	15	1	0	1	8	14	9	5	2	.392/.489/.443	.369	.435	1.1	SS(20): 0.9	1.7
2015	REA	AA	20	405	53	21	7	5	34	49	45	7	2	.265/.354/.407	.272	.289	1.0	SS(85): 6.7	3.1
2016	*PHI*	*MLB*	*21*	*250*	*30*	*10*	*1*	*5*	*23*	*24*	*48*	*4*	*2*	*.243/.320/.369*	*.248*	*.285*	*-0.1*	*SS 1*	*1.0*
2017	*PHI*	*MLB*	*22*	*399*	*48*	*17*	*2*	*10*	*44*	*39*	*76*	*6*	*3*	*.256/.332/.399*	*.269*	*.296*	*0.0*	*SS 2*	*2.0*

Breakout: 9% Improve: 24% Collapse: 2% Attrition: 9% MLB: 30% *Comparables: Mookie Betts, Francisco Lindor, Jurickson Profar*

It's been about 20 years since the Phillies' farm system had a shortstop generating nearly the buzz that Crawford has. That predecessor was only the greatest shortstop in the history of a 130-year-old franchise, so we're obviously starting things off on very rational and grounded footing with comps for Crawford, who seems poised to be the latest injection of youth for the major-league club by some point in 2016. While some wonder if the giant neon signage reading "THE FUTURE" emblazoned with red and white pinstripes could use another few hundred feet of tubing, the naturally counterbalancing "yeah, but" doesn't offer a ton of disincentive. Will Crawford be Carlos Correa? Incredibly unlikely. Does he have the hands and footwork to be a reliable defensive shortstop while showcasing an ever-steadying offensive game, with 10 to 15 home runs a year out on the horizon? He sure does, and his graph is turning parabolic. With no clear obstacle in his way, the big-league shortstop job is his for the taking, and the neon couldn't seem brighter or more inviting.

Luis Encarnacion 1B

Born: 8/9/97 Age: 18 Bats: R Throws: R Height: 6'2" Weight: 185

The Phillies, as an organization, were light on power at nearly every conceivable level in 2015. With Maikel Franco's ascendance to the majors as a full-time player, the farm was left particularly wanting for pop, and one of the best candidates to irrigate that drought-stricken soil by bringing some rain is young Encarnacion, a million-dollar signing out of the Dominican Republic in 2013. Inked on his 16th birthday, it was known from day one that Encarnacion's value lies in his bat. He provides no plus defensive projection, and played exclusively at first base in the Gulf Coast League last year. The power hasn't shown up regularly in games yet, but seeing how Encarnacion is only now the age at which most American high school draftees are selected, his 365 pro plate appearances are nothing less than a head start.

Maikel Franco 3B

Born: 8/26/92 Age: 23 Bats: R Throws: R Height: 6'1" Weight: 215

YEAR	TEAM	LVL	AGE	PA	R	2B	3B	HR	RBI	BB	K	SB	CS	AVG/OBP/SLG	TAv	BABIP	BRR	FRAA	WARP
2013	REA	AA	20	292	47	13	2	15	51	10	31	1	2	.339/.363/.563	.336	.338	0.9	3B(59): 3.3, 1B(8): -0.3	3.7
2013	CLR	A+	20	289	42	23	1	16	52	20	39	0	0	.299/.349/.576	.315	.297	-0.5	3B(64): -4.4	2.2
2014	LEH	AAA	21	556	64	33	4	16	78	30	81	3	1	.257/.299/.428	.247	.276	2.4	3B(107): -3.2, 1B(23): 0.3	0.8
2014	PHI	MLB	21	58	5	2	0	0	5	1	13	0	0	.179/.190/.214	.147	.227	0.5	3B(12): 1.5, 1B(5): -0.3	-0.3
2015	PHI	MLB	22	335	45	22	1	14	50	26	52	1	0	.280/.343/.497	.305	.297	0.8	3B(75): -5.8, 1B(2): 0.2	2.1
2015	LEH	AAA	22	151	15	12	1	4	24	8	25	2	0	.355/.384/.539	.323	.404	1.3	3B(29): -2.1, 1B(4): -0.2	1.4
2016	*PHI*	*MLB*	*23*	*604*	*68*	*33*	*2*	*24*	*85*	*27*	*104*	*1*	*0*	*.270/.306/.466*	*.272*	*.291*	*1.1*	*3B -7*	*1.9*
2017	*PHI*	*MLB*	*24*	*547*	*68*	*29*	*2*	*22*	*74*	*25*	*95*	*1*	*0*	*.266/.303/.456*	*.275*	*.286*	*0.8*	*3B -6*	*0.8*

Breakout: 2% Improve: 36% Collapse: 4% Attrition: 14% MLB: 75% *Comparables: Mike Moustakas, Brett Lawrie, Pablo Sandoval*

Considering the concerns over his approach at the plate and his arm-bar swing mechanics leading up to the season, paired with general Phillies-hitting-prospect cynicism, it seemed entirely possible that Franco was primed to bust more than bust out. Instead, he was an almost singular bright spot on offense and, despite his up-and-down defensive tendencies, appears to be nestling in as a key transitional figure for the club moving forward. The long view would suggest that his peak is close and destined to be short, as a lot of his success is premised on his supersonic bat speed, not typically something that ages well, but there's growing optimism that 2016 will hold big things for Franco, regardless of whether he stays at third or moves across the diamond to first.

Freddy Galvis SS

Born: 11/14/89 Age: 26 Bats: B Throws: R Height: 5'10" Weight: 190

YEAR	TEAM	LVL	AGE	PA	R	2B	3B	HR	RBI	BB	K	SB	CS	AVG/OBP/SLG	TAv	BABIP	BRR	FRAA	WARP
2013	PHI	MLB	23	222	13	5	4	6	19	13	45	1	0	.234/.283/.385	.238	.273	1.0	2B(23): 0.9, 3B(16): -0.3	0.4
2013	LEH	AAA	23	266	26	14	2	3	25	11	51	3	1	.245/.274/.357	.221	.290	0.4	SS(56): -2.5, 2B(3): -0.3	-0.3
2014	CLR	A+	24	20	4	0	2	1	3	0	2	0	0	.200/.200/.550	.248	.176	0.2	SS(2): -0.0, 2B(2): 0.0	0.1
2014	PHI	MLB	24	128	14	3	1	4	12	8	30	1	0	.176/.227/.319	.215	.198	-0.4	SS(25): 1.1, 3B(11): -0.0	-0.1
2014	LEH	AAA	24	149	22	14	1	3	15	11	25	1	1	.267/.322/.452	.261	.308	1.1	SS(30): -2.0, 2B(3): 0.7	0.6
2015	PHI	MLB	25	603	63	14	5	7	50	30	103	10	1	.263/.302/.343	.241	.309	3.4	SS(146): -3.9, 2B(4): 0.1	1.3
2016	*PHI*	*MLB*	*26*	*534*	*59*	*22*	*4*	*12*	*51*	*26*	*98*	*6*	*1*	*.245/.284/.377*	*.229*	*.276*	*1.3*	*SS -7*	*0.3*
2017	*PHI*	*MLB*	*27*	*512*	*54*	*20*	*4*	*12*	*54*	*27*	*94*	*5*	*1*	*.244/.285/.377*	*.238*	*.274*	*1.2*	*SS -7*	*1.7*

Breakout: 7% Improve: 53% Collapse: 7% Attrition: 15% MLB: 96% *Comparables: Marwin Gonzalez, Adeiny Hechavarria, Alexi Amarista*

There's something comforting and absolving about glove-first players. It could be the way we regard their typical offensive shortcomings with the encouragement of supportive parents, heads slightly cocked with a knowing and sad, yet understanding, closed-lip smile as we play armchair coxswain trying to fix the timing issue that's mired them in their latest 0-for-20 slide. This used to be Galvis, and somewhere along the way, the glove became more above-average than special while the slumps at the plate persisted, and the corners of our parental mouths began to droop. Galvis is, in other words, losing his luster and, in a race against time, must be able to reestablish his value as a major-league infielder before the ascendance of J.P. Crawford. After that, maybe he beats out Cesar Hernandez for a starting gig, or maybe that ends his regular playing days in Philadelphia. It's hard to imagine him disappearing entirely—Pete Kozma still pokes his head up each season, after all—but a first-division starter Galvis is not.

Cesar Hernandez 2B

Born: 5/23/90 Age: 26 Bats: B Throws: R Height: 5'10" Weight: 165

YEAR	TEAM	LVL	AGE	PA	R	2B	3B	HR	RBI	BB	K	SB	CS	AVG/OBP/SLG	TAv	BABIP	BRR	FRAA	WARP
2013	PHI	MLB	23	131	17	5	0	0	10	9	26	0	3	.289/.344/.331	.237	.368	-1.2	CF(22): -2.0, 2B(10): -0.1	-0.3
2014	PHI	MLB	24	125	13	2	0	1	4	9	33	1	1	.237/.290/.281	.234	.321	-0.2	3B(14): -0.6, 2B(11): -1.1	-0.2
2014	LEH	AAA	24	171	23	6	3	0	10	15	34	7	4	.256/.322/.333	.230	.328	-0.4	2B(21): -2.5, SS(16): -0.3	-0.3
2014	REA	AA	24	117	13	4	1	3	14	13	13	1	3	.340/.410/.485	.311	.364	0.3	3B(18): -0.4, SS(8): -0.2	1.1
2015	PHI	MLB	25	452	57	20	4	1	35	40	86	19	5	.272/.339/.348	.261	.342	1.7	2B(88): 8.8, SS(12): -0.1	2.5
2016	*PHI*	*MLB*	*26*	*632*	*75*	*24*	*6*	*7*	*50*	*50*	*128*	*21*	*8*	*.269/.329/.365*	*.252*	*.331*	*0.1*	*2B -2, 3B -0*	*1.6*
2017	*PHI*	*MLB*	*27*	*540*	*57*	*20*	*4*	*5*	*48*	*41*	*111*	*17*	*7*	*.266/.323/.358*	*.254*	*.327*	*0.8*	*2B -2, 3B 0*	*1.7*

Breakout: 5% Improve: 51% Collapse: 12% Attrition: 28% MLB: 91% *Comparables: Josh Harrison, Alexi Casilla, Daniel Descalso*

Even if it's difficult to buy into Hernandez as any sort of cornerstone or long-term middle-infield option, his 2015 can't be considered anything less than a pleasant surprise. Coming into the season, Hernandez was the presumed favorite to ascend to the starting role at second base in the event Chase Utley got hurt again (ding) or agreed to be traded (ding ding). Hernandez performed admirably, hitting .289/.343/.361 from the day Utley hit the DL on June 23rd until his season was abruptly concluded by his thumb's dislocation on a play at first base. He may never bop more than five home runs or hit .300 in a season (he needed a well-above-average BABIP just to hit .272 last year), but every year teams do far worse than him for their super-utility quick fixes.

Odubel Herrera OF

Born: 12/29/91 Age: 24 Bats: L Throws: R Height: 5'11" Weight: 200

YEAR	TEAM	LVL	AGE	PA	R	2B	3B	HR	RBI	BB	K	SB	CS	AVG/OBP/SLG	TAv	BABIP	BRR	FRAA	WARP
2013	FRI	AA	21	412	37	12	7	2	30	17	67	15	5	.257/.289/.339	.225	.304	-2.1	2B(93): -0.1, SS(1): -0.0	-0.7
2013	MYR	A+	21	115	13	2	1	1	5	16	19	2	2	.295/.398/.368	.278	.355	-0.1	2B(23): 1.8	0.7
2014	MYR	A+	22	137	26	3	1	0	11	23	21	9	3	.297/.412/.342	.293	.359	2.4	LF(8): -1.6, 2B(6): -1.4	0.7
2014	FRI	AA	22	408	47	16	4	2	48	29	70	12	7	.321/.373/.402	.290	.389	-1.6	2B(91): -8.3, LF(3): -0.3	1.4
2015	PHI	MLB	23	537	64	30	3	8	41	28	129	16	8	.297/.344/.418	.274	.387	4.6	CF(136): -2.0	2.8
2016	*PHI*	*MLB*	*24*	*618*	*71*	*26*	*5*	*8*	*51*	*33*	*138*	*16*	*7*	*.267/.311/.370*	*.241*	*.331*	*3.2*	*CF -1*	*1.2*
2017	*PHI*	*MLB*	*25*	*572*	*60*	*24*	*4*	*8*	*54*	*32*	*126*	*14*	*7*	*.264/.310/.370*	*.248*	*.326*	*3.7*	*CF -1*	*2.1*

Breakout: 9% Improve: 40% Collapse: 8% Attrition: 16% MLB: 72% *Comparables: Billy Hamilton, Danny Santana, Felix Pie*

Few teams have managed to rummage around in the league-wide yard sale that is the Rule 5 draft and emerge with as many impact players as the Phillies in the last decade-plus—credit AGM Mike Ondo for a lot of that—and Herrera is the latest antique vase bought for $2.50 and a smile. Shifted from second base to center field, where he learned on the fly, "El Torito" showed some route and first-step deficiencies that his athleticism compensated for, though those missteps seemed fewer and further between by September. Herrera is bound to see lots more playing time in 2016, though whether 2015 was a fluky peak or the start of a long and successful major-league career remains to be seen.

Rhys Hoskins 1B

Born: 3/17/93 Age: 23 Bats: R Throws: R Height: 6'4" Weight: 225

YEAR	TEAM	LVL	AGE	PA	R	2B	3B	HR	RBI	BB	K	SB	CS	AVG/OBP/SLG	TAv	BABIP	BRR	FRAA	WARP
2014	WPT	A-	21	273	30	15	0	9	40	21	54	3	3	.237/.311/.408	.260	.268	-0.2	1B(37): 0.3	0.2
2015	LWD	A	22	290	39	17	4	9	51	26	50	2	4	.322/.397/.525	.351	.369	-1.6	1B(64): -0.7	2.9
2015	CLR	A+	22	277	47	19	2	8	39	29	49	2	0	.317/.394/.510	.336	.367	-1.7	1B(58): 1.4	2.5
2016	*PHI*	*MLB*	*23*	*250*	*27*	*11*	*1*	*8*	*32*	*18*	*65*	*0*	*0*	*.246/.308/.417*	*.256*	*.303*	*-0.4*	*1B 1*	*0.3*
2017	*PHI*	*MLB*	*24*	*366*	*45*	*18*	*1*	*12*	*45*	*27*	*91*	*0*	*0*	*.256/.318/.426*	*.271*	*.315*	*-0.8*	*1B 1*	*0.5*

Breakout: 7% Improve: 21% Collapse: 5% Attrition: 19% MLB: 39% *Comparables: Ryan Lavarnway, Mark Canha, Ike Davis*

A fifth-round, junior-year sign out of Sacramento State in 2014, Hoskins handled A-ball stops at Lakewood and Clearwater as one would expect of a college bat: with a .900-plus OPS at each. Hoskins features a basic, balanced stance from the right side and an approach that often coaxed younger pitchers in the South Atlantic and Florida State leagues into making mistakes he could lay into. Hoskins does make hard contact, a plus at any stage, but he will need to show an ability to maintain his approach and apply the same contact to more advanced pitching before he seems more viable as a major-league option than, say, Matt Rizzotti once did.

Ryan Howard 1B

Born: 11/19/79 Age: 36 Bats: L Throws: L Height: 6'4" Weight: 250

YEAR	TEAM	LVL	AGE	PA	R	2B	3B	HR	RBI	BB	K	SB	CS	AVG/OBP/SLG	TAv	BABIP	BRR	FRAA	WARP
2013	PHI	MLB	33	317	34	20	2	11	43	23	95	0	0	.266/.319/.465	.278	.349	-1.6	1B(76): -1.1	0.6
2014	PHI	MLB	34	648	65	18	1	23	95	67	190	0	0	.223/.310/.380	.260	.288	-1.5	1B(141): -7.7	-0.3
2015	PHI	MLB	35	503	53	29	1	23	77	27	138	0	0	.229/.277/.443	.250	.272	-2.6	1B(116): -2.0	-0.5
2016	*PHI*	*MLB*	*36*	*591*	*67*	*24*	*1*	*25*	*80*	*50*	*173*	*0*	*0*	*.230/.301/.419*	*.253*	*.288*	*-1.9*	*1B -3*	*-0.1*
2017	*PHI*	*MLB*	*37*	*419*	*51*	*17*	*1*	*16*	*52*	*36*	*126*	*0*	*0*	*.214/.287/.390*	*.247*	*.271*	*-1.6*	*1B -2*	*0.1*

Breakout: 0% Improve: 19% Collapse: 14% Attrition: 11% MLB: 80% *Comparables: Tony Clark, Joe Adcock, Olmedo Saenz*

The trades of Chase Utley, Cole Hamels and Jimmy Rollins left Howard and Carlos Ruiz as the lone remnants of the 2008 champs, and the big flyswatter's continued presence only felt more out of place as the season aged and younger players began filling the vacancies. Howard posted career-worst numbers against left-handed pitching, and Pete Mackanin finally seems as though he'll be the guy to implement a platoon of Howard and Darin Ruf on a regular basis. It's entirely possible that Howard can rebuild some lost value and put up prettier numbers if lefties are removed from his field of view; the Phillies certainly hope he can, as their efforts to trade him to the American League will no doubt continue. Even if he doesn't, 2016 will be his last season in Philadelphia, as his pernicious and perpetually panned contract finally peters out. It's an ignominious end for a former MVP, but it's still entirely possible for him to eclipse 400 home runs before all is totally said and done, even if he'd do it in something other than red pinstripes.

Andrew Knapp C

Born: 11/9/91 Age: 24 Bats: B Throws: R Height: 6'1" Weight: 190

YEAR	TEAM	LVL	AGE	PA	R	2B	3B	HR	RBI	BB	K	SB	CS	AVG/OBP/SLG	TAv	BABIP	BRR	FRAA	WARP
2013	WPT	A-	21	247	30	20	0	4	23	22	57	7	5	.253/.340/.401	.278	.325	-3.4	C(21): -0.4	0.6
2014	LWD	A	22	314	39	19	4	5	25	27	71	3	3	.290/.354/.438	.287	.368	1.0	C(42): -1.5	1.9
2014	CLR	A+	22	90	7	1	0	1	7	5	26	1	0	.157/.222/.205	.163	.214	-1.1		-1.0
2015	CLR	A+	23	281	38	14	3	2	28	29	63	0	1	.262/.356/.369	.282	.344	-1.7	C(46): -0.1	1.5
2015	REA	AA	23	241	39	21	2	11	56	22	43	1	0	.360/.419/.631	.356	.405	0.0	C(48): -4.6	3.1
2016	*PHI*	*MLB*	*24*	*250*	*24*	*12*	*1*	*7*	*29*	*18*	*71*	*0*	*0*	*.235/.296/.385*	*.241*	*.308*	*-0.4*	*C -11, 1B 0*	*-0.7*
2017	*PHI*	*MLB*	*25*	*305*	*34*	*15*	*1*	*8*	*33*	*21*	*90*	*0*	*0*	*.237/.297/.382*	*.248*	*.319*	*-0.6*	*C -14, 1B 0*	*-0.3*

Breakout: 4% Improve: 14% Collapse: 10% Attrition: 25% MLB: 41% *Comparables: Nick Hundley, Michael McKenry, Tom Murphy*

YEAR	TEAM	P. COUNT	FRM RUNS	BLK RUNS	THRW RUNS	TOT RUNS
2015	REA	6622	-3.3	-0.8	0.3	-3.8
2016	*PHI*	*8172*	*-8.7*	*-1.1*	*-0.8*	*-10.6*
2017	*PHI*	*9968*	*-10.1*	*-1.2*	*-0.9*	*-12.2*

Knapp's raw offensive numbers following his midseason promotion to Reading are juicy enough to make Joe Boxscore-Reader wonder if Carlos Ruiz shouldn't be given the unconditional heave-ho over the winter. Truth is, though, Knapp is still a couple of leaps and a handful of bounds from being a major-league catcher on defense, even as his bat progresses. The 2015 Paul Owens Award winner (for best position player in the Phillies' system) did more than just BABIP his way to a hefty slash line in Double-A: He shortened his stroke to emphasize contact later in counts. Knapp is slow to pop and, post-Tommy John surgery, doesn't have the Jorge Alfaro-esque arm to compensate. However, with coaching and experience, things like his receiving and game-calling certainly stand to improve, and plenty of optimism remains that he won't need to be moved off the position.

Jhailyn Ortiz 1B

Born: 11/18/98 Age: 17 Bats: R Throws: R Height: 6'2" Weight: 260

As we creep closer and closer to the moment when someone in professional baseball was born in the year 2000—Ortiz was born in 1998—it's appropriate to think of that early-aughts era of slugging when imagining a player like this in the major leagues someday. All anyone in the know can talk about when Ortiz's name comes up is power, mostly the raw variety, though a fair bit has shown up in amateur game action. He's big, those 260 listed pounds being his weight as a *16-year-old*, which can serve as a springboard of understanding where the chatter about power is coming from. Before sugarplum fairies clad in Giancarlo Stanton jerseys go dancing through your head, however, consider once again Ortiz's age and the amount of work he needs with pitch recognition and swinging for contact. He is a long, long way off, but "potential" is indeed a sexy word—worth $4 million, as far as the Phillies are concerned—and this is one investment the organization feels confident will pay out.

Roman Quinn CF

Born: 5/14/93 Age: 23 Bats: B Throws: R Height: 5'10" Weight: 170

YEAR	TEAM	LVL	AGE	PA	R	2B	3B	HR	RBI	BB	K	SB	CS	AVG/OBP/SLG	TAv	BABIP	BRR	FRAA	WARP
2013	LWD	A	20	298	37	7	3	5	21	27	64	32	9	.238/.323/.346	.263	.297	0.1	SS(65): -18.7	-0.6
2014	CLR	A+	21	382	51	10	3	7	36	36	80	32	12	.257/.343/.370	.259	.316	3.1	CF(69): 0.9, SS(17): -3.1	1.3
2015	REA	AA	22	257	44	6	6	4	15	18	42	29	10	.306/.356/.435	.283	.360	6.2	CF(58): 3.4	2.5
2016	*PHI*	*MLB*	*23*	*250*	*35*	*7*	*2*	*5*	*20*	*16*	*63*	*18*	*6*	*.231/.289/.353*	*.226*	*.288*	*1.6*	*CF 1*	*0.2*
2017	*PHI*	*MLB*	*24*	*344*	*38*	*10*	*3*	*8*	*36*	*22*	*83*	*25*	*9*	*.238/.296/.369*	*.241*	*.290*	*3.5*	*CF 1*	*1.6*

Breakout: 2% Improve: 10% Collapse: 2% Attrition: 3% MLB: 18% *Comparables: Reymond Fuentes, Billy Hamilton, Peter Bourjos*

That Quinn missed a significant chunk of a season due to injury is, sadly, unsurprising at this point. What was heartening, however, is that the time spent on the field was arguably his most productive to date. A tear in his left hip flexor sidelined Quinn from mid-June through the end of the Double-A season, after initial reports suggested only a quad strain, but he returned to make up for some missed plate appearances in the Dominican Winter League. He strikes out more than is desirable, given his prodigious speed, and his stolen-base efficiency took a step backward even prior to the injury, but his switch-hitting and modest defensive ability in center field—his time at shortstop is over—make him the perfect old-school leadoff archetype. Whether he'd assume that role for the Phillies is something that's far too early to call; he'll need a full, healthy season before that's really a discussion worth having.

Cornelius Randolph LF

Born: 6/2/97 Age: 19 Bats: L Throws: R Height: 5'11" Weight: 205

YEAR	TEAM	LVL	AGE	PA	R	2B	3B	HR	RBI	BB	K	SB	CS	AVG/OBP/SLG	TAv	BABIP	BRR	FRAA	WARP
2016	*PHI*	*MLB*	*19*	*250*	*21*	*9*	*1*	*4*	*21*	*18*	*75*	*1*	*1*	*.192/.258/.289*	*.199*	*.261*	*-0.4*	*LF 1*	*-0.8*
2017	*PHI*	*MLB*	*20*	*323*	*34*	*12*	*1*	*7*	*31*	*26*	*92*	*2*	*1*	*.210/.280/.331*	*.228*	*.277*	*-0.6*	*LF 2*	*1.0*

Breakout: 0% Improve: 0% Collapse: 0% Attrition: 0% MLB: 0% *Comparables: Max Kepler, Aaron Hicks, Dalton Pompey*

Back in a different age, when the Phillies would draft at the back end of the first round if they drafted in it at all, the club could be counted on almost sight unseen to draft a toolsy, projectable high school bat. Greg Golson, Adrian Cardenas, Zach Collier, Anthony Hewitt, Larry Greene: These names are all problems, memorable for Phillies fans for all the wrong reasons (save Cardenas, who helped net Joe Blanton in trade en route to a title). What sets Randolph apart is that his hit tool has arrived in professional baseball with a massive head start in refinement, and it is instead his fielding and instincts that will take the most work.

The obvious negative here is that Randolph, who was immediately plopped into left field, has no known position to bank on. The positive is that his floor seems to be "major-league bench bat" right from the get-go. Obviously, the hope for a 10th-overall pick extends a fair bit beyond that, but being able to confidently say that about any 19-year-old is no given. Randolph accrued as many walks as he did strikeouts in the Gulf Coast League and showcased an impressive opposite-field stroke. The Phillies will likely take their sweet time with Randolph, so as to be sure he can hold a position once his time comes, but the bat already has many fans thinking of good times, and the newest top pick is certainly going in the right direction.

Darin Ruf 1B

Born: 7/28/86 Age: 29 Bats: R Throws: R Height: 6'3" Weight: 250

YEAR	TEAM	LVL	AGE	PA	R	2B	3B	HR	RBI	BB	K	SB	CS	AVG/OBP/SLG	TAv	BABIP	BRR	FRAA	WARP
2013	LEH	AAA	26	350	44	22	0	7	46	36	88	1	2	.266/.343/.407	.264	.343	-0.5	LF(60): -4.6, 1B(19): 1.6	0.5
2013	PHI	MLB	26	293	36	11	0	14	30	33	91	0	0	.247/.348/.458	.279	.324	0.7	1B(36): -0.3, RF(29): -1.9	0.9
2014	LEH	AAA	27	91	6	6	0	1	10	6	16	1	0	.265/.308/.373	.252	.309	-1.1	LF(14): -1.0, 1B(8): 0.3	-0.1
2014	PHI	MLB	27	117	13	8	0	3	8	8	32	0	0	.235/.310/.402	.270	.304	0.5	1B(20): 0.5, LF(15): -0.7	0.4
2015	PHI	MLB	28	297	30	12	0	12	39	21	69	1	0	.235/.300/.414	.264	.268	-1.7	1B(66): -2.0, LF(22): -1.6	0.0
2015	LEH	AAA	28	28	3	1	0	0	6	0	2	0	0	.308/.321/.346	.239	.320	-0.6	1B(5): -0.3, LF(2): -0.2	-0.1
2016	*PHI*	*MLB*	*29*	*303*	*36*	*14*	*0*	*13*	*42*	*25*	*78*	*1*	*0*	*.249/.322/.447*	*.271*	*.298*	*-0.2*	*LF -1, 1B -0*	*1.1*
2017	*PHI*	*MLB*	*30*	*425*	*56*	*18*	*0*	*18*	*57*	*38*	*113*	*0*	*0*	*.240/.318/.433*	*.273*	*.289*	*-0.5*	*LF -1, 1B 0*	*0.7*

Breakout: 13% Improve: 31% Collapse: 7% Attrition: 15% MLB: 62% *Comparables: Brandon Moss, Jake Fox, Chris Shelton*

Ruf is nearly 30 years old, with numbers that have declined in various samples since his 2012 debut, but a large swath of Phillies fans would still have you believe there is huge power and production potential in his bat. It may be that nothing teases the mind quite like the promise of power, especially on a club as tater-starved as the Phils have become. Still, Ruf remains in playing-time purgatory, as Ryan Howard still occupies the one position Ruf can be counted on to play without bleeding runs. There is the increased likelihood of a straight platoon for 2016, as Howard continues to decay against lefties and new management becomes less loyal to the old guard. For his part, Ruf did absolutely tear up left-handers in 2015, and perhaps a stricter diet of southpaws is exactly what the doctor ordered to help prettify his numbers. Still, a corner player entering his 30s without a lengthy ledger of success is one on unsure footing, and Ruf's best hope at being an every-day player for the Phillies is almost completely reliant upon Howard's eventual fate, for better or worse.

Carlos Ruiz C

Born: 1/22/79 Age: 37 Bats: R Throws: R Height: 5'10" Weight: 205

YEAR	TEAM	LVL	AGE	PA	R	2B	3B	HR	RBI	BB	K	SB	CS	AVG/OBP/SLG	TAv	BABIP	BRR	FRAA	WARP
2013	PHI	MLB	34	341	30	16	0	5	37	18	39	1	0	.268/.320/.368	.246	.291	4.0	C(86): -7.3	0.7
2014	PHI	MLB	35	445	43	25	1	6	31	46	60	4	2	.252/.347/.370	.281	.281	-4.1	C(109): -8.2	1.6
2015	PHI	MLB	36	320	23	13	1	2	22	28	43	1	1	.211/.290/.285	.219	.242	0.0	C(83): -18.7	-1.9
2016	*PHI*	*MLB*	*37*	*168*	*17*	*8*	*0*	*3*	*17*	*13*	*22*	*1*	*0*	*.259/.332/.378*	*.255*	*.281*	*0.0*	*C -7*	*-0.1*
2017	*PHI*	*MLB*	*38*	*127*	*14*	*6*	*0*	*2*	*12*	*10*	*18*	*0*	*0*	*.246/.322/.358*	*.255*	*.271*	*0.0*	*C -5*	*0.0*

Breakout: 0% Improve: 23% Collapse: 15% Attrition: 8% MLB: 75% *Comparables: Smoky Burgess, Paul Lo Duca, Gregg Zaun*

YEAR	TEAM	P. COUNT	FRM RUNS	BLK RUNS	THRW RUNS	TOT RUNS
2013	PHI	12445	-10.8	0.7	-0.2	-10.3
2014	PHI	15509	-13.0	1.2	0.4	-11.4
2015	PHI	12505	-18.4	0.0	-1.1	-19.5
2016	*PHI*	*6207*	*-7.5*	*0.2*	*-0.2*	*-7.5*
2017	*PHI*	*4695*	*-5.9*	*0.1*	*-0.2*	*-6.0*

There were multiple moments during the 2015 season when Ruiz, notoriously fastidious both behind and at the plate, seemed adrift in thought and in action. It could just be that Chooch's oft-injured body is betraying him more regularly as he enters his age-37 season, with a sub-.300 OBP at the dish and a career-low 19 percent of would-be basestealers caught. The spry Ruiz of yesteryear, who swallowed errant Brad Lidge sliders with ease, has been replaced with one who permitted 35 combined passed balls and wild pitches, a career high despite his lowest innings-caught total in nine seasons. His 11 errors, including seven errant throws, were also a career high. Basically, on all fronts, the season was a disaster for Ruiz, a long-time fan favorite who will continue to see playing time transferred to Cameron Rupp and, eventually, Andrew Knapp or Jorge Alfaro. With an offseason of rest, fans can turn to hoping for a better ending to the Phillies career of a folk hero than 2015 would provide.

Cameron Rupp C

Born: 9/28/88 Age: 27 Bats: R Throws: R Height: 6'2" Weight: 260

YEAR	TEAM	LVL	AGE	PA	R	2B	3B	HR	RBI	BB	K	SB	CS	AVG/OBP/SLG	TAv	BABIP	BRR	FRAA	WARP
2013	LEH	AAA	24	194	18	10	0	6	24	10	55	1	1	.269/.309/.423	.250	.352	-2.2	C(52): 5.9	1.1
2013	REA	AA	24	161	18	6	0	8	21	14	36	0	0	.245/.329/.455	.257	.273	-0.3	C(32): -0.1	0.5
2014	LEH	AAA	25	219	19	8	0	6	19	21	76	0	0	.165/.256/.299	.208	.230	-0.7	C(56): -1.5	-0.5
2014	PHI	MLB	25	64	4	4	0	0	6	4	20	0	0	.183/.234/.250	.161	.275	-0.2	C(18): -1.2	-0.5
2015	PHI	MLB	26	299	24	9	1	9	28	24	71	0	1	.233/.301/.374	.242	.281	-2.4	C(80): -5.8	-0.1
2016	*PHI*	*MLB*	*27*	*449*	*46*	*18*	*1*	*14*	*50*	*31*	*128*	*1*	*1*	*.220/.280/.369*	*.231*	*.281*	*-1.6*	*C -8*	*-0.4*
2017	*PHI*	*MLB*	*28*	*402*	*45*	*15*	*1*	*12*	*44*	*28*	*113*	*0*	*0*	*.213/.274/.358*	*.232*	*.269*	*-1.6*	*C -8*	*0.7*

Breakout: 5% Improve: 25% Collapse: 15% Attrition: 32% MLB: 69% *Comparables: Martin Maldonado, Humberto Cota, Rob Bowen*

YEAR	TEAM	P. COUNT	FRM RUNS	BLK RUNS	THRW RUNS	TOT RUNS
2013	LEH	6849	2.7	0.3	1.3	4.3
2013	PHI	481	0.0	0.0	0.0	0.0
2014	LEH	7335	-0.3	0.0	-0.3	-0.6
2014	PHI	2409	-1.2	0.0	0.1	-1.0
2015	PHI	11024	-5.6	-0.1	0.7	-5.0
2016	*PHI*	*16575*	*-8.2*	*0.0*	*0.3*	*-7.9*
2017	*PHI*	*14856*	*-8.3*	*0.0*	*0.2*	*-8.1*

To look at him, you'd think of Rupp as someone who would profile as more Ryan Doumit on offense than, say, Jose Molina: an imposing, barrel-chested figure who would accidentally hit 15 homers on his way through a season. Instead, despite his stature, Rupp has only been a modest power hitter, save for a seven-homer eruption (please don't stop reading) in August. With passable blocking and receiving skills to go with his near-exceptional arm, the Texas product seems poised to be no worse than a big-league backup for at least a few years, especially as the Phillies prepare to shed The Artist Formerly Known As Carlos Ruiz. Being merely good enough with the bat won't be good enough forever, as the Philly system currently boasts a handful of catching prospects whose defense could match Rupp's, but who bring superior offensive projection. For now, though, he'll likely split time nearly 50-50 with Ruiz until one or the other distinguishes himself or finds his way off the roster.

Nick Williams OF

Born: 9/8/93 Age: 22 Bats: L Throws: L Height: 6'3" Weight: 195

YEAR	TEAM	LVL	AGE	PA	R	2B	3B	HR	RBI	BB	K	SB	CS	AVG/OBP/SLG	TAv	BABIP	BRR	FRAA	WARP
2013	HIC	A	19	404	70	19	12	17	60	15	110	8	5	.293/.337/.543	.303	.371	-0.4	LF(73): 0.1, CF(8): -2.1	2.5
2014	FRI	AA	20	64	4	2	1	0	4	2	21	1	1	.226/.250/.290	.205	.341	0.1	LF(11): -1.5, CF(4): 0.1	-0.4
2014	MYR	A+	20	408	61	28	4	13	68	19	117	5	7	.292/.343/.491	.285	.391	-1.3	LF(44): -0.3, CF(25): -3.5	1.5
2015	REA	AA	21	100	21	5	2	4	10	3	20	3	0	.320/.340/.536	.320	.370	1.5	CF(21): 1.1	1.2
2015	FRI	AA	21	415	56	21	4	13	45	32	77	10	8	.299/.357/.479	.291	.346	0.3	LF(44): -0.1, CF(38): -1.7	2.2
2016	*PHI*	*MLB*	*22*	*250*	*27*	*11*	*2*	*9*	*31*	*8*	*74*	*3*	*2*	*.246/.278/.418*	*.243*	*.318*	*-0.1*	*CF -2, LF -1*	*0.0*
2017	*PHI*	*MLB*	*23*	*363*	*41*	*16*	*3*	*12*	*44*	*13*	*108*	*4*	*3*	*.243/.279/.413*	*.250*	*.317*	*0.0*	*CF -3, LF -1*	*0.6*

Breakout: 3% Improve: 19% Collapse: 1% Attrition: 17% MLB: 41% *Comparables: Trayce Thompson, Jordan Schafer, Marcell Ozuna*

It's going to be tough for Phillies fans to hear "athletic, left-handed outfield bat with big offensive potential" for a little bit without reflexively wincing, but that is indeed the gist with Williams. Like his fellow Hamels trade headliner Jorge Alfaro, Williams' ultimate defensive position remains unknown—he's more of a sure bet in left, but could be athletic enough to make it work in center—and he'll still need good coaching to sharpen his instincts in the field and his eye at the plate. The sobering truth of Williams still being a work in progress was obfuscated by his fantastically hot start upon migrating to the Eastern League, which felt as if it brought his future closer to the present. In reality, Williams still needs polish, but the raw assets that do currently exist carry enough potential after a good buff and wax that he should be expected to capture and hold down an every-day job in Philadelphia somewhere down the line. If he can be a center fielder, he'll obviously carry more value; wherever he does wind up defensively, Phils fans will hope to avoid boarding the Domonic Brown carousel for another spin.

PITCHERS

Mark Appel RHP

Born: 7/15/91 Age: 24 Bats: R Throws: R Height: 6'5" Weight: 220

YEAR	TEAM	LVL	AGE	W	L	SV	G	GS	IP	H	HR	BB/9	K/9	GB%	BABIP	WHIP	ERA	FIP	DRA	WARP	CFIP	MPH
2013	QUD	A	21	3	1	0	8	8	33	30	2	2.5	7.4	54%	.277	1.18	3.82	3.40	4.44	0.3	95	
2014	CCH	AA	22	1	2	0	7	6	39	35	2	3.0	8.8	46%	.300	1.23	3.69	2.99				
2014	LNC	A+	22	2	5	0	12	12	44^{1}	74	9	2.2	8.1	54%	.373	1.92	9.74	5.32	5.33	0.0	96	
2015	CCH	AA	23	5	1	0	13	13	63^{1}	68	7	3.3	7.0	46%	.314	1.44	4.26	4.37	4.86	0.2	104	
2015	FRE	AAA	23	5	2	0	12	12	68^{1}	67	6	3.7	8.0	47%	.303	1.39	4.48	4.36	5.12	0.4	101	
2016	*PHI*	*MLB*	*24*	*6*	*8*	*0*	*24*	*24*	*112*	*113*	*16*	*3.2*	*7.0*	*45%*	*.308*	*1.36*	*4.66*	*4.52*	*5.18*	*0.1*	*123*	
2017	*PHI*	*MLB*	*25*	*6*	*8*	*0*	*23*	*23*	*134*	*136*	*20*	*3.3*	*7.2*	*45%*	*.312*	*1.38*	*4.79*	*5.00*	*5.32*	*0.0*	*127*	

Breakout: 10% Improve: 20% Collapse: 4% Attrition: 17% MLB: 29% *Comparables: Blake Wood, Josh Collmenter, J.R. Graham*

After another disappointing year trudging through the Astros' system, former first-overall pick Appel was sent to the Phillies as part of the return for Ken Giles. After so many chapters, the story remains the same: stuff that ranks among the best in the minors and results that mirror a career minor leaguer. Consistency is an issue, but scouts also bemoan a lack of deception that makes his pitches easy to read despite their quality. New coaches, new scenery and new spiritual mantras may set Appel right, but one thing for certain is that if he shows signs of development, the Philadelphia rotation will provide scant resistance to his joining the major leagues.

Elvis Araujo LHP

Born: 7/15/91 Age: 24 Bats: L Throws: L Height: 6'7" Weight: 270

YEAR	TEAM	LVL	AGE	W	L	SV	G	GS	IP	H	HR	BB/9	K/9	GB%	BABIP	WHIP	ERA	FIP	DRA	WARP	CFIP	MPH
2014	AKR	AA	22	1	0	3	18	0	21	20	2	6.4	9.0	48%	.346	1.67	2.57	4.74	4.65	0.0	104	
2014	CAR	A+	22	1	1	8	25	0	29	23	1	4.0	9.0	60%	.265	1.24	4.03	3.31	4.48	0.1	97	
2015	PHI	MLB	23	2	1	0	40	0	34^{2}	29	1	4.9	8.8	52%	.292	1.38	3.38	3.22	2.70	0.8	101	95.7
2016	*PHI*	*MLB*	*24*	*3*	*1*	*0*	*57*	*0*	*60*	*56*	*7*	*3.7*	*8.1*	*51%*	*.313*	*1.35*	*4.11*	*4.06*	*4.58*	*0.2*	*104*	
2017	*PHI*	*MLB*	*25*	*7*	*6*	*0*	*69*	*15*	*143^{2}*	*130*	*14*	*3.8*	*8.7*	*51%*	*.316*	*1.32*	*3.92*	*4.07*	*4.37*	*1.1*	*99*	

Breakout: 29% Improve: 38% Collapse: 15% Attrition: 28% MLB: 63% *Comparables: Juan Morillo, Nathan Adcock, Frankie De La Cruz*

The Phillies' signing of Araujo in November 2014 caused some humorous, momentary confusion, as he was given a major-league deal despite zero days of service time upon his release by Cleveland. All it really meant, of course, was that Araujo had a reserved spot on the 40-man, safe from Rule 5 plucking. As it turns out, the move was shrewd and prudent: Not only was Araujo protected, he pitched some efficient outings as the lone reliable left-hander once Mario Hollands was ruled out for the year and Antonio Bastardo was shipped away. Araujo's massive stature lends itself to reaction-time reduction for hitters, and that played out in the form of above-average whiff rates on both his fastball and breaking ball. A late-season velocity drop can be explained by fatigue, and Araujo was shelved for the season in late August with a groin strain out of what was called an "overabundance" of caution anyway, so he's expected to be plenty ready for the opportunity in 2016 to build on a successful start to his MLB career.

Alec Asher RHP

Born: 10/4/91 Age: 24 Bats: R Throws: R Height: 6'4" Weight: 230

YEAR	TEAM	LVL	AGE	W	L	SV	G	GS	IP	H	HR	BB/9	K/9	GB%	BABIP	WHIP	ERA	FIP	DRA	WARP	CFIP	MPH
2013	MYR	A+	21	9	7	0	26	25	133^{1}	120	10	2.7	9.4	42%	.300	1.20	2.90	3.27	4.15	1.8	82	
2014	FRI	AA	22	11	11	0	28	28	154	139	18	1.9	7.1	36%	.265	1.11	3.80	3.74				
2015	FRI	AA	23	1	4	0	8	8	43	39	3	3.8	9.0	32%	.308	1.33	3.98	3.60	4.03	0.6	95	
2015	LEH	AAA	23	2	0	0	4	4	26	27	3	1.0	4.2	36%	.273	1.15	2.08	4.08	4.59	0.0	107	
2015	PHI	MLB	23	0	6	0	7	7	29	42	8	3.1	5.0	40%	.330	1.79	9.31	6.78	7.03	-0.7	124	94.5
2015	ROU	AAA	23	3	6	0	12	12	64^{2}	71	16	2.6	7.5	35%	.293	1.39	4.73	6.03	5.73	-0.1	109	
2016	*PHI*	*MLB*	*24*	*8*	*10*	*0*	*27*	*27*	*146^{2}*	*144*	*22*	*2.6*	*6.8*	*35%*	*.295*	*1.26*	*4.55*	*4.44*	*5.07*	*0.4*	*120*	
2017	*PHI*	*MLB*	*25*	*6*	*8*	*0*	*22*	*22*	*130^{2}*	*134*	*21*	*2.8*	*6.9*	*35%*	*.305*	*1.34*	*4.83*	*5.03*	*5.38*	*-0.1*	*128*	

Breakout: 15% Improve: 24% Collapse: 6% Attrition: 16% MLB: 43% *Comparables: Luke Hochevar, Dillon Gee, Graham Taylor*

Asher's first seven major-league starts were a collective disaster, save for a late September outing against the Marlins, and the hope is he has nowhere to go but up. That's a hope worth clinging to more tightly than usual, as Asher's stuff doesn't exactly scream "Will Play Up As a Reliever," and his value as a transitional starter is more valuable to the Phillies than another reliever at this point in time. Hey, the major leagues are hard, and Asher's wake up call to this fact was a bit ruder than most, to be sure. He will need to get ahead of hitters more often, and get one part of his secondary stuff up to put-away status to have a shot of making it past the transitional period. He'll get another look in 2016, but the leash won't be infinite, and it seems he'll need a breakthrough to progress past his current back-end-starter ceiling.

Jesse Biddle LHP

Born: 10/22/91 Age: 24 Bats: L Throws: L Height: 6'5" Weight: 235

YEAR	TEAM	LVL	AGE	W	L	SV	G	GS	IP	H	HR	BB/9	K/9	GB%	BABIP	WHIP	ERA	FIP	DRA	WARP	CFIP	MPH
2013	REA	AA	21	5	14	0	27	27	138^{1}	104	10	5.3	10.0	44%	.278	1.34	3.64	3.88	4.58	1.1	99	
2014	CLR	A+	22	2	0	0	2	2	10	3	0	5.4	8.1	59%	.136	0.90	0.90	3.39	4.36	0.1	102	
2014	REA	AA	22	3	10	0	16	16	82^{1}	78	11	4.8	8.7	44%	.291	1.48	5.03	4.93	4.70	0.4	105	
2015	LEH	AAA	23	2	4	0	9	9	44^{2}	57	4	5.4	6.4	49%	.346	1.88	6.25	4.77	6.55	-1.0	124	
2015	REA	AA	23	7	2	0	15	15	80^{2}	90	7	3.8	6.4	47%	.320	1.54	4.24	4.29	5.17	-0.4	112	
2016	*PHI*	*MLB*	*24*	*1*	*1*	*0*	*3*	*3*	*16*	*16*	*2*	*3.9*	*6.9*	*45%*	*.306*	*1.42*	*4.66*	*4.66*	*5.14*	*0.0*	*122*	
2017	*PHI*	*MLB*	*25*	*2*	*3*	*0*	*8*	*8*	*45*	*44*	*6*	*4.2*	*7.1*	*45%*	*.307*	*1.45*	*4.90*	*5.10*	*5.40*	*-0.1*	*129*	

Breakout: 5% Improve: 10% Collapse: 19% Attrition: 30% MLB: 37% *Comparables: John Lamb, Tyler Wagner, Samuel Deduno*

Of all the rookie pitchers to make a start for the Phillies in 2015—five total—the former first-round pick not being among them stands out as particularly disheartening. The hometown kid has dealt with a bizarre hailstorm-related head injury and a sore elbow in the past two seasons, the latter flaring up both in winter ball in 2014 and at the end of his 2015 effort, eventually requiring him to go under the knife for Tommy John surgery. Biddle just doesn't have the stuff/repeatability/command secret sauce to be effective multiple times through an order, even if he'll touch 94 with his fastball and whip out a beauty of a curveball. A second trip through Double-A was no more successful than the first, and a might-as-well promotion to Triple-A saw even more struggles, so even aside from finding himself once the long road of rehab ends, he's got a lot to prove.

Chad Billingsley RHP

Born: 7/29/84 Age: 31 Bats: R Throws: R Height: 6'1" Weight: 240

YEAR	TEAM	LVL	AGE	W	L	SV	G	GS	IP	H	HR	BB/9	K/9	GB%	BABIP	WHIP	ERA	FIP	DRA	WARP	CFIP	MPH
2013	LAN	MLB	28	1	0	0	2	2	12	12	1	3.8	4.5	45%	.297	1.42	3.00	4.35	5.51	-0.1	115	93.2
2015	LEH	AAA	30	2	2	0	7	6	29^{2}	34	5	3.0	7.0	54%	.305	1.48	4.85	5.11	4.31	0.1	101	
2015	PHI	MLB	30	2	3	0	7	7	37	53	5	1.9	3.6	46%	.353	1.65	5.84	4.84	6.03	-0.4	125	93.2
2016	*PHI*	*MLB*	*31*	*3*	*3*	*0*	*9*	*9*	49^{1}	*54*	*7*	*2.6*	*5.8*	*48%*	*.314*	*1.37*	*4.62*	*4.56*	*5.13*	*0.1*	*122*	
2017	*PHI*	*MLB*	*32*	*9*	*11*	*0*	*29*	*29*	181^{2}	*206*	*25*	*2.6*	*5.7*	*48%*	*.324*	*1.42*	*4.78*	*4.97*	*5.31*	*-0.1*	*126*	

Breakout: 14% Improve: 53% Collapse: 12% Attrition: 8% MLB: 89% *Comparables: J.A. Happ, Kris Benson, Brian Bannister*

It was the right move in the right situation: A team hungry for placeholder arms to eat innings bringing aboard a former All-Star hoping for a pillow contract to begin rebuilding his value is a match made in heaven. Sadly, baseball heaven will have to wait for Billingsley, who made just seven starts for the Phillies before succumbing to injury once more, the final blow dealt in the form of a flexor strain in his troublesome right elbow. Even in his limited time back in the majors, it was apparent that his power stuff was a distant memory, though his post-surgery command of what stuff he did have was a pleasant surprise. As he'll turn 32 in July, time is running short on this reclamation project, but it still feels too far-fetched an idea for his major-league career to be at its end.

David Buchanan RHP

Born: 5/11/89 Age: 27 Bats: R Throws: R Height: 6'3" Weight: 200

YEAR	TEAM	LVL	AGE	W	L	SV	G	GS	IP	H	HR	BB/9	K/9	GB%	BABIP	WHIP	ERA	FIP	DRA	WARP	CFIP	MPH
2013	REA	AA	24	6	11	0	22	22	130^{2}	142	15	2.8	5.9	48%	.304	1.40	4.82	4.58	4.73	0.8	104	
2013	LEH	AAA	24	4	2	0	6	6	39	36	2	2.8	5.1	44%	.274	1.23	3.00	3.90	4.54	0.2	105	
2014	LEH	AAA	25	6	2	0	12	12	57	67	3	3.3	7.3	44%	.356	1.54	3.95	3.69	4.53	0.4	99	
2014	PHI	MLB	25	6	8	0	20	20	117^{2}	120	12	2.4	5.4	54%	.284	1.29	3.75	4.24	4.46	0.5	120	92.6
2015	LEH	AAA	26	4	2	0	10	10	54^{2}	58	2	3.3	4.9	51%	.304	1.43	2.80	3.85	5.24	-0.4	113	
2015	PHI	MLB	26	2	9	0	15	15	74^{2}	109	12	3.5	5.3	51%	.369	1.85	6.99	5.36	7.29	-2.0	124	92.1
2016	*PHI*	*MLB*	*27*	*2*	*3*	*0*	*8*	*8*	*40*	*43*	*5*	*2.8*	*5.6*	*50%*	*.311*	*1.37*	*4.63*	*4.46*	*5.14*	*0.1*	*122*	
2017	*PHI*	*MLB*	*28*	*3*	*3*	*0*	*9*	*9*	*53*	*57*	*7*	*2.7*	*5.8*	*50%*	*.317*	*1.39*	*4.65*	*4.84*	*5.16*	*0.1*	*122*	

Breakout: 15% Improve: 29% Collapse: 17% Attrition: 31% MLB: 56% *Comparables: Sean O'Sullivan, Chris Bootcheck, Dustin Moseley*

Enduring the sophomore slump to end all sophomore slumps, Buchanan would surely love to pretend 2015 never happened. If there is something to build on, however, it would likely be found in his final four starts of the season, each with two or fewer runs allowed despite their relative brevity. Everything prior to that, from the 8.76 April ERA to the severe ankle sprain in Triple-A to the negative-12 Game Score in a mid-August outing in Arizona, held little light. Buchanan wasn't expected to be more than Most Likely to be Serviceable in the yearbook of Phillies starting pitching, but his regression was still a bit disheartening, as it's tough to root against the success of one of the few pitchers going today who could be labeled a "crafty righty." Indeed, that's Buchanan's A game: He aims to keep hitters off-balance and off the barrel with a cutter and curve to offset a modest fastball that doesn't move a ton. He needs a reliable defense and he needs sharp command to be successful, and for most of 2015, he had neither. He'll get another shot to win an Opening Day roster job in the rotation's back end—as he did in 2015 with some particularly impressive work in Florida—and it will be difficult to go anywhere but up.

Jerad Eickhoff RHP

Born: 7/2/90 Age: 25 Bats: R Throws: R Height: 6'4" Weight: 240

YEAR	TEAM	LVL	AGE	W	L	SV	G	GS	IP	H	HR	BB/9	K/9	GB%	BABIP	WHIP	ERA	FIP	DRA	WARP	CFIP	MPH
2013	FRI	AA	22	1	1	0	6	6	29	34	6	4.3	4.0	37%	.298	1.66	7.45	6.40	5.34	-0.1	128	
2013	MYR	A+	22	7	3	0	21	21	116	110	9	2.0	6.2	45%	.285	1.17	3.41	3.83	4.49	1.1	94	
2014	FRI	AA	23	10	9	0	27	26	154^1	129	17	3.0	8.4	39%	.269	1.17	4.08	3.83				
2015	FRI	AA	24	1	0	0	2	2	10	7	2	2.7	12.6	36%	.250	1.00	2.70	4.30	3.14	0.2	84	
2015	LEH	AAA	24	2	1	0	3	3	21^2	17	1	1.2	7.9	28%	.254	0.92	2.49	2.42	2.91	0.5	85	
2015	PHI	MLB	24	3	3	0	8	8	51	40	5	2.3	8.6	38%	.257	1.04	2.65	3.28	2.74	1.4	89	93.6
2015	ROU	AAA	24	9	4	0	18	17	101^2	95	12	2.9	8.2	35%	.291	1.26	4.25	4.40	4.44	1.3	95	
2016	*PHI*	*MLB*	*25*	*7*	*8*	*0*	*23*	*23*	*131*	*115*	*16*	*2.7*	*7.7*	*34%*	*.286*	*1.17*	*4.09*	*3.93*	*4.55*	*1.1*	*106*	
2017	*PHI*	*MLB*	*26*	*6*	*7*	*0*	*20*	*20*	*115^2*	*104*	*15*	*2.9*	*8.1*	*34%*	*.294*	*1.22*	*4.27*	*4.41*	*4.75*	*0.7*	*111*	

Breakout: 16% Improve: 31% Collapse: 12% Attrition: 28% MLB: 46% *Comparables: Michael Bowden, Asher Wojciechowski, Matt Shoemaker*

Of all the pieces the Phillies received from Texas in return for Cole Hamels and Jake Diekman, none came with as little fanfare as Eickhoff, a relative unknown outside of prospect-nerd circles. Flash forward to the present and Eickhoff is the one generating the most excitement following an exceedingly promising four-start stretch in September and October. He dramatically increased his curve usage, and the pitch seemed to get more plus as the starts passed, generating more swings-and-misses and finishing hitters off without balls in play. There's room for his other secondary offerings to improve, and they'll need to if Eickhoff hopes to maintain success multiple times through a batting order now that there's plenty of major-league video on him, but he's the Phillies' de facto no. 2 starter for 2016 without question.

Thomas Eshelman RHP

Born: 6/20/94 Age: 21 Bats: R Throws: R Height: 6'3" Weight: 210

A veritable Tewksbury in Training, Eshelman made a name for himself by walking 17 batters in 362 innings at Cal State Fullerton. It reached the point that by his junior year, he found it nearly impossible: Batters, tired of failing to work counts, gave up and swung at every pitch. Independent of home plate, none of his pitches inspires awe, but his ability to hit spots has served many a Radke and Quisenberry well, limiting baserunners and forcing batters to string together hits. As the third-most interesting prospect in the Giles deal, it'll be fun to watch Eshelman try to put it together.

Jeanmar Gomez RHP

Born: 2/10/88 Age: 28 Bats: R Throws: R Height: 6'3" Weight: 220

YEAR	TEAM	LVL	AGE	W	L	SV	G	GS	IP	H	HR	BB/9	K/9	GB%	BABIP	WHIP	ERA	FIP	DRA	WARP	CFIP	MPH
2013	PIT	MLB	25	3	0	0	34	8	80^2	65	6	3.1	5.9	57%	.243	1.15	3.35	3.83	3.74	1.0	112	93.9
2014	PIT	MLB	26	2	2	1	44	0	62	70	6	3.3	5.5	48%	.318	1.50	3.19	4.34	5.43	-0.7	113	93.6
2015	PHI	MLB	27	2	3	0	65	0	74^2	82	4	2.0	6.0	51%	.317	1.33	3.01	3.28	3.51	1.1	104	94.0
2016	*PHI*	*MLB*	*28*	*3*	*1*	*0*	*60*	*0*	*63^2*	*61*	*7*	*2.5*	*6.3*	*52%*	*.297*	*1.24*	*4.16*	*4.00*	*4.63*	*0.3*	*105*	
2017	*PHI*	*MLB*	*29*	*4*	*3*	*0*	*38*	*8*	*86*	*85*	*9*	*2.6*	*6.6*	*52%*	*.308*	*1.28*	*4.12*	*4.26*	*4.59*	*0.5*	*104*	

Breakout: 16% Improve: 49% Collapse: 18% Attrition: 18% MLB: 90% *Comparables: Anthony Swarzak, Sergio Mitre, Zach Miner*

At some point over the winter before last season, Gomez found an extra mile per hour or two on his heater and breaking ball, elevating him from mop-up duty to unwitting late-inning guy. Ostensibly, Gomez took the job Justin De Fratus was supposed to assume, posting a 1.53 ERA and 23 strikeouts against four unintentional walks in 35 innings across appearances in the eighth and ninth. Ken Giles he is not, and even with the added velocity, Gomez never *looks* all that close to unhittable through a TV screen, but as far as sub-million-dollar free-agent relief signings go, it's greedy to hope for much more. With two more years of team control on the table, it seems the Phillies have found a viable transitional reliever who can be counted on to pitch through just about any situation.

Aaron Harang RHP

Born: 5/9/78 Age: 38 Bats: R Throws: R Height: 6'7" Weight: 260

YEAR	TEAM	LVL	AGE	W	L	SV	G	GS	IP	H	HR	BB/9	K/9	GB%	BABIP	WHIP	ERA	FIP	DRA	WARP	CFIP	MPH
2013	SEA	MLB	35	5	11	0	22	22	120^1	133	21	2.1	6.5	38%	.291	1.34	5.76	4.72	5.08	-0.3	112	93.1
2013	NYN	MLB	35	0	1	0	4	4	23	20	5	4.7	10.2	31%	.268	1.39	3.52	5.28	4.54	0.1	111	92.7
2014	ATL	MLB	36	12	12	0	33	33	204^1	215	15	3.1	7.1	42%	.318	1.40	3.57	3.54	4.27	1.3	112	92.4
2015	PHI	MLB	37	6	15	0	29	29	172^1	189	26	2.7	5.6	39%	.293	1.39	4.86	4.86	4.48	1.1	120	92.4
2016	*PHI*	*MLB*	*38*	*9*	*12*	*0*	*30*	*30*	*180*	*188*	*25*	*2.7*	*6.1*	*39%*	*.306*	*1.34*	*4.59*	*4.49*	*5.10*	*0.4*	*120*	
2017	*PHI*	*MLB*	*39*	*5*	*7*	*0*	*17*	*17*	*99^1*	*108*	*13*	*2.9*	*5.9*	*39%*	*.314*	*1.41*	*4.76*	*4.95*	*5.29*	*0.0*	*124*	

Breakout: 14% Improve: 27% Collapse: 12% Attrition: 13% MLB: 58% *Comparables: John Burkett, Sonny Siebert, Kevin Tapani*

The Phillies were Harang's seventh team in the last six years, and he was brought on for the explicit purpose of taking his turn every fifth day while the club developed and otherwise looked to acquire heirs apparent for the rotation. For a time, it seemed the club might even be able to flip the journeyman at or before the deadline—a 2.02 ERA and 53 strikeouts to 15 walks through May sure seemed like it would be mighty appetizing—but Harang began to combust in June. Over his last 18 starts of the year, Harang posted a 6.86 ERA and allowed his opponents to brand a gruesome .932 OPS on his file in 467 plate appearances. A July DL stint for a bout of plantar fasciitis allowed him enough rest to finish out the season, just not enough to finish it strongly. He's nearing the end of a career that has now spanned 14 seasons, and he's not going to be able to be choosy about the short supply of major-league offers he's likely to receive from here on out, assuming he hasn't retired by the time you read this.

Matt Harrison LHP

Born: 9/16/85 Age: 30 Bats: L Throws: L Height: 6'4" Weight: 240

YEAR	TEAM	LVL	AGE	W	L	SV	G	GS	IP	H	HR	BB/9	K/9	GB%	BABIP	WHIP	ERA	FIP	DRA	WARP	CFIP	MPH
2013	TEX	MLB	27	0	2	0	2	2	10^2	14	2	5.9	10.1	47%	.400	1.97	8.44	5.23	7.50	-0.3	103	94.2
2014	FRI	AA	28	1	0	0	3	3	16	12	0	2.2	5.6	49%	.245	1.00	1.69	2.62				
2014	TEX	MLB	28	1	1	0	4	4	17^1	20	1	6.2	5.2	51%	.317	1.85	4.15	5.01	5.70	-0.2	121	92.9
2015	ROU	AAA	29	1	3	0	5	5	28^2	34	0	3.8	5.7	44%	.351	1.60	5.97	3.70	5.45	0.0	105	
2015	TEX	MLB	29	1	2	0	3	3	16	19	3	3.4	2.8	41%	.291	1.56	6.75	6.04	5.02	0.0	121	90.4
2016	*PHI*	*MLB*	*30*	*2*	*3*	*0*	*8*	*8*	*42^1*	*42*	*5*	*3.0*	*5.9*	*44%*	*.298*	*1.32*	*4.60*	*4.39*	*5.11*	*0.1*	*122*	
2017	*PHI*	*MLB*	*31*	*5*	*6*	*0*	*16*	*16*	*94*	*98*	*12*	*3.1*	*5.7*	*44%*	*.308*	*1.39*	*4.78*	*4.98*	*5.31*	*0.0*	*128*	

Breakout: 12% Improve: 43% Collapse: 20% Attrition: 16% MLB: 91% *Comparables: Roberto Hernandez, Bob Ojeda, Dave Goltz*

Absorbed chiefly as salary relief in the Cole Hamels trade, Harrison arrives in Philadelphia having made just nine combined appearances in the majors in the last three seasons due to myriad and piebald injuries: various back issues, spinal-fusion surgery and, most recently, hyperthyroidism. At this point, his future health and well-being seem more important than an eventual return to baseball, but the man seems committed and has fought his way back before. He's under contract for two more seasons, but any contribution he could make in 2016 would simply be a bonus. When he was at his All-Star best in 2012, Harrison sat 93–94 mph with his fastball and featured a hard, dipping curve and changeup. Following his injuries, he's been clocked more around 89–90, and the curve's usage has become almost token. Root for his comeback, but don't expect the Harrison of old on the mound just yet.

Jeremy Hellickson RHP

Born: 4/8/87 Age: 29 Bats: R Throws: R Height: 6'1" Weight: 190

YEAR	TEAM	LVL	AGE	W	L	SV	G	GS	IP	H	HR	BB/9	K/9	GB%	BABIP	WHIP	ERA	FIP	DRA	WARP	CFIP	MPH
2013	TBA	MLB	26	12	10	0	32	31	174	185	24	2.6	7.0	41%	.307	1.35	5.17	4.25	4.67	0.5	103	93.0
2014	TBA	MLB	27	1	5	0	13	13	63^2	71	8	3.0	7.6	38%	.321	1.45	4.52	4.18	5.31	-0.4	101	92.3
2014	DUR	AAA	27	1	4	0	5	5	18^2	38	1	2.4	7.7	41%	.493	2.30	7.23	3.46	4.70	0.1	100	
2015	ARI	MLB	28	9	12	0	27	27	146	151	22	2.7	7.5	45%	.291	1.33	4.62	4.47	4.79	0.4	109	92.2
2016	*PHI*	*MLB*	*29*	*8*	*10*	*0*	*30*	*30*	*150*	*139*	*20*	*2.5*	*7.2*	*43%*	*.293*	*1.20*	*4.20*	*4.09*	*4.67*	*1.1*	*109*	
2017	*PHI*	*MLB*	*30*	*8*	*9*	*0*	*26*	*26*	*155^2*	*151*	*20*	*2.6*	*7.0*	*43%*	*.301*	*1.25*	*4.33*	*4.49*	*4.82*	*0.8*	*113*	

Breakout: 23% Improve: 47% Collapse: 15% Attrition: 8% MLB: 97% *Comparables: Gil Meche, Adam Eaton, Denny Neagle*

In 2011, Jeremy Hellickson had a 2.95 ERA and won the Rookie of the Year Award. In 2015, he got beat to a 4.62 ERA and won a free breakfast burrito wrap from Taco Bell. His FIP both years was 4.47.

Hellickson's first (and only) year in the desert generated two odd, simultaneous extremes, with career-high marks in homers per nine and groundball rates. Some 44 percent of all hits he allowed were for extra bases. He simply doesn't have the stuff, or the dottable command, to work in the strike zone without getting spun around. When Hellickson was ahead in the count, batters hit .183/.185/.301. When Hellickson was behind, they hit .343/.481/.639. Everybody's better when they're ahead in the count, but for Hellickson the split is extreme: He's one of the league's best pitchers in the one situation and one of the league's worst in the other. What's clear, and disappointing, is this: He's not one of the league's best pitchers.

David Hernandez RHP

Born: 5/13/85 Age: 31 Bats: R Throws: R Height: 6'3" Weight: 245

YEAR	TEAM	LVL	AGE	W	L	SV	G	GS	IP	H	HR	BB/9	K/9	GB%	BABIP	WHIP	ERA	FIP	DRA	WARP	CFIP	MPH
2013	ARI	MLB	28	5	6	2	62	0	62^1	50	10	3.5	9.5	34%	.252	1.19	4.48	4.34	4.28	0.2	90	97.1
2015	ARI	MLB	30	1	5	0	40	0	33^2	33	6	2.9	8.8	40%	.297	1.31	4.28	4.77	5.02	-0.1	102	96.9
2016	*PHI*	*MLB*	*31*	*3*	*1*	*33*	*66*	*0*	*69^1*	*60*	*10*	*2.9*	*8.7*	*38%*	*.285*	*1.18*	*4.19*	*4.06*	*4.68*	*0.2*	*108*	
2017	*PHI*	*MLB*	*32*	*3*	*1*	*0*	*69*	*0*	*65*	*56*	*9*	*2.9*	*8.8*	*38%*	*.289*	*1.18*	*4.13*	*4.29*	*4.61*	*0.2*	*107*	

Breakout: 27% Improve: 44% Collapse: 32% Attrition: 22% MLB: 93% *Comparables: Scott Williamson, Damaso Marte, Joel Hanrahan*

After Hernandez's year in the cold, isolated world of Tommy John rehab, the former setup man was eased back into pitching duties, taking much lower-leverage innings for four months while trying to kick his nasty home run habit. Not to pile on, but allowing a career-high BABIP in a walk year was unfortunate, to say the least. Still, the fastball and slider have the same pre-surgical properties, and while lefties bully his fastball, he'll get to make his case to return to situational late-inning specialist work.

Franklyn Kilome RHP

Born: 6/25/95 Age: 21 Bats: R Throws: R Height: 6'6" Weight: 175

YEAR	TEAM	LVL	AGE	W	L	SV	G	GS	IP	H	HR	BB/9	K/9	GB%	BABIP	WHIP	ERA	FIP	DRA	WARP	CFIP	MPH
2015	WPT	A-	20	3	2	0	11	11	49^1	41	1	3.8	6.6	57%	.282	1.26	3.28	4.02	5.15	-0.1	109	
2016	*PHI*	*MLB*	*21*	*2*	*3*	*0*	*8*	*8*	*35*	*38*	*4*	*4.1*	*5.5*	*47%*	*.312*	*1.54*	*5.17*	*4.87*	*5.71*	*-0.2*	*136*	
2017	*PHI*	*MLB*	*22*	*6*	*10*	*0*	*27*	*27*	*165^2*	*178*	*21*	*4.1*	*5.5*	*47%*	*.312*	*1.52*	*5.18*	*5.44*	*5.72*	*-0.6*	*138*	

Breakout: 0% Improve: 0% Collapse: 0% Attrition: 0% MLB: 0% *Comparables: Sean Nolin, Kyle Drabek, Erik Cordier*

A sleeper in a burgeoning crop of minor-league arms in the Phillies' system, Kilome's raw stuff took a big leap forward in 2015, even if his command of it lagged behind. Adjusting his changeup grip and eschewing his slider for a sharper curveball, Kilome appeared to discover the secondary pitches he needed to pair with fastball velocity that sat rather easily in the mid-90s. While far from a sure thing, Kilome's potential is enough to get some scouts salivating and dropping the coveted "top of the rotation" label on him, even if that kind of signage is a dangerous thing to use on a kid in the New York-Penn League.

Cliff Lee LHP

Born: 8/30/78 Age: 37 Bats: L Throws: L Height: 6'3" Weight: 205

YEAR	TEAM	LVL	AGE	W	L	SV	G	GS	IP	H	HR	BB/9	K/9	GB%	BABIP	WHIP	ERA	FIP	DRA	WARP	CFIP	MPH
2013	PHI	MLB	34	14	8	0	31	31	222^2	193	22	1.3	9.0	47%	.287	1.01	2.87	2.80	2.78	5.7	73	92.9
2014	CLR	A+	35	0	1	0	3	3	10^2	13	1	1.7	6.8	58%	.324	1.41	5.06	3.95	4.48	0.1	103	
2014	PHI	MLB	35	4	5	0	13	13	81^1	100	7	1.3	8.0	51%	.358	1.38	3.65	2.93	5.05	-0.3	91	91.8
2016	*PHI*	*MLB*	*37*	*2*	*2*	*0*	*6*	*6*	*39*	*36*	*4*	*1.4*	*8.3*	*48%*	*.313*	*1.09*	*3.36*	*3.07*	*3.75*	*0.7*	*83*	
2017	*PHI*	*MLB*	*38*	*14*	*11*	*0*	*32*	*32*	*210*	*210*	*23*	*1.5*	*8.1*	*48%*	*.331*	*1.17*	*3.46*	*3.54*	*3.86*	*3.7*	*85*	

Breakout: 12% Improve: 32% Collapse: 19% Attrition: 9% MLB: 83% *Comparables: Connie Johnson, Mike Mussina, Andy Pettitte*

The Cliff Lee Era ended on July 31, 2014, in an abbreviated start against the Nationals that revealed that, sometimes, robots are just as human as the rest of us. His remarkable six-year peak from 2008 to 2013 provided baseball fans with a reinvented strike-throwing machine who worked effortlessly and expediently. Lee won over the notoriously difficult-to-please Philadelphia fans almost from the outset, and the club has perhaps never had a more celebrated free-agent signing than when the lefty was brought back into the fold prior to the 2011 season. Six years feels like too short a time to have spent with Prime Lee, but at least he accomplished the feat of spreading those seasons over four different teams. Every fanbase deserves a little Cliff Lee.

Adam Morgan LHP

Born: 2/27/90 Age: 26 Bats: L Throws: L Height: 6'1" Weight: 195

YEAR	TEAM	LVL	AGE	W	L	SV	G	GS	IP	H	HR	BB/9	K/9	GB%	BABIP	WHIP	ERA	FIP	DRA	WARP	CFIP	MPH
2013	LEH	AAA	23	2	7	0	16	16	71^1	84	10	3.3	6.2	39%	.320	1.54	4.04	4.96	4.76	0.2	112	
2015	LEH	AAA	25	0	6	0	13	13	68^1	81	7	3.6	4.3	39%	.307	1.58	4.74	4.75	6.12	-1.2	122	
2015	PHI	MLB	25	5	7	0	15	15	84^1	88	14	1.8	5.2	31%	.276	1.25	4.48	4.90	4.13	0.9	115	91.6
2016	*PHI*	*MLB*	*26*	*7*	*10*	*0*	*26*	*26*	*130*	*137*	*18*	*2.3*	*5.5*	*33%*	*.303*	*1.32*	*4.66*	*4.51*	*5.18*	*0.2*	*123*	
2017	*PHI*	*MLB*	*27*	*7*	*9*	*0*	*24*	*24*	*141^1*	*152*	*19*	*2.3*	*5.7*	*33%*	*.311*	*1.33*	*4.62*	*4.82*	*5.14*	*0.2*	*122*	

Breakout: 14% Improve: 31% Collapse: 13% Attrition: 23% MLB: 48% *Comparables: Craig Stammen, Ryan Feierabend, Zach Stewart*

Reinvented as a Crafty Lefty in the wake of shoulder injuries that threatened to derail his career completely, Morgan will have to beguile hitters and aim for weak contact, as he's unlikely to regain the oomph his fastball had earlier in his career. Getting ahead in counts will be key, as any batter worth his salt sitting fastball in a favorable count will eat Morgan for lunch and be hungry for seconds. Still, his secondary offerings are not to be slept on, and with the right sequencing and game-calling direction, it's far from laughable to see Morgan play out as a Jason Vargas type as a best-case scenario, assuming his shoulder can withstand a full-season workload going forward. Expect caution in Morgan's usage in 2016, with a start skipped here or there for arm preservation, and only lean on him for fantasy purposes if you feel like living dangerously.

Charlie Morton RHP

Born: 11/12/83 Age: 32 Bats: R Throws: R Height: 6'5" Weight: 235

YEAR	TEAM	LVL	AGE	W	L	SV	G	GS	IP	H	HR	BB/9	K/9	GB%	BABIP	WHIP	ERA	FIP	DRA	WARP	CFIP	MPH
2013	PIT	MLB	29	7	4	0	20	20	116	113	6	2.8	6.6	65%	.306	1.28	3.26	3.57	4.27	0.9	108	95.6
2013	IND	AAA	29	0	1	0	4	4	19	16	1	4.7	5.7	61%	.250	1.37	3.79	4.36	4.80	0.0	112	
2013	ALT	AA	29	1	1	0	4	4	18^2	10	2	2.9	5.3	59%	.154	0.86	2.41	4.50	4.68	0.1	106	
2014	PIT	MLB	30	6	12	0	26	26	157^1	143	9	3.3	7.2	58%	.295	1.27	3.72	3.69	4.26	1.0	107	93.6
2015	PIT	MLB	31	9	9	0	23	23	129	137	13	2.9	6.7	60%	.309	1.38	4.81	4.22	5.33	-0.5	111	94.4
2015	IND	AAA	31	1	1	0	2	2	13^1	13	0	2.7	11.5	60%	.371	1.27	2.03	1.51	2.34	0.4	78	
2016	*PHI*	*MLB*	*32*	*8*	*9*	*0*	*24*	*24*	*144*	*139*	*17*	*2.9*	*7.3*	*60%*	*.310*	*1.28*	*4.20*	*4.12*	*4.67*	*1.0*	*108*	
2017	*PHI*	*MLB*	*33*	*8*	*9*	*0*	*26*	*26*	*150^1*	*146*	*17*	*3.0*	*7.2*	*60%*	*.314*	*1.31*	*4.26*	*4.42*	*4.74*	*0.9*	*110*	

Breakout: 10% Improve: 49% Collapse: 21% Attrition: 13% MLB: 91% *Comparables: Doug Davis, Chuck Finley, Roberto Hernandez*

The difference between the concept and reality of Morton is never more apparent than in his innings count. He *looks* like a workhorse; he's tall, wide and famously uses the same delivery as Roy Halladay—one of the era's most reliable seven-plus-inning starters. The puzzling truth is that Morton has never topped 180 innings in a season, let alone 200. That didn't stop everyone from getting their hopes up when he returned from the disabled list (hip surgery) in late May and went on a tear, working into the seventh inning in four of his first five starts. He then exited his next start in the first inning after allowing nine runs. Rump-rump-ruhhhh. The remainder of Morton's season followed the same tune: a few good followed by a few poor. He's probably just what he is and nothing more: an inconsistent no. 4 who, at the very least, can claim an infinitely better nickname ("Ground Chuck") than Doc ever got.

Edward Mujica RHP

Born: 5/10/84 Age: 32 Bats: R Throws: R Height: 6'3" Weight: 220

YEAR	TEAM	LVL	AGE	W	L	SV	G	GS	IP	H	HR	BB/9	K/9	GB%	BABIP	WHIP	ERA	FIP	DRA	WARP	CFIP	MPH
2013	SLN	MLB	29	2	1	37	65	0	64^2	60	9	0.7	6.4	46%	.263	1.01	2.78	3.69	4.59	0.0	99	94.5
2014	BOS	MLB	30	2	4	8	64	0	60	69	6	2.1	6.4	44%	.332	1.38	3.90	3.73	4.86	-0.3	101	93.3
2015	OAK	MLB	31	2	4	1	38	0	33^2	37	7	1.1	5.9	46%	.286	1.22	4.81	4.86	4.33	0.2	109	92.9
2015	BOS	MLB	31	1	1	0	11	0	13^2	15	3	2.0	5.3	55%	.293	1.32	4.61	5.67	6.54	-0.3	110	92.5
2016	*PHI*	*MLB*	*32*	*3*	*1*	*0*	*55*	*0*	*58*	*54*	*8*	*2.1*	*6.6*	*47%*	*.290*	*1.16*	*4.17*	*4.13*	*4.66*	*0.2*	*107*	
2017	*PHI*	*MLB*	*33*	*3*	*1*	*2*	*58*	*0*	*56*	*55*	*8*	*2.2*	*6.3*	*47%*	*.298*	*1.23*	*4.45*	*4.60*	*4.97*	*-0.1*	*115*	

Breakout: 25% Improve: 46% Collapse: 25% Attrition: 7% MLB: 93% *Comparables: Rod Beck, Jerry Spradlin, Joe Black*

Mujica came full circle in 2015, completing his eight-year transition from mop-up man, to setup man, to closer, to setup man and back to mop-up man. He joined the A's in May (ironically, the only month he pitched well) after the Red Sox tired of his pitch-to-loud-contact approach. In Oakland he continued to help opposing offenses, his splitter in particular dropping less and getting hit harder than in the past. Mujica excelled at starting rallies, with batters posting a 1.119 OPS against him when leading off an inning. There are better ways to gain a manager's trust, and although he may no longer be called on to preserve victories (or even leads), at least he still has epic facial hair.

Hector Neris RHP

Born: 6/14/89 Age: 27 Bats: R Throws: R Height: 6'2" Weight: 215

YEAR	TEAM	LVL	AGE	W	L	SV	G	GS	IP	H	HR	BB/9	K/9	GB%	BABIP	WHIP	ERA	FIP	DRA	WARP	CFIP	MPH
2013	REA	AA	24	6	4	0	46	8	97	89	14	3.6	8.6	35%	.281	1.32	4.55	4.55	4.52	0.6	98	
2014	REA	AA	25	2	0	0	11	0	19^{1}	12	3	4.7	5.6	44%	.176	1.14	1.86	5.68	4.86	0.0	115	
2014	PHI	MLB	25	1	0	0	1	0	1	0	0	0.0	9.0	50%	.000	0.00	0.00	1.10	1.58	0.0	100	94.4
2014	LEH	AAA	25	4	3	2	37	1	58	50	5	2.9	9.0	43%	.287	1.19	4.19	3.77	4.31	0.3	92	
2015	LEH	AAA	26	1	3	1	27	0	37^{1}	38	1	5.8	8.4	36%	.327	1.66	3.62	3.56	4.83	-0.2	107	
2015	PHI	MLB	26	2	2	0	32	0	40^{1}	38	8	2.2	9.1	39%	.280	1.19	3.79	4.75	4.35	0.2	97	95.5
2016	*PHI*	*MLB*	*27*	*3*	*1*	*0*	*55*	*0*	*58*	*52*	*7*	*3.2*	*8.0*	*38%*	*.296*	*1.26*	*4.22*	*3.95*	*4.70*	*0.2*	*109*	
2017	*PHI*	*MLB*	*28*	*2*	*1*	*0*	*33*	*1*	*54^{2}*	*49*	*7*	*3.3*	*8.1*	*38%*	*.296*	*1.27*	*4.33*	*4.50*	*4.82*	*0.1*	*112*	

Breakout: 9% Improve: 15% Collapse: 14% Attrition: 24% MLB: 38% *Comparables: Osiris Matos, Craig Breslow, Ron Flores*

While it's difficult to single out something Neris does exceptionally well, it's equally difficult to tack down a fatal flaw. He'll sit mid-90s with his fastball and showcase a bit of natural cut at times, and he'll fling a slurvy slider or toss a split with heavy arm-side run, too, all of which would combine to suggest the Phillies do indeed have another viable major-league arm in their grasp. Neris was troubled by the home run ball, and too often shied away from challenging left-handed hitters, resulting in a higher platoon-disadvantaged walk rate. He clearly felt more confident challenging right-handers with his arsenal, and commanded the inside of the zone against them particularly well. If the splitter continues to improve, Neris will have added a useful weapon to combat the lefty menace. Despite his lack of flash, Neris has a confident presence on the mound, and feels like a promising asset with room yet to grow even though he's 27 this year.

Aaron Nola RHP

Born: 6/4/93 Age: 23 Bats: R Throws: R Height: 6'1" Weight: 195

YEAR	TEAM	LVL	AGE	W	L	SV	G	GS	IP	H	HR	BB/9	K/9	GB%	BABIP	WHIP	ERA	FIP	DRA	WARP	CFIP	MPH
2014	REA	AA	21	2	0	0	5	5	24	25	4	1.9	5.6	49%	.284	1.25	2.62	4.90	4.54	0.2	102	
2014	CLR	A+	21	2	3	0	7	6	31^{1}	24	4	1.4	8.6	34%	.247	0.93	3.16	3.61	3.74	0.4	80	
2015	LEH	AAA	22	3	1	0	6	6	32^{2}	38	3	2.5	9.1	52%	.365	1.44	3.58	3.16	2.79	0.8	83	
2015	REA	AA	22	7	3	0	12	12	76^{2}	59	4	1.1	6.9	45%	.259	0.89	1.88	2.88	2.54	2.1	77	
2015	PHI	MLB	22	6	2	0	13	13	77^{2}	74	11	2.2	7.9	50%	.289	1.20	3.59	4.06	3.53	1.4	97	93.5
2016	*PHI*	*MLB*	*23*	*8*	*9*	*0*	*26*	*26*	*137^{2}*	*127*	*17*	*2.1*	*7.6*	*48%*	*.299*	*1.16*	*3.91*	*3.77*	*4.36*	*1.5*	*100*	
2017	*PHI*	*MLB*	*24*	*9*	*9*	*0*	*27*	*27*	*158^{2}*	*149*	*21*	*2.1*	*7.5*	*48%*	*.302*	*1.17*	*4.07*	*4.20*	*4.54*	*1.3*	*106*	

Breakout: 23% Improve: 55% Collapse: 19% Attrition: 20% MLB: 83% *Comparables: Shelby Miller, Brian Matusz, Alex Wood*

Nola emerged from behind the curtain of the minor leagues as-advertised: a lanky, command-the-zone-and-conquer righty who won't throw 96, but who will feature three plus pitches just the same. He sits 91-92 mph with his fastball, which doesn't generate a ton of whiffs but moves enough to prevent square contact, and flips a two-plane curve that *does* have opposing hitters chopping air more often. His changeup is probably the most show-me of those pitches, but Nola still commands it well enough to keep a bit of lingering doubt in the minds of most foes. The next challenge is length, as he was only permitted to touch 100 pitches—on the nose, at that—in one of his 13 major-league starts. With good sequencing, there's little doubt Nola's stuff will hold up into a third trip through an order, though how quickly he reaches the point of consistently getting there in starts is to be determined. For 2016, he's the Phillies' staff ace, even if he'll probably perform more like a no. 2 or 3 globally.

Brett Oberholtzer LHP

Born: 7/1/89 Age: 26 Bats: L Throws: L Height: 6'1" Weight: 225

YEAR	TEAM	LVL	AGE	W	L	SV	G	GS	IP	H	HR	BB/9	K/9	GB%	BABIP	WHIP	ERA	FIP	DRA	WARP	CFIP	MPH
2013	HOU	MLB	23	4	5	0	13	10	71^{2}	66	7	1.6	5.7	36%	.260	1.10	2.76	3.68	3.05	1.6	102	92.6
2013	OKL	AAA	23	6	6	0	16	16	80^{1}	77	9	2.8	8.1	51%	.296	1.27	4.37	4.24	4.81	0.8	94	
2014	OKL	AAA	24	1	2	0	5	5	31	35	9	0.9	9.0	44%	.306	1.23	4.65	5.86	5.03	0.3	91	
2014	HOU	MLB	24	5	13	0	24	24	143^{2}	170	12	1.8	5.9	39%	.325	1.38	4.39	3.58	4.38	0.7	101	91.8
2015	FRE	AAA	25	7	4	0	12	12	70	71	9	1.5	6.7	41%	.284	1.19	3.86	4.30	4.09	1.2	91	
2015	HOU	MLB	25	2	2	0	8	8	38^{1}	44	4	4.0	6.3	49%	.328	1.59	4.46	4.46	5.74	-0.3	113	90.9
2016	*PHI*	*MLB*	*26*	*2*	*3*	*0*	*8*	*8*	*40*	*39*	*5*	*2.1*	*6.7*	*42%*	*.303*	*1.22*	*4.00*	*3.91*	*4.44*	*0.4*	*102*	
2017	*PHI*	*MLB*	*27*	*5*	*5*	*0*	*16*	*16*	*92^{1}*	*93*	*11*	*2.2*	*7.3*	*42%*	*.316*	*1.25*	*3.94*	*4.06*	*4.37*	*1.0*	*100*	

Breakout: 20% Improve: 48% Collapse: 19% Attrition: 15% MLB: 81% *Comparables: Wade Miley, Zach McAllister, Clayton Richard*

Oberholtzer might be the only player of value to shake out of the package Houston got for Michael Bourne, though if he does work out, he'll do so in Philadelphia, where he landed in the Ken Giles trade. Oberholtzer is a lefty who doesn't throw hard, has limited stuff and gets hit often, but he doesn't walk all that many. He's kind of boring, to be honest, but boring can be okay. His crowning achievement for 2015 was throwing at Alex Rodriguez, only to have his boss publicly apologize for his actions and demote him to Triple-A after the game. The pitch missed.

Blister problems along with a pretty full rotation in Houston kept Oberholtzer either on the DL or in the minors in 2015, which is for the best; he is an ideal sixth or seventh starter, the fire extinguisher that may or may not have been checked lately. He'll probably be operative if and when the Phillies need to pull the pin.

Nick Pivetta RHP

Born: 2/14/93 Age: 23 Bats: R Throws: R Height: 6'5" Weight: 220

YEAR	TEAM	LVL	AGE	W	L	SV	G	GS	IP	H	HR	BB/9	K/9	GB%	BABIP	WHIP	ERA	FIP	DRA	WARP	CFIP	MPH
2013	AUB	A-	20	0	1	0	5	5	21^1	19	1	4.6	7.2	39%	.271	1.41	3.38	3.80	4.38	-0.2	113	
2014	HAG	A	21	13	8	0	26	25	132^1	142	15	2.7	6.7	44%	.309	1.37	4.22	4.60	4.84	0.8	104	
2015	REA	AA	22	2	2	0	7	7	28^1	32	4	6.0	7.9	41%	.341	1.80	7.31	5.67	3.86	0.3	115	
2015	POT	A+	22	7	4	0	15	14	86^1	70	4	3.0	7.5	46%	.274	1.15	2.29	3.26	3.88	0.8	98	
2015	HAR	AA	22	0	2	0	3	3	15	19	4	5.4	3.6	34%	.294	1.87	7.20	7.74	5.05	0.0	150	
2016	*PHI*	*MLB*	*23*	*6*	*9*	*0*	*22*	*22*	*112^2*	*118*	*15*	*3.9*	*5.9*	*38%*	*.308*	*1.48*	*5.01*	*4.87*	*5.55*	*-0.4*	*133*	
2017	*PHI*	*MLB*	*24*	*5*	*7*	*0*	*17*	*17*	*102*	*109*	*14*	*4.4*	*6.3*	*38%*	*.320*	*1.56*	*5.25*	*5.50*	*5.82*	*-0.6*	*138*	

Breakout: 6% Improve: 14% Collapse: 1% Attrition: 8% MLB: 15% *Comparables: Tyler Wagner, Daniel Corcino, Fernando Nieve*

Velocity: Everybody's got to have it. The Mets made the World Series on the back of an endless supply of starters who threw everything hard; the Royals had a similar story, but with relievers. Successful major-league pitching seasons in this era of baseball are often built on high-velocity arms, and the finer the control on a particular version of 97 mph gas, the better. Pivetta, acquired from the Nationals in the Jonathan Papelbon Trojan Horse, has the big arm and big fastball numbers to one day hack it in the bigs, but command questions temper any expectations beyond that. He throws two fastballs and two breaking balls, plus a changeup, but currently the only plus thing about any of those is the heater velocity. If three of those five can somehow find their way to becoming even average overall pitches, Pivetta's chances of sticking as a starter increase dramatically. Failing that, the bullpen seems the spot. It's still too early to call, and that volatility makes Pivetta equal parts intriguing and worrisome.

Joely Rodriguez LHP

Born: 11/14/91 Age: 24 Bats: L Throws: L Height: 6'1" Weight: 200

YEAR	TEAM	LVL	AGE	W	L	SV	G	GS	IP	H	HR	BB/9	K/9	GB%	BABIP	WHIP	ERA	FIP	DRA	WARP	CFIP	MPH
2013	WVA	A	21	5	5	0	14	14	72^2	79	4	2.5	7.1	56%	.336	1.36	2.72	3.62	4.52	0.5	101	
2013	BRD	A+	21	4	3	0	12	12	67^1	63	4	2.5	5.9	60%	.289	1.22	2.67	3.55	4.34	0.4	103	
2014	ALT	AA	22	6	11	1	30	21	134	151	10	2.9	4.9	57%	.315	1.45	4.84	4.22	4.80	0.4	109	
2015	REA	AA	23	5	4	0	19	8	61	73	8	3.0	6.0	56%	.330	1.52	5.90	4.61	4.81	-0.1	107	
2015	LEH	AAA	23	2	6	0	13	13	68^1	89	3	4.9	4.3	49%	.352	1.84	6.32	4.43	6.54	-1.6	126	
2016	*PHI*	*MLB*	*24*	*6*	*8*	*0*	*22*	*22*	*113^2*	*127*	*14*	*3.2*	*5.0*	*50%*	*.317*	*1.47*	*4.84*	*4.68*	*5.33*	*-0.1*	*127*	
2017	*PHI*	*MLB*	*25*	*6*	*7*	*0*	*20*	*20*	*116^2*	*127*	*14*	*3.3*	*5.4*	*50%*	*.318*	*1.46*	*4.77*	*4.97*	*5.25*	*0.0*	*125*	

Breakout: 11% Improve: 11% Collapse: 4% Attrition: 15% MLB: 22% *Comparables: Tony Pena, Wade Miley, Nick Blackburn*

As the Phillies found out in 2015, "fringe starting pitcher" isn't a bad thing to have in storage. Consider the sheer volume of substandard starting pitching the Phillies trotted out—or, in consideration of your mental health, maybe don't—and it doesn't seem like such a negative to be labeled "passable." Following his 2015 season, it might even seem kind to assign that future to Rodriguez, but the ugly basic numbers obscure the improvements he made following his demotion from Triple-A to Double-A in June. Prior to that, he endured troubling control issues, increasing his walks and his flyball tendency. Being shuffled from the rotation to the 'pen and back to the rotation among those level moves isn't a great foundation for a controlled environment, but outside of a rough trio of starts toward the end of the season when he often started fine and fell victim to repeats of a lineup, Rodriguez showed a return to respectable command and groundball production. The latter is the key to his future success, and worth monitoring as he hopes to rebound in the upper levels of the minors in 2016.

James Russell LHP

Born: 1/8/86 Age: 30 Bats: L Throws: L Height: 6'4" Weight: 205

YEAR	TEAM	LVL	AGE	W	L	SV	G	GS	IP	H	HR	BB/9	K/9	GB%	BABIP	WHIP	ERA	FIP	DRA	WARP	CFIP	MPH
2013	CHN	MLB	27	1	6	0	74	0	52^2	46	7	3.1	6.3	34%	.258	1.22	3.59	4.43	4.07	0.3	106	91.2
2014	ATL	MLB	28	0	0	0	22	1	24^1	21	0	1.5	5.9	42%	.276	1.03	2.22	2.28	2.04	0.7	101	91.1
2014	CHN	MLB	28	0	2	1	44	0	33^1	24	3	4.3	7.0	44%	.219	1.20	3.51	4.24	2.78	0.7	112	91.2
2015	IOW	AAA	29	2	0	3	9	0	11	8	0	3.3	10.6	46%	.308	1.09	2.45	2.33	3.60	0.2	85	
2015	CHN	MLB	29	0	2	1	49	0	34	42	3	2.4	5.3	44%	.336	1.50	5.29	3.93	5.71	-0.4	114	92.3
2016	*PHI*	*MLB*	*30*	*2*	*1*	*3*	*49*	*0*	*52*	*49*	*6*	*2.9*	*6.6*	*43%*	*.290*	*1.27*	*4.35*	*4.17*	*4.86*	*0.0*	*109*	
2017	*PHI*	*MLB*	*31*	*3*	*1*	*1*	*65*	*0*	*52*	*51*	*6*	*3.1*	*6.4*	*43%*	*.297*	*1.32*	*4.46*	*4.63*	*4.98*	*-0.1*	*112*	

Breakout: 34% Improve: 63% Collapse: 16% Attrition: 6% MLB: 89% *Comparables: Rich Monteleone, Lindy McDaniel, Kent Tekulve*

On the one hand, Russell's best role is LOOGY because righties paste him: He's allowed a .275/.337/.464 line to them in his career while striking out just 1.7 for every walk allowed. On the other hand, Russell's best role is longshoreman because only in one season, 2013, has he actually shut lefties down. We need a name for this type of pitcher. Lefty No Outs GuY?

Jake Thompson RHP

Born: 1/31/94 Age: 22 Bats: R Throws: R Height: 6'4" Weight: 235

YEAR	TEAM	LVL	AGE	W	L	SV	G	GS	IP	H	HR	BB/9	K/9	GB%	BABIP	WHIP	ERA	FIP	DRA	WARP	CFIP	MPH
2013	WMI	A	19	3	3	0	17	16	83^1	79	4	3.5	9.8	45%	.325	1.33	3.13	3.33	4.32	0.9	90	
2014	LAK	A+	20	6	4	0	16	16	83	75	3	2.7	8.6	44%	.316	1.20	3.14	3.11	3.87	1.1	85	
2014	ERI	AA	20	1	0	0	2	2	11	10	0	3.3	5.7	40%	.286	1.27	2.45	3.45	4.61	0.1	103	
2014	FRI	AA	20	3	1	0	7	6	35^2	28	3	4.5	11.1	46%	.305	1.29	3.28	3.34				
2015	FRI	AA	21	6	6	0	17	17	87^2	94	7	3.1	8.0	46%	.330	1.41	4.72	3.82	4.02	1.2	94	
2015	REA	AA	21	5	1	0	7	7	45	33	3	2.4	6.8	52%	.256	1.00	1.80	3.42	3.61	0.7	93	
2016	*PHI*	*MLB*	*22*	*6*	*8*	*0*	*22*	*22*	*114^2*	*113*	*15*	*3.0*	*7.4*	*43%*	*.309*	*1.32*	*4.37*	*4.23*	*4.88*	*0.5*	*114*	
2017	*PHI*	*MLB*	*23*	*6*	*8*	*0*	*22*	*22*	*129^2*	*124*	*17*	*3.7*	*8.0*	*43%*	*.310*	*1.37*	*4.53*	*4.72*	*5.06*	*0.3*	*119*	

Breakout: 8% Improve: 14% Collapse: 11% Attrition: 18% MLB: 33% *Comparables: Giovanni Soto, Matt Magill, Jon Moscot*

One of the best descriptors the baseball lexicon has is "wipeout" as it pertains to the quality of a slider. No other pitch gets the label, and Thompson, lucky son of a gun that he is, has a slider worthy of the title. It is his out pitch and bread-and-butter offering, a curveball that evolved from his early days in Little League into a sharper breaking pitch with less downward plane. Thompson will still feature a hook, but it doesn't pack nearly the punch. A near-consensus top-100 prospect entering the season, a lack of added fastball velocity could be perceived as the biggest disappointment attached to his season, but even then, Thompson's growth didn't stall and there's likely more to come. He shouldn't be considered anything less than a summer 2016 rotation candidate, and can be expected to produce mid-rotation-level results in short order.

Alberto Tirado RHP

Born: 12/10/94 Age: 21 Bats: R Throws: R Height: 6'0" Weight: 180

YEAR	TEAM	LVL	AGE	W	L	SV	G	GS	IP	H	HR	BB/9	K/9	GB%	BABIP	WHIP	ERA	FIP	DRA	WARP	CFIP	MPH
2014	VAN	A-	19	1	0	0	17	3	35^2	25	1	7.1	9.1	58%	.255	1.49	3.53	4.77	5.48	0.0	113	
2014	LNS	A	19	1	2	1	13	7	40	45	3	8.8	9.0	55%	.359	2.10	6.30	5.61	5.77	-0.4	134	
2015	DUN	A+	20	4	3	3	31	0	61^1	45	4	5.1	9.0	52%	.272	1.30	3.23	4.08	4.01	0.1	119	
2015	CLR	A+	20	1	0	0	9	0	16	6	0	10.1	9.0	61%	.182	1.50	0.56	4.92	4.67	-0.1	138	
2016	*PHI*	*MLB*	*21*	*3*	*3*	*1*	*42*	*8*	*65^2*	*62*	*7*	*6.2*	*7.1*	*47%*	*.306*	*1.63*	*5.18*	*5.08*	*5.74*	*-0.7*	*135*	
2017	*PHI*	*MLB*	*22*	*3*	*3*	*1*	*33*	*7*	*98*	*90*	*9*	*6.1*	*7.5*	*47%*	*.305*	*1.59*	*5.02*	*5.28*	*5.56*	*-0.5*	*132*	

Breakout: 1% Improve: 1% Collapse: 0% Attrition: 1% MLB: 1% *Comparables: C.J. Riefenhauser, Kevin Siegrist, Trevor Rosenthal*

A back-and-forth conversion project who arrived from Toronto in the Ben Revere trade, Tirado at times flashed stuff that overwhelmed both minor-league hitters and himself. His fastball regularly sat in the mid-90s in relief, with a slider and changeup as companion pieces. The club is considering stretching him back out into a starter, a dangerous proposition when considering the last notable attempt the Phillies made at this was with Phillippe Aumont. It doesn't seem ridiculous to consider his floor as something of a Luis Garcia clone, a high-velocity hucker with little idea where the ball is going when he releases it. If nothing else, that's sure to excite the thrill-seeking-masochist demographic of the fanbase.

Vincent Velasquez RHP

Born: 6/7/92 Age: 24 Bats: B Throws: R Height: 6'3" Weight: 205

YEAR	TEAM	LVL	AGE	W	L	SV	G	GS	IP	H	HR	BB/9	K/9	GB%	BABIP	WHIP	ERA	FIP	DRA	WARP	CFIP	MPH
2013	QUD	A	21	9	4	3	25	16	110	90	7	2.7	10.1	52%	.292	1.12	3.19	2.99	3.90	1.6	76	
2013	LNC	A+	21	0	2	0	3	3	14^2	14	2	4.9	11.7	33%	.353	1.50	6.14	5.00	5.26	0.2	97	
2014	LNC	A+	22	7	4	0	15	10	55^1	45	6	3.7	11.7	44%	.243	1.23	3.74	3.96	4.45	0.7	77	
2015	CCH	AA	23	4	0	0	9	5	33	20	2	3.5	12.3	35%	.246	1.00	1.91	2.63	2.39	0.8	75	
2015	HOU	MLB	23	1	1	0	19	7	55^2	50	5	3.4	9.4	31%	.310	1.28	4.37	3.43	4.69	0.2	94	97.5
2016	*PHI*	*MLB*	*24*	*3*	*3*	*0*	*33*	*6*	*63*	*54*	*7*	*3.2*	*9.0*	*34%*	*.302*	*1.21*	*3.84*	*3.63*	*4.29*	*0.8*	*98*	
2017	*PHI*	*MLB*	*25*	*4*	*4*	*0*	*19*	*12*	*85^1*	*75*	*10*	*3.2*	*9.2*	*34%*	*.310*	*1.23*	*3.90*	*4.03*	*4.36*	*0.7*	*99*	

Breakout: 19% Improve: 46% Collapse: 14% Attrition: 14% MLB: 81% *Comparables: Gio Gonzalez, Matt Harvey, Daniel Hudson*

Velasquez is that shiny new bike you rode to work like five times, the bathroom vanity you bought that is still sitting in your garage, the stack of *New Yorker*s you haven't read. All of these things were brought into your life with the best of intentions, and then at some point they got pushed back and pushed back until they became shadows of the life you thought you'd lead at one time or another.

A prospect with some promise, Velasquez started seven games for the Astros until the return of Scott Feldman from injury and the trade-deadline additions of Scott Kazmir and Mike Fiers pushed him out of the rotation. Rather than sending him down, Houston let Velasquez serve as a sort of mop-up guy to finish the season, then dropped him from the postseason roster, a time when having someone who can throw in the upper 90s would seem pretty useful. Though he didn't exactly light it up as a 23-year-old rookie, there's no reason to believe he won't be given more chances to start games, especially now that he's on a team with little hope of making the playoffs. He simply got lost in the shuffle in 2015. Or maybe Houston kept him on because he's really good at cutting hair or something.

Lineouts

Hitters

NAME	POS	TEAM	LVL	AGE	PA	R	2B	3B	HR	RBI	BB	K	SB	CS	AVG/OBP/SLG	TAv	BABIP	BRR	FRAA	WARP
Brian Bogusevic	LF	LEH	AAA	31	515	65	18	3	12	57	44	97	24	5	.296/.359/.424	.283	.351	1.9	CF(55): -5.6, LF(40): 1.4	2.5
	LF	PHI	MLB	31	61	9	3	0	2	5	3	21	2	0	.259/.295/.414	.244	.371	0.9	RF(14): 1.6, LF(2): -0.0	0.3
Jordan Danks	CF	LEH	AAA	28	448	38	27	0	6	46	34	122	5	3	.257/.318/.368	.255	.352	-0.8	LF(44): -2.7, CF(39): -3.7	0.0
	CF	PHI	MLB	28	4	0	0	0	0	0	0	2	0	0	.000/.000/.000	.003	.000	0.0	LF(1): -0.0	-0.1
Kelly Dugan	OF	LEH	AAA	24	147	11	4	0	2	15	8	34	0	0	.221/.295/.298	.221	.281	-1.9	RF(21): -2.1, LF(14): 0.2	-0.7
	OF	REA	AA	24	192	23	11	1	0	17	13	39	2	0	.315/.391/.393	.290	.405	1.9	RF(37): -1.8	1.0
Jeff Francoeur	RF	PHI	MLB	31	343	34	16	1	13	45	13	77	0	2	.258/.286/.433	.258	.297	-1.4	RF(85): 0.4, LF(20): -2.2	0.2
Tyler Goeddel	UT	MNT	AA	22	533	68	17	10	12	72	48	98	28	9	.279/.350/.433	.297	.326	1.9	LF(61): -5.7, RF(25): -2.0	2.7
Tommy Joseph	1B	LEH	AAA	23	175	9	9	0	3	18	3	33	0	0	.193/.220/.301	.187	.221	-1.1	1B(22): -1.1, C(19): 0.1	-1.1
Scott Kingery	2B	LWD	A	21	282	43	9	2	3	21	18	43	11	1	.250/.314/.337	.251	.287	2.6	2B(65): 0.5	0.8
Darnell Sweeney	UT	OKL	AAA	24	522	69	30	4	9	49	42	116	32	13	.271/.332/.409	.278	.339	0.5	2B(45): -6.6, CF(43): -2.2	1.7
	UT	PHI	MLB	24	98	9	4	1	3	11	13	27	0	2	.176/.286/.353	.239	.218	0.2	LF(12): -2.0, 2B(9): -1.7	-0.3
Carlos Tocci	CF	CLR	A+	19	298	31	9	0	2	18	12	52	3	9	.258/.296/.313	.241	.308	-1.7	CF(68): 3.1	0.5
	CF	LWD	A	19	261	35	14	2	2	25	20	31	14	2	.321/.387/.423	.335	.361	1.8	CF(59): -1.6	3.0

Former Astros first-rounder **Brian Bogusevic** had an impressive and versatile showing as a Triple-A outfielder before his call-up, and he could probably still provide viable emergency depth at 32. ❖ Defensive specialist **Jordan Danks**' four plate appearances sealed a fourth straight season with both Danks brothers appearing in major-league games, but not much else. ❖ Underpowered OBP fiend **Kelly Dugan** will look to stay healthy for a full season and, eventually, join former roommate Aaron Altherr with the big-league club. ❖ The only lament in seeing **Jeff Francoeur**'s comeback play out for just one team was being denied the supernatural two-week offensive frenzy he used to unleash after being traded. ❖ A gifted athlete, **Tyler Goeddel** took a promotion to Double-A and position change to the outfield in stride. The super-utility tools are all there, which is why Philadelphia grabbed him in the Rule 5 draft this winter. ❖ **Tommy Joseph** spent his season playing catch-up from time lost to post-concussion difficulties that will bump him off catching and over to first base. That he got 175 plate appearances at all was far more important than the lackluster offensive performance that accompanied them. ❖ A less-than-impressive pro debut has 2015 second-round pick **Scott Kingery** firmly off the fast track, but the Phillies are flush with second-base types and can afford to be patient. ❖ **Darnell Sweeney** can count himself among those who homered for their first major-league hit, right alongside the fellow he was traded for: Chase Utley. ❖ **Carlos Tocci** finally enjoyed some sustained offensive success in his third try at the South Atlantic League last year before being promoted, but he remains, at 20, the uncertain commodity he's been from the day he was signed.

Pitchers

NAME	TEAM	LVL	AGE	W	L	SV	G	GS	IP	H	HR	BB/9	K/9	GB%	BABIP	WHIP	ERA	FIP	FRA	WARP	CFIP	MPH
Andrew Bailey	NYA	MLB	31	0	1	0	10	0	8^2	9	2	5.2	6.2	43%	.286	1.62	5.19	6.45	4.58	0.0	109	95.5
	SWB	AAA	31	0	0	4	9	0	12^1	12	1	2.2	9.5	35%	.333	1.22	2.19	2.83	3.04	0.2	87	
	TRN	AA	31	1	0	2	11	0	14^1	6	0	3.8	10.7	42%	.194	0.84	0.63	2.15	3.05	0.3	85	
Kevin Correia	PHI	MLB	34	0	3	0	5	5	23^1	37	4	3.1	5.4	45%	.375	1.93	6.56	5.22	6.75	-0.5	118	90.1
	SAC	AAA	34	0	1	0	6	6	37^2	34	4	2.6	6.0	51%	.263	1.19	3.58	4.61	5.40	0.1	107	
Zach Eflin	REA	AA	21	8	6	0	23	23	131^2	136	12	1.6	4.6	44%	.286	1.21	3.69	4.04	4.10	1.2	99	
Ernesto Frieri	TBA	MLB	29	1	0	2	22	0	23^1	20	6	4.2	7.3	30%	.222	1.33	4.63	6.36	5.95	-0.3	112	93.7
Luis Garcia	PHI	MLB	28	4	6	2	72	0	66^2	72	4	5.0	8.5	65%	.340	1.63	3.51	3.72	4.57	0.1	102	98.1
Severino Gonzalez	PHI	MLB	22	3	3	0	7	7	30^2	44	5	2.1	8.2	38%	.394	1.66	7.92	4.53	6.18	-0.4	103	91.9
	LEH	AAA	22	2	7	0	16	16	88	106	8	1.8	4.6	36%	.321	1.41	5.11	4.10	4.78	-0.1	108	
Dalier Hinojosa	PAW	AAA	29	3	1	0	19	0	42	39	2	3.6	8.4	40%	.311	1.33	3.21	3.20	3.44	0.5	94	
	BOS	MLB	29	0	0	0	1	0	1^2	0	0	16.2	10.8	33%	.000	1.80	0.00	7.90	5.28	0.0	102	93.8
	LEH	AAA	29	0	1	0	10	0	13	14	1	3.5	9.0	44%	.342	1.46	5.54	3.31	3.53	0.1	96	
	PHI	MLB	29	2	0	0	18	0	23	15	1	3.1	8.2	47%	.222	1.00	0.78	2.94	1.89	0.8	97	95.8
Ben Lively	REA	AA	23	8	7	0	25	25	143^2	160	14	2.8	7.0	40%	.336	1.43	4.13	4.08	4.27	1.0	101	
Michael Mariot	OMA	AAA	26	4	2	8	42	0	62	52	3	2.3	10.5	41%	.304	1.10	2.32	2.83	1.90	2.3	64	
	KCA	MLB	26	0	0	0	2	0	3	2	1	6.0	3.0	22%	.125	1.33	3.00	8.77	6.40	-0.1	110	95.4
Colton Murray	PHI	MLB	25	0	1	0	8	0	7^2	11	2	2.3	10.6	46%	.375	1.70	5.87	4.99	6.54	-0.2	97	95.7
	LEH	AAA	25	2	2	2	31	0	42	24	2	4.5	8.8	37%	.210	1.07	2.79	3.40	3.83	0.3	97	
	REA	AA	25	6	1	1	21	0	35^2	31	1	2.5	9.1	42%	.300	1.15	2.52	2.46	3.13	0.6	86	
Kenneth Roberts	PHI	MLB	27	1	0	0	6	0	4^1	9	0	2.1	2.1	70%	.450	2.31	10.38	3.39	7.86	-0.2	125	90.8
	ABQ	AAA	27	1	3	0	23	0	31^2	50	3	1.1	8.0	60%	.443	1.71	5.12	3.44	3.42	0.6	82	
	COL	MLB	27	0	1	0	9	0	9^1	13	0	1.9	4.8	49%	.371	1.61	5.79	3.05	4.33	0.0	106	90.8
Jerome Williams	PHI	MLB	33	4	12	1	33	21	121	161	22	2.5	5.5	49%	.333	1.61	5.80	5.27	5.70	-1.0	123	92.5
	REA	AA	33	1	0	0	2	2	11^2	9	1	0.0	6.2	56%	.229	0.77	2.31	3.01	3.39	0.2	90	
Tom Windle	REA	AA	23	4	5	0	34	14	97^1	98	6	4.7	5.9	52%	.306	1.53	4.35	4.36	6.07	-1.6	124	

Former Astros first-rounder **Brian Bogusevic** had an impressive and versatile showing as a Triple-A outfielder before his call-up, and he could probably still provide viable emergency depth at 32. ❖ Defensive specialist **Jordan Danks**' four plate appearances sealed a fourth straight season with both Danks brothers appearing in major-league games, but not much else. ❖ Underpowered OBP fiend **Kelly Dugan** will look to stay healthy for a full season and, eventually, join former roommate Aaron Altherr with the big-league club. ❖ The only lament in seeing **Jeff Francoeur**'s comeback play out for just one team was being denied the supernatural two-week offensive frenzy he used to unleash after being traded. ❖ A gifted athlete, **Tyler Goeddel** took a promotion to Double-A and position change to the outfield in stride. The super-utility tools are all there, which is why Philadelphia grabbed him in the Rule 5 draft this winter. ❖ **Tommy Joseph** spent his season playing catch-up from time lost to post-concussion difficulties that will bump him off catching and over to first base. That he got 175 plate appearances at all was far more important than the lackluster offensive performance that accompanied them. ❖ A less-than-impressive pro debut has 2015 second-round pick **Scott Kingery** firmly off the fast track, but the Phillies are flush with second-base types and can afford to be patient. ❖ **Darnell Sweeney** can count himself among those who homered for their first major-league hit, right alongside the fellow he was traded for: Chase Utley. ❖ **Carlos Tocci** finally enjoyed some sustained offensive success in his third try at the South Atlantic League last year before being promoted, but he remains, at 20, the uncertain commodity he's been from the day he was signed.

Manager

Pete Mackanin

When Ryne Sandberg resigned from his managerial post in late June, the Phillies' new brass designated Mackanin as the interim skipper. The move made sense. Mackanin had been a fixture on the Phillies' staff for most of the post-2008 era, having served as bench coach from 2009 to 2012, then again from 2014 to 2015. He'd also experienced life with the interim label twice before (with the Pirates in 2005 and the Reds in 2007), meaning he was used to inhaling the purgatorial atmosphere that comes with it. Odds are, Mackanin figured he'd finish the season, then move into a consulting or instructional role—or whatever gig good organizational soldiers receive after their useful days are over.

But the next few months deviated from the plan. The Phillies remained in full rebuilding mode, trading veteran mainstays Cole Hamels and Chase Utley, and embracing their young players—even those expected to have marginal big-league futures. Mackanin, to his credit, took the moves in stride. He never complained about playing Aaron Altherr, Darnell Sweeney or Cameron Rupp. Nor did he whine when his rotation was staffed by Aaron Harang, David Buchanan and three rookies. That's not to say this was the ideal arrangement for Mackanin. He's professed his love for analytics before, and once told Prospectus that in-game strategy is a bigger part of managing than most people think. Mackanin didn't have the right talent or means to show his tactical chops and he didn't force the issue. He did, however, do his duty by protecting the kids.

Whereas another interim manager fighting for a shot at the full-time gig might have abused his talented rookie starters, Mackanin allowed Aaron Nola, Jerad Eickhoff and Alec Asher to top the century mark twice in 28 combined starts. On the other side of the ball, Mackanin didn't use many subs or pinch-hitters; he let the kids play. He *did* call for a lot of sacrifices (more than Fredi Gonzalez in nearly half as many games), but that might have been his idea of grooming the kids to have a team-first mentality, or perhaps his way of allowing them to feel good about their contributions, even if they weren't of the most valuable or glamorous sort. (Or maybe he felt playing for one run beat getting zero. Who knows.)

A funny thing happened next. The Phillies improved their record, from a 57-win pace under Sandberg to a 68-win pace under Mackanin. Then another funny thing happened: The Phillies removed the interim tag, giving Mackanin a one-year deal with a club option to remain on board as the club's manager. In all likelihood, Mackanin is going to fill the same role that Rick Renteria did with the Cubs: babysitting until things get interesting, then dismissed for someone with more name value. Mackanin has made the most of limited opportunities, though, so he may stick around longer than expected. It wouldn't be the first time.

PITTSBURGH PIRATES

Essay by Travis Sawchik

Player comments by R.J. Anderson and BP authors

The Pirates just became the 27th team in major-league history to reach the postseason three years in a row. They'll try to become just the 15th to make four in a row. Eight of the 14 previous occurrences came during the wild card era, but the point remains: It's really hard to stay this good for this long. The Pirates have done something.

Their 98 wins last year matched the franchise's highest mark since 1909. Their 280 victories over the past three years are the second most in baseball. And yet, for as much as the Pirates have accomplished over the past three seasons—ending a streak of 20 consecutive losing seasons, a North American pro sports record, and becoming a model organization—they have also won only three postseason games. The buzzsaws Bumgarner and Arrieta left the club, and fan base, unfulfilled.

Can they win their first division title since 1992? Can they avoid the one-game playoff to which they've been shackled the past three years? Can the next three years be better than these past three? Or is this as good as it gets?

A REASON TO BELIEVE the Pirates will continue to contend is that no team has proven better at finding value on the open market than the Pirates. Darned near everything has to go right for the Pirates to succeed, but, under GM Neal Huntington, darned near everything has gone right.

In 2015, they had to fill two starting rotation spots and replace the sizeable void left by Russell Martin, who produced 6.6 WARP in 2014. These are the challenges that send GMs into the marketplace with nine-figure contract offers, which the Pirates simply can't afford. They ended up with two pitchers—Francisco Liriano and A.J. Burnett—who combined for 350 innings of low-3s ERAs, and a catcher (Francisco Cervelli) who out-WARPed Martin for less than a million bucks.

That work alone would have made for a great offseason, but the Pirates also added the steal of the offseason: Jung-ho Kang, the first Korean Baseball Organization position player to jump directly to the majors. In all, the Pirates added or retained all four, and midseason scrap heap pickup J.A. Happ, for a total of $25 million in 2015 salary. They produced 16 WARP. Better, only Kang, at a laughable $2.5 million per year, required a commitment longer than three years.

PIRATES PROSPECTUS

2015 W-L: 98-64, 2nd in NL Central

Pythag	.571	4th	DER	.697	23rd
RS/G	4.30	11th	B-Age	28.1	11th
RA/G	3.68	3rd	P-Age	29.7	27th
TAv	.264	10th	Salary	$90.3M	24th
BRR	6.31	7th	M$/MW	$1.6M	30th
TAv-P	.248	4th	DL Days	1116	18th
FIP	3.39	2nd	$ on DL	10%	7th

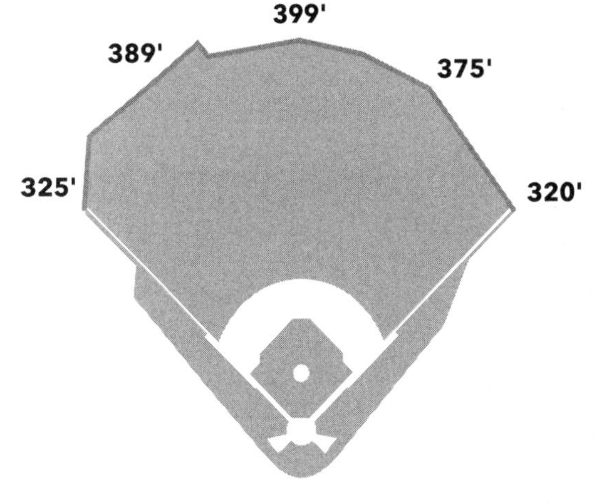

Outfield wall profile: **6'** to **21'**

Three-Year Park Factors

Runs	Runs/RH	Runs/LH	HR/RH	HR/LH
98	105	101	99	101

Top Hitter WARP	5.6	Francisco Cervelli
Top Pitcher WARP	4.2	Gerrit Cole
Top Prospect	Tyler Glasnow	

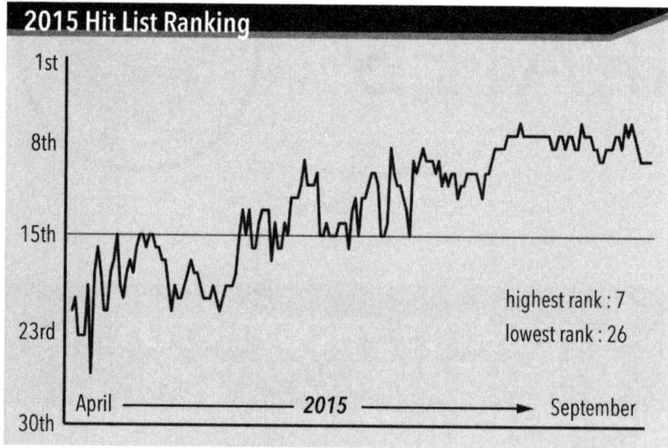

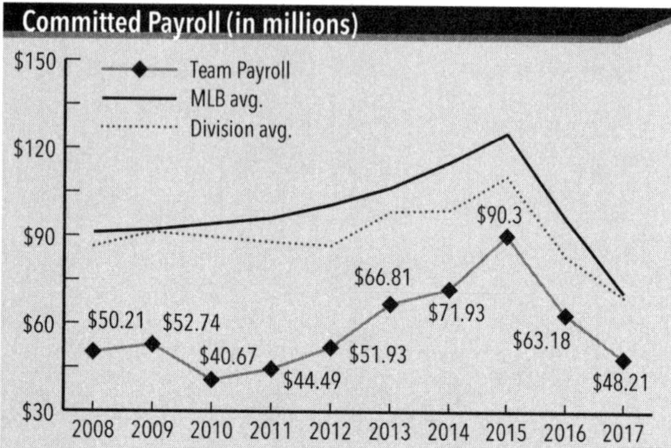

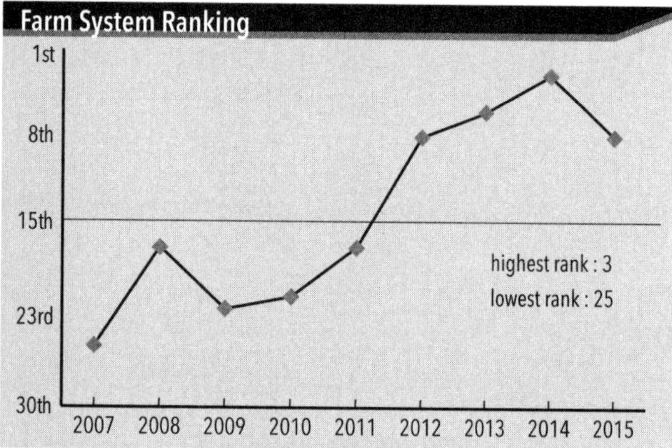

Personnel

President: Frank Coonelly
General Manager: Neal Huntington
Assistant General Manager: Greg Smith
Assistant General Manager: Kyle Stark
Manager: Clint Hurdle

Baseball Prospectus Alumni
Dan Fox
Stuart Wallace

If a team brings back a roster filled with proven performers, we project great things. If a team brings back a front office filled with proven performers, should we project any different?

A REASON TO DOUBT is that Huntington has never faced a challenge like he did this winter. Nine players were arbitration eligible, leading to the non-tendering of Pedro Alvarez, the trade of Neil Walker, and enough raises to put a strain on attempts to resign the eight active Pirates who filed for free agency after the World Series ended. While the Pirates approach their first $100 million payroll in franchise history, the increasing dollars owed to their own players is eroding flexibility in the trade and free agent markets.

"The reality is every offseason is crucial for small- to mid-market teams," Huntington told the *Pittsburgh Tribune-Review* in October, "because the margin for error is small."

Moreover, the gap between the Haves and Have Nots continues to grow with each new TV contract. While the Pirates' local cable TV ratings spiked to a franchise-record high 8.33 average, according to ROOT Sports, their TV deal ranks near the bottom of the sport in annual average dollars. (It expires after the 2018 season.) Meanwhile, the Cardinals signed a 15-year, $1 billion TV rights deal last summer. And the Cubs are reportedly interested in starting their own network, à la the Yankees' YES Network.

Even the Pirates' franchise-record attendance figures last year couldn't keep up with their rivals: Pittsburgh (at 2.48 million paying customers) was outdrawn not just by the Cardinals (3.52 million) and Cubs (2.96 million), but by the Brewers (2.54 million).

There is no help on the way.

A REASON TO BELIEVE is that the Pirates are poised to employ a homegrown, cost-controlled power staff to plow through the NL playoff field. Worse teams than the Pirates have followed that model to the World Series in the past 12 months.

Gerrit Cole blossomed into an ace in 2015, becoming the first Pirates starter since 1991 to finish in the top five in Cy Young voting. (Liriano, who finished ninth in 2013, is the only other Pirates pitcher to get even a single vote in that period.) He'll soon by joined by Tyler Glasnow, one of the dozen best prospects in baseball, with a 2.07 ERA in nearly 400 career minor-league innings. Former second-overall pick Jameson Taillon, two years removed from Tommy John surgery, is also expected in Pittsburgh by the second half. It wasn't long ago that scouts watching Grapefruit League action debated whether they would take Taillon or Cole, and he retains top-50 prospect status despite the injuries.

A REASON TO DOUBT is the Pitch-22 dilemma: While the Pirates are realistic about the unlikelihood of acquiring an ace in free agency—and, thus, have invested in drafting and developing these types of potential top-of-the-rotation arms—that puts them at the mercy of brutal young-arm attrition rates.

The Pirates made a historic commitment to the draft from 2008-2012, spending an MLB-record $51.4 on bonuses before MLB put bonus caps in place. During the period from 2009-2011, the Pirates spent 22 of their first 30 picks on pitchers. The spent more than $25 million on bonuses for the group, of which 17 were high schoolers.

None of these 17 has reached the majors for the Pirates. Taillon has not thrown a minor-league inning since 2013. Stetson Allie, who signed for $2.2 million, gave up pitching to try first base. The Pirates released over-slot signee Zachary Rosenberg ($1.2 million) in April. Only two pitchers drafted in the Huntington Era—Cole and Justin Wilson—have pitched in the majors for the Pirates.

Said Huntington mentor and ex-GM John Hart to the *Tribune-Review* last year, "A truism is if you have 10 (pitching prospects), you can really count on two of them making it. I came up in the (1980s) and never believed it. I said, 'Come on, there can't be that much attrition.' Then bang: This guy gets hurt. This guy doesn't develop a third pitch."

The Pirates bet they could beat those attrition rates, and they did it at the cost of investing elsewhere. Finally, in 2013, they pivoted, investing in athletic, middle-of-the-field players: First-rounders Reese McGuire, Austin Meadows and Cole Tucker. Scouts love them, but the looming threat of a pitching crunch if Taillon and Glasnow don't succeed is terrifying.

A REASON TO BELIEVE the Pirates can match the Cardinals and Cubs? They have a better health care plan.

Finding a way to keep athletes healthy is perhaps the holy grail of sports analytics. In an industry that has spent a handful of billon dollars on injured players over the past decade, if a team found a way to prevent even a fraction of injuries it would be a considerable competitive advantage.

The Pirates, probably more than any other team, have experimented in this field, designing more time off for the players during the season and using technology like the Zephry BioHarness, a wearable monitoring device that gives the training staff readings of players' heart rate and energy consumption. Russell Martin was patient zero in 2014, and by 2015 a third of the club was participating. The training staff gives manager Clint Hurdle a single fatigue number every day for each player to help guide playing-time decisions.

Cole wore the BioHarness and adopted a new shoulder strengthening regimen last year. He threw 200 innings for the first time in his professional career, and credited his health—and his ability to stay in the rhythm of a full season—for the mastery of a back-foot slider that leveled his platoon splits.

In 2014, the Pirates logged the fewest days on the DL. In 2015, they actually managed to lose *negative* value to the disabled list, with the few injuries they dealt with mostly limited to the bottom of the roster. More than 500 of their 799 lost games went to Corey Hart, Andrew Lambo, Brandon Cumpton, Deolis Guerra and Gorkys Hernandez.

A REASON TO DOUBT: The team that lost the *most* player value to injury in 2015, according to Man Games Lost, was the Cardinals. They still won 100 games. The Cardinals' luck and health cannot possibly be any worse next year. Can the Pirates' really be any better?

No one believes every injury can be prevented. Strains and fatigue can be reduced, but there will always be contact injuries, torn UCLs, or the guy who cuts himself making a sandwich. While the Pirates have been innovative on the injury front, they've also been fortunate.

A REASON TO DOUBT is the knowledge that 29 teams are watching and copying.

Before a spring training game in 2014, I found the head of the Pirates analytics department (and former BP staffer) Dan Fox on the warning track behind the batting cages in Ft. Myers, Fla. He told me how the Pirates had come to be at the forefront of identifying pitch framing as a quantifiable, and how that had led them to Russell Martin.

Fox lamented that the advantage was already gone—or soon would be. He had to find the *next* hidden value at the margins.

The Pirates ratcheted up defensive shifts in 2013. By the following season, they could look around and see the rest of the league following suit. They were perhaps the first team to successfully funnel even more grounders into the shift through pitch type and sequencing; they knew the advantage wouldn't last. As hard as it is to find a new J.A. Happ or Edinson Volquez each year, it's just as hard to find a new edge that hasn't been trod flat by the rest of the league.

A REASON TO BELIEVE they can maintain that information edge: They've been asking better questions.

In the Big Data age, teams have the same access to all the same data from StatCast, PITCHf/x, TrackMan, etc. The key is no longer having more data, but asking better questions.

The Pirates have created a rare collaborative culture between their analytics staff and field staff. While teams can copy strategies, it's more difficult to copy personalities, relationships and culture.

"A lot of times a coach or somebody will have something in the back of their head but they won't write an email," Dan Fox told me in *Big Data Baseball*. "They are not going to compose something and give it to you. But they'll come over and say 'From a player-development perspective, track this metric.' I just try to be as available as possible because you never know what you are going to get. They all have these vast databases of player comparisons and situations and strategy I don't have."

The two-way communication has led to better questions, yielding important answers. Perhaps it is a unique, effective culture that will keep the Pirates ahead of the curve, and in contention. At least that's their hope, because everything else is working against them. ■

—Travis Sawchik is staff writer for the Pittsburgh Tribune-Review *and author of* Big Data Baseball.

Hitters

Pedro Alvarez DH

Born: 2/6/87 Age: 29 Bats: L Throws: R Height: 6'3" Weight: 250

YEAR	TEAM	LVL	AGE	PA	R	2B	3B	HR	RBI	BB	K	SB	CS	AVG/OBP/SLG	TAv	BABIP	BRR	FRAA	WARP
2013	PIT	MLB	26	614	70	22	2	36	100	48	186	2	0	.233/.296/.473	.274	.276	0.0	3B(150): 15.3	4.5
2014	PIT	MLB	27	445	46	13	1	18	56	45	113	8	3	.231/.312/.405	.260	.277	-1.1	3B(99): 8.2, 1B(5): -0.6	2.1
2015	PIT	MLB	28	491	60	18	0	27	77	48	131	2	0	.243/.318/.469	.285	.279	0.4	1B(124): 3.5	2.2
2016	*PIT*	*MLB*	*29*	*580*	*72*	*20*	*1*	*28*	*83*	*55*	*167*	*4*	*1*	*.233/.309/.438*	*.262*	*.284*	*-0.4*	*1B 1*	*1.1*
2017	*PIT*	*MLB*	*30*	*489*	*66*	*16*	*1*	*23*	*67*	*50*	*145*	*3*	*1*	*.226/.307/.422*	*.266*	*.280*	*-0.5*	*1B 1*	*0.6*

Breakout: 11% Improve: 62% Collapse: 2% Attrition: 7% MLB: 98% *Comparables: Mike Napoli, Carlos Delgado, Mo Vaughn*

After a gaffe-flooded 2014, Alvarez had to be thrilled to enter spring training with a fresh slate at a new position. The hope was that his athleticism—don't laugh; "El Toro" is more spry than his nickname suggests—would counterbalance his inexperience at the cold corner, eventually allowing him to become an average (or close to it) defender. Nope. Alvarez committed 23 errors, almost as many as he had in 2014—and this time did it without the yips. Do you realize how difficult it is to err that many times at first base? Jose Abreu finished second in the majors—and he had about *half* as many errors. Casey Kotchman committed 18 errors *in his career*. Alvarez started almost all of the Pirates' September games, but completed only three of them. Alvarez's ability to smack 30 home runs and reach base at respectable rates should keep him employed for years to come, but after the Pirates non-tendered him it was probably safe for him to turn his glove into a decorative planter.

Josh Bell 1B

Born: 8/14/92 Age: 23 Bats: B Throws: R Height: 6'2" Weight: 235

YEAR	TEAM	LVL	AGE	PA	R	2B	3B	HR	RBI	BB	K	SB	CS	AVG/OBP/SLG	TAv	BABIP	BRR	FRAA	WARP
2013	WVA	A	20	519	75	37	2	13	76	52	90	1	2	.279/.353/.453	.318	.319	-1.1	RF(83): 1.0	4.1
2014	BRD	A+	21	363	45	20	4	9	53	25	43	5	4	.335/.384/.502	.309	.364	-1.8	RF(62): -8.2	1.5
2014	ALT	AA	21	102	13	2	0	0	7	8	12	4	1	.287/.343/.309	.248	.329	0.3	RF(19): 3.1	0.4
2015	IND	AAA	22	145	20	7	3	2	18	21	15	2	0	.347/.441/.504	.325	.377	-0.1	1B(32): -3.3	0.8
2015	ALT	AA	22	427	47	17	6	5	60	44	50	7	4	.307/.376/.427	.299	.335	-2.1	1B(84): -7.3	1.2
2016	*PIT*	*MLB*	*23*	*250*	*26*	*11*	*2*	*6*	*28*	*19*	*45*	*2*	*1*	*.271/.329/.410*	*.262*	*.310*	*-0.2*	*1B -3*	*0.1*
2017	*PIT*	*MLB*	*24*	*412*	*49*	*20*	*3*	*9*	*46*	*32*	*75*	*3*	*1*	*.275/.333/.419*	*.273*	*.318*	*-0.4*	*1B -5*	*-0.1*

Breakout: 8% Improve: 15% Collapse: 7% Attrition: 22% MLB: 38% *Comparables: Yonder Alonso, Mike Carp, Chris Carter*

Just what should we make of Bell? All he's done throughout his minor-league career is hit—that shiny average he posted in 2015 came with a ridiculous 1:1 walk-to-strikeout ratio—yet there are two major reasons for reservation. Bell is a big, strong-looking fellow who *should* hit the ectoplasm out of baseballs. Instead the limitations of his swings—he doesn't tap into his lower half well, particularly as a righty, as evidenced by a .310 slugging percentage from that side—have led to substandard power numbers for a first baseman. What's worse is Bell's below-average defense, which resulted in 16 errors at first base. (Casey Kotchman made 18 erro—oh, you've heard this one already?) Bell is young enough to outgrow both shortcomings, but as it stands there's a lot of pressure on his bat-to-ball skills translating to the majors—so much that it's hard to feel comfortable about him making an immediate impact when he reaches The Show.

Francisco Cervelli C

Born: 9/4/92 Age: 23 Bats: R Throws: R Height: 6'2" Weight: 215

YEAR	TEAM	LVL	AGE	PA	R	2B	3B	HR	RBI	BB	K	SB	CS	AVG/OBP/SLG	TAv	BABIP	BRR	FRAA	WARP
2013	NYA	MLB	27	61	12	3	0	3	8	8	9	0	0	.269/.377/.500	.321	.275	-0.3	C(16): 3.7, 2B(1): -0.0	1.0
2014	NYA	MLB	28	162	18	11	1	2	13	11	41	1	0	.301/.370/.432	.285	.408	-2.0	C(42): 6.1, 1B(5): -0.0	1.5
2014	TRN	AA	28	20	2	0	0	0	0	4	4	0	0	.133/.350/.133	.198	.182	0.1	C(2): -0.0, 1B(2): -0.1	-0.1
2015	PIT	MLB	29	510	56	17	5	7	43	46	94	1	1	.295/.370/.401	.281	.359	0.0	C(128): 20.5	5.6
2016	*PIT*	*MLB*	*30*	*498*	*49*	*19*	*3*	*8*	*50*	*42*	*102*	*2*	*1*	*.260/.336/.369*	*.255*	*.318*	*-1.0*	*C 20*	*4.2*
2017	*PIT*	*MLB*	*31*	*487*	*56*	*17*	*2*	*8*	*46*	*41*	*105*	*1*	*0*	*.257/.334/.362*	*.259*	*.318*	*-1.2*	*C 19*	*4.0*

Breakout: 2% Improve: 31% Collapse: 8% Attrition: 13% MLB: 81% *Comparables: John Baker, Josh Bard, Jose Lobaton*

YEAR	TEAM	P. COUNT	FRM RUNS	BLK RUNS	THRW RUNS	TOT RUNS
2013	NYA	2156	2.7	0.0	0.0	2.7
2014	NYA	5573	6.3	0.2	0.0	6.5
2015	PIT	17330	18.9	-0.3	-2.1	16.5
2016	*PIT*	*17932*	*19.9*	*-0.2*	*-1.6*	*18.1*
2017	*PIT*	*17554*	*18.3*	*-0.2*	*-1.7*	*16.4*

A little-known clause in 2012's Casey McGehee-Chad Qualls trade stipulated that the Pirates had to employ at least one former Yankees catcher in each subsequent season. Hence Cervelli coming over this winter in exchange for reliever Justin Wilson. His job was to replace one former Yank (Russell Martin) and minimize the role of another (Chris Stewart). It was a risky proposition for the Pirates, since Cervelli had never stayed healthy or productive for a full season. Yet the gamble paid off. In addition to nearly doubling his career plate appearances, Cervelli maintained his production—an impressive accomplishment considering how extra squats often beget worse numbers. He also lived up to his reputation as a quality defender—the third-best framer in the majors, our numbers say—and energetic field general, the latter of which helped with the transition from Martin, widely known as an virtuoso staff-handler. With a year remaining until he hits free agency, Cervelli's time in Pittsburgh is likely near its end; here's hoping he gives Austin Romine a tour of the city before leaving for good.

Elias Diaz C

Born: 11/17/90 Age: 25 Bats: R Throws: R Height: 6'0" Weight: 210

YEAR	TEAM	LVL	AGE	PA	R	2B	3B	HR	RBI	BB	K	SB	CS	AVG/OBP/SLG	TAv	BABIP	BRR	FRAA	WARP
2013	BRD	A+	22	220	30	12	2	2	15	31	33	4	4	.279/.382/.399	.290	.327	-1.5	C(55): -2.1	1.4
2014	IND	AAA	23	37	4	1	0	0	0	3	6	0	1	.152/.243/.182	.172	.185	0.2	C(9): -0.0	-0.2
2014	ALT	AA	23	367	41	20	0	6	54	30	51	3	2	.328/.378/.445	.293	.365	0.8	C(88): 12.5, 1B(1): 1.1	4.5
2015	IND	AAA	24	363	33	16	4	4	47	29	47	1	4	.271/.330/.382	.253	.301	-1.0	C(60): 1.5	1.0
2015	PIT	MLB	24	2	0	0	0	0	0	0	1	0	0	.000/.000/.000	-.003	.000	0.0		0.0
2016	*PIT*	*MLB*	*25*	*33*	*3*	*1*	*0*	*1*	*3*	*2*	*6*	*0*	*0*	*.256/.315/.378*	*.247*	*.298*	*-0.1*	*C -0*	*0.1*
2017	*PIT*	*MLB*	*26*	*204*	*23*	*9*	*1*	*5*	*22*	*15*	*39*	*1*	*1*	*.255/.311/.385*	*.256*	*.296*	*-0.5*	*C -2*	*0.5*

Breakout: 4% Improve: 12% Collapse: 11% Attrition: 27% MLB: 38% *Comparables: Curtis Casali, Tony Sanchez, Dan Butler*

In spite of the fact that Diaz failed to maintain the offensive gains that catapulted him onto prospect lists during the 2014 season, he still looks like a future big-league fixture. Much of the credit for that projection belongs to his defense. He's considered an asset with the mitt, one who pairs a strong arm with skilled receiving and staff-handling (two attributes the Pirates value more than most teams). When Diaz steps to the plate, his best traits are his approach and bat control. He's never going to offer much power (or an outstanding average), but he should do enough at and behind the plate to stick around as a tolerable starter or good backup.

YEAR	TEAM	P. COUNT	FRM RUNS	BLK RUNS	THRW RUNS	TOT RUNS
2014	ALT	11824	9.7	0.1	1.2	10.9
2014	IND	1322	0.2	0.0	-0.1	0.1
2015	IND	8398	1.6	0.4	0.0	2.0
2016	*PIT*	*1207*	*-0.2*	*0.0*	*-0.1*	*-0.3*
2017	*PIT*	*7474*	*-1.6*	*0.0*	*-0.6*	*-2.1*

Willy Garcia OF

Born: 9/4/92 Age: 23 Bats: R Throws: R Height: 6'2" Weight: 215

YEAR	TEAM	LVL	AGE	PA	R	2B	3B	HR	RBI	BB	K	SB	CS	AVG/OBP/SLG	TAv	BABIP	BRR	FRAA	WARP
2013	BRD	A+	20	480	51	21	6	16	60	23	154	13	6	.256/.294/.437	.257	.351	-1.2	RF(114): 15.7, CF(2): 0.4	2.2
2014	ALT	AA	21	474	59	27	5	18	63	24	145	8	4	.271/.311/.478	.277	.361	1.2	RF(103): -1.3, LF(19): 2.7	2.0
2015	IND	AAA	22	291	36	11	4	10	38	12	76	1	4	.246/.285/.424	.250	.305	-3.0	RF(47): 3.3, CF(13): 1.8	0.8
2015	ALT	AA	22	224	26	7	2	5	29	11	47	3	2	.314/.353/.441	.280	.381	-2.2	LF(38): 7.1, CF(11): -0.2	1.5
2016	*PIT*	*MLB*	*23*	*250*	*25*	*10*	*2*	*9*	*31*	*9*	*82*	*2*	*1*	*.235/.266/.401*	*.233*	*.315*	*-0.2*	*RF 0, LF 1*	*0.1*
2017	*PIT*	*MLB*	*24*	*319*	*36*	*13*	*2*	*11*	*39*	*11*	*104*	*2*	*2*	*.240/.273/.410*	*.246*	*.324*	*-0.2*	*RF 0, LF 1*	*1.0*

Breakout: 1% Improve: 8% Collapse: 0% Attrition: 11% MLB: 18% *Comparables: Bryce Brentz, Steven Moya, Carlos Peguero*

Garcia opened the year in Altoona, where he improved each of his slash marks from the previous season. Upon moving to Indianapolis, he did something he hadn't done in years: struggle. In his first month at the level, Garcia batted .222/.241/.284 with 19 more strikeouts than extra-base hits. His performance improved thereafter—he hit .256/.303/.482 through season's end—but complaints about his overaggressive approach remain valid. How valid? His walk rate was roughly comparable to our use of the word "the" in this comment: One in 22 words. Further complicating matters, he fanned about 5.3 times per walk—a poor ratio for elite power hitters, let alone the ones with merely good pop. Garcia's age and defensive versatility earn him leniency, but he's almost certainly looking—nay, *swinging* at a future as a streaky reserve.

Alen Hanson 2B

Born: 10/22/92 Age: 23 Bats: B Throws: R Height: 5'11" Weight: 180

YEAR	TEAM	LVL	AGE	PA	R	2B	3B	HR	RBI	BB	K	SB	CS	AVG/OBP/SLG	TAv	BABIP	BRR	FRAA	WARP
2013	BRD	A+	20	409	51	23	8	7	48	33	70	24	14	.281/.339/.444	.283	.325	2.0	SS(92): 3.5	3.4
2013	ALT	AA	20	150	13	4	5	1	10	8	26	6	2	.255/.299/.380	.273	.306	-0.9	SS(34): -0.8	0.6
2014	ALT	AA	21	527	64	21	12	11	58	31	88	25	11	.280/.326/.442	.279	.321	-0.9	SS(100): -0.0, 2B(17): 1.5	3.3
2015	IND	AAA	22	529	66	17	12	6	43	37	91	35	12	.263/.313/.387	.254	.311	-1.6	2B(111): 11.8, 3B(7): 0.5	2.2
2016	*PIT*	*MLB*	*23*	*231*	*30*	*8*	*3*	*5*	*21*	*12*	*49*	*10*	*4*	*.249/.291/.391*	*.238*	*.293*	*1.0*	*2B 5*	*1.1*
2017	*PIT*	*MLB*	*24*	*393*	*42*	*15*	*6*	*8*	*42*	*22*	*84*	*18*	*7*	*.249/.293/.392*	*.247*	*.293*	*2.6*	*2B 9*	*2.7*

Breakout: 9% Improve: 24% Collapse: 2% Attrition: 12% MLB: 34% *Comparables: Josh Barfield, Stefen Romero, Ryan Brett*

Following years of resistance, the Pirates gave up the ghost on Hanson at shortstop in 2015, moving him across the bag to second base. He was expected to land at the keystone all along, so the positional change didn't do much to harm his stock. What did hurt his standing was the lack of development at the plate, as his first season in Triple-A put his shortcomings on display. Hanson has an average hit tool, yet his below-average on-base skills and power make him a substandard hitter. He does provide value on the basepaths, but his footwork in the field needs improving if he's to become a quality defender. He's still young enough to make the necessary gains, and he'll need to in order to maintain his standing as Josh Harrison's successor.

Josh Harrison UT

Born: 7/8/87 Age: 28 Bats: R Throws: R Height: 5'8" Weight: 195

YEAR	TEAM	LVL	AGE	PA	R	2B	3B	HR	RBI	BB	K	SB	CS	AVG/OBP/SLG	TAv	BABIP	BRR	FRAA	WARP
2013	PIT	MLB	25	95	10	1	2	3	14	2	10	2	0	.250/.290/.409	.238	.253	0.7	RF(14): 0.7, 2B(11): 1.0	0.3
2013	IND	AAA	25	296	50	29	5	4	34	20	39	19	7	.317/.373/.507	.297	.360	1.0	2B(33): 4.1, SS(29): 3.0	3.0
2014	PIT	MLB	26	550	77	38	7	13	52	22	81	18	7	.315/.347/.490	.305	.353	0.4	3B(72): 5.0, RF(26): 4.7	5.1
2015	PIT	MLB	27	449	57	29	1	4	28	19	71	10	8	.287/.327/.390	.264	.336	1.8	3B(72): 2.1, 2B(37): -0.8	1.9
2015	IND	AAA	27	20	0	0	0	0	0	1	2	0	0	.053/.100/.053	.113	.059	0.0	3B(3): 0.5, RF(1): -0.5	-0.3
2016	*PIT*	*MLB*	*28*	*631*	*78*	*36*	*5*	*12*	*60*	*26*	*91*	*18*	*9*	*.282/.320/.424*	*.260*	*.310*	*0.8*	*2B 9, 3B 3*	*3.6*
2017	*PIT*	*MLB*	*29*	*512*	*57*	*29*	*4*	*10*	*56*	*22*	*74*	*14*	*7*	*.277/.316/.420*	*.266*	*.303*	*1.3*	*2B 7, 3B 3*	*2.8*

Breakout: 4% Improve: 48% Collapse: 3% Attrition: 8% MLB: 96% *Comparables: Chone Figgins, Danny Valencia, Casey McGehee*

We've never believed in the vision of Harrison as some kind of idyllic Zobrist-Pedroia-Sandoval mashup. His energy and glove make him a joy to watch, but his swing-happy ways always left us cold. Even when he broke out in 2014, and we wanted to admit we were wrong all along, his approach remained as unlikable as ever.

Luckily for Harrison, the Pirates had no such reservations and gave him an extension worth $27 million before spring training. He responded with a decent, unremarkable effort. His power and BABIP each slipped—a non-worrisome late-season thumb injury shares blame—and as Harrison's BABIP goes, so goes the whole slash line. He looked like what we thought he was: a fun, lovable player who fits perfectly on the Pirates' roster, but imperfectly on an All-Star roster.

Corey Hart DH

Born: 3/24/82 Age: 34 Bats: R Throws: R Height: 6'6" Weight: 240

YEAR	TEAM	LVL	AGE	PA	R	2B	3B	HR	RBI	BB	K	SB	CS	AVG/OBP/SLG	TAv	BABIP	BRR	FRAA	WARP
2014	SEA	MLB	32	255	17	9	0	6	21	16	59	2	0	.203/.271/.319	.246	.244	-0.6	RF(7): -0.6, 1B(2): -0.2	-0.3
2014	TAC	AAA	32	77	8	4	2	4	9	7	13	0	0	.286/.351/.571	.355	.302	-1.5	LF(1): -0.4	0.7
2015	PIT	MLB	33	57	3	1	0	2	9	1	19	0	0	.222/.246/.352	.187	.294	-0.9	1B(8): -0.4, RF(3): 0.5	-0.4
2015	IND	AAA	33	43	4	1	0	2	7	1	15	0	0	.167/.186/.333	.195	.200	1.0	1B(5): -0.1	-0.2
2016	*PIT*	*MLB*	*34*	*250*	*29*	*11*	*1*	*9*	*33*	*17*	*58*	*1*	*0*	*.251/.312/.432*	*.264*	*.292*	*-0.5*	*1B -3, RF 1*	*0.3*
2017	*PIT*	*MLB*	*35*	*58*	*7*	*2*	*0*	*2*	*7*	*4*	*14*	*0*	*0*	*.243/.306/.415*	*.264*	*.286*	*-0.2*	*1B -1, RF 0*	*0.0*

Breakout: 1% Improve: 31% Collapse: 8% Attrition: 21% MLB: 91% *Comparables: Dmitri Young, Garrett Jones, Adam LaRoche*

How do you mend a broken Hart? The Pirates tried micromanagement. For the first time in his career, Hart a) faced more lefties than righties and b) recorded nearly half his at-bats as a pinch-hitter. It didn't matter; he hit the DL in June with an impinged shoulder and, though he went on multiple rehab assignments, he never again donned the pointed P. Maybe it was for the best: Hart didn't perform well when he played, looking less like his past self and more like an old giant with two busted knees and a sign on his back that reads "DFA Me." If nothing else, the injury ensured Hart's stint in Pittsburgh ended on a perfect note: a two-out, two-run homer in the ninth inning that... broke up a 9-0 shutout. Yup, perfect.

Ke'Bryan Hayes 3B

Born: 1/28/97 Age: 19 Bats: R Throws: R Height: 6'1" Weight: 210

YEAR	TEAM	LVL	AGE	PA	R	2B	3B	HR	RBI	BB	K	SB	CS	AVG/OBP/SLG	TAv	BABIP	BRR	FRAA	WARP
2015	WEV	A-	18	52	8	1	0	0	7	6	7	1	1	.220/.320/.244	.296	.250	-1.7	3B(12): 3.1	0.5
2016	*PIT*	*MLB*	*19*	*250*	*21*	*8*	*1*	*3*	*20*	*16*	*69*	*0*	*0*	*.204/.262/.289*	*.200*	*.270*	*-0.4*	*3B 4*	*-0.5*
2017	*PIT*	*MLB*	*20*	*361*	*36*	*13*	*1*	*6*	*33*	*22*	*95*	*0*	*0*	*.215/.270/.320*	*.219*	*.276*	*-0.7*	*3B 6*	*1.4*

Breakout: 0% Improve: 0% Collapse: 0% Attrition: 0% MLB: 0% *Comparables: Maikel Franco, Pablo Sandoval, Giovanny Urshela*

Hayes was the second of the Pirates' two first-round selections, and received consideration for the earlier pick. To paraphrase Cary Grant, you might say the sport doesn't run in his family so much as it gallops. Hayes' father, Charlie, played 14 seasons in the majors, while his older brother Tyree pitched in the minors for six seasons. This apple fell closer to the tree than Tyree did, since Ke'Bryan is an above-average defensive third baseman whose instincts and strong arm atone for his relative immobility (he's already a 30-grade runner). The key difference between father and son is at the plate: Charlie had a career .247 TAv, with some moments here and there, but the younger Hayes has the right approach and swing to project better. If it comes together, he's a starting third baseman.

Jung-ho Kang INF

Born: 4/5/87 Age: 29 Bats: R Throws: R Height: 6'0" Weight: 205

YEAR	TEAM	LVL	AGE	PA	R	2B	3B	HR	RBI	BB	K	SB	CS	AVG/OBP/SLG	TAv	BABIP	BRR	FRAA	WARP
2015	PIT	MLB	28	467	60	24	2	15	58	28	99	5	4	.287/.355/.461	.294	.344	1.7	3B(77): 5.3, SS(60): -8.6	3.2
2016	*PIT*	*MLB*	*29*	*472*	*58*	*22*	*2*	*15*	*57*	*30*	*102*	*5*	*3*	*.269/.334/.438*	*.274*	*.317*	*1.1*	*3B 6, SS -1*	*2.8*
2017	*PIT*	*MLB*	*30*	*325*	*40*	*16*	*1*	*10*	*39*	*21*	*71*	*3*	*2*	*.263/.329/.424*	*.276*	*.315*	*0.9*	*3B 4, SS -1*	*1.3*

Breakout: 3% Improve: 45% Collapse: 1% Attrition: 8% MLB: 98% *Comparables: Adrian Beltre, Ryan Zimmerman, Al Rosen*

In the eight-month period between Kang's signing and his season-ending disassembly—the one where Chris Coghlan tore Kang's meniscus, fractured his tibia and put his status for the beginning of 2016 in doubt—the conversation around him changed. What was once a discussion about whether the Pirates could afford to miss on the $11 million Korean import veered to the other extreme: Would his immediate success in the majors inflate the KBO market to the point that teams like Pittsburgh would be priced out of it? Before Kang went down, he was as instrumental as a Ratatat song, hitting for average, displaying a firm grip on the strike zone and showing pole-to-pole power—all while starting about an equal number of games at shortstop and third base. He resembled, in the simplest terms, a ready-made impact player who was signed through the rest of his prime at arbitration-level prices. Gold frenzies have started over less.

Starling Marte LF

Born: 10/9/88 Age: 27 Bats: R Throws: R Height: 6'1" Weight: 185

YEAR	TEAM	LVL	AGE	PA	R	2B	3B	HR	RBI	BB	K	SB	CS	AVG/OBP/SLG	TAv	BABIP	BRR	FRAA	WARP
2013	PIT	MLB	24	566	83	26	10	12	35	25	138	41	15	.280/.343/.441	.286	.363	3.1	LF(124): -4.2, CF(13): -0.3	2.7
2014	PIT	MLB	25	545	73	29	6	13	56	33	131	30	11	.291/.356/.453	.312	.373	1.5	LF(114): -6.5, CF(28): -2.9	3.3
2015	PIT	MLB	26	633	84	30	2	19	81	27	123	30	10	.287/.337/.444	.281	.333	-1.3	LF(141): -5.4, CF(18): 2.7	2.4
2016	*PIT*	*MLB*	*27*	*611*	*89*	*27*	*7*	*17*	*64*	*31*	*140*	*32*	*12*	*.276/.333/.445*	*.277*	*.336*	*0.3*	*LF -5, CF -2*	*2.3*
2017	*PIT*	*MLB*	*28*	*547*	*66*	*25*	*6*	*15*	*66*	*27*	*132*	*26*	*10*	*.268/.323/.432*	*.276*	*.330*	*1.4*	*LF -4, CF -2*	*1.0*

Breakout: 3% Improve: 54% Collapse: 4% Attrition: 5% MLB: 99% *Comparables: Carlos Gonzalez, Hunter Pence, Yoenis Cespedes*

The biggest drawback to Marte's game has always been his approach at the plate. The man loves to use his bat—so much so that in 2015 he led all National League hitters in both overall swing and chase rates. Predictably, Marte also posted the lowest walk rate of his career. If he could just become more disciplined at the plate, you think to yourself while watching him expand his zone time and again, he would be one of the best players in the majors. Be that as it may, Marte makes up for his excess swinging with one weird trick: getting struck by baseballs. With another 19 bruises in 2015, he pushed his three-year hit-by-pitch total to a majors-leading 60—*seven* more than the next-closest player, Shin-Soo Choo. Marte is already eighth on the Pirates' all-time HBP leaderboard, and he could, in theory, break Jason Kendall's franchise record (177) if his 20-per pace endures through the end of his contract. Seems unlikely, right? Agreed. Here's what's more likely: Marte continues to add more than enough value at the plate, in the field and on the basepaths to overshadow his flaw. He's not one of the game's best players, but he's close.

Andrew McCutchen CF

Born: 10/10/86 Age: 29 Bats: R Throws: R Height: 5'10" Weight: 200

YEAR	TEAM	LVL	AGE	PA	R	2B	3B	HR	RBI	BB	K	SB	CS	AVG/OBP/SLG	TAv	BABIP	BRR	FRAA	WARP
2013	PIT	MLB	26	674	97	38	5	21	84	78	101	27	10	.317/.404/.508	.330	.353	1.0	CF(155): -4.9	6.6
2014	PIT	MLB	27	648	89	38	6	25	83	84	115	18	3	.314/.410/.542	.350	.355	1.1	CF(146): -15.9	6.4
2015	PIT	MLB	28	685	91	36	3	23	96	98	133	11	5	.292/.401/.488	.326	.339	-1.9	CF(152): -16.9	4.8
2016	*PIT*	*MLB*	*29*	*652*	*92*	*32*	*4*	*25*	*92*	*81*	*120*	*16*	*6*	*.295/.390/.502*	*.312*	*.334*	*-0.4*	*CF -12*	*4.7*
2017	*PIT*	*MLB*	*30*	*570*	*82*	*28*	*3*	*20*	*77*	*71*	*106*	*13*	*5*	*.289/.385/.484*	*.315*	*.329*	*0.0*	*CF -10*	*0.7*

Breakout: 4% Improve: 60% Collapse: 1% Attrition: 4% MLB: 98% *Comparables: Frank Robinson, Hank Aaron, Willie Mays*

Our McCutchen comment in last year's Annual was brief enough that we can reproduce it here in its entirety: "Practically the perfect franchise player." If there is a downside to McCutchen's near-idealism, it's that we struggle to find new things to write about him. You can focus on his statistics (he narrowly missed pushing his streak of .300/.400/.500 seasons to four), but that doesn't do him justice. You can focus on the thoughtfulness he shows off the field (including his Players' Tribune article on Little League inequality), but this is a season-preview publication above all and there are certain expectations. So here's our prediction for McCutchen in 2016: He continues to earn kids' admiration for what he does on the field, and parents' for what he does off of it.

Reese McGuire C

Born: 3/2/95 Age: 21 Bats: L Throws: R Height: 6'0" Weight: 181

YEAR	TEAM	LVL	AGE	PA	R	2B	3B	HR	RBI	BB	K	SB	CS	AVG/OBP/SLG	TAv	BABIP	BRR	FRAA	WARP
2014	WVA	A	19	428	46	11	4	3	45	24	44	7	2	.262/.307/.334	.232	.284	0.2	C(84): 1.0	0.6
2015	BRD	A+	20	412	32	15	0	0	34	26	39	14	7	.254/.301/.294	.228	.280	-0.8	C(90): -1.5	0.1
2016	*PIT*	*MLB*	*21*	*250*	*20*	*9*	*1*	*3*	*21*	*10*	*43*	*3*	*1*	*.230/.263/.311*	*.204*	*.265*	*-0.2*	*C 0*	*-0.4*
2017	*PIT*	*MLB*	*22*	*333*	*32*	*13*	*1*	*4*	*29*	*15*	*51*	*4*	*2*	*.239/.276/.328*	*.221*	*.268*	*-0.2*	*C 0*	*1.4*

Breakout: 3% Improve: 5% Collapse: 2% Attrition: 4% MLB: 7% *Comparables: Ramon Cabrera, Rob Brantly, Juan Centeno*

Arguably the top catching prospect in the minors, McGuire showed even less offensive skill in his second full season than he did in his first. If those thoughts seem to clash, it's because there's a big part of the puzzle missing. Here's what a front-office member told Christopher Crawford in May: "He's a special defender. He could come up and hold his own defensively right now; I don't know how many teenagers you could ever say that about." Just what makes McGuire so danged catchy? The union of his strong arm, nimble feet and innate leadership skills. If only McGuire could lead his barrel to the ball—his offensive skill set is reminiscent of Austin Hedges' at the same age, and his High-A performance quite a bit worse. Most prospects fail.

Austin Meadows OF

Born: 5/3/95 Age: 21 Bats: L Throws: L Height: 6'3" Weight: 200

YEAR	TEAM	LVL	AGE	PA	R	2B	3B	HR	RBI	BB	K	SB	CS	AVG/OBP/SLG	TAv	BABIP	BRR	FRAA	WARP
2013	JAM	A-	18	22	8	0	0	2	2	5	4	0	0	.529/.636/.882	.506	.636	0.5	CF(5): 0.5	0.8
2014	WVA	A	19	167	18	13	1	3	15	14	30	2	3	.322/.388/.486	.293	.383	-0.3	CF(38): 1.1	1.2
2015	ALT	AA	20	28	5	2	3	0	1	2	5	1	0	.360/.429/.680	.375	.450	-0.2	CF(6): -0.3	0.4
2015	BRD	A+	20	556	72	22	4	7	54	41	79	20	7	.307/.357/.407	.289	.351	-0.1	CF(114): -15.2	1.8
2016	*PIT*	*MLB*	*21*	*250*	*26*	*11*	*2*	*6*	*27*	*15*	*56*	*4*	*2*	*.256/.305/.390*	*.245*	*.312*	*0.0*	*CF -3*	*0.1*
2017	*PIT*	*MLB*	*22*	*433*	*51*	*18*	*4*	*11*	*50*	*31*	*96*	*7*	*3*	*.268/.325/.418*	*.268*	*.324*	*0.3*	*CF -5, RF 0*	*0.8*

Breakout: 11% Improve: 22% Collapse: 1% Attrition: 9% MLB: 36% *Comparables: Christian Yelich, Joc Pederson, Gregory Polanco*

The Pirates re-routed their usual draft course when they selected a high schooler ninth overall in the 2013 draft, and so far that looks like a good call. In addition to reaching Double-A in his second full season, Meadows improved his career marks to .312/.380/.460. Oh, and he won't turn 21 until May, which makes him about three years younger than the Eastern League's average hitter was last year. Meadows has the tools to support his statistics, too: Scouts think he'll have a plus hit tool and enough glove to stick in center. His power remains more projection than production, but every indication is that he could become an every-day center fielder—likely in time to (STOP READING HERE, PIRATES FANS) replace Andrew McCutchen after the 2018 season.

Jordy Mercer SS

Born: 8/27/86 Age: 29 Bats: R Throws: R Height: 6'3" Weight: 205

YEAR	TEAM	LVL	AGE	PA	R	2B	3B	HR	RBI	BB	K	SB	CS	AVG/OBP/SLG	TAv	BABIP	BRR	FRAA	WARP
2013	IND	AAA	26	109	11	6	1	1	19	12	17	3	1	.333/.404/.448	.293	.392	-0.3	SS(23): 3.6, 2B(2): -0.1	1.2
2013	PIT	MLB	26	365	33	22	2	8	27	22	62	3	2	.285/.336/.435	.274	.330	-4.0	SS(78): -2.6, 2B(26): 3.6	1.6
2014	PIT	MLB	27	555	56	27	2	12	55	35	89	4	1	.255/.305/.387	.256	.285	3.9	SS(144): 10.5, RF(1): -0.0	3.7
2015	IND	AAA	28	26	3	0	0	1	3	1	5	0	0	.240/.269/.360	.240	.263	-0.2	SS(7): 0.5	0.1
2015	PIT	MLB	28	430	34	21	0	3	34	27	73	3	2	.244/.293/.320	.228	.290	2.1	SS(115): 2.8	0.9
2016	*PIT*	*MLB*	*29*	*540*	*56*	*27*	*2*	*11*	*55*	*35*	*95*	*4*	*2*	*.259/.312/.387*	*.248*	*.296*	*0.5*	*SS 4*	*2.5*
2017	*PIT*	*MLB*	*30*	*433*	*47*	*22*	*1*	*8*	*44*	*28*	*77*	*3*	*2*	*.255/.309/.378*	*.251*	*.293*	*0.4*	*SS 3*	*2.4*

Breakout: 2% Improve: 47% Collapse: 9% Attrition: 21% MLB: 97% *Comparables: Brendan Harris, Ronny Cedeno, Cliff Pennington*

He's everything they want, he's everything they need, he makes all the right plays, at exactly the right time, but he means nothing to them, and they don't know why. So goes the ballad of Mercer and the Pirates. He required parts of three seasons in Triple-A before he received a real look in the majors. Then, after bumping Clint Barmes aside and proving he could be an adequate starter in 2013 and 2014, Mercer entered 2015 facing the indignity of being the second-highest-paid shortstop on the roster, behind Kang. Mercer never got his wheels straight after the slight, and later missed a month due to a strained MCL, meaning he could no longer claim durability as a skill. This season will be a pivotal one for Mercer, who is now arbitration-eligible and shockingly close to his 30th birthday. Another clunker and his days as a starting shortstop could be over; another effort more in line with his previous two, though, and he'll probably find himself on a new team—one who we hope gives him the second-division-starter love he deserves.

Michael Morse 1B

Born: 3/22/82 Age: 34 Bats: R Throws: R Height: 6'5" Weight: 245

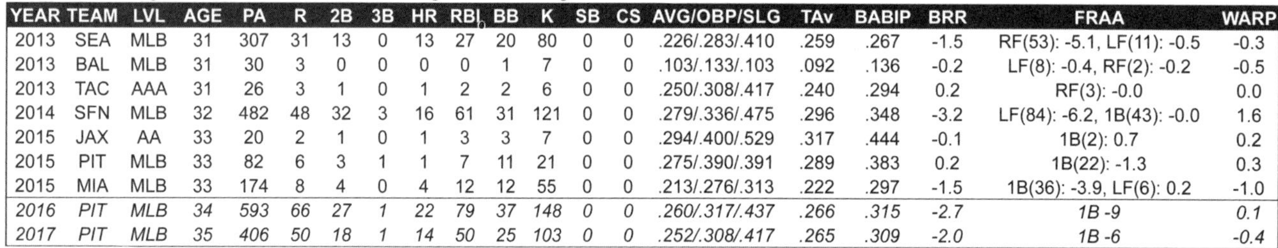

YEAR	TEAM	LVL	AGE	PA	R	2B	3B	HR	RBI	BB	K	SB	CS	AVG/OBP/SLG	TAv	BABIP	BRR	FRAA	WARP
2013	SEA	MLB	31	307	31	13	0	13	27	20	80	0	0	.226/.283/.410	.259	.267	-1.5	RF(53): -5.1, LF(11): -0.5	-0.3
2013	BAL	MLB	31	30	3	0	0	0	0	1	7	0	0	.103/.133/.103	.092	.136	-0.2	LF(8): -0.4, RF(2): -0.2	-0.5
2013	TAC	AAA	31	26	3	1	0	1	2	2	6	0	0	.250/.308/.417	.240	.294	0.2	RF(3): -0.0	0.0
2014	SFN	MLB	32	482	48	32	3	16	61	31	121	0	0	.279/.336/.475	.296	.348	-3.2	LF(84): -6.2, 1B(43): -0.0	1.6
2015	JAX	AA	33	20	2	1	0	1	3	3	7	0	0	.294/.400/.529	.317	.444	-0.1	1B(2): 0.7	0.2
2015	PIT	MLB	33	82	6	3	1	1	7	11	21	0	0	.275/.390/.391	.289	.383	0.2	1B(22): -1.3	0.3
2015	MIA	MLB	33	174	8	4	0	4	12	12	55	0	0	.213/.276/.313	.222	.297	-1.5	1B(36): -3.9, LF(6): 0.2	-1.0
2016	*PIT*	*MLB*	*34*	*593*	*66*	*27*	*1*	*22*	*79*	*37*	*148*	*0*	*0*	*.260/.317/.437*	*.266*	*.315*	*-2.7*	*1B -9*	*0.1*
2017	*PIT*	*MLB*	*35*	*406*	*50*	*18*	*1*	*14*	*50*	*25*	*103*	*0*	*0*	*.252/.308/.417*	*.265*	*.309*	*-2.0*	*1B -6*	*-0.4*

Breakout: 1% Improve: 32% Collapse: 9% Attrition: 20% MLB: 92% *Comparables: Nelson Cruz, Marcus Thames, Dmitri Young*

Give Morse credit for his favorable timing. He waited until *after* signing a two-year deal worth $16 million to suffer through the worst season of his career. The Marlins, optimistic about Justin Bour and always eager to shed an underwater contract, moved quickly to ship it to Los Angeles in the Mat Latos trade. Yes, "it"—Morse himself spent so little time in L.A. that he didn't even have time to see if the Jay Z song was on. The Dodgers spun him to the Pirates for Jose Tabata and *his* problematic contract. Finally able to set down roots in Pittsburgh, Morse played better in the Gaby Sanchez role than Sean Rodriguez and Corey Hart did, and carried the added bonus of looking as if he moonlighted on the set of *Black Sails*.

Kevin Newman SS

Born: 8/4/93 Age: 22 Bats: R Throws: R Height: 6'1" Weight: 180

YEAR	TEAM	LVL	AGE	PA	R	2B	3B	HR	RBI	BB	K	SB	CS	AVG/OBP/SLG	TAv	BABIP	BRR	FRAA	WARP
2015	WEV	A-	21	173	25	10	1	2	9	10	22	7	1	.226/.281/.340	.260	.252	-1.0	SS(38): -6.3	0.0
2015	WVA	A	21	110	14	4	1	0	8	9	8	6	1	.306/.376/.367	.289	.333	-0.4	SS(23): 0.4	0.8
2016	*PIT*	*MLB*	*22*	*250*	*23*	*10*	*1*	*4*	*22*	*12*	*52*	*4*	*1*	*.226/.270/.326*	*.213*	*.271*	*0.1*	*SS -1*	*-0.1*
2017	*PIT*	*MLB*	*23*	*350*	*35*	*14*	*1*	*5*	*32*	*18*	*68*	*6*	*2*	*.234/.281/.335*	*.227*	*.276*	*0.4*	*SS -2*	*1.5*

Breakout: 3% Improve: 8% Collapse: 3% Attrition: 9% MLB: 12% *Comparables: Christian Colon, Carlos Rivero, Chris Taylor*

Newman's professional debut didn't prove it, but the dude can hit. He was the first player in Cape Cod League history to win consecutive batting titles—a product of his disciplined approach and short, simple stroke—and his performance at the University of Arizona seduced many public analysts into ranking him higher than 19th, where the Pirates popped him. His one offensive shortcoming is power, since his swing plane is flat and he doesn't incorporate his lower half. That's okay, because he runs well and should add value on the basepaths. Factor in that scouts consider Newman sticky at shortstop, where the offensive bar is low to begin with, and he could develop into a first-division starter (and big-time draft-night steal) within the next few years.

Gregory Polanco RF

Born: 9/14/91 Age: 24 Bats: L Throws: L Height: 6'5" Weight: 230

YEAR	TEAM	LVL	AGE	PA	R	2B	3B	HR	RBI	BB	K	SB	CS	AVG/OBP/SLG	TAv	BABIP	BRR	FRAA	WARP
2013	BRD	A+	21	241	29	17	0	6	30	16	37	24	4	.312/.364/.472	.311	.350	1.3	CF(56): 0.5	2.3
2013	ALT	AA	21	286	36	13	2	6	41	36	36	13	7	.263/.354/.407	.286	.282	1.7	CF(58): 10.2, RF(6): -0.3	2.8
2014	IND	AAA	22	305	51	17	5	7	51	28	49	16	6	.328/.390/.504	.300	.377	0.7	RF(69): 10.2	3.1
2014	PIT	MLB	22	312	50	9	0	7	33	30	59	14	5	.235/.307/.343	.245	.272	2.3	RF(83): 10.8	1.5
2015	PIT	MLB	23	652	83	35	6	9	52	55	121	27	10	.256/.320/.381	.264	.308	1.3	RF(144): 11.1, LF(8): 0.2	2.8
2016	*PIT*	*MLB*	*24*	*644*	*77*	*30*	*4*	*14*	*68*	*54*	*118*	*27*	*10*	*.260/.323/.398*	*.257*	*.300*	*1.3*	*RF 9*	*2.4*
2017	*PIT*	*MLB*	*25*	*593*	*69*	*27*	*3*	*13*	*64*	*49*	*108*	*25*	*9*	*.259/.323/.395*	*.264*	*.299*	*2.4*	*RF 8*	*2.3*

Breakout: 5% Improve: 53% Collapse: 5% Attrition: 12% MLB: 96% *Comparables: Jose Tabata, Ryan Sweeney, Travis Buck*

Polanco is an anachronism in a generation honeycombed with instant superstars. Over his first season and a half in the bigs, he's followed the traditional, step-by-step maturation path, as opposed to the increasingly crowded shortcut taken by Trout, Harper, Machado and so on. That doesn't mean his progress is always steady and clean: He followed an outstanding August, in which he hit .330 with 10 extra-base knocks, with a brutal September. Nonetheless, it's impressive that Polanco held his own as a 23-year-old, and he's shown enough flashes to think he could still grow into the star many pegged him as during his prospect days. So far as that's concerned, his power could be the determinant. He's tall and long-levered, with well-above-average raw pop—observations that clash with his career .120 ISO, a figure more befitting a second baseman. Power is supposed to be the last thing that clicks in young big-league hitters; for Polanco's sake, here's hoping it does so soon, before folks begin lobbing words like "disappointment" his way.

Aramis Ramirez 3B

Born: 6/25/78 Age: 38 Bats: R Throws: R Height: 6'1" Weight: 205

YEAR	TEAM	LVL	AGE	PA	R	2B	3B	HR	RBI	BB	K	SB	CS	AVG/OBP/SLG	TAv	BABIP	BRR	FRAA	WARP
2013	MIL	MLB	35	351	43	18	0	12	49	36	55	0	1	.283/.370/.461	.288	.308	-2.8	3B(80): -13.1	0.4
2014	MIL	MLB	36	531	47	23	1	15	66	21	75	3	0	.285/.330/.427	.263	.310	-3.0	3B(126): -9.4	0.5
2015	PIT	MLB	37	214	18	13	1	6	33	15	26	0	0	.245/.299/.413	.248	.253	-0.2	3B(48): -2.4, 1B(5): 0.6	0.2
2015	MIL	MLB	37	302	25	18	0	11	42	16	42	1	0	.247/.295/.430	.251	.253	-1.4	3B(74): 2.3	0.8
2016	*PIT*	*MLB*	*38*	*489*	*54*	*26*	*1*	*15*	*61*	*29*	*68*	*2*	*1*	*.268/.323/.430*	*.265*	*.284*	*-2.1*	*3B -11, 1B 0*	*0.3*
2017	*PIT*	*MLB*	*39*	*378*	*44*	*19*	*0*	*11*	*44*	*21*	*55*	*1*	*0*	*.258/.309/.407*	*.261*	*.277*	*-1.8*	*3B -8, 1B 0*	*-0.2*

Breakout: 4% Improve: 18% Collapse: 1% Attrition: 10% MLB: 27% *Comparables: Jose Tabata, Jorge Soler, Billy Butler*

The golden age of piracy is believed to have lasted about 10 years, according to Colin Woodard's book on the subject. The golden age of Ramirez lasted about 12 years, beginning with his departure from the Pirates and ending just after his return at the deadline. It was nothing personal, Pittsburgh; Ramirez announced well before the trade was made that he intended to retire after the 2015 season. Who can blame him for feeling as if he'd accomplished all he could? Hanging around for an additional season or two wouldn't have nudged Ramirez any closer to Cooperstown—he lacks the numbers and the faux platitudes (e.g., "best third baseman of his generation")—meaning a ring was the only reward left for him to chase.

And chase he did. You know that saying about teaching old dogs new tricks? Turns out the secret is using a pennant race as bait. A career third baseman, Ramirez moved across the diamond for his first appearances at the cold corner; that and his willingness to partake in a team-wide costume party by dressing as a Ninja Turtle (Donatello, duh) are testaments to his unselfishness. Ramirez's gaudy career stats—at one point he finished with a better-than-average TAv in 12 consecutive years—are testaments to his remarkable talent. Dude could hit.

Harold Ramirez OF

Born: 9/6/94 Age: 21 Bats: R Throws: R Height: 5'10" Weight: 210

YEAR	TEAM	LVL	AGE	PA	R	2B	3B	HR	RBI	BB	K	SB	CS	AVG/OBP/SLG	TAv	BABIP	BRR	FRAA	WARP
2013	JAM	A-	18	310	42	11	4	5	40	23	52	23	11	.285/.354/.409	.293	.332	1.6	CF(31): -4.4, RF(22): 0.6	2.0
2014	WVA	A	19	226	30	14	1	1	24	11	35	12	3	.309/.364/.402	.283	.365	2.5	CF(24): 1.4, RF(23): -1.4	1.4
2015	BRD	A+	20	344	45	13	6	4	47	25	48	22	15	.337/.399/.458	.330	.385	-0.9	RF(72): 3.5, CF(1): -0.1	3.5
2016	*PIT*	*MLB*	*21*	*250*	*27*	*10*	*2*	*4*	*24*	*12*	*55*	*8*	*5*	*.253/.301/.366*	*.240*	*.311*	*-0.2*	*RF 1, LF 0*	*0.2*
2017	*PIT*	*MLB*	*22*	*378*	*43*	*17*	*3*	*8*	*41*	*22*	*81*	*13*	*8*	*.267/.322/.403*	*.266*	*.322*	*0.6*	*RF 1, LF 0*	*1.0*

Breakout: 4% Improve: 18% Collapse: 1% Attrition: 10% MLB: 27% *Comparables: Jose Tabata, Jorge Soler, Billy Butler*

Ramirez was born 17 days before *The Shawshank Redemption* hit theaters. Hope is a dangerous thing. Hope can drive a man insane. But how can you look at Ramirez—complete with his simple swing, high-contact ways and plus speed—and avoid feeling it? Here's how: by focusing on his negatives. Ramirez doesn't have the chops for center field, nor the arm for right. That leaves him out in left, where his fringe-average power is an awkward fit. In theory, Ramirez's speed could atone for his lacking pop; then again, *in theory* his speed could dissipate quicker than the normal player's due to his thick lower half. See why hope is a dangerous thing? See how hope can drive a man insane? As soon as you find it, you start worrying about losing it.

Sean Rodriguez UT

Born: 4/26/85 Age: 31 Bats: R Throws: R Height: 6'0" Weight: 200

YEAR	TEAM	LVL	AGE	PA	R	2B	3B	HR	RBI	BB	K	SB	CS	AVG/OBP/SLG	TAv	BABIP	BRR	FRAA	WARP
2013	TBA	MLB	28	222	21	10	1	5	23	17	59	1	3	.246/.320/.385	.272	.323	-0.3	LF(47): 0.0, 1B(23): 0.7	0.8
2014	TBA	MLB	29	259	30	13	3	12	41	10	66	2	1	.211/.258/.443	.260	.235	-1.4	2B(23): -0.7, 1B(18): 0.5	0.1
2015	PIT	MLB	30	240	25	12	1	4	17	5	63	2	2	.246/.281/.362	.230	.325	2.2	1B(102): -0.8, LF(16): -1.8	-0.4
2016	*PIT*	*MLB*	*31*	*170*	*18*	*8*	*1*	*4*	*18*	*11*	*39*	*2*	*1*	*.234/.300/.375*	*.240*	*.282*	*0.1*	*LF -0, 2B 1*	*0.3*
2017	*PIT*	*MLB*	*32*	*222*	*25*	*9*	*1*	*5*	*23*	*15*	*53*	*2*	*1*	*.223/.294/.360*	*.242*	*.269*	*0.3*	*LF 0, 2B 1*	*0.7*

Breakout: 0% Improve: 49% Collapse: 5% Attrition: 5% MLB: 90% *Comparables: Bob Horner, Cesar Cedeno, Joe Collins*

Owning your power is a vague concept that has been preached by seemingly everyone over the years, from shamans to Buck O'Neil. Rodriguez seemed to figure out the nuances of power ownership in 2014, as he finished second on the Rays in home runs and posted a career-best .232 ISO—attributes that, when paired with his defensive versatility and baseball acumen (he's a coach's son) made him an attractive little utility player. The Pirates were so intrigued by him that they gave up a decent pitching prospect to gain a year of his services. Good idea, bad results. While Rodriguez's power proved to be a one-year fluke, his approach continued to decay, as he swung more often and made contact less often. If you want to know why he does his best work against lefties, take note of the fact he whiffed on nearly half the swings he took on breaking balls—fueling a career-low walk-to-strikeout ratio that doubled as one of the worst marks in the majors. Even his versatility and baseball IQ went for naught, as he spent most of his time at first base, usually as a late-inning replacement. Perhaps Rodriguez needs a refresher course on what it means to own his power, because he's a much better player than he showed in Pittsburgh.

Chris Stewart C

Born: 2/19/82 Age: 34 Bats: R Throws: R Height: 6'4" Weight: 210

YEAR	TEAM	LVL	AGE	PA	R	2B	3B	HR	RBI	BB	K	SB	CS	AVG/OBP/SLG	TAv	BABIP	BRR	FRAA	WARP
2013	NYA	MLB	31	340	28	6	0	4	25	30	49	4	0	.211/.293/.272	.219	.237	-2.7	C(108): 21.2, 1B(2): -0.0	2.1
2014	PIT	MLB	32	154	9	5	0	0	10	12	27	0	1	.294/.362/.331	.261	.364	0.1	C(46): 4.5	1.2
2015	PIT	MLB	33	172	9	8	0	0	15	6	29	0	0	.289/.320/.340	.243	.348	0.2	C(52): 6.6	1.2
2016	*PIT*	*MLB*	*34*	*125*	*11*	*5*	*0*	*1*	*10*	*9*	*19*	*1*	*0*	*.243/.306/.313*	*.225*	*.276*	*-0.4*	*C 5*	*0.7*
2017	*PIT*	*MLB*	*35*	*129*	*12*	*5*	*0*	*1*	*10*	*9*	*20*	*0*	*0*	*.236/.296/.300*	*.221*	*.269*	*-0.4*	*C 6*	*1.1*

Breakout: 0% Improve: 27% Collapse: 13% Attrition: 20% MLB: 84% *Comparables: Gerald Laird, Jim Essian, Del Crandall*

YEAR	TEAM	P. COUNT	FRM RUNS	BLK RUNS	THRW RUNS	TOT RUNS
2013	NYA	13789	19.9	0.2	0.3	20.4
2014	PIT	5743	4.7	0.0	-0.3	4.4
2015	PIT	5779	6.7	0.0	-0.5	6.2
2016	*PIT*	*4815*	*5.3*	*0.0*	*-0.1*	*5.2*
2017	*PIT*	*4966*	*5.2*	*0.0*	*-0.2*	*5.0*

Stewart is a daguerreotype backup catcher: He can't hit anything except singles, and his livelihood hinges on his defensive talents—which usually means, to paraphrase One Republic: "He'll be doing this, if you ever doubt, 'til the glove runs out, 'til the glove runs out." Unfortunately, the glove might be running out. Stewart's soft hands and strong arm tend to make him a defensive asset. However, in 2015, he committed a career-high nine errors—almost all of the throwing variety. His framing is still good, but by our metrics has slid closer to average in each of the past four years. Teams will tolerate a one-dimensional player so long as that one dimension is good, but Stewart is in danger of becoming a half-dimensional player.

Cole Tucker SS

Born: 7/3/96 Age: 19 Bats: B Throws: R Height: 6'3" Weight: 185

YEAR	TEAM	LVL	AGE	PA	R	2B	3B	HR	RBI	BB	K	SB	CS	AVG/OBP/SLG	TAv	BABIP	BRR	FRAA	WARP
2015	WVA	A	18	329	46	13	3	2	25	16	49	25	6	.293/.322/.377	.269	.336	3.0	SS(68): 2.9	2.3
2016	*PIT*	*MLB*	*19*	*250*	*28*	*10*	*1*	*4*	*18*	*8*	*58*	*9*	*3*	*.230/.258/.325*	*.206*	*.284*	*0.7*	*SS -0*	*-0.1*
2017	*PIT*	*MLB*	*20*	*386*	*37*	*14*	*2*	*6*	*36*	*13*	*83*	*15*	*5*	*.241/.268/.344*	*.222*	*.288*	*1.9*	*SS 0*	*1.9*

Breakout: 0% Improve: 0% Collapse: 0% Attrition: 0% MLB: 0% *Comparables: Eduardo Nunez, Carlos Triunfel, Jonathan Schoop*

It's a good thing Tucker is believed to feature more makeup than a Robert Palmer video, because he'll need that work ethic to fully recover from the shoulder surgery he underwent in August—an operation that is expected to cost him most of, if not the entire 2016 season. The biggest problem with Tucker's game is that every gain has an obvious drawback. He's rawboned to the point where he projects as a slap hitter whose average must stay high to outpace its emptiness; yet bulking up would likely diminish his above-average speed and range, perhaps costing him a future at shortstop. Ideally, Tucker finds the sweet spot between each extreme. But say he doesn't—then what is he? A second-division shortstop? A second or third baseman? A utilityman? A good friend you keep in touch with for years after he's released? Check back in 2018 for the answer.

PITCHERS

Antonio Bastardo LHP

Born: 9/21/85 Age: 30 Bats: R Throws: L Height: 5'11" Weight: 205

YEAR	TEAM	LVL	AGE	W	L	SV	G	GS	IP	H	HR	BB/9	K/9	GB%	BABIP	WHIP	ERA	FIP	DRA	WARP	CFIP	MPH
2013	PHI	MLB	27	3	2	2	48	0	42^{2}	33	2	4.4	9.9	36%	.287	1.27	2.32	2.97	2.87	0.9	92	94.1
2014	PHI	MLB	28	5	7	0	67	0	64	43	4	4.8	11.4	32%	.260	1.20	3.94	3.07	3.36	0.9	87	94.2
2015	PIT	MLB	29	4	1	1	66	0	57^{1}	39	4	4.1	10.0	34%	.246	1.13	2.98	3.35	2.85	1.3	89	95.3
2016	*PIT*	*MLB*	*30*	*3*	*1*	*0*	*52*	*0*	*55*	*43*	*6*	*3.5*	*9.6*	*34%*	*.284*	*1.17*	*3.66*	*3.60*	*4.28*	*0.4*	*96*	
2017	*PIT*	*MLB*	*31*	*3*	*1*	*0*	*57*	*0*	49^{2}	*40*	*6*	*3.7*	*9.7*	*34%*	*.288*	*1.20*	*3.87*	*4.17*	*4.52*	*0.2*	*102*	

Breakout: 24% Improve: 42% Collapse: 34% Attrition: 10% MLB: 93% *Comparables: Francisco Rodriguez, Ryne Duren, Hong-Chih Kuo*

Despite an offseason trade that shipped him across Pennsylvania, the pitcher whose name most sounds like a Danny Trejo character had another typical season. Bastardo is what they call effectively wild: He'll walk four or five batters per nine and post one of the league's highest flyball rates, but he's also an uncomfortable at-bat for righties (against whom he has one of the league's highest HBP rates) and lefties alike. So those walks come with strikeouts; those flyballs don't turn into homers. Bastardo doesn't fit in any specific role—he's not a LOOGY, nor is he quite a high-leverage reliever—yet he should continue to provide value in middle relief for as long as he can miss barrels and, occasionally, miss up and in.

Joe Blanton RHP

Born: 12/11/80 Age: 35 Bats: R Throws: R Height: 6'3" Weight: 215

YEAR	TEAM	LVL	AGE	W	L	SV	G	GS	IP	H	HR	BB/9	K/9	GB%	BABIP	WHIP	ERA	FIP	DRA	WARP	CFIP	MPH
2013	ANA	MLB	32	2	14	0	28	20	132^{2}	180	29	2.3	7.3	45%	.346	1.61	6.04	5.15	6.30	-2.3	110	92.0
2014	SAC	AAA	33	1	0	0	2	2	10^{2}	13	1	2.5	8.4	36%	.375	1.50	5.06	3.89	5.05	0.1	91	
2015	OMA	AAA	34	3	2	0	7	6	39^{1}	34	7	2.3	6.9	42%	.239	1.12	3.89	5.30	4.54	0.4	96	
2015	KCA	MLB	34	2	2	2	15	4	41^{2}	43	6	1.5	8.6	50%	.311	1.20	3.89	3.56	4.83	0.0	89	93.2
2015	PIT	MLB	34	5	0	0	21	0	34^{1}	26	1	2.4	10.2	50%	.287	1.02	1.57	2.14	2.05	1.1	68	93.1
2016	*PIT*	*MLB*	*35*	*3*	*1*	*0*	*52*	*0*	*55*	*55*	*7*	*2.2*	*7.9*	*46%*	*.319*	*1.25*	*3.77*	*3.82*	*4.40*	*0.6*	*99*	
2017	*PIT*	*MLB*	*36*	*9*	*9*	*1*	*39*	*23*	172^{2}	*176*	*23*	*2.3*	*8.2*	*46%*	*.327*	*1.28*	*3.86*	*4.17*	*4.50*	*1.4*	*101*	

Breakout: 11% Improve: 37% Collapse: 14% Attrition: 6% MLB: 80% *Comparables: Chris Capuano, Mickey Lolich, Harvey Haddix*

We're as uncomfortable with this as anyone. Imagine reading in last year's book that Blanton—most recently seen in 2013, when he compiled an ERA higher than Wiz Khalifa's plane—would return and play a pivotal role in a contender's bullpen. You'd have shouted "Tommyrot!" and thrown the book aside. Yet that's what happened. Blanton joined the Pirates in July after an unheralded trade, trimmed his arsenal (more sliders and fewer curveballs) and looked like a different pitcher—maybe because he was. Studies on near-death experiences have shown that those who have them become lighter in heart and soul. To our knowledge, nobody has ever done a study on the effects of near-retirement experiences to see if there's a similar effect, but maybe someone should. Consider pitching guru Jim Benedict a believer—here's what he told David Todd about Blanton: "It's not uncommon for guys who do come back, they go into the bullpen, they're ultra-aggressive, they've already ended it, they're just starting a new chapter."

A.J. Burnett RHP

Born: 1/3/77 Age: 39 Bats: R Throws: R Height: 6'4" Weight: 230

YEAR	TEAM	LVL	AGE	W	L	SV	G	GS	IP	H	HR	BB/9	K/9	GB%	BABIP	WHIP	ERA	FIP	DRA	WARP	CFIP	MPH
2013	PIT	MLB	36	10	11	0	30	30	191	165	11	3.2	9.8	59%	.305	1.21	3.30	2.77	3.84	2.5	81	95.1
2014	PHI	MLB	37	8	18	0	34	34	213^{2}	205	20	4.0	8.0	53%	.302	1.41	4.59	4.11	4.44	0.9	114	94.4
2015	PIT	MLB	38	9	7	0	26	26	164	174	11	2.7	7.8	55%	.336	1.36	3.18	3.39	4.52	1.0	100	93.6
2016	*PIT*	*MLB*	*39*	*9*	*8*	*0*	*23*	*23*	146^{1}	*140*	*15*	*3.1*	*7.9*	*55%*	*.317*	*1.31*	*3.84*	*3.83*	*4.47*	*1.4*	*103*	
2017	*PIT*	*MLB*	*40*	*8*	*8*	*0*	*21*	*21*	123^{2}	*121*	*14*	*3.1*	*8.1*	*55%*	*.323*	*1.33*	*3.94*	*4.26*	*4.59*	*1.1*	*106*	

Breakout: 10% Improve: 33% Collapse: 14% Attrition: 5% MLB: 65% *Comparables: Chuck Finley, Jerry Koosman, Andy Pettitte*

What do you get someone like Burnett for a retirement gift? The Pirates settled on a Batman-themed ATV. The Bat was a fixture during Burnett's two tours in Pittsburgh. When he returned from the disabled list in September, he did so underneath a skyline adorned with bat signals—yes, really—and when the Pirates asked him to design a giveaway t-shirt, he put his name in the shape of the Caped Crusader's logo. Last one: When Burnett went to the All-Star Game (which he regrettably failed to enter), he wore Batman-decorated cleats.

Fittingy, Burnett was the Pirates' Dark Knight. Despite promising he would choose between the Buccos and his kiddos after the 2013 season, he bolted across state for one last payday, later expressing frustration with the Pirates over their negotiation tactics. A year away was enough to melt his heart, as he declined his player option (worth nearly $13 million) and returned to a hero's welcome. Alas, no human can fight crime or throw pitches forever. Burnett retired last winter after 17 seasons—some sensational, but most of which left onlookers puzzled or disappointed—and you get the sense the three he spent in Pittsburgh will be the ones he thinks about when he's cruising around wherever he calls Gotham.

Arquimedes Caminero RHP

Born: 6/16/87 Age: 29 Bats: R Throws: R Height: 6'4" Weight: 245

YEAR	TEAM	LVL	AGE	W	L	SV	G	GS	IP	H	HR	BB/9	K/9	GB%	BABIP	WHIP	ERA	FIP	DRA	WARP	CFIP	MPH
2013	JAX	AA	26	5	2	5	42	0	52^{1}	34	4	3.6	11.7	36%	.261	1.05	3.61	2.68	3.45	0.6	80	
2013	MIA	MLB	26	0	0	0	13	0	13	10	2	2.1	8.3	25%	.235	1.00	2.77	4.10	3.30	0.2	96	98.4
2014	MIA	MLB	27	0	1	0	6	0	6^{2}	8	2	5.4	10.8	37%	.353	1.80	10.80	6.40	7.95	-0.3	101	98.2
2014	NWO	AAA	27	4	1	10	42	0	63	70	7	4.3	11.3	41%	.362	1.59	4.86	4.40	5.05	0.3	90	
2015	PIT	MLB	28	5	1	0	73	0	74^{2}	63	7	3.5	8.8	48%	.276	1.23	3.62	3.83	3.87	0.7	101	100.8
2016	*PIT*	*MLB*	*29*	*3*	*1*	*0*	*54*	*0*	57^{2}	*52*	*6*	*3.3*	*8.4*	*45%*	*.307*	*1.27*	*3.87*	*3.80*	*4.50*	*0.3*	*102*	
2017	*PIT*	*MLB*	*30*	*2*	*1*	*0*	*41*	*0*	*49*	*43*	*6*	*3.7*	*9.2*	*45%*	*.309*	*1.29*	*3.87*	*4.18*	*4.50*	*0.2*	*102*	

Breakout: 23% Improve: 43% Collapse: 13% Attrition: 22% MLB: 70% *Comparables: Fernando Rodney, Derrick Turnbow, Jason Frasor*

Equipped with a million-dollar name and an arm to match, Caminero was purchased from the Marlins in February. His lack of minor-league options proved irrelevant, as he showed enough potential in camp to stick on the active roster all season long. Caminero's signature pitch remained his fastball, which clocked in at an average 98.9 mph—the second-hottest among big-league relievers, behind some guy with the same initials—yet his improvements were rooted in his improved control and arsenal depth. His walk rate was the lowest it had been since 2013, when he was in Double-A, and his increased emphasis on his cutter and splitter palliated his predictability when he did fall behind. None of it made Caminero the perfect reliever—he was too prone to the long ball for someone with his brand of gas—but read the second part of the first sentence again. Caminero turning into a workable middle reliever is a big win.

Gerrit Cole RHP

Born: 9/8/90 Age: 25 Bats: R Throws: R Height: 6'4" Weight: 230

YEAR	TEAM	LVL	AGE	W	L	SV	G	GS	IP	H	HR	BB/9	K/9	GB%	BABIP	WHIP	ERA	FIP	DRA	WARP	CFIP	MPH
2013	IND	AAA	22	5	3	0	12	12	68	44	4	3.7	6.2	50%	.216	1.06	2.91	4.00	4.55	0.4	107	
2013	PIT	MLB	22	10	7	0	19	19	117^{1}	109	7	2.1	7.7	51%	.308	1.17	3.22	2.88	3.69	1.7	92	99.4
2014	PIT	MLB	23	11	5	0	22	22	138	127	11	2.6	9.0	52%	.311	1.21	3.65	3.20	4.18	1.0	91	98.5
2014	IND	AAA	23	3	1	0	4	4	22^{1}	21	1	2.0	6.4	51%	.294	1.16	2.01	3.31	4.44	0.2	98	
2015	PIT	MLB	24	19	8	0	32	32	208	183	11	1.9	8.7	49%	.304	1.09	2.60	2.69	3.33	4.2	82	98.6
2016	*PIT*	*MLB*	*25*	*12*	*9*	*0*	*31*	*31*	*186*	*163*	*17*	*2.2*	*8.4*	*50%*	*.306*	*1.12*	*3.24*	*3.22*	*3.80*	*3.3*	*84*	
2017	*PIT*	*MLB*	*26*	*11*	*9*	*0*	*30*	*30*	189^{1}	*166*	*18*	*1.9*	*8.9*	*50%*	*.311*	*1.09*	*3.13*	*3.36*	*3.67*	*3.4*	*80*	

Breakout: 24% Improve: 60% Collapse: 19% Attrition: 13% MLB: 96% *Comparables: Rich Harden, David Price, Daniel Hudson*

Last year in this space, we wrote that Cole wasn't "in the same class as Matt Harvey and Jose Fernandez just yet." Now he is. Cole put together the finest season of his still-young career, topping 200 innings for the first time and producing new career-best marks in every one-stop pitching metric known to man (and presumably some known only to apes). How did he make the leap? According to Travis Sawchik of the *Pittsburgh Tribune-Review*, Cole placed greater emphasis on taking care of his body. That meant embracing the ancient technique of "cupping," as well as using data collected by a BioHarness—a strap that tracks heart rate and other physiological metrics. Cole has always had the power stuff to be a front-of-the-rotation pitcher, and if his newfound attention to detail proves legitimate, this is the beginning of an era of dominance.

Tyler Glasnow RHP

Born: 8/23/93 Age: 22 Bats: L Throws: R Height: 6'8" Weight: 225

YEAR	TEAM	LVL	AGE	W	L	SV	G	GS	IP	H	HR	BB/9	K/9	GB%	BABIP	WHIP	ERA	FIP	DRA	WARP	CFIP	MPH
2013	WVA	A	19	9	3	0	24	24	111^1	54	9	4.9	13.3	50%	.215	1.03	2.18	3.47	4.08	1.3	88	
2014	BRD	A+	20	12	5	0	23	23	124^1	74	3	4.1	11.4	40%	.260	1.05	1.74	2.63	3.53	2.1	73	
2015	IND	AAA	21	2	1	0	8	8	41	33	1	4.8	10.5	39%	.314	1.34	2.20	2.82	3.49	0.6	92	
2015	ALT	AA	21	5	3	0	12	12	63	41	2	2.7	11.7	42%	.269	0.95	2.43	1.98	1.39	2.6	61	
2016	*PIT*	*MLB*	*22*	*2*	*1*	*0*	*5*	*5*	*25*	*19*	*2*	*3.7*	*9.9*	*38%*	*.292*	*1.19*	*3.46*	*3.24*	*4.05*	*0.4*	*90*	
2017	*PIT*	*MLB*	*23*	*3*	*3*	*0*	*11*	*11*	63^1	*48*	*7*	*4.0*	*10.3*	*38%*	*.290*	*1.21*	*3.68*	*3.96*	*4.31*	*0.6*	*98*	

Breakout: 15% Improve: 22% Collapse: 22% Attrition: 23% MLB: 57% *Comparables: Henry Owens, Tommy Hanson, Keyvius Sampson*

With so many of the Pirates' other heralded arms missing action due to injury, it was only right that Glasnow joined them by sitting out a month with a sprained ankle. When his Double-A season resumed, he went on a rampage, striking out 53 batters in 33 innings while allowing one home run. Glasnow was promptly promoted to Indianapolis, though regrettably, he forgot to bring his newfound understanding of the strike zone with him, culminating in a brutal late-season effort in which he tallied five times as many free passes (five) as he did outs (one). Glasnow responded to that mess by pitching into the eighth inning and not surrendering a walk in his final start of the season—both Triple-A firsts. Glasnow's stuff is of a high enough quality—his fastball and curve both grade as plus or better offerings—that he doesn't need eye-drop precision to succeed. Still, it wouldn't hurt for him to spend a full season in Triple-A before joining the middle of the big-league rotation for the long haul.

John Holdzkom RHP

Born: 10/19/87 Age: 28 Bats: R Throws: R Height: 6'9" Weight: 245

YEAR	TEAM	LVL	AGE	W	L	SV	G	GS	IP	H	HR	BB/9	K/9	GB%	BABIP	WHIP	ERA	FIP	DRA	WARP	CFIP	MPH
2014	IND	AAA	26	2	0	2	18	0	21^2	14	1	4.2	11.2	47%	.260	1.11	2.49	2.99	4.10	0.2	84	
2014	PIT	MLB	26	1	0	1	9	0	9	4	1	2.0	14.0	44%	.200	0.67	2.00	2.10	0.65	0.4	79	97.6
2015	IND	AAA	27	2	0	2	21	0	22^1	16	0	6.9	10.9	50%	.296	1.48	3.22	3.16	4.03	0.1	98	
2016	*PIT*	*MLB*	*28*	*2*	*1*	*0*	*30*	*0*	31^1	*26*	*3*	*3.7*	*8.9*	*47%*	*.301*	*1.25*	*3.66*	*3.65*	*4.25*	*0.3*	*96*	
2017	*PIT*	*MLB*	*29*	*2*	*1*	*3*	*36*	*0*	*41*	*34*	*4*	*4.0*	*9.5*	*47%*	*.307*	*1.28*	*3.77*	*4.07*	*4.38*	*0.2*	*100*	

Breakout: 14% Improve: 16% Collapse: 16% Attrition: 22% MLB: 41% *Comparables: Allan Simpson, Josh Fields, Jess Todd*

When Holdzkom's teammates dubbed him "Sasquatch" in 2014, they had no way of knowing how well the nickname would fit him during the subsequent season. The same onlookers taken by Holdzkom's brilliant big-league cameo—a nine-inning sprint that saw him dominate hitters with little more than a mid-90s cutter—were invariably disappointed by a follow-up effort that saw his command and health prove as elusive as his namesake. He opened 2015 in Indianapolis, walked 13 batters in 11 innings, then sat a month with shoulder fatigue. Holdzkom's control seemed restored upon his return (he walked two and held batters to a .332 OPS in 10 innings), but then his tired shoulder needed *another* nap. He returned in July and repeated the cycle, this time disappearing until September, when he made one last comeback try—a failed effort that cemented 2015 as a lost year. Holdzkom will need his control and health to play nice in 2016; otherwise, folks will begin to question whether his proverbial emergence from the woods was the product of a hoax or fever dream.

Jared Hughes RHP

Born: 7/4/85 Age: 30 Bats: R Throws: R Height: 6'7" Weight: 245

YEAR	TEAM	LVL	AGE	W	L	SV	G	GS	IP	H	HR	BB/9	K/9	GB%	BABIP	WHIP	ERA	FIP	DRA	WARP	CFIP	MPH
2013	PIT	MLB	27	2	3	0	29	0	32	37	2	4.5	6.5	58%	.333	1.66	4.78	4.08	5.99	-0.5	116	94.0
2013	IND	AAA	27	1	0	2	18	1	21	17	0	3.0	7.7	67%	.293	1.14	0.43	2.63	4.05	0.2	90	
2014	PIT	MLB	28	7	5	0	63	0	64^1	51	4	2.7	5.0	66%	.246	1.09	1.96	3.96	3.40	0.9	113	94.7
2015	PIT	MLB	29	3	1	0	76	0	67	70	3	2.6	4.8	65%	.306	1.33	2.28	3.83	4.75	0.0	120	95.2
2016	*PIT*	*MLB*	*30*	*3*	*1*	*1*	*59*	*0*	62^2	*61*	*7*	*2.9*	*5.7*	*64%*	*.294*	*1.29*	*4.25*	*4.32*	*4.95*	*0.0*	*114*	
2017	*PIT*	*MLB*	*31*	*3*	*1*	*1*	*57*	*0*	58^2	*58*	*6*	*2.8*	*6.0*	*64%*	*.303*	*1.30*	*4.16*	*4.53*	*4.85*	*0.0*	*111*	

Breakout: 29% Improve: 51% Collapse: 19% Attrition: 23% MLB: 79% *Comparables: Ryan Mattheus, Javier Lopez, Brandon Medders*

"You seek problems because you need their gifts," wrote Richard Bach. Hughes can relate. His strikeout rate peaked years ago, and in 2015 achieved a spareness that put him in company with Burke Badenhop and Blaine Boyer—who, alliterative names aside, aren't the kind of fellas you wanna hang with when you're years away from free agency. Hughes' inability to rack up strikeouts is a problem, albeit one he seeks by throwing his two-seam fastball close to 80 percent of the time. What gift does he receive in return? A discount rate on double plays. Over the past two seasons, Hughes has succeeded in extirpating twins in about 20 percent of his double-play opportunities—the league-average mark is barely half that. Throwing strikes, keeping the ball within the playing field and turning two more often than a blackjack dealer—yeah, that works, that works just fine for now.

Francisco Liriano LHP

Born: 10/26/83 Age: 32 Bats: L Throws: L Height: 6'2" Weight: 225

YEAR	TEAM	LVL	AGE	W	L	SV	G	GS	IP	H	HR	BB/9	K/9	GB%	BABIP	WHIP	ERA	FIP	DRA	WARP	CFIP	MPH
2013	PIT	MLB	29	16	8	0	26	26	161	134	9	3.5	9.1	52%	.290	1.22	3.02	2.90	3.53	2.7	85	95.5
2013	IND	AAA	29	2	0	0	3	3	16	15	1	0.6	12.9	54%	.350	1.00	3.38	1.52	3.31	0.3	64	
2014	PIT	MLB	30	7	10	0	29	29	162^1	130	13	4.5	9.7	57%	.280	1.30	3.38	3.56	3.99	1.6	93	95.3
2015	PIT	MLB	31	12	7	0	31	31	186^2	155	15	3.4	9.9	54%	.293	1.21	3.38	3.22	3.72	2.9	86	95.4
2016	*PIT*	*MLB*	*32*	*12*	*9*	*0*	*31*	*31*	176^2	*145*	*18*	*3.3*	*9.5*	*54%*	*.300*	*1.19*	*3.47*	*3.46*	*4.05*	*2.6*	*91*	
2017	*PIT*	*MLB*	*33*	*10*	*10*	*0*	*29*	*29*	*178*	*150*	*19*	*3.3*	*9.3*	*54%*	*.304*	*1.21*	*3.60*	*3.87*	*4.20*	*2.1*	*95*	

Breakout: 13% Improve: 44% Collapse: 22% Attrition: 7% MLB: 92% *Comparables: Nolan Ryan, A.J. Burnett, Jose Contreras*

Liriano looked like a goner entering last offseason. He was safely ensconced in the second tier of free-agent starting pitchers—a status that seemed to ensure a better payday than the low-budget Pirates could afford to offer or match. Yet somehow they retained Liriano, snagging him in mid-December on a three-year deal worth $39 million—an AAV that checks in lower than the qualifying offer. Liriano rewarded their investment by pitching as well as he did in 2013 (when he earned down-ballot Cy Young votes), and by making more than 30 starts for the first time since 2010. He still didn't top 200 innings—check last year's Annual for more context on that—but you know it's all good when the point of contention hinges on an arbitrary round number. With two years to go, the Liriano Deal sequel looks almost as good as the original.

Radhames Liz RHP

Born: 10/6/83 Age: 32 Bats: R Throws: R Height: 6'2" Weight: 200

YEAR	TEAM	LVL	AGE	W	L	SV	G	GS	IP	H	HR	BB/9	K/9	GB%	BABIP	WHIP	ERA	FIP	DRA	WARP	CFIP	MPH
2014	BUF	AAA	30	1	0	0	4	4	19	21	3	6.2	5.2	45%	.316	1.79	5.21	6.46	5.29	0.0	126	
2014	NHP	AA	30	2	2	0	8	8	42	32	0	2.4	7.1	44%	.269	1.02	1.93	2.93	4.26	0.4	92	
2015	IND	AAA	31	4	5	0	16	10	64^1	44	0	3.4	10.4	43%	.272	1.06	1.40	2.21	2.05	2.1	74	
2015	PIT	MLB	31	1	4	0	14	0	23^1	26	4	4.6	10.4	39%	.367	1.63	4.24	5.00	6.52	-0.5	102	98.9
2016	*PIT*	*MLB*	*32*	*5*	*4*	*0*	*27*	*11*	*74*	*65*	*7*	*3.2*	*8.2*	*40%*	*.305*	*1.24*	*3.73*	*3.69*	*4.34*	*0.8*	*98*	
2017	*PIT*	*MLB*	*33*	*4*	*5*	*0*	*26*	*13*	*97*	*90*	*12*	*3.3*	*8.3*	*40%*	*.312*	*1.30*	*4.11*	*4.43*	*4.78*	*0.4*	*110*	

Breakout: 10% Improve: 15% Collapse: 8% Attrition: 15% MLB: 33% *Comparables: Matt Kinney, Kei Igawa, Les Walrond*

Signed for $1 million following an impressive, improbable stint in Korea, Liz opened the season in the bullpen, where his power arsenal lent itself to high-leverage dreams. He then allowed the winning run in his first appearance, and from there on was used as rarely as good China, but in paper-plate leverage. He was designated for assignment in May, after which he headed to the minors. While in Indianapolis, Liz tweaked his mechanics and enjoyed a run of success as a starter. The Pirates brought him back to the majors in September based on the strength of that tear, but true to character, he failed to capitalize on the opportunity. It's been five years since Liz appeared in this book, and in that time even Atticus Finch has changed more than Liz.

Jeff Locke LHP

Born: 11/20/87 Age: 28 Bats: L Throws: L Height: 6'0" Weight: 195

YEAR	TEAM	LVL	AGE	W	L	SV	G	GS	IP	H	HR	BB/9	K/9	GB%	BABIP	WHIP	ERA	FIP	DRA	WARP	CFIP	MPH
2013	PIT	MLB	25	10	7	0	30	30	166^1	146	11	4.5	6.8	55%	.278	1.38	3.52	4.00	4.45	0.9	117	93.2
2014	IND	AAA	26	3	1	0	9	9	50	51	5	4.0	6.7	55%	.299	1.46	4.14	4.62	4.81	0.2	109	
2014	PIT	MLB	26	7	6	0	21	21	131^1	127	16	2.7	6.1	53%	.278	1.27	3.91	4.34	4.61	0.3	111	93.1
2015	PIT	MLB	27	8	11	0	30	30	168^1	179	15	3.2	6.9	53%	.312	1.42	4.49	3.98	4.69	0.7	110	93.9
2016	*PIT*	*MLB*	*28*	*8*	*8*	*0*	*24*	*24*	127^1	*122*	*14*	*3.0*	*6.7*	*54%*	*.301*	*1.30*	*4.11*	*4.11*	*4.78*	*0.8*	*112*	
2017	*PIT*	*MLB*	*29*	*7*	*7*	*0*	*21*	*21*	121^1	*117*	*14*	*3.1*	*7.4*	*54%*	*.308*	*1.31*	*4.08*	*4.43*	*4.75*	*0.7*	*110*	

Breakout: 18% Improve: 50% Collapse: 20% Attrition: 21% MLB: 88% *Comparables: Ross Detwiler, Josh Outman, Marc Rzepczynski*

Being a one-time All-Star is like being a one-time Grammy winner: It doesn't matter what happens afterward, you're *always* going to be referred to and introduced by that label. Consider that a happy development for Locke—who, aside from his inflated ERA, had his typical season in 2015: The occasional gem and meltdown sprinkled across a bunch of mediocrity—and a bad development for the Pirates, who now have to decide on an annual basis if keeping him around is worth going through the arbitration process. In a vacuum, they'd probably say yes. But the Pirates don't operate in a vacuum; they have a strapped budget and enough pitching depth that, at some point soon, the answer is going to be no. When it comes to that, at least Locke can use his cool title to find another team.

Mark Melancon RHP

Born: 3/28/85 Age: 31 Bats: R Throws: R Height: 6'2" Weight: 210

YEAR	TEAM	LVL	AGE	W	L	SV	G	GS	IP	H	HR	BB/9	K/9	GB%	BABIP	WHIP	ERA	FIP	DRA	WARP	CFIP	MPH
2013	PIT	MLB	28	3	2	16	72	0	71	60	1	1.0	8.9	62%	.296	0.96	1.39	1.61	2.77	1.6	70	94.8
2014	PIT	MLB	29	3	5	33	72	0	71	51	2	1.4	9.0	60%	.258	0.87	1.90	2.06	1.93	2.2	75	94.4
2015	PIT	MLB	30	3	2	51	78	0	76^2	57	4	1.6	7.3	58%	.251	0.93	2.23	2.85	2.92	1.6	91	93.7
2016	*PIT*	*MLB*	*31*	*3*	*1*	*33*	*59*	*0*	62^2	*53*	*6*	*2.0*	*8.1*	*59%*	*.289*	*1.07*	*3.29*	*3.23*	*3.86*	*0.8*	*84*	
2017	*PIT*	*MLB*	*32*	*3*	*1*	*29*	*58*	*0*	*58*	*51*	*6*	*2.2*	*8.4*	*59%*	*.299*	*1.12*	*3.39*	*3.64*	*3.98*	*0.6*	*87*	

Breakout: 16% Improve: 39% Collapse: 29% Attrition: 7% MLB: 89% *Comparables: Francisco Cordero, Scot Shields, Keith Foulke*

The baseball season lasts a long time. In case you needed more evidence of that statement, consider Melancon's standing at the beginning and end of 2015. Early on, he looked like a cooked squirrel. His velocity was down (his trademark cutter had lost three ticks since the previous April) and he entered May with a collection of ugly statistics: a 5.23 ERA, more hits than innings, nearly as many walks as strikeouts and so on. He was breaths away from losing his closer's job. Then it all clicked. Melancon's velocity climbed throughout the season, right along with his strikeout-to-walk ratio. He'd go on to lead the majors in saves, and he became the first

Pirate to ever notch 50 in a season—sorry about your shattered franchise record, Former All-Star Mike Williams.

We never did get a satisfactory explanation for those early-season blues (the most sensible theory was that Melancon's body was behind schedule after he participated in the all-star series in Japan). Of course, after the season he had, nobody cared to relive the past. But sometimes you have to, and with Melancon's escalating costs, it's hard to ignore how similar his situation is to that of Joel Hanrahan's from a few years back—you know, the former Pirates closer who was traded a year before he hit the open market in a deal that brought Melancon to Pittsburgh? Lightning doesn't usually strike twice, but we ain't talking about lightning.

Juan Nicasio RHP

Born: 8/31/86 Age: 29 Bats: R Throws: R Height: 6'4" Weight: 250

YEAR	TEAM	LVL	AGE	W	L	SV	G	GS	IP	H	HR	BB/9	K/9	GB%	BABIP	WHIP	ERA	FIP	DRA	WARP	CFIP	MPH
2013	COL	MLB	26	9	9	0	31	31	157^2	168	17	3.7	6.8	46%	.303	1.47	5.14	4.23	4.34	1.1	107	95.5
2013	CSP	AAA	26	1	0	0	2	2	11	8	0	0.8	6.5	62%	.250	0.82	0.82	2.39	4.63	0.1	90	
2014	CSP	AAA	27	3	2	1	10	4	35^2	41	4	3.8	9.1	43%	.378	1.57	4.54	4.48	5.20	0.2	97	
2014	COL	MLB	27	6	6	0	33	14	93^2	107	19	3.0	6.1	49%	.298	1.47	5.38	5.42	5.40	-0.8	114	96.2
2015	LAN	MLB	28	1	3	1	53	1	58^1	59	1	4.9	10.0	47%	.360	1.56	3.86	2.85	4.70	0.0	95	98.1
2016	*PIT*	*MLB*	*29*	*3*	*2*	*0*	*51*	*2*	*62^1*	*60*	*7*	*3.4*	*7.6*	*47%*	*.316*	*1.34*	*4.01*	*4.00*	*4.67*	*0.2*	*106*	
2017	*PIT*	*MLB*	*30*	*4*	*4*	*0*	*28*	*12*	*89^1*	*88*	*11*	*3.3*	*7.8*	*47%*	*.318*	*1.35*	*4.07*	*4.42*	*4.74*	*0.4*	*109*	

Breakout: 31% Improve: 53% Collapse: 12% Attrition: 6% MLB: 85% *Comparables: Bud Norris, Cliff Lee, Tom Gorzelanny*

Nicasio's lack of a third pitch and inconsistent command have long foreshadowed a move to the bullpen. The Rockies, in all their infinite wisdom, couldn't figure that out in his first 3 1/2 seasons, finally made him a reliever halfway through last year, saw him pitch quite well in that role... and then promptly gave him away to the Dodgers. It was like the worst episode of *Flip This House* ever. Nicasio was solid but unspectacular for Los Angeles in 2015, walking too many but also missing a ton of bats and recording 17 appearances in which he pitched more than an inning. Given that he has had to overcome minor obstacles, like breaking his neck, and major obstacles, like pitching for Colorado, it's good to see him catch on with a couple of competent clubs in the Dodgers and, now, the Ray Searage Pirates.

Jon Niese LHP

Born: 10/27/86 Age: 29 Bats: L Throws: L Height: 6'3" Weight: 220

YEAR	TEAM	LVL	AGE	W	L	SV	G	GS	IP	H	HR	BB/9	K/9	GB%	BABIP	WHIP	ERA	FIP	DRA	WARP	CFIP	MPH
2013	NYN	MLB	26	8	8	0	24	24	143	158	10	3.0	6.6	53%	.326	1.44	3.71	3.55	4.97	-0.1	109	93.0
2014	NYN	MLB	27	9	11	0	30	30	187^2	193	17	2.2	6.6	50%	.304	1.27	3.40	3.64	4.34	1.0	107	91.3
2015	NYN	MLB	28	9	10	0	33	29	176^2	192	20	2.8	5.8	57%	.300	1.40	4.13	4.44	5.51	-1.0	121	91.8
2016	*PIT*	*MLB*	*29*	*10*	*9*	*0*	*28*	*28*	*168*	*180*	*20*	*2.5*	*5.9*	*55%*	*.317*	*1.34*	*4.17*	*4.24*	*4.85*	*0.9*	*114*	
2017	*PIT*	*MLB*	*30*	*10*	*10*	*0*	*28*	*28*	*168^2*	*183*	*21*	*2.4*	*6.1*	*55%*	*.321*	*1.35*	*4.20*	*4.57*	*4.89*	*0.8*	*115*	

Breakout: 27% Improve: 61% Collapse: 13% Attrition: 10% MLB: 99% *Comparables: Paul Maholm, John Burkett, Nate Robertson*

Niese throws three different fastballs—four-seam, two-seam and the cutter—and it's what the cutter does for the rest of his arsenal that tells the story. Niese's four-seamer generated a respectable 8 percent whiff rate, higher than Noah Syndergaard's or Steven Matz's, and it's all because hitters are expecting a fastball that moves. When it doesn't, there's a problem. Niese throws 69 percent hard stuff, and on 0-0 counts that number ticks up over 72 percent. You know when to get your front foot down; you just don't know where the ball will be when you do. The signs of decline continue: Niese's strikeouts dropped precipitously again, and his ERA rose correspondingly last year. A better infield would have helped Niese survive this, and he's got one now in Pittsburgh.

Rob Scahill RHP

Born: 2/15/87 Age: 29 Bats: L Throws: R Height: 6'2" Weight: 220

YEAR	TEAM	LVL	AGE	W	L	SV	G	GS	IP	H	HR	BB/9	K/9	GB%	BABIP	WHIP	ERA	FIP	DRA	WARP	CFIP	MPH
2013	CSP	AAA	26	5	1	1	23	0	46	53	6	2.2	8.8	59%	.351	1.39	4.50	4.09	4.44	0.4	83	
2013	COL	MLB	26	1	0	0	23	0	33^1	40	5	2.4	5.4	49%	.315	1.47	5.13	4.94	4.95	-0.1	111	97.1
2014	CSP	AAA	27	2	3	2	41	0	58^1	59	6	2.8	8.2	57%	.308	1.32	4.32	4.40	5.06	0.2	92	
2014	COL	MLB	27	1	0	0	12	0	15	17	3	5.4	6.6	43%	.292	1.73	4.80	6.24	6.45	-0.4	113	95.8
2015	PIT	MLB	28	2	4	0	28	0	30^2	33	3	4.7	7.0	60%	.306	1.60	2.64	4.53	5.88	-0.4	111	96.1
2016	*PIT*	*MLB*	*29*	*2*	*1*	*0*	*30*	*0*	*31^1*	*31*	*4*	*2.9*	*7.0*	*56%*	*.310*	*1.31*	*4.07*	*4.16*	*4.73*	*0.1*	*109*	
2017	*PIT*	*MLB*	*30*	*2*	*2*	*0*	*28*	*4*	*59^2*	*58*	*8*	*3.2*	*7.8*	*56%*	*.313*	*1.33*	*4.20*	*4.55*	*4.88*	*0.1*	*112*	

Breakout: 12% Improve: 16% Collapse: 9% Attrition: 12% MLB: 28% *Comparables: Brad Ziegler, Justin Hampson, Brian Slocum*

Acquired in a low-key November trade, Scahill was one of the Pirates' final spring cuts. Then days later, for whatever reason, the Pirates reversed course, bringing him back onto the Opening Day roster in place of Stolmy Pimentel. It proved to be the right call. While both pitchers spent significant time on the disabled list, it was Scahill who showed improvement under the Pirates' instruction—something Pimentel hadn't done enough of during his time in Pittsburgh. Scahill modified his arsenal by emphasizing his sinker, throwing nearly as many during 12 May innings (107) as he had in his previous 48 frames with the Rockies (127). Correspondingly, his groundball percentage increased as his home run rate decreased. The rest of Scahill's peripherals befit a pitcher with a higher ERA, but there's value in having a cheap, groundball-getting reliever lying around—even if he isn't cut out for high-leverage work.

Jameson Taillon RHP

Born: 11/18/91 Age: 24 Bats: R Throws: R Height: 6'5" Weight: 240

YEAR	TEAM	LVL	AGE	W	L	SV	G	GS	IP	H	HR	BB/9	K/9	GB%	BABIP	WHIP	ERA	FIP	DRA	WARP	CFIP	MPH
2013	IND	AAA	21	1	3	0	6	6	37	31	1	3.9	9.0	36%	.288	1.27	3.89	3.18	4.00	0.4	87	
2013	ALT	AA	21	4	7	0	20	19	110^1	112	8	2.9	8.6	52%	.322	1.34	3.67	3.46	4.15	1.4	85	
2016	*PIT*	*MLB*	*24*	*2*	*2*	*0*	*5*	*5*	28^2	*28*	*3*	*2.6*	*6.9*	*44%*	*.308*	*1.25*	*3.68*	*3.81*	*4.30*	*0.3*	*97*	
2017	*PIT*	*MLB*	*25*	*4*	*4*	*0*	*11*	*11*	66^1	*64*	*8*	*2.8*	*7.1*	*44%*	*.307*	*1.29*	*4.02*	*4.35*	*4.70*	*0.4*	*108*	

Breakout: 9% Improve: 17% Collapse: 9% Attrition: 21% MLB: 39% *Comparables: Simon Castro, John Ely, Christian Friedrich*

While Bryce Harper and Manny Machado enjoyed seasons that solidified them as two of the best players in the majors, the pitcher drafted between them endured another lost year. Taillon, who had missed the 2014 season as a result of Tommy John surgery, was on the comeback trail in July when it was announced he would miss the rest of the campaign following another operation—this one to repair an inguinal hernia. He's nearing 30 months without pitching (outside of an extended spring training game) but he could make his big-league debut late in 2016 if he can stay on the mound all year—say, that gives us an idea for a radio-station contest.

Stephen Tarpley LHP

Born: 2/17/93 Age: 23 Bats: R Throws: L Height: 6'1" Weight: 180

YEAR	TEAM	LVL	AGE	W	L	SV	G	GS	IP	H	HR	BB/9	K/9	GB%	BABIP	WHIP	ERA	FIP	DRA	WARP	CFIP	MPH
2014	ABE	A-	21	3	5	0	13	12	66^1	69	4	3.3	8.1	61%	.339	1.40	3.66	3.91	4.44	0.3	106	
2015	WVA	A	22	11	4	0	20	20	116	108	2	1.9	8.1	52%	.305	1.15	2.48	2.85	3.17	2.7	85	
2016	*PIT*	*MLB*	*23*	*6*	*6*	*0*	*18*	*18*	94^2	*100*	*9*	*3.1*	*5.9*	*44%*	*.317*	*1.40*	*4.14*	*4.14*	*4.80*	*0.5*	*112*	
2017	*PIT*	*MLB*	*24*	*9*	*11*	*0*	*30*	*30*	*186*	*199*	*20*	*3.2*	*5.8*	*44%*	*.319*	*1.43*	*4.32*	*4.71*	*5.01*	*0.5*	*118*	

Breakout: 4% Improve: 9% Collapse: 2% Attrition: 9% MLB: 12% *Comparables: Erik Johnson, Jensen Lewis, Nick Tepesch*

"[Expect] the Pirates to get more than Brad Lincoln in return." That's how we ended Travis Snider's comment in the last Annual. Sure enough, the Pirates *did* trade Snider—just before the book hit shelves—and sure enough, the Pirates *did* get more than Lincoln in return. Tarpley, a former third-round pick with a good fastball, was made available in part due to makeup concerns—concerns that either disappeared or were obscured by his stellar performance in his first season with the Pirates, thus proving that production trumps almost all non-legal issues. Anyway, Tarpley will continue working on the three C's of pitching: consistency, command and changeup. If he can nail down those loose boards, he could become a mid-rotation starter; if he can nail down *two* of those loose boards, he could become a late-inning reliever. Whatever his role, Tarpley should break Jeff Karstens' modern franchise record for thickest eyebrows on a pitcher.

Ryan Vogelsong RHP

Born: 7/22/77 Age: 38 Bats: R Throws: R Height: 6'4" Weight: 215

YEAR	TEAM	LVL	AGE	W	L	SV	G	GS	IP	H	HR	BB/9	K/9	GB%	BABIP	WHIP	ERA	FIP	DRA	WARP	CFIP	MPH
2013	RIC	AA	35	2	0	0	2	2	11	10	1	1.6	6.5	38%	.290	1.09	0.82	3.60	4.38	0.1	94	
2013	SFN	MLB	35	4	6	0	19	19	103^2	124	15	3.3	5.8	42%	.320	1.56	5.73	4.88	6.27	-1.7	125	91.9
2014	SFN	MLB	36	8	13	0	32	32	184^2	178	18	2.8	7.4	41%	.294	1.28	4.00	3.82	4.71	0.2	110	92.6
2015	SFN	MLB	37	9	11	0	33	22	135	140	17	3.9	7.2	47%	.299	1.47	4.67	4.55	5.50	-0.8	118	93.6
2016	*PIT*	*MLB*	*38*	*10*	*9*	*0*	*28*	*28*	159^2	*158*	*19*	*3.3*	*6.6*	*44%*	*.304*	*1.36*	*4.36*	*4.36*	*5.07*	*0.4*	*119*	
2017	*PIT*	*MLB*	*39*	*7*	*9*	*0*	*24*	*24*	141^1	*145*	*18*	*3.4*	*6.6*	*44%*	*.314*	*1.41*	*4.49*	*4.89*	*5.22*	*0.1*	*123*	

Breakout: 15% Improve: 30% Collapse: 13% Attrition: 13% MLB: 61% *Comparables: Al Leiter, Mike Hampton, Sam Jones*

When Vogelsong returned to the Giants, he didn't expect to be yo-yo'd between the rotation and bullpen, and the Giants certainly weren't planning for the right-hander to shoulder the third-highest innings load on the staff. He was, at times, San Francisco's second-most-effective starter, but that was more of a commentary on the state of Bruce Bochy's rotation than a compliment to Vogelsong's own work. With waning command of his curve and change, Vogelsong had little but a cutter to lean on when lefties dug into the box. A versatile relief role, in which he could expand his cutter usage while enjoying the platoon advantage more frequently, might be the most fulfilling sunset to this well-traveled career.

Tony Watson LHP

Born: 5/30/85 Age: 31 Bats: L Throws: L Height: 6'4" Weight: 225

YEAR	TEAM	LVL	AGE	W	L	SV	G	GS	IP	H	HR	BB/9	K/9	GB%	BABIP	WHIP	ERA	FIP	DRA	WARP	CFIP	MPH
2013	PIT	MLB	28	3	1	2	67	0	71^2	51	5	1.5	6.8	46%	.227	0.88	2.39	3.17	2.89	1.5	95	96.4
2014	PIT	MLB	29	10	2	2	78	0	77^1	64	5	1.7	9.4	51%	.298	1.02	1.63	2.66	3.28	1.1	76	96.7
2015	PIT	MLB	30	4	1	1	77	0	75^1	55	3	2.0	7.4	50%	.251	0.96	1.91	2.87	2.62	1.9	93	96.3
2016	*PIT*	*MLB*	*31*	*3*	*1*	*2*	*59*	*0*	62^2	*51*	*6*	*2.2*	*8.0*	*50%*	*.279*	*1.06*	*3.45*	*3.41*	*4.04*	*0.7*	*90*	
2017	*PIT*	*MLB*	*32*	*3*	*1*	*1*	*63*	*0*	60^1	*49*	*6*	*2.4*	*8.5*	*50%*	*.285*	*1.08*	*3.45*	*3.71*	*4.04*	*0.6*	*90*	

Breakout: 20% Improve: 40% Collapse: 32% Attrition: 7% MLB: 89% *Comparables: Scot Shields, Darren O'Day, Bobby Jenks*

The one thing separating Watson from recognition as a quality closer is the pesky fact that he's not (and has never been) a closer. That seemed about to change in April, when Mark Melancon scuffled to begin the season, but the Pirates remained steady just long enough for Melancon to regain steadiness. True to history, the duo came together to serve as a dispiriting endgame for opponents. Watson is under team control through 2017, one year longer than Melancon, so—provided his fastball continues to feature more tail than a dragon dance—he should get his chance just in time for a big payday.

Trevor Williams RHP

Born: 4/25/92 Age: 24 Bats: R Throws: R Height: 6'3" Weight: 230

YEAR	TEAM	LVL	AGE	W	L	SV	G	GS	IP	H	HR	BB/9	K/9	GB%	BABIP	WHIP	ERA	FIP	DRA	WARP	CFIP	MPH
2013	BAT	A-	21	0	2	0	10	10	29	26	0	2.5	6.2	61%	.274	1.17	2.48	2.65	4.02	0.2	101	
2014	JUP	A+	22	8	6	0	23	23	129	138	5	2.0	6.3	52%	.322	1.29	2.79	3.17	4.08	1.4	91	
2014	JAX	AA	22	0	1	0	3	3	15	22	0	3.6	8.4	69%	.431	1.87	6.00	2.52				
2015	JAX	AA	23	7	8	0	22	21	117	126	9	2.8	6.8	54%	.320	1.38	4.00	3.75	4.24	0.9	99	
2015	NWO	AAA	23	0	2	0	3	3	14	15	0	4.5	8.4	46%	.341	1.57	2.57	3.46	4.86	0.1	97	
2016	*PIT*	*MLB*	*24*	*7*	*7*	*0*	*23*	*23*	*114²*	*125*	*13*	*3.0*	*5.7*	*50%*	*.321*	*1.42*	*4.27*	*4.34*	*4.94*	*0.5*	*116*	
2017	*PIT*	*MLB*	*25*	*6*	*8*	*0*	*22*	*22*	*131¹*	*145*	*17*	*3.1*	*5.9*	*50%*	*.324*	*1.45*	*4.49*	*4.89*	*5.20*	*0.1*	*123*	

Breakout: 9% Improve: 10% Collapse: 4% Attrition: 9% MLB: 16% *Comparables: Ross Ohlendorf, Tobi Stoner, Chris Rusin*

Williams has steady-eddied his way up to Double-A, and the former second-rounder has posted consistently solid if unremarkable numbers at every stop. His four-pitch arsenal works off a pretty good sinker and also includes an alright slider, a decent changeup, an okay curveball, an adequate personality, tolerable breath, so-so keyboarding skills and an unremarkable understanding of the human heart. Maybe the Pirates get lucky and he turns into something like Jeff Suppan.

Lineouts

Hitters

NAME	POS	TEAM	LVL	AGE	PA	R	2B	3B	HR	RBI	BB	K	SB	CS	AVG/OBP/SLG	TAv	BABIP	BRR	FRAA	WARP
Stetson Allie	1B	ALT	AA	24	469	45	17	0	17	58	47	135	6	3	.205/.293/.372	.243	.256	-2.5	RF(108): 7.9	0.5
Barrett Barnes	OF	ALT	AA	23	146	17	6	0	3	17	16	25	4	4	.246/.338/.365	.273	.283	-0.1	LF(34): -1.6	0.3
	OF	BRD	A+	23	276	45	16	2	6	24	28	41	13	5	.261/.359/.423	.291	.291	-0.3	LF(55): -2.1	1.3
Jaff Decker	OF	IND	AAA	25	265	33	10	1	3	26	36	38	18	3	.266/.370/.362	.283	.302	0.1	LF(43): 1.9, RF(14): -0.6	1.3
	OF	PIT	MLB	25	36	8	1	1	0	1	7	9	0	0	.214/.371/.321	.274	.316	-0.1	LF(4): -0.6, RF(3): 0.3	0.1
Casey Hughston	OF	WEV	A-	21	244	23	9	2	2	28	13	71	4	1	.224/.267/.311	.219	.315	0.7	CF(61): -3.9	-0.6
Travis Ishikawa	1B	PIT	MLB	31	66	5	3	0	1	8	8	17	0	0	.224/.318/.328	.232	.300	0.4	1B(12): 0.0, LF(5): -0.3	-0.1
	1B	SAC	AAA	31	149	17	8	0	4	19	13	41	0	0	.271/.342/.421	.274	.360	1.6	1B(29): 0.4, LF(5): 1.6	0.8
	1B	SFN	MLB	31	6	1	0	0	0	0	1	3	0	0	.000/.167/.000	.090	.000	0.0	LF(1): -0.1	-0.1
Kevin Kramer	MI	WEV	A-	21	209	34	7	3	0	17	25	28	9	4	.305/.390/.379	.307	.358	3.2	2B(44): 7.5, SS(2): -1.1	2.7
	MI	WVA	A	21	56	9	2	1	0	3	5	8	3	0	.240/.321/.320	.246	.286	1.2	2B(8): -0.3, SS(2): -0.6	0.1
Tito Polo	OF	WVA	A	20	414	51	20	2	3	26	28	77	46	13	.236/.313/.328	.258	.292	1.8	CF(86): 1.4, LF(12): 0.2	1.5
Jason Rogers	1B	CSP	AAA	27	147	25	8	0	8	24	24	23	0	0	.344/.449/.607	.349	.370	-0.2	1B(24): 0.9, 3B(6): 0.6	1.7
	1B	MIL	MLB	27	169	22	6	2	4	16	15	34	0	0	.296/.367/.441	.294	.360	0.3	1B(24): -1.8, LF(3): -0.4	0.7
Tony Sanchez	C	IND	AAA	27	371	38	20	2	3	47	45	65	4	3	.236/.342/.342	.254	.284	-0.8	C(70): 4.8	1.6
	C	PIT	MLB	27	9	2	0	0	0	0	1	3	0	0	.375/.444/.375	.404	.600	0.2	C(2): 0.2	0.2
Travis Snider	RF	BAL	MLB	27	236	23	9	2	3	20	23	56	1	0	.237/.318/.341	.248	.309	-1.3	LF(38): -0.7, RF(20): 3.6	0.3
	RF	IND	AAA	27	40	5	1	0	1	4	4	3	0	0	.314/.375/.429	.278	.313	0.8	LF(5): 0.1, RF(2): -0.5	0.2
	RF	PIT	MLB	27	29	1	3	0	1	8	3	10	0	0	.192/.276/.423	.242	.267	0.0	LF(4): 0.1, RF(2): 0.4	0.1

Pitcher-turned-hitter **Stetson Allie** changed positions again, moving from first base to right field; unfortunately, he's also getting progressively worse at baseball. ❖ Former sandwich-round pick **Barrett Barnes** moved to left field and more than doubled his previous career high in plate appearances. He does just enough well to profile as a reserve. ❖ **Jaff Decker** fringy/you already know/he's in the fast lane/from Quad-A to Tokyo. ❖ The last of the Pirates' four top-100 picks, Alabama outfielder **Casey Hughston** could in time possess five average or better tools. ❖ After claiming **Travis Ishikawa** off waivers in July, the Pirates used him almost exclusively as a pinch-hitter against righties, against whom he batted .207/.303/.310. Next they'll sign Ryan Doumit and use him at catcher. ❖ What's the deal with the Pirates drafting UCLA shortstop **Kevin Kramer** hours after taking Kevin Newman? Turns out Kramer, complete with a solid-average hit tool, profiles better as a second baseman. That means Newman and Kramer could soon be making sausages—er, turning double plays. ❖ **Tito Polo** bunts 'n' runs. ❖ It's the sign of a major rebuild when a club's supporters voice such vociferous support for **Jason Rogers**, a 28-year-old, right-handed platoon first baseman. Grasp onto the tiniest straw, right? Anyway, the Marlins traded him, so maybe he really was good. ❖ Scouts used to think **Tony Sanchez** would hit .260 with a dozen homers per season. Don't feel bad, y'all; we once predicted Bobby Estalella would become a reasonable MVP candidate within five years. ❖ The Pirates signed **Travis Snider** to a minor-league deal almost exactly eight months after they traded him to the Orioles for two promising pitching prospects. Way to rub it in.

Pitchers

NAME	TEAM	LVL	AGE	W	L	SV	G	GS	IP	H	HR	BB/9	K/9	GB%	BABIP	WHIP	ERA	FIP	FRA	WARP	CFIP	MPH
Steven Brault	ALT	AA	23	9	3	0	15	15	90	72	1	1.9	8.0	51%	.273	1.01	2.00	2.37	2.45	2.6	76	
	BRD	A+	23	4	1	0	13	13	65^{2}	62	3	2.9	6.2	52%	.292	1.26	3.02	3.44	4.12	0.2	104	
Montana DuRapau	WVA	A	23	1	0	1	11	0	19^{1}	7	2	0.5	8.8	62%	.111	0.41	1.40	3.02	2.60	0.5	76	
	BRD	A+	23	4	1	13	31	0	51^{1}	21	2	1.4	8.2	46%	.154	0.56	1.40	2.48	2.11	1.3	75	
Yeudy Garcia	WVA	A	22	12	5	1	30	21	124^{1}	92	4	3.0	8.1	54%	.259	1.07	2.10	3.33	3.69	2.0	91	
Clay Holmes	BRD	A+	22	0	2	0	6	6	23	18	0	2.7	6.3	67%	.273	1.09	2.74	3.21	4.19	0.1	105	
Nick Kingham	IND	AAA	23	1	2	0	6	6	31^{1}	34	3	2.0	9.2	44%	.337	1.31	4.31	3.22	2.79	0.7	83	
Chad Kuhl	ALT	AA	22	11	5	0	26	26	152^{2}	133	10	2.4	6.0	57%	.265	1.14	2.48	3.68	4.11	1.3	99	
Kyle Lobstein	DET	MLB	25	3	8	0	13	11	63^{2}	78	7	3.3	4.5	54%	.326	1.59	5.94	4.61	5.60	-0.5	120	89.0
	TOL	AAA	25	0	2	0	4	4	17^{2}	26	2	4.6	6.6	43%	.381	1.98	6.62	4.86	5.48	-0.2	112	
Jorge Rondon	NOR	AAA	27	3	1	1	30	0	54	38	0	2.8	7.7	51%	.260	1.02	2.33	2.40	2.89	1.0	85	
	BAL	MLB	27	0	1	0	8	0	13^{1}	20	3	4.1	5.4	42%	.347	1.95	7.43	6.18	-2.33	1.1	119	98.4
	COL	MLB	27	0	0	0	2	0	1	8	0	27.0	9.0	36%	.727	11.00	90.00	10.16	92.47	-1.0	113	98.7
Casey Sadler	IND	AAA	24	6	5	0	13	13	81	72	9	2.8	5.3	54%	.250	1.20	4.22	4.34	5.27	-0.6	115	
	PIT	MLB	24	1	0	0	1	1	5	4	1	1.8	9.0	46%	.250	1.00	3.60	4.36	5.03	0.0	99	92.8

The other pitcher the Pirates received in the Travis Snider trade, **Steven Brault** is an athletic southpaw who could turn into a back-end starter. More importantly: He's from Regis University, which means you're reading this sentence in Regis Philbin's voice. ❖ **Brandon Cumpton's** ascent to the back of a big-league rotation hit a snag in March, when he underwent season-ending Tommy John surgery. It hit another snag in September, as he had an operation on his right shoulder that will cause him to miss the 2016 season, too. Looks like the Pirates are straight outta Cumpton. ❖ We'd never finish the book if we included every short right-handed reliever in A-ball with a low-90s fastball and an impressive strikeout-to-walk ratio. That's why we only make exceptions in special cases—like when the reliever is named **Montana DuRapau**. ❖ For all the Pirates' success in developing international hitters, they've yet to hit on a pitcher. **Yeudy Garcia** has the lively fastball to change that. But there's always a reason you end up in the Lineouts, and Garcia's is lack of command or secondary pitches. ❖ **Clay Holmes** took it slow upon his return from elbow surgery. With further refinement—mostly to his command and off-speed pitches—he could become what baseball people call a workhorse, which, when you think about it, is a really mean and dehumanizing thing to call anyone, let alone an impressionable young man. ❖ The Pirates paid **Mitch Keller** $1 million to skip college. He's probably not regretting his decision after nursing a strained forearm for most of his first pro season. The Pirates probably aren't, either, provided Keller maintains his middle-of-the-rotation upside. ❖ Future mid-rotation starter **Nick Kingham** was four, five seconds from joining the Pirates before he caught a case of the Tommy Johns. The Royal Swine's inauguration has since been rescheduled for sometime late in 2016. ❖ Well-built sinkerballer **Chad Kuhl** has a better Twitter handle (@KuhlWhhip_11) than out pitch. He could thrive as a reliever in front of the shift-heavy Pirates' defense. ❖ **Kyle Lobstein** made it through five good starts before his old-timey K rate caught up with him. If he can't crack it as a regular starter, he could be used in a pinch. ❖ Many a Colorado pitcher has suffered through something like **Jorge Rondon**'s eight-run, no-outs appearance, but the twist was that Rondon's came in Petco. He never did get to see how his high-90s heater would handle altitude, as Colorado released him before the bus got home. ❖ Yet another near-ready starter whose season was derailed by elbow trouble, **Casey Sadler** opted for a PRP injection rather than Tommy John surgery. Modern medicine is evidence that miracles happen every day, but Sadler is probably going to have an elbow zipper by the time you read this. ❖ In Bosnian, **Trey Supak's** surname means... well, we can't print what it means here. Let's just say that if he progresses as planned, a lot of batters will be calling him the English equivalent.

MANAGER

Clint Hurdle

YEAR	TEAM	W	L	Pythag +/-	Avg PC	100+ P	120+ P	QS	BQS	REL	REL w Zero R	IBB	PH	PH Avg	PH HR	SB2	CS2	SB3	CS3	SAC Att	SAC%	POS SAC	Squeeze	Swing	In Play
2013	PIT	94	68	5	89.7	41	0	83	2	465	395	26	285	.207	7	83	36	10	6	93	66.7	35	1	347	100
2014	PIT	88	74	1	93.7	44	0	90	3	452	361	43	317	.218	7	99	41	5	4	101	53.5	18	1	365	135

While the rest of the sport is fixated on hiring first-time managers, Hurdle's success in Pittsburgh is evidence that retreads can learn from their past mistakes. Hurdle's education as a manager is profiled in Travis Sawchik's *Big Data Baseball*. Long story short, Hurdle first learned about analytics while working for MLB Network following his dismissal from the Rockies. He never put that knowledge to use until he realized he was on his last leg with the Pirates. At that point, he accepted the boffins and their teachings, to the degree that he requested a traveling quantitative secretary. As a result, Hurdle's Pirates have become thought leaders in shifting, framing, pitching inside and, most recently, resting their players.

Inspired by the NBA's Golden State Warriors, Hurdle concentrated on protecting his starters against injury and fatigue by leaning on his bench players more often. According to an October article by Henry Druschel, the Pirates' starters had played five games or fewer in the previous week 65 percent of the time—six percentage points more than other teams' starters, on average. The benefits to that mindfulness are unclear—Russell Carleton's past work suggests that, statistically, it's not as large of a deal as you'd expect—but it's another sign that Hurdle has fully bought in to the Pirates' number-crunching ways.

Of course, it's one thing for a manager to accept radical ideology, and it's another for his staff and players to do the same. Fortunately for the Pirates, Hurdle's personality lends itself to buy in. This is the same feller who, in *Sports Illustrated's* MLB preview edition, called Dorothy from *The Wizard of Oz* one of the greatest leaders of all-time. Really. Here's Hurdle's explanation: "She took three people that were missing something and had them look inside themselves to find something they thought they never had. She wanted to go home, that was mission no. 1, but in the end it was all about everyone else."

SAN DIEGO PADRES

Essay by Michael Clair

Player comments by Geoff Young and BP authors

Think back, if you can, to when A.J. Preller was first hired. Here strode a young, almost model-like man in a fitted shirt, saying that he had put the "hardest working group and the hungriest group" together in the front office with their focus set on the World Series.

Those are the kinds of meaningless platitudes we expect our leaders to say when they are introduced to the masses, akin to "As CEO, I believe in work/life balance." The only difference: Preller made all of these things actually happen as he treated the hot stove market like his own private *MLB: The Show* franchise. Or, to use another analogy, if the Moneyball Oakland A's were "card counters at the blackjack table," then Preller was over raising on pocket twos before the flop.

Preller took over a San Diego team that had seemingly decided to mirror the city's lulling weather patterns as their win totals over the previous four seasons were a cool and calm mid-70s: Never quite bad enough to pick up the prime draft pick that comes with being truly awful, nor strong enough to energize a fan base and push for a playoff spot. They were just there—in a gorgeous ballpark with a view of downtown and a wiffle ball field—but there all the same.

Preller tried to change that. Storming the rest of the league, the GM emptied out his minor league system to bring in stars and spectacle. The Padres were no longer going to be the forgotten team on the water; the pleasant vacation spot where people could drop in for a few innings in between going to the beach and drinking copious amounts in the Gaslamp Quarter.

We all wanted to believe. Articles were penned by the dozen about how Preller had won the offseason, that you didn't need a slow, boring rebuild when you could simply take a sledgehammer to your roster in one fell swoop. An outfield filled with three corner outfielders? Sure, that sounded dangerous, but it also sounded incredibly exciting. We hoped that Preller had perhaps just discovered the newest inefficiency which was "why bother with a center fielder if you can just hit home runs all day long."

It didn't work. The team was out of first place by April 23rd, on their way to three fewer victories than 2014 as everything that could go wrong, did.

PADRES PROSPECTUS

2015 W-L: 74-88, 4th in NL West

Pythag	.446	23rd	DER	.697	23rd
RS/G	4.01	23rd	B-Age	27.5	4th
RA/G	4.51	22nd	P-Age	29.2	25th
TAv	0.253	24th	Salary	$108.4M	18th
BRR	3.76	11th	M$/MW	$3.7M	14th
TAv-P	.269	23rd	DL Days	927	12th
FIP	3.96	13th	$ on DL	10%	7th

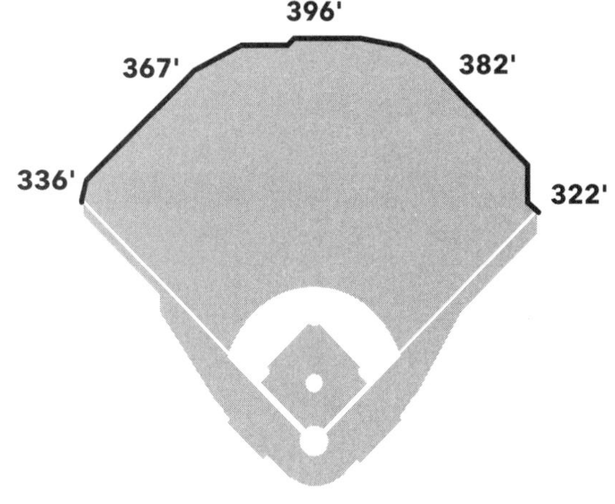

Outfield wall profile: **8'** to **11'**

Three-Year Park Factors

Runs	Runs/RH	Runs/LH	HR/RH	HR/LH
97	105	110	109	113

Top Hitter WARP	3.3	Derek Norris
Top Pitcher WARP	3.5	Tyson Ross
Top Prospect	Manuel Margot	

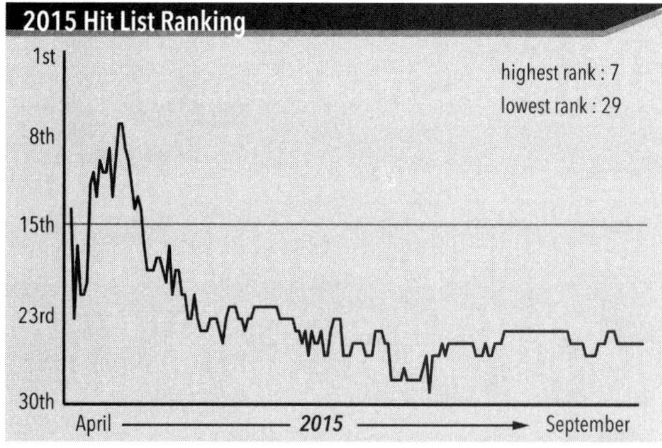

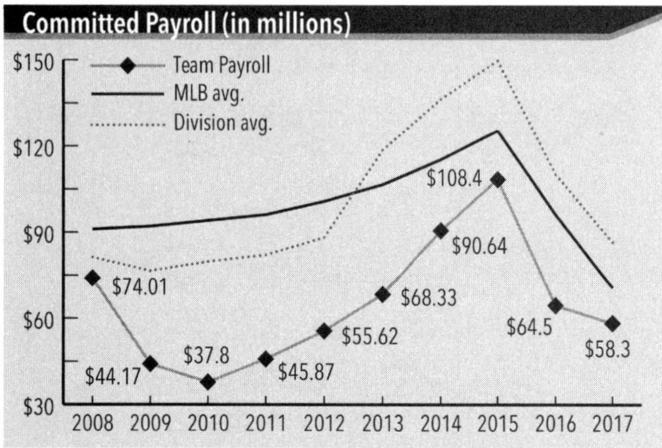

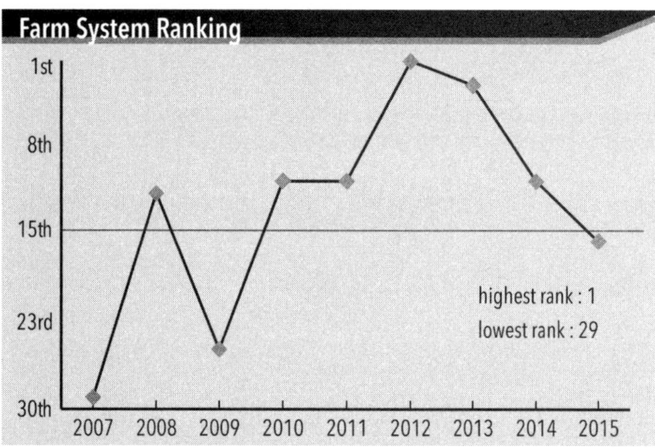

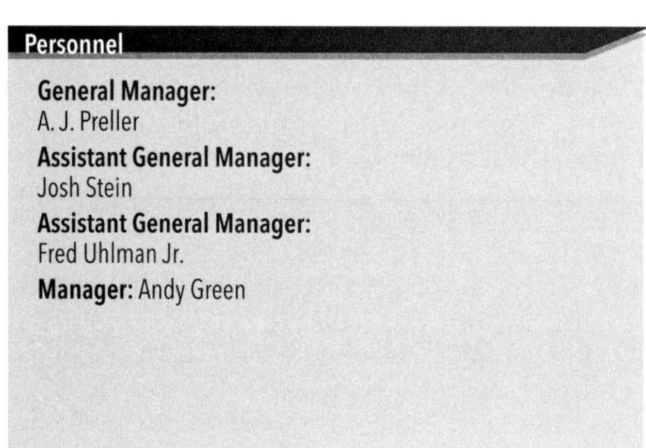
Personnel

General Manager:
A. J. Preller

Assistant General Manager:
Josh Stein

Assistant General Manager:
Fred Uhlman Jr.

Manager: Andy Green

Safe moves proved risky and even the 50/50 swings in luck rarely broke the Padres' way. For every Yangervis Solarte proving that he was worthy of a starting spot, there were multiple Will Middlebrookses continuing to flail at pitches low and away. Even the good news of the amusing minor-league veteran Cody Decker making his big league debut didn't get a storybook ending as he went 0-for-11.

But how did it all go so spectacularly wrong? Let's break down the biggest offseason moves going in reverse order of how successful they ended up:

Wil Myers

If you want a reminder of how we must take the long view of trades, Wil Myers is the perfect test case. After all, when Dayton Moore traded Myers for James Shields and Wade Davis, the baseball internet lost its mind. Since then, the Royals have gone to two World Series and Myers is with his second big league team.

While the outfielder was useful at the plate, still showing signs of his once-the-savior-of-a-franchise status, he once again missed plenty of time and has yet to top 400 plate appearances in a Major League season. The Myers-in-center-field experiment also didn't work out as the combination of Justin Upton, Myers and Matt Kemp in Petco's spacious outfield resembled those early-2000s years when teams thought that defense was as outdated as a flat earth theory.

Of course, the larger issue was what Preller gave up for him. Brought in as part of a three-team deal, Preller traded away prospects Joe Ross, Tyson's brother, and Trea Turner. Ross would go on to post a would-have-been second-best on the team 3.64 ERA in 76 ⅔ innings, while also losing out on the guaranteed revenue from Ross' bobblehead day.

And in the most existential of all possible trades, the Padres sent Turner to the Nationals as the player to be named later that everyone already knew about. Waiting until the deal could officially go through a year after being drafted (a rule that has since been amended), the Padres had to keep Turner in their system, playing him while ostensibly not training him as an undercover operative.

While Myers will likely be moved to first base in 2016 and is still only 25, PECOTA projects Turner to become a 3.5 WARP player by 2017. Considering that only four shortstops were that valuable last year, and the Padres called in Middlebrooks and Gyorko for shortstop duty last year, that could prove a problem.

James Shields

Given the state of the Padres' rotation heading into 2015, signing Shields to a 4-year, $75 million deal actually made a lot of sense. Tyson Ross and Andrew Cashner looked like they could front a rotation, with Ian Kennedy and Odrisamer Despaigne seeming more than capable of holding up the back end. So Preller brought in a pitcher who practically came with a guarantee that he would throw an unlimited number of innings at an above-average rate.

Sure, he was on the wrong side of 30 with a dwindling fastball and strikeout rate, but c'mon, it was only money. And this was Petco Park. What could go wrong? If you haven't been paying attention, everything.

The entire rotation crumbled, with Ross being the only starter to finish the season with an above-average ERA, while Despaigne posted the worst ERA+ for any pitcher with at least 100 innings.

Shields didn't help, either. He surrendered 33 home runs, the most given up by a Padres pitcher since Jake Peavy in 2003. And while Shields' strikeouts spiked to the highest rate of his career, so did his walks. Still, he led the team in innings with 202... even if it was his lowest total since his debut in 2006.

Matt Kemp

Like a failing TV show bringing in a big name star in hopes of goosing ratings and giving the writing staff something to do, the acquisition of Kemp signaled that this was a GM not afraid of taking chances.

While Kemp finished the year with 23 home runs and a nice, round 100 RBI (regardless of your love of advanced stats, there is something inherently beautiful in the 100 RBI season), it wasn't enough. While the three-headed outfield behemoth helped the team to their highest run total since 2012, the team was also 24th in DER and 29th in UZR as they surrendered 160 more runs than they had in 2014.

Unfortunately, the move didn't just cost the team close to $100 million for the duration of his contract, but they also had to give up Yasmani Grandal. The catcher not only had the sixth-highest TAv among catchers with 300 PA, but it came with an MLB-best 25 framing runs above average.

Justin Upton

If we were looking at this trade in the vacuum of a single season, or if the Padres went on to reach the postseason, you could argue that trading for Upton was a stellar deal. After all, he led the team in home runs and slugging percentage, coming one steal away from his third 20-20 season. That's really good! And exciting! What baseball fan out there doesn't like watching Justin Upton come to the plate?

Unfortunately, Upton was with the team for only one season—one season that fell far short of a playoff spot, much less a .500 record. Sure, they'll net a compensation pick when Upton signs a new deal, but the Braves already look to have come out ahead. Last year alone Jace Peterson out-WARPed Jedd Gyorko at second base.

Add in the potential that Mallex Smith and Max Fried offer the Braves in the future, with Smith possibly on the cusp of the Majors next season, and Preller could find himself watching Braves games with his hands over his eyes, as they serve as cruel reminders of what may have been.

Of course, prospects have ways of disappearing into the ether like ghosts in an old house, so one season of watching Justin Upton is better than no seasons watching Upton.

Craig Kimbrel and Melvin Upton

Arguably, and perhaps shockingly, this was the best of the earth-shattering trades that Preller made. Sure, a closer on a sub .500 team doesn't thrill the senses, while Melvin Upton was the trade equivalent of the "Take my wife. No, really, take her," joke, but in a season where chaos reigned, these turned out rather nicely. The Padres didn't even give up all that much, as Cameron Maybin turned in a decent season before heading back to Detroit, Carlos Quentin chose to retire, and Jordan Paroubeck is now in the Dodgers system.

Kimbrel was as advertised, even if he couldn't do much to help the Padres and their 8th-worst bullpen. Sure, just like seemingly every pitcher on the Padres, his ERA and FIP were a run higher than the 2014 version, driven largely by a bizarre uptick in home runs in his move to Petco, but that could simply be small sample hoodwinkery. Even better, once Preller got back to his mad laboratory in the offseason, Kimbrel's trade to Boston netted the team another intriguing shortstop prospect in Javier Guerra and the team's new top prospect in center fielder Manuel Margot. PECOTA projects Margot to be worth nearly three wins by 2017, which could make this whole ordeal all worth it.

Until Margot's ready though, the team has Melvin Upton to man center field. That's right—read that sentence again and remind yourself that it's 2016 and not 2012.

Upton was not only the team's best defensive outfielder, but he posted his best batting average since 2008, OBP since 2011, and SLG since 2012. Granted, it was a limited sample of just 228 PA, but he also upped his line drive percentage to 24.6 percent, over 6 percentage points higher than his career average coming into the season. His numbers were approximately the same as Brett Gardner's. And plenty of people would be excited to see Gardner on their team's roster.

✦✦✦

Despite the less-than-desired outcome, the 2015 season wasn't a total loss. The Padres were exciting again and people wanted to watch them. The team's TV ratings grew 22 percent over the previous year, with April setting an all-time Padres' TV record. Three hundred thousand more fans walked through the turnstiles. Even if you weren't a Padres fan or living in San Diego, it's likely that you were caught in the excitement.

This offseason, Preller's out there again. He could have become gun shy, making only the safest decisions and hoping for a slow, gradual rebuild. But while the Padres may end up regretting some of last year's trades, especially if Ross and Turner continue to develop, Preller's greatest skill may be his willingness to keep churning. To not give up. To not fetishize the young, unproven talent that may never pan out like many teams seem to.

The Diamondbacks may have taken the title of most earth-shattering team this offseason, but Preller has restocked the farm system thanks to trading Kimbrel and Joaquin Benoit, acquired a new left fielder and opened a spot for Cory Spangenberg by dealing Jedd Gyorko, and on and on and on. If death means the lack of action, then the Padres are anything but dead.

Sure, Astros-style total rebuilds have a higher guarantee of future success as your minor league system eventually overwhelms the opposition like hordes of the undead crashing through a barricade. But at the same time, your fan base has to endure years upon years of 60-win seasons with no reason to tune in other than tradition or some sense that this is character building. Life's short. Is that really what you want?

Flags fly forever and there's little more exciting than watching your team make a postseason run. But there's also something to be said for the feeling you have when the season begins, when anything is possible. Your head may say that you want the long, slow, incremental burn but the eight-year-old in your heart wants ice cream for dinner and Justin Upton, Wil Myers and Matt Kemp all in one outfield.

The Padres may not be favorites in 2016, but thanks to Preller's refusal to give in, the future is still bright and the on-field product will be exciting. And isn't that what sports are all about? ■

—Michael Clair writes for MLB.com's Cut4 and believes Craig Counsell's batting stance is arguably the greatest thing in baseball history. Follow him @Clairbearattack.

Hitters

Austin Allen C

Born: 1/16/94 Age: 22 Bats: L Throws: R Height: 6'4" Weight: 225

YEAR	TEAM	LVL	AGE	PA	R	2B	3B	HR	RBI	BB	K	SB	CS	AVG/OBP/SLG	TAv	BABIP	BRR	FRAA	WARP
2015	TRI	A-	21	222	23	10	1	2	34	21	38	1	2	.240/.315/.332	.255	.283	-3.9	C(51): -0.9	0.4
2016	*SDN*	*MLB*	*22*	*250*	*20*	*9*	*1*	*4*	*22*	*13*	*68*	*0*	*0*	*.202/.248/.306*	*.198*	*.261*	*-0.3*	*C -0*	*-0.6*
2017	*SDN*	*MLB*	*23*	*253*	*24*	*9*	*1*	*5*	*23*	*14*	*66*	*0*	*0*	*.208/.255/.319*	*.211*	*.265*	*-0.5*	*C 0*	*1.0*

Breakout: 2% Improve: 3% Collapse: 1% Attrition: 3% MLB: 5% *Comparables: Kyle Phillips, Jett Bandy, Jason Castro*

The Padres grabbed Allen with their fourth-round pick in 2015 out of Florida Tech, the same Division II school that produced Tim Wakefield. A hulking left-handed hitter with pop that failed to materialize in his pro debut, Allen is a catcher for now but could move elsewhere if his defense stalls. He caught just 17 percent of would-be basestealers last year, while leading the Northwest League in stolen bases allowed by plenty. If a move is needed, he'll have to tap into that power potential. His Twitter bio ends with the phrase "Somewhere Hitting Baseballs Hard," so presumably he's working on it.

Alexi Amarista SS

Born: 4/6/89 Age: 27 Bats: L Throws: R Height: 5'6" Weight: 160

YEAR	TEAM	LVL	AGE	PA	R	2B	3B	HR	RBI	BB	K	SB	CS	AVG/OBP/SLG	TAv	BABIP	BRR	FRAA	WARP
2013	SDN	MLB	24	396	35	14	4	5	32	22	57	4	2	.236/.282/.337	.226	.267	2.2	CF(87): 2.9, 2B(23): 0.1	0.4
2014	SDN	MLB	25	466	39	13	2	5	40	29	69	12	1	.239/.286/.314	.243	.271	0.7	SS(73): 3.9, 3B(22): 1.8	1.4
2015	SDN	MLB	26	357	28	10	4	3	30	24	55	5	1	.204/.257/.287	.205	.232	0.9	SS(85): 3.2, LF(11): -0.5	-0.2
2016	*SDN*	*MLB*	*27*	*543*	*52*	*22*	*5*	*8*	*49*	*30*	*84*	*9*	*2*	*.236/.280/.350*	*.223*	*.261*	*1.2*	*SS 6*	*1.3*
2017	*SDN*	*MLB*	*28*	*475*	*46*	*17*	*4*	*7*	*43*	*27*	*76*	*8*	*2*	*.230/.276/.339*	*.225*	*.257*	*1.0*	*SS 5*	*2.8*

Breakout: 4% Improve: 43% Collapse: 3% Attrition: 12% MLB: 99% *Comparables: Luis Rivas, Cesar Izturis, Alex Cintron*

The next time someone tells you that replacement level is a purely theoretical construct with no basis in reality, point to Amarista and say, "Scoreboard." And while you're busting myths, mention that his BABIP is perpetually low due not to bad luck but to a lack of skill at hitting baseballs hard (his average exit velocity was only slightly higher than that of the two fastballs he threw in mop-up duty). Amarista's offensive game keeps deteriorating despite his being at an age where it should be improving. Pitchers continue to expose and exploit his weaknesses, pushing him to the brink of irrelevance. Only Amarista's defensive versatility prevents him from falling over the edge and landing with as much of a thud as anyone dubbed "Little Ninja" can make.

Clint Barmes SS

Born: 3/6/79 Age: 37 Bats: R Throws: R Height: 6'1" Weight: 200

YEAR	TEAM	LVL	AGE	PA	R	2B	3B	HR	RBI	BB	K	SB	CS	AVG/OBP/SLG	TAv	BABIP	BRR	FRAA	WARP
2013	PIT	MLB	34	330	22	15	0	5	23	14	70	0	0	.211/.249/.309	.211	.257	0.7	SS(106): 1.3	-0.1
2014	PIT	MLB	35	116	15	5	0	0	7	9	18	1	1	.245/.328/.294	.240	.294	0.8	SS(27): -2.6, 2B(14): 0.7	0.1
2014	IND	AAA	35	21	3	0	0	1	2	1	1	0	0	.158/.190/.316	.181	.111	0.1	SS(5): -0.8	-0.2
2015	SDN	MLB	36	224	24	14	1	3	16	10	55	0	1	.232/.281/.353	.244	.302	0.8	SS(89): 0.7, 1B(1): 0.0	0.7
2016	*SDN*	*MLB*	*37*	*250*	*22*	*11*	*1*	*5*	*23*	*13*	*55*	*1*	*1*	*.225/.275/.337*	*.219*	*.269*	*0.6*	*SS 0, 1B -0*	*0.2*
2017	*SDN*	*MLB*	*38*	*118*	*11*	*4*	*0*	*2*	*10*	*6*	*26*	*0*	*0*	*.211/.262/.303*	*.211*	*.257*	*0.3*	*SS 0, 1B 0*	*0.6*

Breakout: 1% Improve: 32% Collapse: 14% Attrition: 23% MLB: 82% *Comparables: Alan Trammell, Willie Bloomquist, Juan Castro*

Barmes' bat entered the witness protection program in October 2011, extracted from an abandoned warehouse in Houston under cover of night. It resurfaced in San Diego last April under an assumed identity and found its way back into Barmes' hands. The bat remained there for three months, allowing its wielder to masquerade as a league-average hitter before marshals tracked it down and retrieved it, returning the wayward piece of lumber to a secure location. Barmes was saddened by the loss of his dear friend but understood that it was for the best. The bat was safe again, as were we all in the knowledge that order had been restored.

Christian Bethancourt C

Born: 9/2/91 Age: 24 Bats: R Throws: R Height: 6'2" Weight: 205

YEAR	TEAM	LVL	AGE	PA	R	2B	3B	HR	RBI	BB	K	SB	CS	AVG/OBP/SLG	TAv	BABIP	BRR	FRAA	WARP
2013	MIS	AA	21	388	42	21	0	12	45	16	57	11	7	.277/.305/.436	.273	.294	-0.4	C(85): -2.5	2.0
2013	ATL	MLB	21	1	0	0	0	0	0	0	1	0	0	.000/.000/.000	.053	--	0.0		0.0
2014	GWN	AAA	22	365	33	17	1	8	48	13	61	7	1	.283/.308/.408	.242	.318	0.3	C(80): 1.8	1.1
2014	ATL	MLB	22	117	7	3	0	0	9	3	26	1	1	.248/.274/.274	.210	.322	0.2	C(31): -4.2	-0.5
2015	GWN	AAA	23	218	25	19	0	4	31	12	31	5	0	.327/.359/.480	.292	.365	-0.4	C(48): 1.1	1.8
2015	ATL	MLB	23	160	16	8	0	2	12	5	33	1	1	.200/.225/.290	.201	.242	0.2	C(42): -2.9	-0.5
2016	*SDN*	*MLB*	*24*	*91*	*10*	*5*	*0*	*2*	*9*	*3*	*19*	*1*	*0*	*.255/.280/.398*	*.240*	*.296*	*0.1*	*C -2*	*0.0*
2017	*SDN*	*MLB*	*25*	*286*	*31*	*15*	*1*	*8*	*33*	*9*	*61*	*3*	*1*	*.255/.280/.406*	*.248*	*.296*	*0.4*	*C -7*	*0.5*

Breakout: 9% Improve: 29% Collapse: 8% Attrition: 19% MLB: 52% *Comparables: Miguel Perez, Rob Brantly, J.R. Murphy*

YEAR	TEAM	P. COUNT	FRM RUNS	BLK RUNS	THRW RUNS	TOT RUNS
2013	MIS	11249	-4.9	0.0	0.9	-4.0
2014	ATL	4221	-4.4	-0.1	0.1	-4.4
2014	GWN	11439	-0.1	-0.2	1.4	1.1
2015	ATL	5948	-4.9	-0.2	0.3	-4.7
2015	GWN	6604	0.8	0.3	0.4	1.6
2016	*SDN*	*3356*	*-2.3*	*-0.1*	*0.1*	*-2.3*
2017	*SDN*	*10537*	*-8.0*	*-0.1*	*0.3*	*-7.8*

The definition of insanity is watching Bethancourt play baseball and hoping for different results. The tools and athleticism are there. They've been there since he signed out of Panama, since he played a full season behind the plate at 18 years old, since he was deemed the catcher of the future by former Braves general manager Frank Wren. Applying them on a daily basis, taking charge of a pitching staff and putting in the necessary work continue to be the issues. Bethancourt loses focus behind the plate at times, and inconsistent footwork and accuracy hinder his elite arm strength. He has plus raw power but levels his swing and struggles with pitch recognition. It's been the same stuff for some time now, and, much as it hurts to say this about a 24-year-old, he doesn't have forever to clean it up and become the every-day catcher many expected. If all of this sounds like a change-of-scenery candidate, congratulations, you might be A.J. Preller.

Jabari Blash OF

Born: 7/4/89 Age: 26 Bats: R Throws: R Height: 6'5" Weight: 225

YEAR	TEAM	LVL	AGE	PA	R	2B	3B	HR	RBI	BB	K	SB	CS	AVG/OBP/SLG	TAv	BABIP	BRR	FRAA	WARP
2013	HDS	A+	23	332	42	16	3	16	53	40	85	14	8	.258/.358/.505	.297	.308	-0.4	LF(36): -6.5, RF(22): 3.9	1.7
2013	WTN	AA	23	120	13	3	0	9	21	20	28	1	1	.309/.442/.619	.381	.350	0.0	RF(23): 1.1, LF(2): 0.2	1.9
2014	WTN	AA	24	163	27	7	1	6	22	28	35	4	1	.236/.387/.449	.313	.270	-0.6	RF(21): 0.9, LF(2): -0.2	1.2
2014	TAC	AAA	24	189	23	8	0	12	37	17	57	2	2	.210/.312/.481	.285	.232	1.6	RF(41): -2.4	0.8
2015	WTN	AA	25	248	38	16	2	10	34	31	60	5	0	.278/.383/.517	.338	.340	-2.2	RF(45): -2.4, LF(9): -1.0	2.0
2015	TAC	AAA	25	228	41	8	0	22	47	28	63	3	1	.264/.355/.640	.323	.263	-1.5	RF(34): -4.8, LF(3): 0.2	1.3
2016	*SDN*	*MLB*	*26*	*119*	*16*	*4*	*0*	*6*	*18*	*12*	*36*	*1*	*0*	*.228/.320/.463*	*.281*	*.278*	*-0.1*	*LF -1*	*0.5*
2017	*SDN*	*MLB*	*27*	*327*	*47*	*11*	*1*	*18*	*49*	*35*	*102*	*3*	*1*	*.224/.318/.458*	*.285*	*.275*	*-0.2*	*LF -4*	*0.4*

Breakout: 7% Improve: 22% Collapse: 15% Attrition: 29% MLB: 62% *Comparables: Steven Souza, Russ Canzler, Andrew Lambo*

Blash, 26, might have missed his best chance to get a cup coffee in the big leagues. If so, that would be a shame. It's not that the Mariners turned their backs on a future star: Blash is a one-tool player and his proficient walk rate is more the product of passivity than discernment. Padres fans who remember Paul McAnulty and Kyle Blanks are familiar with the downside of this skill set. It's just that Blash averaged about eight minutes of hang time per homer last season, and his power belongs on the main stage, if only for 24 minutes or so.

Michael Gettys CF

Born: 10/22/95 Age: 20 Bats: R Throws: R Height: 6'1" Weight: 203

YEAR	TEAM	LVL	AGE	PA	R	2B	3B	HR	RBI	BB	K	SB	CS	AVG/OBP/SLG	TAv	BABIP	BRR	FRAA	WARP
2015	FTW	A	19	529	62	27	6	6	44	28	162	20	10	.231/.271/.346	.227	.326	2.4	CF(115): 17.6	1.8
2016	*SDN*	*MLB*	*20*	*250*	*21*	*9*	*1*	*5*	*22*	*8*	*92*	*5*	*3*	*.190/.218/.298*	*.184*	*.281*	*0.1*	*CF 3*	*-0.8*
2017	*SDN*	*MLB*	*21*	*395*	*36*	*16*	*3*	*8*	*37*	*14*	*143*	*8*	*4*	*.202/.233/.321*	*.202*	*.299*	*0.6*	*CF 5*	*1.8*

Breakout: 0% Improve: 0% Collapse: 1% Attrition: 1% MLB: 1% *Comparables: Keon Broxton, Greg Golson, Trayce Thompson*

The toolsy but raw Gettys did fascinating things in his full-season debut. His 21 outfield assists tied for the Midwest League lead, and he turned more double plays than the entire outfields of five teams. On the downside, his quick bat remains unscuffed by baseballs—he struck out in 31 percent of his plate appearances. Although concerns about the hit tool are softened by youth, we all get older, and his ability to adjust will determine how far he goes. The athletic center fielder possesses undeniable physical talent, but his inability to solve even A-ball pitchers makes those tired Drew Stubbs comparisons that have dogged him since he was drafted all the more sobering. Still, there is plenty to dream on, and Stubbs did get his face on some baseball cards.

Ruddy Giron SS

Born: 1/4/97 Age: 19 Bats: R Throws: R Height: 5'11" Weight: 175

YEAR	TEAM	LVL	AGE	PA	R	2B	3B	HR	RBI	BB	K	SB	CS	AVG/OBP/SLG	TAv	BABIP	BRR	FRAA	WARP
2015	FTW	A	18	419	58	12	4	9	49	29	68	15	14	.285/.335/.407	.280	.325	3.2	SS(90): 1.7	3.1
2016	*SDN*	*MLB*	*19*	*250*	*29*	*9*	*2*	*7*	*24*	*11*	*61*	*4*	*4*	*.232/.268/.368*	*.228*	*.281*	*-0.5*	*SS 1, 3B 0*	*0.4*
2017	*SDN*	*MLB*	*20*	*413*	*47*	*17*	*3*	*13*	*49*	*20*	*92*	*7*	*6*	*.248/.287/.408*	*.256*	*.291*	*-0.3*	*SS 1*	*1.9*

Breakout: 0% Improve: 5% Collapse: 0% Attrition: 2% MLB: 7% *Comparables: Addison Russell, Carlos Correa, Manny Machado*

Grand entrances? On May 18th, in his first game of full-season ball, Giron went 6-for-6 with a homer and a stolen base. On July 6th he hit his eighth home run of the year, bringing his line to .331/.383/.534 despite being one of the Midwest League's youngest players. Word got out, and he hit .245/.293/.298 over his final 52 games. Still, the overall numbers are solid for one so young, particularly in a challenging circuit. Giron struggled against same-side pitching, and there are rumblings that he might move to second base at some point. Last year's scorching start provides cause for some excitement, but in an organization less starved for a sustainable answer at shortstop, or less apt to progressively promote its prospects, he wouldn't attract as much attention as he has.

Javier Guerra SS

Born: 9/25/95 Age: 20 Bats: L Throws: R Height: 5'11" Weight: 155

YEAR	TEAM	LVL	AGE	PA	R	2B	3B	HR	RBI	BB	K	SB	CS	AVG/OBP/SLG	TAv	BABIP	BRR	FRAA	WARP
2015	GRN	A	19	477	64	23	3	15	68	30	112	7	9	.279/.329/.449	.280	.342	0.0	SS(112): 9.6, 2B(1): 0.0	4.1
2016	*SDN*	*MLB*	*20*	*250*	*27*	*9*	*1*	*8*	*26*	*11*	*79*	*1*	*1*	*.215/.253/.366*	*.217*	*.281*	*-0.4*	*SS 2, 2B 0*	*0.2*
2017	*SDN*	*MLB*	*21*	*409*	*45*	*18*	*2*	*13*	*48*	*20*	*126*	*2*	*2*	*.227/.268/.388*	*.236*	*.297*	*-0.6*	*SS 3, 2B 0*	*2.1*

Breakout: 2% Improve: 4% Collapse: 0% Attrition: 5% MLB: 6% *Comparables: Nick Franklin, Corey Seager, Javier Baez*

After failing to develop good shortstops internally for the better part of a decade, the Red Sox have had several hits as of late: Jose Iglesias is good, Xander Bogaerts is a star and Deven Marrero exists. The Padres hope that Guerra picked up some of that fairy dust after a breakout season. Already respected for his glove and arm, Guerra rocked 15 homers in Low-A as a rail-thin 19-year-old, belying his origami physique. Guerra also upped his walk rate substantially from a year ago (it would've been hard to lower it), and while he struck out in over a fifth of his PA, he showed decent bat-to-ball ability. Guerra is still probably three-plus years out, but he only has to produce 1.2 WARP to surpass a certain former Dodgers closer as the best Javier Guerra in baseball history.

Austin Hedges C

Born: 8/18/92 Age: 23 Bats: R Throws: R Height: 6'1" Weight: 200

YEAR	TEAM	LVL	AGE	PA	R	2B	3B	HR	RBI	BB	K	SB	CS	AVG/OBP/SLG	TAv	BABIP	BRR	FRAA	WARP
2013	SAN	AA	20	75	4	3	0	0	8	6	9	3	1	.224/.297/.269	.225	.259	0.4	C(18): -0.4	0.1
2013	LEL	A+	20	266	34	22	1	4	30	22	45	5	4	.270/.343/.425	.279	.314	0.7	C(61): 2.7	2.1
2014	SAN	AA	21	457	31	19	2	6	44	23	89	1	3	.225/.268/.321	.210	.269	-1.7	C(106): 38.5	3.5
2015	SDN	MLB	22	152	13	2	0	3	11	8	38	0	0	.168/.215/.248	.191	.202	1.6	C(47): 8.5	0.7
2015	ELP	AAA	22	79	12	8	0	2	15	8	8	1	0	.324/.392/.521	.313	.344	0.0	C(17): 4.3	1.2
2016	*SDN*	*MLB*	*23*	*183*	*15*	*8*	*1*	*3*	*18*	*9*	*42*	*1*	*0*	*.218/.263/.334*	*.213*	*.264*	*-0.3*	*C 8*	*0.8*
2017	*SDN*	*MLB*	*24*	*403*	*41*	*18*	*1*	*9*	*40*	*23*	*91*	*1*	*1*	*.219/.269/.346*	*.227*	*.262*	*-0.8*	*C 18*	*3.5*

Breakout: 4% Improve: 7% Collapse: 2% Attrition: 12% MLB: 14% *Comparables: Rene Rivera, Luke Maile, Carlos Perez*

YEAR	TEAM	P. COUNT	FRM RUNS	BLK RUNS	THRW RUNS	TOT RUNS
2014	SAN	15026	35.4	1.4	4.0	40.8
2015	ELP	2301	3.3	0.0	0.0	3.2
2015	SDN	5804	8.4	0.1	0.3	8.7
2016	*SDN*	*6998*	*8.1*	*0.3*	*0.2*	*8.6*
2017	*SDN*	*15413*	*17.0*	*0.6*	*0.4*	*17.9*

In his much-anticipated debut, Hedges' glove was as good as advertised. He nailed a third of would-be basestealers, which doesn't sound impressive until you realize that he usually caught Tyson Ross, whose track meets have become the stuff of legend. Hedges also ranked among the best at pitch framing despite receiving fewer pitches than those above him. On the downside, his bat was as bad as advertised. His 31 OPS+ tied him (Nick Hundley, 2012) for fourth lowest in Padres history, minimum 150 plate appearances. Although defense will always be Hedges' calling card and should keep him around for a long time, he'll need to start hitting if he's to become more Brad Ausmus than Jeff Mathis.

Travis Jankowski CF

Born: 6/15/91 Age: 25 Bats: L Throws: R Height: 6'2" Weight: 190

YEAR	TEAM	LVL	AGE	PA	R	2B	3B	HR	RBI	BB	K	SB	CS	AVG/OBP/SLG	TAv	BABIP	BRR	FRAA	WARP
2013	LEL	A+	22	556	89	19	6	1	38	54	96	71	14	.286/.356/.355	.281	.350	10.4	CF(117): 9.7	5.1
2014	EUG	A-	23	36	6	0	0	0	1	3	5	4	0	.182/.250/.182	.174	.214	0.4	CF(7): -1.6	-0.4
2014	SAN	AA	23	112	14	4	1	0	10	8	14	10	2	.240/.297/.300	.227	.273	-0.3	CF(28): -0.9	-0.2
2014	LEL	A+	23	25	2	1	0	0	1	6	3	1	0	.167/.375/.222	.271	.200	0.1	CF(3): -0.7, CF(1): -0.7	0.0
2015	ELP	AAA	24	113	19	6	2	0	12	13	10	9	3	.392/.464/.495	.334	.432	1.5	CF(24): 2.4	1.6
2015	SDN	MLB	24	96	9	2	2	2	12	4	24	2	1	.211/.245/.344	.234	.266	0.2	CF(23): -2.5, RF(11): 0.8	-0.2
2015	SAN	AA	24	321	50	11	5	1	13	36	40	23	8	.316/.395/.401	.281	.365	-1.3	CF(62): 2.8	1.8
2016	*SDN*	*MLB*	*25*	*121*	*15*	*4*	*1*	*1*	*9*	*9*	*24*	*6*	*2*	*.250/.310/.345*	*.237*	*.303*	*0.6*		*0.2*
2017	*SDN*	*MLB*	*26*	*349*	*36*	*12*	*4*	*4*	*31*	*26*	*70*	*18*	*6*	*.250/.309/.352*	*.246*	*.301*	*2.6*	*LF 0*	*1.2*

Breakout: 4% Improve: 32% Collapse: 8% Attrition: 35% MLB: 54% *Comparables: Ezequiel Carrera, A.J. Pollock, Matt Angle*

Jankowski is the baseball equivalent of a lanky placekicker, a slap-hitting center fielder who miraculously popped two balls over the fence during his brief Padres debut and whose speed and defense could earn him a bench role. It's not an exciting profile, but being physically able to cover center is in pretty high demand in San Diego these days. If one were to squint, in fact, one could envision him as the Padres' Jarrod Dyson. That is, if Jankowski were more like Dyson, and the Padres were more like the Royals.

Jon Jay CF

Born: 3/15/85 Age: 31 Bats: L Throws: L Height: 5'11" Weight: 195

YEAR	TEAM	LVL	AGE	PA	R	2B	3B	HR	RBI	BB	K	SB	CS	AVG/OBP/SLG	TAv	BABIP	BRR	FRAA	WARP
2013	SLN	MLB	28	628	75	27	2	7	67	52	103	10	5	.276/.351/.370	.263	.325	3.6	CF(152): -6.7	1.8
2014	SLN	MLB	29	468	52	16	3	3	46	28	78	6	3	.303/.372/.378	.277	.363	-1.6	CF(98): -3.9, RF(33): -3.7	1.1
2015	SLN	MLB	30	245	25	5	1	1	10	19	36	0	2	.210/.306/.257	.214	.246	-0.1	CF(54): 1.3, LF(17): 0.0	-0.3
2016	*SDN*	*MLB*	*31*	*435*	*51*	*17*	*3*	*6*	*38*	*30*	*77*	*6*	*3*	*.270/.338/.378*	*.257*	*.315*	*0.5*	*LF 5, CF -1*	*1.8*
2017	*SDN*	*MLB*	*32*	*327*	*37*	*13*	*2*	*5*	*31*	*21*	*59*	*4*	*2*	*.266/.331/.373*	*.261*	*.310*	*0.5*	*LF 4, CF 0*	*1.4*

Breakout: 0% Improve: 52% Collapse: 2% Attrition: 9% MLB: 97% *Comparables: Coco Crisp, Denard Span, Jacoby Ellsbury*

Jay is the textbook example of a second-division starter: He's a quality player who has the chops for center field and delivers better-than-average production at the plate. He's not an All-Star, he's never going to make it into Cooperstown or a Nelly song, but he's a player who can help a team win until something better comes along. So imagine Jay's surprise when, upon returning from his second stint on the disabled list, he received a standing ovation from the St. Louis crowd. It lasted 30 seconds and might have gone longer if not for an obtuse organist stepping all over the moment. Hopefully that hero's welcome heartened him, because the rest of his season had to be frustrating. He dealt with multiple wrist issues and, perhaps relatedly, suffered through the worst season of his career offensively. Anything that can impact a player's swing has to be taken seriously; meaning that, although there's every statistical reason to believe Jay will return to his old form in 2016, don't consider it a foregone conclusion. As such, he could soon begin the next phase of his career as a quality fourth outfielder.

Matt Kemp RF

Born: 9/23/84 Age: 31 Bats: R Throws: R Height: 6'4" Weight: 210

YEAR	TEAM	LVL	AGE	PA	R	2B	3B	HR	RBI	BB	K	SB	CS	AVG/OBP/SLG	TAv	BABIP	BRR	FRAA	WARP
2013	LAN	MLB	28	290	35	15	0	6	33	22	76	9	0	.270/.328/.395	.252	.353	3.6	CF(70): -3.8	0.6
2014	LAN	MLB	29	599	77	38	3	25	89	52	145	8	5	.287/.346/.506	.307	.345	-0.8	RF(59): -0.8, LF(44): -2.1	3.7
2015	SDN	MLB	30	648	80	31	3	23	100	39	147	12	2	.265/.312/.443	.273	.311	1.8	RF(149): 4.5	2.7
2016	*SDN*	*MLB*	*31*	*593*	*78*	*29*	*3*	*26*	*85*	*49*	*144*	*11*	*3*	*.278/.339/.487*	*.289*	*.332*	*1.2*	*RF 4*	*3.9*
2017	*SDN*	*MLB*	*32*	*538*	*71*	*25*	*2*	*20*	*72*	*44*	*136*	*9*	*3*	*.268/.331/.456*	*.284*	*.329*	*1.1*	*RF 4*	*1.6*

Breakout: 0% Improve: 41% Collapse: 5% Attrition: 5% MLB: 99% *Comparables: Hank Aaron, Josh Hamilton, Ryan Braun*

Kemp was the domino that toppled all the others as A.J. Preller rebuilt a moribund Padres franchise, swapping youth for fame without apparent regard for cost. Kemp himself stumbled out of the gate, not hitting his second home run until June 6th. As he had a year earlier, he enjoyed a second-half surge, making his overall line palatable in a Travis Fryman kind of way. Now into his 30s and with arthritic hips, Kemp has slowed on the bases and is—last year's FRAA notwithstanding—a dreadful right fielder. Still, if he keeps those hips in check, he should be able to maintain Fryman levels of production for a while longer. Of course, when you've broken the bank to pay for that, you'd better hope it's a really big bank.

Rymer Liriano RF

Born: 6/20/91 Age: 25 Bats: R Throws: R Height: 6'0" Weight: 230

YEAR	TEAM	LVL	AGE	PA	R	2B	3B	HR	RBI	BB	K	SB	CS	AVG/OBP/SLG	TAv	BABIP	BRR	FRAA	WARP
2014	ELP	AAA	23	71	14	11	1	0	13	8	14	3	1	.452/.521/.661	.371	.583	-1.3	RF(11): -1.4, CF(5): -0.6	0.1
2014	SDN	MLB	23	121	13	2	0	1	6	9	39	4	1	.220/.289/.266	.210	.329	1.1	RF(34): -0.7	-0.4
2014	SAN	AA	23	415	55	20	2	14	53	35	102	17	7	.264/.335/.442	.277	.326	5.3	LF(55): 6.6, CF(37): 5.0	3.7
2015	ELP	AAA	24	549	85	31	3	14	64	64	132	18	8	.292/.383/.460	.289	.376	2.5	RF(102): 13.8, CF(19): -0.9	4.3
2016	*SDN*	*MLB*	*25*	*261*	*30*	*12*	*1*	*7*	*29*	*23*	*77*	*7*	*3*	*.238/.313/.388*	*.251*	*.321*	*0.1*	*LF 1, RF 1*	*0.8*
2017	*SDN*	*MLB*	*26*	*384*	*46*	*17*	*1*	*10*	*42*	*35*	*115*	*10*	*4*	*.238/.316/.382*	*.258*	*.325*	*0.5*	*LF 2, RF 2*	*1.3*

Breakout: 7% Improve: 23% Collapse: 9% Attrition: 33% MLB: 56% *Comparables: Ben Johnson, Steven Souza, Brent Clevlen*

Liriano flashed some promise in his 2014 big-league debut before being squeezed out of last year's plans, thanks to new management's acquisition spree. He nearly duplicated his minor-league line of a year earlier while moving up a level, setting a career high in walks along the way. Liriano finished with a flourish, hitting .341/.412/.561 over the final two months. Although southpaws continue to give him trouble and the stout right fielder (who also played some center field at El Paso last year) doesn't run as much as he once did—an admittedly weird thing to say about a 25-year-old—there is little left for him to prove in the minors. If only the Padres still made trades.

Manuel Margot CF

Born: 9/28/94 Age: 21 Bats: R Throws: R Height: 5'11" Weight: 170

YEAR	TEAM	LVL	AGE	PA	R	2B	3B	HR	RBI	BB	K	SB	CS	AVG/OBP/SLG	TAv	BABIP	BRR	FRAA	WARP
2013	LOW	A-	18	216	29	8	2	1	21	22	40	18	8	.270/.346/.351	.283	.333	2.9	CF(47): 7.3	2.3
2014	SLM	A+	19	56	4	5	0	2	14	2	5	3	2	.340/.364/.560	.320	.333	0.0	CF(16): -0.5	0.5
2014	GRN	A	19	413	61	20	5	10	45	37	49	39	13	.286/.355/.449	.282	.309	2.8	CF(96): 10.3	3.6
2015	PME	AA	20	282	38	21	4	3	33	21	36	19	8	.271/.326/.419	.270	.303	1.9	CF(63): -2.5, RF(1): 0.1	1.1
2015	SLM	A+	20	198	35	6	5	3	17	11	15	20	5	.282/.321/.420	.273	.289	1.5	CF(42): 6.2	1.7
2016	*SDN*	*MLB*	*21*	*250*	*30*	*11*	*2*	*6*	*25*	*13*	*51*	*14*	*5*	*.239/.282/.380*	*.234*	*.278*	*1.1*	*CF 5*	*0.9*
2017	*SDN*	*MLB*	*22*	*436*	*49*	*19*	*5*	*11*	*49*	*29*	*87*	*25*	*10*	*.248/.300/.404*	*.256*	*.285*	*3.4*	*CF 8, LF 0*	*2.7*

Breakout: 4% Improve: 15% Collapse: 0% Attrition: 7% MLB: 19% *Comparables: Melky Cabrera, Mason Williams, Andrew McCutchen*

Traded to Philadelphia for Cole Ham... wait, that *didn't* happen? Well then. In a sense, we didn't learn much new about Margot in 2015. Just like we thought after 2014, he's a potentially elite defensive center fielder with a good feel for hitting, patient approach, above-average speed and doubles power. What we did learn is that Margot can still flash all of these abilities even in the upper minors. While Margot's numbers never quite jump off the page, remember that last year he received more than half of his PA as a 20-year-old in Double-A, where the average player is old enough to rent a car. There's danger in assuming that just because a player holds his own while young he'll thrive once older, but discounting such a factor is equally perilous. If nothing else, we'll get to see how Margot performs without the distraction of leading all 21-year-olds in MLB Trade Rumors this season.

Wil Myers OF

Born: 12/10/90 Age: 25 Bats: R Throws: R Height: 6'3" Weight: 205

YEAR	TEAM	LVL	AGE	PA	R	2B	3B	HR	RBI	BB	K	SB	CS	AVG/OBP/SLG	TAv	BABIP	BRR	FRAA	WARP
2013	TBA	MLB	22	373	50	23	0	13	53	33	91	5	2	.293/.354/.478	.303	.362	0.3	RF(72): -5.0, CF(8): 2.4	2.1
2013	DUR	AAA	22	289	44	13	2	14	57	29	71	7	1	.286/.356/.520	.290	.335	0.3	RF(56): 4.5	2.0
2014	DUR	AAA	23	31	3	1	0	2	6	7	7	3	0	.250/.419/.542	.306	.267	0.2	LF(2): 0.9, RF(2): -0.0	0.3
2014	TBA	MLB	23	361	37	14	0	6	35	34	90	6	1	.222/.294/.320	.233	.286	-2.6	RF(78): 3.6, 1B(2): 0.0	-0.3
2015	SDN	MLB	24	253	40	13	1	8	29	27	55	5	2	.253/.336/.427	.288	.302	0.7	CF(38): -5.4, 1B(22): 0.3	0.9
2016	*SDN*	*MLB*	*25*	*622*	*74*	*29*	*2*	*21*	*78*	*57*	*150*	*11*	*3*	*.257/.326/.430*	*.270*	*.312*	*-0.7*	*1B 5, LF -0*	*2.2*
2017	*SDN*	*MLB*	*26*	*457*	*60*	*21*	*1*	*17*	*60*	*43*	*108*	*8*	*2*	*.258/.330/.441*	*.283*	*.308*	*-0.4*	*1B 3, LF 0*	*0.9*

Breakout: 2% Improve: 53% Collapse: 1% Attrition: 6% MLB: 97% *Comparables: Chris Young, Matt Kemp, Melvin Upton*

Myers started strong with his new team, hitting .291/.340/.493 before tendinitis in his left wrist shelved him for a month. He returned for three games in mid-June, then spent the next 10 weeks on the disabled list recovering from surgery on the same wrist. Primarily a center fielder by necessity before the injuries, Myers saw more action at first base when activated in September. He re-aggravated the wrist a month later, casting further shadows on his future. If 2015 told us anything about Myers it's that he a) can hit when healthy, b) can't stay healthy and c) isn't a big-league center fielder. He remains an intriguing offensive talent, though his monster 2012 campaign has all but disappeared in the rearview mirror.

Derek Norris C

Born: 2/14/89 Age: 27 Bats: R Throws: R Height: 6'0" Weight: 210

YEAR	TEAM	LVL	AGE	PA	R	2B	3B	HR	RBI	BB	K	SB	CS	AVG/OBP/SLG	TAv	BABIP	BRR	FRAA	WARP
2013	OAK	MLB	24	308	41	16	0	9	30	37	71	5	0	.246/.345/.409	.289	.301	0.3	C(91): 1.0, 1B(1): -0.2	2.4
2014	OAK	MLB	25	442	46	19	1	10	55	54	86	2	2	.270/.361/.403	.289	.324	-4.8	C(114): -11.7	1.4
2015	SDN	MLB	26	557	65	33	2	14	62	35	131	4	1	.250/.305/.404	.263	.310	-5.0	C(128): 13.5, 1B(17): -1.6	3.3
2016	*SDN*	*MLB*	*27*	*549*	*61*	*26*	*2*	*17*	*67*	*50*	*127*	*5*	*2*	*.249/.323/.415*	*.267*	*.301*	*-3.4*	*C 2, 1B -4*	*1.8*
2017	*SDN*	*MLB*	*28*	*505*	*61*	*23*	*2*	*15*	*58*	*49*	*122*	*4*	*1*	*.240/.317/.398*	*.268*	*.295*	*-3.2*	*C 1, 1B -3*	*1.0*

Breakout: 3% Improve: 53% Collapse: 6% Attrition: 10% MLB: 99% *Comparables: Miguel Montero, Jason Castro, Joe Torre*

YEAR	TEAM	P. COUNT	FRM RUNS	BLK RUNS	THRW RUNS	TOT RUNS
2013	OAK	10574	1.3	-0.3	0.0	0.9
2013	SAC	285	0.2	0.0	0.0	0.2
2014	OAK	13348	-10.1	-0.4	-1.1	-11.6
2015	SDN	17344	12.2	-0.5	2.4	14.1
2016	*SDN*	*13541*	*2.0*	*-0.4*	*0.5*	*2.1*
2017	*SDN*	*12466*	*0.7*	*-0.3*	*0.3*	*0.7*

A funny thing happened to Norris on his way to the National League: He learned how to throw out baserunners, and forgot how to get on base. He established career highs in several offensive categories, at the expense of a strikeout-to-walk ratio that more than doubled. On defense, he led all big-league catchers in caught stealing by a freakishly large margin. He also improved his pitch-framing during the season, moving from among the worst in May to among the best by the final bell. The Padres sometimes had Norris play first base to save his body from wear and tear, as well as to accommodate Austin Hedges. The gains in power and on defense are encouraging, but Norris must rediscover his plate discipline or risk having that weakness exploited further. Fortunately he's young and talented enough to do that; not making him play 147 games again might help.

Hunter Renfroe RF

Born: 1/28/92 Age: 24 Bats: R Throws: R Height: 6'1" Weight: 215

YEAR	TEAM	LVL	AGE	PA	R	2B	3B	HR	RBI	BB	K	SB	CS	AVG/OBP/SLG	TAv	BABIP	BRR	FRAA	WARP
2013	EUG	A-	21	111	20	9	0	4	18	5	26	2	0	.308/.333/.510	.335	.368	1.1	RF(25): 2.6	1.5
2013	FTW	A	21	72	6	5	0	2	7	4	23	0	0	.212/.268/.379	.230	.293	-1.0	RF(16): -2.2	-0.4
2014	SAN	AA	22	251	17	12	0	5	23	25	53	2	1	.232/.307/.353	.244	.280	-0.5	LF(30): -0.3, CF(22): -2.0	0.0
2014	LEL	A+	22	316	46	21	3	16	52	28	81	9	3	.295/.370/.565	.340	.359	-0.3	RF(49): 0.3, RF(7): 0.3	3.3
2015	SAN	AA	23	463	50	22	3	14	54	33	112	4	1	.259/.313/.425	.259	.316	1.6	RF(79): 13.1, CF(8): -1.7	2.2
2015	ELP	AAA	23	95	15	5	2	6	24	4	20	1	0	.333/.358/.633	.314	.369	0.7	RF(17): 1.1, CF(3): 0.0	0.9
2016	*SDN*	*MLB*	*24*	*250*	*26*	*11*	*1*	*9*	*32*	*15*	*74*	*1*	*0*	*.227/.278/.403*	*.240*	*.289*	*-0.2*	*RF 2, CF -0*	*0.3*
2017	*SDN*	*MLB*	*25*	*389*	*45*	*17*	*2*	*14*	*48*	*23*	*113*	*1*	*0*	*.226/.277/.404*	*.247*	*.285*	*-0.5*	*RF 4, CF 0*	*1.1*

Breakout: 2% Improve: 6% Collapse: 2% Attrition: 11% MLB: 18% *Comparables: Zoilo Almonte, Casper Wells, Bryce Brentz*

Renfroe's tools remain ahead of his production: The bulky right fielder struggled to find a groove in his encore at San Antonio, getting beat by breaking balls early and hitting .224/.278/.324 through May. His tendency to expand the strike zone diminishes the utility of his power: That .711 OPS in 714 career Double-A plate appearances hardly screams middle-of-the-order weapon. Renfroe's bat warmed with the weather and he thrived after a late-season promotion to the PCL, though he didn't control the zone there either. He runs well for a big man and has a right fielder's arm. If he develops a more discerning eye that allows him to tap into his power with greater consistency, he could be a minor star. If not—well, plenty of guys can crush a poorly located fastball. The adjustments have been slow to come, but they are coming. Be patient, and hope Renfroe learns to do the same.

Jose Rondon SS

Born: 3/3/94 Age: 22 Bats: R Throws: R Height: 6'1" Weight: 160

YEAR	TEAM	LVL	AGE	PA	R	2B	3B	HR	RBI	BB	K	SB	CS	AVG/OBP/SLG	TAv	BABIP	BRR	FRAA	WARP
2014	LEL	A+	20	154	18	9	0	1	12	13	23	3	1	.301/.371/.390	.278	.357	-0.3	SS(30): -0.5, SS(3): -0.5	0.8
2014	INL	A+	20	324	40	17	5	0	24	17	50	8	6	.327/.362/.418	.276	.391	0.0		0.0
2015	SAN	AA	21	107	6	2	1	0	9	4	15	1	3	.190/.219/.230	.184	.221	-1.2	SS(27): 1.1	-0.4
2015	LEL	A+	21	264	50	12	3	3	22	21	38	17	6	.300/.360/.414	.291	.345	4.6	SS(53): -4.6	2.0
2016	*SDN*	*MLB*	*22*	*63*	*7*	*2*	*0*	*1*	*5*	*3*	*14*	*1*	*1*	*.223/.269/.321*	*.211*	*.270*	*-0.1*	*SS -0*	*0.0*
2017	*SDN*	*MLB*	*23*	*333*	*33*	*13*	*2*	*5*	*30*	*19*	*68*	*6*	*4*	*.231/.279/.333*	*.226*	*.275*	*0.1*	*SS -1*	*1.4*

Breakout: 3% Improve: 7% Collapse: 7% Attrition: 12% MLB: 13% *Comparables: Cristhian Adames, Ehire Adrianza, Ozzie Martinez*

On May 30th, Rondon channeled his inner Freddie Patek and launched two homers in a game at Stockton, matching his total from the previous two seasons combined. Although he will no more be mistaken for a power threat than Patek was, or currently is, Rondon has good bat-to-ball skills and is a sure-handed defender with a strong enough arm to remain at shortstop. There is nothing exciting about his profile, but he's a solid bet to reach The Show in some capacity, possibly as a starter but more likely in a utility role long term. Changing his last name to Izturis might help.

Yangervis Solarte 3B

Born: 7/7/87 Age: 28 Bats: B Throws: R Height: 5'11" Weight: 195

YEAR	TEAM	LVL	AGE	PA	R	2B	3B	HR	RBI	BB	K	SB	CS	AVG/OBP/SLG	TAv	BABIP	BRR	FRAA	WARP
2013	ROU	AAA	25	577	66	31	0	12	75	39	69	3	0	.276/.323/.403	.259	.294	1.4	2B(88): -2.8, SS(20): -0.4	1.3
2014	SDN	MLB	26	246	30	5	1	4	17	23	24	0	1	.267/.336/.355	.267	.281	-0.1	3B(45): -2.4, 2B(10): -1.4	0.4
2014	NYA	MLB	26	289	26	14	0	6	31	30	34	0	0	.254/.337/.381	.270	.270	-1.1	3B(66): -1.2, 2B(17): -1.3	0.8
2014	SWB	AAA	26	21	3	3	1	0	5	1	2	0	0	.600/.619/.850	.476	.667	0.0	3B(4): -0.1, SS(1): 0.1	0.6
2015	SDN	MLB	27	571	63	33	4	14	63	34	56	1	0	.270/.320/.428	.266	.279	-2.1	3B(92): -3.7, 1B(28): -0.7	1.4
2016	*SDN*	*MLB*	*28*	*606*	*61*	*30*	*3*	*14*	*70*	*43*	*73*	*1*	*0*	*.264/.320/.407*	*.257*	*.279*	*-1.3*	*3B -9*	*0.4*
2017	*SDN*	*MLB*	*29*	*530*	*63*	*25*	*1*	*13*	*59*	*43*	*67*	*0*	*0*	*.257/.320/.397*	*.263*	*.271*	*-1.4*	*3B -8*	*0.3*

Breakout: 3% Improve: 53% Collapse: 5% Attrition: 10% MLB: 93% *Comparables: Alberto Callaspo, Luis Rodriguez, Maicer Izturis*

Solarte improved on his surprising rookie campaign, first in a utility role and then at third base when Will Middlebrooks flailed his way back to Triple-A. Solarte makes contact from both sides of the plate, hitting with greater authority from the left side. Typically more of a doubles hitter, he had as many homers as Justin Upton over the season's final three months. Advanced metrics agree that his defense at the hot corner is not so hot, while fans of fielding percentage—hello, is this thing on?—agree that you should get off their lawn. It's easy to discount his success after he languished in the minors for so long, as there must be a reason for the delayed arrival. Then again, maybe his previous organizations were just wrong, and Solarte is simply the new face of average.

Cory Spangenberg UT

Born: 3/16/91 Age: 25 Bats: L Throws: R Height: 6'0" Weight: 195

YEAR	TEAM	LVL	AGE	PA	R	2B	3B	HR	RBI	BB	K	SB	CS	AVG/OBP/SLG	TAv	BABIP	BRR	FRAA	WARP
2013	LEL	A+	22	253	33	13	6	4	31	23	51	17	3	.296/.364/.460	.299	.368	1.5	2B(52): -6.1	1.3
2013	SAN	AA	22	319	35	10	3	2	20	17	61	19	11	.289/.331/.366	.270	.358	0.9	2B(75): 4.0, LF(1): -0.1	1.7
2014	SAN	AA	23	304	38	17	8	2	22	15	63	14	9	.331/.365/.470	.300	.421	-1.8	2B(48): 0.5, CF(14): 2.6	2.3
2014	EUG	A-	23	25	3	0	1	0	2	0	6	2	0	.200/.200/.280	.156	.263	0.5	2B(4): 0.0, CF(1): -0.1	-0.2
2014	SDN	MLB	23	65	7	2	1	2	9	2	14	4	2	.290/.313/.452	.278	.348	0.2	3B(9): -0.6, LF(4): -1.2	0.1
2015	SAN	AA	24	27	3	0	1	0	1	1	2	1	0	.192/.222/.269	.204	.208	0.4	3B(3): 0.6, 2B(2): 0.0	0.0
2015	SDN	MLB	24	345	38	17	5	4	21	28	75	9	4	.271/.333/.399	.268	.344	4.0	2B(70): -4.6, 3B(19): 0.1	1.2
2016	*SDN*	*MLB*	*25*	*551*	*67*	*23*	*7*	*9*	*47*	*32*	*128*	*19*	*8*	*.261/.306/.387*	*.242*	*.322*	*2.8*	*2B -5, 3B -0*	*0.9*
2017	*SDN*	*MLB*	*26*	*532*	*56*	*21*	*7*	*8*	*52*	*34*	*125*	*18*	*8*	*.258/.308/.381*	*.249*	*.320*	*3.6*	*2B -5, 3B 0*	*1.7*

Breakout: 4% Improve: 29% Collapse: 20% Attrition: 32% MLB: 79% *Comparables: Josh Rutledge, Danny Richar, Tony Abreu*

Spangenberg provided surprising value in his first full season, filling in at second base when Jedd Gyorko forgot how to hit, and getting a few reps at third base as well as the outfield. His offensive game revolves around reaching base and running, although he didn't do as much of the latter as he had in the minors. One aspect of his game that did stow away with him is the ability to hang in against lefties, which gives him (and his manager) additional flexibility. Spangenberg also improved as the season progressed, always an encouraging sign for a rookie. He might never make it as a full-time starter, but he's a good bet to have a long career logging significant playing time in a supporting role. In crucial situations, heroes have been made from similar stuff.

Justin Upton LF

Born: 8/25/87 Age: 28 Bats: R Throws: R Height: 6'2" Weight: 205

YEAR	TEAM	LVL	AGE	PA	R	2B	3B	HR	RBI	BB	K	SB	CS	AVG/OBP/SLG	TAv	BABIP	BRR	FRAA	WARP
2013	ATL	MLB	25	643	94	27	2	27	70	75	161	8	1	.263/.354/.464	.293	.321	2.9	LF(108): 0.5, RF(54): -3.4	3.5
2014	ATL	MLB	26	641	77	34	2	29	102	60	171	8	4	.270/.342/.491	.314	.332	0.4	LF(150): -6.3	4.3
2015	SDN	MLB	27	620	85	26	3	26	81	68	159	19	5	.251/.336/.454	.294	.304	3.8	LF(146): -7.0	3.2
2016	*SDN*	*MLB*	*28*	*614*	*82*	*28*	*3*	*26*	*86*	*62*	*143*	*13*	*4*	*.264/.345/.471*	*.288*	*.311*	*1.6*	*LF -0*	*3.9*
2017	*SDN*	*MLB*	*29*	*559*	*78*	*25*	*2*	*24*	*79*	*56*	*128*	*11*	*4*	*.265/.346/.471*	*.296*	*.309*	*1.7*	*LF 0*	*1.6*

Breakout: 1% Improve: 52% Collapse: 2% Attrition: 3% MLB: 100% *Comparables: Frank Robinson, Matt Holliday, Carlos Gonzalez*

The downside of being blessed with incredible talents and receiving numerous accolades at an early age is that anything short of brilliance can be viewed as failure, reminding us that humans are mortal and life isn't fair. Despite making his third All-Star team last year at age 27, Upton is often labeled a disappointment in the shady alleyways of sports radio. Such is the fate of a former first-overall pick who reached the big leagues as a teenager. Whatever shortcomings Upton might have as a ballplayer stem from inconsistency. He will carry a team with his explosive bat for weeks and then magically disappear. His .182/.277/.309 line in June and July defies probability. Petco Park wasn't a problem: His slugging percentage was 100 points higher there than on the road, and 15 of his first 20 homers came at home (the final six coming elsewhere). Aside from streakiness, Upton's biggest issue is the expectation of people who believed he was a generational talent and who saw visions of Cooperstown in their heads long before they had a right to do so. It's interesting, if not entirely fair, to note that his most similar player by age (per Baseball Reference) has been Ruben Sierra six out of seven years. Upton is not Sierra, though neither man will be enshrined in the Hall of Fame. But the same can be said of almost everyone who has ever played the game, and lamenting that a particular player is merely very good at baseball rather than one of the best in history is a waste of everyone's time and energy.

Melvin Upton CF

Born: 8/21/84 Age: 31 Bats: R Throws: R Height: 6'3" Weight: 185

YEAR	TEAM	LVL	AGE	PA	R	2B	3B	HR	RBI	BB	K	SB	CS	AVG/OBP/SLG	TAv	BABIP	BRR	FRAA	WARP
2013	ATL	MLB	28	446	30	14	0	9	26	44	151	12	5	.184/.268/.289	.212	.266	-1.8	CF(118): -10.1	-2.1
2014	ATL	MLB	29	582	67	19	5	12	35	57	173	20	7	.208/.287/.333	.243	.286	6.1	CF(139): -2.7	1.1
2015	SDN	MLB	30	228	23	12	4	5	17	21	62	9	3	.259/.327/.429	.283	.348	1.5	CF(63): 2.3	1.7
2015	ELP	AAA	30	55	10	2	0	1	6	4	12	4	0	.280/.333/.380	.243	.351	1.4	CF(10): 0.6	0.2
2016	*SDN*	*MLB*	*31*	*560*	*75*	*22*	*4*	*17*	*56*	*51*	*161*	*20*	*6*	*.225/.297/.384*	*.244*	*.291*	*2.2*	*CF -6*	*0.6*
2017	*SDN*	*MLB*	*32*	*380*	*44*	*15*	*2*	*11*	*42*	*36*	*112*	*13*	*4*	*.222/.297/.377*	*.249*	*.291*	*1.9*	*CF -4*	*1.0*

Breakout: 0% Improve: 42% Collapse: 6% Attrition: 6% MLB: 97% *Comparables: Jim Edmonds, Chet Lemon, Rick Monday*

Upton did something unusual last year: He provided value for his team. It wasn't much—certainly not enough to justify his salary—but it was more than he'd done in his first two National League seasons, when his .198/.279/.314 showing created a giant vortex of suck in Atlanta. Moving to the West Coast, he rediscovered the magic that made him less than terrible from 2010 to 2012. After missing the Padres' first 58 games with inflammation in his left foot, he appeared to be his usual unwatchable self for the first month. But then, just before the All-Star break, Melvin Jr. found his long-lost stroke, hitting .289/.349/.480 from July 10th to season's end. Upton can't sustain that over longer periods, and yes, he's overpaid for what he does. But then he showed signs over the final three months that he might not be useless. We take the victories we can.

Brett Wallace 1B

Born: 8/26/86 Age: 29 Bats: L Throws: R Height: 6'2" Weight: 235

YEAR	TEAM	LVL	AGE	PA	R	2B	3B	HR	RBI	BB	K	SB	CS	AVG/OBP/SLG	TAv	BABIP	BRR	FRAA	WARP
2013	HOU	MLB	26	285	35	14	1	13	36	18	104	1	1	.221/.284/.431	.253	.310	-1.0	1B(61): -2.3, 3B(9): -0.5	-0.2
2013	OKL	AAA	26	261	36	16	2	11	37	24	69	1	0	.326/.398/.554	.324	.425	1.0	1B(41): -1.5, 3B(10): -0.8	2.1
2014	BUF	AAA	27	151	12	5	0	7	23	15	33	0	0	.323/.404/.519	.309	.387	-1.4	1B(29): 0.7	0.9
2014	NOR	AAA	27	374	50	12	0	10	35	29	98	0	1	.265/.329/.389	.252	.343	-0.9	1B(72): 2.5, 3B(7): -0.4	0.2
2015	SDN	MLB	28	107	14	6	0	5	16	10	31	0	0	.302/.374/.521	.314	.400	-0.4	1B(17): -0.5, 3B(5): 0.2	0.8
2015	ELP	AAA	28	271	34	13	0	8	37	24	56	1	0	.305/.380/.460	.288	.367	0.4	3B(60): -13.0	0.4
2016	*SDN*	*MLB*	*29*	*101*	*11*	*4*	*0*	*3*	*13*	*7*	*30*	*0*	*0*	*.251/.317/.415*	*.260*	*.331*	*-0.1*	*1B -0*	*0.3*
2017	*SDN*	*MLB*	*30*	*279*	*34*	*12*	*1*	*9*	*33*	*19*	*84*	*0*	*0*	*.248/.312/.401*	*.261*	*.334*	*-0.5*	*1B 0*	*0.5*

Breakout: 5% Improve: 23% Collapse: 7% Attrition: 15% MLB: 61% *Comparables: Josh Fields, Brandon Moss, Wilson Betemit*

Some zombies eat brains. Others, such as Wallace, crave the feel of wood against rawhide and stagger toward a spot on a big-league bench. The erstwhile Cardinals first-round pick terrorized pitchers in a way he seldom had during his first life. He did most of his damage in a pinch-hitting role, batting .349/.440/.698 and leading the majors with four pinch-homers despite not being recalled until mid-June. He also saw sporadic action at both infield corners, but didn't provide much offense when asked to play a defensive position. Minor quibbles aside, for a former top prospect who languished in six different organizations before age 29 and never stuck, 2015 counts as an unqualified success. Searching for someone to give him another chance took perseverance. Finding someone took brains.

PITCHERS

Andrew Cashner RHP

Born: 9/11/86 Age: 29 Bats: R Throws: R Height: 6'5" Weight: 225

YEAR	TEAM	LVL	AGE	W	L	SV	G	GS	IP	H	HR	BB/9	K/9	GB%	BABIP	WHIP	ERA	FIP	DRA	WARP	CFIP	MPH
2013	SDN	MLB	26	10	9	0	31	26	175	151	12	2.4	6.6	53%	.269	1.13	3.09	3.32	3.29	3.4	97	98.0
2014	SDN	MLB	27	5	7	0	19	19	123^1	110	7	2.1	6.8	50%	.275	1.13	2.55	3.06	4.13	1.0	102	97.8
2015	SDN	MLB	28	6	16	0	31	31	184^2	200	19	3.2	8.0	50%	.330	1.44	4.34	3.88	4.89	0.3	104	98.1
2016	*SDN*	*MLB*	*29*	*11*	*10*	*0*	*30*	*30*	*189*	*177*	*21*	*2.7*	*7.4*	*51%*	*.304*	*1.23*	*3.90*	*3.83*	*4.48*	*1.8*	*103*	
2017	*SDN*	*MLB*	*30*	*10*	*10*	*0*	*29*	*29*	*175*	*174*	*19*	*2.6*	*7.3*	*51%*	*.316*	*1.29*	*3.88*	*4.14*	*4.46*	*1.6*	*103*	

Breakout: 19% Improve: 42% Collapse: 21% Attrition: 6% MLB: 98% *Comparables: Anibal Sanchez, Gavin Floyd, John Danks*

We ended last year's comment by declaring that Cashner "is a frontline starter" and he proceeded to prove us wrong. The good news is that he set career highs in starts, innings, and strikeouts. The bad news is that he became very hittable, and only 22 unearned runs kept his ERA+ above 80. He turned lefties into Prince Fielder, which is a neat party trick but isn't conducive to winning. Cashner's velocity and movement didn't change much, leaving unresolved the question of what the problem was. Pitching coach Darren Balsley's response to that question in July was, "I've been thinking about that all year." No solutions were offered or found. Although turning an injury-plagued frontline starter into a healthy back-end guy is another neat party trick, turning him back would be even neater.

Enyel De Los Santos RHP

Born: 12/25/95 Age: 20 Bats: R Throws: R Height: 6'3" Weight: 170

YEAR	TEAM	LVL	AGE	W	L	SV	G	GS	IP	H	HR	BB/9	K/9	GB%	BABIP	WHIP	ERA	FIP	DRA	WARP	CFIP	MPH
2015	EVE	A-	19	3	0	0	8	8	37^{2}	37	2	3.1	10.0	57%	.365	1.33	4.06	3.57	4.10	0.6	94	
2016	*SDN*	*MLB*	*20*	*2*	*3*	*0*	*9*	*9*	44^{1}	*45*	*6*	*3.9*	*7.3*	*43%*	*.317*	*1.45*	*4.84*	*4.66*	*5.48*	*-0.1*	*131*	
2017	*SDN*	*MLB*	*21*	*8*	*11*	*0*	*30*	*30*	186^{2}	*187*	*26*	*3.6*	*7.2*	*43%*	*.313*	*1.40*	*4.65*	*5.01*	*5.27*	*0.0*	*127*	

Breakout: 0% Improve: 0% Collapse: 0% Attrition: 0% MLB: 0% *Comparables: Felipe Rivero, Abel De Los Santos, Adrian Houser*

With a tailing, low-90s heater, a bat-eluding slider and a change that flashes average, De Los Santos has the raw stuff of a big-league starter. Conversely, his upper and lower halves are often out of sync, his change is usually flat and his command below average. An airplane view of the profile suggests that De Los Santos is a reliever-in-waiting, but if he can extract more out of his off-speed while tightening his mechanics, there's more in the tank. It's unfair to use a single player as a measuring stick for an entire player development system, but De Los Santos presents a fascinating case study for San Diego's.

Odrisamer Despaigne RHP

Born: 4/4/87 Age: 29 Bats: R Throws: R Height: 6'0" Weight: 205

YEAR	TEAM	LVL	AGE	W	L	SV	G	GS	IP	H	HR	BB/9	K/9	GB%	BABIP	WHIP	ERA	FIP	DRA	WARP	CFIP	MPH
2014	SDN	MLB	27	4	7	0	16	16	96^{1}	85	6	3.0	6.1	55%	.267	1.21	3.36	3.72	4.19	0.7	116	93.8
2014	ELP	AAA	27	1	3	0	5	5	23^{2}	36	3	4.9	11.0	0%	.440	2.07	7.61	4.67				
2015	SDN	MLB	28	5	9	0	34	18	125^{2}	142	17	2.3	4.9	53%	.298	1.38	5.80	4.80	5.48	-0.8	124	94.1
2016	*SDN*	*MLB*	*29*	*4*	*3*	*0*	*41*	*8*	74^{2}	*76*	*9*	*2.5*	*5.7*	*51%*	*.300*	*1.30*	*4.48*	*4.35*	*5.12*	*0.0*	*122*	
2017	*SDN*	*MLB*	*30*	*6*	*7*	*0*	*24*	*16*	109^{1}	*118*	*15*	*2.7*	*5.3*	*51%*	*.309*	*1.38*	*4.70*	*5.03*	*5.37*	*-0.2*	*128*	

Breakout: 20% Improve: 53% Collapse: 22% Attrition: 8% MLB: 99% *Comparables: Bud Black, Mike Moore, Saul Rogovin*

Armed with an underwhelming arsenal and a propensity for hurling baseballs at a bat's sweet spot from a variety of angles, Despaigne was bumped from the Padres' rotation last July, the hope being that his stuff might be better suited to the bullpen. It was not. Opposing batters went from hitting him hard to hitting him harder. They also attacked when they smelled blood, batting .315/.374/.565 with runners in scoring position and .404/.431/.745 on the rare occasions he was allowed to work in high-leverage situations. Not even his changeup, which he grips as if trying to break his own fingers, was enough to save him. Despaigne is the new Josh Geer, a man who might enjoy marginal success in the PCL for a time if he so chooses.

Robbie Erlin LHP

Born: 10/8/90 Age: 25 Bats: R Throws: L Height: 6'0" Weight: 195

YEAR	TEAM	LVL	AGE	W	L	SV	G	GS	IP	H	HR	BB/9	K/9	GB%	BABIP	WHIP	ERA	FIP	DRA	WARP	CFIP	MPH
2013	TUC	AAA	22	8	3	0	20	20	99^{1}	125	11	3.1	7.6	37%	.352	1.60	5.07	4.38	5.00	0.7	99	
2013	SDN	MLB	22	3	3	0	11	9	54^{2}	53	6	2.5	6.6	39%	.283	1.24	4.12	3.81	3.43	1.0	105	91.7
2014	ELP	AAA	23	0	1	0	2	2	10^{2}	21	2	1.7	6.8	50%	.475	2.16	9.28	5.20	5.31	0.1	97	
2014	SAN	AA	23	0	0	0	3	3	10^{1}	12	1	3.5	8.7	42%	.367	1.55	3.48	3.60				
2014	SDN	MLB	23	4	5	0	13	11	61^{1}	71	6	2.2	6.8	43%	.332	1.40	4.99	3.66	6.02	-0.9	108	91.8
2015	ELP	AAA	24	7	6	0	24	24	125^{1}	151	22	2.7	7.5	47%	.329	1.50	5.60	5.24	5.72	-0.2	108	
2015	SDN	MLB	24	1	2	0	3	3	17	16	1	1.1	5.3	52%	.294	1.06	4.76	3.28	3.32	0.3	105	92.1
2016	*SDN*	*MLB*	*25*	*8*	*8*	*0*	*24*	*24*	136^{2}	*141*	*19*	*2.4*	*7.1*	*45%*	*.314*	*1.30*	*4.27*	*4.19*	*4.89*	*0.6*	*115*	
2017	*SDN*	*MLB*	*26*	*7*	*8*	*0*	*24*	*24*	140^{2}	*144*	*20*	*2.4*	*7.5*	*45%*	*.319*	*1.30*	*4.15*	*4.45*	*4.75*	*0.8*	*112*	

Breakout: 11% Improve: 29% Collapse: 29% Attrition: 29% MLB: 70% *Comparables: Trevor Bell, Scott Baker, Nick Tepesch*

I got hammered in El Paso on tequila and Tabasco
As I tried my best to get the batters out.
But my fastball wasn't poppin' and my curveball wasn't droppin'
Now my future is all clouded up with doubt.

When I got to San Diego just in time to see the day go
There was nearly nothin' left for me to do.
Though I know right where my pants is, I am runnin' out of chances
And that's left me feelin' mighty Padre blue.

My name is Robbie, this ain't no hobby.
I'm just a guy who's tryin' to make the grade.
Yes I'm a pitcher, no belly itcher.
And if I stick around I will get paid—handsomely!

—Probably not Johnny Cash

Ian Kennedy RHP

Born: 12/19/84 Age: 31 Bats: R Throws: R Height: 6'0" Weight: 200

YEAR	TEAM	LVL	AGE	W	L	SV	G	GS	IP	H	HR	BB/9	K/9	GB%	BABIP	WHIP	ERA	FIP	DRA	WARP	CFIP	MPH
2013	SDN	MLB	28	4	2	0	10	10	57^1	52	9	3.9	8.6	44%	.279	1.34	4.24	4.56	3.86	0.7	114	93.2
2013	ARI	MLB	28	3	8	0	21	21	124	128	18	3.5	7.8	38%	.301	1.42	5.23	4.57	5.14	-0.4	111	93.2
2014	SDN	MLB	29	13	13	0	33	33	201	189	16	3.1	9.3	42%	.315	1.29	3.63	3.18	4.25	1.3	94	94.4
2015	SDN	MLB	30	9	15	0	30	30	168^1	166	31	2.8	9.3	41%	.301	1.30	4.28	4.54	5.03	0.0	100	93.8
2016	*SDN*	*MLB*	*31*	*11*	*10*	*0*	*30*	*30*	*180*	*162*	*24*	*2.8*	*8.8*	*41%*	*.303*	*1.21*	*4.00*	*3.90*	*4.60*	*1.5*	*107*	
2017	*SDN*	*MLB*	*32*	*10*	*10*	*0*	*29*	*29*	175^2	*161*	*24*	*2.8*	*8.4*	*41%*	*.303*	*1.22*	*4.01*	*4.28*	*4.61*	*1.4*	*107*	

Breakout: 21% Improve: 57% Collapse: 11% Attrition: 13% MLB: 92% *Comparables: Randy Wolf, Bruce Hurst, Ervin Santana*

Kennedy, along with teammate James Shields, set a new record last year by allowing 19 home runs at Petco Park. His walks decreased, but then, there was no incentive for patience at the plate when he toed the slab: Among ERA qualifiers, only Aaron Harang had a higher OPS against batters that swung at the first pitch. Part of the problem is that anything he threw around the belt—long a target of his—was crushed. Kennedy's pedestrian velocity means he must throw strikes, but there's a difference between throwing strikes and throwing *good* strikes—there were too many of the former and not enough of the latter in 2015. We've seen what he can do when he's more precise with his pitches, and last season we saw what happens when he isn't.

Brandon Maurer RHP

Born: 7/3/90 Age: 25 Bats: R Throws: R Height: 6'5" Weight: 220

YEAR	TEAM	LVL	AGE	W	L	SV	G	GS	IP	H	HR	BB/9	K/9	GB%	BABIP	WHIP	ERA	FIP	DRA	WARP	CFIP	MPH
2013	SEA	MLB	22	5	8	0	22	14	90	114	16	2.7	7.0	45%	.346	1.57	6.30	4.93	6.13	-1.4	110	97.3
2013	TAC	AAA	22	3	4	0	10	10	46^2	48	2	5.0	9.1	39%	.341	1.59	5.21	4.11	5.04	0.3	100	
2014	SEA	MLB	23	1	4	0	38	7	69^2	74	6	2.5	7.1	41%	.308	1.33	4.65	3.52	5.22	-0.5	106	98.8
2014	TAC	AAA	23	1	0	3	12	1	19^1	18	2	3.7	11.2	40%	.333	1.34	2.79	3.80	4.98	0.1	99	
2015	SDN	MLB	24	7	4	0	53	0	51	39	3	2.6	6.9	48%	.243	1.06	3.00	3.34	2.71	1.2	100	97.9
2016	*SDN*	*MLB*	*25*	*3*	*1*	*0*	*51*	*0*	54^1	*52*	*6*	*2.6*	*7.4*	*45%*	*.312*	*1.26*	*3.96*	*3.81*	*4.54*	*0.3*	*105*	
2017	*SDN*	*MLB*	*26*	*4*	*3*	*0*	*29*	*9*	*80*	*78*	*9*	*2.6*	*7.5*	*45%*	*.313*	*1.26*	*3.94*	*4.20*	*4.52*	*0.5*	*104*	

Breakout: 33% Improve: 58% Collapse: 17% Attrition: 18% MLB: 89% *Comparables: Noah Lowry, Vance Worley, Homer Bailey*

Maurer's fastball excited both radar guns and opposing batters during his two years in Seattle. A move to the other end of I-5 yielded results more in line with his stuff, as he dominated until just before the All-Star break. An 8.68 ERA and .985 OPS against over the next month hinted at trouble, which came in the form of right shoulder inflammation. It pushed him to the disabled list in early August for what A.J. Preller called a "two-week breather." Maurer held his breath longer than expected and didn't return. Despite enjoying much greater success out of the bullpen, he has a deep enough repertoire to sustain talk of a return to the rotation.

Brandon Morrow RHP

Born: 7/26/84 Age: 31 Bats: R Throws: R Height: 6'3" Weight: 210

YEAR	TEAM	LVL	AGE	W	L	SV	G	GS	IP	H	HR	BB/9	K/9	GB%	BABIP	WHIP	ERA	FIP	DRA	WARP	CFIP	MPH
2013	TOR	MLB	28	2	3	0	10	10	54^1	63	12	3.0	7.0	39%	.302	1.49	5.63	5.45	5.19	-0.2	108	97.4
2014	TOR	MLB	29	1	3	0	13	6	33^1	37	2	4.9	8.1	52%	.357	1.65	5.67	3.76	5.73	-0.4	106	99.2
2015	SDN	MLB	30	2	0	0	5	5	33	29	3	1.9	6.3	48%	.280	1.09	2.73	3.59	3.82	0.5	104	96.3
2016	*SDN*	*MLB*	*31*	*7*	*8*	*0*	*24*	*24*	*120*	*113*	*15*	*2.8*	*7.4*	*47%*	*.299*	*1.25*	*4.18*	*4.06*	*4.80*	*0.7*	*113*	
2017	*SDN*	*MLB*	*32*	*7*	*8*	*0*	*23*	*23*	136^1	*136*	*18*	*2.8*	*7.2*	*47%*	*.309*	*1.31*	*4.26*	*4.56*	*4.89*	*0.6*	*115*	

Breakout: 20% Improve: 51% Collapse: 21% Attrition: 17% MLB: 93% *Comparables: Ted Lilly, Josh Johnson, Gil Meche*

For five starts, the Padres' signing of Morrow looked like the shrewdest of gambles. He spun seven shutout innings in his debut and pitched deep into games every time out, including what would be his final appearance of the season less than a month later. After landing on the disabled list in May with "shoulder inflammation," he made two rehab starts in early June and one more in late July, before succumbing to surgery in late August. Morrow is expected to be ready for spring training, but given that he has pitched a total of 121 innings over the last three years, it's hard to say what kind of role he can fill as a member of any team's active roster, other than perhaps medical cadaver.

Jacob Nix RHP

Born: 1/9/96 Age: 20 Bats: R Throws: R Height: 6'4" Weight: 220

YEAR	TEAM	LVL	AGE	W	L	SV	G	GS	IP	H	HR	BB/9	K/9	GB%	BABIP	WHIP	ERA	FIP	DRA	WARP	CFIP	MPH
2016	*SDN*	*MLB*	*20*	*2*	*2*	*0*	*15*	*5*	33^1	*39*	*5*	*5.3*	*4.5*	*27%*	*.317*	*1.76*	*6.09*	*5.95*	*7.15*	*-0.7*	*165*	
2017	*SDN*	*MLB*	*21*	*4*	*6*	*1*	*37*	*13*	116^2	*135*	*18*	*4.8*	*4.9*	*27%*	*.318*	*1.68*	*5.77*	*6.26*	*6.77*	*-1.7*	*158*	

Breakout: 0% Improve: 0% Collapse: 0% Attrition: 0% MLB: 0% *Comparables: Josh Stinson, Alex Cobb, Hunter Strickland*

Before the Padres took Nix in the third round last year, he was best known as "the other guy" in the 2014 draft debacle that saw the Astros lose him and Brady Aiken thanks to the latter's balky elbow. With Aiken's deal disintegrating, the team had less money available for Nix, who had reportedly already agreed to terms. After dominoes toppled on Nix's deal, he filed a grievance against the Astros. The two sides eventually reached a financial settlement, and the pitcher ended up plying his trade in IMG Academy's post-graduate program. Heading into the 2015 draft Nix made his feelings about the experience clear: "I hear nothing but good things about 29 teams." He didn't get a long look in his pro debut but features a mid-90s fastball, complemented by a developing curve and change.

Drew Pomeranz LHP

Born: 11/22/88 Age: 27 Bats: R Throws: L Height: 6'5" Weight: 240

YEAR	TEAM	LVL	AGE	W	L	SV	G	GS	IP	H	HR	BB/9	K/9	GB%	BABIP	WHIP	ERA	FIP	DRA	WARP	CFIP	MPH
2013	CSP	AAA	24	8	1	0	15	15	85^{2}	83	6	3.5	10.1	47%	.338	1.35	4.20	3.50	4.36	1.2	79	
2013	COL	MLB	24	0	4	0	8	4	21^{2}	25	4	7.9	7.9	55%	.339	2.03	6.23	6.44	6.80	-0.5	117	94.0
2014	SAC	AAA	25	3	1	0	8	8	46^{1}	45	6	3.3	10.5	42%	.325	1.34	3.69	4.15	4.68	0.6	78	
2014	OAK	MLB	25	5	4	0	20	10	69	51	7	3.4	8.3	48%	.244	1.12	2.35	3.80	3.39	1.1	95	94.0
2015	OAK	MLB	26	5	6	3	53	9	86	71	8	3.2	8.6	43%	.266	1.19	3.66	3.59	3.66	1.2	94	94.5
2016	*SDN*	*MLB*	*27*	*3*	*1*	*0*	*56*	*0*	59^{1}	*50*	*7*	*3.0*	*9.0*	*45%*	*.296*	*1.17*	*3.68*	*3.70*	*4.23*	*0.5*	*96*	
2017	*SDN*	*MLB*	*28*	*6*	*6*	*1*	*32*	*17*	118^{1}	*98*	*12*	*3.0*	*9.3*	*45%*	*.300*	*1.16*	*3.51*	*3.73*	*4.03*	*1.5*	*90*	

Breakout: 29% Improve: 60% Collapse: 19% Attrition: 11% MLB: 91% *Comparables: Tyson Ross, Lance Lynn, Garrett Richards*

Pomeranz started the season with seven shutout innings against the Mariners, then had a few rough outings before landing on the disabled list in mid-May with AC-joint soreness in his left shoulder. Two weeks later he returned as a reliever, pitching well enough (2.61 ERA in 44 appearances) to earn scattered save opportunities. He humiliated left-handed batters (.152/.216/.222), lending further support for a permanent move to the bullpen. A's manager Bob Melvin praised Pomeranz's ability to perform in both roles, expressing hope that "there's even more in the tank than what we've seen this year." Melvin's optimism notwithstanding, Pomeranz was shut down in late September and underwent a "minimally invasive procedure" a month later to treat the same AC joint. He's expected to be ready for spring training.

Kevin Quackenbush RHP

Born: 11/28/88 Age: 27 Bats: R Throws: R Height: 6'4" Weight: 220

YEAR	TEAM	LVL	AGE	W	L	SV	G	GS	IP	H	HR	BB/9	K/9	GB%	BABIP	WHIP	ERA	FIP	DRA	WARP	CFIP	MPH
2013	TUC	AAA	24	8	2	4	28	0	34	33	0	5.0	10.1	49%	.359	1.53	2.91	3.19	4.64	0.2	88	
2013	SAN	AA	24	2	0	13	29	0	31	16	1	2.9	13.4	53%	.246	0.84	0.29	1.77	3.20	0.5	65	
2014	SDN	MLB	25	3	3	6	56	0	54^{1}	42	2	3.0	9.3	41%	.278	1.10	2.48	2.62	2.84	1.1	88	93.4
2014	ELP	AAA	25	0	0	6	13	0	14^{1}	9	0	2.5	7.5	67%	.222	0.91	1.26	2.86	4.48	0.1	107	
2015	SDN	MLB	26	3	2	0	57	0	58^{1}	52	6	3.1	8.9	44%	.291	1.23	4.01	3.59	3.62	0.8	96	92.8
2015	ELP	AAA	26	1	0	2	9	0	11^{2}	6	0	1.5	10.8	39%	.261	0.69	0.77	1.71	2.75	0.3	74	
2016	*SDN*	*MLB*	*27*	*3*	*1*	*35*	*51*	*0*	54^{1}	*46*	*6*	*2.9*	*8.8*	*44%*	*.298*	*1.17*	*3.70*	*3.57*	*4.26*	*0.5*	*94*	
2017	*SDN*	*MLB*	*28*	*3*	*1*	*1*	*50*	*0*	*54*	*47*	*6*	*2.9*	*9.3*	*44%*	*.305*	*1.19*	*3.68*	*3.91*	*4.24*	*0.4*	*94*	

Breakout: 28% Improve: 42% Collapse: 27% Attrition: 19% MLB: 83% *Comparables: Mark Melancon, Steve Cishek, A.J. Ramos*

Quackenbush's sophomore campaign didn't go as planned, starting at a Triple-A level he had mastered a year earlier and revisiting it in mid-June. Pitching as if he'd lost his number one dime, the lefties he handled so well as a rookie gave him fits, and his 5.26 ERA over the final two months failed to excite. He seldom pitched in meaningful situations, sometimes going weeks without appearing in a Padres win. Quackenbush isn't a dominant reliever by any stretch, but he's good enough to serve as a setup man for many teams, should one want to give him the chance.

Colin Rea RHP

Born: 7/1/90 Age: 25 Bats: R Throws: R Height: 6'5" Weight: 220

YEAR	TEAM	LVL	AGE	W	L	SV	G	GS	IP	H	HR	BB/9	K/9	GB%	BABIP	WHIP	ERA	FIP	DRA	WARP	CFIP	MPH
2013	FTW	A	22	2	1	0	16	3	43	34	1	4.6	8.0	42%	.275	1.30	2.09	3.48	4.62	0.2	101	
2013	LEL	A+	22	0	5	0	15	9	43	43	3	8.2	9.4	53%	.345	1.91	6.07	5.59	6.41	-0.1	129	
2014	LEL	A+	23	11	9	0	28	28	139	151	11	2.4	7.6	56%	.332	1.35	3.88	4.02	5.27	-0.1	96	
2015	SAN	AA	24	3	2	0	12	12	75	50	1	1.3	7.2	50%	.233	0.81	1.08	2.35	2.49	2.3	76	
2015	SDN	MLB	24	2	2	0	6	6	31^{2}	29	2	3.1	7.4	50%	.290	1.26	4.26	3.48	4.30	0.3	106	93.3
2015	ELP	AAA	24	2	2	0	6	6	26^{2}	29	2	4.1	6.8	48%	.321	1.54	4.39	4.65	5.60	0.0	106	
2016	*SDN*	*MLB*	*25*	*2*	*3*	*0*	*8*	*8*	*40*	*39*	*5*	*2.9*	*7.1*	*48%*	*.302*	*1.29*	*4.32*	*4.24*	*4.93*	*0.2*	*116*	
2017	*SDN*	*MLB*	*26*	*3*	*4*	*0*	*14*	*10*	65^{2}	*66*	*9*	*3.5*	*7.5*	*48%*	*.314*	*1.39*	*4.58*	*4.90*	*5.23*	*0.0*	*123*	

Breakout: 24% Improve: 35% Collapse: 6% Attrition: 28% MLB: 48% *Comparables: Ryan Cook, Tobi Stoner, John Gast*

Former 12th-round pick Rea dominated Double-A through mid-May, being named Texas League Pitcher of the Week after a 12-strikeout performance against Midland on May 2nd. Back spasms shelved him two weeks later, but he was even better when he returned in mid-June, allowing two runs in four starts before a promotion to El Paso. Triple-A proved more challenging, although after getting chased early in his debut, Rea managed a 2.96 ERA over his final five starts leading up to another promotion. His month in the big-league rotation culminated in seven shutout innings against the Rockies on September 8th. Forearm and elbow soreness kept him from continuing his audition, but he showed enough to merit further looks. His stuff—low-90s fastball, high-80s cutter, developing curve and change—doesn't match his Double-A performance. He profiles as a back-end starter.

Tyson Ross RHP

Born: 4/22/87 Age: 29 Bats: R Throws: R Height: 6'5" Weight: 230

YEAR	TEAM	LVL	AGE	W	L	SV	G	GS	IP	H	HR	BB/9	K/9	GB%	BABIP	WHIP	ERA	FIP	DRA	WARP	CFIP	MPH
2013	SDN	MLB	26	3	8	0	35	16	125	100	8	3.2	8.6	57%	.282	1.15	3.17	3.17	3.42	2.1	86	97.1
2013	TUC	AAA	26	1	1	0	4	2	11^{2}	12	0	4.6	6.9	60%	.343	1.54	4.63	3.57	5.04	0.1	102	
2014	SDN	MLB	27	13	14	0	31	31	195^{2}	165	13	3.3	9.0	59%	.291	1.21	2.81	3.22	3.99	1.9	95	96.3
2015	SDN	MLB	28	10	12	0	33	33	196	172	9	3.9	9.7	62%	.320	1.31	3.26	3.00	3.51	3.5	91	95.6
2016	*SDN*	*MLB*	*29*	*11*	*9*	*0*	*29*	*29*	*174*	*150*	*16*	*3.3*	*9.2*	*61%*	*.315*	*1.23*	*3.49*	*3.41*	*4.03*	*2.6*	*89*	
2017	*SDN*	*MLB*	*30*	*10*	*9*	*0*	*28*	*28*	166^{2}	*147*	*14*	*3.4*	*9.2*	*61%*	*.322*	*1.26*	*3.46*	*3.68*	*3.99*	*2.5*	*88*	

Breakout: 24% Improve: 35% Collapse: 6% Attrition: 28% MLB: 48% *Comparables: Ryan Cook, Tobi Stoner, John Gast*

Ho-hum, the once-inconsistent Ross has become so predictable since coming to San Diego. Only eight men who have pitched at least 500 innings over the last three seasons own a lower ERA than Ross' 3.07. Petco Park helps, though his ERA on the road is a whopping 3.49, a tick better than Jon Lester's. He had trouble controlling his stuff last year, leading the National League in walks and wild pitches. His wildness is mitigated by his ability to keep the ball in the park. Ross allowed nine homers all season, with three coming in the same game. During a 24-start stretch from May 4th to September 5th, opponents took him deep twice. The only things he doesn't do well are field his position and control the running game. If he keeps missing bats and forcing weak contact with his sinker/slider combo, that won't matter too much.

James Shields RHP

Born: 12/20/81 Age: 34 Bats: R Throws: R Height: 6'3" Weight: 215

YEAR	TEAM	LVL	AGE	W	L	SV	G	GS	IP	H	HR	BB/9	K/9	GB%	BABIP	WHIP	ERA	FIP	DRA	WARP	CFIP	MPH
2013	KCA	MLB	31	13	9	0	34	34	228^{2}	215	20	2.7	7.7	43%	.298	1.24	3.15	3.50	3.76	3.2	91	94.7
2014	KCA	MLB	32	14	8	0	34	34	227	224	23	1.7	7.1	47%	.295	1.18	3.21	3.62	3.84	2.7	96	94.7
2015	SDN	MLB	33	13	7	0	33	33	202^{1}	189	33	3.6	9.6	47%	.299	1.33	3.91	4.48	4.72	0.7	100	93.6
2016	*SDN*	*MLB*	*34*	*13*	*12*	*0*	*33*	*33*	*221*	*193*	*28*	*2.6*	*8.5*	*46%*	*.297*	*1.16*	*3.87*	*3.80*	*4.44*	*2.2*	*103*	
2017	*SDN*	*MLB*	*35*	*11*	*11*	*0*	*30*	*30*	*183^{2}*	*169*	*24*	*2.6*	*8.1*	*46%*	*.302*	*1.20*	*4.01*	*4.27*	*4.60*	*1.6*	*107*	

Breakout: 22% Improve: 47% Collapse: 18% Attrition: 6% MLB: 93% *Comparables: Josh Beckett, Steve Carlton, Kevin Millwood*

Shields suffered a severe case of gopheritis on moving to the National League. Despite Petco Park's reputation, he tied for the league lead in homers allowed. He also doubled his 2014 walk rate, and only a late surge by teammate Ross kept him from pacing the circuit in that category as well. What Shields lacks in excellence, he makes up for in durability and consistency. He has made at least 31 starts, thrown at least 202 innings and won at least 11 games in each of the last nine seasons. Mark Buehrle has met the same criteria in seven of those seasons, with four other pitchers doing it six times. In a profession where attrition reigns supreme, there is value in reliability. As number three starters go, a team could do much worse. If only the team were paying him like one.

Austin Smith RHP

Born: 7/9/96 Age: 19 Bats: R Throws: R Height: 6'4" Weight: 220

YEAR	TEAM	LVL	AGE	W	L	SV	G	GS	IP	H	HR	BB/9	K/9	GB%	BABIP	WHIP	ERA	FIP	DRA	WARP	CFIP	MPH
2016	*SDN*	*MLB*	*19*	*2*	*4*	*0*	*9*	*9*	*33*	*40*	*5*	*5.5*	*3.8*	*32%*	*.317*	*1.81*	*6.35*	*6.16*	*7.46*	*-0.9*	*171*	
2017	*SDN*	*MLB*	*20*	*3*	*8*	*0*	*26*	*26*	*156*	*191*	*25*	*4.8*	*4.1*	*32%*	*.321*	*1.75*	*6.05*	*6.58*	*7.11*	*-2.0*	*165*	

Breakout: 0% Improve: 0% Collapse: 0% Attrition: 0% MLB: 0% *Comparables: Hector Rondon, Brandon Maurer, Luis Severino*

Smith, a second-round pick and a first-team All-American out of the same Florida high school that produced Trea Turner, is a big, athletic, hard-throwing right-hander who could add even more velocity and whose other offerings show enough promise to keep him in the rotation. The instructional leagues offered mostly negative feedback in his limited time there, but he has plenty of time to figure out where to orient the breaking ball. He's forever and a day away, but he has a name worth remembering, even if it's a generic one.

Dale Thayer RHP

Born: 12/17/80 Age: 35 Bats: R Throws: R Height: 6'0" Weight: 210

YEAR	TEAM	LVL	AGE	W	L	SV	G	GS	IP	H	HR	BB/9	K/9	GB%	BABIP	WHIP	ERA	FIP	DRA	WARP	CFIP	MPH
2013	SDN	MLB	32	3	5	1	69	0	65	59	8	3.0	8.9	42%	.293	1.25	3.32	3.76	4.07	0.4	91	95.2
2014	SDN	MLB	33	4	5	0	70	0	65^{1}	53	9	2.2	8.5	42%	.250	1.06	2.34	3.82	3.49	0.8	93	94.3
2015	SDN	MLB	34	2	2	0	38	0	37^{2}	37	5	3.6	6.0	41%	.283	1.38	4.06	4.75	4.65	0.0	114	94.0
2016	*SDN*	*MLB*	*35*	*2*	*1*	*0*	*43*	*0*	*45^{2}*	*41*	*6*	*2.8*	*7.5*	*42%*	*.287*	*1.20*	*4.10*	*4.13*	*4.71*	*0.1*	*107*	
2017	*SDN*	*MLB*	*36*	*2*	*1*	*0*	*46*	*0*	*44*	*43*	*6*	*2.9*	*7.3*	*42%*	*.304*	*1.30*	*4.32*	*4.61*	*4.96*	*0.0*	*113*	

Breakout: 22% Improve: 42% Collapse: 21% Attrition: 12% MLB: 77% *Comparables: Joe Borowski, Tyler Walker, John Bale*

Thayer was his usual boring, reliable self through the first third of June. Then something inside him snapped: He unraveled in a couple games against the Dodgers and never recovered, allowing 10 runs in his final 11 appearances. By the end of August he was cleaning out his locker. If baseball's only remaining Dale wants to get more than one last spring training invite, he'll have to figure out why he suddenly can't strike batters out anymore.

Nick Vincent RHP

Born: 7/12/86 Age: 29 Bats: R Throws: R Height: 6'0" Weight: 180

YEAR	TEAM	LVL	AGE	W	L	SV	G	GS	IP	H	HR	BB/9	K/9	GB%	BABIP	WHIP	ERA	FIP	DRA	WARP	CFIP	MPH
2013	TUC	AAA	26	4	3	0	24	0	25^{1}	26	4	4.3	8.5	35%	.297	1.50	3.55	5.27	5.07	0.1	101	
2013	SDN	MLB	26	6	3	1	45	0	46^{1}	33	1	2.1	9.5	46%	.274	0.95	2.14	2.03	2.04	1.4	76	91.7
2014	SDN	MLB	27	1	2	0	63	0	55	44	5	1.8	10.1	38%	.289	1.00	3.60	2.74	3.30	0.8	80	91.5
2015	SDN	MLB	28	0	1	0	26	0	23	25	0	3.9	8.6	34%	.368	1.52	2.35	2.55	4.64	0.0	101	91.3
2015	ELP	AAA	28	5	3	1	40	0	50^{1}	48	5	2.7	12.2	44%	.355	1.25	3.04	3.08	2.04	1.8	66	
2016	*SDN*	*MLB*	*29*	*2*	*1*	*0*	*37*	*0*	*39^{1}*	*33*	*4*	*2.7*	*9.4*	*39%*	*.300*	*1.13*	*3.47*	*3.27*	*4.00*	*0.5*	*88*	
2017	*SDN*	*MLB*	*30*	*2*	*1*	*0*	*43*	*0*	*43^{1}*	*37*	*5*	*2.5*	*9.5*	*39%*	*.307*	*1.14*	*3.47*	*3.68*	*4.00*	*0.5*	*88*	

Breakout: 32% Improve: 52% Collapse: 24% Attrition: 23% MLB: 95% *Comparables: Tony Watson, Mark Melancon, Andrew Bailey*

Although Vincent pitched well for the Padres on the rare occasion he got the chance, he spent most of 2015 at Triple-A El Paso, sentenced for the crime of having options. Given how much the team needed bullpen arms, it was a strange place to keep one of its better relievers. Vincent doesn't throw hard, and his three pitches, fastball, cutter, rare change, have similar velocities; they tried to teach him how to throw a curve as a sort of prison education program, but it didn't take. He's due for parole this year, and soon he'll be free to pitch the sixth and seventh in the majors, where he belongs.

Lineouts

Hitters

NAME	POS	TEAM	LVL	AGE	PA	R	2B	3B	HR	RBI	BB	K	SB	CS	AVG/OBP/SLG	TAv	BABIP	BRR	FRAA	WARP
Carlos Asuaje	2B	PME	AA	23	570	60	23	7	8	61	56	88	9	6	.251/.334/.374	.259	.289	-1.5	2B(106): -17.6, 3B(9): -0.3	-0.7
Auston Bousfield	CF	LEL	A+	21	468	53	12	2	3	32	50	79	22	6	.273/.361/.335	.285	.330	4.2	CF(81): 2.1, LF(4): -0.2	3.2
	CF	SAN	AA	21	81	6	3	0	0	1	8	17	1	0	.247/.321/.288	.222	.321	-0.8	CF(12): -0.3, RF(5): -0.3	-0.4
Franchy Cordero	LF	FTW	A	20	524	59	13	1	5	34	31	121	22	11	.243/.293/.306	.231	.313	3.0	LF(68): -1.5, SS(22): -3.1	-0.6
Alex Dickerson	LF	ELP	AAA	25	519	82	36	9	12	71	45	96	4	0	.307/.374/.503	.308	.360	1.0	LF(95): -8.3, RF(16): -0.2	2.9
	LF	SDN	MLB	25	8	0	0	0	0	0	0	3	0	0	.250/.250/.250	.150	.400	0.0	LF(1): 0.1	-0.1
Rocky Gale	C	ELP	AAA	27	351	34	16	4	1	39	17	59	1	1	.307/.349/.391	.259	.370	-2.4	C(94): 11.2, 3B(3): -0.3	2.4
	C	SDN	MLB	27	10	0	0	0	0	0	0	1	0	0	.100/.100/.100	.038	.111	-0.1	C(6): 0.1	-0.2
Duanel Jones	3B	FTW	A	22	170	22	11	0	7	36	15	36	1	1	.327/.382/.536	.330	.384	-1.7	3B(33): -1.4, 1B(7): 0.5	1.5
	3B	SAN	AA	22	346	39	10	0	7	38	22	65	2	1	.226/.272/.323	.218	.258	-0.7	3B(66): -4.9, 1B(24): 2.7	-1.0
Erik Kratz	C	KCA	MLB	35	5	0	0	0	0	1	0	2	0	0	.000/.000/.000	.091	.000	0.0	C(4): -0.0	-0.1
	C	LEH	AAA	35	97	14	8	1	3	15	18	18	1	0	.312/.433/.558	.346	.362	-0.2	C(11): 3.5, 1B(1): 0.0	1.5
	C	OMA	AAA	35	62	7	2	0	4	12	5	9	0	0	.214/.274/.464	.232	.182	-0.5	C(14): 0.6	0.1
	C	PHI	MLB	35	23	3	2	0	0	2	1	3	0	0	.227/.261/.318	.220	.263	0.1	C(3): 0.5, 1B(2): -0.0	0.0
	C	TAC	AAA	35	43	3	4	0	0	5	3	7	0	0	.205/.279/.308	.203	.250	-0.3	C(4): 0.3, 1B(1): -0.0	-0.2
Taylor Lindsey	2B	ELP	AAA	23	108	8	3	1	0	7	16	18	3	1	.228/.343/.283	.235	.284	-0.1	2B(31): -1.3	-0.1
	2B	SAN	AA	23	225	21	11	0	5	15	23	38	1	0	.171/.258/.302	.219	.184	-0.6	2B(49): 1.4	-0.4
Fernando Perez	2B	LEL	A+	21	492	46	21	3	10	53	39	115	1	1	.224/.291/.352	.243	.279	1.6	2B(101): -8.9, 1B(1): -0.2	-0.4
Josmil Pinto	C	ROC	AAA	26	263	33	9	0	7	31	22	54	0	0	.228/.304/.354	.242	.267	-1.4	C(33): 4.8	0.6
Jose Pirela	2B	NYA	MLB	25	78	7	3	0	1	5	2	16	1	0	.230/.247/.311	.191	.276	-0.5	2B(27): -1.4, LF(2): 0.5	-0.5
	2B	SWB	AAA	25	259	40	14	1	3	23	24	22	5	2	.325/.390/.433	.297	.346	-1.4	3B(20): -1.4, LF(19): 1.2	1.4
Franmil Reyes	OF	FTW	A	19	509	52	25	7	8	62	46	91	10	5	.255/.320/.393	.263	.298	-1.5	RF(95): 2.3, 1B(2): -0.0	1.1
Ryan Schimpf	OF	BUF	AAA	27	122	12	6	0	3	7	11	23	0	2	.200/.270/.336	.230	.224	1.4	RF(10): -1.5, 3B(7): -0.3	-0.2
	OF	NHP	AA	27	307	43	20	0	20	56	42	54	2	1	.271/.378/.581	.325	.267	-1.9	RF(18): -2.3, LF(14): -0.5	2.3
Nick Torres	OF	FTW	A	22	320	45	29	2	2	40	18	52	4	1	.326/.378/.462	.301	.385	4.1	LF(31): -1.9, RF(26): -0.9	2.2
	OF	LEL	A+	22	228	21	15	2	3	30	9	45	5	1	.275/.316/.408	.274	.331	-0.9	RF(25): 3.9, LF(23): 3.4	1.5
Luis Urias	2B	FTW	A	18	224	28	5	1	0	16	16	18	5	10	.290/.370/.326	.267	.318	-1.7	2B(38): 0.9, SS(7): 1.0	1.1
	2B	TRI	A-	18	44	6	1	0	0	1	5	1	3	3	.355/.487/.387	.391	.367	0.2	2B(6): 0.5, 3B(1): 0.0	0.8

Carlos Asuaje is the latest middle infield prospect whose height suggests the Red Sox heavily scout the Shire. He performed reasonably well in Portland en route to being named an Eastern League All-Star. ❖ **Auston Bousfield**, the Padres' fifth-round pick in 2014 out of Ole Miss, is a center fielder with a short stroke whose combination of speed and on-base skills elicits comparisons to Chris Denorfia and who could eventually fill a similar role. ❖ **Franchy Cordero**'s poor plate discipline has kept him from translating raw strength into usable power, which might be workable if he could play a passable shortstop. In left field, where he moved last summer, his offensive entropy is far less charming a quirk. ❖ **Alex Dickerson** rebounded from a lost 2014 with numbers that resembled what he'd done in the past—decent batting average, lots of doubles, some homers—but his brief cameo provided no guarantees that prove the numbers will translate to the show. ❖ **Rocky Gale**, who attended the same high school as Jed Lowrie, provides the defensive consistency his first name would suggest, but also a .610 OPS over six minor-league seasons that fails to earn the sort of vicious connotation conjured by his family name. ❖ **Duanel Jones** started strong in his second Midwest League stint after two dismal years in the California League, but foundered at Double-A (one extra-base hit in his final 34 games) and is ill-equipped to play third base. Other than those little details, he's great. ❖ **Erik Kratz** is just keeping the seat warm at this point, but everything about his intangibles and makeup suggest that he could maybe one day find himself back in a dugout as a coach. ❖ **Taylor Lindsey** has hit .199/.280/.302 in a season's worth of at-bats in the high minors since joining the Padres, which helps explain why he remains in this chapter after the team designated him for assignment in August. ❖ San Diego product **Fernando Perez** began the transition from third base to second in 2014 and stuck at the keystone corner last year in High-A. He also swung at the ball as if battling demons. ❖ Concussions and questions about whether he can catch at all have **Josmil Pinto** hanging in limbo, despite his solid patience and pop. ❖ After another solid season of honing his slap-hitting thing at Triple-A and a bitter cup of coffee in the bigs, **Jose Pirela** was shipped to the Padres for possibly fictional pitching prospect Ronald Herrera. ❖ Teenage behemoth **Franmil Reyes** made slight gains in his second tour of the Midwest League, primarily in terms of tightening his strike zone, but still hasn't tapped into the power expected of such a large young man. ❖ In April, **Ryan Schimpf** homered off Luis Severino, which will make for a great bonding moment with the four Blue Jays who accomplished the same feat in 2015, when they meet thirty years in the future to sip coffee and compare their lives. ❖ **Nick Torres**, a fourth-round pick in 2014 out of Cal Poly San Luis Obispo—the same school that produced Ozzie Smith—tied for sixth in the Midwest League in doubles despite being promoted to High-A in early July. ❖ **Luis Urias** is a diminutive second baseman from Mexico who has good bat-to-ball skills and who held his own in the Midwest League at age 18. His power, equal to a small shrub or a coil of garden hose, suggests a one-dimensional offensive profile that has drawn optimistic comparisons to Marco Scutaro.

Pitchers

NAME	TEAM	LVL	AGE	W	L	SV	G	GS	IP	H	HR	BB/9	K/9	GB%	BABIP	WHIP	ERA	FIP	FRA	WARP	CFIP	MPH
Ryan Butler	LEL	A+	23	3	2	0	12	7	46^{2}	52	2	2.7	6.0	61%	.327	1.41	3.66	4.16	5.86	-0.1	110	
	SAN	AA	23	0	3	0	3	3	17	16	0	4.8	3.7	46%	.286	1.47	4.76	4.06	6.41	-0.2	124	
Leonel Campos	SDN	MLB	27	0	0	0	1	0	1	1	0	9.0	9.0	33%	.333	2.00	9.00	4.16	7.00	0.0	103	96.8
	ELP	AAA	27	2	0	1	38	0	49^{2}	30	2	3.8	12.3	55%	.259	1.03	2.90	2.65	2.30	1.6	69	
Jose Castillo	TRI	A-	19	3	1	0	13	12	52^{1}	54	1	2.8	6.0	62%	.308	1.34	3.61	3.72	5.13	0.2	105	
	FTW	A	19	1	1	0	6	6	27	25	2	5.3	5.3	42%	.284	1.52	4.00	5.06	6.78	-0.6	125	
Rafael De Paula	LEL	A+	24	5	9	0	35	18	120^{1}	125	14	3.5	9.6	34%	.333	1.43	5.01	4.47	4.82	1.1	98	
Jon Edwards	SDN	MLB	27	0	0	0	11	0	10^{2}	6	3	6.8	13.5	25%	.176	1.31	3.38	6.07	4.05	0.1	98	96.8
	TEX	MLB	27	0	0	0	11	0	6	6	1	12.0	9.0	12%	.312	2.33	6.00	7.27	9.09	-0.3	109	96.7
	ROU	AAA	27	2	1	20	32	0	31^{2}	18	1	2.3	12.5	38%	.266	0.82	1.42	1.99	1.65	1.2	56	
Frank Garces	ELP	AAA	25	1	0	3	19	0	21^{2}	17	2	6.2	7.1	38%	.242	1.48	2.91	5.31	6.40	-0.3	116	
	SDN	MLB	25	0	1	0	40	1	38	41	9	5.2	7.1	36%	.291	1.66	5.21	6.48	6.32	-0.7	123	93.8
Tayron Guerrero	ELP	AAA	24	0	0	1	11	0	13^{2}	8	0	7.2	9.9	40%	.267	1.39	3.95	4.04	4.03	0.2	91	
	SAN	AA	24	1	5	13	37	0	42^{1}	33	3	4.3	9.8	48%	.263	1.25	2.76	3.53	4.10	0.4	95	
Justin Hancock	ELP	AAA	24	1	0	0	2	2	10^{1}	15	1	3.5	4.4	40%	.378	1.84	2.61	5.05	5.91	0.0	109	
	SAN	AA	24	7	6	0	22	22	120^{1}	127	8	3.7	6.9	48%	.322	1.46	3.59	3.98	5.04	0.2	106	
Dinelson Lamet	FTW	A	22	5	8	0	26	24	105^{1}	82	9	3.8	10.3	40%	.282	1.20	2.99	3.74	3.87	1.3	96	
Zech Lemond	LEL	A+	22	5	10	0	32	22	130	175	12	3.0	7.0	45%	.374	1.68	5.54	4.58	5.79	-0.1	108	
Marcos Mateo	ELP	AAA	31	3	0	9	25	0	32	20	1	3.4	11.2	42%	.247	1.00	1.69	2.72	2.66	0.9	73	
	SDN	MLB	31	1	1	0	26	0	27	22	5	3.0	11.0	37%	.270	1.15	4.00	4.46	4.11	0.2	89	97.2
Cory Mazzoni	ELP	AAA	25	1	3	5	26	0	34	25	0	3.2	12.2	46%	.298	1.09	3.97	1.95	2.07	1.2	66	
	SDN	MLB	25	0	0	0	8	0	8^{2}	23	2	5.2	8.3	50%	.553	3.23	20.77	6.05	15.14	-1.1	113	96.4
Elliot Morris	SAN	AA	23	5	9	0	21	18	101^{2}	113	6	3.9	6.4	42%	.323	1.54	4.87	4.01	5.38	-0.3	109	
Luis Perdomo	PEO	A	22	5	9	0	17	17	100^{1}	103	7	2.8	9.0	55%	.334	1.34	3.68	3.39	3.70	1.5	94	
	PMB	A+	22	1	3	0	6	5	26^{1}	31	1	2.1	6.2	49%	.345	1.41	5.13	2.98	3.72	0.2	99	
Caleb Thielbar	MIN	MLB	28	0	0	0	6	0	5	5	0	0.0	9.0	73%	.333	1.00	5.40	1.10	1.11	0.2	93	93.5
	ELP	AAA	28	0	0	0	9	0	12^{1}	9	1	3.6	5.1	23%	.211	1.14	0.73	4.98	5.39	0.0	105	
	ROC	AAA	28	5	3	0	29	0	32	30	1	5.1	5.3	44%	.282	1.50	2.81	4.16	5.96	-0.6	121	
Brad Wieck	FTW	A	23	2	0	0	2	2	10^{1}	8	0	2.6	10.5	44%	.296	1.06	2.61	2.53	3.57	0.2	93	
	SAV	A	23	3	5	0	10	10	56	54	2	3.4	11.9	38%	.377	1.34	3.21	2.64	3.23	1.3	86	
	LEL	A+	23	2	6	0	11	11	57	61	6	4.1	8.4	42%	.340	1.53	5.21	4.71	5.50	0.2	106	

Eighth-round draft pick **Logan Allen** landed an overslot deal and then landed in a deal to become San Diego's newest talented lefty prospect. He's a ways off, but it should be interesting to watch Logan's run through the minors. ❖ Former seventh-rounder and Tommy John survivor **Ryan Butler** pumps mid-90s heat but doesn't put the ball past many hitters. His spirit quest will likely end in the bullpen, where the fastball can be fast and the pedestrian secondaries will be less of an obstacle. ❖ After a late-season audition in 2014, **Leonel Campos** returned to Triple-A to refine his game, which he did, improving all his peripherals. The Padres, despite their bullpen woes, rewarded him with a single inning of work for all his efforts. ❖ **Jose Castillo**, who came over in the Wil Myers trade, is a sizable lefty out of Venezuela whose fastball runs in the low-90s with possible room for growth but whose off-speed pitches, health and command have conspired to slow his development. Beware prospects for whom weight is their greatest asset. ❖ Armed with a 92-94 mph fastball and an inconsistent breaking ball, **Rafael De Paula** transitioned to the bullpen last July, where aside from two implosions he pitched well enough. That said, we all deserve to have our outliers tossed out when people judge us; they never are. ❖ **Jon Edwards**, acquired for Will Venable last August, throws baseballs hard and only occasionally in the direction of home plate. ❖ **Frank Garces** quickly set a tone for the season when he intentionally walked the first batter he faced in 2015. He was never called upon to do so again, something his managers, in hindsight, came to largely regret. ❖ **Tayron Guerrero**'s 94–98 mph fastball (best in the Texas League according to *Baseball America*'s annual coaches poll) and above-average slider make for a potent late-innings combination. First, though, he'll have to at least cast some doubt in hitters' minds as to whether they should take the bat off their shoulder. ❖ **Justin Hancock** features a sinking low-90s fastball, along with a decent changeup and breaking ball, but doesn't miss bats enough to slot as more than a back-end starter or middle reliever. His proximity to the majors provides the vast majority of his value to the ballclub. ❖ Four pitches: That was the net result of two years of rehab for poor **Josh Johnson** before he blew out his elbow. He'll spend 2016 working his way back from a third Tommy John surgery, a challenge few pitchers have surmounted. ❖ A 22-year-old out of the Dominican Republic, **Dinelson Lamet** was basically the international equivalent of a senior sign, earning a mere $100,000. Unaware of his station, he subdued Midwest League batters with a mid-90s fastball and slider—especially those of the right-handed persuasion, who hit .153/.282/.227 against him. ❖ **Zech Lemond**'s first name is an onomatopoeia for the sound people make when they watch him pitch. A move to the bullpen would play to his two-pitch strengths and quiet the hecklers. ❖ **Cory Luebke** is still a San Diego Padre. ❖ Long-time minor leaguer and Tommy John survivor **Marcos Mateo** split his season between El Paso and San Diego, enjoying much less success in the latter thanks to an abundance of left-handed hitters who weren't dazzled by his mid-90s heat or his copious sliders breaking inward. ❖ Hard-throwing right-hander **Cory Mazzoni** became the fifth pitcher in MLB history to allow at least 20 runs in fewer than 10 innings, and then followed his act of vandalism by escaping to the disabled list with a strained shoulder. ❖ **Elliot Morris** got devoured by Double-A lefties before missing a month with elbow soreness (he had Tommy John surgery way back in 2011). He was one of the top arms in the Angels' system before heading over in the Huston Street trade, a title worth as much as the Lira at this point. ❖ Energetic string bean **Luis Perdomo** raised his arm slot, improved his performance during a second run at Peoria and gained national acclaim by pumping mid-to-upper-90s gas in the Futures Game. He's made enough progress to convince onlookers he just might stick in the rotation after all. ❖ After spending parts of three seasons in the Twins' bullpen, former St. Paul Saint **Caleb Thielbar** was selected off waivers by the Padres, who sent him to Triple-A El Paso to help bolster the Chihuahuas' staff during their PCL playoff push. ❖ Mountainous left-hander **Brad Wieck** came to the Padres in June as the player to be named later in the much-ignored Alex Torres trade, taking his turn in the Lake Elsinore rotation, where his inability to stand out was made all the more impressive by his large stature.

Manager

Andy Green

In the final days of the Padres' search for a new manager, rumors surfaced that A.J. Preller would pick between two long-time baseball men: either former Twins skipper Ron Gardenhire or Pirates third-base coach Rick Sofield. As he is wont to do, Preller threw everyone a slider and went with Diamondbacks third-base coach Andy Green.

Green, who won't turn 40 until July 2017, has made a quick ascent since retiring after the 2010 season. He spent 2011-2012 managing in Rookie ball, then moved to Double-A, where he subsequently won consecutive Southern League Manager of the Year awards. Last offseason Green interviewed for the Diamondbacks' managerial spot; Chip Hale got the job instead, but he soon added Green as his third-base coach.

A year later, Green has his own team to play with. The book on him is that he's poised beyond his years; that he's a little bundle of energy; and that he's into advanced analytics, to the extent that he handled all the Diamondbacks' defensive positioning. Sounds good on paper, right? So do most first-time managers. The difference is that Green, unlike many of the recent new hires, has a track record indicating he might just be okay at managing. Obviously there's no guarantee those minor-league results translate to the majors, but you can understand why Preller is willing to give Green a look.

SAN FRANCISCO GIANTS

Essay by Erik Malinowski

Player comments by Daniel Rathman and BP authors

On a Saturday in late September, Tim Hudson was holding court with reporters in the visitor's locker room at O.co Coliseum. This was a building—if not a room—that he knew well, going back to the day his big-league career started in the summer of 1999. On this weird and bittersweet afternoon, Hudson had made the penultimate start of his career. He had nothing left to give to the fans who had cheered him as a rookie, nor to his more recent fans across San Francisco Bay. He faced just 11 batters, recorded four outs and was pulled from the game. The A's fans cheered him off, and Hudson came back out for a curtain call. He was really only here to say goodbye.

The game was (technically speaking) meaningless for the Giants—the Dodgers had already clinched the National League West and the wild cards were long gone—yet the day was full of meaning. Hudson was pitching against Barry Zito, his old friend, a former A's teammate and an ex-Giant. His team won in spite of his performance because Jarrett Parker (a 26-year-old rookie with all of 24 big-league plate appearances to his name) happened to slug three home runs. But it was a day to reflect on the older guard whose days in baseball were numbered. "It wasn't quite the pitcher's duel we all envisioned," Hudson told a huddled group of writers. "Today didn't go how I wanted. Didn't throw that many pitches, so maybe next time out I'll be nice and fresh." He cracked a smile as he said this last part.

This entire day—this *feeling* that Hudson's farewell evoked—was very much representative of the 2015 Giants, an above-average, slightly confounding team. There were season-long goodbyes (sometimes painful to watch) and there was youth blossoming, carrying the day in stunning ways and at unexpected times. This is a team with more recent success than any franchise in baseball—the three World Series wins in five years were not some isolated Bay Area fever dream—and yet there is still a hopeful future, thanks to Buster Posey and a core of less-than-hyped position players who have morphed into legit stars. Under Sabean and general Bobby Evans, the Giants don't rebuild. They reload, and never the same way.

✦✦✦

GIANTS PROSPECTUS

2015 W-L: 84-78, 2nd in NL West

Pythag	.548	9th	DER	.717	2nd
RS/G	4.30	11th	B-Age	28.7	21st
RA/G	3.87	7th	P-Age	31	30th
TAv	.274	2nd	Salary	$173.2M	4th
BRR	-1.43	17th	M$/MW	$4.5M	9th
TAv-P	.261	16th	DL Days	952	15th
FIP	3.94	11th	$ on DL	28%	29th

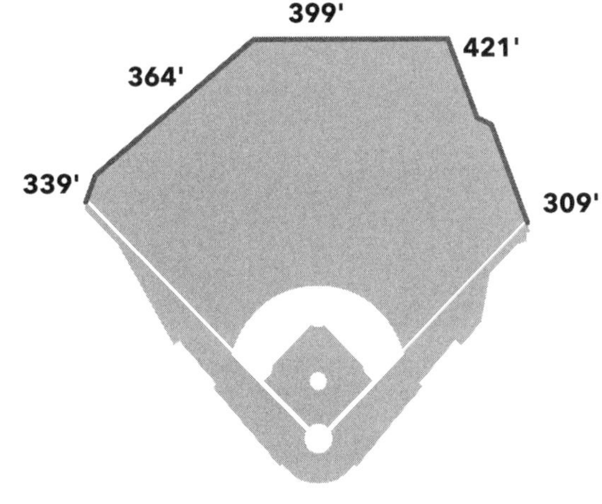

Outfield wall profile: **8'** to **25'**

Three-Year Park Factors

Runs	Runs/RH	Runs/LH	HR/RH	HR/LH
92	99	99	91	88

Top Hitter WARP	7.6	Buster Posey
Top Pitcher WARP	3.8	Madison Bumgarner
Top Prospect	Christian Arroyo	

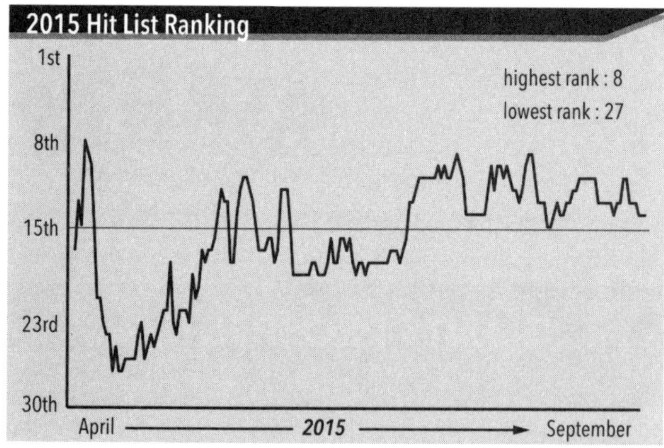

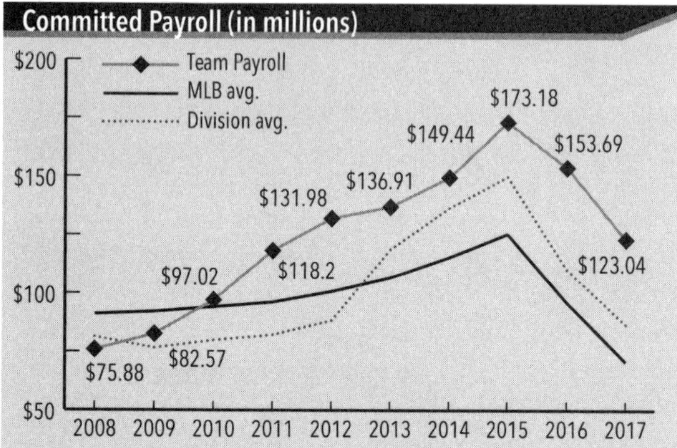

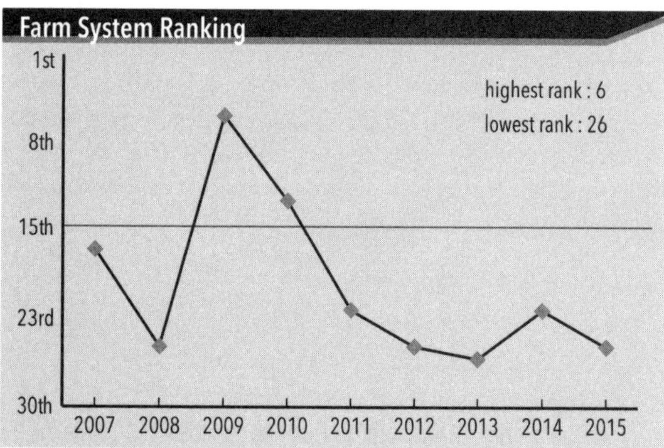

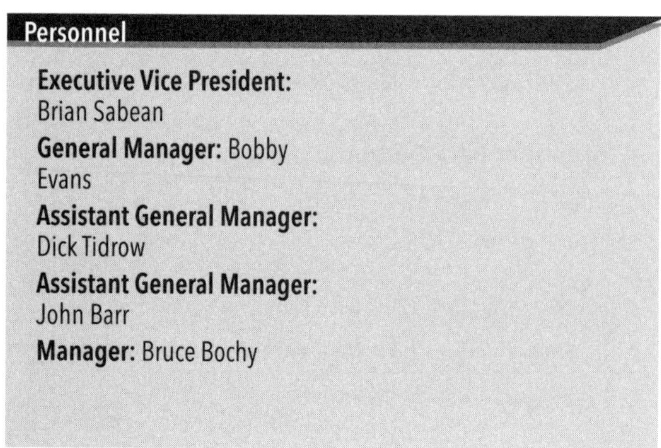
Personnel

Executive Vice President: Brian Sabean

General Manager: Bobby Evans

Assistant General Manager: Dick Tidrow

Assistant General Manager: John Barr

Manager: Bruce Bochy

Here's where we pause to remind you that, lack of playoff qualification aside, the 2015 Giants actually had a pretty good season. By record, they were only four games worse than the 2014 championship team. Their plus-69 run differential was as nice as the 2012 title-winners', and just three runs behind the division-winning Dodgers. As ranked by Defensive Efficiency, the Giants were the second-best fielding team in all of baseball, behind only Toronto. They scored more runs than the Cubs, posted a better on-base percentage than the Yankees, struck out more batters than the Royals and were the only team that broke 100 in ERA+ and OPS+ and didn't make the playoffs. Sure, this is cherry-picking, but there was a lot that undeniably went right for the Giants in 2015. They were within two games of first as late as August 23rd. The division was up for grabs with Labor Day in sight. And third-order winning percentage said the Giants should've ended up five games better than their actual record. That could be bad luck or inopportune run clustering or other extenuating circumstances, but the Giants were as good as they were in 2015 primarily because of their young position players.

To a Giants fan of a decade ago, this is unthinkable—like finding out that while you were at college your dad learned to skateboard. No team in the Bonds and post-Bonds years made developing hitters look so difficult. One of the few Giants signees who panned out was Pedro Feliz, whom the Giants acquired as a 19-year-old free agent out of the Dominican Republic in 1994. By the time he became a regular in the lineup, he was a 28-year-old corner infielder/outfielder who was good for about 20 homers a year and a sub-.300 on-base percentage. After topping out at 2.6 WARP, Feliz signed with the Phillies, was barely above replacement level and won a World Series his first season there. We're not just naming the guy here for nostalgia; Feliz might be the best position player the Giants developed between Bonds' signing (in 1993) and Bonds' retirement (in 2007). (The other candidate for the title is Bill Mueller.) *Pedro Feliz.* Pedro Feliz, whose most lasting contribution to the Giants was his well-timed departure, which cleared the way for a converted catcher named Pablo Sandoval to step in at third base.

Yet the organization survived this drought. They and their general manager thrived. These years were barren for hitting prospects but not for the Giants, who averaged 92 wins per year in Brian Sabean's first eight seasons. This was the first Golden Age of Sabean: The Bonds Era.

Meanwhile, the Giants couldn't develop young pitching, either, which was especially troubling because of how much they had invested in it: 15 of Sabean's first 20 first-round picks as Giants GM were moundsmen. Nearly all—and, most famously, the trio of Jesse Foppert, Kurt Ainsworth and Jerome Williams—flamed out. (Open your window late in the evening and if the wind is carrying along the Bay *just* right, you can still hear that triumvirate giving some Giants fans night terrors.) After Bonds retired, Sabean's Giants somehow figured this out. They built a staff of power arms out of first-rounders Matt Cain, Tim Lincecum and Madison Bumgarner. Still they struggled to develop hitters, but rosters thick with veterans supplemented the pitching and produced the second Golden Age of Sabean: The Pitching Era.

Very few GMs get three golden ages.

✦✦✦

It was Sandoval who broke the hitter-development slump, producing a 124 OPS+ over six full seasons as a homegrown All-Star before cashing in on the East Coast last winter. The Giants of the past would've scrambled to free agency to fill the void he left at third. This is the franchise of Russ Davis and David Bell, of Juan Uribe and Edgardo Alfonzo, of Mark Lewis and Charlie Hayes and Jose Castillo. But that's an old vision of the Giants; 2015 was the year it became apparent that the Giants' future lies in that core of young position players that eluded them for so long.

That includes their new third baseman, Matt Duffy, who had hit zero homers in 501 collegiate at-bats when the Giants drafted him in the 18th round. So of course, Duffy knocked 13 dingers in his age-24 season and finished second in Rookie of the Year voting behind Kris Bryant. Even more face-numbing, his 4.9 bWAR was the second-best mark *ever* for a Giants rookie—better than Posey, Willie Mays, Gary Matthews, Willie McCovey and Orlando Cepeda, all ROY winners themselves. So now with Duffy (11th in WARP among third basemen), Posey (led all catchers with 7.8 WARP), Brandon Crawford (led all shortstops with 4.7 WARP), Brandon Belt (fifth among first basemen with 4.7 WARP), and Joe Panik (led second basemen with .314 TAv), the Giants have a semi-terrifying Cardinals-esque run down the middle of the lineup, from the no. 2 spot to no. 6, all under 30 years old and homegrown through San Francisco's system. Most impressively of all, only Posey was a sure thing on draft day; Panik was a first-rounder viewed by many as an overdraft, Crawford was a fourth-rounder, Belt went in the fifth and Duffy didn't get popped until day three, in the 18th round. They're the core of an offense that matched the Dodgers for the best True Average in the National League.

They've turned into a team that wins more by outslugging other teams rather than allowing fewer runs, if you take my meaning. This is, potentially, the third Golden Age of Brian Sabean: The Homegrown Murderer's Row Era. That and Madison Bumgarner and you've got yourself a shot.

From the Giants' perspective, the best thing that happened to Bumgarner in 2015 was the thing that didn't happen, mainly his right arm spontaneously dissolving off of his rotator cuff joint, falling to the AT&T Park pitcher's mound and bubbling up into a puddle of sea foam and draining into the Bay. I mean, basic science tells us that sort of thing just does not happen from a biological standpoint, but after pitching nearly 270 innings during the course of the 2014 season, you can forgive Giants fans for assuming the most inexplicable scenario would strike their ace. But that didn't happen. Bumgarner was actually *better* in 2015 than the season before, posting career-bests in strikeout rate, walk rate, WHIP, K/9 and ERA+. He started 32 games—his fifth straight season of 30-plus starts—and led the league in complete games with four. Hell, the dude even slugged a career-high five home runs. (Homegrown hitting!)

But more than just the pitching, Bumgarner was also a more emotional, hornery competitor than he's been. You could chalk that up to the Giants ultimately falling short of expectations and almost continually chasing the Dodgers from Opening Day, but his new slew of endorsements and awards and public honors didn't soften him a bit. The single most evocative moment of the entire Giants season might've been Bumgarner's *High Noon*-style staredown of umpire Joe West in an otherwise meaningless September game in San Diego. It was better reality TV than you could find on Bravo or E! (and far more real).

✦✦✦

For the franchise that produced Mel Ott, Mays, McCovey, and the Bonds whose Baseball Reference page gives us the vapors, it feels natural to think of the Giants as a team of mashers, and Sabean has finally brought together a crew of hitters that feels more like the early-to-mid-'90s Yankees (where he cut his teeth before coming westward) or the mid-'00s-to-today Cardinals, with a string of bats that form a gauntlet that can break through on any opposing staff. Thing is, this current situation better last a good while because the Giants' system is basically a whole bunch of tumbleweeds, and tumbleweeds have lousy on-base percentages. The Giants have neither high-ceiling studs—BP's midseason top 50 prospect ranking had nary a Giant within sniffing distance—nor depth. Their top prospect is a 20-year-old shortstop starting his fourth season in the organization and who's never played above Class A. ("Hey, it's not as bad as the Angelszzzzzzz ..." Sabean whispers as he nods off to sleep every night.)

But what the Giants do have right now is a core of young lineup stars under team control for the near future. That gives the farm system time to regenerate. The Giants are young, their stars are making relative peanuts, and the organization as a whole is clicking. They're coming off a dud of a season, and yet the outlook might be better right now than it was entering any even year in recent past. That might sound overly optimistic, but with a recent track record better than any other club, it's foolhardy to think there's anything this team and its president can't do. ■

—Erik Malinowski is a freelance writer based near San Francisco.

HITTERS

Christian Arroyo SS

Born: 5/30/95 Age: 21 Bats: R Throws: R Height: 6'1" Weight: 180

YEAR	TEAM	LVL	AGE	PA	R	2B	3B	HR	RBI	BB	K	SB	CS	AVG/OBP/SLG	TAv	BABIP	BRR	FRAA	WARP
2014	SLO	A-	19	267	39	14	2	5	48	18	31	6	1	.333/.378/.469	.309	.360	0.1	SS(58): 3.9	3.0
2014	AUG	A	19	125	10	3	1	1	14	4	22	1	2	.203/.226/.271	.189	.237	-0.8	2B(26): 6.7, SS(5): -0.1	0.0
2015	SJO	A+	20	409	48	28	2	9	42	19	73	5	3	.304/.344/.459	.304	.355	-2.3	SS(88): -2.4	3.2
2016	*SFN*	*MLB*	*21*	*250*	*20*	*11*	*1*	*4*	*25*	*8*	*57*	*1*	*0*	*.235/.262/.348*	*.223*	*.289*	*-0.3*	*SS 3*	*0.5*
2017	*SFN*	*MLB*	*22*	*399*	*39*	*19*	*2*	*7*	*39*	*15*	*90*	*1*	*1*	*.240/.270/.361*	*.235*	*.293*	*-0.6*	*SS 4*	*2.2*

Breakout: 7% Improve: 12% Collapse: 0% Attrition: 8% MLB: 13% *Comparables: Nick Franklin, Yamaico Navarro, Arismendy Alcantara*

A scout's take on Arroyo is best gauged by the number of adverbs s/he inserts between the helping and main verbs in the sentence "He can hit." This typically ranges from one to three, and is accompanied by some degree of doubt about the Tampa native's ability to play shortstop, which becomes less relevant with each additional "really" in the description of his skills at the plate. Arroyo elicits those compliments because of his precocious pitch recognition and feel for the barrel, both of which suggest that he could catch the express train to the majors. If he reaches his ceiling, Arroyo will be a contact machine who bats near the top of the order and plays above-average defense at the keystone; in other words, he'll be a right-handed version of everything Joe Panik wasn't supposed to be.

Brandon Belt 1B

Born: 4/20/88 Age: 28 Bats: L Throws: L Height: 6'5" Weight: 220

YEAR	TEAM	LVL	AGE	PA	R	2B	3B	HR	RBI	BB	K	SB	CS	AVG/OBP/SLG	TAv	BABIP	BRR	FRAA	WARP
2013	SFN	MLB	25	571	76	39	4	17	67	52	125	5	2	.289/.360/.481	.310	.351	2.5	1B(143): 5.1	4.4
2014	SFN	MLB	26	235	30	8	0	12	27	18	64	3	1	.243/.306/.449	.277	.288	-0.4	1B(59): 8.6, RF(1): -0.0	1.6
2014	FRE	AAA	26	20	2	3	0	2	5	1	5	0	1	.526/.550/1.000	.572	.667	-0.1	1B(4): -0.1	0.7
2015	SFN	MLB	27	556	73	33	5	18	68	56	147	9	3	.280/.356/.478	.317	.363	-1.5	1B(120): 8.0, LF(14): 0.1	4.7
2016	*SFN*	*MLB*	*28*	*609*	*73*	*31*	*4*	*20*	*78*	*61*	*151*	*9*	*3*	*.265/.343/.450*	*.286*	*.331*	*0.1*	*1B 9, LF -1*	*3.7*
2017	*SFN*	*MLB*	*29*	*519*	*68*	*27*	*4*	*17*	*67*	*55*	*129*	*7*	*3*	*.267/.350/.454*	*.301*	*.333*	*0.1*	*1B 8, LF -1*	*1.5*

Breakout: 0% Improve: 50% Collapse: 2% Attrition: 3% MLB: 98% *Comparables: Mark Teixeira, Adrian Gonzalez, Justin Morneau*

Brandon Belt was one of the 10 best hitters (min. 500 PA) in the National League last season. That's not a misprint, so we'll say it again: By TAv, Brandon Belt was one of the 10 best hitters in the National League last season. Shrouded by the San Francisco fog, the Giants first baseman clobbered everything thrown at or below his knees, amassing the league's highest line-drive rate. Belt's (second) breakout can be attributed to a counterintuitive adjustment: He expanded his hitting area to the shins—willingly making more contact on pitches most hitters pound into the dirt—and came out ahead on balance. It's a particularly neat skill considering the downward trajectory of the modern strike zone, and some SABR-savvy teams having been spied pursuing just this trait in free agent hitters. Still an excellent defensive first baseman with a plus arm, Belt is poised to challenge Anthony Rizzo and Joey Votto for All-Star votes, provided his lingering concussion symptoms subside by Opening Day.

Gregor Blanco CF

Born: 12/24/83 Age: 32 Bats: L Throws: L Height: 5'11" Weight: 175

YEAR	TEAM	LVL	AGE	PA	R	2B	3B	HR	RBI	BB	K	SB	CS	AVG/OBP/SLG	TAv	BABIP	BRR	FRAA	WARP
2013	SFN	MLB	29	511	50	17	6	3	41	52	95	14	9	.265/.341/.350	.259	.328	0.2	CF(76): -4.1, LF(72): -1.1	0.8
2014	SFN	MLB	30	444	51	18	6	5	38	41	77	16	5	.260/.333/.374	.271	.311	4.0	CF(72): -1.5, LF(64): 0.1	2.0
2015	SFN	MLB	31	372	59	19	3	5	26	40	59	13	5	.291/.368/.413	.299	.338	4.3	CF(44): -3.2, LF(38): 3.4	2.8
2016	*SFN*	*MLB*	*32*	*535*	*65*	*21*	*5*	*6*	*42*	*52*	*106*	*18*	*7*	*.253/.329/.359*	*.253*	*.308*	*2.8*	*LF 6, CF -2*	*2.1*
2017	*SFN*	*MLB*	*33*	*408*	*44*	*15*	*4*	*5*	*37*	*39*	*83*	*12*	*5*	*.245/.320/.350*	*.256*	*.299*	*2.6*	*LF 4, CF -1*	*1.7*

Breakout: 1% Improve: 45% Collapse: 1% Attrition: 10% MLB: 95% *Comparables: Robin Yount, Coco Crisp, Johnny Damon*

A combination of injuries and Angel Pagan's collapse served to make Blanco the league's most important fourth outfielder last year, and he filled those shoes with aplomb. The Venezuelan credited Aoki and Joe Panik for inspiring a couple of swing adjustments that produced a better contact rate and more hard grounders, both driving factors behind his career-best performance in all three slash stats. Now much more adept at hitting breaking balls, Blanco isn't spooked when a southpaw toes the rubber, and his relatively narrow platoon splits enhance his utility. A plus defender in the corners, he's somewhat challenged in center, so it's tempting to call him a "tweener." But there's a fine line between "tweener" and "useful regular," and if the offensive gains he made last year are real, Blanco will be on the right side of it.

Kyle Blanks 1B

Born: 9/11/86 Age: 29 Bats: R Throws: R Height: 6'6" Weight: 265

YEAR	TEAM	LVL	AGE	PA	R	2B	3B	HR	RBI	BB	K	SB	CS	AVG/OBP/SLG	TAv	BABIP	BRR	FRAA	WARP
2013	TUC	AAA	26	46	8	3	0	1	4	6	10	0	0	.237/.370/.395	.271	.296	-0.5	1B(7): 0.6, LF(5): 0.1	0.1
2013	SDN	MLB	26	308	31	14	0	8	35	21	85	1	1	.243/.305/.379	.256	.317	1.5	RF(37): 1.6, LF(35): 1.4	0.8
2014	SAC	AAA	27	28	4	0	0	1	3	6	3	0	0	.429/.536/.571	.401	.444	0.3	1B(5): -0.6, LF(1): 1.3	0.6
2014	OAK	MLB	27	56	9	1	0	2	7	8	13	0	0	.333/.446/.489	.356	.419	-2.2	1B(17): 0.6, RF(1): -0.0	0.4
2014	SDN	MLB	27	10	1	0	0	0	0	0	3	0	0	.200/.200/.200	.159	.286	0.0	1B(3): 0.2, LF(1): -0.0	-0.1
2014	ELP	AAA	27	99	15	5	0	9	20	10	24	0	0	.265/.364/.651	.295	.250	-0.2	1B(20): 0.6, LF(3): 0.1	0.1
2015	ROU	AAA	28	69	8	7	0	3	11	6	20	0	0	.293/.391/.569	.333	.389	-0.7	1B(13): -0.1	0.5
2015	TEX	MLB	28	71	10	5	0	3	6	4	20	1	0	.313/.352/.522	.301	.409	-0.2	1B(13): 0.8, LF(3): -0.6	0.4
2016	*SFN*	*MLB*	*29*	*138*	*15*	*6*	*1*	*5*	*18*	*11*	*38*	*0*	*0*	*.248/.316/.425*	*.271*	*.314*	*-0.1*	*LF -0, 1B 0*	*0.6*
2017	*SFN*	*MLB*	*30*	*250*	*31*	*11*	*1*	*8*	*31*	*20*	*70*	*0*	*0*	*.240/.309/.414*	*.274*	*.307*	*-0.3*	*LF -1, 1B 0*	*0.5*

Breakout: 5% Improve: 34% Collapse: 9% Attrition: 17% MLB: 71% *Comparables: Josh Phelps, Nelson Cruz, Mike Carp*

The Kyle Blanks Tour took its act to Arlington last year (after a brief stop in Round Rock). For the second season, Blanks offered a tantalizing glimpse into his power potential, especially against left-handed pitching, but failed to stay healthy long enough to make any kind of appreciable impact. The Achilles woes that hampered him in 2014 ended his season in 2015 as well, with Blanks opting for surgery in early September. He is expected to be healthy in time for spring training, although where the oft-injured Blanks fits in on the Giants isn't entirely clear, particularly since he is only average at best against righties.

Marlon Byrd RF

Born: 8/30/77 Age: 38 Bats: R Throws: R Height: 6'0" Weight: 245

YEAR	TEAM	LVL	AGE	PA	R	2B	3B	HR	RBI	BB	K	SB	CS	AVG/OBP/SLG	TAv	BABIP	BRR	FRAA	WARP
2013	PIT	MLB	35	115	14	9	0	3	17	6	20	0	0	.318/.357/.486	.291	.365	-0.6	RF(27): 0.9, LF(2): -0.2	0.6
2013	NYN	MLB	35	464	61	26	5	21	71	25	124	2	4	.285/.330/.518	.311	.350	0.1	RF(111): -3.0, CF(2): 0.2	3.0
2014	PHI	MLB	36	637	71	28	2	25	85	35	185	3	2	.264/.312/.445	.286	.341	-3.7	RF(149): 13.2	3.9
2015	CIN	MLB	37	388	46	13	3	19	42	23	101	2	1	.237/.286/.448	.272	.273	-0.3	LF(88): -3.0, RF(4): 0.2	1.0
2015	SFN	MLB	37	156	12	12	2	4	31	6	44	0	0	.272/.301/.463	.292	.356	0.4	RF(37): 1.5	1.0
2016	*SFN*	*MLB*	*38*	*531*	*53*	*23*	*4*	*16*	*64*	*25*	*136*	*2*	*2*	*.249/.290/.405*	*.255*	*.308*	*-1.0*	*LF -3, RF 1*	*0.9*
2017	*SFN*	*MLB*	*39*	*409*	*44*	*18*	*3*	*11*	*45*	*18*	*107*	*1*	*1*	*.239/.278/.383*	*.252*	*.300*	*-0.8*	*LF -2, RF 1*	*0.7*

Breakout: 0% Improve: 10% Collapse: 14% Attrition: 25% MLB: 79% *Comparables: Alfonso Soriano, Reggie Sanders, Roberto Clemente*

The demand for right-handed power hitters has outstripped the supply in recent years, which helps explain why Byrd has nabbed everyday playing time long past his productive-regular shelf life. A consummate journeyman who's appeared for six different National League teams in the past five years, Byrd now fits best with a junior-circuit club that could deploy him on the short side of a DH/outfield timeshare. There's still a useful player here, and now that he's no longer strapped to a multi-year contract, perhaps Byrd will find a team that can properly use him.

Hunter Cole UT

Born: 10/3/92 Age: 23 Bats: R Throws: R Height: 6'1" Weight: 190

YEAR	TEAM	LVL	AGE	PA	R	2B	3B	HR	RBI	BB	K	SB	CS	AVG/OBP/SLG	TAv	BABIP	BRR	FRAA	WARP
2014	SLO	A-	21	104	17	5	0	4	10	8	20	1	0	.239/.311/.424	.270	.261	-0.5	LF(8): -0.3, 3B(3): 0.1	0.2
2015	SJO	A+	22	245	28	11	5	6	37	19	42	4	3	.313/.373/.493	.330	.358	-0.3	RF(20): -1.7, 2B(15): 2.8	2.5
2015	RIC	AA	22	208	23	16	4	3	21	14	46	1	1	.292/.338/.464	.308	.368	-0.5	RF(40): 2.0	1.6
2015	AUG	A	22	46	4	6	0	0	5	5	12	2	1	.275/.370/.425	.303	.393	-0.8	2B(10): 0.1	0.3
2016	*SFN*	*MLB*	*23*	*250*	*24*	*12*	*3*	*5*	*26*	*15*	*64*	*1*	*1*	*.240/.290/.382*	*.243*	*.305*	*-0.1*	*RF -1, 2B 1*	*0.3*
2017	*SFN*	*MLB*	*24*	*318*	*34*	*15*	*3*	*6*	*32*	*21*	*84*	*1*	*1*	*.240/.295/.375*	*.251*	*.311*	*-0.2*	*RF -1, 2B 1*	*0.9*

Breakout: 1% Improve: 14% Collapse: 2% Attrition: 3% MLB: 20% *Comparables: J.D. Martinez, Rene Tosoni, Preston Tucker*

The draft-and-follow era in baseball is consigned to the history books, but Cole and the Giants offered a nod to the good ol' days two summers ago. Selected in the 26th round out of the University of Georgia, Cole, then a junior, was under no pressure to sign. Instead, he dragged negotiations to the mid-July deadline while living a rake's life in the Cape Cod League, increasing his leverage with every wood-bat hit. The Giants ultimately caved, and a year later, they were thrilled they did, as the ex-Bulldog rocketed through the system to Richmond. A third baseman in college, Cole fits better in the outfield as a pro, which puts the onus on the development of his bat. There's average power and hit potential here, albeit from a long swing, and Cole's breaking-ball recognition needs work before the Giants can consider a promotion. Still, Cole looks the part of another late-round gem, a useful reserve who might have low-end-regular upside if he

Brandon Crawford SS

Born: 1/21/87 Age: 29 Bats: L Throws: R Height: 6'2" Weight: 215

YEAR	TEAM	LVL	AGE	PA	R	2B	3B	HR	RBI	BB	K	SB	CS	AVG/OBP/SLG	TAv	BABIP	BRR	FRAA	WARP
2013	SFN	MLB	26	550	52	24	3	9	43	42	96	1	2	.248/.311/.363	.247	.290	2.1	SS(147): -1.5	1.6
2014	SFN	MLB	27	564	54	20	10	10	69	59	129	5	3	.246/.324/.389	.269	.307	-0.2	SS(149): 9.9	3.9
2015	SFN	MLB	28	561	65	33	4	21	84	39	119	6	4	.256/.321/.462	.291	.294	-0.9	SS(140): 6.1	4.7
2016	*SFN*	*MLB*	*29*	*609*	*63*	*27*	*5*	*13*	*62*	*49*	*126*	*5*	*3*	*.240/.305/.379*	*.249*	*.285*	*0.2*	*SS 5*	*2.8*
2017	*SFN*	*MLB*	*30*	*521*	*58*	*24*	*4*	*11*	*54*	*42*	*108*	*3*	*3*	*.241/.305/.380*	*.257*	*.288*	*0.3*	*SS 4*	*2.8*

Breakout: 2% Improve: 44% Collapse: 4% Attrition: 9% MLB: 99% *Comparables: Michael Young, Asdrubal Cabrera, Bobby Crosby*

If Crawford weren't a shortstop—and a very good one, at that—he might have washed out of the majors early or stalled on the way there. As it was, the Giants were so impressed with his glovework that they rushed him up before he was ready to hit. Crawford's swing was mechanically flawed—hindered first by an armbar and later by a tendency to drop his hands—blemishes that only outstanding defensive players can survive. But the Giants were patient, figuring that they'd benefit from a vacuum in the middle infield while making their hitting coaches earn their pay.

Then, before the 2015 season, Brian Sabean went out on a limb, telling reporters that the former UCLA Bruin was on the verge of stardom. Executives don't often make bold proclamations about their major-league players, but Sabean knew what outsiders didn't: Hensley Meulens and Co. had mended Crawford's swing by lowering his hands to shorten his path to the ball. Sure enough, Crawford crushed hard stuff both in and away, batting .330 against sinkers and slugging .612 on four-seamers. He led the Giants in big flies and might have lapped the injury-ravaged field if not for his own stints on the DL. And he made his first All-Star Game appearance, just as his boss suggested he would, earning a six-year, $75 million extension by proving Sabean right.

Matt Duffy 3B

Born: 1/15/91 Age: 25 Bats: R Throws: R Height: 6'2" Weight: 170

YEAR	TEAM	LVL	AGE	PA	R	2B	3B	HR	RBI	BB	K	SB	CS	AVG/OBP/SLG	TAv	BABIP	BRR	FRAA	WARP
2013	AUG	A	22	339	48	14	3	4	43	45	41	22	6	.307/.405/.418	.321	.346	5.8	SS(74): 12.9	5.6
2013	SJO	A+	22	115	17	6	1	5	14	7	16	3	1	.292/.342/.509	.302	.306	0.0	SS(25): 0.6	1.1
2014	SFN	MLB	23	64	5	2	0	0	8	1	14	0	1	.267/.302/.300	.242	.348	-0.5	2B(9): 1.5, SS(7): -0.3	0.2
2014	RIC	AA	23	417	53	24	4	3	62	42	66	20	4	.332/.398/.444	.308	.391	1.9	SS(89): 6.1, 3B(3): -0.1	4.7
2015	SFN	MLB	24	612	77	28	6	12	77	30	96	12	0	.295/.334/.428	.283	.336	2.9	3B(134): 0.4, 2B(9): -0.1	3.8
2016	*SFN*	*MLB*	*25*	*671*	*80*	*31*	*6*	*12*	*62*	*43*	*120*	*14*	*2*	*.278/.327/.402*	*.268*	*.325*	*1.5*	*3B 2*	*2.8*
2017	*SFN*	*MLB*	*26*	*591*	*66*	*27*	*5*	*10*	*61*	*39*	*107*	*12*	*2*	*.275/.326/.399*	*.274*	*.322*	*1.4*	*3B 2*	*1.8*

Breakout: 1% Improve: 43% Collapse: 8% Attrition: 26% MLB: 95% *Comparables: Kyle Seager, Lonnie Chisenhall, Brent Morel*

There's a drug of sorts—Giants devil magic, it's come to be called—that turns underappreciated college infielders into first-division regulars for the team that shares its name. In the 18th round of the 2012 draft, the Giants saw through a batting line that featured zero long balls in three seasons and decided that devil magic was right for Duffy. And, since it worked so well on Belt, Crawford and Joe Panik, they determined that Duffy—an even longer shot to become an everyday contributor—could use a double dose.

To make Giants devil magic, mix thorough scouting with quality coaching. Duffy's greatest asset coming out of Long Beach State was his defense at shortstop, but the Giants had Crawford there and trouble afoot at third base. Weeks later, Duffy, who'd played third just three times in the minors, was a natural at the hot corner, ready to supplant a hapless Casey McGehee and trade Web Gems with Nolan Arenado when the Rockies were in town.

You'll also need a heaping helping of clubhouse culture, the positive kind, where rookie onboarding means advice and encouragement, where humbling happens on the field, where veterans step aside gracefully when spring chickens cluck for their jobs. When Duffy arrived in the summer of 2014, Hunter Pence told him "We need you." "Play big," the team's other leaders advised. So he did. Since 2011, the only freshman position players who've surpassed Duffy's WARP are Jose Abreu, Kris Bryant, Yoenis Cespedes, Bryce Harper, Yasiel Puig, and Mike Trout—chiseled specimens who fill out every wrinkle of a uniform. They're the sort of players who make the field look small. At 170 pounds dripping wet, Duffy's size belies his game.

Those three ingredients are great, but Giants devil magic isn't for everyone. Players with world-class tools don't need it; those who lack feel for the game can't use it. Duffy's speed isn't a shade over 60-grade and his power—obscured by Long Beach State's home park and a digestive disorder before his junior season—looked fringy at best. But his baseball acumen and instincts qualified him for treatment, and the results spoke for themselves. He became the first rookie since 1950 to hit at least 12 homers and go 12-for-12 or better stealing bases, joining the likes of Jackie Robinson and Sam "The Jet" Jethroe on a list of nine.

Aramis Garcia C

Born: 1/12/93 Age: 23 Bats: R Throws: R Height: 6'2" Weight: 220

YEAR	TEAM	LVL	AGE	PA	R	2B	3B	HR	RBI	BB	K	SB	CS	AVG/OBP/SLG	TAv	BABIP	BRR	FRAA	WARP
2014	SLO	A-	21	76	5	3	0	2	12	5	19	0	0	.229/.289/.357	.217	.286	-0.1	C(18): 0.0	0.0
2015	SJO	A+	22	84	10	4	0	0	5	9	22	1	0	.227/.310/.280	.223	.321	0.1	C(19): 0.9	0.1
2015	AUG	A	22	363	42	15	1	15	61	35	77	0	1	.273/.350/.467	.313	.312	-3.4	C(72): 0.6	3.4
2016	*SFN*	*MLB*	*23*	*250*	*23*	*9*	*1*	*7*	*28*	*17*	*74*	*0*	*0*	*.211/.268/.355*	*.227*	*.272*	*-0.3*	*C 1*	*0.3*
2017	*SFN*	*MLB*	*24*	*252*	*27*	*9*	*1*	*7*	*27*	*17*	*75*	*0*	*0*	*.208/.263/.350*	*.228*	*.269*	*-0.5*	*C 1*	*1.1*

Breakout: 8% Improve: 11% Collapse: 3% Attrition: 12% MLB: 17% *Comparables: Michael McKenry, Max Stassi, Jonathan Lucroy*

YEAR	TEAM	P. COUNT	FRM RUNS	BLK RUNS	THRW RUNS	TOT RUNS
2016	*SFN*	*8937*	*0.0*	*0.0*	*0.0*	*0.0*
2017	*SFN*	*9016*	*0.0*	*0.0*	*0.0*	*0.0*

Few players were responsible for as much action in as little time as Garcia was during his High-A stint last year. In 19 games in the squat for San Jose, he threw out 16 runners attempting to steal... and also allowed seven passed balls. Scouts' reviews matched the numbers, gawking at Garcia's plus-plus cannon while lamenting his form as a blocker, so while the hose will buy the 2014 second-rounder time, he must improve his lateral agility to be more than a fringy defender. At the plate, Garcia has the quick, smooth swing typical of players whose hit tools mature at 55-grade or above, and solid-average raw power that stems more from natural strength than an uppercut hack. The building blocks for an everyday catcher are present, but the two-way development spells a slow burn through the upper minors while Garcia puts them all together.

Grant Green UT

Born: 9/27/87 Age: 28 Bats: R Throws: R Height: 6'3" Weight: 180

YEAR	TEAM	LVL	AGE	PA	R	2B	3B	HR	RBI	BB	K	SB	CS	AVG/OBP/SLG	TAv	BABIP	BRR	FRAA	WARP
2013	OAK	MLB	25	16	0	0	0	0	1	0	6	0	0	.000/.000/.000	.027	.000	0.0	2B(5): -1.1	-0.5
2013	SLC	AAA	25	28	2	1	0	0	3	3	7	0	1	.333/.393/.375	.285	.444	0.0	3B(4): -0.1, 2B(2): 0.3	0.2
2013	ANA	MLB	25	137	16	8	1	1	16	10	38	0	0	.280/.336/.384	.260	.391	-0.9	2B(40): -4.4	-0.2
2013	SAC	AAA	25	415	66	27	3	11	50	27	70	4	1	.325/.379/.500	.313	.376	-0.6	2B(73): -11.0, 1B(1): -0.1	2.3
2014	SLC	AAA	26	214	38	17	3	5	42	13	31	4	2	.333/.379/.525	.297	.374	1.0	SS(18): -1.3, 3B(15): -1.8	1.3
2014	ANA	MLB	26	103	7	5	0	1	11	2	20	1	4	.273/.282/.354	.250	.325	-2.0	LF(17): -2.8, 2B(10): 0.2	-0.3
2015	ANA	MLB	27	44	6	0	0	1	3	2	14	0	1	.190/.227/.262	.156	.259	-0.3	2B(11): -0.6, 1B(5): -0.3	-0.5
2015	SLC	AAA	27	414	59	26	7	5	43	18	70	2	3	.306/.337/.449	.263	.359	2.2	LF(39): -2.8, 1B(23): -2.1	0.4
2016	*SFN*	*MLB*	*28*	*250*	*26*	*12*	*2*	*4*	*22*	*11*	*57*	*2*	*2*	*.256/.293/.377*	*.245*	*.318*	*-0.9*	*LF -1, 1B -1*	*-0.2*
2017	*SFN*	*MLB*	*29*	*270*	*27*	*13*	*2*	*4*	*26*	*13*	*64*	*1*	*1*	*.248/.289/.364*	*.245*	*.312*	*-0.9*	*LF -1, 1B -1*	*0.1*

Breakout: 4% Improve: 18% Collapse: 14% Attrition: 30% MLB: 45% *Comparables: Eric Patterson, Lou Montanez, Rusty Ryal*

Green hit his annual home run on August 30th last year in what turned out to be his second-to-last game of the season, as a sore Achilles kept him from seizing a rare opportunity for big-league playing time with Johnny Giavotella out of the lineup. The former first-rounder has proven that he can rake in the minors, with more than 1,600 plate appearances of .311/.354/.474 hitting in Triple-A, but he'll still be in the waiting room pounding cups of coffee until the next opportunity arises.

Jalen Miller SS

Born: 12/19/96 Age: 19 Bats: R Throws: R Height: 5'11" Weight: 175

YEAR	TEAM	LVL	AGE	PA	R	2B	3B	HR	RBI	BB	K	SB	CS	AVG/OBP/SLG	TAv	BABIP	BRR	FRAA	WARP
2016	*SFN*	*MLB*	*19*	*250*	*20*	*8*	*1*	*3*	*18*	*12*	*79*	*3*	*1*	*.184/.225/.262*	*.182*	*.258*	*0.2*	*SS -3, CF 0*	*-1.2*
2017	*SFN*	*MLB*	*20*	*372*	*32*	*13*	*2*	*4*	*29*	*18*	*114*	*5*	*2*	*.196/.235/.280*	*.194*	*.271*	*0.4*	*SS -4, CF 0*	*1.3*

Breakout: 0% Improve: 0% Collapse: 0% Attrition: 0% MLB: 0% *Comparables: Argenis Diaz, Adrian Cardenas, Charlie Culberson*

The Giants love high school shortstops, and in Miller they got one scouts believe can actually stick at the six spot. Drawing parallels to fellow Georgia high schooler Brandon Phillips, Miller has smooth actions on the dirt and quick, strong wrists at the plate. Those traits nabbed the Clemson signee a $1.1 million bonus, almost double the slot value of the 95th-overall selection, even though his 5-foot-10 frame leaves little room for projection. Miller will take a methodical path through the minors, but the Giants believe he can develop 15-homer power in time, which—coupled with an otherwise well-rounded profile—could make him a first-division regular at a premium position.

Angel Pagan CF

Born: 7/2/81 Age: 34 Bats: B Throws: R Height: 6'2" Weight: 200

YEAR	TEAM	LVL	AGE	PA	R	2B	3B	HR	RBI	BB	K	SB	CS	AVG/OBP/SLG	TAv	BABIP	BRR	FRAA	WARP
2013	SFN	MLB	31	305	44	16	3	5	30	23	36	9	4	.282/.334/.414	.277	.307	2.6	CF(71): -4.6	1.3
2013	FRE	AAA	31	22	1	0	0	0	3	2	2	0	0	.278/.364/.278	.237	.294	0.2	CF(5): -0.5	0.0
2014	SFN	MLB	32	413	56	21	2	3	27	25	53	16	6	.300/.342/.389	.277	.339	0.3	CF(91): -0.5	2.0
2015	SFN	MLB	33	551	55	21	3	3	37	32	93	12	4	.262/.303/.332	.236	.310	0.6	CF(124): -10.6	-0.7
2016	*SFN*	*MLB*	*34*	*660*	*75*	*30*	*7*	*7*	*52*	*44*	*100*	*18*	*7*	*.264/.311/.369*	*.250*	*.301*	*1.3*	*CF -8*	*0.9*
2017	*SFN*	*MLB*	*35*	*498*	*48*	*21*	*5*	*3*	*41*	*32*	*79*	*12*	*5*	*.249/.296/.338*	*.239*	*.290*	*1.3*	*CF -6*	*1.1*

Breakout: 1% Improve: 28% Collapse: 13% Attrition: 18% MLB: 91% *Comparables: David DeJesus, Coco Crisp, Felipe Alou*

Pagan batted third on Opening Day last year, went on to make over 550 plate appearances, and compiled a .635 OPS. To illustrate how appalling that is, the previous player to meet all of those criteria was Terry Pendleton 30 years earlier. Worse, futility at the plate wasn't even half the story of Pagan's putrid 2015. He added patella tendinitis to a mounting chart of leg injuries, then returned to watch helplessly as sinking liners fell steps in front of him and gappers squeaked by to the wall. There's no dodging the fact that Pagan was one of baseball's very worst regulars last season, one who'd have trouble securing any paycheck were he not already owed $11.25 million. The Giants are no strangers to excising pricey outfield lemons, having done so with Aaron Rowand in 2011. If a few months of rest don't put some hop back in Pagan's step, they might be forced to go there again.

Joe Panik 2B

Born: 10/30/90 Age: 25 Bats: L Throws: R Height: 6'1" Weight: 190

YEAR	TEAM	LVL	AGE	PA	R	2B	3B	HR	RBI	BB	K	SB	CS	AVG/OBP/SLG	TAv	BABIP	BRR	FRAA	WARP
2013	RIC	AA	22	599	64	27	4	4	57	58	68	10	5	.257/.333/.347	.260	.285	-0.8	2B(117): -7.6, SS(20): 1.3	1.0
2014	FRE	AAA	23	326	50	14	4	5	45	27	33	3	2	.321/.382/.447	.289	.346	-0.6	2B(61): -5.0, SS(10): -0.8	1.4
2014	SFN	MLB	23	287	31	10	2	1	18	16	33	0	0	.305/.343/.368	.262	.343	1.1	2B(70): -4.0	0.5
2015	SFN	MLB	24	432	59	27	2	8	37	38	42	3	2	.312/.378/.455	.314	.330	-1.1	2B(99): -6.5	2.8
2016	*SFN*	*MLB*	*25*	*568*	*62*	*26*	*4*	*7*	*49*	*41*	*72*	*3*	*2*	*.273/.328/.381*	*.259*	*.300*	*0.0*	*2B -8*	*1.3*
2017	*SFN*	*MLB*	*26*	*514*	*55*	*24*	*3*	*7*	*49*	*36*	*66*	*3*	*1*	*.266/.320/.379*	*.262*	*.292*	*-0.1*	*2B -8*	*1.0*

Breakout: 1% Improve: 34% Collapse: 9% Attrition: 26% MLB: 83% *Comparables: Aaron Hill, Dustin Ackley, Blake DeWitt*

Marco Scutaro's comment in last year's annual was more prescient about Panik's 2015 prospects than the upstate New Yorker's own. We called Panik an "awesomely boring" two-win regular in the latter and—citing the career-ending back woes that befell his predecessors Scutaro and Freddy Sanchez—advised Panik to find a chiropractor in the former. The St. John's product blew past our value projection in less than two-thirds of a season, then spent the summer nursing a lower-back injury that wouldn't go away. This time, we'll learn our lesson and hedge our bets: Panik will be a repeat All-Star—unless his back decides he won't.

Jarrett Parker OF

Born: 1/1/89 Age: 27 Bats: L Throws: L Height: 6'4" Weight: 210

YEAR	TEAM	LVL	AGE	PA	R	2B	3B	HR	RBI	BB	K	SB	CS	AVG/OBP/SLG	TAv	BABIP	BRR	FRAA	WARP
2013	RIC	AA	24	524	72	18	5	18	57	60	161	13	11	.245/.355/.430	.293	.343	1.2	RF(110): 12.8, CF(17): -1.6	4.3
2014	RIC	AA	25	419	52	20	6	12	58	45	103	11	4	.275/.370/.463	.293	.353	-0.5	RF(70): -3.8, CF(30): -3.7	1.6
2014	FRE	AAA	25	89	13	5	0	3	10	9	23	1	2	.278/.360/.456	.306	.358	1.1	RF(22): 1.3	0.9
2015	SFN	MLB	26	54	11	2	0	6	14	5	21	1	1	.347/.407/.755	.413	.500	-0.5	RF(9): -1.2, LF(5): 0.3	0.9
2015	SAC	AAA	26	504	74	25	3	23	74	62	164	20	7	.283/.375/.514	.322	.398	-1.8	RF(61): 1.9, LF(48): -3.3	4.0
2016	*SFN*	*MLB*	*27*	*384*	*47*	*14*	*3*	*14*	*48*	*37*	*131*	*8*	*4*	*.231/.314/.414*	*.264*	*.327*	*0.1*	*LF -2, RF 1*	*1.1*
2017	*SFN*	*MLB*	*28*	*424*	*54*	*16*	*3*	*16*	*54*	*41*	*147*	*8*	*4*	*.229/.313/.415*	*.273*	*.326*	*0.4*	*LF -3, RF 1*	*0.9*

Breakout: 4% Improve: 12% Collapse: 10% Attrition: 26% MLB: 44% *Comparables: Jai Miller, Andrew Brown, Alex Castellanos*

Chartered flights, 40,000-seat stadiums, five-star hotels, six-figure paychecks—the major-league life is certainly a small step up from the minor-league slog, usually accompanied by one giant leap in competition. But sometimes, for a few days in September, a lucky long-time minor leaguer gets to play under the big-league lights without facing big-league pitching. Parker was blessed with such fortune during a weekend in Oakland, and he made the most of it, showing off his Bondsian raw power against mediocre fastballs from hurlers who belonged in Nashville. He homered thrice in the Barry Zito game, his fourth-fifth-sixth in his first 27 career ABs. But little else about Parker's game resembles Bonds'—or even Kevin Maas'!—a contrast that became starker with each breaking ball he chased after his fireworks display. Dead-red thump alone gives the Virginia product a shot as a fourth outfielder, but he's as likely to be hitting bombs for the Yomiuri Giants as he is for the San Francisco outfit long term.

Hunter Pence RF

Born: 4/13/83 Age: 33 Bats: R Throws: R Height: 6'4" Weight: 220

YEAR	TEAM	LVL	AGE	PA	R	2B	3B	HR	RBI	BB	K	SB	CS	AVG/OBP/SLG	TAv	BABIP	BRR	FRAA	WARP
2013	SFN	MLB	30	687	91	35	5	27	99	52	115	22	3	.283/.339/.483	.294	.308	-0.4	RF(162): 10.4	4.8
2014	SFN	MLB	31	708	106	29	10	20	74	52	130	13	6	.277/.332/.445	.288	.318	2.0	RF(161): 2.8, CF(1): -0.0	3.9
2015	SFN	MLB	32	223	30	13	1	9	40	16	48	4	1	.275/.327/.478	.288	.320	1.2	RF(51): 9.9	2.3
2015	SAC	AAA	32	20	6	0	0	2	5	2	4	0	0	.294/.350/.647	.344	.250	-0.6	RF(5): -0.4	0.1
2016	*SFN*	*MLB*	*33*	*596*	*70*	*26*	*5*	*19*	*75*	*44*	*119*	*12*	*4*	*.267/.322/.438*	*.277*	*.307*	*0.4*	*RF 9*	*3.5*
2017	*SFN*	*MLB*	*34*	*446*	*55*	*19*	*3*	*14*	*54*	*33*	*93*	*7*	*3*	*.266/.322/.430*	*.282*	*.311*	*0.3*	*RF 6*	*1.6*

Breakout: 0% Improve: 27% Collapse: 4% Attrition: 6% MLB: 96% *Comparables: Dave Winfield, Michael Cuddyer, Magglio Ordonez*

Pence has been the Giants' spiritual leader since he arrived at the 2012 trade deadline, so it's fitting that when injuries marred the right fielder's year, the shepherd led the flock onto the DL. From a broken forearm to wrist tendinitis to a strained oblique, the league's leading iron man heading into the season frequented the training room before bagging it in mid-September. Pence was as good as ever in his brief spurts on the field, hitting for power, running well and tracking down gappers with his tongue out. He's at the age now when a decline can't be ruled out, but none of his 2015 ailments are of the lingering sort. Chances are he'll return to four-win form, making Pence a viable contender to be the NL's Comeback Player of the Year.

Buster Posey C

Born: 3/27/87 Age: 29 Bats: R Throws: R Height: 6'1" Weight: 215

YEAR	TEAM	LVL	AGE	PA	R	2B	3B	HR	RBI	BB	K	SB	CS	AVG/OBP/SLG	TAv	BABIP	BRR	FRAA	WARP
2013	SFN	MLB	26	595	61	34	1	15	72	60	70	2	1	.294/.371/.450	.296	.312	-4.5	C(121): 20.0, 1B(21): -1.2	6.2
2014	SFN	MLB	27	605	72	28	2	22	89	47	69	0	1	.311/.364/.490	.316	.319	-3.5	C(111): 23.8, 1B(35): 1.4	8.2
2015	SFN	MLB	28	623	74	28	0	19	95	56	52	2	0	.318/.379/.470	.320	.320	-1.8	C(106): 17.2, 1B(42): -1.6	7.6
2016	*SFN*	*MLB*	*29*	*617*	*75*	*31*	*2*	*20*	*83*	*57*	*79*	*1*	*1*	*.301/.368/.475*	*.303*	*.318*	*-2.8*	*C 23, 1B -1*	*7.5*
2017	*SFN*	*MLB*	*30*	*563*	*75*	*28*	*1*	*18*	*72*	*51*	*76*	*0*	*0*	*.296/.362/.461*	*.308*	*.317*	*-2.8*	*C 19, 1B -1*	*3.7*

Breakout: 2% Improve: 49% Collapse: 2% Attrition: 3% MLB: 98% *Comparables: Joe Mauer, Brian McCann, Justin Morneau*

YEAR	TEAM	P. COUNT	FRM RUNS	BLK RUNS	THRW RUNS	TOT RUNS
2013	SFN	16776	19.4	0.5	-0.1	19.8
2014	SFN	14256	23.6	0.2	-1.3	22.5
2015	SFN	13948	12.7	0.1	0.9	13.7
2016	*SFN*	*16508*	*22.0*	*0.3*	*-0.3*	*22.0*
2017	*SFN*	*15052*	*15.6*	*0.2*	*-0.3*	*15.5*

If footspeed weren't a factor, Posey might be the league's best-rounded player. He's a saint in the squat—plus at every part of his defensive job description—and a savant with the stick, able to drive the ball to all fields without a visible hole in his swing. When you're as good at as many baseball things as Posey is, it's difficult to find ways to improve. It turns out, though, that Posey is good at that, too. Not yet content with the maturity of his approach at the plate, he began to swing more often, a perilous decision that for most hitters shaves walks and breeds strikeouts. But Posey is not most hitters: His selective aggression resulted in *more* free passes and fewer punchouts, and produced his best offensive season since he was the NL MVP in 2012. With across-the-board excellence and the clubhouse leadership BBWAA writers worship, he's a strong bet to contend for that award again this year.

Christopher Shaw 1B

Born: 10/20/93 Age: 22 Bats: L Throws: R Height: 6'4" Weight: 255

YEAR	TEAM	LVL	AGE	PA	R	2B	3B	HR	RBI	BB	K	SB	CS	AVG/OBP/SLG	TAv	BABIP	BRR	FRAA	WARP
2015	SLO	A-	21	200	22	11	0	12	30	19	41	0	0	.287/.360/.551	.305	.310	-1.8	1B(31): 1.3	1.1
2016	*SFN*	*MLB*	*22*	*250*	*24*	*9*	*1*	*7*	*27*	*13*	*74*	*0*	*0*	*.209/.254/.352*	*.220*	*.266*	*-0.3*	*1B 0*	*-0.7*
2017	*SFN*	*MLB*	*23*	*323*	*35*	*12*	*1*	*10*	*35*	*19*	*91*	*1*	*0*	*.214/.265/.360*	*.232*	*.269*	*-0.5*	*1B 0*	*0.4*

Breakout: 1% Improve: 3% Collapse: 0% Attrition: 4% MLB: 4% *Comparables: Jerry Sands, C.J. Cron, Jesus Aguilar*

The Giants relish the opportunity to see collegiate prospects in the wood-bat Cape Cod League, often weighting performance there more heavily than the spring season. It makes sense, then, that Shaw, who paced the Cape with eight homers in 2014, grabbed their attention at the end of the first round. Unlike the typical Giants position-player prospect, Shaw boasts plus-plus raw power. What he lacks is footspeed, which limits him to first base, and patience at the plate, which puts extra pressure on his ability to make contact. The Boston College product has above-average bat speed and excellent balance in his swing, reasons to be bullish that his power will play, but as with most first-base-only prospects, everything has to go right offensively for a first-division regular to emerge.

Andrew Susac C

Born: 3/22/90 Age: 26 Bats: R Throws: R Height: 6'1" Weight: 215

YEAR	TEAM	LVL	AGE	PA	R	2B	3B	HR	RBI	BB	K	SB	CS	AVG/OBP/SLG	TAv	BABIP	BRR	FRAA	WARP
2013	RIC	AA	23	310	32	17	0	12	46	42	68	1	0	.256/.362/.458	.310	.299	-0.6	C(71): 1.9, 1B(9): -0.7	3.1
2014	SFN	MLB	24	95	13	8	0	3	19	7	28	0	0	.273/.326/.466	.291	.368	0.5	C(29): -2.2	0.5
2014	FRE	AAA	24	253	34	9	0	10	32	34	50	0	0	.268/.379/.451	.295	.305	0.4	C(56): 9.9	3.2
2015	SFN	MLB	25	148	14	7	2	3	14	14	43	0	0	.218/.297/.368	.254	.299	-0.8	C(40): 0.5	0.5
2015	SAC	AAA	25	32	6	3	0	1	2	3	10	0	0	.321/.406/.536	.335	.471	-0.3	C(7): -0.5	0.3
2016	SFN	MLB	26	174	19	8	1	5	21	17	46	0	0	.234/.318/.400	.263	.296	-0.1	C 1	0.9
2017	SFN	MLB	27	231	28	10	1	7	26	23	62	0	0	.229/.312/.387	.266	.293	-0.2	C 1	1.0

Breakout: 5% Improve: 34% Collapse: 12% Attrition: 21% MLB: 79% *Comparables: Welington Castillo, Geovany Soto, Josmil Pinto*

YEAR	TEAM	P. COUNT	FRM RUNS	BLK RUNS	THRW RUNS	TOT RUNS
2013	RIC	8907	2.3	-0.3	0.0	2.0
2014	FRE	6308	8.4	-0.4	1.2	9.2
2014	SFN	3009	-1.8	-0.1	-0.1	-2.0
2015	SAC	869	0.3	0.0	0.0	0.3
2015	SFN	4737	0.0	0.0	-0.5	-0.5
2016	SFN	5669	0.9	-0.2	0.1	0.7
2017	SFN	7530	0.6	-0.2	0.0	0.4

It's hard enough to hit in the majors when you play every day, have a defined role and are able to make adjustments within and between games. As the Giants roster evolved, Susac wasn't given those luxuries, moving from Triple-A to backup duty to a quasi-platoon role to bench-bat scraps to the DL. He started hot but was caught in between when pitchers changed speeds, lagging behind quality fastballs, leaking his hips early on soft stuff, and taking to pinch-hitting like toddlers take to tetanus shots. A living, breathing chicken-and-egg problem, Susac has the raw power and catch-and-throw skills to become at least an average regular, but he might need to play regularly to show them off.

Kelby Tomlinson 2B

Born: 6/16/90 Age: 26 Bats: R Throws: R Height: 6'3" Weight: 180

YEAR	TEAM	LVL	AGE	PA	R	2B	3B	HR	RBI	BB	K	SB	CS	AVG/OBP/SLG	TAv	BABIP	BRR	FRAA	WARP
2013	SJO	A+	23	148	13	7	0	0	16	12	32	5	1	.276/.338/.328	.261	.359	-0.2	SS(30): -2.2	0.4
2013	RIC	AA	23	116	13	5	0	0	4	16	27	3	1	.198/.313/.250	.238	.275	0.9	SS(32): -1.7	0.1
2014	RIC	AA	24	494	63	9	6	1	32	44	82	49	12	.268/.340/.323	.251	.325	1.0	2B(73): 0.5, SS(50): -2.1	1.2
2015	SAC	AAA	25	149	21	1	1	2	15	7	22	5	3	.316/.354/.382	.266	.360	0.2	2B(16): 2.2, SS(15): 0.7	0.9
2015	RIC	AA	25	289	43	18	3	1	28	25	37	16	6	.324/.387/.431	.316	.372	3.3	2B(49): 2.4, SS(25): -1.9	3.1
2015	SFN	MLB	25	193	23	6	3	2	20	14	40	5	4	.303/.358/.404	.294	.382	1.3	2B(50): -1.1, SS(1): -0.0	1.2
2016	SFN	MLB	26	157	18	5	1	1	11	11	34	6	2	.252/.308/.339	.239	.316	0.5	2B 0	0.4
2017	SFN	MLB	27	383	38	13	4	3	32	27	88	15	6	.247/.304/.333	.240	.315	1.8	2B 1	1.6

Breakout: 8% Improve: 31% Collapse: 1% Attrition: 26% MLB: 43% *Comparables: Eric Patterson, Kevin Russo, Eric Young*

Tomlinson hails from tiny Elgin, Okla., where the mayor recently celebrated the installation of a traffic light as a sign of growth. It's a podunk so anonymous that Wikipedia doesn't list a single famous native or resident. A 12th-round pick out of Texas Tech, the bespectacled Tomlinson didn't figure to change that, resembling a future English teacher more than a budding big leaguer. But the wiry infielder is faster and stronger than he looks, able to punch the ball into right field often enough to bat .280 or better. The secondary skills lag behind the hit tool, as Tomlinson offers minimal power and below-average instincts at the keystone, but there's enough here for a utility profile—which in turn is enough to put Elgin on the map.

Mac Williamson RF

Born: 7/15/90 Age: 25 Bats: R Throws: R Height: 6'5" Weight: 240

YEAR	TEAM	LVL	AGE	PA	R	2B	3B	HR	RBI	BB	K	SB	CS	AVG/OBP/SLG	TAv	BABIP	BRR	FRAA	WARP
2013	SJO	A+	22	599	94	31	2	25	89	51	132	10	1	.292/.375/.504	.332	.345	2.8	RF(115): 4.1	6.5
2014	SJO	A+	23	100	16	7	0	3	11	13	14	6	1	.318/.420/.506	.325	.353	0.9		0.9
2015	RIC	AA	24	290	41	16	2	5	42	25	53	3	1	.293/.366/.429	.303	.351	-1.8	RF(55): 1.0	1.8
2015	SFN	MLB	24	34	2	0	1	0	1	0	8	0	0	.219/.235/.281	.189	.280	-0.4	LF(6): -0.4, RF(3): -0.1	-0.3
2015	SAC	AAA	24	227	35	12	0	8	31	26	55	1	0	.249/.370/.439	.318	.307	1.6	LF(30): -3.3, RF(16): 1.2	1.8
2016	SFN	MLB	25	250	26	11	1	7	30	18	65	1	0	.245/.316/.399	.264	.309	-0.2	RF 1, LF -1	0.8
2017	SFN	MLB	26	345	41	14	2	9	38	28	91	1	0	.240/.319/.388	.271	.309	-0.5	RF 2, LF -1	0.8

Breakout: 6% Improve: 25% Collapse: 8% Attrition: 34% MLB: 59% *Comparables: Nolan Reimold, Steven Souza, Michael Taylor*

A surprisingly nimble athlete, considering his size, Williamson is a physical specimen who has the makings of a plus defensive right fielder. His profile is less robust at the plate, where above-average bat speed is tempered by poor breaking-ball recognition. Williamson has the raw power to sting the ball when he squares it up, but he might always be susceptible to right-handed sliders, a flaw that has reduced many an Adonis to Quad-A material. The Wake Forest product's stellar Arizona Fall League campaign stirred hope that he can eventually solve spin, so while Williamson would ideally start on the short end of a timeshare, he might grow into a serviceable regular in time.

Pitchers

Jeremy Affeldt LHP

Born: 6/6/79 Age: 37 Bats: L Throws: L Height: 6'4" Weight: 225

YEAR	TEAM	LVL	AGE	W	L	SV	G	GS	IP	H	HR	BB/9	K/9	GB%	BABIP	WHIP	ERA	FIP	DRA	WARP	CFIP	MPH
2013	SFN	MLB	34	1	5	0	39	0	33^{2}	27	2	4.5	5.6	57%	.245	1.31	3.74	4.42	3.75	0.3	115	94.0
2014	SFN	MLB	35	4	2	0	62	0	55^{1}	47	1	2.3	6.7	68%	.279	1.10	2.28	2.83	3.05	1.0	104	93.9
2015	SFN	MLB	36	2	2	0	52	0	35^{1}	43	6	3.6	5.3	57%	.308	1.61	5.86	5.54	6.34	-0.7	122	92.9
2016	*SFN*	*MLB*	*37*	*2*	*1*	*1*	*38*	*0*	*40^{1}*	*38*	*4*	*2.9*	*6.3*	*60%*	*.294*	*1.26*	*4.10*	*4.06*	*5.06*	*-0.1*	*118*	
2017	*SFN*	*MLB*	*38*	*2*	*1*	*1*	*51*	*0*	*44^{1}*	*46*	*6*	*3.1*	*6.1*	*60%*	*.306*	*1.38*	*4.37*	*5.04*	*5.39*	*-0.3*	*126*	

Breakout: 21% Improve: 45% Collapse: 21% Attrition: 5% MLB: 77% *Comparables: Gary Lavelle, Roberto Hernandez, Salomon Torres*

After losing a literal coin-flip to be the Royals' Opening Day starter in 2003, Affeldt spent the first five years of his career bouncing between the rotation and bullpen. Those were bleak times in Kansas City, but when the dark clouds parted and the World Series came to western Missouri, there was Affeldt, on the mound for the Giants, pitching 2 1/3 critical innings in the winner-take-all Game Seven. It took years for Affeldt to carve out his niche, but he found it in San Francisco, where his infamous 57-foot fastballs—he dubbed them "scuds"—were comic relief and where not even the freakiest of freak injuries could derail him. Amid the Giants' three championships, Affeldt emerged as one of the best postseason pitchers of his generation, his 22 straight scoreless playoff appearances second only to Mariano Rivera. The lefty's retirement ensures that Rivera will keep the record at 23. But it also means that Affeldt—the unsung hero of that Game Seven in his first home park—will ride off into the sunset with his streak forever intact.

Tyler Beede RHP

Born: 5/23/93 Age: 23 Bats: R Throws: R Height: 6'4" Weight: 200

YEAR	TEAM	LVL	AGE	W	L	SV	G	GS	IP	H	HR	BB/9	K/9	GB%	BABIP	WHIP	ERA	FIP	DRA	WARP	CFIP	MPH
2015	SJO	A+	22	2	2	0	9	9	52^{1}	51	2	1.5	6.4	64%	.295	1.15	2.24	3.43	4.66	0.6	97	
2015	RIC	AA	22	3	8	0	13	13	72^{1}	62	4	4.4	6.1	60%	.269	1.34	5.23	4.21	5.81	-0.9	121	
2016	*SFN*	*MLB*	*23*	*5*	*6*	*0*	*18*	*18*	*90*	*91*	*11*	*3.4*	*5.8*	*57%*	*.304*	*1.39*	*4.52*	*4.57*	*5.49*	*-0.2*	*132*	
2017	*SFN*	*MLB*	*24*	*6*	*8*	*0*	*22*	*22*	*129^{1}*	*135*	*18*	*4.0*	*6.3*	*57%*	*.313*	*1.49*	*4.70*	*5.42*	*5.71*	*-0.6*	*137*	

Breakout: 9% Improve: 16% Collapse: 1% Attrition: 12% MLB: 18% *Comparables: Daniel Corcino, Tyler Wagner, Fernando Nieve*

All players evolve between college and the majors, but few first-round picks pull the sort of complete 180 that has defined Beede's first two years in the pros. A scintillating but erratic power pitcher in college, Beede joined the Giants and quickly discovered that his first professional employer valued consistency and command over fastball velocity and pure stuff. To his credit, the Vanderbilt product beat back concerns about his coachability by buying into the plan to morph into a finesse hurler. Yet as he learned to repeat his arm slot and command sinkers and cutters around the zone, he seemed to forget how to miss bats. If the 2015 version provided a peek into the final product, the chase for consistency has turned Beede into a garden-variety back-end worm-burner, the opposite of what scouts who liked him in college thought he was destined to be.

Phil Bickford RHP

Born: 7/10/95 Age: 20 Bats: R Throws: R Height: 6'4" Weight: 200

YEAR	TEAM	LVL	AGE	W	L	SV	G	GS	IP	H	HR	BB/9	K/9	GB%	BABIP	WHIP	ERA	FIP	DRA	WARP	CFIP	MPH
2016	*SFN*	*MLB*	*20*	*2*	*3*	*0*	*10*	*10*	*34^{2}*	*36*	*4*	*5.1*	*6.3*	*21%*	*.317*	*1.62*	*5.08*	*5.06*	*6.34*	*-0.4*	*147*	
2017	*SFN*	*MLB*	*21*	*4*	*8*	*0*	*29*	*29*	*179*	*182*	*25*	*4.4*	*6.6*	*21%*	*.308*	*1.50*	*4.72*	*5.46*	*5.89*	*-0.7*	*138*	

Breakout: 1% Improve: 1% Collapse: 0% Attrition: 0% MLB: 1% *Comparables: Luis Severino, Kendry Flores, Kyle Lobstein*

Bickford flunked a marijuana test days before the draft, but his control and athleticism convinced the Giants to look past that transgression and make him the first JuCo first-rounder in the organization's history. While he looks more like a Santa Cruz surfer than a San Francisco pitcher, he wields a fastball with explosive late life, a potential plus weapon even when it sits 90-91. Scouts also see the makings of a plus slider. Some voice doubts about Bickford's future as a starter, citing a downtrend in his velocity within outings and a still-fledgling changeup. Following in Beede's footsteps as an ex-Jays draftee who wound up in orange and black, Bickford carries more upside but also more risk. Despite an outstanding debut in the Arizona League, he probably won't sniff the majors until 2018.

Ty Blach LHP

Born: 10/20/90 Age: 25 Bats: R Throws: L Height: 6'2" Weight: 200

YEAR	TEAM	LVL	AGE	W	L	SV	G	GS	IP	H	HR	BB/9	K/9	GB%	BABIP	WHIP	ERA	FIP	DRA	WARP	CFIP	MPH
2013	SJO	A+	22	12	4	0	22	20	130^{1}	124	8	1.2	8.1	48%	.304	1.09	2.90	3.23	4.76	2.0	82	
2014	RIC	AA	23	8	8	0	25	25	141	142	8	2.5	5.8	47%	.295	1.28	3.13	3.70	4.44	1.1	97	
2015	SAC	AAA	24	11	12	0	27	27	165^{1}	189	16	1.7	5.1	49%	.311	1.33	4.46	4.33	5.37	0.4	106	
2016	*SFN*	*MLB*	*25*	*1*	*1*	*0*	*3*	*3*	*15*	*16*	*2*	*2.1*	*5.0*	*46%*	*.304*	*1.29*	*4.28*	*4.31*	*5.27*	*0.0*	*126*	
2017	*SFN*	*MLB*	*26*	*2*	*3*	*0*	*7*	*7*	*38^{2}*	*43*	*6*	*2.4*	*5.0*	*46%*	*.306*	*1.38*	*4.62*	*5.35*	*5.69*	*-0.2*	*137*	

Breakout: 16% Improve: 22% Collapse: 9% Attrition: 25% MLB: 32% *Comparables: Josh Geer, Elih Villanueva, Cesar Valdez*

The Giants forgot to spray themselves with injury-bug repellent, but for all the bumps and bruises, sprains and strains that ravaged their roster, the front office never dipped into its pipeline for a starting pitcher. All nine of the starters Bruce Bochy deployed began the 2015 season on an active roster or the major-league disabled list, leaving Blach waiting in Sacramento for a call-up that never came. At this point, the former Creighton Bluejay is what he is: a four-pitch finesse lefty with a compact motion and just enough command to get by. The sink on his fastball and the fade on his changeup imperil nearby worms, so he could be a passable fifth starter in front of rangy infielders. Unfortunately for his fallback options, he lacks the swing-and-miss breaking ball to be more than a long man if moved to the bullpen.

Ray Black RHP

Born: 6/26/90 Age: 26 Bats: R Throws: R Height: 6'5" Weight: 225

YEAR	TEAM	LVL	AGE	W	L	SV	G	GS	IP	H	HR	BB/9	K/9	GB%	BABIP	WHIP	ERA	FIP	DRA	WARP	CFIP	MPH
2014	AUG	A	24	1	3	1	33	0	31^{1}	16	1	4.0	18.4	39%	.333	0.96	3.73	1.45	3.24	0.6	47	
2015	SJO	A+	25	2	1	0	20	5	25	13	2	9.0	18.4	47%	.324	1.52	2.88	3.74	3.07	0.7	78	
2016	*SFN*	*MLB*	*26*	*2*	*1*	*1*	*31*	*1*	*36^{2}*	*29*	*4*	*5.0*	*11.2*	*37%*	*.317*	*1.35*	*3.87*	*3.67*	*4.76*	*0.1*	*110*	
2017	*SFN*	*MLB*	*27*	*3*	*1*	*2*	*53*	*2*	*60*	*49*	*8*	*5.5*	*11.6*	*37%*	*.321*	*1.42*	*3.94*	*4.52*	*4.84*	*0.1*	*112*	

Breakout: 8% Improve: 12% Collapse: 6% Attrition: 18% MLB: 26% *Comparables: Juan Jaime, Carlos Guevara, Ian Thomas*

Black can throw that speedball by you, but much like his triple-digit heat, his glory days might pass you by in the wink of a young girl's eye. The Scranton native beat the odds by recovering his premium velocity after a torn labrum, which severely delayed his professional debut. He's also got a Tommy John surgery on his medical chart, so there's no guarantee his body will ever withstand the toll of a full season. The hard stuff is closer-caliber right now, though, so even a hint of improved control and a fringy breaking ball could prompt a rapid promotion to the majors lest his arm fail him before he gets there.

Clayton Blackburn RHP

Born: 1/6/93 Age: 23 Bats: L Throws: R Height: 6'3" Weight: 230

YEAR	TEAM	LVL	AGE	W	L	SV	G	GS	IP	H	HR	BB/9	K/9	GB%	BABIP	WHIP	ERA	FIP	DRA	WARP	CFIP	MPH
2013	SJO	A+	20	7	5	0	23	23	133	111	12	2.4	9.3	49%	.280	1.10	3.65	3.86	4.70	2.2	79	
2014	RIC	AA	21	5	6	0	18	18	93	94	1	1.9	8.2	57%	.341	1.23	3.29	2.54	4.03	1.2	83	
2015	SAC	AAA	22	10	4	0	23	20	123	127	6	2.3	7.2	52%	.323	1.29	2.85	3.55	3.98	2.2	89	
2016	*SFN*	*MLB*	*23*	*1*	*1*	*0*	*3*	*3*	*16*	*15*	*2*	*2.4*	*7.0*	*50%*	*.309*	*1.23*	*3.74*	*4.10*	*4.64*	*0.1*	*108*	
2017	*SFN*	*MLB*	*24*	*4*	*4*	*0*	*12*	*12*	*73^{1}*	*74*	*10*	*2.6*	*7.0*	*50%*	*.313*	*1.30*	*3.92*	*4.53*	*4.86*	*0.4*	*114*	

Breakout: 17% Improve: 28% Collapse: 18% Attrition: 30% MLB: 57% *Comparables: Wade LeBlanc, Matt Magill, Wade Davis*

A minor shoulder injury sidelined Blackburn for the first month of the 2015 campaign, and it continued to bother the burly Texan in his first few weeks in the Sacramento rotation. Once the hindrance wore off, Blackburn's command returned, and he resumed generating groundballs while keeping hitters on their heels. That recipe works at any level, even the hitter-friendly Pacific Coast League, which the former 16th-rounder solved to the tune of a 1.71 ERA in 10 second-half starts. Blackburn's menu is average across the board, and cynics say the absence of a kill pitch will undo him. Optimistic evaluators, on the other hand, see a back-end innings-chewer who has always been young for his levels and brings a sub-3 career ERA and five Ks per walk to his impending big-league debut.

Madison Bumgarner LHP

Born: 8/1/89 Age: 26 Bats: R Throws: L Height: 6'5" Weight: 235

YEAR	TEAM	LVL	AGE	W	L	SV	G	GS	IP	H	HR	BB/9	K/9	GB%	BABIP	WHIP	ERA	FIP	DRA	WARP	CFIP	MPH
2013	SFN	MLB	23	13	9	0	31	31	201^{1}	146	15	2.8	8.9	49%	.252	1.03	2.77	3.03	3.04	4.5	83	93.7
2014	SFN	MLB	24	18	10	0	33	33	217^{1}	194	21	1.8	9.1	46%	.296	1.09	2.98	3.02	3.95	2.2	81	94.1
2015	SFN	MLB	25	18	9	0	32	32	218^{1}	181	21	1.6	9.6	43%	.282	1.01	2.93	2.90	3.56	3.8	79	94.3
2016	*SFN*	*MLB*	*26*	*13*	*10*	*0*	*33*	*33*	*208*	*169*	*20*	*1.8*	*9.3*	*45%*	*.296*	*1.01*	*2.92*	*2.89*	*3.70*	*3.9*	*79*	
2017	*SFN*	*MLB*	*27*	*13*	*10*	*0*	*30*	*30*	*192^{2}*	*166*	*21*	*1.9*	*9.0*	*45%*	*.303*	*1.07*	*3.01*	*3.48*	*3.81*	*3.5*	*83*	

Breakout: 15% Improve: 53% Collapse: 15% Attrition: 10% MLB: 98% *Comparables: Felix Hernandez, Don Drysdale, Dwight Gooden*

After famously receiving a Chevy truck "with technology and stuff" from a rattled pitch man, Bumgarner showed up to spring training driving a Ford and appeared in their commercials all season. While the North Carolina country boy switched pickup allegiances, what didn't change—amid alarm bells over his historic October workload—was his performance. Bumgarner's regular-season innings total, and his earned runs, homers and walks allowed, barely budged. The lefty also raised his strikeout rate by spinning more curveballs and trading a little velocity for a lot more two-plane movement on his cutter. He was, in other words, better than ever, no worse for the 270-inning wear. So perhaps it's fitting that Bumgarner drives an F-150 instead of a Colorado: He's not some journeyman trying to "Find New Roads"; he's a "Built Ford Tough" ace ready to contend for the NL Cy Young.

Matt Cain RHP

Born: 10/1/84 Age: 31 Bats: R Throws: R Height: 6'3" Weight: 230

YEAR	TEAM	LVL	AGE	W	L	SV	G	GS	IP	H	HR	BB/9	K/9	GB%	BABIP	WHIP	ERA	FIP	DRA	WARP	CFIP	MPH
2013	SFN	MLB	28	8	10	0	30	30	184^{1}	158	23	2.7	7.7	39%	.260	1.16	4.00	3.90	4.05	1.9	103	93.6
2014	SFN	MLB	29	2	7	0	15	15	90^{1}	81	13	3.2	7.0	46%	.265	1.25	4.18	4.55	4.84	-0.1	114	93.8
2015	SFN	MLB	30	2	4	0	13	11	60^{2}	71	12	3.0	6.1	36%	.304	1.50	5.79	5.57	7.49	-1.8	124	93.2
2015	SAC	AAA	30	1	2	0	5	3	19^{2}	18	2	1.8	10.1	38%	.296	1.12	3.20	3.45	3.38	0.5	82	
2016	*SFN*	*MLB*	*31*	*9*	*9*	*0*	*26*	*26*	*156*	*137*	*18*	*2.7*	*7.0*	*40%*	*.279*	*1.17*	*4.00*	*3.96*	*4.93*	*0.7*	*118*	
2017	*SFN*	*MLB*	*32*	*10*	*11*	*0*	*29*	*29*	*175*	*162*	*24*	*2.7*	*6.8*	*40%*	*.286*	*1.23*	*4.06*	*4.69*	*5.01*	*0.6*	*120*	

Breakout: 11% Improve: 31% Collapse: 30% Attrition: 12% MLB: 93% *Comparables: Bartolo Colon, Brad Penny, Jarrod Washburn*

Sturdy frame, easy delivery, six straight seasons of 200 or more frames—Cain was the sort of pitcher who's supposed to never break down. Then bone spurs cost him the second half of 2014, and a strained flexor tendon shelved him for the first half of last year. Flexor strains are a fickle injury that can sap a pitcher's command long after the pain fades, and the Giants, who still owe the right-hander nearly $50 million, can only hope a winter of rest restores Cain's vintage form. If The Horse is done (or done*ish*) at 31, he'll serve as a sobering reminder that no pitcher, no matter his build, no matter how effortlessly he lights up the gun, offers any assurance of long-term health.

Santiago Casilla RHP

Born: 7/25/80 Age: 35 Bats: R Throws: R Height: 6'0" Weight: 210

YEAR	TEAM	LVL	AGE	W	L	SV	G	GS	IP	H	HR	BB/9	K/9	GB%	BABIP	WHIP	ERA	FIP	DRA	WARP	CFIP	MPH
2013	SFN	MLB	32	7	2	2	57	0	50	39	2	4.5	6.8	55%	.262	1.28	2.16	3.64	3.58	0.6	107	96.2
2014	SFN	MLB	33	3	3	19	54	0	58^{1}	35	3	2.3	6.9	57%	.211	0.86	1.70	3.15	2.37	1.5	99	96.6
2015	SFN	MLB	34	4	2	38	67	0	58	51	6	3.6	9.6	48%	.298	1.28	2.79	3.66	4.53	0.1	94	95.9
2016	*SFN*	*MLB*	*35*	*3*	*1*	*25*	*57*	*0*	*60^{2}*	*48*	*6*	*3.1*	*8.4*	*51%*	*.279*	*1.14*	*3.58*	*3.62*	*4.45*	*0.3*	*100*	
2017	*SFN*	*MLB*	*36*	*3*	*1*	*25*	*61*	*0*	*55^{2}*	*49*	*7*	*3.3*	*8.2*	*51%*	*.291*	*1.24*	*3.87*	*4.46*	*4.81*	*0.0*	*109*	

Breakout: 24% Improve: 43% Collapse: 26% Attrition: 14% MLB: 90% *Comparables: Jose Valverde, Roberto Hernandez, Heath Bell*

A few bad apples can taint any reliever's otherwise gold 'n' delicious season, and Casilla learned that the hard way in 2015, allowing half of his earned runs in three dreadful appearances that accounted for just one of his 58 innings. Installed as the full-time closer midway through 2014, the right-hander has done the job well, though he appeared to respond to disaster by altering his pitch mix and working higher in the zone. The revised approach boosted Casilla's strikeout rate, but upticks in walks and homers joined in, yielding a net negative to his peripherals. Nonetheless, despite the abundant competition for saves in San Francisco, the ninth inning should be Casilla's to lose if he stays by the Bay.

Samuel Coonrod RHP

Born: 9/22/92 Age: 23 Bats: R Throws: R Height: 6'2" Weight: 225

YEAR	TEAM	LVL	AGE	W	L	SV	G	GS	IP	H	HR	BB/9	K/9	GB%	BABIP	WHIP	ERA	FIP	DRA	WARP	CFIP	MPH
2015	AUG	A	22	7	5	0	23	22	111^{2}	103	3	2.7	9.2	50%	.319	1.23	3.14	2.97	3.17	2.6	85	
2016	*SFN*	*MLB*	*23*	*5*	*5*	*0*	*24*	*16*	*82*	*80*	*9*	*3.3*	*7.4*	*42%*	*.315*	*1.34*	*4.02*	*4.08*	*4.96*	*0.3*	*116*	
2017	*SFN*	*MLB*	*24*	*7*	*9*	*1*	*40*	*26*	*178^{1}*	*174*	*22*	*3.3*	*7.2*	*42%*	*.309*	*1.34*	*4.04*	*4.68*	*4.99*	*0.4*	*118*	

Breakout: 3% Improve: 6% Collapse: 5% Attrition: 7% MLB: 13% *Comparables: Jonathan Sanchez, Bruce Billings, Erik Johnson*

There are two Samardzijas in baseball circles: Jeff, the pitcher, is better known than his older brother, Sam, an agent who is gradually building his portfolio of clients. Sam Samardzija has advised Coonrod since the latter was at SIU-Carbondale, where he showed the stuff but not the strike-throwing ability that now makes him one of the organization's top pitching prospects. Coonrod's electric arm-speed enables him to reach the high-90s without much effort, and he pairs that heat with an above-average slider. After emerging as the only Sally League pitcher to both strike out more than 100 batters and exceed a strikeout per inning, Coonrod worked out of the bullpen in the California League playoffs. He could rise to the majors quickly in a late-inning capacity, but patience with the development of his changeup might instead yield a mid-rotation starter.

Kyle Crick RHP

Born: 11/30/92 Age: 23 Bats: L Throws: R Height: 6'4" Weight: 220

YEAR	TEAM	LVL	AGE	W	L	SV	G	GS	IP	H	HR	BB/9	K/9	GB%	BABIP	WHIP	ERA	FIP	DRA	WARP	CFIP	MPH
2013	SJO	A+	20	3	1	0	14	14	68^{2}	48	1	5.1	12.5	44%	.324	1.27	1.57	2.94	4.77	1.1	82	
2014	RIC	AA	21	6	7	0	23	22	90^{1}	78	7	6.1	11.1	47%	.326	1.54	3.79	3.96	4.67	0.5	104	
2015	RIC	AA	22	3	4	0	36	11	63	47	2	9.4	10.4	36%	.292	1.79	3.29	4.84	8.18	-2.7	145	
2016	*SFN*	*MLB*	*23*	*1*	*0*	*0*	*22*	*0*	*23^{1}*	*20*	*2*	*5.8*	*9.2*	*37%*	*.311*	*1.51*	*4.42*	*4.15*	*5.34*	*0.0*	*127*	
2017	*SFN*	*MLB*	*24*	*3*	*5*	*0*	*14*	*14*	*83*	*71*	*10*	*6.6*	*9.8*	*37%*	*.312*	*1.58*	*4.57*	*5.25*	*5.52*	*-0.2*	*131*	

Breakout: 23% Improve: 35% Collapse: 13% Attrition: 28% MLB: 62% *Comparables: Bill Bray, Mike Morin, Daniel Schlereth*

Gaylord Perry once walked 115 batters in a big-league season. He went on to win 314 games, earn a plaque in Cooperstown, and announce Crick's selection as the 49th-overall pick in the 2011 draft. Since Crick's professional debut the Texan has more than doubled Perry's walk allowance from that 1973 campaign in four fewer frames, none of them above Double-A. After years of debate about the live-armed righty's future role, the question now is whether Crick's wildness will prevent him from holding down any job.

Put it this way: In the summer of 2014, pundit speculation suggested Crick as trade bait if the Giants wanted to acquire Chase Utley. And in the summer of 2015, pundit speculation suggested Crick as trade bait if the Giants wanted to acquire Chase Utley. Now go read Chase Utley's comment in this book to see how much Crick's stock has dropped.

Johnny Cueto RHP

Born: 2/15/86 Age: 30 Bats: R Throws: R Height: 5'11" Weight: 220

YEAR	TEAM	LVL	AGE	W	L	SV	G	GS	IP	H	HR	BB/9	K/9	GB%	BABIP	WHIP	ERA	FIP	DRA	WARP	CFIP	MPH
2013	CIN	MLB	27	5	2	0	11	11	60^{2}	46	7	2.7	7.6	53%	.236	1.05	2.82	3.78	3.07	1.3	105	95.4
2014	CIN	MLB	28	20	9	0	34	34	243^{2}	169	22	2.4	8.9	48%	.238	0.96	2.25	3.28	2.81	5.9	89	95.9
2015	CIN	MLB	29	7	6	0	19	19	130^{2}	93	11	2.0	8.3	45%	.234	0.93	2.62	3.22	2.58	3.8	84	95.3
2015	KCA	MLB	29	4	7	0	13	13	81^{1}	101	10	1.9	6.2	43%	.343	1.45	4.76	4.03	4.93	0.1	109	95.0
2016	*SFN*	*MLB*	*30*	*11*	*9*	*0*	*29*	*29*	*174*	*142*	*16*	*2.1*	*7.9*	*46%*	*.283*	*1.05*	*3.29*	*3.28*	*4.13*	*2.4*	*93*	
2017	*SFN*	*MLB*	*31*	*11*	*10*	*0*	*29*	*29*	*175^{1}*	*152*	*20*	*2.1*	*7.9*	*46%*	*.290*	*1.10*	*3.34*	*3.85*	*4.19*	*2.4*	*95*	

Breakout: 13% Improve: 52% Collapse: 22% Attrition: 14% MLB: 95% *Comparables: Whitey Ford, A.J. Burnett, Warren Spahn*

Cueto spent the last few months of his Redlegs career doing his usual thing: embarrassing hitters while delivering his three fastball varieties, his slider and his Bugs Bunny changeup from four distinct dreadlock-flailing hesitation deliveries. Then the Royals gave up a clutch of talented young arms for his services down the stretch, and the wheels came off. During a five-game run Cueto suffered diminished velocity and was torched at a .390/.411/.675 rate. His fastball eventually came back, and Cueto went on to make two dominant postseason starts alongside two forgettable ones. That late-season wobble brought on yet another unfortunate whisper campaign about size and durability and hidden injuries, just in time for his first big dive into the free agent pool. Cueto has taken at least 30 turns in six of his eight big league seasons and possesses some of baseball's filthiest stuff. While his overall numbers last year didn't match his breakout 2014 they were still ace-caliber. The opt-out in his new Giants contract puts him in position to hit free agency after 2017 with a bit more momentum.

Chris Heston RHP

Born: 4/10/88 Age: 28 Bats: R Throws: R Height: 6'3" Weight: 195

YEAR	TEAM	LVL	AGE	W	L	SV	G	GS	IP	H	HR	BB/9	K/9	GB%	BABIP	WHIP	ERA	FIP	DRA	WARP	CFIP	MPH
2013	FRE	AAA	25	7	6	0	19	19	108²	129	14	3.8	8.0	48%	.350	1.61	5.80	4.98	5.09	0.7	103	
2014	FRE	AAA	26	12	9	0	28	28	173	152	16	2.7	6.5	51%	.266	1.17	3.38	4.50	5.14	1.2	102	
2014	SFN	MLB	26	0	0	0	3	1	5¹	6	0	5.1	6.8	53%	.353	1.69	5.06	3.29	5.36	0.0	109	92.5
2015	SFN	MLB	27	12	11	0	31	31	177²	169	16	3.2	7.1	54%	.299	1.31	3.95	4.05	4.71	0.7	113	91.7
2016	*SFN*	*MLB*	*28*	*5*	*3*	*0*	*48*	*8*	*84¹*	*77*	*8*	*2.9*	*6.9*	*52%*	*.298*	*1.24*	*3.89*	*3.83*	*4.81*	*0.2*	*112*	
2017	*SFN*	*MLB*	*29*	*5*	*6*	*0*	*14*	*14*	*84²*	*83*	*11*	*3.3*	*7.2*	*52%*	*.309*	*1.35*	*4.16*	*4.81*	*5.15*	*0.1*	*121*	

Breakout: 9% Improve: 25% Collapse: 11% Attrition: 19% MLB: 50% *Comparables: Rick VandenHurk, Cha Seung Baek, Tanner Roark*

When a rookie is touted as having "no-hit stuff," it's usually said figuratively, anticipating a historic outing to come. Heston, a sinker-baller whose curveball proved better than advertised, was seldom the subject of such praise... until he blanked the Mets with *literal* no-hit stuff in June. It turns out, though, that when it comes to projecting future performance, the figurative label means more than the literal one. Heston averaged just 4 2/3 innings per start over the season's last two months. Honestly, expectations were so low for this slow-burn 12th rounder that the one super-cool start puts the Giants into "house money" territory here. Heston will come to spring training with no assurance of a job in his sophomore season.

Tim Hudson RHP

Born: 7/14/75 Age: 40 Bats: R Throws: R Height: 6'1" Weight: 175

YEAR	TEAM	LVL	AGE	W	L	SV	G	GS	IP	H	HR	BB/9	K/9	GB%	BABIP	WHIP	ERA	FIP	DRA	WARP	CFIP	MPH
2013	ATL	MLB	37	8	7	0	21	21	131¹	120	10	2.5	6.5	57%	.281	1.19	3.97	3.43	3.90	1.6	105	91.9
2014	SFN	MLB	38	9	13	0	31	31	189¹	199	15	1.6	5.7	54%	.300	1.23	3.57	3.51	4.46	0.8	109	91.1
2015	SFN	MLB	39	8	9	0	24	22	123²	134	13	2.7	4.7	57%	.300	1.38	4.44	4.56	5.19	-0.2	129	90.3
2016	*SFN*	*MLB*	*40*	*7*	*7*	*0*	*20*	*20*	*118²*	*114*	*12*	*2.3*	*5.5*	*55%*	*.293*	*1.22*	*3.97*	*4.00*	*4.91*	*0.5*	*116*	
2017	*SFN*	*MLB*	*41*	*10*	*12*	*0*	*31*	*31*	*197*	*203*	*24*	*2.5*	*5.2*	*55%*	*.299*	*1.31*	*4.17*	*4.82*	*5.16*	*0.3*	*123*	

Breakout: 16% Improve: 40% Collapse: 19% Attrition: 8% MLB: 80% *Comparables: Kevin Brown, Tom Glavine, Warren Spahn*

Longtime nemesis Jimmy Rollins once observed that Hudson was a pitcher who wanted foes to feel confident, who wanted opponents to dig in eager to hit, because he knew their zeal would be their undoing. The *Moneyball*-era A's ace arrived in the majors at 23 and matured quickly, realizing that his path to stardom was his cunning mound presence and first-rate sinker, that groundballs and wily sequencing were the market inefficiencies in an era when strikeouts and intimidation came to dominate the game. Along the way, Hudson survived Tommy John surgery in his early 30s and a gruesome ankle injury at 38, neither enough to derail his pursuit of a World Series ring.

If Hudson falls short of enshrinement in Cooperstown—and Jay Jaffe's JAWS places him on the periphery—the time he missed recovering from those ailments will be the main reason why. He retired as the active leader in wins, and one of 15 pitchers ever to defeat all 30 teams. He was kind to the media and even more generous to teammates, the sort of magnanimous clubhouse presence who inspired articles about mentoring young starters nearly every spring. All of this must have awed scouts who once saw a diminutive right-hander at Auburn University and recommended him as a senior sign, projecting a future swingman or long reliever. If those scouts were confident of one thing, it was that Hudson would not make history, that 17 major-league seasons and a chance at Cooperstown were a pipe dream. In other words, as Rollins would tell you, Hudson always had them right where he wanted them.

Jordan Johnson RHP

Born: 9/15/93 Age: 22 Bats: R Throws: R Height: 6'3" Weight: 175

YEAR	TEAM	LVL	AGE	W	L	SV	G	GS	IP	H	HR	BB/9	K/9	GB%	BABIP	WHIP	ERA	FIP	DRA	WARP	CFIP	MPH
2015	SJO	A+	21	2	3	0	6	6	31¹	34	3	2.9	9.5	44%	.344	1.40	4.31	3.87	4.34	0.5	93	
2016	*SFN*	*MLB*	*22*	*2*	*3*	*0*	*9*	*9*	*41²*	*42*	*7*	*3.4*	*7.9*	*40%*	*.317*	*1.39*	*4.63*	*4.67*	*5.62*	*-0.2*	*136*	
2017	*SFN*	*MLB*	*23*	*5*	*8*	*0*	*24*	*24*	*139²*	*149*	*27*	*3.2*	*7.8*	*40%*	*.322*	*1.42*	*4.70*	*5.40*	*5.71*	*-0.5*	*138*	

Breakout: 1% Improve: 3% Collapse: 1% Attrition: 3% MLB: 5% *Comparables: Adam Wilk, Josh Lindblom, Andrew Heaney*

After a run of churning out top-notch starters on the strength of shrewd first-round drafting, the Giants have hit a pitcher-development lull. Since 2010, the only steady rotation member they've graduated is Chris Heston, who pitched his rookie season at the age of 27. And while the Giants have resumed investing premium draft currency into power arms, their next homegrown mid-rotation-or-better starter might not be Beede or Bickford or Crick or Stratton, but a 23rd-rounder who struck out fewer than five batters per nine innings in his junior season at Cal State-Northridge. Johnson, who shot up from the complex league to High-A after his velocity spiked into the mid-90s, shoots that gas with a loose, easy arm action and complements it with a slurvy breaking ball that has the spin to miss bats. Command remains a hurdle, in part because Johnson has yet to harness his newfound velocity, but this is a popup prospect with staying power. He could reach Double-A by the end of the year.

George Kontos RHP

Born: 6/12/85 Age: 31 Bats: R Throws: R Height: 6'3" Weight: 215

YEAR	TEAM	LVL	AGE	W	L	SV	G	GS	IP	H	HR	BB/9	K/9	GB%	BABIP	WHIP	ERA	FIP	DRA	WARP	CFIP	MPH
2013	FRE	AAA	28	3	2	4	18	0	23^{2}	19	3	1.1	9.9	45%	.250	0.93	4.18	3.40	4.16	0.3	72	
2013	SFN	MLB	28	2	2	0	52	0	55^{1}	60	7	2.9	7.6	39%	.323	1.41	4.39	4.05	5.18	-0.4	103	92.7
2014	SFN	MLB	29	4	0	0	24	0	32^{1}	24	1	3.1	7.5	39%	.267	1.08	2.78	2.86	2.90	0.6	99	93.2
2014	FRE	AAA	29	3	3	4	30	0	47^{2}	41	4	2.1	11.0	41%	.303	1.09	2.08	3.05	4.56	0.5	72	
2015	SFN	MLB	30	4	4	0	73	0	73^{1}	57	9	1.5	5.4	44%	.219	0.94	2.33	4.05	3.08	1.4	109	93.5
2016	*SFN*	*MLB*	*31*	*2*	*1*	*0*	*44*	*0*	46^{2}	*41*	*5*	*2.3*	*6.9*	*42%*	*.281*	*1.13*	*3.75*	*3.73*	*4.66*	*0.2*	*108*	
2017	*SFN*	*MLB*	*32*	*2*	*1*	*0*	*38*	*0*	44^{2}	*42*	*6*	*2.4*	*6.7*	*42%*	*.290*	*1.22*	*4.04*	*4.67*	*5.02*	*-0.1*	*117*	

Breakout: 18% Improve: 28% Collapse: 27% Attrition: 21% MLB: 67% *Comparables: Brian Tallet, Geoff Geary, Kameron Loe*

When the Giants acquired Kontos four years ago, he was a strike-throwing slider fiend, vulnerable to left-handed batters because everything he threw moved toward them. He's since widened his pitch mix to incorporate more sinkers and cutters, both of which burned worms at greater-than-50 percent rates and helped Kontos strand his first 26 inherited runners of the year. That streak notwithstanding, the righty lacks the oomph to survive mistakes and his margin for error is too slim for setup duty. He's best utilized as a multi-inning middle reliever, gobbling up low-leverage frames so that superior arms are well rested when the game is on the line.

Tim Lincecum RHP

Born: 6/15/84 Age: 32 Bats: L Throws: R Height: 5'11" Weight: 170

YEAR	TEAM	LVL	AGE	W	L	SV	G	GS	IP	H	HR	BB/9	K/9	GB%	BABIP	WHIP	ERA	FIP	DRA	WARP	CFIP	MPH
2013	SFN	MLB	29	10	14	0	32	32	197^{2}	184	21	3.5	8.8	47%	.300	1.32	4.37	3.71	4.24	1.6	99	92.9
2014	SFN	MLB	30	12	9	1	33	26	155^{2}	154	19	3.6	7.7	49%	.299	1.39	4.74	4.28	5.47	-1.3	115	92.2
2015	SFN	MLB	31	7	4	0	15	15	76^{1}	75	7	4.5	7.1	45%	.300	1.48	4.13	4.31	5.31	-0.3	117	90.0
2016	*SFN*	*MLB*	*32*	*5*	*5*	*0*	*14*	*14*	77^{2}	*73*	*9*	*3.4*	*7.7*	*47%*	*.305*	*1.31*	*4.03*	*4.02*	*4.98*	*0.3*	*117*	
2017	*SFN*	*MLB*	*33*	*10*	*11*	*0*	*30*	*30*	189^{2}	*186*	*26*	*3.4*	*7.5*	*47%*	*.307*	*1.36*	*4.13*	*4.77*	*5.10*	*0.4*	*120*	

Breakout: 17% Improve: 58% Collapse: 12% Attrition: 8% MLB: 93% *Comparables: Ervin Santana, Mark Langston, Floyd Bannister*

There is comfort, sometimes, in learning the culprit behind a previously unexplained downfall, because the first step to correcting a problem is identifying it. After three and a half rocky seasons, Lincecum was diagnosed with a degenerative condition in both of his hips, and a torn labrum in his left one, which shortened his freakishly long stride and prevented him from generating the torque that once fueled his power stuff. He turned to Alex Rodriguez's old surgeon, Dr. Marc Philippon, for help, hoping that medical advances could end his mid-career crisis and enable him to pitch effectively deep into his 30s. Lincecum is all-in on the surgery; his father, instrumental in designing his unique mechanics, is confident that it's the miracle cure to his son's prolonged malaise. Now comes the moment of truth: If the righty shows no signs of his vintage form this year, it's probably safe to say that he never will.

Javier Lopez LHP

Born: 7/11/77 Age: 38 Bats: L Throws: L Height: 6'4" Weight: 220

YEAR	TEAM	LVL	AGE	W	L	SV	G	GS	IP	H	HR	BB/9	K/9	GB%	BABIP	WHIP	ERA	FIP	DRA	WARP	CFIP	MPH
2013	SFN	MLB	35	4	2	1	69	0	39^{1}	30	1	2.7	8.5	65%	.261	1.07	1.83	2.38	3.02	0.7	88	88.9
2014	SFN	MLB	36	1	1	0	65	0	37^{2}	31	2	4.5	5.3	68%	.238	1.33	3.11	4.30	3.41	0.5	121	88.2
2015	SFN	MLB	37	1	0	0	77	0	39^{1}	19	1	3.7	5.9	69%	.173	0.89	1.60	3.39	2.10	1.2	111	86.8
2016	*SFN*	*MLB*	*38*	*2*	*1*	*2*	*44*	*0*	46^{2}	*41*	*5*	*3.4*	*6.7*	*68%*	*.282*	*1.25*	*4.05*	*4.09*	*5.01*	*0.0*	*112*	
2017	*SFN*	*MLB*	*39*	*4*	*2*	*1*	*90*	*0*	48^{2}	*45*	*6*	*3.4*	*6.3*	*68%*	*.286*	*1.31*	*4.19*	*4.83*	*5.18*	*-0.2*	*116*	

Breakout: 23% Improve: 41% Collapse: 27% Attrition: 6% MLB: 87% *Comparables: Scott Downs, Al Worthington, Randy Choate*

National League lefty swingers have had more than half a decade to solve Lopez, but even the circuit's elite remain a step behind the low-slot specialist. His latest tactic is relying more on a bowling-ball sinker that like-handed foes beat into the dirt 77 percent of the time. While the slider is Lopez's best swing-and-miss pitch, the sinker is a more trustworthy friend, always there at the knees when called upon and rarely hit farther than the dirt. With four World Series rings, Lopez is, deservedly, the sparkliest LOOGY ever, and he's defied Father Time to remain the league's best even as he approaches the big 4-0.

Mac Marshall LHP

Born: 1/27/96 Age: 20 Bats: R Throws: L Height: 6'0" Weight: 181

YEAR	TEAM	LVL	AGE	W	L	SV	G	GS	IP	H	HR	BB/9	K/9	GB%	BABIP	WHIP	ERA	FIP	DRA	WARP	CFIP	MPH
2015	SLO	A-	19	0	0	1	5	2	13^{2}	18	1	6.6	11.9	45%	.436	2.05	6.59	4.33	4.95	0.0	102	
2016	*SFN*	*MLB*	*20*	*2*	*2*	*1*	*22*	*4*	35^{1}	*35*	*5*	*4.8*	*7.3*	*35%*	*.317*	*1.53*	*4.80*	*4.94*	*5.82*	*-0.3*	*139*	
2017	*SFN*	*MLB*	*21*	*2*	*2*	*1*	*31*	*7*	99^{2}	*101*	*14*	*4.2*	*7.3*	*35%*	*.316*	*1.49*	*4.53*	*5.22*	*5.49*	*-0.3*	*132*	

Breakout: 0% Improve: 0% Collapse: 0% Attrition: 0% MLB: 0% *Comparables: Rafael Dolis, Brett Oberholtzer, Johnny Cueto*

Parkview High School in Georgia boasts four major-league alumni, all of them position players, unless you count Jeff Francoeur's two innings on the bump. The best bet to begin balancing the scales is Marshall, whose post-draft agreement with the Astros was collateral damage in the Brady Aiken debacle and who had to wait an extra year for his overslot payday. Athletic southpaws with present-plus changeups are typically a hot commodity, but Marshall has some history of elbow soreness and is six feet tall on the nose, faults that kept him on the board for the Giants at 126th overall. The cambio is the calling card here, with an average curve playing second fiddle and a low-90s fastball holding back the mix. Marshall can reach 93 on a warm day, but the utility of his four-seamer trails its velocity and might ultimately relegate him to bullpen work, even though he has the secondary stuff to start.

Adalberto Mejia LHP

Born: 6/20/93 Age: 23 Bats: R Throws: L Height: 6'3" Weight: 195

YEAR	TEAM	LVL	AGE	W	L	SV	G	GS	IP	H	HR	BB/9	K/9	GB%	BABIP	WHIP	ERA	FIP	DRA	WARP	CFIP	MPH
2013	SJO	A+	20	7	4	0	16	16	87	75	11	2.4	9.2	38%	.277	1.13	3.31	4.20	5.04	1.1	91	
2014	RIC	AA	21	7	9	0	22	21	108	119	9	2.6	6.8	36%	.326	1.39	4.67	3.78	4.35	1.0	95	
2015	RIC	AA	22	5	2	0	12	9	51^1	38	2	3.2	6.7	46%	.238	1.09	2.45	3.41	4.49	0.2	104	
2016	*SFN*	*MLB*	*23*	*3*	*3*	*0*	*15*	*9*	*53^1*	*53*	*6*	*2.8*	*6.5*	*37%*	*.306*	*1.30*	*4.06*	*4.09*	*4.98*	*0.2*	*118*	
2017	*SFN*	*MLB*	*24*	*8*	*9*	*0*	*35*	*25*	*172^1*	*180*	*25*	*3.1*	*6.4*	*37%*	*.310*	*1.39*	*4.35*	*5.03*	*5.34*	*-0.2*	*128*	

Breakout: 11% Improve: 12% Collapse: 8% Attrition: 15% MLB: 26% *Comparables: Nick Martinez, Zach Lee, Eric Jokisch*

Getting suspended and getting hurt are two ways to dim one's prospect stock, and Mejia managed to do both in the same year. He's still a left-hander with three average to solid pitches, however, and those types tend to make it, even if their developmental paths are paved with gravel. The Dominican already knows how to add and subtract from his fastball, which flashes plus sink and run, but he needs to learn how to work effectively in all four quadrants. There's a no. 4 starter here if he does, and he could arrive as soon as this summer.

Steven Okert LHP

Born: 7/9/91 Age: 24 Bats: L Throws: L Height: 6'3" Weight: 210

YEAR	TEAM	LVL	AGE	W	L	SV	G	GS	IP	H	HR	BB/9	K/9	GB%	BABIP	WHIP	ERA	FIP	DRA	WARP	CFIP	MPH
2013	AUG	A	21	2	2	2	44	0	60^2	55	3	3.6	8.8	48%	.302	1.30	2.97	3.42	4.31	0.3	95	
2014	RIC	AA	22	1	0	5	24	0	33	24	3	3.0	10.4	43%	.266	1.06	2.73	3.23	3.95	0.3	80	
2014	SJO	A+	22	1	2	19	33	0	35^1	33	2	2.8	13.8	46%	.308	1.25	1.53	2.52	4.34	0.2	74	
2015	SAC	AAA	23	5	3	3	52	0	61^1	62	7	4.3	10.1	46%	.337	1.48	3.82	4.35	4.71	0.3	97	
2016	*SFN*	*MLB*	*24*	*1*	*0*	*0*	*18*	*0*	*18^2*	*17*	*2*	*3.3*	*8.6*	*43%*	*.310*	*1.28*	*3.89*	*3.79*	*4.79*	*0.0*	*111*	
2017	*SFN*	*MLB*	*25*	*1*	*0*	*1*	*20*	*0*	*25^1*	*25*	*3*	*4.1*	*9.0*	*43%*	*.329*	*1.43*	*4.01*	*4.62*	*4.94*	*0.0*	*114*	

Breakout: 11% Improve: 18% Collapse: 5% Attrition: 16% MLB: 27% *Comparables: Joe Paterson, David Carpenter, Mark Melancon*

Okert followed up a brilliant 2014 Arizona Fall League showcase with a good-but-not-great season in Triple-A, but was passed over for Josh Osich when the Giants had an opening for a bullpen lefty. Whereas Osich thrives on the sheer power of his fastball, Okert brings more deception to the table, using a deep stab at the back of his delivery and a low-three-quarter release point to spice up a four-seamer that registers 91 more often than 97. Okert's waning feel for his slider and changeup led to his slide down the depth chart, but he could win an Opening Day gig if he gets on top of the ball consistently this spring.

Joshua Osich LHP

Born: 9/3/88 Age: 27 Bats: L Throws: L Height: 6'2" Weight: 230

YEAR	TEAM	LVL	AGE	W	L	SV	G	GS	IP	H	HR	BB/9	K/9	GB%	BABIP	WHIP	ERA	FIP	DRA	WARP	CFIP	MPH
2013	RIC	AA	24	2	3	3	22	0	29^2	26	2	3.6	8.5	51%	.300	1.28	4.85	3.53	4.47	0.1	96	
2013	SJO	A+	24	3	1	12	34	0	40^1	32	1	2.2	10.7	41%	.304	1.04	2.45	2.46	4.67	0.5	78	
2014	RIC	AA	25	1	0	0	28	0	33^1	28	4	5.4	7.3	56%	.264	1.44	3.78	5.18	4.78	0.0	110	
2015	RIC	AA	26	0	1	19	31	0	34	23	1	2.6	9.0	60%	.242	0.97	1.59	2.62	2.89	0.7	82	
2015	SFN	MLB	26	2	0	0	35	0	28^2	24	4	2.5	8.5	49%	.247	1.12	2.20	3.93	3.98	0.2	100	97.8
2016	*SFN*	*MLB*	*27*	*2*	*1*	*0*	*40*	*0*	*42*	*37*	*4*	*2.9*	*7.8*	*51%*	*.299*	*1.21*	*3.71*	*3.52*	*4.60*	*0.2*	*106*	
2017	*SFN*	*MLB*	*28*	*2*	*1*	*1*	*39*	*0*	*43^2*	*41*	*5*	*3.2*	*8.3*	*51%*	*.312*	*1.30*	*3.74*	*4.33*	*4.64*	*0.1*	*107*	

Breakout: 6% Improve: 15% Collapse: 22% Attrition: 30% MLB: 49% *Comparables: Joe Paterson, Cody Eppley, Cesar Jimenez*

Here's a complete list of left-handed relievers whose fastballs traveled faster than Osich's did in 2015: Aroldis Chapman, Jake Diekman, Enny Romero and Zach Britton. Two closers and two non-closers, fitting because the Idahoan's odds of earning ninth-inning duty are about one-in-two. Armed with a blistering four-seamer that features late sink, a plus cutter that he deployed more often down the stretch, and a show-me changeup to keep right-handed batters on their heels, Osich's stuff screams "high-leverage arm." So, too, does his entrance song, "The Fireman" by George Strait, and if Osich can sharpen his command in the lower third of the zone, he'll soon be making his rounds all over the league, putting out old flames.

Jake Peavy RHP

Born: 5/31/81 Age: 35 Bats: R Throws: R Height: 6'1" Weight: 195

YEAR	TEAM	LVL	AGE	W	L	SV	G	GS	IP	H	HR	BB/9	K/9	GB%	BABIP	WHIP	ERA	FIP	DRA	WARP	CFIP	MPH
2013	BOS	MLB	32	4	1	0	10	10	64^2	56	6	2.6	6.3	30%	.256	1.16	4.04	3.82	3.60	1.0	101	92.8
2013	CHA	MLB	32	8	4	0	13	13	80	74	14	1.9	8.6	36%	.278	1.14	4.28	4.13	4.15	0.7	87	93.1
2014	BOS	MLB	33	1	9	0	20	20	124	131	20	3.3	7.3	42%	.301	1.43	4.72	4.83	4.93	-0.2	112	92.4
2014	SFN	MLB	33	6	4	0	12	12	78^2	65	3	1.9	6.6	40%	.270	1.04	2.17	3.00	3.26	1.5	102	92.1
2015	SFN	MLB	34	8	6	0	19	19	110^2	99	12	2.0	6.3	40%	.263	1.12	3.58	3.89	4.04	1.3	107	92.4
2015	SAC	AAA	34	0	3	0	6	6	32^1	39	5	2.5	7.8	34%	.340	1.48	6.12	4.90	5.14	0.2	101	
2016	*SFN*	*MLB*	*35*	*9*	*9*	*0*	*26*	*26*	*148^1*	*135*	*16*	*2.3*	*7.0*	*39%*	*.293*	*1.17*	*3.79*	*3.78*	*4.71*	*1.0*	*110*	
2017	*SFN*	*MLB*	*36*	*9*	*10*	*0*	*27*	*27*	*158^1*	*155*	*22*	*2.4*	*6.7*	*39%*	*.300*	*1.25*	*3.98*	*4.59*	*4.94*	*0.7*	*116*	

Breakout: 17% Improve: 41% Collapse: 23% Attrition: 12% MLB: 90% *Comparables: Roy Oswalt, Don Sutton, Paul Byrd*

Few pitchers present a bigger contradiction between stuff and mound demeanor than Peavy, whose fiery outbursts and furious soliloquies mask a finesse approach that no longer intimidates his foes. Close-up shots of the right-hander are a telecast producer's worst nightmare, because he's liable to drop an f-bomb or five whether the preceding pitch resulted in an untimely homer or a dazzling double play. The former outcome becomes more predictable when Peavy sees opponents for the third time: Eight of the

12 big flies he allowed were launched in the sixth or seventh frames, and he remains a flyball-heavy pitcher prone to middle-middle mistakes as he fatigues. Peavy's backloaded contract pays him $15 million this year, so he won't just be one of the league's most entertaining fourth starters; he'll also be one of its priciest.

Sergio Romo RHP

Born: 3/4/83 Age: 33 Bats: R Throws: R Height: 5'11" Weight: 185

YEAR	TEAM	LVL	AGE	W	L	SV	G	GS	IP	H	HR	BB/9	K/9	GB%	BABIP	WHIP	ERA	FIP	DRA	WARP	CFIP	MPH
2013	SFN	MLB	30	5	8	38	65	0	60^1	53	5	1.8	8.7	42%	.276	1.08	2.54	2.82	3.97	0.5	84	90.1
2014	SFN	MLB	31	6	4	23	64	0	58	43	9	1.9	9.2	38%	.233	0.95	3.72	3.91	3.37	0.8	88	90.0
2015	SFN	MLB	32	0	5	2	70	0	57^1	51	3	1.6	11.1	47%	.331	1.06	2.98	1.94	3.66	0.7	70	89.4
2016	*SFN*	*MLB*	*33*	*3*	*1*	*8*	*53*	*0*	*55^2*	*44*	*6*	*2.1*	*9.4*	*44%*	*.289*	*1.03*	*3.05*	*3.17*	*3.87*	*0.6*	*83*	
2017	*SFN*	*MLB*	*34*	*3*	*1*	*7*	*68*	*0*	*58^2*	*50*	*7*	*2.2*	*8.7*	*44%*	*.292*	*1.10*	*3.30*	*3.83*	*4.19*	*0.5*	*93*	

Breakout: 20% Improve: 49% Collapse: 30% Attrition: 8% MLB: 97% *Comparables: Skip Lockwood, Jonathan Papelbon, John Wetteland*

In some corners of the world, left-handedness is considered a vice. It's associated with clumsiness and frailty, and so abhorred that children are banned from using their portside appendage to write. Unfortunately for Romo, 21st-century America isn't such a place, and while Major League Baseball has pioneered cultural changes before, it's not about to deny lefties the right to bat. Opposing managers would do well to take heed of that freedom, because when Romo had the platoon advantage at his side last year, he struck out 64 and (unintentionally) walked one. If a lefty-loathing loony wins the White House before Romo hangs 'em up, he'll be a Cy Young contender. As it is, he's a matchup setup man who helps ensure the skipper gets his cardio in walking to and from the mound.

Jeff Samardzija RHP

Born: 1/23/85 Age: 31 Bats: R Throws: R Height: 6'5" Weight: 225

YEAR	TEAM	LVL	AGE	W	L	SV	G	GS	IP	H	HR	BB/9	K/9	GB%	BABIP	WHIP	ERA	FIP	DRA	WARP	CFIP	MPH
2013	CHN	MLB	28	8	13	0	33	33	213^2	210	25	3.3	9.0	50%	.314	1.35	4.34	3.75	4.21	1.8	92	97.2
2014	CHN	MLB	29	2	7	0	17	17	108	99	7	2.6	8.6	54%	.306	1.20	2.83	3.07	3.73	1.4	91	96.8
2014	OAK	MLB	29	5	6	0	16	16	111^2	92	13	1.0	8.0	49%	.262	0.93	3.14	3.33	3.00	2.5	83	97.3
2015	CHA	MLB	30	11	13	0	32	32	214	228	29	2.1	6.9	41%	.303	1.29	4.96	4.20	4.32	1.8	103	96.8
2016	*SFN*	*MLB*	*31*	*12*	*10*	*0*	*29*	*29*	*194^1*	*178*	*21*	*2.1*	*7.8*	*45%*	*.304*	*1.15*	*3.52*	*3.51*	*4.39*	*2.1*	*101*	
2017	*SFN*	*MLB*	*32*	*11*	*11*	*0*	*30*	*30*	*184^2*	*179*	*23*	*2.1*	*7.6*	*45%*	*.311*	*1.20*	*3.57*	*4.12*	*4.45*	*1.9*	*103*	

Breakout: 25% Improve: 57% Collapse: 22% Attrition: 16% MLB: 97% *Comparables: Bert Blyleven, Mickey Lolich, Steve Carlton*

Samardzija made a number of approach adjustments under the tutelage of Don Cooper, and none of them seemed to work out well. He virtually ditched his splitter against right-handed batters, leaning ever harder on his slider. He scaled back his sinker and went to the cutter much more. The result: career lows (as a starter) in strikeout and groundball rates. Samardzija has always been a one-trick pony, but the one trick was missing bats, which is the best trick any pitcher can do. His repertoire is all power and similar lanes. When the White Sox tried to give his game some nuance, they ended up robbing him of his greatest strength.

Daniel Slania RHP

Born: 5/24/92 Age: 24 Bats: R Throws: R Height: 6'5" Weight: 275

YEAR	TEAM	LVL	AGE	W	L	SV	G	GS	IP	H	HR	BB/9	K/9	GB%	BABIP	WHIP	ERA	FIP	DRA	WARP	CFIP	MPH
2013	SLO	A-	21	1	1	3	12	0	13^2	13	1	2.0	9.2	38%	.308	1.17	3.95	3.10	3.85	0.1	86	
2014	AUG	A	22	2	5	12	43	0	58^2	56	5	3.2	7.1	40%	.290	1.31	3.99	4.25	4.79	0.2	103	
2014	RIC	AA	22	0	0	0	10	0	11^1	10	0	2.4	2.4	34%	.244	1.15	0.79	3.62	4.89	0.0	114	
2015	SJO	A+	23	4	5	16	59	0	71^1	70	7	1.9	11.4	41%	.339	1.19	3.53	3.20	2.60	2.1	72	
2016	*SFN*	*MLB*	*24*	*3*	*1*	*3*	*60*	*0*	*64*	*62*	*9*	*3.1*	*8.0*	*34%*	*.313*	*1.31*	*4.18*	*4.21*	*5.14*	*-0.2*	*121*	
2017	*SFN*	*MLB*	*25*	*1*	*0*	*1*	*28*	*0*	*34^2*	*34*	*5*	*3.1*	*8.5*	*34%*	*.317*	*1.33*	*4.08*	*4.70*	*5.02*	*-0.1*	*118*	

Breakout: 3% Improve: 4% Collapse: 9% Attrition: 11% MLB: 15% *Comparables: Daniel Stange, Chris Rearick, Kam Mickolio*

As lazy comps go, Jonathan Broxton for Slania at least has the benefit of double meaning. They're both right-handed relievers, and they both look like their ideal offseason weekends involve football on the tube and bags of Cheez Doodles by their sides. From there, to go from modern-day Broxton to Slania, you'll have to subtract a little oomph from the fastball and add a bit of dart to the slider. Throw in a fringe-average splitter and glue on Jeff Karstens' eyebrows, and finally, a week of Weight Watchers will complete the transformation from veteran to soon-to-be rookie.

Hunter Strickland RHP

Born: 9/24/88 Age: 27 Bats: R Throws: R Height: 6'4" Weight: 220

YEAR	TEAM	LVL	AGE	W	L	SV	G	GS	IP	H	HR	BB/9	K/9	GB%	BABIP	WHIP	ERA	FIP	DRA	WARP	CFIP	MPH
2013	SJO	A+	24	1	0	9	20	0	21	10	1	2.1	9.9	51%	.196	0.71	0.86	3.06	4.67	0.3	79	
2014	RIC	AA	25	1	1	11	38	0	35^2	25	3	1.0	12.1	41%	.275	0.81	2.02	2.09	3.38	0.6	58	
2014	SFN	MLB	25	1	0	1	9	0	7	5	0	0.0	11.6	56%	.312	0.71	0.00	0.53	0.44	0.3	85	100.1
2015	SFN	MLB	26	3	3	0	55	0	51^1	34	4	1.8	8.8	40%	.240	0.86	2.45	2.93	2.64	1.3	86	99.3
2015	SAC	AAA	26	1	1	5	15	0	21^2	14	0	1.2	10.4	69%	.275	0.78	1.66	1.85	2.46	0.7	70	
2016	*SFN*	*MLB*	*27*	*2*	*1*	*0*	*35*	*0*	*37^1*	*30*	*3*	*2.3*	*8.9*	*45%*	*.299*	*1.07*	*3.14*	*2.91*	*3.94*	*0.5*	*87*	
2017	*SFN*	*MLB*	*28*	*2*	*1*	*1*	*37*	*2*	*49^1*	*41*	*5*	*2.2*	*9.4*	*45%*	*.305*	*1.08*	*3.01*	*3.48*	*3.78*	*0.7*	*83*	

Breakout: 18% Improve: 34% Collapse: 24% Attrition: 22% MLB: 74% *Comparables: Santiago Casilla, Andrew Brown, Evan Scribner*

You only get one chance to make a first impression, and Strickland flubbed his by serving up a half-dozen moonshots on the post-season stage in 2014. That gopherballing reputation stayed glued to the righty when he entered contests in his first full big-league season, but the issue was well behind him. Strickland learned that country hardball doesn't fly in the majors when the hardballs fly a country mile, so he traded some straight four-seamers for two-seamers and got less predictable with his locations. That's all it took to turn the late-blooming Georgian into a quality setup man.

Andrew Suarez LHP

Born: 9/11/92 Age: 23 Bats: L Throws: L Height: 6'2" Weight: 210

YEAR	TEAM	LVL	AGE	W	L	SV	G	GS	IP	H	HR	BB/9	K/9	GB%	BABIP	WHIP	ERA	FIP	DRA	WARP	CFIP	MPH
2016	*SFN*	*MLB*	*23*	*2*	*2*	*0*	*11*	*7*	*36^{2}*	*37*	*5*	*3.1*	*6.9*	*43%*	*0.311*	*1.36*	*4.46*	*4.35*	*5.44*	*-0.1*	*131*	
2017	*SFN*	*MLB*	*24*	*7*	*9*	*1*	*38*	*25*	*173^{2}*	*173*	*27*	*3.2*	*7.4*	*43%*	*0.308*	*1.35*	*4.35*	*5.01*	*5.31*	*-0.1*	*128*	

Breakout: 2% Improve: 3% Collapse: 0% Attrition: 1% MLB: 3% *Comparables: Joel Carreno, David Huff, Cory Luebke*

College lefties with four average-or-better pitches always garner attention on draft day, and Suarez was no exception. After spending the first 22 years of his life in Miami, Suarez soared from the ACC to the Cal League in a few months' time, using his fastball and whichever specialty pitch(es) were working on any given day to flummox low-minors competition. Therein lies the rub, however, because the southpaw's curveball, slider and changeup come and go from start to start. Newfound consistency and continued good health (he's three years removed from shoulder surgery) could make Suarez a no. 4 starter by 2017.

Lineouts

Hitters

NAME	POS	TEAM	LVL	AGE	PA	R	2B	3B	HR	RBI	BB	K	SB	CS	AVG/OBP/SLG	TAv	BABIP	BRR	FRAA	WARP
Ehire Adrianza	2B	SAC	AAA	25	195	16	6	1	3	15	17	37	6	1	.316/.384/.415	.295	.389	0.3	SS(43): 2.5, 2B(1): 0.2	1.8
	2B	SFN	MLB	25	134	11	7	1	0	11	15	20	3	2	.186/.303/.265	.225	.226	-0.1	SS(20): 0.1, 2B(20): 0.6	0.1
Trevor Brown	C	SAC	AAA	23	314	35	17	0	2	27	21	53	1	0	.261/.319/.343	.247	.313	2.1	C(72): 8.4	2.0
	C	SFN	MLB	23	43	1	3	0	0	5	3	8	1	1	.231/.279/.308	.225	.281	0.4	C(13): -1.8	-0.1
Everth Cabrera	SS	BAL	MLB	28	105	7	2	0	0	4	5	22	2	0	.208/.250/.229	.172	.263	-0.7	SS(27): -1.8, 2B(2): -0.0	-0.8
	SS	NOR	AAA	28	25	3	1	0	0	1	1	7	0	0	.208/.240/.250	.214	.294	0.2	2B(4): 1.0, SS(2): -1.0	0.0
	SS	SAC	AAA	28	119	14	3	0	0	7	9	16	7	2	.231/.297/.259	.215	.272	0.3	SS(12): 0.3, 2B(12): 0.1	-0.1
Daniel Carbonell	OF	RIC	AA	24	214	18	3	2	1	12	4	53	9	1	.146/.173/.194	.145	.190	2.6	LF(39): -5.0, CF(17): -0.3	-2.5
	OF	SJO	A+	24	282	35	14	2	6	27	13	51	9	7	.279/.327/.419	.311	.324	-1.0	LF(62): 7.7, CF(3): -0.3	2.9
Steven Duggar	OF	SLO	A-	21	267	40	12	1	1	27	35	52	6	3	.293/.390/.367	.283	.373	1.4	RF(52): 9.9, CF(7): -0.8	2.3
C.J. Hinojosa	INF	SLO	A-	20	203	24	18	1	5	19	8	15	2	3	.296/.328/.481	.289	.298	-0.2	SS(47): -0.0	1.5
Hak-Ju Lee	SS	DUR	AAA	24	360	33	15	1	3	27	35	105	20	3	.220/.303/.304	.233	.319	1.5	SS(94): -5.9, 2B(1): -0.0	0.0
Nick Noonan	INF	SAC	AAA	26	70	6	1	0	2	10	5	15	1	0	.266/.314/.375	.245	.313	-0.2	SS(17): -1.1, 3B(1): 0.0	0.0
	INF	SFN	MLB	26	24	2	1	0	1	3	2	8	0	0	.091/.167/.273	.153	.077	0.5	SS(5): -0.3, 1B(3): -0.1	-0.2
	INF	SWB	AAA	26	269	28	13	0	1	26	17	68	1	1	.262/.308/.328	.255	.352	0.1	SS(60): 4.1, 2B(4): -0.2	1.3
Austin Slater	INF	RIC	AA	22	218	21	11	1	0	13	14	48	1	1	.296/.350/.362	.266	.388	0.5	2B(54): 4.1	1.2
	INF	SJO	A+	22	265	25	15	1	3	34	10	44	4	3	.292/.321/.396	.258	.340	0.4	2B(42): -0.5, SS(7): 0.4	0.7

It's tough to say what's more impressive, that **Ehire Adrianza** worked a walk in more than 11 percent of his plate appearances, or that he posted a lower True Average than Jake Peavy while doing so. ❖ **Trevor Brown** wasn't in the squat regularly until 2014, but he's already a solid receiver and thrower who could become someone's personal catcher someday. ❖ Signed to a minor-league deal in July, **Everth Cabrera** couldn't hit well enough in Triple-A to unseat Adrianza as the Giants' backup shortstop, which tells you all you need to know about his fall from grace. ❖ Professional baseball players can make a living with noodle arms and turtle speed, but, as $1.4 million Cuban signee **Daniel Carbonell** learned in the middle of the Cal League playoffs, a defective hit tool is a one-way ticket to the unemployment line. ❖ Top-shelf wheels and range in center field will eventually get **Steven Duggar** to the majors, but he'll have to refine his swing to be more than a reserve at the highest level. ❖ The Giants' biggest-ever foray into the international amateur market brought them **Lucius Fox**, who signed for $6.5 million and could one day be a table-setting shortstop with plus-plus speed and the athleticism to be a plus defender. ❖ A highly regarded prep-schooler ahead of the 2012 draft, **C.J. Hinojosa** didn't live up to expectations at Texas, with whispers of poor conditioning deflating his performance on both sides of the ball. There might yet be a bat-first keystoner here if he puts it all together after a solid professional debut. ❖ A former top prospect, **Hak-Ju Lee** is just looking for the opportunity to remain in professional baseball. Scouting may be the only viable alternative. ❖ Of the Giants' six first-round picks in the 2007 draft, **Nick Noonan** has the third-most major-league service time; it's anyone's guess whether he or Charlie Culberson will finish second when all is said and done. ❖ An outfielder at Stanford, **Austin Slater** impressed evaluators with his smooth transition back to the dirt, giving him a chance to stick in a super-utility role.

Pitchers

NAME	TEAM	LVL	AGE	W	L	SV	G	GS	IP	H	HR	BB/9	K/9	GB%	BABIP	WHIP	ERA	FIP	FRA	WARP	CFIP	MPH
Michael Broadway	SAC	AAA	28	2	0	13	40	0	48^{1}	25	0	1.5	11.9	42%	.243	0.68	0.93	1.45	0.82	2.3	47	
	SFN	MLB	28	0	2	0	21	0	17^{1}	20	1	3.6	6.8	41%	.345	1.56	5.19	3.80	6.43	-0.4	109	97.5
Cory Gearrin	SAC	AAA	29	2	2	0	33	0	43	38	4	2.9	9.6	46%	.293	1.21	2.72	3.86	3.70	0.7	86	
	SFN	MLB	29	0	0	0	7	0	3^{2}	1	0	2.5	12.3	100%	.143	0.55	4.91	1.25	-0.50	0.2	95	94.4
Joan Gregorio	RIC	AA	23	3	2	1	37	9	78^{2}	64	6	3.7	8.2	38%	.272	1.22	3.09	3.69	3.86	0.8	96	
Cody Hall	SFN	MLB	27	0	0	0	7	0	8^{1}	10	1	4.3	7.6	52%	.321	1.68	6.48	4.84	5.04	0.0	105	96.3
	SAC	AAA	27	1	3	3	43	0	67^{2}	67	3	3.5	7.3	42%	.306	1.37	3.46	3.70	5.07	0.1	101	
Chase Johnson	RIC	AA	23	1	1	0	3	3	13^{2}	16	0	5.3	11.9	48%	.400	1.76	5.93	2.39	4.03	0.1	96	
	SJO	A+	23	8	3	0	20	18	111	95	5	2.8	9.0	57%	.304	1.16	2.43	3.39	3.96	2.1	89	
Derek Law	RIC	AA	24	0	1	13	28	0	25^{2}	31	1	2.8	11.2	45%	.400	1.52	4.56	2.22	2.56	0.6	78	
Tyler Rogers	SJO	A+	24	5	1	1	42	0	79^{1}	57	4	2.3	9.8	66%	.269	0.97	1.47	3.10	3.25	1.8	80	
	RIC	AA	24	0	1	0	10	0	10^{2}	10	1	4.2	12.7	28%	.375	1.41	5.91	3.36	3.25	0.2	87	
Michael Santos	AUG	A	20	0	2	0	9	9	36^{2}	38	2	2.5	5.6	57%	.310	1.31	3.44	4.00	5.00	0.1	105	
Jacob Smith	SJO	A+	25	4	4	16	56	0	84^{1}	50	7	2.2	12.6	40%	.246	0.84	2.35	2.88	1.62	3.4	59	
Chris Stratton	SAC	AAA	24	4	5	0	17	17	98	88	6	3.7	6.6	47%	.281	1.31	3.86	4.30	5.59	0.0	108	
	RIC	AA	24	1	5	0	9	9	50	40	3	4.0	7.0	48%	.252	1.24	4.14	3.87	4.88	0.0	109	

Michael Broadway can sling it up there at 97 mph, but he's yet to figure out where "there" is supposed to be. ❖ The UCL in **Cory Gearrin**'s right elbow went *poof!* in 2014, but he resurfaced in September with the textbook ROOGY starter kit: a side-slinging delivery and a fastball and slider that dive in opposite directions as they reach the plate. ❖ Draw a stick figure with a baseball cap, and you'll have a reasonable depiction of **Joan Gregorio**, who's more twiggy than projectable, and whose long levers detract from his command, pointing toward a future in middle relief. ❖ **Cody Hall** has the stuff to stick as a middle reliever, and if he does, his (plumbing warehouse) rags to (big-league) riches story will be a readymade movie screenplay. ❖ **Chase Johnson** reaches the mid-90s with excellent armspeed but his mechanics are tough on the elbow and won't support a starter's workload. ❖ Just another hard-throwing righty in a pipeline clogged with them, **Derek Law** needs to iron out his command post-Tommy John surgery to state his case for a big-league trial. ❖ Austin Peay State, whose sports teams are dubbed the Governors, has produced four big-league relievers, but interestingly enough, no governors. A submariner likely to begin 2016 in Double-A, **Tyler Rogers** could make it 5-0 by next year. ❖ Lost seasons spell trouble for any pitching prospect, but **Michael Santos** flashed the makings of a plus fastball and curve in his brief 2015 campaign, enough to dream on a rotation future if everything breaks right. ❖ More than just another bullpen power arm, **Jacob Smith** has a deceptive delivery and feel for a hard cutter and sweeping slider, which overmatched High-A hitters and earned him a 40-man roster spot. ❖ **Chris Stratton** has a clean delivery and a starter's mindset, but his fastball-slider tandem would play better in short bursts.

MANAGER

Bruce Bochy

YEAR	TEAM	W	L	Pythag +/-	Avg PC	100+ P	120+ P	QS	BQS	REL	REL w Zero R	IBB	PH	PH Avg	PH HR	SB2	CS2	SB3	CS3	SAC Att	SAC%	POS SAC	Squeeze	Swing	In Play
2013	SFN	76	86	3	96.1	79	2	80	2	524	429	64	258	.213	4	64	24	3	1	86	76.7	25	2	329	119
2014	SFN	88	74	1	94.7	59	1	86	6	475	412	35	233	.222	4	52	24	4	2	66	68.2	20	5	268	97
2015	SFN	84	78	-5	90.8	37	0	78	3	557	474	28	224	.249	1	87	32	6	3	60	75.0	12	1	309	106

Bochy is a future Hall of Famer, a three-time world champion who signed an extension in spring through the 2018 season, giving him at least three more years to add to his trophy case. Should he secure another pennant, he would become the 15th skipper to snag five (the others are in Cooperstown). Another World Series win would join Bochy to Walter Alston and Joe Torre as managers hired since World War II who enjoyed four title parades. Essentially, no matter when Bochy retires, no matter what he does until then, he's going down as one of the most successful managers in modern history.

Yet all his accomplishments haven't caused Bochy to grow a big head—er, ego. When he was hospitalized in February so doctors could insert two stents, he received a text from Jeremy Affeldt asking what was going on. Bochy replied: "Heart procedure. Watched your bullpen," according to Duane Kuiper. Obviously his people skills remain sharp, but they aren't the only reason he excels. Bochy is a hit-and-run fanatic who loathes sacrificing with his positional players. He also runs one of the tightest bullpen operations around and has coerced consistently good performances from a group of relievers who, frankly, you wouldn't suspect were capable of consistently good performances.

Part of that success stems from Bochy's willingness to walk to the mound a lot. No manager lifted relievers after one batter more often last season than he did, and the gap between him and the second-place finisher was twice as large as the gap between the second-place finisher and the third-place finisher. Correspondingly, the Giants led the majors in relief appearances with zero runs allowed, while tying for last in outs per game—an unsurprising fact, given the Giants had only three qualified relievers who recorded more than three outs per appearance, including longman Yusmeiro Petit.

All Bochy's matchups cause the latter parts of Giants games to drag. But so long as the seasons continue to result in deep postseason runs, he'll have all the time he wants in San Francisco.

SEATTLE MARINERS

Essay by Meg Rowley

Player comments by Mike Gianella, Brendan Gawlowski, and BP authors

Fandom is a balancing act; a careful, at times fraught, attempt to find the equilibrium between optimism and new, awful, unexpected ways to be disappointed. What side the scale tips toward colors that season. The balance is difficult to strike in the offseason. Each spring, a heady combination of free-agent signings and distance from the daily follies of our team at play make it easy to believe that this is our year. It isn't until we begin to mark time in innings played, and wins and losses, that we experience the bitter realization that our team really can lose that way. That this isn't our year, so much as it is like every other failed year. By that standard and almost any other, few teams find themselves afflicted by disappointment as often as the Seattle Mariners.

For a lot of years the Seattle Mariners were just bad. They were bad for the first 18 years of the franchise. Beginning in 1995, they were briefly spectacular, buoyed by the irrepressible cool of Ken Griffey Jr., and later, the euphoria of a 116 win season. Then they were bad again. The mid-2000s were the sort of plodding bad that keeps good free agents away, inviting a cast of characters who seemed as likely to be extras in a movie about baseball as they were to be actual major leaguers paid for baseball services rendered. Ownership's interests were solely pecuniary, maddeningly indifferent to nostalgia or aspiration. The King's Court Era brought a new, sadder sort of bad, the kind of nadir typified by a 1-0 loss and a starting pitcher's head hung. Willie Bloomquist figured prominently. Where other teams seemed to regularly unlock the alchemy of drafting and development, the Mariners appeared flummoxed. Fans, ever yearning for some sustained evidence of vigor, wondered what, apart from winning a staring contest with gloom, they stood to gain.

✦✦✦

Every season offers great moments. That's almost assured in a sport where even the best teams rarely win more than 100 games. It's the distribution of those moments that colors our collective imaginations. They shape what we see in our minds' eye when team logos flicker across TV screens. The cracks in a franchise's facade emerge when the good will of fans is stretched too tightly over moments strewn too far apart. The mood

MARINERS PROSPECTUS

2015 W-L: 76-86, 4th in AL West

Pythag	.453	22nd	DER	.702	17th
RS/G	4.05	21st	B-Age	28.6	20th
RA/G	4.48	20th	P-Age	28.2	13th
TAv	.264	10th	Salary	$123.2M	11th
BRR	-13.64	28th	M$/MW	$4M	12th
TAv-P	.268	22nd	DL Days	751	10th
FIP	4.11	21st	$ on DL	5%	3rd

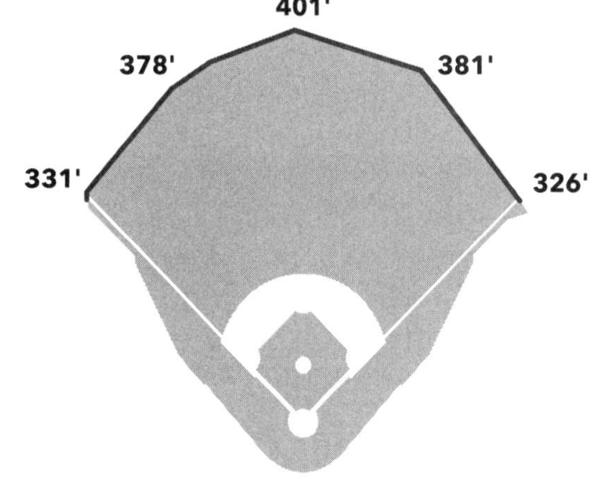

Outfield wall profile: **8'**

Three-Year Park Factors

Runs	Runs/RH	Runs/LH	HR/RH	HR/LH
97	109	109	111	109

Top Hitter WARP	5.4	Nelson Cruz
Top Pitcher WARP	3.3	Felix Hernandez
Top Prospect	Alex Jackson	

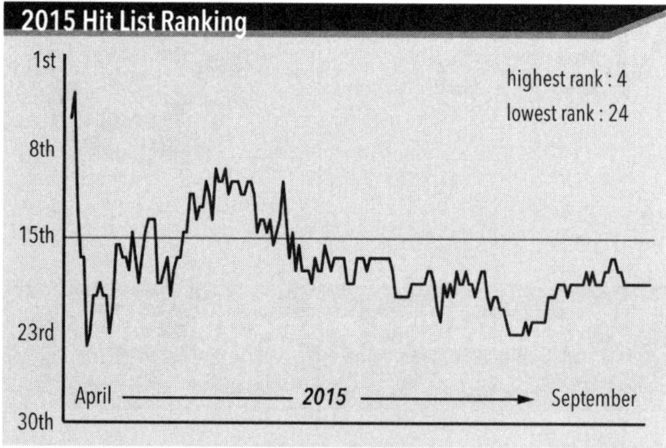

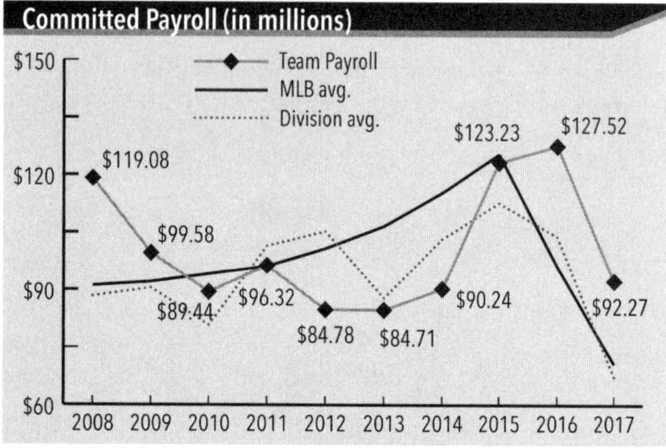

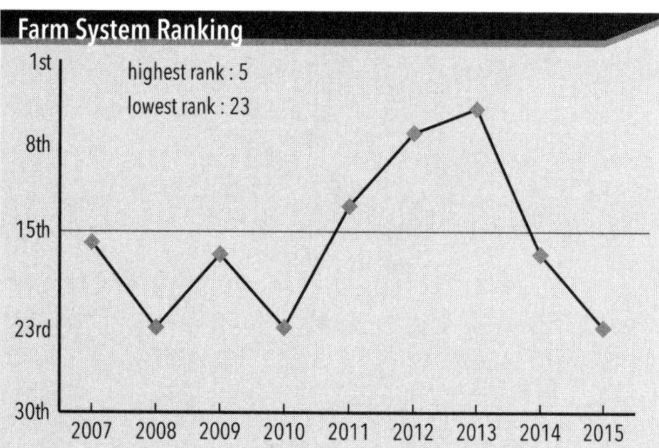

Personnel

General Manager: Jerry Dipoto
Assistant General Manager: Jeff Kingston
Manager: Scott Servais

Baseball Prospectus Alumni
Caleb Peiffer

in the ballpark becomes taut. Fans file in, but can reach out and touch empty seats around them. The bones of the park show through where families and old timers and drunken 20-somethings should be. Jerseys from other franchises creep into the stands until they stand out on broadcasts.

We are left feeling the absence. Of belief. Of October baseball. Of former players resplendent in the pinstripes of another teams' uniform. And piercing through all of that are a few scattered memories, screaming through the doldrums. The dearth of recent celebrations only serves to underscore how far into the past one has to look to find the highlights. Time works on the great moments of every season. The marginalia of each year are erased, leaving the story of a franchise sketched out in thin chapters and rising action unrealized, Chekhov's gun laying dust-covered on the mantle. We are forced to sit with the uncomfortable realization that they were all captured in standard definition, before our legends' hair had thinned. When they are too scattered and too distinct, they grant permission for resentment, even bitterness.

Baseball should be fun. It should thrill and excite and offer the promise of delaying disappointment until the last possible instant. It should afford its acolytes the chance to freewheel into optimism, immune from what is likely as we search for what is transcendent. Mariners baseball has remained dispiritingly, almost perpetually, earthbound. Jack Zduriencik promised a new sort of regime: Driven by analytics. Nimble. Decisive. Despite the turbulence of his reign, the indifferent suitors and regrettable free agents, success always lingered hazily in the distance. But the team's failure to reach escape velocity turned all that energy inward, tunneling into the faithful, bringing with it the scattered, great moments but also faith's dirge: doubt.

And then the brief reprieve. The introduction of a second wild card spot has made it possible for a middling performance to be good enough provided it is punctuated with a few extended stretches of very good. And in 2014, the Mariners were precisely that. The emergence of Kyle Seager as one of the best all-around third basemen in the game coupled with a good year of Robinson Cano to breathe new life into the offense. Felix Hernandez had arguably his best season as a pro. The bullpen, so often leaky, was among the best in the American League. That it happened in a year where the team was predicted to be bad seemed proof that there was more to the band of misfits Zduriencik had assembled than met the eye. The Mariners missed the playoffs by one game. The relief of baseball actually mattering on the very last day of the season was a hell of a drug. The city was keen for more. As if unshackled, they sprinted toward the next year, cocky and sure 2015 would be the season.

Entering 2015, the Mariners found themselves suddenly in vogue; in his AL West preview for Grantland, Ben Lindbergh said their greatest strength was "their lack of weaknesses." Apart from Nelson Cruz, there weren't many splashy signings, mostly because the club held no vacancies. The Mariners were healthy. They lacked obvious holes. The fans, weary after years spent collecting chits the club had yet to repay, allowed themselves to crow. They leaned on the final day of the season prior and puffed up their chests in anticipation of a cessation of irrelevance. They penciled in October baseball. The King won on Opening Day.

Then the Mariners found new, awful, unexpected ways to disappoint. They vacillated between shocking degrees of competence and bumbling doldrums. They were good at one thing and bad at another, and instead of the quick death of years past, strung their fans along. Not because they were playing the meaningful baseball of 2014, but because the mediocrity of the American League had not yet made clear just how meaningless this baseball was. And there was Captain Jack, an Ahab searching for right handed power, trying to hold a crumbling, empty empire together with little more than his hands and Felix Hernandez, until the ship began to crack and splinter beneath his feet.

Strategies were discarded before they took root, ripped out in hopes the ground would prove more fecund for other gritty varieties of veterans. It did not. Seth Smith and Franklin Gutierrez were useful, but other platoon pieces were never given the chance to gel. The club abandoned some ingredients in the experiment (Rickie Weeks) and refused to play others (Justin Ruggiano). The drafting and development failures of the past reared their heads, like particularly vindictive versions of the ghosts of Christmas Past and Future. The minors offered no spirited young reserves, ready to stand for battle. The front office showed a maddening tendency to identify the roster's weaknesses, only to fail to commit to its own solutions. It traded for Welington Castillo to spell Mike Zunino, only to trade Castillo away for Mark Trumbo. It all smacked of a man tinkering around the edges, outmatched by his own mess. Jack had outplayed himself. Finally confronted with the manifestations of years of slow collapse, all he could do was weight his pockets with failed closers and journeymen, and wade out, waiting for the end to come.

✦✦✦

Ownership's patience finally depleted, the Mariners exiled Zduriencik to television, and appointed Jerry Dipoto. Where Zduriencik was all harsh edges, Jerry is cheerful optimization. Where Jack was unreadable, Dipoto is your indomitable high school chemistry teacher, keen to tell you how he assembled this great baseball experiment. The contours of his plan conform to the dimensions of Safeco. The needs Dipoto identified are logical: playing better defense, getting on base, controlling the strike zone. He's sought to lengthen the line-up while keeping the long term financial commitments short. To wrench the team free from black holes. He's endeavored to raise the floor while slyly speculating on how high the ceiling can go. Confronted with limited talent and treasure to effect these changes, he has largely focused his offseason on players who personify one facet of the plan and placed concurrent bets on regression to make up the rest. It all makes a tremendous amount of sense.

The question doesn't seem to be whether Dipoto can properly identify what is needed to win at Safeco; it's whether he'll be able to make good on it in time to leverage the best of what remains of the Felix-Cano-Cruz-Seager core. But the parallels between this incarnation of the Mariners and the last are there for the fan brave (or damaged) enough to look. The promises of change are discomfiting in their familiarity. The accolades heaped on a baseball town yearning to be free did nothing to dispel the specter of irrelevance for the previous administration. The last flurry of activity brought Chone Figgins. The great fear among fans of the franchise isn't that the team will fail but that Jerry Dipoto's great machine will prove to be assembled from the same frayed wires and broken down gears. That he will reveal his own white whales as crippling to the franchise as Zduriencik's.

One of the tricky things about new general managers is that the moment we are presented with the clearest articulation of their baseball philosophy is also the moment when we are most limited in our capacity to judge and evaluate. It takes a long time to, as Dipoto would say, "get to know their baseball." So we are left with our memories and our doubt. We long to push ahead, but lack the landmarks requisite to navigate. Our task becomes not letting that doubt consume us. Zduriencik was revealed to be a false dawn, but Dipoto is a new day. The outcome might be exactly the same, but the fresh process means it will almost certainly feel different. The stakes for the franchise aren't just the next few years. The stakes are the fans' ability to build new moments to push back the doubt, a slow the reclamation of optimism amidst all the new ways to be disappointed. Maybe it will all hang together. Maybe Dipoto's bets will cash out, and he'll be able to begin to repay some of the years of bad and worse. Maybe the farm will be replanted and redeveloped, and Mariners fans will learn what good prospects can do. Maybe. In this moment, stuck between the unknowable future and the regrettable past, the great fear is that the new, awful, unexpected way to be disappointed is actually that this is all just a little bit of history repeating. That, dressed up with better hair and cloaked in the vocabulary of BABIP and OBP, this is simply another ill-constructed machine. Maybe it is. But maybe, after careful evaluation and warm, microbrewfilled nights, fans will get to know Mariners baseball, and like what they see. Maybe, finally, the Mariners will transcend. ■

—Meg Rowley lives in Seattle, a city that both blessed and cursed her with Mariners fandom. She is an author of Baseball Prospectus and Lookout Landing, *and her work previously appeared on Just A Bit Outside.*

HITTERS

Nori Aoki RF

Born: 1/5/82 Age: 34 Bats: L Throws: R Height: 5'9" Weight: 180

YEAR	TEAM	LVL	AGE	PA	R	2B	3B	HR	RBI	BB	K	SB	CS	AVG/OBP/SLG	TAv	BABIP	BRR	FRAA	WARP
2013	MIL	MLB	31	674	80	20	3	8	37	55	40	20	12	.286/.356/.370	.269	.295	-4.2	RF(149): 2.2, CF(2): -0.1	1.7
2014	KCA	MLB	32	549	63	22	6	1	43	43	49	17	8	.285/.349/.360	.267	.314	3.6	RF(119): -6.9, LF(5): -0.2	1.0
2015	SFN	MLB	33	392	42	12	3	5	26	30	25	14	5	.287/.353/.380	.272	.298	-1.3	LF(86): -0.3, RF(2): -0.4	1.1
2016	*SEA*	*MLB*	*34*	*649*	*77*	*25*	*3*	*6*	*50*	*48*	*65*	*21*	*9*	*.266/.330/.354*	*.258*	*.283*	*-0.6*	*LF 3*	*2.1*
2017	*SEA*	*MLB*	*35*	*428*	*45*	*16*	*2*	*4*	*37*	*31*	*46*	*12*	*6*	*.259/.322/.344*	*.251*	*.278*	*0.0*	*LF 2*	*1.3*

Breakout: 2% Improve: 35% Collapse: 7% Attrition: 10% MLB: 92% *Comparables: Juan Pierre, Luis Castillo, Jason Kendall*

A couple of years ago, Giants radio broadcasters Dave Flemming and Jon Miller invented a synonym for BABIP: Magic wandoo. It isn't a number per se, but a way of celebrating players who put just enough English on grounders to elude shortstops' gloves, or just enough topspin on ducksnorts to find grass instead of leather. Aoki, who flirted with a .300 average despite the lowest hard-hit rate in the National League, was the magic wandoo champion of 2015. The ex-Royal was a handy leadoff man for a Giants club that spent just $4.7 million in a crazed market that awarded Nick Markakis nearly 10 times that much. The two were virtually equal in value last season, and Aoki should be a bargain again in 2016 as long as he doesn't misplace his magic wandoo.

Braden Bishop CF

Born: 8/22/93 Age: 22 Bats: R Throws: R Height: 6'1" Weight: 190

YEAR	TEAM	LVL	AGE	PA	R	2B	3B	HR	RBI	BB	K	SB	CS	AVG/OBP/SLG	TAv	BABIP	BRR	FRAA	WARP
2015	EVE	A-	21	248	34	8	1	2	22	5	33	13	3	.320/.367/.393	.285	.368	1.2	CF(51): 9.6, LF(2): -0.2	2.5
2016	*SEA*	*MLB*	*22*	*250*	*21*	*9*	*1*	*3*	*20*	*7*	*63*	*4*	*1*	*.213/.246/.302*	*.202*	*.268*	*0.0*	*CF 3, LF -0*	*-0.4*
2017	*SEA*	*MLB*	*23*	*308*	*29*	*11*	*1*	*5*	*27*	*9*	*75*	*5*	*2*	*.223/.257/.320*	*.211*	*.274*	*0.2*	*CF 3, LF 0*	*1.3*

Breakout: 0% Improve: 1% Collapse: 1% Attrition: 1% MLB: 2% *Comparables: Charlie Blackmon, A.J. Pollock, Colin Curtis*

A somewhat divisive player among evaluators, Seattle's third-round pick brings 70-grade speed and a hard-nosed mentality to center field. There isn't much pop in the stick, though, and Bishop's ultimate role hinges on how often he'll make hard contact. Regardless, he's the rare minor leaguer already using his platform as a professional athlete for the greater good. In honor of his mother, who was diagnosed with early-onset Alzheimer's, Bishop started #4MOM to raise awareness of the disease. His campaign swept through the Pac-12 and into the Northwest League last year, culminating in the feel-good moment of the summer. On #4MOM day, with mom in attendance and most of the crowd and Mariners brass donning purple T-shirts for the occasion, Bishop lined just his second professional homer. He's a fourth outfielder if everything works out, but he's an easy guy to root for.

Willie Bloomquist SS

Born: 11/27/77 Age: 38 Bats: R Throws: R Height: 5'11" Weight: 200

YEAR	TEAM	LVL	AGE	PA	R	2B	3B	HR	RBI	BB	K	SB	CS	AVG/OBP/SLG	TAv	BABIP	BRR	FRAA	WARP
2013	RNO	AAA	35	23	5	0	1	0	9	2	2	0	0	.429/.478/.524	.310	.474	0.7	2B(5): 0.1, SS(1): 0.0	0.3
2013	ARI	MLB	35	150	16	5	1	0	14	8	11	0	2	.317/.360/.367	.262	.341	2.2	2B(15): -0.6, SS(9): -1.4	0.5
2014	SEA	MLB	36	139	15	6	0	1	14	4	32	1	1	.278/.297/.346	.250	.356	-0.4	SS(16): -2.1, 2B(10): -0.6	-0.1
2015	SEA	MLB	37	72	2	1	0	0	4	2	13	1	1	.159/.194/.174	.163	.196	-0.1	2B(8): -0.2, SS(7): 0.4	-0.5
2016	*SEA*	*MLB*	*38*	*250*	*24*	*9*	*1*	*1*	*17*	*11*	*43*	*3*	*3*	*.255/.291/.324*	*.229*	*.303*	*0.2*	*SS -1, 2B -1*	*-0.2*

Breakout: 1% Improve: 20% Collapse: 27% Attrition: 29% MLB: 76% *Comparables: John McDonald, Jose Vizcaino, Alan Trammell*

The stinging winter rains foretell what we all already know: Willie Bloomquist is gone. But there will be another Willie Bloomquist; there always is. He may have a different name, and a different face, and a different team. But the soul of a Bloomquist is not hindered by mere corporoeality, not as long as there are children searching vainly for heroes.

Robinson Cano 2B

Born: 10/22/82 Age: 33 Bats: L Throws: R Height: 6'0" Weight: 210

YEAR	TEAM	LVL	AGE	PA	R	2B	3B	HR	RBI	BB	K	SB	CS	AVG/OBP/SLG	TAv	BABIP	BRR	FRAA	WARP
2013	NYA	MLB	30	681	81	41	0	27	107	65	85	7	1	.314/.383/.516	.324	.327	-0.9	2B(153): -0.4, SS(1): -0.0	6.3
2014	SEA	MLB	31	665	77	37	2	14	82	61	68	10	3	.314/.382/.454	.317	.335	2.8	2B(150): 2.7	6.3
2015	SEA	MLB	32	674	82	34	1	21	79	43	107	2	6	.287/.334/.446	.285	.316	-2.6	2B(149): -2.0	3.1
2016	*SEA*	*MLB*	*33*	*677*	*80*	*37*	*3*	*22*	*89*	*52*	*99*	*5*	*3*	*.293/.351/.468*	*.297*	*.317*	*-0.4*	*2B -1*	*5.2*
2017	*SEA*	*MLB*	*34*	*576*	*72*	*31*	*2*	*17*	*71*	*39*	*85*	*3*	*2*	*.286/.339/.446*	*.287*	*.312*	*-0.3*	*2B -1*	*1.9*

Breakout: 0% Improve: 25% Collapse: 4% Attrition: 5% MLB: 96% *Comparables: Chase Utley, Ben Zobrist, Aramis Ramirez*

In 2014, despite a dip in his power, Cano still delivered significant value to the Mariners in the first year of his 10-year, $240 million megadeal. However, like a lot of sequels, 2015 failed to impress audiences and critics alike. *Seattle Cano II: Robinson's Boogaloo* featured Cano's worst batting average and on-base percentage since 2008, along with the second-worst WARP of his career. Some of this was the result of a groundball rate that was over 50 percent for the second year in a row, but the real culprit was an elevated swinging-strike rate that cut into his production across the board. On a personal level, Cano had a difficult year. His grandfather passed in March; Cano called him a "second father" in a midseason interview with *USA Today*. He also had a stomach parasite, leading to a severe case of acid reflux, that took some time to manage. A vastly improved slash line after the break hints that while Cano might never sock 25 home runs again, his personal struggles were legitimate and he's far from finished. *Seattle Cano X* might be direct-to-DVD, however.

Steve Clevenger C

Born: 4/5/86 Age: 30 Bats: L Throws: R Height: 5'10" Weight: 210

YEAR	TEAM	LVL	AGE	PA	R	2B	3B	HR	RBI	BB	K	SB	CS	AVG/OBP/SLG	TAv	BABIP	BRR	FRAA	WARP
2013	ABE	A-	27	20	4	0	0	0	1	2	0	0	0	.389/.450/.389	.352	.389	-0.3	C(3): -0.1, 1B(2): 0.1	0.2
2013	CHN	MLB	27	9	1	0	0	0	0	1	3	0	0	.125/.222/.125	.155	.200	0.4	3B(2): 0.0	0.0
2013	NOR	AAA	27	82	12	2	0	2	11	10	9	0	0	.324/.402/.437	.290	.344	-1.0	C(11): -0.4, 1B(8): 0.2	0.4
2013	BAL	MLB	27	15	1	1	0	0	2	0	2	0	0	.267/.267/.333	.195	.308	0.0	C(4): 0.2	0.0
2013	IOW	AAA	27	61	14	5	0	3	11	9	7	0	0	.327/.426/.596	.374	.333	-0.5	C(11): -0.7, 3B(2): -0.1	0.8
2014	BAL	MLB	28	97	8	8	1	0	8	8	19	0	0	.225/.289/.337	.239	.286	-0.9	C(25): 0.8, 1B(3): -0.0	0.2
2014	NOR	AAA	28	254	28	13	0	2	30	23	30	1	0	.305/.366/.389	.257	.338	-2.4	C(48): -7.3, 1B(3): 0.2	-0.1
2015	NOR	AAA	29	301	28	11	0	4	32	32	37	0	1	.305/.375/.393	.279	.335	-1.7	C(61): -2.0, 2B(1): -0.2	1.4
2015	BAL	MLB	29	105	11	4	2	2	15	4	13	0	0	.287/.314/.426	.250	.314	-0.8	C(9): -0.1, 1B(1): -0.0	0.0
2016	*SEA*	*MLB*	*30*	*60*	*5*	*3*	*0*	*1*	*6*	*5*	*10*	*0*	*0*	*.253/.310/.359*	*.249*	*.295*	*-0.1*	*C -1*	*0.0*
2017	*SEA*	*MLB*	*31*	*236*	*24*	*10*	*1*	*3*	*21*	*17*	*43*	*0*	*0*	*.245/.298/.341*	*.237*	*.287*	*-0.7*	*C -6*	*0.2*

Breakout: 2% Improve: 17% Collapse: 7% Attrition: 19% MLB: 43% *Comparables:* *Jose Morales, Guillermo Rodriguez, J.R. Towles*

YEAR	TEAM	P. COUNT	FRM RUNS	BLK RUNS	THRW RUNS	TOT RUNS
2013	IOW	1508	-0.3	0.0	-0.5	-0.9
2013	BAL	584	0.2	0.0	0.0	0.2
2013	NOR	1299	-0.3	-0.1	0.0	-0.4
2014	BAL	2965	1.5	0.0	-0.4	1.1
2014	NOR	6451	-6.7	0.0	-0.5	-7.1
2015	BAL	957	-0.1	0.0	0.0	-0.1
2015	NOR	8315	-0.6	0.4	-0.1	-0.3
2016	*SEA*	*2258*	*-1.3*	*0.0*	*-0.1*	*-1.4*
2017	*SEA*	*8869*	*-5.7*	*0.2*	*-0.5*	*-6.0*

Ah, the ol' Triple-A/backup-catcher-turned-starting-DH trick. Clevenger toiled at Norfolk for most of yet another season, earning only a Memorial Day vacation in Baltimore before the Orioles recalled him for good in late summer. In 10 torrid games as the every-day DH in August, he lifted his career OPS by some 50 points on the strength of a .387 BABIP, then collapsed to a .216/.245/.353 September line that was more familiar to his fans. The Mariners acquired him in December, which saves Clevenger from a life of being Baltimore's last reminder of the Jake Arrieta trade. It's unlikely he'll make enough of an impression to remind M's fans of Mark Trumbo, or Welington Castillo, or Yoervis Medina, or Steve Clevenger.

Austin Cousino CF

Born: 4/17/93 Age: 23 Bats: L Throws: L Height: 5'10" Weight: 178

YEAR	TEAM	LVL	AGE	PA	R	2B	3B	HR	RBI	BB	K	SB	CS	AVG/OBP/SLG	TAv	BABIP	BRR	FRAA	WARP
2014	EVE	A-	21	309	40	17	1	6	28	28	54	23	4	.266/.341/.402	.273	.310	3.2	CF(62): -8.0	0.9
2015	CLN	A	22	257	23	11	2	0	12	19	46	9	4	.190/.253/.254	.201	.235	3.7	CF(54): 0.8	-0.4
2016	*SEA*	*MLB*	*23*	*250*	*24*	*9*	*1*	*3*	*17*	*12*	*67*	*5*	*2*	*.194/.235/.282*	*.192*	*.250*	*0.1*	*CF -2*	*-1.1*
2017	*SEA*	*MLB*	*24*	*397*	*36*	*14*	*2*	*5*	*32*	*21*	*101*	*9*	*4*	*.203/.249/.293*	*.202*	*.258*	*0.7*	*CF -3*	*1.0*

Breakout: 3% Improve: 3% Collapse: 0% Attrition: 2% MLB: 3% *Comparables:* *Daniel Robertson, Darin Mastroianni, Fernando Perez*

Seattle's third-rounder in 2014, Cousino spent the first half of the season in the infirmary. He may have been rushed back to the front, needing a "big" final week to claw his way to a .500 OPS in 57 games at Low-A Clinton. Better known for his wheels and solid glove in center than his prowess at the plate, Cousino still has his supporters inside and outside the organization. With a pretty swing and above-average bat speed, he still has the tools to carve out a big-league career as a dependable fourth outfielder.

Nelson Cruz DH

Born: 7/1/80 Age: 35 Bats: R Throws: R Height: 6'2" Weight: 230

YEAR	TEAM	LVL	AGE	PA	R	2B	3B	HR	RBI	BB	K	SB	CS	AVG/OBP/SLG	TAv	BABIP	BRR	FRAA	WARP
2013	TEX	MLB	32	456	49	18	0	27	76	35	109	5	1	.266/.327/.506	.294	.295	-0.9	RF(102): -6.2	1.6
2014	BAL	MLB	33	678	87	32	2	40	108	55	140	4	5	.271/.333/.525	.313	.288	-4.0	LF(60): -0.5, RF(11): -0.4	4.2
2015	SEA	MLB	34	655	90	22	1	44	93	59	164	3	2	.302/.369/.566	.331	.350	-0.2	RF(80): -4.0	5.4
2016	*SEA*	*MLB*	*35*	*655*	*84*	*29*	*1*	*33*	*99*	*49*	*160*	*4*	*3*	*.258/.317/.477*	*.287*	*.296*	*-1.6*	*RF -2*	*2.9*
2017	*SEA*	*MLB*	*36*	*554*	*74*	*22*	*1*	*26*	*79*	*40*	*138*	*3*	*2*	*.248/.307/.451*	*.277*	*.288*	*-1.4*	*RF -1*	*1.0*

Breakout: 1% Improve: 24% Collapse: 4% Attrition: 5% MLB: 95% *Comparables:* *Hank Aaron, Jermaine Dye, Jayson Werth*

If the baseball universe didn't exactly chortle over the signing of a 34-year-old, one-dimensional slugger to a four-year contract, it at least let out a few hearty guffaws. Cruz had a great year in 2014, but the move to a pitchers' paradise in Seattle and the backlog of week-long hamstring pulls suggested that Cruz would "only" hit 25-30 home runs in his new venue. Not only did Cruz continue to rake at Safeco, but he bested his career high in home runs just 137 games into the 2015 season. While Cruz did hit more home runs on the road, his slugging percentage was higher at Safeco in 2015 than it was at Camden Yards in 2014. While his defense has deteriorated to the point where he shouldn't even be allowed to practice it, there's cause for optimism that the last year of his deal won't actually be an unmitigated disaster.

Franklin Gutierrez RF

Born: 2/21/83 Age: 33 Bats: R Throws: R Height: 6'2" Weight: 200

YEAR	TEAM	LVL	AGE	PA	R	2B	3B	HR	RBI	BB	K	SB	CS	AVG/OBP/SLG	TAv	BABIP	BRR	FRAA	WARP
2013	SEA	MLB	30	151	18	7	0	10	24	5	43	3	1	.248/.273/.503	.289	.283	-0.5	RF(21): -2.0, CF(17): 0.2	0.6
2013	TAC	AAA	30	213	27	16	0	3	25	15	60	4	2	.211/.272/.340	.217	.286	1.1	RF(25): -2.9, CF(2): -0.4	-0.9
2015	TAC	AAA	32	209	34	12	0	7	31	23	43	2	0	.317/.402/.500	.315	.379	1.2	LF(29): -0.6, CF(1): 0.3	1.7
2015	SEA	MLB	32	189	27	11	0	15	35	14	54	0	0	.292/.354/.620	.334	.340	-0.7	LF(42): 3.8, RF(4): -0.1	2.2
2016	*SEA*	*MLB*	*33*	*171*	*20*	*8*	*0*	*5*	*18*	*10*	*42*	*1*	*0*	*.238/.289/.392*	*.250*	*.288*	*-0.3*	*LF 1*	*0.4*
2017	*SEA*	*MLB*	*34*	*211*	*23*	*10*	*0*	*6*	*23*	*14*	*54*	*1*	*0*	*.226/.281/.365*	*.239*	*.278*	*-0.5*	*LF 2*	*0.7*

Breakout: 0% Improve: 19% Collapse: 7% Attrition: 12% MLB: 75% *Comparables: Ryan Spilborghs, Jacob Cruz, Mitch Maier*

Injuries are a part of the game, but Gutierrez's injury history reads like a Greek tragedy of the first order. Gutierrez missed all of 2014 with ankylosing spondylitis, a debilitating arthritic condition of the spine. It was an open question as to whether he would even recover, let alone set foot on a baseball field again. But after a year and a half of rehabilitation, Guti not only made it back, he mashed the you-know-what out of the ball, crushing as many homers as he did the previous four years combined. To call his small-sample slugging percentage a fluke is accurate but misleading; it insinuates a return to career norms. But beneath the hospital blankets and casts, Gutierrez has transformed as a ballplayer, losing defensive prowess and accumulating power. The question, as always, is how long can he stay on the field and on his feet, before Zeus comes and strikes him down with the next tragic malady.

Chris Iannetta C

Born: 4/8/83 Age: 33 Bats: R Throws: R Height: 6'0" Weight: 230

YEAR	TEAM	LVL	AGE	PA	R	2B	3B	HR	RBI	BB	K	SB	CS	AVG/OBP/SLG	TAv	BABIP	BRR	FRAA	WARP
2013	ANA	MLB	30	399	40	15	0	11	39	68	100	0	1	.225/.358/.372	.275	.284	-3.1	C(113): -20.3	-0.1
2014	ANA	MLB	31	373	41	22	0	7	43	54	91	3	0	.252/.373/.392	.298	.329	-0.3	C(104): -9.6	2.1
2015	ANA	MLB	32	317	28	10	0	10	34	41	83	0	1	.188/.293/.335	.230	.225	-0.8	C(85): 13.9, 1B(2): 0.0	1.9
2016	*SEA*	*MLB*	*33*	*498*	*56*	*18*	*1*	*13*	*52*	*70*	*128*	*2*	*1*	*.219/.335/.360*	*.261*	*.278*	*-1.6*	*C -4*	*1.7*
2017	*SEA*	*MLB*	*34*	*388*	*47*	*13*	*1*	*9*	*39*	*54*	*101*	*0*	*0*	*.212/.327/.343*	*.254*	*.271*	*-1.3*	*C -4*	*1.1*

Breakout: 2% Improve: 25% Collapse: 3% Attrition: 10% MLB: 90% *Comparables: Darren Daulton, Gary Carter, Norm Cash*

YEAR	TEAM	P. COUNT	FRM RUNS	BLK RUNS	THRW RUNS	TOT RUNS
2013	ANA	15249	-17.8	-0.3	-1.1	-19.1
2014	ANA	13871	-7.3	-0.3	0.5	-7.1
2015	ANA	11581	14.4	-0.1	-1.1	13.2
2016	*SEA*	*19037*	*-1.9*	*-0.3*	*-1.0*	*-3.2*
2017	*SEA*	*14845*	*-2.2*	*-0.3*	*-0.8*	*-3.4*

As a catcher who takes walks and hits the occasional bomb, Iannetta carries unconventional value in an age when defensive skills such as pitch-framing are at a premium. Formerly below average in framing metrics, Iannetta focused on improving and did just that, ranking fifth in the AL in 2015 with 99 extra strikes, a total made more impressive by the fact that he started just 80 games behind the dish. One can only imagine the value he would have provided had he not been channeling Mario Mendoza at the plate for most of the season. Jerry Dipoto stressed on-base skills in his inaugural speech after taking over as Mariners GM, and proved it by signing him before stepping down from the podium.

Alex Jackson RF

Born: 12/25/95 Age: 20 Bats: R Throws: R Height: 6'2" Weight: 215

YEAR	TEAM	LVL	AGE	PA	R	2B	3B	HR	RBI	BB	K	SB	CS	AVG/OBP/SLG	TAv	BABIP	BRR	FRAA	WARP
2015	EVE	A-	19	197	31	11	1	8	25	21	61	2	4	.239/.365/.466	.290	.326	0.4	RF(38): 5.4, CF(3): 1.1	1.7
2015	CLN	A	19	121	10	6	0	0	13	6	35	1	1	.157/.240/.213	.187	.230	0.5	RF(18): -0.2, LF(10): -2.8	-1.0
2016	*SEA*	*MLB*	*20*	*250*	*19*	*8*	*1*	*5*	*23*	*12*	*90*	*0*	*0*	*.178/.235/.283*	*.194*	*.261*	*-0.4*	*RF 1, LF -0*	*-1.1*
2017	*SEA*	*MLB*	*21*	*331*	*33*	*11*	*1*	*8*	*31*	*18*	*119*	*1*	*0*	*.187/.248/.303*	*.206*	*.272*	*-0.7*	*RF 2, LF -1*	*0.8*

Breakout: 0% Improve: 0% Collapse: 0% Attrition: 0% MLB: 0% *Comparables: Jamie Romak, Chris Parmelee, Lorenzo Cain*

Baseball had never been hard for Jackson. An elite catcher renowned for hitting massive home runs as a prep in California, Jackson was considered the top high school bat in the 2014 draft. The Mariners popped him with the fourth pick, shifted him to the outfield, and watched him play well in the AZL. If not for accidentally using his face to catch a sinking line drive, Jackson would have been promoted to short-season ball as an 18-year-old.

Then, for one month, Jackson could do nothing right. Aggressively assigned to Low-A Clinton out of spring training, he looked lost, making poor contact and, a third of the time, none at all. Along the way, he hurt his shoulder, giving the organization an opportunity to gracefully demote him to a more developmentally appropriate affiliate. In short-season ball, a mostly healed Jackson played like the talented teenager he was. There were moments of frustration: too many whiffs, an eagerness to expand the zone, mental mistakes on the bases and in the field. He was also one of the best hitters in the circuit, slugging eight homers and taking plenty of good at-bats against pitchers two or three years his senior.

While Jackson's frigid start to 2015 put his stock on hold, it's the anomaly of his baseball life. With a strong right arm and a plus power projection very much in play, Jackson has the tools to develop into a first-division right fielder. He looks a bit less likely to reach that ceiling than he did a year ago, but a strong 2016 season—and a new player development staff placing a stronger emphasis on contact—would help re-establish him as one of the top corner outfield prospects in baseball.

Drew Jackson SS

Born: 7/28/93 Age: 22 Bats: R Throws: R Height: 6'2" Weight: 200

YEAR	TEAM	LVL	AGE	PA	R	2B	3B	HR	RBI	BB	K	SB	CS	AVG/OBP/SLG	TAv	BABIP	BRR	FRAA	WARP
2015	EVE	A-	21	266	64	12	1	2	26	30	35	47	4	.358/.432/.447	.352	.414	5.0	SS(58): -1.8	4.1
2016	*SEA*	*MLB*	*22*	*250*	*28*	*9*	*1*	*3*	*19*	*15*	*62*	*16*	*3*	*.222/.271/.310*	*.218*	*.282*	*1.9*	*SS -1*	*0.3*
2017	*SEA*	*MLB*	*23*	*329*	*33*	*12*	*1*	*5*	*29*	*21*	*80*	*22*	*5*	*.228/.281/.323*	*.228*	*.287*	*3.4*	*SS -1*	*1.8*

Breakout: 6% Improve: 14% Collapse: 5% Attrition: 13% MLB: 22% *Comparables: Jose Pirela, Trevor Plouffe, Danny Worth*

The MVP of the Northwest League, Jackson is a better prospect in the field than at the plate. That may sound odd for a player who hit .358 with solid walk and strikeout numbers, but his batting line isn't particularly impressive for a 22-year old in short season ball and it's nothing that Mike Zunino, Chris Taylor and Jamodrick McGruder haven't topped in Everett recently. Jackson simply doesn't have the power or barreling ability of an impact offensive player. Meanwhile, defensively, his tools are strong enough to still make him one of Seattle's best prospects. A plus runner, Jackson has a quick first step at shortstop and a plus-plus arm. He's a natural coming in on the ball and he has above-average range to both sides. He did make 11 errors last summer, a high number that may be partially attributable to playing his home games on a choppy infield baked by an unusually hot summer. Regardless of the cause, Jackson's mistakes should dwindle with repetition. He has enough stick to reach the majors in some capacity, and could develop into an average regular if he hits a little bit.

Adam Lind 1B

Born: 7/17/83 Age: 32 Bats: L Throws: L Height: 6'2" Weight: 195

YEAR	TEAM	LVL	AGE	PA	R	2B	3B	HR	RBI	BB	K	SB	CS	AVG/OBP/SLG	TAv	BABIP	BRR	FRAA	WARP
2013	TOR	MLB	29	521	67	26	1	23	67	51	103	1	0	.288/.357/.497	.301	.324	-3.2	1B(76): -1.2	2.3
2014	TOR	MLB	30	318	38	24	2	6	40	28	48	0	0	.321/.381/.479	.306	.369	2.9	1B(47): -1.2	2.0
2015	MIL	MLB	31	572	72	32	0	20	87	66	100	0	0	.277/.360/.460	.294	.309	-0.2	1B(138): -6.8	1.9
2016	*SEA*	*MLB*	*32*	*488*	*55*	*21*	*1*	*16*	*62*	*41*	*98*	*0*	*0*	*.265/.327/.428*	*.275*	*.303*	*-0.2*	*1B -5*	*0.9*
2017	*SEA*	*MLB*	*33*	*462*	*57*	*20*	*1*	*14*	*55*	*38*	*95*	*0*	*0*	*.257/.317/.411*	*.267*	*.297*	*-0.4*	*1B -5*	*0.0*

Breakout: 1% Improve: 30% Collapse: 3% Attrition: 8% MLB: 95% *Comparables: Mike Sweeney, Paul Konerko, Michael Cuddyer*

Lind isn't complicated. He bludgeons right-handed pitching, flails helplessly against southpaws, and is a health risk due to his back. When he's limber and shielded from lefties, he's an easy two-win player and someone who can provide above-average production for a contender on the cheap. He's basically Lucas Duda without the lucky 2015 season against lefties to inflate his perceived value (and before you argue, Duda had a 31.8 percent strikeout rate and .378 BABIP versus southpaws). In fact, Lind had a better OPS against righties than Adrian Gonzalez, Buster Posey, Brandon Belt, Lucas Duda, Albert Pujols, and Carlos Santana—which makes him one of the most underrated hitters in the game. Some days.

Tyler Marlette C

Born: 1/23/93 Age: 23 Bats: R Throws: R Height: 5'11" Weight: 195

YEAR	TEAM	LVL	AGE	PA	R	2B	3B	HR	RBI	BB	K	SB	CS	AVG/OBP/SLG	TAv	BABIP	BRR	FRAA	WARP
2013	CLN	A	20	297	36	17	2	6	37	24	53	10	4	.304/.367/.448	.291	.360	0.4	C(73): 1.3	2.6
2014	HDS	A+	21	339	51	23	0	15	49	24	61	9	2	.301/.351/.519	.289	.332	0.0	C(70): 0.6, C(7): 0.6	2.7
2014	WTN	AA	21	36	3	2	0	2	2	4	10	0	1	.250/.333/.500	.288	.300	-0.4	C(9): -0.1	0.2
2015	WTN	AA	22	188	15	13	1	3	12	10	31	0	0	.258/.298/.393	.233	.299	-0.5	C(40): -0.7, 1B(1): -0.0	0.1
2015	BAK	A+	22	162	17	5	1	5	20	12	35	2	1	.216/.284/.365	.268	.250	-0.9	C(33): -0.3	0.7
2016	*SEA*	*MLB*	*23*	*250*	*24*	*11*	*1*	*7*	*28*	*13*	*63*	*1*	*1*	*.228/.270/.367*	*.234*	*.280*	*-0.3*	*C -7, 1B -0*	*-0.4*
2017	*SEA*	*MLB*	*24*	*272*	*29*	*11*	*1*	*7*	*29*	*15*	*71*	*2*	*1*	*.224/.268/.358*	*.230*	*.280*	*-0.4*	*C -7, 1B 0*	*0.2*

Breakout: 7% Improve: 21% Collapse: 5% Attrition: 19% MLB: 31% *Comparables: Jeff Mathis, Jonathan Lucroy, Austin Romine*

YEAR	TEAM	P. COUNT	FRM RUNS	BLK RUNS	THRW RUNS	TOT RUNS
2015	WTN	5873	0.5	0.0	-0.5	0.1
2016	*SEA*	*8557*	*-5.4*	*-0.2*	*-1.0*	*-6.6*
2017	*SEA*	*9296*	*-6.1*	*-0.2*	*-1.0*	*-7.3*

Marlette took his time getting going last season, weathering the Mariner Organization Flu for two months, but the underlying tools supporting his game haven't diminished. He has an efficient swing with above-average bat speed, good feel for the barrel and just enough loft to suggest he could hit for some power. Behind the plate, Marlette looks, well, like the stocky converted infielder he is. His footwork remains a work in progress, and in a time where framing is more valuable than ever, he'll have to work hard to improve his presentation. At 23, he has plenty of time to develop into an offense-minded backup.

Ketel Marte SS

Born: 10/12/93 Age: 22 Bats: B Throws: R Height: 6'1" Weight: 165

YEAR	TEAM	LVL	AGE	PA	R	2B	3B	HR	RBI	BB	K	SB	CS	AVG/OBP/SLG	TAv	BABIP	BRR	FRAA	WARP
2013	HDS	A+	19	92	18	0	2	1	8	4	11	4	3	.256/.289/.337	.244	.284	1.6	SS(15): -1.1, 2B(2): 0.3	0.3
2013	CLN	A	19	406	61	15	5	0	29	15	39	16	8	.304/.330/.370	.263	.336	-1.3	SS(70): 2.7, 2B(24): -1.7	1.7
2014	TAC	AAA	20	90	16	5	0	2	9	8	13	6	0	.313/.367/.450	.297	.343	1.2	SS(19): 3.3	1.2
2014	WTN	AA	20	472	63	27	6	2	46	19	65	23	10	.302/.329/.404	.265	.346	0.2	SS(102): -4.5, 2B(7): 2.0	2.0
2015	SEA	MLB	21	247	25	14	3	2	17	24	43	8	4	.283/.351/.402	.289	.341	-0.5	SS(51): 4.6, 2B(4): 0.4	2.2
2015	TAC	AAA	21	287	41	12	2	3	29	20	32	20	3	.314/.359/.410	.279	.345	3.3	SS(49): 0.1, 2B(14): 0.3	2.1
2016	*SEA*	*MLB*	*22*	*562*	*63*	*24*	*4*	*5*	*42*	*25*	*103*	*20*	*7*	*.262/.294/.354*	*.239*	*.308*	*-0.3*	*SS 2*	*1.7*
2017	*SEA*	*MLB*	*23*	*589*	*59*	*24*	*4*	*7*	*53*	*29*	*104*	*22*	*8*	*.263/.300/.359*	*.244*	*.307*	*0.7*	*SS 2*	*3.0*

Breakout: 5% Improve: 34% Collapse: 12% Attrition: 24% MLB: 54% *Comparables: Tyler Pastornicky, Jose Ramirez, Jose Altuve*

Marte's big deficiency going into the season was his plate discipline, but he made strides in this area: Not only did he refine his knowledge of the strike zone, he also fought off tough pitches in the zone while waiting for a hitter's pitch. There was some talk that Marte would play center field upon his promotion, but instead teammate Brad Miller was pushed to the outfield and Marte was handed the shortstop job. The knock on him defensively was on his arm, but the overall package played in his short stint. Marte has no power to speak of, and it is quite possible that we've seen the best his offense has to offer, but a .270 TAv with 20-25 steals and good defense aren't worthless in this era. If Marte can merely duplicate his 2015 production, the M's would be content to add his name to the bottom of lineup and worry about other things.

Leonys Martin CF

Born: 3/6/88 Age: 28 Bats: L Throws: R Height: 6'2" Weight: 200

YEAR	TEAM	LVL	AGE	PA	R	2B	3B	HR	RBI	BB	K	SB	CS	AVG/OBP/SLG	TAv	BABIP	BRR	FRAA	WARP
2013	TEX	MLB	25	508	66	21	6	8	49	28	104	36	9	.260/.313/.385	.256	.319	4.1	CF(127): 8.1, RF(21): -1.5	2.4
2014	TEX	MLB	26	583	68	13	7	7	40	39	114	31	12	.274/.325/.364	.259	.336	4.3	CF(152): 18.4	4.3
2015	TEX	MLB	27	310	26	12	0	5	25	16	69	14	5	.219/.264/.313	.210	.270	1.4	CF(92): 11.6	0.7
2015	ROU	AAA	27	43	7	3	0	2	4	5	4	2	1	.297/.372/.541	.346	.281	0.8	CF(8): 2.1, RF(1): -0.0	0.8
2016	*SEA*	*MLB*	*28*	*524*	*63*	*21*	*4*	*10*	*48*	*33*	*110*	*27*	*10*	*.251/.303/.373*	*.246*	*.299*	*2.2*	*CF 11*	*2.6*
2017	*SEA*	*MLB*	*29*	*469*	*51*	*19*	*4*	*9*	*48*	*30*	*97*	*23*	*9*	*.249/.304/.375*	*.247*	*.296*	*2.9*	*CF 10*	*2.9*

Breakout: 2% Improve: 44% Collapse: 4% Attrition: 11% MLB: 90% *Comparables: Angel Pagan, Aaron Rowand, Desmond Jennings*

One the few bright spots for the Rangers in 2014, Martin left the team during its playoff run after losing his starting job to Delino DeShields. The Cuban was demoted after a miserable start to the season: The hits didn't fall, and the consequent pressing cut into his walk rate as well, until he just stopped reaching base. He still has speed and remains an excellent defensive center fielder, so he can provide value even without a gaudy batting average. It made perfect sense for the Mariners, devoid of outfield defense as they were, to obtain him in a buy-low proposition.

Jesus Montero DH

Born: 11/28/89 Age: 26 Bats: R Throws: R Height: 6'3" Weight: 235

YEAR	TEAM	LVL	AGE	PA	R	2B	3B	HR	RBI	BB	K	SB	CS	AVG/OBP/SLG	TAv	BABIP	BRR	FRAA	WARP
2013	SEA	MLB	23	110	6	1	1	3	9	8	21	0	1	.208/.264/.327	.227	.231	-0.4	C(26): -8.2	-0.8
2013	TAC	AAA	23	82	12	6	2	1	9	8	24	0	0	.247/.317/.425	.256	.347	-0.3	1B(16): -0.4, C(1): -0.0	0.0
2014	SEA	MLB	24	17	1	0	0	1	2	0	3	0	0	.235/.235/.412	.236	.231	0.0	1B(1): 0.0	0.0
2014	TAC	AAA	24	409	55	24	1	16	74	37	79	1	0	.286/.350/.489	.296	.320	-3.6	1B(44): -3.9	1.4
2015	TAC	AAA	25	430	70	18	6	18	85	29	71	3	1	.355/.398/.569	.329	.394	-0.8	1B(82): 6.6	4.2
2015	SEA	MLB	25	116	11	6	0	5	19	4	32	0	0	.223/.250/.411	.234	.267	-1.0	1B(27): -4.0	-0.7
2016	*SEA*	*MLB*	*26*	*272*	*29*	*11*	*1*	*9*	*35*	*17*	*60*	*0*	*0*	*.262/.308/.429*	*.268*	*.305*	*-0.4*	*1B -2*	*0.4*
2017	*SEA*	*MLB*	*27*	*305*	*37*	*12*	*1*	*11*	*38*	*20*	*69*	*0*	*0*	*.257/.306/.423*	*.266*	*.301*	*-0.6*	*1B -2*	*0.2*

Breakout: 2% Improve: 49% Collapse: 1% Attrition: 7% MLB: 79% *Comparables: Chris Shelton, Mitch Moreland, Mark Trumbo*

Douglas Adams once wrote, "A life that is burdened with expectations is a heavy life." This quote could easily have been written with Montero in mind. The former top prospect has spent years struggling to put the pieces back together after it became apparent that he was never going to fake being a catcher. While Montero must take ownership for some of these failings, he was pushed hard at every level by both the Yankees and the Mariners in an effort to try and make him something he was not time and time again. The biggest what-if of Montero's career revolves around the notion that perhaps if the Yankees had given up on the idea of Montero catching earlier he could have concentrated on his hitting and become a solid citizen in the majors. He had his best year in the minors at Tacoma at the remotely tender age of 25, so while Montero is never going to scale the heights, he could emerge somewhere in the majors, even if only as a part-time power bat.

Gareth Morgan OF

Born: 4/12/96 Age: 20 Bats: R Throws: R Height: 6'4" Weight: 220

YEAR	TEAM	LVL	AGE	PA	R	2B	3B	HR	RBI	BB	K	SB	CS	AVG/OBP/SLG	TAv	BABIP	BRR	FRAA	WARP
2016	*SEA*	*MLB*	*20*	*250*	*17*	*7*	*1*	*5*	*22*	*8*	*99*	*0*	*0*	*.170/.200/.267*	*.173*	*.259*	*-0.3*	*CF -1, LF 2*	*-1.4*
2017	*SEA*	*MLB*	*21*	*341*	*30*	*10*	*2*	*7*	*30*	*14*	*134*	*1*	*0*	*.185/.223/.291*	*.190*	*.283*	*-0.4*	*CF -1, LF 2*	*1.1*

Breakout: 0% Improve: 0% Collapse: 0% Attrition: 0% MLB: 0% *Comparables: Keon Broxton, Jordan Schafer, Dexter Fowler*

Those looking for evidence of a sophomore breakout from last season's second-round pick will take no solace in Morgan's stat line. Once again, he struggled to translate his immense raw power into game action, and his 36.9 percent strikeout ratio topped the league among players with 150 plate apperances. Still, club officials say Morgan made progress in his second spin through the AZL, looking more comfortable and taking better at-bats as the season progressed. The Mariners will probably keep him at their complex until he hits in games, with an eye toward a late season promotion to short-season ball.

Tyler O'Neill OF

Born: 6/22/95 Age: 21 Bats: R Throws: R Height: 5'11" Weight: 210

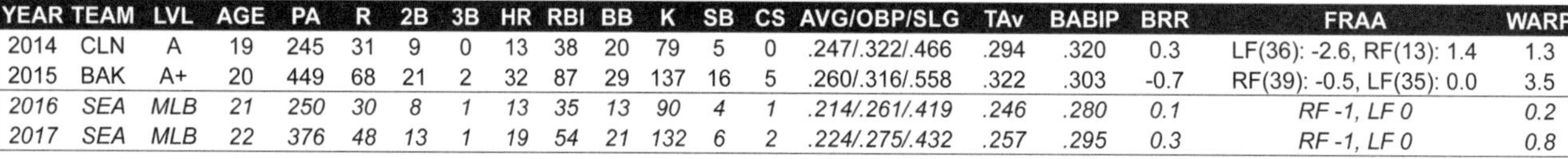

YEAR	TEAM	LVL	AGE	PA	R	2B	3B	HR	RBI	BB	K	SB	CS	AVG/OBP/SLG	TAv	BABIP	BRR	FRAA	WARP
2014	CLN	A	19	245	31	9	0	13	38	20	79	5	0	.247/.322/.466	.294	.320	0.3	LF(36): -2.6, RF(13): 1.4	1.3
2015	BAK	A+	20	449	68	21	2	32	87	29	137	16	5	.260/.316/.558	.322	.303	-0.7	RF(39): -0.5, LF(35): 0.0	3.5
2016	*SEA*	*MLB*	*21*	*250*	*30*	*8*	*1*	*13*	*35*	*13*	*90*	*4*	*1*	*.214/.261/.419*	*.246*	*.280*	*0.1*	*RF -1, LF 0*	*0.2*
2017	*SEA*	*MLB*	*22*	*376*	*48*	*13*	*1*	*19*	*54*	*21*	*132*	*6*	*2*	*.224/.275/.432*	*.257*	*.295*	*0.3*	*RF -1, LF 0*	*0.8*

Breakout: 4% Improve: 18% Collapse: 12% Attrition: 13% MLB: 36% *Comparables: Domingo Santana, Jay Bruce, Javier Baez*

O'Neill is as intense as they come. He's a gamer and a workout warrior with big arms, a big swing and, at least on occasion, a big temper. Famously, he missed several weeks in 2014 after an ill-advised swipe at a concrete wall left him with a broken hand. Lazy as it is, it's tempting to compare O'Neill's personality with his physical tools. He has a cannon for an arm, plus-plus raw power and a violent swing that produces whiffs and homers in bunches. At this stage of his development, he thinks he can smash everything out of the park, and last year, Cal League pitchers didn't exactly prove him wrong. The fourth-youngest player in the league, O'Neill topped the circuit in homers, providing at least temporary justification for all of those strikeouts.

Following a successful stint on the Canadian national team, O'Neill will head to Double-A for a steady diet of advanced breaking balls. He's a tough prospect to bet on, as his power and lack of plate discipline are respectively tantalizing and concerning in roughly equal measure. Whether he can tame his instinct to swing at everything that moves enough to provide value as a power-hitting right fielder remains an open question. He may ultimately hack himself into a Pegueroan Quad-A career, but optimists can take comfort in his makeup and track record of success against older competition. The Brett Lawrie comps are already stale.

D.J. Peterson 1B

Born: 8/29/90 Age: 25 Bats: R Throws: R Height: 6'1" Weight: 195

YEAR	TEAM	LVL	AGE	PA	R	2B	3B	HR	RBI	BB	K	SB	CS	AVG/OBP/SLG	TAv	BABIP	BRR	FRAA	WARP
2013	CLN	A	21	107	16	5	1	7	20	7	24	1	0	.293/.346/.576	.321	.324	-0.1	3B(21): -1.0	0.9
2013	EVE	A-	21	123	20	6	0	6	27	13	18	0	1	.312/.382/.532	.331	.326	-0.6	3B(24): -2.7, 1B(1): -0.0	0.9
2014	HDS	A+	22	299	51	23	1	18	73	23	65	6	0	.326/.381/.615	.318	.372	1.3	3B(37): -1.8, 1B(8): 1.1	2.5
2014	WTN	AA	22	248	32	8	0	13	38	22	51	1	1	.261/.335/.473	.286	.283	-0.8	3B(45): -1.1, 1B(9): 0.5	1.3
2015	WTN	AA	23	393	39	19	2	7	44	31	90	5	0	.223/.290/.346	.238	.279	-0.9	1B(57): 1.3, 3B(28): -2.1	-0.5
2016	*SEA*	*MLB*	*24*	*250*	*26*	*10*	*1*	*10*	*32*	*13*	*71*	*1*	*0*	*.223/.268/.394*	*.242*	*.275*	*-0.3*	*1B 1, 3B -1*	*0.0*
2017	*SEA*	*MLB*	*25*	*335*	*40*	*13*	*1*	*13*	*42*	*20*	*95*	*1*	*0*	*.223/.273/.398*	*.246*	*.274*	*-0.6*	*1B 1, 3B -1*	*0.4*

Breakout: 2% Improve: 8% Collapse: 14% Attrition: 24% MLB: 26% *Comparables: Neftali Soto, Cody Decker, Tyler Moore*

Peterson had arguably the worst 2015 season of any top 100 prospect who managed to stay (relatively) healthy. He tweaked his swing mechanics a couple of times throughout the year, first in an effort to reach the majors quicker, then to emulate the swing he had in college. Neither clicked, and his slugging percentage fell below Jesus-Montero-at-the-major-leagues level. It's also increasingly clear that his defensive future is at first base, which isn't unexpected but does put additional pressure on his bat to develop. He still has plus raw power, along with the bat speed and hand-eye coordination to be an average regular at first, but he'll have to prove that last season was an anomaly. Peterson's ceiling remains unchanged from this time last year, but his likelihood of reaching it has diminished considerably.

Herschel Powell CF

Born: 1/14/93 Age: 23 Bats: L Throws: L Height: 5'10" Weight: 185

YEAR	TEAM	LVL	AGE	PA	R	2B	3B	HR	RBI	BB	K	SB	CS	AVG/OBP/SLG	TAv	BABIP	BRR	FRAA	WARP
2013	VER	A-	20	245	30	7	3	0	14	26	34	14	6	.283/.364/.344	.290	.337	2.0	CF(46): 6.2, LF(8): 0.7	2.5
2014	STO	A+	21	69	11	3	1	0	11	8	4	0	2	.377/.449/.459	.316	.404	0.3	CF(11): -0.6, RF(3): 1.8	0.8
2014	BLT	A	21	312	43	7	4	3	17	53	49	16	13	.335/.452/.429	.327	.404	-2.0	CF(66): -0.2	3.0
2015	DUR	AAA	22	246	22	10	3	2	18	32	41	7	6	.257/.360/.364	.258	.309	-2.3	CF(29): 2.7, LF(22): -0.8	0.5
2015	MNT	AA	22	276	44	6	6	1	22	29	38	11	8	.328/.408/.416	.302	.385	1.6	CF(34): -0.2, RF(17): 3.6	2.5
2016	*SEA*	*MLB*	*23*	*250*	*30*	*8*	*2*	*3*	*20*	*25*	*52*	*6*	*4*	*.253/.331/.352*	*.251*	*.311*	*-0.5*	*CF 2, LF -0*	*0.7*
2017	*SEA*	*MLB*	*24*	*382*	*41*	*11*	*3*	*5*	*34*	*36*	*79*	*8*	*7*	*.245/.321/.339*	*.242*	*.298*	*0.0*	*CF 2, LF 0*	*1.4*

Breakout: 2% Improve: 23% Collapse: 5% Attrition: 17% MLB: 45% *Comparables: Ezequiel Carrera, L.J. Hoes, Desmond Jennings*

Gritty. Tenacious. Spunky. Relentless. Now that we have all the size-related superlatives out of the way we can talk directly about baseball's newest Boog. Powell blew through the competition at Double-A, displaying the contact and on-base chops of a top-of-the-order hitter. He was promoted to Durham, where he continued to get on base but struggled a bit more on balls in play. Powell has a compact swing from the left side, but don't let his size fool you; he has a decent jab and can punch the ball into the gaps. He does all the things fans love, including diving in the outfield and running fast. That said, he needs to become a better baserunner instead of just a fast runner. A second-tier starter in the outfield seems like an reasonable expectation.

Stefen Romero RF

Born: 10/17/88 Age: 27 Bats: R Throws: R Height: 6'2" Weight: 220

YEAR	TEAM	LVL	AGE	PA	R	2B	3B	HR	RBI	BB	K	SB	CS	AVG/OBP/SLG	TAv	BABIP	BRR	FRAA	WARP
2013	TAC	AAA	24	411	51	23	4	11	74	28	87	8	4	.277/.331/.448	.273	.331	0.6	LF(73): -3.1, 2B(2): -0.2	1.2
2013	HDS	A+	24	21	1	1	0	0	2	2	1	0	0	.278/.381/.333	.229	.294	-0.1	3B(4): 0.3	0.0
2014	TAC	AAA	25	163	26	7	2	12	36	8	28	1	3	.358/.387/.669	.356	.368	-2.5	RF(30): -0.2, LF(3): -0.1	1.8
2014	SEA	MLB	25	190	19	6	2	3	11	4	48	0	4	.192/.234/.299	.196	.244	0.3	RF(42): -0.9, LF(11): -0.5	-1.0
2015	SEA	MLB	26	24	6	1	0	1	3	3	6	0	0	.190/.292/.381	.255	.214	-0.1	LF(6): -0.8, RF(5): 0.3	0.0
2015	TAC	AAA	26	516	77	37	4	17	79	29	85	10	1	.292/.333/.494	.290	.320	-2.0	RF(76): -2.3, LF(17): -0.3	2.0
2016	*SEA*	*MLB*	*27*	*133*	*14*	*6*	*1*	*4*	*16*	*6*	*31*	*1*	*1*	*.243/.283/.405*	*.250*	*.288*	*0.3*	*RF -0*	*0.2*
2017	*SEA*	*MLB*	*28*	*277*	*31*	*12*	*2*	*8*	*32*	*13*	*66*	*3*	*2*	*.235/.279/.389*	*.245*	*.281*	*0.8*	*RF 0*	*0.7*

Breakout: 4% Improve: 14% Collapse: 20% Attrition: 31% MLB: 53% *Comparables: Delwyn Young, Jorge Piedra, Scott Cousins*

On June 3, 2014, Romero came off the bench to deliver a three-run homer, breathing life into a Mariners rally that culminated in a come-from-behind win in Atlanta. Manager Lloyd McClendon rewarded him with a rare start the following afternoon and, the Mariners offense being what it was, hit him cleanup. With a triple and a single, Romero contributed to both runs in a 2-0 Seattle victory, an effort that lifted his season OPS to .632. It proved to be his apex: He had just nine hits over the rest of the 2014 season and played in only 13 empty September games for the team last year. As the new front office reworks the roster, emphasizing athleticism in the outfield, it appears that Romero's days in the organization are numbered. To the extent that anyone remembers him, his legacy in Seattle will be as a poor-hitting corner outfielder who couldn't quite cut it in the big leagues.

Kyle Seager 3B

Born: 11/3/87 Age: 28 Bats: L Throws: R Height: 6'0" Weight: 210

YEAR	TEAM	LVL	AGE	PA	R	2B	3B	HR	RBI	BB	K	SB	CS	AVG/OBP/SLG	TAv	BABIP	BRR	FRAA	WARP
2013	SEA	MLB	25	695	79	32	2	22	69	68	122	9	3	.260/.338/.426	.290	.290	0.9	3B(160): 3.4	4.9
2014	SEA	MLB	26	654	71	27	4	25	96	52	118	7	5	.268/.334/.454	.306	.296	-0.8	3B(157): 20.7	7.4
2015	SEA	MLB	27	686	85	37	0	26	74	54	98	6	6	.266/.328/.451	.279	.278	-2.3	3B(160): 12.6, SS(1): 0.0	4.7
2016	*SEA*	*MLB*	*28*	*708*	*83*	*35*	*2*	*23*	*90*	*57*	*122*	*8*	*5*	*.265/.329/.437*	*.278*	*.292*	*-0.9*	*3B 12*	*4.7*
2017	*SEA*	*MLB*	*29*	*588*	*75*	*29*	*2*	*20*	*74*	*50*	*101*	*6*	*4*	*.260/.328/.435*	*.279*	*.285*	*-0.5*	*3B 10*	*2.5*

Breakout: 0% Improve: 41% Collapse: 4% Attrition: 6% MLB: 97% *Comparables: Edwin Encarnacion, Pablo Sandoval, George Brett*

The esoteric argument about whether or not Seager was worth a $100 million contract extension has faded into the rearview mirror, as Seager put up another strong campaign for the Mariners. He has been so solid for so long now that he often gets ignored when the top third basemen in the game are mentioned. Seager has swatted 20 or more home runs and slugged .420 or better for four seasons running. Add in two consecutive seasons of stellar defense at the hot corner, and Seager is likely to be one of the best players at the position for at least a few more seasons. On a team already locked into players heading into their twilight, Seager's stability through his prime is a major plus.

Seth Smith LF

Born: 9/30/82 Age: 33 Bats: L Throws: L Height: 6'3" Weight: 210

YEAR	TEAM	LVL	AGE	PA	R	2B	3B	HR	RBI	BB	K	SB	CS	AVG/OBP/SLG	TAv	BABIP	BRR	FRAA	WARP
2013	OAK	MLB	30	410	49	27	0	8	40	39	94	0	0	.253/.329/.391	.265	.320	1.1	LF(50): 1.5, RF(9): -0.8	1.1
2014	SDN	MLB	31	521	55	31	5	12	48	69	87	1	1	.266/.367/.440	.310	.305	-1.6	LF(102): 0.5, RF(43): -2.0	3.4
2015	SEA	MLB	32	452	54	31	5	12	42	47	99	0	0	.248/.330/.443	.281	.298	2.6	LF(65): 0.2, RF(55): -1.8	2.0
2016	*SEA*	*MLB*	*33*	*407*	*42*	*22*	*3*	*10*	*47*	*41*	*88*	*1*	*0*	*.248/.329/.408*	*.269*	*.298*	*0.5*	*RF -0*	*1.3*
2017	*SEA*	*MLB*	*34*	*427*	*49*	*23*	*3*	*9*	*45*	*41*	*93*	*0*	*0*	*.250/.326/.393*	*.264*	*.305*	*0.4*	*RF 0*	*0.9*

Breakout: 0% Improve: 27% Collapse: 7% Attrition: 8% MLB: 95% *Comparables: Rico Carty, Hideki Matsui, Carl Yastrzemski*

It's unfortunate when a player gets blamed for the extension he's offered, but it's also seemingly inevitable. So it went with Seth Smith, to whom the Padres decided to give a two-year, $13 milllion contract extension through 2016. He'll spend neither of those years as a Padre; the Mariners acquired Smith in the offseason after the Padres acquired somewhere in the neighborhood of 4,347 outfielders. Smith is what he is: a reliable platoon option who is an above-average hitter against right-handers and a solid if unspectacular corner outfielder. In retrospect, Smith's deal was probably a misstep, but unlike many misguided contract extensions, Smith was less of an overpay, and more of an unnecessary luxury.

Jesus Sucre C

Born: 4/30/88 Age: 28 Bats: R Throws: R Height: 6'0" Weight: 225

YEAR	TEAM	LVL	AGE	PA	R	2B	3B	HR	RBI	BB	K	SB	CS	AVG/OBP/SLG	TAv	BABIP	BRR	FRAA	WARP
2013	TAC	AAA	25	95	10	3	0	0	8	7	10	1	1	.299/.351/.333	.277	.338	1.5	C(23): 6.6	1.4
2013	SEA	MLB	25	29	1	0	0	0	3	2	1	0	0	.192/.241/.192	.162	.192	0.3	C(8): 1.9	0.1
2014	TAC	AAA	26	181	13	7	1	2	16	4	29	0	1	.274/.293/.360	.232	.317	0.3	C(47): 9.1	1.2
2014	SEA	MLB	26	64	4	2	0	0	5	0	17	0	0	.213/.213/.246	.175	.295	-0.3	C(21): 2.8	0.0
2015	SEA	MLB	27	142	9	6	0	1	7	6	21	0	0	.157/.195/.228	.165	.181	0.4	C(50): 3.5, P(2): -0.0	-0.3
2015	TAC	AAA	27	26	4	0	0	0	2	3	8	0	0	.261/.346/.261	.298	.400	0.2	C(6): -0.2	0.2
2016	*SEA*	*MLB*	*28*	*30*	*2*	*1*	*0*	*0*	*2*	*1*	*5*	*0*	*0*	*.229/.264/.308*	*.211*	*.267*	*0.0*	*C 1*	*0.1*
2017	*SEA*	*MLB*	*29*	*165*	*14*	*6*	*1*	*2*	*13*	*7*	*32*	*0*	*0*	*.218/.251/.296*	*.203*	*.256*	*0.1*	*C 4*	*1.1*

Breakout: 3% Improve: 22% Collapse: 14% Attrition: 28% MLB: 56% *Comparables: Drew Butera, Mike Rabelo, Josh Bard*

No one expects a second-string catcher to hit, and there is probably something to be said for a steady defensive hand behind the dish as opposed to a thumper with an iron glove, but even then no-hit doesn't mean zero actual hitting. Sucre's .165 TAv would have put him 31st among major-league *pitchers* (min. 10 PA). Based on Baseball Prospectus' framing metrics, Sucre does offer a good deal of value with his defense when he is starting. His 3.4 framing runs added by count was good for 28th in baseball, which is particularly impressive considering given his limited innings. The conundrum for a major-league team is that Sucre's bat is so bad that it is difficult to justify starting or even playing him, despite his possessing receiving skills of quite of deserving candidate.

YEAR	TEAM	P. COUNT	FRM RUNS	BLK RUNS	THRW RUNS	TOT RUNS
2013	SEA	1064	1.2	0.0	0.0	1.2
2013	TAC	3341	6.4	0.0	0.1	6.5
2014	SEA	2576	2.5	0.1	0.0	2.5
2014	TAC	5608	7.9	0.2	1.3	9.4
2015	SEA	6224	2.7	0.0	0.4	3.1
2015	SEA	6224	2.7	0.0	0.4	3.1
2015	TAC	895	-0.1	0.0	0.0	-0.1
2016	*SEA*	*1185*	*0.7*	*0.0*	*0.1*	*0.8*
2017	*SEA*	*6517*	*3.5*	*0.0*	*0.4*	*3.9*

Chris Taylor SS

Born: 8/29/90 Age: 25 Bats: R Throws: R Height: 6'1" Weight: 195

YEAR	TEAM	LVL	AGE	PA	R	2B	3B	HR	RBI	BB	K	SB	CS	AVG/OBP/SLG	TAv	BABIP	BRR	FRAA	WARP
2013	HDS	A+	22	319	62	16	7	7	44	44	62	20	2	.335/.426/.524	.320	.407	5.2	SS(61): 1.2, 2B(2): 0.0	4.1
2013	WTN	AA	22	300	46	12	4	1	16	40	55	18	3	.293/.391/.383	.296	.368	5.3	SS(39): 4.7, 2B(25): -0.5	3.3
2014	TAC	AAA	23	346	63	22	7	5	37	35	74	14	6	.328/.397/.497	.317	.412	2.1	SS(53): 3.7, 2B(21): 1.9	4.3
2014	SEA	MLB	23	151	16	8	0	0	9	11	39	5	2	.287/.347/.346	.291	.398	2.4	SS(47): 4.0	1.8
2015	TAC	AAA	24	396	56	20	6	4	32	50	61	16	8	.300/.391/.429	.280	.355	-0.4	SS(72): 4.2, 2B(13): -0.9	2.6
2015	SEA	MLB	24	102	9	3	1	0	1	6	31	3	2	.170/.220/.223	.172	.254	-0.6	SS(28): -0.6, 2B(4): -0.2	-0.7
2016	*SEA*	*MLB*	*25*	*64*	*8*	*3*	*1*	*1*	*5*	*6*	*15*	*2*	*1*	*.253/.326/.353*	*.254*	*.331*	*0.2*	*SS 1*	*0.4*
2017	*SEA*	*MLB*	*26*	*300*	*32*	*12*	*3*	*3*	*27*	*27*	*71*	*10*	*4*	*.255/.325/.358*	*.255*	*.330*	*1.4*	*SS 4*	*1.9*

Breakout: 4% Improve: 26% Collapse: 18% Attrition: 41% MLB: 78% *Comparables: Chase d'Arnaud, Brandon Crawford, Brock Holt*

Taylor was an exciting concept heading into 2015: Not only did the Mariners have a two-win shortstop, they had two! Surplus value at any position, given their generally moribund offense, was a happy dream. Sadly, it proved just that. His gap power and fast hands were lauded last year in this space, but pitchers made the adjustments that major-league pitchers generally do and Taylor had the bat knocked out of his hands before getting demoted to Triple-A. Taylor's glove work will bring him back to the majors, either as a starter or as a utility infielder, but in the meantime a third shortstop stole the job. He'll have to bide his time, waiting for another chance.

Austin Wilson OF

Born: 2/7/92 Age: 24 Bats: R Throws: R Height: 6'4" Weight: 249

YEAR	TEAM	LVL	AGE	PA	R	2B	3B	HR	RBI	BB	K	SB	CS	AVG/OBP/SLG	TAv	BABIP	BRR	FRAA	WARP
2013	EVE	A-	21	226	22	11	3	6	27	17	42	2	4	.241/.319/.414	.297	.277	-0.3	RF(45): 0.2, CF(3): 0.1	1.3
2014	CLN	A	22	299	38	17	3	12	54	26	65	1	1	.291/.376/.517	.321	.346	1.0	RF(51): 2.2, LF(9): 0.0	2.9
2015	BAK	A+	23	442	51	17	2	10	48	31	115	8	7	.239/.342/.374	.273	.315	-2.2	RF(78): 8.5, CF(17): -0.2	2.1
2016	*SEA*	*MLB*	*24*	*250*	*24*	*9*	*1*	*6*	*26*	*14*	*74*	*1*	*1*	*.208/.277/.341*	*.230*	*.276*	*-0.4*	*RF 2, CF -1*	*-0.1*
2017	*SEA*	*MLB*	*25*	*336*	*37*	*13*	*1*	*9*	*35*	*18*	*100*	*2*	*1*	*.212/.281/.349*	*.235*	*.282*	*-0.6*	*RF 2, CF -1*	*0.8*

Breakout: 1% Improve: 9% Collapse: 1% Attrition: 8% MLB: 12% *Comparables: Andrew Lambo, Bronson Sardinha, Steven Souza*

When Seattle snagged Wilson in 2013, he instantly became one of the best athletes in the system. At 6-foot-4 and 250 pounds, he's a muscle of a man with a plus arm, plus raw power and above-average speed. Still, the Mariners couldn't have expected him to move quickly: Wilson's hitting mechanics were a mess and he had trouble translating his raw power into game production.

Stanford's head coach, Mark Marquess, teaches all of his players a flat, inside-out swing designed to help kids slap line drives to the opposite field; it's a sound strategy in the college game but a poor fit for a player like Wilson, who is built to drive the ball. The Mariners have spent the past two and a half years re-programming his swing, getting him to lengthen his stroke, quiet his mechanics, pull the ball, keep his head still.

A glance at his stat line suggests he hasn't progressed much, but it's really a case of two steps forward and one step back. By nature, Wilson is a hard worker and a perfectionist. He has the fortitude to try to make an adjustment and the athleticism to pull it off. Mechanical changes aren't easy, and he's endured weeks of terrible at-bats while ironing out the kinks. Consequently, he's climbed slowly, mashing the ball in stretches when everything clicks and showing enough potential to justify all the work the Mariners have put into his game. There's still a chance he develops into a first-division right fielder; just don't expect to see him in the big leagues until 2017 at the earliest.

Mike Zunino C

Born: 3/25/91 Age: 25 Bats: R Throws: R Height: 6'2" Weight: 220

YEAR	TEAM	LVL	AGE	PA	R	2B	3B	HR	RBI	BB	K	SB	CS	AVG/OBP/SLG	TAv	BABIP	BRR	FRAA	WARP
2013	SEA	MLB	22	193	22	5	0	5	14	16	49	1	0	.214/.290/.329	.247	.267	-0.8	C(50): 5.6	1.1
2013	TAC	AAA	22	229	38	12	3	11	43	17	66	0	0	.227/.297/.478	.285	.269	2.1	C(50): 14.4	3.4
2014	SEA	MLB	23	476	51	20	2	22	60	17	158	0	3	.199/.254/.404	.241	.248	1.5	C(130): 19.4	3.6
2015	SEA	MLB	24	386	28	11	0	11	28	21	132	0	1	.174/.230/.300	.196	.239	-1.1	C(112): 7.3	-0.1
2015	TAC	AAA	24	43	7	2	0	3	8	0	8	0	0	.317/.349/.585	.288	.333	-0.2	C(4): -0.3	0.2
2016	*SEA*	*MLB*	*25*	*60*	*6*	*2*	*0*	*2*	*7*	*3*	*19*	*0*	*0*	*.207/.266/.381*	*.235*	*.262*	*0.0*	*C 2*	*0.3*
2017	*SEA*	*MLB*	*26*	*273*	*31*	*10*	*1*	*11*	*33*	*14*	*87*	*1*	*1*	*.202/.258/.376*	*.231*	*.255*	*0.1*	*C 8*	*2.0*

Breakout: 1% Improve: 43% Collapse: 5% Attrition: 14% MLB: 95% *Comparables: Jarrod Saltalamacchia, Jesus Flores, Earl Williams*

YEAR	TEAM	P. COUNT	FRM RUNS	BLK RUNS	THRW RUNS	TOT RUNS
2013	SEA	7049	6.2	-0.1	-0.3	5.8
2013	TAC	7146	15.9	-0.9	-0.4	14.6
2014	SEA	17328	20.4	-1.1	0.4	19.7
2015	SEA	14437	9.9	0.0	-0.8	9.1
2015	TAC	577	-0.2	0.0	0.0	-0.2
2016	*SEA*	*2219*	*2.0*	*-0.1*	*-0.1*	*1.9*
2017	*SEA*	*10091*	*8.5*	*-0.3*	*-0.4*	*7.8*

At least he outhit Jesus Sucre!

For defensive specialists, there is always a fine line between acceptable and unacceptable offensive output. Zunino not only crossed that line last year, but he poured gasoline on it and lit it on fire. His defense and his framing were still fairly positive, but, yes, that's really a .196 TAv. Always one to swing first and look for the ball second, Zunino sort of compensated for this prior to 2015 with his prodigious home run power. That power disappeared last year. Things got so bad for Zunino that the Mariners decided to shut him down early and send him to instructional league in an effort to revamp his swing. He's certainly young and talented enough to recover, but it is entirely possible that his offensive limitations and near-Incaviglian minor-league education will keep him from ever being an every-day player.

PITCHERS

Joaquin Benoit RHP

Born: 7/26/77 Age: 38 Bats: R Throws: R Height: 6'4" Weight: 250

YEAR	TEAM	LVL	AGE	W	L	SV	G	GS	IP	H	HR	BB/9	K/9	GB%	BABIP	WHIP	ERA	FIP	DRA	WARP	CFIP	MPH
2013	DET	MLB	35	4	1	24	66	0	67	47	5	3.0	9.8	44%	.256	1.03	2.01	2.90	2.58	1.6	77	96.9
2014	SDN	MLB	36	4	2	11	53	0	54^{1}	28	3	2.3	10.6	38%	.203	0.77	1.49	2.29	1.78	1.8	74	96.9
2015	SDN	MLB	37	6	5	2	67	0	65^{1}	36	7	3.2	8.7	48%	.182	0.90	2.34	3.77	2.52	1.7	93	96.8
2016	*SEA*	*MLB*	*38*	*3*	*1*	*3*	*49*	*0*	51^{2}	*40*	*6*	*2.9*	*9.3*	*44%*	*.259*	*1.11*	*3.77*	*3.80*	*4.14*	*0.4*	*92*	
2017	*SEA*	*MLB*	*39*	*2*	*1*	*2*	*48*	*0*	47^{1}	*41*	*6*	*3.2*	*8.6*	*44%*	*.272*	*1.23*	*4.10*	*4.15*	*4.50*	*0.1*	*102*	

Breakout: 19% Improve: 33% Collapse: 25% Attrition: 6% MLB: 84% *Comparables: Tom Gordon, J.J. Putz, Joel Peralta*

Benoit was quietly been one of baseball's best relievers during his two years in San Diego, holding batters to a .155/.229/.279 line. The shoulder issues that dogged him in 2014 didn't resurface, and he led the Padres in appearances last season. It's hard to find fault with a guy whose WHIP rose to 0.90, but there were signs of erosion: Home runs and walks decreased, strikeouts decreased, calendar turned. Still, his stuff hasn't deteriorated, and he's everything you dream of in a high-leverage reliever: dominant, durable, capable of closing if needed. With their refurbished relief corps, the main concern for the Mariners is that they may need to rely on him too much.

Jacob Brentz LHP

Born: 9/14/94 Age: 21 Bats: L Throws: L Height: 6'2" Weight: 195

YEAR	TEAM	LVL	AGE	W	L	SV	G	GS	IP	H	HR	BB/9	K/9	GB%	BABIP	WHIP	ERA	FIP	DRA	WARP	CFIP	MPH
2015	EVE	A-	20	1	1	1	5	4	14	9	0	5.1	9.0	43%	.257	1.21	3.86	3.53	4.78	0.1	102	
2016	*SEA*	*MLB*	*21*	*1*	*2*	*0*	*17*	*5*	*31^2*	*38*	*5*	*5.4*	*4.6*	*34%*	*.301*	*1.79*	*6.30*	*6.27*	*6.86*	*-0.8*	*159*	
2017	*SEA*	*MLB*	*22*	*3*	*4*	*1*	*31*	*11*	*104*	*127*	*16*	*5.2*	*4.8*	*34%*	*.311*	*1.80*	*5.90*	*5.94*	*6.42*	*-1.3*	*149*	

Breakout: 0% Improve: 0% Collapse: 0% Attrition: 0% MLB: 0% *Comparables: Angel Nesbitt, Gregory Infante, Jairo Diaz*

Part of the haul for two months of Mark Lowe, Brentz may prove to be the jewel of the deal. The southpaw touches the mid-90s with a sinking two-seamer and he complements the pitch with a tumbling curve and fading changeup, each of which flashes average. Just as impressive is his ability to throw all three for strikes while maintaining the arm speed he uses on his fastball. Brentz is not without warts. His command comes and goes, and while his best curves miss bats, the pitch is often soft and loopy. Still, a 21-year-old with a good changeup is a valuable commodity and as a player relatively new to the mound—he was primarily an outfielder in high school—he has a lot of room to grow.

Steve Cishek RHP

Born: 6/18/86 Age: 30 Bats: R Throws: R Height: 6'6" Weight: 215

YEAR	TEAM	LVL	AGE	W	L	SV	G	GS	IP	H	HR	BB/9	K/9	GB%	BABIP	WHIP	ERA	FIP	DRA	WARP	CFIP	MPH
2013	MIA	MLB	27	4	6	34	69	0	69^2	53	3	2.8	9.6	55%	.278	1.08	2.33	2.49	2.86	1.5	76	94.8
2014	MIA	MLB	28	4	5	39	67	0	65^1	58	3	2.9	11.6	46%	.331	1.21	3.17	2.14	3.37	0.9	70	94.6
2015	SLN	MLB	29	0	0	1	27	0	23^1	18	2	5.0	7.7	43%	.254	1.33	2.31	4.36	3.14	0.4	112	93.2
2015	MIA	MLB	29	2	6	3	32	0	32	37	2	3.9	7.9	49%	.350	1.59	4.50	3.54	5.81	-0.4	101	93.1
2016	*SEA*	*MLB*	*30*	*2*	*1*	*37*	*49*	*0*	*51^2*	*46*	*6*	*3.5*	*9.1*	*48%*	*.288*	*1.28*	*3.98*	*4.02*	*4.38*	*0.2*	*94*	
2017	*SEA*	*MLB*	*31*	*2*	*1*	*13*	*48*	*0*	*47*	*44*	*5*	*3.7*	*8.8*	*48%*	*.297*	*1.34*	*3.93*	*3.97*	*4.32*	*0.2*	*93*	

Breakout: 30% Improve: 51% Collapse: 30% Attrition: 16% MLB: 92% *Comparables: Brian Wilson, Scott Williamson, Mike MacDougal*

Cishek had an oddball 2015. He started the season as the Marlins' closer, but lost that gig quickly and went to the minors to work on fixing his arm slot. He returned a week and a half later and pitched well enough to catch the Cardinals' eye at the deadline. Them being the Cardinals and all, he went on to cut his pre-trade ERA in half. This wasn't your normal case of regression to the mean, however. Cishek posted *worse* peripherals in St. Louis, a development he owed to declining control. To recap: His ERA was bad when his periphs were pretty good, and his ERA was good when his periphs were pretty bad. Makes sense. The Mariners, somewhat optimistically, signed him to be their closer for 2016, or at least to begin with.

Justin De Fratus RHP

Born: 10/21/87 Age: 28 Bats: B Throws: R Height: 6'4" Weight: 225

YEAR	TEAM	LVL	AGE	W	L	SV	G	GS	IP	H	HR	BB/9	K/9	GB%	BABIP	WHIP	ERA	FIP	DRA	WARP	CFIP	MPH
2013	LEH	AAA	25	3	0	0	13	0	19	18	0	2.8	8.1	62%	.321	1.26	1.89	2.68	4.16	0.1	92	
2013	PHI	MLB	25	3	3	0	58	0	46^2	45	3	4.8	8.1	46%	.316	1.50	3.86	3.98	4.31	0.2	107	95.8
2014	LEH	AAA	26	0	0	3	15	0	16	20	1	2.2	7.3	45%	.396	1.50	4.50	3.48	4.39	0.1	95	
2014	PHI	MLB	26	3	1	0	54	0	52^2	45	4	2.1	8.4	41%	.272	1.08	2.39	3.08	3.36	0.7	95	94.3
2015	PHI	MLB	27	0	2	0	61	0	80	92	9	3.6	7.7	46%	.335	1.55	5.51	4.31	4.75	0.0	108	94.6
2016	*SEA*	*MLB*	*28*	*2*	*1*	*0*	*40*	*0*	*42*	*42*	*5*	*3.3*	*7.5*	*46%*	*.294*	*1.36*	*4.36*	*4.34*	*4.73*	*0.0*	*107*	
2017	*SEA*	*MLB*	*29*	*2*	*1*	*0*	*37*	*0*	*40*	*41*	*5*	*3.7*	*7.4*	*46%*	*.298*	*1.43*	*4.42*	*4.47*	*4.80*	*0.0*	*110*	

Breakout: 27% Improve: 49% Collapse: 15% Attrition: 15% MLB: 78% *Comparables: Wesley Wright, Kevin Jepsen, Evan Meek*

De Fratus was curiously transplanted into a long-relief role after appearing to settle into short-relief scenarios in 2014, and his numbers dropped off precipitously as a result. Only Travis Wood, a former full-time starter who also made nine starts in 54 appearances, threw more pitches in relief than De Fratus in 2015. Apparently unwilling to give the long-relief transition another year to ferment, the Phillies outrighted De Fratus off the 40-man roster following the season, and he elected free agency, then signed a one-year deal with the Mariners. If limited to more typical short-relief outings, De Fratus can hold the mid-90s with his fastball and sling an above-average slider, and given that he'll be just 28, he's a good bet to stick in a major-league role this season.

Edwin Diaz RHP

Born: 3/22/94 Age: 22 Bats: R Throws: R Height: 6'3" Weight: 165

YEAR	TEAM	LVL	AGE	W	L	SV	G	GS	IP	H	HR	BB/9	K/9	GB%	BABIP	WHIP	ERA	FIP	DRA	WARP	CFIP	MPH
2014	CLN	A	21	4	4	2	38	0	66^1	52	1	4.5	10.4	61%	.305	1.28	2.71	2.90	4.20	0.5	91	
2015	BAK	A+	22	4	3	2	28	1	55	46	0	2.3	11.5	58%	.341	1.09	2.13	2.16	2.10	1.9	66	
2015	WTN	AA	22	0	2	7	22	0	25	22	0	3.6	15.5	46%	.407	1.28	1.80	1.18	0.47	1.2	57	
2016	*SEA*	*MLB*	*22*	*7*	*7*	*0*	*22*	*22*	*113^2*	*107*	*13*	*3.5*	*8.3*	*38%*	*.292*	*1.33*	*4.26*	*4.23*	*4.59*	*0.7*	*107*	
2017	*SEA*	*MLB*	*23*	*6*	*7*	*0*	*21*	*21*	*122*	*117*	*16*	*3.9*	*8.5*	*38%*	*.296*	*1.39*	*4.33*	*4.37*	*4.67*	*0.6*	*109*	

Breakout: 7% Improve: 10% Collapse: 9% Attrition: 14% MLB: 25% *Comparables: Scott Barnes, Anthony Swarzak, Derek Holland*

The top arm in Seattle's system, Diaz entices evaluators with a sinking, mid-90s fastball and an above-average slider. His changeup has also improved since he was drafted back in 2012, and the righty has no. 2 upside if he can execute the pitch consistently going forward. Still, he's not a lock to wind up in a big-league rotation. Beyond concerns about his changeup, Diaz must prove that he can throw quality strikes with stiff and unconventional arm action, and that his rail-thin frame won't be an impediment to logging 180 innings. It's not unreasonable to project him as a back-end reliever or this generation's Rich Harden, capable of producing a dazzling run of starts in between extended trips to the shelf. Perhaps that's not such a bad outcome; baseball loves its history and the game glorifies the bright flames who burn out quickly.

Paul Fry LHP

Born: 7/26/92 Age: 23 Bats: L Throws: L Height: 6'0" Weight: 190

YEAR	TEAM	LVL	AGE	W	L	SV	G	GS	IP	H	HR	BB/9	K/9	GB%	BABIP	WHIP	ERA	FIP	DRA	WARP	CFIP	MPH
2014	CLN	A	21	4	4	2	38	0	66^1	52	1	4.5	10.4	61%	.305	1.28	2.71	2.90	4.20	0.5	91	
2015	BAK	A+	22	4	3	2	28	1	55	46	0	2.3	11.5	58%	.341	1.09	2.13	2.16	2.10	1.9	66	
2015	WTN	AA	22	0	2	7	22	0	25	22	0	3.6	15.5	46%	.407	1.28	1.80	1.18	0.47	1.2	57	
2016	*SEA*	*MLB*	*23*	*3*	*1*	*3*	*61*	*0*	*65*	*59*	*8*	*3.6*	*10.1*	*50%*	*.306*	*1.32*	*3.91*	*3.93*	*4.27*	*0.7*	*95*	
2017	*SEA*	*MLB*	*24*	*1*	*1*	*1*	*24*	*0*	*42*	*40*	*5*	*3.7*	*10.5*	*50%*	*.319*	*1.35*	*3.75*	*3.79*	*4.10*	*0.3*	*91*	

Breakout: 3% Improve: 5% Collapse: 4% Attrition: 4% MLB: 10% *Comparables: Jack Leathersich, Cory Burns, Donnie Joseph*

From an organizational perspective, it's a bad sign when your lone representative in the Cal League's All-Star Game is a former 17th-rounder working middle relief. That's to take nothing away from Fry, a southpaw who's grown significantly since he was drafted from St. Clair County Community College in 2013. He had never worked with a real pitching coach prior to joining the Mariners' organization, and the club's development staff helped smooth his delivery and increase the tilt and movement on his pitches. The results have been excellent, as his one-two punch now consists of a low-90s tailing fastball and a knockout slider that flashes plus. Fry breezed through High-A, and after striking out 43 Double-A hitters in 25 innings he's in line to reach Seattle this season. Not too shabby for a guy who couldn't get a sniff from Division III colleges coming out of high school.

Luiz Gohara LHP

Born: 7/31/96 Age: 19 Bats: L Throws: L Height: 6'3" Weight: 210

YEAR	TEAM	LVL	AGE	W	L	SV	G	GS	IP	H	HR	BB/9	K/9	GB%	BABIP	WHIP	ERA	FIP	DRA	WARP	CFIP	MPH
2014	EVE	A-	17	0	6	0	11	11	37^1	46	6	5.8	8.9	60%	.348	1.88	8.20	6.25	5.88	0.0	120	
2015	EVE	A-	18	3	7	0	14	14	53^2	67	4	5.4	10.4	53%	.404	1.84	6.20	4.27	5.10	0.2	103	
2016	*SEA*	*MLB*	*19*	*2*	*5*	*0*	*13*	*13*	*51^1*	*59*	*9*	*5.2*	*6.4*	*46%*	*.307*	*1.74*	*6.14*	*6.05*	*6.51*	*-0.8*	*156*	
2017	*SEA*	*MLB*	*20*	*5*	*10*	*0*	*27*	*27*	*159^2*	*185*	*29*	*4.7*	*6.6*	*46%*	*.309*	*1.68*	*5.73*	*5.76*	*6.07*	*-1.2*	*146*	

Breakout: 0% Improve: 0% Collapse: 0% Attrition: 0% MLB: 0% *Comparables: Jenrry Mejia, Jason Garcia, Adrian Houser*

Scouts and evaluators have been drooling over Gohara's potential for so long that it's hard to remember he's only 19. With a mid-to-upper-90's fastball and an otherwise unrefined arsenal, he's like the first kid in middle school to grow facial hair: By looking 16, he disappoints people by behaving like the 13-year-old he is. If Gohara's off-speed pitches or command ever catches up to his fastball, the Mariners would have a top-shelf starter on their hands. As is, the big lefty's curve loops, his change doesn't change much and he struggles to repeat his delivery. It'll be interesting to see if the Mariners challenge him with another tough assignment or if they let him sharpen his secondaries against kids (nearly) his own age for once.

Felix Hernandez RHP

Born: 4/8/86 Age: 30 Bats: R Throws: R Height: 6'3" Weight: 225

YEAR	TEAM	LVL	AGE	W	L	SV	G	GS	IP	H	HR	BB/9	K/9	GB%	BABIP	WHIP	ERA	FIP	DRA	WARP	CFIP	MPH
2013	SEA	MLB	27	12	10	0	31	31	204^1	185	15	2.0	9.5	53%	.313	1.13	3.04	2.63	3.35	3.8	71	94.5
2014	SEA	MLB	28	15	6	0	34	34	236	170	16	1.8	9.5	57%	.258	0.92	2.14	2.59	2.69	6.1	72	94.9
2015	SEA	MLB	29	18	9	0	31	31	201^2	180	23	2.6	8.5	58%	.289	1.18	3.53	3.69	3.64	3.3	89	94.5
2016	*SEA*	*MLB*	*30*	*13*	*10*	*0*	*30*	*30*	*210*	*185*	*22*	*2.2*	*9.2*	*57%*	*.292*	*1.13*	*3.40*	*3.38*	*3.76*	*3.4*	*83*	
2017	*SEA*	*MLB*	*31*	*13*	*10*	*0*	*30*	*30*	*186*	*177*	*21*	*2.2*	*8.9*	*57%*	*.304*	*1.20*	*3.43*	*3.47*	*3.79*	*3.2*	*84*	

Breakout: 17% Improve: 54% Collapse: 16% Attrition: 13% MLB: 96% *Comparables: Adam Wainwright, Jose Rijo, Jon Lester*

If Felix Hernandez were a sitcom instead of a pitcher, he'd have reached the stage where loyal viewers notice that the show has gone downhill but refuse to stop watching because they have faith in the writers. Felix had always thrived despite a long, steady descent in his velocity, but last year finally saw some erratic results that led to his highest ERA since way back in 2007. There were varying theories on what was wrong with Felix—including an inconsistent release point, an early-season ankle injury that impacted his performance all year, and theories that he was masking a more serious injury—but no definitive answers. While many oohed and aahed at his decline, Felix's DRA was much closer to previous seasons' DRAs than his ERA was to past season's ERAs. In other words, this could be the beginning of a long and gradual decline but it could also be a blip on the radar. If Felix is healthy, he will be more like *Seinfeld* than *How I Met Your Mother*, and should produce quality content—even if it isn't top flight stuff like during the peak of the show—for many years to come.

Hisashi Iwakuma RHP

Born: 4/12/81 Age: 35 Bats: R Throws: R Height: 6'3" Weight: 210

YEAR	TEAM	LVL	AGE	W	L	SV	G	GS	IP	H	HR	BB/9	K/9	GB%	BABIP	WHIP	ERA	FIP	DRA	WARP	CFIP	MPH
2013	SEA	MLB	32	14	6	0	33	33	219^2	179	25	1.7	7.6	50%	.252	1.01	2.66	3.47	3.05	4.9	86	92.7
2014	SEA	MLB	33	15	9	0	28	28	179	167	20	1.1	7.7	52%	.287	1.05	3.52	3.28	3.89	2.0	88	92.1
2015	SEA	MLB	34	9	5	0	20	20	129^2	117	18	1.5	7.7	53%	.271	1.06	3.54	3.71	3.41	2.5	89	92.1
2016	*SEA*	*MLB*	*35*	*12*	*11*	*0*	*31*	*31*	*195^1*	*176*	*24*	*1.7*	*7.9*	*52%*	*.277*	*1.09*	*3.72*	*3.75*	*4.08*	*2.4*	*92*	
2017	*SEA*	*MLB*	*36*	*12*	*10*	*0*	*29*	*29*	*182^1*	*168*	*24*	*1.7*	*7.9*	*52%*	*.281*	*1.12*	*3.67*	*3.70*	*4.02*	*2.6*	*90*	

Breakout: 23% Improve: 44% Collapse: 25% Attrition: 14% MLB: 90% *Comparables: Koji Uehara, Roy Oswalt, Johan Santana*

The first three months of the season were forgettable for Iwakuma, who started off slow and then strained a lat muscle. After a rusty first start back, he was himself again, posting both an ERA and a FIP south of three the rest of the way.He doesn't have the stuff to get consideration for Cy Young votes, but he's always in consideration to be in consideration; he rarely walks batters, and his split-finger gets groundballs when hitters do make contact. After failing to crack the rotation his first season in Seattle, he's been a bargain for the team in both his posting and his reasonable extension. His relatively light workload on both sides of the Pacific should make the slope of his aging curve a gentle one, though his ability to stay on the mound will finally settle the age-old question of whether the Dodgers or the Mariners are better at conducting physicals.

Nate Karns RHP

Born: 11/25/87 Age: 28 Bats: R Throws: R Height: 6'3" Weight: 225

YEAR	TEAM	LVL	AGE	W	L	SV	G	GS	IP	H	HR	BB/9	K/9	GB%	BABIP	WHIP	ERA	FIP	DRA	WARP	CFIP	MPH
2013	HAR	AA	25	10	6	0	23	23	132^{2}	109	14	3.3	10.5	47%	.289	1.18	3.26	3.60	4.04	1.8	82	
2013	WAS	MLB	25	0	1	0	3	3	12	17	5	4.5	8.2	37%	.316	1.92	7.50	8.35	10.52	-0.8	114	96.2
2014	TBA	MLB	26	1	1	0	2	2	12	7	3	3.0	9.8	47%	.148	0.92	4.50	5.74	4.04	0.1	97	96.2
2014	DUR	AAA	26	9	9	0	27	27	145^{1}	142	16	3.8	9.5	47%	.323	1.40	5.08	4.03	4.48	1.1	98	
2015	TBA	MLB	27	7	5	0	27	26	147	132	19	3.4	8.9	43%	.285	1.28	3.67	4.06	4.13	1.6	97	94.6
2016	*SEA*	*MLB*	*28*	*4*	*4*	*0*	*10*	*10*	*60*	*54*	*7*	*3.3*	*8.7*	*44%*	*.284*	*1.26*	*4.05*	*4.02*	*4.41*	*0.5*	*101*	
2017	*SEA*	*MLB*	*29*	*4*	*4*	*0*	*12*	*12*	*69^{2}*	*62*	*8*	*3.6*	*8.9*	*44%*	*.285*	*1.28*	*3.99*	*4.03*	*4.34*	*0.6*	*100*	

Breakout: 26% Improve: 51% Collapse: 11% Attrition: 19% MLB: 76% *Comparables: Dan Meyer, Collin McHugh, Sam LeCure*

A 27-year-old rookie, Karns entered spring training vying for the temporary fifth starter's spot in the Rays' rotation. To sum up how Tampa Bay's month of March went, Karns ended up starting the second game of the season and spent most of the year as the club's no. 3 guy. The right-hander held his own. His fastball-slash-curveball combination was enough to stymie most lineups at least twice through the order, which was usually all first-year manager Kevin Cash asked of him. That said, he proved to be worthy of more on several occasions. The changeup is definitely his third option, and he has trouble getting started, perhaps a byproduct of his body type. Even with just two pitches—both are plus—he has the durability and control to project as a middle-of-the-rotation type going forward.

Wade Miley LHP

Born: 11/13/86 Age: 29 Bats: L Throws: L Height: 6'0" Weight: 220

YEAR	TEAM	LVL	AGE	W	L	SV	G	GS	IP	H	HR	BB/9	K/9	GB%	BABIP	WHIP	ERA	FIP	DRA	WARP	CFIP	MPH
2013	ARI	MLB	26	10	10	0	33	33	202^{2}	201	21	2.9	6.5	54%	.296	1.32	3.55	3.95	4.37	1.3	107	94.0
2014	ARI	MLB	27	8	12	0	33	33	201^{1}	207	23	3.4	8.2	52%	.317	1.40	4.34	3.95	4.29	1.2	103	94.0
2015	BOS	MLB	28	11	11	0	32	32	193^{2}	201	17	3.0	6.8	50%	.307	1.37	4.46	3.78	3.95	2.5	101	93.8
2016	*SEA*	*MLB*	*29*	*11*	*11*	*0*	*31*	*31*	*186*	*181*	*20*	*2.8*	*7.4*	*52%*	*.292*	*1.29*	*4.05*	*4.02*	*4.41*	*1.6*	*102*	
2017	*SEA*	*MLB*	*30*	*9*	*9*	*0*	*26*	*26*	*151^{2}*	*161*	*18*	*3.0*	*7.2*	*52%*	*.308*	*1.39*	*4.15*	*4.19*	*4.52*	*1.1*	*105*	

Breakout: 29% Improve: 51% Collapse: 19% Attrition: 7% MLB: 97% *Comparables: Shawn Hill, Kevin Correia, Anibal Sanchez*

After providing Red Sox fans with Honda Civic–like production in a rotation full of broken-down luxury cars, Miley is set to disappoint an entirely new fanbase. Boston acquired and extended him to provide average innings in bulk, and that's exactly what he did; the Mariners, who relied too heavily on rookie starters in 2015, did the same. It's his price that may rankle: Miley's best-in-(disappointing)-class performance comes not at the cost of a Mike Leake–sized contract, but of two young, cost-controlled assets in Roenis Elias and electric closer Carson Smith. If the Mariners' sketchy bullpen coughs up leads in the eighth, fans will blame this trade; they'll also probably forget to praise Miley for getting them through seven.

Mike Montgomery LHP

Born: 7/1/89 Age: 26 Bats: L Throws: L Height: 6'4" Weight: 200

YEAR	TEAM	LVL	AGE	W	L	SV	G	GS	IP	H	HR	BB/9	K/9	GB%	BABIP	WHIP	ERA	FIP	DRA	WARP	CFIP	MPH
2013	DUR	AAA	23	7	8	0	20	19	108^{2}	111	9	4.0	6.4	50%	.305	1.46	4.72	4.36	4.85	0.2	114	
2014	DUR	AAA	24	10	5	0	25	25	126	117	9	3.4	7.0	51%	.285	1.31	4.29	3.99	4.76	0.6	108	
2015	TAC	AAA	25	4	3	0	11	11	65^{1}	59	3	2.6	8.0	51%	.299	1.19	4.13	3.43	3.61	1.4	85	
2015	SEA	MLB	25	4	6	0	16	16	90	92	11	3.7	6.4	53%	.291	1.43	4.60	4.64	5.05	0.0	113	93.4
2016	*SEA*	*MLB*	*26*	*3*	*2*	*0*	*47*	*3*	*61^{2}*	*61*	*7*	*3.1*	*6.6*	*51%*	*.286*	*1.33*	*4.44*	*4.34*	*4.79*	*0.1*	*113*	
2017	*SEA*	*MLB*	*27*	*4*	*5*	*0*	*14*	*14*	*79^{2}*	*84*	*11*	*3.3*	*6.6*	*51%*	*.297*	*1.42*	*4.61*	*4.64*	*4.97*	*0.1*	*117*	

Breakout: 14% Improve: 31% Collapse: 10% Attrition: 28% MLB: 60% *Comparables: Clay Hensley, Joe Saunders, Adam Warren*

It was an extremely long journey to the majors for the former top Royals prospect, but Montgomery finally made his debut in 2015, seven years after he was drafted and two organizations later. Montgomery showed some promise early, including back-to-back shutouts in his fifth and sixth starts. But the same issues that plagued him throughout his minor-league career emerged soon afterward: Montgomery keeps the ball down in the zone and generates a significant number of groundballs, but he doesn't have much in the way of an out pitch and still struggles to maintain his consistency from game to game and inning to inning. He could survive at the back end of a big-league rotation, but it is more likely that if he survives it will be as a spot starter and middle-to-long relief type.

Andrew Moore RHP

Born: 6/2/94 Age: 22 Bats: R Throws: R Height: 6'0" Weight: 185

YEAR	TEAM	LVL	AGE	W	L	SV	G	GS	IP	H	HR	BB/9	K/9	GB%	BABIP	WHIP	ERA	FIP	DRA	WARP	CFIP	MPH
2015	EVE	A-	21	1	1	0	14	8	39	37	2	0.5	9.9	46%	.340	1.00	2.08	2.29	1.75	1.5	64	
2016	*SEA*	*MLB*	*22*	*2*	*2*	*1*	*20*	*5*	*35^1*	*35*	*5*	*2.7*	*8.4*	*36%*	*.302*	*1.30*	*4.27*	*4.23*	*4.67*	*0.1*	*108*	
2017	*SEA*	*MLB*	*23*	*3*	*3*	*1*	*32*	*12*	*126^1*	*135*	*20*	*2.7*	*8.1*	*36%*	*.312*	*1.37*	*4.32*	*4.36*	*4.72*	*0.2*	*109*	

Breakout: 2% Improve: 5% Collapse: 4% Attrition: 9% MLB: 11% *Comparables: Cam Bedrosian, Ross Detwiler, Abel De Los Santos*

Well regarded for his command and intense conditioning regimen, Moore uses an up-tempo delivery to extract every bit of velocity he can out of his modest frame. He sits in the low-90s with his fastball, and he's an improved secondary pitch from a real breakout. Players with average tools and a plausible chance to take a step forward make for exciting picks in, say, the sixth round. As a second-rounder though, Moore lacks the upside or the polish of most players drafted in his orbit. He has the dedication and mentality to make the most of his skills but his ceiling is a back-end starter and he probably won't miss enough bats to make it work there. For where he was picked, it's an underwhelming profile, particularly for a team that didn't have a first-rounder in last year's draft.

Vidal Nuno LHP

Born: 7/26/87 Age: 28 Bats: L Throws: L Height: 5'11" Weight: 210

YEAR	TEAM	LVL	AGE	W	L	SV	G	GS	IP	H	HR	BB/9	K/9	GB%	BABIP	WHIP	ERA	FIP	DRA	WARP	CFIP	MPH
2013	SWB	AAA	25	2	0	0	5	5	25	14	2	0.7	10.8	44%	.211	0.64	1.44	2.08	3.52	0.4	67	
2013	NYA	MLB	25	1	2	0	5	3	20	16	2	2.7	4.1	36%	.219	1.10	2.25	4.53	3.46	0.3	117	90.2
2014	NYA	MLB	26	2	5	0	17	14	78	86	15	3.0	6.9	39%	.301	1.44	5.42	5.20	5.47	-0.7	111	91.4
2014	ARI	MLB	26	0	7	0	14	14	83^2	71	10	2.2	7.4	39%	.257	1.09	3.76	3.87	3.48	1.3	103	91.4
2015	ARI	MLB	27	0	1	0	3	0	14^1	10	1	3.1	11.9	44%	.273	1.05	1.88	2.46	0.66	0.7	76	91.4
2015	SEA	MLB	27	1	4	0	32	10	74^2	80	14	2.0	7.5	43%	.300	1.30	4.10	4.77	5.11	-0.2	101	91.8
2015	RNO	AAA	27	3	3	0	8	8	50^2	51	7	1.4	7.3	54%	.288	1.16	3.38	4.31	3.60	1.1	86	
2016	*SEA*	*MLB*	*28*	*2*	*2*	*0*	*6*	*6*	*30*	*28*	*4*	*2.3*	*7.7*	*43%*	*.279*	*1.20*	*4.17*	*4.14*	*4.55*	*0.2*	*105*	
2017	*SEA*	*MLB*	*29*	*3*	*3*	*0*	*13*	*8*	*55^2*	*55*	*8*	*2.5*	*7.7*	*43%*	*.289*	*1.26*	*4.19*	*4.23*	*4.57*	*0.3*	*106*	

Breakout: 23% Improve: 55% Collapse: 15% Attrition: 20% MLB: 89% *Comparables: Chris Young, David Phelps, Matt Belisle*

For the second time in two seasons, Nuno was traded midseason, this time from the Diamondbacks to the Mariners as part of a six-player swap. Nuno's desirability as a trade chip stems mostly from the fact that he is a left-handed pitcher who inhales oxygen, but the hope was that the spacious dimensions at Safeco would keep his home run tendencies in check. It worked, but only when he was pitching at Safeco. He surrendered 10 home runs in 39 innings on the road, a number that can't merely be explained away by small sample size. At worst, it is easy to envision Nuno as a LOOGY for the next 5-10 years, based on his radical splits.

James Paxton LHP

Born: 11/6/88 Age: 27 Bats: L Throws: L Height: 6'4" Weight: 235

YEAR	TEAM	LVL	AGE	W	L	SV	G	GS	IP	H	HR	BB/9	K/9	GB%	BABIP	WHIP	ERA	FIP	DRA	WARP	CFIP	MPH
2013	TAC	AAA	24	8	11	0	28	26	145^2	158	10	3.6	8.1	51%	.338	1.48	4.45	3.92	4.91	1.2	97	
2013	SEA	MLB	24	3	0	0	4	4	24	15	2	2.6	7.9	59%	.203	0.92	1.50	3.28	1.47	1.0	89	97.9
2014	TAC	AAA	25	0	1	0	3	3	10^1	13	2	5.2	12.2	53%	.393	1.84	4.35	5.25	5.08	0.1	100	
2014	SEA	MLB	25	6	4	0	13	13	74	60	3	3.5	7.2	57%	.270	1.20	3.04	3.31	3.75	0.9	101	97.8
2015	SEA	MLB	26	3	4	0	13	13	67	67	8	3.9	7.5	50%	.289	1.43	3.90	4.28	4.96	0.1	106	97.2
2016	*SEA*	*MLB*	*27*	*8*	*8*	*0*	*23*	*23*	*131*	*130*	*15*	*3.2*	*7.5*	*52%*	*.297*	*1.35*	*4.24*	*4.22*	*4.60*	*0.8*	*106*	
2017	*SEA*	*MLB*	*28*	*8*	*9*	*0*	*26*	*26*	*153^2*	*158*	*19*	*3.4*	*7.6*	*52%*	*.305*	*1.41*	*4.22*	*4.27*	*4.58*	*0.9*	*106*	

Breakout: 26% Improve: 51% Collapse: 21% Attrition: 27% MLB: 84% *Comparables: Roberto Hernandez, Tyson Ross, Bobby Parnell*

Here's a useful spiritual exercise. Each time you get cut off on the freeway, each time your friend cancels on you or your child screams at you, remember: James Paxton probably just got hurt again. Last year was a house of horrors for the Mariners' starter, who injured his forearms during an agility exercise in February, strained a tendon in his left middle finger in May, and tore a fingernail on his hand in September. The tendon injury was the worst of the three, knocking Paxton out of game action for all but 67 major-league innings. Paxton will be 27 on Opening Day, so while there's still some shine on his potential, it's developing a patina.

Donn Roach RHP

Born: 12/14/89 Age: 26 Bats: R Throws: R Height: 6'0" Weight: 195

YEAR	TEAM	LVL	AGE	W	L	SV	G	GS	IP	H	HR	BB/9	K/9	GB%	BABIP	WHIP	ERA	FIP	DRA	WARP	CFIP	MPH
2013	SAN	AA	23	8	12	0	28	28	142^2	138	7	2.5	4.9	65%	.278	1.25	3.53	3.56	4.62	0.7	108	
2014	ELP	AAA	24	4	6	0	19	13	77^1	98	2	4.7	5.1	59%	.352	1.78	5.24	4.72	4.62	0.7	115	
2014	SDN	MLB	24	1	0	0	16	1	30^1	36	2	4.5	5.0	65%	.333	1.68	4.75	4.72	6.10	-0.6	127	91.4
2015	CHN	MLB	25	0	1	0	1	1	3^1	8	0	2.7	2.7	69%	.500	2.70	10.80	3.46	11.91	-0.3	112	90.9
2015	IOW	AAA	25	7	2	0	15	15	89	83	6	1.6	3.3	66%	.258	1.11	2.33	4.37	5.59	0.0	110	
2015	LOU	AAA	25	2	4	0	7	7	42	57	2	1.5	3.9	60%	.342	1.52	6.00	3.49	4.55	0.1	110	
2015	BUF	AAA	25	0	0	0	3	1	12	10	0	2.2	1.5	67%	.233	1.08	1.50	3.57	4.64	0.0	112	
2016	*SEA*	*MLB*	*26*	*6*	*6*	*0*	*40*	*16*	*112*	*126*	*14*	*2.6*	*4.3*	*62%*	*.289*	*1.41*	*4.97*	*4.91*	*5.34*	*-0.6*	*127*	
2017	*SEA*	*MLB*	*27*	*3*	*4*	*0*	*15*	*10*	*75^2*	*89*	*11*	*2.8*	*4.3*	*62%*	*.298*	*1.49*	*5.11*	*5.16*	*5.49*	*-0.4*	*132*	

Breakout: 13% Improve: 21% Collapse: 9% Attrition: 28% MLB: 37% *Comparables: Tim Dillard, Dallas Beeler, Doug Mathis*

The soft-tossing sinkerballer took a more eventful trip from Chicago to Toronto than Frank Gallagher, and ended up being unceremoniously dumped just days before the Blue Jays clinched their division title. In fact, from November 3, 2014 to September 30, 2015, Roach allowed an earned run for every time he was designated for assignment (four). It's hard to keep going with that ratio for many reasons, the least of which is the constant ribbing from a revolving door of teammates who think they're the first ones to make that super-original marijuana joke.

Evan Scribner RHP

Born: 7/19/85 Age: 30 Bats: R Throws: R Height: 6'3" Weight: 190

YEAR	TEAM	LVL	AGE	W	L	SV	G	GS	IP	H	HR	BB/9	K/9	GB%	BABIP	WHIP	ERA	FIP	DRA	WARP	CFIP	MPH
2013	OAK	MLB	27	0	0	0	18	0	26^2	26	3	2.4	6.4	35%	.271	1.24	4.39	3.90	5.28	-0.2	108	91.1
2013	SAC	AAA	27	3	1	1	31	0	44^2	32	2	1.8	11.7	36%	.278	0.92	2.22	2.16	3.81	0.7	59	
2014	SAC	AAA	28	4	1	16	40	0	47	39	4	1.7	13.8	38%	.337	1.02	3.06	2.38	3.87	0.7	39	
2014	OAK	MLB	28	1	0	0	13	0	11^2	11	4	0.0	8.5	37%	.226	0.94	4.63	5.99	4.72	0.0	97	93.6
2015	OAK	MLB	29	2	2	0	54	0	60	58	14	0.6	9.6	40%	.286	1.03	4.35	4.30	4.60	0.1	81	93.3
2016	*SEA*	*MLB*	*30*	*1*	*0*	*0*	*22*	*0*	*23^1*	*20*	*3*	*1.9*	*9.6*	*39%*	*.281*	*1.09*	*3.56*	*3.54*	*3.92*	*0.3*	*87*	
2017	*SEA*	*MLB*	*31*	*2*	*1*	*1*	*32*	*0*	*39^2*	*36*	*5*	*2.0*	*9.7*	*39%*	*.288*	*1.12*	*3.44*	*3.48*	*3.79*	*0.4*	*83*	

Breakout: 25% Improve: 51% Collapse: 18% Attrition: 8% MLB: 85% *Comparables: Mike Adams, Casey Fien, Jason Motte*

Thanks to Scribner's freakish control, he became the second man in MLB history to allow at least 10 homers in a season while walking fewer than five batters (Zach Stewart did it in 2012). Although the 16-to-1 strikeout-to-walk ratio looks great, the .238 ISO doesn't. Nor does this: If you split Scribner's season exactly down the middle, you get a 2.01 ERA and .322 SLG over his first 27 games, but a 6.91 ERA and .655 SLG against over his last 27. He also melted in anything other than low-leverage situations. Still, there are worse ways to fill out a bullpen and worse fates for a former 28th-round pick. A torn lat sustained at the end of August brought his season to a premature close.

Taijuan Walker RHP

Born: 8/13/92 Age: 23 Bats: R Throws: R Height: 6'4" Weight: 235

YEAR	TEAM	LVL	AGE	W	L	SV	G	GS	IP	H	HR	BB/9	K/9	GB%	BABIP	WHIP	ERA	FIP	DRA	WARP	CFIP	MPH
2013	TAC	AAA	20	5	3	0	11	11	57^1	54	5	4.2	10.0	49%	.331	1.41	3.61	3.99	4.69	0.6	90	
2013	WTN	AA	20	4	7	0	14	14	84	58	6	3.2	10.3	47%	.259	1.05	2.46	2.84	3.37	1.4	77	
2013	SEA	MLB	20	1	0	0	3	3	15	11	0	2.4	7.2	39%	.250	1.00	3.60	2.28	2.10	0.5	102	98.0
2014	TAC	AAA	21	6	4	0	14	14	73	68	13	3.1	9.1	37%	.281	1.27	4.81	5.30	5.28	0.4	101	
2014	SEA	MLB	21	2	3	0	8	5	38	31	2	4.3	8.1	49%	.282	1.29	2.61	3.71	3.96	0.4	103	98.2
2015	SEA	MLB	22	11	8	0	29	29	169^2	163	25	2.1	8.3	41%	.291	1.20	4.56	4.04	4.17	1.7	93	97.2
2016	*SEA*	*MLB*	*23*	*9*	*9*	*0*	*28*	*28*	*148^1*	*136*	*18*	*2.4*	*8.3*	*41%*	*.284*	*1.18*	*3.92*	*3.87*	*4.27*	*1.5*	*98*	
2017	*SEA*	*MLB*	*24*	*9*	*9*	*0*	*26*	*26*	*157^1*	*154*	*21*	*2.5*	*8.2*	*41%*	*.296*	*1.25*	*3.99*	*4.03*	*4.35*	*1.3*	*100*	

Breakout: 27% Improve: 56% Collapse: 17% Attrition: 17% MLB: 86% *Comparables: Gerrit Cole, Alex Wood, Shelby Miller*

After years of justifiable hype, Walker finally logged significant major-league innings for the first time, at the tender age of 22. The results were mixed, but most of Walker's high ERA was fueled by his first nine starts, when he posted a 7.33 ERA. The Mariners worked with Walker to remedy a flaw in his delivery and encouraged him to use his curve more, with positive results. From May 29th forward, Walker posted a 3.62 ERA and cut his walk rate to 1.2 per nine innings. His first-pitch strike percentage increased significantly and his swinging strike percentage increased, as well. He was shut down early due to an innings limit, but, health permitting, is ready to take another step forward.

Nick Wells LHP

Born: 2/21/96 Age: 20 Bats: L Throws: L Height: 6'5" Weight: 185

YEAR	TEAM	LVL	AGE	W	L	SV	G	GS	IP	H	HR	BB/9	K/9	GB%	BABIP	WHIP	ERA	FIP	DRA	WARP	CFIP	MPH
2015	EVE	A-	19	1	0	0	4	3	18	6	0	2.0	8.0	36%	.136	0.56	1.00	2.66	3.91	0.3	92	
2016	*SEA*	*MLB*	*20*	*2*	*2*	*0*	*16*	*5*	*33^2*	*36*	*5*	*3.7*	*6.4*	*25%*	*.298*	*1.50*	*5.17*	*5.08*	*5.50*	*-0.3*	*132*	
2017	*SEA*	*MLB*	*21*	*4*	*5*	*1*	*28*	*15*	*133^1*	*146*	*19*	*3.3*	*6.3*	*25%*	*.300*	*1.46*	*4.76*	*4.80*	*5.06*	*-0.1*	*122*	

Breakout: 0% Improve: 0% Collapse: 0% Attrition: 0% MLB: 0% *Comparables: Daniel Norris, Felipe Rivero, Edwin Escobar*

Drafted two years ago out of the ardently named Battlefield High and sent to Seattle in the Mark Lowe trade, Wells is a projectable lefty who hasn't quite grown into his body yet. On the mound, he hits the low-90s, throws strikes and spins a 12-6 curve with consistent shape. That gives him a chance to start if he can fill out his slender frame and sharpen the movement on his off-speed pitches. He's far away but worth a follow.

Anthony Zych RHP

Born: 8/7/90 Age: 25 Bats: R Throws: R Height: 6'3" Weight: 190

YEAR	TEAM	LVL	AGE	W	L	SV	G	GS	IP	H	HR	BB/9	K/9	GB%	BABIP	WHIP	ERA	FIP	DRA	WARP	CFIP	MPH
2013	TEN	AA	22	5	5	3	47	0	56	51	2	3.4	6.4	58%	.274	1.29	3.05	3.13	4.10	0.2	100	
2014	TEN	AA	23	4	5	2	45	0	58^1	75	3	2.8	5.4	56%	.369	1.59	5.09	3.74				
2015	SEA	MLB	24	0	0	0	13	1	18^1	17	1	1.5	11.8	53%	.348	1.09	2.45	2.01	3.69	0.2	80	98.6
2015	TAC	AAA	24	1	2	4	25	0	31^2	34	2	2.6	10.5	54%	.376	1.36	3.41	3.13	2.65	0.9	73	
2015	WTN	AA	24	0	0	5	15	0	16^2	11	0	0.0	9.7	54%	.268	0.66	2.16	1.68	1.90	0.5	71	
2016	*SEA*	*MLB*	*25*	*1*	*1*	*0*	*27*	*0*	*28*	*28*	*3*	*2.9*	*8.1*	*52%*	*.308*	*1.33*	*3.97*	*3.92*	*4.33*	*0.2*	*98*	
2017	*SEA*	*MLB*	*26*	*2*	*1*	*0*	*29*	*0*	*37*	*38*	*4*	*3.1*	*8.6*	*52%*	*.320*	*1.39*	*3.93*	*3.98*	*4.29*	*0.2*	*97*	

Breakout: 21% Improve: 27% Collapse: 13% Attrition: 31% MLB: 41% *Comparables: Michael Tonkin, Aaron Loup, Kam Mickolio*

Zych is not only the final player listed alphabetically in the Baseball Encyclopedia, but also the rare bird who made his first professional start in the big leagues. Held back by control problems throughout his time in the Cubs organization, Zych smoothed his delivery and dialed back his pronounced head snap at the tail end of the 2014 season, just in time for the Mariners to grab him and reap the benefits. Now, he's throwing strikes and getting whiffs with a tailing low-to-mid-90s fastball and an above-average slider. Of the 497 relievers the Mariners trotted to the mound over the season's final two months, Zych has the best chance to stick around.

LINEOUTS

Hitters

NAME	POS	TEAM	LVL	AGE	PA	R	2B	3B	HR	RBI	BB	K	SB	CS	AVG/OBP/SLG	TAv	BABIP	BRR	FRAA	WARP
Leon Landry	CF	TAC	AAA	25	211	33	5	0	8	27	18	31	11	4	.262/.322/.417	.280	.268	0.2	CF(24): -3.8, LF(14): -0.2	0.4
	CF	WTN	AA	25	36	8	2	0	0	6	3	8	4	1	.333/.389/.394	.276	.440	0.8	RF(3): -1.1, LF(2): -0.3	0.1
Luis Liberato	OF	CLN	A	19	32	3	1	1	0	0	2	10	1	0	.133/.188/.233	.161	.200	0.5	CF(7): -0.6	-0.3
	OF	EVE	A-	19	215	34	10	5	5	31	24	47	10	3	.260/.341/.453	.287	.318	1.9	CF(21): 1.8, LF(18): 1.3	1.7
Erick Mejia	SS	CLN	A	20	27	5	0	1	0	3	0	4	0	0	.269/.269/.346	.259	.318	0.4	SS(6): 0.9	0.3
	SS	EVE	A-	20	149	24	5	1	0	11	16	22	18	0	.282/.361/.336	.257	.339	4.0	2B(25): 1.9, SS(10): -0.9	0.9
Shawn O'Malley	OF	SEA	MLB	27	57	10	1	0	1	7	12	14	3	0	.262/.418/.357	.320	.357	1.0	CF(14): -1.3, LF(4): 0.2	0.5
	OF	TAC	AAA	27	344	50	11	5	5	39	19	47	20	7	.297/.345/.413	.266	.335	1.1	2B(57): -8.1, CF(11): -1.5	0.2
Luis Sardinas	2B	CSP	AAA	22	416	51	17	5	1	33	20	54	16	4	.282/.319/.359	.229	.325	2.1	SS(73): -1.0, 2B(30): -0.4	0.2
	2B	MIL	MLB	22	105	8	0	1	0	4	6	25	0	0	.196/.240/.216	.188	.260	-0.1	2B(16): 0.7, SS(14): 0.3	-0.3
Justin Seager	1B	BAK	A+	23	315	20	17	1	2	22	24	88	2	0	.191/.277/.281	.213	.268	-0.8	1B(60): 0.3, 3B(1): -0.6	-1.4
Tyler Smith	SS	WTN	AA	23	520	40	24	2	3	32	61	85	10	4	.271/.361/.354	.274	.328	-0.6	SS(87): -2.3, 2B(34): 0.4	2.5

Leon Landry's ability to cover center field and hit right-handers should get him a big-league cameo at some point. That's as exciting as chalk but it could be enough to technically win the Brandon League deal. ❖ A fast center fielder with a plus arm and just enough power to keep pitchers nervous, **Luis Liberato** is toolsy but raw. Check back again in 2018; he could be leading off and swiping bags in Double-A, or out of baseball altogether. ❖ A plus runner with enough arm and plenty of range to hang at short, **Erick Mejia** will rocket through the system list if he can maintain Erick-level power in the upper minors. ❖ **Shawn O'Malley** is a career minor leaguer (read: old) whose speed and on-base skills could make him a useful bench player for a number of big-league teams. ❖ **Luis Sardinas** is nothing but Cesar Izturis reincarnated. Although that's borderline offensive—given the .250/.290/.330 profile—it does mean that he should get hundreds inexplicable plate appearances for a half-dozen teams over the next decade. ❖ For three years now, Mariners fans have scoured **Justin Seager**'s page in the hope that he's following in the footsteps of his brothers. To save you the trouble: He is not. ❖ **Tyler Smith** and fellow slick-fielding, light-hitting shortstop Jack Reinheimer were drafted three rounds apart in 2013, and the two soon became fast friends. Last June, the Mariners traded Reinheimer, simultaneously showing their faith in Smith while reminding the youngster what a cruel game baseball can be.

Pitchers

NAME	TEAM	LVL	AGE	W	L	SV	G	GS	IP	H	HR	BB/9	K/9	GB%	BABIP	WHIP	ERA	FIP	FRA	WARP	CFIP	MPH
Dan Altavilla	BAK	A+	22	6	12	0	28	28	148^1	138	11	3.2	8.1	37%	.300	1.29	4.07	4.15	4.98	1.3	101	
Jonathan Aro	BOS	MLB	24	0	1	0	6	0	10^1	15	2	3.5	7.0	19%	.371	1.84	6.97	5.23	7.03	-0.3	107	94.6
	PAW	AAA	24	0	1	2	26	0	51^2	43	2	1.7	9.2	37%	.297	1.03	3.14	2.42	2.01	1.5	73	
	PME	AA	24	3	2	0	8	0	22^1	15	0	3.2	7.7	41%	.227	1.03	2.82	2.78	4.04	0.1	98	
Anthony Bass	TEX	MLB	27	0	0	0	33	0	64	66	5	2.8	6.3	50%	.303	1.34	4.50	3.70	4.30	0.3	103	95.9
Charlie Furbush	SEA	MLB	29	1	1	0	33	0	21^2	9	2	2.1	7.1	50%	.125	0.65	2.08	3.70	1.68	0.8	99	93.8
Mayckol Guaipe	SEA	MLB	24	0	3	0	21	0	26^2	34	5	4.4	7.4	52%	.372	1.76	5.40	5.69	6.67	-0.6	111	95.9
	TAC	AAA	24	0	4	5	38	0	47	49	3	1.9	6.9	38%	.319	1.26	2.87	3.60	3.83	0.7	87	
Logan Kensing	TAC	AAA	32	2	0	1	19	0	32^1	29	1	2.8	7.0	54%	.289	1.21	2.23	3.57	4.34	0.3	94	
	SEA	MLB	32	2	1	0	19	0	15^1	12	2	4.1	7.6	41%	.238	1.24	5.87	4.47	3.58	0.2	104	94.3
Cody Martin	NAS	AAA	25	4	4	0	11	11	60	59	6	4.7	8.7	47%	.308	1.50	5.10	4.67	5.41	0.1	104	
	ATL	MLB	25	2	3	0	21	0	21^2	24	4	2.9	10.0	33%	.357	1.43	5.40	4.45	6.69	-0.5	89	92.4
	GWN	AAA	25	1	3	1	7	6	34^1	24	2	2.4	8.7	51%	.244	0.96	2.10	2.87	2.77	0.8	83	
	OAK	MLB	25	0	2	0	4	2	9	16	4	5.0	3.0	38%	.333	2.33	14.00	10.22	8.93	-0.4	136	90.4
Rob Rasmussen	SEA	MLB	26	2	1	0	19	0	14^1	25	2	5.0	10.0	37%	.469	2.30	10.67	4.36	7.34	-0.4	103	95.6
	TOR	MLB	26	0	0	0	1	0	1	1	0	0.0	9.0	33%	.333	1.00	0.00	1.10	3.20	0.0	100	94.5
	BUF	AAA	26	4	1	1	34	1	42	26	1	4.3	8.6	47%	.221	1.10	2.36	2.99	3.79	0.3	96	
David Rollins	SEA	MLB	25	0	2	0	20	0	25	37	3	2.9	7.6	41%	.405	1.80	7.56	4.18	6.33	-0.5	104	95.6
A.J. Schugel	RNO	AAA	26	2	7	0	9	9	38	65	4	4.0	6.4	44%	.427	2.16	10.18	5.05	6.21	-0.3	109	
	MOB	AA	26	7	2	0	12	12	77^1	74	5	1.7	6.1	52%	.295	1.15	2.21	3.46	3.55	1.3	92	
	ARI	MLB	26	0	0	0	5	0	9	17	2	5.0	5.0	61%	.385	2.44	5.00	6.61	11.44	-0.7	118	94.2
Ryan Yarbrough	BAK	A+	23	4	7	0	16	16	81^1	86	7	2.0	8.2	55%	.321	1.28	3.76	3.93	4.38	1.2	93	

Dan Altavilla pairs a mid-90s fastball with an above-average slider, a combination that will prove more alluring when he's shifted to the bullpen. ❖ Before you ask: **Jonathan Aro** is no replacement for departed closer Fernando Rodney; his last name isn't even pronounced that way. ❖ **Anthony Bass** managed to put together a serviceable if unspectacular season in the Ranger bullpen. His best feature is his ability to go multiple innings per appearance; dominating those innings is not his second-best feature. ❖ **Charlie Furbush** was fulfilling his usual role as Head Lefty of the Mariners' bullpen, but a slightly torn rotator cuff ended his 2015 at the halfway mark and hurls 2016 into doubt. ❖ In what might be his only positive split, **Mayckol Gauipe** posted a 9.28 K/9 ratio in medium leverage situations last year. To keep him optimally concerned, Mariners coaches will take turns reminding him about things like the national debt and the growing threat of antibiotic-resistant germs. ❖ **Danny Hultzen**, Ryan Anderson and Roger Salkeld walk into a bar. The bartender asks, "why the long face?" The three don't answer, instead nursing their Bud Lights and staring silently into the middle distance. ❖ A journeyman reliever, **Logan Kensing**'s journey took him to Seattle briefly in 2015 before the Mariners dropped him off on the side of the road in October. ❖ **Cody Martin**, who attended the same high school as former M's outfielder Dave Henderson, saw his middling stuff get smacked around while attempting to fulfill a variety of roles as a rookie. He can definitely strike out Henderson, though. ❖ A second-round pick, **Nick Neidert** looked sharp in the AFL, flashing the mid-90s heater and surprisingly advanced changeup that earned him an above-slot bonus. A quick Google image search reveals that he was also the youngest-looking player eligible for selection in last year's draft. ❖ It would be hyperbolic to say that **Rob Rasmussen** couldn't get anybody out in his big-league trial last year, but not by much. ❖ A Rule 5 pick from the Astros, **David Rollins** followed a fine spring by being sentenced to 80 days of writing "Stanozolol" on lined paper. The M's stuck with him and he'll fight for a role in this year's 'pen. ❖ Things you can get for 7.99: a whole pie at Marie Callender's, a one-month subscription to Netflix, a large three-topping from Domino's, *The Polar Express* on Blu-Ray at Amazon and, in the case of **A.J. Schugel**—who has that very ERA in 127 career Triple-A innings—a pretty disastrous debut in the big leagues. ❖ Dylan Thompson did all of the right things after the Mariners drafted him last summer, meaning that he threw hard, threw strikes, and enticed at least a couple of executives to say nice things about his hammer-curve. Still, despite a relatively refined arsenal for a high school pitcher, he's years away from the big leagues. ❖ Talk to the right guy, and he might convince you that **Ryan Yarbrough**'s low-90s fastball and above-average command makes him the top lefty in Seattle's system. That's faint praise, and he'll need to sharpen his curve to be more than an up-and-down guy.

Manager

Scott Servais

Yet another new skipper appointed without previous managerial experience. Servais can instead credit his 20-year relationship with Jerry Dipoto and Dipoto's feud with Mike Scioscia as the top reasons he received the nod.

After catching in parts of 11 big-league seasons, Servais retired and has worked in a variety of player-development roles for various organizations. He's never managed, though, and while his communication skills have been praised, there are obvious differences between instructing recent draftees and motivating a player with eight years of major-league service time. Servais has never had to work with disillusioned veterans, or many players who out-gross him. Likewise, he has never had to worry about in-game strategy, how to respond to an eight-game losing streak or where to look for the right way to tell a reliever he's been designated for assignment. You learn those things on the bench, not the backfield.

That isn't to say Servais can't or won't succeed. Just that he doesn't seem like the most qualified candidate from any angle, other than "gets along well with the general manager." Obviously, communication between the dugout and front office is important, and it's something the Mariners haven't had a lot of in recent years—heck, the Mariners haven't had much of *anything* in the dugout except change, with no manager lasting more than three seasons since Lou Piniella left following 2002. Maybe Servais becomes Seattle's Weaver, Stengel or, hell, Scioscia. But based on his curriculum vitae, it seems more likely that the Mariners are searching for another manager come 2017 or 2018.

ST. LOUIS CARDINALS

Essay by Dayn Perry

Player comments by R.J. Anderson and BP authors

"The coldest of cold comforts is the comfort that does not exist, save for in the foul-smelling nooks of one's own head." - Cicero, probably

"'Tis lame-wad in the extreme for a nine of baseball-ists to toil at the row for so long, only to have a more slackened side dry-gulch them when the Acadian broadleafs of the White Mountains are turning the color of the sun's blood." - Nathan Hale, probably

In the sense that anything is possible, the two quotes above are factual and accurate, and they give rise to next 1,900 words or so, which your scribe is undertaking in exchange for redeemable U.S. currency.

So, the 2015 Cardinals ... They won 100 games, the most in baseball. They did so despite playing an unbalanced schedule in sans-merci NL Central. They posted a winning record in every month of the season until an 0-3 mark in October, when seeding was already locked in place and most teams could hardly be bothered. Of the 19 teams they played in the regular season, they posted a losing record against just three of them. They spent 175 days in first place.

The royal we could go on, of course. As you know, though, the Cardinals went into the playoffs with a compromised rotation (Adam Wainwright was in the bullpen, Carlos Martinez had already been lost for the season to shoulder woes, and Michael Wacha had been in a diminished state for much of the second half), and they were defenestrated by the rival Cubs in the NLDS. If you're a Cardinals rooter, then a more lacerating conclusion to a brilliant season is hard to conjure up.

Mostly because I'm in need of a transition paragraph, this raises the matter of those other teams who have lorded over the regular season only to see their efforts come to grief in whatever playoff structure was in place at the time. Now, this isn't to say that the team that posts the highest regular season winning percentage is, ipso facto, the best team in baseball for a given season. For instance, the Blue Jays this past season posted a substantially better run differential than the Cardinals, and the Cardinals had just the 10th best mark in baseball according to the third-order standings. However, wins at a certain point become the

CARDINALS PROSPECTUS

2015 W-L: 100-62, 1st in NL Central

Pythag	.591	2nd	DER	.703	15th
RS/G	3.99	24th	B-Age	28.4	17th
RA/G	3.24	1st	P-Age	28	10th
TAv	.262	14th	Salary	$122.1M	12th
BRR	-6.06	23rd	M$/MW	$2.1M	27th
TAv-P	.249	6th	DL Days	936	13th
FIP	3.50	5th	$ on DL	28%	29th

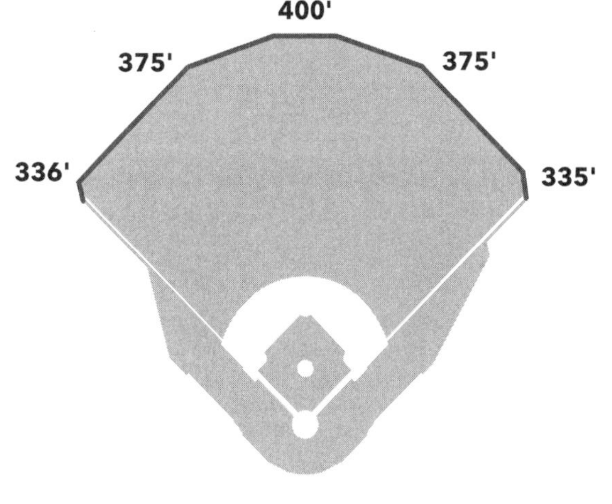

Outfield wall profile: **8'**

Three-Year Park Factors

Runs	Runs/RH	Runs/LH	HR/RH	HR/LH
98	102	105	95	103

Top Hitter WARP	5.9	Jason Heyward
Top Pitcher WARP	2.7	Jaime Garcia
Top Prospect		Alex Reyes

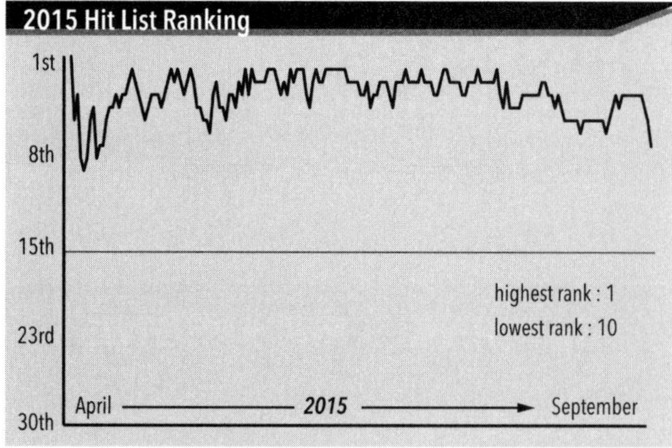

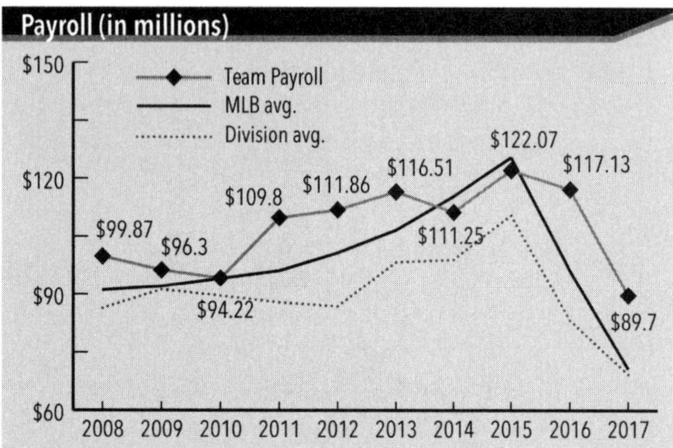

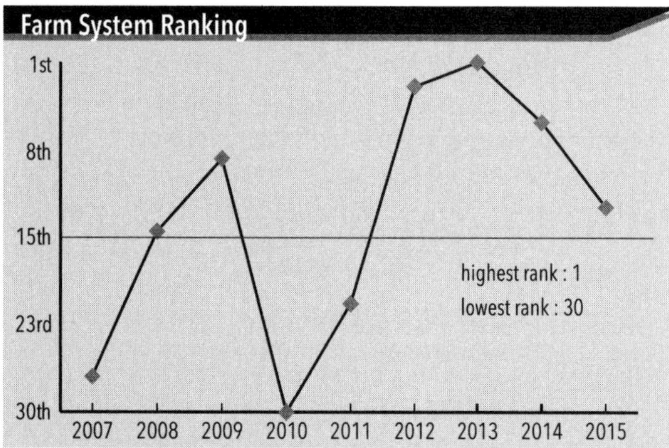

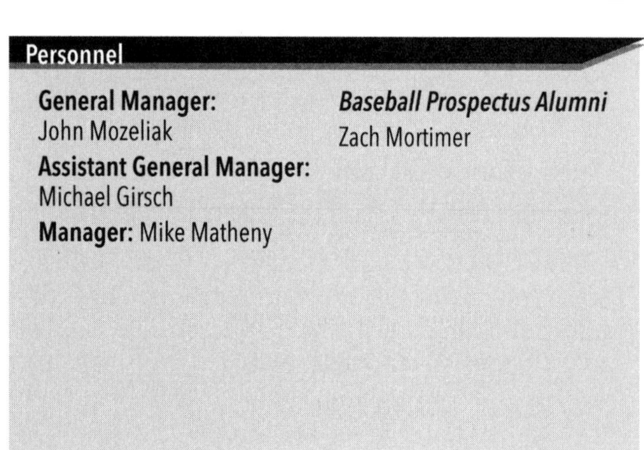
Personnel

General Manager:
John Mozeliak

Assistant General Manager:
Michael Girsch

Manager: Mike Matheny

Baseball Prospectus Alumni
Zach Mortimer

currency of a season, so wins and their grim counterparts inform what follows.

Let us now announce via implied megaphone those teams who have posted the highest regular season winning percentage in a given year but been vanquished by the forces of sample size in the postseason (with possible assists from those rank handmaidens, Fatigue and Malady) ...

- 1906 Chicago Cubs: 116-36, lost World Series to White Sox
- 1913 New York Giants: 101-51, lost World Series to Athletics
- 1914 Philadelphia Athletics: 99-53, lost World Series to Braves
- 1916 Brooklyn Robins: 94-60, lost World Series to Red Sox
- 1918 Chicago Cubs: 84-45, lost World Series to Red Sox
- 1921 New York Yankees: 98-55, lost World Series to Giants
- 1922 New York Yankees: 94-60, lost World Series to Giants
- 1924 New York Giants: 93-60, lost World Series to Senators
- 1925 Washington Senators: 96-55, lost World Series to Pirates
- 1926 New York Yankees: 91-63, lost World Series to Cardinals
- 1931 Philadelphia Athletics: 107-45, lost World Series to Cardinals
- 1933 Washington Senators: 99-53, lost World Series to Giants
- 1934 Detroit Tigers: 101-53, lost World Series to Cardinals
- 1935 Chicago Cubs: 100-54, lost World Series to Tigers
- 1943 St. Louis Cardinals: 105-49, lost World Series to Yankees
- 1945 Chicago Cubs: 98-56, lost World Series to Tigers
- 1946 Boston Red Sox: 104-50, lost World Series to Cardinals
- 1952 Brooklyn Dodgers: 96-57, lost World Series to Yankees
- 1953 Brooklyn Dodgers: 105-49, lost World Series to Yankees
- 1954 Cleveland Indians: 111-43, lost World Series to Giants
- 1957 New York Yankees: 98-56, lost World Series to Braves
- 1959 Chicago White Sox: 94-60, lost World Series to Dodgers
- 1960 New York Yankees: 97-57, lost World Series to Pirates
- 1962 San Francisco Giants: 103-62, lost World Series to Yankees
- 1963 New York Yankees: 104-57, lost World Series to Dodgers
- 1964 New York Yankees: 99-63, lost World Series to Cardinals
- 1965 Minnesota Twins: 102-60, lost World Series to Dodgers
- 1969 Baltimore Orioles: 109-53, lost World Series to Mets
- 1971 Baltimore Orioles: 101-57, lost World Series to Pirates
- 1972 Pittsburgh Pirates: 96-59, lost NLCS to Reds
- 1973 Cincinnati Reds: 99-63, lost NLCS to Mets
- 1974 Los Angeles Dodgers: 102-60, lost World Series to Athletics
- 1977 Kansas City Royals: 102-60, lost ALCS to Yankees
- 1979 Baltimore Orioles: 102-57, lost World Series to Pirates
- 1980 New York Yankees: 103-59, lost ALCS to Royals
- 1981 Cincinnati Reds: 66-42, didn't make postseason because of special playoff structure
- 1982 Milwaukee Brewers: 95-67, lost World Series to Cardinals

- 1983 Chicago White Sox: 99-63, lost ALCS to Orioles
- 1985 St. Louis Cardinals: 101-61, lost World Series to Royals
- 1987 Detroit Tigers: 98-64, lost ALCS to Twins
- 1988 Oakland Athletics: 104-58, lost World Series to Dodgers
- 1990 Oakland Athletics: 103-59, lost World Series to Reds
- 1991 Pittsburgh Pirates: 98-64, lost NLCS to Braves
- 1992 Atlanta Braves: 98-64, lost World Series to Blue Jays
- 1993 Atlanta Braves: 104-58, lost NLCS to Phillies
- 1995 Cleveland Indians: 100-44, lost World Series to Braves
- 1996 Cleveland Indians: 99-62, lost ALDS to Orioles
- 1997 Atlanta Braves: 101-61, lost NLCS to Marlins
- 1999 Atlanta Braves: 103-59, lost World Series to Yankees
- 2000 San Francisco Giants: 97-65, lost NLDS to Mets
- 2001 Seattle Mariners: 116-46, lost ALCS to Yankees
- 2002 New York Yankees: 103-58, lost ALDS to Angels
- 2003 Atlanta Braves, New York Yankees: 101-61, lost NLDS to Cubs; lost World Series to Marlins
- 2004 St. Louis Cardinals: 105-57, lost World Series to Red Sox
- 2005 St. Louis Cardinals: 100-62, lost NLCS to Astros
- 2006 New York Mets, New York Yankees: 97-65, lost NLCS to Cardinals; lost ALDS to Tigers
- 2008 Los Angeles Dodgers: 100-62, lost NLCS to Phillies
- 2010 Philadelphia Phillies: 97-65, lost NLCS to Giants
- 2011 Philadelphia Phillies: 102-60, lost NLDS to Cardinals
- 2012 Washington Nationals: 98-64, lost NLDS to Cardinals
- 2014 Los Angeles Angels: 98-64, lost ALDS to Royals
- 2015 St. Louis Cardinals: 100-62, lost NLDS to Cubs

Woe betide the squads above! Out of 111 World Series, 62 have been won by a team other than the the one with the best record. Stated another way, the team that posted the best record in the regular season has won the World Series just 44.1 percent of the time.

As you would expect, that percentage falls as layers are added to the postseason. From 1969 through 1993—the divisional era in which we had two playoff rounds—just 36 percent of best-in-regular-season teams won the World Series. Since 1995, when the Division Series came into being, that figure has fallen to 19 percent. Lo and also behold: Since a third round was added to the postseason just four teams—the '98 Yankees, '07 Red Sox, '09 Yankees, and '13 Red Sox—have both notched the best regular season record and won the World Series.

On a certain level, this is feature, not bug. If postseason outcomes were strongly correlated with regular season outcomes, then the sport would lose quite a bit of autumn intrigue. Still, speaking subjectively it seems that as MLB has added more and more obstacles between regular-season supremacy and trophy-hoisting, something baseball-ish has been lost.

This is not a lamentation specific to the 2015 Cardinals. Rather, this is a general complaint that what was built from the rudiments over the course of a regular season that spans half a calendar year is so quickly forgotten if the team of note manages to lose three of five or four of seven in October. It's baseball's everyday-ness, its tidal certainty during the spring and summer that appeals to so many of us, and it says here that the team that comes out the other side of that six-month battle royal ought to have more of a to-do made about it.

Let them have a trophy—a trophy celebrating the team that authored the best record during the regular season! Something similar is of course done in the NHL with the Presidents' Trophy and in the English Premiership with ... something. A fatted calf, maybe. The point is there is precedent for handing out laurels based on regular season excellence alone.

Among major sports leagues, baseball is singular in its sprawl (more than 2,400 regular season games) and in the utter unpredictability of its postseason. So think of honoring the regular season winner as a nod to the former and a complement—rather than a counterweight—to the latter.

If any sport should have a trophy that exalts the best of the marathonic (not a word, probably, but should be) regular season, it's baseball. Consider this the belated embrace of one of its most obvious native characteristics. If you're reading this, then you probably appreciate this about baseball—that it's always there. If you're YouTube commenter or someone similarly miserable, then this numbers among the demerits that makes baseball not football enough. Let this stand as a stinging rebuke of that ilk.

To be sure, bestowing greatness upon the team with the best regular season record isn't entirely fair, as we're comparing across leagues and operating in the era of unbalanced schedule. But an impossible precision isn't really the goal of this. Seed the playoffs according to record all the way through the World Series (thus ending the "This Time It Counts" All-Star Game contrivance), and there's a light dusting of incentive for excellent teams to do something more than trot out the back of the engorged September roster in the final days of the regular season.

Alas and alack, it is too late for the 2015 Cardinals to claim the Weaver Trophy, which is what I'm calling it for now, being that the Weaver Trophy does not exist. (It's for Earl Weaver, you see, who helmed many a regular-season colossus in Baltimore. Come to think of it "The Colossus Trophy" would be another good name.) Whatever we call it, let us proclaim the accomplishments of the team that wins the most games in a season.

No doubt, as part of the pushback against doing this, the "participation trophy" argument would surely be invoked, possibly in a Facebook thread that calls upon an elementary-school basketball anecdote. This, though, isn't that. This is rewarding the utter persistence and thoroughgoing excellence of the team that outlasted all others over the span of 162 games. If we're going to give the ultimate belt and title to a team that won 11 or 12 games in October or November before any of nine other clubs did, then why not this? Sometimes—19 percent of the time, as noted—a team will hoist both the Weaver Trophy and the World Series Trophy, in which case the privileges of conquest shall flow like rivers of honey made of cash. Fans of said team would be empowered all across the Internet, which is all any of us have ever wanted.

The point of it all will always be to win the World Series, and winning the World Series will never be dislodged from its perch. Heck, the players themselves may wind up caring not especially much about the Weaver Trophy—or The 2001 Mariners Trophy or The Whoa Those Mid-90s Indians Teams Trophy. Or—forthwith we're about to bring this sucker full circle—The 2015 Cardinals Trophy. This, though, carves out an honor for a baseball achievement that in a basic regard in the most baseball-ish of achievements. Herein: Make this happen.

Hey, look, a concluding quote …

"Worldly justice, salve of humankind: thine name is 'Make-Believe Sports Trophy.'" - King Solomon, probably.

—Dayn Perry a Mississippi native and BP alumnus who lives in Chicago with his wife, male spawn, and dog. He's a baseball writer for CBSSports.com. He has written three books all by himself, two of which he has yet to renounce.

Hitters

Matt Adams 1B

Born: 8/31/88 Age: 27 Bats: L Throws: R Height: 6'3" Weight: 260

YEAR	TEAM	LVL	AGE	PA	R	2B	3B	HR	RBI	BB	K	SB	CS	AVG/OBP/SLG	TAv	BABIP	BRR	FRAA	WARP
2013	SLN	MLB	24	319	46	14	0	17	51	23	80	0	1	.284/.335/.503	.289	.337	-1.6	1B(74): -0.6	1.1
2014	SLN	MLB	25	563	55	34	5	15	68	26	114	3	2	.288/.321/.457	.281	.338	-2.6	1B(133): -2.5	1.2
2015	SLN	MLB	26	186	14	9	0	5	24	10	41	1	0	.240/.280/.377	.242	.285	0.1	1B(46): -0.6	-0.2
2016	*SLN*	*MLB*	*27*	*556*	*63*	*30*	*2*	*21*	*75*	*29*	*124*	*3*	*1*	*.272/.312/.457*	*.267*	*.318*	*-1.5*	*1B -1*	*1.0*
2017	*SLN*	*MLB*	*28*	*420*	*52*	*22*	*1*	*15*	*55*	*25*	*96*	*2*	*1*	*.268/.313/.450*	*.270*	*.317*	*-1.3*	*1B -1*	*0.7*

Breakout: 5% Improve: 52% Collapse: 8% Attrition: 10% MLB: 95% *Comparables: Mike Jacobs, Adam Lind, Adrian Gonzalez*

An old chum with outsized expectations—this is Albert Pujols' successor, after all—Adams entered the season with Adrian Gonzalez's 2006 (.300/.362/.500) serving as his top PECOTA comparison. Before he could prove the comp deadly (in)accurate, he strained his quad in late May and landed on the disabled list for the next three-plus months. When Adams returned in September, he was inserted into a four-way timeshare at the cold corner, further limiting his opportunity to make up for a slow start. If there's anything to take away from his 2015—and there's not much, considering the sample size and his lengthy layoff—it's that his power failed to spring back to its old levels. That's a potentially unsettling development if it carries into 2016, seeing as how Adams' walk-resistant ways lay more stress upon his average and slugging percentage than if he had, say, Gonzalez's discerning eye. As such, Adams will need his bat to play as large as he does if he's to remain the Cardinals' most-days first baseman for the foreseeable future.

Matt Carpenter 3B

Born: 11/26/85 Age: 30 Bats: L Throws: R Height: 6'3" Weight: 215

YEAR	TEAM	LVL	AGE	PA	R	2B	3B	HR	RBI	BB	K	SB	CS	AVG/OBP/SLG	TAv	BABIP	BRR	FRAA	WARP
2013	SLN	MLB	27	717	126	55	7	11	78	72	98	3	3	.318/.392/.481	.312	.359	8.4	2B(132): 4.5, 3B(42): 0.4	7.3
2014	SLN	MLB	28	709	99	33	2	8	59	95	111	5	3	.272/.375/.375	.288	.318	-1.6	3B(156): -3.8, RF(2): -0.2	3.7
2015	SLN	MLB	29	665	101	44	3	28	84	81	151	4	3	.272/.365/.505	.317	.321	-0.6	3B(146): -11.2, 2B(11): -0.2	4.9
2016	*SLN*	*MLB*	*30*	*650*	*83*	*37*	*4*	*14*	*68*	*76*	*114*	*4*	*3*	*.276/.365/.433*	*.283*	*.317*	*1.7*	*3B -5*	*3.0*
2017	*SLN*	*MLB*	*31*	*546*	*68*	*31*	*3*	*11*	*60*	*64*	*98*	*3*	*2*	*.269/.359/.420*	*.281*	*.312*	*1.4*	*3B -5*	*2.2*

Breakout: 1% Improve: 51% Collapse: 6% Attrition: 7% MLB: 97% *Comparables: Morgan Ensberg, Chipper Jones, Sal Bando*

ST. LOUIS, 2017 — Nearly two years after being reprimanded for improperly accessing another team's proprietary databases, the Cardinals avoided a second scandal when an investigative body found no merit to recent accusations against the player development department. "We have determined, throughout the course of our year-long audit that [the Cardinals] have done nothing unethical, nothing immoral," lead investigator Conrad Metcalf said on Thursday. "The fact they have a lot of players like Carpenter in their system—players with uncertain defensive positions, players whose offensive value is tied to their batting average and on-base percentages, and players who tend to become more valuable than first thought—appears to be a coincidence, or a product of their scouting predilections. Not—I'll repeat—*not* the product of cloning. We found no evidence, no proof that suggests anything different. If Carpenter *is* considered the prototype, then it's merely as a theoretical one, not something literal." Various charges had been lodged against the Cardinals in the preceding years due to the production of a seemingly never-ending line of similar players. As one baseball source, who sought anonymity out of fear of retribution, said, "It's like they have a [freaking] assembly line of those guys. Just blip, bloop, blip, bloop all [freaking] day long." The Cardinals issued no comment on the investigation or its findings.

Greg Garcia SS

Born: 8/8/89 Age: 26 Bats: L Throws: R Height: 6'0" Weight: 190

YEAR	TEAM	LVL	AGE	PA	R	2B	3B	HR	RBI	BB	K	SB	CS	AVG/OBP/SLG	TAv	BABIP	BRR	FRAA	WARP
2013	MEM	AAA	23	424	50	23	4	3	35	49	70	14	2	.271/.377/.384	.290	.331	2.4	SS(73): -4.8, 2B(21): -2.4	2.5
2014	MEM	AAA	24	441	60	12	3	8	40	41	95	7	5	.272/.358/.382	.274	.342	-1.6	2B(90): 4.7, SS(13): -0.9	2.2
2014	SLN	MLB	24	18	2	1	0	0	1	1	6	0	0	.143/.333/.214	.230	.250	-0.2	2B(4): -0.5, SS(1): 0.0	-0.1
2015	SLN	MLB	25	87	7	5	0	2	4	10	12	0	0	.240/.337/.387	.278	.262	0.9	SS(12): 0.7, 2B(10): -1.7	0.4
2015	MEM	AAA	25	389	47	19	2	0	36	48	55	16	3	.294/.391/.364	.287	.351	3.6	SS(69): -5.4, 2B(19): -1.0	2.3
2016	*SLN*	*MLB*	*26*	*201*	*20*	*9*	*1*	*2*	*18*	*18*	*40*	*4*	*1*	*.252/.335/.351*	*.249*	*.307*	*0.1*	*3B 0, SS -1*	*0.4*
2017	*SLN*	*MLB*	*27*	*373*	*40*	*17*	*2*	*4*	*33*	*32*	*74*	*6*	*2*	*.249/.327/.350*	*.249*	*.301*	*0.3*	*3B 0, SS -1*	*0.5*

Breakout: 1% Improve: 26% Collapse: 13% Attrition: 29% MLB: 48% *Comparables: Justin Sellers, Eric Sogard, Jason Bartlett*

A lot of questions go through your head while watching the Cardinals play—like, were Hector Luna's most ardent supporters called the St. Lunatics?—but one of the nagging ones is why they elided Garcia throughout the 2015 season in favor of Pete Kozma. Garcia has proved the same thing in each of his three stints at Memphis: He's ready for a big-league bench job. His strike-zone management and barrels-o'-singles approach buoy his offensive production, and he's played enough positions in the minors that a manager can feel comfortable inserting him at any of the premium infield spots. Besides, Garcia is unlikely to improve much more, so the Cardinals would be wise to use what's left of his prime years.

Randal Grichuk LF

Born: 8/13/91 Age: 24 Bats: R Throws: R Height: 6'1" Weight: 195

YEAR	TEAM	LVL	AGE	PA	R	2B	3B	HR	RBI	BB	K	SB	CS	AVG/OBP/SLG	TAv	BABIP	BRR	FRAA	WARP
2013	ARK	AA	21	542	85	27	8	22	64	28	92	9	5	.256/.306/.474	.285	.272	3.0	RF(95): 17.8, CF(23): -2.1	4.6
2014	SLN	MLB	22	116	11	6	1	3	8	5	31	0	2	.245/.278/.400	.244	.316	-1.5	RF(28): -0.1, CF(5): 1.0	0.0
2014	MEM	AAA	22	472	73	23	2	25	71	28	108	8	5	.259/.311/.493	.280	.289	-0.9	LF(53): -2.0, CF(36): -5.3	1.4
2015	SLN	MLB	23	350	49	23	7	17	47	22	110	4	2	.276/.329/.548	.316	.365	-1.5	LF(49): -2.7, CF(37): 1.5	2.6
2016	*SLN*	*MLB*	*24*	*547*	*64*	*27*	*5*	*23*	*75*	*26*	*136*	*6*	*4*	*.251/.293/.457*	*.263*	*.296*	*-2.0*	*CF -2*	*1.7*
2017	*SLN*	*MLB*	*25*	*515*	*63*	*25*	*5*	*20*	*69*	*26*	*130*	*6*	*4*	*.247/.291/.448*	*.264*	*.294*	*-1.7*	*CF -2*	*1.5*

Breakout: 4% Improve: 28% Collapse: 20% Attrition: 29% MLB: 82% *Comparables: Travis Snider, Fernando Martinez, Dayan Viciedo*

Halfway through the season, MLB.com's Mike Petriello declared Grichuk "might be the first Statcast star." Petriello's observation, which was one shared by others, was prompted by Grichuk's exit velocity—like, he hits the ball hard. Randal Grichuk, Stathead Celeb. It's an odd development.

A decade ago, Grichuk (and those of his ilk) would have been, at best, tolerated by the analytics community. He *does* hit the ball hard—the product of his forceful, torque-heavy swing—but he also chucks the bat at everything with two seams, and comes up empty about a third of the time. Aside from the aesthetics, there's further reason to be skeptical: He'd never shown this kind of power before. His best minor-league ISO was .238, set five years ago in the Midwest League. Heck, Grichuk's minor-league numbers were such that he entered the year projected to be a below-average hitter. There's every statistical reason to think he's not *this* good, and if he's not *this* good, he projects to a sub-.300 OBP.

So what should we believe about Grichuk? That he's the new, right-handed Josh Hamilton, whose breakout transcends the norm? Or that he's a souped-up Justin Ruggiano, who didn't move out of apartment 4OF following his big year? Based on Grichuk's Statcast data, you might think the former. Here's the catch, though: That Statcast data isn't all that notable. He hit the ball pretty hard—but you would have known that by his numbers—but he didn't even lead all Cardinals rookie outfielders in exit velocity. (Who did that? Pham, Thomas.) Yes, sample size matters and all that good stuff ... still, the lesson is to be careful with your data—no matter how new or cool it is—because it'll only ever tell you what it knows you to want hear.

Grichuk could prove to be the banana pudding, but we'll give it another season before anointing him.

Jedd Gyorko 2B

Born: 9/23/88 Age: 27 Bats: R Throws: R Height: 5'10" Weight: 205

YEAR	TEAM	LVL	AGE	PA	R	2B	3B	HR	RBI	BB	K	SB	CS	AVG/OBP/SLG	TAv	BABIP	BRR	FRAA	WARP
2013	SDN	MLB	24	525	62	26	0	23	63	33	123	1	1	.249/.301/.444	.264	.287	0.2	2B(117): -4.1, 3B(13): 1.0	1.3
2014	ELP	AAA	25	28	7	2	0	1	5	4	4	0	0	.292/.393/.500	.310	.316	0.2	2B(6): 0.2	0.0
2014	SDN	MLB	25	443	37	17	1	10	51	36	100	3	2	.210/.280/.333	.243	.253	0.2	2B(109): -4.4	0.0
2015	ELP	AAA	26	69	8	1	0	4	9	7	11	0	1	.279/.362/.492	.271	.283	0.2	2B(16): -0.1	0.3
2015	SDN	MLB	26	458	34	15	0	16	57	27	107	0	1	.247/.297/.397	.252	.290	-1.1	2B(93): -0.5, SS(29): -1.5	0.7
2016	*SLN*	*MLB*	*27*	*206*	*23*	*9*	*0*	*7*	*26*	*14*	*45*	*1*	*0*	*.246/.305/.413*	*.254*	*.283*	*0.0*	*SS -1, 2B -0*	*0.6*
2017	*SLN*	*MLB*	*28*	*278*	*34*	*11*	*0*	*10*	*34*	*20*	*61*	*1*	*1*	*.240/.301/.402*	*.253*	*.278*	*-0.1*	*2B -1*	*0.7*

Breakout: 2% Improve: 48% Collapse: 2% Attrition: 5% MLB: 100% *Comparables: Kelly Johnson, Chad Tracy, Richie Hebner*

Gyorko's bat again arrived late to the party, though this time there was no plantar fasciitis to blame. After a refresher at Triple-A he picked up his game and finished with decent numbers. In their perpetual quest for a competent shortstop, the Padres tried him there down the stretch, and he didn't embarrass himself. Although his range isn't great, he is more athletic than his body type suggests, with his sure hands and accurate arm being assets on either side of the bag. Gyorko's plate discipline shows no signs of improving, but he generates good power for a middle infielder, which makes him useful down in the order—much as Khalil Greene was a decade ago—despite his .293 career OBP. He followed the Greene template all the way down to getting traded to St. Louis.

Matt Holliday LF

Born: 1/15/80 Age: 36 Bats: R Throws: R Height: 6'4" Weight: 250

YEAR	TEAM	LVL	AGE	PA	R	2B	3B	HR	RBI	BB	K	SB	CS	AVG/OBP/SLG	TAv	BABIP	BRR	FRAA	WARP
2013	SLN	MLB	33	602	103	31	1	22	94	69	86	6	1	.300/.389/.490	.300	.322	3.0	LF(136): -9.4	3.1
2014	SLN	MLB	34	667	83	37	0	20	90	74	100	4	1	.272/.370/.441	.292	.298	3.2	LF(150): -12.4	2.6
2015	SLN	MLB	35	277	24	16	1	4	35	39	49	2	1	.279/.394/.410	.299	.335	-1.4	LF(64): -6.5	0.9
2016	*SLN*	*MLB*	*36*	*620*	*76*	*32*	*1*	*20*	*80*	*68*	*108*	*4*	*2*	*.275/.366/.451*	*.290*	*.310*	*1.3*	*LF -7*	*3.3*
2017	*SLN*	*MLB*	*37*	*388*	*51*	*19*	*1*	*11*	*46*	*41*	*69*	*2*	*1*	*.266/.355/.423*	*.282*	*.303*	*0.7*	*LF -4*	*1.5*

Breakout: 2% Improve: 27% Collapse: 3% Attrition: 9% MLB: 87% *Comparables: Sid Gordon, Carlos Beltran, Lance Berkman*

Durability streaks are like gossamers in the grass: hard to build, easy to destroy. That is to say, it wasn't surprising that Holliday's streak of 10 consecutive 500-PA seasons ended in 2015. The culprit was a strained quad, which forced him to the shelf twice for a combined two and a half months. When Holliday was well, he posted his usual numbers but for an ISO that was the lowest of his career by more than 30 points. Seeing as how Holliday has been one of the game's most consistent and productive hitters for a decade, we're willing to cut him some slack. Now 36 and entering a potential walk year, it's time to stop taking his plate appearances for granted—Lord knows how many he has left, even if his 2016 goes well.

Carson Kelly C

Born: 7/14/94 Age: 21 Bats: R Throws: R Height: 6'2" Weight: 200

YEAR	TEAM	LVL	AGE	PA	R	2B	3B	HR	RBI	BB	K	SB	CS	AVG/OBP/SLG	TAv	BABIP	BRR	FRAA	WARP
2013	PEO	A	18	168	18	6	0	2	13	13	25	0	0	.219/.288/.301	.242	.248	0.2	3B(31): -4.6	-0.3
2013	SCO	A-	18	299	35	16	1	4	32	20	31	1	0	.277/.340/.387	.260	.301	-0.9	3B(64): -8.7	-0.1
2014	PEO	A	19	415	41	17	4	6	49	37	54	1	0	.248/.326/.366	.264	.274	-2.2	C(79): -0.9	1.5
2015	PMB	A+	20	419	30	18	1	8	51	22	64	0	0	.219/.263/.332	.223	.239	-1.0	C(104): -0.8	0.0
2016	*SLN*	*MLB*	*21*	*250*	*21*	*10*	*1*	*5*	*25*	*13*	*50*	*0*	*0*	*.217/.262/.332*	*.212*	*.251*	*-0.3*	*C -0*	*-0.2*
2017	*SLN*	*MLB*	*22*	*314*	*33*	*13*	*1*	*8*	*32*	*16*	*63*	*0*	*0*	*.220/.267/.353*	*.223*	*.249*	*-0.7*	*C 0*	*0.0*

Breakout: 2% Improve: 6% Collapse: 0% Attrition: 4% MLB: 6% *Comparables: Tucker Barnhart, Bryan Anderson, Carlos Perez*

YEAR	TEAM	P. COUNT	FRM RUNS	BLK RUNS	THRW RUNS	TOT RUNS
2016	*SLN*	*9034*	*0.0*	*0.0*	*0.0*	*0.0*
2017	*SLN*	*11340*	*0.0*	*0.0*	*0.0*	*0.0*

Catching prospects move slowly by rule (seriously, it's in Leviticus); there's just so much to learn on the mental side, and so much to handle on the physical side, that only the best get to the majors within their first few seasons as a professional. Kelly, then, is doing well by reaching High-A in his third full year—especially given he's a converted infielder, which, in theory, should mean he moves at the same pace as dial-up internet. Thanks to his agility, strong arm and soft hands, his defense has improved to the point where he should be an average-at-worst defender. Unfortunately, he hasn't made the same progress at the plate, where his bat looked slow (and weak) throughout 2015. The good news for Kelly is the majors are full of backup catchers whose mitts outweigh their bats; the bad news is so are the minors. Kelly is still young enough to figure it all out, but these days he looks more likely to succeed Cruz than Molina, and more likely to succeed Ed Easley and/or Cody Stanley than either.

Yadier Molina C

Born: 7/13/82 Age: 33 Bats: R Throws: R Height: 5'11" Weight: 220

YEAR	TEAM	LVL	AGE	PA	R	2B	3B	HR	RBI	BB	K	SB	CS	AVG/OBP/SLG	TAv	BABIP	BRR	FRAA	WARP
2013	SLN	MLB	30	541	68	44	0	12	80	30	55	3	2	.319/.359/.477	.297	.338	-5.6	C(131): 24.8, 1B(5): -0.2	6.6
2014	SLN	MLB	31	445	40	21	0	7	38	28	55	1	1	.282/.333/.386	.256	.307	-2.5	C(107): 2.6, 1B(1): 0.0	1.8
2015	SLN	MLB	32	530	34	23	2	4	61	32	59	3	1	.270/.310/.350	.239	.295	-4.9	C(134): 10.1	1.9
2016	*SLN*	*MLB*	*33*	*538*	*56*	*29*	*1*	*12*	*62*	*33*	*60*	*3*	*1*	*.288/.334/.422*	*.266*	*.304*	*-3.8*	*C 12*	*3.7*
2017	*SLN*	*MLB*	*34*	*434*	*49*	*23*	*0*	*8*	*46*	*25*	*51*	*2*	*1*	*.281/.324/.400*	*.260*	*.300*	*-3.2*	*C 9*	*2.5*

Breakout: 2% Improve: 23% Collapse: 2% Attrition: 6% MLB: 94% *Comparables: Kenji Johjima, Ramon Hernandez, Yogi Berra*

YEAR	TEAM	P. COUNT	FRM RUNS	BLK RUNS	THRW RUNS	TOT RUNS
2013	SLN	17446	21.7	1.6	0.4	23.7
2014	SLN	14449	0.6	0.3	1.7	2.7
2015	SLN	18104	7.6	0.4	1.1	9.1
2016	*SLN*	*18321*	*10.8*	*0.7*	*1.5*	*13.0*
2017	*SLN*	*14781*	*7.9*	*0.5*	*1.1*	*9.5*

We're supposed to start every Molina comment by praising his defense, so let's do that now. He remains an above-average receiver and marksman (in 2015 he nailed 41 percent of attempted thieves), and all indications are he'll continue to share the shining with his pitching staff, resulting in high-quality game-calling. But we have to ask, is this the beginning of the end? Molina's offensive numbers looked more like those from a decade ago, when he paired an empty average with emptier on-base and slugging percentages, than the last few seasons, when he was a legitimate above-average hitter. Another factor is that he's not *just* 33 years old, he's 33 years old with more than 12,000 regular-season innings behind the plate, as well as another 86 postseason appearances. Add it up and he's caught more innings through age 32 than Bengie and Jose had combined. We're not saying Molina is definitely done or shouldn't start—again, he's a brilliant defender—but we're bearish on an offensive rebound, and it's probably time for the Cardinals to work on Plan B.

Brandon Moss RF

Born: 9/16/83 Age: 32 Bats: L Throws: R Height: 6'0" Weight: 210

YEAR	TEAM	LVL	AGE	PA	R	2B	3B	HR	RBI	BB	K	SB	CS	AVG/OBP/SLG	TAv	BABIP	BRR	FRAA	WARP
2013	OAK	MLB	29	505	73	23	3	30	87	50	140	4	2	.256/.337/.522	.328	.301	-1.9	1B(111): -5.0, RF(27): 0.2	3.5
2014	OAK	MLB	30	580	70	23	2	25	81	67	153	1	0	.234/.334/.438	.290	.283	0.7	1B(67): -3.2, LF(56): -1.5	2.6
2015	SLN	MLB	31	151	11	7	1	4	8	17	42	0	1	.250/.344/.409	.271	.337	-1.7	1B(32): -0.3, LF(10): -0.3	0.1
2015	CLE	MLB	31	375	36	17	1	15	50	32	106	0	0	.217/.288/.407	.244	.265	-3.4	RF(79): 2.3, 1B(10): 1.2	0.0
2016	*SLN*	*MLB*	*32*	*345*	*43*	*16*	*1*	*16*	*51*	*34*	*93*	*1*	*1*	*.246/.328/.466*	*.277*	*.297*	*-1.1*	*1B -1, LF 0*	*1.3*
2017	*SLN*	*MLB*	*33*	*382*	*51*	*16*	*1*	*16*	*52*	*38*	*106*	*0*	*0*	*.240/.323/.441*	*.273*	*.296*	*-1.4*	*1B -1, LF 0*	*1.0*

Breakout: 1% Improve: 26% Collapse: 3% Attrition: 6% MLB: 95% *Comparables: Nelson Cruz, Marcus Thames, Michael Morse*

Health is the next great separator in sports analytics, according to everyone with a pulse. That's why the trade that sent Moss to Cleveland in exchange for a minor-league second baseman caused us to pause. Just what did the deal say about the state of his troublesome hip? After all, Moss relies on his power—generated by his hips—and on-base skills to remain employable, and without the former, the latter comes into question as well. Those concerns seemed foolish during his hot April, but regained validity as he endured a shaky second half that resulted in a measly .138 ISO (and that's *with* a post-trade bounce). While no one can say for certain whether those struggles stemmed from his achy hip, there's reason beyond his flat pop to doubt he'll ever return to his well-above-average form. Namely, Moss turned 32 in September, which translates to, oh, about 38 in Dunn years.

Michael Ohlman C

Born: 12/14/90 Age: 25 Bats: R Throws: R Height: 6'5" Weight: 215

YEAR	TEAM	LVL	AGE	PA	R	2B	3B	HR	RBI	BB	K	SB	CS	AVG/OBP/SLG	TAv	BABIP	BRR	FRAA	WARP
2013	FRD	A+	22	424	61	29	4	13	53	56	93	5	0	.313/.410/.524	.313	.389	-2.1	C(46): -0.5	3.4
2014	BOW	AA	23	454	40	25	1	2	33	43	86	0	0	.236/.310/.318	.242	.292	-2.4	C(91): -2.1	0.4
2015	SFD	AA	24	417	53	17	0	12	69	46	77	0	1	.273/.356/.418	.277	.315	-0.8	C(97): -2.0	2.3
2016	*SLN*	*MLB*	*25*	*32*	*3*	*1*	*0*	*1*	*3*	*3*	*8*	*0*	*0*	*.238/.307/.358*	*.240*	*.300*	*-0.1*	*C -1*	*0.0*
2017	*SLN*	*MLB*	*26*	*211*	*23*	*10*	*1*	*4*	*21*	*18*	*52*	*0*	*0*	*.234/.303/.356*	*.245*	*.297*	*-0.5*	*C -7*	*0.0*

Breakout: 3% Improve: 9% Collapse: 10% Attrition: 23% MLB: 31% *Comparables: Adam Moore, Dan Butler, Tim Federowicz*

YEAR	TEAM	P. COUNT	FRM RUNS	BLK RUNS	THRW RUNS	TOT RUNS
2014	BOW	12883	0.3	-1.2	-1.7	-2.6
2015	SFD	13428	-0.9	-1.0	-0.7	-2.6
2016	*SLN*	*1170*	*-0.8*	*-0.1*	*-0.1*	*-1.1*
2017	*SLN*	*7714*	*-5.9*	*-0.8*	*-0.9*	*-7.5*

For all the caveats in this book about players' future defensive homes—"*if* he can improve his reads," "*if* he can learn the footwork," and so on—Ohlman is evidence that sometimes none of it matters. He's an inconsistent thrower and substandard receiver whose size is likely to prevent him from gaining low strikes. So why hasn't Ohlman moved to first base? Because while his bat is the best part of the package, it isn't so good as to play at a less-demanding defensive position. Ohlman is probably a year or two from sliding there anyway, but for now the Cardinals will continue to hold out hope he can make it as a backup catcher.

Brayan Pena 1B

Born: 1/7/82 Age: 34 Bats: B Throws: R Height: 5'9" Weight: 240

YEAR	TEAM	LVL	AGE	PA	R	2B	3B	HR	RBI	BB	K	SB	CS	AVG/OBP/SLG	TAv	BABIP	BRR	FRAA	WARP
2013	DET	MLB	31	243	19	11	0	4	22	6	26	0	2	.297/.315/.397	.260	.315	-2.9	C(64): 4.6, 1B(1): -0.1	1.3
2014	CIN	MLB	32	372	23	18	1	5	26	20	42	2	3	.253/.291/.353	.240	.273	-6.5	1B(53): -1.7, C(46): 0.5	-0.6
2015	CIN	MLB	33	367	17	17	0	0	18	29	34	2	0	.273/.334/.324	.242	.303	-3.5	C(86): -8.5, 1B(5): -0.1	-0.4
2016	*SLN*	*MLB*	*34*	*151*	*13*	*7*	*0*	*1*	*12*	*8*	*16*	*1*	*0*	*.259/.299/.339*	*.228*	*.280*	*-1.4*	*C -1*	*-0.1*
2017	*SLN*	*MLB*	*35*	*248*	*24*	*11*	*0*	*2*	*20*	*12*	*28*	*1*	*1*	*.253/.291/.331*	*.226*	*.275*	*-2.4*	*C -2*	*-0.4*

Breakout: 1% Improve: 27% Collapse: 10% Attrition: 13% MLB: 87% *Comparables: Brian Harper, Del Crandall, Brian Schneider*

The 34-year-old Pena has now played in 629 games with four teams over 11 seasons, posting a career WARP of zero. Another way to describe that is "replacement level," which sounds like a pejorative until your starting catcher gets hurt and you actually need a replacement. Sabermetric theory holds that replacements are readily available, but in the real world you want that replacement to already know the pitching staff and their handshakes and the names of the clubhouse assistants, and if he can be warm, funny and loved by his teammates and fans, even better. That's why Pena, a mediocre receiver with limited on-base skills and no power, will once again have a big league job this summer no matter what the numbers say.

Jhonny Peralta SS

Born: 5/28/82 Age: 34 Bats: R Throws: R Height: 6'2" Weight: 215

YEAR	TEAM	LVL	AGE	PA	R	2B	3B	HR	RBI	BB	K	SB	CS	AVG/OBP/SLG	TAv	BABIP	BRR	FRAA	WARP
2013	DET	MLB	31	448	50	30	0	11	55	35	98	3	3	.303/.358/.457	.293	.374	-2.8	SS(106): 8.6, LF(3): -0.1	4.0
2014	SLN	MLB	32	628	61	38	0	21	75	58	112	3	2	.263/.336/.443	.285	.292	-3.1	SS(152): 5.2	4.4
2015	SLN	MLB	33	640	64	26	1	17	71	50	111	1	4	.275/.334/.411	.273	.311	-1.7	SS(148): 6.6	4.1
2016	*SLN*	*MLB*	*34*	*608*	*64*	*30*	*1*	*16*	*71*	*47*	*115*	*3*	*2*	*.263/.324/.409*	*.262*	*.303*	*-2.1*	*SS 5*	*3.5*
2017	*SLN*	*MLB*	*35*	*533*	*60*	*25*	*1*	*11*	*55*	*41*	*101*	*1*	*1*	*.253/.312/.379*	*.254*	*.295*	*-1.8*	*SS 5*	*2.4*

Breakout: 0% Improve: 39% Collapse: 6% Attrition: 12% MLB: 94% *Comparables: Miguel Tejada, Mark DeRosa, Ty Wigginton*

From the spelling of his first name to his defensive reputation and career arc, nothing is ever what it seems with Peralta—not even his contract. Most free-agent pacts are structured so the dollars are paid out evenly or at an escalating rate, as a means for teams to save coins using the time value of money. Peralta's is not. Halfway through his four-year deal, he's already made nearly 60 percent

($30.5 million) of the contract's total payout ($53 million). It's turned out to be a beneficial arrangement for both sides, since Peralta makes more money than he would have otherwise, and the Cardinals will have less of their budget promised to shortstop entering his mid-30s. Not that Peralta's age is affecting him yet. He had another solid season at the plate (his fourth above-average effort in five tries), and his ability to actually improve as a shortstop in his 30s (and with his body type!) gives hope to every old Buick out there. Peralta's contract didn't look like a steal at the time, but it's proved to be a bargain of a deal, albeit an unusual one.

Thomas Pham CF

Born: 3/8/88 Age: 28 Bats: R Throws: R Height: 6'1" Weight: 175

YEAR	TEAM	LVL	AGE	PA	R	2B	3B	HR	RBI	BB	K	SB	CS	AVG/OBP/SLG	TAv	BABIP	BRR	FRAA	WARP
2013	SFD	AA	25	188	27	6	6	6	28	20	42	6	3	.301/.388/.521	.303	.371	0.0	CF(36): 3.1, RF(1): -0.0	1.7
2013	MEM	AAA	25	113	6	6	1	1	13	7	25	2	1	.264/.310/.368	.261	.338	0.3	CF(28): 0.8, LF(2): -0.1	0.5
2014	SLN	MLB	26	2	0	0	0	0	0	0	2	0	0	.000/.000/.000	-.003	--	0.0	LF(2): -0.0, RF(1): -0.0	-0.1
2014	MEM	AAA	26	390	63	16	6	10	44	38	81	20	2	.324/.395/.491	.318	.397	-1.3	CF(59): -1.0, LF(29): 0.0	3.5
2015	MEM	AAA	27	196	29	10	1	6	39	22	36	9	0	.327/.398/.503	.339	.379	2.2	CF(42): -4.8, LF(2): 0.4	2.0
2015	SLN	MLB	27	173	28	7	5	5	18	19	41	2	0	.268/.347/.477	.298	.333	2.1	CF(33): -2.7, LF(18): -0.7	1.0
2016	*SLN*	*MLB*	*28*	*219*	*28*	*9*	*3*	*5*	*22*	*19*	*51*	*5*	*1*	*.267/.334/.421*	*.268*	*.332*	*0.8*	*CF -1, LF 1*	*1.0*
2017	*SLN*	*MLB*	*29*	*375*	*44*	*16*	*5*	*9*	*42*	*32*	*88*	*8*	*2*	*.262/.328/.416*	*.269*	*.327*	*1.4*	*CF -1, LF 1*	*1.5*

Breakout: 6% Improve: 27% Collapse: 14% Attrition: 26% MLB: 57% *Comparables: John Mayberry, Chris Denorfia, Ryan Spilborghs*

The late-blooming Pham—he was part of the same 2006 draft class as Chris Perez, who, um, retired this year following a seven-year big-league career—spent most of the first half in a familiar place: on the disabled list. He made his season debut in June when his strained quad healed, and showed enough to earn multiple recalls, including in July as a stand-in starter. In addition to one of the most pun-friendly surnames in the game, Pham possesses a stellar defensive reputation thanks to his good range, strong arm and penchant for making Vine-worthy grabs. His offensive game isn't as prone to retweets, but he could pass as an everyday player for a few seasons if his gap-to-gap approach translates. Oh, and if he can prevent his recurring health woes from, you know, recurring.

Stephen Piscotty RF

Born: 1/14/91 Age: 25 Bats: R Throws: R Height: 6'3" Weight: 210

YEAR	TEAM	LVL	AGE	PA	R	2B	3B	HR	RBI	BB	K	SB	CS	AVG/OBP/SLG	TAv	BABIP	BRR	FRAA	WARP
2013	PMB	A+	22	264	30	14	2	9	35	18	27	4	5	.292/.348/.477	.296	.300	1.1	RF(59): -1.8	1.4
2013	SFD	AA	22	207	17	9	0	6	24	19	19	7	3	.299/.364/.446	.292	.304	-4.3	RF(48): 1.0	0.7
2014	MEM	AAA	23	556	70	32	0	9	69	43	61	11	5	.288/.355/.406	.277	.313	-1.0	RF(113): 1.7, LF(8): 0.1	2.2
2015	SLN	MLB	24	256	29	15	4	7	39	20	56	2	1	.305/.359/.494	.314	.372	-1.9	LF(55): -5.7, RF(15): -0.9	1.0
2015	MEM	AAA	24	372	54	28	2	11	41	46	62	5	6	.272/.366/.475	.310	.304	-2.3	RF(61): 4.8, LF(10): -1.1	2.8
2016	*SLN*	*MLB*	*25*	*597*	*64*	*32*	*3*	*14*	*68*	*45*	*99*	*7*	*4*	*.267/.328/.415*	*.267*	*.301*	*-2.7*	*RF 4*	*2.0*
2017	*SLN*	*MLB*	*26*	*575*	*67*	*30*	*2*	*13*	*62*	*45*	*100*	*6*	*4*	*.261/.324/.401*	*.265*	*.298*	*-2.4*	*RF 4*	*1.6*

Breakout: 3% Improve: 31% Collapse: 12% Attrition: 33% MLB: 78% *Comparables: Thomas Neal, Mitch Moreland, Desmond Jennings*

The Cardinals have this habit of bletting their position-player prospects, leaving them on the vine until they're so ripe you'd swear they must be rotting. Piscotty is the latest example. He dominated Memphis in 2014, and appeared ready to take over in right field following Oscar Taveras' passing. Instead the Cardinals acquired Jason Heyward. Okay, but he was the first man up following an injury, right? Nope. When injuries struck throughout the first half, the Cards turned to Bourjos, Grichuk and Pham in that order. Piscotty didn't get the call until late July, after he'd received nearly 400 more plate appearances in Triple-A. Guess what? He was fine, good even. Piscotty started at least once at four different positions, and finished fifth among rookies in True Average. Maybe we oversimplify things by saying the Cardinals sure know how to pick them—maybe knowing *when* to pick them is just as important? After all, proper bletting makes certain fruit sweeter.

Nick Plummer OF

Born: 7/31/96 Age: 19 Bats: L Throws: L Height: 5'10" Weight: 200

YEAR	TEAM	LVL	AGE	PA	R	2B	3B	HR	RBI	BB	K	SB	CS	AVG/OBP/SLG	TAv	BABIP	BRR	FRAA	WARP
2016	*SLN*	*MLB*	*19*	*250*	*21*	*8*	*1*	*3*	*19*	*20*	*80*	*2*	*1*	*.182/.253/.269*	*.191*	*.260*	*-0.3*	*CF -2*	*-1.2*
2017	*SLN*	*MLB*	*20*	*338*	*33*	*10*	*2*	*5*	*28*	*27*	*104*	*3*	*2*	*.193/.264/.290*	*.205*	*.268*	*-0.2*	*-*	*-0.9*

Breakout: 0% Improve: 0% Collapse: 0% Attrition: 0% MLB: 0% *Comparables: Dalton Pompey, Aaron Hicks, Andrew McCutchen*

Watching Plummer hit, it's hard to understand how he developed his sweet swing and discerning approach while growing up in Michigan—a short-season state that hadn't seen a prepster go in the first round since 1997—and how, with those attributes in tow, he slipped to 23rd overall. Perhaps the dreaded cold-state bias was in play, but the more reasonable explanation places the blame on Plummer's otherwise polarizing profile. Scouts aren't sure if he'll stick in center field long term due to his less-than-ideal range, which, when combined with his below-average arm strength, could precipitate a move to left. Add in varying opinions about Plummer's future power production—he has the requisite hand speed, yet not the swing plane—and there's a lot of pressure on him hitting for average and getting on base. Good thing those qualities should serve as his biggest strengths.

Charlie Tilson CF

Born: 12/2/92 Age: 23 Bats: L Throws: L Height: 5'11" Weight: 175

YEAR	TEAM	LVL	AGE	PA	R	2B	3B	HR	RBI	BB	K	SB	CS	AVG/OBP/SLG	TAv	BABIP	BRR	FRAA	WARP
2013	PMB	A+	20	39	1	1	1	0	0	5	6	0	0	.294/.385/.382	.290	.357	-0.9	CF(9): 0.8	0.3
2013	PEO	A	20	411	49	8	6	4	30	25	58	15	6	.303/.349/.388	.269	.349	2.5	CF(71): -3.9, LF(17): 0.1	1.7
2014	PMB	A+	21	402	54	8	8	5	36	24	76	10	7	.308/.357/.414	.281	.377	3.8	CF(83): -10.8	1.5
2014	SFD	AA	21	145	19	4	1	2	17	6	28	2	3	.237/.269/.324	.221	.284	2.8	CF(26): -3.2, LF(6): 1.2	-0.1
2015	SFD	AA	22	594	85	20	9	4	32	46	72	46	19	.295/.351/.388	.276	.333	4.8	CF(128): 2.6	3.7
2016	*SLN*	*MLB*	*23*	*250*	*29*	*8*	*3*	*3*	*19*	*12*	*49*	*10*	*4*	*.258/.296/.354*	*.230*	*.310*	*0.6*	*CF -2, LF 0*	*-0.1*
2017	*SLN*	*MLB*	*24*	*402*	*41*	*12*	*5*	*5*	*37*	*20*	*75*	*16*	*7*	*.259/.300/.359*	*.236*	*.305*	*1.9*	*CF -3, LF 0*	*0.1*

Breakout: 6% Improve: 19% Collapse: 4% Attrition: 9% MLB: 30% *Comparables: Billy Hamilton, Peter Bourjos, Engel Beltre*

The most-used comparison for Tilson is Brett Gardner. In a sense, the comp works as a reference point: Both players are short, left-handed-hitting outfielders with strong jawlines, similar builds and high motors who rely upon hitting for average and reaching base to prop up their offensive games. But in another sense, the comp fails by leaving out Tilson's rawness, which almost ensures he'll never reach Gardner's level. He needs to improve his technique on every side of the ball, whether it's tightening his strike zone, bettering his reads on the basepaths or taking sharper routes in the field. If Tilson can do all this, he could develop into every team's dream: a leadoff-hitting center fielder. If he doesn't, he's probably a fourth outfielder—just like most young players burdened with the Gardner comp.

Kolten Wong 2B

Born: 10/10/90 Age: 25 Bats: L Throws: R Height: 5'9" Weight: 185

YEAR	TEAM	LVL	AGE	PA	R	2B	3B	HR	RBI	BB	K	SB	CS	AVG/OBP/SLG	TAv	BABIP	BRR	FRAA	WARP
2013	SLN	MLB	22	62	6	1	0	0	0	3	12	3	0	.153/.194/.169	.143	.191	0.6	2B(18): 0.8	-0.4
2013	MEM	AAA	22	463	68	21	8	10	45	41	60	20	1	.303/.369/.466	.307	.332	0.7	2B(102): 11.1	4.9
2014	SLN	MLB	23	433	52	14	3	12	42	21	71	20	4	.249/.292/.388	.241	.275	6.7	2B(107): -4.3	0.6
2014	MEM	AAA	23	80	16	4	0	3	13	5	9	6	0	.360/.400/.533	.351	.381	1.0	2B(18): 1.4	1.3
2015	SLN	MLB	24	613	71	28	4	11	61	36	95	15	8	.262/.321/.386	.259	.296	2.3	2B(147): 11.1	3.1
2016	*SLN*	*MLB*	*25*	*630*	*81*	*27*	*5*	*15*	*61*	*36*	*99*	*21*	*6*	*.264/.315/.405*	*.254*	*.292*	*4.2*	*2B 7*	*3.4*
2017	*SLN*	*MLB*	*26*	*568*	*63*	*24*	*4*	*13*	*61*	*32*	*88*	*18*	*5*	*.255/.305/.388*	*.250*	*.281*	*4.4*	*2B 6*	*2.6*

Breakout: 0% Improve: 56% Collapse: 8% Attrition: 14% MLB: 99% *Comparables: Blake DeWitt, Josh Barfield, Jose Lopez*

Wong's second full season in the majors went better than his first. He wasn't demoted to the minors midway through, didn't have to share reps with Mark Ellis, and did improve on his overall offensive marks. If there was a drawback, it was that he was miserable against left-handed pitchers—to the extent that he recorded only 15 more hits against them than he had in 2014, in 93 more at-bats. On the plus side, Wong's numbers versus righties (.276/.340/.432) represented his ideal production: good average, solid on-base skills and more power than you'd expect from someone whose listed height and weight are the same as Omar Vizquel's. Add in his good defense at the keystone and, even if he continues to look more like a platoon player than an everyday starter, you have a solid youngster who won't qualify for arbitration until after the 2016 season.

Pitchers

Matt Belisle RHP

Born: 6/6/80 Age: 36 Bats: R Throws: R Height: 6'4" Weight: 225

YEAR	TEAM	LVL	AGE	W	L	SV	G	GS	IP	H	HR	BB/9	K/9	GB%	BABIP	WHIP	ERA	FIP	DRA	WARP	CFIP	MPH
2013	COL	MLB	33	5	7	0	72	0	73	76	6	1.8	7.6	50%	.321	1.25	4.32	3.01	3.69	0.8	83	93.5
2014	COL	MLB	34	4	7	0	66	1	64^2	74	5	2.6	6.0	48%	.322	1.44	4.87	3.71	3.48	0.8	106	94.2
2015	SLN	MLB	35	1	1	0	34	0	33^2	34	1	4.0	6.7	55%	.314	1.46	2.67	3.67	4.85	-0.1	109	93.5
2016	*SLN*	*MLB*	*36*	*2*	*1*	*0*	*35*	*0*	*37*	*37*	*4*	*2.9*	*7.0*	*51%*	*.314*	*1.31*	*3.84*	*3.93*	*4.55*	*0.2*	*103*	
2017	*SLN*	*MLB*	*37*	*2*	*1*	*0*	*49*	*0*	*48^1*	*50*	*6*	*2.8*	*7.1*	*51%*	*.325*	*1.36*	*4.01*	*4.42*	*4.75*	*0.1*	*108*	

Breakout: 25% Improve: 44% Collapse: 33% Attrition: 5% MLB: 86% *Comparables: LaTroy Hawkins, Salomon Torres, Hoyt Wilhelm*

At last freed from Coors Field and that monstrosity named "Dinger," Belisle did the exact opposite of what you would have expected from him: He broke. Whereas he had been classified as a workhorse during his six seasons in Colorado, which comprised five consecutive 60-plus-inning seasons, he couldn't even reach 50 in St. Louis. Instead he experienced life on the disabled list for the first time since 2008, sitting out more than two months due to an inflamed elbow. When he was healthy, he didn't look like the same pitcher whose career was built on throwing so-so stuff for strikes, as evidenced by a walk total that rivaled his past amounts in half as many innings. We used to wonder what Belisle would do once he escaped Coors; now 35 and declining in health and control, we wonder if he has much time left to do anything.

Jonathan Broxton RHP

Born: 6/16/84 Age: 32 Bats: R Throws: R Height: 6'4" Weight: 305

YEAR	TEAM	LVL	AGE	W	L	SV	G	GS	IP	H	HR	BB/9	K/9	GB%	BABIP	WHIP	ERA	FIP	DRA	WARP	CFIP	MPH
2013	CIN	MLB	29	2	2	0	34	0	30^{2}	27	4	3.5	7.3	47%	.261	1.27	4.11	4.65	4.90	-0.1	109	96.8
2014	MIL	MLB	30	0	1	0	11	0	10^{1}	9	1	1.7	10.5	54%	.296	1.06	4.35	2.62	2.49	0.3	68	97.4
2014	CIN	MLB	30	4	2	7	51	0	48^{1}	32	3	3.2	6.9	46%	.221	1.01	1.86	3.50	2.44	1.2	106	96.0
2015	MIL	MLB	31	1	2	0	40	0	36^{2}	41	5	2.5	9.1	52%	.346	1.39	5.89	3.73	4.90	-0.1	90	97.1
2015	SLN	MLB	31	3	3	0	26	0	23^{2}	20	2	4.6	9.9	62%	.295	1.35	2.66	3.58	4.15	0.2	97	97.3
2016	*SLN*	*MLB*	*32*	*3*	*1*	*0*	*49*	*0*	52^{1}	*47*	*6*	*3.0*	*8.1*	*53%*	*.303*	*1.22*	*3.67*	*3.82*	*4.38*	*0.3*	*99*	
2017	*SLN*	*MLB*	*33*	*3*	*1*	*3*	*57*	*0*	53^{2}	*48*	*6*	*3.0*	*8.2*	*53%*	*.304*	*1.23*	*3.74*	*4.11*	*4.46*	*0.3*	*102*	

Breakout: 24% Improve: 51% Collapse: 26% Attrition: 10% MLB: 97% *Comparables: Tippy Martinez, Pedro Feliciano, Randy Myers*

Broxton looked like your archetypical buy-low candidate at the deadline. His ERA was nearing 6.00 and he'd allowed more than one home run per nine, but those who glanced at his peripherals and saw his continued ability to miss bats had legitimate reasons to believe better days were ahead. After the deal, he started using his slider more and enjoyed a surprising amount of success when contrasted with his stint in Milwaukee. Broxton isn't fit for ninth-inning duty anymore, yet his deep release point and power arsenal make it likely he'll stick around for a few more seasons as a big-name middle reliever.

Randy Choate LHP

Born: 9/5/75 Age: 40 Bats: L Throws: L Height: 6'1" Weight: 210

YEAR	TEAM	LVL	AGE	W	L	SV	G	GS	IP	H	HR	BB/9	K/9	GB%	BABIP	WHIP	ERA	FIP	DRA	WARP	CFIP	MPH
2013	SLN	MLB	37	2	1	0	64	0	35^{1}	26	0	2.8	7.1	68%	.260	1.05	2.29	2.54	2.39	0.9	106	88.5
2014	SLN	MLB	38	2	2	0	61	0	36	27	2	3.2	8.0	63%	.260	1.11	4.50	3.55	2.80	0.7	100	87.1
2015	SLN	MLB	39	1	0	1	71	0	27^{1}	29	2	1.6	7.2	63%	.329	1.24	3.95	3.71	4.50	0.1	103	85.9
2016	*SLN*	*MLB*	*40*	*2*	*1*	*1*	*36*	*0*	37^{2}	*34*	*4*	*2.8*	*7.2*	*64%*	*.292*	*1.21*	*3.94*	*3.94*	*4.66*	*0.1*	*106*	
2017	*SLN*	*MLB*	*41*	*5*	*2*	*2*	*110*	*0*	*55*	*51*	*7*	*2.9*	*7.3*	*64%*	*.296*	*1.24*	*4.10*	*4.51*	*4.85*	*0.0*	*111*	

Breakout: 13% Improve: 32% Collapse: 30% Attrition: 9% MLB: 79% *Comparables: Al Worthington, John Franco, Marv Grissom*

Death, be not proud, though some have called thee
Mighty and dreadful, for thou art not so;
For those whom thou think'st thou dost overthrow
Die not, poor Death, nor yet canst thou kill me
—Randol Doyle Choate

Or maybe it was John Donne. But hey, put Choate in a cabin for a few days with a legal pad and some pencils and who knows what he'd come up with. Choate had a historic 2015. He became the game's all-time *and* single-season leader in fewest innings per appearance, thereby cementing his status as the Barry Bonds of LOOGYs. It was odd, then, that he accomplished those historic feats—okay, certain people's concept of historic feats—during one of the worst seasons of his career. He allowed lefties to post an OPS more than 150 points higher than they had in any season since his rebirth in 2009—a bad development, considering he was used as true to the definition as any LOOGY in history. Seeing as how he celebrated his 40th birthday in September, it's time to ponder: Does the lefty to end all lefties have anything left...y?

Tim Cooney LHP

Born: 12/19/90 Age: 25 Bats: L Throws: L Height: 6'3" Weight: 195

YEAR	TEAM	LVL	AGE	W	L	SV	G	GS	IP	H	HR	BB/9	K/9	GB%	BABIP	WHIP	ERA	FIP	DRA	WARP	CFIP	MPH
2013	PMB	A+	22	3	3	0	6	6	36	38	1	1.0	5.8	43%	.316	1.17	2.75	2.74	4.11	0.3	94	
2013	SFD	AA	22	7	10	0	20	20	118^{1}	132	8	1.4	9.5	49%	.366	1.27	3.80	2.43	3.39	2.2	72	
2014	MEM	AAA	23	14	6	0	26	25	158	158	21	2.7	6.8	48%	.291	1.30	3.47	4.93	5.47	0.5	108	
2015	MEM	AAA	24	6	4	0	14	14	88^{2}	61	9	1.6	6.4	38%	.211	0.87	2.74	4.17	3.85	1.6	89	
2015	SLN	MLB	24	1	0	0	6	6	31^{1}	28	3	2.9	8.3	40%	.287	1.21	3.16	3.61	5.17	-0.1	96	92.0
2016	*SLN*	*MLB*	*25*	*4*	*3*	*0*	*30*	*8*	63^{2}	*62*	*8*	*2.3*	*6.9*	*41%*	*.302*	*1.23*	*3.92*	*4.03*	*4.64*	*0.3*	*108*	
2017	*SLN*	*MLB*	*26*	*5*	*6*	*0*	*17*	*17*	98^{1}	*97*	*14*	*2.5*	*7.4*	*41%*	*.307*	*1.27*	*4.12*	*4.54*	*4.88*	*0.5*	*114*	

Breakout: 15% Improve: 30% Collapse: 12% Attrition: 32% MLB: 52% *Comparables: Asher Wojciechowski, Adam Wilk, Michael Bowden*

What do teams want from their back-end starters? Sounds like the introduction of a kitschy *Cosmo* article, but it's a fair inquiry. Most would answer health, innings and the ability to keep games close. If the Cardinals agree, then they must have been pleased with Cooney's July stint in the rotation. He worked into the sixth inning and allowed two earned runs or fewer in four of his five tries—almost as if to say, Yeah, I'm ready for this. Rest assured Cooney *is* ready for this. He's gimmicky and low on sizzle (his arsenal is average throughout) but reliable and high on polish. Cooney is then, in a sense, the kind of pitcher whose starts you can skip without regret, not because they're bad but because if you've seen a few you've seen them all.

Jack Flaherty RHP

Born: 10/15/95 Age: 20 Bats: R Throws: R Height: 6'4" Weight: 205

YEAR	TEAM	LVL	AGE	W	L	SV	G	GS	IP	H	HR	BB/9	K/9	GB%	BABIP	WHIP	ERA	FIP	DRA	WARP	CFIP	MPH
2015	PEO	A	19	9	3	0	18	18	95	92	2	2.9	9.2	37%	.330	1.29	2.84	2.83	2.90	2.3	86	
2016	*SLN*	*MLB*	*20*	*4*	*4*	*0*	*15*	*15*	*70*	*70*	*6*	*3.4*	*6.9*	*30%*	*.317*	*1.37*	*3.91*	*3.85*	*4.61*	*0.6*	*107*	
2017	*SLN*	*MLB*	*21*	*8*	*9*	*0*	*29*	*29*	179^{1}	*176*	*19*	*3.2*	*7.1*	*30%*	*.313*	*1.34*	*3.96*	*4.38*	*4.67*	*1.0*	*109*	

Breakout: 5% Improve: 6% Collapse: 1% Attrition: 2% MLB: 6% *Comparables: Jarrod Parker, Justin Nicolino, Roberto Osuna*

A product of the same high school as Lucas Giolito and Max Fried, Flaherty doesn't come equipped with their ceilings or Q Scores. Still, he possesses a real chance of becoming noteworthy in his own right. His arsenal comprises three pitches that could grade as average or better, as well as a curve that ought to work as a show-me offering. Flaherty's delivery, frame and pitching know-how are just as important to his future success, and each indicates he should in time mature into an innings-gulping mid-rotation fixture. Basically, Flaherty possesses everything you want from a non-elite teenage starter, meaning his biggest blemish is that he's a non-elite teenage starter.

Jaime Garcia LHP

Born: 7/8/86 Age: 29 Bats: L Throws: L Height: 6'2" Weight: 215

YEAR	TEAM	LVL	AGE	W	L	SV	G	GS	IP	H	HR	BB/9	K/9	GB%	BABIP	WHIP	ERA	FIP	DRA	WARP	CFIP	MPH
2013	SLN	MLB	26	5	2	0	9	9	55^{1}	57	6	2.4	7.0	64%	.300	1.30	3.58	3.69	4.90	0.0	104	90.9
2014	SLN	MLB	27	3	1	0	7	7	43^{2}	39	6	1.4	8.0	54%	.270	1.05	4.12	3.79	4.07	0.4	89	92.7
2015	SLN	MLB	28	10	6	0	20	20	129^{2}	106	6	2.1	6.7	62%	.267	1.05	2.43	3.03	3.28	2.7	96	92.3
2016	*SLN*	*MLB*	*29*	*9*	*7*	*0*	*24*	*24*	*144*	*136*	*14*	*2.3*	*7.3*	*61%*	*.309*	*1.20*	*3.52*	*3.53*	*4.19*	*1.9*	*96*	
2017	*SLN*	*MLB*	*30*	*10*	*9*	*0*	*28*	*28*	*166^{2}*	*159*	*18*	*2.3*	*7.5*	*61%*	*.312*	*1.21*	*3.60*	*3.96*	*4.28*	*1.9*	*98*	

Breakout: 15% Improve: 49% Collapse: 23% Attrition: 6% MLB: 99% *Comparables: Rick Reuschel, Charles Nagy, Jon Matlack*

Two years had passed since we'd last seen Garcia appear more than a handful of times in a season. Fortunately, that trend ended in 2015, as he started 20 times and proved he could coerce grounders as well as ever before. Oh sure, Garcia still missed time with injuries: He didn't join the active roster until late May due to last year's thoracic outlet syndrome surgery, and he later missed most of July with a strained groin. But he was hearty and hale more often than not, and asserted that by finishing second among starters in groundball percentage. The key to Garcia's groundwork? His entire arsenal. Garcia topped the 55 percent grounder-per-BIP mark with each of his four main pitches, according to Brooks Baseball. His body remains as trustworthy as a mountebank, but the Cardinals nonetheless exercised their $11.5 million club option on his services. Garcia will need another season like 2015 if they're to do the same thing next fall with his $12 million option for 2017.

Marco Gonzales LHP

Born: 2/16/92 Age: 24 Bats: L Throws: L Height: 6'1" Weight: 195

YEAR	TEAM	LVL	AGE	W	L	SV	G	GS	IP	H	HR	BB/9	K/9	GB%	BABIP	WHIP	ERA	FIP	DRA	WARP	CFIP	MPH
2013	PMB	A+	21	0	0	0	4	4	16^{2}	10	1	2.7	7.0	33%	.214	0.90	1.62	3.36	4.14	0.1	97	
2014	SFD	AA	22	3	2	0	7	7	38^{2}	33	2	2.3	10.7	45%	.304	1.11	2.33	2.19				
2014	PMB	A+	22	2	2	0	6	6	37^{2}	34	1	1.9	7.6	53%	.303	1.12	1.43	2.67	3.97	0.4	88	
2014	MEM	AAA	22	4	1	0	8	8	45^{2}	43	7	1.8	7.7	43%	.279	1.14	3.35	4.77	5.11	0.3	94	
2014	SLN	MLB	22	4	2	0	10	5	34^{2}	32	4	5.5	8.0	39%	.283	1.53	4.15	4.72	5.06	-0.1	114	91.9
2015	SLN	MLB	23	0	0	0	1	1	2^{2}	7	1	3.4	3.4	43%	.462	3.00	13.50	8.41	17.51	-0.4	111	91.7
2016	*SLN*	*MLB*	*24*	*5*	*4*	*0*	*33*	*11*	*82*	*82*	*10*	*3.0*	*6.9*	*40%*	*.311*	*1.34*	*4.15*	*4.19*	*4.89*	*0.3*	*114*	
2017	*SLN*	*MLB*	*25*	*7*	*8*	*0*	*23*	*23*	*137^{2}*	*137*	*18*	*3.4*	*7.6*	*40%*	*.316*	*1.37*	*4.26*	*4.69*	*5.02*	*0.4*	*118*	

Breakout: 19% Improve: 26% Collapse: 9% Attrition: 18% MLB: 49% *Comparables: Tyson Ross, Jason Windsor, Edinson Volquez*

You wouldn't know it based on his numbers, yet Gonzales entered the season ranked as the Cardinals' top pitching prospect by most evaluators (including ours). An athletic changeup artist who can swing the bat (relatively) well and field his position, he was supposed to be an easy-to-project mid-rotation starter. But a pair of shoulder-related shutdowns limited him to 18 minor-league appearances on the season, in which he posted some gnarly numbers, including a 5.45 Triple-A ERA and 2.1 strikeout-to-walk ratio. Gonzales did reach the majors for a September spot start, but was sent home afterward with the hope that he would use the early jump on the offseason to rebuild his arm strength and regain his past crispness. If Gonzales accomplishes both feats, he'll be in position to claim a big-league job.

Mitchell Harris RHP

Born: 11/7/85 Age: 30 Bats: R Throws: R Height: 6'4" Weight: 215

YEAR	TEAM	LVL	AGE	W	L	SV	G	GS	IP	H	HR	BB/9	K/9	GB%	BABIP	WHIP	ERA	FIP	DRA	WARP	CFIP	MPH
2013	SCO	A-	27	4	1	1	20	0	33^{1}	22	0	4.1	7.8	40%	.247	1.11	0.81	2.89	4.04	0.1	101	
2014	SFD	AA	28	2	0	1	33	0	43^{2}	38	5	2.7	7.0	40%	.258	1.17	3.92	3.94				
2014	PMB	A+	28	0	2	0	8	0	12^{2}	8	1	4.3	6.4	28%	.200	1.11	4.26	4.42	4.49	0.0	105	
2015	MEM	AAA	29	0	4	4	25	0	26^{2}	30	1	3.4	6.8	44%	.341	1.50	3.38	3.82	4.42	0.2	93	
2015	SLN	MLB	29	2	1	0	26	0	27	30	4	4.3	5.0	48%	.289	1.59	3.67	5.42	5.33	-0.2	123	96.5
2016	*SLN*	*MLB*	*30*	*1*	*0*	*0*	*22*	*0*	*23^{2}*	*24*	*3*	*3.3*	*6.0*	*44%*	*.301*	*1.38*	*4.42*	*4.60*	*5.21*	*-0.1*	*121*	
2017	*SLN*	*MLB*	*31*	*1*	*0*	*0*	*23*	*0*	*29^{2}*	*29*	*4*	*3.3*	*6.5*	*44%*	*.299*	*1.35*	*4.42*	*4.88*	*5.21*	*-0.1*	*122*	

Breakout: 7% Improve: 8% Collapse: 8% Attrition: 12% MLB: 17% *Comparables: Carlos Muniz, Randy Williams, Ryan Braun*

When Harris was drafted from the Naval Academy in 2008, he applied for a waiver that would have allowed him to honor his commitment *after* chasing his big-league dreams. The waiver was denied, and so he reported for duty and served most of his five-year commitment without throwing a professional pitch. Harris returned to the organization as a free man in 2013, and it didn't take long for his sea legs to dry out. He reached the majors in April, showing a mid-90s fastball and nifty cutter. Yet good story and stuff aside, it's hard to ignore the shakiness of his performance. Harris walked almost as many batters as he struck out. His groundball rate is fine but, unlike another man forced by a higher power to live on a boat, he didn't show a preference for dealing in pairs, as his double-play percentage was nothing special. There's no doubting that Lieutenant Harris has the nerves to pitch in high-leverage situations; for now, though, he seems like a better fit in low-leverage spots, or Memphis.

Mike Leake RHP

Born: 11/12/87 Age: 28 Bats: R Throws: R Height: 5'10" Weight: 190

YEAR	TEAM	LVL	AGE	W	L	SV	G	GS	IP	H	HR	BB/9	K/9	GB%	BABIP	WHIP	ERA	FIP	DRA	WARP	CFIP	MPH
2013	CIN	MLB	25	14	7	0	31	31	192^{1}	193	21	2.2	5.7	50%	.285	1.25	3.37	4.01	4.22	1.6	112	92.6
2014	CIN	MLB	26	11	13	0	33	33	214^{1}	217	23	2.1	6.9	55%	.298	1.25	3.70	3.85	4.17	1.6	104	93.2
2015	CIN	MLB	27	9	5	0	21	21	136^{2}	123	14	2.2	5.9	52%	.262	1.15	3.56	3.97	3.33	2.8	104	93.2
2015	SFN	MLB	27	2	5	0	9	9	55^{1}	51	8	2.4	4.7	53%	.254	1.19	4.07	4.86	4.02	0.7	133	93.0
2016	*SLN*	*MLB*	*28*	*11*	*10*	*0*	*29*	*29*	*174*	*171*	*19*	*2.1*	*5.7*	*53%*	*.298*	*1.22*	*3.96*	*4.03*	*4.71*	*1.2*	*110*	
2017	*SLN*	*MLB*	*29*	*10*	*11*	*0*	*29*	*29*	*178*	*178*	*21*	*2.1*	*6.1*	*53%*	*.304*	*1.24*	*3.96*	*4.36*	*4.71*	*1.2*	*110*	

Breakout: 14% Improve: 57% Collapse: 19% Attrition: 4% MLB: 94% *Comparables: Scott McGregor, John Smiley, Frank Viola*

The Giants ventured into the deadline pitching fray for the second straight year, but the returns on their 2015 acquisition weren't good. Billed as a durable starter who'd savor the move from Great American Ball Park to AT&T, Leake missed time with a hamstring strain, then gave up homers at a higher pace in San Francisco than he had in Cincinnati. The disappointing summer by the bay might have dimmed Leake's stock, but he reached free agency much younger than his available colleagues, a product of his non-stop route from Arizona State to the majors. Walt Jocketty should get a kickback on Leake's new $80 million deal.

Lance Lynn RHP

Born: 5/12/87 Age: 29 Bats: R Throws: R Height: 6'5" Weight: 240

YEAR	TEAM	LVL	AGE	W	L	SV	G	GS	IP	H	HR	BB/9	K/9	GB%	BABIP	WHIP	ERA	FIP	DRA	WARP	CFIP	MPH
2013	SLN	MLB	26	15	10	0	33	33	201^{2}	189	14	3.4	8.8	45%	.314	1.31	3.97	3.25	4.14	1.9	97	95.1
2014	SLN	MLB	27	15	10	0	33	33	203^{2}	185	13	3.2	8.0	46%	.290	1.26	2.74	3.32	3.67	2.8	97	95.4
2015	SLN	MLB	28	12	11	0	31	31	175^{1}	172	13	3.5	8.6	46%	.319	1.37	3.03	3.47	4.26	1.6	97	95.1
2016	*SLN*	*MLB*	*29*	*10*	*8*	*0*	*26*	*26*	*154*	*143*	*15*	*3.1*	*8.3*	*46%*	*.314*	*1.27*	*3.59*	*3.61*	*4.27*	*1.9*	*97*	
2017	*SLN*	*MLB*	*30*	*8*	*8*	*0*	*23*	*23*	*137*	*132*	*15*	*3.3*	*8.3*	*46%*	*.322*	*1.32*	*3.74*	*4.12*	*4.45*	*1.4*	*102*	

Breakout: 24% Improve: 45% Collapse: 20% Attrition: 4% MLB: 95% *Comparables: Anibal Sanchez, Francisco Liriano, Daisuke Matsuzaka*

Between his monk-like devotion to routine and his reliever-like inability to harness a pitch to neutralize lefties, we're beginning to think we've identified the motivation behind Lynn's consistency: He just hates change. Would explain the remarkable consistency of his FIPs and his groundball rates over the past three years, and perhaps his decision to sign away his arbitration years (for $22 million) to the Cardinals. The closest thing to a detour was his trip to the DL with a strained forearm in June, the first time he'd tapped out since joining the Cardinals' rotation in 2012. Lynn returned 17 days later and went back to doing what he always does. Maybe he'll surprise us and get a new haircut or glove in 2016.

Tyler Lyons LHP

Born: 2/21/88 Age: 28 Bats: L Throws: L Height: 6'4" Weight: 200

YEAR	TEAM	LVL	AGE	W	L	SV	G	GS	IP	H	HR	BB/9	K/9	GB%	BABIP	WHIP	ERA	FIP	DRA	WARP	CFIP	MPH
2013	SLN	MLB	25	2	4	0	12	8	53	49	5	2.7	7.3	50%	.282	1.23	4.75	3.70	4.24	0.4	103	92.4
2013	MEM	AAA	25	7	2	0	17	16	100^{1}	85	6	1.7	7.7	52%	.280	1.04	3.32	3.38	4.55	1.2	86	
2014	MEM	AAA	26	8	2	0	14	14	81^{1}	94	9	2.0	8.3	44%	.348	1.38	4.43	3.96	4.85	0.8	83	
2014	SLN	MLB	26	0	4	0	11	4	36^{2}	33	4	2.7	8.8	43%	.284	1.20	4.42	3.62	4.44	0.1	96	92.9
2015	MEM	AAA	27	9	5	0	16	16	94^{2}	104	12	1.2	9.1	46%	.336	1.24	3.14	3.69	2.60	3.1	73	
2015	SLN	MLB	27	3	1	0	17	8	60	59	12	2.2	9.0	42%	.281	1.23	3.75	4.56	5.50	-0.4	97	92.8
2016	*SLN*	*MLB*	*28*	*3*	*2*	*0*	*43*	*3*	58^{2}	*56*	*7*	*2.2*	*7.8*	*44%*	*.310*	*1.20*	*3.67*	*3.67*	*4.35*	*0.2*	*99*	
2017	*SLN*	*MLB*	*29*	*5*	*5*	*0*	*16*	*16*	*92*	*87*	*13*	*2.3*	*8.5*	*44%*	*.311*	*1.20*	*3.78*	*4.15*	*4.48*	*0.8*	*103*	

Breakout: 22% Improve: 44% Collapse: 7% Attrition: 15% MLB: 64% *Comparables: Marco Estrada, Collin McHugh, Matt Shoemaker*

The unluckiest man in the minors? Probably not, but you can't blame Lyons if he feels that way. For a fourth consecutive season, he spent most of his time in Memphis. Predictably, Lyons continued to dominate against Triple-A batters, reasserting that they were no match for his above-average control and deep arsenal—led by a slider that boasts one of the highest spin rates in the game. In most other organizations, Lyons would be entering his second or third full season as a back-end starter. In St. Loo, he's still waiting on his first. It should be coming soon, since he's out of options; the question is which organization will give him his lucky break.

Seth Maness RHP

Born: 10/14/88 Age: 27 Bats: R Throws: R Height: 6'0" Weight: 190

YEAR	TEAM	LVL	AGE	W	L	SV	G	GS	IP	H	HR	BB/9	K/9	GB%	BABIP	WHIP	ERA	FIP	DRA	WARP	CFIP	MPH
2013	MEM	AAA	24	2	2	0	4	4	25	34	2	1.1	6.5	40%	.376	1.48	4.32	3.65	4.78	0.2	93	
2013	SLN	MLB	24	5	2	1	66	0	62	65	4	1.9	5.1	70%	.311	1.26	2.32	3.41	4.56	0.0	107	92.6
2014	SLN	MLB	25	6	4	3	73	0	80^{1}	77	7	1.2	6.2	57%	.289	1.10	2.91	3.35	3.51	1.0	99	91.6
2015	SLN	MLB	26	4	2	3	76	0	63^{1}	77	7	1.8	6.5	58%	.345	1.42	4.26	3.81	5.65	-0.7	105	91.6
2016	*SLN*	*MLB*	*27*	*3*	*1*	*0*	*54*	*0*	*57*	*57*	*6*	*2.1*	*6.3*	*59%*	*.307*	*1.23*	*3.79*	*3.85*	*4.50*	*0.3*	*102*	
2017	*SLN*	*MLB*	*28*	*4*	*3*	*1*	*45*	*6*	*73*	*72*	*8*	*2.3*	*6.8*	*59%*	*.310*	*1.23*	*3.76*	*4.15*	*4.47*	*0.5*	*101*	

Breakout: 25% Improve: 52% Collapse: 19% Attrition: 16% MLB: 86% *Comparables: Tony Pena, Dave Bush, Ryan Rowland-Smith*

The top selling point on Maness throughout his minor-league days was his command—he could, in so many words, split an amoeba in half. Having proved that reputation correct, he's since added a few more features to the back of his box. Most notably, he has proved to be a rubber-armed groundball specialist. Last year he generated more than 55 percent grounders for a third consecutive season, while only one right-hander appeared in more games than he. Maness continues to contend with an image problem—he looks like a Quad-A reliever due to his substandard height and stuff—but none of those advertising concepts matter in the majors, where production trumps presentation. Although Maness isn't pretty, his statline is, and that's what'll keep him busy for the foreseeable future.

Carlos Martinez RHP

Born: 9/21/91 Age: 24 Bats: R Throws: R Height: 6'0" Weight: 185

YEAR	TEAM	LVL	AGE	W	L	SV	G	GS	IP	H	HR	BB/9	K/9	GB%	BABIP	WHIP	ERA	FIP	DRA	WARP	CFIP	MPH
2013	SFD	AA	21	1	0	0	3	3	11^{2}	11	1	0.8	6.9	57%	.278	1.03	2.31	3.14	4.14	0.1	94	
2013	SLN	MLB	21	2	1	1	21	1	28^{1}	31	1	2.9	7.6	55%	.345	1.41	5.08	3.06	4.38	0.1	100	100.2
2013	MEM	AAA	21	5	3	0	13	13	68	54	3	3.6	8.3	56%	.268	1.19	2.51	3.75	4.78	0.6	93	
2014	MEM	AAA	22	1	0	0	2	2	10^{1}	6	0	0.9	6.1	48%	.207	0.68	0.00	2.63	5.00	0.1	93	
2014	SLN	MLB	22	2	4	1	57	7	89^{1}	90	4	3.6	8.5	55%	.333	1.41	4.03	3.15	3.92	0.7	92	100.3
2015	SLN	MLB	23	14	7	0	31	29	179^{2}	168	13	3.2	9.2	56%	.318	1.29	3.01	3.24	4.31	1.5	92	99.0
2016	*SLN*	*MLB*	*24*	*8*	*7*	*0*	*24*	*24*	*127^{1}*	*114*	*12*	*3.0*	*8.5*	*56%*	*.310*	*1.22*	*3.43*	*3.50*	*4.09*	*1.8*	*90*	
2017	*SLN*	*MLB*	*25*	*7*	*6*	*1*	*40*	*19*	*137*	*124*	*14*	*2.9*	*9.1*	*56%*	*.319*	*1.23*	*3.41*	*3.76*	*4.07*	*1.7*	*90*	

Breakout: 21% Improve: 48% Collapse: 16% Attrition: 18% MLB: 97% *Comparables: Rich Harden, Jaime Garcia, Tommy Hanson*

For a pitcher of his prospect pedigree and faux-lineage—Pedro Martinez has taken Little Pedro under his wing as though Carlos were his real boy—the relief stats were always a bit disappointing. Elite young pitchers don't strike out 7.9 batters per nine out of the bullpen; heck, badly flawed young pitchers don't even strike out 7.9 batters per nine out of the bullpen these days. But Martinez's excellent changeup was buried in a bullpen role, and in his first full year as a starter we saw emerge a pitcher with the stuff, stamina, and repertoire to make an All-Star team. Which he did. He actually improved his strikeout rate to a career high, and recorded a quality start in nearly 70 percent of his games. He's the kind of pitcher a team wants starting Game Two in a playoff series.

Alas, he saved the only negative of the year for his last start in September, which he exited due to a season-ending shoulder strain—an injury that seems preferable to a torn UCL or labrum, and that isn't expected to impact his 2016 season. Not every short, lanky pitcher runs into durability problems, but it's a cliche for a reason. Until the often-dominant Martinez—whose delivery features significant recoil during the follow-through stages—works a full season or two without incident, both his boosters and his skeptics will be saying "I told you so."

Alex Reyes RHP

Born: 8/29/94 Age: 21 Bats: R Throws: R Height: 6'3" Weight: 175

YEAR	TEAM	LVL	AGE	W	L	SV	G	GS	IP	H	HR	BB/9	K/9	GB%	BABIP	WHIP	ERA	FIP	DRA	WARP	CFIP	MPH
2014	PEO	A	19	7	7	0	21	21	109^{1}	82	6	5.0	11.3	40%	.295	1.31	3.62	3.45	4.30	1.0	94	
2015	PMB	A+	20	2	5	0	13	13	63^{2}	49	0	4.4	13.6	46%	.371	1.26	2.26	1.75	1.51	2.4	71	
2015	SFD	AA	20	3	2	0	8	8	34^{2}	21	1	4.7	13.5	44%	.286	1.12	3.12	2.32	2.57	1.0	77	
2016	*SLN*	*MLB*	*21*	*6*	*5*	*0*	*18*	*18*	*88^{2}*	*75*	*9*	*4.5*	*10.0*	*36%*	*.319*	*1.35*	*3.70*	*3.77*	*4.41*	*0.9*	*100*	
2017	*SLN*	*MLB*	*22*	*9*	*10*	*0*	*31*	*31*	*200^{2}*	*162*	*22*	*4.7*	*10.7*	*36%*	*.313*	*1.33*	*3.77*	*4.14*	*4.49*	*1.4*	*102*	

Breakout: 8% Improve: 9% Collapse: 3% Attrition: 6% MLB: 15% *Comparables: Keyvius Sampson, Trevor Bauer, Trevor May*

As part of the book-making process, we make it a point to talk to scouts, executives and anyone else who might provide insight on certain players and situations. For the sake of this comment, we've fabricated an interview with singer Rob Thomas—you know, for educational purposes. So Mr. Thomas, what do you make of Reyes' fastball? "Man, it's a hot one." Sure is—reports have him touching into the upper 90s when he needs it. His command tends to waver when he throws too hard, though, leading to pitches located in the batter's hot zones, right? "Like seven inches from the midday sun." You might say that; you definitely might say that. What advice would you give Reyes to avoid falling into those ruts, being a world-traveled and -renowned performer and whatnot? "I hear you whisper and the words melt everyone." Huh. Well, that's poetic, and correct—his low-effort fastball *is* good enough to overpower the opposition, so there's no point in going full bore when he doesn't need to. Okay, last one: what do you make of his curveball? "It's just like the ocean, under the moon." How is it ... oh, because it's so wavy? Man, you sure know your stuff, Mr. Thomas. Thanks for your time.

Trevor Rosenthal RHP

Born: 5/29/90 Age: 26 Bats: R Throws: R Height: 6'2" Weight: 220

YEAR	TEAM	LVL	AGE	W	L	SV	G	GS	IP	H	HR	BB/9	K/9	GB%	BABIP	WHIP	ERA	FIP	DRA	WARP	CFIP	MPH
2013	SLN	MLB	23	2	4	3	74	0	75^{1}	63	4	2.4	12.9	46%	.341	1.10	2.63	1.88	3.99	0.5	59	100.2
2014	SLN	MLB	24	2	6	45	72	0	70^{1}	57	2	5.4	11.1	39%	.318	1.41	3.20	2.96	3.44	0.9	87	99.7
2015	SLN	MLB	25	2	4	48	68	0	68^{2}	62	3	3.3	10.9	47%	.337	1.27	2.10	2.45	3.59	0.9	77	100.3
2016	*SLN*	*MLB*	*26*	*3*	*1*	*35*	*58*	*0*	*61^{2}*	*49*	*6*	*3.1*	*10.5*	*45%*	*.311*	*1.14*	*3.01*	*3.09*	*3.61*	*1.0*	*76*	
2017	*SLN*	*MLB*	*27*	*5*	*3*	*40*	*60*	*4*	*83*	*65*	*8*	*3.2*	*11.0*	*45%*	*.314*	*1.14*	*2.98*	*3.26*	*3.58*	*1.4*	*75*	

Breakout: 36% Improve: 63% Collapse: 19% Attrition: 8% MLB: 93% *Comparables: Carlos Marmol, Jose Arredondo, Brandon Beachy*

You know your closer is pitching well when his paternity leave is used as a brickbat by neanderthals. Such was the case with Rosenthal, who, in addition to welcoming his second daughter to the world in late August, enjoyed what might have been his best season yet. His walk rate, which had reached danger-zone levels in 2014, regressed most of the way back to his 2013 marks, when he controlled his gas better than OPEC. That was the only big change in his peripherals, as he continued to evade lumber and pile up strikeouts en route to the lowest ERA of his career. If the Cardinals have a complaint about Rosenthal's 2015, it's that it served as his lead-in to his arbitration eligibility—i.e., he'll make enough to buy a bigger crib.

Kevin Siegrist LHP

Born: 7/20/89 Age: 26 Bats: L Throws: L Height: 6'5" Weight: 215

YEAR	TEAM	LVL	AGE	W	L	SV	G	GS	IP	H	HR	BB/9	K/9	GB%	BABIP	WHIP	ERA	FIP	DRA	WARP	CFIP	MPH
2013	SFD	AA	23	1	1	1	13	0	20	8	2	3.2	15.8	42%	.207	0.75	2.25	2.06	3.06	0.4	60	
2013	SLN	MLB	23	3	1	0	45	0	39^2	17	1	4.1	11.3	41%	.195	0.88	0.45	2.26	1.73	1.4	80	98.4
2014	SLN	MLB	24	1	4	0	37	0	30^1	32	5	4.7	11.0	33%	.338	1.58	6.82	4.59	5.82	-0.5	96	96.6
2015	SLN	MLB	25	7	1	6	81	0	74^2	53	4	4.1	10.8	32%	.271	1.17	2.17	2.93	3.66	0.9	81	96.5
2016	*SLN*	*MLB*	*26*	*2*	*1*	*0*	*45*	*0*	47^2	*35*	*5*	*3.2*	*10.0*	*33%*	*.282*	*1.10*	*3.22*	*3.38*	*3.84*	*0.6*	*84*	
2017	*SLN*	*MLB*	*27*	*4*	*2*	*1*	*53*	*4*	68^2	*49*	*7*	*3.5*	*10.8*	*33%*	*.282*	*1.10*	*3.14*	*3.45*	*3.75*	*1.0*	*81*	

Breakout: 35% Improve: 57% Collapse: 20% Attrition: 17% MLB: 90% *Comparables: Carlos Marmol, Antonio Bastardo, Daniel Bard*

For the first time under Matheny's watch, the Cardinals had two relievers finish in the top 10 in the majors in appearances: Maness and Siegrist, who topped the leaderboard. Siegrist is the third St. Louis southpaw to answer 80+ calls in a season, following Steve Kline (89 apps in '01) and Ray King (86 in '04), but make no mistake: He's different than them. For one, Kline and King were employed under Tony La Russa, who inflated relief appearances like Dickens inflated word counts. For another, both of those fellers were used as lefty specialists; Siegrist wasn't—in fact, he faced roughly two-thirds *right*-handed batters. The reasons behind Siegrist's odd usage are straightforward, if unusual: His top secondary pitch is a circle-change and he has performed considerably worse versus same-handed batters. Against righties, meanwhile, he has allowed a lower OPS over the past three years than Brad Ziegler and Luke Gregerson. Such reverse splits are rare, but *The Book* tells us that left-handers' platoon splits are reliable after 450 same-side matchups; Siegrist is a bit more than halfway there. Improved fastball command or a decent breaking ball could make Siegrist a valuable two-way threat, but for now he'll settle for working more days than God as one of the best left-on-right relievers in the game.

Miguel Socolovich RHP

Born: 7/24/86 Age: 29 Bats: R Throws: R Height: 6'1" Weight: 195

YEAR	TEAM	LVL	AGE	W	L	SV	G	GS	IP	H	HR	BB/9	K/9	GB%	BABIP	WHIP	ERA	FIP	DRA	WARP	CFIP	MPH
2014	LVG	AAA	27	2	2	3	51	0	59^1	68	5	2.9	10.3	42%	.375	1.47	3.64	3.46	4.65	0.5	77	
2015	SLN	MLB	28	4	1	0	28	0	29^2	25	1	3.0	8.2	50%	.276	1.18	1.82	2.79	3.10	0.6	96	93.3
2015	MEM	AAA	28	2	2	0	21	0	32^2	18	1	3.3	9.9	49%	.224	0.92	2.48	2.99	3.21	0.7	80	
2016	*SLN*	*MLB*	*29*	*1*	*0*	*0*	*22*	*0*	23^2	*21*	*2*	*2.9*	*8.4*	*46%*	*.298*	*1.20*	*3.57*	*3.42*	*4.24*	*0.3*	*96*	
2017	*SLN*	*MLB*	*30*	*1*	*0*	*0*	*23*	*0*	*31*	*28*	*4*	*3.1*	*9.0*	*46%*	*.309*	*1.25*	*3.72*	*4.09*	*4.42*	*0.2*	*101*	

Breakout: 12% Improve: 22% Collapse: 34% Attrition: 33% MLB: 60% *Comparables: Blake Parker, Chris Leroux, Marcus McBeth*

Socolovich is the Cardinals at their most maddening. When he signed a minor-league pact in November, he looked like pure org filler—after all, he'd returned stateside only a year earlier, having spent 2013 with the Hiroshima Carp. So much for that noise. Socolovich did more than appear in a few stray games; he appeared in a few stray games and posted top-notch results. How he did it isn't clear. Socolovich doesn't throw hard or feature killer secondary pitches (though his changeup is good), and while the delivery is deceptive, it doesn't explain everything or atone for his below-average command. So what does? Cardinals Devil Magic.

Sam Tuivailala RHP

Born: 10/19/92 Age: 23 Bats: R Throws: R Height: 6'3" Weight: 195

YEAR	TEAM	LVL	AGE	W	L	SV	G	GS	IP	H	HR	BB/9	K/9	GB%	BABIP	WHIP	ERA	FIP	DRA	WARP	CFIP	MPH
2013	PEO	A	20	0	3	1	28	0	35^1	31	0	5.1	12.7	58%	.365	1.44	5.35	2.55	4.05	0.4	82	
2014	SLN	MLB	21	0	0	0	2	0	1	5	2	18.0	9.0	0%	.600	7.00	36.00	33.10	46.08	-0.5	111	99.8
2014	SFD	AA	21	2	1	1	17	0	21	18	0	3.9	12.9	56%	.375	1.29	2.57	1.69				
2014	PMB	A+	21	0	1	3	29	0	37^2	29	1	4.3	15.3	47%	.364	1.25	3.58	1.93	3.15	0.7	62	
2015	SLN	MLB	22	0	1	0	14	0	14^2	13	2	4.9	12.3	49%	.314	1.43	3.07	3.84	5.34	-0.1	90	99.3
2015	MEM	AAA	22	3	1	17	43	0	45	28	2	5.2	8.6	43%	.228	1.20	1.60	4.20	4.86	0.2	100	
2016	*SLN*	*MLB*	*23*	*1*	*0*	*0*	*18*	*0*	*19*	*17*	*2*	*3.8*	*9.0*	*43%*	*.315*	*1.33*	*3.79*	*3.83*	*4.49*	*0.1*	*101*	
2017	*SLN*	*MLB*	*24*	*1*	*0*	*0*	*22*	*0*	*26*	*23*	*3*	*3.6*	*9.8*	*43%*	*.318*	*1.29*	*3.69*	*4.06*	*4.37*	*0.2*	*98*	

Breakout: 9% Improve: 10% Collapse: 7% Attrition: 12% MLB: 18% *Comparables: Matt Stites, Rich Thompson, Stephen Pryor*

Few teams have gotten more mileage from hitter-to-pitcher conversions than the Cardinals. Both Jason Motte and Trevor Rosenthal were drafted as position players, only to transition to the mound and later ascend to the closer's role. Whether Tuivailala, a former infielder, will reach the same heights is to be determined by his refinements in the finer aspects of pitching. There's no questioning his arm strength—his fastball was clocked over 100 mph in May—but he needs to work on his command (he has walked more than five batters per nine innings for his career) and consistency of his breaking balls. The recent failures of similar relievers, like Juan Jaime and Jose Dominguez, prove that elite heat isn't enough to guarantee success—not even in a middle-relief role. Still, Tuivailala is young and he's under the careful watch of the Cardinals, so he has a real chance to make this work, and soon.

Carlos Villanueva RHP

Born: 11/28/83 Age: 32 Bats: R Throws: R Height: 6'2" Weight: 215

YEAR	TEAM	LVL	AGE	W	L	SV	G	GS	IP	H	HR	BB/9	K/9	GB%	BABIP	WHIP	ERA	FIP	DRA	WARP	CFIP	MPH
2013	CHN	MLB	29	7	8	0	47	15	128^2	117	14	2.8	7.2	43%	.283	1.22	4.06	3.84	4.03	1.2	97	90.8
2014	CHN	MLB	30	5	7	2	42	5	77^2	89	6	2.2	8.3	45%	.342	1.39	4.64	3.10	4.57	0.0	93	92.0
2015	SLN	MLB	31	4	3	2	35	0	61	50	6	3.1	8.1	42%	.265	1.16	2.95	3.77	4.06	0.5	100	90.8
2016	*SLN*	*MLB*	*32*	*3*	*1*	*0*	*57*	*0*	*60*	*54*	*6*	*2.7*	*7.5*	*43%*	*.298*	*1.20*	*3.70*	*3.67*	*4.39*	*0.6*	*99*	
2017	*SLN*	*MLB*	*33*	*6*	*5*	*1*	*55*	*12*	135^2	*121*	*15*	*2.6*	*7.7*	*43%*	*.293*	*1.18*	*3.74*	*4.11*	*4.44*	*1.0*	*100*	

Breakout: 23% Improve: 54% Collapse: 23% Attrition: 9% MLB: 96% *Comparables: Stan Williams, Grant Jackson, Bert Blyleven*

Part of the Cardinals' design to add length to their bullpen, Villanueva belongs to a species so rare in modern times that it might be classified as a cryptid, alongside the akkorokamui and the igopogo: the multi-inning reliever. Were it not for the Giants' Yusmeiro Petit, Villanueva would be the NL's undisputed king of long relief. Both he and Petit show the positives that come from thinking outside the box. Neither is fit to start or pitch in high-leverage situations, but both provided value to their teams by doing what they do best: going through a lineup one, maybe one-and-a-half times, and saving other relievers from having to pitch. With the bullpen game becoming so specialized, why not carry someone whose utility benefits everyone else? Only 32, Villanueva figures to have a job until his arm loses elasticity.

Michael Wacha RHP

Born: 7/1/91 Age: 24 Bats: R Throws: R Height: 6'6" Weight: 210

YEAR	TEAM	LVL	AGE	W	L	SV	G	GS	IP	H	HR	BB/9	K/9	GB%	BABIP	WHIP	ERA	FIP	DRA	WARP	CFIP	MPH
2013	MEM	AAA	21	5	3	0	15	15	85	65	9	2.0	7.7	38%	.241	0.99	2.65	3.90	4.53	1.0	86	
2013	SLN	MLB	21	4	1	0	15	9	64^{2}	52	5	2.6	9.0	46%	.275	1.10	2.78	2.90	2.75	1.6	88	97.0
2014	SLN	MLB	22	5	6	0	19	19	107	95	6	2.8	7.9	44%	.288	1.20	3.20	3.14	3.74	1.4	99	96.3
2015	SLN	MLB	23	17	7	0	30	30	181^{1}	162	19	2.9	7.6	48%	.272	1.21	3.38	3.90	3.92	2.4	103	97.1
2016	*SLN*	*MLB*	*24*	*12*	*10*	*0*	*31*	*31*	*195^{1}*	*171*	*21*	*2.6*	*7.5*	*46%*	*.286*	*1.16*	*3.69*	*3.75*	*4.38*	*2.1*	*101*	
2017	*SLN*	*MLB*	*25*	*11*	*11*	*0*	*31*	*31*	*199^{2}*	*177*	*23*	*2.5*	*7.6*	*46%*	*.288*	*1.17*	*3.74*	*4.12*	*4.44*	*1.8*	*103*	

Breakout: 24% Improve: 54% Collapse: 11% Attrition: 7% MLB: 98% *Comparables: Chad Billingsley, Matt Cain, Mat Latos*

From a rate-stat perspective, Wacha had the same season that he did in 2014: His four big per-nine measures (that's hits, walks, home runs and strikeouts, kids) *combined* to change by 0.8 ticks. From a more narrative-driven position, Wacha's season featured too *much* change. He entered June with a 2.27 ERA and appeared in his first All-Star Game a few weeks later. But any talk about his Cy Young candidacy was muted by an awful September that saw him allow 25 hits, 21 runs, 18 walks and seven homers in 24 innings. Was his slide caused by fatigue? Hangover? Envy of Trevor Rosenthal's paternity leave? Heaven only knows. Because this isn't meant to be a jeremiad, let's focus on some positives. For one, Wacha continued to look like an above-average starter using eyes or numbers. For another, he accomplished a very important feat by making 30 starts for the first time in his career. You'll understand the significance of that achievement if you open your copies of last year's book to page 378. We'll save you the effort: "The aftereffects of the scapular stress fracture Wacha suffered in 2014 are unpredictable, and could bother him all the time or never again." It was the latter in 2015. The Cards hope it stays that way in 2016.

Adam Wainwright RHP

Born: 8/30/81 Age: 34 Bats: R Throws: R Height: 6'7" Weight: 235

YEAR	TEAM	LVL	AGE	W	L	SV	G	GS	IP	H	HR	BB/9	K/9	GB%	BABIP	WHIP	ERA	FIP	DRA	WARP	CFIP	MPH
2013	SLN	MLB	31	19	9	0	34	34	241^{2}	223	15	1.3	8.2	50%	.305	1.07	2.94	2.52	3.50	4.1	78	93.6
2014	SLN	MLB	32	20	9	0	32	32	227	184	10	2.0	7.1	49%	.267	1.03	2.38	2.85	2.49	6.4	91	92.8
2015	SLN	MLB	33	2	1	0	7	4	28	25	0	1.3	6.4	52%	.287	1.04	1.61	2.16	4.22	0.3	99	93.1
2016	*SLN*	*MLB*	*34*	*14*	*10*	*0*	*32*	*32*	*214^{1}*	*193*	*19*	*1.9*	*7.4*	*50%*	*.302*	*1.11*	*3.24*	*3.28*	*3.88*	*3.6*	*86*	
2017	*SLN*	*MLB*	*35*	*13*	*11*	*0*	*31*	*31*	*198*	*180*	*19*	*2.0*	*7.6*	*50%*	*.305*	*1.13*	*3.32*	*3.64*	*3.97*	*3.3*	*88*	

Breakout: 20% Improve: 48% Collapse: 22% Attrition: 10% MLB: 97% *Comparables: Roger Clemens, Chris Carpenter, Pascual Perez*

For most of the year, it looked like Wainwright's part in the 2015 season would last approximately as long as Miles Archer's in *The Maltese Falcon*. He exited his fourth start of the season with a torn Achilles tendon, an injury that was expected to sideline him for nine-to-12 months. Yet there he was, some five months later, marching to the mound to make a relief appearance—hey, who said Marcus Stroman was the only pitcher with superhuman healing powers? Wainwright pitched out of the bullpen just three times during the regular season, but showed enough command and stuff—including his signature curveball—to earn a spot on the Cardinals' postseason roster as a reliever. (And he was good.) Given what we saw from Wainwright, we expect him to rejoin the rotation heading forward—and for him to do so without showing any ill effects from the injury or the layoff.

Jordan Walden RHP

Born: 11/16/87 Age: 28 Bats: R Throws: R Height: 6'5" Weight: 250

YEAR	TEAM	LVL	AGE	W	L	SV	G	GS	IP	H	HR	BB/9	K/9	GB%	BABIP	WHIP	ERA	FIP	DRA	WARP	CFIP	MPH
2013	ATL	MLB	25	4	3	1	50	0	47	39	4	2.7	10.3	33%	.292	1.13	3.45	2.79	3.16	0.8	76	98.7
2014	ATL	MLB	26	0	2	3	58	0	50	33	2	4.9	11.2	45%	.272	1.20	2.88	2.76	2.58	1.2	93	98.7
2015	SLN	MLB	27	0	1	1	12	0	10^{1}	7	0	3.5	10.5	42%	.269	1.06	0.87	2.00	3.47	0.2	90	97.7
2016	*SLN*	*MLB*	*28*	*2*	*1*	*0*	*43*	*0*	*45*	*38*	*5*	*3.4*	*9.4*	*43%*	*.301*	*1.22*	*3.51*	*3.66*	*4.18*	*0.4*	*91*	
2017	*SLN*	*MLB*	*29*	*3*	*1*	*1*	*56*	*0*	*49^{1}*	*44*	*6*	*3.9*	*9.5*	*43%*	*.308*	*1.32*	*3.99*	*4.38*	*4.75*	*0.1*	*106*	

Breakout: 26% Improve: 52% Collapse: 31% Attrition: 11% MLB: 95% *Comparables: Scott Williamson, Mark Littell, Ricky Bottalico*

Thoreau wrote: "The grand necessity, then, for our bodies, is to keep warm, to keep the vital heat in us." Walden's body has had trouble keeping warm. His latest injury (biceps inflammation) did more than run his streak to four consecutive seasons with a DL stint, it all but wiped out his year. Consider Walden's decision to sign a multi-year extension with the Cardinals before appearing in a game with them a smart and fortuitous twist—in addition to the obvious benefits, he was able to rest and rehab without fear of losing his 2016 paycheck. The looming concern now is whether Walden's injury will threaten his vital heat—the mid-90s fastball he jumps at hitters with to set up his slider. Here's hoping not.

Luke Weaver RHP

Born: 8/21/93 Age: 22 Bats: R Throws: R Height: 6'2" Weight: 170

YEAR	TEAM	LVL	AGE	W	L	SV	G	GS	IP	H	HR	BB/9	K/9	GB%	BABIP	WHIP	ERA	FIP	DRA	WARP	CFIP	MPH
2015	PMB	A+	21	8	5	0	19	19	105^{1}	98	2	1.6	7.5	46%	.303	1.11	1.62	2.28	2.47	2.6	83	
2016	*SLN*	*MLB*	*22*	*5*	*5*	*0*	*16*	*16*	75^{1}	*77*	*6*	*2.6*	*6.1*	*42%*	*.315*	*1.31*	*3.66*	*3.68*	*4.38*	*0.8*	*99*	
2017	*SLN*	*MLB*	*23*	*8*	*10*	*0*	*31*	*31*	197^{1}	*201*	*19*	*2.9*	*6.5*	*42%*	*.315*	*1.34*	*3.83*	*4.23*	*4.58*	*1.2*	*105*	

Breakout: 5% Improve: 9% Collapse: 3% Attrition: 9% MLB: 14% *Comparables: Trevor Rosenthal, Tyler Robertson, Andre Rienzo*

The Matt Carpenter comment alluded to the Cardinals' "type" of position player; they have one when it comes to pitchers, too. They don't seem to care about size, not so long as the pitcher has the requisite athleticism, and they seem to ignore the long-held scouting belief that breaking balls are innate while changeups can be learned through repetition. All that is evident through some of their recent top picks, including 2014 first-rounder Weaver, who, like Wacha and Gonzales before him, came by way of a major collegiate program armed with a slender frame, a good fastball-changeup combination and an iffy breaking ball. Now a full season into his career, Weaver looks like he'll be pitching in the majors soon. He doesn't have the highest ceiling—most peg him as a middle-of-the-rotation starter—but look how much those cost on the open market. The Cardinals' ability to consistently produce pitchers of similar quality without ever picking in the top half of the draft is incredible—and a testament not only to their scouting and development chops, but to their willingness to eschew conventional wisdom.

Jake Woordford RHP

Born: 10/28/96 Age: 19 Bats: R Throws: R Height: 6'4" Weight: 210

YEAR	TEAM	LVL	AGE	W	L	SV	G	GS	IP	H	HR	BB/9	K/9	GB%	BABIP	WHIP	ERA	FIP	DRA	WARP	CFIP	MPH
2016	*SLN*	*MLB*	*19*	*2*	*2*	*1*	*20*	*5*	34^{2}	*39*	*5*	*4.1*	*5.2*	*46%*	*.317*	*1.57*	*5.10*	*5.32*	*5.95*	*-0.5*	*143*	
2017	*SLN*	*MLB*	*20*	*2*	*3*	*0*	*19*	*8*	*90*	*101*	*13*	*3.8*	*5.6*	*46%*	*.320*	*1.54*	*4.96*	*5.50*	*5.79*	*-0.4*	*140*	

Breakout: 0% Improve: 0% Collapse: 0% Attrition: 0% MLB: 0% *Comparables: Dan Cortes, Chris Tillman, Andrew Faulkner*

The Cardinals drafted Woodford with their second first-round pick on the strengths of his athleticism, frame and potentially above-average fastball and slider. Basically, he looks like a fairly safe bet (for a high school pitcher) to turn into at least a back-end starter. The big caveats being that pitchers get hurt and Woodford is years away from contributing. But that last part is okay because linear time is a man-made construct, and in a different, parallel lifetime you already know how this turned out.

LINEOUTS

Hitters

NAME	POS	TEAM	LVL	AGE	PA	R	2B	3B	HR	RBI	BB	K	SB	CS	AVG/OBP/SLG	TAv	BABIP	BRR	FRAA	WARP
Harrison Bader	OF	PEO	A	21	228	34	11	2	9	28	15	44	15	6	.301/.364/.505	.310	.344	3.4	CF(42): 8.8, LF(7): 4.0	3.6
	OF	SCO	A-	21	30	6	2	0	2	4	0	5	2	0	.379/.400/.655	.356	.409	0.5	LF(4): -0.1, RF(3): -0.4	0.4
Aledmys Diaz	SS	MEM	AAA	24	58	12	3	0	3	6	6	5	0	1	.380/.448/.620	.381	.372	0.0	SS(14): -3.3	0.7
	SS	SFD	AA	24	409	47	25	2	10	46	29	62	6	5	.264/.324/.421	.269	.294	-0.4	SS(91): -1.8	1.8
Ed Easley	C	MEM	AAA	29	323	26	12	0	4	36	39	44	1	2	.251/.345/.337	.266	.283	-1.9	C(52): 0.6, 1B(9): 0.2	1.3
	C	SLN	MLB	29	7	0	0	0	0	1	0	1	0	0	.000/.000/.000	.116	.000	-0.1	C(3): -0.1	-0.1
Dan Johnson	1B	LOU	AAA	35	40	3	0	0	0	2	10	9	1	0	.069/.325/.069	.188	.100	-0.7	1B(7): 0.7	-0.3
	1B	MEM	AAA	35	403	51	19	1	15	62	45	64	0	1	.260/.345/.449	.299	.275	-1.4	1B(75): -7.7	1.2
	1B	SLN	MLB	35	21	1	0	0	0	2	2	4	0	0	.158/.238/.158	.146	.200	-0.6	1B(6): 0.2	-0.3
Magneuris Sierra	OF	PEO	A	19	190	19	1	3	1	7	7	52	4	5	.191/.219/.247	.177	.260	-1.2	CF(50): 5.9	-0.6
Cody Stanley	C	MEM	AAA	26	303	36	11	0	7	45	24	49	2	1	.241/.304/.359	.242	.264	-2.6	C(55): -1.7, LF(3): -0.2	0.1
	C	SLN	MLB	26	10	2	1	0	0	3	0	3	0	0	.400/.400/.500	.317	.571	0.1	C(2): -0.0	0.1
Breyvic Valera	UT	PMB	A+	23	62	9	3	1	0	7	11	2	0	3	.353/.468/.451	.346	.367	-1.7	2B(8): 0.4, SS(3): -0.3	0.6
	UT	SFD	AA	23	401	37	9	2	3	31	34	27	2	4	.236/.301/.297	.220	.246	0.0	2B(37): 1.0, SS(28): 2.1	-0.4
Jacob Wilson	3B	MEM	AAA	24	342	41	14	1	11	56	23	68	2	1	.231/.292/.391	.252	.256	0.4	3B(80): 3.8, 2B(9): -0.4	1.2
	3B	SFD	AA	24	141	18	6	0	7	21	17	25	0	2	.225/.326/.450	.275	.222	-0.9	2B(19): -0.3, 3B(12): -0.0	0.5

Harrison Bader was the 100th pick in the draft; a nice, round number for a nice, well-rounded future fourth outfielder. ❖ Rough professional debut aside, second-rounder **Bryce Denton**has a real chance to become an above-average hitter. Alas, he has an imaginary chance to stick at third base. ❖ About as close as the Cardinals get to a "You only moved the headstones!"-level mistake, **Aledmys Diaz** hasn't impressed since signing a four-year, $8 million contract prior to the 2014 season. The expectation now is that he could turn into an extra infielder. Diaz passed through waivers untouched in July, so the rest of the league might find that evaluation a tad optimistic. ❖ Nondescript third catcher **Ed Easley** was drafted ahead of Jordan Zimmermann, Giancarlo Stanton and Freddie Freeman, among others. What we're saying is, nobody knows nothing about nothing. ❖ It might be winter for the Great Pumpkin. **Dan Johnson's** latest big-league cameo included no dramatic moments nor indication that he belongs in the majors. ❖ Scouting the stat line is a crime punishable by snark, especially when it means giving up on a teenager with as many tools as **Magneuris Sierra** (that's mahg-nair-EE) after a rough virginal go in A-ball. Still, a performance like Sierra's is a good way to slow the hype train. Another good way is pointing out that there is no such thing as a hype train. ❖ Part of the same signing class as Alex Reyes and Magneuris Sierra, **Edmundo Sosa** is arguably the top shortstop prospect in the system. As you would expect, he's an instinctual defender and a gap-to-gap hitter with a good approach. Oh, and FYI: He wasn't yet a month old when the Unabomber was arrested. ❖ Catcher **Cody Stanley** received an 80-game suspension after failing a second PED test. The time off won't help him win the backup job, but it will allow him to sharpen his carpet-cleaning skills. ❖ Double-A is the baseball equivalent of the page-69 test: if you don't like what you see there, you probably won't like what comes afterward. Too bad for switch-hitting utilityman **Breyvic**

Valera, who, despite recording more walks than strikeouts for the third consecutive season, underwhelmed in his second tour of Springfield. ❖ Third baseman **Jacob Wilson** has earned Dan Uggla comparisons throughout his career due to their shared alma mater, offensive approaches and unusual defensive profiles. You might laugh, but Uggla has a World Series ring, more than $75 million in total earnings and (presumably) the right of refusal to star in any future "Popeye" movie; Wilson won't amass half that.

Pitchers

NAME	TEAM	LVL	AGE	W	L	SV	G	GS	IP	H	HR	BB/9	K/9	GB%	BABIP	WHIP	ERA	FIP	FRA	WARP	CFIP	MPH
Jayson Aquino	LYN	A+	22	1	3	0	6	6	33	31	1	1.4	5.5	57%	.286	1.09	2.45	2.89	3.52	0.5	94	
	BRD	A+	22	2	6	0	13	13	78^{2}	77	5	2.2	5.7	65%	.281	1.22	3.78	3.64	3.82	0.6	100	
	DUN	A+	22	2	2	0	5	5	25^{2}	27	2	2.1	5.6	64%	.305	1.29	2.81	3.63	3.82	0.2	100	
Austin Gomber	PEO	A	21	15	3	0	22	22	135	97	10	2.3	9.3	43%	.246	0.97	2.67	3.06	2.52	3.9	81	
Nick Greenwood	SLN	MLB	27	0	1	0	1	0	0	2	1			0%	1.000				14.26		106	89.1
	MEM	AAA	27	13	6	0	32	22	129	166	16	1.7	4.2	46%	.325	1.48	5.79	4.98	5.87	-0.5	110	
Corey Littrell	PMB	A+	23	9	9	0	27	17	130^{1}	125	5	1.5	6.4	50%	.296	1.12	2.69	2.77	2.69	2.8	85	
Chris Perry	SFD	AA	24	1	3	1	18	0	28	27	1	5.8	7.7	50%	.321	1.61	6.11	4.08	5.77	-0.3	114	
	PMB	A+	24	1	3	11	25	0	32	15	0	4.5	9.6	45%	.205	0.97	1.97	2.82	3.64	0.2	98	
Zach Petrick	MEM	AAA	25	7	7	0	28	28	157^{1}	181	14	1.7	6.5	45%	.327	1.33	4.52	3.99	4.08	2.6	90	

Jayson Aquino had a very busy 2015; after the Rockies traded him to the Blue Jays, the Jays sold him to the Pirates, who later sold him to Cleveland, who gifted him to the Cards. His strikeout rate isn't great for a High-A veteran, and he's changed hands more often than Buster Bluth, so buyers beware. ❖ **Austin Gomber's** goatee is outré in an organization that favors beards. But, as with most 22-year-old rebels, he conforms to the Cardinal Way where it counts by having a good fastball and changeup and plenty of pitching know-how. Poseur. ❖ **Nick Greenwood** came over from the Padres in the Ryan Lud—uh, the Corey Kluber trade. Fitting, since Greenwood is the antithesis of Kluber: He's a high-effort southpaw with so-so stuff, a low ceiling and human emotions. ❖ Southpaw **Corey Littrell's** command and *littrelly* big curveball give him a chance to overcome his velocity-challenged fastball. ❖ The only thing keeping **Chris Perry** from claiming a middle-relief job is his well-below-average control. Right, and the only thing keeping him from floating into space is gravity. ❖ Originally an undrafted free agent, **Zach Petrick** commands his three fringe-average or better pitches well enough to envision him taking turns at the back of a rotation, or pitching in middle relief, or walking on the beach on a desert island while the tide high fives the shore and birds sing "Shama Lama Ding Dong. ❖ **Ronnie Williams** is short and slender with a good fastball. That's enough in most orgs to earn a sentence to life in the 'pen. Here? Williams will avoid the bully until the Cardinals are convinced his consistency and command have peaked.

MANAGER

Mike Matheny

YEAR	TEAM	W	L	Pythag +/-	Avg PC	100+ P	120+ P	QS	BQS	REL	REL w Zero R	IBB	PH	PH Avg	PH HR	SB2	CS2	SB3	CS3	SAC Att	SAC%	POS SAC	Squeeze	Swing	In Play
2014	SLN	90	72	7	94.0	60	2	91	2	485	393	35	251	.225	2	48	25	9	7	97	66.0	24	2	306	112
2015	SLN	100	62	2	94.5	64	0	106	1	515	434	37	270	.218	4										

Matheny is a litmus test for how people view managers. To the casual observer, Matheny is a managing prodigy. He's the only manager in baseball history to lead his team to four consecutive postseasons to begin his career; he's won the division in each of his last three tries; and he's yet to win fewer than 88 games in a season. Matheny turns 46 in September, but he's already notched as many postseason trips as Buck Showalter, Clint Hurdle and Bob Melvin, and he's one away from tying Joe Maddon and Joe Girardi. If he's not the Mike Trout of managers, he's the closest thing from a surface-level perspective.

To the analytically inclined observer, Matheny is a managing fraud. In October, Ben Lindbergh wrote an article on Grantland judging managers' bullpen management using a system called BMAR—basically a randomized distribution of relief performance that weighs platoon splits. Lindbergh found that no manager performed worse than random chance in 2015 ... except for Matheny, who was 18 percent *worse* than optimal usage. This wasn't a one-year aberration, either. Matheny ranked last from 2012 on as well, inserting the optimal relievers just 7.5 percent of the time. To think, Matheny did this *while* using Randy Choate as a literal left-handed one-out guy. Imagine if he hadn't. Yikes.

Matheny has other flaws, too. According to Craig Edwards of Viva El Birdos, the Cardinals led the majors in high-leverage plate appearances afforded to their pitchers. Why? In part because Matheny is dedicated to allowing his starters to chase the win statistic, rather than going to his bullpen to secure the team win. We won't even address how Matheny overworked certain relievers throughout the season.

In short, Matheny's success has come from riding the uniform tails of his talented rosters, not from his own doing. Yet, for all the negatives, there is a positive to end on: Matheny seems like a genuinely good, likable people person, someone who is easy to work for and with. That doesn't excuse his flaws or make him a good manager, but it does explain why the Cardinals hired him—and why they've stuck with him for four seasons.

TAMPA BAY RAYS

Essay by Chris Mosch

Player comments by Tommy Rancel and BP authors

When Matt Silverman replaced Andrew Friedman as the general manager of the Tampa Bay Rays, one of his first statements was that he didn't expect to hold the position for the next 10 years. Silverman, who had served as the team president and dabbled in the baseball parts of the organization before, was effectively keeping the seat warm for the next young executive who would rise from within the front office. This was a reorganization of roles rather than a new direction, and, in time, Silverman would reorganize himself back into his previous role.

It was a reminder that the Rays' front-office structure has always been about more than one person. Losing Friedman hurt. But despite the split of Tampa Bay's Big Three, Silverman and principal owner Stuart Sternberg didn't plan to shake up the structure that had realized so much success. The best test of just how successful Friedman's tenure in Tampa Bay had been would be whether the culture he had created could outlast him.

✦✦✦

It has always been difficult to take the pulse of the Rays front office. We have a broad understanding of how it operates, but the secrecy of the details has been something of a legend—itself a strategy, a tactic, a defining feature of what the front office values. This opacity clouds the lens through which we view the operation, but we do know a few things.

We know they've built a successful organization with no financial flexibility. We know they are constantly experimenting and trying new things. We know that, whatever next big thing they are working on, they're hiding it from the public and from every other team.

In recent years the Rays have arguably overtaken the Athletics as the pundits' favorite innovators. Maybe it's Billy Beane fatigue. Maybe it's the intrigue that secrecy produces. But for whatever reason, the Rays under Friedman emerged as the team we most often looked to when trying to identify "The New *Moneyball*." As Sam Miller once put it, "[Friedman's] Rays have been experimental and at the vanguard of various 'trends'—at various times shifting, locking up pre-arb players ever earlier, building around defense, resisting multi-year contracts to relievers, or giving what figuratively seem like literally millions of

RAYS PROSPECTUS

2015 W-L: 80-82, 4th in AL East

Pythag	.501	16th	DER	.716	3rd
RS/G	3.98	25th	B-Age	28.5	19th
RA/G	3.96	10th	P-Age	26.4	2nd
TAv	.259	19th	Salary	$77.3M	28th
BRR	-11.80	27th	M$/MW	$2M	28th
TAv-P	.253	8th	DL Days	1790	29th
FIP	3.88	10th	$ on DL	23%	25th

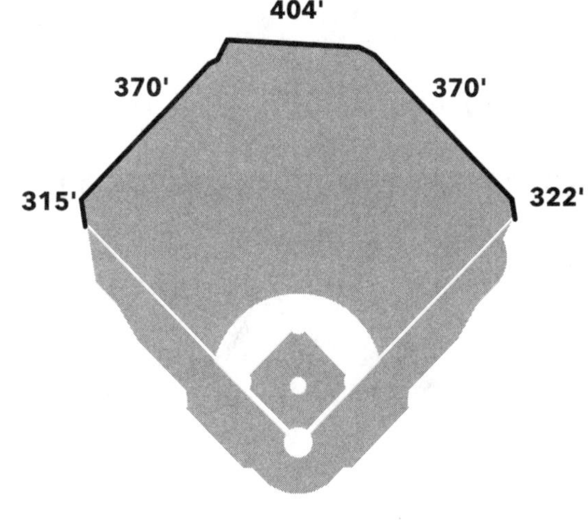

Outfield wall profile: **5'** to **11'5"**

Three-Year Park Factors

Runs	Runs/RH	Runs/LH	HR/RH	HR/LH
100	109	112	111	116

Top Hitter WARP	5.2	Kevin Kiermaier
Top Pitcher WARP	4.9	Chris Archer
Top Prospect	Blake Snell	

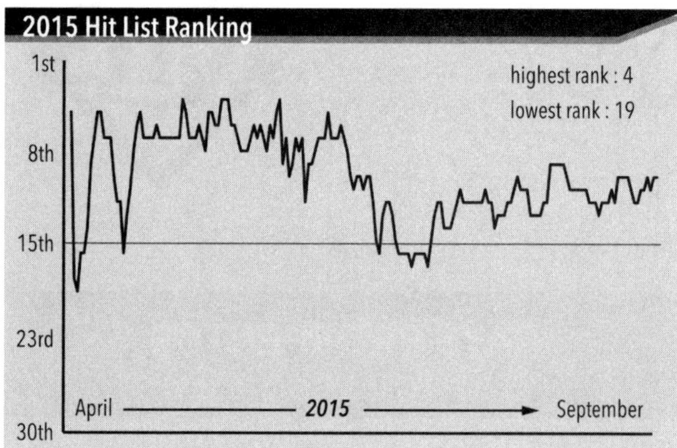

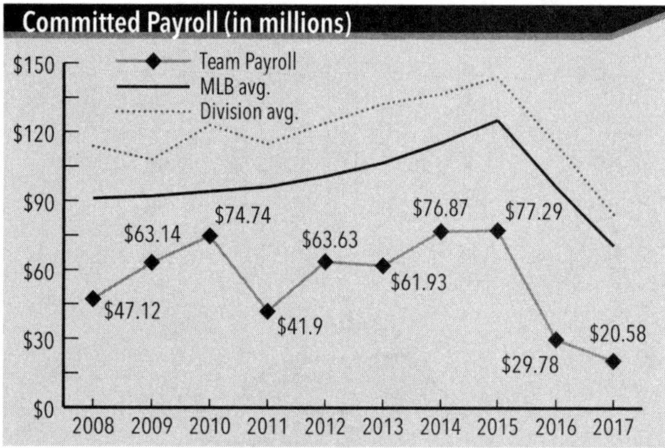

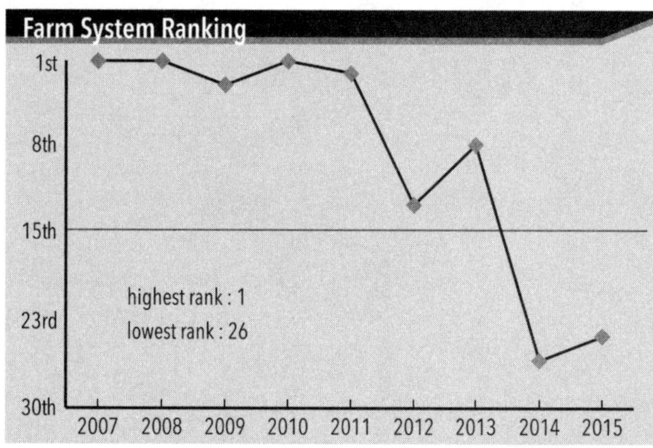

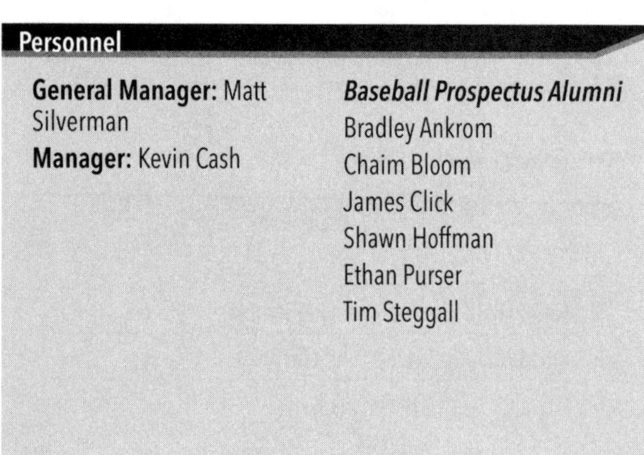

at-bats to Jose Molina—that have become routine, even over-fished, around the league years later. We tend to see his Rays as the first clinical trial for the strategies that will soon be ubiquitous, so we pay a ton of attention to him."

It didn't take long after Friedman went west to realize the Rays would keep on Raysing, would keep clearing salary and keep the revolving door of players spinning. Ben Zobrist and Wil Myers were shipped out, the latter for an old-for-his-level prospect, Steven Souza, who lacked Myers' pedigree but had more team control and was revered by every projection system (presumably their internal system as well).

When the season started, they added a new unorthodox strategy to their list. The times-through-the-order penalty is an effect known by any sabermetric scribe; increased familiarity that hitters gain with a starting pitcher over the course of a game degrades that hurler's effectiveness. New manager Kevin Cash was proactive in giving his starters a quicker hook than we've ever seen. Nate Karns, Alex Colome and Matt Andriese each made starts in the first half where they were pulled after two times through the order despite a low pitch count and no runs allowed. In Tampa Bay, 18 (batters) overtook 100 (pitches) as the magic number for considering a pitching change. The front office supported the effort shuttling relievers with remaining options back and forth between Tampa Bay and Triple-A Durham, keeping the bullpen fresh. It helped keep the Rays in the AL East race into July, despite myriad injuries to the projected rotation. The Rays were still innovating.

✦✦✦

"We have to find [the next big thing]. And if we do, I promise you we're not going to talk about it." —Andrew Friedman, The Extra 2%: How Wall Street Strategies Took a Major League Baseball Team from Worst to First

It was the most fitting quote Jonah Keri could have used to lead into the "Mystery Men" chapter of his book, *The Extra 2%*. Within the chapter, Keri delved into the importance that Sternberg, Silverman and Friedman placed on secrecy. The lengths to which the Wall Street trio went to keep their information confidential is what made them more fascinating than any other front office.

It was how, in 2008, they dove headfirst into PITCHf/x analysis by poaching analyst Josh Kalk from the public realm of baseball research—with hardly anybody noticing. They barred the former math professor from revealing his new employer and kept him off their staff directory. New hires were welcomed with non-disclosure agreements. Cozying up to reporters was proscribed. Nothing the team was working on was ever leaked. The Rays were a black box, and over the years the public had come to understand that when a member of the front office said something mildly interesting, chances were far more likely it was an attempt to misdirect than an actual revalation.

Remember back in 2009, when Sternbeg said there was no $7 million closer showing up in Tampa Bay? Then five days later, the club swapped Jesse Chavez for Rafael Soriano and signed the veteran reliever to a one-year, $7.25 million deal. Or remember when—amidst rumors to the contrary at the 2010 Winter Meetings—Joe Maddon insisted Matt Garza would definitely pitch for the Rays the following season? The team shipped the starting pitcher to the Cubs weeks later.

If the Rays wouldn't even be straight up with the public about which players they were pursuing or planning to keep at a given time, there was no chance they would give a glimpse at actual strategy. So if I showed you this quote from Silverman after the 2015 season, you wouldn't put much stock in it, right?

"Several years ago it seemed like there was a reward to patience at the plate, especially in knocking out a starting pitching and getting to a team's bullpen earlier. Today bullpens are incredibly formidable, and a number of teams are adjusting and taking a more aggressive approach throughout and trying to hit the strikes they see. It's a different ballgame."

Silverman hinted to *Tampa Bay Times* beat writer Marc Topkin that one of the teams reconsidering its hitting philosophy was Silverman's Rays, which fit very snugly into the Who Will Be The New Royals narrative that was running rampant. But by now we know better than to fall into that trap, right? We've been trained by now to interpret quotes from Tampa Bay's head honchos with doubt and skepticism.

This time might be different.

Go back through the archives and you'll find the first trace of the Rays talking about adopting a new aggressive approach on August 6th. Cash had told Topkin that the team had discussed on the previous homestand the need to "be more aggressive." Hitting coach Derek Shelton added that the key was "making sure there is a consistent message throughout the lineup." But even those quotes are unconvincing on their own.

What might really pique your interest is an in-game interview with Shelton on October 1st. The Rays had long been out of the playoff hunt, and the most optimistic takeaway from a bleak second half had been that the offense—putrid for most of the season—had shown signs of life over the final two months.

Shelton opined that the offensive turnaround had been a product of a more aggressive approach at the plate. This wasn't your typical clichéd quote from a hitting coach about his guys just trying to put good at-bats together. Shelton mentioned a specific meeting that took place between the front office, coaching staff and players that called for a teamwide shift in offensive philosophy. "The biggest thing is the players bought into it," Shelton said. "We told them we were going to take them out of their comfort zones and we have, and we've seen good results."

Subsequent reporting by Roger Mooney of *The Tampa Tribune* confirmed that members of the baseball operations department had laid out this new approach during the meeting. They wanted to stick a nail in the coffin of the old Rays strategy of working deep counts for the sake of driving up pitch counts and drawing walks. If hitters saw a fastball they liked early in the count, they were encouraged to jump on it.

The exact date of this meeting is difficult to pinpoint, but for the purpose of determining a cutoff, I chose July 24th—the start of the homestand mentioned in the August 6th article.

As a team, the Rays increased their first-pitch swing rate from 30 percent before July 24th (ranked ninth in baseball during that span) to 33 percent after July 24th (third). Their swing rate when they were ahead in the count bumped up from 47 percent (10th) to 50 percent (second). After the meeting, no team in baseball swung at more fastballs than the Rays.

The lineup had already begun to lean toward a more aggressive style due to personnel changes (trading Ben Zobrist, acquiring Asdrubal Cabrera) and injuries (such as the one that shelved the normally passive Desmond Jennings). But the mid-season shift wasn't a matter of different personnel. There were eight hitters who ranked among Tampa Bay's top 12 in plate appearances both before and after July 24th. Among them, only Kevin Kiermaier became less aggressive on first pitches and ahead in the count.

For once, the Rays were acting as something closer to copycats than trendsetters. This aggressive approach was a strategy a handful of other organizations had also taken up. The Astros, for instance, led all teams in first-pitch swing rate in 2015. Baseball Prospectus author Matt Trueblood wrote before and during the 2015 season that the league as a whole has become more aggressive early in counts. Deep counts—three-ball and two-strike counts, especially—were producing diminishing returns, increasing the "cost" of a first-pitch take. For the first time in decades, hitters are now just as well off swinging at the first pitch as they are taking it.

If this turns out to be just another attempt by the Rays to misdirect the public, it's one hell of a ruse. Even the normally reticent Kevin Kiermaier went public:

"If (an opposing) pitcher throws 70, 80, 90 pitches, who cares? We don't. We're not going to take fastballs to let our starting pitcher rest and get time before he goes back (to the mound)," Kiermaier told Mooney. "Hit pitches that you're supposed to hit. Hit fastballs early in the count, no matter if he's thrown five pitches this inning and you're the third hitter. If you make an out and the pitcher throws seven pitches, so what?"

The shift in strategy is intriguing in and of itself, but the more perplexing question is why the Rays suddenly strayed from their past policies. Why telegraph ahead of the attack? The dedication to secrecy was a Wall Street tactic originally stressed by Sternberg; there's little reason to believe Friedman's departure should have made the front office more transparent.

Sorting through the Rays' ulterior motives has always been something of a futile effort. But what this does signal is that what classifies as a "secret" or "next *Moneyball*" is changing. Over the past few years, the intellectual gap between front offices has shrunk considerably. Most teams are now armed with executives with Ivy League degrees, computer programmers capable of building databases from the ground up and analysts who can sift through big data. It's becoming harder than ever to distinguish front offices from one another, which, combined with the game's copycat nature, is making it nearly impossible to sustain an upper hand for long.

Teams still differentiate themselves through varying philosophies about roster construction and how to allocate resources, but it's not as if there are still front offices out there that don't know the value of pitch framing. Heck, by the end of the season, Joe Maddon, the long-time Rays manager who had jumped to the Cubs, was utilizing a similarly quick hook with *his* back-end starters.

It's what has made the refusal to acknowledge even the most basic facts in the past somewhat frustrating. After all, the games are played on the field, right in front of all of us, and there are more eyes on what's going on in the game than ever before. We can see the Rays shift their infielders more than any other team. We can see their drastic outfield alignments and positioning assignment card that Kiermaier keeps in his back pocket. We can see their pitchers throw an inordinate number of same-side changeups, pitch up in the zone, lead the league in flyballs induced. We can see what's going on when Cash brings in his closer in the eighth inning against the heart of the opposing lineup or pulls his starters immediately after the second trip through the order. And, yes, we can pick up on Rays hitters going from passive to hyperaggressive almost overnight.

So maybe that's why the Rays didn't care to keep this one under wraps. Maybe they knew some blogger would write about it during the offseason, or that some other team's intern had probably noticed anyway. Maybe they felt that reinforcing buy-in from the players was more important. By making it a story, players like Kiermaier were forced to defend the strategy to reporters, talking about what "we" are going to do and making it something the players could bond over and rally around. Sound communication and commitment from players is essential for a team that implements so many unorthodox on-field strategies. It's likely why Silverman solicited the opinions of veterans Evan Longoria and Alex Cobb before tabbing Cash as Maddon's successor, along with other moves involving field staff hires last offseason.

Because clearly, the Rays and Cubs aren't the only front offices that know about the TTO penalty. That they were the first clubs to regularly factor it into their manager's bullpen usage (and have their pitchers buy into it) says more about the communication and overarching philosophy in place throughout the organization. It's these types of "soft factors," along with keeping players healthy and improved player development, that are areas for the most progressive organization to find the next breakthrough.

✦✦✦

Last spring, articles started circulating about neuroscouting, a tool in amateur evaluation and player development that a select group of teams have used to try to get ahead of the rest of the league. In one of those articles, Alex Speier of *The Boston Globe* detailed how Mookie Betts had been one of the first amateur prospects the Red Sox put through the rigorous tests back in 2011. Theo Epstein, overseeing the efforts during that pilot program with the Red Sox, and now president of baseball operations with the Cubs, joked with Speier at the time that he couldn't talk about the inner workings of the program "because then I'd have to kill you." Epstein's current employers, the Cubs, were one of the two teams in addition to the Red Sox rumored to be using neuroscouting programs last year, according to an article written in April by the Associated Press.

The other team was the Rays. Matt Silverman didn't respond to the Associated Press' request for comment. ■

—Chris Mosch formerly wrote the weekly Ducks on the Pond column for Baseball Prospectus and now works as a baseball operations intern for the Los Angeles Angels..

HITTERS

Willy Adames SS

Born: 9/2/95 Age: 20 Bats: R Throws: R Height: 6'1" Weight: 180

YEAR	TEAM	LVL	AGE	PA	R	2B	3B	HR	RBI	BB	K	SB	CS	AVG/OBP/SLG	TAv	BABIP	BRR	FRAA	WARP
2014	BGR	A	18	114	15	5	2	2	11	15	30	3	0	.278/.377/.433	.292	.379	2.1	SS(25): -3.0	0.8
2014	WMI	A	18	400	40	14	12	6	50	39	96	3	6	.269/.346/.428	.307	.353	0.7	SS(97): -0.7	3.8
2015	PCH	A+	19	456	51	24	6	4	46	54	123	10	1	.258/.342/.379	.275	.356	-0.6	SS(97): 4.8	3.0
2016	*TBA*	*MLB*	*20*	*250*	*23*	*9*	*2*	*5*	*23*	*21*	*82*	*1*	*0*	*.213/.282/.339*	*.226*	*.307*	*0.0*	*SS 0*	*0.3*
2017	*TBA*	*MLB*	*21*	*447*	*49*	*19*	*5*	*9*	*46*	*40*	*148*	*1*	*1*	*.225/.297/.368*	*.241*	*.326*	*-0.2*	*SS 1*	*1.2*

Breakout: 3% Improve: 4% Collapse: 0% Attrition: 5% MLB: 6% *Comparables: Addison Russell, Corey Seager, Nick Franklin*

From learning English in less than a year to his sometimes overeager approach on the diamond, Adames takes no half steps. Playing at High-A as a teenager, he held his own despite the competition and conditions. He has more power than Port Charlotte's humidity allowed him to show, and he can go chalk to chalk. On the flipside, his style of attack leaves him prone to the punch out, and elbow problems late in the year caused him some issues. He is assertive on the basepaths, even if that fails to show up in the stolen-base column. Defensively, he made 23 errors in 97 games; however, that had more to do with his enthusiasm to make the miracle play rather than a lack of skill at the position. And he's as affable as he is talented.

Jake Bauers 1B

Born: 10/6/95 Age: 20 Bats: L Throws: L Height: 6'1" Weight: 195

YEAR	TEAM	LVL	AGE	PA	R	2B	3B	HR	RBI	BB	K	SB	CS	AVG/OBP/SLG	TAv	BABIP	BRR	FRAA	WARP
2014	FTW	A	18	467	59	18	3	8	64	51	80	5	6	.296/.376/.414	.284	.347	0.9	1B(103): 8.6	2.7
2015	PCH	A+	19	249	33	14	2	6	38	29	33	2	3	.267/.357/.433	.298	.291	1.2	1B(52): -5.0	0.9
2015	MNT	AA	19	285	36	18	0	5	36	21	41	6	3	.276/.329/.405	.267	.307	2.3	1B(61): -1.7	0.6
2016	*TBA*	*MLB*	*20*	*250*	*24*	*11*	*1*	*6*	*27*	*17*	*56*	*1*	*1*	*.236/.291/.367*	*.237*	*.283*	*-0.4*	*1B -1*	*-0.4*
2017	*TBA*	*MLB*	*21*	*447*	*52*	*21*	*1*	*12*	*51*	*33*	*101*	*3*	*2*	*.250/.309/.398*	*.253*	*.300*	*-0.9*	*1B -2, RF 0*	*0.0*

Breakout: 3% Improve: 5% Collapse: 0% Attrition: 13% MLB: 17% *Comparables: Freddie Freeman, Anthony Rizzo, Jon Singleton*

Bauers has a patient approach and exhibits more control over the bat than Dracula. Those virtues hold true even against fellow lefties, something seldom seen for a player of his handedness and age. But he's limited physically, with marginal athletic tools. He's not fast. He has a sturdy lower base and strong hands, but may never pop 20 home runs in a season. He's a first baseman who probably needs to go to the outfield for his bat to play. It's an unusual profile without much definition at this point.

Tim Beckham 2B

Born: 1/27/90 Age: 26 Bats: R Throws: R Height: 6'0" Weight: 195

YEAR	TEAM	LVL	AGE	PA	R	2B	3B	HR	RBI	BB	K	SB	CS	AVG/OBP/SLG	TAv	BABIP	BRR	FRAA	WARP
2013	DUR	AAA	23	522	71	25	7	4	51	44	108	17	7	.276/.342/.387	.250	.348	2.4	SS(106): -2.6, 2B(15): 0.9	1.6
2013	TBA	MLB	23	8	1	0	0	0	1	0	0	0	0	.429/.375/.429	.349	.375	0.1	2B(3): 0.1, SS(1): -0.0	0.1
2014	DUR	AAA	24	65	8	2	0	0	4	2	14	0	2	.258/.281/.290	.191	.333	-0.2	2B(7): -1.0, SS(5): -0.3	-0.5
2015	DUR	AAA	25	45	5	6	0	0	4	5	10	2	1	.308/.378/.462	.286	.400	-0.3	3B(7): -0.9, 2B(2): 0.2	0.1
2015	TBA	MLB	25	223	24	7	4	9	37	13	69	3	1	.222/.274/.429	.254	.279	-1.2	2B(38): -1.9, SS(28): -1.8	0.0
2016	*TBA*	*MLB*	*26*	*231*	*26*	*9*	*2*	*4*	*20*	*15*	*59*	*4*	*2*	*.240/.293/.367*	*.237*	*.305*	*-0.8*	*2B -0, SS -1*	*0.3*
2017	*TBA*	*MLB*	*27*	*371*	*39*	*15*	*3*	*7*	*37*	*23*	*99*	*7*	*3*	*.238/.290/.365*	*.235*	*.307*	*-0.9*	*2B -1, SS -1*	*0.3*

Breakout: 5% Improve: 41% Collapse: 4% Attrition: 35% MLB: 59% *Comparables: Jason Donald, Danny Richar, Chris Nelson*

In case you hadn't heard, Beckham is actually Former Top Overall Pick Tim Beckham, the man who failed to live up to expectations while others in his class surpassed theirs. With that obligatory mention out of the way, we can make an assessment based on talent level and production. These days, Beckham is a decent middle man with the chops to back up shortstop and second base, sort of in between the Reid Brignac the world deserved and the one it got. He showed surprising pop in the majors considering his marginal outputs in the minors; however, it came at the expense of discipline. Barry Larkin he is not, or even Barry Bonnell, but if you take away the ancient draft history, you have a suitable 12th or 13th man.

Ryan Brett 2B

Born: 10/9/91 Age: 24 Bats: R Throws: R Height: 5'9" Weight: 180

YEAR	TEAM	LVL	AGE	PA	R	2B	3B	HR	RBI	BB	K	SB	CS	AVG/OBP/SLG	TAv	BABIP	BRR	FRAA	WARP
2013	PCH	A+	21	225	38	11	4	4	22	15	27	22	7	.340/.396/.490	.307	.377	1.0	2B(47): -3.7	1.5
2013	MNT	AA	21	114	19	6	1	3	16	8	14	4	0	.238/.289/.400	.257	.247	1.8	2B(25): 0.4	0.5
2014	MNT	AA	22	459	64	25	6	8	38	24	74	27	7	.303/.346/.448	.282	.350	4.4	2B(100): 2.0	3.0
2015	TBA	MLB	23	4	0	1	0	0	0	1	0	0	0	.667/.750/1.000	.575	.667	0.0	2B(3): -0.0	0.1
2015	DUR	AAA	23	354	48	18	1	5	30	15	64	4	3	.247/.288/.354	.246	.288	0.8	2B(68): 3.7, CF(8): -0.5	0.8
2016	*TBA*	*MLB*	*24*	*250*	*30*	*12*	*1*	*5*	*23*	*10*	*54*	*7*	*2*	*.253/.289/.383*	*.241*	*.303*	*0.4*	*2B 2, CF -0*	*0.7*
2017	*TBA*	*MLB*	*25*	*262*	*28*	*12*	*2*	*6*	*27*	*12*	*56*	*7*	*2*	*.248/.289/.378*	*.240*	*.295*	*0.7*	*2B 2, CF 0*	*0.7*

Breakout: 4% Improve: 20% Collapse: 7% Attrition: 29% MLB: 44% *Comparables: Devon Travis, Micah Johnson, Taylor Featherston*

A third-round pick in 2010, Brett was a surprise addition to the Rays' roster in April, though less so once a dozen of his teammates landed on the disabled list. Perhaps feeling left out, Brett dislocated his shoulder after just four plate appearances and was disabled himself until late May. When he did return, it was to Triple-A. Much of the profile remains the same: His limited frame puts a cap on things like power and his arm strength, which restricts his positioning on the diamond. He received some reps in center field as well, an unsurprising move considering his athletic ability and his organization's versatility fetish. His style of play and size make rodent-based comparisons apt. Is Brett a rat? A gritty hard worker who is fearless and has to scrap for everything? Or is he more squirrel? Quick and shifty with the ability to escape danger and use his size and speed to his advantage as he outwits potential predators? Perhaps he is a bit of both; or maybe he is actually a prairie dog.

Curtis Casali C

Born: 11/9/88 Age: 27 Bats: R Throws: R Height: 6'2" Weight: 230

YEAR	TEAM	LVL	AGE	PA	R	2B	3B	HR	RBI	BB	K	SB	CS	AVG/OBP/SLG	TAv	BABIP	BRR	FRAA	WARP
2013	PCH	A+	24	184	15	6	1	5	22	18	31	1	0	.267/.342/.406	.255	.302	-1.7	C(37): -0.4	0.5
2013	MNT	AA	24	145	25	11	0	5	31	21	18	0	0	.383/.483/.600	.385	.418	-0.7	C(25): 0.9	2.5
2014	TBA	MLB	25	84	10	3	0	0	3	8	23	0	0	.167/.268/.208	.199	.245	1.0	C(29): 0.3	0.0
2014	MNT	AA	25	96	7	5	0	1	13	23	16	0	0	.314/.500/.429	.353	.396	-1.0	C(15): -0.4	1.2
2014	DUR	AAA	25	183	11	10	0	3	15	22	50	0	0	.237/.335/.359	.233	.324	-1.5	C(41): -1.1	0.0
2015	TBA	MLB	26	113	13	6	0	10	18	8	34	0	0	.238/.304/.594	.318	.241	-0.9	C(37): 1.4	1.3
2015	DUR	AAA	26	132	14	4	0	4	13	17	29	1	0	.205/.326/.348	.276	.241	-1.6	C(24): 0.3	0.6
2016	*TBA*	*MLB*	*27*	*411*	*46*	*17*	*1*	*13*	*50*	*44*	*108*	*0*	*0*	*.235/.326/.396*	*.264*	*.294*	*-0.7*	*C -4*	*1.5*
2017	*TBA*	*MLB*	*28*	*385*	*48*	*15*	*0*	*12*	*43*	*41*	*101*	*0*	*0*	*.231/.322/.382*	*.258*	*.290*	*-1.0*	*C -5*	*0.9*

Breakout: 9% Improve: 27% Collapse: 14% Attrition: 30% MLB: 64% *Comparables: Chris Gimenez, Max Ramirez, Tony Sanchez*

YEAR	TEAM	P. COUNT	FRM RUNS	BLK RUNS	THRW RUNS	TOT RUNS
2014	DUR	5893	-0.7	0.0	0.2	-0.5
2014	MNT	1604	-0.7	0.2	0.1	-0.4
2014	TBA	3404	1.0	-0.2	0.0	0.8
2015	DUR	3480	0.5	-0.1	0.0	0.4
2015	TBA	4392	1.7	0.0	0.0	1.7
2016	*TBA*	*15881*	*-2.8*	*-0.3*	*-1.0*	*-4.1*
2017	*TBA*	*14871*	*-3.5*	*-0.2*	*-1.0*	*-4.8*

Here is a fun fact to share at your next social gathering: Casali was one of a dozen American League catchers to belt double-digit home runs. In fact, his slugging percentage ranked third in the whole American League (if you're feeling intellectually dishonest and set the minimum at 110 plate appearances). (Actually, those facts will get you nowhere in real life, but for purposes of this book it is noteworthy.) Previously seen as a defense-first backstop, Casali made the most of his limited time with the unforeseen display of power. The downside was a disregard for patience and an increase in strikeouts. He remains a steady defender, better at the stationary aspects (framing and calling) than when in motion (blocking and throwing). The home run rate is unsustainable, but even a modest improvement puts him in the mix for an increased role.

Hank Conger C

Born: 1/29/88 Age: 28 Bats: B Throws: R Height: 6'2" Weight: 220

YEAR	TEAM	LVL	AGE	PA	R	2B	3B	HR	RBI	BB	K	SB	CS	AVG/OBP/SLG	TAv	BABIP	BRR	FRAA	WARP
2013	ANA	MLB	25	255	23	13	1	7	21	17	61	0	1	.249/.310/.403	.259	.307	-0.2	C(71): 17.1	2.9
2014	ANA	MLB	26	260	24	12	0	4	25	22	57	0	2	.221/.293/.325	.232	.275	0.8	C(79): 23.7	3.2
2015	HOU	MLB	27	229	25	11	0	11	33	23	63	0	1	.229/.311/.448	.262	.271	-2.9	C(69): 1.8, LF(1): -0.0	1.0
2016	*TBA*	*MLB*	*28*	*148*	*16*	*6*	*0*	*5*	*17*	*12*	*34*	*0*	*0*	*.235/.303/.390*	*.248*	*.277*	*-0.2*	*C 7*	*1.3*
2017	*TBA*	*MLB*	*29*	*182*	*22*	*7*	*0*	*6*	*21*	*15*	*43*	*0*	*0*	*.230/.299/.381*	*.244*	*.273*	*-0.2*	*C 9*	*1.4*

Breakout: 2% Improve: 43% Collapse: 6% Attrition: 14% MLB: 93% *Comparables: Ronny Paulino, Chris Snyder, Jason Castro*

YEAR	TEAM	P. COUNT	FRM RUNS	BLK RUNS	THRW RUNS	TOT RUNS
2013	ANA	9108	17.3	-0.3	0.1	17.2
2014	ANA	10278	23.8	-0.1	-0.8	22.9
2015	HOU	8425	3.6	0.1	-1.9	1.8
2016	*TBA*	*5769*	*7.7*	*0.0*	*-0.4*	*7.3*
2017	*TBA*	*7109*	*9.1*	*0.0*	*-0.5*	*8.5*

Conger just may be the American Dream. He's a guy who's pretty good at his job and who everybody likes. As humans, these are two good goals to achieve, and because of it, he'll most likely find work until his body tells him he can't any more. He's a capable backup, has a nickname for everyone, and dances like a robot in the dugout every time a teammate hits a home run. Not since The Fonz has someone so successfully made a career out of simply being a cool dude. Kids with egos want to grow up to be Mike Trout. Kids with a solid understanding of how the world works want to grow up to be Hank Conger.

Logan Forsythe 2B

Born: 1/14/87 Age: 29 Bats: R Throws: R Height: 6'1" Weight: 205

YEAR	TEAM	LVL	AGE	PA	R	2B	3B	HR	RBI	BB	K	SB	CS	AVG/OBP/SLG	TAv	BABIP	BRR	FRAA	WARP
2013	TUC	AAA	26	33	6	2	2	2	5	8	7	0	0	.360/.515/.840	.378	.438	0.6	SS(4): -0.1, 2B(3): -0.1	0.6
2013	SDN	MLB	26	243	22	6	1	6	19	19	54	6	1	.214/.281/.332	.234	.255	1.5	2B(34): 0.4, LF(11): -1.3	0.1
2014	TBA	MLB	27	336	32	12	1	6	26	25	71	2	0	.223/.287/.329	.240	.268	0.0	2B(74): 2.8, 3B(6): -0.1	0.4
2015	TBA	MLB	28	615	69	33	2	17	68	55	111	9	4	.281/.359/.444	.290	.323	-2.9	2B(126): -5.0, 1B(26): 0.6	2.8
2016	*TBA*	*MLB*	*29*	*553*	*69*	*24*	*3*	*14*	*55*	*49*	*115*	*8*	*3*	*.253/.330/.396*	*.264*	*.300*	*-0.7*	*2B 0, 3B 2*	*2.4*
2017	*TBA*	*MLB*	*30*	*530*	*63*	*23*	*2*	*12*	*57*	*47*	*113*	*6*	*2*	*.248/.326/.386*	*.260*	*.298*	*-0.6*	*2B 0, 3B 1*	*1.9*

Breakout: 1% Improve: 40% Collapse: 3% Attrition: 4% MLB: 99% *Comparables: Ben Zobrist, Neil Walker, Marcus Giles*

Here is a comp for Forsythe that you will not see above these words: Young Jeezy. The similarities start with their winter-inspired nicknames. Jeezy is commonly known as The Snowman while Forsythe also is known as a snowman; more specifically, Frosty. The pair of Southern gentlemen understand their roles in the game, whether it be Jeezy riding shotgun on a Jay Z track or Forsythe holding his own as an every-day second baseman for the first time. Both hail from south of the Mason-Dixon line: Jeezy was born in South Carolina, but claims Atlanta as his stomping grounds. Though Forsythe was born in Tennessee, and played college ball in Arkansas, the lovely town of Forsyth, Georgia is located about an hour south of Jeezy's headquarters. The duo, however, part ways in future trajectory. Forsythe blossomed on both ends of the field in 2015. He was a key contributor at the keystone and at the plate. In addition to hitting for decent average, he hit for more power than expected. As for Jeezy, at this stage of his career, he appears to be all out of hits.

Nick Franklin 2B

Born: 3/2/91 Age: 25 Bats: B Throws: R Height: 6'1" Weight: 190

YEAR	TEAM	LVL	AGE	PA	R	2B	3B	HR	RBI	BB	K	SB	CS	AVG/OBP/SLG	TAv	BABIP	BRR	FRAA	WARP
2013	TAC	AAA	22	177	28	9	0	4	20	30	20	7	0	.324/.440/.472	.339	.350	0.9	2B(23): 1.2, SS(15): -1.1	2.2
2013	SEA	MLB	22	412	38	20	1	12	45	42	113	6	1	.225/.303/.382	.260	.290	-1.3	2B(96): 13.3, SS(3): 0.5	2.5
2014	TAC	AAA	23	333	45	16	1	9	47	47	60	9	5	.294/.392/.455	.310	.340	1.2	2B(34): -5.5, SS(34): 3.2	2.9
2014	SEA	MLB	23	52	3	0	1	0	2	3	21	1	0	.128/.192/.170	.147	.222	0.1	SS(7): 0.5, 2B(5): 0.4	-0.4
2014	TBA	MLB	23	38	4	2	0	1	4	3	11	1	0	.206/.263/.353	.234	.261	0.1	2B(7): -0.4, SS(3): -0.2	0.0
2014	DUR	AAA	23	113	8	2	0	2	9	10	34	2	0	.210/.288/.290	.216	.297	0.2	2B(16): 0.4, SS(7): 0.8	-0.1
2015	DUR	AAA	24	221	26	10	1	11	30	27	48	4	3	.266/.353/.500	.294	.296	-2.2	2B(24): -0.8, SS(17): -2.0	0.9
2015	TBA	MLB	24	109	11	4	1	3	7	7	37	1	0	.158/.213/.307	.175	.213	0.3	2B(17): 0.1, SS(11): -0.7	-0.7
2016	*TBA*	*MLB*	*25*	*128*	*16*	*5*	*0*	*4*	*13*	*13*	*33*	*2*	*1*	*.232/.314/.387*	*.253*	*.289*	*-0.3*	*2B 2*	*0.6*
2017	*TBA*	*MLB*	*26*	*224*	*27*	*9*	*1*	*7*	*25*	*24*	*58*	*4*	*1*	*.231/.314/.385*	*.252*	*.289*	*-0.4*	*2B 3*	*0.9*

Breakout: 2% Improve: 43% Collapse: 11% Attrition: 18% MLB: 87% *Comparables: Danny Espinosa, Ian Kinsler, Luis Valbuena*

Picture the commerical where Matthew McConaughey is driving down an open highway only to encounter a bull named Cyrus standing in the middle of the road blocking his path. McConaughey acknowledges Cyrus' superiority, turns around, and takes the long way instead. Now picture Nick Franklin standing at the plate with a bat in his hand. The bat is his Lincoln MKC and the field is his road. Cyrus in this scenario is the ability to hit the ball, and he is always standing 60 feet, six inches in front of Franklin. The ambisinister switch-hitter failed to claim one of the two open middle-infield jobs in spring training, spending most of his season in the minors. The same mechanical maladies that plagued him from both sides of the plate in Seattle have not been cured in Tampa Bay. Meanwhile, neither his glove nor his arm are strong enough to overlook the lack of production. It may be time to turn around and look for a different path.

Casey Gillaspie 1B

Born: 1/25/93 Age: 23 Bats: B Throws: L Height: 6'4" Weight: 240

YEAR	TEAM	LVL	AGE	PA	R	2B	3B	HR	RBI	BB	K	SB	CS	AVG/OBP/SLG	TAv	BABIP	BRR	FRAA	WARP
2014	HUD	A-	21	308	27	16	1	7	42	42	65	2	3	.262/.364/.411	.268	.321	-2.5	1B(63): 0.2	0.3
2015	BGR	A	22	268	37	11	0	16	44	28	43	4	0	.278/.358/.530	.307	.275	-3.1	1B(60): 1.6	1.5
2015	PCH	A+	22	45	3	0	1	1	4	4	9	0	0	.146/.222/.268	.181	.161	-0.7	1B(12): -0.6	-0.5
2016	*TBA*	*MLB*	*23*	*250*	*27*	*8*	*1*	*10*	*32*	*20*	*67*	*0*	*0*	*.215/.283/.387*	*.239*	*.257*	*-0.4*	*1B 1*	*-0.1*
2017	*TBA*	*MLB*	*24*	*317*	*39*	*12*	*1*	*12*	*39*	*26*	*83*	*0*	*0*	*.225/.295/.396*	*.248*	*.270*	*-0.7*	*1B 1*	*0.1*

Breakout: 5% Improve: 9% Collapse: 3% Attrition: 11% MLB: 16% *Comparables: Matt Clark, Andy Wilkins, Chris Parmelee*

Gillaspie, a Wichita State product, started the season back in the midwest as a member of the Bowling Green Hot Rods. The 20th pick in the 2014 draft showed his first-round talent and earned a midseason promotion to High-A Charlotte. In his first game with the Stone Crabs, he defeated the Florida humidity with an opposite-field grand slam. Unfortunately, his season was interrupted by a broken bone: He did make up for some lost time during the fall in Arizona, showing previews of the plus power he is projected to have going forward. A switch-hitter, he has more pop from the left side, but with more empty swings. The right-side stroke is geared more toward contact, often solid. Conor's little brother is a big kid, which limits his positioning, but he flashes some athleticism in the field. All signs continue to point toward a useful big leaguer.

Brandon Guyer LF

Born: 1/28/86 Age: 30 Bats: R Throws: R Height: 6'2" Weight: 200

YEAR	TEAM	LVL	AGE	PA	R	2B	3B	HR	RBI	BB	K	SB	CS	AVG/OBP/SLG	TAv	BABIP	BRR	FRAA	WARP
2013	DUR	AAA	27	405	73	23	6	7	41	29	62	22	3	.301/.374/.458	.285	.346	0.7	RF(41): 0.2, LF(29): -0.1	2.5
2014	DUR	AAA	28	26	8	2	2	0	1	6	4	0	0	.400/.538/.700	.395	.500	0.2	RF(1): 0.2, LF(1): -0.0	0.5
2014	TBA	MLB	28	294	37	15	1	3	26	16	52	6	1	.266/.334/.367	.276	.322	3.5	LF(62): 0.2, CF(11): -0.8	1.5
2015	TBA	MLB	29	385	51	21	2	8	28	25	61	10	4	.265/.359/.413	.279	.303	1.6	LF(60): 4.9, RF(41): -3.8	1.8
2016	*TBA*	*MLB*	*30*	*234*	*27*	*11*	*2*	*5*	*26*	*15*	*43*	*6*	*2*	*.266/.336/.412*	*.270*	*.308*	*1.3*	*CF 1, LF 1*	*1.3*
2017	*TBA*	*MLB*	*31*	*380*	*45*	*18*	*2*	*9*	*42*	*23*	*73*	*9*	*3*	*.263/.331/.410*	*.269*	*.305*	*2.2*	*CF 1, LF 2*	*1.9*

Breakout: 1% Improve: 31% Collapse: 4% Attrition: 17% MLB: 69% *Comparables: Ryan Spilborghs, Daniel Nava, Matt Diaz*

If you remember back to last year's annual, Guyer's comment ended with the following: "All this may leave some yearning for more Guyer, but not everyone in the band can be the lead singer; somebody's got to man the rhythm section." In 2015, Guyer had a Bruno Mars–like beat, which is to say: He was on point with the funk. Pressed into extended duty to cover multiple injuries, the man with blue-eyed soul was above-average in all facets of the game. As a right-handed batter, he continued to excel against southpaws while holding his own against the orthodox side. On the basepaths he's an athletic runner with good feel and instincts, and those traits carry over into the outfield, where he can hold down all three positions. Though not quite a one-man band, Guyer has perhaps played himself in position to get the occasional solo.

John Jaso DH

Born: 9/19/83 Age: 32 Bats: L Throws: R Height: 6'2" Weight: 205

YEAR	TEAM	LVL	AGE	PA	R	2B	3B	HR	RBI	BB	K	SB	CS	AVG/OBP/SLG	TAv	BABIP	BRR	FRAA	WARP
2013	OAK	MLB	29	249	31	12	0	3	21	38	45	2	1	.271/.387/.372	.291	.331	-0.7	C(48): -6.2, 1B(1): -0.0	1.0
2014	OAK	MLB	30	344	42	18	3	9	40	28	60	2	0	.264/.337/.430	.294	.300	-2.2	C(54): -13.5	0.5
2015	TBA	MLB	31	216	23	17	0	5	22	28	39	1	2	.286/.380/.459	.300	.336	-1.9	LF(7): -0.8, RF(1): -0.0	0.9
2015	PCH	A+	31	23	3	2	0	0	0	2	4	0	0	.286/.348/.381	.252	.353	-0.4	LF(1): -0.3, 1B(1): -0.1	-0.1
2016	*TBA*	*MLB*	*32*	*250*	*32*	*13*	*1*	*6*	*25*	*29*	*44*	*2*	*1*	*.261/.353/.411*	*.277*	*.300*	*-1.1*	*LF -5, 1B 0*	*0.4*
2017	*TBA*	*MLB*	*33*	*205*	*25*	*10*	*1*	*5*	*22*	*23*	*38*	*1*	*0*	*.250/.340/.393*	*.267*	*.290*	*-0.9*	*LF -4, 1B 0*	*0.6*

Breakout: 1% Improve: 30% Collapse: 1% Attrition: 7% MLB: 95% *Comparables: Joe Mauer, Kent Hrbek, Mike Sweeney*

Jaso returned to the Gulf Coast after a three-year stay on the West Coast. Despite the absence, some things were the same as ever: He was an above-average performer against right-handed pitching and missed time with injuries. Luckily for him, this injury was to his wrist and not his head. After leading off with a walk on Opening Day, he was injured sliding into second base while trying to advance. His first official at-bat of the season came three months later.

From there he was as expected, displaying patience and power from the strong side of a designated-hitter platoon. For the first time in his career, he did not make an appearance at catcher, but he did make his debut in the outfield. The shift from behind the dish should keep him in the lineup more, where his bat can continue to flourish on appropriate evenings. It was likely key to his signing with the DH-less Pirates.

Desmond Jennings CF

Born: 10/30/86 Age: 29 Bats: R Throws: R Height: 6'2" Weight: 210

YEAR	TEAM	LVL	AGE	PA	R	2B	3B	HR	RBI	BB	K	SB	CS	AVG/OBP/SLG	TAv	BABIP	BRR	FRAA	WARP
2013	TBA	MLB	26	602	82	31	6	14	54	64	115	20	8	.252/.334/.414	.287	.295	5.7	CF(136): -1.8	4.0
2014	TBA	MLB	27	542	64	30	2	10	36	47	108	15	6	.244/.319/.378	.263	.296	1.1	CF(118): -1.2	1.8
2015	DUR	AAA	28	25	2	2	0	0	0	4	5	0	0	.143/.280/.238	.183	.188	0.1	LF(4): -0.2	-0.2
2015	TBA	MLB	28	108	9	2	1	1	7	8	17	5	3	.268/.324/.340	.254	.309	-0.7	LF(21): 1.7, CF(10): -0.9	0.2
2016	*TBA*	*MLB*	*29*	*518*	*69*	*23*	*4*	*12*	*50*	*48*	*108*	*18*	*6*	*.251/.328/.400*	*.262*	*.296*	*2.1*	*LF 3*	*2.2*
2017	*TBA*	*MLB*	*30*	*400*	*47*	*17*	*3*	*9*	*43*	*37*	*85*	*13*	*5*	*.245/.321/.391*	*.258*	*.291*	*2.1*	*LF 2*	*1.5*

Breakout: 4% Improve: 37% Collapse: 3% Attrition: 8% MLB: 95% *Comparables: Andy Dirks, Bobby Kielty, David Murphy*

For all those still waiting for Jennings to turn into a dynamic two-way player who steals 50 on the basepaths and steals hits in the field: go home, you're drunk. Last season was the most disappointing yet for the underachieving outfielder, this time adding injury to insult. A knee injury suffered in 2014 never went away, and the Rays moved him from center field back to left, like a kid jiggling a video game cartridge to no avail. He spent several weeks on the DL in early 2015 with that bum knee before undergoing surgery. He returned briefly, only to hit the shelf for good in late August with futher knee issues and... a tooth infection. This is Desmond Jennings.

Kevin Kiermaier RF

Born: 4/22/90 Age: 26 Bats: L Throws: R Height: 6'1" Weight: 215

YEAR	TEAM	LVL	AGE	PA	R	2B	3B	HR	RBI	BB	K	SB	CS	AVG/OBP/SLG	TAv	BABIP	BRR	FRAA	WARP
2013	MNT	AA	23	417	65	14	9	5	28	31	61	14	11	.307/.370/.434	.302	.354	2.5	CF(89): 13.8	5.0
2013	DUR	AAA	23	154	24	7	6	1	13	14	26	7	1	.263/.338/.423	.258	.315	3.6	CF(38): 10.3	1.9
2014	DUR	AAA	24	143	28	7	2	3	13	12	23	11	1	.305/.362/.461	.280	.350	1.5	CF(33): 4.8	1.4
2014	TBA	MLB	24	364	35	16	8	10	35	23	71	5	4	.263/.315/.450	.286	.306	-1.4	RF(68): 6.7, CF(42): 3.9	2.8
2015	TBA	MLB	25	535	62	25	12	10	40	24	95	18	5	.263/.298/.420	.259	.306	2.5	CF(148): 31.1, RF(2): -0.1	5.2
2016	*TBA*	*MLB*	*26*	*637*	*80*	*27*	*11*	*14*	*62*	*36*	*121*	*19*	*7*	*.268/.314/.422*	*.262*	*.311*	*0.4*	*CF 29*	*5.6*
2017	*TBA*	*MLB*	*27*	*545*	*60*	*24*	*9*	*12*	*60*	*32*	*105*	*16*	*6*	*.263/.310/.418*	*.260*	*.307*	*1.0*	*CF 25*	*4.5*

Breakout: 6% Improve: 57% Collapse: 11% Attrition: 19% MLB: 95% *Comparables: Leonys Martin, Cameron Maybin, Peter Bourjos*

Affectionately known as the "Outlaw" for his gunslinger mentality on the field, Keirmaier also failed to reach base in 70 percent of his plate appearance, putting extra emphasis on the first syllable of the nickname. He is more of a no. 9 hitter than he is a no. 1. He makes up for the offense with tremendous speed, and in turn, his ability to track down balls in center field at a historical rate. He also has a flair for the dramatic play, though there are times it appears he is trying to rob home runs on pop flies to shallow center. Nonetheless, a pre-arbitration 31st-rounder with the ability to play perhaps the best center field in the game is fun stuff.

James Loney 1B

Born: 5/7/84 Age: 32 Bats: L Throws: L Height: 6'3" Weight: 235

YEAR	TEAM	LVL	AGE	PA	R	2B	3B	HR	RBI	BB	K	SB	CS	AVG/OBP/SLG	TAv	BABIP	BRR	FRAA	WARP
2013	TBA	MLB	29	598	54	33	0	13	75	44	77	3	1	.299/.348/.430	.282	.326	-2.7	1B(154): -1.6	1.5
2014	TBA	MLB	30	651	59	27	0	9	69	41	80	4	0	.290/.336/.380	.271	.319	-5.5	1B(152): -5.3	0.2
2015	TBA	MLB	31	388	25	16	0	4	32	23	34	2	4	.280/.322/.357	.243	.298	-5.7	1B(101): 1.1	-0.8
2016	*TBA*	*MLB*	*32*	*599*	*58*	*28*	*1*	*11*	*63*	*38*	*77*	*3*	*2*	*.277/.323/.388*	*.254*	*.303*	*-4.5*	*1B -5*	*-0.5*
2017	*TBA*	*MLB*	*33*	*443*	*49*	*21*	*0*	*7*	*44*	*28*	*60*	*2*	*1*	*.279/.325/.381*	*.253*	*.310*	*-3.3*	*1B -4*	*-0.5*

Breakout: 0% Improve: 30% Collapse: 6% Attrition: 8% MLB: 91% *Comparables: Sean Casey, Mark Grace, Doug Mientkiewicz*

The light-hitting Loney put together another season in which he posted an aspartame batting average, with top-shelf ability to put the bat on the ball and minimal pop. It's a middle infielder's profile at a power position. After appearing in at least 144 games over the last seven seasons, he landed on the disabled list twice (oblique and broken finger) which limited him to 104, but truth be told, it should have been fewer considering his platoon splits. With holes elsewhere, however, the Rays lacked a suitable alternative for most of the year. His best asset defensively is his plus arm, which he uses to toss pickoff throws back to the pitcher. Although he lacks superior range, his glove work around the bag is a boost to his infield mates. He drives 54 mph in a 55 mph zone, just in case. He waits 45 minutes after eating to go swimming. He watches paint dry just for fun. He is James Loney: the least interesting man in baseball.

Evan Longoria 3B

Born: 10/7/85 Age: 30 Bats: R Throws: R Height: 6'2" Weight: 210

YEAR	TEAM	LVL	AGE	PA	R	2B	3B	HR	RBI	BB	K	SB	CS	AVG/OBP/SLG	TAv	BABIP	BRR	FRAA	WARP
2013	TBA	MLB	27	693	91	39	3	32	88	70	162	1	0	.269/.343/.498	.309	.312	-0.8	3B(147): 6.1	6.2
2014	TBA	MLB	28	700	83	26	1	22	91	57	133	5	0	.253/.320/.404	.284	.285	1.7	3B(155): 3.6	4.5
2015	TBA	MLB	29	670	74	35	1	21	73	51	132	3	1	.270/.328/.435	.275	.309	0.5	3B(148): 9.1	4.2
2016	*TBA*	*MLB*	*30*	*644*	*79*	*30*	*1*	*26*	*89*	*61*	*133*	*3*	*1*	*.261/.336/.455*	*.284*	*.294*	*0.2*	*3B 8*	*4.4*
2017	*TBA*	*MLB*	*31*	*564*	*73*	*25*	*1*	*20*	*72*	*52*	*117*	*2*	*1*	*.254/.328/.428*	*.273*	*.290*	*-0.1*	*3B 7*	*2.9*

Breakout: 1% Improve: 53% Collapse: 3% Attrition: 9% MLB: 99% *Comparables: David Wright, Chipper Jones, Aramis Ramirez*

It has been a while since former Rays skipper Joe Maddon unveiled his five stages of player development. Step one is simple: Just happy to be here. This is followed by the more rigorous step two: Survival mode. Once a player has survived, he reaches the ever-important stage three of feeling that he belongs. Stage four is all about maximizing monetary value. Maddon, himself, apparently reached this stage after the 2014 season, when he cashed out of Tampa Bay for bigger bucks. With financial security, a player can focus on the fifth and final stage, which is winning. Longoria skipped a few stages along the way.

Sure, he was happy to be here when he arrived in 2008. Survivor mode was never a thing for him; regarding stage three, Longoria knew he belonged almost immediately, as the Rays attempted to bypass stage four by signing him to a $44 million extension less than a week into his big-league career. Years later he was rewarded with a second contract that included eight zeros. Entering his age-30 season, Longoria has but one stage to conquer, but some wonder if he has enough to get there. His power production has waned in recent seasons. It is unlikely he has that "breakout" campaign at this point. Breaking balls away are a continuous bugaboo and he struggled turning on pitches inside. He also dealt with a few undisclosed injuries throughout the season. To his credit, he did not use injury as an excuse, and missed just two games as he continued to shed the "fragile" label that was unfairly put upon him.

Yet despite the decline, he remains an above-average two-way player and relishes his role as face of the franchise. He is the go-to-guy in the clubhouse when things go wrong and an ambassador for the club off the field. When it is all said and done, Longoria will be regarded as the first homegrown star produced by the Tampa Bay franchise, and his impact will be much greater than what he did as a 29-year-old on an 80-win team. The number "3" currently worn on the back of the area's youth will be synonymous with the birth of many fans' love of the game. Longoria's first four stages went by like a blur. Now, with clear vision, the rest of his career is set on reaching nirvana.

Mikie Mahtook OF

Born: 11/30/89 Age: 26 Bats: R Throws: R Height: 6'1" Weight: 200

YEAR	TEAM	LVL	AGE	PA	R	2B	3B	HR	RBI	BB	K	SB	CS	AVG/OBP/SLG	TAv	BABIP	BRR	FRAA	WARP
2013	MNT	AA	23	568	71	30	8	7	68	43	102	25	8	.254/.322/.386	.261	.303	-0.1	RF(85): 1.8, CF(43): 0.2	1.5
2014	DUR	AAA	24	550	56	33	6	12	68	46	137	18	5	.292/.362/.458	.272	.380	3.2	CF(74): -1.1, RF(41): 3.6	3.0
2015	TBA	MLB	25	115	22	5	1	9	19	6	31	4	3	.295/.351/.619	.352	.338	-0.6	LF(16): 0.4, CF(13): -0.8	1.4
2015	DUR	AAA	25	418	35	27	3	4	45	22	98	10	1	.249/.304/.366	.251	.323	-2.0	RF(43): -2.5, CF(34): 6.5	0.6
2016	*TBA*	*MLB*	*26*	*143*	*15*	*7*	*1*	*3*	*16*	*8*	*38*	*4*	*1*	*.245/.298/.393*	*.249*	*.315*	*0.2*	*LF 2*	*0.4*
2017	*TBA*	*MLB*	*27*	*327*	*36*	*16*	*2*	*8*	*35*	*21*	*87*	*8*	*3*	*.238/.299/.387*	*.247*	*.307*	*0.8*	*LF 4*	*0.9*

Breakout: 6% Improve: 18% Collapse: 9% Attrition: 18% MLB: 35% *Comparables: Josh Kroeger, Jeff Baker, John Mayberry*

Mahtook, a former first-round pick out of LSU, saved his best work for the biggest stage. Not previously known for his power—although there has always been some positive projection—he slugged nine home runs in limited major-league action while performing well at all three outfield positions. As was the case coming into 2015, Tampa Bay has a few players who fit a similar profile. Fortunately for Mahtook's future fortunes, he is the cheapest among that group, and he has the highest upside.

Brad Miller SS

Born: 10/18/89 Age: 26 Bats: L Throws: R Height: 6'2" Weight: 200

YEAR	TEAM	LVL	AGE	PA	R	2B	3B	HR	RBI	BB	K	SB	CS	AVG/OBP/SLG	TAv	BABIP	BRR	FRAA	WARP
2013	WTN	AA	23	175	27	7	1	6	25	20	30	4	3	.294/.379/.471	.313	.333	-0.4	SS(29): -2.0, 2B(6): -0.8	1.3
2013	TAC	AAA	23	122	26	5	1	6	28	15	18	2	1	.356/.426/.596	.369	.373	1.8	SS(22): 3.3, 2B(3): 0.3	2.5
2013	SEA	MLB	23	335	41	11	6	8	36	24	52	5	3	.265/.318/.418	.279	.294	2.3	SS(68): -6.0, 2B(13): 0.2	1.6
2014	SEA	MLB	24	411	47	15	4	10	36	34	95	4	2	.221/.288/.365	.263	.268	0.9	SS(107): 0.4, 2B(13): 0.1	1.9
2015	SEA	MLB	25	497	44	22	4	11	46	47	101	13	4	.258/.329/.402	.273	.307	-2.6	SS(89): -0.2, CF(20): -1.4	2.0
2016	*TBA*	*MLB*	*26*	*522*	*68*	*21*	*5*	*15*	*56*	*46*	*104*	*10*	*4*	*.259/.327/.420*	*.268*	*.299*	*0.0*	*SS 0*	*3.1*
2017	*TBA*	*MLB*	*27*	*449*	*55*	*18*	*4*	*14*	*54*	*39*	*89*	*8*	*3*	*.250/.318/.417*	*.265*	*.284*	*0.3*	*SS 0*	*2.4*

Breakout: 1% Improve: 52% Collapse: 3% Attrition: 10% MLB: 99% *Comparables: Asdrubal Cabrera, Stephen Drew, Troy Tulowitzki*

Miller found himself forcibly evolving yet again. After spending half of the previous year as a super-sub, the athletic-but-inconsistent former shortstop was thrust into center field by exeunt Austin Jackson. The metrics weren't impressed, nor were the fans who witnessed every balky route, but again Miller's raw skills made up for his outfield naivete. On offense, an offseason conditioning program designed to add muscle seemed to add some pop to his bat, but the end result was yet another decent, but not amazing, performance. He follows fellow middle infielder Nick Franklin to Tampa, where he's expected to be given an actual position to play.

Logan Morrison 1B

Born: 8/25/87 Age: 28 Bats: L Throws: L Height: 6'2" Weight: 240

YEAR	TEAM	LVL	AGE	PA	R	2B	3B	HR	RBI	BB	K	SB	CS	AVG/OBP/SLG	TAv	BABIP	BRR	FRAA	WARP
2013	MIA	MLB	25	333	32	13	4	6	36	38	56	0	0	.242/.333/.375	.262	.281	-0.1	1B(79): -0.5	0.4
2013	JUP	A+	25	27	0	0	0	0	3	4	0	0	1	.174/.296/.174	.218	.174	-1.4	1B(3): 0.3	-0.2
2013	JAX	AA	25	35	5	0	0	2	7	2	4	0	0	.182/.229/.364	.212	.148	0.1	1B(7): -0.2	-0.2
2014	TAC	AAA	26	77	13	2	0	3	8	11	8	2	0	.308/.416/.477	.324	.315	0.3	1B(6): 0.3	0.7
2014	SEA	MLB	26	365	41	20	0	11	38	24	59	5	2	.262/.315/.420	.282	.287	-2.5	1B(79): -3.8, RF(8): 0.8	0.6
2015	SEA	MLB	27	511	47	15	3	17	54	47	81	8	4	.225/.302/.383	.254	.238	-3.2	1B(140): -5.0, RF(3): 0.0	-0.7
2016	*TBA*	*MLB*	*28*	*526*	*62*	*22*	*2*	*19*	*67*	*49*	*92*	*6*	*3*	*.244/.321/.423*	*.267*	*.264*	*-2.1*	*1B -0*	*1.0*
2017	*TBA*	*MLB*	*29*	*451*	*59*	*19*	*2*	*17*	*58*	*44*	*80*	*5*	*2*	*.247/.325/.426*	*.269*	*.268*	*-1.8*	*1B 0*	*1.4*

Breakout: 0% Improve: 36% Collapse: 3% Attrition: 7% MLB: 94% *Comparables: James Loney, Willy Aybar, Dan Johnson*

Morrison, the perennial victim of knee maladies throughout his career, managed to stay on the field for most of year, and Mariners fans' hearts never got the chance to grow fonder. Never a strict platoon player in the past, he struggled significantly against left-handed pitching, posting an awful .185 TAv against southpaws while failing to hit a home run. Ironically, the team had the reserves in place for just such an emergency, but platoon failures in left and right field used them up. Even in the game's current, somewhat power-deprived context, Morrison's output isn't acceptable for a modern first sacker. Fortunately for him, the Rays have low standards for the position.

Justin O'Conner C

Born: 3/31/92 Age: 24 Bats: R Throws: R Height: 6'0" Weight: 190

YEAR	TEAM	LVL	AGE	PA	R	2B	3B	HR	RBI	BB	K	SB	CS	AVG/OBP/SLG	TAv	BABIP	BRR	FRAA	WARP
2013	BGR	A	21	439	49	17	0	14	56	31	111	5	0	.233/.290/.381	.244	.283	1.4	C(62): 0.4	0.9
2014	PCH	A+	22	340	40	31	2	10	44	15	78	0	0	.282/.321/.486	.269	.343	-1.4	C(68): -0.3	1.6
2014	MNT	AA	22	84	9	4	0	2	3	1	20	0	0	.263/.298/.388	.246	.328	0.6	C(14): -1.0	0.1
2015	MNT	AA	23	444	50	27	3	9	53	13	129	10	2	.231/.255/.371	.228	.308	1.3	C(92): -0.8	0.3
2016	*TBA*	*MLB*	*24*	*250*	*22*	*11*	*1*	*7*	*27*	*6*	*82*	*2*	*1*	*.211/.233/.351*	*.208*	*.285*	*-0.1*	*C -6*	*-1.0*
2017	*TBA*	*MLB*	*25*	*281*	*28*	*13*	*1*	*8*	*30*	*9*	*92*	*2*	*1*	*.210/.240/.349*	*.212*	*.286*	*-0.2*	*C -7*	*-1.1*

Breakout: 2% Improve: 4% Collapse: 8% Attrition: 13% MLB: 13% *Comparables: Lucas May, Ali Solis, Welington Castillo*

YEAR	TEAM	P. COUNT	FRM RUNS	BLK RUNS	THRW RUNS	TOT RUNS
2014	MNT	1903	-1.7	-0.1	0.6	-1.1
2015	MNT	13671	0.9	-2.9	2.0	0.1
2016	*TBA*	*8790*	*-5.4*	*-1.8*	*0.9*	*-6.3*
2017	*TBA*	*9871*	*-6.4*	*-1.9*	*0.9*	*-7.4*

Ask anyone about O'Conner and you will quickly learn there is absolutely, positively nothing wrong with his arm. A true 80-grade bow from behind the plate, there are some that believe the backstop is major-league ready as a defender right now. In addition to shutting down more robbery attempts than Dick Tracy, the former first-round pick draws favorable reviews for his work as a game-caller and overall handling of a staff. He is also improving as a receiver. O'Conner's work in front of the dish, however, is worrisome. Much of the goodwill earned from a breakout campaign in 2014 was washed away by an abysmal approach in Double-A. Not known for his patience to begin with, he regressed further in this area while struggling to making contact. The contact he did make was somewhat loud, especially relative to his position. On the other hand, if Fetty Wap howled over a DJ Premier beat, that too would be loud; sometimes loud is not enough to make something good. As it stands, O'Conner still projects as a primary catcher with a game-changing throwing arm and occasional pop. If he can clean up some of the ancillary, yet important, items on offense, the ceiling goes up.

Rene Rivera C

Born: 7/31/83 Age: 32 Bats: R Throws: R Height: 5'10" Weight: 215

YEAR	TEAM	LVL	AGE	PA	R	2B	3B	HR	RBI	BB	K	SB	CS	AVG/OBP/SLG	TAv	BABIP	BRR	FRAA	WARP
2013	TUC	AAA	29	276	36	18	0	5	38	17	42	0	2	.343/.382/.474	.289	.388	-1.9	C(68): 10.0, 1B(3): -0.4	2.9
2013	SDN	MLB	29	71	4	3	1	0	7	2	16	0	0	.254/.268/.328	.224	.321	-1.4	C(21): 6.0	0.6
2014	SDN	MLB	30	329	27	18	1	11	44	27	76	0	0	.252/.319/.432	.276	.301	-1.3	C(89): 26.9, 1B(3): -0.1	4.8
2015	TBA	MLB	31	319	16	14	0	5	26	11	86	0	0	.178/.213/.275	.176	.230	-2.8	C(107): 6.0, 1B(7): -0.1	-1.0
2016	*TBA*	*MLB*	*32*	*59*	*5*	*3*	*0*	*1*	*6*	*3*	*14*	*0*	*0*	*.227/.275/.350*	*.223*	*.278*	*-0.3*	*C 3*	*0.3*
2017	*TBA*	*MLB*	*33*	*232*	*23*	*10*	*0*	*5*	*22*	*13*	*57*	*0*	*0*	*.221/.269/.337*	*.217*	*.271*	*-1.3*	*C 10*	*0.8*

Breakout: 6% Improve: 25% Collapse: 18% Attrition: 25% MLB: 81% *Comparables: Chad Moeller, Miguel Ojeda, Koyie Hill*

YEAR	TEAM	P. COUNT	FRM RUNS	BLK RUNS	THRW RUNS	TOT RUNS
2013	SDN	2846	5.9	0.0	0.2	6.1
2013	TUC	8813	5.4	0.1	4.0	9.5
2014	SDN	11771	22.5	0.7	2.8	26.0
2015	TBA	12905	5.2	0.0	1.2	6.4
2016	*TBA*	*2330*	*2.1*	*0.0*	*0.3*	*2.4*
2017	*TBA*	*9153*	*7.9*	*0.0*	*1.1*	*9.0*

With quick reflexes, easy hands and the ability to steal outs from behind the plate, you might comp Rivera to the fictional Kitty Softpaws. Neither poses a threat to the opposition offensively, given they both lack claws. Following a breakout season at the plate in 2014, the Rays handed the career backup the starter's role in hopes of finding the next Jose Molina. Well, good job there, as he was a near facsimile. He was a solid defender who did a good job "presenting" strikes, to borrow a rave from Chris Archer. Meanwhile, he failed to recapture his inflated home run rate of a season ago and barely reached base 20 percent of the time. His OBP was lower than Molina's worst as a Ray by 17 points, and only 213 points higher than Molina's 2015 line. By season's end, he was relegated to part-*part*-time duty as Archer's semi-personal catcher. As long as he can flick it and pick it as a backstop, he should have a job; however, he'll never become Puss in Boots.

Daniel Robertson SS

Born: 3/22/94 Age: 22 Bats: R Throws: R Height: 6'1" Weight: 205

YEAR	TEAM	LVL	AGE	PA	R	2B	3B	HR	RBI	BB	K	SB	CS	AVG/OBP/SLG	TAv	BABIP	BRR	FRAA	WARP
2013	BLT	A	19	451	59	21	1	9	46	41	79	1	7	.277/.353/.401	.272	.324	-0.6	SS(99): -8.3	1.6
2014	STO	A+	20	642	110	37	3	15	60	72	94	4	4	.310/.402/.471	.308	.349	3.0	SS(115): 0.8, 2B(7): -0.7	6.2
2015	MNT	AA	21	347	49	20	5	4	41	33	58	2	3	.274/.363/.415	.306	.324	0.8	SS(69): 3.6	3.6
2016	*TBA*	*MLB*	*22*	*250*	*26*	*11*	*1*	*5*	*22*	*18*	*56*	*0*	*0*	*.238/.306/.356*	*.245*	*.294*	*-0.4*	*SS -1, 2B -0*	*0.6*
2017	*TBA*	*MLB*	*23*	*429*	*48*	*19*	*2*	*9*	*43*	*29*	*94*	*0*	*0*	*.244/.309/.367*	*.251*	*.299*	*-1.0*	*SS -1, 2B -1*	*1.2*

Breakout: 6% Improve: 27% Collapse: 8% Attrition: 19% MLB: 38% *Comparables: Ivan De Jesus, Eugenio Suarez, Marcus Semien*

For now, he's still the guy they got for Zobrist, but Robertson should make his own name in Tampa Bay before long. His scouting report has more fives than a fictional phone number, with the occasional four or six just to throw people off. He might even end up playing the five spot on the field, though the Rays are keeping him at the six for now and will most likely try him at the four as the first alternative. A heads-up player with natural instincts, he is on his way to becoming a polished, if flashless, major leaguer. Just don't think about comparing him to... well, you know who.

Richie Shaffer 3B

Born: 3/15/91 Age: 25 Bats: R Throws: R Height: 6'3" Weight: 220

YEAR	TEAM	LVL	AGE	PA	R	2B	3B	HR	RBI	BB	K	SB	CS	AVG/OBP/SLG	TAv	BABIP	BRR	FRAA	WARP
2013	PCH	A+	22	519	55	33	1	11	73	35	106	6	0	.254/.308/.399	.258	.299	-2.5	3B(107): 1.5	1.4
2014	MNT	AA	23	491	58	28	4	19	64	56	119	4	0	.222/.318/.440	.267	.261	-0.5	3B(109): -2.7	1.6
2015	MNT	AA	24	175	22	10	0	7	27	23	49	3	0	.262/.362/.470	.305	.340	-2.5	3B(34): -5.6	0.5
2015	DUR	AAA	24	282	42	17	1	19	45	31	74	1	1	.270/.355/.582	.324	.303	-1.3	3B(42): -4.7, 1B(19): -0.5	2.0
2015	TBA	MLB	24	88	11	3	0	4	6	10	32	0	1	.189/.307/.392	.266	.256	-0.4	1B(10): 0.1, 3B(8): -0.3	0.1
2016	*TBA*	*MLB*	*25*	*168*	*19*	*7*	*0*	*7*	*22*	*14*	*52*	*0*	*0*	*.217/.289/.408*	*.249*	*.274*	*-0.3*	*RF 1, LF -0*	*0.2*
2017	*TBA*	*MLB*	*26*	*344*	*42*	*15*	*1*	*13*	*43*	*28*	*105*	*1*	*0*	*.213/.283/.396*	*.244*	*.270*	*-0.7*	*RF 2, LF -1*	*0.4*

Breakout: 7% Improve: 17% Collapse: 18% Attrition: 30% MLB: 51% *Comparables: Mat Gamel, Mike Olt, Brandon Wood*

Every year, Shaffer—who swings the bat like you'd expect a Tarantino bad guy to—hits a little bit better, and every year his first-round power shows up more frequently in games. The athletic former Clemson Tiger has played mostly third base in the minors, but was shifted across the diamond in anticipation of a call-up. He is spry enough to handle either corner of the infield and has the arm to range into the outfield as well. The Rays value versatility, so it might take some time to find a permanent home, but they also value lineup-altering power, so they'll at least find him an apartment.

Grady Sizemore LF

Born: 8/2/82 Age: 33 Bats: L Throws: L Height: 6'2" Weight: 205

YEAR	TEAM	LVL	AGE	PA	R	2B	3B	HR	RBI	BB	K	SB	CS	AVG/OBP/SLG	TAv	BABIP	BRR	FRAA	WARP
2014	LEH	AAA	31	51	5	1	0	1	2	5	7	0	0	.283/.353/.370	.265	.316	0.8	CF(5): -1.3, LF(3): -0.2	0.0
2014	BOS	MLB	31	205	14	10	2	2	15	19	41	5	0	.216/.288/.324	.231	.266	-0.9	LF(24): 0.7, CF(18): 1.0	-0.2
2014	PHI	MLB	31	176	21	9	2	3	12	14	35	1	1	.253/.313/.389	.269	.306	2.2	LF(28): -1.7, RF(12): -2.3	0.3
2015	PCH	A+	32	25	4	4	0	0	2	2	5	0	0	.261/.320/.435	.316	.333	0.5	LF(4): -0.7	0.2
2015	TBA	MLB	32	192	20	12	0	6	27	14	37	3	3	.257/.318/.429	.262	.293	-0.1	LF(29): -0.4, RF(14): -0.4	0.3
2015	PHI	MLB	32	104	4	5	0	0	6	6	23	0	0	.245/.288/.296	.228	.320	-0.3	RF(28): -1.9, LF(3): 0.1	-0.4
2016	*TBA*	*MLB*	*33*	*308*	*30*	*15*	*1*	*7*	*32*	*22*	*72*	*4*	*2*	*.234/.294/.368*	*.240*	*.289*	*0.2*	*RF -3, LF 1*	*0.0*
2017	*TBA*	*MLB*	*34*	*264*	*27*	*13*	*1*	*5*	*25*	*18*	*64*	*2*	*1*	*.225/.283/.345*	*.230*	*.284*	*0.2*	*RF -3, LF 1*	*-0.4*

Breakout: 0% Improve: 31% Collapse: 6% Attrition: 8% MLB: 93% *Comparables: Jim Northrup, Jay Johnstone, Jason Michaels*

Like LeBron James' hairline, Sizemore refuses to believe he is done. Let us give him credit for keeping the dream alive well past the point anyone thought he could. The 33-year-old with the 73-year-old knees logged nearly 300 plate appearances for two teams across two leagues with essentially replacement-level success. He showed signs of life during his tenure with the Rays as a left-handed platoon bat, feasting on fastballs and fasting on pitches with tilt. The performance will likely earn him a non-roster invite to an American League camp this year; playing the outfield at this point would be harmful to person and team alike. There are some holding hope for one last sizzle out of Sizemore. Meanwhile, Anthony Hamilton is still waiting for Charlene to come home. Neither appears likely at this point.

Steven Souza RF

Born: 4/24/89 Age: 27 Bats: R Throws: R Height: 6'4" Weight: 225

YEAR	TEAM	LVL	AGE	PA	R	2B	3B	HR	RBI	BB	K	SB	CS	AVG/OBP/SLG	TAv	BABIP	BRR	FRAA	WARP
2013	HAR	AA	24	323	54	23	1	15	44	41	76	20	6	.300/.396/.557	.348	.360	0.5	RF(72): 0.4, CF(5): 0.4	3.9
2014	SYR	AAA	25	407	62	25	2	18	75	52	75	26	7	.350/.432/.590	.347	.398	0.0	RF(63): 5.0, CF(27): 2.5	5.7
2014	WAS	MLB	25	26	2	0	0	2	2	3	7	0	0	.130/.231/.391	.225	.071	0.0	RF(8): -0.1, LF(4): -0.3	-0.1
2015	TBA	MLB	26	426	59	15	1	16	40	46	144	12	6	.225/.318/.399	.259	.318	2.2	RF(103): -1.8	0.8
2016	*TBA*	*MLB*	*27*	*619*	*84*	*27*	*1*	*25*	*82*	*65*	*177*	*22*	*8*	*.252/.337/.444*	*.282*	*.324*	*2.0*	*RF -1*	*3.0*
2017	*TBA*	*MLB*	*28*	*534*	*71*	*23*	*1*	*20*	*69*	*55*	*152*	*18*	*7*	*.247/.331/.431*	*.274*	*.318*	*2.4*	*RF -1*	*2.1*

Breakout: 8% Improve: 36% Collapse: 6% Attrition: 21% MLB: 80% *Comparables: Casper Wells, Kyle Blanks, Nelson Cruz*

PECOTA did Souza no favors. Brought in to replace former top prospect and Rookie of the Year Wil Myers, the old-for-his-levels rookie was given a .297 TAv projection with 3.7 WARP. He ended the season with a slightly below-average TAv and wasn't productive or present long enough to post a single win above replacement. He dealt with two hand-related injuries; the more serious one, a broken bone, zapped a month of playing time. Around the injuries, Souza struggled to make contact and was prone to stretches of high strikeouts and no production. The power potential is evident; he has tremendous strength and will work a count—sometimes to his detriment, as he shows a tendency to let hittable pitches pass. Failure to meet lofty expectations aside, Souza is an enjoyable character, works hard on his craft, and still has a (slightly less enthusiastic) admirer in PECOTA.

Garrett Whitley OF

Born: 3/13/97 Age: 19 Bats: R Throws: R Height: 6'0" Weight: 200

YEAR	TEAM	LVL	AGE	PA	R	2B	3B	HR	RBI	BB	K	SB	CS	AVG/OBP/SLG	TAv	BABIP	BRR	FRAA	WARP
2015	HUD	A-	18	48	3	0	1	0	4	5	12	3	1	.143/.250/.190	.207	.200	-0.2	CF(12): -1.3	-0.3
2016	*TBA*	*MLB*	*19*	*250*	*24*	*8*	*1*	*5*	*20*	*16*	*82*	*5*	*3*	*.184/.240/.286*	*.194*	*.256*	*-0.1*	*CF 1*	*-0.8*
2017	*TBA*	*MLB*	*20*	*310*	*31*	*10*	*2*	*6*	*28*	*21*	*99*	*7*	*4*	*.195/.255/.309*	*.207*	*.269*	*0.3*	*CF 1*	*-0.7*

Breakout: 0% Improve: 0% Collapse: 0% Attrition: 0% MLB: 0% *Comparables: Dalton Pompey, Byron Buxton, Aaron Hicks*

The Rays drafted Whitley 13th overall in June's draft. While his cold-weather location—upstate New York—might put him developmentally behind his peers, his talent is worth a little extra wait. He flashes average-or-better tools across the board, projecting to hit for power while also impacting the game on the bases and in center field with plus speed. He struggled to make contact in his first attempt at pro ball, something some evaluators expressed concern over. Check back with us around 2020, when we should have a better idea of the type of prospect he will be.

PITCHERS

Matt Andriese RHP

Born: 8/28/89 Age: 26 Bats: R Throws: R Height: 6'3" Weight: 215

YEAR	TEAM	LVL	AGE	W	L	SV	G	GS	IP	H	HR	BB/9	K/9	GB%	BABIP	WHIP	ERA	FIP	DRA	WARP	CFIP	MPH
2013	SAN	AA	23	8	2	0	15	15	76	71	3	2.0	7.5	61%	.298	1.16	2.37	2.70	3.93	1.0	88	
2013	TUC	AAA	23	3	5	0	12	10	58^2	64	2	1.8	6.4	57%	.332	1.30	4.45	3.30	4.55	0.7	86	
2014	DUR	AAA	24	11	8	0	28	25	162^1	153	18	2.7	7.2	53%	.291	1.24	3.77	4.24	4.65	0.9	105	
2015	TBA	MLB	25	3	5	2	25	8	65^2	69	8	2.5	6.7	50%	.298	1.32	4.11	4.11	4.57	0.2	106	93.9
2015	DUR	AAA	25	3	3	0	13	12	65	65	2	1.4	9.6	50%	.344	1.15	2.35	1.94	1.24	2.8	63	
2016	*TBA*	*MLB*	*26*	*4*	*3*	*0*	*56*	*5*	80^1	*81*	*9*	*2.5*	*7.2*	*50%*	*.295*	*1.29*	*4.11*	*4.04*	*4.40*	*0.2*	*101*	
2017	*TBA*	*MLB*	*27*	*5*	*6*	*0*	*17*	*17*	*100*	*105*	*13*	*2.7*	*7.0*	*50%*	*.300*	*1.34*	*4.33*	*4.30*	*4.64*	*0.5*	*108*	

Breakout: 15% Improve: 28% Collapse: 19% Attrition: 30% MLB: 66% *Comparables: Adam Warren, Matt Maloney, Charles Brewer*

The Rays treated Andriese's right arm like a yo-yo, doing around-the-worlds and sending him up and down multiple times throughout the season. Making matters even tougher, they bounced him from the rotation to the bullpen nearly as often. When working on a consistent basis, the former third-round selection flashes back-of-the-rotation potential. Throwing with control, he works primarily off of a low-90s heater followed by decent cutter and a useable curveball. He also has what can be described as a bulldog mentality on the mound. Provided he is not worked like a toy attached to a string, he should be a viable contributor moving forward.

Chris Archer RHP

Born: 9/26/88 Age: 27 Bats: R Throws: R Height: 6'3" Weight: 190

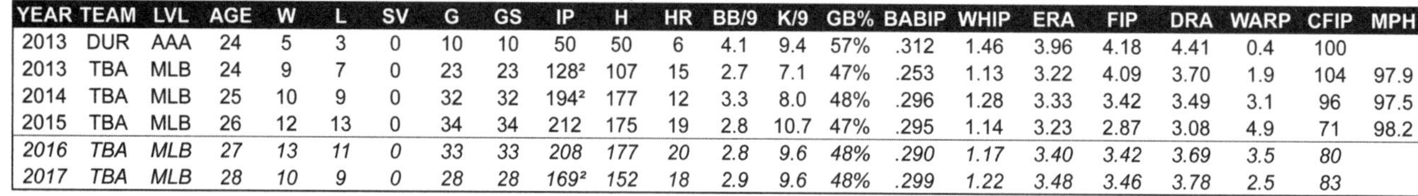

YEAR	TEAM	LVL	AGE	W	L	SV	G	GS	IP	H	HR	BB/9	K/9	GB%	BABIP	WHIP	ERA	FIP	DRA	WARP	CFIP	MPH
2013	DUR	AAA	24	5	3	0	10	10	50	50	6	4.1	9.4	57%	.312	1.46	3.96	4.18	4.41	0.4	100	
2013	TBA	MLB	24	9	7	0	23	23	128^2	107	15	2.7	7.1	47%	.253	1.13	3.22	4.09	3.70	1.9	104	97.9
2014	TBA	MLB	25	10	9	0	32	32	194^2	177	12	3.3	8.0	48%	.296	1.28	3.33	3.42	3.49	3.1	96	97.5
2015	TBA	MLB	26	12	13	0	34	34	212	175	19	2.8	10.7	47%	.295	1.14	3.23	2.87	3.08	4.9	71	98.2
2016	*TBA*	*MLB*	*27*	*13*	*11*	*0*	*33*	*33*	*208*	*177*	*20*	*2.8*	*9.6*	*48%*	*.290*	*1.17*	*3.40*	*3.42*	*3.69*	*3.5*	*80*	
2017	*TBA*	*MLB*	*28*	*10*	*9*	*0*	*28*	*28*	169^2	*152*	*18*	*2.9*	*9.6*	*48%*	*.299*	*1.22*	*3.48*	*3.46*	*3.78*	*2.5*	*83*	

Breakout: 19% Improve: 49% Collapse: 18% Attrition: 7% MLB: 88% *Comparables: Ubaldo Jimenez, J.P. Howell, Alex Cobb*

This is where it pays to have the advanced stuff: By wins and losses, Archer is getting worse; by ERA, he's staying exactly the same; but by cFIP and DRA, he has turned into an ace. We're obviously the sort who opt for the latter, and we suspect you are, too. Archer's arsenal is so dirty he could sneak into the Mets' rotation and nobody would even notice until he asked for his paycheck. He's a budding star, with a fastball like the sun, and a breaking ball that bends like the moon, and a changeup that's getting closer like an asteroid that will eventually end all life on this planet. Even if that last one is still a work in progress, his command of the one-two is so good that he can attack hitters with a predictability that borders on disrespect, like a raccoon in your garbage can: It knows you can see it, and you both know what it is about to do, but it does not give a damn and will be successful in messing you up.

Andrew Bellatti RHP

Born: 8/5/91 Age: 24 Bats: R Throws: R Height: 6'1" Weight: 190

YEAR	TEAM	LVL	AGE	W	L	SV	G	GS	IP	H	HR	BB/9	K/9	GB%	BABIP	WHIP	ERA	FIP	DRA	WARP	CFIP	MPH
2013	PCH	A+	21	6	3	2	22	0	55	39	2	2.8	8.5	34%	.248	1.02	2.95	2.80	3.75	0.5	82	
2013	MNT	AA	21	1	1	1	14	0	26^2	32	6	3.7	6.1	34%	.302	1.61	7.09	5.84	4.39	0.0	108	
2014	MNT	AA	22	2	6	6	46	0	71	69	6	2.8	10.1	36%	.326	1.28	3.68	2.96				
2015	TBA	MLB	23	3	1	0	17	0	23^1	16	4	3.9	6.9	38%	.194	1.11	2.31	5.20	4.25	0.1	108	95.2
2015	DUR	AAA	23	2	1	1	20	4	46^1	50	5	2.9	8.5	32%	.336	1.40	5.24	3.70	3.67	0.5	95	
2016	*TBA*	*MLB*	*24*	*2*	*1*	*0*	*31*	*0*	32^1	*32*	*4*	*3.3*	*7.9*	*33%*	*.296*	*1.36*	*4.31*	*4.32*	*4.60*	*0.1*	*105*	
2017	*TBA*	*MLB*	*25*	*1*	*0*	*0*	*18*	*0*	34^1	*35*	*5*	*3.8*	*7.7*	*33%*	*.300*	*1.45*	*4.63*	*4.59*	*4.94*	*-0.1*	*114*	

Breakout: 8% Improve: 14% Collapse: 6% Attrition: 10% MLB: 23% *Comparables: Rich Thompson, Eury De La Rosa, Osiris Matos*

Although he might not stand out from any other average reliever, Bellatti could turn out to be the new prototype for the middle man. He's stuck between not good enough to be a starter and not consistent enough to be trusted in high leverage (at least not yet), but there's an increased need in Tampa for the hybrid—a long reliever not just used to cover injury or blowouts but to float the Rays when they use the Rule of 18 to pull pitchers after two trips through the lineup. Bellatti is a former starter who made 37 appearances between Triple-A and the majors in 2015, racking up 69 innings—just under two frames per. He's got great stuff for the half-marathon role: His fastball has some giddyup in limited doses, and he has a pair of secondary offerings that allow him to pitch multiple frames without becoming predictable. This sounds like a decent starter until you mix in the control slash command issues and the flyball/homer tendencies. Bellatti may or may not be the one to truly take hold of this perceived new role, but he does make you wonder if there are more of him out there.

Brad Boxberger RHP

Born: 5/27/88 Age: 28 Bats: R Throws: R Height: 6'2" Weight: 225

YEAR	TEAM	LVL	AGE	W	L	SV	G	GS	IP	H	HR	BB/9	K/9	GB%	BABIP	WHIP	ERA	FIP	DRA	WARP	CFIP	MPH
2013	TUC	AAA	25	2	4	5	42	0	57^{1}	50	3	3.0	14.0	35%	.376	1.20	3.61	2.14	3.39	1.2	44	
2013	SDN	MLB	25	0	1	1	18	0	22	19	3	5.3	9.8	49%	.296	1.45	2.86	4.38	5.47	-0.2	98	94.5
2014	TBA	MLB	26	5	2	2	63	0	64^{2}	34	9	2.8	14.5	44%	.227	0.84	2.37	2.87	2.44	1.6	55	95.6
2015	TBA	MLB	27	4	10	41	69	0	63	54	9	4.6	10.6	37%	.292	1.37	3.71	4.23	4.66	0.0	89	95.1
2016	*TBA*	*MLB*	*28*	*3*	*1*	*30*	*61*	*0*	*64^{2}*	*52*	*8*	*3.4*	*11.2*	*40%*	*.290*	*1.18*	*3.57*	*3.60*	*3.88*	*0.8*	*84*	
2017	*TBA*	*MLB*	*29*	*3*	*1*	*12*	*50*	*0*	*55*	*46*	*7*	*3.5*	*10.6*	*40%*	*.288*	*1.22*	*3.71*	*3.70*	*4.03*	*0.5*	*88*	

Breakout: 28% Improve: 45% Collapse: 38% Attrition: 20% MLB: 93% *Comparables: Edwar Ramirez, Jose Valverde, Ernesto Frieri*

The first three autocompleted words or phrases that populate after Boxberger's name in a Google search are: "closer," "contract" and "blown saves." Sounds about right. After working as a setup man in 2014, Boxberger became Tampa Bay's de facto closer in 2015 after Jake McGee underwent offseason surgery and several veterans failed to reclaim their past glory. His AL-leading 41 saves demonstrate that he handled the job more often than not, but when you take 10 losses as the last man on the mound, that image tends to stick in people's minds. Using his mid-90s fastball and plus changeup, Boxberger continued to rack up the strikeouts, but the free passes he had curtailed in 2014 returned. Couple the extra baserunners with a flyball profile and you see how Him + Small Margins might = A Mess. Still, a 28-year-old who can work late in games, and is not yet arbitration-eligible, is a valuable member of the bullpen whether it be in or out of the Capital-C Closer's role.

Xavier Cedeno LHP

Born: 8/26/86 Age: 29 Bats: L Throws: L Height: 6'0" Weight: 215

YEAR	TEAM	LVL	AGE	W	L	SV	G	GS	IP	H	HR	BB/9	K/9	GB%	BABIP	WHIP	ERA	FIP	DRA	WARP	CFIP	MPH
2013	WAS	MLB	26	0	0	0	11	0	6	5	0	1.5	9.0	69%	.312	1.00	1.50	1.52	-0.33	0.4	103	93.5
2013	SYR	AAA	26	2	0	4	39	0	34^{1}	23	2	4.2	11.8	51%	.276	1.14	1.31	2.83	3.70	0.4	77	
2013	HOU	MLB	26	0	0	0	5	0	6^{1}	10	0	9.9	4.3	56%	.400	2.68	11.37	6.39	13.18	-0.7	126	90.9
2014	WAS	MLB	27	0	0	0	9	0	7	10	1	0.0	6.4	40%	.375	1.43	3.86	3.53	6.02	-0.1	103	93.5
2014	SYR	AAA	27	5	1	4	35	0	39^{1}	22	3	2.7	13.0	61%	.247	0.86	2.29	2.37	3.32	0.7	51	
2015	TBA	MLB	28	4	1	1	61	0	43	37	3	2.5	9.0	56%	.296	1.14	2.09	2.92	2.38	1.2	90	91.1
2015	WAS	MLB	28	0	0	0	5	0	3	3	1	6.0	12.0	25%	.286	1.67	6.00	7.83	12.95	-0.3	96	91.3
2016	*TBA*	*MLB*	*29*	*3*	*1*	*0*	*56*	*0*	*59^{1}*	*54*	*7*	*3.1*	*9.3*	*54%*	*.297*	*1.26*	*3.80*	*3.83*	*4.11*	*0.4*	*89*	
2017	*TBA*	*MLB*	*30*	*4*	*1*	*1*	*70*	*0*	*59^{2}*	*55*	*7*	*3.0*	*9.2*	*54%*	*.295*	*1.25*	*3.84*	*3.82*	*4.15*	*0.4*	*91*	

Breakout: 21% Improve: 38% Collapse: 28% Attrition: 28% MLB: 77% *Comparables: Nick Hagadone, Tom Wilhelmsen, Donnie Veal*

Cedeno arrived in Tampa Bay from Washington via a brief layover at LAX. Initially thought of as a disposable bottom-of-the-roster type, the lefty turned out to be the steadiest piece of an otherwise uneven bullpen. Fitting the typical southpaw reliever profile, he attacked hitters—mostly of the same hand—with upper-80s velocity and sweeping breaking balls. He displayed improved control and sequencing, resulting in a punchout per frame and a healthy strikeout-to-walk ratio. His unassuming persona and contract make him the ideal candidate to stick as a second lefty in a bullpen, with the ability to get outs 16-to-21 in a game.

Alex Cobb RHP

Born: 10/7/87 Age: 28 Bats: R Throws: R Height: 6'3" Weight: 205

YEAR	TEAM	LVL	AGE	W	L	SV	G	GS	IP	H	HR	BB/9	K/9	GB%	BABIP	WHIP	ERA	FIP	DRA	WARP	CFIP	MPH
2013	TBA	MLB	25	11	3	0	22	22	143^{1}	120	13	2.8	8.4	57%	.279	1.15	2.76	3.39	3.50	2.4	85	93.3
2014	TBA	MLB	26	10	9	0	27	27	166^{1}	142	11	2.5	8.1	56%	.282	1.14	2.87	3.26	3.33	3.0	93	94.0
2016	*TBA*	*MLB*	*28*	*2*	*2*	*0*	*6*	*6*	*31^{2}*	*29*	*3*	*2.6*	*8.4*	*58%*	*.294*	*1.21*	*3.72*	*3.53*	*4.02*	*0.4*	*89*	
2017	*TBA*	*MLB*	*29*	*5*	*4*	*0*	*13*	*13*	*74^{1}*	*74*	*9*	*2.6*	*8.1*	*58%*	*.304*	*1.28*	*3.91*	*3.90*	*4.23*	*0.8*	*96*	

Breakout: 26% Improve: 58% Collapse: 21% Attrition: 8% MLB: 93% *Comparables: Erik Bedard, Dustin McGowan, Brandon McCarthy*

Stories are often told of Cobb, son of man and nymph, a warrior, a seer and augur. What little we know has been passed down through the generations, told from father to child, embellished and dramatized into unrecognizable myth. Some say that he learned the language of birds from the god Apollo, or that he slew the Gorgon by meeting her gaze. Others tell of a brute who ate rocks and drank sand. What little truth the scholars have extracted is this: that he was a man, that he was a hero and that he accidentally tread on an asp on the shores of Libya, forcing him to miss all of 2015 with Tommy John surgery.

Alex Colome RHP

Born: 12/31/88 Age: 27 Bats: R Throws: R Height: 6'2" Weight: 220

YEAR	TEAM	LVL	AGE	W	L	SV	G	GS	IP	H	HR	BB/9	K/9	GB%	BABIP	WHIP	ERA	FIP	DRA	WARP	CFIP	MPH
2013	DUR	AAA	24	4	6	0	14	14	70^1	63	5	3.7	9.2	42%	.301	1.31	3.07	3.49	4.19	0.7	93	
2013	TBA	MLB	24	1	1	0	3	3	16	14	2	5.1	6.8	45%	.255	1.44	2.25	5.08	5.20	-0.1	111	96.7
2014	PCH	A+	25	0	1	0	3	3	11	7	0	4.1	8.2	45%	.241	1.09	1.64	2.94	4.28	0.1	98	
2014	TBA	MLB	25	2	0	0	5	3	23^2	19	1	3.8	4.9	40%	.247	1.23	2.66	3.88	3.07	0.5	116	96.2
2014	DUR	AAA	25	7	6	0	15	15	86	84	2	3.1	7.6	42%	.319	1.33	3.77	3.25	4.48	0.7	98	
2015	TBA	MLB	26	8	5	0	43	13	109^2	112	9	2.5	7.2	41%	.317	1.30	3.94	3.52	4.09	1.1	97	96.6
2016	*TBA*	*MLB*	*27*	*3*	*1*	*0*	*56*	*0*	*59^1*	*57*	*6*	*2.9*	*7.4*	*41%*	*.290*	*1.28*	*4.04*	*4.02*	*4.32*	*0.4*	*98*	
2017	*TBA*	*MLB*	*28*	*4*	*4*	*0*	*18*	*12*	*80^2*	*78*	*9*	*3.0*	*7.4*	*41%*	*.290*	*1.30*	*4.11*	*4.07*	*4.40*	*0.6*	*100*	

Breakout: 19% Improve: 47% Collapse: 15% Attrition: 24% MLB: 75% *Comparables: David Phelps, Troy Patton, Adam Warren*

After a few seasons alternating between Durham and St. Petersburg, as well as the rotation and the bullpen, Colome found his home as a reliever in Hi-Leverage City. The stuff is apparent, with a fastball in the mid-90s and a slider that confuses hitters like Big Sean lyrics. His changeup flashes the same baffling ability but at a lesser frequency. With a full offseason, as well as camp, to get even more acclimated to his new job, he might make like a solar system and plan it (planet) out. Whatever that means.

Danny Farquhar RHP

Born: 2/17/87 Age: 29 Bats: R Throws: R Height: 5'9" Weight: 185

YEAR	TEAM	LVL	AGE	W	L	SV	G	GS	IP	H	HR	BB/9	K/9	GB%	BABIP	WHIP	ERA	FIP	DRA	WARP	CFIP	MPH
2013	TAC	AAA	26	0	1	6	15	0	20	17	1	1.8	13.5	50%	.340	1.05	2.25	1.82	3.88	0.3	62	
2013	SEA	MLB	26	0	3	16	46	0	55^2	44	2	3.6	12.8	43%	.336	1.19	4.20	1.89	2.58	1.4	61	96.5
2014	SEA	MLB	27	3	1	1	66	0	71	58	5	2.8	10.3	45%	.298	1.13	2.66	2.89	3.83	0.6	86	95.1
2015	SEA	MLB	28	1	8	1	43	0	51	53	9	3.0	8.5	40%	.306	1.37	5.12	4.58	5.23	-0.3	100	95.2
2015	TAC	AAA	28	1	1	3	27	1	38	40	3	2.4	9.7	38%	.359	1.32	3.08	3.26	2.87	1.0	76	
2016	*TBA*	*MLB*	*29*	*3*	*1*	*0*	*61*	*0*	*64^2*	*61*	*8*	*3.0*	*9.3*	*41%*	*.301*	*1.27*	*3.88*	*3.97*	*4.17*	*0.6*	*92*	
2017	*TBA*	*MLB*	*30*	*2*	*1*	*1*	*45*	*0*	*56^1*	*52*	*7*	*3.3*	*9.5*	*41%*	*.300*	*1.29*	*3.92*	*3.88*	*4.21*	*0.3*	*93*	

Breakout: 29% Improve: 55% Collapse: 14% Attrition: 23% MLB: 94% *Comparables: Brad Brach, Chris Resop, Jason Motte*

Farquhar was supposed to be a key component of one of the best bullpens in baseball, but like a lot of Mariners relievers he slipped badly. A dip in velocity and a loss in movement on his cutter, which had been his bread-and-butter pitch in 2014, led to fewer strikeouts and all the home runs. It reached the point where fans were giving him back his autographs. Farquhar will get a fresh start with Tampa Bay and an opportunity to rediscover the magic; he's a reliever, so there's no reason to believe he will and no reason to believe he won't.

Steven Geltz RHP

Born: 11/1/87 Age: 28 Bats: R Throws: R Height: 5'10" Weight: 210

YEAR	TEAM	LVL	AGE	W	L	SV	G	GS	IP	H	HR	BB/9	K/9	GB%	BABIP	WHIP	ERA	FIP	DRA	WARP	CFIP	MPH
2013	DUR	AAA	25	5	3	3	41	0	67	35	8	3.2	10.7	32%	.189	0.88	2.82	3.49	3.83	0.7	82	
2014	TBA	MLB	26	0	1	0	11	0	8^1	6	3	5.4	15.1	25%	.231	1.32	3.24	7.00	6.76	-0.2	88	95.0
2014	DUR	AAA	26	3	3	1	29	0	41^2	27	3	3.7	13.0	32%	.276	1.06	2.38	2.71	3.65	0.6	66	
2015	TBA	MLB	27	2	6	2	70	2	67^1	45	8	3.5	8.2	36%	.216	1.05	3.74	4.08	3.08	1.3	97	94.5
2016	*TBA*	*MLB*	*28*	*3*	*1*	*0*	*61*	*0*	*64^2*	*53*	*8*	*3.3*	*8.9*	*34%*	*.267*	*1.19*	*4.00*	*4.08*	*4.30*	*0.4*	*96*	
2017	*TBA*	*MLB*	*29*	*3*	*1*	*1*	*50*	*0*	*61^2*	*51*	*8*	*3.5*	*9.1*	*34%*	*.269*	*1.22*	*4.09*	*4.07*	*4.40*	*0.2*	*100*	

Breakout: 16% Improve: 30% Collapse: 27% Attrition: 23% MLB: 65% *Comparables: Danny Farquhar, Craig Breslow, Nick Vincent*

Geltz continues to defy the odds as a true underdog story. Besides retiring 32 straight batters after being kissed by Paula Abdul (he caught her ceremonial first pitch), the undersized and undrafted right-hander out of a small upstate New York town was among the most-used relief pitchers in the American League in 2015. Plenty of that was out of sheer necessity—including two spot starts—but Geltz held his own nonetheless. He uses a three-pitch medley, led by a mid-90s fastball that lives above the belt loops. He spins a slider as well as an off-speed pitch, but neither grades out as above-average. With spotty command and a flyball profile, home runs are likely to always be an issue, and the free passes are more frequent than you would like. His best role is as the fourth or fifth right-hander out of the 'pen. Just the fact that he has a role is impressive unto itself.

Brandon Gomes RHP

Born: 7/15/84 Age: 31 Bats: R Throws: R Height: 5'11" Weight: 190

YEAR	TEAM	LVL	AGE	W	L	SV	G	GS	IP	H	HR	BB/9	K/9	GB%	BABIP	WHIP	ERA	FIP	DRA	WARP	CFIP	MPH
2013	TBA	MLB	28	3	1	0	26	0	19^1	18	4	3.3	13.5	26%	.326	1.29	6.52	3.85	5.33	-0.2	71	94.2
2013	DUR	AAA	28	0	0	0	9	0	10^1	7	1	0.9	12.2	33%	.261	0.77	2.61	2.33	3.63	0.1	75	
2014	TBA	MLB	29	2	2	0	29	0	34	28	5	2.9	6.4	33%	.235	1.15	3.71	4.63	4.00	0.2	108	93.3
2014	DUR	AAA	29	0	2	0	27	0	37^1	36	4	2.9	10.1	36%	.320	1.29	3.62	3.63	4.13	0.3	85	
2015	TBA	MLB	30	2	6	1	63	0	59	55	10	2.3	6.7	38%	.260	1.19	4.27	4.73	4.54	0.1	106	93.4
2016	*TBA*	*MLB*	*31*	*3*	*1*	*1*	*52*	*0*	*55*	*54*	*8*	*2.9*	*7.6*	*37%*	*.287*	*1.31*	*4.42*	*4.51*	*4.71*	*0.0*	*107*	
2017	*TBA*	*MLB*	*32*	*2*	*1*	*0*	*35*	*0*	*38^2*	*39*	*6*	*2.9*	*7.4*	*37%*	*.287*	*1.33*	*4.53*	*4.49*	*4.83*	*0.0*	*111*	

Breakout: 16% Improve: 28% Collapse: 15% Attrition: 14% MLB: 55% *Comparables: Greg Aquino, Scott Dohmann, Chris Resop*

Gomes is known in some circles as "Diners, Drive-Ins and Dives," because fans get disgusted and change the channel when he comes in. Despite clearing waivers last winter, he was somehow pegged for high-leverage duty once the season started despite no increase in skill or ability. Such were the Rays. He does not possess ideal size for a pitcher. His fastball is ordinary and he lacks a plus secondary offering. Yes, he can throw strikes; however, he lacks the command to stay away from nitro zones. He signed with the Cubs in the offseason, so when hungry NL power hitters come to the plate, Gomes can take them right to flavor town, 90 mph at a time.

Taylor Guerrieri RHP

Born: 12/1/92 Age: 23 Bats: R Throws: R Height: 6'3" Weight: 195

YEAR	TEAM	LVL	AGE	W	L	SV	G	GS	IP	H	HR	BB/9	K/9	GB%	BABIP	WHIP	ERA	FIP	DRA	WARP	CFIP	MPH
2013	BGR	A	20	6	2	0	14	14	67	54	5	1.6	6.9	67%	.266	0.99	2.01	3.77	4.27	0.8	90	
2015	PCH	A+	22	2	2	0	12	10	42	37	0	2.4	9.4	63%	.322	1.14	2.14	2.00	2.23	1.2	80	
2015	MNT	AA	22	3	1	0	8	8	36	28	2	2.0	7.0	67%	.241	1.00	1.50	3.39	3.57	0.6	92	
2016	*TBA*	*MLB*	*23*	*3*	*4*	*0*	*13*	*13*	*53*	*53*	*6*	*3.0*	*6.8*	*60%*	*.292*	*1.33*	*4.37*	*4.39*	*4.65*	*0.3*	*108*	
2017	*TBA*	*MLB*	*24*	*7*	*9*	*0*	*29*	*29*	*182*	*191*	*22*	*3.1*	*6.7*	*60%*	*.300*	*1.40*	*4.48*	*4.44*	*4.77*	*0.5*	*111*	

Breakout: 10% Improve: 12% Collapse: 6% Attrition: 14% MLB: 24% *Comparables: Simon Castro, Adam Warren, Alex Cobb*

Guerrieri's right arm might as well be nicknamed the Commodore: It's been brought along easier than a Sunday morning. Despite the Tommy John scar, he proved durable in 2015 (though far from a brick house), as the Rays kept him on a strict pitch count rather than let him go all night long. The fastball lives in the low- to mid-90s and he spins a changeup that can dance on the ceiling. He's also unafraid to use the breaking ball once, twice or even three times a plate appearance. As he steps out of the shadow of the infirmary, he should be truly given a chance to pitch this season, and could be saying "hello" to the big leagues sooner than later.

Brent Honeywell RHP

Born: 3/31/95 Age: 21 Bats: R Throws: R Height: 6'2" Weight: 180

YEAR	TEAM	LVL	AGE	W	L	SV	G	GS	IP	H	HR	BB/9	K/9	GB%	BABIP	WHIP	ERA	FIP	DRA	WARP	CFIP	MPH
2015	BGR	A	20	4	4	0	12	12	65	53	3	1.7	10.5	39%	.299	1.00	2.91	2.40	1.40	2.8	69	
2015	PCH	A+	20	5	2	0	12	12	65^{1}	57	2	2.1	7.3	49%	.291	1.10	3.44	2.72	2.83	1.3	87	
2016	*TBA*	*MLB*	*21*	*5*	*6*	*0*	*17*	*17*	86^{1}	*85*	*10*	*3.0*	*8.0*	*37%*	*.300*	*1.32*	*4.01*	*4.04*	*4.31*	*0.8*	*97*	
2017	*TBA*	*MLB*	*22*	*8*	*9*	*0*	*27*	*27*	163^{2}	*163*	*20*	*3.1*	*7.9*	*37%*	*.298*	*1.33*	*4.13*	*4.10*	*4.44*	*1.1*	*102*	

Breakout: 31% Improve: 32% Collapse: 2% Attrition: 5% MLB: 37% *Comparables: Luis Severino, Keyvius Sampson, Roman Mendez*

Have you ever felt so confident in your ability that you imagine yourself walking on clouds while singing love songs in a boy band? That's how Honeywell feels every fifth day from April to October. Described by one person as "confident, hyper-critical and humble at the same time," the 21-year-old right-hander is coachable and shows surprising maturity—the type to buy a crock pot and start a family. He is a student of the craft with a keen understanding of pitching nuances. He has at least two plus offerings, in a low-to-mid-90s fastball that can spike higher and a changeup. He also spins a curveball in the 70s. However, The Pitch is the screwball he learned from Uncle Mike Marshall's blueprint. When it works as intended, observers are left looking like they just contracted the stomach flu. Young Honeywell is certainly a bird of a different feather, one who should be strutting like a peacock in a few years.

Jake McGee LHP

Born: 8/6/86 Age: 29 Bats: L Throws: L Height: 6'3" Weight: 230

YEAR	TEAM	LVL	AGE	W	L	SV	G	GS	IP	H	HR	BB/9	K/9	GB%	BABIP	WHIP	ERA	FIP	DRA	WARP	CFIP	MPH
2013	TBA	MLB	26	5	3	1	71	0	62^{2}	52	8	3.2	10.8	43%	.286	1.18	4.02	3.44	3.96	0.5	81	98.9
2014	TBA	MLB	27	5	2	19	73	0	71^{1}	48	2	2.0	11.4	38%	.280	0.90	1.89	1.76	1.69	2.5	61	99.1
2015	TBA	MLB	28	1	2	6	39	0	37^{1}	27	3	1.9	11.6	39%	.276	0.94	2.41	2.30	2.77	0.9	70	98.1
2016	*TBA*	*MLB*	*29*	*2*	*1*	*4*	*46*	*0*	48^{2}	*40*	*5*	*2.6*	*10.7*	*40%*	*.286*	*1.11*	*3.25*	*3.18*	*3.57*	*0.7*	*73*	
2017	*TBA*	*MLB*	*30*	*4*	*2*	*10*	*68*	*0*	61^{2}	*51*	*7*	*2.7*	*10.3*	*40%*	*.285*	*1.13*	*3.30*	*3.29*	*3.63*	*0.8*	*75*	

Breakout: 22% Improve: 52% Collapse: 31% Attrition: 9% MLB: 100% *Comparables: Frank Francisco, Steve Cishek, Bobby Jenks*

McGee remains one of the best relievers in baseball, even though his name is rarely brought up in the discussion about the best relievers in baseball. The broad-shouldered southpaw chucks fastballs in the mid-90s with extreme accuracy. The singular "fastball" actually comprises a quartet as he can locate it to the four quadrants of the zone at will. He can also spin the occasional upper-70s curveball, mostly to show he can, but also to make Manny Machado's knees buckle once in a while. But it's also right to be a little nervous: He began the season on the DL after a winter scope of his elbow. This likely cost him velocity early on, as his routine was thrown off, and killed any chance of him reclaiming the closer's role and gathering its customary accolades. He rounded out the season in similar fashion, missing more than a month with a torn meniscus. With free agency looming, 2016 is very important year for Clockhands.

Matt Moore LHP

Born: 6/18/89 Age: 27 Bats: L Throws: L Height: 6'3" Weight: 210

YEAR	TEAM	LVL	AGE	W	L	SV	G	GS	IP	H	HR	BB/9	K/9	GB%	BABIP	WHIP	ERA	FIP	DRA	WARP	CFIP	MPH
2013	TBA	MLB	24	17	4	0	27	27	150^{1}	119	14	4.5	8.6	41%	.259	1.30	3.29	3.98	3.78	2.0	103	95.1
2014	TBA	MLB	25	0	2	0	2	2	10	10	1	4.5	5.4	42%	.281	1.50	2.70	4.76	5.28	-0.1	108	94.4
2015	TBA	MLB	26	3	4	0	12	12	63	74	9	3.3	6.6	42%	.332	1.54	5.43	4.79	6.08	-0.8	115	94.7
2015	DUR	AAA	26	2	3	0	7	7	40^{1}	35	6	2.7	12.9	46%	.330	1.17	3.57	3.26	1.75	1.5	70	
2015	PCH	A+	26	0	0	0	3	3	11	9	1	3.3	7.4	50%	.258	1.18	1.64	4.07	3.78	0.1	99	
2016	*TBA*	*MLB*	*27*	*8*	*10*	*0*	*29*	*29*	*145*	*137*	*18*	*3.5*	*8.1*	*42%*	*.289*	*1.33*	*4.36*	*4.33*	*4.65*	*0.8*	*108*	
2017	*TBA*	*MLB*	*28*	*8*	*9*	*0*	*26*	*26*	156^{2}	*151*	*20*	*3.6*	*8.2*	*42%*	*.295*	*1.36*	*4.30*	*4.27*	*4.59*	*0.9*	*107*	

Breakout: 22% Improve: 52% Collapse: 22% Attrition: 11% MLB: 92% *Comparables: Ricky Romero, Erik Bedard, Alex Cobb*

Instead of a feel-good story, Moore's initial return from Tommy John surgery read like the script from a horror film. His fastball lacked the velocity it once had and his location caught more barrels than strike zone. Things were so bad he was soon optioned to

Triple-A Durham to read self-help books and drink thoughtfully. He appeared to be much more comfortable after figuring out who moved his cheese. In each of his final four starts, Moore went at least six innings, a particularly magic number for the pitch count–challenged hurler. No longer just a young thunder, he augments the now-modest fastball with a cutter and curveball in addition to the changeup. The arsenal is mostly there, but control will be his biggest obstacle outside of health. He goes into this season another year removed from surgery, with a normal winter's workouts and an Eckhart Tolle paperback.

Jake Odorizzi RHP

Born: 3/27/90 Age: 26 Bats: R Throws: R Height: 6'2" Weight: 190

YEAR	TEAM	LVL	AGE	W	L	SV	G	GS	IP	H	HR	BB/9	K/9	GB%	BABIP	WHIP	ERA	FIP	DRA	WARP	CFIP	MPH
2013	DUR	AAA	23	9	6	0	22	22	124^{1}	101	12	2.9	9.0	37%	.282	1.13	3.33	3.45	3.98	1.5	87	
2013	TBA	MLB	23	0	1	1	7	4	29^{2}	28	3	2.4	6.7	34%	.287	1.21	3.94	3.92	4.26	0.2	103	93.9
2014	TBA	MLB	24	11	13	0	31	31	168	156	20	3.2	9.3	32%	.295	1.28	4.12	3.78	4.21	1.2	92	92.8
2015	TBA	MLB	25	9	9	0	28	28	169^{1}	149	18	2.4	8.0	40%	.271	1.15	3.35	3.58	3.76	2.6	91	93.6
2016	*TBA*	*MLB*	*26*	*12*	*11*	*0*	*32*	*32*	*192*	*173*	*22*	*2.7*	*8.5*	*37%*	*.282*	*1.20*	*3.81*	*3.82*	*4.10*	*2.3*	*93*	
2017	*TBA*	*MLB*	*27*	*9*	*9*	*0*	*27*	*27*	*161^{2}*	*149*	*21*	*2.6*	*8.4*	*37%*	*.283*	*1.21*	*3.95*	*3.92*	*4.25*	*1.6*	*97*	

Breakout: 33% Improve: 64% Collapse: 17% Attrition: 8% MLB: 89% *Comparables: Alex Cobb, Daniel Hudson, J.P. Howell*

The Shang Tsung of the Rays, Odorizzi's ability to adapt and absorb the talents and tips of those around him has morphed him into a solid middle-of-the-rotation starter. The days of simply throwing low-90s fastballs and upper-70s curves are gone. Though the fastball still hovers around his birth year, he now augments it with a pair of pitches about five or six years his senior. The addition of a mid-80s cutter has all but replaced the need or want to toss a breaking ball—though the big hook still remains on the books. The cutter induced groundballs and served as a weapon against same-siders. Meanwhile, going against the platoon, the split/change he sponged from Alex Cobb continued to generate outs, working in tandem with the fastball to create a speed trap. Carlos Pena once said going from a changeup to a fastball was akin to driving in a school zone and then switching to NASCAR. If that is true, Odorizzi could navigate a school bus on the banks of Daytona International Speedway.

Erasmo Ramirez RHP

Born: 5/2/90 Age: 26 Bats: R Throws: R Height: 5'11" Weight: 200

YEAR	TEAM	LVL	AGE	W	L	SV	G	GS	IP	H	HR	BB/9	K/9	GB%	BABIP	WHIP	ERA	FIP	DRA	WARP	CFIP	MPH
2013	TAC	AAA	23	3	3	0	7	7	43^{2}	43	4	2.9	8.7	44%	.315	1.31	3.09	3.87	4.64	0.5	88	
2013	SEA	MLB	23	5	3	0	14	13	72^{1}	79	12	3.2	7.1	44%	.300	1.45	4.98	4.86	4.59	0.3	109	95.0
2014	TAC	AAA	24	6	5	0	15	14	86^{1}	92	8	1.4	7.0	41%	.313	1.22	3.65	3.94	4.91	0.9	87	
2014	SEA	MLB	24	1	6	0	17	14	75^{1}	82	13	4.1	7.2	40%	.307	1.54	5.26	5.40	6.41	-1.5	118	94.0
2015	TBA	MLB	25	11	6	0	34	27	163^{1}	145	16	2.2	6.9	49%	.272	1.13	3.75	3.74	3.85	2.2	100	94.1
2016	*TBA*	*MLB*	*26*	*9*	*10*	*0*	*29*	*29*	*153^{2}*	*151*	*18*	*2.6*	*7.2*	*46%*	*.291*	*1.28*	*4.17*	*4.18*	*4.45*	*1.2*	*103*	
2017	*TBA*	*MLB*	*27*	*8*	*9*	*0*	*25*	*25*	*145^{2}*	*152*	*20*	*2.6*	*7.4*	*46%*	*.302*	*1.34*	*4.32*	*4.28*	*4.61*	*0.8*	*107*	

Breakout: 33% Improve: 66% Collapse: 14% Attrition: 10% MLB: 90% *Comparables: Alex Cobb, Joe Blanton, Ivan Nova*

A decimated starting rotation gave the Rays a late-spring opportunity to trade option-carrying Mike Montgomery for an optionless Ramirez. He allowed 15 earned runs in his first five innings with the Rays, not the best way to make an introduction. But with some alterations to pitch selection and usage, Ramirez rewarded his new club with a surprisingly stellar campaign. Employing a Hi-Lo strategy that would make Bob Barker proud, the short right-hander used his fastball and plus changeup to adjust speeds and alter eye levels, leading to weak contact. Just what Tampa Bay needed: another team-controlled starting pitcher under the age of 30.

Drew Smyly LHP

Born: 6/13/89 Age: 27 Bats: L Throws: L Height: 6'3" Weight: 190

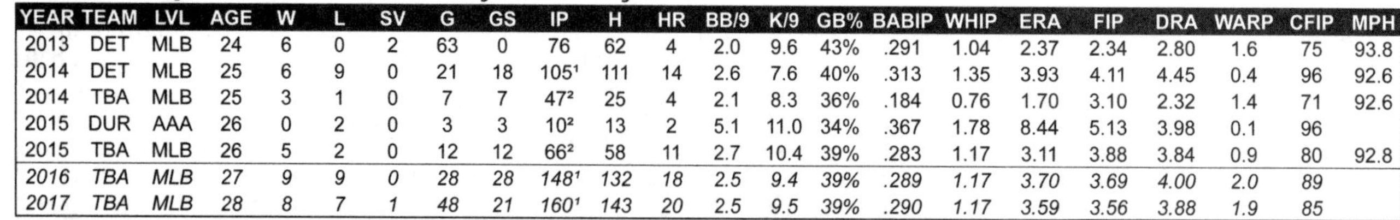

YEAR	TEAM	LVL	AGE	W	L	SV	G	GS	IP	H	HR	BB/9	K/9	GB%	BABIP	WHIP	ERA	FIP	DRA	WARP	CFIP	MPH
2013	DET	MLB	24	6	0	2	63	0	76	62	4	2.0	9.6	43%	.291	1.04	2.37	2.34	2.80	1.6	75	93.8
2014	DET	MLB	25	6	9	0	21	18	105^{1}	111	14	2.6	7.6	40%	.313	1.35	3.93	4.11	4.45	0.4	96	92.6
2014	TBA	MLB	25	3	1	0	7	7	47^{2}	25	4	2.1	8.3	36%	.184	0.76	1.70	3.10	2.32	1.4	71	92.6
2015	DUR	AAA	26	0	2	0	3	3	10^{2}	13	2	5.1	11.0	34%	.367	1.78	8.44	5.13	3.98	0.1	96	
2015	TBA	MLB	26	5	2	0	12	12	66^{2}	58	11	2.7	10.4	39%	.283	1.17	3.11	3.88	3.84	0.9	80	92.8
2016	*TBA*	*MLB*	*27*	*9*	*9*	*0*	*28*	*28*	*148^{1}*	*132*	*18*	*2.5*	*9.4*	*39%*	*.289*	*1.17*	*3.70*	*3.69*	*4.00*	*2.0*	*89*	
2017	*TBA*	*MLB*	*28*	*8*	*7*	*1*	*48*	*21*	*160^{1}*	*143*	*20*	*2.5*	*9.5*	*39%*	*.290*	*1.17*	*3.59*	*3.56*	*3.88*	*1.9*	*85*	

Breakout: 25% Improve: 55% Collapse: 17% Attrition: 6% MLB: 91% *Comparables: Jeff Francis, Max Scherzer, James Shields*

Smyly, a lanky left-hander, is already used to pitching with diminished stuff. He took that to the extreme last year, pitching with a partially torn rotator cuff. Rather than going under the knife like some injury experts expected, he opted for rehabilitation instead, missing about three months before making a successful return in August. He made nine starts over the final six weeks of the season, allowing one earned run or fewer in five of those games. He also produced the best strikeout rate of his career while maintaining a walk rate of fewer than three free passes per nine. Nice set of PECOTA comps.

Blake Snell LHP

Born: 12/4/92 Age: 23 Bats: L Throws: L Height: 6'4" Weight: 180

YEAR	TEAM	LVL	AGE	W	L	SV	G	GS	IP	H	HR	BB/9	K/9	GB%	BABIP	WHIP	ERA	FIP	DRA	WARP	CFIP	MPH
2013	BGR	A	20	4	9	0	23	23	99	90	8	6.6	9.6	57%	.318	1.65	4.27	4.52	5.24	0.0	119	
2014	PCH	A+	21	5	6	0	16	16	75^1	69	1	4.4	9.2	54%	.325	1.41	3.94	3.19	4.38	0.5	100	
2014	BGR	A	21	3	2	0	8	8	40^1	26	1	4.2	9.4	69%	.253	1.12	1.79	3.14	4.42	0.4	98	
2015	PCH	A+	22	3	0	0	4	2	21	10	0	4.7	11.6	59%	.227	1.00	0.00	2.17	2.82	0.4	87	
2015	DUR	AAA	22	6	2	0	9	9	44^1	29	2	2.6	11.6	55%	.276	0.95	1.83	2.12	1.39	1.8	64	
2015	MNT	AA	22	6	2	0	12	12	68^2	45	5	3.8	10.4	48%	.260	1.08	1.57	3.26	2.56	1.9	80	
2016	*TBA*	*MLB*	*23*	*2*	*1*	*0*	*36*	*0*	*37*^{2}	*34*	*4*	*4.2*	*9.1*	*51%*	*.294*	*1.37*	*4.18*	*4.12*	*4.46*	*0.0*	*102*	
2017	*TBA*	*MLB*	*24*	*4*	*4*	*0*	*13*	*13*	*76*^{1}	*70*	*9*	*4.4*	*9.2*	*51%*	*.298*	*1.40*	*4.17*	*4.14*	*4.45*	*0.5*	*102*	

Breakout: 20% Improve: 34% Collapse: 13% Attrition: 34% MLB: 53% *Comparables: Wade Davis, Trevor May, Jeurys Familia*

Coming off a year in which he was named the organization's minor-league pitcher of the year, Snell elevated to another plane, dominated three levels, and won it again. Already talented, his biggest difference was an increase in maturity, preparation and openness to coaching. He's also matured physically since being drafted out of high school in 2011; once seen as a finesse southpaw, his arsenal now includes a fastball around 92-95 mph, with the ability to touch higher early in games. From there he possesses a plus changeup, a big breaking curveball and an occasional mid-80s slider. The menage of pitches is nasty enough to make Nikki blush.

Chase Whitley RHP

Born: 6/14/89 Age: 27 Bats: R Throws: R Height: 6'3" Weight: 215

YEAR	TEAM	LVL	AGE	W	L	SV	G	GS	IP	H	HR	BB/9	K/9	GB%	BABIP	WHIP	ERA	FIP	DRA	WARP	CFIP	MPH
2013	SWB	AAA	24	3	2	3	29	5	67^2	61	3	2.8	8.2	44%	.310	1.21	3.06	3.06	3.94	0.7	86	
2014	NYA	MLB	25	4	3	0	24	12	75^2	94	10	2.1	7.1	46%	.353	1.48	5.23	4.16	5.62	-0.8	103	93.1
2014	SWB	AAA	25	3	2	0	10	6	31^1	22	0	2.3	10.6	56%	.286	0.96	2.01	1.76	3.63	0.5	65	
2015	NYA	MLB	26	1	2	0	4	4	19^1	20	3	2.3	7.4	51%	.293	1.29	4.19	4.55	5.08	0.0	103	91.5
2015	SWB	AAA	26	2	0	0	3	3	17	13	0	3.2	6.9	35%	.265	1.12	2.12	2.69	3.78	0.2	96	
2016	*TBA*	*MLB*	*27*	*2*	*2*	*0*	*24*	*4*	*42*	*41*	*5*	*2.6*	*7.7*	*46%*	*.296*	*1.28*	*4.07*	*4.07*	*4.36*	*0.4*	*100*	
2017	*TBA*	*MLB*	*28*	*2*	*2*	*0*	*18*	*4*	*50*^{1}	*51*	*6*	*2.9*	*7.7*	*46%*	*.302*	*1.34*	*4.13*	*4.09*	*4.42*	*0.3*	*101*	

Breakout: 15% Improve: 33% Collapse: 21% Attrition: 35% MLB: 69% *Comparables: Josh Lindblom, Phil Coke, Zach Putnam*

On May 4th, Whitley threw seven shutout innings against the Blue Jays, with six strikeouts and no walks. Ten days later he tore his UCL and it's unclear when we'll see him again, as he's the sort of pitcher who could easily just fall off the map. The walking definition of "just a guy," the right-handed swingman throws 90 mph without any outstanding breaking pitches or major accomplishments. His minor-league track record is strong enough, but he's not especially talented and has yet to distinguish himself in the big leagues. He's not *Waterworld*-Kevin Costner bad, but he's post-*Waterworld*-Kevin Costner forgettable.

LINEOUTS

Hitters

NAME	POS	TEAM	LVL	AGE	PA	R	2B	3B	HR	RBI	BB	K	SB	CS	AVG/OBP/SLG	TAv	BABIP	BRR	FRAA	WARP
Patrick Leonard	4C	MNT	AA	22	514	72	32	3	10	43	54	129	11	3	.256/.350/.408	.285	.337	2.7	3B(82): 0.4, 1B(25): -3.1	2.7
Luke Maile	C	DUR	AAA	24	337	38	9	1	5	29	35	50	1	1	.207/.298/.296	.215	.231	0.8	C(84): 13.6	1.3
	C	TBA	MLB	24	35	2	3	0	0	2	0	8	0	0	.171/.171/.257	.128	.222	0.1	C(15): 0.0	-0.3
Taylor Motter	UT	DUR	AAA	25	558	74	43	1	14	72	57	95	26	8	.292/.366/.471	.304	.332	-0.7	RF(62): 2.2, 3B(25): 1.3	4.2
Andrew Velazquez	2B	PCH	A+	20	203	29	9	2	0	10	15	53	5	8	.290/.343/.360	.285	.406	-0.7	3B(18): -1.8, SS(14): -1.1	1.1
Justin Williams	OF	BGR	A	19	406	43	25	2	7	42	13	76	3	1	.284/.308/.413	.264	.334	0.6	RF(95): 13.2, CF(1): -0.1	2.4
	OF	PCH	A+	19	84	8	5	0	0	6	1	14	3	1	.241/.250/.301	.194	.290	-0.7	RF(14): -0.9, LF(5): 0.3	-0.6
Kean Wong	2B	PCH	A+	20	438	46	14	3	1	36	29	65	15	6	.274/.319/.332	.252	.320	1.9	2B(95): 8.5	1.9

The third catcher taken in the 2015 draft, **Chris Betts** was essentially the first catcher taken in this year's draft, as the team physical revealed that he'd need Tommy John surgery. ❖ After nearly falling off the prospect lists during a rough start to his fourth season, **Patrick Leonard** heated up in the second half, and restored hope that he might see the majors by part six. ❖ A polished defender behind the plate and a species of flowering plant in the dogbane family, **Luke Maile** made his major-league debut and could stick as a glove-first reserve. ❖ **Taylor Motter** had a breakout season at the plate and can play multiple positions. Somewhere, someone is unfairly comparing him to Ben Zobrist. ❖ **Adrian Rondon**, a talented former bonus baby, struggled in his first foray into professional baseball, but remember he was born *after* the (Devil) Rays played their first game. ❖ A shoulder strain and broken hamate kept **Andrew Velazquez** off the field for a large part of the year, and limited his explosiveness for the rest. Minor ailments aside, he still projects to become a useful piece at the highest level. ❖ **Justin Williams** has flashed a big bat and big arm, sometimes even in games. He also had to be reminded to run to first on occasion. ❖ **Kean Wong**, the younger brother of Kolten, maintained a solid, if mostly empty, average around a wrist injury. The package is more solid than spectacular at the keystone.

Pitchers

NAME	TEAM	LVL	AGE	W	L	SV	G	GS	IP	H	HR	BB/9	K/9	GB%	BABIP	WHIP	ERA	FIP	FRA	WARP	CFIP	MPH
Grant Balfour	TBA	MLB	37	0	0	0	6	0	4^{1}	3	1	8.3	0.0	25%	.133	1.62	6.23	9.57	7.05	-0.1	122	91.8
Buddy Borden	PCH	A+	23	9	7	0	28	17	127^{1}	104	9	4.1	6.7	41%	.259	1.27	2.97	3.98	4.90	-1.0	113	
Jacob Faria	PCH	A+	21	10	1	0	12	10	74^{1}	51	1	2.7	7.6	40%	.253	0.98	1.33	2.53	3.03	1.3	89	
	MNT	AA	21	7	3	0	13	13	75^{1}	52	5	3.6	11.5	33%	.278	1.09	2.51	2.85	1.77	2.9	71	
Chih-Wei Hu	PCH	A+	21	0	3	1	5	4	18^{1}	23	1	3.9	9.8	55%	.407	1.69	7.36	3.00	3.55	0.2	87	
	FTM	A+	21	5	3	0	15	15	84^{2}	79	5	2.0	7.8	40%	.303	1.16	2.44	2.99	3.54	1.0	86	
Enny Romero	DUR	AAA	24	1	1	1	17	3	46^{1}	48	5	3.3	8.7	44%	.326	1.40	4.86	3.78	3.96	0.3	98	
	TBA	MLB	24	0	2	0	23	0	30	39	1	3.9	9.3	49%	.400	1.73	5.10	2.77	5.62	-0.3	100	98.8
Jaime Schultz	MNT	AA	24	9	5	0	27	27	135	105	11	6.0	11.2	42%	.306	1.44	3.67	4.07	4.30	1.0	100	
Ryne Stanek	MNT	AA	23	4	3	1	16	8	61^{2}	52	7	4.5	6.0	52%	.250	1.35	4.09	5.01	5.76	-0.7	116	
	PCH	A+	23	4	2	0	9	9	50^{2}	33	2	2.7	6.8	59%	.228	0.95	1.78	3.07	3.43	0.6	95	

Once paid to get outs in high-leverage situations, the Rays paid **Grant Balfour** to go away (twice). ❖ Acquired from the Pirates, **Buddy Borden** tossed a no-hitter in the Florida State League and flourished as a starter after bouncing between roles. His sturdy frame and three-pitch mix may earn him some sleeper hype. ❖ Using his long frame to generate downward plane, **Jacob Faria** knows how to use his largely average array of pitches to generate weak contact and quick outs. If he can grow six inches, he's got Chris Young's career to model himself after. ❖ **Grayson Garvin** is the tooth fairy. He seems like a nice character; everyone has kind words for him. Alas, nobody has ever seen him. He missed 2015 with a torn left lat muscle. ❖ **Chih-Wei Hu**, sent over from the Twins for Kevin Jepsen, arrives with plus pitchability and makeup. He also controls upwards of five pitches, but not the blender that caused a laceration and forced him to miss time. Why the blender would do such a thing? Hu knows. ❖ The time is up for **Enny Romero**, starting-pitching prospect. However, the time for Enny Romero, major-league reliever and per diem recipient, may be now. ❖ **Jamie Schultz** is a small right-hander with a big strikeout rate and bigger control issues. The stuff is also larger than his size, but inconsistency could lead to a life in relief. ❖ After missing all of 2014 with a muscle flexor strain, **Burch Smith** missed all of 2015 with a torn ligament. If there's any silver lining, it's that moving to the 60-day DL allowed him to make the major-league minimum, a 500 percent raise. The hope is that he'll make his half-million the old-fashioned way this season. ❖ The same questions evaluators had about **Ryne Stanek** heading into the 2013 draft—health and ability to start—remain. A full-time move to the bullpen, where his stuff may play up and injury risk move down, seems likely.

MANAGER

Kevin Cash

YEAR	TEAM	W	L	Pythag +/-	Avg PC	100+ P	120+ P	QS	BQS	REL	REL w Zero R	IBB	PH	PH Avg	PH HR	SB2	CS2	SB3	CS3	SAC Att	SAC%	POS SAC	Squeeze	Swing	In Play
2015	TBA	80	82	-1	90.6	46	1	68	3	530	416	23	179	.219	3	62	40	25	4	29	65.5	17	0	290	82

In his first season as manager, the most interesting thing about Cash—whose jejune pressers were the opposite of his predecessor's, much to the media's chagrin—was how he handled the pitching staff. Confronted with an injury-ravaged rotation (and roster, really), Cash's solution was to limit his weakest starters' exposure. As a result, no team restricted its rotation to fewer batters faced after the second time through the order than the Rays did. Yet that answer had its own drawbacks—like, say, having to use Brandon Gomes and other Triple-A arms more often than they merited, as well as overtaxing the few reliable relievers on the roster. Even Matthew Silverman admitted after the season that the Rays lacked the optimal personnel to do it right. You might ask why the Rays didn't adjust their personnel or their strategy to make life easier on the youngest manager in the game, but perhaps it's as simple as Silverman having 2016 in the employee pool for when the 38-year-old Cash would turn gray.

The rest of Cash's season had its share of highlights and frayed ends. He showed an appreciation for playing matchups, double-stealing and shifting like an autumn breeze. At the same time, it's beyond us why Cash asked James Loney to attempt six steals (one of which resulted in a fractured finger), or what he preached in camp that inspired his charges to record the majors' second-most outs on the basepaths. But by now Cash is probably tired of being questioned publicly, since a number of Rays did it throughout the season—another sharp contrast to the He Who Must Not Be Named era.

Brad Boxberger made the most inflammatory comments when he blamed his second-half demise on unusual usage. Boxberger overstated his case—he fingered two seventh-inning appearances, in June and in April, as the cause—but it was his act, not his facts, that made the episode noteworthy. (Ditto for Nate Karns, who questioned the aforementioned bullpen-centric strategy after his relief blew a game.) Factor in the Rays' dispiriting deadline trades—raffling off clubhouse favorite David DeJesus and setup man Kevin Jepsen to teams the Rays were competing with for a playoff spot—and the front office did Cash few favors when it came to gaining and maintaining the clubhouse's respect and approval. Nonetheless, Cash showed plenty of confidence and creativity (perhaps too much of each, if you polled his players), and he deserves credit for milking a solid record from a skeleton crew. For his sake, though, you have to hope the front office does a better job heading forward.

TEXAS RANGERS

Essay by Kate Morrison

Player comments by Mike Gianella, Kate Morrison, and BP authors

It wasn't a question of whether Cole Hamels was going to be traded, but a question of where, and for how much.

Hamels was a known commodity, an ace in an era where it takes generally takes great luck (in the draft) or nine figures (in free agency) to land one. You know what you're going to get from Hamels: a devastating changeup from the left side, a steadying presence in the rotation, a greater chance of victory any time he's on the mound. A bulldog mentality. Postseason experience and success. A few thousand more T-shirt sales. And, perhaps most importantly, a key upgrade for the 2015 pennant race—which made the Rangers one of the last teams that baseball writers, executives or fans would expect to land him.

The Rangers weren't in the 2015 pennant race. They had been longshots from Opening Day, with Prince Fielder a question mark after a career-threatening neck injury and with Shin-Soo Choo coming off an awful season on both sides of the ball—the two superstars the Rangers had counted on to carry them in 2014[1]. BP authors collectively predicted the Rangers to finish in last place in the AL West before the season started, and then things got worse: Yu Darvish went down to Tommy John surgery, Derek Holland to a shoulder problem, and former top prospect Jurickson Profar was put on the Well, We Don't Really Know-Day DL. The team that had lost more than 2,100 days to the DL last year was ahead of its own pace. The Astros had hit the "production" part of their 2017 plan early, the Angels were playing like their payroll had promised, and even the Mariners—our authors' preseason pick—were interesting.

So, 24 hours before the 2015 trade deadline, the Rangers had a 1-in-150 chance of winning the AL West, according to BP's playoff odds. They were about 1-in-20 to win one of the two Wild Card slots. They were eight games out of first place and six out of second place. If anybody had an immediate and pressing need for Cole Hamels, it wasn't the Rangers—it was the Astros, who tried and were (reportedly) blocked. Or the Giants, or the Cubs, or the Dodgers.

1 The Rangers counted on their contribution in 2014 to the tune of trading Ian Kinsler for Fielder, six years of his contract, and $30 million, and signing Choo to a seven-year, $130 million deal.

RANGERS PROSPECTUS

2015 W-L: 88-74, 1st in AL West

Pythag	.511	14th	DER	.706	11th
RS/G	4.64	3rd	B-Age	28.8	24th
RA/G	4.52	23rd	P-Age	28.4	16th
TAv	.264	10th	Salary	$143.7M	8th
BRR	20.46	1st	M$/MW	$3.3M	17th
TAv-P	.266	20th	DL Days	1722	28th
FIP	4.31	26th	$ on DL	20%	21st

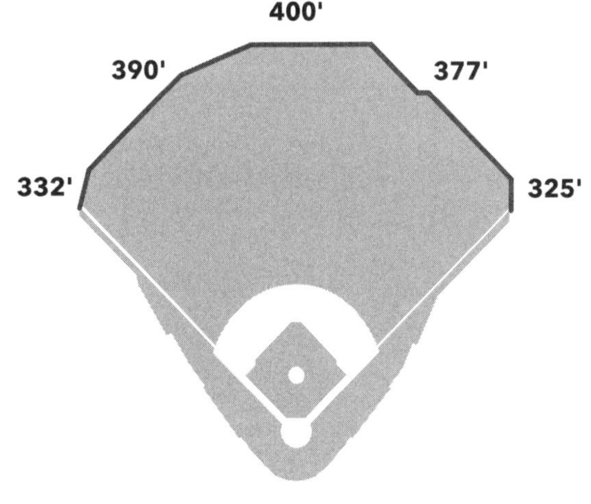

Outfield wall profile: **8'** to **14'**

Three-Year Park Factors

Runs	Runs/RH	Runs/LH	HR/RH	HR/LH
105	119	118	110	113

Top Hitter WARP	4.5	Shin-Soo Choo
Top Pitcher WARP	2.4	Colby Lewis
Top Prospect	Nomar Mazara	

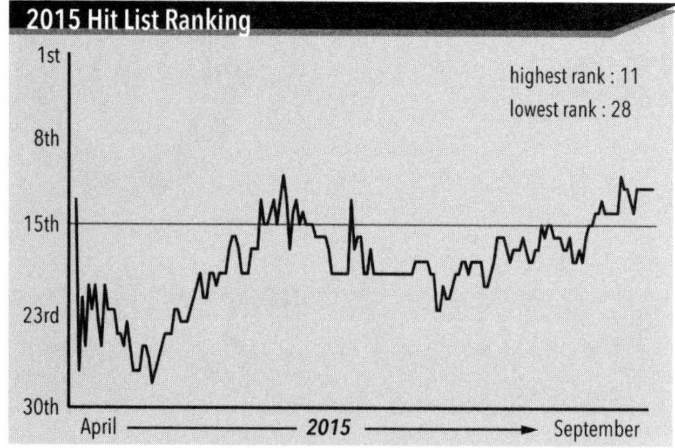

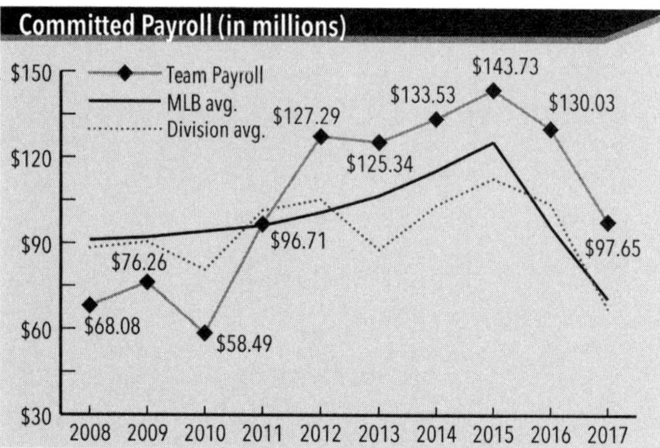

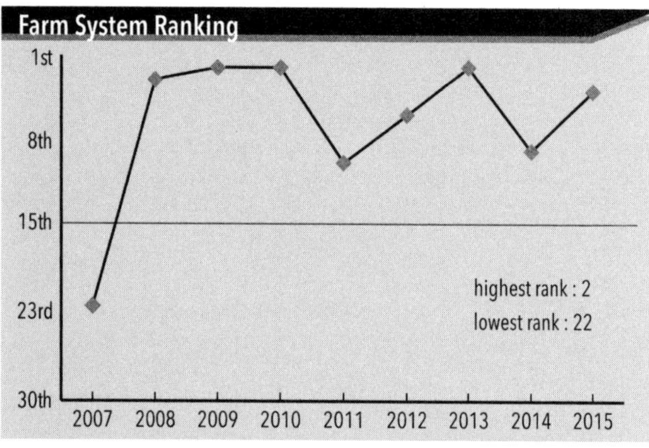

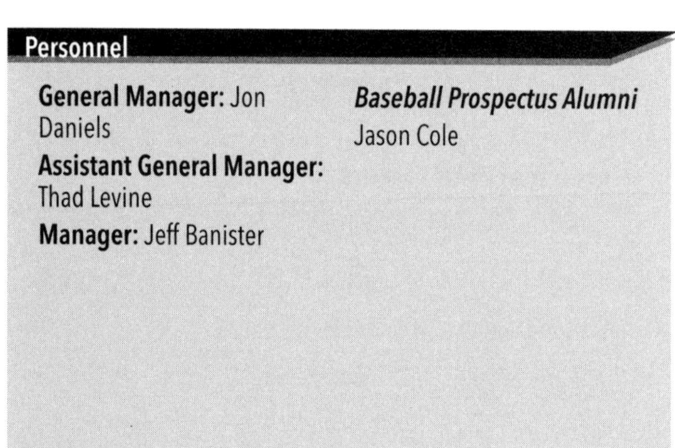

Personnel

General Manager: Jon Daniels

Assistant General Manager: Thad Levine

Manager: Jeff Banister

Baseball Prospectus Alumni

Jason Cole

But there was another question besides where Hamels would fit: What would he cost? To that, the baseball world had a much more unified answer: Talent, young talent, lots of young talent. And if the Rangers seemed like an odd fit for Hamels, they were a great match for the Phillies, because the Rangers, more than any team in baseball over the past decade, have had talent, young talent, lots of young talent. Nobody should have been surprised that the Rangers could offer enough to get Hamels. And, the way that the Rangers front office has worked, year in and year out, with the now-obvious belief in the ceiling of their organization, we shouldn't have been surprised that they would.

✦✦✦

Even in third place the Rangers were outplaying their expectations, thanks to a strategy based around the front office's strengths. While the Rangers have a well-publicized affinity for upside-heavy signings and draft picks, they also have developed the ability to find high-floor players at any round of the draft. This surplus of unheralded players, guys who hover around replacement level, meant the Rangers could run a kind of plug-and-play team, a lineup of prospects testing their wings outside the nest, an interchangeable collection of "who-is-that-guy?"s who could be replaced the second the league figured them out. They found enough pieces on waivers and cheap trades and in the edges of their farm system to stay afloat in a division where the hot-starting teams were starting to fade. Fielder and Choo bounced back enough to anchor a first-division lineup. DeShields emerged as one of the best Rule 5 picks in modern history and stole the center-field job.

But despite their luck with the replacement parts, the Rangers needed pitching. Teams closer to the playoffs were favored—after all, who would send away that much talent to "waste" a summer of Hamels near the bottom of a division?

The answer is, the team that could most afford him. This will be the ninth year that Baseball Prospectus ranks team farm systems each spring, and in that time the Rangers have had a remarkable run of producing talent: Look at the chart to the left.

And they've done it while competing almost every year—typically a drain on organizational talent, as teams trade prospects or give up draft picks to acquire the final pieces, and draft low in the first round when they do have picks. All this means that the Rangers could acquire a player like Hamels without leaving the cupboard bare. How do they do it?

Since Jon Daniels arrived in October 2005, the main focus on the developmental side of the organization has been building a renewable resource out of the farm. While giving up Nick Williams, Jorge Alfaro, Jerad Eickhoff, Jake Thompson and Alec Asher will dramatically affect the Rangers' depth charts in the coming seasons, the additions of Cole Hamels and, crucially, Jake Diekman impacted how the Rangers performed in crunch time in 2015.

The package gives us a snapshot at their drafting, signing and development strategy:

The High-Variance Upside Play

Nick Williams is a classic high-ceiling, low-floor prospect with the talent to be a superstar and the strong likelihood of busting completely. The Rangers love to draft guys like him[2] out of high school, particularly in the top rounds, on the theory that the more lottery tickets you've got, the greater your chances of owning an island. It's an act of faith to take something as unrefined as Williams and believe that you, and your organization, can develop him into something great. After acing the Double-A test last year, Williams is on the road to success, and his sky-high ceiling makes him a covetable asset for a Phillies team trying to pull itself out of the basement.

The International Scouting and Signing

The Rangers have never relied too much on the draft, because they couldn't. Before 2014, the last time they had a top-10 draft pick was 2003, when they picked John Danks ninth overall out of Round Rock High School. The Rangers' org-rankings dynasty was built on the blockbuster Mark Teixeira trade, but has since relied on the club's ability to beat everybody else to the best international prospects. It's there that the most aggressive teams can separate themselves from other teams, taking long positions on players with enormous volatility. The breakdown of the Rangers' top 10 (or 11, depending on the year) prospects, as ranked by BP authors since 2008:

	2008	2009	2010	2011	2012	2013	2014	2015
Trade	5	4	2	1	0	0	0	1
International	0	2	3	5	7	6	5	2
Draft	6	5	6	5	4	4	5	7

They've found top prospects from Curaçao (Jurickson Profar), Venezuela (Rougned Odor and Martin Perez), Cuba (Leonys Martin), Mexico (Christian Villanueva), the Dominican Republic (Roman Mendez and Ronald Guzman), and Colombia (Jorge Alfaro). Of those eight, five have major-league service time, one is still a top prospect, one is biding his time behind Kris Bryant in Chicago, and one still has potential. Odor was a major contributor to the 2015 club; Alfaro, as a key trade piece for Hamels, was, too.

Low-Variance Pitching

Eickhoff has already made considerable contributions to the Philadelphia rotation, and is a great example (along with non-traded Chi Chi Gonzalez) of the Rangers' pitching philosophy: Draft mostly college or junior college arms. Asher is another of these community college arms, with a lower ceiling but higher floor for the Phillies' future. Why go low-variance on pitching? Older, more developed arms are easier to push through a system fast. Drafting college arms also allows them to sign more teenage Latin American pitchers, leaning on their strength in that area. These college arms don't typically offer ace futures, but a lot of value can be squeezed out of fringe MLB arms—either in helping a staff gut through a hot Arlington summer, or in trade to a team looking for cost-controlled pitch depth.

Guess what? Trades!

In the disaster 2014 season, Texas turned reclaimed closer Joakim Soria into Jake Thompson and Corey Knebel. Thompson turned into part of Hamels, and Knebel turned into part of Yovani Gallardo. Even if these prospects aren't making it to the big leagues with the Rangers, they're making the Rangers' big-league team better. This has consistently been one of Daniels' favorite ways to acquire assets, a strategy that goes back to his second year as general manager, when he traded Teixeira for a full package of prospects from the Atlanta Braves. While none of those prospects was traded for other assets[3], they made the big-league team better through their contribution.

While a trade of this magnitude might have bankrupted many other teams' farms, the Rangers will, once again, be in the top 10 of Baseball Prospectus' organizational rankings this spring. Some of this is, yes, luck—prospects bust all the time for no particular reason. A lot of it, however, is a dedication to scouting and development, making sure that out of every year's influx of potential, more than one or two of these talents realize. The Rangers managed to get a bona fide ace without giving up either of their top two prospects.

Trades are bets. One team is betting that its acquisition will be at least as valuable, if not more, than what it is giving up, or, at least, more valuable to them. The Rangers have gotten burned on trades before (two particular deals with the Chicago Cubs come to mind[4]), but they've been both willing and able to make those deals, something that not many clubs can say year after year. If there's one thing Jon Daniels has shown himself extremely willing to do in his 10 years as general manager, it's take the big risk, and be prepared for when it doesn't work out. Part of why Daniels has been able to take these risks is the long leash given by ownership. While other clubs' management groups may have meddling owners, the Rangers' Ray Davis and Bob

2 I expanded on this in the early 2015 series "Every Team's Moneyball" on Baseball Prospectus, but here are some more of these raw but talented athletes the Rangers have had varying levels of success with: Jake Skole, Jamie Jarmon, Jordan Akins, Lewis Brinson, Eric Jenkins, and more.

3 Matt Harrison's inclusion in the Hamels trade was a salary dump, not an asset acquisition.

4 In 2012, Ryan Dempster for 3B Christian Villanueva and RHP Kyle Hendricks. In 2013, Matt Garza for 3B Mike Olt, RHP Carl Edwards, Jr., RHP Justin Grimm, and RHP Neil Ramirez. Neither trade worked out particularly well for the Rangers.

Simpson trust the judgment of Daniels and his lieutenants, and have been rewarded with a few coin flips away from the ultimate pennant. All GMs are fundamentally bettors, but JD bets on himself, on his player development staff, and on his team itself.

The Rangers went 39-22 after the trade deadline and won the AL West. ■

—Kate Morrison is a freelance writer and minor-league evaluator, and a member of Baseball Prospectus' prospect team.

HITTERS

Hanser Alberto SS

Born: 10/17/92 Age: 23 Bats: R Throws: R Height: 5'11" Weight: 215

YEAR	TEAM	LVL	AGE	PA	R	2B	3B	HR	RBI	BB	K	SB	CS	AVG/OBP/SLG	TAv	BABIP	BRR	FRAA	WARP
2013	MYR	A+	20	104	6	5	0	0	7	4	8	3	1	.258/.301/.309	.193	.281	-0.8	SS(29): 4.5	0.1
2013	FRI	AA	20	384	37	6	4	4	40	16	41	13	5	.213/.253/.287	.206	.227	0.8	SS(98): 6.7	0.2
2014	MYR	A+	21	285	37	15	3	5	43	10	25	10	4	.271/.301/.408	.248	.280	1.3	SS(64): 0.8, 3B(5): 0.3	1.0
2014	FRI	AA	21	190	23	6	1	2	15	6	17	6	4	.275/.314/.354	.259	.296	1.1	SS(50): 8.3	1.8
2015	TEX	MLB	22	104	12	2	1	0	4	2	17	1	0	.222/.238/.263	.197	.268	0.4	2B(24): 2.1, SS(8): -0.0	-0.1
2015	ROU	AAA	22	330	42	19	4	4	32	9	33	5	5	.310/.331/.435	.281	.335	2.2	SS(65): 4.5, 2B(10): -1.3	2.4
2016	*TEX*	*MLB*	*23*	*150*	*14*	*6*	*1*	*2*	*13*	*4*	*21*	*2*	*1*	*.245/.269/.344*	*.216*	*.269*	*0.0*	*SS 1, 3B -1*	*-0.1*
2017	*TEX*	*MLB*	*24*	*390*	*37*	*14*	*3*	*5*	*35*	*12*	*54*	*6*	*3*	*.245/.274/.344*	*.225*	*.269*	*0.3*	*SS 3, 3B -2*	*0.1*

Breakout: 9% Improve: 26% Collapse: 7% Attrition: 21% MLB: 44% *Comparables: Erick Aybar, Donovan Solano, Jose Iglesias*

Quickly, here's the baseball part of this comment: Alberto's never going to hit for average, or for power, or for entertainment, but his talented glove and good attitude make him a valuable bench player on a team in need of versatility. Here's the non-baseball part: If videos could be embedded into books, this chapter would have just one: Hanser Alberto and Joey Gallo's post-homer celebration. Described by Jeff Passan as "the first celebratory sack-tap I've ever seen," it's part weird-brotherhood, part trust-exercise, part utter nonsense, and it's one of the best things about Gallo's homers, other than the homers themselves. This celebration (both parts) will most likely happen in Triple-A to start 2016, but keep an eye out for it on regional cable in June or July.

Elvis Andrus SS

Born: 8/26/88 Age: 27 Bats: R Throws: R Height: 6'0" Weight: 195

YEAR	TEAM	LVL	AGE	PA	R	2B	3B	HR	RBI	BB	K	SB	CS	AVG/OBP/SLG	TAv	BABIP	BRR	FRAA	WARP
2013	TEX	MLB	24	698	91	17	4	4	67	52	97	42	8	.271/.328/.331	.251	.312	6.8	SS(146): -4.5	2.4
2014	TEX	MLB	25	685	72	35	1	2	41	46	96	27	15	.263/.314/.333	.240	.305	5.8	SS(153): -5.4	1.5
2015	TEX	MLB	26	661	69	34	2	7	62	46	78	25	9	.258/.309/.357	.246	.283	5.7	SS(160): 12.7	3.8
2016	*TEX*	*MLB*	*27*	*615*	*75*	*27*	*3*	*5*	*46*	*48*	*79*	*27*	*10*	*.273/.333/.362*	*.250*	*.302*	*4.0*	*SS -2*	*2.6*
2017	*TEX*	*MLB*	*28*	*600*	*65*	*27*	*4*	*6*	*54*	*48*	*78*	*25*	*10*	*.273/.336/.368*	*.259*	*.302*	*4.9*	*SS -2*	*3.0*

Breakout: 3% Improve: 56% Collapse: 0% Attrition: 2% MLB: 100% *Comparables: Barry Larkin, Harvey Kuenn, Alan Trammell*

Even among those with an analytical bent, there is often a misguided expectation that a player holding his own at a very young age sees an inevitable, exponential improvement during his pre-peak years. Andrus has been dinged frequently over the years for not developing more power or becoming something along the lines of Jose Reyes 2.0, and the expectations of a $120 million, eight-year contract extension certainly have not helped. The reality is that, while there is probably little if any growth left in Andrus' profile, a shortstop who has averaged two-plus WARP over the past three seasons still has suitable value, particularly in a modern hitting environment teeming with easy outs. That extension doesn't look like the albatross it might have become when Andrus signed it in 2013, and since it isn't a backloaded deal, the Rangers have the flexibility to move on if Jurickson Profar ever gets healthy or if another option emerges down the road.

Adrian Beltre 3B

Born: 4/7/79 Age: 37 Bats: R Throws: R Height: 5'11" Weight: 220

YEAR	TEAM	LVL	AGE	PA	R	2B	3B	HR	RBI	BB	K	SB	CS	AVG/OBP/SLG	TAv	BABIP	BRR	FRAA	WARP
2013	TEX	MLB	34	690	88	32	0	30	92	50	78	1	0	.315/.371/.509	.312	.322	-1.7	3B(146): 0.3	5.7
2014	TEX	MLB	35	614	79	33	1	19	77	57	74	1	1	.324/.388/.492	.319	.345	-1.5	3B(136): -6.0	4.8
2015	TEX	MLB	36	619	83	32	4	18	83	41	65	1	0	.287/.334/.453	.279	.295	3.0	3B(142): -2.3	3.3
2016	*TEX*	*MLB*	*37*	*643*	*77*	*32*	*2*	*24*	*90*	*42*	*79*	*1*	*0*	*.296/.345/.480*	*.291*	*.305*	*0.0*	*3B -5*	*3.4*
2017	*TEX*	*MLB*	*38*	*500*	*63*	*23*	*1*	*17*	*63*	*31*	*64*	*0*	*0*	*.278/.326/.443*	*.279*	*.290*	*-0.3*	*3B -4*	*1.8*

Breakout: 0% Improve: 22% Collapse: 7% Attrition: 11% MLB: 81% *Comparables: Aramis Ramirez, Alex Rodriguez, Magglio Ordonez*

Beltre has been so darned good for so long that it was sometimes difficult to envision him being anything other than Beltre. In 2015, the time finally came, and it was like watching your old cat struggle to jump up on the bed. Some of the decline arose from a sprained left thumb that he suffered in late May, but even after returning from the disabled list he openly admitted that he was still having some difficulty swinging the bat. However, even without the injury, Beltre has reached the age where it is no longer a certainty that he will automatically bounce back to his prior levels of performance. Only seven third basemen post-World War II have posted a bWAR of 6.1 after turning 37. He has one more year on his contract with the Rangers, and is likely to start at third base, but after that it is an open question of where he lands and where he plays. FRAA has rated him negatively the past four seasons (other systems are more kind), and if he loses too much at third, his bat might not be enough to carry him for long at another position. Perhaps he will defy the odds and be productive at the position into his early 40s, but a sharp decline is the more likely scenario.

Lewis Brinson CF

Born: 5/8/94 Age: 22 Bats: R Throws: R Height: 6'3" Weight: 170

YEAR	TEAM	LVL	AGE	PA	R	2B	3B	HR	RBI	BB	K	SB	CS	AVG/OBP/SLG	TAv	BABIP	BRR	FRAA	WARP
2013	HIC	A	19	503	64	18	2	21	52	48	191	24	7	.237/.322/.427	.268	.362	-0.1	CF(119): 3.3	2.3
2014	HIC	A	20	186	36	8	1	10	28	18	46	7	4	.335/.405/.579	.329	.413	3.0	CF(43): 5.9	2.9
2014	MYR	A+	20	199	17	8	1	3	22	15	50	5	5	.246/.307/.350	.251	.323	-0.9	CF(33): 2.7, LF(3): 0.2	0.5
2015	HDS	A+	21	298	51	22	7	13	42	31	64	13	6	.337/.416/.628	.363	.402	0.9	CF(51): -1.3, LF(7): 1.1	4.3
2015	FRI	AA	21	121	14	8	1	6	23	6	28	2	1	.291/.328/.545	.301	.333	-0.3	CF(22): 3.8, LF(3): 0.4	1.3
2015	ROU	AAA	21	37	9	1	0	1	4	7	6	3	0	.433/.541/.567	.431	.522	0.3	LF(7): 0.1, CF(1): -0.2	0.8
2016	*TEX*	*MLB*	*22*	*250*	*33*	*10*	*1*	*9*	*27*	*18*	*80*	*5*	*2*	*.235/.295/.404*	*.247*	*.316*	*0.1*	*CF 2, LF 0*	*0.8*
2017	*TEX*	*MLB*	*23*	*404*	*48*	*16*	*2*	*13*	*48*	*29*	*126*	*9*	*4*	*.237/.299/.399*	*.254*	*.320*	*0.4*	*CF 4, LF 0*	*1.4*

Breakout: 3% Improve: 26% Collapse: 2% Attrition: 13% MLB: 48% *Comparables: Michael Choice, Chris Young, Domingo Santana*

If they gave out awards for the longest legs in the minor leagues, Brinson would certainly be in contention for them, as well as for "Most Improved, Center Field Division." He came into 2015 needing to prove that last year's improvement at the plate wasn't an anomaly, and he did just that. He hit extremely well across High-, Double- and Triple-A, helping power the Round Rock Express to a near-championship. In addition to his always-stellar defense, Brinson showed an impressive amount of power last season. His steps forward put him among the upper echelon of Rangers prospects.

Robinson Chirinos C

Born: 6/5/84 Age: 32 Bats: R Throws: R Height: 6'1" Weight: 210

YEAR	TEAM	LVL	AGE	PA	R	2B	3B	HR	RBI	BB	K	SB	CS	AVG/OBP/SLG	TAv	BABIP	BRR	FRAA	WARP
2013	TEX	MLB	29	30	3	3	0	0	0	2	6	0	0	.179/.233/.286	.183	.227	-0.4	1B(4): -0.1, 3B(3): 0.0	-0.3
2013	ROU	AAA	29	311	35	10	2	8	40	38	55	2	0	.257/.356/.400	.287	.294	1.7	C(51): -6.0, 3B(10): -1.2	1.6
2014	TEX	MLB	30	338	36	15	0	13	40	17	71	0	1	.239/.290/.415	.267	.265	-0.3	C(91): -5.2	1.2
2015	TEX	MLB	31	273	33	16	1	10	34	28	62	0	0	.232/.325/.438	.265	.270	-1.3	C(78): -6.4	0.6
2016	*TEX*	*MLB*	*32*	*403*	*43*	*17*	*1*	*11*	*44*	*33*	*89*	*1*	*0*	*.235/.309/.382*	*.246*	*.277*	*-0.7*	*C -10*	*0.1*
2017	*TEX*	*MLB*	*33*	*392*	*44*	*15*	*1*	*9*	*40*	*32*	*89*	*0*	*0*	*.224/.300/.355*	*.240*	*.269*	*-0.8*	*C -10*	*-0.4*

Breakout: 3% Improve: 26% Collapse: 2% Attrition: 13% MLB: 48% *Comparables: Michael Choice, Chris Young, Domingo Santana*

YEAR	TEAM	P. COUNT	FRM RUNS	BLK RUNS	THRW RUNS	TOT RUNS
2013	ROU	7158	-4.5	-0.1	-0.9	-5.6
2013	TEX	413	-0.5	0.0	0.0	-0.5
2014	TEX	13110	-9.3	0.5	2.6	-6.3
2015	TEX	10786	-5.4	0.1	0.1	-5.2
2016	*TEX*	*15503*	*-10.5*	*0.1*	*0.7*	*-9.7*
2017	*TEX*	*15073*	*-10.9*	*0.0*	*0.6*	*-10.3*

Once a corner-infield backup who could chip in catching on the sabbath, Chirinos continued to solidify his role as a solid if not spectacular backstop for the Rangers in 2015. With Jorge Alfaro now in the Phillies' system, Chirinos will have first crack at the head of a job-sharing arrangement at a minimum and could crack 100 games for the first time if his health permits. What you've seen of his offensive performance is assuredly what you'll get.

Shin-Soo Choo RF

Born: 7/13/82 Age: 33 Bats: L Throws: L Height: 5'11" Weight: 210

YEAR	TEAM	LVL	AGE	PA	R	2B	3B	HR	RBI	BB	K	SB	CS	AVG/OBP/SLG	TAv	BABIP	BRR	FRAA	WARP
2013	CIN	MLB	30	712	107	34	2	21	54	112	133	20	11	.285/.423/.462	.318	.338	1.1	CF(150): -4.8, LF(3): 1.3	6.2
2014	TEX	MLB	31	529	58	19	1	13	40	58	131	3	4	.242/.340/.374	.266	.308	0.3	LF(64): -8.3, RF(12): 0.7	0.4
2015	TEX	MLB	32	653	94	32	3	22	82	76	147	4	2	.276/.375/.463	.295	.335	2.7	RF(148): 6.5	4.5
2016	*TEX*	*MLB*	*33*	*632*	*85*	*28*	*3*	*16*	*65*	*76*	*140*	*9*	*5*	*.263/.368/.414*	*.280*	*.325*	*1.3*	*RF 9*	*4.0*
2017	*TEX*	*MLB*	*34*	*555*	*71*	*25*	*2*	*13*	*61*	*59*	*124*	*6*	*4*	*.262/.356/.405*	*.277*	*.324*	*1.3*	*RF 8*	*3.1*

Breakout: 0% Improve: 23% Collapse: 3% Attrition: 5% MLB: 98% *Comparables: Bobby Abreu, J.D. Drew, Al Kaline*

While even the most foolhardy analyst wouldn't paint Choo's 2014 as anything but an unmitigated bust, the other side of this coin is that his money-making 2013 was an improbable outcome for a then-30-year-old outfielder with his skill set. Choo bounced back in 2015 to a rather happy medium. A hot second half brought his TAv and ISO right in line with career norms. The stolen bases are gone and are unlikely to return, but if he can continue to hit like he did in 2015, they won't be missed much. The numbers won't look this pretty by the time Choo's contract is over, but at least for now the overall package is more than adequate for Texas' purposes.

Carlos Corporan C

Born: 1/7/84 Age: 32 Bats: B Throws: R Height: 6'2" Weight: 240

YEAR	TEAM	LVL	AGE	PA	R	2B	3B	HR	RBI	BB	K	SB	CS	AVG/OBP/SLG	TAv	BABIP	BRR	FRAA	WARP
2013	HOU	MLB	29	210	16	5	0	7	20	10	60	0	0	.225/.287/.361	.242	.288	-1.8	C(57): 2.9, 1B(1): -0.0	0.6
2014	HOU	MLB	30	190	22	6	0	6	19	14	37	0	0	.235/.302/.376	.250	.264	-1.6	C(54): 5.1	1.1
2015	TEX	MLB	31	121	10	4	0	3	15	6	40	0	0	.178/.244/.299	.205	.242	-0.4	C(31): -2.0	-0.4
2016	*TEX*	*MLB*	*32*	*250*	*25*	*9*	*1*	*6*	*26*	*15*	*63*	*0*	*0*	*.225/.285/.355*	*.225*	*.277*	*-1.2*	*C 1*	*0.2*
2017	*TEX*	*MLB*	*33*	*165*	*17*	*6*	*0*	*4*	*16*	*9*	*43*	*0*	*0*	*.215/.275/.333*	*.221*	*.269*	*-0.8*	*C 1*	*0.0*

Breakout: 6% Improve: 27% Collapse: 15% Attrition: 20% MLB: 76% *Comparables: Miguel Ojeda, Chad Moeller, Eli Whiteside*

YEAR	TEAM	P. COUNT	FRM RUNS	BLK RUNS	THRW RUNS	TOT RUNS
2013	HOU	7794	4.2	0.1	-0.2	4.1
2014	HOU	7042	7.0	0.1	-0.3	6.8
2015	ROU	423	0.0	0.0	0.0	0.0
2015	TEX	4899	-1.6	0.0	0.0	-1.6
2016	*TEX*	*9438*	*2.7*	*0.0*	*-0.5*	*2.3*
2017	*TEX*	*6225*	*1.5*	*0.0*	*-0.3*	*1.2*

"When they gave us homework where you had to pick a career, doctor or dentist or whatever, I would chose baseball," Corporan told the *Houston Chronicle* in 2011. "My teacher told me 'That's not a real career.' I said, 'That's what I'm going to do. I'm a baseball player.'" Converted from shortstop to catcher in college, he has hardly lit the baseball world on fire. Last season was Corporan's worst in the majors by far, as even his once-reliable pitch framing deserted him, but there is something to be admired in his fulfillment of his dream, even if it was only for the briefest of moments in the baseball firmament.

Delino DeShields CF

Born: 8/16/92 Age: 23 Bats: R Throws: R Height: 5'9" Weight: 210

YEAR	TEAM	LVL	AGE	PA	R	2B	3B	HR	RBI	BB	K	SB	CS	AVG/OBP/SLG	TAv	BABIP	BRR	FRAA	WARP
2013	LNC	A+	20	534	100	25	14	5	54	57	91	51	18	.317/.405/.468	.296	.387	7.1	2B(107): -9.5	3.4
2014	CCH	AA	21	507	75	14	2	11	57	61	112	54	14	.236/.346/.360	.274	.293	8.7	CF(78): -5.1, LF(29): -3.0	2.3
2015	TEX	MLB	22	492	83	22	10	2	37	53	101	25	8	.261/.344/.374	.259	.334	4.3	CF(87): -0.7, LF(35): -0.5	1.7
2015	ROU	AAA	22	27	2	3	0	0	2	1	6	0	0	.308/.333/.423	.296	.400	-1.2	CF(2): -0.1, LF(1): -0.2	0.0
2016	*TEX*	*MLB*	*23*	*652*	*85*	*26*	*7*	*7*	*48*	*63*	*145*	*39*	*12*	*.247/.329/.357*	*.243*	*.307*	*3.4*	*CF -1*	*1.5*
2017	*TEX*	*MLB*	*24*	*623*	*68*	*24*	*7*	*8*	*56*	*63*	*139*	*37*	*11*	*.243/.329/.356*	*.249*	*.301*	*5.0*	*CF -1*	*1.7*

Breakout: 1% Improve: 27% Collapse: 4% Attrition: 13% MLB: 52% *Comparables: Andrew McCutchen, Anthony Gose, Dexter Fowler*

Entering 2015, conventional wisdom said that Rule 5 pick DeShields might stick with the Rangers as a fourth outfielder/pinch-running type, assuming that he stuck at all. Conventional wisdom didn't foresee Leonys Martin cratering and forcing the Rangers to push Son of DeShields into an every-day role in center field. It certainly didn't see it working. DeShields got on base at an acceptable clip and provided the Rangers with table-setting speed at the top of the order. His defense was far from optimal, or optimized, but the move back to center field from second base comes with a learning curve, especially in spacious Arlington. There is a chance he sticks as a starter, but there is a fine line between players like Dee Gordon and players like Eric Young Jr.

Prince Fielder 1B

Born: 5/9/84 Age: 32 Bats: L Throws: R Height: 5'11" Weight: 275

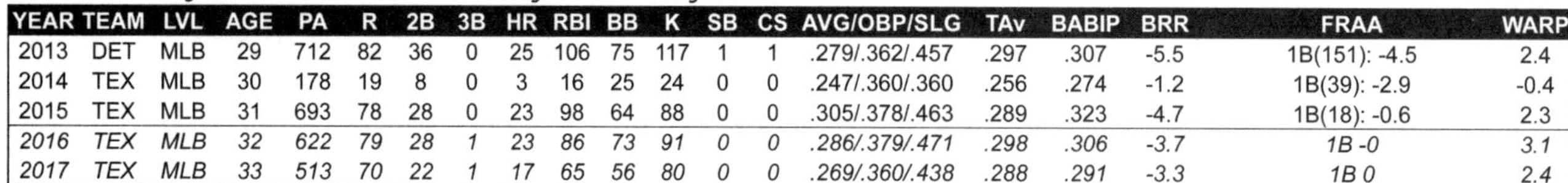

YEAR	TEAM	LVL	AGE	PA	R	2B	3B	HR	RBI	BB	K	SB	CS	AVG/OBP/SLG	TAv	BABIP	BRR	FRAA	WARP
2013	DET	MLB	29	712	82	36	0	25	106	75	117	1	1	.279/.362/.457	.297	.307	-5.5	1B(151): -4.5	2.4
2014	TEX	MLB	30	178	19	8	0	3	16	25	24	0	0	.247/.360/.360	.256	.274	-1.2	1B(39): -2.9	-0.4
2015	TEX	MLB	31	693	78	28	0	23	98	64	88	0	0	.305/.378/.463	.289	.323	-4.7	1B(18): -0.6	2.3
2016	*TEX*	*MLB*	*32*	*622*	*79*	*28*	*1*	*23*	*86*	*73*	*91*	*0*	*0*	*.286/.379/.471*	*.298*	*.306*	*-3.7*	*1B -0*	*3.1*
2017	*TEX*	*MLB*	*33*	*513*	*70*	*22*	*1*	*17*	*65*	*56*	*80*	*0*	*0*	*.269/.360/.438*	*.288*	*.291*	*-3.3*	*1B 0*	*2.4*

Breakout: 1% Improve: 33% Collapse: 2% Attrition: 6% MLB: 95% *Comparables: Edwin Encarnacion, Adrian Gonzalez, Mark Teixeira*

After having bones in his neck fused together in 2014, there were more questions surrounding Fielder's 2015 return than any other position player in the game. Those concerns were gently but firmly quashed. Fielder charged out of the gate, slashing .339/.403/.521 in the first half before cooling off after the All-Star Game. The overall results were solid, if more similar to his "off" 2013 line rather than his 2007-2012 peak. Fielder's defense has never been even charitably described as adequate, and he'll probably spend the majority of his 30s as a designated hitter. But with his recovery from cervical fusion surgery behind him, he could age better than we always feared for a man of his girth. He's big, sure, but he has always been in better physical condition than the shape suggests.

Joey Gallo 3B

Born: 11/19/93 Age: 22 Bats: L Throws: R Height: 6'5" Weight: 230

YEAR	TEAM	LVL	AGE	PA	R	2B	3B	HR	RBI	BB	K	SB	CS	AVG/OBP/SLG	TAv	BABIP	BRR	FRAA	WARP
2013	HIC	A	19	446	82	19	5	38	78	48	165	14	1	.245/.334/.610	.316	.305	3.1	3B(100): -7.4	3.7
2014	FRI	AA	20	291	44	10	0	21	56	36	115	2	0	.232/.334/.524	.306	.322	-1.3	3B(53): -0.8, 1B(7): -0.1	2.1
2014	MYR	A+	20	246	53	9	3	21	50	51	64	5	3	.323/.463/.735	.400	.370	1.0	3B(54): 4.9	5.2
2015	ROU	AAA	21	228	20	9	0	14	32	27	90	1	0	.195/.289/.450	.267	.258	-1.9	3B(33): 0.2, LF(14): 0.8	0.7
2015	FRI	AA	21	146	21	10	1	9	31	24	49	1	0	.314/.425/.636	.359	.453	0.6	3B(19): 1.4, LF(6): 0.6	2.2
2015	TEX	MLB	21	123	16	3	1	6	14	15	57	3	0	.204/.301/.417	.246	.356	0.4	LF(19): 0.2, 3B(15): 0.0	0.2
2016	*TEX*	*MLB*	*22*	*232*	*32*	*7*	*1*	*15*	*38*	*26*	*93*	*1*	*0*	*.217/.307/.480*	*.272*	*.303*	*0.0*	*1B -1, LF -2*	*0.6*
2017	*TEX*	*MLB*	*23*	*384*	*58*	*12*	*2*	*25*	*64*	*46*	*151*	*3*	*0*	*.220/.317/.489*	*.285*	*.303*	*-0.1*	*1B -1*	*1.6*

Breakout: 5% Improve: 41% Collapse: 1% Attrition: 11% MLB: 65% *Comparables: Giancarlo Stanton, Javier Baez, Chris Davis*

There might not be anyone unaware of Gallo's potential at this point, but his disappointing Triple-A and big-league debuts have some jumping off the talent wagon at ankle-breaking speed. (His 46.3 percent strikeout rate was a record for a season with 120-plus plate appearances.) But fear not, fans of power! Gallo has traditionally struggled in his early exposure to any new level. Additionally, despite the Swiss cheese swing, he has emerged as a potentially competent left fielder, adding even more to his potential value. He still has the work ethic and athleticism noted in prior years' books, and if trends hold, 2016 will be a very big year for him.

Chris Gimenez C

Born: 12/27/82 Age: 33 Bats: R Throws: R Height: 6'2" Weight: 225

YEAR	TEAM	LVL	AGE	PA	R	2B	3B	HR	RBI	BB	K	SB	CS	AVG/OBP/SLG	TAv	BABIP	BRR	FRAA	WARP
2013	TBA	MLB	30	4	0	1	0	0	0	1	1	0	0	.333/.500/.667	.334	.500	-0.8	C(1): -0.0, 3B(1): -0.0	0.0
2013	DUR	AAA	30	375	43	16	0	3	22	57	63	1	1	.224/.350/.305	.237	.270	-1.6	C(56): 0.7, RF(19): -1.4	0.0
2014	CLE	MLB	31	10	0	0	0	0	0	1	3	0	0	.000/.100/.000	.068	.000	0.0	1B(5): -0.2, C(2): -0.1	-0.2
2014	TEX	MLB	31	118	13	10	0	0	11	11	26	0	1	.262/.331/.355	.248	.346	0.0	C(26): 2.5, 1B(5): -0.2	0.6
2014	ROU	AAA	31	156	18	4	2	6	22	19	30	0	1	.284/.365/.478	.293	.317	0.0	C(18): -1.6, 1B(14): -0.5	0.8
2015	ROU	AAA	32	277	28	10	0	6	33	24	62	2	0	.243/.315/.356	.254	.298	-2.3	C(26): 0.9, 1B(20): -1.2	0.3
2015	TEX	MLB	32	113	19	6	1	5	14	10	19	2	0	.255/.330/.490	.279	.270	0.1	C(36): 0.4	0.8
2016	*TEX*	*MLB*	*33*	*181*	*18*	*7*	*0*	*3*	*18*	*18*	*39*	*1*	*0*	*.236/.316/.352*	*.239*	*.286*	*-0.2*	*C -0*	*0.4*
2017	*TEX*	*MLB*	*34*	*273*	*30*	*10*	*1*	*5*	*26*	*26*	*60*	*0*	*0*	*.228/.305/.341*	*.237*	*.277*	*-0.4*	*C -1*	*0.3*

Breakout: 3% Improve: 6% Collapse: 12% Attrition: 19% MLB: 26% *Comparables: Raul Casanova, Eric Munson, Mike Rivera*

YEAR	TEAM	P. COUNT	FRM RUNS	BLK RUNS	THRW RUNS	TOT RUNS
2013	DUR	6997	1.2	-0.6	-0.7	0.0
2014	ROU	2563	-2.0	0.0	0.8	-1.2
2014	TEX	3591	2.9	-0.2	-0.1	2.5
2014	TEX	3591	2.9	-0.2	-0.1	2.5
2014	CLE	61	0.0	0.0	0.0	0.0
2015	ROU	3578	0.9	0.0	0.0	1.0
2015	TEX	4512	0.5	0.0	-0.4	0.1
2016	*TEX*	*6757*	*-0.5*	*-0.2*	*-0.3*	*-0.9*
2017	*TEX*	*10187*	*-1.2*	*-0.3*	*-0.4*	*-2.0*

Small sample sizes can be fun. In 36 major-league games last year, Gimenez posted his best slugging percentage since 2008 and his best ISO since 2007 (min. 100 PA). This came after a minor-league performance that was serviceable but certainly didn't lead to any "Free Chris Gimenez" campaigns on the internet, not even among the most ardent Rangers diehards in Tarrant County. Buried behind Robinson Chirinos and Carlos Corporan to start the season, Gimenez benefited significantly from Chirinos' health woes down the stretch, starting in 35 of the Rangers' final 59 regular-season games and earning two playoff starts in the ALDS to boot. If statistics lie, then when it comes to part-time players and late-season call-ups, they are Pinocchio before he ultimately learns his lesson and turns into a real live boy.

James Jones CF

Born: 9/24/88 Age: 27 Bats: L Throws: L Height: 6'4" Weight: 200

YEAR	TEAM	LVL	AGE	PA	R	2B	3B	HR	RBI	BB	K	SB	CS	AVG/OBP/SLG	TAv	BABIP	BRR	FRAA	WARP
2013	WTN	AA	24	405	44	14	10	6	45	40	72	28	9	.275/.347/.419	.273	.330	-2.6	RF(53): 0.3, CF(18): -0.6	1.0
2014	TAC	AAA	25	173	24	6	3	2	15	13	31	7	3	.282/.341/.397	.269	.341	1.8	CF(32): -0.4, RF(6): 0.3	0.9
2014	SEA	MLB	25	328	46	9	5	0	9	12	67	27	1	.250/.278/.311	.236	.318	3.4	CF(85): -10.9, RF(9): -0.5	-0.8
2015	TAC	AAA	26	310	47	12	7	1	28	38	43	25	4	.272/.365/.381	.269	.318	1.7	CF(62): -2.0, RF(7): 0.3	1.2
2015	SEA	MLB	26	31	1	1	0	0	0	2	13	1	1	.103/.161/.138	.120	.188	0.2	CF(20): -1.4, RF(6): -0.2	-0.5
2016	*TEX*	*MLB*	*27*	*250*	*31*	*9*	*4*	*2*	*18*	*18*	*50*	*15*	*3*	*.250/.307/.351*	*.235*	*.307*	*0.8*	*CF -5, RF -0*	*-0.3*
2017	*TEX*	*MLB*	*28*	*274*	*27*	*10*	*4*	*2*	*23*	*20*	*56*	*16*	*4*	*.250/.307/.348*	*.239*	*.308*	*1.4*	*CF -5, RF 0*	*-0.2*

Breakout: 2% Improve: 23% Collapse: 12% Attrition: 22% MLB: 56% *Comparables: Jerry Owens, Charles Thomas, Ezequiel Carrera*

Fifteen to 20 years ago, when home runs were flying out of ballparks at record-breaking rates, players like Jones were an afterthought, particularly when **everyone** with a bat could seemingly clear the fence on any given swing. Now, with offense down on the whole and pitching reigning supreme, players with his game-changing speed profile are tantalizing, or at least tempting. Alas, while the idea of a 50-to-60-steal monster on the bases whets the appetite, Jones appears to be settling as a pinch-runner at best. His acceptable minor-league walk rates have not translated to the majors, and despite his speed, his defense profiles as below average, by FRAA and by non-BP metrics as well. Without the ability to serve as defensive replacement, he's the 40th man on an expanded roster, a baseball player who only exists in fall.

Patrick Kivlehan OF

Born: 12/22/89 Age: 26 Bats: R Throws: R Height: 6'2" Weight: 215

YEAR	TEAM	LVL	AGE	PA	R	2B	3B	HR	RBI	BB	K	SB	CS	AVG/OBP/SLG	TAv	BABIP	BRR	FRAA	WARP
2013	HDS	A+	23	302	48	13	2	13	59	26	65	10	3	.320/.384/.530	.314	.373	-3.0	3B(66): 4.4	2.9
2013	CLN	A	23	247	26	12	1	3	31	17	42	5	3	.283/.344/.386	.271	.333	-2.1	3B(49): -0.1	0.8
2014	WTN	AA	24	431	60	23	7	11	68	44	78	9	4	.300/.374/.485	.304	.348	0.2	3B(58): -8.9, 1B(26): 1.1	2.4
2014	HDS	A+	24	157	24	9	2	9	35	12	32	2	0	.282/.331/.563	.291	.298	0.1	3B(12): 0.4, 1B(9): -0.6	0.7
2015	TAC	AAA	25	518	58	25	1	22	73	36	113	14	3	.256/.313/.453	.272	.289	-5.4	LF(48): 0.8, 1B(30): -0.1	0.9
2016	*TEX*	*MLB*	*26*	*250*	*27*	*10*	*1*	*8*	*30*	*16*	*63*	*4*	*1*	*.243/.296/.402*	*.247*	*.296*	*0.1*	*LF 1, 1B -0*	*0.2*
2017	*TEX*	*MLB*	*27*	*307*	*36*	*12*	*1*	*10*	*36*	*20*	*78*	*4*	*1*	*.240/.293/.398*	*.251*	*.294*	*0.2*	*LF 1, 1B 0*	*0.3*

Breakout: 2% Improve: 9% Collapse: 12% Attrition: 23% MLB: 33% *Comparables: Cole Garner, Roger Kieschnick, John-Ford Griffin*

Kivlehan is a test of temperament. Optimists see a late bloomer who can play five positions, and a guy who translated above-average raw power into 22 homers just four seasons after reviving his baseball career (he was a football player in college). Skeptics will note that Kivlehan should really only play in left, and that he was just an average hitter as a 25-year-old last season. Sadly, the glass is probably two-thirds empty. Kivlehan brings relentless intensity and focus to the game, and he has improved significantly since the Mariners tabbed him in the fourth round in 2012. At this point, though, he's a mistake hitter who can be beat by gas and breaking balls alike, who will chase pitches above the letters and below the knees in equal measure. Athletes who start playing baseball later than their peers sometimes break out late, and there's always a chance that Kivlehan takes an unexpected step forward. More likely, he'll collect a few big-league paychecks as an up-and-down guy, never making enough hard contact to stick.

Nomar Mazara RF

Born: 4/26/95 Age: 21 Bats: L Throws: L Height: 6'4" Weight: 195

YEAR	TEAM	LVL	AGE	PA	R	2B	3B	HR	RBI	BB	K	SB	CS	AVG/OBP/SLG	TAv	BABIP	BRR	FRAA	WARP
2013	HIC	A	18	506	48	23	2	13	62	44	131	1	2	.236/.310/.382	.254	.301	-2.5	RF(114): 1.7	0.5
2014	FRI	AA	19	97	10	7	1	3	16	9	22	0	0	.306/.381/.518	.313	.377	-3.1	RF(23): -3.0	0.1
2014	HIC	A	19	461	68	21	2	19	73	57	99	4	3	.264/.358/.470	.291	.304	-3.5	RF(91): -7.5	1.2
2015	FRI	AA	20	470	57	22	2	13	56	47	92	2	0	.284/.357/.443	.280	.329	-4.5	RF(62): 0.4, LF(32): 0.1	1.5
2015	ROU	AAA	20	88	11	4	0	1	13	5	10	0	0	.358/.409/.444	.322	.400	0.1	RF(14): 1.0, LF(1): 0.3	0.9
2016	*TEX*	*MLB*	*21*	*250*	*25*	*11*	*1*	*7*	*29*	*19*	*64*	*0*	*0*	*.236/.298/.382*	*.240*	*.292*	*-0.4*	*RF -1, LF 0*	*-0.1*
2017	*TEX*	*MLB*	*22*	*439*	*52*	*19*	*2*	*13*	*51*	*36*	*109*	*0*	*0*	*.242/.309/.400*	*.255*	*.298*	*-0.9*	*RF -2, LF 1*	*0.5*

Breakout: 3% Improve: 11% Collapse: 0% Attrition: 5% MLB: 16% *Comparables: Caleb Gindl, Billy Butler, Wil Myers*

Some baseball players have to work themselves up to a feverish level of intensity to perform at their best. Mazara is not one of them. Tall, lean and always chill, Mazara earns top billing on the Texas farm due to his prodigious power, his preternatural hitting ability, and his willingness to demonstrate a work ethic that's turned him from "DH-kinda-guy" to "can actually not kill you in the outfield right now, as a 20-year-old." It'll be interesting to see what the Rangers do with him positionally, but if this year is anything like last, that question will be answered sooner rather than later.

Mitch Moreland 1B

Born: 9/6/85 Age: 30 Bats: L Throws: L Height: 6'2" Weight: 230

YEAR	TEAM	LVL	AGE	PA	R	2B	3B	HR	RBI	BB	K	SB	CS	AVG/OBP/SLG	TAv	BABIP	BRR	FRAA	WARP
2013	TEX	MLB	27	518	60	24	1	23	60	45	117	0	0	.232/.299/.437	.269	.255	-2.1	1B(146): 3.6, RF(1): -0.0	1.2
2014	TEX	MLB	28	184	18	9	1	2	23	12	43	0	0	.246/.297/.347	.237	.315	-0.9	1B(22): -0.8, LF(2): 0.0	-0.4
2015	TEX	MLB	29	515	51	27	0	23	85	32	112	1	0	.278/.330/.482	.284	.317	-2.1	1B(120): -7.8	0.8
2016	*TEX*	*MLB*	*30*	*523*	*60*	*25*	*1*	*18*	*65*	*39*	*111*	*1*	*0*	*.255/.315/.429*	*.260*	*.292*	*-1.8*	*1B -3*	*0.3*
2017	*TEX*	*MLB*	*31*	*481*	*60*	*22*	*1*	*16*	*59*	*39*	*100*	*0*	*0*	*.251/.315/.418*	*.264*	*.287*	*-1.9*	*1B -3*	*0.3*

Breakout: 2% Improve: 45% Collapse: 1% Attrition: 11% MLB: 93% *Comparables: Chad Tracy, Glenn Davis, Benny Ayala*

Someday in the very near future, the comments in this Annual will degenerate into nothing save for hashtag shorthand, and #OffensiveThreatMitchMoreland will suffice. Moreland bounced back from a serious ankle injury in 2014 to live up to his Twitter hashtag, putting up the best TAv of his career and delivering his second 20-plus-home-run campaign over the past three years. While the raw numbers looked great, Moreland's BABIP, his infield-fly percentage and his homer-per-fly rate all point to the possibility that 2015 might be closer to ceiling than norm. Moreland is a viable platoon option against right-handers, but most hashtags quickly revert to irony.

Rougned Odor 2B

Born: 2/3/94 Age: 22 Bats: L Throws: R Height: 5'11" Weight: 190

YEAR	TEAM	LVL	AGE	PA	R	2B	3B	HR	RBI	BB	K	SB	CS	AVG/OBP/SLG	TAv	BABIP	BRR	FRAA	WARP
2013	MYR	A+	19	425	65	33	4	5	59	26	67	27	8	.305/.369/.454	.293	.355	1.4	2B(84): 8.2	3.6
2013	FRI	AA	19	144	20	8	2	6	19	9	24	5	2	.306/.354/.530	.314	.337	-0.4	2B(30): 3.4	1.6
2014	TEX	MLB	20	417	39	14	7	9	48	17	71	4	7	.259/.297/.402	.255	.294	1.6	2B(110): 2.8	1.4
2014	FRI	AA	20	138	21	2	1	6	17	7	22	6	3	.279/.314/.450	.274	.294	0.0	2B(31): 2.9	0.9
2015	ROU	AAA	21	124	26	12	2	5	19	12	10	3	1	.352/.426/.639	.342	.355	1.0	2B(28): -1.3	1.4
2015	TEX	MLB	21	470	54	21	9	16	61	23	79	6	7	.261/.316/.465	.278	.283	4.2	2B(119): 4.5	3.1
2016	*TEX*	*MLB*	*30*	*523*	*60*	*25*	*1*	*18*	*65*	*39*	*111*	*1*	*0*	*.255/.315/.429*	*.260*	*.292*	*-1.8*	*1B -3*	*0.3*
2017	*TEX*	*MLB*	*31*	*481*	*60*	*22*	*1*	*16*	*59*	*39*	*100*	*0*	*0*	*.251/.315/.418*	*.264*	*.287*	*-1.9*	*1B -3*	*0.3*

Breakout: 7% Improve: 58% Collapse: 4% Attrition: 11% MLB: 87% *Comparables: Xander Bogaerts, Starlin Castro, Manny Machado*

Odor's hyper-aggressive approach led to an early demotion to Triple-A, and for some it was proof he had been rushed to the majors. He wasn't down at Round Rock for long, though, and returned with a better measure of the strike zone. In 367 plate appearances after his recall, Odor put up a .292/.334/.527 line with 15 home runs and a .235 ISO. The cherry was a strong showing in the ALDS, including a home run against the Blue Jays in a losing effort. He'll be 22 on Opening Day, and even in the unlikely event he doesn't improve he'll be one of the best keystoners in baseball. Even without walks, the ceiling is perennial All-Star.

Jurickson Profar 2B

Born: 2/20/93 Age: 23 Bats: B Throws: R Height: 6'0" Weight: 200

YEAR	TEAM	LVL	AGE	PA	R	2B	3B	HR	RBI	BB	K	SB	CS	AVG/OBP/SLG	TAv	BABIP	BRR	FRAA	WARP
2013	TEX	MLB	20	324	30	11	0	6	26	26	63	2	4	.234/.308/.336	.248	.280	-0.8	2B(32): -2.3, SS(18): 1.5	0.2
2013	ROU	AAA	20	166	27	7	2	4	19	21	24	6	1	.278/.370/.438	.289	.310	1.5	SS(30): 1.1, 2B(7): -1.8	1.3
2015	HIC	A	22	35	2	1	0	1	5	1	9	0	0	.273/.314/.394	.262	.348	-0.1		0.0
2016	*TEX*	*MLB*	*23*	*131*	*16*	*6*	*1*	*3*	*13*	*12*	*23*	*2*	*1*	*.253/.324/.395*	*.255*	*.287*	*0.0*	*2B -1, LF -0*	*0.2*
2017	*TEX*	*MLB*	*24*	*265*	*32*	*12*	*2*	*6*	*30*	*24*	*47*	*4*	*2*	*.257/.329/.407*	*.266*	*.291*	*0.1*	*2B -3, LF 0*	*0.7*

Breakout: 6% Improve: 37% Collapse: 12% Attrition: 28% MLB: 61% *Comparables: Casey Kotchman, Daric Barton, Billy Butler*

In January, it looked like Profar was almost completely recovered from a torn teres muscle in his shoulder, but a setback in his rehab led to surgery and cost him a second year of action. He showed flashes of brilliance in the Arizona Fall League, fueling hopes that a full recovery is not just a possibility but has already happened. He's more than a year younger than Kris Bryant.

Ryan Rua LF

Born: 3/11/90 Age: 26 Bats: R Throws: R Height: 6'2" Weight: 205

YEAR	TEAM	LVL	AGE	PA	R	2B	3B	HR	RBI	BB	K	SB	CS	AVG/OBP/SLG	TAv	BABIP	BRR	FRAA	WARP
2013	HIC	A	23	430	70	24	1	29	82	49	91	13	2	.251/.356/.559	.332	.253	0.3	2B(87): 4.3, 3B(8): -1.2	4.9
2013	FRI	AA	23	95	19	2	1	3	9	7	24	1	0	.233/.305/.384	.244	.288	0.8	3B(23): -2.9	-0.1
2014	TEX	MLB	24	109	11	7	0	2	14	2	18	1	0	.295/.321/.419	.269	.341	0.9	LF(17): -2.2, 1B(9): 0.3	0.2
2014	ROU	AAA	24	241	31	13	2	8	36	21	42	1	2	.313/.382/.505	.310	.355	-1.2	3B(27): -0.4, LF(24): -2.8	1.6
2014	FRI	AA	24	288	34	13	1	10	38	30	55	5	3	.300/.375/.475	.309	.349	-0.7	3B(50): -4.2, 1B(6): -0.3	1.7
2015	TEX	MLB	25	86	10	5	0	4	7	3	32	0	0	.193/.221/.398	.223	.255	0.0	LF(22): -0.1, RF(4): -0.9	-0.3
2015	ROU	AAA	25	165	18	5	0	6	22	18	45	3	0	.197/.303/.359	.255	.239	-1.0	LF(10): 1.2, 3B(9): 0.6	0.2
2016	*TEX*	*MLB*	*26*	*137*	*16*	*6*	*0*	*5*	*18*	*10*	*34*	*1*	*0*	*.243/.308/.421*	*.259*	*.291*	*-0.1*	*LF -2, RF -1*	*0.0*
2017	*TEX*	*MLB*	*27*	*296*	*37*	*13*	*1*	*11*	*37*	*24*	*73*	*2*	*1*	*.242/.310/.419*	*.266*	*.292*	*-0.3*	*LF -4, RF -2*	*0.2*

Breakout: 5% Improve: 27% Collapse: 10% Attrition: 26% MLB: 62% *Comparables: Allen Craig, Justin Huber, Brandon Jones*

Rua was in line for a starting job until a broken bone in his heel and a severe ankle sprain said otherwise. His season sank like Artax after he returned in June, but it was hard to tell how much of this was due to legitimate issues at the plate versus rust and lack of reps. The Rangers didn't waste much effort finding out, sending him back to Triple-A, where he did little to instill regret. He's got power and not much else.

Justin Ruggiano RF

Born: 4/12/82 Age: 34 Bats: R Throws: R Height: 6'1" Weight: 210

YEAR	TEAM	LVL	AGE	PA	R	2B	3B	HR	RBI	BB	K	SB	CS	AVG/OBP/SLG	TAv	BABIP	BRR	FRAA	WARP
2013	MIA	MLB	31	472	49	18	1	18	50	41	114	15	8	.222/.298/.396	.253	.260	1.0	CF(84): -4.2, LF(23): -1.2	0.5
2014	IOW	AAA	32	25	3	1	0	0	0	3	6	0	0	.143/.280/.190	.194	.200	0.3	RF(5): -0.5	-0.2
2014	CHN	MLB	32	250	29	13	1	6	28	18	70	2	4	.281/.337/.429	.290	.375	0.5	RF(34): -2.9, CF(18): -0.9	1.1
2015	LAN	MLB	33	60	12	4	1	4	12	3	14	2	0	.291/.350/.618	.354	.324	1.6	LF(16): -1.4, RF(2): -0.2	0.7
2015	TAC	AAA	33	205	27	9	0	10	29	23	51	6	4	.296/.385/.514	.306	.364	-0.5	LF(17): -2.9, CF(11): -0.8	0.9
2015	SEA	MLB	33	81	8	4	0	2	3	11	27	3	2	.214/.321/.357	.245	.317	-0.5	CF(15): -1.4, RF(11): -0.4	-0.2
2016	*TEX*	*MLB*	*34*	*203*	*26*	*10*	*1*	*7*	*26*	*17*	*53*	*5*	*3*	*.254/.323/.435*	*.267*	*.315*	*0.3*	*CF -1, RF -1*	*0.6*
2017	*TEX*	*MLB*	*35*	*180*	*22*	*8*	*1*	*6*	*22*	*15*	*48*	*4*	*3*	*.244/.310/.408*	*.255*	*.307*	*0.5*	*CF -1, RF -1*	*0.4*

Breakout: 1% Improve: 27% Collapse: 9% Attrition: 19% MLB: 85% *Comparables: Brian Daubach, Marcus Thames, Nelson Cruz*

Ruggiano made his debut in 2007 and still has fewer than 1,400 career plate appearances. That says a lot about what the mid-30s outfielder isn't, but perhaps sells short what he does bring. He's is a career .272/.336/.520 hitter against southpaws and has performed even better over the past two seasons. He's decent in a corner, can fake it in center and... well, that's it really, but it's something! Short-side platoon outfielders who don't dazzle with the glove aren't hot commodities, but Ruggiano showed enough with the Dodgers to get another spin around the league. He's in the constantly-proving-himself phase of his career, though, so another bad month or two could mean the end.

Drew Stubbs CF

Born: 10/4/84 Age: 31 Bats: R Throws: R Height: 6'4" Weight: 205

YEAR	TEAM	LVL	AGE	PA	R	2B	3B	HR	RBI	BB	K	SB	CS	AVG/OBP/SLG	TAv	BABIP	BRR	FRAA	WARP
2013	CLE	MLB	28	481	59	21	2	10	45	44	141	17	2	.233/.305/.360	.254	.319	2.4	RF(105): 4.9, CF(43): 3.5	2.0
2014	COL	MLB	29	424	67	22	4	15	43	30	136	20	3	.289/.339/.482	.269	.404	2.1	CF(113): -6.5	1.2
2015	ROU	AAA	30	30	6	1	0	0	0	3	7	4	0	.222/.300/.259	.261	.300	1.0	CF(3): -0.4, LF(3): -0.1	0.1
2015	COL	MLB	30	114	14	3	2	5	10	9	50	2	1	.216/.286/.431	.230	.362	0.1	CF(25): 1.1, LF(13): -1.1	-0.1
2015	TEX	MLB	30	26	6	1	0	0	0	5	10	3	0	.095/.269/.143	.166	.182	0.9	CF(17): -1.2, LF(8): -0.6	-0.3
2015	ABQ	AAA	30	165	22	4	3	2	20	24	39	6	3	.263/.376/.380	.263	.347	-1.1	CF(34): 0.3	0.5
2016	*TEX*	*MLB*	*31*	*250*	*32*	*9*	*1*	*6*	*22*	*22*	*78*	*10*	*2*	*.228/.302/.355*	*.236*	*.316*	*0.8*	*CF -1, LF -1*	*0.0*
2017	*TEX*	*MLB*	*32*	*168*	*19*	*6*	*1*	*4*	*17*	*16*	*53*	*6*	*2*	*.222/.300/.348*	*.240*	*.310*	*0.7*	*CF -1, LF -1*	*0.1*

Breakout: 0% Improve: 40% Collapse: 7% Attrition: 7% MLB: 93% *Comparables: Reggie Sanders, Rick Monday, Mike Cameron*

Since 1937, nine hitters have topped a .400 BABIP in at least 400 plate appearances. On average, those hitters have lost 72 points of BABIP the following season. Stubbs was one of those nine in 2014, making it all but inevitable he was going lose a lot of hits. The Rockies cut his playing time and then cut him loose, and the Rangers picked him up for the stretch run as a bat/glove/runner off of the bench; you can't *prove* he didn't at least do two of those. He's now the short side of a platoon that you try not to think about too much.

Will Venable CF

Born: 10/29/82 Age: 33 Bats: L Throws: L Height: 6'3" Weight: 205

YEAR	TEAM	LVL	AGE	PA	R	2B	3B	HR	RBI	BB	K	SB	CS	AVG/OBP/SLG	TAv	BABIP	BRR	FRAA	WARP
2013	SDN	MLB	30	515	64	22	8	22	53	29	118	22	6	.268/.312/.484	.281	.313	2.1	RF(97): -2.4, CF(80): -3.4	2.0
2014	SDN	MLB	31	448	47	13	2	8	33	33	107	11	6	.224/.288/.325	.234	.283	-1.0	CF(76): -1.8, RF(75): 0.9	-0.3
2015	SDN	MLB	32	308	34	10	3	6	30	25	73	11	1	.258/.318/.378	.246	.328	1.7	CF(57): -2.2, RF(16): -1.7	0.1
2015	TEX	MLB	32	82	6	3	0	0	3	12	21	5	0	.182/.325/.227	.226	.267	0.1	LF(28): 1.1, CF(6): -0.4	0.0
2016	*TEX*	*MLB*	*33*	*378*	*49*	*15*	*4*	*10*	*37*	*28*	*85*	*14*	*4*	*.250/.311/.400*	*.249*	*.299*	*0.6*	*CF -1, LF 1*	*0.8*
2017	*TEX*	*MLB*	*34*	*303*	*34*	*11*	*3*	*7*	*32*	*23*	*71*	*10*	*3*	*.238/.302/.376*	*.245*	*.291*	*0.6*	*CF -1, LF 1*	*0.4*

Breakout: 0% Improve: 23% Collapse: 7% Attrition: 9% MLB: 96% *Comparables: Aaron Rowand, Gary Matthews, Jacque Jones*

Once viewed as a potential late bloomer (think Raul Ibanez with less power and more speed), Venable regressed in 2014 and found himself near the bottom of San Diego's outfield pile. Injuries to said pile allowed him to claw back to the surface, but doing so wore him out: His slugging percentage failed to live up to the potential of 2013. It turns out his 2013 power production had benefited not just from Petco's tightened dimensions, but also a flurry of fence-scraping home runs. Fence-scraping is a tough talent to maintain. He could be a second-division or platoon starter for a number of teams, but it's just as likely he settles in as a fourth outfielder who can man both corner-outfield positions and play center field in a pinch.

Pitchers

Alexander Claudio LHP

Born: 1/31/92 Age: 24 Bats: L Throws: L Height: 6'3" Weight: 185

YEAR	TEAM	LVL	AGE	W	L	SV	G	GS	IP	H	HR	BB/9	K/9	GB%	BABIP	WHIP	ERA	FIP	DRA	WARP	CFIP	MPH
2013	FRI	AA	21	1	5	0	21	0	31^{2}	28	2	3.1	8.2	61%	.302	1.23	2.84	3.18	4.06	0.2	92	
2013	HIC	A	21	3	1	11	24	0	47	22	2	1.3	11.9	66%	.208	0.62	1.15	1.84	3.23	0.8	57	
2014	FRI	AA	22	2	2	0	8	6	37^{1}	31	1	0.5	5.3	52%	.246	0.88	2.17	2.53				
2014	MYR	A+	22	4	0	4	17	2	49^{1}	38	2	1.6	10.2	64%	.298	0.95	1.09	2.44	3.57	0.8	65	
2014	TEX	MLB	22	0	0	0	15	0	12^{1}	14	0	2.9	10.2	58%	.389	1.46	2.92	1.86	5.43	-0.1	92	86.9
2015	ROU	AAA	23	3	1	0	29	0	40	43	2	1.6	7.9	57%	.347	1.25	2.92	3.10	3.37	0.8	82	
2015	TEX	MLB	23	1	1	0	18	0	15^{2}	12	4	3.4	7.5	52%	.190	1.15	2.87	6.10	3.95	0.1	100	86.2
2016	*TEX*	*MLB*	*24*	*1*	*0*	*0*	*23*	*0*	*24*	*24*	*3*	*2.7*	*7.5*	*55%*	*.294*	*1.29*	*4.17*	*4.20*	*4.38*	*0.2*	*99*	
2017	*TEX*	*MLB*	*25*	*2*	*1*	*1*	*28*	*2*	*55*	*56*	*7*	*3.2*	*7.8*	*55%*	*.302*	*1.38*	*4.48*	*4.36*	*4.71*	*0.1*	*107*	

Breakout: 22% Improve: 37% Collapse: 12% Attrition: 30% MLB: 57% *Comparables: Zach Putnam, Daniel Herrera, Eury De La Rosa*

Changeup artist Claudio spent the year as an occasional member of the Texas bullpen, finishing on the 60-day DL with a groin strain. He's a groundball specialist who simply can't survive his mistakes, with more than a quarter of the flyballs he allowed landing in the seats. Those blew up his FIP and hint at regression, but a sterling minor-league track record offers hope.

Yu Darvish RHP

Born: 8/16/86 Age: 29 Bats: R Throws: R Height: 6'5" Weight: 220

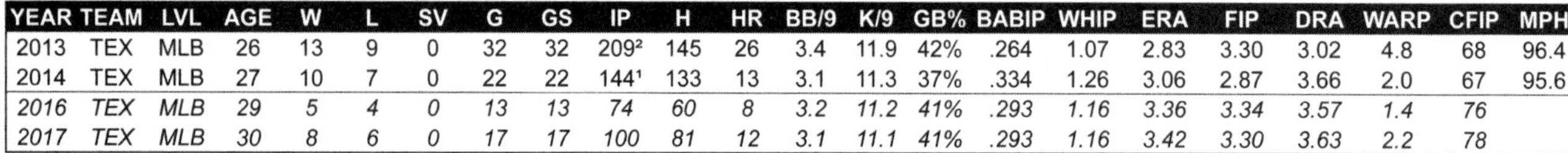

YEAR	TEAM	LVL	AGE	W	L	SV	G	GS	IP	H	HR	BB/9	K/9	GB%	BABIP	WHIP	ERA	FIP	DRA	WARP	CFIP	MPH
2013	TEX	MLB	26	13	9	0	32	32	209^{2}	145	26	3.4	11.9	42%	.264	1.07	2.83	3.30	3.02	4.8	68	96.4
2014	TEX	MLB	27	10	7	0	22	22	144^{1}	133	13	3.1	11.3	37%	.334	1.26	3.06	2.87	3.66	2.0	67	95.6
2016	*TEX*	*MLB*	*29*	*5*	*4*	*0*	*13*	*13*	*74*	*60*	*8*	*3.2*	*11.2*	*41%*	*.293*	*1.16*	*3.36*	*3.34*	*3.57*	*1.4*	*76*	
2017	*TEX*	*MLB*	*30*	*8*	*6*	*0*	*17*	*17*	*100*	*81*	*12*	*3.1*	*11.1*	*41%*	*.293*	*1.16*	*3.42*	*3.30*	*3.63*	*2.2*	*78*	

Breakout: 20% Improve: 52% Collapse: 22% Attrition: 3% MLB: 96% *Comparables: Max Scherzer, Kerry Wood, Jake Peavy*

Welcome to Episode 10,343 of "Why Can't We Have Nice Things?" starring Yu Darvish. One of the best pitchers in the game since his debut stateside, Darvish took a leave of absence early in 2014 with what was hoped to be nothing more than elbow inflammation. But it foreshadowed a partially torn ligament that was discovered when he was preparing for spring training last year. Something in the darkness hissed the name "Dr. Andrews," and he was promptly taken away. Rangers fans are already preemptively drooling at the possibility of a Darvish/Hamels jab-hook, but it won't be fully ready by Opening Day and it might come with an innings restriction.

Jake Diekman LHP

Born: 1/21/87 Age: 29 Bats: L Throws: L Height: 6'4" Weight: 205

YEAR	TEAM	LVL	AGE	W	L	SV	G	GS	IP	H	HR	BB/9	K/9	GB%	BABIP	WHIP	ERA	FIP	DRA	WARP	CFIP	MPH
2013	LEH	AAA	26	1	0	11	30	0	30	31	1	7.2	11.1	62%	.380	1.83	5.70	3.67	4.46	0.1	101	
2013	PHI	MLB	26	1	4	0	45	0	38^{1}	34	1	3.8	9.6	53%	.311	1.30	2.58	2.47	2.48	1.0	89	99.1
2014	PHI	MLB	27	5	5	0	73	0	71	66	4	4.4	12.7	44%	.363	1.42	3.80	2.62	4.02	0.4	75	99.5
2015	TEX	MLB	28	0	0	0	26	0	21^{2}	13	2	2.9	8.3	60%	.200	0.92	2.08	3.57	2.27	0.6	94	99.5
2015	PHI	MLB	28	2	1	0	41	0	36^{2}	40	3	5.9	12.0	55%	.381	1.75	5.15	3.68	5.04	-0.1	90	99.0
2016	*TEX*	*MLB*	*29*	*3*	*1*	*0*	*53*	*0*	56^{1}	*53*	*6*	*4.1*	*10.0*	*52%*	*.310*	*1.39*	*3.95*	*3.86*	*4.17*	*0.4*	*90*	
2017	*TEX*	*MLB*	*30*	*3*	*1*	*1*	*58*	*0*	*54*	*48*	*6*	*4.1*	*10.4*	*52%*	*.306*	*1.36*	*3.91*	*3.80*	*4.13*	*0.4*	*90*	

Breakout: 30% Improve: 56% Collapse: 21% Attrition: 24% MLB: 96% *Comparables: Boone Logan, Jerry Blevins, C.J. Wilson*

Diekman is one of those tantalizing live arms who cooks with serious gas (hitting 98 on the gun at times) but who has also had trouble maintaining any control or command. After he was traded to the Rangers in the Cole Hamels deal, his new team asked him to concentrate on throwing the heater, particularly against righties. The result was a significant drop in his walk rate, and while all the usual sample-size caveats apply, that ups the odds of him breaking through LOOGY limitations.

Sam Dyson RHP

Born: 5/7/88 Age: 28 Bats: R Throws: R Height: 6'1" Weight: 210

YEAR	TEAM	LVL	AGE	W	L	SV	G	GS	IP	H	HR	BB/9	K/9	GB%	BABIP	WHIP	ERA	FIP	DRA	WARP	CFIP	MPH
2013	JAX	AA	25	3	7	0	16	15	75^1	72	0	2.7	4.9	64%	.287	1.26	2.63	3.14	4.52	0.1	116	
2013	MIA	MLB	25	0	2	0	5	1	11	16	2	4.1	4.1	70%	.341	1.91	9.00	6.11	8.57	-0.5	120	96.1
2013	NWO	AAA	25	1	3	0	5	5	31	23	1	3.5	4.6	62%	.232	1.13	2.61	4.21	5.18	0.2	108	
2014	MIA	MLB	26	3	1	0	31	0	42	41	1	3.2	7.1	67%	.310	1.33	2.14	3.13	3.16	0.7	103	98.8
2014	NWO	AAA	26	2	1	1	13	0	25^1	21	0	3.6	7.1	66%	.296	1.22	2.49	3.54	5.33	0.0	106	
2015	TEX	MLB	27	2	1	2	31	0	31^1	24	1	1.1	8.6	76%	.277	0.89	1.15	2.08	0.85	1.4	74	98.6
2015	MIA	MLB	27	3	3	0	44	0	44	41	3	3.5	8.4	65%	.302	1.32	3.68	3.55	4.19	0.3	99	98.5
2016	*TEX*	*MLB*	*28*	*2*	*1*	*0*	*48*	*0*	*51*	*51*	*5*	*3.1*	*7.1*	*68%*	*.294*	*1.33*	*4.15*	*4.12*	*4.36*	*0.3*	*98*	
2017	*TEX*	*MLB*	*29*	*3*	*2*	*0*	*37*	*5*	*69*	*67*	*7*	*2.9*	*7.6*	*68%*	*.296*	*1.30*	*3.99*	*3.87*	*4.19*	*0.5*	*93*	

Breakout: 28% Improve: 41% Collapse: 18% Attrition: 22% MLB: 73% *Comparables: Bryan Morris, Bobby Parnell, Javy Guerra*

Categorized in the past as a groundball specialist who could never strike out enough batters to ever be a top-line reliever, Dyson finally shed that label in a big way. He struck out nearly a batter per inning while maintaining his stellar grounder rate. Improved command in the zone combined with increased usage of a changeup allowed him to keep hitters off-balance, leading to more swings and misses and a move from the middle of the bullpen to the back end of it. He was quietly one of the most important deadline acquisitions in baseball, particularly for a team whose starters often failed to go deep into games and required strong bridge innings to get to the ninth.

Sam Freeman LHP

Born: 6/24/87 Age: 29 Bats: R Throws: L Height: 5'11" Weight: 165

YEAR	TEAM	LVL	AGE	W	L	SV	G	GS	IP	H	HR	BB/9	K/9	GB%	BABIP	WHIP	ERA	FIP	DRA	WARP	CFIP	MPH
2013	MEM	AAA	26	7	2	2	49	0	69^2	57	4	3.5	8.5	48%	.273	1.21	2.97	3.71	4.89	0.3	97	
2013	SLN	MLB	26	1	0	0	13	0	12^1	8	0	3.6	5.8	40%	.216	1.05	2.19	2.94	2.78	0.3	109	98.0
2014	MEM	AAA	27	0	1	0	16	0	20^1	25	1	3.1	11.5	48%	.393	1.57	3.54	2.96	4.93	0.1	84	
2014	SLN	MLB	27	2	0	0	44	0	38	34	2	4.5	8.3	61%	.294	1.39	2.61	3.76	3.73	0.4	105	96.1
2015	TEX	MLB	28	0	0	0	54	0	38^1	31	4	5.9	9.4	50%	.273	1.46	3.05	4.57	3.66	0.5	105	96.7
2016	*TEX*	*MLB*	*29*	*2*	*1*	*0*	*48*	*0*	*51*	*48*	*6*	*4.0*	*7.9*	*52%*	*.286*	*1.39*	*4.48*	*4.42*	*4.66*	*0.0*	*108*	
2017	*TEX*	*MLB*	*30*	*2*	*1*	*0*	*44*	*0*	*45*	*45*	*6*	*3.9*	*8.1*	*52%*	*.303*	*1.44*	*4.48*	*4.35*	*4.66*	*0.0*	*107*	

Breakout: 12% Improve: 41% Collapse: 26% Attrition: 15% MLB: 97% *Comparables: Gavin Floyd, Jason Hammel, Bob Rush*

Freeman is one of those odd ducks in baseball: a left-hander whose rising fastball and sinking splitter are far more effective against right-handed batters than against lefties. The Rangers picked him up for a player-or-maybe-just-cash-to-be-named later from the Cardinals just before Opening Day, and after a brief trip to Round Rock he found a strong grip on a big-league bullpen job in Texas. There was once a time where one lefty was enough, and a non-LOOGY like Freeman wouldn't survive long. He has a place in any seven-man 'pen, though, so long as he doesn't walk every fourth lefty he sees.

Yovani Gallardo RHP

Born: 2/27/86 Age: 30 Bats: R Throws: R Height: 6'2" Weight: 205

YEAR	TEAM	LVL	AGE	W	L	SV	G	GS	IP	H	HR	BB/9	K/9	GB%	BABIP	WHIP	ERA	FIP	DRA	WARP	CFIP	MPH
2013	MIL	MLB	27	12	10	0	31	31	180^2	180	18	3.3	7.2	51%	.299	1.36	4.18	3.87	4.34	1.2	103	93.0
2014	MIL	MLB	28	8	11	0	32	32	192^1	195	21	2.5	6.8	54%	.294	1.29	3.51	3.91	4.38	1.0	108	93.7
2015	TEX	MLB	29	13	11	0	33	33	184^1	193	15	3.3	5.9	51%	.303	1.42	3.42	3.97	4.04	2.2	108	93.2
2016	*TEX*	*MLB*	*30*	*11*	*11*	*0*	*30*	*30*	*180*	*187*	*20*	*3.0*	*6.3*	*52%*	*.295*	*1.38*	*4.35*	*4.39*	*4.55*	*1.2*	*106*	
2017	*TEX*	*MLB*	*31*	*8*	*9*	*0*	*25*	*25*	145^1	*154*	*18*	*3.0*	*6.3*	*52%*	*.298*	*1.40*	*4.58*	*4.45*	*4.79*	*0.6*	*113*	

Breakout: 12% Improve: 41% Collapse: 26% Attrition: 15% MLB: 97% *Comparables: Gavin Floyd, Jason Hammel, Bob Rush*

Gallardo is one of those pitchers who seems like he's at least 35 years old, and has stories from the good old days before the internet and cell phones when movies played on expensive premium-cable channels at set times. But he wasn't a grizzled 35-year-old in 2015, but rather an in-his-prime 29-year-old. Some of this misperception is because he has logged nearly 1,500 innings in his career, but most of it is due to the fact that Gallardo is no longer the ace he never quite was. His sub-six strikeout rate in 2015 speaks to a diminished pitcher, but a combination of increased changeup and slider usage (instead of his curve) and careful innings rationing allowed him to be an effective back-end option. He posted the best DRA of his career despite the low whiff rate, and he'll continue to thrive on any team that doesn't ask for more than five or six solid innings.

Chi Chi Gonzalez RHP

Born: 1/15/92 Age: 24 Bats: R Throws: R Height: 6'3" Weight: 210

YEAR	TEAM	LVL	AGE	W	L	SV	G	GS	IP	H	HR	BB/9	K/9	GB%	BABIP	WHIP	ERA	FIP	DRA	WARP	CFIP	MPH
2013	SPO	A-	21	0	4	0	9	9	23^2	30	1	2.7	7.6	69%	.382	1.56	4.56	3.19	4.14	0.3	95	
2013	MYR	A+	21	0	0	0	5	5	19	15	1	4.3	7.1	59%	.264	1.26	2.84	3.88	4.91	0.1	109	
2014	MYR	A+	22	5	2	0	11	11	65^1	56	3	2.2	6.8	55%	.262	1.10	2.62	3.62	4.51	0.5	99	
2014	FRI	AA	22	7	4	0	15	14	73^1	67	3	3.1	7.9	55%	.300	1.25	2.70	3.09				
2015	ROU	AAA	23	8	7	0	16	16	88^1	95	3	3.2	5.7	54%	.325	1.43	3.57	3.96	5.31	0.3	105	
2015	TEX	MLB	23	4	6	0	14	10	67	49	6	4.3	4.0	50%	.206	1.21	3.90	4.94	3.49	1.2	125	94.3
2016	*TEX*	*MLB*	*24*	*3*	*4*	*0*	*11*	*11*	58^1	*61*	*7*	*3.5*	*5.5*	*51%*	*.285*	*1.43*	*4.81*	*4.94*	*5.00*	*0.1*	*118*	
2017	*TEX*	*MLB*	*25*	*4*	*5*	*0*	*15*	*15*	89^2	*94*	*11*	*3.6*	*6.0*	*51%*	*.293*	*1.45*	*4.84*	*4.71*	*5.03*	*0.1*	*119*	

Breakout: 9% Improve: 32% Collapse: 22% Attrition: 30% MLB: 72% *Comparables: Jarred Cosart, Aaron Laffey, Kameron Loe*

Gonzalez threw a three-hit complete-game shutout in his second appearance as a big leaguer. The magic didn't last, and he hopped between Triple-A and the majors instead of following the instant-phenom path we've become greedy for. A medium-sized righty, he gets plus-sized life on his fastball, but his off-speed pitches linger in the same general vicinity, both velocity-wise and location-wise. He can only get away with operating in those narrow bands when he's at peak command.

A.J. Griffin RHP

Born: 1/28/88 Age: 28 Bats: R Throws: R Height: 6'5" Weight: 230

YEAR	TEAM	LVL	AGE	W	L	SV	G	GS	IP	H	HR	BB/9	K/9	GB%	BABIP	WHIP	ERA	FIP	DRA	WARP	CFIP	MPH
2013	OAK	MLB	25	14	10	0	32	32	200	171	36	2.4	7.7	33%	.242	1.12	3.83	4.58	3.88	2.5	102	91.5
2016	TEX	MLB	28	2	2	0	6	6	35^{2}	34	6	2.4	7.6	33%	.271	1.21	4.48	4.67	4.67	0.2	110	
2017	TEX	MLB	29	10	11	0	31	31	195^{1}	187	33	2.4	8.0	33%	.277	1.22	4.58	4.45	4.77	0.7	114	

Breakout: 17% Improve: 49% Collapse: 15% Attrition: 16% MLB: 83% *Comparables: David Phelps, Josh Collmenter, John Maine*

One missed season isn't always enough, and Griffin joined the growing list of pitchers for whom Tommy John surgery became a series of setbacks and delays. In May he experienced shoulder soreness during a simulated game and was shut down for a few weeks, before making two rehab starts in the California League and two more in the PCL in June. After his second start for Nashville, he was reinstated from the disabled list but optioned to the same team. Further shoulder issues landed him back on the shelf, which makes his future blurrier than photos of the Lake Merritt Monster.

Cole Hamels LHP

Born: 12/27/83 Age: 32 Bats: L Throws: L Height: 6'3" Weight: 200

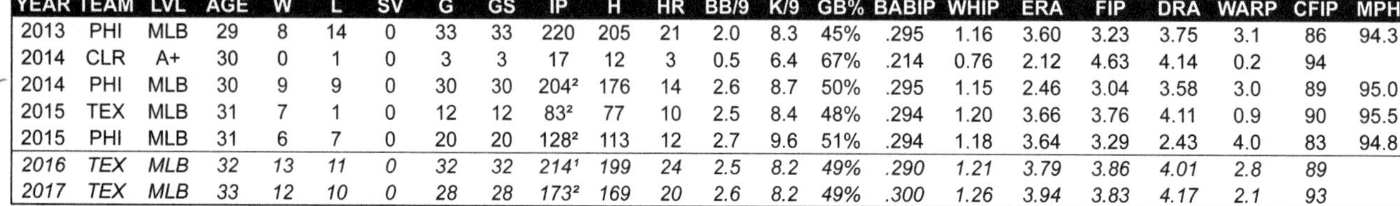

YEAR	TEAM	LVL	AGE	W	L	SV	G	GS	IP	H	HR	BB/9	K/9	GB%	BABIP	WHIP	ERA	FIP	DRA	WARP	CFIP	MPH
2013	PHI	MLB	29	8	14	0	33	33	220	205	21	2.0	8.3	45%	.295	1.16	3.60	3.23	3.75	3.1	86	94.3
2014	CLR	A+	30	0	1	0	3	3	17	12	3	0.5	6.4	67%	.214	0.76	2.12	4.63	4.14	0.2	94	
2014	PHI	MLB	30	9	9	0	30	30	204^{2}	176	14	2.6	8.7	50%	.295	1.15	2.46	3.04	3.58	3.0	89	95.0
2015	TEX	MLB	31	7	1	0	12	12	83^{2}	77	10	2.5	8.4	48%	.294	1.20	3.66	3.76	4.11	0.9	90	95.5
2015	PHI	MLB	31	6	7	0	20	20	128^{2}	113	12	2.7	9.6	51%	.294	1.18	3.64	3.29	2.43	4.0	83	94.8
2016	TEX	MLB	32	13	11	0	32	32	214^{1}	199	24	2.5	8.2	49%	.290	1.21	3.79	3.86	4.01	2.8	89	
2017	TEX	MLB	33	12	10	0	28	28	173^{2}	169	20	2.6	8.2	49%	.300	1.26	3.94	3.83	4.17	2.1	93	

Breakout: 12% Improve: 37% Collapse: 30% Attrition: 6% MLB: 90% *Comparables: Josh Beckett, Bob Gibson, Kelvim Escobar*

A year and a half of pointless internet bickering (is there any other kind?) over whether the Phillies *had* to trade Hamels mercifully ended when the Rangers sent a bushel of prospects for him in July. He is now one of three pitchers who has logged 200 or more innings in every year since 2010, along with Felix Hernandez and James Shields. In no way is Hamels in King Felix's class for dominance, nor even in that of Shields in durability, but his fortitude and consistency and near-ace-if-not-quite-ace stuff are underrated assets. (It's difficult to appreciate the absence of something, but when that thing is Joe Blanton starts, we should make the effort.) Hamels' DRA was the lowest of his career, so while the move to Arlington and the American League will ding his ERA, the overall value proposition remains quite strong.

Derek Holland LHP

Born: 10/9/86 Age: 29 Bats: B Throws: L Height: 6'2" Weight: 215

YEAR	TEAM	LVL	AGE	W	L	SV	G	GS	IP	H	HR	BB/9	K/9	GB%	BABIP	WHIP	ERA	FIP	DRA	WARP	CFIP	MPH
2013	TEX	MLB	26	10	9	0	33	33	213	210	20	2.7	8.0	43%	.307	1.29	3.42	3.46	4.10	2.1	90	96.3
2014	TEX	MLB	27	2	0	0	6	5	37	34	0	1.2	6.1	42%	.296	1.05	1.46	2.21	3.08	0.8	90	94.9
2014	ROU	AAA	27	2	1	0	4	4	15^{1}	20	5	4.7	11.2	52%	.349	1.83	5.87	7.03	5.46	0.1	102	
2015	TEX	MLB	28	4	3	0	10	10	58^{2}	59	11	2.6	6.3	43%	.281	1.30	4.91	5.27	5.01	0.0	108	95.8
2016	TEX	MLB	29	9	9	0	26	26	156	154	19	2.6	7.5	45%	.293	1.27	4.07	4.12	4.26	1.6	98	
2017	TEX	MLB	30	10	10	0	28	28	169	172	21	2.6	7.6	45%	.300	1.30	4.17	4.04	4.36	1.5	100	

Breakout: 21% Improve: 44% Collapse: 18% Attrition: 6% MLB: 97% *Comparables: Anibal Sanchez, Erik Hanson, Yovani Gallardo*

Maybe he was rushed back from the shoulder strain that tore out half the calendar. Maybe it was the rust of two straight misspent summers. Maybe it was the mustache. But after his first four starts returning from the disabled list in August, the last weeks of summer camp proved tough for Holland. Command was an issue, especially with his four-seam and two-seam fastballs. When he concentrated on aiming, his velocity plummeted and he was eminently hittable. He should be fine, but he is one of those rare veterans whose spring training performance bears watching.

Luke Jackson RHP

Born: 8/24/91 Age: 24 Bats: R Throws: R Height: 6'2" Weight: 205

YEAR	TEAM	LVL	AGE	W	L	SV	G	GS	IP	H	HR	BB/9	K/9	GB%	BABIP	WHIP	ERA	FIP	DRA	WARP	CFIP	MPH
2013	MYR	A+	21	9	4	0	19	19	101	79	6	4.2	9.3	48%	.284	1.25	2.41	3.55	4.57	0.9	96	
2013	FRI	AA	21	2	0	0	6	4	27	13	0	4.0	10.0	48%	.213	0.93	0.67	2.17	3.83	0.4	85	
2014	FRI	AA	22	8	2	1	15	14	83^{1}	58	5	2.6	9.0	44%	.242	0.98	3.02	2.92				
2014	ROU	AAA	22	1	3	0	11	10	40	56	9	6.3	9.7	45%	.395	2.10	10.35	6.72	6.09	-0.1	122	
2015	ROU	AAA	23	2	3	0	39	5	66^{1}	62	3	4.7	10.7	54%	.335	1.46	4.34	3.43	3.73	1.2	85	
2015	TEX	MLB	23	0	0	0	7	0	6^{1}	5	1	2.8	8.5	53%	.222	1.11	4.26	4.21	2.00	0.2	102	98.8
2016	TEX	MLB	24	1	0	0	19	0	20^{2}	20	2	4.0	8.5	48%	.303	1.43	4.34	4.11	4.53	0.1	104	
2017	TEX	MLB	25	3	3	0	17	10	67^{1}	64	9	3.9	9.4	48%	.301	1.38	4.27	4.14	4.46	0.4	103	

Breakout: 15% Improve: 25% Collapse: 11% Attrition: 27% MLB: 49% *Comparables: Alex Torres, Chris Dwyer, Jose Cisnero*

A rough first trip through Triple-A became a rough second trip through Triple-A, providing a rare moment of frustration for the Rangers' player development department. A midseason conversion to relief provided that same relief to his ERA, but the right-hander with the #flow still struggled with command and the long ball. The good news is that the stuff that brought him to Round Rock, including an upper-90s fastball and good curve, is still present. If that's all there is, and the secondaries never come around, he'll make a fine reliever.

Ariel Jurado RHP

Born: 1/30/96 Age: 20 Bats: R Throws: R Height: 6'1" Weight: 180

YEAR	TEAM	LVL	AGE	W	L	SV	G	GS	IP	H	HR	BB/9	K/9	GB%	BABIP	WHIP	ERA	FIP	DRA	WARP	CFIP	MPH
2015	HIC	A	19	12	1	0	22	15	99	92	5	1.1	8.6	61%	.314	1.05	2.45	2.62	1.80	3.8	68	
2016	*TEX*	*MLB*	*20*	*4*	*3*	*1*	*30*	*8*	*64^{2}*	*68*	*8*	*2.6*	*7.1*	*52%*	*.305*	*1.34*	*4.23*	*4.25*	*4.46*	*0.5*	*102*	
2017	*TEX*	*MLB*	*21*	*4*	*4*	*1*	*27*	*12*	*111*	*120*	*16*	*3.1*	*7.5*	*52%*	*.313*	*1.43*	*4.65*	*4.52*	*4.90*	*0.1*	*114*	

Breakout: 5% Improve: 8% Collapse: 2% Attrition: 5% MLB: 12% *Comparables: Noah Syndergaard, Matt Wisler, Robbie Erlin*

An unknown commodity outside of serious prospect circles entering the year, Jurado quietly established himself last year. His 2.45 ERA was good for fifth best in the South Atlantic League (min. 90 innings), and his K/BB rate was tops. His sinking fastball hits anywhere from 89 to 95 mph, and is complemented by a curve and a changeup that, while promising, are both in need of refinement. Developmentally, Jurado's range of outcomes stretch from mid-tier starting pitcher to decent middle reliever to high school social studies teacher, but his performance in the minors has at a minimum put him on the map for even non-serious prospect types.

Keone Kela RHP

Born: 4/16/93 Age: 23 Bats: R Throws: R Height: 6'1" Weight: 230

YEAR	TEAM	LVL	AGE	W	L	SV	G	GS	IP	H	HR	BB/9	K/9	GB%	BABIP	WHIP	ERA	FIP	DRA	WARP	CFIP	MPH
2013	SPO	A-	20	1	2	2	12	0	16^{2}	17	1	3.2	14.0	67%	.381	1.38	3.78	2.60	3.62	0.2	81	
2013	HIC	A	20	2	2	1	12	0	18^{2}	18	0	2.9	9.6	51%	.340	1.29	2.41	2.62	4.13	0.1	90	
2014	FRI	AA	21	2	1	5	36	0	38^{2}	22	1	6.3	12.8	50%	.259	1.27	1.86	2.86				
2014	MYR	A+	21	0	1	5	8	0	10^{1}	9	0	3.5	11.3	37%	.333	1.26	2.61	2.16	4.24	0.1	89	
2015	TEX	MLB	22	7	5	1	68	0	60^{1}	52	4	2.7	10.1	54%	.314	1.16	2.39	2.61	2.98	1.2	74	98.6
2016	*TEX*	*MLB*	*23*	*3*	*1*	*0*	*53*	*0*	*56^{1}*	*50*	*6*	*3.3*	*9.8*	*53%*	*.299*	*1.24*	*3.53*	*3.63*	*3.73*	*0.8*	*81*	
2017	*TEX*	*MLB*	*24*	*3*	*1*	*1*	*55*	*0*	*59*	*49*	*6*	*3.2*	*10.4*	*53%*	*.291*	*1.18*	*3.44*	*3.33*	*3.64*	*0.8*	*78*	

Breakout: 26% Improve: 41% Collapse: 16% Attrition: 21% MLB: 75% *Comparables: Dominic Leone, Tim Collins, Chris Perez*

Only two dedicated relievers pitched more innings for the Rangers than Kela, and one was long-man Anthony Bass. Kela surprised out of spring training, adding a viable changeup to his heavy, shifting fastball and his developing breaking pitch. The breaker settled into a distinctive curveball and the fastball was lassoed and controlled. The Rangers used him in high leverage as the season progressed, but they also acquired two alternatives at the trade deadline, so the faith was hedged.

Colby Lewis RHP

Born: 8/2/79 Age: 36 Bats: R Throws: R Height: 6'4" Weight: 245

YEAR	TEAM	LVL	AGE	W	L	SV	G	GS	IP	H	HR	BB/9	K/9	GB%	BABIP	WHIP	ERA	FIP	DRA	WARP	CFIP	MPH
2013	FRI	AA	33	0	1	0	5	5	18	23	4	2.0	7.5	37%	.328	1.50	7.00	4.95	4.25	0.2	96	
2014	TEX	MLB	34	10	14	0	29	29	170^{1}	211	25	2.5	7.0	35%	.339	1.52	5.18	4.49	5.12	-0.7	103	91.3
2015	TEX	MLB	35	17	9	0	33	33	204^{2}	211	26	1.8	6.2	35%	.290	1.24	4.66	4.15	4.05	2.4	101	90.8
2016	*TEX*	*MLB*	*36*	*9*	*9*	*0*	*28*	*28*	*148^{1}*	*159*	*19*	*2.2*	*6.5*	*35%*	*.298*	*1.32*	*4.36*	*4.35*	*4.56*	*1.0*	*105*	
2017	*TEX*	*MLB*	*37*	*7*	*8*	*0*	*21*	*21*	*125*	*137*	*18*	*2.1*	*6.6*	*35%*	*.302*	*1.34*	*4.51*	*4.39*	*4.72*	*0.6*	*110*	

Breakout: 29% Improve: 48% Collapse: 15% Attrition: 10% MLB: 82% *Comparables: John Lackey, Harry Brecheen, Ron Guidry*

There is arguably no greater sign of human progress in the early 21st century than the fact that Colby Lewis had 17 wins and wasn't even mentioned in passing as a Cy Young candidate. Not that Lewis wasn't a credible candidate for inclusion on a 10-man team-MVP ballot: He chewed up innings and kept Texas in ballgames. On a Darvish-less staff—and with the Rangers' strong offense backing him up—having an arm that could simply munch innings was enough. His 23 starts of six or more innings, 18 of which were quality starts, achieved exactly that.

Nick Martinez RHP

Born: 8/5/90 Age: 25 Bats: L Throws: R Height: 6'1" Weight: 200

YEAR	TEAM	LVL	AGE	W	L	SV	G	GS	IP	H	HR	BB/9	K/9	GB%	BABIP	WHIP	ERA	FIP	DRA	WARP	CFIP	MPH
2013	FRI	AA	22	2	0	0	5	4	32	11	1	2.0	6.5	49%	.123	0.56	1.12	2.68	3.99	0.4	92	
2013	MYR	A+	22	10	7	0	22	21	119^{1}	106	5	2.9	7.9	54%	.294	1.21	2.87	3.27	4.43	1.2	91	
2014	TEX	MLB	23	5	12	0	29	24	140^{1}	150	18	3.5	4.9	35%	.289	1.46	4.55	4.97	4.98	-0.4	124	93.7
2015	ROU	AAA	24	1	1	0	6	6	31	32	1	2.0	5.2	43%	.320	1.26	2.90	3.73	5.03	0.2	103	
2015	TEX	MLB	24	7	7	0	24	21	125	135	16	3.3	5.5	44%	.293	1.45	3.96	4.95	5.47	-0.7	119	92.3
2016	*TEX*	*MLB*	*25*	*7*	*7*	*0*	*50*	*16*	*127*	*134*	*16*	*3.2*	*5.7*	*41%*	*.291*	*1.42*	*4.82*	*4.87*	*5.00*	*0.1*	*119*	
2017	*TEX*	*MLB*	*26*	*6*	*8*	*0*	*21*	*21*	*124^{2}*	*130*	*17*	*3.1*	*6.2*	*41%*	*.290*	*1.39*	*4.92*	*4.77*	*5.10*	*0.0*	*122*	

Breakout: 19% Improve: 45% Collapse: 24% Attrition: 24% MLB: 84% *Comparables: Brad Bergesen, Homer Bailey, Zach Duke*

Martinez started the 2015 campaign with a bang, giving up a single earned run in 26 April innings. But with his customarily low strikeout rate intact, no one was fooled into believing that this was the turning over of a new leaf. He throws four pitches in the zone, if not for strikes, but hitters can lay off of his off-speed stuff and wait on his underwhelming fastball. Arlington can't even be blamed in this case, since his home/road splits favored his outings in Texas significantly last year. His DRA was awful and other metric-oriented numbers like FIP and SIERA back up the fact that Martinez was lucky more than good. With Hamels in the fold, Darvish almost healthy, and a rich crop of prospects either in Texas or on the way, Martinez is likely to find himself back in Round Rock waiting for his next stroke of luck.

Michael Matuella RHP

Born: 6/3/94 Age: 22 Bats: R Throws: R Height: 6'6" Weight: 220

Had Matuella been healthy at the time of the 2015 draft, he would have been gone before Texas' first pick rather than falling to 78th overall. The former Blue Devil was plagued by arm soreness and durability issues before going under the knife, but he also wielded two plus pitches in his fastball and slider, with a promising changeup. If Matuella can come back from Tommy John surgery with the same kind of stuff he showed in college, this could be an absolute steal of a choice—and his Twitter account is amazing, to boot. Matuella spent his time post-draft hanging and working out with the Frisco RoughRiders, a possible hint as to how quickly Texas would like to move him when he's pitching again.

Ross Ohlendorf RHP

Born: 8/8/82 Age: 33 Bats: R Throws: R Height: 6'4" Weight: 240

YEAR	TEAM	LVL	AGE	W	L	SV	G	GS	IP	H	HR	BB/9	K/9	GB%	BABIP	WHIP	ERA	FIP	DRA	WARP	CFIP	MPH
2013	SYR	AAA	30	4	6	0	14	13	74^2	65	5	3.6	8.6	42%	.284	1.27	4.22	3.50	4.19	0.7	93	
2013	WAS	MLB	30	4	1	0	16	7	60^1	56	8	2.1	6.7	41%	.268	1.16	3.28	4.00	3.65	0.8	106	96.2
2015	TEX	MLB	32	3	1	1	21	0	19^1	21	4	3.3	8.8	36%	.309	1.45	3.72	4.91	4.82	0.0	94	96.4
2015	ROU	AAA	32	4	5	0	27	0	36^2	39	2	3.2	10.8	40%	.374	1.42	4.17	3.05	3.00	0.9	77	
2016	*TEX*	*MLB*	*33*	*2*	*2*	*0*	*18*	*6*	*41^2*	*43*	*5*	*3.2*	*7.9*	*38%*	*.307*	*1.39*	*4.25*	*4.25*	*4.45*	*0.3*	*101*	
2017	*TEX*	*MLB*	*34*	*6*	*5*	*1*	*39*	*15*	*125^1*	*133*	*17*	*3.1*	*8.3*	*38%*	*.316*	*1.40*	*4.28*	*4.16*	*4.48*	*0.7*	*102*	

Breakout: 15% Improve: 28% Collapse: 14% Attrition: 18% MLB: 51% *Comparables: Raul Valdes, John Maine, Chris Jakubauskas*

Limited by a chronic back injury in 2014, Ohlendorf entered the season as a footnote, a contingency plan, a glass case with a switch inside, a raven perched atop a bookcase. For most of the year, it looked like the Rangers wouldn't have to employ this particular metaphor, but not only did Ohlendorf find his way back to the majors, but he found himself throwing key innings for Texas down the stretch and in the ALDS. He did the thing many converted starters do, abandoning his complete arsenal and relying primarily on the two true pitches. At the age of 33, he's unlikely to suddenly emerge as a high-end stopper, but the sudden uptick in velocity is likely to keep him in someone's big-league bullpen for the next couple of seasons at a minimum.

Luis Ortiz RHP

Born: 9/22/95 Age: 20 Bats: R Throws: R Height: 6'3" Weight: 230

YEAR	TEAM	LVL	AGE	W	L	SV	G	GS	IP	H	HR	BB/9	K/9	GB%	BABIP	WHIP	ERA	FIP	DRA	WARP	CFIP	MPH
2015	HIC	A	19	4	1	0	13	13	50	45	1	1.6	8.3	45%	.306	1.08	1.80	2.50	2.81	1.4	80	
2016	*TEX*	*MLB*	*20*	*2*	*3*	*0*	*9*	*9*	*34*	*37*	*4*	*3.3*	*6.5*	*38%*	*.304*	*1.44*	*4.58*	*4.51*	*4.77*	*0.1*	*111*	
2017	*TEX*	*MLB*	*21*	*6*	*8*	*0*	*29*	*29*	*177^2*	*190*	*23*	*3.1*	*6.6*	*38%*	*.301*	*1.41*	*4.63*	*4.50*	*4.82*	*0.4*	*113*	

Breakout: 5% Improve: 7% Collapse: 1% Attrition: 4% MLB: 9% *Comparables: Jarrod Parker, Justin Nicolino, Arodys Vizcaino*

The arm issues that caused Ortiz to fall in the 2014 draft cropped up again in the middle of the season, wasting a perfectly good summer. When he *was* pitching, however, he dominated the South Atlantic League. With stamina still a concern, it wouldn't be surprising to see him back with Hickory to start the year, but he'll likely face the challenge of High Desert by summer.

Martin Perez LHP

Born: 4/4/91 Age: 25 Bats: L Throws: L Height: 6'0" Weight: 195

YEAR	TEAM	LVL	AGE	W	L	SV	G	GS	IP	H	HR	BB/9	K/9	GB%	BABIP	WHIP	ERA	FIP	DRA	WARP	CFIP	MPH
2013	TEX	MLB	22	10	6	0	20	20	124^1	129	15	2.7	6.1	49%	.292	1.34	3.62	4.26	4.33	0.9	109	95.8
2013	ROU	AAA	22	5	1	0	6	6	36	29	1	2.0	7.0	59%	.280	1.03	1.75	3.21	4.85	0.3	98	
2014	TEX	MLB	23	4	3	0	8	8	51^1	50	3	3.3	6.1	53%	.315	1.34	4.38	3.72	4.43	0.2	102	93.4
2015	TEX	MLB	24	3	6	0	14	14	78^2	88	3	2.7	5.5	60%	.326	1.42	4.46	3.37	4.09	0.9	109	94.3
2015	ROU	AAA	24	0	1	0	4	4	20	27	2	0.9	7.7	55%	.397	1.45	4.95	3.50	3.78	0.4	87	
2016	*TEX*	*MLB*	*25*	*9*	*10*	*0*	*29*	*29*	*153^2*	*162*	*17*	*2.7*	*6.2*	*56%*	*.300*	*1.36*	*4.26*	*4.33*	*4.46*	*1.2*	*103*	
2017	*TEX*	*MLB*	*26*	*9*	*9*	*0*	*27*	*27*	*160^2*	*169*	*18*	*2.5*	*6.7*	*56%*	*.305*	*1.33*	*4.16*	*4.05*	*4.36*	*1.4*	*100*	

Breakout: 22% Improve: 49% Collapse: 21% Attrition: 16% MLB: 89% *Comparables: Luke Hochevar, Dana Eveland, Noah Lowry*

Sidelined by Tommy John surgery back in May 2014, Perez returned to the majors on July 17th with a decent if not spectacular outing against the Astros. For the most part, this is how most of his starts (including a playoff go against the Blue Jays) went. He played as a severe groundball pitcher without any of kind swing-and-miss stuff. He kept the ball in the park but with a strikeout rate under six per nine, he was significantly held at the whim of his defense. If there was a silver lining in his performance, it was that both his fastball velocity and his swinging-strike rate improved as the season continued, and his performance in September showed flashes of dominance. One would like to say that this will be Perez's first full season post-Tommy John, but it would also be his first full season in the majors. Rangers fans have been forced to be patient, but what they've gotten hasn't been bad and better things may still be to come.

Tanner Scheppers RHP

Born: 1/17/87 Age: 29 Bats: R Throws: R Height: 6'4" Weight: 200

YEAR	TEAM	LVL	AGE	W	L	SV	G	GS	IP	H	HR	BB/9	K/9	GB%	BABIP	WHIP	ERA	FIP	DRA	WARP	CFIP	MPH
2013	TEX	MLB	26	6	2	1	76	0	76^2	58	6	2.8	6.9	51%	.252	1.07	1.88	3.77	3.05	1.4	100	99.2
2014	TEX	MLB	27	0	1	0	8	4	23	31	6	3.9	6.7	54%	.333	1.78	9.00	6.77	7.91	-0.9	114	97.6
2015	ROU	AAA	28	0	2	2	13	0	14	11	0	5.1	7.1	51%	.282	1.36	1.93	3.96	5.06	0.0	102	
2015	TEX	MLB	28	4	1	0	42	0	38^1	37	6	5.4	7.5	40%	.274	1.57	5.63	5.43	5.35	-0.3	109	97.3
2016	*TEX*	*MLB*	*29*	*3*	*1*	*3*	*53*	*0*	*56^1*	*57*	*7*	*3.7*	*7.1*	*46%*	*.296*	*1.42*	*4.63*	*4.64*	*4.82*	*0.0*	*110*	
2017	*TEX*	*MLB*	*30*	*3*	*1*	*1*	*55*	*0*	*53^2*	*52*	*6*	*4.1*	*7.4*	*46%*	*.291*	*1.42*	*4.64*	*4.51*	*4.83*	*-0.1*	*110*	

Breakout: 30% Improve: 49% Collapse: 20% Attrition: 17% MLB: 79% *Comparables: Santiago Casilla, Vinnie Chulk, Jeremy Accardo*

It was another inconsistent season for Scheppers, whose performance on the field never seems to match his raw stuff. Some of the problem has been injuries, which have shaved a couple of miles off what was once a high-90s fastball, but some of it has been the product of a continually devolving pitch repertoire. He relied far more on his slider than ever before, with suboptimal results: His whiff rates dropped on every type of pitch except a rarely used changeup. The stuff is still there for him to emerge as a shutdown reliever, but the stuff has always been there. The shutting-down part is the challenge.

Dillon Tate RHP

Born: 5/1/94 Age: 22 Bats: R Throws: R Height: 6'2" Weight: 165

YEAR	TEAM	LVL	AGE	W	L	SV	G	GS	IP	H	HR	BB/9	K/9	GB%	BABIP	WHIP	ERA	FIP	DRA	WARP	CFIP	MPH
2016	*TEX*	*MLB*	*22*	*2*	*3*	*0*	*9*	*9*	*33^1*	*34*	*5*	*3.8*	*6.0*	*58%*	*.274*	*1.45*	*5.14*	*5.31*	*5.29*	*-0.1*	*126*	
2017	*TEX*	*MLB*	*23*	*4*	*6*	*0*	*29*	*29*	*177*	*182*	*26*	*3.9*	*6.7*	*58%*	*.280*	*1.47*	*5.19*	*5.05*	*5.34*	*-0.3*	*127*	

Breakout: 1% Improve: 1% Collapse: 1% Attrition: 1% MLB: 2% *Comparables: Pedro Beato, Travis Wood, T.J. House*

Texas was rewarded for a miserable, injury-ridden 2014 with the fourth-overall pick. After getting his jersey, Tate pitched only nine professional innings amid concerns about overwork, partially because of a minor trap muscle injury and partly because his senior year was his first as a starter. At UC Santa Barbara, Tate featured a mid-to-high-90s fastball with arm-side movement and a slider with two-plane break that he could both spot and bury. His other two pitches, a curveball and a changeup, are decidedly weaker, but even if they fail to surface he's got the repertoire of a potentially dominant reliever. Tate will enter 2016 on a full offseason of rest, ready to really start his professional career.

Nick Tepesch RHP

Born: 10/12/88 Age: 27 Bats: R Throws: R Height: 6'4" Weight: 240

YEAR	TEAM	LVL	AGE	W	L	SV	G	GS	IP	H	HR	BB/9	K/9	GB%	BABIP	WHIP	ERA	FIP	DRA	WARP	CFIP	MPH
2013	TEX	MLB	24	4	6	0	19	17	93	100	12	2.6	7.4	48%	.309	1.37	4.84	4.22	4.65	0.3	102	94.2
2014	TEX	MLB	25	5	11	0	23	22	126	128	15	3.1	4.0	43%	.272	1.37	4.36	5.03	4.57	0.3	127	92.6
2014	ROU	AAA	25	6	1	0	7	7	45^2	36	1	1.8	8.1	55%	.280	0.99	1.58	2.91	4.73	0.5	79	
2016	*TEX*	*MLB*	*27*	*2*	*2*	*0*	*6*	*6*	*34^1*	*37*	*4*	*2.9*	*5.6*	*46%*	*.295*	*1.41*	*4.78*	*4.67*	*4.96*	*0.1*	*117*	
2017	*TEX*	*MLB*	*28*	*9*	*11*	*0*	*29*	*29*	*181^2*	*197*	*25*	*2.7*	*6.1*	*46%*	*.299*	*1.39*	*4.72*	*4.59*	*4.90*	*0.4*	*116*	

Breakout: 23% Improve: 50% Collapse: 20% Attrition: 26% MLB: 85% *Comparables: Anthony Swarzak, Kyle Gibson, Nick Blackburn*

A borderline fifth-starter candidate entering the year, Tepesch started the season in the minors, but then had his option reversed due to inflammation in the ulnar nerve (elbow). Rehab was attempted, but it turned out that he had thoracic outlet syndrome, a tightening of the nerve bundle in the technically titled shoulder-armpit area. It required surgery and ended his year. Former inductees into the TOS club include Chris Young (good news!), Shaun Marcum (bad news!) and Jaime Garcia (news still pending!). Blood clotting is a potential outcome, so Tepesch's recovery from what can be a life-threatening condition trumps any concern over whether or not he will ever make it back onto the mound.

Shawn Tolleson RHP

Born: 1/19/88 Age: 28 Bats: R Throws: R Height: 6'2" Weight: 220

YEAR	TEAM	LVL	AGE	W	L	SV	G	GS	IP	H	HR	BB/9	K/9	GB%	BABIP	WHIP	ERA	FIP	DRA	WARP	CFIP	MPH
2014	TEX	MLB	26	3	1	0	64	0	71^2	56	10	3.5	8.7	40%	.245	1.17	2.76	4.26	3.04	1.3	91	94.8
2015	TEX	MLB	27	6	4	35	73	0	72^1	66	9	2.1	9.5	44%	.294	1.15	2.99	3.41	3.79	0.8	78	95.3
2016	*TEX*	*MLB*	*28*	*3*	*1*	*25*	*58*	*0*	*61^1*	*55*	*8*	*2.7*	*8.9*	*43%*	*.286*	*1.20*	*3.82*	*3.93*	*4.03*	*0.6*	*87*	
2017	*TEX*	*MLB*	*29*	*3*	*1*	*6*	*52*	*0*	*54^1*	*48*	*7*	*3.1*	*8.9*	*43%*	*.280*	*1.23*	*4.19*	*4.06*	*4.42*	*0.2*	*98*	

Breakout: 29% Improve: 50% Collapse: 29% Attrition: 8% MLB: 92% *Comparables: Bill Bray, David Aardsma, Chris Ray*

Cast off by the Dodgers after the 2013 season, Tolleson was a fastball-reliant pitcher who could blow the ball by less-experienced hitters but lacked the plus off-speed offering to handle big leaguers. The Rangers worked with him on establishing a changeup, and it became a legitimate weapon that upgraded him from a middling middle man to a viable stopper. The Rangers' bullpen was filled with success stories like this, solid pitchers with shortcomings who were converted into more valuable assets due to solid coaching. Tolleson was the most successful example of this formula coming to fruition.

Tom Wilhelmsen RHP

Born: 12/16/83 Age: 32 Bats: R Throws: R Height: 6'6" Weight: 220

YEAR	TEAM	LVL	AGE	W	L	SV	G	GS	IP	H	HR	BB/9	K/9	GB%	BABIP	WHIP	ERA	FIP	DRA	WARP	CFIP	MPH
2013	TAC	AAA	29	0	1	0	8	2	12	19	3	3.8	11.2	42%	.485	2.00	10.50	6.07	4.95	0.1	96	
2013	SEA	MLB	29	0	3	24	59	0	59	45	2	5.0	6.9	44%	.253	1.32	4.12	3.72	2.99	1.1	113	98.8
2014	SEA	MLB	30	3	2	1	57	2	79^{1}	47	6	4.1	8.2	53%	.204	1.05	2.27	3.76	2.81	1.6	103	98.0
2015	SEA	MLB	31	2	2	13	53	0	62	56	3	4.2	8.7	45%	.308	1.37	3.19	3.30	3.75	0.7	95	97.5
2016	*TEX*	*MLB*	*32*	*2*	*1*	*0*	*48*	*0*	*51*	*47*	*6*	*4.0*	*7.7*	*47%*	*.282*	*1.36*	*4.34*	*4.46*	*4.55*	*0.1*	*102*	
2017	*TEX*	*MLB*	*33*	*2*	*1*	*3*	*44*	*0*	*50^{1}*	*49*	*6*	*3.9*	*7.8*	*47%*	*.295*	*1.42*	*4.48*	*4.36*	*4.70*	*0.0*	*106*	

Breakout: 26% Improve: 44% Collapse: 29% Attrition: 16% MLB: 92% *Comparables: Jared Burton, Ramon Ramirez, Brad Ziegler*

If someone decided to make a poster festooned with the words "closers are made and not born," there would surely be a picture of Wilhelmsen and his wonderfully goofy smile plastered upon it. Shunted into a middle-relief role behind "proven" closer Fernando Rodney and wunderkind Carson Smith, he made his way back into the stopper role by the end of the season and acquitted himself respectably. He'll never be an elite stopper in the mold of Aroldis Chapman, but holding closers up to this standard is bound to leave you sad and disappointed. Wilhelmsen will otherwise leave you happy.

Lineouts

Hitters

NAME	POS	TEAM	LVL	AGE	PA	R	2B	3B	HR	RBI	BB	K	SB	CS	AVG/OBP/SLG	TAv	BABIP	BRR	FRAA	WARP
Jairo Beras	OF	HIC	A	20	350	45	18	2	9	43	19	88	9	4	.291/.332/.440	.286	.372	0.6	RF(70): 2.2, CF(8): 0.6	
Patrick Cantwell	C	FRI	AA	25	221	22	3	2	3	19	16	43	0	0	.187/.256/.268	.196	.221	0.9	C(54): -0.2	
	C	ROU	AAA	25	52	4	0	1	0	3	2	12	0	1	.136/.240/.182	.167	.188	0.2	C(14): 1.7, RF(1): -0.1	
Ryan Cordell	UT	FRI	AA	23	242	26	5	3	5	18	12	73	10	1	.217/.263/.335	.207	.293	1.0	CF(27): 1.6, 3B(16): -1.2	
	UT	HDS	A+	23	319	58	13	5	13	57	28	53	10	5	.311/.376/.528	.310	.342	2.9	CF(32): -3.0, 3B(17): 0.7	
Michael De Leon	SS	HIC	A	18	337	29	11	2	1	29	23	47	1	1	.222/.277/.281	.222	.258	0.4	SS(74): 6.0, 2B(6): -0.4	
Travis Demeritte	INF	HIC	A	20	198	27	12	1	5	19	25	69	10	1	.241/.343/.412	.295	.371	0.5	2B(43): 5.9, 3B(3): 0.4	
	INF	SPO	A-	20	22	0	0	0	0	0	2	11	0	2	.150/.227/.150	.138	.333	-0.3	2B(5): -1.4	
Ronald Guzman	1B	HDS	A+	20	452	54	25	7	9	73	27	101	3	0	.277/.319/.434	.257	.343	-1.2	1B(106): 0.1	
	1B	HIC	A	20	104	10	3	0	3	14	6	15	2	0	.309/.346/.433	.287	.338	-0.2	1B(24): -0.6	
Josh Morgan	SS	HIC	A	19	416	59	15	1	3	36	45	53	9	4	.288/.385/.362	.298	.330	2.0	3B(50): 2.0, SS(44): -0.7	
Guilder Rodriguez	2B	FRI	AA	31	148	15	4	0	0	13	20	23	6	2	.248/.347/.280	.251	.298	0.7	2B(12): 0.3, 3B(12): 0.4	
Ryan Strausborger	OF	ROU	AAA	27	381	54	21	2	10	34	24	66	27	5	.278/.329/.438	.286	.317	1.2	RF(50): 1.0, CF(27): 0.3	
	OF	TEX	MLB	27	51	9	0	0	1	3	3	11	2	1	.200/.240/.267	.208	.229	0.8	LF(18): 1.1, RF(1): -0.1	
Yeyson Yrizarri	SS	ROU	AAA	18	34	2	1	1	0	4	1	5	0	1	.273/.294/.364	.195	.321	-0.5	SS(9): -1.2	
	SS	SPO	A-	18	257	27	10	1	2	29	6	46	8	6	.265/.290/.339	.240	.318	0.0	SS(57): 0.3, 2B(5): -0.8	

Jairo Beras' raw power is tantalizing, but his swing mechanics bear a passing resemblance to a face-painted skirmisher in a battle scene from *Braveheart*. ❖ A classic catch-and-throw backstop, **Patrick Cantwell** can swing a bat but can't well. ❖ **Ryan Cordell** has a bat that could take him places, but the trick is going to be finding a tolerable place for him on the defensive spectrum. If Double-A proves easier the second time around, the answer may be all of them. ❖ **Michael De Leon** has the defensive ability to play anywhere on the diamond. How the switch-hitter develops his offense will dictate how many positions he'll play in the majors: probably three or four, a couple of times a week. ❖ After leading all Single-A hitters with home runs in 2014, **Travis Demeritte** spent half his 2015 suspended for using Furosemide, a drug that treats chronic heart failure, swelling, and high strikeout rates. Side effects may include loss of development time. ❖ The Rangers spent all year tinkering with **Ronald Guzman**'s swing and approach at the plate. Despite their best efforts, he remains Ronald Guzman. ❖ A speed-demon prep outfielder, 2015 second-round draftee **Eric Jenkins** fits right into the talented-but-raw profile Texas loves to hoard in the upper rounds. He showed more polish than expected in his professional debut, despite the strikeouts, and will likely get a chance to progress in Low-A Hickory this season. ❖ What **Josh Morgan** may lack in flashy tools or discernible power he makes up for with a solid all-around game, highlighted by a terrific batting eye. He could be a top-of-the-lineup middle infielder in the majors in a few years if everything breaks right. ❖ After 14 years in professional baseball—and 14 major-league plate appearances—**Guilder Rodriguez** has retired. The Rangers hope to bring him back as a coach somewhere in the organization. ❖ A long-time minor-league grinder, **Ryan Strausborger** got his major-league chance after injuries to Josh Hamilton and Leonys Martin. Though he couldn't sandwich together many hits, his pinch-running in important situations allowed him to occasionally play the hero. ❖ **Yeyson Yrizarri** is yet another Rangers shortstop prospect, with a blunderbuss for an arm and a boat oar for a bat. Politicians will be running for president all over again before his scheduled ETA of 2019, but you should be able to remember his name.

Pitchers

NAME	TEAM	LVL	AGE	W	L	SV	G	GS	IP	H	HR	BB/9	K/9	GB%	BABIP	WHIP	ERA	FIP	FRA	WARP	CFIP	MPH
Andrew Faulkner	TEX	MLB	22	0	0	0	11	0	9^2	8	2	2.8	9.3	48%	.240	1.14	2.79	4.66	4.01	0.1	97	95.6
	FRI	AA	22	7	4	1	28	15	92^1	84	9	4.6	8.8	42%	.291	1.42	4.19	4.34	5.14	-0.4	107	
Phil Klein	ROU	AAA	26	2	1	0	18	10	63^2	49	2	3.8	8.2	42%	.272	1.19	2.97	3.60	4.50	0.7	96	
	TEX	MLB	26	1	0	0	11	2	17^1	23	4	5.2	6.2	41%	.317	1.90	6.75	6.45	7.31	-0.5	113	93.8
Will Lamb	FRI	AA	24	1	1	0	22	0	26	27	0	3.8	8.3	38%	.333	1.46	3.12	3.07	4.32	0.2	97	
	ROU	AAA	24	2	3	0	25	0	31	32	3	4.4	7.8	43%	.312	1.52	5.52	4.76	5.72	-0.2	107	
Jose Leclerc	FRI	AA	21	6	8	0	26	22	103	97	8	6.4	8.6	33%	.310	1.65	5.77	4.71	6.35	-1.4	119	
Brett Martin	HIC	A	20	5	6	0	20	18	95^1	92	6	2.5	6.8	49%	.306	1.24	3.49	3.67	4.55	0.7	101	
David Martinez	ROU	AAA	27	0	0	0	9	2	16^2	17	4	6.5	4.3	38%	.250	1.74	4.32	8.28	7.81	-0.4	129	
	FRI	AA	27	3	5	22	40	0	50^2	47	1	2.5	7.3	32%	.307	1.20	2.84	2.76	3.04	1.1	83	
Yohander Mendez	HIC	A	20	3	3	3	21	8	66^1	57	2	2.0	10.0	54%	.312	1.09	2.44	2.41	2.24	2.1	74	
Connor Sadzeck	HDS	A+	23	2	1	0	11	8	40^2	32	4	5.3	10.6	46%	.277	1.38	3.98	4.69	4.98	0.3	100	
	FRI	AA	23	1	1	0	7	6	19^2	22	1	7.8	7.3	42%	.344	1.98	9.61	5.53	7.67	-0.6	129	

A cross-fire lefty with strikeout stuff, but a tendency to allow innings to get away from him, **Andrew Faulkner** needs to refine his breaking ball soon or his dreams of being a starter may lay dying. ❖ The Rangers' rotation woes forced them to give big **Phil Klein** his fifth professional start in the majors. It didn't go so well, but his conversion in the minors held enough promise for him to possibly get another shot in 2016. ❖ A 6-foot-6 southpaw with control issues, **Will Lamb** struggled all year at Triple-A and never was promoted, even with the Rangers' early bullpen struggles. He'll need to pitch better or grow taller to make next year's annual. ❖ **Jose Leclerc**, whose last name is French for "The Clerk," has shown flashes of greatness on the mound, a phrase that insinuates a lot of non-greatness in between. He'll continue to hunt for consistency as he molds himself into a relief prospect worth caring about. File the name away. ❖ **Brett Martin** soared up the organization's charts last season, partially because of his projectable profile and stuff, and partially because everyone else got promoted or traded. ❖ Cut by the Astros after two brief stints in the majors in 2013–2014, **David Martinez** struggled all year at Triple-A and failed to make it back to the bigs. ❖ A good-sized left-hander, **Yohander Mendez** has a deceptive delivery and a solid three-pitch arsenal, including perhaps the best changeup in the organization. After an excellent but intermittent season, physical development and health are the keys for him to make the next step. ❖ With a fastball that can touch 98 mph, **Connor Sadzeck** is a tantalizing prospect, but his messy secondary offerings and lack of command make him more project than projectable.

Manager

Jeff Banister

Over his 52 years, Banister has survived cancer, broken bones, temporary paralysis and decades in the Pirates organization during the lean years; deductive reasoning suggests he has more makeup than Revlon. Comparatively, Banister must have found turning around the Rangers to be a cupcake.

Banister's greatest strength, besides his calmness, was his willingness to adapt. Stylistically, the Rangers continued to resemble Ron Washington's teams: They bunted, stole bases and, even when they didn't steal, wreaked havoc on the basepaths—all because those were the strategies that fit the roster. Banister was also flexible enough to trust and rely upon young, unproven players. Rougned Odor, Delino DeShields and Keone Kela all played significant roles in the Rangers' success, and are better off for it. Additionally, Banister's top relievers by season's end were Shawn Tolleson, Sam Dyson and Jake Diekman—a trio that, collectively, hadn't pitched in the postseason or qualified for arbitration.

Another thing Banister showed a penchant for was challenging plays; no manager issued more, according to Baseball Savant. The downside to Banister's compulsive urge to ask for an official review was that he finished with the lowest percentage of overturns among those who finished in the top five, succeeding on fewer than 32 percent of his tries. Failing on a challenge is probably less costly than, say, failing to make a pitching change or something along those lines, but it remains noteworthy. The good news is, even after review, the Rangers have to be happy with their decision to hire Banister.

TORONTO BLUE JAYS

Essay by Dustin Parkes

Player comments by Bret Sayre and BP authors

If we were to read all the motivational quotes ever written on the subject of opportunity, we'd find one unifying theme: It is up to us to create our own. Baseball, though, is quite outside the purview of the great motivators. There is no conjuring of chances. Skill is necessary to seize a moment, but more than anything else, the opportunities granted a baseball player are dependent on the whims of management, the structures of batting orders, the rotations of starting pitchers, the strike zones of umpires and the absolutely uncontrollable randomness that permeates this wonderfully imperfect game.

The Devil Rays had Jose Bautista on their 25-man roster for three weeks in 2004 before selling him to the Royals for $50,000. His roster spot was taken by Joey Gathright. In 1,329 plate appearances in the major leagues, Gathright recorded one home run (oddly enough, while playing for the Royals two years later). From 2010 to 2015, Bautista hit 227 home runs, 28 more than the no. 2 batter over that period; from 2010 to 2015, Joey Gathright had one major-league plate appearance.

Baseball is strange. Really strange. But for all the weird things in the sport's history, the weirdest happened last season. It occurred in Toronto during the seventh inning of a game on October 14th. That's not hyperbole. What happened in Game Five of the ALDS between the Blue Jays and Rangers makes you reevaluate the frequency with which you use words ending in "-est." Even The New Yorker's Roger Angell, who, at the age of 95, has probably seen more baseball than 99.9 percent of the humans on earth, wrote that the inning "will stand as one of the strangest runs of events in the annals."

With the score tied at two in the deciding game, the seventh inning began with a single by Rougned Odor. The Rangers' second baseman had been nickel-and-diming Toronto pitchers for singles and stolen bags all series. His pedaling down the baselines wasn't restricted to counting stats, either. Odor was having the kind of series that gets celebrated by those who emphasize the importance of scrappiness. His talents lie beyond raw speed and determination; he's an incredibly clever player, one who gives credence to the idea that the baserunner has as much say in being advanced as the hitter putting the ball in play. Despite the next two batters' inability to get on

BLUE JAYS PROSPECTUS

2015 W-L: 93-69, 1st in AL East

Pythag	.633	1st	DER	.721	1st
RS/G	5.50	1st	B-Age	29.6	28th
RA/G	4.14	12th	P-Age	30.1	29th
TAv	.281	1st	Salary	$125.9M	10th
BRR	18.6	2nd	M$/MW	$2.5M	20th
TAv-P	.252	7th	DL Days	748	8th
FIP	4.06	17th	$ on DL	9%	6th

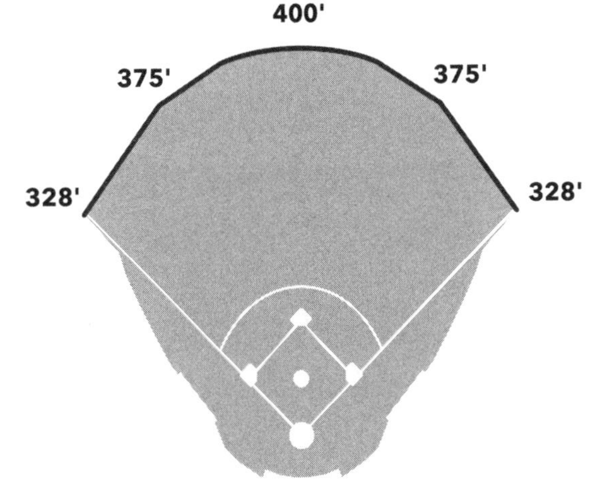

Outfield wall profile: **10'**

Three-Year Park Factors

Runs	Runs/RH	Runs/LH	HR/RH	HR/LH
103	116	110	121	114

Top Hitter WARP	7.6	Josh Donaldson
Top Pitcher WARP	3.5	Marco Estradae
Top Prospect		Anthony Alford

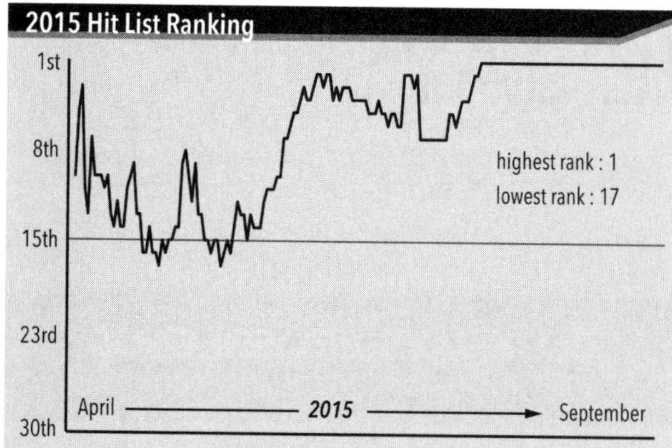

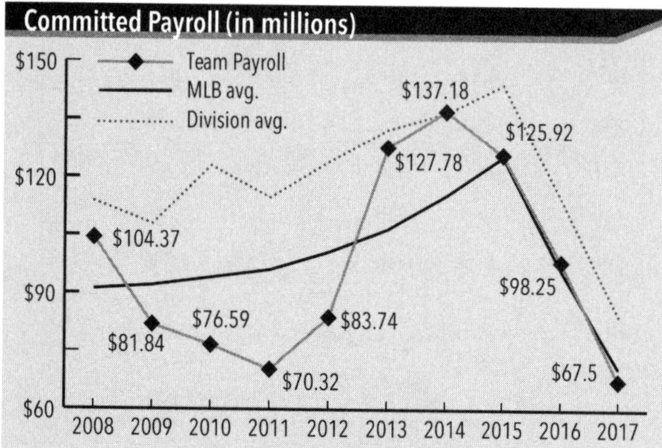

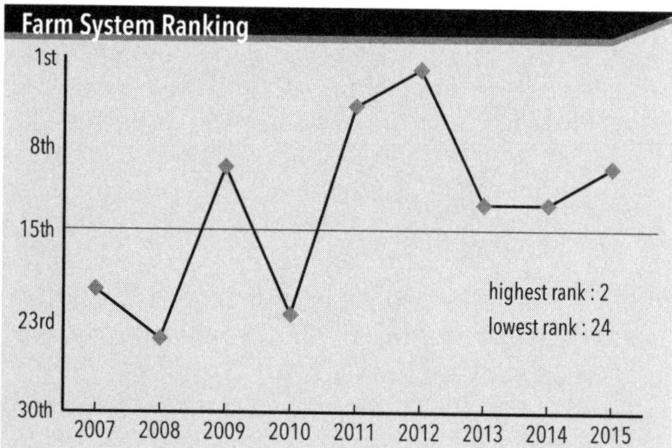

Personnel

President: Mark Shapiro
General Manager: Ross Atkins
Assistant General Manager: Andrew Tinnish
Manager: John Gibbons

Baseball Prospectus Alumni
Dan Evans
Jason Paré

base or even get the ball out of the infield, Odor moved from first to third.

That brought up Shin-Soo Choo to face Aaron Sanchez. Russell Martin has caught more than 10,000 innings in his career. Only Yadier Molina has caught more this century. Yet something happened during this at-bat that he had never seen, much less done. A routine toss by Martin back to Sanchez ricocheted off Choo's bat as he stood in the box minding his own business.

The ball rolled meekly down the third-base line as if Elvis Andrus had gotten all of it, and Odor, once again more alert than any other player on the field, scrambled home with body language that simultaneously conveyed franticness and disbelief at the fortuitous moment.

Umpires conferred. The television commentators had no answers despite a plethora of replays. Fans at the stadium questioned what exactly had happened.

What happened, the officials would soon confirm, was that the Rangers had scored the go-ahead run by a method endorsed by the rules but condemned by anyone with a sense of justice who was not adorned in a Rangers jersey.

Cue: outrage. For 18 minutes, the game was halted as fans at the Rogers Centre threw everything they could find on the field. A television replay showed a thrown can of beer spraying all over a baby. It was doubly painful: Embarrassment soon replaced anger as the primary emotion across the country.

The rest of Canada has a reputation for hating the city of Toronto, while Toronto has a reputation for not realizing that the rest of the country is there at all. A similar relationship exists between Blue Jays fans and the rest of baseball. Many of the team's supporters are of the belief that Major League Baseball is out to get the franchise, and that a grand conspiracy—typically based on a bad call from an umpire—is in place to halt any progress the team makes. This is, of course, delusional. There's certainly not enough ill will or concern about playoff television ratings in the U.S. to prompt an institution more than 100 years old to risk its entire existence just to stack the odds unfairly against one organization.

But try telling that to the heat-seeking missile that is a Blue Jays fan whose team, after waiting 22 years to return to the playoffs, was suddenly down a run with only three innings remaining. The vulgar protest did nothing to change the score line, though, and after the delay Choo struck out swinging to end what was perhaps the lowest point in the team's history.

Leading off the bottom of the seventh was Martin, who still appeared to be more shaken by the events of the top half than he was eager to find redemption. He grounded the fourth pitch he saw from Cole Hamels up the middle, well within the range of Andrus at shortstop. Only, not so much. The typically elite fielder made a last-second decision to try to get square with the ball rather than scoop it on the run. It bounced off the heel of his glove and

Martin was safe at first. Next up was Kevin Pillar, who also fell behind in the count before offering up a dribbler to the Rangers' infield. This time the ball rolled to first baseman Mitch Moreland, who tried to catch Martin at second rather than taking two steps to get the easy out at first. His throw to Andrus bounced in the dirt; suddenly, the Blue Jays had two men on with none out.

Ryan Goins laid down a bunt, but it was hit a bit too hard down the third-base line; he spoke up when a whisper was needed. Adrian Beltre scooped it on the run and had a real chance to get pinch-runner Dalton Pompey at third. His throw to Andrus covering the bag was perfect, but again, the ball bounced off the heel of the shortstop's glove. Three men on. Three straight errors.

The Rangers finally got the lead runner on a force at home when the next batter, Ben Revere, kicked a pitch straight to Moreland, but that still left the bases loaded for Josh Donaldson. The eventual MVP's bloop hit should have been caught by Odor at second, but his feet, which had run havoc on the Blue Jays for the entire series, looked like they were encased in stone. He didn't move, and the ball fell to his left. Pillar scored the tying run, Goins advanced to third and Revere was forced out at second, though only because he assumed the ball was going to be caught.

Have you ever seen Angels In The Outfield? My favorite scenes are when you can't see the heavenly host involving themselves in the play. That's what we were seeing in Toronto. Baseball, with all its randomness, is the only sport angels could interrupt and still go incognito.

The next batter was Jose Bautista.

His arms are an extension of his body. The bat, an extension of his arms. He is one with his swing, but not in a spiritual sense. He is a thinking man's power hitter. His strength isn't brutish or mysterious; it's calculated. Every time Jose Bautista makes contact, there's a lesson in leverage, a testament to torsion.

Imagine if you'd never seen Bautista before, but merely read his statistical breakdown over the last five years. What would you picture in your mind? He is a slingshot when you expect a battering ram. He looks nothing like what fans expect a power hitter to look like: Constantly stretching, his flexible frame is long and lean. His is a sinewy presence at the plate. His bat doesn't crack baseballs with raw power; it launches them like a catapult. As a pitch comes in, Bautista pushes off his front foot, accumulates weight on his back leg, then torques his whole body forward in a coordinated motion.

If baseballness approached godliness, Bautista's unlikely story would make him the patron saint of the unfulfilled. Toiling in unrealized potential for a number of years (and teams), he didn't find consistent success until the age of 29, when he emerged out of relative obscurity to hit 54 home runs. It's a bit like muddling through college algebra freshman year, then proving the Beal Conjecture as a sophomore. Then, just in case the math community labels you a fluke, you solve a new unsolvable problem every year after that.

If there's anything more surprising than Bautista's rise through the ranks of the best power hitters in baseball, it's the ease with which he's accepted his stardom. That Bautista's miraculous transformation came while wearing the uniform of the Toronto Blue Jays has obviously endeared him to the team's fan base, but the rest of baseball has often been rubbed the wrong way by what seems like an undying sense of entitlement. Bautista doesn't suffer fools, and there are few as foolish to the slugger as an umpire who makes a questionable call or a pitcher who responds enthusiastically to collecting an out. While the fiery Latino ballplayer is a stereotype baseball fans would do well to excise, its existence doesn't make it less true that Bautista plays with more visible emotion than most.

With the game tied at three, two men on and one out in the bottom of the seventh, Jose Bautista hit a home run.

Seldom can an instance of collective exuberance be so well captured by the same individual who caused the sheer joy being experienced. Bautista did it all, though, first by hitting the home run, and then by tossing his bat, not just in celebration, but to offer an exclamation point to the cheers that erupted in the stadium.

There was an immediate response on the field. Both benches cleared, and yet another delay occurred in what ended up being a 53-minute inning. Misanthropes, including members of the opposing team and broadcast booth mainstays, would later cite baseball's "unwritten rules" to condemn Bautista's bat flip. Baseball has always frowned on open celebrations that might bring further shame to vanquished foes. There's little doubt that "unwritten rules" have remained unwritten through baseball's storied history because if they were ever written down, we'd quickly realize how stupid they are. However, those silly "unwritten rules" added to the experience of Bautista's homer.

If everyone flipped his bat after hitting a home run, Bautista's display would have been meaningless. Thankfully, they don't. It was a special occasion made more exceptional by the slugger's immediate reaction, as spontaneous as fans' response: leaping off bar stools, jumping on living-room couches, extending hands for high fives from friends and family and nearby strangers. It was justice and redemption. After more than 20 years, what Toronto fans wanted to have happen actually seemed to align with fate.

Baseball is the only sport in which you can't ensure your best player is given the opportunity to win it for you. In basketball, you can give the ball to LeBron James. In football, you can set Tom Brady free with two minutes remaining. In hockey, you can pass to Sidney Crosby in overtime. In baseball, you leave it up to fate and a batting order. That's how a seemingly meaningless single in the second inning can have a profound impact on a game or an entire season.

Nine days after all that happened in Toronto, Jose Bautista would watch from the on-deck circle as Josh Donaldson grounded out to third base in the ninth inning of Game Six of the ALCS. It ended the Blue Jays' season. He didn't get the opportunity to extend it. The chance may never come again. ■

—*Dustin Parkes is the Executive Producer of Arts & Culture for the* National Post.

HITTERS

Anthony Alford CF

Born: 7/20/94 Age: 21 Bats: R Throws: R Height: 6'1" Weight: 205

YEAR	TEAM	LVL	AGE	PA	R	2B	3B	HR	RBI	BB	K	SB	CS	AVG/OBP/SLG	TAv	BABIP	BRR	FRAA	WARP
2014	LNS	A	19	25	3	1	0	1	3	0	8	4	0	.320/.320/.480	.287	.438	0.8	CF(4): -0.4	0.2
2015	LNS	A	20	232	49	14	1	1	16	39	60	12	1	.293/.418/.394	.287	.419	6.5	CF(46): -3.7	1.7
2015	DUN	A+	20	255	42	11	6	3	19	28	49	15	6	.302/.380/.444	.299	.374	4.1	CF(55): 0.8	2.4
2016	*TOR*	*MLB*	*21*	*250*	*30*	*10*	*2*	*5*	*21*	*25*	*72*	*7*	*2*	*.223/.305/.345*	*.235*	*.304*	*0.4*	*CF 1*	*0.4*
2017	*TOR*	*MLB*	*22*	*393*	*46*	*17*	*3*	*9*	*41*	*42*	*113*	*11*	*4*	*.236/.321/.378*	*.250*	*.321*	*1.2*	*CF 2*	*1.4*

Breakout: 5% Improve: 9% Collapse: 0% Attrition: 5% MLB: 17% *Comparables: Anthony Gose, Byron Buxton, Joc Pederson*

To say, before 2015, that Alford hadn't quite gotten his minor-league career going was like saying Nicolas Cage hadn't quite gotten his acting career going at the release of *Fast Times at Ridgemont High*. After six weeks Alford had 170 plate appearances, matching his *combined* total of the three prior years, but what really stood out at that point was his .439 on-base percentage. With his days as a wide receiver and part-time prospect behind him, Alford has quickly torn off the "raw" label people like us slapped on him when he was taken in the third round of the 2012 draft. His plus-plus speed is present and his above-average raw power is not, but the hit tool and approach that can tie it all together were on display for much of the season. When a team goes all-in and trades its entire farm system, the guys left behind are a mix of can't-let-'em-goes and nobody-wants-'ems. Rest assured that Alford isn't in the latter group.

Jose Bautista RF

Born: 10/19/80 Age: 35 Bats: R Throws: R Height: 6'0" Weight: 205

YEAR	TEAM	LVL	AGE	PA	R	2B	3B	HR	RBI	BB	K	SB	CS	AVG/OBP/SLG	TAv	BABIP	BRR	FRAA	WARP
2013	TOR	MLB	32	528	82	24	0	28	73	69	84	7	2	.259/.358/.498	.307	.259	-1.5	RF(109): -0.2, 3B(3): -0.3	3.3
2014	TOR	MLB	33	673	101	27	0	35	103	104	96	6	2	.286/.403/.524	.332	.287	-2.8	RF(131): 6.7, CF(12): -0.5	6.5
2015	TOR	MLB	34	666	108	29	3	40	114	110	106	8	2	.250/.377/.536	.316	.237	0.3	RF(118): -4.8	4.5
2016	*TOR*	*MLB*	*35*	*664*	*100*	*26*	*1*	*37*	*108*	*103*	*107*	*7*	*2*	*.264/.382/.516*	*.316*	*.263*	*-1.4*	*RF -3*	*0.4*
2017	*TOR*	*MLB*	*36*	*556*	*88*	*21*	*1*	*30*	*87*	*85*	*95*	*5*	*2*	*.257/.375/.500*	*.307*	*.260*	*-1.3*	*RF -3*	*1.4*

Breakout: 1% Improve: 25% Collapse: 4% Attrition: 7% MLB: 96% *Comparables: Barry Bonds, Carlos Beltran, Brian Giles*

Awesome. Distasteful. Aggressive. Disrespectful. Demonstrative. Fun. *Super* aggressive. Awful. Meme-worthy. Egregious. All of these, and more, were used to describe one of the most poignant moments of the season, a huge home run in a huge spot of a huge game, with all discussion reduced to a single bat flip, a bat flip so intense it got its own t-shirt. While that's the lasting visual memory of Bautista's 2015 season, it's the continued consistency that defines his career. He's the quintessential late bloomer in a modern-day Murderer's Row full of them: Bautista, Josh Donaldson and Edwin Encarnacion *combined* for 8.1 WARP prior to their age-27 seasons. Bautista's is a Hall of Fame-worthy second act, as he is lapping the league in homers since 2010 with 227 (no one else even has 200) and trails only Joey Votto in walks. All this while playing plus defense in right field (though FRAA marked him negative last year for the first time in his Toronto tenure, not an unexpected outcome for someone now solidly into his mid-30s). Bautista has one year remaining on an extension that was widely panned back in 2011 for being unnecessarily risky and expensive. Nobody knows anything: $64 million over the last five years looks absurdly team-friendly now, and Toronto's team option at $14 million for this season was a laughably easy decision.

Ezequiel Carrera CF

Born: 6/11/87 Age: 29 Bats: L Throws: L Height: 5'10" Weight: 185

YEAR	TEAM	LVL	AGE	PA	R	2B	3B	HR	RBI	BB	K	SB	CS	AVG/OBP/SLG	TAv	BABIP	BRR	FRAA	WARP
2013	CLE	MLB	26	5	1	0	0	0	1	0	1	0	0	.500/.500/.500	.291	.667	0.6	RF(1): -0.1	0.1
2013	PHI	MLB	26	16	2	0	0	0	0	1	4	0	0	.077/.250/.077	.146	.111	0.0	RF(5): 0.2, CF(1): 0.1	-0.1
2013	COH	AAA	26	464	57	16	5	5	31	38	87	43	12	.248/.312/.346	.245	.301	2.7	CF(41): 5.7, LF(38): 2.8	1.6
2014	TOL	AAA	27	434	68	15	5	6	41	48	65	43	13	.307/.387/.422	.281	.355	1.5	CF(69): -0.6, RF(25): -1.0	2.2
2014	DET	MLB	27	73	12	4	1	0	2	3	14	7	1	.261/.301/.348	.244	.327	0.9	CF(38): 0.1, LF(1): -0.4	0.2
2015	BUF	AAA	28	133	18	5	0	1	10	12	16	6	2	.276/.349/.345	.267	.313	-1.0	CF(25): -2.6, RF(4): 0.6	0.3
2015	TOR	MLB	28	192	27	8	0	3	26	11	45	2	1	.273/.321/.372	.253	.349	1.4	LF(46): -1.7, RF(35): -1.1	0.0
2016	*TOR*	*MLB*	*29*	*63*	*8*	*2*	*1*	*1*	*5*	*4*	*12*	*3*	*1*	*.256/.313/.360*	*.238*	*.301*	*0.3*	*RF -0, LF 1*	*0.1*
2017	*TOR*	*MLB*	*30*	*264*	*27*	*9*	*2*	*3*	*23*	*19*	*50*	*13*	*4*	*.248/.306/.346*	*.233*	*.293*	*1.7*	*RF -1, LF 2*	*0.3*

Breakout: 2% Improve: 23% Collapse: 15% Attrition: 22% MLB: 51% *Comparables: Craig Gentry, Julio Borbon, Jerry Owens*

Once signed as part of Omar Minaya's inaugural international class for the New York Mets, the Venezuelan outfielder finally managed to drag his career WARP into positive territory in 2015 by being nearly league average at the plate in a reserve role. Carrera is an extreme groundball hitter, which was much more helpful when he was fast, and he's able to play all three outfield positions, though that really depends on your definition of "play." With little power to speak of, Carrera is running out of chances to prove he should be on a major-league roster, even in a reserve role.

Chris Colabello 1B

Born: 10/24/83 Age: 32 Bats: R Throws: R Height: 6'4" Weight: 235

YEAR	TEAM	LVL	AGE	PA	R	2B	3B	HR	RBI	BB	K	SB	CS	AVG/OBP/SLG	TAv	BABIP	BRR	FRAA	WARP
2013	MIN	MLB	29	181	14	3	0	7	17	20	58	0	1	.194/.287/.344	.240	.253	-0.9	1B(26): 0.1, RF(11): -0.3	-0.3
2013	ROC	AAA	29	391	58	25	0	24	76	43	89	2	1	.352/.427/.639	.350	.413	-2.0	1B(67): -1.4, RF(14): -1.4	3.9
2014	ROC	AAA	30	238	28	13	0	10	38	21	55	0	0	.268/.336/.469	.266	.313	-0.6	1B(54): 4.7, RF(2): -0.1	0.8
2014	MIN	MLB	30	220	17	13	0	6	39	14	66	0	2	.229/.282/.380	.245	.308	0.2	1B(23): -0.4, RF(19): -0.9	-0.2
2015	TOR	MLB	31	360	55	19	1	15	54	22	96	2	0	.321/.367/.520	.304	.411	1.0	1B(34): -0.0, LF(33): -3.6	1.9
2015	BUF	AAA	31	95	14	3	0	5	18	11	19	0	0	.337/.421/.554	.367	.390	-0.2	1B(12): -1.0, RF(2): 0.2	1.1
2016	*TOR*	*MLB*	*32*	*247*	*30*	*12*	*0*	*10*	*35*	*19*	*69*	*1*	*0*	*.263/.325/.459*	*.275*	*.329*	*0.2*	*1B -0, RF -2*	*0.7*
2017	*TOR*	*MLB*	*33*	*338*	*44*	*15*	*0*	*13*	*44*	*26*	*97*	*0*	*0*	*.255/.317/.434*	*.266*	*.326*	*0.2*	*1B 0, RF -2*	*0.6*

Breakout: 0% Improve: 20% Collapse: 7% Attrition: 9% MLB: 77% *Comparables: Shelley Duncan, Marcus Thames, Randy Ruiz*

Some stories are great, like they were scripted by the most unabashedly optimistic (or corny) of Hollywood screenwriters. Colabello has one of those, what with his seven seasons in independent baseball, but the most impressive thing to say about him now is that in 2015, he played well enough for The Story not to be the whole story. He showed a more aggressive approach with Toronto than he had with Minnesota, raising his swing rate by five percentage points and jumping on the first pitch more often. In fact, his 1.316 OPS on the first pitch was third in the American League among those with at least 50 one-pitch at bats. Colabello also received good fortune in spades during the 2015 season. He was the beneficiary of playing time because Jose Bautista was unable to play the field for most of May, as well as the beneficiaray of a .411 BABIP. The last time someone had a higher BABIP in at least 300 plate appearances was 1924, when Rogers Hornsby posted a .422 mark.

Josh Donaldson 3B

Born: 12/8/85 Age: 30 Bats: R Throws: R Height: 6'0" Weight: 220

YEAR	TEAM	LVL	AGE	PA	R	2B	3B	HR	RBI	BB	K	SB	CS	AVG/OBP/SLG	TAv	BABIP	BRR	FRAA	WARP
2013	OAK	MLB	27	668	89	37	3	24	93	76	110	5	2	.301/.384/.499	.326	.333	-2.9	3B(155): -1.8, 1B(1): -0.0	6.2
2014	OAK	MLB	28	695	93	31	2	29	98	76	130	8	0	.255/.342/.456	.305	.278	-2.5	3B(150): 16.2	6.9
2015	TOR	MLB	29	711	122	41	2	41	123	73	133	6	0	.297/.371/.568	.324	.314	4.0	3B(150): 1.2	7.6
2016	*TOR*	*MLB*	*30*	*683*	*91*	*36*	*2*	*31*	*103*	*68*	*127*	*6*	*1*	*.279/.355/.501*	*.299*	*.303*	*-0.6*	*3B 9*	*5.7*
2017	*TOR*	*MLB*	*31*	*591*	*82*	*29*	*2*	*25*	*84*	*57*	*112*	*4*	*1*	*.270/.345/.475*	*.288*	*.296*	*-0.8*	*3B 7*	*4.3*

Breakout: 0% Improve: 20% Collapse: 7% Attrition: 9% MLB: 77% *Comparables: Shelley Duncan, Marcus Thames, Randy Ruiz*

This was not the year we learned anything new about Donaldson. It wasn't the year he was proclaimed a bust. It wasn't the year we learned Donaldson could play plus defense at the hot corner. It wasn't the year we learned he was a late bloomer capable of MVP-caliber production, or that he could sustain elite-level performance. He did more or less exactly what we already knew he was capable of, and he did it in the middle of possibly the best lineup baseball has seen this decade, playing in a park built for sluggers. So, yes, he led the American League in both runs and RBI (becoming the first to eclipse 120 in each category since Albert Pujols in 2009), and smashed 40-plus home runs for the first time—both of which led to his MVP Award—but we still learned nothing new. Even with defense that will continue to decline, arbitration numbers that are likely to skyrocket and his 30th birthday behind him, the Blue Jays have already reaped the rewards of Donaldson's 2014 acquisition and will continue to do so for longer than that haircut of his remains in style.

Edwin Encarnacion 1B

Born: 1/7/83 Age: 33 Bats: R Throws: R Height: 6'1" Weight: 230

YEAR	TEAM	LVL	AGE	PA	R	2B	3B	HR	RBI	BB	K	SB	CS	AVG/OBP/SLG	TAv	BABIP	BRR	FRAA	WARP
2013	TOR	MLB	30	621	90	29	1	36	104	82	62	7	1	.272/.370/.534	.319	.247	1.8	1B(79): -4.3, 3B(10): 1.3	4.4
2014	TOR	MLB	31	542	75	27	2	34	98	62	82	2	0	.268/.354/.547	.310	.260	-0.1	1B(80): -5.3, LF(2): -0.1	2.8
2015	TOR	MLB	32	624	94	31	0	39	111	77	98	3	2	.277/.372/.557	.324	.267	-1.6	1B(59): 0.1	4.7
2016	*TOR*	*MLB*	*33*	*654*	*92*	*31*	*1*	*35*	*105*	*74*	*94*	*5*	*2*	*.269/.356/.512*	*.302*	*.264*	*-0.1*	*1B -1*	*5.7*
2017	*TOR*	*MLB*	*34*	*546*	*78*	*24*	*1*	*26*	*80*	*58*	*86*	*2*	*1*	*.252/.336/.469*	*.283*	*.254*	*-0.3*	*1B -1*	*4.3*

Breakout: 1% Improve: 21% Collapse: 11% Attrition: 14% MLB: 97% *Comparables: Mark Teixeira, Lance Berkman, Albert Pujols*

In this era of decreased contact, the power hitter without a large strikeout total has gone the way of the buffalo. (Both the animal and the city, as the entire Bisons team combined for just 59 home runs in 2015.) Encarnacion, however, remains in the wild, a throwback to days that seem impossible in Play Index searches. Since 2012, there have been 14 seasons of more than 30 home runs and fewer than 100 strikeouts, and he of the parrot-perch home run trot has four of them. He's also the first to do it in four consecutive seasons since Albert Pujols from 2008 to 2011 (and also 2001 to 2007, but who's counting?). Encarnacion enters his final year before free agency as not only one of the best power hitters in the game, but one of the most consistent as well. His *worst* TAv in the last four years was a .307 mark in 2014. He'll be at full strength after offseason surgery to repair a sports hernia, searching for that Nelson Cruz bling come next winter.

Ryan Goins 2B

Born: 2/13/88 Age: 28 Bats: L Throws: R Height: 5'10" Weight: 185

YEAR	TEAM	LVL	AGE	PA	R	2B	3B	HR	RBI	BB	K	SB	CS	AVG/OBP/SLG	TAv	BABIP	BRR	FRAA	WARP
2013	BUF	AAA	25	418	42	22	1	6	46	29	85	3	5	.257/.311/.369	.242	.316	0.6	SS(101): 5.1, 2B(9): -1.6	1.3
2013	TOR	MLB	25	121	11	5	0	2	8	2	28	0	0	.252/.264/.345	.231	.315	-1.4	2B(32): 0.6, SS(2): -0.2	-0.1
2014	TOR	MLB	26	193	14	6	3	1	15	5	42	0	1	.188/.209/.271	.191	.237	-0.7	2B(57): 2.1, SS(15): -0.3	-0.7
2014	BUF	AAA	26	402	36	21	2	0	30	28	64	4	4	.284/.337/.353	.248	.342	0.2	SS(51): 0.7, 2B(49): 2.1	1.2
2015	TOR	MLB	27	428	52	16	4	5	45	39	83	2	1	.250/.318/.354	.238	.304	3.9	2B(66): -3.5, SS(58): 0.4	0.5
2015	BUF	AAA	27	21	1	1	0	0	3	0	5	0	0	.350/.333/.400	.262	.438	0.0	SS(4): 0.1, 2B(2): -0.1	0.1
2016	*TOR*	*MLB*	*28*	*341*	*34*	*15*	*2*	*4*	*28*	*20*	*71*	*2*	*1*	*.244/.289/.347*	*.226*	*.293*	*0.5*	*SS 1, 2B -0*	*5.7*
2017	*TOR*	*MLB*	*29*	*464*	*45*	*21*	*3*	*6*	*41*	*27*	*99*	*2*	*1*	*.238/.284/.342*	*.225*	*.289*	*0.7*	*SS 2, 2B 0*	*4.3*

Breakout: 3% Improve: 20% Collapse: 16% Attrition: 31% MLB: 57% *Comparables: Matt Kata, Willie Harris, Omar Quintanilla*

You'd barely know Ryan Goins was a baseball player by looking at him. You'd certainly never guess that he still holds the single-season home run record at a Division I university. In fact, he hit more homers in the 2009 season for Dallas Baptist (22) than he has in his entire minor-league career, spanning 2,640 plate appearances. Yet after Devon Travis was officially lost for the season on July 28th, Goins played a quiet yet important role for the hard-charging Jays. He hit .282/.371/.398 from that point forward, playing very capable defense at both second and short. He credits his turnaround at the plate to quieting his pre-swing movement; it resulted in drawing walks at more than double his career rate. If this improvement can be sustained, Goins can continue to be a vital utilityman going forward.

Vladimir Guerrero Jr. OF

Born: 3/16/99 Age: 17 Bats: R Throws: R Height: 6'0" Weight: 220

YEAR	TEAM	LVL	AGE	PA	R	2B	3B	HR	RBI	BB	K	SB	CS	AVG/OBP/SLG	TAv	BABIP	BRR	FRAA	WARP

Breakout: X% Improve: XX% Collapse: X% Attrition: XX% MLB: XX% *Comparables: XXXXX XXXX, XXXXX XXXXX, XXXXX XXXXXX*

The title of "most talented player available in the 2015 J2 class" was up for debate, but "most famous" never was. Fortunately for the Junior Impaler, Guerrero possesses many of the same tools at the plate as his father, including extreme bat-to-ball ability for a 16-year-old. However, the similarities in the batter's box are flanked by stark differences in the field, as his speed and arm grades register as fringe-average at best. If you squint, he's his father in the batter's box and his uncle riding on top of his father's shoulders everywhere else.

Maicer Izturis 2B

Born: 9/12/80 Age: 35 Bats: B Throws: R Height: 5'8" Weight: 185

YEAR	TEAM	LVL	AGE	PA	R	2B	3B	HR	RBI	BB	K	SB	CS	AVG/OBP/SLG	TAv	BABIP	BRR	FRAA	WARP
2013	TOR	MLB	32	399	33	12	0	5	32	27	38	1	5	.236/.288/.310	.224	.249	2.3	2B(59): -3.7, 3B(36): -2.4	-0.6
2014	TOR	MLB	33	38	3	1	0	0	1	2	4	1	0	.286/.324/.314	.243	.323	0.1	2B(10): -0.8	0.0
2016	*TOR*	*MLB*	*35*	*250*	*25*	*12*	*0*	*3*	*21*	*18*	*30*	*4*	*2*	*.255/.311/.348*	*.237*	*.279*	*1.1*	*2B -2, SS -0*	*0.3*

Breakout: 1% Improve: 31% Collapse: 5% Attrition: 15% MLB: 87% *Comparables: David Eckstein, Mark Loretta, Alex Cora*

"After Endy Chavez was released at the end of spring training last season, he became the last position player left standing who once donned Montreal Expos laundry" is what we might have said about Izturis if injuries hadn't prevented him from getting into a single game during the 2015 season. That season was also the final year of an embarrassing three-year contract he received from Alex Anthopolous and company, another in a long line of examples proving that reserves should not get multi-year deals.

Munenori Kawasaki 2B

Born: 6/3/81 Age: 35 Bats: L Throws: R Height: 5'11" Weight: 175

YEAR	TEAM	LVL	AGE	PA	R	2B	3B	HR	RBI	BB	K	SB	CS	AVG/OBP/SLG	TAv	BABIP	BRR	FRAA	WARP
2013	BUF	AAA	32	81	9	0	0	0	3	14	12	3	0	.250/.400/.250	.234	.313	-0.9	SS(12): -0.4, 2B(11): -0.7	-0.1
2013	TOR	MLB	32	289	27	6	5	1	24	32	41	7	1	.229/.326/.308	.245	.269	0.9	SS(60): -2.4, 2B(18): 1.1	0.5
2014	BUF	AAA	33	129	12	11	1	0	9	8	17	1	1	.276/.320/.388	.253	.320	-0.3	SS(28): -0.8, 2B(13): 1.7	0.4
2014	TOR	MLB	33	274	31	7	1	0	17	22	49	1	0	.258/.327/.296	.240	.323	1.3	2B(64): 2.9, 3B(19): 2.0	0.9
2015	TOR	MLB	34	34	6	2	0	0	2	4	6	0	1	.214/.313/.286	.214	.273	0.1	2B(17): 1.0, 3B(3): -0.0	0.0
2015	BUF	AAA	34	227	18	8	0	0	8	24	32	8	4	.245/.332/.286	.258	.291	-1.4	2B(34): 0.8, SS(26): 2.9	0.9
2016	*TOR*	*MLB*	*35*	*250*	*23*	*9*	*2*	*1*	*18*	*22*	*43*	*4*	*2*	*.236/.310/.308*	*.225*	*.276*	*0.4*	*2B 2, SS -1*	*0.4*
2017	*TOR*	*MLB*	*36*	*101*	*10*	*3*	*1*	*0*	*7*	*9*	*18*	*1*	*1*	*.231/.305/.296*	*.220*	*.274*	*0.2*	*2B 1, SS 0*	*0.1*

Breakout: 0% Improve: 26% Collapse: 7% Attrition: 18% MLB: 72% *Comparables: Kazuo Matsui, Ramon Vazquez, Johnny Pesky*

Despite his TAv falling back into the abyss and his playing time almost completely evaporating in 2015, Kawasaki still managed to lead the team in HARP (Happiness Above Replacement Player). Whether it's his post-game interviews, his car commercials for Bob Bannerman Motors or his interpretative dance moves, the city of Toronto loves the utility infielder almost as much as he loves everything. However, the simple facts that he had more bunts than line drives and didn't play an inning at shortstop in 2015 highlight why he'll need all of his personality to keep finding jobs going forward.

Russell Martin C

Born: 2/15/83 Age: 33 Bats: R Throws: R Height: 5'10" Weight: 205

YEAR	TEAM	LVL	AGE	PA	R	2B	3B	HR	RBI	BB	K	SB	CS	AVG/OBP/SLG	TAv	BABIP	BRR	FRAA	WARP
2013	PIT	MLB	30	506	51	21	0	15	55	58	108	9	5	.226/.327/.377	.260	.266	0.4	C(120): 13.3, 3B(3): -0.3	3.7
2014	PIT	MLB	31	460	45	20	0	11	67	59	78	4	4	.290/.402/.430	.309	.336	-1.1	C(107): 20.9	6.6
2015	TOR	MLB	32	507	76	23	2	23	77	53	106	4	5	.240/.329/.458	.275	.262	-0.9	C(117): 13.9, 2B(2): -0.2	4.4
2016	*TOR*	*MLB*	*33*	*551*	*66*	*23*	*1*	*19*	*69*	*61*	*109*	*6*	*4*	*.238/.332/.411*	*.268*	*.266*	*-0.4*	*C 20*	*0.4*
2017	*TOR*	*MLB*	*34*	*480*	*61*	*19*	*1*	*15*	*56*	*50*	*97*	*4*	*3*	*.232/.324/.392*	*.260*	*.263*	*-0.1*	*C 17*	*0.1*

Breakout: 1% Improve: 23% Collapse: 1% Attrition: 7% MLB: 94% *Comparables: Gary Carter, Justin Morneau, Mike Sweeney*

YEAR	TEAM	P. COUNT	FRM RUNS	BLK RUNS	THRW RUNS	TOT RUNS
2013	PIT	16495	10.6	0.4	1.7	12.7
2014	PIT	14470	15.1	-0.1	2.4	17.5
2015	TOR	15667	11.6	-0.5	2.5	13.6
2016	*TOR*	*18439*	*15.7*	*-0.3*	*2.8*	*18.2*
2017	*TOR*	*16071*	*12.8*	*-0.3*	*2.3*	*14.9*

It was a successful homecoming (of sorts) for Martin in 2015, who nudged out the prior record-holder for most WARP recorded by a Canada-born player for the lone remaining team calling the Great White North home. When the tattooed one who now sits in second place was traded, a crying child became a YouTube sensation; Martin's tenure is sure to end with a misty-eyed salute from an entire stadium. Of course, the $75 million remaining on his contract means that reaction won't be warranted for quite some time. He continued to be a well-above-average framer and threw out baserunners at a career-high 44 percent clip, but he also showed up as the worst catcher in baseball at preventing wild pitches and passed balls via our new advanced catcher metrics. At the plate, Martin crushed left-handers to the tune of a .937 OPS with more walks than strikeouts, but his .306 on-base percentage without the platoon advantage was a far cry from the .363 mark he's put up over the last two seasons. His reputation for leadership and his demeanor on the field mean he'll continue to have perceived value (and maybe real value) even as his measurables give way to the all-consuming specter of age.

Max Pentecost C

Born: 3/10/93 Age: 23 Bats: R Throws: R Height: 6'2" Weight: 191

YEAR	TEAM	LVL	AGE	PA	R	2B	3B	HR	RBI	BB	K	SB	CS	AVG/OBP/SLG	TAv	BABIP	BRR	FRAA	WARP
2014	VAN	A-	21	87	15	2	3	0	9	2	18	2	1	.313/.322/.410	.265	.388	0.3	C(6): -0.1	0.3
2016	*TOR*	*MLB*	*23*	*250*	*19*	*9*	*1*	*4*	*22*	*10*	*71*	*1*	*1*	*.201/.238/.299*	*.190*	*.266*	*-0.2*	*C -0*	*-1.2*
2017	*TOR*	*MLB*	*24*	*276*	*26*	*11*	*1*	*5*	*25*	*12*	*77*	*1*	*1*	*.209/.247/.315*	*.202*	*.273*	*-0.3*	*C 0*	*-1.0*

Breakout: 0% Improve: 0% Collapse: 0% Attrition: 0% MLB: 0% *Comparables: Steve Pearce, Sean Halton, Darin Ruf*

YEAR	TEAM	P. COUNT	FRM RUNS	BLK RUNS	THRW RUNS	TOT RUNS
2016	*TOR*	*3354*	*0.0*	*0.0*	*0.0*	*0.0*
2017	*TOR*	*3708*	*0.0*	*0.0*	*0.0*	*0.0*

Pentecost wasn't passed over much, going 11th overall in 2014, but now he has a right shoulder that can't quite get right. He ended the season just as he started: on the sidelines, recovering from surgery. When healthy, he's an athletic catcher and a strong hitter, albeit with middling power, but if he returns with a diminished arm, he may no longer be a potential starter behind the plate and would need to max out on offense to avoid bustdom. His potential has the Jays seeing visions and dreaming dreams, though, and there's significant advantage to be gained if they can get him through his injuries so he bears his first fruits in Toronto.

Kevin Pillar CF

Born: 1/4/89 Age: 27 Bats: R Throws: R Height: 6'0" Weight: 205

YEAR	TEAM	LVL	AGE	PA	R	2B	3B	HR	RBI	BB	K	SB	CS	AVG/OBP/SLG	TAv	BABIP	BRR	FRAA	WARP
2013	BUF	AAA	24	218	30	19	4	4	27	12	39	8	5	.299/.341/.493	.294	.350	1.9	LF(21): 0.9, CF(20): -1.1	1.9
2013	TOR	MLB	24	110	11	4	0	3	13	4	29	0	1	.206/.250/.333	.219	.257	-1.7	LF(33): 1.1, RF(1): -0.1	-0.3
2013	NHP	AA	24	327	44	20	2	5	30	19	31	15	8	.313/.361/.441	.284	.336	1.3	CF(53): 7.9, LF(20): 1.1	2.9
2014	TOR	MLB	25	122	19	9	0	2	7	4	28	1	2	.267/.295/.397	.261	.333	-0.1	LF(30): -0.8, CF(16): 0.6	0.3
2014	BUF	AAA	25	434	57	39	3	10	59	21	48	27	6	.323/.359/.509	.296	.345	3.2	LF(47): 1.2, CF(31): -3.0	3.3
2015	TOR	MLB	26	628	76	31	2	12	56	28	85	25	4	.278/.314/.399	.257	.306	6.1	CF(142): 8.9, LF(14): 4.3	3.8
2016	*TOR*	*MLB*	*27*	*528*	*59*	*32*	*2*	*12*	*58*	*22*	*83*	*19*	*5*	*.276/.311/.420*	*.258*	*.307*	*1.7*	*CF 5, LF 0*	*2.6*
2017	*TOR*	*MLB*	*28*	*551*	*61*	*32*	*2*	*12*	*61*	*25*	*87*	*19*	*6*	*.273/.311/.413*	*.257*	*.305*	*2.4*	*CF 5, LF 0*	*2.7*

Breakout: 5% Improve: 37% Collapse: 8% Attrition: 19% MLB: 88% *Comparables: Jon Jay, Charlie Blackmon, Nate Schierholtz*

There's a certain profile we expect out of prospects who we throw the fourth-outfielder tag on, and Pillar has them all. Below-average power? Check. Strong instincts and makeup? Check. Can play center field in a pinch? Check. Of course, the profile blows up when the player shows Gold Glove–caliber defense in the majors. Even the Blue Jays, who drafted him in the 32nd round back in 2011 and have the most information on Pillar's skill set, only gave him 43 percent of his minor-league starts in center. With both the scouts and stats converging to grade Pillar's glove a true plus-plus, the question becomes: How long can he keep this up before he loses a step? He's 27 already, after all, and at the plate, he is exactly what he was expected to be: a high-contact, low-OBP hitter without much power. If he can maintain his range, he's an incredibly valuable controlled asset. If last year was the blip, it was a really fun blip.

Dalton Pompey LF

Born: 12/11/92 Age: 23 Bats: B Throws: R Height: 6'2" Weight: 195

YEAR	TEAM	LVL	AGE	PA	R	2B	3B	HR	RBI	BB	K	SB	CS	AVG/OBP/SLG	TAv	BABIP	BRR	FRAA	WARP
2013	LNS	A	20	511	68	22	9	6	40	63	106	38	10	.261/.358/.394	.266	.329	2.7	CF(102): -7.8, RF(6): -0.9	1.3
2014	TOR	MLB	21	43	5	1	2	1	4	4	12	1	0	.231/.302/.436	.257	.308	0.8	LF(9): -0.5, CF(5): -0.2	0.1
2014	BUF	AAA	21	56	15	5	0	0	5	3	10	6	0	.358/.393/.453	.300	.442	0.7	CF(11): -0.4	0.5
2014	NHP	AA	21	127	20	5	3	3	12	14	18	8	5	.295/.378/.473	.304	.330	2.3	CF(30): 0.5	1.3
2014	DUN	A+	21	317	49	12	6	6	34	35	56	29	2	.319/.397/.471	.306	.380	6.6	CF(70): 3.4	3.6
2015	NHP	AA	22	148	26	2	3	6	22	11	23	7	3	.351/.405/.545	.342	.387	2.0	CF(22): -1.5, LF(7): -0.5	1.8
2015	BUF	AAA	22	295	44	7	4	1	18	36	41	16	7	.285/.372/.356	.272	.332	2.1	CF(43): -3.2, LF(22): 1.3	1.2
2015	TOR	MLB	22	103	17	8	0	2	6	7	23	5	1	.223/.291/.372	.233	.275	-0.4	CF(21): 0.2, LF(6): 0.2	0.0
2016	*TOR*	*MLB*	*23*	*98*	*13*	*4*	*1*	*2*	*9*	*9*	*22*	*4*	*1*	*.252/.320/.389*	*.251*	*.310*	*0.4*	*CF -1*	*0.2*
2017	*TOR*	*MLB*	*24*	*408*	*46*	*16*	*4*	*8*	*42*	*36*	*95*	*18*	*6*	*.247/.317/.384*	*.249*	*.308*	*2.5*	*CF -4*	*0.8*

Breakout: 1% Improve: 28% Collapse: 3% Attrition: 12% MLB: 56% *Comparables: Ryan Kalish, Desmond Jennings, Dexter Fowler*

Another victory for backyard scouting (Pompey's high school is a 34-kilometer drive from Rogers Centre), the Blue Jays came into last season with high expectations for the well-regarded outfielder after he blew through the minors in 2014. They jettisoned those expectations after a rough eight-game stretch at the end of April in which Pompey got on base just twice (he was hitting .255/.339/.455 up to that point). Then Kevin Pillar ended up in center field, a million GIFs were birthed and the rest is history. Pompey will still play the entire 2016 season at the age of 23, and is still just as likely to be Toronto's center fielder of the future as anyone else in the organization, but he may need more seasoning in Buffalo. Maybe some Frank's RedHot?

Ben Revere CF

Born: 5/3/88 Age: 28 Bats: L Throws: R Height: 5'9" Weight: 170

YEAR	TEAM	LVL	AGE	PA	R	2B	3B	HR	RBI	BB	K	SB	CS	AVG/OBP/SLG	TAv	BABIP	BRR	FRAA	WARP
2013	PHI	MLB	25	336	37	9	3	0	17	16	36	22	8	.305/.338/.352	.250	.344	1.5	CF(87): 8.8	1.8
2014	PHI	MLB	26	626	71	13	7	2	28	13	49	49	8	.306/.325/.361	.261	.330	6.5	CF(141): -7.5	1.9
2015	TOR	MLB	27	246	35	9	1	1	19	13	28	7	2	.319/.354/.381	.268	.355	3.9	LF(56): -7.2, CF(1): -0.1	0.4
2015	PHI	MLB	27	388	49	13	6	1	26	19	36	24	5	.298/.334/.374	.268	.328	5.9	LF(56): 2.7, CF(42): -0.1	2.1
2016	*TOR*	*MLB*	*28*	*660*	*81*	*21*	*7*	*4*	*48*	*31*	*62*	*39*	*9*	*.292/.327/.370*	*.248*	*.313*	*5.6*	*LF -1, CF 0*	*1.7*
2017	*TOR*	*MLB*	*29*	*561*	*56*	*17*	*5*	*4*	*48*	*24*	*54*	*30*	*8*	*.283/.316/.356*	*.241*	*.304*	*5.6*	*LF -1, CF 0*	*1.1*

Breakout: 1% Improve: 48% Collapse: 2% Attrition: 11% MLB: 95% *Comparables: Juan Pierre, Shannon Stewart, Lew Ford*

The debate of the age-27 power breakout continues across baseball, and those who believe in the magic number can add Revere's 2015 season to the victory column, as his .071 ISO was 30 percent higher than his previous career high. Aside from the power surge (modest though it may be by anybody else's standards), Revere did exactly what you'd expect after his July trade to Toronto, as his batting average on groundballs and bunts jumped up on the artificial turf and he continued to play merely passable defense in left field. Revere's game is still "make contact first, ask questions later," and the 85 percent clip at which his plate appearances ended with a ball in play ranked behind only Daniel Murphy last season.

Michael Saunders RF

Born: 11/19/86 Age: 29 Bats: L Throws: R Height: 6'4" Weight: 225

YEAR	TEAM	LVL	AGE	PA	R	2B	3B	HR	RBI	BB	K	SB	CS	AVG/OBP/SLG	TAv	BABIP	BRR	FRAA	WARP
2013	SEA	MLB	26	468	59	23	3	12	46	54	118	13	5	.236/.323/.397	.281	.298	2.1	CF(78): -3.3, RF(34): -0.3	2.1
2014	TAC	AAA	27	71	11	3	1	1	9	16	15	0	0	.327/.479/.473	.372	.436	1.0	RF(10): -0.9	1.0
2014	SEA	MLB	27	263	38	11	3	8	34	26	59	4	5	.273/.341/.450	.318	.327	0.1	RF(68): -2.9, CF(12): -0.3	1.8
2015	TOR	MLB	28	36	2	0	0	0	3	5	10	0	0	.194/.306/.194	.210	.286	-0.7	RF(6): 1.4, LF(3): -0.4	-0.1
2015	DUN	A+	28	33	2	3	0	0	2	3	8	0	0	.233/.303/.333	.218	.318	-0.5	LF(4): -0.4, RF(2): -0.6	-0.2
2016	*TOR*	*MLB*	*29*	*130*	*16*	*6*	*1*	*4*	*14*	*14*	*32*	*3*	*1*	*.242/.323/.406*	*.261*	*.297*	*0.2*	*RF -1, LF -0*	*0.2*
2017	*TOR*	*MLB*	*30*	*179*	*22*	*8*	*1*	*5*	*21*	*19*	*45*	*3*	*2*	*.235/.317/.399*	*.256*	*.292*	*0.4*	*RF -1, LF -1*	*0.3*

Breakout: 4% Improve: 44% Collapse: 3% Attrition: 7% MLB: 94% *Comparables: Michael Cuddyer, Xavier Nady, Austin Kearns*

It turns out that irrigation systems care not for your park-neutral statistics. The British Columbia native ended up in the perfect situation—great home park, fantastic lineup, 70-grade Chinatown—last offseason after spending years in one of the worst. One sprinkler head, one knee surgery, one bone bruise and zero extra-base hits later, Saunders heads into 2016 again looking to prove that the vast dimensions of Safeco Field are the reason he was not a beloved household name and fantasy outfielder. However, as surprising as it may have sounded if we'd said this last year, he will have a very tough competition with the emergent Chris Colabello for a starting spot in his final year before free agency.

Justin Smoak 1B

Born: 12/5/86 Age: 29 Bats: B Throws: L Height: 6'4" Weight: 230

YEAR	TEAM	LVL	AGE	PA	R	2B	3B	HR	RBI	BB	K	SB	CS	AVG/OBP/SLG	TAv	BABIP	BRR	FRAA	WARP
2013	SEA	MLB	26	521	53	19	0	20	50	64	119	0	0	.238/.334/.412	.281	.278	-5.1	1B(125): -8.8	0.2
2013	TAC	AAA	26	22	2	2	0	0	1	0	5	0	0	.238/.273/.333	.266	.313	0.3	1B(3): -0.2	0.0
2014	SEA	MLB	27	276	28	13	0	7	30	24	66	0	1	.202/.275/.339	.235	.243	-0.4	1B(79): -3.3	-0.8
2014	TAC	AAA	27	249	29	13	0	7	40	33	41	0	2	.337/.422/.502	.353	.376	-0.9	1B(42): -1.8	2.6
2015	TOR	MLB	28	328	44	16	1	18	59	29	86	0	0	.226/.299/.470	.267	.254	-2.4	1B(110): 2.2	0.6
2016	*TOR*	*MLB*	*29*	*486*	*55*	*22*	*1*	*18*	*63*	*52*	*106*	*0*	*0*	*.237/.322/.416*	*.263*	*.272*	*-2.6*	*1B -5*	*0.1*
2017	*TOR*	*MLB*	*30*	*412*	*54*	*19*	*0*	*16*	*53*	*45*	*88*	*0*	*0*	*.243/.329/.426*	*.268*	*.277*	*-2.3*	*1B -4*	*0.3*

Breakout: 6% Improve: 45% Collapse: 7% Attrition: 7% MLB: 97% *Comparables: Mitch Moreland, Kevin Youkilis, Edwin Encarnacion*

If you could go back in time and tell the 2010 version of yourself that this former elite prospect would have the most valuable season of his career at 28 and that he'd be worth less than a win in said season, you'd get slapped. Twice. First by yourself for being an idiot, and then by Jack Zduriencik for making *him* look like an idiot. But it's tough sledding when you're a poor defensive first baseman who doesn't get on base, even if you come with above-average power. With just one season left until free agency, Smoak will likely open the season sharing time with Chris Colabello, who that 2010 version of yourself may have seen with the Worcester Tornadoes. High draft picks and former top prospects will always get chances, but Smoak's may be running out faster than he can swing at a breaking ball.

Rowdy Tellez 1B

Born: 3/16/95 Age: 21 Bats: L Throws: L Height: 6'4" Weight: 245

YEAR	TEAM	LVL	AGE	PA	R	2B	3B	HR	RBI	BB	K	SB	CS	AVG/OBP/SLG	TAv	BABIP	BRR	FRAA	WARP
2014	LNS	A	19	49	6	0	0	2	7	7	10	0	0	.357/.449/.500	.369	.433	0.3	1B(8): -0.1	0.7
2015	LNS	A	20	299	36	19	0	7	49	24	56	2	2	.296/.351/.444	.290	.346	-4.4	1B(50): 2.0	1.0
2015	DUN	A+	20	148	17	5	0	7	28	14	28	3	0	.275/.338/.473	.275	.293	0.6	1B(24): 0.6	0.5
2016	*TOR*	*MLB*	*21*	*250*	*25*	*10*	*1*	*8*	*30*	*17*	*65*	*0*	*0*	*.229/.280/.388*	*.235*	*.277*	*-0.4*	*1B 0*	*-0.3*
2017	*TOR*	*MLB*	*22*	*404*	*48*	*17*	*1*	*14*	*49*	*30*	*100*	*1*	*0*	*.241/.297/.403*	*.249*	*.290*	*-0.9*	*1B 0*	*0.1*

Breakout: 2% Improve: 5% Collapse: 0% Attrition: 3% MLB: 20% *Comparables: Chris Marrero, Anthony Rizzo, Matt Davidson*

If you're into sluggers with soft bodies (dibs on the band name), you need to be tracking Tellez. Saying he's a 30th-round pick from 2013 understates his status: He received the largest third-day bonus of any player under the current CBA ($850,000). The facts that Tellez is limited to and limited at first base do not preclude him from being among the Blue Jays' top prospects, as his hit tool projects as average at worst and his power is easily plus. Baseball history is littered with bat-only prospects who didn't measure up, but if Tellez continues to improve his in-game power, he may hit himself out of that fate.

Josh Thole C

Born: 10/28/86 Age: 29 Bats: L Throws: R Height: 6'1" Weight: 205

YEAR	TEAM	LVL	AGE	PA	R	2B	3B	HR	RBI	BB	K	SB	CS	AVG/OBP/SLG	TAv	BABIP	BRR	FRAA	WARP
2013	BUF	AAA	26	167	18	5	1	7	31	14	25	0	1	.322/.383/.510	.293	.345	-2.2	C(37): 0.8, 1B(1): 0.1	1.2
2013	TOR	MLB	26	135	11	3	1	1	8	12	25	0	0	.175/.256/.242	.190	.213	0.4	C(39): 0.2, 1B(2): -0.2	-0.3
2014	TOR	MLB	27	150	11	4	0	0	7	14	25	0	3	.248/.320/.278	.224	.306	-1.2	C(53): 0.5	0.0
2015	BUF	AAA	28	170	12	5	0	0	17	20	20	0	0	.228/.320/.262	.243	.264	-1.6	C(45): 9.6	1.3
2015	TOR	MLB	28	52	5	2	0	0	2	3	9	0	0	.204/.250/.245	.174	.250	0.1	C(18): 0.5	-0.2
2016	*TOR*	*MLB*	*29*	*91*	*9*	*4*	*0*	*1*	*8*	*8*	*14*	*0*	*0*	*.245/.313/.345*	*.235*	*.274*	*0.0*	*C 1*	*0.3*
2017	*TOR*	*MLB*	*30*	*131*	*14*	*5*	*0*	*2*	*12*	*11*	*20*	*0*	*0*	*.239/.304/.338*	*.231*	*.270*	*0.1*	*C 1*	*0.3*

Breakout: 7% Improve: 47% Collapse: 8% Attrition: 16% MLB: 95% *Comparables: Dioner Navarro, Tim McCarver, Jordan Pacheco*

Instead of teaching your kids to be left-handed, maybe you should teach them how to catch a knuckleball. Thole's OPS+ progression in his three seasons in Toronto has gone 38, 72, 38, which is both very bad and something that might give Sir Mix-A-Lot nightmares. Without the disguise of The Only Person Able To Properly Catch R.A. Dickey protecting him, the Illinois native would likely have been riding buses in one form or another last year. We're glad he didn't because then we wouldn't have this fun fact: He collected 40 percent of his base hits while facing an 0-2 count.

YEAR	TEAM	P. COUNT	FRM RUNS	BLK RUNS	THRW RUNS	TOT RUNS
2013	BUF	4934	1.3	0.3	-0.9	0.6
2013	TOR	4676	0.3	0.5	-0.1	0.8
2014	TOR	5839	0.7	0.1	-0.4	0.4
2015	BUF	5996	9.4	0.3	-0.2	9.6
2015	TOR	1983	0.4	0.2	-0.1	0.6
2016	*TOR*	*3474*	*1.1*	*0.2*	*-0.2*	*1.1*
2017	*TOR*	*5010*	*1.2*	*0.3*	*-0.3*	*1.2*

Devon Travis 2B

Born: 2/21/91 Age: 25 Bats: R Throws: R Height: 5'9" Weight: 190

YEAR	TEAM	LVL	AGE	PA	R	2B	3B	HR	RBI	BB	K	SB	CS	AVG/OBP/SLG	TAv	BABIP	BRR	FRAA	WARP
2013	LAK	A+	22	237	38	11	2	10	34	18	32	8	1	.350/.401/.561	.340	.371	2.4	2B(53): -5.5	2.5
2013	WMI	A	22	339	55	17	2	6	42	35	32	14	3	.352/.430/.486	.341	.375	3.3	2B(68): 9.3	5.2
2014	ERI	AA	23	441	68	20	7	10	52	37	60	16	5	.298/.358/.460	.276	.327	2.7	2B(95): 2.8, CF(3): -0.6	2.5
2015	TOR	MLB	24	238	38	18	0	8	35	18	43	3	1	.304/.361/.498	.307	.347	1.4	2B(62): -0.3	1.9
2015	BUF	AAA	24	38	5	1	0	0	0	6	9	1	0	.219/.342/.250	.236	.304	0.8	2B(5): -0.1	0.1
2016	*TOR*	*MLB*	*25*	*429*	*49*	*21*	*2*	*12*	*52*	*31*	*78*	*7*	*2*	*.271/.327/.429*	*.267*	*.307*	*1.3*	*2B 0*	*2.2*
2017	*TOR*	*MLB*	*26*	*510*	*62*	*25*	*3*	*14*	*61*	*38*	*92*	*8*	*3*	*.270/.327/.428*	*.267*	*.305*	*1.6*	*2B 0*	*2.7*

Breakout: 2% Improve: 23% Collapse: 16% Attrition: 35% MLB: 85% *Comparables: Johnny Giavotella, Jason Kipnis, Danny Richar*

Even with the star power in the Blue Jays' lineup, it was The Little Second Baseman Who Could who finished the 2015 season behind only Josh Donaldson in WARP per game. Travis' pop surprised even his biggest advocates from his prospect days, as his .194 isolated power ranked sixth among all keystoners, nestled between Stephen Drew and Andres Blanco. No, seriously. He didn't hit cheapies, either, as not one of his eight home runs was classified as "just enough" by ESPN's Home Run Tracker. The former Seminole will look to put his left-shoulder woes behind him in 2016, and he should start spring training without impediment after September exploratory surgery.

Troy Tulowitzki SS

Born: 10/10/84 Age: 31 Bats: R Throws: R Height: 6'3" Weight: 215

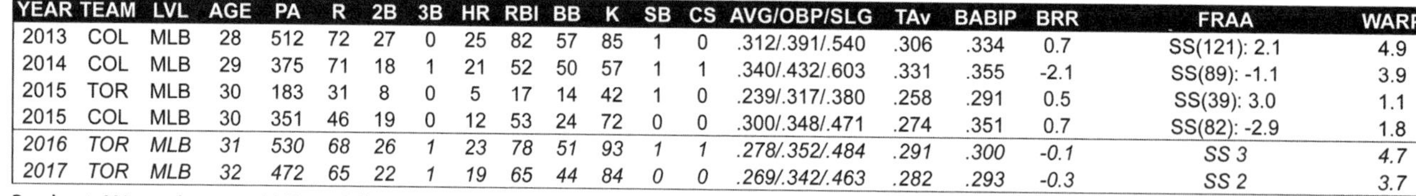

YEAR	TEAM	LVL	AGE	PA	R	2B	3B	HR	RBI	BB	K	SB	CS	AVG/OBP/SLG	TAv	BABIP	BRR	FRAA	WARP
2013	COL	MLB	28	512	72	27	0	25	82	57	85	1	0	.312/.391/.540	.306	.334	0.7	SS(121): 2.1	4.9
2014	COL	MLB	29	375	71	18	1	21	52	50	57	1	1	.340/.432/.603	.331	.355	-2.1	SS(89): -1.1	3.9
2015	TOR	MLB	30	183	31	8	0	5	17	14	42	1	0	.239/.317/.380	.258	.291	0.5	SS(39): 3.0	1.1
2015	COL	MLB	30	351	46	19	0	12	53	24	72	0	0	.300/.348/.471	.274	.351	0.7	SS(82): -2.9	1.8
2016	*TOR*	*MLB*	*31*	*530*	*68*	*26*	*1*	*23*	*78*	*51*	*93*	*1*	*1*	*.278/.352/.484*	*.291*	*.300*	*-0.1*	*SS 3*	*4.7*
2017	*TOR*	*MLB*	*32*	*472*	*65*	*22*	*1*	*19*	*65*	*44*	*84*	*0*	*0*	*.269/.342/.463*	*.282*	*.293*	*-0.3*	*SS 2*	*3.7*

Breakout: 0% Improve: 39% Collapse: 3% Attrition: 2% MLB: 98% *Comparables: Hanley Ramirez, Chase Utley, David Wright*

Those of you who had July 2015 in your Tulowitzki trading pool, please stand up and collect your prize. The first five months of the 2015 season flew in the face of what we were trained to believe, as the superstar-when-healthy shortstop was both healthy and only pretty good. A tough adjustment period in his first trip through the American League caused him to miss even his 10 percent PECOTA TAv projection. This was highlighted by a more aggressive approach (his swing rate of 46 percent was his highest since 2007) that pushed his walk rate to a career low and his strikeout and whiff rates through the roof. We'd be foolish to declare a precipitous decline for the player who might have been the most valuable in the National League just one season ago, and he's still just 31, but these are warning signs not to be ignored. Tulowitzki already had a tough road ahead of him to make a Hall of Fame case because players are rarely healthier in their 30s than in their 20s, but an earlier-than-expected performance decline will push it from challenging to impossible.

Richard Urena SS

Born: 2/26/96 Age: 20 Bats: B Throws: R Height: 6'1" Weight: 170

YEAR	TEAM	LVL	AGE	PA	R	2B	3B	HR	RBI	BB	K	SB	CS	AVG/OBP/SLG	TAv	BABIP	BRR	FRAA	WARP
2014	VAN	A-	18	37	3	2	1	0	5	3	5	1	0	.242/.297/.364	.261	.276	0.0	2B(5): -0.2, 3B(3): -0.9	0.0
2015	DUN	A+	19	128	9	3	1	1	8	3	26	3	1	.250/.268/.315	.228	.309	0.0	SS(30): -2.7	-0.2
2015	LNS	A	19	408	62	13	4	15	58	13	84	5	5	.266/.289/.438	.254	.299	1.9	SS(89): -9.7	0.6
2016	*TOR*	*MLB*	*20*	*250*	*26*	*9*	*1*	*8*	*26*	*5*	*68*	*1*	*1*	*.221/.238/.373*	*.213*	*.268*	*-0.2*	*SS -5, 2B -0*	*-0.6*
2017	*TOR*	*MLB*	*21*	*408*	*43*	*16*	*3*	*14*	*49*	*9*	*104*	*2*	*1*	*.231/.250/.393*	*.226*	*.274*	*-0.5*	*SS -8, 2B 0*	*-0.4*

Breakout: 0% Improve: 3% Collapse: 0% Attrition: 3% MLB: 5% *Comparables: Nick Franklin, Adam Jones, Chris Owings*

One of the top talents in the 2012 J2 class, Urena signed for $750,000, but remained overshadowed by Franklin Barreto, whom the Jays signed a day earlier. With Barreto in Oakland after last year's Josh Donaldson trade, though, Urena now checks in as Toronto's shortstop of the future because every organization is legally required to have one. At the plate, he is aggressive and generates surprising pop with his combination of bat speed and strong wrists. In the field, he has the arm and actions to stick at the six, with his range being the one big defensive question mark. Speaking of aggressive, the Blue Jays promoted him to the Florida State League in July, where he was the second-youngest hitter to appear in the league. (The youngest, Luis Espiritu, was only in the league for 10 days and batted just eight times.) Five-tool shortstops are enticing, but there is no shortage of roadblocks that could derail Urena from that future.

PITCHERS

Mark Buehrle LHP

Born: 3/23/79 Age: 37 Bats: L Throws: L Height: 6'2" Weight: 240

YEAR	TEAM	LVL	AGE	W	L	SV	G	GS	IP	H	HR	BB/9	K/9	GB%	BABIP	WHIP	ERA	FIP	DRA	WARP	CFIP	MPH
2013	TOR	MLB	34	12	10	0	33	33	203^{2}	223	24	2.3	6.1	48%	.305	1.35	4.15	4.13	4.11	2.0	106	86.8
2014	TOR	MLB	35	13	10	0	32	32	202	228	15	2.0	5.3	45%	.316	1.36	3.39	3.69	4.12	1.7	110	86.9
2015	TOR	MLB	36	15	8	0	32	32	198^{2}	214	22	1.5	4.1	48%	.285	1.24	3.81	4.23	4.68	0.8	118	86.5
2016	*TOR*	*MLB*	*37*	*10*	*9*	*0*	*27*	*27*	167^{1}	*187*	*21*	*2.0*	*4.6*	*47%*	*.292*	*1.34*	*4.58*	*4.62*	*4.70*	*0.8*	*110*	
2017	*TOR*	*MLB*	*38*	*7*	*7*	*0*	*18*	*18*	108^{2}	*125*	*13*	*2.0*	*4.8*	*47%*	*.302*	*1.38*	*4.67*	*4.46*	*4.79*	*0.5*	*112*	

Breakout: 8% Improve: 38% Collapse: 22% Attrition: 13% MLB: 85% *Comparables: Rick Reuschel, Derek Lowe, Bret Saberhagen*

Life can be cruel when you try to cut corners. Buehrle finished what should have been his final start of the year a mere two innings shy of a 15th consecutive 200-inning season. He could have settled, at that point, for joining Don Sutton, Phil Niekro, Gaylord Perry and Greg Maddux as the only post-expansion pitchers with 14, but he took the mound on the final day of the season, on one day's rest no less, in a last effort to crack 200. He was serenaded by misfortune and disappointment. Error, out, single, single, error, out, walk, homer, double, single, then a seat in the dugout to watch all those runners come around off Ryan Tepera. He got awfully comfortable on that seat too, as he was left off the playoff roster in both the Division and League Championship series. On the bright side, Buehrle cracked 88 mph with his fastball for the first time since the 2012 season. At press time, he was rumored to be deciding between the Cardinals and retirement. Better for our room of joke-writers if it had been the Padres, but alas.

Brett Cecil LHP

Born: 7/2/86 Age: 29 Bats: R Throws: L Height: 6'3" Weight: 220

YEAR	TEAM	LVL	AGE	W	L	SV	G	GS	IP	H	HR	BB/9	K/9	GB%	BABIP	WHIP	ERA	FIP	DRA	WARP	CFIP	MPH
2013	TOR	MLB	26	5	1	1	60	0	60^{2}	44	4	3.4	10.4	53%	.267	1.10	2.82	2.91	2.37	1.6	81	94.9
2014	TOR	MLB	27	2	3	5	66	0	53^{1}	46	2	4.6	12.8	55%	.344	1.37	2.70	2.37	2.94	1.0	75	95.4
2015	TOR	MLB	28	5	5	5	63	0	54^{1}	39	4	2.2	11.6	54%	.280	0.96	2.48	2.31	2.61	1.4	66	94.8
2016	*TOR*	*MLB*	*29*	*3*	*1*	*2*	*48*	*0*	51^{1}	*42*	*5*	*2.8*	*10.3*	*54%*	*.284*	*1.13*	*3.29*	*3.30*	*3.44*	*0.8*	*70*	
2017	*TOR*	*MLB*	*30*	*5*	*3*	*2*	*58*	*6*	81^{1}	*65*	*8*	*2.9*	*10.6*	*54%*	*.285*	*1.12*	*3.36*	*3.19*	*3.51*	*1.3*	*72*	

Breakout: 34% Improve: 60% Collapse: 12% Attrition: 13% MLB: 97% *Comparables: Adam Ottavino, Nick Masset, Aaron Heilman*

There were a lot of performances that fueled Toronto's charge from peripheral contender (they hovered around .500 for much of July) to division winner, but Cecil's looks most impressive. The consistently underrated southpaw was removed from the closer role after a June 21st implosion against the Orioles raised his ERA to 5.96 on the season. From that point on, The Goggled One went into Terminator mode, allowing no earned runs and just four walks while striking out 44 in 31 innings to close out the season. When Cecil tore his calf muscle in Game Two of the ALDS, his presence against left-handed batters was sorely missed, especially against the Royals. The key to his success continues to be a heavy reliance on his curveball, which is strong against right-handers and completely unfair against lefties. In his three years as a full-time reliever, Cecil has thrown that curve to same-side hitters 424 times and given up *two* extra-base hits, neither of them in 2015.

Jesse Chavez RHP

Born: 8/21/83 Age: 32 Bats: R Throws: R Height: 6'2" Weight: 160

YEAR	TEAM	LVL	AGE	W	L	SV	G	GS	IP	H	HR	BB/9	K/9	GB%	BABIP	WHIP	ERA	FIP	DRA	WARP	CFIP	MPH
2013	SAC	AAA	29	2	2	0	5	5	30	35	1	1.5	7.8	41%	.351	1.33	2.70	2.87	4.43	0.4	83	
2013	OAK	MLB	29	2	4	1	35	0	57^{1}	50	3	3.1	8.6	47%	.281	1.22	3.92	3.04	3.18	1.0	89	94.8
2014	OAK	MLB	30	8	8	0	32	21	146	142	17	3.0	8.4	43%	.302	1.31	3.45	3.92	4.35	0.7	95	93.6
2015	OAK	MLB	31	7	15	1	30	26	157	164	18	2.8	7.8	45%	.312	1.35	4.18	3.82	4.42	1.1	97	94.1
2016	*TOR*	*MLB*	*32*	*5*	*3*	*0*	*52*	*8*	94^{1}	*94*	*12*	*3.0*	*7.9*	*44%*	*.296*	*1.33*	*4.25*	*4.24*	*4.38*	*0.8*	*99*	
2017	*TOR*	*MLB*	*33*	*4*	*4*	*0*	*22*	*11*	*86*	*88*	*12*	*3.1*	*8.0*	*44%*	*.304*	*1.37*	*4.49*	*4.29*	*4.63*	*0.4*	*106*	

Breakout: 16% Improve: 46% Collapse: 18% Attrition: 9% MLB: 82% *Comparables: Tim Stauffer, Dustin McGowan, Carlos Torres*

Chavez, who is built like a quart carton of milk, has an expiration date of June 21st. His ERA over the last two years through then is 2.62 in 171 innings; opponents hit .237 against him. After that date his ERA is 5.41, with opponents adding 52 points of batting average and 125 points of slugging. He ended 2014 in the bullpen and last year on the disabled list thanks to a non-displaced fracture in his ribs on the right side. Nobody seems to know how the injury happened, but given that he had never worked more than 123 innings in any of his 11 seasons preceding 2014, maybe his body can't bear the burden of being a full-time starter. The Blue Jays presumably did not trade Liam Hendriks for Chavez just to put him in the bullpen, though.

Steve Delabar RHP

Born: 7/17/83 Age: 32 Bats: R Throws: R Height: 6'5" Weight: 220

YEAR	TEAM	LVL	AGE	W	L	SV	G	GS	IP	H	HR	BB/9	K/9	GB%	BABIP	WHIP	ERA	FIP	DRA	WARP	CFIP	MPH
2013	TOR	MLB	29	5	5	1	55	0	58^{2}	50	4	4.4	12.6	32%	.338	1.35	3.22	2.75	3.33	0.9	67	97.4
2014	BUF	AAA	30	2	2	1	24	0	28	21	3	5.8	12.2	33%	.295	1.39	2.89	4.29	4.28	0.2	90	
2014	TOR	MLB	30	3	0	0	30	0	25^{2}	19	3	6.7	7.4	37%	.235	1.48	4.91	5.61	4.41	0.0	120	95.7
2015	BUF	AAA	31	3	1	1	24	0	25^{1}	12	1	3.6	10.7	46%	.196	0.87	1.42	2.49	2.29	0.7	76	
2015	TOR	MLB	31	2	0	1	31	0	29^{1}	28	5	4.3	9.2	43%	.291	1.43	5.22	4.81	5.38	-0.2	101	96.0
2016	*TOR*	*MLB*	*32*	*2*	*1*	*0*	*48*	*0*	51^{1}	*46*	*7*	*4.0*	*9.2*	*39%*	*.284*	*1.33*	*4.26*	*4.41*	*4.40*	*0.2*	*98*	
2017	*TOR*	*MLB*	*33*	*2*	*1*	*1*	*46*	*0*	48^{1}	*45*	*6*	*4.2*	*9.2*	*39%*	*.293*	*1.39*	*4.51*	*4.32*	*4.66*	*0.0*	*105*	

Breakout: 17% Improve: 35% Collapse: 18% Attrition: 13% MLB: 66% *Comparables: Jason Bulger, Scott Dohmann, Matt Daley*

The former All-Star spent another season straddling the line between the majors and Triple-A, though fortunately they remained less than 100 miles apart in Delabar's case. The big right-hander has historically been able to ride an effective (and sometimes nasty) split-finger to a reverse split, but he struggled while spotting hitters the platoon split in 2015: While a .783 OPS against left-handed batters doesn't seem awful, it's nearly 150 points above his career mark and it's where he needs to make his money. Speaking of making his money, Delabar was eligible for arbitration for the first time this offseason, and he'll walk the fine line between bullpen depth and nontender candidate henceforth.

R.A. Dickey RHP

Born: 10/29/74 Age: 41 Bats: R Throws: R Height: 6'3" Weight: 215

YEAR	TEAM	LVL	AGE	W	L	SV	G	GS	IP	H	HR	BB/9	K/9	GB%	BABIP	WHIP	ERA	FIP	DRA	WARP	CFIP	MPH
2013	TOR	MLB	38	14	13	0	34	34	224^{2}	207	35	2.8	7.1	42%	.265	1.24	4.21	4.61	3.84	2.9	105	85.2
2014	TOR	MLB	39	14	13	0	34	34	215^{2}	191	26	3.1	7.2	45%	.263	1.23	3.71	4.35	3.80	2.6	109	84.7
2015	TOR	MLB	40	11	11	0	33	33	214^{1}	195	25	2.6	5.3	43%	.257	1.19	3.91	4.45	3.92	2.8	116	84.6
2016	*TOR*	*MLB*	*41*	*12*	*11*	*0*	*32*	*32*	201^{2}	*193*	*27*	*2.9*	*6.0*	*43%*	*.268*	*1.27*	*4.73*	*4.74*	*4.85*	*0.6*	*116*	
2017	*TOR*	*MLB*	*42*	*10*	*10*	*0*	*26*	*26*	*156*	*156*	*20*	*3.0*	*5.8*	*43%*	*.279*	*1.34*	*4.89*	*4.68*	*5.01*	*0.2*	*120*	

Breakout: 7% Improve: 53% Collapse: 13% Attrition: 5% MLB: 78% *Comparables: Tim Wakefield, Early Wynn, Phil Niekro*

The only more predictable correlation than economic growth to Presidential approval ratings is Dickey's ERA to his knuckleball velocity. Halfway through last season, the ageless and UCL-less one was sporting a 76 mph knuckler (a far cry from the 78 mph of his Cy Young season) and an ERA north of 5.00. Yet in his final 16 starts, the pitch jumped to 77 mph, his walk rate dropped by more than half and that ERA was a sparkling 2.78. Of course, nothing is both as easy and difficult as telling a pitcher, "Hey throw harder," but Dickey is very aware of the difference one or two ticks can have on his success. The 41-year-old is in the last year of his contract, but history has shown that age has little effect on his kind: Tim Wakefield maintained his late-career performance level through age 44, and Charlie Hough through 45.

Marco Estrada RHP

Born: 7/5/83 Age: 32 Bats: R Throws: R Height: 6'0" Weight: 200

YEAR	TEAM	LVL	AGE	W	L	SV	G	GS	IP	H	HR	BB/9	K/9	GB%	BABIP	WHIP	ERA	FIP	DRA	WARP	CFIP	MPH
2013	MIL	MLB	29	7	4	0	21	21	128	109	19	2.0	8.3	39%	.262	1.08	3.87	3.83	3.72	1.8	90	91.2
2014	MIL	MLB	30	7	6	0	39	18	150^2	137	29	2.6	7.6	34%	.257	1.20	4.36	4.85	4.70	0.0	110	91.1
2015	TOR	MLB	31	13	8	0	34	28	181	134	24	2.7	6.5	34%	.216	1.04	3.13	4.38	3.40	3.5	105	91.4
2016	*TOR*	*MLB*	*32*	*11*	*10*	*0*	*31*	*31*	*176^2*	*161*	*25*	*2.7*	*6.9*	*34%*	*.262*	*1.21*	*4.53*	*4.53*	*4.66*	*1.0*	*110*	
2017	*TOR*	*MLB*	*33*	*9*	*9*	*0*	*35*	*26*	*175*	*161*	*25*	*2.6*	*6.9*	*34%*	*.265*	*1.21*	*4.59*	*4.40*	*4.72*	*0.7*	*112*	

Breakout: 9% Improve: 46% Collapse: 28% Attrition: 8% MLB: 91% *Comparables: Ted Lilly, Freddy Garcia, Bert Blyleven*

With his highest walk rate since 2010 and his lowest strikeout rate ever, of course Estrada put together a career year that culminated in two playoff victories. It was great timing, as he more than doubled his prior career earnings with a two-year, $26 million contract in free agency off the efficacy of his changeup, though that figure surely would have been larger without the Blue Jays' qualifying offer hanging around his neck. Beyond his go-to pitch, Estrada scaled back on his curveball usage in favor of a cutter, which was certainly not the reason he found success. Sure, the cutter isn't designed to miss bats (which it didn't), but it's also supposed to induce weak contact (which it didn't). There are plenty of reasons not to get hung up on his shiny ERA in a tough division last year, but the biggest of all might be (and there's no way you realized this) that he's already 32. That next velocity drop could be his last.

Jeff Francis LHP

Born: 1/8/81 Age: 35 Bats: L Throws: L Height: 6'5" Weight: 220

YEAR	TEAM	LVL	AGE	W	L	SV	G	GS	IP	H	HR	BB/9	K/9	GB%	BABIP	WHIP	ERA	FIP	DRA	WARP	CFIP	MPH
2013	CSP	AAA	32	2	2	0	11	6	37^1	42	1	2.2	8.0	58%	.336	1.37	4.34	3.03	4.52	0.4	84	
2013	COL	MLB	32	3	5	0	23	12	70^1	89	12	3.1	8.1	48%	.344	1.61	6.27	4.51	4.95	-0.1	96	89.4
2014	OAK	MLB	33	0	1	1	9	0	13^1	11	1	2.0	6.8	46%	.250	1.05	6.07	3.53	3.40	0.2	98	90.6
2014	CIN	MLB	33	0	1	0	1	1	5	5	1	0.0	7.2	25%	.267	1.00	5.40	4.10	4.65	0.0	97	90.1
2014	NYA	MLB	33	1	0	0	2	0	1^2	2	1	0.0	5.4	50%	.200	1.20	5.40	9.76	6.27	0.0	117	90.3
2014	LOU	AAA	33	4	3	0	8	8	48^2	52	3	2.2	8.3	53%	.338	1.32	3.33	3.11	4.01	0.6	80	
2015	BUF	AAA	34	6	3	0	19	14	92	84	3	1.3	7.7	50%	.295	1.05	2.35	2.39	1.97	3.0	73	
2015	TOR	MLB	34	1	2	0	14	0	22	27	3	3.7	8.6	44%	.364	1.64	6.14	4.33	5.71	-0.3	100	89.7
2016	*TOR*	*MLB*	*35*	*5*	*5*	*0*	*26*	*14*	*88*	*93*	*11*	*2.6*	*7.4*	*47%*	*.308*	*1.35*	*4.14*	*4.16*	*4.28*	*0.9*	*96*	
2017	*TOR*	*MLB*	*36*	*7*	*7*	*1*	*34*	*21*	*142*	*156*	*17*	*2.6*	*7.8*	*47%*	*.322*	*1.38*	*4.14*	*3.95*	*4.28*	*1.2*	*95*	

Breakout: 12% Improve: 29% Collapse: 19% Attrition: 13% MLB: 77% *Comparables: Vicente Padilla, John Wasdin, Chris Jakubauskas*

It may have been a few years too late, but 2015 marked the first season that Francis appeared solely as a reliever in the major leagues. He hasn't been a league-average pitcher since 2007 and he's barely thrown 500 innings since undergoing shoulder surgery during the spring of 2009, so it's not such a shock that he got pounded last year, reliever or no. This failed Canadian homecoming is probably why the veteran retired in December.

J.A. Happ LHP

Born: 10/19/82 Age: 33 Bats: L Throws: L Height: 6'5" Weight: 205

YEAR	TEAM	LVL	AGE	W	L	SV	G	GS	IP	H	HR	BB/9	K/9	GB%	BABIP	WHIP	ERA	FIP	DRA	WARP	CFIP	MPH
2013	BUF	AAA	30	0	2	0	3	3	13^1	17	2	5.4	8.8	44%	.385	1.88	6.75	5.00	4.71	0.0	108	
2013	TOR	MLB	30	5	7	0	18	18	92^2	91	10	4.4	7.5	38%	.288	1.47	4.56	4.34	4.48	0.5	110	93.8
2014	TOR	MLB	31	11	11	0	30	26	158	160	22	2.9	7.6	42%	.297	1.34	4.22	4.29	4.55	0.5	104	95.1
2015	SEA	MLB	32	4	6	0	21	20	108^2	121	13	2.7	6.8	44%	.319	1.41	4.64	4.09	5.09	-0.1	106	94.6
2015	PIT	MLB	32	7	2	0	11	11	63^1	52	3	1.8	9.8	44%	.299	1.03	1.85	2.21	1.89	2.4	63	94.7
2016	*TOR*	*MLB*	*33*	*11*	*10*	*0*	*31*	*31*	*176^2*	*179*	*23*	*2.8*	*7.4*	*42%*	*.295*	*1.32*	*4.25*	*4.29*	*4.39*	*1.5*	*100*	
2017	*TOR*	*MLB*	*34*	*9*	*9*	*0*	*28*	*28*	*172^2*	*179*	*21*	*2.7*	*7.4*	*42%*	*.302*	*1.34*	*4.29*	*4.10*	*4.43*	*1.3*	*101*	

Breakout: 22% Improve: 54% Collapse: 14% Attrition: 10% MLB: 90% *Comparables: Randy Wolf, Luis Tiant, Jerry Koosman*

An afterthought of a deadline acquisition in Pittsburgh last year, Happ brought a 4.64 ERA with him from Seattle, a figure that was on pace to be his highest mark since 2012. The assumption at the time was that he'd fill in for a few weeks at the back of the rotation before moving aside when the games became important. Instead, Happ's relationship with the Pirates evolved like one ripped from a horrible rom-com: Weariness turned to wonderment, sourness to sweetness and so on, all while they were entrapped in a cockamamie story about how pitching coach Ray Searage turned a frog into a prince; it's a shocker Happ's final start didn't end with an embrace in the middle of a raging storm.

The problem with the narrative was that many of Happ's supposed revelations occurred *before* the trade. He had lowered his arm slot, closed his landing and altered his pitch selection before ever donning a Pirates uniform. The real difference between Happ as an M and Happ as a P was his increased willingness to pitch inside, a philosophy preached by Searage and embraced by the Pirates' statistical boffins, who pledge that pitching inside leads to better results. It sure did for Happ.

But what Happ's late-season dominance teaches us is not that Searage is a pitching genius (though he is) or that Happ is now a middle- instead of a back-of-the-rotation starter (though he'll get the chance to prove that in Toronto); rather, it's that we tend to oversimplify these ascents. Happ needed more than one tweak, more than one adjustment to enjoy his excellent stretch run, yet most of his hard work was overlooked in favor of the easy explanation. These players are human. They strive to be the best. Those hours spent perfecting their craft are often in vain—otherwise everyone would enjoy stretches like Happ's—but they count the same as ours do. We shouldn't forget that.

Jonathan Harris RHP

Born: 10/16/93 Age: 22 Bats: R Throws: R Height: 6'4" Weight: 175

YEAR	TEAM	LVL	AGE	W	L	SV	G	GS	IP	H	HR	BB/9	K/9	GB%	BABIP	WHIP	ERA	FIP	DRA	WARP	CFIP	MPH
2015	VAN	A-	21	0	5	0	12	11	36	48	1	5.2	8.0	43%	.388	1.92	6.75	4.02	5.74	-0.2	109	
2016	*TOR*	*MLB*	*22*	*2*	*3*	*0*	*8*	*8*	*31^{2}*	*37*	*5*	*5.4*	*5.3*	*34%*	*.304*	*1.79*	*6.14*	*5.99*	*6.23*	*-0.4*	*148*	
2017	*TOR*	*MLB*	*23*	*5*	*8*	*0*	*26*	*26*	*153^{2}*	*175*	*24*	*4.8*	*6.1*	*34%*	*.306*	*1.67*	*5.68*	*5.48*	*5.76*	*-0.7*	*138*	

Breakout: 0% Improve: 0% Collapse: 0% Attrition: 0% MLB: 0% *Comparables: Tyler Wagner, David Phelps, Tyler Cloyd*

When he's not playing a Doctor of Intergalactic Environmental Psychology on the boob tube, Harris is enjoying his role as the top pitching prospect in the Blue Jays' farm system. The 29th-overall pick in the 2015 draft out of Missouri State features a fastball that generates plus movement to match his plus velocity, making it difficult to elevate, and a bevy of other pitches that flash potential anywhere from average to plus. His slider and changeup show the most promise, but, especially compared to many high-end college arms, they still have a way to go in command and consistency. A mid-rotation future looks reachable, but don't expect him to move particularly quickly.

LaTroy Hawkins RHP

Born: 12/21/72 Age: 43 Bats: R Throws: R Height: 6'5" Weight: 220

YEAR	TEAM	LVL	AGE	W	L	SV	G	GS	IP	H	HR	BB/9	K/9	GB%	BABIP	WHIP	ERA	FIP	DRA	WARP	CFIP	MPH
2013	NYN	MLB	40	3	2	13	72	0	70^{2}	71	6	1.3	7.0	51%	.301	1.15	2.93	3.03	3.98	0.5	93	96.0
2014	COL	MLB	41	4	3	23	57	0	54^{1}	52	3	2.2	5.3	48%	.275	1.20	3.31	3.36	2.75	1.2	104	95.8
2015	TOR	MLB	42	1	0	1	18	0	16^{1}	22	1	1.7	7.7	54%	.382	1.53	2.76	2.74	5.58	-0.2	92	95.5
2015	COL	MLB	42	2	1	2	24	0	22^{1}	22	3	1.6	8.1	57%	.306	1.16	3.63	3.65	2.82	0.5	90	95.7
2016	*TOR*	*MLB*	*43*	*2*	*1*	*6*	*37*	*0*	*39^{1}*	*40*	*5*	*2.4*	*6.7*	*52%*	*.293*	*1.30*	*4.18*	*4.33*	*4.32*	*0.2*	*97*	
2017	*TOR*	*MLB*	*44*	*2*	*1*	*7*	*46*	*0*	*43^{2}*	*47*	*5*	*2.4*	*6.7*	*52%*	*.305*	*1.35*	*4.33*	*4.14*	*4.48*	*0.1*	*102*	

Breakout: 11% Improve: 14% Collapse: 21% Attrition: 20% MLB: 49% *Comparables: Doug Brocail, Mike Timlin, Darren Oliver*

To get a sense of how strange baseball will be without Hawkins, consider these three facts about his major-league debut. First, he gave up a home run to Harold Baines, and Baines would go on to hit 86 more dingers after that. Second, Hawkins recorded an out against Andy Van Slyke, which may or may not have been more impressive than the two outs he recorded against Scott Van Slyke in 2014. Finally, after Hawkins was battered around for seven runs in less than two innings, he was replaced by Rich Robertson. This is not the third interesting fact. That would be the pitcher who replaced Robertson, also making his major-league debut: Twins pitching saint Brad Radke, who fell off the Hall of Fame ballot in his first year of eligibility, 2012. In the end, Hawkins' Game Score of 13 in that first major-league start barely outpaced the 11 teams Hawkins would play for in his 21-year career.

Happy trails to the only pitcher to appear in every single edition of this Annual.

Drew Hutchison RHP

Born: 8/22/90 Age: 25 Bats: L Throws: R Height: 6'3" Weight: 195

YEAR	TEAM	LVL	AGE	W	L	SV	G	GS	IP	H	HR	BB/9	K/9	GB%	BABIP	WHIP	ERA	FIP	DRA	WARP	CFIP	MPH
2013	BUF	AAA	22	0	3	0	5	5	19	28	2	2.8	9.5	27%	.433	1.79	6.63	4.05	4.17	0.2	91	
2014	TOR	MLB	23	11	13	0	32	32	184^{2}	173	23	2.9	9.0	37%	.293	1.26	4.48	3.87	3.68	2.5	92	95.2
2015	TOR	MLB	24	13	5	0	30	28	150^{1}	179	22	2.6	7.7	40%	.343	1.48	5.57	4.39	5.80	-1.4	104	95.3
2016	*TOR*	*MLB*	*25*	*9*	*8*	*0*	*24*	*24*	*136^{2}*	*140*	*19*	*2.8*	*7.9*	*39%*	*.302*	*1.33*	*4.28*	*4.35*	*4.41*	*1.2*	*102*	
2017	*TOR*	*MLB*	*26*	*8*	*8*	*0*	*24*	*24*	*139^{2}*	*146*	*19*	*2.8*	*8.4*	*39%*	*.314*	*1.35*	*4.26*	*4.08*	*4.39*	*1.1*	*101*	

Breakout: 33% Improve: 66% Collapse: 16% Attrition: 6% MLB: 99% *Comparables: Ervin Santana, Brett Myers, Jake Peavy*

When your parents told you life wasn't fair, you blew them off for being jaded. You stared into the world developing in front of your own barely pubescent eyes knowing that the world was made for you if you did your part. You're not like those other Millennials, you said. That selfie stick makes you look ridiculous, you said. Yet the bus came three minutes early as you tried to get home from the shelter where you volunteer (looks great on the resume) and there was no service as you scrambled to figure out when the next one was coming. That extra hour of studying you did for the history midterm ended up being from the wrong chapter; you were supposed to be reading about the Panic of 1837. And despite the worst DRA in baseball among pitchers who threw at least 150 innings, Hutchison had as many wins as Matt Harvey, Chris Sale and Cole Hamels. You probably should have gotten that haircut.

Aaron Loup LHP

Born: 12/19/87 Age: 28 Bats: L Throws: L Height: 5'11" Weight: 205

YEAR	TEAM	LVL	AGE	W	L	SV	G	GS	IP	H	HR	BB/9	K/9	GB%	BABIP	WHIP	ERA	FIP	DRA	WARP	CFIP	MPH
2013	TOR	MLB	25	4	6	2	64	0	69^{1}	66	5	1.7	6.9	61%	.299	1.14	2.47	3.35	3.43	1.0	95	94.4
2014	TOR	MLB	26	4	4	4	71	0	68^{2}	50	4	3.9	7.3	56%	.246	1.17	3.15	3.86	2.74	1.5	104	95.0
2015	TOR	MLB	27	2	5	0	60	0	42^{1}	47	6	1.5	9.8	59%	.339	1.28	4.46	3.70	5.10	-0.2	88	96.1
2016	*TOR*	*MLB*	*28*	*3*	*1*	*0*	*58*	*0*	*61^{2}*	*60*	*7*	*2.7*	*7.7*	*58%*	*.291*	*1.27*	*4.13*	*4.07*	*4.27*	*0.4*	*95*	
2017	*TOR*	*MLB*	*29*	*3*	*1*	*2*	*62*	*0*	*60*	*57*	*7*	*2.9*	*8.2*	*58%*	*.295*	*1.28*	*4.02*	*3.85*	*4.16*	*0.4*	*92*	

Breakout: 27% Improve: 50% Collapse: 22% Attrition: 15% MLB: 87% *Comparables: Brandon League, Kevin Jepsen, Tony Pena*

The hard-throwing reliever is a great example of why you can't be blinded by strikeout-to-walk ratio, and why FIP should include hit-by-pitches. As a southpaw, Loup's job—more often than not—is to face and retire left-handed batters. For his career, he has allowed a .555 OPS to them. You'd think that posting 19 strikeouts against just one walk in 77 plate appearances with the platoon advantage would be an improvement on even that solid figure. However, he also hit *six* of those batters, which takes a big chunk out of that nifty ratio. The Louisiana native was arbitration-eligible for the first time this offseason, and should find himself back in his familiar (and best) role this year: second lefty in the bullpen.

Roberto Osuna RHP

Born: 2/7/95 Age: 21 Bats: R Throws: R Height: 6'2" Weight: 230

YEAR	TEAM	LVL	AGE	W	L	SV	G	GS	IP	H	HR	BB/9	K/9	GB%	BABIP	WHIP	ERA	FIP	DRA	WARP	CFIP	MPH
2013	LNS	A	18	3	5	0	10	10	42^{1}	39	6	2.3	10.8	51%	.311	1.18	5.53	3.69	4.10	0.6	83	
2014	DUN	A+	19	0	2	0	7	7	22	28	3	3.7	12.3	37%	.446	1.68	6.55	4.07	3.89	0.3	85	
2015	TOR	MLB	20	1	6	20	68	0	69^{2}	48	7	2.1	9.7	36%	.238	0.92	2.58	2.99	2.97	1.4	75	98.3
2016	*TOR*	*MLB*	*21*	*3*	*1*	*25*	*53*	*0*	*56^{2}*	*50*	*7*	*2.6*	*9.5*	*37%*	*.288*	*1.16*	*3.56*	*3.72*	*3.71*	*0.8*	*79*	
2017	*TOR*	*MLB*	*22*	*4*	*3*	*7*	*48*	*9*	*98^{1}*	*89*	*12*	*2.6*	*9.6*	*37%*	*.296*	*1.20*	*3.79*	*3.60*	*3.95*	*0.9*	*86*	

Breakout: 17% Improve: 25% Collapse: 6% Attrition: 13% MLB: 45% *Comparables: Clayton Kershaw, Noah Syndergaard, Shelby Miller*

We're accustomed to raising our eyebrows when a player is plucked from the minors without any experience above High-A. We did it with Rick Porcello and, most recently, Jose Fernandez. However, Osuna is special even among those special cases, as he only threw 64 innings in A-ball (compared to 125 for Porcello and 134 for Fernandez). He spent the entire regular season as the youngest player in the majors and rode his 96 mph fastball to the closer's role and a handful of Rookie of the Year votes. With two bat-missing secondary pitches, Osuna is a rarity in today's bullpen; in fact, he was one of only four relievers to have a 40 percent whiff rate on both a changeup and a breaking ball while throwing at least 100 of each. The Blue Jays now have the eternal "dominant reliever or unknown-quality starter?" dilemma on their hands. We know the difficulties of fighting inertia with pitchers (not to mention managers). The odds are extremely high that he'll get the one more save he needs to tie his uncle, Antonio, for the family saves title.

Sean Reid-Foley RHP

Born: 8/30/95 Age: 20 Bats: R Throws: R Height: 6'3" Weight: 220

YEAR	TEAM	LVL	AGE	W	L	SV	G	GS	IP	H	HR	BB/9	K/9	GB%	BABIP	WHIP	ERA	FIP	DRA	WARP	CFIP	MPH
2015	LNS	A	19	3	5	0	17	17	63^{1}	57	3	6.1	12.8	46%	.355	1.58	3.69	3.44	3.80	0.8	95	
2015	DUN	A+	19	1	5	0	8	8	32^{2}	25	1	6.6	9.6	45%	.279	1.50	5.23	3.81	5.26	-0.4	116	
2016	*TOR*	*MLB*	*20*	*4*	*5*	*0*	*18*	*18*	*68*	*64*	*8*	*6.1*	*8.8*	*40%*	*.299*	*1.62*	*4.85*	*4.96*	*4.91*	*0.2*	*115*	
2017	*TOR*	*MLB*	*21*	*6*	*8*	*0*	*28*	*28*	*168^{1}*	*151*	*17*	*6.0*	*9.7*	*40%*	*.300*	*1.56*	*4.65*	*4.47*	*4.71*	*0.5*	*111*	

Breakout: 1% Improve: 2% Collapse: 0% Attrition: 0% MLB: 2% *Comparables: Keyvius Sampson, Trevor Cahill, Trevor May*

Opinions on Reid-Foley's arm action map very well to opinions on whether he remains a starting pitcher. Opinions on whether his last name sounds more like a midsize Philadelphia accounting firm or a really bad pseudonym for Cactus Jack are also split, but don't map to anything. Teams scurried away in the 2014 draft despite Reid-Foley's top-notch stuff, but the Blue Jays have worked on cleaning up the delivery. Still, his inability to repeat his motion led to a walk rate that eclipsed 15 percent and a late-season demotion back to Low-A, where he had started the year. Reid-Foley should bring his mid-90s fastball back to the Florida State League this year in his quest to become just the second Guam-born player to make the majors.

Ben Rowen RHP

Born: 11/15/88 Age: 27 Bats: R Throws: R Height: 6'3" Weight: 195

YEAR	TEAM	LVL	AGE	W	L	SV	G	GS	IP	H	HR	BB/9	K/9	GB%	BABIP	WHIP	ERA	FIP	DRA	WARP	CFIP	MPH
2013	ROU	AAA	24	3	1	3	20	0	32	18	0	1.7	8.4	78%	.212	0.75	0.84	2.26	4.15	0.4	72	
2013	FRI	AA	24	3	0	10	31	0	33^{2}	23	1	2.9	7.5	67%	.253	1.01	0.53	2.76	4.08	0.2	94	
2014	TEX	MLB	25	0	0	0	8	0	8^{2}	10	0	4.2	7.3	61%	.357	1.62	4.15	2.93	3.28	0.1	100	81.4
2014	ROU	AAA	25	3	0	5	34	0	47	47	2	1.7	5.9	62%	.290	1.19	3.45	3.89	5.19	0.1	96	
2015	BOW	AA	26	2	0	1	20	0	27^{2}	24	1	1.0	5.9	63%	.284	0.98	2.28	2.87	3.55	0.3	92	
2015	BUF	AAA	26	0	1	1	14	0	18	12	0	1.0	5.5	74%	.226	0.78	2.00	2.60	2.97	0.3	89	
2016	*TOR*	*MLB*	*27*	*1*	*1*	*0*	*29*	*0*	*30^{2}*	*30*	*4*	*2.7*	*5.8*	*62%*	*.277*	*1.29*	*4.55*	*4.61*	*4.69*	*0.0*	*107*	
2017	*TOR*	*MLB*	*28*	*1*	*1*	*0*	*27*	*0*	*36^{1}*	*37*	*5*	*2.8*	*6.7*	*62%*	*.294*	*1.34*	*4.56*	*4.37*	*4.70*	*0.0*	*107*	

Breakout: 8% Improve: 20% Collapse: 22% Attrition: 29% MLB: 48% *Comparables: Blake Parker, Robbie Weinhardt, C.C. Lee*

Aside from being just about the last person on the planet you'd expect to have "Ramon" as a middle name (here's hypothesizing that he'd have more than one major-league stint if he used that instead of "Ben"), Rowen also failed to be as interesting as he could be by posting a 17 percent strikeout rate in the minors as a 26-year-old in 2015. If this was all you knew about him, you'd already be on the next comment, but the back of his baseball card won't tell you that he's a submariner who gets groundballs by the bushel. It also won't tell you that he's never thrown a pitch faster than 82 mph in the majors. He may not be a true knuckle-dragger like Chad Bradford, but Rowen is the type of player you should be praying gets extended time in the majors in 2016.

Aaron Sanchez RHP

Born: 7/1/92 Age: 23 Bats: R Throws: R Height: 6'4" Weight: 200

YEAR	TEAM	LVL	AGE	W	L	SV	G	GS	IP	H	HR	BB/9	K/9	GB%	BABIP	WHIP	ERA	FIP	DRA	WARP	CFIP	MPH
2013	DUN	A+	20	4	5	0	22	20	86^{1}	63	4	4.2	7.8	61%	.250	1.19	3.34	3.67	4.29	0.6	100	
2014	TOR	MLB	21	2	2	3	24	0	33	14	1	2.5	7.4	67%	.157	0.70	1.09	2.83	0.87	1.5	98	99.4
2014	BUF	AAA	21	0	3	0	8	6	34^{1}	36	4	4.5	7.1	62%	.317	1.54	4.19	4.87	4.76	0.1	108	
2014	NHP	AA	21	3	4	0	14	14	66	52	2	5.5	7.8	69%	.279	1.39	3.82	4.16	4.80	0.2	109	
2015	TOR	MLB	22	7	6	0	41	11	92^{1}	74	9	4.3	5.9	62%	.247	1.28	3.22	4.58	4.29	0.7	117	98.2
2016	*TOR*	*MLB*	*23*	*3*	*1*	*0*	*53*	*0*	*56^{2}*	*52*	*7*	*3.9*	*6.5*	*63%*	*.271*	*1.36*	*4.72*	*4.83*	*4.84*	*-0.1*	*114*	
2017	*TOR*	*MLB*	*24*	*4*	*5*	*0*	*31*	*14*	*104^{1}*	*101*	*12*	*4.0*	*7.2*	*63%*	*.290*	*1.41*	*4.69*	*4.50*	*4.81*	*0.2*	*113*	

Breakout: 24% Improve: 42% Collapse: 26% Attrition: 31% MLB: 76% *Comparables: Jaime Garcia, Vin Mazzaro, Aaron Poreda*

The hard-throwing right-hander set out in 2015 to finally put the starter/reliever debate to rest, yet here we are again. After two months of wildly outperforming his peripherals in the rotation, Sanchez returned to the bullpen after missing seven weeks with a right-lat strain and impressed yet again. His FIP of 3.10 throwing in short bursts was miles ahead of his 5.21 FIP in the rotation, which was not terribly surprising considering he threw some sort of fastball nearly 80 percent of the time. Even if the changeup never comes along—and it certainly didn't last year—Sanchez's curve is going to be what makes him a very important arm. Don't let his diminished usage of the hammer fool you; it's still an unfair weapon against right-handed batters, flashing the same easy plus grades it got back in his prospect days. In fact, righties swung at his curve 76 times in 2015 and got exactly two hits: a Caleb Joseph double (sure) and an Adonis Garcia single (obviously). He'll enter spring training with the goal and intent of throwing every fifth day, but his repertoire and bullpen success may again leave him on the outside looking in.

Bo Schultz RHP

Born: 9/25/85 Age: 30 Bats: R Throws: R Height: 6'3" Weight: 220

YEAR	TEAM	LVL	AGE	W	L	SV	G	GS	IP	H	HR	BB/9	K/9	GB%	BABIP	WHIP	ERA	FIP	DRA	WARP	CFIP	MPH
2013	RNO	AAA	27	0	2	0	17	0	19^{2}	29	4	3.2	10.5	48%	.431	1.83	5.49	5.10	4.86	0.0	93	
2013	MOB	AA	27	5	4	1	20	16	85	62	3	3.1	5.5	55%	.231	1.07	2.86	3.42	4.37	0.3	111	
2014	RNO	AAA	28	10	8	0	28	23	135^{1}	174	17	3.1	5.5	56%	.334	1.63	6.18	5.23	5.67	0.2	116	
2014	ARI	MLB	28	0	1	0	4	0	8	13	1	1.1	5.6	50%	.414	1.75	7.88	3.85	7.23	-0.3	103	98.1
2015	TOR	MLB	29	0	1	1	31	0	43	32	7	2.9	6.5	48%	.208	1.07	3.56	4.83	3.63	0.6	109	98.2
2015	BUF	AAA	29	2	1	7	16	0	21^{1}	15	1	3.0	7.6	47%	.246	1.03	1.69	3.06	3.31	0.3	90	
2016	*TOR*	*MLB*	*30*	*1*	*0*	*0*	*29*	*0*	*30^{2}*	*32*	*4*	*3.2*	*5.8*	*50%*	*.286*	*1.40*	*4.91*	*4.81*	*5.03*	*-0.1*	*118*	
2017	*TOR*	*MLB*	*31*	*2*	*2*	*0*	*23*	*5*	*53*	*59*	*8*	*3.3*	*6.0*	*50%*	*.301*	*1.49*	*5.17*	*4.97*	*5.30*	*-0.2*	*125*	

Breakout: 4% Improve: 10% Collapse: 0% Attrition: 8% MLB: 13% *Comparables: Justin Lehr, Jason Stanford, Tim Dillard*

This former Northwestern Wildcat appears to be a generic middle reliever with a big fastball, but he's got an even bigger story. He didn't go to college to play baseball, although he did walk on his freshman year; he went to become a sports journalist and interned for ESPN Radio, *Outdoor Life* and *Men's Journal*. He went undrafted after he started pitching during his junior year. He played in the Williamsburg Softball League for a bar called the Turkey's Nest. He's worked out with his younger and much more famous high school teammate, Clayton Kershaw. He tried to be a submariner for a couple of years. He was out of baseball in 2011. He started touching the high 90s in 2012 and that heater has given him the chance for a number of wordy internet writers to profile him and teach the story of one of baseball's most unlikely characters.

Marcus Stroman RHP

Born: 5/1/91 Age: 25 Bats: R Throws: R Height: 5'8" Weight: 180

YEAR	TEAM	LVL	AGE	W	L	SV	G	GS	IP	H	HR	BB/9	K/9	GB%	BABIP	WHIP	ERA	FIP	DRA	WARP	CFIP	MPH
2013	NHP	AA	22	9	5	0	20	20	111^{2}	99	13	2.2	10.4	46%	.301	1.13	3.30	3.33	3.72	1.9	71	
2014	TOR	MLB	23	11	6	1	26	20	130^{2}	125	7	1.9	7.6	55%	.306	1.17	3.65	2.87	3.28	2.4	92	95.9
2014	BUF	AAA	23	2	4	0	7	7	35^{2}	32	1	2.3	11.4	54%	.348	1.15	3.03	2.12	3.60	0.6	65	
2015	TOR	MLB	24	4	0	0	4	4	27	20	2	2.0	6.0	64%	.237	0.96	1.67	3.51	2.73	0.7	103	94.4
2016	*TOR*	*MLB*	*25*	*11*	*9*	*0*	*31*	*31*	*164^{1}*	*161*	*18*	*2.4*	*7.5*	*56%*	*.295*	*1.25*	*3.86*	*3.88*	*4.00*	*2.2*	*89*	
2017	*TOR*	*MLB*	*26*	*10*	*9*	*0*	*28*	*28*	*174^{2}*	*173*	*19*	*2.3*	*8.1*	*56%*	*.303*	*1.24*	*3.80*	*3.62*	*3.94*	*2.3*	*88*	

Breakout: 29% Improve: 55% Collapse: 23% Attrition: 16% MLB: 95% *Comparables: Sonny Gray, Daniel Hudson, Matt Harvey*

If you're one of #The6 people on Twitter who isn't familiar with Drake, you may think Stroman is responsible for Toronto's most recent nickname. No matter how it started, it ended up being appropriate for the diminutive hurler. Stroman was expected to miss the entire season after tearing his ACL during a bunt drill in March, yet only ended up missing #The6 months, returning in time to make four September starts. He continues to be one of the best modern examples of "tunneling," as his excellent release-point repeatability makes it extremely difficult for hitters to identify which of #The6 pitches Stroman throws is coming at them. Despite not returning with his best swing-and-miss stuff (as evidenced by #The6 strikeouts per nine), he relied heavily on his sinker to generate a very good groundball rate. The ability to use high-end movement to keep the ball on the ground is even more important for Stroman, given that he resides below #The6-foot-plus ideal for pitchers. The Long Island native and recent college graduate—he finished his degree at Duke last summer while rehabbing his knee injury—will front a suddenly deep rotation in #The6 this season.

Pat Venditte BHP

Born: 6/30/85 Age: 31 Bats: B Throws: B Height: 6'1" Weight: 180

YEAR	TEAM	LVL	AGE	W	L	SV	G	GS	IP	H	HR	BB/9	K/9	GB%	BABIP	WHIP	ERA	FIP	DRA	WARP	CFIP	MPH
2013	TRN	AA	28	1	2	0	8	0	11^1	13	1	2.4	10.3	30%	.375	1.41	3.97	2.97	4.17	0.1	86	
2014	SWB	AAA	29	2	5	0	26	2	56^1	54	4	2.7	8.5	32%	.305	1.26	3.36	3.36	4.15	0.5	86	
2014	TRN	AA	29	0	1	1	15	0	22	11	2	2.0	12.3	26%	.200	0.73	0.82	2.49	3.76	0.3	71	
2015	OAK	MLB	30	2	2	0	26	0	28^2	22	3	3.8	7.2	33%	.235	1.19	4.40	4.12	3.31	0.5	104	88.1
2015	NAS	AAA	30	1	0	0	23	1	40^2	27	2	3.3	8.9	36%	.234	1.03	1.55	3.53	4.06	0.5	90	
2016	*TOR*	*MLB*	*31*	*1*	*0*	*0*	*19*	*0*	20^2	*19*	*3*	*3.3*	*7.5*	*32%*	*.277*	*1.30*	*4.42*	*4.64*	*4.55*	*0.1*	*105*	
2017	*TOR*	*MLB*	*32*	*1*	*0*	*0*	*18*	*0*	27^2	*27*	*4*	*3.3*	*8.3*	*32%*	*.292*	*1.33*	*4.47*	*4.27*	*4.60*	*0.0*	*106*	

Breakout: 7% Improve: 17% Collapse: 10% Attrition: 14% MLB: 32% *Comparables: Dale Thayer, Rafael Martin, Jumbo Diaz*

It's easy to focus on the freakishness of an ambidextrous pitcher and forget that Venditte can pitch. As a May 12th *ESPN the Magazine* article noted, this is no novelty act for the switch-pitcher, who has been doing it since he was seven. His stuff isn't overpowering from either side, but it's good enough to get big-league hitters out, even if the peculiar nature of his talents kept him from getting a shot until just before his 30th birthday. He was far more effective working as a lefty in his debut, consistent with his minor-league track record. He'll need to solve righties at the highest level, and he'll never be a dominant late-innings guy, but Venditte is more than a curiosity and can add value to a bullpen with his versatility.

LINEOUTS

Hitters

NAME	POS	TEAM	LVL	AGE	PA	R	2B	3B	HR	RBI	BB	K	SB	CS	AVG/OBP/SLG	TAv	BABIP	BRR	FRAA	WARP
D.J. Davis	CF	LNS	A	20	554	77	19	7	7	59	39	119	21	10	.282/.340/.391	.259	.353	3.4	CF(75): -9.5, LF(31): -2.3	0.7
Matthew Dean	1B	DUN	A+	22	521	53	27	3	14	63	36	139	3	1	.253/.313/.410	.261	.328	-4.9	1B(79): -1.6, 3B(13): 1.5	0.2
Matt Dominguez	3B	CSP	AAA	25	287	37	21	1	6	30	15	37	0	0	.281/.324/.434	.249	.305	-3.6	3B(67): -1.2, 1B(2): -0.0	0.1
	3B	FRE	AAA	25	188	14	9	0	4	26	4	28	0	0	.251/.289/.371	.237	.276	-1.2	3B(38): 4.6, 1B(4): -0.5	0.4
Roemon Fields	CF	BUF	AAA	24	27	1	1	0	0	1	3	4	2	0	.217/.308/.261	.212	.263	-0.9	CF(4): 0.1, LF(2): 0.1	-0.1
	CF	DUN	A+	24	287	34	10	4	1	21	16	52	21	9	.269/.312/.348	.241	.330	0.8	CF(65): 8.8	1.4
	CF	NHP	AA	24	225	28	2	1	1	11	18	34	23	5	.257/.321/.292	.246	.305	3.0	CF(43): 0.4, LF(5): 1.7	0.9
Jake Fox	C	NHP	AA	32	122	15	10	0	5	19	12	27	1	0	.278/.361/.509	.306	.329	0.3	1B(4): -0.3, RF(1): -0.0	0.7
Caleb Gindl	OF	BUF	AAA	26	335	29	12	2	4	27	25	54	2	2	.228/.287/.319	.234	.263	-1.4	RF(34): 4.7, LF(32): 1.7	0.2
Matt Hague	1B	BUF	AAA	29	596	70	33	1	11	92	61	65	5	1	.338/.416/.468	.333	.370	0.7	1B(68): -6.8, 3B(62): -2.9	4.9
	1B	TOR	MLB	29	15	1	1	0	0	0	2	4	0	0	.250/.400/.333	.236	.375	0.1	1B(3): 0.2, 3B(1): 0.0	0.0
A.J. Jimenez	C	BUF	AAA	25	98	6	7	1	0	9	9	12	2	0	.218/.296/.322	.236	.250	0.1	C(23): 1.4	0.3
	C	NHP	AA	25	21	0	0	0	0	0	0	6	0	0	.095/.095/.095	.096	.133	0.0	C(4): -0.0	-0.3
Junior Lake	LF	BAL	MLB	25	22	2	3	0	0	0	0	9	0	0	.136/.136/.273	.167	.231	0.9	LF(4): -0.8, CF(2): -0.1	-0.2
	LF	CHN	MLB	25	62	2	4	0	1	5	4	20	4	0	.224/.274/.345	.225	.324	-0.5	RF(10): 0.0, LF(6): -0.4	-0.2
	LF	IOW	AAA	25	231	37	10	0	7	31	30	53	9	9	.315/.404/.472	.325	.396	-2.9	LF(31): 3.4, RF(14): 0.7	2.3
	LF	NOR	AAA	25	61	2	3	0	0	5	10	16	3	2	.300/.410/.360	.322	.429	-0.7	LF(15): -0.5	0.4
Mitch Nay	3B	DUN	A+	21	437	32	18	5	5	42	32	75	0	1	.243/.303/.353	.234	.282	-1.1	3B(100): -4.0	-0.4
Dwight Smith	OF	NHP	AA	22	512	74	26	2	7	44	47	64	4	3	.265/.335/.376	.257	.294	-0.3	LF(85): 3.8, RF(14): -0.7	1.3

No one ever said it would an easy developmental path for **D.J. Davis**, and his 2014 season bore that out, but his second year in the Midwest League showed signs of progress—particularly in his approach and willingness to lay off chase pitches—for the 80-grade runner. He even succeeded in more than half of his stolen-base attempts! ❖ If Blue Jays first-base prospects were Matryoshka dolls, **Matt Dean** would be the one that resides inside Rowdy Tellez; he's a step down in both physical size and ability to hit anything that wiggles. ❖ Getting released by the Brewers in 2015 seems like a pretty good way to sum up a lot of things for **Matt Dominguez**, but his glove and first-round pedigree will earn him more chances, and more Lineouts, in the future. ❖ Expectations are something that undrafted free agents rarely develop, but in his 18 months in the Blue Jays' system, **Roemon Fields** has done that with near-elite speed that allows him to wreak havoc on the basepaths and track down flyballs by the bushel in center field. ❖ He hit 10 home runs in spring training that one time, was the Atlantic League Player of the Year, and once hit a 387-foot dinger off Wade Davis, but **Jake Fox** will probably be remembered most for not being a catcher. ❖ After posting a .606 OPS in Triple-A as a 26-year-old, **Caleb Gindl** can take solace in the fact that no one can take the two home runs he hit off Bronson Arroyo away from him, even if it was back in 2013. He'd be in a pickle if someone put them on a high shelf, though. ❖ The first Buffalo Bison to ever win the International League MVP was Beauty McGowan in 1936, and he got 12 more major-league at-bats before he retired. **Matt Hague** got 11 after his 2015 MVP season, so let's start the internet campaign now. ❖ In each of the last two seasons, **A.J. Jimenez** has seen his OPS fall by around 100 points, and he was merely league average at his best. He's now facing a lifetime of being called "defense-minded." ❖ After nine seasons of pro ball, it's hard to believe that **Junior Lake** is still just 25, but that's how math and 16-year-old signees work. He might be toiling in the minors for another nine years if his secondary skills stay on their current plateau. ❖ The biggest problem with 2012 supplemental first-rounder **Mitch Nay**'s performance in the Florida State League is that he hit like a defensive specialist at the hot corner and played defense like an impact hitter. ❖ A high school teammate of Reds first-round pick Tyler Stephenson at Kennesaw Mountain High School in Georgia, **Reggie Pruitt** is a 24th-round draft pick in name only, as he received a $500,000 bonus. He's a plus-plus runner and his ability to cover Landis impressive, which could lead to plus defense in center (and has already led to a mind-bogglingly bad play on words). ❖ Dwight Smith played eight years in the big leagues and finished second in the NL in the Rookie of the Year voting in 1989. **Dwight Smith Jr.** played left field last year at Double-A, but not well enough not to devote this Lineout to his dad.

Pitchers

NAME	TEAM	LVL	AGE	W	L	SV	G	GS	IP	H	HR	BB/9	K/9	GB%	BABIP	WHIP	ERA	FIP	FRA	WARP	CFIP	MPH
Shane Dawson	LNS	A	21	12	4	0	19	17	101^{2}	95	7	2.1	8.7	47%	.318	1.17	3.01	3.19	2.62	2.8	82	
	DUN	A+	21	3	2	0	5	5	26	20	2	2.8	7.6	40%	.240	1.08	3.12	3.74	3.75	0.2	99	
Chad Girodo	DUN	A+	24	2	2	0	20	0	27^{1}	17	1	2.3	10.5	52%	.250	0.88	1.32	2.29	1.98	0.8	75	
	NHP	AA	24	2	0	2	21	0	29	26	0	0.6	7.1	58%	.306	0.97	0.62	1.89	2.72	0.6	80	
Conner Greene	LNS	A	20	7	3	0	14	14	67^{1}	75	4	2.5	8.7	38%	.364	1.40	3.88	3.22	3.37	1.3	91	
	NHP	AA	20	3	1	0	5	5	25	25	1	4.3	5.4	55%	.304	1.48	4.68	4.15	5.36	-0.2	115	
	DUN	A+	20	2	3	0	7	7	40	36	1	1.8	7.9	55%	.297	1.10	2.25	2.34	2.82	0.8	87	
Roberto Hernandez	HOU	MLB	34	3	5	0	20	11	84^{2}	90	9	2.8	4.5	52%	.290	1.37	4.36	4.45	5.23	-0.3	121	91.5
Clinton Hollon	VAN	A-	20	2	2	0	9	9	45^{1}	37	1	3.0	7.9	46%	.283	1.15	3.18	3.31	3.94	0.8	92	
	LNS	A	20	1	1	0	3	3	13^{1}	11	0	4.7	3.4	41%	.250	1.35	4.05	4.67	6.31	-0.2	120	
Chad Jenkins	BUF	AAA	27	8	6	1	41	11	93^{2}	98	5	2.5	5.8	46%	.299	1.32	2.98	3.47	4.07	0.5	99	
	TOR	MLB	27	0	0	0	2	0	3^{2}	3	1	7.4	4.9	33%	.182	1.64	4.91	8.01	6.57	-0.1	110	92.3
Ryan Tepera	BUF	AAA	27	3	1	3	21	0	34	16	1	3.4	9.8	56%	.190	0.85	1.06	2.51	2.39	0.8	78	
	TOR	MLB	27	0	2	1	32	0	33	23	8	1.6	6.0	47%	.169	0.88	3.27	5.74	3.90	0.3	109	97.4

A seventh-round pick out of Kennesaw State, **Travis Bergen** had an impressive yet abbreviated debut in the Northwest League, relying on his relatively advanced command rather than his more pedestrian raw stuff to strike out 11 of the 19 batters he faced. ❖ He may have been limited to just three games last year due to another elbow injury, but when healthy, **Ryan Borucki** features a plus fastball, a change that can flash the same and 70-grade love of Johnny Manziel. ❖ There has never been a player from Lethbridge College in the majors (even though 10 have been drafted), and **Shane Dawson** is both left-handed and upright, which gives him a fighting chance to make Kodi the Kodiak proud. Was that a dead giveaway that the school is in Alberta? ❖ Two years after being a ninth-round senior sign, **Chad Girodo** held southpaws to a .266 OPS across three levels (including a September stop in Triple-A) with a fastball that barely cracked 90 and a sweeping slurve that is very tough to pick up out of his sidearm motion. ❖ At 20 years old, **Conner Greene** raced through three levels of the minors in 2015 on the strength of his fastball, spending the final month in Double-A. He's also a model and actor who guest-starred in the Charlie Sheen sitcom *Anger Management*, so he's probably received more medical advice from Jenny McCarthy than you have. ❖ What can be said about **Roberto Hernandez** that hasn't already been angrily yelled at televisions by Houston dads in 2015? He drew a walk as a batter in 2015, so we'll go with that. ❖ Tommy John surgery and a 50-game suspension for amphetamines have made the first three seasons of **Clinton Hollon**'s professional career *interesting*, but this isn't quite what the Blue Jays had in mind when they selected him 47th overall in 2013. ❖ Even a career 3.31 ERA in a tough home park and a tough division wasn't enough to get **Chad Jenkins** more than two appearances with the Blue Jays in 2015. Maybe he should try striking out more than a batter every other inning, or going by his given name, Chadwick. ❖ A star high school quarterback turned 2015 draft pop-up prospect, **Justin Maese** went 5-0 with a 1.01 ERA in the Gulf Coast League last summer, and he was born on the same day the Braves played their last game in Fulton County Stadium. ❖ It often takes a long time for pitchers as tall as 6-foot-8 **Matt Smoral** to get their limbs under control and throw strikes consistently. The hourglass sand will run especially quickly for the southpaw if he continues to average barely 30 innings per season. ❖ Longing to become the best pitcher out of Sam Houston State since Steve Sparks, **Ryan Tepera** was the most unknown of all the pitchers who appeared in the playoffs, only surfacing as part of the unsteady bridge to Cliff Pennington in the Blue Jays' lopsided ALCS Game Four loss.

MANAGER

John Gibbons

YEAR	TEAM	W	L	Pythag +/-	Avg PC	100+ P	120+ P	QS	BQS	REL	REL w Zero R	IBB	PH	PH Avg	PH HR	SB2	CS2	SB3	CS3	SAC Att	SAC%	POS SAC	Squeeze	Swing	In Play
2013	TOR	74	88	-2	92.3	56	1	67	6	487	391	33	102	.220	3	87	38	25	3	44	65.9	26	0	353	99
2014	TOR	83	79	-2	96.6	68	4	86	7	449	367	23	176	.220	9	64	16	14	5	61	57.4	34	1	309	102
2015	TOR	93	69	-10	92.8	58	1	84	5	469	384	20	88	.225	3	70	18	17	4	51	70.6	34	1	281	77

Tough luck has been the theme throughout Gibbons' managerial career. In his first go with the Blue Jays, he led his teams to 80-, 87- and 83-win seasons before getting fired after a 35-39 start to his fourth full year. Rough. Gibbons returned to the helm five years later, and continued to experience disappointments. The Blue Jays entered the 2013 season with all kind of high expectations—they'd acquired Jose Reyes, R.A. Dickey, Josh Johnson and Mark Buehrle—and finished with 74 wins. The 83-win follow-up in 2014 didn't do much for anyone either, leaving Gibbons' long-term future in doubt.

The way 2015 started, you would have thought Gibbons would be on his way out by fall. The Blue Jays rolled into the All-Star break with a 45-46 record and a 4 1/2-game deficit in the standings. Toronto then acquired Troy Tulowitzki, David Price and various others, setting up a second-half run for the ages. The Blue Jays won 11 consecutive games to welcome in August, and would go 48-23 in the second half—outscoring their opponents by nearly 150 runs, or three-plus per victory.

As easy as it would be to credit Toronto's stars for all the winning, Gibbons played a role as well. He batted Josh Donaldson second all year, toyed with Tulowitzki in the leadoff spot and successfully ran platoons at other positions. He also deserves credit for how he incorporated and trusted young players. The Blue Jays broke camp with a majors-leading six rookies on their roster, and two of them eventually played crucial roles in the bullpen. Not every manager would willingly insert a 20-year-old as closer, no matter how uncowed the guy seemed. Gibbons did—and then used him unflinchingly.

Alas, Gibbons' Blue Jays came up short in the playoffs, losing the American League Championship Series in six games to the Royals. Still, odd usage of Price aside, Gibbons finished the postseason on a high note. Lest anyone forget, he sent Roberto Osuna to the mound with the game tied in the eighth inning. In a league where most managers refuse to call upon their closers in the *ninth* inning of a tied game, Gibbons showed no fear—and, as if nature wanted to keep him in line, he lost because of it. Don't feel too bad for Gibbons though. He seemed to enjoy the journey. During the in-game interview phase of an elimination game, Gibbons joked that Dioner Navarro is "hard to score on a home run."

WASHINGTON NATIONALS

Essay by Chelsea Janes

Player comments by Dan Rozenson and BP authors

On the late-February day when the 2015 Washington Nationals first convened in full, the reigning National League Manager of the Year tacked a color-coded chart to the bulletin board in the back of the Space Coast Stadium clubhouse. The chart outlined the day's activities, his daily ordinance for regimen, a testament to the disciplined approach Matt Williams preached through 96 wins a year before: Trust the process. Control what you can. Look to tomorrow, and do it all again.

But the quote of the day that glared from the top of the page that day deviated from those principles, eschewed such determined short-sightedness.

"The road to the World Series begins here," it read. The expectations for these Washington Nationals were officially decreed, unavoidable now, irrevocable once chiseled in the cork.

Those expectations—that this team could bring D.C. its first World Series title since 1924—had hovered unspoken for some time.

They originated in that 96-win 2014 team, which was bumped by the eventual World Series champions in the National League Division Series. All five members of that starting rotation, the best statistical starting rotation in baseball, would be back in 2015.

They were solidified on a chilly winter Sunday on which the Nationals scooped up a former Cy Young Award winner with a record $210 million contract—evidence that Washington's traditionally conservative-spending owners wanted more.

They became impossible to ignore the day before Williams tacked them up, when Bryce Harper uttered a phrase that would be used against him when things fell apart. What did he think when Max Scherzer signed with the Nationals?

"Where's my ring?" Harper laughed. He had just reported to spring training for what would become one of the most prolific offensive seasons in baseball history—one that still wouldn't be enough to earn the jewelry he was looking for, or even a playoff berth.

Though no one articulated as much quite so boldly, nearly everyone who examined Washington's roster shared the 22-year-old's optimism. Vegas rated the Nationals as the favorites to win the Word Series. Experts

NATIONALS PROSPECTUS

2015 W-L: 83-79, 2ND IN NL EAST

Pythag	.546	10th	DER	.700	20th
RS/G	4.34	10th	B-Age	28.3	14th
RA/G	3.92	8th	P-Age	28.5	19th
TAv	.268	5th	Salary	$162M	6th
BRR	7.07	6th	M$/MW	$4.3M	10th
TAv-P	.253	8th	DL Days	1452	27th
FIP	3.48	4th	$ on DL	20%	21st

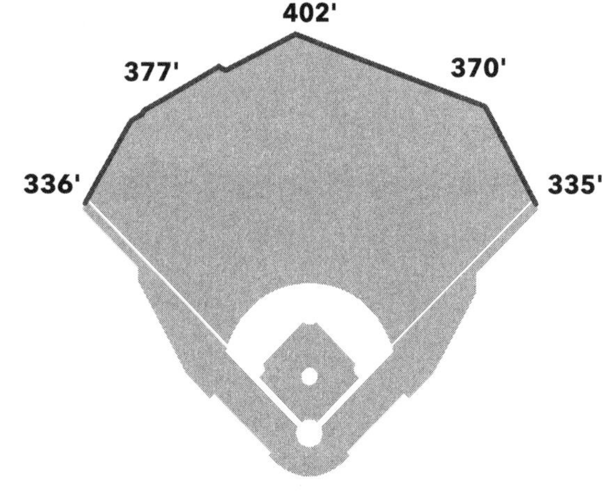

Outfield wall profile: **8'** to **14'**

Three-Year Park Factors

Runs	Runs/RH	Runs/LH	HR/RH	HR/LH
97	102	108	109	117

Top Hitter WARP	11.2	Bryce Harper
Top Pitcher WARP	6.2	Max Scherzer
Top Prospect	Lucas Giolito	

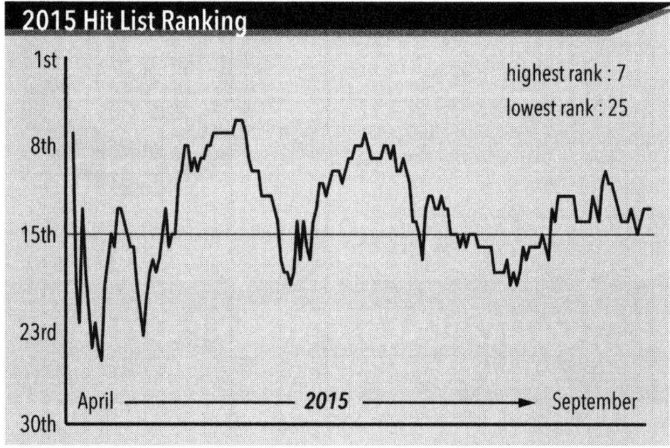

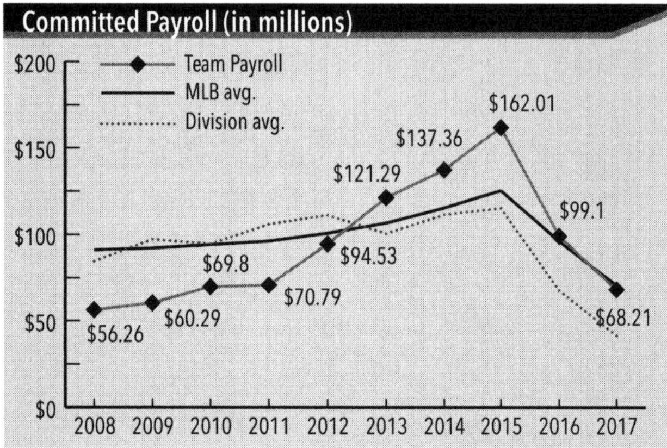

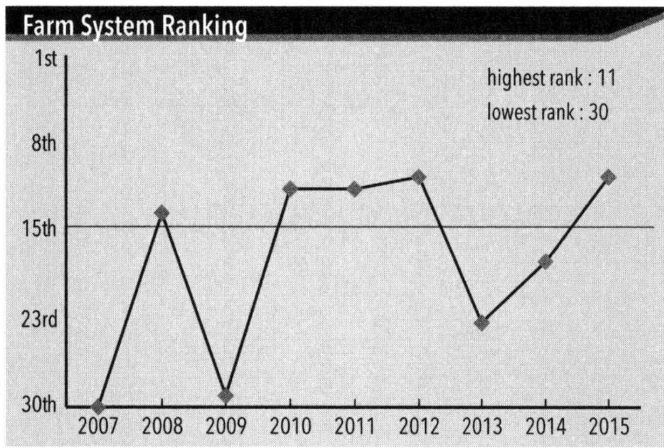

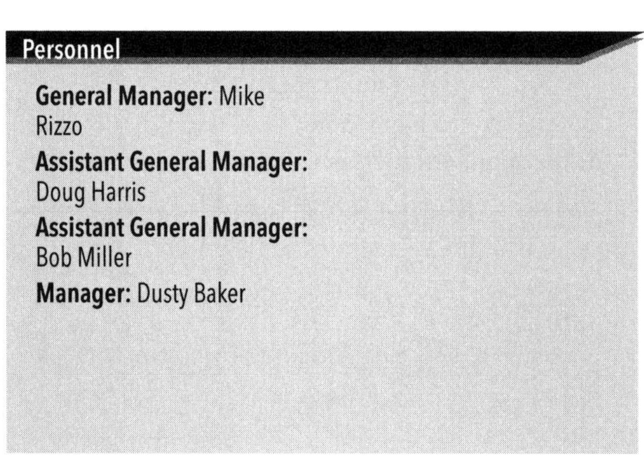
Personnel

General Manager: Mike Rizzo

Assistant General Manager: Doug Harris

Assistant General Manager: Bob Miller

Manager: Dusty Baker

from media outlets paraded them as a safe bet. Stoic Jordan Zimmermann, one of four key figures and two homegrown stars nearly certain to depart after the season, said in spring training that if this Nationals core were ever going to win a World Series, this would be the year.

Those expectations seem foolishly optimistic now, desecrated by the failures that followed. Not only did the Nationals not meet expectations, they did not even threaten them. Then they imploded.

Built to win, but not built to last

No teams play without cracks in the foundation. Over the course of 162 games, the teams that patch them, fill them—or at least keep them from growing—last deep into October. At some point, all but one team is undone in the end, whether by a sliver of ineptitude or gaping instabilities. (Even the Mets, who charged through October with an overachieving second baseman and the hardest throwing group of young starters many can remember, were undone by the Royals' relentless contact and pesky speed.)

As the Nationals embarked on that title-bound path Williams foresaw, two questions needed answering: One, was the bullpen good enough to win meaningful games late and playoff games later? Two, would an injury-prone roster stay healthy?

Begin with the latter, because most of the initial expectations came with a caveat that resembled a hypothesis. If the Nationals can stay healthy, then few teams could beat them. They did not stay healthy.

Stephen Strasburg sprained his ankle during conditioning drills. He tried to pitch through the pain, compensated subconsciously, and back trouble followed. He landed on the disabled list twice, not right until August, just in time to give the Nationals two months of sparkling Strasburg gems that reminded them what could have been.

Jayson Werth had shoulder surgery in January, too late to be ready for spring training, or even Opening Day. He returned, then was hit by a pitch on his beleaguered left wrist a few months later. A career .270 hitter, Werth played 88 games and hit .221.

Denard Span had core surgery a few days after the spring training opener, rushed back, hit the disabled list. He ended up in surgery again. Third baseman Anthony Rendon sprained the MCL in his left knee in early March. He missed the start of the regular season, and was never the same again. Ryan Zimmerman played through plantar fasciitis until he couldn't, returned to form by August, then pulled his oblique in early September. He never played again.

The expectations were built around a lineup with Span and Rendon at the top, Werth and Zimmerman in the middle. The lineup the Nationals built their hopes on—some combination of Span, Rendon, Werth, Harper, Zimmerman, Ian Desmond, Wilson Ramos, and Yunel Escobar—materialized twice, for two days in late August.

But thanks to a combination of superstars and

substitutes, the Nationals lurched through a 6-13 start and lunged their way into first place in the National League East by the time Rendon, Werth and Zimmerman returned after the All-Star break.

Meanwhile, Harper and Scherzer made history. Scherzer compiled one of the most dominant stretches any starter has in decades as he won National League Pitcher of the Month in May and June. In one two-start stretch, he allowed one bloop hit and one hit batsman, struck out 16, then threw a no-hitter. He carried a no-hitter into the fifth in his next start. Scherzer would struggle in the second half before steadying in August, but he was brilliant when no one else in the rotation could be, so the Nationals survived.

As Scherzer carried the rotation, Harper shouldered the lineup and the burden of his expansive expectations. He compiled a Herculean offensive season in which he showed an older hitter's patience as he capitalized on the few pitches he saw in the zone. During one May stretch he hit six home runs in three games, one of them a walk-off winner. Once, he went a whole game without swinging at a single pitch. By season's end he had the highest OPS a 22-year-old has had since Ted Williams in 1941. He contended for the batting title until the last day of the season. He hit 42 home runs, hit .330, and drove in 99 runs. When the rest of the lineup sputtered around him, Harper kept pushing the Nationals offense along.

Deadline decisions

So, at first, the Nationals overcame injuries, the unfathomable first-half offensive struggles of stalwart shortstop Ian Desmond, and limited production from offense-first catcher Wilson Ramos. They clung to first until the regulars returned, just before the trade deadline. At that time, General Manager Mike Rizzo and the Nationals stayed patient. They had four All-Star-caliber players—Span, Rendon, Werth and Zimmerman—rejoining them. Add an arm or two to the bullpen, and voila! World Series contenders once more, in spite of it all.

So instead of gutting his arsenal of top prospects to land an elite reliever like Craig Kimbrel or Aroldis Chapman, Rizzo chose then-Phillies All-Star closer Jonathan Papelbon, who came with more baggage, but at a lower price.

At first, on paper, Papelbon gave the Nationals a one-two punch in the back of the bullpen with Drew Storen. Storen had 21 saves at the time, and was a legitimate All-Star candidate in the midst of his best season ever. Storen—a homegrown National, too—was not happy about the move to set-up, but seemed determined to take it out on his opposition, striking out nearly every hitter he faced in the aftermath of the switch.

Would hothead Papelbon disrupt Storen and team chemistry? Or would he be the edge, the World Series tested enforcer the polite and professional Nationals needed? The bullpen struggled all season. If he could get outs, most figured, he would be better than the late-inning alternatives.

With Papelbon in the mix, the Nationals arrived at Citi Field for a series with the Mets on trade deadline day. Externally, confidence was waning in the Mets front office, the consensus being that it would not make the moves necessary to push the Nationals in this unanticipated division race after a megadeal fell apart with to embarrassing effect: A young shortstop was left crying on the edge of the infield about a flight to Milwaukee he never had to take.

At about 2:30 p.m. on Friday, July 31, the Nationals had a three-game lead in the division. They had just acquired Papelbon. The Mets had made small moves, but not the big one most thought they needed to make this a race. Advantage, Nationals.

By midnight that Friday night, the Mets had made the season-altering acquisition of Yoenis Cespedes. The difference atop the division was down to two games, because that once-teary shortstop hit a walk-off home run. Two days later, the division was tied. Citi Field, Queens, and the city woke up. The Mets soon took over, and never let go.

After that weekend, the Nationals' road wound away from the World Series and toward the quicksand of doubt and distrust failure always seems to stir.

Williams did not use Storen or Papelbon in those three games, losing the first two with less established relievers in the game. As it happened, Storen was unavailable to pitch one of those nights, though Williams did not admit that fact to evidence until later, when the court of public opinion had already decided against him. From then on, every decision he made earned doubt, and nearly all of them seemed to backfire, because pitchers young and old struggled to get the ball to Storen and Papelbon, who eventually began to struggle themselves.

The bullpen falls apart

After that series, almost fully healthy, the Nationals did not take off in August. They headed toward another pivot-point series with the Mets in early September within striking distance, still able to salvage things after all. In those three games, they carried leads into the sixth inning or later in all three. They lost all three. In one, the Nationals watched a six-run lead succumb to the collective wildness of their middle relief corps, then watched Storen and Papelbon concede it late. In another, they watched Stephen Strasburg work seven brilliant innings, only to allow a game-tying home run late. That day, Storen allowed a go-ahead run to Cespedes, after which he slammed the door to the cubby atop his locker in frustration. It bounced back against his thumb, which broke, and ended his season in the process.

The crack in the foundation that had loomed there

from the start—the one the Nationals never patched successfully and therefore allowed to settle and expand—doomed them. The Nationals' bullpen gave way. The veterans Rizzo brought in did not succeed. The young pitchers he trusted got hurt or faltered.

So August and September fell away, missed opportunity after missed opportunity, with no visible urgency from the Nationals. Williams stuck to stoicism so determinedly he grew robotic.

"All we can do is look to tomorrow," he would say. True, and with the mindset unchanged, most tomorrows went the way of yesterdays. Expectations burned out as summer turned to autumn, and from the ashes rose rumblings of a clubhouse no longer loyal to its manager, of a manager out of touch with his frustrated team.

Dysfunction funneled to a few moments on the final home Sunday of the season—a subdued fan appreciation day most thought would be a playoff sendoff, not a shuttering up for winter.

On that day, Desmond walked off the field at Nationals Park to a standing ovation from the fans who knew their longest-tenured star would likely not play for them again. Naturally, in a season so filled with complication, a touching moment was followed by painful one.

After Harper did not run out a pop up at top speed, Papelbon put his hands around the neck of the best young talent in the league. Williams let him return to the mound the next inning, but did not let Harper return. He admitted later he did not know the extent of the trouble, though his coaches had been intricately involved in breaking it up. Williams, who was given an extension on that first day of spring training, watched—seemingly helplessly—as losing devolved to embarrassment.

The Nationals' road did not lead to the World Series. It led, fittingly, to Citi Field, to a chilly autumn Sunday afternoon where it all ended after 83 wins and 79 losses, to a quiet visitor's clubhouse full of players long resigned to the fact that this was the dead end they never imagined.

There was Werth, the veteran, sitting and reflecting, staring blankly. There was Harper, the future, nursing a bruise he received from a Jacob deGrom fastball the day before. Despite being nearly unable to walk, he'd homered after the blow. He finished at 99 runs batted in, a few points off from the batting title. There was Desmond, the cornerstone, the homegrown talent, the only former Expos draft pick left playing for the franchise, struggling to compose himself in front of his locker. He and Zimmermann and Span had planned a different ending to these Nationals' narrative. His road will lead him elsewhere now, because an era ended when this season did. A transition began.

Williams became the face of the crisis, the only man who touched everything, the most easily blamed when everything went wrong. Just more than 12 hours after Desmond's teary goodbye, Williams was gone, too, fired less than 12 months after winning the league's manager of the year award.

Expectations come from somewhere. They are not often heaped on the untalented, the unprepared, or the undeserving. They are therefore a great honor—and a massive burden. Williams and the Nationals acknowledged this. They had no choice. The first day of spring training was supposed to being a journey that would end in early November, with a trophy and with rings. Instead, that journey ended a month too soon, with a frustrated clubhouse, a managerial vacancy, and a longer-than-anticipated winter to wonder when the road to the World Series might lead to D.C. again. ■

—Chelsea Janes is the Nationals beat reporter for the Washington Post *and a former Yale softball player with a career .175 average, still banking on intangibles.*

HITTERS

Ian Desmond SS

Born: 9/20/85 Age: 30 Bats: R Throws: R Height: 6'3" Weight: 215

YEAR	TEAM	LVL	AGE	PA	R	2B	3B	HR	RBI	BB	K	SB	CS	AVG/OBP/SLG	TAv	BABIP	BRR	FRAA	WARP
2013	WAS	MLB	27	655	77	38	3	20	80	43	145	21	6	.280/.331/.453	.273	.336	0.2	SS(158): 1.4	3.8
2014	WAS	MLB	28	648	73	26	3	24	91	46	183	24	5	.255/.313/.430	.271	.326	1.8	SS(154): 6.6	4.4
2015	WAS	MLB	29	641	69	27	2	19	62	45	187	13	5	.233/.290/.384	.254	.307	2.5	SS(155): -1.4	2.4
2016	*WAS*	*MLB*	*30*	*600*	*71*	*28*	*2*	*20*	*72*	*40*	*153*	*17*	*5*	*.252/.305/.416*	*.257*	*.308*	*0.8*	*SS 2*	*-0.6*
2017	*WAS*	*MLB*	*31*	*549*	*64*	*25*	*1*	*17*	*64*	*36*	*145*	*14*	*5*	*.246/.299/.401*	*.256*	*.307*	*1.1*	*SS 1*	*-0.4*

Breakout: 1% Improve: 52% Collapse: 2% Attrition: 9% MLB: 97% *Comparables: Jhonny Peralta, Alfonso Soriano, Ernie Banks*

Desmond entered 2015 with little interest in restarting contract negotiations with the Nationals, hoping to play his way into better money in the offseason. (Last year in this space, we praised his ambition.) For much of the season, that looked like an unwise choice. Desmond's shockingly poor first-half offense (.211/.255/.334) and defensive woes (eight errors in a 12-game span in April) brought about wild midseason trade rumors, as sources close to the team suggested Desi's lurking free agency got inside his head. But the Nationals kept their veteran shortstop for the second half, and he rebounded offensively (.777 OPS) and settled defensively. The early-season struggles may have spooked us for a time, but it's clear that Desmond remains a perennial 20/20 threat at a premium position, and he has missed just 38 games due to injury since 2010.

Wilmer Difo SS

Born: 4/2/92 Age: 24 Bats: B Throws: R Height: 6'0" Weight: 195

YEAR	TEAM	LVL	AGE	PA	R	2B	3B	HR	RBI	BB	K	SB	CS	AVG/OBP/SLG	TAv	BABIP	BRR	FRAA	WARP
2013	AUB	A-	21	136	15	3	4	1	6	10	17	3	2	.217/.291/.333	.257	.243	-0.4	SS(18): -3.3, 2B(13): 1.5	0.2
2013	POT	A+	21	20	2	1	0	0	1	2	3	0	1	.222/.300/.278	.202	.267	-0.5	SS(4): -0.8, 2B(1): -0.0	-0.2
2013	HAG	A	21	56	7	2	0	2	11	5	13	4	1	.220/.286/.380	.259	.250	2.1	3B(11): 0.7, SS(1): -0.6	0.4
2014	HAG	A	22	610	91	31	7	14	90	37	65	49	9	.315/.360/.470	.294	.333	6.5	SS(70): 1.1, 2B(66): 3.7	5.6
2015	POT	A+	23	83	13	7	0	3	14	8	13	4	1	.320/.386/.533	.337	.356	0.4	SS(19): -2.8	0.8
2015	HAR	AA	23	381	48	21	6	2	39	12	79	26	1	.279/.312/.387	.251	.349	0.7	SS(77): 4.8, 2B(11): -0.7	1.7
2015	WAS	MLB	23	11	1	0	0	0	0	0	2	0	0	.182/.182/.182	.141	.222	-0.8	2B(2): 0.0	-0.2
2016	*WAS*	*MLB*	*24*	*259*	*31*	*11*	*2*	*5*	*22*	*10*	*58*	*11*	*2*	*.241/.275/.361*	*.226*	*.293*	*1.6*	*2B 1, SS 0*	*0.5*
2017	*WAS*	*MLB*	*25*	*419*	*43*	*19*	*3*	*9*	*43*	*17*	*95*	*18*	*3*	*.246/.281/.374*	*.239*	*.300*	*3.1*	*2B 1, SS 0*	*0.9*

Breakout: 2% Improve: 11% Collapse: 5% Attrition: 23% MLB: 35% *Comparables: Trevor Plouffe, Grant Green, Carlos Triunfel*

Simultaneously on time (given his age) and way ahead of schedule (given his very limited experience in the high minors), Difo arrived suddenly in mid-May and left just as quickly. Speed is a theme in his game, too: He's quick to the ball with the bat, a demon on the bases and puts strong zip on his throws. The exciting blend of tools has a lot in common with fellow young shortstop Trea Turner, and what makes their positional battle so interesting is that they both could play second base if needed to clear space for the other—although word on the inside is Difo would probably make that move before Turner.

Danny Espinosa 2B

Born: 4/25/87 Age: 29 Bats: B Throws: R Height: 6'0" Weight: 210

YEAR	TEAM	LVL	AGE	PA	R	2B	3B	HR	RBI	BB	K	SB	CS	AVG/OBP/SLG	TAv	BABIP	BRR	FRAA	WARP
2013	WAS	MLB	26	167	11	9	0	3	12	4	47	1	0	.158/.193/.272	.178	.202	-0.3	2B(43): -0.3, SS(1): -0.1	-1.0
2013	SYR	AAA	26	313	32	12	1	2	22	19	101	6	1	.216/.280/.286	.210	.324	1.3	2B(41): -1.9, SS(35): -0.8	-0.8
2014	WAS	MLB	27	364	31	14	3	8	27	18	122	8	1	.219/.283/.351	.233	.319	-1.3	2B(89): -0.4, SS(12): -0.0	-0.2
2015	WAS	MLB	28	412	59	21	1	13	37	33	106	5	2	.240/.311/.409	.264	.299	3.1	2B(81): 9.1, 3B(16): -0.2	2.6
2016	*WAS*	*MLB*	*29*	*539*	*59*	*24*	*2*	*15*	*56*	*38*	*158*	*9*	*3*	*.222/.291/.369*	*.236*	*.291*	*0.5*	*2B 5, 3B -0*	*1.3*
2017	*WAS*	*MLB*	*30*	*494*	*56*	*22*	*1*	*13*	*53*	*37*	*145*	*8*	*2*	*.216/.290/.361*	*.241*	*.284*	*0.5*	*2B 4, 3B 0*	*1.0*

Breakout: 2% Improve: 41% Collapse: 10% Attrition: 19% MLB: 95% *Comparables: Keith Ginter, Felipe Lopez, Geronimo Pena*

For a couple of shaky seasons, Espinosa's most notable contribution to the team came in the form of showing up to spring training with Sam Elliott's moustache from *The Big Lebowksi*. Fortunately, Espinosa abided in 2015, rediscovering his swing and providing steady defense in an unexpectedly prominent role. In particular, his performance against right-handed pitching (.709 OPS, 26 percent strikeout rate) showed significant improvement over the prior season (.532 OPS, 39 percent strikeouts) and put to rest discussion about him becoming a dedicated right-handed hitter. He went from a non-tender candidate in the winter to a plausible extension candidate by the All-Star break.

This resurgence made it all the more frustrating for Espinosa when Matt Williams benched him from July 27th onward, when the Nationals' roster healed up. *The Washington Post*'s Barry Svrluga reported that Espinosa "seethed" when Williams broke playing-time pledges to him, giving him just over a dozen starts in the club's final 65 games. "This was typical [of Williams], and it ate at the clubhouse culture," Svrluga wrote. If Espinosa's strikeouts return en masse, he might be squeezed out of a job for cause, but as it is his infield versatility, pop and ability to switch-hit make him a valuable part of a good team's depth chart.

Brian Goodwin CF

Born: 11/2/90 Age: 25 Bats: L Throws: R Height: 6'0" Weight: 195

YEAR	TEAM	LVL	AGE	PA	R	2B	3B	HR	RBI	BB	K	SB	CS	AVG/OBP/SLG	TAv	BABIP	BRR	FRAA	WARP
2013	HAR	AA	22	533	82	19	11	10	40	66	121	19	11	.252/.355/.407	.286	.321	2.0	CF(116): -3.2	3.0
2014	SYR	AAA	23	329	31	10	4	4	32	50	95	6	4	.219/.342/.328	.253	.320	0.1	CF(65): 1.1, RF(14): 0.2	0.8
2015	HAR	AA	24	472	58	17	4	8	46	38	93	15	7	.226/.290/.340	.239	.269	-0.6	CF(87): -1.8, RF(22): 2.3	0.1
2016	*WAS*	*MLB*	*25*	*250*	*29*	*9*	*2*	*5*	*21*	*25*	*68*	*5*	*3*	*.218/.299/.342*	*.235*	*.285*	*0.1*	*CF -0, RF 1*	*0.2*
2017	*WAS*	*MLB*	*26*	*302*	*33*	*10*	*2*	*6*	*29*	*30*	*83*	*6*	*3*	*.216/.298/.343*	*.242*	*.284*	*0.4*	*CF 0, RF 1*	*0.3*

Breakout: 8% Improve: 26% Collapse: 5% Attrition: 29% MLB: 42% *Comparables: Brian Bogusevic, Chris Denorfia, Jeff Salazar*

As a wise and handsome baseball scout used to say for an influential online publication, "Prospects will break your heart." It was another year of hope and another step back for the speedy center fielder Goodwin. His swing mechanics still fail him, as he struggles to get his hands in a launch position when they need to be. He's especially vulnerable against left-handed pitching. As he enters his age-25 season, it's difficult to see a path to a consistent role without a miracle "click."

Bryce Harper LF

Born: 10/16/92 Age: 23 Bats: L Throws: R Height: 6'3" Weight: 215

YEAR	TEAM	LVL	AGE	PA	R	2B	3B	HR	RBI	BB	K	SB	CS	AVG/OBP/SLG	TAv	BABIP	BRR	FRAA	WARP
2013	WAS	MLB	20	497	71	24	3	20	58	61	94	11	4	.274/.368/.486	.303	.306	-0.6	LF(97): 4.1, RF(16): 0.5	3.8
2014	WAS	MLB	21	395	41	10	2	13	32	38	104	2	2	.273/.344/.423	.290	.352	-1.9	LF(90): 1.6, RF(10): -0.6	1.9
2015	WAS	MLB	22	654	118	38	1	42	99	124	131	6	4	.330/.460/.649	.386	.369	5.1	RF(140): 6.2, CF(13): 0.8	11.2
2016	*WAS*	*MLB*	*23*	*630*	*90*	*28*	*3*	*30*	*97*	*82*	*133*	*8*	*4*	*.282/.378/.516*	*.312*	*.318*	*0.8*	*RF 4, CF 0*	*5.7*
2017	*WAS*	*MLB*	*24*	*580*	*90*	*26*	*3*	*28*	*90*	*78*	*118*	*7*	*4*	*.284/.383/.519*	*.324*	*.317*	*0.9*	*RF 4, CF 0*	*5.3*

Breakout: 3% Improve: 57% Collapse: 2% Attrition: 5% MLB: 99% *Comparables: Mike Trout, Jason Heyward, Bernie Carbo*

To give some perspective on just how valuable this Most Valuable of Players was: He produced more WARP than the next six players on his team combined. He doubled both his walk rate and his isolated power from the previous year. He made improvements across the board, but especially in areas of prior weakness—soft pitches and left-handed pitchers. His .986 OPS against lefties would have been fifth in the majors on its own, and he showed superior bat control against all pitch types. There's no safe way to pitch him anymore. To think, other players have called him overrated.

Spencer Kieboom C

Born: 3/16/91 Age: 25 Bats: R Throws: R Height: 6'1" Weight: 230

YEAR	TEAM	LVL	AGE	PA	R	2B	3B	HR	RBI	BB	K	SB	CS	AVG/OBP/SLG	TAv	BABIP	BRR	FRAA	WARP
2014	HAG	A	23	361	50	28	4	9	61	21	67	2	2	.309/.352/.500	.294	.358	-0.9	C(86): 0.8	3.1
2015	POT	A+	24	285	30	16	1	2	26	36	30	1	1	.248/.344/.346	.256	.273	-2.4	C(69): 5.3	1.5
2016	*WAS*	*MLB*	*25*	*250*	*22*	*12*	*1*	*5*	*26*	*16*	*56*	*0*	*0*	*.231/.283/.354*	*.227*	*.279*	*-0.5*	*C 1*	*0.3*
2017	*WAS*	*MLB*	*26*	*210*	*21*	*10*	*0*	*4*	*20*	*14*	*48*	*0*	*0*	*.223/.274/.344*	*.227*	*.271*	*-0.5*	*C 1*	*0.1*

Breakout: 8% Improve: 12% Collapse: 13% Attrition: 25% MLB: 32% *Comparables: Bobby Wilson, Jett Bandy, Jason Jaramillo*

YEAR	TEAM	P. COUNT	FRM RUNS	BLK RUNS	THRW RUNS	TOT RUNS
2016	WAS	9027	0.0	0.0	0.0	0.0
2017	WAS	7574	0.0	0.0	0.0	0.0

Though Kieboom is best known as Lucas Giolito's personal catcher, roomie and uncanny look-alike, there are other reasons why the Nationals added him to their 40-man roster. Like, most importantly, his bat. While his swing has a hitch that makes him prone to swinging and missing, there's enough strength present that he's able to go kaboom when he makes contact. Add in a mitt that's more than passable behind the plate—especially as it pertains to receiving—and you have a ready-made backup who is familiar with the club's future ace. Nice.

Jose Lobaton C

Born: 10/21/84 Age: 31 Bats: B Throws: R Height: 6'1" Weight: 215

YEAR	TEAM	LVL	AGE	PA	R	2B	3B	HR	RBI	BB	K	SB	CS	AVG/OBP/SLG	TAv	BABIP	BRR	FRAA	WARP
2013	TBA	MLB	28	311	38	15	2	7	32	30	65	0	1	.249/.320/.394	.280	.300	-3.2	C(96): 4.3	2.2
2014	WAS	MLB	29	230	18	9	0	2	12	15	61	0	0	.234/.287/.304	.224	.318	-1.0	C(64): 3.9	0.5
2015	WAS	MLB	30	155	11	4	0	3	20	15	40	0	0	.199/.279/.294	.226	.253	-0.5	C(42): 4.2	0.6
2016	*WAS*	*MLB*	*31*	*162*	*16*	*7*	*0*	*3*	*15*	*16*	*39*	*0*	*0*	*.231/.310/.347*	*.241*	*.291*	*-0.7*	*C 3*	*0.6*
2017	*WAS*	*MLB*	*32*	*154*	*16*	*6*	*0*	*3*	*14*	*15*	*39*	*0*	*0*	*.220/.296/.330*	*.236*	*.283*	*-0.7*	*C 2*	*0.4*

Breakout: 3% Improve: 33% Collapse: 11% Attrition: 22% MLB: 87% *Comparables: Miguel Ojeda, Dioner Navarro, Josh Bard*

YEAR	TEAM	P. COUNT	FRM RUNS	BLK RUNS	THRW RUNS	TOT RUNS
2013	TBA	11772	4.5	0.5	-1.3	3.7
2014	WAS	8464	2.4	0.2	0.5	3.1
2015	WAS	5681	5.0	-0.1	-0.2	4.7
2016	*WAS*	*6096*	*2.8*	*0.1*	*-0.2*	*2.7*
2017	*WAS*	*5780*	*2.4*	*0.1*	*-0.2*	*2.2*

Did you know that the Nationals tried signing Jose Molina before they traded for Lobaton? No? Well, Lobaton must've, because he spent 2015 imitating his one-time mentor. For those unfamiliar with Molina—and, by extension, Ben Lindbergh—that meant combining a blatant disregard for offense with an eternal thirst for stealing strikes. Did Lobaton frame? Boy, did he ever. He framed on the left, framed on the right, framed on the bed and framed on the floor. As a result, Lobaton finished with 39 extra strikes on the season—or 15 more than Wilson Ramos compiled in about three times as many opportunities. The thing about impersonations, though, is that they're seldom as good as the original. That's true here, too. So if Lobaton wants to stick around through his 40th birthday, like Molina did, he might want to incorporate more offense back into his game.

Tyler Moore 1B

Born: 1/30/87 Age: 29 Bats: R Throws: R Height: 6'2" Weight: 220

YEAR	TEAM	LVL	AGE	PA	R	2B	3B	HR	RBI	BB	K	SB	CS	AVG/OBP/SLG	TAv	BABIP	BRR	FRAA	WARP
2013	WAS	MLB	26	178	16	9	0	4	21	8	58	0	0	.222/.260/.347	.238	.311	-0.2	LF(29): -5.7, 1B(14): -1.7	-1.0
2013	SYR	AAA	26	200	26	14	1	10	46	23	39	1	0	.318/.395/.584	.336	.354	-1.3	LF(21): 1.1, 1B(19): -0.2	2.0
2014	WAS	MLB	27	100	8	2	0	4	14	7	29	0	0	.231/.300/.385	.256	.293	0.0	1B(24): 0.5, LF(4): 0.2	0.2
2014	SYR	AAA	27	354	45	21	0	10	44	47	77	0	2	.265/.367/.434	.278	.323	-3.7	1B(64): -4.1, LF(15): -0.8	0.3
2015	WAS	MLB	28	200	14	12	0	6	27	11	45	0	0	.203/.250/.364	.230	.234	-1.8	1B(39): -2.8, LF(20): -1.7	-0.9
2016	*WAS*	*MLB*	*29*	*334*	*38*	*16*	*0*	*13*	*45*	*28*	*89*	*0*	*0*	*.240/.307/.427*	*.262*	*.292*	*-0.8*	*1B -1, LF -1*	*0.5*
2017	*WAS*	*MLB*	*30*	*405*	*50*	*18*	*0*	*15*	*51*	*35*	*112*	*0*	*0*	*.230/.300/.408*	*.261*	*.284*	*-1.2*	*1B -2, LF -2*	*0.0*

Breakout: 7% Improve: 27% Collapse: 7% Attrition: 17% MLB: 61% *Comparables: Mike Carp, Chris Shelton, Brandon Moss*

Out of options in 2015, Moore stayed on the big-league club with little to contribute. Relegated to pinch-hit duty when the starters were healthy, the glove-less Moore ran his three-year totals to .216/.264/.362 and 106—as in 106 more strikeouts than walks. It's worth remembering that Moore reached the majors in the first place by overachieving for several seasons in the minors. The scouts might have been right all along: Moore just doesn't have the hand-eye coordination to hit top-tier arms.

Wilson Ramos C

Born: 8/10/87 Age: 28 Bats: R Throws: R Height: 6'0" Weight: 230

YEAR	TEAM	LVL	AGE	PA	R	2B	3B	HR	RBI	BB	K	SB	CS	AVG/OBP/SLG	TAv	BABIP	BRR	FRAA	WARP
2013	WAS	MLB	25	303	29	9	0	16	59	15	42	0	1	.272/.307/.470	.268	.270	-1.1	C(77): 6.9	2.3
2014	WAS	MLB	26	361	32	12	0	11	47	17	57	0	0	.267/.299/.399	.250	.290	1.9	C(87): -1.0	1.4
2015	WAS	MLB	27	504	41	16	0	15	68	21	101	0	0	.229/.258/.358	.231	.256	-1.4	C(125): 4.0	1.0
2016	*WAS*	*MLB*	*28*	*458*	*52*	*18*	*0*	*17*	*58*	*29*	*82*	*0*	*0*	*.254/.301/.422*	*.257*	*.274*	*-0.1*	*C 2*	*2.2*
2017	*WAS*	*MLB*	*29*	*430*	*53*	*16*	*0*	*16*	*54*	*28*	*81*	*0*	*0*	*.250/.299/.414*	*.263*	*.273*	*-0.3*	*C 2*	*1.8*

Breakout: 1% Improve: 49% Collapse: 2% Attrition: 7% MLB: 100% *Comparables: Matt Wieters, Jonathan Lucroy, Miguel Montero*

YEAR	TEAM	P. COUNT	FRM RUNS	BLK RUNS	THRW RUNS	TOT RUNS
2013	WAS	10425	6.7	-0.2	0.4	6.9
2014	WAS	11905	-2.6	-0.1	0.7	-2.0
2015	WAS	16690	0.6	0.4	1.2	2.2
2016	*WAS*	*15649*	*0.5*	*0.1*	*1.2*	*1.8*
2017	*WAS*	*14708*	*-0.5*	*0.1*	*1.1*	*0.7*

"Ramos will be one of the best-hitting catchers in baseball if he can just stay healthy!"—Ancient wisdom passed down through many generations

Ramos defied the odds last year, staying on the field all year but also hitting well below his career averages. Indeed, he arguably had the worst year of any catcher in the majors with as much playing time as he received. That's not to say the season was a total loss: He remained a capable defender and pitch framer who made the pitching staff better. Ramos enters a contract year with one last chance to show he belongs in the top tier of backstops.

Jakson Reetz C

Born: 1/3/96 Age: 20 Bats: R Throws: R Height: 6'1" Weight: 195

YEAR	TEAM	LVL	AGE	PA	R	2B	3B	HR	RBI	BB	K	SB	CS	AVG/OBP/SLG	TAv	BABIP	BRR	FRAA	WARP
2015	AUB	A-	19	132	18	4	0	0	5	13	37	3	0	.212/.326/.248	.223	.316	0.2	C(33): -0.7	0.0
2016	*WAS*	*MLB*	*20*	*250*	*19*	*8*	*1*	*4*	*21*	*15*	*81*	*1*	*0*	*.189/.245/.277*	*.191*	*.269*	*-0.3*	*C -0*	*-0.8*
2017	*WAS*	*MLB*	*21*	*252*	*25*	*9*	*1*	*4*	*22*	*17*	*80*	*1*	*0*	*.200/.261/.302*	*.211*	*.278*	*-0.5*	*C 0*	*-0.4*

Breakout: 0% Improve: 0% Collapse: 0% Attrition: 0% MLB: 0% *Comparables: Lou Marson, Christian Vazquez, Wilin Rosario*

YEAR	TEAM	P. COUNT	FRM RUNS	BLK RUNS	THRW RUNS	TOT RUNS
2016	*WAS*	*8928*	*0.0*	*0.0*	*0.0*	*0.0*
2017	*WAS*	*9017*	*0.0*	*0.0*	*0.0*	*0.0*

Much younger than other catching prospects in the system, Reetz offers more impact potential with his bat and a higher overall ceiling. The former football player is strong and athletic, with a good arm, and the chance to hit 15-plus homers per year. Getting comfortable with a revamped swing and staying healthy are the first orders of business for 2016.

Anthony Rendon 3B

Born: 6/6/90 Age: 26 Bats: R Throws: R Height: 6'1" Weight: 210

YEAR	TEAM	LVL	AGE	PA	R	2B	3B	HR	RBI	BB	K	SB	CS	AVG/OBP/SLG	TAv	BABIP	BRR	FRAA	WARP
2013	WAS	MLB	23	394	40	23	1	7	35	31	69	1	1	.265/.329/.396	.261	.307	1.3	2B(82): 0.7, 3B(15): 0.2	1.3
2013	HAR	AA	23	152	17	11	2	6	24	30	25	1	0	.319/.461/.603	.376	.352	-0.5	3B(24): 4.7, 2B(5): -0.9	2.8
2014	WAS	MLB	24	683	111	39	6	21	83	58	104	17	3	.287/.351/.473	.301	.314	4.9	3B(134): 1.3, 2B(28): -2.4	5.4
2015	HAR	AA	25	27	1	3	0	0	0	3	4	0	0	.250/.333/.375	.271	.300	-0.2	2B(5): 0.6, 3B(1): 0.4	0.2
2015	WAS	MLB	25	355	43	16	0	5	25	36	70	1	2	.264/.344/.363	.262	.321	-0.2	2B(59): -1.7, 3B(28): 0.8	1.0
2015	POT	A+	25	20	2	2	0	0	1	3	2	0	0	.471/.550/.588	.398	.533	0.0	3B(4): -0.1	0.3
2016	*WAS*	*MLB*	*26*	*613*	*79*	*33*	*2*	*17*	*66*	*58*	*107*	*7*	*3*	*.269/.343/.431*	*.274*	*.303*	*1.9*	*3B 6*	*3.5*
2017	*WAS*	*MLB*	*27*	*515*	*65*	*27*	*2*	*16*	*63*	*48*	*86*	*6*	*2*	*.260/.334/.431*	*.279*	*.285*	*1.6*	*3B 5*	*2.7*

Breakout: 2% Improve: 58% Collapse: 3% Attrition: 9% MLB: 99% *Comparables: Ian Kinsler, Kelly Johnson, Martin Prado*

"Anthony will be good. It's just a question of a few days," manager Matt Williams said of Rendon's spring MCL sprain. But that tweak, and the oblique strain he suffered during rehab, kept him out of action until early June, and after straining his quadriceps he played sporadically for the two months after that. The second clause of Williams' statement being disproved, Rendon went about refuting the first, matching glove-first types like Elvis Andrus and Juan Lagares in ISO. It became obvious that inconsistent playing time and pain threw off his hitting rhythm. The swell in his strikeout rate was caused less by chasing than by far more empty cuts at pitches in the zone.

He also played second base much more than expected: 59 games versus 19 at third. If there's one positive to come from 2015 for Rendon it's the Yunel Escobar trade. He's now freed to resume his duties at third base. The Nationals can only hope he finds the good health he left there.

Clint Robinson 1B

Born: 2/16/85 Age: 31 Bats: L Throws: L Height: 6'5" Weight: 245

YEAR	TEAM	LVL	AGE	PA	R	2B	3B	HR	RBI	BB	K	SB	CS	AVG/OBP/SLG	TAv	BABIP	BRR	FRAA	WARP
2013	NHP	AA	28	332	41	14	2	11	43	40	50	1	2	.270/.364/.446	.288	.294	-0.4	1B(70): -9.1, RF(1): -0.1	0.3
2013	BUF	AAA	28	130	13	9	0	2	12	19	33	0	0	.213/.323/.352	.248	.276	-0.4	1B(32): -0.0, LF(2): 0.0	-0.1
2014	LAN	MLB	29	10	3	0	0	0	2	1	1	0	0	.333/.400/.333	.252	.375	0.3	1B(3): -0.1	0.0
2014	ABQ	AAA	29	499	77	31	5	18	80	64	84	0	0	.312/.401/.534	.308	.350	-1.1	1B(99): -4.1, RF(2): -0.1	2.8
2015	WAS	MLB	30	352	44	15	1	10	34	37	52	0	0	.272/.358/.424	.287	.298	-2.2	1B(44): -0.1, LF(27): -3.3	0.9
2016	*WAS*	*MLB*	*31*	*116*	*12*	*5*	*0*	*3*	*13*	*13*	*22*	*0*	*0*	*.247/.332/.393*	*.262*	*.284*	*-0.3*	*LF -1*	*0.4*
2017	*WAS*	*MLB*	*32*	*308*	*37*	*14*	*1*	*8*	*33*	*33*	*58*	*0*	*0*	*.242/.327/.382*	*.265*	*.279*	*-1.0*	*LF -1*	*0.6*

Breakout: 1% Improve: 15% Collapse: 8% Attrition: 18% MLB: 36% *Comparables: Cole Gillespie, Rico Washington, Jeff Salazar*

After nearly 4,000 plate appearances in the minor leagues and two fleeting tastes of the majors, Robinson earned a chance to prove he was the positionless left-handed bat we all thought he could be. (Actually, to say he was positionless sells him short. He was granted the honor of becoming the first Nationals position player pitcher on May 12th. He struck out Aaron Hill and threw a scoreless, nine-pitch inning.) At the dish, he showed a steady approach with decent power and plenty of patience, the latter of which we probably could have guessed from his resume.

Pedro Severino C

Born: 7/20/93 Age: 22 Bats: R Throws: R Height: 6'2" Weight: 200

YEAR	TEAM	LVL	AGE	PA	R	2B	3B	HR	RBI	BB	K	SB	CS	AVG/OBP/SLG	TAv	BABIP	BRR	FRAA	WARP
2013	HAG	A	19	302	28	19	2	1	45	13	54	1	0	.241/.274/.333	.244	.291	0.9	C(81): 0.8	1.1
2014	POT	A+	20	326	41	15	1	9	36	21	57	2	0	.247/.306/.399	.256	.276	-0.7	C(93): 1.7	1.5
2015	WAS	MLB	21	4	1	1	0	0	0	0	1	0	0	.250/.250/.500	.233	.333	0.1	C(2): 0.1	0.0
2015	HAR	AA	21	357	33	13	0	5	34	19	51	1	2	.246/.288/.331	.232	.276	-1.5	C(91): -1.9	0.2
2016	*WAS*	*MLB*	*22*	*30*	*3*	*1*	*0*	*1*	*3*	*1*	*7*	*0*	*0*	*.226/.262/.340*	*.216*	*.267*	*-0.1*	*C -1*	*-0.1*
2017	*WAS*	*MLB*	*23*	*276*	*28*	*12*	*0*	*6*	*27*	*13*	*60*	*0*	*0*	*.227/.269/.344*	*.228*	*.266*	*-0.7*	*C -7*	*-0.7*

Breakout: 2% Improve: 5% Collapse: 5% Attrition: 10% MLB: 12% *Comparables: John Hicks, J.T. Realmuto, Miguel Montero*

YEAR	TEAM	P. COUNT	FRM RUNS	BLK RUNS	THRW RUNS	TOT RUNS
2015	HAR	12147	-2.8	0.2	0.4	-2.2
2016	*WAS*	*1102*	*-0.8*	*0.0*	*0.1*	*-0.8*
2017	*WAS*	*10125*	*-8.3*	*0.0*	*0.5*	*-7.8*

After a solid year in Double-A—including three baserunners gunned down in his first game—the Nationals' most mature catching prospect earned a September call-up and his first major-league hit. Severino's defense draws high marks from both team and outside scouts, who are quick to praise his footwork, blocking ability and arm strength. His pitch framing has improved, too. The flip side is a bat that will struggle to stand up at the highest level. His power is minimal and a decent average would be optimistic. Even to make it as a backup, he needs more work on his swing and approach.

Denard Span CF

Born: 2/27/84 Age: 32 Bats: L Throws: L Height: 6'0" Weight: 210

YEAR	TEAM	LVL	AGE	PA	R	2B	3B	HR	RBI	BB	K	SB	CS	AVG/OBP/SLG	TAv	BABIP	BRR	FRAA	WARP
2013	WAS	MLB	29	662	75	28	11	4	47	42	77	20	6	.279/.327/.380	.251	.313	0.3	CF(153): 8.6	2.4
2014	WAS	MLB	30	668	94	39	8	5	37	50	65	31	7	.302/.355/.416	.288	.330	6.8	CF(147): 8.1	5.6
2015	WAS	MLB	31	275	38	17	0	5	22	25	26	11	0	.301/.365/.431	.305	.318	2.3	CF(61): 2.2	2.6
2016	*WAS*	*MLB*	*32*	*534*	*64*	*27*	*4*	*6*	*44*	*41*	*64*	*19*	*4*	*.275/.331/.384*	*.258*	*.301*	*2.3*	*CF 5*	*2.6*
2017	*WAS*	*MLB*	*33*	*367*	*39*	*18*	*2*	*4*	*34*	*28*	*48*	*12*	*3*	*.266/.320/.371*	*.259*	*.293*	*1.8*	*CF 3*	*1.5*

Breakout: 1% Improve: 41% Collapse: 2% Attrition: 12% MLB: 96% *Comparables: Johnny Damon, Shane Victorino, Coco Crisp*

Who among you picked Denard Span to put together back-to-back .300 seasons? (Put your hands down, liars.) Span's impressive overall contributions were cut short by injuries to begin (abdominal muscle) and end (hip and back) the season. He has developed a mastery of the strike zone—25 walks to 26 strikeouts—to add to his base-stealing and outfield range, but the toll of playing center field for so long seems to be hitting his body hard, and the Nationals opted not to make him a qualifying offer when he hit free agency. The talent and work ethic are hard to ignore, but so is the continued injury risk.

Andrew Stevenson OF

Born: 6/1/94 Age: 22 Bats: L Throws: L Height: 6'0" Weight: 185

YEAR	TEAM	LVL	AGE	PA	R	2B	3B	HR	RBI	BB	K	SB	CS	AVG/OBP/SLG	TAv	BABIP	BRR	FRAA	WARP
2015	HAG	A	21	153	28	3	2	1	16	8	16	16	4	.285/.338/.358	.282	.311	2.7	CF(35): 0.7	1.2
2015	AUB	A-	21	80	11	1	2	0	9	7	12	7	3	.361/.413/.431	.294	.426	1.2	CF(16): 2.9, LF(3): 1.6	1.1
2016	*WAS*	*MLB*	*22*	*250*	*27*	*9*	*1*	*4*	*20*	*11*	*58*	*12*	*4*	*.224/.264/.324*	*.211*	*.275*	*0.8*	*CF 2, LF 0*	*-0.2*
2017	*WAS*	*MLB*	*23*	*276*	*27*	*10*	*1*	*4*	*25*	*13*	*61*	*13*	*5*	*.233/.275/.332*	*.224*	*.284*	*1.6*	*CF 2, LF 0*	*-0.1*

Breakout: 0% Improve: 3% Collapse: 2% Attrition: 4% MLB: 6% *Comparables: Mason Williams, A.J. Pollock, Rafael Ortega*

Without a first-round pick in last year's draft, the Nats had to wait patiently before selecting Stevenson, a speed-first contact hitter with a center-field profile and "baseball rat" makeup. He'll need to keep his body quieter through the zone as he faces higher-quality pitching, and his arm strength lags behind his plus range, but his speed-and-D profile ought to grant him a future as a reserve if all else fails. Whether he can start will be easier to tell once there's a full season of work to judge, but the flowing blonde hair grades as a 65 or better already.

Michael Taylor CF

Born: 3/26/91 Age: 25 Bats: R Throws: R Height: 6'3" Weight: 210

YEAR	TEAM	LVL	AGE	PA	R	2B	3B	HR	RBI	BB	K	SB	CS	AVG/OBP/SLG	TAv	BABIP	BRR	FRAA	WARP
2013	POT	A+	22	581	79	41	6	10	87	55	131	51	7	.263/.340/.426	.265	.331	7.5	CF(117): 24.8, RF(4): 0.4	5.4
2014	SYR	AAA	23	52	7	3	1	1	3	7	14	3	1	.227/.333/.409	.259	.310	0.8	CF(12): 2.5	0.5
2014	HAR	AA	23	441	74	17	2	22	61	50	130	34	8	.313/.396/.539	.324	.421	3.5	CF(87): 20.5, RF(1): 0.6	7.0
2014	WAS	MLB	23	43	5	3	0	1	5	3	17	0	2	.205/.279/.359	.235	.333	-0.8	CF(10): -0.2, RF(5): 0.4	-0.1
2015	WAS	MLB	24	511	49	15	2	14	63	35	158	16	3	.229/.282/.358	.240	.311	-0.4	CF(96): 0.9, LF(38): 4.3	0.9
2015	SYR	AAA	24	32	4	1	0	1	4	4	10	2	1	.385/.452/.538	.374	.563	0.2	CF(6): -1.4, RF(1): 0.1	0.4
2016	*WAS*	*MLB*	*25*	*613*	*82*	*24*	*2*	*19*	*61*	*48*	*192*	*24*	*6*	*.235/.298/.386*	*.246*	*.317*	*-0.5*	*CF 13*	*2.6*
2017	*WAS*	*MLB*	*26*	*569*	*66*	*23*	*1*	*17*	*65*	*45*	*174*	*22*	*6*	*.233/.297/.385*	*.252*	*.311*	*0.3*	*CF 12*	*2.4*

Breakout: 4% Improve: 28% Collapse: 11% Attrition: 35% MLB: 75% *Comparables: Kirk Nieuwenhuis, Trayvon Robinson, Cameron Maybin*

Denver air or not, the 493-foot home run Taylor hit on August 20th—the longest of the 2015 season tracked by Statcast—showed that this defense-first outfielder has the bat speed to make an impact if his development continues. Pressed into regular service ahead of schedule because of Denard Span's injuries, Taylor showed off tools that add up to a likely starter with room for growth. He'll be a 20/20 threat for the foreseeable future, and his plus-plus defensive range will make it easier to part ways with Span. Better pitch recognition is the only thing separating Taylor from a higher slot in the order. And a more encouraging set of PECOTA comps.

Trea Turner SS

Born: 6/30/93 Age: 23 Bats: R Throws: R Height: 6'1" Weight: 175

YEAR	TEAM	LVL	AGE	PA	R	2B	3B	HR	RBI	BB	K	SB	CS	AVG/OBP/SLG	TAv	BABIP	BRR	FRAA	WARP
2014	FTW	A	21	216	31	14	2	4	22	24	48	14	3	.369/.447/.529	.338	.478	2.8	SS(36): 0.8	3.0
2014	EUG	A-	21	105	14	2	0	1	2	11	19	9	1	.228/.324/.283	.271	.278	0.7	SS(14): 1.4	0.7
2015	SAN	AA	22	254	31	13	3	5	35	24	48	11	4	.322/.385/.471	.297	.389	1.6	SS(57): 5.4	2.8
2015	WAS	MLB	22	44	5	1	0	1	1	4	12	2	2	.225/.295/.325	.259	.296	0.1	2B(12): 0.6, SS(6): -0.1	0.2
2015	HAR	AA	22	41	6	4	1	0	4	1	8	4	0	.359/.366/.513	.303	.438	0.2	SS(10): -1.0	0.3
2015	SYR	AAA	22	205	31	7	3	3	15	13	41	14	2	.314/.353/.431	.291	.381	2.0	SS(44): 5.2, 2B(2): -0.3	2.2
2016	*WAS*	*MLB*	*23*	*550*	*71*	*23*	*3*	*12*	*52*	*38*	*139*	*21*	*7*	*.263/.315/.397*	*.256*	*.335*	*1.6*	*SS 8*	*3.6*
2017	*WAS*	*MLB*	*24*	*535*	*62*	*22*	*3*	*13*	*59*	*39*	*139*	*21*	*6*	*.259/.315/.396*	*.264*	*.332*	*2.4*	*SS 8*	*3.6*

Breakout: 4% Improve: 34% Collapse: 6% Attrition: 16% MLB: 62% *Comparables: Junior Lake, Aaron Cunningham, Marcus Semien*

Turner didn't wow at the plate when he was called up at the end of August, but don't let the numbers fool you. He is ready to compete for a starting-shortstop position in the majors, a thought that startles the Nationals' front office. He just finished his first full season of pro ball—only half of which was technically with their organization—and he's already pushing to be a starting regular at a prime position. For Steven Souza, *this*?

But there's no catch. Turner's superb contact and speed, solid glovework and range, and plus instincts add up to a dependable cog in the lineup. He won't hit many home runs, but his gap power and stolen-base threat will give him some punch beyond line-drive singles.

Drew Ward 3B

Born: 11/25/94 Age: 21 Bats: L Throws: R Height: 6'3" Weight: 215

YEAR	TEAM	LVL	AGE	PA	R	2B	3B	HR	RBI	BB	K	SB	CS	AVG/OBP/SLG	TAv	BABIP	BRR	FRAA	WARP
2014	HAG	A	19	478	45	26	3	10	73	42	121	2	2	.269/.341/.413	.260	.353	-5.0	3B(92): -0.8	0.8
2015	POT	A+	20	426	47	19	2	6	47	39	110	2	1	.249/.327/.358	.256	.333	-0.9	3B(95): -3.1	0.7
2016	*WAS*	*MLB*	*21*	*250*	*21*	*10*	*0*	*5*	*25*	*17*	*81*	*0*	*0*	*.210/.267/.322*	*.212*	*.295*	*-0.5*	*3B -2*	*-0.8*
2017	*WAS*	*MLB*	*22*	*390*	*41*	*18*	*1*	*9*	*40*	*27*	*126*	*0*	*0*	*.214/.274/.348*	*.229*	*.298*	*-1.0*	*3B -3*	*-0.9*

Breakout: 0% Improve: 0% Collapse: 0% Attrition: 2% MLB: 2% *Comparables: Alex Liddi, Will Middlebrooks, Mat Gamel*

It's hard to avoid the "country strong" cliche with Ward, a native of an Oklahoma town with 300 souls. For now, he's still trying to tap into his raw power during games, so he and the player development staff are taking baby steps, focusing foremost on working the gaps. He's a big body without ideal footwork at third base, but he's looked more comfortable at the position recently and wants to stay at that corner. Whether that wish will be enough to prevent a move to first is an open question. Ultimately, Ward's power is the key to success. Just know that.

Jayson Werth RF

Born: 5/20/79 Age: 37 Bats: R Throws: R Height: 6'5" Weight: 240

YEAR	TEAM	LVL	AGE	PA	R	2B	3B	HR	RBI	BB	K	SB	CS	AVG/OBP/SLG	TAv	BABIP	BRR	FRAA	WARP
2013	POT	A+	34	20	6	1	0	2	8	2	0	0	0	.556/.600/.944	.464	.500	-0.8	RF(6): 1.3	0.5
2013	WAS	MLB	34	532	84	24	0	25	82	60	101	10	1	.318/.398/.532	.325	.358	3.2	RF(126): -0.9	4.8
2014	WAS	MLB	35	629	85	37	1	16	82	83	113	9	1	.292/.394/.455	.319	.343	2.5	RF(139): -1.4	5.1
2015	WAS	MLB	36	378	51	16	1	12	42	38	84	0	1	.221/.302/.384	.254	.253	1.9	LF(76): -8.8, RF(14): -2.0	-0.4
2015	SYR	AAA	36	26	2	2	0	0	5	1	2	1	0	.391/.423/.478	.344	.409	0.0	LF(5): -0.4	0.2
2016	*WAS*	*MLB*	*37*	*586*	*69*	*27*	*1*	*18*	*71*	*67*	*126*	*6*	*1*	*.256/.346/.416*	*.274*	*.303*	*2.2*	*LF -16*	*1.2*
2017	*WAS*	*MLB*	*38*	*449*	*55*	*20*	*0*	*12*	*49*	*49*	*100*	*3*	*1*	*.241/.329/.384*	*.266*	*.290*	*1.5*	*LF -12*	*0.1*

Breakout: 0% Improve: 23% Collapse: 10% Attrition: 13% MLB: 82% *Comparables: Raul Ibanez, Luis Gonzalez, Carlos Beltran*

Aw, we'd been doing so well. It had been years since the mention of "Werthless," the vastly overpaid and overly hairy outfielder out to destroy team payroll with the one-two punch of being unavailable and unproductive. But he reappeared for a time last year, struggling to regain his form after wrist fractures kept him out of action for much of the first half. His OPS didn't creep up over .600 until August 27th, and his defense has only become more of a liability each season.

On the other hand, the fan-favorite garden gnome showed up by year's end. In his final 50 games, he managed a slug-dependent .805 OPS and 10 home runs, giving hope that the remainder of the infamous contract will still provide enough production to justify regular playing time.

Werth has a history of serving as counterweight to his teams' managers and front offices, more recently confronting manager Matt Williams about his poor performance: "When exactly do you think you lost this team?" the outfielder asked, a drop-the-mic moment that might as well have served as Williams' walking papers. One way or another, he's going to be a major part of this team for two more years. For Dusty Baker's sake, here's hoping Werth is healthy, productive and happy.

Ryan Zimmerman LF

Born: 9/28/84 Age: 31 Bats: R Throws: R Height: 6'3" Weight: 220

YEAR	TEAM	LVL	AGE	PA	R	2B	3B	HR	RBI	BB	K	SB	CS	AVG/OBP/SLG	TAv	BABIP	BRR	FRAA	WARP
2013	WAS	MLB	28	633	84	26	2	26	79	60	133	6	0	.275/.344/.465	.284	.316	0.9	3B(141): 1.5	3.9
2014	WAS	MLB	29	240	26	19	1	5	38	22	37	0	0	.280/.342/.449	.294	.313	-3.1	LF(30): -0.3, 3B(23): 0.9	1.2
2015	WAS	MLB	30	390	43	25	1	16	73	33	79	1	0	.249/.308/.465	.283	.268	0.3	1B(93): -8.3, LF(1): -0.0	0.5
2016	*WAS*	*MLB*	*31*	*550*	*64*	*28*	*1*	*20*	*73*	*50*	*109*	*3*	*1*	*.263/.328/.444*	*.275*	*.295*	*-0.9*	*1B -9*	*0.7*
2017	*WAS*	*MLB*	*32*	*437*	*55*	*22*	*1*	*15*	*54*	*40*	*90*	*1*	*0*	*.250/.317/.424*	*.272*	*.284*	*-1.0*	*1B -7*	*0.0*

Breakout: 1% Improve: 36% Collapse: 4% Attrition: 3% MLB: 94% *Comparables: Seth Smith, Ted Kluszewski, Rafael Palmeiro*

Moving Zimmerman to first base was supposed to take his mind off distractions, keep him healthy, and let him do what he does best: bang. Unfortunately for Zim, the move was accompanied by a stubborn case of plantar fasciitis that bothered him on both sides of his game and forced him to miss two months of action. (His 4-for-46 slide in the two weeks leading up to the DL trip might have been a tip-off that he wasn't playing at 100 percent.) He also missed much of September with an oblique injury. But underneath all the pain, the barrel-to-ball ability he's had his whole career is still there, as his second half numbers (.311/.372/.652) will attest. Washington's longest-tenured player figures to stay a middle-of-the-order bat if his body will let him, but he's now seen the DL in five consecutive seasons, so who can be certain about anything except that the sun will rise tomorrow. Probably, anyway.

PITCHERS

A.J. Cole RHP

Born: 1/5/92 Age: 24 Bats: R Throws: R Height: 6'5" Weight: 200

YEAR	TEAM	LVL	AGE	W	L	SV	G	GS	IP	H	HR	BB/9	K/9	GB%	BABIP	WHIP	ERA	FIP	DRA	WARP	CFIP	MPH
2013	HAR	AA	21	4	2	0	7	7	45^{1}	31	3	2.0	9.7	39%	.248	0.90	2.18	2.68	3.77	0.8	72	
2013	POT	A+	21	6	3	0	18	18	97^{1}	96	12	2.1	9.4	38%	.317	1.22	4.25	3.69	4.01	1.5	77	
2014	SYR	AAA	22	7	0	0	11	11	63	69	9	2.4	7.1	40%	.316	1.37	3.43	4.48	4.56	0.4	101	
2014	HAR	AA	22	6	3	0	14	14	71	79	1	1.9	7.7	40%	.342	1.32	2.92	2.58	3.96	1.0	80	
2015	SYR	AAA	23	5	6	0	21	19	105^{2}	91	9	2.9	6.5	36%	.256	1.18	3.15	3.90	4.36	0.4	103	
2015	WAS	MLB	23	0	0	1	3	1	9^{1}	14	1	1.0	8.7	41%	.394	1.61	5.79	2.95	5.97	-0.1	96	93.5
2016	*WAS*	*MLB*	*24*	*3*	*2*	*0*	*29*	*6*	*54*	*53*	*6*	*2.7*	*7.0*	*35%*	*.306*	*1.29*	*4.05*	*3.98*	*4.62*	*0.2*	*106*	
2017	*WAS*	*MLB*	*25*	*4*	*5*	*0*	*15*	*15*	*87^{2}*	*92*	*11*	*3.1*	*7.1*	*35%*	*.321*	*1.39*	*4.40*	*4.67*	*5.02*	*0.2*	*117*	

Breakout: 14% Improve: 23% Collapse: 18% Attrition: 30% MLB: 52% *Comparables: Kyle Hendricks, David Huff, Tim Cooney*

Seemingly forever on the verge of arriving, Cole made his long-awaited debut in Atlanta on April 28th—and proceeded to surrender 10 baserunners in two innings because his sinker was up and lacked life. He made good use of his time at Triple-A in the second half of the year. His 1.89 ERA from June 24th on—as well as just two homers allowed in 67 innings and an uptick in fastball speed—spoke to a mechanical adjustment in his stride, allowing him to keep the ball out of the hitting zone consistently. That he's still eligible to make this year's Top 101 prospects for a fifth straight season is mildly damning. That our prospect team left him off this year is much worse.

Erick Fedde RHP

Born: 2/25/93 Age: 23 Bats: R Throws: R Height: 6'4" Weight: 180

YEAR	TEAM	LVL	AGE	W	L	SV	G	GS	IP	H	HR	BB/9	K/9	GB%	BABIP	WHIP	ERA	FIP	DRA	WARP	CFIP	MPH
2015	HAG	A	22	1	2	0	6	6	29	24	1	2.5	7.1	52%	.274	1.10	4.34	3.48	4.05	0.4	95	
2015	AUB	A-	22	4	1	0	8	8	35	38	1	2.1	9.3	56%	.346	1.31	2.57	2.60	2.44	1.1	81	
2016	*WAS*	*MLB*	*23*	*3*	*3*	*0*	*10*	*10*	*46^{2}*	*48*	*7*	*3.4*	*6.9*	*44%*	*.311*	*1.40*	*4.70*	*4.67*	*5.33*	*0.0*	*127*	
2017	*WAS*	*MLB*	*24*	*8*	*11*	*0*	*30*	*30*	*189^{2}*	*193*	*28*	*3.3*	*6.7*	*44%*	*.308*	*1.39*	*4.72*	*5.04*	*5.35*	*-0.1*	*128*	

Breakout: 2% Improve: 2% Collapse: 0% Attrition: 1% MLB: 2% *Comparables: Joel Carreno, Jesse Hahn, David Huff*

The Nationals finally got a look at their 2014 first-round pick in June, fresh off his recovery from pre-draft Tommy John surgery. Fedde breezed through short-season Auburn and looked comfortable at Low-A Hagerstown, with his 93 mph moving heater leading the way. Fedde is able to generate that power from a lanky frame without adopting a theatrical windup, which the Nats hope will spare him the durability concerns that surround most wispy pitchers. His low-80s slider flashes plus and is further along developmentally than his changeup, which is still a work in progress. As with all young pitchers, he has the chance to be a mid-rotation starter if things go well.

Doug Fister RHP

Born: 2/4/84 Age: 32 Bats: L Throws: R Height: 6'8" Weight: 210

YEAR	TEAM	LVL	AGE	W	L	SV	G	GS	IP	H	HR	BB/9	K/9	GB%	BABIP	WHIP	ERA	FIP	DRA	WARP	CFIP	MPH
2013	DET	MLB	29	14	9	0	33	32	208^{2}	229	14	1.9	6.9	56%	.332	1.31	3.67	3.29	3.92	2.5	95	91.5
2014	WAS	MLB	30	16	6	0	25	25	164	153	18	1.3	5.4	51%	.262	1.08	2.41	3.90	3.74	2.1	111	90.5
2015	WAS	MLB	31	5	7	1	25	15	103	120	14	2.1	5.5	47%	.310	1.40	4.19	4.58	6.12	-1.4	118	88.9
2016		*MLB*	*32*	*6*	*6*	*0*	*17*	*17*	*107^{1}*	*104*	*13*	*2.0*	*6.3*	*50%*	*.298*	*1.19*	*4.05*	*4.00*	*4.62*	*0.8*	*108*	
2017		*MLB*	*33*	*11*	*12*	*0*	*31*	*31*	*197^{1}*	*203*	*25*	*2.0*	*6.0*	*50%*	*.307*	*1.25*	*4.23*	*4.50*	*4.83*	*1.0*	*114*	

Breakout: 13% Improve: 43% Collapse: 26% Attrition: 14% MLB: 95% *Comparables: Phil Niekro, Frank Lary, Doug Drabek*

It was almost unthinkable after his fantastic 2014 season, but Fister could very well be done as a regular starting pitcher. He has never been a power pitcher, and his long limbs give him a deep release point that mitigates his declining velocity to some degree,

but he may finally have found a speed at which his pitches are no longer effective. By the third time through the order, his sinker was averaging no more than 86 mph, and the Nationals' front office grew concerned by midseason that something had to change. Fister was moved to a middle/long relief role, where he fared much better and figures to stay for the foreseeable future. This is an established pitcher just into his 30s, a pitcher who would likely have made $75 million or so if he'd hit free agency one year earlier than he did. Your reminder that the unreliability of pitching prospects is more about the first P in TINSTAAPP than the second.

Lucas Giolito RHP

Born: 7/14/94 Age: 21 Bats: R Throws: R Height: 6'6" Weight: 255

YEAR	TEAM	LVL	AGE	W	L	SV	G	GS	IP	H	HR	BB/9	K/9	GB%	BABIP	WHIP	ERA	FIP	DRA	WARP	CFIP	MPH
2013	AUB	A-	18	1	0	0	3	3	14	9	1	2.6	9.0	67%	.250	0.93	0.64	3.31	3.83	0.1	93	
2014	HAG	A	19	10	2	0	20	20	98	70	7	2.6	10.1	51%	.262	1.00	2.20	3.16	3.98	1.5	73	
2015	HAR	AA	20	4	2	0	8	8	47^1	48	2	3.2	8.6	56%	.341	1.37	3.80	3.18	3.85	0.5	95	
2015	POT	A+	20	3	5	0	13	11	69^2	65	1	2.6	11.1	54%	.352	1.22	2.71	1.96	0.88	3.2	66	
2016	*WAS*	*MLB*	*21*	*6*	*6*	*0*	*21*	*21*	*101^1*	*94*	*11*	*3.2*	*8.3*	*48%*	*.314*	*1.29*	*3.90*	*3.78*	*4.50*	*0.9*	*102*	
2017	*WAS*	*MLB*	*22*	*8*	*10*	*0*	*29*	*29*	*181^2*	*178*	*22*	*3.4*	*8.3*	*48%*	*.324*	*1.35*	*4.14*	*4.40*	*4.78*	*0.8*	*110*	

Breakout: 8% Improve: 13% Collapse: 5% Attrition: 11% MLB: 23% *Comparables: Jake McGee, Danny Duffy, Justin Nicolino*

It's full speed ahead for the top pitching prospect in baseball, whose pre-draft Tommy John surgery seems a distant memory. Giolito's mid-90s fastball and low-80s curveball wreaked havoc at High-A Potomac, as he overwhelmed hitters with his ability to change speeds and eye levels. He surrendered just one home run in 70 innings. (This despite sometimes having his pitch selection dictated to him by the Nationals' development-focused front office—though that oversight was finally drawn way back last year.)

He later moved to Harrisburg, where he showed that he's human after all, and that he needs to continue to work on his command, as well as the finer bits of pitching—holding runners on, fielding his position and rolling his R's. There's no rush to bring Giolito up just yet—other than the tick, tick, tick of every arm's countdown clock—but he'll be agitating for a rotation spot in the very near future.

Gio Gonzalez LHP

Born: 9/19/85 Age: 30 Bats: R Throws: L Height: 6'0" Weight: 210

YEAR	TEAM	LVL	AGE	W	L	SV	G	GS	IP	H	HR	BB/9	K/9	GB%	BABIP	WHIP	ERA	FIP	DRA	WARP	CFIP	MPH
2013	WAS	MLB	27	11	8	0	32	32	195^2	169	17	3.5	8.8	44%	.286	1.25	3.36	3.38	4.07	2.0	93	95.1
2014	WAS	MLB	28	10	10	0	27	27	158^2	134	10	3.2	9.2	48%	.294	1.20	3.57	3.00	3.78	2.0	92	94.5
2015	WAS	MLB	29	11	8	0	31	31	175^2	181	8	3.5	8.7	55%	.341	1.42	3.79	3.08	4.22	1.7	94	94.4
2016	*WAS*	*MLB*	*30*	*12*	*10*	*0*	*31*	*31*	*195^1*	*168*	*19*	*3.1*	*8.6*	*52%*	*.300*	*1.20*	*3.61*	*3.51*	*4.14*	*2.7*	*94*	
2017	*WAS*	*MLB*	*31*	*11*	*10*	*0*	*31*	*31*	*200^2*	*180*	*20*	*2.9*	*8.4*	*52%*	*.309*	*1.22*	*3.63*	*3.84*	*4.16*	*2.5*	*94*	

Breakout: 15% Improve: 49% Collapse: 19% Attrition: 15% MLB: 94% *Comparables: Ubaldo Jimenez, Bob Gibson, A.J. Burnett*

For a pitcher so frustratingly inconsistent from start to start, and even inning to inning, Gonzalez's main rate statistics have been steady every year. Part of that consistency lies in one simple truth: Gio ain't a tinkerer. That makes his tweaks stick out even more, like the groundball rate spike he enjoyed in 2015, anchored mostly by a shift toward using his sinker more and four-seamer less against right-handed hitters. Other than that, the basic ingredients are unchanged, and he remains a maddening, yet valuable piece of the Nats' rotation.

Trevor Gott RHP

Born: 8/26/92 Age: 23 Bats: R Throws: R Height: 6'0" Weight: 190

YEAR	TEAM	LVL	AGE	W	L	SV	G	GS	IP	H	HR	BB/9	K/9	GB%	BABIP	WHIP	ERA	FIP	DRA	WARP	CFIP	MPH
2013	FTW	A	20	2	2	4	27	0	31^2	23	1	3.4	9.4	56%	.278	1.11	2.56	2.99	4.29	0.2	90	
2014	SAN	AA	21	0	0	0	10	0	11^2	11	0	6.9	8.5	60%	.314	1.71	4.63	3.55				
2014	LEL	A+	21	2	4	16	29	0	31^1	28	3	2.6	8.9	58%	.288	1.18	3.16	3.96	4.88	-0.1	88	
2014	ARK	AA	21	2	1	2	13	0	17^2	11	0	3.6	9.2	58%	.256	1.02	1.53	2.27				
2015	ARK	AA	22	1	0	8	18	0	19^2	19	0	3.2	9.2	64%	.358	1.32	3.20	2.48	3.89	0.2	93	
2015	ANA	MLB	22	4	2	0	48	0	47^2	43	2	3.0	5.1	58%	.266	1.24	3.02	3.71	3.18	0.9	113	98.7
2016	*WAS*	*MLB*	*23*	*2*	*1*	*0*	*41*	*0*	*43^1*	*41*	*5*	*3.2*	*6.8*	*56%*	*.301*	*1.31*	*4.17*	*4.12*	*4.76*	*0.1*	*110*	
2017	*WAS*	*MLB*	*24*	*2*	*1*	*1*	*41*	*0*	*45^1*	*44*	*5*	*3.3*	*6.9*	*56%*	*.306*	*1.33*	*4.23*	*4.50*	*4.83*	*0.0*	*111*	

Breakout: 24% Improve: 31% Collapse: 21% Attrition: 32% MLB: 56% *Comparables: Scott Feldman, Eric O'Flaherty, Fabio Castro*

Pitchers like Gott who utilize a big burst to the plate are typically jettisoned to the bullpen due to the perceived "effort" in their deliveries, leaving aside the fact that the effort in question comes from the *lower* half, which is a much more sustainable place to carry the burden of pitching mechanics than a shoulder or an elbow. In the case of Gott, however, the bullpen assignment is more than justified by the lack of depth in his arsenal. He threw his four-seam fastball 84 percent of the time last year, averaging a beastly 97 mph on the pitch, but his breaking ball has yet to enter the circle of trust. Opposing batters enjoy the luxury of sitting on the heat and redirecting its kinetic energy toward outfields around the league. Gott's heat was enough to rack up impressive strikeout totals in the minors, but the big boys don't play; he'll need to develop *something* else if he wants to be more than a seventh guy in the majors.

We had a joke here about a man named "Gott" playing for the Angels, subsequently ruined by his trade to the Nationals for Yunel Escobar. Baseball is cruel.

Matt Grace LHP

Born: 12/14/88 Age: 27 Bats: L Throws: L Height: 6'3" Weight: 205

YEAR	TEAM	LVL	AGE	W	L	SV	G	GS	IP	H	HR	BB/9	K/9	GB%	BABIP	WHIP	ERA	FIP	DRA	WARP	CFIP	MPH
2013	POT	A+	24	3	0	0	14	0	28^{1}	26	0	2.2	7.6	70%	.302	1.16	3.18	2.71	4.29	0.2	86	
2013	HAR	AA	24	6	3	1	28	0	38	42	2	1.7	7.3	69%	.342	1.29	3.79	3.01	4.36	0.2	93	
2014	SYR	AAA	25	2	0	0	28	0	41^{2}	28	1	2.8	6.5	65%	.237	0.98	1.30	3.31	4.35	0.2	95	
2014	HAR	AA	25	3	1	3	22	0	35^{1}	32	0	3.1	8.2	74%	.291	1.25	1.02	2.56	4.13	0.3	86	
2015	SYR	AAA	26	0	2	1	38	0	48^{2}	43	1	3.0	5.7	64%	.280	1.21	2.40	3.14	4.37	0.0	104	
2015	WAS	MLB	26	2	1	0	26	0	17	26	0	4.2	7.4	59%	.426	2.00	4.24	3.10	7.33	-0.5	108	93.9
2016	*WAS*	*MLB*	*27*	*1*	*0*	*0*	*23*	*0*	*24*	*25*	*3*	*3.0*	*6.6*	*62%*	*.316*	*1.35*	*4.10*	*4.29*	*4.68*	*0.1*	*107*	
2017	*WAS*	*MLB*	*28*	*2*	*1*	*1*	*24*	*3*	*47*	*48*	*5*	*3.3*	*6.8*	*62%*	*.321*	*1.40*	*4.32*	*4.60*	*4.93*	*0.1*	*114*	

Breakout: 10% Improve: 19% Collapse: 10% Attrition: 24% MLB: 35% *Comparables: Jack Cassel, Daniel Moskos, David Martinez*

The former UCLA southpaw bounced up and down between Triple-A and The Show a couple of times, earning a role as a lefty specialist. Aside from one dreadful outing against Cincinnati on May 31st (he allowed four runs on six strikes and was demoted afteward), he was mostly effective, posting a 2.25 ERA before the Very Bad Day and a 1.80 afterward. His sinking fastball and decent slider are enough to hold him against lefties, but there's no third pitch and thus no bigger role ahead. That's too bad, because we had a killer Amazin' Grace joke all ready to go.

Casey Janssen RHP

Born: 9/17/81 Age: 34 Bats: R Throws: R Height: 6'4" Weight: 205

YEAR	TEAM	LVL	AGE	W	L	SV	G	GS	IP	H	HR	BB/9	K/9	GB%	BABIP	WHIP	ERA	FIP	DRA	WARP	CFIP	MPH
2013	TOR	MLB	31	4	1	34	56	0	52^{2}	39	3	2.2	8.5	49%	.254	0.99	2.56	2.77	2.37	1.4	83	92.2
2014	TOR	MLB	32	3	3	25	50	0	45^{2}	47	6	1.4	5.5	38%	.273	1.18	3.94	4.17	3.67	0.5	111	91.4
2015	WAS	MLB	33	2	5	0	48	0	40	38	5	1.8	6.1	34%	.264	1.15	4.95	4.11	4.19	0.2	107	90.4
2016	*WAS*	*MLB*	*34*	*6*	*7*	*0*	*97*	*50*	*50*	*46*	*6*	*2.3*	*6.7*	*38%*	*.285*	*1.17*	*4.04*	*4.02*	*4.62*	*0.2*	*107*	
2017	*WAS*	*MLB*	*35*	*3*	*1*	*11*	*64*	*0*	*59^{1}*	*56*	*7*	*2.5*	*6.6*	*38%*	*.292*	*1.22*	*4.12*	*4.38*	*4.71*	*0.1*	*108*	

Breakout: 10% Improve: 32% Collapse: 39% Attrition: 3% MLB: 90% *Comparables: Dave Smith, LaTroy Hawkins, Mike Jackson*

Casey Janssen used to throw 93, used to miss bats, used to come in for the ninth inning. And Rick Santorum and Mike Huckabee used to get to stand on the main stage at GOP debates. Sometimes big shifts can happen in four years, and for Janssen the the big shift involved a flattening curveball, slowing fastball and achy shoulder. Righties hit .284/.302/.500 against him, which is a fancy way of saying that his ceiling is a seventh-inning guy on a bad team.

Shawn Kelley RHP

Born: 4/26/84 Age: 32 Bats: R Throws: R Height: 6'2" Weight: 220

YEAR	TEAM	LVL	AGE	W	L	SV	G	GS	IP	H	HR	BB/9	K/9	GB%	BABIP	WHIP	ERA	FIP	DRA	WARP	CFIP	MPH
2013	NYA	MLB	29	4	2	0	57	0	53^{1}	47	8	3.9	12.0	34%	.312	1.31	4.39	3.66	3.95	0.4	76	94.9
2014	NYA	MLB	30	3	6	4	59	0	51^{2}	45	5	3.5	11.7	36%	.315	1.26	4.53	3.04	2.83	1.0	76	95.6
2015	SDN	MLB	31	2	2	0	53	0	51^{1}	41	4	2.6	11.0	44%	.301	1.09	2.45	2.60	2.72	1.2	74	94.4
2016	*WAS*	*MLB*	*32*	*3*	*1*	*0*	*55*	*0*	*57^{2}*	*47*	*6*	*3.0*	*10.3*	*41%*	*.302*	*1.15*	*3.35*	*3.25*	*3.87*	*0.7*	*80*	
2017	*WAS*	*MLB*	*33*	*3*	*1*	*1*	*58*	*0*	*56^{1}*	*48*	*6*	*3.1*	*9.8*	*41%*	*.313*	*1.21*	*3.49*	*3.68*	*4.03*	*0.6*	*84*	

Breakout: 25% Improve: 43% Collapse: 25% Attrition: 3% MLB: 86% *Comparables: Frank Francisco, Scott Williamson, Michael Wuertz*

Kelley's Padres career got off to a miserable start, with his ERA sitting at 9.35 in mid-May. After working with pitching coach Darren Balsley to keep his front shoulder closed and fix his landing, he held hitters to a .441 OPS over the final four and a half months and struck out a third of the batters he faced. Kelley got cuffed around with runners in scoring position, but he was rarely in that position and it hasn't been a problem in the past. He missed three weeks in April with a left calf strain and three more in September with a right forearm strain that was not considered serious. His fastball/slider combo is tough against righties and lefties alike, making him a legitimate late-innings option and possible closer material. Assuming, at least, that his Nationals career doesn't get off to a miserable start.

Reynaldo Lopez RHP

Born: 1/4/94 Age: 22 Bats: R Throws: R Height: 6'0" Weight: 185

YEAR	TEAM	LVL	AGE	W	L	SV	G	GS	IP	H	HR	BB/9	K/9	GB%	BABIP	WHIP	ERA	FIP	DRA	WARP	CFIP	MPH
2014	AUB	A-	20	3	2	0	7	7	36	15	0	3.8	7.8	62%	.167	0.83	0.75	3.14	4.34	0.2	103	
2014	HAG	A	20	4	1	0	9	9	47^{1}	27	1	2.1	7.4	65%	.211	0.80	1.33	2.91	4.37	0.5	88	
2015	POT	A+	21	6	7	0	19	19	99	93	5	2.5	8.5	47%	.321	1.22	4.09	2.95	2.64	2.5	84	
2016	*WAS*	*MLB*	*22*	*5*	*5*	*0*	*16*	*16*	*82^{1}*	*80*	*9*	*3.3*	*7.0*	*47%*	*.308*	*1.34*	*4.23*	*4.11*	*4.83*	*0.4*	*113*	
2017	*WAS*	*MLB*	*23*	*8*	*10*	*0*	*29*	*29*	*180*	*178*	*21*	*3.7*	*7.2*	*47%*	*.314*	*1.40*	*4.47*	*4.76*	*5.10*	*0.3*	*120*	

Breakout: 5% Improve: 7% Collapse: 7% Attrition: 12% MLB: 17% *Comparables: Frank Francisco, Scott Williamson, Michael Wuertz*

The fact that he sits at 96-97 dominates the conversation, but Lopez is more than just a pretty radar gun reading. He puts a ton of rotation on the ball, giving the heater late life and run. His short curve and slow change are decent, too, though they don't give him the same kind of arsenal that, say, Giolito has; think, instead, more along the lines of Yordano Ventura. The Nats want him to repeat his mechanics better, and if he learns to, it's easy to see a mid-rotation future. All goes well, and he'll debut sometime in 2017. In other words, expect to see him in 2018.

Tyler Mapes RHP

Born: 7/18/91 Age: 24 Bats: R Throws: R Height: 6'2" Weight: 205

YEAR	TEAM	LVL	AGE	W	L	SV	G	GS	IP	H	HR	BB/9	K/9	GB%	BABIP	WHIP	ERA	FIP	DRA	WARP	CFIP	MPH
2014	AUB	A-	22	1	1	5	15	0	21^2	20	1	2.5	5.8	58%	.297	1.20	1.25	3.72	4.39	0.0	105	
2015	POT	A+	23	6	3	1	30	8	90^2	94	3	1.7	7.0	59%	.324	1.22	2.38	2.78	2.87	1.8	87	
2016	*WAS*	*MLB*	*24*	*4*	*2*	*2*	*49*	*5*	*72*	*76*	*8*	*2.7*	*5.8*	*55%*	*.314*	*1.35*	*4.25*	*4.21*	*4.84*	*0.2*	*113*	
2017	*WAS*	*MLB*	*25*	*3*	*2*	*1*	*29*	*4*	*73^1*	*77*	*8*	*3.0*	*6.0*	*55%*	*.317*	*1.39*	*4.36*	*4.65*	*4.97*	*0.0*	*116*	

Breakout: 6% Improve: 6% Collapse: 0% Attrition: 1% MLB: 7% *Comparables: Jon Link, Ryan Kelly, Kyle McClellan*

With a fastball that tops out at 93 and a buckshot slurve as his main secondary pitch, it's easy to see how two years in a row nobody thought to draft him until the late rounds. But Mapes has impressed at the lower levels; the team store at High-A Potomac even stocks his jerseys now. Don't expect the big-league team to follow suit just yet. Though his fastball has heavy sink, his secondaries will probably top out as fringe-average offerings. As such, he'll walk the line between back-end starter and swingman.

Rafael Martin RHP

Born: 5/16/84 Age: 32 Bats: R Throws: R Height: 6'3" Weight: 220

YEAR	TEAM	LVL	AGE	W	L	SV	G	GS	IP	H	HR	BB/9	K/9	GB%	BABIP	WHIP	ERA	FIP	DRA	WARP	CFIP	MPH
2013	POT	A+	29	0	0	2	17	0	26	12	1	4.8	11.4	38%	.193	1.00	1.04	3.04	4.35	0.2	89	
2014	SYR	AAA	30	1	1	10	25	0	33^2	20	0	1.9	11.2	39%	.260	0.80	0.80	1.49	3.47	0.5	58	
2014	HAR	AA	30	2	1	1	11	0	20	15	1	2.2	9.0	44%	.264	1.00	2.70	2.90	4.14	0.1	88	
2015	WAS	MLB	31	2	0	0	13	0	12^1	12	4	3.6	18.2	32%	.381	1.38	5.11	4.78	6.83	-0.3	70	91.1
2015	SYR	AAA	31	5	5	12	46	0	56	41	4	2.6	10.9	28%	.278	1.02	3.21	2.57	1.29	2.2	63	
2016	*WAS*	*MLB*	*32*	*1*	*0*	*0*	*14*	*0*	*14^1*	*11*	*1*	*2.9*	*10.4*	*30%*	*.294*	*1.09*	*3.22*	*2.62*	*3.71*	*0.3*	*79*	
2017	*WAS*	*MLB*	*33*	*1*	*0*	*0*	*22*	*0*	*29^2*	*23*	*3*	*2.8*	*10.6*	*30%*	*.294*	*1.09*	*3.33*	*3.50*	*3.84*	*0.4*	*82*	

Breakout: 13% Improve: 25% Collapse: 13% Attrition: 22% MLB: 48% *Comparables: Yhency Brazoban, Jim Miller, Joe Nelson*

How in the world does a guy with a 90 mph fastball get four misses out of every 10 swings? With a quirky, quick and deceptive delivery that slings the heater in with some late life. Martin made his major-league debut at age 30 and struck out five in two innings; that would foreshadow one of the oddest seasons in baseball, as he became the first pitcher in history to strike out 18-plus batters per nine (min. 10 innings). Despite that, he was not very good, spending most of the year in the minors, where his strikeout rates were as pedestrian as his velocity readings. He'll compete for a middle-relief spot on the 25-man roster, and eventually see his unexplainable record fall.

Jonathan Papelbon RHP

Born: 11/23/80 Age: 35 Bats: R Throws: R Height: 6'4" Weight: 225

YEAR	TEAM	LVL	AGE	W	L	SV	G	GS	IP	H	HR	BB/9	K/9	GB%	BABIP	WHIP	ERA	FIP	DRA	WARP	CFIP	MPH
2013	PHI	MLB	32	5	1	29	61	0	61^2	59	6	1.6	8.3	42%	.296	1.14	2.92	3.02	2.99	1.2	86	94.5
2014	PHI	MLB	33	2	3	39	66	0	66^1	45	2	2.0	8.5	44%	.247	0.90	2.04	2.50	2.00	2.0	90	93.8
2015	WAS	MLB	34	2	2	7	22	0	23^2	22	4	1.5	6.1	50%	.250	1.10	3.04	4.89	4.83	0.0	112	94.3
2015	PHI	MLB	34	2	1	17	37	0	39^2	31	3	1.8	9.1	53%	.267	0.98	1.59	3.04	2.28	1.1	84	93.8
2016	*WAS*	*MLB*	*35*	*3*	*1*	*35*	*55*	*0*	*57^2*	*51*	*7*	*2.2*	*8.0*	*48%*	*.292*	*1.13*	*3.74*	*3.68*	*4.31*	*0.4*	*97*	
2017	*WAS*	*MLB*	*36*	*2*	*1*	*20*	*49*	*0*	*50^2*	*47*	*6*	*2.2*	*7.2*	*48%*	*.292*	*1.17*	*4.01*	*4.25*	*4.62*	*0.2*	*106*	

Breakout: 21% Improve: 39% Collapse: 31% Attrition: 13% MLB: 93% *Comparables: Mike Adams, Francisco Cordero, Akinori Otsuka*

On the back nine of a storied career, Papelbon's legacy is beginning to take shape. He is an alternate-universe Mariano Rivera who, despite putting up impressive stats every year, intentionally makes teammates uncomfortable with remarkable effectiveness. He's as "proven" as a closer can get, but he's as unpredictable as ever. He hasn't pitched in the postseason since a series-ending blown save/loss in 2009, and the underperformance of his two teams last year seemed to uncork very deep frustrations. He now represents a type of player that baseball has had fewer of lately: The established veteran whose behavior jeopardizes his roster spot despite his on-field performance. He has the third-best ERA+ in major-league history, and he might not get a single Hall of Fame vote when he retires .

Oliver Perez LHP

Born: 8/15/81 Age: 34 Bats: L Throws: L Height: 6'3" Weight: 220

YEAR	TEAM	LVL	AGE	W	L	SV	G	GS	IP	H	HR	BB/9	K/9	GB%	BABIP	WHIP	ERA	FIP	DRA	WARP	CFIP	MPH
2013	SEA	MLB	31	3	3	2	61	0	53	50	6	4.4	12.6	31%	.361	1.43	3.74	3.28	4.62	0.0	79	95.3
2014	ARI	MLB	32	3	4	0	68	0	58^2	50	5	3.7	11.7	47%	.312	1.26	2.91	3.20	3.82	0.5	86	94.0
2015	ARI	MLB	33	2	1	0	48	0	29	25	2	3.4	11.5	45%	.311	1.24	3.10	3.06	3.68	0.4	85	94.8
2015	HOU	MLB	33	0	3	0	22	0	12	14	2	3.0	10.5	32%	.343	1.50	6.75	3.94	5.54	-0.1	92	94.6
2016	*WAS*	*MLB*	*34*	*3*	*1*	*0*	*50*	*0*	*53*	*46*	*6*	*3.2*	*10.0*	*41%*	*.316*	*1.21*	*3.54*	*3.47*	*4.08*	*0.5*	*89*	
2017	*WAS*	*MLB*	*35*	*3*	*1*	*1*	*60*	*0*	*50^2*	*46*	*6*	*3.7*	*9.7*	*41%*	*.322*	*1.31*	*3.97*	*4.20*	*4.57*	*0.2*	*102*	

Breakout: 25% Improve: 44% Collapse: 20% Attrition: 7% MLB: 81% *Comparables: John Bale, Tim Byrdak, Kerry Wood*

If you take a Stretch Armstrong doll, remove the goo from three of its joints (choice of joints not terribly important) so they just kind of flop around, and teach it to throw left handed, you have basically created the 2015 edition of Oliver Perez. And like that Stretch Armstrong doll, he'll still be around long after we're all gone. Signing with the Nationals means that Mets fans will have to watch him more often than ever in 2016.

Yusmeiro Petit RHP

Born: 11/22/84 Age: 31 Bats: R Throws: R Height: 6'1" Weight: 250

YEAR	TEAM	LVL	AGE	W	L	SV	G	GS	IP	H	HR	BB/9	K/9	GB%	BABIP	WHIP	ERA	FIP	DRA	WARP	CFIP	MPH
2013	FRE	AAA	28	5	6	0	15	15	87^2	92	16	1.3	9.3	38%	.315	1.20	4.52	4.31	4.41	1.2	82	
2013	SFN	MLB	28	4	1	0	8	7	48	46	4	2.1	8.8	33%	.313	1.19	3.56	2.83	2.76	1.2	85	90.2
2014	SFN	MLB	29	5	5	0	39	12	117	97	12	1.7	10.2	36%	.290	1.02	3.69	2.75	3.62	1.5	73	91.2
2015	SFN	MLB	30	1	1	1	42	1	76	75	11	1.8	7.0	34%	.278	1.18	3.67	4.12	4.59	0.1	105	90.7
2016	*WAS*	*MLB*	*31*	*3*	*2*	*0*	*48*	*3*	*64*	*58*	*8*	*2.1*	*8.2*	*34%*	*.298*	*1.14*	*3.72*	*3.65*	*4.26*	*0.9*	*96*	
2017	*WAS*	*MLB*	*32*	*5*	*4*	*0*	*25*	*12*	*92^2*	*87*	*12*	*2.0*	*8.2*	*34%*	*.306*	*1.17*	*3.82*	*4.03*	*4.37*	*0.9*	*99*	

Breakout: 24% Improve: 44% Collapse: 19% Attrition: 19% MLB: 86% *Comparables: Buddy Carlyle, Colby Lewis, Kiko Calero*

If a pitching genie granted you one wish for a world-class offering of your choosing, which type would you pick? Petit serves as fairly sound evidence that you ought not select a curveball. The right-hander spins a dandy, high-70s hook that held foes to an .089 average and .139 slugging percentage last year, produced 41 strikeouts in the 101 at-bats it terminated, and remains one of baseball's best-kept secrets. What's not a secret is that the rest of Petit's menu is blander than airline breakfast, an assortment of fastballs, cutters and changeups that each yielded a slugging percentage above .600. The net result was a replacement-level long reliever, the sort who grows on Triple-A trees, even if his curveball does not.

Felipe Rivero LHP

Born: 7/5/91 Age: 24 Bats: L Throws: L Height: 6'2" Weight: 200

YEAR	TEAM	LVL	AGE	W	L	SV	G	GS	IP	H	HR	BB/9	K/9	GB%	BABIP	WHIP	ERA	FIP	DRA	WARP	CFIP	MPH
2013	PCH	A+	21	9	7	0	25	23	127	122	7	3.7	6.4	47%	.299	1.37	3.40	3.92	4.48	0.6	106	
2014	HAR	AA	22	2	7	0	10	10	43^2	45	4	3.7	7.8	52%	.304	1.44	4.12	4.18	4.54	0.3	99	
2015	WAS	MLB	23	2	1	2	49	0	48^1	35	2	2.0	8.0	47%	.250	0.95	2.79	2.67	2.18	1.5	90	98.4
2016	*WAS*	*MLB*	*24*	*2*	*1*	*0*	*45*	*0*	*48*	*45*	*5*	*2.9*	*7.5*	*48%*	*.307*	*1.27*	*3.91*	*3.85*	*4.46*	*0.3*	*102*	
2017	*WAS*	*MLB*	*25*	*3*	*3*	*0*	*25*	*10*	*78^1*	*74*	*9*	*3.4*	*7.7*	*48%*	*.312*	*1.32*	*4.11*	*4.37*	*4.69*	*0.4*	*108*	

Breakout: 23% Improve: 34% Collapse: 5% Attrition: 18% MLB: 51% *Comparables: Felix Doubront, Jason Windsor, Arodys Vizcaino*

Rivero had 11 stops in his pro career before Washington, including Fall League and winter ball action, and in five of those stops he allowed at least six runs per nine. (Only once was he below four.) But a move to relief last year served him and the club well, as he escaped a disastrous stint in Triple-A and helped rescue a Nationals bullpen badly in need of an effective lefty. All three of his pitches—96 mph fastball, changeup, and a relatively soft slider—get whiffs, and he commands all well enough to avoid hard contact. Among all southpaw relievers, he had the 11th-best OPS allowed against right-handed batters; he was the ninth-best against lefties. Only Aroldis Chapman was better against both orientations than Rivero was.

Tanner Roark RHP

Born: 10/5/86 Age: 29 Bats: R Throws: R Height: 6'2" Weight: 235

YEAR	TEAM	LVL	AGE	W	L	SV	G	GS	IP	H	HR	BB/9	K/9	GB%	BABIP	WHIP	ERA	FIP	DRA	WARP	CFIP	MPH
2013	WAS	MLB	26	7	1	0	14	5	53^2	38	1	1.8	6.7	50%	.243	0.91	1.51	2.39	2.16	1.7	95	95.0
2013	SYR	AAA	26	9	3	2	33	11	105^2	85	6	1.7	7.2	47%	.255	0.99	3.15	3.01	3.93	1.0	85	
2014	WAS	MLB	27	15	10	0	31	31	198^2	178	16	1.8	6.3	42%	.270	1.09	2.85	3.44	3.70	2.7	107	93.8
2015	WAS	MLB	28	4	7	1	40	12	111	119	17	2.1	5.7	49%	.293	1.31	4.38	4.73	5.22	-0.4	115	95.6
2016	*WAS*	*MLB*	*29*	*10*	*10*	*0*	*29*	*29*	*165^1*	*160*	*20*	*2.2*	*6.4*	*46%*	*.296*	*1.21*	*4.11*	*4.01*	*4.69*	*1.2*	*110*	
2017	*WAS*	*MLB*	*30*	*8*	*8*	*0*	*36*	*21*	*152^2*	*155*	*20*	*2.2*	*6.6*	*46%*	*.308*	*1.26*	*4.23*	*4.50*	*4.83*	*0.7*	*113*	

Breakout: 19% Improve: 40% Collapse: 17% Attrition: 13% MLB: 73% *Comparables: Craig Stammen, Bronson Arroyo, Darrell Rasner*

The problem with "sit tight, kid, something will open up" is that, by the time it does, you just might have already been exposed as not really all that. After the Nationals signed Max Scherzer, they told the overachieving Roark to sit tight, something will open up. It did, when Stephen Strasburg got injured, but by that point Roark had struck out seven batters in 20-plus relief innings. He still got the part, but bounced back and forth the rest of the way, never looking right as a reliever and never looking settled in as a starter. In only one of his 12 starts did he get as many as 10 swinging strikes—something he achieved in nine of 31 starts the year before. The guy who appeared to be baseball's most overqualified sixth starter in April seemed perfectly qualified for thankless swingman duties by the end. He's still a bubble candidate for the rotation, but with young talent on Washington's doorstep, a 30-start season is a fool's bet.

Joe Ross RHP

Born: 5/21/93 Age: 23 Bats: R Throws: R Height: 6'4" Weight: 205

YEAR	TEAM	LVL	AGE	W	L	SV	G	GS	IP	H	HR	BB/9	K/9	GB%	BABIP	WHIP	ERA	FIP	DRA	WARP	CFIP	MPH
2013	FTW	A	20	5	8	0	23	23	122^1	124	7	2.9	5.8	52%	.298	1.34	3.75	3.89	4.80	0.6	106	
2014	LEL	A+	21	8	6	0	19	19	101^2	101	6	2.5	7.7	54%	.325	1.27	3.98	3.83	5.03	0.5	92	
2014	SAN	AA	21	2	0	0	4	3	20	23	2	0.4	8.6	47%	.339	1.20	3.60	2.67				
2015	WAS	MLB	22	5	5	0	16	13	76^2	64	7	2.5	8.1	54%	.265	1.11	3.64	3.45	3.38	1.5	98	96.3
2015	SYR	AAA	22	3	1	0	5	5	24^2	15	2	2.6	5.5	55%	.188	0.89	2.19	3.85	4.16	0.1	102	
2015	HAR	AA	22	2	2	0	9	9	51^1	46	3	2.1	9.5	50%	.323	1.13	2.81	2.80	2.78	1.3	81	
2016	*WAS*	*MLB*	*23*	*8*	*8*	*0*	*26*	*26*	*137^2*	*129*	*16*	*2.8*	*7.4*	*52%*	*.302*	*1.24*	*3.97*	*3.92*	*4.54*	*1.2*	*105*	
2017	*WAS*	*MLB*	*24*	*7*	*8*	*0*	*24*	*24*	*139^1*	*135*	*18*	*3.1*	*7.8*	*52%*	*.314*	*1.31*	*4.21*	*4.47*	*4.81*	*0.7*	*112*	

Breakout: 17% Improve: 30% Collapse: 21% Attrition: 28% MLB: 63% *Comparables: Alex Sanabia, Drew Pomeranz, Randall Delgado*

Tyson's little brother joined the rotation midseason and showed a mature approach even as a rookie, using a low-90s sinker effectively to both sides of the plate. His slider was devastating, especially against right-handed hitters (.211 SLG, 47 percent whiff/

swing). Yet his changeup was as firm as suggested, and as a result he struggled to get lefties out. As such, the development of his camby will determine if he's a no. 2 or no. 4 starter. (Odd numbers needn't apply.) Ross has already conquered one aspect of the job that his brother never could: Just one baserunner successfully stole on Joe, three dozen fewer than took bases from Tyson.

Max Scherzer RHP

Born: 7/27/84 Age: 31 Bats: R Throws: R Height: 6'3" Weight: 215

YEAR	TEAM	LVL	AGE	W	L	SV	G	GS	IP	H	HR	BB/9	K/9	GB%	BABIP	WHIP	ERA	FIP	DRA	WARP	CFIP	MPH
2013	DET	MLB	28	21	3	0	32	32	214^1	152	18	2.4	10.1	38%	.259	0.97	2.90	2.77	2.29	6.8	68	96.9
2014	DET	MLB	29	18	5	0	33	33	220^1	196	18	2.6	10.3	38%	.315	1.18	3.15	2.87	3.04	4.7	68	96.3
2015	WAS	MLB	30	14	12	0	33	33	228^2	176	27	1.3	10.9	38%	.268	0.92	2.79	2.79	2.77	6.2	66	97.4
2016	*WAS*	*MLB*	*31*	*15*	*10*	*0*	*33*	*33*	*221*	*173*	*24*	*2.0*	*10.7*	*38%*	*.300*	*1.00*	*2.91*	*2.81*	*3.36*	*5.1*	*70*	
2017	*WAS*	*MLB*	*32*	*13*	*9*	*0*	*30*	*30*	*189*	*155*	*21*	*1.8*	*10.4*	*38%*	*.308*	*1.02*	*3.01*	*3.15*	*3.47*	*4.2*	*73*	

Breakout: 21% Improve: 52% Collapse: 20% Attrition: 9% MLB: 95% *Comparables: Javier Vazquez, Billy Pierce, Ron Guidry*

Scherzer spent nearly half the season as a below-average pitcher, surrendering a 4.45 ERA in 15 starts from July 7th to September 23rd. Wrapped around were the other 19 starts, in which Mad Max was unstoppable: three starts with Game Scores above 95, two no-hitters and a 1.66 ERA. His final start of the season, a 17-strikeout virtual perfect game (save for an infield error), might be the most dominant pitching performance in the sport's history. It's undeniably close.

Two versions of Scherzer, as different as his eye colors. What made the difference? He becomes susceptible to the home run ball when his mechanics fail him and cause him to miss location. In the summer stretch of mediocrity, hitters slugged 20 of their 27 homers against him.

Sammy Solis LHP

Born: 8/10/88 Age: 27 Bats: R Throws: L Height: 6'5" Weight: 230

YEAR	TEAM	LVL	AGE	W	L	SV	G	GS	IP	H	HR	BB/9	K/9	GB%	BABIP	WHIP	ERA	FIP	DRA	WARP	CFIP	MPH
2013	POT	A+	24	2	1	0	13	12	57^2	58	3	3.0	6.2	48%	.314	1.34	3.43	3.63	4.60	0.4	97	
2015	WAS	MLB	26	1	1	0	18	0	21^1	25	2	1.7	7.2	46%	.329	1.36	3.38	3.49	4.79	0.0	101	96.7
2015	SYR	AAA	26	0	0	2	9	0	13^1	8	0	3.4	7.4	50%	.222	0.98	2.03	2.86	3.78	0.1	96	
2015	HAR	AA	26	0	3	2	11	1	13^1	19	0	3.4	7.4	39%	.413	1.80	6.75	3.19	4.60	0.0	103	
2016	*WAS*	*MLB*	*27*	*1*	*0*	*0*	*18*	*0*	*19^1*	*20*	*2*	*2.9*	*6.9*	*45%*	*.317*	*1.34*	*4.13*	*3.92*	*4.72*	*0.1*	*108*	
2017	*WAS*	*MLB*	*28*	*3*	*2*	*0*	*27*	*7*	*68^1*	*68*	*8*	*2.9*	*7.4*	*45%*	*.314*	*1.31*	*4.13*	*4.40*	*4.72*	*0.2*	*108*	

Breakout: 9% Improve: 23% Collapse: 7% Attrition: 13% MLB: 33% *Comparables: Hector Ambriz, Mike Bolsinger, Mike Ekstrom*

It's always hard to confidently blame injuries for bad performances—when did the pains start, how long did they linger, and so on—but it's tempting to give Solis a bit of a pass for some of his worst outings last year. On May 22nd, the Nationals announced he had shoulder inflammation. In the two outings before the announcement, he allowed five runs; in the two upon his return (to Double-A Harrisburg), he allowed five more. Otherwise, he had a 2.25 ERA across three levels. So it's not Rolaids-hardware level or anything, but the bottom line is that Solis is useful when he's healthy. He's just never healthy enough to be useful.

Drew Storen RHP

Born: 8/11/87 Age: 28 Bats: B Throws: R Height: 6'1" Weight: 195

YEAR	TEAM	LVL	AGE	W	L	SV	G	GS	IP	H	HR	BB/9	K/9	GB%	BABIP	WHIP	ERA	FIP	DRA	WARP	CFIP	MPH
2013	WAS	MLB	25	4	2	3	68	0	61^2	65	7	2.8	8.5	44%	.319	1.36	4.52	3.59	5.19	-0.4	94	96.1
2014	WAS	MLB	26	2	1	11	65	0	56^1	44	2	1.8	7.3	54%	.259	0.98	1.12	2.68	2.48	1.4	94	95.6
2015	WAS	MLB	27	2	2	29	58	0	55	45	4	2.6	11.0	44%	.301	1.11	3.44	2.82	3.16	1.0	78	96.3
2016	*WAS*	*MLB*	*28*	*3*	*1*	*0*	*50*	*0*	*53*	*43*	*6*	*2.5*	*9.1*	*47%*	*.291*	*1.09*	*3.42*	*3.47*	*3.94*	*0.6*	*86*	
2017	*WAS*	*MLB*	*29*	*3*	*1*	*14*	*61*	*0*	*55*	*47*	*6*	*2.6*	*9.0*	*47%*	*.300*	*1.14*	*3.58*	*3.79*	*4.13*	*0.5*	*90*	

Breakout: 21% Improve: 51% Collapse: 29% Attrition: 7% MLB: 95% *Comparables: Jesse Orosco, Doug Corbett, Tug McGraw*

Thank goodness the boos Storen heard in the second half probably blended in with the characteristic "Drooo!!" he was used to hearing in Nationals Park. Storen started the season in the closer role and dominated, allowing runs in just five of his first 43 appearances. But soon after his *de facto* demotion to a setup role at the trade deadline, Storen's command betrayed him. He allowed earned runs in four straight outings, then walked in the tying run in the Nationals' epic September 8th collapse against the Mets—a game that all but ended the Nationals' NL East chances and Matt Williams' managerial career.

Inevitably, observers have attributed this drop-off—and his subsequent hand injury from slamming his locker shut one bad outing later—to a wounded ego stemming from losing the closing job. It's not the first time the Nationals have given Storen less deference than the Proven C patch normally affords; he had lost the ninth inning once before, to Rafael Soriano; and was demoted in 2013, a move that was controversial both in the Nats clubhouse and on his dad's Twitter timeline. Storen can still pitch effectively, but if closers need unshakeable confidence to get the job done, it's hard to see how being in this organization can help.

Stephen Strasburg RHP

Born: 7/20/88 Age: 27 Bats: R Throws: R Height: 6'4" Weight: 230

YEAR	TEAM	LVL	AGE	W	L	SV	G	GS	IP	H	HR	BB/9	K/9	GB%	BABIP	WHIP	ERA	FIP	DRA	WARP	CFIP	MPH
2013	WAS	MLB	24	8	9	0	30	30	183	136	16	2.8	9.4	52%	.263	1.05	3.00	3.18	3.28	3.6	85	98.0
2014	WAS	MLB	25	14	11	0	34	34	215	198	23	1.8	10.1	48%	.315	1.12	3.14	2.91	3.85	2.5	78	97.3
2015	WAS	MLB	26	11	7	0	23	23	127^1	115	14	1.8	11.0	45%	.311	1.11	3.46	2.84	3.96	1.6	73	98.0
2016	*WAS*	*MLB*	*27*	*10*	*8*	*0*	*26*	*26*	*156*	*127*	*18*	*2.2*	*9.9*	*48%*	*.301*	*1.05*	*3.25*	*3.14*	*3.74*	*2.9*	*82*	
2017	*WAS*	*MLB*	*28*	*11*	*9*	*0*	*30*	*30*	*184^2*	*160*	*23*	*2.1*	*9.8*	*48%*	*.313*	*1.09*	*3.36*	*3.53*	*3.87*	*2.9*	*85*	

Breakout: 28% Improve: 54% Collapse: 17% Attrition: 6% MLB: 99% *Comparables: Hideo Nomo, Daisuke Matsuzaka, Jake Peavy*

Strasburg's Jekyll and Hyde season is a cautionary tale about trying to pitch through pain. His year began with rumors of nagging injuries—rumors that only intensified as the right-hander posted a 6.55 ERA through the end of May. His velocity was healthy, and his control was fine, but he struggled to command his secondary pitches and was forced to pound fastball after fastball into the zone. In the entire month of May—five full starts—he got just 20 swinging strikes.

But two mid-year DL stints gave him the chance to rest and become whole, and Strasburg came back as dominant as ever. His full-season pace from June through late September put his ERA under 2.00 and would pace almost 300 strikeouts against just 32 walks. On September 15th alone, he got *27* swinging strikes. In his healthy appearances, Strasburg was the same old pitcher the Nats relied on since his debut. There's no reason to doubt that will continue, other than the permanent doubt that a pitcher's good health will continue.

Matt Thornton LHP

Born: 9/15/76 Age: 39 Bats: L Throws: L Height: 6'6" Weight: 235

YEAR	TEAM	LVL	AGE	W	L	SV	G	GS	IP	H	HR	BB/9	K/9	GB%	BABIP	WHIP	ERA	FIP	DRA	WARP	CFIP	MPH
2013	CHA	MLB	36	0	3	0	40	0	28	25	4	3.2	6.8	45%	.266	1.25	3.86	4.72	4.40	0.1	111	96.6
2013	BOS	MLB	36	0	1	0	20	0	15^{1}	22	0	2.9	5.3	61%	.386	1.76	3.52	2.88	3.29	0.2	114	96.3
2014	NYA	MLB	37	0	3	0	46	0	24^{2}	23	0	2.2	7.3	57%	.299	1.18	2.55	2.75	3.02	0.4	102	97.1
2014	WAS	MLB	37	1	0	0	18	0	11^{1}	10	0	1.6	6.4	56%	.294	1.06	0.00	2.48	2.13	0.3	102	97.8
2015	WAS	MLB	38	2	1	0	60	0	41^{1}	33	2	2.4	5.0	46%	.231	1.06	2.18	3.55	3.01	0.8	113	95.8
2016	*WAS*	*MLB*	*39*	*2*	*1*	*0*	*38*	*0*	*40*	*40*	*5*	*2.8*	*6.3*	*49%*	*.302*	*1.31*	*4.29*	*4.31*	*4.92*	*0.0*	*111*	
2017	*WAS*	*MLB*	*40*	*3*	*1*	*1*	*63*	*0*	45^{1}	*48*	*6*	*2.7*	*6.0*	*49%*	*.312*	*1.37*	*4.57*	*4.87*	*5.24*	*-0.2*	*120*	

Breakout: 15% Improve: 46% Collapse: 13% Attrition: 9% MLB: 77% *Comparables: Scott Downs, Rheal Cormier, Gene Garber*

From the surface, it doesn't appear much has changed for the 39-year-old Thornton, who was once again an effective relief option. Yet plug your nose and dive in, and you'll find some tweaks. He responded to a cooler fastball by changing to a two-seamer for the first time in his career. He also dug into his past to bring back a long-forgotten splitter. That combination left him with fewer strikeouts, sure, but he has also allowed just two home runs over the past two seasons. Maybe you don't believe in home run suppression as a skill, and want more of a sample before you trust Thornton. That's fair. But by the time we have enough innings to say for sure, Thornton will be about 45—or just outside of a LOOGY's expected prime.

Blake Treinen RHP

Born: 6/30/88 Age: 28 Bats: R Throws: R Height: 6'5" Weight: 230

YEAR	TEAM	LVL	AGE	W	L	SV	G	GS	IP	H	HR	BB/9	K/9	GB%	BABIP	WHIP	ERA	FIP	DRA	WARP	CFIP	MPH
2013	HAR	AA	25	6	7	0	21	20	118^{2}	125	9	2.5	6.5	58%	.310	1.33	3.64	3.79	4.57	0.8	99	
2014	SYR	AAA	26	8	2	0	16	16	80^{2}	78	4	2.2	7.1	58%	.301	1.21	3.35	3.31	4.29	0.7	91	
2014	WAS	MLB	26	2	3	0	15	7	50^{2}	57	1	2.3	5.3	60%	.333	1.38	2.49	3.06	4.50	0.1	114	98.0
2015	WAS	MLB	27	2	5	0	60	0	67^{2}	62	4	4.3	8.6	65%	.328	1.39	3.86	3.52	4.17	0.4	97	98.9
2015	SYR	AAA	27	0	0	0	5	0	12	6	0	0.8	10.5	71%	.214	0.58	0.00	1.07	1.91	0.4	70	
2016	*WAS*	*MLB*	*28*	*1*	*0*	*0*	*23*	*0*	*24*	*23*	*2*	*3.0*	*7.4*	*62%*	*.314*	*1.29*	*3.91*	*3.58*	*4.48*	*0.2*	*101*	
2017	*WAS*	*MLB*	*29*	*3*	*2*	*0*	*17*	*7*	53^{1}	*51*	*6*	*3.2*	*7.8*	*62%*	*.316*	*1.30*	*3.98*	*4.24*	*4.56*	*0.4*	*104*	

Breakout: 21% Improve: 43% Collapse: 12% Attrition: 24% MLB: 73% *Comparables: Dan Meyer, Troy Patton, Chad Qualls*

Treinen is one half of an elite relief pitcher. Against right-handed batters, his heavy power sinker generated 80 percent groundballs and just a .211 SLG. Against lefties, however, that became 60 percent grounders and a .575 SLG. His big slider gets lots of whiffs, but he lacks the ability to finish at-bats against southpaws and ends up walking many of them. Overall, they stung him for a .934 OPS. So what's Treinen to do? He could try again on that changeup development, or he could settle for being a ROOGY. But nobody wants to be a ROOGY.

LINEOUTS

Hitters

NAME	POS	TEAM	LVL	AGE	PA	R	2B	3B	HR	RBI	BB	K	SB	CS	AVG/OBP/SLG	TAv	BABIP	BRR	FRAA	WARP
Osvaldo Abreu	SS	HAG	A	21	513	74	35	4	6	47	50	89	30	11	.274/.357/.412	.285	.327	3.4	SS(79): -12.1, 2B(42): -0.9	2.3
Rafael Bautista	CF	AUB	A-	22	34	6	3	0	0	4	1	7	3	0	.273/.294/.364	.224	.346	1.0	CF(7): 0.3	0.1
	CF	POT	A+	22	226	23	7	2	0	8	11	22	23	4	.272/.318/.325	.253	.301	0.0	CF(52): -3.2	0.2
Cutter Dykstra	2B	HAR	AA	26	278	27	11	1	5	29	25	67	6	4	.256/.324/.368	.268	.328	-2.5	LF(20): -1.8, 3B(20): -2.3	0.0
	2B	SYR	AAA	26	190	11	1	0	1	7	30	50	2	3	.185/.323/.210	.215	.264	-0.9	2B(50): 1.6	-0.3
Chris Heisey	LF	BUF	AAA	30	67	5	0	0	2	2	9	16	0	0	.155/.269/.259	.212	.175	0.1	LF(11): -0.1, CF(4): -1.0	-0.3
	LF	LAN	MLB	30	72	8	2	0	2	9	15	17	0	1	.182/.347/.327	.266	.211	-0.7	RF(12): -0.1, LF(12): -0.7	0.0
	LF	OKL	AAA	30	262	46	8	1	15	41	39	57	3	0	.241/.370/.495	.310	.255	2.5	CF(53): 0.7, RF(4): -0.3	2.4
Victor Robles	CF	AUB	A-	18	167	29	5	4	2	16	8	21	12	4	.343/.424/.479	.334	.383	1.1	CF(37): 2.6, RF(1): -0.2	2.2
Logan Schafer	RF	CSP	AAA	28	282	29	15	2	1	17	14	35	3	1	.258/.292/.342	.244	.291	0.2	CF(59): 16.8, RF(7): 1.1	2.2
	RF	MIL	MLB	28	143	17	6	1	1	6	12	29	1	0	.221/.299/.311	.231	.280	1.1	CF(49): -2.5, LF(1): -0.0	-0.1
Max Schrock	2B	AUB	A-	20	186	31	10	4	2	14	13	16	2	1	.308/.355/.448	.299	.329	0.5	2B(30): -5.3, SS(10): 1.6	1.0
Dan Uggla	2B	WAS	MLB	35	141	12	4	2	2	16	19	40	0	1	.183/.298/.300	.241	.253	0.2	2B(31): -0.5, 1B(1): -0.0	0.1
Rhett Wiseman	OF	AUB	A-	21	231	25	12	0	5	35	18	52	6	2	.248/.307/.376	.253	.303	-0.4	RF(52): 2.5	0.5

Give **Osvaldo Abreu** credit for making the most of his fringy skill set, as he showed some impact with his legs and steady defense at second base—though a choppier ability at shortstop. ❖ **Rafael Bautista** has speed, range and a wiry frame reminiscent of parent club outfielder Michael Taylor, but his swing repels homers like diethyltoluamide. ❖ **Cutter Dykstra** has done everything he can to earn a chance at the big leagues, except convince absolutely anybody that he actually has the offensive skill set to succeed there. ❖ The Dodgers designated **Chris Heisey** for assignment on August 7th, only to reacquire him from the Blue Jays on September 1st. The six hits he registered from there on out made all the difference. ❖ **Nate McLouth** was not extended a qualifying offer. ❖ Second-round selection **Blake Perkins** is a tools-first investment with potential to switch-hit at the top of the order and start in center, but there's still a lot of physical and baseball projection. ❖ The 18-year-old **Victor Robles** has earned far more attention in two years than you expect from a $225,000 Dominican signee. His combination of bat speed, barrel-to-ball ability, baserunning and defense give him strong impact potential, though it's years away. ❖ **Logan Schafer** couldn't eclipse the .300 OBP mark in Colorado Springs, nor could he launch more than a single homer. That faint noise you heard was Ben Revere and Juan Pierre high-fiving and trying to stifle a giggle. ❖ A steal in the 13th round, **Max Schrock** has packed into his diminutive frame several tools that project as average or better. You'll see him get reps across the diamond to aid his development, but his future lies at second. ❖ For now, last summer's J2 signee **Juan Soto** is notable for being the Nationals' biggest international signing since Esmailyn Gonzalez, whose age fraud put Washington's international scouting department on its heels for years. In time, Soto might be notable as a left-handed corner bat with a feel for hitting. ❖ Unproductive though **Dan Uggla** was in his limited playing time, the Nationals could sort of rationalize keeping him as long as another team was paying his contract. Now he doesn't have that luxury. ❖ In contrast to the two outfielders that the Nats chose ahead of him, Vanderbilt product **Rhett Wiseman** lacks standout tools and profiles more in a corner, but he has better pop potential.

Pitchers

NAME	TEAM	LVL	AGE	W	L	SV	G	GS	IP	H	HR	BB/9	K/9	GB%	BABIP	WHIP	ERA	FIP	FRA	WARP	CFIP	MPH
Dakota Bacus	HAR	AA	24	6	3	0	22	11	89^{2}	87	7	2.9	5.3	51%	.285	1.29	3.51	4.11	5.29	-0.6	115	
	POT	A+	24	2	0	3	8	5	27	23	1	3.3	9.7	53%	.293	1.22	2.33	2.92	2.85	0.6	87	
Aaron Barrett	WAS	MLB	27	3	3	0	40	0	29^{1}	28	1	2.1	10.7	45%	.351	1.19	4.60	2.24	3.79	0.3	81	96.4
Erik Davis	HAR	AA	28	1	0	3	24	0	34	32	2	4.8	9.0	42%	.323	1.47	2.65	3.62	4.29	0.1	101	
	SYR	AAA	28	0	2	0	11	0	11^{2}	19	0	6.9	8.5	58%	.463	2.40	8.49	3.59	5.37	-0.1	109	
Abel De Los Santos	WAS	MLB	22	0	0	0	2	0	1^{2}	2	1	5.4	16.2	25%	.333	1.80	5.40	9.16	9.85	-0.1	99	97.1
	HAR	AA	22	4	4	8	39	0	57^{2}	53	6	1.9	8.6	37%	.285	1.13	3.43	3.39	2.90	1.1	83	
Jake Johansen	POT	A+	24	1	7	1	24	0	48	60	6	5.1	9.0	55%	.358	1.81	5.44	4.69	5.43	-0.7	111	
Taylor Jordan	SYR	AAA	26	5	6	0	19	19	103^{2}	92	4	2.3	5.3	49%	.265	1.15	2.95	3.41	4.18	0.6	101	
	WAS	MLB	26	0	2	0	4	1	17	20	0	3.2	5.8	48%	.333	1.53	5.29	2.93	4.82	0.0	110	94.4
Nicholas Lee	POT	A+	24	1	1	9	20	0	28	20	1	4.5	9.0	53%	.268	1.21	2.57	3.32	3.92	0.1	98	
	HAR	AA	24	2	0	1	20	0	24	20	0	7.1	10.9	44%	.339	1.62	3.75	3.48	5.33	-0.2	113	
Mariano Rivera	AUB	A-	21	1	2	5	19	3	33	51	1	0.8	7.1	55%	.388	1.64	5.45	2.70	2.82	0.8	86	
Jefry Rodriguez	HAG	A	21	1	5	0	10	10	42^{2}	45	3	5.3	5.7	52%	.304	1.64	6.75	5.52	7.27	-1.0	126	
	AUB	A-	21	3	5	0	13	13	68^{2}	72	4	4.3	8.8	43%	.351	1.53	4.59	3.94	4.32	0.6	100	
John Simms	POT	A+	23	6	6	0	15	14	88^{2}	70	7	2.5	4.9	40%	.236	1.07	2.74	4.14	4.95	-0.3	110	
	HAR	AA	23	2	3	0	8	8	45	49	3	3.0	6.8	50%	.336	1.42	4.40	3.82	4.43	0.2	103	
Craig Stammen	WAS	MLB	31	0	0	0	5	0	4	2	0	6.8	6.8	55%	.182	1.25	0.00	3.91	2.23	0.1	103	93.6
Austin Voth	HAR	AA	23	6	7	0	28	27	157^{1}	134	10	2.3	8.5	47%	.284	1.11	2.92	3.07	3.01	3.5	84	

The immediate future for **Dakota Bacus** lies in the bullpen, where the organization hopes his 89 mph fastball will live a bit closer to 92 and get some separation from his hard slider. ❖ **Aaron Barrett** pitched effectively in late relief until Tommy John surgery turned his radio off in August. ❖ Tyler Clippard look-alike **Erik Davis** struggled with control as he returned from elbow surgery, but he saw a bit of playing time thanks to his plum spot on the 40-man roster. ❖ **Abel de los Santos**' move to relief added a few ticks, made his average command less of a concern, and paved the way for a nice career in middle relief. Sure, it's a demotion when the pitching coach tells you that you're not going to start anymore, but most of us are trying too hard to be something we're not anyway. ❖ The Nationals stress **Jake Johansen**'s tools over his results, but he's 25 years old and still trying to find success in a High-A bullpen. ❖ **Taylor Jordan** hasn't changed, but the depth chart ahead of him has. He's just about crowded out. ❖ **Nicholas Lee** is a power lefty with two solid pitches. If he cuts down on the walks, he'll get a shot. If he doesn't, he'll still get a shot, being, as he is, a power lefty with two solid pitches. ❖ Fourth-rounder and sinuous right-hander **Mariano Rivera III** profiles as a solid relief pitcher—although he favors a straight fastball and power slider to his dad's cutter. (His dad didn't have a cutter at that age, either.) ❖ Now that he's finally stopped getting taller, **Jefry Rodriguez** can work on repeating his mechanics more consistently to let his live fastball and curve play up to his potential as a useful arm—albeit out of the 'pen, most likely. ❖ **John Simms** was slow to get rolling last spring after offseason hip surgery, but a strong performance in the Arizona Fall League puts him on the Nationals' depth chart as back-end rotation depth this year. ❖ It's a bit of a stretch to say the Nationals' bullpen fell apart because of **Craig Stammen**'s early season-ending injury, but they sure did miss having a reliable multi-inning option like him. ❖ **Austin Voth** doesn't have a pitcher's body, doesn't have even 90 mph in his right arm, and doesn't have anything left to prove in the minors.

MANAGER

Dusty Baker

YEAR	TEAM	W	L	Pythag +/-	Avg PC	100+ P	120+ P	QS	BQS	REL	REL w Zero R	IBB	PH	PH Avg	PH HR	SB2	CS2	SB3	CS3	SAC Att	SAC%	POS SAC	Squeeze	Swing	In Play
2013	CIN	90	72	-5	95.3	61	2	94	6	461	389	28	232	.248	5	61	32	6	2	118	72	37	2	314	111

This spot seemed reserved for Bud Black, who had reportedly agreed to take the job a week before the Nationals introduced Baker as their new skipper—the franchise's sixth on a permanent basis since relocating to D.C. What happened? The Nationals low-balled Black by offering him a one-year deal—yes, a one-year deal in an era when every Tom, Dick and Harry receives a two- or three-year pact. Black was so put off by the offer that the Nationals had to circle back to Baker, their other finalist. Going from Black to Baker is a downgrade in the analytical community's eyes. Black is revered for his process-oriented ways, while Baker is detested for his old-school approach. Yet there are many positives to consider—and not just that Baker claims to have once shared a joint with Jimi Hendrix.

For starters, Baker has had more regular-season success than many of the so-called top managers, including Joe Maddon and Bruce Bochy—and no, that's not all Barry Bonds' doing. Baker won 51.3 percent of his games with the Cubs and Reds—or just below Maddon's career 52.5 percent mark. What's more, Baker isn't replacing a top manager. Instead he is taking over for Matt Williams, who, in spite of compiling a winning record over two seasons, might have a worse strategical reputation. It's not as if Williams atoned for his tactical shortcomings with great interpersonal skills, either. Reports surfaced late in the season that the clubhouse had turned on Williams, with veteran Jayson Werth berating him in front of the rest of the team. Baker might not make the best in-game decisions, but he's regarded as a good leader and player's manager who isn't likely to lose the clubhouse within 24 months.

Of course, you might argue that Baker's people skills are useless if he's making poor tactical calls. Fair enough. But being good at one part of the game is better than being bad at both. In that sense, the Nationals upgraded when they hired Baker—even if they took the scenic route to do it.

The Average Within

by Jonathan Judge

To watch baseball is to keep track of baseball. In the 19th Century, Henry Chadwick started by keeping track of raw *counts*: strikeouts, hits and outs, among others. But Chadwick soon started to focus on the *rate* at which these events were happening. To do this, he divided the number of hits a batter made by his times at bat (so-called "batting average") and the number of runs properly charged against the pitcher per nine innings of work ("earned run average"). These *rate statistics* tracked a player's results as a function of their playing time.

Chadwick had little use for walks, but researchers soon began tracking them as part of a batter's on-base percentage. People then began to distinguish different categories of hits from each other. In the 1950s, Branch Rickey tracked what he called "Extra Base Percentage," and baseball later settled on "slugging percentage," which multiplies a hitter's percentage of at-bats that result in singles, doubles, triples and home runs by the raw number of bases awarded for each hit type. What had been a simple arithmetic average had now become a weighted average.

But progress continued, as it often does. In the 1980s, Pete Palmer popularized the idea of "linear weights": average run values for each type of batting event that together provide a more accurate summary of a batter's expected production.[1] And in 2007, Tom Tango, Mitchel Lichtman and Andrew Dolphin published *The Book,* which, among other things, better calibrated these linear weights, and proposed the statistic of weighted on-base average (wOBA), incorporating those updated linear weights into a useful rate statistic. (True Average is our equivalent of wOBA at Baseball Prospectus).

Two aspects of this history stand out. The first is the transition of baseball statistics from a focus on raw counts to the player's *expected value*, as measured by progressively more complex rate statistics. The second is that the value measure is always some form of average, computed by totaling a player's assigned numbers of interest and dividing them by the number of opportunities. Mathematically speaking, this approach makes sense, because the "expected value" of any normal data set is its average.

1 John Thorn and Palmer's book, *The Hidden Game of Baseball*, has recently been re-released, and is well worth a read for its history alone.

Except for one annoying problem: A typical sample of player "averages" in baseball often doesn't reflect an individual player's expected value at all. The noise surrounding a play largely consumes the value of the player inside of it. Right now, we focus our descriptive statistics on the average outcomes that coincide with player participation. What we should be doing is focusing on the averages *within* those outcomes: the average of their true contributions to each play. In particular, I want to describe how we've started tracking those unique contributions at Baseball Prospectus, and why doing so is an important step in making baseball statistics more accurate.

The Noise, and the Signal[2]

In *The Book*, Tango et al. discussed the difference between players' "true talent" and the outcomes of their various plate appearances over a season. Specifically, they observed that players with particularly good or bad performances in the prior year tend to revert toward the league average in the following season.

This trend is everywhere in baseball, and it is ongoing. Take, for example, the batters who featured the most extreme on-base percentages in 2014. Taking the absolute value of their distances from the league mean (AKA the league average), look how those players performed the following season:

Player	Distance from Mean, 2014	Distance from Mean, 2015
Troy Tulowitzki	10%	2%
Jonathan Schoop	8%	2%
Andrew McCutchen	8%	7%
Victor Martinez	8%	3%
Justin Turner	8%	4%
Jose Bautista	8%	5%
Mike Zunino	7%	10%
Russell Martin	7%	0%
Paul Goldschmidt	7%	11%
Giancarlo Stanton	7%	2%
Jayson Werth	7%	3%
Adrian Beltre	6%	1%
Anthony Rizzo	6%	6%
Mike Moustakas	6%	2%
Freddie Freeman	6%	4%

2 My apologies to former BP Managing Partner, Mr. Nate Silver.

Of the 15 batters listed, 12 reverted toward the league mean, two went further away and one stayed about the same. The same is true of many pitcher statistics. Take the rate of home runs allowed, for example:

Pitcher	Distance from Mean, 2014	Distance from Mean, 2015
Marco Estrada	86%	19%
Garrett Richards	60%	14%
Anibal Sanchez	58%	66%
Jake Peavy	58%	3%
Jake Arrieta	58%	61%
Chris Young	55%	16%
Miguel Gonzalez	55%	49%
Clayton Kershaw	46%	42%
Colby Lewis	45%	14%
Dan Haren	44%	46%
Jacob deGrom	42%	25%
Jose Quintana	42%	31%
Carlos Carrasco	40%	12%
Chase Anderson	39%	6%
J.A. Happ	38%	7%

Of the 15 pitchers listed, 12 reverted toward the league mean, and only three went in the other direction, with two of those moving only slightly. We can keep doing this with various other statistics, but you get the idea.

To address this issue, Tango et al. proposed to "regress" all players by adding an additional number of hypothetical plate appearances to approximate the player's true ability. For example, to reach a batter's "true wOBA talent," they proposed adding about 220 "average" plate appearances to a batter's seasonal wOBA.

Adjustments like this are helpful, but the more interesting question is why we tolerate baseball's descriptive statistics being so consistently inaccurate in the first place. As "averages," these statistics are supposed to reflect the expected value of players. And yet, these statistics—batting average, earned run average, and wOBA/True Average, among many others—consistently overestimate players' contributions to each play. As a result, they tend to beat a steady retreat from their initial estimates, both in subsequent years and especially inside the same season.[3]

The most likely "true" measurements of these players' performances are in fact readily derivable, and in real time. But as with so many things in baseball, it requires a more sophisticated approach than we've been using to date. To find this *average within*, we need to rethink the way we credit baseball players for their on-field accomplishments, and use a method that dynamically implements this approach as events occur.

The Concept of Partial Credit

Let's start by talking about *why* this issue exists. In fact, let's just talk generally about professional baseball players.

Major-league players are incredibly gifted. You know this, at least intuitively, but do you ever think about how ridiculously talented baseball players are? Researchers have studied this repeatedly, and with varying degrees of vigor, but they consistently reach similar conclusions: Baseball players are special. Really special. One study found that the average professional baseball player had 20/15 vision, with many demonstrating vision as good as 20/9.2.[4] But physical ability is only part of the equation. Others have suggested that the psychological focus necessary to be a high-level baseball player is a one-in-a-million proposition.[5] Regardless of which source you trust, and how much hyperbole you tolerate, most seem to agree on one thing: Professional baseball players by definition do amazing things, particularly if they are good enough to stick around in the majors for any period of time.

So, let's take this prior knowledge and apply it to an actual game situation. A batter steps up with the go-ahead runs in scoring position and laces a single between infielders, thereby causing the winning runs to score. Why did that happen? Because that batter truly did something unique? Or did he merely do something that successful major-league hitters by definition are capable of doing on a regular basis?

Now turn the question around. What if the pitcher instead had struck that batter out and preserved the win for his team? What is the most likely explanation for that event? That this pitcher reached down deep inside for a clutch moment? Or is it that if the pitcher *couldn't* strike a guy out when it mattered, he wouldn't be playing professional baseball in the first place?

The point is that our current method of scoring accomplishments—taking the arithmetic average of all outcomes for a particular player—tends to vastly over-credit the players involved for their actual contributions to each play. This also explains why stretches of "clutch" hitting and "shutdown" pitching so often fail to replicate themselves over time: There was often nothing "clutch" or "shutdown" about the performance to begin with. Baseball's "all-or-nothing" method of assigning credit for play outcomes made sense before the age of computers, but is difficult to defend when our methods are now so much more sophisticated.

This doesn't mean that some players aren't significantly better than others, or that certain players don't sustain excellent performance over time, relative to their peers. It also doesn't mean that averages of raw outcomes aren't worth tracking. But we need to start compiling statistics

3 Technically, these measures are providing an "expected value"—the results of the plate appearances involving the player in some form or another; except that no one actually interprets these statistics in so limited a matter.

4 http://goo.gl/SSMcgQ

5 Dave Ritterspusch of the Baltimore Orioles, quoted in Stadler, *The Psychology of Baseball: Inside the Mental Game of the Major League Player* (p. 119) (2007).

that reflect a *proper skepticism* about the extent to which an individual player's ability in fact drove their results, mindful that much of what we see is the give-and-take among a super-population of athletes and nothing more. To derive these averages *within* the raw outcomes, we can apply that skepticism on a real-time basis. That, in turn, allows us to make better decisions, sooner, on which performances to trust and which ones to question.

But what does it mean to be "properly skeptical" of a statistic? And how do we do it? To answer that question, we'll turn to Mr. James, Mr. Stein and, especially, Mr. Efron.

The Paradox, and the Solution

In 1977, Dr. Bradley Efron, along with Carl Morris, published an important article in the magazine *Scientific American*, entitled "Stein's Paradox in Statistics."[6] The article is considered a classic in the statistics literature, but appears to have gone largely unnoticed in mainstream baseball research. This is odd, because the article's primary proof involves the unreliability of baseball batting averages as a true indicator of batter ability.

The batting average study—which Efron and Morris had previously discussed in more academic articles—compared the averages of various professional hitters after 40 at-bats (about 10 percent of the 1970 season) versus their cumulative seasonal batting averages at the end of that same year. The authors found, not surprisingly, that a hitter's raw batting average after 40 at-bats was not predictive of much of anything over the rest of the season. This, for the reasons we've already discussed, seems to defeat the purpose of tracking a player's "average" at all, so the authors set out to find a better solution.

The solution lay in something the authors called "Stein's Paradox." In the 1950s, Charles Stein infuriated the statistical establishment by finding that, when three or more relevant events occur, the raw average of their outcomes is no longer the best estimate of their expected value. Rather, the best path to the true value was through application of a "shrinkage factor" that deliberately biased the averages toward the so-called "grand mean"—the overall average of all subjects in a given study.[7] The formula for deriving this shrinkage factor is known as the James-Stein estimator.

"Stein's paradox is that . . . the James-Stein estimators give better estimates of true batting ability than the individual batting averages." In fact, applying Stein's paradox, even so early in the season, gave values that were 3.5 times more accurate in forecasting the end-of-season batting averages for these players. As the authors put it, "we have not just been lucky." Rather, they had hit upon the *average within* the raw averages: the batter's true typical contribution to the outcomes of his at-bats. While it is obvious that shrinking player performance toward the league mean will help with average players, the authors found, to their surprise, that "the estimator does at least marginally better no matter where the true means are."

The Stein-James estimator has amazing qualities. It adjusts dynamically to the data, and doesn't require you to know the "true" average of the data. If player performances overall tend to be clustered toward the league mean, the estimator will shrink outliers further inward; if, on the other hand, player performances vary widely, it tends to respect those variances. At all times, the formula permits any player to demonstrate he is sincerely better (or worse) than league average, because the shrinkage factor is applied to the actual arithmetic average of each player's assigned outcomes. But it is only with sustained performance different from the league average over time that a player will be viewed as truly different from his or her peers.

Mixed Models and the Way Forward

As many of you know, Baseball Prospectus spent the 2015 season rolling out new statistics based on "mixed" models: models that incorporate both fixed (for us, external) and random (usually player) effects. We did so first with catcher framing;[8] we then adopted contextual FIP (cFIP);[9] and then, most ambitiously, we created Deserved Run Average (DRA),[10] which relies upon a series of (predominantly mixed) models to provide a comprehensive assessment of the runs that a pitcher "deserved" to give up, adjusted for the context of each batter faced.

Of all the comments we have received about these efforts, one has stuck with me. To paraphrase it: "Why are you doing this? What need are you addressing and how is this important?" It's an incredibly important question, and up until now, we have answered it primarily with respect to the strength of the individual models themselves: the consistency of our catcher framer ratings; the strong explanatory power of DRA; and the ability to predict future performance, such as with our models for passed balls and wild pitches.

But the fundamental and overall answer to that person's question is the entire point of this article. Mixed models are superior to existing options because, unlike raw averages, linear constants or post-hoc adjustments, they explicitly incorporate the principles of the Stein-James estimator on a real-time basis.

In a mixed model, the contributions of individual players—be it hitting, pitching or fielding—are dynamically shrunk toward the league mean, based on the inherent characteristics of the data. The end result is an estimate that not only shrinks each player's contribution toward

6 Efron & Morris, "Stein's Paradox in Statistics," *Scientific American* (1977), available at http://goo.gl/YfhJSD.

7 Unlike certain other contexts, the terms "shrinkage" and "bias" are often viewed as positives in the field of statistics.

8 http://www.baseballprospectus.com/article.php?articleid=25514

9 http://www.hardballtimes.com/fip-in-context/

10 http://www.baseballprospectus.com/article.php?articleid=26195

his most likely ability level, but can further control for the (shrunken) contributions of other players of interest, including those of the opposing or fellow players on the team. We can go even further and adjust for external factors like stadium, temperature and the platoon effect. In sum, mixed models are superior not because Jonathan Judge says so, but because they rely upon fundamental and demonstrably true statistical facts.

Let's close with a few examples of how our mixed models here at BP have been using shrinkage to provide more reliable estimates. It makes sense to start with the same metric Efron and Morris did: batting average. If, in fact, our mixed model methods appropriately shrink batter values, then we should see results similar to those of Morris and Efron. To do that, we generated random samples[11] of 10 percent of the 2015 season, considering all batters with at least 10 at-bats, and compared those to those players' final batting averages this past year. Final seasonal batting averages have their problems too, but they at least benefit from a full season's sample size.

We'll start with the simplest possible mixed model, fitting only the likelihood of a batter getting a hit. Both the raw sample and the mixed-model estimate based on 10 percent of the season will be compared to each batter's final batting average during the season. Our goal is to minimize "error," or the distance between the sample's batting average estimate and the batter's final seasonal batting average. This means that less error is better. Here is how that turns out:

Sample	Sum of Squared Errors (SSE)	Root Mean Squared Error (RMSE)
Raw 10% of AB	14.79	.15
Modeled 10% of AB	3.7	.07

In their article, Efron and Morris found that a properly shrunk estimator of batting average was about 3.5 times better than the raw number, using the sum of squared errors. Here, the ratio of the squared errors between the raw batting averages through 10 percent of the season is 14.79 to 3.7, which is actually *four* times better. A fourfold improvement in accuracy, working with just the first few weeks of the season! Our basic mixed-model format performs even better than the James-Stein estimator itself. For those of you who prefer the RMSE as a metric, the advantage is clear there as well.

Now that we know our method is sound, let's apply it to something more rigorous: catcher framing. Catcher framing was the first mixed model we released, and we can do a similar comparison here: The average error between a catcher's partial and final called-strike rates, comparing both his raw and modeled called-strike rates. To keep it fair, we'll do a very simple model that leaves out the probability of the pitch being a strike, and track only the identity of the catcher, batter, pitcher and umpire on each pitch. Following the same general method as before, this time we'll present the results as a graph across the entire season. On the graph, "CS" represents the called strike rate. Again, we are measuring error, so lower is better.

Mixed Model vs Raw Framing

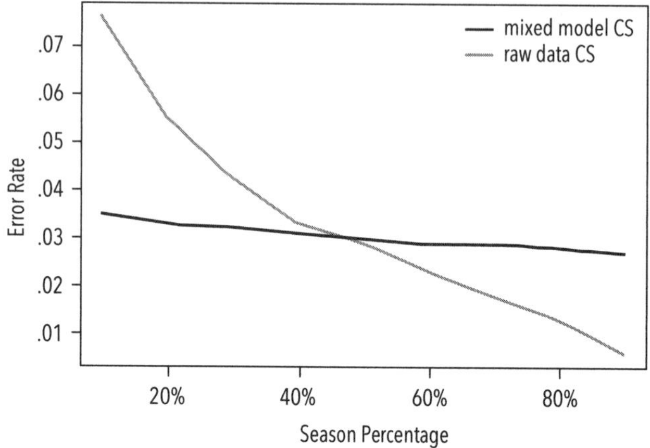

You'll notice that, as before, the shrunken estimate is once again skeptical about the meaningfulness of early-season breakouts/slumps. At the 10 percent mark of the season, the difference is particularly drastic: a 4 percent difference in the estimated called-strike ability for a catcher between the raw and modeled averages. Since each 1 percent in called-strike rate is worth about 10 runs, that equates to a difference of almost 40 runs, or nearly five wins of difference between the mixed model's ability to (correctly) predict a catcher's end-of-year called-strike rate and the raw numbers, even after only a few weeks of the season. That's kind of a big deal, and we're only talking about one statistic here.

You probably also noted that the mixed model's advantage in predicting the raw, end-of-season called-strike rate disappears about halfway through the season. Does this mean that mixed models are only useful before the All-Star break? No. Remember that the mixed model's primary virtue is its consistency: It largely pegs each catcher at a valid rate early on, and only needs to modify that opinion slightly as the season goes on. That consistency is highly desirable. Moreover, it is obvious that the raw called-strike rate will surpass the modeled called-strike rate at some point because it has to converge with itself. The real question is whether end-of-season raw called-strike rate is actually better than the mixed model at estimating catcher framing talent. If not, catching up to the final raw values is ultimately a sign of weakness, not strength.

11 Random samples of 10 percent of the season, taken with replacement, are more reliable estimates of performance than just taking the first 10 percent of the season, as Efron and Morris did. We took 2,500 random samples of each estimate for the raw averages, 10 samples of the modeled averages and averaged their error values. The difference in sampling volumes accounts for how long each sample takes to reasonably stabilize.

We can test this by comparing the end-of season called-strike rate of catchers who appeared in both 2014 to 2015, both from raw called-strike percentage and the mixed-model's estimates:

Cumulative Called-Strike Average	Root Mean Squared Error (RMSE), 2014-15
Raw Full Season	.046
Modeled Full Season	.014

As you can see, by incorporating the shrinkage concepts of James-Stein, the mixed model not only provides much better information, earlier, but also itself converges on a more accurate and consistent value.

These examples are the mere tip of the iceberg. Mixed models underlie our statistics of cFIP, Deserved Run Average (DRA) and thus also BP's pitcher wins above replacement player (PWARP), and catcher blocking (PBWP). More extensions will come this year as these concepts are rolled out into other important areas of baseball research.

A Look Back, and Forward

We traditionally have discussed player "regression" or "shrinkage" in terms of future projection. But projections, to be most effective, need to be based on accurate descriptions of what actually happened. Thus, if we want more accurate baseball decisions, and in particular, if we want more accurate baseball forecasts, we need to improve our underlying descriptive statistics. By using mixed models as the primary driver of our next-generation statistics here at BP, we feel we can be more accurate about more things than ever before. ■

—Jonathan Judge is a trial lawyer who enjoys analytics, law, baseball and their various combinations.

The Psychology of Scott Boras

by Jeff Passan

One recent October, Scott Boras was talking about a player with a sex addiction, and it was hysterical for reasons well beyond the most powerful man in baseball marveling at the voluminous breasts of the player's wife. Somehow, as is always the case with Boras, he took the subject at hand and tied it in a fashion uniquely his to the game he loves.

"When he's focused on the playoffs instead of sex, holy shit," Boras said. "What kind of player is he? You'd better know that. You'd better know he's a different kind of cat. And because of that, you know the value is greater."

I've known Boras for a dozen years now, and by know I mean that I've seen the parts he self-selected for consumption. He partitions himself so as to appeal to journalists, owners, executives and especially the players who entrust their careers to him. In his reign as baseball's majordomo, thought leader and head provocateur for going on a quarter-century, Boras hears every whisper and shout, sheathes the information and unleashes it at the right time, whether for giggles at a press conference or to sway hundred-million-dollar contract negotiations.

All of this is part of Boras' genius, the calculation—plenty would call it manipulation, especially because the nefariousness of the word hews to Boras' reputation—one element of a bigger, longer play. Boras considers himself an attorney or a representative instead of an agent, much as he considers his finest clients "generational talents" or "premium players" instead of just stars. And this is because everything in his sphere returns to a fact he holds dear: The way to the wallet is through the mind.

Boras is evermore on a quest to infiltrate and better understand the psychology of the baseball world. Nothing interests him like the mind of a player. He spent four years as one in the minor leagues, and failure always fascinated him. The statistics with which we judge players—the same ones he wields to bludgeon owners into making his 5 percent that much heartier—are, to Boras, only as useful as what spawns them.

"We have an intellectual knowledge, a psychological knowledge," Boras said. "All the statistical data we use for WAR goes south because it completely forgets the inner workings of the player. Sabermetrics is psychologically void. Much like a farm boy who had acres and acres of grapes, you're sitting there with the vine and you know the fruit is coming. But there is a process of fermenting into the wine. What barrels you use. The kind of oak. The seasonal component of outside factors. All of these things relate to players, and the factors are psychology. The rain that makes the player grow is psychology. There are those who start with a really fine character base and then the game takes them in a direction. Success may. Failure may."

When Boras, 63, gets rolling on a subject, the material rolls off his tongue like a stump speech. The pauses between sentences aren't to gather his thoughts; they're to breathe and prepare for another blitzkrieg. For 35 years now, Boras has honed his worldview from tussling with billionaires, placating millionaires and absorbing every possible insult from those whose net worth includes no illion. To the latter crowd, Boras is alternately, and sometimes simultaneously, the Devil, the worst person in sports, a greedy bastard, a parasite, the reason ticket prices are so high or some other villain colored by the bleating of the uninformed.

In truth, the reality of Boras isn't best reflected in anything he does himself. It's in a question more fundamental than existential: What does it say about the game of baseball that a man like Scott Boras is its supreme entity?

✦✦✦

In a 2011 article for Baseball Prospectus, Vince Gennaro looked at every free agent contract signed from 2003-2010. Even though Boras negotiated just 6 percent of the deals, he handled more than 20 percent of the money teams guaranteed players. The average Boras client made $25.8 million more than those of his non-Boras counterparts. Gennaro attributed 39 percent of the premium to Boras himself, the same share as Gennaro assigned to the players' WARs.

Anyone who tries to understate Boras' place in baseball today suffers from jealousy, delusion or both. Thanks to profiles from *The New Yorker, Esquire, ESPN the Magazine, Sports Illustrated,* the *Washingtonian, LA Weekly, OC Weekly* and the *Boston Globe Magazine*, among dozens of other publications, his story by now is boilerplate: Raised on a farm—hence the earlier metaphor—outside of Sacramento. Smart kid. Scholarship to play baseball at the University of the Pacific. Bum knees, bad glove killed his minor-league career. Went back to Pacific, earned Ph.D. in pharmacology and law degree. Got into agent business to help out buddies and former teammates. Changed sports forever.

The proliferation of this account comes right from the playbook of another master at the craft, Donald Trump, to whom Boras—famously a staunch Democrat in the red worlds of baseball and Orange County, California—may dry heave if ever compared. This, from Trump's 1987 book, *The Art of the Deal*, embodies so much of what made Boras' career: "The key to the way I promote is bravado. I play to people's fantasies. People may not always think big themselves, but they can still get very excited by those who do. That's why a little hyperbole never hurts. People want to believe that something is the biggest and the greatest and the most spectacular."

Baseball's first agent was Christy Walsh, the marketing genius behind Babe Ruth. A movie producer named Frederick Stephani bought the rights to an amateur pitcher named Paul Pettit for $85,000 and profited $15,000 when the Pirates made him the first six-figure bonus baby in 1950. The advent of a real players' union in 1966 brought with it more representation, whether the kind Ron Shapiro or flashy Dennis Gilbert, who made his riches selling life insurance. Boras wasn't the first lawyer. He was just the first to approach the system with the cynicism of the union's forebear, Marvin Miller, and the nihilism of a man with nothing to lose.

After fetching his buddies well-above-market contracts, Boras turned his attention to the draft. His draft-bonus-record deals from 1988-1991 went from incremental to exponential—Andy Benes at $247,500 in the first year to Brien Taylor at $1.5 million in the last. He sent Jason Varitek, J.D. Drew and Matt Harrington to independent ball. He existed to sniff out loopholes in contract language. "Boras is always the guy with the ace showing," Scott Raab once wrote, though I'm not sure that's true. For all of his bullets, Boras prefers playing a 7-2 offsuit through the river.

"The career choice and challenge," he said, "was never about money."

He's insistent about this, and for the well-worn axiom in front offices that every time Boras opens his mouth a lie escapes, I believe him. The money—the goo-gobs of it that shattered the illusion of sport as game and forever cemented it as business—is nothing more than a proxy. It represents the respect and fairness that Boras sees as more than personal markers. Money, to him, is the game's greatest opportunity to better itself.

"I've always felt baseball was an entity where the lions ate their young. I want it to be a system where the lions are protecting their young," Boras said. "Because the truth of the matter is the young are great athletes whether or not they play baseball. Whether or not they play baseball is going to be the product of an environment we create to attract them. Remember, with so few stars that we have—and it's those stars, maybe 50 people, who create the agenda of who people think of and idolize and pay to see—we need to get it right."

In the time since Scott Boras became Scott Boras, the offseason became more important than the regular season. Baseball's retraction into a parochial sport from February through October cedes the first week of November, when the free-agent-and-trade free-for-all that consumes the next three months renders fans of all kinds drunk on rumors, supposition, mock deals and all the other bullshit that 99 percent of the time amounts to nothing. The offseason is a daily blue-balling of fans, and they love it. The excitement of what might be always beats the reality of what is.

To call Boras the architect of this is too strong, because Miller did dream up the system. Boras brute-forced it into its current incarnation. Everything in baseball—transactions, partnerships, game times, even on-field rule changes—is rooted in economics, and Boras' fingerprints are everywhere. At least 60 homegrown amateurs a year get $1 million in the draft. The best players regularly break the $200 million threshold in free agency, and the $400 million mark is Boras' next target. Even the opt-out clause, his little stroke of genius in his truest opus, the 10-year, $252 million Alex Rodriguez contract, is now almost standard among "generational talents" and "premium players."

Boras' stubbornness led to losses. Harrington's tortuous and tortious journey left in its wake the story of all draft-disaster stories, and Stephen Drew and Kendrys Morales' careers were left in limbo after they declined qualifying offers. Boras soldiers on undaunted, still as interested in fomenting change as he was in the early '80s, when remnants of pre-Miller baseball remained in place because the labor wars ensured progress came at a Molina's pace.

He still wants to overhaul the draft, particularly at the top, where the slotting system agreed to in the 2012 collective-bargaining agreement killed the players' ability to receive anything close to the $15.5 million Boras landed for Stephen Strasburg or the $9.9 million he got for Bryce Harper. The $63 million Boston spent on draft-aged Yoan Moncada more than proved that the artificial capping of amateur players' bonuses neuters free-market value. Boras' argument dovetails with his point about enticing the best athletes to play baseball. "I've never, ever agreed on spending a lot of money on third-, fourth-, fifth-round picks," he said. "I've agreed on spending major money to attract the top five or 10 of every draft. If you're that great and a baseball player, our industry holds something for you. It's not going to cost this industry any more money. It's just appropriate allocation."

Look past the bluster, past the verbiage, past the overuse

of acronyms he and only he understands, and substance exists in Boras' perspectives. He knows the game and knows it well. And it's why, when he starts talking about psychology, I'm inclined to listen. If Boras is a blowhard, at least his blowhardery comes laced with logic.

When he says the following—"I enjoy telling people I have a sports fitness institute and have 10 trainers; I have guys from MIT, Yale, Harvard, Stanford; I have people with perfect SAT scores"—what he means is: cracking psychology is a job for many. Boras Corporation employs about 80 people, and those who aren't recruiting are helping create a player profile that Boras eventually uses to sell to teams.

The Boras logo is ubiquitous around major-league stadiums, a dead giveaway for polo-shirted underlings who prowl the country to recruit new clients and check in on old ones. Sometimes these visits yield new information that Boras will enter into his secret sauce. Boras is convinced his algorithm for player value contains a proper psychological component. This is the holy grail, taking the seemingly immeasurable and trying to quantify it, and Boras puts a massive premium on it.

"The character and psychology of a player may mean as much as 25 to 30 percent of his value going forward," he said. "And we have a record of his ethic. What he does. How he does it. How he manages failure. How he manages success. How he manages situationally. With authority. With teammates. Leadership. Patterns of consistency. All the things that are hugely important to delivering length and consistency of performance."

It's a marketing trick, of course, one that helps sell clients as generational and premium and whatever other adjectives he dreams up in the coming years. And yet Boras almost certainly does know his players better than the teams that send scouts out for half-assed reconnaissance missions, or that rely on secondhand word and hearsay to form character opinions. Boras' bias aside—never shall anyone forget the Oliver Perez–Sandy Koufax comparisons—his pitches continue to work, which doesn't make them right so much as compelling.

In trying to convince teams after the 2014 season that starting pitcher Max Scherzer was on a career upswing at age 30, Boras invoked character, intelligence and work ethic as much as a right arm that throws 98 mph. The Washington Nationals gave Scherzer a seven-year, $210 million deal, nearly 50 percent more than he'd turned down less than a year earlier from Detroit.

Boras wants everyone to believe he knows more than teams because it gives him perceived power, and if the Nationals bought his Scherzer spiel, it reinforces the power vacuum he occupies. All it takes is a few, and whether or not he can figure out what's inside of players' minds, nobody can argue Boras took up residence in teams' heads long ago with a lease that ends no time soon.

+++

Here's what Scott Boras' existence says about baseball: It's working.

Even though the sentiment about Boras stretches across almost every front office—some amalgamation of disdain and begrudging respect for his skill—he plies his trade like anyone else. Boras works the same job as Joel Wolfe, who negotiated the biggest contract ever, the same job as Casey Close, who has exceeded Boras dollar for dollar in recent years. For however much Boras lives to upend systems, his ethos comes from neither greed nor the Seventh Circle; he works for the players and the sport, because both need an appropriate counterbalance to the owner-sympathetic public.

It's something I've never understood, this idea that players chasing money are unbecoming while owners doing the same get a free pass. Boras refuses to let Marvin Miller's work die that way. Reform is risky business, and the last person in baseball as loathed as Boras was Miller, who shepherded the sport—all major American professional sports, really—into what we see today.

In March 2012, Boras flew to New York, checked into the Four Seasons and waited outside the hotel for a man whom he'd sent a car to pick up. Marvin Miller was 94 years old, and never had Boras taken the time to sit down with him and hear first-hand accounts of the fights about which Boras only could dream. They sipped soup and rapped the rap of iconoclasts.

"He realized stars and talent run the game," Boras said. "That's what I learned from Marvin. That's what we all learned from him."

Mentioning the two in the same sentence is an act of heresy to most of Boras' competitors, even if Boras more than anybody has personified the principle for which Miller fought: Players deserve choices, and choices in a free market can breed staggering growth.

More than $2 billion in signed contracts later, Boras is still espousing those principles. This is the natural evolution of Miller. The game's power brokers cannot help but hear Boras. They may not listen, but they hear, and his words worm their way into psyches. During meetings with owners, he preys on their insecurities in the most acute way possible: asking if they want to be losers. Boras traffics in loaded phraseology, and none gutshots billionaires like the L-word. Once, after Boras went all *Glengarry Glen Ross* during a free-agent meeting, an owner said: "That was really good. That was really strong." And though he didn't sign the player Boras was trying to close, the owner's verbal applause reinforced the game's constant do-si-do with Boras. It's still trying to wrap its mind around him as much as he is with it.

Everyone takes comfort, then, in the odd rituals that exist only in the Boras bubble, like the polo shirts or acronyms or State of the Boras addresses. Yes, every year at the Winter Meetings, baseball's gathering of the masses at an oversized hotel that plays bubbling cauldron to the hot stove's bullshit stew, one of Boras' public-relations people sends out a mass text giving a time and a location for any interested media to congregate and listen to Boras' musings on the baseball world.

At the Gaylord Opryland Resort and Convention Center, a redneck fever dream come to life, Boras parked himself near a column and immediately watched a semicircle of reporters descend around him. The 2015 offseason was slogging along, and Boras was calling the shots on more than a half-dozen unsigned free agents. Perhaps he would let slip something substantive.

By now, those in attendance should know better. Boras long ago mastered the ability of acting like he's answering a question when in reality he's guiding it to a place more conducive to his comfort. He speaks with such conviction that it lends gravitas to generalities. And when he gets clever with his wordplay—to wit: "From the past approach of the Cubs, I would say that they've certainly got off the frontage road where all the stop signs are and they're on the good freeway to a better team"—it's enough to fool you into thinking he might actually say something later.

Boras knows better. He says what he wants when he wants to whom he wants, every syllable deliberate, every intention premeditated. He stands in a blue blazer, dark jeans and shoes with an extra-bright shine, surrounded by the Gaylord's Christmastime holly and cheer, brow sweaty from the camera lights, voice box working overtime, duties never over. He'll do this until he can't anymore because this is who Scott Boras is, what Scott Boras is, one and the same. The unlikely lion trying to protect all the young, and not just its own, one roar at a time. ■

—Jeff Passan is the author of The Arm: Inside the Billion-Dollar Mystery of the Most Valuable Thing in Sports, *to be published in April by HarperCollins. He is the MLB columnist for Yahoo Sports*

Dear WAR

by Russell A. Carleton

Dear WAR,

We need to talk. I've been giving this a lot of thought lately and I think we need to break up. I need to see other stats.

I'm sorry if this comes totally out of left field. I know how you are, and I probably caught you in the middle of incorporating information on Daniel Murphy's defensive value or something like that. I want you to know that it's not about anything you did. It's not about that silly little argument we once had about where to set your replacement level. And yeah, I know it sounds so cliché, but really, truly, it's not you. It's me.

I know we had some crazy days (and nights) together. I remember back in 2012 when you and I were hanging out in my mom's basement and we really bonded over the Mike Trout–Miguel Cabrera MVP vote. We stayed up all night making fun of Murray Chass that one time, remember? I really do treasure those memories. We made some magic between the spreadsheets. Honestly. I'm not breaking up with you because you didn't spend enough time with me on your park factors or because I didn't like your—um, shall we say, positional adjustments. I can even get past the thing where you like FIP and I like ERA. To-may-to, to-mah-to. No couple agrees on everything. I don't want you walking away from this feeling like you've been hit with a 96 mph fastball. I don't want you blaming yourself for things that you could have done.

This is about me. I need to do this.

At the time we met, you were exactly what I needed. It felt nice to know that in this cruel world where everyone gets judged by surface-level stuff like RBIs and wins, there was a stat like you that really knew how to look at the whole player. I thought it was really sweet that you understood why Andrelton Simmons and his defense were so important to me. It's still such an endearing quality about you and I hope you never change that. You saw below the surface to what was really deep inside. Maybe I never quite understood you as well, but I knew a good one when I saw one. And you were it.

I don't know when I started noticing it, but when I was with you, I feel like I stopped growing as a sabermetrician. Remember when we started playing that game where we'd talk about a player and then give him a rating from zero to 10 on your WAR scale and we both agreed that Mike Trout was the only perfect 10 out there? You were always into putting numbers on everything. He's a two. He's a five. He's just Uggla. I know you were just calling things like you saw them, but one day when you were out on one of your trips to Fenway Park, or maybe it was to whatever they're calling SkyDome now, I had a question creep into my head: What would happen if you weren't there anymore?

At first I figured that I'd be lonely and adrift. I mean, there have been other stats in my life, and so as not to embarrass any of them, I'll only refer to them by their initials. Back in the early 2000's, I had my flings with O.B.P. and O.P.S. and I even went out with your older brother V.O.R.P. once. But those were all ex-lovers from long ago. Without you, would my life or Jonny Gomes' place in the cosmos have any meaning?

Then I started thinking it through and a few things started to bother me. Yes, you were helpful in figuring some things out in my life. How to properly value baserunning and how to adjust for Petco Park and all that. But then, I remembered that there were a lot of issues where you weren't really willing to "go there." Remember that time a couple years ago when I asked you about Sonny Gray and you just kinda shrugged? I asked where you thought he would be with a little more maturity and major-league experience. It was a really important question to me and you said that stuff wasn't a big deal.

Not a big deal?

At the time, I pushed that to the side because I told myself I was in love with you, but it gnawed at me. I get that you are really good at sizing people up for what they really are, but why can't we also talk about the future? It was clear that Gray had a bright sunshiny day in front of him if he could nail down a few things, but you didn't want to talk about that. I want someone who believes that people can grow and change. I mean, isn't that the real question?

You seemed so intent on putting a number on everyone and that became *his* number. I stopped thinking about how, in a different set of circumstances—maybe just a few years of learning or maybe a new pitch—that same guy could be something entirely different. A strange thing happens when you start putting numbers on people. It's easy to pretend that those numbers have been etched into concrete. It's like giving a child an IQ test in second grade and then pretending that she or he is a "100" until time shall end. That just isn't how things work.

And then there's the clubhouse chemistry thing. You've always said "context doesn't matter," and I get where that comes from, but I'm not so sure about it. We always made fun of teams that signed guys for more than we figured they were worth, just based on all that chemistry stuff. Maybe it actually does matter. Maybe it doesn't. But I need to break free from you so that I can go find out for myself.

Right now, I'm sure you're saying that you can't be all things to all people and that I'm being too demanding of one stat. And that's probably true. I mean, you've said that you have no way to get good data (always the data!) about that chemistry thing and so you don't even bother. What I realized was that I spent so much time being into you that I started pushing all those questions aside. Problem is that I'm starting to realize that those are *really* important questions. Maybe they were *the* questions all along, and I didn't even realize it. Like I said, it's not you, it's me.

But that's why we need to break up. When I started thinking about what would happen if you didn't come back, I realized that yeah, it would be strange for a bit, but I also realized that I'd have a lot more room to grow as a person. If I keep spending all my time with you, there's a lot that I'll miss out on.

I still want to talk sometimes. I don't think you're a useless piece of trash. I do really like you, and I'm happy you came into my life. I just feel that spending all my time with you is holding me back from understanding things that I really want to understand. If I keep this up, I'm probably not going to get to explore those.

I hope that after this, we can still be friends. I do still love hearing you talk about how awesome Mike Trout is. Your joy brings me joy. I value your perspective on life and baseball, and I know you're going to make some other sabermetrician very happy at some point. These kinds of break-ups are always tough, because it's not that I hate you. It's that I just need to keep growing. To really grow, I need to let you go.

So WAR, I guess this is goodbye. Or at least, so long and thanks for all the Trout. I'll check in on you at all your usual hangouts, and I promise that if I find anything interesting out there, I'll tell you all about it.

Peace, Love, Happiness, Banana Pudding,

Russell A. Carleton ■

—Russell Carleton owns his own basement in Atlanta.

Top 101 Prospects

by Jeffrey Paternostro and Wilson Karaman

1. Corey Seager, SS, Los Angeles Dodgers
It's dangerous to read too much into a month's worth of major-league plate appearances, especially when that month is September. Maybe Corey Seager took advantage of 40-man roster fodder and teams with one foot on the golf course to hit .337/.425/.561 as the 2015 season waned, but that's pretty consistent with what he has done at every other stop in his professional career. He hits for average. He hits for power. He may not be a shortstop forever, as he is a very large human, but the bat is good enough to play anywhere. Regardless, Seager will be the Dodgers shortstop in 2016, and he may very well be the best one in the National League from the moment he sets foot on the field Opening Day.

2. Byron Buxton, OF, Minnesota Twins
It may be an exercise in hyperbole to refer to our no. 2 prospect as a "post-hype sleeper" (especially since he's been our no. 1 prospect the last two years), but in an industry always on the lookout for the next new hotness, Buxton qualifies as old news. It doesn't help his Q rating (or for the Millennials reading, his Klout score) that he missed most of 2014 with a wrist injury and then a concussion, or that he looked overmatched at times in his first taste of the majors. As the old scouting adage goes, "tools play," and Buxton's selection rivals your local Ace Hardware. He may not be the next Andre Dawson, as we opined in 2013, but Buxton still looks like an impact major leaguer.

3. Lucas Giolito, RHP, Washington Nationals
Last year was a good one for the Giolito clan. Showtime announced a Twin Peaks revival (Lucas' uncle co-created it with David Lynch, and his grandfather played Dr. Will Heyward, the remarkably normal town coroner), and the youngest Giolito made it all the way to Double-A, striking out better than a batter per inning and flashing true top-of-the-scouting-scale stuff along the way. He is now more than three years removed from the UCL tear that kept him from going first overall in the 2012 draft, and with an invitation to Nationals spring training already secured, Giolito may soon be on the hunt for some cherry pie and a damn fine cup of coffee in the nation's capital.

4. J.P. Crawford, SS, Philadelphia Phillies
Crawford will inevitably draw comparisons to Jimmy Rollins, his predecessor in Philadelphia (future histories will gloss over the Freddy Galvis epoch). Both were early-round picks and African-American shortstops out of high schools in California. Sure, it's not fair to saddle him with this comp: Rollins is a first-ballot Hall of Very Good player who won an MVP and made multiple All-Star games. Crawford may not reach those lofty heights, but he is a true five-tool player and the total package at shortstop.

5. Nomar Mazara, OF, Texas Rangers
Texas invested more than $5 million in Mazara, setting the record for a bonus given to a 16-year-old amateur the year before international bonus pools were implemented. He's rewarded their investment with a quick ascent through Texas' system, showing a rare set of offensive tools on a long-levered, 6-foot-5 frame. Mazara has a pure left-handed stroke that should produce both contact and home run power at above-average outputs. The fluidity of his swing path—supplied by long arms and a physical frame—gives an effortless look to a left-handed stroke that elicits some Will Clark comparisons. Mazara throws well but only moves fairly to decently defensively; while he ultimately could wind up in either outfield corner, it's the hitting tools that give him legitimate middle-order, All-Star upside. It also makes him one of baseball's best prospects entering his age-21 season. Mazara had a successful 20-game stint at Triple-A to end 2015. It isn't unreasonable to foresee him mashing his way into the Rangers' lineup at some point in the upcoming season.

6. Julio Urias, LHP, Los Angeles Dodgers
Following prospects is a great way to be continuously aware of your own encroaching mortality. Urias is not the youngest player on this list, but he did spend most of last season as an 18-year-old, and he finished it in Triple-A. This isn't just age-relative-to-league novelty: The stuff is potentially elite, and he has pitchability beyond his years. Urias was dominant in 2015 while only facing two batters who were younger than him (both during rehab). His combination of youth, polish and stuff draws comparisons to Felix Hernandez, in part because he is very good and in part because there's no one else similar in recent history. The cold water: Unlike Felix at the same age, Urias has never thrown even 90 innings in a season, and may not be able to handle a full 200-inning workload until 2018. But he will be getting major-league hitters out well before then.

7. Yoan Moncada, 2B, Boston Red Sox
The Red Sox paid $31.5 million dollars for the 19-year-old Moncada ($63 million if you include the 100 percent tax Boston had to pay for exceeding their bonus pool), giving a glimpse into a world where the top amateur talent is allowed to freely negotiate their services with teams, a scenario more horrifying to baseball owners than anything dreamed up by David Cronenberg. So far Moncada has looked well worth the money (which is more than you could say for Crash), showing five average-or-better tools in the South Atlantic League. Moncada has work to do at second base and may fit better at third, where he would have more than enough arm for the position. At either spot, the bat has the potential to anchor the middle of a major-league lineup.

8. Joey Gallo, 3B, Texas Rangers
Shortly after he was called up to the majors, Gallo hit a home run off Clayton Kershaw. The box score describes it as going out to deep right field, but that dry recitation of the facts does it no justice. It was a moment that makes you understand why Russian audiences nearly rioted after hearing The Rites of Spring for the first time. It was an ode to atonality on the baseball diamond, a burst of free jazz. Unfortunately, in Gallo's other 122 major-league plate appearances, his bat was more of a wind instrument, as he struck out 57 times (including in all three of his other plate appearances against the Dodgers that day). The swing-and-miss issues continued after his demotion to Triple-A. He wields true 80 raw power, and we live in an era when teams stomach even a 30 percent strikeout rate if the player can play third base and hit majestic dingers that cause those in atten-

dance to reconsider centuries of acceptable artistic form and their place in the universe. But any more whiff than that and you're looking at just another Quad-A Salieri.

9. Steven Matz, LHP, New York Mets
It seems odd to call someone who made three playoff starts for the National League pennant winner a prospect, but Prospect List protocol demands it. A torn lat muscle and a stiff back in the second half kept Matz from accruing enough service time to graduate, but he did pitch enough for the Mets to show off three average-or-better major-league offerings, including a plus-plus fastball and plus curve. He also has begun to work on the vaunted "Warthen Slider," which you may remember from such 70-grade offerings as Matt Harvey's and Jacob deGrom's.

10. Alex Reyes, RHP, St. Louis Cardinals
Reyes has one of the most electric right arms in the minors. His fastball sits in the upper 90s and touches triple digits. He pairs that with a potential wipeout curve that he can throw for strikes or bury to put away hitters. He struggles at times to harness both pitches, and his command of the fastball is presently below average. The optimist might say that just means he has a chance to get even better, and minor-league hitters were no match for him in 2015 as it stood. The pessimist might point to the command troubles and the lack of an average changeup projection, and see "only" a good late-inning arm. Both would probably agree he has one of the highest ceilings of any current pitching prospect.

11. Tyler Glasnow, RHP, Pittsburgh Pirates
Last season was more of the same for the Pirates' top prospect, for both good and ill. Glasnow continued to show a fastball that can touch the high 90s and a curve that will flash plus. When both are working, he looks like a guy who will strike out a batter per inning in the majors, much like he's done at every other stop so far. Glasnow does struggle from tall-pitcher syndrome at times (he's listed at 6-foot-8), where his delivery can get out of whack, causing both his control and command to suffer. The stuff is good enough that even with those issues, he should pitch in the middle of a major-league rotation for a while, perhaps as soon as this year, but the ceiling if he ever works out the mechanical issues is as high as any arm on this list.

12. Orlando Arcia, SS, Milwaukee Brewers
With improvements across the board in 2015, Arcia turned himself into an archetypal shortstop prospect. He is smooth in the field, equipped with a plus arm and plus projection in the glove. The hitting took a large step forward as well. Arcia has always been able to put bat to ball, but he added strength in 2015 and can now get the ball over the infielders. He's not a double-digit home run threat yet, but pitchers will need to be careful challenging him, because he can drive the ball in both gaps and let his plus-plus legs wreak havoc from home to third. The defense/speed combination was likely going to make him a useful major leaguer regardless, but now he bats second instead of eighth.

13. Trea Turner, SS, Washington Nationals
In a scene that Tom Stoppard probably left on the cutting-room floor, Turner spent the first half of 2015 playing for an organization that had already traded him. Everyone knew this; most just nodded along politely and hoped he didn't twist an ankle. He didn't, and even got a new rule named after him. (Draftees can now be traded after the World Series rather than their teams having to wait a year to move them. See Dansby Swanson's inclusion in the Shelby Miller trade this offseason for an example.) Despite his high overall ranking, Turner could get overlooked on a list this deep in shortstop talent. He is a very good runner, but doesn't have Ozhaino Albies' or Jorge Mateo's gaudy stolen-base totals. He is a solid defender, but isn't a potential Gold Glover like Orlando Arcia or Raul Mondesi. And he can hit, but the offensive profile isn't as tantalizing as J.P. Crawford's. Unlike those five names, Turner is already a major leaguer. The Nationals brought in Stephen Drew to provide a little competition, but Turner should reach his rightful place before too long.

14. Manuel Margot, OF, San Diego Padres
Margot's high ranking here is thanks in part to a renewed emphasis on defense across the game. This is not to suggest that potentially plus center-field gloves were ever at risk of becoming passé in scouting circles, but it's easier to get on the bandwagon in an era when the Royals have won back-to-back pennants. Margot won't be hitting in the eight hole, either: He's shown some bat-to-ball ability and gets more power out of his sub-six-foot frame than you'd expect. The party piece here is the speed/defense combination, which should get plenty of work in the still-spacious Petco outfield.

15. Lewis Brinson, OF, Texas Rangers
Have bat, will travel. Brinson made five stops in 2015, playing in three different time zones from April 9th more or less straight through to the end of the year. No matter how short or long his stay, he impressed the locals by putting balls over the fence, socking 20-plus home runs in less than a season's worth of games. He also cut his strikeouts to a relatively reasonable rate in this day and age. You'd like to see him do more outside the very friendly confines of High Desert, but last year was a breakout from start to finish. Feel free to dream on some 20/20 seasons from a plus center fielder.

16. Raul Mondesi, SS, Kansas City Royals
One of two players on this list to play in the 2015 World Series, Mondesi did not fair as well as Matz, striking out against Noah Syndergaard in his one plate appearance. He does head back to Northwest Arkansas with a big ring, a large playoff share and one of the odder Baseball Reference pages out there. Mondesi struggled in his first taste of the Texas League, as you might expect from a 19-year-old who has never been even league average on offense at any of his full-season stops. But the Royals may continue to be aggressive with his development track, as the glove will play in the high minors even if the bat is presently overmatched. If he does learn to hit, and the tools are certainly there, Mondesi is a slam-dunk first-division shortstop.

17. Jose Berrios, RHP, Minnesota Twins
The flip side of Tyler Glasnow, Berrios gets knocked for the usual short-pitcher reasons. It starts with phrases like "fastball lacks downward plane" and usually ends with "may be best suited to relief." A lot of scouting is about comps, and there aren't many short, slim, right-handed starters in baseball. Berrios might bust the quota with three potential plus pitches, including a devastating changeup. There is a track record of durability here too, at least by pitching-prospect standards. Berrios tossed 166 innings in the upper minors this year, four fewer than Dylan Bundy has thrown in his entire professional career. That sure looks like a starting-pitcher profile, even if he doesn't look like most starting pitchers.

18. Aaron Judge, OF, New York Yankees
Judge should make his debut in the Bronx sometime in 2016, but it feels like a man of his proportions and potential needs a nickname. For opposing pitchers he might very well be "Judge Dredd," or when he fires one back up the box, "Judge Holden." Or maybe his 6-foot-7 frame holds "the long arms of the law." (When they get extended the 70-grade raw power definitely plays.) All right, these aren't as good as "Death to Flying Things" (although Judge should be a good defensive right fielder), so maybe we'll just let his bat do the talking when he gets to East 161st Street.

19. Tim Anderson, SS, Chicago White Sox

"Raw" isn't the first adjective that usually comes to mind when discussing a prospect who hit over .300 in Double-A, but Anderson is unusual. A basketball state champion in high school, he didn't play baseball until his junior year, and spent two years in junior college before being drafted. He still gets by even as he's catching up, in part due to his loud athletic tools. His stats grow harder to hand wave as his competition improves, even though his approach is still quite unrefined. Anderson may require a longer adjustment period against major-league pitching than other prospect bats in this range, and questions about his long-term position remain, but given how rapidly his skills have matured in pro ball, this might be the last time "raw" shows up in his scouting reports.

20. Brendan Rodgers, SS, Colorado Rockies

Rodgers was the third straight shortstop taken to start the 2015 draft, but he may end up the best of the troika. He won't get to the majors as quickly as Dansby Swanson or Alex Bregman, the two SEC players picked ahead of him, but with a potential plus hit–plus power offensive profile and a glove that will keep him on the left side of the diamond, Rodgers may be worth the extra wait. Fortunately, time is one thing the Rockies have had plenty of lately.

21. Blake Snell, LHP, Tampa Bay Rays

Snell vaulted to the top of our Tampa Bay Top 10 list after burning through three levels of the minors with a 1.41 ERA. Minor-league ERA not your thing? Understandable. He also fanned 163 batters in 134 innings while giving up only 84 hits. The stuff more than matches the gaudy stats: Snell features a 92–94 mph fastball with excellent movement and life and pairs it with a plus slider and a potentially solid-average change. The only quibble is that you'd like to see him iron out his control issues before he debuts in the Trop, which will likely be sometime in 2016.

22. Austin Meadows, OF, Pittsburgh Pirates

Meadows has yet to grow into the power some forecast for him as a top-10 pick in 2013, but there is little else here to complain about. He's so far assuaged concerns that he can stick in the middle of the diamond, and his swing still draws raves from scouts. He may never develop even average home run power, but he should knock plenty of doubles. That, combined with his overall hitting acumen and ability to play center field, has drawn comparisons to Christian Yelich.

23. Bradley Zimmer, OF, Cleveland Indians

Zimmer struggled in his first taste of Double-A this season, but the Indians' 2014 first-round pick can take some positives away from his first full year as a pro. His defense in center field improved to the point where he may be at least average there over the middle term, and his solid-average power continued to show up in games, even against more advanced arms. While he doesn't have the vaulted ceiling of some of the other prospects in this area of the list, Zimmer is a polished player on both offense and defense, and all of his tools grade out at average or better. If he continues to improve in center field, his broad base of skills would make him a first-division starter there, and if forced to a corner, his plus arm and sufficient pop would still qualify him to play every day.

24. Jeff Hoffman, RHP, Colorado Rockies

Hoffman made his professional debut last year after recovering from the Tommy John surgery that knocked him down draft boards in 2014. The reports on his stuff continue to wow, even if the results weren't as dominant as you might expect from the kind words. He can touch 99 with his fastball and shows a potentially plus change and curve as well. Dealt from the Blue Jays to the Rockies at the deadline as part of the Troy Tulowitzki deal, Hoffman sits near the top of a suddenly thriving Colorado system. He will be two years removed from surgery in 2016, and no one would be shocked if he moves into the top tier of prospect arms on our 2017 list.

25. Nick Williams, OF, Philadelphia Phillies

Williams was Texas' second-round pick in 2012, and was considered one of the best athletes in the draft. Even on a field of professionals he clearly displays the most athleticism on the diamond, and that shows up in nearly every aspect of his game. In years past he hasn't managed to turn those raw tools into polished skills, but Williams made real strides in that regard last season, and it culminated in him being a centerpiece of the prospect package the Phillies received from the Rangers in return for Cole Hamels. He has freakish bat-to-ball skills that allow him to reach base despite rarely walking. He has also hit double-digit home runs in every full season he's played. Williams has the raw speed to handle center field, and is slowly starting to figure out how to take good routes. Naysayers will continue to question his strike-zone control and lackluster approach until he proves it in the majors.

26. Franklin Barreto, SS, Oakland Athletics

For the next couple of years Barreto, who spent last season at High-A, will be known as "that guy the A's got back for MVP Josh Donaldson." He's less-catchily known as a prospect with an advanced feel for hitting and more power than you'd expect from a player listed at 5-foot-9 (which means there's no way he's actually 5-foot-9). Defensively, he is more of a mixed bag. Barreto has the arm for shortstop, but there are questions about whether he will develop the instincts and actions for the position. The bat looks like it will play elsewhere on the infield, even if the approach will confuse the people who think Moneyball was only about taking walks.

27. Dansby Swanson, SS, Atlanta Braves

Let's play two truths and a lie:

Dansby Swanson was the no. 1 overall pick by the Diamondbacks, a college shortstop who should move quickly through the minors and be a solid regular in the majors, although he lacks the loud tools and overall ceiling of many of the players taken behind him.

Dansby Swanson was the first player dealt under the new Trea Turner Rule when he was included in Arizona's package sent to the Braves for Shelby Miller.

"Dansby Swanson" is the name of a popular recurring character, a bit of an upper-class twit, played by a young Hugh Laurie in some of his early sketch-comedy work.

28. Jose De Leon, RHP, Los Angeles Dodgers

De Leon was a breakout star in the Dodgers' system in 2015. He features an explosive fastball that shows good late life, and his changeup has improved to the point where he is comfortable throwing it to both right-handed and left-handed batters. De Leon's delivery produces extension and deception, which makes the whole package play up. But don't take our word for it, just ask Cal and Texas League hitters, who struck out 35 percent of the time against De Leon last season.

29. Victor Robles, OF, Washington Nationals

All prospect rankings involve a certain amount of dreaming, but if you are going to dream, find a player on whom you can dream big. Robles offers some of the most vivid, 35mm Eastmancolor dreams in the minors right now. The 18-year-old raked in the New York–Penn League last summer, forcing scouts to re-evaluate their expectations. The performance alone would be noteworthy in a league filled with experienced college arms, but Robles pencils in three future 70-grade tools (hit, run, arm) on the scouting sheet as well. He is a long way from the majors, but he has an impact profile both in center field and at the plate.

30. Robert Stephenson, RHP, Cincinnati Reds

A lot of what we wrote for Tyler Glasnow also applies to Stephenson. The Reds' top prospect has two potential 70-grade offerings in his fastball and curve, but like his NL Central counterpart, struggles to command them. With Glasnow, the difficulty is getting his long levers to repeat his mechanics; with Stephenson, it's due to what we called a "grip and rip mentality" on the mound in his pre-2015 scouting report. Last year, he got all the way to Triple-A and struck out more than a batter per inning between the Southern and International Leagues, but the command and control issues lingered. Stephenson struggled with walks and was a bit more hittable at times than you would think given the arsenal. There is a no. 2 starter in here with further refinement, with a mid-rotation or late-inning relief profile otherwise.

31. David Dahl, OF, Colorado Rockies

Dahl missed a month in 2015 after having his spleen removed, the result of a bad outfield collision in New Britain. He was one of the youngest players in the Eastern League and more than held his own on the field. Dahl is a true center fielder with advanced instincts to match his plus speed and strong arm. At the plate he struggled with more advanced sequencing from Double-A arms and was vulnerable to fastballs out of the zone with two strikes. When he does make contact, he does so with exclamation marks, and he may grow into more power as he matures. He needs to make adjustments to his approach to fully tap into his offensive potential, but the defense and athleticism should make him a good regular in center even if the bat never fully develops.

32. Sean Newcomb, LHP, Atlanta Braves

This isn't a Top 101 of prospects who were traded to the Braves this offseason, but it's understandable that you might think so. Newcomb, the grand prize sent to in Atlanta in the Andrelton Simmons deal, garners comparisons to Jon Lester due to his size, handedness and low-effort delivery. Lefties with potential plus-plus velocity are a rare commodity, but Newcomb has struggled with his control and command so far as a professional. Still, he's not just an arm-strength guy; he shows a full four-pitch mix and more feel than you'd expect from a cold-weather, small-college arm. If he gets a better handle on his mechanics and the strike zone, there is front-of-the-rotation upside here.

33. Jon Gray, RHP, Colorado Rockies

The career of a Colorado Rockies pitching prospect is only slightly less tenuous than that of a Spinal Tap drummer. While Gray can do his level best to stay away from gardening shears, he couldn't avoid breathing in the thin air of Albuquerque and Denver in 2015. Gray's fastball sits around 95, and his plus slider will be a bat-misser at the highest level, but command and altitude issues led to more loud contact than you would expect from an arm with his arsenal. He's already logged innings in the majors and has the frame to pitch 200 of them per season, but he will need to refine his changeup and improve his fastball command (and avoid spontaneously combusting, natch) to reach his no. 3 starter upside.

34. Jake Thompson, RHP, Philadelphia Phillies

Thompson is the second of three prospects on this list that came over from Texas in the Cole Hamels deal. He doesn't have the upside of Nick Williams or Jorge Alfaro, but Thompson's a future major-league starter who will show you a plus fastball and slider to go with an average curveball and changeup. He is a strike-thrower as well, but his command lags behind his control, and that makes the whole arsenal a little more hittable than it should be based on the raw scouting grades. Still, the stuff is good enough that Thompson should settle into the middle of the Phillies' rotation as soon as the end of 2016, and he has the frame for eating up innings once he arrives there.

35. Rafael Devers, 3B, Boston Red Sox

It's unusual even this far down the list to find a plus hit–plus power bat like Devers. Granted, he's still very young and a ways away from contributing to the big club in Boston, but you don't have to squint too hard to see an impact major-league hitter given the above-average bat speed and backspin Devers produces at the plate. If he were a lock to stay on the left side of the infield, that's a borderline All-Star profile, but he's already stout at just 18 years old and struggles with his footwork. When he moves across the diamond to first base, the bat will be just "good" there.

36. Ryan McMahon, 3B, Colorado Rockies

You can nitpick McMahon's performance the last two seasons if you like. In 2014 he played his home games in Asheville, which has one of the most inviting right-field porches in minor-league baseball. And in 2015 he played all of his games in the Cal League, which is the Cal League. There is 20–home run power in his bat in any park or league, though, and McMahon is a polished third baseman with a plus arm, so he will contribute on the defensive side as well. Perhaps someday he'll do enough to please you.

37. Ozhaino Albies, SS, Atlanta Braves

One of the few 2016 Braves prospects who was also a 2015 Braves prospect, Albies made a smooth transition to full-season ball as an 18-year-old, hitting .300 in the South Atlantic League. The diminutive switch-hitter is never going to be much of a power threat (you'd be forgiven for suspecting his one career home run was an inside-the-park job), but he offers major-league tools everywhere else. In a perfect world Albies is a good glove up the middle while swiping 30-plus bases and serving as a table-setter for the rest of the lineup. In several other worlds, he's a reboot of Casey Candaele.

38. Braden Shipley, RHP, Arizona Diamondbacks

For variety's sake, here are some potential no. 3 starter Mad Libs:

Shipley features a plus fastball that sits in the mid-90s and complements it with (pitcher's name)(scouty verb)
a plus changeup that could be a swing-and-miss offering in the bigs. His(best off-speed pitch) (synonym for MLB)
curveball lags behind his other two offerings, but could get to average with further(third pitch) development. The command profile here is only fringe -average, due to issues
(noun that ends in "ment")(probably "fringe")repeating his delivery. Shipley is a potential manatee on the mound, capable of taking (pitcher's name)(strong animal)the ball every fifth day and logging innings in the middle of a major-league rotation.

39. Alex Bregman, SS, Houston Astros

When the Astros selected Bregman with the second pick in the 2015 draft, they got a proven, polished performer from the best baseball conference in NCAA. You will find plenty of shortstops with louder tools on this list, but Bregman's floor is likely higher than all of them. He shows a plus hit tool and a solid glove for the position, and may start his first full professional season in Double-A. He also gets high marks for makeup and is a top-step player through and through. While he may not be a future All-Star, Bregman could be contributing to a major-league team as soon as this September.

40. Grant Holmes, RHP, Los Angeles Dodgers
Holmes is one of the more underrated pitching prospects in baseball. He is outshone in his own system by the top-end arm strength of Jose De Leon and the combination of youth, stuff and pitchability of Julio Urias. He even got overlooked among the 2014 prep-arm draft class due to the lack of projection in his 6-foot-1 frame. The Dodgers may have gotten a steal with the 22nd-overall pick as a result. Holmes features a plus fastball and curve, but needs to refine his command and changeup to reach his projection as a mid-rotation starter. You may have heard some of this before.

41. Gleyber Torres, SS, Chicago Cubs
After graduating Addison Russell, Kris Bryant and Kyle Schwarber in 2015, it would be forgivable if the Cubs system were down a bit this year. Their player-development system doesn't rebuild, though; it reloads. Torres may remind you of Starlin Castro, although not so much Castro the wizened veteran but Castro the prospect. He shows the same precocious hitting ability (Torres hit .293 as the youngest player in the Midwest League), and there are also questions about whether he sticks at shortstop long term. Torres cost the current Cubs front office a few pretty pennies more than the $45,000 that Jim Hendry and company paid for Castro, but if he can produce the same results at the plate, it's unlikely there will be much quibbling over the $1.7 million "splurge."

42. Raimel Tapia, SS, Colorado Rockies
Tapia is a divisive prospect, even within Baseball Prospectus. He has bat-to-ball skills border on the preternatural. His ability to get the barrel on almost any pitch leads to some bad contact and chasing, though. He is still raw in center field, but his plus foot speed should let him play at least average there with further development of his reads and routes. The bat would be pushed in a corner, as the power projection is muddied a bit by his stints in Asheville and the Cal League. In short, Tapia has more development room than you would think for a player set to start the 2016 season in Double-A, but the bat is so tantalizing that it keeps him in the top half of this list.

43. Aaron Blair, RHP, Atlanta Braves
Hey, another Braves prospect who wasn't a Braves prospect at the beginning of last season! Blair lacks the upside of Sean Newcomb or Touki Toussaint, but he is a major-league-ready arm with mid-rotation upside. He has a prototypical starter's frame (6-foot-5, 230 pounds) and he's made 52 starts over the last two seasons. He may lack a high-end swing-and-miss offering against major-league hitters (though both the curve and change have a chance to be above average), but he has four major-league pitches and a body built to sweat out 200 innings.

44. Anthony Alford, OF, Toronto Blue Jays
Alford cost the Jays almost twice the third-round slot on a two-sport deal out of the 2012 draft (he was a highly regarded quarterback prospect at Southern Miss), and it started to pay off in 2015. He always had five-tool potential, and it showed up at the plate in a big way in his first extended taste of full-season ball. Alford displayed above-average bat speed and an improving approach, and his athleticism already plays well in center. Although he lost some development time due to his dalliance with college football, he will find himself in 2016 a level-appropriate 22-year-old in the Eastern League.

45. Sean Manaea, LHP, Oakland Athletics
Manaea certainly looks the part of a top pitching prospect. He's got the prototypical workhorse-starter build. The fastball can touch 97 from the left side and sits comfortably plus with good movement. He complements that with a slider and change, both of which could be at least average. However, there are a whole bunch of "cans" and "coulds" with this profile. The Manaea described above doesn't show up in every start, and recently he hasn't been showing up much at all. An abdominal injury followed by a groin injury limited him to under 100 innings in 2015, even after he popped up healthy in the crisp baseball of autumn. If you shook a Magic 8 Ball and asked it about Manaea, you'd get an "Outlook Cloudy" or "Ask Again Later."

46. Andrew Benintendi, OF, Boston Red Sox
A bit of a surprise pick by the Red Sox at no. 7 in the 2015 draft, Benintendi hit the ground running, putting pitchers in both the New York–Penn and the South Atlantic League to the sword. There is no one carrying tool here, and the ceiling isn't as high as it usually is for a seventh-overall pick, but nothing grades out as worse than average, and he gets more power out of his 5-foot-10 frame than you'd expect. His advanced approach makes the whole offensive profile play up, and he should stick in center field. The lack of a long professional track record or standout tool injects some risk into the profile, but there isn't much more Benintendi could have done in 2015 to quell any remaining doubts.

47. Cody Reed, LHP, Cincinnati Reds
Reed moved from the land of burnt ends to the land of "chili" last summer as part of the Johnny Cueto deal. The tall, lanky lefty was in the midst of a breakout season in the Royals' system at the time, and he continued his success in Pensacola for the Reds. He has an electric fastball from the left side, which sits 92-95 as a starter and has touched 99 in short bursts. Reed pairs that with a sharp-breaking, upper-80s slider. He still has occasional issues with control and command, which plagued him more prominently in 2013 and 2014, due to a bit of a crossfire delivery and timing issues with his lightning-fast arm action. He may be best suited as a reliever long term, but his fastball-slider combo could make him an elite late-inning arm.

48. Archie Bradley, RHP, Arizona Diamondbacks
Last year was a bit of a lost season for the Diamondbacks' top prospect. His major-league debut was marred by a line drive off his face and general control struggles led to his demotion back to Triple-A. Shoulder issues followed, and cost him most of the summer. He showed flashes of what made him a top-10 national prospect at the end of the year in Reno, but this was the second straight year in which Bradley spent more time off the field than on it. At his best, he features a mid-90s fastball and a hammer curve, but much to Riverdale's dismay, he has rarely been at his best lately.

49. Josh Bell, OF, Pittsburgh Pirates
We've been waiting for years for Bell's raw plus power to start showing up in games. It didn't get all the way there in 2015, but the hit tool took a huge step forward against upper-level pitching. He hit .317 between the Eastern and International Leagues and walked as often as he struck out. Although he has yet to post double-digit home runs in a professional season, Bell shows power from both sides of the plate, and even if it only plays as average in the end, his 2015 makes you feel more confident that his bat will play in right field (where he isn't great defensively, although his arm is good) or first base (where it doesn't really matter).

50. Jesse Winker, OF, Cincinnati Reds
"Left-field profile" is a pejorative in scout circles, a little like calling a movie "one of Adam Sandler's better ones." The implication is that the player does not have the athleticism for center or the arm for right. Left fielders have to hit. Fortunately, Winker hasn't had much of a problem with that so far. The raw power won't wow you, but Winker should deliver plenty of doubles, hit for a good average and show a strong approach that ties the whole offensive package together.

51. Jameson Taillon, RHP, Pittsburgh Pirates
Nowadays we all but expect top pitching prospects to lose a year to Tommy John surgery somewhere along the road, but two years without a line on the baseball card will raise an eyebrow. Taillon missed all of 2014 for the de rigueur elbow surgery, and his path back last season was further marred by a hernia that kept him off the mound. Before his injury issues, Taillon had stuff that would easily put him among the top tier of prospects on this list, and he ended 2013 on the cusp of the majors. This ranking may look too low in six months, or it may look too high. It could also look juuuuuuuuuust right.

52. Brent Honeywell, RHP, Tampa Bay Rays
Most of the press around Honeywell is concerned with his screwball, taught to him by his uncle, Mike Marshall. It's a pitch worth the column inches, already a bat-missing offering in the minors, but Honeywell is far from a one-trick pony, with a plus fastball and two other major-league-quality secondaries in his arsenal as well. That is a quality mid-rotation profile, if a unique one nowadays. Honeywell also does not lack for moxie, something else he may have picked up from Uncle Mike.

53. Clint Frazier, OF, Cleveland Indians
If you remember nothing else about Frazier, highly regarded 2013 prep bat, you probably remember that he had near-elite bat speed and bright red hair. In 2016, he still swings a fast stick and is still very ginger. The plus-plus bat speed and lift from his swing plane translated into real over-the-fence power in the Carolina League last season, and he cut his strikeout rate to a more acceptable level. There is still too much swing and miss in the zone from Frazier, and questions linger about his pitch recognition and whether he will be able to play center field in the majors, but oh man does that bug-zapper bat speed seduce.

54. Willy Adames, SS, Tampa Bay Rays
Adames rose to national prominence as the main prospect sent to Tampa in the David Price deal. That brings with it additional attention and expectations, so it is easy to view his 2015 season (.258/.342/.379 in High-A) as a disappointment. But Adames will play the entire 2016 season as a 20-year-old, and the underlying skill set that makes him a potentially above-average regular at shortstop are still present. If his lack of foot speed forces him to second or third (the arm should play at the latter), the bat will have to take a step forward.

55. A.J. Reed, 1B, Houston Astros
Reed is the best first-base prospect in the minors. While that isn't quite the dictionary definition of "damning with faint praise," you can probably find it in a thesaurus. He will have to do more than just hit; he'll have to mash for the bat to play even average for the position. Fortunately, the skill set fits the bill. Reed socked 34 home runs across two levels in 2015, and the scouting reports back up the statistical performance, raving about his power to all fields and epic batting-practice displays. The swing that generates this power is long enough that even with his advanced approach, there will be strikeout issues that cut into his average, but the potential 30–home run pop and OBP skills should make up for that deficiency. Reed doesn't offer much outside of the bat, even considering the already low bar at first base, so it's not the worst thing in the world that he'll have the DH option available to him in the majors.

56. Javier Guerra, SS, San Diego Padres
Guerra entered 2015 as one of our "prospects on the rise" in a very, very deep Red Sox system. He enters the 2016 season in the Padres system (he was part of the package for Craig Kimbrel), and as one of the best shortstop prospects in the game. Guess he rose. What changed? The slick glove that brought Guerra to our attention in the first place remains. Everything he does in the field is loose and smooth, and he shows both the range and arm the position demands. The bat was the real revelation. In his full-season debut, the 19-year-old Panamanian knocked 15 home runs in the South Atlantic League, and while the power may not reach quite those heights at higher levels, he's always shown above-average bat speed and a frame that could add strength as he ages. Guerra still needs refinement in his approach, but given the defensive projection, if he turns into even an average hitter in the majors, he's a slam-dunk first-division shortstop.

57. Willson Contreras, C/3B, Chicago Cubs
Contreras didn't get cut from BP's Cubs top-prospects list coming into the 2015 season because he wasn't in legit consideration in the first place. It's a tribute both to how outstanding their system is and how large a step forward Contreras took in 2015 that he lands just outside the top 50 a year later. Contreras came somewhat late to catching, as the Cubs signed him as an infielder out of Venezuela, and he spent his first three professional seasons playing mostly first and third. But he's taken well to the tools, and is a good bet to be at least an average defender behind the plate. That said, it was the development of his bat over the last year that marks him as the best catching prospect in baseball. Contreras hit .333 in Double-A and set a career high with 34 doubles; his approach and plate discipline took a step forward as well. It was a true breakout season, and another voyage of self-discovery could rocket him into the top echelon of prospects next year, assuming he doesn't hit his way to Wrigley first.

58. Hunter Harvey, RHP, Baltimore Orioles
As you may have gathered, we are now in the middle of the "oft-injured pitching prospect with potentially great stuff" range. A healthy Harvey was a top-20 prospect entering 2015, but was plagued by general discomfort in his forearm area throughout the season. If that sounds like a precursor to Tommy John surgery, well, it often is. That would at least clarify the situation for him, although it would also cost him all of 2016 as well. If a healthy Harvey gets back on the mound, hopefully his top-of-the-rotation stuff returns with him. He's a potential no. 2 starter, but that whole "when healthy" thing is a chilling qualifier for any pitching prospect.

59. Dillon Tate, RHP, Texas Rangers
The consensus best pitcher in the 2015 draft class, Tate failed to slip past the Rangers at no. 4, who paid $4.2 million to procure his services. He features a mid-90s fastball that can touch 98 and a potentially plus-plus slider that will generate whiffs against both righties and lefties. The changeup has a ways to go, but that's how it is for most amateur arms; he didn't need it much to get Big West hitters out. Tate also has a chance to become the most famous alumnus of Claremont High School, a title currently held by The Mountain Goats' frontman, John Darnielle. It's not a great chance, though; We Shall All Be Healed is a really good record.

60. Max Kepler, OF, Minnesota Twins
Kepler has always looked the part of a big, slugging corner outfielder, but the production from the German has never matched the body. That finally changed in 2015, as he set a career high in extra-base hits with 56, and even got a brief cup of coffee with the Twins in September. Kepler is still playing some center field, but it's more of a dalliance given his burgeoning physique and, maybe more importantly, the existence of Byron Buxton, so it would be helpful if some of those 2015 doubles turn into home runs. At this point along his development path, power will be the last piece of the puzzle, as he has an extremely advanced approach, can hit for average and runs just well enough nip 15 bases a year.

61. Brett Phillips, OF, Milwaukee Brewers
The centerpiece of the Carlos Gomez trade, Phillips is a hard-nosed center fielder with a free safety's mentality and an arbalest for a right arm. He improved his approach at the plate and grew into his swing last year, and now combines an ability to make in-swing adjustments with some natural loft and pull-side pop to project as an average contributor at the plate with additional value added on the basepaths. Phillips didn't show much of that pop outside of the launching pad in Lancaster (15 home runs in 66 games in the Cal League, one home run in 54 elsewhere), but he doesn't need to hit for much power to be a productive regular in center field given the rest of the skill set.

62. Nick Gordon, SS, Minnesota Twins
Son of Flash, brother of Dee, Nick garners all the positive epithets we often hear about a prospect with major-league bloodlines. You will hear things like "high baseball IQ" and "good feel for the game." As far as the tools go, he doesn't have his older brother's elite speed, but he's athletic enough to stick on the left side of the diamond and could even end up above average there due to his strong fundamentals at shortstop and a plus arm. He's more advanced in the field than at the plate, but he showed some feel for hitting and a bit of gap-to-gap power in his 2015 Midwest League campaign.

63. Francis Martes, RHP, Houston Astros
Acquired at the 2014 trade deadline as part of the return for Jarred Cosart, Martes blew through three levels as a 19-year-old last year, finishing in the Texas League. Along the way he struck out nearly a quarter of the batters he faced on the strength of a fastball-curve combo that flashes plus-plus. He is only 6-foot-1 and struggles at times with mechanical inconsistency, so there will always be bullpen whispers, but Martes has the frame to handle a starter's workload and already shows a solid change. He needs further refinement on the mound, but this is a potential front-of-the-rotation arm. The fallback position of relief ace who sits in the upper 90s isn't too shabby either.

64. Mark Appel, RHP, Philadelphia Phillies
We have around 100 words or so to describe the player in question in these blurbs, so some summarizing is always necessary. Focus on a couple high points, stick in a developmental opportunity, maybe a quick projection and on to the next one. Appel confounds that modality. Getting any agreement on him from scouts and evaluators, even on velocity readings, which vary from day to day, is a difficult task. Forget about reaching any sort of détente around his pitch grades or ultimate projection. The best reports show Appel with three plus offerings (though not always in the same start) and a possible no. 2 starter outcome. Others teem with complaints about inconsistency in the stuff from start to start, inning to inning, even pitch to pitch, and predict a consignment to the bullpen. "The truth is probably somewhere in the middle" is an awfully pat conclusion in most instances, but here the middle is a vast expanse that covers most of the outcomes likely for prospects good enough to make this list in the first place. We could go on, but we are already stretching the patience of our lovely editors and their "around 100 words" diktat.

65. Jorge Mateo, SS, New York Yankees
The Yankees have spent millions in the international market over the last few seasons, blowing past their cap in both 2013 and 2014, but their best IFA prospect might be one they paid just a quarter of a million dollars in 2012. Mateo is an 80 runner fully capable of stolen-base titles. He offers a potentially solid glove at shortstop as well. The bat is still quite raw, and may never win him a Silver Slugger, but he can challenge the old adage that "you can't steal first." Every ball in play is a potential single, and every ball up the alleys a potential triple.

66. Jacob Nottingham, C, Oakland Athletics
Nottingham was dealt from Houston to Oakland in the Scott Kazmir trade while in the midst of a breakout season with the bat. Granted, he did a fair chunk of damage in the Cal League, which is quite hitter-friendly, but the swing backs up a plus power projection to go with the A-ball production. Behind the plate he's a mixed bag, with a strong arm but raw receiving skills. Prep catchers can take longer to develop, and the happy dreams of a 20-homer catcher are enough to give Nottingham more time behind the dish.

67. Ian Happ, OF, Chicago Cubs
It is not mere happenstance that finds Happ on this year's 101. He's another polished college bat who the Cubs happily added to their system, selecting the Cincinnati outfielder with the ninth-overall pick in the 2015 draft. If you happened upon him in his professional debut last summer, you saw a switch-hitting outfielder who never looks hapless from either side of the plate, and shows enough present-day feel and approach to move quickly through the minors. Happ is not quite athletic enough for center field, and has run out to all three outfield positions so far in his brief pro career. There is some thought that he might be able to play second base, so there is no need for the Cubs to make a decision about his ultimate defensive home haphazardly.

68. Luis Ortiz, RHP, Texas Rangers
A 2014 first-round pick, Ortiz performed very well in his first full professional season. He posted very impressive strikeout and walk rates, especially for a 19-year-old in a full-season league. Ortiz has a workhorse frame, but needs to monitor his weight to avoid being compared to less complimentary animals. His delivery is unorthodox, but as his control numbers suggest, he fills the zone quite well. A potential mid-rotation starter, Ortiz has a heavy sinker-slider mix with a changeup that can get to average. A 2017 debut at absolute earliest, Ortiz likely will be capped at Double-A Frisco this year while logging more innings.

69. Dylan Bundy, RHP, Baltimore Orioles
Much of what was written for Hunter Harvey would fit under Bundy's name as well. He did pitch in 2015, but he only threw 22 innings, and dealt with shoulder issues for much of the season. This comes on the heels of arm issues in 2014, and Tommy John surgery that cost him all of 2013. You might forget that he pitched a bit in the majors in 2012 after signing a big-league deal out of the draft, but the Orioles are probably well aware, as he enters 2016 out of options. If he's not on the DL, he'll have to be on the major-league staff somewhere, but balancing the building of his arm strength with keeping his rights will be a sticky wicket for the Baltimore front office and field staff. Why go through all this trouble for an oft-injured pitcher? Bundy showed three potentially plus pitches at his height as a prospect. The number of arms even on this list with that résumé is very, very short.

70. Jorge Alfaro, C, Philadelphia Phillies
It feels like #TheLegend has been tantalizing us with his potential for years now. Alfaro's loud tools are fun to talk about, but they needed to show up in actual baseball games more consistently, and that still didn't happen in 2015. Granted, Alfaro missed a lot of time with an ankle injury, but a leg issue for a catching prospect, one about whom there were already whispers regarding his long-term future behind the plate, is very concerning. Alfaro the player may never live up to Alfaro the prospect, but this is a prospect list, and it is tough to ignore a potential five-tool catcher.

71. Jorge Lopez, RHP, Milwaukee Brewers
Lopez was nowhere near our 2015 Top 101 list, and only clocked in at seventh overall in a shallow Milwaukee system. The stuff

projected as average across the board at best, and his performance in the Carolina League was uninspiring. He looked like a prototypical projectable guy who hadn't yet projected, physically or astrally. Flash forward 12 months and Lopez's fastball now sits 92-94, touching the upper 90s, with a curve that dismays opponents. He dominated Double-A and got two starts for the Brewers as they played out the string. He'll likely be back in their rotation at some point in 2016, and while his occasional control issues may keep him from being a front-line arm, he could end up a useful mid-rotation starter, something that seemed very unlikely this time last year.

72. Brandon Drury, 2B, Arizona Diamondbacks
Anytime a former 13th-rounder makes his big-league debut, someone somewhere in an amateur-scouting department gets an extra half-hour of free continental breakfast at the closest Days Inn. Drury has a legitimate shot at helping the big club in a significant way in 2016. He'll show four average-or-slightly-better tools, with the power potential standing out as an expected strength despite curiously poor home run totals in the high minors. A competent defender at second or third, he's capable of occupying prime real estate on the depth chart for the next several years.

73. Anderson Espinoza, RHP, Boston Red Sox
Remember what you were doing at 17? If your answer doesn't involve hitting triple digits with your fastball on the back end of a seven-figure bonus, then you and Espinoza might not have a whole lot to talk about. The Venezuelan wunderkind forced his way stateside in his first professional season, then proceeded to whiff a batter an inning while allowing all of three earned runs in his first 40 frames of Rookie ball. That's a 0.68 ERA if you're scoring at home. Espinoza's heater already shows projection as an elite major-league weapon, and he backs it up with startlingly advanced feel for a pair of potentially plus secondaries. Still, his slight build and the natural attrition rate of young pitchers are reasons enough to keep expectations in check, kind of like your junior prom date did when you were the kid's age.

74. Billy McKinney, OF, Chicago Cubs
If "left-field profile" is pejorative, "tweener" is an epitaph. But we come to praise McKinney, not to bury him. He is, after all, the 74th-best prospect in baseball. True, he doesn't have the foot speed for center field, nor the arm for right, and his yearly total of dingers should just barely creep into double digits once his game power fully develops. What he can do is engage that most primal of baseball skills: See ball, strike ball. If we were to rank these same 101 prospects just on their hit tools, McKinney would be much higher, and not just because there are a lot of pitchers. He could be a perennial .300 hitter in an era when that is a very rare thing. That may be enough to carry a left-field profile and avoid the tweener tag.

75. Reynaldo Lopez, RHP, Washington Nationals
A pop-up prospect in the New York–Penn League in 2014, Lopez proved more hittable over a full season at High-A last year. At its best his fastball sits in the high 90s and hops to the arm side in the nick of time. Physical gains also had his curveball snapping harder and avoiding more bats for Potomac. He struggles at times to repeat a delivery that can get overwhelmed by his top-shelf arm speed, but the cadence and raw material for a solid command profile are present. The Nationals have built his workload cautiously, and figure to polish him at Double-A this spring.

76. Reese McGuire, C, Pittsburgh Pirates
McGuire lacks the offensive upside of the other catching prospects on the 101, but he's by far the best defender of the group. He struggled with the bat in the Florida State League last year, but he offers a plus defensive projection behind the plate with a plus arm and advanced receiving skills. He's a good athlete for a catcher as well, and may grow into more game power over time. His stock is down until he starts to hit a bit more, but the glove alone gives him a good shot at a major-league career, even if it's the one-day-a-week kind.

77. Amir Garrett, LHP, Cincinnati Reds
Garrett advanced one level to pitch the entirety of 2015 at age-appropriate High-A, and he put together an eerily consistent season compared to 2014, save for an impressively slashed home run rate. Although he'll pop the mid-90s from a tough left-handed angle, he still hasn't quite figured out how to fully channel his premium athleticism into a consistent delivery. That hasn't necessarily mattered thus far, as he's shown plenty of raw stuff to get by in the lower minors, but 2016 will bring with it a stronger challenge at Double-A and a chance for Reds brass to figure out Garrett's place among the organization's expanding hierarchy of interesting pitching prospects.

78. Yadier Alvarez, RHP, Los Angeles Dodgers
We've reached the point in gluttonous Dodgers spending where they could throw eight figures at the shruggy emoticon guy and nobody would so much as raise an eyebrow. Their outlay for the 19-year-old Cuban wasn't quite that random, but it was certainly aggressive given Alvarez's poor production in junior-league play. A well-timed growth spurt helped his velocity spike into the high 90s when he defected last year, and he tantalizes with premium arm speed and flashes of a wipeout slider. The mechanics are raw enough to be served on lightly toasted rye bread, however, and he struggles mightily to repeat his delivery and command the baseball right now. The upside is massive, and the risk would be too, if risk mattered to the Dodgers.

79. Austin Riley, 3B, Atlanta Braves
A two-way player in high school more generally regarded as a future hurler heading into the draft, Riley heard his name on day one thanks to an Atlanta front office that preferred the raw thunder in his bat. He didn't disappoint after signing, slugging a dozen rhombuses and 14 doubles in his 60 games of Rookie ball. He generates plus-or-better power with an easy, country-strong swing, though an Ugglan strikeout rate warrants caution. His strong arm and surprising agility for a big man lend hope that he can stay at the hot corner long term, while his dreamy blue eyes and plus baseball name round out the package of a potential franchise cornerstone.

80. Harold Ramirez, OF, Pittsburgh Pirates
A 2011 bonus baby out of Colombia, Ramirez would have comfortably led the offense-challenged Florida State League in hitting had he tallied a qualifying number of at-bats. The well-rounded outfielder failed to do so, however, because the team held him back for extensive conditioning work after he showed up last spring heavily emphasizing the "round." And the "heavily." (He was overweight.) Questions of focus and dedication notwithstanding, Ramirez can really hit. His barrel-delivery and feel for contact are both well above average, and his frame suggests ample power should be on the way as his approach matures. His body type and lack of arm strength may force him to left field, but the Pirates aren't likely to mind if he reaches his offensive potential.

81. Jose Peraza, SS, Cincinnati Reds
When a top prospect is traded twice in the space of four months, it tends to elicit sidelong glances. Why was the player deemed expendable? The focus turns to what he can't do. There are things Peraza can't do, to be sure. He won't walk much or hit for any sort of power. That profile can be tough at the highest level, because major-league arms will challenge you if the worst they can expect is a line-drive single. Peraza can give you those

those, though. He can also run and has experience at all three up-the-middle positions. If he improves at shortstop, he's an everyday player; he's also a guy worth trading for twice.

82. Kolby Allard, LHP, Atlanta Braves
Allard is a true oddity on this list. Not that the ranking is out of place or anything: He was the best prep arm in the 2015 draft, synecdochally speaking. The little lefty will flash three plus pitches and also gets high marks for command and pitchability given his age. No, the weird thing is that he is listed as a Braves prospect, but as far as we here at Baseball Prospectus can tell, at no point in time has Allard played any of his amateur baseball in the state of Georgia. We'll continue to investigate.

83. Albert Almora, OF, Cubs
Almora's well-rounded skill set hasn't quite coalesced at the superstar speed of some of his fellow 2012 first-rounders, but it's getting there. An aggressive approach has frequently undercut his promising hit tool and limited his solid power potential as he's journeyed up the ranks. But while the power remains nascent he made notable progress in upping his previously abysmal walk rate at Double-A last year, and he continued to make contact at a fine clip. He shines in the field, and though he lacks for much more than average raw foot speed he is blessed with an innate ability to anticipate and read contact. It remains an open question whether the offensive package is likely to get to first-division caliber, but the defense and drive should be more than enough to grant him an audition to find out in the near future.

84. Taylor Guerrieri, RHP, Tampa Bay Rays
Guerrieri's stuff may merit a higher place on this list, but he's yet to have the opportunity to show that stuff across a full season: The 78 innings he threw in 2015 were a career high, and he was drafted all the way back in 2011. Most of the other first-round prep arms from that draft have already debuted in the majors or are knocking on the door (e.g. Jose Fernandez, Joe Ross, Dylan Bundy, Archie Bradley and Robert Stephenson), while Guerrieri has thrown just 36 innings above A-ball. The fastball-curve combo both show up as plus, but given his durability issues and lack of an above-average future projection for the change, he may end up as a late-inning reliever.

85. Daz Cameron, OF, Houston Astros
Writing about teenage prospects will make you feel old, as we've mentioned before. Writing about teenage prospects whose father's career you remember from start to finish will make you feel... really old. Daz is the son of former All-Star Mike, and the Astros gave him $4 million in last year's draft, tying him for the fifth-highest bonus paid. Daz may not offer the same speed-power combo his father did, and he'll almost certainly never hit four home runs in a game, but he has a good shot to stick in center field, and he has a broad set of offensive tools to bet on with an up-the-middle defensive profile.

86. Dominic Smith, 1B, New York Mets
Unix programmers follow a guiding philosophy of DOTADIW (Do One Thing And Do It Well). Meet Smith. Dude can hit. He's a first-base-only prospect, and he has yet to show much in the way of game power in his first two professional seasons, but he has preternatural bat-to-ball skills and started driving the ball into the left-center gap more in 2015. It's still a difficult profile, and he has a high-maintenance body even for first base, but when you watch him swing the bat, those thoughts drift further from your mind. Now if only we could get you all using mutt for email.

87. Michael Fulmer, RHP, Detroit Tigers
Various arm and leg issues cost Fulmer large chunks of 2013 and 2014. He shook them off in 2015, and showed why he was a supplemental first-round pick. The fastball is still a plus offering that can touch the mid-90s consistently, and his slider took a large step forward. The changeup lags behind, and this was the first full (ish) healthy season Fulmer has pitched, so there will be lingering questions about whether he is a major-league starter. He looks built for a 200-inning workload, so he could turn into a mid-rotation stalwart with further command and changeup refinement, but he may be best suited as a late-inning reliever where the fastball-slider combination could play up further in short bursts.

88. Daniel Robertson, SS, Tampa Bay Rays
We hope you're not tired of reading about shortstops yet, because we have a few more to go. Robertson technically qualifies: Sent to Tampa in the Ben Zobrist deal with Oakland, he demonstrates below-average range at the position, although both the A's and the Rays have never been shy about playing shortstops who are stretched. He has the arm for third, but he has yet to show the over-the-fence power for a corner (outside of the Cal League, anyway). If he does find himself banished from shortstop, there still might be enough OBP and doubles power in the profile to carve out a career as a regular.

89. Kyle Zimmer, RHP, Kansas City Royals
Zimmer has now compiled a stellar 3.28 ERA in parts of four professional seasons, but he's also logged more days on the disabled list than innings on the mound. Last year, a setback in rehabbing his surgically repaired shoulder delayed his debut and ultimately cost him two more months of development, after which the organization conservatively limited his innings in a relief role for the bulk of the season. When he did toe the rubber he still showed the same premium velocity and hammer curveball that got him drafted as the fifth-overall pick back in the day. Short of hiring away the white-gloved Stanley Cup bodyman to shadow him, it's unclear what else the Royals can do to keep their top pitching prospect on the mound for a full season. They'll try again in 2016.

90. Hunter Renfroe, OF, San Diego Padres
"Right-field profile" doesn't get the same bad press as the other corner outfield spot, but it puts similar pressure on the bat to perform. Our vision of a right fielder is more in line with a baseball player who oozes tools. Sure, maybe he isn't quite athletic enough for center (Renfroe certainly isn't), but we are more likely to find a big arm and some lift in the swing next to the no. 9 on your scorecard (Renfroe gives you both). There's enough swing and miss here that the 70-grade raw power may only play as 60 against major-league pitching, but, coupled with his above-average athletic tools for a corner, that should make him a solid regular for the Friars as soon as the second half of 2016.

91. Yusniel Diaz, OF, Los Angeles Dodgers
A legend of the Cuban junior leagues, Diaz signed with the Dodgers for eight figures because of course he did. He's a center fielder by trade, with four above-average tools and raw power that may evolve into a fifth depending on how his body develops. He already shows solid command of the zone, leading evaluators to believe that outstanding hand-eye coordination can help him play as a top-of-the-order asset who gets on base and steals some bags. That assumes, of course, that the Dodgers haven't bought all of the free agents by then and left him as a superfluous—if quite rich—career minor leaguer.

92. Gary Sanchez, C, New York Yankees
This is Sanchez's sixth appearance on a BP Top 101, so it falls to him to show the kids how to fix the copier and where we keep the K-Cups. He took steps forward on both sides of the ball in 2015, and the plus power and plus-plus arm that have kept him on every new iteration of this list are still very much present.

Evaluations differ on whether he is a catcher long term, but the Yankees have an opening for him behind the plate in 2016, albeit as a backup, so we prospect writers should at least be able to avoid the seven-year itch. Maybe Sanchez should avoid any subway grates around the D train just to be on the safe side though.

93. Kyle Tucker, OF, Houston Astros

Tucker's swing was the subject of much internal discussion here at BP Towers. It's difficult to find a modern comp for it, as nowadays no one loads their hands quite as low as he does. The result was email threads filled with grainy film of Ted Williams and Stan Musial. Needless to say, those are a couple of wildly unfair names to drop in the commentary for any hitter, much less an 18-year-old, even one highly regarded enough as an amateur to get picked fifth overall. Tucker needs to work out the occasional timing issues with his left hook of a swing and add more physical strength in order to generate enough power for his right-field projection. He remains one of the most intriguing amateur bats in the 2015 class, and he can always pick up some free pointers from older brother, Preston.

94. Alex Jackson, OF, Seattle Mariners

The 20-year-old Jackson is a bit young for the "post-hype sleeper" designation, but hitting just .157/.240/.213 in the Midwest League after getting pegged as the sixth-overall draft pick will dissipate your hype quickly. He fared better in the Northwest League, where he was hardly an old man, and showed more of the power that made him such a highly regarded amateur talent. Jackson is limited to right field, so he will have to hit a lot, but the pedigree and potential are still there.

95. Franklyn Kilome, RHP, Philadelphia Phillies

Kilome may very well be the rawest arm on this list. He's a 6-foot-6 string bean who has yet to throw a pitch in full-season ball. The stuff that earns him this spot only shows up in flashes right now. That's the (possibly temporary) bad news. The good news is he has plus-plus arm strength and bumped the upper 90s last summer for Williamsport. He will also flash a plus curve. The development path will be long for Kilome, but there may be projection left in his frame, and the upside is very, very high.

96. Amed Rosario, SS, New York Mets

Rosario has turned into a very different type of prospect than the Mets might have figured when they gave the Dominican shortstop $1.7 million in 2012. Scouts thought he might grow into serious game power but out of the position. Rosario hasn't really put on mass, and hit zero home runs in the Florida State League (where he was the youngest every-day player) last year, but he has made huge strides with his defense. Rosario now looks like he could be an above-average glove, and he does have incredibly quick wrists that should at least give him gap power as he continues to physically mature. He may not be the prospect we expected, but he's still a good one. If you were just here for the shortstops, you can quit now. No more, promise.

97. Eddy Julio Martinez, OF, Chicago Cubs

Martinez might want to steer clear of the Swan Oyster Depot for a while after backing out of a deal with San Francisco to take $3 million from the Cubs. It's not the end of the world (Chicago has almost as many Michelin stars as offensive stars nowadays), but the 20-year-old Cuban outfielder still has a ways to go developmentally before he'll be scoring reservations at Alinea or 42 Grams. Martinez is likely to start 2016 in South Bend (best restaurant according to TripAdvisor: LaSalle Grill), where he will start to answer the questions about his power potential and ultimate defensive home in the outfield.

98. Michael Kopech, RHP, Boston Red Sox

Kopech's dominant season in the South Atlantic League was cut short in July by a 50-game suspension for using a banned amphetamine. If you insist the two are related we will point you to that XKCD comic about correlation versus causation (no. 552; there truly is an XKCD for every situation). Even in an abbreviated stint, Kopech showed a fastball that could bump the upper 90s and a potentially plus power curve. The mechanics (like much of the rest of the profile) are a bit raw and he may eventually settle in as a power arm in the bullpen. Given that he won't turn 20 until a month into the 2016 season, Kopech still has plenty of time to try sticking as a starter.

99. Trent Clark, OF, Milwaukee Brewers

Clark's is an unusual profile among first-round prep picks, especially one likely to end up in a corner spot. He has an advanced approach and impressive pure hitting ability for his age, but lacks big-time athletic tools. Without much in the way of projected power or enough speed for center field, Clark will have to hit his way to the majors. Fortunately, he may very well have been the best overall high school hitter in last year's draft class.

100. Conner Greene, RHP, Toronto Blue Jays

The Jays nabbed Greene as a projectable Southern California prep arm in the seventh round of the 2013 draft. He, uh, projected, climbing three levels of the minors in his full-season debut. The skinny 6-foot-3 right-hander can run his fastball up to 98 and sits comfortably at 92-94. The curveball and changeup will both flash average, but are in need of further development. Greene got all the way to Double-A, but he is still a bit of a raw athlete on the mound. The stuff is good enough that with more development time he could round into a mid-rotation starter, although the top-end velocity he showed last year would also be alluring in a late-inning role.

101. Forrest Wall, 2B, Colorado Rockies

If Trent Clark was considered the best pure hitter among the prep bats in 2015, Wall got similar accolades in 2014. He has a swing geared to spray line drives all over the outfield and has one of the best pure hit tools in the minors. He's inexperienced at second base, only being forced there after undergoing labrum surgery in high school, which has left his arm well below average. He has the foot speed to play in center field, though so far the Rockies have left him at the keystone, where he projects as an average defender. Wall's swing is geared for contact over power, so his average raw power may end up playing more fringy in games. Having conquered the lefty's paradise in Asheville, he will head to the Cal League in 2016. Life can be tough out there for second-base prospects, but Wall is a good one.

Team Codes

CODE	TEAM	LG	AFF.	Name
ABE	Aberdeen	NYP	Orioles	IronBirds
ABQ	Albuquerque	PCL	Rockies	Isotopes
AKR	Akron	EAS	Indians	RubberDucks
ALT	Altoona	EAS	Pirates	Curve
ANA	Los Angeles	AL	-	Angels
ANG	AZL Angels	AZL	Angels	-
ARI	Arizona	NL	-	D-backs
ARK	Arkansas	TEX	Angels	Travelers
ART	Artemisa	CNS	-	
ASH	Asheville	SAL	Rockies	Tourists
AST	GCL Astros	GCL	Astros	GCL Astros
ATH	AZL Athletics	AZL	Athletics	-
ATL	Atlanta	NL	-	Braves
AUB	Auburn	NYP	Nationals	Doubledays
AUG	Augusta	SAL	Giants	GreenJackets
BAK	Bakersfield	CAL	Mariners	Blaze
BAL	Baltimore	AL	-	Orioles
BAT	Batavia	NYP	Marlins	Muckdogs
BGR	Bowling Green	MID	Rays	Hot Rods
BIL	Billings	PIO	Reds	Mustangs
BIN	Binghamton	EAS	Mets	Mets
BIR	Birmingham	SOU	White Sox	Barons
BLJ	GCL Blue Jays	GCL	Blue Jays	GCL Blue Jays
BLT	Beloit	MID	Athletics	Snappers
BLU	Bluefield	APP	Blue Jays	Blue Jays
BLX	Biloxi	SOU	Brewers	Shuckers
BNC	Burlington	APP	Royals	Royals
BOI	Boise	NWL	Rockies	Hawks
BOS	Boston	AL	-	Red Sox
BOW	Bowie	EAS	Orioles	Baysox
BRA	GCL Braves	GCL	Braves	GCL Braves
BRD	Bradenton	FSL	Pirates	Marauders
BRI	Bristol	APP	Pirates	Pirates
BRO	Brooklyn	NYP	Mets	Cyclones
BRR	AZL Brewers	AZL	Brewers	-
BRV	Brevard County	FSL	Brewers	Manatees
BUF	Buffalo	INT	Blue Jays	Bisons
BUR	Burlington	MID	Angels	Bees
CAR	Carolina	CAR	Braves	Mudcats
CCH	Corpus Christi	TEX	Astros	Hooks
CDR	Cedar Rapids	MID	Twins	Kernels
CFG	Cienfuegos	CNS	-	
CHA	Chicago	AL	-	White Sox
CHB	Chiba Lotte	NPB	-	Marines
CHN	Chicago	NL	-	Cubs
CHR	Charlotte	INT	White Sox	Knights
CHT	Chattanooga	SOU	Twins	Lookouts
CHU	Chunichi	NPB	-	Dragons
CIN	AZL Reds	AZL	Reds	-
CIN	Cincinnati	NL	-	Reds

CODE	TEAM	LG	AFF.	Name
CLE	Cleveland	AL	-	Indians
CLE	AZL Indians	AZL	Indians	-
CLN	Clinton	MID	Mariners	LumberKings
CLR	Clearwater	FSL	Phillies	Threshers
COH	Columbus	INT	Indians	Clippers
COL	Colorado	NL	-	Rockies
CRD	GCL Cardinals	GCL	Cardinals	GCL Cardinals
CSC	Charleston	SAL	Yankees	RiverDogs
CSP	Colorado Springs	PCL	Brewers	Sky Sox
CUB	AZL Cubs	AZL	Cubs	-
DAN	DSL Angels	DSL	Angels	DSL Angels
DAR	DSL Astros Orange	DSL	Astros	DSL Astros Orange
DAS	DSL Astros	DSL	Astros	DSL Astros
DAT	DSL Athletics	DSL	Athletics	DSL Athletics
DAY	Daytona	FSL	Reds	Tortugas
DBA	DSL Orioles2	DSL	Orioles	DSL Orioles2
DBL	DSL Blue Jays	DSL	Blue Jays	DSL Blue Jays
DBR	DSL Braves	DSL	Braves	DSL Braves
DBW	DSL Brewers	DSL	Brewers	DSL Brewers
DCA	DSL Cardinals	DSL	Cardinals	DSL Cardinals
DCU	DSL Cubs	DSL	Cubs	DSL Cubs
DDI	DSL D-backs	DSL	D-backs	DSL D-backs
DDO	DSL Dodgers	DSL	Dodgers	DSL Dodgers
DDR	DSL Rays	DSL	Rays	DSL Rays
DEL	Delmarva	SAL	Orioles	Shorebirds
DET	Detroit	AL	-	Tigers
DGI	DSL Giants	DSL	Giants	DSL Giants
DIA	AZL D-backs	AZL	D-backs	-
DIN	DSL Indians	DSL	Indians	DSL Indians
DME	DSL Mets1	DSL	Mets	DSL Mets1
DML	DSL Marlins	DSL	Marlins	DSL Marlins
DMR	DSL Mariners	DSL	Mariners	DSL Mariners
DNV	Danville	APP	Braves	Braves
DOD	AZL Dodgers	AZL	Dodgers	-
DOR	DSL Orioles1	DSL	Orioles	DSL Orioles1
DPA	DSL Padres	DSL	Padres	DSL Padres
DPH	DSL Phillies	DSL	Phillies	DSL Phillies
DPI	DSL Pirates1	DSL	Pirates	DSL Pirates1
DRD	DSL Reds	DSL	Reds	DSL Reds
DRG	DSL Rangers	DSL	Rangers	DSL Rangers
DRJ	DSL Rojos	DSL	Reds	DSL Rojos
DRN	DSL Rangers2	DSL	Rangers	DSL Rangers2
DRO	DSL Rockies	DSL	Rockies	DSL Rockies
DRS	DSL Red Sox	DSL	Red Sox	DSL Red Sox
DRX	DSL Red Sox2	DSL	Red Sox	DSL Red Sox2
DRY	DSL Royals	DSL	Royals	DSL Royals
DTI	DSL Tigers	DSL	Tigers	DSL Tigers
DTW	DSL Twins	DSL	Twins	DSL Twins
DUN	Dunedin	FSL	Blue Jays	Blue Jays

CODE	TEAM	LG	AFF.	Name
DUR	Durham	INT	Rays	Bulls
DWA	DSL Nationals	DSL	Nationals	DSL Nationals
DWS	DSL White Sox	DSL	White Sox	DSL White Sox
DYA	DSL Yankees1	DSL	Yankees	DSL Yankees1
DYN	DSL Yankees2	DSL	Yankees	DSL Yankees2
DYT	Dayton	MID	Reds	Dragons
ELP	El Paso	PCL	Padres	Chihuahuas
ELZ	Elizabethton	APP	Twins	Twins
ERI	Erie	EAS	Tigers	SeaWolves
EUG	Eugene	NWL	Cubs	Emeralds
EVE	Everett	NWL	Mariners	AquaSox
FKU	Fukuoka	NPB	-	Hawks
FRD	Frederick	CAR	Orioles	Keys
FRE	Fresno	PCL	Astros	Grizzlies
FRI	Frisco	TEX	Rangers	RoughRiders
FTM	Fort Myers	FSL	Twins	Miracle
FTW	Fort Wayne	MID	Padres	TinCaps
GIA	AZL Giants	AZL	Giants	-
GJR	Grand Junction	PIO	Rockies	Rockies
GRB	Greensboro	SAL	Marlins	Grasshoppers
GRF	Great Falls	PIO	White Sox	Voyagers
GRL	Great Lakes	MID	Dodgers	Loons
GRN	Greenville	SAL	Red Sox	Drive
GRV	Greeneville	APP	Astros	Astros
GWN	Gwinnett	INT	Braves	Braves
HAB	La Habana	CNS	-	
HAG	Hagerstown	SAL	Nationals	Suns
HAR	Harrisburg	EAS	Nationals	Senators
HDS	High Desert	CAL	Rangers	Mavericks
HEL	Helena	PIO	Brewers	Brewers
HIC	Hickory	SAL	Rangers	Crawdads
HNS	Hanshin	NPB	-	Tigers
HOU	Houston	AL	-	Astros
HRO	Hiroshima Toyo	NPB	-	Carp
HUD	Hudson Valley	NYP	Rays	Renegades
IDA	Idaho Falls	PIO	Royals	Chukars
IND	Indianapolis	INT	Pirates	Indians
INL	Inland Empire	CAL	Angels	66ers
IOW	Iowa	PCL	Cubs	Cubs
JAX	Jacksonville	SOU	Marlins	Suns
JCY	Johnson City	APP	Cardinals	Cardinals
JUP	Jupiter	FSL	Marlins	Hammerheads
KAN	Kannapolis	SAL	White Sox	Intimidators
KCA	Kansas City	AL	-	Royals
KNC	Kane County	MID	D-backs	Cougars
KNG	Kingsport	APP	Mets	Mets
LAK	Lakeland	FSL	Tigers	Flying Tigers
LAN	Los Angeles	NL	-	Dodgers
LEH	Lehigh Valley	INT	Phillies	IronPigs

CODE	TEAM	LG	AFF.	Name
LEL	Lake Elsinore	CAL	Padres	Storm
LEX	Lexington	SAL	Royals	Legends
LKC	Lake County	MID	Indians	Captains
LNC	Lancaster	CAL	Astros	JetHawks
LNS	Lansing	MID	Blue Jays	Lugnuts
LOU	Louisville	INT	Reds	Bats
LOW	Lowell	NYP	Red Sox	Spinners
LTU	Las Tunas	CNS	-	
LVG	Las Vegas	PCL	Mets	51s
LWD	Lakewood	SAL	Phillies	BlueClaws
LYN	Lynchburg	CAR	Indians	Hillcats
MCO	DSL Mariners2	DSL	Mariners	DSL Mariners2
MEM	Memphis	PCL	Cardinals	Redbirds
MET	DSL Mets2	DSL	Mets	DSL Mets2
MHV	Mahoning Valley	NYP	Indians	Scrappers
MIA	Miami	NL	-	Marlins
MID	Midland	TEX	Athletics	RockHounds
MIL	Milwaukee	NL	-	Brewers
MIN	Minnesota	AL	-	Twins
MIS	Mississippi	SOU	Braves	Braves
MNT	Montgomery	SOU	Rays	Biscuits
MOB	Mobile	SOU	D-backs	BayBears
MOD	Modesto	CAL	Rockies	Nuts
MRL	GCL Marlins	GCL	Marlins	GCL Marlins
MRN	AZL Mariners	AZL	Mariners	-
MSO	Missoula	PIO	D-backs	Osprey
MTS	GCL Mets	GCL	Mets	GCL Mets
MYR	Myrtle Beach	CAR	Cubs	Pelicans
NAS	Nashville	PCL	Athletics	Sounds
NAT	GCL Nationals	GCL	Nationals	GCL Nationals
NBR	New Britain	EAS	Rockies	Rock Cats
NEX	Nexen	KBO	Heroes	
NHP	New Hampshire	EAS	Blue Jays	Fisher Cats
NIP	Nippon Ham	NPB	-	Fighters
NOR	Norfolk	INT	Orioles	Tides
NWA	NW Arkansas	TEX	Royals	Naturals
NWO	New Orleans	PCL	Marlins	Zephyrs
NYA	New York	AL	-	Yankees
NYN	New York	NL	-	Mets
OAK	Oakland	AL	-	Athletics
OGD	Ogden	PIO	Dodgers	Raptors
OKL	Oklahoma City	PCL	Dodgers	Dodgers
OMA	Omaha	PCL	Royals	Storm Chasers
ONE	Connecticut	NYP	Tigers	Tigers
ORI	GCL Orioles	GCL	Orioles	GCL Orioles
ORM	Orem	PIO	Angels	Owlz
ORX	Orix	NPB	-	Buffaloes
PAW	Pawtucket	INT	Red Sox	Red Sox
PCH	Charlotte	FSL	Rays	Stone Crabs
PDR	AZL Padres	AZL	Padres	-
PEN	Pensacola	SOU	Reds	Blue Wahoos
PEO	Peoria	MID	Cardinals	Chiefs
PHI	Philadelphia	NL	-	Phillies
PHL	GCL Phillies	GCL	Phillies	GCL Phillies
PIR	GCL Pirates	GCL	Pirates	GCL Pirates
PIT	Pittsburgh	NL	-	Pirates
PMB	Palm Beach	FSL	Cardinals	Cardinals
PME	Portland	EAS	Red Sox	Sea Dogs
POT	Potomac	CAR	Nationals	Nationals
PRI	Princeton	APP	Rays	Rays
PUL	Pulaski	APP	Yankees	Yankees
QUD	Quad Cities	MID	Astros	River Bandits
RAK	Rakuten	NPB	-	Golden Eagles
RAY	GCL Rays	GCL	Rays	GCL Rays
RCU	Rancho Cucamonga	CAL	Dodgers	Quakes
REA	Reading	EAS	Phillies	Fightin Phils
RIC	Richmond	EAS	Giants	Flying Squirrels
RNG	AZL Rangers	AZL	Rangers	-
RNO	Reno	PCL	D-backs	Aces
ROC	Rochester	INT	Twins	Red Wings
ROM	Rome	SAL	Braves	Braves
ROU	Round Rock	PCL	Rangers	Express
ROY	AZL Royals	AZL	Royals	-
RSX	GCL Red Sox	GCL	Red Sox	GCL Red Sox
SAC	Sacramento	PCL	Giants	River Cats
SAN	San Antonio	TEX	Padres	Missions
SAV	Savannah	SAL	Mets	Sand Gnats
SBN	South Bend	MID	Cubs	Cubs
SCO	State College	NYP	Cardinals	Spikes
SDN	San Diego	NL	-	Padres
SEA	Seattle	AL	-	Mariners
SEI	Seibu	NPB	-	Lions
SFD	Springfield	TEX	Cardinals	Cardinals
SFN	San Francisco	NL	-	Giants
SJO	San Jose	CAL	Giants	Giants
SLC	Salt Lake	PCL	Angels	Bees
SLM	Salem	CAR	Red Sox	Red Sox
SLN	St. Louis	NL	-	Cardinals
SLO	Salem-Keizer	NWL	Giants	Volcanoes
SLU	St. Lucie	FSL	Mets	Mets
SPO	Spokane	NWL	Rangers	Indians
STA	Staten Island	NYP	Yankees	Yankees
STO	Stockton	CAL	Athletics	Ports
SWB	Scranton/WB	INT	Yankees	RailRiders
SYR	Syracuse	INT	Nationals	Chiefs
TAC	Tacoma	PCL	Mariners	Rainiers
TAM	Tampa	FSL	Yankees	Yankees
TBA	Tampa Bay	AL	-	Rays
TCV	Tri-City	NYP	Astros	ValleyCats
TEN	Tennessee	SOU	Cubs	Smokies
TEX	Texas	AL	-	Rangers
TGR	GCL Tigers	GCL	Tigers	GCL Tigers
TOL	Toledo	INT	Tigers	Mud Hens
TOR	Toronto	AL	-	Blue Jays
TRI	Tri-City	NWL	Padres	Dust Devils
TRN	Trenton	EAS	Yankees	Thunder
TUL	Tulsa	TEX	Dodgers	Drillers
TWI	GCL Twins	GCL	Twins	GCL Twins
VAN	Vancouver	NWL	Blue Jays	Canadians
VCU	VSL CHN	VSL	Cubs	VSL Cubs
VER	Vermont	NYP	Athletics	Lake Monsters
VIS	Visalia	CAL	D-backs	Rawhide
VPH	VSL PHI	VSL	Phillies	VSL Phillies
VSE	VSL SEA	VSL	Mariners	VSL Mariners
VTB	VSL TB	VSL	Rays	VSL Rays
VTI	VSL DET	VSL	Tigers	VSL Tigers
WAS	Washington	NL	-	Nationals
WEV	West Virginia	NYP	Pirates	Black Bears
WIL	Wilmington	CAR	Royals	Blue Rocks
WIS	Wisconsin	MID	Brewers	Timber Rattlers
WMI	West Michigan	MID	Tigers	Whitecaps
WNS	Winston-Salem	CAR	White Sox	Dash
WPT	Williamsport	NYP	Phillies	Crosscutters
WSX	AZL White Sox	AZL	White Sox	-
WTN	Jackson	SOU	Mariners	Generals
WVA	West Virginia	SAL	Pirates	Power
YAK	Hillsboro	NWL	D-backs	Hops
YAN	GCL Yankees1	GCL	Yankees	GCL Yankees
YAT	GCL Yankees2	GCL	Yankees	GCL Yankees2
YKL	Yakult	NPB	-	Swallows
YKO	Yokohama DeNa	NPB	-	BayStars
YOM	Yomiuri	NPB	-	Giants

PECOTA Leaderboards

Hitters

HR

Rank	NAME	Team	HR
1	Chris Davis	BAL	38
1	Giancarlo Stanton	MIA	38
3	Jose Bautista	TOR	37
4	Edwin Encarnacion	TOR	35
5	Miguel Sano	MIN	33
5	Nelson Cruz	SEA	33
7	Kyle Schwarber	CHN	32
7	Kris Bryant	CHN	32
7	Anthony Rizzo	CHN	32
10	David Ortiz	BOS	31
10	Josh Donaldson	TOR	31
10	Jose Abreu	CHA	31
13	Bryce Harper	WAS	30
13	Adam Jones	BAL	30
13	Paul Goldschmidt	ARI	30
13	Mike Trout	ANA	30
13	Mark Trumbo	BAL	30
18	Khris Davis	MIL	29
18	Joc Pederson	LAN	29
18	Evan Gattis	HOU	29

RUNS

Rank	NAME	Team	R
1	Mike Trout	ANA	107
2	Jose Bautista	TOR	100
3	Joc Pederson	LAN	97
4	Paul Goldschmidt	ARI	95
5	Mookie Betts	BOS	94
6	Giancarlo Stanton	MIA	93
7	Andrew McCutchen	PIT	92
7	Edwin Encarnacion	TOR	92
7	Jose Altuve	HOU	92
10	Josh Donaldson	TOR	91
10	Jacoby Ellsbury	NYA	91
10	Anthony Rizzo	CHN	91
10	Curtis Granderson	NYN	91
14	Jason Heyward	CHN	90
14	Bryce Harper	WAS	90
14	Joey Votto	CIN	90
14	Billy Hamilton	CIN	90
18	Carlos Gomez	HOU	89
18	Kris Bryant	CHN	89
18	Starling Marte	PIT	89

BATTING AVERAGE

Rank	NAME	Team	AVG
1	Miguel Cabrera	DET	.317
2	Jose Reyes	COL	.308
3	Jose Altuve	HOU	.305
4	Buster Posey	SFN	.301
5	Corey Dickerson	COL	.299
5	Mookie Betts	BOS	.299
5	Mike Trout	ANA	.299
8	Michael Brantley	CLE	.297
9	Adrian Beltre	TEX	.296
10	Andrew McCutchen	PIT	.295
11	Robinson Cano	SEA	.293
12	Ben Revere	TOR	.292
13	Joey Votto	CIN	.291
13	Dustin Pedroia	BOS	.291
15	Paul Goldschmidt	ARI	.290
15	Melky Cabrera	CHA	.290
17	Jose Abreu	CHA	.289
18	Ryan Braun	MIL	.288
18	Nolan Arenado	COL	.288
18	Yadier Molina	SLN	.288
18	Victor Martinez	DET	.288

RBI

Rank	NAME	Team	RBI
1	Jose Bautista	TOR	108
2	Giancarlo Stanton	MIA	106
3	Edwin Encarnacion	TOR	105
4	Chris Davis	BAL	103
4	Josh Donaldson	TOR	103
6	Anthony Rizzo	CHN	100
7	Jose Abreu	CHA	99
7	Nelson Cruz	SEA	99
7	Paul Goldschmidt	ARI	99
10	Adam Jones	BAL	98
11	Miguel Cabrera	DET	97
11	Bryce Harper	WAS	97
13	Kris Bryant	CHN	96
13	David Ortiz	BOS	96
15	Miguel Sano	MIN	95
16	Kyle Schwarber	CHN	94
17	Mike Trout	ANA	93
18	Andrew McCutchen	PIT	92
19	Adrian Beltre	TEX	90
19	Nolan Arenado	COL	90
19	Kyle Seager	SEA	90
19	Evan Gattis	HOU	90

STOLEN BASES

Rank	NAME	Team	SB
1	Billy Hamilton	CIN	67
2	Dee Gordon	MIA	56
3	Jarrod Dyson	KCA	54
4	Ben Revere	TOR	39
4	Delino DeShields	TEX	39
4	Jose Altuve	HOU	39
7	Billy Burns	OAK	38
8	Jacoby Ellsbury	NYA	35
9	Starling Marte	PIT	32
10	Anthony Gose	DET	31
11	Carlos Gomez	HOU	29
11	Charlie Blackmon	COL	29
11	Jose Reyes	COL	29
14	A.J. Pollock	ARI	28
15	Elvis Andrus	TEX	27
15	Gregory Polanco	PIT	27
15	Leonys Martin	SEA	27
18	Lorenzo Cain	KCA	26
19	Mookie Betts	BOS	25
19	Jean Segura	MIL	25
19	Byron Buxton	MIN	25

ON-BASE PERCENTAGE

Rank	NAME	Team	OBS
1	Joey Votto	CIN	.421
2	Miguel Cabrera	DET	.402
3	Mike Trout	ANA	.390
3	Andrew McCutchen	PIT	.390
5	Paul Goldschmidt	ARI	.388
6	Jose Bautista	TOR	.382
7	Prince Fielder	TEX	.379
8	Bryce Harper	WAS	.378
9	Buster Posey	SFN	.368
9	Shin-Soo Choo	TEX	.368
11	Matt Holliday	SLN	.366
12	Matt Carpenter	SLN	.365
12	Freddie Freeman	ATL	.365
14	Carlos Santana	CLE	.364
14	Mookie Betts	BOS	.364
16	David Ortiz	BOS	.363
17	Joe Mauer	MIN	.362
18	Giancarlo Stanton	MIA	.360
19	Kris Bryant	CHN	.359
19	Yasiel Puig	LAN	.359

Hitters cont.

SLUGGING PERCENTAGE

Rank	NAME	Team	SLG
1	Mike Trout	ANA	.546
2	Giancarlo Stanton	MIA	.545
3	Miguel Cabrera	DET	.542
4	Paul Goldschmidt	ARI	.531
5	Corey Dickerson	COL	.524
6	Chris Davis	BAL	.523
7	Bryce Harper	WAS	.516
7	Jose Bautista	TOR	.516
9	Jose Abreu	CHA	.514
9	David Ortiz	BOS	.514
9	Carlos Gonzalez	COL	.514
12	Nolan Arenado	COL	.513
13	Edwin Encarnacion	TOR	.512
14	Kris Bryant	CHN	.510
15	Ryan Braun	MIL	.509
16	Andrew McCutchen	PIT	.502
17	Josh Donaldson	TOR	.501
18	Miguel Sano	MIN	.500
19	Anthony Rizzo	CHN	.495
20	Matt Kemp	SDN	.487
20	Kyle Schwarber	CHN	.487
20	Yasiel Puig	LAN	.487

STRIKEOUT RATE

Rank	NAME	Team	SOR
1	Ben Revere	TOR	.094
2	Andrelton Simmons	ANA	.095
3	Jose Reyes	COL	.098
4	Nori Aoki	SEA	.100
4	Victor Martinez	DET	.100
6	Michael Brantley	CLE	.108
7	Jose Altuve	HOU	.111
8	Yadier Molina	SLN	.112
8	Martin Prado	MIA	.112
10	J.B. Shuck	CHA	.113
11	Erick Aybar	ATL	.118
12	Ian Kinsler	DET	.119
12	Dustin Pedroia	BOS	.119
14	Omar Infante	KCA	.120
14	Yangervis Solarte	SDN	.120
14	Denard Span	WAS	.120
17	Albert Pujols	ANA	.121
18	Jose Ramirez	CLE	.122
19	Adrian Beltre	TEX	.123
20	Nick Markakis	ATL	.127
20	Daniel Murphy	NYN	.127
20	Joe Panik	SFN	.127

TRUE AVERAGE

Rank	NAME	Team	TAv
1	Mike Trout	ANA	.331
2	Miguel Cabrera	DET	.326
3	Joey Votto	CIN	.321
4	Giancarlo Stanton	MIA	.317
5	Jose Bautista	TOR	.316
5	Paul Goldschmidt	ARI	.316
7	Bryce Harper	WAS	.312
7	Andrew McCutchen	PIT	.312
9	Kris Bryant	CHN	.307
10	Jose Abreu	CHA	.305
11	Buster Posey	SFN	.303
12	Edwin Encarnacion	TOR	.302
12	Yasiel Puig	LAN	.302
14	George Springer	HOU	.300
14	Anthony Rizzo	CHN	.300
16	Josh Donaldson	TOR	.299
17	Ryan Braun	MIL	.298
17	David Ortiz	BOS	.298
17	Prince Fielder	TEX	.298
20	Robinson Cano	SEA	.297
20	Freddie Freeman	ATL	.297

ISOLATED SLUGGING

Rank	NAME	Team	ISO
1	Giancarlo Stanton	MIA	.279
2	Chris Davis	BAL	.266
3	Miguel Sano	MIN	.253
4	Jose Bautista	TOR	.252
5	Mike Trout	ANA	.247
6	Kris Bryant	CHN	.244
7	Edwin Encarnacion	TOR	.243
8	Paul Goldschmidt	ARI	.241
9	Carlos Gonzalez	COL	.236
9	David Ortiz	BOS	.236
11	Bryce Harper	WAS	.234
11	Kyle Schwarber	CHN	.234
13	Khris Davis	MIL	.231
14	Chris Carter	HOU	.230
15	Adam Duvall	CIN	.229
15	Anthony Rizzo	CHN	.229
17	George Springer	HOU	.227
18	Jose Abreu	CHA	.225
18	Corey Dickerson	COL	.225
18	Miguel Cabrera	DET	.225
18	Nolan Arenado	COL	.225
18	Evan Gattis	HOU	.225

WALKS

Rank	NAME	Team	BBR
1	Joey Votto	CIN	.180
2	Jose Bautista	TOR	.155
3	Carlos Santana	CLE	.155
4	Chris Iannetta	SEA	.141
5	Joc Pederson	LAN	.139
6	Paul Goldschmidt	ARI	.138
7	Alex Avila	CHA	.137
8	Jon Singleton	HOU	.137
9	Yasmani Grandal	LAN	.133
10	Mike Napoli	CLE	.130
11	Bryce Harper	WAS	.130
12	Andrew McCutchen	PIT	.124
13	Dexter Fowler	CHN	.123
14	Nick Swisher	ATL	.123
15	Miguel Cabrera	DET	.122
16	Mike Trout	ANA	.122
17	Kyle Schwarber	CHN	.121
18	Giancarlo Stanton	MIA	.121
19	Miguel Sano	MIN	.120
20	Shin-Soo Choo	TEX	.120

RUNS ABOVE AVERAGE

Rank	NAME	Team	RAA
1	Yasmani Grandal	LAN	30.7
2	Buster Posey	SFN	22.0
3	Russell Martin	TOR	18.2
4	Francisco Cervelli	PIT	18.1
5	Travis d'Arnaud	NYN	16.0
6	Jonathan Lucroy	MIL	14.9
7	Yadier Molina	SLN	13.0
8	Miguel Montero	CHN	10.8
9	Austin Hedges	SDN	8.6
10	Yan Gomes	CLE	8.2
11	Jason Castro	HOU	7.8
12	Austin Barnes	LAN	7.5
13	Hank Conger	TBA	7.3
14	Tony Wolters	CLE	7.2
14	Martin Maldonado	MIL	7.2
16	Brian McCann	NYA	6.2
17	Chris Stewart	PIT	5.2
18	Luke Maile	TBA	4.7
19	J.R. Murphy	MIN	4.5
20	Roberto Perez	CLE	4.3

Hitters cont.

AL WARP

Rank	NAME	Team	WARP
1	Mike Trout	ANA	7.9
2	Miguel Cabrera	DET	5.9
3	Josh Donaldson	TOR	5.7
4	Kevin Kiermaier	TBA	5.6
5	Manny Machado	BAL	5.3
6	Russell Martin	TOR	5.2
6	Robinson Cano	SEA	5.2
8	Byron Buxton	MIN	5.1
9	Jose Bautista	TOR	5.0
10	Kyle Seager	SEA	4.7
10	Troy Tulowitzki	TOR	4.7

NL WARP

Rank	NAME	Team	WARP
1	Buster Posey	SFN	7.5
2	Yasmani Grandal	LAN	6.6
3	Paul Goldschmidt	ARI	6.2
4	Giancarlo Stanton	MIA	6.0
5	Bryce Harper	WAS	5.7
6	Joey Votto	CIN	5.4
7	Kris Bryant	CHN	5.2
8	Travis d'Arnaud	NYN	4.9
9	Andrew McCutchen	PIT	4.7
10	Nolan Arenado	COL	4.4

CATCHER WARP

Rank	NAME	Team	WARP
1	Buster Posey	SFN	7.5
2	Yasmani Grandal	LAN	6.6
3	Russell Martin	TOR	5.2
4	Travis d'Arnaud	NYN	4.9
5	Francisco Cervelli	PIT	4.2
6	Jonathan Lucroy	MIL	4.1
7	Yadier Molina	SLN	3.7
8	Brian McCann	NYA	3.5
9	Yan Gomes	CLE	3.4
10	Miguel Montero	CHN	3.3

1B WARP

Rank	NAME	Team	WARP
1	Paul Goldschmidt	ARI	6.2
2	Miguel Cabrera	DET	5.9
3	Joey Votto	CIN	5.4
4	Jose Abreu	CHA	4.1
5	Edwin Encarnacion	TOR	4.0
5	Anthony Rizzo	CHN	4.0
7	Brandon Belt	SFN	3.7
8	Prince Fielder	TEX	3.1
8	Freddie Freeman	ATL	3.1
10	Adrian Gonzalez	LAN	3.0

2B WARP

Rank	NAME	Team	WARP
1	Robinson Cano	SEA	5.2
2	Dustin Pedroia	BOS	3.9
2	Ben Zobrist	CHN	3.9
4	Ian Kinsler	DET	3.6
4	Josh Harrison	PIT	3.6
6	Rougned Odor	TEX	3.5
7	Kolten Wong	SLN	3.4
8	Jason Kipnis	CLE	3.2
9	Neil Walker	NYN	3.1
10	Jose Altuve	HOU	3.0

3B WARP

Rank	NAME	Team	WARP
1	Josh Donaldson	TOR	5.7
2	Manny Machado	BAL	5.3
3	Kris Bryant	CHN	5.2
4	Kyle Seager	SEA	4.7
5	Nolan Arenado	COL	4.4
5	Evan Longoria	TBA	4.4
7	Anthony Rendon	WAS	3.5
8	Adrian Beltre	TEX	3.4
9	David Wright	NYN	3.1
10	Matt Carpenter	SLN	3.0
10	Justin Turner	LAN	3.0

SS WARP

Rank	NAME	Team	WARP
1	Troy Tulowitzki	TOR	4.7
2	Carlos Correa	HOU	4.3
3	Andrelton Simmons	ANA	3.8
4	Jean Segura	MIL	3.7
5	Trea Turner	WAS	3.6
6	Corey Seager	LAN	3.5
6	Jhonny Peralta	SLN	3.5
8	Jose Reyes	COL	3.1
8	Brad Miller	TBA	3.1
8	Ian Desmond	WAS	3.1

LF WARP

Rank	NAME	Team	WARP
1	Yoenis Cespedes	NYN	4.0
1	Kyle Schwarber	CHN	4.0
3	Alex Gordon	KCA	3.9
3	Justin Upton	SDN	3.9
5	Christian Yelich	MIA	3.6
6	Michael Conforto	NYN	3.4
7	Matt Holliday	SLN	3.3
8	Corey Dickerson	COL	3.0
8	Khris Davis	MIL	3.0
10	David Peralta	ARI	2.9

CF WARP

Rank	NAME	Team	WARP
1	Mike Trout	ANA	7.9
2	Kevin Kiermaier	TBA	5.6
3	Byron Buxton	MIN	5.1
4	Andrew McCutchen	PIT	4.7
5	Lorenzo Cain	KCA	3.9
6	Carlos Gomez	HOU	3.6
7	Adam Eaton	CHA	3.3
8	Jason Heyward	CHN	3.2
9	Jacoby Ellsbury	NYA	3.1
10	Adam Jones	BAL	2.9

RF WARP

Rank	NAME	Team	WARP
1	Giancarlo Stanton	MIA	6.0
2	Bryce Harper	WAS	5.7
3	Jose Bautista	TOR	5.0
4	Mookie Betts	BOS	4.6
5	George Springer	HOU	4.0
5	Shin-Soo Choo	TEX	4.0
7	Matt Kemp	SDN	3.9
8	Hunter Pence	SFN	3.5
9	Ryan Braun	MIL	3.4
10	Kole Calhoun	ANA	3.3

AL ROOKIE WARP

Rank	NAME	Team	WARP
1	Byron Buxton	MIN	5.1
2	Ryan LaMarre	BOS	0.8
3	Ryan Brett	TBA	0.7
3	Luke Maile	TBA	0.7
5	Reymond Fuentes	KCA	0.6
5	Joey Gallo	TEX	0.6
7	Rob Refsnyder	NYA	0.5
7	Dusty Coleman	KCA	0.5
9	Mikie Mahtook	TBA	0.4
10	Terrance Gore	KCA	0.3
10	Matthew Duffy	HOU	0.3
10	Lane Adams	KCA	0.3

NL ROOKIE WARP

Rank	NAME	Team	WARP
1	Trea Turner	WAS	3.6
2	Corey Seager	LAN	3.5
3	Austin Barnes	LAN	2.2
4	Jarrett Parker	SFN	1.1
5	Micah Johnson	LAN	1.0
5	Hector Olivera	ATL	1.0
7	Mac Williamson	SFN	0.8
7	Rymer Liriano	SDN	0.8
7	Scott Schebler	CIN	0.8
10	Alex Dickerson	SDN	0.7
10	Matt Clark	MIL	0.7

BIGGEST WARP DECLINE

Rank	NAME	Team	WARP 2015	WARP 2016	WARP DIFF
1	Bryce Harper	WAS	11.2	5.7	-5.5
2	Eddie Rosario	MIN	2.4	-1.0	-3.4
3	Nolan Arenado	COL	7.4	4.4	-3.0
3	Paul Goldschmidt	ARI	9.2	6.2	-3.0
5	Mike Moustakas	KCA	4.6	1.8	-2.8
5	Lorenzo Cain	KCA	6.7	3.9	-2.8
5	Curtis Granderson	NYN	5.5	2.7	-2.8
8	Jason Heyward	CHN	5.9	3.2	-2.7
9	Ender Inciarte	ATL	4.1	1.5	-2.6
9	A.J. Pollock	ARI	5.4	2.8	-2.6

BIGGEST WARP IMPROVEMENT

Rank	NAME	Team	WARP 2015	WARP 2016	WARP DIFF
1	Byron Buxton	MIN	0.6	5.1	4.5
2	Trea Turner	WAS	0.2	3.6	3.4
3	Yan Gomes	CLE	0.4	3.4	3.0
4	Jonathan Lucroy	MIL	1.4	4.1	2.7
5	Chase Utley	LAN	0.1	2.6	2.5
5	Anthony Rendon	WAS	1.0	3.5	2.5
5	Jacoby Ellsbury	NYA	0.6	3.1	2.5
8	Matt Holliday	SLN	0.9	3.3	2.4
9	Steven Souza	TBA	0.8	3.0	2.2
10	Robinson Cano	SEA	3.1	5.2	2.1
10	Carlos Santana	CLE	0.4	2.5	2.1

Pitchers

WINS

Rank	NAME	Team	W
1	David Price	BOS	14
1	Jon Lester	CHN	14
1	Jake Arrieta	CHN	14
1	Clayton Kershaw	LAN	14
5	Chris Sale	CHA	13
5	Felix Hernandez	SEA	13
5	Gio Gonzalez	WAS	13
5	Max Scherzer	WAS	13
9	Garrett Richards	ANA	12
9	Zack Greinke	ARI	12
9	John Lackey	CHN	12
9	Collin McHugh	HOU	12
9	Dallas Keuchel	HOU	12
9	Michael Pineda	NYA	12
9	Francisco Liriano	PIT	12
9	Gerrit Cole	PIT	12
9	James Shields	SDN	12
9	Hisashi Iwakuma	SEA	12
9	Jeff Samardzija	SFN	12
9	Madison Bumgarner	SFN	12
9	Adam Wainwright	SLN	12
9	Michael Wacha	SLN	12
9	Cole Hamels	TEX	12

ERA, STARTERS

Rank	NAME	Team	ERA
1	Clayton Kershaw	LAN	2.48
2	Chris Sale	CHA	2.89
3	Max Scherzer	WAS	2.91
4	Madison Bumgarner	SFN	2.92
5	Matt Harvey	NYN	2.94
6	Jose Fernandez	MIA	3.03
7	Jake Arrieta	CHN	3.05
8	Jacob deGrom	NYN	3.06
9	Corey Kluber	CLE	3.10
10	Carlos Carrasco	CLE	3.14
10	Noah Syndergaard	NYN	3.14
12	Jon Lester	CHN	3.18
13	Zack Greinke	ARI	3.24
13	David Price	BOS	3.24
13	Gerrit Cole	PIT	3.24
13	Adam Wainwright	SLN	3.24
17	Stephen Strasburg	WAS	3.25
18	Hyun-jin Ryu	LAN	3.29
18	Johnny Cueto	SFN	3.29
20	Felix Hernandez	SEA	3.40
20	Chris Archer	TBA	3.40

WHIP

Rank	NAME	Team	WHIP
1	Clayton Kershaw	LAN	0.87
2	Matt Harvey	NYN	0.99
3	Max Scherzer	WAS	1.00
4	Madison Bumgarner	SFN	1.01
5	Chris Sale	CHA	1.02
6	Jake Arrieta	CHN	1.03
7	Jose Fernandez	MIA	1.04
8	Johnny Cueto	SFN	1.05
8	Stephen Strasburg	WAS	1.05
10	Noah Syndergaard	NYN	1.06
10	Jacob deGrom	NYN	1.06
12	Jon Lester	CHN	1.08
13	Hisashi Iwakuma	SEA	1.09
14	Hyun-jin Ryu	LAN	1.10
15	Masahiro Tanaka	NYA	1.11
15	Adam Wainwright	SLN	1.11
17	Zack Greinke	ARI	1.12
17	Jason Hammel	CHN	1.12
17	Gerrit Cole	PIT	1.12
20	David Price	BOS	1.13
20	Raisel Iglesias	CIN	1.13
20	Michael Pineda	NYA	1.13
20	Felix Hernandez	SEA	1.13

STRIKEOUTS

Rank	NAME	Team	SO
1	Clayton Kershaw	LAN	243
2	Chris Sale	CHA	237
3	Max Scherzer	WAS	230
4	Felix Hernandez	SEA	208
5	Jose Fernandez	MIA	207
6	David Price	BOS	205
6	Jake Arrieta	CHN	205
8	Jon Lester	CHN	201
9	Chris Archer	TBA	195
10	Gio Gonzalez	WAS	192
11	Madison Bumgarner	SFN	189
12	Carlos Carrasco	CLE	186
12	Francisco Liriano	PIT	186
14	Tyson Ross	SDN	184
15	James Shields	SDN	183
16	Zack Greinke	ARI	181
16	Matt Harvey	NYN	181
18	Ubaldo Jimenez	BAL	177
18	Cole Hamels	TEX	177
20	Danny Salazar	CLE	176

ERA, RELIEVERS

Rank	NAME	Team	ERA
1	Aroldis Chapman	CIN	2.56
2	Kenley Jansen	LAN	2.61
3	Andrew Miller	NYA	2.71
4	Dellin Betances	NYA	2.80
5	Trevor Rosenthal	SLN	3.01
6	Silvino Bracho	ARI	3.04
7	Sergio Romo	SFN	3.05
8	Cody Allen	CLE	3.06
9	David Robertson	CHA	3.12
9	Carter Capps	MIA	3.12
11	Will Smith	MIL	3.13
12	Michael Broadway	SFN	3.14
12	Hunter Strickland	SFN	3.14
14	Wade Davis	KCA	3.15
14	Sean Doolittle	OAK	3.15
16	Jeurys Familia	NYN	3.16
17	Kevin Siegrist	SLN	3.22
17	Rafael Martin	WAS	3.22
19	Koji Uehara	BOS	3.23
20	Carson Smith	BOS	3.25
20	Jake McGee	TBA	3.25

SAVES

Rank	NAME	Team	SV
1	Wade Davis	KCA	43
2	Kenley Jansen	LAN	40
3	Craig Kimbrel	BOS	39
3	Francisco Rodri-guez	DET	39
5	Hector Rondon	CHN	38
5	Aroldis Chapman	CIN	38
7	David Robertson	CHA	37
7	Ken Giles	HOU	37
7	Glen Perkins	MIN	37
10	Zach Britton	BAL	35
10	Jeurys Familia	NYN	35
10	Trevor Rosenthal	SLN	35
10	Roberto Osuna	TOR	35
14	Jason Motte	COL	34
15	Huston Street	ANA	33
15	David Hernandez	PHI	33
15	Mark Melancon	PIT	33
15	Jonathan Papelbon	WAS	33
19	Brad Ziegler	ARI	32
19	Jason Grilli	ATL	32
19	Cody Allen	CLE	32
19	Sean Doolittle	OAK	32

PITCHERS CONT.

STRIKEOUTS PER 9 IP

Rank	NAME	Team	SO9
1	Chris Sale	CHA	11.0
2	Clayton Kershaw	LAN	10.8
3	Max Scherzer	WAS	10.7
4	Carlos Carrasco	CLE	10.1
4	Corey Kluber	CLE	10.1
6	Jose Fernandez	MIA	9.9
6	Stephen Strasburg	WAS	9.9
6	Danny Salazar	CLE	9.9
9	Rich Hill	OAK	9.6
9	Chris Archer	TBA	9.6
11	Francisco Liriano	PIT	9.5
12	Noah Syndergaard	NYN	9.4
12	Lance McCullers	HOU	9.4
14	Drew Smyly	TBA	9.3
14	Madison Bumgarner	SFN	9.3
16	Felix Hernandez	SEA	9.2
16	Tyson Ross	SDN	9.2
16	David Price	BOS	9.2
16	Jake Arrieta	CHN	9.2
20	Matt Harvey	NYN	8.9
20	Jon Lester	CHN	8.9
20	Jacob deGrom	NYN	8.9
20	Mike Fiers	HOU	8.9
20	Carlos Rodon	CHA	8.9

WALKS PER 9 IP

Rank	NAME	Team	BB9
1	Phil Hughes	MIN	1.5
1	Bartolo Colon	NYN	1.5
3	Clayton Kershaw	LAN	1.6
4	Michael Pineda	NYA	1.7
4	David Price	BOS	1.7
6	Hisashi Iwakuma	SEA	1.8
6	Matt Harvey	NYN	1.8
6	Madison Bumgarner	SFN	1.8
6	Hyun-jin Ryu	LAN	1.8
6	Masahiro Tanaka	NYA	1.8
11	Adam Wainwright	SLN	1.9
11	Chris Sale	CHA	1.9
11	Max Scherzer	WAS	1.9
14	Jordan Zimmermann	DET	2.0
14	Mark Buehrle	TOR	2.0
14	Dan Haren	CHN	2.0
14	Wei-Yin Chen	BAL	2.0
18	Jose Quintana	CHA	2.1
18	Jon Lester	CHN	2.1
18	Jeff Samardzija	SFN	2.1
18	Ryan Merritt	CLE	2.1
18	Johnny Cueto	SFN	2.1
18	Noah Syndergaard	NYN	2.1
18	Stephen Strasburg	WAS	2.1
18	Gabriel Ynoa	NYN	2.1
18	Rick Porcello	BOS	2.1

HOME RUNS PER 9 IP

Rank	NAME	Team	HR9
1	Clayton Kershaw	LAN	0.80
1	Tyson Ross	SDN	0.80
3	Jake Arrieta	CHN	0.81
4	Jose Fernandez	MIA	0.82
4	Adam Wainwright	SLN	0.82
4	Sonny Gray	OAK	0.82
4	Gerrit Cole	PIT	0.82
8	Johnny Cueto	SFN	0.83
8	Mike Pelfrey	DET	0.83
10	Madison Bumgarner	SFN	0.84
11	Carlos Martinez	SLN	0.85
12	Jesse Hahn	OAK	0.86
13	Jacob deGrom	NYN	0.87
13	Jarred Cosart	MIA	0.87
15	Jaime Garcia	SLN	0.88
15	Lance Lynn	SLN	0.88
15	Zack Greinke	ARI	0.88
18	Jose Quintana	CHA	0.89
18	Matt Harvey	NYN	0.89
18	Chris Archer	TBA	0.89
18	Dallas Keuchel	HOU	0.89
18	Gio Gonzalez	WAS	0.89

FIELDING INDEPENDENT PITCHING

Rank	NAME	Team	FIP
1	Clayton Kershaw	LAN	2.44
2	Max Scherzer	WAS	2.80
3	Madison Bumgarner	SFN	2.87
4	Jose Fernandez	MIA	2.92
5	Chris Sale	CHA	2.93
6	Matt Harvey	NYN	3.01
7	Jake Arrieta	CHN	3.08
8	Jacob deGrom	NYN	3.13
9	Stephen Strasburg	WAS	3.14
10	Corey Kluber	CLE	3.19
11	Jon Lester	CHN	3.22
11	Gerrit Cole	PIT	3.22
13	David Price	BOS	3.23
13	Carlos Carrasco	CLE	3.23
15	Noah Syndergaard	NYN	3.24
16	Zack Greinke	ARI	3.25
17	Hyun-jin Ryu	LAN	3.26
18	Johnny Cueto	SFN	3.28
19	Adam Wainwright	SLN	3.30
20	Tyson Ross	SDN	3.39

FIP IN CONTEXT

Rank	NAME	Team	CFIP
1	Clayton Kershaw	LAN	57
2	Chris Sale	CHA	63
3	Max Scherzer	WAS	70
4	Carlos Carrasco	CLE	71
4	Corey Kluber	CLE	71
6	David Price	BOS	72
7	Jake Arrieta	CHN	75
8	Jose Fernandez	MIA	77
9	Matt Harvey	NYN	78
10	Madison Bumgarner	SFN	79
11	Chris Archer	TBA	80
12	Michael Pineda	NYA	81
12	Jon Lester	CHN	81
14	Jacob deGrom	NYN	82
14	Stephen Strasburg	WAS	82
16	Dallas Keuchel	HOU	83
16	Jose Quintana	CHA	83
16	Felix Hernandez	SEA	83
19	Gerrit Cole	PIT	84
20	Noah Syndergaard	NYN	85
21	Masahiro Tanaka	NYA	86
21	Adam Wainwright	SLN	86
21	Hyun-jin Ryu	LAN	86
21	Danny Salazar	CLE	86
21	Zack Greinke	ARI	86
26	Marcus Stroman	TOR	89
26	Drew Smyly	TBA	89
26	Clay Buchholz	BOS	89
26	Tyson Ross	SDN	89
26	Cole Hamels	TEX	89

Pitchers cont.

WARP, STARTERS

Rank	NAME	Team	WARP
1	Clayton Kershaw	LAN	5.5
2	Max Scherzer	WAS	4.4
2	Chris Sale	CHA	4.4
4	Jake Arrieta	CHN	4.1
5	David Price	BOS	4.0
6	Jon Lester	CHN	3.8
7	Jose Fernandez	MIA	3.7
8	Matt Harvey	NYN	3.6
9	Madison Bumgarner	SFN	3.4
10	Carlos Carrasco	CLE	3.3
10	Felix Hernandez	SEA	3.3
10	Gerrit Cole	PIT	3.3
10	Zack Greinke	ARI	3.3
14	Adam Wainwright	SLN	3.1
14	Michael Pineda	NYA	3.1
14	Chris Archer	TBA	3.1
14	Dallas Keuchel	HOU	3.1
18	Corey Kluber	CLE	2.9
18	Stephen Strasburg	WAS	2.9
20	Jose Quintana	CHA	2.8
20	Hyun-jin Ryu	LAN	2.8
20	Jacob deGrom	NYN	2.8
20	Noah Syndergaard	NYN	2.8

WARP, RELIEVERS

Rank	NAME	Team	WARP
1	Mychal Givens	BAL	0.8
2	Shawn Armstrong	CLE	0.6
2	Sean Nolin	OAK	0.6
4	Brian Johnson	BOS	0.5
5	Nick Rumbelow	NYA	0.4
5	Mike Wright	BAL	0.4
5	Dylan Bundy	BAL	0.4
5	A.J. Achter	ANA	0.4
9	Alex Meyer	MIN	0.3
10	Austin Adams	CLE	0.2
10	Nick Maronde	CLE	0.2
10	Anthony Zych	SEA	0.2
10	Alexander Claudio	TEX	0.2
10	Branden Pinder	NYA	0.2
10	James Pazos	NYA	0.2
10	Ryan O'Rourke	MIN	0.2

WARP, ROOKIES

Rank	NAME	Team	WARP
1	Steven Matz	NYN	1.8
2	John Lamb	CIN	1.3
2	Jonathan Gray	COL	1.3
4	Zach Davies	MIL	1.1
4	Josh Smith	CIN	1.1
6	Jorge Lopez	MIL	0.9
7	Silvino Bracho	ARI	0.8
8	Akeel Morris	NYN	0.7
8	Manny Banuelos	ATL	0.7
10	Spencer Patton	CHN	0.6
10	Michael Mariot	PHI	0.6

BIGGEST WARP DECLINE

Rank	NAME	Team	WARP 2015	WARP 2016	WARP DIFF
1	Zack Greinke	ARI	7.6	3.3	-4.3
2	Jake Arrieta	CHN	7.4	4.1	-3.3
3	Sonny Gray	OAK	5.6	2.4	-3.1
3	Dallas Keuchel	HOU	6.2	3.1	-3.1
5	Shelby Miller	ARI	4.6	1.6	-2.9
6	Marco Estrada	TOR	3.5	1.0	-2.5
7	Clayton Kershaw	LAN	7.9	5.5	-2.4
8	R.A. Dickey	TOR	2.8	0.6	-2.2
8	Cole Hamels	TEX	4.8	2.6	-2.2
8	Mike Leake	SLN	3.3	1.2	-2.2

BIGGEST WARP IMPROVEMENT

Rank	NAME	Team	WARP 2015	WARP 2016	WARP DIFF
1	Adam Wainwright	SLN	0.3	3.1	2.9
2	Jose Fernandez	MIA	1.2	3.7	2.5
3	Patrick Corbin	ARI	0.6	2.3	1.7
4	Derek Holland	TEX	0.1	1.6	1.5
4	Marcus Stroman	TOR	0.7	2.2	1.5
6	Andrew Cashner	SDN	0.4	1.8	1.4
6	Phil Hughes	MIN	0.1	1.5	1.4
6	Ian Kennedy	SDN	0.1	1.5	1.4
9	Steven Matz	NYN	0.4	1.8	1.3
10	Stephen Strasburg	WAS	1.6	2.9	1.2
10	Erik Johnson	CHA	0.0	1.3	1.2
10	James Shields	SDN	0.7	1.9	1.2
10	Kevin Gausman	BAL	0.9	2.1	1.2
10	Jonathan Gray	COL	0.1	1.3	1.2

Contributors and Acknowledgements

R.J. Anderson lives in Florida and joined Prospectus in 2011. In the past, Anderson's work has appeared on ESPN.com and Wired, as well as in *Newsweek*. His nightmares include a busted ex-Mariners' middle-infield prospect. No, the other one.

Nick Ashbourne is a sabermetrically inclined hired gun based out of Toronto. He writes about the Blue Jays for Sportsnet, about his countrymen for Canadian Baseball Network and about the Yankees for Baseball Prospectus. His first favorite baseball player was Raul Mondesi.

Paul Boye (@paul_boye) is a University of Scranton alum and writer-at-large in New York City whose work has appeared on ESPN.com, Sports On Earth, MLB Properties publications and more Phillies blogs than he can count. His appearance in this book is the publishing equivalent of "first-time caller, long-time listener."

J.P. Breen is the Editor-in-Chief at BP Milwaukee and a regular author at Baseball Prospectus. He's also a graduate student at the University of Chicago.

Ben Carsley is the Managing Editor of BP Boston, host of the TINO podcast and a senior author on the BP Fantasy Team. When he's not writing about baseball, he is generally cooking, sampling IPAs, arguing about sandwiches and catering to his niche Twitter following of William Faulkner-loving Red Sox fans with a high tolerance for sarcasm.

Patrick Dubuque is a semi-professional dilettante and raconteur, and has contributed words to Baseball Prospectus, Lookout Landing, The Hardball Times and other ordinarily respectable establishments. He lives in Seattle with his wife, two children and the burden of trivializing the heavy weight of mortality.

Like Brigadoon without a soundtrack or a burr, **Ken Funck** is a mysterious visitor from a simpler past who has appeared every winter since 2009 to contribute to the Baseball Prospectus annuals. Ken manages Business Intelligence systems, blogs about politics and lives outside Madison, Wisconsin with his ever-supportive wife Stephanie, their son Max (at least on holiday breaks), their daughter Abby, one cat, two dogs and nowhere near enough time on his hands.

Brendan Gawlowski covers prospects and player development for Baseball Prospectus. He also writes about the Mariners on Lookout Landing.

Mike Gianella has been writing about fantasy baseball since 2007 and doing so at Baseball Prospectus since 2013. By day he is a data sciences project manager for a healthcare provider. Gluttons for punishment can follow Mike on Twitter at @MikeGianella.

Craig Goldstein is an author and editor at Baseball Prospectus and The Dynasty Guru. His work has appeared in Vice Sports, Fox Sports MLB and SB Nation MLB. He lives and works in Washington, DC, where he spends just the right amount of time thinking about the dangers of coconut crabs and bobbit worms.

Bryan Grosnick (@bgrosnick) is a columnist for Baseball Prospectus Boston, a contributor to Baseball Prospectus and the lead writer for the sabermetrics blog Beyond the Box Score. He lives with his beautiful wife Sarah in Michigan, where they can be found running toward things but also occasionally climbing up and down things.

Wilson Karaman is a former political kingmaker turned stay-at-home dad. He scouts the California League and writes regularly for Baseball Prospectus.

David Lee is a member of the Baseball Prospectus prospect team and a baseball writer for *The Augusta Chronicle* in Augusta, Ga. Consider him the odd evaluator/storyteller combination, spending his life behind home plate at some ballpark in the Southeast.

Sam Miller is the Editor-in-Chief of Baseball Prospectus, the co-host of the Effectively Wild podcast and the co-author with Ben Lindbergh of *The Only Rule Is That It Has To Work*, a chronicle of their summer running a real-life professional baseball team. It will be published in May. This is his third year co-editing the Baseball Prospectus annual.

Kate Morrison is a freelance writer, minor league evaluator and analyst, and (day job alert!) social media coordinator based out of Dallas, and has been with Baseball Prospectus since 2014. In the summers, Kate can be found at the ballpark, and in the winters, making idle comparisons between hockey and baseball.

Tommy Rancel is a writer/analyst for ESPN Insider. In addition to the Baseball Prospectus annual, he has written for Bloomberg Sports, FanGraphs and Gammons Daily. He lives in the Tampa Bay area with his wife Jamie and their four children: Alexis, Vincent, Jarek and Brooklyn.

Daniel Rathman is a real-estate market researcher based in San Francisco. He holds degrees in economics from Tufts University and urban planning from New York University. He'll never back down from a Seinfeld trivia challenge.

Dan Rozenson is a young professional and graduate student based out of Washington, DC. He is a contributor to Baseball Prospectus and does PITCHf/x research and analysis for Brooks Baseball.

Bret Sayre is the Managing Editor of Baseball Prospectus. He's known to be a bit verbose, so he's really trying to keep this brief. By day, he is quite adept at telling investment professionals what not to do. By night, he is a full-time family man, part-time cook, part-time nurse, full-time baseball writer and part-time musician. As an 8-year-old boy, he was knocked over by a man in his 30s as he tried to catch a dead ball thrown by Kevin Mitchell at Shea Stadium. Now, he lives in New Jersey with his wife, Carolyn, his son, Joshua, and his daughter, Alyson, who cheered for the Royals this past October because she thought they were all princes.

Matt Sussman (Bats: R, Throws: L) is an IT professional in Toledo, Ohio and makes merry for the Prospectus Hit List. Among these contributors he is undoubtedly the best curler.

David G Temple is an IT professional and part-time writer. His work has appeared at FiveThirtyEight, FanGraphs, NotGraphs, The Classical and The Hardball Times. He is the Managing Editor of TechGraphs and once did a podcast that people seemed to like.

Doug Thorburn is a pitching junkie. He writes the Raising Aces column at Baseball Prospectus, a series which studies the science of pitching though the trifocal lens of mechanics, stuff and stats. Thorburn has trained in the arts of coaching and scouting, he directed the motion analysis program at the National Pitching Association and he also co-authored a book about pitching: *Arm Action, Arm Path, and the Perfect Pitch*.

Matt Trueblood contributes to Baseball Prospectus and BP Wrigleyville, mostly by digging into the statistical bedrock of baseball, slightly past the point at which the rest of the world loses interest. More of his time and attention, though, go to his wife and three sons, who too often give up their shares of his time and good humor so he can write semi-coherently.

Jason Wojciechowski is a labor lawyer in Los Angeles and the occasional proprietor of the A's blog Beaneball.

Bradley Woodrum has an MFA in Creative Writing and an MA in Economics. His writing credits include FanGraphs, The Hardball Times, ESPN, DRaysBay and presently Banknotes Industries. He has also authored hundreds of little poetical sticky notes he hides around the office.

Will Woods is a copywriter in his native New York City. He learned most of what he knows about baseball as a backup catcher at Tufts University. He grew up with the 1990s Mets, from whom nobody learned much of anything.

Geoff Young founded Ducksnorts, publishing under that title from the time Greg Maddux won his 183rd game to the time Stephen Strasburg won his sixth. He has contributed to Baseball Prospectus, The Hardball Times, ESPN.com, Padres Public and many other outlets. This is his fifth appearance in the BP annual. Geoff lives in San Diego with his patient wife, Sandra, and believes that pitcher wins are best used to measure spans of time.

Acknowledgements

Nick Ashbourne: Nick's writing would be significantly worse without the skill and experience of his editors and the patience and understanding of his family. Special thanks go to Tom Dakers, the first person to offer him a chance to write baseball; Bob Elliott, the unofficial uncle of everyone in Canadian baseball; Ben Nicholson-Smith, a great editor and champion for concise writing; Esmee Robinson, a supportive and wonderful girlfriend despite being a baseball heretic.

Paul Boye: My parents and grandparents for believing in me and my writing beyond all reason. Michael Baumann and the rest of Do Stuff for being OG. My lovely Kerry. Bill Baer, Liz Roscher, Pat Gallen, Emma Span, David Roth and Mike McCormick for all enabling my writing at various points in my life and career. Matt Kaufman and Justin Levine. The Aquinas, Dr. Kim Pavlick and Dr. Matt Reavy. *The Scranton Times-Tribune* and Terry Bonifanti. Baseball Info Solutions and Ben Jedlovec. The Camden Riversharks and Jordan Johnson.

J.P. Breen: Craig Goldstein and Sarah Davies Breen.

Ben Carsley: My Red Sox-crazed family, the ever-patient Allyson Clancy, Bret Sayre, Craig Goldstein, Mauricio "Marco" Rubio, Joe Hamrahi, Jim Walsh, Jason Parks, Spike Lundberg, Tim Britton, Brian MacPherson, Marc Normandin, Matt Collins, Mike Curtin, Xander Bogaerts, Mary Donovan, Daniel Ohman and the C-4 Content Team.

Patrick Dubuque: R.J. Anderson, Chris Crawford, Craig Goldstein, Rob McQuown, Eno Sarris, Nathan Bishop, Brendan Gawlowski and the Lookout Landing Slack channel, Kjersten Dubuque, Plato.

Ken Funck: Ben Lindbergh, Steven Goldman, John Perrotto, Christina Kahrl, Rany Jazayerli, Doug Ross, Zach Eveland, Lorrie Moore, Doyle Walls, Robert Hasman, Jill Jokela, Jimmy Perry.

Brendan Gawlowski: Patrick Dubuque for his steady editorial hand on this project, and for just being a great guy; Rich Gawlowski, Jon Shields, Nathan Bishop, Jason Churchill, Nick Faleris and too many other friends and sources to name in full. Finally, Sierra for encouraging me to spend so much time on the I-5 corridor.

Mike Gianella: Brendan Gawlowski and Kate Morrison, whose excellent collaborative skills and superior knowledge made my job that much easier. A special thanks to my wife Colleen for all the times she took my daughters out so I could have the time to write, along with the peace and quiet to do so.

Craig Goldstein: Laurie Gross, Harvey Goldstein, Alexis Goldstein, Katherine Pappas, Bret Sayre, Ian Miller, Riley Breckenridge, Jason Parks, The BP Prospect Team, Marc Normandin, R.J. Anderson, Chris Crawford, Ben Carsley, Jacob Raim, Zach Mortimer, Jason Cole, Mike Ferrin, Spike Lundberg, Matt Sussman, Tommy Rancel, Geoff Young, and Holly Hollenbeck.

Bryan Grosnick: Sarah Grosnick (first, always), Steven Martano, Neil Weinberg, Kevin Ruprecht, Ben Carsley, R.J. Anderson, Jason Lukeheart, Matt Lyons, Andrew Kinsman, Ryan Romano, Eno Sarris, and the data providers at BP, Baseball-Reference, FanGraphs, and Brooks Baseball.

Wilson Karaman: My wife for putting up with my frequent late night excursions down the rabbit hole, my kids for pushing me to be a more efficient writer and manager of time, my parents and grandparents for investing in my education, my 6th and 12th grade English teachers for learnin' me how to research and write, and my editors at BP for making me a better writer with every column I submit.

David Lee: Scouts are the lifeblood of the game, and they're also a major reason why I'm where I am today. I appreciate those willing to talk and answer questions while watching batting practice during those scorching hot summer afternoons. A big thank you also goes to my family for putting up with me during the writing process and each baseball season.

Sam Miller: Tom Keown, Leland Bailey, Noah Clark, Michael Conlan, Mark Reynolds, Spencer Silva, Brett Handerson, Kortney Hebert and Zak Welsh.

Kate Morrison: To my mother, for instilling in me the love of the game; to Michael Baumann, Katy Clarke, Patrick Dubuque, Erik Malinowski, Or Moyal, Harry Pavlidis, Jen Mac Ramos, Jarrett Seidler, and everyone else who has encouraged me, pushed me, listened to me, worked with me, or otherwise impacted my work in ways I can't fully articulate—thank you.

Tommy Rancel: Jamie, Alexis, Vincent, Jarek, Brooklyn, Adam Sobsey, Josh Vitale, Khaled bin Abdul Khaled, R.J. Anderson, Craig Goldstein, D.F. Jonez, Jonah Keri, Erik Hahmann, Jason Collette, Keith Law, Christopher Crawford, LaJethro Jenkins, Rebecca Basse, Carlos Alvarez.

Daniel Rathman: R.J. Anderson, Grant Brisbee, Evan Brunell, Chris Crawford, Craig Goldstein, Joe Hamrahi, Wilson Karaman, Chris Kusiolek, Ben Lindbergh, Rob McQuown, Harry Pavlidis and Wendy Thurm.

Dan Rozenson: Harry Pavlidis, Dan Brooks, Kate Morrison, Craig Goldstein, Mike Ferrin, Mike DeBartolo, Mark Scialabba, Doug Harris, Tucker Blair, Doug Thorburn.

Bret Sayre: Carolyn, Alyson, and Joshua, for always making me smile and keeping me sane. Lynn and Peter Sayre. The entire Baseball Prospectus family. Joe Hamrahi, Jason Parks, Marc Normandin and Ray Guilfoyle. The Gentlemen of TINO (R.I.P. Mau). The FFF Crew. Ryan Westmoreland. Howard Johnson. Jack Johnson (the boxer). All of my friends and family not mentioned above. Sam, Jason, Patrick and editors everywhere for making us all look better than we are.

Matt Sussman: Brittany Sussman, Maxwell Sussman, Brooks Baseball, and the Play Index. Exactly those four. It's the Mount Rushmore of thank yous.

David Temple: Birdie, Paul Swydan, Carson Cistulli, all the fine folks at Crawfish Boxes, Michael Clair, Bill Parker, and Michael Bates.

Matt Trueblood: Maria, Emerson, Sorkin, and Lincoln Trueblood; Todd and Margie Trueblood, Ben Lindbergh, Bret Sayre, Sahadev Sharma, Brett Taylor; Don Wycliffe, Phil Ponce, Dan McGrath, Randy Minkoff, Sue Castorino-Minkoff, David Kaplan; Ken Maeda, Scott Kramer, Mikey Poley, Brandon Lee; the doctors, nurses, and support staff at Children's Hospital Minneapolis, Ronald McDonald House Charities, nurses and support staff of Pediatric Home Services, Bryan and Cindy Novak (and family); the Minnesota Twins media relations staff; the makers of Mountain Dew® KickStart.

Jason Wojciechowski: Jim Walsh, Dave Pease, Rob McQuown, Bryan Davidson, Paul Boye, Bryan Grosnick, Geoff Young, Matt Trueblood, Wilson Karaman, Kate Morrison, Craig Goldstein, Matt Sussman, R.J. Anderson, Ben Carsley, Bradley Woodrum, Chris Crawford, Harry Pavlidis, Jonathan Judge, Austen Rachlis.

Bradley Woodrum: I want to thank the love of my life and the most impressive person I've ever known, Patrick Dubuque. He brought me into this project, and his self-loathing, mournful writing has sustained me through many tough times. I should also mention my wife and kid, who support me financial and emotionally and stuff.

Will Woods: The entire BP prospect staff, especially Jeffrey Paternostro and Jeff Moore; your work is indispensable. Thanks also to Ben Lindbergh for everything.

Geoff Young: Ken Arneson, Barry Bloom, Corey Brock, James and Jo Ellen Canine, Bill Center, John Conniff, Patrick Dubuque, Craig Elsten, Sean Forman, Brendan Gawlowski, Craig Goldstein, John Hickey, Wilson Karaman, Jeremy Koo, Patrick Kurish, David Laurila, Jane Lee, Dennis Lin, Patrick Macnee, Kiley McDaniel, Leonard Nimoy, Dustin Palmateer, Dave Pease, SABR, Eno Sarris, Bret Sayre, Sahadev Sharma, Jim Stiglich, Susan Slusser, Didi Tanadjaja, Sandra Tokashiki, Alan Torres and anyone else inadvertently missed.

Index of Names

Baseball's Many Physical Dimensions

Unlike any other professional sport, baseball's contest is played upon fields that vary in size from park to park. With the exception of the infield diamond, where strict rules regulate the location and height of the pitcher's mound and distance between the bases, no two baseball fields are alike. From the geometry of the field to the distance and height of the outfield walls, the 30 cathedrals of Major League Baseball exhibit unique and distinguishing physical characteristics.

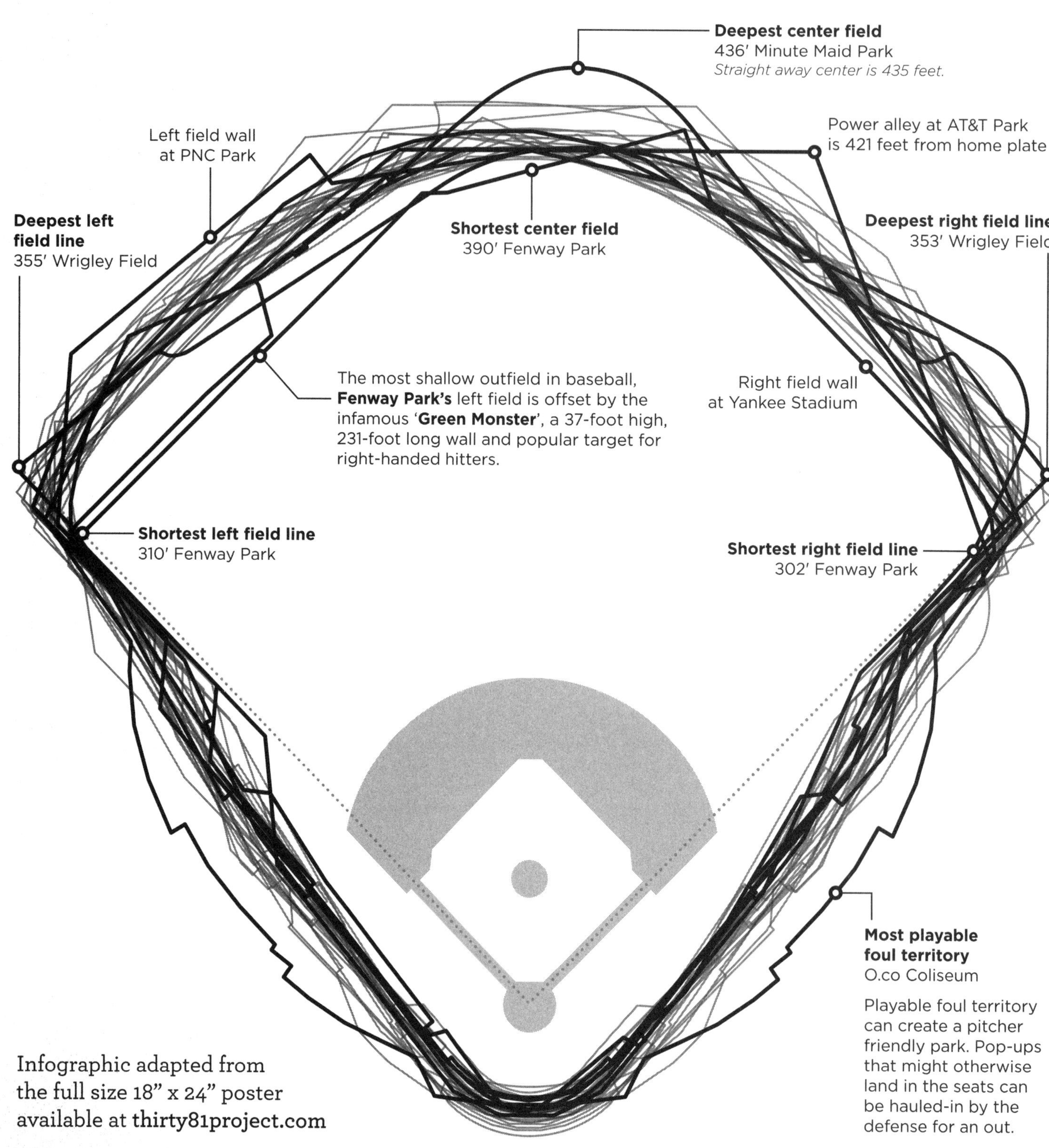

Deepest center field
436′ Minute Maid Park
Straight away center is 435 feet.
Left field wall
at PNC Park
Power alley at AT&T Park
is 421 feet from home plate
Deepest left
field line
355′ Wrigley Field
Shortest center field
390′ Fenway Park
Deepest right field line
353′ Wrigley Field
The most shallow outfield in baseball, **Fenway Park's** left field is offset by the infamous '**Green Monster**', a 37-foot high, 231-foot long wall and popular target for right-handed hitters.
Right field wall
at Yankee Stadium
Shortest left field line
310′ Fenway Park
Shortest right field line
302′ Fenway Park
Most playable
foul territory
O.co Coliseum
Playable foul territory can create a pitcher friendly park. Pop-ups that might otherwise land in the seats can be hauled-in by the defense for an out.

Infographic adapted from
the full size 18" x 24" poster
available at thirty81project.com

THIRTY81 Project